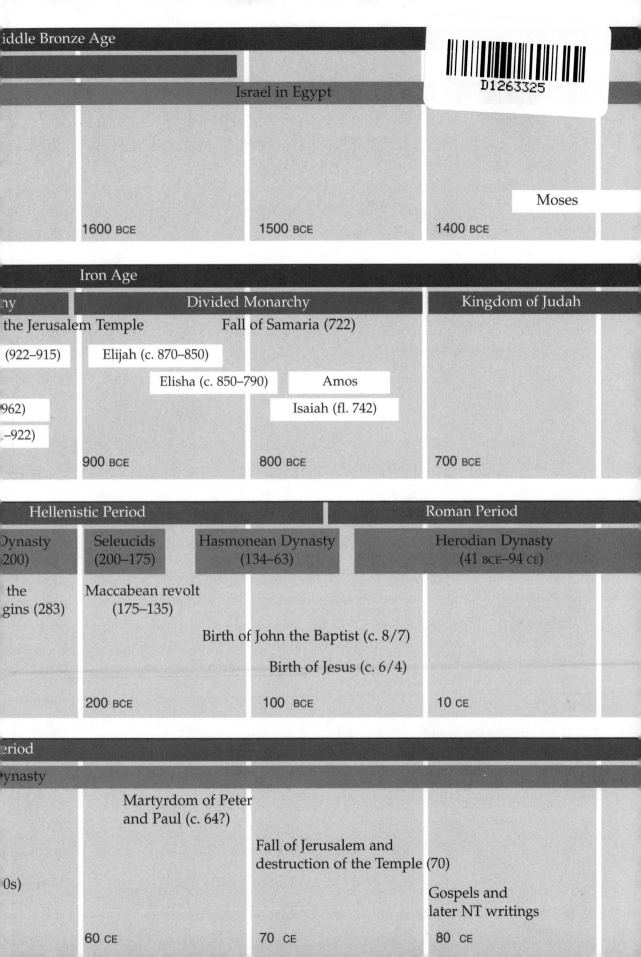

iddle Bronze Age

Israel in Egypt

Moses

1600 BCE   1500 BCE   1400 BCE

Iron Age

| hy | Divided Monarchy | Kingdom of Judah |

the Jerusalem Temple   Fall of Samaria (722)

(922–915)   Elijah (c. 870–850)

Elisha (c. 850–790)   Amos

962)   Isaiah (fl. 742)

–922)

900 BCE   800 BCE   700 BCE

Hellenistic Period   Roman Period

|)ynasty 200) | Seleucids (200–175) | Hasmonean Dynasty (134–63) | Herodian Dynasty (41 BCE–94 CE) |

the   Maccabean revolt
gins (283)   (175–135)

Birth of John the Baptist (c. 8/7)

Birth of Jesus (c. 6/4)

200 BCE   100 BCE   10 CE

eriod

ynasty

Martyrdom of Peter
and Paul (c. 64?)

Fall of Jerusalem and
destruction of the Temple (70)

Gospels and
later NT writings

0s)

60 CE   70 CE   80 CE

THE COLLEGEVILLE PASTORAL DICTIONARY OF BIBLICAL THEOLOGY

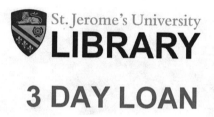

The Collegeville Pastoral Dictionary of Biblical Theology

Carroll Stuhlmueller, C.P.
General Editor

Dianne Bergant, C.S.A.
Demetrius R. Dumm, O.S.B.
Mark R. Francis, C.S.V.
Leslie J. Hoppe, O.F.M.
Kathleen Hughes, R.S.C.J.
Irene Nowell, O.S.B.
Barbara E. Reid, O.P.
Robert J. Schreiter, C.PP.S.
Donald Senior, C.P.
Editors

A Liturgical Press Book

THE LITURGICAL PRESS
Collegeville, Minnesota

Nihil obstat: Robert C. Harren, J.C.L., *Censor deputatus.*
Imprimatur: ✢ John F. Kinney, Bishop of St. Cloud, January 15, 1996.

Cover design by Ann Blattner

The copyediting of this book was accomplished by Catherine M. Hally, M.S.H.R., and Annette Kmitch.

1	2	3	4	5	6	7	8

Library of Congress Cataloging-in-Publication Data

The Collegeville pastoral dictionary of biblical theology / Carroll
    Stuhlmueller, general editor ; Dianne Bergant . . . [et al.] editors.
    . . .
        p. cm.   MAY 2 9 1996
    ISBN 0-8146-1996-7
    1. Bible—Dictionaries. 2. Bible—Theology—Dictionaries.
  I. Stuhlmueller, Carroll. II. Bergant, Dianne.
  BS417.C735 1996
  230—dc20
                                            95-40743
                                            CIP

Contents

Carroll Stuhlmueller, C.P. (1923–1994) vii
  Donald Senior, C.P.

Using the Dictionary: An Introduction ix
  Donald Senior, C.P.

The Bible and Its Books xii
  Barbara E. Reid, O.P.

English Versions of the Bible xv
  Demetrius R. Dumm, O.S.B.

History of the Major Religious Movements in the Bible:
Old and New Testaments xxii
  Barbara E. Bowe, R.S.C.J.

Biblical Interpretation Through the Ages xxxi
  Dale Launderville, O.S.B.

Archaeology and Biblical Interpretation xxxix
  Leslie J. Hoppe, O.F.M.

The Bible and Culture xlvi
  Robert J. Schreiter, C.PP.S.

Biblical Theology li
  Leslie J. Hoppe, O.F.M.

Entries 1

Contributors 1115

Carroll Stuhlmueller, C.P.
1923–1994

The *Collegeville Pastoral Dictionary of Biblical Theology* is from start to finish a tribute to Fr. Carroll Stuhlmueller, C.P. It was his idea in the first place. His vision and energy persuaded the many contributors to join the project. And, above all, his unique and powerful blend of biblical scholarship and pastoral dedication embodied the very purpose of this work.

For those of us who knew him as a friend and colleague, Carroll left an indelible impression. His life as a priest and biblical scholar spanned a crucial period in the Church, particularly in North America. Carroll's strong, genuine piety, his vigorous scholarship, and his open, gentle spirit made him a leading and beloved figure in the biblical renewal. He was one of the first contributors, general editor, and then long time member of the editorial board of *The Bible Today.* He was President of the Catholic Biblical Association and an active member all his life. His more than twenty-three books and innumerable articles in scholarly and popular journals, his record of thousands of lectures, retreats, and tapes are testimony to his prodigious contribution to biblical scholarship and to his life-long ministry of the Word.

In many ways this dictionary was to be the crowning achievement of his career. Carroll guided the editorial board through the design of the entries and in the selection of contributors. He himself wrote the article on "glory" as a guide for the rest of us— ironically it turned out to be the only article in this dictionary that would bear his name. Just as the authors were completing their work and the avalanche of manuscripts were beginning to arrive, Carroll's own health—so vigorous throughout his ministry—began to break. In February 1994, with some eighty percent of the work on the dictionary completed, God called Carroll home.

It is testimony both to the esteem in which Carroll was held by his friends and fellow workers and the importance of this project, that there was never any question of abandoning the work. Four of his colleagues in the biblical department at Catholic Theological Union, Dianne Bergant, C.S.A.; Leslie Hoppe, O.F.M.; Barbara Reid, O.P.; and myself agreed to take up the remaining tasks of the general editorship that Carroll left behind. Numerous entries that Carroll had planned to do himself had to be reassigned and the host of details in editing and coordinating over five hundred entries attended to.

On behalf of the general editing team, I would like to thank, first of all, Michael Naughton, O.S.B., and Mark Twomey of The Liturgical Press for never losing faith in this project and for their unfailing support. Carroll Stuhlmueller had an association with The Liturgical Press and St. John's Abbey that stretched over thirty-five years; having this dictionary published by that great Catholic press was a source of joy for him. And we also want to thank our many generous colleagues who contributed to the dictionary and in a special way to those who gave priority to unexpected assignments so that the dictionary's publication schedule would not be inordinately disrupted. Above all, special thanks is due to Sr. Catherine Hally, M.S.H.R. In the last few months of his life, Catherine served as a special editorial assistant to Carroll. She had just completed her graduate work in Scripture at Catholic Theological Union and was preparing to return to her teaching ministry in Kenya. Her gracious, friendly spirit and expert editorial hand were a great support to Carroll at a time when his own energy was ebbing. The very day that Carroll suffered his fatal stroke, Catherine learned that she had been elected as the Provincial superior of her community in Ireland. Despite the enormous responsibilities of her new office, Catherine still found time to complete the painstaking task of copyediting the entire five thousand-page manuscript. She did it, she said, "out of tribute to Carroll."

This entire work is a tribute to Carroll Stuhlmueller, C.P., on behalf of all those who strive to direct biblical scholarship where it belongs—in the service of God's people.

DONALD SENIOR, C.P.
CATHOLIC THEOLOGICAL UNION

Using the Dictionary:
An Introduction

The *Collegeville Pastoral Dictionary of Biblical Theology* is designed to bring the best of biblical scholarship and pastoral theology to the service of the Church and its ministry. Each word of the title proclaims the purpose of this resource. It is a product of The Liturgical Press in Collegeville, Minnesota, and draws on its great tradition of making the Bible and theology accessible to the Church, as evidenced in its extraordinary publishing record over the past several decades. It is a "Dictionary" in that it distills important information and provides it in article form for easy reference by the reader. Yet this is a "Pastoral" Dictionary, intended not primarily for the scholar or academician (although we hope they might also find it useful), but for priests, religious, teachers at all levels, and educated laity who in a variety of settings want to deepen their understanding of the Bible and its proper place within the life of the Church.

The specific focus of this Pastoral Dictionary is "Biblical Theology." The Catholic perspective (one shared by many other Christian traditions) understands the biblical Word not in isolation but in the context of the Church's ongoing life and teaching. Only in the context of the living Church, which, under the guidance of the Spirit, both received and produced the Bible, can the biblical message be authentically understood and interpreted. At the same time, the biblical word both nourishes and challenges the Church and the Church must be receptive to and allow its life to be guided by its Sacred Scriptures. This perspective has been a hallmark of Catholic theology and was reaffirmed in the Second Vatican Council's decree on Divine Revelation, *Dei verbum:* "It is clear, therefore, that, in the supremely wise arrangement of God, sacred Tradition, sacred Scripture and the Magisterium of the church are so connected and associated that one of them cannot stand without the others. Working together, each in its own way under the action of the one Holy Spirit, they all contribute effectively to the salvation of souls" (Dogmatic Constitution on Divine Revelation, no. 10).

Therefore the articles in this Dictionary not only consider the Bible in itself, but where appropriate also trace biblical themes and motifs as they have become absorbed and interpreted within the teaching of the Church and its pastoral practice. At the same time, the emphasis of the Dictionary is emphatically biblical. The choice of topics for the Dictionary has been charted according to the biblical terrain and practical pastoral issues, thus less focus will fall on topics that are more exclusively the domain of systematic or moral theology or specific to periods of later Church history.

THE DESIGN OF THE DICTIONARY

Four types of articles make up the contents of the Dictionary:

(1) *Introductory Articles.* A series of introductory articles stand at the head of the Dictionary. Their purpose is to introduce the reader to key background issues for situating the Bible in its own historical context and for proper interpretation of the Bible within the context of Church life. Individual articles trace the "anatomy" of the Bible through its various literary expressions; the history of major religious movements and motifs within the Bible; a consideration of the various approaches to biblical interpretation; the impact of diverse cultural contexts on the Bible itself and on ways it has been understood and used within Church life.

A chart of biblical history and a map of the biblical lands are printed on the inside covers. These will be handy reference as readers make their way through various articles in the Dictionary.

(2) *Major Articles.* Major articles on a select number of topics have multiple, distinct components, usually contributed by three different scholars. The article on "Law," for example, considers the role of the Mosaic Law within the Hebrew Scriptures, various New Testament perspectives on the law such as those in the Gospel of Matthew and in Paul, and a "pastoral-liturgical" section that traces the role of law with the life of the Church. In some instances, a particular topic may only have two segments, as for example that on "Son of God," which explains this important title in its biblical (mainly, New Testament) and its doctrinal development in the theology of the Church.

In accord with the purpose of this Dictionary, treatment of such major issues is thematic and explanatory—attempting to provide the reader with solid information about the topic and point to some of its significance for Christian life and practice.

(3) *Secondary Articles.* These articles focus on a particular topic, issue, or biblical motif, tracing its context and meaning in the Bible and, where appropriate, suggesting theological and pastoral implications. The selection of topics was prompted by two sources: one was key biblical issues or motifs that could not be ignored; the other stimulus came from the spiritual and pastoral experience of the Church where certain issues with evident biblical connection suggested an entry. So, for example, the Dictionary includes an article on "Tribes" a topic that may not seem to have pressing pastoral significance, yet was too important within the Bible to omit and one that, with reflection, can have significance for our understanding of the Church today. And so, too, the phenomenon of speaking in tongues probably does not rate as a major biblical motif, yet it has pastoral significance in many quarters and so has an article devoted to it ("Tongues, the gift of").

(4) *Brief Entries.* A limited number of entries are quite brief and intended to provide essential information on pertinent biblical subjects. Some, for example, would identify biblical figures whose names frequently appear in the liturgy or symbolism of the Church, such as "Abraham," "Solomon," or "Baal"; others provide succinct information on biblical cities or objects or events that also pick up symbolic meaning in Christian tradition, such as entries on "Bethlehem," "rock," or "flood."

USING THE DICTIONARY

The authors and editors of the Dictionary hope it will be useful in multiple ways and in a variety of settings. Our assumption is that most readers will consult this work from a certain "practical" vantage point. Here are some examples:

Preaching and Liturgy Preparation

Someone preparing a sermon or homily on a particular passage may decide initially to develop a particular theme prompted by the biblical passage in the Lectionary or some other chosen text. They can turn to the Dictionary to refresh and inform their understanding. Preaching on one of the gospel miracle stories, for example, would suggest turning to the major article on "Healing" to review how this motif stretches across the entire span of the Scriptures and into the sacramental life of the Church. Leads and explicit cross references to related motifs in other articles invite the reader to move even further along this track.

Someone preparing to lead a retreat could get assistance from various articles relating to the subject of a particular presentation or sermon. Just paging through the rich array of biblical themes and topics in the Dictionary might also spark new ideas for retreat sermons or meditations.

Those responsible for preparing a parish liturgy might also want to have the dictionary within reach. For example, a proposal to highlight certain season symbols such as "water" or "ashes" in the environment of a worship space during Lent could be prepared for by reading these articles and understanding more deeply the place of these symbols within the Bible and church tradition. A presentation on the use of the psalms for a prayer service could draw on the dictionary's major article on that topic.

Classroom Teaching and Learning

There is no doubt that the Dictionary will be a valuable resource for college, seminary, and even upper level secondary school courses on the Bible or religion. Each article and entry places biblical motifs, events, and personages within the broader context of the Scripture and Church life and attempts to do so in a way that is intelligent but not overly technical. Teachers can find easily accessible information to use in their classes. For example, every religion teacher knows what a synagogue is, but the dictionary provides a major article on this intriguing institution that traces its evolution in detail and relates it to the development of the Church's own liturgy. Turning to the Dictionary can provide just the ready information a teacher would need to add depth and interest to a presentation without having to take the time to gather material from several sources.

The Dictionary can do the same for student projects and papers. It is a mature and reliable reference work but not one that will overwhelm or discourage a student, as reference tools designed for scholars might.

Bible Study and Reflection

A commitment to reading the Scriptures thoughtfully and prayerfully is one of the signs of renewed life in the modern Church. Whether on one's own or together with a prayer or study group, the reader of the Bible will find the Dictionary an invaluable aid. Many readers, especially those coming to the Scriptures for the first time, can be discouraged by stumbling over terms or viewpoints that seem incomprehensible. And a lot of Bible study groups can become an occasion for shared ignorance rather than a pooling of wisdom.

Someone reading one of the Synoptic Gospels, for example, might wonder what Jesus meant by the "reign of God"—the Dictionary has a major article that explains this complicated metaphor in its biblical context and in its use in church tradition. Assigning members of a parish Bible study group specific questions to research on behalf of the group often proves to be a good strategy for involving people in group, while at the same time meeting the group's goal of understanding the Scriptures more deeply.

These are just some illustrations of what the Dictionary might offer. No doubt readers will discover other ways of absorbing the wealth of information and insight contained in the more than five hundred entries in this book. Those of us who have had the privilege of contributing to its contents hope that this volume will prove a welcome and well-worn feature on your bookshelf.

DONALD SENIOR, C.P.

The Bible and Its Books

The Bible is not one book, but a collection of books that were written by different authors in various places over a period of centuries. There is a great variety among their theologies and literary styles, although they are united in that they all testify to the faithfulness of God and serve to build up the believing community.

The selection of the particular books which now form the Bible was a lengthy process. Judaism and Christianity alike chose some books and excluded others in forming the canon. The word "canon" comes from the Greek word *kanōn*, derived from the Semitic word for "reed" (*qaneh* in Hebrew), a measuring tool. Thus, a canonical book is one that is inspired by God and provides a valuable measure for the life of faith. The official determination of the books that constitute the Jewish canon came at the end of the first century CE. For Christians, this decision was made officially at the Council of Trent (1546 CE). In both cases, the books ultimately declared canonical had been recognized for centuries as authoritative.

The three major sections of the Hebrew Bible are the Law, the Prophets, and the Writings. The first division, the Law, also known as the Torah (the Hebrew word for "Law"), or the Pentateuch (first five books), consists of Genesis, Exodus, Leviticus, Numbers, and Deuteronomy. The second section, the Prophets, includes the "Former Prophets," also termed "Deuteronomistic History": Joshua, Judges, 1 and 2 Samuel, 1 and 2 Kings; and the "Latter Prophets": Isaiah, Jeremiah, Ezekiel, Hosea, Joel, Amos, Obadiah, Jonah, Micah, Nahum, Habakkuk, Zephaniah, Haggai, Zechariah, Malachi. These latter are often referred to as the Major (Isaiah, Jeremiah, Ezekiel) and Minor Prophets (the "Twelve"). The Writings include Psalms, Proverbs, Job, Song of Songs, Ruth, Lamentations, Ecclesiastes, Esther, Daniel, Ezra-Nehemiah, and 1 and 2 Chronicles.

There was no debate about the inclusion of these thirty-nine books in the Jewish canon; thus they are termed by Roman Catholics "protocanonical." There are seven other books that are included in the Roman Catholic and Orthodox Christian canon of the First Testament: Tobit, Judith, 1 and 2 Maccabees, Wisdom, Ecclesiasticus, Baruch, and additional passages in Daniel and Esther. Because of the controversy over their inclusion, Roman Catholics and Orthodox Christians designate these books "deuterocanonical." They are regarded as "apocryphal" by Jews and Protestant Christians. The term "apocrypha" comes from the Greek *apokryphos,* meaning "concealed" or "hidden." Originally, the word was used to refer to books that were sacred, and thus, to be concealed from the common believer. By the time of Jerome (fourth century CE) the term came to mean noncanonical books similar to those included in the Scriptures. Five books considered apocryphal by Roman Catholics and Protestants are regarded as canonical by Orthodox Christians: 1 and 2 Esdras, the prayer of Manasseh, Psalm 151, 3 Maccabees.

The reason for these variations among Christian canons of the First Testament is that the earliest Christians were Greek-speaking and used as their Scriptures a Greek translation of the Hebrew Bible. This Greek translation, begun in the third century BCE in Alexandria, is known as the Septuagint (LXX), a name derived from the tradition that it was produced by seventy Jewish translators. This Alexandrian Greek Bible contained the seven books regarded as deuteroncanonical by Roman Catholics and Orthodox Christians. At the time of the Reformation, Protestants reverted to the shorter canon of thirty-nine books held as canonical by Jews.

Roman Catholic, Protestant, and Orthodox Christians all agree today on the twenty-seven books of the Second Testament: the Gospels of Matthew, Mark, Luke, John, Acts of the Apostles, Romans, 1 and 2 Corinthians, Galatians, Ephesians, Philippians, Colossians, 1 and 2 Thessalonians, 1 and 2 Timothy, Titus, Philemon, Hebrews, James, 1 and 2 Peter, 1, 2, and 3 John, Jude, and Revelation.

There is another body of early Jewish literature not considered canonical by either Jews or Christians, but which greatly influenced both. These works, written between 200 BCE and 100 CE, are designated "Apocrypha" by Roman Catholics. Protestants refer to them as "Pseudepigrapha," a name that reflects the questionability of their proclaimed authorship. Because of the use of the name "Apocrypha" by Protestants for books considered "deuterocanonical" by Roman Catholics, a less confusing title for the works written between the two Testaments is "Intertestamental Literature." This body of early Jewish literature includes such works as the books of Enoch, Jubilees, the Testaments of the Twelve Patriarchs, Sibylline Oracles, the Assumption of Moses, the Letter of Aristeas, 3 and 4 Maccabees, the Prayer of Manasseh, 1 and 2 Esdras, 2 and 3 Baruch, Psalms of Solomon.

A large number of manuscripts from both this group of writings and those that would eventually be declared canonical were discovered at Qumran beginning in 1947. Of the biblical books, only Esther is absent from among the scrolls and fragments. In addition, there are various documents pertaining to the sectarians, for example, The Manual of Discipline or the Rule of the Community, Hymns of Thanksgiving, the Damascus Covenant, and the Rule for the War. It is not clear if the Qumran community made distinctions between these and the biblical works.

There are further Christian writings dating from the second through the ninth centuries CE, in Greek, Latin, Syriac, Coptic, Arabic, Slavonic, and Anglo-Saxon, that reveal much information about the beliefs and practices of early Christians. Among these works are Gospels, Acts of Apostles, Epistles, and Apocalypses. They include the Protoevangelium of James; the Infancy Gospel of Thomas; the Gospels of Peter, Nicodemus, Thomas, Philip, and Mary; the Acts of John, Peter, Paul, Andrew, and Thomas; the Third Letter of Paul to the Corinthians; The Epistle to the Laodiceans; the Letters of Paul and Seneca; the Apocalypses of Peter, Paul, James, and Mary, to name a few.

It is not entirely clear what criteria were used for deciding canonicity. With regard to the Jewish canon, some have thought that a book's relation to the Law was a measure for its inclusion. Another factor was its use in the liturgy. For the Christian canon, in addition to widespread liturgical use, a book's apostolic origin and orthodox content were determinative. It is thought that the emergence of Christian literature, beginning to rival the Jewish Scriptures as sacred, was the impetus for the closing of the Jewish canon. It is also possible that disputes within Judaism prompted the fixing of the canon of the First Testament.

The composition of the books of the Bible spans over a millennium. Although the most ancient biblical poetry probably dates back to the twelfth century BCE (the Song of Miriam in Exod 15:1-18 and the Song of Deborah in Judges 5), the actual writing of the First Testament probably began at the time of the monarchy (approximately 1000 BCE). The latest books in the Jewish and Protestant First Testament canon, Daniel and Esther, were composed during the second century BCE. In the Roman Catholic canon the latest are 2 Maccabees and Wisdom, which date to approximately 100 BCE.

Following several decades of oral preaching and teaching, Christian traditions were set to writing. This was prompted by the death of the eyewitnesses of Jesus' mission, the rapid and wide geographical spread of Christianity, and the catechetical needs of the communities. The letters of Paul are the earliest compositions, dating mostly to the fifth decade of the first century CE. Paul's First Letter to the Thessalonians is the earliest, written in 50 or 51 CE. The first Gospel to take written shape was that of Mark, in the late 60s, followed by the Gospels of Matthew and Luke (and his second volume, Acts of the Apostles) about a decade later, and finally, that of John in the last quarter of the first century. The non-Pauline letters and the Book of Revelation were also written toward the end of the first century, possibly the beginning of the second.

As the revealed Word of God, the Bible is essential for the ongoing story of the people of God. God's Spirit, at work in the whole process of the formation of the biblical tradition within the believing community, and its commitment to writing by human authors, continues to guide the lives of believers today.

BARBARA E. REID, O.P.

English Versions of the Bible

Consideration of English versions or translations of the Bible necessarily raises a prior question about the possibility of a truly successful translation. There is an old Latin adage: *"Omnis, traductor, traditor,"* that is, "Every translator is a traitor." This is a rather drastic but realistic expression of the difficulties that must be faced by biblical translators.

First of all, there is the problem of choosing between a literal translation, which tries to find an exactly equivalent English word for the original, and a freer translation, which seeks to discover the thought of the original and then render it in idiomatic and more readable English. Obviously, there are many possibilities between a rigidly literal version and one that is so free that it amounts to paraphrase. In fact, most of these possibilities are found among the many English translations of the Bible.

Secondly, there is the problem of acknowledging the impossibility of ever achieving a translation into "timeless English," although such a claim has occasionally been made. This is due to the fact that English is a living language and that the meaning of words is constantly changing. Moreover, it is impossible to control or even predict where the change of meaning will occur or at what pace it will happen. Accordingly, even the most excellent translation will inevitably require revision or updating in the course of time.

Thirdly, the intended use of a biblical text will be a factor in deciding how literal or free a translation should be. Some translations may be good for private reading but not for public proclamation. For example, the use of elisions, such as "isn't" or "doesn't," creates problems in public reading. Some versions are also better for situations where the text is to be set to music, such as in liturgical usage.

Finally, the quality of an English version of the Bible will depend upon the accuracy of the original language text from which the translation is made. Some older English versions, which were excellent as far as quality of translation is concerned, were nonetheless marred because the Hebrew or Greek text being translated was full of errors. Since the art of text criticism is a relatively recent phenomenon and since it is constantly refining the accuracy of the original texts, English versions will need to be revised periodically simply in order to respond to these advances in scholarship. With these considerations in mind, one can appreciate the need for ever new translations and revisions of the Bible and also assess more securely the relative merits of the attempts that have been made.

ANGLO-SAXON AND MIDDLE ENGLISH VERSIONS

The earliest known examples of "English" translations of the Bible are the interlinear Anglo-Saxon paraphrases on the Latin Vulgate, particularly of the Psalter and the Gospels. Other translations were made at this time (eighth to eleventh centuries) but most of this work has been lost.

This situation changed significantly during the time of Middle English, represented by Chaucer (late fourteenth century). At this time, the first translation of the complete Bible appeared. It is associated with John Wycliffe. Since he was very critical of the Catholic Church of his day, he is sometimes considered the first Protestant, but such a conclusion is probably anachronistic. A revision of this Bible was produced shortly afterward by John Purvey, who was Wycliffe's secretary.

THE FIRST PRINTED BIBLES

The almost simultaneous advent of printing and the Protestant Reformation gave a new impetus to Bible translations. The most influential among the early printed English Bibles was William Tyndale's translation. It was made from the original languages, in part at least in protest against the Vulgate, which was the official Bible of the Catholic Church. His NT appeared in 1525 and the OT was published in 1531. He had become a convinced Protestant, as is evident from the anti-Catholic notes on his text. He died a Protestant martyr. His translation had great influence on subsequent Protestant versions.

Miles Coverdale published a complete printed Bible in 1535. It was translated from various sources, including Luther's German version, and was in part a reprint of Tyndale's translation. He placed the Apocrypha (deuterocanonical books) at the end of the NT to reflect the general Protestant conviction of their lesser value.

The Great Bible, attributed to John Rogers, was a patchwork of earlier versions. It appeared in 1539. It is noteworthy because it became the official Bible in Protestant England and its Psalter was adopted for the *Book of Common Prayer*. The Geneva Bible (1560), a revision of Tyndale and the Great Bible, was prepared at Geneva during the reign of Catholic Queen Mary. This became a very popular Bible in England and was used, for example, by Shakespeare. The Bishops' Bible (1568) was another revision of the Great Bible but, though more official, it never replaced the popular Geneva Bible.

THE KING JAMES VERSION (KJV)

By all odds, the most famous Protestant version of the Bible was this revision of the Bishops' Bible which gradually supplanted the Geneva Bible as the most popular English version ever. Since it was commissioned by King James I, it came to be considered the Authorized Version (AV) even though it was never declared such in any official manner. It was published in 1611 and is the result of a collaborative effort of the best English scholars of that day.

All agree that this version has come to be a classic of English literature and that it has exercised a powerful influence on subsequent English literary works. This is probably due as much to its familiarity as to any inherent virtues of style. In any case, it cannot be considered such a standard today, for it represents English usage of the early seventeenth century which is so archaic now that many of its words no longer have the meaning that they had at that time. Moreover, the Greek NT text which was available to the KJV revisers is now acknowledged to be marred by many scribal errors in the centuries of its transmission. The Hebrew text consulted for the OT was likewise seriously defective. This was of course no fault of those scholars since more accurate texts were not then available, but it does remind us that the KJV is far from being the best English Bible available today.

It is worth noting that the KJV included the Apocrypha (deuterocanonical books), although it placed them between the two Testaments. It eliminated the often contentious notes of its predecessors. Moreover, one finds, at the end of the Lord's Prayer, a doxology which scholars now recognize to be a scribal addition, namely, "For thine is the kingdom, and the power, and the glory, forever" (Matt 6:15).

CATHOLIC TRANSLATIONS FROM THE VULGATE

Since the Catholic Church had used the Latin Vulgate with confidence throughout the Middle Ages, it is not surprising that the earliest Catholic translations were from that version. At first sight, it might appear that such a translation could not possibly be as good as one from the original languages. However, since the Hebrew and Greek texts available were at least as corrupt as the Vulgate, such a conclusion would be at least doubtful.

The first post-Reformation Catholic translation was prepared by Gregory Martin during his exile on the continent. The NT version was published at Rheims in 1582, while the OT appeared at Douay in 1609. It is worth noting that this translation ante-dated the KJV, although only the Rheims NT was actually consulted by the KJV revisers. Martin's English style is quite literal, replete with Latinisms, and is now archaic. A revision of the Douay-Rheims Bible was made by Richard Challoner between 1749 and 1763. This remained the standard Catholic Bible in English for the next two centuries.

Eventually, a thorough revision of the Douay-Rheims-Challoner version was sponsored by the Episcopal Committee of the Confraternity of Christian Doctrine in 1936; the NT was published in 1941. Though the Hebrew and Greek texts were consulted, this was still technically based on the Latin Vulgate in accordance with longstanding Vatican directives. A similar OT revision was begun but, when Pope Pius XII (in 1943) permitted direct recourse to the original languages, that project was abandoned. This courageous move made excellent sense since it was clear that the now carefully corrected Hebrew and Greek texts were far more accurate than the Vulgate text.

A British Catholic scholar, Ronald Knox, prepared a translation of the complete Bible from the Latin Vulgate between 1944 and 1950. This rather amazing achievement was noteworthy for its fine English style and its complete break with "Bible English." It suffered, however, from the weaknesses of the Vulgate, from Knox's lack of expertise in Hebrew and, for American readers, from frequent Britishisms.

THE REVISED VERSION (RV) AND THE AMERICAN STANDARD VERSION (ASV)

By 1870, it was recognized that, because of significant changes in English usage and advances in scholarship, a revision of the venerable KJV was imperative. The intention of the revisers, most of whom were British Anglican scholars, was to make changes only where clearly unavoidable. However, it soon became evident that this would be a rather thorough revision. Typical changes were: "who" for "which" in reference to persons; "know" and "knew" for "wot" and "wist." Surprisingly, "Jehovah" was used in the OT where the KJV had used "Lord."

At a late stage, American Protestant scholars were invited to participate in the preparation of the RV but most of their suggested changes ended up in an appendix. Accordingly, the Americans decided to prepare their own revision, partly because American English had begun to depart significantly from British usage. Since the American scholars had agreed not to publish their revision for at least twenty years (to avoid direct competition), this American Standard Version did not appear until 1901. Textual scholarship was developing so rapidly at that time that the ASV NT was already based on a much better Greek text than the RV. Examples of changes in English usage were: "Holy Spirit" for "Holy Ghost" and "precede" for "prevent." However, neither the RV nor the ASV was able to seriously challenge the established and familiar KJV.

PRIVATE TRANSLATIONS

Private translations of the Bible were attempted by various scholars in the early 1900s. Notable among these was the work of James Moffatt whose translation of the NT was published in London in 1913. The OT version appeared in 1924–25 in New York. Moffatt responded to the desire for a less literal version and his translation has been quite influential; however, it could never compete with the institutionally sponsored versions.

Another highly regarded translation was prepared by a group of American scholars, the best known of whom was E. J. Goodspeed. His version of the NT was published in 1923 and the OT, translated by his colleagues, appeared in 1927. This translation was entitled *The Complete Bible: An American Translation*. Since it was published by the University of Chicago Press, it came to be known as the "Chicago Bible." As a translation, it was both scholarly and idiomatic and is probably the best of the private translations.

The English Jesuit Cuthbert Lattey and others published a NT translation from the Greek called the *Westminster Version* in 1935. The OT translation was never completed. A similar attempt was made by the American Catholic scholars James Kleist and Joseph Lilly, whose work appeared between 1950 and 1954. Both of these efforts are noteworthy mainly to illustrate the yearning among Catholics at that time for a better translation than the official Douay-Rheims-Challoner version.

THE REVISED STANDARD VERSION (RSV)

This revision of the Bible is in the tradition of the KJV. It was begun in 1937 by a group of thirty-two scholars under the leadership of Luther Weigle. Their stated intention was to update the wording but retain the style of the KJV. The NT appeared in 1946 and the complete Bible was published without the Apocrypha in 1952, and with these books in 1956. Though advertised as a revision, it amounted to a fresh translation and, though it tended to be fairly literal, it nonetheless created a great deal of controversy.

The principal objections came from conservative Protestant circles where certain changes, though fully justified by scholarly standards, caused shock and scandal. The most notable of these was the change from "virgin" to "young woman" in translating the Hebrew *'almah* in Isaiah 7:14. On the other hand, more liberal readers objected to the retention of "thou" and "thee" in discourse involving the divinity. Nonetheless, this version gained in popularity and, though it did not displace the venerable KJV, it easily outsold its nearest modern competitors.

A Catholic edition of the RSV, with a few changes (e.g., "brethren" for "brothers" in

referring to Jesus' relatives) was published in England in 1966. Later, a Catholic edition without any changes was published in the United States.

THE NEW WORLD TRANSLATION

This Bible translation was prepared by the Watchtower Bible and Tract Society ("Jehovah's Witnesses") and appeared in 1950 (NT) and 1961 (OT). It is worth mentioning primarily as a warning against relying on it since it is probably the only modern Bible translation where theological views seem to have played a pervasively negative role. For example, there is no objective justification for translating "Lord" in the NT as "Jehovah."

THE JERUSALEM BIBLE (JB)

The JB is so named because it was based on a French translation prepared under the auspices of the Ecole Biblique in Jerusalem. The French edition, which appeared in fascicles beginning in 1948 and then as a complete Bible in 1961, was based on excellent Hebrew and Greek texts, though some think it favored the Septuagint too often over the Hebrew text in the OT.

The English version, which translated the French edition with an eye on the original texts, was prepared by a group of British scholars under the guidance of Alexander Jones and appeared in 1966. It is judged to be a rather free version and borders at times on paraphrase. One unique feature of this version is the use of "Yahweh" as God's name in the OT. It is quite sensitive to Catholic concerns, explaining for example that the "brothers of the Lord" could be near relatives. As might be expected, there are occasional Britishisms, e.g., "goal" for "jail" and "corn" for "wheat."

This version has been justly praised for its extensive and helpful footnotes. These offer explanations of obscure passages and assist the reader where local geography or cultural peculiarities need to be clarified.

Nor are they tendentious. The Apocrypha are included in the traditional Catholic manner as in the Vulgate.

A revision of the JB, based on a thoroughly revised French edition, was prepared under the leadership of Henry Wansbrough and was published as the *New Jerusalem Bible* (NJB) in 1985. The footnotes are updated and some errors in the JB are corrected. It tries also to be more sensitive about inclusive language.

THE NEW AMERICAN BIBLE (NAB)

The NAB is a Catholic version which succeeded the Confraternity Bible translated from the Vulgate (see above). Since work on the Confraternity OT was abandoned in 1943 when recourse to the original language texts was permitted, this new translation from the Hebrew and Greek began with the OT, which appeared in separate segments between 1952 and 1969. Work on a NT translation from the Greek was also progressing during this period, so the entire Bible was published in 1970.

This translation was prepared by some fifty scholars, most of them Catholics, from the best critically edited Hebrew and Greek texts. Newly available information from the Qumran texts was also consulted. The translators made a special effort to be sensitive to future liturgical usage also.

This translation generally steers a middle course between literal fidelity and readability. One welcome change was the use of proper names derived from the Hebrew rather than from the Latin, for example, "Isaiah" for "Isaias," "Elijah" for "Elias," etc. Moreover, the names of biblical books were changed to agree with the more proper usage of the Protestant Bibles, for example, "Chronicles" for "Paralipomenon," "Sirach" for "Ecclesiasticus," "Revelation" for "Apocalypse," etc. Its concern for tradition is evident, however, in the rendering of *'almah* as "virgin" in Isaiah 7:14.

The NT translation for this edition had been rushed somewhat to have it available

for the new Lectionary that followed the liturgical reforms of Vatican Council II and was soon found to be less than satisfactory. Accordingly, a thorough and greatly improved revision of the NT was prepared and was published in 1987. All NAB Bibles since that time contain this version of the NT. A Catholic Study Bible using this revised NAB and containing almost six hundred pages of introduction was published in 1990.

THE NEW AMERICAN STANDARD BIBLE (NAS)

The NAS was prepared by fifty-eight anonymous scholars and was published between 1963 and 1970. It claimed to be in the tradition of the ASV but it was in fact a fresh translation designed to satisfy conservative Protestant congregations. It omitted the Apocrypha entirely. Its conservative nature is illustrated by the capitalization of all pronouns referring to God and of all OT references thought to be messianic. In general, this translation favors the very literal tradition of Fundamentalist Protestantism and its literary style suffers accordingly.

THE NEW ENGLISH BIBLE (NEB)

The NEB was prepared in England under the editorship of C. H. Dodd and was published between 1961 (NT) and 1970 (complete Bible). The Apocrypha are included between the two Testaments. This translation was intended to be an entirely new version that would consciously avoid "Bible English" as much as possible. Compared to other translations, it should probably be characterized as liberal, even bordering on paraphrase. For example, John 1:1 reads: "When all things began, the Word already was." Since it was prepared primarily by British scholars for British readers, it uses spellings and expressions that are unfamiliar to American readers. Some examples are: "corn" for "wheat," "cairn" for "heap," and "thirty pounds" for "300 denarii." The great merit of the NEB is its lively English style and it is especially well suited for private reading.

THE GOOD NEWS BIBLE (ALSO KNOWN AS TODAY'S ENGLISH VERSION)

This version was prepared by a group of scholars commissioned by the American Bible Society. The NT appeared in 1968 and the entire Bible, including the Apocrypha, was published in 1979. The translators deliberately chose a style that would be suitable for an elementary school reading level. It is also sometimes described as "newspaper English." As might be expected, it is a very free translation that frequently amounts to paraphrase. In keeping with its title, "gospel" is consistently translated as "good news." It has been a popular version and is more useful for private reading than for study.

THE NEW INTERNATIONAL VERSION (NIV)

The NIV was designed specifically for the use of conservative Evangelical Protestants and was sponsored by the New York Bible Society International. The NT was published in 1973 and the complete Bible appeared in 1978. This is a new translation which is based on very good critical texts and which tends to be moderate and traditional while striving for a contemporary English style. It emphasizes the messianic meaning of relevant OT texts and, contrary to the best scholarly opinion, continues to translate *almah* as "virgin" in Isaiah 7:14. It is generally considered to be a reliable and readable translation.

THE NEW KING JAMES VERSION (NKJV)

The NKJV was published under the auspices of Thomas Nelson Publishers and appeared in 1979 (NT) and 1982 (complete Bible). It does not include the Apocrypha. The aim of the translators was to produce a text that would be modern but would retain some of the lyrical qualities of the KJV. This would presumably satisfy the nostalgic yearnings of those accustomed to the KJV and at the same time would eliminate some of that version's more obvious deficiencies. Accordingly, such forms as "thee" and "thou" are studiously avoided. However, the treatment of messianic passages in the OT is clearly influenced by Christian theology. Moreover, the translators surprisingly relied on a Greek text of the NT which does not benefit from modern text criticism and is generally considered deficient.

THE REVISED ENGLISH BIBLE (REB)

This Bible is a revision and updating of the NEB. The process of revision, which began in 1973, was at first an exclusively Protestant undertaking but eventually some Catholics were also invited to participate. This revision was published in 1989 and is available with or without the Apocrypha. The aim of the revisers was to take advantage of advances in text criticism and new discoveries in Bible lands as well as to respond to valid criticisms of the NEB.

In particular, an attempt was made to use more inclusive language, especially where a suitable synonym could be used for "man/men" when the meaning is generic. The "thou" and "thee" forms that had been used in prayers were now completely abandoned. On the other hand, some of the more innovative renderings of the NEB were modified, such as John 1:1 which had read, "When all things began, the Word already was," and now reads, "In the beginning the Word already was." In general, this version is highly readable and, in comparison with the NEB, is somewhat more restrained in its paraphrasing tendencies.

THE NEW REVISED STANDARD VERSION (NRSV)

The NRSV was prepared, beginning in 1973, by a group of scholars working under the auspices of the National Council of Churches. Some Catholic scholars were also invited to participate. This version is intended to be a revision in the tradition of the KJV, RV/ASV and RSV. It was published in 1990 and offers editions with or without the Apocrypha.

This version, like the RSV, strives for a rather literal translation without sacrificing good English style. The "thou/thee" language which the RSV had used in prayers was now completely abandoned. In spite of the attacks on the RSV, the translation of "young woman" was retained in Isaiah 7:14. But the most noticeable change in the NRSV is its determined use of inclusive language. In all cases where "man/men" has a generic sense, a gender-neutral substitute is provided. Moreover, where "brothers" or "brethren" is found, as in the Pauline letters, "brothers and sisters," or some similar substitution, is used. A footnote alerts the reader to the change. Only a few sporadic attempts are made to deal with "vertical" exclusive language, i.e., the use of masculine pronouns in references to the divinity. Overall, this is considered a very accurate and readable translation. In November 1991 it was approved by the American Bishops for use by Catholics in the USA.

JEWISH TRANSLATIONS

The need for an English translation for Jewish communities in England and America was not urgent until the mid-nineteenth century when Jews became more numerous in these countries. The first significant translation was made by Isaac Leeser whose Pentateuch was published in 1845, followed by the complete Hebrew Scriptures in 1853–54. His scholarship was primarily that of his German origin but he was also influenced to some degree by the KJV.

Leeser's translation remained dominant in England and America until 1917 when a new translation was published under the auspices of the Jewish Publication Society of America. For this reason it is generally identified as the JPS version. This version was influenced by the RV and tended to be quite literal. The Jewish scholars who prepared it under the leadership of Max Margolis were careful to eliminate Christian influences reflected in the RV, particularly in the messianic texts.

Finally, a more independent translation representing the best contemporary scholarship was sponsored by the Jewish Publication Society of America and appeared in complete form in 1982. It is known as the New JPS version. Harry Orlinsky spearheaded this effort and was joined by many other eminent Jewish scholars. This translation tends to be fairly literal and adheres closely to the Hebrew Massoretic text.

CONCLUSION

From this sketchy survey it should be obvious that those who are interested in the sacred writings of the Judaeo-Christian tradition enjoy a kind of embarrassment of riches in regard to texts available for their use. Moreover, these versions represent almost every possible blend, from the very literal to the very readable. The English language will certainly continue to evolve, and more accurate original texts will be prepared, but the inevitable future translations will have a solid foundation on which to build.

DEMETRIUS R. DUMM, O.S.B.

History of the Major Religious Movements in the Bible: Old and New Testaments

INTRODUCTION

The biblical tradition as we know it is not *one* single story of faith, but many. The Bible contains a variety of diverse traditions reflecting the beliefs and religious practices of the people of Israel and of their early Christian descendants. These span a period of time from the second millennium BCE to the second century CE. Gathered together and complied into a single collection, these diverse traditions of faith mirror the multi-faceted and dynamic process of theological reflection carried on in the communities of ancient Israel throughout its long history, and later in the circles of the followers of Jesus during the first and early second centuries CE.

Diverse oral and literary forms convey this experience of faith and give expression to its content. Poetry, narrative and song, proverb, parable, legend and mythic tale, sayings, oracles, and apocalyptic visions—all these biblical forms of expression (and more) lend themselves to the articulation of faith in the God who is experienced in Israel and early Christianity. The richness and variety of both theological content and literary form convey in themselves the infinite character of God's presence throughout biblical history, and the multiple ways God has been revealed to people of faith throughout the centuries.

At the heart of the biblical tradition is the certainty that God is revealed and accessible in the created world and through the events of history. The biblical God is not a deity who is remote and unconcerned with human existence. Rather, the God of Israel, the God revealed in Jesus, pitches a tent among us (Sir 24:8; John 1:14) and is named Emmanuel, God-with-us (Isa 7:14; Matt 1:23). Our access to knowing and experiencing this infinite God is, however, always mediated to us through our limited human experience, and it is, therefore, inextricably intertwined with our social-historical context in every period of history.

The sweep of biblical history, from its early beginnings in the Middle Bronze age to the early second century CE, can be conveniently divided for the purposes of tracing the major religious movements of both ancient Israel and early Christianity. In the history of Israel, five distinct periods of social-historical as well as religious development are evident: the pre-monarchical period from ca. 1250–1000 BCE, the period of the united monarchy from 1000–922 BCE, the period of the divided monarchy from 922–587 BCE, the Exile from 587–537 BCE, and the post-exilic period from 537 BCE to the beginning of the Christian era.

The early Christian movement can likewise be divided between its Palestinian geographical origins and its movement into the urban centers of the Greco-Roman world, although in both contexts there existed a variety of Christian expressions of faith and religious self-understandings. The Bible witnesses to this long process of faith experience and reflection, and affirms with tenacious certainty that the God of the Bible is actively involved in this historical process.

OLD TESTAMENT RELIGIOUS MOVEMENTS

Pre-Monarchical Israel ca. 1250–1000 BCE

The historical origins of Israelite faith can be traced to the beginnings of the formation of a people who shared a common social-political, egalitarian ideal based on and supported by their collective belief in a God whom they addressed and worshiped as Yahweh. The biblical story roots this new social, political, and religious entity called "Israel" in Yahweh's liberating action which delivered a people from the oppressive power of Egyptian enslavement (Exodus 1–15). The Exodus from Egypt and the consequent migration of peoples into the land of Canaan, therefore, mark the decisive beginning of Israel's own story of faith as told in Exodus through Judges.

Competing theories about the actual nature of Israel's beginnings in the land abound, and caution must attend any general conclusions drawn about this period. Nevertheless, there is agreement that a new social-political and religious movement began to take shape in Palestine around 1250 BCE. This movement, grounded in its common faith in Yahweh (see Joshua 24), seems to have rejected both the social-political organization of the Canaanite city-states as well as their supporting deities, like Baal and Asherah (e.g., Josh 24:23). Convinced instead that their God, Yahweh, was a champion of liberation and social equality, these early Israelites forged a loosely confederated union of clans, bound together not so much by actual kinship as by common vision of a new society which attracted members from the indigenous population of Canaanites. At times the various tribes cooperated for purposes of common defense (see Judges 5), and were linked by covenant to God and to one another.

Much of this new social and religious vision was grounded in the tradition of Moses' leadership. The Mosaic covenant at Sinai (see Exodus 19–24) articulated the values of Israelite faith. Those gathered together under the banner of this faith expressed their desire to be a covenant people bound in fidelity to Yahweh. The ethical and religious basis for their faith called this people to be holy, as their God was holy (Exod 19:5-6; Lev 19:1-2), and bound them to ethical principles which protected the weak and powerless: the orphan, the widow, strangers, the poor. Rejecting the structures of power evident in the stratification of Canaanite society, they sought a different mode of social organization grounded in the

covenant stipulations. This was a covenant bond conditioned by the people's obedience and grounded in their continued fidelity to Yahweh (Exod 19:5-6). Walter Brueggemann has termed their attempt "a precarious social experiment based on a precarious theological vision."

Leadership in this social and religious movement was, at first, in the hands of local figures—elders, judges—persons whose leadership strengthened the more "democratic" features of the covenant community and discouraged the centralization of power in the hands of a select elite. The book of Judges, however, provides a sharp critique (albeit from hindsight) of the degree to which these figures failed to provide adequate leadership for the new community.

Cultic practices were centered in various shrines and ancient sanctuaries throughout the tribal lands, especially in the premonarchic sanctuaries at Shiloh, Shechem, and Beth-shemesh. The ancestral stories in Genesis provide later explanatory traditions for the existence of cultic centers that developed in the monarchy, for example at Bethel (Gen 28:10-17). Priestly clans traced their origins back to Moses and took leadership in the care and functioning of the ancient sanctuaries. (e.g., Eli and Samuel 1 Samuel 2–3). Whether, or in what fashion, the disparate tribes gathered yearly for cultic celebration and the renewal of the covenant stipulations, as von Rad argued and Joshua 24 narrates, remains uncertain. What is certain is that the sociopolitical and religious movement known as Yahwism offered a compelling alternative to the social and religious structures of the Canaanite city-states.

The Period of Monarchy 1000–587 BCE

The rise of the monarchy in Israel marked a radical change in both the embodiment of its covenant vision as well as in its social-political structures. The various forces which contributed to the unification of the Israelite tribes and to the establishment of the monarchy under Saul, David, and Solomon are complex and much debated, but chief among them was the consolidation of the Philistine threat and the need for a more centralized effort to counter Philistine power.

In general, the "revisionist" traditions reflected in 1 Samuel 7–8, 10, 12 and Deuteronomy 17:14-20 all criticize the tribal insistence on a king and their desire "to be like all the nations" (1 Sam 8:20). From a theological perspective, this desire reflected a movement toward religious assimilation and syncretistic practices, which implied a relaxation, even abandonment, of older covenant loyalties. The ensuing development of the royal bureaucracy: census and taxation, military conscription, forced labor, and the further stratification of society all moved in a direction different from the original vision of the covenant community based as it was on the radical freedom of God and God's power of liberation for the people.

With the defeat of the Philistines and the definitive establishment of the united monarchy under David (2 Samuel 5–6), a new theology of covenant and people had to emerge. The earliest of the written sources in the Pentateuch, the so-called Yahwist source, shaped a story of Israel's beginnings which celebrated the promise made to Abraham in the ancient past that Yahweh would give to Abraham and Sarah and to their descendants land, power, and progeny (Gen 12:1-3; 15:5-7). Reflecting the position and optimism of the Davidic empire, the Yahwist source saw in the establishment of the Davidic dynasty the final fulfillment of the promises to Abraham of old. In its ideal vision, this tradition of the Davidic covenant gave to the king the solemn responsibility for safeguarding the covenant norms, but the reality fell far short of the ideal.

With Solomon, the move toward royal establishment was finally complete. The chilling "warning" by Samuel in 1 Samuel 8:10-18 describes the actual abuses of power later associated with Solomon's rule. Whereas the Mosaic covenant traditions celebrated the freedom of Yahweh's presence with the people symbolized in the pillar of cloud and fire in the wilderness, the Davidic expression embodied in Solomon's empire located Yahweh's presence in the Davidic dynasty and in the permanent establishment of the Temple in Jerusalem as the house of Yahweh. Moreover, David had sought to combine the ancient priestly traditions associated with Abiathar and the sanctuary at Shiloh together with the Zadokite priests of Jerusalem, but Solomon rejected Abiathar and with him the ties to the older cultic and Mosaic covenant traditions associated with the Ark enshrined at Shiloh.

One only needs to read the Hebrew Psalter to glimpse how central was the temple cult during the period of the monarchy. Jerusalem's Temple functioned as a symbol of the heart and center of Israelite faith, the place where one encountered the God of the covenant. The Temple was celebrated as the "house of the LORD" (Pss 84:5; 122:1), God's very "dwelling place" (Ps 84:2). Even one day in the courts of the Temple were considered as a thousand elsewhere (Ps 84:11). The procession to the Temple on the great festivals, the atoning rituals and sacrificial offerings all celebrated in word and action that Yahweh was Israel's protector, the one who continued to give life and abundance to the people, and their only true king.

With the division of the kingdom in 922 BCE (1 Kings 12) the ten northern tribes established both an alternative political center in Samaria as well as alternative cultic centers in the various shrines of the northern kingdom. No longer would the Temple in Jerusalem unite the former tribes. Instead, Jeroboam erected in Dan and Bethel altars with golden calves as pedestals for the invisible presence of God to rest. This action was, of course, judged by later writers as idolatry and reason alone, in the judgment of the Deuteronomistic historians, for the eventual destruction of the northern kingdom at the hands of the Assyrians in 722 BCE.

The Prophetic and Deuteronomistic Traditions

The period of the Israelite monarchy was synonymous with the flourishing of the prophetic traditions in Israel. Persistent conflicts between prophet and king, between the Mosaic covenantal vision in conflict with the vision of the royal establishment, marked Israel's religious drama from 1000 BCE to 597 BCE. The prophetic voices were shrill and uncompromising, pleading for justice and faithfulness to God. "Woe to the complacent in Zion" Amos warned (Amos 6:1).

These guardians and messengers of covenant faith challenged king, prophet, and priest alike in their insistence on the heart of the covenant vision (e.g., Hos 8:1-4; 9:7-8; 4:4-5). God's people were to be a holy people (Exod 19:5-6) because their God was holy. Just, compassionate, steadfast in love, merciful—as God was with them, so they were to be with others. But in the place of holiness the prophets found perversion of justice, idolatry, abuse of the poor and the weak, and empty ritual devoid of faith. Amos and Hosea warned the northern kingdom of the impending divine judgment but to no avail.

Nevertheless, prophetic faith found reason to hope even in the midst of despair. God would not revoke the promise nor withdraw divine favor from Israel. God would indeed chasten and punish the people but a remnant would be spared (Isa 7:3; 11:10-16; Mic 4:6-7; Jer 23:3-4). However, security was to be found neither in political power nor in cultic life. Even the Temple itself, viewed as the bastion of God and an indestructible refuge, came under Jeremiah's vehement attack (Jeremiah 7 and 26) on very the eve of its destruction. Hope was not lost, though, and Jeremiah even foresaw the possibility of a new covenant that would be written on the heart (Jer 31:31-34).

In this way prophecy in Israel challenged the royal and priestly establishment to be guardians of covenant faith. The prophets kept before king and people the religious vision of a community belonging to God whose institutions and cultic life would embody God's own justice and holiness.

Related to this prophetic vision was the religious perspective of the Deuteronomistic history, the historical account in the Books of Deuteronomy through 2 Kings. Together these books present a theological reflection on Israel's history grounded in the conviction that disobedience to Yahweh and the covenant obligations have warranted punishment from God. The traditions reflected in the Deuteronomistic history were formulated in the late seventh century on the eve of the Exile and revised in the light of the exilic period. These traditions provided a theological explanation for the destruction of Jerusalem and for the disaster of the Exile. The Deuteronomistic historians did not relinquish hope in God's promise to David to establish an eternal covenant with the house of Judah, but they reintroduced the ancient covenant stipulation of the *conditional* nature of this covenant bond. Apostasy, infidelity, violation of covenant justice had brought destruction for Israel and Judah; only repentance and recommitment could restore God's favor.

The Exile 597–538 BCE and Post Exilic Restoration

The Exile marked a watershed in the history of Israel's faith. With the Temple destroyed, the city of Jerusalem in ruins, the nation brought to its knees, only the combined religious imagination of both priest and prophet could restore hope for a broken people. Two prophets of the Exile in different ways embodied these voices of hope for Israel. Ezekiel conveyed the priestly viewpoint, that hope rested in a restored Temple and cult wherein the glory of God would reside and be celebrated (Ezek 40–48). From this new Temple would spring the waters of life and God's holiness and glory would be restored to the land.

The priestly leadership of the exilic community likewise gathered together the ancient traditions to create the collection of writings in the Pentateuch as we now have it. Their faith was shaped by the great myths of Babylon which influenced their own stories of creation and the flood. Their ordered account of the drama of the earth's beginnings ("And evening came . . . and morning followed . . . the first day, . . . the second day . . ., etc.") was a powerful antidote to the sense of chaos created by the Exile. Their theological vision assured the people that even the Exile could not cancel God's eternal covenants made with Noah (Gen 9:16), with Abraham (Gen 17:13), with the people (Exod 31:16), with the priests (Lev 24:8), and with Moses (Exod 19:6).

The anonymous prophet known as "Second Isaiah" (Isaiah 40–55) evoked the ancient symbols of the Exodus to proclaim a new exodus which would mark the return of the exiles to Zion. The punishment they had endured was finished and a new beginning was about to dawn. This prophet envisioned the renewed community in Zion as a center to which all the nations would stream. There Yahweh alone would be proclaimed as God and lord of history, the holy one (Isaiah 43).

But the grand vision of Second Isaiah met the harsh reality of the task of rebuilding the community in the land now under Persian rule. By 515 BCE the second Temple was completed and became once again a focal point of Jewish life in Palestine, although on a less grandiose scale than the prophet Ezekiel had earlier envisioned. Moreover, under the leadership of Ezra and Nehemiah, the Jewish minority consolidated their efforts to strengthen Jewish identity by a more narrow and defensive outlook toward its communal life. To maintain their Jewish identity strict observance of the Torah was essential. Intermarriage was forbidden and those who had foreign wives were encouraged to divorce them (Ezra 10:1-17). Led by their priests and scribes, the post-Exilic community had become a theocracy and covenant faith had become synonymous with faithful observance of the Law in its entirety.

Apocalyptic Traditions

The experience of Exile and its aftermath also prompted a new religious perspective to emerge in Israel. Already dawning in the prophetic visions of Ezekiel, Zechariah, and Third Isaiah this new religious expression gathered momentum during the turbulent years of Seleucid rule in Palestine and find expression especially in the book of Daniel 7–12. Apocalypticism, from the Greek word meaning "unveiling," revelation, is both a socio-political and religious perspective that sees the present world, and its political rulers, as doomed to imminent destruction by the powers of God. This destruction will usher in a completely new world in which the apocalyptic community will be rescued from its current alienation and suffering and rewarded for its steadfast adherence to God.

In this manner, the Book of Daniel provided hope and consolation for the Jewish community persecuted and struggling to survive under the oppressive policies of Antiochus Epiphanes in 168 BCE. Apocalypticism, with its urgent longings for the in-breaking of God's rule, became the dominant mode of expectation in Palestinian Judaism and one that eventually found resonance in the proclamation of Jesus of Nazareth.

Wisdom Traditions

No survey of the religious movements in Israel would be complete without attention to the diverse traditions gathered together under the title of "Wisdom." This Sapiential tradition was part of Israel's religious consciousness from the very beginning but in the literary framework of the biblical Torah and Prophets it has occupied a subordinate position in relationship to the drama of salvation history. Nevertheless, the Wisdom traditions provide an essential corrective and complement to what some have called the "saving tradition" in Israel's faith.

Wisdom is the name given to the religious conviction which says that God's revelation comes not primarily through dramatic acts in history, but through the ordinariness of everyday life. Wisdom recognizes that God is revealed first and foremost in the whole of creation, and in the essential harmony and order that is constitutive of it. The traditions of wisdom in Israel appear to be less concerned with the dramatic historical moments of Exodus and Exile than with the dailiness of ordinary life and how God is to be encountered in the fabric of life and relationships day in and day out. The Wisdom traditions recognize the essential ambiguity of life, the eternal paradox at the heart of creation. They shy away from the uncompromising clarity of prophetic judgment which draws a sharp line between black and white, blessing and curse, evil and good. The Wisdom tradition acknowledges that all life is marked by an area of gray. Life is essentially a mystery which human beings can never comprehend.

The origins and expressions of wisdom are as diverse as creation itself. Proverbial wisdom drawn from Egypt and elsewhere, family and tribal wisdom preserved in oral memory from the period of the Judges, courtly and royal wisdom fashioned in the urban bureaucracy of the monarchy, scribal wisdom—all these make up the variety of wisdom in Israel. The disputations of Job's struggle to understand the problem of suffering, the proverbial sayings gathered together in the Book of Proverbs, together with the philosophical skepticism of Qoheleth, all reflect the different dimensions of wisdom. Essential in this tradition of Jewish faith was the gradual development of the figure of wisdom personified (Proverbs 1–8; Wisdom 7–9; Sirach 24) which became a primary resource for the early Christian community's developing Christological speculation. Despite its less dominant role in the biblical tradition, wisdom embodies an essential dimension of OT faith.

NEW TESTAMENT RELIGIOUS MOVEMENTS

Introduction

The twenty-seven books of the NT canon contain the literary expression of early Christian faith as it developed from the public ministry of Jesus (ca. 30 CE) until the early decades of the second century. Compared with the long evolution and development of faith in Israel's history, these writings are much less diverse and multifaceted than the Hebrew Scriptures. At the same time, the NT writings reproduce the various ways in which early Christians reflected on the life, death, and ministry of Jesus and the implications they drew from this reflection for their own lives and faith.

Various forms of oral and literary expression stand side by side in the NT as they did in the OT texts: biographical narratives, letters, hymns, sayings, parables, revelation discourse, beatitudes and woe oracles, prayers and doxologies—all combine to portray early Christian faith in the person of Jesus and his message. This early Christian movement began in the rural areas of Palestine but quickly established itself not only in the heart of Jerusalem and the Jewish Diaspora, but in the major urban centers of the Gentile, Greco-Roman world.

Jesus and the Reign of God

The Synoptic Gospels of Matthew, Mark, and Luke, each with its unique theological perspective, narrate the story of Jesus for the communities of their day. Their portraits of Jesus share many similarities as well as differences, but together they capture the essential quality of the life and death of Jesus, his words and deeds as they were already being interpreted in the early Church. Two different dimensions of the portrait of Jesus stand together in these sources. We see Jesus on the one hand as the apocalyptic prophet, like his forerunner John the Baptist. As prophet, Jesus is one who challenged the Jews of his day to repentance in the face of the immanent and dramatic coming of the reign of God (Mark 1:14-15).

On the other hand, much of the tradition reflected in the Synoptics portrays Jesus as the wisdom sage who teaches that God's power is already, but mysteriously, accessible within the domain of ordinary history. Like the seed growing secretly or the leaven at work within the dough, God's reign is a present but imperceptible reality. Both the parables of Jesus and the many aphorisms attributed to him challenge his hearers to reconsider how they view the world and God's place within it. Many scholars today speak of the "subversive" character of the wisdom of Jesus which challenged the accepted world view and modes of thinking of his day.

In this sense, there is an unmistakable prophetic quality in the words and deeds of Jesus. He embodied God's own compassion, justice, and holiness which were contained and celebrated in the covenant vision of Israel's past. Jesus put himself on the side of those who were excluded from the mainstream of Jewish society. He welcomed to his circle tax collectors and sinners, the poor, Gentiles, women and any whom society relegated to the margins. In a particular way he seemed determined to challenge the religious and social boundaries that rendered some as accepted and approved while others were banished to the margins by virture of their sins, their infirmities, or their religious laxity. The man from Nazareth extended to all the mercy and compassion of God.

In the generation after his death, the followers of Jesus proclaimed his resurrection and vindication by God. "He has been raised; he is not here!" (Mark 16:6). For many, Jesus' resurrection confirmed their hope that the end time had begun, the new age had dawned.

Johannine Traditions

The Fourth Gospel, the "maverick gospel" as Robert Kysar has called it, contains a unique perspective on the life and message of Jesus and provides a unique example of early Christian faith. For the Johannine Christians living in the last decade of the first century, the memory of Jesus was preserved and interpreted primarily through the categories of the Jewish Wisdom tradition and its counterpart in the Hellenistic philosophical speculation on the *logos*. The prologue of John's Gospel proclaims Jesus as the Word made flesh who pitched a tent among us and this text echoes what had been said long ago of the figure of Lady Wisdom in Sirach 24:8. As *logos*, Jesus is the word of God, the revealing word who mediates to the world God's own life.

As Wisdom did, so Jesus also speaks in enigmatic self-proclamations which point to the intimacy, even identity, between Jesus and the God of Israel (e.g., John 5). With a myriad of metaphors Jesus is presented in the Gospel as light, life, bread, the shepherd, the one sent by God for the life of the world. No longer the apocalyptic prophet, nor even the wisdom sage of the Synoptic Gospels, in John's Gospel, Jesus is the very Wisdom of God incarnate.

Those gathered together by their faith in Jesus have become truly children of God (John 1:12) who possess the power of the spirit-paraclete. Theirs is a mutually egalitarian community of service, modeled on the master who washed the feet of his disciples (John 13). Women, it seems certain, provided significant leadership in the community. Few structures and a complete absence of hierarchical patterns make the ecclesiology of John's Gospel unique. The criterion for all service and leadership among Johannine Christians is nothing less than intimacy with Jesus reflected in the quality of one's love.

The later Johannine letters attest that this ideal for Christian community was, in fact, unrealizable without some concrete structures for ministry and some more specific formulations of conduct and ethical norms. Nevertheless, the commandment of love remained at the core of Johannine faith.

The Christian Mission, Pauline Christianity, and Beyond

The rapid spread of Christianity from Palestine to the whole of the Mediterranean world is a phenomenon unexplainable except by the powerful attraction of the good news proclaimed by Christian missionaries. Their message promised that faith in the Risen Jesus, and baptism in his name, brought freedom, forgiveness, and the possibility of new life in the community of believers, the body of Christ. The Acts of the Apostles as well as Paul's own letters attribute this extraordinary success of the Christian mission to the power of the Spirit which, as Acts 2 narrates, was poured out in that great Pentecost event. The prophecy of Joel 3:1-2 was at last realized.

No figure dominates the story of the Christian mission more than Paul of Tarsus. Pharisee turned follower of Christ, Paul's leadership and influence on the beginnings of Christianity are enormous. Because of the revelation Paul received of the Risen Christ on the Damascus road, he was radically transformed from an energetic Jewish Pharisee to a missionary disciple of Christ. The resurrection of Jesus was proof for Paul that the new age had begun, that new creation which Isaiah promised was indeed at hand. Christ was the "first fruits," the "down payment" but soon all would follow and be gathered together to God.

In the interim Christians themselves were empowered by the Spirit, for they were Christ's body. This identity conveyed a holiness and righteousness before God that the Law could not provide, and one which they must therefore safeguard. Christians were bound to live their lives in imitation of Christ and invited to celebrate their oneness in the Lord's supper as they awaited his final coming in their midst. Paul's letters are filled with wisdom and advice for these fledging communities not to lose hope in Christ's coming again (Thessalonians), not to give in to lives of slavery to the law (Galatians), and not to put false hope in spiritual elitism but to demonstrate in all things a communal concern based in an ethic of love (1 Corinthians).

Paul recognized the role of leadership in the community but grounded such activity in the gifts of the Spirit given to the community for the common good of all. Paul was a product of his own time and his writings convey the socially conservative rhetoric of one who accepted the basic structures of society without challenge. He benefitted himself from the patronage and support of many wealthy Christians, for example Gaius (Rom 16:23) and Stephanus (1 Cor 16:15).

Paul's gospel was rooted in the Cross of Christ and the mystery of life through death that it symbolized. All of Paul's writings expressed the urgency that marked his life—the conviction that the time was short and the Lord was very near. In the generations after Paul the Christian communities focused to a greater degree in ways to accommodate themselves to the secular world while at the same time maintaining their Christian identity. They concerned themselves with establishing institutional structures that could support the growth of the community, and with formulating their beliefs about the Christ.

Revelation and the Enduring Vision of the End Time

The last book of the NT canon, the Book of Revelation, draws on the tradition of apocalyptic images and prophetic visions in an effort to address the suffering Christian communities of Asia Minor at the end of the first century. Its perspective views the political power of the Roman Empire as a "beast" to be battled and resisted by Christians. To die at the hands of this "beast" is ultimate victory, for martyrdom unites one with Christ, the victorious lamb that was slain.

In its final chapters, the Book of Revelation offers a picture of the end time that echoes Isaiah's dream of the new heaven and the new earth (Isa 65:17). But in the vision of Revelation the new Jerusalem descends from on high to this world, making the whole of creation the temple of God's presence. The seer claims that justice reigns in this city, for God will "wipe away every tear . . ., and there shall be no more death or mourning" (Rev 21:4). Nevertheless, the future envisioned by this prophet of God is yet to be achieved.

CONCLUSION

The richness of the biblical tradition is like a great mosaic whose tiny pieces, taken together, produce a masterpiece. Only in its totality and diversity can this mosaic be truly revelatory of God. However, the humanness of its expressions, the limits as well as the power of its language and metaphors, are everywhere apparent to the reader. The Bible cannot capture or contain the God it proclaims, it can only convey the faith of others and challenge us to find our own.

BARBARA E. BOWE, R.S.C.J.

Biblical Interpretation Through the Ages

The interpretation of the Christian Bible during the past two millennia relates the story of the Bible's forming believers and the believers' shaping and filtering of the message of the Bible. This act of interpretation is an interchange between the reader and the sacred text within a particular historical context. The sacred text, through which the living God instructs and empowers the believers, communicates eternal, divine truths by means of human language and according to the limitations and constraints of the process by which humans communicate. This survey of the history of interpretation of the Bible will be divided into four periods: (1) the early Church, (2) the Middle Ages, (3) the Reformation to the Enlightenment, and (4) Critical Method in the nineteenth and twentieth centuries.

EARLY CHURCH

In the apostolic and post-apostolic ages, the Christian communities sought to understand who Jesus was through the interpretation of the events of his life and of OT prophecies. The preaching of the apostles drew upon OT texts (e.g., Psalms 2; 110) which identified Jesus as the Messiah. Credal formulae capsulized the saving significance of Jesus' death and resurrection. A collection of Jesus' sayings (Q—Quelle) formed a primary source for the Gospel accounts. The crowning achievement of the interpretive process of the Church of the first two centuries was the composition of the Gospels and Letters. An important result of this process of reflection and writing of the early Church was that it helped to clarify the early Christians' identity.

By 140 CE, the NT writings as we know them were complete. But until the latter part of the fourth century, the Church did not officially recognize these twenty-seven writings as constituting a closed collection.

Such a canonical corpus emerged as the early Church responded to threats from Gnostic groups which forced it to identify those writings that were useful for upbuilding the community, were of apostolic origin, or were in conformity with the "rule of faith."

The Gnostic Marcion's (ca. 85–160 CE) limitation of sacred Christian writings to ten letters of Paul and a shortened version of the Gospel of Luke provoked a response from Christian communities which treasured the OT and the other NT writings. Marcion's attack against OT portrayals of the wrath of God and the other NT writings as insufficiently spiritual revealed his adherence to the Gnostic doctrine of matter as evil. The balance for the Christian between reverence for creation and hope in a destiny transcending death ran the risk of slipping into a Gnostic-like, world-denying asceticism. Thus, the identification of writings in conformity with the rule or standard of the faith, coupled with a faithful interpretation of them, enabled Christian communities to learn and be strengthened by the Word of God. The rule of faith functioned as a negative principle that identified those writings which undermined the faith, but it did not presume to capsulize the multivalent mystery of faith in propositional form.

By the end of the second century CE, the canonical writings began to appear in the format of a list. This list was not promulgated by Church councils in the East or West until the end of the fourth century. But during the second to the fourth centuries, the twenty-seven canonical writings were being read within liturgical, catechetical, and school settings. The aim of the interpreters was primarily theological and was closely related to the moral and spiritual concerns of the interpreter's audience. Although aware of the historical dimension of these writings and the events related therein, the early Christian interpreters were not preoccupied with discovering the meaning that the original authors of these canonical writings intended.

The principle that the rule of faith should guide the interpretation of Scripture was first articulated by Irenaeus. His interpretive framework saw the OT as prophetic of Christ and Christ as summing up the future. Irenaeus' form of typological exegesis at times resembled allegorization. Thus, the conflict between the allegorical exegesis of Alexandria and the literal exegesis of Antioch was implicit in Irenaeus' scheme of reconciling the two Testaments with reference to Christ's headship.

The distinction between Alexandrian and Antiochene exegesis is most evident by contrasting the work of Origen (ca. 185–251) with that of Theodore of Mopsuestia (ca. 350–428). Origen, one of the foremost scholars of the early Church who did extensive text critical work in preparing the Hexapla, is primarily concerned with the hidden or spiritual meaning of Scripture, while Theodore searches out the literal, narrative meaning prior to launching into typological or symbolic interpretations. Origen searched out the spiritual or heavenly meaning of texts when (1) the literal meaning contradicted commonsense or reason, (2) the text portrayed the God of the OT as less ethical than the God of the NT, (3) the anthropomorphic or metaphoric God-language demanded a figurative interpretation, or (4) the linkage between events and characters of the OT and NT could best be effected on the level of the spiritual meaning. Theodore, on the other hand, saw the two Testaments as distinct dispensations wherein God addressed humans in their particular circumstances. For example, Moses' lifting his arms at the battle with Amalek is an action primarily linked with the Israelite battle plan rather than shaped in a hidden way as a symbol of Christ's crucifixion. While Origen tends to dissolve the Hebrew Scriptures within the NT, Theodore tries to keep the two Testaments distinct, except for types within the OT which foreshadow NT events and personages.

Theodore's interpretation of John's Gospel accents his reluctance to depart from the literal interpretation of the narrative into the hidden meaning (theoria). John's account of the cleansing of the Temple takes place at the beginning of Jesus' ministry (John 2:13-22), whereas in the Synoptics this event occurs just prior to his arrest (Mark 11:15-19). Theodore holds firmly to the historicity of the Johannine order on the basis of the fact that John includes many historical details absent from the Synoptic accounts. By contrast, Origen, who treasures John's Gospel as the "spiritual" Gospel, is more disposed to solve contradictions between John and the Synoptics by appealing to the hidden, spiritual meaning: the level which he regarded as revealing more significant truth.

Other notable interpreters of the early Church fell between the extremes mapped out by Origen and Theodore. Although Jerome (340–420) employed both literal and spiritual exegesis, his training by Apollinarus of Laodicea led him to be more attentive to the literal, historical level of narratives. However, Augustine (354–430) was only able to become a Christian when he found the allegorical method. It equipped him with the tools for combating the Manicheans who, for example, dismissed such OT figures as the patriarchs because of their immoralities (e.g., polygamy, lying). Augustine exhorted interpreters to discern the mind of the sacred writers under the guidance of the law of love and the tradition of the Church.

As a whole the early Church writers were primarily concerned about the application of scriptural principles to theological, moral, and spiritual issues. The detailed application of these principles occupied early Church writers rather than an antiquarian goal of discovering what the authors intended to communicate to their original audiences. An important objective for Clement and Origen was to make the Christian message intellectually respectable to the Alexandrian populace of their day. Their translation of the Platonic quest for truth into the arena of scriptural interpretation became a basis upon which Scripture could be interpreted for its own sake; such interpretation without a precisely defined moral or spiritual goal could be formative of believers and lead them to a fuller participation in the mystery of God.

In the transition to the early Middle Ages, the four senses to be found regularly in scriptural passages were summarized by John Cassian (d. 435): (1) the historical, (2) the allegorical, (3) the anagogical, and (4) the tropological or moral. The four senses are most clearly exemplified by reference to the city of Jerusalem in Galatians 4:21-31: (1) the historical = the city of Jerusalem, (2) the allegorical = the Church of Christ, (3) the anagogical = the heavenly city which is the mother of us all, and (4) the tropological or moral = the human soul. Although the usual practice was only to search out the historical and allegorical senses, each passage could have a multiplicity of meanings. Most theologians of the first millennium regarded Scripture as functioning symbolically like a medieval cathedral, for within its pages lay hidden God's Word whose richness could not be adequately communicated by human words.

MIDDLE AGES

With the age of doctrinal controversy behind them, interpreters in the early Middle Ages, such as Gregory the Great (Pope from 590–604), could rely on the foundational credal formulations and so focus their attention on the moral and spiritual dimensions of the scriptural texts. Gregory imagined the interpretive enterprise as analogous to the construction of a building: one first lays the historical foundation and then pursues the typical sense in order to strengthen one's faith; finally, the moral teaching graces the entire structure. Gregory conceived of the Scriptures as a school for training in the love of God and one's neighbors.

As the rule of faith became more focussed by credal formulations and as the tradition of intepretation grew, many commentators, such as Bede (d. 735), came to be mediators and synthesizers of the learning of previous great commentators. The interpretations assumed the form of glosses and catenae which were penciled in the margins or between the lines of the scriptural text. The glosses were notations to assist the memory of the teacher; the catenae were chains of interpretation of a passage drawn from the early Church writers. In the early Middle Ages through the Carolingian revival (ninth through eleventh centuries), such interpretation was carried out upon the Vulgate text within monasteries and cathedral schools.

In the monastic cloister, the practice of divine reading (*lectio divina*) ideally proceeded through four stages: from reading to meditation to prayer to contemplation. The contemplative milieu in which *lectio divina* was practiced established a more leisurely, measured pace to the interpretive enterprise than was found in the cathedral schools. Since the cathedral schools were charged with improving the education of the clergy, the focus of their work was more vocational than contemplative. To equip a cleric with the necessary information and doctrines for leading a parish, the Scripture instructors needed to be more systematic in their interpretation than their monastic counterparts. For monastic commentaries rarely covered a scriptural book from beginning to end. The primary goal of interpretation for a monastic such as Gregory the Great was to come to greater love of God and one's neighbor by meditative reading of God's Word.

The cathedral schools grew in influence during the twelfth to the fifteenth centuries. Increasing attention was paid to establishing the correct text and translation. In the Abbey of St. Victor in Paris, Hugh (d. 1141) set out to learn Hebrew in order to pay closer attention to the literal, historical sense. For example, in his interpretation of messianic prophecy, Hugh claimed that the prophet addressed his words to his own historical situation but that his words also pointed to the coming of Christ: a level of meaning in Scripture akin to the modern notion of *sensus plenior* (i.e., the fuller meaning of words or phrases known to the divine author but not to the human author at the time of writing). Hugh's disciple, Andrew, was successful in mastering Hebrew; he also conceived of the biblical authors as researchers and recipients of traditions rather than as mere amanuenses of the divine author in a purely mechanical fashion.

The cathedral schools also promoted the practice of recording in the glosses "Questions" about contradictions or other textual problems. These questions later were circulated independently. The development of these questions was fostered by the dialectical model of learning practiced in the liberal arts. Students were encouraged to ask questions rather than to be mere docile recipients of information. The contrast between the interpretive methods of the monastic cloister and the cathedral school was immortalized in the disputations between Bernard of Clairvaux (1090–1193) and Peter Abelard (1079–1142). Bernard espoused contemplation as the primary goal of scriptural interpretation whereas Abelard focused upon the tensions which existed between church doctrine and biblical revelation. Abelard argued that the biblical interpreter must employ subtle logic in order to grasp the truth of biblical revelation.

The rediscovery of Aristotle in twelfth century Europe posed a challenge to the Platonic framework which had supported the allegorical interpretation of Scripture. In Platonic realism the truth lay hidden behind the earthly shadows: an approach to truth supportive of a symbolic understanding of reality. By contrast, Aristotelian nominalism located the essence of a thing within the thing itself rather than in some imaginary world of forms. The Aristotelian approach supported the renewed emphasis upon the literal sense in the twelfth century. By the thirteenth century, Aquinas located the original intention of the author in the literal sense even if the author was employing metaphors or speaking in the genres of prophecy or parable.

The mendicant orders of Franciscans and Dominicans promoted greater attention to the literal sense by developing biblical concordances, dictionaries, and geographies of Palestine. Such data-gathering, greatly facilitated by numbering the chapters of the biblical books, enabled commentators to explore problems more fully upon the literal level before resorting to solutions on the allegorical level. Perhaps as a consequence of the Dominicans' mission of combating popular heretical preachers, Aquinas focused upon the literal sense and argued that there was no multiplicity of meanings for a given passage. For scholastics like Aquinas, Scripture had become a tool which assisted in moving into problems of logic and theology, the area which challenged their intellectual creativity in place of the earlier practice of propounding multiple allegorical meanings.

In the high Middle Ages, questions began to arise over the relationship of scriptural to ecclesiastical authority. William of Ockham (1285–1347) argued that theological truth cannot be reached by logical deduction from the propositions of Scripture but must be derived from the tradition of the Church. Such a stance gave free rein to papal decretals and thus encouraged greater centralization of the Church. From this same period, John Wycliffe (1330–1384) contended that there were no real contradictions within the biblical text. If correctly interpreted, the biblical account of the world could stand together with the philosophical. This understanding undergirded the belief to emerge fully at the time of the Reformation that Scripture was authoritative and all-sufficient apart from the ecclesiastical tradition.

THE REFORMATION TO THE ENLIGHTENMENT

The cornerstone of Luther's reform movement was the doctrine of justification by faith: i.e., the individual believer could stand upright before God by means of the salvation freely bestowed through Jesus' death and resurrection. Emphasis upon the freedom of conscience and the private judgment of the individual led to a marked shift in human self-understanding. The emphasis which Luther placed upon the individual's responsibility to decide for Christ by hearing the Word shifted authority to the individual, away from the communitarian basis for biblical intepretation, which had been the practice in the early Church and in the monastic traditions.

In order to gather individuals into a community of believers, it was essential that they hear the summons of the Word. Luther espoused the search for a simple, solid literal sense of a scriptural passage which would call individuals to faith. Although he disallowed the multiple means spawned by the allegorical method, Luther maintained a Christological goal as the fulfillment of the OT history of faith. Also he discovered examples of gospel and law in the OT. Thus, Luther maintained the importance of the OT for Christian theology even though he interpreted it historically.

The capacity to examine the literal sense of Scripture was further enhanced by the philological accomplishments of the Christian humanists. Most notable among them was Erasmus (1469–1536) who was responsible for establishing the Greek text whose later editions became known as the Textus Receptus. This text underlay the venerable King James translation. These philological efforts focused attention not merely upon the literal sense but also upon the fact that the more original text should form the basis of an authoritative translation. In the Counterreform, the Council of Trent designated an official version of the Vulgate as authoritative for Roman Catholics. The Protestant Second Helvetic Confession (1566) required belief in the divine inspiration of the traditional Hebrew text; but the French Oratorian priest, Richard Simon (1638–1712), opposed this identification of the traditional Hebrew text as the true text and argued for the task of reconstructing and revocalizing the text on the basis of manuscript evidence.

In the seventeenth and eighteenth centuries, reason gained its autonomy vis-à-vis the authority of Scripture. The roles were reversed such that Scripture was credible for many only to the extent that it could defend itself on rational grounds. For interpreters in the Middle Ages, the primitive, barbarous incidents contained in the OT demanded a justification. But in the seventeenth century, under the questioning of the deists, believers were further expected to provide a rational explanation for phenomena such as miracles. Descartes' dictum that truth can be reached only through methodical doubt was *prima facie* inimical to the reception of truth through revelation. This methodical doubt lay at the heart of the scientific, empirical method. When such a method was applied to history so as to examine the truth-value and meaning of documentary evidence, then the question arose how matters of faith would ever surface in a method which denied the reality of anything that could not verify itself before the tribune of reason. Unqualified positivism was hostile to the faith. However, the historical-critical method could be harnessed in the service of the faith if the excesses of skepticism could be curbed. Under such conditions then, it is understandable that there was a necessary tension between historical and theological exegesis: if the voice of one becomes too strong, that of the other will be muffled through neglect.

In the eighteenth century, questions were raised about the unity of authorship of the Pentateuch. The Jewish and Christian traditions had maintained that Moses was the author of the Pentateuch. However in 1753, Jean Astruc, a physician at the court of Louis XIV, argued that the Pentateuch consisted of two distinct memoirs which could be distinguished on the basis of the usage of divine names. The German Orientalist, J. D. Michaelis (1717–1791), likewise criticized Mosaic authorship of the Pentateuch as he researched the ancient Israelite social world which produced the Pentateuchal legislation. The critical examination of the

OT reflected the fact that the OT had lost its place in Christian theology and thus could be examined like any other ancient document. By searching for the sources of a document and tracing out the history of its formation, scholars could provide rational explanations to skeptical deists for problematic features of texts.

Critical Method in the Nineteenth through the Twentieth Centuries

The German university of the nineteenth century provided a milieu free of the control of the Church for the implementation of the historical-critical method. This method was not a radical innovation but rather was continuous with the increasing emphasis placed upon the literal sense of Scripture by the scholastics in the twelfth century. However, the modern context, in which the natural sciences began to command respect, set faith and reason at loggerheads such that the untrammeled exercise of reason could undermine faith.

De Wette (1780–1849) is regarded as the founder of the historical-critical method for biblical scholarship. He urged the examination of the literary character of biblical books and the discovery of the intellectual milieu and social circumstances of the author. The discovery of sources and attention to their authorship would lead to the reconstruction of the history of the text. This source-critical approach was applied to the Pentateuch by Reuss (1804–1891) and by K. H. Graf (1815–1869). But the classic formulation of the documentary hypothesis came from Julius Wellhausen (1844–1918). He identified and dated four documents which came together over the course of Israel's history to form the Pentateuch: the Jahwist (870 BCE), the Elohist (770 BCE), the Deuteronomist (621 BCE), and the Priestly Writer (550 BCE). The general outline of Wellhausen's documentary hypothesis has survived to the present.

In the NT, the source-critical method has been applied to the Synoptic Gospels to sort out the literary relationships between these three documents. After charting out these relationships, two questions present themselves: (1) Was Mark or Matthew written first? (2) Did Luke use Matthew? The two leading solutions to the Synoptic problem answer these questions in opposite ways. J. J. Griesbach (1745–1912) hypothesized that Matthew was the first Gospel written and was used by Luke; then Mark conflated and abbreviated Matthew and Luke in writing his Gospel. The other solution, also formulated in the nineteenth century, was proposed by H. J. Holtzmann (1863) as the Two-Source Theory. This solution argues that Mark was written first and that Luke and Matthew did not know one another's work but that they both used Mark and a collection of Jesus' sayings known as Q.

The effort to reconstruct the history of the text so as to know more clearly the relationship of the text to the events and persons it purports to describe received a new direction from the method known as form-history or form criticism. Introduced by H. Gunkel (1862–1932) in his work on the patriarchal narratives of Genesis, form-history seeks to identify oral and literary forms and genres which then may be linked to particular settings in which they typically functioned. For example, a lament psalm has a typical structure and tone; its life setting is one of misfortune or disorientation for an individual who brings his or her troubles before God in the sanctuary. The identification of a genre such as a NT parable allows one to move behind the Gospel text and reconstruct an oral stage of transmission of the parable as preached by Jesus to its incorporation into the written Gospel text. In the NT, M. Dibelius (1883–1947) and R. Bultmann (1884–1976) stand out as leading contributors to the development and application of this method to the Gospels. The form critical method as applied to the Synoptic Gospels has regularly resulted in the identification of three stages or levels in the tradition: (1) the life-setting of Jesus, (2) the life-setting of the early Church, and (3) the life-setting of the evangelist. Unfortunately for many Gospel passages, the reconstruction of these three stages must remain hypothetical.

The application of form criticism to the Bible has often resulted in attention being focused on small units, resulting in the atomization of the text. Regarding the final composition as more than a compilation of disparate pieces glued together, W. Marxen promoted in Gospel research a method known as redaction criticism. The redactor or editor is not a mindless compiler but is rather an author with an ideology and techniques to guide the process of composition. This method has been profitably applied to the books of the NT and OT alike.

In an attempt to bring together the historical method and the theological dimensions of the OT traditions, G. von Rad composed two volumes of his *Old Testament Theology* in which he traced out not only the history of the religion of the Israelite community but also the story of the confession of the faith of this community. The conjoining of critical history with kerygmatic history represents an effort to write an OT theology which can present its case before the tribune of critical reason and yet can be nurturing of the faith of the believing community.

In the NT, Bultmann sought to present a kerygmatic theology which would prove credible to a skeptical modern audience. His demythologization program sought to remove time-conditioned elements of the ancient worldview which he judged not to be essential to the gospel message but which proved to be a stumbling block to many of his contemporaries' accepting the gospel. This process of demythologizing has been criticized as reductionistic. Also Bultmann's radical skepticism regarding the historicity of the Gospel traditions has been challenged for emphasizing the Christ of faith to such an extent that the Jesus of history appears to be of little or no consequence. In his concern about the composition of the traditions contained in the Gospel narratives, Bultmann ascribed considerable creativity to the Church and the evangelists. He maintained then that the picture we have of Jesus stems, for the most

part, from the memory of the believing community rather than from "objective" historical reporting.

The unavoidable subjectivity which enters into the reconstruction of the history of biblical traditions has led some interpreters to question whether the authority of Scripture has been subtly shifted from the canonical biblical text to the scholar's reconstruction of the history of the tradition or the milieu in which the text purportedly was created. B. Childs has championed an approach to the biblical text which he labels "canonical." Rather than being another form of criticism on par with form or redaction criticism, "canonical criticism" is simply an approach which demands that primary attention be paid to the final redaction of the biblical text rather than to the stages by which the text might have come into existence. Childs endorses the historical method, but wishes to qualify its efforts by dogmatically claiming at the outset that the final form of the text has more truth-value for the believing community than any strata which can reasonably be shown to be nearer to the event or person described. One problem which Childs' approach seeks to alleviate is the propensity of the historical method to ignore or suppress theological questions.

James Sanders' version of canonical criticism locates the canonical principle within the historical process by which the text came into existence. He attempts to explicate the dynamics of canonical authority by recreating the interchange between the authoritative oral or written word and the community which lies at the heart of the formation of a tradition. He does not single out the final redactional level as the authoritative text.

Efforts of historians to understand the milieu which influenced the original author in composing a text have been assisted by the methods and findings of sociologists, anthropologists, and other social scientists. Many biblical documents directly supply information about the political and religious dimensions of the situations they describe, but they frequently either neglect or conceal information about the everyday life of the people. By the use of social scientific method and of comparative data from ancient and contemporary societies, much light can be shed on the social structure and function of ancient societies. Recent studies on ecstatic behavior and role theory are examples of how social science has assisted in understanding the role of the OT prophet. Also studies in genealogies and in Marxist theory have brought to light previously unrecognized aspects of ancient Israelite society.

DALE LAUNDERVILLE, O.S.B.

Archaeology and Biblical Interpretation

Biblical archaeology is a scholarly discipline that has made significant contributions to the study of the Bible. As the methods of excavation and interpretation become more sophisticated there is potential for even greater contributions. Archaeology provides a picture of the cultural setting in which the biblical tradition emerged. Excavation of sites in the Middle East has yielded texts and inscriptions that make it possible to view ancient Israel against its ancient Near Eastern cultural background. Excavation projects in Palestine have broken out of their narrow historical interest and have helped to provide a more complete picture of ancient Israel, early Judaism, and early Christianity than literary sources alone. The literary sources represent the perspectives of an elite group while the material remains can help create a more balanced and accurate view.

THE DISCIPLINE OF BIBLICAL ARCHAEOLOGY

The Task of Biblical Archaeology

Biblical archaeology is the branch of biblical studies that uses the results of relevant archaeological research to illuminate the world of the Bible. The biblical writers provide a theological explanation for the events that they narrate. The contribution of archaeology is to provide the cultural and social setting of the biblical stories. Once biblical archaeology was narrowly historical in its orientation. Its focus was on the reconstruction of the political history of ancient Israel. The objective of most excavations was to establish the chronology of sites to support the historical value of the biblical narratives.

Under the influence of New World archaeology, biblical archaeology has broadened its concerns beyond chronology to the sociology, economy, politics, ecosystems, and population patterns to reconstruct the entire culture of ancient Palestine from the prehistoric era down to the end of the Byzantine period (seventh century CE). Accompanying this shift in interest, biblical archaeologists have employed improved techniques of retrieval, recording, and analysis of data. The stratigraphic method of excavation developed in the 1950s has now been supplemented by scientifically more sophisticated procedures of excavation and interpretation. One result of this scientific sophistication is the interdisciplinary approach of archaeology today. Besides field archaeologists, excavation projects often employ specialists from the natural and social sciences.

Assumptions Behind Biblical Archaeology

The development of the technical side of archaeological method has been accompanied by important changes in the presuppositions with which biblical archaeologists have approached their work. Archaeology deals with the material remains of antiquity. The Bible is one of antiquity's literary legacies. In the past, data that came from the former were seen as providing an independent and objective support for the latter with the implication that faith was either dependent upon or perhaps enhanced by a demonstration that the events narrated in the Bible actually happened. Today biblical archaeologists see the complementary relationship that exists between the literary and nonliterary sources of knowledge of the biblical era and its people. They excavate not to prove the historicity of biblical narratives but to explain the meaning of these texts by understanding the people who produced, received, and transmitted them. This understanding is provided by the interpretation of the material remains that these people left behind.

Because of the narrower interests of early archaeologists, sites with connections to the

Hebrew Scriptures were once the prime focus of attention. Because of the theological concerns that have characterized NT research it was believed that archaeology could have little more than tangential value for understanding the beginnings of the Christian movement; as a result, NT archaeology scarcely qualified for the status of an academic discipline. Similarly the wealth of literary sources from early Judaism seemed to make excavation of Jewish sites an unnecessary luxury. Today some of the most productive archaeological research under way is connected with sites from the Roman and Byzantine periods that witnessed the development of rabbinic Judaism and the early Church. The historian of early Judaism and Christianity can no longer depend solely on written sources since archaeology has provided so much new data. The new information provided by archaeological research must be evaluated and studied as seriously as have been the literary sources.

The Nature of Biblical Archaeology

The most noteworthy area of discussion among archaeologists in recent years has been focused on the very nature of the discipline. William G. Dever has called for an end to what he considers the domination of archaeology by biblical studies. Dever believes this is necessary so that archaeology develops its own identity as an academic discipline so that it will be able to reach its own wider goals without having its agenda set by biblical studies. He further suggests that scholars abandon the term "biblical archaeology" for "Syro-Palestinian archaeology" to eliminate any possible misunderstanding of the archaeological enterprise as serving to enhance the Bible's credibility. The term "Syro-Palestinian archaeology" carries no theological freight.

Dever defines Syro-Palestinian archaeology as that branch of general archaeology that deals with the geographical, cultural, and chronological entity that embraced the land bridge between Egypt and Mesopo-

tamia with a succession of cultures from the middle of the fourth millennium BCE to the end of the Byzantine period (seventh century CE). He considers archaeology to be a secular, academic discipline whose assumptions, methods, and goals are determined by archaeology itself rather than by the concerns of religious belief or even biblical scholarship. While some of Dever's colleagues consider his suggestion regarding the name of their enterprise to be merely a semantic exercise, Dever considers it vital to ensure that archaeology achieve an independence that is necessary to the scholarly maturation of the discipline whose purpose should be to understand the phenomenon of cultural process and change.

The Contributions of Biblical Archaeology

Although Dever calls for the end to what he sees as biblical studies' domination of archaeology, he nonetheless believes that archaeology has much to contribute to biblical studies. Dever describes five general areas within which archaeology can make significant contributions. First, by recovering the remains of many ancient Near Eastern peoples, archaeology provides many opportunities for cross-cultural comparison. Second, archaeology can provide a cultural context for events narrated in the Bible in a way that these narratives cannot do themselves. Third, archaeology's recovery of the material remains of ancient cultures provides a supplement to the literary remains already available. Fourth, archaeology sometimes provides a perspective different from the literary texts making possible a more balanced view of events narrated in the Bible. Fifth, archaeology sometimes provides data that can aid the interpretation of an obscure text.

More than any other field of study, archaeology has made it possible for people to recognize how ancient cultures conditioned the human expression of the word of God. Excavations have shown that the form in which we encounter divine revelation is time-conditioned. It is possible to recognize the way of the human dimension of the word of God only if one is familiar with that human dimension. Archaeology uncovers that human dimension through the excavation and interpretation of the material remains of the ancient societies of the biblical period.

TEXTS, DOCUMENTS AND INSCRIPTIONS

Archaeological excavations in the Middle East have shown that the Israelites lived, wrote, and thought in ways similar to the peoples that surrounded them. During excavations in Syria from 1964 to 1976, an important cultural center from the third millennium came to light: the city of Ebla. The principal find was the city's archives. Archaeologists recovered almost seventeen thousand tablets. Though little more than preliminary work has been done in the interpretation of these tablets, it is obvious that they will have a major impact on our understanding of the history, religion, and culture of the ancient Near East of the Early Bronze Age (3150–2200 BCE). The language of Ebla is related to ancient Hebrew; therefore, the Ebla tablets may become an important source for understanding biblical Hebrew. Many words appear only once in the Hebrew Bible. The Ebla texts may be helpful in learning the meaning of some of these more obscure words.

Biblical interpreters are confident about the potential contribution of the Ebla archives to our understanding of biblical Hebrew because of their experience with the tablets found early in this century at Ras Shamra, the site of the ancient city of Ugarit. This city on the Mediterranean coast north of Palestine flourished from 2000 to 1200 BCE. The tablets found there date from the fourteenth century BCE—some two hundred years before the appearance of ancient Israel. The tablets from Ugarit have been of immense help in understanding Hebrew poetry. Ugaritic parallels have illumined obscure passages, especially in the psalms and in Job.

The Ugaritic texts also preserved the Canaanite myths of the Baal cycle along with other Canaanite religious texts. These stories of ancient Canaan have helped interpreters understand the allusions in the Bible to the non-Yahwistic religious traditions of the region. It is now apparent how ancient Israel's beliefs were forged in contact with these religious traditions.

Other finds in the Eastern Mediterranean region have contributed to more nuanced appreciation of the biblical tradition. For example, texts from Mari, an eighteenth century BCE site on the Euphrates, have contributed to our understanding of the phenomenon of prophecy in the ancient Near East. Further east along the Tigris River is the site of ancient Nuzi. This site flourished in the sixteenth and fifteenth centuries BCE. Its texts revealed ancient Near Eastern customs and legal practices that biblical traditions reflect. Excavations in the territory of the second millennium Hittite Empire in Asia Minor uncovered texts that help us understand the biblical covenant. The way that the Bible describes ancient Israel's covenant with God resembles the pattern of Hittite treaties. Finally, archives found at the fourteenth-century site of Amarna in Egypt describe the political, social, and military chaos that reigned in Canaan just before the arrival of the Israelite people. These texts make several references to the "Hapiru," people with loyalties to established political and social entities. The emergence of the Hapiru people in Canaan may represent a preliminary stage in a process that eventually ended with the Israelite settlement in Canaan.

Unfortunately Palestine has not yielded the number of inscriptional and documentary finds attested elsewhere in the Near East. The most important of these is the stele of Mesha, king of Moab. The stele describes the defeat of Israel by the Moabites in 840 BCE from the perspective of the Moabites. (See 1 Kgs 3:1-27 for the biblical point of view.) The text inscribed on the stele shows that the Moabites' conception of their god Chemosh was similar in some ways to the Israelite conception of Yahweh. Another inscription from the biblical period in Israel is one found in the Siloam tunnel. It describes how the tunnel was dug (see 2 Kgs 20:20).

The textual finds from Palestine would be few and unimportant compared with those from other areas in the ancient Near East were it not for the Dead Sea Scrolls. The discovery of these scrolls in 1947 was the single most important find relating to the Bible.

The finds from Qumran help illuminate Palestinian Judaism in the period just before the birth of Jesus. Another cache of manuscripts found about the same time in Egypt help clarify the first centuries of Church history. The finds come from the town of Nag Hammadi along the Nile in central Egypt. They comprise some 1240 pages of material written in Coptic that reflect the beliefs of Christian gnostics of the second and third centuries CE. One of these works, the Gospel of Thomas, contains sayings of Jesus in a more primitive form than in the canonical gospels. These may preserve memories of Jesus not in the NT.

ARCHAEOLOGY AND THE OLD TESTAMENT

The work of biblical archaeologists is complicated because they turn up few texts or inscriptions from the biblical period. Biblical archaeology is silent for the most part. This calls for interpretive skills from those who uncover material remains from biblical sites. Interpretation of material remains involves a much more complex and expensive set of procedures than the interpretation of texts. The way archaeologists interpret these material remains depends in part on the interests and theological orientation of archaeologists.

For example, at one point in the development of biblical archaeology the question of history was paramount. Some archaeologists were convinced that archaeology could support the historicity of the biblical narratives about the settlement of the Is-

raelite tribes in Canaan. The biblical stories themselves (the Books of Joshua and Judges) present different pictures of how the Israelites came to possess the land. Historians have developed different hypotheses. Archaeology would settle the issue. Unfortunately this did not happen.

Excavations that took place from 1950 to 1972 produced evidence that both supports and contradicts the biblical material. While the Bible says that the Israelite tribes camped at Kadesh Barnea before entering Canaan (Num 33:16-36; Deut 1:45), archaeology can provide no evidence that people lived at this site before the time of David. The Book of Joshua describes the fall of Jericho and Ai (Joshua 2–8), but archaeological evidence shows that there was no major city at Jericho at the time the Israelites entered Canaan and that Ai was unoccupied from the third millennium until later than 1200 BCE. On the other hand, the Bible says that both Lachish (Josh 10:31-32) and Hazor (Josh 11:11) were destroyed violently. Archaeology supports this but cannot identify the Israelites as those responsible for the destruction.

These results were problems for those who believed with George E. Wright that "in biblical faith everything depends on whether the central events actually occurred." What archaeology of the settlement has done is to help move biblical theology from the "recital of the acts of God" to an evaluation of biblical speech about God. Archaeology has shown that a conception of biblical theology as "history interpreted by faith" is based on dogmatic not historical grounds. The task of biblical theology is to consider how the Bible portrays God. It then clarifies the meaning and truth claims of this biblical portrait from a modern critical perspective. Archaeology has its contribution to make in this task. It can offer some help in clarifying how the Bible portrays God.

Even if archaeology could prove that every biblical narrative were historically reliable, still this would not exhaust the meaning of these narratives. Biblical narratives were intended to serve other functions. The stories of the conquest served as motivation for ethical conduct. They were probably associated with the liturgical celebration of Israel's acquisition of its land. They formed part of a larger work whose concern was to provide a religious explanation for the fall of Jerusalem and the exile of some Judahites to Babylon. In these and other functions of the stories of the settlement, historicity is not an issue. The value of these narratives, then, is not properly understood if people read them as historiography whose accuracy is provable through archaeology.

For more than a century the general goal of archaeological investigation in Palestine had as its primary purpose the correlation of literary with nonliterary or material remains to support, correct, and supplement the supposed historiography of the Bible. This aim has been at least partially successful, but there can be another purpose for archaeology.

The Bible is the product of elite groups in ancient Israel. The focus of the biblical traditions is on public happenings, great political events, and the deed of prominent figures like leading priests, kings, and prophets. Almost completely lacking in the Bible are the reminiscences and reflections of private people. There is little in the Bible like diaries, biographies, journals, and other literary forms that can give us some hint of what ordinary people thought of their religious traditions and how they lived their lives. Here is where archaeology can be very helpful. Excavation of domestic and industrial buildings, the recovery and analysis of tools, pottery, pollens, and the examination of jewelry and other domestic artifacts can begin to fill the gaps left by the biblical tradition.

For example, Tirzah, once the capital of the northern kingdom, produced evidence of two types of domestic buildings. There was unmistakable evidence of larger homes for the rich and the more simple structures for the poor. This not only shows that there was some town planning in the cities of an-

cient Israel but also that there was social stratification in ancient Israelite society.

Another area where archaeology can be very helpful is in the reconstruction of the liturgy of ancient Israel. Earlier purely literary studies stressed the unique features of ancient Israelite religion. Again dogmatic concerns were responsible for this approach. People assumed that the locus of divine revelation was in those elements that differentiated the religion of ancient Israel from the religion of its neighbors. The results of archaeology have shifted the focus to those features that ancient Israel shared with other ancient Near Eastern religions in general and with the Canaanite religion of the Late Bronze Age (1550–1200 BCE) in particular.

Archaeology of public and domestic shrines confirms that many ancient Israelites revered other deities, specifically Canaanite fertility gods. Among these were Asherah, the "Mother Goddess." Artifacts discovered at Kuntillet 'Ajrud suggest that some people thought of Asherah as Yahweh's consort while other Israelites thought of her as the consort of Baal, the Canaanite storm god. Until the Exile, Asherah and Baal were potent rivals of Yahweh for the loyalty of the Israelites. On a popular level, the claims of Canaanite religion to harness the very life-giving forces of nature for the benefits of worshipers made Baalism an attractive alternative to Yahwistic religion with its ethical demands.

The pervasive character of Canaanite fertility religion in ancient Israel is not an unheard of idea. Archaeology serves to confirm what the Bible consistently underplays. The prophetic protest against Canaanite religious practice was directed at the genuine threat that non-Yahwistic religion posed to ancient Israel. Archaeology supplies the social, religious, and cultural context for the prophetic protest against Canaanite religion.

Archaeology also makes it clear that worship was a local affair for most people. They worshiped at the many open-air sanctuaries in the land or in their own household shrines. These local temples and shrines continued in use after Solomon. Most rituals comprised of the offering of food and drink: grain, olive oil, wine, sheep. These were the principal agricultural products of Canaan long before the emergence of Israel.

Scholars who ignore the results of archaeological work will continue to minimize the affinity and even continuity of ancient Israelite religion with that of Canaan. Still archaeology makes it difficult to continue a one-sided emphasis on the uniqueness of ancient Israel. Recent archaeology has shown that in terms of material culture and the behavior it reflects, there is little difference between Canaanite and Israelite religion—at least in practice. The rituals were almost the same.

ARCHAEOLOGY AND THE NEW TESTAMENT

Archaeology relating to the NT has its own set of problems. First, the theological emphasis in NT interpretation has led to ignoring the archaeological record. Second, the material culture of the first Christians was not different from that of other Jews in Palestine. Christians did not develop their own symbol system until much later. In fact, if one had nothing but the archaeological record to go by, one would conclude that Christianity was imported into Palestine by the Byzantines in the fourth century CE.

Belarmino Bagatti, O.F.M., excavated at both Nazareth and Capernaum. His work at these sites led him to describe a phenomenon that he calls Jewish Christianity that he asserts existed in Palestine during the first centuries of the Christian era. For example, he maintains that graffiti and other remains found at Nazareth confirm the use of a synagogue for Christian worship. He deciphered one graffito on one pillar from this Jewish-Christian synagogue that he read as "Hail Mary."

Excavations at Capernaum beneath a fifth-century Byzantine church by Virgilio Corbo, O.F.M., and Stanislao Loffreda, O.F.M., have led them to conclude that this church was built over a private home that shows evidence of having been modified for public worship already in the first century CE. Again graffiti etched on the walls lead the excavators to posit this as a shrine in honor of St. Peter.

Excavations of the Churches of the Holy Sepulchre and the Nativity have led to the conclusion that both sites were venerated within less than two hundred years after Christ. Still archaeology cannot decide whether this veneration represented a historical memory or the localization of pious belief.

Excavations at Sepphoris, the capital of Lower Galilee in Jesus' day, have revealed a cosmopolitan city in which Jew and Gentile were able to live together in peace and mutual understanding. (Sepphoris did not join in the first revolt against Rome in 67–70 CE.) Herod Antipas built the city when Jesus was growing up in Nazareth just a few miles away. This had led some to speculate that Joseph may have been a laborer on this building project. Also, the discovery of a Roman theater there has led to the suggestion that Jesus' criticism of the scribes and Pharisees as "hypocrites" is the use of a metaphor from the theater since one Greek term for actor is "hypocrite." Of course, archaeology cannot prove either assertion.

What NT archaeology can do for NT interpretation is not to prove any historical questions, but to reconstruct the cultural and social setting of first century Palestine. The preliminary results of the archaeology of this period show that Judaism at this time was a far more diverse religious phenomenon than usually thought. For too long people have understood the Judaism of Jesus' day according to the patterns set by rabbinic Judaism that emerged later. The results of archaeological work supplemented by renewed study of textual material (the so-called Intertestamental literature) shows that early Judaism displayed a remarkable variety of belief and practice determined largely by local variation. The emergence of the Jesus-movement is more understandable against this background.

This diversity and regionalism continued beyond the first century CE. For example, excavations of synagogues of the Roman and Byzantine Periods reveal a marked difference in the ways religious Jews interpreted the prohibition of images. Some synagogues have simple geometric patterns serving as ornamentation. Others will have animal, human, and even mythological figures serving as decorative motifs. Still others will confine their ornamentation to Jewish symbols like the menorah or Torah shine. In several cases there is a combination of geometric, figurative, and Jewish symbols.

Biblical archaeology concerns itself with more than the occupation history of sites. It tries to understand the site's religion, politics, economics, aesthetics, and every other aspect of its culture based on material remains excavated at the site. The growing sophistication of the archaeological enterprise means that it is no longer practiced by biblical scholars as an avocation. Excavation and interpretation of the data recovered is the province of trained archaeologists. Future prospects of this discipline include a more nuanced understanding of the cultures that produced the Bible.

LESLIE J. HOPPE, O.F.M.

The Bible and Culture

WHAT IS CULTURE?

"Culture" has become an increasingly important word in the vocabulary of the Church since the Second Vatican Council. It first came to prominence in the Pastoral Constitution on the Church in the Modern World, *Gaudium et spes*, where it is defined as "all those things which go to the refining and developing of man's diverse mental and physical endowments." It goes on to say that "the word 'culture' often carries with it sociological and ethnological connotations; in this sense one can speak about a plurality of cultures" (no. 53).

Before Vatican II, "culture" appeared in Church documents in what is now known as its classical sense, that is, as referring to the highest artistic and poetic achievements of a people. Seen this way, certain educated and aesthetically refined people "have" culture, while uneducated and unrefined people do not. A certain group of artists and intellectuals are "shapers" of culture, while the rest are consumers of it. This classical sense of culture continues in the Church and the larger society.

Alongside this sense is one that *Gaudium et spes* adopts and brings to the forefront; namely, a historical or anthropological sense of culture. This sense reflects the first part of the definition given above: all of those things that go into making us human, who we are. More specifically, that includes our *worldview* (how we see and interpret the world around us, what values guide our lives), our *behavior* (our ways of interacting, the rituals that mark important moments in our lives), and our *material dimension* (language, clothing, food, etc.). Moreover, culture thus understood is specific to certain social groups, and their difference from other groups is marked off by worldview, behavior, and material artifacts. This results in a plurality of cultures. This historical sense of culture, with the idea that each of these cultures has a certain integrity and value of its own, is a fairly recent development in human history. It arose first in Germany in the second half of the eighteenth century, and came to be widespread in the nineteenth century as European nations described the peoples they were colonizing outside Europe and the Americas. Although it originally was intended as a way of preserving local distinctiveness against the homogenizing influences of industrialization and the Enlightenment, it is understood today especially as the right of a people to shape their own lives and to underscore the intrinsic value of such social formations.

Culture in this historical sense has become important for the Church since the Second Vatican Council because of the rapid spread of Christianity through the world. For the first time in its history, the Church is truly universal, a worldwide Church. In becoming such a reality, it now embraces thousands of cultures. The restored understanding of the Church sees the local (particular) Church as embodying the fullness of the Church in communion with other local Churches; the location of the particular Church within concrete cultures, therefore, gives those cultures a new significance. This has led to understanding a new need for the evangelization of cultures as the mission of the Church in the world. This has become a prime theme in the pontificates since the Second Vatican Council. What it means is that human beings are not brought to the Gospel as isolated entities. All of us are embedded in concrete cultures that shape us profoundly, but do not completely determine us. Hence evangelization of cultures—purifying what is good in cultures, speaking in judgment on those elements that are not good—is an essential part of the Church's evangelizing mission.

Where does the Bible fit into all of this? There are three dimensions to the answer to that question. There is, first of all, the Bible as a cultural process and a cultural document itself. Although divinely inspired, it comes down to us through human media, which makes it embedded, like us, in cultures. Second, the Bible itself has had a profound influence on shaping the cultures of Jews and Christians through the centuries, both within their immediate communities and in their wider societies, especially when either of these groups represented the majority of the population. And third, in the new reality of the Church as a worldwide phenomenon, we have to come to terms with readings of the Bible coming from many more perspectives than was the case in the past. We will now explore each of these dimensions.

THE BIBLE AS A CULTURAL PROCESS AND CULTURAL DOCUMENT

The Bible is, of course, not one book, but a library of books composed over a millennium. As a result, there were many different hands at work, representing many different historical periods and cultures.

The very composition of the books of the Bible represents a process of making culture and changing culture. First of all, scholars since the second half of the nineteenth century have pointed out that significant sections of the Old Testament are not completely original compositions. Barely beneath the surface of the creation story in Genesis 1 lies a Babylonian creation story. The Code of Hammurabi can be seen behind parts of the Mosaic lawgiving. The Song of Songs has antecedents in Egyptian love poetry. The demonology and visions of the end of the world owe something to their Babylonian and Zoroastrian forebears. All of this is said not to downplay the biblical books as original and creative media of God's revelation. It is only to say that the biblical writers took stories and literary forms already familiar to their hearers and recrafted them for a new purpose. Indeed we should not only not be surprised by this process but actually expect it. A totally new story has less chance of finding a place in the hearers' mental universe. Christian missionaries were to learn much later that when material is totally new, it is difficult to comprehend and is frequently misunderstood.

Second, scholars during this same period have found the biblical writers often reworking the material into new forms to suit the changing circumstances in which their hearers found themselves. Many texts enjoyed a long history of oral transmission before being committed to print. What happens to orally transmitted texts is that they do change in significant ways even while remaining substantially the same. This is done not only to make the texts easier to recall, but to keep them relevant to their hearers. The complex history of the composition of the Gospels is a case in point. Scholars generally believe that different oral sources were drawn upon, that parts or even whole Gospels may have been written down, only to be revised, and that the compositions of earlier Gospels influenced later ones. All of this takes place in a cultural context, involving different hands, changing circumstances, and sometimes translation from one language to another.

The historical understanding of culture may be a modern concept, but the peoples of the Bible were clearly aware of what we would call cultural difference. At times the Israelites can be fiercely tribal, disparaging the ways of their neighbors. Yet there are also touching stories of reaching across those cultural boundaries, such as the stories of Ruth and Naomi, Elijah and the widow in Zarephath, Rahab and the spies of Joshua, and Jesus and the Syro-Phoenician woman. Quite frequently it is the women who establish intercultural understanding. The more universal vision of the later prophets presents another picture of Israel and the nations (where "nations" might be roughly understood as equivalent to the modern sense of cultures), where Israel becomes a light to the nations, the goal of their own fulfillment.

The New Testament struggles with cultural questions too, especially in redefining the boundary between Jew and Greek or Gentile in the young community. The sorting out at the Council of Jerusalem (Acts 15) of what religious duties were in fact specific (as we would say) to specific cultures has remained for Christians one of the points of orientation for understanding the relation of Gospel and culture to this day. Similarly, Paul's speech in Athens at the Aeropagus (Acts 17) represents an attempt to recast his preaching in a different cultural medium.

The Bible therefore manifests the ongoing presence of many cultural processes—borrowing, emending, enlarging, interpreting, and translating—and as such is a deeply cultural document itself. Again, this should not be surprising for Christians, who see the Incarnation—the Word's taking on human form (John 1:14)—as being at the very center of God's activity in history.

THE BIBLE AS SHAPER OF CULTURE

Because Jews and Christians believe that the Bible (in its respective versions) contains the revealed word of God, its contents have had deep and enduring influence on their communities and the larger societies in which they participated. The Christian practice of transcribing the Scriptures on individual sheets of parchment and then sewing them together along one side—creating the codex or book—made them more transportable and easier to search through for specific passages. That influenced the shaping of the book as the predominant form of writing over the scroll.

There are three ways that the Bible shaped culture that will be explored here: the Bible in art and literature, the Bible as creator of social groups and movements, and the Bible in translation.

The stories and the figures of the Bible have had an incalculable effect on the art and literature of the Christian world. So much of the pictorial art of Europe up to the time of the Renaissance was devoted to de-

picting scenes from the Bible. Copies of the Bible itself and liturgical books were adorned with biblical scenes. The most popular book before the time of movable type was the *biblia pauperum*, or paupers' Bible, made up of block prints of stories from the Bible. The great churches of Europe were decorated with paintings and sculptures recounting the stories of the Bible from creation to apocalypse, and were further adorned in the high Middle Ages with exquisite stained glass windows that gave a luminacy to those same stories. Altar paintings, and later paintings commissioned by the wealthy and kept in their homes, presented biblical figures and scenes from the life of Christ. Such art was meant to instruct those who gazed upon it. But the scenes of the Last Judgment on the tympana above the western doors of Romanesque and Gothic cathedrals also embued a morality in those who entered the portals.

Hence this art was not only ecclesiastical, but shaped the rest of people's lives as well. This is clear in music recounting biblical stories that has moved people far beyond the confines of the Church—be it Handel's *Messiah* or Andrew Lloyd Weber's *Jesus Christ Superstar*. Similarly the Bible as literature has shaped Christian cultures as well. From the retelling of the Gospel stories in the apocrypha or the eighth-century Frankish accounts, to stories that take up biblical motifs of exodus and liberation, death and resurrection; or stories that capture the imagination of people at a certain time, such as Salome at the end of the nineteenth century, the Bible has shaped Western European literature like no other single source.

The influence of the Bible on culture reaches beyond the so-called high cultural products such as art and literature. It is also to be seen more directly in the shaping of social life. European pre-Christian festivals celebrating the old and new year were replaced by Christmas and Easter, respectively. These festivals now reach beyond societies where Christians are in the majority, to places like Japan where Christmas is celebrated with increasing enthusiasm.

But beyond such wide-ranging influences as holy days that become holidays, social movements influenced by the Bible have made a perduring impact on life in North America and beyond. The two most notable kinds of movements emerging from readings of the Bible are utopian and apocalyptic movements.

Utopian (literally "no place") movements preach a withdrawal from society, either to escape the sinfulness of the world, or to recreate the so-called primitive Church of Acts 4. Many monastic foundations had their origins in such inspiration, and monasteries were the carriers of classical culture in Europe from the sixth to the fourteenth centuries. Others have been more short-lived, in a variety of forms. Such communities, often lay and married, flourished on the American frontier. Some, such as the Oneida community in New York or the Amana colonies in Iowa, have lasted over generations. Others do not outlive their founding leader.

Apocalyptic movements harbor dark visions of the end of the world, based on such accounts in the New Testament, especially Mark 13 and Revelation. Some, such as the Seventh Day Adventists, evolve into a denomination and continue to influence the culture through their missionary work. Others end in violence and destruction, such as the Peoples' Temple in Guyana in 1979 or the Branch Davidian sect in Waco, Texas, in 1993. Because of their violent demise, these movements have effects on their cultures going far beyond their immediate adherents. In unstable or uncertain times in cultures apocalyptic movements tend to arise. They occur among displaced or disadvantaged peoples in majority cultures, and among whole groups in minority cultures (the Ghost Dance Religion that ended at Wounded Knee, South Dakota, in 1890 is an example).

A third way in which the Bible has influenced and shaped culture has been through its translations. In oral societies, the translation and publication of the Bible has been a means to give a common language to a group of dialects. Saint Cyril and Saint Methodius' translation did that for Slavic peoples in the ninth century; Martin Luther's translation of the Bible into a Saxon dialect gave a common language to the German-speaking peoples in the sixteenth century. In the nineteenth and twentieth centuries grammars and dictionaries for more than a thousand languages were developed by missionaries and Bible translators as preludes for preparing editions of the Bible. In so doing, they helped preserve languages and cultures in the midst of rapid and sometimes debilitating change.

NEW WAYS OF READING THE BIBLE

One of the most fascinating results emerging from the world Church is the plurality of readings of the Bible that emerge out of the crucible of cultures. At a time when academic exegesis had advocated historical and literary critical readings of the biblical text, fresh readings have been appearing from different parts of the world. Some of those readings may be questionable, and say more about the reader than the text; but most have enriched the life of the Church immeasurably. Here are a number of examples:

Oppressed peoples have often taken biblical passages to speak aloud of their plight in coded fashion. Thus, "crossing over the Jordan" for African slaves in the pre-Civil War period in the United States was code for crossing north of the Mason-Dixon line to freedom.

Oppressed peoples today in many parts of the world have taken over the Exodus story to inspire their own escape from oppression to freedom. Liberation theologies have given new meaning to this story. But not all oppressed people do so: many native peoples of North America and Palestinian Christians identify with the Canaanites whose land was taken from them, and look instead to the return from Exile for their inspiration. Nor are oppressed Coptic Christians in Egypt keen on the Exodus story.

In other instances, less read parts of the Bible become especially attractive to certain peoples. In the African independent Churches, for example, Proverbs and James are favorite texts for preaching, because proverbs play such a large role in African culture and James' practicality is much admired.

Sometimes texts too well known take on new vibrancy in another situation. Under the Somoza regime in Nicaragua in the 1970s, reciting the *Magnificat* (Luke 1:46-55) in public was forbidden because of its subversive reference to the mighty being brought down from their thrones.

Also, biblical stories that have lost their relevance in one culture retrieve their liveliness in another. Africa rediscovered the healing stories of Jesus at a time when they were often explained away in Western pulpits and classrooms.

Yet other biblical texts take on new importance. The Wisdom literature of the Bible has become especially important for dialogue with the great religious traditions of Asia.

Finally, some stories get reversed in another culture. The parable of the two sons in Matthew 21:23-28 is exactly reversed in some Asian cultures, because no son would ever disagree with his father to his face, for that would dishonor him.

Thus, in the long history of interaction of Bible and culture, we find ourselves living today at a time when new treasures of interpretation are being brought out with the old.

ROBERT J. SCHREITER, C.PP.S.

Biblical Theology

THE ECLIPSE OF BIBLICAL THEOLOGY

Biblical theology was once an important subdiscipline of biblical studies. In the last fifty years that has changed. There were several reasons for this change though the most significant was a perceived disharmony between the critical methods of biblical interpretation and the presuppositions that come from faith. Some scholars prefer to treat the Bible as an ancient literary product whose claims on people today are concerns of the Church and Synagogue—not the academy.

Some biblical scholars no longer regard theology as the central focus of biblical studies. Many do not even regard theology as a necessary dimension of biblical studies. Scanning titles of learned articles and monographs written on biblical topics makes it clear that today most scholars focus their research in literary criticism and sociological analysis. Few focus their research on theological questions except as an exercise in the history of religion. There are fewer still who study the Bible as a source for the development of a biblical theology.

What is the reason for the eclipse of biblical theology? Perhaps there is just an inherent contradiction between the dogmatic convictions behind the theological enterprise and the historical method used in biblical studies. The historical method does not provide the certainty that some believers seek. It offers only relative degrees of probability. Basic to the method used in biblical studies is the principle of criticism according to which any conclusion is subject to revision in the light of new evidence. For some, dogmatic convictions make it difficult to use the critical and historical method. Theology has long since lost its position as "the queen of the sciences." Now its role in biblical studies is in doubt because of presuppositions that some scholars view as incompatible with the critical method.

Most believers appreciate how contemporary biblical scholarship has shown what the Scriptures meant in their historical and cultural setting. Still, some consider biblical studies less helpful in showing how the Scriptures confront the contemporary believer as the Word of God. They regard critical scholarship as a better guide to the intellectual, social, political, and cultural thought of antiquity than it is for the development of a contemporary spiritual theology.

Modern biblical scholarship owes its existence, in part, to the need of biblical interpreters to be part of the larger community of scholars. Its development was part of an attempt to place the study of the Bible on an objective, scientific footing. To accomplish this biblical scholars developed approaches that tried to respond to the demands of a scientific method rather than to confessional considerations. Still, the methods of study used by biblical scholars can result directly in the discovery of truth necessary for authentic religious living.

Genuine and lasting commitment to God is a primary concern of the Bible. The Scriptures describe the many ways that the people of ancient Israel, early Judaism, and early Christianity tried to live in the presence of God. The Bible testifies to the attempts of believers to commit themselves to a life of holiness because they recognized that such a life is the only appropriate response to God. Both those who lived in accord with the Torah and those who believed in Jesus saw themselves as "a chosen race, a royal priesthood, a holy nation, God's own people" (1 Pet 2:9; see Exod 19:6).

THE CONTRIBUTION OF BIBLICAL SCHOLARSHIP

Though biblical theology is not the direct interest of most biblical scholars today, does this mean that biblical scholarship has nothing to offer those concerned with finding in the Bible support for their religious commitments? Despite the unwillingness of many scholars to make theology a focus in their work, biblical studies and its critical method can inform those who want to find in the Bible the words of "spirit and life."

The first task of biblical theology is a critical evaluation of biblical speech about God and the response that this speech evokes. A biblical theology does not simply say that this is what ancient Israel or the early Church believed or this is how the Israelites or the first Christians responded to their experience of God. A biblical theology needs to evaluate what the Bible says about the shape of the human response to God to see what light it can shed on the contemporary experience of the divine. A biblical theology needs to evaluate current affirmations, patterns, and assumptions of spiritual theology in the light of the biblical tradition. It should help believers mediate between the religious experience of past and present.

This is where the critical method of biblical scholarship can make a significant contribution. It holds that every conclusion is subject to revision in the light of new evidence. This demand for evidence can save biblical theology from simple fadism. The critical method makes it possible for the Bible to be a genuine source in the development of a spiritual theology. How can the critical method accomplish this?

The critical method helps develop a biblical theology because it leads readers to be sensitive to the contours of biblical texts. This prevents a flat, one-dimensional, and uninformed reading of the Bible. Using the critical method in the construction of a biblical theology makes possible a creative conversation between the experience that lies behind the biblical text and the experience of contemporary believers. It allows the Bible to be more than a collection of edifying or sometimes disedifying stories. The historical method opens believers to possibilities of interpretation that are not immediately self-evident.

Another characteristic of historical criticism that makes it helpful in the development of a biblical theology is its adaptability. Since all conclusions are subject to revision and reexamination in the light of new evidence, historical criticism is free from the dogmatism that looks upon new insights as potential threats. Feminist critics, though highly critical of the results of critical scholarship, use critical methods to argue for their new understanding of the text. The foundational expressions of liberation theology derive from the biblical tradition. These include God as liberator from the Exodus tradition, the command to do justice from the legal and Prophetic traditions, and Jesus as proclaimer of God's reign from the gospel tradition. Biblical interpreters from a liberation perspective may assert that usual patterns of interpretation have robbed these motifs of their force. To make this objection and to move readers beyond these patterns is to use the critical method.

The most important contribution that historical criticism has made to the advancement of biblical studies is that it provides a framework within which interpreters from different confessions or no confession at all have been able to speak constructively with each other. By requiring evidence and some measure of probability for each assertion, the critical method makes exchange possible and productive. It allows for the experience of many different people to come into play during the interpretive process.

There are problems in relating the historical-critical method with the development of a biblical theology, but to ignore the critical method in favor of a supposed direct encounter with the Word of God is to isolate spiritual theology from all that is interesting and important in biblical studies today. We should not make biblical theology a reservation apart from the mainstream of biblical studies. The critical method supplies a framework for discussion and enrichment that cannot take place unless we are willing to listen to those who do not hold certain confessional tenets or do not share certain assumptions about spiritual theology. Openness to revision is the hallmark of the critical method. The reward for this openness is new insight.

TWO EXAMPLES

Two examples should clarify how critical method can inform biblical theology. One concerns the definition of the various literary forms in the Bible and the social function these forms have. We know that appreciation of a text's form helps us to have realistic expectations about what we can learn from that text. Literary theory helps us recognize that a text is not an exact mirror of objective reality. This makes it possible for us to appreciate it as a medium of human expression.

Form critics have told us that the story of Jacob's struggle at the Jabbok River as narrated in Genesis 32 is an etiological saga. They warn us not to expect historical data from a saga because as a literary form it is concerned more with the present than it is with the past. They have also taught us that etiologies do more than supply answers to questions of curious people about the origins of things. In particular, the story of Jacob's struggle does more than explain the origin of the name Israel. It explains who Israel is. Israel is the one who has wrestled with God. Israel—the individual and the nation—has experienced God directly and immediately and has not only lived but has been blessed. Generations of believers have read Genesis 32 and affirmed that what happened to Jacob was true because the same thing has happened to them. That is what a saga does—it helps believers to see how God touches human life and becomes part of human experience.

Second, the critical method has taught us also that the stories in the Bible are more complex than if they were ordinary historical documents. Even if the details of a particular story are verifiable, the story's value goes beyond its usefulness in reconstructing history. The same story may provide motivation for obedience, support for the political claims of some segment of ancient society, and a paradigm for the understanding of later events. Often the historical character of biblical stories is hardly a consideration in the Bible itself. Consider the way this story of ancient Israel's Exodus from Egypt functions in the varied literary contexts in which it appears in the Bible. Legal traditions use it as a way to motivate Israel to obey. Second Isaiah uses the Exodus story as a way to interpret Judah's experience toward the end of the Exile. The ritual connected with this story in the Book of Exodus led later generations to identify themselves as having been slaves in Egypt.

DEVELOPING A BIBLICAL THEOLOGY

There are five principles that guide the development of a biblical theology. Each of these takes seriously contemporary biblical scholarship. The first of these is obvious: the substance of authentic biblical theology ought to be the biblical text itself. The Church has a defined body of Sacred Scripture that it accepts as normative for faith and life. Some maintain that it is impossible to maintain the dogmatic conception of the canon since it is not intrinsic to the biblical writings. Still one can justify concentration on the canon by asserting that this does nothing more than recognize the historical importance of the canonical texts. Fortunately the Church has not defined the meaning of many texts within the body of the Scriptures. Exegetical insight can roam freely over these texts.

Still, the Bible makes claims on believers. These claims are not only in the moral realm. Believers also experience these claims in terms of their religious language, imagery, and style. Christians need to be careful to enjoy the rich imagery and lush religious language of the Hebrew Bible. For example, one motif underused by Christian theology is that of the Temple. The Temple as the means of intimacy with God, its role as an asylum for the just and a place of vision offer intriguing possibilities to those who will take the time with this motif.

A second principle is that the binding substance of any authentic Christian biblical theology is the centrality of Jesus. The Jesus that biblical studies offers us is the Jesus who emerges from the pages of the New Testament, who lived and died in first century Palestine, who advised his disciples not to do away with one letter or even the smallest part of a letter of the Torah (Matt 5:17-18), the form of whose teachings was shaped by the cultural, religious, and social currents of the Judaisms of his day. It is the Jesus whose followers tried to understand in terms of their ancestral religious traditions. For his disciples Jesus was "the Holy One of God" (John 6:69), "the prophet" (Matt 21:11), "the Messiah" (Matt 16:16), "the Lamb of God" (John 1:29), "the priest according to the order of Melchizedek" (Heb 7:15-22). It is the Jesus some of whose followers tried to understand in terms of the cultural and religious traditions of the Greek world. This Jesus was "the image of the invisible God, the firstborn of all creation" (Col 1:15). Also, the followers of Jesus were able to find images at home in both the Jewish and Hellenistic traditions. Jesus was "the Lord," "the Savior," or simply "the Word."

In developing a biblical theology, there is a need to avoid the error made by some Christians who tried to write a theology of the Old Testament. Several of these scholars asserted that the "profoundest meaning" of the Hebrew Bible is disclosed by its relationship to the New Testament. It is probably more accurate to say that the "profoundest meaning" of the New Testament is disclosed by its relationship to the Hebrew Bible.

A third principle of a biblical theology is that for the Bible ethical performance is more important than religious belief. The religious truths of the Bible serve to pattern the way of life that is at the heart of biblical religion. The affirmations of the Bible are rhetorical devices to motivate behavior. The Cain and Abel story comments on the law of fugitives. The Abraham story supports the law of circumcision. The Exodus story underscores the laws of the Passover, the offering of firstfruits, and the redemption of the firstborn. The many stories of sin and rebellion comment on the laws of atonement. The central importance of ethics in the biblical tradition is most obvious in the parables of Jesus. Analysis of the biblical text ought to lead to an evaluation of clarification of the propriety of these ethical affirmations for the contemporary world.

A fourth principle of a biblical theology revolves around the recognition that there are ideological uses of God-language in the Bible. When we read that the conquest of Canaan and the disposition of its inhabitants by the Israelites was the consequence of a divine command, surely we are suspicious that we are dealing with ideological rhetoric and not the certainty of dogmatic affirmation. The priests use statements about God to support participation in their rituals. The prophets do the same to support their conception of how Israelite society ought to be structured. While we ought to avoid reducing a text to the ideological function it may have, ignoring such a function is naive.

The fifth principle of a biblical theology involves the recognition that the Bible offers several ways of understanding our life with God. The effort to find the one and only valid biblical theology is doomed to failure. The goal of a contemporary biblical theology is to evaluate the religious perspectives in the text. The biblical tradition is the product of human imagination, drawing on the ingredients of human experience and faith. It does not have the logical necessity of the coherent philosophical system. While the Church has accepted the biblical tradition as normative for its own life, Catholics recognize that the components of the tradition have a view of reality that is limited, partial, and relative because the biblical text is the product of the human mind. Nonetheless, they treasure these traditions because they have broadened the horizons of generations of believers. These traditions, however, make their greatest contribution when they stimulate our imagination.

Finally, what binds biblical scholars and those who read the Bible to nourish their faith is a fascination with the Bible. This fascination offers the common ground necessary for biblical scholarship to use its methods not simply to reconstruct the history of the religion practiced by the ancient Israelites, early Jews, and first Christians. Contemporary biblical scholarship can offer believers invaluable assistance as they develop an authentic biblical theology.

LESLIE J. HOPPE, O.F.M.

A

AARON

Aaron plays two major roles in the Bible: Moses' brother and colleague in the Exodus,* and the first priest and progenitor of a priestly family within the tribe of Levi.

Old Testament

Aaron in the Exodus. Aaron acted as partner and helper to Moses* in Egypt. When Moses complained that he was inadequate to speak God's message, God assigned Aaron the Levite as his spokesperson to the people (Exod 4:14-16). God arranged a meeting of Aaron and Moses in the desert, then they brought God's word and signs to the people (Exod 4:27-31). Together they spoke before Pharaoh (Exod 7:1-2), where Aaron worked a wonder and the first two plagues against Egypt (Exod 7:8–8:15). He stood beside Moses during the battle with the Amalekites (Exod 17:8-10), at the meeting with Jethro (Exod 18:12), and at Sinai (Exod 19:24; 24:1, 9). Northern traditions (E, D), however, did not count him blameless. Aaron fashioned a golden calf to worship their God when Moses was on Sinai (Exodus 32). Later he and Miriam challenged Moses' sole leadership, an action that brought punishment (Num 12:1-15), even though Aaron escaped total rejection. Both stories are omitted in southern traditions (J, P). Finally, Aaron as partner of Moses appears in Micah 6:4, Psalms 77:21 and 105:26-27.

Aaron as Priest. The P tradition paints a different picture: Aaron as the first high priest, chosen by God through Moses (Exod 28:1-2). His consecration occurred in stages: purification, investiture, anointing with oil (Exod 29:4-7; 40:12-15; Lev 8:6-12); ordination sacrifices follow (Aaron was sprinkled with blood) and a presentation of bread to him for an offering (Exod 29:19-24; Lev 8:22-23, 26-27). One of his vestments was a diadem inscribed with the words "Sacred to the LORD" (Exod 39:30); a sign of his consecration, it attested to his role as priest. Around 200 BCE Sirach remembered Aaron as ordained and anointed in a lasting covenant for a lasting priesthood (Sir 45:15).

Priestly narratives also illustrate his stature. Korah the Levite was punished for his rebellion against Aaron's priestly prerogatives: only Aaron's descendants are tabernacle priests, while other Levites shall be their servants (Numbers 16–18). When Moses sinned by striking the rock twice for water, the innocent Aaron was also barred from entering the land (Num 20:2-13). Aaron died on Mount Hor and Moses took Aaron's garments and invested Eleazar his son as priest (Num 20:22-29).

The Aaron of History? Many scholars consider the priestly Aaron as a post-exilic invention, even though priests existed during the monarchic era; they imply that high priestly status reversed an ancient, more egalitarian approach to God. However, contemporary Jewish scholars argue that P is rooted in Judah during the reigns of Ahaz and Hezekiah, and reflects a situation where Aaronite priests ministered in the first Temple. Some neglected data from earlier traditions might corroborate this view. God spoke to Moses of "your brother, Aaron the Levite" (Exod 4:14 [J]; see also Exod 6:20 [P]); Levite clearly indicates priestly identity. The golden calf story portrays Aaron as a worship leader, a priestly activity (Exod 32:1-5, 21-24 [E]). In D, when Aaron died his son Eleazar succeeded him "in priestly office" (Deut 10:6). So we find two portraits of Aaron, with separable but reconcilable emphases: partner and priest. For Israel's religion this theory suggests that distinct priestly roles developed before the Exile; it also avoids a stereotypical denigration of post-exilic Jewish religion.

New Testament

Although Aaron is mentioned five times, only one reference connects him with the Exodus: Stephen mentions him as innocent in the golden calf episode (Acts 7:40). Luke refers to his priestly role: Elizabeth was descended "from the daughters of Aaron" (Luke 1:5). The author of Hebrews compares Aaron's high priesthood with that of Jesus, and finds Aaron's less effective and temporary (Heb 5:4; 7:11). Among the objects in the holy of holies was "the staff of Aaron that had sprouted" (Heb 9:4; see Num 17:16-26). Aaron's priestly family forms part of Jesus' religious background, while the author of Hebrews compares and subordinates his priesthood to that of Jesus.

Pastoral-Liturgical Tradition

The NT never connects Aaron's priestly line with Christian ministry, but theologians have referred to him as a model (Origen, *Homilies on Leviticus*). The Roman consecratory prayer for the Ordination of Presbyters includes the reference "You shared among the sons of Aaron the fullness of their father's power, to provide worthy priests in sufficient number for the increasing rites of sacrifice and worship" (22).

See: ANOINTING, CONSECRATION, EGYPT, EXODUS, MOSES, PRIEST, SACRIFICE, TEMPLE

JOHN C. ENDRES, S.J.

ABEL

Abel is presented in Scripture as the one who offered a sacrifice acceptable to God. As such, he is considered a type of Christ's perfect sacrifice.

Old Testament

All of the biblical references to Abel presuppose the original story that appears in Genesis 4:1-16. Abel, a shepherd, is contrasted with his older brother, Cain, a farmer. The nature of the contrast is expressed in the different divine reaction to each's offering: "The LORD looked with favor on Abel and his offering, but on Cain and his offering he did not" (Gen 4:4b-5a).

It should be noted, first of all, that there can be no question of a literal understanding of this text since there was no domestication of animals or development of agriculture at the beginning of the human race.

On a theological level, the story serves to document the general theme of continued sinfulness after the fall of Adam and Eve.* However, there is also a deeper motif that involves the meaning of divine acceptance. A traditional explanation has assumed that Abel's offering was *objectively* better than Cain's. In that case, it would be a simple matter of relative generosity. In fact, however, the text seems to suggest that Cain's fault is not lack of generosity but refusal to allow God to show approval in God's own free way.

Accordingly, Abel becomes a model of all who trust God enough to believe that their offering has been accepted even when the evidence is not what they expected, whereas Cain stands for all who demand approval on their own terms and, when that approval seems lacking, turn their anger at God against their fellow human beings, such as a brother.

New Testament

In Matthew 23:35 (see also Luke 11:51), Jesus places the scribes and Pharisees in the company of those who murdered the prophets. Abel is listed among these because he is considered to be the first example of the sacrifice of innocent blood. As such, he is a type of Christ and of all other innocent victims of violence.

Abel appears again in Hebrews 11:4 where he heads a long list of OT persons who showed heroic courage because of their faith.* This conclusion is based on the author's conviction that all good and lasting deeds must derive from faith which alone puts human beings in touch with the reality of divine goodness. When it is said that Abel "though dead, still speaks" (11:4), the reference is probably to the fact that his innocent blood continues to cry out for justice (Gen 4:10).

In Hebrews 12:24, Abel's pure sacrifice is said to be eclipsed by the sacrifice of Christ, whose blood "speaks more eloquently than that of Abel." No doubt this is due to the far superior status of Christ, but it is also because Christ's blood cries out for mercy rather than for vengeance.

Pastoral-Liturgical Tradition

The sacrifice of Abel has been depicted occasionally in Christian art and his name appears sporadically in liturgical texts. At present, he holds a place of honor in Roman Canon I with Abraham and Melchizedek as OT types of the perfect sacrifice of Christ.

See: ABRAHAM, ADAM AND EVE, BLOOD, FAITH, MELCHIZEDEK, SACRIFICE, TYPE

DEMETRIUS R. DUMM, O.S.B.

ABOMINATION OF DESOLATION

Old Testament

In Daniel 11:31 we read that an impious king would defile the sanctuary, abolish the daily sacrifice, and set up "the abomi-

nation that makes desolate" (NAB: the horrible abomination). It is clear from the context that the reference is to the actions of the Syrian king Antiochus Epiphanes. The same episode is described more directly in 1 Maccabees 1:54: "On the fifteenth day of the month of Chislev in the year one hundred and forty-five [that is, December 167 BCE] the king erected the horrible abomination upon the altar of holocausts, and in the surrounding cities of Judah they built pagan altars." Most probably, the abomination was a pagan altar that was superimposed on the altar of holocausts in the Jerusalem Temple,* but it has also been interpreted as a statue of a pagan god. The Hebrew expression *siqqus mesomem* involves a word play on the name of the Syrian god Baal Shamem. The abomination is also mentioned in Daniel 9:27 and 12:11 (compare also 8:13, "the desolating sin"). It remained in the Temple for three years, until Jerusalem was recaptured by Judas Maccabee (1 Macc 4:36-59). Then its stones were carried away to "an unclean place."

New Testament

After the Maccabean period, the prophecies of Daniel were still taken to refer to future events. In the first century CE, they were thought to predict the destruction of Jerusalem by the Romans. The abomination of desolation appears again in Mark 13:14: "When you see the desolating abomination standing where he should not (let the reader understand) then those in Judea must flee to the mountains. . . ." The most striking thing about this citation is that the participle "standing" is masculine, though the word for "abomination" is neuter. The "abomination" here has traditionally been interpreted as the antichrist, but the reference may have been to the Roman general Titus. The parallel passage in Luke 21:20 reads: "When you see Jerusalem surrounded by armies, know that its desolation is at hand. Then those in Judea must flee to the mountains. . . ." The parallel in Matthew 24:15 cites Daniel explicitly and

3

uses the neuter participle to agree with "abomination."

Pastoral-Liturgical Tradition

Like many apocalyptic* symbols, the "abomination of desolation" has a deliberate ambiguity that lends itself to reinterpretation and reapplication. The original referent in Daniel was quite specific. The traditional Christian interpretation as the antichrist,* however, pushes the phrase into the realm of eschatological myth, as a motif associated with the end of the world. Attempts to predict when this will come, or to identify the abomination with a historical individual, have been notoriously unsuccessful, although the phrase can be marvelously apt to describe various offensive objects that "stand where they should not be." (A hotel on the Mount of Olives is a well-known, humorous example.) The passage dealing with the abomination in Matthew 24 has traditionally been read on the last Sunday of the liturgical year. The passage as a whole serves to evoke a sense of an ending and the threat of catastrophe that is never absent from human life.

See: ANTICHRIST, APOCALYPTIC, ESCHATOLOGY

JOHN J. COLLINS

ABRAHAM

In Genesis, Abraham is presented as that man who was, more than any other human being, called, tested, and approved by God. Because of his indomitable trust in God's goodness and promises, he reversed the sinful current that began with Adam and Eve's sin. Paul therefore sees him as an example of salvation by faith rather than works.

Old Testament

Though the monumental figure of Abraham, Israel's primary patriarch, impacts the entire OT, his essential story is found in Genesis 12–25. Few scholars would still maintain that this story was simply created to provide Israel with a heroic ancestor. However, it is equally true that the person-age described emerges as a powerful symbolic as well as historical figure. And what Abraham symbolizes is nothing less than the proper relationship of a human being to the creator.

Abraham Called. God called Abraham in summary fashion and Abraham's response was unconditional: "The LORD said to Abram: 'Go forth from the land of your kinsfolk and from your father's house to a land that I will show you'. . . . Abram went as the Lord directed him, . . . " (Gen 12:1-4). No questions are asked; no answers are provided. The career of Abraham is thus definitively established as a departure from the static, familiar past and an entrance into a dynamic, unknown future. The patriarch agrees to be God's traveler and that forever specifies the vocation of his believing descendants.

The journey was not, however, an aimless wandering. God knew the destination and God declared it to be the stuff of dreams: "I will make you a great nation, and I will bless you. . . . All the communities of the earth shall find blessing in you" (Gen 12:2-3). What God planned for Abraham was so good and so generous that he would be known henceforth as the very model of a blessed person. In the ensuing years, God would expand on this promise so that it would include numberless posterity and secure possession of land. God told Abraham that the deepest desires of the human heart can be realized and Abraham dared to believe that divine promise.

Abraham Tested. As God spoke ever more expansively about the promises, Abraham seemed to be trapped in an ever clearer awareness of the futility of his trust: "O Lord GOD, what good will your gifts be, if I keep on being childless. . . ?" (Gen 15:2). God's answer was a solemn covenant* with Abraham (15:7-21). But a child was still not provided. Finally, the aged Abraham is pictured offering exquisite hospitality to three strangers (Genesis 18), thereby symbolizing his continued willingness to entertain divine mystery and to persevere in his journey into the unknown. Against all expectation, an heir was provided and the puzzle appeared to be solved. But the real test was still to come.

The climax of Abraham's career came when God commanded him to sacrifice* his son, Isaac:* "Take your son, Isaac, your only one, whom you love, and go to the land of Moriah. There you shall offer him up as a holocaust on a height that I will point out to you" (Gen 22:2). God had asked Abraham to leave his home, thus sacrificing his past; God was now asking him to sacrifice his future.

In Jewish tradition, this sacrifice of Isaac, called the *Akedah* or the "binding of Isaac," has been rightly considered one of the central events of salvation history for it was the supreme example of Abraham's trust in God's promises. When Abraham, in response to Isaac's question about the lack of a victim, responded, "God himself will provide the sheep for the holocaust" (Gen 22:8), he was in effect turning his whole being and all his hopes over to God's care. He "died" that God might give him life.

Abraham Approved. God in fact intervened to prevent the sacrifice of Isaac, declaring: "I know now how devoted you are to God, since you did not withhold from me your beloved son" (Gen 22:12). The promises are then divinely reaffirmed as God gives Abraham new life, expressed in the images of future posterity and land.

Other OT Texts About Abraham. Abraham's exemplary faith and special relationship with God are invoked frequently in the history of Israel. Time and again, the OT writers recall that God had sworn to give the land to their fathers, Abraham, Isaac, and Jacob (e.g., Deut 9:5). And in the Exile* the Israelites are reminded that God, who called Abraham "my friend" (Isa 41:8), cannot abandon them. Abraham is also extolled by Sirach in his praise of Israel's ancestors (Isa 44:19-21).

However, the primary significance of Abraham for Israel, and indeed for the whole human race, is found in his relationship to the "history" that preceded him. For Abraham is presented as the one who reversed a tragic history of sin and death. Adam had rebelled against the creator; Cain refused to entertain the mystery of "non-acceptance" and murdered Abel; even Noah was more concerned with preservation than with renewal. But in Abraham God found the person whose generosity would allow the revival of the original divine plan. God's image shone again in this radically obedient servant. The effects would be truly a blessing on all the nations of the earth.

New Testament

It is scarcely surprising that the name of Abraham is encountered frequently in the NT since he was such a dominant figure in the history of Israel. Specifically, the Christian communities claimed a share in the promise of God to Abraham (e.g., Luke 1:55, 73). They considered the special heirs of this promise to be the followers of Jesus who, through faith, were able to understand the deeper, spiritual meaning of God's word to Abraham (e.g., Matt 3:9; John 8:39-40). This new understanding of the promise is expressed most clearly in Paul's writings.

Abraham in Romans. After presenting his revolutionary teaching about justification through faith independently of the works of the Law, Paul searches for support in the Scriptures. He claims to find it in the story of Abraham. Paul's attention is drawn in particular to Genesis 15, where God's solemn covenant with Abraham is described. Abraham had just pointed out to God that he was childless and had suggested ruefully that perhaps one of his servants might become his heir. God summarily blocks this avenue.

The whole unqualified promise was then repeated by God: "'Look up at the sky and count the stars, if you can. Just so,' he added, 'shall your descendants be'" (Gen 15:5). The promise was indeed extravagant and it stood on God's word alone. Then came the words that Paul is searching for (as he recorded them in Rom 4:3): "Abraham believed God, and it was credited to him as righteousness." Paul wastes no time in driving home his point: "when one does not work, yet believes in the one who justifies the ungodly, his faith is credited as righteousness" (Rom 4:5). Quite simply, Abraham was found righteous before God not because of his works, but because of his faith. (A similar line of argument is found in Gal 3:6ff.)

If Abraham's righteousness did not derive from his works or law-observance, perhaps it was due to his circumcision.* This too is rejected. For a careful reading of Genesis reveals that Abraham's circumcision was mentioned only after the declaration of his righteousness (Gen 17:10-11). Paul concludes: "And he received the sign of circumcision as a seal on the righteousness received through faith while he was uncircumcised" (Rom 4:11). This rite merely confirmed the prior and decisive declaration of righteousness through faith.

This line of reasoning led Paul to a stunning conclusion, namely, that the righteousness of Abraham, which was credited to him because he believed in the God who promises, antedated and transcended both Law and circumcision and is therefore available to all without exception on condition that they believe as Abraham did. In this sense Abraham can be called "the father of us all" (Rom 4:16), Gentile as well as Jew. Accordingly, the promise is now seen to embrace a universal progeny, and the "land" becomes the totality of messianic blessings culminating in eschatological glory.

Paul then examines more closely the motivation for Abraham's faith: "He is our father in the sight of God, in whom he believed, who gives life to the dead and calls into being what does not exist" (Rom 4:17). In other words, Abraham discounted the evidence of death in his mortal body and all about him as he trusted absolutely in the promise of his life-giving creator. In this he is a model for all Christians who now have even greater evidence of God's life-giving power manifested in the resurrection of Jesus (4:24). Accordingly, to be justified is to possess the gift of life in its fullest and richest meaning.

Paul again invokes the figure of Abraham in Romans 9, where he considers the thorny question of the meaning of Israel's election. He points out that physical descendance from Abraham is of little consequence. What does matter is to be "children of the promise" (9:8), and this happens only where there is faith, as Paul has made clear in Romans 4.

Abraham in Hebrews and James. Abraham's name appears frequently in the Letter to the Hebrews but in most instances it is only to recall common Christian convictions about his faith or about the promises entrusted to him. In Hebrews 7, he serves as a kind of foil to Melchizedek* who is the center of attention. In Hebrews 11, Christian insight is attributed to Abraham who is said to have felt like an alien in the promised land because he knew that our true homeland is heaven.

In the Letter of James 2:21-24, we find a clarification of Paul's argument in Romans 4 from the story of Abraham: "Was not Abraham our father justified by works when he offered his son Isaac upon the altar?" (2:21). In other words, Abraham's obedience in offering Isaac (a good work) proves that faith is shown to be authentic only when good works flow from it. Therefore, good works are the necessary effect of good faith.

Pastoral-Liturgical Tradition

The early Fathers of both East and West extolled the witness of Abraham, particularly in the sacrifice of Isaac. This was recognized as a foreshadowing of God's offering of his Son, Jesus, who also carried the wood for his own sacrifice. It is for this reason also that Abraham's name appears in Canon I of the Roman Mass, where his sacrifice is recalled as a preparation for the perfect sacrifice of Jesus.

Various elements of the story of Abraham appear in the liturgical readings also, particularly as the second reading for the

Easter Vigil and the annual OT reading for the Second Sunday of Lent. Finally, Abraham's name is invoked in the funeral liturgy to reassure the faithful about the trustworthiness of God's promise of eternal life.

See: ABEL, ADAM AND EVE, CIRCUMCISION, COVENANT, ELECTION, FAITH, HOSPITALITY, JUSTIFICATION, LAND, LAW, LIFE, MELCHIZEDEK, MESSIAH, PROMISE, RESURRECTION, SACRIFICE

DEMETRIUS R. DUMM, O.S.B.

ADAM AND EVE

Adam and Eve, though portrayed as the first created man* and woman* from whom all humankind descended, really represent every man and every woman. Their story is both particular and universal. It unfolds in a land beyond this world and at a time outside of history. It is the story of the dawn of life* and the foreboding of death, of belonging and of alienation, of innocence and of sin. This story about beginnings traditionally has been used to explain some of the fundamental questions of human existence.

Old Testament

The Hebrew word 'ādām (meaning red or ruddy) serves as a collective noun (humankind, Gen 1:26), as reference to a male individual (the man, Gen 2:8) and as a proper name (Adam, Gen 5:1). In most Bibles today, what appears as the proper name "Adam" is usually a translation of the general reference "the man." Such differing uses of the word have left the creation narratives open to a variety of interpretations. The Hebrew is quite clear with reference to the woman, however. First she is called (identified as) woman (Gen 2:23), and then called by the name Eve (Gen 3:22). The most commonly known characterizations of Adam and Eve are found in the second account of creation* and the report of the first sin (Gen 2:4b–3:24). Most of the other biblical references to them allude to this tradition (e.g., Hos 6:7; Tob 8:6; Sir 33:10). Although in the first account of creation 'ādām was created in the image of God (Gen 1:27-28), the word appears only in these two verses and is a clear reference to the entire race and not to its first member, unless one believes that the first human being was an androgyne. The first account goes on to distinguish the couple as "male and female," not as Adam and Eve.

Adam was also the name of a city on the east bank of the Jordan River. It was the place where the waters were dammed, thus enabling Joshua to lead the people into the land (Josh 3:16).

Creation and Relationship (Gen 2:4b-25). According to the second account, Adam and Eve were created at different times, in different ways, out of different material. Several literary features mark this as an imaginative story rather than a factual account. The man was made first, formed by God out of the dust* of the ground ('ªdāmâ—the reddish clay which, when tilled, will yield necessary sustenance) and then quickened by the breath of life (v. 7). The anthropomorphic description of God is plain, and the assonance in 'ādām/'ªdāmâ is unmistakable. (Creation from clay mixed with divine blood was a common theme in both Egypt and Mesopotamia.) The story goes on to show that, like the man, the trees (v. 9) and the wild animals and birds of the air (v. 19) were also "formed" from the "ground."

Despite the affinity between the man, the earth, and the other animals that inhabited the earth, the man was set apart from the other creatures. Only he had the breath of life breathed into him. His uniqueness is also evident in the singular role he played in relation to the rest of creation. Originally there was neither "field shrub" nor "grass of the field" because "God had sent no rain" and "there was no man to till [from 'ābad, to serve] the ground" (v. 5). The 'ªdāmâ could not be productive without the services of 'ādām. Similarly, the animals too were somehow dependent on the man. The story states that God formed the animals from the same ground so that the man

7

would not be alone. But, though they shared his origin, they were not his counterpart, much less his succor (a better translation of 'ēzer than helpmate. See Exod 18:4; Deut 33:26; Ps 20:3). His prominence is demonstrated further when the animals are named by him (v. 19f.), since the right to name* implies authority over what is named, even to the extent of playing some part in determining its very being.

A distinct and totally different kind of creative act produced the woman. She was built by God from one of the man's ribs (v. 22). (The name of the Sumerian goddess Ninti can mean "Lady of the rib" or "Lady of life." The play on words is lost when translated into Hebrew, but in part, the meaning has been retained in the image of the rib and in part, in the name Eve, Mother of the Living.) The poetic character of the account is apparent in the play on the words "bone and flesh" (v. 23a). Built from his rib, she certainly was his bone, but the word-pair is an example of a particular poetic pattern which expresses something in its totality (e.g., flesh and blood; young and old; east and west). Bone and flesh refers to power and limitation respectively and, in this poetic form, implies the total range of human potential. A further play on her origin from him is found in 'iššâ (woman) and 'îš (man). Though the two words are not etymologically linked, the assonance is clear. From the very beginning, the man and woman belong together. They are of the same bone and flesh, and they are husband and wife (v. 24).

Sin and Punishment (Gen 3:1-24). The account of creation ends with mention of the couple's nakedness and lack of shame. Their innocence was not because of naivete. "His woman" (Gen 2:24f.) suggests sexual intimacy. Shame was related to nakedness only after they had sinned (v. 10). With few exceptions nakedness was a sign of dispossession, deprivation, and powerlessness (see Isa 20:2; Hos 2:5; Job 22:6). It was not primarily the *cause* of shame, it *signified* an existing shameful situation. In this narrative, nakedness as part of sexual intimacy and nakedness related to sin are not the same.

The temptation is portrayed as a dialogue between the serpent and the woman. The cunning ('ārûm) of the serpent (v. 1) and the nakedness ('ārôm) of the couple create yet another assonance. This and the serpent's faculty of speech are further evidence of the mythic character of the story. Wanting to be like God, knowing "what is good and what is bad" (v. 5), the couple disregarded the order about eating the fruit of the tree and the attendant threat of death (see 2:16f.). Their eyes were opened and indeed they did know good from bad. Several consequences flowed from their action: their nakedness now signified their shameful situation (vv. 7, 10); they knew alienation from God (v. 8) and from each other (v. 12), and even the earth refused to yield its fruits (v. 18); and they were denied access to the tree of life and all the promise that it held (v. 22).

The separate and dissimilar punishments for the man and the woman, though probably descriptions of life in ancient Israel, are related to the account of their distinctive creations. While the same Hebrew word translates as the "pain" of pregnancy and the "toil" of farming, the woman's punishment resulted from her "origin" ('iššâ/'îš) and the man's from his ('ādām/'adāmâ). Now life was fraught with pain for both the man and the woman, and this pain touched the very core of their beings. Their punishments were related to conditions of life, not to death. Death would be the end to their suffering, which would last until they "return[ed] to the ground from which [they] were taken" (v. 19, see 2:7). An instance of the man's authority over the woman was his power to name her Eve (v. 20).

Another Version (Genesis 1). This version is less a story about Adam and Eve than it is an account of the creation of the entire universe. The creation of and role played by humankind (1:26-30) is one piece of this account. Unlike the descriptions of the creation of other animals ("Let the water teem. . . . Let the earth bring forth . . .," vv. 20, 24), the verb that begins the report of this particular divine act expresses direct and deliberate action ("Let us make . . .," v. 26). All of the other living things were made "according to their kind" (a better translation than "every kind" or "all kinds," vv. 11f., 21, 24f.), but humankind was created in God's image, according to God's likeness (v. 26f.). In addition to the charge to reproduce (a comparable order was given to other creatures, v. 22), the man and the woman were given authority over the earth and the animals (v. 28). However, their privilege and authority were not absolute. They were images of God, not gods in their own right.

Theological Significance. The story of Adam and Eve addresses some historically unanswerable yet unavoidable questions. The poetical, sometimes mythological, language and imagery implicitly suggests that its message is for all people of all times. The etiological explanations answer some of the ultimate human questions that plague every human being, questions about the origin of life, the place of human beings in creation, the relationship between man and woman, sexual attraction and marriage, the reason for death, and the source of sin. The way Israel answered these questions constitutes its own anthropological understanding.

Although these traditions have much in common with the creation myths of other cultures, significant differences do exist. Both traditions maintain that the man and the woman were created directly and solely by God, since there is no other deity who might be involved. Human beings were not generated by some life-giving force within water or the earth. The ground did not play an active role in the creation of the man, nor did the man in the creation of the woman. The traditions further attest both to the affinity that human beings have with the rest of creation and to the place of honor that they enjoy among all creatures. Their distinction gives them both privilege and responsibility ("subdue," "have dominion," "guard," and "till"). They were

not created to do the menial work of the gods, as some Mesopotamian traditions state. Their labor was for their own sake and for the sake of the natural world.

In both accounts the man and the woman, though different, are depicted as counterparts. Essentially the same (image of God, "bone of my bone") their relationship is one of intimacy and mutuality. Natural sexual attraction prompts human beings to disengage themselves from their families of origin in order to enter into families of procreation.

Unlike other ancient myths that tell of humans being tricked out of immortality by a capricious god, Israel's story puts the blame on humans themselves. Because of their sin, they were denied access to the tree of life. However, one understands that sin (e.g., pride, disobedience, etc.), the source of the temptation, was something that was, in itself, good (the tree of knowledge), and the tempter was cunning not evil.

See: CREATION, DEATH, HUMANKIND, IMAGE OF GOD, LIFE, MAN/MEN, SIN, WOMAN/WOMEN

DIANNE BERGANT, C.S.A.

New Testament

Adam as a Type of Christ. In the NT Adam is given far more attention than Eve and the most important passage dealing with Adam occurs in Romans 5. Paul has already discussed the reality of justification and is now prepared to consider the special fruit of God's mercy, which is hope. Hope rather than victory takes center stage because, although Jesus is now in glory, the believer must still struggle and strive to persevere.

It is, however, a struggle that is joyful and confident because the power given to the Christian by Jesus is more than adequate to cancel the old legacy of death and to permit a free choice of justice and life. In Christ, the believer replaces helplessness with confidence.

Paul illustrates all this by invoking both a similarity and a contrast between Adam and Christ. Adam and Christ are alike because each stands at the beginning of a new race. Therefore, Adam is considered "a type of the one who was to come" (Rom 5:14). But in all other respects they are dissimilar. For with Adam the reign of sin* began and that brought with it the bitter experience of death, whereas Christ initiated a new tradition of forgiveness and life.

Paul does not speculate about the exact connection between sin and death but the effect of their reign was a general human condition of bondage and helplessness. In this sense, Paul provides a basis for the traditional doctrine of original sin even though the phrase "in whom [i.e. Adam] all sinned" (Rom 5:12) can no longer be sustained as a basis for that teaching since the phrase should be translated, "inasmuch as all sinned." At most one can say that Paul here affirms a real but mysterious connection between the sin of Adam and the general sinfulness of the human race prior to the victory of Christ.

Jesus challenged the universal reign of sin and death as he won a victory that stamps the new age which he inaugurated with the surpassing sign of God's gracious gift of love: "For if by that one person's transgression the many died, how much more did the grace of God and the gracious gift of the one person Jesus Christ overflow for the many" (Rom 5:15). The victory of Christ, therefore, completely eclipsed the former dominance of sin and death.

Paul continues the contrast between Adam and Christ in terms of disobedience and obedience: "For just as through the disobedience of one person the many were made sinners, so through the obedience of one many will be made righteous" (Rom 5:19). This suggests that the sinful choice of Adam, which remains a real option for all humans, involves a foolish and selfish grasp for freedom that disregards the claims of the creator and is doomed from the start. By contrast, Jesus' obedience accepts the design of God and converts both human life and human death into an opportunity for authentic freedom and glory.

The reign of sin and death is thus replaced by the reign of God's love in the gift of Jesus himself.

Adam and Bodily Resurrection. Paul refers again to the special relationship between Adam and Christ when he takes up the important question of the fact and nature of the bodily resurrection of the faithful in 1 Corinthians 15. Paul's position is stated clearly: "For since death came through a human being, the resurrection of the dead came also through a human being. For just as in Adam all die, so too in Christ shall all be brought to life . . . " (15:21-22).

The "death" for which Adam was responsible involves much more than physical death; it includes a pride and selfishness that are ultimately suicidal. By contrast, Jesus brings a "life" that does not exclude physical death but uses it and all human life as an occasion for love and trust and thereby fulfills God's gracious purpose, which is to provide a radical new kind of life that is totally impervious to death. At present we see the full realization of this only in Christ himself but this victory will be shared in due time by all who have imitated Christ's love and trust. In the meantime, these believers must be patient and persevering.

The skeptical Corinthians, influenced no doubt by the Hellenistic disdain for the body (see Acts 17:32), question the very notion of a risen body (1 Cor 15:35). After pointing out the fact of continuity and transformation in nature (e.g., seed and plant), Paul appeals to Scripture as he recalls the story of Adam's creation: "So, too, it is written, 'The first man, Adam, became a living being,' the last Adam a life-giving spirit" (1 Cor 15:45).

By quoting the passage from Genesis 2:7, Paul acknowledges the reality of a certain kind of life received by all humans on the level of Adam's life. However, we now realize that a new kind of life is available through the sacrifice of Jesus in whom "the life-giving spirit" of God brings about a radical new creation: "The first man was from the earth, earthly; the second man, from heaven" (Gen 15:47). This new creation, being essentially spiritual, will overcome all earthly resistance and will replace corruption with incorruptibility (15:50-55). The power that makes this possible is the gift of God's love manifested in Jesus and empowering the faithful to live in unselfishness and trust. This is the import of Paul's statement in 2 Corinthians 5:17: "So whoever is in Christ is a new creation: the old things have passed away; behold, new things have come."

Eve and Church Order. Eve appears anonymously in 1 Corinthians 11:7-12. There Paul is apparently concerned about assuring proper masculine and feminine distinction in the liturgical assembly. He supports his position by alluding to the creation story: "A man . . . should not cover his head, because he is the image and glory of God, but woman is the glory of man. For man did not come from woman, but woman from man; nor was man created for woman, but woman for man . . . "(1 Cor 11:7-9). In the context of the creation story, woman would be man's "glory" by accepting her vocation as his helpmate (Gen 2:18). Both man and woman then would glorify God by responding to their respective vocations. This is given further emphasis by the reminder that woman (Eve) was created from man (Adam; Gen 2:21-22) and therefore was intended to be his helpmate.

Paul's argument from Scripture is faulty because he makes no distinction between the first story of creation (Gen 1:1–2:4a) where man (generic) is made in God's image, and the second story of creation (Gen 2:4b-25) where woman is derived from man (specific). In any case, Paul is concerned primarily about the pragmatic matter of order in the liturgical assembly and scarcely intends to establish a principle valid for all times. He seems more interested in assuring the place of God and Christ in any church order: "But I want you to know that Christ is the head of every man, and a husband is the head of his wife,

and God the head of Christ" (1 Cor 11:3). Furthermore, in the same context he clearly declares the essential equality of man and woman: "Woman is not independent of man nor man of woman in the Lord. For just as woman came from man, so man is born of woman; but all things are from God" (1 Cor 11:11-12).

The author of 1 Timothy also invokes the name of Eve in dealing with church order: "I do not permit a woman to teach or to have authority over a man. She must be quiet. For Adam was formed first, then Eve. Further, Adam was not deceived, but the woman was deceived and transgressed" (2:12-14). Paul's church was less restrictive in this matter (see 1 Cor 11:5). Moreover, the dubious reasoning in this passage is corrected by other texts (e.g., Rom 5:14) where the culpability of Adam is clearly recognized.

Eve as a Type of Mary. Some believe that the Gospel of John recognizes Eve as a type of Mary when, in 2:4 and 19:26, Jesus addressed his mother as "woman." Such an unusual way of speaking suggests a connection between Mary, mother of Jesus, and Eve, "mother of all the living" (Gen 3:20). As mother of the "last Adam" (1 Cor 15:45), Mary would be the new "Eve," not indeed at Cana, but truly when she participates in the "hour" of Jesus and is pictured standing by the cross. Thus the basis is being laid for the recognition of Mary as Mother of the Church.

See: BODY, DEATH, GLORY, HOPE, JUSTIFICATION, LIFE, LOVE, MAN/MEN, MARY, MERCY, OBEDIENCE, RESURRECTION, SIN, TYPE, WOMAN/WOMEN

DEMETRIUS R. DUMM, O.S.B.

Pastoral-Liturgical Tradition

Adam and Eve have had enduring importance in the Christian tradition because they have come to stand as prototypes of what it means to be human, both as a symbol of what God intended human persons to be, and as a meditation on our deep alienation from God (original sin). Appropriately, then, the story of Adam and Eve is invoked in the Easter Vigil liturgy, since that story speaks of our original destiny, our fall from that high calling, and that "happy fault which merited so great a Redeemer" (Easter Vigil hymn to the paschal candle). Because Adam and Eve play such an important role in inaugurating the history of salvation, the Eastern Churches have kept a feast in their honor (in the Greek Church, the Sunday before Christmas). Latin medieval theologians played on the palindrome of "Eva" ("Ave") to show that Eve's name prefigured the salutation of Gabriel to Mary, initiating the incarnation.

Although both Genesis accounts stress the creation of male and female (Gen 1:27; 2:22), the male-centered bias of the tradition has focused on Adam rather than Adam and Eve together. Eve was frequently pictured as the temptress of Adam who led him into sin.* The one countervailing force was the depiction of Adam and Eve in their Edenic state as the prototype of marriage. It is only in the last part of the twentieth century that feminist scholarship has recovered Eve as important for Christian understandings of the human, and not just as justification for the oppression of women.

Adam and Eve, portrayed as parents of all human beings, have been symbols of both the origins and the unity of humankind. By standing at the very beginning of humanity, they offer a picture of what God intended humanity to be. The Eastern Church has emphasized their creation in the very image of God (Gen 1:27). This image has been tarnished by sin, but is restored in Christ in such a way that the image comes to partake in the divine nature it reflects. The Western Church was more preoccupied with the ethical dimensions of the relationship, and emphasized the specific capacities accorded to Adam and Eve in the garden: freedom from disordered desire (freedom from concupiscence), freedom from suffering, and freedom from death. In theological terms, they lived in a state of sanctifying grace, union with God.

In their free act to disobey God's injunction, Adam and Eve fell from grace and became subject to concupiscence, suffering, and death. These Western elaborations on the story of Adam and Eve were absent in the earliest centuries of Christian tradition. Indeed, the exact nature of their fall from grace was not the object of much speculation; rather, the account of Paul in Romans 5 was implicitly accepted. The Eastern Church has largely continued to follow that path. The Western Church owes its greater elaboration of the meaning of the sin of Adam and Eve to Augustine's debates with the followers of Pelagius. The followers of Pelagius saw the meaning of Adam and Eve's fall as largely exemplary of what happens to humans, and advocated that through asceticism humans could gain communion with God. Both out of his own experience and his reading of Romans 5 Augustine argued vehemently against the Pelagian position. The fall from grace has affected human ability to turn to God freely in a profound and complete way. It is only through the acceptance of God's grace that humans are able to do so. This alienation from God is not something absorbed from the environment, but is transmitted to each human at the moment of conception. That it is transmitted means that sinfulness (the state of original sin) is not constitutive of being human as such. Indeed, Christian teaching (for Roman Catholics, formulated in the canons of the Council of Trent) is that the guilt of original sin is removed in baptism, although its effects (concupiscence, suffering, and death) linger.

Augustine's teaching was affirmed at the Synods of Carthage (418) and Orange (529). Questions raised by Nominalists about how human beings become implicated in original sin and by the Protestant reformers about the nature of human depravity led the Council of Trent to reaffirm Catholic teaching in 1546. That formulation of the doctrine remained intact down into the twentieth century. Under the growing acceptance of evolutionary theory about the origins of humankind, the literal reading of Genesis 1–3 made the Christian account of human origins and sinfulness seem improbable. Evolutionary theory proposed that the human species was not a separate creation as depicted in the Genesis accounts, but a gradual evolution from other animal species. Moreover, parallel evolutions could have happened (polygenism), rather than evolution toward a single pair (monogenism). And given the evolutionary schema, ethical development would not have been adequate to give credence to the "original sin" story in Genesis 2–3. The Roman Catholic Church, bound most closely to Augustine's theology, struggled mightily with this dilemma in the early and middle part of the twentieth century. The Pontifical Biblical Commission required a literal reading of the Pentateuch in 1909, but Pius XII opened the door to other methods of exegesis in 1943. But seven years later, the encyclical *Humani Generis* appeared to close the door again on a broader interpretation. The Pastoral Constitution on the Church in the Modern World (no. 13), by speaking of the sinfulness of humankind without direct reference to the Adam and Eve story, seemed to make possible new interpretations. Consequently there was a great deal of theological speculation on the nature of human sinfulness, consonant with the concerns of the tradition (the unity of humankind, sinfulness affects all, it is God's help that rescues us from this state) and the exigencies of contemporary understandings of the origin of the human. All of these give broader, non-literal interpretations to the Adam and Eve story. No single theological proposal has won widespread acceptance. Important in all of them, however, is the preservation of the aforementioned values of the tradition and a credibility within contemporary understandings of the origin of the human species.

See: BAPTISM, DEATH, GRACE, HUMANKIND, JESUS CHRIST, SIN

ROBERT J. SCHREITER, C.PP.S.

ADOPTION

Old Testament

Adoption. Adoption refers to the act of taking for one's own by selection or assent, especially with reference to family membership and inheritance. References to adopted persons appear in the OT but no laws regulating adoption practices are given except those related to the Israelite system of levirate marriage (Deut 25:1-10). Adoption laws are evident, however, in other Semitic traditions, for example, in Hammurabi's Code and the Nuzi tablets of the fifteenth century BCE.

Genesis 15:1-3 records Abraham's lament that he has no natural child, but only an adopted heir, but there are few other Israelite examples of adoption. In Exodus 2:10, Moses becomes the adopted child of Pharaoh's daughter, reflecting similar practices among the Egyptians. And Esther 2:7, 15 describes the adoption of Esther by Mordecai, confirming the Persian custom as well.

Metaphors of Adoption. More important in the OT are the metaphors of adoption describing the relationships of individuals and groups to God. Psalm 2:7, "You are my son, today I have begotten you," reflects the formula of adoption whereby the newly enthroned Israelite king becomes God's son (see also 2 Sam 7:14; Ps 89:26-27). The relationship of the whole nation of Israel to God was also expressed with the metaphors of adoption-sonship as, for example, in Hosea 11:1 or Exodus 4:22. Israel's adoption and election by God gave them both special privileges and special responsibilities to live in fidelity to the covenant which sealed their special status as God's chosen people.

New Testament

Jesus, Son of God. The metaphor of adoption in the NT is applied indirectly to Jesus as God's son and also to Christians who, through faith, become children of God. The earliest Christological formulations (e.g.,

Rom 1:3-4) claim that Jesus had been installed as the Son of God through the resurrection of the dead, although the technical Greek term for adoption—*huiothesia*—is nowhere used of Jesus. Mark 1:11 (and parallels) designate the baptism of Jesus as the moment of the revelation of his sonship, although they could imply as well that the baptism was the beginning of that sonship manifested in the descent of the Spirit and the voice which said, "You are my beloved Son; with you I am well pleased."

Christians as Adopted Children of God. Through faith in the Son and resurrected One, Christians receive "sonship" (their identity as daughters and sons) and the capacity to cry, "Abba, Father" (Gal 4:5-7; Rom 8:15; Eph 1:5). Using the metaphors of legal inheritance and the manumission of slaves, Paul speaks of our adoption by God through Jesus (Gal 4:1-7) and specifies that this new status bestows on us the Spirit (Rom 8:16). As adopted children of God, we participate in the freedom and full inheritance of God's promise. Not that we are yet perfect; no, our adoption is to be completed in the future with the final redemption of our bodies in the resurrection (Rom 8:22-23). Until then, we live in hope waiting for the fulness of God's gift of adoption to be revealed.

Pastoral-Liturgical Tradition

Adoption in Christological Controversies. The Christological heresy known as Adoptionism maintained that Christ in his humanity is not the true but only the adoptive son of God. Early tendencies in this direction are found in Nestorius and the Antiochene school. The fullblown heresy originated in Spain in the eighth century and was revived later in the twelfth century.

The Rite of Baptism celebrates the adoption of the baptized Christian into the family* of God. Initiates receive a new status—not that of a slave, but that of a child—together with the gift of the Spirit which empowers them to cry to God, "Abba."

See: BAPTISM, ELECTION, FAMILY

BARBARA E. BOWE, R.S.C.J.

AGONY

The term "agony" is used only once in the NT. Describing Jesus' intense prayer on the eve of his death, Luke portrays him as being "in such agony" (22:44). Luke's reference to Jesus' profuse sweat "like drops of blood falling on the ground" adds to this powerful portrayal of anguished prayer. The Greek term *agonia* comes from the root word *agon* meaning a "contest" or "struggle," often used of an athletic contest (as in Heb 12:1). The noun *agonia* or "agony" retains this connotation of intense struggle. This nuance fits Luke's portrayal of Jesus in his passion* narrative. He prays to be delivered from the final "trial" or "test" *(peirasmos)* that will be inflicted by the power of evil and urges the disciples to do the same (Luke 22:40, 46). Like a mighty champion preparing intensely for a momentous contest, Jesus prays for the strength to endure his struggle with death* and the power of evil. There is little doubt that Luke intends this portrait of Jesus as instruction for the Christian reader. The power of evil, the threat of suffering* and death—these "test" the faith of Jesus' followers. To find strength one must pray earnestly. Jesus tells his disciples, "It is you who have stood by me in my trials" (22:28), and the disciples themselves are instructed to pray in the Lord's prayer: "do not subject us to the final test" (11:4).

See: DEATH, PASSION, SUFFERING

DONALD SENIOR, C.P.

ALMSGIVING

The sharing of one's goods with those in need is a strong and continuing tradition of the Bible and of the Church.

Old Testament

The sharing of one's resources with the needy is provided for in the OT, but there is no Hebrew term for "almsgiving" as such. One of the words the Greek Septuagint used to translate terms for "mercy" and "righteousness," *eleemosyne*, eventually came to be understood in the sense of "benevolent activity"; in the NT this is the regular term for almsgiving. The oldest texts of the Hebrew Bible have sparse mention of almsgiving; there is an increase of interest later, especially in the Hellenistic period when class distinctions became more pronounced.

Law Codes. The needs of the poor are addressed in the Deuteronomic Code (Deuteronomy 12–26) and the Holiness Code (Leviticus 17–26). The Deuteronomic Code enshrines the ancient hope of a society in which there will be no class of "the poor." Provision is made for those without land—the Levite, the slave, the alien, the orphan and the widow—to have regular access to food, not as a dole but as a right, through the provision of the third-year tithe (Deut 14:28-29). At harvest time, the reaper is not to be so conscientious that there is nothing left for the poor to glean (Deut 24:19-22). Every seven years there was to be a relaxation of debts (15:1) so that no one would become hopelessly mired in poverty.

The motivation for sharing blessings was the example of God, who shared his bounty with the Israelites (Deut 16:17), and the promise that sharing would bring continued blessings (Deut 15:10). The vision found in 15:4 that this sharing of God's bounty would eradicate poverty is contradicted by 15:11: "The needy will never be lacking in the land." This may be an editorial comment from a later time, when the utopian society had not materialized.

A separation of rich and poor is more pronounced in the Holiness Code (Leviticus 17–26), laws from the period of the monarchy collected at the time of the Exile. Those who find themselves "reduced to poverty and unable to hold out beside you" (Lev 25:35) are to be accorded charity until they can get back on their feet. If this is ineffective, the debtor will become technically a slave, but one who is treated with respect as a servant of God whom he saved from slavery in Egypt (v. 42). The provision for gleaning by the needy is also present in this Code (Lev 19:9; 23:22). Besides the Sabbatical year, the Holiness Code makes provision for a Jubilee year, occurring every fifty years, when all property would return to the original owner (vv. 8-34).

Sources of Divine Blessings. Almsgiving will continue to be viewed as a response to and imitation of God's largesse toward the Israelites. As time goes on, the benefits of almsgiving to the giver are stressed more and more: "He who gives to the poor suffers no want" (Prov 28:27). The two aspects are occasionally combined: "the just man is kindly and gives, . . . Neither in my youth, nor now that I am old, have I seen a just man forsaken nor his descendants begging bread" (Ps 37:21, 25; see Ps 112:9). The failure of conventional wisdom in this regard is portrayed in the example of Job, the proverbial just man, who was "eyes to the blind and feet to the lame" (Job 29:12-16), but who suffered calamity.

But sometimes almsgiving is presented as simply the right thing for a servant of God to do (Prov 3:27). It makes a person happy (3:21) and glorifies the Maker (v. 31). The idea that God is especially served in the poor is expressed beautifully in Proverbs 19:17: "He who has compassion on the poor lends to the Lord." But at the same time to be poor and forced to beg is seen as a great curse (1 Sam 2:36; Ps 109:10).

Besides almsgiving as such, other practices of compassionate sharing are urged and praised. The just man is one who "is gracious and lends" (Ps 112:5); the opposite of this is not failure to lend but usury: "If you lend money to one of your poor neighbors among my people, you shall not act like an extortioner toward him by demanding interest from him" (Exod 22:24). Almsgiving is also disguised in the generosity expected in true hospitality (Deut 10:18) and on the occasion of special sacrifices* (1 Sam 9:13) and feasts. When David brought the ark of the covenant to Jerusalem, "He then distributed among all the people, to each man and each woman in the entire multitude of Israel, a loaf of bread, a cut of roast meat, and a raisin cake" (2 Sam 6:19). On the great day of the promulgation of the Law, Ezra urged the multitude to share food and drink with "those who had nothing prepared" (Neh 8:10), which is probably a gracious way of including those who had nothing they could prepare.

Late sources indicate that almsgiving became a principal work of charity in the Hellenistic period. The imitation of God is more explicit than before: this practice makes one "like a son to the Most High" (Sir 4:10). The benefits are also described in more elaborate terms: "Water quenches a flaming fire, and alms atone for sins" (3:29; see Dan 4:24). Almsgiving even staves off the power of death and *sheol*: "Almsgiving frees one from death, and keeps one from going into the dark world" (Tob 4:10). Even before death the remembrance of one's generosity will gain assistance for the giver in a later time of need. Threats are employed too: the ungenerous will be vulnerable to the curses of the poor, whose prayers receive attention in heaven (Sir 3:30; 4:5-6). The material gift is not enough; it must come from a generous heart, "A grudging gift wears out the expectant eyes" (18:17).

In what seems to be the latest development in the spirituality of almsgiving in the OT, giving to the poor is equated with sacrifice in the Temple: "In works of charity one offers fine flour, and when he gives alms he presents his sacrifice of praise" (Sir 35:2; see Tob 4:11). In the triad of prayer, fasting, and almsgiving, the latter "accompanied by righteousness" is best (Tob 12:8).

New Testament

The early Christian community was heir to the attitudes toward almsgiving developed in the OT. The NT writings, produced during a relatively short period of time, reflect especially the context of the Hellenistic period, by which time almsgiving had become a standard sign of an upright religious life.

Mark of Christian Discipleship. The Synoptic story of the rich man (Mark 10:17-22; Matt 19:16-22; Luke 18:18-23) reaches its climax in the response to Jesus' challenge: "You are lacking in one thing. Go, sell what you have, and give to [the] poor and you will have treasure in heaven; then come, follow me" (Mark 10:21). The man cannot bring himself to part with his possessions, and turns away sad. In Luke's Gospel, he is contrasted to the tax collector in the Temple and the little children and matched with the Pharisee who went home unjustified (18:14).

In the Sermon on the Mount, Jesus speaks of the traditional triad of piety—almsgiving, prayer, fasting—as "deeds of righteousness" (Matt 6:1). Underneath his emphasis on the danger of ostentation in observance is the implication that these practices are focal to Christian piety as they were to Jewish. Earlier in the Sermon, Christian discipleship is expressed as open-handedness to the borrower as well as to the one who cannot pay back (5:40-42). Paul presents as a sign of a religious spirit "giving away everything" (1 Cor 13:3). He stresses, of course, that only with love* does this really have meaning. Judas, an earlier example, spoke of concern for the poor, but it was a cover for other plans (John 12:5-6). Giving to the needy should be an expression of love; vice versa, without this giving, love is suspect (1 John 4:17).

The Lucan writings disclose a particular interest in almsgiving. "Sell your belongings and give alms" sounds a unique note in Luke's version of the Lilies of the Field sermon (Luke 12:33; see Matt 6:19). Several motives are noted for almsgiving. Zacchaeus sees it as a proof of his sincerity (Luke 19:8). Tabitha and Cornelius are commended for their generosity; the latter's prayer and almsgiving "have ascended as a memorial offering before God" (Acts 10:4; see 9:36). The crippled beggar expects alms from Peter and John and receives what they are able to give (3:6). The problem of daily distribution of food to the poor widows prompts the appointment of the seven Hellenist leaders (6:3).

Blessed Are the Poor. Poverty is no longer a sign of God's disfavor. The poor are even "blessed" (Luke 6:20). A poor widow is singled out for praise (Mark 12:41-44). At the final judgment, it will be revealed that those who helped the needy were really helping the "Son of Man" (Matt 25:44). God chose the poor and it is wrong to dishonor them (Jas 2:5-6). When arranging a banquet, in fact, it is the poor and the needy who should be invited (Luke 14:13). This doctrine counteracts a traditional attitude which interpreted riches and possessions as a sign of God's approval. But neither does it mean that poverty is a guarantee of divine approval. What is said about the poor is best understood in connection with what is said about the rich. Riches are good, but they may endanger salvation* by creating an illusion of self-sufficiency and independence from God (Mark 10:25). The rich must learn to share, to understand that "It is more blessed to give than to receive" (Acts 20:35).

The reward to be pursued is not wealth in this life but treasure in heaven. God will not be outdone in generosity. "Give and gifts will be given to you; a good measure, packed together, shaken down, and overflowing, will be poured into your lap" (Luke 6:38). The benefits begin already: giving alms cleanses the sinner from the inside (Luke 11:41). The proper relationship to wealth and possessions is a spirit of detachment (Matt 10:8) which, based on a reliance on God's loving providence, makes one truly "blessed."

The Collection for Jerusalem. A pervasive theme of Paul's missionary work among the Gentile communities in Asia Minor and Europe is the collection for the "holy ones" *(hagioi)*, the poor members of the Jerusalem Church. In Paul's vision, the collection is not only a response to need, but a symbol of the union between the new Greek-speaking communities and the mother Church. He described this as a fitting gift of material blessings in return for the spiritual blessings of the gospel (Rom 15:25-27).

Two different collections can be identified. The first was organized by Barnabas and Saul in Antioch in response to a famine (Acts 11:28-30). Whether on this visit or later, the Jerusalem leaders encouraged Paul to "be mindful of the poor," which he says dovetailed exactly with his own intentions (Gal 2:10). The other collection was taken up in Galatia, Corinth, Macedonia, and Achaia and delivered by Paul on his final trip to Jerusalem (Acts 24:17; 1 Cor 16:1-4).

Paul's thought on the collection for Jerusalem is developed in 2 Corinthians 8–9. He strongly urges generosity, convinced that this will both be a concrete expression of discipleship of Jesus (8:8-9) and a means of strengthening the bonds between Jewish and Gentile Christians. These chapters sparkle with key theological terms: *charis* (grace), *koinonia* (fellowship), *agape* (love), *eucharistia* (thanksgiving). Paul views the alms for Jerusalem as a "service" *(diakonia:* 8:4; 9:1) and, in a subtle play on words, implies that it is an act of divine worship*: "the administration of this public service *(leitourgia)* is not only supplying the needs of the holy ones but is also overflowing in many acts of thanksgiving *(eucharistia)* to God" (9:12).

Paul applies considerable pressure in his appeal, presenting the example of the generosity of the Macedonians (8:1-2), sending respected emissaries to the Corinthians (8:16-23), and reminding them of their reputation (9:1-4). Still, he does not want to coerce them, stressing that he is only "giving counsel" (8:10). They must be free and joyful in their charity, for "God loves a cheerful giver" (9:7). Though he praises the Macedonians for giving beyond their means, Paul appeals to the relatively wealthy Corinthian church primarily in terms of the principle of equality, by which those who have more should share with those who have less (8:12-15).

See: DISCIPLE/DISCIPLESHIP, EUCHARIST, GRACE, LOVE, MERCY, POOR, PRAYER, RICH, SACRIFICE, SALVATION, WORSHIP

JEROME KODELL, O.S.B.

Pastoral-Liturgical Tradition

The story of almsgiving in the Church is impressive. It is a subject on which a number of biblical texts have been quoted in sermons and books: Matthew 9:14, echoing Hosea 6:6 ("I want mercy, not sacrifice"); Sirach 3:29 ("alms atone for sins"); Tobit 12:8-9 ("prayer and fasting are good, but better . . . is almsgiving"). Two texts seem to have exerted the most influence: first, the parable of the last judgment in Matthew 25:31-46 ("as often as you did it for one of my least"), but also James 1:27, which describes pure religion as "caring for orphans and widows in their distress."

We must also mention the pervasive influence of the Eucharist, where rich and poor alike share the same food. When this solidarity was lacking, it was no longer the Lord's Supper (1 Cor 11:20-22; cf. Jas 2:2-7). Another connection between the Eucharist and the table of the poor can be seen in the role of deacons. Collections for the poor* were made during the liturgy everywhere and are mentioned by many of the Fathers.

From the beginning, almsgiving (a category embracing all corporal works of mercy) has been interpreted mainly in two ways. First, on the basis of Matthew 25:40, it was perceived as an act of service to Christ. Cyprian repeatedly states that when we give alms, we give to Christ (*De oper.* 12, 16, 23), as does Augustine (*Serm.* 15.8), following Origen (*In Mt* Latin, 72). On the basis of Matthew 9:14, Augustine compares alms with sacrifices (*City of God* 10.5-6). Thomas Aquinas, inspired by Matthew 25, concludes that caring for the needy is in

some sense a liturgy (Summa Theologiae, IIa IIae, q. 188, a. 2). Christ's identification with the poor came to be an object of spiritual experience. Martin of Tours gave his cloak to a beggar who turned out to be Christ. Elizabeth of Hungary gave bread to her Lord. John of God rescued from the sidewalk a sick person in whom he saw Jesus. Vincent de Paul spoke of our Lord in the poor.

Second, almsgiving was seen as a factor for spiritual growth. This interpretation appears with various nuances. (1) Based on Luke 6:36 ("Be compassionate, as your Father is compassionate"), Clement of Alexandria, Chrysostom, and Leo the Great write that in our generosity we imitate God. They were to some extent prepared to understand the Gospel in this sense by the stress that some Hellenistic philosophies had laid on imitating God as a way of becoming godlike. (2) On a different level, almsgiving was related to prayer. Augustine wrote that almsgiving helps our prayer life (*Letter* 130 to Proba). Perhaps under his influence the sixteenth-century Dominican, Louis of Granada, included a section on almsgiving in his treatise on prayer. Others speak of the intercessory power of the poor. Based on Luke 16:9 ("Make friends through the use of goods . . . so that they may welcome you"), Gregory the Great wrote that the poor intercede for us and are our advocates (*Hom. in Ev.* 40.10). (3) More common was the notion of almsgiving as atonement. Fathers, penitential books, and medieval theologians included almsgiving among the forms of doing penance for one's sins (cf. Prov 15:27; Sir 3:29). In fact, alms, prayer, and fasting were combined in the observance of Lent. Occasionally, a reward in heaven for almsgiving was mentioned. Jonas of Orléans (ninth century) modified this traditional topic when he wrote that while monks and virgins, because of their renunciation, will be seated with the Lord at the last judgment, lay Christians will be saved if they give alms to Christ's poor (*On the Formation of the Laity* 3.18). Unhappily, some of those who preached to the bourgeoisie in the seventeenth and eighteenth centuries laid too much stress on this motive of personal interest, in language that the middle class understood all too well.

Almsgiving eventually lost its connection with justice and charity in the strong sense of Aquinas. In the eighteenth and nineteenth centuries it became a matter of benevolence or philanthropy. It has been remarked that some of those who distributed blankets to the destitute on Christmas were relatives of the laissez-faire industrialists who had abandoned their impoverished workers. Alms may have been something of a tranquilizer to soothe bad consciences. This would never have happened if almsgiving had not lost its meaning as a service rendered to Christ in the person of the poor and as an act of Christian solidarity.

See: CONSCIENCE, EUCHARIST, POOR

JOHN MANUEL LOZANO

ALTAR

In every celebration of the Eucharist the Church makes remembrance of two discrete historical moments when the presider prays the institution narrative. The words of these short paragraphs evoke the memories of both the Last Supper and Calvary. The Last Supper gives our celebration of the Eucharist its ritual form (meal), while the events of Calvary give the Eucharist its sacramental content (sacrifice). These two historical referents also correspond to the dual meaning attributed to the "altar-table" used in Christian liturgy.

Throughout its history, the Church's celebration of the Eucharist has gravitated between these two symbolic poles. Likewise, its theological apprehension of the Eucharist has often embraced one bloc of sacramental referents in preference over the other. It should not be surprising, then, that the appearance of the altar-table has changed, too, as the Church's understanding of its worship and its own self-understanding have shifted from age to age.

In the Apostolic and post-Apostolic age, when the Church's numbers were still rela-

tively small, its relationship to Judaism more compatible, and its self-identity still more markedly eschatological,* the setting for its Eucharist was the home, where the Church assembled around a simple "dining table" provided by the host or hostess. For most of this period, too, the structure of the Eucharist was more fluid, varying in detail from place to place, but marked everywhere by greater freedom from texts and rubrics than later practice allowed. This less fixed structure was suited to the less formal setting; both combined to express a less institutional, more evangelical self-identity. The altar was a table. The Eucharist was a meal. The sacrificial understanding of the Eucharist and the symbolic meaning of table as altar were not absent, but were less developed than they would become in later ages.

In the centuries after the official establishment of Christianity the Church became more comfortable in its role as partner with the state. The local assembly had formerly distinguished itself from the larger society. Now the Church, less distinguishable from the society in which it had a larger part, differentiated between itself, "here below," and the assembly of heaven, made up of angels and saints.

Parallel to these shifts in the Church's self-identity came a shift in the environment of the Church's worship. The liturgy which had formerly been celebrated in "house-churches" moved into more spacious basilicas. The rites of the Church developed more elaborate ceremonial, often borrowing elements from the imperial cult. With time the table of the Lord's Supper evolved into a more fixed and permanent altar of sacrifice.

During roughly the same period the "cult of martyrs" influenced the shape of the Church's liturgical time and space. The Church's "liturgical year" became more complex as the calendar absorbed annual commemorations of the martyrs' "birthdays" into eternal life. These commemorations, originally celebrated at the tombs of the martyrs, were later moved from the

19

cemeteries into the basilicas themselves in order to protect and preserve the dignity and formality which the liturgy was acquiring. In other instances, basilicas were built above the martyrs' tombs.

The remains of the martyrs—their "relics"—were understood to have a kind of sacramental significance flowing from the Church's conviction that the martyr's death was a participation in the death of Christ. This link was expressed by enshrining relics, at a first stage in caskets placed under the altar, and later by enclosing the relics in the altar itself by means of an altar stone. With time, the placement of relics in the altar became an essential ritual ingredient in the dedication of altars. Consequentially it became more and more appropriate to fashion altars from stone.

The evolution of the liturgy from the Middle Ages through the Gothic into the Baroque period witnessed additional changes in the altar's appearance. The action of the liturgy, with the loss of Latin as a vernacular language, was more exclusively reserved to the performance of the bishop or priest presider. Church sanctuaries became the domain of the ordained while the laity, restricted to the nave, were reduced to passive forms of participation. The altar migrated toward the back wall of the apse and came to be eclipsed by an elaborate "retable"—paintings or carved figures of the Blessed Mother or the saints—or "baldachino"—a fixed and permanent canopy—built upon, behind, or above the altar itself. In addition to the "high altar," "side altars" multiplied in transepts and nave to accommodate multiple "private masses."

In the sixteenth century it became customary to place the tabernacle for the reserved Eucharist in the center of the high altar, with the retable serving as its decorative backdrop. The altar, formerly the locus of the Church's supper-sacrifice, now became, in addition, a throne for the reserved sacrament.

The Liturgical Movement of the twentieth century witnessed a renewed appreciation for the ancient forms and theories of the Church's worship. Scholarly historical research recovered the notion of the Eucharist as banquet and the altar as table. Some churches returned to fashioning altars from wood.

The liturgical renewal initiated by the Second Vatican Council precipitated a more profound restoration of the ritual shape of the Eucharist. The altar was moved away from the back wall so that the presider faced the assembly during the Eucharistic Prayer (once again proclaimed in the language of the people). The reserved sacrament in the tabernacle was given an honored place away from the altar.

In addition, Vatican II endorsed the identification of the altar of the Church's sacrifice with the table of the Church's banquet:

> The Christian altar is by its very nature a table of sacrifice and at the same time a table of the paschal banquet:—a unique altar on which the sacrifice of the cross is perpetuated in mystery throughout the ages until Christ comes;—a table at which the Church's children assemble to give thanks to God and receive the body and blood of Christ (*Rite of Dedication of a Church and an Altar*, Chapter IV: Dedication of an Altar, #4).

The Church's vocabulary about the Eucharist is enlarged beyond "Holy Sacrifice of the Mass" to include "the Lord's Supper" and "the Breaking of Bread" (cf. *Catechism of the Catholic Church*, 1329).

Beyond its functional features, the altar, standing in the midst of the assembly, has symbolic significance as well. In the course of its life the altar will be anointed, incensed, clothed, and kissed. It is approached and touched with reverence. Worshipers in many places honor it by bowing. All of these gestures make sense only in light of the symbolic meaning of the altar.

The altar is not only the table at which the sacrifice of Christ is made present again in the ritual form of the Passover supper. In the style of a symbol, the altar itself is a sacrament of Christ: our priest, our altar and our Lamb of sacrifice.

The altar cannot be reduced to its ritual purpose as though it were simply an instrument at the service of liturgy. It is not the Church's workbench. Rather, the Church relates to the altar sacramentally, attributing meaning to it and deriving meaning from it. It is "a sign of Christ . . . a table of joy . . . a place of communion and peace." It is "a source of unity and friendship" and "the center of our praise and thanksgiving." It is, finally, a sacrament on earth of Christ himself, "high priest and living altar" (cf. Prayer of Dedication, *Rite of Dedication of a Church and an Altar*).

See: EUCHARIST, MEAL, SACRIFICE, TEMPLE

BRIAN J. FISCHER

AMEN

Amen, a word ubiquitous in the Christian liturgy, is derived from Hebrew usage: it means both "Yes, it is true," and "Let this come to pass, so be it." It is thus a word which expresses at one and the same time assent and personal participation, faith and religious commitment—though generally one or other of these denotations predominates.

Amen in the Scriptures

The most frequent use of *Amen* in both the OT and the NT is as a communal acclamation at the end of a prayer* spoken on the community's behalf. Typical of this liturgical usage is the dialogue between Ezra and the assembly: "Ezra blessed the Lord, the great God, and all the people answered, 'Amen, Amen,' lifting up their hands; and they bowed their heads and worshiped the Lord with their faces to the ground" (Neh 8:6). Equivalent usage is found in 1 Chronicles 16:36, Tobit 8:8, and Judith 15:10. The psalms, particularly those of praise and thanksgiving, regularly join "Amen" to their doxological refrains, for example, "Blessed be the Lord, the God of Israel, who alone does wondrous things. Blessed be his glorious name for ever; may his glory fill the whole earth! Amen! Amen!" (Ps 72:18-19). Solemn curses uttered in the assembly were similarly ratified with the acclamation "Amen," as Deuteronomy 27:15 attests.

In the NT *Amen* is used in three distinct ways. (1) There is the use of the *Amen* which the evangelists record on Jesus' lips, not at the end but at the beginning of important teachings, for example in Matthew 5:18 and 18:3, and again—and doubled—in John 1:51 and 5:19. This use of *Amen*, echoing familiar liturgical usage, has the effect of signaling the hearer to pay special attention to what is to follow because Jesus himself has already ratified it as true and Jesus commits himself to its content. (2) Secondly, the community gradually came to realize that Jesus, himself, not just his words, was the perfect Amen, the Amen of God and this they expressed thus: "The Son of God, Jesus Christ, whom we preached among you . . . was not Yes and No; but in him it is always Yes. For all the promises of God find their Yes in him. That is why we utter the Amen through him, to the glory of God" (2 Cor 1:19-20; cf. Rev 3:14). This theological affirmation is significant both because it suggests the relationship between Jesus and the One he called Abba, and because it expresses the Christian theology of prayer which is always "through Christ and with him and in him." (3) Finally, there is ample evidence that when Christians assembled for worship they adopted the use of this Hebrew acclamation to assent to prayer spoken on their behalf (1 Cor 14:16; Rev 5:14; 19:4) and to conclude doxology (Rom 1:25; 2 Pet 3:18; Heb 13:21; Gal 1:5) even when it occurred outside of worship* in regular discourse and writing, but in these instances, the "Amen" of the OT is now transformed because of the One who stands before the throne of grace interceding on our behalf.

Pastoral-Liturgical Tradition

The effect of speaking one's *Amen*, whether individually or, more frequently, in the liturgical assembly, is to ratify, confirm, acclaim, and solemnize what has gone before—and to do so through the mediation of Jesus Christ. To say "Amen" is to express a sacred commitment to live what has just been proclaimed. Such was the insight of the modern liturgical movement with its emphasis on full, conscious, and active participation in the liturgy, a goal expressed in the oft-quoted line of the Constitution on the Sacred Liturgy that active participation is the right and the duty of each Christian in virtue of their baptism. Active participation, however, has sometimes been misinterpreted to refer to the externals of worship, the responses, the singing, the warmth of the assembly's greeting of peace, and so on. Yet it is interior participation which the council (Vatican II) wished to foster, interior participation which the word "Amen" describes, for, as the Scriptures make clear, *Amen* is both an acclamation *and* a commitment, a way of saying "that is true" and at the same time affirming "Yes I will." "Amen" is an external expression of an internal attitude. And as Jesus, the Amen of God, is faithful to his word, so the Christian pledges, with each "Amen" that same faithfulness to live the implications of what we celebrate.

See: FAITH, PRAYER, WORSHIP

KATHLEEN HUGHES, R.S.C.J.

ANCESTORS

Old Testament

Among the many names for ancestors, the ancients called them "patriarchs" (Acts 2:29), that is, the head of one's father's house, "ancestors" (Lev 26:45; Ezra 4:15), "forefathers" (Jer 11:10), "progenitors" (2 Tim 1:3), or just "fathers" (Gen 31:3; 47:30). Because of social conventions, these were all male figures performing the public role as head of the household (see article on "father").

Ancestors, Clan Membership, and Personal Identity. In the ancient world, the family* constituted the dominant social institution. Family structure then differed greatly from the nuclear family of modern industrial nations, for it comprised many generations living under one roof. Married sons remained in the father's compound with their wives, children, and servants. These extended families were related to other families of the same clan through a common ancestor, thus reinforcing a sense of blood solidarity.

Men young and old are known in terms of their fathers (e.g., "Simon, son of John"). An essential part of their personal identity resides precisely in blood descent from a certain person, for sons were expected to carry on their fathers' skills or trade and to embody their virtues and vices; sons were chips off the old block. Hence, Genesis narrates the aetiology or ancestry of the tribes surrounding Israel to indicate their legacy of territory, bodily characteristics, virtues and vices, and the like.

Ancestors and Legacies. Membership in a family's household and clan meant survival in the ancient world. Blood ties translated into fellowship, which meant certain rights to food, support, defense, honor, status, and the like. The remote ancestor of the clan was credited with leaving a certain legacy to it. As head and source of blessings or curses, the ancestor bequeathed an inheritance of rights to land, cattle, wells, etc., to his descendants. Abraham's descendants inherited at least the promise of "the land" (Gen 12:7; 15:18-20); Jacob's offspring claimed rights to his well (John 4:7, 12). Conversely, if the ancestor lost property, reputation, and even grace, this loss too was handed on to his successors, as in the case of Esau (Genesis 27). Adam was understood as the ancestor who lost God's great gifts of grace, eternal life, Paradise, etc., and lost them not just for himself, but for his clan. Inasmuch as he was the ultimate ancestor of all, he lost them for all his descendants (Rom 5:12-21).

Ancestors and Immortality. Given the brief average life spans in the ancient world, an elder who saw his great-grand-children would be truly blessed. The psalmist accounts it a special blessing to see "your children's children" (Ps 128:8). Conversely, when God threatens to visit judgment on a whole household, the threat encompassed "the children and the children's children, to the third and fourth generation" (Exod 34:7), thus wiping out the clan. Yet when the clan thrived, a certain sense of immortality was gained for the ancestors as their name and their seed prospered on earth. Hence child-lessness became a major stigma. Reverence for the dead ancestors was a major duty of the clan.

New Testament

Genealogies. A genealogy* was the social means of claiming a certain role and status in society because of blood ties to a specific ancestor or patriarch. This would have been especially true of the royal and priestly clans. Josephus tells us that even in his day "they [the priests] took precautions to ensure that the priests' lineage should be kept unadulterated and pure" (*Apion* 1.30); not only the males' but the females' pedigree must be inspected, "even obtaining the genealogy from the archives." Josephus boasts of an elite status in his society because he was descended from the highest priestly castes on his father's side and from the Hasmonaean royal family on his mother's side (*Life* 1–3). Jesus likewise was related to priests through his mother's side (Luke 1:5) and to the house of David on his father's side (Luke 1:27).

Blessings and Curses through the Patriarch. The dominant NT portrait of Jesus casts him in the role of an ancestor, the new head of the clan. What he achieves by way of immortality, covenant blessings, and the like, he wins for his family and clan in perpetuity (1 Cor 15:22-23; Rom 5:12-21). Hence the early disciples of Jesus could interpret his significance for them in terms of

his role as the new patriarch, the founder of the clan, the second Adam. His characteristic faith in God and obedience to God's will become the legacy of salvation to be imitated by his followers.

Pastoral-Liturgical Tradition

There is a definite stream of material in the NT which tends to undermine the traditional value placed on blood ties to ancestors. True offspring of Abraham come only from one seed, Isaac (Gal 3:16-17), or are recognized only by doing what he (Abraham) did (John 8:39); legitimacy is not automatic because of blood ties (John 1:12-13). Thus new criteria for membership in the community develop which are more inclusive, namely, sharing Abraham's faith in God.

The genealogy of Jesus in Matthew 1:1-16 contains the mention of four women who seem to cast dishonor on Jesus' ancestry: Tamar, Rahab, Ruth, and Bathsheeba. Some were foreign women; some dishonored the clan because of sexual impropriety. Ordinarily genealogies would suppress such unfavorable, shameful information, but the bold inclusion of these ancestors in Jesus' lineage indicates both God's ethnic inclusivity of Gentiles in a new covenant tribe gathered around Jesus, and the profound meaning of Jesus' name as the one who saves his people from their sins. Thus these ancestors symbolize new values in the clan of Jesus.

The Twelve apostles take on the imagery and function of the twelve sons of Jacob and become ancestors in their own right. Jesus assigns them leadership roles (Luke 22:29-30), which they fulfill in Acts of the Apostles (2:14; 3:1; 15:6-11) and Galatians (2:1-11). Revelation identifies them as the new heads of the twelve tribes (21:14), even as Ephesians acclaims them as the foundation stones of the new Temple (2:20-21). Legends record the pride of many original churches at being founded by a specific apostle, whereby the honor of the ancestor is bequeathed to clan members. Thus we begin to value the succession of doctrine and authority bequeathed by the apostles.

See: ADAM AND EVE, FAMILY, GENEALOGY

JEROME H. NEYREY, S.J.

ANGEL

Old Testament

There are several terms in the OT for angels who make up the heavenly retinue: "host of heaven," *ṣĕbāʾ haššāmayim* (1 Kgs 22:19); "assembly of the holy ones," *biqhal qĕdošîm* (Ps 89:6); "his angels," *mĕl ʾākāyw* (Ps 148:2); "his ministers," *mĕšārtāyw* (Ps 103:21); and "sons of God," *bĕnê-hā ʾĕlohîm* (Gen 6:2; Job 1:6) or *bĕnê ʾēlîm* (Pss 29:1; 89:7). Although they are different from angels, later tradition also includes in the ranks of angels "cherubim" and "seraphim." The six-winged seraphim (Isa 6:2-6) attend the divine throne and praise God with cries of "Holy, holy, holy." The cherubim* were also winged (Exod 37:9). They act as God's steed (Ps 18:11), appear as part of God's throne (Ps 99:1; 2 Kgs 19:15), and guard the way to the tree* of life (Gen 3:24).

Pre-exilic traditions envision angels primarily as God's court attendants, whose function is to praise, adore, and do God's bidding (Ps 148:2). Angels surround God's throne (Deut 22:19), and constitute the heavenly army (Deut 33:2). In the Exilic period, angelology becomes more fully developed, perhaps due to Babylonian and Persian influence.

The most frequently used term for "angel" in the OT is *malʾāk* or *malʾāk YHWH*, "angel of the LORD." The root meaning of the word is "messenger," i.e., one sent from God. With few exceptions (in Hag 1:13; Isa 44:26; 2 Chr 36:15, *malʾāk* refers to a prophet; in Mal 2:7 to a priest), God's messenger is a heavenly envoy. Angels act on God's behalf toward human beings and convey messages from God. In this way God actively directs earthly doings.

In the majority of instances where God's messenger acts, it is to assist human beings.

Angels go before God's people, as in the Exodus journey (Exod 14:19; 23:20-23; 32:34; 33:2; Num 20:16; see also Gen 24:7, 40; Zech 12:8). Angels save God's faithful ones from mortal danger, as in the rescue of Azariah and his companions from the fiery furnace (Dan 3:49) and Daniel from the lions (Dan 6:23). In only a few instances does God's angel act as an agent of punishment or destruction (2 Sam 24:16-17; 2 Kgs 19:35).

Angels who speak on God's behalf convey divine commands, interpret events, and predict happenings. God's angel issues commands to Hagar to arise and care for Ishmael (Gen 21:17-19), to Abraham not to harm Isaac (Gen 22:12), to Jacob to "Leave this land and return to the land of your birth" (Gen 31:13), to Elijah to get up and eat when he is sleeping under the broom tree (1 Kgs 19:4-8) and to intercept the messengers of Samaria's king (2 Kgs 1:3-4). Commands issued by God's angel may also involve a call, as with Moses in Exodus 3:1-12 and Gideon in Judges 6:11-17.

There are instances where an angel imparts to a human being the divine interpretation of past or present happenings (Num 22:31-35; 2 Macc 3:22-34). The visions of Ezekiel (Ezekiel 40–48), Daniel (Dan 8:15–12:13), and Zechariah (Zech 1:7–6:15) are interpreted by an angel. In the Book of Tobit, the angel Raphael serves throughout as an interpreting guide to Tobias. Angels also predict future happenings: the birth of Ishmael (Gen 16:1-16); the birth of Isaac (Gen 18:1-16); the birth of Samson (Judg 13:2-23); Enoch's ascension (2 Enoch 1:1-10). Interpreting angels clarify the meaning of some occurrence in the divine drama of salvation, and emphasize the importance of the event. By relating the divine perspective on the earthly happenings, they make it clear to the readers what explanation of the narrated events they are to adopt.

God and the divine messenger are not always clearly distinguished, as in Genesis 16:11-13. The "angel of the LORD" speaks to

Hagar (v. 11), who then relates that "the LORD" spoke to her (v. 13). When YHWH or heavenly messengers are seen by mortals they appear in human form. The "three men" that appear to Abraham (Gen 18:2) are YHWH (Gen 18:1, 33) and two angels (referred to interchangeably as "men" [Gen 19:5, 10, 12] and "angels" [Gen 19:1, 15, 16; Heb 13:2]; see also Judg 13:3, 6). The angel who rescues Shadrach, Meshach, and Abednego (Dan 3:95) first seemed to king Nebuchadnezzar one of "four men" walking in the fire (Dan 3:92).

When angels appear as men, they are identified by radiance or brilliant dress, as the man "whose appearance was that of bronze" (Ezek 40:3) and the two young men "remarkably strong, strikingly beautiful, and splendidly attired" (2 Macc 3:26). It is seldom that a heavenly messenger is identified by name. Gabriel (Dan 8:16; 9:21; Luke 1:19, 16), Raphael (Tob 5:4-5), and Michael (Dan 10:13, 21; 12:1; Jude 1:9; Rev 12:7) are the exceptions.

Speculation about angels becomes even more prevalent in the Intertestamental period, particularly in apocalypses. Other terms for angels emerge, such as "watchers" (Jub 4:15, 22), "spirits" (1 Enoch 15:4; 1QH 1:11), "glorious ones" (2 Enoch 21:1; 1QH 10:8), "authorities" (1 Enoch 61:10) and "powers" (2 Enoch 20:1). Dualistic notions of "bad" and "good" angels develop. The War Scroll from Qumran (1QM) describes how all the heavenly powers, angels both good and evil, will be engaged in the final battle when the forces of darkness will finally be defeated.

New Testament

The word "angel" comes from the Greek term *angelos*, "messenger." Four times in the NT *angelos* refers to human messengers (Luke 7:24; 9:52; Gal 4:14; Jas 2:25). Otherwise, the "angel of the Lord" (*angelos kyriou*) is a heavenly envoy.

The functions of NT angels correspond to those of the OT. The heavenly court that praises God is glimpsed when the angel of the Lord had finished speaking of Jesus' birth to the shepherds,* "There was a multitude of the heavenly host with the angel, praising God and saying: 'Glory to God'" (Luke 2:13-14). In Luke 12:8-9 Jesus speaks of the angelic throng when he says, "everyone who acknowledges me before others the Son of Man will acknowledge before the angels of God. But whoever denies me before others will be denied before the angels of God." The "elect angels" join God and Christ Jesus as heavenly witnesses to the actions of presbyters (1 Tim 5:21). The angels who surround God's throne are frequently mentioned in Revelation (ex., 4:9; 5:11; 7:11).

As in the OT, God's messenger acts as a rescuing agent. When the devil tries to tempt Jesus into throwing himself down from the parapet (Luke 4:10; Matt 4:6), he quotes Psalm 91:11, "He will command his angels concerning you, to guard you." At the end of the temptations angels ministered to Jesus (Mark 1:13; Matt 4:11). At his arrest, Jesus is aware of the help available to him, "Do you think that I cannot call upon my Father and he will not provide me at this moment with more than twelve legions of angels?" (Matt 26:53). At his agony, "an angel from heaven" appeared to Jesus to strengthen him (Luke 22:43). Twice the apostles are rescued from prison by an angel (Acts 5:19; 12:6-11).

Less frequently, an angel plays the role of destroyer or punisher. The gruesome death of Herod comes at the hand of "the angel of the LORD," who "struck him down because he did not ascribe the honor to God, and he was eaten by worms and breathed his last" (Acts 12:23).

A series of commands issued by the angel of the Lord in dream* appearances is found in Matthew 1–2. The angel instructs Joseph to take Mary into his home, explaining that her child has been conceived through the holy Spirit (Matt 1:20-21). The angel commands Joseph to take Jesus and his mother to Egypt (Matt 2:13), where they remained until the angel ordered Joseph to return to

Israel (Matt 2:20). The early mission of the Church was also directed by angelic commands (Acts 5:20; 8:26).

Angels who interpret past or present events are found in a number of key NT incidents. The birth of Jesus is explained by angels to the shepherds (Luke 2:8-15). Angels at the empty tomb speak about Jesus' resurrection. In Matthew 28:2-3 there is a single messenger (*angelos kyriou*); in Mark 16:5 the figure is a young man (*neaniskos*), recognizable as an angel by his white robe; in Luke 24:4 the two men (*andres dyo*) are identifiable as angels by their brilliant apparel (see also Luke 24:23). In John 20:12-13 the two angels (*dyo angelous*) do not explain the empty tomb; they merely ask Mary why she is weeping. Jesus' ascension is interpreted by angels: "two men dressed in white garments" (Acts 1:10). A heavenly envoy explains Cornelius' vision* in Acts 10. He is identified alternately as an "angel of God" (Acts 10:3, 7) and as "a man in dazzling robes" (10:30).

Predictions of future events by angels include the birth of John the Baptist (Luke 1:5-23) and the birth of Jesus (Luke 1:26-38). Paul's safety in the midst of a storm at sea* is foretold by an angel (Acts 27:23).

Angels are part of the retinue of the Son of Man at his coming, "When the Son of Man comes in his glory, and all the angels with him, he will sit upon his glorious throne and all the nations will be assembled before him" (Matt 25:31; similarly Matt 16:27; Mark 8:38; Luke 9:26; 2 Thess 1:7). Angels will also be sent out to "gather [his] elect from the four winds" (Mark 13:27). The angels do not, however, know the time of the second coming (Mark 13:32; Matt 24:36). They will be present at the judgment (Luke 12:8-9) and will separate the wicked from the righteous (Matt 13:39, 41, 49; 24:31; Mark 13:7). God's angels rejoice over repentant sinners (Luke 15:10). Jesus warns against despising "little ones" because "their angels in heaven always look upon the face of my heavenly Father" (Matt 18:10). The angels carry away the poor Lazarus after his death, to be with Abraham (Luke 16:22). Angels do not marry (Matt 22:30; Luke 20:36).

In the Fourth Gospel there is an enigmatic saying of Jesus, "Amen, amen, I say to you, you will see the sky opened and the angels of God ascending and descending on the Son of Man" (John 1:51). The allusion to Jacob's ladder (Gen 28:12) is clear; the exact meaning of the saying is not. The Johannine Jesus is the point of contact between the divine and the earthly realms, yet here the angels seemingly play a role in that communication. In another Johannine instance of divine communication with Jesus, a voice from heaven speaks, and some in the crowd believe an angel had spoken to Jesus (John 12:29).

In Acts of the Apostles, the first Christian martyr, Stephen, during his trial before the Sanhedrin, has a face like that of an angel (6:15). When Peter, who had been released from prison by an angel (Acts 12:7), appeared at the gate of the house of Mary, those inside would not believe it was he, but rather thought, "It is his angel" (Acts 12:15). When Paul is on trial "for hope in the resurrection of the dead," he incites a great dispute between the Pharisees and the Sadducees, for the latter "say that there is no resurrection or angels or spirits, while the Pharisees acknowledge all three" (Acts 23:8).

Paul lists angels with principalities, powers, and creatures, all of whom are incapable of separating the believer from the love of Christ (Rom 8:38). Twice Paul uses the phrase "angels and humans" to express totality (1 Cor 4:9; 13:1). Paul believes that Christians will participate in Christ's judgment of the world and of angels (1 Cor 6:2-3). Angels were thought to have acted as God's intermediaries in giving the Law to humankind (Acts 7:53; Gal 3:19; Heb 2:2). Referring to this belief, Paul admonishes the Galatians, "Even if we or an angel from heaven should preach [to you] a gospel other than the one that we preached to you, let that one be accursed!" (Gal 1:8). When addressing the Corinthians on problems in their liturgical assemblies, Paul advises, "a woman should have a sign of authority on her head, because of the angels" (1 Cor 11:10). It is not clear whether angels were thought to be present in the worship assembly nor is it apparent what their function would be in relation to the women prophets.

Colossians 2:18 warns against "worship of angels." It is not certain here whether angels are the object or the subject of worship. If the former, the admonition is clear: only God and Christ are to be worshiped. If the latter, then Christians are being told not to engage in ascetic practices that would enable them to worship with the angels; no angelic mediation is needed in worship.

Hebrews gives a developed presentation of Christ's superiority to the angels. The author queries, "For to which of the angels did God ever say: 'You are my son; this day I have begotten you'?" (Heb 1:5) and "to which of the angels has [God] ever said: 'Sit at my right hand until I make your enemies your footstool'? Are they not all ministering spirits sent to serve, for the sake of those who are to inherit salvation?" (1:13-14). Although in his incarnation Christ was made "for a little while lower than the angels," all things are now subject to him (2:7).

There are several NT references to Satan and his angels. In Matthew's scene of the last judgment, the Son of Man commands those on his left, "Depart from me, you accursed, into the eternal fire prepared for the devil and his angels" (Matt 25:41). Paul mentions "even Satan disguises himself as an angel of light" (2 Cor 11:14). He describes his sufferings, "a thorn in the flesh was given to me, an angel of Satan, to beat me, to keep me from being too elated" (2 Cor 12:7). References to God punishing fallen angels are found in 2 Peter 2:4 and Jude 6. Revelation 12 describes a war in heaven between Michael and his angels and the dragon and its angels. The dragon "who is called the Devil and Satan, who de-ceived the whole world, was thrown down to earth, and its angels were thrown down with it" (Rev 12:9).

Abundant references to angels as divine messengers and ministers of God's judgment are found in the book of Revelation. A letter is sent to the angel of each of the seven churches (Rev 2:1, 8, 12, 18; 3:1, 7, 14). Seven angels blow seven trumpets (8:6, 7, 8, 10, 12; 9:1, 13; 10:7; 11:15). Three angels announce the good news of the fall of Babylon (14:6-13). Seven angels with seven plagues administer the final cataclysm (15:1–16:21).

Pastoral-Liturgical Tradition

With the development of scientific knowledge and historical and literary critical methods of biblical interpretation, many regard angels as a literary fiction rather than actual beings. Nonetheless, later tradition has developed notions of angels as invisible spirits, without corporeality, who were created before the world. Although all angels were created good, some rebelled against God. According to some traditions their sin was sexual transgression; more often it is thought to be pride.

The notion of guardian angels evolved to the point that each person and nation was thought to have their own angelic protector. The Church celebrates the feast of the Guardian Angels on October 2, praying, "send your holy angels to watch over us . . . defend us always by their protection and let us share your life with them forever."

The idea that angels would come at death to lead the soul into the next world can be traced back to the early Church Fathers (e.g., Tertullian, *De anima* 53.6). In the Rite of Funerals, as the body is being led from the church at the conclusion of the Funeral Liturgy, the assembly prays, "May the angels lead you into paradise" or "May the choir of angels welcome you."

An intercessory role is envisioned for angels in the Confiteor, where, after confessing sins, the worshiper prays, "and I ask blessed Mary, ever virgin, and all the angels and saints, and you my brothers and sisters to pray for me to the Lord our God."

See: CHERUBIM, PRAISE, SATAN, SON OF MAN, THRONE OF GOD, VISIONS, WORLD

BARBARA E. REID, O.P.

ANOINTING

To anoint means to touch some person or thing with a substance (oil, water,* blood,* fat, mud) to effect a change, either external or internal. Perhaps the most common substance for anointing is oil, which was used for cleansing not only in religious rites but also for athletic events, civil ceremonies, treatment of wounds (Isa 1:6; Luke 10:34), personal hygienic and cosmetic treatments (Ezek 16:9; Ruth 3:3), preparation for a celebration (Jdt 16:7), welcoming a guest (Luke 7:46), and preparing a body for burial (Mark 14:8). Anointing with oil usually was associated with joyful situations (Ps 45:8), so it was not practiced when fasting (2 Sam 12:20) or when mourning (2 Sam 14:2; Dan 10:3; Jdt 10:3). In oracles of doom one effect is that anointing will cease (Deut 28:40; Mic 6:15). Besides these secular activities, which often carry a religious meaning, anointing often accompanies religious ritual employed to effect a change in spiritual and/or physical reality of a person or thing. These uses in biblical texts provide background for contemporary sacramental and religious rituals which involve anointing.

Old Testament

The common Hebrew word for anointing, *mashach,* usually implies a legal act to symbolize or effect holiness or some new kind of reality. Often it means to pour oil over the head of a special person to be instituted into a certain office, but it also is applied to things; in both situations, anointing frequently comprises part of a service of consecration.* Some early texts attribute anointing rituals to kingship, while most anointing passages appear in priestly prescriptions, which aim for the continuance of God's holiness in Israel.

Royal Anointing. Like their counterparts among the Hittites (and possibly the Jebusites in Jerusalem), Israel's first two kings were consecrated in an anointing by a prophet: Samuel poured oil on Saul's head and proclaimed, "The LORD anoints you" (1 Sam 10:1); the same prophet anointed David (1 Sam 16:13). Anointing consisted of pouring oil from a horn or a vessel over the head of the designated person. In Solomon's case, Zadok the priest* performed the anointing, while the prophet Nathan was present (1 Kgs 1:39). Other royal anointings were effected by the people: the Judahites anointed David in Hebron (2 Sam 2:4); later the elders of Israel followed suit (2 Sam 5:3); Absalom's followers also anointed him (2 Sam 19:11); Jehu was anointed king of Israel in private, by a prophet whom Elisha sent (2 Kgs 9:6). In the Chronicler's post-exilic retelling, the whole assembly had anointed Solomon as the Lord's prince (1 Chr 29:22). In later centuries, anointing was usually reserved for the Davidic line.

To speak of a king as "anointed by the LORD" implied that God had anointed the person for a special mission; any human who poured the oil would act only as a mediator. So God had brought this person to a new state of life which demanded respect and protection. David refused to take advantage of Saul because he was "the LORD's anointed," and thus would be protected by God (1 Sam 24:7; 26:9, 11, 23; 2 Sam 1:14, 16). A royal psalm reports God's word about David: "with holy oil I have anointed him, that my hand may be always with him" (Ps 89:21); this anointing signifies election by God and promises divine protection (see also Ps 2:2, 9). Before David's anointing by Samuel, the prophet looked at David's older brother Eliab and thought, "Surely the LORD's anointed is here" (1 Sam 16:6); so anointing corresponds to election by God. Later, when David had survived various rebellions, Abishai argued that Shimei should be put to death for cursing "the LORD's anointed," i.e., David (2 Sam 19:22). David's "Last Words" refer to him as: "Anointed of the God of Jacob / favorite of the Mighty One of Israel" (2 Sam 23:1); poetic parallelism compares anointing with divine favor. A result of David's anointing was that "the spirit of the LORD spoke through [him]" (2 Sam 23:2); one is reminded of the divine anointing of Cyrus the Persian, addressed by God as "his anointed" for the task of returning exiled Jews to Jerusalem (Isa 45:1, 4); both kings experienced divine anointing for a special task. The titles Messiah—from Hebrew—and Christ[os]—from Greek—both draw their meaning from this sense of "anointing" for the service of God's plans.

Prophetic Anointing. One text implies a human anointing of a prophet: a voice from God ordered Elijah to anoint Elisha as prophet (1 Kgs 19:16). Later, post-exilic Isaiah spoke of himself as anointed by God: "The spirit of the LORD is upon me, because the LORD has anointed me" (Isa 61:1; see also Luke 4:18). Both cases introduce another aspect of anointing: hearing God's word in order to proclaim it.

Priestly Anointing. For priests the rite of anointing usually accompanies a ceremony of ordination* and/or consecration for God's service; like royal anointing, it implies both a new role and the imposition of responsibility for effecting and preserving holiness for Israel (the cleansing aspects of oil may be associated with purificatory rites). In P's description of priestly ordination (Leviticus 8–9), Aaron's consecration as high priest included an anointing after the stages of purification and investiture (Lev 8:12; Exod 29:7; Num 35:25). On the contrary, Exodus 28:41; 30:30 and 40:12-15 stipulate anointing for all the priests, sons of Aaron; the first and third texts join anointing to consecration, while the second calls it an anointing for priesthood. Elsewhere, in a prescription about sacrificial portions (the "anointed part") for the

priests, the command is dated to the day that God "anointed them" (Lev 7:35-36). Although the variations are minor, they raise a question about the antiquity of the practice of anointing priests (versus anointing of Aaron alone). It seems that the high priest was often designated the "anointed priest" (Lev 4:3, 5, 16; 6:15), whose anointing ceremony was more elaborate than that of regular priests (Lev 8:12). Finally, two high priests are occasionally cited as examples of high priestly ordination without anointing—Eleazar, installed as Aaron's successor (Num 20:26-28) and Joshua, first high priest after the Exile (Zech 3:1-9); however, though both texts lack the anointing, it is not clear that either describes an ordination.

After the Exile, the Chronicler's priestly viewpoint still conceives of a popular anointing of Zadok as priest, along with Solomon (1 Chr 29:22); this text also suggests that anointing of high priests happened during the monarchy. Sirach in his praise of Israel's ancestors describes Aaron as anointed by Moses "with the holy oil, in a lasting covenant . . . that he should serve God in his priesthood" (Sir 45:15). Finally, Daniel 9:25-26 mentions two anointed leaders: "the one who is anointed and a leader" may refer to Cyrus or to Joshua, the high priest (Dan 9:25); an anointed who was "cut down" probably points to the deposed high priest, Onias III, who was murdered in 171 BCE (Dan 9:26).

Anointing of Sacred Objects. In the J and E epic traditions, Jacob poured oil on top of a stone that he set up at Bethel to mark the site of his dream (Gen 28:18; in 31:13 the word "anointed" appears); by doing this he consecrated a stone pillar, a fixture of Canaanite shrines which took on a new meaning in Israelite religion. In priestly lore, anointing oil was mixed according to a unique recipe; it should never be used for ordinary bodily anointing, nor should its mixture be duplicated for perfumes (Exod 30:22-33; the prohibition implies that theft of formulas was a problem). Other texts specify various objects to be consecrated by use of this oil: the tabernacle (Exod 30:26; 40:9; Lev 8:10-11; Num 7:1), the ark (Exod 30:26), the altar of holocausts (Lev 8:11; in Exod 29:36 and Num 7:10 only the outer altar is included), the laver, a large basin for purification rites (Lev 8:10-12), the table for the bread of presence and the menorah and the incense altar (Exod 30:27), and the priestly vestments (Lev 8:30). Anointing for both priests and furniture effects a type of contagious holiness for the tabernacle and all that it includes.

New Testament

The range of meanings approximates that of the OT world, but there are significant differences: anointings of people constitute either their Christian identity or aim at their healing. Royal anointings in the OT now apply to Jesus, especially as God's anointed one, but possibly also to his anointing by various women. Most anointings lead to some change of life-pattern or purpose or experience.

Anointings of Jesus by Women. Many of the secular uses of anointing with oil (greeting, celebrating, preparing a body for burial) are witnessed in the NT, and several of them receive a spiritual interpretation when Jesus is involved. After a sinful woman anointed Jesus' feet, a Pharisee challenged Jesus for not keeping separation from her; in his reply, Jesus compared her loving actions with his host's neglect: "You did not anoint my head with oil, but she anointed my feet with ointment" (Luke 7:46). Jesus linked her gesture of love to forgiveness of sins, then said: "Your faith has saved you; go in peace" (Luke 7:50).

Similar motifs appear in the story of Jesus' anointing by a woman before his passion. This story appears in three Gospels: in two of them she brought myrrh in an alabaster jar and anointed his head (Mark 14:3-9; Matt 26:6-13); a different tradition identifies her as Mary of Bethany who anoints his feet with expensive perfume (John 12:1-8; the woman in Luke also

anointed his feet). In these three stories Jesus interprets the act of anointing as an anticipation of his own burial (Mark 14:8; Matt 26:12; John 12:7). Others suggest that it includes a recognition of Jesus' messianic dignity (see 1 Sam 10:1; 2 Kgs 9:6), an interpretation comparable to the notion that Jesus was anointed by God.

Jesus Anointed by God's Spirit. Luke often speaks of Jesus as anointed by God. At the outset of his ministry in the synagogue at Nazareth, Jesus read aloud the text of Isaiah 61:1-2 and applied that prophetic anointing to his own experience of God's power; thus anointing serves to authorize his own prophetic preaching (Luke 4:16-24). A similar reflection occurs in Peter's speech to the household of Cornelius, where he takes up both earlier texts (Isa 61:1-2 and Luke 4:18) and applies them to Jesus: "God anointed Jesus of Nazareth with the Holy Spirit and power. He went about doing good and healing all those oppressed by the devil, for God was with him" (Acts 10:38). These stories establish the linkage between anointing by God and Jesus' mission of word and deed. Another story describes the prayer of the community after Peter and John had been released by the Sanhedrin; their prayer recalls words of Psalm 2:1-2 (the powers gathered against the Lord and "his anointed") and applies it to the opposition by Pontius Pilate, Herod, the Gentiles, and peoples of Israel (Acts 4:26-27). Luke saw Jesus' anointing as leading to the same opposition that was experienced by historical Israel's leaders.

The author of Hebrews introduced Jesus as the final word of God who has been enthroned as Messiah, Anointed one. He quotes from several psalms as examples of God's speaking about Jesus. God says, "You loved justice and hated wickedness; therefore God, your God, anointed you with the oil of gladness above your companions" (Heb 1:9; Ps 45:7-8). Originally a psalm for a royal wedding, it now relates to Jesus' anointing and his status as Messiah. Though the author draws on royal imagery, he uses it to develop his notion of Jesus as High Priest; so priestly anointing finds a reflection in this book.

Christians as God's Anointed. At the beginning of 2 Corinthians Paul tried to resolve the crisis that arose when he changed his travel plans. Describing his own sincerity and constancy in their regard, he concluded with an explanation of their relationship in God: "But the one who gives us security with you in Christ and who anointed us is God; he has also put his seal upon us and given the Spirit in our hearts as a first installment" (2 Cor 1:21-22). All of the verbs Paul used refer to God's action of establishing the Corinthians in a new existence; more specifically, he proclaimed God's ongoing work in the baptized. The word "anointed" describes one aspect of their Christian initiation and life. The Christian, then, is an anointed one, in Greek a *christos*, an indirect link to the name given them.

A similar notion of the Christian's anointing by God appears in the First Letter of John. As a defense against the power of the antichrists, he tells them, "you have the anointing that comes from the holy one" (1 John 2:20). Moreover, the anointing remains with them and teaches them (1 John 2:27); it should confirm the author's account of the tradition. Most important, this anointing apparently refers to the Spirit, the Paraclete who is to guide and teach the community. When they face the opposition of deceivers, this community can rely on the anointing of the Spirit to protect and teach them. Anointing has changed their lives and it continues to direct them.

Anointing and Healing. Jesus touched ears and eyes with spittle in two healing* scenes (Mark 7:33; 8:23); he also combined saliva with dirt to make a clay compound with which he "anointed" a blind man (John 9:11). His healing ministry carried over to his disciples; one text states that the Twelve "anointed with oil . . . and cured" many sick (Mark 6:13). Since this text parallels curing with the driving out of demons, the anointing apparently meant more than simple cleansing of the wound: it symbolized the healing presence and power of Jesus.

Perhaps the best known instance of anointing for healing comes from the Letter of James, where the sick in the community should summon the presbyters, who will "pray over him and anoint [him] with oil in the name of the Lord, and the prayer of faith will save the sick person, and the Lord will raise him up. If he has committed any sins, he will be forgiven" (Jas 5:14-15). In this scene the anointing with oil has connotations of healing and sanctifying the person: it effects physical and spiritual healing, as well as forgiveness of sins. The polyvalent symbolism of this anointing seems appropriate to a culture which did not pretend to make radical distinctions between material and spiritual realms (so it would more easily have dealt with "psychosomatic" illness).

See: ALTAR, BLOOD, CONSECRATION, ELECTION, HEALING, HOLY/HOLINESS, JESUS CHRIST, MESSIAH, MONARCHY, ORDINATION, PRIESTHOOD, WATER

JOHN C. ENDRES, S.J.

Pastoral-Liturgical Tradition

In the pastoral-liturgical traditions of the Christian churches, anointing is a symbolic action, an enacted prayer. Sacramental liturgies of anointing disclose spiritual reality through the visible application of oil on the Christian people and on certain objects that are designated for use in worship. In the Roman Catholic Church, the current rites of Christian initiation, rites for the sick, rites for the ordination* of bishops and presbyters, and rites for the dedication of a church building and its altar include acts of ritual anointing with oil. Because of the centrality of ritual anointings within its tradition of public worship, the Roman Catholic Church also celebrates a distinctive rite for the episcopal blessing of holy oils within the liturgy of Holy Week, the Chrism Mass.

The blessing of holy oils in the Chrism Mass manifests the complementary emphases in spiritual meaning that underlie the various acts of anointing. In some ritual anointings, therapeutic meanings predominate; spiritual cleaning and healing are the purpose of the embodied prayer. In others the dominant meaning is the disclosure of spiritual transformation, glorification, or even divinization. In the Roman liturgy, three holy oils are blessed: the oil of catechumens, the oil for the sick, and holy chrism. The first two oils are used in prayer settings in which therapeutic concerns for cleansing and strengthening persons is uppermost. Holy chrism is used in settings celebrating the mystery of spiritual transformation. The oils set aside for liturgical use are pure plant or vegetable oils, commonly but no longer necessarily olive oil. What distinguishes holy chrism from the first two oils is the addition of fragrance, commonly but again not necessarily balsam. This complementary emphasis on therapeutic and transformative intent is analogous to the virtually universal cultural applications of oils and ointments on the body, sometimes to heal, cleanse, or protect the skin and sometimes for purposes of the enhancement of physical beauty.

Anointing with holy oils is embodied prayer; in the liturgical tradition ritual anointing is surrounded and supported by silent and verbal prayer and the reading of scriptural texts that help the assembled church situate its acts in the larger context of God's creative and redemptive design. Because different liturgical traditions East and West vary in their particular ritual practices, this brief account will focus on the rites of anointing in current use in the Roman Catholic tradition.

The rites of Christian initiation make use of two oils. When adult candidates for baptism* are being prepared, provision is made for one or more anointings with the oil of catechumens. These anointings take place in gatherings where baptized Christians pray that the candidates may have the spir-

itual strength to overcome the attractions of sin and evil and to turn to the gospel way of life. In catechumenal liturgies an officially designated (normally ordained) minister anoints the hands and the breast of the candidate, saying, "We anoint you with the oil of salvation . . . in the name of Christ our savior. May he strengthen you with his power. . . ."

The scented chrism is used in the culminating rites of Christian initiation normally celebrated at the Easter Vigil. The initiand is anointed twice with holy chrism after emerging from the triple water bath or immersion. In the first of these post-baptismal anointings the presiding presbyter anoints the crown of the head. The Church's accompanying prayer recalls the mystery of Jesus as the Christ, the Messiah, the Anointed One of God, and identifies the new Christian with that mystery: "As Christ was anointed Priest, Prophet, and King . . . so may you always live as a member of his body." The second anointing with holy chrism, identified in later liturgical history with the sacrament of confirmation, follows immediately in the current order of Christian initiation of adults. In this anointing, the presiding priest or bishop uses the holy chrism to make the sign of the cross on the forehead of the initiand and proclaims, "N., be sealed with the gift of the holy Spirit." This gift of the Spirit to Christian believers is explicated in a subsequent prayer which recalls the prophet Isaiah's description of the Messiah, the chosen one of God who would enjoy the gifts of wisdom and understanding, right judgment and courage, knowledge, reverence, and wonder and awe in the presence of God (Isa 11:2-3). The verbal proclamation is sustained by olfactory experience; the fragrance of the holy chrism surrounds and pervades the ritual space.

The anointings of Christian initiation help the Church to celebrate God's work of healing and transforming the created world. Believers find latent manifestations of the living God who gives life, who heals, and who divinizes in the natural plant oils they take up into their worship. Believers also affirm and confirm the meaning and direction of their own lives. In these successive anointings with holy oils, the Church symbolically recalls the story of Jesus's messianic vocation, his victory over sin, death, and the powers of this world and his glorious vindication.

All other liturgical anointings find their grounding in these anointings of Christian initiation. Later anointings explicate aspects of the mystery of Christian life already given their central expression in these initiatory anointings.

Oils for the anointing of the sick are blessed for the Church's use with the petition, "Make this oil a remedy for all who are anointed with it; heal them in body, in soul, and in spirit, and deliver them from every affliction." Candidates for this liturgical anointing are baptized Christians who suffer from serious bodily or mental illnesses or from the infirmities of age, as well as those anticipating imminent surgery. The anointing normally takes place in a gathering which includes family members, friends, and care givers, as well as ordained ministers. Scripture reading—most commonly one of the many biblical narratives of healing—contextualizes the community's enacted prayer. Biblical proclamation of God's healing power is followed by the silent prayer of the assembly and the priestly laying on of hands. Then the presbyter anoints the forehead, the hands, and perhaps other areas of pain or injury with the oil of the sick, praying, "May the Lord in his love and mercy help you with the grace of the holy Spirit. May the Lord who frees you from sin save you and raise you up." Here the therapeutic intent of the Church's prayer is evident. But it does not overshadow the Church's confidence in the spiritual transformation that is at work in the mystery of suffering. As the general introduction to the Roman rite observes, the sick have a distinctive ministry to the rest of the Church, to show "that our mortal lives must be redeemed through the mystery of Christ's death and resurrection."

Liturgical rites for the ordination of presbyters and bishops currently each contain within them an embodied prayer of an anointing. Historically, anointings during ordination rites appeared relatively late in the liturgical tradition, unlike the anointings for Christian initiation and for the sick, which are attested to in the earliest periods of the Church. Since the middle ages, the ordination of presbyters has included an anointing of their hands, while an anointing of the bishop's head is part of the liturgy for the ordination of bishops.

Holy chrism is used for each of these ritual anointings. But the meaning of this chrismation is consecratory rather than initiatory. Each candidate for ordination is already a sharer in the divine life of the Christian people who, filled with the holy Spirit, are the body of Christ, a royal, priestly, and prophetic people. The ordained are consecrated, that is, set apart for service within this holy community. The earliest ministerial consecrations evidently took the simple form of communal prayer and the laying on of hands by those already holding episcopal office. In medieval France, the religious sensibilities of the people led them to elaborate the ceremonial aspects of most Christian liturgical acts. Their growing consciousness of the presbyter as a *sacerdos*, a priest who offered the sacrifice of Christ on the altar, found its expression in the desire to anoint and so set apart as specially holy the hands of the priest who held the eucharistic sacrifice.

In that same milieu, the OT account of Moses' consecration of Aaron and his sons by ritual anointing (Leviticus 8) generated a parallel action of anointing with oil during the liturgical consecration of a Christian bishop. Episcopal consecration sets apart for leadership within the Church one who has already been set apart for priestly service to the community of believers. Today, while the consecrating bishop anoints the new bishop's head with the fragrant chrism, he prays for an intensification of the one same Spirit of his baptism: "God has brought you to share the high priesthood of Christ. May he pour out on you the oil of mystical anointing and enrich you with spiritual blessing."

Two other ritual anointings with holy chrism are part of the Roman Catholic liturgical tradition, both occurring on the occasion of the dedication of a church building, the place where the Christian people will gather for worship. These anointings are also consecratory, and they too call up memories of the OT account of the consecration of the Tent of Meeting (Exodus 30). The bishop pours chrism on the middle of the altar table and at its four corners and then proceeds to spread the fragrant oil on the entire table on which the Eucharist will be offered. Then the bishop, often with the assistance of priests, anoints the four walls of the church, marking them multiple times with the sign of the cross. He prays: "May God in his power make them [altar and walls] holy, visible signs of the mystery of Christ and his Church." But during the anointings the assembly sings, "See the place where God lives among his people; there the Spirit of God will make his home among you; the temple of God is holy and you are that temple." The antiphon confirms the fundamental mystery of Christian faith celebrated in the initiatory anointings with holy chrism and in the consecratory anointings of the place of worship: the Spirit of God has been poured out on the Christian community which is the body of Christ.

See: BLESSING, CONSECRATION, SEAL

MARY COLLINS, O.S.B.

ANTICHRIST

The coming of the antichrist has provoked fascination, revulsion, and speculation in every age and particularly in times of crisis. While the antichrist symbolizes the powers of the universe that are arrayed against God and the Christ and the Church

in every age, the actual word is found only in the Johannine Epistles in the Bible (1 John 2:18, 22; 4:3; 2 John 7). There the antichrist is presupposed to be a familiar and even traditional figure. Clearly it depends on a rather wide OT background (see R. E. Brown, *The Epistles of John* [AB 30; Garden City, N.Y.: Doubleday, 1982] 333–337). This includes the sea monster, the Satan,* the human-ruler embodying evil, and the false prophet, which were combined in different ways in Christian reflections.

Old Testament

The biblical description of Yahweh's victory over Rahab the dragon and Leviathan the sea* beast* (Isa 51:9; Pss 74:13-14; 89:11; Job 26:12) is influenced by the ancient myths of the creator god (Babylonian Marduk or Canaanite Baal) struggling and conquering Tiamat the dragon of chaos. For Job 40:25–41:26 the monster is still alive and "king over all the sons of pride." For Isaiah the monster is demythologized and becomes the political power of Egypt ("Rahab quelled" Isa 30:7; cf. Isa 27:1; Ezek 29:3).

Eventually the Satan (Job 1:6; Zech 3:1) was identified as the devil and serpent of Genesis 3:1-15 whose hostility against people continues. He becomes the angel prince of Persia fighting Israel's angel Michael (Dan 10:13; 12:1). In *Jubilees* 1:20 he is Belial who has gained power over all human beings and in Qumran writings (1QS 1:18, 24; 2:5, 19; 1QM 1:1-2) the spirit of iniquity leading people away from God's paths and from Christ and his apostles.

Deuteronomy (13:2-6; 18:15-20) describes, in contrast to the prophet like Moses, the coming of a prophet doing signs and wonders while leading the people to other gods. In the Qumran literature we find the Man of Lies, the Wicked Priest, the Mocker who leads Israel astray (1QpHab 2:1-2; CD 1:10).

New Testament

The coming of the human Jesus gave a new focus as the anti-God of the OT becomes the anti-Christ who will be finally conquered in the great eschatological battle. New titles include "false Christs" (Mark 13:22), "the lawless one" (2 Thess 2:3-9), "the one doomed to perdition" (2 Thess 2:3), and "the two beasts" (Rev 13:1-18).

The Synoptic Gospels refer to the notion of the antichrist in the apocalyptic* chapters which picture the end and the signs of the end. They mention false Christs and prophets leading astray with signs and wonders (Matt 24:11, 24; Mark 13:22). The Synoptic Gospels also speak of the "strong one" whose demons Jesus drives out and whose kingdom Jesus destroys (Matt 12:29; Mark 3:27). In the Fourth Gospel he is called "the ruler of this world" (John 12:31).

In the Pauline letters there are warnings against Satan (1 Thess 2:18), Beliar (2 Cor 6:15), and rulers of the present darkness and the spiritual hosts of evil (Eph 6:12). In 2 Thessalonians 2:1-12 Paul refutes the claim that the Day of the Lord has already come by reminding the Thessalonians of what he has already taught them: the coming of the antichrist is the valid sign of the parousia. The description of how the Lord Jesus "will kill with the breath of his mouth and render powerless" the lawless one (2:8) recalls Isaiah 11:4; Job 4:9; and Revelation 19:15. The widespread interpretation attested by the Church Fathers of a Jewish antichrist leading a powerful army against Christians led to some shocking consequences.

The most extensive use of the OT categories is found in the Book of Revelation. There the abrupt introduction of the beast in 11:7 presupposes acquaintance with the OT tradition and prepares the way for chapters 12, 13, 17, and 20. These in turn contain almost every aspect of the Jewish portrait of future evil culminating in the casting into hell* of Gog and Magog whom Satan inspired to attack Jerusalem (20:1-10).

The author of 1 John believed that the time of his writing was "the last hour" (2:18). He asserts, "Just as you heard that the antichrist was coming, so now many antichrists have appeared." In 2 John 7 "the deceitful one and the antichrist" are "those who do not acknowledge Jesus Christ as coming in the flesh." This view seems to contrast sharply with that of 2 Thessalonians 2:1-12. Most probably the Johannine letters reflect a polemic against the false teachers who have seceded openly and joined the ranks of Satan, the great liar. False teachers are mentioned in Acts 20:30; 1 Timothy 1:3; and 2 Peter 2:1. But John's reinterpretation associates them with the ultimate opposition to Christ. For John, to deny the Son is to deny the Father because the Son is the true way to know the Father (1 John 2:23). One must test the spirits and discriminate among the inspirations which different teachers claim (1 John 4:1-6).

See: ANGEL, APOCALYPTIC, BEASTS/MONSTERS OF THE DEEP, CHAOS, DAY OF THE LORD, HELL, PAROUSIA, POWER, PROPHET, SATAN, SEA

SEAN P. KEALY, C.S.SP.

Pastoral-Liturgical Tradition

The figure of the antichrist developed in the Patristic and Medieval tradition is an integral part of the Christian apocalyptic* vision of world history. As the Church's reflection on the mystery of Christ expanded, so did the tendency to reflect on Christ's negative counterpart, the antichrist. This tendency is fed by the ongoing experience of evil despite the claims of redemption in Christ; and it draws from myth, legend, and folklore to create an elaborate vision of this final enemy of Christ and of humanity. In the post-biblical tradition the antichrist is sometimes thought of as an individual or as a series of individuals, and sometimes as a collective symbol for all that is hostile to Christ and God. At times it is viewed as a future reality associated with the end of time; at other times, it is envisioned as the symbol of evil powers that are universally present in history.

Antichrist and Polemics. The early Medieval view of the antichrist as an individual human being with satanic connections who would come at the end of history as the final enemy of Christ gave way in the late thirteenth century and later to a polemic tendency which viewed the papacy or even particular popes as the antichrist. This polemic was continued and intensified in the writers of the Protestant Reformation who often identified the Roman Catholic Church with the antichrist.

Didactic Function. While most Patristic treatments of the antichrist are found in the context of biblical commentaries, the Medieval period developed its views of the antichrist extensively in the form of sermons for didactic purposes. Here the notion of antichrist was extended to allow the preacher to show that every sinful Christian was, in fact, part of the antichrist. This moralizing tendency together with the conviction that the end was near created the situation in which the figure of the antichrist could function as a strong motivational force in living the Christian life.

Antichrist and Literature. Particularly in the Middle Ages the figure of the antichrist became significant in the legends, poems, and dramas which served as an important means of educating the illiterate classes of Medieval Europe. The antichrist was thought of as a man begotten of a human couple through Lucifer's power. The entire career of the antichrist was developed as a parody of the history of Christ. Even the relation of Christ to the Church as Head to body is paralleled in the relation of the antichrist to the body of Satan.*

Pastoral Dimension. The appearance of this tradition at so many different levels of literature suggests the power it has acquired at the level of popular spirituality. R. K. Emmerson suggests the significance of the antichrist rests in the fact that it represents the total corruption of humanity standing in opposition to the complete, positive fulfillment of humanity which Christians see in Christ (*Antichrist in the Middle Ages*, Seattle: University of Washington Press, 1981, p. 203). Today we might think of this in terms of C. G. Jung's theory of the shadow side of reality. The significance of this tradition is related to the broader apocalyptic sense of moral urgency concerning the quality of human life. The sense of a future provides the basis for a hopeful outlook. Knowing something about the enemy that stands in the way of the future enables one to be ready to meet the enemy.

See: APOCALYPTIC, JESUS CHRIST, MYTH, REDEMPTION, SATAN

ZACHARY HAYES, O.F.M.

ANTIOCH

Young among the great cities of the East, Antioch-on-the-Orontes (mod. Antakya) was founded in only 300 BCE by Seleucus I Nicator who made it the capital of Syria. An important and commercial center, it attracted an ever increasing population. By the time of Augustus it is estimated that its Jewish inhabitants numbered about 20,000. At that stage Syria had become a Roman province, and Jewish rights guaranteed by legislation were defended by successive emperors. Josephus asserts that Gentiles at Antioch found Judaism so attractive that many became proselytes (*J.W.* 7:45). Herod the Great reciprocated by building colonnades on both sides of the main street (*J.W.* 16:148).

As far as Luke's source can be reconstructed from Acts 11:19-30, it seems that Gentiles at Antioch were converted by missionaries from Cyprus and Cyrene. Partly at least because of his Cypriot origins, Barnabas was sent from Jerusalem to take charge of the new Church. He recruited Paul,* and their ministry was so successful that a later editor noted that a new name—"Christians"—was coined for their converts.

The presence of both Jews and Gentiles in the community gave rise to a debate concerning the necessity of circumcision for Gentiles, which was settled in Jerusalem by a decision favoring the Law-free form of Christianity espoused by Paul (Gal 2:1-10). In order to mitigate the consequences, Gentiles were asked to respect certain Jewish food laws (Acts 15:28-29).

It was this tolerant community that sent Paul on his first two missionary journeys (Acts 13:1-3). Subsequently, however, nationalistic pressures made it imperative for Judaeo-Christians in Palestine to reassert their Jewish identity. Envoys from James in Jerusalem ensured a similar hardening of attitude among Jewish members of the Church at Antioch, and Gentile believers were no longer accepted as equals. This forced Paul to recognize that once Law was permitted any role in a Christian community it became the central feature (Gal 2:11-21). In consequence, as a missionary, he could no longer represent Antioch; in subsequent letters he insists that he is "an apostle of Christ Jesus" (1 Cor 1:1; cf. 1 Thess 1:1).

Thereafter, it would seem, the Church at Antioch was controlled by conservative Jewish Christians. They, however, lost their key reference points when James died in 66 and Jerusalem was destroyed in 70. Moreover, the composition of the community changed with the advent of Gentile converts. It seems likely that at this stage radically conservative Jewish Christians returned to the synagogue. Moderate conservatives, however, stayed in the Church and strove to build a new community together with Gentiles and liberal Jewish Christians. An extraordinary theologian, the product of a school of scribes (Matt 13:52), realized that this would be possible only if the different words and deeds of Jesus, on which the various groups relied, were combined into one Gospel. Unity and truth demanded the integration of the *whole* tradition. His achievement is the Gospel of Matthew.

See: CIRCUMCISION, COMMUNITY, JEW, LAW, PAUL, PROSELYTES

JEROME MURPHY-O'CONNOR, O.P.

APOCALYPTIC

From the Greek, *apokalypsis*, revelation. The term means both a theological worldview and a literary genre. As a worldview, it is a form of eschatology* characteristic of some Jewish and Jewish-Christian theology of the Intertestamental and early Christian period, and it continues to reappear regularly in Christianity. It is thought to have evolved from both OT prophecy* and the wisdom tradition, and to be found especially meaningful in times of perceived crisis and diminishment.

Apocalyptic theology can be described as biblical prophecy pushed to its extreme. Whereas biblical prophecy opened the horizon of God's future as the time when the reign of God would hold sway, apocalyptic theology sees a definitive break in history before the inauguration of God's reign in a renewed and restored creation.

The apocalyptic worldview has a number of distinct characteristics. First, a catastrophic eschatology: history is moving toward its consummation in cosmic struggle, which will mean a period of intense suffering, upheaval, and confusion for all, even the faithful. It is no wonder that this anticipated struggle is sometimes compared to the anguish of a woman in labor (John 16:21; Rom 8:22-23). Second, dualism: cosmic dualism, in which the powers of good and evil are locked in combat; moral dualism, by which humanity can be effectively divided into good and bad; and temporal dualism, in which there is a keen sense of break and discontinuity between this age, in which evil holds sway, and the age to come, in which God's justice will be vindicated. Third, the time of suffering in this age will give way to happiness and restoration to wholeness for the faithful. This restoration can take the specific form of bodily resurrection, sometimes only of the faithful deceased (2 Macc 7:14), sometimes extended to all, for eternal happiness of the just and eternal punishment of the wicked (John 5:28-29). Thus the real purpose of apocalyptic writing is the encouragement and consolation of the just during their time of suffering (Luke 21:28).

Apocalyptic literary genre exhibits the above characteristics in the form of secret revelations given by a heavenly messenger to a privileged earthly recipient who is charged to communicate them to those who can hear (Daniel 7). Visions, future predictions, reviews of history, and heavenly journeys are often included, besides moral instruction as to how to remain faithful in time of trial. Apocalypses are often pseudonymous, that is, they purport to be from another author, usually someone of significant stature in the tradition.

Such late OT and Intertestamental writings as Daniel, Ezekiel, 4 Ezra, 2–3 Baruch, 1–2 Enoch, and the Book of Jubilees are predominantly apocalyptic in form, or contain major apocalyptic portions.

Old Testament

Apocalyptic literature had its roots in OT prophecy. After the fall of Jerusalem and the end of the independent monarchy in 586 BCE, it appeared as an explanation and foretelling of world destruction. The major apocalyptic sections of the OT are found in Isaiah 24–27, Ezekiel 38–39, Zechariah 12–14, and Daniel. These passages announce the catastrophic end of the world, but also victory over death and the forces of evil. The descriptions are frequently allegorical visions that depict the defeat of the enemies of Israel (Ezekiel). At other times they report the cleansing of the sinful but repentant Israel (Zechariah).

The apocalyptic message in Daniel is visionary in form and character. Knowledge hidden from the beginning of time is revealed to him by a heavenly mediator. Ancient prophecies are scrutinized in search of an explanation for the turmoil that the people are undergoing. At the heart of apocalyptic hope is the belief that something is about to happen that will shake the earth at its foundations and be cosmic in scope. The mixture of historical and cosmic elements produces imagery that is both bizarre and majestic. Because this literature grows out of political turmoil and personal danger, the real identity of the author is concealed beneath the pseudonym Daniel. Such imagery and pseudonymity enabled

this protest literature to survive undetected in the midst of persecution.

New Testament

Among Christian writings, the Apocalypse of the NT is the clearest example, but there are other postbiblical Christian apocalyptic books such as the Shepherd of Hermas and the Apocalypse of Peter. But writings that are predominantly in another literary genre can also contain apocalyptic segments, e.g., the so-called "Synoptic apocalypse": Matthew 24, Mark 13, and Luke 21. Paul, too, incorporates elements of apocalyptic theology in his letters, e.g., 1 Thessalonians 4:16-17; 2 Thessalonians 2:1-12.

Synoptic Gospels. The Synoptic apocalypse is set at that moment in Jesus' life in which he has entered Jerusalem in an authoritative manner and claimed authority in the Temple by disrupting the business activities there (Matt 21:12-13; Mark 11:15-19; Luke 19:45-48). After engaging in debate with his opponents, and in Matthew and Luke pronouncing some parables that directly challenge the authority of the Temple leaders, Jesus proceeds to act as heavenly revealer for his disciples, telling them of the catastrophic events to come.

In all three discourses, the prediction of the destruction of Jerusalem and the Temple is confusingly merged with descriptions of the eschatological struggle of the end times. Probably these texts were all written after the destruction of the city and the defeat of the Jewish uprising in 70 CE, so that they describe the horror of that event as prelude and example of end time desolation. Terrible wars and cosmic upheavals (Matt 24:4-8; Mark 13:5-8; Luke 21:8-11) will be preceded by persecution and trials (Matt 24:9-14; Mark 13:9-13; Luke 21:12-19), destruction of homes, and many driven off as refugees (Matt 24:15-22; Mark 13:14-20; Luke 21:20-24). Finally, the messianic figure of the Son of Humanity (Man) will appear in the sky and begin the gathering of the faithful to accompany him in glory (Matt 24:30-31; Mark 13:26-27; Luke 21:27).

The sign of the fig tree putting forth its leaves in spring is given as parable* of how to read the signs of the times: just as the new fig leaves are the sign of the coming of summer, so are these events the sign of the coming apocalyptic tribulation (Matt 24:32-33; Mark 13:28-29; Luke 21:29-31). Finally all three discourses conclude with various warnings to remain watchful, since one of the characteristics of the apocalyptic end time is its sudden appearance that will take the unprepared by surprise.

Mark's discourse shows the least knowledge of the actual destruction of Jerusalem, and it is sometimes thought that it was written before the event. However, its beginning point is still "not one stone left upon another" in the Temple (Mark 13:1-4). More probable is the theory that Mark wrote his apocalyptic discourse from afar, but having heard of the event. Luke's account seems at points actually to describe what really happened: Jerusalem surrounded by armies, its inhabitants put to death by the sword and sent off into foreign slavery, and the city overrun by Gentiles (Luke 21:20, 24). All three evangelists, however, use apocalyptic theology and worldview to express the horror of the destruction of Jerusalem as sign and preparation for the endtime. There are other apocalyptic statements attributed to Jesus in the Gospels, such as Mark 9:1; Luke 22:16.

Paul. Paul, too, had his own kind of apocalyptic worldview. Noteworthy is his discussion of the general resurrection of the body in 1 Corinthians 15, within which he situates God's raising of Jesus as firstfruits, the sign that the rest of the harvest is to follow. 1 Thessalonians 4:13-18 deals with the question of community members dying, by speaking in apocalyptic language of the Lord's descent from heaven to raise the dead and take the faithful living with him literally up into the clouds. 2 Thessalonians 2:1-12 speaks of a personified "mystery of lawlessness" that must appear and be destroyed by Christ at his final coming, and rejects the interpretation that "the day of the Lord" has already arrived. Toward the end of his life, Paul speaks with less certainty about details, but with the same conviction of God's ultimate triumph, as we wait in eager expectation for deliverance and adoption (Rom 8:18-25).

1 Peter. This letter under the authority of Peter envisions suffering for those who call themselves Christian, and it is not clear to what extent the persecution they seem to be undergoing is merged with the endtime. As in Mark 13, the two themes become indistinguishable. They undergo a "trial by fire" for the name of Christ (1 Pet 2:7; 4:12-14), but "the end of all things" is also in view (1 Pet 4:7).

The Apocalypse. The best NT example of apocalyptic literature is Revelation, or what is simply called the Apocalypse. As in the Synoptic apocalypse, here the heavenly revealer is Jesus. But this time, the risen exalted Christ appearing in glory, after dictating messages of encouragement and warning to the seven churches, paves the way for a series of heavenly revelations of eschatological turmoil that climax in the defeat of evil and the triumph of God in the heavenly Jerusalem.

Interpretation. Much apocalyptic literature is probably the product of visionary experience on the part of the author, though the details are often indicative of literary embellishment. Apocalyptic expression probably arises from the experience of desperation, whether caused by persecution, discouragement, or disillusionment with the present order. The question whether Jesus himself was an apocalyptic preacher has been much debated, and is closely tied to the historical reliability of the Gospels, particularly Mark, who portrays him most strongly in that mode. While Gospel scholarship of the earlier part of this century was more inclined to a positive judgment on this issue, more recent opinion has swung in the direction of attributing to Jesus a prophetic and wisdom theology, to which the apocalyptic flavor was added by later oral tradition or by the Gospel writers themselves.

Apocalyptic theology in Judaism* was eventually absorbed into more moderate rabbinic Judaism with its lowered eschatological profile. In Christianity it was absorbed into more moderate forms of ecclesiastical Christianity that continued to use some of the language and reverence some of the texts, but with little interest in or understanding of the worldview that produced them.

Apocalyptic theology is one way among many in which the early Church expressed its faith in the power of God for deliverance and salvation. Nonetheless, beginning already with the Montanist movement in the second half of the second century, apocalyptic expectation is periodically renewed, because it appeals to the hope for a better world, whether here or to come. But because it is so vulnerable to psychic and emotional imbalance, the consequences are, unfortunately, often disastrous.

See: ESCHATOLOGY, JERUSALEM, JESUS CHRIST, JUDAISM, JUSTICE, PARABLE, PROPHECY/PROPHET, RESURRECTION, TEMPLE, SON OF MAN, VISIONS, WISDOM

CAROLYN OSIEK, R.S.C.J.

Pastoral-Liturgical Tradition

Apocalyptic literature appears throughout all of Christian history down to the present. At times this literature maintains the interest in history which played a dominant role in early apocalyptic. At other times, perhaps because of the delay of the expected end, the sense of urgency diminishes and the historical focus shifts to concern for personal morality and the promise of the afterlife. But despite this shift, as B. McGinn argues, the characteristic pattern of crisis, judgment, and salvation is retained (*Vision of the End*, New York: Columbia University Press, 1979, p. 15). Even though the use of the apocalyptic genre itself moved in several directions, the interest in interpreting history was never lost to Christian thought even when it was not always carried out in a specifically apocalyptic genre. Thus, in the high Middle Ages, Dante could write the most extravagant apocalyptic account of a tour of the other world in his *Divine Comedy* and St. Bonaventure could produce a major, Medieval theology of history in the form of collations *On the Six Days of Creation*.

The following uses of apocalyptic can be distinguished in Christian history:

(1) *Criticism.* Although apocalyptic is used at times in support of political powers, it frequently provides a perspective from which criticism of the structures of society or of the Church could be carried out.

(2) *Hope.* In a special way, apocalyptic provides a sense of belonging to a larger historical pattern of reality and hence offers a framework for defining a sense of personal meaning. The hope that humanity can be radically transformed for the better is one of the great theological contributions of apocalyptic. The transcendence of death in the form of bodily resurrection is seen by some as the supreme achievement of apocalyptic thought. Ultimately, the message of apocalyptic is one of hope in the final victory of the good.

(3) *Moral decision.* One of the persistent functions of apocalyptic is to call people to decision with respect to good and evil. Endurance in suffering for the sake of the good will be rewarded and persistence in evil will be punished.

(4) *Values.* In J. Collins' formulation, the principal purpose of apocalyptic is "to foster the cherishing of values which transcend death and thereby the experience of transcendent life" ("The Symbolism of Transcendence in Jewish Apocalyptic," *Biblical Research* 19, 1974, p. 7). In this sense, apocalyptic calls one to recognize that death is not the ultimate disaster.

ZACHARY HAYES, O.F.M.

APOSTASY

Old Testament

In its biblical usage, *apostasy* designates an act of rebellion against God and the laws of God, or the abandonment of faith in the God of the covenant. The call to fidelity to Yahweh and warnings against those who forsake their God lie at the heart of the biblical tradition. But the communal context of this fidelity is no less significant. Abandoning God, therefore, is to abandon the covenant community. In this sense, apostasy can refer both to political or religious renunciation of this firmly held allegiance.

For example, Joshua 22:22 records the response of the transjordanian Israelite tribes who claim they have committed no rebellion nor apostasy against the Deuteronomic law (Deut 12:13-14) in building an altar of witness in Transjordan. Disclaiming apostasy, they reaffirm their allegiance to Yahweh and to the Tribal alliance. In another text, the Chronicler (2 Chr 33:19) remembers the apostasy of the evil king, Manasseh (687–642 BCE), who led all of Judah to rebel against Yahweh and to turn to "other gods." See also 2 Chronicles 29:19 which describes the earlier apostasy of King Ahaz (735–715 BCE).

Within the Prophetic tradition, Jeremiah, especially, denounces the apostasy and faithlessness he perceives in Judah. Jeremiah 2:19 warns, "Your own wickedness chastises you, your own infidelities punish you." Throughout this entire chapter, Jeremiah laments bitterly the foolishness of Judah's rebellion. With poignancy and power, he uses the image of a cistern to describe the futility of their apostasy (Jer 2:13): "they have forsaken me, the source of living waters. They have dug themselves cisterns, broken cisterns that hold no water." On another occasion, the prophet spares no rebuke as he warns of lions, wolves, and leopards who will ravage them and punish them for their numerous rebellions (Jer 5:6).

Throughout the OT tradition, apostasy is understood as rebellion against the God who entered into covenant with Israel. To renounce this God was also to renounce the covenant community. While multiple images and metaphors are used to refer to apostasy, the metaphor of "harlotry" is prominent among them (see especially Hosea).

New Testament

The notion of apostasy in the Christian tradition follows the Jewish idea of infidelity to God and abandonment of the laws and obligations incumbent upon the covenant community. Only two texts in the NT, however, employ the technical Greek term for apostasy: Acts 21:21 and 2 Thessalonians 2:3. Hebrews 6:6, on the other hand, warns against "falling away," which implies a voluntary (or involuntary) abandonment of one's faith.

In Acts 21:21, the term *apostasia* appears in the context of Jewish accusations against Paul. They accuse Paul of teaching Jews to forsake their heritage and to denounce the Torah obligations. In their minds, therefore, Paul's proclamation of a gospel of "freedom from the law" (Gal 5:1-6) constitutes apostasy.

2 Thessalonians 2:3, drawing on the prophecies of Daniel 11, speaks of a general apostasy which was to precede the End Time. The author warns the Thessalonians not to be disturbed if lawlessness and rebellion seem to prevail, for such apostasy is merely in keeping with God's plan for the events of the End Time. In typical apocalyptic language, then, the author assures those in Thessalonica that the victory of the Lord Jesus will soon be manifest.

Hebrews 6:6 graphically depicts Christian apostasy, or "falling away," as "recrucifying the Son of God [for themselves] and holding him up to contempt." For such persons, there is no hope of repentance, so heinous is the offense committed against Christ and the Christian community. This text portends the on-going and often vigorous debates in the second and third centuries about the possibility, or impossibility, of repentance after apostasy, a problem compounded by the threats of persecution if one did not renounce Christ.

Pastoral-Liturgical Tradition

Apostasy as Deadly Sin. Early Christian tradition viewed apostasy as the complete abandonment of Christ and his Church. Together with murder and fornication, apostasy committed by a baptized person was judged, at first, to be unpardonable. The author of 1 John 5:16 may have had apostasy in mind when he argued that, "There is such a thing as deadly sin" (literally, "sin unto death").

The Lapsi Controversy. Later tradition devised elaborate systems of public penance to atone for apostate acts. During the period of intense persecution under the emperor Decius (249–251 CE), apostasy, brought on by threat of death or torture, was especially widespread. Controversy arose over these *lapsi* (Lat., "the fallen") and whether they could be readmitted to the Church after repentance and probation. Cyprian (Bishop of Carthage), together with the Roman presbyter Cornelius, argued in favor of their readmittance, while Novatian and his followers took the rigorist position denying forgiveness to the *lapsi*. This dispute eventually lead to an open schism. The moderate position in favor of readmittance prevailed, opening up the way for on-going debate concerning issues of guilt and forgiveness for apostasy.

Today, Catholic theologians still differ in their assessment of apostasy and in their judgment about whether or not one who repudiates the faith is, thereby, always guilty of sin. All, however, recognize the forces in modern secular society which threaten and challenge persons of faith to abandon their beliefs.

See: FAITH, REPENTANCE

BARBARA E. BOWE, R.S.C.J.

APOSTLE

Old Testament

Neither the word nor the concept is prevalent in the OT, though certainly the prophets and others thought of themselves as official messengers and representatives of God. Isaiah 61:1-3 is a good example, in which the prophet sees himself as sent by God to announce the good news of healing, consolation, and liberation. It is no accident that Luke found this passage perfect to express the mission of Jesus (Luke 4:17-19).

New Testament

The Gospels. The word apostle acquired a special meaning in the NT period, but just what that meaning was is debated. An uncritical reading of the Synoptic Gospels often confuses it with "disciple,"* one who follows and learns. Apostle, however, denotes the next step: the one who has learned by following is now sent out to convey the message to others and draw them into the circle of those who have received the good news.

In the Gospels, the word apostle is limited to the Twelve, who are personally called by Jesus in a solemn moment and whose names are preserved, though not in the same order (Matt 10:2-4; Mark 3:16-19; Luke 6:13-16; Acts 1:13). There is confusion at the end of the list between Thaddeus (Matthew and Mark) and Judas (=Jude) the son of James (Luke and Acts). Obviously, preservation of the names was important to early Christians.

The Gospel of Mark. In Mark, Jesus calls the Twelve first of all as companions, and only then to be sent out to preach and cast out demons (Mark 3:13-14). They are not called apostles, but only the Twelve. The phrase "Whom he also named apostles" is missing from many manuscripts of Mark 3:14. Most likely it is an interpolation from Luke 6:13. Later the Twelve are sent out on a mission expedition with explicit instructions (Mark 6:7-13). Only when they have returned and are giving a report on their work are they called *apostles* by the narrator—for the only time in Mark's Gospel (6:30).

The Gospel of Matthew. At the time of their calling, Matthew refers to the group first as the Twelve disciples, his more common term for them throughout (10:1; see Matt 9:10; 12:1-2; 17:6; 21:1; 26:40, and many more). But when giving the list of their names beginning in the next verse, he refers to them for the only time as the Twelve *apostles* (10:2).

Without repeating Mark's characterization of them as those called first to be with Jesus, Matthew passes immediately to their mission to exorcise and to heal (Matt 10:1). Immediately after calling them, Jesus sends them out two by two on a mission similar to that in Mark (Matt 10:5-15). Thus while the group of the Twelve around Jesus is very important for both Mark and Matthew, calling them apostles is not; it happens only once in each Gospel, either when they have just functioned as missionaries (Mark), or when they are chosen by Jesus (Matthew).

The Gospel of Luke and Acts of the Apostles. In the Gospel of Luke, after spending the night in prayer, Jesus calls to himself twelve disciples and, without commissioning them for any formal mission at this point, chooses them and names them apostles (Luke 6:12-16). Only in Luke does Jesus himself name them apostles at the time of their calling (Luke 6:13), but he reserves the specifics of their mission until later. Then he summons the Twelve and authorizes them to exorcise, preach, and heal (Luke 9:1-6).

But for Luke, having only the Twelve formally sent on mission is not sufficient; a further seventy[-two] are also organized and sent out (Luke 10:1-12), though they are not called apostles, and Jesus rejoices when they return and report in (Luke 10:17-20). By focusing on the call of the Twelve whom Jesus names apostles even without describing their role in the same context, Luke reveals his interest in focusing on the apostles themselves even apart from their mission. By later telling that Jesus appointed not only twelve but seventy[-two] more, he shows how important an organized mission strategy is to him.

In Acts, "the apostles" are the core of the group of 120 gathered together in Jerusalem (Acts 1:15). One of the first things they must do is to elect someone to replace Judas, someone who was a co-witness of Jesus' entire ministry, death, and resurrection (Acts 16:26). That done, the number twelve is again complete, a number no doubt important for its symbolism of the twelve tribes of Israel (see Matt 19:28; Luke 22:30; Acts 26:7; Rev 21:12) as well as its cosmic symbolism (see Rev 12:1).

The apostles appear frequently in Jerusalem through the first eight chapters of Acts. By Acts 15:2 they are joined by "the presbyters," an undefined leadership group; after 16:4 they cease to be mentioned. It would seem that by "the apostles" Luke has in mind the Twelve, with the sole exception of Acts 14:4, 14 where Paul and Barnabas are also called apostles, but nowhere else. Acts 1:15-26 makes clear how Luke sees the twelve apostles: as official witnesses of the life, death, and resurrection of Jesus, replacing the twelve tribes of Israel in the new Israel, the Church.

The Gospel of John. In John's Gospel there are occasional mentions of names of those closest to Jesus, names that match those in the Synoptic lists (e.g., Andrew and Simon Peter; Philip [John 1:40-45]; Thomas [John 20:24-29]). There are two mentions of the Twelve (John 6:67, 71; 20:24). But there is no list, no commissioning, no description of their tasks, unless one wants to consider the brief commissioning of Peter in John 21:16-17. The word apostle appears only once in a non-technical context (John 13:16), though the consciousness of being sent is all-pervasive. John the Baptist is the one sent to bear witness (John 1:6; 3:28). It is primarily, however, Jesus who is sent into the world by God (John 3:16-17; 4:34; 5:36-38; 11:42; ch. 17 throughout; 20:21; see Heb 3:1), though the disciples are also sent "to reap what [they] have not sown" (John 4:38).

After the resurrection Jesus sends the disciples to continue the movement whereby God has sent Jesus into the world (John 20:24). While discipleship is of crucial importance to John, the circle of disciples is indefinite, without formal delineation of a smaller group. The Twelve are part of the circle, but seem not to have a distinctive role. While the awareness of being sent by God into the world is of crucial importance, there is almost no language or title of formal commissioning.

Paul. No one in the NT is so frequently called an apostle, and except for Acts 14:4, 14, it is by self-designation, either of himself alone (Rom 1:1; 11:13; 1 Cor 1:1; 9:1; 15:9; 2 Cor 1:1; Gal 1:1; Eph 1:1; Col 1:1; 1 Tim 1:1; 2:7; 2 Tim 1:1) or himself among others (1 Cor 4:9; 1 Thess 2:7). Paul understands himself to be a fully-qualified apostle because he has seen Jesus in direct revelation (1 Cor 9:1; Gal 1:15-16).

He knows of a resurrection appearance to the Twelve (1 Cor 15:5), but also of another to "all the apostles," who seem not to be identical to the Twelve (1 Cor 15:7). He acknowledges the preeminence of the apostles in the Jerusalem Church (Gal 1:17-19), but includes as one of them James, the brother of the Lord, who is not on the Synoptic list. Moreover, Paul calls others apostles besides the Jerusalem leaders and himself: his relatives Andronicus and Junia (Rom 16:7); Epaphroditus (Phil 2:25—translated "messenger" in the revised NAB); some unnamed co-workers (2 Cor 8:23); those with whom he disagrees at Corinth (2 Cor 11:5; 12:11; cf. Rev 2:2). Given Paul's touchiness about the title for himself, he would hardly have used it loosely of others.

What are we to make of the discrepancy between Luke's limited use of apostle primarily for the Twelve, and Paul's use of the word for many others? Over the years, there have been two alternative interpretations. The traditional one follows Luke and assumes that in the earliest Church only the Twelve were considered apostles in the fullest sense, with the addition of Paul as a special exception. In this case, the use of the word for others is only in a derivative sense.

The second interpretation, and probably more historically accurate, is that in fact there were many missionaries who bore the title of apostle, Paul and the Twelve being among them—which is not to deny the special place of the Twelve as Jesus' closest companions and first witnesses. It is Luke, then, who restricts his use of the term for the most part to the Twelve. This interpretation is supported by the fact that some post-NT writings of the late first and early second century, especially the Didache, also know of other missionaries who are called apostles.

The Church was built upon the apostles and prophets, with Jesus Christ as capstone (Eph 2:20; see Rev 21:14). Whatever the number and identity of apostles in the early Church, it is they who laid the foundations and built the solid walls within which faith in the risen Christ was first nourished and transmitted.

See: CHURCH, DISCIPLE, GOOD NEWS, MINISTRY, MISSION, PREACHING, TEACH/TEACHING, WITNESS

CAROLYN OSIEK, R.S.C.J.

ARAB(S)

The Bible rarely uses the term Arab(s) as a generic term for the inhabitants of the Syrian or Arabian desert. Usually the Bible refers to the peoples of these regions by their tribal names such as the Midianites, the Sabeans, the people of the East (Kedemites), and the Dedanites. The genealogies of Genesis include Arabian peoples among the descendants of Abraham (Gen 25:13-16) and therefore assume that the Arabs are related to the Israelites.

The term "Arab" derives from a Semitic root that means "steppe" or "desert." When the Bible uses this term, it often is not an ethnic designation but a geographic one. It refers to the people who live in the Arabah, the desert to the south of ancient Israel where nomads lived. Several texts remember the Arabs as nomads or tent dwellers: Judg 5:6; 8:11; Pss 83:6; 120:5; Jer 49:29, 31; Ezek 38:11; 2 Macc 12:10-12.

There are some favorable references to Arabian tribes in the OT. The story of Moses remembers the Midianites as a pastoral people among whom Moses finds both a refuge and a wife (Exod 2:15-22). These people also supplied a guide for the Israelites for their journey in the wilderness (Num 10:29-32). Arab caravaners were trading partners of Solomon (1 Kgs 10:15; 2 Chr 9:14). Their wares included precious stones and metals (Isa 60:6; Jer 6:20; Ezek 27:22), livestock (2 Chr 17:11; Isa 60:7; Ezek 27:20), textiles (Ezek 27:20), and slaves (Joel 3:8). Solomon's wisdom is compared to that of the people of the East [Kedemites] (1 Kgs 4:30; 5:10). The "ravens" of the Elijah story (1 Kgs 17:4, 6) were probably Arabs of the desert who fed Elijah during his stay in the desert. [A slight emendation of the Hebrew text can support the translation of "Arab" for "raven."] The Nabateans, an Arab tribe that settled east of the Jordan, controlled trade there from the fourth century BCE into the Roman period. The Maccabees had friendly relations with them (1 Macc 5:25; 9:35).

Most of the biblical references to Arabs and Arabian tribes are negative. Several texts mention the Arabs' raiding activity: 2 Chronicles 21:16; 26:7; Isaiah 21:13-17. Gideon led several Israelite groups against a coalition of Arab tribes whose raids threatened the Israelite settlements in the central highlands (Judges 6–8). Raiding remained the traditional sport of the Arabs of the desert into modern times. Jeremiah 3:2 implies that the Arabs were little more than wayside bandits. During the restoration following the Exile,* Arabs were among the groups that hindered the progress of the Jewish community in Jerusalem (Neh 2:19; 4:7; 6:1-6).

The "Arabians" of Acts 2:11 were Jews who lived in Arab cities—probably those of the Nabateans. Paul says that he went to Arabia after his experience on the road to Damascus (Gal 1:17). This was probably the Syrian desert. The term "Arabia" was probably quite fluid and referred to no specific geographical region since Paul places Mount Sinai in Arabia (Gal 4:25).

Living in the harsh environment of the desert made frugality, hardiness, and hospitality qualities prized by the Arabs. Their nomadic existence in search of pasture and water for their flocks made them a fiercely independent people who resisted the imposition of discipline from the outside.

See: DESERT

LESLIE J. HOPPE, O.F.M.

ARK OF THE COVENANT

Old Testament

The English word "ark" has traditionally translated two Hebrew words. The first, *tebah,* refers to Noah's ark (Genesis 6–9) and to Moses' little boat of papyrus reeds (Exod 2:3, 5). The second, *'arôn,* indicates a box or chest, as in Genesis 50:26 where it refers to the coffin of Joseph. However, ark refers mainly to one of Israel's most sacred objects whose origin and early significance are not entirely clear. This box is variously called the "ark of God" or the "ark of the LORD Sabaoth" or "the ark of the covenant/testimonies"; the different names reflect its changing theological significance.

Numbers 10:33-36, thought by some to reflect one of the most ancient traditions, calls this box "the ark of the covenant of the LORD," a title which links it to the covenant* at Sinai. During the desert journey, the ark served both as a divine guide and as the reference point for the invisible presence of God within the community of Israel. Numbers 10:35 also connects the ark to the theme of the Lord as warrior, for, "whenever the ark set out, Moses would say, 'Arise, O LORD, that your enemies may be scattered. . . .'" At the conclusion of the wilderness journey, the ark leads the people through the Jordan (Joshua 3–4) and comes to rest at Gilgal (Josh 4:19), then, per-

45

haps, at Shechem (Josh 8:30-35), before moving to Bethel (Judg 2:1; 20:26-28), and later to Shiloh (1 Sam 3:3). Although the early traditions do not specifically link the ark and the tent* of meeting, the link seems reasonable. Both serve as places of divine presence and as a source for oracles* (Exod 33:7-9; Judg 20:27-28; 1 Sam 3:21).

At times the ark is carried into battle as a palladium to guarantee safety and victory (2 Sam 11:11; cf. also Num 14:40-45; Josh 6:4). In 1 Samuel 4:3-11, however, the ark is lost to the Philistines, a sign of God's rejection, yet the Philistines find that this object of holiness brings them a curse and return it to the land of Israel. After David's capture of Jerusalem, he searches out the neglected ark and brings it to the royal city as a symbol of the ancient faith and the locus of God's presence (2 Samuel 6; 7:6; Psalm 132). By this act, David transforms Jerusalem into the new religious and cultic center.

1 Samuel 4:4 speaks of "the ark of the LORD of hosts, who is enthroned upon the cherubim." The word "hosts" refers to the heavenly armies, the image of God as warrior. The reference to cherubim also suggests the cherubim throne in which the sides of the chair were formed by two of these animals and the seat by their wings. When Solomon sets up the cherubim throne in the holy of holies, the ark rests in front of the two cherubim as the footstool (1 Chr 28:2; see also Pss 99:5; 132:7). This throne for the unseen God presents both a sense of immanence and transcendence, an important image for the enthroned God of Jerusalem's royal theology.

Except for an oblique reference in 2 Chronicles 35:3, the ark is not mentioned in the historical books after Solomon. Only Jeremiah among the prophets makes reference to the ark, and he insists that Jerusalem itself will become "the throne of the LORD" in place of the ark (Jer 3:16-17). As such, it reflects the later theologies which move away from the anthropomorphic notion of God sitting enthroned in the Temple. In the Deuteronomistic theology, which influenced the Book of Jeremiah, the Temple becomes the place of God's name. In the Priestly tradition, found also in the Book of Ezekiel, God's glory dwells in the Temple. Both theologies focus on this box as "the ark of the covenant" and the repository for tablets of the law (e.g., Exod 25:21-22 and Deut 10:1-5). The Priestly tradition also gives special significance to the *kapporet*, a cover of pure gold for the ark, variously translated as "mercy seat" or "propitiatory" because the Hebrew word contains both the meaning "to cover" and "to make atonement."

New Testament and Pastoral-Liturgical Tradition

The ark of the covenant was lost either at the time of the destruction of Jerusalem (586 BCE) or before. Perhaps because of this, the NT contains only two references. Hebrews 9:4 contrasts the Temple liturgy of atonement at the ark with the sacrifice of Christ. Revelation 11:19 places the ark within the temple of the heavenly Jerusalem, but makes nothing more of it.

The ark maintains a vital place in the Jewish imagination and theology and becomes the name of the receptacle for the Torah in the synagogue, the holiest shrine of these buildings. Unlike Noah's ark which has served as an image of the Church throughout the tradition, the ark has not played a large role in Christian symbolism except as a title for Mary who bore the Word of God. For Christians the ark of the covenant mainly evokes the literal object of Israel's religion. Both the irony of a throne for an invisible God and its connections to the tablets of the Ten Commandments continue to evoke a sense of mystery and awe. A recent movie about the search for the lost ark demonstrates its hold on the popular mind.

See: CHERUBIM, COVENANT, GLORY, JERUSALEM, NAME, ORACLE, TEMPLE, TENT

HARRY HAGAN, O.S.B.

ARMAGEDDON

The only occurrence of the word Armageddon is in Revelation 16:16, where it is named as the site for the decisive battle at the end of the world and the triumphant final judgment* of the King of Kings (Rev 16:13-21; 19:11-21). The dominant theme of Revelation 16 is God's judgment on the whole earth and on the wicked in particular, symbolized by seven bowls of wrath. Quite abruptly as the evil forces gather for the great day of battle (16:14), Jesus himself appears. Having warned the community as he had warned Sardis and Laodicea (3:2, 18) that he comes like a thief, he pronounces a beatitude on those who watch (16:15). Then the author of Revelation suddenly switches to describe again the gathering together of the kings of the whole world for the final war "in the place that is named Armageddon in Hebrew" (16:16). No Greek equivalent is given for Armageddon, in contrast to Abaddon, whose Greek counterpart Apollyon is provided in Revelation 9:11. The name Armageddon suggests the Hebrew *har měgiddō*, "mountain of Megiddo," the scene of many key battles in antiquity.

Megiddo, one of the fortress cities of Solomon, stood at the entrance of a key pass between the coastal plains of Palestine and the interior plain of Esdraelon (1 Kgs 9:15) and the northern tribes. It lay on the great highway from Egypt to Damascus. No wonder an ancient Egyptian once remarked: "The capture of Megiddo is as the capture of a thousand towns" (ANET 237). It is told that Napoleon once recalled the biblical passage as he stood on this hill and commented that "all the armies of the world could manoeuvre for battle here." Of the roughly two hundred battles fought there one can recall how, at a time when Israel had neither shield nor spear, the Lord helped Deborah rout Sisera with his chariots of iron in what became a highly symbolic victory over evil (Judg 5:19). Already in 1498 BCE one of the great Pharoahs had defeated the Hyksos there to found a world empire. There Jehu fought Ahaziah (2 Kgs 9:27) and good king Josiah lost his life to Pharaoh Neco (2 Kgs 23:29), a tragedy which was long remembered (Zech 12:11).

A problem is that there is no Mount Megiddo. No such place is found in any ancient map nor is it mentioned in the OT. Although a seventy foot tell stood on the plain of Esdraelon when the author of Revelation was writing, it could not properly be called a mountain. It is, however, not far from the Carmel range of mountains. In addition, some twelve different spellings are found in the manuscripts of Revelation 16:16. This has given rise to other suggested meanings such as "his fruitful mountain," or "city of desire," that is, Jerusalem (Joel 3:2) or "destroying mountain" (Jer 51:25). An interesting suggestion is the "mount of assembly," where, according to Isaiah 14:13, the morning star, the king of Babylon (Lucifer in the Vulgate), boasts he will set up his throne above the stars of God. This is the equivalent of Mount Sapon of Canaanite mythology or Mount Aralu of the Babylonians or Mount Olympus of the Greeks. The problem is that the exact transliteration of Isaiah's Hebrew does not correspond.

Certainly Megiddo was for the author of Revelation the best symbol for the final defeat of evil. Possibly he was influenced by Ezekiel who places the final battle with Gog and Magog in the mountains of Israel (Ezek 38:6-9). Clearly this kind of battle should not be sought on a map like Verdun or Waterloo; but rather, should be understood symbolically. In the apocalyptic* tradition the valley of Jehosaphat (literally, "Yahweh judges"), popularly identified with the Kidron Valley in Jerusalem, was to be the place of final conflict and judgment (Joel 4:2-3; Zech 12:2-9; Isa 29:1-8; 4 Ezra 13:1-38).

Pastoral-Liturgical Tradition

In general one should insist that the Bible does not give detailed chronological or topographical information about the times or places of the great final judgment. In fact there is an insistence in the Synoptic Gospels that no one knows the hour, "neither the angels in heaven, nor the Son, but the Father alone" (Matt 24:36; Mark 13:32) and that its coming will be like that of a thief in the night (Matt 24:42-44; Luke 12:35-40). The aim of the biblical writer is to remind people that the struggle with evil will continue right to the end and that the powers of evil will seem to grow even more formidable. Nevertheless evil ultimately will be defeated no matter how powerful it may seem. Jesus will return triumphant (Matt 24:43; Luke 12:39).

See: JUDGMENT, MOUNTAIN, PAROUSIA, SON OF MAN, WATCH, WRATH OF GOD

SEAN P. KEALY, C.S.SP.

ART, BIBLE AND

When Israel was in the desert, the ark was the dwelling place of the invisible God. To assure loyalty to Yahweh Exodus 20:4-5 prohibits the making of graven images and any worship of them. Consequently the impression has been that art was absent from Israel's life. However, when Israel became a people of land, monarchy, and temple, art assumed a limited role. In Solomon's Temple the cherubim are depicted as well as the twelve oxen supporting the molten sea. Care is taken in both the utensils and the vesture used in sacrifice to assure their artistic quality.

Synagogue art functioned to complement study, oral interpretation, and conversation; to edify those gathered in prayer; and to support the memory of Israel. Walls, pillars, and floors were used to depict scenes from the Bible and the experience of Judaism as it was lived out in various regions and as it was touched by adherents of Roman and early Christian religion. Synagogue art included scenes from Exodus: Miriam and Moses; the figure of Moses over the Red Sea; the crossing of the Red Sea in twelve paths; the portable well in the desert; the figure of Esther. Midrashic interpretation combined with images of Jonah in the belly of the sea monster as well as Jonah, naked, blissfully asleep under the gourd for eternal life. The tent of meeting, the lion of Judah, the bull of Ephraim, the eagle, the peacock and birds of Paradise, the bird in the cage, and the palm tree and branches all inspired Jewish faith. The seven branch candlestick might appear in murals and on medallions. In short, synagogue art was a graphic support for study and prayer in Judaism.

Christian art, drawn from the symbol system of the Bible, served to express the victory of Christ, to inspire hope, and to support the liturgical actions of baptism, Eucharist, and Roman/Christian devotion to the dead, especially martyrs. While some Christian texts expressed worry over idolatry and gave the impression of an aniconic stance, Christian art developed both in relationship to the Roman religion and in continuity with the OT persons, events, and symbols of faith.

Heraldic symbols appeared on signet rings. These included the chi-rho, the ship, the anchor, the lyre, the dove, and the fish. Sarcophagi art in the catacombs depicted Christ as Orpheus, the Shepherd, and Helios. Instead of the cross, pre-Constantinian Church art expressed the deliverance of Christians in the victory of Christ and the role of Christ in Roman terms. Christ became the orant, the shepherd with the ram, and the philosopher offering new wisdom. Due to the influence of the twenty-third psalm in the baptismal and Eucharistic mysteries, the figure of the Good Shepherd was prominent on baptistry walls (e.g., in the house church of Dura-Europus). Christ was also pictured as the Victor/risen One who had ascended and was ruler of the universe. Finally, Christian art used biblical figures and events to support living faith. These included: the binding of Isaac, an event showing God's mercy and the hope of Jews and Christians; Daniel in the lions den; Moses atop Sinai; Job; the Magi coming to the infant; the wedding feast at Cana; the healing stories (the paralytic, the woman with the issue of blood, the demoniac, the blind man, the multiplication of the loaves and fishes, the Samaritan woman, etc.). Art expressed deliverance, healing, and rescue from death.

Post-Constantinian Christian art focused more on the life of Jesus and on the events of his passion. Soon Christ was pictured not as the teacher, but as triumphant in majesty; not as the risen Christ, but as pantocrator. From the sixth century CE on, the crucifixion came into Christian art.

Art is an important complement to liturgical action and biblical text. Art can support the devotion and faith, memory, and imagination of assemblies. Liturgical spaces need not be bare places. Nor are they museums. Art is to aid liturgy, to evoke memory, and to trigger imagination. Good art is done by skilled crafters of fonts and baptistries, ambos, altar tables, tabernacles, etc. Significant art is also attentive to the culture of those engaging in worship and prayer, catechesis and formation. It respects the genius of various cultural heritages and the rich heritage of biblical persons and events.

See: BAPTISM, DEATH, EUCHARIST, HOPE, TEACH/TEACHING

JOHN J. O'BRIEN, C.P.

ASCENSION

The Ascension is the traditional name given to the transit of the risen Christ to the glory of God after the resurrection.* Usually the word denotes the final departure of the risen Jesus after his appearances to the gathered disciples, as presented in Luke 24:51-53 and Acts 1:6-11. Although the conventional, *post*-biblical term has always been "ascension," a word implying an action (as expressed in the credal affirmation, "he ascended into heaven"), the biblical references to this transit most frequently denote a passive occurrence, an assumption, as expressed in Acts 1:9, "he was lifted up, and a cloud took him from their sight." This is an instance of the "divine passive," in which the movement is described not so much as an action of Jesus but as something done to him by God the Father. This parallels the way NT authors refer to the resurrection, sometimes with the active "he rose," more often with the passive "he was raised."

Old Testament

The only OT traditions that relate in any way to ascension are the references to the assumptions of Enoch and Elijah. Genesis 5:23-24 notes cryptically, "The whole lifetime of Enoch was three hundred and sixty-five years. Then Enoch walked with God, and he was no longer here, for God took him." Sirach 49:14b interprets this as a physical transfer: "he was taken up bodily." Hebrews 11:5 explicitly sees this rapture as a bypassing of death.

A similar transfer of the prophet Elijah is presented more graphically in 2 Kings 2:9-11. Just before Elijah departs from Elisha, he asks his successor what he might do for him "before I am taken up from you." Elisha asks for a double portion of his spirit.* Elijah assures him, "If you see me taken up from you, your wish will be granted; otherwise not." As they continue to walk and converse, a fiery chariot and flaming horses come between them "and Elijah went up [in the LXX, "was taken up,"] to heaven in a whirlwind." Subsequently Elisha strikes the Jordan with his master's mantle, the waters part, he crosses over, and fifty guild prophets observe that "the spirit of Elijah rests on Elisha." Sirach recapitulates this tradition: "You were taken aloft in a whirlwind, in a chariot with fiery horses" (48:9). 1 Maccabees 2:58 expresses the tradition in this way: "Elijah, for his burning zeal for the law, was taken up to heaven." These references to the assumptions of Enoch and Elijah have three important aspects in common: (1) a physical transfer of a human being from earthly existence to the realm of God, (2) a preference for the passive verb *analambanomai* to describe the transfer in the Greek versions, and (3) no mention of death as part of the process.

New Testament

What distinguishes the ascension of Christ from any previous account (pagan or biblical or intertestamental) of a celestial "translation" of a human being is that the ascension of Jesus is subsumed wholly into the larger fact of his resurrection. Indeed, ascension is essentially a spatial image to express the reality of the final withdrawal of the risen Jesus' physical presence from the assembled disciples. And the resurrection of Christ is no mere physical and spatial transfer but a transformation from death to a sharing in the divine glory, which the NT writers understand as happening instantly, "on the third day." Jesus' passage from earthly existence to the heavenly is complete with the resurrection, and his post-Easter appearances are understood to emanate from that realm of glory. "Was it not necessary that the Messiah should suffer these things and enter into his glory?" the risen Jesus asks the Emmaus disciples (Luke 24:26), implying that his entry into glory has already occurred, even before his final departure from them near Bethany (24:51).

Texts that Proclaim Exaltation without Reference to Ascension. Discussion of the ascension must distinguish this specific notion of a visible transfer to heaven from the more abstractly conceived process of *exaltation*. The NT can speak of the post-burial existence of Christ simply as being taken up into the divine glory without specifying the mode of transfer. Sometimes that exaltation is proclaimed even without explicit mention of resurrection, as in the hymn of Philippians 2:8-11 ("because of this [obedient death on a cross], God greatly exalted him . . ."). Similarly, see 1 Timothy 3:16, where Jesus is described as "taken up [*analēmpthē*, the verb used in the Greek OT to describe Elijah's assumption] in glory," again without explicit reference to resurrection. In the same way, the "lifted-up" sayings (using a different Greek word, *hypsothēnai*) in John 3:14; 8:28; and 12:32, 34, taken together, appear to refer to Jesus' being "lifted up" both in crucifixion and in exaltation.

The preaching in Acts sometimes makes the connection between resurrection and exaltation (Acts 2:32-33; 5:30-31). And sometimes the risen Lord's celestial existence is referred to without reference to ascension (1 Thess 1:10; 4:16; Rev 1:12-18; 3:21b; 6:1b-7; 7:17).

Non-narrative Assertions About the Ascension. The number of NT texts that make assertions about the ascension of Christ are few. There are a handful of passages that *allude* to Jesus' exaltation as an ascension without using the actual word for "ascend" (*anabainein*) (Heb 4:14; 9:24; 1 Pet 3:22). Others do use the word "ascend" (Rom 10:6-8; Eph 4:7-11; John 20:17). Finally, there are the three canonical NT texts that actually narrate the ascension: Luke 24:50-51; Acts 1:9-11; and Mark 16:19.

The Three New Testament Narratives of the Ascension. Apart from the canonical Appendix to Mark (to be considered in a moment), the only Gospel narrative of the ascension of Jesus is Luke 24:50-51:

> Then he led them out as far as Bethany, raised his hands, and blessed them. As he blessed them he parted from them *and was taken up to heaven*. They did him homage and then returned to Jerusalem with great joy, and they were continually in the temple praising God.

The Greek manuscripts contain several variant readings in these verses, the most important of which is the very clause that describes the ascension. The second half of verse 51, *anephereto eis ton ouranon* ("and he was taken up to heaven"), does not appear in the Western text-tradition. The clause does, however, appear in all the other major Greek manuscripts. Though the question is still debated, most scholars accept the longer reading. However the text-critical question is resolved, the fact remains that even the shorter reading means to narrate the final departure; the implied author of Luke-Acts is thereby alluding to the ascension, which is clearly presented as such at the beginning of his second volume.

The situation and gestures of this final scene of Luke's Gospel recall the description of the high priest Simon II in Sirach 50:1-24 in several ways. Like Simon, Jesus' presence occasions worship (Sir 50:17, 22), he raises his hands in blessing (Sir 50:20), and this is followed by references to the community blessing God and rejoicing (Sir 50:22-23).

This scene fittingly rounds off the narrative of the Third Gospel. What the priest Zechariah was unable to do at the beginning (i.e., bless the people, Luke 1:22), Jesus does at the end. And the mention of Bethany (24:50) helps the implied reader recall the entry of Jesus into Jerusalem (Luke 19:29) and see in this moment a triumphal exit.

Yet this final departure of the risen Christ from his gathered disciples is narrated in quite another way at the beginning of Acts. In his introductory remarks to Theophilus, Luke speaks of Jesus' continuing to appear to the disciples and teaching them for an interval of forty days. He caps this with a final scene of instruction in which Jesus tells his followers to remain in Jerusalem to await the promise of the Father, the holy Spirit, who will empower them to witness to the ends of the earth. Then the departure is described:

> When he had said this, as they were looking up, he was lifted up [epērthē] and a cloud took him from their sight. While they were looking intently at the sky as he was going, suddenly two men dressed in white garments stood beside them. They said, "Men of Galilee, why are you standing there looking at the sky? This Jesus who has been taken up from you to heaven [analēmphtheis aph' hymōn eis ton ouranon] will return in the same way as you have seen him going into heaven."

While it is clear that Luke 24 and Acts 1 present the same event, the final departure of Jesus from his gathered disciples, the second account contains several variations, two of them quite striking: the time (Easter night in Luke; forty days later in Acts) and the description (a simple reference to ascension in Luke; and in Acts, an array of

what J. Fitzmyer has called "apocalyptic* stage props"—movement upward into the heavens, a cloud as vehicle, and interpreting angels).

Some scholars explain the differences in the accounts by suggesting that Luke has expanded the time phase of Luke 24 to the round, and biblically suggestive, number of forty in order to associate the ascension closely with the outpouring of the Spirit on the fiftieth day, Pentecost.* The apocalyptic stage props serve (1) to recall the transfiguration (another mountain episode when the disciples could not pray, as now they can), (2) to look forward to the outpouring of the Spirit and the mission that follows, (3) to recount the departure of Jesus in a way that recalls 2 Kings 2:9-12, another narrative about the transmission of spirit for prophetic succession, and (4) to point toward the parousia (described already in Luke 21:27 as coming "in a cloud," alluding to the cloud imagery of Dan 7:13, but in the singular, to prepare for Acts 1:9). Thus Luke is able to speak of one reality, the final departure of Jesus from his assembled followers, from two interpretive points of view. Luke 24 alludes to the ascension as a fitting ending of the story of Jesus. Acts 1 narrates the same event as the beginning of the story of the mission of the Church, initiated by the risen Lord and empowered by the gift of the Spirit.

Finally, the NT presents a third telling of the ascension in Mark 16:19: "So then the Lord Jesus, after he spoke to them, was taken up into heaven and took his seat at the right hand of God."

Note that this verse is part of the so-called Longer Ending or Appendix of Mark (Mark 16:9-20). Since these twelve verses are missing in Codex Vaticanus and Codex Sinaiticus and use a non-Marcan vocabulary, scholarly consensus does not consider this passage to be part of the Gospel of Mark. It is understood to be a résumé of the appearances of the risen Lord reflecting Luke and John. The passage is nonetheless canonical, having been part of the canon accepted at the Council of Trent. What is notable in the verse about the ascension is that the event is here narrated as occurring on Easter Sunday evening, apparently indoors (see v. 14, "as the eleven were at table"), and is expressed in two clear biblical allusions: 2 Kings 2:11 ("he was taken up to heaven") and Psalm 110:1 ("the right hand of God"). The allusions have led some to conclude that Mark 16:19 reflects not Luke but an earlier, independent tradition.

Thus the NT canon gives us three narratives of the Ascension of Christ, each expressing in various ways the single reality that is both Jesus' final withdrawal from physical presence to his assembled disciples and, at the same time, an expression of his risen state which celebrates his victory and points toward Pentecost and parousia.

See: APOCALYPTIC, ELIJAH/ELISHA, GLORY, HOLY SPIRIT, MOUNTAIN, MISSION, PAROUSIA, PENTECOST, RESURRECTION, TRANSFIGURATION, WITNESS

M. DENNIS HAMM, S.J.

Pastoral-Liturgical Tradition

Luke's chronology depicting Jesus' ascension forty days after the resurrection was never a literal framework for early Christian worship or belief. Christ's ascension was an integral part of the paschal mystery: passion, resurrection, and ascension were understood as a single reality. Thus Justin Martyr (*First Apology* 1.50) and Irenaeus (*Demonstration* 83–85) could speak about the ascension without presuming the existence of a separate feast. Theologically the ascension symbolized the exaltation of Christ (Chrysostom, Sermon for the Ascension) and the glorification of those united to Christ (Augustine, Sermon for the Ascension).

At the end of the fourth century a separate feast emerged. The *Apostolic Constitution* (ca. 380 CE ?) witnesses to a celebration of the ascension on the fortieth day after Easter (V.20.2). According to Egeria (ca. 384 CE), Jerusalem celebrated the outpouring of the Spirit and the ascension together fifty

days after Easter (ch. 43); forty days after Easter there was a special gathering at Bethlehem (ch. 43). Scholars are divided whether the latter was a celebration of the ascension. Chrysostom's sermon on the ascension (ca. 386 CE) treated it as a well-established feast, noting that although ascension and Pentecost were separate, they were two facets of the same reality. By ca. 388 CE Gregory of Nyssa preached an ascension sermon that did not look forward to Pentecost. By the fifth century the Jerusalem liturgy (*Armenian Lectionary* 57) commemorated Christ's ascension on the fortieth day after Easter. Evidence from this period also suggests that a fast resumed after this feast. Thus the Church begins speaking of the "great forty days of *pascha.*" These developments contributed to a fracturing of the fifty days and the historicization of the paschal mystery.

The ascension eventually acquired a three day preparatory fast that developed into the Rogation days. A vigil celebration evolved by the eighth century; an octave soon followed. This fragmentation of the Easter season became complete with the emergence of "ascension-tide." In the popular imagination this period commemorated the historical ascent of Christ forty days after the resurrection (ritualized by the extinguishing of the paschal candle after the ascension Gospel), and the historical interlude before Pentecost.

Recent reforms integrate the ascension back into the Easter season. Ascension-tide and the extinguishing of the paschal candle have been eliminated. Today's liturgy stresses the intimate relationship between passion, resurrection, ascension, and the outpouring of the Spirit. This non-literal approach to the ascension is underscored by the *General Norms for the Liturgical Year and Calendar* (no. 7) which notes that if the ascension is not observed as a holy day, it is moved to the following Sunday. Ascension Preface II well summarizes the theology of this feast: "In his risen body he plainly showed himself to his disciples* and was taken up to heaven* in their sight to claim for us a share in his divine life."

See: GLORY, JESUS CHRIST, RESURRECTION

EDWARD FOLEY, CAPUCHIN

ASSYRIA

The name Assyria derives from the city Ashur that was located on the right bank of the Upper Tigris River. Later the name of the city was extended to a territorial state and world empire that emerged during the second millennium BCE in Mesopotamia. One feature of the territory occupied by the Assyrian state was that it had no natural borders and was therefore open to attack. In the second millennium there was a continuing struggle for power in Mesopotamia between Babylon, Larsa, Assyria, and Mari. Assyrian power peaked in the middle of the thirteenth century before giving way to Babylon.

After a period of retrenchment, Assyria began to reassert itself by taking offensive operations against its neighbors in the tenth century BCE. This brought it into contact with the Israelite kingdoms. The main objective of the first Assyrian campaigns was to stop the incursions of its neighbors into its territory and to get booty and prisoners for various building projects. Though the Bible does not mention it, Ahab of Israel (869–850 BCE) participated in a coalition of states from Syria-Palestine that halted the Assyrian march into that region. The Assyrian Chronicles state that Ahab contributed two thousand chariots and ten thousand foot soldiers to the forces of the coalition.

In the first half of the eighth century BCE, Assyria again moved against Syria-Palestine. The Assyrians thoroughly defeated the Arameans, but they were unable to capitalize on their victories because their attention was diverted to the north by the Kingdom of Urartu that challenged Assyrian hegemony. The primary beneficiaries of these developments were the two Israelite kingdoms. Aram was the chief rival of the Kingdom of Israel for dominance in Syria-Palestine. The rise of Assyria neutralized the Aram's power. When Assyria itself had to direct its attention away from the region in the ninth century BCE, Israel had a free hand in Syria-Palestine. This was the time of Israel's greatest economic prosperity and political power (2 Kgs 14:23-29). Judah too enjoyed the respite from the Assyrian threat (2 Chronicles 26).

This peace was short-lived. The second half of the eighth century witnessed a more ominous movement into the region by the Assyrians. They were no longer satisfied with taking treasure and prisoners. They sought a more permanent arrangement by which conquered kingdoms became satellites with only a semblance of independence. Assyrian rule was harsh and spawned futile revolts. Among these was the revolt of the Kingdom of Israel in 721 BCE (2 Kgs 17:1-6). Israel paid for its folly by the dismemberment of its territory and incorporation into the Assyrian provincial system. The Kingdom of Israel ceased to exist and many of its leading citizens were deported to various corners of the Assyrian Empire (2 Kgs 17:23).

Judah resisted the temptation to join these futile revolts and remained a compliant and even loyal vassal of Assyria. Isaiah advised Ahaz not to rely on Assyrian protection when Judah faced menacing threats by Aram and Israel who wanted Judah to join their revolution (Isa 7:3-9). In 704 BCE Judah could no longer resist the temptation to revolt. The Assyrians defeated Judah in 701 BCE but allowed it to resume its vassal status (2 Kgs 18:13–20:21).

Internal conflicts began to weaken the Assyrian Empire seriously. It became clear to Judah that the Assyrian hegemony was at an end. Under King Josiah (640–609 BCE), Judah fought with the Babylonians against Assyria. Though Josiah died in battle (2 Kgs 23:29-30), the end of the Assyrian Empire was assured and the neo-Babylonian Empire was born.

The OT reflects the dominant role that Assyria played in the life of the Israelite kingdoms for some two hundred years. Reports of the conflicts with Assyria take up sizeable portions of the Deuteronomistic and Chronicler's Histories (2 Kings 15–20; 2 Chronicles 28–33). Prophetic literature did not ignore Assyria. In particular Isaiah sees Assyria as God's instrument of judgment against the Israelite kingdoms (Isa 10:5). The prophet promised that once this judgment came upon the kingdoms, God would defeat Assyria (Isa 10:12; 14:25). Also the Assyrians would recognize Yahweh's power and join Judah in the service of its God (Isa 19:23-25). Nahum is not so sanguine about such a possibility. His oracles exult in Assyria's defeat. The Book of Jonah, however, has the king and citizens of Nineveh, the capital of Assyria, repent at the preaching of Jonah.

The importance of Assyria in the cultural development of Israel and Judah was profound. Assyria was the conduit for diffusing Babylonian culture in the ancient Near East (just as Rome would later be the conduit for Greek culture). Culturally Israel was oriented toward Mesopotamia, and the two hundred years of Assyrian hegemony in the territory of the Israelite kingdoms were decisive for the biblical tradition.

The Assyrians are responsible for our understanding of ancient Mesopotamian culture and history. Much of the early literature produced in the region survives in copies made by Assyrian scribes. The dictionaries compiled by these scribes have helped interpret the ancient languages of Mesopotamia. The Assyrian King List and Chronicles provide a scheme for dating events in the ancient Near East and reconstructing its history. Finally it was the Assyrians who were able to establish a genuine world state in which the peoples of the world were to live in security under a single government. Ancient Israel's experience of the Assyrian Empire led certain prophetic circles to begin thinking of a universal reign of God. This idea, of course, is a basic metaphor in the NT. The evange-

lists portray Jesus as the one whom God called to inaugurate the reign of God.

See: BABEL/BABYLON

LESLIE J. HOPPE, O.F.M.

ATHENS

Athens was the capital of the ancient Greek province of Attica and the locale of part of Paul's ministry in Achaia. Although the Golden Age of Athens was five centuries before his arrival, it was still an impressive city in Paul's day. On the Acropolis, rising three hundred feet from the Attic plain, he would have seen the Parthenon, dedicated to the goddess Athena, built with an unsurpassed architectural mastery of curvature and perspective, all in dazzling white Pentellic marble. Also on the Acropolis would have been visible the Erechtheum, built over the holy spot where Athena's gift of the olive tree won her the favor of patronage of the city over Poseidon. The Temple of Athena Nike, or "Victory" and the Propylaea, the great ceremonial entryway on the west end of the Acropolis, would also have commanded the attention of the first century visitor.

Paul's visit to Athens, around 50 CE, follows a hasty departure from Thessalonica and Beroea, when Jews of Thessalonica set these cities in turmoil against Paul (Acts 17). Paul's friends took him to Athens, where he awaited his associates Silas and Timothy. In Paul's first letter to the Thessalonians (3:1) he refers to his stay in Athens while Timothy strengthened and encouraged the community in Thessalonica. While in Athens, Paul "debated in the synagogue with the Jews and with the worshipers, and daily in the public square with whoever happened to be there" (Acts 17:17).

The agora, or marketplace, with its enclosed stoas, provided the central gathering place for Greek philosophers. On one occasion some of the Epicurean and Stoic philosophers invited Paul to address them at the Areopagus, the hill northwest of the Acropolis on which the supreme council had met in classical times. Paul's speech at the Areopagus (Acts 17:22-34) is the center-piece in Luke's construction of Paul's mission in Achaia, and is regarded by many as the climax of the Acts of the Apostles. Paul is portrayed as a great Athenian orator in the citadel of Hellenistic religiosity. He employs language and concepts from Greek philosophers and poets (Acts 17:28) to speak to his Gentile audience of the one God; the god whom they unknowingly worship (Acts 17:23), and who Paul now reveals.

Paul met with little success in Athens. For the most part the Athenians misunderstood his preaching, thinking him to be promoting two new deities, "Jesus" and "Anastasis" ("Resurrection"). Although Athenians were tolerant of other peoples' gods and "used their time for nothing else but telling or hearing something new" (Acts 17:21), they were, in fact, a people with a more classical conservatism, placing value in what was ancient, not in new gods or new ideas. In the end, "some did join him, and became believers. Among them were Dionysius, a member of the Court of the Areopagus, a woman named Damaris, and others with them" (Acts 17:34). Following this, Paul left Athens and went to Corinth (Acts 18:1), where he founded one of his most significant communities.

In later Church tradition, Dionysius the Areopagite became the patron saint of Athens. Eusebius, writing in the fourth century, asserts that Dionysius was also the first bishop of Athens. The earliest evidence for a Church in Athens is the letter to Athenian Christians by Dionysius, the bishop of Corinth, dated approximately 170 CE.

See: CITY, CORINTH, PAUL

BARBARA E. REID, O.P.

ATONEMENT

This entry consists of three parts. The OT section explores ancient Israel's language, theology, and rituals that centered on atonement. The NT section examines the reinterpretation of these by Paul, Mark, Matthew, and the author of Hebrews. The Pastoral-Liturgical section considers atonement both as the reconciliation of humanity to God through the death of Christ and as human acts of reparation.

Old Testament

Atonement is the act of restoring a disordered relationship between God and humans. The disordered state is a consequence of sin* (Gen 3:14-24); impure and unethical human actions are responsible for unleashing chaotic or impure forces within the human community (e.g., 2 Sam 12:7-12). The danger to individuals and the community from sin requires that steps be taken to reconcile the sinner to God. The most important steps take on ritual form in which God forgives the sinner; the ritual actions are neither magical in character nor human productions designed to placate a wrathful God. These ritual actions create the setting in which God intervenes to break the connection between sin and punishment. This encounter with a forgiving, holy God leads to a deepening as well as a restoring of the relationship.

The primary Hebrew term denoting "atonement" is *kipper*. The etymology of *kipper* consists of three main possibilities: (1) the Akkadian *kuppuru*, "to cleanse, to purify"; (2) the Arabic *kafara*, "to cover"; and (3) a denominative of the Hebrew *kōper*, "ransom." In the Mesopotamian cultic context, *kuppuru* denotes ritual actions of cleansing the cult of impurities. In Mesopotamia, impurity was regarded as a demonic force such that purificatory rites were frequently carried out to protect the sanctuary. The corpse of a sacrificial animal functioned as an absorbent material which gathered the impurities adhering to the sanctuary; the defiled corpse was then disposed of apart from the purified sanctuary. The Arabic term *kafara*, whose usage most closely parallels that of the Hebrew *kipper*, refers to "covering over" the sin so that the sinner and the sinful community were protected from the sphere of sin. The derivation of the verb *kipper* from the noun *kōper* involves bringing the non-cultic term for "ransom-money" into the sphere of the divine-human relationship where the holy God becomes angry with a wayward people; *kipper* refers to a restoring of the relationship rather than to an assuaging of God's anger. The most commonly accepted etymology is the Arabic *kafara*. However, a harmonization between the usage of the Akkadian *kuppuru* and that of the Arabic *kafara* may possibly be found in the action of "rubbing": the "rubbing off" of impurities with *kuppuru* and the "rubbing on" of protection with *kafara*.

God's Presence. As an element in the cultic actions designed to restore the divine-human relationship, the altar served as a symbol of God's presence. In the Priestly theology, God could countenance a modicum of impurity, but the build-up of impurities within the Israelite community threatened to drive God from their midst. The sins of the community could be of both an ethical and a cultic nature. Wherever these sins were committed within the Israelite community, the effects impinged upon the sanctuary as impurities and threatened to make the sanctuary uninhabitable for God. The ritual actions associated with *kipper* were designed to purify the sanctuary of these impurities.

Sin Offering. The primary cleansing agent is the blood of sacrificial animals in the *ḥaṭṭā't* (sin or purificatory) offering. In most expiatory offerings, the blood was placed upon the horns of the altar. This action symbolized the removal of sin and impurity from the altar so that Israel could once again gain access to God. The base of the altar was also the place at which the sacrificial blood was poured out; this symbolized the return or restoration of the life of the sacrificial animal to its creator. According to Leviticus 17:11, God instructed Moses: "Since the life of a living body is in its blood, I have made you put it on the altar, so that atonement may thereby be made for your own lives, because it is the blood, as the seat of life, that makes atonement." God gave the blood, which was the

bearer of life, to the Israelites to place upon the altar so that they could gain reconciliation. In the expiatory offerings, the blood was not functioning apotropaically nor did it serve as a propitiatory libation poured out to a vengeful deity such as was the case in other ancient Near Eastern cultures where the underworld deities delighted in blood.

The blood rites for the sin offering assumed a "smaller form" for the unwitting sins of a ruler but a "larger form" for the unwitting sins of the priest and the congregation as a whole. In the sin offering, the blood was never placed upon a human person but only upon cultic objects. In the smaller version, the blood was placed on the horns of the altar and the rest was poured out at the base of the altar (Lev 4:25). In the larger version, the blood was sprinkled seven times before the curtain of the holy of holies, then some was placed on the horns of the altar, and the remainder was poured out at the base of the altar (Lev 4:6-7, 17-18). Some commentators interpret these actions as protective measures for Yahweh: i.e., to prevent the holy God from striking out at impurities, the blood drives away the impurities analogous to the manner in which the "blood on the lintel" prevented the Destroyer from attacking the first-born of the Hebrews in Egypt (Exod 12:23). However, the picture of Yahweh as a vulnerable Deity residing in the holy of holies and taking defensive measures against demonic forces stands in tension with Israel's monotheistic understanding.

The expiatory offerings were efficacious for inadvertent sins, but they needed to be preceded by contrition or remorse for lesser sins and by public confession for more serious sins (1 Sam 7:6; 1 Kgs 8:33-34; Lev 16:21). It was assumed that such contrition and confession had taken place apart from the sanctuary prior to bringing a sin offering (Num 5:7; Lev 5:5). Thus, the process for forgiving sins was personal or juridical rather than magical.

A significant gesture for the atonement to be effected by the sin offering was the laying on of hands. Although some questions remain about the precise significance of this action, it does not symbolize the shifting of guilt nor the transfer of the sin itself to the sacrificial animal. It does, however, seem to symbolize the identification of the sinner with the animal which is about to die; the animal then vicariously bears the sins of the offerer; the sinners are to see themselves undergoing death in the slaughter of the animal in order to restore the relationship with God. In the bull offered by the high priest for his inadvertent sins, he lays one hand on the bull before slaughtering it (Lev 4:4). In the offering of the bull for the inadvertent sins of the whole community, the elders lay their hands on the head of the bull (Lev 4:15); the ruler does likewise in offering a goat for his inadvertent sins (Lev 4:23-24). These offerings, where sinners acknowledge their sinfulness before a holy God, were meant to symbolize a moving beyond or a freeing from whatever might separate them from God. For deliberate, high-handed sins, the annual ritual of the Day of Atonement was necessary, or otherwise no sacrificial means of expiation would suffice.

Purification. The concept of atonement also has a role to play in determining whether impure individuals are fit to re-enter the Israelite community. The need to maintain boundaries is one of the highest duties of the priests. To neglect, scorn, or treat lightly such a task meant a serious deficiency in reverence for God. This task of maintaining boundaries took on specific form with regard to death, sex, and contagious illnesses. Any Nazirite who was near someone at the time of that person's death had to undergo a lengthy ritual to restore the condition of being a Nazirite (Num 6:9-12). A woman who gives birth must purify herself (Lev 12:1-8). Discharges from the genital area by either a man or a woman must be purified (Lev 15:1-33). A leper must also undergo a cleansing process in order to be fit to re-enter the community (Lev 14:1-32). The common denominator

for contact with a corpse, sexual emissions, and skin diseases is not immediately apparent, but perhaps it is the repulsive aspect of each and the threatening character of death, disease, and fertility cults which led the Israelites to label these phenomena impure.

Another ritual of cleansing individuals so that they do not defile the cult and disorder Israel's relationship with God is the ordination of priests (Lev 8:1-36; Exod 29:1-46). The ritual of taking the blood from the sacrificial animal and placing it upon the lobe of the right ear, the thumb of the right hand, and the large toe of the right foot of the one to be ordained (Lev 8:24) resembles the placing of blood upon the leper who is to be declared clean (Lev 14:14). This similarity suggests that the rite of ordination was not for imparting special graces to the person but rather a cleansing so that the person would be fit to draw near to the altar of God.

Intercession and Expiation. Besides contrition for sins, an important non-cultic means of atonement for the Israelites before God was intercession. After the idolatrous worship of the "golden calf," Moses said to the people, "You have committed a grave sin. I will go up to the LORD, then; perhaps I may be able to make atonement for your sin" (Exod 32:30). Abraham likewise interceded for the people of Sodom; in the course of his bargaining with God, he says, "Please, let not my LORD grow angry if I speak up this last time" (Gen 18:32). Abraham undertakes the dangerous role of approaching an angry God who intends to punish for sins. The use of words by a heroic intercessor to stay God's just punishment was another, yet exceptional, means of suspending or breaking the connection between sin and punishment and thereby providing an opportunity for renewing Israel's relationship with God.

Atonement between Israel and God was most frequently effected by God's acting through priestly expiatory offerings. As a ritual of riddance, the scapegoat ritual was also important for cleansing the sanctuary on the Day of Atonement (Lev 16:20-28). A prerequisite to the authenticity and effectiveness of these rituals was the sinners' repentance. The priestly cultic theology revered the sanctuary as a meeting place of God and humans; as a copy of the heavenly sanctuary, the earthly sanctuary and its rituals were not human constructs. As the dwelling place of God in Israel, the sanctuary for the priestly theology was the goal of creation (Exod 40:34-38). To keep the Israelite community free from impurities would allow God to continue to abide in their midst. Through this priestly understanding of the cult, the Israelites were offered an explanation of why they receive blessings and punishments. To maintain and deepen its relationship with God, Israel needed the cult, the priesthood, and its expiatory rituals.

See: ALTAR, BLOOD, CLEAN/UNCLEAN, DAY OF ATONEMENT, EXPIATION, HAND, ORDINATION, PRIEST, RECONCILIATION, REPENTANCE, SACRIFICE, SIN, TENT, WORSHIP

DALE LAUNDERVILLE, O.S.B.

New Testament

The Anglo-Saxon compound term at-one-ment connotes peace and unity. The etymology of this word also indicates reconciliation following estrangement, the restoration and renewal of a broken relationship. After the rupture caused by sin, atonement creates harmony. Atonement provides the means for interrupting the sin-guilt-punishment or retribution cycle that characterizes the human condition. In addition, atonement means the reconciliation or peaceful relationship between God and us enjoyed once satisfaction for sin* has been made.

Several Greek words appear in the NT to convey the notion of atonement (*halaskethai, katharizein, katallasso*). Yet this is not a concept that is well developed or emphasized in the NT writings. Building on the OT description of the celebration of Yom Kippur (Lev 16:1-34; 23:26-32; Num 29:7-11), the NT writers described the life

and ministry, the death, and resurrection of Jesus as a means of atonement for sins and reconciliation with God. They also interpreted the final day of judgment as a time when faith in Jesus as the Christ will be the salvation that includes atonement for sin. When Jesus returns in glory to judge the world, the faithful will be judged righteous and punishment for sin will have been satisfied.

The Gospels. The Synoptic Gospels portray Jesus' death as atonement. For example, the oldest Gospel, Mark, perhaps referring to Jesus' own view of himself, describes Jesus' ministry as a giving of his life as a "ransom for many" (Mark 10:45). The notion of "ransom" includes a substitution of animal or human life or some valued offering to redeem or "buy back" one who is condemned. According to Mark, the "many" would be condemned, but Jesus substituted his own life for theirs and thus won for all freedom and life.

This is the interpretation of Jesus' death that prevails in Mark, Matthew and Paul. Jesus' blood is the "blood of the covenant, which will be shed for many" (Mark 14:24). The concept appears to have been based on the Torah's description of the sacrifice for sin (see Exod 32:30-35) cultically symbolized in the Day of Atonement (Lev 23:26-32). It is also prevalent in the prophet Isaiah's description of the servant of God who ransoms the Gentiles by suffering on their behalf. This is, of course, a concept that greatly influenced the NT writers' interpretation of the mission of Jesus.

The concept is, surprisingly, absent from Luke's interpretation of Jesus' life and death. For Luke, Jesus is a just yet suffering "martyr," a "witness" testifying to the fidelity of God even in the midst of great suffering. But the notion of Jesus' atoning for our sins is not present in Luke.

Nor is John much influenced by the OT atonement concept. Jesus freely lays down his life for his friends and thus shows the extent of his love (John 10:17; 13:1). Jesus is victorious in death and over death. John reminds us that "unless a grain of wheat falls to the ground and dies, it remains just a grain of wheat; but if it dies, it produces much fruit" (John 12:24). Jesus' death is life-giving: the OT concept of atonement is not prominent in John.

The Letters of Paul. For Paul, the first Christian writer, the concept of atonement is important. Jesus Christ is God's mercy revealed to a sinful world. Jesus suffered and died "for our sins" (Gal 1:4; see 1 Cor 15:3). Paul insists that all have sinned and are subject to the wrath of God. Nevertheless, all are justified through Jesus Christ whom God gave as expiation to justify all who have faith (see Rom 3:25-26). Paul further states that "you have been purchased at a price" (1 Cor 6:20; 7:23). By his death, Jesus Christ has ransomed or purchased sinners so that now we live "for God" (see Rom 6:10-11).

For Paul, the Law held us captive but Christ ransomed us from the Law and now we have been adopted by God. This is one aspect of Christ's work as described in Galatians: "Christ ransomed us from the curse of the law by becoming a curse for us" (3:13), and "God sent his Son, . . . born under the law, to ransom those under the law, so that we might receive adoption" (4:4-5).

The Letter to the Hebrews. It is in the letter to the Hebrews that the concept of atonement, linked to the image of Christ as high priest, is most clearly expressed. Christ had to become human in all things, including being subject to sin and death, in order to free all humans from the power of sin and death. Becoming like us in every way, Christ is "a merciful and faithful high priest before God to expiate the sins of the people" (Heb 2:17).

The most eloquent description of Christ's role as high priest atoning for the sins of people occurs in chapters four and five of Hebrews:

> We have a great high priest, . . . Jesus, the Son of God, . . . For we do not have a high priest who is unable to sympathize with our weaknesses, but one who has similarly been tested in every way, yet without sin. So let us confidently approach the throne of grace to receive mercy and to find grace for timely help. Every high priest is taken from among men and made their representative before God, to offer gifts and sacrifices for sins. He is able to deal patiently with the ignorant and erring, for he himself is beset by weakness. . . . In the days when he [Christ] was in the flesh, he offered prayers and supplications with loud cries and tears to the one who was able to save him from death, and he was heard because of his reverence. Son though he was, he learned obedience from what he suffered; and when he was made perfect, he became the source of salvation for all who obey him (4:14-16; 5:1-2, 7-9).

Some of the same thoughts are expressed again in Hebrews 10:19-21, where we read:

> since through the blood of Jesus we have confidence of entrance into the sanctuary by the new and living way he opened for us through the veil, that is, his flesh, and since we have a "great priest over the house of God," let us approach with a sincere heart and in absolute trust, with our hearts sprinkled clean from an evil conscience.

Conclusion. The English term "atonement" which can translate several Greek terms, does not often appear in the major translations. (For example, "atone" or "atonement" does not appear at all in the RSV.) Yet the concepts signified by this interesting word—the satisfaction for sin and reconciliation with God—are part of the very basic interpretation of the life and death of Jesus according to Paul, Mark, Matthew, and the author of Hebrews.

See: EXPIATION, JUSTIFICATION, PRIEST, RECONCILIATION, REDEMPTION, SALVATION

MARY ANN GETTY

Pastoral-Liturgical Tradition

The understanding of the atonement found in the Christian tradition embraces two dimensions of that concept. On the one hand, it involves the reconciliation of humanity to God through the sacrificial death of Christ. It is Christ who, through his death, atones for our sins.* On the other hand, atonement refers to the human activity in response to Christ's atoning activity whereby human beings undertake acts of reparation for the damage caused by sin.

In the elaboration of the first dimension of atonement—Christ's death as atonement for sin—the early Church drew especially on the Pauline writings. The Fathers expanded upon the Pauline understanding, however, by imagining the reconciliation of humanity as a struggle between God and Satan. Satan had acquired a proprietary right over humankind, as it were, because of human sin. Some versions of this went so far as to propose Christ's death as a ransom paid to Satan to free humankind from its bondage. In Christ's death, however, Satan was tricked by the resurrection of Christ.

The defining understanding of the atonement for the Western Church was the work of Anselm (ca. 1033–1109), who in his *Cur Deus homo* (Why Did God Become Human?) developed the idea of atonement as vicarious satisfaction. Rather than offering ransom to the devil, Christ in his death offered infinite satisfaction to the infinite offense to the honor of God rendered by human sin. Based on Paul's understanding of atonement, Anselm combined the newly retrieved sense of Roman law with the codes of honor of Germanic military culture. It produced the judicial metaphors that have marked Western atonement theology ever since. Such legal language strikes many who live in democracies where the rule of law is presumed as stifling and remote. But in Anselm's time, such adjudication of offense by legal rather than by physical means was liberating.

Subsequent understandings of the atonement through the Middle Ages and the Reformation brought certain refinements to

Anselm's theory, but did not alter it significantly. Aquinas stressed the suitableness (*convenientia*) of Christ's death as atoning rather than its necessity. Luther emphasized Christ's willingness in bearing the punishment for sin.

Abelard prefigured modern attenuation of Anselm's theory inasmuch as he stressed Christ's death as an example of love which inspires Christians to similar acts of atonement. Modern theories of the atonement tread more lightly in the question of the necessity of Christ's death for atonement. Some feminist theologians have suggested that for God to demand the death of Jesus is analogous to child abuse. On the other hand, in reaction to what it saw as a modernist erosion of biblical faith, Protestants who formed the Fundamentalist movement insisted on the atoning death of Christ as one of the fundamentals of Christian belief.

The Roman Catholic Church has not solemnly defined any of the ways used to speak of God's activity in the death of Jesus for our behalf.

Alongside this theological tradition was the human response to God's atoning action in Christ. In the early Church, the martyr's death was seen as an atoning act, at first for the sins of the martyr through the imitation of Christ's death, and later for the sins of the Church. Attention likewise focused upon atonement for the sins the Christian committed after having been cleansed from sin in baptism. The development of the sacrament of reconciliation (whose purpose here is clearer in its older name, Penance) created a ritual space wherein Christians could undertake atoning activity for the damage done by their sins, which had now been forgiven in the atoning death of Christ. Such atoning activity expanded into and fused with ascetical activity, especially in the monasteries.

Undertaking reparational activity for the effects of one's sins came to take on an ever-increasing role in the spiritual life, especially in the West. In the modern period, a spirituality that fostered a mystical participation in the passion of Christ motivated another framework for atonement, atoning not only for one's own sins, but also for the sins of the world. The modern devotion to the Sacred Heart, promoted so effectively by St. Margaret Mary Alacoque (1647–1690), focused atonement on modern indifference to Christ and to offenses against the Blessed Sacrament. The devotional practice of receiving the Eucharist on nine consecutive first Fridays of the month, the centerpiece of Sacred Heart devotion, has persisted in many places down to the present time. Sacred Heart devotion grew from the eighteenth century and was the single most popular devotion (alongside devotion to Mary) from that time into the 1950s.

While the theology of atonement was best understood on a metaphysical level, and its devotional counterpart on a ritual level, atonement today is most frequently understood psychologically, as the assuagement of guilt. There are, however, exceptions, mainly in the instances of monstrous human transgression, where more ritual or cosmic understandings continue to be invoked. An example would be the Carmel of the Precious Blood established on the site of the former concentration camp at Dachau to atone for the crimes committed there. In such instances of unspeakable suffering, those cosmic proportions of atonement spoken of by Patristic and Medieval theologians become actual for modern sensibilities.

See: DEATH, GOD, JESUS CHRIST, RESURRECTION, SATAN, SIN

ROBERT J. SCHREITER, C.PP.S.

ATONEMENT (DAY OF)

Old Testament

The Day of Atonement was an annual day of fasting, public assembly, and special sacrifices* whose purpose was the purification of the officiating high priest, the Temple, and the people. It began in the evening of the ninth of Tishri, the seventh month, and ended in the evening of the tenth (Lev 16:29; 23:27). This was the only day of the year on which the high priest entered the holy of holies and stood before the mercy seat on which was enthroned the glory of God.

A solemn Sabbath-like day on which no work occurred, the Day of Atonement was the only day on which the Mosaic Law demanded that non-Israelite ("resident alien") and Israelite alike "mortify himself," i.e., fast from all food (Lev 16:29). According to Leviticus 23:26-32, failure to observe these regulations was punished by death. In addition to the animal sacrifices described below, Numbers 29:7-11 calls for grain offerings. The blowing of the shofar, the ritual horn, further distinguished this day (Lev 25:9) from other observances.

There is no mention of the Day of Atonement in the pre-exilic literature. Ezekiel 45:18-20 describes a ritual limited to priests in which two bulls were sacrificed to purify the Temple and to remove the effects of any sin* committed out of "inadvertence or ignorance." This may echo a purification rite used in the first Temple. The Day of Atonement is not mentioned explicitly in post-exilic Ezra and Nehemiah. Nehemiah 9:1 mandates a day of fasting and penance on the "twenty-fourth day of this month," but it is not clear that the month in question is Tishri.

Descriptions of activities associated with the Day of Atonement occur only in the Priestly tradition. The most substantial text is Leviticus 16. Three important rituals are detailed there.

First, the high priest, dressed in linen garments, sacrificed a young bull (v. 6), the sin offering designated for priests in Leviticus 4:3-12. He then entered the holy of holies. There he offered incense before the mercy seat where the Glory of God was enthroned. The cloud of incense shielded the priest from the power of God's holiness and preserved his life (Lev 16:12-13). The high priest sprinkled the mercy seat with the blood of the sacrificed bull to expiate his own sins and the sins of his household (v. 11), the members of the Aaronite priesthood.

Second, the priest went out to the people. In their presence, he distinguished by lot between two goats; one was selected for the Lord, the other, "for Azazel." The goat selected for the Lord the high priest sacrificed for the sins of the people (vv. 7-9). He carried its blood back into the holy of holies and sprinkled it on the mercy seat (v. 15); he also splashed it on the horns of the golden altar of incense (Exod 30:10).

Third, the priest returned to the people. He laid his hands on the goat selected for Azazel and pronounced over it the sins of the people of Israel (vv. 20-21). Given its parallelism with the proper name YHWH, Azazel is best understood as the name of a demon who, in folklore, was a particular threat to any community who stood outside the protection of its national deity. Removal of guilt restored this protective relationship. A member of the assembly led this goat, bearing the guilt of the nation, into the desert, the traditional dwelling place of demons (Isa 13:21; 34:11-14; Tob 8:3; Mark 1:12-13 and parallel passages; Matt 12:43). This goat could not be sacrificed because it was now unclean.

Once these rituals were concluded, the priest traded his penitential linen tunic for his more elaborate liturgical robes to offer burnt offerings at the great altar. Also offered were the fat of the bull and the goat (Lev 16:23-25). The other remains of these animals were carried outside and burned. The person charged with this duty along with the man who had led the goat for Azazel into the desert were deemed uncleaned; they had to purify themselves by bathing and washing their clothes before they could rejoin the community.

Leviticus 16 achieved its final form late in the post-exilic period. This text is the product of much editorial activity. There are several doublets (vv. 6 and 11; 9b and 15; 4 and 32) and two conclusions (v. 29a and v. 24);

verses 29b-34 resemble Leviticus 23:27-32. The connection (vv. 1-2) with the death of Aaron's sons (Lev 10:1-5) is artificial.

The earliest layer of material probably describes an annual rite used by the priests to purify themselves and the Temple, a concern of Ezekiel 45:18-20. During the late post-exilic period, this in-house activity was expanded to include the whole community. To it was also joined the "goat for Azazel" tradition. This expansion of a private priestly ritual into a solemn day of penance and fasting reflects the post-exilic preoccupation with the reality of human sinfulness and the demands of divine justice. The extension of obligation to the entire nation may be later than Nehemiah.

Leviticus 14:4-9 reports a practice analogous to the "goat for Azazel" tradition. There, after the sores of leprosy had healed, the victim of the disease could transfer the impurity which had caused it to a bird; once the bird had flown away, carrying away the cause of the disease, the leper was declared clean.

The rituals described in Leviticus 16 have parallels in extra-biblical religious texts as well as in the OT itself. In Babylon, e.g., during the celebration of the New Year in the month of Nisan, the body of a beheaded sheep was rubbed against the temple of Nabu to take away the impurities that had accumulated there over the past year; the animal was then thrown into the Euphrates River.

New Testament

There is not explicit reference to the Day of Atonement in the New Testament. However, the annual atonement rituals are certainly the presumed background in Hebrews 9:6-12. This passage suggests a contrast between the high priest and Jesus, the authentic high priest (Heb 2:17). The rites the high priest performed hidden from view in the holy of holies, Jesus accomplished publically on the cross. Further, the death of Jesus accomplished once and for all what the Day of Atonement rituals were able to guarantee only on a year-to-year basis (9:7). The high priest of Leviticus used the blood of a bull and goat, but Jesus used his own blood (9:12-14) to achieve forgiveness of sin. Romans 3:25 suggests that the crucified Christ has become the new mercy seat, the public assurance of forgiveness of sin.

See: BLOOD, GLORY, HOLY/HOLINESS, PRIEST/PRIEST-HOOD, SACRIFICE

KATHLEEN S. NASH

B

BAAL

Old Testament

Baal means "lord" or "ruler." It is the name of one of the major gods of the Canaanite* pantheon. Baal is the storm god and the god of fertility.*

Canaanite Myth and Worship. In the Canaanite myth Baal is the son of the father god El. Two stories illustrate his prominence. In the first story Baal fights with the sea god Yam. In the struggle Baal wins, confines the sea to its limits, and allows the dry land and the rest of creation to appear. The image of storm versus sea as the origin of creation reflects the experience of the people who lived between the Arabian desert and the Mediterranean.

In the second story Baal fights with the god of death, Mot. In this story Baal is defeated and Mot takes him to the underworld. Because Baal is the source of the rain and thus the provider of fertility for the earth,* the land withers and becomes barren. Baal's sister-bride Anath, however, is murderously angry with Mot. She pursues Mot, kills him, and plows pieces of his body into the earth. Then Baal rises from death and is reunited with Anath. The rains return and the land flourishes with growth. The myth reflects the cycle of dry season and wet season in Canaanite experience.

In the worship of Baal the story is retold and the action of ritual sexual intercourse is performed as a kind of sympathetic magic intended to remind Anath and Baal to unite again with each other so that the rains may come and the earth be fertile again.

Prophetic Struggle. Throughout Israel's history in the land there is a struggle against worship of Baal. Concepts relating to the Baal myth are transformed and proclaimed of Yahweh. Yahweh defeats the sea and brings forth ordered creation. The Genesis account transcends the battle motif. Yahweh creates simply by word (Gen 1:1-2, 6-9). Other accounts echo the battle of the myth more closely (Job 26:12-13; 38:8-11; Pss 74:12-15, 89:10-12; Isa 27:1; 51:9). Yahweh's power, however, is never in doubt. Psalm 104 describes the sea monster as only a creature of Yahweh (104:26).

The people, however, are inclined to combine worship of Yahweh with worship of Baal. The fertility rites are seen as insurance to secure good crops. The prophets consistently condemn this infidelity on the part of God's people. Elijah confronts the prophets of Baal with a contest and, after his victory, slits the throats of 450 of them (1 Kgs 18:16-40). In Hosea, God divorces his wife Israel because she has committed adultery by going over to Baal instead of remaining faithful to her true husband, Yahweh. She has believed that Baal gave her grain and wine and oil. Therefore God will take them away from her so that she will return to her first husband (Hos 2:8-15). Names honoring Baal are found throughout the pre-exilic period: JeruBa'al, IshBa'al, MeriBa'al (Judg 7:1; 2 Sam 2:8; 9:6).

See: CANAAN, CREATION, EARTH, EL/ELOHIM, ELIJAH/ELISHA, FERTILITY, IDOLATRY, LAND, SEA, SEXUALITY

IRENE NOWELL, O.S.B.

BABEL/BABYLON

Babylon, the ancient city of enmity with the Jewish people, is important in the OT and NT for historical and theological reasons. It represented oppression and destruction, but it now serves the Church as an image of hope that God can overcome such obstacles.

Old Testament

Babylon is important in the Bible for historical, theological, and symbolic reasons. Babel is the Hebrew name for this ancient Mesopotamian city, situated between the Tigris and Euphrates Rivers in present-day Iraq. The OT uses the name for both the region and for its major city. At the height of its glory, the city was famous for its architecture and for its hanging gardens, which were considered one of the wonders of the ancient world. Historically, Babylon served as the capital for various royal dynasties, whose influence was widely felt in the ANE. One of the most famous figures associated with it is Hammurabi (eighteenth century BCE), whose great code of law influenced the development of other ANE law codes, including parts of the OT (e.g., Exod 21:23-25).

The OT most frequently mentions Babylon in passages recounting the military and political threat which its rulers posed to Judah (2 Kgs 20:16-18). The most consequential act of Babylon against the Jewish people was the attack and siege of Judah and its capital, Jerusalem, beginning in 598 BCE. When the appointed Jewish regent, Zedekiah, rebelled against the Babylonian King Nebuchadnezzar, the latter exacted a devastating destruction on Jerusalem (587/586 BCE), which leveled the Temple and the city and forced thousands of inhabitants into exile. The Exile* is memorialized in Psalm 137:1-4: "By the streams of Babylon we sat and wept when we remembered Zion. . . . Though there our captors asked of us the lyrics of our songs . . . How could we sing a song of the LORD in a foreign land?" Jeremiah, a prophet of the Exile, frequently mentions Babylon and its king. He prophesied about the catastrophic events that befell Jerusalem (Jer 20:4-6; 27:1-22), and about the vengeance of God against Babylon for its destruction of Judah (Jer 50:1-46; see Isa 13:19).

Babylon serves a theological purpose in the famous story about the tower of Babel preserved in Genesis 11:1-9. The author used the story as an etiological legend, that is, a tale which tries to explain the origin of the differences in human languages. Through a play on the Hebrew word "confuse" *(balal)* and the name Babel, the author taught that it was humankind's arrogance in trying to build a building to heaven that caused the originally unified languages in the world to become diffused. The English word "babble" still refers to confused or incoherent speech. Although the story grew out of the reputation which Babylon had for large pyramidal temples called "ziggurats," the writer used it to illustrate the evil of human pride and its consequences.

The name Babylon is also used as a reference to God's just judgment against Judah's wickedness. Despite the profound grief felt by the Jews at the destruction of Jerusalem, the prophetic literature at times refers to Babylon as an instrument of God's will. The text of Jeremiah (Jer 25:1-11) refers to Judah's disobedience to God and even goes so far as to call the king of Babylon "my servant" (Jer 25:9; 27:6), while the Book of Ezekiel refers to Israel as a "rebellious house" against which the king of Babylon acted (Ezek 17:11-18).

Late OT traditions developed a more symbolic use of the name. The Book of Daniel, for example, uses Babylon as a symbol of the oppression and persecution directed against the Jews in the time of Antiochus IV Epiphanes (second century BCE). In stories that purport to be about the historical Babylon, the image of Babylon symbolically represents oppression experienced at any given time (e.g., Daniel 5).

New Testament

There is no explicit mention of the tower of Babel in the NT, though some see in the Pentecost story (Acts 2:1-13) a reversal of the language divisions created at Babel. With the coming of the holy Spirit, human communication was again reestablished and the gospel could be spread to all lands, thus fostering hope for reunification of all peoples of the earth.

Babylon is used in the NT in two senses, historically and symbolically. The Gospel of Matthew uses the Babylonian Exile as a historical limit in the genealogy of Jesus Christ (Matt 1:1-17). This designation acknowledges the importance of the Exile in Israel's history. It also helped Matthew to establish three uniform periods in Israel's history, each with fourteen generations, reinforcing Jesus' position as the royal Messiah in David's line, and thus the hope of Israel.

The primary NT use of Babylon is symbolic. Based upon the OT reference to the city as a means of destruction and oppression, Babylon was transformed among Christians into a symbol of any oppression which they experienced. Thus, it became a code name for Rome (e.g., 1 Pet 5:13). The Book of Revelation especially makes Babylon a symbol of Roman oppression and persecution (Rev 14:8; 16:19). It is described graphically as a whore, "Babylon the great, the mother of harlots and of the abominations of the earth" (Rev 17:5), referring to the corruption of true religion by the pagan cultic worship of the emperor. This crude feminine image is used in the great prophecy of destruction foretold of Babylon (Rev 18:1-24). There the evil city is destroyed in a scene which provides a dramatic contrast to the victory of another symbolic city, the heavenly Jerusalem (Rev 21:9-27). This biblical "tale of two cities"

boldly imparted a message of hope for the persecuted Christians. The NT thus gives testimony to the surviving potency of this symbol.

Pastoral-Liturgical Tradition

Babylon continues to function as a symbol primarily in two ways. First, it represents corruption. Early Protestant reformers at times even used Babylon, with its NT association with Rome, as a symbol of the perceived corruption of the Roman Church. Secondly, it is used to evoke the experience of exile. Through the ages, Babylon has been used to represent the traumatic experience of being ousted from one's homeland and forced to live in slavery. Readings about Babylon from Daniel and Revelation are found in the lectionary near the end of the liturgical year, a time when the Church recalls with hope Christ's victory over all evil and oppression. Psalm 137 is found in three places in the lectionary, each time with the refrain: "Let my tongue be silenced, if I ever forget you [Jerusalem]!" The symbol still serves as a reminder to be faithful, even in the experience of oppression, war, destruction, and exile. The tower of Babel also continues to function as a symbol of human arrogance and pride. Many artists have painted interpretations of this biblical scene, the most memorable being that of Pieter Brueghel the Elder (1563).

See: EXILE, JEW

RONALD D. WITHERUP, S.S.

BAPTISM

Baptism derives its meaning from the symbolic meaning of water* as source of life and cleansing. In the OT, when used by God's command, water could effect ritual purification and be the source of inner forgiveness in messianic times. John's baptism initiated these times, preparing the way for Jesus' baptism in the holy Spirit.*

Old Testament

The word "baptism" is derived from the Greek verb *baptizo* which means "to plunge" or "dip into." As in many ancient religions, such an action had a symbolic inner value because of the cleansing properties of water. The actual word is rare in the OT. Elisha cured Naaman the Syrian of leprosy by commanding him to wash in the Jordan river: "Go and wash seven times in the Jordan, and your flesh will heal, and you will be clean" (2 Kgs 5:10). After much hesitation, Naaman obeyed the prophetic voice of God: "Naaman went down and plunged [lit. was baptized] into the Jordan seven times at the word of the man of God. His flesh became again like the flesh of a little child, and he was clean" (2 Kgs 5:14). The word of God effected a new power in water to go beyond its external cleansing to a real inner cure. This example suggests that water plus the word of God can be the source of a new inner change (2 Kgs 5:13-15).

The Law required many purifications, some with specially prepared water, to purify people from ritual uncleanness and prepare them for worship (e.g., Num 19:11-22). Here again, the obedience to God's voice in the Law gave water a special power. However, the prophets announced that a full inner purification from sin would only come in the last times: "On that day there shall be open to the house of David and to the inhabitants of Jerusalem, a fountain to purify from sin and uncleanness" (Zech 13:1). Ezekiel associated this purification with the eschatological gift of the holy Spirit: "I will sprinkle clean water upon you to cleanse you from all your impurities,. . . . I will give you a new heart and place a new spirit within you" (36:25-26). The Qumran community practiced many daily water purifications in order to preserve continual ritual purity. These repeated washings were neither initiation rites nor channels of forgiveness from God. This could only be obtained by inner humble obedience to God. Close to NT times, Judaism required Gentile proselytes (Matt 23:15) to undergo a baptism of initiation before they could be circumcised and become converts. This had a once and for

all symbolic nature of renewal and moral regeneration.

New Testament

John the Baptist* announced that the long awaited reign of God was drawing near (Matt 3:2). To be Jews and sons of Abraham was not enough to prepare for the coming reign preceded by God's judgment or wrath (Matt 3:7). John required a baptism of initiation. This baptism was not a repeated purification but a decisive step like that of a proselyte seeking to become a Jew. Only such a change would make a person a member of the true Israel as a real son of Abraham (Matt 3:9-11). Confession of sins preceded this baptism as a sign of sincere repentance (Matt 3:6; Mark 1:5). The result of such a baptism was forgiveness of sins in preparation for the new age (Mark 1:4; Luke 3:3). Matthew does not mention forgiveness at this point to stress that full forgiveness of sins will only come through Jesus' blood (26:28). The Baptist required definite changes in life-style and stressed ascetic practices such as fasting and special prayers (Mark 2:18; Matt 9:14; Luke 5:33). Yet Luke draws more attention to moral regeneration characterized by good works such as sharing with the hungry and needy along with uprightness in one's profession even for soldiers or tax collectors (3:10-14). After his own baptism, Jesus joined the Baptist and continued this apostolate as a colleague and disciple (John 3:22; but cf. 4:2 which seems to attempt to separate Jesus from John's work). Yet the close association of Jesus and the Baptist is confirmed by the fact that Jesus' most important disciples had first of all been disciples of the Baptist before Jesus met them (John 1:35-49; see Acts 1:21-22).

Written from the perspective of Jesus' death and resurrection as constitutive actions of the reign of God, the Gospels are careful to distinguish the baptism of John from that of Jesus. This was especially necessary since there were disciples of John the Baptist after Jesus' death who continued to cling to the Baptist's teachings (Acts 18:24-

26; 19:1-7). Mark has the Baptist proclaim, "I have baptized you with water; he will baptize you with the holy Spirit" (1:8). Jesus calls his own death a "baptism" into which James and John must be plunged along with him if they are to be part of the reign of God (10:38). In the longer ending of Mark we find a statement about the necessity of baptism: "Whoever believes and is baptized will be saved" (16:16). However, it is absent in important Greek manuscripts and is probably an early second century addition to the Gospel. Matthew's Gospel more carefully separates Jesus' baptism from that of John. The Baptist announces that one greater than he will come who will baptize with the holy Spirit and fire (3:11). Full forgiveness of sin will only come about through Jesus' death as participated in through the Last Supper (26:28). Matthew's Gospel leads to a climax in a final mountain enthronement and commission scene. Jesus announces that he now has all power in heaven and on earth and transfers this to the eleven: "Go, therefore, and make disciples of all nations, baptizing them in the name of the Father, and of the Son, and of the holy Spirit, teaching them to observe all that I have commanded you" (28:19-20). Previous to Jesus' death and resurrection, the apostles could not have this power nor were they to go beyond the Jewish people (10:1-7). However, Jesus' triumphant resurrection opens up the gospel to the world. The traditional liturgical formula comes from Matthew's Gospel and derives its power from the words of the risen Christ. However, the Gospel text was written toward the end of the first century and earlier forms of baptism may have been employed (see further on Acts). Jesus' words reflect his own baptismal experience with the voice from the Father and the descent of the holy Spirit (3:16-17). A disciple is plunged/baptized into the same relationship with the Father and holy Spirit. Along with baptism, the disciple learns Jesus' teachings as a model for a new life: "Teaching them to observe all that I have commanded you" (Matt 28:20).

Luke-Acts further disassociates Jesus from John's baptism. The holy Spirit descends on Jesus more as a result of his prayer than the baptism of John (3:21). Luke has the Baptist carefully assure the people that he is not the one to come and that his baptism is distinct from Jesus' coming baptism with the holy Spirit and fire (Acts 3:15-17; see also 1:5; 11:16). This baptism of the Spirit and fire takes place in the first Pentecost following the continued prayer of Jesus' disciples and family (2:1-4). In Acts, only those who were not previously disciples before Jesus' death undergo a water baptism. Thus Ananias baptizes Paul; Peter baptizes Cornelius and his companions; Philip baptizes Samaritans; Paul "rebaptizes" former disciples of the Baptist (19:6). The baptismal formula in Acts is baptism in the name of Jesus, the Lord Jesus, or Jesus Christ (2:38; 8:16; 10:48). Sometimes the holy Spirit comes before the actual baptism, and sometimes afterward (8:17; 10:44-48). This coming is often signaled by some kind of charismatic gift such as tongues or prophecy (1:4; 10:44-46; 19:6). At other times it is only stated that the person was baptized or received the holy Spirit. At times, baptism and the reception of the Spirit are separated (8:14-17; 10:44-48). In the first case, that of the Samaritans, Luke may be stressing that the laying on of hands by Peter and John is important to establish direct lines and discipleship with Jesus.

Paul's writings contain the earliest Christian descriptions of baptism, even though he builds on previous tradition. While Christ has objectively accomplished the whole work of salvation, the individual can enter subjectively into it only through baptism and faith. Baptism is a washing away of sin: "You have been washed, you were sanctified, you were justified in the name of the Lord Jesus Christ and in the Spirit of our God" (1 Cor 6:11). The much later Letter to Titus calls it "the bath of rebirth and renewal by the holy Spirit" (3:5). The words "in the name of the Lord Jesus Christ" in 1 Corinthians 6:11 refer to an old baptismal formula also found in Acts. "Lord" is part of a baptismal confession of faith that Jesus is Lord, as found more explicitly in Philippians 2:11 and Romans 10:9.

The baptismal action is not just an external ritual but a personal adhesion to Christ: "All you who were baptized into Christ have clothed yourselves with Christ" (Gal 3:27). "Into Christ" also means incorporation into a community where previous ethnic, social, or sex inequalities are destroyed (Gal 3:28). This community is a "body of Christ" made possible through union with Christ and the gift of the holy Spirit: "For in one Spirit we were all baptized into one body, whether Jews or Greeks, slaves or free persons and we were all given to drink of one Spirit" (1 Cor 12:13). The much later Letter to the Ephesians also emphasizes the ecclesial aspect with the words: "Love your wives, even as Christ loved the church and handed himself over for her to sanctify her, cleansing her by the bath of water with the word" (5:26).

However, to be joined to Christ means to be joined to the central event of his death and resurrection by dying and rising with him: "You must think of yourselves being dead to sin and living for God in Christ Jesus" (Rom 6:11). Thus the plunging into water symbolizes that the believer has been "buried with him through baptism into death" and the coming up from the water signifies that "just as Christ was raised from the dead by the glory of the Father, we too might live in newness of life" (Rom 6:4). Romans emphasizes the future implications of baptism: "If we have died with Christ, we believe that we shall also live with him" (6:8). At the same time, the letter brings out the present implications in a regenerated life style. It refers to the "pattern of teaching to which you were entrusted" (6:17). This means the new way of life and worship which Christian teachers taught the catechumens over a period of time before the baptism ritual.

Romans 10:9 seems drawn from the baptismal event: "If you confess with your mouth that Jesus is Lord and believe in your heart that God raised him from the dead, you will be saved." Later letters of the Pauline corpus become less future oriented and emphasize strongly the *present* implications of baptism. The Letter to the Colossians states: "If you were raised with Christ, seek what is above" (3:1). Thus the resurrection has more present emphasis and is followed by very practical details about living the Christian life (3:5-18). What to avoid is part of the symbolic baptismal death (3:5ff.) and putting off the old garments. The new life is symbolized by putting on the new clothes (3:10ff.). Ephesians follows the same pattern, referring to the way catechumens were taught (4:21ff.).

See: DEATH, JOHN THE BAPTIST, REIGN OF GOD, REPENTANCE, RESURRECTION

JOSEPH A. GRASSI

Pastoral-Liturgical Tradition

To speak of the practice of baptism in the Church is to seek to understand what it means to be a disciple of the perfect disciple, the well-beloved child of God, who so loved the world that he went to his death that the world might have life and have it in abundance. Jesus Christ, the perfect disciple, was raised to life by the power of God; his abiding presence empowered a community, and his earthly life and ministry became the model for all who would attach themselves to this community, claim to be his followers, and pledge themselves to continue his saving work on earth. Such is the mystery of relationship with God and God's people, of death and life, of discipleship and mission which is expressed in Christian baptism.

What is unmistakable from the survey of baptismal evidence in the two testaments is that as the early Christian community adopted and adapted common initiatory practices to its own ends it was responding to three different kinds of questions—questions of readiness, of ritual, and of interpretation. What kind of preparation is needed in order to hear and believe the good news of Jesus Christ and to join oneself to the community of Jesus' faith-filled disciples? How shall this experience of conversion* be brought to public, ritual expression? What new and deeper theological meanings do these evolving ritual patterns convey? These same questions are necessarily the preoccupation of every culture and every age. Many traditions and patterns have emerged in the past twenty centuries; this article will examine only the general patterns of baptismal preparation, ritual, and meaning in the Western Roman tradition.

In the post-apostolic Church a pattern of preparation, baptism, and incorporation into the life of the community is already discernible in the scriptural evidence. There was an initial proclamation of the good news which contained most—if not all—of the following elements: Jesus the Christ, one sent by God, fulfilled the ancient prophecies; he went about doing good and healing those who were in need; this man was put to death and raised to life; and, as Lord of the living and the dead, he has sent his Spirit to forge a new community (see, for example, Acts 2:14ff.; 10:34ff.). Some who listened to this good news were "cut to the heart" (Acts 2:37), a sign of first faith and the beginning of conversion. More ample catechesis about the life, death, and rising of Jesus followed. Those who welcomed the message were baptized, and took up life among the community of believers (Acts 2:43-47; 4:32-34). Readiness for baptism presumed the proclamation of the good news, faith, and conversion of life; baptism with water* and word followed the determination of readiness and made one a full participant in the community's life and mission.

The content of the proclamation and the length of the period of testing for signs of genuine conversion of life have varied from community to community and from age to age as has the way the community has celebrated baptism. The shape of baptism from the beginning included a water bath joined to a ritual word, but the manner of baptism varied depending on circumstances. Immersion, dipping, or simply pouring water over the candidate were various forms of baptism depending on the climate, the availability or scarcity of water, cultural sensitivities to nudity, and so on. The ritual word, at first a Christological statement of belief, for example, "Jesus is Lord," was soon supplanted by a trinitarian formula. Such was surely true of the community of Matthew (Matt 28:19). Water and word were nearly always joined to an apostolic laying on of hands or to the manifestation of the Spirit's presence and energy in pneumatic and miraculous gifts or simply in the mystery of the community's daily living in charity, joy, and peace.

What did the community understand to be the meaning of its baptismal action? According to an ancient adage, the law of prayer is the law of belief. In other words, the celebration of baptism gave rise to theological reflection. The Acts of the Apostles and the letters are sprinkled with language of burial, purification, and regeneration. The symbolic power of water, interpreted in light of the Christ event, gave rise to early interpretation of the water bath as a rite of passage which plunged the candidate into the death and rising of Christ in the power of the Spirit. Various theological interpretations are suggested in the baptismal metaphors employed: dying and rising with Christ, death to sin, purification of hearts as well as bodies, the beginning of a new life in Christ Jesus, and membership in a single body.

The expansion of the early community as well as the rigor of its life in an age of persecution gave rise to a more elaborate and robust preparation for initiation. The *Didache*, a proto-Church Order of the late first century, appears to contain a standard catechetical instruction, although it is silent on the process of catechesis or the ministers who were involved. Further evidence of initial baptismal development is found in the legislation of early Church Councils: a longer period of preparation, an extended fast prior to baptism, some criteria for admission to the sacrament, and hints of a developing catechetical process.

By the third century rigorous and lengthy baptismal preparation and a highly elaborate ritual had evolved. The *Apostolic Tradition* of Hippolytus (Rome, ca. 215) describes a strict examination prior to entry into a three-year catechumenate, a second demanding examination prior to election,* a final period of intense preparation and prayer, and a highly developed initiation ritual. To the liturgical baptismal core of water and word had been joined an all-night vigil, readings and instruction, a prayer over the water, renunciations, several anointings, triple questions and immersions, a final anointing, clothing, episcopal laying on of hands with prayer, another anointing and signing, prayers of the community, the exchange of peace, and participation in the Eucharistic banquet. In addition, the *Apostolic Tradition* names a variety of different ministries associated with the process: friends, family, catechists, sponsors, deacons, presbyters, and the bishop all have a role in the initiation of new members. There appears to be similar evidence for the development of a more elaborate catechumenal process in Egypt, Palestine, and Syria as well.

A variety of factors led to the decline of the catechumenate as well as to the dismemberment of the original unity of the water bath, sealing, and table-fellowship. When the age of persecution ended and the Church was officially recognized as a state religion it was now no longer dangerous but positively advantageous to be a Christian. Defective motivation flooded the catechumenate with ambitious inquirers who, at the same time, were in no hurry to complete the process of initiation and assume the obligations of full membership. In an attempt to rescue the catechumenate, its three year duration was collapsed into an intense six to eight week preparation for baptism coinciding with the time of Lent. Eventually, and spurred by the rise of infant baptism, the entire catechumenal process disappeared, but the various rituals once attached to its several periods and stages were joined into a single liturgical rite which sometimes made little sense, as for example, when the exorcisms originally part of an adult rite were pronounced over infants.

The growth of the Church also led, in the West, to the separation of the several sacraments of initiation. As exemplified in the *Apostolic Tradition,* laying on of hands and prayer, the ritual which followed baptism, was an episcopal ceremony. Full ritual immersion in baptism took place under the direction of presbyters and deacons apart from the community because of the nudity entailed. Those baptized quasi-privately were clothed and led to the bishop who waited with the community to complete their incorporation publicly with prayer, laying on of hands and then participation in the Eucharistic banquet. As numbers increased, it became impossible for the bishop to be present at every celebration of initiation. In his absence, baptism was followed by Eucharist; the episcopal ceremonies simply were postponed by days or weeks until the bishop could complete the ceremony. Eventually even more time elapsed, and a rite of episcopal laying on of hands with prayer, now quite independent of baptism, demanded a theological rationale.

Thus, confirmation became a distinct sacrament, and gradually it lost its initiation moorings entirely as it was called a sacrament of Christian maturity, or, in this century, a sacrament of Catholic Action. "Strengthening" became the language associated with confirmation—strengthening to preach the gospel, to give witness, to maintain one's baptismal purity in the face of the sinfulness of the world. Confirmation, then, was deliberately postponed until the age of reason, variously computed between seven and the end of adolescence. And, in a final dismemberment of the ancient unity of the three sacraments of initiation, the Eucharist, too, was also postponed out of exaggerated medieval reverence for the sacred species.

These several historical developments help to explain many of the decisions of the Second Vatican Council and subsequent ritual revisions of initiation. Furthermore, the simple biblical-liturgical pattern of water, word, and spirit presence has, over the centuries, regularly acquired preparatory and explanatory rites including additional prayers, renunciations, exorcisms, and blessings, anointing with oil, laying on of hands, the clothing of the candidate in a white garment, and lighting of a baptismal candle. Even foot washing and tonsure have found their way into the baptismal ritual in the course of its history. Just as the ritual attracted additional rites and prayers to itself, so too, in the course of its history, it sometimes needed to be pruned. Such was also a goal of the revisions of Vatican II.

The Constitution on the Sacred Liturgy (CSL 64–71) proposed the following: a restoration of the ancient catechumenate, incorporation of local customs of initiation in mission lands, development of several forms of baptism (simple, solemn, suited to infants, for large numbers, for catechist presiders, in emergency), development of a rite of incorporation into full communion for candidates from other Christian bodies whose baptism is valid, and a revision of confirmation which would restore its intimate connection to baptism.

The contemporary theology of baptism is developed in the general introduction to the *Rite of Christian Initiation of Adults* (see RCIA 1–6). In the celebration of baptism one is freed from the power of darkness, joined to Christ's death, burial and resurrection, given the spirit of adoption, and incorporated into the entire people of God who live in memory of the Lord's death and resurrection. Baptism incorporates us into Christ, forms us as God's people, pardons all our sins, rescues us from darkness, bestows dignity upon us as children of God, makes us a new creation by water and the Spirit, and pledges us to a life of discipleship—of shared beliefs, common life, community prayer, and a passion for mission. Baptism draws us into the very life of God.

The effects of baptism are expressed in more condensed fashion in the prayer which accompanies the post-baptismal anointing: "The God of power and Father of our Lord Jesus Christ has freed you from sin and brought you to new life through water and the Holy Spirit. He now anoints you with the chrism of salvation, so that, united with his people, you may remain for ever a member of Christ who is Priest, Prophet, and King" (RCIA 227).

Confirmation is distinguished from baptism in this way: the anointing with oil—the sealing of confirmation—makes us more completely images of the Lord and fills us with the Spirit of God to bear witness before all the world and to work to bring the body of Christ to fullness. Confirmation is a modest ritual reminder of baptism, deepening and prolonging the effects of baptism and "in-spiriting" recipients to take more seriously the obligation, as members of Christ, to extend the reign of God.

The Eucharist also may be understood in relation to baptism. At once sacrament, sacrifice, and meal, the Eucharist is the most perfect symbolic expression that we are in communion with Christ and with one another. The Eucharist sustains the community with the food of eternal life and shows forth the unity of God's people. The three sacraments of initiation—baptism, confirmation, and Eucharist—combine to bring us to the full stature of Christ and to enable us to carry out the mission of the entire people of God in the Church and in the world. These sacraments commit us to a vocation: to live as children of God, brothers and sisters of one another, freed from sin and the power of evil; joined to Christ; empowered by the Spirit; within a community of disciples, a priestly people, all of whom owe our allegiance to God in Christ and all of whom are witnesses to these realities before the world.

In contemporary sacramental theology, baptism and confirmation are rejoined as ritual moments in a single, whole initiatory celebration which comes to fullest ritual expression at the Eucharistic banquet. As baptism incorporates one into Christ and Christ's body, so in Eucharistic communion that reality finds its most perfect expression. The reception of communion may thus be understood as the repeatable sacrament of Christian initiation, one's daily dip in the baptismal font.

See: CHURCH, COMMUNITY, WATER

KATHLEEN HUGHES, R.S.C.J.

BARRENNESS

Barrenness, the state of being sterile or childless, is a biblical concept with physical and figurative dimensions. Both OT and NT relate this image to God's power to create life. The concept has special pastoral potential during the Advent season.

Old Testament

Barrenness is a common motif in the OT and is often contrasted with fertility.* In the context of a society where being fertile, bearing many children (especially males), and raising a large family was considered a sign of prosperity and blessing, barrenness symbolized a defective life. It was a terrible curse (Lev 20:20-21). The OT uses the concept primarily in two ways: physically, relating it to the condition of women who are unable to bear children; and figuratively, applying the concept more broadly to sterility of land or nation.

Physical Barrenness. The background of barrenness in the OT is the divine command to all living creatures at the beginning of creation to "be fertile and multiply" (Gen 1:22, 28). Barrenness opposes this basic orientation. Sometimes barrenness is stated as a simple fact with no reason given for its cause. Sarai, Abram's wife, is an example. Genesis 11:30 baldly states: "Sarai was barren; she had no child" (see also the wife of Manoah, Judg 13:2). At other times the OT states that barrenness is specifically a result of God's own action, as in the case of Hannah, the wife of Elkanah. Elkanah is said to offer a double portion of sacrifices to God for Hannah, "because he loved her, though the Lord had made her barren" (1 Sam 1:5). Elkanah's other wife, Peninnah,

reinforces this judgment about Hannah's barrenness in 1 Samuel 1:6: "Her rival, to upset her, turned it into a constant reproach to her that the Lord had left her barren." Regardless of the cause of barrenness the OT uniformly looks upon barrenness as a sign of disfavor and a curse to be removed. Even virginity can be lamented as a barren state as seen in the tragic story of the unnamed daughter of Jephthah (Judg 11:37-40) who mourns for her virginity prior to her premature death.

From its pre-scientific perspective the OT views physical barrenness as virtually a female phenomenon (except Deut 7:14 which seems to acknowledge that males can also be sterile). The result of this state for women is envy, jealousy, and hurtful rivalry. Genesis 30:1 describes this fearful state in the contrast between Leah, who bears three children, and her sister Rachel, who produces none: "When Rachel saw that she failed to bear children to Jacob, she became envious of her sister." The same situation is found in the story of Hannah and Peninnah (1 Sam 1:1-20). Hannah becomes so distraught at her barrenness and her rival's fecundity that she can only pour out her bitterness to God in tears and prayers, pleading to grant her request to conceive a male child.

The OT also describes the lengths to which women try to overcome barrenness. "Sarai said to Abram: 'The LORD has kept me from bearing children. Have intercourse, then, with my maid; perhaps I shall have sons through her'" (Gen 16:2). This same motif appears in the story of Rachel, Jacob's wife (Gen 30:1-8). Rachel cries out to her husband, "Give me children or I shall die!" (Gen 30:1). But when Jacob becomes angry and insists that he cannot accomplish what God has thus far not fulfilled, Rachel makes an offer similar to Sarai's: "Here is my maidservant Bilhah. Have intercourse with her, and let her give birth on my knees, so that I too may have offspring, at least through her" (Gen 30:3). Even Leah, Rachel's fecund sister, offers Jacob her own maidservant Zilpah after

Leah stops bearing her own children (Gen 30:9). Though this practice often yielded the desired result of children, it sometimes produced animosity. When Sarai's maidservant, Hagar the Egyptian, becomes pregnant, Sarai herself becomes incensed at the fact that Hagar "looked on her mistress with disdain" (Gen 16:4). Sarai proceeds to abuse Hagar so much that she runs away into the wilderness, only to be told by God that she should return and take Sarai's abuse because God promises to make her own descendants "too many to count" (Gen 16:6-10).

Another aspect of physical barrenness in the OT is that God alone can overcome it. If God is typically seen as the source of one's barrenness, God is also seen as the one who has the power to heal sterility. Genesis 25:21 testifies to this belief: "Isaac entreated the LORD on behalf of his wife, since she was sterile. The LORD heard his entreaty, and Rebekah became pregnant." Hannah, too, entreats God in prayer: "O LORD of hosts, if you look with pity on the misery of your handmaid, if you remember me and do not forget me, if you give your handmaid a male child, I will give him to the LORD . . ." (1 Sam 1:11). Time and again God is praised for granting the request to bear children (e.g., Gen 16:11; 30:6, 17, 22-24). Fertility overcomes barrenness and demonstrates God's blessing. Yet barrenness itself can be more than the absence of progeny.

In the OT physical barrenness is often a vehicle through which the God of creation acts to fulfill the promise of a covenant with chosen human instruments. Despite the advanced age of Abraham and his wife Sarah, God promises to grant them a male child, Isaac, through whom they will receive innumerable descendants (Gen 17:2-19). Additionally, barrenness is sometimes an opportunity for God's love to be demonstrated, as in the case of Leah: "When the LORD saw that Leah was unloved, he made her fruitful . . ." (Gen 29:31).

Barrenness can also be the occasion for God to choose an unlikely person for special, sacred duties, as in the case of Samson's birth from the sterile wife of Manoah: "Though you are barren and have had no children, yet will you conceive and bear a son. . . . for this boy is to be consecrated to God from the womb. It is he who will begin the deliverance of Israel from the power of the Philistines" (Judg 13:3-5). Thus, barrenness does not disqualify one from a fulfilling life.

The OT often shows how barrenness provides conditions for God's special intervention and action in the world. When the barren Hannah finally gives birth to Samuel, she takes him to the Temple to fulfill her promise to dedicate him entirely to the service of God (1 Sam 1:24-28; see v. 11). At the conclusion of her worship she cries out to God in a great prayer which foreshadows the *Magnificat* (Luke 1:46-55): "My heart exults in the LORD. . . . The barren wife bears seven sons while the mother of many languishes. The Lord puts to death and gives life; he casts down to the nether world and raises up again" (1 Sam 2:1, 5b-6). We see that barrenness can be a way in which God accomplishes a divine plan beyond the comprehension of human beings. It is the nature of God to make the barren fertile, to provide descendants where there are none, and to have mercy on those who languish in hopelessness.

Figurative Barrenness. It is an easy shift in the OT from the physical reality of barrenness to a broader figurative use. Just as women could be viewed as barren, sterile, or fruitless if they had no children, so could land (desert, wasteland) or a nation be viewed as barren. Ancient Israel was largely desert. It was well known that lack of water and fertilization kept the land from being "fruitful," from bearing produce for the nourishment of people (e.g., 2 Kgs 2:19). A further extension of the figurative use of barrenness is a connection between it and wickedness. Psalm 107:33-35 indicates that God has the power to impose barrenness because of people's evil deeds or to remove it: "He changed rivers into desert, water springs into thirsty ground, fruitful land into salt marsh, because of the wickedness of its inhabitants. He changed the desert into pools of water, waterless land into water springs . . ." (see also Ps 28:4). An explicit connection between death, physical barrenness, and desert is made in Proverbs 30:15b-16: "Three things are never satisfied, four never say 'Enough!' The nether world, and the barren womb; the earth, that is never saturated with water, and fire. . . ." Being barren, whether physically or figuratively, is like being dead. Barrenness produces no life.

Jeremiah makes harsher use of the figurative dimension of barrenness. In a stinging prophecy against Babylon Jeremiah foretells the coming destruction which will make the once fertile and powerful nation barren and desolate: "Your mother shall be sorely put to shame, she that bore you shall be abashed. See, the last of the nations, a desert, dry and waste. Because of the LORD's wrath she shall be empty, and become a total desert" (Jer 50:12-13). Synonymous with barrenness, then, can be the emptiness, desolation, and destruction of a people unable to bear the fruit of a righteous life.

New Testament

The NT mirrors the OT in the employment of this image. Though barrenness is not as prominent in the NT as in the OT, one finds evidence of both the physical condition and figurative usage of the idea.

Physical Barrenness. As with the OT, the NT also contains stories of barren women who miraculously become vehicles for the accomplishment of God's will. The most prominent example is Elizabeth, the relative of Mary, the mother of Jesus. Zechariah and Elizabeth are described as righteous and obedient in God's eyes, yet their lives are haunted by the specter of infertility: "But they had no child, because Elizabeth was barren and both were advanced in years" (Luke 1:7). This almost stereotypical situation becomes the fertile field for God's seed to bear fruit. During Mary's own reve-

lation that she is to become miraculously pregnant with the Son of God, the angel Gabriel also tells her: "And behold, Elizabeth, your relative, has also conceived a son in her old age, and this is the sixth month for her who was called barren; for nothing will be impossible with God" (Luke 1:36-37; see also Matt 1:18-25). Both women are barren from different perspectives. Mary is barren by virtue of being a virgin (Luke 1:27); Elizabeth is barren because of her sterility and old age. Yet God effects miraculous fertility in both. The fruits of their wombs, John the Baptist and Jesus, will serve the advancement of God's reign and the salvation of God's people. As with the OT, barrenness can yield abundant progeny through God's power!

The NT also speaks explicitly of some figures of barrenness in the OT. Paul especially employs OT figures to communicate his message, as when he commends the faith of Abraham who trusted God's promise of progeny despite the apparent barrenness of Sarah: "He did not weaken in faith when he considered his own body as [already] dead (for he was almost a hundred years old) and the dead womb of Sarah" (Rom 4:19). Paul strongly commends this "hoping against hope" because it is the challenge of faith and the trust in God's power to transform barrenness into new life.

Another example of this usage is found in Luke's portrayal of Jesus' way of the cross (Luke 23:26-32). The women of Jerusalem come out to weep over him as he proceeds to his crucifixion. Jesus turns their concerns around and warns them to weep for themselves and their children, for more horrible things will befall the people who reject the Messiah. So devastating will that time be that barrenness, normally seen as a curse, will be considered a blessing: "people will say 'Blessed are the barren, the wombs that never bore and the breasts that never nursed'" (Luke 23:29).

Figurative Barrenness. The NT most frequently speaks figuratively of barrenness as unfruitfulness. The Word of God can become barren if it bears no fruit because it succumbs to worldly enticements (Mark 4:19), and Christians should devote themselves to doing good deeds so that their lives do not become "unproductive" (Titus 3:14). A barren fig tree, itself the symbol of a curse, is in turn cursed by Jesus as a sign of the impending destruction to come upon Israel for its failure to bear the fruit of righteousness (Matt 21:18-19; cf. 21:43). In Luke Jesus uses the same image of a barren fig tree that can be made fruitful only through proper fertilization (13:6-9). God has the patience of a gardener giving a barren tree one more chance to bloom (see also Jas 5:7). But if it does not bear fruit, it will be destroyed. Likewise, the lesson is that barrenness of faith can also lead to one's destruction.

Pastoral-Liturgical Tradition

Modern sensitivities to the patriarchal prejudices of the past make the subject of barrenness a delicate topic. Lack of progeny can no longer be viewed as a curse or a sign of God's disfavor. Yet the image of barrenness can still function in pastoral and liturgical settings because of its potency as a symbol of negative and positive possibility. Negatively, barrenness can be a metaphor for an empty, dry, directionless life, a life led without faith. It goes nowhere and yields nothing. Positively, barrenness can be a recognition of sinfulness and the need to be transformed by God's grace.

The Church's annual celebration of the Advent season holds particular promise for this concept. Many of the biblical readings of Advent employ images of God's power transforming the desert wasteland into a lush source of life-giving prosperity (e.g., Isa 35:1-2, 6; 43:19-20; 51:3). Barrenness can contain the seeds of a renewed hope that God will raise up descendants to carry on the commitment of faith and that justice itself can spring up from the parched earth (Isa 61:9-11). The inclusion of women whose ability to bear children was somehow blocked in the genealogy of Jesus' ancestry (Matt 1:1-16) may also relate to this motif. As in ages past, barrenness of whatever kind, rather than being an obstacle for new life, can be the very source of it through God's power (Ps 80:9-20).

See: BABEL/BABYLON, BLESSING, COVENANT, FERTILITY, GENEALOGY, ISRAEL, LIFE, PROMISE, SARAH, TEMPLE

RONALD D. WITHERUP, S.S.

BEASTS/MONSTERS OF THE DEEP

Beasts, especially sea monsters, were a regular part of the ancient Near Eastern world view. Sometimes they were given proper names.

Old Testament

The mythologies of the peoples surrounding Israel often mention monsters of the deep. In Egypt, Apophis, the giant serpent, embodied the powers hostile to the sun. She attacked the sun in the evening, just before his descent into the underworld, and was fought off by Seth, who was in the bow of the sun boat. Her blood made the heavens red. Apophis became the model of all enemies of the gods and was equated with Seth as enemy of Osiris and persecutor of the young Horus.

In *Enuma elish,* the twelfth century BCE Akkadian epic exalting the storm god Marduk, Marduk's enemy is Tiamat, salt sea personified. With freshwater sea, Apsu, she pre-existed the world of gods and of human beings. Eight monsters—snake, "savage snake," hairy hero, "big demon," savage dog, scorpion-man, fish-man, and bull-man—accompanied her in battle. Marduk slays her in single combat and from her body makes the universe.

In other Mesopotamian myths precreation waters are not personified. In Canaan, the Ugaritic texts portray Sea (masculine in contrast to Tiamat) as the enemy of the storm god Baal Hadad. Among Sea's allies against the storm god are El's Flood Rabbim, the Dragon (= Heb. *tannin*), the crooked serpent (the same adjective modifies Leviathan in Isa 27:1), Shalyat the seven-headed (*ANET,* 137); some of the titles may in fact be epithets of Sea. In the Mot cycle, Baal is said to slay

"Lotan, the twisting serpent, the scaly serpent, Shalyat with the seven heads" (*ANET*, 138). Thus ancient Near Eastern literature speaks of monsters of the deep, which are part of the inert pre-creation state. They are hostile to society and to the gods.

Lotan (= OT Leviathan), one of the monsters in the Ugaritic texts, appears in the OT. (The change in spelling is because Hebrew does not reduce the diphthong.) The Bible takes over the monster enemy of the storm god Baal in order to glorify the storm god Yahweh. Leviathan occurs in Psalm 74:13-14: "You stirred up the sea by your might; you smashed the heads of the dragons in the waters. You crushed the heads of Leviathan, and made food of him for the dolphins." The monster Leviathan is integrated into the Israelite national story by being identified with the Red Sea. Just as the Red Sea kept Israel from entering its land and thus existing fully, so Leviathan stands between Israel and its land. The monster is many-headed, an ally of sea (or perhaps an epithet of sea). Psalm 104:26 shows a thoroughly tamed Leviathan; it is a sign of the complete victory of Yahweh over primordial darkness and waters: "And [the sea] where ships move about with Leviathan, which you formed to make sport of it." The monster is just another fish in the harmonious universe that has been made for the human race.

In Job Leviathan is a primordial monster and retains his aspect of menace: "Let them curse it [the day of Job's birth] who curse the sea, the appointed disturbers of Leviathan." In the Yahweh-Job encounter (ch. 41) that is the climax of the book, Leviathan is the beast of the creation battle. In splendid poetry God admiringly describes this magnificent remnant of the chaotic period: "Clubs he esteems as splinters; he laughs at the crash of the spear. His belly is sharp as pottery fragments; he spreads like a threshing sledge upon the mire" (41:21-22). If God wishes to keep this great symbol of evil and disorder within the universe, what is it to Job?

The most straightforward mythological use of the Leviathan myth* is in Isaiah 27:1:

"On that day the LORD will punish with his sword that is cruel, great, and strong, Leviathan the fleeing serpent, Leviathan the coiled serpent, and he will slay the dragon that is in the sea." Leviathan here represents the evil destined to be punished by direct divine intervention for the sake of Israel. His slaying means the total victory of Yahweh over evil.

Another word for dragon is *tannin*, which is used in parallel with Leviathan in Psalm 74:13. Isaiah 51:9, "Was it not you [God] who crushed Rahab, you who pierced the dragon [*tannin*]? Was it not you who dried up the sea, the waters of the great deep?" The text refers to the primordial battle of the storm god and the monsters of the deep. The battle that brought the world into existence is equated with the battle at the Red Sea that brought Israel into existence. As often, creation is the removal of the obstacles to the emergence of human community; Yahweh gets rid of the sea that keeps Israel from entering its land.

Jeremiah 51:34 speaks generally of a monster, not necessarily of the primordial sea dragon: "He has swallowed me like a dragon: he has filled his belly with my delights, and cast me out." Sometimes the dragon is a symbol of Egypt, the "great crouching monster amidst your Niles" (Ezek 29:3; see 32:2).

In Daniel 7:3 four beasts—a lion with eagle's wings, a bear, a leopard, and an unnamed but terrifying animal—came up out of the sea. They represent, in the conventional listing of the time, the four great empires—Babylon, Media, Persia, Greece. The beasts (Greek *therion*) serve as models for the depiction of the two beasts (*therion*) from the sea in Revelation 13.

New Testament

The NT does not conceptualize evil in the same way as does the OT. Mark portrays a demonic world, but the other Gospels stress that resistance to the message of Jesus comes from within human beings not from outside them. Before embarking on his public ministry, Jesus is tempted, being "with the beasts" for forty days (Mark 1:12-13; Matt 4:1-11; Luke 4:1-13). The desert with its exotic animals in the OT is a place of God's absence, and sometimes even of a kind of pre-creation disorder (see esp. Isa 43:16-21).

The Book of Revelation borrows from Daniel 7 the image of the symbolic beasts climbing up out of the sea. Chapter 12, which some scholars believe was originally a Jewish story about the imperiled community, identifies the enemy of the Church as a "huge red dragon, with seven heads and ten horns [see Dan 7:20], and on its heads were seven diadems" (12:3). The same chapter identifies the dragon as "the Devil and Satan, who deceived the whole world" (v. 9. The figure of Satan in the OT varies from a judicial figure in the heavenly court to an enemy of the human race [see Job 1–2, Zech 3:1-2, and Wis 2:24]). This chapter goes beyond Daniel by bringing together into one figure the primordial dragon of pre-creation chaos and the devil.

In Revelation 13 the dragon takes his stand on the sands of the seashore; from the sea, the domain of the dragon, two beasts arise. The beasts are generally taken to represent the Roman Empire and its priesthood and correspond to the beast-empires of Daniel 7. As in Daniel, the beasts are eventually overthrown but, unlike Daniel, the sea dragon itself, which symbolizes a yet more profound evil, is finally destroyed (ch. 20). Thus the NT explains the relative evil of the empire opposing the Christian community and the absolute evil behind it.

Pastoral-Liturgical Tradition

Ancient Near Eastern traditions of primordial sea monsters were assimilated in Daniel and especially Revelation to OT traditions of the Satan or judicial prosecutor in the heavenly court. This assimilation contributed to the figure of the devil, who played an important role in the liturgy, especially baptismal liturgy, and in theology. When baptismal candidates began the catechumenate, they were told: "If you see any

evil thought coming to your spirit, know that it is the serpent of the sea who is setting snares for you" (Cyril of Alexandria). In the exorcisms of Holy Saturday, the candidate renounced the wiles of Satan.

Modern pastoral practice about evil in the world should follow the example of the Bible. Ordinarily in the Bible human beings are the source of evil in the world; biblical exhortations assume that people are capable of good or evil acts. Yet the Bible sometimes speaks of an agent of evil extrinsic to human beings, correctly recognizing that there is an inherent evil in the world, prior to the decision of any individual human being. Pastors should emphasize that this residual evil can not be exactly described. The Bible itself portrays it in a variety of ways, even borrowing from ancient Near Eastern myths. The eclectic approach implies that evil in the world can be only partially understood.

See: CHAOS, SATAN, SEA

RICHARD J. CLIFFORD, S.J.

BEATITUDES

A beatitude is a literary form common in both the OT (esp. in the Wisdom literature and the psalms) and NT which consists of a short cry of joy like "Happy you!" which can be expanded to include a reason for the person's good fortune. The word beatitude comes from the Latin *beatus* meaning happy or blissful, an adjective representing the Hebrew 'ashrê and the Greek *makarios*. These terms are to be distinguished from the passive participle *blessed*, often used in older English translations for the just-mentioned set of terms as well as for Latin *benedictus*, Hebrew *bārûk*, Greek *eulogētos*, thus leading to some confusion of blessing and beatitude. Properly the participle form is used only of God and is an invocation or wish. The adjective is used only of human beings and recognizes an existing state of happiness, represents an approving proclamation of fact, and contains an evaluative judgment. It is a proclamation of happiness, not merely a promise (though in the beatitudes of Jesus a promise is joined to it). It is a formula of congratulation or felicitation.

Old Testament

In the OT beatitudes occur primarily in the Wisdom literature as a form of gnomic or proverbial saying, as well as in the psalms as a prayer form. Beatitudes are pronounced upon people who are righteous, who keep their hands from doing evil and do not profane the Sabbath—such persons may look forward with confidence to such earthly rewards as peace, prosperity, the satisfactions of family life, the joys of temple worship, and renewal of strength (see Pss 41:1; 65:4; 84:5; 106:3; 112:1; 128:1; Prov 8:32; Isa 32:20; 56:1-2) (*IDB*). Note that these rewards are not yet understood by Israel's consciousness as taking place in an eschatological future, but as in the here and now. Even punishment from the Lord was regarded as a blessing. Psalm 94:12 proclaims blessed those whom the Lord disciplines. The pleasures of a full and happy life are the goal of human existence. But these are related to God's presence to the just. The psalms declare blessed all who take refuge in God (Ps 2:12); one whose sin is forgiven (Ps 32:1-2); one who trusts in God (Pss 40:4-5; 84:12); and those who fear the Lord and greatly delight in God's commands (Ps 112:1).

An important further literary step is when beatitudes are grouped together in artistically shaped lists. This occurs in Sirach 25:7-10 where ten happy conditions are laid down. At the top of the ladder-like list, which seems to move from lower to higher values, stand wisdom and fear of the Lord. A similar list of wisdom beatitudes, even more spiritual-intellectual in character, has been found at Qumran ("Péricopé des Béatitudes en Ben Sira et Matthieu [Planche I]" *RB* 98 [1991] 80–106). These lists of beatitudes formally prepare the way for the lists of beatitudes in the NT.

New Testament

The preaching of Jesus begins as a cry of joy, as good news (Matt 5:3-11; Luke 6:20-22). This joy is based on the nearness of the reign of God. The famous series of beatitudes just referred to has, according to scholars, a complex evolution. Luke gives four of them, and the first three of these are short and based on Isaiah 61:1-4. These probably go back to Jesus himself and represent a kind of messianic manifesto for God's care for the poor, the hungry, and those who weep (probably three adjectives for the same group of people). The fourth of Luke's list probably comes from the early Christian community and represents their first experiences of persecution. Matthew's much longer list of eight, nine, or ten (scholars count them variously) adds some desirable qualities: being just, pure of heart, merciful, and a peacemaker. He thereby makes the list into a program of Christian life, a series of virtues. These additional beatitudes are in some measure derived from the psalms.

Each of these beatitudes is composed in such a way as to involve the literary style of synthetic parallelism: one line of congratulations followed by a second line containing a reason for the congratulations, namely, a divine reward or blessing. All of the rewards will find their realization in the greatest blessing of all, the reign of God. The passive voice of the verb in many of the reward clauses is a theological passive. It is God who will comfort, fill, have mercy, call people children of God. All of the reward verbs are in the future tense, except the first and last. Even these two can be understood to imply a future realization. Thus the perspective of an eschatology oriented toward the future predominates throughout the entire series.

Other early beatitudes derived from the Q source, and thus likely going back to Jesus himself, concern the scandal which Jesus' ministry represented for many ("blessed is the one who takes no offense at me" Matt 11:6; Luke 7:23); the happiness of those who have lived in the new era of salvation (Matt 13:16; Luke 10:23); and the need for watchfulness ("blessed are those servants whom the master finds vigilant on his arrival" Luke 12:37-38, 43; see Matt 24:46). A uniquely Matthean beatitude concerns the special grace of revelation accorded to Peter (Matt 16:17).

Luke shows some of his special interests in the beatitudes proper to his Gospel, his interest in women, especially Mary the mother of Jesus, and his interest in hospitality or meals. Of Mary it is said "Blessed are you who believed" (1:45), and blessed is her womb (11:27). "Blessed are those who hear the word of God and observe it" (11:28). "Blessed are the barren" (23:29). Relating to meals we find: "Blessed indeed will you be because of their inability to repay you," followed by, "Blessed is the one who will dine in the kingdom of God" (14:14-15).

John has two beatitudes. The first concerns the relation of faith to action: "If you understand this, blessed are you if you do it" (13:17). The second concerns the relation of faith to sight: "Blessed are those who have not seen and have believed" (20:29).

The most famous beatitude in Acts runs: "It is more blessed to give than to receive" (20:35). In 26:2 Paul congratulates himself at the beginning of his great speech of self-defense.

In Romans, after citing Psalm 32:1-2, Paul asserts that makarisms or beatitudes are evidence of divine favor (Rom 4:7-9). Paul also blesses the persevering widow in 1 Corinthians 7:40. In the Pastoral Letters God is blessed (1 Tim 1:11; 6:15). In James blessed are those who persevere in time of trial (1:12) and in their activity (1:25). The first letter of Peter summarizes its message in a beatitude with an unusual form: "Even if you should suffer because of righteousness, blessed are you" (1 Pet 3:14; 4:14 is similar).

The Book of Revelation contains a series of seven beatitudes which have an integrity all their own. Blessed are they who read and listen (1:3), blessed are the dead who die in the Lord (14:13), blessed is the one who watches (16:15), blessed are those called to the wedding feast of the Lamb (19:9), "blessed is the one who keeps the prophetic message of this book" (22:7). Perhaps most important and most developed is the blessing on those who are present for the millennium, the thousand year reign of the saints on earth with Christ. "Blessed and holy is the one who shares in the first resurrection. The second death has no power over these; they will be priests of God and of Christ, and they will reign with him for the thousand years" (20:6). The last blessing sounds strange at first, refers to the martyrs, yet will be of great comfort to those who do house work: "Blessed are they who wash their robes so as to have the right to the tree of life and enter the city through its gates" (22:14). All seven of these beatitudes reflect the apocalyptic outlook of the sacred author which is based on his experience of persecution and which is wholly oriented toward the coming of Christ in glory with the heavenly Jerusalem, that is, the reign of God to earth. This orientation and hope is the specific content of the New Testament beatitudes taken as a whole.

Pastoral-Liturgical Tradition

The main beatitudes of Jesus as listed in Matthew 5:3-12 are frequently read in the liturgy of the Roman Rite according to the 1970 lectionary. The two most strategic and prominent uses are as the gospel for the great feast of All Saints (November 1) and for the Fourth Sunday of the Year (A), which falls between the Christmas-Epiphany cycle and the Lent-Easter cycle. The meaning of the first use may be understood in this way. The beatitudes here represent the program of Christian life, a list of peculiarly Christian virtues (though of course with OT roots). They thus at the same time represent the program of Christian personal holiness, heroic virtue (including suffering persecution for justice and/or for the faith). Heroic virtue is the definition of sanctity according to Pope Benedict XIV. The meaning of their second use is this: after the cycles of redemption and initiation into Christ, the liturgy begins the long, slow cycle of Christian nurture, the living out of what was begun at Easter. The continuous reading of Matthew's Gospel which gives prominence to matters of ethics and justice, in such a way as to give prominence to the Sermon on the Mount of which the beatitudes constitute the exordium or solemn introduction, plays an important role in this process of Christian nurture. To be sure, ethics and law are not the whole of this process. The grace and work of the holy Spirit, the sacraments, personal prayer, the life of the community all play a role. But the beatitudes and their sequence are there to hold up a pattern of Christian life.

The use of the Lucan form of the beatitudes (Luke 6:20-26) is much less prominent in the liturgy. It is used as the Gospel text for Wednesday of the Third Week of the Year.

The Matthean beatitudes are also used in the common of saints, in Masses connected with the sacraments of confirmation and marriage, and in funeral and other masses for the dead. They are also read at special Masses for persecuted Christians and for peace and justice. All these different and varied uses flow from the basic principles already given, as well as from some particular part of the content of the beatitudes. For example, the promise after each beatitude (e.g., "they shall see God") is appropriate to those who have died in Christ. Again, the fourth, eighth, and ninth beatitudes are obviously appropriate to those who hunger for justice and who suffer persecution. In sum, wherever it is a question of a program of Christian life and its destiny, the beatitudes may be called upon to serve.

See: BLESSING, JOY, PRAYER

BENEDICT T. VIVIANO, O.P.

BETHANY

A village some two miles east of Jerusalem (John 11:18), Bethany is located at the foot of the eastern slope of the Mount of Olives. Bethany was the home of Jesus' friends Mary, Martha, and Lazarus (John 11:1), and was the place where Jesus would spend the night when he was in the vicinity of Jerusalem (Mark 11:11; Matt 21:17).

Several significant gospel events take place in Bethany. Both Mark (11:1) and Luke (19:29) describe Jesus' entry into Jerusalem as proceeding from Bethpage and Bethany at the Mount of Olives. This marks the beginning of Jesus' Jerusalem ministry in the Synoptic Gospels. In contrast to the fourth evangelist, who shows Jesus making several trips to Jerusalem during his ministry, the first three Gospel writers present Jesus as making only one fateful journey to Jerusalem.

The anointing of Jesus for his burial takes place at Bethany (Mark 14:3; Matt 26:6; John 12:1). Mark (14:3) and Matthew (26:6) locate the incident in the home of Simon the leper. They tell how an unnamed woman entered and broke an alabaster jar of costly perfumed oil on Jesus' head. Against the objections of some in attendance, Jesus declares his approval of her action and interprets it: "She has done a good thing for me. . . . She has anticipated anointing my body for burial" (Mark 14:6, 8). In the Gospel of John (12:1-8) it is Mary of Bethany who performs this action six days before Passover, at a meal she and Martha and Lazarus host for Jesus in their house. Luke relates one other episode in which Martha and Mary host Jesus (Luke 10:38-42), but he does not in this instance name their village.

The closing verses of Luke's Gospel (24:50-53) identify Bethany as the site of the ascension. The resurrected Jesus led his disciples "as far as Bethany, raised his hands, and blessed them. As he blessed them he parted from them and was taken up to heaven" (24:50-51).

In the Gospel of John the first mention of Bethany is John 1:28, where John the Baptist's activity is said to have "happened in Bethany across the Jordan." This site does not correspond to the village of that name elsewhere in the Gospels. Some manuscripts read "Bethabara" in place of "Bethany."

The last of the signs performed by Jesus in the Fourth Gospel takes place in Bethany.

Jesus raises Lazarus, who has been dead four days (John 11:1-44), an action that provokes the Sanhedrin to begin plotting Jesus' death (John 11:45-54). The fourth evangelist also uses this incident to stage a significant theological discussion between Martha and Jesus about the resurrection, which leads to her proclamation of Jesus as the Messiah.

The Gospel associations with Bethany are significant. It is the place where Jesus enjoys respite, hospitality, and friendship. It is where God's power works in Jesus to restore Lazarus to life and where a believer recognizes Jesus' true identity to proclaim him Messiah and to anoint him for burial. From Bethany comes Jesus' symbolic entrance into Jerusalem, and from there his earthly presence departs.

See: ANOINTING, ASCENSION, JERUSALEM, MESSIAH, MINISTRY, PASSION, PASSOVER, POWER, RESURRECTION

BARBARA E. REID, O.P.

BETHEL

Bethel marks the intersection of two great ancient highways fifteen miles north of Jerusalem. Founded after 2000 BCE when it was called Luz, Bethel—like its sister-city Dan—is a border city, a holy city.

Old Testament

Bethel belongs to the heartland of Israel where some of the Bible's most told traditions developed. Nearby Bethel are Jericho and Ai, where villagers celebrated Yahweh's gift of new land to them by telling stories like those in Joshua 2–8. Bethel was also part of the territory where the ark stories (1 Samuel 4–6; 2 Samuel 6) and the stories of Samuel were told.

Jacob's Ladder. Hebrews laid claim to Bethel with the stories of the covenant with Abraham and Sarah (Gen 11:27–13:18) and Jacob's Ladder (Gen 28:10-22). These ancestors celebrated their commitment to El the creator by erecting a great stone there. Their stories found their way into the Bible through what scholars call the Elohist traditions. In his story, Jacob does not actually see a ladder, but Esagila, a ziggurat or great stepped-platform which the gods use to enter and leave Babylon. Genesis 11:1-9 satirizes the same ziggurat as the Tower of Babel. The stories confer the status of the Gate *(Bab)* of God *(Elyon)* in Mesopotamia on the House *(Beth)* of God *(El)* in Syria-Palestine.

The Golden Calf. Around 925 BCE northern Israel declared its independence from southern Judah. Jeroboam, Israel's first king, designated Bethel as the place where the revolution would be commemorated as a new exodus from slavery. A gold bull was installed as a pedestal on which Yahweh could stand victorious (1 Kgs 12:26-32). Prophets like Elijah and Elisha also sanctioned Bethel's new status (2 Kgs 2:1-25).

Understandably, Judah's kings and prophets (Hos 4:15) did not consider Bethel a house of God, but caricatured it as a house *(Beth)* of sacrilege *('Awen).* They did their best to destroy or discredit it. Twice, Judah's armies overran Bethel (1 Kgs 12:33–13:34; 2 Chr 13:1-23; 2 Kgs 22:1–23:30). Propaganda like the Story of the Golden Calf (Exod 32:1-35), which compares Israel's secession from Judah with Aaron's rebellion against Moses, and Amos' verdict against Bethel's priest (Amos 7:10-17) was Judah's most consistent weapon against the venerable sanctuary. Nonetheless, its reputation remained intact. Even the Assyrians who conquered Israel in 721 BCE publicly acknowledged Yahweh's sanctuary there (2 Kgs 17:24-28).

New Testament

Acts 10:1–11:18 parallels Jacob's dream at Bethel and Peter's vision at Joppa. Like Jacob, Peter is an ancestor. Also like Jacob, Peter experiences in a dream the divine presence coming and going in a strange new place and awakes to approve the community there.

Pastoral-Liturgical Tradition

Preserving Israel's traditions of Bethel as a holy city, Christians built churches and monasteries dedicated to Abraham and Jacob there. The Lectionary understands the dedication of each new church to repeat Jacob's dedication of the sanctuary at Bethel. Continuing Judah's indictment of it as a place of sacrilege, the Lectionary cites Amos' interdiction of Bethel (Amos 7:10-17) as a precedent of Jesus' commission of the Twelve (Mark 6:7-13) to cities who treat them inhospitably.

See: ELIJAH/ELISHA, JACOB

DON C. BENJAMIN, O.CARM.

BETHLEHEM

The modern West Bank city of Bethlehem lies eight kilometers (about six miles) south of Jerusalem, clinging to the side of the great central ridge that moves south from Jerusalem to Hebron and flattens into the Negev desert region. To the east of Bethlehem begins the Judean wilderness descending rapidly in elevation to the rift valley. The city has a spectacular vista onto its desert wastes.

This town has a long and significant history. The first known reference to Bethlehem is found in the Amarna letters (ca. 1250 BCE): a local vassal complains to the Pharaoh that the people of Bethlehem had allied themselves with the "Habiru" (a possible reference to the Hebrews).

A number of biblical incidents are connected with Bethlehem. According to Genesis 35:19, Rachel died near Bethlehem and was buried here (her grave is still venerated in Bethlehem). In the gruesome story of the Levite and the concubine, both the young Levite and his terribly abused companion are from Bethlehem (Judges 17–19). Ruth's father-in-law Elimelech was also a citizen of Bethlehem.

Bethlehem's most important claim to fame in the Hebrew Scriptures is its association with David. This was David's home and it was here that the prophet Samuel selected David to be anointed as future king from among his brothers (1 Sam 16:1-13). Some of David's "mighty men" also came from Bethlehem (2 Sam 23:24),

and once when it was under Philistine control three of David's men slipped into the city and brought back water from the cistern near Bethlehem's gate for which David longed (2 Sam 23:16). When the kingdom was divided after Solomon's death, Rehoboam made Bethlehem one of the fortified cities of Judah (2 Chr 11:6).

Matthew and Luke identify Bethlehem as the birthplace of Jesus, and John's Gospel may also affirm the same tradition (see John 7:42). The evangelists highlight the town's connection with David. Matthew sees Jesus' birth as the fulfillment of Micah 5:2-5, whose words are freely adapted to praise Bethlehem as "by no means least among the rulers of Judah" (see Matt 2:6). Both Gospels portray Jesus as the Davidic Messiah and consider his birth in Bethlehem as a sign of his royal status. In Matthew the chief priests and the scribes summoned by Herod know that the Messiah is to be born in Bethlehem. The wise men offer Jesus royal homage but, like Pharaoh, Herod tries in vain to destroy the child. Joseph is directed to flee with his family to Egypt.

Luke refers repeatedly to Jesus' royal status in his infancy narrative and to Bethlehem as the "City of David" (Luke 2:4, 11). The angel Gabriel announces to Mary that her son "will be great and will be called Son of the Most High, and the Lord God will give him the throne of David his father . . ." (Luke 1:32). The humble circumstances of Jesus' birth and the first homage offered by the shepherds signify that Jesus' royal status will confound the usual expectations of royal power.

Matthew and Luke have differing traditions about Jesus' connection to Bethlehem. For Matthew Jesus and his family reside in Bethlehem; they go to Nazareth only because they fear Herod's son Archelaus, who had succeeded his father as ruler of Judea (Matt 2:22-23). In Luke's account, Mary and Joseph reside in Nazareth and come to Joseph's ancestral home Bethlehem only because of the census (Luke 2:1-7). This disparity has led some interpreters to conclude that the location of Jesus' birth at

Bethlehem is a theological assertion rather than a historical tradition. Jesus, in fact, would have been born a Galilean. Locating Jesus' birth at Bethlehem enables the gospel tradition to affirm Jesus' Davidic ancestry and his messianic nature.

However, there is no decisive argument for doubting the historical basis of the gospel tradition on this point. Matthew's Gospel, for example, ascribes Davidic ancestry to Jesus only through Joseph and his acceptance of Mary's child into his family. This is a strange complication introduced by the evangelist if, in fact, he had located Jesus' birth at Bethlehem for the theological purpose of being able to affirm Jesus' Davidic ancestry. The disparities between the two infancy narratives about how Jesus and his family got to Bethlehem could also be seen as reflecting a historical tradition in that the two independent accounts with different sources and different theological purposes yet agree on Bethlehem as the locale of Jesus' birth.

Whatever judgment one may make about their historicity, the enticing accounts of Jesus' birth and the drama and warmth of these stories have fixed Bethlehem forever in Christian imagination as the humble birthplace of God's Son. Bethlehem was an object of Christian reverence from the earliest centuries. Helena, the mother of Constantine, constructed a basilica there in the fourth century and it was later enhanced under Justinian in the sixth century. Jerome and Paula established a monastic community in Bethlehem and much of his famed work of biblical translation and commentary took place here. The sixth century basilica has remained intact, although ravaged by earthquake, fire, and pillaging over the centuries. Today, as from the beginning of Christian history, it is a place of pilgrimage.

See: JESUS CHRIST, MESSIAH

DONALD SENIOR, C.P.

BISHOP

To speak of the origin of bishops in the Catholic Church is a difficult task, for even in the NT we do not find a clearly formulated description or definition of Christian ministerial offices. "Bishop" is the usual translation of the Greek *episkopos.* Certainly the ministry of leadership in the early Church took various forms which were later combined in the office of *presbyter/episkopos.* For example the Church at Phillipi seems to have had a *presbyteros/episkopos* structure at an early stage (see Phil 1:1), while the Church at Corinth seems to have been directed by Paul himself as the founding apostle. By the end of the first century, however, even the Corinthian Church's ministry was administered by a *presbyteros/episkopos* structure. In the NT there is certainly a close connection between *presbyteros* and *episkopos,* for the terms seem to have been used interchangeably. In the Pastoral Letters *episkopos* is used in the singular, whereas *presbyteros* appears in the plural. It is likely that by the end of the first century, the *episkopos* was chosen from among the elders in the community for roles of leadership and administration in the local church, but there is no clear evidence in the NT that the presbyters were subordinate to a single *episkopos* or overseer, as was the case in the second and third centuries.

The First Letter to Timothy (3:1-7) and the Letter to Titus (1:7-9) speak of the requirements for the episcopal office rather than the roles to be carried out, but it may be inferred that the bishop's principal functions were administrative supervision and pastoral care (teaching, counseling, representing, and judging). Since the *episkopos* was responsible for the overall welfare of the local church, he was also probably the leader of worship, though no biblical texts confirm that presumption. Most likely the episcopal office had a Jewish origin. Many recent scholars maintain that in light of the office of "overseer" *(megaqqar)* in the Qumran community, the episcopal office was adapted by the early Church from Judaism and its office of pastoral care, just as the office of presbyters or elders *(zeqenim)* was adapted from the organization of the synagogue.

Supervision seems to have been the main function of the *episcopoi* in the first decades of the Church. Although that function included responsibility for temporalities, it was primarily centered on spiritual values and was concerned with keeping all the baptized in communion with the Christian faith proclaimed by those who witnessed to the life, death and resurrection of Jesus Christ.

It was Ignatius of Antioch (ca. 105) who first attributed to the *episkopos* the key office in the local Church. By the end of the second century, the bishop was generally recognized as the major leader in each local Christian community. By that time also the term *episkopos*, as well as *presbyter*, was linked to *hiereus, sacerdos*, and *pontifex*. In other words, a priestly interpretation in the Jewish and Greek sense became prominent. Leadership in liturgy began to be the foundation for Church leadership rather than Church leadership being the foundation for leadership in liturgy. In *The Apostolic Tradition* of Hippolytus, a highly traditional work reflecting Roman practice in the early third century, we have the ordination ritual for an *episkopos, presbyter*, and deacon. The rite notes that the *episkopos* is ordained for pastoral leadership and because of his exemplary Christian life. Leadership in liturgy is not the central focus of the rite.

From the beginning of the third to the middle of the fifth century, the *episkopos* was the principal leader of the Christian community. He alone presided at the Eucharist; he was the primary minister in the sacraments of baptism and public penance. This gradual emphasis on his liturgical roles, along with an increased solemnization of the ordination rite, shifted the foundation for Christian ministry away from leadership in the community to liturgical ordination. The ordained *episkopos* was looked upon as the successor of the apostles and therefore as the primary symbol and source of orthodoxy in the local Church.

With the expansion of Christianity into more rural areas throughout the Middle Ages, various episcopal roles were taken over by presbyters so that the presbyter was thought to possess the fullness of the priesthood. In the East the bishop continued to be the principal priest in the local Church, but in the West, from 1100 onwards, the bishop, *qua* bishop, was thought simply to have a greater title of honor and jurisdiction; he was not more a priest than the presbyter. The only functions specifically reserved to the bishop were the right to confirm the newly baptized and to ordain other ministers. Throughout the High Middle Ages theologians disputed the nature of the episcopacy; the majority maintained that the sacrament of orders did not include the bishop as the highest degree.

The Protestant Reformers challenged the traditional doctrine of episcopacy and sometimes rejected it. Although they saw the pastoral office as of divine institution, they saw it as actualized primarily in the priesthood of all believers.

The Council of Trent took for granted that there was a hierarchy of orders and a hierarchy of jurisdiction, but it did not settle the issue of the episcopacy as a distinct but essential stage in the sacrament of orders, nor did it specify how it related to the papacy. Vatican I defined the pope's universal episcopate but it did not develop a more thorough theology of the episcopacy, a task which was left to the fathers of Vatican II.

Throughout the history of the episcopacy, three essential functions of the local bishop have been constant. He has always had an office of teacher, involving preaching, explaining, and preserving the apostolic faith. He has been a leader, maintaining the local Church in unity in spite of diversity among the members. And he has been a sanctifier, transmitting the grace of Christ which makes the Church a chosen race, a royal priesthood, a consecrated nation and a people set apart to sing the praise of God (1 Pet 2:9). These are the functions that are affirmed by the documents of Vatican II and the revised ritual of episcopal ordination.

Vatican II affirmed the sacramental nature of the episcopate and noted that bishops form a college, as did the apostles; they continue to govern the Church collegially. Individual bishops have an identity rooted in Christ who was priest, teacher, and ruler. They become members of the college by ordination. The college acts collegially when it is solemnly assembled, as at an ecumenical council, or when it is dispersed throughout the world, provided the bishop of Rome, who is the head of the college, at least accepts the action as a collegial action. Full authority in the Church may be exercised by the college acting as a college or by the bishop of Rome acting as vicar of Christ and head of the college.

The basic understanding of ordination that the Church had in the early centuries has been restored in the last fifty years. In an apostolic constitution *Episcopalis consecrationis* (1944), Pope Pius XII asserted that the two bishops who accompany the primary bishop ordaining a new member of the episcopal college are themselves consecrators and not mere assistants. He went on in 1947 to decree that the imposition of hands and the accompanying prayer are the essential rites in the ordination liturgy. In an encyclical issued in 1957, he reminded bishops that in addition to their responsibility for their proper dioceses, they are also responsible collegially for the evangelization of the world.

In accord with the directive of the Constitution on the Sacred Liturgy, a revised ritual for ordinations was promulgated by Pope Paul VI on June 18, 1968. In the past the Roman Pontifical spoke of priests and deacons being ordained but bishops being consecrated; now the term "ordination" is applied to all three degrees of the one sacrament. In the new rite all the bishops present impose hands on the bishop-elect. The principal ordaining bishop then places the open book of Gospels on the candidate's head; two deacons hold it in place during the prayer of ordination. The new bishop's head is then anointed with sacred chrism; this rite is then followed by the presentation of the book of Gospels, the episcopal ring, the miter, and the crozier.

By a decree of the Congregation for Divine Worship and the Discipline of the Sacraments, issued on June 29, 1989, a revised edition of the rites for ordination of bishops, presbyters, and deacons was issued; however there were no significant changes made in the rite for the ordination of bishops. On September 14, 1984, the Congregation for Divine Worship promulgated a thorough revision of the *Ceremonial of Bishops*. The text contains eight parts and three appendices: I. General Norms, II. The Mass, III. Liturgy of the Hours and Celebrations of the Word of God, IV. Celebrations of the Mysteries of the Lord during the Cycle of the Year, V. Celebration of the Sacraments, VI. Celebration of Sacramentals, VII. Notable Days in the Life of a Bishop, VIII. Rites for Plenary and Provincial Councils and for Diocesan Synods. The appendices give the norms for the vesture of prelates, a table of precedence of liturgical days, and rules governing ritual Masses, votive Masses, and Masses for the Dead.

See: CHURCH, COMMUNITY, DEACON, MINISTRY, ORDINATION, PRIEST

R. KEVIN SEASOLTZ, O.S.B.

BLASPHEMY

Blasphemy, or cursing God, is the most serious crime mentioned in the Bible. God is cursed for not being the kind of God this higher power should be. In effect, human beings want to be God. This is complicated by the fact that Jesus "blasphemed" and defended his claim both for himself and for others.

Old Testament

The prohibition against blasphemy first appears in the Code of Holiness in Leviticus 17–26 simply as a story of a half-Egyptian man who "quarreled publicly with another Israelite and cursed and blasphemed the LORD's name" (Lev 24:11). What he actually said is not recorded. The man was stoned to death and this set a precedent.

The best remembered instance of blasphemy is found in the story of the servants of the Assyrian king who blasphemed God as they besieged Jerusalem (2 Kings 18). They derided God as impotent to withstand the Assyrian gods or armies. Isaiah 36–37 repeats that story as a reminder of God's saving action.

The prophets denounced their people for "breaking faith with me" (Ezek 20:27). This denunciation seems to be addressed to the heart of the crime of those who are covenanted to God yet break faith and seek other gods. Breaking faith seems the capital crime.

New Testament

In the Synoptics "blasphemy" is an accusation directed against both the scribes and Jesus. The principal story in which Jesus is accused of blasphemy is that of the paralytic whose sins Jesus forgives (Matt 9:1-7; Mark 2:3-12; Luke 5:18-26). In all three texts blasphemy is mentioned; Mark and Luke specify it further: "Who but God can forgive sins?" (Mark 2:7; Luke 5:21). The scribes and Pharisees understand blasphemy as a claim to do something which the God of Israel alone can do.

In John 10:33-39, we read that at the end of the violent confrontation with the Jews in Jerusalem Jesus asserted: "The Father and I are one" (John 10:30). The Jews justified themselves by trying to stone him: "We are not stoning you for a good work but for blasphemy. You, a man, are making yourself God" (John 10:34).

In all these instances Jesus was the one accused of blasphemy; basically he claimed the power attached to God's name. Furthermore, Jesus involved all who hear the word of God in this blasphemy. "Is it not written in your law, 'I said, You are gods'? If it calls them gods to whom the word of God came, and scripture cannot be set aside, can you say that the one whom the Father has consecrated and sent into the world blasphemes because I said, 'I am the Son of God'?" (John 10:34-36). Blasphemy and truth have come very close to each other.

Jesus also accused the scribes of blasphemy. In Mark 3:20-30, when Jesus is ac-cused by the scribes of being possessed by Beelzebul, he accuses them of blasphemy. "'Amen, I say to you, all sins and all blasphemies that people utter will be forgiven them. But whoever blasphemes against the holy Spirit will never have forgiveness, but is guilty of an everlasting sin.' For they had said, 'He has an unclean spirit'" (Mark 3:28-29). In the Greek text the "everlasting sin" seems to have something to do with the apocalyptic age, a concept which is important in Mark. Revelation 13:6; 16:9, 11, 21 use the same word in an apocalyptic sense to describe the punishment of those who blasphemed God. The basis for the severe judgment of this everlasting sin is some motivation within the blasphemer, a motivation which is not clear. It seems that there is blasphemy which is forgivable and there is blasphemy which is not.

Acts sometimes speaks of more conventional blasphemy as abusive speech (Acts 13:45; 18:6; 26:11). In Romans 2:24 Paul accuses the Jews by quoting Isaiah 52:2: "Because of you that name of God is reviled [blasphemed] among the Gentiles." 1 Timothy 1:20; 6:1; Titus 2:5; and James 2:7 all mention blasphemy as some irreverent speech about God. The specific offense is not clear.

Pastoral-Liturgical Tradition

The biblical data in reference to blasphemy is not clear. In the earliest tradition it is obviously a capital crime, a violation of fidelity to the covenant, since it is punishable by death. However, in the NT its meaning becomes ambiguous when the one who has the Spirit of Truth is accused of blasphemy. In the history of the Church the line between heresy and orthodoxy is also hard to distinguish. Heresy is denounced by the early Fathers as the most heinous of crimes. At a later period we encounter the exaggerations of the Spanish Inquisition. On the other hand, a pluralism which is so bland that it finds truth irrelevant or unattainable cannot be sustained.

See: CURSE, SIN

JAMES A. FISCHER, C.M.

BLESSING

A blessing is a powerful prayer* in which the purpose, power, and favor of God are invoked for our safety, well-being, and strength. Blessings are found in various contexts throughout both OT and NT and have become a distinctive form of both Jewish and Christian prayer.

Old Testament

In the OT the word for blessing seems to have a clear meaning. However, its connotations are varied. In contemporary societies, blessings may be more or less formalized and superficial invocations of the goodness of God upon people or actions. In more oral and communitarian societies, the words of blessings have much deeper meaning. Like curses, they are expected to accomplish what they say. They are not to be used lightly for they include inevitable results. The Hebrew adjective, "blessed" is most often used in the sense of "happy," "fortunate."

Historical Situation. The notion of "blessing" is used most frequently (over two hundred times) in the tribal stories of the OT. The remembrance of promised blessings or the handing on of blessings were very important events in the daily life of the people.

The first concentration of the use of the word is in the ancestral stories. These accounts begin with the foundational blessing of Abraham and his descendants:

> I will make of you a great nation,
>   and I will bless you;
> I will make your name great,
>   so that you will be a blessing.
> I will bless those who bless you
>   and curse those who curse you.
> All the communities of the earth
>   shall find blessing in you
>   (Gen 12:2-3).

This unrevoked promise continues in the stories of Isaac and of Jacob (see Genesis 26–28; 30–32) and in the great blessing of Genesis 49. In these ancestral pronounce-ments the blessing of God will result in an unspecified glory, the giving of numerous progeny to the ancestor, a promise of protection against curses, and, most surprisingly, a blessing upon all the communities of the earth who will be blessed in Abraham and his descendants. This blessing remained in the tradition as the perpetual and central relationship between God and the people.

A second concentration of words is found in the stories of the Exodus. These references to God blessing the people are much more sparse. Deuteronomy 11:26-31 concludes a sermon with a set of blessings on those who keep the Law. At the end of its exhortatory sermons Deuteronomy 28:1-6 has a series of blessings. Such blessings are attached to the keeping of the Law, not to the ancestral promises. This suggests that a shift has occurred in the way people expected blessings to be allocated.

A third series of uses of blessing is found in the stories of the kings, especially David. 1 Kings 2:45 states, "But King Solomon shall be blessed, and David's throne shall endure before the LORD forever." Although it speaks of blessing, this is a self-serving excuse on the lips of Solomon which tries to justify his killing of Shimei. The actual promises to David are always put in the declarative form of "your house shall endure forever."

The Psalms. "Bless" and "blessings" are favorite expressions in the psalms. God is frequently asked to bless the entire people or particular individuals and the people are frequently exhorted to bless God. In the later Greek translation, "bless" is literally "speak well of." The psalms speak well of the good God.

> Bless the LORD, O my soul!
>   O, LORD, my God, you are great indeed!
>   (Ps 104:1).

In such creation hymns all creatures are called upon to bless God for having made them and endowed them with wonder. The history of the chosen people is also material to praise God for protection and graciousness.

Sometimes the blessing is upon the people, often in the form of a priestly blessing.

> May the LORD bless you from Zion,
>   the maker of heaven and earth
> (Ps 134:3).

Prophetic Blessings. Such blessings are less frequent, though they sometimes occur. Blessings upon the people are prayers that the good things of God will continue to flow upon the people. The action, however, is always in both directions. People bless God; God blesses the people. Blessings are limited to this one people. A prophetic psalm reads:

> May God have pity on us and bless us;
>   may he let his face shine upon us.
> So may your way be known upon earth;
>   among all nations, your salvation.
> May the peoples praise you, O God
>   may all the peoples praise you
> (Ps 67:2-4).

Wisdom Literature. This literature takes for granted that God will bring good to all who call upon God. "Blessed" or "happy" came to be a common designation of anyone who prospered and consequently of anyone who seemed to be just.

> Happy the man who follows not
>   the counsel of the wicked. . . .
> He is like a tree
>   planted near running water,
> That yields its fruit in due season,
>   and whose leaves never fade.
> [Whatever he does, prospers]
> (Ps 1:1, 3).

Such is the keynote at the beginning of the book of Psalms.

The Problem of Retribution. The implicit equivalence of good living with prosperity and of evil-doing with punishment is ingrained in many parts of the common lore of Israel. One of the noblest statements of ethics anywhere is found in the so-called Code of Holiness, Leviticus 19–26. Chapter 26:3-13 sets out the blessings on those who observe the Code: "If you live in accordance with my precepts and are careful to observe my commandments, I will give you rain in due season" (Lev 26:3). The blessings include: abundant crops, peace, freedom from ravenous beasts, routing your enemies, numerous progeny, stores of food, my Dwelling among you. On the other hand: "But if you do not heed me and do not keep all these commandments, if you reject my precepts and spurn my decrees, refusing to obey all my commandments and breaking my covenant, then I, in turn, will give you your deserts" (Lev 26:14). Punishment includes: sickness, enemies who destroy crops, subjection, an iron sky and a bronze earth, wild beasts, the sword, lack of bread, cannibalism, devastation of sanctuaries, exile.

Such a listing of blessings and curses was common in ancient treaties. The gods of both parties were called upon to witness to the oaths; the benefits and penalties were expressed in horrendous specifics. The Holiness Code was intended to be taken seriously even if, as with the later Sermon on the Mount, it seemed too idealistic for human action.

The sentiments expressed by retribution can be admired, but the danger lurking behind a rigid mentality is easy enough to see. Equating justice and blessings can easily become a matter of mechanical logic; attributing evil to misfortune is too automatic. The close relationship between language and deed tended to make blessings and curses automatic. In some ancient societies the magic of curses was well understood. Whether or not the Israelites thought this way is not clear. The chosen people struggled with the concept of retribution throughout their history. Any solution that seemed to infringe upon the freedom of God was rejected.

The Prophetic View of Retribution. Words of blessing are surprisingly infrequent in the prophets—only about twenty occurrences in the prophetic corpus and some are merely variations on the traditional wish: "May the

LORD bless you" (Jer 17:7; 31:23). Isaiah, in whose message the greatest number occur, several times alludes to the patriarchal blessing for the race (Isa 19:25; 44:3; 51:2; 61:9). In one song of redemption other nations are gathered under this blessing: "On that day Israel shall be a third party with Egypt and Assyria, a blessing in the midst of the land, when the LORD of hosts blesses it: 'Blessed be my people Egypt, and the work of my hands Assyria, and my inheritance, Israel'" (Isa 19:24-25).

Curses and blessing together are used only in Zechariah and Malachi. In Zechariah 8:13 the promise of restoration through Israel reads: "Just as you were a curse among the nations, O house of Judah and house of Israel, so will I save you that you may be a blessing; do not fear, but let your hands be strong."

In Malachi 2:3 it is the curse which is emphasized:

And if you do not lay it to heart,
to give glory to my name, says the LORD
of hosts,
I will send a curse upon you
and of your blessing I will make a curse.

This divergence from the retributive use of curses and blessings for performance seems deliberate and somewhat puzzling. Our contemporary analysis of prophetic messages claims that the true prophets almost always spoke of condemnation and consolation. Both go together, and that seems somewhat analogous to the curses and blessing approach. However, they are no longer tied to the behavior of the people. The blessings, especially, are seen as pure gifts of the good God.

See: CURSE, PSALMS, RETRIBUTION

JAMES A. FISCHER, C.M.

New Testament

The NT uses of blessing (*eulogein*) and cursing (*katarasthai*) terminology cut to the heart of the saving message and actions of Jesus Christ. Two of the first clusters of uses in the gospels are related to (1) Jesus' central messages, the near coming of the reign of God to earth as the greatest of divine historical blessings on God's people, and (2) to the central action of Jesus' saving death and resurrection, as symbolically represented in the ritual of the Eucharist.

The relation to the reign of God is made in the great judgment parable when the Son of Man as king issues an invitation to those on his right: "Come, you who are blessed by my Father. Inherit the kingdom prepared for you" (Matt 25:34). But it is found already at Jesus' entry to Jerusalem, as the crowds greet him with words from Psalm 118:26: "Blessed be he who comes in the name of the Lord! Blessed is the kingdom of our father David that is to come!" (Mark 11:9-10; see Matt 21:9; Luke 19:38; John 12:13). The same cry will greet the Messiah at his (second) coming (Matt 23:39; par. Luke 13:35).

The Eucharistic blessing presents a more complicated picture. The Christian Eucharistic meal, we know, is a great blessing of the present era of salvation, precisely because it is a foretaste or anticipation of the reign of God (Mark 14:25; Matt 26:29; Luke 29:18). But the story of the Last Supper, the institution of the Eucharist, presents us with a number of questions related to blessing. Why do Mark and Matthew say that Jesus *blessed* the bread, but *gave thanks* over the cup? Why do Paul (1 Cor 11:24) and Luke (22:17, 19) drop the term blessing in their accounts of the Last Supper, using only thanksgiving there, yet bring the blessing back in other Eucharistic contexts: Luke 24:30; 1 Cor 10:16; 14:16; not to mention the blessing in the pre-eucharistic context of the feeding of the multitudes (Mark 6:61; 8:7; Matt 14:19; Luke 9:16)? Why is Jesus' thanksgiving over the cup *longer* than his blessing over the bread? How do we move from the Last Supper to the Christian Eucharist? That is, why do we have a Eucharistic Prayer (or canon) at Mass rather than just the words of institution?

The answer to these questions takes us to the period of transition from the OT to the

NT by way of the evolution of Jewish prayer forms. The standard OT formula for blessing God is the stable *bārûk YHWH*, Blessed be the Lord (third person). Only in a few late texts (1 Chr 29:10; Ps 119:12; 1 Macc 4:30), do we find the formula "Blessed be you, O Lord" (*bārûk 'attâ, YHWH*; second person, direct address). These late texts give us a clue to the formation of the liturgical blessings in the synagogues that was going on at the same time. These blessings take the stable form: Blessed are you, O Lord our God, [who bring forth bread from the earth]. They also indicated a shift from blessings as public statements to blessings as personal address, expressing a bold, direct, immediate relation to God. The short formula just cited is later called a *hatimah* (seal) because it sometimes concludes a longer prayer.

Now we must return to our questions about the Eucharist. In Mark and Matthew, Jesus blesses the bread in that he recites the short blessing formula, or *hatimah*, just cited at the start of the meal. He gives thanks over the cup because he recites, at the close of the meal, the lengthy *birkat ha-mazon* (grace after meals) which consists of three parts: blessing, thanksgiving,* and supplication or petition. Paul and Luke drop the blessing terminology because, like the early Christian text called the Didache, they sense that God's new act in Christ requires thanksgiving first of all and then only secondarily blessing and petition. Jesus' words over the cup are longer than those over the bread because it was customary to pray briefly at the beginning of a Jewish meal and at length at the end. The NT Eucharistic texts are brief. They do not cite in full Jewish prayers which their first readers knew by heart. The NT is not a manual of rubrics. But our earliest Eucharistic Prayers outside the NT (Didache, Apostolic Constitutions, Hippolytus, Addai and Mari) give us the impression that they grew out of a rearranged *birkat ha-mazon* (Jewish grace after meals) with the thanksgiving placed first, and then the blessing and the prayers of supplication. Within this long prayer, Jesus'

words of institution were, at some point, inserted. That is how we get from the Last Supper to the Eucharistic Prayers.

To these two principal NT developments in the realization of blessing may be added some others which are found particularly in the Lucan and Pauline literature. The first is ethical. It is a striking fact that in Luke's reproduction of Jesus' ethical instruction, in Jesus' boldest teaching, the love of enemies, a phrase is found which is not present in Matthew's version: "Bless those who curse you" (Luke 6:28,-Q; cf. Matt 5:44). This is strong language since the Bible sees all God's power engaged in blessings and curses. At one stroke the whole OT tradition of balanced blessings and curses is swept away, replaced by blessing only (see 2 Cor 1:17-20). This strong accent on the positive is, however, tempered elsewhere by woes (Luke 6:24-26; 10:13; 11:42-52; 17:1; 21:23; 22:22) and by anathemas (Gal 1:8-9; 1 Cor 16:22; but cf. 12:3; Rom 9:3; Jas 3:9). Does this abolition of cursing go back to Jesus himself or is it a Lucan gloss? This question cannot be settled with certainty but Paul and other early Christian authors seem aware of this elimination of cursing (Rom 12:14; 1 Cor 4:12; 1 Pet 3:9 bis; Jas 3:9-10). This fact points to the authenticity of this teaching or at least to its presence in Q. (The prohibition begins in Job 31:30.)

Another use of the blessing motif may be called a "triple play" or framing technique. Luke uses blessing language in relation to each of the three great poems which punctuate his infancy narrative: Mary says, "All generations will call me blessed" in her *Magnificat* (1:48); Zechariah begins his hymn with, "Blessed be the Lord" (1:68); and Simeon introduces his hymn by blessing God (2:28; see 1:64); he then blesses Jesus' parents (2:34), as Elizabeth had declared Mary blessed (1:42). All this blessing at the beginning of Luke's Gospel is matched by a triple use of blessing language in the last paragraph of the Gospel (24:50-53), not always clear in modern translations: "Then he led them out as far as Bethany, raised his hands, and blessed them. As he blessed them he parted from them and was taken up to heaven. They did him homage and then returned to Jerusalem with great joy, and they were continually in the temple praising [blessing] God." Luke ends his Gospel as he had begun it (1:9), in the Jerusalem temple, a place where God was traditionally blessed. This triple pattern is also found at the beginning of the great prayer or doxology with which the letter to the Ephesians opens: "Blessed be the God and Father of our Lord Jesus Christ, who has blessed us in Christ with every spiritual blessing in the heavens" (1:3). In this very Jewish *berakah* there is yet a hint of the Trinity in this verse, which becomes explicit in the development (vv. 5-13). (This prayer-vision of Ephesians plays a programmatic role in the Second Vatican Council's view of the Church.) Similar usage occurs in 2 Corinthians 1:3; 1 Peter 1:3.

Still another special Lucan-Pauline twist on the blessing theme is built directly on the OT to make a Christian point. In Genesis Abraham is thrice said to be a source of blessing for all the nations of the earth (12:3; 18:18; 22:18). The NT takes this seriously as a promise of the extension of God's covenant with Abraham to all nations. Peter's speech (Acts 3:25-26) uses this blessing to interpret the presence of Jesus among the Jewish people and as a basis for an appeal for their moral conversion. Paul, in Galatians 3:8, 9, 14, extends the blessing of Abraham to the Gentiles through Christ to the Gentiles explicitly. Hebrews 6:14 derives the immutability of God's promise from the same passage and Hebrews 7:1, 6, 7 makes Melchizedek a type of Christ blessing Abraham and his descendants (based on Genesis 14).

It remains to note that the Blessed One serves as a way of referring to God in Mark 14:61, a formula which recalls the (later?) rabbinic usage of The Holy One Blessed be He (*ha-Qodesh baruk-hu*). Paul refers to God Blessed forever as a concluding doxology. Blessing is a liturgical honor received by

Christ the Lamb in Revelation 5:12. The next verse extends this to Father and Son. Revelation 7:12 reserves it for God alone. With these references blessing is located in the context of liturgical praise and prayer.

For NT uses of the beatitude formula of blessing, see the article under that word. For the NT, the definitive blessing is bestowed upon humankind in Jesus Christ and in the reign whose coming he announced and anticipated. In the times between these two divine gifts, the time of the Church, other blessings are the gift of the holy Spirit, the sacraments, the Scriptures, charity and support within the community of faith and hope, ecstatic prayer, healing, and peace. The experience of blessing brings us close to the heart of religion, the goodness and power of the creating and redeeming God.

See: BEATITUDES, EUCHARIST, PRAYER

BENEDICT T. VIVIANO, O.P.

Pastoral-Liturgical Tradition

Blessing is a distinctive form of biblical-liturgical prayer within the Christian churches. In the Roman Catholic tradition, blessing enjoys a broad scope. The natural world of creation, the cultural world of human social existence, and the ecclesial community with its identity as a holy people chosen for mission provide the Church with limitless occasions for the prayer of blessing. Some of these occasions for blessing, central to the self-understanding of the Christian people, have given rise to official rites of blessing. These liturgical blessings can be found in the general Roman Catholic liturgical books (the Orders for Mass, for the Christian Initiation of Adults, for the Pastoral Care of the Sick, for Christian Funerals, for Ordinations, for Christian Marriage, for Penance, and in the Pontifical) and in a special collection, the *Book of Blessings,* a volume that the National Conference of Catholic Bishops has supplemented with the book *Catholic Household Blessings and Prayers.* The phenomenon of blessing will be considered first, followed by reflection on its religious significance.

For convenience, it is possible to consider liturgical blessings in three sub-groups: ecclesial blessings, blessings of creation, and blessings of human social existence. In the group of ecclesial blessings are the blessing of the baptismal waters, the blessing of the oils for the sick and for catechumens, the consecratory blessings of holy chrism, the Eucharistic bread and wine, and candidates for ordination, the nuptial blessing, the blessings for catechumens during the time of their preparation for baptism, the blessing of penitents, and the blessing of mourners on the occasion of a funeral. Perhaps the most frequent form of liturgical blessings is the blessing that precedes the dismissal of each liturgical assembly. Less familiar because less frequent are the blessings of objects used in the liturgy (e.g., sanctuary furniture, church bells, cemeteries and grave sites), blessings of buildings set apart for the use of the Christian people (e.g., schools, seminaries), the solemn blessings of an abbot or abbess, solemn blessings of assemblies of the sick gathered at pilgrimage sites like Lourdes, blessings of other pilgrim groups, and commissioning blessings of Christian missionaries and catechists.

What characterizes these blessings as ecclesial is that their occasion is the affirmation and intensification of the spiritual identity and mission of the Christian people. Another group of blessings celebrates the goodness of the world as the gift of the creator; the blessing of animals, fields, and harvested foods are prominent here. Blessings directed to human social existence include blessings that affirm domestic and family life (e.g., homes, children, engaged couples, meals), civic life (e.g., hospitals, media centers, means of transportation), human labor (e.g., tools, work sites), education (e.g., libraries, schools and universities), and recreation (e.g., gyms and athletic fields) as part of God's design.

As prayers of the gathered community, liturgical blessings take a ritual form, involving patterned gestures, words, and differentiation of roles. The minister of a blessing will, according to the occasion, lay hands on the persons or things being blessed or extend hands over them. Or a minister's hand may trace the sign of the cross on or over the subject of blessing; sometimes a hand-held crucifix or the Eucharistic host reserved in a monstrance may be used. Less frequently, the minister may sprinkle the subjects of blessing with holy water or incense them. In such circumstances, what is implied at least tacitly is a ritual purification of the subject of blessing. Silent prayer in the assembly may accompany the gesture; it is always summed up in an oral prayer that typically names the occasion and invokes the presence and action of the trinity of divine persons revealed in Jesus. The words of blessing may be as metaphorically rich and expansive as the Eucharistic Prayer or as brief as the common formula, "May almighty God bless you, in the name of the Father and of the Son and of the holy Spirit." Since blessing is the prayer of the Church, the silent prayer and spoken "Amen" of the Christian people are part of this liturgical action.

The multiplicity and diversity of occasions for blessing prompts the Church's theologians to ask questions like "What do we think we are doing when we bless someone or some thing or even bless God?" and "What do we think God is doing when we pray in this way?" The message of biblical revelation, enunciated most clearly in the narratives of the Book of Genesis, is that it is God who blesses or acts graciously toward this world and its inhabitants. God's favor is made known through a good word, a "benediction," which has an irrevocable effect. When the Church blesses persons or things, it remembers God's blessing with gratitude and in so doing celebrates in particular situations the divine intention: that creation is good, that human social existence is good, that a people has been chosen and sanctified to be a light to the world on the way of salvation. When the Church blesses God, it is praising the God who blesses us.

Because ritual communication is symbolically condensed, even truncated, the full religious significance of the Church's prayer of blessing can be missed or misunderstood. The most common faulty perception is that blessing involves humans in the wielding of divine power. In this regard, recalling biblical teaching about blessing can be helpful for grasping the point of praying a blessing. The deeds of God—the created world, the cultural world of human social existence, and the works of redemption—are holy. When we interact in each of these arenas—which taken together comprise the whole of human existence—we must begin by openly acknowledging God's holiness and God's design; we must pray a blessing. In so acknowledging God's presence, these realities become available to us for our benefit.

In the Roman tradition liturgical ministry is hierarchically ordered, so that the bishop, priest, and deacon in turn are designated as preferred ministers for blessings. This provision reflects the expectation that the one who presides in the Church gathered for public worship is ordained. But in actual fact, not all liturgical blessing is reserved to the ordained. *Catholic Household Blessings and Prayers,* with its affirmation of lay leadership in the prayer of blessing, the provision that lay catechists may preside at the blessing of catechumens in the Rite of Christian Initiation of Adults, and the acknowledgement in the *Book of Blessings* that laity may appropriately preside at many blessings in virtue of their baptism confirms the truth that blessing is ecclesial and not exclusively sacerdotal prayer.

Finally, it should be noted that the major and occasional ritual blessings of the Roman liturgical books are meant to be celebrated, a style of performance that involves music, movement, gesture and posture, attention to ritual setting, ritual clothing, and so on. Such full performance of the prayer of blessing gives rise to feast, fiesta, and festival.

See: CONSECRATION, PRAYER

MARY COLLINS, O.S.B.

BLOOD

This entry consists of two articles. The first focuses on the atoning and cleansing function of blood in the ancient Israelite sacrificial system. The second presents the NT association of blood and redemption.

Old Testament

Blood is essential to the physical life of humans and animals. In its critical role for sustaining life, blood took on special significance for the Israelites both in the popular imagination and in the official cult. The near magical quality of blood for fending off death* appears in a few OT texts, which function is the correlate of its more usual one as the bearer of life.

Sacrificial Blood. As an apotropaic agent, the blood placed on the lintel of Hebrew homes in Egypt prevented the Destroyer from killing the first-born among the Hebrew slaves (Exod 12:7, 13, 22). This Passover* ritual in which blood protected against harmful spirits probably originated among seminomadic shepherds who ritualized the danger to newborn lambs during the annual spring migration to new pastures. The blood would propitiate the death-threatening deities. The feeding of blood to underworld deities in rites of death was also known in ancient Greece. In the *Odyssey* 11:50, 96, the dead are depicted as clamoring around a sacrifice offered by Odysseus so that they might partake of the blood. Might not the psalmist be referring to practices of apostates in Israel who pour out blood to underworld deities when he says: "They multiply their sorrows who court other gods. Blood libations to them I will not pour out, nor will I take their names upon my lips" (Ps 16:4)? In the ancient Near East, blood did not play an important role in the sacrificial systems outside of Israel except for propitiating the deities of the underworld.

In Israel, the blood of sacrificial animals had to be regularly poured out at the base of the altar (Lev 4:7, 18, 25, 30) and thereby be returned to God. The blood was not food for God (Ps 50:13). Rather the blood as bearer of life was given to God in atonement* for the sins of humans. God says,

"Since the life of a living body is in its blood, I have made you put it on the altar, so that atonement may thereby be made for your own lives, because it is the blood, as the seat of life, that makes atonement" (Lev 17:11). Everyone, non-Israelites as well as Israelites, was to refrain from eating blood (see Gen 9:4). In the context of Leviticus 17, the danger of eating blood presents itself most acutely on hunting expeditions where the slaughter takes place outside the sanctuary. In priestly terminology, the sacrificial slaughter is a peace offering *(selamim)* rather than a holocaust *('ola)* or a sin offering *(hatta't)*, for the hunters partake of the flesh of the animal. But the hunters must be careful to offer the blood to God as an expiation for their serious offense of taking the life of an animal. Those humans who are carnivorous depart from the example of the original, ideal human in Genesis 1:29-30 and have been commanded to live by the Noachic precepts (Gen 9:4-5; Acts 15:20) so as to guard against scorning the sanctity of life.

In holocausts and sin offerings, an animal taken into the sacral sphere was either to be totally consumed by fire or to have select parts eaten by priests. The blood was always poured out at the base of the altar. In sin offerings for the high priest and congregation, the blood was sprinkled seven times on the veil of the holy of holies and placed on the horns of the altar of incense before the major portion of the blood was poured out at the base of the altar of holocausts (Lev 4:5-7, 17-18). The blood, as the bearer of life of the animal, substituted for the blood of the sinful human. Transgressions against God demanded serious acts of reparation; symbolically, the human sinner was offering his or her own life to God in order to make amends and to ward off punishment. The offering of animals in the guilt offerings, sin offerings, and holocausts accentuated the seriousness of sin; the breach in the relationship with God demanded that the sinner symbolically lay down his or her life through the sacrificial animal so as to re-establish the relationship with God.

The most important expiatory sacrifices were the offering of the bull, the ram, and the goat on the Day of Atonement. The high priest sprinkled the blood of the bull and the goat on the *kapporet*, "the mercy-seat" (Lev 16:14) and thereby brought reconciliation between the Israelites and God. After sprinkling the mercy-seat, the high priest placed blood on the horns of the altar and then sprinkled the altar (Lev 16:17-19). Such sprinkling and anointing with blood highlighted the cleansing properties of blood. Blood functioned in a similar fashion in the cleansing of a leper (Lev 14:14) and in the ordination of a priest (Exod 29:20-21; Lev 8:23-24): i.e., the leper and the one to be ordained had blood placed on the lobe of the right ear, the thumb of the right hand, and the large toe of the right foot. The blood removed the impurities which would defile the Israelite community and its cult.

Further Concepts. In Exodus 24:3-8, Moses sprinkled one-half of the blood of oxen on the assembled Israelites, and the other half he poured against the altar. This sacrificial ritual was part of a covenant ceremony in which the Israelites bound themselves to God. The use of blood to seal a covenant in which the parties to the covenant were sprinkled with blood was unique to this passage in the OT. Among later Arabic tribes, there were initiation rites in which the blood of a sacrificial animal bound the initiate to the tribal deity.

The conception of blood as the bearer of life is not too removed from the understanding of blood as an independent agent which can make claims even after it has been shed or poured out. After Cain had slain Abel, God confronted Cain, saying: "What have you done! Listen: your brother's blood cries out to me from the soil!" (Gen 4:10). Within an Israelite clan, a redeemer of blood was obliged to exact the blood of a murderer for the blood shed by a murdered brother (Num 35:19). Because manslaughter or unintentional murder was not a capital offense in Israel (Num 35:22-24), Israel established cities of refuge to which the manslayer could flee from the anger of the redeemer of blood (Num 35:25).

Blood also functioned as an apocalyptic portent. In Joel's account of the Day of the Lord, this catastrophic event was envisioned as one in which "the sun will be turned to darkness, and the moon to blood" (3:4).

In summary, blood played an essential role in ancient Israel in keeping the Israelites' relationships with God and with one another intact. The atoning and cleansing functions of blood highlighted the seriousness and the cost of the Israelites' remaining obedient to God.

See: ALTAR, ATONEMENT, CLEAN/UNCLEAN, CONSECRATION, COVENANT, DAY OF ATONEMENT, DAY OF THE LORD, PRIEST, RECONCILIATION, REDEMPTION/REDEEMER, SACRIFICE

DALE LAUNDERVILLE, O.S.B.

New Testament

The NT word for blood means exactly that and only that. The theological and pastoral significance comes from its symbolic use and social connotations.

Physical Blood. References to physical blood occur in various stories. So we have the woman with a hemorrhage (Mark 5:25, 29; Luke 8:43, 44); the bloody sweat of Jesus in the garden (Luke 22:44); the shedding of blood in cult (Acts 15:20, 29; 21:35; 22:30; Eph 3:13; Heb 9:14). These we understand readily enough as references to blood in a literal sense.

Blood Guilt. Guilt that involves the shedding of blood is the worst kind. It is surprising how often the NT uses blood in this sense: Judas is guilty of the blood of Jesus (Matt 23:30; Mark 23:35; 27:4; Luke 11:50, 51; 13:1); the priests want to have nothing to do with the blood money of the bribe (Acts 1:19). Christians may be guilty of the blood of Christ if they abuse the Eucharist (1 Cor 11:27).

Flesh and Blood. As in our own language, "flesh and blood" means our total

being or that of someone close to us. The expression is used in Matthew 16:17; John 1:13; 1 Corinthians 15:20; Galatians 1:16; Hebrews 2:14.

Redeeming Blood. The instincts involved here go back a long way. To people living in an agricultural and pastoral society blood speaks of the sharing of all life. Such people live with animals, domesticated or wild. The community of all living things stands out. Some must die but it is a sacred event for their blood to be shed. So also people who give their blood to save others are not simply heroes; they are sacred.

All of the earliest traditions concerning Jesus see a cosmic meaning in the life and death of this one man. He was locked in combat with the mythical demon, the real force of evil which exists in our world. He conquered evil in a radical sense and that has affected us all.

Paul. Paul was the first to write of this meaning of the death of Jesus. As early as 1 Corinthians, probably about 56 CE, he wrote: "The cup of blessing that we bless, is it not a participation in the blood of Christ? The bread that we break, is it not a participation in the body of Christ?" (1 Cor 10:16; see also 1 Cor 11:17-34 for his treatment of the Eucharistic meal).

The context of these quotations is clearly the ritual celebration of a commemorative meal as practiced at Corinth. The later Synoptic accounts use approximately the same formulas in telling the story of the Last Supper. The exact words bear evidence of having been accommodated to a liturgical celebration, rather than a verbatim report of what Jesus said. The substance is accurate, but the expressions already bear an interpretation. Paul was not innovating at Corinth.

It is noteworthy that this earliest written explanation of how the death of Jesus affects us is put in terms of bread that we eat and blood that we drink. The bread is the easier symbol to understand since its meaning of life-giving is clearer and more joyfully acceptable. The blood symbol, however, contains deeper meaning. As in the more general symbolism of blood among people in such a society, the notions of a cultic shedding of blood in a common sacrifice and the connection with some sort of blood-guilt are apparent. Paul insists that we participate in the blood of Christ; we may need to answer for the body and blood of the Lord (1 Cor 11:27).

The thought is developed further in the letter of Paul to the Romans. "They are justified freely by his grace through the redemption in Christ Jesus, whom God set forth as an expiation, through faith, by his blood, to prove his righteousness because of the forgiveness of sins previously committed, through the forbearance of God" (Rom 3:24-25). Here the redemption is clearly "by his blood." Redemption is something which God does freely out of his love for us. Yet the free choice of God also demanded a visible sign of acceptance of his will. It was by the acceptance of this shedding of blood that the Father manifested his own goodness and that of us also.

By the time the later Pauline letters were written the Pauline expressions had almost become a formula which could be used without further explanation. "In him we have redemption by his blood, the forgiveness of transgression, in accord with the riches of his grace, that he lavished upon us" (Eph 1:7; see also Col 1:19-20). Redemption and blood have become indissolubly united in the Christian interpretation of the final victory over evil. At times, the Cross has become a stand-in for this same bloody consummation (see 1 Cor 1:17, 18; Gal 5:11; 6:12, 14; Eph 2:16; Phil 2:8; 3:18). It is in the great hymn to Christ, the victor in Philippians 2, that this becomes very clear: "He humbled himself, becoming obedient to death, even death on a cross" (Phil 2:8).

Why God the Father should have wanted the bloody death of his Son we do not really know. God is free. As Paul is well aware in Romans, God does not need our advice or our justification. However, for Paul both the once for all death on the cross and the constantly re-enacted Eucharist must be in the blood. It is easy for Paul, then, to carry this into our own lives and see our carrying of the Cross even to the shedding of the blood as a necessary part of our union with the cosmic Redeemer.

Synoptics. The Synoptic Gospels stand as witnesses to the earlier tradition which lies behind them as well as to the developing liturgical usage and interpretation. "Then he took a cup, gave thanks, and gave it to them, saying, 'Drink from it, all of you, for this is my blood of the covenant, which will be shed on behalf of many for the forgiveness of sins'" (Matt 24:27-28; see also Mark 14:24; Luke 22:20). It is not only the affirmation that what is in the cup is his blood; it is also the interpretation that this blood will be shed for many for the forgiveness of sins. That is what the Jewish tradition along with the other great religions had always seen as central to any religious duties: the union with a savior.

John. John's Gospel makes a unique approach. It has no story of the institution of the Eucharist at the Last Supper. Instead John expands the discourse on the Bread of Life. "He gave them bread from heaven to eat," seems to be the keynote from which John develops the theme that the multitude needs a heavenly source of wisdom and life (John 6:31). The bread symbol is central and most easily understood. However, as the discourse in John develops the association of blood comes into the picture from the liturgical usage. When the final dispute breaks out over "How can this man give us his flesh to eat?" (John 6:52), the text has Jesus saying, "Amen, amen, I say to you, unless you eat the flesh of the Son of Man and drink his blood, you do not have life within you" (John 6:53). From then on the eating of the flesh and the drinking of the blood are correlative. The symbolism has shifted somewhat from the Synoptic usage. In the institution texts blood was associated with the forgiveness of sins; in John the first association is with life (John 6:53-56). The giving of eternal life is central in John; it does entail the forgiveness of sins, but that is not pointed out explicitly in these texts. So also the First Letter of John observes: "But if we walk in the light as he is in the light, then we have fellowship with one another, and the blood of his Son Jesus cleanses us from all sin" (1 John 1:7; see also 1 John 5:6, 7).

Apostolic Writings. In the apostolic writings at the end of the NT period the association of blood and redemption is taken for granted as the starting point of practical theology. The First Letter of Peter begins with a reference to the sprinkling of the blood of Jesus Christ (1 Pet 1:2) and goes on to remind his readers that "you were ransomed from your futile conduct, handed on by your ancestors, not with perishable things like silver or gold but with the precious blood of Christ as of a spotless unblemished lamb" (1 Pet 1:18-19). The Letter to the Hebrews makes even greater use of the OT references: "Therefore, Jesus also suffered outside the gate, to consecrate the people by his own blood" (Heb 3:12; see also Heb 13:20). In Revelation it is the saints who have "washed their robes and made them white in the blood of the Lamb" (Rev 7:14; see also Rev 1:5; 5:9; 6:10, 12; 8:7, 8; 11:6; 12:11; 14:20; 16:3, 4, 6; 17:6; 18:24; 19:2, 13).

This is a necessary part of the apocalyptic vision which sees the return of all living things to God.

See: EUCHARIST, FORGIVENESS, SACRIFICE, SIN

JAMES A. FISCHER, C.M.

BODY

Body seems a simple enough word to us in the Roman Catholic theological tradition. It is paired with soul as the other part of the totality of an individual. This is not the usage of the Bible. To the biblical writers body is always one with the totality. Hence, when the word is used in transferred meanings, we may think that we have a quite clear idea of what is being said. The theological implications may shatter on the basic reality of oneness. This is so especially in the NT; the OT has far less problems since the word is not often used in a metaphorical or symbolic way.

Old Testament

The OT has no single word for body. Sometimes names for various parts of the body are used in the Hebrew text which we translate as "body": belly (Mic 6:7), back (Gen 47:18), flesh (Prov 5:11; Isa 10:18), or a more vague "what is palpable" (Dan 5:21). Much of this is a question of translation. Sometimes the translators even use body to translate what in our thinking would not be physical body; e.g., soul (Num 19:13). The Hebrews thought of what they could observe in action without our philosophical or scientific undergirding of parts of the human composite.

Consequently, they do not use the word body to express such ideas as a social body or a corporate body. "People," "nation," "tribe" were more often the word. When Isaiah needs to picture the people of Israel, he thinks of a vine, but not a body (Isa 5:1-7). A number of such comparisons infiltrate the NT, but there is no OT body imagery similar to Pauline usage.

New Testament

Fortunately, the NT uses only one Greek word, *soma,* for body. It has one clear meaning—the physical body; all other meanings are metaphorical extensions of it.

Soma. Soma sometimes refers to the physical body as in the Gospel stories about the corpse of John the Baptist (Matt 14:12), the woman with the hemorrhage (Mark 5:29), the anointing of Jesus by Mary (Matt 26:12; Mark 14:8), or the crucifixion and burial (Matt 27:58, 59; Mark 15:43, 45; Luke 23:52, 55; 24:3, 23; John 19:31, 38, 40; 20:12). Matthew 27:52 has a curious addition to the death of Jesus, "the bodies of many saints who had fallen asleep were raised." We do not know what to make of this, whether it is a factual report or a symbol. The latter is more probable.

Transferred meanings. Transferred meanings of body are rather easily made. Two sets of sayings in Matthew and Luke make use of body comparisons. The so-called sayings on the lilies of the field contrast spiritual goods with bodily ones: "Therefore I tell you, do not worry about your life, what you will eat [or drink], or about your body, what you will wear. Is not life more than food and the body more than clothing?" (Matt 6:25). The second use compares the way the eye works to spiritual insight: "The lamp of the body is the eye. If your eye is sound, your whole body will be filled with light" (Matt 6:25; see Luke 11:34, 36). Luke is more concerned about the negative aspect of darkness invading the body if there is no spiritual insight: "Take care, then, that the light in you not become darkness" (Luke 11:35). Hence, there is an easy application to the need for perseverance, "I tell you, my friends, do not be afraid of those who kill the body but after that can do no more" (Luke 12:4; see Matt 10:28).

Paul. When we come to Paul, the matter becomes much more complex. Paul is typically Semitic, not Hellenistic, in his holistic way of speaking of the body. He never thinks of the body as distinct from the soul, the Spirit, the breath of life; nor can he think of body parts as having individual functions as a podiatrist or ophthamologist might do. Body can only be described by what we do and manifest in our total physical makeup. So flesh, blood, Spirit, body, soul, and breath all represent human activities and can be used of the total creature. On the other hand, there are conflicts in the way we act and these same terms can describe both good and bad tendencies within us.

Paul sometimes uses body in its physical sense. He boasts of bearing the marks of Jesus on his body (Gal 6:17); he uses the conventional "present in body" to denote physical presence (Rom 1:24; 1 Cor 5:3; 2 Cor 12:2, 3). But more often he makes use of transferred meanings. To express his Christian conviction of a future life, he refers to his body as a temporary home (2 Cor 5:6, 8). God can make other kinds of bodies. So Paul speaks in his resurrection theology of spiritual bodies (1 Cor 15:35,

40). So also Paul can emphasize that repulsive word "cross" to concentrate attention on redemption through the body of Christ. "In the same way, my brothers, you also were put to death to the law through the body of Christ" (Rom 7:4; see also Col 1:22).

The unity of the body of Christians among themselves is an easy application from this viewpoint. The elaborate explanation of the functioning of eyes, ears, feet in 1 Corinthians 12:14-24 is a simple illustration of the need for Christians to function as one in Christ. "As the body is one though it has many parts, and all the parts of the body, though many, are one body, so also Christ" (1 Cor 12:12). In a somewhat similar way: "Do you not know that your body is a temple of the holy Spirit within you, whom you have from God, and that you are not your own?" (1 Cor 6:19). This same body metaphor is used, though less extensively, in Romans 12:4-8.

The body of Christ as affecting individual Christians in their way of acting physically is first alluded to in 1 Corinthians 6:15, "Do you not know that your bodies are members of Christ?" In the later Captivity Letters the insight is developed that Christians united as Church act as the body of Christ. "Rather, living the truth in love, we should grow in every way into him who is the head, Christ, from whom the whole body, joined and held together by every supporting ligament, with the proper functioning of each part, brings about the body's growth and builds itself up in love" (Eph 4:15-16). So the body of Christ affects the way in which we suffer (Col 1:24), love (Eph 5:30), and minister (Eph 4:12). Of body in this sense it is Christ who is the head (Col 1:18; Eph 1:22-23).

Paul, however, is no dreamer. Like the wise men of the OT he is acutely aware of the conflicts within ourselves. These can be illustrated by what we see in our physical actions. The body (or sometimes "the flesh" as he calls it) can stand for everything perverse deep within us. "For if you live according to the flesh, you will die, but if by the spirit you put to death the deeds of the body, you will live" (Rom 8:13). Paul himself had experience of that conflict. He ends the self-revelation of his weakness by crying: "Miserable one that I am! Who will deliver me from this mortal body?" (Rom 7:24).

On the other hand, redemption is seen as affecting us totally and the body shares in this glory. 1 Corinthians 15 is a protest against those who would spiritualize our resurrection into a mystical experience. It is not just spiritual salvation for our souls; it is the reality of glorified total existence. "So also is the resurrection of the dead. It is sown corruptible; it is raised incorruptible. It is sown dishonorable; it is raised glorious. It is sown weak; it is raised powerful. It is sown a natural body; it is raised a spiritual body. If there is a natural body, there is also a spiritual one" (1 Cor 15:42-44).

This is extended to all creation. In one startling passage Paul says, "We know that all creation is groaning in labor pains even until now; and not only that, but we ourselves, who have the firstfruits of the Spirit, we also groan within ourselves as we wait for adoption, the redemption of our bodies" (Rom 8:22-23; see also 1 Thess 5:23; Rom 8:10; 1 Cor 6:13; 7:34; 15:40; 2 Cor 4:10; Phil 1:20; 3:21; Col 2:17). The unity of our bodily existence embraces not only everything we do but all creation; and that is all redeemed in glory.

The Eucharist is a particular point of emphasis for application of the body imagery to a spiritual reality. It was obviously difficult to explain the sayings of Jesus about giving his body and blood (see 1 Cor 11:24 for the words of institution; the Gospel passages in Matt 26:26; Mark 14:22; and Luke 22:19 are all influenced by later liturgical formulas). The reality was firmly in the tradition, but the significance had to be developed. Paul addresses the question in 1 Corinthians in discussing the abuses connected with the celebration of a cultic meal. He uses the body comparison as a reminder of how individual parts are always united. "As the body is one though it has many parts, and all the parts of the body, though

many, are one body, so also Christ" (1 Cor 12:12). This is not simply an image; the warnings against abuses invoke the reality of blood guilt. "Therefore, whoever eats the bread or drinks the cup of the Lord unworthily, will have to answer for the body and blood of the Lord" (1 Cor 11:27; see also 11:29).

Apostolic Writings. In the later apostolic writings "body" is not much used. It occurs in the conventional physical sense in Hebrews 10:5; 13:3, 11; James 2:16; 3:3, 6; Jude 9. It is related to redemption through the body of Jesus in 1 Peter 2:24; Hebrews 10:5, 10 and in the punch line of James 2:26: "For just as a body without a spirit is dead, so also faith without works is dead."

Pastoral-Liturgical Tradition

It is noteworthy that the use of body to explain the faith concentrated largely on the emphasis of spiritual realities which were almost as palpable as a physical body. Christianity was not presented in the beginning as a philosophical explanation; it was simply a matter of past experience and future hope and that of the most earthy sort. Converts accepted as a savior a Jew who had been crucified; they understood the resurrection teaching not simply as a factual report but as a statement of the reality of the presence of the resurrected Lord among them and a hope of future sharing in complete human life. It was presence, the presence of the Lord Jesus, which differentiated those of the Way from those who found God in the Temple or from the Gentiles who desperately strove to find God anywhere, the "Unknown God" whom Paul mentioned in Athens (Acts 17:23).

In Medieval times it was the Eucharist which was stressed as the great unifying and ennobling ideal in society. The "real presence" was the nub of this belief. While theologians struggled with a philosophical explanation which was finally termed "transubstantiation," it was the people who united in the *Corpus Christi* celebrations, in various societies of the Blessed Sacrament and devotions to the Eucharistic presence, such as building cathedrals. Perhaps it was overdone at times, but it certainly united people in the awareness of the presence of Jesus among us.

Vatican II has stressed the unity of all humans beyond the simple bounds of the Church. Yet it has recognized the unique role of the Church as the worshiping community. The liturgy is the center and summit of all the activity of the Church. The center of the liturgy is the act of making Christ's body and blood physically present in a sacrificial manner upon our altars. And this has extended his presence into all things physical. The council's (Vatican II) concern with the world and its environment derives from this conviction of the abiding presence of God in all physical and spiritual things. Body (like blood) is not a medical concept; it is a spiritual vision of the wholeness of all creatures, "For in him all the fullness was pleased to dwell, and through him to reconcile all things for him, making peace by the blood of his cross [through him], whether those on earth or those in heaven" (Col 1:19-20).

See: BLOOD, FLESH, LIFE, SOUL, SPIRIT

JAMES A. FISCHER, C.M.

BODY OF CHRIST

Drawing on Paul's bold metaphor, the term "body of Christ" remains one of the most powerful and fruitful metaphors for the mystery of the Church.

New Testament

The NT image of "the Body of Christ" expresses its theological meaning on three mutually interpenetrating levels.

The Historical Body. On the first and basic level the image refers to the crucified Jesus. Paul has this reference in mind when he writes, "You died to the Law through the body of Christ" (Rom 7:4). Paul here is also alluding to the participation or solidarity of believers with Jesus in this crucifixion, as he explicitly describes in Galatians

2:19, "I have been crucified [literally, "concrucified"] with Christ", but this solidarity presupposes the historical dying body of Jesus. Colossians 1:22 repeats the idea, "Now, you are reconciled in the body of his flesh through death."

For Paul the mortal body of Christ does not represent an immaculate sacrifice* but rather a place where the power of sin is concentrated and eventually destroyed through the death of that body. The involved context of Romans 7:4 presupposes some identification of the body of Christ with the tyrannical Law, which must die to bring about the widow's liberation. Romans 8:3 speaks of the earthly life of Jesus as the very "likeness [better translated: "model," *homoiôma*] of sinful flesh" (see also Gal 3:13).

1 Peter expresses the same associations while nuancing the presence of sin in the body of Christ. After insisting on the impeccable conduct of Jesus (1 Pet 2:22-23), the letter continues, "He carried our sins in his body on the cross, in order that we, having died to sin, might live for justice" (2:24). 1 Peter insists on the distinction between *our* sins and *his* body. The allusion throughout this section is to the innocent suffering servant of Isaiah 53, who carries our infirmities in a process of vicarious redemption.

In a curious "misquotation" of Psalm 40 (LXX 39), Hebrews refers to the "body" prepared by God for Christ as the replacement of "sacrifice and offerings" (10:5). The author then concludes, "We have been sanctified once and for all through the offering of the body of Jesus Christ" (10:10).

The meaning of "body" in these texts is essentially the Jewish sense which is basically the same as "person." As translating the Hebrew *basar* along with several other words, the Greek word *sôma* in the Septuagint most generally means the human being, usually as an object of some action (Lev 14:9; Job 7:5). At times *sôma* functions like a personal pronoun (Job 6:4) or a reflexive pronoun (Prov 11:17; Dan 3:95). Only in late OT writings, especially those outside the Hebrew canon, is *sôma* spoken of as a part of the human being, e.g., as distinguished from *psychê* (see 2 Macc 7:37; Wis 8:20). In some texts of the NT where *sôma* is contrasted specifically with *melos* ("member", Matt 5:29), the word "body" takes on a specifically Hellenistic sense of "totality." However, none of these later Greek nuances are present in the above NT texts about the body of Christ.

The Social Body. In contrast, Paul and the deutero-Pauline authors draw from a specifically Greek or Hellenistic background of the term when they refer to the Christians as a body (Rom 12:4-5; 1 Cor 10:17; 11:29; 12:13, 25) and specifically "the body of Christ" (1 Cor 12:27; Eph 4:12; Col 2:17). Nowhere in the OT does "body" have this meaning.

On the other hand, examples abound of Greek and Roman writers who use *sôma* or *corpus* to refer to a group of people or some other totality of individual things. Philosophers discussed the difference between a "body" in which the parts or members do not exist on their own (the body of an animal) and one in which they do (the body of the senate). Philo noted that the cosmos could be called the greatest body of all. In these writings "body" is distinguished from "member" as "totality" is from "part."

Troubled by their factious spirit, in 1 Corinthians Paul repeatedly reminds the Corinthians that they are a body (12:12-29). In so doing he stresses the very need for differences in the community, particularly differences arising from the gifts of the Spirit and the corresponding roles within the community (12:14-20, 29-30). At the same time Paul can stress the mutual dependence of all members of the community (12:21-22). With this same imagery Paul likewise warns against seeking any hierarchy of honor within the community (12:23-26). This body Paul calls "the body of Christ" (12:27) or simply "Christ" (12:12).

In this identification, however, Paul must develop a "corporate" concept different than that used in his Hellenistic culture. For Paul, Christ exists before the community came to be. Hence the community as a totality of individuals do not make the body of Christ, but rather the body of Christ makes the community, the body constitutes the members, not vice versa. Paul stresses the divine origin of this body. "God has set each member of the body in the place he wanted it to be" (12:18). "God constructed the body" (12:24). Individuals are "incorporated" into the body, a process which Paul describes in terms of baptism and the Spirit: "It was in one Spirit that all of us . . . were baptized into one body" (1 Cor 12:13). The Spirit is the source of the mutually supportive roles by which the members function as a body (12:7-11).

The idea of the community being formed into the body of Christ is basically the ecclesial spinoff of Paul's idea of existence "in Christ," the idea of participating in the redemption that took place first in Christ and that now can begin in us to the extent we live by the Spirit in the risen Lord (Romans 8). When dealing again with the diverse and mutually dependent functions in the community, Paul can say, "We are all one body in Christ" (Rom 12:4). The motif "in Christ" by itself, however, is used to minimize differences among Christians (Gal 3:28), whereas, "the body of Christ" or "the body in Christ" accommodates differences in an organic unity.

By speaking of the community as the body of Christ, Paul can likewise insist on the need for selfless love and care within the community. Harming a member of the community is equivalent to harming Christ (1 Cor 8:12). Paul sees the duty of sexual morality likewise as a consequence of this existence as a member of Christ (1 Cor 6:15).

More so than any other image, the body of Christ evokes a strong sense of unity among all Christians. As used by Paul the word "church" (*ekklêsia*) does not of itself suggest a single universal reality. In fact Paul frequently refers to the many churches. Behind these churches, distinguished usually according to cities, the very work of Paul along with a variety of motifs in his letters suggest some network uniting these churches into something analogous to Israel as a People of God, even though scattered throughout the world. Among these motifs, "the body of Christ" is one of the most expressive. Never used in the plural, explicitly emphasizing the intense internal unity of a community, this theme in Paul implies a way in which the various churches around the world form a totality unified in the very unity of Christ himself.

In Colossians and Ephesians this theme of universal Church* unity becomes explicit. In Colossians "the Church" appears on three levels, a house church (4:15), a city church (4:16), and most striking as a universal Church, which, as such, is consistently and explicitly identified with the body of Christ (1:18, 24). Ephesians, where again we see the identification of the Church with the body of Christ (1:22; 5:23), speaks of the Church only as a universal reality (see also 2:10, 21; 5:24-32).

In these two letters likewise the priority of Christ over the Church becomes explicit in the image of Christ as "head" of this body (Col 1:18; Eph 1:22; 5:23). The description of Christ as head of his body the Church is clearly meant to evoke the biological relationship between head and torso, a relationship used in Hellenistic writing to describe that of the emperor to the state. However, the Greek of the NT frequently echoes its Jewish background, where the Hebrew word for "head," *rosh*, rings with a nuance of "source." Christ is the origin of the Church.

In both Ephesians and Colossians the ecclesial Body of Christ is growing and developing, through the pastoral service of leaders (Eph 4:11-13) and by the loving energy of each and every member (Eph 4:15-16). Paul, or someone writing in Paul's name, describes this dynamic process as nothing other than continuation of the redemptive mission of the historical Christ, "In my own flesh I fill up what is lacking in the sufferings of Christ for the sake of his body, the church" (Col 1:24).

The Body of the Lord's Supper. When Jesus broke and distributed bread at the beginning of his last supper, he identified the bread, "This is my body" (Matt 26:26; Mark 14:22; Luke 22:19; 1 Cor 11:24). According to the Jewish concept of "body," Jesus was identifying the broken bread with himself—not a part of himself, but his human totality. The words of Jesus were the equivalent of "This is me." Spoken with the gesture of offering food on the night before his death, the words pick up the sense of a selfless gift for the sake of the disciples.

When the tradition behind Luke and Paul adds the words describing the body as "given for you" or simply "for you," this tradition simply renders explicit the sense implied in Jesus' gesture. The bread represents Jesus giving himself for the sake of the disciples, as one devotes oneself "for" another.

By the time these words were written down in the NT, they were brought into immediate parallel with the words Jesus spoke at the end of the dinner, as he distributed the final cup of wine, "This is my blood, the blood of the covenant, to be poured out in behalf of many" (Matt 26:28; Mark 14:24) or, "This cup is the new covenant in my blood, which will be shed for you" (Luke 22:20; see 1 Cor 11:25). The reference to violent death is unmistakable ("blood shed"). The death as covenant sacrifice with atoning power is likewise clear in these words. The words and gestures with the bread and those with the wine were no longer seen as two separate gestures but one single gift. The "body" of Jesus is thus presented as a representation of Jesus' sacrificial death on the cross.

The stylized description of Jesus' words and gestures suggests that the farewell dinner of Jesus had been ritualized by the communities for whom these Gospels were written. The words found in Luke and Paul, "do this in remembrance of me," confirms this suggestion. Paul in fact gives us a description of this ritualized repetition of Jesus' distribution of his "body" and "blood," which he names "the Lord's Supper" (1 Cor 11:17-34; see 10:16-17).

Actually what Paul describes are abuses at the Lord's Supper, specifically the selfish divisions which are addressed all through 1 Corinthians. In the strongest terms Paul calls the Corinthians to a loving unity by reminding them that the Lord's Supper is precisely the celebration of the body of Christ.

With deliberate ambiguity Paul shifts between the "Eucharistic" body and the social body of Christ in order to insist on the inseparable character binding the two. Speaking of the Lord's Supper in chapter 10, Paul describes the Corinthians as participating in the Blood and Body of Christ through the cup and the bread (10:16). Referring then to the community, he immediately declares, "We all are one body" (10:17). In the next chapter, again speaking of the Lord's Supper and describing the Corinthians' selfish and unsharing comportment at this event, Paul warns against becoming "guilty of the body and blood of the Lord" (11:27). Two verses later when he pinpoints their failure as "not recognizing the body" (11:29), Paul almost certainly is again referring to the community and the failure of the Corinthians to see that they are the body of Christ. The shift from one meaning of "body" to the other is the same as that in chapter 10 only with an ambiguity that suggests the mutual dependence. Only as one body of Christ can they worthily celebrate the "Eucharistic" body of Christ. Conversely the Corinthians become one body "because all eat of the one bread" (10:17).

If the body of Christ in the Lord's Supper blends with the historical body of Christ which carried our sins on the cross, so likewise the Body of Christ in the Lord's Supper blends with the communitarian body of Christ. Each level draws its meaning from the other and completes the other.

See: BAPTISM, BLOOD, CHURCH, COMMUNITY, COVENANT, EUCHARIST, FLESH, MEAL, PEOPLE OF GOD, REDEMPTION, SACRIFICE, SPIRIT, WORLD

VINCENT P. BRANICK

Pastoral-Liturgical Tradition

In John, as in the Pauline teaching in the NT, the body of Christ refers to the physical humanity of Jesus, the Word* made flesh (John 1:14). Paul teaches that insofar as Jews or Gentiles enter into the mystery of the incarnation and life, passion, and resurrection of Christ, they are delivered from the body of sin and death. Through faith in the Christ they are incorporated into the Church,* the body of Christ, and share in the Body of Christ, the Eucharist.* From the first to the ninth centuries the Body of Christ referred to both the Church and to the Eucharist.

The Human Body of Christ. In Paul's theology the reality of Jesus' bodiliness is the basis for the Christian community. When the Word became flesh, when Christ put on the garment of his body, his humanity revealed his solidarity with the human race and the invisible power of God to offer salvation for humanity. Through the body that the Word assumed, Jesus healed so that humanity might be healed. Through his bodily death and resurrection the Christ raised our human solidarity to a spiritual unity with himself; he incorporated us into the Church; he gave us a pledge of resurrection.

The body *(soma),* refers to the whole person and the potential of the whole personality which was made by and for God. This sense of body knits together all the themes of Pauline theology. "It is from the body of sin and death that we are delivered; it is through the body of Christ on the Cross that we are saved; it is into His body the Church that we are incorporated; it is by His body in the Eucharist that this community is sustained; it is in our body that its new life has to be manifested; it is to a resurrection of this body to the likeness of His glorious body that we are destined" (Robinson).

The Church as the Body of Christ. What Christ in his body did on the cross is reproduced in the life of Christians, the Body of Christ. Paul would say that Christians have put off the body of flesh *(sarx),* that they

105

have been circumcised in the circumcision of Christ (Col 2:11), that they have died in, with, and through the crucified body of Christ. Thus the Church, beginning in holy baptism and continuing in both the Eucharist and in shared life together, shares in his death "once for all" (Rom 6:10). Baptized into one body (1 Cor 12:13), all Christians have been made dead to the Law (Rom 7:4) and have begun to walk a new way that builds up the body of Christ (Eph 4:12-16). To share in the body of Christ means that the Church must grow to fill out the whole Christ, the fullness of the cosmic Christ (Eph 1:23). The lives of Christians will be marked by the nail marks of the Cross (Gal 2:20; 6:14-17) and apostolic suffering (Phil 3:7-11; Col 1:24).

The Body of Christ as the Eucharist.
Those who have been incorporated into the body of Christ through baptism share an interdependent life. Their union is due to their sharing in the one Spirit (1 Cor 12:13). Thus the members engage one another in order that they may be transformed, may walk in the likeness of Christ (2 Cor 3:18). This communal life of the body of Christ is sustained and renewed in the celebration of the Eucharist. To share in the Eucharist is to have participation or shared life in the Body of Christ (1 Cor 10:16). This ritual action becomes a source of union with Christ and one another; ritual behavior requires that the assembled body of Christ overcome division (1 Cor 11:18-22). Furthermore, sharing in the Lord's body is to share in his life and to continue the new covenant* at the table of the Lord (1 Cor 11:23-25). The Eucharist is the ritual act in which the Church concretizes its connection with the risen Lord. The Eucharist becomes a memorial of the sacrificial death of Jesus (1 Cor 11:25) and it points the Church toward an eschatological proclamation of the Lord's death until he comes again (1 Cor 11:26).

The nature of the Eucharistic action both demands and causes the Church to put on the qualities of its head and Lord (Col 1:18; Eph 1:22; 4:15). Eucharistic hospitality requires that the assembly attend to the needs of one another when it gathers (1 Cor 11:17-34). It calls for a hospitality that acknowledges a variety of gifts among its members (1 Cor 12:4-13) and that it attend to its least and suffering members (1 Cor 12:26). Compassion, mutual support and concern, a spirit of welcome to strangers and guests, a spirit of love all flow from an active participation in the Eucharistic Body of Christ (Rom 12:4-13).

The Body of Christ in the World Today.
The body of the risen Christ remains the source of holiness for the Church as it attends to the indwelling of Christ in its members and as its members actively share in the sacraments, especially the Eucharist. Sharing at the table of the Eucharist challenges the Church to encourage the gifts of all, to eliminate forms of discrimination (Gal 3:27-29), to widen doorways of welcome in order to be in solidarity with other Christians, and to relate the action of the Eucharist to the deepest hungers of the suffering least and poor in the world. When the local Church or the world Church excommunicates itself from the heartache of the world today and closes in on itself, it ceases to be a leaven in the world and it fails to fulfill its task of proclaiming the death of the Lord until he comes again. Both the local Church and the world Church then show their nakedness and shame since they may have put off Christ, and may have drifted back into a bodiliness that is distant from God. In these instances the Church is called to repentance and a conversion that calls forth a largesse of heart.

See: CHRIST, CHURCH, COMMUNITY, COVENANT, FOOD, JUSTICE, MEAL

JOHN J. O'BRIEN, C.P.

BOOK OF LIFE

The book of life is the heavenly register of the elect, the righteous, or the citizens of God's kingdom. It records the names of those favored by God and privileged to live in the heavenly Jerusalem.

Two distinct ideas may have contributed to the image of the book of life in the Bible. First, there is the belief (already well developed in antiquity) that all human activity is not only observed by the deity but also recorded in heaven. In ancient Egypt, for example, the god Thoth was credited with keeping records for the gods. Israel too assumed that a record of human deeds was kept in heaven (Ps 139:16; Dan 7:10).

Second, membership in any community must be delimited. It is important to know who belongs and who does not. This is one of the functions of the genealogies* recorded in Scripture (Gen 5:1-32; 10:1-32; 11:10-30; Exod 6:14-25). Membership within Israel became especially important after the Exile, when the purity of the people and the priesthood was at stake (Ezra 2:59-63; 10:1-44; Neh 7:6-65; 10:31; 13:1-3, 23-30).

In the OT the only occurrence of the expression "book of life" occurs in Psalm 69:29. Here the psalmist prays that the wicked "be erased from the book of the living, and not be recorded with the just!" To be erased from the book of the living is to die.

Scattered throughout the OT, however, are references to a record of those who have a special relationship with God. In Exodus 32:32 Moses begs God to "strike me out of the book that you have written." Isaiah 4:3 speaks of those "marked down for life in Jerusalem." Ezekiel 13:9 threatens the false prophets that they shall not "be recorded in the register of the house of Israel." See also Daniel 12:1; Malachi 3:16; and Psalm 87:6.

The NT continues the tradition of a heavenly record of the elect (Luke 10:20; Phil 4:3; Heb 12:23). This image is especially notable in the Book of Revelation. A distinction is made between those recorded in the book of life (the persevering faithful) and those not found there (Rev 3:5; 13:8; 17:8). This heavenly book will become especially significant at the Last Judgment. Then it will be opened, and all shall be judged according to their deeds. Those whose names do not appear in this register will be thrown into the pool of fire (Rev 20:12, 15), while those listed will be able to enter the new Jerusalem (Rev 21:27).

The book of life symbolizes divine omniscience and providence.* Those who are faithful are recognized and rewarded by God. However, this is no divine bookkeeper who eagerly awaits a mistake in order to pounce and punish. Rather we are assured of God's interest in humanity and of the accomplishment of the divine purpose. One might catch a hint of predestination (Rev 13:8; 17:8; 20:15). Yet the emphasis is not on a predetermined list but on the divine remembrance of the faithful. For it is possible to be eliminated from the book of life (Exod 32:32; Ezek 13:9; Rev 3:5), just as it is possible to be added to its register (Ps 87:6).

See: EXILE, GENEALOGY, ISRAEL, PRIEST/PRIESTHOOD, PROVIDENCE

TIMOTHY A. LENCHAK, S.V.D.

BORN AGAIN

In the OT, God gives birth to his people through the Exodus and a rebirth through the return from Exile. The prophets of Israel announce a future rebirth of Israel. The NT, especially the Fourth Gospel, teaches that this is fulfilled through Jesus' baptism of the holy Spirit.

Old Testament

The OT does not use the precise expression "born again." God himself gave birth to the people of Israel. God commanded Moses to tell Pharaoh, "Israel is my son, my first-born" (Exod 4:22). God proved Israel to be this child through the miraculous Exodus from Egypt, yet God complained, "You were unmindful of the Rock that begot you, you forgot the God who gave you birth" (Deut 32:18). However, Israel's later return from the Exile will be like a new birth. Using the image of a miraculous heart transplant, the prophet Ezekiel announces that the Spirit of God will give the people a new heart and a new life (36:26-28). In the Exile, the people will be figuratively dead in their graves, yet the Spirit will bring their dry bones to life again and return them to their own land (Ezek 37:1-14). Jewish writers close to NT times used the rebirth image to describe Gentile proselytes' conversion to Judaism: they should start life over again as if new born children.

New Testament

The Gospels of Matthew, Mark, and Luke contain no exact expression of new or second birth. However, they often refer to a return to childhood. This implies a new beginning and a break from the past. In Matthew, Jesus introduces his discipleship discourse by presenting the model of children: "Amen, I say to you, unless you turn and become like children, you will not enter the kingdom of heaven" (18:3). In Mark, Jesus embraces and blesses little children as models for discipleship (9:33-37; 10:13-16). In Luke, Jesus' own birth becomes a model for believers. Luke also presents children as models for discipleship to introduce his journey narrative (9:46-48). Then he repeats the theme near the end of that narrative in 18:15-17. The Synoptic Gospels also present the equivalent of a new birth in the seed parables where the divine seed or word of God entering into peoples' hearts is the principle of a new moral life (Matt 13:18-23 and parallels).

The words "born again" occur in John only where Jesus tells Nicodemus, "Amen, Amen, I say to you, no one can see the kingdom of God without being born from above" (3:3). On Jesus' lips, the words have a double meaning, either "born from above" or "born again." Without enlightenment, Nicodemus understands them in pure earthly terms and asks Jesus, "How can a person once grown old be born again? Surely he cannot re-enter his mother's womb and be born again, can he?" (3:4). Jesus explains the higher sense of a new birth made possible by a divine principle: "Amen I say to you, no one can enter the kingdom of God without being born of water* and Spirit" (3:5). A birth from the flesh and a birth from the Spirit are entirely distinct (3:6). John's Gospel

later shows that this Spirit will come through Jesus' death. The water issuing from his side will be a sign of this effect (19:34; see Jesus' promise in 7:37-39).

Other NT texts describe the divine principle of new birth in various ways, either through the divine Word or the Spirit. The First Letter of John emphasizes the outward manifestation in lifestyle: "No one who is begotten by God commits sin, because God's seed remains in him; he cannot sin because he is begotten by God" (3:9). Paul emphasizes the action of the Spirit: "As proof that you are children, God sent the spirit of his Son into our hearts, crying out, 'Abba, Father'" (Gal 4:6; see Rom 8:15-16). A "born again" Christian is therefore not a special type of believer in contrast to other Christians. The Spirit brings about a moral regeneration and a transformed lifestyle. Paul sees every Christian as "born again" in his description of baptism.* He writes to the Romans: "you have become obedient from the heart to the pattern of teaching to which you were entrusted" (6:17). This "pattern of teaching" was given during the time that adult catechumens learned the Christian way of life through special teachers who lived for a time in the neophytes' homes so that they could learn by living example. The actual baptismal rite was the culmination of a long period of preparation and initiation. Paul considered the holy Spirit to be a dynamic transformational force that embodied God's own love for people, especially those who seemed less deserving: "The love of God has been poured out into our hearts through the holy Spirit that has been given to us" (Rom 5:5). This love, which is the love of Christ, prompted him even to die for sinners and the unjust (Rom 5:6-10).

The Letter to Titus emphasizes the moral transformation brought about by the Spirit: "He [God our Savior] saved us through the bath of rebirth and renewal by the holy Spirit" (3:5). The Letter of James emphasizes new birth through the word as the source of productive action: "He willed to give us birth by the word of truth that we may be a kind of firstfruits of his creatures" (1:18). Believers must be "doers of the word and not hearers only" (1:22). The First Letter of Peter describes practical love of others as a result of the word's power to effect a true rebirth: "Since you have purified yourselves by obedience to the truth for sincere mutual love, love one another intensely from a [pure] heart. You have been born anew, not from perishable but from imperishable seed, through the living and abiding word of God" (1:22-23). Consequently, believers should be like newborn infants who long for pure spiritual milk (2:2).

Pastoral-Liturgical Tradition

"Born again" terminology is part of effective teaching when explained in terms of Spirit, word, and moral transformation. The liturgy emphasizes this theme by calling upon believers to renew frequently their own baptismal promises. This takes place whenever a baptism is performed. Lent and Easter are times of intense effort to join with catechumens in dedicated prayer and action. Each Sunday is a weekly Easter celebration when the baptismal action is renewed through repentance, forgiveness, and union with Christ.

See: BAPTISM, EXILE, EXODUS, FATHER, SPIRIT, WATER, WORD

JOSEPH A. GRASSI

BREAD

Bread is a major element in human diet. Indeed bread is used in the Bible as a general term for food (2 Sam 9:10; 2 Kgs 25:3). When God comes in judgment on Israel, God withholds this "staff of life" (Lev 26:26). Thus bread came to be used in the Bible to depict some human conditions or situations, e.g., "the bread of tears" (Ps 80:6); "the bread of wickedness" (Prov 4:17); "the bread you need" (Isa 30:20); "our daily bread" (Matt 6:11; Luke 11:3).

Old Testament

Symbol of Hospitality. Bread serves as a symbol of bonding both strangers and friends. Thus Melchizedek offers the victorious Abram bread and wine* (Gen 14:18). Similarly Abraham welcomes his heavenly visitors by providing bread in the form of rolls (Gen 18:6). By sharing bread offered by another, one enters into a relationship with the host. To betray a host is to violate the sacredness of the relationship implied in the sharing of bread. The psalmist captures this dimension when he laments: "Even my friend who had my trust and partook of my bread, has raised his heel against me" (Ps 41:10).

Symbol of Covenant-making. One way of ratifying a covenant was a communal meal where bread obviously figured prominently. Thus Laban and Jacob seal their relationship by sharing a meal together: "When they had eaten [bread], they passed the night on the mountain" (Gen 31:54). The covenant-making on Mount Sinai takes place with a variety of traditions and not surprisingly a communal meal has a conspicuous place. One such tradition represents the Lord as the tribal leader who accepts Moses and the clan leaders into his family. By sharing a communal meal, Israel commits itself to the Lord (Exod 24:9-11).

Liturgical Use. It is significant that bread used in liturgy had to be made of wheat, not barley flour (Exod 29:2, 40). Since wheat was a more precious commodity than barley, only the former was deemed worthy in religious services. Since leavened bread smacked of impurity, only unleavened bread was permitted in liturgy (Exod 23:18; 34:25). The showbread was extremely meaningful. According to Leviticus 24:5-9 twelve cakes of pure wheaten flour were arranged in two lines on a table before the holy of holies and were renewed on every Sabbath. It is likely that the bread symbolized the God of Israel as the provider of bread. The twelve cakes recalled the covenant between the Lord and the twelve tribes of Israel. Bread functioned as a way of reminding Israel of its allegiance to the Lord and the terms of the covenant.

New Testament

The Messianic Banquet. The OT speaks on more than one occasion of the consummation of God's plan for his people in terms of a banquet (Isa 25:6-8; 65:13-14). The NT frequently makes use of the same image to describe the consummation of God's reign (Matt 8:11-12; Luke 13:28-29; Rev 3:20). In his parable of the great dinner, Luke makes special mention of bread: "One of his fellow guests . . . said to him, 'Blessed is the one who will dine [lit. eat bread] in the kingdom of God'" (Luke 14:15). This image of eating bread conjures up the OT notions of covenantal friendship and community. Eating bread in the reign of God is the fulfillment of the believer's aspirations. Bread thereby reconfirms the link between God and the individual in the setting of community.

The Loaves Section (Mark 6:31–8:26). In this section Mark makes frequent mention of bread. In the first multiplication of loaves and fish Jesus has compassion on the crowds and goes on to feed more than five thousand with five loaves and two fish. The miracle displays Jesus' messianic mission, and the setting in the desert (Mark 6:35) recalls the Lord's providing for Israel in the desert, viz., the manna (Exod 16:32). Unlike the first feeding that took place in Jewish territory (Mark 6:34-44), the second feeding in Mark 8:1-10 occurs in Gentile territory. Jesus' feeding of both Jews and Gentiles demonstrates the universal thrust of his mission. The bread captures the Markan Jesus' intent to meet the needs of both Jews and Gentiles. For Mark, not to understand the loaves is not to understand Jesus' mission. Mark makes this point in 6:52: "They had not understood the incident of the loaves."

In the account of the leaven (Mark 8:14-21) Jesus warns the disciples against imitating the leaven of the Pharisees and Herod, i.e., their inimical attitude toward Jesus. Finally, in the story of the Syrophoenician woman (Mark 7:24-30) the request for bread is a request for Jesus to meet the needs of Gentiles as well as Jews. In these instances, therefore, bread is employed to identify the person and mission of Jesus.

The Eucharist. In 1 Corinthians 11:17-34 Paul takes up the issue of Eucharist* in Corinth and, in so doing, mentions the tradition he had received for the words of institution. In the same letter (10:16-17) he underlines the role of the bread in the context of the Christian community: "Because the loaf of bread is one, we, though many, are one body, for we all partake of the one loaf." Here Paul speaks of common-union or shared-union (koinonia). By sharing the one loaf, i.e., the one bread that is the body of Christ, believers do in fact become a body or community. Though they are diverse because of a multiplicity of gifts, they are also a unity. For Paul sharing the bread in the Eucharist is sharing the concerns and needs of the community. To that extent this bread has the capacity to draw believers together despite their apparent differences.

In their descriptions of the Last Supper the Synoptics link the words of institution with the person and career of Jesus. In Mark 14:22-24 the loaf is now Jesus' very self, his body. For Mark this is the body that will be handed over, beaten, and finally killed. The loaf of bread is now a powerful symbol of Jesus' death for others. In Matthew 26:26-28 the broken loaf is proclaimed the broken body of Jesus. Matthew, however, underlines the covenantal dimension of the Eucharist. By eating of the bread and drinking of the cup, the disciple shares in that bond that surpasses Israel and Sinai. In Luke 22:19-20 Jesus says: "'This is my body, which will be given for you. . . .' And likewise the cup: 'This cup is the new covenant in my blood. . . .'" By using the words "for you," the Lucan Jesus makes clear that Jesus' death is not an arbitrary tragedy but a self-giving for those he loves. Both the bread and the cup remind the believer that Jesus' death is for him/her.

In the Gospel of John there is no institution of the Eucharist at the Last Supper. However, this Gospel develops the miracle of the loaves and fish in terms of Jesus as the heavenly bread (John 6:35-59). Jesus describes himself as the bread of life. It is no longer a question of the manna* or "bread from heaven" or even "the bread of God." By accepting Jesus as the bread of life, the believer will no longer hunger. Toward the end of the discourse Jesus announces: "For my flesh is true food, and my blood is true drink" (John 6:55). This is probably the Eucharistic formula used in the Johannine community. Finally the discourse concludes with: "whoever eats this bread will live forever" (John 6:58). There is thus a decided contrast between the Christian community that possesses the "bread from heaven" and the Jewish opponents of Jesus whose ancestors fed on the manna but subsequently died. For John the symbol of bread is Christologically central to the entire mystery of Jesus.

"Breaking of the bread" (Acts 2:42, 46; 20:7, 11; 27:35) is probably a technical term for Eucharist. Originally this gesture began a festive Jewish meal and perhaps is the sense of the passage describing the Risen One at Emmaus: "he was made known to them in the breaking of the bread" (Luke 24:35). It is worth noting that in Acts 2:42 the breaking of the bread is associated with the teaching of the apostles, the communal life, and the prayer.

See: COVENANT, DESERT, EUCHARIST, MANNA

JOHN F. CRAGHAN

Pastoral-Liturgical Tradition

Because of its association with Jesus' table fellowship at the Last Supper and during his public ministry, bread became one of the central symbols of Eucharistic worship. The word "bread," used as a synecdoche for food in general, also highlights the divine/human cooperation necessary for God to nourish humanity, both physically and spiritually. Just as God provides the grain, and human labor and skill produce bread, the "staff of life," so the divine, life-giving presence is manifested to the world through the lives of human beings. For Christians, Jesus Christ as "the bread of life" is the primordial paradigm of this divine/human "working together" or synergism. It is not surprising, therefore, that a brief examination of how Eucharistic bread was regarded by the Church through the centuries illustrates developments in both Christology and ecclesiology.

The Subapostolic and Patristic Period (Second to Seventh Centuries). While Jesus most probably identified himself with unleavened wheat bread at the Last Supper, evidence from the first several centuries suggests that Christians did not attach particular importance to the use of unleavened bread at the Eucharist.* Because the faithful brought bread from their own homes and presented the loaves at the Eucharistic assembly along with other gifts for the poor, it is most probable that this bread was leavened.

While the early Church was not overly concerned with the leavened or unleavened nature of the bread, what was done ritually with it became the focus of liturgical/theological examination. Both in the writings of the NT and those of the subapostolic period, the "breaking of the bread" was synonymous with the Eucharistic worship of the Church. This action of breaking the bread is beautifully highlighted in the ninth chapter of the Didache, a document which dates from the first part of the second century: "Just as the bread broken was first scattered on the hills, then was gathered and became one, so let your Church be gathered from the ends of the earth into your kingdom" (9:4). This emphasis on the unity of the Church founded on Christ, symbolized by the breaking and sharing of the "eucharistized" bread identified with the presence of the risen One, reflects an understanding of Eucharist as corporate worship which both celebrates and promotes the oneness of all who believe in Christ.

Because of the sacrificial interpretation attached to Eucharistic worship during the later patristic period, the elements of bread and wine over which the thanksgiving of the community was said were increasingly referred to as the *oblata* or *prosphorá* (offerings). While the bread was still generally leavened, care was taken to enlist the skill of master bakers in its preparation and it thus became distinguishable from the ordinary bread brought by the faithful from their homes. In the mosaics in the Italian city of Ravenna which date from this period, we see loaves presented at worship by the Emperor Justinian in the form of a complicated braided chaplet or crown *(corona)* which took great skill to produce. Joseph Jungmann and other scholars of liturgical history see this new emphasis on the "specialness" of the Eucharistic bread as reflecting the heightened concern on the part of orthodox Christians to emphasize the divinity of Christ in the face of the Arian heresy.

From the Early Middle Ages to Vatican II. The trend to distinguish between ordinary bread and the bread used at the Eucharist continued, especially in the West. Decrees of local church councils from the ninth century onward began to stipulate that the bread of Eucharist be unleavened and of the purest ingredients. The sacrificial nature of the Eucharist continued to be emphasized. This is reflected by the proleptic term used to describe the bread before consecration: the *hostia* ("victim"). Because most of the faithful no longer communicated, except at great feasts, the dimensions of the "host" shrunk to the size of a *denarius* or large coin for the priest which was broken and consumed entirely by him at communion. The faithful were accommodated by separate, even smaller communion wafers. The production of these hosts was almost universally reserved to priests and religious (monks and nuns) in order to safeguard the purity of the elements. While the Council of Florence (1439) recognized the legitimacy of the Eastern practice of using leavened bread for the Eucharist, the Roman Rite has maintained the use of unleavened bread to this day.

Pastoral Notes. The liturgical renewal promoted by the Second Vatican Council has once again recovered an emphasis on the symbolic value of bread as real food whose focus is the unity of the assembly in Christ. While in no way forbidding the use of wafer-like "hosts," the *General Instruction of the Roman Missal* once again emphasizes the sign value of the breaking of the bread, reflected in the NT and the writing of the early Church as a constitutive part of the Rite of Mass. "The nature of the sign demands that the material for the Eucharistic celebration truly have the appearance of food . . . it should be made in such a way . . . that the priest is able actually to break the host into parts and distribute them to at least some of the faithful. The action of the breaking of the bread, the simple term for the Eucharist in Apostolic times, will more clearly bring out the force and meaning of the sign of the unity of all in the one bread and of their charity, since the one bread is being distributed among the members of one family" (GIRM 283).

See: CHURCH, EUCHARIST, JESUS CHRIST, PRIEST, WORSHIP

MARK R. FRANCIS, C.S.V.

C

CALL/VOCATION

The notion of call or vocation is used to express the communication of God's intention. This applies to creation in general, the whole of God's people, and to specific individuals. In the OT the desired response to God's call is faithfulness to the covenant. Individuals who are called are usually asked to accept a new position of leadership, often as a prophet. In the NT the call is to the discipleship of Jesus. In subsequent Christian tradition the notion of call has been applied not only to the call to faith, but also as a call to a specific ministry or to a specific way of living the Christian life.

Old Testament

While we do not find in the OT a specific word corresponding to our noun "vocation," we can recognize as vocation passages those in which God called or summoned individuals or groups to be instruments of the divine purpose in the world. Such passages occur throughout the three major divisions of the OT: (1) Historical Books, (2) Wisdom Books, and (3) Prophetic Books.

Historical Books. In the context of the first creation* story, human beings were called by God into existence in the divine image and likeness (Gen 1:26-28). On the first three days of creation, God subdued the dark, windy, watery chaos and brought out of the formlessness and void an ordered universe fit for habitation. God exercised dominion over the chaos. On the second three days, God filled this universe with moving, living beings. Appearing on the sixth day, human beings are, on the one hand, part and parcel of the world, fully and deeply integrated into it, and, on the other, the climax of God's creative activity. As divine image, all human beings, men and women, are called (1) to accept that imagehood in faith* and (2) to live it out in giving life and in sharing God's dominion (see also Psalm 8). It is the task of dominion to maintain an orderly creation in which peoples and nature can live in harmony and right relationship (Psalms 93, 96–99); two terms which frequently occur to describe this condition are peace and justice. The human vocation in the world can thus be summed up: to share God's dominion in being life-giving, peace-making, and justice-doing.

The stories that follow in the primal history (Adam and Eve, Cain and Abel, Noah and the Flood, the Tower of Babel) show that humans were not faithful to their call. In rejecting imagehood (Gen 3:5), they brought death and broke down the harmony and unity of creation. While curse, the power of death, became stronger and spread over the earth, it will not have the last word. God's purpose is for blessing, the power of life in all its manifestations. The turning point comes with the call of Abraham (Gen 12:1-4).

Abraham was called to leave behind his past, his land, and his family, the two realities which, then as now, make life both possible and meaningful, and to set out into a new and unknown future which God would give. God would be present to Abraham and give him a new land and a new family, but this is not just for Abraham. In and through him and his family, God's purpose of blessing will embrace all the communities of the earth. Abraham responded with faith and obedience; the reeducation of humans in the path of blessing had begun.

A further step along this path appears in the call of Moses (Exodus 3–4). The Israelites, groaning under the oppression of Egypt, cried out to God in their distress; God heard their cry and called Moses to go to Pharaoh and lead the people out of Egypt (Exod 3:10). Through fear and a sense of his own inadequacy, Moses raised a number of objections, but God turned these aside with the assurance, "I will be with you" (Exod 3:12).

In a real sense, the people Israel were called also: "If you hearken to my voice [i.e., hear my call] . . . you shall be to me a kingdom of priests, a holy nation" (Exod 19:5-6). Yahweh delivered Israel from oppression; then, facing certain death at the hand of the Egyptians, Israel was blessed with unexpected life (Exodus 13–15). Israel was called to respond to this God in two ways: (1) they were to worship only Yahweh as their God (Exod 20:2-3); and (2) they were to live this out in their behavior toward each other. If they truly worship Yahweh, the God who frees from oppression and death, they must not become sources of oppression and death to others. Being called to worship Yahweh has serious social ramifications. This call of Yahweh and Israel's response find expression and embodiment in the covenant at Sinai.

After about two hundred years of living in the land of Israel in a loose tribal organi-zation, the people realized that if they were to survive, some changes were needed. God called Samuel to be a key instrument in this period of transition. From his youth, Samuel had been raised by Eli at the shrine of Shiloh, and while sleeping there one night, he heard his name called. Thinking it was Eli, three times Samuel went to him. Samuel, we are told, "was not familiar with the LORD" (1 Sam 3:7); we can presume, however, that he was familiar with Eli. The voice of God and the voice of Eli must have sounded much the same. It was Eli who realized what was happening. The next time Samuel responded with obedience, "Your servant is listening." Samuel mediated the word of Yahweh to the people and was acknowledged as a prophet (1 Sam 3:20). When later the cry went up for a king, Samuel played an important role, eventually anointing David to this office (1 Samuel 8; 16).

Wisdom Books. In the Wisdom writings, the call of God is presented as coming to us through the Wisdom Woman (Prov 1:20-33; 4:5-9; 8:1-36; 9:1-18). Wisdom cries aloud at the crossroads, the heights, the city gates (1:20-21; 8:1-3), i.e., in the midst of our every-day lives. Her call is addressed to men and women, the whole human family (8:4, 32). We learn wisdom through our faith-rooted (Prov 1:7) observation and reflection on the world of creation and of human experience (Prov 8:12). Wisdom leads to life, peace, and justice (Prov 3:16-18; 8:20). Wisdom, the feminine face of God turned to creation and humanity, calls us to reject folly and choose the path of wisdom. It is an urgent matter of life and death (Prov 8:35-36).

Prophetic Books. The element of call appears in a number of the classical prophets. Amos, a shepherd and dresser of sycamore trees (Amos 7:14), was called from his home in Tekoa in southern Judah to go and speak the word of the Lord in the northern kingdom of Israel. He denounced the gross injustices and oppression of the poor* that lay at the heart of that society (e.g., 2:6-7; 4:1-3; 8:4-8) and announced the coming judgment of God (e.g., 3:13-15; 7:11, 17). Hosea was called to marry Gomer, and his troubled marriage became a living symbol of God's love for the idolatrous Israel (Hosea 1–3). From his own experience Hosea was able to speak for the heart of God, betrayed by the beloved (Hos 11:8-9).

The Books of Isaiah, Jeremiah, and Ezekiel contain longer sections which can be termed more properly "call narratives." Isaiah (6:1-13) was praying before Yahweh in the Temple of Jerusalem. He was caught up into the heavenly throne room where he had an overwhelming experience of God's holiness. In the light of this, Isaiah was aware of his own deep sinfulness and unworthiness, but this was no obstacle to God. In a symbolic action, Isaiah's lips were cleansed with a burning coal so he could go and speak God's word to the people, words of challenge, judgment, and hope.

Jeremiah had a strong sense of being called, even from his mother's womb (Jer 1:4-10). Like Moses, Jeremiah was overcome by a sense of fear and inadequacy, but he too was assured, "Have no fear before them, for I am with you to deliver you" (Jer 1:8). Jeremiah too spoke words of judgment and condemnation, but also words of encouragement and hope. Unlike some of the earlier prophets, Jeremiah's whole life was caught up in his calling. Ezekiel, Jeremiah's younger contemporary, received his call among the exiles in Babylon (Ezekiel 1–3). Like Isaiah, he was overwhelmed by an experience of God's glory and holiness, but God's power (spirit) raised him up and sent him to speak to Israel. And again, his words were harsh words of challenge and encouraging words of hope.

Conclusion. Throughout the OT God's call rings out, addressed at times to all humans (creation, wisdom) and at times to chosen individuals (Abraham, Moses, Samuel, the prophets). Certain constants appear especially as this call affects the past, the present, and the future. The past is a place of security and comfort, but also of brokenness. Those called by God must, to some degree, abandon their past. Things will not be the same. That call then demands a response in the present; two dimensions of that response recur: (1) there is often a sense of unworthiness, weakness, sinfulness, resistance, but (2) this is overcome by faith, obedience, and trust in God's presence and strength. Finally, God's call is not directed to individuals for their own sakes. Each call or vocation also implies and involves a mission* to the future. Here too a double aspect recurs: (1) sinfulness is to be identified, recognized, and left behind (2) for the sake of furthering the wholeness, life, peace, and justice which represent God's purpose for Israel, humanity, and all of creation.

See: BLESSING, COVENANT, CURSE, DEATH, FAITH, HOLY/HOLINESS, JUSTICE, LIFE, MISSION, PEACE, PROPHET, WISDOM

MICHAEL D. GUINAN, O.F.M.

New Testament

The Christian tradition affirms that Israel's God, and the God of Jesus, is a God of self-disclosure who continues to be revealed in the world and to communicate with human persons in every age. Moreover, it attests that in Jesus of Nazareth this God was revealed once and for all in a son (Heb 1:1-2). God's revelation and self-disclosure is often depicted in the biblical tradition, both in the OT and NT, by means of narratives describing the "call" of individuals or groups to follow God's direction in their lives. The OT prophetic call stories (e.g., Moses [Exod 3:4-10]; Amos 7:15; Isa 1:1-8; Jer 1:4-10) are prime examples of this conviction that God is close to humanity and invites persons to respond and follow the divine call. Not only individuals but whole communities can experience the gracious invitation of God to be God's own people.

In both the OT and NT, God calls persons in the midst of their everyday activities and ordinary moments of their lives. Moses was caring for Jethro's flock; Amos, dressing the sycamore trees; Isaiah, fulfilling his usual duties in the Temple; Peter, James, and John, tending their nets; and the Samaritan woman, drawing water at the well. These stories all attest that God's call breaks in and arrests us, not outside our ordinary human experience but precisely within it.

Jesus, the One: Sent, not Called. Nowhere, however, is a call of Jesus described or narrated in the NT. Jesus' relationship with God is seen as unique. With language that would be discussed and debated for centuries to come, the NT speaks of Jesus' unique relationship with God in the images of servant (Matt 12:18; Acts 4:27, 30), of son (Mark 1:11; Matt 3:17; 16:16; John, passim), of judge (John 5:27, 30), of one who is "equal to the Father" and "one with" him (John 10:30). John's Gospel in particular affirms that Jesus is not someone who was called by God. He is the son "sent" from God into the world for the world's salvation (John 3:16-17). He is, moreover, the "only begotten" son of God (John 1:18; 3:16-18).

The Call of Discipleship. Discipleship in the NT is a way of life in response to Jesus' call to "follow." The numerous accounts of Jesus' encounters with individuals and groups demonstrate the importance of Jesus' own *initiative* in calling people to follow him. John's Gospel makes explicit this aspect of Jesus' mission: "It was not you who chose me, but I who chose you" (John 15:16). Like the prophetic call stories of the OT, the Gospel accounts portray Jesus' compelling invitation to various persons to come and follow him.

The first circle of disciples gathered around Jesus in response to Jesus' explicit invitation to them: "Come after me, and I will make you fishers of men" (Mark 1:17; Matt 4:19; Luke 5:10). In a similar fashion, the call of Matthew [or Levi] highlights the immediate and unconditional nature of the response which Jesus' call evokes in those whom he invites to follow (Matt 9:9; Mark 2:4). In addition, negative examples of discipleship and of inappropriate responses to Jesus' invitation to follow in his way rein-

force the Gospel portrayal of the demanding quality of the call to Christian discipleship.* Luke 9:57-62 (see Matt 8:19-22) recounts objections and conditions of some "would be" disciples in response to Jesus' call: "Let me go first and bury my father," or "First let me say farewell to my family at home." In the case of the OT call of Elisha (1 Kgs 19:20) such conditions were permitted, but Jesus' reply to these conditions is unequivocal: "No one who sets a hand to the plow and looks to what was left behind is fit for the kingdom of God" (Luke 9:62). Jesus' call to follow him demands absolute priority over all kinship ties and familial responsibilities.

Special emphasis is given to Jesus' calling of the Twelve. All three Synoptic Gospels recount this solemn moment (Mark 3:13-19; Matt 10:1-4; Luke 6:12-16). The circle of the Twelve, who symbolize the reconstituted twelve tribes of Israel, the new covenant* community, carry the responsibility for the first missionary efforts and thereby guarantee the continuity between the mission of Jesus and that of the early Church. Their calling and appointment by Jesus is singled out in the tradition as exemplary for other Christians. And the betrayal of this call by Judas, one of the Twelve, is therefore all the more scandalous (Mark 14:10-11; Matt 26:14-16; Luke 22:3-6).

The call to follow Jesus is ultimately a call to discipleship in the way of the Cross (Mark 8:34). Taking up one's Cross daily is the explicit requirement for all who respond to the call. For his first disciples, as for Christians in every age, therefore, response to Jesus' call entails certain costs. Those who first followed the call left their families, occupations, and possessions to join Jesus on the way that led to Jerusalem. Only by means of this 'costly following' will the disciple gradually be conformed to the way of the Master who came "not to be served but to serve and to give his life as a ransom for many" (Mark 10:45).

Matthew's Gospel, moreover, reminds Christians that call and response are not automatic. In fact, the Gospel claims that

"Many are invited but few are chosen" (Matt 22:14). This climactic saying at the end of the parable of the wedding feast highlights the perseverance demanded in response to the gospel call. It calls for a perseverance throughout one's life so that at the moment of judgment there will be a final and perfect incorporation into the company of all those who have faithfully heard and obeyed the call.

Pauline Tradition. Paul's letters speak often both of the call that all believers have received from God as well as of his own particular call to be an apostle. It was according to the divine will and purpose, Paul claims, that God called people to be "conformed to the image of his Son" (Rom 8:29). Jew and Greek alike received the call (1 Cor 1:24) to be God's people in Christ, a people who are not only called, but also "predestined, . . . justified, and . . . glorified" (Rom 8:30). For Paul, God's call comes through the preaching of the gospel, that is, through the "word of the cross" which is a stumbling block to some but the very power of God for those who are being saved (1 Cor 1:18).

Paul regularly addresses Christians as "those who have been sanctified in Christ Jesus, called to be holy" (Rom 1:6-7; 1 Cor 1:2). God calls Christians to holiness marked by freedom (Gal 5:13) and a holy way of life (1 Thess 4:7). Each local church (*ekklesia*) is the body of Christ, those called into a fellowship together in which their common calling marks them as unique. The spirit is the animator of their fellowship and the power at work in their midst bestowing different gifts for the upbuilding of the body (1 Cor 12:1-31). Moreover, Christians in their daily lives must consider their calling as a way to discern right action for their common lives (1 Cor 1:16; 11:29).

In addition to the universal call extended by God to all people, Paul recognized the particular way in which God calls some –individuals. Few things were more important to Paul than that his own claim to apostolic calling was equal with that of the first apostles (Rom 1:1-5; Gal 1:1). On the road to Damascus he experienced a unique call from God that radically reordered his life and mission. Paul's description of this call in Galatians highlights its specific features. Paul claims that his calling (like Jeremiah's before him) originated even before his birth (Gal 1:15), and was made known to him through a revelation. Paul did nothing to invite or to deserve his call; in fact, one could argue that his calling came despite his fierce resistance to the newness of God's plan in Christ Jesus. As a result of his Damascus road encounter with the risen Christ, Paul embarked on the mission* to which he was called: to preach the gospel of Christ among the Gentiles. That is, he in turn became the mediator of God's call to others. This same apostolic commission claims all those who have been called into the way of discipleship.

Post-Pauline Tradition. Baptismal catechesis in the early Church, moreover, continued to reflect the language of God's calling to believers. You were "called out of darkness to God's own light" is the way in which the author of 1 Peter reminds his addressees of their unique status as Christians (1 Pet 2:9). Ephesians, too, repeats this reminder: "Live in a manner worthy of the call you have received" (Eph 4:1). Thus, the initial moment of God's calling influences the whole life of Christian disciples and prepares them for the final moment when they will come before God as people not only called, but also chosen.

See: CONVERSION, DISCIPLE/DISCIPLESHIP, ELECTION

BARBARA E. BOWE, R.S.C.J.

Pastoral-Liturgical Tradition

The idea of a person being called by God has been central to all forms of Christian anthropology since Apostolic times, thanks to Paul, but also under the influence of other biblical texts (Mark 1:16-20; Matt 19:21; Acts 13:1-3).

Historical Development. At first, only two kinds of call, both present in Paul, were distinguished: a call to faith and a call to ministry in the Church. In contrast, the idea of a call to martyrdom seems to have played no significant role in Christian literature: sufferings were caused by human evil and were countered by God with a gift of supernatural strength.

Athanasius' *Life of Antony* (no. 2) opened new ground by explicitly stating something already found in the Christian Scriptures. Besides the calls to faith and to ministry, there is also a vocation to a way of life: Antony followed a divine call when he embraced monasticism. Since Athanasius' book soon became a "best seller," this idea spread to other *Lives*. One point it stressed was that in the awakening of a call to monasticism, the Scriptures played a decisive role.

While the call to faith receded into the background when Christianity became a matter of birth, the two calls to ministry and to religious life were all that people had in mind when they spoke of vocations. Even until recently, the various "theologies of vocation" were modeled on these two particular calls. What about a call to marriage or to secular life in general? Very seldom has such a call been envisioned. The reason is that, since the fourth century, the Fathers kept repeating that virginity was the original call to humankind in Eden and that with sexual relationships came sin. So, it was concluded, Christians must look to celibacy or virginity as *the* call, and only if they were not able to follow it should they be allowed to marry. Therefore, as many texts up to the early twelfth century state, marriage was tolerated for "the weak."

With the "return to nature" that came with the twelfth-century renaissance, the status of secular Christians began to improve. Francis of Assisi, by proposing the whole gospel as a rule for all and by accepting secular and married people into his movement, took a decisive step toward their full recognition.

Another more positive line of thought followed the reaffirmation of a universal call to Christian perfection. Origen had already stated that renunciation was not perfection itself, but a means to reach it (*Comm. in Matt.* 19). Thomas Aquinas set the horizons for acknowledging a secular call by restating the universal call to perfection and distinguishing between the counsels (renunciation), to which a minority are called, and the spirit of the counsels, to which all are called. It took considerably longer to explicitly spell out the connection between the common call to perfection and the vocation to different ways of life and service. Francis de Sales and some Jesuit writers began to speak about it. Vatican II made it clear (Dogmatic Constitution On the Church, 40–41).

Theology. The statement that each person has a divine call implies both a dynamic view of the self and an image of God as not only the source of our being, but also as the term of our deepest orientation. The Greek philosophers had already reflected on the possibility of intellectual and moral growth *(paidagogia)*. Modern thought insists on the innate tendency of humans to grow on all levels. Christian theology adds a deeper dimension to this human potential by stressing a divine call to grow. Jesus spoke of a God who is closely associated with our future: "The kingdom of God is at hand, repent and believe in the gospel" (Mark 1:15). To repent means to break with our sinful past and to believe is to enter into God's future, or into God our future. Jesus sets human beings in the presence of a God who is not only transcendent, but who "is coming," who is never totally revealed. And this God is not some merely objective goal or utterly remote absolute: God calls us, attracts us to share in the divine glory.

There is, then, a universal vocation to the fullness of love, which implies an overall development of the person. Each one must reach his/her own perfection by following her/his own way of life and service. The call is not purely external (a voice that reaches us from outside); it is inside ourselves. Our call is present in the gifts we receive from God. Paul, who related the gifts Israel received to its call (Rom 11:29), spoke of gifts enabling or empowering us for a way of life (1 Cor 7:7) and for service (1 Cor 12:8-11). Call and vocational charisms go together.

To "hear a call" usually means to discover gifts and aptitudes that already exist in us and, through them, to discern in faith the deep orientation of our persons and lives. Since conservation in being is a constant creation, God's creative action orients us toward a fullness of sharing in the divine glory and inclines us toward a concrete way of reaching it and of serving others on their way to God.

As regards the call to a way of life (e.g., single/married), the response to it depends only on our free choice. When it comes to a call to the ordained priesthood, however, the Church and/or the Order have something to say in the matter. The Christian community has the right to choose its ministers. The Church did so from the very beginning. In the same way, an Order or Secular Institute has the right to accept or not accept its candidates. A simple inclination does not confer any right to ordination or profession. In these two instances vocation is only fully meaningful when it is acknowledged by the community.

See: FAITH, GIFTS, LOVE, MINISTRY

JOHN MANUEL LOZANO

CALVARY

Calvary is the name of the place where Jesus was executed by the Romans. The word itself derives from the Latin word for skull. The other name for this spot, Golgotha, derives from the Aramaic word for skull (Matt 27:33; Mark 15:22; John 19:17). The name of the place may reflect either the physical appearance of the site in antiquity or its use as a place of execution. It is not possible to be sure.

This site of Jesus' execution was outside the city of Jerusalem (Matt 27:32; Mark 15:21) and near the tomb of Jesus (John 19:41). This accords with Roman and Jew-ish practice. The Romans preferred to stage crucifixion just outside the city walls on a main road. The purpose of such an exhibition was to provide an object lesson for those who would flout Roman law and authority. The Jews buried their dead outside the city walls to avoid contact with the dead that brought ritual impurity. The proper location of graves and cemeteries would have been an important matter in Jerusalem, the site of the Temple. Priests and worshipers needed to concern themselves with this matter (Lev 21:1; Num 5:2).

Little is known about the site of Jesus' execution other than its name. Since Matthew says that the cross could be seen from a distance (27:55), it may be that the spot was elevated. The reference to the passers-by in Matthew 27:39 suggests that the site was near a road. Though a church has stood on a reputed site of Calvary since the fourth century, it is impossible to be certain that the Church of the Holy Sepulchre stands on the place where Jesus was crucified and buried.

In the nineteenth century, a British general, Cyrus Gordon, suggested an alternative that was outside the present city walls of Jerusalem. He noticed that the face of a hill near the Church of St. Stephen looked like a skull. He also found a first century CE tomb nearby. He was convinced that this was the place that the Byzantines located Calvary and the tomb of Jesus. He argued that the Church of the Holy Sepulchre is based on a tradition that developed first in the Crusader Period (eleventh century CE) and that it placed the tomb of Jesus inside the city walls.

Excavations in Jerusalem during the 1960s confirm that the site where the Church of the Holy Sepulchre stands was outside the city walls in Jesus' day. [The current walls of the Old City of Jerusalem date from the sixteenth century CE.] Excavations have also shown that the site was an abandoned stone quarry into which several tombs had been cut before the city expanded to the north in 41 CE. While this is circumstantial evidence, it does refute Gordon's claims that the Church of the Holy Sepulchre could not occupy the site of Calvary and the tomb.

The site identified by Gordon attracts Protestant evangelicals. It is the only "holy site" that they control. Most archaeologists and historians support the Church of the Holy Sepulchre at the likely spot of Calvary.

See: JERUSALEM, JESUS CHRIST, PRIEST, TEMPLE

LESLIE J. HOPPE, O.F.M.

CANAAN

The name Canaan refers not to a national state but to a territory. [The title "king of Canaan" given to Jabin in Judg 4:2 is inaccurate. Josh 11:1 is probably correct when it calls Jabin "king of Hazor."] This territory lies between Egypt and Syria and was the place where the ancient Israelites* settled in the thirteenth century BCE and established their national state two hundred years later. Before the emergence of the Israelite national state that encompassed the entire region, Canaan was organized into many small city-states ruled by petty kings. The Amarna Letters (fourteenth-century BCE letters sent by Canaanite rulers to the Pharaoh who had nominal hegemony in the region) show that these city-states cooperated very little. On the contrary, they were engaged in almost constant conflict with each other.

The lack of any central government made the region vulnerable to outsiders. Both the Philistines and the Israelites took advantage of this to begin settling in the region. These threats led to some alliances among the Canaanite city-states (Josh 9:1-2; 10:1-5), but this concerted action was not enough to stop the Israelites. The Book of Joshua lists thirty-one Canaanite rulers that the Israelites managed to defeat (Josh 12:7-24). That there were so many petty states in this limited area is evidence of the political fragmentation that made it possible for invading populations to settle in Canaan with some measure of impunity.

Because Canaan refers to a region rather than a political entity with defined borders

there is some ambiguity about the actual extent of its territory. Genesis 10:19 sets specific boundaries for Canaan, but elsewhere the Bible speaks with less precision. The same is true for other ancient Near Eastern texts. Some texts use the term broadly; others show a more discriminating use. While Canaan refers to a discrete territory, it is not possible to determine precise boundaries based on currently available sources.

It is an understatement to say that the OT is hostile to the indigenous population of Canaan. This is clear from the genealogy that Genesis provides for the Canaanites. According to Genesis 9:18, Canaan was a son of Ham and therefore a brother to Egypt, Cush [Ethiopia], and Put [Lybia] (Gen 10:6). The Canaanites were, however, a Semitic people like the Israelites. Noah curses Canaan for an offense committed against him and condemns Canaan to be a slave (Gen 9:20-26). Deuteronomy is more severe as it urges the annihilation of the Canaanites (Deut 20:16-18).

The animosity that the biblical tradition harbors against the Canaanites reflects social and religious conflicts. Canaanite society was stratified. A small privileged class burdened the larger peasant class with taxation, military service, and other controls. The Israelites attempted to establish a society in which these controls were denied to any human being as given over exclusively to their God.

Canaanite religion focused on maintaining fertility through the annual rains that made life possible in a region without a system of rivers like Egypt or Mesopotamia. The storm god Baal and his consort Anat made possible the regular cycles of rain that brought fertility to the crops and herds. The myths and possibly the rituals of Canaanite underscored the role of sexuality in the life cycles of nature. Israelite religion demanded the exclusive service of Yahweh. The stories about Yahweh and the rituals of Yahwistic religion eliminated this dominant aspect of Canaanite religion since Yahweh did not have a consort. Still the strong inclination of Israelite farmers to ensure their success by serving Baal is evident from the Elijah stories (see especially 1 Kgs 18:20-46).

Despite the religious conflict with Canaan, ancient Israel inherited a significant religious legacy from the Canaanites. Its principal shrines such as Bethel were once places associated with Canaanite religion. Israel's principal feasts (Exod 23:14-17) were probably harvest festivals whose origin was in Canaanite religion. The Passover celebrated the barley harvest. The Feast of Weeks marked the wheat harvest. The Feast of Booths came during the fall fruit harvest. The Bible reinterprets Canaanite religious belief and practice and makes them vehicles for expressing its faith in Yahweh.

Nowhere is this debt to the Canaanites more obvious than in the images used in the psalms. For example, Psalm 29 is either borrowed from the Canaanites or it was at least written in imitation of their hymns to Baal, the Canaanite god of the storm. For example, the description of Mount Zion as in the "far north" (Ps 48:1) makes no geographic sense. In Canaanite mythology Mount Zaphon ("north") was the home of Baal. According to Israelite religious belief, Mount Zaphon's recesses have been transferred from Baal to Yahweh whose heavenly home is Mount Zion in Jerusalem. Psalm 104 addresses Yahweh, "You make the clouds your chariot" (v. 3) while Canaanite myths call Baal "the rider of the clouds." In verse 7 thunder is Yahweh's voice while in Canaanite religious texts thunder is Baal's voice. According to verse 13 Yahweh waters the mountains from his palace while Canaanite mythology describes an opening in Baal's palace through which he waters the earth.

The Bible adopts Canaanite religious language not merely to claim Baal's prerogatives for Yahweh as a chauvinistic exercise, but to broaden the horizons of Israelite religious belief. Such usage is meant to imply that the sphere of Yahweh's activity is wider than ancient Israel's historical experience. Yahweh is master of nature as well as Israel's Lord. The discovery of ancient texts from Ras Shamra (Ugarit) has led to a great appreciation of the significant debt that ancient Israelite religion and culture owe to the Canaanites.

See: BAAL, CONQUEST

LESLIE J. HOPPE, O.F.M.

CANTICLE

Canticles are biblical poems found outside the Psalter which are recited or sung during the Liturgy of the Hours. They are drawn from both the OT and the NT. The word "canticle" comes from the Latin word *canticulum,* which means "a little song." Canticles often resemble psalms in form and content.

In the Roman rite the most familiar canticles come from the Gospel of Luke: the Canticle of Zechariah or *Benedictus* (Luke 1:68-79) is recited during morning prayer; the Canticle of the Blessed Virgin Mary or *Magnificat* (Luke 1:46-55) is recited during evening prayer; and the Canticle of Simeon or *Nunc Dimittis* (Luke 2:29-32) is recited during night prayer.

The *Benedictus* is both a prayer of thanksgiving and a prophecy. Zechariah, the father of John the Baptist, was a priest who took on the role of a prophet, for he initiated a new age of prophecy with this prayer. The *Benedictus* is a thanksgiving for God's continual acts of salvation. It directs us to John the Baptist, the herald of the Messiah. References to the child actually occur in only two verses (vv. 76-77). However, these link John with both the promises of the past and with his role as prophet of future salvation. Zechariah and John the Baptist together provide a priestly and prophetic witness to the fact that the messianic age has arrived.

The *Magnificat* is a hymn of praise which expresses delight in God and thanksgiving for the divine power to change human society. It reflects many of the themes and interests of the prayer of Hannah (1 Sam 2:1-10). Both show a special sensitivity toward the weak and the underprivileged. The *Magnificat* is Mary's response to both the angel's announcement that she will give birth to the "Son of the Most High" and to Elizabeth's greeting, which confirmed that message. Mary's pregnancy is not actually mentioned in this prayer, although there are allusions to it in "the Mighty One has done great things for me" and "from now on all ages will call me blessed." The great deeds of God will continue in a new form through the child whom Mary will bear.

The *Nunc Dimittis* is a prayer of confidence which is an appropriate act of submission to God at the end of each day. Like Zechariah, Simeon was a priest endowed with a spirit of prophecy. This short prayer expresses strong trust in God, who is now fulfilling the promises to Israel and accomplishing a new act of salvation. The child Jesus is the "glory for your people Israel" as well as "a light for revelation to the Gentiles" (Luke 2:32). This language not only echoes that of Isaiah 42:1-4; 49:1-6, but also reflects a major concern of Luke's Gospel: Jesus is savior not only of Israel but also of the Gentiles.

Other canticles from both testaments also appear in the Liturgy of Hours: during morning prayer an OT canticle is recited between two psalms, and during evening prayer a NT canticle is recited after two psalms. The number of canticles used has increased greatly since Vatican II's reform of the liturgy.

See: PRAYER

TIMOTHY A. LENCHAK, S.V.D.

CELIBACY

Although "celibacy" is not strictly a biblical word, it is closely related to "virginity"* which, though it usually refers only to women, can also mean simply a chaste life without marriage and can thus apply to both men and women.

In the OT, celibacy was not considered desirable. An exception seems to be the case of Jeremiah. In the NT, Christ speaks of those who choose celibacy for the sake of the reign of God, and Paul writes at some length about the merits of such a state of life. In Church tradition, celibacy has been essential to the religious state and, after a halting beginning, has become normative for diocesan clergy, particularly in the Latin Church.

Old Testament

Celibacy is virtually unknown in the OT writings. Everyone was expected to marry and produce children. Failure to do so was considered cause for mourning (see Judg 11:37). One notable exception seems to occur in the case of the prophet Jeremiah who wrote: "This message came to me from the LORD: Do not marry any woman; you shall not have sons and daughters in this place" (16:1-2). From the context it is clear that this prohibition extended to all the joys and sorrows of the people and was given in view of the terrible fate that awaited Israel. As such, it was a prophetic and eschatological sign. Some suggest that it may in fact have been merely symbolic since, if historical, it would have had to be a premonition from the very youth of Jeremiah when he would normally have contemplated marriage.

New Testament

References to celibacy in the NT are infrequent but they are significant precisely because they are unexpected in a setting that is still profoundly Jewish.

Matthew 19:12. In the context of a discussion about marriage in which Jesus strictly forbids divorce, the disciples wonder why anyone in that case would even consider marriage. Jesus points out that marriage without the possibility of divorce may indeed be hard to accept but that it is possible for "those to whom that is granted" (19:11). He then continues: "Some are incapable of marriage because they were born so; some, because they were made so by others; some, because they have renounced marriage for the sake of the kingdom of heaven. Whoever can accept this ought to accept it" (19:12).

Jesus thus notes two cases in which, at least from the male perspective, the incapability of marriage is involuntary (physical disability and castration) and then speaks of a voluntary renunciation of marriage. Such a decision, which would have been unthinkable in that culture, is said to be made "for the sake of the kingdom of heaven." This can mean either "because of the kingdom," i.e., because of one's total commitment to the demands of the in-breaking reign of God through Jesus' proclamation, or "in view of the kingdom," i.e., because of the need to prepare for the reign that is to come. In fact, it can, and probably does, include both meanings. It is a question then of a single-minded absorption in the affairs of the reign to the point that marriage would be experienced as a distraction or hindrance. Jesus makes it clear, however, that this is only for those who have received a special call and that marriage remains a normal and praiseworthy alternative.

It has been noted that, in the context of marriage and divorce, the option of celibacy offered by Jesus might refer only to the innocent and unwilling partners in a divorce who would thus be counseled to remain unmarried. However, this seems very unlikely since the answer of Jesus in verse 11 appears to refer clearly to those who are contemplating marriage.

There is also a powerful indirect witness to the value of celibacy in the NT portrayal of Jesus as celibate. Even though this is never explicitly stated, it would appear extremely unlikely that a supposed marriage of Jesus could have gone unnoticed and unrecorded. The virginity of Mary is also clearly affirmed in the infancy narratives of both Matthew (1:18-23) and Luke (1:27, 34-35). The example of Jesus and Mary will be in fact a dominant influence in the adoption of a celibate way of life by Christians in subsequent centuries.

Paul provides important evidence about the existence and meaning of celibacy in the Christian community of Corinth. He broaches the subject in response to a question that has apparently been presented to him concerning marriage and virginity: "Now in regard to the matters about which you wrote: 'It is a good thing for a man not to touch a woman'" (1 Cor 7:1). In other words, Paul wishes to defend the choice of a celibate state. He makes it quite clear that this does not mean that marriage is less worthy; in fact, it is the norm. However, he does affirm that some, like himself, have a special gift of continence (7:7) and he recommends imitation.

After discussing other marital problems, Paul returns to the subject of marriage and virginity: "So this is what I think best because of the present distress: that it is a good thing for a person to remain as he is. Are you bound to a wife? Do not seek a separation. Are you free of a wife? Then do not look for a wife" (7:26-27). Paul's rather surprising advice derives from his awareness of "the present distress." "Distress" translates a Greek word that normally means "necessity" and suggests a situation of great pressure or urgency. There is a hint about the nature of this urgency in Paul's further comment: "I tell you, brothers, the time is running out" (7:29). The urgency then comes from a conviction that the end of the world is imminent. This awareness is in harmony with other references in Pauline literature to an imminent parousia (e.g., Phil 4:5).

This sense of time slipping away should profoundly influence the Christian's attitude toward the realities that will disappear with earthly time. And so Paul urges a diffident attitude toward marriage, grief, and joy (vv. 29-30) and concludes: "the world in its present form is passing away" (7:31). It is often assumed that Paul was simply mistaken about the imminent end of all things. But it is quite possible that he was keenly aware of the special situation that exists between the first and second coming of Christ. This whole period can in fact be aptly described as the "last days" and therefore Paul's comments would be valid for the entire period of the Christian Church.

In any emergency situation, it is important to be clear about what can and should be preserved. If one's house is on fire, it helps to be clear about what must be saved. And so Paul addresses the matter of cares and anxieties that may become dangerous distractions from what is essential: "I should like you to be free of anxieties" (7:32). He then makes it clear that he is referring to excessive preoccupations that detract from one's ability to be attentive to the primary relationship to the Lord. One may be anxious about pleasing the Lord or about pleasing other human beings, such as a wife or husband. It has been suggested that Paul may be warning against all forms of anxiety, including anxiety to please the Lord. But this is unlikely in view of verse 34 where the result of being anxious about the things of the Lord is said to be holiness.

It seems fairly clear, therefore, that the point Paul wants to make concerns excessive preoccupation about matters of this passing world and he concludes that, all other things being equal, the virgin or celibate will be able to avoid such distractions more easily than a married person. Since in any given situation things are frequently not equal, a married person may indeed be more attentive to the Lord than a celibate. One may surmise that, ultimately, Paul is more concerned about attention to the Lord than about the relative merits of one's state of life.

Pastoral-Liturgical Tradition

In surveying Church tradition one must distinguish carefully between celibacy in religious congregations of men or women and among the diocesan clergy.

Celibacy in Religious Congregations. There has never been any serious question about the appropriateness and indispensability of celibacy for the members of religious communities of men or women. This was especially true of the earliest monastic witnesses, whether in the somewhat fluid conditions of the Egyptian desert or in the later more organized situation of life under a monastic rule. In more recent congregations that are no longer strictly monastic the adherence to celibacy has remained constant. In all these cases, celibacy has been understood as a special devotion to a gospel idealism that includes a single-minded, prayerful dedication to the primacy of divine claims on individual human lives. These claims must be recognized by all believers but they are honored in a more intense and dramatic way by properly motivated celibates.

Celibacy in the Diocesan Clergy. This matter is addressed already in the Pastoral Letters of the NT where the authors explicitly recognize the right of a bishop to be married (1 Tim 3:2; Titus 1:6) and undoubtedly this right would have been extended a fortiori to the clergy generally. This makes it clear that there is no essential link between celibacy and diocesan priesthood. Moreover, this situation appears to have continued for the first several centuries of the Church's existence. No doubt many members of the clergy chose to be celibate but there appears to have been no explicit or universal legislation in this regard.

This situation changed during the fourth century. Church legislation began to favor the celibate state for clergy and especially for bishops. Norms varied from region to region but the move toward obligatory celibacy for diocesan clergy became ever more evident. For example, the Spanish council at Elvira in 300 CE decreed continence for all members of the clergy. As a general rule, the Eastern Church was more lenient than the Latin Church in this regard.

This practice of clerical celibacy in the West during subsequent centuries generally followed the rhythm of laxity and reform that was generally evident in the Church. After the dissolution of the Carolingian empire there was frequent disregard of the rule. However, in the reforms of Pope Gregory VII sacerdotal celibacy was forcefully restored. This trend was confirmed by the Second Lateran Council

(1139) which declared clerical marriages to be not only illicit but invalid. Another period of decline in the practice of clerical celibacy occurred during the turmoil occasioned by the Black Death plague and the Hundred Years' War. Then, in the Protestant Reformation, this law was explicitly rejected by the Reformers.

The Council of Trent, in reacting to the Reformation, examined this matter very carefully. While rejecting the opinion of those who maintained that celibacy was required of clerics by divine rather than merely ecclesiastical law, it nonetheless strongly re-affirmed the value of such a Church Law. Furthermore, the Council made clear that this law did not imply a pejorative judgment on the state of Christian marriage.

The Second Vatican Council, while acknowledging the somewhat different discipline in the Eastern Church, strongly re-affirmed the decrees of the Council of Trent in regard to the clergy of the Latin Church. In its *Decree on the Ministry and Life of Priests*, the Council recognized that celibacy is not essential to the priestly state but declared that it is most suitable to that state and that, when lived sincerely and generously, it can greatly enhance the fruitfulness of priestly ministry. The fulcrum of this argument seems to lie in the conviction that gospel ministry demands a total and single-minded devotion to the reign of God as it breaks in constantly on human history and that the traditional and time-honored expression of such complete devotion is the freely chosen condition of celibate living.

See: MARRIAGE, MARY, MOTHER OF JESUS, PAROUSIA, REIGN OF GOD, VIRGIN

DEMETRIUS R. DUMM, O.S.B.

CHAOS

Chaos is a Greek term occurring in Hesiod's *Theogony* and in other Greek literature to describe the state before God created the world. The word itself does not occur in the Greek Bible but the concept of a pre-creation state is common in the ancient Near East and in the Bible.

Old Testament

Chaos can only be understood against the background of ancient Near Eastern cosmogonies. Egyptians characterized the pre-creation universe with four concepts—the Flood, the Waters, the Darkness, and Chaos. Creation always involved differentiation of an original monad; the creator god was "the god who became millions." Chaos or nothingness was always at the margin of the universe and could be experienced within ordinary life, e.g., in the groundwater that one encountered when digging a well and in the night.

In Mesopotamian literature of the third and early second millennium, the Nippur tradition had a primeval city of gods prior to the cosmic marriage between Heaven (An) and Earth (Ki). In the Eridu tradition, chaos was the state before Enki filled the Tigris and Euphrates with the underground waters. In literature from the eighteenth century BCE, intensely theo- and templocentric, chaos was the period when there were no temples and reeds and mud to make them, and when there were no kings and human race to build them and animals to offer in sacrifice. Chaos was the opposite of civilized life as the people of Mesopotamia experienced it.

The two most "philosophical" Akkadian cosmogonies, Atrahasis and *Enuma elish*, have more than one state or period of time prior to the definitive created world. Atrahasis opens "when gods were man" (v. 1), i.e., when the lower class gods worked. Human beings are created as substitute workers after the gods' rebellion but the creation is flawed: excessive noise provokes the gods to wipe out the first batch of human beings with the exception of Ea's client Atrahasis. From him the gods create a new society, this time with inherent population controls to ensure there will be no disturbing noise. "Chaos" in Atrahasis is specific: the period when human population was out of control, not suitable for the available space.

Enuma elish, probably of the eleventh century BCE, exalts Marduk by telling how he created the world and thus exercises legitimate kingship. The god's claims are justified by a theogony (tablet I) and a cosmogony (tablets IV–VI). Before the theogony, there is only primal sea, Apsu (fresh water) and Tiamat (salt water); neither has the prefix of divinity and transitive verbs are not used in their descriptions. There are no temples and destinies have not been assigned. After the gods appear, there is a conflict between them and Apsu/Tiamat in which Ea slays Apsu. The peace from that victory is only temporary and Ea's son Marduk must vanquish Tiamat. Marduk's creation of the world (including human beings) finally establishes definitive order. Chaos in *Enuma elish* designates primarily the initial period of limitless waters and inertia. There are no active deities. There was a second state prior to Marduk's creation, when the divine but not the human world existed, but the term chaos is probably not applicable to the period.

In Canaan, the Ugaritic texts attest the storm god Baal's victories over his enemies Sea and Death (Mot). Sea is apparently sea threatening to flood land, and Mot (Death), infertile desert encroaching on the fertile land. Though Baal does not construct the universe after his victory (unlike Marduk), some scholars believe a genuine cosmogony results from his victory, since he becomes king and builds the temple that symbolizes social and agricultural order. Baal's victory must have been accompanied by the installation of the human king and the stabilizing of political and social order. Chaos in these texts is infertility and social disorder.

The preeminent cosmogony in the OT is Genesis 1. Its depiction of chaos is the most famous in the Bible: "In the beginning, when God created the heavens and the earth, the earth was a formless wasteland, and darkness covered the abyss, while a mighty wind swept over the waters. Then God said, 'Let there be light', and there was light" (Gen 1:1-3). "Formless wasteland"

translates *tohu wabohu*. *Tohu* occurs twenty times in the OT (only two other times with its alliterative partner *bohu*) and means desert, waste, devastation, i.e., not abstract nothingness but a menace. "Darkness" is not neutral, mere absence of light, since God must make its opposite, light, before creating further. "Mighty wind" is better translated "wind of God" and suggests that, even before creation, God controlled chaos.

Chaos in Genesis 1 is impersonal; it is not endowed with will and there is no battle. It is essentially thick night and limitless waters, the opposite of the highly differentiated and beautiful universe that is to arise in the following six days. It is the negation of light, dry land, vegetative, marine, and bird life, animals, and especially human society (the man and woman stand for society).

Since not all cosmogonies are conflictual, pre-creation chaos need not be a particularly disordered period. Genesis 2–11, for instance, is a single cosmogony, with the same plot as Atrahasis and the Sumerian Flood Story, i.e., creation of humans, their fault, the flood, and a re-creation. The story is not built on the chaos-creation contrast of Genesis 1 since humans in Genesis 2 are not created in response to "chaos" or crisis. Unlike comparable Akkadian accounts, culture is created in the pre-flood era (Gen 4:17-26). There is a fault in the pre-Flood population, but it is in human beings not God. God does not adjust a previously faulty balance between land and population.

In other religious literature a possible return to chaos is suggested by the yearly need to enthrone the god (and the king) at the onset of the fall rains. Presumably the god was defeated by the gods of chaos during the arid summer months and arose to power with the return of fertility. In Israel's monotheism, Yahweh did not have to effect fresh victories over chaos. Israel could, however, celebrate Yahweh's creation victory over chaos and enthronement as a reenactment of a once for all primordial victory. Several psalms, e.g., 77, 89, 93, 114, speak of Yahweh conquering sea and leading Israel into the land or installing the king. In these psalms chaos is symbolized by sea but its real meaning is political and social disorder.

In a famous passage, Jeremiah parodies Genesis 1, threatening a return to chaos if Israel continues to sin: "I looked at the earth, and it was waste and void *(tohu wabohu)*, at the heavens, and their light had gone out" (Jer 4:23). The return to chaos will be effected by "the enemy from the north," Jeremiah's term for a human king sent by Yahweh as avenger for Israel's rebellion against God. Chaos here is reversal of fertility and the destruction of towns (social disorder).

A similar view of chaos as imminent threat is found in the Book of Job. In reply to Job's criticism that the world is without order and without justice, God describes the land monster Behemoth (40:15-24) and the sea monster Leviathan (ch. 41). Leviathan is an ally of Sea against Baal in the Ugaritic texts and in Isaiah 27:1 (the same monster is tamed in Ps 104:26). Yahweh deliberately parades before Job Leviathan, a vestige of chaos, to show that human beings must reckon with chaos even in the world Yahweh created. How dare Job demand an antiseptic and reasonable world?

Chaos is equated with the political power of Israel's enemies in the Zion psalms, 46, 48, and 76. Zion has been established at creation as God's residence. Israel's enemies may rage at Zion's base but will never succeed in taking it. God will defeat them at the very base of the mountain.

Similarly in Daniel, second-century Jews are told that the four great empires they have suffered under (Babylonia, Media, Persia, Greece) are commissioned by chaotic power; the four beasts came up out of the sea (Dan 7:2-3). The reign of the four beasts will ultimately be ended by the native Jewish dynasts, ruling in the name of Yahweh.

The Deuterocanonical 2 Maccabees, probably of the first century BCE, reinterprets pre-creation chaos as nothingness. The mother exhorts her seventh son to endure martyrdom: "I beg you, child, to look at the heavens and the earth and see all that is in them; then you will know that God did not make them out of existing things; and in the same way the human race came into existence" (7:28). The mother's point is God's total ownership of humans; even a mother who knows her child intimately must admit her son came from outside her (see vv. 22-23). The text does not provide a philosophical argument for creation from nothing but rather, a motive for remaining faithful to one's creator.

An interpretation of chaos from about the same time is found in Wisdom 11:17: "your almighty hand, that had fashioned the universe from formless matter *(amorphou hyles)*." The author accepts the popular Greek view that the world is made of pre-existing matter that is shaped by God.

In the OT, then, chaos is the opposite of the order that God imposes on the world in creating. It is night and waters in Genesis 1 which make human life and community impossible. God removes the destructive potential of chaos not by annihilation but by rearrangement. Darkness becomes part of day-night, and water goes into sea or satisfies the thirst of animals and humans (especially in Psalm 104). Chaos is the opposite of human society. Enemy armies can be instruments of chaos, somehow representing social disorder.

New Testament

Chaos as a cosmogonic concept is not prominent because the NT makes limited reference to ancient Near Eastern cosmogonies. The Gospel of Mark, it is true, assumes a demon-filled universe but only as a vivid illustration of human alienation. The apocalyptic description of the end of the world in Mark 13 (and parallels) uses language from ancient cosmogonies to show recreation. The powers and principalities of this age arise themselves against God who defeats them in order to bring in the new age. The NT authors use language from the OT such as that of Isaiah 40–66,

Zechariah 9–14, and Daniel 7–12. These and other passages describe God directly intervening to destroy an unjust social order and create a new one.

The clearest reference to chaos in the NT is in the Book of Revelation. In chapters 12–13, the great dragon is described with some of the traits of Sea, the enemy of Baal in Ugaritic texts and of Yahweh in some psalms and Second Isaiah. The dragon lives in the sea (13:1) and commissions the two beasts who will persecute the Church. The scene is like that of Daniel 7:2-3. In chapter 20, the dragon is killed by Christ and in the new creation "the sea is no more" (21:1). Only in this new creation of Christ is chaos completely overcome. Revelation made use of cosmogonic language to portray the persistence of evil.

Pastoral-Liturgical Tradition

Christian liturgy affirmed God as creator in the language of the OT. Only a few early authors, e.g., Justin (*Apol.* 1.59) and Clement of Alexandria (*Strom.* 5.14), accepted the Platonic view that God created out of pre-existing matter. This material view of chaos was rejected by Theophilus of Antioch (*Ad Autolycus* 2.4) of the late second century and received its death blow in the conflict with gnosticism. *Creatio ex nihilo*, creation from nothing, became the standard formula of the Church, expressing better than any other God's mastery in creation.

The formula, creation out of nothing, should not make one forget that pre-creation chaos is primarily a threat against human society. God makes society flourish by removing obstacles. The obstacles can be variously symbolized—thick night that prevents people from facing one another, vast waters that prevent one from taking a standpoint, and from talking, listening, or breathing. Since culture, e.g., tools, kingship, laws, are part of creation, chaos is their absence. The Bible occasionally expresses the persistence of evil by admitting that there is still some primordial evil. Only in Revelation is it expressly stated

that all vestiges of the evil of primeval chaos will be eliminated.

See: BEASTS/MONSTERS OF THE DEEP, CREATION, SEA

RICHARD J. CLIFFORD, S.J.

CHARISM

The term charism comes from the Greek word *charisma*, often translated "gift," and is found almost exclusively in the NT, especially in the Pauline literature. Charism comes from the same root as the related Greek words, *chairō* ("I rejoice") and *charis* ("thanks," "grace," "favor"). In the OT the concept of charism emerges as a principle of power for those who have received the Spirit of the Lord. The concentration of the Spirit's power is a distinctive sign of the "charismatic leader," to use Max Weber's well known expression. In the NT the theme of charism appears mainly in the Pauline literature. Paul devotes his attention to the individual spiritual gifts that have been given to believers by the Spirit. Paul puts forth criteria for judging the great variety of gifts, their relative importance, and their proper exercise. Each charism is to be exercised for the edification of the community, and each is to be motivated by love, which is itself the greatest of the gifts. While charisms are essential to the Church's nature, there have been tensions between charismatic individuals and ecclesiastical authorities.

Old Testament

Although the term charism does not occur in the OT, the concept can be related to the powerful effect of the divinely given Spirit of the Lord. In the period of the Judges and early monarchy, certain individuals are portrayed as being empowered by the spirit of the Lord to do extraordinary feats. Primarily, this divine spiritual impulse enabled such leaders as Othniel (Judg 3:10), Gideon (Judg 9:39), Jephthah (Judg 12:29), Samson (Judg 14:6, 19; 15:14), and Saul (1 Sam 11:6) to be victorious militarily against the enemies of Israel. "The spirit of God rushed" upon Saul and he delivered the inhabitants of Jabesh-gilead who were besieged by the Ammonites (1 Sam 11:6). Having demonstrated by the deeds he did that the spirit of the Lord was with him, Saul was accepted as the first king of Israel. In the case of Samson, the forcefulness of the spirit's empowerment is demonstrated particularly in his extraordinary physical strength. "The spirit of the Lord came upon Samson, and although he had no weapons, he tore the lion in pieces as one tears a kid" (Judg 14:6). With the Judges, the gift of the spirit seemed to have been bestowed upon these charismatic leaders at specific times; it was a passing phenomenon. With the dawn of the monarchy, the spirit was understood to reside permanently in the king, even though extraordinary deeds were generally not attributed to the kings after Saul.

New Testament

In the NT charism or gift is used occasionally in the broad sense referring to the "one person Jesus Christ" (Rom 5:15), "eternal life" (Rom 6:23), or to "the gifts and call of God" to Israel (Rom 11:29). More frequently, the focus is on specific spiritual gifts. Two Greek expressions used for "spiritual gifts" are *pneumatika* and *pneumatikon charisma*, both suggesting the origin of the individual gifts, namely the Spirit *(pneuma)*.

Classification and Variety of Spiritual Gifts. There are a number of lists of spiritual gifts in the Pauline literature, no two of which are the same (1 Cor 12:4-11, 28-30; Rom 12:6-8; Eph 4:1-12; 1 Pet 4:10-11). The variations among the lists indicate that the passages cited should not be taken as exhaustive. Notable is the tremendous variety of gifts found in the early Christian communities. There are gifts of utterance, including prophecy, exhortation, instruction, tongues, and the ability to interpret tongues. The gifts of ministry named are care for the needy, financial contribution, acts of mercy, administration, and teaching. And there are the gifts of healing and performing miracles.

Paul mentions the active presence of the Spirit, the gift of "prophetic utterances," and the importance of testing "everything" in his earliest letter, 1 Thessalonians (5:19-21), but he does not use the technical term charism until 1 Corinthians. It is in 1 Corinthians 12–14 that one finds Paul's most extended discussion of the spiritual gifts. Paul responds to concerns in Corinth brought to his attention. The Corinthians appeared to have been so richly blessed by manifestations of the Spirit, such that Paul writes: "You are not lacking in any spiritual gift" (1 Cor 1:7). However, the proper exercise and evaluation of these gifts by the Corinthians was problematic and required Paul's lengthy instruction about the purpose and the proper exercise of the gifts.

Purpose and Evaluation of the Gifts. Some basic tenets about the spiritual gifts emerge from 1 Corinthians 12–14. First, the variety of charisms, though many, are from one source: the same Spirit, the same Lord, the same God (see 1 Cor 12:4-6). Originating from one source, the exercising of the gifts is to foster unity, not division. Second, Paul stresses that every person has received some "manifestation of the Spirit" (12:7). Paul puts forth these basic theological tenets, aware that some Corinthians were "speaking by the spirit of God" without professing faith in Jesus (1 Cor 12:3) or were placing undue importance on the exercise of tongues (1 Corinthians 14). Paul counters whatever spiritual elitism is in the community by reminding them that all have made the baptismal confession: "Jesus is Lord" (12:3). He also instructs the believers that all gifts are for the edification of the community (1 Cor 12:7). Each spiritual gift is given for the common good; they are for service (12:5) and not for self aggrandizement or boasting. Using the image of the human body (an organic unity of diverse parts), Paul argues that the exercise of gifts cannot lead to "divisions in the body, but that the parts [should] have the same concern for one another" (12:25). As a common endeavor, all are encouraged to "strive eagerly for the spiritual gifts" (14:1).

Apostles, Prophets and Teachers. Paul orders the gifts in 1 Corinthians 12:28, where he ranks apostleship first. This was indeed Paul's own calling as well as that of other men and women in the early church (see for example Andronicus and Junia, Rom 16:7).

Second are prophets, followed by teachers. Prophecy was a prominent feature of the early Church (Acts 11:27-28; 13:1-2; 15:32; 21:8-9, 11), a role exercised not only by men such as Paul, but also by women (see 1 Cor 11:5 and Acts 21:9 which mentions the "four daughters [of Philip the evangelist] gifted with prophecy"). When a person in the assembly prophesies, all the believers are to discern (1 Cor 14:29; 1 Thess 5:21). The faith of the whole community is the measure by which prophecy is to be evaluated. Paul ranks prophecy above tongues, the last of the gifts mentioned in the list, because "whoever prophesies builds up the church" (14:4), whereas the one who speaks in tongues builds up him/herself. Furthermore, in the liturgical assembly everything, especially prophecy and tongues, "must be done properly and in order" (14:39).

The third charism mentioned in 1 Corinthians 12:28 is teaching, a gift differing from prophecy by being exercised outside the liturgical assembly. An important criterion for the fruitful exercise of any of the gifts is whether or not it edifies the community and is motivated by love.

The Greatest of the Gifts. The beneficial exercise of all the spiritual gifts is determined according to Paul ultimately by the one who follows the "more excellent way" (1 Cor 12:3), that of love. It is no accident that the hymn to love in 1 Corinthians 13 is placed between chapters 12 and 14. Love is the foundation, the more basic, pervasive, and enduring value that gives all other charisms their effectiveness. Paul does not define love, but personifies it with an impressive list of fifteen verbs. Love is patient,

kind, not jealous, not pompous, not inflated, not rude, etc. (1 Cor 13:4-7; see also 8:1). These qualities were virtues evidently neglected by the Corinthians. At the end of the chapter Paul ranks love as the greatest of the three gifts, faith, hope, and love.

The Gift of Tongues. Tongues, also called glossolalia, is a series of utterances called by Paul "mysteries in spirit" (14:2), spoken to God and not to human beings. Because tongues is unintelligible speech, it does not edify the community unless it is interpreted for the benefit of those present. Therefore, the one who speaks in tongues is instructed to pray for the gift to interpret (14:13). If there is no interpreter then the person with the gift of tongues "should keep silent in the church and speak to himself and to God" (14:28). Related to tongues is the prayer of the Spirit who "intercedes with inexpressible groanings" for the person (Rom 8:26). Spirit-inspired speech also occurred, for example, at the Pentecost event, when the apostles spoke in such a way that each one present was able to understand in his or her native tongue (Acts 2:8).

See: APOSTLE, FRUITS OF THE SPIRIT, LOVE, PENTECOST, PROPHET

JOHN L. GILLMAN

Pastoral-Liturgical Tradition

Throughout much of its history, the Church has had a love/hate relationship with charismatic persons, groups, and events. This ambivalence is already evident in the NT, in polemical passages like Matthew 7:15-20, where "false prophets" are explicitly condemned and *all* Christian prophecy is implicitly critiqued. Matthew's community was clearly concerned to fix and stabilize the tradition of Jesus' teaching. Indeed, the whole project of writing the narrative, canonical Gospels can be construed as an effort to limit the charismatic innovations of prophets, men and women who claimed to teach authoritatively in the name of the risen One, under the direct impulse of the Spirit and without any mandate or approval from the community's local leadership.

Historical Struggles between Charisms and Offices: Even before Matthew's Gospel was written, the struggle between gifted charismatics and pastoral authorities (whether local and residential or itinerant and "apostolic") was an issue for Christians. Paul dealt with it, especially at Corinth, by countering the potential divisiveness and elitism of the charismatics with an inclusive definition of charism valid for all Christians. For Paul (see Rom 6:23), charism (*charisma*) is the divine, eternal life that claims and possesses believers now in their history and bodily existence, and is manifested in various gifts (*charismata*) whose purpose is to serve and build up Christ's body, the Church. Thus the whole Church is charismatic, its life characterized by an interplay of mutual ministries that complement rather than compete with one another.

Still, historically, this Pauline perspective has not always succeeded in preventing conflict between the so-called "hierarchy of charisms" and the institutional hierarchy of office-holders in the Church. Through the ages, many movements have arisen (e.g., Montanism, Gnosticism, and Manichaeism in the early Church; Albigensianism and Catharism in the medieval Church), all of which reasserted the role of charismatic gifts (e.g., prophecy, teaching, healing) that emerge independently from the Church's office-holders. While these movements came to be viewed as heretical, they had the positive effect of causing the Church at large to reflect on the ongoing value and necessity of charismatic gifts among its members.

Charisms as Essential to the Church's Nature. In our own time, both theologians and the magisterium have explicitly affirmed charisms as a necessary and permanent part of the Church's life (thus Pius XII in *Mystici Corporis* [AAS 35 (1943), 200f.]; Vatican II, Dogmatic Constitution on the Church 11, 12, 23, 34). In the view of theologians like Karl Rahner, charisms belong to the intrinsic nature of the Church as "sacrament of the world," as the visible presence of God's eschatologically victorious grace which is offered to all human beings and signals God's plan to unite all humankind in lasting bonds of justice, mercy and love. Because they are thus essential to the Church's very definition and existence, Church authorities must not merely tolerate but critically encourage charisms (see 1 Thess 5:19-21). New and hitherto unknown charisms must be allowed to emerge—as they did, for instance, in the period following the Council of Trent, when new communities of men and women arose in response to new pastoral needs. Charisms must thus be re-valued in our day as the necessary (if not always comfortable) complement of ecclesiastical office, as an essential aspect of the Church's mission as the "holy people of God"* called to witness to God's lavish gifts of nature and grace.

See: CHURCH, BODY OF CHRIST, PEOPLE OF GOD, PROPHECY

NATHAN D. MITCHELL

CHERUBIM

Old Testament and New Testament

The cherubim of the OT bear little resemblance to the Baroque image of babies with little wings. In Genesis 3:24, God stations the cherubim at the gate of the garden of Eden with a sword, flaming and turning, so that Adam and Eve cannot return and eat of the tree of life. The image suggests fierce guardians, much like Cerberus, the guardian of Hades in Greek mythology.

The prophet Ezekiel identifies his fantastic vision of the four living creatures as cherubim (Ezekiel 10; see also Ezekiel 1; 43). As a main feature, these fantastic creatures have the face of a lion, an ox, an eagle, and a human being. This particular mixture is found in the griffin, a composite animal of the divine bestiary in Mesopotamia. These fantastic beasts, which had a human face, the body of a lion or bull, and the wings of a bird, guarded the entrances of palaces and temples and are related to the sphinx of Egypt. In addition to their role as guardians for buildings, two of these winged creatures were placed side by side to form a throne for kings or gods as pictured on an ivory plaque from Megiddo (1350–1150 BCE) and on the sarcophagus of Ahiram of Byblos (late second millennium).

The cherubim throne for the "the LORD Sabaoth" mentioned in 1 Samuel 4:4 seems to predate the kingdom, yet it is the cherubim's presence in the Temple which has won them an enduring place in the imagery of Western tradition. Archaeologists have found examples of a cherubim throne among the artifacts of the Canaanite culture. These pieces of ivory show each side of the throne is formed by a cherub, an animal with wings and a human face; the seat is created by joining the inner wings of the cherubim.

According to 1 Kings 6:23-28, Solomon places two cherubim in the holy of holies which are interpreted as the throne for the unseen God. They were ten cubits high and measured ten cubits from tip to tip of their outstretched wings; thus they would have just fit into the inner chamber, a cube of twenty cubits. The outer wing of each touched the wall, and the inner wing touched each other and formed the seat of the throne with the ark resting before them as a footstool. The wings of the beast also suggest the ability of the deity to move, and in Ezekiel 10:18-19; 11:2-4, the glory of the Lord rose up from the Temple with the cherubim below. The theme of mobility is also found in 2 Samuel 22:11 where God rides on a cherub and flies on the wings of the wind.

In the later Priestly tradition, the cherubim face one another more as guardians of the ark of the covenant and especially of its covering called the "mercy seat" or "propitiatory" where blood was sprinkled on the Day of Atonement (Exod 25:18-20; see also Heb 9:5, the sole reference in the NT).

The seraphim, so often connected to the cherubim in the later tradition, would also seem to be fantastic creations. Their name, connected both to "burning" and to "serpents," suggests "fiery serpents." They make only one clear, but famous, appearance in the Bible. Isaiah describes them as part of his smoke filled vision in which each had six wings, a pair for flying and a pair to cover their face and feet as they cried out: "Holy, Holy, Holy is the LORD of Hosts" (Isa 6:2-4). The same word is used for the bronze serpent in the desert (Num 21:6, 8; see also Deut 8:15; Isa 14:29; 30:6).

Pastoral-Liturgical Tradition

In the Christian tradition, the cherubim and seraphim have been taken from the fantastic bestiary and tamed by humans. The presentation of angels in general as human beings with wings is a Roman transposition of these creatures from their native middle-eastern context. Theological tradition has rarefied the notion of angels, and artists, too often, have reduced these wondrous beings to prettiness in order to fill the heavens with something more than clouds. The tradition, unfortunately, has lost sight of the fantastic and the fierce image communicated by these wondrous creatures which formed and guarded the place of God's presence and mercy. Ezekiel's fantastic vision is remembered mainly for the four realistic faces which became icons for the Gospels: the human for Matthew, the bull for Mark, the ox for Luke, and the eagle for John. The Gospels would be well served by remembering the whole brilliance and wondrous majesty of Ezekiel's vision.

See: ANGEL, ARK OF THE COVENANT, TEMPLE

HARRY HAGAN, O.S.B.

CHRISTIAN

This term used throughout the centuries as the most common designation for followers of Jesus appears only three times in the NT. "Christianos" seems to be derived originally from a Latin term, i.e., one who belongs to "Christ." This derivation coincides with the information in Acts 11:26 where Luke notes that it was in Antioch where the disciples were first called "Christian," presumably by those outside the community. So, too, in Acts 26:28 King Agrippa sarcastically chides Paul, "Are you so quickly persuading me to become a Christian?"

A significant use of the term is found in 1 Peter 4:16: "Yet if any of you suffers as a Christian, do not consider it a disgrace, but glorify God because you bear this name." Here the possibly derisive use of this term by outsiders (note: to suffer "as a Christian"; to "bear this name") is now accepted by the author of the letter as a badge of honor which binds together the followers of Jesus. The Roman historian Tacitus writing in the early second century confirms that the name is meant to be derogatory when he refers in his *Annals* to the "Christians" who had been made scapegoats by Nero as "hated for their abominable crimes." His text also indicates what was probably true from the beginning, namely that outsiders considered the name "Christ" as a proper name for Jesus and were unaware of its significance as a messianic title. Tacitus explains that "their name comes from Christ" who had been executed by Pontius Pilate. Similar references are found in other second and third century Roman authors such as Suetonius, Pliny the Younger, and Lucian of Samosota.

It is wonderfully ironic that a name begun in derision and perhaps often used by those who inflicted violence on the Christian community would become for the disciples of Jesus themselves a term that aptly expresses the essence of Christian faith, namely belonging to Jesus.

See: CHURCH, DISCIPLE, WITNESS

DONALD SENIOR, C.P.

CHURCH

Our English word church imports its meaning from the Greek word in the NT, *ekklêsia*. In turn the NT writers developed this special religious significance of the word *ekklêsia* from the Greek OT, where this word, along with *synagôgê*, translated the Hebrew word *qāhāl*.

Old Testament

From its inception Israel appears as "a people" or "nation." Scholars disagree on the historical accuracy of the Genesis stories depicting Israel as biologically descending from Abraham, Isaac, and Jacob-Israel. However, the religious meaning of the stories is clear. Children of Israel are members of a family; they are brothers and sisters. They stand beloved before God as a group united in the corporate personality of their patriarch. Together as a people they are the children of God (Hos 11:1).

From Sinai/Horeb on, the covenants renew and give full expression to this basic solidarity of Israel. What is new with the covenants is the picture of Israel "gathering," assembling to listen to the words of God and to ratify its part in the ensuing treaty. The day of the covenant at the base of Horeb (Sinai), will be remembered as "the day of the assembly" (*qāhāl*; Deut 9:10; 10:4; 18:16).

At times physically gathered together as a *qāhāl* (Deut 31:28-30), at other times as a motley nation migrating through the desert (Num 20:4), Israel understands itself as "the assembly of God," the *qĕhal Yahweh*. It is God who calls them together and thus gives Israel its identity. This *qĕhal Yahweh* is holy also because God is in its midst (Num 16:3).

When Israel celebrated its identity and its covenants, it did so above all by a cultic assembly which seemed to represent its foundational assembly. The presence of "all Israel" at the dedication of Solomon's Temple is described as the *qĕhal Israel*. The anguished petitioner of Psalm 22 proclaims the name of God and invites divine praise in the "assembly" (*qāhāl*; Ps 22:23-26; see also Ps 149:1). The reading and renewal of the Torah under the leadership of Ezra after the Babylonian captivity is described as proclamation to "the assembly [*qāhāl*] of men, women, and children" (Neh 8:2). Israel became Israel in the most intense way when it assembled.

To some extent, especially from the Temple's destruction in the sixth century BCE on, the very act of assembling before God was more significant than priestly acts of sacrifice. Jews dispersed around the world could be Jews by assembling, by gathering especially to listen to the words of the Torah just as their ancestors gathered and listened to the original proclamation. The practice gives rise to the institution of the synagogue.

New Testament

Although today we clearly distinguish between "church" and "synagogue," the two concepts start out basically identical. The Greek words *ekklêsia* and *synagôgê* both translate the Hebrew *qāhāl*, with no apparent difference of meaning. If the word *synagôgê* was appropriated by the later Jews for their assembly as the word *ekklêsia* became the property of Christians (although see Jas 2:2), the ensuing distinctions between the two words and their English translations is imposed by later usage not by their original meaning.

In effect any understanding of the Church in the NT must encompass a wide trajectory in which the early Christians both distanced themselves and appropriated elements of the synagogue as they drew boundaries around themselves in order to define themselves as an identifiable group.

Jesus and His Disciples. As followers of an eminent teacher of the Law, the disciples of Jesus looked much like the rabbinic schools of NT times with two very important exceptions. First, these disciples responded to the initiative of Jesus calling them rather than selecting their own teacher (Mark 1:16-20). Second, Jesus demanded a loyalty to his person far beyond the demands normal for a rabbi of the day. It was his person far more than his teaching that focused the group. The loyalty demanded by Jesus excluded any rival loyalty, even the most serious obligations to one's family (Matt 8:21-22; Luke 9:59-62).

The Gospel of Mark recalls how new social relations precisely modeled on the family molded the school into a group (Mark 10:29-30). Yet again this "group" differed from most groups in two important ways. First, a hierarchy of authority was emphatically excluded. In order to be first, one had to be last. The servant was the image of the leader (Mark 9:33-35; 10:42-45). Second, despite efforts by the disciples, Jesus resisted drawing clear boundaries distinguishing members from non-members (Mark 9:38-40). Thus this early "church" was more a movement within Judaism rather than a socially definable group or sect.

The very idea of clear boundaries dividing insiders from outsiders ran counter to the primary sense of Jesus' mission. He came to call sinners. Unlike the table fellowship of the Pharisees which symbolized an exclusive fellowship of the pure, table fellowship with Jesus meant the unconditional offering of God's mercy to all sinners (Mark 2:15-17).

Paul. Paul's letters give us an insight into the transformation which the "Jesus movement" underwent in the decades immediately following the death and resurrection of Jesus. For one thing the Jesus movement became heavily populated by Gentiles, people with little interest in adopting Jewish practices. For another thing, the movement became urbanized, having to deal therefore with wealth and social strata, the need to identify one's groups in order to deal harmoniously with population density, and the inevitable imitation of other clubs "around the corner."

Paul's churches appear rooted in urban households (Rom 16:5; 1 Cor 16:19; Philemon 2). Most voluntary associations of the time faced a crucial challenge of finding a place to meet. Paul met that challenge by directing his initial efforts to the conversion of wealthy households, who would then host the developing Christian community (1 Cor 1:14-16; Rom 16:23). The dining room or *triclinium* became the setting for Christian cult. Here took place the "Lord's

Supper," followed most probably by a sharing of spiritual gifts (1 Cor 11:14).

Boundaries arise in the Pauline churches, although they remained soft. The "uninitiated" could be present at Christian cult (1 Cor 14:23-25). The non-believing spouse of a Christian was in some way drawn into the circle of holiness (1 Cor 7:12-14). However, Paul makes a clear distinction between "a brother" and an "outsider" and views expulsion of a member from the Christian group as a radical form of discipline (1 Cor 5:11-13).

Like the households and urban clubs of his day, the churches of Paul develop a defined authority structure. Again two major differences distinguish leadership of the "Jesus clubs" from other groups. First, this leadership formed in the interplay of local authorities, who managed the life of the particular urban group, and itinerant authorities, like Paul himself, who linked the urban Christian group to the larger movement. The "apostles" and perhaps also the "prophets" and "teachers" mentioned by Paul in his list of fledgling offices (1 Cor 12:28; see also Rom 12:6-7) represent the itinerant group. The "assistants" and "administrators" (1 Cor 12:28) and above all one who "contributes in generosity," one who "is over others" (better translated, "the patron"), and one who "does acts of mercy" (Rom 12:8) represent the resident authorities in the local church, whose very functions required a substantial economic basis. More than likely, this resident group consisted primarily of the heads of households like Stephanas (1 Cor 16:15-16) or Nympha (Col 4:15) who opened their expensive homes to the community and acted much like the patrons of contemporary Hellenistic clubs.

A second way in which this early Christian authority structure differed from its Hellenistic counterpart—Gentile or Jewish—was by the stress Paul continues against developing a hierarchy of honor. The patrons and founders of Hellenistic clubs were decorated by their groups with extravagant titles and accorded special privileges within the life of those clubs. Reminiscent of the instructions of Jesus, Paul insisted on avoiding decorative honors and stressed the mutual dependence of all members (1 Cor 12:21-26). Paul described his own "office" in terms of a dialectic of power and weakness, honor and dishonor (1 Cor 4:9-13). Since Paul gives us no word to the contrary, we can suppose that the resident patron or household head—man or woman—presided over the Lord's Supper and the sharing of gifts that took place in his or her home. Nowhere does Paul lift this "office" above other gifts. He rather insists on the image of a body where every part has its function and all functions depend on each other in organic unity (1 Cor 12:12-22). More than likely the "bishops and deacons" of Philippi (Phil 1:1) were similar to the patron/leaders of Corinth.

Although the Pauline church had no priests, no physical sacrifice, no sacred processions or sacred sanctuaries, Paul was conscious of the deeply religious significance of his churches. Like the Jews of the Diaspora who could not offer physical sacrifices, the members of Paul's churches worshiped God in a spiritual way. Their very lives (bodies) constituted a "living sacrifice" (Rom 12:1). Their gathering was "the temple of God" (1 Cor 3:16-17). Through the Spirit, God was constantly revealing gifts to this community (1 Corinthians 2). They were, in fact, the body of Christ* (1 Cor 12:27). God was present among them and by them.

The perspective of the impending return of Jesus dominated Paul's thinking, including his views of the churches. For Paul "the time is short." "The form of this world is already passing away" (1 Cor 7:29, 31; see 1 Thess 4:15). Paul therefore did not call his churches to engage in the reform of worldly institutions. Rather the churches were to represent to the world a kind of "beachhead" of God's reign. Members were to live the life of love (agapê) which is the truly eschatological gift (1 Corinthians 13). They were already in that "pneumatic" state which characterizes the risen body (compare 1 Cor 2:14-16 with 1 Cor 15:42-44).

In effect Paul recreated something like the Jewish synagogue, a symbolic gathering of God's chosen people to listen to God as they prepared for an ultimate gathering. Instead of concentrating on the Law, however, the Pauline churches concentrated on their own gathering, building up that body, exercising above all the gift of love. Christ had replaced the Law, and the body of Christ was in fact the community. Like the synagogue, the Christian church was rooted in the patron family yet represented a city-wide group. Like the synagogue, the church was a part of a much larger picture, a world-wide people of God, who saw their home in Jerusalem. By his letters, by his emissaries, by his greetings and news from one group to another, and especially by his effort to bring a collection to Jerusalem, Paul reminded his local churches of their world-wide network and of their roots in Jerusalem.

The Synoptics. Although the Gospels of Matthew, Mark, and Luke focus on the stories of Jesus, the manner in which the stories are told provide precious, although incomplete, insights into the communities telling those stories and, hence, into the further development of the Christian churches.

Mark's Gospel chose to highlight the warnings of Jesus against developing a hierarchy of honor. We can infer that the tendency toward such a development was real in the Marcan church. Even the twelve apostles in Mark's Gospel appear as weak persons incapable of grasping the suffering mission of Jesus—unlikely founders and models for a later community. The rehabilitation of the twelve is hinted at only by the promise of Jesus "to go before" them—in effect, to shepherd them as a shepherd goes before his flock—into Galilee (Mark 14:28; 16:7).

In the Marcan account we see a community which has discarded all Jewish food laws (Mark 7:15-19). The Last Supper of Jesus was vividly recalled as a covenantal

act and was probably repeated by the Marcan community (Mark 14:24). In general, however, this community was one whose eyes were fixed on the future and imminent return of Jesus as the glorious Son of Man (Mark 13:24-27) who alone would lift the veil of mystery and suffering enveloping the followers of Jesus (Mark 13:5-23).

Matthew's Gospel excised the Marcan disregard for food laws (compare the parallel in Matt 15:10-20) presumably because the Matthean Church practiced such Jewish rules and in general held the Torah in great esteem (Matt 5:17-19). As it appears indirectly in this Gospel, the Matthean Church looks like a Judeo-Christian group working hard to integrate its Israelite heritage with its new faith in Jesus (Matt 13:52), explaining OT texts as prophecies of Jesus (Matt 1:22; 2:5; etc.), upholding the "fulfilled" validity of the Torah, and above all seeing Jesus as the Jewish Messiah (Matt 1:1).

As Matthew understands it, openness to Gentiles came about because of a historical event, the emphatic rejection by the Jews of their Messiah (Matt 27:20-25). Jesus came for the tribes of Israel (Matt 10:5-6), but Israel's refusal meant that the kingdom was taken from them (Matt 21:43) and offered to "all nations" (Matt 28:18-19).

The anti-Pharisaic material in Matthew (Matt 15:12-14; 16:12; 21:43) bespeaks the definitive break between the Church and the synagogue. This break entails similarities and dissimilarities between the two institutions. Like the Pharisees who possessed the keys of the kingdom (Matt 23:13), so does the "chief rabbi" of Jesus' Church (Matt 16:19; see Isa 22:22)—although Christians are not to use the rabbinic titles of "rabbi," "father," and "master" (Matt 23:8-11). As the synagogue concentrated its meeting on the Torah, the Christian assembly concentrates on the ethical teachings of Jesus which replaces "what was said of old" (Matt 5:21-48). The ultimate mission of the disciples is "Teach all nations to carry out everything I have commanded you" (Matt 28:20). Like the synagogue, the Christian *ekklêsia* is the gathering where a member can exercise his or her duty of fraternal correction. Only when the offenders ignore the admonition of the *ekklêsia* are they to be treated like Gentiles (Matt 18:15-18).

As seen in its emphasis on the Church's power "to loose and bind," the Matthean Gospel clearly is struggling with the paradox of sinfulness within the community. Although the community, according to Matthew, was now given the kingdom, and in some ways represents the first phase of the kingdom, this community was not the gathering of equally pure but rather constituted a mixture of good and bad which must remain so until the final judgment (Matt 13:24-30, 36-43).

As Matthew remembers them, the disciples were not the blinded followers of the Marcan account, but rather a group who understood well the teaching of Jesus (Matt 13:51) and in general exemplified faith. Matthew limits the disciples to the symbolic number of twelve—even if he has to rename Levi to identify him with one of the Twelve. Like the twelve patriarchs of Israel (Matt 19:28; Luke 22:30), these apostles represent the whole people. Peter clearly speaks for this group and functions as a foundation for Jesus' *ekklêsia* (Matt 16:13-19). But what is said of Peter is said of the Twelve (Matt 18:18), and what is said of the Twelve is symbolically a statement about the whole new people of God.

If anything expresses the significance of the Church in Matthew's Gospel, it is the promise, "Where two or three are gathered in my name, there am I in their midst" (Matt 18:20). In this way the final words of Jesus as Emmanuel are fulfilled, "Know that I am with you always until the end of the world" (Matt 28:20).

Luke retells the stories of Jesus to a Christian community disillusioned in its hope for an early parousia of Jesus. Hence Luke must complete the stories of Jesus with stories of the early Church as it settles in for a long "time of the Gentiles" (Luke 21:24). Jesus' proclamation was only the beginning. The Church now continues the same proclamation in the same Spirit that animated Jesus. The Gospel of Luke is completed by the Acts of the Apostles.

Already in the Gospel, Luke prepares us for his budding ministers. Jesus has several levels of disciples. The closest are the Twelve, but the seventy-two likewise form a wider circle. Around the seventy-two is the unnamed group of listeners who, by accepting the teaching of the seventy-two, accept Jesus (Luke 10:16). Personal reception of Jesus' emissaries (Matt 10:40) is replaced by adherence to their teaching. Personal emissaries are of course limited to a generation, teaching can last through the centuries. Thus a principle of Christian identity, one not limited to the first generation, has been established: fidelity to apostolic teaching.

The Acts of the Apostles continues the development of a hierarchy of ecclesial status. The apostles remain on top, and adherence to their teaching is one of the main characteristics of the Christian community (Acts 2:42-47). Soon the seven table assistants are added to the organization under the apostles (Acts 6:1-6). "Prophets and Teachers" appear later in Antioch who by solemn gesture, the laying on of hands, confer authority on Barnabas and Saul (Acts 13:2-3). Saul (Paul) is healed, instructed, and "confirmed"—by the laying on of hands—by Ananias, the Jewish Christian of Damascus (Acts 9:5-19). Saul is then introduced to the apostles by the Jewish Christian leader, Barnabas (Acts 9:27). Paul and Barnabas in turn appoint "elders" in each church they found (Acts 14:22). It is with the presbyters (also called "overseers") of Ephesus that Paul caucuses on his final return to Jerusalem rather than meet with the whole Church of Ephesus (Acts 20:17-38).

Besides the "laying on of hands" the double Lucan account relates details suggesting the development of ritual, especially that of the Lord's Supper. Jesus' last supper incorporates the line, "Do this in memory of me" (Luke 22:19). Luke is careful to present Paul as "breaking bread" on the first day of the week in a Christian gathering which included "much talk" (*eph' hikanon homilêsas*; Acts 20:7-12).

For Luke, Jerusalem is the place of salvation and the origin of the gospel's radiation. Yet of its nature the gospel is intended for all peoples, not simply because the Jews rejected Jesus, but because Jesus, from the beginning, is "a light to all the nations" (Luke 2:32). The "Jewish/Gentile" issues regarding the Law more or less disappear in Luke. The fight between Peter and Paul on this matter (Gal 2:11-14) is smoothed over (Acts 15:36-39). However, Luke testifies to the Gentile churches' appropriation of a basically Jewish institution, the presbyterate, and to the Jewish ritual of "laying on of hands." Luke's Church is one of synthesis and adaptation.

Deutero-Paul. The importance of the presbyterate appears in the Pastoral Letters (1 and 2 Timothy, Titus), where presbyters (also called overseers) of the local churches form the highest teaching authority and are charged with management of the community. This official appears to be the evolved form of the earlier "patron/administrator" of the Pauline churches, only now he has assumed the teaching functions within the Church. In the pastorals this official has his office from an appointment by Timothy or Titus (1 Tim 5:22; Titus 1:5), who in turn are sent by Paul. Thus the picture of the "apostolic succession of bishops" arises.

In Colossians and Ephesians we see the development of the Church into a clearly universal entity. In the earlier letters of Paul, the Church was primarily a city-wide association—perhaps composed of individual house churches*—and this Church was opened to a network of churches ultimately rooted in Jerusalem. In Colossians and Ephesians the Church is one. It is the body of Christ (Col 1:18, 24; Eph 5:3). Colossians actually maintains reference to three levels of church: house church (Col 4:15), city-wide church (Col 4:16), as well as universal (Col 1:18, 24). Ephesians speaks only of a universal Church.

Ephesians develops the ecclesiology of Colossians and describes the Church as the "wife of Christ" much as Israel was the (unfaithful) wife of God (Eph 5:22-33; see Ezekiel 16; Hosea 3). By implication the Church is the New Israel. Unlike Colossians, Ephesians develops the role of the Christian apostles and prophets into that of "the foundation" on which the Church is built (Eph 2:20; compare Col 2:7) as well as the exclusive recipients of God's revelation of the mystery (Eph 3:1-6; compare Col 1:16-17).

John. In the Fourth Gospel the Church is conspicuous by its absence. The descriptions of Jesus' baptism and the Lord's Supper disappear. But John does provide a discourse about regeneration of "water and the Spirit" (John 3:5) as well as discourse about the bread of life which, as the flesh of Jesus, must be eaten (John 6:51-58). In effect, John seems to be interested in developing the meaning of such ecclesial practices rather than linking them to some foundational action of Jesus.

In John the Twelve are hardly mentioned (John 6:67-71; 20:24). However, a Beloved Disciple appears and acts as the perfect disciple, related to Jesus as Jesus is related to the Father (John 1:18; 13:23). This Beloved Disciple is the eyewitness through whom believers may come to know the truth of Jesus (John 21:34).

In John the dialectic with the Jewish traditions comes to acute hostility. True worship is neither in Jerusalem nor on the Samaritan mountain but in Spirit and Truth (John 4:21-24). Jesus as the good Shepherd leads his own out of "the court of the sheep" (*hê aulê tôn probatôn*) and forms a new flock (John 10:1-5, 16). The Jewish leadership ("the Jews") have judged themselves in rejecting the Light of the World and now have only the devil as their Father (John 8:12-59).

If Israel was the (unfruitful) vineyard of God (Isa 5:1-7), Jesus is the true vine and disciples draw life from him like the branches on a stock (John 15:1-17). Here is the essence of the Johannine view of Church. It is unity of life formed by each disciple's union with Jesus. It is a unity of life dominated by the imperative, "Love one another" (John 5:12).

Outside of that vine, however, is only the hatred of "the world" (15:18-25). This is "the world" for which Jesus does not pray (17:9). The command to love your enemies disappears. The boundaries defining the group of Jesus' followers now become a rampart.

John understood the crucifixion not as an act of sacrifice or even as a moment of intense suffering, but rather as the gesture that would gather the children of God into a unity (John 11:51-52). On Calvary the undivided garment of Jesus, literally, the garment in which they made no "schism," recalls the divided robe of the prophet Ahijah which he tore into pieces precisely to prophesy the division of the people of God (1 Kgs 11:30). The unnamed mother of Jesus, identified as "woman", recalls the image of Jerusalem which gives birth to a nation (Isa 54:1-3; 66:7-13) and perhaps even "the woman" of Adam whom he called Eve because "she was the mother of all the living" (Gen 3:20). On Calvary "the woman" is identified as the mother of the disciple in close correspondence (*hoi men . . . de;* John 19:25) with the action of the soldiers. Finally closely connected (*meta touto;* John 19:28) with the identification of "the woman," Jesus completes the entire scene and "*conferred* the Spirit" (*paredôken to pneuma*). Although the word "Church" is never used in this scene, John appears to be describing its origin.

See: APOSTLE, BODY OF CHRIST, COMMUNITY, HOUSE CHURCH, MINISTRY

VINCENT P. BRANICK

Pastoral-Liturgical Tradition

Both the liturgical texts and the writings of early Christians describe Church in continuity with the scriptural heritage. The Church is the assembly of God called together by the Spirit in order to follow the teachings and lifestyle of Jesus, and to do the public work of worship* in memory of Jesus.

While early Christians expected an imminent second coming, what they became were households of disciples who renounced dominative power, and eliminated social barriers. They were an egalitarian community of brotherhood and sisterhood, ministers of healing and peace, whose lives and service were characterized by love. Entrance into this community was the result of the gift of God manifested in faith and in baptism.

Church as the People of God in Human History. Just as the mystery of Christ can be described "from above" (Fourth Gospel), in other words, as the Word coming forth from God, so also the Church can be seen as originating "from above." Therefore, the Church is a people fashioned by the grace of God, convoked and sustained by the Spirit, and achieving the plan of salvation designed by God. But in complementary fashion, the mystery of Christ can be described "from below" (Synoptic Gospels) and the Church can be seen as a historical, human, and empirical body of believers living out the mystery of Christ in diverse places, cultures, and situations. Consequently the Church is primarily the local church, a people of holiness (1 Pet 2:9-10), a spiritual house and a holy priesthood persevering in prayer and in praising God (Acts 2:42-47). The local Church, in communion with other local churches, is a pilgrim people of God called out of darkness into marvelous light. Both its spiritual, divine origin, and historical pilgrimage interact as Church worship and service in and to the world develop.

Gradually, then, a Church identity develops as the Church extends the mission of Jesus to the four ends of the known world (Acts) and as it is rooted in local communities (Pauline correspondence). Its goal is salvation offered according to the designs of the divine plan of salvation for humanity and the cosmos. This salvific grace is offered in love in order that the Church might point to the in-breaking of God's reign and as the Church is a cause of that reign's becoming. God's benefaction is manifested in the local Church as it worships, evangelizes, and serves. This new Israel, "while going forward in this present world, goes in search of a future and abiding city" (Heb 13:14) (*Constitution on the Church*, no. 9).

Church as Mystery. The local Church, in continuity with the Scriptures, draws its inspiration from various metaphors. No one image fully describes the Church, but a skein of images interact in order to disclose and uncover the mystery of Church. Furthermore, they invite a deeper experience of Church as each community is shaped by the Word of God and the Liturgy of the Eucharist. Consequently the Church is described as a sheepfold, a flock guided by Christ and its human shepherds; a tract of land, the field of God (1 Cor 3:9); a choice vineyard (Matt 21:33-43); the edifice of God as well as the holy temple, the Holy City, the New Jerusalem; our mother (Gal 4:26); the bride; and the body of Christ.* (*Constitution on the Church*, no. 6). These images become ingrained in the imagination and memory of local Churches. While one image or one set of images linked together may appeal to one local Church, other images or sets of images may shape the identity of another local Church. Thus the mystery of Church retains its unity with other churches, yet a rich diversity develops among local Churches through their use of images. This is reinforced as the images are used in the Liturgy of the Eucharist and in the Liturgy of the Hours. The experience of worship shapes each local Church's experience and enables its reflection and belief.

Church as Community. Although the Church has often drawn its vitality from monastic centers of devotion and preaching as well as from sanctuaries and places of popular piety and pilgrimage, the local Church has been and is a structured communion under the guidance of a pastor and in unity with the bishop, the vicar of Christ. This experience of Church finds its source and summit in the celebration of the Eucharist on the Lord's Day (*Constitution on the Liturgy*, no. 10). In the Liturgy of the Eucharist Christ is present in the assembly, the Word proclaimed, the priest, and reserved sacrament. The public work of the Church manifests the Church fully as the assembly offers its prayer and praise to God. Sharing at the Lord's table enables the assembly's communion and energizes the people of God to fulfill their ecclesial tasks: to evangelize, to engage in supporting the conversion process of catechumens, to reconcile those out of communion with them, to be nourished and strengthened to bring the gospel into the marketplace. The bonds of grace also shape the local Church so that it can be a sacrament of God for one another and for the locale in which it exists. This causes the local Church to reflect on its models of ministry and to develop its ministries according to the pattern of its worship. The local Church is not a part of a pre-existing whole, that is, the local Church in worship and in ministerial structure is not a branch office of a corporation with its headquarters in Rome. Instead the local Church is a concrete realization of all that the one Church is. In the local Churches and out of them the one and holy catholic Church comes to exist. Consequently the local Church is required to think consciously about its structures and its models of ministry. The Liturgy of the Eucharist, the sacrament of communion, offers a paradigm for ecclesial ministry and mission. The Liturgy of the Eucharist is the work of the entire assembly. While various ministers enable that communal worship, all ministers remain a part of the assembly and function so that the entire assembly can give praise and thanks to God. So, too, the inner life of the Church and the mission of its people to the world interact not only according to their charisms,* but also in communion and cooperation with one another. The model of ministry, a model of collaboration, is a direct reflection and consequence of its liturgical celebration. At every Eucharist the assembly invokes the Spirit to come down upon them so that the bread and the cup may be transformed and that they may become "one body, one spirit in Christ." The Spirit is active in fashioning an ecclesial and Eucharistic Body of Christ. In addition, communion is fostered as the assembly takes responsibility for its members in initiation (through sponsors, godparents and ecclesial testimony, and affirmation of faith in the catechumens), in marriage (through pastors and laity cooperating in preparing couples for the liturgy and vocation of marriage), in orders (through ecclesial acknowledgement of the readiness of candidates for ordination and through affirmation that such persons have been chosen by God), in reconciliation (through ecclesial acknowledgement of communal and social sin), and in pastoral care of the sick (through communal celebration of anointing and through pastoral visitation).

How local churches sufficiently blessed with clergy develop a communion of life and a shared community of affection will influence the younger churches. These younger churches are often intentional communities which rely on mutual support, shared reflection on the Word of God, and prayer. Their development and their maturity can be helped or hindered by the models of communion, collaboration, and community they see in the long established churches. In turn, their experience of Church will also be instructive for older churches.

Church as Universal. While nineteenth-century ecclesiology focused on the essence of Catholicism and Church from Protestant and Catholic perspectives, the Church finds itself in a different place at the close of the twentieth century. A new sense of the Church universal is happening. Unity is not based on the dependency of younger churches on those of the North Atlantic nor directions from authority in Rome. Each local Church risks a narrow vision based on ethnic, racial, political, or nationalistic viewpoint. Furthermore, both younger and older churches risk becoming separatist or sectarian. However, unity now requires an active sharing of all local Churches in communion with and under the presidency of the Bishop in Rome. In their particular ways, both Paul VI and John Paul II recognized the significance of this shift from the northern to the southern hemispheres. Papal visits to other local and regional Churches indicate an appreciation of the polycentric nature of the Church today. To some degree papal visits to other churches are in continuity with the traditional role the Church in Rome played in late antiquity. Rome became known as a Church of charity, faith, and love. It was sought out in moments of conflict because it became known for its fairness in arbitration and its advocacy on behalf of other churches.

The shift from a Eurocentric to a universal sense of Church is due to a number of historical and ecclesially self-conscious factors. The decline of classicist culture gave rise to a historically conditioned and empirically based ecclesiology. The demise of European colonialism was accompanied by the creation of the United Nations. Second, the Church at Vatican II took steps in the direction of de-Europeanization. It admitted the vernacular in worship, set up the international Synod of Bishops, and developed the role of regional and national bishops' conferences. Third, the majority of bishops now reside in the southern hemisphere and, by the end of the century, seventy percent of the Church will be in the southern hemisphere. For the first time in its history, the Church is becoming a world Church. Its task is to balance unity amid plurality, universality in the midst of particularity.

There are significant implications for the new situation in which the Church finds itself. First, the Church finds itself carefully reflective on its relationship to other religions. This includes the relationship of the Church to Judaism. Vatican II acknowledged a spiritual bond between Judaism and Christianity. It also rejected any charge of deicide against Judaism and the Church deplored any hatred or persecution against Jews at any time and from any source.

Second, the Church, especially through theological dialogue and the active steps of John Paul II, has begun to give priority to the unity of the Christian Churches. Since no church is simply a coalition for action, the importance of doctrine cannot be by-passed. Some measure of doctrinal accord will be necessary even if complete agreement on all matters of doctrine may be unattainable. Whatever agreement exists, for example, on the basic essentials of Christian faith, the practice of valid baptism, the communal Scriptures and the ancient creeds, etc., needs to be admitted and each Church needs to see what hierarchy of importance it gives to Christian doctrines.

On a practical level, interchurch unity has been fostered by communal prayer and study, by interfaith marriages, and by members of various Churches participating in social justice, advocacy, and charitable effort. How various Churches deal with reception of doctrinal agreement and a spiritual assimilation of unity in the life of the Churches will be important.

Church as Global. The challenge facing the Church is: how will it be midwife to a new world, a new heaven, and a new earth? While each Church worships and acts in memory of Jesus and each Church exists as an embodiment of the one Church, the Church points toward the future of humanity. A crucial test will be one of credibility, i.e., how does the Church operate in fact? A reflective praxis by the younger churches of the southern hemisphere and the minority churches of North America creates some suspicion regarding the theological assumptions of the dominant churches and the example witnessed in everyday life. In addition, the newer churches find themselves in a process of inculturation of liturgy and patterns of thought and leadership. How can the Church adapt and appropriate local culture and maintain its basic heritage of faith

in Christ? How will the Church embody the simplicity and poverty of the gospel as it advocates a nuanced and varied option for the poor and the young? How will the Church become advocate for the earth and stem the process of geocide? The way the Church embraces a crucified, suffering humanity will determine whether it can be midwife for the future.

See: BODY OF CHRIST, COMMUNITY, PEOPLE OF GOD, REIGN OF GOD

JOHN J. O'BRIEN, C.P.

CIRCUMCISION

Old Testament

General. Although female circumcision is known in some cultures, the term usually refers to male circumcision and consists in the complete or partial cutting off of the foreskin of the penis. It was widely practiced from ancient times, being known among the Egyptians at least as far back as 4000 BCE. Although it came to be promoted as a hygienic measure, this is a more recent development; among earlier peoples it was a rite which carried important social or religious meanings, often having the significance of an initiation of sorts. For many tribes it was performed at the time of puberty or was a premarital rite (as suggested in the Shechem incident of Gen 34:14-18) and thus initiated the male into manhood or adult life.

Abraham. The primary OT text is Genesis 17, in which God renews the covenant made with Abraham and enjoins circumcision on him and all his male descendants as a sign of the covenant (vv. 9-11). Since the rite is to be the sign of the covenant, specific mention is made of Isaac (as yet unborn), with whom God's covenant will be renewed (vv. 19, 21). Ishmael, the future father of the Arab nations, is said to have been thirteen years of age at the time (vv. 23, 25), which no doubt reflects the practice of the Arabs, who circumcise as a puberty rite. Genesis 17 is a late narrative; it is assigned to the Priestly Code, generally dated to exilic or post-exilic times (see also Sir 44:20). Pertinent legislation is found in Exodus 12:44, 48; Leviticus 12:3; Numbers 9:14.

Development. Although the Abraham text is late, the antiquity of the rite in Israel is attested by the use of flint knives for the operation (Josh 5:2; see Exod 4:25), a practice known also in ancient Egypt. Through much of the OT period most of Israel's neighbors practiced circumcision, so that the Philistines, who did not, were often referred to as "uncircumcised" (Judg 14:3; 15:18; 1 Sam 14:6; etc.). This explains why the two hundred foreskins David counted out to Saul as the "bridal price" for Michal (1 Sam 18:22-27) proved that David had killed two hundred Philistines. A text as late as Jeremiah 9:24-25 speaks of the Egyptians, Edomites, Ammonites, and Moabites, along with Israel, as being circumcised. In exilic times, when Judah was surrounded by people who did not practice it, circumcision came to be considered the distinctive mark of the Jew. This, along with its being administered on the eighth day, instead of as a puberty or pre-marriage rite, allowed it to be seen as the sign of the covenant and of entry into the people.

Metaphorical Use. The lack of circumcision is often used in a metaphorical sense to designate that which is not fit for use, as when Moses' lips or fruit of trees are referred to as uncircumcised (Exod 6:12, 30; Lev 19:23). More often the metaphorical usage suggests lack of moral uprightness, as when Jeremiah speaks of uncircumcised ears or of God enacting judgment because "all these nations, like the whole house of Israel, are uncircumcised in heart" (Jer 6:10; 9:24-25; see Lev 26:41), or when Ezekiel complains that "foreigners, uncircumcised both in heart and flesh" have been brought into the sanctuary (Ezek 44:7, 9). Conversely, Moses can call Israel to "circumcise" the heart (Deut 10:16) or promise that God will do that for them (30:6), where the complementary expressions ("be no longer stiff-necked" and "that you may love the Lord, your God") indicate the significance

of this spiritual circumcision. Jeremiah exhorts in similar terms as the means of turning away God's wrath (Jer 4:4).

New Testament

Circumcision comes up in at least three contexts in the NT.

John and Jesus. John the Baptist was circumcised on the eighth day, at which time his name was imposed and Zechariah's speech was restored (Luke 1:59). Jesus also, as a Jew and the child of observant Jewish parents, was circumcised and named on the eighth day (Luke 2:21).

Gentile Converts. Circumcision comes up importantly in the controversy in the early Church over the question of observance of the Mosaic Law.* Once Gentiles began to be admitted to baptism the question arose whether they had to observe the provisions of the Mosaic Law, especially circumcision. The problem appears prominently in Paul's letters to the Galatians and to the Romans, where he argues, against the so-called "Judaizers," that salvation comes through faith in Jesus Christ, that to seek justification in external observances of the Law is the equivalent of rejecting faith in Christ. In Romans 4 Paul gives prominent attention to the Abraham narrative, arguing that the promises were made to Abraham before he was circumcised and that he was justified by his faith; circumcision was received subsequently "as a seal on the righteousness received through faith when he was uncircumcised" (Rom 4:9-11), and the Law, coming in four hundred thirty years later, does not annul the promise (Gal 3:17). Acts 15 recounts that men from Judea began to teach the recent Gentile converts at Antioch that they had to be circumcised to be saved, that Paul and Barnabas took the matter to the Church leaders in Jerusalem (vv. 1-2), and that this occasioned what we call the "council of Jerusalem." The council did not deal merely with the question of circumcision but more broadly with that of the issue of Gentile converts and the Mosaic Law. The decision was that the Law should not be imposed on them, though four provisions to ease table fellowship between Gentiles and Jews were adopted. Hence Paul's formula "in Christ Jesus, neither circumcision nor uncircumcision counts for anything, but only faith working through love" (Gal 5:6).

Metaphorical Use. In the NT circumcision is used metaphorically in much the same way as in the OT. Stephen accuses his persecutors of being "uncircumcised in heart and ears" (Acts 7:51) and Paul says that "circumcision is of the heart, in the spirit, not the letter" (Rom 2:29). But when he claims "for we are the circumcision," the contrast is between worshiping "through the Spirit of God" and putting "our confidence in flesh" (Phil 3:3; see Col 2:11).

Pastoral-Liturgical Tradition

Although circumcision is not practiced as a religious rite in the Church, baptism takes its place as a rite of initiation, for women as well as for men. The single rite for all corresponds to Paul's dictum that in Christ Jesus "there is . . . not male and female" (Gal 3:27-28). All those things said of circumcision in the metaphorical sense, exhortations to live in truth the implications of becoming a member of the people of God, to be the "true circumcision," i.e., to live in the spirit of dedication and holiness that should characterize one called to God's covenant, remain valid.

See: ABRAHAM, BAPTISM, COVENANT, LAW, NATIONS, PHILISTINES

JOSEPH JENSEN, O.S.B.

CITY

The emergence of cities in the Middle East goes back beyond 3000 BCE. Although cities varied in nature and function over the ages and in various cultures, there are some consistent features. The gathering of peoples into a more or less permanent settlement provided for defense in time of attack, enabled the distribution of goods, served as the seat of government, and was often the location for a central sanctuary

and cult. Therefore in the city there flourished occupations and crafts that went beyond agriculture, leading the way to the development of a truly urban population.

Many cities in the ancient Middle East and throughout the Mediterranean world enjoyed a degree of political independence, forming quasi city-states. Many cities would form the center around which were clustered outlying villages and farms. During periods of invasion, the people in the outlying areas would seek refuge within the fortified walls or ramparts of the city.

The ancient city had certain common features frequently alluded to in the Bible. Fortified cities would have an encircling wall or earthen rampart. The gates of the city were carefully constructed to ensure security as well as access, and the inevitable flow of traffic and activity around the city gates made them a natural meeting place. Many cities were dominated by an acropolis or high point which was the center of defense and, in many cases, contained the fortified palace of the ruler as well as the location of the sanctuary. Granaries or silos would be built in the city to store grain for barter and redistribution. Providing water for the city population as well as having an adequate supply during time of siege led to the development of elaborate water systems such as those found at Megiddo, Hazor, and Jerusalem. In contrast to the flimsy construction of the ordinary citizens' dwellings, public buildings such as the Temple, the palace, and the homes of the elite were built of cut stones and decorated wood. All of these features of the city become biblical images in both the OT and NT.

At the time of the conquest, the region of Israel* was inhabited by a number of Canaanite* cities. While most of the population was agrarian and semi-nomadic or located in small farming hamlets, there were early Israelite cities which reflected many of the same features described above. Greek culture was more self-conscious about the life of the city; the *polis* was viewed as the ideal community in which government, religion, commerce, and culture all thrived. Alexander's conquest of the entire Mediterranean area in the third century BCE brought the Greek ideal of the city into the world of the Bible. Herod the Great was devoted to building cities in the Greek (and similar Roman) pattern: his cities at Caesarea, Samaria, and to a large extent Jerusalem itself included not only government and religious buildings but large forums or the "agora" for commerce, as well as theaters and gymnasiums. In addition to Jerusalem, Jesus and the early Christian community would have experienced this same taste of urban life if they ventured into Sepphoris (near Nazareth) or Tiberias (on the sea of Galilee near Capernaum)—neither of which are mentioned in the Gospels.

The dominating presence of Jerusalem* brings the city into the theological perspective of the Bible. Once David established Jerusalem as the capital of the united Kingdom and located the Temple there, Jerusalem becomes a symbol of Israel's hope as well as the locus of its anguish. The division of the kingdom into north and south after Solomon's reign as well as the later alienation of the Samaritans blunted Jerusalem's historical role for these populations, but within the Bible's theological perspective Jerusalem remains dominant. In Jerusalem dwells the living God within the Temple and there, too, is God's Son the King. At Jerusalem the priests offer sacrifice and prayers to God on Israel's behalf. Thus this city becomes a symbol of the gathered people of God, united in faith and peace. Jerusalem becomes the object of pilgrimage and longing for all Jews (see Psalms 2; 87; 122; 125; 128; 129).

At the same time, Jerusalem becomes a symbol of its hopes dashed and unrealized. It is besieged by enemies, its walls leveled, and the Temple itself destroyed by its traditional foes. The infidelity of the monarchs and the people provoke divine anger against Jerusalem and result in God's judgment against the city (Jer 9:7-11; 13:9, 27; Ezek 5:5-17). During the Exile, the return to Jerusalem and the longing to rebuild the city become poignant biblical themes (see Psalm 137).

This ambivalent role of Jerusalem is clearly seen in the NT. Luke, for example, emphasizes that from Jerusalem and its Temple would come the Messiah; the infancy narrative ends with Jesus being presented in the Temple and he pulls away from his parents to return to the Temple, his "father's house" (Luke 1–2). In the same way, the Temple and the city of Jerusalem would be both the endpoint of Jesus' own mission and the starting point for the community formed in his name (Luke 24; Acts 1–2). The early Christian mission would begin "from Jerusalem" and extend to the ends of the earth (Luke 24:47; Acts 1:8).

Paul, too, pays homage to the crucial role of Jerusalem, seeing the origin of his mission there (Rom 15:19), returning there to confer with the apostles (Gal 1:18; 2:1), and asking the Gentile communities to make a monetary offering to the Church of Jerusalem as a sign of their debt to this mother church (Rom 15:25-29; 1 Cor 16:1-4; 2 Cor 8–9). Jerusalem also plays a role in the theology of Hebrews as the now heavenly realm where the sacrifice of the risen and exalted Christ is enacted (Heb 12:22).

The Book of Revelation capitalizes on the symbolic role of Jerusalem. The endpoint of all salvation history is the new city, Jerusalem, that descends from heaven and becomes the dwelling place of God and of the saved (Revelation 21–22). The typical features of the ancient city are cited and transformed: the gleaming walls of precious jewels; its resplendent gates and decorations; its abundant water supply; its role as a haven of peace and security; its beauty and cleanliness. In this city there is no Temple because the victorious Christ, the Lamb of God, is its Temple and here there is no darkness for the glory of God is its light.

Thus in the overall span of the Bible, the movement is from the desert to, ultimately, the city. Put in other terms, the biblical drama of salvation entails the gathering of all God's people into a community of peace. Thus for the Bible the arena of salvation and the ultimate sacred place is the "city," despite its violence, conflicts, and inequities.

See: JERUSALEM

DONALD SENIOR, C.P.

CLEAN/UNCLEAN

The words "clean," "wise," and "honorable" are parallel labels describing either physical conditions or human behavior that the Bible approves. "Unclean," "foolish," and "shameful" are parallel labels describing conditions or behavior that the Bible censures. Proverbs, Qoheleth, and Job concentrate on wise and foolish human behavior. Exodus, Leviticus, and Numbers concentrate on clean and unclean physical conditions. Anthropologists describe both these ways of classifying conditions and behavior in ancient Israel and other Mediterranean cultures as "codes of honor and shame."

Old Testament

In the OT, "clean" and "unclean" have little to do with hygiene. They are labels that defined the status of a household in the village. They do not say as much about what a household was actually doing or not doing, but rather how villagers reacted to it. The labels "clean" and "unclean" are analogous to credit ratings today and distinguished households in good social and economic standing from those that were not.

The bodies of the men and women of a household were considered as microcosms. They were households in miniature. The penis, vagina, mouth, eyes, anus, ears, nose, and nipples were the borders where these human bodies interacted with the outside world. Consequently, emissions from these orifices were important, but were not the only sources of information on the status of the body of the household itself with respect to the outside world. Menstruation, vaginal hemorrhage, distillation from the penis, semen, and afterbirth were unclean because they were either typically female, were associated with death, or were uncontrollable. Saliva, mucus, sweat, breast milk, pus, and blood from circumcision were clean because they were either typically male, were associated with life, or were controllable. Deuteronomy (Deut 23:10-15) labels excrement as unclean, but Leviticus labels it as clean.

Labels teach each generation a specific way of looking at life. In the world of the Bible, some formal education did take place in schools whose teachers explained to students why certain ways of doing things were clean, and others were unclean. But most education was informal, and labeling was the principal means of informal education. Villagers applied labels with words, gestures, facial expressions, or tone of voice.

"Clean" behavior entitled a household to life. The clean ate moderately, did not get drunk, worked hard, made good friends, sought advice before acting, held their temper, paid their taxes, and imposed fair legal judgments. The clean were careful in dealing with one another during menstruation, sexual intercourse, childbirth, and death. And they were equally conscientious about what food they ate, what clothes they wore, what animals they herded, and what crops they planted in their fields. Clean households could care for their own members and were prepared to help their neighbors. "Clean" was the label for a household in good standing, licensed to make a living in the village and entitled to its support. Only the clean were entitled to buy, sell, trade, marry, arrange marriages, serve in assemblies, and send warriors to the tribe. Only the clean were entitled to make wills, appoint heirs, and serve as legal guardians to care for households endangered by drought, war, and epidemic. The clean were in place and functioning well.

"Unclean" behavior sentenced a household to death by placing its land and children in jeopardy. The unclean ate too much, drank too much, were lazy, quarrelsome, selfish, and thought nothing about lying to the village assembly. They were thoughtless in their sexual relationships, and disrespectful of the newborn and the dead. The herds of the unclean were mangy, and their farms run down. Unclean households did not fulfill their responsibilities to their own members or their neighbors. "Unclean" is the label for households on probation. The unclean were out of place and not functioning properly. Consequently, both their contributions to the village and their eligibility for its support were suspended. The label "unclean" downgraded the status of a household, until it proved that it was again contributing to the village.

New Testament

Some NT households changed the OT norms for deciding clean and unclean status: "nothing that enters one from outside can defile that person; but the things that come out from within are what defile" (Mark 7:15, also Rom 14:13-23; Titus 1:10-16). Some did not (Acts 10:1–11:18). The norms most often discussed in the NT for determining whether a household is clean or unclean are circumcision, diet, and sexual relationships.

The circumcision of males as the most significant indication of the status of a clean OT household was soon replaced in NT households by the baptism of both females and males (Gal 3:25-29). Soon, it was necessary to be baptized, rather than to be circumcised, in order to be saved or to be clean. Practices in the dominant Greco-Roman or Hellenistic culture that Alexander brought to the eastern Mediterranean after 333 BCE played an important role in redefining "clean" and "unclean" in NT households. Ritual bathing, for example, was virtually mandatory in a Hellenistic culture, while circumcision or any other physical mutilation was prohibited.

Diet also distinguished clean OT households from unclean households. Soon, however, the diet of some NT households became virtually no different from the diet of other Hellenistic households. Some NT households remained clean and in good standing even when they served pork and other meats butchered at public sanctuaries (1 Cor 8:1-13). Yet some NT households continued to consider such a diet to be unclean (Acts 10:1-33).

As more Gentiles became Christians, marriages between Christians who were Jews and Christians who were Gentiles, and marriages between Christians and Gentiles who were not Christian, were approved or clean. Most other sexual relationships prohibited in OT households remained unclean for NT households as well (1 Cor 7:1-16; Acts 15:22-35).

Pastoral-Liturgical Tradition

Of all of the traditions on clean and unclean in the OT, virtually only those dealing with leprosy appear in the Lectionary. In contrast, the Lectionary reads most NT adaptations of these OT traditions that play a more important role in defining the status of Christians in their communities. The clean enjoyed a wide range of social and economic blessings, the unclean were excommunicated.

Patristic traditions like the *Epistle of Barnabas*, *2 Clement*, and the *Shepherd of Hermas* use "clean" and "unclean" to label those eligible to participate in the liturgy. Only the clean or those "in the state of grace" participated fully in the Eucharist.

But they also use the labels for Christians committed to an ascetical way of life like hermits, monks, or nuns. While technically Christian asceticism embraces the disciplining or cleaning of all the senses, sexuality became the central focus. The Stoics, who had dedicated themselves to cleaning their lives of joy, grief, or any other emotion, exercised a significant influence in polarizing sexual activity and holiness or cleanness in this Christian tradition. Like Stoics, Christians labeled only sexual activity necessary for procreation as clean. Eventually, Christians went on to label sexual activity on days when the Eucharist was celebrated as unclean and to prohibit sexual activity for the clergy at any time.

Therefore, "clean" came to mean not simply "ascetic," but "celibate."

See: LEPROSY

DON C. BENJAMIN, O. CARM.

CLOUD

Many ancient people believed that the divine presence was such an awe-inspiring splendor that one had to ward it off. Usually the cloud is part of that cosmic scenario that manifests the divine presence but preserves the divine transcendence. The cloud is also a powerful symbol of God's involvement with humans.

Old Testament

God's Protective Presence. God's concern for Israel frequently took on military contours. God used clouds as military hardware in order to defend the people. Elsewhere God is spoken of in a military context as "one who rides the clouds/skies in his majesty" (see Deut 33:26). What is at stake here is God's concerted intervention on behalf of the people.

The linkage of cloud and protective presence is to be especially noted in the Exodus experience. The Bible uses two expressions in this regard: (1) column of cloud by day and column of fire by night (Exod 13:21-22) and (2) column of cloud and fire (Exod 14:24). The use of cloud together with fire is Israel's manner of describing Yahweh's participation in the key events of the Exodus and the desert wandering. When the Egyptians pursue the Israelites with their horses, chariots, and charioteers, Yahweh exercises his sovereignty in the cloud by vanquishing the enemy. Earlier in this same scene, in order to protect Israel from attack, the column of cloud took up a position in the rear to separate the two camps (Exod 14:19-20). Cloud powerfully demonstrates Yahweh's intent to become involved in the life and death struggles of Israel.

Divine Presence in the Desert. Yahweh is present in the volcanic eruption at the covenant-making process on Mount Sinai (Exod 19:16-18). Cloud is also used as a symbol of God's glory.* This is a rich priestly term for demonstrating the unique way in which God influences human existence. The cloud of glory is associated with the cloud on Mount Sinai. "After Moses had gone up, a cloud covered the mountain. The glory of the LORD settled upon Mount Sinai" (Exod 24:15-16).

This description of God's manifestation at Sinai becomes a model for all subsequent Israelite worship. Just as the cloud covers the mountain and Yahweh's glory settles there (Exod 24:15-16), similarly the cloud covers the sanctuary or tent of meeting: "Then the cloud covered the meeting tent, and the glory of the LORD filled the Dwelling" (Exod 40:34). On the seventh day Yahweh summons Moses from the midst of the cloud (Exod 24:16). On the eighth day Moses calls Aaron, his sons, and the elders of Israel (Lev 9:1). According to Exodus 24:17 Yahweh's glory (linked with the cloud) appears as a consuming fire. In Leviticus 9:24 fire advances from God's presence and consumes the first sacrifice. Sinai becomes the model for Israel's worship and, significantly, the cloud is in evidence.

The Jerusalem Temple. The dedication of Solomon's Temple is a key event recounted in both First Kings and Second Chronicles. According to 1 Kings 8:10 and 2 Chronicles 5:14, the cloud so filled the Temple that the priests could no longer perform their ministry. The cloud, and with it God's glory, manifests not only the divine presence but also Yahweh's taking possession of the Temple (see Exod 40:34-35; Ezek 43:1-5). More than likely, censors in the Temple (1 Chr 28:17) created such glory. In this connection one may note that on the Day of Atonement the high priest effects a cloud of incense in the holy of holies to conceal God's majesty and thus prevent his own death (Lev 16:13).

Punitive Presence. Finally, there are some texts where cloud is associated with darkness, gloom, and somberness. In these contexts cloud suggests not the presence, but the absence of Yahweh. For example, Ezekiel employs the parable of the shepherds to condemn Israel's leaders and to announce his intention to rescue the scattered people from their misery: "I will rescue them from every place where they were scattered when it was cloudy and dark" (Ezek 34:12). Given a plague of locusts, the prophet Joel proclaims the Day of the Lord, i.e., a time of God's judgment on the people: "a day of darkness and of gloom, a day of clouds and somberness!" (Joel 2:2).

New Testament

Transfiguration of Jesus. While both Matthew and Mark as well as Second Peter preserve the tradition of Jesus' transfiguration (Matt 17:1-8; Mark 9:2-8; 2 Pet 2:17-18), it is Luke who provides more OT links to cloud, glory, Sinai, and divine presence. The mountain (Luke 9:28) is the Lucan place par excellence for communion with God. Moses and Elijah appear in glory (see Exod 34:30-35) and discuss Jesus' *exodos* or departure (Luke 9:31-32). The word conjures up Israel's Exodus from Egypt during which Yahweh's glory was perceived. The three disciples see Jesus' glory, i.e., the risen Lord (Luke 9:32). "While he was still speaking, a cloud came and cast a shadow over them, and they became frightened when they entered the cloud" (Luke 9:34). As at Sinai, the cloud functions as an indicator of God's presence and glory. While the text is not totally clear, apparently only Jesus, Moses, and Elijah enter the cloud. It is difficult not to find an allusion to Moses' entering the cloud in Exodus 24:18. In sum, the cloud functions within the context of divine presence and Jesus' anticipated resurrection glory.

Parousia. In the eschatological discourse, Jesus announces his parousia* or second coming and the cosmic signs associated with it: "And then they will see 'the Son of Man coming in the clouds' with great power and glory" (Mark 13:26; see Matt 24:30; Luke 21:27). Here Jesus returns for judgment and the deliverance of the disci-

ples. "The Son of Man coming in the clouds" refers to Daniel 7:13 where "one like a son of man" approaches God to receive kingship. Here, however, Jesus returns from heaven for judgment. One should note that Luke 21:27 uses the singular "cloud" rather than the plural "clouds" mentioned by Matthew and Mark. Probably Luke links Jesus' discourse with the ascension of Jesus in Acts. There a cloud takes Jesus from the sight of his disciples (Acts 1:9). Next the two men assure these disciples that Jesus will return in the same way (Acts 1:11). For Luke the ascension prefigures the parousia.

At the trial of Jesus both Matthew and Mark have Jesus refer to Daniel 7:13 (as well as Ps 110:1). When asked whether he is the Messiah, the son of the Blessed One/ the Son of God, Jesus responds: "I am; and you will see the Son of Man seated at the right hand of the Power and coming with the clouds of heaven" (Mark 14:62; see Matt 26:64. Luke omits the reference to the clouds; see Luke 22:69). Jesus' answer places the clouds from Daniel 7:13 in the context of exaltation and triumph. Having been exalted at God's right hand (Ps 110:1) through the resurrection, Jesus vows to return as the triumphant king. Fittingly the clouds capture the OT element of divine presence and divine involvement.

Paul offers a rather vivid description of the parousia: "Then we who are alive, who are left, will be caught up together with them [Christians who have died] in the clouds to meet the Lord in the air" (1 Thess 4:17). Once again clouds manifest God's presence. Christians alive at the time of the parousia are caught up in the clouds because they too participate in the status of the glorified Jesus.

Pastoral-Liturgical Tradition

Divine Presence. The biblical tradition, that clouds are the instrument of divine presence, still has validity. Both the awesome power of the storm and the "ordinary" character of less violent clouds can easily remind the believer of divine presence. However, the challenge inherent in the symbol is to activate the imagination to uncover and develop the metaphor of "God with us." Perhaps the greatest challenge in this quest is to discover God present in other people. Such presence is readily linked to the cloud's association with revelation, e.g., on Mount Sinai. This God chooses to share himself/herself in and through humans. The discovery or recovery of the goodness of others is a movement that catapults one into the realm of the sacred. God's glory is reflected in all and sundry. By ferreting out the manifold divine presence, the believer enters into the cloud with Moses.

Divine Justice. God's presence in the pillar of cloud (and the pillar of fire) is a justice-oriented presence. Through the cloud Yahweh provides for his oppressed people. Cloud, therefore, must remind the believer that every form of injustice is by definition the absence, not the presence of God. To reach out to the marginalized, the victims of "the system," etc., is to concretize one dimension of the imagery of the cloud. This aspect is not far removed from the parousia of Jesus where the One in the clouds comes in judgment of the evil and deliverance of the good. Fundamentally to do justice, especially on behalf of the downtrodden, is to develop a proleptic parousia, viz., Jesus has anticipated his return in the clouds because believers have already demanded justice.

See: ASCENSION, DAY OF THE LORD, EXODUS, GLORY, PAROUSIA, SON OF MAN, TEMPLE, TRANSFIGURATION

JOHN F. CRAGHAN

COMMUNITY

The term community does not formally appear in the Bible, although there are many terms for assembly, convocation, association, meeting, people of God,* household of God, and the like. The NT names the disciples of Jesus as "church" and "synagogue." Hence when readers examine the notion and reality of community in the Bible, they must take special care to examine the specific how and why ancient Jews and Christians assembled together, which will be different from modern associations.

Old Testament

Although some of the terms seem familiar to us, ancient social institutions differed from our own. Jews and Christians belonged to only two basic social institutions, kinship (the family/household) and politics. In reality, the stronger by far was the family, with its immediate kinship network.

Community and Family. The notion of community was rooted in the sense of belonging to a large extended family.* Individual households included parents, their married children, wives and offspring, slaves and servants, all under one house. One's primary identity rested in this family, with its extended relationships to tribe or clan. From this came a sense of sharing the wealth of the family (e.g., its wells, fields, animals, etc.), its network of support and defense, its honor and respect. Ideal marriages were between cousins, thus cementing the network of trust and support, wealth and power, among families and tribes. One's basic notion of community, then, was that of kinship, with its rich and overlapping strands of shared identity, trust, honor, and support.

Communities which are kinship-based tended to gather for rituals important to the survival or cohesion of the family. Most important would be marriages, which joined houses and clans together, and burials, which confirmed the importance of family members. Festive meals, especially such as harvest festivals or Passover, were other occasions to gather. It would be anachronistic to imagine community public worship either in temple or synagogue by a family, such as we experience in parishes today.

Community and Political Institutions. Politics, the second major institution, touched the lives of Israelites and Christians less immediately and forcefully. The tribes of Israel were basically kinship groups, but they were occasionally summoned to gather as an assembly for military purposes or to support the political ascendancy of a ruler. It is important to note that the basic Hebrew word for assembly (qahal) contains the notion of invited participation or summoning. This suggests that such large gatherings were irregular and exceptional; Israelites gathered at someone's command or request for joint military purposes or raiding. At such assemblies, the tribes were represented by their male leaders (2 Chr 5:2), elders (Jer 26:17), captains (Judg 20:2), and warriors. Thus one should not think of them in modern democratic terms, for only males and males of high status within the kinship groups participated.

New Testament

Community as Fictive Family. People belonged to groups outside the family network, which are properly understood as fictive families. The community of Jesus' disciples describes itself as a (fictive) family. With his blood relatives standing outside a house, Jesus turns to those inside listening to his teaching and says, "Here are my mother and my brothers. Whoever does the will of God is my brother, and sister, and mother" (Mark 3:34-35). Hence Paul spoke of himself as the "father" of the community (1 Cor 4:14-15) and his co-workers as "brothers" (1 Cor 1:1; Phil 2:25). He likewise identifies the members of the Church as kin (1 Thess 4:6; 1 Cor 5:11). He expects community members to extend the same respect, support, and indulgence to fictive kin as to blood kin (see 1 Cor 8:11, 13; Rom 14:10-15). At Corinth Stephanus' whole household joined the Church (1 Cor 1:16; see Acts 16:15) and that kinship group became (fictive) kin with others in the household of God.

Christian Borrowing of Jewish Terminology. The Hebrew terms for community are quite varied, the most common and important one being qahal or invited gathering. In the Greek translation of the Hebrew bible qahal was rendered either as ekklesia or synagoge. In the Greek world, ekklesia or "church" normally refers to a political group which enjoys citizenship in a city-state. When Christians take up this term to describe their communities, they do so as citizens of a new political entity, the reign of God. Their "commonwealth is in heaven" (Phil 3:20); no longer strangers and sojourners in this world, they have become "fellow citizens and members of the household of God" (Eph 2:19). Although ancient Jews and Christians gathered in a synagogue, synagoge refers to a general meeting of people, not necessarily a religious gathering. As part of the daily public life, adult male Jews gathered in the market places under the stoas to trade, read, gossip, etc. This gathering might occasionally be on the Sabbath around the reading of Torah, and it too would tend to be a gathering of males. Cities have many such meeting places, even specific buildings for such gatherings (Acts 9:2). In a heterogeneous situation, members gathered in terms of predictable social distinctions. We know of a specific synagogue of the Freedmen (Acts 6:9) and synagogues based on ethnic lines, such as the synagogue of the Cyrenians and Alexandrians (Acts 6:9b). Christian meetings were also called a synagogue (Jas 2:2).

Pastoral Notes: Community and Social Relations

Social relations in the community of the disciples of Jesus mirrored the pattern of relations in the family. Ideally all members of this fictive family were to be treated with due honor, support, and protection as members of the same household. Hence the sharing of fellowship (koinonia) characterized them. Greek and Hebrew widows were both supported (Acts 6:1-6). Non-elite members should be treated with special respect (1 Cor 12:24-25). Acts of the Apostles describes the community sharing resources like a true family (2:44; 4:34). Such is the ideal. Although fellowship characterizes Christian social relations, we should not imagine an egalitarian or communistic group. The same social structures and classifications found in the family characterize the fictive family or Christian community as well; and family structures were definitely not egalitarian.

Community: A Structured Reality. Although membership in "the Way" was open to all ethnic groups and to both sexes (Gal 3:28), gender specific roles characteristic of the culture persisted within the community. Paul the apostle acted as founder and father (1 Cor 3:10; 4:15), with authority appropriate to a male elder. In time leadership roles became more formalized as recognizable offices (bishop, deacon, elder: 1 Tim 3:1-13; 5:17-21), with specific rights and duties. Other males and females enjoyed roles in the group shaped by the gender conventions of the day (e.g., 1 Cor 14:33-36; 1 Tim 2:11-12). Within the group were rich and poor (Jas 2:1-7), master and slave (Philemon; 1 Cor 7:17-24), who, rhetoric notwithstanding, shared unequal status and support. Elites at the community's *agape* meal liberally ate meat and drank wine, while poorer members went hungry (1 Cor 11:20-22). Rich members sat, while poorer ones stood. Instead of the mutual support given family members, community members took other members to court (1 Cor 6:1) or acted in ways that shamed the honor of this new family (1 Cor 5:1-2). Instead of the expected concern for the welfare of members of the family, some acted arrogantly in disregard of others (1 Cor 8:9-13). Yet the community ideally understood itself in terms of a family with all its cultural notions of mutual honor, support, and defense.

Altruism, Not Individualism. Modern notions of a community as a voluntary association of strong individuals are foreign to ancient Jewish and Christian communities. Family ideology indicates that individuals should always "seek the good of the group" (1 Cor 10:24), and not pursue individualistic objectives. Josephus expressed this well when he spoke of what characterizes Jews: "For we are born for fellowship, and he who sets its claims above his private interests is specially acceptable to God" (Josephus, *Apion* 2.196).

Strong individualists at Corinth flaunted concern for group values, both by an unseemly marriage (5:1-2) and by eating proscribed foods (8:1-2, 7-11). Paul points out how the incestuous marriage harmed the community, as leaven pollutes flour (5:6-8); the unscrupulous eating of idolmeat caused scandal to some, destroying the weak kinsman for whom Christ died (8:11). Promoting one's interests, then, offends the group, and so comes under censure.

Paul counters the problems he discovers with an appeal to what unifies the Church, builds it up, and reaffirms the complex set of roles and statuses established by God. In short he envisioned the community's values and structures mirroring those of an extended family, in particular, concern for the good of the group over individualistic desires. He reminds elitists in regard to their own bodies that, "you are not your own" because "you were bought with a price" (1 Cor 6:19-20; 7:23); that is, individuals are embedded in the household of Christ. Paul always speaks of himself as "servant of God" or "steward of God's mysteries."

Non-individualistic community values are expressed in the importance given to authority in ancient families and fictive family communities. God ascribes to certain peoples a distinctive role and status. In regards to the basic institution of the family, according to God's commandment parents are to be honored (Mark 7:10). Families in this cultural perspective also admit different roles to husbands and wives, roles which are supported in the codes of household duties frequent in Christian preaching (Eph 5:21-33; Col 3:18-19; 1 Peter 3:1-7). Individuals, then, must respect the role and status of others in the group, whom God has so placed (1 Cor 12:18). The notion of faithfulness or loyalty further illustrates the importance of authority in group relations. Sons must honor and obey fathers; likewise slaves their masters. Even Jesus is praised for his faithfulness to God (Heb 3:1-3) and his obedience to him (Heb 5:8; Rom 5:14-21). Family values thus became community virtues.

See: BODY OF CHRIST, CHURCH, FAMILY, MARRIAGE

JEROME H. NEYREY, S.J.

Pastoral-Liturgical Tradition

Community, as it refers to Church, is the gift of God whereby people are called together to share in the life of the Trinity. While there is a plurality of local Churches, the one Church* of Christ is a people made one in the unity of Father, Son, and Spirit (*Constitution on the Church*, no. 4). The worldwide Church, a network of local Churches and communities, participates in the one Christ. Community comes about because each Church vitally belongs to Christ (1 Cor 3:23; 15:23) and is composed of Christ (1 Cor 6:15; 12:27). As the triune persons are related to one another, and are one, so also community establishes the unity of the Church. The Church as community is called to a shared life whereby divine life is mediated through the Word of God and the Lord's Supper. Participation in the triune life enables local Churches to be in cross reference to one another. This enables them to create bonds of love through sharing in the one bread and table, to create mutual esteem through a baptismal dignity and equality, and to do the mission of Christ through an ecclesial mediation of salvation. The local Church, a community alive in Christ (2 Cor 2:14-16), is knit together in God and in Christ, the head of the Body (Gal 2:19-20).

Community as Shared Life. The local Church shares in the Christian vocation to participate in the life of Jesus Christ (1 Cor 1:9; see Phil 2:1; 2 Cor 13:11-13). This is evident in the local community's participation in the Eucharist and it is highlighted in the celebration of Holy Thursday Eucharist which begins the paschal triduum. The gospel narrates the action of Jesus at the Last Supper when he washed the feet of his disciples (John 13:4-8). This action, although an example and an expression of humility, carried a profound significance. To share in the foot washing was to have participation in the glorious Passover of Christ. The shared life of Christians in community has consequences for their life together and for their service to the world.

The NT word that describes this is *koinonia*, often rendered as participation or fellowship in English. The *koinon-* word group does not specify anything specifically Christian or religious. Ordinarily the word refers to an inner relationship. This is seen in Acts 2:42, the idealized Lucan picture of Christian community shaping its inner life. It is also seen in Galatians 2:9 where the pillars of the Jerusalem Church gave Paul and Barnabas the right hand of fellowship.

To have a share in Christ's life and in the Christian community entails a transformation of the members of the Body of Christ. This includes a life led in the light (1 John 1:3, 6, 7); a life without sin (1 John 3:8-10); a sharing in affliction (Phil 4:14); a sharing of resources for other churches (Rom 12:13, 15, 26-27; 2 Cor 8:4); a shouldering of one another's burdens (Gal 6:6); a reciprocity and an exchange of gifts (Phil 1:5; 4:15); a sharing in the sufferings of Christ (Phil 3:10; 2 Cor 1:7), as well as in the Spirit (Phil 2:1; 2 Cor 13:13). To have fellowship in the Christian community also points the churches to the eschatological object of fellowship through blessing (1 Cor 9:23) and the glory not yet revealed (1 Pet 5:1; Rom 8:17).

Community as Participation in Communal Meal. Community is not only expressed in the common meal of the Eucharist; it is also the means by which community is created, fostered, and sustained. The basis for Eucharistic fellowship is Jesus himself. Not only was Jesus a footwasher. His entire life manifested a devotion to his Father; a share in divine life; a beneficent concern for the poor, the marginalized, the sick and troubled; and a service which proclaimed the breakthrough of the reign of God into the lives of his people. His ministry was highlighted by communal meals as signs of a new fellowship. Thus his table sharing points to his ultimate self-gift, his own death. The Eucharist becomes the ritual expression of his costly discipleship (1 Cor 11:23-26) and a pledge of his presence in the community until he comes again. The Eucharist manifests his presence in the midst of the assembly. It challenges the local Church to enter into his life and his cross (1 Cor 1:18). While the Eucharist can become an empty ritual used to avoid his presence (1 Cor 11:20-22), its transforming symbols invite the community to a corresponding transformation in their lives. The consequences of the Eucharist challenge the community to enter into a relationship that welcomes strangers, that builds up the body in love (1 Cor 14:17, 26; 16:14), that enables Christians to make ties of friendship and shared purpose. Sharing in the Eucharist calls the community to live out Christ's mission so that the community encourages mutual respect for one another's dignity, acts in solidarity with other churches who share the one bread, and does the work of justice.

Community as Shared Resources. Christian community is demonstrated by a sharing of personnel and material goods. Although the biblical teachings do not condemn riches or wealth, they do counsel a sharing of money for the support of the community (Acts 4:36-37). Generosity is the result of faith, not self-interest. It is for the sake of more needy members of the community, especially those who might find themselves without the ability to provide for themselves (Acts 2:45; 4:21-35). Care must be given to the needy at one's doorstep (Luke 16:19-31). The custom of presenting bread and wine along with material goods for the poor demonstrates that the Eucharistic community will not brook social and economic disunity (1 Cor 11:1-34). Resources need to be put aside so that new ministries might develop to care for minority members of the Church (Acts 6:1-7). Churches with sensitivity to poorer churches will gladly share their resources (Phil 4:10-18) so that the gospel may be preached and so that weaker churches may survive. The poor, the recipients of contributions, will pray for those who are generous and will manifest Christ who had nowhere to lay his head (Luke 9:58). When communities share resources, they relearn compassion, gratitude, and stewardship.

Since God is a benefactor, community draws people into the divine life. It enables them to develop bonds of hospitality and warmth; it motivates them to do the mission of Christ and to share their resources for the needy and for a global economy that will ensure the freedom and dignity of all peoples.

See: BODY OF CHRIST, CHURCH, RICH

JOHN J. O'BRIEN, C.P.

COMPASSION

Compassion is generally thought to be a human sentiment. However, from a biblical point of view, it is first a divine attribute.

Old Testament

Several Hebrew words are translated "compassion" or "compassionate." Most prominent is *rhm* with the primary meaning of "cherishing," "soothing" or "a gentle attitude of mind." It refers to tender parental love. In all but five of the almost fifty appearances of the verb, the subject is God. Furthermore, the adjective *rahûm* is used only of God and, with few exceptions, the noun *rahᵃmîn* denotes a divine quality. The root also yields *rehem*, one of the two Hebrew nouns translated as "womb." This cluster of words, which suggests a bond like the one between a mother and the child of her womb or between those who came from the same womb, expresses Israel's preferred way of understanding God's compassion.

The passages wherein *rhm* or its derivatives are found fall into four thematic categories: covenant renewal, mercy* after wrath, repentance of sin, national restoration.

Covenant Renewal. Exodus 32–34 recounts Israel's apostasy, the punishment God meted out as retribution, God's subsequent forgiveness, and the mediatorial role that Moses played in the restoration of covenantal relationship. The sin was Israel's desire for some tangible sign of God's presence in its midst. Constructing an image constituted a failure in trust that struck at the very heart of covenant relationship. This is the context within which the compassion of God is proclaimed.

Exodus 33:18-23 anticipates the theophany which is recounted in chapter 34. Moses seeks an unmediated revelation of God. Although this is denied him, he is granted a glimpse of God's goodness along with the proclamation of God's name, "LORD." The name is a revelation of God's essential being and explicitly identifies God as "mighty, compassionate and gracious, slow to anger and rich in steadfast love and faithfulness" (Exod 34:6). This statement, which appears to be a technical covenantal characterization of God, is not found in the accounts that relate the initial covenant experience. It appears only after Israel's apostasy.

Mercy after Wrath. To claim that God acts compassionately toward sinners is not to deny the fury of God that is inflamed in the face of sin. This is a wrath of judgement, and not merely of temper. It is a wrath that does not persist; God punishes first, and then shows compassion (Lam 3:22, 32; Dan 9:9). Israel acknowledged its guilt and God's response in its prayers for mercy (Pss 77:10; 79:8). The Bible states that even before the people entered the land of Canaan, they were warned of God's wrath, yet they were also promised God's compassion if they followed God's decrees (Deut 13:18). When David sinned by conducting a census of the people, he chose the punishment wherein he felt that the compassion of God would be most evident (2 Sam 24:14; 1 Chr 21:13).

One of the most moving images of God's compassion toward suffering sinners is found in that part of Jeremiah known as the Book of Consolations. The tenderness with which God speaks of this sorrowing repentant people is particularly noteworthy in chapter 31. This poetry also highlights the role that repentance plays in moving God from anger to compassion. The Prophetic books abound with references to God's anger giving way to compassion (Isa 30:18),

treading their guilt underfoot in the process (Mic 7:19).

It is perhaps in the writings of the prophet Hosea that God's longing to be compassionate is most poignantly depicted. Hosea is told by God to name Gomer's second child, a daughter, *Lō-ruhāmâ* (not-receiving compassion) and the second son, *Lō-ammî* (not my people) (Hos 1:6f.), symbolic names representing some aspect of the relationship between God and Israel. After the people had suffered for a time and have repented of their unfaithfulness, the names were changed to *Ammî* and *Ruhāmâ* (receiving compassion) (Hos 2:3). The covenant relationship is reestablished and depicted as marital intimacy (Hos 2:21). The notion of marital reconciliation which flows from God's compassionate forgiveness is found in Isaiah as well. It augments the Isaian description of the restored nation (Isa 54:7-10). Here too is a promise that, once reestablished, the covenantal relationship will endure.

God is characterized as both a compassionate father (Jer 31:9) and a compassionate mother (Isa 49:15). The loving attachment itself is explicitly related to the womb, because of its generative properties. Like the womb, divine compassion is life-giving. Compassion is the forerunner and enabler of restoration, of re-birth.

Repentance of Sin. God's willingness and longing to show compassion is dependent upon sinners' admission of guilt and their conversion (Prov 28:13). Several passages state that God refuses to withdraw the fury of divine wrath if there is no repentance. This was true of the northern kingdom of Israel (Isa 9:16), of Assyria, its conqueror (Isa 27:11), and of the southern kingdom of Judah as well (Jer 13:14). Just as God's response to infidelity is wrath, so God's response to repentance is divine compassion.

National Restoration. The greatest suffering that the nation underwent was the overthrow of the Davidic monarchy, the capture and destruction of the city of Jerusalem, and the exile to Babylon of a significant portion of the population of Judah in the sixth century BCE. The extent of this catastrophe, perceived as the consequence of the consuming force of divine fury, became the measure of God's compassion once the nation had repented.

Again, it is primarily in the writings of the prophets that this trust in God's compassion is clearly articulated. The destroyed cities would be rebuilt (Jer 30:18; Dan 9:18; Zech 1:16), leaders would be raised up (Jer 33:26), and the nation itself would again prosper (Ezek 39:25) as if it had never known misfortune (Zech 10:6). God's compassion and a return to fidelity to God's Law will bring new life (Ps 119:77, 156). These last passages illustrate the ultimate goal of God's compassion—restoration. Restoration would demonstrate that God's love is not defeated by human unfaithfulness. On the contrary, God's love is a vibrant creative force that is always straining toward some kind of union. The compassion of God is more than comforting, it is creative. As the womb brings to birth life with all of its possibilities, so divine compassion brings to rebirth life that was threatened or perhaps even lost.

The Compassion of Jesus. The NT writers may have preferred *éleos* (mercy) when speaking of compassion, but forms of the verb *oiktirō* (sympathetic) also appear in several passages, notably: "Be compassionate *(oiktirmōnes)* as your Father is compassionate *(oiktirmōn)*" (Luke 6:36; Matt 5:48). This word is used in referring to the compassion of God and to the compassion that Christians should have toward each other. However, it never refers to the compassion of Jesus, either historical or risen. Another word, *splánchnon*, is used there instead.

God's compassion occurs frequently in the writings of Paul. Explaining the relationship between God's promises to Israel and divine freedom, Paul quotes Exodus 33:19: "For to Moses he says, I will show mercy *(eleēso)* to whom I show mercy; and I will be compassionate *(oikteiréso)* to whom I am compassionate" (Rom 9:15). God is re-

ferred to as "the Father of compassion," (2 Cor 1:3) whose compassion is the inspiration for Christian sacrifice (Rom 12:1). The sense of God's *raḥ*ᵃ*mîm* lies behind this use of *oiktirmói*.

Splánchnon, a word that essentially means the "inward parts" of a sacrifice, almost always appears in the plural form. In early Greek it referred to the lower part of the body, especially the womb or the loins. Later it came to denote impulsive passions as distinct from the sensibilities of the heart. Apart from its use in the description of the tragic end of Judas (Acts 1:18), *splánchnon* denotes profound feelings or emotion. Twice is it found in the NT with *oiktirō* (Phil 2:1; Col 3:12) describing the kind of attachment Christians must have toward each other. It seems that for Paul emotions that might be regarded as personal inclinations are really expressions of being "in Christ" (Phil 1:8).

It is the use of the verb that is most interesting. With the exception of its appearance in three parables, its subject is always Jesus. It is used to describe the deep-seated emotion elicited in him by the desperate straits of others and it seems to characterize the messianic quality of the actions that flow from this passion, thus giving the emotion itself messianic character. Profoundly moved, Jesus heals the blind (Matt 20:34), the lepers (Mark 1:14), the boy with a demon (Mark 9:22), and unnamed illnesses of the crowds (Matt 9:36 [Mark 3:34]; 14:14). He multiplies loaves and fishes (Matt 15:32 [Mark 8:2]) and raises a boy from the dead (Luke 7:13).

The verb appears in Jesus' parables that tell of a loving father who is overwhelmed to see his prodigal son returning (Luke 15:20), of an unselfish Samaritan who is willing to care for one who otherwise would most likely spurn him (Luke 10:33), and of an employer who, while exacting justice, is moved to pity (Matt 18:27). The first parable is a characterization of the compassionate God. The second offers Christians an ideal after which they should model themselves. The story itself ends with such an exhortation (Luke 10:37). The third narrative both characterizes God as compassionate and exhorts Christians to act toward others with the same compassion God has shown them (Matt 18:33). Clearly, this deep-seated emotion is a profoundly religious sentiment.

The verb appears in characterizations of the reign of God, indicating its messianic connotations. The miracles of Jesus have long been understood as signs of the in-breaking of God's reign. Each miracle in its own way gives us a glimpse of the meaning of that reign, showing that the domination of sin and death, the presence of which causes the profound emotion in Jesus, has come to an end, and that the power of God in Jesus is at hand with new hope and new life.

Eleos, the word used most frequently in the NT for compassion or mercy, denotes emotion roused by undeserved suffering in others. When referring to God, it is understood in the Hebrew sense of steadfast love, the covenantal faithfulness of God that can be traced throughout the history of salvation. It carries this meaning in both the Canticle of Mary, known as the *Magnificat* (Luke 1:50, 54), and in the Canticle of Zechariah (Luke 1:72, 78). However, it is also used to describe God's disposition toward sinners. As with *rah*e*mîm,* the contexts of this word yield the notion of new life or rebirth through the mercy of God (Eph 2:4; Titus 3:5; 1 Pet 1:3). It seldom appears without either a direct or an indirect reference to the divine/human relationship.

This mercy is implored of Jesus when someone begs him for a cure. This same mercy becomes part of an early Christian formula for greeting and blessing (Gal 6:16; 1 Tim 1:2; 2 Tim 1:2; etc.). It takes on an eschatological meaning when it is promised to those who show compassion to others (Matt 5:7). Thus compassion in Jesus, as well as in the followers of Jesus, is a harbinger of the reign of God.

See: COVENANT, ESCHATOLOGY, MERCY, REPENTANCE, RETRIBUTION

DIANNE BERGANT, C.S.A.

Pastoral-Liturgical Tradition

Compassion is the capacity to be moved by another's misfortune and to feel sorrow for it because we see it as our own. A moral sentiment essential for the virtue of justice, compassion is an affective stance toward life which flows from the ability to imagine oneself sharing the predicament of another. Based on the kinship we have with others as members of a common humanity and children of God, compassion leads, where possible, to acts of care on behalf of those who suffer; however, even where alleviation is not possible, compassion remains an appropriate response to another's affliction.

In this respect, compassion is an integral part of the distinctive Christian love of *agape,* a love which is essentially other-regarding and requires a willingness to sacrifice self-interest for the well-being of others. Similarly, compassion is entailed by charity, the friendship love we have for God, and, consequently, for all those loved by God, even our enemies. As Aquinas comments, "loving someone deeply makes us love their children too, however unfriendly they may be towards us" (S.Th., II-II, 25, 8). Thus, compassion is rooted in a deep sensitivity to the mystical unity of all life and leads to the heartfelt conviction that because all creatures are esteemed by God, their well-being cannot be disregarded.

Rationale for Compassion. Christians are obliged to cultivate compassion as the appropriate attitude to the misfortune of others in light of the general gospel summons to live in keeping with the character of God. Throughout the Gospels, Jesus is continually drawn into somebody else's pain; he walks straight into life's brokenness and comes to know our affliction. Encountering the vast human spectacle of suffering* and grief, Jesus is moved; he sees the wreckage of life and is touched in the center of his being (Matt 9:36). In Jesus the cry of human suffering becomes God's own because when confronted with the sorrow and exhaustion of life, God does not turn away:

God opens his heart and becomes one with our pain. That is the divine compassion, the tenderness of heart exhibited by a God who is infinitely sensitive to every sorrow the world has ever known. The gospel message is this: we have a God of a suffering heart. In the passion of Jesus, God risks the intimacy of entering our pain. In Jesus too God becomes the Good Samaritan (Luke 10:29-37), the one who binds up our wounds, but the gospel paradox is that God can be a balm for all wounds foremost because in Christ God knows what it is to suffer and be pained; God's power to heal is inseparable from God's power to feel.

In the Catholic moral tradition, Aquinas saw compassion as part of the virtue of charity. He defined compassion as *misericordia,* a "mercy of heart" that "comes from one's heart being miserable at the sight of another's distress" (S.Th., II-II, 30, 1). A person's ability to be compassionate for the distress of another is determined by the depth of their "affective union" with one who suffers. The sadness we feel over another's misfortune is commensurate with our sensitivity to human solidarity. Aquinas reasoned that we have compassion only when we are able to see another's misfortunes as our own, and this requires that we see the other not as a stranger to us, but as a friend, another self (S.Th., II-II, 30, 2). Like Aristotle, Aquinas too noted that we are more likely to feel compassion for others if the evil which befalls them comes not by choice but by chance; this is especially true for someone who has always striven for what is good, "yet meets with nothing but evil; hence, Aristotle's remark that 'mercy is especially called for when misfortune afflicts one who has not deserved it'" (S.Th., II-II, 30, 1).

Pastoral Applications. Compassion is the courage to be intimate to another's pain. It demands that we risk a heart like the crucified one. It asks that we be willing to absorb the suffering of others as our own and allow our hearts to be reshaped by their pain. It means practicing a love expansive enough to hold within its embrace the sorrow and loss of others until they can walk straight again. Interestingly, our capacity for compassion pivots on our attitude to suffering. A compassionate person can be no coward to sorrow; indeed, compassion belongs to those who have been wounded by some pain and have used it to draw them more deeply into life. For Christians, suffering should not shrivel our hearts but make them more expansive. Like Christ who was "like us in all things but sin" (Eucharistic Prayer IV), Christians are called to befriend others in their affliction.

In this respect, the Eucharist is crucial for cultivating compassion. As we gather to commemorate the compassion of a God who suffered and died for us, we pray that we too might make ourselves available to the struggles and pains of the world. Our gratitude and humility before the tender mercies of a God who "always loved those who were his own in the world" and never failed to show them "the depth of his love" (Eucharistic Prayer IV), moves us to show mercy for the misery of another, even to the point of making our heart a home for their grief. In this way we imitate the love of a God who continues to befriend all those in need.

See: BODY OF CHRIST, CHARITY, FRIEND, LOVE, MERCY

PAUL J. WADELL, C.P.

CONFIDENCE

Trust in God may be easy when all goes well, but the authors of both the OT and NT present strong arguments for confidence even in times of uncertainty and trial. God intervened effectively in Israel's history, often in moments of greatest danger, and continues to be mysteriously present in the Temple, or in heaven, with compassion and love for those in need. Past fidelity is the key to future salvation;* God will not abandon those who cry for help. Jesus too is a source of confidence, because of his teaching about God's omniscient care, the wondrous cures he wrought for those with faith, and the great sacrifice of self for the remission of sin. The apostles and early disciples preached the word of God with boldness and confidence because of their extraordinary experience of salvation in Christ.

Old Testament

Vocabulary. Hebrew words that express confidence are primarily *baṭaḥ*, and *kesel*. The verb *baṭaḥ* means "to trust, have confidence in," and is used with reference to God, other persons, things, or even absolutely: "I am confident" (Isa 12:2). *Beṭaḥ* is a noun with the basic meaning of "security" and signifies absence of danger (Deut 12:10) or lack of worry: "my body, too, abides in confidence" (Ps 16:9). *Kesel* comes from a root which originally means "to be plump," with a negative connotation of being sluggish or stupid (Qoh 7:25; Job 4:6), and a positive one of being cared for: "For the LORD will be your confidence" (Prov 3:26).

Psalms of Trust. Profound assurance of God's abiding, protective love is expressed in Israel's psalms of trust (e.g., Psalms 4; 11; 16; 23; 27:1-6; 62). They contain absolute statements of confidence in God's providence: "The LORD is my shepherd, I shall not want" (Ps 23:1), or that God alone is the source of true security (Pss 4:9; 62:2-3). Sometimes they give reasons for having confidence in God, such as the divine presence in the Temple, in Israel, even in heaven (Pss 27:4f.; 121:4; 11:4), or God's sense of justice, which means effective aid for those who do right (Pss 4:4; 11:7), and for those who are oppressed (Ps 4:2). Other reasons include God's omniscient scrutiny of people's hearts (Ps 11:5), divine power and kindness (Ps 62:12f.), faithfulness (Ps 91:4), and will for fullness of life (Ps 16:9-11).

Psalms of Lament. Expressions of confidence occur also in psalms of lament.* During a crisis, perhaps a grave illness, defeat in battle, a natural calamity, or hostility from others, the psalmist calls upon God for salvation, and adduces reasons why the request should be granted—divine compassion, faithfulness, previous assistance, the people's innocence or repentance. All this inspires confidence and trust even while suffering (Pss 3:5-7; 28:7; 44:7-9). Indeed, confidence is necessary and appropriate especially in times of difficulty, for when all goes well what assurance have we that our trust is a true act of faith, of authentic interaction with God?

Historical Traditions. In its long history with God, Israel had to deal with the issue of confidence time and again. It is hinted at that even Moses doubted when he struck the rock in the desert. He struck it twice, and water did come forth, but God said: "Because you were not faithful to me in showing forth my sanctity before the Israelites, you shall not lead this community into the land I will give them" (Num 20:12). This story is especially significant because the same word "rock" *(selaʿ)* was often applied to God as an expression of unshakable confidence (Pss 18:3; 31:4).

Trust in God was the whole issue between Isaiah and king Ahaz. Threatened by a coalition from Syria and the northern kingdom of Israel, Ahaz had turned to pagan Assyria for help. Isaiah confronted him, predicted the defeat of those enemies, and urged him to confide in God alone (Isa 7:3-9). Ahaz refused, and was given the promise of Immanuel ("God with us," Isa 7:10-16). A later king, Hezekiah, did confide in God in spite of taunts by the powerful troops of Sennacherib (2 Kgs 18:19) and saw them withdraw from Jerusalem because of divine intervention (2 Kgs 19:35f.)!

Critique of Misplaced Confidence. The danger of seeking one's security outside of God was all too common. Ezekiel 29:16 denounces Israel for trusting in Egypt; Psalm 40:5 warns against confiding in "idolatry or . . . falsehood." Job denies that he put his "trust in gold" or called fine gold his "security" (Job 31:24), but others had done just that. He was, however, accused of letting his *piety* be "a source of confidence" (Job 4:6).

On other occasions it seemed that the people of Israel were *too* confident. Because God resided in the Temple all would be well, no matter how they lived their personal lives. Jeremiah—like other prophets—strove mightily to counteract such presumption, shouting at one point, "Put not your trust in the deceitful words: 'This is the Temple of the Lord! The Temple of the Lord! The Temple of the Lord!' Only if you thoroughly reform your ways and your deeds . . . will I remain with you in this place . . . (Jer 7:4-7). The Book of Job reminds us that the hope of the godless shall perish and that their "confidence is but a gossamer thread" (Job 8:13f.). Micah 2:8 also threatens "those who go their way in confidence."

Instead, we find our security by accepting God in humility, patience, and honesty (Isa 30:15; Prov 10:9).

Abandonment. Allied with confidence in God is the issue of abandonment. The Israelites were assured that God would not abandon them (Deut 4:31; 1 Sam 12:22; Ps 94:14), though in fact they were abandoned to their enemies at times as divine punishment (Isa 2:6; Neh 9:28; Ps 78:62). They often abandoned the Law (2 Chr 12:1; Ezra 9:10; 1 Macc 1:52) and even God by turning to idols (Judg 2:13; 2 Chr 24:24; Hos 4:10), but were urged to abandon their wickedness and to repent (Wis 12:2, 20).

New Testament

Several Greek words express the idea of confidence. *Parresia* means "plainness of speech, boldness," and refers to outspokenness based on security; thus it also means "assurance, confidence." This connection is brought out well in Ephesians 3:11f., which speaks of "Christ Jesus our Lord, in whom we have boldness of speech and confidence of access through faith in him." The verb *tharreo* means to be courageous (2 Cor 5:6) or confident (2 Cor 7:16). *Pepoithesis* is a late Greek noun meaning "confidence" in God (Eph 3:12), in others (2 Cor 8:22), or in oneself (2 Cor 10:2). Another word in this context is *pistis*, "faith," used to signify confidence or trust (Heb 10:22). The verb *peitho* means "to convince, persuade," and in the passive, "to be confident," for instance, in God's grace (Phil 1:6), in other people (2 Cor 2:3), and in oneself (Phil 1:25).

The Synoptic Gospels. Jesus demands total confidence on the part of those who would be healed. He asks, "Do you believe I can do this?" (Matt 9:28); he says to the centurion, "As you have believed, let it be done for you" (Matt 8:13), and declares to others, "your faith [i.e., confidence] has saved you" (Matt 9:22; Mark 10:52). Speaking on prayer he says: "Therefore I tell you, all that you ask for in prayer, believe that you will receive it and it shall be yours" (Mark 11:24). During the storm on the sea Jesus asks, "Why are you terrified, do you not yet have faith?" (Mark 4:40), and in speaking about the birds of the air and lilies of the field: "If God so clothes the grass of the field, which grows today and is thrown into the oven tomorrow, will he not much more provide for you, O you of little faith?" (Matt 6:30/Luke 12:28).

John. This Gospel explores the profound dimensions of faith required for a true relationship with Jesus, but the demand for confidence in him remains. The royal official is rewarded with the cure of his son because he "believed what Jesus said to him and left" (John 4:50). Jesus strengthens Martha's confidence before raising her brother Lazarus from the dead: "Did I not tell you that if you believe you will see the glory of God?" (John 11:40). Confidence in Jesus is part of that faith which will bring us to eternal life (John 3:16).

Acts. The apostles and disciples preach about Jesus with great confidence: "They were all filled with the holy Spirit and continued to speak the word of God with boldness" (Acts 4:31). The book concludes with a description of Paul as a prisoner in Rome and states that "with complete assurance and without hindrance he proclaimed the kingdom of God and taught about the Lord Jesus Christ" (Acts 28:31).

Pauline Letters. Paul expresses great confidence, not only in the power of God's grace (2 Cor 3:4; Phil 1:6) through faith (Eph 3:12), but also in the goodness and fidelity of the community (2 Cor 7:16; Gal 5:10), as well as in himself (2 Cor 10:2; Phil 1:25). He dares to hope "that with all boldness, now as always, Christ will be magnified in my body, whether by life or by death" (Phil 1:20). He abjures, on the other hand, confidence in the "flesh" (Phil 3:3).

Hebrews. The Letter to the Hebrews exhorts us to "hold fast to our confidence" (3:6), to "confidently approach the throne of grace" (4:16) "with a sincere heart and absolute trust" (10:22) in Christ, the high priest. Our confidence is secure because of Christ's eternal priesthood and eternal sacrifice (7:24f.).

See: COMPASSION, FAITH, FAITHFULNESS, SALVATION

JOSEPH F. WIMMER, O.S.A.

CONQUEST

This term refers to the process by which the Israelite tribes came to occupy Canaan. There are problems in reconstructing the history of this process. The literary record, preserved in the Bible, cannot be used for historical reconstruction since the writers of the narratives relating to this period knew little or nothing about the origins of Israel in Canaan. Still the narratives can provide some information relevant to the rise of early Israel. The biblical narratives divide the history of early Israel into the periods of the patriarchs, the Exodus, the conquest, and the judges. Contemporary historians recognize that these periods were devised by those who wrote these narratives many centuries after the "events" they describe.

The archaeological record is not entirely helpful in reconstructing the story of how Israel got its land because the archaeological record is silent, i.e., few texts or inscriptions contemporary with the strata from this early period have been found. This makes the interpretation of the results of excavations difficult. The period that witnessed the emergence of early Israel was of a turbulent time of mass migrations by various peoples. What archaeological remains can be related to early Israel is sometimes a matter of guess work.

Because of this uncertainty three theories attempt to explain how Israel got its land. The first is the invasion or conquest model. This model is based on the narratives of the Book of Joshua. It holds that the twelve Israelite tribes invaded Canaan from Transjordan toward the end of the thirteenth century BCE. The tribes engaged in a concerted effort aimed at the total destruction of the indigenous population of Canaan. The Israelite conquest was completed in the space of a few years with an initial campaign in central Canaan followed by later campaigns in the south and north. The conquest ended with the Israelite tribes dividing Canaan among themselves.

Opposing this model is one that sees the process in terms of a gradual infiltration or immigration. Here the settlement of the Israelite tribes in Canaan is the result of a series of uncoordinated movements from the eighteenth to the eleventh centuries BCE. The indigenous population was never annihilated by the incoming Israelites since conflicts were only sporadic. The immigrating Israelites managed to live peaceably with the Canaanites for the most part. David absorbed the Canaanites into his kingdom and this caused a cultural and religious struggle that continued throughout the time of the monarchy. The story of the conquest with its description of Joshua's victories over the Canaanites was simply a propaganda tool in the hand of Yahwists who objected to the syncretistic tendencies of some in monarchic Israel.

A third approach is provided by the revolt model that posits that many native Canaanite peasants revolted against their political leadership and joined forces with the invading Israelites from the Transjordan. This model interprets the available biblical and archaeological evidence with sociological and anthropological categories. It takes into account the social, economic, and political circumstances of thirteenth century Canaan and concludes that the area was ripe for revolt. Yahwism provided the religious legitimation for a revolution of the marginalized elements of Canaanite society against an unjust and repressive social and political system.

None of these models has won universal approval. Each fails in some way to consider relevant biblical and archaeological data. What is emerging in the attempts to understand the origins of early Israel is the recognition that the events described in the Bible need to be analyzed as a part of the wider history of the eastern Mediterranean region. In particular more attention needs to be focused on the role of Egypt in the region since Egyptian imperial power dominated Canaan from the late sixteenth century BCE and peaked in the thirteenth and early twelfth centuries. The collapse of the Egyptian hegemony in Canaan permitted the expansion of settlement and population in the region. The Israelite tribes took advantage of these circumstances and began to move into the lowlands of Canaan where they came into conflict with the Philistines and other groups seeking control of the same territory. The origins of early Israel must be sought within the framework of the political process that occurred in Canaan. This process included the end of Egyptian power and the consequent struggle for power in Canaan between the Israelite tribes who lived in the highlands and the Philistines and others who controlled the lowlands.

No matter what shape the reconstruction of ancient Israel's settlement in Canaan takes, there is one theological problem that cannot be avoided. It is clear that to some extent ancient Israel had to fight for the land that was to be the scene of its subsequent history. In particular, the establishment of David's empire that finally secured Israel's hold on Canaan was the result of violence. The Bible asserts that this violence was not only in accord with the divine will but actually commanded by God (e.g., Josh 8:1-2). How can this violence be considered God's will? Most often it is Christians who

ask this question because they are scandalized by a God who calls for the death of innocent people. This is a strange question coming from Christians who believe it was God's will that Jesus suffer and die as an innocent victim. The violence that marked the settlement of the Israelite tribes in Canaan is no more a theological problem than is the suffering that Jesus experienced.

The violence by which Israel acquired its land was evil. Innocent people did die. What the Bible affirms is that despite this evil, the divine will achieves its purposes. Human sin* cannot frustrate God. That is the consistent affirmation of the Scriptures. Second the Bible affirms that Israel's acquisition of its land was not its own achievement despite the military victories of its militia. The land was a gift of God that Israel could not have acquired on its own.

See: CANAAN, EGYPT, JOSHUA, JUDGES, PHILISTINES

LESLIE J. HOPPE, O.F.M.

CONSCIENCE

When modern Christians think of "conscience," they tend to understand it as an agent (or "voice"*) of God fixed innately inside each person and, hence, a reliable indicator of proper behavior. Although commonly discussed today, conscience is a rare term in the Bible, and we cannot assume that ancient biblical notions correspond to modern understandings. The word occurs only in the NT; nearly half of the instances are found in the letters of the Apostle Paul, and most of these are clustered around a single controversy: whether Christians in the ancient city of Corinth should eat meat prepared in a pagan fashion, offered to Greek and Roman gods (1 Corinthians 8 and 10). Perhaps the most significant difference between modern and ancient understandings is that according to Pauline thought the conscience can err (e.g., 1 Cor 8:7-13 and 10:28-30; see also Titus 1:15, although deutero-Pauline), whereas people today generally have a high degree of confidence in the accuracy of the conscience's ability to suggest the right action.

New Testament

Syneidēsis. *Syneidēsis* (alternatively, *synoida*) is the Greek word translated as "conscience" or "consciousness," coined from the Greek verb "to know" plus the preposition "with," and equivalent to *conscientia* in Latin. No single definition of conscience covers every usage in the NT. Before NT times, the closest Hebrew analogy would be "heart,"* considered by the Israelites and other ancient Mediterranean peoples as the organ that generates thoughts (not emotions, as popularly regarded today). Job claims that "my heart does not reproach me for any of my days" (Job 27:6). The Septuagint uses *syneidēsis* in one place (rendered in the NAB as "thoughts"): "Even in your thoughts do not make light of the king, / nor in the privacy of your bedroom revile the rich, / Because the birds of the air may carry your voice, / a winged creature may tell what you say" (Eccl 10:20). However, few people stopped to consider the existence of a "conscience" before the advent of Greek philosophy. Greek thinkers such as Socrates considered self-knowledge a prerequisite for the "good" life, exhorting critical introspection and knowledge of one's soul in the Socratic goal to "know thyself." Greek (and Roman) poets personified conscience in mythology as "The Furies," avenging deities from whom no criminal could escape. By the first century CE, Jewish authors such as Philo of Alexandria and Josephus began writing reflectively about conscience, borrowing ideas current in Hellenistic popular philosophy ("popular" in the sense of nontechnical). It is not surprising, therefore, to find another first-century Jew, Paul, also influenced by his Greco-Roman milieu.

In Paul's Letters. Although Paul presumes the existence of a conscience in each individual, he nowhere engages in a systematic treatment to defend this view. Of the Gentiles, he writes: "They show that the demands of the law are written in their hearts, while their conscience also bears witness and their conflicting thoughts accuse or even defend them on the day when, according to my gospel, God will judge people's hidden works through Christ Jesus" (Rom 2:15-16). In this discussion (the only one that approaches theoretical or "dogmatic" speculation), he defines the faculty of *syneidēsis* eschatologically, as an inner judge that will accuse or excuse both Jew and Gentile in the final day of judgment when Christ returns. Paul argues that even Gentiles, who did not receive the Torah, nevertheless can access Torah ("a law") in their hearts and thus will be held accountable despite their living under pre-revelatory and ignorant times. In this regard, the argument of Romans 2:1-16 contradicts the theme of Paul's Areopagus speech written by Luke in Acts 17:30-31, which claims that "God has overlooked the times of ignorance."

In other places Paul appeals to the conscience (both his and of others) to argue that he has behaved ethically in his apostolic mission, using conscience as a witness for his defense against detractors and adversaries. With forensic rhetoric he utters words similar to those in an oath, "I speak the truth in Christ, I do not lie; my conscience joins with the holy Spirit in bearing me witness that I have great sorrow and constant anguish in my heart" (Rom 9:1-2). The juridical imagery echoes throughout Pauline apologies (1 Cor 4:4; 2 Cor 1:12; 4:2; 5:11; Acts 23:1; 24:16).

The most involved discussion of conscience falls under the rubric of communal ethics, and is found in the idol meat controversy recorded in 1 Corinthians 8 and 10. Paul faces a congregation with problems: two distinct groups differ in their understanding of conscience. The "strong" equate conscience with the person, and argue that since knowledge edifies the person, it also edifies the conscience. Therefore one may eat idol meat, and so learn that "there is no idol in the world" (1 Cor 8:4). The "weak" believers, however, lack this higher form of knowledge and possess a lower kind; they deem conscience to be only painful knowledge of one's transgression, which ought to be avoided at all costs. When they see a "strong" Christian eating idol meat, "weak" Christians wrongly revert to their old pagan beliefs that the food has religious significance; but then "when they eat meat sacrificed to idols, their conscience, which is weak, is defiled" (1 Cor 8:7). Paul urges the Corinthians toward reconciliation, using the Jewish ethic of loving one's neighbor (1 Cor 10:24; see Lev 19:18). Therefore, although identifying himself with the "strong," Paul rejects the identification of conscience with the person and insists that the conscience is separate from a person and must be allowed to govern an individual's behavior—even if the conscience errs, as in the case of the "weak" conscience, which wrongly interprets the sacrificing of meat to idols as efficacious under Greco-Roman polytheism. Paul then turns the whole topic into an argument for limiting the personal liberty of the "strong" conscience for the benefit of those fellow Christians with weaker consciences (1 Cor 10:23-30). This ethic appears again in Romans 13—Paul's theological defense of the Roman Empire—in which the apostle directs Christians to pay taxes to Caesar (Rom 13:5-7) so as to "owe nothing to anyone, except to love one another; for the one who loves another has fulfilled the law" (Rom 13:8; see Mark 12:31, where the wisdom of the Jewish love ethic would later be attributed to Jesus).

In Other NT Letters. As the Church became more institutionalized with a threefold hierarchy of bishops, elders, and deacons, the letter writers after Paul began to downplay the apocalyptic fervor of Paul's understanding of conscience and to underscore the present requirements of conscience in Church order and discipline. The deutero-Pauline author of 1 Timothy, for example, writes: "The aim of this instruction is love from a pure heart, a good conscience, and a sincere faith" (1 Tim 1:5; see also 1:19). The author further exhorts: "Similarly, deacons must be dignified, not deceitful, not addicted to drink, not greedy

for sordid gain, holding fast to the mystery of the faith with a clear conscience" (1 Tim 3:8-9). A similar use of conscience as a tool of instruction toward proper behavior is found in 1 Peter: "Slaves, be subject to your masters with all reverence, not only to those who are good and equitable but also to those who are perverse. For whenever anyone bears the pain of unjust suffering because of consciousness [*syneidēsis*] of God, that is a grace" (1 Pet 2:18-19).

A final use of "conscience" is found in relation to worship and cultic activity. For example, the author of Hebrews writes: "This is a symbol of the present time, in which gifts and sacrifices are offered that cannot perfect the worshiper in conscience" (Heb 9:9; see also 9:14; 10:2, 22; 2 Tim 1:3; and 1 Pet 3:21 in relation to baptism).* The call is to have a clear conscience when worshiping God, either in personal prayer or in public ritual.

See: HEART, SPIRIT, LAW, RECONCILIATION, VOICE OF GOD

J. ALBERT HARRILL

Pastoral-Liturgical Tradition

Conscience has been understood and defined in many different ways within the Christian tradition. Frequently, terms like "heart"* and "loins" have been used to express what conscience is, but what is common about all these expressions is the fact that they point to the innermost nature of the human person. The phenomenon of conscience has been discovered in every culture, and thus conscience is considered a universal characteristic of humanity.

Aspects of Conscience. Catholic theologians have generally distinguished three interrelated aspects of conscience. The first aspect is called *synderesis*, which is actually a variation of the Greek word for conscience (*syneidēsis*). *Synderesis* is understood as the habit of conscience or the basic sense of responsibility that is characteristic of the human person. By *synderesis* one has an immediate experience in the depths of one's personality of the moral quality of one's concrete actions. This experience is not primarily of moral rules or norms but of an attraction to value (good) or an aversion from disvalue (evil). This aspect of conscience, then, points to the fact that persons have both an intellectual and affective receptivity for moral values, and this receptivity is the basis for the general sense of personal moral responsibility.

The second aspect of conscience relates to the effort to perceive specific values in a concrete situation. Frequently, theologians call this aspect of conscience "moral science" because it is concerned with the discernment, appreciation, and balancing of individual values that pertain to life situations. This category of moral knowledge not only draws upon individual experience and discernment but also upon the knowledge that is found in the community, revelation, and authority. The specific knowledge that is arrived at by this aspect of conscience is conceptual and objective, and it is at this level that moral disagreement between people of goodwill is most apparent.

The third aspect of conscience is the actual act of conscience in which the person judges a specific act to be morally right or wrong. It is at this level that an individual applies one's general sense of moral responsibility and specific knowledge of moral values to a concrete act. The judgment that is arrived at can be either antecedent *(conscientia antecedens)* or subsequent *(conscientia consequens)* to the performing of the act. Though this act of conscience is always necessarily incomplete and partial because of the limiting circumstances of the individual and though conscience can even be invincibly erroneous *(error invincibilis)*, nevertheless this aspect of conscience becomes the definitive norm *(regula proxima moralitatis)* for the individual decision. Consequently, as the final subjective norm for moral action the judgment of conscience must be unambiguous so that a well-grounded uncertainty is excluded *(certitudo moralis)*.

The Development and Formation of Conscience. All three aspects of conscience develop over the life-span of an individual's life. However, it is particularly the second aspect of conscience, where a person discerns individual values, that development and formation of conscience is absolutely crucial. Constant training in the cognitive perception and in the affective appreciation of values becomes an essential element of all good decision making.

See: CHURCH, IMAGE OF GOD, LIBERTY

JAMES J. WALTER

CONSECRATION

Consecration as a liturgical act involves the permanent dedication of some person or thing for sacred use. In the current Roman liturgy, rites exist for the consecration of the Eucharistic bread and wine, the consecration of chrism, the consecration of a bishop, presbyter, and deacon, and the consecration of a female virgin. In other eras and cultures, the Christian Churches have had expanded repertoires of liturgical consecrations. For example, church buildings, altars,* altar vessels, and even church bells were consecrated, that is, irrevocably set apart for exclusive divine service. More recently, such rites are called rites of dedication and the occasions are understood as occasions for the prayer of blessing. The distinction seems to acknowledge a change in religious sensibilities and theological understanding that will be explored below.

Each of the consecrations named above is effected through the prayer of the Church. The consecratory prayer is voiced by the ordained minister who extends hands over the subject of consecration, and it is affirmed by the "Amen" of the assembly. Five of the consecrations are reserved to an ordained bishop; but an ordained priest may be the minister of Eucharistic consecration, i.e., he may pray the Eucharistic anaphora or prayer of thanksgiving.

The content of the consecratory prayers provides a sound source for understanding the religious significance of an act of liturgical consecration. Each of the consecratory prayers narrates some aspect of the deeds of God in the history of salvation (e.g., God's use of the fruits of creation for saving action; the election of leaders for the chosen people; the mystery of Christ's saving death and resurrection; God's choice of a virginal spouse in Mary), and then situates within that trajectory of divine saving action the present consecratory event in the Church's life. The first part of a prayer of consecration sets the consecratory act within the history of God's choice or election; the contemporary ecclesial consecration is then expressed as response to God's continuing choice. The prayer moves, like every prayer of blessing, from thankful remembering to confident invocation that the living God will act again in familiar ways. The outcome of the prayer of consecration is understood as a permanent separation of the person or thing so consecrated from mundane existence.

Ritual anointings* with holy chrism sometimes accompany the prayer of consecration of a person; for example, when a bishop and priest are consecrated, they are also anointed, but the anointing is not done for the consecration of a deacon or a virgin. However, not all ritual anointings are part of liturgical rites of consecration. So church walls and the altar table are anointed, but are said to be dedicated. And Christian initiation included a chrismation of the subject's head (long before a comparable chrismation was introduced for episcopal consecration, according to the witness of liturgical documents), but such initiatory anointing has not ordinarily been interpreted by theologians as a consecration.

By contrast, very early documents of the Roman liturgy called solemn prayer with episcopal hand-laying at the ordination of a presbyter or a bishop a consecration, even when there was no physical anointing. Only in the middle ages did the ordination of bishop and presbyter in the West begin to include anointings: for the bishop, the crown of his head; for the presbyter his hands, to consecrate them and him for the offering of the Eucharistic sacrifice. At pre-

sent, these ritual anointings persist, but for the presbyter the consecratory meaning no longer focuses on the hands.

The distinctions between consecration, dedication, and blessing are not merely elusive; they are sometimes inconsistent, and this inconsistency reflects shifting theological world views in the course of development of the liturgical tradition and systematic theology. A heightened attention to rites of consecration is characteristic of a perception that the world and baptized laity who conduct the business of the world are profane, i.e., outside the sphere of the holy. Accordingly, much cultic activity is directed to claiming things for divine service, setting them apart from the *saeculum* by consecrating them.

The Scriptures witness to the idea that the priestly writers of the OT understood consecration to be their identifying prerogative. They were consecrated and had the power of consecration. A theology of sacerdotal consecration underscored their religious conviction that God's original choice of a covenant people had been refined by the further choice of a distinct tribe of priests who were God's own portion. The destruction of the Jerusalem Temple in 70 CE disrupted the centrality of this sacerdotal interpretation within Judaism.

About the same time, the author of the Letter to the Hebrews proposed a Christian reinterpretation of the OT theology of priesthood. With the proclamation of the gospel of God's salvation in Jesus Christ, the familiar focus on temple and priestly cult as the zone of the sacred where the holiness of God was manifest gave way to an understanding of the world as a new creation in which the power of evil was being overcome by the victory of Christ. Baptized disciples of Jesus, filled with the Spirit of Jesus, were themselves temple and priesthood, the dwelling of God in the midst of the *saeculum* to whom they were to announce the good news of salvation. Within this Christian world view, baptism itself became the operative consecration or setting apart of a chosen people for divine service.

That original Christian world view, supported by the doctrine of redemptive incarnation, found little cultural support in the dominant philosophies of the Mediterranean world, which denigrated things material and carnal. Christian understandings of creation and redemption were compromised and then began to give way under the force of complex historical and cultural circumstances. Baptism of whole populations without prior evangelization and catechesis, the limited access to literacy and so to study of the apostolic faith, a theocratic understanding of tribal leadership, and the harsh circumstances of daily life among the newly baptized peoples beyond the Alps set the stage for a reappropriation of a sacerdotalism inspired by the OT. The ordination of ministers came to be understood as high priestly and priestly consecrations setting celibate Church officeholders apart from the baptized for the exercise of divine authority over secular rulers and the exercise of sacred power in the Church. Consecratory acts tended to multiply in the medieval ecclesial environment; medieval liturgical books reflect this.

In the high middle ages, Thomas Aquinas enunciated as the principle guiding rites of consecration, "We consecrate those things which we make use of in the Eucharist" (*Summa Theologica* III, 83, 3; see also 78 and 82). That principle does not cover actual liturgical practice, however, and a comprehensive theology of consecration must take account of the full liturgical practice of the Church. Given the recovered emphasis on the role of the assembly in the celebration of the Eucharist in the current Roman Missal, such a theology of consecration will necessarily take Christian initiation as its starting point.

See: CHURCH, EUCHARIST, HOLY/HOLINESS, JESUS CHRIST, ORDINATION, SPIRIT

MARY COLLINS, O.S.B.

CONSECRATION TO GOD

Consecration means to set someone or something aside as holy,* and so to dedicate it to God. In the OT, the person or object that is consecrated is usually connected in some way to worship;* this meaning emerges mostly in traditions which emerge from priestly circles (whose members were born into priestly families rather than having made vocational choices). In addition, individuals who were not priests occasionally engaged in Nazarite consecration to God, either temporarily or for life. Finally, a few texts in the NT speak of Christ consecrating early Christians to God.

The rituals of consecration in the liturgy permanently dedicate a person or thing for sacred use. A contemporary theology of consecration needs to regard Christian initiation as its starting point.

Old Testament

Consecrate refers to two different Hebrew words: *kiddesh* and *nazar*. *Kiddesh*, "to consecrate," seems to be a stronger form of the verb *kadash*, "to be holy"; its use attributes holiness to persons, places, things, or even times. So the notion of consecration relates directly to holiness, being set aside or apart for God. OT translations render this word in various ways; when the NAB translation of *kiddesh* used in this article seems inaccurate, an alternative translation is included in parentheses, usually from the NRSV or NJPS. *Nazar*, by contrast, indicates a voluntary and personal setting aside or dedicating of self to God.

Kiddesh. Some uses of *kiddesh*, "to consecrate," are found in stories from the historical books. In early Israel, Micah's mother "consecrated the silver to the LORD as my gift in favor of my son" (Judg 17:4). Some time later, when the inhabitants of Kiriath-Jearim brought the ark into the house of Abinadab, they appointed (consecrated) "his son Eleazar as guardian" (1 Sam 7:1). After completing the Temple,* Solomon dedicated it: "on that day the king consecrated the middle of the court facing the temple of the LORD" (1 Kgs 8:64; 2 Chr 7:7). In these cases, human beings consecrate some thing or person to God.

Elsewhere, it is God who makes holy/ consecrates. After the Temple dedication Solomon heard God's response: "I have consecrated this temple which you have built . . ." (1 Kgs 9:3; 2 Chr 7:16, 20). God also consecrated Jeremiah (Jer 1:5; NAB reads: "I dedicated you").

This notion of consecration may derive from traditions about Israel's formation in the generation of the Exodus. When they came to Sinai, Moses ascended the mountain and heard God speak about Israel's election. After his descent, God instructed him to consecrate the people as a preparation for a theophanic experience of God on the third day: "Go to the people and have them sanctify [consecrate] themselves today and tomorrow" (Exod 19:10, 14). Two aspects of such consecration were washing their garments and abstaining from sexual intercourse (Exod 19:14-15). It seems that God's promise to them, that they will be a "holy people" (Exod 19:6), leads to reciprocal acts, in which they consecrate themselves as a people to God. Places can also be consecrated, generally as reminders of other consecrations: Moses heard that he must also consecrate this mountain (Exod 19:23).

Another important consecration occurs after the Passover regulations in Exodus 12, when God commands Moses: "Consecrate to me every first-born that opens the womb among the Israelites" (Exod 13:2). The obligation to consecrate the firstborn reminds Israel how God passed over their firstborn in Egypt and how they were elected by God; in later Priestly theology, the Levites are accepted as substitutes for the firstborn males (Num 3:11-13). Consecration describes both God's action toward Israel and Israel's response to their God; God's holiness touches them and they mutually set themselves aside for holiness.

Many texts that use the word "consecrate" concern worship and are derived from priestly traditions (e.g., Exod 25–31, 35–40; Leviticus 8–10), where consecration appears together with notions of ordination* and anointing.* Directions for Aaron's priestly vestments are intended to "set him apart [to consecrate him] for his sacred service as my priest" (Exod 28:3). There follow lengthy instructions about the ritual for consecration of Aaron and his sons as priests (Exod 28:41; 29:1, 33, 44; 30:30; 40:13). This seven-day ritual also includes the consecration of objects important for worship: wave-offerings (Exod 29:27), the altar (Exod 29:36), the meeting tent (Exod 29:44), the ark, the table, the lampstand, altar of incense, altar of burnt offering, the basin (Exod 30:26-28), the tabernacle (Exod 40:9). Consecration makes these objects holy in a contagious sense: "whatever touches them shall be sacred" (Exod 30:29). The execution of these divine commands to Moses occurs especially in Leviticus 8:10-12, 15, 30. Priestly consecration may also suggest legitimation: when Ezekiel describes the Zadokite priests* of the new Israel, he speaks of the "consecrated priests" (Ezek 48:11); they did not stray, as the Levites had.

Nazar. Another word for consecration is derived from *nazar*, "to separate or dedicate." Curiously, Aaron wore something on his head that is often translated "diadem," though it was a *nezer* (from *nazar*); it was a "sign of consecration" (Exod 39:30; Lev 8:9) and bore on it the words, "Sacred to the LORD" (Exod 39:30).

This part of priestly garb may suggest some comparison with the Nazarites, who provide another example of consecration to God. In Israel there were two types of Nazarites: life-long, probably dedicated by their mothers as thanksgiving for pregnancy, like Samson (Judg 13:7) and Samuel (1 Sam 1:11, 21); and temporary, resulting from a type of vow and constituting a period of ascetic behavior (Num 6:1-21). Both men and women were allowed to take Nazarite vows (Num 6:2), and some important Jewish women of the second Temple period were known to have been temporary Nazarites (Queen Helena of Adiabene and Berenice, sister of King Agrippa II). In fact, this ascetical practice apparently became widespread in the late second Temple era; it was known during the time of the Maccabees (1 Macc 3:49) and from Rabbinic writings.

Temporary Nazarites seem to have shared the holiness of priests for their time of dedication, and all Nazarites seem to have shared in two obligations: refraining from wine or fruit of the vine (Num 6:3-4; Judg 13:4; 1 Sam 1:11) and from cutting their hair (Num 6:5; Judg 13:5; 1 Sam 1:11). Temporary Nazarites were also prohibited from contact with a corpse, even of their own family (Num 6:6-8). Since the rules for temporary Nazarites occur in priestly legislation some speculate that the priests favored the temporary type of Nazarites over the permanent Nazarite vow of earlier times as a way of regulating them. The distinctive marks of a Nazarite's dedication to God, especially uncut hair, are external signals, unlike the behavioral transformation required for true holiness in the priests' Holiness Code: Leviticus 19, for example, provides a consistent ethic of community relations and care of the underprivileged as the requisite for holiness (Lev 19:2). In its best context, the Nazarite vow demonstrates gratitude to God for a child (Samson, Samuel); at its worst, it could function as a temporary external sign of dedication to God which did not emphasize the behavioral holiness legislated for the priests.

New Testament

Consecration. Consecration is one translation of the Greek word *hagiazo*, "to make holy/consecrate." Early Christians viewed consecration not as a voluntary human act but as a gracious act of God or Jesus. In the Gospel of John consecration has three different connotations: God consecrates Jesus (John 10:36); Jesus consecrates himself on behalf of his followers (John 17:19), whom he begs God to consecrate (John 17:17). In Acts, Luke views those who have followed Christ as receiving an "inheritance" among the "consecrated" (Acts 20:32; 26:18). The

Letter to the Hebrews proclaims that Jesus has sanctified us for worship in the heavenly realm, where he now exists. In that context, the author speaks of Christians as those who have been consecrated by the priestly act of Jesus offering his body (Heb 2:11; 10:10, 14, 29) or by the shedding of his blood (Heb 13:12).

Nazarites. The NT also witnesses to the continuation of the Nazarite movement at the end of the Second Temple era. John the Baptist was probably a Nazarite; the angel who foretold his birth to Zechariah said that he would "never drink wine or strong drink" (Luke 1:15). Paul apparently had taken this vow, for we hear that "at the port of Cenchreae he shaved his head because of a vow he had taken" (Acts 18:18). Later Paul was asked by the Jerusalem leaders to give evidence that he had not renounced Jewish customs; as proof they asked him to accompany four men who had taken a Nazarite vow and to "pay the fee for the shaving of their heads" (Acts 21:23-24). It appears, however, that these examples of Nazarite vows are regarded as Jewish forms of behavior without making explicit any particular connection with holiness.

See: ALTAR, ANOINTING, ARK OF THE COVENANT, BLESSING, ELECTION, FIRST-BORN, HOLY/HOLINESS, ORDINATION, PRIESTHOOD, TEMPLE, VOWS, WORSHIP

JOHN C. ENDRES, S.J.

CONSOLATION

In times of grief or personal catastrophe people reach out to console one another, as witnessed in both Testaments. The consolation provided may be sexual union with one's spouse, visits by relatives or friends, the physical touch of an embrace, words of comfort, the willingness to listen, the offer of food or drink, whatever might relieve the pain and provide hope. It is the gift of love.

God also consoles. Prophets are acutely aware of Israel's sinfulness, but promise that after due punishment the people will receive divine consolation. The psalmist, in time of affliction, trusts in God and hopes to be comforted.

In the NT, "consolation" may be a general term for the blessings of the messianic age; it can also refer to the rewards of fidelity and include life after death. It is often used by Paul as "encouragement," to which he exhorts the new converts, explaining that it is a gift of God mediated to us through Jesus, the Scriptures, the missionaries, and one another.

Old Testament

The primary Hebrew word for consolation is the verb *niham* (in the Piel) or nouns formed from this root, and is translated "console," "comfort," "encourage," depending on the context. Consolation is called for at death or in other calamities, and is granted by relatives and friends (Gen 37:35; 1 Chr 7:22), but also by God (Deut 32:36; Pss 23:4; 94:19).

Historical Traditions. Human consolation at the death of a loved one predominates. Sexual union with his wife Rebekah gave Isaac "solace" after the death of his mother (Gen 24:67). When David and Bathsheba's child died, both parents were greatly grieved, but David "comforted" his wife, and she conceived and bore a son, Solomon (2 Sam 12:24). In a gesture that led to marriage, Boaz consoled the widow Ruth (Ruth 2:13). Promises can also be consoling; just before his death Joseph "reassured" his brothers that he would provide for them and their children (Gen 50:21). A connection is made between consolation and the production of wine (probably intended by relating the name Noah to "relief . . . out of the ground"; see Gen 5:29 and 10:20). Divine consolation is mentioned too; God "shall have pity" on the faithful Israelites (Deut 32:36).

Wisdom Literature. Qoheleth laments the victims of violence who have none to "comfort" them (Qoh 4:1). Job's friends came to bring him "sympathy and comfort" (Job 2:11), but he found the best conso-lation in a good conscience (Job 6:10). He had sought "comfort" from his bed, but was frightened by nightmares (Job 7:13). At the end of his ordeal imposed by God, Job was "comforted" by relatives and friends who came to dine with him and offered him gifts (Job 42:11).

Psalms. God is the good shepherd whose rod and staff "give courage" (Ps 23:4); one can hope in time of affliction that God would again "comfort" (Pss 71:21; 86:17); indeed, a simple divine promise brings consolation (Ps 119:50; see 119:76, 82). With trust the psalmist prays, "When cares increase within me, your comfort gives me joy" (Ps 94:19); see Psalm 135:14.

Prophets. Sometimes in anger at Israel God's "eyes are closed to compassion" (Hos 13:14). Jeremiah threatens death and lack of burial for the sinful inhabitants of Judah: "They will not break bread with the bereaved to console them; they will not give them the cup of consolation to drink over the death of father or mother" (Jer 16:7). The Book of Lamentations, written soon after the Exile of 587 BCE, still smarts from the pain of the destruction of Jerusalem and the lack of consolation (Lam 1:2, 9, 16, 17, 21). But after Israel has suffered for its sins, God consoles: "I will console and gladden them after their sorrows" (Jer 31:13); see Isaiah 12:1. This thought is deeply embedded in the Book of Consolation written during the Exile (Isa 40:1; 49:13; 51:3, 12; 52:9); also Ezekiel 14:22-23; Zechariah 1:13. The Spirit of God is upon the anointed prophet to "comfort" all who mourn (Isa 61:2). Postexilic Jerusalem is personified as a mother, and the prophet exclaims, "Oh, that you may suck fully of the milk of her comfort. . . . As a mother comforts her son, so will I comfort you" (Isa 66:11, 13).

New Testament

The Greek word underlying "consolation" is *parakaleō*, a verb that signifies "to call to oneself," and may be translated "to comfort," "encourage." Nouns formed from it, *paraklēsis* and *paraklētos*, also have several meanings, including "consolation," "encouragement," and "advocate."

Synoptic Gospels. Simeon was awaiting the "consolation of Israel" (Luke 2:25). This reflects Palestinian usage which, on the basis of Isaiah 40:1-2 and 61:2, considered the coming messianic age as the "consolation of Israel," parallel to waiting for the "redemption of Jerusalem" (Luke 2:38; see Isa 52:9; 2 Bar 44:7 speaks of the "consolation of Zion"). The woe of Luke 6:24 declares that the rich have already received their "consolation"; they have no claim for a future reward. In the parable of the rich man and Lazarus, the rich man was tormented in the netherworld, while Lazarus was "comforted" in the bosom of Abraham (Luke 16:25). The reward promised by the Beatitudes for those who mourn is that they "will be comforted" (Matt 5:4), namely by participation in the reign of God definitively inaugurated by Jesus. The passive verbal form, "will be comforted," is a theological passive, that is, their "comfort" will be brought about by God.

Acts of the Apostles. The "consolation of the Holy Spirit" (Acts 9:31) is the divine guidance experienced by those drawn to join the early Church through the apostolic preaching.

Paul. Many of the Pauline letters speak of "solace" or "encouragement" that the apostle receives from the fidelity of the newly formed Christians (1 Thess 3:7; 2 Cor 7:4, 13). He also hopes to encourage them, either directly (2 Cor 1:4) or through fellow missionaries (Eph 6:22; Col 4:8), asks them to "be encouraged" (Col 2:2), to "console one another" (1 Thess 4:18), and reminds them that encouragement comes from God (2 Cor 1:4; 7:6), the "God of all encouragement" (2 Cor 1:3; see Rom 15:5), "our Lord Jesus Christ himself and God our Father" (2 Thess 2:16-17). Encouragement is derived from the Scriptures (Rom 15:4; see Heb 6:18) and is based on the salvific deeds of Christ (Phil 2:1). Those who share in the sufferings also share in "the encouragement" (2 Cor 1:7), now and in the future.

John. Jesus promises to send another Advocate, the "Spirit of truth" (John 14:15-17; 15:26-27; 16:7-14), the "holy Spirit" (John 15:26), also sent by the Father, to dwell in the disciples, guide them, bear witness to Jesus, teach them, and remind them of all that Jesus had told them. The Holy Spirit is presented here as the spiritual presence of Jesus in the hearts of the disciples while Jesus is at the same time definitively with the Father. According to the First Letter of John, Jesus himself is presented as an "Advocate" (Greek, *paraklētos*) with the Father (1 John 2:1), referring to Jesus' continuing intercession for us in his exalted state with the Father.

See: BLESSING, HOPE

JOSEPH F. WIMMER, O.S.A.

CONVERSION

There are few concepts in contemporary Christian spirituality which have attracted more attention, reflection, and writing than the word conversion. The basic meaning of conversion, elements or features typically associated with it, and some of the classic patterns it assumes are the topic of frequent discussion and sometimes debate. Lives of individuals which exemplify the dynamics of conversion are regularly the subject of anthologies and biographies. Religious denominations describe those in their membership who have transferred their affiliation from another religious tradition as "converts." Fundamentalist Christians speak of having a "born again" experience which they label "conversion."

Among Roman Catholics, burgeoning interest in spirituality has developed alongside a thriving movement of liturgical renewal. Among the developments of the latter, the recent recovery of the catechumenal process in the revised *Rite of Christian Initiation of Adults* has been the occasion for renewed reflection on the journey of conversion in general and, in particular, on the dynamics of the conversion process which leads to full ecclesial incorporation in the sacraments of initiation and which is celebrated each time the community gathers for prayer.

Such contemporary interest is not a new phenomenon, however. Conversion has been a feature of the holy life from ancient times and its meaning is illumined in both Old and New Testament passages.

Old Testament

In the OT, the concept of conversion is communicated by the Hebrew word *shub* which means "to turn" as in Isaiah 6:10 where the act of turning, of changing one's whole orientation, is described as a prelude to healing: "Make the mind of this people dull, and stop their ears, and shut their eyes, so that they may not look with their eyes, and listen with their ears, and comprehend with their minds, and turn and be healed." *Shub* also connotes a "turning again" or a "return" as in Psalm 51:13: "I will teach transgressors your ways, and sinners will *return* to you." Similarly, conversion includes reversal, coming home, or restoration of a previous state as in Isaiah 55:7: "let the wicked forsake their way, and the unrighteous their thoughts; let them return to the Lord, that he may have mercy on them, and to our God for he will abundantly pardon."

While we regularly think of conversion as applying to humankind, the OT also indicates that God engages in "turning": "Lord, you were favorable to your land; you restored the fortunes of Jacob. You forgave the iniquity of your people; you pardoned all their sin. You withdrew all your wrath; you turned from your hot anger" (Ps 85:1-3). God's change of direction is sometimes described as influenced by human behavior: "Do not let anything devoted to destruction stick to your hand, so that the Lord may turn from his fierce anger and show you compassion, and in his compassion multiply you, as he swore to your ancestors" (Deut 13:17; see also Hosea 11).

Although the word *shub* appears infrequently in the OT, the complex reality of conversion and change of heart is a challenge habitually preached by the prophets and sometimes even placed on the lips of the Almighty: "Turn to me and be saved, all the ends of the earth" (Isa 45:22). In some cases the divine invitation to conversion takes the form of a plea: "I formed you, you are my servant; O Israel, you will not be forgotten by me. I have swept away your transgressions like a cloud, and your sins like mist; return to me, for I have redeemed you" (Isa 44:21b-22).

"Turning" appears to be the heart of conversion, turning away from sin and the company of sinners, from evil of every kind, from idols of one's own creation, and turning to the living God, desiring a change of heart, choosing life, and embracing friendship with God. Humankind and God are in relationship with one another; the act of turning has to do with either the rejection and destruction of relationship or its restoration and deepening.

New Testament

In the NT, the word "conversion" appears only in Acts 15:3, a passage which reports the conversion of the Gentiles. There are, however, two Greek words which communicate the concepts of conversion and repentance: *metanoia* and *epistrophe*. These words are nearly interchangeable, yet there is a subtle difference in their use: *metanoia* has more to do with the internal process of conversion; *epistrophe* suggests the external effects of the process of conversion, the inevitable and radical changes in one's existence and way of life which follow the internal acceptance of the invitation to conversion. True conversion incorporates both interior and exterior movements.

While conversion in the OT and in Rabbinic writings appears to be a precondition for the coming of the Messiah, what clearly marks the NT's prophetic call to a change of heart is that the Messianic Age has already dawned in the presence and power of Jesus Christ. Jesus' public ministry begins with such an announcement: "The time is fulfilled, and the kingdom of God has come near; repent, and believe in the good news" (Mark 1:15 and paralls.). Indeed, John the Baptist, the last of the great prophets, stands at the threshold of this new age, crying out for a change of heart in preparation for Jesus' appearing (Mark 1:1-8; Matt 3:1-12; Luke 3:1-20).

Jesus' life and ministry was a continuous invitation to repentance,* to the restoration of friendship—even intimacy—with God, and to the acceptance of whatever changes such friendship might entail. In the Gospels, one's acceptance of Jesus' invitation invariably led to faith* and to a life of discipleship.* Implied in many encounters is a turning or a return to relationship together with embracing its inevitable consequences, for example, leaving everything (Luke 5:11) or taking up one's cross (Matt 10:38).

In the record of the early Church, apostolic preaching takes up the refrain: "Repent, and be baptized everyone of you in the name of Jesus Christ so that your sins may be forgiven; and you will receive the gift of the Holy Spirit. For the promise is for you, for your children, and for all who are far away, everyone whom the Lord our God calls to him" (Acts 2:38-39). Indeed, the Acts of the Apostles is filled with examples of individuals and groups who experience conversion. Together such stories as those of Saul/Paul (9:1-22), the jailor at Philippi (16:27-34), the eunuch on the road from Jerusalem to Gaza (8:26-39), and the crowds moved to baptism on Pentecost (2:5-47) suggest a typical pattern of conversion: hearing the voice of God or a mediated word of life; initial openness and acceptance; some active personal engagement in the process of transformation; ritualizing the decision; living out that decision over a lifetime of gradual transformation. The lifetime journey that conversion launches is nothing less than transformation into the image of the divine: "All of us, with unveiled faces, seeing the glory of the Lord as though reflected in a mirror, are being transformed into the same image from one degree of glory to another; for this comes from the Lord, the Spirit" (2 Cor 3:18). This biblical pattern of conversion remains the norm to this day.

Pastoral-Liturgical Tradition

Both theological reflection and liturgical reform have influenced our contemporary understanding of conversion.

Perhaps most influential among systematic theologians who have addressed the process of conversion is Bernard Lonergan who distinguishes several levels of the phenomenon: the intellectual, the moral, and the religious. The person converted, according to Lonergan, apprehends differently, values differently, and relates differently because the person *is* different. The words of the Second Letter to the Corinthians are apt: "If anyone is in Christ, there is a new creation; everything old has passed away; see, everything has become new!" (2 Cor 5:17) Nothing less than a new world order is the inescapable result of intellectual conversion to truth, of moral conversion to values, and of religious conversion which Lonergan describes as "an undertow of consciousness, a fated acceptance of a vocation to holiness." As a person undergoes the process of conversion, *everything* changes both in one's interior experience and one's way of being in the world.

As interest in spirituality has become both popular and widespread in our day, Lonergan is one of numerous writers who have attempted to supply a theological framework for the life of communion with God and its external manifestations. Happily, a concurrent revival of interest in the Church's liturgy has provided a communal counterpoint to the individual's spiritual quest.

In the liturgical reforms of the Second Vatican Council, the restoration of a catechumenate as part of the process of becoming a Catholic Christian has been a major impetus for a reexamination of the meaning of conversion and for the application of its consequences to all Christians, not just potential members. Conversion no longer implies a once-for-all decision; it is now common currency to describe the whole of the Christian life as a journey of conversion. This metaphor communicates that conversion is a life-long striving for holiness in the midst of others which plays itself out at the levels of intellect and affection, which implies particular ethical choices and issues in a commitment to mission. It is this journey, this longing for the holy life, this deepening of relationship which is brought to public, ritual expression each time the community gathers to celebrate the paschal mystery of Jesus' death for the life of the world and its participation in dying and rising with Christ.

The *Rite of Christian Initiation of Adults* (RCIA) makes of the conversion journey an experience of mutual ministry between catechumens and members of the community: "The initiation of catechumens is a gradual process that takes place within the community of the faithful. By joining the catechumens in reflecting on the value of the paschal mystery and by renewing their own conversion, the faithful provide an example that will help the catechumens to obey the Holy Spirit more generously" (RCIA 4).

Conversion is thus a process which entails a gradual reorientation of one's mind and heart. It is accomplished in the midst of others and includes the development of a faithful relationship with God, the discovery of community, the gradual assimilation of the community's ways of worship, and a commitment to the community's mission of extending the reign of God. The RCIA (75) amply illustrates this multi-faceted nature of conversion in its summary of the aims of the catechumenal period, an extended period during which potential members of the Church are given spiritual formation and guidance, aimed at forming them in the Christian life: (1) suitable teaching which will lead to a profound sense of the mystery of salvation in which they desire to participate; (2) famil-

iarity with the Christian way of life and a progressive change of outlook and conduct; (3) gradual introduction to the community's liturgical treasury; (4) dedication to work actively with others in continuing Christ's saving mission.

All of the elements of biblical conversion appear to be incorporated into the RCIA's catechetical formation: turning to God in faith and trust and gradually developing friendship with God as one disentangles oneself from everything that is not of God in one's life. At every step of the process the catechumen's experience of the "turning" process is celebrated in rite and prayer. Blessings, scrutinies, exorcisms, and celebrations of the word of God help the catechumen to nurture an evangelical life completely in accord with the Spirit of Christ.

The liturgical celebration of conversion is not limited to Christian Initiation. Each time the community assembles for the celebration of the Eucharist, it celebrates its own conversion journey as well, and it acknowledges the paradox of the Christian life: that we are saved yet sinners, liberated yet ever in need of deeper conversion. Each time we gather we rehearse the wonderful works of God and give praise and thanksgiving that we have been counted worthy to stand in God's presence and to serve. At every celebration we acknowledge that God never ceases to call us to a new and more abundant life, that as sinners we are invited to trust in God's mercy, that the covenant of friendship with God is a bond that need never be broken, and that now, today, the always present *hodie* of the liturgy, is the day to return, to be renewed in Christ. A time of grace and reconciliation is always at hand. With each celebration of the liturgy we beg that the Spirit of God, the spirit of transformation, will change the elements of bread and wine and will change the community to be the very holiness of God.

Eucharist is a foretaste of the eternal banquet when no more "turning" will be needed, when the journey of conversion will be completed, when God will be all in all.

See: BAPTISM, RECONCILIATION

KATHLEEN HUGHES, R.S.C.J.

CORINTH

From the time of Homer the adjective used to describe Corinth was "wealthy" (*Iliad* 2:570). A great manufacturing city, its location on the six kilometer-wide isthmus linking mainland Greece to the Peloponnese gave it control over both north-south and east-west trade, the latter through its harbors at Lechaeum and Cenchreae. Destroyed by the Romans in 146 BCE, its economic potential led to its restoration as *Colonia Laus Julia Corinthiensis* by Julius Caesar in 44 BCE. For the most part the new settlers were former slaves from Greece, Syria, Judea, and Egypt, whose enterprise and industry quickly led to the reestablishment of trade and commerce. In less than half a century the city had made itself capable of hosting once again the Isthmian Games, a panhellenic festival second only to the Olympic Games.

The proverb "Not for everyone is the journey to Corinth" (Strabo, *Geography* 8:6.20; Horace, *Letters* 1:17.36) graphically illustrates the intensely competitive ethos of Corinth where only the strong and ruthless could prosper. Wealth, however, can vanish as quickly as it came, and so the dominant mythical figure associated with Corinth was Sisyphus, the craftiest of men (*Iliad* 6:154). Condemned to a pointless task he symbolized the futility of existence. The ephemeral success of the trickster was all that could be hoped for. Contrary to a very popular view, Aphrodite was not the patroness of Corinth. Neither were there one thousand sacred prostitutes devoted to her service; this legend arose because of a mistake by Strabo (*Geography* 8:6.20).

Paul's* choice of Corinth as one of his principal missionary centers was well motivated. It was open to new ideas, and offered him superb communications. Moreover, if Christianity could be implanted in a city so hostile to spiritual values, it would demonstrate its power to change the world (2 Cor 3:2). Visitors who saw the gospel in action might become its missionaries.

During his eighteen months (Acts 18:11) in Corinth—spring 50 to late summer 51 CE—Paul worked with tent-makers (Acts 18:1-3) who, among other jobs, supplied tents for visitors to the Isthmian Games (celebrated in spring 51) and the shopkeepers who served them. The occasion influenced his imagery in 1 Corinthians 9:24-25.

The names of sixteen of Paul's converts can be gleaned from Acts 18:2-17, 1 Corinthians 16:15-19, and Romans 16:1-3, 21-23. Since some were converted with their households, and presumably all were married, the minimum membership of the community must have been between forty and fifty. Some were wealthy, but the majority were poor (1 Cor 1:26-28). Such inequality, when combined with the lack of a house big enough to accommodate comfortably the whole Church (1 Cor 14:23; Rom 16:23), gave rise to jealousy and strife and to the formation of party factions (1 Cor 1:12; 3:3-4). Such tensions were exacerbated by Judaizing missionaries from Jerusalem. The ensuing theological ferment forced Paul to explore a wide range of subjects in a series of at least five letters of which only three have been preserved in 1 and 2 Corinthians.

See: COMMUNITY, HOUSE CHURCH, PAUL

JEROME MURPHY-O'CONNOR, O.P.

COSMOS

The term "cosmos" or "world" has important NT roots and takes on various meanings within Christian tradition.

New Testament

Cosmos (in Greek, *kosmos*, which is nearly always translated by "world") occurs in the NT a total of 187 times. Over half its instances are in the Johannine corpus. The Pauline writings use it frequently, comprising about one-quarter of its occurrences. The Synoptics and the rest of the NT make up the remainder. The range of meaning of cosmos in the NT is not broad. It refers to the physical universe created by God, the world* inhabited by human beings, or rational creatures at enmity with God. Accordingly cosmos is used of creation* in either a physical or spatial sense, and of humanity in either a neutral or pejorative manner. Generally speaking, both usages, the cosmological and theological, are set within the framework of God's salvific work: the entire cosmos, rational creatures as well as the physical universe, stands in need of the redemption wrought by Christ.

Johannine Usage. The fullness of theological usage of cosmos appears in the Johannine writings. The cosmos is the locus of redemption, where the Word becomes flesh and enters into human history. John's usage is thoroughly Christocentric; the cosmos is always seen in relation to Christ. The Word existed before the cosmos began (John 17:5, 24) and was created through him. Yet the cosmos does not know the Word (John 1:9-10; 3:19). But neither does it know the Father (John 17:25), who sent the Son into the cosmos to save it, proving his love for it (John 3:16-17; 12:47; cf. 16:28). The Son saves the cosmos by taking away its sin (John 1:29; 1 John 2:2); he calls the cosmos to believe in him, who is its light (John 8:12; 9:5; 12:46). Indeed, he is its Savior (John 4:42; 1 John 4:14) and its very life (John 6:33, 51).

Christ and the cosmos are in conflict (1 John 4:4-6). The cosmos is under the power of Satan, whom Christ judges and has conquered by the power of the Cross (John 12:21; 14:30; 16:11, 33; 1 John 4:3; 5:19; Rev 11:15). The Word's entrance into the cosmos divides it (John 9:39). The cosmos is especially used to mean those human beings who are hostile to Christ, for while the entire world (cosmos) goes after Christ, it clearly rejects him and his disciples (John 12:19; 7:7; 15:18; 3:19). This should not surprise the faithful (1 John 3:13), especially since they have the spirit of truth, whom

the cosmos cannot accept (John 14:17). Neither Christ nor his reign, then, belongs to the cosmos (John 8:23; 17:16; 18:36; 1 John 4:17). Accordingly the faithful are no longer of the cosmos, but rather are in Christ; those who hate their lives in this world (cosmos) save them (John 12:25; 15:18-19; 17:14). Because Christians still exist in the cosmos, they can expect to suffer (John 16:33). Christ has prayed for their protection (John 17:9, 11, 15) but has not taken them out of the cosmos.

By their unity the faithful are to bring the cosmos to believe that the Father sent the Son and loves the cosmos (17:21-23; 1 John 4:14). The faithful conquer the cosmos in Christ (1 John 5:4-5). Thus, while the faithful are not of the cosmos they do interact with it. The faithful are not to love the cosmos because it is at enmity with God and is passing away (1 John 2:17). The faithful are to love neither the things of the cosmos nor its allurements, for the cosmos has rejected Christ (1 John 2:15-17). Love of Christ is incompatible with love of the cosmos.

The cosmos is used by John to indicate that part of creation capable of responding to the Word and his offer of salvation. Cosmos is often personified in order to convey this. For example, it is said to hate Jesus and not to recognize him (e.g., 1 John 3:1). In particular cosmos is used to mean those who reject Christ and the faithful and persist in unbelief, listening only to themselves (John 17:6-9; 1 John 4:5). Yet the offer of salvation never ceases (John 12:32; 1 John 2:2), for it is the will of both the Father and the Son to save it. Paradoxically, Christ's saving the cosmos means putting it out of existence. Those who do accept Christ and his offer of salvation no longer belong to the cosmos even though they must continue to live in it.

The cosmos was created by God, but it offers nothing from the Father (1 John 2:16). Before the incarnation it was in darkness (John 1:5), and even after it preferred to be so (John 3:16). One of John's favorite themes is that of Christ as the light of the world (cosmos) (e.g., John 9:5; 12:35-36).

Along the same line, he is portrayed by John as the Savior of the whole world [cosmos] (John 4:42), which could not possibly contain a record of all that he did (John 21:25). Thus the Word became flesh for the sake of the life of the cosmos, that is, to bring all humanity, which is at enmity with God, to redemption. Christ is in the cosmos to show humanity its way from the world (cosmos) to the Father.

Pauline Usage. Cosmos occurs in the Pauline corpus forty-seven times. It is used in much the same way as in the Johannine literature, although not quite so sharply focused or as fully developed. In a cosmological sense, Paul speaks of the creation of the cosmos (Rom 1:20), which is passing away (e.g., 1 Cor 7:31). In a theological sense, Paul uses cosmos to mean the abode of humanity (in a neutral sense, Rom 1:8; 1 Cor 14:10; Col 1:6), and to mean rational creatures in conflict with God. For example, the cosmos' wisdom is absurdity with God, who turns it to folly (1 Cor 3:19; 1:20).

The faithful cannot escape corruption in the cosmos (1 Cor 5:10) because it is a place of sin (Rom 5:12-13). Christians are not to be taken in by the ways of the *cosmos*, which is ruled by certain powers opposed to Christ (Gal 4:3; Col 2:8, 20). The faithful are said to have been chosen by God before the world (cosmos) began (Eph 1:4). The apostles are said to be a "spectacle to the universe [cosmos], to angels and men alike," and to be the cosmos' refuse (1 Cor 4:9-13). To the cosmos Christians are foolish and weak (1 Cor 1:27-28). Paul assures the faithful, however, that they have God's spirit, which is clearly not that of the cosmos (1 Cor 2:12; 3:19; 2:6-7, 14). God's standards are not those of the cosmos: worldly sorrow brings death, but Godly sorrow leads to conversion and salvation (2 Cor 7:10). The cosmos makes demands and brings distractions (1 Cor 7:32-34).

God judges the whole cosmos, which stands convicted (Rom 3:6, 19). The faithful, who are set apart from the cosmos, will also judge it (1 Cor 6:2; 11:32). For Paul, Christ was reconciling the cosmos to God, and Christians have been entrusted with this mission (2 Cor 5:19). The cosmos belongs to the faithful because they are Christ's (1 Cor 3:22); they shine like stars in it (Phil 2:15). Perhaps the attitude that best sums up Paul's perspective on the cosmos is his boast that the world [cosmos] has been crucified to him and he to it (Gal 6:14).

In the Remainder of the NT. In the Pastoral and Catholic Letters, Hebrews, Acts, and the Synoptic Gospels, cosmos is used to indicate the physical universe created by God, the sphere of humanity, and those at enmity with God. As in the rest of the NT, in these works, love of the cosmos is enmity to God. Friendship with the cosmos and God are mutually exclusive (Jas 4:4). The faithful are to flee the cosmos, which is corrupted by lust (2 Pet 1:4; 2:20). Christians should be unspotted by the cosmos (Jas 1:2). James speaks of the tongue as a "whole universe [cosmos] of malice" (3:6). The cosmos is not worthy of those who suffer and die for the faith (Heb 11:38). As in the Johannine and Pauline literature, Christ came into the cosmos to save sinners (1 Tim 1:15; Heb 10:5), and was chosen to do so before its foundation (1 Pet 1:20).

As might be expected, cosmos is used to speak of the created universe (Matt 13:35; 24:21; 25:34; Luke 11:50; Acts 17:24), and humanity (Matt 4:8; 26:13; Mark 14:9; 16:15; 2 Pet 2:5; 3:6; 5:9; 1 Tim 3:16). Jesus calls the disciples the light of the world (cosmos) (Matt 5:14). All three Synoptics are clear that there is no profit in gaining the whole world (cosmos) if it means loss of oneself (Matt 16:26; Mark 8:36; Luke 9:25). In this same vein, Jesus speaks disparagingly of unbelievers in this cosmos who run after worldly things, making it plain that his disciples are not to do so (Luke 12:30).

The use of cosmos in these sections of the NT does not add anything to its usage in John and Paul. It is noteworthy that the NT's theology of the cosmos is consistent throughout. God created it in all its vastness. The cosmos' hostility to Christ is a primary theme; the conflict between the cosmos and the faithful is also an essential one. Overall, the NT concern with the cosmos is in relation to Christ. Unredeemed humanity is called to die to the cosmos and to accept its Savior. Those who come to believe in him are to live accordingly.

See: CREATION, LIGHT AND DARKNESS

SUSAN F. MATHEWS

Pastoral-Liturgical Tradition

In the Christian tradition, cosmos has been the rubric under which Christians have sought to discern the meaning and the connectedness of the entire universe, and the place and role of the human being within it. Understanding the cosmos is grounded therefore in the doctrine of creation.* It is God who has created the cosmos and has pronounced it good. Because the cosmos is both created and sustained in communion with God, it is inherently a meaningful place and carries within it (to use Augustine's words) "traces of God."

Christian speculations about the make-up of the cosmos (called "cosmologies") have regularly drawn upon those ideas in their environments, from the Platonic and Aristotelian cosmologies of the Patristic and Medieval periods, to the hermetic ones of early modernity and models from astrophysics in the twentieth century. In all of these, however, the belief that it is God who creates and sustains the universe has been brought to bear on those theories.

Three aspects of the cosmos in Christian tradition deserve to be highlighted. The first is the relation of the liturgy to the cosmos. This has been especially evident in the Byzantine liturgical tradition, where the Divine Liturgy is understood to mirror the heavenly liturgy before the throne of God. Participation in the Divine Liturgy, therefore, binds one in a communion with the entire cosmos, with the heavenly hosts, and so with God. Similarly, Vatican II's Constitution on the Sacred Liturgy speaks of the earthly liturgy as a foretaste of the heavenly liturgy (no. 8).

Secondly, the Christian understanding of the cosmos has been at the basis of a variety of mysticisms, stretching from the early Middle Ages down to the present. Among them are a sense of the connectedness of the universe, and the place of the human being as a "microcosm" within the "macrocosm" of the universe. One finds the former reflected in the Neoplatonic vision of John Scotus Erigena (ca. 810–ca. 877), in the revelations of Hildegard of Bingen (1098–1179), and in the fusion of modern science with a Christocentric worldview by Pierre Teilhard de Chardin (1879–1955). Certainly the greatest representative of the microcosm-macrocosm view is Nicholas of Cusa (1401–1464), which forms the basis of a profoundly sacramental view of the world.

Thirdly, a renewed interest in the cosmos can be found in the ecology movement. Here a theology of a deeply organic unity of the earth and all living things that dwell upon it is seen as the key to developing sustainable forms of human society. Rather than instrumentalizing our understanding of nature, such ecological theologies, represented especially in the work of Thomas Berry (b. 1914), show how inextricably human society and nature are bound up with one another.

See: CREATION

ROBERT J. SCHREITER, C.PP.S.

COVENANT

Covenant is a central theological idea in the OT, which uses this term to speak of God's special relationship to ancient Israel. Covenant is a far less central notion in the NT, which contrasts the OT covenant with the new relationship with God available to believers through Jesus Christ. The Christian theological tradition uses covenant as a metaphor in speaking of the sacraments of baptism, Eucharist, and matrimony.

Old Testament

Central to Israel's faith, life, and worship is the conviction that God, at a particular time and place, freely chose to enter into communion with Israel,* to constitute it as the people of God, and to impose upon it specific obligations. The dominant symbol used by Israel to describe this special relationship is that of covenant, which is understood to be a two-sided agreement, containing both promise and demand: "I will be your God and you shall be my people" (Jer 7:23; 11:4; 24:7; Ezek 11:20; 14:11; Hos 2:25). This powerful idea of covenant with God gave purpose to their life and meaning to their history.

The Idea of the Covenant. The idea of covenant (*berith* in Hebrew) was in widespread use in the ancient Near East long before Israel adopted it to represent its special relationship with God. Reflecting the need for human beings to work together effectively, covenants were solemn agreements between covenanting partners, usually specifying the rights and duties of each. Their primary goal was peace. References to such agreements are abundant in the OT. There were covenants between equal individuals or groups and also between unequal partners where the more powerful assures protection to the weaker, while the latter promises fidelity and service. Frequently such covenants were accompanied by a litany of blessings that would accrue to those who kept the agreement and curses that would befall those who violated it. In a time when written documents were rare or non-existent, these covenants were usually oral, and the spoken word was accorded a ritual solemnity. The blessings or curses would inevitably affect the person to whom they were directed. Written forms are best exemplified in treaties preserved in Hittite documents from 1450–1320 BCE. The ceremonies accompanying the making of a covenant suggest that it was regarded as a permanent commitment. Sometimes one or both partners passed through the pieces of an animal that had been cut in two, thus symbolizing that if they should break the covenant they would suffer the same fate as the slain animal. The commitment also could be sealed by eating a meal, or by tasting the preservative salt together. A tree might be planted or a stone set up to serve from then on as a witness to the pact. Loyalty, service, and solidarity were the appropriate responses to the union created by covenant.

Such is the rich idea of covenant that Israel appropriated and adapted to describe its new religious reality. Clearly the covenant between God and Israel is not understood to be a covenant between equal partners, and it differs from all human covenants because it is none other than God who initiates it.

The Covenant at Sinai. The covenant that established the relationship between God and Israel is the covenant at Sinai, described in Exodus. God's name and God's plan to deliver the Hebrews from Egypt and to bring them into the land of Canaan are first revealed to Moses* after the experience or the burning bush (Exodus 3), and the covenant that occurs at Sinai is portrayed as the purpose and consummation of this deliverance. "You have seen for yourselves how I treated the Egyptians and how I bore you up on eagle wings and brought you here to myself. Therefore, if you hearken to my voice and keep my covenant, you shall be my special possession, dearer to me than all other people, though all the earth is mine. You shall be to me a kingdom of priests, a holy nation" (Exod 19:4-6). It is clear that the election of Israel is a free act of God, not in any way deserved by Israel (Deut 9:4), but solely the result of God's love and fidelity to the oath sworn to their fathers (Deut 7:8).

After the ritual preparation of the people, God appears in the storm and the earthquake and imposes upon Israel the obligation of the covenant (Exodus 19–20). The Pentateuch furnishes many formulations of these obligations that make up the Law.* Indeed, the whole of Israelite law, which develops over a period of time, is intimately linked to the Sinai covenant and has as its major purpose to actualize the Israelites' personal response to it in their everyday life. Israel is to worship God alone, to reject any idolatry, and to observe the standards of cult and conduct befitting their character as God's people (Exod 20:3). The people express their willingness to abide by these obligations: "Everything the LORD has said, we will do" (Exod 19:8). This is a solemn and permanent commitment that will forever affect their history. They are assured of God's blessings* if they obey; if they break their word, they bring upon themselves curses* (Deuteronomy 28). It is within this context that the true nature of sin is to be understood. It is infidelity to the covenant, apostasy.

Exodus preserves two different traditions for the conclusion of the Sinai covenant. One is a ritual meal in which Moses, Aaron* and his sons, and seventy of the elders* of Israel, representing the entire people, share a common meal and contemplate God (Exod 24:1-2; 9-11), by that symbolizing covenant union. In the second, a ritual of blood, Moses first raises twelve sacred pillars for the twelve tribes and an altar for sacrifice; then he sprinkles the blood of sacrificed animals on the altar, which represents God, and on the people, symbolizing that God and Israel share the same blood bond (Exod 24:3-8).

The Covenant in the History of Israel. In subsequent history the memory of this solemn pact was maintained through diverse objects. The ark of the covenant, a small portable box, conveys God's presence; the two stone tablets that the ark contained, their covenant obligations before God (Exod 25:10-22; Deut 9:9, 11, 15). The Tent of Meeting is the place of the encounter between God and Israel, mediated through Moses (Exod 33:7-11). These symbols eventually evolve into the Temple,* the central scene of Israelite worship. In this way is perpetuated the connection between later Israelite worship and the initial act that produced it, the covenant at Sinai.

Renewals of the covenant are recorded in the OT, but it is not possible to ascertain how frequently these ceremonies occurred. One such ceremony is described in Deuter-

onomy where the ritual blessings for the observance of the covenant and the imprecations for its violation are accepted by the people (Deuteronomy 27). It is probable that the covenant was renewed at certain critical junctures in the history of the people. After the entry into Canaan, Joshua* recites the great delivering deeds of God and in response the people renew their commitment to God alone (Josh 24:1-28). This ceremony may also reflect the adoption of the covenant commitment by all the tribal groups of the amphictyony that comprised Israel at this time, for it is clear that outsiders were constantly absorbed into the covenant community where the decisive requirement for admission was not kinship but willingness to submit oneself to the God of the covenant. A covenant renewal ceremony was part of the dedication of Solomon's Temple (1 Kings 8). Similar renewals were conducted under Joash (2 Kgs 11:17), by Josiah (2 Kgs 11:17), and by Ezra (Nehemiah 8).

The OT also speaks of covenants between God and particular individuals, suggesting that the idea of the covenant with Israel as a whole was extended to certain key leaders. God made a covenant with David and David's house, establishing for them an eternal dynasty (Ps 89:20-38; 2 Sam 7:8). For their part, David and his descendants are bound to serve God's Law; if they do not, they will be punished, although the dynasty will remain. God also makes a covenant with Levi, promising an eternal priesthood to him (Jer 33:18).

In remarkable fashion the historians of Israel prevent the whole record of Israel's life and experience in the context of the Sinai covenant. The Yahwist (or "J") retrojects the covenant idea into the patriarchal period, portraying the covenant with Abraham* as the original basis of the special relationship between God and Israel. God promises to Abraham many descendants and for these descendants the land of Canaan. The condition for this is faith or trust (Genesis 12; 15). Going back even further in history, the Priestly tradition (or "P") traces God's plan back to the time of creation. After the catastrophic flood, God makes a covenant with Noah (Gen 6:18), thus giving the concept of covenant universal scope. Not only Israel, but the whole of humanity stands in covenant relationship with God. "P" then focuses on God's selection of Abraham and his offspring, making circumcision the sign of the covenant (Gen 17:9-14), and proceeds to the Sinai covenant that established Israel as the people of God. The Deuteronomic historian presents the whole history of Israel, from Moses to the end of the nation (Joshua–2 Kings), as an account of the people's constant betrayal of God's fulfilled promises for them. The destruction of Samaria and Jerusalem is seen as the consequence of their infidelity to their covenant obligations (2 Kgs 17:7-23; 23:26-27).

Prophetic Insights. The word covenant is not common among the eighth and seventh century BCE prophets. However, the Sinai covenant is at the heart of prophetic preaching. As they reflected on the special relationship between God and Israel against the backdrop of human experience in their day, the prophets discovered new images to describe its intimacy. The relationship is one of shepherd to flock, vine dresser to vine, potter to clay, father to son, husband to wife. All these images stress God's love and tender care for Israel. The Deuteronomic (or "D") outlook reflects these prophetic insights. While emphasizing the demands of the covenant, it puts them in the perspective of the love of God (Deut 4:37; 7:8; 10:15) and pleads with the people for a response of love on their part (Deut 6:5; 10:12). Thus will the people show that they are observing God's commands not through fear but by their own free decision. The prophets also clarify the nature of true worship. God rejects the people's external offering when it does not correspond to the required conduct, especially with respect to the practice of justice and concern for neighbor (Isa 1:10-20; Jer 7:21-28; Amos 5:14-15, 21-28). In this way the prophets attack the legalistic distortion of the covenant relationship that assumes that God must serve the interests of the people if they make the proper offerings.

The New Covenant. Based on the covenant obligations, the prophets denounce Israel's infidelities and speak of the catastrophes that will inevitably follow the betrayal of their word. However, they also move beyond this assessment and proclaim that although Israel has broken the covenant and has suffered the consequences for this, God's covenant plan remains and will be effected in an eschatological new covenant. Hosea speaks of a new marriage in which God will give Israel the bridal gifts of justice, love, mercy, fidelity, and knowledge of God and will reestablish peace between human beings and all creation (Hos 2:20-25). Jeremiah foresees in the future a new covenant which will be written on the heart and not on stone tablets as was the old covenant. Instruction will not be external but will come from within, as God teaches each individual Israelite (Jer 31:31-34). Ezekiel proclaims an eternal covenant in which God will bestow upon the people a new heart and a new spirit (Ezek 36:26). This will be an everlasting covenant of peace (Ezek 37:26). Second Isaiah widens the circle beyond Israel to include all peoples. He introduces a mysterious figure, the servant of God, whom he calls "a covenant of the people." This designation refers to the function of the servant: he is to be a light to the nations, to open the eyes of the blind, to free those who are imprisoned, to restore the land (Isa 42:6-7; 49:6); yet simultaneously he will justify "the many" through his suffering (Isaiah 53). As covenant-mediator the servant will bring Israel and the world into a voluntary embracing of full covenant relationship with God. Thus, in the eschatological age, God's covenant plan will realize its culmination.

See: BLESSING, CURSE, ELECTION, LAW

MARILYN M. SCHAUB

New Testament

Despite the use of the Latin word for covenant *(testamentum)* in the very title of the NT (for somewhat obscure reasons), the NT surprisingly is not permeated by references to covenants. The NT employs the Greek word for covenant *(diathēkē)* thirty-three times, often in passages referring to the OT. Half of the references occur in one book of the NT, the Letter to the Hebrews. The NT citations of covenant can be divided into four categories: (1) secular usage; (2) OT traditions, (3) Last Supper traditions, and (4) the covenantal theology of Hebrews.

Secular Usage. Common secular Greek use of *diathēkē* referred to one's last will and testament. This same use is found in two passages in the NT. Paul writes, "In human terms I say that no one can annul or amend even a human will once ratified" (Gal 3:15). Paul employs this image of a last will and testament in the context of reaffirming God's faithfulness to the covenant promises made to Abraham,* but it clearly refers to the common term for a will. The Letter to the Hebrews also employs the term in similar fashion, though in a theological context which will be discussed below. "Now where there is a will, the death of the testator must be established. For a will takes effect only at death; it has no force while the testator is alive" (Heb 9:16-17). This secular usage is the most elementary use of *diathēkē* in the NT.

OT Traditions. The NT also employs *diathēkē* in contexts which refer explicitly to various OT covenants. Minor attention is given to expressions like "the ark of the covenant" (Heb 9:4; Rev 11:19) and "tablets of the covenant" (Heb 9:4; see Exod 16:34). More importantly, the term *diathēkē* is intimately connected to themes of promise,* blood, Law, and the various agreements which God made with the people of Israel* through their history. Paul speaks of his own special love for Israel in a passage which explicitly connects Israel's covenants of old

(plural form) with their relationship to the coming of Jesus: "They are Israelites; theirs the adoption, the glory, the covenants, the giving of the law, the worship, and the promises; theirs the patriarchs, and from them, according to the flesh, is the Messiah" (Rom 9:4-5; see "covenants of promise" in Eph 2:12). For Paul, the relationship between the Law, the OT covenants, and the promises of God is a complex one which does not annul the validity of the covenants of old (Gal 3:15-22). These covenants remain as a testimony to God's faithfulness to the chosen people throughout the ages. If the coming of Jesus results in a new covenant, "it is not that the word of God has failed" (Rom 9:6), but that God brings the chosen people into a new relationship in which the Law is superseded by the faith that comes from righteousness (Galatians 3).

The NT contains other explicit references to OT covenants, especially the covenant with Abraham (e.g., Luke 1:72-73). The Acts of the Apostles refers to "the covenant of circumcision"* (7:8) and places this covenant in its proper perspective in salvation history: "You are the children of the prophets and of the covenant that God made with your ancestors when he said to Abraham, 'In your offspring all the families of the earth shall be blessed'" (3:25). This agreement God made with Abraham is used in Peter's speech in Solomon's Portico (Acts 3:11-26) to remind the Israelites that the coming of Jesus as the Messiah fits into this context as the final fulfillment* of God's promises. Consequently, the OT covenants prepare for and provide a pattern for the new agreement made between God and human beings in Jesus Christ.

References in the NT to OT covenants inevitably lead to a contrast. Paul's viewpoint is particularly instructive. In language which specifically alludes to OT themes, Paul speaks of his ministry as part of a new agreement between God and human beings, a covenant "not on tablets of stone but on tablets that are hearts of flesh" (2 Cor 3:3; see Jer 31:33; Ezek 11:19). Paul expands the contrast when he speaks of the ministry he and his coworkers have received from God: "our qualification comes from God, who has indeed qualified us as ministers of a new covenant, not of letter but of spirit; for the letter brings death, but the Spirit gives life" (2 Cor 3:5b-6, see vv. 7-11). The expression "new covenant" is actually an OT term (Jer 31:31-34) which speaks of a radical new way in which God will relate to the chosen people in a covenant of interiority. The roots of the contrast are already found in the OT in this passage from the prophet Jeremiah. Because the people of Israel could not remain faithful to the obligations of the previous covenants God made with them (Jer 2:26-27), the prophet harkens to a future new covenant which will be based on internal conviction rather than external obligation. Paul takes this contrast further by applying it to the transformation that has come to the covenant between God and Israel in the Christ-event. In Jesus, the new people of God find the fulfillment of all the promises of old. Rather than a covenant of legal observation, faith will be the new way in which people fulfill the obligations of the new covenant. The spirit of the Law transcends the letter of the Law, and the tablets of the heart replace the tablets of stone.

Paul employs another image to reinforce this contrast in covenants by means of an allegory on Christian freedom (Gal 3:21-31). Utilizing the OT covenant of Abraham, the allegory contrasts Abraham's progeny by the slave woman, Hagar, with Isaac,* his son by his wife Sarah (unnamed in this passage). Being children of the freeborn woman is superior to being children of a slave. Likewise, Paul insists that Christians are born of freedom and not of slavery (v. 31), and are thus set free to live according to the obligations of the new covenant of faith, not being bound to the legal observances of the former covenant.

The NT use of OT concepts of covenant is a mixture of recollection and contrast. If the NT continues to remind Christians of their ancestral heritage in the people of Israel and God's covenants with them, it also makes clear that the coming of Jesus Christ implies a transformation of this relationship.

Last Supper Traditions. The Last Supper traditions of the NT preserve two somewhat different viewpoints. The NT is consistent in preserving the memory that Jesus, on the night before his death, ate a final meal with his disciples during which he pronounced words over a cup of blessing. These words constitute a memorial which forms the heart of the new relationship between God and God's people. Mark and Matthew preserve one form of the tradition while Paul and Luke preserve another.

Mark 14:24 records the following words of Jesus at the Last Supper: "This is the blood of the covenant which will be shed for many." Matthew 26:27-28 contains similar words with the addition of the phrase "for the forgiveness of sins," in order to emphasize that Jesus' death has sacrificial, atoning value which results in reconciliation. Two observations are important. Both passages leave out the adjective "new" to describe this covenant, and both connect this covenant with the shedding of blood. The tone of these passages is shaped by strong OT imagery. Just as the OT covenants were sealed by blood, as a reminder of the awesome obligations contained therein (e.g., Exod 24:8), so this covenant is ratified by blood. This covenant which Jesus enacts by his suffering and death is in line, then, with those of the OT. Jesus himself becomes the sacrifice which seals the covenant and makes it efficacious, achieving salvation* and redemption for "many," a typical Hebraic expression for "everyone."

Paul preserves a somewhat nuanced tradition of the words of the Last Supper: "This cup is the new covenant in my blood. Do this, as often as you drink it, in remembrance of me" (1 Cor 11:25; cf. Luke 22:20). Here the actual expression "new covenant" is used, and it establishes the tradition for contrasting this particular covenant with all other preceding ones. By this direct allusion to the new covenant promised by the prophet Jeremiah (31:31-34), Paul emphasizes the radical contrast between this covenant (of promise, spirit, heart, freedom) to the patriarchal covenants of old (of Law, flesh, stone, slavery). Paul also adds a liturgically influenced formula which notes the importance of continual remembrance of Jesus' action: "For as often as you eat this bread and drink this cup, you proclaim the death of the Lord until he comes" (1 Cor 11:26). The eschatological dimension of this saying is consistent with the hopeful stance of the early Christians to await the parousia* in confidence and faith, for Christ's return in glory would provide the ultimate fulfillment of the covenant with God in the establishment of God's reign.

Covenantal Theology in the Letter to the Hebrews. Hebrews requires a separate treatment of covenant not only because it uses the concept more frequently than any other NT writing, but also because it significantly transforms the notion into a virtual "theology" of covenant. Whereas the Pauline writings refer to the contrast between previous covenants and the new covenant, Hebrews unabashedly carries the contrast to its ultimate conclusion. The new covenant is infinitely superior to the old.

There are multiple aspects to the superiority of the new covenant. Hebrews 7 lays out an understanding of Melchizedek,* the mysterious royal and priestly figure of the OT (Gen 14:22), as the typological forerunner of Jesus Christ. Just as God had made Melchizedek a priest forever by the oath sworn to him, so "to the same degree has Jesus [also] become the guarantee of an [even] better covenant" (7:22). This covenant is better because it is eternal and is not based upon continual sacrifices made in the Temple, but on the one eternal sacrifice made by Christ himself. This high priesthood of Jesus has made him a perpetual mediator between God and humanity:

"Now he has obtained so much more excellent a ministry as he is mediator of a better covenant, enacted on better promises" (8:6). Another passage makes it clear that it is Jesus' own death which enables this new position of mediation to take place and that the result is eternal life: "For this reason he is mediator of a new covenant: since a death has taken place for deliverance from transgressions under the first covenant, those who are called may receive the promised eternal inheritance" (9:15). This is also where Hebrews utilizes a pun on the meaning of *diathēkē* as both will/testament and covenant (9:16-17 discussed above). Only Jesus' death itself ensures the efficacy of this new covenant.

Hebrews continues to explain the relationship between these two covenants in a section which employs the entire "new covenant" passage of Jeremiah 31:31-34 (Heb 8:8-12; see also 10:16), quoting from the Septuagint. It is the longest single quote of the OT found in the NT, and demonstrates how instrumental this passage is to the author of Hebrews in shaping a profound theology of covenant. The author labels the OT Mosaic covenant "the first covenant" (8:7; 9:1) and criticizes the inability of the previous covenant to be effective. "For if that first covenant had been faultless, no place would have been sought for a second one. . . . When he speaks of a 'new' covenant, he declares the first one obsolete. And what has become obsolete and has grown old is close to disappearing" (8:7, 13). The exaltation of the second, new covenant necessitates the denigration of the first, old covenant. Obsolescence leads to the need for a replacement. But one should also emphasize that this understanding of superiority is based upon a very "high Christology" (i.e., emphasizing the divinity of Christ and underplaying his humanity) in which Jesus is the new and eternal high priest (e.g., 4:14-15; 9:11-14; 10:11-14). From this perspective, when God spoke to the Israelites of old and made a covenant with them, it was only a pale reflection of the glories which were to come in Jesus (1:1-2).

The new covenant, consequently, is both a fulfillment and a surpassing of previous promises. He who was "far superior to the angels"* (1:4) was also superior to Moses* (3:1-6a). He alone, by virtue of his identity, mission, and sacrifice, constitutes the source for the new covenant's preeminence.

With the Letter to the Hebrews, the entire NT teaching on covenant reaches its apex. Although this theology of covenant is firmly rooted in the covenantal traditions of the OT and builds upon them, the NT development finds its terminus far beyond the OT vision. The covenant of interiority promised by the prophet Jeremiah (see also Ezek 36:26-27) has arrived in Jesus Christ.

See: ABRAHAM, ARK OF THE COVENANT, BLOOD, CIRCUMCISION, EUCHARIST, FAITH, FLESH, FULFILLMENT, HEART, ISRAEL, JESUS CHRIST, LAW, LIFE, MELCHIZEDEK, MESSIAH, MINISTRY, MOSES, PROMISE, RECONCILIATION, SLAVERY, WORSHIP

RONALD D. WITHERUP, S.S.

Pastoral-Liturgical Tradition

The notion of a covenant between God and a special people is clearly found in the theology and sacramental practice of the early Church and of the Church today. This is especially evident in the sacraments of baptism, Eucharist, and marriage. In baptism a person enters into a covenant relationship with God and the Church. Through the celebration and reception of the Eucharist the new covenant in Christ's blood is reaffirmed, participated in, and celebrated by the whole community of the baptized and the individual Christian. And the mutual love and fidelity of wife and husband reflects the covenant between Christ and the Church.

Baptism. In the OT, circumcision* was the ritual act by which a Jewish male entered into the community of the covenant (see Gen 17:1-14), whereas in the NT baptism became the rite by which the Christian enters into the new covenant community of the Church. The early Jewish Christian communities practiced both circumcision and baptism. Paul objected to requiring circumcision of Gentile converts and appealed to the apostles in Jerusalem. The resulting Council of Jerusalem decided that Gentiles need not be circumcised; baptism was deemed to be sufficient (see Acts 15:1-35). Although the term "covenant" is not necessarily used in later Patristic writings about baptism, it is clear that baptism is an act of God in Christ to the people of the new covenant. Through baptism the believer participates in the paschal mystery of Christ's passion, death, and resurrection and becomes both an adopted child of God and a member of the Church of Christ. These themes are found in the General Introduction to the Rites of Christian Initiation, reformed by the Second Vatican Council: "Through baptism men and women are incorporated into Christ. They are formed into God's people and they obtain forgiveness* of all their sins. They are rescued from the power of darkness and brought to the dignity of adopted children (Rom 8:15; Gal 4:5), a new creation through water and the holy Spirit. Hence they are called and are indeed the children of God (1 John 3:1)" (Christian Initiation, General Introduction, no. 2). The General Introduction goes on to note that through baptism women and men are incorporated into the Church, built in the Spirit into a dwelling place for God (see Eph 2:22) and into a holy nation and a royal priesthood (see 1 Pet 2:9) (General Introduction, no. 4). The baptismal rites use two further figures of the OT for the covenant, especially in the prayers for blessing the baptismal water and of the choice of Scripture readings (Gen 9:9-17) and the passage through the Red Sea (Exod 24:1-11).

Eucharist. The covenant of the OT is ratified and reaffirmed by sacrifice* and by the sprinkling of the blood of the sacrificial victim over the people. The new covenant is ratified and reaffirmed by the celebration of the Eucharist. The blood of the new covenant is that of Christ, shed for the forgiveness of sins of all God's people. The words of institution for the cup explicitly speak of it as "the blood of the new and everlasting covenant." The new covenant of which Jeremiah (31:31) speaks is accomplished and made effective by Christ's sacrificial death on the cross. In the celebration of the Eucharist and the reception of Communion the Church enters into the sacrifice of Christ and shares in the benefits of the new covenant of love. The promise* of the new covenant is reaffirmed: by eating the bread of life and drinking from the cup of salvation we are given the foretaste and promise of eternal life (John 6:53-58). The death and resurrection lie at the apex of all the covenants God has made with us, as Eucharistic Prayer IV reminds us: "Again and again you offered a covenant to [us] and through the prophets you taught [us] to hope for salvation . . . in the fullness of time you sent your only Son to be our Savior. . . . In fulfillment of your will he gave himself up to death . . . he destroyed death and restored life" (Eucharistic Prayer IV, Preface). Not only did the OT covenants and covenant renewals involve the use of blood, they also often involved a covenant meal* whereby the participants partook of the sacrificial victim or food that was offered. The Eucharist is celebrated in the context of a meal, as was the covenant memorial of the Passover;* Christ becomes our food, our nourishment. It is the "sacred banquet in which Christ is received, the memory of his passion is renewed, the mind is filled with grace, and the pledge of future glory is given to us." This banquet meal effects communion between God and the individual participants, while, at the same time, uniting the individuals into the one body of Christ, the Church.

Marriage. Saint Paul sees Christian marriage as an image of Christ's relationship to the Church. The total self-giving of husband to wife and wife to husband is a sign of Christ's total gift of himself to the Church—the sacrificial covenant of love accomplished on the cross (see Eph 5:2, 21-33). In the contemporary marriage rite this gift of self, which lies at the core of the new covenant of Christ, is expressed in the ex-

change of consent between the man and the woman. Rather than being merely a legal expression of a marriage contract, it is truly an expression of a covenant between the husband and wife, mirroring that of Christ and the Church: "I, N., take you, N., to be my (husband/wife). I promise to be true to you in good times and in bad, in sickness and in health. I will love you and honor you all the days of my life." The notions of permanence and fidelity in the marriage vows reflect the same two aspects of God's covenant with the Church. Marriage as a reflection of Christ's covenant is also given expression in the second nuptial blessing: "Father, to reveal the plan of your love, you made the union of husband and wife and an image of the covenant between you and your people . . . marriage is a sign of the marriage between Christ and the Church." The covenant of marriage is not merely between the husband and wife, for God is also a party to their covenant, as the nuptial blessing says: "Lord, grant that as they begin to live this sacrament they may share with each other the gifts of your love and become one in heart and mind as witnesses to your presence in their marriage" (Nuptial Blessing, no. 2).

See: ABRAHAM, BAPTISM, BLOOD, CIRCUMCISION, EUCHARIST, LOVE, MARRIAGE, VOWS

ALAN F. DETSCHER

CREATION

The creation of the universe has fascinated people from the beginning of time. This interest can be traced from the mythology of the ancient Near Eastern myths, through the traditions of both biblical testaments, down to the teachings of contemporary theologians.

Old Testament

The First Testament uses several verbs to describe God's primordial creation activity. *bārā'*, "to create" (Gen 1:1, 21, 27; Isa 42:5; 43:1; etc.), is considered a technical term and is used only when speaking of a new and extraordinary or epochal creation by

God. The following words express an element of relationship between the creator and the creation: *'āśâ*, "to make" (Gen 1:7, 16, 25, 26; 2:4, 18; Isa 44:2; 45:12, 18; etc.) usually implies making something out of existing material; *qānāh*, "to establish" (Ps 139:13; Prov 8:22) always means "to establish for oneself"; *yātsar*, "to form" (Gen 2:7f., 19; Isa 43:1, 7; 44:2, 21, 24), suggests the activity of a potter shaping and fashioning clay by hand. These words are used interchangeably or in poetic parallel construction which prevents interpreters from making precise distinctions among them. The imagery used to refer either to the events of creation or to the creator governs the choice of vocabulary.

The titles for God as creator are derived from these same verbs. Creator, from *bārā'*, only appears twice (Isa 40:28; 43:15). Maker, the more commonplace title, is derived from one of the other three verbs: from *'āśâ* (Job 4:17; 32:22; 35:10; Pss 95:6; 149:2; Isa 51:13); from *qānāh* (Gen 14:19, 22); from *yātsar* (Isa 49:9, 11). However, God is more frequently described as creating than called the creator. This creative activity is often referred to as stretching out the heavens (Isa 40:22; 44:24; 45:12; 51:13), firmly establishing the earth* (Pss 75:4; 93:1; 96:10; 104:5), or conquering the mythological beasts (Ps 74:13-15; 89:10f.; Isa 51:9f.; Job 9:13).

Creation and History. A careful reading of the stories of creation found in the first two chapters of the Book of Genesis shows that creation was less a calling forth out of nothingness than an ordering of primordial chaos.* This is especially apparent in the first account (Gen 1:1–2:4a). There we read that God put order in a world that was a "formless wasteland" where "darkness covered the abyss" (1:2). God first separated the light from darkness (1:4), then the waters above the firmament from the waters below (1:6-7). Having caused the dry land to appear (1:9), God set about populating the waters and the sky (1:21) and then the earth (1:25, 27).

The ancient Israelites probably drew upon several earlier Near Eastern myths* of creation as they shaped their own account of primordial events. Chief among these versions was the Babylonian epic *Enuma Elish*. In it the young warrior Marduk engaged in fierce combat with the monster Tiamat. The account of this battle between the forces of two gods follows a mythical pattern that was very common in the ancient Near Eastern world. One of the gods was the embodiment of order and the other was a comparable embodiment of chaos. Chaos was conquered and its forces were restrained. The victorious warrior-god restored the cosmic order that had been threatened, entered triumphantly into the city, constructed and took up residence in the temple-palace and, thereby, established peace.

Although Israel significantly reshaped this story to fit its monotheistic faith, traces of the pattern are scattered throughout the First Testament. Allusions to the battle as well as to the victorious procession and establishment of the temple-palace are found primarily in the poetic literature (Pss 24:1-2, 7-10; 74:12-17; 89:10-14; Isa 27:1). In many places it is difficult to distinguish between primordial events and remembered incidents in the unique history of Israel. Historical battles were believed to have cosmic repercussions, and the cosmogonic victory that established universal world order also set the parameters of specific national and social order. This is especially clear in Psalm 24 which praises the triumphant march of God who, as primordial creator and national warrior, entered both the cosmic temple and the promised land. There the oppressive powers of Egypt and the Canaanite states are regarded as the concrete embodiment of cosmic chaos. The psalm attributes to Israel's God the characteristics of the valiant warrior, and it celebrates the exultant march of God and the people of God into the place where God would reign supreme.

Just as "the beginning" is depicted as the establishment of order in the natural world, so at "the end" the order will be overturned and the created world will be subject to natural disaster (Gen 7:17-23; Isa 24:3-5). Historical disasters were also described as the disruption of the cosmic order (Jer 4:23f.). For the ancients, the created world was not merely the stage on which the drama of history unfolded. Creation and history were intimately united. For this reason, their faith in God's ultimate victory led them to speak of political restoration as a "new creation" (Isa 65:17; 66:22). This theme dominates the message of Second Isaiah, who brings creation and history together as does no other prophet (40:12-31; 42:5-9; 51:9-11). Thus the goal of history is the return to the original plan of the creator, a plan of natural order and harmony as delineated in the creation accounts.

Creation and Life. The Israelites came to believe that their God was the great Creator-God, the one responsible for the world and everything in it. Observing the regularity in creation, they concluded that there was some kind of order inherent in nature itself. They believed that, if they could discover how this order operated and then harmonize their lives with it, they would be successful and at peace. The ability to perceive this order and to live in accord with it was known as wisdom. They reasoned further that, if it takes human wisdom to learn how to live orderly lives within this ordered world, there must be some kind of divine wisdom that first established and now sustains the created order. Thus we see the very close relationship between creation theology and wisdom thinking.

There are both wisdom allusions in creation accounts and creation concerns in the Wisdom literature. First, the orderly manner in which God separated primordial matter and then caused life to appear in the world as recorded in Genesis 1 attests to that tradition's wisdom interests. Furthermore, the drama reported in Genesis 2–3 revolves around the "tree of the knowledge of good and evil" (2:9, 16f.; 3:1-13), clearly a wisdom theme. On the other hand, the primordial origin and extraordinary character of wisdom is highlighted in Proverbs 8:22-31. Begotten of God (v. 22), Wisdom is present at the creation of all else, even in some way taking part in God's creative activity (v. 30, see also Wis 7:22). This same connection between Wisdom and creation is made in Sirach, a much later Wisdom book (24:2-6).

It is perhaps in the Book of Job that the relationship between creation and wisdom takes on new meaning. Throughout the dialogues, Job cries out against what he perceives to be God's inability to sustain order. He even pleads for the return of cosmic chaos (3:3-10). When God finally does reply, there is no mention of justice (or wisdom) but only of the grandeur of creation. Questioning Job about primordial events is God's way of defending divine justice. Only divine wisdom was able to bring the world into existence; only divine wisdom can sustain this world and everything within it. The lesson of wisdom that Job must learn is a lesson about creation and about the creator.

Praise is a sentiment that wells up within believers when they are overwhelmed by the wonders around them. They stand in awe before the splendor of creation and they are drawn out of ourselves. This same sentiment is found in those psalms referred to as hymns of praise. The psalmist does not seem able to find words adequate to describe the grandeur of creation (Psalms 8; 29; 104; 148) and so all of the forces of nature are called upon to join in glorifying God. Underlying such sentiments of praise is the belief that God is the creator of all things and that all that God has created is beautiful, deserving of our respect, and a reminder of the majestic creator.

The Creator. The language and imagery of the Bible tell more about Israel's notions of God than about the primordial events themselves. The story of the cosmic struggle between two warring gods, a theme found in the traditions of most ancient Near Eastern cultures, was adjusted significantly to conform to monotheism. Whatever force posed a challenge for others was clearly subservient to Israel's God who, though sometimes depicted as a warrior (Ps 24:8), enjoyed sovereign rule. The somewhat detached creation (*bārā'*) by mere word suggests that God's omnipotence transcends a more direct or immediate involvement. As mentioned above, most of the other verbs used to speak of creation also denote some kind of relationship between the creator and creation. The biblical contexts within which these verbs are found indicate that the relationship is marked by divine generosity and concern. Israel's Creator-God was dependable, not capricious as were the gods worshiped by some other people. The Wisdom literature and the psalms reflect praise of a wise and generous creator whose architectural blueprint is incomprehensible and whose artistry is awe-inspiring. This creator chose the man and the woman to govern the created world in God's place (Gen 1:28), and to live in covenant with this world and all the creatures of it (Gen 9:9-17).

See: ADAM AND EVE, CHAOS, EARTH, FLOOD, MYTH

DIANNE BERGANT, C.S.A.

New Testament

The NT understanding of creation is firmly based on the traditions of the OT affirming God as sole creator and the goodness of creation. The Greek verb *ktizo* is used only of God and reflects the Hebrew verb *bārā'* in the OT. Not surprisingly however, these traditions are understood in new ways in the light of the Christ event which is portrayed as the culminating moment in the creative salvific activity of God.

The Gospels. In the Gospel tradition Jesus does not speak explicitly about creation as such. Rather he is rooted in OT ideas and preaches to the disciples the goodness of creation and God's providential care for the world: "Notice the ravens, they do not sow nor reap, they have neither storehouse nor barn, yet God feeds them. How much more important are you than birds!" (Luke 12:24). In his conflict with the authorities over ritual purity he took the argument of the goodness of creation to its logical conclusion and declared all foods clean (Mark 7:19). In 1 Timothy 4:4 this position is very clearly and positively stated: "For everything created by God is good and nothing is to be rejected when received with thanksgiving." Another aspect of creation which is present in the Gospels is its situation in time: God is not only creator but also Lord of history who in time reveals the great divine plan for the salvation of the world. Jesus rejoices that the revelation of this plan is given to the childlike and hidden from the wise and learned. This is how it is willed by his "Father, LORD of heaven and earth" (Matt 11:25). The plan of God as intended from the beginning is referred to elsewhere in the Gospels as for example when Jesus speaks of marriage (Mark 10:6) or in the story of the last judgment when the righteous are told: "Inherit the Kingdom prepared for you since the foundation of the world" (Matt 25:34). The command of Jesus to the disciples, "Go into the whole world and proclaim the gospel to every creature" (Mark 16:15), illustrates that the good news of salvation is intended for everyone, everywhere and embraces all of creation.

Creation in Christ. Paul too affirms the traditional Biblical stance on creation when he attempts dialogue with the philosophers of Athens (Acts 17:24) and when he and Barnabas are almost worshiped by the delighted townspeople of Lystra after the healing of the crippled man (Acts 14:15-17). The evidence about God in creation is invoked again in Romans 1:20-25 when the Gentiles are upbraided for their failure to recognize God at work in the natural order and for even going so far as to worship the creature rather than the creator.

However, Paul not only restates traditional OT views, he also emphasizes the importance of Christ's role in creation. In this he appears to be making use of the mediatory role ascribed to *wisdom* in Proverbs 8:22-31 and in Wisdom 7:22. In this he is not unique, for in John 1:3, 10 and Hebrews 1:2, 10-12 similar statements on the function of the pre-existent Christ are to be found. Even so, it is in the letters of Paul that it is most strongly stated.

Thus in 1 Corinthians 8:6: "There is for us . . . One LORD, Jesus Christ through whom all living things are and through whom we exist." In Colossians this is developed to show that creation is not only through Christ but also *for* him: the plan of creation even in its supernatural dimensions comes to its fullness in him. "For in him were created all things in heaven and on earth, the visible and the invisible, whether thrones or dominations or principalities or powers; all things were created through him and for him. He is before all things and in him all things hold together" (Col 1:16-17). That our election in Christ was God's intention from the very beginning is stated in Ephesians 1:3: "God chose us in him before the foundation of the world, to be holy and without blemish before him."

Christ's involvement in creation serves to highlight its meaning and purpose. Through the passage of time all of created reality moves toward its final consummation. The life, death, and resurrection of Jesus has not done away with the effects of sin, yet in him the destiny of glory which awaits the world has been manifested. This means that creation too "awaits with eager expectation the revelation of the children of God . . . so that creation itself would be set free from slavery to corruption and share in the glorious freedom of the children of God" (Rom 8:19-21). Needless to say this process which is like the act of giving birth is not without its pain, which we all share in (Rom 8:22-23).

New Creation. The understanding of Christ's role in creation opens up another aspect of Paul's thought which pertains to the role and identity of the Christian. By baptism Christians come to life* in Christ and so they are a new creation. This means

that former ways of living and distinctions on the basis of the Law are no longer acceptable or relevant. "For neither does circumcision mean anything nor does uncircumcision, but only a new creation" (Gal 6:15). Being a new creation brings with it the responsibility of living in a new way, involving us in the reconciling ministry of Christ. "So whoever is in Christ is a new creation: the old things have passed away, behold new things have come. All of this is from God who has reconciled us to himself through Christ and given us the ministry of reconciliation" (2 Cor 5:17-18).

By virtue of his death Christ has destroyed the enmity that existed between Jew and Gentile, creating in himself "one new person, thus establishing peace" (Eph 2:15). This peace comes to fruition when Christians grow in the awareness that they have indeed put on a new self, "having been created in God's way, in righteousness and holiness of truth" (Eph 4:24). The community at Colossae is also urged to accept the consequences of their new life: "Stop lying to one another, since you have taken off the old self with its practices and have put on the new self, which is being renewed, for knowledge, in the image of its creator" (Col 3:9-10).

New Heavens and New Earth. The journey toward the complete fulfilment of God's plan of creation, which Paul speaks about, is seen elsewhere in the NT where the writers look forward to "a new heaven and a new earth" echoing an idea found in Isaiah 65:17; 66:22. In 2 Peter 3:13 this is the reality which the community awaits and it is exhorted to do so in a spirit of patience and right conduct. In Revelation the vision of the heavenly liturgy presented in chapters 4–5 focuses on the praise offered to God and the Lamb. In Revelation 4:11 the twenty-four elders representing the whole people of God give thanks for the gift of creation, while in 5:13 "every creature in heaven and on earth and in the sea, everything in the universe" proclaims the praise of God and the Lamb. After the depiction of God's final victory over the forces of evil that have marred human history and distorted creation, God's eternal reign appears. It is "a new heaven and a new earth, . . . a new Jerusalem" where God's dwelling is with the human race. "God will wipe every tear from their eyes, and there shall be no more death or mourning, wailing or pain, for the old order has passed away" (Rev 21:4).

As the Bible began with creation it is fitting that it should end with that creation being fully renewed. As Christians we look forward to that day with hope, striving to live by the values of the reign of God and rejoicing in the beauty and wonder of the world that surrounds us.

See: EARTH, GLORY, HEAVEN, LIFE, WISDOM

SEAN GOAN, C.P.

Pastoral-Liturgical Tradition

Three things especially have marked the theology of creation throughout the ages. First of all, from the earliest part of the post-Apostolic period, Christians have affirmed the *creatio ex nihilo,* or creation from nothing. This means that the world was not created out of some pre-existent material; rather, everything that is owes its existence to God. In insisting on creation from nothing, Christians want to confess the sovereignty of God over all of creation, and that all creation belongs to God and not to some other being. Even though there is evil in the world, that evil does not ultimately hold sway over creation: it will someday be overcome by God's saving power.

Second, the world that God has created is good. This not only echoes a theme that reverberates throughout the first Genesis account of creation (Gen 1:1–2:4), but also makes an important point; namely, that even though there is sin and evil in the world, the world is intrinsically good and was created neither evil nor sinful. Evil, Christians maintain, entered somehow into the world after God had created it. Consequently, all creation, both living and inanimate, is to be treated as good and as a gift from God.

Third, Catholic Christians have maintained that through creation God can be known by the light of natural reason. In other words, creation itself is revelatory of God to us, even prior to the revelation given to Israel and in Jesus Christ. This teaching was reaffirmed at the First Vatican Council (DS 3004). This belief has been important in upholding a fundamentally sacramental understanding of nature, whereby God's creation mirrors forth God's own glory. Such a belief has not been as widely held in most Protestant circles, mainly because of doubts about the capacities of human reason unaided by grace.

For much of Christian history, the creation story given in Genesis 1:1–2:4 was taken, at least implicitly, to be a largely literal account of how the world came to be. It was only with the emergence of evolutionary theory in the middle of the nineteenth century that such belief came to be questioned. If the evolutionary account was correct, then the world was considerably older than the Bible seemed to say, and plants and animals—not to mention humans only gradually and slowly evolved into the forms in which they are known today. Beginning in the late nineteenth century and well into the twentieth, a considerable struggle went on among Christians in their efforts to reconcile their faith with scientific theory. One group of conservative Christians has affirmed the literal truth of the Genesis account in the face of scientific discovery, maintaining that God created the world as we now know it a little over four thousand years ago, and in the space of six days. This position is known as "creationism." It sees evolution as only a theory that cannot be proven definitively. Most modern Christians, however, would view the evolutionary account of creation as the likely fact, and hold the account of creation given in Genesis 1–2 as a theological, rather than historical perspective. Thus the way God calls all creation into being in the Genesis account is meant to underline God's sovereign power; the six days of creation merely underscore the orderly and purposeful way in which the creation of the world was undertaken. Such a theological reading accords better with the story and allays the problem of harmonizing apparent contradictions, such as how God created light before the sun was created.

In the wake of trying to understand an evolutionary worldview from a Christian perspective, the ancient Patristic view of the *creatio continua* or continuous act of creation has been retrieved for modern Christians. Creation is thus seen as a dynamic, ongoing process whereby the presence and designs of God continue to unfold. The writings of the French palaeontologist and mystic Pierre Teilhard de Chardin (1879–1955) have been central to this new understanding of creation. Teilhard saw the evolving world being lured forward to its Omega Point, which is Christ, relying here especially on the cosmic vision of Ephesians 1:10.

In the latter third of the twentieth century, concerns for a better treatment of the environment have fueled a new interest in the theology of creation. Of special concern has been the mandate given to the first humans to dominate the earth (Gen 1:26) as having been a warrant to use the goods of creation without concern for the environment. Since the 1970s these ecological concerns have been translated into a theology of creation that emphasizes care for the earth rather than a careless exploitation of it. It has also spawned a spirituality that aims at a more wholistic lifestyle and society. In this view, care and co-responsibility for God's creation are stressed above the call to increase, multiply, and dominate the earth.

Closely connected to this ecological concern is another, older issue that gained new vitality after the Second Vatican Council; namely, the just distribution of the goods of the earth. Thomas Aquinas had already affirmed the principle of just distribution as being prior to any proprietary right; popes from Leo XIII to John Paul II have reaffirmed in their social encyclicals that just distribution supersedes private property as an absolute right. Justice is there-fore integral to a contemporary theology of creation.

See: ADAM AND EVE, EARTH, WORLD

ROBERT J. SCHREITER, C.PP.S.

CUP

Old Testament

The cup overflowing represents the largess of the host, that is God, in Psalm 23:5. The image, however, is a traditional motif of the ancient Near East, and a number of statues of deities and human beings can be found holding a cup overflowing as an image of the abundance of life. Psalm 16:5 refers to God "my allotted portion and my cup," which again fits this theme of abundance, as opposed to Psalm 11:6 where a scorching wind shall be the allotted cup for the wicked.

In Psalm 116:13, "the cup of salvation" is typically seen as a reference to libation, an offering made to a deity by pouring out wine (Exod 29:40-41; Num 28:7-8). The psalmist makes this offering to repay the vow undertaken during time of trouble.

Other references are linked to wine.* Jeremiah 16:7 makes reference to the "cup of consolation" given to mourners. However, the link to wine is mainly negative and suggests drunkenness as judgment and punishment. In Jeremiah 25:15-29, the nations are given "this cup of foaming wine" so that they will "be convulsed and go mad." In Psalm 75:9, the wicked of the earth shall drink the cup "even to its dregs" (see also Ps 60:5; Isa 51:17, 22; Jer 49:12; Ezek 23:31; Hab 2:16). The theme of judgment is continued in the Book of Revelation (14:10; 16:19; 17:4; 18:6). All of this suggests the high sense of shame connected with drunkenness in this culture.

New Testament

In the NT, the cup has four contexts. As the cup of cold water, it represents the simplest and most basic act of charity which guarantees the reward of belonging to Christ (Matt 10:42; Mark 9:41). As a utensil associated with purification, it serves as an example of hypocrites who cleanse the outside but not the inside (Matt 23:25-26; Mark 7:4). Echoing the image of the cup of wrath and punishment in the OT, Jesus asks James and John if they can drink the cup that he will drink (Matt 20:22-23; Mark 10:38-39; Luke 11:39), and in the garden, Jesus asks that the cup that he must drink be taken away but adds: "Not what I will, but what you will" (Mark 14:36; Matt 26:39; Luke 22:42; see also John 18:11). The context of suffering is linked also to the Eucharist.* Unlike the libation in which the cup held the wine to be spilled as sacrifice, the Eucharistic cup preserves the blood* poured out in sacrifice (Matt 26:27; Mark 14:23-24; Luke 22:17, 20; 1 Cor 11:25-28). Paul contrasts this "cup of the Lord" with the "cup of demons" (1 Cor 10:21), for, as he says, "The cup of blessing that we bless, is it not a participation in the blood of Christ?" (1 Cor 10:16). The "cup of blessing" is also the name of the third cup of wine consumed at the Passover, which adds another overtone to this meal. Paul also equates this cup with the name "New Testament," which is later applied to the canon: "This cup is the new covenant (Latin: *novum testamentum*) in my blood" (1 Cor 11:25). Finally, by drinking the cup, the Christian "proclaims the death of the Lord until he comes" (1 Cor 11:26).

Pastoral-Liturgical Tradition

In the early Church when Eucharist was celebrated in private homes, an ordinary vessel was used for the wine. Gradually there developed a special pedestal cup, with or without handles, for use only at the Eucharist, and the Latin church applied the Greek word *kalix* (from which comes the English "chalice") to designate this special cup. Also during this early period, the deacon became the minister of the cup. Artists in every age have fashioned these special cups; among the masterpieces produced is the Tassilo chalice of 788 CE. During the Middle Ages, the Celtic and Christian traditions came together in the troubador tradition to produce the various stories telling of the search for the Holy Grail, the cup used by Christ at the Last Supper. Like many stories of journey, the theme is maturation, but in this context, the journey seeks more than psychological maturation.

All of the biblical connotations can enrich the understanding of the Eucharistic cup. Given the prejudice of our age, the tendency will be to discount the dimensions of judgment and punishment although the priest's secret prayer acknowledges the reality. Finally, while the turn to simpler designs and materials for chalices is appropriate in this age, simplicity unfortunately suggests to some that anyone is capable of an artist's craft and genius.

See: BLOOD, DRUNKENNESS, EUCHARIST, JUDGMENT, SACRIFICE, WINE

HARRY HAGAN, O.S.B.

CURSE

Cursing is the invoking of some extreme evil upon a human being. Although the Bible often uses the word popularly to refer to outbreaks of emotion, as in the dramatic story of Shimei cursing David (2 Sam 16:5-14) or in Peter's denial that he knew Jesus (Matt 26:74; Mark 14:71), the biblical use of the word generally has far more serious meaning. The drama of life is a struggle between good and evil. The curse is intended to trigger a retribution which is beyond recall. The curse calls on a mysterious power, either of God or of the devil. In the OT the first curse is on the serpent in the Garden of Eden. This spreads to blessings and curses attached to various treaties and covenants and becomes enshrined in law as a prohibition against wishing ill of anyone. In the NT the excesses of cursing others is reproved; "love your enemies" is much more to the fore. Only in Revelation does the consciousness of the need to curse cosmic evil come back strongly. In our pastoral history we have come close to invoking curses to counter blindness to real evil; our culture today leads us to ignore curses. Yet blessing* remains a more powerful cure than cursing.

Old Testament

The OT begins with the most serious curse of all. "Then the LORD God said to the serpent:* 'Because you have done this, you shall be banned from all the animals and from all the wild creatures. On your belly shall you crawl, and dirt shall you eat all the days of your life. I will put enmity between you and the woman, and between your offspring and hers; He will strike at your head while you strike at his heel'" (Gen 3:14-15). This represents the fundamental concept of an evil operating in human life which cannot be eliminated by human power. Later in this symbolic story, God curses the ground which Adam will need to till (Gen 3:17). The misfortune has arisen from a temptation to be like God and must inevitably lead to punishment.

The role of magic in cursing cannot be ignored. In the ancient Middle East standardized curses against those who broke the pledges were attached to treaties. They are found in the Execration Texts of Egypt, which are curses against rebellious cities in Palestine. Even today they are found in the taboos and sanctions imposed by witch doctors in some tribal cultures, or at least remembered in some of our own traditions such as the "evil eye" or the "voodoo doll." In all cases it is the mysterious power beyond recall which makes curses so threatening.

Curses and Blessings. Good and evil are almost always included in cursing. God promises protection to Abraham; blessings for those who bless him and curses for those who curse him (Gen 12:3; 27:29). Most vivid is the story of Balaam, the pagan diviner, who was summoned by the king of Moab to curse the Israelites as they approached the Promised Land (Num 22:1–24:25). Balaam was unable to curse the Israelites and was forced to bless them. The story is remembered later in Deuteronomy 23:5 and Joshua 24:9.

The later Israelite legislation is relatively mild, unlike that against blasphemy.* Leviticus 19:14 reads: "You shall not curse the deaf, or put a stumbling block in front of the

194

blind, but you shall fear your God. I am the LORD." Leviticus 20:9 has, "Anyone who curses his father or mother shall be put to death; since he has cursed his father or mother, he has forfeited his life." Jesus comments on this law in the NT (Matt 15:4; Mark 7:10). The obligation of honoring father and mother sprang from the common-sense realization that if society were to be preserved, family loyalty must prevail. So it appears in the later observation of Proverbs 20:20, "If one curses his father or mother, his lamp will go out at the coming of darkness."

Ecclesiastes could observe dourly of the need to protect one's neighbors, "Do not give heed to every word that is spoken lest you hear your servant speaking ill of you for you know in your heart that you have many times spoken ill of others" (Eccl 7:21-22). One must avoid even the first suggestion of wrongdoing. "Even in your thoughts do not make light of the king, nor in the privacy of your bedroom revile [curse] the rich, because the birds of the air may carry your voice, a winged creature may tell what you say" (Eccl 10:20).

Only in Job is anyone tempted to curse God and there it is done for dramatic effect to describe a man driven to the extreme of despair. In the initial story his wife said to him, "Are you still holding to your innocence? Curse God and die." But he said to her, "'Are you going to speak as senseless women do? We accept good things from God; and should we not accept evil?' Through all this, Job said nothing sinful" (Job 2:9-10). Job is aware of the power of curses and blessings and will not tempt fate.

The Prophets. The prophets are singularly innocent of the vocabulary of cursing despite all their denunciations. Jeremiah bewails the fate that "all curse me" (Jer 15:10). Isaiah predicts that the Assyrian in his defeat will "curse his king and his gods" (Isa 8:21; see NAB 14:21).

New Testament

The NT has references to the law of honoring father and mother. Matthew 15:4 and Mark 7:20 both have Jesus reproving the

Pharisees and scribes for violating this inevitable law. "And why do you break the commandment of God for the sake of your tradition? For God said, 'Honor your father and your mother,' and 'Whoever curses father or mother shall die'" (Matt 14:3-4). Mark quotes the same commandment but attributes it to Moses. The more characteristic attitude of the NT is found in Luke's saying: "But to you who hear me I say, 'Love your enemies, do good to those who hate you, bless those who curse you, pray for those who mistreat you'" (6:27-28). Paul quotes a similar saying in Romans 12:14, "Bless those who persecute you, bless and do not curse them."

Paul never uses the word in a derogatory sense. This is surprising since his fierce picture of the wrath of God in Romans 1 would lead to the belief that God would curse the Gentiles. In his summary of human sinfulness shortly thereafter he does refer to those whose "mouths are full of bitter cursing" (Rom 3:14). He is also aware of the saying, "Cursed be everyone who does not persevere in doing all the things written in the book of the law" (Gal 3:10), but then surprisingly we read that "Christ ransomed us from the curse of the law" (Gal 3:13). Here the true meaning of curse emerges. Paul's opponents, whoever they were, seem to have attributed some inflexible meting out of punishment on those who did not observe the Law as they understood it. This punishment was inevitable. Paul, however, sees Christ as the savior who removed this inevitability.

The Book of James contains the ancient wisdom belief that the tongue is a restless evil which cannot be controlled. "With it we bless the Lord and Father, and with it we curse human beings who are made in the likeness of God. From the same mouth come blessing and cursing" (Jas 3:9-10).

The Book of Revelation deals with the final assessment of the human drama. It has unmeasured curses for those who have defied the power of God for good. In the New Jerusalem "Nothing accursed will be found there anymore" (Rev 22:3). All evil will be banished. "Outside are the dogs, the sorcerers, the unchaste, the murderers, the idol worshipers, and all who love and practice deceit" (Rev 22:15). The great woes pronounced on Babylon the Great (Rev 17:1-6), the Beast and the Harlot (Rev 17:7-18), the kings of the earth, ship captains, the merchants, etc., are depicted in this highly colored denunciation as specifications of the cursing of evil which will finally be conquered entirely.

Pastoral-Liturgical Tradition

The idea of curses, which have inevitable effects, seems pervasive in most societies. It relies on an unspoken conviction of a law of retribution* which can be invoked but not rescinded. Such a theology has at times been very strong in the Church and has led to an automatic imposition of sanctions which could be invoked or suspended by some law or ritual. Hence, rituals for exorcisms and an official ministry of exorcist have been employed against such curses.

Our problem with cursing suggests that we do not want to admit the palpable existence of evil. Yet we too have our own witchcraft to invoke to turn away evils we cannot control. Vatican II and many pastoral letters of Bishops have protested against a materialistic way of life fueled by a scientific age. We believe that we should be able to control both prosperity and want; we believe that we cannot but go on struggling as though we were gods.

The belief in curses testifies to a recognition of a power greater than ourselves that we attempt to invoke to our own advantage but which turns out to our destruction. On the other hand, the evil of the real curse lies in that presumption of our ability to act like God either in judging or in punishing. The Christian attitude which comes from the Bible is to bless and not to curse, and to leave the final recompense to God.

See: BLASPHEMY, RETRIBUTION

JAMES A. FISCHER, C.M.

D

DAVID

Information regarding this hero-figure, depicted as one of Yahwism's greatest leaders and champions, comes exclusively from the Bible. The character is portrayed as the youngest of the Bethlehemite Jesse's eight sons (1 Sam 17:12-14; see Ruth 4:18-22; 1 Chr 2:1-15; Matt 1:2-6; Luke 3:31-38); a musician (1 Sam 16:23) who is anointed by Samuel (1 Sam 16:1-13) and becomes a youthful giant-slayer (1 Sam 17:1–18:5). He finds his way into Saul's house where he befriends Saul's son Jonathan and marries his daughter Michal (1 Samuel 18–20). Relations with Saul soon sour, and David is driven into exile where he roams the Judean wilderness and becomes an ally of the Philistines (1 Samuel 21–26), Saul's and Israel's archenemies.

Probably with Philistine sponsorship, David turns misfortune to success by becoming leader first of Ziklag (1 Sam 27:6), then of the ancient Yahwist center, Hebron (2 Sam 2:11), and finally of Jerusalem that he conquered with his own troops and made the neutral capital outside the territories of Judah and Israel that he led simultaneously (2 Sam 5:5-8). In Jerusalem, the story portrays David as displacing Saul (2 Samuel 6) and achieving kingship and divinely sanctioned dynasty (2 Samuel 7). Again, misfortune is near. His adulterous union with Bathsheba leads to the death of her husband, his soldier Uriah (which David arranges), and of the illegitimately conceived child (2 Samuel 11–12). His successor son, Solomon, the text insists, was conceived and born after David married Bathsheba (2 Sam 12:24).

The sordid episodes stand as precursors to David's family fates: son Amnon rapes a sibling, Tamar, and is killed by his brother Absalom; Absalom overthrows David and takes the royal harem but is eventually murdered by David's forces (2 Samuel 9–19); and son Adonijah attempts succession after the aged David is no longer capable of ruling, only to be assassinated by his brother, Solomon, for requesting rights to David's concubine, the Shunamite Abishag (1 Kings 2).

The theme and plot of the narrative in the Books of Samuel has been modified in antiquity and in modern scholarship. These directly affect the image of David. Early editors are probably responsible for the Solomonic sections in Samuel. These shift the emphasis away from the religious issues raised by centralizing under David to succession that is a later and distinct issue. The Chronicler also portrays none of David's failings and instead focuses on his contribution as the Temple* planner (1 Chr 29:28, 39), a role that the author of Samuel twice denies (2 Samuel 7; 24). Further passage of time improves his image even more.

In later OT writings and the Psalter, David is God's chosen one, the head of the Davidic dynasty, the author of psalms, and a king with eschatological significance. In the NT he is the ancestor of Jesus and in many ways the paradigm for Christ's kingship, a perception that grew in early Christianity.

In spite of total silence in extrabiblical ancient Near Eastern sources, modern scholars customarily find a historical David and place his life near the end of the tenth century BCE. Although the dating rests on tenuous reconciling of Egyptian and biblical sources, the acceptance by William F. Albright and others has led to it being almost universally accepted.

Several branches of modern scholarship today doubt the historical accuracy of much of the accounts. The stories, as reported, seem to envisage movement toward, and achieving of, high centralization, i.e., full statehood and monarchy, in Israel during David's time. He is called "king" and he becomes a model for successor-kings. Archaeologists, however, have found few or no signs of full centralization during the late tenth century BCE. Similarly, investigations by biblical scholars have moved in several directions away from such literal readings of the Samuel account.

Literary approaches to the Bible, influenced by newer forms of criticism developed in other disciplines, rely on the final forms of biblical texts rather than on the "original" or "historical" accounts sought by nineteenth and early twentieth century source and historical critical methods. Scholars who employ these approaches argue that the story, its characters, themes, and plots bear religious significance without being historical records or paradigms.

Simultaneously but independently of the literary studies, since the mid-1970s historical studies on the OT have turned toward different approaches. Social world studies of biblical antiquity have led this movement. In them, emphasis is placed on the social environment represented in the stories and on historical settings more than individual personalities and events that may or may not have occurred as described in the Bible. Accordingly, David's role, more exactly the role of the David-figure, has been scrutinized. The role and its place in the development of centralized leadership and institutions have been clarified.

Seen against the background of the social world of the period, the time attributed to David appears as a transition between former tribal organization and high centralization, but neither was fully in place. His role appears chiefly, similar to a paramount chieftaincy, which arose as an intermediate stage between the tribal period depicted in the Book of Judges and the full kingship attributed to David in the Books of Samuel. The excessive claims in the David narratives, therefore, represent later reflections from different perspectives where theological and political purposes combine to influence the authors. Textual, archaeological, and comparative sociological information—the three primary databases for social world studies—separately and in unison support such an interpretation.

The religious implications of the reconstruction are considerable. David appears as a clever, committed mediator and leader who forms consensuses according to the values of the tenth century. Quandaries and uncertainties abound in the society so that the religion of ancient Israel, like others, is a quest for knowing the divine will rather than a pattern of guaranteed certainties that leaders and peoples embrace unerringly.

Commentators have noted the paucity of references to the deity in the David narratives, especially in the so-called Court History in 2 Samuel 9–20. They have also noted the contradictions within the stories of David's rise where even the question of centralization caused Samuel to waver. These and other ambiguities probably accurately represent the religion of the transitional period where more than one alternative, none of them immediately or divinely compelling, offered themselves to Israel.

David's ability to forge consensuses for sometimes one and sometimes another alternative makes him a classical figure. Like other classics, his role stretches the imagination and fits a variety of situations. In those situations, Israel turned repeatedly to the David figure and made him a hero in the new settings that history offered.

See: JERUSALEM, SOLOMON, TEMPLE

JAMES W. FLANAGAN

DAY OF THE LORD

Old Testament

The earliest reference to the Day of the Lord in the OT is found in Amos 5:18-20: "Woe to those who yearn for the day of the Lord! What will this day of the Lord mean for you? Darkness and not light! . . . Will not the day of the Lord be darkness and not light, gloom without any brightness?" It is apparent from this passage that the expectation of a "day of the Lord" was widespread in the eighth century BCE when Amos spoke, and that it was generally expected to be a joyful occasion. Yet the precise connotation of the phrase is disputed. Some scholars have taken it as a day of battle when the Lord would defeat the enemies of Israel (compare "the day of Midian," Isa 9:3). More likely, however, it was a cultic festival (perhaps Tabernacles, the "feast of Yahweh," Lev 23:39) that celebrated the sovereignty of the Lord and was taken to imply that Israel would benefit from the sovereignty. The passage immediately following in Amos goes on to say "I hate, I spurn your feasts, I take no pleasure in your solemnities" (5:21). Amos saw that Israel was not being governed by the sovereignty of God, and he wanted to undermine the assumption that the Lord would support Israel unconditionally.

After Amos, there are many references to "the day of the Lord" in the prophets. Sometimes it is a day of universal judgment.* According to Isaiah 2:12, "The Lord of hosts will have his day against all that is proud and arrogant, all that is high, and it will be brought low." Zephaniah, who prophesied in the late seventh century BCE, uses the motif extensively to pronounce judgment on both Judah and the other nations. Ezekiel 7:10 relates the day of the Lord to the destruction of Jerusalem by the Babylonians, but it also could refer to a day of destruction of other individual nations: Isaiah 13:6, 9 (Babylon), Isaiah 34:8 (Edom), Jeremiah 46:10 (Egypt), Ezekiel 30:3 (Egypt), Obadiah 15 (Edom)—it is also a day of judgment for all the nations. In Joel 1–2 the day of the Lord takes the form of a plague of locusts.

In the postexilic period, eschatological passages are often introduced by the expression "on that day." The expression occurs more than a dozen times in Zechariah 12–14. In Zechariah 14:1-2 "a day shall come for the Lord when the spoils shall be divided in your midst. And I will gather all the nations against Jerusalem for battle . . ." Here the "day" is a day of battle and destruction in the indefinite future. In Malachi 3:1-2 the emphasis is on the cultic connotations of the "day" but the effects are similar: "suddenly there will come to the Temple the Lord whom you seek . . . but who will endure the day of his coming and who can stand when he appears? For he is like the refiner's fire. . . ."

In later Jewish writings the expression "day of the Lord" is not especially frequent, but we often find references to a decisive "day" or "time" that has similar connotations. In Daniel 12, the archangel Michael will arise "at that time" and the resurrection* will follow. The Qumran War Scroll tells how "on the day the Kittim fall, there shall be battle and terrible carnage before the God of Israel." There are occasional similar expressions in the Pseudepigrapha (e.g., 2 Bar 55:6, "the day of the Mighty One").

Amos' reinterpretation of the Day of the Lord, then, had a lasting effect in the biblical tradition. The phrase became synonymous with judgment and destruction, and increasingly came to denote a final definitive divine intervention in human affairs.

New Testament

In the NT, Revelation 16:14 refers to a battle involving the kings of the whole world "on the great day of God the almighty." More typically, however, the "day of the Lord" refers to the second coming of Christ. Paul tells the Thessalonians not to worry about times and seasons for "you yourselves know very well that the day of the Lord will come like a thief at night" (1 Thess 5:2) and 2 Thessalonians 2:2 tells people "not to be shaken out of your minds suddenly or to be alarmed either by a 'spirit,' or by an oral statement, or by a letter allegedly from us to the effect that the day of the Lord is at hand." (Compare the warning against false signs of the day of the Son of Man in Luke 17:24.) Nonetheless Paul repeatedly refers to the day of the Lord, or the day of our Lord Jesus Christ (1 Cor 1:8; 5:5; 2 Cor 1:14) or the day of Christ (Phil 1:6, 10; 2:16), as the definitive day of judgment.

The classic NT passage on the day of the Lord, however, is found in 2 Peter 3:1-13. The letter warns that scoffers will say "where is the promise of his coming," but with the Lord one day is like a thousand years and a thousand years like one day. The apparent delay in the parousia* is only to allow time for repentance, "but the day of the Lord will come like a thief, and then the heavens will pass away with a mighty roar and the elements will be dissolved by fire and the earth and everything done on it will be found out." Here the day of the Lord is the end of the world, but it will be followed by "new heavens and a new earth on which righteousness dwells."

Pastoral-Liturgical Tradition

The expectation of the great and terrible "day of the Lord" has cast a long shadow over Christian history. Perhaps the most vivid expression can be found in the medieval Latin hymn, "Dies irae, dies illa," which until recently was chanted at solemn requiem Masses. The idea that the world will one day be dissolved into ashes is a sobering reminder of the fragility of human life and indeed of the planet earth itself.

The NT passages, however, highlight another way in which the expectation of the

Day of the Lord has been played out. Already in the first century CE people were anxious to know the time of the Lord's coming. Attempts to predict the day flourished in the Middle Ages and continue down to the present day in some fundamentalist circles. The NT is unequivocal on this question. It is given to no one to know the day or the hour. The day of the Lord will come as a thief in the night. While the belief that this world will pass and be subject to judgment* is an integral part of Christian tradition, speculation about the exact time has no place in Christian faith.

See: ESCHATOLOGY, JUDGMENT

JOHN J. COLLINS

DEACON

Deacon (Greek *diakonos* and cognates) is a term which takes on a unique coloration in the NT period especially in relation to the ministry* of Jesus and the way it was viewed in the emerging Christian communities. There seems little in the socio-cultural world of Greece and Rome which lead to this emphasis because here service was seen as a menial task and the goal of the individual was the development of personality and the exercise of power. Even within the OT, it is difficult to find a precedent for the unique development of the term within early Christianity.

Old Testament

In the Septuagint, *diakonos* occurs only seven times and is generally used to refer to the servants or attendants of the king, especially during the Persian period (Esth 1:10; 2:2; 6:3, 5), while *diakonia* occurs even less frequently and simply with reference to the service thus rendered. Judaism, however, did develop a deeper concept of service, especially in relation to the service rendered to God by all people which found expression in the term *douleuein* (Pss 100:2; 102:22). In the specific context of the cult, the verb *leitourgein*/worship (Ezek 40:46; 44:11, 15, 17, 19) was used to designate the role of priests* and Levites who ministered before

God on behalf of the people (Deut 17:12; 1 Sam 2:11). During the Exilic period, a new perspective was offered by the great poet whose voice we hear in the latter chapters of the Book of Isaiah and who sang of the ideal Israelite, the servant *(pais)*, the one chosen by God to carry out the liberation of all humanity according to God's visioning (Isa 42:1-7; 49:1-6; 50:4-9; 52:13–53:12). It was this and related imagery from the poet/prophet which most profoundly shaped the early Christian reflection on the person and mission* of Jesus.

New Testament

Within the NT, the noun *doulos* and verb *douleuein* are used generally to refer to bonded service whether to a human master (Matt 6:24) or to other powers (Rom 6:6; Gal 4:8). Occasionally they are found in the more metaphorical context of bondage to Jesus but then with the sense of a bondage freely chosen (Rom 1:1; 1 Cor 7:22; Col 4:12; 2 Pet 1:1). *Leitourgein*, on the other hand, occurs rarely. The word group used most consistently to refer to service and ministry within the NT and therefore expressive of the new emerging Christian consciousness is that of *diakonein, diakonia,* and *diakonos* and it is within this wider context that our understanding of deacon must be considered.

The Unique Pattern of the Life of Jesus. Within each of the Synoptic Gospels, toward the end of the ministry of Jesus, that ministry is summed up in the words of Jesus as one of service. In both Mark and Matthew, Jesus claims that he did not come "to be served but to serve and to give his life as a ransom for many" (Matt 20:28; Mark 10:45). The Lucan text differs slightly but the message is similar: "I am among you as the one who serves" (Luke 22:27). The action of the washing of the feet of the disciples in John (13:1-20) is a symbolic representation of that same belief. The life of Jesus was one of freely chosen service, of *diakonia*. The evangelists took a term which carried the general sense of "waiting at table" and used it in a new manner to characterize the uniqueness of the ministry of Jesus.

This ministry was one authorized by God as the baptism scenes in each story make manifest by way of their recalling the servant theme of Isaiah 42:1 (Matt 3:13-17; Mark 1:9-11; Luke 3:21-22). It was a ministry of prophetic proclamation of the *basileia,* the way of God designed for humanity, which challenges all human relationships, beliefs, and structures that fail to lead to the fullness of human freedom and human life for all (Matt 4:17; 15:6-9; 23:4-7, 23). It found particular expression in the healing activity of Jesus whereby the *basileia* of God was made experientially available and the power of God touched the lives of those oppressed and marginalized and brought wholeness and life (Matt 9:22; Mark 5:1-20; Luke 7:11-17).

A Pattern for the Followers of Jesus. Within the story of Jesus, those who would follow him as disciples are called to pattern their lives on his (Matt 16:24-26; Mark 8:34-37; Luke 9:23-25), to be as servants/*diakonoi* like the one who serves (Matt 20:25-27; Mark 9:35). The last great parable of Matthew's Gospel delineates the nature of this service (Matt 25:31-46) and a number of those faithful to Jesus, especially women, manifest a service like that of Jesus (Matt 8:15; 27:55; Luke 8:3; 10:40), a service which is named in the same way as the ministry of Jesus. Just as a general term was used in a new way to designate the uniqueness of the ministry of Jesus, so too it was similarly applied to those whose ministry within the Jesus story was patterned on that of Jesus.

A Pattern for the Early Church. Within the letters addressed by Paul and others to the various Christian churches, it is clear that the early Church was seen to be characterized by gifts/*charismata* and service/*diakonia:* "there are different gifts but the same Spirit; there are different ministries but the same Lord" (1 Cor 12:4-5; see also Eph 4:11-12; 1 Pet 4:10-11). Ministry was therefore the role of all depending on their various gifts. The service of individuals and groups was seen as *diakonia* (Acts 6:1; 12:25) and Paul calls himself and others who worked with him *diakonos/diakonoi* (1 Cor 3:5; 2 Cor 3:6). As well as the variety of gifts and ministries already noted, this ministry includes collection for the poor in Jerusalem (Rom 15:25) and preaching* (2 Cor 11:7-8). In the case of Stephanus, oversight of the community is presented as a "service of the holy ones" (1 Cor 16:15-16). Once again, we see *diakonein* and cognates being used to describe the unique understanding of ministry that was emerging in the early Christian churches. It was not a ministry associated with the cultus and hence the apparent avoidance of *leitourgein*, nor was it the service of God evoked by the use of *douleuein*, but rather it incorporated the service of both God and the human community through the preaching of the liberating gospel message of Jesus and the actualizing of this in the everyday lives of its recipients.

Within the ambience of the ministry of all, Paul uses the term *diakonos* to refer to individuals who seem to have a leadership role within a particular church. Phoebe is called a deacon in the Church of Cenchreae (Rom 16:1) and the subsequent use of *prostatis* in relation to her points to her leadership role. The letter to the Philippians is addressed to the "holy ones in Christ Jesus who are in Philippi, with the overseers and ministers" (Phil 1:1), but there is nothing within the letter itself to shed further light on the nature of these roles. Here, however, for the first time within the NT these roles are linked.

Toward the end of the NT period, the term *diakonos*/deacon is used in a way which begins to suggest a more specific office within emerging church structures. In 1 Timothy, the letter writer lists the qualities which are necessary to serve as bishop* or overseer within the "church of God" (1 Tim 3:1-7). These are followed immediately by the qualities which must characterize deacons (1 Tim 3:8-13), strengthening the link already suggested in Philippians but still providing

little information about the nature of the service. It is clear, however, that women as well as men functioned within the latter group as 1 Timothy 3:11 lists those qualities specific to the women. That same verse, on the other hand, with its unique requirements for women, may provide a hint of the gradual alienation of women from key ministerial roles within the church as clearer structures of leadership were developed.

The term deacon/*diakonos* used to designate one of the earliest ordered roles within the Church's ministry likewise shares in the uniqueness of this word group within the NT. The role of the deacon must therefore be patterned on Jesus, on those who followed Jesus within his ministry, and on those who ministered following his death and resurrection. As well as providing a model, the ministry of Jesus which challenged structures of domination and oppression that were life-destroying remains within the NT text to act as a foil for or critique of this emerging structure lest it violate the *basileia* vision which he both preached and actualized. Rather it is this very vision which the new order or office itself must enable.

See: BISHOP, DISCIPLE, MINISTRY, MISSION, PRIEST, SERVANT

ELAINE M. WAINWRIGHT

Pastoral-Liturgical Tradition

In the post-apostolic period, deacons were important ministers in the Church, even more visible in the community than presbyters. With the eventual clear specification of episcopal and presbyteral roles, however, the diaconate lost its independent status in the Western Church and became a simple step of ascent to the priesthood. In his apostolic constitution *Sacramentum ordinis* (Nov. 30, 1947), Pope Pius XII affirmed that deacons no less than priests* and bishops* receive the sacrament of holy orders by the imposition of hands.

The Second Vatican Council decreed that the diaconate should be restored as a permanent and independent order in the Western Church (*Dogmatic Constitution on the*

Church, no. 29). This directive was carried out by Pope Paul VI in a motu proprio *Sacrum diaconatus ordinem* (June 18, 1967), which decreed that two types of deacons would exist: celibate deacons, for whom the minimum age would be twenty-five, and married deacons, for whom the minimum age would be thirty-five and who must have their wives' consent to the ordination* in writing.

Ordination to the diaconate remains a requirement for those to be ordained presbyters. Through ordination to the diaconate one becomes a cleric and is incardinated into a particular church for whose service he is ordained. Deacons are to be ordained by their proper bishop or with dimissorial letters from the proper bishop. Transitional deacons should have completed at least five years of philosophical and theological study before ordination. They are to have pastoral experience in the diaconate before they are ordained priests. They must have previously received and exercised the ministries of lector and acolyte; there should be a six-month interval between their installation as acolyte and ordination as deacon.

National bishops' conferences may decide whether to restore the permanent diaconate in their territories; their decisions must be approved by the Holy See. Permanent deacons are to be given sound theological and pastoral formation. Young men should spend three years in a house of formation prior to ordination.

Deacons share in the teaching office of the Church. They have the faculty to preach everywhere unless restricted by the ordinary. As clerics they must obey the regulations of the episcopal conference regarding participation in radio and television programs which treat questions of Catholic doctrine or morals. Regarding their liturgical office, they may administer baptism solemnly, distribute Holy Communion, carry viaticum to the dying, expose the Blessed Sacrament and give Benediction, officiate at and bless marriages if properly delegated, preside at funerals and burials, deliver homilies, preside over worship and prayer, and administer those sacramentals and give those blessings which are permitted by law. A report of the Catholic Theological Society of America, commissioned by the bishops of the United States, recommended that deacons be empowered to administer the sacrament of the anointing of the sick and that they be given faculties to administer the sacrament of penance in the context of their ministry* to the sick and the dying, but no action has been taken on those recommendations.

The diaconate has traditionally been associated with the ministry of charity. Although it has been thought of primarily as a ministry to the poor, it should be viewed in a wider context as a ministry of the Church's temporalities. Since administration of those temporalities has come to encompass complex planning, social welfare, insurance, and the rehabilitation of the destitute, deacons should be well informed about social issues and structures that facilitate a positive response to those issues.

The rite for the ordination of deacons, originally promulgated in 1968, was revised and promulgated on June 29, 1989. Of special note is the requirement, mandated by Pope John Paul II, that even candidates who have taken perpetual vows in a religious institute must make a promise of celibacy within the ordination rite.

Although there seems to be solid basis in both the NT and tradition for ordaining women to the diaconate, the question is still being studied by the Holy See.

See: CHURCH, COMMUNITY, MINISTRY, SERVANT

R. KEVIN SEASOLTZ, O.S.B.

DEAD SEA SCROLLS

The term "Dead Sea Scrolls" refers to a collection of texts found in caves near the Wadi Qumran beginning in 1947. The Wadi Qumran is a river bed that directs the water run-off to the Dead Sea during the rainy season. The discovery of the first texts was completely accidental. Once the value of these first texts became clear, the local bedouin made a thorough search of caves for every scrap of material, for which they were well paid. The Scrolls are now in the possession of the Israeli Department of Antiquities. Though most major documents have been published, there are still many fragments that await reconstruction, deciphering, and publication.

The Importance of the Scrolls

The finds were particularly significant because of the paucity of textual material found in Palestine. The dry climate in the Dead Sea region helped preserve the Scrolls from early antiquity. Second, the texts revealed the existence of a Palestinian Jewish community that flourished from about 150 BCE to 70 CE. This period corresponds to the time that witnessed the ministry of Jesus and the rise of early Christianity. Third, the ideology of this community was apocalyptic* in tone with several similarities to Christianity.

The Literature

The literature found at Qumran falls into three categories. First there is biblical literature. Several complete scrolls of the Book of Isaiah have been found at Qumran. At least some fragments of every other book of the Hebrew Bible except Esther have been found as well. Comparing the Qumran texts of the Hebrew Bible with the Masoretic text (the surviving Hebrew version of the Hebrew Bible) reveals no striking discrepancies. What is important to note is that when readings in the Qumran texts differ from those of the Masoretic text, they usually agree with readings from the Septuagint. Before the discovery of the Scrolls, common opinion held that at least some portions of the Septuagint reflected a careless translation of the Hebrew original. Now it is obvious that those who made the Greek translation found in the Septuagint used Hebrew text tradition different from the one preserved by the Masoretes. This accounts for the differences between the Hebrew Bible and the Septuagint.

A second category of literature found at Qumran are non-canonical Jewish religious texts. These texts include some books today classified as the apocrypha and pseudepigrapha of the OT. Examples of these texts found at Qumran include the Book of Sirach and the Testaments of the Twelve Patriarchs. It is difficult to be certain about the status the people of Qumran accorded these texts. Their presence shows that they helped shape the religious perspectives of the people at Qumran though the rabbis at a later date did not include them in their canon.

The third and most important category of texts found at Qumran are religious texts created by and for the religious community that lived in a settlement close to the caves where the texts were found. It is assumed that the people living in the settlement produced these texts and that these people were the Essenes mentioned by Josephus, although the word Essene never appears in the texts themselves. These texts include rules that regulate the life of the community, commentaries on biblical texts, and collections of biblical texts with and without commentaries.

The Beliefs of the Qumran Community

It is difficult to overestimate the value of these texts for understanding the religious milieu in Palestine at the time of the ministry of Jesus and the rise of Christianity. Analysis of the Dead Sea Scrolls helped to illustrate the diversity that was early Judaism. The texts reveal a community that saw itself as the true Israel. It was a group made up principally of priests who believed that the worship in the Temple was hopelessly corrupt because of the moral failures of the priests of the Temple and because of the incorrect calendar used by them. The community of Qumran was waiting for the day when they would be empowered to take over the direction of worship in the Temple and restore it to the authentic service of God. That day would be preceded by a terrible conflict with the powers of darkness. The people of Qumran, "the children of light" would be led to victory by God.

Analysis of the Qumran commentaries on biblical texts reveals the method of interpretation that was characteristic of the period and which is evident in the NT. It is interpretation that pays no heed to the historical circumstances of the text to be interpreted. It shows that the experience of the Qumran community shaped its method of interpretation. Obviously the community looked on itself as composed of outsiders with definite eschatological expectations. The people of Qumran were waiting for God's final intervention in Israel's life since it would vindicate them. The Qumran method of biblical interpretation was based on the experiences of the community and arose from the linguistic possibilities in the actual wording of the text. A similar pattern of biblical interpretation is evident in the NT as it reinterprets OT texts to give expression to its faith in Jesus as the suffering Messiah.

Like other Jews of the period, the Qumran people believed that true piety involved obedience to the Torah. It was the interpretation of the Torah that separated the people of Qumran from other Jews. The people of Qumran believed that only their sages, in particular the Teacher of Righteousness, knew how to expound the Torah and the Prophets correctly. They also believed that God chose each member of their community for salvation through participation in the community's life. The Qumran community believed that it was living in the final days before God's decisive intervention in Israel's life. They looked forward to this day because they were confident in the correctness of their beliefs and in their eventual salvation.

Qumran and Christianity

The relationship of the first Christians to the people of Qumran has been the subject of an inordinate amount of fanciful speculation. After years of study, the consensus is that the Dead Sea Community and Christianity were both reinterpretations of early Judaism's traditions. Their similarities derive from their common origins in the ancestral religion of the Jews. Their differences reflect the diverse experiences of the two groups. No one has successfully proven that Qumran had a direct impact on the development of Christianity's beliefs and practices.

See: APOCALYPTIC, JUDAISM

LESLIE J. HOPPE, O.F.M.

DEATH

The certainty of death has plagued the human race from the beginning. Despite its inevitability, human beings have been reluctant to accept the fact of their mortality. Ancient myths include tales of a search for the source of life. Even the Bible tells of a tree of life placed by God in the midst of the garden in Eden (Gen 1:9). Many societies believed in life after this life. Funeral customs* often anticipated this afterlife. Although its early writings mention Sheol,* the place of the dead, it is not until Israel incorporated the Greek notion of the immortal soul* into its teachings that it began to develop its own ideas about an afterlife.

Old Testament

Ultimate Destiny. The Bible first mentions death in the account of the creation and sin* of the first man and woman. There we read that God warned that eating of the tree of knowledge of good and evil would doom the sinner to death. Belief that death is the punishment* for sin grew out of this part of the story. However, elements of that very narrative cause one to question any simple understanding of the origin of death. First, the man is made of the dust* of the ground, a clear reference to the ground of the grave, thus marking his inherent perishability. Furthermore, the punishment meted out, pain in childbirth and domination of the woman by the man as well as the hardship in agriculture, obviously endures only *until* death (Gen 3:16-19). This part of the narrative asserts that death is the termination of the punishment that each will suffer rather than the punishment itself. The story actually recounts how humankind was made of the stuff of the grave (dust) yet given access to a mysterious source of life (the tree). Not satisfied being dependent on God, the man and the woman sinned and were subsequently denied access to the tree of life and thus were made subject to the consequences of mortality.

In the Book of Sirach, a much later writing, a Hellenized author provides a quite literal reading of this creation story and even blames the woman for committing the first sin and bringing the punishment of death upon the entire human race (Sir 25:23). It is important to note that this book contains some of the harshest statements about women found in the entire Bible. Since this section of the book is less an explanation of the origin of death than it is a harangue against women in general, it cannot be considered fundamental teaching on punishment for sin. The author of the Book of Wisdom also reads the Genesis tradition literally, but blames the envy of the devil for the entry of death into the human drama (Wis 2:24).

If it was the dust of the ground that destined human beings to death, it was the breath of life that animated the earth creature in the first place (Gen 2:7) and that holds death at arms length throughout the few years allotted to each person. The ephemeral nature of breath well describes the transitoriness of life. Again and again the Bible insists that when God withdraws this breath, all flesh will perish and return to the dust (Job 34:15; Pss 104:29; 146:4). Just as breath became a symbol for life, dust became a symbol for death (Job 10:9; 17:16; 20:11; 21:26; 30:19; Pss 22:16, 30).

The relationship between life* and death is also found in the Bible's teaching on wisdom and ethics. There we find distinctions made between two ways of living, the way of wisdom which will be blessed with long and prosperous life and the way of folly which leads to suffering and misfortune and finally to death (Prov 8:33-36; 10:2; 14:12). From this view of life developed the notion that any diminishment of happiness or good fortune was in fact a form of death.

Thus, from the beginning death has had a hold on everyone, and over time it takes more and more control until it finally takes over completely.

Fate of the Dead. Despite the fact that Israel did not develop a teaching about an afterlife until quite late in its history (second century BCE), it did not presume that the dead were completely annihilated. It seems that they perceived existence after death as some form of weakened life that took place in a shadowy nether world called Sheol. This was probably some kind of underworld where the dead were cut off from all of the cherished activities of life, especially the praise of God (Ps 6:6): "there will be no work, nor reason, nor knowledge, nor wisdom in the nether world" (Qoh 9:10). In this weakened state, they were referred to as "shades" (Job 26:5; Ps 88:11; Prov 2:18; Isa 14:9; 26:14, 19). Sheol was neither a place of reward nor of punishment, although sometimes it is described as a place of corruption (Job 17:14). However, the dead do not appear to have been completely separated from the living. For example, after the prophet Samuel died, King Saul was overwhelmed by the threatening military power of the Philistines. In desperation and in violation of covenant law, he engaged a medium who was successful in conjuring up the spirit of the prophet in order to benefit from the counsel of this dead man (1 Samuel 28). It was precisely because of their belief in the mysterious powers of the dead that the Israelites denounced this or any form of divination (Deut 18:10f.; 1 Sam 15:23; Isa 2:6).

Insistence on proper burial is further evidence of belief in some kind of existence after death. It was important that the deceased be secured in a grave, which was regarded by some as the entrance to Sheol, lest they disrupt the balance between the land of the living and the land of the dead. Proper burial also provided the living an opportunity to benefit from the deceased ancestors should there be some extraordinary need of assistance. For example,

Rachel could be heard near her tomb weeping over the devastation of her children, the northern kingdom (Jer 31:15). Besides, since death was considered the weakest form of life, it was conceivable that at some later time God could restore one to full life (Ps 30:4; 86:13; 1 Sam 2:6). Although such an idea is usually found in poetic sections, its very suggestion suggests that death was not perceived as total obliteration.

Death and the Justice of God. Death as punishment for sin does not seem to pose a problem for Israel when the deceased had lived a wicked life. However, when death appeared to be untimely or the abrupt and painful termination of the life of a righteous person, the justice of the situation was thrown into question. Such is precisely the dilemma that faced Job. The first words out of his mouth after his period of mourning was condemnation of his life and a desire for the lease of death (ch. 3). Here death is seen as the only avenue out of his extreme and inexplicable suffering (the end of suffering as in Gen 3:19). Job's attitude appears to change further in the book to the point that he almost seems to taunt God with his own death. If God does not act soon in correcting the injustice of Job's situation, it will be too late and God will have to live with the guilt of having inflicted an innocent man with unbearable suffering. "For soon I shall lie down in the dust; and should you seek me I shall then be gone" (7:21).

The justice or wisdom of God is also challenged in the Book of Qoheleth (Ecclesiastes). This is a man who was troubled about the inevitability of death and the sense of futility it often imparts. He realized that regardless of how one lives, whether honorably or in sin, death is the ultimate fate of all. It cancels everything. Any advantage that one might have had because of righteousness, wisdom, or wealth is only temporary and, therefore, questionable. Death and the total relinquishment that it demands forced Qoheleth to question the value of any human accom-

plishment and to wonder if perhaps life itself might be nothing more than "a chase after the wind" (Qoh 1:14, 17; 2:11, 17, 26; 4:4, 6, 16; 6:9).

Neither Job nor Qoheleth was fixated on death. Actually, it was their fierce commitment to life that elicited such protest in the face of the apparent inequity of the human situation. Believing that the order of the universe was established by God at creation, they denounced the bewildering disarray that characterizes so much of life and they chafed at death when it deprived a righteous person from enjoying the rewards of upright living, as it so often does.

Survival after Death. The earliest Israelites believed in a kind of collective immortality. They held that as long as the nation continued, the deceased members of the community would not completely perish. They also maintained that they were indisputably joined, in the intricate web of life, with both their ancestors and their descendants. For them to die childless meant that this connection was jeopardized. Not only would one fail to survive into the future through continuation of the family blood line, but also there would be no one to perform the necessary funeral rites which enabled one to rest in peace with the ancestors. Among other things, children guaranteed a certain kind of family survival after death.

The earliest testimony to belief in personal life after death is found in the Book of Daniel (12:1-3). This passage also contains a clear identification of the afterlife as a place of retribution, where the good will be rewarded and the evil punished. The book probably originated during the religious oppression inflicted by Antiochus IV Epiphanes around 164 BCE. During this crisis, not only were the righteous suffering (the problem of Job), but their torments were brought on precisely because they were righteous, observing the customs of their faith. These people were revered as religious martyrs. In a most profound way, the justice of God was on trial in this persecution and in the deaths that resulted from it. The same religious confrontation is chronicled in the Books of Maccabees. There we find examples of heroic dedication in the face of certain death along with unyielding confidence in some kind of life after death (2 Macc 7:9, 11, 14, 23, 29, 36; 12:43-46; 14:46). The writers who chronicled this period of Israel's history sought to show that the ways of God and the virtue of the faithful ultimately would be vindicated. One can clearly see that the Israelite belief in an afterlife originated in reliance on the justice of God.

The Wisdom of Solomon builds on this elementary belief in an afterlife. While the book does not mention resurrection of the body, as some of the other texts do, it introduces the Greek notion of immortality. As was the case with both Daniel and Maccabees, the concern here is with the blameless righteous who have suffered an untimely or ignominious death. Those who died for the cause of religion were not to be viewed as afflicted or destroyed. The author insists that they are at peace in the hand of God, and their hope is full of immortality (Wis 3:3f.). This book also develops the concept of immortality out of a second Israelite theme, that of the Wisdom Woman (see Prov 8:22-31). Meditating on the tradition of Solomon's prayer for wisdom (see 1 Kgs 3:5-14), the author depicts the king's devotion to her and the immortality that he looked forward to because of this devotion (8:13, 17).

Although the concept of immortality is Greek, in the Bible the argument proceeds from Jewish theological thinking. It is righteousness, a fundamental covenant concern, that assures immortality or incorruptibility (Wis 4:1; 6:18f.), not an immaterial soul. The philosophical concepts of Hellenism provided Israel with the language and the classifications that assisted in its theological development, but they did not determine this development.

See: DUST, ESCHATOLOGY

DIANNE BERGANT, C.S.A.

New Testament

Death always carries the major overtone that it had acquired in the OT tradition: the end of human relationship to others and even to God. Hence the good news of the gospel can be proclaimed as the end of the power which death has in human life:* "Indeed, just as the Father possesses life in himself, so has he granted it to the Son to have life in himself" (John 5:26). At the same time that the NT announces that death has been conquered in Christ (1 Cor 15:54-55), the isolation of the unbeliever from God presents an even starker image of death than anything found in the OT. There is no further hope for persons who have cut themselves off from God's new offer of salvation either through willful disbelief or sin (John 8:24). Revelation uses the expression "second death" to refer to the ultimate fate of those who reject salvation (Rev 20:6). This state includes the punishment for sin which follows God's judgment* (see Matt 25:46).

Death as a Phenomenon in Human Life. The whole range of human experiences with death appear in the NT. A few holy people have the privilege of dying in a special relationship of peace with God (e.g., Simeon in Luke 2:26-32). Jesus must have surprised the audience by extending this privilege to the poor beggar, Lazarus, taken by angels to rest in Abraham's bosom (Luke 16:22). God does indeed hear the cry of the poor. Other holy people, some of the prophets, John the Baptist, and Jesus suffer a violent death at the hands of evil persons who cannot tolerate their message of goodness and justice. Jesus warns that his followers may face a similar fate (e.g., Matt 5:11-12). Exemplified by Stephen (Acts 7:54–8:1), such deaths are eloquent testimony of the power of faith to overcome the fear of death which leads most persons to give in to the threats of evil persons. Jesus' own victory in the face of death is so great that he promises the repentant criminal, who comes to Jesus' defense, a place with God that day (Luke 23:39-43).

The NT recognizes that most people do not experience death as an affirmation of the special relationship with God that comes from a life of faithful witness. Death, which always reminds us of human sinfulness, comes as a painful interruption. Jesus promised that God would heal that pain (Matt 5:4). As evidence that God does not rejoice in the human suffering which such deaths bring, Jesus takes away the sting of death in some of its most painful contexts: the young girl lost to her parents (Mark 5:21-43) or the only son of the widow (Luke 7:11-17). Jesus' friends are not immune. Martha and Mary wonder why Jesus permitted Lazarus to die rather than heal his illness (John 11:1-44). The miracle proves that God's power is greater than death, not that Christians will be spared the pain of the human experience of death.

Paul voices another dimension of the human anxiety about death when he confronts his own death while in prison (Phil 1:12-26). He has no doubt that if he dies he will be with Jesus. But Paul sees the rivalries that have broken out among Christians because he is in prison. Will the young Philippian Church be able to survive his death? Death forces all humans to leave behind unfinished projects and relationships. Will what we have given our life to accomplish survive? Paul concludes that he must have faith that God will send him back to the Philippians if that is necessary. Otherwise, his death may be a sacrificial offering that will purify their faith (Phil 2:16-17).

Death as an Expression of Separation from God. The Bible never treats human death as a mere accident of human biology. The other things in nature die as a matter of course (Matt 6:30). But humans are created in God's image. Death, evil, and suffering remind us that the world of human experience is marked by sin. Humans are "dead through sin" when they are closed to the love, mercy, and justice that come from God (e.g., Eph 2:1-2). Paul reverses this metaphor when he speaks of baptism as dying to sin in order to live in Christ (Rom 6:3-5). Humans are given a fundamental choice. They can lead a life that is separated from God, that is, they can live in a way that leads to death, or they can find new life in Christ (Rom 6:13-23).

John's Gospel poses this fundamental choice between life and death as the question of whether or not a person will believe that Jesus' word is the word of God. The believer has already passed from death and sin to eternal life (John 5:24; 8:21-24, 34-47). Jesus' unbelieving audience thinks that such words are nonsense. They can only evaluate death as the termination of a life measured in years. Jesus speaks God's life-giving word which exists before all creation and even before Israel's most famous hero of faith, Abraham (John 8:48-59). Ironically, the crowd tries to execute Jesus for blasphemy.

Matthew 4:15-16 and Luke 1:79 quote the prophecy of Isaiah: "On those who inhabit a land overshadowed by death, light has arisen" (9:1) to describe the ministry of Jesus. What was lost to God is now restored.

Because death symbolizes separation from God, Paul can even speak of the Law as bringing death through the sin which humans commit (1 Cor 15:56; Rom 7:10). Paul insists that Scripture shows us a humanity which continuously turned away from God's will as expressed in the Law. Humanity deserved condemnation and death. Instead, God provided a new way for persons to move from sin and death to life with God, faith in Jesus (Rom 1:18–3:26).

Death Personified and the Adam Story. When Paul speaks of the power which sin and death have over human life, death is described as an enemy force which will only be completely defeated at the second coming of Christ (1 Cor 15:51-58). Death will be forced to give up its prisoners when the faithful are resurrected* to be with Christ. Romans 7:13-25 personifies sin as a power which works through human desires and the divided human will to lead people to disobey the law of God even when they acknowledge that it is good.

Paul describes this conflict as one that occurs within the individual between the mind or reason and desires that arise out of the physical human being. Without the assistance of Christ, sin wins and leads us to death. Consequently, Paul can even speak of the person as trapped in a mortal body (Rom 7:24).

Paul uses the story of Adam's fall to speak of both aspects of the experience of sin and death: first, all human beings are under sin and thus separated from God; second, freedom from sin and death comes to us as the free gift of Christ (Rom 6:21-23). Paul compares Adam and Christ. Adam's trespass was the entry of sin and death into the world. But the universal experience of sin that began in Adam is nothing compared with the experience of redemption that has come to all persons in Jesus, "so that as sin reigned through death, grace may reign by way of justice leading to eternal life, through Jesus Christ our Lord" (Rom 5:21).

Paul expands on the Adam/Christ parallel in defending the Christian message of resurrection* against skeptics at Corinth (1 Cor 15:20-24). We do not see those who have died in Christ resurrected now because the final victory over death remains to be won at the end time (1 Cor 15:25-28). The risen Christ is the first fruits of many more who will share this triumph over death. Paul interprets the two accounts of God making Adam alive in Genesis (Gen 1:26f.; 2:7) as prefiguring the two Adams (1 Cor 15:45-49). Genesis 2:7 refers to the earthly Adam. The NAB has translated Paul's adjective *psychikos* (literally "psychic" or "ensouled") as "natural." This translation might mislead some readers into thinking that Paul is treating human death as merely a natural phenomenon associated with our material nature. But Genesis 1:27 refers to Christ as the spiritual Adam, the image of God into which believers are transformed. Thus, there is more to salvation than simply escaping or returning from death. Salvation will mean acquiring a new, divine reality that is shaped like that of Christ.

The imagery of death as humanity's mythic enemy who must be defeated and subjected by the victorious Christ is developed in Revelation. Christ, first born from the dead, is the victorious ruler over all earthly powers. Christ holds the keys of Hades and death (Rev 1:18). Death rides forth against humanity like an invading army (Rev 6:7-8). At the final victory, death, Hades, and all who belong to them are cast into the lake of fire (Rev 20:14-15). For those who remain alienated from God this condemnation is the "second death."

The Death of Christ. Though it is easy for twentieth century readers to think of the death of Christ as a political execution, the NT insists on a different perspective. Leaders who found Christ's views threatening decided to have Jesus killed (e.g., John 11:45-53). Yet, the real truth about Jesus' death is its sacrificial character. Jesus offers himself on behalf of all of sinful humanity, for "the Son of Man has not come to be served but to serve—to give his life in ransom for the many" (Mark 10:45). Jesus' sinlessness and special relationship to God gives his death a special character: "For our sakes God made him [Jesus] who did not know sin, to be sin, so that in him we might become the very holiness of God" (2 Cor 5:21). The sinfulness of the world, which separates humanity from God, has been overcome by Jesus' death.

Hebrews uses imagery from the OT sacrificial cult to argue for the special character of Jesus' offering. Sinless and perfectly obedient to God, Jesus makes a sacrifice for sin that does not have to be repeated as Jewish rituals were (Heb 7:26-28; 9:11-14). Christ's death becomes the offering which creates a new covenant, a new people of God (9:15-28). This understanding is also captured in the Eucharistic formula which speaks of the cup as "blood of the covenant" (Mark 14:24; see also Matt 26:28; 1 Cor 11:25).

The sacrificial understanding of Christ's death is the first item in our earliest Christian creed: "I handed on to you first of all what I myself received, that Christ died for our sins in accordance with the scriptures" (1 Cor 15:3). NT formulae often proceed from the affirmation of Christ's death to his resurrection or exaltation to God's right hand (Rom 4:25; 1 Thess 4:14; Phil 2:9-10). John's Gospel combines death and exaltation so closely that the cross itself is spoken of as glorification. The cross is not a place of suffering or degradation but the place where God's glory in Jesus becomes visible (John 3:14-15; 8:28; 13:31-32).

The death of Jesus plays an important role in the spiritual life of NT Christians. It provides the model for the relationships of love and service to others that are the core of Christian ethics (cf. Phil 2:1-11). The sufferings which Paul has endured as an apostle have marked his body with the marks of Christ's crucifixion (Gal 6:17).

See: ADAM AND EVE, BAPTISM, EUCHARIST, GLORY, IMAGE OF GOD, JUDGMENT, LAW, LIFE, RESURRECTION, SALVATION, SIN

PHEME PERKINS

Pastoral-Liturgical Tradition

The theological tradition is dominated by the concept of death as the separation of soul and body. This definition was shaped largely through the influence of Greek philosophy and provided Christians with a way of conceptualizing personal existence after death in the form of a spiritual soul. Since the soul is thought to maintain an intrinsic ordering to the body, the condition of all who have died is essentially incomplete (interim state) until the soul is reunited with the body (resurrection of the body). This was generally thought to happen for the individual at the time of the general resurrection at the end of history. The concept of the separated soul and the interim state provided the context for understanding the significance of many practices of piety such as suffrages for the dead, indulgences, etc.

Related Themes. The theological tradition commonly links the phenomenon of human death with the reality of sin.* Already in the sixth century, the Council of Orange described death as a result of Adam's sin (DS 371–372). This was reaffirmed by the Council of Trent (DS 1512). When this position is viewed in the context of the traditional doctrine of the preternatural gifts, it becomes clear that immortality is not thought of as a natural condition of humanity *(non posse mori)*, but as a special gift of grace *(posse non mori)*.

It has been common in the tradition also to envision death as the definitive end of an individual's personal history. However law and medical science might define death, the theological tradition is convinced that there is a point of no return for the human person even though we may not know precisely where that point is. Whatever lies beyond that point is qualitatively different from historical existence. Survival is not an extension of historical existence after death, but is a move into a new dimension of being. Hence, Christian tradition has resisted all forms of re-incarnationalism.

Contemporary Reformulations. Death has become a much-discussed topic particularly since the 1950s. It was felt necessary to come to a deeper understanding of death as a human reality. The work of K. Rahner has set new directions in this area. The critical insight of Rahner's phenomenology of death is the awareness that death is not simply a passive fate to be suffered but is a process in which the human person is actively engaged. In this view, death is the privileged and decisive act of human freedom which is prepared for during life and which determines one's eternal destiny.

From this perspective, theologians have reformulated the traditional concerns of the theology of death. The relation between sin and death is seen in terms of the distortions which sin brings to all our human relations. In a world marked by sin, we experience death differently than we would in a world untouched by sin. It is not the simple fact of death that is the result of sin but the darkness and anguish associated with death.

Rahner's phenomenological understanding of death is developed by L. Boros and

G. Greshake into a consistent theory of death as "final decision." In this context, the traditional concerns of judgment* and purgation are seen not as things that happen after death but as dimensions of the experience of death itself. The argument that even the resurrection* takes place in death had been disputed among German theologians in the 1970s. The Congregation for the Doctrine of the Faith expressed its concern that new forms of eschatological interpretation should not make the prayers and rites of the Church "meaningless and unintelligible" (AAS 71 [1979] 941).

The reformulation of the theology of death attempts to take into account also the fact that Christ's death has been understood to have salvific meaning. This meaning is seen to lie not so much in the violence which was inflicted on him, but in his personal, active appropriation of his destiny, including his violent death. From the side of history, his death was painful, dark, and ambiguous. Only from the perspective of the Easter faith was it possible to see his death as salvific and to believe that God had accepted the whole of Jesus' human reality into the fullness of life with God. And from that perspective, it becomes possible for Christians to see in Jesus' death the actualization of the deepest possibilities of human death and hence to view death not as a threat of annihilation but as the condition for that total fullness of being which constitutes salvation.

Pastoral-Liturgical Implications. Christian theology sees death as the possibility of either eternal communion with God or eternal failure and isolation. Hence, from a pastoral perspective, the question of "how" a person dies takes on great importance. This is a significant point at which pastoral practice can be shaped by insights gained from clinical experience in work with the dying (see the work of E. Kübler-Ross and R. Moody). Theology and empirical experiences underscore the importance of the attitudes and values one brings to the process of dying and to death itself. A responsible faith in eternal life

should make it possible to approach death without the sense that one must cling to historical existence at all cost.

Moving back from the moment of death and using the death-resurrection framework of Christology, we can reflect on the presence of "death in the midst of life" and integrate sickness and dying more realistically into the experience of living. In this sense, the way we deal with the limitations placed on us by the presence of others throughout life is a "little dying" in which we rehearse the death that meets us at the end.

This dialectical relation between death and life is associated in the Pauline tradition with the meaning of baptism which may be seen as a movement into the death and resurrection of Christ and hence as a participation in the salvific power of his death which opens us to "newness of life" (Rom 6:3-5, 8).

Christians may approach death with a firm hope that eventually death will be definitively overcome (1 Cor 15:26; Rev 20:14; 21:4).

It is clear that the shift in the theological understanding of death cannot be without implications for our understanding of practices of Christian piety. The more radical form of the theory of "final decision" as presented by G. Greshake offers no convincing rationale for the practice of suffrages for the dead. The moderate form of the theory, however, as represented by Rahner, interprets such matters as purgation and prayer for the dead in terms of a process of maturation. In this sense, the theory seems to stand firmly within the framework of theological possibilities suggested by the teaching of the Magisterium.

See: BODY, SIN, SOUL

ZACHARY HAYES, O.F.M.

DECAPOLIS

This Greek term used once in Matthew (4:25) and twice in Mark (5:20; 7:31) refers to the league of "ten cities" founded in the wake of Alexander's incursion into the

Middle East. These small city-states in the Hellenistic mold covered a broad region stretching from the land east of the Sea of Galilee down to the northern extremity of the Dead Sea. Only one of the cities, Scythopolis, was located on the western bank of the Jordan. These mainly Gentile cities were absorbed briefly into Israel* in the first century BCE under the Hasmoneans but regained a certain autonomy under Roman rule when Pompey (63 BCE) reestablished the league under the overall supervision of the Governor of Syria. This would have been their status during the first century CE. Pella, the city alleged to be a place of refuge for Jewish Christians during the revolt against Rome in 66 CE, is one of the cities of the Decapolis.

In the Gospels, the Decapolis is accurately portrayed as Gentile, and therefore foreign territory. Matthew lists the Decapolis in a string of far flung locations from which the crowds come streaming to Jesus at the beginning of the Sermon on the Mount (Matt 4:25), a harbinger of the ultimately universal scope of Jesus' mission (see 28:16-20). Matthew's inspiration for this epic scene may already be present in Mark 5:1-20. Jesus performs a powerful exorcism in the country of the Gerasenes (some ancient manuscripts read "Gadarenes"); the precise location of Gerasa on the shore of the Sea of Galilee is disputed but there is little doubt that Mark wants to locate Jesus' miracle in the Decapolis. The amazing transformation of the man possessed by "legion" climaxes with his being sent on mission to the Decapolis (5:20).

In 7:31 Mark places Jesus again in the "region of the Decapolis" as he completes his great missionary journey that arches from Tyre and Sidon in the west around through the Decapolis in the east and back to the district of Dalmanutha on the western shore of the Sea (8:10). Mark locates the healing of a man who was both deaf and mute (7:31-37) as well as the second great feeding of the multitudes (8:1-20) in the Decapolis. The entire section of the Gospel from 4:35 to 8:10 presents Jesus on mission,

moving back and forth across the lake and beyond the boundaries of Israel, bringing his liberating power of healing to both Jew and Gentile. Thus the Gospels draw on the historical fact of the Decapolis as a Gentile territory as a symbolic means of foreshadowing the inclusive mission of the post-Easter community.

See: MISSION, NATIONS

DONALD SENIOR, C.P.

DESERT

Desert generally designates a barren or partially barren geographical area characterized by low rainfall. More often than not, desert means wilderness. According to the Bible it is in such desolate areas that humans can have special relationships with God. In the Christian Tradition, the desert has become a powerful symbol of the place of inward pilgrimage leading to the experience of God.

Old Testament

Place of Hardships. The desert is an ongoing reminder of the reality of danger and death. It is a place to which fugitives and bandits like David fled (1 Sam 23:24). It is the haunt of dangerous wild animals (Isa 30:6) and the abode of demons (Isa 34:14). According to Jeremiah 4:26 it is Yahweh's wrath that transforms the garden land into a desert. To lose one's way in the desert is to anticipate an almost certain death (Job 6:18).

Scene of God's Protection. Despite the hardships mentioned above, Israel experienced God's unique protection in the desert during the Exodus.* Although the people grumble against the Lord in Exodus and Numbers, the primary focus is God's graciousness while the secondary focus (subsequently developed by Israel's theologians) is the rebellion of the people. At Marah, for example, the people were unable to drink the water since it was too bitter. Yahweh then points out a certain piece of wood to Moses. "When he threw this into the water, the water became fresh" (Exod 15:25). Similarly, when the people needed food, Yahweh supplied the quail and the manna* (Exod 16:1-36). Since it was the task of the wife/mother to provide food and drink, the biblical text accentuates the feminine aspect of the God of Israel. In the desert, therefore, Mother Yahweh met the needs of her family.

In the desert Yahweh also provides protection by means of military victory and tribal organization. When Israel's traditional enemies, the Amalekites, threaten Israel's existence, Aaron* and Hur prop up a rock for Moses to sit on and thus defeat the enemy. "And Joshua mowed down Amalek and his people with the edge of the sword" (Exod 17:13). When Moses is unable to satisfy all the legal needs of his people, Yahweh intervenes by having Moses' father-in-law instruct him about appointing minor judges (Exod 18:13-27). The desert is indeed the place where the God of Israel succors his people.

Place of Covenant-making. Sinai is undoubtedly the best known desert area in the Bible. It is in this wilderness that Yahweh enters into a special relationship, a covenant, whereby Israel becomes Yahweh's people. According to one tradition the desert is that place of intimacy where Yahweh "bore you up on eagle wings and brought you here to myself" (Exod 19:4). At Mount Sinai God manifests himself in a variety of forms. He is present in a volcanic eruption (Exod 19:18), a violent storm (Exod 19:16), and in the more peaceful setting of a communal meal (Exod 24:11). The number and variety of the traditions demonstrate the importance and centrality of this desert place.

Since covenant necessarily entails obligations, it is not surprising that the desert provides the fitting location for commands and prohibitions. Hence at Mount Sinai God proclaims the Decalogue or Ten Commandments to Israel (Exod 20:1-7; Deut 5:6-21), as well as many other laws (Exod 20:22–23:19). The desert is now the place where the terms of the relationship between Yahweh and Israel are spelled out.

It is in the desert that Moses receives instructions for the building of the desert sanctuary. The desert is the apt place for linking God's holiness with such institutions as priesthood and sacrifices. While Sinai is not the place for the covenant, it is the place par excellence for Yahweh's manifestation.

It should be noted that some Sinai scenes reflect not only the participation of the desert community but also their generosity (Exod 35:20-29). In fact, the community is so generous that Moses must put a halt to their contributions (Exod 36:2-6). The outcome of the offerings and the manual labor is God's presence in the midst of the community. The presence of Yahweh then determines the pace of the trek through the desert.

Scene of Israel's Fidelity. In the eighth century BCE the prophet Hosea had to confront the sinfulness of his people, more specifically, their practice of Canaanite fertility or nature religion. He comes to understand Israel's apostasy by reflecting on his own marriage. His wife, Gomer, who is described as "a harlot's wife" (Hos 1:2), has been unfaithful. She has probably become a devotee of the fertility religion and receives hire (Hos 2:14) for her sexual favors. Despite such infidelity Hosea continues to love Gomer and longs for the time when they will be reunited.

For Hosea Gomer stands for his own people. Just as Gomer has betrayed Hosea, so Israel has sinned against her husband, that is, Yahweh. In hopes of reconciliation the prophet recalls the desert, the place of the honeymoon in the covenant-making setting of Sinai. He reflects on Israel's generous and faithful response in those days and looks for their return. "So I will allure her; I will lead her into the desert and speak to her heart. From there I will give her the vineyards she had. . . . She shall respond there as in the days of her youth, when she came up from the land of Egypt" (Hos 2:16-17).

For Hosea the desert is not a place for on-going withdrawal but an ideal place to seek God. It is the place where estranged lovers may be reconciled. It is the whole atmosphere of Israel's original fidelity in the desert that sparks the hope for reunion. (See 1 Kgs 19:1-18 where the ninth-century BCE prophet Elijah flees to the desert in order to sustain himself in his mission against Jezebel and her imposition of her brand of Canaanite religion.)

The prophet Jeremiah was influenced by Hosea's marriage analogy and the significance of the desert. In the late seventh century BCE Jeremiah had to face the inroads of Canaanite religion and the impending destruction of Judah. In contrast to Judah's present condition he recalls the loving devotion of the desert days. "I remember the devotion of your youth, how you loved me as a bride, following me in the desert, in a land unsown" (Jer 2:2). Unlike Hosea, Jeremiah never announces that Israel will or should return to the desert. Rather, the ideal is the attitude that Israel had toward Yahweh during the wandering in the desert. It is that "following me in the desert" that Jeremiah wishes to see his people recover.

Scene of Israel's Infidelity. Whereas both Hosea and Jeremiah reflected Israel's fidelity in the desert experience, the prophet Ezekiel accentuated Israel's infidelity during that time. In the first half of the sixth century BCE Ezekiel preached to an exilic audience that Judah would fall. In order to demonstrate the imminence of the collapse he courageously proclaims that there was no time at which Israel was truly faithful to Yahweh. Hence Israel of the sixth century BCE was identical to Israel of the thirteenth century BCE in terms of rebellion and unfaithfulness.

When the desperate exiles gather around Ezekiel, they anticipate good news since Yahweh was the God who delivered them from Egypt and led them through the desert. However, the prophet counters by announcing that Israel sinned in Egypt (Ezek 20:8-9). He then proceeds to tell them that the first generation in the desert also sinned. "But the house of Israel rebelled against me in the desert. They did not observe my statutes . . . " (Ezek 20:13). To confound confusion, Ezekiel also states that the second generation in the desert also was unfaithful. "But their children rebelled against me; they did not observe my statutes or keep my ordinances . . . " (Ezek 20:21). In that very setting where the exiles insisted on Israel's fidelity, the prophet must proclaim Israel's infidelity. (For other witnesses to Israel's sinfulness in the desert see Psalms 78 and 106.)

The reasons for Israel's forty-year wandering in the desert are given by a variety of biblical sources, e.g., Numbers 13–14 and the author of Deuteronomy 1:19-46. Although aware of these traditions, the author eliminates every link with war and conquest in the story of the spies and insists that the sin of the desert community is in the disparaging of the Promised Land. Although the report about the land is positive, the desert community responds: "The land that we explored is a country that consumes its inhabitants" (Num 13:32). In addition, this community wishes it had died in Egypt or in the desert (Num 14:3). Despite the positive reports by Joshua and Caleb, the community prefers the rumor that life outside the land is preferable to life inside the land. The desert wandering, therefore, is apt punishment for the unwillingness to see the Promised Land as the goal of their stay in the desert.

Second Desert Experience. Around the middle of the sixth century BCE the anonymous prophet of the Exile, Second Isaiah, offers a message of hope to his despairing audience in Babylon. He begins by announcing the decision of God's council to create a highway across the desert that will transport the exiles back to the land of Israel. "A voice cries out: in the desert prepare the way of the LORD! Make straight in the wasteland a highway for our God!" (Isa 40:3). The prophet regards this desert march as a second exodus. Thus the God who acted on behalf of the wilderness generation will reenact and heighten the drama of that scene on behalf of the exilic generation.

The miracles of the desert experience will reoccur. "The desert and the parched land will exult; the steppe will rejoice and bloom. . . . Streams will burst forth in the desert, and rivers in the steppe" (Isa 35:1, 6). Because of the abundance of water there will be extraordinary fertility: "I will plant in the desert the cedar, acacia, myrtle, and olive . . . " (Isa 41:19). The splendor of paradise will be once again in evidence: "Her deserts he shall make like Eden, her wasteland like the garden of the LORD . . . " (Isa 51:3). This miracle, while it builds upon the first desert experience, clearly outstrips it.

New Testament

John the Baptist. Luke writes: "and he [the Baptist] was in the desert until the day of his manifestation to Israel" (Luke 1:80). As Luke will later mention, this statement anticipates the Baptist's proclamation of a new manner of salvation that will be available to humans. Given the OT background on the desert as the place of God's dealings with Israel, Luke's emphasis on the Baptist's locale is not surprising.

Later Luke, like Matthew, Mark, and John (Matt 3:3; Mark 1:2-3; John 1:23), will refer to the prophetic message of Second Isaiah to establish a link between the mission of the Baptist and the start of John's proclamation of the good news. It is from the desert that God's initiative will advance. "A voice of one crying out in the desert: 'Prepare the way of the Lord, make straight his paths'" (Luke 3:4). In this use of Isaiah 40:3 the evangelists were not alone in connecting the desert with God's new enterprises. The Dead Sea Scrolls show the Qumran community using this same text to prepare for God's new coming through the study and observance of the Law and the Prophets. Clearly the desert and God's plan for Israel were intimately bound together.

Jesus' Temptation. All three Synoptic writers state that Jesus was tempted in the desert after his baptism. The desert seems to hold a twofold significance for Jesus. As in Hosea, the desert conjures up a place of contact with God. As elsewhere in the Bible, the desert is the dwelling place of wild animals and demons. Through his baptism Jesus has received his mission from the Father. In the temptation scene Jesus must resolve the manner in which he will accomplish that mission. While a positive formulation of that mission is not forthcoming in this scene, its negative implications are clear.

In both Matthew and Luke there is a threefold temptation of Jesus. When the tempter suggests that Jesus turn stones into loaves of bread (Matt 4:3) or a stone into a loaf of bread (Luke 4:3), Jesus quotes Deuteronomy 8:3, viz., that humans do not live on bread alone—a reference to the manna in the desert. When the tempter urges Jesus to throw himself down from the parapet of the Temple (Matt 4:5; Luke 4:9), Jesus cites Deuteronomy 6:16, viz., that one is not to tempt the Lord—a reference to the water from the rock. What these texts show is that, whatever God has in mind for Jesus, it does not involve this form of mission. Ultimately Jesus is experiencing the temptations of Israel in the desert. However, where Israel failed, Jesus has succeeded.

Paul refers to the temptation in the desert when confronting the dangers of overconfidence in Corinth. What happened to the Israelites in the desert could happen to the Christians in Corinth. "These things happened to them as an example, and they have been written down as a warning to us, . . ." (1 Cor 10:11).

Pastoral-Liturgical Tradition

First Sunday of Lent. This Sunday in all three cycles recounts Jesus' temptation in the desert. It powerfully recalls the symbolism of desert, especially in coping with temptations. The believer easily recalls Israel's infidelity in the desert. However, the believer is also challenged to remember God's fidelity in the desert. While one easily becomes aware of one's weaknesses, one must always bear in mind that the desert is a place of grace as well.

Communing with God. The prophets Elijah and Hosea view the desert, especially the desert of Sinai, as that particular locus where God communicates with humans. To that extent the desert becomes that area where one can break free of distractions and concerns to focus on the God of Israel and his Son. Every place, therefore, that helps to overcome the frantic pace of daily living and provides a sense of intimacy with God is to be welcomed. To that extent the desert is no longer a given geographical area but a powerful metaphor of communing with God. The words of Hosea come quickly to mind: "I will lead her into the desert and speak to her heart" (Hos 2:16).

See: COVENANT, DEAD SEA SCROLLS, EXODUS, MANNA

JOHN F. CRAGHAN

Pastoral-Liturgical Tradition

In the third and fourth centuries, the desert became one of the most powerful Christian symbols. At the end of the age of martyrs, it was a place that enabled people to live a full Christian life that became a paradigm for all: monasticism. This implied a change from the perspective of Paul, for whom the desert belonged to the prophetical past. For Antony of Egypt and his followers, to follow Christ meant going into solitude. His models were Elijah and the Baptist, not Moses. The desert visibly embodied the anchorites' pilgrimage* toward God and opposed a dynamic understanding of the gospel to the static way of the city, where the Church was now settling down in triumph. The desert was also threatening, not only because it was boundless and thus seemed inhuman to Hellenistic sensibilities (cf. John Cassian on *the desert vastness*), but also because in popular thought it was the haunt of demons. The first communities of Macrina and Basil (in fourth-century Asia Minor) and of Mary and Pachomius (fourth-century Egypt) had to be established in solitary places. In the more fertile and populated West, beginning with Benedict and Scholastica (sixth-century Italy), monks and nuns sought out a mountain top, another privileged place of encounter with God. In order to capture one aspect of the desert—distance from other human beings—enclosure was soon established. Pachomius' early settlement— a whole village sometimes open to all—became, with his disciples, a space reserved for the monks alone who, recalling the original Exodus, now called themselves "the true people of God in the desert."

Religious have been the guardians of the desert's lost paradise. Often, however, they seem to have forgotten their primitive symbol. Periodically, a desert movement would spring up here and there in the West, preaching a return to solitude: Carthusians, Camaldolese, Cistercians. In the twelfth and thirteenth centuries, religious life began a return to the city. Servites, Augustinians, and Carmelites came down from their mountain fastness to cities. Teresa and John of the Cross (sixteenth-century Spain) brought their Carmelites back to the desert. Paul of the Cross (eighteenth-century Italy) went back and forth between the desert and the city.

At a time when most Americans were in transition from Great Plains settlements to urban life, the Trappists (mid-nineteenth century) brought us back to the ideal of a remote solitude. Thomas Merton (d. 1968), at a time when the myth of the American paradise had already been lost, popularized this symbol and made it attractive.

After Vatican II, the desert is again exerting a strong attraction in the U.S. Carmelites, but also members of apostolic Congregations, are establishing hermitages; spirituality centers are opening in American deserts. The desert is no longer so much a threatening place, now that the devils seem to have moved away (though one still has to face the dark side of oneself), as it is a place of inward pilgrimage leading to the experience of God. The symbol has been reinterpreted in a sense closer to that of Gregory of Nyssa in his *Life of Moses*.

See: SOLITUDE

JOHN MANUEL LOZANO

DIASPORA/DISPERSION

The word Diaspora is derived from the Greek verb *diaspeiro*, which means "to disperse." In a biblical context, it refers to those Jews who, over the centuries, have left their homeland, either forcibly or willingly, to take up residence in many parts of the world. In the OT, this refers particularly to the large communities of Jews in Mesopotamia and, later, in Egypt. The term is not common in the NT and when it does appear it refers usually to Christians living as pilgrims away from their heavenly homeland.

Old Testament

The earliest instance of significant dispersion of Israelites outside of Palestine occurred at the time of the Assyrian conquest of the northern ten tribes in the eighth century BCE (734–721). At that time a significant number of Jews were deported to Assyria but they seem to have been largely absorbed into the local population. A much larger deportation occurred at the time of the Babylonian conquest of Israel in the sixth century BCE (598–587). These deportees became a large colony in Mesopotamia which retained its identity and had a profound influence on the subsequent history of Israel.

With the guidance and encouragement of the prophet Ezekiel, the Jews of Babylon developed a vibrant spirituality which found expression in study of the Torah, in the collection and preservation of sacred books, and in the production of the Babylonian Talmud. Since temple worship was no longer possible, they organized highly successful centers for prayer and study which were the forerunners of the synagogue. It is to these devout Israelites that the promises of restoration in Second Isaiah are directed. Some of these Jews returned to Palestine

after the Persian conquest of Babylon (sixth century BCE) where they rebuilt the Temple and effected a modest restoration of religious observance.

The Assyrian and Babylonian deportations were forced and can therefore qualify as the punishment that is envisaged in Deuteronomy 4:27: "The LORD will scatter you among the nations. . . ." Later migrations were voluntary and were even viewed with pride as a sign of vitality and as a significant source of support for the relatively impoverished homeland. This was particularly the case after Alexander the Great's conquest of the Persians (323 BCE), which brought to the area a cosmopolitan spirit as well as a facility for travel.

Large Jewish colonies developed at this time in Alexandria, Rome, and Antioch, while smaller groups appeared in other places. They maintained contact with Jerusalem but they were also open to the more liberal spirit of Hellenism. Some of the later Wisdom literature was clearly influenced by this spirit (e.g., Qoheleth, Sirach, and Wisdom). The Books of Tobias, Judith, and Esther reflect the experience of Jews living in exile* and offer encouragement to them.

One of the most significant products of the Diaspora was the translation of the OT into Greek (the Septuagint), which took place in Alexandria after 300 BCE and which profoundly influenced the early Christian Church. Thus, the dispersion of the Jews, which began as cruel deportation, ended as a highly successful sowing of Jewish ideas and ideals in most parts of the then known world.

New Testament

The word Diaspora occurs only three times in the NT. In John 7:35, its meaning is not altogether clear. Jesus had just said that he would go away and that those who sought him would be unable to find him. Thereupon, "the Jews said to one another, 'Where is he going that we will not find him? Surely he is not going to the dispersion among the Greeks to teach the Greeks, is he?'" These "Greeks" could be Greek-speaking Jews, but it is much more likely that they are Gentiles and the question would then suggest that Jesus might go to live with Jews outside Palestine (in the Diaspora) and teach the Gentiles. This was, apparently, a misunderstanding of Jesus' meaning.

The term Diaspora occurs in a quite different sense in 1 Peter 1:1, where we read: "Peter, an apostle of Jesus Christ, to the chosen sojourners of the dispersion in Pontus, Galatia, Cappadocia, Asia, and Bithynia. . . ." The letter is addressed to Christians converted mainly from paganism who live in the northern provinces of Asia Minor which were apparently in the orbit of Rome's (and Peter's) influence. They are said to be "of the dispersion" but only by analogy with the Jewish Diaspora because they are, along with all other Christians, a minority in the foreign land of this world as opposed to their true homeland, which is heaven (see 2:11).

This term occurs again in the address of the letter of James: "James, a slave of God and of the Lord Jesus Christ, to the twelve tribes in the dispersion, greetings" (1:1). These addressees are called "the twelve tribes," not in the original sense of Israel, but as the Christian Church understood the new Israel to be. It is not clear whether they are Jewish or Gentile Christians. They are said to be "in the dispersion" either because, as in 1 Peter 1:1, they are away from their heavenly home, or because they are living as a minority in the Greco-Roman world.

Several texts in Acts refer to the Diaspora by using the corresponding Greek verb. Typical of these is Acts 8:4: "Now those who had been scattered went about preaching the word." In Acts 8:1 and 11:19, it is noted that this dispersion was caused by the persecution of Christians in Jerusalem, notably at the time of Stephen's martyrdom. It is generally concluded that those scattered were Greek-speaking Jewish Christians. According to Acts, their dispersion was a providential development that promoted the expansion of the Christian Church (11:21). No doubt this is already suggested by the presence of so many Diaspora Jews at the dramatic event of Pentecost (Acts 2:5-11).

Pastoral-Liturgical Tradition

The term Diaspora rarely appears in later Christian tradition and when it does it refers primarily to the phenomenon of Jewish survival in all parts of the world. Christian spirituality has certainly been aware of the pilgrim status of believers in this passing world, but this is not usually referred to as a Diaspora.

See: EXILE, PENTECOST, SYNAGOGUE

DEMETRIUS R. DUMM, O.S.B.

DISCIPLE/DISCIPLESHIP

The concept of discipleship is of prime importance in Christian tradition. Its roots can be found in the OT, where Israel is portrayed as a disciple, a learner, of God. Frequently the godhead who instructs Israel is personified as Wisdom Woman. There are also references in the OT to disciples of prophets. In the NT discipleship is commitment to Jesus and his mission. The Christian, who always remains a disciple, does not gather disciples to him or herself. Rather, in living as a follower of Jesus she or he attracts others to follow him. For the early Christians discipleship often became synonymous with martyrdom. In later tradition, perfect discipleship came to be interpreted as renunciation of all to follow Christ.

Old Testament

The theme of discipleship is so central in the NT that it comes as a bit of a surprise to realize that it is scarcely found in the OT at all. The word "disciple" *(talmid)*, which means basically a "learner," occurs only once and informs us that among the musicians of the Temple there were teachers and disciples (1 Chr 25:8). We can, however, distinguish in the OT a narrow and a broad usage of the concept: (1) in the narrow or strict sense, a disciple is one who follows the instruction of another who is accepted as teacher and leader; (2) in the broad or wide sense, Israel is to be the disciple of God, the Teacher, from whom they are to receive instruction.

Disciple in the Strict Sense. We often meet followers (as individuals or groups) of prophetic figures. The early prophets* appeared almost invariably with other persons closely associated with them and their work. Samuel first had his sons with him (1 Sam 7:17–8:3) but appeared later with a larger band over which he presided (1 Sam 19:19-24). Prophetic bands were present at Saul's election (1 Sam 18:5, 10), but no specific leader is mentioned. Elijah had Elisha as a follower (1 Kgs 19:19-21), just as Elisha had Gehazi (2 Kgs 4:2). At times other bands of prophets appeared with them (2 Kgs 2:3, 5, 15). Among the later prophets, Isaiah's wife was called a prophetess (8:3), and he entrusted his instruction to his "disciples" for a later day. Jeremiah shared his mission with Baruch who not only wrote down the prophet's words but even delivered them in the Temple when Jeremiah was not able to do so in person (Jer 36:4-8). It is a common opinion among scholars that these disciples of the prophets played a significant role in handing on their oracles which now survive in the books that bear their names.

A second area in which we can speak more properly of disciples is that of wisdom.* Education began in the home, "Hear your father's instruction and reject not your mother's teaching" (Prov 1:8). A father not only instructed from his own experience but cited the teaching he had received from his father (Prov 4:4, 11). Appeal was also made to the ancestors of former generations: "Will they not teach you and tell you and utter their words of understanding" (Job 8:10). The student was admonished to obey now and avoid later regret, "Why did I not listen to the voice of my teachers, nor to my instructors incline my ear!" (Prov 5:13). Of Qoheleth (Ecclesi-astes) it is said, "Besides being wise, Qoheleth taught the people knowledge" (Qoh 12:9). Ben Sira, writing about 180 BCE, invited students to "come aside to me and take up lodging in the house of instruction" (Sir 51:23); he compared himself to a rivulet from the stream of wisdom, and his students to plants in his garden (Sir 24:28-31). We are very close here to the situation in Jesus' time when disciples would attach themselves to prominent teachers (rabbis).

Disciple in the Broad Sense. One of the most basic obligations of Israel was to be disciples of God. "I, the LORD, your God, teach you what is for your good, and lead you on the way you should go" (Isa 48:17). At the consecration of the Temple in Jerusalem, Solomon prayed that God would teach the people the right and good way to live (1 Kgs 8:36; 2 Chr 6:27). All Israel's children "shall be taught by [disciples of] the LORD, and great shall be the peace of your children" (Isa 54:13). Israel might be afflicted, but they could hope that in the future their Teacher would no longer be hidden, but "with your own eyes you shall see your Teacher" (Isa 30:20).

When Israel entered the land and began to dwell there, they had to be on their guard not to "learn to imitate the abominations of the peoples there" (Deut 18:9; 20:18). If Israel was to be faithful, they were not to "learn from the ways of the nations" (Jer 10:2). These other nations, rather, were to learn from Israel how to swear by Yahweh's name so that they might live (Jer 12:16-17). They would say, "Come, let us climb the Lord's mountain, that he may instruct us . . . for from Zion shall go forth instruction [torah]" (Isa 2:3; Mic 4:2). Throughout the psalms, Israel prayed, "O Lord, teach me your ways" (Ps 25:4-5; see also 27:11; 119:12, 26, 64, 66, 68, 73, 108, 124, 135, 171; 143:10).

When God instructed the people it was done through intermediaries. Moses received from God the tablets with the commandments for the instruction of Israel (Exod 24:12). Throughout the Book of

Deuteronomy, Moses calls the people to "hear the statutes and decrees which I am teaching you to observe" (Deut 4:1, 5, 10, 14; 6:1). Aaron, the priests, and Levites were also given the charge to teach/instruct the people in the laws that God gave through Moses (Lev 10:11; Deut 24:8; 33:10; 2 Kgs 12:3; 2 Chr 15:3; Ezek 44:23). Prophets instructed the people in God's ways (Judg 13:8); Isaiah's words were recorded as instruction *(torah)* for a later time (Isa 8:16). After the Exile, Ezra "set his heart on the study and practice of the law of the Lord and on teaching statutes and ordinances in Israel" (Ezek 7:10). Finally, God's teaching comes to us through the feminine figure of Wisdom who calls to us through creation and our everyday lives (Prov 1:20-33; 4:5-9; 8:1-36; 9:1-18; Wis 6:22–9:18; Sir 24:1-31; 51:13-30).

Once Israel had learned from God, they were, in turn, to teach others: "Therefore, take these words of mine into your heart and soul. . . . Teach them to your children, speaking of them at home and abroad, whether you are busy or at rest" (Deut 11:19; 6:6-9). After learning of God's forgiveness, the psalmist promised, "I will instruct you [others] and show you the way you should walk" (Ps 32:8); and, "I will teach transgressors your ways" (Ps 51:15). "Come, children, hear me; I will teach you the fear of the Lord" (Ps 34:12). What we learn from God is to be shared.

Conclusion. The disciple as a follower of some human teacher, while not absent in the OT, is relatively insignificant. On the other hand, the disciple as Israel, learners of the divine Teacher, looms quite large. In the NT, both of these aspects will come together in the disciples of Jesus, God become human.

See: PRIEST, PROPHET, WISDOM

MICHAEL D. GUINAN, O.F.M.

New Testament

The discipleship that Jesus called for differs from discipleship as it developed among the rabbis. The Jewish student chose his rabbi; his objective was to absorb his rabbi's teaching and to imitate his life. When he had applied himself sufficiently he could himself become a rabbi. For his part, Jesus took the initiative in calling his disciples. The disciples' commitment was to the person of Jesus and the disciples' duty was to proclaim Jesus. The Christian always remains a disciple; he never becomes a rabbi (Matt 23:8).

Discipleship in Mark. In Mark most of Jesus' teaching is given after the midpoint of the Gospel (the confession at Caesarea Philippi), but in the area of discipleship much is also given by way of foreshadowing. Soon after the action gets under way, Mark shows Jesus calling his first disciples. Passing along the Sea of Galilee Jesus saw Simon and Andrew casting a net. He called them, and immediately they left their nets and followed him. Similarly, James and John left their father and the hired servants and followed him (1:20).

Here Mark shows in a concrete way what the call to discipleship can mean. The story is like a woodcut in that only the important features are presented; nothing is said about time or exact place, or about any other details. Discipleship always begins with Jesus looking at a person and calling him. The call* of the disciples is related without any indication that the fishermen might have had time for reflection or might have had to overcome certain difficulties before responding. Discipleship is a new manner of acting and thinking which is sustained by the event of grace. And we see that Jesus did not encounter persons in some special religious sphere, but in the midst of everyday life where they really live.

In Mark, Jesus' explicit teaching is given after the midpoint and that teaching is devoted especially to discipleship. Moreover, it is imparted in close conjunction with the passion predictions while Jesus and his disciples are "on the way" to Jerusalem, a journey which is bracketed by the healing of two blind men.

At Caesarea Philippi Peter acknowledged Jesus as the Christ. Immediately Jesus went on to say that to be the Christ means to suffer: "He began to teach them that the Son of Man must suffer greatly" (8:31). Then Jesus went on to say that to be a disciple also means to suffer: "Whoever wishes to come after me must deny himself, take up his cross, and follow me" (8:34). There are two more passion predictions with the same message (9:31 and 10:32). From the prediction of the passion, therefore, one moves directly to the nature of discipleship.

Mark reserves the teaching on discipleship to a place toward the end of his Gospel because the only way the disciples could discover who Jesus is and who they are was to walk the way of Jesus to the end. They could not understand Jesus prior to his cross and resurrection; therefore, it is fitting that the teaching on discipleship should be imparted as Jesus and his disciples were walking toward the scene of those events.

In Mark, the disciples are characterized by lack of understanding or incomprehension, and this is never explicitly dispelled anywhere in the Gospel. Despite all Jesus had taught them, despite their intimate association with him, and despite all they had seen him do, the disciples could not understand Jesus prior to his climactic fate on the cross.

By the arrangement of his Gospel, Mark brings home to his readers that there is no real comprehension of Jesus apart from knowledge of his final fate on the cross and the subsequent resurrection. By the same token, there is for us no Jesus apart from faith. Jesus' words and deeds were marked by ambiguity, open to different interpretations, and that ambiguity is transferred to the time frame of Mark and his readers. Christian disciples must continue to walk by faith even on the Easter side of resurrection.

Discipleship in Matthew. Matthew too stresses Jesus' initiative in calling his disciples. Jesus saw, Jesus summoned, and at once those summoned left behind everything in order to follow him in total allegiance (4:18-20, 21-22). Peter and Andrew, James and John, were persons accounted as being upright citizens. But Matthew as a toll-collector was looked upon by Jewish society as no better than a thief.

In describing Jesus' ministry to Israel (4:17–11:1), Matthew describes the disciples as persons of "little faith," which manifests itself in crises of trust. They did not understand at once what Jesus taught them, or left untapped the authority Jesus would have made available to them. Jesus did not condone bouts of little faith but he did not abandon his disciples at such times.

In the latter half of the second part of his story (11:2–16:20), Matthew tells of Israel's repudiation of Jesus. In contrast to Israel, the disciples stand out as the recipients of divine revelation. In the third part of his Gospel (16:21–28:20), Matthew tells of Jesus' journey to Jerusalem and of his suffering, death, and resurrection. Parallel to this, he shows how the disciples were led to appropriate Jesus' evaluative point of view according to which suffering sonship is a summons to suffering discipleship. Servanthood constitutes the essence of discipleship.

Thus in 16:21 we read that "Jesus began to show his disciples that he must go to Jerusalem and suffer greatly." This is followed immediately by his words: "Whoever wishes to come after me, must deny himself, and take up his cross." These two passages, taken together, lead to the conclusion that Jesus revealed to his disciples, in all he said and did, that God had ordained that he should go to Jerusalem to suffer, and that his way of suffering is a summons to his disciples also to go the way of suffering (i.e., the way of servanthood). For "the Son of Man does not come to be served but to serve and to give his life as a ransom for many" (20:29). Here Matthew alerts the reader that suffering, defined as servanthood, is the essence of discipleship and that Jesus would show the disciples in what he said and did that this is in fact the case.

Discipleship in Luke/Acts. In the NT we find mention of "the disciples" without always a clear indication that they are disciples of Jesus as distinguished from the followers of John the Baptist (Matt 9:14), or even of the Pharisees (Matt 22:16). Sometimes the term refers to the apostles,* as in Matthew 10:1: "his twelve disciples," and sometimes to all of his followers in general, as in Luke 6:17: "crowd of his disciples"; but in many cases it is impossible to say whether it refers to the smaller or the larger group. Only in Luke 10:1-17 is mention made of a very special group of seventy-(two) disciples who formed a group distinct both from the twelve apostles and from the followers of Jesus in general. The instructions given in 10:3-12 to these seventy(two) disciples, when they were sent out two by two, is substantially the same as that given to the Twelve in Matthew 10:5, when they were sent out to preach.

In Acts the term, "the disciples of the Lord" (9:1) or simply "the disciples" (6:1), is practically equivalent to the term, "the Christians" (11:26), a term which the NT avoids. Apart from the special instructions given to that particular group of Jesus' disciples who were to assist him in his preaching and his ministry, the teaching which Jesus gave "to his disciples" is meant for all his followers, of all times and places.

Summary. In the Sermon on the Mount (Matthew 5–7), Jesus "speaks past" his story characters and addresses his implied readers (present day disciples) directly. He indicates the quality of life that is indicative of disciples who live in the sphere of God's end-time rule. Jesus calls this the "greater righteousness" (5:20). "Righteousness" (*dikaiosynē*) is a term that Jesus predicates to both God and humans. The "greater righteousness" is doing the will of God as Jesus teaches it. One does God's will when one is perfect, that is, not flawless but wholehearted in one's devotion to God (5:48), and one is such when one loves God with heart, soul, and mind, and loves the neighbor as self (22:27). At the center of the greater righteousness, then, is undivided fealty toward God and selfless love of the neighbor (5:21–6:18).

Through the call of Jesus, disciples have entered into the sphere of God's end-time rule. The kinds of persons Jesus' disciples must strive to be also comes to light in the Beatitudes (5:3-10). For example, "the poor in spirit" are those who may or may not be economically deprived, but who in any case stand before God with no illusions of self-righteousness or self-sufficiency. "Those who mourn" are those who grieve over sin and evil in the world. "The meek" are those who are lowly and powerless, whose only hope is God.

See: APOSTLE, CHRISTIAN, FAITH, JESUS CHRIST, JOHN THE BAPTIST, PHARISEE, RESURRECTION, SERVANT, SUFFERING

AUGUSTINE STOCK, O.S.B.

Pastoral-Liturgical Tradition

The NT figure of the disciple soon became in the Church the prototype of all Christians. Initially, Jesus' sayings on the conditions for discipleship were more influential than the stories of the call of the first disciples. Origen used some of these sayings (*Exhortation to Martyrdom,* 12, 14, 37) to encourage Christians in danger of suffering martyrdom for their faith. Ignatius of Antioch had already referred to those who died for their faith as "followers of Christ" (*Rom* 5:3, *Magn.* 9:1). Indeed, martyrs soon came to be regarded as those who most fully embodied the call to discipleship. When the "Age of Martyrs" ended, many Christians felt called by the same Gospel texts to embrace a new exemplar form of discipleship: monasticism. In their *Lives* of monks, Athanasius of Alexandria, Jerome, and others explained the monastic call by quoting those same passages of the Gospels. A new prototype of discipleship for all was born.

At about this time the expression "apostolic life" was coined. It appears for the first time in the second *Catechesis* of Theodore, a disciple of Pachomius (fourth-century Egypt), then in Epiphanius (*Haer.* 61), and would be repeated dozens of times more until the twelfth century. What we now call discipleship was for many centuries known as an imitation of the apostles' lives. In every case, the "apostolic life" was meant to express something thought to be central to the gospel. For the earliest solitaries it meant renunciation, and for members of communities from Pachomius and Augustine, to the clerical reformers of the eleventh century and the canons regular of the twelfth, it meant communion of heart and possessions. The core of gospel spirituality had passed on from ascetic renunciation to communion of life, and the early Jerusalem Church became the new inspiring model. In the thirteenth century it would change again. An early Dominican source defines the apostolic life as following Christ in poverty and preaching the gospel.

Basil of Caesarea and his sister Macrina (fourth century) wanted to take the whole gospel as a rule; hence Basil, in his *Asketikon*, described the life of his sisters and brothers as a "life faithful to the gospel." However, it seems that, at least while he was living in his community before becoming a bishop, Basil could not figure out how to relate the gospel as professed by all Christians with the gospel life as practiced by his followers. He thought it very difficult to live according to the gospel in a secular setting. For him, nevertheless, a disciple is no longer mainly characterized by either ascetic renunciation or by communion, but rather by embracing the entire spirituality and life described in the Gospels. In the thirteenth century, this idea of gospel-life was even more central to Francis of Assisi, for whom fidelity to the gospel was the only thing that mattered. He could therefore open up his gospel movement to include the laity.

For John of the Cross (2 *Ascent* 7.4-10) and Teresa of Jesus (*Castle* 3, 1.6), discipleship embraces the whole of human existence. But John, who made this idea central to his spiritual theology, transferred it even to the realm of interiorized spirituality. He

uses the Gospel texts on the call to discipleship to urge us to seek God alone above all creatures, including even the deepest prayer experiences. Discipleship was once again for all, since all are called to love God with all their heart.

It is interesting to note that while in the Gospels discipleship or "following Christ" originally meant that everyone should share in Jesus' expectation of God's reign, in post-biblical tradition the emphasis was on the generosity ("leaving all things") required as a pre-condition. In the martyrs, that generosity was actualized at the moment of their dying for Christ, while in monasticism, it was actualized by a life that involved renunciation. In the latter, it became something objective, a way of life, even though it was rooted in a spiritual attitude. With John of the Cross, it again became a disposition of the spirit.

The Lutheran martyr and master of spirituality, Dietrich Bonhoeffer, placed discipleship once more at the center of the life of the Church (*The Cost of Discipleship*). He did so to encourage Christians to resist the temptation to join the new paganism (Nazism) and to be ready to accept martyrdom instead, just as Origen had done centuries earlier. Bonhoeffer praised the Catholic Religious Orders for keeping the ideal of discipleship alive, but criticized the Catholic Church for restricting it to religious. Yet the Church has persisted in proposing religious as models for all Christians: their lives were a kind of challenging parable or, as Vatican II repeatedly put it, a sign for the whole Church (Dogmatic Constitution on the Church, no. 44; see no. 41). Had not Thomas Aquinas written that while the material embodiment of the "counsels" is proper of religious, the "spirit of the counsels" is for all?

It is nonetheless true that all too often from the fourth century to the beginning of the twelfth, secular Christians were viewed as people who were unable to renounce all, and were hence called "children" or "the weak." They therefore tended to appear as rather imperfect disciples. Vatican II has striven to strike a balance between the view of Christianity as discipleship (Dogmatic Constitution on the Church, no. 41) and the traditional understanding of religious life as a public form of following Christ (Dogmatic Constitution on the Church, no. 41; Decree on the Renewal of Religious Life, no. 1). The council relates the way of religious life to the way of common discipleship in two ways: first, religious life is a special sign of common discipleship; second, religious aim at following Christ more closely. No doubt many will find the second argument less satisfactory.

At a time when the figure of Jesus is extremely attractive to many, while the prevailing trend is toward various forms of materialism (consumerism, hedonism, etc.), it is most important that we return to the gospel spirituality of discipleship. It is the very core of Christian life. In proclamation, catechesis, and Christian education, the emphasis should be on what is specifically Christian: sharing Jesus' faith and expectations, imitating his freedom to rise above all immediate concerns, his solidarity with the outcast, his filial relationship with a sovereign yet caring God. This is what makes us disciples and hence, Christians.

See: CALL/VOCATION, ELECTION

JOHN MANUEL LOZANO

DOVE

Old Testament

As part of all creation pointing to God, there were many features of the various species of dove that lent themselves to higher symbolism. Some were migratory and therefore their spring return and song was a sign of new life, fertility, and renewal: "The song of the dove is heard in our land" (Cant 2:12). Doves were gentle, tending to pair together, hence they were a sign of peace and love. In the Canticle, the beloved is called, "my dove" (2:14; 5:2; 6:9). Her eyes are like those of a dove (1:15; 4:1). To find out if the Deluge had ended, Noah sent out a dove three times (Gen 8:8-12). The swift fluttering action of doves made

them an apt symbol of the Spirit's action in creation (Gen 1:2) and its renewal after the Flood (Gen 8:1). In these texts, the creative wind or Spirit* of God is described as hovering or sweeping over the waters.

Since doves were especially esteemed, they were the only birds that could be used in sacrifice. The poor were allowed to substitute them for the larger and more costly animals used in holocausts and sin offerings (Lev 1:14; 5:7). These sacrifices were required after childbirth (Lev 12:6-8), cure from leprosy or flow of blood (Lev 14:22-32; 15:14-30), and at the end of a Nazarite vow (Num 6:10). Because of the need for these sacrificial birds, they were sold in the Temple area (Matt 21:12). The dove could also be a symbol for Israel, God's beloved people. The psalmist prays, "Give not to the vulture the life of your dove" (Ps 74:19; see 68:14).

New Testament

At Jesus' baptism, a dove appeared over his head (Mark 1:10; Matt 3:16; Luke 3:22; John 1:32). Mark seems to present this as part of a private experience of Jesus in view of that Gospel's messianic secret. Matthew describes it as a public event witnessed by the Baptist. Luke emphasizes the physical reality of the dove by noting that it descended in "bodily form" (3:22). In John, the dove is a special sign promised by God that was witnessed by the Baptist (1:32-33). John emphasizes the dove's abiding over Jesus to show the fulfillment of Isaiah's prophecy of the coming of the *abiding* Spirit of God over the descendant of David (11:1-2).

The biblical background of the dove symbol may be the fluttering dove/Spirit of God's creation (Gen 1:1; 8:1) that started anew with the baptism of Jesus. Or it may be a symbol of God's love for his people or his Son in view of other OT texts (cf. above). In other NT texts, the doves are the offering that Jesus' parents brought to the Temple when they presented him to the Lord (Luke 2:24). Jesus advises his disciples to be "as shrewd as serpents and simple as doves" (Matt 10:16).

Pastoral-Liturgical Tradition

The dove has remained a symbol of the holy Spirit as well as Christian love. The dove image is frequently found near the baptismal fount, over the altar, or in representations of the Trinity.

See: BAPTISM, JOHN THE BAPTIST, SACRIFICE, SPIRIT

JOSEPH A. GRASSI

DREAMS

Consideration of dreams as a means of divine revelation is treated differently in various stages of the biblical narrative. Some texts seem to represent belief in this type of experience as authentic revelation. In other texts there is suggestion of folklore in the narratives, and in some cases resistance to belief in such experience. While the ancient Near Eastern neighbors of Israel had books of dream interpretations and professional dream interpreters, such extensive use of this method of revelation is not characteristic of biblical religion.

Old Testament

Dreams or dream-like experiences occur more often in the OT than in the NT. The communication is sometimes direct and straightforward, or it may be symbolic and in need of interpretation. The early tradition offers instances of both types of messages. The form of the narratives uses such stereotyped language as "during sleep," or "when night fell." Dreamers are usually passive; they see a vision or hear a voice speaking to them. God is active and gives the message. Sometimes a prominent leader might go to a shrine or holy place in hope of receiving a divine communication. This is called incubation and often involves conversation between the person and the Lord. Solomon's dream at Gibeon was such an experience (1 Kgs 3:4-15). In contrast, at Gilboa Saul sought consultation through dreams, among other things, but did not receive the dream-revelation (1 Sam 28:6).

Direct Communication. During the travels of Abraham in the Negev he stayed for a time in Gerar where he referred to Sarah as his sister. Abimelech, king of Gerar, took her, but in a dream God warned him of impending death for having taken another man's wife (Gen 20:3). The narrative is thought to have characteristics of the Elohist documents in its high sense of morality and revelation through the mediation of a dream. It is a story which likely shows protection of Sarah because of her important function in salvation history, and so it was preserved in light of the promise.

Another brief instance of direct communication in a dream was the warning to Laban against harming Jacob because of his flight (Gen 31:24). The process of salvation history was to remain in progress. Two other dream sequences are part of this narrative and both are partly direct and partly symbolic in nature. Jacob's departure from Beersheba brought him to a Canaanite shrine where he dreamed of a stairway between earth and heaven (Gen 28:12). The direct communication came in the words of God, and reiteration of the patriarchal promise emphasized the continuity of God's presence with the chosen people. The fact of the dream's occurrence at a shrine might suggest the notion of an incubation, but the promise was not attached to that place, but to the patriarchal line through Isaac by reference to Beersheba as the point of departure. In his old age Jacob would return to Beersheba on his way to Egypt, and in a dream he would be assured of return to his land (Gen 46:1-4). In the context of his flight from Laban, Jacob related a previous dream involving the symbol of streaked and speckled goats, but also relating God's direct command to him to return to the land of his birth (Gen 31:10-13). All of that worked toward the fulfillment of the promise.

Two other examples of direct communication can be noted. The first, the call of Samuel, does not use the word "dream," but the incident happened during sleep and involved a direct message from God concerning the family of Eli (1 Sam 3:11-14). This situation also moved toward the phenomenon of prophecy,* for as a result Samuel became acknowledged as a prophet of God. The second, the dream of Solomon at Gibeon, was more clearly an incubation involving a conversation between the king and the Lord (1 Kgs 3:5-14). Solomon's famous prayer for wisdom comes from this passage. The narrator also referred to Solomon's unacceptable idolatrous practices and the Lord's reiteration of the call to covenant morality that was an integral part of their relationship.

Symbolic Dreams. Among the best-known dreams in the Bible are the dreams in the Joseph story (Genesis 37–50). The dreams of Joseph himself were symbolic, but the meaning was immediately clear to his family (Gen 37:5-11). The dreams of Pharaoh's chief cup bearer, chief baker, and of Pharaoh himself were also symbolic, but they required the use of Joseph's gift of interpretation. Joseph was ultimately acknowledged as wise and discerning and endowed with the spirit of God. Thus Joseph came to be in charge of the whole land of Egypt and would eventually save the line of Jacob for the transmission of God's promise to future generations.

In the time of the Judges the conflict between Israel and Midian provided the setting for the Midianite's dream which was interpreted in favor of Israel (Judg 7:13-14). The barley bread was taken to be Israel who would advance on the Midianite tents and overcome them. Gideon took it as a message of victory for his troops, so he pursued the battle. The message to Gideon was in the form of direct communication from the Lord, but the dream about victory was in symbolic form and called for interpretation.

Even in the early tradition the relative value of dreams in comparison with direct communication was the point of the Lord's word to Aaron and Miriam (Num 12:6-8). Moses' preeminence was emphasized by his direct communication with the Lord, in contrast to prophetic communication through the mediation of dreams. Connection between prophecy and dreams is seen in Deuteronomy 13:2-6, where even such revelation is subject to the scrutiny of established revelation.

Elihu's acceptance of Job's terrifying dreams showed that some accepted their validity (Job 7:14; 33:15). Nebuchadnezzar's dream of a large and terrifying statue related in the Book of Daniel combines the symbolic with elements of folklore and ancient concepts of world history (Dan 3:31-35). The story is meant to show the superiority of the God of Israel and the God-given wisdom of Israel's sages over the gods and the wisdom of other nations. Thus the faith and courage of the writer's contemporaries could be strengthened for living in their current time while looking toward the final triumph of God's reign. If that section reflects events of the Hellenistic era, then it also reflects the valuation of dreams as the Lord's protection of Israel.

Resistance to Dreams. An implicit resistance to dreams can be surmised from the valuation of dreams as less important than direct communication. Even more clear is the strong resistance of Jeremiah in his tirade against prophets who prophesied lies in his day (Jer 23:25-40). He identified dreams with lies which are not consistent with the truthful speaking of the word of God. Jeremiah continued thus against the professional prophets and dreamers who served the kings of Judah.

In the wisdom tradition Qoheleth spoke of the futility and emptiness of dreams (Qoh 5:2). Dreams led to the proliferation of empty wordiness, and for the Preacher such futility is the mark of the fool. What profits is the fear of God. Ben Sira also rejected the efficacy of dreams and included them with the anxieties of life that drive away rest even at night (Sir 34:1-7; cf. 31:1). All people are upset by them and terrified by what disturbs their sleep, though sinners lose by suffering greater anxiety because of what they gained unjustly.

Finally, in contrast to the Lord who does good things for his people, diviners and dreamers offer deceitful dreams and empty comfort. Zechariah envisioned a new order of things in which the divine victory would restore all things to proper perspective (Zech 10:1-3).

Dreams in Similes. The term "dream" is often used as a comparison for what is fleeting, ephemeral, or perishing. The wicked perishes like a vision of the night (Job 20:8), and all the nations who war against God's people will come to nothingness as does a dream (Isa 29:7). The Psalter has poetic uses of such similes for the fate of the wicked who are made desolate (Ps 73:20). It also uses the term for returning exiles for whom coming back to Zion had far exceeded their expectations and seemed too good to be believed (Ps 126:1).

New Testament

The NT tradition has very few references to dreams or night visions, and this may reflect the conviction that such methods were not necessary. The two instances in Matthew's Gospel which use the word "dream" itself center on the birth narrative (Matt 1:20; 2:12, 13, 19) and on one brief reference at the time of the trial of Jesus (Matt 27:19). Those connected with the birth narrative have sometimes been considered legendary, but even if that is true they can be seen to focus on the central event of salvation history and bespeak God's active involvement in bringing his promise to fulfillment.

At the time of Mary's pregnancy, Joseph had a dream in which an angel gave him assurance that Mary's child was the savior. The evangelist commented on these events as fulfillment of prophecy (Matt 1:20). After the birth of the child wise men or astrologers from the East were warned in a dream not to return to Herod (Matt 2:12). Immediately Joseph was directed by an angel in a dream to take the family to Egypt (Matt 2:13) where they remained until a similar command called them back to their own land after Herod's death (Matt 2:19). Another dream was the reason Joseph avoided settling in Judaea but went instead

to Nazareth (Matt 2:22). This cycle of dreams had the function of protecting the well-being of the child and assured the progress of salvation history. Whether they are a matter of literary form or of theological commentary, they make the point of God's direct involvement in fulfillment of his word. The only other incident in Matthew is a brief mention about a dream of Pilate's wife while Pilate presided at Jesus' trial. Reference to this is made without comment.

While Paul does not mention dreams in his letters, there are references in Acts to communications he had at night. They use the characteristic language of dream references, and it is generally thought they can be considered dreams. A night vision which summoned him and his companions to Macedonia was taken as a summons from God (Acts 16:9-10). Paul was directed to settle for a time in Corinth (Acts 18:9-11), to keep up his courage and to proceed to Rome (Acts 23:11), and not to give up hope of survival in the face of shipwreck (Acts 27:23-26). Whatever was the source of information of Paul's visions, they emphasize God's protection of the apostle at an important point in the transmission of the gospel message.

Though dreams in the NT are few, it can be noted that they could be eliminated entirely, but more likely are viewed very critically. As the OT tradition purified the phenomenon of the superstition exercised in the ancient world, so the NT made dreams ancillary and peripheral to the essential message of the good news. Jude 8 even relegated them to the realm of hallucination or auto-suggestion which distorted true revelation and misguided the community.

Pastoral-Liturgical Tradition

The high level of discipline required for the proper understanding of the dream as revelatory experience did not survive for very long. Gradually belief in dreams returned, sometimes betraying unmasked paganism. Among the martyrs dreams often revealed agitation in the face of martyrdom, but uncertainty of interpretation led to anxiety about correct understanding. The appearance of books of dream interpretation paved the way for the credence of dreams as powers of divination, and since such practices were known to exist among leaders in the Christian community the door was opened to crass superstition and dream manticism.

In our day there is widespread interest in dreams and books of dream interpretations. These psychic phenomena often occur during sleep and are thought to rise from the sub-conscious or unconscious levels of the personality. Earlier civilizations often regarded these experiences as contact with invisible realms. Today they are frequently explored psychologically as a means of self-discovery. In any case, interpretation lacks certainty, and great discernment is needed before giving affirmation to such phenomena.

See: MAGIC AND DIVINATION, PROMISE, PROPHET, VISIONS, WORD

BETTY JANE LILLIE, S.C.

DRUNKENNESS

The Bible does not condemn wine* itself. However, its intoxicating power and the disgraceful conduct that drunkenness frequently provokes is recorded throughout both Testaments. Drunkenness undermines inhibitions and leaves one open to every type of dissolute behavior. It was also associated with the worship of idols and, therefore, strongly denounced.

Old Testament

The reason for indulging in the exhilaration of wine may be legitimate, even religious, celebration. However, inebriation can render one unrestrained or defenseless and, thereby, prone to indulge in one's own questionable inclinations or to become the victim of the harmful designs of another. The first account of drunkenness in the Bible is found in the story of Noah (Gen 9:21-27). The narrative suggests that an innocent Noah was ignorant of the power of the fruit of the vine. We are told that when he was overcome by it he "lay naked inside his tent" (v. 21). Although the Bible does not explicitly criticize him for his over-indulgence (it condemns Canaan for lack of respect [vv. 25-27]), it describes the vulnerability in which his actions placed him and the ridicule from his own son that he sustained because of it.

On the other hand, the great David was well aware of the power of strong drink. Having impregnated Bathsheba, the wife of Uriah the Hittite, David sought to conceal his adulterous sin by persuading the loyal soldier to go to his wife and have relations with her. David hoped that the child she was carrying then would be presumed to be Uriah's and he himself would be free of suspicion (2 Samuel 11). However, he underestimated the loyalty of this soldier. Uriah did not accede to the king's plan, even after David succeeded in making him drunk. Unlike Noah, whose honor was compromised by his drunkenness, Uriah did not succumb to the king's deception. (He was later put in the front lines and there killed, 11:14-17.) However, this account demonstrates how one person's susceptibility to alcohol can become the weapon of another.

Such was the case with Holofernes, one of the generals of Nebuchadnezzar, king of Assyria. Intending to seduce the noble Jewish woman Judith, he gave a banquet at which he was overcome by the wine (Jdt 12:10-20). Judith did not make him drunk, but she was well aware of his designs on her and the lack of restraint which characterized the celebrations of the Assyrians. She had prepared herself and her maid for an opportune moment which she would seize. Holding herself in readiness, when the moment came she took advantage of Holofernes' incapacity and cut off his head with his own sword (13:1-10). Thus, his drunkenness was his downfall. Drunken stupor was also the occasion of the murder of Elah, king of Israel (1 Kgs 16:9), and Ben-hadad, king of Aram (1 Kgs 20:16).

The evils of drunkenness are also recounted in the writings of the prophets. Isaiah hurled biting words at "those who demand strong drink as soon as they rise in the morning, and linger into the night while wine inflames them" (5:11). Neither the priests nor the prophets "of the drunkard Ephraim" (the northern kingdom) who "stagger from strong drink" were beyond his condemnation (28:1, 3, 7). A later prophet continuing the tradition of Isaiah of Jerusalem derided the religious leaders of his time. He declared that because of their drinking, they acted like dumb relentless dogs (56:9-12). One of the most abhorrent practices against which the prophets railed was Israel's participation in the fertility cults with their licentious abandon. The prophet Hosea was especially troubled by this kind of violation of the covenant. He decried the people's idolatry and the intoxication that was part of it (Hos 4:11-14).

While the Wisdom writings acknowledge the recuperative powers of wine (Prov 31:6-7), this same tradition counsels against giving wine to kings and princes lest their ruling ability be impeded (31:4-5). Wisdom was less concerned with violation of religious or societal law than it was with prudence and practicality in social life. Drunkenness prevented one from living a balanced respectable life. This tradition characterizes drunkenness as foolishness (Sir 31:31; Prov 20:1) which will eat up one's money (21:17; 23:20f.). It takes over one's senses and subjects the drunkard to erratic behavior (23:29).

New Testament

One of the most important themes of the NT is that of the approaching return of Christ and the imminent nature of the reign of God. Although this reign had been inaugurated by the life, death and resurrection of Jesus, it had not yet fully appeared. The exact time of Christ's coming was secret and so Christians were continually admonished to be prepared and to watch (Matt 24:42-44; 25:23; Mark 13:33-37; Luke 12:35-40). Uncompromising vigilance was required since Christ would come like a thief in the night (Luke 12:39f.). Therefore, drunkenness, which impedes one's perception and generates a false sense of control, was forbidden. One who was intoxicated would be incapable of reading the signs of the times and would be unprepared for the final coming.

Drunken behavior was regarded as unbecoming a bishop, since it restricted his ability to discern and to govern and it gave bad example to the rest of the community (1 Tim 3:3; Titus 1:7). More than this, it was forbidden of anyone desirous of membership in the community and entrance into the reign of God (1 Cor 5:11; 6:10; Rom 13:13; Gal 5:21; 1 Pet 4:3). It appears that this vice was so common in the broader society that it even crept into the communal meal of the Corinthian community. Paul roundly condemned such behavior, which not only caused a division within the community between those who had means and those who did not, but it also prevented the ones intoxicated from entering deeply into the mystery of the Lord's Supper (1 Cor 11:21).

Although it was common, drunkenness was so repugnant in the society that those seeking to discredit Jesus accused him of being a drunkard (Matt 11:19; Luke 7:34). Later at the time of Pentecost when, as a result of being filled with the Spirit of God, the followers of Jesus went forward proclaiming the good news* in various tongues, their ecstatic behavior was misunderstood and they too were accused of being drunk. In their defense, Peter was quite clear in insisting that the outpouring of the Spirit and its manifold manifestations had nothing to do with drunkenness (Acts 2:13-21). Still, the headiness that results from intoxication is employed metaphorically to describe the exuberance that flowed from being filled with the Spirit, since both cause one to act out of a kind of ecstasy (Eph 5:18).

See: WINE

DIANNE BERGANT, C.S.A.

DUST

The Hebrew word for dust (*ʿāpār*) denotes the dry surface of the ground out of which God formed the first man (Gen 2:7). It also describes the ground of the grave, and for this latter reason it acquired the added connotation of commonness or worthlessness and even death itself.

Essentially, dust is a form of common dirt, the dry loose earth on the surface of the ground (see Exod 8:13; Matt 10:14; Acts 13:51). It can also refer to the powder of something that has been pulverized (see Exod 32:20). However, it is as the material integral to or associated with the beginning and the end of human existence that it is most commonly identified.

In the second account of creation (Gen 2:4b–3:24), God is figuratively portrayed as fashioning the first man in a way much like an artisan would shape a pot out of some kind of clay. The material that God used in this act of creation was this very loose and very common dust, although several major editions translate the Hebrew word as "clay." The choice of *ʿāpār* rather than *hômer* (clay) may reflect the ancient author's intent to relate this story of creation with the later report of the punishment that God passed on this man, and subsequently on all human beings who followed, immediately after the sin: "For you are dust and to dust you shall return" (3:19). The story in its entirety declares that the man's origin was from the dust and his final destiny would be in the dust as well. It is probably in this association with death that dust is most commonly understood. It became a reference to the place of death (see Job 7:21; 20:11, 21, 26) and it frequently symbolizes death itself (see Ps 104:29; Eccl 3:20).

The ephemeral quality of human existence is aptly characterized by the amorphous nature of dust (see Ps 103:14). This characterization is found especially in the Wisdom tradition which poses questions about the meaning of human life in the face of persistent ambiguity and impermanence (see Job 4:19; Sir 10:9; 17:27).

As an expansion of this basic meaning, dust came to be understood as a symbol for humiliation or self-abnegation. It was a part of the serpent's condemnation (Gen 3:14); it was thrown at David as a sign of dishonor (Ps 89:40); licking the dust was a sign of abasement (see Isa 49:23; Ps 72:9; Mic 7:17). Coupled with *ʾēper* (ashes) it symbolized the lowly character of human beings (see Gen 18:27; Job 30:19; 42:6; Sir 10:9; 17:27; 40:3). It was also a way of representing grief (Ps 44:26), and throwing dust on one's head was an important part of the rituals of mourning (see Josh 7:6; Job 2:14).

The tradition of the first man's creation from dust was used by Paul in his teaching to the Christians at Corinth about the resurrection (1 Cor 15:45-49). Just as in resembling Adam, the man of dust, we are of dust, so in resembling Christ, the man of heaven, we will become heavenly. Because we are mortal we already bear the image of Adam, but we can also bear the image of Christ and transcend our earthly existence. It is clear that in this thinking, our identity as heavenly persons is more significant than an identity as merely creatures of the dust.

See: ADAM AND EVE, DEATH

DIANNE BERGANT, C.S.A.

E

EARTH

The Bible understands the universe as composed of heaven and earth. God is the creator of this universe and therefore its God (Gen 1:1; 24:3). The earth then belongs to God (Ps 24:1). The earth is also the place of human habitation and the setting of history. The Bible looks forward to the creation of a new heaven and new earth (Isa 65:17; 66:22; 2 Pet 3:13; Rev 21:1). Christian worship uses earthly elements in its quest to express the human relationship with God.

Old Testament

Although stories of how the earth came to be are fundamentally important to the religions of the ancient Near East, ancient Israel apparently did not formulate an independent creation story. The oldest Yahwistic traditions depict Israel's God as a redeemer rather than a creator. Eventually Israel came to understand the earth as the handiwork of God, then Israel thought of its redeemer as the creator.

To speak of Yahweh as creator, Israel adopted the mythological language relating to Baal, who the Canaanites believed to be the Lord of the earth. To people like the Canaanites and Israelites with an agricultural economy, the earth on which the crops grow, the animals graze, and people live has great importance. Human beings may venture on the sea, but the sea is not their real home. The earth is where people live and die. The stories of Baal revolve around this god's attempts to become the lord of the earth. Baal has to overcome the waters (sea and river) who also wish to control the earth. Baal overcomes the waters and rules the dry earth. All that is necessary for the survival of plants, animals, and human beings are under Baal's control.

The story of creation in Genesis begins with the spirit of God hovering over the waters of chaos (Gen 1:1-2). God makes the earth arise from what was a formless wasteland. The earth then was the raw material for creation. It existed in chaos upon which God imposed order. Genesis makes no attempt to account for the presence of the earth as a formless wasteland before creation. It describes how God made the earth a place where it was possible for human beings to live. All that is necessary for life and survival on the earth is given over to God's human creature to control (Gen 1:28).

Besides the didactic and "historical" description of the creation of the earth in Genesis 1, ancient Israel celebrated God's creation in hymns of praise such as Psalm 104. This hymn portrays creation as complete and eternal. It continues in existence even when God turns away from it (Ps 104:29). This is clear from what the psalm says about the earth. The psalmist also uses the mythological motif of a divine struggle with chaos. Upon God's rebuke of the waters, they flee and the mountains and valley appear. According to Psalm 104:9, the waters can never again return to earth to the original chaos. God set up borders that these waters cannot cross. God also provided the earth with a firm foundation that cannot be shaken (Ps 104:5).

Ancient Israel imagined the earth to be a flat disk (Isa 42:5) resting on a foundation or pillars (Job 9:6). It is surrounded by the ocean (Pss 24:2; 136:6). It has four corners (Isa 11:12; Ezek 7:2; Job 37:3; 38:13) and an edge (Isa 24:26) or ends (Isa 40:8; Job 28:4; Ps 48:11; Jer 6:22; 25:32). It also has a center or navel (Ezek 38:12). Except for the implication that Jerusalem is the earth's center, ancient Israel's view of the world did not differ from that of other ancient Near Eastern peoples.

There are a few references to the expanse of the earth as the ancient Israelites conceived of it. For example, Psalm 72:8 asserts that the dominion of the king is from sea to sea from the Euphrates to the ends of the earth. A bit more explicit is the assertion that the "whole earth" over which God will become king extends from the eastern sea (probably the Persian Gulf) to the western sea (the Mediterranean Sea, Zech 14:8-9).

God has given the surface of the earth to human beings and animals for their dwelling place (Gen 1:24, 28). Plants grow from its surface (Gen 1:11-12, 29; Amos 7:2) and insects can cover its surface (Exod 10:5, 12, 15). God makes rain fall on the earth so that earth may be fruitful (Hos 6:3; Ps 147:8; Job 5:10). God gave human beings the commission to have dominion over everything that lives on the earth (Gen 1:28-29).

Though God supplies the rain, the fertility of the earth is dependent upon what human beings do. Israel's infidelity causes Yahweh's care and providence to be withdrawn (Deut 11:1-17). In particular, blood shed on the earth brought infertility (Gen 4:11-12; Num 35:33-34).

The earth recognizes the power of God. It trembles and quakes before God (Isa 13:13; Jer 10:10; Joel 2:10; Ps 18:8). When God comes down on the earth, the mountains melt like wax (Mic 1:3-4). The earth is still when God speaks words of judgment from the heavens (Ps 76:9). Along with the heavens, the earth serves as a witness in the prophetic lawsuit against Israel (Isa 1:2; Mic 6:2; see also Deut 31:28; Ps 50:4). On the Day of the Lord, the earth will mourn (Isa 24:4) and stagger like a person who is drunk (Isa 24:20). Israel's view of the eschaton involves God's creation of a new heaven and a new earth (Isa 65:17; 66:22). This is a motif that the NT adopts as its own (2 Pet 3:13; Rev 21:1).

See: CREATION, HEAVEN

LESLIE J. HOPPE, O.F.M.

New Testament

In the NT the word earth (Greek: *ge*) reflects the OT usage of two distinct Hebrew words: *'adamah* meaning earth, soil, or dust, and *'eretz* meaning land. This results in a variety of usages in the NT, though the context usually makes clear which is to be understood. The word shall be examined under the following headings:

(1) Earth as soil, dust, or land.
(2) Earth as the place of human habitation and the theatre of history.
(3) Earth in relation to heaven.

Earth as Soil, Dust, or Land. This meaning of the term is found as part of the practical imagery used by Jesus in the parables. In Mark 4 the image of the seed growing in the soil occurs both in the parable of the sower (4:3-8) and in the parable of the seed growing by itself (4:26-29). In the former the seed that falls on good soil bears fruit, while in the latter the productive nature of the land is highlighted. In John 12:24 the image of the seed falling to the earth and dying is used to convey the fruitfulness of the death of Jesus. While in these parables the benefits of the earth are shown, in Luke 6:46-49 Jesus uses the image in a non-agricultural context to bring out a different meaning. Here he contrasts the wisdom of building on a foundation of rock with the foolishness of "building a house upon the ground without a foundation. When the river burst against it, it collapsed at once and was completely destroyed." On another occasion we are told that Jesus wrote on the ground with his finger (John 8:6-8).

The Greek word *ge* is sometimes used to translate "land." This can be in a generic sense to differentiate between land and sea (Matt 14:34; Mark 4:1) or sometimes to refer to a district or region. So, for example, when Jesus raised the official's daughter to life, "the news of this spread through the whole land" (Matt 9:26). Also in Mark 15:33 at the point of Jesus' death on the cross "darkness came over the whole land until three in the afternoon."

By extension "land" came to refer to "the Promised Land" (the OT *'eretz-yisrael*). This is referred to as the "land of promise" in Hebrews 11:9 and in Acts 7:3 as "the land that I will show you" (quoting Gen 12:1). In the Sermon on the Mount the meek (i.e., those who are slow to anger) are told that "they will inherit the land" (Matt 5:5). Here Matthew is relying on Psalm 37:11 where this phrase occurs. In the psalm it obviously refers to the Promised Land but in the context of the Sermon on the Mount the meaning has shifted to embrace the idea of "the reign of God."

The Earth as Place of Human Habitation. With this usage the earth (sometimes translated as world) is the theatre of human history and therefore the focus of God's salvific activity which is supremely manifested in Jesus. The disciples who follow him are to be "salt of the earth and light of the world" (Matt 5:13). These metaphors emphasize a specific mission in the world which involves believers in an active role of witnessing to the power of the gospel. Elsewhere Jesus' mission is depicted in terms that highlight the tension which is inherent in the proclamation of God's reign. This proclamation will inevitably lead to conflict with those who are opposed to its values.

This is stated dramatically in the Gospels: "Do not think that I have come to bring peace upon the earth. I have come to bring not peace but the sword" (Matt 10:34). In Luke this tension is expressed through the image of fire, "I have come to set the earth on fire, and how I wish it were blazing already" (12:49). This is a purifying fire which will meet with acceptance or rejection, and as a source of conflict it will even divide families. This division is not Jesus' intention for the earth but is rather an inevitable consequence of his message. As history unfolds believers are invited to trust in the faithfulness of God who will not be slow to answer the prayer for justice. Jesus expresses a fear that they will not persevere in their task: "I tell you, he will see to it that justice is done for them speedily. But when the Son of Man comes, will he find faith on earth?" (Luke 18:8).

The movement of history is such that the earth as we know it will come to an end. The NT looks forward to the second coming of Christ when the complete victory of God over evil and death will be finally achieved. In the writing of the first century this was often spoken about in the language of the apocalyptic genre, and the destruction of the Jerusalem Temple by the Romans in 70 CE was interpreted in this light. So in Luke 21:23 Jesus speaks of a "terrible calamity that will come upon the earth." However he encourages the disciples not to be overwhelmed by events: "For that day will assault everyone who lives on the face of the earth. Be vigilant at all times and pray that you will have the strength to escape the tribulations that are imminent and to stand before the Son of Man" (Luke 21:35). In the Book of Revelation this unfolding of history is portrayed in a similar way and the theme of endurance is emphasized here too. "Because you have kept my message of endurance, I will keep you safe in the time of trial that is going to come to the whole world to test the inhabitants of the earth" (Rev 3:10). Elsewhere in Revelation the physical earth is depicted as cooperating in the work of salvation as it protects the woman who symbolizes the Church (see Rev 12:9). In contrast with this, society's attraction to evil, symbolized by the beast, is stated thus: "Fascinated, the whole world followed after the beast" (Rev 13:3).

Earth in Relation to Heaven. Given the limitations of history and the effects of sin it is not surprising that the earth is often spoken about in terms of its relationship to heaven. On occasion this is simply by way of considering the whole of creation as made up of heaven and earth. Jesus gives thanks to God who is "Lord of heaven and earth" (Matt 11:25). The NT reflects the cosmology of the ancient Near East which considered the world as divided into "the heavens, the earth, and the sea" (Acts 4:23). Or, as written in Revelation 5:3, "No one in heaven, on earth or under the earth was able to open the scroll." Not surprisingly this subdivision tends to attribute higher value to the heavenly realm. In Acts 7:49 (which is quoting Isa 66:1-2) the heavens are considered as God's throne while the earth is his footstool (see also Matt 5:34-35). Jesus encourages the disciples by emphasizing the necessary bond between the two realms. They are to pray that "God's will be done on earth as in heaven" (Matt 6:10), and they are to have confidence that when "two of you agree on earth about anything for which they are to pray, it shall be granted to them by my heavenly Father" (Matt 18:19). So too the importance of the leadership role assigned to Peter is expressed in terms of binding and loosing on earth and in heaven (see Matt 16:19).

In other places the earth is considered negatively as the place where sin dwells (Mark 2:10). In the Gospel of John, which uses dualistic metaphors to express the life that God offers, the earth is representative of what is from below. "The one who is of the earth is earthly and speaks of earthly things. But the one who comes from heaven is above all" (John 3:31). Jesus, when he is "lifted up from the earth" (John 12:32), will be the source of salvation for all. However,

the Fourth Gospel in no way disparages the created order: "For God so loved the world that he gave his only Son" (John 3:16). Jesus' task was to glorify God on earth (17:4) and when he was leaving his disciples he prayed not that they be taken out of the world but that they be kept from the evil one, "For they do not belong to the world any more than I belong to the world" (John 17:16). The notion of belonging to the world is a Johannine metaphor for unbelief and being cut off from God.

Paul too sometimes uses the contrast between heaven and earth to emphasize the distinction between the temporal and the eternal, the divine and the merely human. "For we know that if our earthly dwelling, a tent, should be destroyed, we have a building from God, a dwelling not made with hands, eternal in heaven" (2 Cor 5:1). So for this reason believers are urged to "think of what is above, not of what is on earth" (Col 3:2). The emphasis here is on the values that are appropriate to living according to their new life in Christ. It is not to be read as a downgrading of human existence as such. In trying to express the reality of the resurrection Paul again resorts to language which relies on the contrast between the earthly and the heavenly. "The first man [Adam] was from the earth, earthly; the second man [Christ] from heaven. . . . Just as we have borne the image of the earthly one, we shall also bear the image of the heavenly one" (1 Cor 15:47-49). This distinction is also found in other places in the NT. The author of Hebrews notes that our ancestors in the faith "acknowledged themselves to be strangers and aliens on earth" because of their desire for a better homeland, "a heavenly one" (Heb 11:13, 16). In the Letter of James the wisdom which is "from above" is sharply contrasted with that which is "earthly" and believers are urged to pursue the former (see Jas 3:15-17).

It has already been noted that in the Book of Revelation the earth is the place where human history unfolds. However, in the eschatological orientation of the book this history is passing away and a new era is anticipated. The present order which is corrupted by sin will come to an end when "heaven and earth flee from the one who sits upon the throne" (Rev 20:11). Here the ultimate victory of God is celebrated: "Then I saw a new heaven and a new earth. The former heaven and the former earth had passed away and the sea was no more" (Rev 21:1). This marks the beginning of the vision of the heavenly Jerusalem when God's dwelling will be with the human race.

The NT shares with the OT a sense of the goodness of creation and can celebrate that "the earth and its fullness is the Lord's" (1 Cor 10:6). The natural world with all its blessings is a gift from the Lord of heaven and earth and is to be rejoiced in as such. However, the earth as it is now constituted is deeply affected by the results of sin and the ravages of human history. It is passing away and Christians look forward to the consummation of all history when all things in heaven and on earth will be summed up in Christ (Eph 1:10). As we await that time our calling remains focused on working for the reign of God and being "the salt of the earth and the light of the world."

See: CREATION, ESCHATOLOGY, HEAVEN, REIGN OF GOD

SEAN GOAN, C.P.

Pastoral-Liturgical Tradition

Christian worship is earthy as well as spiritual. In the liturgy we express and experience our relationship with God not only in our hearts and minds, but also with our whole bodies, and as well through other persons and the whole of creation.

We worship, usually, in a church building, which is constructed of stone and brick, wood and metal, glass and plastic; our churches are built on and into the earth. In the Rite of Dedication of a Church the plot of land on which the new church will be erected is blessed, the foundation stone is put in place with prayer, the interior of the church is sprinkled with holy water, the altar and walls are anointed with oil, incense is burned and candles lighted, the chalice and paten are blessed.

Our worship also involves linens of cotton, wool, and other materials, books, candles, and crosses. Churches are decorated with statues, pictures and icons, metalwork and woodwork. There are doors and windows and pews. Organs, guitars and other instruments are crafted from wood, metal, gut, and synthetics.

The central symbols of our worship come from the earth: the water of baptism, bread and wine of Eucharist, oils used for baptism, confirmation, ordination, and anointing of the sick. These sacramental symbols are carried or enclosed in fonts made of stone or metal; in cups of metal, ceramic or glass; on plates of wood, metal or other materials; in vials of glass. Other important liturgies employ palms or other branches, and ashes made by burning leftover branches.

In the liturgy of Christian burial the place of committal is blessed, and the body of the dead person (or the ashes) is committed to the earth (or the deep or other resting place) "for we are dust and unto dust we shall return."

Prayers are provided by the Church for earth-related concerns. For example, the Roman Missal of 1970 includes Masses and prayers for productive land, after the harvest, in time of famine or for those who suffer from famine, in time of earthquake, for rain, for fine weather, and to avert storms.

In the Book of Blessings (1990) there are prayers and liturgies of blessing for a variety of buildings, for an athletic field, for various means of transportation, for boats and fishing gear, for tools and other equipment for work, for animals, fields and flocks, for seeds at planting time, at harvest time, and for the food we eat.

Our ancestors in the faith were much more attuned to the earth than we are today. The Roman Ritual of 1614, for example, contained a wealth of blessings for the earth and things of the earth: for ale, beer, and wine; for animals, bees, cattle, fowl, goats, horses, lambs, sheep, swine, and even silkworms; for bread, butter, cakes, cheese, eggs, fruit, grapes, herbs, lard, oats; for fields, fire, chalk, lilies, medicine, mountain-meadows, gold, incense and myrrh, pastures, seedlings, vineyards, and many other things. The same liturgical book provided for processions for averting tempests, for fine weather, for rain, and in time of famine.

At times during the liturgical year the Christian people have sometimes abstained from eating animals or animal products.

Today many questions are being raised regarding the place of earth—creation—in Christian theology and in our liturgy. For example, the prayers and practices of the past arise out of the worldview of an agricultural society; this is still an important influence today. Yet large segments of the human population are no longer closely connected to agriculture. How can we both respect those who are still engaged in farming and fishing, and as well reflect the experience and thinking of those who live in cities?

Some believe that the liturgical use of the earth in the past has expressed a utilitarian and human-centered view of creation. That is, creation has not been respected for its own sake, but only to the extent that is of use to humankind; this is a "human-centered" view of things. In reaction, some today wish to honor creation for its own sake by speaking of "creation-centered theology."

In addition, traditional practices and views imply that the relationship between humankind and the earth is one of human domination. Today, many would prefer to speak of human stewardship or care for the earth. Even these views tend to separate humanity from the rest of creation, and place it in a position of superiority vis-à-vis the earth; some feel that even these views are unfaithful to God's intention in creation.

The words "environment" and "creation" may be used in ways that imply different kinds of relationship between earth and humanity. The former term can be understood to separate humankind from the rest of creation, whereas the latter includes humans with other animals and with the plants, earth, sky, and waters. These issues are the subject of much discussion today.

In the past, earth was considered to share in the fallenness of original sin; earth, as well as humanity, was considered to be basically sinful and in need of redemption. The liturgies of the Church, therefore, were full of prayers of exorcism, in which God was asked to rid the earth of this fallenness. Today we are much more positive about humankind and about the earth and no longer feel a need for prayers of exorcism. Instead, we are inclined to liturgies of blessing, recognizing the fundamental goodness of all of God's creation.

In the liturgy, the earth is often mediated through human labor and creativity. Bread is derived from grain sown, grown, harvested, milled, and baked by women and men. Wine too is the product of human labor and creativity. Oil is pressed from olives or seeds. Today some feel that this work of co-creation with God ought to be better recognized in our liturgies.

See: CREATION

J. FRANK HENDERSON

ECSTASY

Ecstasy is a mental state that involves a suspension of consciousness. It is an effect of possession by a spiritual power. This possession may be voluntary or involuntary, spontaneous or induced, partial or complete. Ecstasy is a term that covers a variety of conditions: trance, possession, dreams, visions, frenzy, auditions. The purpose of ecstasy is to make communication with God possible. Sometimes ecstasy refers to patterns of behavior manifested by a person who is communicating with the divine world. Among these characteristics are visions, compulsive actions, loss of consciousness, and slurred speech. These behaviors are the clues that the one exhibiting them has been caught up with the divine.

The Ancient Near East

There are several examples in ancient Near Eastern literature of ecstatic experiences depicted in a positive light. Eighteenth century BCE texts from Mari (a city of the middle Euphrates) describe how various gods invade people without their consent. The king is to recognize the words these people speak as direct communications from the gods. In the story of Wen-Amon that dates from the twelfth century BCE, the attitude of the Prince of Byblos changed toward Wen-Amon because of the words of someone who unintentionally became ecstatic during a sacrificial feast and spoke positively of Wen-Amon. The prince assumed that the ecstatic utterance was a message from the gods. During a siege, Zakir, king of Hamath (ninth century BCE), prays to his god Baalshamem who responds by speaking through a group of seers in ecstasy.

The Old Testament

There are several instances in the Bible when certain activities take on the characteristics of ecstasy. Abram is in a trance when God speaks with him (Gen 15:12). Numbers 11:25-29 speaks about the spirit that was on Moses resting on the elders so that they prophesied. David's dancing before the ark may have been a technique for inducing ecstasy (2 Sam 6:12-23). Both Amos (Amos 7–9) and Isaiah (Isaiah 6) appear to have ecstatic experiences that led them to their prophetic ministries. Ezekiel has several ecstatic experiences as he describes the spirit's lifting him, falling on him, transporting him, and entering him (Ezek 2:2; 3:14, 23-27; 8:3; 11:1, 5; 37:1).

Ecstasy appears in the Bible as technique associated with prophecy but used by non-Israelite prophets to make possible communication with their god. The prophets of Baal from Phoenicia and Syria organized themselves in groups. They danced and even wounded themselves so as to bring themselves into a state of ecstasy (1 Kgs 18:28-29). At one time biblical scholarship was concerned with making a clear distinction between these experiences and those characteristic of Israelite prophets. Some scholars simply denied that the prophets whose oracles are found in the Bible were ecstatics. Others said that while the prophets may have had ecstatic experiences, they delivered their oracles after such experiences. A third approach was to focus on the content of the oracle and away from the ecstatic means by which the oracle came to the prophet.

Ecstatic behaviors apparently were recognized as signs of divine choice and a mark of authority. That is certainly the impression one has when reading the account of the elders in Numbers 11. A similar impression is left by the account of Saul's election (1 Sam 9:1–10:13). Saul is told that he will meet a band of men who will be acting like prophets. The story does not describe the specifics of their behavior. When he does meet them, they are playing musical instruments. Perhaps they were trying to induce a trance. It had to be the type of trance that allowed them to carry on a semblance of normal activity. When Saul met this group the spirit of Yahweh possessed him (1 Sam 10:5-6). This is a sign that God chose him to be king. Saul began acting like a prophet though the text does not describe the exact nature of his actions. People recognized his actions as prophet-like and asked, "Is Saul also among the prophets?" (1 Sam 10:11). As the story makes clear, Saul's spirit possession was a sign of God's choice of Saul as king not as a prophet. These stories show that there was some identifiable behavior that people recognized as prophetic and that they evaluated positively. Unfortunately the precise nature of these behaviors is not clear.

The question "Is Saul also among the prophets?" is asked a second time (1 Sam 19:24). The question is posed during the story of David's rise to power. At one point in the story Saul again exhibited a type of behavior that people recognized as typical of prophets. He stripped off his clothes and "remained in a prophetic state" all night before Samuel. This time Saul's behavior was uncontrolled. His ecstasy is driving him mad (1 Sam 18:10-11). Not all people in Israel then evaluated ecstasy in the same way. Some saw ecstasy as an expected part of the prophet's behavior. It was a sign of divine election. Others saw ecstatic behavior as a sign of mental illness. This shows that it is difficult to generalize about this phenomenon. Its appearance was ambiguous.

The call narratives of some prophets appear to reflect some type of ecstatic experience—especially those that relate a visionary experience of God. Several prophets describe a summons into the deliberations of the divine council: Micaiah ben Imlah (1 Kgs 22:19), Isaiah (Isaiah 6), and Ezekiel (Ezekiel 1). Elements of ecstatic experience surface throughout the Book of Ezekiel. There are visions (ch. 1), transportations (ch. 10), dumbness (3:26), and paralysis (3:25). Sometimes these have been seen as signs of psychological abnormality. It is clear that they represent typical ways of legitimating the prophet's word by showing that he was chosen by God to deliver that word. The prophet's ecstatic experiences prove that the prophet is genuine.

The function of stories about ecstatic behavior was to legitimate an individual as an authentic intermediary between God and Israel. For the most part, Israel tolerated the behaviors broadly described as ecstatic because of the stress caused by the social change experienced in Israelite society and the threats brought to bear on that society by aggressive and powerful neighbors. When prophecy arose in ancient Israel, instability marked its society. The prophets served as intermediaries who sought to restore Israelite society by renewing its contacts with its national God. Ecstasy was simply one of the mechanics of mediation.

Ancient Israelite society assumed that God chose human intermediaries directly. The choice is obvious because of some mystical experience that an individual undergoes. Sometimes a person will try to induce such an experience. The Bible does not view such attempts sympathetically as is evident from the descriptions of the prophets of Baal (1 Kgs 18:25-29). Apparently ancient Israel considered inducing ecstatic experience as compromising Yahweh's freedom. In fact, the call narratives of the prophets usually show them resisting the choice that God made. Sometimes this occurs because of their feelings of moral inadequacy (Isa 6:5). Other times it is a feeling of incompetence (Jer 1:6). Supported by their ecstatic experience, the prophets engage in efforts to cause social change, to reaffirm traditional values, and to reestablish social stability.

New Testament

In the NT ecstatic experiences mark special moments such as the events surrounding the birth of Jesus. The figure of Zechariah stands out here (Luke 1:67-79). Jesus has several ecstatic experiences: the Spirit's descent at his baptism (Mark 1:9-11), his being led by the Spirit into the desert (Luke 4:1), the transfiguration (Mark 9:2-8). Several important figures of the early Church experience ecstasy: the apostles on Pentecost (Acts 2:2-4), Stephen's vision during his martyrdom (Acts 7:55), and Peter's trance (Acts 10:10). Certainly Paul's conversion took place during ecstasy (Acts 9; 22; 26). Paul says that he speaks with tongues (1 Cor 14:6, 18), hears voices (2 Cor 12:9), that he journeyed to the third heaven (2 Cor 12:2-4). John says that he was "caught up in spirit" on the Lord's day when he had his visions (Rev 1:10).

The Bible does not define ecstasy nor describe it in specific terms. It simply assumes that the force of ecstatic experience can overtake a person. That is the significance of phrases such as "the spirit rested on them" (Num 11:25-26); "the spirit entered into me" (Ezek 2:2); the spirit of the Lord is upon me (Isa 61:1); the spirit clothed itself with . . . (see Judg 6:34; 1 Chr 12:19; 2 Chr 24:20); "the spirit lifted me up" (Ezek 8:3). While these expressions do not necessarily imply ecstasy, they do show that people believed that God could come to possess a person for the sake of communicating with the wider community. In other words, ecstasy has a social function in the Bible.

Pastoral-Liturgical Tradition

Today people who consider ecstatic experiences as authentic encounters with God tend to consider these to be individual matters. A notable exception are claims made by visionaries who assert that Jesus or Mary has given them a particular message for the Church. Charismatics, both Protestant and Catholic, also claim to convey important messages to believers. The Church usually takes an active role in evaluating the credentials of ecstatics when they claim to have a message to convey. Still some groups will support particular ecstatics without relying on the opinions of ecclesiastical authorities. This is true when the ecstatic delivers a message that is in conformity with those groups' expectations and beliefs. Even when these groups reject a particular ecstatic messenger, they see this as a rejection of an individual who may be misguided or a fraud. They do not see this as a rejection of a belief that Jesus or Mary can chose an individual as an intermediary.

Just as people in ancient Israel were able to recognize prophetic behavior because it followed a predictable pattern, so groups that accept ecstatic messengers have specific expectations about their behaviors. They have notions about how intermediaries should act and speak. That is why the behaviors of visionaries and their messages are stereotypical. People who expect visions know how visionaries are to act and what they are to say.

Stories about genuinely ecstatic behavior occupy a small space in the Bible. Current anthropological studies are providing a framework to understand the few stories that do occur. Ecstatic behavior fulfills a certain function in society, and in ancient Israel it served to legitimate prophets and their message. The personal experiences that the prophets had of God are most easily described in terms that evoke the idea of ecstasy. While the function that ecstasy had in ancient Israelite religious life needs to be recognized, still what was important about the prophets was the content of what they preached. Focusing on this content should not result in dismissal of the role that ecstasy had in the biblical tradition. Still this role is subordinate to the prophetic word itself. This word calls people of every age to examine the quality of their relationship with God. It is a relationship whose health is based not on the number and quality of religious experiences but on fidelity to the commitment that every believer has made to recognize the absolute claim God has on our life.

See: PROPHECY/PROPHET, VISION

LESLIE J. HOPPE, O.F.M.

EDEN

Eden has come to be a synonym for paradise. The word itself is a form of the Hebrew word for "delight" and is close to the Akkadian *edinu,* meaning plain or steppe. Although the rivers in the garden bear the names of genuine rivers, this garden of delight is difficult to locate.

It is not clear whether Eden and the garden are identical or distinct. The Genesis story first says that God planted a garden *in* Eden (an ancient land in the east) and there placed the man (2:8). It then states that God settled the man in the garden *of* Eden (v. 15). Eden also appears in some of the later prophets where it is identified as the garden of the Lord (Isa 51:3) or the garden of God (Ezek 28:13). (The notion of sacred groves, where human beings might enjoy communion with God, was popular in the ancient Near East.) In the Genesis account, both the double mention of placing the man in the garden and the discrepancy about the garden itself suggest the presence of different versions of the story. The report of the trees in the garden is further evidence of various versions. The tree of life holds the place of honor in the middle of the garden. The mention of the tree of the knowledge of good and bad seems to be a literary afterthought (v. 9). This suggests that an early version or source had only the tree of life and the second tree was added to the story in order to explain why humankind was barred from that first tree.

The trees play important roles in the drama. Since the man was made of the dust of the ground (perishable material), immortality could only be achieved through the agency of some other being. The tree of life was such an agent. Eating of it would guarantee further life. The second tree represents something entirely different. "Good and bad" is an expression that includes the entire range of reality between the complementary pair. (Other examples include flesh and blood, east and west.) Knowledge of good and bad denotes comprehensive knowledge in general.

A river sprang up in the garden and then divided into four branches after it flowed out of it. Two of these branches, the Tigris and the Euphrates, are well known even today. The locations of Havilah (v. 11) and of Cush (v. 13) are uncertain and so the locations of the Pishon and the Gihon have baffled interpreters down through the ages. The highly symbolic character of the entire narrative would suggest that this was no ordinary river. Rather, it was the primordial river from which flows all (four) rejuvenating waters. Therefore, neither it nor all of its branches can be geographically located.

In the beginning of the narrative, God plants a garden and there places the man to till it and to guard it (2:8, 15). At the end of the narrative, the man and the woman are driven from the garden and God stations the cherubim to guard the way to the tree of life (3:24). The role of the man was to till the ground and thus, in cooperation with God who sends rain, to enable the barren earth to bring forth life (2:5). At the end of the account, he and his wife are driven from the garden of delight, which he was to till (see 2:15), back into the wilderness where the ground will bring forth thorns and thistles (3:18). The man and the woman no longer have access to the sacred grove where they enjoyed communion with God.

See: CREATION, DEATH, HUMANKIND, SIN

DIANNE BERGANT, C.S.A.

EGYPT

Humans have lived in Egypt since 10,000 BCE. In the fourth millennium BCE, Egypt became the first national state. It was a great civilization for about two thousand years before the rise of the Davidic monarchy in Israel. The pyramids were standing for fifteen hundred years when Solomon began to build the Temple. The social, political, and cultural achievements of Egyptian civilization are beyond calculation. Still the influence of Egypt on other ancient peoples in general and ancient Israel in particular was not commensurate with these achievements.

One reason for the surprising meager influence that Egypt had over ancient Israel was the geographical isolation of Egypt. The settled area of Egypt is a strip of arable land ranging between three and five miles wide on either side of the Nile. Deserts separated it from other cultural centers. Egypt did develop commercial ties with the coastal cities of Phoenicia north of Israel, and Egypt's political influence over ancient Israel was strong at times. Under Thutmoses III (1502–1448 BCE) Egypt gained control over Canaan,* though it controlled the region through local rulers. The breakdown of Egyptian hegemony in Canaan in the thirteenth century BCE helped make possible the settlement of the Israelites there. Culturally Israel was oriented toward the East and the Semitic Mesopotamian civilizations.

For the biblical tradition Egypt is a paradox. The core memory of this tradition centers on the liberation that Israel's ancestors experienced from slavery in Egypt. The first victory that Yahweh won for Israel was over Pharaoh and his army at the Red Sea

(Exodus 15). Still Deuteronomy admonishes, "You shall not abhor any of the Egyptians, because you were an alien residing in their land" (23:7b). Perhaps the reason for this ambivalence was because Egypt served as a place of refuge. Abraham (Gen 12:10-20) and Jacob's families (Genesis 46) went to Egypt in time of famine. After the fall of Jerusalem, some Judahites who could not accept the Babylonian hegemony went to Egypt (Jer 41:11-18). There was a Jewish colony at Elephantine and another at Leontopolis. The Ptolemaic period witnessed significant Jewish settlement in Egypt, with Alexandria having a sizeable Jewish population. The Gospel of Matthew has Joseph taking Mary and Jesus to Egypt to avoid Herod's plot against the child (2:13-15).

The most significant area of Egyptian influence in ancient Israel was in the Wisdom tradition. Proverbs 22:17–24:22 is a slightly reworked version of an Egyptian sapiential text entitled "The Wisdom of Amenemope." The conduit for this text and other wisdom material that reflect the Egyptian sapiential tradition may have been the Egyptian scribes that help set up the royal administration of David and Solomon. At least one of Solomon's officials bears an Egyptian name (1 Kgs 4:3).

A most significant aspect of Egyptian religious belief was its notion of the afterlife. No other ancient civilization had such an elaborately developed belief in life after death. Survival after death depended on the preservation of the body, so the Egyptians perfected the process of mummification. Egyptian religion was a complex matter. Amenhotep IV [Ikhnaton] (1377–1358 BCE) tried to simplify it by promoting the worship of a single god, Aton. He was unsuccessful. After his death, the Egyptians reverted to their traditional patterns of worship and attempts were made to obliterate Amenhotep's name from all records.

See: EXODUS, PASSOVER

LESLIE J. HOPPE, O.F.M.

EL/ELOHIM

Old Testament

El is a generic Semitic word meaning "god." It may come from a root meaning "power."

Ugaritic/Canaanite Background of El. In the Canaanite pantheon El is the father god. He is the creator and the king of all creation. He is the most high god who rules the other gods. He is called the Father of Years and the Bull. His consort is Asherah of the Sea. In the Ugaritic texts found at Ras Shamra, however, El is old and his power seems to be diminishing in favor of his son Baal.*

Early Use of the Name El. In the stories of the ancestors the image of El merges with the God of Abraham, Isaac, and Jacob. The El titles that are connected to specific sanctuaries in Canaan*—El Elyon of Jerusalem (Gen 14:18), El Roi of Beer-lahai-roi (Gen 16:7-14), El Olam of Beersheba (Gen 21:33), El Bethel (Gen 31:13; 35:7)—are seen as titles of the one god whose proper name is Yahweh.* El is the God of Israel (Gen 33:20), the God of the family rather than of a specific sanctuary.

El Shaddai is the most frequent title given to God in the ancestral stories (Gen 17:1; 28:3; 35:11; 43:14; 48:3; 49:25). This title, which seems to come from the root meaning "breasts," is interpreted as "God of the mountains." The Greek translation of the OT renders the term as *pantokrator*, "Almighty." It is this title which is specifically linked to Yahweh in the Mosaic stories of the gift of God's proper name: "As [El Shaddai] I appeared to Abraham, Isaac and Jacob, but my name [Yahweh] I did not make known to them" (Exod 6:3).

The term El is applied to the God of Israel throughout the OT. The characteristics of the Canaanite El are appropriated by Yahweh: creator, father, king. The image of the Ancient One in Daniel's vision is modeled on the figure of the old and regal Canaanite god (Dan 7:9-10).

Elohim. Elohim is also a generic word meaning "god." In the Hebrew Bible Elohim is the most common term used for God, appearing over 25,000 times. The word is plural in form, which may reflect a polytheistic background. It is used as a plural to refer to gods of the other nations (Exod 12:12; Josh 24:14-15). It is also used in a singular sense referring to individual pagan gods: Dagon of the Philistines (Judg 16:23-24), Astarte of Sidon, Chemosh of the Moabites, and Milcom of the Ammonites (1 Kgs 11:33), Baalzebub of Ekron (2 Kgs 1:16).

In the Hebrew Bible the sense of Elohim is always singular when it refers to Israel's God. The plural form is often interpreted as a plural of majesty. The plural form sometimes carries over into the verb as in Genesis 1:26: "Let us make [humans] in our image." The plural suggests a heavenly council of lesser gods, "sons of God" *(bene 'elohim)*, such as is found in the prologue to the Book of Job (Job 1:6). In Psalm 82 human judges are given the rank of gods: "You are gods, all of you sons of the Most High" (Ps 82:6; cf. 82:2). The plural form is ambiguous in the temptation story. The serpent says, "You will be like *'elohim*" (Gen 3:5). This can mean "like gods" or "like God."

The word *'elohim* is sometimes used in the sense of powerful or superhuman. At the beginning of creation a *ruah 'elohim*, either a "mighty wind" or the "Spirit of God," hovers over the waters of primeval chaos (Gen 1:2).

New Testament

The common NT term for God, *theos,* is the Greek term which corresponds to the Hebrew word *'elohim*. The God of Abraham, Isaac, and Jacob (Matt 22:32) is the one God who is now revealed in Christ (John 1:18). Christ is the image of God (Col 1:15), Emmanuel, God-with-us (Matt 1:23). Through him we come to know the everlasting God (see John 17:3).

See: BAAL, CANAAN, GOD, YAHWEH

IRENE NOWELL, O.S.B.

ELDERS

The "elder," whether understood as a designation for an older and wiser member of the community or as a more formalized designation of a leadership role within the community, is an important term in the Bible.

Old Testament

The Meaning of the Word. The most common word for "elder" in the OT is *zaqen,* "bearded" and thus "older." It occurs some 178 times, and has two major meanings. In about one third of the texts, it signifies either old age or an older person. In the remaining texts, it designates an official role, the elder. In nearly every case, this latter usage is tied to an explicit role or place, i.e., *the* elder, or elder *of.* . . . Thus it refers to the holder of an official position or title, and not just a revered senior citizen.

Old Age. Long life was a major ideal for the ancient Israelite. "I shall dwell in the house of the LORD for many long years" (Ps 23:6); "My son, keep in mind my commands, for many days and years of life, and peace, will they bring you" (Prov 3:2). Such a wish is common in the Psalms (Pss 21:5; 116:9) and in Deuteronomy, where the command to obey the law is often accompanied by "so you may live long in the land" (Deut 5:16; 6:3; 8:1; 11:21; 22:6-7). The prophets, too, express a dramatic vision of long life: "No longer shall there be in it, an infant who lives but a few days, or an old man who does not round out his full lifetime; he dies a mere youth who reaches but a hundred years" (Isa 65:20; see 53:10).

But old age is also seen as a time of physical failure and decline and is often lamented (Gen 18:12; 1 Kgs 1:4; Ruth 1:11). Qoheleth 12 is a long poem about the weaknesses of aging. Getting old brings fear and pessimism: "Seventy is the sum of our years, or eighty, if we are strong, and most of them are fruitless toil and they pass quickly and we drift away" (Ps 90:10); "Cast me not off in my old age, as my strength fails, forsake me not" (Ps 71:9; see

71:18). At the same time, old age brings wisdom (Ps 119:100; Job 32:4-7) and a time of respect and blessing (Exod 20:12; Prov 23:22). Characteristics include health (Deut 34:7), many children (Gen 50:23; Job 42:16-17), righteousness (Ps 92:15), and wealth (Gen 24:1). Indeed, Abraham epitomizes blessing on old age: God does not call him until he is 75, and he dies content when he is 175 years old (see Gen 25:7-8). Because old age is both a blessing and a time of physical and mental dissolution, the command to honor and respect parents and the old is taken very seriously (Lev 19:32).

The Office of Elder. Because of the shortness of ancient lifespans, the wisdom and leadership of the older members of tribe and society were valued highly. Like many other nations around it (Babylon, Ugarit, Phoenicia, Moab), Israel institutionalized the role of the elder in local government. David's gifts to elders in the towns of Judah (1 Sam 30:26-31) make it clear these elders were part of every town's administration. They are sometimes found together with a governor or royal appointee (2 Kgs 10:5; Isa 3:14), but in smaller towns usually functioned alone (1 Kgs 21:8; 2 Kgs 23:1; Deut 21:1-9). In the capital cities of Samaria and Jerusalem, they may even have become part of a hereditary nobility (2 Kgs 10:1; Lam 2:9-10). In the postexilic period, we find other terms for leading citizens, and there is no mention of elders in either Ezra or Nehemiah. This suggests the role of the elders died out after the Exile.

Elders played several roles in town affairs. They formed a council of advisors on issues (Jer 18:18; Ezek 7:26) or to handle crises (Lev 4:15; Deut 21:1-9). They served as judges of local issues, particularly those based on traditional family matters or relationships. Thus, for example, laws in Deuteronomy deal with a rebellious son (Deut 21:19), the protection of a virgin (Deut 22:15), and levirate marriage customs (Deut 25:9). This latter function provides the setting for the most touching story of elders dealing with personal issues, the Book

of Ruth. Boaz agrees to marry Ruth in the council of elders meeting at the city gate and his declaration is ratified by them (Ruth 4:1-12). These judicial roles were limited by the offices of royal judges appointed to settle disputes the elders could not reach agreement on (Deut 16:18-19), that involved more than one community (Deut 21:1-3), or were on appeal (Deut 19:18-19); and by the priestly areas of judgment in ritual and purity matters (Leviticus 13–14; Ezek 44:24); and of course by the role of the king himself, the supreme judge of the land (1 Kgs 3:16-28). Finally, elders are mentioned in connection with sharing the religious leadership of the people in the early traditions. They appear with Moses and Aaron at Mount Sinai (Exod 24:1, 9) and the Spirit came upon them to assist Moses in Numbers 11.

An office of elders is also noted for the whole people, or on occasion for a tribe. These "elders of the nation" seemed to have been chosen as advisors to national policy makers. They are consulted in times of war (1 Kgs 20:7), and apparently even had a strong influence over such political decisions as rejecting or supporting the king (2 Sam 3:17; 2 Kgs 6:32). If they are the same as "the people of the land" (Jer 26:17), they were a major force in limiting or maintaining the king's ability to act (see 2 Kgs 21:24). Such a national group of elders remains somewhat shadowy, however. They appear mostly in the Pentateuch and historical books as upholders of the covenant (Deut 31:9; Josh 8:33). They are so idealized that their historical role is problematic.

Pastoral Analysis. Just as old age is honored in the OT because it carries on the traditions of the people and reflects wisdom, practical prudence, and experience, so the office of elder reflects a deep respect for lessons learned by hard experience, care and concern to maintain and uphold the practices of the nation and its religious law, and especially of justice and covenant rights for all. In ancient times when life was short and disasters often turned life upside down in villages and small nations, the office of elders maintained confident continuity with the ways of our forbears and provided a chance for every member of the community to be heard and to express a viewpoint on common matters. All ministerial office in Judaeo-Christian tradition owes much to those elements of service to, and respect for, every member of the community of faith that elders represented by their office.

See: COMMUNITY, GATE, JUDGES, MINISTRY, PRIEST

LAWRENCE BOADT, C.S.P.

New Testament

Presbyteros, the Greek word translated as "elder" or "presbyter" in the NT, has various referents. It is used in its masculine form to refer to men of considerable age in comparison with a younger generation (Acts 2:17; 1 Tim 5:1), while the feminine refers to older women (1 Tim 5:2). It also designates an official within Judaism as well as early Christianity. Finally, the seer writing the Book of Revelation uses the term in relation to heavenly beings.

Jewish Officials. It is within the Gospels and the early and later chapters of Acts (Acts 4:5, 8, 23; 6:12; 23:14; 24:1; 25:15) that we encounter *presbyteroi* with reference to officials within Judaism. They were members of local councils presiding over Jewish communities within cities and villages (Luke 7:3), formed the governing body in local synagogues, and were lay members of the Sanhedrin along with the priests, scribes, and perhaps even some Pharisees. Their task seems to have been primarily judicial as the phrase "traditions of the elders" (Matt 15:2; Mark 7:3) suggests. In the Matthean Gospel they are generally linked with the "chief priests," and in Mark and Luke with the "chief priests and scribes" as the group responsible for the arrest (Matt 26:3-4, 47; Mark 14:43; Luke 22:52) and trial of Jesus (Matt 26:57; 27:1, 12, 20; Mark 14:53; 15:1).

Within the Early Christian Churches. The ease with which the writer of the Acts of the Apostles moves between the use of *presbyteroi* or "elders" in relation to Jewish officials on the one hand (Acts 4:5-6, 8, 23; 6:12) and its use as a designation of particular members of the emerging Christian community on the other (Acts 11:30; 14:23; 15:2) suggests the influence of the earlier structure on the shaping of latter. Interestingly, although Luke recounts the appointment of "elders" within the churches of Antioch by Paul and Barnabas, there is no reference to "elders" in the Pauline letters which may point to the later emergence of this group out of the earlier charismatic and diaconal foundations of the Church (1 Cor 12:4-5). Within Acts, the Christian elders perform the administrative function of the distribution of famine relief in the churches of Judea (11:30); and they are members—with the apostles under the leadership of James (21:18)—of a distinctive body in the founding Church of Jerusalem: "When they arrived in Jerusalem they were welcomed by that church, as well as by the apostles and the presbyters" (15:4; see also 15:2, 6, 22, 23). One task of this group is decision-making in relation to the nature of the Church's mission (16:4), which further underlines the patterning of this structure along the lines of the judicial function of the Jewish elders.

A similar influence is observed in the Letter of James which manifests profound links with Judaism. James advises his communities to call for the "elders" of the Church when anyone is sick (5:14). They are to pray over the sick person and to anoint that person with oil. Their function is liturgical in a way that may have been similar to that of the elders in the synagogue, but James makes no reference to their teaching.

Within the Pastoral Letters, written toward the end of the NT period, we catch a glimpse of the development of administration and leadership within the Christian communities along more structured lines. In the opening chapter of the Letter to Titus, he is encouraged to appoint elders in every town on the island of Crete (Titus 1:5) and is guided as to their requisite qualities: "blameless, married only once, with believing children who are not accused of licentiousness or rebellious" (1:6). This advice is followed immediately by a list of the qualities necessary in the bishop, which raises questions as to the relationship between the presbyters or elders and the bishop. Many scholars suggest that the latter may have been selected from the group of elders, especially since both are required to be irreproachable or blameless and a close connective link is made between the two lists of qualities.

The term *presbyteros* is generally used inclusively of women and men in Greek texts. The tendency within the Pastoral Letters to restrict the ministerial roles of women is therefore evidenced in the above texts which imply that the elders were males. These very explicit restrictions, however, together with evidence of female elders within councils of Jewish communities in the Diaspora, point to the possibility of their contributing as elders within the early Christian communities. This would be particularly so if the group of elders was made up of the leaders of house churches, since there is NT evidence of women holding such positions (Acts 12:12; 16:14-15; Luke 10:38; Rom 16:2; Col 4:13).

The collegial nature of the group of elders is further indicated in 1 Timothy 4:14 where the term *presbyterion* or council of elders is used. This group was responsible for laying hands on Timothy for the ministry to which he is exhorted: "reading, exhortation, and teaching" (1 Tim 4:13). Later in the same letter, reference is made to the preaching and teaching role of the elders as specific tasks within their general role of governing or presiding over the Church (1 Tim 5:17).

NT evidence that would enable us to make explicit claims about the developing role of "elder" within early Christian communities is slight indeed. Even more slight is information that would allow us to distinguish clearly between the roles of bishop, deacon, and elder. We have seen above that the elders had presiding and juridical roles which later came to be associated with the bishop, as well as administrative and ministerial roles that are commonly thought of as diaconal tasks. One thing, however, is clear, namely that the early Christian communities drew on the gifts of women and men in the community whose wisdom and perhaps even age equipped them for leadership and service. As roles became more clearly defined, the churches drew upon patterns of leadership within their Jewish foundations and yet shaped these according to the needs of a community continuing the mission of Jesus.

See: ANOINTING, APOSTLE, BISHOP, DEACON, JUDAISM, MISSION, PHARISEE, PRAYER, PRIEST, SCRIBE, SYNAGOGUE

ELAINE M. WAINWRIGHT

Pastoral-Liturgical Tradition

The English word "elder" is a translation of the Greek *presbyteros* and the Latin *presbyter,* but it is used above all in Protestant circles not to designate a priest but rather one who holds any office in the Church. It is used notably in the Presbyterian and Mormon Churches. Although the term regularly appears in Christian literature in the first two centuries following the death of Christ, the office of elder more or less disappeared once the threefold ministry of bishop, presbyter, and deacon was stabilized in Christian communities (ca. 180 CE). During the Protestant Reformation it was revived by certain Churches. According to Presbyterian theory of Church governance, there are two catagories of elders: teaching elders, usually called ministers, who are ordained and set apart for pastoral office; and ruling elders, who are lay persons generally chosen by the congregation to assist the minister in supervising and administering the Church. In those Churches that reject the idea of ordination and the distinction between clergy and laity, the term usually signifies anyone who presides at worship or has a function in governing the Church. Generally elders may be men or women.

In the Church of Jesus Christ of Latter-day Saints, or the Mormon Church, an elder is a male member who is at least twenty years old. At the age of twelve, all worthy male Mormons become deacons, and before the age of twenty they become priests. At twenty they become elders in the Melchizedek priesthood, and in later life they might become high priests or members of the seventy. Among Methodists ordained clergy are often called elders. In the Lutheran Church the terms "elder" and "deacon" are often used interchangeably to designate those who advise and assist the pastor in administering the Church.

Roman Catholics do not use the term elder, but the role that elders play in Protestant Churches would be carried out by Roman Catholic lay men and women who are parish trustees or members of the finance committee, parish council, or other parish committees.

The Code of Canon Law prescribes that the pastor establish a finance council which has a consultative vote and assists the pastor in the administration of parish temporalities. The diocesan bishop may establish a policy that every parish also have a pastoral council to promote pastoral action. These roles would be filled by elders in Protestant Churches. If there is a dearth of priests in a Catholic diocese, a lay person or a group of lay people may be appointed to exercise pastoral care within a parish, but a priest with the powers and faculties of a pastor must supervise their pastoral care. Lay people may also fulfill important liturgical roles which would be exercised by elders in Protestant Churches. They may preside at prayer services, proclaim the Word of God, give reflections on the Word, and distribute the Eucharist. Although the terms "elder" and "elderly" are related, the elderly are more often the object of ministry in the Roman Catholic Church than they are the subjects of active ministry in their parishes. However, efforts are being made to utilize their gifts and above all their experience in the life of Roman Catholic parishes.

See: CHURCH, COMMUNITY, GIFTS, MINISTRY

R. KEVIN SEASOLTZ, O.S.B.

ELECTION

The theme of election, the choice by God of a specific people, is at the heart of biblical theology. Taken by itself, it might suggest superiority and, subsequently, engender attitudes of elitism. Understood appropriately, it makes no claims of merit and insists that the choice is due to God's graciousness alone. Election as people of God requires a style of life that reflects this office. It is as much a responsibility as it is a privilege.

Old Testament

At the core of Israelite faith is the conviction that God had chosen Israel* from among all other peoples, had entered a unique relationship with it, and had imposed specific obligations upon it. This conviction is known as the biblical doctrine of election. Throughout its history Israel reflected on this choice and posed many questions. What motivated God to make this selection? From what kind of historical situation had God first summoned it? How would the continuity of God's choice be assured? What did this election mean for Israel's thought and life? What was God's plan for other nations? The OT materials address these questions.

To express its theological ideas Israel often appropriated terminology familiar in human life. In everyday language election, or choice, refers to a selection from among many possibilities, which is the result of a reflective decision. The Hebrew word for choose is *bahar*, with its related forms. Related to it are other words that express a similar idea, such as know (Amos 3:2; Jer 1:5) or take (Exod 6:7). When these terms are used of God, they express God's supreme and unlimited power to make a totally free choice of persons, places, or things, a choice that is above questioning by any human being. It is in this sense that

Amos portrays God as selecting Israel from among all the available nations or peoples: "You alone have I favored, more than all the peoples on earth" (Amos 3:2).

God's Choice of a People. God's choice of Israel marks the beginning of its history as God's people (Ezek 20:5). The classic formulation of election occurs in Deuteronomy: "For you are a people sacred to the Lord, your God; he has chosen you from among all the nations on the face of the earth to be a people peculiarly his own" (Deut 7:6). This is the only book in the Pentateuch that uses the word "elect" or "election" (bahar) to describe this idea. However, although the word appears rather late (Deuteronomy was written ca. 623 BCE), the tradition that Israel was specially chosen by God goes back to Israel's earliest historical memories (Judg 5:5, 11; Exod 19:5).

When the OT attempts to address God's motivation in making this choice, the notion that Israel somehow deserved it is nowhere advanced. Indeed Deuteronomy stresses the opposite point, repeatedly insisting that election is the result of God's initiative, not of any characteristics of Israel: "It was not because you are the largest of all the nations that the LORD set his heart on you and chose you, for you are really the smallest of the nations" (Deut 7:7). Only one positive reason is advanced: God's incomprehensible free decision of love (Deut 10:15).

What this election means for Israel is addressed in different ways. Israel is to be God's special possession (Exod 19:5), who by their way of life will image God. Israel is to be "holy" (Deut 7:6), which essentially means to be set apart (cf. Num 23:9). Israel is also to be a "kingdom of priests" (Exod 19:6). Possibly there is already present in this last description the idea of being set apart for the priestly service of mediation, an understanding that will become explicit in Second Isaiah's depiction of God's elect whom he calls the "servant" of God (Isa 42:1). None of these designations is meant to describe privilege or superiority. Rather the stress is on Israel's responsibility, a responsibility shared by no other nation. Israel is to recognize no other God but God and to obey God's commandments or Law (Deut 4:39-40). Clearly, Israel's election is intimately connected with the covenant: "If you hearken to my voice and keep my covenant, you shall be my special possession" (Exod 19:5). Implicit in this formulation is that the failure of Israel to live up to its covenant commitment, the purpose for which it was chosen, can result in its non-election.

God's Choice of Individuals. God is also said to favor certain individuals within the chosen people. The prehistory of the human race described in the early chapters of Genesis gives a foretaste of the doctrine of election in its description of God's special favor accorded Abel (Gen 4:4), Enoch (Gen 5:24), Noah (Gen 7:1), and Shem (Gen 9:26). But it is specifically with the patriarchs that the plan of election emerges. Abraham is selected to be specially blessed and this blessing will continue through his descendants (Gen 12:2-3). In the patriarchal stories three themes are pursued. The first is God's constant fidelity to the promises made to Abraham. The second is the total freedom of God concerning the way in which the promise is fulfilled. Repeatedly the one chosen is not the natural heir, the elder son. Isaac is chosen over Ishmael, Jacob over Esau, Judah over Reuben. In this way, it is made clear that the initiative in the election is always God's, following no automatic pattern. The third is that election calls for a response from the human side, an attitude of humble obedience and unconditional trust that must be maintained no matter how severe the testing.

The idea of election (although not the word) appears in the raising up of individual judges who are to serve the needs of the people and in the calling of the prophets who are selected for the specific task of proclaiming God's Word to their contemporaries. The king also is said to receive his office through divine election

(Deut 17:14-15). Sometimes God's choice of a king was made known through the word of a prophet or through another person attested by God. God's choice falls upon Saul (1 Sam 10:24) and upon David (1 Samuel 16), and the election of David is extended to his entire dynasty (2 Sam 7:11-16; Ps 89:20-38). In the northern kingdom also there are many references to how designation by a prophet precedes the king's accession (1 Kgs 11:29-30; 14:14; 2 Kgs 9:1-2). The divine election is applied to Moses and to Aaron (Ps 105:26), to the priesthood of the house of Eli (1 Sam 2:28), and to the tribe of Levi (Deut 18:5; 21:5). In none of these individual selections is there any hint of blind favoritism by God. Always the choice is for service. This point is forcefully illustrated in the fact that God's choice is said to fall for a particular purpose on Nebuchadnezzar, Cyrus, the Assyrians, and the Chaldeans.

The Deuteronomic tradition emphasizes that the divine choice also falls upon a particular place, Jerusalem, not that it is a site sacred in itself but so that there God's name may dwell and God may be worshiped (Deut 12:5, 11).

Distortion of the Idea of Election. When dissociated from its concomitant obligations, the idea of election becomes distorted and even dangerous, producing a false sense of superiority over other peoples. This occurred in Israel. The idea of being God's chosen people became transformed into a reassuring conviction that God was Israel's patron deity whose function was to guarantee its prosperity and continued existence amid all threats by surrounding nations. Gone was the sense of Israel's covenant responsibilities "to do right and to love goodness, and to walk humbly with your God" (Mic 6:8). Therefore the preexilic prophets almost never speak of Israel's election. Amos does so, but only to refute the people's self-satisfied claim on God's protection: "You alone have I favored, more than all the families of the earth; therefore I will punish you for all your crimes" (Amos 3:2). He further attacked their exclusivist interpretation of election by claiming that God was also concerned with the nations they considered to be their enemies (Amos 9:7). Indeed because Israel had so betrayed its obligations, the prophets challenge the very assumption that Israel the nation can any longer be identified with the people of God. Amos unequivocally proclaims the end of the kingdom of Israel (Amos 7:7-9) and Jeremiah declares the same outcome for Judah (Jer 6:30; 14:19). Because election is God's free choice, it can be abrogated any time.

The New Eschatological Election. What is truly remarkable is the prophets' equally strong conviction that while the nation Israel will be destroyed, God's plan for election will continue in a new form. In the eschatological age rebellious Israel will be transformed by the power of God into the new Israel, the obedient Israel. It is in Second Isaiah that the idea of election reaches a culmination. In powerful and creative language he focuses on the election of the new Israel as an election for service to the world. Indeed, he uses the terms "servant" and "chosen" almost interchangeably (Isa 41:8-9; 44:1-2). Through its witness Israel will completely fulfill its destiny as the chosen servant of God in the Gentile world (Isa 43:10). In this context Second Isaiah introduces a mysterious figure whom God calls "my servant" (Isa 42:1; 49:3; 52:13), "my chosen one" (Isa 42:1). He is endowed with the Spirit of God to establish justice on earth, to be a covenant of the people and a light for the nations, to open the eyes of the blind, to deliver prisoners (Isa 42:1-7; 49:6), and ultimately to bring deliverance by his suffering (Isaiah 53). The role of the servant is thus to bring about an order where depth of life will characterize the whole human race as each and all are renewed by the divine presence. In this way will the ultimate purpose of God's election be fulfilled.

See: COVENANT

MARILYN M. SCHAUB

New Testament

Meaning. Early Christians continued Israel's belief in a God whose free gift of election calls people to faith and to membership in the community of God's people. Divine election in Christian understanding builds upon its Jewish model expressed in the classic text of Deuteronomy 7:6: "For you are a people sacred to the LORD, your God; he has chosen you from all the nations on the face of the earth to be a people peculiarly his own." Several different Greek terms in the NT denote God's act of choosing either individuals or groups for special relationship with God. "Election" *(eklogē)* and "elect" *(eklektos)* convey the idea of God's calling out some among others and connote the divine act of choosing *(eklegomai)*. Elsewhere the related verbs *hairetizō* (Matt 12:18) and *haireō* (2 Thess 2:13—"to choose") signal God's special choice of certain persons. Always, however, this choice entails obligations on the person or group chosen. To belong to God in the special relationship of election demands that one imitate the very character and qualities of God.

Christians understood divine election as a constitutive element within the totality of God's plan and will for creation (Rom 8:28-30). God's plan, however, was never seen as arbitrary or random but as the manifestation of God's love and mercy and the sign of God's unmerited bestowal of graciousness in and for creation. Those called to an elect status retain the freedom to receive or to reject God's offer. Moreover, the certainty of one's ultimate inclusion within God's elect remains fundamentally an *eschatological* reality determined by one's faithful obedience to God's call throughout one's life, and especially during times of distress and tribulation (Matt 24:22, 24, 31; 1 Cor 1:18).

The Christian Community as God's Elect. Just as Israel had understood itself as a people sacred to Yahweh, so too early Christians saw themselves as the continuation of God's holy and elect people. And so, the author of 1 Peter can remind the Christians of his day living in Asia Minor: "But you are a 'chosen race, a royal priesthood, a holy nation, a people of his own, so that you may announce the praises' of him who called you out of darkness into his wonderful light" (1 Pet 2:9). Here, especially, the connection between election and the call to holiness can be seen. Moreover, the responsibility of those elect ones to announce to the world the good news of God's action, that is, the call to mission incumbent on the elect is undeniable.

Jesus the Elect One. As the servant and anointed one of God, par excellence, Jesus is God's beloved who accomplishes, once and for all, God's saving plan in human history (John 1:34; Luke 9:35—some mss.). Initially, the early Christians identified Jesus with the Servant of Deutero-Isaiah (Isa 42:1-4; 49:1-7; 50:4-11; 52:13–53:12) who was called the "chosen one of God" (Isa 42:1). Again, drawing on the metaphor of Isaiah 28:16, the author of 1 Peter describes Jesus as the "cornerstone, chosen and precious" (1 Pet 2:6) and calls upon Christians to "Come to him, a living stone, rejected by human beings but chosen and precious in the sight of God" (1 Pet 2:4). The polyvalent quality of this Isaian servant image allows it to be applied both to Jesus and to the Christian community as a whole in the same way that the Servant of Isaiah symbolized both an individual prophetic figure as well as the people of Israel collectively. In Christian understanding, nevertheless, Jesus above all others stands as God's elect and chosen one.

Synoptic Tradition. The "elect" in the Synoptic Gospels are those who remain steadfast in the tribulations of the end time (Matt 24:22, 24, 31; Mark 13:20, 22, 27; Luke 18:7) and are, thereby, revealed as God's truly elect ones. Unlike those who fall away and follow after false prophets, these elect are gathered from the four winds by the Son of Man through the activity of his angels (Matt 24:31). Not all who have been called will be included in this final number, for, as Matthew reminds his readers

"Many are called but few are chosen [elect]" (Matt 22:14).

Pauline Tradition. Paul's understanding of election includes his own experience of being called and chosen for God's work: "But when [God], who from my mother's womb had set me apart and called me through his grace . . ." (Gal 1:15). This radical encounter that Paul had with the risen Lord on the road to Damascus became the grounding of his apostolic life, the source of his convictions about God's offer of life to Jew and Gentile alike, and the fundamental insight of his pastoral theology.

Paul's own sense of having been set apart by God was not unique, but an example of God's choice of others as well. He reminds the Christians in Thessalonica of their chosen status (eklogē), an identity that calls them into the work of the gospel (1 Thess 1:4-8). Paul's shorthand expression to capture this new identity and elect status is simply to be "in Christ," a phrase he uses repeatedly and one that signals election as surely as any of the more technical terms for election and calling. To be "in Christ" assumes that one now shares both a real and symbolic incorporation into Christ's Body through baptism. Moreover, the company of the elect include both the living and the dead, those who have died "in Christ" (1 Thess 4:13-18). These are the holy ones (hagioi) who share God's promised reward (1 Thess 3:13).

Paul is likewise certain that the basis for election has nothing whatsoever to do with one's social status, spiritual merit, or any other claim believers might propose for their deserving election. God's choice is utterly free, gratuitous, and impartial. For example, Paul is quick to disabuse the Corinthians' false sense of importance about their election: "Rather God chose [lit. "elected"—eklegomai] the foolish of the world to shame the wise, and God chose the weak of the world to shame the strong, and God chose the lowly and despised of the world, those who count for nothing, to reduce to nothing those who are some-thing, so that no human being might boast before God" (1 Cor 1:27-28).

In Romans 8:28-39, Paul gathers together a cluster of terms all of which express his understanding of God's election. God "calls, knows beforehand, predestines, justifies, glorifies" those whom God wills. In this letter, too, Paul addresses the difficult question of the permanence of Israel's elect status within the new covenant community. At the same time, he affirms God's faithfulness to those who have been chosen but acknowledges that "Not all who are of Israel are Israel" (Rom 9:6), that is, membership in the elect community is not gained merely through lineage but is accomplished only through God's mercy. Moreover, the Gentile mission does not cancel Israel's claim to elect status, but this status may find representation only in a faithful remnant who will be "grafted in" to the elect community at the end of time (Rom 11:23).

Election, in Paul's understanding, is linked to holiness, to freedom, and to suffering. As Leviticus had enjoined the Israelite community "be holy as I am holy" (Lev 11:44), so Paul's exhortations call Christians to holiness which must be both a sign and a consequence of their election. "For God did not call us to impurity but to holiness" (1 Thess 4:7; elsewhere e.g., 1 Thess 3:13; 4:3; 1 Cor 6:11). In his Letter to the Galatians, Paul underscores that to be called in Christ is to be called for freedom (Gal 5:13-15). Freedom from the obligations of the Mosaic Law, however, is not indiscriminate libertinism, but freedom constrained by the demands of love for the neighbor. Finally, for Paul election is linked irrevocably with suffering. Election "in Christ" is, for Paul, therefore, always election in Christ crucified. That is why Paul sends Timothy to Thessalonica to strengthen and encourage the faithful who lived amid affliction. "For you yourselves know that we are destined for this" (1 Thess 3:3). And for the Christians in Philippi, the story of Jesus' suffering and death (Phil 2:6-11) becomes the model for their lives. In Paul's life, too, the "upward calling" includes "sharing in Christ's sufferings by being conformed to his death" (Phil 3:10-14). To count oneself among the elect in Christ is to be called into holiness and freedom, but always, for Paul, into the shadow of the Cross.

Election in the Johannine Tradition. The author of the Gospel of John uses the language of election most explicitly in the Last Discourse: "It was not you who chose me, but I who chose you to go and bear fruit that will remain" (John 15:16). Through Jesus, the Word made flesh, God reveals the divine mystery in the world and summons all to belief. The elect, therefore, are all those who respond in faith and who bear fruit. No one is excluded from this universal invitation, but no one can come to Jesus without the Father drawing them (John 6:44). Three times in the great prayer of Jesus in John 17 (17:2, 6, 9), Jesus speaks of those whom the Father "has given him," namely those who have become part of the circle of disciples, those who have believed in the one sent by God. Despite its implicit election language, John's Gospel stresses more the freedom operative in each one's response to Jesus and the corresponding challenge to believe and, thereby, to have eternal life.

The Book of Revelation acknowledges those in the company of the Lamb "who is Lord of lords and king of kings" (Rev 17:14) as those who are "called, chosen, and faithful." These are the elect, those whose names are written "from the foundation of the world" in the book of life (Rev 3:5; 13:8; 17:8; 20:12, 15). For this author, perseverance in times of persecution and, ultimately, martyrdom seal the identity of the elect.

See: CALL/VOCATION, CONVERSION, DISCIPLE/DISCIPLESHIP

BARBARA E. BOWE, R.S.C.J.

Pastoral-Liturgical Tradition

The theology of election in the Church tradition has been inextricably bound up with the theology of predestination since the time of Augustine. In his debates with the Pelagians, Augustine maintained that our predestination to eternal salvation rests on a free act of election by God. Aquinas, too, tried to maintain the distinction between election and predestination, seeing election as an act of the will prior to predestination, which is an act of the intellect. However, from the time of Augustine down to Friedrich Schleiermacher at the beginning of the nineteenth century, election and predestination were used as rough equivalents of each other.

Concern about the nature and the extent of God's election of individuals became much more focused in the Reformation, particularly as the Church was no longer seen as the mediator of that election. John Calvin's reading of Augustine led him to an extreme view, in which certain persons are elected by God without reference either to faith or to works. Consequently, one could never be assured of one's election to eternal salvation. The followers of Arminius softened that position somewhat, leaving room for the perseverance in faith and the performance of good works as signs of election.

Schleiermacher reestablished a focus on God's election of humanity by trying to bring together the Lutheran concern for the universality of God's grace with the Calvinist concern for the unconditioned character of God's grace. His proposal helped separate out once again election from questions of predestination. Karl Barth moved that further in the twentieth century by emphasizing the incarnation of Christ as God's act of election of humanity.

In the latter part of the twentieth century, concern about election has voiced itself in negative commentary on the doctrine. NT emphasis on the election of the Church over (or against) Israel was seen to have fueled the persistent anti-Semitism found in Christianity. Although biblical election can be understood as a call to special responsibility, it is too often taken to mean an ascribed superiority of the elect over all others. This latter understanding of election was also seen to have informed an especially imperialistic form of mission in the nineteenth and early twentieth century. It is also suspected of shaping attitudes of superiority in Christianity toward other religions, thus calling into question Christian aspirations to interreligious dialogue. Feminist theologians frequently regard the doctrine of election as inherently exclusionary of those not elected, and therefore also almost inevitably hierarchical. Moreover, being chosen rather than choosing seems also, once more, to take away true subjecthood from women.

Despite all these reservations about election as a way of talking about how God intervenes in or is involved in our history, there are positive things about the doctrine that perdure. If election is understood as vocation and responsibility rather than privilege to the detriment of others, it becomes a highly efficacious way of understanding the role and task of the Christian in the world. Those who experience God's grace in their lives feel themselves called to participate all the more in the building up of God's reign. The doctrine of election has also appeared in another kind of way in the latter part of the twentieth century, namely, in belief in the preferential option for the poor. Here God chooses the poor in a special way to hear God's Word and to witness to it in the world. Finally, election may also be understood as a special form of belonging to God—a belonging in the sense both of deep communion with God, and the vocation to manifest what God means for the world.

The doctrine of election finds ritual expression in the Rite of Christian Initiation of Adults. At the beginning of Lent, the Rite of Election takes place. Having heard the testimony of godparents and catechists, and having listened to the catechumens reaffirm their intention to enter the Christian community, the Church elects the catechumens, i.e., declares that they may proceed toward initiation in the sacred mysteries to be celebrated at Easter. This ritual action enacts the Christian understanding of God's choosing persons to be in full communion with the Holy Trinity.

See: CALL/VOCATION, GRACE

ROBERT J. SCHREITER, C.PP.S.

ELIJAH/ELISHA

Elijah and Elisha were ninth-century BCE prophets who ministered in the northern kingdom. Traditions about them are preserved in the Books of Kings: 1 Kings 17–19, 21; 2 Kings 1:1–2:18 (Elijah); and 2 Kings 2:19–8:15 (Elisha). Elijah called Elisha to be a prophet* and the latter received a double portion (the inheritance of the eldest son) of Elijah's spirit when Elijah was taken by the fiery chariot (2 Kgs 2:1-18). Elijah is a solitary figure who lived in caves while Elisha stayed in the cities and appears in the company of "the sons of the prophets" (2 Kgs 16:3, 19, 32; 2 Kgs 2:3-15; 4:3). Neither prophet left written works of their own. The stories in Kings are more in the form of anecdotes that try to show the importance of the events in which the prophets participated. A most important motif in these stories is the absolute claim that Yahweh has on Israel.

There are four stories in which Elijah is the protagonist: the contest with the prophets of Baal and its aftermath (1 Kgs 16:29–19:18), Naboth's vineyard (1 Kings 21), Ahaziah's inquiry (2 Kgs 1:2–2:17), and Elijah's relationship with Elisha (1 Kgs 19:19-21; 2 Kgs 2:1-18). These stories portray Elijah as a worker of miracles and as an opponent of Baal worship and the oppressive social system that it supported.

The miraculous is a thread that is woven through the Elijah stories though the tradition remembers Elisha as an even greater worker of wonders. Several miracles occur in connection with the great drought that Elijah announces to Ahab (1 Kgs 17:1). Ravens feed the prophet during the famine caused by the drought (1 Kgs 17:6). Later a widow from Zarephath cooks for the prophet from the oil and flour that he miraculously provided. When her son dies, the prophet restores him to life (1 Kgs 17:7-24).

Israelite farmers were attracted to the service of the Baals worshiped by the indigenous population of Canaan* because Baal was associated with the rains that were necessary for successful farming in the region. The introduction of the Baal from Tyre to Israel following the marriage of Ahab and Jezebel, a Tyrian princess, marked a new turn in the conflict between Yahweh and Baal. The Tyrian Baal supported a hierarchical social system that led to injustice exemplified by the judicial murder of Naboth and the confiscation of his ancestral land holdings (1 Kings 21). That is why Elijah is both the opponent of Baalism and a champion of justice. Yahwism supported a social system that protected the rights of simple peasants. Even Ahab recognized these rights (1 Kgs 21:1-4). It was Jezebel who thought that the respect that her husband grudgingly gave to Naboth's rights was foolish (1 Kgs 21:5-7).

Because the stories about Elijah do not report his death, but his going up to heaven in a whirlwind (2 Kgs 2:11), there arose the belief that Elijah would return before the Day of the Lord (Mal 3:23; Sir 48:10). Some of Jesus' contemporaries believed that Jesus was Elijah come back to the earth (Matt 16:14; Mark 6:15; Luke 9:8, 19), though Jesus asserted that John the Baptist* was Elijah (Matt 11:14; Mark 9:12-13).

Elijah appeared with Moses during the transfiguration of Jesus (Matt 17:3; Mark 9:4; Luke 9:30). The Letter of James proposes Elijah as a model of prayer since his prayer began and ended a drought (Jas 5:17; see 1 Kings 18).

The stories about Elisha fall into two categories: personal and political. The prophet worked miracles to help ordinary people in times of personal crisis. For example, he raised the Shunammite's only son from the dead (2 Kgs 4:18-37). These miracles underscore the power of Israel's God over the forces of nature and thus they provide an indirect challenge to Baalism that Elijah attacked more directly. The effect of these stories is to portray Elisha as a greater wonder worker than Elijah and so later tradition remembered him (Sir 48:12-14).

Elisha intrudes into domestic and international politics. He helped bring Hazael to the throne of Damascus (2 Kgs 8:7-15) and Jehu to the throne of Israel (9:1-13). The prophet urged Jehu to "destroy the house of Ahab" (2 Kgs 9:7). A century later Hosea condemns the blood-bath that followed (Hos 1:4). Some people, agreeing with Hosea, find the moral tone of the Elisha stories unattractive because the prophet is an advocate of violence.

The notion that John the Baptist was Elijah who was to come first as the harbinger of God's final intervention may have led Mark to portray Jesus as another Elisha. Of course, the evangelist portrays Jesus as a wonder worker even greater than Elisha. Though both work a miracle through which many people are fed (2 Kgs 4:42-44; Mark 6:32-44), Jesus feeds more people with fewer loaves, and has a great amount left over. In Kings the forerunner-successor pair (Elijah/Elisha) tried to extend God's rule to Israel and beyond. In Mark another forerunner-successor pair (John/Jesus) attempt to do the same.

Whether Mark consciously depicted the ministries of John and Jesus according to the pattern set by the Elijah/Elisha cycle, the liturgy takes full advantage of the similarities. Texts from this cycle appear nine times in the Sunday lectionary. Most often texts from the Kings' account of the prophets are chosen because of the Gospel pericope. For example, on the Tenth Sunday of Ordinary Time in Cycle C, the Gospel lesson is the raising of the widow's son (Luke 7:11-17). The first lesson for that Sunday narrates Elijah's raising of a widow's son (1 Kgs 17:17-24).

Elijah and Elisha represent the perspective of those in ancient Israel who held that Yahweh has an exclusive claim on Israel's loyalties. This claim extended to every area of life. Sometimes these prophets are portrayed as militant monotheists who resisted the syncretism that infected the royal establishment of the Northern Kingdom. It is important to recognize that their monotheism did not concern itself with the existence of other gods as much as it was the affirmation that Yahweh alone was the source of Israel's prosperity and peace.

See: BAAL, MIRACLE

LESLIE J. HOPPE, O.F.M.

EMMANUEL

New Testament

Matthew 1:22-23. These verses, containing the only explicit use of "Emmanuel" in the NT, clearly allude to the oracle of Isaiah 7:1-17 in its Greek version. In this oracle, Isaiah foretells the collapse of the coalition forged by King Rezin of Aram (Syria) and King Pekah of Israel (Ephraim) against King Ahaz of Judah. Isaiah assures Ahaz implicitly that the Davidic dynasty will continue. The child to be born of the young woman (*ha'almah*, Isa 7:14) will be God's sign to Ahaz pledging fulfillment of this prophecy.

Matthew, however, fixes upon the Greek translation of *'almah* ("young woman") as *parthenos* (which he understands as "virgin") and shifts the focus of this prophecy to emphasize the mode of the child's birth. The child (for Matthew, Jesus) is to be born of a virgin (*parthenos*).

Emmanuel in Matthew. By noting that Joseph names Mary's son "Jesus," whereas the prophecy as Matthew cites it states that "they shall call his name Emmanuel," Matthew turns the name "Emmanuel" into a theological title for Jesus. The significance of this title for Jesus, "God with us," is brought out in Matthew 18:20 and even more clearly at the end of Matthew's Gospel.

In Matthew 18:20, Jesus promises that "where there are two or three gathered together in my name, there am I in the midst of them." This statement has a remarkable similarity to that in the Mishnah of the Talmud, which speaks of God's presence (*Shekinah*) among those who study the Mosaic Law: "if two sit together and words of the Law [pass] between them, the Divine Presence abides between them" (Pirke Aboth 3:2).

At the end of Matthew's Gospel, the risen Jesus is not shown ascending into heaven. Instead, he declares, "I am with you all days, until the end of the world" (Matt 28:20). This is a powerful theological statement, since it refers back to Matthew 1:23 and identifies Jesus as God.

Christ's Presence Elsewhere in the NT. The presence of Christ not only with believers but in believers is noted in the Pauline corpus in such passages as Romans 8:10; Galatians 2:20; Colossians 1:27. Paul says, "if Christ is in you, although the body is dead because of sin, the spirit is alive because of righteousness" (Rom 8:10). And Paul emphasizes this presence by asserting "I live, no longer I, but Christ lives in me" (Gal 2:20). The author of Colossians also alludes to "Christ in you" (Col 1:27).

John's Gospel proclaims that "the Word became flesh and made his dwelling among us" (John 1:14). John also accentuates the fact that God "remains" with Jesus' disciples. Jesus tells his followers that they will come to know the Spirit of truth, "because it remains with you and will be in you" (John 14:17). Jesus promises that "whoever loves me will keep my word, and my Father will love him, and we will come to him and make our dwelling with him" (John 14:23). Comparing himself to a vine, Jesus bids his disciples, "Remain in me, as I remain in you" (John 15:4).

Pastoral-Liturgical Tradition

Israel's longing for a new manifestation of God's presence with the chosen people finds expression in the beautiful Advent hymn, "O Come, O Come Emmanuel," which gives voice to Israel's plea for deliverance and then joyfully announces that Emmanuel has indeed been born and resides with his people.

See: FULFILLMENT, JESUS CHRIST, NAME, PROPHECY, VIRGIN

NEIL J. MCELENEY, C.S.P.

EPIPHANY

The word *epiphany* comes from the Greek word *epiphaneia*, meaning "appearing," "appearance," or "manifestation." It is these three words that will be found in English translations of the Bible; rarely is *epiphaneia* translated "epiphany." The word is used almost exclusively of divine manifestations on earth.

Old Testament

In the Greek OT *epiphaneia* translates the Hebrew *yārē'*, and almost always refers to God's self-manifestation, particularly in saving deeds toward Israel. King David prays, "What other nation on earth is there like your people Israel, which God has led, redeeming it as his people; so that you have made yourself renowned by doing this magnificent deed, and by doing awe-inspiring things *[epiphaneian]*?" (2 Sam 7:23).

The most frequent instances of *epiphaneia* occur in 2 Maccabees, which recounts "the story of Judas Maccabeus and his brothers, of the purification of the great temple, the dedication of the altar, the campaigns against Antiochus Epiphanes and his son Eupator, and of the heavenly manifestations *[epiphaneias]* accorded to the heroes who fought bravely for Judaism, so that, few as they were, they seized the whole land, put to flight the barbarian hordes, regained possession of the world-famous temple, liberated the city, and reestablished the laws that were in danger of being abolished, while the Lord favored them with all his generous assistance" (2:19-22). The author of Maccabees contrasts the manifestations of the God of Israel to the exploits of the Syrian ruler Antiochus IV (175–163 BCE), who assumed the epithet "Epiphanes," "the Manifest" ("God" understood). When Heliodorus was sent to plunder the treasury in Jerusalem, "the Lord of spirits who holds all power *manifested* himself in so striking a way that those who had been bold enough to follow Heliodorus were panic-stricken at God's power and fainted away in terror" (2 Macc 3:24). And "when

Judas' first cohort appeared, the enemy was overwhelmed with fear and terror at the *manifestation* of the All-seeing" (2 Macc 12:22). Later Judas and his men "laid low at least thirty-five thousand, and rejoiced greatly over this *manifestation* of God's power" (2 Macc 15:27. See also 2 Macc 5:4; 14:15; 3 Macc 2:9; 5:8, 51).

A different connotation of *epiphaneia* is found in the woes delivered by the prophet Amos, where God rejects the "grand peace offerings" *(sōterious epiphaneias)* that Israel would proffer (Amos 5:22).

The verb *epiphainein* is used only of God's self-manifestation. In Genesis 35:7, "Jacob named the place Bethel, for it was there that God had revealed himself to him." Similar references to God's appearing are found in Zephaniah 2:11; Jeremiah 36(29):14; 2 Maccabees 3:30. Several times *epiphainein* is translated as God's "shining forth" or "letting his face shine upon" one (Num 6:25; Deut 33:2; Pss 30[31]:16; 66[67]:1; 79[80]:3, 7, 19; 117[118]:27; 118[119]:135).

The adjective *epiphanēs* describes God's glorious name (1 Chr 17:21; Mal 1:14), the great day of the Lord (Joel 2:11), the glorious Lord (2 Macc 15:34), the manifest Lord God (3 Macc 5:35), the glorious old age of Eleazar (2 Macc 6:23), and the notable temple to Bacchus (2 Macc 14:33).

New Testament

In the NT *epiphaneia* is used exclusively of Christ's "appearing." In one instance, 2 Timothy 1:10, it refers to Jesus' birth, his first appearance on earth. The apostle asserts that God's grace is "now made manifest through the appearance *[epiphaneia]* of our savior Christ Jesus." Twice the verb *epiphainein*, "to appear" or "to show oneself," is used in reference to Jesus' incarnation. In the canticle of Zechariah the tender mercy of God is extolled, "by which the daybreak from on high will visit us to shine on *[epiphanai]* those who sit in darkness and death's shadow, to guide our feet into the path of peace" (Luke 1:78-79). Titus is advised to reject "godless ways and worldly desires and to live temperately, "For the grace of God has appeared [*epephanē*] saving all" (Titus 2:11).

In all other NT instances, *epiphaneia* refers to Christ's manifestation at his second coming. The community at Thessalonica is assured, "then the lawless one will be revealed, whom the Lord [Jesus] will kill with the breath of his mouth and render powerless by the *manifestation* of his coming" (2 Thess 2:8). Timothy is exhorted, "keep the commandment without stain or reproach until the *appearance* of our Lord Jesus Christ" (1 Tim 6:14). Timothy is also charged, "in the presence of God and of Christ Jesus, who will judge the living and the dead, and by his *appearing* and his kingly power: proclaim the word" (2 Tim 4:1-2). The reward for fidelity will be a "crown of righteousness" which "the Lord, the just judge will award to . . . all who have longed for his *appearance*" (2 Tim 4:8). Titus is reminded "to reject godless ways and worldly desires and to live temperately, justly, and devoutly in this age, as we await the blessed hope, the *appearance* of the glory of the great God and of our savior Jesus Christ" (Titus 2:12-13).

In one instance the verb *epiphainein* is used of the sun and stars. In the storm and shipwreck saga of Acts 27, "neither the sun nor the stars were visible [*epiphainontōn*] for many days" (27:20). The adjective *epiphanēs* occurs once, describing the remarkable day of Christ's coming, "The sun shall be turned to darkness, and the moon to blood, before the coming of the great and splendid [*epiphanē*] day of the Lord" (Acts 2:20).

See: FACE OF GOD, GLORY, PAROUSIA, VISITATION OF GOD, VOICE OF GOD

BARBARA E. REID, O.P.

Pastoral-Liturgical Tradition

The early Christian community did not celebrate any specific manifestation feasts* like Epiphany or Christmas. Rather, the multiple manifestations of Christ, from birth to Ascension, were summed up in the weekly Sunday assembly. It is only in the third century that a specific feast of Epiphany emerged on January 6.

There is much speculation why January 6 was chosen as the date for this feast in the East. Pagan precedents, including the nativity of the Sun God (Aion) and various water festivals celebrated on this date, are sometimes thought to be the determining factor. Such suggestions remain inconclusive, although images of the birth of light, revelation, and water central to the pagan festivals reoccur in the emerging Christian feasts.

The first evidence for a feast of Epiphany comes from Clement of Alexandria (d. ca. 215), who mentions that the gnostic Basilidians commemorated the baptism of Christ on this day (*Stromata* 1.21.146). With the exception of Palestine in the fourth century, all Eastern Churches celebrated Christ's baptism, not the nativity, on January 6. Thomas Talley (*Origins of the Liturgical Year*) suggests that this may reflect the influence of the Gospel of Mark on an emerging African calendar: a Gospel that does not begin with nativity but with baptism as the initial revelatory event in Jesus' mission. In some places in the East January 6 was also a baptismal feast and called the "Feast of Lights" (Gregory of Nazianzus, *Oratio* 39.1).

The eastern manifestation feast of January 6 is more primitive than the western counterpart on December 25. In 274 CE the Emperor Aurelian established a feast of the birth of the sun on the solstice, December 25. The western feast builds on this pagan festival. First evidence for a Christian feast of nativity on December 25 appears in the Chronograph of 354 whose internal evidence suggests that the feast was celebrated as early as 330 in Rome. One context for the emergence of this feast was the Council of Nicea (325), which affirmed that God became man at the incarnation. The theological instinct to emphasize the wedding of divinity and humanity at incarnation was supported by a festival that celebrated nativity as the first revelation of Christ's divinity. This western feast influenced eastern calendars by the fourth century. The Syrian *Apostolic Constitutions* (ca. 380?) includes December 25 in its list of festivals, and Chrysostom (d. 407) apparently introduced this feast into Antioch circa 386. There is similar evidence from the 380s in Constantinople and Cappadocia.

The earliest mention of a January 6 feast in the West comes from Gaul circa 360. This festival commemorated the visit of the Magi,* Jesus' baptism, and the miracle at Cana. The West did not maintain January 6 as a feast of the Lord's baptism, but transformed it into a second nativity festival. It was distinguished from December 25th by focusing on the Magi or the "manifestation of Christ to the Gentiles" as exemplified by the preaching of Leo (d. 460) and Augustine (d. 430). This focus on the Magi in the West could be considering a move toward historicization, similar to that which occurred with the feast of the Ascension in the same century.

Attention to the adoration of the Magi gave way to focus on the Magi themselves. Though the Scriptures do not name them, note their number, or assert their royal heritage, all three of these transformations took place especially under the influence of Psalm 71:10 ("The kings of Tharsis . . . of the Arabians and of Seba shall bring gifts"). Eventually a separate feast developed for "Sts. Balthasar, Melchior and Gaspar" on July 23. Their "relics" were brought to Cologne in 1164 where they are still venerated today.

Focus on the Magi contributed to the structural separation of January 6 from December 25 in the West. A vigil developed by the sixth century, and an octave by the eighth century. By the high Middle Ages the intervening Sundays between Epiphany and Lent were counted as Sundays after Epiphany.

In recent western reforms Epiphany has been reintegrated into the "season of manifestation." In 1955 the octave of Epiphany was suppressed. Epiphany is now officially part of what the Roman Rite calls the "Christmas Season." *The General Norms for the Liturgical Year and Calendar* outlines the sweep of this season: "The Church holds most sacred the memorial of Christ's birth and early manifestation" (32). The octave of Epiphany and "Sundays after Epiphany" are suppressed. The Christmas season extends from Evening Prayer I of Christmas until the first Sunday after Epiphany or January 6 inclusive (33). The significance of Epiphany for the Church requires that it is celebrated on January 6 unless it has been assigned to the Sunday falling between January 2 and January 8 (37), as is the case in the United States.

Reintegrating Epiphany into the Christmas season allows the feast to function again as part of the yearly cycle of manifestations instead of simply a chronological celebration of the appearance of three mythic kings. Some liturgical texts do seem to focus on the Magi, e.g., "Father, you revealed your son to the Nations by the guidance of a star" (opening prayer, *Roman Missal*). More critical is the preface for Epiphany, subtitled "Christ the light of the Nations." The central text is "Today you revealed in Christ your eternal plan of salvation and showed him as the light of all peoples. Now that his glory has shone among us you have renewed humanity in his immortal image."

The readings for the day (Isa 60:1-6; Psalm 72; Eph 3:2-3, 5-6; Matt 2:1-12) need to be considered in the context of the entire season. Read in tandem with all the readings for the major feasts of the season, these texts appear as an integrated part of a continuing revelation: in nativity (December 25), to shepherds (Christmas Mass at dawn), in the context of believing family (Sunday in octave of Christmas, cycle A) which includes further revelations to the Jews (cycles B and C), to the nations (Epiphany), and in baptism (Baptism of the Lord). That ends the season, but not the revelatory cycle that continues in an elision with "ordinary time": the second Sunday of the year shows the continuation of the revelation through the witness of John the Baptizer (cycle A), the call of the first disciples (cycle B), and the first miracle (cycle C).

See: BAPTISM, JESUS CHRIST, LIGHT AND DARKNESS, MAGI, MIRACLE, NATIONS

EDWARD FOLEY, CAPUCHIN

EPISTLE/LETTER

An "epistle" is a literary composition possibly but not necessarily occasioned by a concrete situation, and intended for a wide public. A "letter" is a non-literary means of communication intended only for the person or persons to whom it is addressed. Letters are found within the OT writings (Jer 29:1-33); writing letters was a popular practice in the Hellenistic world. Paul* introduced it into the Christian movement, pioneering letter as a means to communicate with communities that he had founded in Asia Minor and Greece. He wrote 1 Thessalonians on his second missionary journey (51 CE) and the rest of his letters—Galatians 1 and 2 Corinthians, Philippians, Philemon, Romans—on his third missionary journey (52–56 CE). Romans is most like an epistle. Colossians is a letter; Ephesians is an "encyclical" epistle. Hebrews is a treatise, not a letter; the Pastorals—1 and 2 Timothy, Titus—are church orders in letter form. In Revelation (2:1–3:21) the letters to seven churches, or more accurately to their "angels," are simply literary introductions to the entire work which is cast in an epistolary framework.

Paul wrote letters to address the conflicts and problems that arose in the communities he founded, as well as to defend himself against attacks from other Christian missionaries. The concrete situation, as well as the contemporary style of writing letters, determined the literary form of his letters. Six elements normally appear in the identical sequence: address, greeting, thanksgiving, message, final greeting, benediction.

In the address Paul introduces himself as the sender, mentions his cosenders, and names those to whom the letter is written. How he describes himself sets a tone for the letter. Normally, Paul refers to his apostolic authority, because, as an apostle, he is entitled to address the community, admonish its members, and tell them how to resolve their difficulties. Paul often mentions his coworker(s) who may also have contributed to the contents of the letter. In greeting the community, Paul uses the same basic formula: "Grace to you and peace from God our Father and the Lord Jesus Christ" (2 Cor 1:2). Sometimes Paul expands the greeting with statements about God and Jesus Christ.

In the thanksgiving Paul discloses his reason for writing the letter, its dominant themes, and his attitude toward the community addressed, while providing valuable insights into his person and life. In 1 Thessalonians he devotes almost three-fifths of the letter to thanksgiving, and in 2 Corinthians he develops the thanksgiving into an extended blessing (1:3-11). Paul gives thanks for the community and prays that they may continue to grow by God's power at work in them until its final revelation at the end-time. In Galatians, however, Paul substitutes an angry rebuke (1:6-9) for his customary thanksgiving.

Without any set pattern Paul addresses his message to the particular issues that face this community at this time. Modeling his message on his "good news," Paul normally begins with statements about God's action in Jesus Christ and then moves to exhortations and instructions about how the community is concretely to live that good news. In the final greetings Paul frequently includes news about himself and those with him, as well as advice for specific individuals in the community. Paul concludes each letter with a simple benediction: "The grace of our Lord Jesus Christ be with you" (1 Cor 16:23). As in the initial greeting, this solemn closing expresses Paul's prayer that the community develop and grow in the Lord. Paul writes as a man of prayer and frames his letters with prayer.

Address, greeting, thanksgiving, message, final greeting, benediction—these six elements in the same sequence constitute the literary form of a Pauline letter. It is difficult to say whether Paul wrote his letters in his own hand, dictated them word-by-word to someone else, gave the sense of his message to a coworker who formulated the letter, or at times simply instructed a coworker to write in his name. He may have used different methods for different letters. But Paul claimed the letters as his own. At times he added a statement in his own hand to assure the community that he was the author (e.g., 1 Cor 16:21; Gal 6:11). Christians today who read the letters or pray with them must approach them as letters—not as more literary epistles (Ephesians), or as vivid stories about Jesus (Matthew; Mark; Luke; John), or as treatises about the risen Lord (Hebrews), or as apocalyptic visions of the end time (Revelation).

See: APOSTLE, COMMUNITY, GOOD NEWS, PAUL

WILLIAM G. THOMPSON, S.J.

ESCHATOLOGY

This entry consists of three parts. The OT section describes ancient Israel's expectations about the end as they relate to the nation of Israel, the cosmos, and the individual. The NT section explores the variety of ways Christ is associated with the final establishment of God's power at the consummation of history. The Pastoral-Liturgical section examines how an original expectation of Christ's imminent return became transformed into an expectation of Christ's return in the distant future.

Old Testament

Eschatology literally means "talk about the end." In biblical theology the term refers to various kinds of expectation about the future. It will be helpful to distinguish between national, cosmic, and personal eschatology.

National Eschatology. The earliest "talk about an end" in the OT is found in the prophet Amos (eighth century BCE). The prophet sees a basket of ripe fruit and is told, "The time is ripe to have done with

my people Israel; I will forgive them no longer" (Amos 8:2. The Hebrew involves a word play on *qayis*, ripe fruit, and *qes*, end). Amos predicted that the northern kingdom of Israel would be brought to an end: "The eyes of the Lord God are on this sinful people and I will destroy it from off the face of the earth" (9:8). His prophecy was exceptional in its finality, but it was fulfilled when the Assyrians destroyed Samaria in 722 BCE. The northern kingdom, as such, was never restored.

While predictions of doom are characteristic of OT prophecy (cf. Jer 28:8), most of the prophets entertained some hope for the future. Hosea, whose career must have overlapped with that of Amos, spoke movingly of a new Exodus, when the Lord would again woo Israel in the wilderness (Hosea 2). Yet the same prophet could say, "Where are your plagues, O death! where is your sting, O nether world! My eyes are closed to compassion" (13:14). There is a tension here between the prophet's trust in divine mercy and his realistic appraisal of the political and military situation in which he lived. The northern kingdom was in fact doomed. The hopes of Israel, however, lived on in the southern kingdom of Judah. So a later editor could soften Amos's message and assure his readers that "I will not destroy the house of Jacob completely, says the Lord" (Amos 9:8).

The existence of Judah was also precarious. At the time of the Assyrian crisis at the end of the eighth century BCE, the prophet Isaiah predicted that Judah would be like an oak whose trunk remains when its leaves have fallen (Isa 6:13). Isaiah, however, foresaw that a remnant would return (hence the name of his son Shear-jashub, 7:3). In the Book of Isaiah we also first meet with messianic prophecy: the expectation of a utopian age under an ideal king: "a shoot shall sprout from the stump of Jesse. . . . Then the wolf shall be a guest of the lamb and the leopard shall lie down with the kid" (Isa 11:1-9). Some scholars think that this passage is a later addition to the Book of Isaiah, but it is quite conceivable in the time of the prophet. The language, of course, is poetic and not to be taken literally. It expresses the human yearning for peace and harmony, which the ideology of kingship in the ancient Near East always promised but could never deliver.

The survival of Judah was more seriously threatened a century after the time of Isaiah by the Babylonian invasion. This time Jerusalem would be destroyed. The prophets Jeremiah and Ezekiel were blunt in their warnings. Jeremiah declared that no descendant of the current king, Jehoiachin, would ever again sit on the throne of David (23:30). Ezekiel echoed the words of Amos: "The end has come upon the four corners of the land! Now the end is upon you . . ." (7:2-3). Yet we are told that in the darkest days of the siege of Jerusalem Jeremiah purchased the field of a relative in Anathoth because "houses and fields and vineyards shall again be bought in this land" (32:15). Also attributed to Jeremiah is the prophecy of a new covenant when God would place the Law within the people and write it upon their hearts (Jer 31:31-34). At the end of the Book of Ezekiel we also find prophecies of restoration. (The authenticity of these prophecies is disputed.) The most vivid is the vision of a valley full of dry bones that come back to life (Ezekiel 37). The bones are identified as "the whole house of Israel" and the prophet is told to prophesy: "O my people, I will open your graves and have you rise from them and bring you back to the land of Israel" (37:12). Resurrection* here is a metaphor for the restoration of Israel from the Exile.

The hope for restoration figures prominently in the period after the Exile. The so-called Second Isaiah envisaged the return from Babylon as a new Exodus across the desert (Isaiah 40). The prophet Haggai expected that the earth would be transformed when the Temple was rebuilt. No great transformation took place. Increasingly, the eschatological hopes were assigned to the indefinite future. In the prophetic books we find several passages with the phrase "In days to come . . ." or "in the last days" (e.g.,

Isa 2:2; Mic 4:1; Hos 3:5; Ezek 38:16). These passages were probably inserted by editors in the postexilic period. Some messianic prophecies are also late additions (e.g., Jer 23:5-6). The hope of restoration became a standard part of Jewish religion even when it was not expected in the near future.

The hope for national restoration persisted into the NT period. The Book of Daniel predicts that "the God of heaven will set up a kingdom which will never be destroyed or delivered up to another people" (2:44) and that "the people of the holy ones of the Most High" will be given an everlasting kingdom (7:27). While this kingdom is not further described, it presumably involves a restoration of the Jewish kingdom on earth. In the first century BCE the apocryphal Psalms of Solomon predict the coming of a Davidic Messiah. In the apocalypse of 4 Ezra (2 Esdras 7:28), from about 100 CE, the Messiah will reign on earth for four hundred years before the final transformation. By this period, however, Jewish eschatology had become much more complex, and involved much more than national restoration.

Cosmic Eschatology. When Amos was contemplating the imminent destruction of Israel, he saw in a vision a fire that "devoured the great abyss and was consuming the land" (7:4). He is assured by the Lord that this would not be, but the vision functions as a metaphor for what would actually happen. Later prophets often use cosmic imagery to express the enormity of their situations. So Jeremiah "looked at the earth, and it was waste and void; at the heavens, and their light had gone out!" (Jer 4:23). An oracle preserved in Isaiah 13 describes the fall of Babylon as an eclipse of the heavenly bodies, and another anonymous, postexilic oracle in Isaiah 34 says that because of the Lord's anger against Edom "the heavens shall be rolled up like a scroll and all their host shall wither away." In all these cases it is clear that the language is metaphorical, and that an end of the physical world is not at issue.

This is still true in Isaiah 65:1: "Lo, I am about to create new heavens and a new earth." The language of a new creation is used to express the hope for radical change. In Isaiah 65 the prophet hopes for a utopian state where no one would die prematurely. Yet this state would be similar to life as we know it: "they shall live in the houses they build, and eat the fruit of the vineyards they plant," and die at a ripe old age. What concerns the prophet is not the future of the physical world but the conditions of human life.

The hope for a new erection, in the sense of a radical change in the human condition, could also be expressed through the language of ancient myth. Speaking of the restoration from the Exile, Second Isaiah recalls God's battle with the monster Rahab and the mythical dragon. No such battle is reported in Genesis, but there are allusions to it in the poetic books (Job 26:12; Ps 89:11). We know that other Near Eastern peoples envisaged creation as a battle between the creator and a monster (e.g., the Babylonian creation story, *Enuma Elish*, tells of a battle between Marduk and the monster Tiamat). The Israelites evidently had a similar story. In the postexilic period, the imagery of this myth was used to describe what would happen in the future. So in Isaiah 27:1 we read that "on that day, the Lord will punish with his sword that is cruel, great and strong, Leviathan the fleeing serpent, Leviathan the coiled serpent; and he will slay the dragon that is in the sea." Leviathan here is not any particular historical enemy of Israel. It represents everything that is wrong with this world. The same section of Isaiah (Isaiah 24–27, written after the Exile) says that God "will destroy the veil that veils all peoples . . . he will destroy Death forever" (25:7-8). Death, like Leviathan, was a figure in ancient Canaanite myth. In this case the symbolism is transparent.

The mythical and cosmic imagery of postexilic prophecy expresses a concern that goes beyond the welfare of the people of Israel and addresses the human condition at large. Even when the later prophets are concerned with Israel's enemies, we still find a tendency to universalization. Ezekiel 38–39, probably an addition to the book, uses the fictional Gog from the land of Magog as a symbol for Gentile power, which will eventually be crushed in the land of Israel. Joel 4 assembles all the nations for judgment in the valley of Jehoshaphat. The theme of universal judgment plays a prominent part in the apocalyptic* literature that appears in the second century BCE and is represented in the OT by the Book of Daniel.

Daniel reflects a very specific crisis in the history of Judaism: the persecution by Antiochus Epiphanes, which is described in the Books of Maccabees. In Daniel 7, however, Epiphanes and all Gentile kingdoms are cloaked in the imagery of ancient myth: they are beasts that come up out of the sea. The judgment in Daniel 7 is not only on the enemies of the Maccabean period but on all Gentile power. The figure who comes in triumph in Daniel's vision, however, is not the national Messiah of Israel but a heavenly "one like a son of man" who comes on the clouds of heaven. Later in Daniel the heavenly victor is identified as the archangel Michael (Dan 12:1). In Jewish writings of the NT period (the Similitudes of Enoch, 4 Ezra) this "Son of Man" figure is identified as the Messiah, but he is also a heavenly figure and represents a transformation of the messianic hope.

Even Daniel does not envisage the end of the physical world. That idea first appears in Jewish sources in the Book of Enoch, an apocryphal work preserved in Ethiopic, some parts of which are older than Daniel. There we read that "the world will be written down for destruction . . . and the first heaven will vanish and pass away, and a new heaven will appear" (1 Enoch 91:15-16). By the end of the first century CE the end of the world was an established part of Jewish eschatology. The clearest expression is in 4 Ezra 7:30, which says that after the messianic age the world will be turned back to primeval silence for seven days. Then it will be aroused, that which is corruptible will perish, and the earth will give up its dead.

Personal Eschatology. The end of the world, as we find it in 4 Ezra, is closely bound up with the idea of resurrection.* Only those who are raised from the dead can pass over to the new world. The idea of resurrection was firmly rejected in much of the OT. It is a commonplace in the psalms that the dead do not praise the Lord. Even in Sirach, at the beginning of the second century BCE, we read that "whether one has lived a thousand years, a hundred, or ten, in the nether world he has no claim on life" (Sir 41:4).

There are only a few hints in the OT of a hope for life beyond death (other than the pale survival of the shade in Sheol). The psalmist expresses confidence that God will not abandon his soul to the nether world (Ps 16:10), but the deliverance envisaged is probably temporary. We have seen that resurrection is used as a metaphor for the restoration of Israel in Ezekiel 37 and that Isaiah 25 affirms that God will destroy death. The first clear occurrence of a belief in the resurrection of individuals, however, is in Daniel 12:2: "Many of those who sleep in the dust of the earth shall awake; some shall live forever, others shall be an everlasting horror and disgrace." The context of this passage is the persecution of the Jews by Antiochus Epiphanes. According to traditional Jewish belief, those who kept the law of God would prosper in this life. In the time of persecution it was precisely those who kept the Law who were put to death. We also find affirmations of resurrection in the same context in 2 Maccabees 7 (the story of the mother and her seven sons). The hope for immortality is also presented in a context of persecution in the Wisdom of Solomon.

In the Book of Daniel the resurrection is part of the cosmic upheaval at the end of a period of crisis. It is not something that happens to individuals in isolation. This is also the case in other apocalyptic writings, from the Book of Enoch to 4 Ezra. The ex-

pectation of resurrection is the clearest point of distinction between apocalyptic eschatology and the older eschatology of the prophets. It came to be widely accepted in Judaism after the Maccabean period. The emergence of this belief is probably the most significant shift in the history of Jewish eschatology. The Jewish people in the NT period continued to hope for national restoration. The judgment of the dead, however, would be a judgment of individuals. Eschatology would henceforth concern not only the welfare of the nation on earth but the eternal salvation* or damnation of the individual.

See: JUDGMENT, MESSIAH, RESURRECTION

JOHN J. COLLINS

Eschatology, from the Greek *eschatos*, last, having to do with beliefs and ideas about the end time, and with the valuation of time and history in this perspective. Most religious traditions have some set of beliefs about an ultimate future of the individual and of the earth, whether that future is envisioned as eternal, cyclic, or limited.

New Testament

Christian eschatology is dominated by the theme of the significance of the past, historical figure of Jesus of Nazareth inasmuch as he is also the risen and exalted Christ who has a future role to play as the one who will return at a determined time in the future (John 21:22-23; Acts 1:11). The precise manner of his return varies considerably. For some, he will be the inaugurator of a new era in history. Thus Christian eschatology looks to the future, but in light of the past event of Jesus. The flow of time is thus sanctified and brought into the process of future fulfillment. NT eschatology is therefore "proleptic" or "inaugurated," expressing both the "already" of Jesus' first coming, and the "not yet" when the full meaning of that coming will be revealed.

Apocalyptic. One NT form of eschatology, apocalyptic,* structures language and thinking about the end around a perceived present crisis that gives signs in the form of visions and secret revelations about what is to come, necessitating cataclysmic upheaval of cosmic proportions that will bring great suffering and turmoil before the final resolution of conflict in God's defeat and destruction of the powers of evil and establishment of a new heavenly era. Here, the final coming of Christ (his "parousia"*) is accompanied by cosmic signs of great power (Matt 24:29-31; Mark 13:24-27; 1 Thess 4:16-17; Rev 1:7). This return will be sudden and unannounced, taking the unprepared by complete surprise (Matt 24:36-41; Mark 13:33; 2 Pet 3:10); hence the need for constant preparedness (Matt 24:42-51; Mark 13:35-37; Luke 21:34-36). Often too it includes the bodily resurrection* of the dead, in which the resurrection of Christ was but the first sign (1 Cor 15:23; Rev 20:4-5). Sometimes, however, the return of Christ is envisioned in less spectacular ways (John 14:3; Titus 2:13; Heb 9:28). But apocalyptic eschatology, while not the only form of eschatology in the NT, is so prevalent there and its symbolism so widespread that it is often difficult to distinguish it from other kinds of eschatology.

Synoptic Gospels. The eschatology of the Synoptic Gospels highlights the reign of God* (Matthew: reign of heaven) as the elusive mystery that, from its humble and unobtrusive beginnings, grows like the mustard seed into a great thing (Matt 13:31-32; Mark 4:30-32). Thus it is at the same time the imminent reality hidden in the midst of daily life (Mark 4:26-28; Matt 13:33), the mysterious presence that requires conversion* (Mark 1:14), yet also the consummation in the glorious age to come (Luke 21:25-31). The reign of God will ultimately be the era in which God's interests will triumph, but the seeds of that era are already present when disciples turn to God in faith.

Banquet. The banquet is a frequent eschatological symbol, since solemn feasting is an ancient and traditional way of imagining

heavenly happiness. This is how Matthew speaks of the inclusion of the Gentiles in the reign of heaven (Matt 8:11-12), and Luke of the reward of the faithful disciples as they will be constituted judges (Luke 22:28-30). In both Matthew and Luke, Jesus tells a story about a banquet whose invited guests are replaced by others (Matt 22:1-14; Luke 14:15-24). In Matthew's version, it is a king's wedding feast for his son, which enhances the Christological allusion and combines the banquet motif with another traditional eschatological theme, marriage (see Rev 21:2-4). Luke's version begins with an explicit reference to the eschatological banquet (Luke 14:15). The Last Supper is also understood by the Synoptics to be an eschatological meal that inaugurates the period of expectation for Jesus' return (Matt 26:29; Mark 14:25; Luke 22:15-16), and Paul interprets every Eucharistic celebration as such (1 Cor 11:26, 29).

Gospel of John. The Gospel of John contains several distinct eschatological models. What has been called a "realized eschatology" brings expectation of the future into the present for those who believe in Jesus: what is promised is also fulfilled in the presence of Jesus, who is Way, Truth, and Life (John 14:6), and Resurrection (John 11:25). To believe in him and in God is to have eternal life (John 17:3). Yet, John has echoes of apocalyptic eschatology in the raising of the dead from their tombs (John 5:28-29; 6:39-40). Still another form of Johannine eschatology has been called "heavenly eschatology": here, especially in the Last Supper Discourse (chs. 14–17), the theme is that Jesus, the one from heaven, returns there as in a homecoming, and goes to prepare a place for those who believe in him and are his disciples (John 14:2-4, 28; 16:28).

Paul. Pauline eschatology generally follows the apocalyptic mode, with Paul's own particular emphases and interpretations. For him, the first Adam from the earth brought sin and therefore death into the world; the last Adam, Christ, brings release from this condemnation by opening the way to resurrection and spiritual transformation (Rom 5:12-21; 1 Cor 15:42-50). Though earlier in his ministry Paul anticipates a dramatic appearance of Christ (1 Thess 4:13-18; 2 Thess 2:7-10; 1 Cor 15:51-52), as he writes to the Romans, his fiery language has changed to deep and patient expectation (Rom 8:18-25).

1 and 2 Peter. In the Petrine Letters, too, the sense of expectation is profound and affective (1 Pet 1:8-12; 4:7), except for the apocalyptic flash of 2 Peter 3:7-12, and perhaps merges with an envisioned persecution, just as the Synoptic apocalyptic theology is inseparable from the catastrophic scene of the destruction of Jerusalem. In the face of scoffers who would deny the reason for Christian hope in the coming of Christ, the author of 2 Peter reassures readers that their hope must remain alive (2 Pet 3:1-13), which does not indicate a major crisis of "the delay of the parousia" in the early Church, as has sometimes been thought by modern biblical scholars.

Final Opposition and Judgment.* The appearance of a personalized superhuman opponent of Christ and his kingdom as a sign just before the endtime is sometimes presumed: Paul's "lawless one" (2 Thess 2:3-12), 1 John's "antichrist"* (1 John 2:18, 22; 4:3), or the beast of Revelation (Rev 13:1-8), though this individualized opponent figure is by no means a constant feature of NT eschatology, but a deepening of the awareness of the contingency of history.

A key concept surrounding projected events of the endtime has to do with the judgment of nations and groups as well as assignment of individuals to different eternal destinies, depending on how they have lived their lives (Matt 25:31-46; 2 Cor 5:10; 2 Tim 4:1, 8; 1 Pet 4:5-6, 17-19; Heb 9:27; Rev 11:18). Typically, John claims that this judgment takes place here and now as each one responds to the confrontation with the person of Jesus (John 3:17-21). In some strands of this tradition, Jesus' closest disciples, or the saints in general, will co-preside with Christ in the final judgment (Matt 19:28; Luke 22:30; 1 Cor 6:2-3; Rev 3:21; 20:4; see Dan 7:22). This participation of the faithful in the judgment of others is one way of envisioning the righting of wrongs, an answer to the perennial problem: Why does God allow the innocent to suffer at the hands of the wicked?

Millennium. A much popularized eschatological feature that appears only in the Book of Revelation is the millennium, the thousand-year reign on earth of the deceased but now resurrected faithful with Christ before the rest of the dead are resurrected for judgment (Rev 20:1-6). Several important early Church writers were captivated with this idea, but it was soon repudiated in its literal sense. Like all explicit eschatological imagery, this is another way of imagining a time and place in which truth and justice will triumph, and the faithful who have suffered will be vindicated.

There is no single NT eschatology, but a variety of ways of envisioning and talking about a consummation of history in which finally God's power will be established in the person of the exalted Christ. It would be a mistake to literalize any of the details. Together, they create a scenario by which Christian hope has been nourished over the centuries, even as it continues to be.

See: ADAM AND EVE, ANTICHRIST, APOCALYPTIC, BEASTS/MONSTERS OF THE DEEP, CONVERSION, GOSPEL, JERUSALEM, JESUS CHRIST, JUDGMENT, MARRIAGE, MINISTRY, PAROUSIA, REIGN OF GOD, RESURRECTION, SAINTS, VISIONS

CAROLYN OSIEK, R.S.C.J.

Pastoral-Liturgical Tradition

The development of eschatological thought in the history of the tradition is uneven and at times obscure. In the earliest period after the completion of the NT the concerns of Christian writers remained closely linked to those of the Scriptures. Christians expected the return of the Lord. But there is evidence of a two-fold tradition, one of near-expectation and one of distant-expectation. In both cases eschatological awareness is linked to the puzzling fact that, despite what Christians have claimed about Jesus, history continues to run its course and does not seem to be empirically very different from pre-Christian history.

The Patristic era gave rise to various forms of millenarianism as well as to the theory of universal restoration (*apokatastasis*). The former, which held that Christ would reign on earth with his elect for a thousand years prior to the end of history, was derived from a too-literal interpretation of texts such as Revelation 20. A metaphorical approach to such texts suggested by Origen in the East and Augustine in the West offered an alternate possibility for dealing with such issues. The theory of universal restoration, found in Origen as well as in other Eastern writers, was rejected by the Council of Constantinople in 553 CE. Neither of these views would disappear completely, and both can be found among eschatological patterns down to the present.

In the twelfth century there were attempts to develop a theology of history by authors such as Rupert of Deutz and Honorius of Autun. In this period the work of Joachim of Fiore is particularly important. He developed a new style of interpreting the Scriptures, and his doctrine of the three ages of history would play a significant role in subsequent Western reflection, particularly in various forms of utopian thought.

Aside from such historically oriented models, Medieval and Baroque eschatology devoted much energy to the study of the destiny of the individual person as theologians developed extensive speculations about the nature of the separated soul, the interim period, the nature and location of purgatory, the resurrected body, and the understanding of heaven as beatific vision. At the same time in literature and at the popular level, eschatology took the form of an elaborate geography of other-worldly places.

Despite some attempts in the nineteenth century to develop theology in dialogue with the then current Romantic philosophies of history, the dominant style of Roman Catholic eschatology would remain the style bequeathed by Baroque Catholicism and sharpened by nineteenth century Neo-Scholasticism. Hence for recent generations of Catholics, eschatology was simply the doctrine about the "last things" presented as the final tract in the Neo-Scholastic handbook tradition of the late nineteenth and early twentieth century.

Under the impact of biblical studies and contemporary philosophies of history and utopian thought, theology currently has moved away from this physical style with its individualistic focus to a style that is more anthropological in tone and reflects a stronger concern for the social and collective aspects of the broader tradition. This shift in approach coheres with an understanding of eschatological language which sees it not as descriptive of places and events but basically as a metaphorical suggestion of creation's final relation with God.

In the aftermath of the Christian-Marxist dialogues of the 1960s there is a notable tendency to develop eschatology in the context of a philosophy of hope and to search out the relation between common human hope and the biblical vision of hope for the fulfillment of God's creation. A significant concern of these discussions was the Marxist sense that it is the Christian belief in a transcendent future that effectively alienates Christians from concern for engagement in world-building. This led to discussions of the relation between human action and divine agency and of the relation between humanly-created futures and a divine future.

From a totally different perspective and independently of the biblical renewal, evolutionary and cosmological concerns are reflected in the attempt of Teilhard de Chardin to bring the vision of faith into closer relation with the concerns of contemporary science. His work inspired attempts to relate the sense of cosmic, evolutionary history with the biblical sense of an open-ended future in a cosmic process that finds its ultimate fruit in the mystery of Christ. This suggested the need for a new model for doing theology and has given rise to attempts to redefine the relation of natural evolution to what in Teilhard's language is called *Christification* (= the transforming union of the world with God through love). These challenges were picked up by K. Rahner and others in the 1960s. More recently R. Pendergast and T. Berry have suggested ways in which the vision of contemporary scientific cosmology might become the primary matrix for defining the problems of human and cosmic history from a theological perspective.

The teaching of Vatican II represents an important instance of magisterial teaching attempting to deal with the theological implications of the renewal of eschatological thought. The council makes a significant distinction between the Church and the reign of God, seeing the former as the historical instrument of the latter. While the council clearly sees the reign of God as a transcendent future that cannot be identified with any empirical, social configuration (Dogmatic Constitution on the Church, nos. 8, 44, 48-51), it attempts to draw from its vision of the reign of God the motivation for Christian engagement in the processes of world-building (e.g., Pastoral Constitution on the Church in the Modern World, no. 39).

In the years since the closing of Vatican II we have seen the rise of a number of theological projects inspired by eschatological thought and metaphors: theology of the world, theology of liberation, and theology of revolution. While none of these attempts can claim theological adequacy, by developing the implications of the biblical eschatological vision, they have brought significant enrichment to many areas of Christian theology.

In summary, two major directions of development characterize the current state of the question:

(1) Theologians have developed a basic reinterpretation of the traditional themes of individual eschatology and of universal or collective eschatology. While the form of individual eschatology familiar from the handbooks might be too limited in its vision, still the issues of individual destiny must be dealt with. The individual and collective dimensions must be maintained in an irreducible dialectical relation with each other.

(2) The development of historical and cosmological themes is situated in the context of a Christian theology of hope. If questions about personal and collective destiny are questions about a future, they cannot be isolated from the human sense of historicity or from the cosmic context within which human historical consciousness is located. Eschatology must deal with the question of history without allowing Christian hope to be reduced simply to a principle of inevitable evolutionary progress, whether cosmic, cultural, or ethical. Christian hope must reckon with the possibility that humanity can act in opposition to the creative aim of God. Finally, the transcendent future opened to humanity by God is not simply identical with any humanly created future. Theology at this level must deal with the relation between eschatology and creation theology, and with the problem of human freedom and its relation to the divine manner of activity.

See: JUDGMENT

ZACHARY HAYES, O.F.M.

ETHIOPIA

In the Bible Ethiopia is known as Cush (as it is in Egyptian, Babylonian, and Assyrian sources), and to the Greeks as Aithiopia (red face or burnt face), and so identified in Homer [Od. 1:22-24] and Herodotus [iii.94]. Eratosthenes (ca. 200 BCE) refers to the area as Nubia (Strabo, Geog. xvii.1, 2). These terms originally designated the entire area south of the First Cataract of the Nile, including what is now Sudan, Ethiopia, and Eritrea. In the narrower sense it refers to the highlands east of the Nile, the territory now known as Ethiopia.

The earliest references to Cush occur in Egyptian records during the reign of Pharaoh Sesostris (1971–1928 BCE) who completed the conquest of Nubia. Egypt,* whose southern border was at the First Cataract, at Aswan, expanded into the southern area for economic and imperial reasons, and maintained its control until approximately 1000 BCE. Independence came to Cush at about the same time it came to Israel under David and Solomon, and probably for the same reason, the simultaneous decline in power of both Egypt and Babylonia/Assyria.

With the ebb of Egyptian control the area achieved self-rule, and under the Nubian/Ethiopian Pharaoh Sheshonk we hear of an invasion of Israel during the reign of Rehoboam, Solomon's successor. During the next century Ethiopian Kings Piankhy, Shabataka, and Tirhaka became major players in the Fertile Crescent and Tigris/Euphrates Valley.

By 350 CE, a dynasty of Southwest Arabian origin took control under King Azana and established its capital at Aksum. The new rulers converted to Christianity and Monophysite Coptic religion became the state religion. Church and state were closely linked and the Ethiopian Church looked to Alexandria for religious authority. The Aksumite Kingdom was deeply influenced by early semitic language and cultural roots going back to the tenth preChristian century and Judeo-Christian influences from their formative years.

The thirteenth century saw the establishment of the Solomonic dynasty, which reigned uninterruptedly until 1974 when Haile Selassie was deposed. The Ethiopian epic Kebra Nagast (Glory of the Kings) was composed in the fourteenth century and contained the legend of Solomon and the Queen of Sheba, the birth of their son King Menelik I, and the removal of the ark of the covenant to Ethiopia. The sacred literary language of Ethiopia is Ge'ez, a semitic tongue that shares many words with Hebrew and Arabic.

Old Testament

In the Hebrew Bible Ethiopia is always referred to as Cush. It is mentioned twice in Genesis, and although its location is disputed by some, it seems clear that Ethiopia is involved. Reference to Cush and the Gihon River (Gen 2:13) points in this direction, and the fact that the term in Ethiopic for the Nile springs is Gijon supports this view.

In the geography of the nations in Genesis 10, we read of the sons of Ham: Cush, Mizraim, and Put. In Egyptian sources, Mizraim, Put, and Cush are used to describe the area from Lower Egypt to the area of Ethiopia and the headwaters of the Nile.

Some suspect that Moses was not only raised in Egypt, but that he had Nubian/ Ethiopian connections. The episode of his Cushite wife (Num 12:1), a suspicion by some that Zipporah and the Cushite were one and the same; and the fact Aaron's grandson was named Pinehas (Egyptian for Nubian) raises interesting questions. Cushan appears as a synonym in parallelism with Midian in Habakkuk (3:7), and in the Septuagint it is rendered as Aithiopon.

The visit of the Queen of Sheba to Solomon suggests contact with Southwestern Arabia and Ethiopia. The invasion of Israel by Sheshonk (probably an Ethiopian Pharaoh) after the death of Solomon included Ethiopian troops (2 Chr 12:3), and not too many years later there is a reference to Zerah the Ethiopian with his army and chariots.

By 700 BC we hear of Tirhaka, the Ethiopian king of the dynasty that had thrown off Egyptian control, actively involved in the area (2 Kgs 19:9; Isa 37:9), in connection with an Assyrian invasion (701 BCE).

Isaiah (43:3) speaks of the wealth of Ethiopia; Nahum (3:9) of its strength. Zephaniah (3:10) speaks of exiles returning from Ethiopia; Daniel (11:43) refers to "the treasures of the . . . Ethiopians." Jeremiah is rescued from prison by Ebed Melech, an Ethiopian mercenary (38:7ff.) and as part of a polemic against his own people's stubborness could say: "Can an Ethiopian change his skin?" (3:28). Amos, in a similar vein, cries out: "Are you not like the sons of the Ethiopians?" (9:7).

When Babylonia sacks Jerusalem and puts an end to Judah, some of the exiles flee to Egypt as far south as Tahpanhes (Jer 44:1) which is in the Ethiopia area.

New Testament and Midrash

Unlike the OT, which has many references to Ethiopia and Ethiopians, there is only one in the NT (Acts 8:27), the episode of the Ethiopian eunuch, an official of the court of the Queen of Ethiopia who is "on a pilgrimage to Jerusalem." He is encountered by Philip, reading the prophet Isaiah in his chariot, asks for exegesis, and as a result is persuaded to become a Christian. This would mark the first link of Ethiopia to Christianity, the only mention in the Gospels. The referral to the Ethiopian Queen as Candace is an interesting example of the inclusion of an Ethiopic term characteristic of the Aksumite kingdom. It is, as well, another link in the chain of evidence that establishes continuing links between Ethiopia and Jerusalem.

In Talmudic and Midrashic literature there are a few more references, perhaps five or six. There is one reference to a historical figure, Zerah, King of Ethiopia. It is in connection with a legendary account of the hoard of gold gathered by Joseph, taken when the Israelites left Egypt, and then plundered by the various Empires ruling Jerusalem. In this context Ethiopia is considered among the major powers with Egypt, Assyria, Babylonia, Persia, Greece, and Rome (Pesahim 119a). Other references deal with the size of Ethiopia (Pesahim 94a), the black skin of an Ethiopian as a sign of distinction (Berakhot 45b) or in a derogatory sense (ibid. and Kid. 49a). In the former case the reference to Moses and his Ethiopian wife is used as evidence for the beauty of Zipporah. In this connection we can also cite the passage "I am black and beautiful" from the Song of Songs (1:5).

See: EGYPT

HAYIM GOREN PERELMUTER

EUCHARIST

The Eucharist is a specifically Christian event with its origins in the life, death, and resurrection of Jesus. As such, it did not exist in OT times, but like so many other realities in the NT, it has deep roots there, and Christians can see how it was foreshadowed in the OT.

Old Testament

The traditional liturgical text Paul cites in 1 Corinthians 11:23-25 includes several terms rich with OT meaning and two major OT themes. The terms are body,* remembrance* or memorial, cup,* and blood.* The themes are those of sacrifice and covenant. The sacrificial offering implied in the words "This is my body that is for you" (1 Cor 11:24) evokes the OT peace offerings made in thanksgiving (Lev 7:11-15; 22:29). These sacrifices point to the thanksgiving sacrifice of the NT in which the bread* (Lev 7:12-13) is the body or person of Christ. The "new covenant" referred to in the words "This cup is the new covenant in my blood" (1 Cor 11:25) evokes the Mosaic covenant initiated at Sinai with a blood offering (Exod 24:3-8) and communion sacrifice (Exod 24:9-11), as well as Jeremiah's announcement of "a new covenant" with God's Law written upon the heart (see Jer 31:31-34).

In 1 Corinthians, Paul further develops this earliest OT typology. Applying the NT terms "baptism," "spiritual food," and "spiritual drink" to OT realities (1 Cor 10:1-5), Paul showed how being "under the cloud" (see Exod 13:21-22; Pss 78:14; 105:39) and passing "through the sea" (see Exod 14:15-16; Ps 78:13) foreshadowed Christian baptism, and how the quail and the manna (see Exod 16:4-35; Pss 78:24-30; 105:40) and the water from the rock (see Exod 17:1-7; Pss 78:15-16; 105:41), foreshadowed the spiritual food and drink of the Eucharist. Pursuing the same typology with the example of those who "sat down to eat and drink, and rose up to revel" (1 Cor 10:7; see Exod 32:6; Num 25:1-9), Paul showed that the Eucharist would do them no good if they indulged in immorality (1 Cor 10:6-13).

The Synoptic Gospels enlarged the OT typological repertoire by introducing the theme of the Suffering Servant of the Lord, the imagery of the eschatological banquet, and the Feast of the Unleavened Bread and the Passover. The theme of the Suffering Servant is evoked in the words accompanying the cup, "which will be shed for many" (Mark 14:24) and "shed on behalf of many for the forgiveness of sins" (Matt 26:28). For Mark and Matthew, the Songs of the Suffering Servant, especially Isaiah 52:13–53:12, point to Jesus and his fulfillment of the Servant's "passion" in his own passion and in the Eucharist. The imagery of the eschatological banquet (Isa 25:6; 55:1-2; 65:13-14) is recalled in Jesus' reference to drinking the fruit of the vine "new in the kingdom of God" (Mark 14:25; Matt 26:29; see Luke 22:18) and to not eating the Passover again "until there is fulfillment in the kingdom of God" (Luke 22:16). The Isaian eschatological banquet thus points to the eschatological dimension of the Eucharistic banquet.

The typology of the Suffering Servant and the imagery of the eschatological banquet were introduced in the liturgical text itself. The Synoptic Gospels also enrich our typological understanding by associating Jesus' Last Supper and the Lord's Supper with the Feast of the Unleavened Bread and the Passover (Mark 14:1, 12, 14; Matt 26:2, 17-19; Luke 22:1, 7-13, 15). The important point in this is not whether Jesus' Last Supper was actually a Passover meal, but that the Synoptic Gospels went out of their way to present it as such. In the Synoptics, the Lord's Supper, celebrated weekly on the first day of the week, is thus filled with the meaning of Passover and the Feast of the Unleavened Bread. So it is that the great Passover texts of the OT (e.g., Exod 12:1-28; Deut 16:1-8) announce and prepare the NT Passover of Jesus' passion-resurrection and its celebration in the Eucharist.

John's Gospel further enriches the OT repertory of "Eucharistic" texts by developing the Exodus and manna* typology and introducing the imagery of the banquet of wisdom. The Exodus and manna typology is essential for understanding some key elements in Jesus' discourse on the bread of life (John 6:31-35, 48-51, 57-58). John presupposes the similarities and emphasizes the differences between the old and the new manna. Those who ate of the old manna died, but those who eat the new manna, which is the very person and flesh of Jesus, will never die. The manna of the Exodus (see Pss 78:24; 105:40; Exod 16:4, 13-15; Num 11:7-9) is superceded by the manna provided by Jesus in word and sacrament. The same Johannine passages (John 6:31-35, 48-51, 57-58) present the nourishment Jesus provides as fulfilling the OT banquet of wisdom (Prov 9:1-6; Sir 24:19-24). The OT feast of wisdom is thus fulfilled in the banquet of Eucharistic wisdom.

New Testament

Institution. The most important text on the Eucharist in the NT is the account of its institution in an old liturgical formula used at the Lord's Supper. The text appears in four different forms, reflecting diverse theological and pastoral concerns (1 Cor 11:23-25; Mark 14:22-25; Matt 26:26-29; Luke 22:19-20), but with the basic elements reaching back to the very earliest years of Christianity. The four forms of the text can be grouped in pairs, the Pauline and Lukan representing the Antiochene tradition at two different stages of its development, and the Markan and Matthean representing the Jerusalem or Palestinian tradition.

Already in earliest tradition, the liturgical text for the Lord's Supper was associated with Jesus' Last Supper "on the night he was handed over" (1 Cor 11:23), assuring that the Lord's Supper would always be seen in the context of Jesus' passion and death and the Last Supper in that of his resurrection and risen life. There is no separating Jesus' passion from the resurrection, and there is no separating the table of the risen Lord from the table of Jesus' passion and death. In the Synoptic Gospels, the institution is part of the Last Supper account and plays a major role interpreting the passion-resurrection of Jesus and assuring that Jesus' death would be understood actively as the giving and offering of his life and not passively as its taking away. The liturgical text has also left its mark on several other meal stories in the NT, notably the six accounts of the breaking of bread, popularly referred to as "the multiplication of loaves" (Mark 6:34-44; 8:1-10; Matt 14:13-21; 15:32-39; Luke 9:10-17; John 6:1-15), investing these and other events with Eucharistic significance.

In each of its forms, the institution narrative includes two parts, the first dealing with the bread and the second with the cup. Each part includes a narrative statement of what Jesus did, followed by a direct quotation of what he said. For example, the narrative statement in 1 Corinthians 11:23-24a indicates that "the Lord Jesus . . . took bread, and after he had given thanks, broke it." Each action verb refers to the entire Eucharistic event and not to a particular rubric. Two of them, "after he had given thanks" and "broke it," eventually gave rise to the names Eucharist, first attested in the Didache 9.1, and the Breaking of Bread (Luke 24:35; Acts 2:42). After the narrative statement, Jesus declares, "This is my body which is for you" (1 Cor 11:24b), then follows the command, "Do this in remembrance of me" (1 Cor 11:24c). It would take many centuries to specify and clarify the various elements contained in "This is my body."

According to this liturgical text, which articulates the most essential aspects of the Eucharist, Jesus asks the participants to do what he did that the memorial of him might be realized. He asks them to take bread, give thanks and break bread in such a way that they too would be able to say, "This is my body that is for you," associating themselves with his body or person and allowing him to be visible and active in them. This mode of presence would later be called sacramental. The pattern of narrative and quotation is then repeated for the cup

of the new covenant sealed in his blood or life (1 Cor 11:25). The cup is understood not as an object but as an event, as when people speak of gathering for a special cup. The covenant refers to the set of relationships binding the members of the community to one another in Christ. The covenant is new by reason of the interior transformation brought about by sharing in Jesus' passion-resurrection and because of its universality, excluding no one by reason of nationality, peoplehood, race, sex, or social status.

Paul. As a liturgical text, the tradition Paul quotes in 1 Corinthians 11:23-25 is far more than a historical narrative of the Eucharist's institution. It contains a tremendous prophetic challenge. Doing "this in remembrance" of the Lord Jesus has implications for the relationships among the community members and between them and others (1 Cor 11:2-34). It also excludes immoral behavior (1 Cor 10:1-13) and relationships incompatible with it (1 Cor 10:14-22) and demands respect for the conscience of others (1 Cor 10:23-33). When seriously celebrated, the Eucharist holds enormous potential for transforming all aspects of life, both personal and social. By quoting the text in 1 Corinthians 11:23-25, Paul demonstrates the inconsistencies between the behavior of the assembly and its very purpose and then appeals to the Eucharist's transforming power. Paul's special contribution to Eucharistic theology is to spell out the connection between the Eucharistic liturgy and Christian ethics.

To achieve this, Paul emphasizes both the memorial and proclamation aspects of the Eucharist. It is likely that the repetition of the words "Do this in remembrance of me" in 1 Corinthians 11:25 was effected by Paul, who also added "as often as you drink it" (1 Cor 11:25). Paul insists that a real celebration of Eucharist is in fact a memorial of Jesus' supreme gift of himself as realized in his passion and symbolically and sacramentally communicated in the Eucharist. But, to be such, the participants have to discern the body (1 Cor 11:29), setting aside all divisions (1 Cor 11:18-19) in their commitment to the Church of God (1 Cor 11:22). Earlier, Paul showed that they would not benefit from spiritual food and drink if they indulged in immorality (1 Cor 10:1-13). Now he adds that "whoever eats the bread and drinks the cup of the Lord unworthily will have to answer for the body and blood of the Lord" (1 Cor 11:27) and be under divine judgment (1 Cor 11:29-32).

Such is the context in which Paul introduces the name "Lord's Supper" (1 Cor 11:20), telling the Corinthians that their assembly, where "each one goes ahead with his own supper, and one goes hungry while another gets drunk" (1 Cor 11:21) could not be called the Lord's Supper. The expression Lord's Supper, in which the Greek word for "Lord's" is an adjective *(kuriakos)* and not a noun *(kurios)*, refers to a supper reflecting the qualities of Jesus' risen life. The risen Jesus has a spiritual body (1 Cor 15:44), which is spirit-filled and spirit-giving (1 Cor 15:45-49) and which transcends all human divisions and gathers all in unity.

Paul also emphasizes how the Lord's Supper, properly celebrated as Jesus' memorial, is a proclamation. By eating this bread and drinking this cup, the participants "proclaim the death of the Lord until he comes" (1 Cor 11:26). As a memorial, the Eucharist recalls an event from the past and makes it present. As a proclamation, it announces a future event and initiates it. The risen Lord does not die in himself since he lives eternally with God. He dies in those who celebrate the Eucharist and offer their own lives as the Lord Jesus did "the night he was handed over." They thus make Christ's passion present in history until his full return in glory.

Synoptic Gospels and Acts. Like Paul, who developed the ethical implications and formative potential of the Eucharist, each of the Synoptic Gospels makes a special contribution to the development of Eucharistic theology. Mark shows how it is related to the following of Christ in his mission. Matthew focuses on its relationship to the forgiveness of sins in the community of disciples. Luke-Acts develops its relationship to various issues and challenges in the life of the Church.

Mark's special emphasis appears in a phrase, "and they all drank from it" (Mark 14:23), inserted in the liturgical text, recalling an earlier exchange between Jesus and the sons of Zebedee. When James and John asked to sit one at Jesus' right and the other at his left when he came into his glory, Jesus asked if they could drink the cup he drank and be baptized with the same baptism with which he was baptized, that is, if they could drink the cup and be baptized in the baptism of his passion (Mark 10:35-38). When they said they could, Jesus promised they would do so. Mark's presentation of the Last Supper shows the Twelve, including James and John, drinking the cup that Jesus drank. At the Last Supper, the followers joined Jesus in the commitment to serve that he demonstrated in his passion by giving "his life as a ransom for many" (Mark 10:45), that is, for all human beings.

Mark also related the Eucharist to the mission of the Church (Mark 6:6b–8:21). Two stories of breaking of bread dominate this part of the Gospel. In the first (Mark 6:34-44), the disciples ask Jesus to send the crowd away to buy themselves something to eat, since it was late, and they were in a deserted place. Jesus shows the disciples that in their mission very little bread is needed to nourish a vast crowd and leave an abundance of bread broken for sharing with others. So it is that all are wonderfully nourished. The story is situated on the Galilean side of the sea and reflects the origins of the Eucharist in Judaeo-Christian and male-oriented communities. Hence the five thousand men *(andres)*.

The second story (Mark 8:1-10) is situated on the Decapolis side of the sea, and the breaking of bread is for four thousand people, including both Jews and Gentiles, men and women. The difficult transition from the Church's Jewish and male origins to its Jew-Gentile and male-female openness is symbolically mediated by the request of a Greek woman, "a Syrophoenician by birth," that Jesus drive a demon from her daughter. An exchange of sayings between Jesus and the woman addresses the request in terms of bread and those for whom it is intended (Mark 7:24-30).

Matthew's particular emphasis appears in the phrase, "for the forgiveness of sins" (Matt 26:28), added to the basic liturgical text. As elsewhere (e.g., Matt 5:3-12; 6:9-13), Matthew respects a traditional text but adds a new element at the end of one of its sections. For Matthew, the forgiveness of sins is associated with Jesus' mission (Matt 1:21), not with that of John the Baptist (contrast Matt 3:11 and Mark 1:4), and is effected by Jesus' personal gift of "his life as a ransom for many" (Matt 20:28), that is, as a ransom for all. The disciples, whom Matthew explicitly mentions in the text of the Last Supper (contrast Matt 26:26 and Mark 14:22), receive that forgiveness of sins in the Eucharist when they drink from the cup (Matt 26:27) of Jesus' "blood of the covenant . . . shed on behalf of many for the forgiveness of sins" (Matt 26:28). Mark showed how in the Eucharist the followers join Christ in his self-sacrificing mission. Matthew shows how the disciples participate in the forgiveness of sins that is realized in Jesus' atoning sacrifice.

Matthew's presentation of the two stories of the breaking of bread (Matt 14:13-21; 15:32-39) is also very different from that of Mark. Mark, who incorporates the mission to the Gentiles in the story of Jesus' life and mission, develops the relationship between the Eucharist and the development of the universal mission of the Church. Matthew, for whom the mission to the Gentiles was undertaken only after Jesus' resurrection (see Matt 28:16-20), shows its relationship to Jesus' messianic work and the formation of his disciples. Before the resurrection, the disciples, like Jesus (Matt 15:24), were sent only "to the lost sheep of the house of Israel" (Matt 10:6).

Luke's contribution to Eucharistic theology also appears in his account of the Last Supper (Luke 22:14-38), a farewell discourse, in which Jesus relates the Last Supper to future challenges of the Church in the Lord's Supper. The Last Supper is emphasized as Jesus' final meal with the apostles, distinct from its eschatological fulfillment in the reign of God (Luke 22:14-18). The Lord's Supper, to be celebrated in memory of him, is then presented as the beginning of that eschatological fulfillment (Luke 22:19-20). Pursuing the same distinction, the discourse presents the betrayal associated with the Last Supper (Luke 22:21-23) and that taking place in the Lord's Supper (Luke 22:24-30), and the same for the denial (Luke 22:31-34, 35-38). Throughout this presentation, as in the meal's preparation, Luke emphasizes the role of the apostles assembled in solidarity with Jesus. The Last Supper is the Passover of the Church as well as his own.

For Luke, the Last Supper is the climax in a whole series of meals, which focused on issues and problems in the life of the community (Luke 5:27-32; 7:36-50; 9:10-17; 10:38-42; 11:37-54; 14:1-24; 19:1-10). The Lord's Supper also stands at the head of a new series of meals with the risen Lord, showing how the risen Lord is recognized in "the breaking of the bread" (Luke 24:13-35), the Lucan expression for Eucharist, and providing the grounds for the mission "to all the nations" (Luke 24:36-53). Luke's second volume, The Acts of the Apostles, situates "the breaking of the bread" among the distinguishing elements of the Christian community (Acts 2:42, 46), and shows it to be the basis for apostolic witness (Acts 10:41) and the source of life (Acts 20:7-12) and salvation (Acts 26:33-36).

John. John also contributes much to the NT theology of the Eucharist but, unlike Paul and the Synoptic Gospels, he does not quote a liturgical text used at the Lord's Supper, nor does he present Jesus' Last Supper as a Passover meal (see John 13:1). Instead, John situates the actual death of Jesus on preparation day for Passover (John 19:14), when the paschal lambs were slaughtered (see John 1:29, 36). In John, the principal event at the Last Supper is the washing of feet (John 13:1-20), a purification rite (John 13:4-10) in which Jesus shows himself as a model of loving service for the disciples (John 13:1, 12-17), contrasted with the betrayal of Judas (John 13:2, 10-11, 21-30) and the initial resistance of Simon Peter (John 13:6-9). The washing of feet is followed by a great farewell discourse spelling out basic attitudes inspired by the Eucharist for the life and development of the Church (John 14:1–16:33) and concluding with a solemn prayer (John 17:1-26).

John had already situated the origins of the Eucharist in the breaking of bread with the disciples for a crowd of five thousand (John 6:1-15). Situated "on the mountain" (John 6:3) and as "the Jewish feast of Passover was near" (John 6:4), the event marks a major revelatory moment whose implications are afterwards spelled out in a great discourse, climaxing with a challenging section on the Eucharistic presence and nourishment as the very flesh of Jesus. Like John's statement on the incarnation, the Word made flesh in the prologue (John 1:14), the insistence on Jesus giving his flesh for the life of the world (John 6:51) and on having to eat his flesh and drink his blood (John 6:52-56) are meant to obviate any proto-Gnostic tendencies arising in the community. Like Luke, John also associates the Eucharist with the post-resurrection manifestation of Jesus as risen Lord (John 21:1-23).

See: BLOOD, BODY, BREAD, COVENANT, CUP, ESCHATOLOGY, MEAL, PASSOVER, REMEMBRANCE, VINE, WINE

EUGENE LAVERDIERE, S.S.S.

Pastoral-Liturgical Tradition

As we have already seen in the NT material, the Lord's Supper or Eucharist (Greek = thanksgiving) was the most characteristic form of worship among the first followers of Jesus. It finds its origin in the Jewish practice of prayerful thanks and praise at table, especially during festive communal meals. Jesus' command to share bread* and wine* in his memory in the context of a last Passover meal with his disciples has been faithfully obeyed by Christians down through the ages. Beginning with the joyful experience of reconciliation in the presence of the risen Lord eating with his disciples on "the first day of the week" (Luke 24; John 21) to the progressively more elaborate developments of Eucharistic worship in the succeeding centuries, the weekly celebration of the Lord's Supper is both the very epiphany of the risen Christ's presence to believers and the place where the Church assembled in the name of the risen One most profoundly identifies itself as his body* in the world. For this reason the Eucharist is regarded by the Constitution on the Sacred Liturgy of Vatican II as "the summit toward which the activity of the Church is directed; at the same time it is the fount from which all the Church's power flows" (CSL 10). While the centrality of the Eucharist among Christians—at least in the Catholic tradition—has never been questioned, the celebration of the Eucharist has been influenced by the historical, cultural, and philosophical context in which the Church has moved and developed. Whatever the formal changes in its celebration occasioned by time and place, the celebration of the Eucharist as the preeminent occasion when God is thanked and blessed for the life, death and resurrection of Jesus Christ, when the holy Spirit is invoked to transform both the elements and the assembly who share in the Eucharist into the body and blood of Christ, anticipating that final and everlasting banquet of God's reign at the end of time when we shall see God face to face.

The Eucharist Before the Council of Nicaea (325). The first followers of Jesus, regarding themselves as faithful Jews, most probably continued praying in both synagogue and Temple in addition to their coming together in private homes for the Eucharist, known first as "the breaking of bread" (Acts 2:46). This informal, domestic context of the Eucharist in house churches as a meal shared by the community is reflected by both the NT and contemporary documents of this early period. The first extra-biblical witness to early Eucharistic practice is the Didache (ca. 100 CE), which clearly describes the cultic meal of bread and wine celebrated by the Christian community now separated from the synagogue but heavily indebted to the style of a Jewish Prayer of blessing and thanks at table. This prayer lovingly describes God's marvelous action on behalf of the world in Jesus Christ (chs. 9-10; 14). It is clear, though, that the prayer also indicates that sharing this meal was the final step in incorporating believers into the Church; therefore, those who partake of the Eucharist must be baptized (9:5). It also offers a recurrent petition for the unity of all who share in this meal to be fully realized at the final coming of Christ. A more detailed account of the primitive Eucharist is found in the writings of Justin Martyr (ca. 150 CE). In his *First Apology* he recounts the gathering of the community on the Lord's Day (Sunday), the two parts of the service—the reading from the Hebrew Scriptures and the "memoirs of the apostles" together with a homily related to the preceding readings as well as prayers of petition, and the formal prayer of thanks over bread and wine as well as the sharing in the "eucharistized" elements of bread and wine. That the Eucharist recalled the death of the Lord (see 1 Cor 11:26) and gave strength for withstanding persecution was a theme in the writing of Ignatius of Antioch (ca. 115 CE).

By the beginning of the third century, the organization of the Church and the way in which it gathered to celebrate the Eucharist continued to become more formal, reflecting the ministerial roles found throughout the Mediterranean basin now composed of the three orders of bishop, presbyter, and deacon. This church order is reflected in the first detailed description of the Eucharistic celebration found in the *Apostolic Tradition* attributed to St. Hippolytus of Rome written at the beginning of the third century.

The great prayer of thanksgiving found in this document is the source of the Second Eucharistic Prayer of the present Roman Sacramentary. While not proposed by Hippolytus as an invariable text, this anaphora (Eucharistic Prayer) was offered by the bishop on behalf of the entire priestly assembly of baptized who thank God for having "counted them worthy to stand in God's presence." It also reflects the classic components of Eucharistic praying: remembering God's mighty works, especially the paschal mystery of Jesus Christ *(anamnesis)*, petitioning the holy Spirit *(epiclesis)* to transform the bread and wine into the body and blood of Christ and for the unity of the whole Church as a result of its sharing in the sacred elements.

The Eucharist in the High Patristic Age (Fourth to Seventh Centuries). With the legalization of the Christian Church under Constantine in 313 and the establishment of Christianity as the faith of the Empire in 384 under Theodosius, the style of Eucharistic celebration and the theology used to describe it necessarily changed to reflect this new relationship. The Church was no longer a small and persecuted sect but a triumphant and established power in its own right within the Empire. The leaders of the Church found themselves increasingly responsible for the stability and welfare of both Christian and pagan citizens in a society on the verge of collapse due to the decline of imperial power. Thus, bishops, presbyters, and deacons became civil as well as religious leaders and wore tokens of authority traditional for imperial functionaries. This is the origin of stoles, miters, and some of the other special vesture for the clergy.

Not surprisingly, the numbers of those seeking to become Christian swelled during this period and the Church had to adopt new pastoral strategies for dealing with the changed situation. From the small, intimate gatherings of previous centuries the Eucharist now was grandly celebrated in basilicas—formerly royal audience halls or law courts—now designed for Christian use because they were capable of holding large groups of the faithful. As the numbers in attendance increased, so did the formality of worship. While retaining the essential two part schema of the liturgy of the word and liturgy of the sacrament, the Eucharistic celebration in the patristic basilicas adopted signs and symbols from the imperial court to help the large assemblies of Christians participate in the sacred actions. Processions, litanic prayer, lights, incense, responsorial chant, came into the Christian liturgy during this period as reflections of the surrounding "imperial" culture.

This was also the period of the initial development of the principal liturgical families of both the East and West around the Patriarchates of the Empire. In the East, Antioch on the Orontes, Alexandria in Egypt, Constantinople on the Bosphorus, and Jerusalem all developed their own characteristic way of praying and liturgical calendars reflecting a rooting of Christianity in the language and mores of local Churches. In the West, although all employed the Latin language, the principal patriarchal rite of Rome was complemented by distinctive local rites throughout the former Western Empire such as the Ambrosian Rite of Milan, the Celtic Rite of the British Isles, the Gallican Rite of Gaul (present day Southern France), and the Mozarabic Rite of Visigothic Spain.

The formalization of the rite as well as the typological interpretation of Scripture supported by the pervasive Neo-platonism of the period aided in the gradual but steady sacralization of the both the place where the liturgy was celebrated and those who were the principal ministers. Images of altar, sacrifice, and priesthood used metaphorically in the previous period now became more literally understood as the fulfillment of the types or figures announced in the Hebrew Scriptures. The Eucharistic elements themselves became an object of reflection that often seemed far removed from their origin as part of the meal of the Christian assembly. Thus St. Ambrose (ca. 390) could ascribe the power of consecration of these elements to the words of Christ in the Eucharistic prayer (*De sacramentis* IV:15-16).

This tendency toward the objective sacralization of the liturgy in general and the elements in particular was balanced during this period by the fact that the action of the giving thanks with bread and wine for God's mighty deeds in Christ was understood to be the sacrificial action of the priestly community by virtue of their baptism into Christ. Indeed, according to St. Augustine the Eucharist is a sacrifice because the very mystery celebrated is that of the Church offering itself as the body of Christ to the Father (*City of God*, Bk 10). There is such an intense identification of the Church as body of Christ with the Eucharist as Body of Christ that Augustine will insist that, "if you then are the body and members of Christ, your mystery is laid on the table of the Lord; it is your mystery you receive" (*Sermo* 272).

The Eucharist During the Middle Ages and Reformation (Eighth to Sixteenth Centuries).

After the fall of Rome and the conversion of much of Northern Europe to Christianity from the seventh to the tenth centuries, the Eucharist, now increasingly referred to in the West as the Mass—from the diaconal dismissal at the end of the celebration "*Ite, missa est*" (Go, you are sent forth)—became more and more removed from the laity. This was largely due to the fact that the Western Church opted to retain Latin as the liturgical language—a language that had become incomprehensible to all but the educated clergy—rather than following the strategy of the Eastern Churches which translated the Bible and the liturgy into the languages of the people. In the West commentators on the Mass such as Amalarius of Metz (ca. 780–850) began to regard the Mass as an allegory of the life of Christ.

The understanding of sacraments in general and the Eucharist in particular explained by Neo-platonic categories such as figure or type, began to give way to a sacramental objectivism that sought to affirm the physical presence of Christ in the Eucharist in ways heretofore unheard of. This tendency reaches its climax in Berengar's Oath of 1059 which juxtaposes the terms "sacramental" and "real" in a way that would have appeared bizarre to theologians of the Patristic period. This oath affirmed that "the bread and wine which are placed on the altar are after consecration not only a sacrament but also the real body and blood of our Lord Jesus Christ" and that these are "held and broken by the hands of priests and are crushed by the teeth of the faithful." The use of the neologism "transubstantiation" by the Fourth Lateran Council in 1215 and its further development by scholastic theologians such as St. Thomas Aquinas was a means of going beyond the crude "butcher shop" realism inadvertently promoted by formulations like that of Berengar.

Medieval commentators also emphasized the sacrificial nature of the Eucharist as a re-presentation of Christ's death on the cross. Consequently the celebration of the Mass took on a decidedly penitential overtone. Because of feelings of unworthiness, the number of people receiving communion also dramatically declined and drinking from the chalice became reserved to the presiding clergy only. Communion for laypeople was accomplished primarily visually, by gazing on the elements elevated by the priest after words of consecration had been pronounced. This mode of participation in the Eucharist naturally obscured its rooting in the human action of sharing a meal—and much of the critique of the Mass by the Protestant Reformers centered directly or obliquely on this issue.

In response to the challenge of the Reformers, the Counter Reformation set in motion by the Council of Trent in the sixteenth century largely sought to reaffirm traditional Catholic teaching in light of what the fathers of the council regarded as heretical innovation. Thus, much of the medieval development surrounding the celebration of the Eucharist was reaffirmed against the teaching of the Reformers while the Mass itself was purged of the more notorious abuses which had scandalized Catholics as well as Protestants.

The Eucharist as Sacrament, Sacrifice, and Meal. One of the overarching goals of the liturgical reform of Vatican II was to recover the rich Eucharistic tradition of the first Christian centuries and to balance these biblical and patristic insights with the later medieval developments. The affirmation that the celebration of the Eucharist is an action of the whole church and that the baptized assembly ought to participate in this action in a full, active, and conscious manner (CSL 14) is a hallmark of the reform. Thus, in his encyclical *Eucaristicum mysterium* of 1967, Pope Paul VI neatly summarized the doctrinal themes present in the conciliar and postconciliar understanding of the Eucharist: "the Mass, the Lord's Supper, is at once and inseparably: the sacrifice in which the sacrifice of the cross is perpetuated; the memorial of the death and resurrection of the Lord who said: 'Do this in memory of me' (Luke 22:19); the sacred banquet in which, through the communion of the body and blood of the Lord, the people of God share the benefits of the paschal sacrifice, renew the New Covenant with us made once and for all by God in Christ's blood, and in faith and hope foreshadow and anticipate the eschatological banquet in the Father's kingdom as they proclaim the death of the Lord 'until he comes'" (EM 3a).

See: BREAD, EPIPHANY, HOSPITALITY, MEAL, MYSTERY, REMEMBRANCE, SACRIFICE, SPIRIT OF GOD, SIGN, THANKSGIVING, TYPE, VESTURE, WINE

MARK R. FRANCIS, C.S.V.

EXAMPLE

Semitic thought sees example more in terms of a relationship between master and disciple than as an artistic model to be copied. God offers a covenant to chosen leaders, and as they respond to the divine will they forge a path for others, who are not to "turn aside" from it. This creates a community of like-minded members, the people of God. In the NT Jesus reveals the gospel of divine salvation by his actions and words and demands of his hearers faith and discipleship. As they strive to be true to his teaching and way of life they too establish community through mutual support and love.

Old Testament

Vocabulary. Hebrew does not have a specific word to signify "example"; at best this is a relatively rare meaning of 'oth, "sign, portent" (see Num 5:22; Sir 44:16). The Israelites preferred to speak dynamically about following in someone's footsteps. To a certain extent this implied imitation, but even more, obedience and fidelity to the way of life pointed out. Words such as halāk ("walk"), derek ("way"), 'orah ("path"), 'ahrê ("after"), kēn ("thus") are important in this context, as in Judges 2:17: "They were quick to stray from the *way* their fathers had taken, and did not follow their *example* of obedience" (lit. "do thus"), or 1 Samuel 8:3: "His sons did not follow his *example*" (lit. "walk in his ways").

Pentateuch. Although YHWH is the central hero of the patriarchal and Mosaic narratives, virtuous actions such as the faith and reverential obedience of Abraham (Gen 15:6; 22:12) or the purity of Joseph (Gen 40:12) provide good examples for others to follow. The text of Leviticus 17:2, "Be holy, for I, the LORD your God, am holy," does not call for direct imitation but for a strengthening of the covenant bond between God and the "chosen people" through mutual fidelity.

Historical Books. In the Deuteronomistic history all the kings of northern Israel are severely criticized for continuing the political and religious schism inaugurated by Jeroboam (1 Kings 12). They are accused of following his bad example, "*imitating* all his sins" (see 1 Kgs 15:3, 26, 34; 16:7). In 2 Maccabees there are several instances of good example, especially that of ninety-year-old Eleazar, who explains: "I will leave to the young a noble *example* of how

to die willingly and generously for the revered and holy laws" (2 Macc 6:28). The seven brothers are also willing to die for their faith as they find strength from their mother and in one another (see 2 Macc 7:37).

Wisdom Literature. Many proverbs portray wise and foolish activity with the implication that the one should be imitated and the other rejected. They include the world of nature, such as ants (Prov 6:6-11), birds (Sir 27:9), or lions (Prov 28:1; 30:30), as well as humans, especially the wise. The figures of Tobit, Esther, and Judith also serve as models of virtue (see Jdt 8:24).

New Testament

"Example" is expressed by Greek words such as hypodeigma, "model" or "pattern" (John 13:15; Heb 4:11); hypogrammos, "model text" to be copied in writing (1 Pet 2:21); and typos, "model" or "image," the visible impression of a stamp or stroke (e.g., Phil 3:17; 1 Tim 4:12). In Hellenistic philosophy these words often portray the concept of a visual pattern to be repeated as a copy, but their biblical usage is heavily influenced by the Septuagint and the thought-world of the OT with its emphasis on the obedience of discipleship. Yet the idea of imitating a model is also present.

Synoptic Gospels Good example abounds in the words and deeds of Jesus. He exemplifies prayer (Luke 3:21; 6:12; Mark 14:32-42), simplicity of life (Mark 8:34f.; Luke 9:58), forgiveness (Luke 7:36-50), compassion by his acts of healing (e.g., Mark 1:40-45; 2:1-12). His sermons, especially the parables, often present paradigms for imitation, such as humble faith "*like* a child" (Mark 10:15), or mercy *like* the good Samaritan (Luke 10:37).

Paul. Pauline literature emphasizes example as calling forth discipleship. The Christians of Rome are praised because they "have become obedient from the heart to the *pattern* of teaching" which they had learned (Rom 6:17); the teaching constitutes a certain form or model which would shape the conduct of their lives. Yet Paul teaches not simply by words but also by example. He practices what he preaches, and urges others to imitate his trust in divine grace and energetic cooperation with its inspiration "according to the *model* you have in us" (Phil 3:17). Even his economic self-support through work is to be a *"model"* for the community to do the same (2 Thess 3:9). The evaluation of the Thessalonians as having become "imitators of us and of the Lord" (1 Thess 1:6-7) or the call to the Corinthians to "be imitators of me as I am of Christ" (1 Cor 11:1) is to be understood in the same way. Paul had learned a new way of life from Christ whose disciple he became, and the congregations are being encouraged to follow his example of obedient service and faith. They are also asked to imitate the example of Christ, or at least to "have the same attitude" of humility and love that characterized Christ's incarnation and self-emptying on the cross (Phil 2:5). The Christians themselves are to be "a *model* for all the believers" (1 Thess 1:6-7) by their fidelity. Although they might have the right to eat food offered to idols, Paul asks them to refrain from doing so if their example were to scandalize the weaker ones (1 Cor 8:13). The purpose of providing good example is always the same, the building up of community.

The Pastoral Letters. Christ's patience with Paul, the foremost of sinners, is to serve "as an *example* for those who would believe" so that they too might hope for forgiveness and through faith enter into everlasting life (1 Tim 1:16). Timothy is admonished to "set an *example* for those who believe, in speech, conduct, love, faith, purity" (1 Tim 4:12), and Titus is to preach and show himself "a *model* of good deeds in every respect," with integrity of teaching, dignity, and sound speech (Titus 2:7f.).

The Catholic Letters. James asks his hearers to consider the courage of the prophets and take them "as an *example* of hardship and patience" (Jas 5:10). Peter addresses the slaves, admonishes them to be subject to their masters, and adduces Christ's suffering for them, "leaving you an *example* that you should follow in his footsteps" (1 Pet 2:21).

John. At the Last Supper Jesus washes the feet of the disciples and offers himself as a *"model* to follow, so that as I have done for you, you should also do" (John 13:15). This is the concrete demonstration of the general admonition to love one another "as I have loved you" (John 13:34). By following Christ's example the people will create a distinctive community: "This is how all will know that you are my disciples, if you have love for one another" (John 13:35).

See: COMMUNITY, COVENANT, DISCIPLESHIP, OBEDIENCE, TYPE

JOSEPH F. WIMMER, O.S.A.

EXCOMMUNICATION/ANATHEMA

New Testament

Anathema. In the NT anathema designates something or someone accursed, that is, separated from the community. This technical term appears primarily in Paul (Rom 9:3; 1 Cor 12:3; 16:22; Gal 1:8, 9), although Acts 23 records its use among Paul's Jewish opponents, and in Mark 14:71 Peter is said to have invoked a curse upon himself in his denial of Jesus. Beyond the use of this technical term, Christians demonstrated their concern for maintaining the holiness of the community in many ways. The NT evinces various procedures for intra-communal reconciliation* and forgiveness* as well as for temporary or permanent exclusion of members from the community. These practices laid the basis for the development in the Church of formal procedures for excommunication.

Jewish Disciplinary Practice. Jews of the first century employed a usual penalty of exclusion from the synagogue for serious offenses against the religious or moral norms of the group. Various degrees of punishment existed ranging from temporary dismissal to indefinite or permanent exclusion. At Qumran (1QS 5.26–6.1) members of the community were to accuse other companions before the whole congregation *only* after they had first admonished them in the presence of witnesses (see Matt 18:15-17) in an effort to convince them of their error so that they might repent. The Gospel of John (9:22; 12:42; 16:2) reflects the Jewish practice in the late first century which imposed a more formal synagogue ban (*birkat haminim* of the "Eighteen Benedictions") that ostracized heretics or sectarians (including Christians) from the synagogue. Christian discipline was undoubtedly influenced by these Jewish practices.

Pauline Tradition. Paul pronounces a curse, "Let that one be accursed!" on anyone who should preach a gospel different from his own (Gal 1:8, 9) or on any Christian who fails to love the Lord (1 Cor 16:22), but in these texts he never specifies how the curses are to be interpreted in practice within the community. In 1 Corinthians 12:3, Paul seems to be answering the attacks of his opponents when he claims that "nobody speaking by the spirit of God says, 'Jesus be accursed.'" Paul can even go so far as to say that he would allow himself to become accursed (Rom 9:3) if such action could win the conversion of the Jews to Christ.

Paul's position on the practice of excommunication is clarified in 1 Corinthians 5:1-13 when he responds to a case of incest reported to him. The offender, because of his blatant (5:2, 6) and persistent immorality, should be expelled (5:2, 13) and "delivered to Satan," that is, to the non-Christian world where Satan reigns. (See the similar punishment given Hymenaeus and Alexander in 1 Tim 1:19-20.) Contrast, however, Paul's exhortations toward forgiveness of the sinful person in 2 Corinthians 2:6-11. No consistent procedures, therefore, are yet evident in Paul. 2 Thessalonians 3:10 urges the withholding of food from those who do not work, a practice known also at Qumran, and both 2 Thessalonians 3:14-15 and Titus 3:9 counsel social ostracism toward those who are disobedient or heretical. The

author of 2 John 10 exhorts Christians to refuse hospitality to those espousing a different doctrine, and 3 John presents the case of just such a refusal by Diotrephes who, thereby, stands condemned by the Elder.

Matthean Tradition. The origins of Christian excommunication are often seen in the reference to "binding and loosing" in Matthew 16:19; 18:18 (cf. John 20:23). Together with the "power of the keys" (see Isa 22:22), in Matthew 16:19 Peter is given authority "to bind and loose." These terms refer both to authoritative teaching and to judgments about inclusion or exclusion from the community. The same power "to bind or loose" is given to the entire community in Matthew 18:18 where it more clearly refers to disciplinary actions taken by the local community. Matthew 18, moreover, underscores the need for repeated efforts by the community to persuade the offender to repent. A threefold procedure for correction is offered: first, one to one, then with two or three witnesses, and finally before the whole assembly. Only after all these attempts have failed should someone be excluded. Such a serious punishment was not taken lightly nor exercised without extreme caution.

See: BLESSING, CURSE

BARBARA E. BOWE, R.S.C.J.

EXILE

The practice of removing conquered peoples was common in the ancient Near East. The Israelites experienced it several times. After Tiglath-Pileser III of Assyria (745–727 BCE) subjugated the Gilead and Galilee, he removed some the citizens of the northern kingdom to Assyria (2 Kgs 15:29). Sargon (722–705 BCE) did the same when he completed the conquest of the Northern Kingdom. According to the Assyrian Chronicles, Sennacherib (705–681 BCE) claims to have captured 200,150 people after crushing Hezekiah's rebellion in 701 BCE. (The Bible does not mention this deportation.) The

Babylonians deported a part of the population from Judah three separate times. The first exile took place in 597 BCE and involved the royal family, some of the army, and some artisans (2 Kgs 24:14-16). In 587 BCE, after crushing Judah's futile revolt, Nabuchadnezzar (605–562 BCE) deported more of its population (2 Kgs 25:11-12). Jeremiah (52:30) mentions a third deportation by the Babylonians.

The practice of the deportation of conquered peoples undoubtedly sought to make resistance and revolution less likely. Exile detached people from their land and suppressed their national identity. The number of people exiled by the Babylonians according to the Bible did not exceed fifty thousand. Obviously this was not the entire population. Those sent into exile were the royal family and other leaders of the society. The conquerors assumed that it was these people that would have fomented revolution. Simple farmers and villagers remained in the land (2 Kgs 25:12). Jeremiah 40 assumes that Judah's population was large even after the Exile and asserts that the Babylonians appointed Gedaliah, a Judean noble, to administer the territory of the former kingdom. A certain Ishmael, a member of the royal family, assassinated Gedaliah (2 Kgs 25:25). Jeremiah 41–44 and 2 Kings 25:26 assume that the entire Judean population fled after Gedaliah's death. This is unlikely. Judeans continued to live in the land while many of their leaders were in exile.

In describing the conditions following the deportation of people from the northern kingdom, the Bible says that the Assyrians brought in people from various parts of their empire to repopulate the region (2 Kgs 17:24). The text makes no note of a similar repopulation in Judah. This probably reflects the concern of postexilic Judah to present itself as authentic Israelites while the people of Samaria were considered the descendants of the foreign population introduced by the Assyrians. The Bible is written from a Judean perspective for the most part. These details reflect the conflicts between Samaria and Judah beginning in the last part of the sixth century BCE.

The Bible also ignores the fate of the exiles from the former northern kingdom. This has produced the many ludicrous theories about the identification of the supposed "lost tribes" of Israel. These tribes were never lost since Mesopotamia had a large population of people whose origins could be traced to the Assyrian and Babylonian exiles into the Muslim period. The Bible simply chooses to ignore the Assyrian exiles because its interest was with the people from the former southern kingdom.

Little is known about the condition of the exiles. The conclusions that can be drawn from the scant information given in the Bible show that the exiles were not prisoners or slaves. Babylonian texts show that they were landowners and business people. They enjoyed some freedom of actions (Jer 29:5-6). They lived in their own communities and settlements (Ezek 8:1; 20:1; Ezra 8:15-17). Two texts hint at the existence of Jewish temples in exile (Ezek 11:16; Ezra 8:17). Conditions were such that when the Persians gave the Jews the opportunity to return to the homeland, many refused to go. Babylon remained an important center of Judaism into the Medieval period.

The exilic period is important in the religious development of Judaism. It was the time when ancient Israel's religious traditions were collected. It provided the impetus for committing these traditions to writing. The codification of the law as it now exists in the Torah began during the Exile. The works of the preexilic prophets were put into order at this time. Two of the greatest prophetic texts, the Book of Ezekiel and Isaiah 40–55, were written during the Exile. Once these traditions took written form, there arose a scribal class whose task it was to interpret these for the people (Nehemiah 8). It has been suggested that the synagogue developed during the exilic period as a substitute for the Temple. There is, however, no evidence to support this hypothesis.

The Exile became an important theological motif in the Bible. The Bible tries to explain the Exile as the consequence of Israel's sin. Such an explanation was necessary since the usual explanation for the fall of Jerusalem would have been that the city's patron deity Yahweh was defeated in heavenly combat with Marduk, the patron deity of Babylon. The Bible demythologizes the explanation of the Exile by asserting that the Exile happened because of what Judah did. It also was a catalyst for new reflection on Israel's identity. At this time, practices like the Sabbath observance, dietary laws, and circumcision became important since their observance was independent of Judah's presence in its land.

While the Bible preserves Judah's grief (Lamentations) and confession of its guilt, it also emphasizes God's forgiveness (Jer 31:34; Ezekiel 33–39; Isaiah 40–55). The Exile was a serious breach in Judah's self-confidence in its position as God's Chosen People, but it did not destroy its faith in God. Judah's faith proved to be capable of handling the disaster that was the Exile. Judah believed that there was a way out of the Exile. Its literary production at this time is testimony to that. Some of these texts do not describe the precise contours of the future: Lamentations and the Deuteronomistic History. Others give a highly idealistic picture of the expected restoration: Isaiah 40–55 and Ezekiel. The Priestly and Deuteronomic legislation provide an exact picture of how the restored Israel should pattern its new life.

See: ASSYRIA, BABYLON, LAND, SAMARIA/SAMARITAN

LESLIE J. HOPPE, O.F.M.

EXODUS

God's liberation of the Hebrew people from enslavement to the Egyptians is the central saving event of the OT and is seen in Christian tradition as a prefiguration of the salvation accomplished by Christ. The Exodus (lit. "the going out") from Egyptian bondage led to the formation of the Hebrew people as a nation, Israel.* The detailed narrative of the Exodus event is found in Exodus 1–15, particularly Exodus 12:37–15:21. References to the Exodus abound in the remainder of the Pentateuch, the Prophets, and the Writings.

In the NT, although the word "Exodus" occurs only three times (Heb 11:22; 2 Pet 1:15; Luke 9:31), allusions to this paradigmatic saving event are numerous. Christians, understanding themselves as the "new people of God" (e.g., 1 Pet 2:9-10; Exod 19:6), reappropriated the language and imagery of Exodus to interpret their understanding of the Christ event.

In pastoral and liturgical tradition, the Exodus continues to play a key role, as it is seen to prefigure the Christian spiritual journey. The crossing of the Red Sea and the gift of manna are particularly highlighted as prefiguring the sacraments of Baptism and Eucharist. The release of the Christian from the tyranny of sin is analogous to the freedom gained by the Hebrews from Egyptian bondage. From the Patristic period to the present, Exodus symbols have been employed to speak of God as a liberating God, who, out of great love and compassion, acts within history and within all seemingly hopeless situations to free people from oppression.

Old Testament

The Exodus features in each section of the OT. The marvelous event is recounted in Exodus 1–15. Leviticus, Numbers, and Deuteronomy also allude to it, and in some instances, shed further light on it. The Former Prophets, e.g., Samuel, feature God leading the Israelites out of other various oppressive situations that can also be understood as exodus experiences in the broadest sense of the word. The Latter Prophets, particularly Ezekiel and Deutero-Isaiah, announce a new exodus inaugurated by Cyrus that would gather the Israelites from among the nations, specifically Babylon, where they had been scattered after the fall of Jerusalem in 587 BCE. This new exodus enables the Israelites to become truly a light to the nations. In the Writings, particularly the psalms, God's people also cry out to God to deliver them from oppression. There is not only a sense of urgency in their pleas but also an expression of confidence.

Pentateuch. Exodus, the name of the second book of the Pentateuch in the OT, is a story about God's love and compassion for a particular group of people, the Hebrews,* whom God led out of Egyptian oppression and bondage. Hence, Exodus is not only a book but also refers to a historical event. Because the details recounted about the Exodus are not altogether historically accurate, and are not verifiable archaeologically, questions remain about the historicity of the event.

In the Pentateuch Exodus 1:1–12:36 describes the Hebrew people's oppressive situation prior to their departure out of Egypt. Exodus 12:37–14:31 traces the people's exodus that occurs in two stages: (1) the march from Rameses to Succoth (Exod 12:37–13:16) and (2) the journey along an indirect road from Succoth to the Red Sea (Exod 3:17–4:31). Exodus 15:1-21 features Moses' and Miriam's songs that commemorate the Exodus event. God had promised to rescue the Israelites from the forced labor and slavery of the Egyptians (Exod 6:7). The Exodus from Egypt, under the direction of Moses, fulfills God's promise.

Deuteronomy 7:7-8 expresses the divine motivation behind the Exodus:

> It was not because you are the largest of all the nations that the Lord set his heart on you and chose you, for you are really the smallest of all nations. It was because the Lord loved you and because of his fidelity to the oath he had sworn to your fathers, that he brought you out with his strong hand from the place of slavery, and ransomed you from the hand of Pharaoh, king of Egypt (Deut 7:7-8).

The oath that God swore to the Israelites' ancestors was the promise of land (Gen 17:8; 26:3; 28:13; see also Exod 6:23). Exodus from Egypt and deliverance from bondage must happen if God is to fulfill the divine plan and oath. By means of the Exodus ex-

perience, God is able to enter into a special relationship with the Israelites:

> I will take you as my own people, and you shall have me as your God. You will know that I, the Lord, am your God when I free you from the labor of the Egyptians and bring you into the land which I swore to give to Abraham, Isaac, and Jacob. I will give it to you as your own possession—I, the Lord! (Exod 6:7-8).

And God will dwell among them (Exod 29:45-46).

Freed from bondage, the Israelites live under divine promise and sovereignty while sharing in an intimate and mutual relationship with their God (see also Lev 25:38; 26:45). The Exodus also declares God's sovereignty to the foreign nations, specifically Egypt (Exod 7:5).

The Exodus enables the Israelites to become God's servants (Deut 6:12-15) and, under God's directives, they are to keep the Passover and the Festival of Unleavened Bread as a reminder not only of their liberation but also of God who accomplished the great deed (Exod 12:1-20; Deut 16:1-8). God reminds the Israelites repeatedly that Yahweh is their God, who is the one that brought them out of Egypt (see e.g., Exod 20:2-3; Lev 19:36; 25:35; Num 15:41). Furthermore, Moses encourages the Israelites that when they do come into the land and have eaten their fill, they are to take care not to forget God who brought them "out of the land of Egypt, out of the house of slavery" (Deut 6:12). Yet, history shows that the Israelites do forget God in their prosperity, and as a consequence they experience divine chastisement. Psalm 107 captures the situation vividly.

With respect to the Pentateuchal account of the Exodus, one can say that this experience becomes the heart of Israel's revelation and faith and serves a fourfold theological function. It (1) reveals who God is; (2) establishes a mutual, intimate relationship between God and the Israelites; (3) acts as a witness to and reminder of God's divine power, sovereignty, compassion, and love;

(4) celebrates God as a liberating God who makes and keeps promises, who not only hears the cry of the oppressed but also does something about it.

Prophets. The Former Prophets also feature God freeing the Israelites from other experiences. For example, Yahweh saves David from the grasp of all his enemies and from the hand of Saul. 2 Samuel 22:1-51, David's Song of Thanksgiving, describes the experience vividly.

The Latter Prophets, namely Ezekiel and Deutero-Isaiah, allude to a "new exodus" when the Exile will come to an end. The Latter Prophets attribute Jerusalem's fall to the Israelites' forgetfulness of Yahweh, their apostasy, and their wicked deeds of injustice and unrighteousness. Following the fall of Jerusalem in 587 BC, many of the Israelites were deported to Babylon; others sought refuge in foreign nations such as Egypt.

As in the former days, the Israelites feel the weight of their oppression, but this time it is not because of a foreign enemy; rather, it is because of their own crimes and sins (Isa 6:8-30; Ezek 33:10). Yet, God remains faithful to the Israelites and promises to put an end to their exile (Ezek 20:33-38; 34:1-13).

In Ezekiel 20:33-38, God's "bringing out" will be a great act of deliverance but it will take place in conjunction with judgment. Before God allows a new entry into the Promised Land to take place, the Israelites will enter into judgment with God "face to face" (Ezek 20:35), who will separate the faithful ones from those who have "rebelled" and "transgressed" against God. (Ezek 20:38). There is also an element of purification that must happen. All idols are to be destroyed (Ezek 20:39). Then God will bring the people back to Israel, and by this deed they shall know that God is the Lord (Ezek 20:42).

In Isaiah 40–55, the prophet describes the wonders of the future "new exodus" that, in fact, does come to pass under the leadership of Cyrus of Persia. Like the first exodus, the new one will be a display of God's great strength and compassion. Unlike the first

exodus where Moses shepherded the people, the new exodus will find God shepherding the Israelites (Isa 40:11; 52:12; Ezek 34:11-16). God will gather them (Ezek 34:24), cleanse them (Ezek 34:25), give them a new heart (Ezek 34:26), put God's Spirit within them (Ezek 34:27), make an everlasting covenant with them (Ezek 37:26; Isa 55:3), bring them into the land of their ancestors (Ezek 34:28a), enter into relationship with them (Ezek 34:28b), and fill them with all good gifts (Ezek 34:29-30; Isa 54:11-17).

Writings. In the Writings, the hope of deliverance from affliction is the object of the people's prayer in the psalms. In Psalm 25 the psalmist cries out:

> Look toward me and have pity on me,
> for I am alone and afflicted.
> Relieve the troubles of my heart,
> and bring me out of my distress.
> Put an end to my affliction and suffering,
> and take away all my sins
>
> (Ps 25:16-18).

In Psalm 31:5 the psalmist addresses God with confidence: "You will free me from the snare they set for me / for you are my refuge."

In summary, the Israelites' experience of exodus is central to their knowledge of and relationship with their God. As an encounter of divine intervention in the midst of human history, the Exodus event offers hope because it is concerned with liberation from oppression in its various forms. It is a sign of divine love and compassion and a plan for universal salvation as all of creation groans and eagerly awaits liberation (Rom 8:19-23).

See: ANCESTORS, BABYLON, COMPASSION, EGYPT, EXILE, HEBREW, HOPE, ISRAEL, LAND, LIBERTY, LOVE, MOSES, NATIONS, PASSOVER, POWER, PROMISE, SALVATION, SLAVERY

CAROL J. DEMPSEY, O.P.

New Testament

The Greek term *exodos* occurs three times in the NT. In Hebrews 11:22 it refers to the Exodus of the Hebrew slaves from Egypt.

In 2 Peter 1:15 the meaning of the word broadens to connote departure from life, i.e., death. In Luke 9:31 the term carries a double connotation: not only does it refer to Jesus' death, but to its liberating effects for God's people.

Beyond these three instances, there are numerous allusions to the Exodus throughout the NT. These are particularly evident in Jesus' instructions to his disciples when sending them forth on mission, in the Gospel narratives of the feeding of the crowd in the desert, and in the Last Supper accounts. Exodus motifs are especially prominent in the Gospels of Matthew and John. Paul also draws on Exodus imagery in his first letter to the Corinthian community.

Hebrews 11:22. In Hebrews 11, a chapter that rehearses the examples of faith provided by the ancients, there is this reference: "By faith Joseph, near the end of his life, spoke of the Exodus of the Israelites and gave instructions about his bones" (v. 22). Here, Exodus is understood as the historic saving event in which God brought the Israelites* out of Egyptian bondage into the Promised Land. The author of Hebrews brings this paradigmatic event to mind to exhort Christian believers to the same conviction exhibited by their ancestors in the faith.

2 Peter 1:15. A second instance is 2 Peter 1:15, "I shall also make every effort to enable you always to remember these things after my departure [*exodos*]." In this case, *exodos* denotes "death." The author of the letter, purportedly the apostle Peter, is leaving his last testament on the occasion of his imminent death. This connotation of *exodos* is also found in Wisdom 3:2 and 7:6 (LXX). Wisdom 3:2 speaks of the souls of the just, "They seemed, in the view of the foolish, to be dead; and their passing away [*exodos*] was thought an affliction." Wisdom 7:5-6 asserts, "For no king has had a different beginning of existence; there is for all one entrance into life, and one way out [*exodos*]" (NRSV).

Luke 9:31. The final example is found in Luke 9:31 in the account of the transfiguration. Luke relates that when Jesus went up the mountain to pray, Moses and Elijah appeared in glory and were conversing with him about "his *exodos* that he was going to accomplish in Jerusalem." There are several possible interpretations of the word *exodos* in this instance. One level of meaning is that this is a reference to Jesus' death, akin to the use of *exodos* in 2 Peter 1:15. On another level, Jesus' *exodos* is his "departure," which includes the whole complex of events that forms his transit to God: his passion, death, burial, resurrection, and ascension/exaltation. Luke presents salvation history as a course of events following a schedule of times set by God and moving along a "way" (*hodos*) leading to the Gentiles. Accordingly, Luke depicts Jesus' entire life and ministry as a course or "way" (this motif is also found in Mark 8:27; 9:33, 34; 10:17, 32). The beginning of Jesus' public ministry is termed *eisodos* ("entrance" or "coming") in Acts 13:24, "John heralded his coming by proclaiming a baptism of repentance to all the people of Israel." Corresponding to this, the beginning of the final events of Jesus' journey is signaled with *exodos* in Luke 9:31. Luke also uses *hē hodos* in Acts 9:2; 19:9, 23; 22:4; 24:14, 22 to designate Christianity as a way of life, a way that imitates the way of Jesus. Thus, the term *exodos* designates a step along the "way" of salvation history. Jesus' death and its attendant events are understood as the great liberating action for his people, just as was the Exodus of old.

Although the word "Exodus" is found only three times in the NT, there are numerous allusions to the Exodus experience and its themes.

Missionary Instructions. In the Gospel of Mark, Jesus' instructions to his disciples as he sends them out on mission contain overtones of the Israelites' preparation for their Exodus journey. The latter were told to eat the Passover meal "with your loins girt, sandals on your feet and your staff in hand, you shall eat like those who are in flight"

(Exod 12:11). Similarly, Jesus directed his disciples to take nothing for the journey but a walking stick and to wear sandals (Mark 6:8-9). By contrast, Matthew's version (10:9) says that the disciples are not to take sandals or a staff; likewise Luke 9:3 prohibits a staff; sandals are not allowed in Luke 10:4.

Feeding in the Desert. Another Gospel incident that recalls the Exodus is the feeding of Jesus' followers in the desert (Mark 6:32-44; 8:1-10; Matt 14:13-21; 15:32-39; Luke 9:10-17; John 6:1-15). Like the Israelites who were fed manna in the desert, and who all had their fill (Exodus 16), so the crowd that followed Jesus to a deserted place were fed until all were satisfied. In the Gospels the leftovers are collected (Mark 6:43 and pars.), whereas Moses adjures the Israelites not to keep any of the manna over until the next day except on the sixth day when they were to gather enough for the Sabbath as well (Exod 16:19-30).

The Last Supper. In the Synoptic accounts of Jesus' last meal with his disciples (Mark 14:22-26; Matt 26:26-29; Luke 22:15-20) the Exodus motifs abound. The meal takes place at the feast of Passover. The bread is reminiscent of the manna and the "blood of the covenant" recalls Exodus 24:8, where Moses ratified the covenant by sprinkling the blood of oxen on the altar and on the people. The overtones of hope and liberation as Jesus speaks of newness in the coming reign of God evoke the memory of the liberation of the Israelites from oppression in Egypt.

Matthean Allusions. The first evangelist, in particular, highlights Exodus themes in his Gospel account. One of Matthew's specific theological concerns is to show Jesus as the fulfillment of the Law and the Prophets, even as he supersedes them. Thus, Matthew constructs explicit parallels between Jesus and Moses in his accounts of Jesus' infancy, temptation, Sermon on the Mount, multiplication of loaves, and transfiguration. In Matthew 2:13-23 Jesus recapitulates the Exodus journey of his people,

with the flight to and exit from Egypt. In the account of the temptation (Matt 4:1-11), the desert setting, the forty-day duration (paralleling the forty years of desert wandering), and the quotations from Deuteronomy recall Exodus themes.

In the transfiguration (Matt 17:1-8) there are numerous parallels with the Sinai theophany and the Exodus-wilderness events described in Exodus 24 and 34. Elements found in both Matthew 17 and Exodus 24 include: a high mountain (Matt 17:1; Exod 24:12); a reference to six days (Matt 17:1; Exod 24:16); three companions (Matt 17:1; Exod 24:1, 9); the voice of God coming from a cloud (Matt 17:5; Exod 24:16); entering the cloud (Matt 17:5; Exod 24:18). The radiance of Jesus' face (Matt 17:2) parallels that of Moses in Exodus 34:29-30, 35. The fear of the disciples (Matt 17:6) is like that of Aaron and the people of Israel in Exodus 34:30. Peter's proposal to build tents is reminiscent of the tent of meeting of Exodus 27:21.

Johannine Allusions. The fourth evangelist also draws numerous connections between Jesus and the Exodus experience. He punctuates his account with frequent references to Passover (2:13, 23; 6:4; 11:55; 12:1; 13:1; 18:28, 39; 19:14), with a view to portraying Jesus as replacing in himself the Jewish feast. He presents Jesus as the Paschal Lamb (1:29, 36) whose death coincides with the slaughter of the Passover lambs in the Temple (19:14, 42). In the discourse on the bread of life, references to the manna in the wilderness are made explicit (6:31, 49). Allusions to Moses bringing forth water from the rock are found in John 7:37-39 and 19:34. John 3:14-15 constructs a parallel with Numbers 21:4-9: "just as Moses lifted up the serpent in the desert, so must the Son of Man be lifted up, so that everyone who believes in him may have eternal life."

Paul. Paul alludes to the Passover/Exodus experience in his first Letter to the Corinthians. He exhorts them, "Clear out the old yeast, so that you may become a fresh batch of dough, inasmuch as you are unleavened. For our paschal lamb, Christ, has been sacrificed" (5:7). In his warnings to the Corinthian community against overconfidence (1 Cor 10:1-13), he invokes the memory of their ancestors who "were all under the cloud and all passed through the sea, and all of them were baptized into Moses in the cloud and in the sea. All ate the same spiritual food, and all drank the same spiritual drink, for they drank from a spiritual rock that followed them, and the rock was the Christ. Yet God was not pleased with most of them, for they were struck down in the desert. These things happened as examples for us, so that we might not desire evil things as they did" (10:1-6).

See: COVENANT, DEATH, DESERT, EGYPT, ELIJAH/ELISHA, FAITH, HOPE, ISRAELITE, LAMB OF GOD, LAND, LAW, LIBERTY, LIFE, MANNA, MISSION, MOUNTAIN, MOSES, PASSION, PASSOVER, ROCK/STONE, SALVATION, SEA, SERPENT, TENT, TRANSFIGURATION, WATER, WAY

BARBARA E. REID, O.P.

Pastoral-Liturgical Tradition

Interpretations of the story of the Exodus fall into three categories: social-historical, typological, and sacramental. The first provides a theological interpretation of a paradigmatic event in the history of Israel. The second provides a theological interpretation of the Exodus as a prefiguring of present and future events in the personal and communal lives of a believing people. The third interprets Exodus as a prefiguration of the spiritual journey into the Christian community through the rites of Christian initiation: baptism and Eucharist.

The Exodus event has continued to provide Christians with language and imagery to interpret their own spiritual journey. The persons and revelatory signs of the social-historical journey of the Hebrews have been seen to prefigure God's offer of liberation in Jesus. God's revelatory presence in Exodus provided hope for the oppressed Hebrews. Jesus became the ultimate source of hope and perseverance for present and all future generations. Through Jesus, the New Moses, the people of God participated in the "true Exodus" that delivered the people from oppression and the enslavement of sin and the devil (1 Cor 10:1-11).

Exodus symbolism has been reappropriated in sacramental theology. The Gospel of John (6:30-35) drew an analogy between the manna in the desert and Jesus, the Bread of Life. The bread and cup shared at the Last Supper were a sign of the "new covenant" sealed in the suffering, death, and resurrection of Jesus Christ (1 Cor 10:2-4). These analogies gave rise to a sacramental interpretation of the crossing of the Red Sea as a figure of baptism. The Eucharist was prefigured in Exodus by the manna in the desert and the rock of Horeb (Exod 16:1–17:7). The whole process of Christian initiation celebrated during the paschal liturgies was prefigured by the "sacrament of Exodus." Early Christian traditions compared the initiation of the catechumens in the early Church to the "sacrament" that the Exodus people received at the crossing of the Red Sea. As the Hebrews were freed from the tyranny of Pharaoh by the destruction of his army in the Red Sea, so the catechumens were set free from the tyranny of Satan by his destruction in the waters of baptism.

During the Patristic period, the story of Exodus was appropriated analogously by Tertullian, Origen, St. Basil, St. Gregory of Nyssa, St. Cyril of Jerusalem, and Didymus the Blind as a figure of baptism. By baptism, the Christian was freed from the tyranny of the demon. The entire story of Exodus was perceived as a type of baptism: Egypt was a type of the evil world; Pharaoh was Satan, the devil, or the demon; the waters of the Red Sea were a type of the waters of baptism which broke the demon's tyrannical hold on the people of God.

In Patristic theology, the pillar of cloud that guided the people by day and in the Exodus story was interpreted as the visible sign of the Holy Spirit. Origen validated his sacramental interpretation of Exodus by citing Paul's reference to the event: "they were all baptized in the cloud and the sea" (1 Cor 10:2-3). In his fifth *Homily on Exodus*, Origen rendered a sacramental interpretation of

Paul's reference: "That which the Jews consider to be the crossing of the Sea, St. Paul calls Baptism. That which they believe to be a cloud, St. Paul proves to be the Holy Spirit. . . ." Origen's interpretation of the cloud as a symbol of the Holy Spirit would be echoed in St. Ambrose's *De Mysteriis*.

In a parallel fashion the pillar of fire that guided the people by night in the Exodus account was interpreted in John's Gospel as a prefiguration of Christ, the light of the World (8:12). St. Ambrose's *De Sacramentis* identified the pillar of fire as "Christ the Lord, who has scattered the darkness of paganism and has spread the light of thought and of spiritual grace in the heart of men" (*De sacr.* 1.22).

In theological literature from the medieval to the mid-twentieth century, there appear few, if any, references to the Exodus outside of sacramental or liturgical theology. The use of typological and sacramental analogy effectively de-emphasized the social-historical liberation of the Hebrew people and supported an exclusively religious interpretation of Exodus. It was this purely religious liberation that was emphasized when preaching to people who were enslaved or colonized. In contrast, the historical literature recording European colonization of Africa and the United States often used popularized notions of "chosen people" and "Manifest Destiny," traceable to the Exodus event, to legitimize the appropriation of land and the conquest of the indigenous peoples of Africa and the Americas.

The revival and emphasis on the social-historical significance of the Exodus as a paradigm of human liberation surfaced primarily among oppressed races, cultures, and peoples. Africans finding themselves enslaved within Christian households of America interpreted the Exodus event through the framework of their own physical enslavement.

African-American spirituals and poetry reveal their use of analogy to interpret the Exodus event in the context of their own slavery. The God who had intervened in human history to liberate the Hebrews would also liberate them physically, spiritually, and socially. An analysis of Exodus-related themes in the spirituals reveals frequent reference to Egypt as a place of enslavement and oppression. The Red Sea was the place where God gave the victory to the oppressed. Canaan was the promised land of the North. Pharaoh was the symbol of oppression overcome and destroyed. Pharaoh's daughter was a good woman arising from bad stock who protected Moses; and Moses, the most popular of the spiritual figures, symbolized the deliverance of a whole people and the opportunity for each person to be free (e.g., "Go Down Moses").

This popular folk theologizing, found in songs and preaching within the African American context, was given formal theological voice by the writing of Black and Latin American theologians in the mid-twentieth century. James Cone and Gustavo Gutierrez, the theological fathers of the contemporary Black and Latin American Liberation movements respectively, used human experience as the starting point. They focused on the social-historical context of the political struggles of the oppressed peoples in their contexts (Black Americans, and the poor of Peru). Interestingly, while Exodus is cited in the popular folk theologies of liberation, both Cone and Gutierrez initially used a strong Christocentric emphasis in their initial works. Both saw the liberation of the oppressed as a central theme of Jesus' ministry. Gutierrez's inaugural work, *A Theology of Liberation*, made scant reference to Exodus. He used numerous biblical references from both the OT and NT, indicating that liberation was a central theme of the whole Bible, not solely that of Exodus. Cone does not make significant mention of Exodus until his fourth book, *God of the Oppressed*. Both agree, however, that Exodus reveals a God who took sides with the oppressed, i.e., a God who participated in the Hebrews' journey of liberation. The work of Cone and Gutierrez signaled a revival of liberation as a theological paradigm.

Two documents from the Congregation for the Doctrine of the Faith, "Instruction on Certain Aspects of the 'Theology of Liberation'" and "Instruction on Christian Freedom and Liberation" (ICFL) also explore the relation of the Exodus theme to liberation theology. While maintaining a primacy of order for religious liberation, they both maintain that Exodus is a legitimate primary source for liberation theology. They further note that the theme of liberation is at the heart of both the OT and NT. Exodus is not simply about a spiritual liberation, nor is it the legitimate basis for an exclusively social-political approach to liberation. Exodus "has a meaning which is both religious and political." God sets his people free and gives them descendants, a land, and a law, but within a covenant and for a covenant (ICFL, no. 44). The Church must participate in assisting human beings in their liberation from the power of sin and the Evil One which oppress them, and bring them into communion of Love of God (ICFL, no. 53). While asserting the primacy of order of religious and moral conversion, i.e., the need for the moral conversion of the heart (ICFL, no. 63), the Church still recognizes the need to eliminate unjust structures. "Those who suffer oppression on the part of the wealth or the politically powerful should take action, through morally licit means, in order to secure structures and institution in which their rights will be truly respected" (ICFL, no. 75).

See: LIBERTY

JAMIE T. PHELPS

EXPIATION

Expiation connotes cleansing, purification, or removal of sin by satisfaction and forgiveness. Although it does appear in both Testaments, the concept of expiation is not given much emphasis, especially in the NT. Its background relates to the conviction that God is faithful to the covenant made with human beings, but that human beings are not. This infidelity, often called "sin,"* must somehow be amended. Many ancient religions include the need for such satisfaction from both human and divine viewpoints. God is said to exact satisfaction for transgressions in the form of appeasement or propitiation; humans offer expiation and make sacrifice as a means of having their sins removed. But in the Bible, only God can and does supply the means of expiation. No appeasement is demanded by God. Humans realize that their sacrifices and offerings are inadequate. Yet God has given a way of being reconciled and restored to grace through Jesus Christ.

Old Testament

In the OT, terms for expiation (most often derivatives of the Hebrew *kipper*) occur in reference to averting threatened punishment for sin (Prov 16:14; Deut 32:43). God is not indifferent to sin. Expiation is a means by which human beings can restore the broken relationship caused by sin. The obvious example is that of the scapegoat loaded with the sins of the Israelites, exiled from the community, and set loose in the desert. Observing *Yom Kippur* or Day of Atonement,* the Israelites felt that they were cleansed of both sin and guilt. They were thus restored to a right relationship with God and became once again a covenant people.

New Testament

Terms for expiation in the NT are likewise relatively infrequent. Whereas in the OT the concept usually appears in a cultic or liturgical context, in the NT expiation has a more real, operative, theological sense. God has given us Jesus by whom and in whom our sins are expiated (Rom 3:25). All who had been threatened with the wrath of God are, because of Christ, now subject to God's patient endurance (Rom 2:4). It is the graciousness of God that causes our sins to be removed or expiated (Luke 18:13; 1 John 2:2; 4:10). In the Letter to the Hebrews, Jesus is described as making expiation for our sins in his role as high priest (2:17).

Pastoral-Liturgical Tradition

The notion of somehow making satisfaction for sins has left a lasting impression on pastoral-liturgical theology. For example, expiation has been seen as one of the four principal forms of Christian prayer.* But the notion of expiation is always shaped by the conviction that it is God who freely bestows the covenant and is faithful to that covenant. It is not God who requires appeasement. The means of expiation for sin is given by God in Jesus Christ, our high priest, who stands before God as our sinless representative and intermediary.

See: ATONEMENT, COVENANT, PRAYER, SACRIFICE, SIN, WRATH OF GOD

MARY ANN GETTY

F

FACE OF GOD

Old Testament

In both the OT and the NT the "face of God" connotes God's personal presence (Pss 16:11; 21:7). In the OT the Hebrew words *pānîm* and *'ap,* like the Greek word *prosōpon* in the NT, literally denote "face," or "countenance." Because the face reflects one's whole appearance, these terms also carry the wider connotation of "person" or "personal presence."

Prayer is referred to as seeking the face of God: "Your presence *[panîm],* O Lord, I seek" (Ps 27:8; similarly Ps 105:4). Entreating God's favor in prayer is "softening God's face." The prophet Zechariah (8:21) describes how, in the days of the Messiah, the inhabitants of many different cities will approach one another, saying, "Come! let us go to implore the favor of the LORD" (literally, "let us go to soften the face of God"; similarly 1 Sam 13:12; 2 Kgs 13:4; 2 Chr 33:12; Jer 26:19).

The prayer that God may "let his face shine upon us" (Pss 67:2; 80:3, 8), like the priestly blessing of Numbers 6:25, is an entreaty for God's grace and favor. Conversely, when God's face is hidden or turned away, this connotes divine displeasure and the absence of God's protection (Deut 31:17-18). So the psalmist prays, "Hide not your face from me in the day of my distress" (Ps 102:3; similarly Ps 22:25).

"Seeing God face to face" is an expression that describes intense, personal encounters with the divine. The OT traditions are not uniform on whether it is permissible to see the face of God and live. During Moses' encounter with God on the mountain he requests, "Do let me see your glory!" (Deut 33:18). God replies, "I will make all my beauty pass before you, and in your presence I will pronounce my name, 'LORD' . . . but my face you cannot see, for no man sees me and still lives" (Deut 33:19-20; similarly, Judg 6:22; 13:22). But in Deuteronomy 34:10 the Israelites eulogize Moses as a unique prophet, "whom the LORD knew face to face." And in Deuteronomy 5:4 Moses' experience extends to all the Israelites, "The LORD spoke with you face to face on the mountain from the midst of the fire."

Jacob was also said to have seen God face to face, but he, too, is aware of the peril involved. He named the place of his nocturnal wrestling with God's messenger "Peniel, 'Because I have seen God face to face,' he said, 'yet my life has been spared'" (Gen 32:31).

In other instances, to "see God's face" means being received favorably. Elihu speaks to Job of one who shall pray and whom God will favor, who shall "see God's face with rejoicing" (Job 33:26). In Genesis 33:10 Jacob likens his favorable reception from Esau to having seen the face of God.

In some instances "to see the face of God" has the cultic sense, "to visit the sanctuary for worship" (e.g., Ps 42:3). And ritual sacrifices are brought "before the face of God" (Exod 23:15; 34:20; Isa 1:12). Israel may have taken over these expressions from non-Israelite cults that had an idol in the Temple for veneration.

New Testament

The references to the face of God in the NT follow closely the OT concepts. Acts 2:28 quotes Psalm 16:11 where the "face of God" connotes the divine presence. 1 Peter 3:12 quotes Psalm 33:17 to remind believers that God's favor is upon those who pursue the virtuous life, while "against evildoers the LORD sets his face."

Hebrews 9:24 contains an allusion to the cultic sense of coming before the face of God in the Temple. Christ is said to have entered into the heavenly sanctuary, "that he might now appear before God [lit. "the face of God"] on our behalf."

As for seeing God's face, this privilege is already accorded the angels of "the little ones," who "always look upon the face of my [Jesus'] heavenly Father" (Matt 18:10). Revelation 22:4 asserts that in the end time the righteous will see God "face to face" and bear the divine name on their foreheads. The beatitudes also promise that the single-hearted shall see God (Matt 5:8). Meanwhile, Paul says, "we see indistinctly, as in a mirror, but then face to face" (1 Cor 13:12). And 1 John 3:2 promises, "We shall be like him [God], for we shall see him as he is."

See: ANGELS, BLESSING, GLORY, MOSES, PRAYER, TEMPLE, WORSHIP

BARBARA E. REID, O.P.

FAITH

For the OT the notion of faith centers on the belief in God's reliability. Ancient Israel believed that it could depend upon God completely because of God's fidelity. In the NT, faith is identified with accepting Jesus as coming from God. In later Christian tradition, faith is an infused theological virtue that makes it possible for human beings to understand divine truth. Still, it remains a moral reality since it is perfected through love.

Old Testament

The ancient Israelites were firmly convinced that God had intervened to save and guide them in former times of oppression and danger. They learned to fear, trust,* and love this divine person who had been so faithful to them from the very beginning. Faith in the OT is primarily trust, but it includes a cognitive element, the knowledge of God through communal and personal religious experience and the living of a faithful life. It is extended to God as person, as one who seeks a relationship with human beings; it is a mutuality of life with God who is accepted as creator, covenant partner, savior, and guide. Exactly what that entails is learned gradually, especially through the experience of worship and through the ministry of the prophets, with their emphasis on social justice. Eventually the Israelites came to realize that other gods are only vain idols and do not really exist, in contrast to the "true" God of transcendent liberty, creative power, justice, and loving compassion.

Vocabulary. Although the complexity of a faith relationship with God is expressed by many verbs, such as "love," "fear," "trust," "obey," and with many images, e.g., God as "rock," "fortress," "light," "savior," "judge," there is one Hebrew root which specifies this relationship more directly, namely, 'aman.

Used in the Niphal, a passive form (ne'eman), it may refer to a "faithful" messenger (Prov 25:13), a "reliable" witness (Isa 8:2), "trustworthy" men (Neh 13:13). When referring to God, it means "reliable" or "faithful" (Deut 7:9; Isa 49:7).

The Hiphil, a declarative form (he'emin), means "believe" or "trust," with human reality as an object (Jer 12:6; Prov 14:15), or God (Pss 106:12, 24; 78:32).

'Emeth, a noun from the same root, is said of "true" human speech (1 Kgs 10:6; Zech 8:16), an "unmistakable" token (Josh 2:11), "trustworthy" men (Exod 18:21). God is an *'el 'emeth*, a "faithful God" (Ps 31:6), one who "keeps faith forever" (Ps 146:6), praised for the divine qualities of "kindness" and "truth" (Pss 115:1; 138:2), where "truth" clearly means "fidelity." God's "truth" in Psalms 25:5; 26:3; and 86:11 ("Teach me, O LORD, your way, that I may walk in your truth"), is not to be taken abstractly; it refers either to divine faithfulness or instruction, the Torah. The contrast in Jeremiah 10 of "true God" to pagan gods who do not even exist does involve some definition of divinity (Jer 10:10).

'Emunah means "steadfastness," "honesty," and is often contrasted with *sheqer*, "falsehood" or "deception." A "truthful witness does not lie" (Prov 12:17); God's eyes "look for honesty" (Jer 5:3); judges are to "act faithfully" (2 Chr 19:9). People who are just shall live "because of" their "faith" (Hab 2:4). *'Emunah* is also applied to God, who rules with justice and "constancy" (Ps 96:13) and performs works that are "trustworthy" (Ps 33:4). God is an *'el 'emunah*, a "faithful God" in whom there is no deceit (Deut 32:4).

'Amen has the force of a jussive, "may it be!" In Deuteronomy 27 the people are told to answer "Amen" to the various curses, condemning themselves should they become guilty. The "Amen" of Jeremiah 28:6 is interpreted by what follows, "thus may the LORD do!" The expression *'elohe 'amen* ("God of amen") appears twice in Isaiah 65:16 and signifies that God will certainly carry out what is sworn.

Although variously nuanced, the different forms of *'aman* converge on the meaning "reliability." They assure us that we can depend on God completely because God always has been and always will be faithful, with a divine fidelity that calls forth our own.

Pentateuch. The "word of the LORD" appears to Abraham in a vision, tells him not to fear, promises to be his shield, and predicts that his descendants will be as numerous as the stars in the sky. Abraham "put his faith in the LORD, who credited it to him as an act of righteousness" (Gen 15:6). Abraham's faith expresses a personal relationship; it is directed to "the LORD" rather than to the "word of the LORD" because the latter implies the former: the extraordinary promise is reliable because of the One who made it. Genesis 15 describes a covenant* of grace, for God, in a rite similar to that of Jeremiah 34:18, symbolically walks through a row of cut meat (v. 17) to emphasize divine assurance, while Abraham is simply called upon to accept this covenant in faith. He manifests his fidelity by believing God's promises and by his willingness to carry out God's will, be it the command to leave his native land and kinsfolk for "a land that I will show you" (Gen 12:1), or the directive to sacrifice his son on an altar (Genesis 22). Abraham's "faithful heart" is commemorated in Nehemiah 9:8, and his "loyalty" in Sirach 44:20. In the NT, both Paul and James cite Genesis 15:6 as part of their reflections on faith (Gal 3:6; Jas 2:23).

At the Exodus the Israelites sometimes "feared the LORD and believed in" God and Moses (Exod 14:31), but at other times were criticized for refusing "to believe in me despite all the signs I have performed among them" (Num 14:11). They would not "trust" God though they were carried like a child in God's arms (Deut 1:32); the "Rock" was a "faithful God, without deceit," yet was still treated basely by the people (Deut 32:4-5). Faith is the proper response to God's mighty deeds, but it is not forced; it is invited, yet too often rejected by sinful human willfulness.

Historical Books. God's faithfulness receives special emphasis in the Davidic covenant, the promise that the dynasty of David would "endure forever" (2 Sam 7:16). Allusions to this are made in 1

Samuel 25:28; 1 Kings 8:26; 11:38, and also in Psalm 89. The Davidic covenant with its assurance of permanent royal rule forms the basis of later messianic expectations.

The Deuteronomistic meditation on the fall of Samaria, 2 Kings 17, lists the sins of Israel and Judah, and includes their lack of faith: they were "as stiff-necked as their fathers, who had not believed in the LORD, their God" (v. 14).

Prophets. The prophets often indict their audiences for lack of faith but also offer them hope. Hosea accuses Israel and Judah of rebellion against "the Holy One, who is faithful" (Hos 12:1), and though there is "no fidelity . . . in the land" (Hos 4:1), a time will come when "I will espouse you in fidelity and you shall know the LORD" (Hos 2:22). Isaiah denounces Jerusalem, the "faithful city," for having become "an adulteress" (Isa 1:21), but he also promises a time of restoration when she shall again be called "city of justice, faithful city" (v. 26). His warning to Ahaz, "Unless your faith is firm, you shall not be firm" (Isa 7:9), is a call to trust in God at a time of military peril, especially God's promise to the dynasty of David, and not rely on dangerous foreign powers like Assyria; a similar thought is expressed in Isaiah 28:16. The coming Messiah will be characterized by justice and "faithfulness" (Isa 11:5). Habakkuk looks at the sad state of Jerusalem conquered by the Babylonians (probably in 598 BCE), is tempted to question God's ways, but concludes that the just shall live "because of" their "faith" (Hab 2:4), that is, they shall continue to be in right relationship with God if they trust and remain faithful in spite of their present unhappy experience (see Ezek 18:9). Jeremiah promises divine pardon if even one person in Jerusalem "lives uprightly and seeks to be faithful" (Jer 5:1). He contrasts idols that cannot save with the "true God," "the living God," the eternal Ruler (Jer 10:10) who "made the earth" in power, wisdom, and skill (v. 12). Though the emphasis is still on trust, this passage in Jeremiah helps to define God as the object of faith not only because of God's past fidelity to Israel, but because of a number of divine qualities—life, eternal royalty, justice, wisdom, creative power—characteristics of the "true" God. Deutero-Isaiah promises restoration to the exiles in Babylon and encourages them to trust in God, besides whom there is no other, a God who had chosen them "to know and believe in me and understand that it is I" (Isa 43:10), the "God of truth" (lit. "the God of amen," Isa 65:16).

Psalms. God is reliable and worthy of trust. This basic insight is found throughout the psalms.

Laments express hope for a positive response because of God's "faithfulness" (Pss 36:6; 71:22; 143:1), "kindness and constancy" (Ps 25:10), for God is a "faithful God" (Ps 31:6). Psalm 85:11 personifies "kindness and truth," "justice and peace," as characteristics of future divine salvation; see also Psalm 43:3 ("Send forth your light and your fidelity"). At times the psalmist asks, "Guide me in your truth and teach me, for you are God my savior" (25:5; see 26:3; 86:11). The "truth" in question may simply be God's "fidelity" as in Psalm 43:3, or perhaps the guidance God gives through the Torah, precepts commended in other texts such as Psalms 111:7; 119:43, 66, 86, 138, 142, 151, 160.

Historical psalms depict the wonders of the Exodus whereby the Israelites "believe" God's words and sing God's praises (Ps 106:12), but they also portray a refusal to believe in spite of signs (Pss 78:32; 106:24).

Royal psalms proclaim God's fidelity to the house of David and to the divine promise that it would last forever (Pss 89:3, 29, 34, 38, 50; 132:11).

Hymns extol God's "faithfulness" (Ps 100:5) and "salvation" (40:11). God abounds "in kindness and fidelity" (Ps 86:15), two divine qualities that are often mentioned together (e.g., Pss 92:3; 98:3), or "kindness" and "truth" (Pss 115:1; 138:2), where "truth" according to the context signifies "faithfulness." God, who "keeps faith forever" (Ps 146:6; see 117:2) and whose works are "trustworthy" (Ps 33:4) or "faithful" (Ps 111:7), who rules with "constancy" (Ps 96:13), establishes "true" ordinances (Ps 19:10) and "trustworthy" decrees (Pss 19:8; 93:5).

See COVENANT, FEAR, GRACE, KNOWLEDGE, LOVE, OBEDIENCE

JOSEPH F. WIMMER, O.S.A.

New Testament

Meaning. The classical Greek terms denoting "faith"—the noun, *pistis* (trust, faith); the adjective, *pistos* (trustworthy, faithful); and the verb, *pisteuein* (to believe, to have confidence in, to accept as true)—had no specifically religious connotation in classical Greek. The Septuagint employed these terms, however, to express Israel's trust and confidence in Yahweh, the faithful one. The NT, especially the letters of Paul and others, uses this word group frequently with reference to the Christian's response to God, manifest in the person of Jesus. To have faith in Jesus is, therefore, to adhere to the totality of Jesus' person: his words and his deeds, and to accept them as true, as come from God.

Synoptic Tradition. As in the OT, the primary object of faith is God, as Jesus commands in Mark 11:22: "Have faith in God." Christian faith in God, however, soon expressed itself exclusively in the acceptance of and belief in Jesus as the Anointed One, the Son of God. In the Gospels, moreover, Jesus calls people to faith in himself (Matt 10:32-33), or better, to faith in the power of God at work in him. For example, he chides the disciples in the boat, "Do you not yet have faith?" (Mark 4:40), and questions the two blind men, "Do you believe that I can do this?" (Matt 9:28). In contrast to Mark and Matthew, Luke's Gospel sometimes uses "faith" in a more general sense, as faithfulness or trustworthiness, as in Luke 16:10-12.

Christians are also challenged to put their faith in the gospel, the good news. On the lips of Jesus, this invitation signals the call to believe in the announcement of the imminent coming of God's reign among them (Mark 1:15). In the postresurrection communities, however, this same call to believe in the "gospel" demands faith, that is, acceptance and acknowledgment of the kerygma, the proclamation of the saving deeds of God in Christ (1 Thess 1:5).

And in Matthew 21:32, Jesus admonishes the chief priests and the elders of the Jews because they have failed to believe in John the Baptist as one who came "in the way of righteousness" and was, therefore, a herald of God's presence among them. Tax collectors and prostitutes believed before the leaders of the Jews.

The miracles of Jesus are often performed in direct response to faith (Mark 2:5; 5:34; 10:52), and lack of faith is an obstacle to God's power being revealed (Matt 13:58; Mark 6:5). In fact, Jesus assures his followers that all things are possible to those who have faith (Mark 9:23). And faith itself is sufficient even to "move mountains" (Matt 17:20; 21:21). But, in many gospel stories, non-Jews demonstrate greater faith than the disciples themselves: for example, the Roman centurions in Matthew 8:10; Mark 15:39; Luke 7:9; the Syro-Phoenician (Canaanite) woman in Mark 7:24-30; Matthew 15:21-28; tax collectors and prostitutes in Matthew 21:32.

Matthew's Gospel contains a special emphasis on the call to faith, evident in the Matthean redaction of several Markan texts wherein Matthew adds an additional reference to faith (Matt 8:13; 9:28). And this Gospel repeatedly admonishes the disciples, and therefore indirectly the Matthean community, for their "little faith" (Matt 6:30; 8:26; 14:31; 16:8; 17:20). It is all the more striking, therefore, that the Canaanite woman, a Gentile and an outsider, is praised in the Gospel for her "great faith" (Matt 15:28).

Faith in the power of God at work in Jesus leads not only to physical healings and the exorcism of demons, but ultimately to the forgiveness of sin, for example in Mark 2:5 and Luke 7:48-50.

The Acts of the Apostles. In Acts, the profession of faith becomes a prerequisite for baptism, and a necessary condition of salvation. The object of faith in Acts is the preaching of the apostles (Acts 9:42; 16:30-32; 18:8). Such a faith response is always a free act, however, and is never imposed on those who hear the word (Acts 2:41; 6:7). Faith is gift of God and comes through the power of the Spirit on Jew and Gentile alike, as Peter attests in Acts 11:15, 17: "As I began to speak, the holy Spirit fell upon them [i.e., Gentiles] as it had upon us at the beginning. . . . If then God gave them the same gift he gave to us when we came to believe in the Lord Jesus Christ, who was I to be able to hinder God?" In another example, the textual variant in the Western text of Acts 8:37, which adds a reference to the affirmation of faith by the Ethiopian eunuch—"I believe that Jesus Christ is the Son of God"—confirms the developing importance in the early Church of the profession of faith spoken in the context of the baptismal ritual.

Pauline Tradition. For Paul, faith is the *sine qua non* of salvation and the means by which we are incorporated into the body of Christ. Faith finds expression in response to hearing the gospel, the proclamation of the kerygma of the death, resurrection, and exaltation of Christ: "Thus faith comes from what is heard, and what is heard comes through the word of Christ" (Rom 10:17). This word is, for Paul, the "gospel." It is a word of freedom (Gal 1:6-9) and anyone proclaiming a different "word" Paul says is accursed. It is a word grounded in the "folly of the Cross"* (1 Cor 1:21) and faithful reception of this word means participation in the Cross (Rom 6:8; 8:17-18; Phil 1:29; 3:10). Finally, it is a word that leads to salvation if it is accepted in faith.

As in the Synoptic tradition, the object of faith for Paul is, properly, God (1 Thess 1:8). But faith in God is now summoned,

once and for all, in response to God's self-revelation in the death and resurrection of Christ (1 Thess 4:14), God's total revelation of love for creation. Paul insists that faith is not a matter of words or intellectual assent to a body of truths. Instead, he speaks of the "obedience of faith" (Rom 1:5; 16:26) which implies a total commitment to the one in whom one believes. Faith finds appropriate expression, therefore, in public confession (Rom 10:9) and demands faithful obedience to the person in whom one believes (2 Cor 10:5-6). The followers of Christ in Thessalonica, therefore, can be called simply "believers" (1 Thess 1:7).

Faith has both a present and future dimension. Persons who hear the gospel, and in that hearing encounter the risen Christ, are called to believe in the one who is proclaimed, to confess that belief, and to receive baptism as the ritual expression of their faith and entry into new life. Paul reminds the Church at Rome, "Or are you unaware that we who were baptized into Christ Jesus were baptized into his death? We were indeed buried with him through baptism into death, so that, just as Christ was raised from the dead by the glory of the Father, we too might live in newness of life" (Rom 6:3-4).

Faith has also a future dimension since the Christian is called to believe in the promises of God for the future, as Paul affirms in 1 Thessalonians 4:14: "For if we believe that Jesus died and rose, so too will God, through Jesus, bring with him those who have fallen asleep." Faith stands, therefore, as the key element in the triad of "faith, hope, and love" (1 Thess 1:3; 5:8; 1 Cor 13:13). Despite Paul's claim that love is the greatest of these (1 Cor 13:13), it is faith that "works through love" (Gal 5:6), and it is faith in Christ, as the "first fruits" (1 Cor 15:20) of those who have been raised from the dead, that inspires hope for the future.

In all his letters, Paul underscores the dynamic quality of faith. Faith "works" in those who believe (1 Thess 2:13), and, as noted above, it works through love. Faith, moreover, must be "strengthened and encouraged" (1 Thess 3:2). Faith progresses and increases (Phil 1:25; 2 Cor 10:15) as Christians "struggle together for the faith of the gospel" (Phil 1:27). The quality of faith differs in different individuals. In some, faith is weak (Rom 14:1) or deficient (1 Thess 3:10), in others, faith is firm (1 Cor 16:13; 2 Cor 1:24). These expressions indicate that Paul understands faith in terms of a capacity to respond to the mystery of God revealed in Christ; this capacity he terms "the obedience of faith."

By far, the most developed reflection on faith in the Pauline letters concerns the relationship between faith and righteousness. Against his Judaizing opponents in Galatia who place their trust in works of the Law to achieve righteousness before God, Paul claims emphatically, again and again, that "a person is not justified by works of the law but through faith in Jesus Christ" (Gal 2:16; see Rom 3:21-22). His aim in this section of Galatians is primarily to counter his opponents who want to impose on Gentile converts the demands and obligations of Torah observance as a means to righteousness. Paul is convinced, on the contrary, that righteousness is made possible *only* through the death/resurrection of Jesus Christ, and that persons have access to righteousness only through faith, that is, through God's gift. Their acceptance of this gift is manifest in their adherence to Christ. Paul in no way eliminates the importance of a lived response in faith; adherence to Christ demands a life of holiness marked by moral virtue. The gift of faith, furthermore, renders one a child of God (Gal 3:26; 4:6-7) and a member of Christ's body (Rom 12:3, 9-11; 1 Cor 12:12-13).

Johannine Tradition. In the Johannine tradition, faith is an essential theme, a fact which is demonstrated by the more than one hundred occurrences in the Gospel and Letters of the verb, *pisteuein*—to believe. In the Gospel, persons are consistently challenged to accept or reject the revelation of God manifest in Jesus who is the Word (John 1:1-18), the One Sent (John 3:17; 8:29; 11:42; 16:27; 17:21), the perfect revelation of the Father (John 14:8-9). In the First Letter of John, the author insists further that belief in Jesus demands an acknowledgment that Jesus has come "in the flesh" (1 John 4:2) against those who would deny his humanness.

Believing is linked in the Johannine tradition with other terms that have virtually the same meaning: seeing and knowing. In John 12:42, the terms seeing and believing are linked explicitly, as Jesus says, "Whoever believes in me believes not only in me but also in the one who sent me, and whoever sees me sees the one who sent me." Together, these terms play throughout the Gospel and convey the essential challenge of the good news which is to accept the revelation of God present in Jesus. The author of the Gospel makes this aim explicit in the concluding verse of John 20:31— "these are written that you may believe that Jesus is the Messiah, the Son of God, and that through this belief you may have life in his name." The gospel witness is, therefore, a proclamation that summons people to belief.

The consequences of belief or non-belief in the Gospel are equally clear. Belief in Jesus is demonstrated in the Gospel by giving testimony (witness) to others (John 1:7, 15, 32). John the Baptist is the herald and witness *par excellence,* but the Samaritan woman (John 4:39), the royal official (John 4:53), the man born blind (John 9), the Beloved Disciple (John 20:8), and Mary Magdalene (John 20:18) all are examples in the Gospel of persons whose faith is also demonstrated by a confession of faith, a public acknowledgment of their acceptance of Jesus.

Belief, demonstrated in this way, guarantees that one has entered eternal life (John 6:40, 47). Confrontation with the Word, therefore, whether in the person of Jesus or by means of the testimony of another, summons people to faith. For this reason the Son was sent into the world, because "God so loved the world" and willed that all might have eternal life (John 3:16) through

299

him. The fate of those who encounter the Word, however, rests with their capacity either to accept or to reject the revelation in Jesus: "Whoever believes in him will not be condemned, but whoever does not believe in him has already been condemned, because he has not believed in the name of the only Son of God" (John 3:18; see John 3:36). Faith, that is, acceptance of the Word, grants to the believers the "power to become children of God" (John 1:12).

The author of the Gospel, however, consistently criticizes faith based solely on "signs." Jesus' miracles, or "signs" as John always calls them, are of no real significance in themselves. Their value derives from their ability to point beyond themselves to the glory of God revealed in Jesus—the revealing Word. Faith, true faith in the Johannine sense, must not be dependent on signs but on the word of testimony. Jesus challenges Nathanael to see beyond the marvelous disclosure about his "sitting under the fig tree" (John 1:50). Again, Jesus refuses to entrust himself to those in Jerusalem who believed only because of his signs (John 2:23). The royal official (and, implicitly, the hearers of the gospel) are chided for this faith based on signs: "Unless you people see signs and wonders, you will not believe" (John 4:48). And in the climactic scene of the resurrection appearance to Thomas and the other disciples, Jesus blesses those who "have not seen and have believed" (John 20:29).

Faith in Jesus as the One Sent requires that the believer follow the pattern of Jesus' life. He is the shepherd who "lays down his life for the sheep" (John 10:11, 15, 17, 18). His commandment "to love one another" (John 13:34; 15:12-17) is "new" (see Lev 19:18) in that it calls for the kind of loving Jesus demonstrated by washing the feet of the disciples. Faith in Jesus, therefore, is a lived faith by which the believers are willing to lay down their very lives for one another, as Jesus had done. The Johannine letters underscore this theme even more emphatically (1 John 2:3, 9-10; 3:11, 16, 23).

Perseverance in faith, especially in the face of hostility from non-Christians and possible martyrdom at the hands of the State, is a dominant theme throughout the Book of Revelation. Having described, for example, the great beast with ten horns and the evil wrought in its name, the author proclaims, "Anyone destined to be slain by the sword shall be slain by the sword. Such is the faithful endurance of the holy ones" (Rev 13:10). These faithful martyrs are praised and blessed in Revelation 14:13, "Blessed are the dead who die in the Lord from now on" (see Rev 22:7, 14).

Hebrews. "Faith is the realization of what is hoped for and the evidence of things not seen" (Heb 11:1). This classic definition of faith from the Letter to the Hebrews opens a chapter that praises the faith of the ancestors in Judaism. The author of Hebrews uses "faith" in the sense of fidelity, trust, obedience, whose sole object is God. The OT examples, therefore, illustrate faithfulness to the covenant with God, a faithfulness demonstrated in specific behavior. Faith's opposite, on the other hand, is rejection of God's promises.

Christ is "the leader and perfecter of faith" (Heb 12:2), the one who inaugurates "something better for us" (Heb 11:40), better than the examples of faith of old. He is the one who enables Christian faithfulness as both model and "pioneer" (Heb 12:2). Christ, therefore, is not so much the object of faith in Hebrews as the one who makes faith possible.

Letter of James. The apparent dichotomy between Paul and James over the question of faith and works is just that, apparent and not real. James exposes the futility of empty faith, "faith without works" as he calls it (Jas 2:17). But he is not speaking here of "works of the law" as a means of righteousness, as Paul does in Galatians. His concern is to counter those who may be *misinterpreting* Paul, thereby claiming that they have no obligation to show concern and care for their fellow Christians. Both Paul and James call for a faith that shows itself through love (Gal 5:6; 1 Cor 13:1-13) and demands acts of compassion toward the neighbor (Rom 12:9-17).

See: CONFIDENCE, HOPE

BARBARA E. BOWE, R.S.C.J.

Pastoral-Liturgical Tradition

Faith is the theological virtue infused in us by God that enables us to have knowledge of God and some understanding of the truths of God. Since the purpose of any virtue is to direct an act to its most proper end and to achieve its own special excellence, it is through faith that our minds are involved in the perfecting activity of assenting to and contemplating the truth we find in God. Faith is necessary for what is entailed in the fullest possible development of our nature. Since we are called to share the divine life and goodness, the most perfect development of our intelligence and understanding comes not through considering purely human truths, but in pondering the supernatural truth and goodness of God. The absolute need for faith corresponds to the supernatural possibilities to which God calls us. Because God summons us to the beatific vision, we must be able to grasp the truths in which our fullness consists.

We do so by the grace of faith, the infused supernatural virtue which makes us capable of understanding, however imperfectly and incompletely, the truths of God. Faith precedes understanding because without the grace of faith we would not be able to grasp sufficiently the love God has for us and the happiness to which God calls us. If we are to learn about God and grow in our understanding of the mystery of God, belief is essential. It is the openness and susceptibility to God that allows us to be influenced by God and come to deeper understanding of the things of God.

Faith, then, is the virtue by which we become learners of God through the guidance of God. The special activity of faith is to learn about God by being taught by God.

Faith is prior to understanding because it disposes us to learn the truths of salvation, truths we grasp not by our own powers, but through the agency of God. Aquinas holds that "No one of us can attain to this vision of God except by being a learner with God as our teacher. . . . Thus in order that we come to the full, beatific vision, the first requisite is that we believe God, as a learner believing the master teaching him or her" (S.Th., II-II, 2, 3).

If from God's side faith means God instructing us, primarily through Scripture and the Spirit, in the truths necessary for blessedness, from our side to have faith is to assent to the truths of God as worthy of belief and essential for salvation. Faith is a virtue of the intellect by which we subscribe to the credibility and truthfulness of all things pertaining to God, especially those crucial to salvation. Through faith our minds are focused on God as the source of all goodness and truth, and as the ultimate end of our life, the one in whom we shall find complete joy, peace, and satisfaction (S.Th., II-II, 4, 5). To have faith is to yield to God as one eminently worthy of belief and to see in God the truth that perfects not only our mind, but our whole person; in this respect, faith constitutes an overall stance of a person to be centered on God, to contemplate the things of God, and to seek to know and understand God. The assent of faith is not to something completely and perfectly known, or to something already wholly present, but represents both a desire and a willingness to yield to the truth of God; thus, persons of faith favor belief over unbelief and allow themselves to be influenced favorably by anything that supports belief (S.Th., II-II, 1, 4).

The key mark of faith is to believe in God's overwhelming desire to save us. Faith assents not to the trivial but to the essential, and indeed the essence of faith is a firm disposition to yield our hearts to God's desire to love and befriend us in Christ and the Spirit. The assent of faith focuses primarily on the qualities of God that pertain to salvation. Its interest is God actively seeking our well-being. The principal truth of faith to which the mind yields is that God exists and cares for us, which is why Aquinas says the specific focus of faith is not just God, but God as provident (S.Th., II-II, 1, 7). What we are to affirm is not only the existence of God, but the character of God as one whose every activity is to be involved in history on our behalf.

Since the object of faith is everything by which we reach beatitude, e.g., Christ's incarnation, passion, death, and resurrection, it is through the assent of faith that we not only live on the path to salvation, but participate, however incompletely, in eternal life now. Faith comprises everything that contributes to blessedness, but to enter a life of faith is to anticipate and share the perfection of happiness to which our life tends. Through faith we begin to live now all that we hope will be perfectly ours with God. Like hope and charity, faith is the theological virtue which connects our present life to our future glory by allowing the vision of God's love to shape who we are and inform all we do. If the object of faith is all we can possibly hope for—absolute blessedness with God and all the saints— through faith the life of beatitude begins because it is to live now as true and absolutely compelling the joy that will be ours in glory (S.Th., II-II, 4, 1).

Faith as an Infused Virtue. Faith is as much a gift as an achievement. Faith works under the influence of God assisting us through grace. Faith is impossible without grace because the special excellence of faith involves knowing something utterly beyond the powers of our nature. Faith begins in grace and grows from grace; indeed, grace is required not only when faith begins, "but as long as it perdures" (S.Th., II-II, 4, 4). This is why faith has traditionally been understood as an infused, rather than acquired, virtue (S.Th., II-II, 6, 1). Though the notion of infused supernatural virtue is problematic, it is a way the Catholic tradition has addressed the fact that left to ourselves we are absolutely incapable of knowing God in a way adequate for salvation. It is by the infused virtue of faith that the disparity between what we need to know about God and our limited capacity to understand is bridged. The dilemma is that the most excellent and perfecting activity of our minds lies completely beyond the power of our nature. How can we who are not God grasp the truth of God? We do so through faith, the gift by which we are rendered capable of knowing God. Consequently, to have the virtue of faith is to assent to the truths necessary for salvation; however, we can only practice the virtue of faith because we have first received the gift of faith.

Nonetheless, we are to act on and respond to the gift we have received, and in this respect faith, like any other virtue, is to be nurtured and developed. What God's grace enables through the infused virtue of faith, we are to embrace by an ongoing and active assent to the truths of faith. Faith is not meant to be dormant, but to shape, change, and direct our lives. We are to live what God's grace enables us to understand. To have the virtue of faith is to commit ourselves to growing deeply into the truths of God, it is to strengthen and constantly ratify the assent which grace makes possible. If the infused virtue of faith is God's gift to us, the activity of faith is our grateful response. Put differently, there is a purpose given with the infused virtue of faith, namely that we devote ourselves to a deeper knowledge of God. That we can do so is a gift of God; however, whether we do depends on whether we develop the virtue or let it die.

Consequences of Faith and Sins Against Faith. The principal consequence of faith is understanding. If we develop the faith God entrusts us with, we come to a more penetrating knowledge of God. Faith is assent for the sake of understanding, and the deeper our possession of faith the more excellent our understanding of God. Aquinas defines the understanding which comes from faith as "a certain intimate knowing" of God that comes from entering more deeply into the truth of God (S.Th., II-II, 8, 1). Understanding is knowledge of God derived from sharing in the life of God. If faith is necessary for understanding divine things, a vital, active faith increases understanding by allowing us to see more deeply into the mystery of God. Thus, through faith we gain "a capacity for insight or intimate penetration" into the being of God (S.Th., II-II, 8, 6). Understanding is connected to faith and grows from faith inasmuch as it brings a firmer grasp or greater certitude of the truths proposed for belief (S.Th., II-II, 8, 8).

Still, deeper understanding of God does not signify complete comprehension of God; in fact, a central paradox of faith is that "in this life the better we know God the more we understand that [God] surpasses whatever the mind grasps" (S.Th., II-II, 8, 7). Short of the beatific vision, we can never know the essence of God or perfectly apprehend the nature of God. The heart of faith is to believe for the sake of understanding, realizing that what we know about God can never equal the mystery of God.

Disbelief is the primary sin against faith, but it is important to understand it properly. Since faith is a gift of grace, no one can be faulted for a gift he or she may not have received. But we are held accountable for neglecting or refusing to act on grace, and in this respect disbelief is a sin. Every sin consists in turning away from God, and disbelief is the sin by which we turn away from God by shunning or ignoring the truths of God. Disbelief separates us from God by preventing true knowledge of God (S.Th., II-II, 10, 3). Most often, the sin of disbelief is expressed through a stubborn resistance to faith, an unwillingness to believe, or a hardening of our minds to the truths of God. The latter occurs when we actively oppose the growth of faith after it has been accepted (S.Th., II-II, 10, 5).

But we can also sin by weakening the gift of faith instead of safeguarding it. Heresy,

for example, is a corruption of faith brought about by believing wrongly about a particular truth of faith (S.Th., II-II, 11, 1). Similarly, blasphemy has traditionally been seen as a sin against faith because to blaspheme God is to disparage the excellence of God, and thus no longer hold God as worthy of belief. Aquinas defined blasphemy as the sin which "vilifies the divine goodness" (S.Th., II-II, 13, 2) and "casts slurs on the divine honor" (S.Th., II-II, 13, 3). Blasphemy is a species of infidelity because it reviles God who is the source of all goodness, belittling God for the sake of dishonoring and weakening belief in God (S.Th., II-II, 13, 1).

Still, faith is more commonly weakened through distraction and neglect. We can have the gift of faith, but fail to attend to God in our lives, diverting our attention to lesser things. In this case, faith is diminished when we grow preoccupied with things we love more than God (S.Th., II-II, 15, 2). To practice the virtue of faith is to remain steadfastly attentive to God as the supreme excellence of life. Through faith our mind stays fixed on God; however, if we become attentive to many things other than God, making them the center or focus of our lives, faith grows dull and can even be lost. If we habitually neglect the things of the Spirit, we can become indifferent to the blessedness God wants for us. For instance, excessive attention to material things or sensuality makes us forgetful of God and lessens our appreciation for the superior excellence of God (S.Th., II-II, 15, 3).

Pastoral Applications. Even though faith is an intellectual activity inasmuch as it is an assent of the mind to the truths of God, it is also a moral reality inasmuch as faith is perfected through love. Faith implies commitment to God and involvement with God, but this suggests that the credibility of faith is established through deeds that honor God by imitating God. To have faith is to assent not to the idea of God, but to the character of God, which is why faith is incomplete without good works, especially justice (Jas 2:14-17).

But to assent to the truths of God is also to have our self formed according to the stories of God, particularly the saga of Israel and Jesus. The Eucharist is the central context for our formation in faith because it is there that we hear and encounter the truths we assent to live. The saga of creation, covenant, redemption, and restoration is not a narrative we are to view from afar, but precisely the story that should govern our understanding of ourself. To assent to the truths of faith is to let these stories of God constitute and shape our world. These are the truths by which we pledge to know life now, and that is why it is in light of them that we understand best what our being in the world involves. "We recall Christ's death, his descent among the dead, his resurrection, and his ascension to your right hand" (Eucharistic Prayer IV), not as nostalgic consolation, but in order to enter the paschal mystery and allow Jesus to relate to us redemptively everyday.

To live in faith is to yield to the stories of God, to inhabit them, and to read our lives by them. To live in faith is to appropriate these stories, striving to embody their viewpoints, values, and vision as our own. To assent to the truths of faith portrayed in the Scripture is to allow them to become the interpretative framework for our world. For instance, when in Eucharist we hear of Jesus forgiving sins and setting people free, we are to realize that Jesus summons us to repentance and new life now. The connection between faith and Eucharist is that in the Eucharist we enter into the narratives we take to be normative for our lives, allowing them to mold and shape us, especially in the attitudes and virtues of Jesus. This is why through faith we participate already in eternal life. By assenting to the truths of God we encounter in the Eucharist, we participate in the saving life of Christ, making him the one in whom and through whom we live. Thus, the Eucharist enhances the vitality of Christian faith because it releases Jesus from the confinement of the past that he can live in us now, calling us from sin and working in us the redemption God wants for the world. To assent in faith is to yield—perhaps more aptly to surrender—to redemption for the sake of joy.

See: GRACE, MYSTERY, TRUTH

PAUL J. WADELL, C.P.

FAITHFULNESS

Faithfulness is the virtue of truth, especially the truth of maintaining the loyalty one has pledged to another. In the Bible it pertains to both God and us, but in different ways. Our faithfulness to God and God's promises is always uncertain; we do not control either our own ability to remain loyal or an ability to make the promises come true. God, on the other hand, both knows and is almighty. At times, it appears that God is unfaithful and God's promises are not fulfilled. Then we must take the risk that God not only knows, but God accomplishes good.

Old Testament

Faithfulness is implicit in the covenants* which God made with Abraham and the patriarchs, Moses and David. "I am your God, you are my people," is endlessly repeated as an unshakeable truth. Whatever the people think of God or whatever the people do, God remains their God and they remain God's people. The relationship may change in its actual working, but it is never abolished. So God is hailed as faithful:

> Praise the LORD, all you nations;
>   glorify him, all you peoples!
> For steadfast is his kindness toward us,
>   and the fidelity of the LORD endures
>   forever
>
> (Ps 117).

God, Emmanuel: "God with us" is always present. God's presence is not contingent on our success; it is simply there. God's plans stretch from end to end; it is only in the final apocalyptic judgment that we shall perceive God's presence in all human affairs.

Our principal duty is to be faithful to God each in one's own measure. Since the OT is mainly the story of the chosen people, it is a drama of the faithfulness and unfaithfulness of that people to the covenant conditions which God laid down. God's presence is to be acknowledged and glorified in all our living, good or bad. Yet that fidelity does not bind God to a literal fulfillment of the promises, especially as people interpret them. Thus David can be promised an absolute succession to his throne (2 Sam 7:12-16) and yet fulfillment of the promise is seemingly dependent on Solomon's fidelity (1 Kgs 9:6-9). The Babylonian Exile and the elimination of Davidic monarchy came as a shock to the people; they fully expected that God would fulfill the promise despite all that they had done. Lamentations is a dirge over Jerusalem, full of questioning about the goodness or justice of God. When logic had no answer to the Exile, the risk of faith in God's faithfulness still prevailed. "The favors of the LORD are not exhausted, his mercies are not spent; they are renewed each morning, so great is his faithfulness" (Lam 3:22-23).

Most of the references to faithfulness as such in the OT occur in the Wisdom literature of Psalms and Proverbs. These are primarily observations on the value of human faithfulness among ourselves.

New Testament

The adjective "faithful" occurs frequently in the NT, describing an absolute condition of salvation. Both Matthew and Luke report the saying that keynotes the parable of the unfaithful servant. "Who, then, is the faithful and prudent servant, whom the master has put in charge of his household to distribute to them their food at the proper time?" (Matt 24:45; see Luke 12:42).

It is Paul who is most insistent on faithfulness. Faith is the beginning of salvation for us. It is not that he uses the word faithfulness as such, but it is the attitude that he takes. Jesus is the one who is perfectly faithful (2 Cor 1:20), as God is faithful (1 Thess 5:24). But Paul is a realist and knows that

we cannot impose on God our ideas of how God should be faithful. The long meditation in Romans 9–11, where Paul struggles with the contemporary fact that his chosen people have rejected the gospel, leads him to conclude that God is still faithful to the promises, but in ways which we do not understand. "I ask, then, has God rejected his people?" (Rom 11:1). His answer is that "the gifts and the call of God are irrevocable" (Rom 11:29). But he cannot explain this. "For who has known the mind of the Lord or who has been his counselor?" (Rom 11:34). God's fidelity is a mystery which will be revealed only at the end.

In the later essay called the Letter to the Hebrews, Jesus is introduced into the priestly class as a human being, "therefore, he had to become like his brothers in every way, that he might be a merciful and faithful high priest before God to expiate the sins of the people" (Heb 2:17). Nothing can change this, not even human failure. "Jesus Christ is the same yesterday, today, and forever" (Heb 13:8). The Letter to the Hebrews, as is well known, is a strong exhortation and warning to remain faithful. "Let us hold unwaveringly to our confession that gives us hope, for he who made the promise is trustworthy" (Heb 10:23).

In Revelation Jesus is called "The Amen, the faithful and true witness, the source of God's creation" (Rev 3:14). Later in the song of victory John writes, "Then I saw the heavens opened, and there was a white horse; its rider was [called] 'Faithful and True'" (Rev 19:11). The victory comes to those who have remained faithful despite all the persecutions and dread of inevitable failure.

Pastoral-Liturgical Tradition

The members of the Church have been called "the faithful" from very early on (see Acts 10:45; 2 Cor 6:15; Eph 1:1). The name has been maintained throughout history both in pious reading and in the actual hearts of people. In disaster the most common reflection of acceptance has been: "God knows best." The saying reflects a willingness both to admit that one's knowledge of God's fidelity is limited and to take the risk that God's fidelity includes a goodness of love which cannot be questioned. There have been devotions which stress the need for depending on God for the gift of perseverance. These include the practice of receiving Holy Communion on nine first Fridays and societies reminding people to pray for a happy death. It is the final gift for which we hope, and we hope for it as a gift, not as a human achievement for which we work.

See: COVENANT, FAITH, SALVATION

JAMES A. FISCHER, C.M.

FAMILY

The peoples of the Bible were formed in traditional cultures in which the extended family held a central and revered place. The family and household are the setting for many biblical narratives and much biblical imagery. Familial relationships and the drama of family life are also used symbolically in both OT and NT to express the experience of faith and the relationship of God to Israel, Jesus, and the early Church.

Old Testament

The Setting. In order to understand the structure of the Israelite family as it has been depicted in the biblical texts, it is important to appreciate the conditions under which people lived during the second and first millennia BCE and their struggles to survive. The ancient peoples were very dependent on land—for grazing livestock and for growing crops—yet the land of Israel was not particularly fertile. Its southern area is desert, its middle portion is rocky hill country, only the northern section is what one would describe as fertile. Under such conditions, crop farming and the raising of sheep and cattle demanded much effort from many people. The ancient Israelites depended on large families to plant and harvest the crops and to shepherd the cattle, thus ensuring survival.

Large families were also essential to ensure that at least some members would survive periods of drought and famine, pestilence and plague. Otherwise an entire family, an entire people, could be wiped out. If there were many children in a family, some, at least, would survive.

Other factors that threatened the survival of the ancient Israelites and made large families necessary were the fact that (1) many women died during childbirth; (2) many children died as infants; (3) the people were often subject to attack from hostile aggressors. If some children were to survive to adulthood, there must be many children in the first place.

Israel produced large families by practicing polygamy and by holding motherhood in high regard. Polygamy as practiced in ancient Israel permitted one man to legitimately take more than one woman as his wife, thus making it possible for the man to have many children. Because of the high esteem in which motherhood was held, women were motivated to bear many children even at the cost of great physical pain and serious personal risk. When one turns from these sociological considerations regarding ancient Israel to the biblical texts themselves, one can trace how these conditions might easily have been responsible for how families are depicted in the Bible.

Whether or not it is appropriate to describe ancient Israelite society as patriarchal—because of the practice of polygamy by males and other social customs such as, for example, Levirate marriage—is debated. Patriarchy implies father as head of family, and by extension, males as generally superior to females. Most historians believe that ancient societies did not originally possess strict divisions between men and women's labor. Women may have worked closer to home because of children, but they too worked to help provide for the family's needs. Only when everyone worked could a family hope to survive. Later on, perhaps because of a perceived need to protect women during periods of severe plague or disease, women came to be seen as needing protection and, therefore, as weaker and inferior. Historians hypothesize that when women no longer needed protection from unusual life-threatening conditions, men nevertheless continued to regard them as weaker and inferior. What had been functionally appropriate during the biblical period was eventually ideologized.

The Ancestors. Genesis 12–50 relates narratives about the ancestors, the people who eventually, according to the biblical account, become the people of Israel. The stories detail the family of Abraham and Sarah. In Abraham (and Sarah), all the families of the earth shall find blessing (Gen 12:3).

Abraham and Sarah have one child, Isaac (Gen 21:2). Isaac eventually marries Rebekah and together they bear Esau and Jacob (Gen 25:19-26). Jacob in his turn marries Leah and then Rachel, the two daughters of Jacob's maternal uncle Laban (Gen 29:14-30). Jacob's two wives and their maids bear him thirteen children, twelve sons and a daughter (Gen 30:21 and 35:22-26). One of Jacob's sons, Joseph, is responsible for saving the family from a famine (Gen 45:11); he occasions the family's traveling southwest into Egypt (Gen 46:1-7).

A close examination of the narratives reveals a patriarchal family structure. The male was head of the household and bearing sons was considered more valuable than bearing daughters. If a husband died before he had begotten a son, his brother was to take to himself the dead man's wife in order to raise up a son for his dead brother (Deut 25:5-10; cf. Genesis 38). Genealogies detail almost exclusively male lineage: father begets son (e.g., Genesis 5; 10–11; 1 Chronicles 1–2). Land transfer normally takes place from father to son, or at least to the closest male relative (Num 27:1-11). The daughters of a father who had not begotten any sons could inherit property, but they must marry men of their own tribe so that their father's property would remain "in the family" (e.g., Num 36:1-12).

The biblical narratives suggest that ancient Israelite society condoned polygamy. God had promised to make Abraham into a great nation, but since his wife Sarah was barren she gave her handmaid Hagar to her husband. Hagar conceived and bore Ishmael (Gen 16:1-4, 13). Since Laban tricked Jacob into marrying his elder daughter Leah, Jacob determined to work another seven years to secure Rachel as his wife (Gen 29:28). When these two women were not themselves bearing children, they each gave over their maidservant to Jacob and each of the maidservants had children by him (Gen 30:3-13). Though a man might have more than one wife at a time, a woman could not have more than one husband at a time (e.g., Deut 22:22). A woman could remarry only if her first husband had either died or divorced her (Gen 24:1-2); a wife could not initiate a divorce.

The House of David. Just as the family of Abraham and Sarah is the recipient of the divine promise to Israel of land and people, the house of David represents the promise of monarchy and dynasty in Israel.

The narratives about the family of David (2 Samuel through 1 Kings 2) illustrate what has come to be called Deuteronomistic theology of retribution. When one is faithful to God and obedient to divine Law, blessings will surely follow; however, the one who is unfaithful will inevitably experience curses. David is depicted as essentially faithful to God. It is for this reason that he is granted a dynasty. When a portion of the kingdom is taken from David's descendants, it is understood as a punishment for Solomon's and Rehoboam's sins. One tribe, Judah, is preserved "for the sake of David." It remains under the governing authority of the family of David (e.g., 1 Kgs 11:12-13, 32, 34; 15:4; 2 Kgs 19:34; 20:6; cf. 1–2 Chronicles).

David sinned against God by taking for himself Uriah's wife Bathsheba (2 Samuel 11; see Deut 22:22) and by having Uriah killed. As a consequence, the prophet Nathan warned David that the sword would not depart from his family (2 Sam 12:10). 2 Samuel 13–1 Kings 2 details David's many family problems. The first child conceived from the sexual union of David and Bathsheba dies. David's daughter Tamar is raped by her half-brother, Amnon (2 Sam 13:1-17). Another son, Absalom, sees to it that Amnon dies for this offense (2 Sam 13:32). Next, Absalom flees his father's wrath (2 Sam 13:34, 37) and then returns to conspire against David (2 Sam 15:1-6). Absalom symbolizes his intent by violating David's concubines (2 Sam 16:21-22). Joab, David's general, puts an end to Absalom's revolt by killing him (2 Sam 18:14). Finally, because David's son Adonijah wishes to take his father's woman, Abishag—understood as a move to take over David's kingdom—Solomon has Adonijah killed (1 Kgs 2:24).

David and his sons are polygamists. Among David's wives were Michal (1 Sam 18:27), Ahinoam and Abigail (1 Sam 25:43), and Bathsheba (2 Sam 11:27; cf. 2 Sam 5:13). Solomon not only took Pharaoh's daughter for a wife (1 Kgs 3:1), he took many other foreign wives (1 Kgs 11:1-3). Most of the descendents of David who ascend the throne of Judah are specified by the names of their mothers. One is not only one's father's son; he is also the son of a particular one of his father's wives, and this woman is named (e.g., 1 Kgs 15:2; 22:42; 2 Kgs 8:26).

The Prophets. The Prophetic literature uses the family symbolically. Hosea marries a woman who becomes a harlot; this symbolizes Yahweh's covenant relationship with Israel (Hosea 1–3). Hosea also understands Israel as God's "son" (11:1). Moreover, Hosea's children are each given symbolic names; Jezreel (the valley of Israel's defeat), Lo-ruhama (not-compassionate), and Lo-ammi (not-my-people). Their names are later changed to signify Israel's changed relationship with their God: "Yahweh will sow" (the new meaning of Jezreel), "Compassionate," and "You are my people."

Isaiah's children, like Hosea's, bear symbolic names: "Shear-yashub" meaning "a remnant shall return" (Isa 7:3; cf. 10:21) and "Maher-shalal-hash-baz" meaning "the spoil speeds, the prey hastes" (Isa 8:1).

The prophet Jeremiah likewise understands the relationship between Israel and Yahweh in marital terms. He compares Israel's first devotion to Yahweh "as the love of a bride" (Jer 2:2). In chapter 16 Jeremiah remains unmarried to symbolize Judah's imminent and inevitable exile to Babylonia. This is a time not of blessing but of punishment, not of fertility but of sterility. Hence Jeremiah is deprived of a family of his own to symbolize the fall of Judah.

Ezekiel continues the tradition of using marriage symbolism to depict Israel's relationship to Yahweh. The faithless harlot spouse is Israel (Ezekiel 16; cf. Ezekiel 23). Elsewhere Ezekiel himself becomes a widower but is exhorted not to mourn his wife's death. This symbolizes either the fact that (1) the destruction of Jerusalem's temple is deserved or (2) Israel's time of mourning in exile will be shortlived (Ezekiel 24).

See: FATHER, MARRIAGE, MOTHER

ALICE L. LAFFEY

New Testament

Family values and structures are inherently conservative and so change very little over time. Hence the observations here are equally applicable to families in both the OT and NT.

Ancient Family, Extended but Not Nuclear. Unlike modern nuclear families where married children leave parents and establish their own households, in the ancient family married children continued living with their parents in the same house, now enlarged to accommodate the new couple, their children, servants, and possessions. The ancient extended family consisted of father (or patriarch) and his wife(s), children, married sons and their wives, children, slaves, and concubines (Gen 46:5-7). This extended family network could also include not only siblings, but uncles and cousins, who might be called "brothers and sisters." Thus Jesus' extended family is described: "Is he not . . . the son of Mary, and the 'brother' of James and Joses and Judas and Simon? And are not his 'sisters' here with us?" (Mark 6:3).

The terminology of "family" reflects different aspects of the social reality. It may be called a "house" *(byt, oikia)*, "father's house" *(mishpahah; patria)*, or "clan." Indeed, *oikia* may mean household, family, and retainers. For example, the "house of so-and-so" = the household of a leading patriarch (Gen 17:23; Judg 4:17); the "house of Pharaoh or Saul" = dynasty or palace entourage (Gen 12:17; 2 Sam 7:11-14; 9:2); and "house of Judah or Jacob" = clan or tribe (2 Sam 2:4; Isa 2:5).

Members' identities as well as their safety and sustenance derived from membership in an extended family. Children were generally identified in terms of their father, e.g., "Phineas, son of Eleazar the priest" (Josh 22:13); "Abner, son of Ner" (1 Sam 26:14); "Hosea, son of Beeri" (Hos 1:1). Membership in the extended family indicated honor and status as well as certain rights and duties. Insult or injury to any member of the family was judged as an affront to the whole family, and thus collectively avenged (Neh 4:14; 2 Kgs 9:26). Similarly, the debts of the father may result in the whole family being sold into servitude (Matt 18:25). Comparably, it is not uncommon to read that a whole family became believers of Jesus and so were saved collectively (Acts 11:14; 16:33). Blessings accruing to one member extend to all (1 Cor 7:14).

Family and the Moral Division of Labor. In antiquity family members were socialized to certain tasks and roles according to cultural definitions of gender. In the article on "father," we cite an important passage from Philo about the customary division of life into spheres both male and female (*Special Laws* 3.169). Although Philo described the urban life of elite families, most families were peasant farmers living outside cities. Yet the principles were the same: male members of the family attended to public tasks, such as herding, plowing, soldiering, etc.; female family members were in charge of clothing production, child care, and food preparation. It is hardly accidental that we read stories of so many women at the common well, a place to which women would go in groups at specific times of the day when they would be away from the company of men (Gen 24:11; 29:6-7; Exod 2:15-17; John 4:7-26). If houses were large enough, there would even be distinctive women's quarters, shielded from the world of men's affairs. This common spatial arrangement describes Greek, Egyptian, as well as Jewish houses (Lysias 1.9; Diodorus Siculus 17.50.3; Philo, *Leg.All.* 3.98; *Sac.* 103; *Agr.* 79; *Migr.* 96; *Somn.* 2.9, 55, 184; *Vit.Cont.* 32; *Leg.* 358). Kings, of course, had many wives, who lived in the exclusive women's quarters guarded by a eunuch (see Esth 2:3-14; 2 Sam 16:22).

Hence it is not surprising to find in the NT pairs of stories and parables respecting this male/female moral division of labor in the family: (1) a male shepherd searches for a lost sheep on the public hillside, while a female sweeps her private home for a lost coin (Luke 15:3-10); (2) two men plow in the fields and one is taken; and two women grind grain at home and one is taken (Matt 24:40-41). We note this balance among family members in Jesus' remarks about concern for food and clothing: men are told not to worry about what to eat (sowing, harvesting), while women were consoled over what to wear (spinning, weaving; Matt 6:25-31).

Role and Status/Rights and Duties. In Israelite and Christian families, respect is the right of the father (patriarch or head of the clan); custom enjoins "honor" for such a figure. His wife, mother of his children, enjoyed a comparable status in the spheres of her influence. Alternately, the parents' duty was to nurture their offspring, as well as socialize them into their proper roles in the clan and village. Their children thus owed them honor and respect for the fundamental gift of life, a debt that could never be repaid: "What can you give them for all they gave you?" (Sir 7:28). How shameful, then, was the behavior of the son who demanded an inheritance which he squandered in idle luxury on those outside the household

(Luke 15:13). He dishonored his father by taking his inheritance before the parent's death; he did not take provision for the care of his parents in their old age; nor did he use his wealth to benefit his family . . . shame on all sides. First-born sons, heirs to the estate, enjoyed higher rank and status than their siblings. The exceptions in the case of Jacob and Esau, Joseph and his brothers, David and his siblings, etc., only prove the rule. The reciprocal rights and duties of family members are carefully enshrined in the codes of household duties (haustafeln) found in Ephesians 5:21–6:9; Colossians 3:18–4:1 and 1 Peter 2:13–3:7.

Economics and the Family. Inasmuch as most families consisted of landowning peasants or tenant farmers, they strove to be self-sufficient (autarcheia, Phil 4:11; 1 Tim 6:6), more so when they were nomadic herders. They produced and consumed all basic necessities: clothing, food, tools, dwellings, etc. Families practiced altruistic generosity among their members, giving without thought of return (see Luke 11:11-12). Yet with non-family neighbors, transactions were always balanced, quid pro quo affairs (see Luke 6:32-34). If a clan member is forced to sell land, the family has first rights to "redeem what is sold" (Lev 25:25; Jer 32:6-15).

Fathers would automatically teach their sons their own skills and trades. For example, Joab was the father of a family of craftsmen (1 Chr 4:14); Mareshah, the father of linen workers (1 Chr 4:21); and Cozeba, Joash, and Saraph, the fathers of potters (1 Chr 4:23). James and John were fishermen, like their father Zebedee (Mark 1:19-20), just as Jesus took up Joseph's trade of carpentry (Mark 6:3; Matt 13:55). A man's sons would work the family fields and herd its flocks.

Family and Marriage. Genesis records polygynous marriages among the patriarchs. Abraham had two wives, Hagar the Egyptian and Sarah (Gen 16:3); Jacob married two sisters, Rachel and Leah (Gen 29:18-30; see also Gen 4:19; 22:20-24; 25:1, 6). King David and other rulers had harems of wives and concubines for purposes of alliances or display of status (2 Sam 5:13-16). This form was gradually replaced with monogamous marriages. By NT times, a bishop must be married to but one woman (1 Tim 3:2).

Marriage* and marriage strategies had little to do with modern notions of romance or individual choice, for they were contracted between families and clans for economic and political reasons that would strengthen the well-being of the families or clans joined by such marriages. At certain periods in Israel's history exogamous marriages served to link the newly arrived clans of Israel with their neighbors, thus assuring them safety among former strangers or enemies (see Gen 41:45; Exod 2:21). Solomon stabilized his kingdom by marriages with foreign women, thus securing political and economic alliances (1 Kgs 11:1-2).

But post-exilic Judaism adopted a strategy of endogamous marriages in light of its concern to keep pure the worship of God. Ezra and Nehemiah record oaths taken by Israelite men to put away foreign wives and thus marry within orthodox families and clans (Ezra 10:5; Neh 10:28-30; 13:23-27). Nevertheless, family strategies might prevail, as in the case of Timothy, son of a Jewish mother and a Greek father (Acts 16:1). Yet endogamy became the ideal even for Christians, both for first marriages (2 Cor 6:14-15) and the remarriage of widows (1 Cor 7:39).

Forms of marriage customs often enshrine values that find expression in social structures. Endogamous marriages place a strong value on shared religious and political ideologies, which could only be weakened by marriage to outsiders. Endogamous marriages enshrine group solidarity, unity, and exclusivity even as they devalue novelty or risk. Israelite marriages, moreover, required the eldest son to remain in the father's house after marriage, thus keeping him firmly under paternal authority and emphasizing this quality of parent-children relationships.

Inheritance laws favored the eldest son with special property rights, thus underscoring a sense that all the children are not equal (see Luke 15:29, 31).

Symbolic Use of "Family." Family describes households, clans, and even nations, as expressed by the phrase "the house of Israel" (Lev 10:6; Num 20:29; 1 Sam 7:3). When extended broadly, it serves to identify both the mutual rights and duties of members and the unity of the social group. The same concept extends into NT times as the early Church described itself as the "household of God" (Eph 2:19; 1 Tim 3:15; 1 Peter 4:17) or the "household of the faith" (Gal 6:10). In the Gospels we read of distinctions made between blood relatives and fictive kin (Mark 3:31-35); not all are "seed of Abraham" by mere physical descent, but those who share his faith and do what he did (John 8:39-40).

Allegiance to Jesus seems to have caused serious divisions in family loyalties, pitting children against their parents (Matt 10:34-36). Jesus said, "Whoever loves father or mother more than me is not worthy of me" (Matt 10:37). Indeed, some passages expect disciples to have "given up house or brothers or sisters or mother or father or children or lands" for Jesus' sake (Mark 10:29). New disciples would gain a fictive family with other disciples (Mark 10:30), valuing and being valued as kin, and so supported like kin.

For purposes of proselytizing, Jesus and the early Church challenged old family values and structures. But new disciples of Jesus were quickly cautioned to maintain certain conventions, such as the prohibition against divorce (Mark 10:1-12; 1 Cor 7:10-14). From being disturbers of family values and structures, the early Christians became their strong defenders.

See: FATHER, MARRIAGE

JEROME H. NEYREY, S.J.

Pastoral-Liturgical Tradition

Development of the Modern Family Structure. The Roman world that received the gospel had no word that directly corresponds to the contemporary notion of family. The Latin term *familia* is better translated as "household." It encompassed all that was under the authority of the head of the household, the *paterfamilias*, and included servants, slaves, and even livestock as well as wife and children. Among the very wealthy, such households could number well over a hundred members. The *paterfamilias* owned the *familia* and therefore was not considered part of it. The advent of Christianity did little to change this basic social structure.

By the end of the fourth century, however, Germanic peoples had begun to migrate into the provinces of the Roman Empire. These societies had familial structures and customs quite different from those of Rome. Marriage* was less formal, and could be initiated by capture or purchase as well as mutual consent of the partners. Polygyny was relatively common, especially among the rich. Divorce was easy to obtain, and only women could be charged with the crime of adultery. As these peoples accepted Christianity, conflicts inevitably arose between their traditional practices and the developing Church teaching regarding marriage and family. Gradually, however, Church and society influenced each other. By the beginning of the ninth century, a new understanding of family had finally emerged, one which emphasized a stable, coresidential, primary descent group. Aided by the moral teachings of the Church and the developing canon law, a common meaning of family was created that would remain relatively unchanged until the present day.

In ensuing centuries, this basic understanding underwent further modification. The agrarian culture of the Middle Ages and the early modern period encouraged large extended families. With the advent of industrialization, families moved from rural areas into the city. The family likewise changed from being a unit of production to one of consumption. This resulted in a movement from extended families to smaller, nuclear families, with the father* usually working outside of the home and the mother* responsible for the tasks of nurture and socialization of the children. The so-called sexual revolution of the last third of the twentieth century has also challenged the traditional understanding of the family. Divorce and remarriage have tended to complicate the relationships among family members. A variety of non-traditional domestic partnerships have further called into question the traditional definition of family. Finally, new birth technologies, with the possibility of donor gametes, have also challenged the understanding of what it means to be parent and family.

Church Teaching. Confronted with these attempts to expand the meaning of family, the Church has tried to conserve and strengthen the traditional understanding. Recent reaffirmations of the Church's teaching on homosexuality, divorce, and so-called free unions, as well as its condemnation of in vitro fertilization and related technologies, are at least in part attempts to strengthen marriage and the traditional family. It has based this defense both on natural law and on its belief that the family is a particular manifestation of the Church itself, a domestic church.

Basing their understanding on natural law, theologians have traditionally described the family as a natural society whose primary purpose is the begetting and education of offspring. Only a stable family, that is, one created from a permanent, faithful, and indissoluble marriage, is the sort of community appropriate for this purpose. Since Pope Leo XIII, the social encyclicals have emphasized the fact that the family is the most primary unity of human society. Pope Leo himself described the family as "a true society anterior to every kind of state or nation, with rights and duties of its own, totally independent of the commonwealth." Similarly, Pope John XXIII listed the right to set up a family as a fundamental right. He then calls upon the larger society to ensure that "careful provision . . . be made for the family both in economic and social matters as well as in those which are of a cultural and moral nature, all of which look to the strengthening of the family and helping it carry out its function." In more personalist terms, the Second Vatican Council's Pastoral Constitution on the Church in the Modern World described the family as a "school of deeper humanity."

In the years since the Second Vatican Council, this natural law conception has been supplemented by a more spiritual, biblically-based understanding of the purpose of the family as domestic church. Using Ephesians 5 as a basis, the Pastoral Constitution suggests that the family is a participation in the covenant uniting Christ and the Church. It manifests Christ's living presence to the world by means of love, fruitfulness, and faithfulness. In this way it gives witness to the genuine nature of the Church. Similarly, the Dogmatic Constitution on the Church states that the family "loudly proclaims both the present virtues of the kingdom of God and the hope of a blessed life to come." More recently, Pope John Paul II's Apostolic Exhortation on the Family (*Familiaris consortio*) suggests that the family shares in the life and mission of the Church by its being a believing and evangelizing community. The Pope calls on the family to become a witness to the Church itself, enabling the Church to develop more familial structures.

Holy Family. Although not completely unknown in the late Middle Ages, devotion to the Holy Family as the model of the Christian family did not really develop until the Counter-Reformation, fostered especially by the Jesuits and the Sulpicians. In the nineteenth century, witnessing the break-up of family life, Pius IX fostered confraternities under the patronage of the Holy Family. His successor, Leo XIII, suggested that all Catholic homes be consecrated to the Holy Family. In 1921, Benedict XV instituted the universal feast of the

Holy Family, to be celebrated the Sunday after Epiphany. In 1969, the feast was transferred to the Sunday after Christmas.

See: FATHER, MARRIAGE, MOTHER

THOMAS NAIRN

FATHER

In the patriarchal societies of biblical times, the father played a very significant role in the family as well as in the broader social groups. The role of father was also taken over by the religious imagination of the people and frequently applied to God.

Old Testament

The term "father" is essentially relational; though it implies a mother, the term is comprehensible only with a man's begetting of son(s) and/or daughter(s). Since the ancient Israelites did not believe in life after death, having children was the means whereby a man might hope to continue his existence after his death; he would live on in his offspring. Ancient Israel possessed a patriarchal culture: a culture in which the *pater*, or father, was *arche*, the head. The father was head of the family and, by extension, of the clan or tribe. The biblical account traces human origins to one father and mother, Adam and Eve (Genesis 1–2); the bearing of children was key to the perpetuation of the human race.

Genealogies. The genealogies in Genesis 5 and 10 trace lineage from the first father Adam through his male descendants, from father to sons who themselves become the fathers of other sons. The genealogies function in the biblical texts both to connect characters, time periods, and events, and to distance them. From Adam to Noah is ten generations; from Noah's son Shem to Abram is ten generations. Rarely do wives or daughters appear in the genealogies (but see Num 26:59).

Paternity. In order to ensure that a man would become a father, Israelite law allowed him to have more than one wife. This would ensure that, if one or more of a man's wives proved to be barren, or if she/they should die in childbirth, he might still have sons by another one of his wives. (Male fertility was assumed.) The practice of polygamy provided the likelihood that a man would beget many sons; even if several of them died of natural causes or in war before manhood, he would have sons to continue his memory on earth after his death. Moreover, if a man should die without having become the father of a son, the brother of the deceased, or his closest kin, should take the widow for his own wife and raise up the first son of that new union for the dead man. This would guarantee that the deceased's memory would continue by means of a male offspring (Deut 25:5-10; see also Genesis 38).

Most characters in the Bible are identified as being the son (or daughter) of their father. For example, the first time both Abraham and David are introduced in the narrative, they are identified as their fathers' sons. Abraham is the son of Terah (Gen 11:27); David is Jesse's son (1 Sam 16:1).

The Patriarchs. Genesis 12–50 has often been described as the "patriarchal history," that is, the record of the chief fathers of the Israelite people. These include Abraham, his son Isaac, Isaac's sons Esau and especially Jacob, and Jacob's twelve sons. Though Abraham and Isaac have more than one son, only one of each of their sons, according to the biblical account—Isaac and not Ishmael, Jacob and not Esau—becomes the chief father of other sons. Jacob's twelve sons are credited with being the fathers of families who become the tribes of Israel.

Fathers as Heads of Houses. That the father was head of the household is clear from the frequency of biblical references to one's father's house. At the Lord's directive Abraham departed from his father's house (Gen 12:1; 20:13; 24:7); Rebekah dwelt in her father's house, which is also understood to be Abraham's father's house (Gen 24:23, 38, 40); Jacob referred to his home as his father's house (Gen 28:21); Laban referred to Jacob's home as Jacob's father's house (Gen 31:30); both Leah and Rachel had dwelt in their father's house (Gen 31:14); Tamar returned to her father's house after her husbands' deaths (Gen 38:11). These are but examples of a pattern of language that designated the father as head/ owner of the house.

Eponymous Names. Many of the fathers in the OT become fathers of a people, and the people take on their father's name. For example, Ishmael is the father of the Ishmaelites (e.g., Gen 25:18); Esau, the father of the Edomites (e.g., Gen 36:9); Jacob, renamed Israel, the father of the Israelites (Gen 32:29-33; 35:10); Moab, the father of the Moabites (e.g., Gen 19:34-37); Ammon, the father of the Ammonites (e.g., Gen 19:38). Moreover, the sons of Jacob become the fathers of tribes whose names are derived from their respective fathers (e.g., the sons of Levi, the Levites; the sons of Benjamin, the Benjaminites; the sons of Dan, the Danites, etc.).

The God of the Fathers. Scholars suggest that the primary religious experience of the Israelite people was the Exodus; having suffered oppression in Egypt, they experienced a God who delivered them from bondage and brought them into the land of Canaan. This God eventually came to be understood as the same God whom Abraham, Isaac, and Jacob worshiped and is identified in the biblical texts as "the God of our fathers" (e.g., Gen 49:25; Exod 3:13; 18:4; Deut 1:11, 21; 4:1; 6:3; 12:1; 26:7; 27:3; 29:24) or the "God of Abraham, Isaac, and Jacob" (e.g., Gen 32:10; 48:15; Exod 3:6; 4:5; 6:3). This God of our fathers made a covenant with our fathers (e.g., Gen 15:18; 17:2, 4, 7, 10, 19, 21; Exod 2:24; 6:4-5). The sign of the covenant, circumcision, did not necessitate fatherhood but maleness and, therefore, potential fatherhood. In Deuteronomy 32:6 God is portrayed as Israel's father (cf. Ps 103:13).

Our Father David. The Davidic dynasty is composed of David, David's son, and David's son's son through generations of sons who ruled the land of a united Israel and then the southern kingdom of Judah. Historians affirm that the Davidic dynasty was able to survive for almost four hundred years partially because of the strength of dynasty. Precisely because each new king stood against the backdrop of a long tradition of fathers who had ruled before them, their own rule was made more secure. Both the account in 1–2 Kings and the account in 1–2 Chronicles take pains to show how the next ruler on the throne of Judah was a son of David (e.g., 1 Kgs 2:12; 11:43; 14:31; 15:3, 11, 24; 22:51; 2 Kgs 8:24; 9:28; 12:22; 14:20; 15:7, 38; 16:20; 20:21; 21:18, 26; 23:30; 24:6).

The Law. The Law gave to fathers both responsibilities and privileges. Children were to honor their father and their mother (Exod 20:12; Lev 19:3; Deut 5:16; 27:16); the person who struck his father or mother would be put to death (Exod 21:15); the person who cursed his father or mother would be put to death (Exod 21:17; Lev 20:9); a daughter taken as a captive of war was to be allowed to mourn her father and mother before being taken as a sexual partner by her Israelite captor (Deut 21:13). A son was forbidden under penalty of death to have intercourse with his mother or with his father's wife, for he would thus disgrace his father (Lev 18:7-8; 20:11).

A father and mother who had a disobedient, stubborn, and rebellious son, a son who drank and ate excessively, was to bring him before the elders at the city gates and there to testify against him; such a disobedient son deserved to be and was to be stoned by the men of the city (Deut 21:18-21). A man who took a woman not yet betrothed and had intercourse with her was required by law to give the father of the woman fifty sheckels of silver and to marry her; furthermore, he was not allowed ever to divorce her (Deut 22:28-29). A father might refuse to give his unbetrothed daughter to the man who had seduced her, but the man would still have to pay the marriage price to the girl's father (Exod

22:16). The father and mother of a young woman whose virginity was questioned by her husband might, if in fact their daughter was still a virgin, present the tokens of the girl's virginity to the elders, and the husband who had falsely accused his wife was then to be whipped and fined a hundred sheckels of silver; these latter were to be paid to the girl's father. As for the husband, he could never divorce the woman (Deut 22:15-19).

Specific privileges and responsibilities applied to fathers who were priests. The daughter of a priest would dishonor her father if she committed fornication; she was to be punished by being burned to death (Lev 21:9). Although priests were forbidden to make themselves unclean by having contact with a dead person, they would be able to have contact with their closest relatives, that is, their father or mother or son or daughter or brother or unmarried sister (Lev 21:2). The one exception was the high priest who was not allowed to make himself unclean even for his father or mother (Lev 21:11).

The biblical texts portray a patriarchal culture in which the father is head of the household and, by extension, the male God Yahweh is also depicted as Father. Nevertheless, an explanation for this form of social organization may be found in the living conditions of the second and first millennia BCE. Careful attention to all the biblical texts suggests that the role of mother was also held in high esteem (e.g., the laws cited above) and that even God is occasionally depicted as acting mother-like (e.g., Isa 66:13).

See: FAMILY, MARRIAGE, MOTHER

ALICE L. LAFFEY

Since the cultural role of father changed little from OT to NT times, we shall not divide this analysis in the usual way. In a culture where kinship is the major social institution, fathers enjoy a social role worthy of respect. Because honor is the pivotal value of the biblical world, we examine the cultural definition of a father and the ways in which it was accorded respect.

Right of Fathers: Honor Thy Father

Since honor is not real unless acknowledged by others, the honorable role and status of a father depends upon public respect. Fathers first and foremost expected respect from their children. The Ten Commandments enshrine this injunction: "Honor your father and mother" (Exod 20:12; Deut 5:6; Mal 1:6; Eph 6:1-3). Children's honor of their fathers was particularly manifested by obedience to them (Gen 27:8, 13, 43; 28:7; Col 3:21; Eph 6:1) and by the support given an aged parent (Sir 3:11-16). Because fathers give the gift of life to their children, they remain always in his debt and can never repay that all-encompassing benefaction.

Alert to all forms of disrespect to one's father, the Bible explicitly censures the ways in which this figure can be dishonored: cursing one's father (Exod 21:17; Lev 20:9; Prov 20:20; 30:11); shaming him (Prov 28:7); dishonoring him (Deut 27:16; Micah 7:6); robbing him (Prov 28:24); mocking him (Prov 30:17); striking him (Exod 21:15); not obeying him (Prov 5:13). A father is particularly shamed by a rebellious son (Deut 21:18-21) and by an unchaste daughter (Deut 22:21; see Gen 19:31-35; Lev 21:11, 19; Deut 27:20). Hence it is a father's right to be treated honorably by his children as this is culturally defined. This honor then translates into public respect for him as well (see 1 Tim 3:4-7).

Duties of Fathers

Ascribed his role and status by God, a father enjoys publicly acknowledged rights and duties. Since in biblical culture the roles of father and offspring were socially defined, certain things were generally expected of a father. In particular an honorable father was duty bound to socialize his children into those traditional roles and values which he himself had learned. Besides redeeming his first born (Exod 13:13), a father ensured that his son was circumcised into the covenant (Gen 21:4; Lev 12:3).

It was a father's duty to instruct his children in the ways of Yahweh; one law states that apostate children were to be denounced publicly and killed (Deut 13:6-10). Needless to say, fathers were expected to feed their children (Matt 7:9-11), as well as nurture and protect them (Deut 1:31; Hos 11:1-3). It is a father's duty, moreover, to instruct his son in social expectations of the village and family (Prov 1:8; 4:1; 23:22) and to discipline and chastise him (Heb 12:5-9; Prov 3:11-12). Likewise it falls to the father to oversee the chastity of his wife and the virginity of his daughter; it was the duty of Miriam's father "to spit in her face" so as to teach her her place in that society (Num 12:14). He should not let his daughters be seduced (Lev 19:29; Exod 21:7), but must defend their honor (Deut 22:13-21).

In the NT, the lists of household duties in Ephesians 5:21–6:9; Colossians 3:18–4:1 and 1 Peter 2:13–3:7 encapsulate the rights of fathers: "Children, obey your parents." Admitting their duty to discipline their children, the same lists warn fathers not to be too strict (Eph 6:4; Col 3:21). Yet, as we saw, discipline was a culturally expected duty of an honorable father.

Fathers and Cultural Definitions of Male Gender

Every father is obviously a male; but in the ancient world there were social expectations of where males belonged and what tasks they did or roles they played, all of which were quite different for mothers or females. This is typically described in terms of the gender division of labor, and embodies the values of honor and shame. For example, Philo compares and contrasts the spheres of fathers/mothers or males/females: "Market-places and council-halls and law-courts and gatherings and meetings where a large number of people are assembled, and open-air life with full scope for discussion and action—all these are suitable to men both in war and peace. The women are best suited to the indoor life which never strays from the house, within which the middle door is taken by the maidens as their boundary, and the outer door by those who have reached full womanhood" (*Special Laws* 3.169). Fathers, who represent their households in the public arenas, are expected to take public and vocal roles in trade in the market places, at religious associations such as synagogue meetings, and in contracts and legal proceedings at the city gates or under the stoa. They labor in public areas, such as herding and shepherding flocks on hillsides or plowing and sowing fields or soldiering or trading abroad. It is important to note the cultural definition of maleness and so fatherhood, for such definitions will necessarily change with shifts in culture. Biblical notions relative to that ancient culture can be culturally irrelevant elsewhere.

Fathers and Sons: Personal Identity

The biblical world differs from our modern world in that people were not individualistic but family and group-oriented. They took their basic identity from the clan and household into which they were born. Hence, when men are identified in the Bible, they are known in terms of their fathers, presuming that the son is of the same trade or social rank as the father: Joshua, son of Nun (Deut 1:38; Josh 2:1); Jonathan, son of Saul (1 Sam 14:1); Ahimelek the priest, son of Ahitub (1 Sam 23:6); Solomon, son of David (Prov 1:1); Simon, son of Jonah (Matt 16:17).

To know the father is also to know the son, for all expect him to be a chip off the old block. Moreover, honor resides in blood; and so sons participate in the clan's honor into which they are born, which helps to explain the importance given to biblical genealogies.

Fathers and Cultural Notions of Sexual Generation

Before modern biology identified the female ovum in 1827, it was thought that a father contributed in his semen all substance necessary for generation of children. The semen, moreover, was thought to contain a miniature person, a *homunculus*, which helps to explain the sanctity accorded semen in the story of Onan (Gen 38:8-10). Since men usually married young maidens before the onset of menarche, they were credited both with opening the womb and with causing the woman's fertility, thus enhancing the cultural myth of male potency and power.

The generation of many sons greatly increased a father's honor. In a world without retirement funds or social security, a father's sons were his protection in old age (Sir 3:11-16); they were the extra hands needed for planting, raiding, and defense. They increased the father's productivity, aided in his defense, provided marriages with which to seal alliances, and so added to his honor (see Ps 128:3). Numerous sons imply a sort of immortality, for if a man's semen contained actual miniature humans, those same sons themselves contained their sons and so on. So all future generations are contained in one patriarch's semen. And the father's name and memory live on in his sons and their sons.

Fathers and Family

Since marriage was an economic, political, and sexual relationship, fathers might allow their sons to marry outside the clan (exogamy) to make alliances and gain advantages. But by Herod's time, marriage strategy had become endogamous, and the marriages were arranged between cousins or members of the same clan or extended family, either blood or fictive family (2 Cor 6:14; 1 Cor 7:39). The eldest married son continued to live in his father's house subject to his authority, thus perpetuating a predisposition toward respect for authority. Inheritances were unequal, with the eldest son inheriting the father's land or the largest portion of his estate (see Luke 15:12, 31); this in turn tended to perpetuate the sense of inequality in social role and status in those societies. Both strategies increased the importance of the father's role as patriarch of the clan and concentrated honor and power.

Metaphorical Sense of Fatherhood

Various aspects of cultural fatherhood give rise to metaphorical uses of "father." As a father begets children, so a man might be called "father" for founding a sect or group (the Rechabites; Jer 35:1-11), establishing certain trades (herdsmen, musicians, and metalworker; Gen 4:20-21), and confirming the priesthood (1 Macc 2:54). Certain figures, from whom clans were named, were designated "father" (Moab; Gen 19:37). Men might take mentors and call them "fathers" (Judg 17:10; 19:19), just as Elisha took Elijah (2 Kgs 2:11-12). A king once acknowledged a prophet as father because of his duty to instruct the sons of Israel (2 Kgs 13:14). Joseph described himself as Pharaoh's father because he administered the royal household (Gen 45:8). Sometimes men took patrons and called them father, as David took Saul (1 Sam 24:11; see 2 Kgs 5:13; Isa 22:21). Thus the exercise of the teaching, advising, protecting role of a blood father might lead to its honorary ascription to a man other than a biological parent, a tradition which Jesus criticized when he commanded his disciples to call no man "father" but God in heaven (Matt 23:9).

In the NT, where notions of membership in clan and tribe are broadened, fatherhood is redefined in regard to adoption by God and descent from Abraham. Gentile Christians cannot claim covenant honor or membership through blood descent from a Jewish father. But John and Paul accord them full membership in the fictive family of the Church because of their imitation of the deeds of father Abraham, namely, faith in God (John 8:39-40; Rom 4:12, 17; Gal 3:8-9). By imitating Abraham, they prove themselves his spiritual children and so share in his blessings. God adopts Gentiles by treating them in the same way as ethnic Jewish sons, such as Jesus. God pours the holy Spirit into them, thus empowering them to recognize God as "Abba! Father!" (Gal 4:5-7) and themselves as offspring of God.

See: FAMILY, MARRIAGE

JEROME H. NEYREY, S.J.

Pastoral-Liturgical Tradition

Notion of Fatherhood. The understanding of father that has been used in the pastoral tradition of the Church has come more from the philosophical and medical writers in the early centuries of the Common Era than it has from the Bible. Three centuries before the development of Christian thought, Aristotle had identified the father as the generator or, more precisely, the "principle" of the child. Using an agrarian model of human conception, he taught that the father provided in his semen (lit. "seed") the homunculus or the "form" of the human person. The mother* was considered merely a passive partner, her womb furnishing the "fertile field" in which the seed was planted and her menstrual blood providing the "matter" to aid in the growth of the homunculus into a person.

This notion of father as principle of the children, combined with a belief that males were more rational than females, grounded the understanding of paternal authority that acknowledged the father not only as provider and protector of the family* but as its ruler. In the Roman Empire, for example, the head of the household, the *paterfamilias*, exercised near absolute authority over the entire household—wife, children, and slaves. Since the *paterfamilias* owned the *familia*, he was not considered part of it. In the Middle Ages, even though the understanding of family had changed, theologians still maintained a similar theory of paternal rule based on their understanding of natural law. Thomas Aquinas, for example, taught that a man rules his wife by means of a political dominance, since he rules according to the laws of matrimony, and rules his children by means of kingly dominance, as a king rules his subjects. Vestiges of this notion are still present in Pope Leo XIII's encyclical, On the Condition of Labor *(Rerum novarum)*, when he quotes Thomas's dictum that "the child belongs to his father" in an attempt to refute the Socialist theory of the centrality of the state over the family.

Responding to contemporary society that acknowledges a greater flexibility in the roles of father and mother, the Church has replaced its natural law understanding with a more personalist one, though vestiges of the former remain. For example, Pope John Paul II, in his Apostolic Exhortation on the Family, states that the father "must ensure the harmonious development of all members of the family" by exercising "responsibility for life," by "commitment to education," by "work which is never a cause of division in the family but promotes its unity and stability," and by "the witness he gives of an adult Christian life."

God as Father. The understanding of father described above influenced the Christian idea of the fatherhood of God. The Greeks were able to conceive of Zeus as the "father of gods and human beings," and the Hebrews could speak of God as the father of Israel (Hos 11:1-4). To acknowledge God as father, then, came easily to early Christian teachers. This designation, however, did not necessarily entail an explicit belief in the Trinity. The earliest source of this doctrine is found in the theology of Athenagoras (ca. 170), who states that the son is the mind of the father who "came forth to serve as Ideal Form" for creation.

Over the centuries, an elaborate theology of the Trinity—and a concomitant naming of the First Person of the Trinity as Father—developed, based on the understanding of generation described above. Pseudo-Dionysius, for example, would demonstrate God's goodness and perfection by showing that God the Father communicated "himself" in the highest degree by generating an equal in the Son. Because of this generation, the attribute of power was explained as appropriately given to the Father. In calling God Father, therefore, theologians expressed the belief found in the Creed that all life comes from God, both the interior life of the Trinity and created life.

Early in the history of the Church, this belief led to a reflection of the fatherhood of God in relation to human fatherhood. St. Athanasius wrote that God alone is father, properly speaking. Any human fatherhood is merely an imperfect participation in God's divine fatherhood. In subsequent theological reflection, the understanding of God as father became so central that other names for God either receded in the background or were altogether lost. The metaphorical nature of the term "father" as applied to God was forgotten. Recent critical and constructive work has returned to the ancient tradition of using many names to describe God.

Joseph as Model of Fathers. Devotion to Joseph as head of the Holy Family and foster father of Jesus and the liturgical celebration of his feast can be documented in the Eastern Church as early as the fourth century. In the West, he appears in martyrologies by the eighth and ninth centuries, his feast being celebrated on March 19. In an effort to strengthen the Christian family, Pope Pius IX extended his feast to the whole Church in 1847. In 1870, he proclaimed St. Joseph patron of the universal Church. His successor, Pope Leo XIII, acknowledged the fittingness of this title, since the "Church is his numberless family, scattered throughout all lands, over which he rules with a sort of paternal authority, because he is the husband of Mary and the father of Jesus."

Ecclesiastical Uses of the Term. The term "father" as a sign of respect was given in the early Church to bishops as teachers possessing authority over the faithful. The term "abbot," coming from the Hebrew word for father, was used as early as the fourth century to describe Egyptian hermits who served as teachers of young monks. It designated their spiritual fatherhood and authority over those in their charge. The term was also used in the Rule of St. Benedict to refer to heads of monasteries. In modern times, the term father became a title used for priests. This custom began in Ireland, and because of

Irish immigration, spread to other English-speaking countries.

See: FAMILY

THOMAS NAIRN

FEAR

The concept of fear in the Bible is related to a wide range of emotions, vacillating between simple anxiety, absolute terror or dread, and respect or reverence. It is used in the OT, NT, and Pastoral-Liturgical tradition both in secular and theological contexts. At times it refers to the panic or fright one experiences when facing an impending disaster or a power greater than oneself. On other occasions it is used in expressions like "the fear of Yahweh" or "the fear of God." When used in this theological sense it can refer to many different emotions, from fear or terror to reverence and awe.

Old Testament

The English word fear is used to translate several different Hebrew words and their derivatives. The range of meaning of these words is quite extensive, from simple anxiety or terror to reverence and respect. Fear occurs in the human sphere and in one's encounter with the divine.

Secular Sphere. In the secular sphere, human beings are afraid whenever they encounter someone or something that threatens their life, security, or well-being. Isaac was afraid that the men of Gerar would kill him if he admitted that Rebekah was his wife (Gen 26:7). Joseph's brothers were "apprehensive" that they would be seized as slaves because the money they had paid for grain was found later in their bags (Gen 43:18).

Religious Sphere. Taken out of context, the term "the fear of God" is ambiguous. It can evoke terror or dread when it is used of the sinner who knows that severe punishment is at hand from one more powerful. The fear of God can also involve awe, reverence, or love for the one who creates and sustains the universe. After their act of dis-

319

obedience in the garden, the first couple hid themselves from God. When God asks where they are, the man answers, "I was afraid, because I was naked, so I hid myself" (Gen 3:10). Moses fears God's response to the sin of worshiping the golden calf, "For I dreaded the fierce anger of the LORD against you: his wrath would destroy you" (Deut 9:19).

The understanding that God severely punishes the sinner found its way into Israelite eschatology and its understanding of the Day of the Lord. Fear is the appropriate emotion for the sinner approaching judgment. The prophet Joel states, "Let all who dwell in the land tremble, for the day of the LORD is coming; yes, it is near, a day of darkness and of gloom" (Joel 2:1-2).

At times fear gives way to reverence, awe, and love. There is usually great mystery that accompanies God's self disclosure in a theophany. The typical human response to the holiness of God is fear. On most occasions, however, the familiar "Fear not!" is addressed by God or God's representative to the human beings involved. When Gideon became fearful, having seen the angel of God face to face, "The LORD answered him, 'Be calm, do not fear. You shall not die'" (Judg 6:23). According to Isaiah 41:10, the Lord reassures the chosen people by saying, "Fear not, I am with you; be not dismayed; I am your God." One should not fear because faith in the power of the holy God of Israel delivers one from worldly fears. "Even though I walk in the dark valley I fear no evil; for you are at my side with your rod and your staff that give me courage" (Ps 23:4).

In the Wisdom literature of ancient Israel one learns that "The beginning of wisdom is the fear of the LORD and knowledge of the holy One is understanding" (Prov 9:10). The avoidance of evil or sin and the hatred of both lead one to be called upright. "He who walks uprightly fears the LORD, but he who is devious in his ways spurns him" (Prov 14:2). In post-exilic Israel this idea becomes more legalistic and the one who fears God is the one who keeps the Law and is faithful to

it. "The fear of the LORD is pure, enduring forever; the ordinances of the LORD are true, all of them just" (Ps 19:10).

New Testament

The English word fear is used to translate at least three Greek words and their derivatives. The majority of uses in the NT parallel those in the OT. Fear can be used to refer to anxiety, to terror or dread, or to awe and reverence. One learns that anxiety is to be rejected, that terror or dread frequently accompanies the manifestation of divine power, and that fear of God cannot be separated from faith as the basic attitude of the one who depends totally on God.

Secular Sphere. In the secular sphere, human beings are afraid whenever they encounter someone or something which threatens their life, security, or well-being. When Joseph "heard that Archelaus was ruling over Judea in place of his father Herod, he was afraid to go back there" (Matt 2:22). According to Acts 5:26 the captain and the court officers went and brought the apostles before the Sanhedrin, "but without force, because they were afraid of being stoned by the people."

Religious Sphere. A different type of fear is created when individuals witness divine activity in the world. Fear is often associated with the appearance of angels. A divine messenger says to Mary, "Do not be afraid, Mary, for you have found favor with God" (Luke 1:30). The shepherds watching over their flocks are told by an angel, "Do not be afraid; for behold, I proclaim to you good news of great joy that will be for all people" (Luke 2:10).

The power of God that is actively at work in the miracles of Jesus also causes fear. After the stilling of the storm the disciples "were filled with great awe" (Mark 4:41). Similarly, when the crowd caught sight of the man who had been possessed by an unclean spirit "they were seized with fear" (Mark 5:15). Initial fear often evolves into reverence and awe, as in the response of the onlookers to Jesus' raising of the widow of

Nain's son: "Fear seized them all, and they glorified God" (Luke 7:16). As in the OT, the security of knowing that God is in control of events often turns fear into confidence and joy. Upon discovering that Jesus' body was not in the tomb, the women "went away quickly from the tomb, fearful yet overjoyed, and ran to announce this to his disciples" (Matt 28:8).

The OT expression "the fear of God" appears several times in Luke's writings. In Mary's canticle one learns that God's "mercy is from age to age to those who fear him" (Luke 1:50). The corrupt and unjust judge "neither feared God nor respected any human being" (Luke 18:2, 4). Cornelius, on the other hand, is described as "devout and God-fearing" (Acts 10:2). Later in the same chapter one reads that "God shows no partiality. Rather, in every nation whoever fears him and acts uprightly is acceptable to him" (Acts 10:35).

The followers of Jesus are told not to be dominated by worldly cares or anxieties, however, they are still to fear evil in all its forms and to fear the punishment that awaits the sinner. "Do not be afraid of those who kill the body but cannot kill the soul; rather, be afraid of the one who can destroy both soul and body in Gehenna" (Matt 10:28). In numerous NT texts fear of eternal punishment is the motivation for moral behavior. In 1 John 4:18, however, one reads, "There is no fear in love, but perfect love drives out fear because fear has to do with punishment, and so one who fears is not yet perfect in love." The followers of Jesus are challenged to overcome fear and to be motivated by trust and love.

Pastoral-Liturgical Tradition

The uses of anxiety and fear in the documents of Vatican II parallel those in the OT and NT. Fear can be used to refer to anxiety, to terror or dread, or to awe and reverence. One can be perplexed about current trends in the world (Pastoral Constitution on the Church 3, 3) or anxious about whether one will have financial security in later years (Decree on the Ministry and

Life of Priests 21, 37). Faith provides the answer (Pastoral Constitution on the Church 18, 27) to fear of the arms race (ibid. 81, 30) or fear of death (ibid. 18, 5). In a passage about the people of God (Dogmatic Constitution on the Church 9, 2) one reads that "at all times and in every race, anyone who fears God and does what is right has been acceptable to him." This is acknowledged as a paraphrase of Acts 10:35.

See: ANGEL, JUDGMENT, KNOWLEDGE, MYSTERY, POWER, SIN, WISDOM, WORSHIP, WRATH OF GOD

DENNIS M. SWEETLAND

FEAR OF GOD

Fear associated with the deity is prominent in religions of the ancient Near East, and is a major theme of both Testaments. This feeling can embrace two seemingly contradictory movements as it attempts to define this human encounter with God. First, there are retreat and terror before the awesomeness of divinity; second, there is attraction and even love for this reality that can reveal itself in a personal way, provide help and guidance, and assure life. As the sense of fright diminishes, "fear of God" can equivalently mean "religion" or "piety" and embrace the further elements of worship and obedience.

Old Testament

By far the most common Hebrew root for "fear" is *yr*'. If its etymology remains a problem, its importance to the OT is certain. With its derivatives, particularly *yir'â* (noun) and *yārē'* (verbal adjective), it appears 435 times in the biblical text, most often in the Psalter (83), Deuteronomy (44), and the Wisdom literature (48). There are also many occurrences in Isaiah (34) and Jeremiah (23). Almost eighty percent of these passages have God as the object of fear. Depending on its context, it can suggest the range of ideas and feelings associated with fear. When the man hears God in the garden, he becomes afraid because of his nakedness (Gen 3:10). Sarah is afraid of God because she lied (Gen 18:15). The court officials of Abimelech are horrified because of what was told them about God's threat to the king in a dream (Gen 20:8). On the other hand, reverential fear of God leads the midwives to refuse to obey the pharaoh's command (Exod 1:17). And the marvels that God works cause all to fear and trust God (Pss 40:4; 65:9).

Close to the sense and usage of yr° is the root *paḥad*, "trembling, dread." The terror of the Lord's majesty in judgment is something to hide from (Isa 2:10, 19, 21; cf. 19:16); but King Jehoshaphat wishes that the fear of God be upon his people to encourage them to serve God faithfully (2 Chr 19:7). Another such term is *gwr*, "dread, be afraid of, revere," used in parallel with yr° in Psalms 22:24 and 33:8, where a reverential fear for God is encouraged. Other associated terms describe different reactions to the appearance/presence of the numinous, such as *ḥyl*, "shudder, writhe" (Exod 15:14; Ps 77:17) and *ḥrd*, "tremble" (Exod 19:16; Job 37:1). Yr° will also appear with words for loving and serving God: *ʾhb*, "love" (Deut 10:12); *ʿbd*, "serve" (Deut 6:13; 10:12, 20; Josh 24:14; 1 Sam 12:14); *dbq*, "cling to" (Deut 10:20). "Keeping the commandments" (Deut 5:29) and "walking in [God's] ways" (Deut 8:6) are other examples of how to fear God.

Fear, as a retreat from God, comes in response to the divine word or the divine presence. In the former case, it most often is concerned with the threat of punishment for sins (Gen 3:10; 20:8; Deut 9:19), a theme that reaches its most important expression in the prophetic announcement of the "day of the Lord" (Isa 2:19, 21). Fear also arises in response to the sheer magnificence and awesomeness of a theophany (Gen 28:17; Exod 3:6; Deut 5:5; Ps 99:3). There is a close connection between God's holiness and fear (Exod 15:11). God is called "fearful" (Pss 47:3; 68:36). The presence of the numinous is frightening since it is assumed that death must follow (Exod 20:18), even if this presence is experienced in a dream (Gen 28:17).

God's presence is revealed, as well, in his mighty acts and these, too, cause fear. First among these acts are all the works of creation, which lead the psalmist to praise (Ps 33:8). The same response is encouraged by Jeremiah (5:22-24; 10:7). The narrative of the deliverance from Egypt concludes on this note of fear, but links it with faith (Exod 14:31). Even unbelievers tremble. Merely upon recalling the events in Egypt the Philistines become afraid (1 Sam 4:7).

God's punishment of sin is revealed in mighty acts as well. At that future day of judgment the nations shall fear before the Lord's signs and wonders just as peoples once did at the time of the Exodus (Mic 7:15-17; see Exod 15:14-16; Isa 19:16; 25:3; Zech 9:5). The whole earth will experience fear at the judgment (Ps 76:9; Isa 41:5), and such fear even becomes a petition in prayer (Ps 67:8). The reaction of the righteous to God's judgment of the wicked first inspires fear, then joy (Ps 52:8; 64:10-11). In Jonah, the pagan sailors' fear is followed by sacrifices (Jonah 1:16). The themes of judgment and creation are intertwined in Psalm 65:6-9, where fear is joined with praise.

In summary, then, though many passages describe a fear that inspires retreat from the numinous, withdrawal from the divine presence is not the final intent. Such fear should lead to faith, sacrifice, joy, and praise.

Fear takes on an ethical sense in the Elohist passages of the Pentateuch. The E version of the "wife-sister" story (Gen 20:1-18) emphasizes obedience to God's commands and respect for strangers as aspects of the fear of God (vv. 8, 11). The story of Abraham's sacrifice (Genesis 22) stresses fear as obedience to God. The "God-fearers" (Exod 18:21) are people whose lives are oriented to the divine will. Fidelity to the covenant is another area where fear can denote a positive movement toward God. Deuteronomy clearly links fear of God to covenant loyalty and worship (Deut 5:29; 6:13, 24; 14:23). Indeed, "fear" is for all practical purposes synonymous with "love" and "serve" (Deut 10:12, 20). As such, fear can be learned; the "lesson" is appropriate conduct (Deut 17:19), or worship (Deut 14:23), or the law (Deut 4:10; 31:12). In the Deuteronomistic literature, fear is most often linked to worship (1 Sam 12:14, 24; 1 Kgs 8:40, 43). Fear of God, then, is more than just an attitude, but involves moral and cultic obligations.

Among the Wisdom books, Proverbs identifies fear as an object of reflection. It is the beginning of knowledge (1:7; 9:10) and equated with knowledge (2:5). It also has a moral dimension and is linked with proper behavior (15:33; 24:21), which leads to various rewards (10:27; 14:26-27; 15:16). Ecclesiastes' linking of fear with obedience to God is set against the background of the numinous (3:14), whose actions can neither be described nor forecast. With Sirach this fear is again associated with keeping the commandments (1:26), but also with love (2:15) and hope (34:16). A more religious and cultic understanding of fear is revealed in another context, the psalms, where "those who fear the Lord" are identified as the community that worships and praises the Lord (Pss 15:4; 22:24, 26; 31:20; 66:16).

New Testament

The Greek verb *phobeomai* (95 times) and the noun *phobos* (47 times), with a few other derivatives from the same stem, are the NT's words for "fear." They appear mainly in the Gospels and Acts, with the noun more common in the Pauline letters. The verb *sebomai,* "worship," is used six times in Acts to describe the "God-fearers" (13:43, 50; 16:14; 17:4, 17; 18:7). This suggests that this group did not merely honor God but worshiped God (five more instances use *phobeomai*). The NT understanding of fear follows that of the OT, but with more emphasis on the relationship that faith and love have to fear.

It is the concrete manifestation of the incomprehensible, divine power in Jesus that inspires fear among all who witness it. So in response to the wonders that Jesus performs over nature, such as the stilling of the storm (Mark 4:41; Luke 8:25), or Jesus walking on the water (Matt 14:26; John 6:19), the disciples are afraid. The Transfiguration inspires great fear among the three disciples (Mark 9:6; attributed to entrance into the cloud in Luke 9:34; and to the voice from the cloud in Matt 17:6). The miracle stories are filled with references to the fear that comes over the eyewitnesses (the cure of the demoniac, Mark 5:15; Luke 8:37; the raising of the widow's son, Luke 7:16; the healing of the paralytic, Matt 9:8; Luke 5:26). Even those cured can become afraid (Mark 5:33). The resurrection causes fear among the women who came to the tomb (Mark 16:8) since they had not yet seen the risen Lord. In addition, fear comes upon those who are visited by the angel of the Lord in Luke's infancy narrative (1:12; 2:9). This fear, however, is different from that which seizes the wicked at the judgment (Luke 21:26; Heb 10:27, 31; Rev 18:10, 15), since the latter fear does not lead to praise of God (Matt 9:8).

The command "Do not fear" is meant to dissolve the fear at the mighty works of Jesus (Matt 14:27; Mark 6:50; Luke 5:10) and, at times, it even leads to belief in the One at work in Jesus (Matt 14:28-33). Once Jesus makes himself known as the risen One, fear gives way to worship (Matt 28:9-10).

Fear still can have a role in the Christian life. The early Christians are described as "walking in the fear of the Lord" (Acts 9:31). Holiness and fear are intertwined (2 Cor 7:1). Fear can be a salutary reminder of the dependence of one's faith on grace and the threat of divine judgment (Rom 11:20); it also represents the profound awe and reverence that should characterize the service of God (1 Cor 2:3; Phil 2:12; 2 Cor 7:15). Fear can sum up the hope Christians have after death (2 Cor 5:11) and growth in this kind of fear comes because of suffering (2 Cor 7:11). The Christian is not subject to a servile fear (Rom 8:15), but, rooted in the saving work of Jesus, is free from the fear of death (Heb 2:15) and enabled to proclaim the gospel (Phil 1:14).

See: DAY OF THE LORD, HOLY/HOLINESS

THOMAS P. MCCREESH, O.P.

323

FEASTS

Various Jewish feasts are referred to in both Testaments of the Bible. They recall and celebrate God's gracious action toward human beings. Some feasts were familial celebrations that took place at home; others required pilgrimage to the Temple* in Jerusalem. Certain feasts were observed regularly at set times; others were occasional. These festivities were reminders to believers to live always in a spirit of thanksgiving to God, and transported them beyond daily drudgeries.

Old Testament

References to festive occasions with a religious orientation appear throughout the Old Testament. Many are familial events: the weaning of a child (Gen 21:8); marriage (Gen 29:21-22; Judges 14; Tobit 10); funerals (Gen 23:1-2; 50:1-14). Others extend beyond the family to a large work force and celebrate agricultural or pastoral events. Judges 21:19-24 describes a vintage festival at Shiloh. In 1 Samuel 25 and 2 Samuel 13:23-29 the completion of sheep shearing occasions a festival. Other feasts concerned the entire nation: the dedication of a temple (1 Kings 8), the coronation of a king (1 Kgs 1:39-40; 2 Kgs 11:12-13), victory in war (1 Sam 18:6-7). All these events were opportunities for thanksgiving, feasting, dancing, and singing.

Fixed Feasts (Lev 23:2). The general word for feast originally designated a fixed place or a fixed time; it then came to mean a meeting or an assembly to celebrate a feast.

The Sabbath,* observed as a time of rest every seventh day, is mentioned in all the Pentateuchal traditions (Exod 16:22-30; 20:8-11; 23:12; 31:12-17; 34:21; 35:2-3; Lev 19:3; 23:3; 26:2; Num 15:32-36; 28:9-10; Deut 5:12-15). It celebrated the rule of the God of Israel over creation (Gen 2:2-3; Exod 20:8-11) and was a memorial of the Exodus which had brought the Hebrew slaves from a place of bondage to a place of rest (Deut 5:12-15; Exod 23:12). It is an ancient feast; according to Exodus 16:22-30, for example,

its observance in the biblical tradition predates the Sinai covenant. Only very late in the history of biblical Israel did Sabbath observance become a sign of its relationship with the Lord (Exod 31:16-17). The command to keep the Sabbath obligated all circumcised males, slaves and resident strangers alike; failure to do so brought death (Num 15:32-36).

The day of the new moon,* the first day of each lunar month, was observed as a religious feast, set apart as a day of rest (Amos 8:5). Special sacrifices, more numerous than those prescribed for the Sabbath, were offered (Num 28:11-15). This ancient observance was taken over by the Yahwist cult to celebrate the permanence of the covenant and the fidelity of Israel's God. The day of the new moon that began the seventh month, the month of Tishri, was called the "Feast of the Trumpet." Its particular importance (Lev 23:23-25; Num 29:1-6) probably derives from its place as the seventh in a series of seven. On this day were offered more sacrifices than on any of the new moon observances.

Every seventh year was designated a year of rest for the land and for the people. Agricultural land was left uncultivated (Exod 23:10-11; Lev 25:1-7), an affirmation that the whole land belonged to the God of Israel. The poor, along with livestock, had access to whatever vegetation grew on this fallow land (Exod 23:10-11; Lev 25:6). Israelite slaves were set free (Exod 21:2-6; Deut 15:12-18), and debts were cancelled or suspended (Deut 15:1-11). Leviticus 26:27-39 interprets the Babylonian Exile as God's punishment for the violation of the sabbatical year (see Jer 34:8-22).

Mention of the Jubilee year, the year following a series of seven sabbatical years, occurs only in the Priestly tradition (Lev 25:8-55; 27:17-24). It had the same requirements as the sabbatical year: freedom for slaves, restoration of ancestral land to its original owners, rest for the land. This feast, perhaps created on analogy with the feast of Weeks, may never have been actually observed in biblical Israel.

The Pilgrimage Feasts. Three times a year Israelite males were obliged to journey first to local sanctuaries or shrines, then, after the Deuteronomic reform of Josiah, to the Jerusalem Temple to observe these feasts (Exod 23:14, 17; 34:32; Deut 16:16-17). The word *ḥag*, from the verb "to dance, to dance or turn around" (Ps 107: 27), refers to the processions and dances that were part of the pilgrimage ritual. Moslems today still refer to the pilgrimage to Mecca as the *haj*.

The oldest liturgical calendars (Exod 23:14-17; Exod 34:18-23) mention three pilgrimage feasts: the feast of Unleavened Bread (March–April), the observance of the grain harvest (May–June), and the celebration of the summer-fruit harvest (September–October). The Deuteronomic calendar (Deut 16:1-17) adds the Passover,* celebrated in the same month as Unleavened Bread. Unlike the other calendars, and in tune with the particular concerns of Deuteronomic theology, this calendar specifies that the pilgrimage be to "the place where [the LORD] will choose," i.e., Jerusalem. The later Priestly calendar (Leviticus 23) lists specific dates on which the pilgrimage festivals are to be observed. It describes liturgical practices from the late monarchy and for the first time combines the feasts of Passover and Unleavened Bread.

Passover and Unleavened Bread (Exodus 12; 23:15; 34:18, 25; Lev 23:5-8; Num 9:1-14; 28:16-25; Deut 16:1-8; Ezek 45:21-24). The history of the origin and the development of both feasts is complex and unclear. The feast of Passover was at first a feast of pastoralists, celebrated in the spring when ewes and nannies dropped their offspring and before the flocks were moved to new pasturage. The sacrifice of the lamb and use of blood were apotropaic rites designed to protect the flocks against evil spirits and demons and to secure their continued fertility. The feast of Unleavened Bread, on the other hand, originated among agriculturalists and originally celebrated the beginning of the barley harvest in early spring.

Because they both occurred in the spring, the two feasts were eventually combined. They were also reinterpreted and grounded in Israel's interpretation of its history; thus they became a commemoration of the Exodus and of the establishment of Israel as the people of God. Under this schema, the Passover began at sunset of the fourteenth of Nisan; the feast of Unleavened Bread began the following day and lasted through the twenty-first of the month.

Feast of Weeks (Pentecost) (Exod 34:22; Num 28:26; Deut 16:10). This one-day feast marked the beginning of the wheat harvest in May/June. Because it depended on the ripening of crops, at first it had no set date (Exod 23:16; 34:22). Once Passover was joined to the feast of Unleavened Bread and given a fixed date, the date of this feast also became fixed. It occurred fifty days after the feast of Unleavened Bread, seven full weeks from the day following the Sabbath on which the first sheaf of barley had been offered to God; in the Greek tradition, its name "Pentecost" is derived from the Greek work for "fifty" (Tob 2:1; 2 Macc 12:31-32). The feast concluded the barley harvest and is thus organically related to the feast of Unleavened Bread (Deut 16:9-10) and indirectly to Passover. From this association it acquired a historical context and was celebrated as the commemoration day for the covenant at Sinai. In the Exodus narrative, the date on which the Israelites arrived at Sinai coincides with the occurrence of this feast.

Feast of Sukkoth (Booths or Tabernacles). Originally called "the Feast of Ingathering," this feast marked the conclusion of the summer fruit harvest, in particular, the grape harvest and the processing of new wine (Deut 16:13-18). It was initially celebrated with singing, dancing, and drinking of the new wine in local areas, outdoors at the threshing floors and wine presses (Judg 21:19-21). That this was the most important pilgrimage feast in biblical Israel is evident from references to it as "the feast" (1 Kgs 8:2, 65; Ezek 45:25) and the "Feast of the LORD" (Lev 23:39; Num 29:12).

The later liturgical calendars (Deut 16:13-16; Lev 23:34) and related texts (Ezra 3:4; Zech 14:16-18) call the feast Sukkoth. This name derives from the custom, still practiced in Palestine, of building temporary huts in fields and vineyards for use by workers during the harvest.

Like the agricultural feasts of Unleavened Bread and Weeks, this feast was not at first observed on a set date because it depended upon the ripening of crops. The earliest calendars only note that it was celebrated in the fall at the end of the year (Exod 23:16; 34:22). A date was fixed during the late monarchy; in Leviticus 23:34 and Ezekiel 45:25, the feast begins on the fifteenth day of the seventh month, Tishri (September/October).

The earliest systematic description of the feast is recorded in Deuteronomy 16:13-14: it entailed a pilgrimage to Jerusalem and seven days of merrymaking and elaborate sacrifices (Num 29:12-34). Leviticus 23:34-36 adds an eighth day of rest and worship with more sacrifices (Num 29:35-38). According to Nehemiah 8:13-18, during the post-exilic period, the people gathered in Jerusalem began to observe the feast in a novel manner; for its duration, they dwelt in huts (sukkôt) to commemorate the only dwellings available to their ancestors during the wilderness period after the Exodus. Leviticus 23:40-41 records a final development in the observance of the feast; the people gathered foliage to carry in procession. According to 2 Maccabees 10:6-8, this element of the Sukkoth celebration was incorporated into the rededication of the Jerusalem Temple.

Like the feasts of Passover, Unleavened Bread, and Weeks, this feast was eventually linked with the Exodus; however, unlike these feasts, Sukkoth remained essentially an agricultural feast. The huts came to represent the tents in which the Israelites had lived after their liberation from Egypt (Lev 23:43). In the Prophetic literature, the feast became associated with the time when God would provide economic prosperity and political autonomy for faithful Israel (e.g., Joel 3–4; Zech 14:17-18), the occasion of a worldwide pilgrimage to the Jerusalem Temple (Zech 14:16).

Post-exilic Feasts. After the Exile, three new feasts appeared. Although the Day of Atonement (Leviticus 16) was developed late in this period, its rituals have deep roots in earlier practices. Using the blood of sacrificed animals, the high priest removed from the Temple, from the people, and from the members of the priesthood the guilt of sin that had accrued during the previous year. As a dramatic portrayal of the removal of this guilt, the "goat for Azazel," bearing the sins of the people, was led off into the desert. This was the only day on which the Mosaic Law required fasting; it was also the only day of the year the high priest was allowed to enter the holy of holies.

The feast of Hanukkah, "Dedication," commemorated a significant victory in the second century BCE Maccabean revolt. Antiochus Epiphanes had desecrated the Jerusalem Temple by setting up a pagan altar in the holy of holies; on 25 Kislev (December), 167 BCE, he offered upon it sacrifices to Olympiad Zeus. Three years later to the day the Hasmonean, Judas Maccabee, purified and re-dedicated the Temple (1 Macc 4:36-59; 2 Macc 10:6-8), which he had captured from the Syrian forces. Annual observance of the feast began in 152 BCE with the high priesthood of Jonathan.

The Feast of Purim, "Lots," celebrated on the fourteenth day of the Adar (February–March) for one or two days, originated in an unknown Jewish community in the east (present-day Iran or Iraq) and commemorates the escape of that community from a planned genocide or pogrom. The book of Esther, the fictional narrative based on that escape, provides the script for the celebration; it tells how Esther and Mordecai delivered their Jewish community from the machinations of the evil Haman who cast lots to determine the day on which the community would be destroyed (9:24-26). The Feast of Nicanor (1 Macc 7:49), the commemoration of a Maccabean victory (1

Macc 7:26-50) on the thirteenth of the same month, may have been combined with the feast of Purim.

See: DAY OF ATONEMENT, EXILE, JUBILEE YEAR, MOON, PASSOVER, SABBATH

KATHLEEN S. NASH

New Testament

References to many of these same feasts appear in the NT. Passover,* Unleavened Bread, Succoth, Dedication, Pentecost,* and Sabbath* all provide a backdrop to NT events. The fourth evangelist, in particular, presents Jesus as reinterpreting these Jewish feasts in his person and his ministry. Festive meals take on a new significance in the NT and in Christian tradition. Apocalyptic victory is anticipated as cause for festivity in the Book of Revelation.

Liturgical Feasts as Historical Markers. The OT meaning of *ḥag* as a solemn liturgical festival, such as Sabbath, Passover, or Succoth on the Jewish calendar (see Exod 23:12-19; 34:18-26; Lev 23:1-34), is carried over into the NT as *heortē*, the feast, principally in the Synoptic passion narratives and John.

In describing the events of Jesus' passion, all the evangelists set the arrest, interrogation, and trial before Pilate, and the execution and burial within the context of the Jewish week of Passover observances (Mark 14:1-2; Matt 26:2, 17; Luke 22:1-2; John 12:1; 13:1). At this festival the Roman governor releases a prisoner (Mark 15:6; Matt 27:15; Luke 23:16-20). Passover is not as a single day, but includes a week of preparations (Lev 23:5-8). John implies that Jesus shared the Passover meal with his disciples before the final day of that week (John 13:1-2; 18:28; 19:42). Likewise, Luke places the Passover meal on the feast of Unleavened Bread, on which the passover lamb had to be sacrificed (Luke 22:1, 7-8).

John takes regular note of festivals on the Jewish calendar as the backdrop for the ministry and death of Jesus. At Passover Jesus goes up to Jerusalem and drives sellers out of the Temple (John 2:13-22). Jesus goes up to Jerusalem at another feast and cures the man paralyzed for thirty-eight years on the Sabbath (John 5:1-18). The multiplication of the loaves and fishes occurs in Galilee at the time of Passover (John 6:4). Fearing for his life, Jesus avoids Jerusalem, but nevertheless eventually goes there for the week-long pilgrimage-festival of Succoth, or Tabernacles. During the feast he teaches and on the last day calls on all who are thirsty to drink from him (John 7:2, 14, 37). Jesus is shown again in Jerusalem at the Feast of the Dedication, most likely Hanukkah, where he encounters the heightened hostility of his challengers (John 10:22). At Passover time (John 11:55; 12:1) Jesus returns to Bethany and raises Lazarus (John 11:1-44). This inaugurates the final events in Jesus' life, which are collapsed into about a three-week period. From the six days before Passover (John 12:1) to the first day of the week at which Jesus is revealed to Magdalene and the male disciples (John 20:1, 19) until eight days later at the encounter with Thomas (John 20:26), it is this single festival period within which the narrative of John 13–20 is organized.

Events in Acts of the Apostles are marked by major Jewish festivals. The coming of the Spirit occurs at the time of Pentecost (Acts 2:1) when Jerusalem is full of pilgrims celebrating. Persecution of the Jerusalem community's leadership is inaugurated by Herod in the days of Unleavened Bread or Passover. James is killed and Peter arrested (Acts 12:1-4). When Paul enters new missionary territory, he typically presents himself in the local synagogue on the Sabbath (Acts 13:14, 42; 14:1; 17:1-2; 18:4). Paul wants to reach Jerusalem by Pentecost (Acts 20:16). To prove his orthodoxy and loyalty to Mosaic Law, Paul undertakes financial sponsorship for the liturgical rite of purification in the Temple of four men whose Nazarite vow has reached its term at Pentecost (Acts 21:20-24). This effort backfires, and Paul's presence in the Temple provokes a riot (Acts 21:27-36). After his arrest that day by Roman authorities (Acts

21:33), Paul's missionary career ends and he is never again a free man.

Domestic Feasts. The domestic meaning of feast is associated with events in family or social life, such as circumcising and naming a child (Luke 1:59; 2:21), and purification after childbirth (Luke 2:22). Some of Paul's struggles with his Gentile communities concern circumcision and the sharing of meals with Gentiles at the feast of the Lord's Supper. The community's worship in Pauline house-churches became a cause of scandal because the banquet that preceded the Eucharist divided the community. Some people were invited to eat, others uninvited were left hungry, and others became drunk (1 Cor 11:17-34). Paul condemned these abuses as a violation of the meaning of the Lord's Supper, and advised separating the festive meal from the liturgical celebration.

Observance of the Sabbath. The sanctity of the weekly observance of Sabbath during which no work is to be done (Exod 31:12-17; Lev 23:3) is often a principle of contention between Jesus and his adversaries in the Synoptic healing stories. The debate concerns the definition of what work is forbidden on the weekly feast. Jesus often heals on the Sabbath when people are gathered for prayer. These acts of mercy confront the legal reductionism possible in any institution. Mark's report of Jesus' first miracle is a Sabbath expulsion of a demonic spirit (Mark 1:21-28). Jesus heals a man with a withered hand in the synagogue on the Sabbath (Mark 3:1-6).

Jesus' challenge represents the view of the Jewish-Christians: "Is it lawful on the sabbath to do good or to do harm, to save life or to kill?" (Mark 3:4). Matthew adds the common-sense observance of Jesus that if a domestic animal falls into a pit on the Sabbath, the owner pulls it out anyway. "Of how much more value is a man than a sheep" (Matt 12:12). Jesus heals a bent-over woman in the synagogue on the Sabbath, and this provokes controversy (Luke 13:10-17). If the Sabbath is meant to be a weekly celebration of people's relation with God, so the healings of Jesus belong on a day of remembrance and celebration of God's goodness.

Celebratory Festal Meals. The first sign of Jesus and keynote of his public ministry is the abundance of wine that prolongs the marriage feast at Cana (John 2:1-11). The wedding feast, a type of messianic banquet associated with Jewish apocalyptic, is featured at the end of Matthew in two parables. The kingdom of heaven is compared to a king giving a marriage feast for his son (Matt 22:1-14; Luke 14:15-24), and to ten maidens who went out to meet the bridegroom at the wedding festivities (Matt 25:1-13). The imaginative imagery associated with Jewish and Christian eschatology is dominated by fearful images of persecution, flight, judgment, heavens shaking, and the awesome appearance of the Son of Man (Mark 13:1-37). However, the apocalyptic image of feasting at a wedding is a joyful image of the end time, at which servants greet their long-awaited master (Luke 12:35). In the multiplication of loaves and fishes on the hillside (Matt 15:29-37) Jesus provides a feast that alludes to prophetic imagery of the great banquet, sign of the fulfillment of God's promises to restore his people after exile (Isa 25:6-10).

Luke often associates the ministry of Jesus with a festive meal, a reception (*dochē*), or a dinner (*deipnon*). After Jesus invites the tax-collector to be his follower, Levi prepares a celebratory meal (Luke 5:29). That Jesus eats with sinners is a cause of scandal to religious leaders, but Jesus says that his mission of healing and calling to repentance is directed to those with whom he sits at table (Luke 5:29-31). Jesus teaches the values of humble service, noncompetitiveness for power and honor by reflecting on the behavior of guests who seek the best places at a formal dinner (Luke 14:7-11). Disinterested service is described by the metaphor of inviting to a feast the poor and outcast rather than family or rich neighbors (Luke 15:12-14). Repentance of the wayward son inspires killing the fatted calf, and giving a feast to which family and friends are invited (Luke 15:23-24). Jesus affirms the repentance of Zaccheus by celebrating a meal with him (Luke 19:1-10)

The Solemn Liturgical Celebrations in the Book of Revelation.

The Book of Revelation presents images of solemn liturgical festivals as images for the reordering of the universe. These visions express a conviction that the community's enemies will eventually be defeated, and the victory after persecution and martyrdom will be cause for a festival. The seer beholds a throne surrounded by elders; four living creatures sing a ceaseless hymn (Rev 4:1-11). The number of the saved, 144,000 victorious martyrs, utter liturgical acclamations and prayers of praise (Rev 7:9-12; 14:1-2). When the Lamb opens the seventh seal, there is silence in heaven for half an hour (Rev 8:1-5). Repeated trumpet blasts (Rev 8:6) recall the Jewish festival of Rosh Hashanah, announcing the passage of the old year and the joyful coming of the new time. The solemn disclosure of the ark of the covenant within the heavenly temple is accompanied by theophanic thunder and lightning (Rev 11:15-19).

A new festival hymn is sung by the redeemed who have abstained from sexual contact and thus prepared themselves to come into God's presence (Rev 14:2-4; Exod 19:15). Vested angels exit the Temple with bowls of incense from which arise the smoke of God's glory that fills the Temple (Rev 15:1-8). A festal Alleluia chant, acclamation, and response is preparation for the wedding day of the Lamb, whose bride is wearing linen (Rev 19:1-8). As a final disclosure of the feast that awaits the community, the seer is shown the splendor of the heavenly Jerusalem, bride of the Lamb, descending from God (Rev 21:9-10).

See: ANGEL, CIRCUMCISION, ESCHATOLOGY, EXILE, GALILEE, HEALING, MERCY, MINISTRY, NAME, PARABLE, PASSION, PAUL, REPENTANCE, SPIRIT, TEMPLE

MARIE-ELOISE ROSENBLATT, R.S.M.

Pastoral-Liturgical Tradition

Christianity emerged in a rich cultural milieu that observed a variety of feasts and calendars. There was no such thing as a particular Christian calendar or feast in the beginning. Various civil and religious calendars provided the backdrop for emerging Christianity which some scholars believe began without any reference to year. One might suggest that in the beginning there was no feast other than Eucharist. Thus Cyrille Vogel could comment that the real surprise is not that the liturgical year developed so slowly, but that it developed at all, since every celebration of the Eucharist is a celebration of the life, death, and resurrection of Jesus. The followers of Jesus never intended to create a cycle of festivals in imitation of Judaism or any other institution. Rather, the community was committed to keeping alive the memory of Jesus' living, dying, and rising. This commitment to what later generations have called the paschal mystery can be the only motivation behind the emergence of a Christian calendar. Specific temporal commemorations or festivals emerged in the Christian community only to enhance the community's understanding and acceptance of this central mystery.

The first Christians accepted the seven-day cycle of the Jews and observed the Sabbath. Early on, however, their distinctive belief in the resurrection of Jesus provided the impetus for shifting allegiance from the last day of the week to the first. Sunday became the original Christian feast and the preferred day for Eucharist. There also developed an annual observance of the death of Jesus, which could have been celebrated from the very beginning at Passover.* No other distinctive Christian feasts are detectable until the late second century. This is probably due to the rich significance of the Sunday gathering and the annual Christian *Pascha,* as well as a strong belief in the imminent return of Christ. The emergence of an annual cycle of Christian feasts signified a shift in community consciousness away from this dominant eschatological perspective.

During the second century the Christian fast days of Wednesday and Friday (*Didache* 8) became Eucharistic days in some places. Though evidence for an annual nativity celebration on January 6 emerges in the third century, the feast could reach back into the second century. This century also provides the first evidence for an annual commemoration of a martyr, Polycarp of Smyrna. Like the other memorials of martyrs that would follow, this commemoration was a celebration of the paschal mystery, honoring one who mirrored Jesus' martyrdom.

The fourth century witnessed significant developments. Most important for the West was an annual memorial of the nativity (25 December). There also developed a preparatory period (Advent) and a series of post-nativity feasts and commemorations. Christmas, surrounded by this constellation of feasts and seasons, became the second great axis in the liturgical year next to Easter. Easter was already celebrated for fifty days in the second century, and acquired a preparatory fast as early as the third century. Eventually this simple fast expanded into Triduum, Holy Week, Lent and a pre-Lenten period. The great period of fifty days encompassing Ascension and stretching to Pentecost* completed the season.

Significant changes also occurred during this period in the type of saints who were honored. Previously only martyrs were the focus of commemorations. When persecutions ceased in the fourth century, communities began honoring confessors who had survived the persecutions as well as bishops. The fifth century provides the first evidence of a feast for Mary (August 15).

The rise of liturgical books in the fifth and sixth centuries had a decided effect on the development of the liturgical year. Until this phenomenon it was difficult to speak of an autonomous liturgical calendar. Rather, the few universal feasts such as Easter and the Nativity, plus a few local feasts, were wed to whatever calendar system was operative in a given place and time. As various liturgical books emerged in the early middle ages, they created the opportunity to break away from the structure of civil calendars. Readings and prayers for the various celebrations had to be arranged according to some coherent schema. While early examples followed the format provided by civil calendars, later liturgical books broke with this tradition. Some recognize Easter as the beginning of the year; others begin with the feast of the Nativity. By the ninth century Rome had accepted the First Sunday of Advent as the beginning of the liturgical year.

The emergence of liturgical books helped to distinguish between two distinct but complementary cycles within the Christian calendar: the temporal and the sanctoral. The temporal cycle is a series of Christological festivals revolving around the two major axes of Easter and Nativity. The sanctoral cycle encompasses the feasts of various saints, usually on fixed dates corresponding to the day of their death. While the two axes of the temporal cycle (Easter-Christmas) were established relatively early, this cycle underwent significant growth in the middle ages. Besides the stabilization of the various seasons before and after Easter and Christmas, this included the emergence of a series of festivals based on theological concepts such as Trinity Sunday on the octave of Pentecost in the tenth century. As the temporal cycle expanded, so did the sanctoral cycle enlarge. The primitive tradition of celebrating only the feasts of local martyrs was displaced by the trend to incorporate saints of every kind from Rome or other places into local calendars. By the year 1000 there was a group of saints that achieved almost universal recognition and were incorporated into virtually every Christian Calendar in the West. Eventually the sanctoral cycle and special "feasts of ideas" like the Immaculate Conception dominated the calendar, obscuring its Christological core and the central rhythms of the paschal mystery.

Various calendar reforms have occurred over the centuries. The 1969 reform was based on five principles: (1) lessen the number of devotional feasts, (2) scrutinize the history of the lives of the saints, (3) retain only saints of significance for the universal Church, (4) examine the days on which the sanctoral celebrations were observed, and (5) include saints from every race and period of time. Unfortunately the current calendar remains a largely male and clerical reserve.

The underlying theology of the current calendar is found in the *General Norms for the Liturgical Year and the Calendar:* "The Church celebrates the memory of Christ's saving work on appointed days in the course of the year. Every week the Church celebrates the memorial of the resurrection on Sunday, which is called the Lord's Day. This is also celebrated, together with the passion of Jesus, on the great feast of Easter once a year. Throughout the year the entire mystery of Christ is unfolded, and the birthdays of the saints are commemorated" (n. 1).

See: EUCHARIST, JESUS CHRIST, MYSTERY, PASSION, SABBATH

EDWARD FOLEY, CAPUCHIN

FERTILITY

Fertility, the quality of being prolific, fruitful, or bearing many children, has both biological and symbolic dimensions in the OT and NT. Fertility is a blessing from God, part of God's promise to the chosen people to be the ancestors of many nations. It remains a symbol of hope in the pastoral and liturgical life of the Church.

Old Testament

The OT understanding of fertility must be placed in the context of the pagan culture of the ANE. In the time of the ancestors the ancient world was filled with various pagan religions that emphasized the precariousness of human existence. Ancient peoples believed that they would survive only by appeasing gods who controlled the universe. Fertility was an essential aspect

of survival. The ability to produce a large, prosperous family helped to ensure the survival of individuals and of the entire tribe or nation. To assist in achieving this goal pagan religions fostered cult prostitution. They believed that having ritual intercourse with sacred cult prostitutes (of both sexes) could unite them with the prolific powers of the gods and assure their own fertility. Fertility of people, animals, and land was a sign of blessing from the gods. Barrenness* was a curse (Gen 20:17-18). The rhythmic cycle of the seasons, of life and death, of famine and feast, was the foundation of this world view in which gods and goddesses of fertility were worshiped and offered sacrifices at sacred shrines.

The OT itself shows some remnants of these cultic practices. Examples are found in the mention of the Mesopotamian god of fertility, Tammuz (Ezek 8:14), and in allusions to the Canaanite goddess of fertility, Asherah (Exod 34:13; 2 Kgs 21:7). When the Hebrew people conquered the land of Canaan, they adopted and adapted many of the cultural and religious practices of their environment, though these were often at odds with their own religious outlook. The use of "sacred pillars" *(massebah),* stones similar to phallic symbols used in fertility rites, is specifically condemned (Exod 34:13; Lev 26:1; Deut 7:5; 12:3). Engaging in cult prostitution is proscribed as one of the dangerous and idolatrous "practices of the nations" (1 Kgs 14:24; 15:12). The temptation to engage in these pagan rituals was ever-present and was consistently decried as idolatry.

In contrast to the pagan outlook in which fertility was a product of appeasing gods and goddesses, the religion of Israel emphasized that fertility was a gift from God, the creator of the heavens and the earth. "Be fertile and multiply" is the dual command God gives at creation (Gen 1:22, 28), a command repeated over and over again (e.g., 8:17; 9:1, 7). The OT perspective emphasizes that fertility is a blessing from God. If conjugal love is exalted (Sir 40:20), it is only in the context of marriage that it finds fruitful blessing (Gen 2:21-24). The act of procreation is seen as a sacred part of marriage, a share in God's own generative power. Often fertility is part of the promise of a covenant between God and one of God's chosen people (e.g., Lev 26:9).

The Hebrews viewed fertility as literally stemming from the "loins" of men (Gen 35:11). A man's semen (*zera*'=seed) symbolized his "descendants" (e.g., Gen 12:7; 13:15-16). God promises Abraham: "I am making you the father of a host of nations. I will render you exceedingly fertile; I will make nations of you; kings shall stem from you" (Gen 17:5b-6; see 15:5; 17:20; 35:11). When Isaac blesses Jacob he calls upon God's fertile power: "May God Almighty bless you and make you fertile, multiply you that you may become an assembly of peoples" (Gen 28:3). Women also receive this promise of innumerable descendants, as Hagar does in Genesis 16:10-11.

The OT frequently contrasts fertility with barrenness. God's power can overcome barrenness and put in its place the ability to have children. "[God] establishes in her home the barren wife as the joyful mother of children" (Ps 113:9). That ancient Israelites highly prized children, especially males, is not surprising since the survival of the family was at stake. Fertility guaranteed someone to fulfill God's promises. The psalms praise the gift of children and the fertile wife: "Behold sons are a gift from the LORD; the fruit of the womb is a reward" (Ps 127:3) and "Your wife shall be like a fruitful vine in the recesses of your home; your children like olive plants around your table" (Ps 128:3). The OT sometimes even boldly depicts the prolific ability of the Hebrews, as in the Book of Exodus where the robust Hebrew wives are contrasted with the weak Egyptians: "But the Israelites were fruitful and prolific. They became so numerous and strong that the land was filled with them. . . . the more they were oppressed the more they multiplied and spread" (Exod 1:7, 12).

God's blessing of fertility does not only make people fecund. The OT also emphasizes that God makes the land bear fruit as well. For example, Deuteronomy 28:11 ties fertility of people and land together: "The LORD will increase in more than goodly measure the fruit of your womb, the offspring of your livestock, and the produce of your soil, in the land which he swore to your fathers he would give you" (see Lev 26:10). Sometimes this concept is used as a metaphor. Isaiah, for example, uses the image of a "vineyard on a fertile hillside" to represent God's chosen people (Isa 5:1-7). The transformation of the desert into an orchard (Isa 32:15) or some seeds into a fertile field (Ezek 17:3-8; 19:10) constitutes a powerful symbol of God's ability to make the chosen people of the covenant fertile and fruitful in every way. God's word, too, is praised as fruitful: "For just as from the heavens the rain and snow come down and do not return there till they have watered the earth, making it fertile and fruitful, . . . so shall my word be that goes forth from my mouth; it shall not return to me void, but shall do my will, achieving the end for which I sent it" (Isa 55:10-11).

New Testament

The NT seldom uses the concept of fertility in a literal fashion to describe prolific procreation. Most often the NT uses the common concept of being fruitful to describe metaphorically the growth of the Church and the spread of the Word of God.

In a few instances the NT alludes to biological fertility or to the promises made to the ancestors. The discourse of Stephen, for instance, mentions the procreative ability of the Hebrews while they were in Egypt (Acts 7:17), while the Letter to the Hebrews recalls the promise of progeny God made to Abraham (Heb 6:13-14; see Gen 22:17). The Acts of the Apostles also draws attention to the growth of the Church in sheer numbers, because of the work of the holy Spirit (6:1; 9:31), and to God's generous blessing of fertility upon the land by sending rain and causing fruitful harvests (14:17).

Most frequently, the NT uses the concept of fruitfulness metaphorically. Provided it lands on rich soil, the seed of the Word of God sprouts in abundance (Mark 4:20; Matt 13:23; Luke 8:15). The Acts of the Apostles also calls attention to the spreading of the gospel and the growth of the Word of God (6:7; 12:24) as examples of the "fertility" of Christianity (see Col 1:6). Paul, too, emphasizes that God is the source of this fruitfulness: "I planted, Apollos watered, but God caused the growth. Therefore, neither the one who plants nor the one who waters is anything, but only God, who causes the growth" (1 Cor 3:6-7).

While he emphasizes God's role in this productivity, Paul also charges Christians to commit themselves fully to the ethical demands of the gospel "in order that we might bear fruit for God" (Rom 7:4). Bearing fruit (*karpophoreō*) is an expression for living the righteous life. The Gospel of Matthew, in particular, uses the image of fruit (*karpos*) to describe the effective result of the proper, ethical life. John the Baptist warns, "Produce good fruit as evidence of your repentance" (Matt 3:8), and Jesus teaches in the Sermon on the Mount, "By their fruits you will know them. . . . A good tree cannot bear bad fruit, nor can a rotten tree bear good fruit" (Matt 7:16-18; see 12:33).

The strongest word of all is Jesus' dire warning to the people of Israel who reject Jesus and his teachings: "Therefore, I say to you, the kingdom of God will be taken away from you and given to a people that will produce its fruit" (Matt 21:43). From Matthew's perspective, the fruitfulness of God's reign shines forth not only from God's own power, who is the source of all "fertility" and productivity, but also from the ethical commitment of disciples to live out the demands of the gospel. The transformation in the NT of the concept of fertility into a symbolic metaphor, then, is both a reminder of promise and a call to commitment.

Pastoral-Liturgical Tradition

Fertility always holds some attraction to Christians as a biological concept because of its ties to the mystery of human sexuality and to the sacrament of matrimony. Modern science has made significant advances in assisting married couples who have difficulty in conceiving, though many of these advances have led to complex moral dilemmas. Since fertility is so bound to the divine command to populate the earth and subdue it (Gen 1:28), it is also a concept which leads one to reflect on ecology, the right relationship of humans to the earth we have been given as our "garden." Fertility cannot be a call to irresponsible parenthood nor to an abuse of earth's resources.

As powerful as the biological image of fertility remains, the most viable pastoral application of this biblical concept is its metaphorical use. Though most modern people are far removed from the land and the agricultural rhythms of ancient peoples' lives, nevertheless we remain attracted to this symbol of hope and trust in God's power to grant new life. The liturgical season of Lent especially offers an opportunity to rediscover the language of fertility. Lent is a time of repentance and renewal, a time when the Church reflects on the mystery of rebirth through the death and resurrection of Jesus at the same time the earth comes alive again in spring. It is also a time to meditate upon our ancestors whom we have followed in faith and whose progeny we are.

In every age the Church is called to remain faithful to the Word of God as it grows in our midst to a great harvest (Mark 4:26-29). Though some plant the seed and others water the garden, God causes the growth (1 Cor 3:6). In the symbol of fertility, God's people continue to find reason for hope, that the will of God who is the source of all life will ultimately be accomplished in the reign of eternal life.

See: ANCESTORS, BARRENNESS, CANAAN, COVENANT, GENEALOGY, PROMISE, SEED

RONALD D. WITHERUP, S.S.

FINGER OF GOD

Finger of God occurs in the OT as a figurative expression for the power* of God. In this sense it is similar to OT references to the hand of God, which also represents divine power. The only significant NT use appears in Luke 11:20 and suggests God's direct intervention. In post-NT Christian writings the holy Spirit is identified as the Finger of God.

Old Testament

"Finger of God" appears in several OT texts, usually as a figurative expression for the power of God. It occurs in Exodus 8:15 at the end of the report about the third (gnat) plague. After Pharaoh's magicians are unable to match the actions of Aaron, the magicians, referring to Aaron's staff (mentioned in v. 13), say to Pharaoh, "This is the finger of God" (Exod 8:15). Later in Exodus one reads that "when the LORD had finished speaking to Moses on Mount Sinai, he gave him the two tablets of the commandments, the stone tablets inscribed by God's own finger" (Exod 31:18). Moses is pictured as affirming this action of God in Deuteronomy 9:10 when he says, "the LORD gave me the two tablets of stone inscribed by God's own finger." In Psalm 8:4 the psalmist praises God for creating the heavens, "the work of your fingers." While "finger of God" appears infrequently in the OT, "the hand of God," a more common expression referring to God's power, occurs more than two hundred times.

New Testament

In the NT the expression "finger of God" appears only in Luke 11:20 and implies that Jesus drives out demons "by the finger of God." Jesus' words allude to the story of the third plague in Exodus 8:15 and suggest that the exorcisms he is able to perform are accomplished by God's direct intervention. The phrase is usually understood to be expressing the ease with which Jesus has expelled the demon.

In Matthew's parallel verse (Matt 12:28) it is suggested that Jesus casts out demons by the "Spirit of God." This variance in expression will be important for post-NT writings as will be seen below.

Pastoral-Liturgical Tradition

In the writings of the Fathers of the Church, relying on the parallel mentioned above between Matthew 12:28 and Luke 11:20, the holy Spirit is identified as the Finger of God. Writing in the fourth century, St. Ambrose (*On the Holy Spirit,* Book 3, ch. 4.17) uses the traditional analogy of the Son and Spirit as the Father's hand (see Matt 26:64) and finger. This image does not imply that they are merely a small portion of God. Rather, it expresses the unity of power among the three in all their actions.

This understanding of the expression is found in the liturgical tradition several centuries later. In the Vesper hymn for Pentecost, the *Veni Creator Spiritus* of Rhabanus Maurus (766–856), the Spirit is referred to as the "Finger of God's Right Hand."

The only use of the expression "finger of God" in the Vatican II Documents is in the Dogmatic Constitution on the Church, no. 5, where it is a quotation of Luke 11:20 and is used to speak of the miracles of Jesus as a sign that the reign of God is already on earth.

See: MIRACLE, POWER, REIGN OF GOD, SIGN, SPIRIT

DENNIS M. SWEETLAND

FIRE

Fire has many common uses in the Bible. It is used to cook food (2 Chr 35:13), for heat and light (Isa 44:16, 19), as a weapon of war (Num 31:10; Judg 9:52; 2 Kgs 25:9), and as a means of signaling from one city to the next (Jer 6:1). The more important occurrences of the word, however, are symbolic. Fire symbolizes the presence of God and God's protection. Fire is a natural symbol of both anger* and judgment.* It also connotes testing and purification.

Old Testament

Theophany. "Our God is a consuming fire" (Deut 4:24). Fire is a frequent element in theophanies. It is an integral part of the central theophany in the OT, the manifestation of God's presence on Mount Sinai to make covenant with Israel (Exodus 19–20; Deuteronomy 4–5). At the sealing of the Sinai covenant God's glory appears like a devouring fire (Exod 24:17). God also appears in the form of fire to make covenant with Abraham (Gen 15:17). A burning bush manifests God's presence in the call of Moses (Exod 3:2). In the Exodus event God leads and protects Israel by means of a column of fire (Exod 13:21-22). The glory of God which fills the tabernacle appears like a fire at night (Exod 40:38). To Ezekiel the divine presence appears like one in human likeness who looks like fire from the waist down (Ezek 1:27; 8:2).

God's arrival is often announced with the image of fire. Fire goes before the divine presence (Ps 50:3). Lightning and coals of fire accompany God (Pss 18:13-15; 29:7). Mountains melt like wax at God's approach (Mic 1:4). Seraphim, fiery creatures (perhaps serpents), proclaim the divine holiness at the call of Isaiah (Isa 6:2-7); at the call of Ezekiel the divine presence arrives in a huge cloud with flashing fire accompanied by cherubim with burning coals moving among them (Ezek 1:4-13). In Daniel's vision the Ancient One sits on a throne of fire from which flows out a surging stream of fire (Dan 7:9-10). In a later vision to Daniel the angel Gabriel appears with a face like lightning and eyes like fiery torches (10:6).

The perpetual fire on the altar symbolizes the faithful presence of God (Lev 6:2, 5-6). The author of 2 Maccabees claims that the sacred fire was preserved during the Exile and rediscovered by Nehemiah centuries later (2 Macc 1:18-23, 31-36).

Fire is the ordinary way of offering sacrifice (Lev 1:7-17; 2:2-11) and signifies God's acceptance of the sacrifice. Fire confirms the installation of Aaron as high priest (Lev 9:24). At the call of Gideon (Judg 6:21) and in the contest between Elijah and the prophets of Baal, God consumes the sacrifice in fire (1 Kgs 18:38). God sanctifies the threshing floor (1 Chr 21:26) and takes possession of the Temple in the form of fire (2 Chr 7:1).

What is left over from the sacrifice must be consumed by fire (Exod 12:10; Lev 4:11-12). Incense is also offered by fire (Exod 30:7-8; Lev 16:12-13). The Nazarite's consecrated hair is burned with fire (Num 6:18).

Fire can also signify illicit sacrifice. Sacrifices to Moloch, burning children in the fire, are forbidden in the Law (Lev 18:21; Deut 12:31; 18:10). But people continue the abominable practice (2 Kgs 16:3; 21:6) that is rigorously condemned by the prophets (Jer 7:31; Ezek 20:26, 31). God rejects the sacrificial fire of sinful priests (Mal 1:10). Nadab and Abihu, Aaron's sons, are punished for offering "strange fire" to God (Lev 10:1-2).

Fire is God's servant (Ps 104:4). Fire is called to praise God (Ps 148:8). God's word burns like fire (Jer 20:9). Elijah is taken up to heaven in a chariot of fire (2 Kgs 2:11). God's presence cannot be equated with fire, however. When Elijah goes to Mount Horeb, God is not in the fire, but in the tiny whisper (1 Kgs 19:12).

Protection. God destroys enemies before Israel as a consuming fire (Deut 9:3). Elisha is protected from the Aramean soldiers by fiery chariots (2 Kgs 6:17). God will protect the remnant in Zion by a new pillar of fire (Isa 4:5-6). The new Jerusalem will be surrounded by a wall of fire (Zech 2:9). God's jealousy burns like fire to deliver the land from those who have plundered it (Ezek 3:5). God's presence also protects the faithful from threatening fire (Ps 66:12; Isa 43:2). The three young men thrown in the fire by Nebuchadnezzar are untouched by the flames in the white-hot furnace (Dan 3:23-24, 49-50).

Anger and Judgment. God's anger is symbolized by fire (Nah 1:6). God comes from afar to destroy Assyria with a tongue like consuming fire (Isa 30:27, 30, 33), and Babylon like flames among stubble (Isa 47:14). Amos announces God's destruction of six foreign nations and the land of Judah by fire because of their wickedness (Amos 1:3–2:5). God's wrath is a fire which devours those who turn to other gods (Deut

32:22; Jer 11:16). The wicked must be consumed by fire (2 Sam 23:7; Ps 83:14-15; Isa 10:17). God rains fiery coals upon them (Ps 11:6) and burns them as though in a furnace (Ps 21:10). They perish before God as wax melts before the fire (Ps 68:3). What peoples build by violence will be food for flames (Hab 2:13). God's people themselves will be a flame to devour their enemies (Obad 1:17-18; Zech 12:6).

God's wrath also flames against the chosen people when they are unfaithful (Ps 78:21; Isa 5:24; Jer 4:4; Amos 5:6). Drought devours the land like fire (Joel 2:19-20; Amos 7:4-6). A locust invasion crackles and destroys like fire (Joel 2:3-5). Ezekiel burns his hair as a sign that the city of Jerusalem will be destroyed by fire (Ezek 5:1-4). The psalmist pleads that the fire of God's wrath be turned against the wicked and not upon God's people (Ps 79:5-6; see 140:11).

God punishes Sodom and Gomorrah with fire (Gen 19:24). The fire of lightning is one of the plagues (Exod 9:23-24). Fire comes forth from God's presence to consume Nadab and Abihu (Lev 10:1-2). When the people complain in the desert God's wrath flares up and the fire of God consumes the outskirts of the camp (Num 11:1-3). Fire from God consumes the followers of Korah who challenge Moses and Aaron (Num 16:35). Achan, who steals booty from Jericho, is burned along with his family and all his possessions (Josh 7:15, 24-25). Fire destroys the soldiers of Amaziah who come to summon Elijah (2 Kgs 1:10, 12).

Wickedness itself burns like fire (Isa 9:17). Adultery is like fire which burns the one who embraces it (Prov 6:26; see Sir 6:2). The scoundrel is a furnace, breathing fire (Prov 16:27). Wicked rulers of Israel are like a blazing oven (Hos 7:4-7). The enemies attack like fire among thorns (Ps 118:12; cf. Ps 80:17). They even burn the sanctuary of God (Ps 74:7; Isa 64:10). But charity heaps coals of fire on an enemy's head (Prov 25:22).

Testing and Purification. God tests people like precious metal in the fire (Zech 13:9). In the time of Jeremiah God declares the testing a failure: "The wicked are not drawn off," so they shall all be rejected (Jer 6:27-30). Through Ezekiel God says that the whole house of Israel has become dross to be smelted off in the furnace (Ezek 22:17-22). On the Day of the Lord God's messenger will refine the Levites with fire (Mal 3:2-3).

Fire is also a means of purification. Moses burns the golden calf, grinds it into powder, mixes it with water and makes the people drink it (Exod 32:20). Contaminated clothes are to be burned in the fire (Lev 13:52, 55, 57). Fire purifies what is brought back from combat (Num 31:22-23; Isa 9:4). The idols of foreign nations are to be burned in fire (Deut 7:5, 25; 12:3; 2 Kgs 23:11). Cities that turn to other gods must be burned (Deut 13:13-19). Joshua burns the cities he conquers along with the booty and their weapons of war (Josh 6:24; 8:8, 19). God too burns the weapons of war (Ps 46:10). The demon Asmodeus is driven away from Sarah when Tobiah burns the fish's heart and liver (Tob 6:8; 8:2-3). After the desecration by the Seleucids the Temple is purified and reconsecrated by the burning of incense and the lighting of lamps (1 Macc 4:50; 2 Macc 10:3). Isaiah's lips are cleansed by the burning ember that he might proclaim God's word (Isa 6:5-7).

Eschatological Symbolism. The Day of the Lord will be signaled by wonders in the heavens and on the earth: blood, fire, and columns of smoke (Joel 3:3). The fire of God's jealousy will devour the whole land (Zeph 1:18; 3:8). In the great final battle God will visit Ariel [Jerusalem] with whirlwind and the flame of consuming fire (Isa 29:6). Then in the restoration of Zion God shall come in fire to judge all humanity; the wicked shall be condemned to eternal fire (Isa 66:15, 24).

New Testament

The usage of the term "fire" in the NT is similar to that of the OT. It has the same common uses: to cook food (John 21:9), for heat and light (Mark 14:54; Acts 28:2).

Theophany. The Spirit comes to the disciples in the upper room in the form of tongues of fire (Acts 2:3). The event is seen as a fulfillment of Joel's vision of the last days (Joel 3:3; Acts 2:19). The Letter to the Hebrews reverses Psalm 104:4 and describes the angels as fiery flames (Heb 1:7). The same author calls upon the fiery theophany at Sinai as a contrast to the new Mount Zion (Heb 12:18) and reminds the readers that "our God is a consuming fire" (Heb 12:29; Deut 4:24). Echoing the vision of Daniel, the Book of Revelation describes Christ with eyes of fiery flame (Rev 1:14; 2:18; 19:12). Fiery lightning comes from God's throne. In attendance are the seven burning spirits of God (Rev 4:5). Before the throne is a sea of glass mingled with fire (Rev 15:2).

Testing and Purification. John announces that Jesus will baptize in the holy Spirit and fire (Matt 3:11; Luke 3:16). His mission is to purify the earth with fire (Luke 12:49). Fire will test the quality of everyone's building upon Christ the foundation (1 Cor 3:13, 15). Christian faith tested by trials is more precious than fire-tried gold (1 Pet 1:7; see 4:12). Grace too is like gold refined by fire (Rev 3:18).

Eschatological Judgment. Several OT examples of judgment by fire are found again in the NT. The disciples want to cast fire on Jesus' enemies in imitation of Elijah but he prevents them (Luke 9:54; cf. 2 Kgs 1:10, 12). Sodom and Gomorrah are used as an example of the fate awaiting the wicked at the day of judgment (Luke 17:29; Jude 7; see Gen 19:24). Paul borrows the proverbial saying that charity heaps coals of fire upon an enemy's head (Rom 12:20; Prov 25:22).

Fire will be the punishment for evil. The wicked, symbolized as trees that do not bear good fruit, chaff from the threshing floor, or as weeds, will be cast into the fire of judgment (Matt 3:10, 12; 7:19; 13:40; Luke 3:9, 17). Anyone who does not remain attached to Jesus the vine will be burned like a withered branch (John 15:5). Hell or Gehenna is described as a place of fire (Matt 5:22; 13:42, 50; 18:8-9; Mark 9:43-48). Those who failed to minister to the least of Jesus' followers will be sent into the eternal fire prepared for the devil and his angels (Matt 25:41).

Fire is especially prominent in the description of the final judgment in the Book of Revelation. The angel of God will hurl burning coals from the censer upon the earth as a beginning of the final days (Rev 8:5) and fire will destroy the heavens and the earth (8:7-8; see 2 Pet 3:7, 10, 12). The horses bearing the plagues of the last judgment breathe fire, smoke, and sulfur which will kill one-third of the human race (Rev 9:17-18). Fire from the mouths of the two martyrs devours their enemies (11:4-5). The beast whose number is 666 can also make fire come upon the earth (Rev 13:13). Whoever worships the beast will be tormented in burning sulfur (Rev 14:10). The sun is given power to burn people with fire (16:8-9). Babylon, the beast, the false prophet, the devil, death, Hades, and the wicked will all be destroyed by fire (17:16; 18:8; 19:20; 20:10, 14-15; 21:8).

Pastoral-Liturgical Tradition

In liturgical practice fire remains a sign of the divine presence. The sanctuary lamp indicates the presence of Christ in the reserved Eucharist. Candles draw attention to the divine presence in the midst of the community assembled for worship.

Fire as a sign of theophany is celebrated at the Easter Vigil. Fire is blessed to symbolize the glory of the risen Christ who is light of the world. The Easter candle, lit from the new fire, leads the procession of God's people. Everyone shares the candle flame as everyone shares the hope of resurrection. The great hymn of the Exsultet proclaims the Easter event and petitions God to accept the Easter candle and to keep it burning until Christ, the Morning Star, returns in glory to dispel night forever.

See: APOCALYPTIC, COVENANT, ESCHATOLOGY, EXODUS, JUDGMENT, WRATH OF GOD

IRENE NOWELL, O.S.B.

FIRST-BORN, FIRST-FRUITS

Old Testament

First-born Children. "First-born" or *bekor* refers in OT tradition to male children who occupy this family position of social privilege and material advantage. Primogeniture determines the size of one's inheritance, greater than that of one's younger siblings, a double portion of what the others receive (Deut 21:15-17). The first-born can be linked to the father, as Reuben is to Jacob by his wife Leah (Gen 29:32; 49:3). Or the child is related to the mother, the first opening her womb (Exod 13:2), as Joseph to Jacob's wife Rachel (Gen 30:25). The first-born obtains legal rights by the fact of being born first, not because of personal accomplishments. That legal protection was necessary to counteract favoritism is suggested in the mandate prescribed for a man with two wives. He cannot treat the son of the loved wife in preference to the *bekor* of his disliked wife, but must acknowledge the legal status of his first-born, no matter the feelings toward the disliked wife (Deut 21:15-17).

The social, legal, and moral tensions over the designation of primogeniture are dramatized in the patriarchal history by a number of episodes. Ishmael, conceived by Sarah's maid Hagar, is Abraham's first-born by surrogate. Once Sarah bears her own first-born child, Isaac, she is hostile toward Hagar and Ishmael and insists they be driven out (Gen 16:1-6; 21:9-21). Sarah asserts that her rights as wife protect the inheritance of her own son Isaac, for "the son of this slave woman shall not be heir with my son Isaac" (Gen 21:10). In the case of first-born twins, such as Esau and Jacob, the elder Esau is technically the *bekor*. Jacob, aided by his mother Rebekah, impersonates Esau to gain the one-time, irrevocable blessing of their father Isaac (Gen 27:1-29). Jacob, as the legal *bekor*, then inherits the family property, and bears the special blessing through which God renews and fulfills the promise to Abraham.

Joseph is loved more dearly than his brothers because he is the son of Jacob's old age (Gen 37:3), but also because Joseph is the first-born of Rachel, Jacob's best-loved wife (Gen 29:18-20). The younger Joseph eventually supplants Reuben, *bekor* of Jacob and Leah, and proves to be the savior of the entire family because of his position of power and responsibility in Egypt during a period of famine in Canaan. He forgives his brothers and provides for their survival (Gen 45:1-15).

Subversion of the status of the first-born son is something of a literary convention in biblical narrative. This suggests that the working out of God's covenant* is mysterious and does not always conform to human law* or expectation. Abel is preferred by God to the first-born Cain (Gen 4:1-5). Jacob, the younger twin, tricks his elder brother Esau out of his birthright and connives to receive their father Isaac's blessing (Gen 24:27-34; 27:1-40). David is the youngest of Jesse's sons chosen to be anointed king of Israel by Samuel (1 Sam 16:1-13; 17:12-14). Solomon, second child of Bathsheba and David (2 Sam 12:24), is not the first-born of David's sons. David has begotten other sons by his previously taken wives, including his first-born Amnon (2 Sam 3:2-5). It is Amnon who rapes his half-sister Tamar (2 Sam 13:1-22), and is killed by Absalom (2 Sam 13:23-38). After Absalom's death (2 Sam 18:9-17), Adonijah has ambitions to become David's successor, but Bathsheba and the prophet Nathan succeed in having David name Solomon as his successor (2 Kgs 1:1-40).

Assignment of the favored position of eldest son is understood to express God's election of the entire community of Israel, which is named God's first-born son (Exod 4:22). God will console Israel after their tears and bring them back to their land because Israel is loved by God as a father's first-born (Jer 31:9). David, who personifies Israel, is invoked by the psalmist as God's first-born in a celebration of the king's messianic status. He is anointed with favor, and will be honored as the greatest king. God will be faithful in covenant to him and to his descendants (Ps 89:28-29).

Dedication and Offering of the First-Born Child to God. God commands that every first-born should be consecrated to him, "for it belongs to me" (Exod 13:1). Another motive for the dedication is the remembrance of God's sparing of the children of Israel and the slaying of all first-born children and animals among the Egyptians (Exod 11:4-6; 12:29). The Israelites' first-born sons must be bought back or redeemed from God by the family's substitute sacrificial offering of an animal (Exod 13:13). The ransom can also be paid for a one-month old boy in silver shekels (Num 18:16).

The Levites are consecrated to the service of God as the institutionalized substitute for the first-born males among the people, to be assistants to Aaron and his sons in the services performed at the tent of meeting (Num 8:5-19). They serve from age twenty-five to fifty (Num 8:23-25). The number of Levites is determined by a census of the first-born males among the people of Israel, and the number of first-born Israelites in excess of the number of Levites are ransomed with silver shekels (Num 3:40-51). Levites do not inherit property (Deut 12:12; 14:27). Symbolizing the dedication of all first-born sons, they belong to the community. Every third year, the community brings tithes* of its produce and puts them in the community store so that the Levite, alien, orphan, and widow can eat (Deut 14:28). Families are responsible for providing for the Levites' material needs, just as they take care of the alien, orphan, and widow (Deut 26:11, 13).

The spirit of thanksgiving that inspires dedication of a first-born to God is dramatized in the story of Samuel's birth. His mother Hannah begs for a son (1 Sam 1:11) and vows to dedicate him to God. When her *bekor*, Samuel, is weaned, Hannah takes him to the Temple, offers flour and wine, sacrifices a three-year-old bull, but does not redeem her son by taking him back. She leaves Samuel in the service of God as a permanent act of thanksgiving (1 Sam 1:27), making clear that the animal is not a substitute offering to fulfill a requirement, but a free gesture of generosity. She fulfills the Law both literally and symbolically.

Dedication of First-born Animals. According to God's word to Moses, the first-born, both of humans and animals, is specially designated as the one consecrated to God (Exod 13:2; 22:29). First-born animals, such as cattle and sheep, are to be offered to God and killed as sacrificial offering in remembrance of God's rescue of the Israelites from Egypt, precipitated by God's slaying of the first-born in Egypt (Num 3:11-16). The cattle of the Levites become a substitute for the offering of the first-born of cattle belonging to the rest of the people (Num 3:40, 45). Some valuable work animals, such as an ass, can be redeemed by the sacrifice of a lamb (Exod 13:13). The sacrifice of male instead of female animals ensures economic protection of herds, for fewer males are needed for breeding.

Dedication of First-fruits of Produce. At the harvest time, a sheaf of grain is to be brought to the priest the day after the Sabbath to be presented as a wave-offering to God (Lev 23:9-15). Offering of first-fruits is an act of thanksgiving for having been rescued from Egypt and brought into a fruitful land whose harvest is seen as a direct gift from God (Deut 26:1-11). The pilgrimage festivals of Passover, Pentecost, and Succoth are linked with harvest times during the year at which offerings of choicest first-fruits of the field are brought to God, both of grain and fruit (Exod 23:14-19; Lev 34:22-26). Priests and Levites, dependent on the community, live on the oblations offered to God, and they receive the first-fruits of grain, wine, and oil, and shearing of the flock (Num 18:12-13; Deut 18:1-5). In the restoration of the Temple cult after the return from the Exile, Israelites offer to God the first fruit of fields, trees, first batch of dough, and first press of wine and olive oil (Neh 10:36-38).

New Testament

The theme of first-born and first-fruits in the OT is used theologically and metaphorically in the NT. The terms are applied to the humanity of Jesus and his role as savior, and they interpret what resurrection means. Jesus is the first child of Mary, her *prototokos* (Luke 2:7), or first-born son consecrated to God. In obedience to Mosaic Law, she and Joseph go to Jerusalem, present him to the Lord, and make the substitute offering of turtle doves to redeem him (Luke 2:22-24). Witnesses to the death of Jesus will look upon him whom they have pierced (John 19:37). In this scene, John alludes to the sadness over the loss of Jerusalem, as intense as mourning the loss of a first-born and only son, as part of a mysterious process of cleansing the people from sin (Zech 12:10; 13:1).

Encouraging those who suffer persecution, Paul says that Jesus is the first-born of many children (Rom 8:29) who are destined to share the same call, holiness, and glory as the resurrected Jesus. Christ's resurrection makes him the first-fruits or *aparchē* of all who have died, and this generates a process that encompasses all other believers (1 Cor 15:20, 23). For another pastoral theologian, Jesus is the first-born of all creation (Col 1:15) as well as the first-born from the dead (Col 1:18).

Those who share the first-fruits of the Spirit are organically related to all of creation, and pray with longing for an eventual redemption of the body (Rom 8:22-24). In speaking to Gentile converts, Paul refers to his own Jewish community which has made everyone else holy, since they are like the first-fruit offering of a batch of dough that consecrates all the rest of the dough (Rom 11:16; Num 15:18-21; Neh 10:37). Paul celebrates his success with the Greeks by calling a convert "first-fruits" (Rom 16:5). The community born from the preaching of the truth is made up of believers who are the first-fruits of God's creatures (Jas 1:18).

Pastoral-Liturgical Tradition

The theme of the first-born reflects a male-oriented culture, and illustrates the secondary status of women in the biblical tradition. The importance of first-born women, such as Miriam, sister of Moses (Exod 2:7; 6:20; Num 12:1-16) is suppressed in the transmission of the biblical narrative. The issue of determining who is truly the first born son of Abraham lies at the heart of Paul's pastoral struggle in Galatians to provide biblical justification for calling Gentiles inheritors of God's promises along with the Jews. He offers a multi-leveled allegory on the difference between the slave Hagar's son, Ishmael, and the free woman Sarah's son, Isaac (Gal 4:21-31; Gen 16:1-16; 21:1-21). Gentiles are related to Abraham and Sarah because, like Isaac, they are children of the promise. They are truly heirs of Abraham through their faith in Jesus. They enjoy freedom from literal observance of Mosaic Law.

Unfortunately, aspects of Paul's complex reasoning about who is first-born have been used to support a supercessionist theology that regards Judaism as inferior to Christianity. The tendency to assert the superior status of Christianity can be reinforced by an unhistorical reading of many NT passages, including Hebrews. The Jewish-Christian pastor, wanting to encourage his community (Heb 13:22), regards Jesus as the personification of Wisdom, the full manifestation of God's glory (Heb 1:1-3). Jesus has the status of God's first-born son (Heb 1:6). Jesus, the new High Priest, mediates a new covenant in the presence of the firstborn enrolled in heaven (Heb 12:22-24). There is need to acknowledge the historical fact of alienation between the larger Jewish community and the Jewish-Christians who felt shamed and reproached by rejection of their views (Heb 13:13-14). However, this historical moment is not normative for defining present relations between Judaism and Christianity.

Vatican II in *Nostra Aetate* (1965) challenged older supercessionist views and acknowledged the integrity of God's covenant with the Jewish people. This ecumenical vision has been foundational for improved Christian-Jewish relations. Such a corrected perspective becomes vital in preaching on the Passion narrative, especially during the services of Holy Week.

See: BLESSING, CONSECRATION, COVENANT, ELEC-
TION, HOLY/HOLINESS

MARIE-ELOISE ROSENBLATT, R.S.M.

FLESH

The Bible shows little interest in a philosophical diagnosis of human beings and
even less of an interest in flesh as a medical
or anatomical part. "Flesh" represents an
acute observation of how human beings
act, especially of the deep conflict going on
inside. Good and evil were not abstractions; they were actions that could be seen.
Flesh could be a symbol term for good or
bad actions; all flesh could worship God,
but flesh could also war against the spirit.
The flesh is the battleground; the victory
comes when the Word becomes flesh. It is
against such a background of clashing
human drives that the word flesh must
be understood in its biblical sense. The
Pastoral-Liturgical tradition reflects ambivalence toward the flesh despite belief in
the incarnation.

Old Testament

The basic attitudes of the biblical people
toward life were grounded largely in their
creation stories. God made Adam out of
the clay of the ground and blew into his
nostrils the breath of life, and so he became a living being (Gen 2:7). Later "the
man called his wife Eve, because she became the mother of all the living" (Gen
3:20). The earthy origin stresses the unity
of us all.

In the biblical world "flesh and bone" becomes the most appropriate way of expressing kinship. "All flesh" is an appropriate
way of saying "all of us." It can embrace not
only humans, but all living things—the angels (Ezek 10:12) as well as the sacrificial
animals to whom it is often applied. It is
also the final way of referring to the total
human being. When Satan in the story of
Job proposes the final test, he suggests to
God: "put forth your hand and touch his
bone and his flesh, and surely he will blaspheme you to your face" (Job 2:5).

The psalms are particularly conscious of
this fleshly concern. Worship had to be a
fleshly response in a definite place.

> My soul yearns and pines
> for the courts of the LORD.
> My heart and my flesh
> cry out for the living God
> (Ps 84:2).

Even the weakness of the flesh had its
place. "To you all flesh must come because
of wicked deeds" (Ps 65:3). The flesh was
mortal and trembled before God (Ps
119:120). Yet there was a confidence that
even flesh would somehow survive death
and not undergo corruption (Ps 16:9). Job in
his extremity knows this and calls upon his
vindicator that "from my flesh I shall see
God" (Job 19:26).

Ezekiel sees the conversion of his own
people to true worship in terms of a "fleshly
heart." "I will give them a new heart and
put a new spirit within them; I will remove
the stony heart from their bodies, and replace it with a natural heart" (Ezek 11:19). In
the Hebrew text the word for natural is
fleshly. Ezekiel likes the thought so much
that he repeats it in 36:26.

It is this understanding of the flesh (or the
body, which often means the same) that
makes it a battleground. As we see life, God
is battling a cosmic evil. Isaiah announces
the great judgment scene of the contest between Yahweh and the pagan gods to explain events. "A voice says, 'Cry out!' I
answer, 'What shall I cry out?' 'All mankind
[flesh] is grass, and all their glory like the
flower of the field'" (Isa 40:6). So be it; no
one can explain it; God must make the victory of justice come about in the flesh.

Flesh in the OT is the link that we have
with the earth, with each other, and eventually with God. The OT knows nothing of
an asceticism that punishes or down-
grades the body. The joys of eating and
drinking, of loving and begetting children,
of singing and dancing, are celebrated
often. Yet there is a realistic awareness that
flesh is mortal and subject to disorder. In

the long run, however, it is flesh that brings us back to God and to one another: "To you all flesh must come because of wicked deeds" (Ps 65:3).

New Testament

Flesh receives a profound new dignity in the NT when the Word became flesh, a truth which is most dramatically asserted in John (John 1:14). On the other hand, the battleground was revisited in the light of a new contemporary paganism. Hellenistic culture both exalted the flesh in art and games and entertainment and conversely despised it as inferior to soul or spirit.

John is especially aware of this antithesis between the flesh and the spirit. Jesus says to Nicodemus, "What is born of flesh is flesh and what is born of spirit is spirit" (John 3:6). Even more absolutely in the discourse on the bread of life he says to the disciples, "It is the spirit that gives life, while the flesh is of no avail" (John 6:63). To his opponents he says, "You judge by appearances [flesh], but I do not judge anyone" (John 8:15). In all these cases flesh stands for a human way of thinking. On the other hand he insists in the bread of life discourse that this bread is his flesh for the life of the world (John 6:51; see also 6:52-56). The repeated insistence on this precise word flesh leaves no doubt about its literal meaning.

Paul, however, is the principal agent for making the flesh a vital element in the explanation of redemption. The evil we were redeemed from was not some petty crime; it was the evil that lurked in the world. Flesh and spirit are not just opposites; they are mortal enemies. They fight within us. It is in Galatians that his insight becomes clear after he has argued that we were redeemed by faith, not by the Law, and then sees the practical consequence in the disagreement at hand. "For you were called for freedom, brothers. But do not use this freedom as an opportunity for the flesh; rather, serve one another through love. . . . I say, then: live by the Spirit and you will certainly not gratify the desire of the flesh. For

the flesh has desires against the Spirit, and the Spirit against the flesh; these are opposed to each other, so that you may not do what you want. . . . Now those who belong to Christ [Jesus] have crucified their flesh with its passions and desires" (Gal 5:13, 16-17, 24). The whole of Pauline theology is here.

The flesh is the attitude we take in thinking that we can accomplish happiness or responsible living by ourselves. Speaking of his own experience in Romans, Paul says, "For I know that good does not dwell in me, that is, in my flesh. The willing is ready at hand, but doing the good is not" (Rom 8:18-19). Even after his thanks for salvation at the end of the soliloquy, he adds: "Therefore, I myself, with my mind, serve the law of God but, with my flesh, the law of sin" (Rom 7:25). This is not simply fleshly lust of which he speaks; it is the law of doing it oneself that drives on this disorder.

Yet the redemption is at hand and wrought through the flesh. "For what the law, weakened by the flesh, was powerless to do, this God has done: by sending his own Son in the likeness of sinful flesh and for the sake of sin, he condemned sin in the flesh, so that the righteous decree of the law might be fulfilled in us, who live not according to the flesh but according to the spirit" (Rom 8:3-4).

So the redemption for Paul is something that was worked in the total Christ and which must affect us in the same way. The resurrection of the flesh is a necessity for both him and us. In his defense of the teaching on the bodily resurrection in 1 Corinthians 15, Paul insists first on the reality of Christ's resurrection with its redeeming value. The final victory over evil comes through the resurrection. "For just as in Adam all die, so too in Christ shall all be brought to life, but each in proper order" (1 Cor 15:22-23a). How this shall happen Paul confesses he does not know. But there are different kinds of bodies. "Not all flesh is the same, but there is one body for human beings, another kind of flesh for animals, another kind of flesh for birds, and another for fish. There are both heavenly bodies and earthly bodies, but the brightness of the heavenly is one kind and that of the earthly another" (1 Cor 15:39-40).

In the later Christian writings of the NT these ideas were taken for granted. The Letter to Timothy cites a Christian hymn: "Undoubtedly great is the mystery of devotion, who was manifested in the flesh, vindicated in the spirit, seen by angels, proclaimed to the Gentiles, believed in throughout the world, taken up in glory" (1 Tim 3:16). Redemption was not seen as redemption from the flesh or the suppression of our fleshly selves; rather it was seen as the great harmony of all things bringing us back into the original unity with God.

See: BLOOD, BODY, LIFE, SOUL, SPIRIT

JAMES A. FISCHER, C.M.

Pastoral-Liturgical Tradition

The complexity of attitudes toward the flesh that runs through both the OT and NT continues in the pastoral-liturgical tradition. While an emphasis on the incarnation* and its consequences has remained a constant theme in Christian theology and practice, there continues an ambivalence toward the flesh that has persisted into the present. More recent emphasis on a holistic attitude toward the body have attempted to integrate more fully the flesh and the spirit.

Historical Background. The significance of the Word become flesh is the key issue in early Christian controversies against such heresies as Gnosticism, which rejected the idea that the divine became incarnate. The affirmation at Chalcedon (451) that Jesus Christ was "true God and true man" remains the standard against which doctrinal statements about Christ are measured. Christ is also the model for humanity and the particular way in which he lived in the flesh has provided the inspiration for the celibate life as the highest form of Christian witness. Matthew 19:21 ("sell what you have and give it to the poor") was often cited as inspiration.

In addition, the influence of Greek thought in the early Church cannot be overstated. The neo-platonic ordering of the cosmos, with material reality existing as the result of a fall from divine grace, and the body's subordination to the soul, was powerfully influential in the development of a theology of the person and of Christian life. The monastic traditions provided models of the Christian life; by the fourth century, clerical celibacy had become the norm and virginity was praised as a higher calling than married life. Asceticism, the mortification of the flesh, became the means of disciplining the weak human body. In the thinking of Augustine (354–430), inspired by St. Paul, the sinfulness of humanity found itself in *concupiscence*, the lust of the flesh *against* the spirit. The idea that original sin was inherited through sexual intercourse remained predominant well into the twentieth century.

While the idea that the flesh is sinful in itself has always been judged as heretical, contrary to both the goodness of created reality and the incarnation, neither is the flesh seen as unambiguously good. Even before clerical celibacy became normative, sexual abstinence before celebrating Mass (for clergy) or receiving communion (for laity) was strongly encouraged. Fasting as a means of bodily mortification during certain liturgical seasons and before receiving the Eucharist has been a long-standing practice, although this has become less common in the present. These ascetic practices have been interpreted by some as signifying a hatred of the flesh, but a closer reading reveals more complex meanings: the need to discipline the often unruly body, the desire to imitate the life of Jesus, the desire to live a life contrary to secular culture. Alongside these practices of bodily mortification has been a profound respect for and appreciation of the body, found in commentaries on the Song of Songs, meditations on the suffering Christ, and admonitions to care for the poor and the oppressed.

This ambivalence toward the flesh was frequently expressed in a similarly ambivalent attitude toward women. A dualistic association of men with spirit and women with flesh has pervaded much of Christian spirituality. Women were able to achieve spiritual equality with men through denial of their capacity for childbearing, in becoming "spiritually male." The exclusion of women from liturgical leadership, while officially based in tradition, is also rooted in a long historical and psychological association of women with uncontrollable bodily functions and a fear of the flesh.

Contemporary Issues. The dualistic conception of the person as body and soul, or flesh and spirit, has, in the twentieth century, and especially in the light of Vatican II, given way to a more holistic understanding. Seeing the flesh as the primary location of sin, especially sexual sin, had the effect of implicitly denying the goodness of the flesh as created by God. In its emphasis on the dynamic relationship between Church and world, Vatican II sought to redefine the world and the flesh as the locus of revelation.

The changes in liturgical practice have been for many the most obvious of the fruits of Vatican II. The use of the vernacular language, the greater participation of the congregation in the liturgy, and the expansion of ministries to the laity are all in large part expressions of a renewed appreciation for the "fleshly" dimension of human existence. The importance of the sacraments and the visible community of the Church have always been hallmarks of the Roman Catholic tradition. The reform of the sacraments, emphasizing their connections with the stages of human life, and an understanding of the Church as "People of God" have served to reintegrate the spiritual with the material.

Contemporary spirituality has been profoundly affected by this renewed emphasis on the body. While the decline in vocations to vowed religious life may indicate to some a decline in the spiritual vitality of the Church, others would point to the growth in lay ministries and a renewed interest in spirituality among the laity as signs of a deeply incarnational religious conviction. In addition, the practices of other religious traditions in prayer and meditation, such as yoga, and those of secular culture on healthy living, have broadened the understanding of Christian spirituality to include the body in new ways.

Vatican II's turn to the world has also resulted in a greater concern for social justice. Liberation theology, whose concern is liberation from *all* forms of oppression—economic, racial, sexual, political—proclaims that care for the suffering flesh of humanity is central to the mission of Christianity in the world.

It should be clear from the above that the flesh is at the center of Christian life in the incarnation. Yet it is an ambiguous reality: mortal, beautiful, weak. The importance of the flesh for liturgy, spirituality, and the moral life is based in that paradox that God comes to us in the flesh, which is "folly to the Jews and a scandal to the Greeks."

See: BODY, SOUL, WOMAN/WOMEN

SUSAN A. ROSS

FLOOD

The narrative of a primordial flood not only preserves the memory of some disastrous deluge but also reminds believers that God's punishment can be quite severe in the face of grave sin. Because he was just, Noah* and all those with him in the ark were saved. The ark was to become a symbol of salvation in both Jewish and Christian tradition.

In the traditions of many early civilizations, a flood narrative was, in fact, the actual creation narrative. In these literatures, destructive waters was seen as the primeval flood and the individual saved from these waters was the first created human being. This understanding suggests that both the creation and the flood were regarded as primeval happenings, not as historical events. The same view is borne out in the biblical material. Present-day scholars agree that the narrative of the flood and the eventual recession of the waters also comprise a kind of creation story coming from the same theological tradition and highlighting much of the same theology as found in Genesis 1.

Ancient Israel's flood account contains some of the very vocabulary found in its creation report. For instance, the abyss was in place before God separated the waters (Gen 1:2). This same abyss burst open causing the flood (Gen 7:11), and was closed when God decreed its end (8:2). Both narratives mention a wind that swept over the cosmic abyss (1:1; 8:1). In both accounts, God intends that the animals "be fertile and multiply" (1:22; 8:17). Finally, the same blessing and a commission to rule over the animals is given to humankind in both passages (1:28; 9:1-2). These similarities suggest a correlation between the creation account and the story of the flood and strengthen the already accepted contention that the two narratives not only come from the same tradition but should be understood in relation to each other.

Literary studies have shown a correlation between the account of the creation and appointment of the world (see Gen 1:1–2:4a) and the construction and appointment of the wilderness sanctuary (see Exod 39:42–40:33). This point is further borne out by the fact that both the creation narrative and the list of stipulations regarding the sanctuary end with reference to the Sabbath, the sign of completion (see Gen 2:2–3; Exod 31:12–17). Characteristically, rest signifies the conclusion of creation. It indicates that the order established by God is permanent and will not be disturbed by some additional creative act. (Since in this tradition creation is really a primeval and not a historical event, it should not be perceived as ongoing.) By giving liturgical meaning to this rest, the writer not only took it out of the primeval realm but also invested the Sabbath with cosmic significance.

The flood was perceived as punishment for the "wickedness on earth" (6:5). The magnitude of devastation matches the gravity of human wickedness, for "no desire that [the human] heart conceived was ever anything but evil" (6:5). The Lord regretted having made humankind, and not only humankind, "but also the beasts and the creeping things and the birds of the air" (v. 7). One might wonder why the rest of the natural world had to suffer because of human iniquity. It was because the earth itself was defiled by the sinfulness of the people who lived on it (6:11-13). Just as creation included a triumph over primordial chaos and the subsequent ordering of the universe, so the return of primordial chaos (7:11) reversed the ordering of nature.

The biblical flood narrative is not merely a story of the return of primordial chaos; it is a story of deliverance. God directed Noah, the only one who found favor with the Lord, to build an ark so that he and his family and some of the animals might escape the punishing waters of the flood. Just as there is a correspondence between the creation and appointment of the universe and the construction and appointment of the wilderness sanctuary, so there are similarities between the protecting ark and the sanctuary. Both were constructed according to divine specifications. Furthermore, after the flood, the restored earth emerged on the first day of the liturgical year, the same day on which the sanctuary was established and consecrated (see Gen 8:13; Exod 40:2). Distinguishing between clean and unclean animals as they enter the ark (Gen 7:2-3) is a practice with obvious liturgical significance. Like the wilderness sanctuary, as well as the tabernacle and temple that eventually replaced it, the ark was a haven of purity and order in the midst of a world of defilement and chaos.

Much has been written about the covenant that God made with Noah (Gen 9:8-17). Actually, the covenant was between God and *all* living beings (vv. 9-10, 12, 15, 17) and between God and the earth (vv. 13, 16), not a divine covenant with human beings and through them with the rest of creation. The covenant was really a promise that chaotic waters would never again return to destroy, not merely human beings, but all of creation. The bow in the sky was an eternal sign of that promise, and it was a reminder to God, not to humankind. Since the ancient story of creation frequently included some kind of cosmic battle between chaos and a warrior god, the bow was probably a reference to the weapon of the divine warrior, who was victorious over the forces of primeval chaos. This interpretation is supported by several Mesopotamian artifacts depicting a creator god with arrows in a quiver. Hanging the bow in the sky would be a sign that the primeval war was over and that all of creation could rest secure. Like the divine rest after creation (Gen 2:2-3), retirement of the bow heralded the establishment of order.

The NT writers used the imagery and the theology of this account in their own Christian teaching. For them, the flood continued to be a symbol of divine punishment (see Matt 24:38-39; Luke 17:27). The focus there, however, is on the unexpected nature of its coming. Just as the women and men of Noah's time were taken by surprise, so will the sudden advent of the Son of Man find people unprepared. In a significantly different interpretation, the flood waters also prefigured the waters of baptism (1 Pet 3:21). Here the waters are neither punishment nor cleansing. They are a passage into a new life.

See: CREATION, NOAH

DIANNE BERGANT, C.S.A.

FOLLY

The English word folly is used to translate several uncomplimentary terms. These words are often used in the OT Wisdom literature to describe persons lacking wisdom and the senseless behavior of such persons. Folly is opposed to wisdom, and the fool is the reverse of the wise, upright, or prudent person. The type of behavior the fool engages in is usually seen as immoral or self-defeating. In the NT these words are used in a similar fashion. Immoral behavior and arrogant self-praise are seen as folly. However, one must admit to being a fool (i.e., without true wisdom) in order to be wise in God's sight.

Old Testament

In the OT wisdom and folly are essentially directed toward one's relationship with God, especially one's moral conduct. The wise are not necessarily intellectuals; they are religious individuals who live up to their obligations to God and their neighbors. The fool is not necessarily stupid; the fool simply refuses to serve God and by OT standards this is folly. Wise persons are seen as good and foolish ones as wicked. According to the wise, all people belong to one group or the other, for there is no middle ground.

An image that plays an important part in the vocabulary of Israel's sages is the path or way* to life.* Those who rely on their own ingenuity soon become hopelessly lost. The wise journey toward their ultimate destination with confidence that they will reach that place safely, whereas fools lose their way. In the Wisdom books the folly of pride, laziness, passion, deceit, gossip, etc., is often noted. These vices are opposed to virtues such as generosity, faithfulness, self-control, industry, and sobriety.

Because God is just, the righteousness of the wise must be rewarded and the evil actions of the fool must be punished. For the wisdom writer, as for most of the OT authors, there is no final judgment, therefore no reward or punishment, after death. What one discovers then is that virtue, with which wisdom is identified, brings reward in this life while folly brings punishment ("death," "the rod," "downfall," "trouble"). The author of Proverbs 1–9 describes the happy results of wisdom and the disastrous consequences of folly by opposing Wisdom, personified and divinized, to Dame Folly in three passages (1:20-33; 8:1-36; 9:1-6, 13-18). Because "the woman Folly is fickle, she is inane, and knows nothing" (Prov 9:13), individuals are urged to "forsake foolishness that you may live; advance in the way of understanding" (Prov 9:6).

The word folly, as noted above, is used to translate many different Hebrew words that occur most often in the Wisdom literature of ancient Israel. The range of meaning of these terms varies from the simply naive to the obstinate to the depraved person or individual characterized by irrational madness. While most individuals who engage in folly are beyond help, the folly of a naive, untutored individual is seen as a challenge. This individual can still be influenced for good. "Forsake foolishness that you may live; advance in the way of understanding" (Prov 9:6). A person characterized by obstinacy can also change. "Folly is close to the heart of a child, but the rod of discipline will drive it far from him" (Prov 22:15).

At times folly is attributed to the fact that one is innately stupid. "As a dog returns to his vomit, so the fool repeats his folly" (Prov 26:11). More often, however, it is seen as the intentional, evil behavior of God's enemies. An extreme type of fool combines folly and wickedness. This person is a source of contention in society, hates correction, and would be unable to find wisdom even if it were sought. "Beyond intrigue and folly and sin, it is arrogance that men find abominable" (Prov 24:9).

In the OT there is a contrast between God and God's wisdom and the fool and his folly. "The fool says in his heart, 'There is no God'" (Ps 14:1). It never crosses the fool's mind that "the beginning of wisdom is fear of the LORD" (Prov 9:10).

New Testament

In the Synoptic Gospels, as in the OT, folly is used to refer to immoral behavior. In Mark 7:22 the term folly appears last in a list of evil acts or vices that come from within a person and serve to defile that person. It is usually understood as referring to the stupidity of the individual who lacks moral judgment.

In Matthew 7:26 one finds emphasis on the importance of moral behavior consistent with the teaching of Jesus. Those who listen to Jesus but do not act on his words are called fools. Likewise, those who invert the order of values by their teaching are seen as fools (Matt 23:17). The familiar biblical contrast between folly and wisdom is found in Matthew 25:2, 3, 8. The foolish virgins are those who failed to exhibit the constant watchfulness demanded by the coming of the "son of man" and are seen as short-sighted and foolish.

In Luke 11:40 Jesus refers to the Pharisees as fools because of their false piety. They are filled with pride and self-importance, concerned with outward purity but ignoring inward greed and covetousness. The parable of the rich fool (Luke 12:16-21) indicates that one who has a true sense of values realizes that life is not measured in terms of possessions. It is folly to prepare for one's own comfort but not for one's ultimate destiny. The rich man is implicitly depicted as selfishly enjoying his riches without thought for his needy neighbors or concern about God. Such an attitude is folly in the eyes of God.

The wisdom/folly contrast is found also in 1 Corinthians 1:18-31 where Paul writes about the "foolishness of God." What God has done in Christ crucified is a direct contradiction of human ideas of wisdom and power, yet it achieved what human wisdom and power fail to achieve. True wisdom is to be found paradoxically where one would least expect to find it. Those individuals who are arrogant and self-assertive, wise in their own eyes and in the eyes of the world, are seen as fools. "For the foolishness of God is wiser than human wisdom" (1 Cor 1:25) and "the wisdom of this world is foolishness in the eyes of God" (1 Cor 3:19). One must become foolish by worldly standards in order to be wise in a Christian sense (1 Cor 4:10).

In 2 Corinthians 11:1–12:13 Paul speaks about foolish boasting. Within this section one finds the repetition of key words; fool (11:16, 17, 19, 21; 12:6, 11), foolish (11:16), and foolishness (11:1). Paul sees this arrogant self-praise, in which one claims to live and be saved by one's own resources, as a radical sin. While self-praise was viewed negatively by the OT (e.g., Prov 27:2; Jer 9:22-23), by NT times certain types of self-praise (e.g., defending one's good name) were considered acceptable. Paul admits that he acts the fool by engaging in self-praise; however, given the position of his opponents, this tactic appears to have been necessary. Paul contrasts arrogant self-praise with boasting in the Lord, which is to acknowledge that we live only from God and for God.

See: JUDGMENT, LIFE, POWER, WAY, WISDOM

DENNIS M. SWEETLAND

FRIENDSHIP

Friendship as a treasured human experience and as a way of describing the relationship between God and humanity has deep roots within the biblical and Christian tradition.

Old Testament

General. The Bible touches on friends and friendship mainly in passing, without extended investigation or reflection. Individual human friendships are spoken of, friendship in the vertical dimension (divine-human) is acknowledged, and the Wisdom writers offer sage advice about making, keeping, and treating friends. Friendship and love can be closely related and this is reflected in Hebrew terminology. One of the terms for "friend" is 'oheb, the active participle of the verb "to love"; the root covers a broad spectrum, being used to refer to the physical and affectionate aspects of love, as well as to friendship in the broader, more platonic sense. This corresponds fairly well to the common Greek terms for "love" (*philein*) and "friend" (*philos*). The most common Hebrew term for friend, *rea*ʿ, suggests the idea of companionship but also a broader range of meanings. Usually these two terms have more or less the same meaning: *rea*ʿ is used of Job's friends (Job 2:11; 16:20; 19:21; etc.), 'oheb of Haman's (Esth 5:10, 14; 6:13); and the terms

sometimes appear in close conjunction or in parallel (cf. Ps 38:12; 88:19; Lam 1:2). Other terms used may not denote any particular closeness; in many texts "associate," "neighbor," or "fellow" would be equally appropriate translations.

David and Jonathan. The best example of a close personal friendship is that between David and Jonathan. It is said that Jonathan "loved [David] as he loved himself" (1 Sam 18:1). They entered into a covenant, and Jonathan gave David articles of clothing and his weapons as a sign of friendship. When Saul turned against David, Jonathan supported him against his father (19:1-7; 20:1–21:1). When Jonathan and Saul were killed in battle with the Philistines, David composed a beautiful elegy in which he extolled their bravery and spoke movingly of his love for Jonathan and grief at his death (2 Sam 1:19-27).

Friend of God. Abraham, Israel's great ancestor, is referred to in two late texts as God's friend (2 Chr 20:7 and Isa 41:8—'oheb in each case) and, in the Greek addition to Daniel of the Septuagint, as "your beloved" (Dan 3:35). This terminology suggests God's love for him and may indicate why God's choice fell on him. Of Moses, Israel's great leader and law-giver, it is said that God spoke to him face to face "as one man speaks to another [his friend]" (Exod 33:11, where the term is *rea*ʿ). While this metaphorical description of God's manner of dealing with Moses stops short of calling him God's friend, it suggests an intimate relationship. Sirach says of Moses that he was dear to God and to people (Sir 45:1).

Practical Advice. The Wisdom writers show themselves somewhat cautious on the subject of friendship and sometimes even a little cynical. There is danger in going surety for a friend (Prov 6:1-5; 17:18; Sir 29:16-20); the rich and generous are sure to have many friends (Prov 14:20; 19:4, 6) and their experience is much different than that of the poor (Prov 19:7; Sir 13:20); some people make fickle friends (Sir 6:8-10; 37:1-2, 4). Nevertheless, friendship is to be valued. Sirach, in particular, has lengthy passages offering detailed advice about dealing with friends. New ones should be put to the test before being trusted (Sir 6:7, 13), but a true friend is a treasure beyond price (6:14-16), an ally in time of struggle (37:5-6); depth of commitment is revealed in time of adversity, when true friends stand fast and false ones fall away (Prov 17:17; 18:24; Sir 12:8-9; 22:23). A good friend should be clung to (Prov 27:10; Sir 9:10). Wisdom dictates that a friend be one like oneself (Sir 13:14-15), especially in being one who fears God (Sir 6:17; 9:15-16; 37:12).

New Testament

General. The term most often translated "friend" in English is *philos*, but it occurs not at all in Mark and only once in Matthew—although Matthew uses another term (*hetairos*, which more properly means "companion" or "comrade") three times: twice in parables and once for Jesus' address to Judas in Gethsemane (Matt 26:50). In Luke it is more frequent, being used in Jesus' parables, in which examples of behavior common among friends illustrate Jesus' teachings (e.g., the parable of "the friend at midnight" [11:5-8] and of the lost sheep and lost coin [15:3-10]). Outside the parables Luke quotes Jesus as telling us that we should invite the poor to our banquets rather than friends who will repay us (Luke 14:12-14) and warning that his followers will be betrayed by their friends (Luke 21:16). John uses the term half a dozen times, often in very important contexts (see below).

Friends of Jesus in the Synoptics. Of special interest is the sort of people Jesus made his friends. A constant accusation on the part of Jesus' adversaries was his companionship with those known as sinners and those who did not observe the Mosaic Law (Matt 9:10-13; 11:19—Matthew's only use of *philos;* Mark 2:15-17; Luke 5:29-32; 7:34; 15:1-2; 19:7). While accusations may have been prompted by hostility and envy, there is little doubt that Jesus accepted table fel-

lowship with people despised by others. It was such accusations that prompted some of his parables of mercy. Jesus graciously received women into his company, and the "ministering women" who followed him are frequently mentioned (Matt 27:55-56; Mark 15:40-41; Luke 8:2-3; 23:49, 55-56); he received with kindness the sinful woman (Luke 7:36-50) and the Samaritan woman (John 4:7-42). In all of this Jesus was setting an example of loving behavior for his disciples and his future Church.

John. It is especially John who develops the nature of the relationship between Jesus and his disciples and others. At the Last Supper Jesus calls the Twelve his friends, indicates that he is to lay down his life for them, thus giving the highest proof of love possible, distinguishes their relationship with him from that of master and slave, and reminds them that he had chosen them and not the other way around; he exhorts them to imitate him in manifesting toward one another the love he has manifested toward them (15:9-17). Jesus refers to Lazarus as "our friend" and is said to love him, as well as his sisters, Mary and Martha (11:3, 5, 11, 36). The one disciple especially beloved of Jesus is never named but stands as representative of every faithful disciple (13:23; 19:26; 20:2; 21:7, 20).

See: ABRAHAM, APOSTLE, DISCIPLE, LOVE, MOSES, NEIGHBOR, WOMAN/WOMEN

JOSEPH JENSEN, O.S.B.

Pastoral-Liturgical Tradition

The status of friendship in the Christian life results from being created in the image of a God whose very life is a community of friendship love called Trinity. The doctrine of the Trinity tells us that God is a community of persons who love one another with the benevolence and reciprocity constitutive of friendship. In God person *is* community inasmuch as Father, Son, and Spirit are identified through the relationship each has with the other. The Trinitarian life of God demonstrates that God lives because God loves, and the same will be true for us who are God's images; thus, we have life as God has life, through relationships of love that establish and sustain community. In this respect, the rationale for friendship in the Christian life is derived from an analogy between the divine nature and human nature, which argues that we are most genuinely human when we do in our life what God does in the divine life. For us to live is for us to image God, and we best image God when we make of our life a community of friendship love in which good will and affection are given and received. Consequently, friendship is central to the Christian life, first because, like God, love is in our nature and is our most perfecting activity, and second because like God we are inherently relational. Friendship is indispensable to our humanity because human existence does not precede relationships, but is constituted by relationships; friendship matters because it is only through love that we live.

Distinguishing Marks of Friendship. Friendship is love, but not every love is friendship. The love that is friendship is defined by three characteristics: benevolence or well-wishing, mutuality or reciprocity, and the capacity to look upon the friend as another self, a capacity derived from participating in the good upon which a friendship is based. The first mark of friendship is benevolence. Benevolence is not only wishing others well, but actively seeking their good. A friend is one who wants what is best for another precisely because he or she loves the other. Friendship reverses the direction of love's concern. Its interest is not one's own pleasure, but the happiness and well-being of the friend. With benevolence the strategy of friendship is to find one's own good through devotion to the good of another. Friendship is a way of life in which two or more people work for each other's well-being and are dedicated to prospering one another's good.

Benevolence is necessary for friendship but not sufficient. To be friendship, the good will one offers another must be returned in kind. Friendship is mutual or reciprocal love in which each person knows the good they offer another is also the good the other wishes for them. This second characteristic of friendship attests that friends are those who recognize each other's love and share it, the exchange of which is the soul of the relationship.

Finally, because friendships are relationships established and sustained by persons who enrich one another in the good or purpose which is the center of the friendship, eventually each friend sees the other as "another self." The third mark of friendship is that through the love that bonds the friends, each becomes like the other not only in interests and ideals, but also in goodness and character. Friends see one another as "another self" because through their friendship they are shaped and identified by the good that forms their relationship; thus, through the life of the friendship each comes to see the other as a reflection or "mirror image" of oneself. This does not mean that the friends become identical, for indeed we can only have a friendship with someone who is other, but that delighting in a shared good makes possible the union of hearts that is friendship's perfection. What friendship achieves is not an identity of selves, but the most genuine differentiation fostered by a love for the most genuine good.

The Three Types of Friendship. Following Aristotle (386–322 BCE), three kinds of friendship have been identified, each defined by what attracts persons and binds them together in friendship. There are friendships of usefulness or advantage, friendships of pleasure, and friendships of virtue or character. Friendships of usefulness describe relationships formed around tasks or projects in which each person is useful to the other and needs the other. An example of a friendship of usefulness would be relationships we have with people with whom we work. There are clear limits and well-defined expectations in the relationship and it normally ends when the work project is completed. Friendships of pleasure are relationships we have with people with whom we enjoy doing things, such as going to the theater or hobbies. While it is true that relationships based on goodness or virtue are friendships in the best sense, friendships of usefulness and pleasure are necessary ingredients to a balanced and healthy life; indeed, not every relationship could sustain the intensity and depth of virtue friendships.

Still, friendships based on virtue have the highest moral value because the center of the friendship is mutual love for the most excellent goods, especially the goodness of God, and the activity of the friendship is the development and enhancement of virtue in the friends. Such relationships are integral to the Christian moral life because we cannot become good without them; in fact, it is in such relationships that we are trained and tutored in the virtues. We need friends not only as the people with whom we learn and practice virtue, but also as the people in company with whom we are formed in the good. This is why friendship is not just a relationship, but a moral enterprise. Friendships of virtue are born from a mutual love for the most noble goods, and their purpose is to be the context within which those who are devoted to the good seek it for one another and thus are transfigured in goodness themselves.

Friendship in the Christian Tradition. Within the Christian tradition, there have been two very different responses regarding the value and fittingness of friendship. The first, represented foremost by Soren Kierkegaard (1813–1855 CE) and Anders Nygren (1890–1978 CE), is most often associated with Protestant theologians who charge that friendship is at odds with the distinctively Christian love of agape because friendship is a preferential love based on an attraction we feel for some but not for others, and agape is a universal love open to everyone, a love not motivated by consideration of what might be lovable or attractive in another, and not dependent on

reciprocity. From this perspective, friendship may remain a necessary good in a flourishing life, but it is not a specifically Christian good; indeed, in light of the qualities of agape, the love of friendship is inherently lacking.

A second strand in the Christian tradition, exemplified by Augustine (354–430 CE) and Aelred of Rievaulx (1110–1167 CE), sees friendship not in antithesis to agape, but the relationship in which Christian love is learned. In this approach, friends are brought together by a mutual love for God and a desire to follow Christ, and their friendship is the setting in which they learn the ways of God and imitate the love of Christ; in short, friendships centered in Christ are not impediments to agape, but schools of discipleship in which the friends learn to love all whom God loves, even their enemies.

This is evident in Augustine's explication of friendship. He argued that the author and giver of friendships is God; we do not choose our friends, God does, which is why every friend is both the gift and the work of God's love. For Augustine, friends are brought together by God to help one another seek God and return to God. Divine gifts, they represent the very concrete and personal way God loves and redeems. Furthermore, Augustine reasoned that every genuine friendship ought to be modeled on the Trinitarian friendship of God. The friendship between Father, Son, and Spirit is the grace in which authentic friendship is rooted, the love to which it must conform, and the community in which it is perfected. This is why Augustine concluded that what distinguishes Christian friendships is that they are means of growing together in the love of God. Far from being hindrances to Christian love, they are centers of conversion in which Christians move to God by being transformed in their mutual love for Christ.

A similar approach is taken by the twelfth-century Cistercian monk, Aelred of Rievaulx. In his *Spiritual Friendship*, Aelred speaks of Christ as a partner to every genuine friendship and says the friends reach fullness of life in God through their discipleship friendship in Christ. Spiritual friendship is Christocentric because the friends journey to God through the friendship they have with one another in Christ; it is the history of their friendship in Christ that makes possible their union with God. Lastly, for Aelred the union of the friends in Christ prefigures the union of all humanity in God. In Christian friendship, preference signals not a narrowing of one's world, but an endless extension of it as one learns to love all those loved by God. This is why Aelred held that in the love Christians have for one another, they see the kingdom fellowship to which God's love inexorably tends, that community of perfect love in which each beholds the other as God does, and where the happiness of one is the happiness of all. Thus, the reign of God is not the end of spiritual friendship but its fulfillment; indeed, it is a community of perfect friendship, humanity of one heart and mind with God.

It was Thomas Aquinas (1225–1274 CE), however, who radicalized the notion of friendship by speaking of it not only as a relationship we have with other people, but also as the relationship we are called to have with God. For him, to be Christian is to live in friendship with God and to consider this extraordinary possibility the ordinary way of understanding our lives. In his *Summa Theologiae*, Aquinas identifies charity as the central virtue and core activity of the Christian life, and defines it as a "certain friendship with God" which is "begun here in this life by grace, but will be perfected in the future life by glory" (S.Th., I–II, 65, 5). For Aquinas, the Christian life is meant to be an ever deepening friendship with a God who is our happiness, a relationship of love given and love received, a sharing in which we delight in God and God delights in us.

Too, for Aquinas charity is not only a means to happiness, but is the life of happiness because friendship with God is the relationship through which men and women reach the highest possible development proper to a human being. Thomas reasoned that happiness is not so much a state, but whatever activity brings men and women to the fullness for which they were created. Charity-friendship with God is happiness because it is precisely the love relationship by which union with God is achieved; in short, charity is not something other than happiness, but is the way of life that is happiness.

Finally, for Aquinas charity is beatitude because it is the love that works the changes essential for redemption. Every love changes us, but charity changes us unto God. We cannot love God and remain the same, and that is our hope. As Thomas saw it, to love God in charity is to become like God in goodness. There is a terrible vulnerability to any love because to love is to become like the one we love; indeed, it is to lose one kind of self and take on another. Nowhere is this transformation more drastic than in charity, for charity fosters a vulnerability to God so exhaustive that we ultimately become one with God.

Pastoral Applications. Friendship is central to the Christian life not only because the social nature of existence requires that we find life in relationship to others, but more pointedly because we are to model in our lives the friendship love we see in God. In this respect, the Church is to be a community of friends whose lives are centered on "the love of God poured out in our hearts" (Rom 5:5). This demands an understanding of friendship and an appreciation for the skills of achieving it that are far more profound than the rather trivial notions of friendship dominant in society; in this sense, Christian friendship is countercultural. Since the quality and depth of any friendship depends on the kind of good on which the friendship is based, the Church needs to show that friendships centered on Christ have the utmost moral and spiritual possibilities, and needs to witness what counts as genuine friendship and the commitment and skill required for sustaining it.

Finally, the Eucharist is pivotal for nurturing the community of Christian friendship. Most importantly, the Eucharist commemorates the befriending activity of God throughout history, principally in Christ and the Spirit, and testifies that even though we often reject God's offer of friendship, "God does not abandon us to the power of death," but constantly reaches out in covenant that this friendship may be restored (Eucharistic Prayer IV). The Eucharist is a people's grateful praise for the sacrificial love by which lost friendship is healed: "Therefore we offer you, God ever faithful and true, the sacrifice which restores us to your friendship" (Eucharistic Prayer of Reconciliation I). The Eucharist is a community's ritual activity in which the virtues of Christian friendship are learned and acquired. Growth in virtue occurs through the relationships we have with people who are one with us in what we consider important. At Eucharist we gather with all those who see in the breaking of the bread how we slowly come to embody the love in which we are completed. The Eucharist is the primary sacrament of Christian friendship because it teaches that such love is not something we can offer ourselves, but is the gift we can only receive from a God whose love continually offers it.

See: COMMUNITY, FRIENDSHIP, LOVE

PAUL J. WADELL, C.P.

FRUITS OF THE SPIRIT

In this entry on fruits of the Spirit there will also be a discussion of virtues and vices. The combination of these two themes is warranted because of the close proximity of both themes in select biblical texts. The classic reference for a listing of the fruits of the Spirit is Galatians 5:22, where love, peace, and joy are the first three of nine fruits identified. These fruits of the Spirit are also characteristically called a "catalog" of virtues. In the immediately preceding verses (Gal 5:19-21) there is a catalog of "works of the flesh," which can aptly be labeled vices. The vices mentioned include impurity, idolatry, rivalry, envy, and the like. In general the biblical writers say relatively little about virtue or the virtues beyond an occasional listing of qualities which later Christian tradition has identified or classified as virtues.

The term "virtue" is the translation for the Greek *aretē*, which broadly means excellence of any kind, whether that of a person, animal, or a thing. For instance, virtue can refer to the sharpness of a knife, the swiftness of a runner, or the bravery of a warrior. Applied to persons, virtues refer in a more particular sense to specific moral habits or practical skills of the good life, as well as to dispositions that help mold character. Perhaps the wide spectrum and lack of precision of *aretē* in the Greek world contributed to the sparse use of the concept in the NT. *Aretē* is found in only four NT texts where it is variously translated "excellence" (Phil 4:8), "praises" (1 Pet 2:9), "power" (2 Pet 1:3), and "virtue" (2 Pet 1:5).

After a rather brief paragraph on the connotations of fruit in the OT, the theme of fruits (of the Spirit) will be explored in the NT where it is more extensively utilized. It is also in the NT where the few catalogs of virtues and vices, typical of Greek philosophy, especially the late Stoic school, are found. Much more attention has been given to the virtues and vices in the pastoral and liturgical tradition. Up until modern times efforts have been made to categorize and to prioritize them. In the Vatican II documents the virtuous life was addressed as the universal call to holiness of all the faithful, each according to his or her vocation.

Old Testament

Fruits as Produce or Offspring. In the OT the literal use of fruit is common enough. Fruits from the land of Canaan are brought to Moses as a sign of its fertility (Num 13:27; Deut 1:25). In favorable conditions the rain and soil yield produce; plants and trees bear fruit (Deut 11:17; see Lev 25:3; Ezek 36:8). In an analogous way, children are called the fruit of the body. They are the "fruit of the womb" (Gen 30:2), and as such a "gift from the Lord" (Ps 127:3; see Ps 132:11; Isa 13:18; Luke 1:42).

Fruits Used in a Symbolic Sense. A more symbolic usage comes into play with the frequent occurrence of fruit to designate the results or consequences of one's actions. The words of people have their fruit (Prov 12:14). In several instances fruit represents the divine judgment brought to bear on human actions. The Lord "rewards everyone according to his ways, according to the merit [lit. "fruit"] of his deeds" (Jer 17:10). The wayward are those who have eaten the "fruit of falsehood" (Hos 10:13). On a theological level, creation itself is portrayed as fruit of the divine: "The earth is replete with the fruit of your [God's] works" (Ps 104:13). Also, divine justice is presented as having its fruit (Amos 6:12). Correspondingly, on a human level, fruits, understood as the results of one's activity, are subject to God's scrutiny. The fruits produced lead to either reward or punishment. On a divine level, the fruits of God in creation are to lead to praise.

Virtues and Vices. Over half of the occurrences of virtue in the OT are found in Proverbs and Ezekiel. Virtue is the opposite of doing evil or iniquity (Prov 18:26). Virtue saves the upright person from death (Prov 10:2; 11:4, 6), exalts a nation (Prov 14:34), enables a person to save him/herself, though not others (Ezek 14:14, 20), brings continued life (Ezek 18:22), and provides an unforgettable example to others (2 Macc 6:31; see Sir 44:10). The person who pursues virtue is loved by the Lord (Prov 15:9), and is rewarded on the basis of his/her virtue (2 Chr 6:23). The virtuous wife is acclaimed as being the source of the "radiance of her home" (Sir 26:16). A virtuous name will never be annihilated (Sir 41:11). However, "if a virtuous man turns away from virtue and does wrong . . . he shall die . . . and his virtuous deeds shall not be remembered" (Ezek 3:20). Finally, the mention of virtue is combined with the image of fruit in Proverbs 11:30: "The fruit of virtue is a tree

of life." A familiar theme throughout Proverbs 11 and other OT passages is that virtue is its own reward, vice its own punishment. The life of the virtuous is an example for others; such a life is remembered, rewarded, and loved by the Lord.

If virtue brings life, vice brings death, as the psalmist dramatically affirms: "Vice slays the wicked" (Ps 34:22). The only other OT text where the NAB uses vice is Sirach 10:13, where pride is named a reservoir of sin, "a source which runs over with vice."

An important text identifying what were later called the four cardinal virtues is Wisdom 8:7. For the person who loves justice, "the fruits of her works are virtues; for she teaches moderation and prudence, justice and fortitude." This fourfold grouping goes at least as far back as Plato.

New Testament

Bearing Good Fruit, a Sign of Conversion and Discipleship. Both the literal and the figurative use of fruit carry over into the NT. Here attention will be on the latter. Starting with Matthew, one notices that the judgment theme predominates. Evidence for one's *metanoia* (or repentance) is to be found in the "good fruit" one produces, as John the Baptist emphasizes (Matt 3:8). On the other hand, "bad fruits" are signs of non-repentance (3:10) and false prophets (7:15-20). "By their fruits you will know them" (7:20; see 12:33). As the value of a tree is manifest by the quality of its produce, so too the authenticity of one's conversion is displayed by the acts or fruits a person produces.

The inner power enabling a person to bear good fruit is spelled out figuratively by the "vine and branches" imagery in John 15, and literally by the expression "fruits of the Spirit" in Paul. In John 15:1-2 the Johannine Jesus identifies himself with the true vine that enables all those branches remaining in him to bear fruit. "Just as a branch cannot bear fruit on its own unless it remains on the vine, so neither can you unless you remain in me" (John 15:4). John also emphasizes that faithful discipleship, particularly losing one's life for Christ, produces fruit. Using an analogy from nature, Jesus lays down a radical condition for the disciple: "Unless a grain of wheat falls to the ground and dies, it remains just a grain of wheat; but if it dies it produces much fruit" (John 12:24).

The Fruits of the Spirit Listed. Paul not only names the power, namely the Spirit, empowering the believer to bear fruit, he also specifies the kind of fruit the Spirit-filled person produces. In Galatians 5:19-22 he contrasts sharply two kinds of deeds: the works of the flesh and the fruits of the Spirit. Those controlled by such vices as hatred, jealousy, drinking bouts, and orgies fall under an eschatological warning. They will not inherit the reign of God. On the other hand those who live in the Spirit are freed from the desires of the flesh and belong to Christ. The expression "reign of God," frequently found in the Synoptics, but rarely in Paul, suggests that Paul is employing early Christian catechetical teaching.

Named as fruits of the Spirit, a concept unique in Paul, are nine qualities (not an exclusive list): love, joy, peace, patience, kindness, generosity, faithfulness, gentleness, and self control. These are identified as fruits because they are benefits given by the Spirit to those who belong to Christ. The common source of these fruits also highlights their unity. Though these benefits are also called virtues by later Christian tradition, they are not to be understood in the Greek sense as qualities of personal behavior that can be chosen and appropriated, nor are they good deeds in the sense of Jewish ethics. Instead, they are benefits or gifts. A close analogy to Paul's "fruits of the Spirit" is the Philonic expression "fruits of the soul," referring to virtues, and the Philonic definition: "the contemplative life is a fruit of knowledge."

Love, the First of the Fruits, the Greatest Gift. Love, the first of the fruits mentioned, is acclaimed in 1 Corinthians 13 as the "greatest of these" (faith, hope, and love). The three gifts are classified in later Chris-

tian tradition as the three theological virtues. Paul enlarges upon the divine origin of love in Romans 5:5: "The love of God has been poured out into our hearts through the Holy Spirit that has been given to us."

The Virtues Bring God's Peace. Another list of virtues, typical of late Stoic philosophy, is found in Philippians 4:8-9. In this passage, the only Pauline use of the Greek *aretē* (virtue), translated by "excellence," is found. "Whatever is true, whatever is honorable, whatever is just, whatever is pure, whatever is lovely, whatever is gracious, if there is any excellence [*aretē*] and if there is anything worthy of praise, think about these things." For the person who does these things, Paul writes, "the God of peace [the third fruit mentioned in Gal 5:22] will be with you" (Phil 4:9). By using concepts typical of Stoic philosophy, and hence familiar to the Philippians, Paul exhorts them at least to live up to the ideals of their fellow citizens. It is not so much the content of the virtues themselves, but the motivation and the benefit, namely God's peace, which are more specifically Christian. This passage suggests that the social context is one locus which determines for the individual or community what it is that is virtuous.

Beyond the Pauline literature, another list of virtues, beginning with faith and culminating with love, is given in 2 Peter 1:5-7: "Make every effort to supplement your faith with virtue [*aretē*], virtue with knowledge, knowledge with self-control, self-control with endurance, endurance with devotion, devotion with mutual affection, mutual affection with love." The fruitfulness of these virtues is knowledge of Christ (1:8), their absence is spiritual blindness (1:9). See also Ephesians 5:9 where the "fruitless works of darkness" are contrasted with light which "produces [lit. "the fruit of light is . . ."] every kind of goodness and righteousness and truth."

The Vices Listed and the Consequences. Lists of vices, a common feature of Hellenistic Judaism, occur frequently in a variety of

Pauline contexts (1 Cor 5:9-11; 6:10-11; 2 Cor 12:20-21; Gal 5:9-21; Rom 1:29-31; Col 3:5, 8; Eph 5:3-5; 1 Tim 1:9-11; 2 Tim 3:2-5; Titus 3:3; see also Matt 7:21-22; 1 Pet 2:1; 4:3; Rev 21:8; 22:15). The variety of vices among the lists shows that Paul does not intend to be either systematic or exhaustive. A sampling of vices/evildoers mentioned are unnatural relations between those of the same sex (Rom 1:26-27), greed, murder, envy, gossip (Rom 1:29), robbers, idolaters (1 Cor 5:9), slanderers, drunkards (1 Cor 5:11), fornicators, adulterers, boy prostitutes (1 Cor 6:9), impurity, licentiousness, sorcery, rivalry, jealousy (Gal 5:19-20). Several of the vices are mentioned repeatedly, others only once. In giving these lists, Paul makes some important observations. He tells the Galatians that what constitutes proper behavior is self-evident: "Now the works of the flesh are obvious" (Gal 5:19); similarly the Romans are told that even pagans have an innate awareness of behavior to avoid, hence "they have no excuse" (Rom 1:20). The Corinthians are instructed not to associate with "anyone named a brother" who is immoral (1 Cor 5:11); furthermore, they are warned that evildoers will not "inherit the kingdom of God" (1 Cor 6:10). The unrepentant give cause for Paul to mourn (2 Cor 12:21). Since the vices Paul lists are frequently found in other sources of the period, Paul is not establishing a novel ethical code. He is instructing believers at least to avoid the behavior that violates public behavior. Further, Paul is clear about the negative consequences that fall upon believers who are evildoers and upon the Christian communities to which they belong.

Pastoral-Liturgical Tradition

Virtues: Traditional and Contemporary. In the first three centuries of Christianity there was little attempt to establish fixed list of virtues and vices. In the fourth century Ambrose adopted and named as "cardinal" the four virtues previously identified as central by Plato in Book IV of the *Republic:* prudence, justice, courage, and temperance (PL 14:280–282). According to

Augustine, virtue is a fixed disposition of the soul, bestowed as a gift from God; it is the art of living rightly. Influenced by Aristotle, Thomas Aquinas understood the virtues as habits, i.e., actions controlled by the will and ordered to one's chosen objectives. Further, Aquinas correlated the cardinal virtues with the functions of reason and subordinated these to the three theological virtues of faith, hope, and charity. In his view the latter have God as their object and are caused or infused directly by God. The former are natural virtues, not in the sense that they are innate, but in the sense that they come into being through the intention to do good and the consequent action. The "form" of all the virtues is charity, for it transforms the other virtues to their proper end and enables people to realize their destiny, life with God.

In more recent times there has been a renewed interest in the virtues. One development is the endeavor to link the formation and exercise of virtues by the individual with the moral communities in which he or she lives. Groups ranging from the family to the church community, and to society at large have a significant role in establishing virtues for their members. However, the fragmentary nature of many contemporary groups to which people belong hinders this role. A further issue is the effort to identify certain virtues with particular stages of life. Authors such as Erik Erikson and Donald Capps have correlated the following life-cycle stages with saving virtues: infancy—hope; early childhood—will (courage); play age—purpose (and dedication); school age—competence (and discipline); adolescence—fidelity; young adulthood—love; adulthood—care; mature adulthood—wisdom.

Heroic Virtue and the Universal Call to Holiness. Extraordinary virtue or heroic virtue has been part of the tradition going back to the early Church, and before that to Aristotle. In early Christian tradition those who manifested heroic virtue were the martyrs, the first to be venerated as saints.

Since then the Church has singled out and canonized as saints great numbers of women and men whose virtuous lives were outstanding. The person of heroic virtue is one who consistently and faithfully fulfilled his or her duties and obligations. In the liturgical calendar many of these saints are commemorated on particular days as examples of virtuous living for the faithful.

In the Vatican II documents, what had traditionally been described as heroic virtue has been named the universal call to holiness for all the faithful. The document *Lumen Gentium* affirms that the "holiness of the Church is unceasingly manifested . . . through those fruits of grace that the Spirit produces in the faithful" (ch. 5, par. 39). All Christians "are invited and bound to pursue holiness and the perfect fulfillment of their proper state in life" (ch. 5, par. 42). That person is holy who lives the theological and other virtues to an eminent degree.

Vices: Traditional and Contemporary. The counterpart to the classification of virtues has been the categorizing of sins or vices. Most notable is the traditional list of seven deadly sins (pride, envy, anger, sloth, greed, gluttony, and lust). The composition of this list is usually attributed to Gregory the Great. These sins are still treated in recent discussion from the perspectives of both personal fault and of social evils. But the question has been raised: How adequate is the traditional list for the contemporary world? It has been suggested that it belies the preoccupations and distortions of the society that produced it. Authors such as Judith Shklar and Mary Daly hold that the traditional list is largely a product and reflection of a male-dominated society. Common vices in today's society are identified as cruelty, hypocrisy, snobbery, betrayal, and misanthropy. Of these, Karl Menninger insists that the chief is cruelty, especially cruelty to children.

See: CREATION, GIFTS, GRACE, HOLY/HOLINESS, JOY, KNOWLEDGE, LIFE, LOVE, PRIDE, SIN, SPIRIT

JOHN L. GILLMAN

FULFILLMENT

Fulfillment, the accomplishment or realization of a goal or a promise, has two senses in the Bible, human and divine. The biblical emphasis, especially in the NT, is on God's ability to fulfill the promises of the covenants. The NT underscores the belief that Jesus Christ is the fulfillment of all of God's promises to Israel. The Church continues to give witness to this belief in its pastoral and liturgical life.

Old Testament

Christians tend to view the OT as the book of promise, compared with the NT, the book of fulfillment. But the OT contains passages that reflect both the human and divine senses of fulfillment.

The human perspective is intimately tied to the covenantal language of observing the statutes, regulations, and commandments of God's covenant. A covenant consists of both promise and obligation. Accomplishment of the obligations, or obedience to the stipulations, assures the continual validity of the agreement, as in Deuteronomy 4:40: "You must keep his statutes and commandments which I enjoin on you today, that you and your children after you may prosper . . ." (see also 1 Chr 22:13).

Most often, however, the divine perspective is the dominant motif of fulfillment. God is said to fulfill the promise of a threat (Lam 2:17) or to accomplish the words revealed by a prophet. Fulfillment and prophecy go hand in hand in the biblical world. Deuteronomy 18:21-22 delineates the clear criterion, albeit from a negative vantage point, for determining the truth of a prophecy: "know that, even though a prophet speaks in the name of the LORD, if his oracle is not fulfilled or verified, it is an oracle which the LORD did not speak." The OT occasionally speaks of the fulfillment of prophetic utterances (1 Kgs 2:27; 2 Chr 36:21; Ezra 1:1), but most often the message of fulfillment is contained in the general attitude that God's word is efficacious (Isa 55:10-11) or that God accomplishes the wishes of those who seek God's help. Psalm 145:19 proclaims, "He fulfills the desire of those who fear him, he hears their cry and saves them." Despite the effectiveness of the OT perspective on fulfillment, it is only in the NT that the interplay between prophecy and fulfillment achieves its greatest impact.

New Testament

The NT also shows vestiges of the human dimension of fulfillment. Acts 14:26 speaks of the human accomplishments of Paul and Barnabas in spreading the gospel of Jesus Christ, though the success is attributed to God's grace. Obedience to certain stipulations of the Law, most especially love of neighbor, is also commended as an important accomplishment of God's will by human beings (Rom 13:8; Gal 5:14; Jas 2:8). It is, however, the new law of Christ which is essential to fulfill. Paul asserts, "Bear one another's burdens, and so you will fulfill the law of Christ" (Gal 6:2). He also urges those called to ministry to fulfill their ministerial duties (Col 4:17), but elsewhere acknowledges that it is really God in the minister who effectively accomplishes the divine will (2 Thess 1:11).

As important as the human act of accomplishment may be, the NT emphasizes much more strongly that fulfillment is a divine attribute that mysteriously exists in the world. The Gospels and Acts provide many examples of this phenomenon.

The ministry of Jesus is overshadowed by the notion of the fulfillment of God's promises to the chosen people, for he proclaims, "This is the time of fulfillment. The kingdom of God is at hand" (Mark 1:15). Luke's portrayal of Jesus also affirms that Jesus has come to fulfill what God has promised. The time (kairos) of Jesus is the appointed time of fulfillment. At the outset of his ministry Jesus goes to the synagogue in Nazareth, reads from the prophet Isaiah, and says to the assembly: "Today this scripture passage is fulfilled in your hearing" (Luke 4:16-21). This act of perceived arrogance leads to his rejection by his own

home town and foreshadows his final rejection by the Jewish leaders in Jerusalem (Luke 22–23). Accomplishing God's will can exact a costly price.

The NT often cites "the Scriptures" in general (meaning, the OT) as the object of fulfillment (e.g., Mark 14:49; John 17:12). In Luke's Gospel Jesus once mentions a threefold division of the Scriptures that must be fulfilled: "that everything written in the law of Moses and in the prophets and psalms must be fulfilled" (Luke 24:49). Most often the NT singles out the prophetic writings for fulfillment, especially those that lend themselves to messianic interpretation (Luke 24:25-27; John 12:38).

The Gospel of Matthew raises the theme of prophecy and fulfillment to new heights in the NT. Only Matthew uses the frequent technique of "formula citations" in which a prophetic quote is introduced by the following or similar formula: "All this took place to fulfill what the Lord had said through the prophet" (e.g., 1:22; 2:15, 17; 13:35). It is no exaggeration to say that everything that happens in Matthew's Gospel occurs under the aegis of fulfilling God's will. It is seen from the beginning of Jesus' ministry in Matthew, when he is baptized to "fulfill all righteousness" (3:15), to the carrying out of the passion, "all this has come to pass that the writings of the prophets may be fulfilled" (26:56; see also v. 54). Jesus not only fulfills prophetic predictions by his life and death, but he also fulfills every aspect of the sacred writings and of the Law itself: "Do not think that I have come to abolish the Law or the prophets. I have come not to abolish but to fulfill" (5:17). As God's chosen and obedient Son, Jesus in Matthew's Gospel has the ability to interpret properly, and establish with new authority, the true direction of the Law. In his very life, death, and resurrection he fulfills the Sacred Scriptures, and he accomplishes all that his heavenly Father asked him to do (24:34).

The NT also contains two other noteworthy aspects of fulfillment. Luke connects discipleship to faith by means of fulfillment. This is accomplished through the image of Mary, the mother of Jesus, who serves as a model disciple. Elizabeth, Mary's relative, praises Mary's great achievement in assenting to God's will: "Blessed are you who believed that what was spoken to you by the Lord would be fulfilled" (Luke 1:45). The one who hears and does the Word of God is thus an instrument of fulfilling God's will. The opposite of this type of faith in God's promises is the lack of trust that Zechariah exhibits when the angel Gabriel tells him his wife is to bear a son, despite their advanced age: "But now you will be speechless and unable to talk until the day these things take place, because you did not believe my words, which will be fulfilled at their proper time" (Luke 1:20).

The Gospel of John adds another aspect to fulfillment in the person of Jesus. Like the other Gospels, John shows how Jesus fulfills the prophetic writings (John 12:38), but he also emphasizes that Jesus' own words find fruition in the course of the gospel story. At his arrest, when Jesus intercedes for his disciples so that they are not arrested, the fourth evangelist asserts, "This was to fulfill what he had said, 'I have not lost any of those you gave me'" (18:9; also v. 32). For John, Jesus fulfills not only the writings of old but all of his own teachings, too.

A final aspect of NT teaching on fulfillment is that God's will is sometimes accomplished ironically by the very people who hope to thwart it. This is most clearly seen in the passion of Jesus. Acts makes this judgment explicit in one of Paul's addresses at a synagogue: "The inhabitants of Jerusalem and their leaders failed to recognize him, and by condemning him they fulfilled the oracles of the prophets that are read Sabbath after Sabbath" (Acts 13:27). This illustrates the basic NT stance that God's will is accomplished in due time regardless of the human attempts to ignore it or worse, sabotage it.

The NT teaching on fulfillment, then, involves numerous aspects of accomplishment but the emphasis is clearly upon God's will. Jesus himself is the primary source of fulfillment as he inaugurates the final days which lead to the reign of God. The NT does not claim that every prophecy ever uttered has been fulfilled, but it does teach that, in Jesus Christ, the fulfillment of the ages has come to pass.

Pastoral-Liturgical Tradition

The centerpiece of the Church's reflection on God's fulfillment of promises is the person of Jesus Christ. The Church continues to preserve the tension between promise and fulfillment every time it celebrates Eucharist and proclaims the memorial acclamation, "Christ has died, Christ is risen, Christ will come again." The statement mirrors the salvific deed God has already accomplished in Christ, but also states the expectation of the parousia and the promised reign which has yet to be fulfilled. The liturgical season that best expresses the Church's proclamation of God's fulfillment is Advent/Christmas. The infancy narratives of Matthew (chs. 1–2) and of Luke (chs. 1–2) spell out a profound theological understanding of fulfillment by describing how the coming of Jesus accomplishes Israel's hopes through the ages. Indeed, the Church consecrates its entire day with morning, evening, and night prayers which incorporate three great hymns from Luke's infancy narratives that extol God's faithful fulfillment of promises. These are the *Benedictus* (Luke 1:68-79), the *Magnificat* (Luke 1:46-55), and the *Nunc Dimittis* (Luke 2:29-32), respectively, which are inserted into the daily prayer life of the Church through its "Liturgy of the Hours." The words of Zechariah praise God because "He has raised up a horn for our salvation within the house of David his servant, even as he promised through the mouth of his holy prophets from of old" (Luke 1:69-70). There are also visual and musical references to the notion of fulfillment during the Advent/Christmas season. Visually, the liturgical season reinforces the message by the presence of creche scenes which recount the story of Jesus' birth. Musically, the strains of G. F. Handel's famous oratorio, "The Messiah," echo throughout the season to provide a sacred musical backdrop for the divine scenario of promise and fulfillment. Christians believe they live in the time of fulfillment even as they await the full coming of God's reign.

See: COVENANT, FAITH, LAW, OATH, OBEDIENCE, PROMISE, PROPHET, REIGN OF GOD, TIME, WILL OF GOD, WORD

RONALD D. WITHERUP, S.S.

FULLNESS

Fullness pertains to the state of being complete, satiated, or lacking nothing. The Bible uses fullness to express both common and theological concepts. In the NT this notion takes on specific Christological meaning which holds great importance for the Church's understanding of the nature of Christ. This Christological significance remains prominent in the Church's contemporary life.

Old Testament

The OT uses the notion of fullness, derived from the verb "to fill" *(mala')*, exclusively in the common sense of completeness or entirety. When 1 Chronicles 16:32 speaks of "the sea and what fills it," it means *everything* that is found in the sea (also Ps 96:11). Likewise, the common expression "the earth and its fullness" (Ps 24:1; 50:12; Deut 33:16; 1 Cor 10:26) refers to everything that exists on the earth. In either case the notion of fullness is usually tied to the fact that everything belongs to God the creator because God alone is the source of everything in the universe, and the one who sustains all life. Another example of this common sense is found in Psalm 16:11, which contains the phrase "fullness of joy," standing for complete, utter joy.

The notion of fullness in the OT is not restricted to natural objects such as earth and sea. God is also the subject of the verb "to fill." Jeremiah calls attention to God's om-

nipresence in the universe, "Can a man hide in secret without my seeing him? says the LORD. Do I not fill both heaven and earth? says the LORD" (Jer 23:24). This text allies God's fullness to presence in a way that expounds the basic OT understanding that God, the creator, permeates the universe.

New Testament

In the NT, though the Greek word "fullness" *(plēroma)* may have roots in speculative Greek philosophy, it is also used to express the common notion of completion or entirety. When Paul refers to the "full number of the Gentiles" (Rom 11:12, 25), meaning all the Gentiles, it is in the context of the relationship between the salvation of the Jews and the Gentiles. The failure of Israel to respond properly to the gospel redirects the message to the Gentiles so that their conversion,* in turn, may make the Jews jealous and contribute to their own salvation at a later time (Rom 11:11, 26). Paul's realization that Christ's message of salvation is meant for *all*, including the Gentiles, demonstrates strikingly how extensive God's love really is. Colossians 3:11 illustrates this insight: "Here there is not Greek and Jew . . . but Christ is all and in all" (see also Gal 3:27-28). Fullness in this context implies an all-encompassing incorporation into Christ and relates to the deeper, Christological meaning discussed below.

Although the NT makes use of this common understanding of fullness, its occurrence with two other concepts reveals a more profound meaning which has wider ramifications. The two concepts are time and Christology.

Time. The NT uses the expression "the fullness of time" (Gal 4:4; Eph 1:10) to delineate the eschatological time of God's definitive action in the world. The clause, "But when the fullness of time had come, God sent his Son, born of a woman" (Gal 4:4), not only expresses the achievement of the correct chronological time for the event, but also connotes the appointed time *(kairos)* in God's plan of salvation. The plan is specifically mentioned in Ephesians: "In all wisdom and insight, he [God] has made known to us the mystery of his will in accord with his favor that he set forth in him [Christ] as a plan for the fullness of time to sum up all things in Christ, in heaven and on earth" (Eph 1:8b-10). The fullness of time is consecrated or sacred time, the time of Christ's coming with the gift of salvation, the time for God's eternal plan to come to fruition.

Christology. By far the most important NT use of fullness, either as a noun or in its verbal form (to fill), is in relation to Christology. This use centers primarily on three NT books: the Gospel of John, Colossians, and Ephesians. All three writings are known for their "high Christology" (i.e., emphasis on the divinity of Christ, as opposed to "low Christology," emphasizing the humanity of Christ). Although these passages are abstract and often difficult to interpret precisely, the basic meaning seems clear: Jesus Christ is the full embodiment of God, and his fullness overflows into our lives.

John 1:16 makes reference to Christ with the words, "From his fullness we have all received, grace in place of grace." This statement is part of the prologue of the Gospel (1:1-18) in which Jesus Christ is shown to exist with God from the beginning of time, and to be the replacement of the previous covenant with Israel. It is this special cosmic status with God that enables us to receive testimony of the Word-made-flesh (1:14). For John, Jesus Christ embodies all that the Father embodies because of the unique intimacy that exists between them. In Jesus' words, "The Father and I are one" (John 10:30); thus, Jesus *is* the fullness of the Father (see John 1:1).

The Letter to the Colossians has an even more expansive notion of Christ's fullness. It states of Christ: "He is the head of the body, the church. He is the beginning, the firstborn from the dead, that in all things he himself might be preeminent. For in him all the fullness was pleased to dwell" (Col 1:18-19). The context for this passage is a great hymn that exalts the role of Christ in the life of the universe and in the Church. By virtue of his resurrection, Jesus has become the preeminent one, the head of the body. Colossians 2:9-10 enhances this understanding more explicitly: "For in him dwells the whole fullness of the deity bodily, and you share in this fullness in him, who is the head of every principality and power." This fullness refers not simply to divine attributes but to God's very nature, God's essence. Christ's preeminence is not merely a matter of status. It is a matter of substance. Christ has power over all the other powers of the cosmos. Christ's fullness is consequently a partaking in God's reign over the universe, even as it is also a grace shared with the Church.

A more problematic reference in Colossians is Paul's apparent statement of making up for some lack in Christ's sufferings: "Now I rejoice in my sufferings for your sake, and in my flesh I am filling up what is lacking in the afflictions of Christ on behalf of his body, which is the Church" (Col 1:24). Since it is clear in the NT that the sufferings of Christ are fully sufficient themselves for achieving the intended salvation of all God's people, this passage probably refers to Paul's uniting of his own sufferings to those of Christ (see Phil 3:10).

Ephesians, which is closely related to Colossians, represents the crowning achievement of this effusive Christological development. One passage extols "the God of our Lord Jesus Christ, the Father of glory" because of the special status bestowed on Christ (1:15-23). God "put all things beneath his feet and gave him as head over all things to the Church, which is his body, the fullness of the one who fills all things in every way" (1:22-23). He who is complete in every way, because of the abundance of grace showered upon him by his heavenly Father, is also the one who is able to make all things complete, lacking for nothing. Indeed, the purpose of Christ's resurrection and ascension to power is precisely "so that he might fill all things" (4:10). Just because this fullness is a gift of

God's grace and satiates us does not mean that members of the Church have no role to play in this divine plan. The Church is also told to strive in ministry to live up to that fullness that comes from Christ, so that we ourselves may attain "the full stature of Christ" and no longer be infants in the eyes of God (4:13). The great prayer for the readers (3:14-21) includes the wish "that you may be filled with all the fullness of God" (v. 19), a sentiment that hopes for the satiation of every need and desire of the members of Christ's body, the Church. This may be similar to the expression, "the fullness of Christ's blessings" (Rom 15:29) in the context of Paul's impending visit to the Church gathered at Rome. He expresses confidence that, once he is free to make his visit, it will become another sign of Christ's abundant blessings upon the Church.

In sum, the NT sees fullness primarily as a Christological attribute that demonstrates the unique relationship between Jesus and God the Father. The universe has never before seen such intimacy, in which the Creator's own fullness resides in the person of Christ. The extent of this fullness is expressed by the sentiment of Colossians 3:11: "But Christ is all and in all."

Pastoral-Liturgical Tradition

The abstract nature of fullness makes it a difficult concept to apply pastorally. Its philosophical roots and its application to Christology may make it an unattractive concept to the contemporary Christian. Nonetheless, its importance remains felt in the life of the Church. The hungers of the human family, whether physical, emotional, or spiritual, always leave people feeling empty and unfulfilled. Human yearnings continue to gnaw at modern Christians, just as they have always done to people through the ages. The Christian belief that, in Jesus Christ, the fullness of time has come, and the definitive act of God's revelation has taken place, provides the basic orientation for contemporary faith. The completeness of God's action in Jesus

means that there can be no more lacking fulfillment in the universe. The fullness of Christ makes up for any lack we may have as individuals or as a people. In Christ the fullness of God has been revealed. The universe is fully suffused with God's grandeur and is alive with Christ's grace. Jesus' saying, "whoever sees me sees the one who sent me" (John 12:45), gives assurance of this completeness. A popular Irish prayer expresses this belief well in spatial terms: "Christ before me, Christ behind me, Christ beside me, Christ above me, Christ below me, Christ all around me!"

See: FULFILLMENT, JESUS CHRIST, MYSTERY, TIME

RONALD D. WITHERUP, S.S.

FUNERAL CUSTOMS

The proverb "death is the echo of life" primarily suggests that the manner of a person's death often reflects the manner of that person's life. Honorable people like Sarah and Abraham experienced a peaceful and honorable death (Gen 23:1; 25:8). Dishonorable people like Absalom generally died a shameful death (2 Sam 18:9-17). Beyond this moral sense, though, death echoes life in that the values that govern life in each culture are reflected in its funeral customs as well.

The core values of kinship and family-centeredness that dominate life in Mediterranean culture also characterize its funeral customs. It was important to be buried with one's family in the family tomb (see 2 Sam 21:12-14). The recurrent phrases "gathered to his people" (Gen 25:8; 35:29; 49:29, 33) and "slept with his fathers" (1 Kgs 2:10; 11:43; 14:31; 15:8) reflect a belief that the family extends beyond death. Not to be buried with one's family was a calamity surpassed only by the shame of not being buried at all (Isa 14:20; Eccl 6:3; Jer 22:19). This fate was reserved for sinners (Deut 28:25-26)

In the Christian tradition, the experience of death is understood in the light of Jesus' death and resurrection. The *Order of Chris-*

tian Funerals embodies this understanding in the liturgy.

Old Testament

As one might expect from a high context document like the Bible, there is precious little information about funeral customs in ancient Israel. It seems that the eldest son or closest relative present closed the eyes of the deceased at death (Gen 49:6). The body was washed and anointed in preparation for burial. Jacob and Joseph were embalmed (perhaps more correctly, mummified) quite likely because this was the customary practice in Egypt where they died (Gen 50:2-3, 26). Otherwise, embalming was not customary among the Israelites.

Families and professionals (see Jer 9:17) lamented for the deceased person. King David's decision to lament while his stricken child was sick but to cease lamenting when the child died seems unusual (2 Sam 12:15-23) but is understandable from a Middle Eastern cultural perspective. Fasting, lamenting,* and mourning in the Bible are protest strategies calculated to stir another person to action. David sought to stir God to rescue the young child. When the child died, David recognized that he had failed to persuade God to save the child's life. The protest strategies serve no purpose now. Instead of lamenting, David seeks to comfort himself and Bathsheba and hopes that God will bless their union with a new child. God does not disappoint them.

The OT suggests that people were buried where they died (e.g., Miriam [Num 20:1]; Aaron [Num 33:39]; Moses [Deut 34:6]) and often near a tree (Gen 35:8; 1 Sam 31:12-13) likely reminiscent of divine presence (Gen 21:32-33) or immortality (Gen 2:9). Still, multiple burials in family caves, as with Abraham and his descendants at Machpelah (Gen 50:12-13), was the prevalent practice.

"Bench" tombs located near the family patrimony were also common. Usually such a tomb consisted of a central court surrounded by burial chambers, each of which contained waist-high "benches" on which to place a body. To make room for new burials, skeletal remains and other objects were relocated to a repository (a pit) in the center of the room or under a bench.

Pottery and other objects found in the tombs were placed there sometimes for the deceased but more often for those who visited the tomb to use for cultic or other purposes.

New Testament

Accounts of the death and burial of Jesus reflect the cultural beliefs and practices of that day. People lamented for him (Luke 23:27, 48; see also Luke 8:52). Jesus' body may have been washed (Acts 9:37) before Joseph of Arimathea, a disciple, wrapped it in a linen shroud and placed it in his own new tomb, hewn in the soft limestone rock (Matt 27:59-60). Friends came to the tomb after the Sabbath intending to anoint the body (Luke 24:1).

Joseph's may have been a family tomb or perhaps a "personal" tomb (taking Matthew's description of him as "rich" to suggest social prestige). It was part of the intricate cemetery complex that surrounded the walled city of Jerusalem. In antiquity, people were normally buried outside the city walls.

The entrance to this tomb was sealed by a circular, disk-like stone that was set into a groove carved in front of the rectangular shaped entrance to the tomb. The stone could be rolled in one direction or the other to seal or open the entrance. Even a small sized stone, e.g., four feet in diameter and six to eight inches thick, would be difficult if not impossible for one person alone to roll away. The stone served to protect the contents of the tomb from thieves.

Though not mentioned in the NT, the practice of secondary burial was very common in the first century CE. Joseph's tomb would have had niches in which a corpse would remain for about one year. When the flesh had rotted, the bones would be gathered and placed into a stone "bone box" called an ossuary. The name or names of the deceased whose remnants were thus gathered would be inscribed on the box. This practice made it possible for the same family tombs to be used for many generations.

In summary, the funeral practices of both the OT and NT reflect the group-centered nature of Mediterranean culture. Just as Mediterranean personalities needed others to shape their identity in life, so in burial, family ties remained unbroken by burying deceased family members in the same family tomb. While Joseph's magnanimous offer to bury his master's body in his personal tomb is honorable and noteworthy, the fact that Jesus died away from his hometown and was not buried in the family tomb can be interpreted as the ultimate disgrace of his shameful end. Yet this dark picture of the final days of Jesus' life would be totally wiped out by the brilliance of Jesus' resurrection* from death by his Father. This is a family honor no earthly family member could possibly match.

See: DEATH

JOHN J. PILCH

Pastoral-Liturgical Tradition

For the Christian, the experience of death,* no less than the experience of life, is understood in the light of Christ's paschal mystery. Indeed, for the believer death is the ultimate passage into the fullness of life with Christ.

The Constitution on the Sacred Liturgy of the Second Vatican Council called for a revision of the funeral rites of the Church that would "express more clearly the paschal character of Christian death" and "correspond more closely to the circumstances and traditions found in various regions" (no. 81). The article concludes by singling out the use of liturgical color as an example of the adaptation being called for.

The Order of Christian Funerals (OCF), published on October 1, 1989, is the revised vernacular edition for use in dioceses of the United States of the *editio typica* of the *Ordo Exsequiarum,* promulgated on August 15, 1969, for implementation on June 1, 1970. Upon the death of a Christian, the OCF asserts, not only does the Church "intercede on behalf of the deceased," but it also "ministers to the sorrowing and consoles them in the funeral rites" (art. 4). This consolation is "rooted in the hope that comes from faith in the saving death and resurrection of the Lord Jesus Christ" (art. 8). Not only pastors, but the whole Christian community has a role in the ministry of consolation (art. 9). While this ministry is expressed in a particular way by participation in the funeral rites according to a variety of liturgical roles, liturgical ministry does not exhaust the forms of the community's consolation (art. 10–15).

The "General Introduction" of the OCF makes provision for the selection of "rites and texts that are most suitable to the situation: those that most closely apply to the needs of the mourners, the circumstances of the death, and the customs of the local Christian community" (art. 43). The provision of a wider variety of texts for different circumstances and the flexibility of the various ritual parts of the OCF enhances the adaptability of the rites to particular conditions. In principle, local adaptations should always be made with the goal of expressing the paschal character of Christian ritual and the Church's hope in the resurrection.

The funeral rites are divided into three principal parts: the vigil for the deceased, the funeral liturgy itself, and the rite of committal. Other, secondary, "related rites and prayers" are also provided with the recognition that local, cultural circumstances will govern their use (art. 100). These rites are explicitly suggested as "models," meant for adaptation: prayers after death, gathering in the presence of the body, and transfer of the body to the church or to the place of committal. In addition, morning and evening prayer from the Office for the Dead are provided for optional use.

While the "Related Rites and Prayers" are proposed not for celebration with the whole Christian community but only with the family and close friends of the deceased, they include a ritual signal of their importance. The only ritual among all of those in the OCF that begins with the sign of the cross is the rite for "Gathering in the Presence of the Body" (art. 112). Here the OCF seems to mirror the Paschal Triduum, which, although it is celebrated across several days, is considered one organic liturgy, beginning with the sign of the cross at the Mass of the Lord's Supper and concluding with the dismissal at the conclusion of the Easter Vigil.

The very structure of the OCF implies that the rites will be adapted to particular circumstances, by providing two models of each of the three principal parts. The two forms of the vigil are the "Vigil for the Deceased," and "Vigil for the Deceased with Reception at the Church" (art. 51). The two forms of the funeral liturgy are the "Funeral Mass" and the "Funeral Liturgy outside Mass" (art. 128). The two forms of the rite of committal are the "Rite of Committal" and "Rite of Committal with Final Commendation" (art. 205).

In addition, Part II of the OCF provides "Funeral Rites for Children," including a "Vigil for a Deceased Child," the "Funeral Liturgy," and a "Rite of Committal." Explicit permission is granted to adapt both these rites and the "Related Rites and Prayers" of Part I to the "circumstances" and "the particular needs and customs of the mourners" (art. 234–235).

The flexibility of the OCF is further enhanced by an ample selection of Scripture texts to be used in the rites (Part III), and by a wide variety of prayers and other presidential texts suited to different circumstances (Part V). Both the Scripture selections and the prayer text options are considered variable within all of the rites of the OCF (art. 344 and 397).

Customs are by their nature local, varying from place to place. They can be particular to an individual ethnic group, national region, or even a specific parish. In acknowledging the importance of custom, the OCF implicitly suggests that no two celebrations of the rites will ever unfold in exactly the same form.

An example of ethnic custom that might be incorporated into the rites would be the Hispanic tradition of the *novenario*, the family novena prayed for nine nights following the burial of the deceased. This custom generally includes the rosary and Marian litany prayed around an *altarcito*, a small family altar at which a picture of the deceased is enshrined with candles. The *novenario* might include hymns, intercessions, or it could include some part of vespers.

In the African-American community it is not uncommon to celebrate the funeral liturgy in the evening. Indeed, this practice is currently spreading beyond the African-American community, perhaps as a result of changes in the communion fast. This shift will imply changes in the forms of and relationship among the vigil service, the funeral liturgy and the rite of committal.

The liberal permissions for adaptation found within the General Introduction to the OCF, in the pastoral introductions to each of its various parts, and in many of the rubrics scattered throughout the rites reveal a conviction earlier implied in the Constitution on the Sacred Liturgy of Vatican II (nos. 81, 82: see also nos. 37–40); that is, that Christian faith is expressed through the media of culture and custom, and that culture and custom give form or "flesh" to the faith of the Church. While the "substantial unity" of the Roman rite is to be preserved, its liturgical expression will, by necessity, vary according to the culture and customs of the place where it is celebrated.

See: DEATH

BRIAN J. FISCHER

G

GALILEE/SEA OF GALILEE

The name Galilee comes from the Hebrew *galil* whose basic meaning appears to be "something round." From there it was an easy step to "circuit" and what is enclosed therein, a "region," e.g., "the region of the Philistines" (Josh 13:2). This generic term then became a proper name, "the land of Galilee" (1 Kgs 9:11), which became *Galilaia* in Greek.

The geographical limits of Galilee are striking and obvious. Three valleys—the Litani river on the north, the Jordan river on the east, and the Jezreel valley on the south—mark off a rectangle roughly ninety by fifty kilometers. It is divided into two almost equal zones on the basis of altitude (*J. W.* 3:35) by a fault line running from Akko to just north of the Sea of Galilee. Upper Galilee averages three hundred to six hundred meters higher than Lower Galilee. The good land in the wide valleys of the latter was owned by absentee landlords and worked by tenants (Mark 12:1-12), who paid forty to sixty-five percent of their produce in taxes. The fertility of the plain of Ginnosar near the lake was extraordinary (*J. W.* 3:516–521).

The political limits of Jewish Galilee (*J. W.* 3:35–40) never corresponded to its geographical limits, particularly on the north and west. Neither the coast nor the hinterland of Tyre ever had a significant Jewish presence. The number of Jews in the interior is a debated question at all periods prior to its conquest by Aristobulus I (104–103). In the first century BCE the situation is clear. The population must have been predominantly Jewish for Rome to assign it to the control of Jerusalem in 63.

The exercise of power by upstarts such as Antipater and his son Herod the Great (40–4) was resisted by the Hasmonean nobility of Galilee, and Herod had to act with his customary decisive brutality to establish his dominion there after being named king by the Romans. Thereafter Galilee gave no further trouble, and its 204 towns and villages prospered (Josephus, *Life*, 235). When Herod died there was an uprising, which the Romans quickly surpressed, destroying Sepphoris, the capital of Galilee, in the process (*J. W.* 2:68).

Under his father's will Herod Antipas inherited Galilee, which he ruled until 39 CE. He had a nominal overlord in the governor of Syria, but he was not subject to the direct control that the Romans exercised in Judea and Samaria. Tax collectors in Galilee, therefore, were working for a Jewish sovereign, not for the oppressor as in Judea. Antipas immediately began to rebuild Sepphoris (*Ant.* 18:27); the availability of permanent work there explains why Joseph settled in nearby Nazareth (Matt 2:22-23). The city had not long been completed when Antipas undertook the construction of Tiberias, a new city on the west shore of the lake (*Ant.* 18:36-38), which then became the capital (*Life* 37).

The Sea of Galilee in the OT is known as the Sea of Kinnereth (Num 34:11), a name that is imaginatively associated with *kinnor,* "harp." For some the lake is shaped like a harp, whereas for others the music of its waters resembles the sound of a harp. The surface is over two hundred meters below sea-level. The lake is twenty kilometers long and twelve kilometers at its widest point. Sudden strong winds cause the waves to rebound off the opposite shore quickly creating very turbulent seas. Small boats caught in the cross waves are at high risk (Mark 4:37).

Fishing was the most important industry in Galilee, because fish was part of the staple diet of rich and poor (Luke 11:11; 24:42). Four of Jesus' disciples operated as a partnership (Luke 5:7, 10) with employees (Mark 1:20). Thus they worked under contract with the state to whom they paid twenty-five to forty percent of their catch. Fish was processed at Taricheae/Magdala (Strabo, *Geography* 16:2.45) not far south of Capernaum. The move of Peter and Andrew to this latter city (Mark 1:29) was probably for tax reasons, since their place of origin, Bethsaida (John 1:44), was outside the territory of Antipas.

As a frontier village Capernaum needed a garrison (Matt 8:5) and a tax-collector (Matt 9:9). The one-story multiple family dwelling units were built of undressed rounded black basalt stones (Mark 2:1-12). Their cobbled floors easily hid coins (Luke 15:8). Such houses graphically illustrate the poverty of the inhabitants, which explains why they needed a Gentile centurion to build them a synagogue (Luke 7:5). The synagogue was also of basalt and measured eighteen by twenty-four meters. It was here that Jesus preached (Mark 1:21).

See: SEA

JEROME MURPHY-O'CONNOR, O.P.

GATE

Gates as Protection

In the ancient world every viable city had a wall to protect it. The city gate provided the passageway between the protection of life inside and the dangers lurking outside. The gate was potentially the weakest point in the wall, and cities adopted various strategies to strengthen them. Towers on either side provided high ground to shoot at enemies attacking with fire or battering-rams. Larger cities built two sets of gates separated by a chamber with guardrooms on the sides. From a second story of the gatehouse guards could watch through the night when the gates were closed (Josh 2:5). Large cities, such as Jerusalem, had several gates; some were only a narrow passage for pedestrian traffic. The gates themselves were typically of wood, in some cases strengthened with metal. Affixed to posts, they turned in holes made in the threshold and lintel and were secured by bars (Ps 147:13). Better houses also had wooden doors which formed or should have formed a further wall of protection (Genesis 19; Judges 19). In poorer houses the door was the only opening to the light.

The Gate as the Center of Civic Life

With no open space inside the walls, the area in front of the gates served as the town square. There markets were set up and contracts were made (Gen 23:10, 18). Threshing took place on its well-trodden ground (1 Kgs 22:10). News, gossip, and fame was reported (Ps 69:13; Prov 31:23, 31). The poor and the disabled took their place at the gate (Prov 22:22; Amos 5:12). Here the elders of the town met to sort out legal matters and disputes (Ruth 4; Ps 127:5; Isa 29:21). The elders also heard court cases at the gates and in some instances carried out executions (Deut 21:19; 22:15, 24; 25:7).

Gate as a Part for the Whole

The gates of a city or temple or the like may serve as a part for the whole (metonomy). Psalm 9:14-15, for example, contrasts the "gates of death" with "the gates of the daughter of Zion." The focus on the image of the "gate" emphasizes the idea of entering into death or life (see also Ps 107:18; Isa 38:10 and Ps 87:2; Jer 1:15).

Inside Looking Out

The gate or the door serves as one of those pervasive images of separation between the inside and the outside. Many passages presume a stance of being inside and safe looking outside toward danger. Most importantly at the Passover (Exod 12:21-23), the Israelites mark the lintels with blood, the sign of life, and those inside remain unharmed; within the tradition, this space becomes repeatable and transcends time and place as a promise to future generations. Deuteronomy 6:9 commands the Israelites to write the words of the covenant "on the doorposts of your houses and on your gates," and so they fastened to their doorposts a mezuzah, a small box containing Deuteronomy 6:4-9; 11:13-21 and the divine name "Shaddai" written on a piece of parchment, and thereby established the boundaries of the house as a place of covenant. Later in Deuteronomy anyone living "within your gates" becomes a part of your community with legal claims. Therefore, "the Levite, who has no share in the heritage with you, and also the alien, the orphan and the widow who belong to your community [lit. who are within your gates] may come and eat their fill" (Deut 14:29; also 16:11, 14).

Acts 5:19; 12:6-11; and 16:26-27 reverse the presupposition and tell of prison doors opening by themselves to free the apostles, Peter, and Paul, respectively. The door that opens by itself for god-like human beings is a recurring feature in stories from the ancient world. The stories from Acts, however, demonstrate that the gospel and its preachers cannot be contained by human space or power.

Outside Looking In

In other situations, the character stands outside looking in and seeking entrance that will bring a change of worlds or transformation. Jacob awakes from his vision in the night of angels going up and down to proclaim that this is "the gateway of heaven" (Gen 28:17). Babylon makes the most famous claim in this regard, for its name translates "gate [bab] of the gods [ilani]." The psalmist calls for the gates of the Temple to lift up so that the Lord of Hosts can enter in (Ps 24:7-10). The gate that Jesus calls narrow creates a vision of the Kingdom's demand to enter a new and different world. At the same time, Jesus promises that if you knock, "the door will be opened to you" (Luke 11:9-10; Matt 7:7). In Acts 14:27, Paul tells of "the door of faith," and Colossians 4:3 asks God to open "a door for the word, to speak of the mystery of Christ" (see also 1 Cor 16:9; 2 Cor 2:12).

Doors form part of the eschatological vision which draws a sharp line between the inside and outside, between the just and the unjust, between belonging and abandonment. The foolish virgins who come with no oil return to find the door locked and the wise inside with the Bridegroom (Matt 25:10; see Luke 13:24-27). Revelation 3:7 borrows from Isaiah 22:22 and proclaims the Messiah as "the holy one, the true, who holds the key of David, who opens and no one shall close, who closes and no one shall open."

The Book of Revelation borrows from Isaiah and Ezekiel to create a vision of the twelve jeweled gates of the New Jerusalem that never close (Isa 54:12; 60:11; Ezek 48:30-34; Rev 21:12-13, 15, 21). Isaiah captures the hope by saying: "You shall call your walls 'Salvation' and your gates 'Praise'" (Isa 60:18).

Doors as the Space Between

In Hosea 2:17, God promises to make the valley of Achor, a place of Israel's sin, into "a door of hope" and thereby transforms the "outside" into the door itself. In the metaphor "I am the door" (John 10:7, 9), Jesus places himself between the inside and the outside and becomes the mediating term between two worlds. As such, Christ suggests that Christian ministry takes place at this middle point.

See: CITY, JERUSALEM

HARRY HAGAN, O.S.B.

GEHENNA

Gehenna as the fiery place of eternal punishment is the final stage of a basic three-fold development in the Bible. The word itself comes from the Hebrew *ge-hinnom,* meaning "valley of Hinnom." Sometimes it is referred to as the "valley of the sons of Hinnom." Located southwest of Jerusalem, this valley or ravine ran into the Kidron Valley and at one time was part of the boundary between the tribes of Judah and Benjamin (Josh 15:8; 18:15-16).

In the first stage, during the time of the monarchy and especially in the days of Ahaz and Manasseh, this valley acquired a terrible reputation as the center of an idolatrous cult where sacrifices, including children, were offered to Moloch (2 Kgs 16:2-3; 21:6; 2 Chr 28:3-4; 33:6).

The second stage begins with the prophet Jeremiah's strong judgment and condemnation of the Valley of Hinnom (Jer 7:32; 19:1-9). This judgment was remembered later on during the Intertestamental period when a concept of hell* as a fiery lake or abyss emerged (Dan 7:10; 1 Enoch 18:11-16; 27:1-3; 90:26), and then Gehenna was used metaphorically as a designation for hell or eternal damnation. It was the place where the last judgment was to take place.

The final stage of development is the NT understanding of Gehenna. Important here is the clear distinction the NT makes between hades and Gehenna. Hades is the place where the ungodly are sent only temporarily and the judgment is provisional (Acts 2:27-31; Rev 20:13-14). Gehenna, on the other hand, is the place of permanent punishment and the judgment is final (Mark 9:43-48). Explicit NT references to Gehenna are found in the Synoptic Gospels and the Letter of James (Matt 5:22, 29, 30; 10:28; 18:9; 23:15, 33; Mark 9:43, 45-46; Luke 12:5; Jas 3:6). Jesus makes threatening references to Gehenna when he calls his hearers and disciples to accountability. Anger that leads to public humiliation will be liable to fiery Gehenna (Matt 5:22). Bearing physical pain or loss of a limb or an eye out of commitment to the reign of God is nothing when compared to being cast into Gehenna and condemned to eternal punishment (Matt 5:29, 30; 10:28; 18:9; Luke 12:5). Civil and religious leaders who fail in their responsibilities and encourage others to do likewise are destined for the everlasting judgment of Gehenna (Matt 23:15, 33). The point Jesus is making here by referring to the punishment of Gehenna is that this will be the consequence of failure to accept the reign of God. Jesus is teaching by clearly contrasting the choices available to a hearer. These are life or death choices and there is no turning back.

See: HELL, JUDGMENT, JERUSALEM, REIGN OF GOD

EUGENE HENSELL, O.S.B.

GENEALOGY

A genealogy is the record of the descent of a person, group, or tribe from their ancestors.* A genealogy may be segmented (taking account of several figures within a single generation) or linear (moving from one generation to the next by means of a single figure in each generation). It may go forward (descending) or backward (ascending). The genealogies in the Bible are mainly linear and descending. The genealogies of Jesus in Matthew 1:1-17 and Luke 3:23-38 trace his descent to Abraham and Adam, respectively.

Old Testament

The Hebrew Bible contains more than twenty genealogical lists. The most extensive is 1 Chronicles 1–9, which descends from Adam to David. But before focusing on these it may be helpful to summarize some principles derived from research on oral genealogies in modern cultures and written genealogies in the ancient Near East. Since genealogies are more statements about relationships in the present than records motivated by antiquarian interest, one must look to the present function of the genealogy in the domestic, political-legal, or religious sphere. Moreover, in the oral stage genealogies are flexible and fluid. The details may be changed to suit new circumstances, and a person may have more than one genealogy. When committed to writing, genealogies tend to lose their fluidity and be taken more seriously as historical documents.

The main purpose of the biblical genealogies is to establish descent and thereby the identity of the persons who are listed. Genesis 4:17-26 contains two genealogies: from Cain to the sons of Lamech (4:17-24), and from Adam through Seth to Enosh (4:25-26). Genesis 5 begins with the characteristic heading: "This is the book of the generations of Adam" ("the record of the descendants of Adam" in the NAB). It then descends from Adam to Noah in linear fashion. Other genealogies in Genesis list the descendants of Noah (10:1-32), the generations from Shem to Abraham (11:10-32), and the descendants of Jacob (46:8-27). Exodus 6:16-25 gives the descendants of Levi down to Aaron, and Ruth 4:18-22 goes from Perez to Jesse, the father of David. In post-exilic times as Israel began to reconstitute itself in its homeland, there was great emphasis on descent and identity (see Ezra 2; 10; Nehemiah 13), and so family lists were drawn up. The primary interest of the books of Chronicles was David and his dynasty. The narrative of David is prefaced by nine chapters of genealogies based largely on the already existing biblical books that trace Israel's history from Adam to David (1 Chronicles 1–9). Early Jewish writers such as the authors of *Jubilees* (see 4:7-33; 8:5-8) and *Biblical Antiquities* filled out the biblical genealogies with names found in no biblical texts. Thus around Jesus' time a certain fluidity remained even with regard to genealogies long committed to writing.

New Testament

The descending genealogy of Jesus in Matthew 1:1-17 traces his descent through Abraham and David. That Jesus came at the "right time" is indicated by the three-fold sequence of fourteen generations: from Abraham to David (1:2-6a), from David to the Exile (1:6b-11), and from the Exile to Joseph (1:12-16). The names up to 1:12 can be traced to 1 Chronicles 2–3 and Ruth 4:18-22. The literary pattern ("A became the father of B") also follows Ruth 4. But the origin of the names from 1:13 (Abiud) to 1:16 (Jacob) remains a mystery.

An unusual feature of the genealogy in Matthew 1:1-17 is the appearance of five women: Tamar (Genesis 38), Rahab (Joshua 2; 6), Ruth, Bathsheba (2 Samuel 11–12), and Mary. It is difficult to discover a common factor among the women beyond a certain "irregularity," which in turn prepares for the irregular birth of Jesus in Matthew 1:18-25.

Whereas Matthew sought to emphasize Jesus' place within Israel, Luke in 3:23-38 stressed the universal significance of Jesus by following Jesus back to Adam: "the son of Adam, the son of God" (3:38). Luke gives Joseph's father's name as Heli and traces Jesus' Davidic descent from Nathan (see 2 Sam 5:14; 1 Chr 3:5; 14:4) rather than Solomon. He also goes back beyond Abraham to the generations from Terah to Adam (3:34b-38).

Both evangelists place Jesus in line with David and Abraham. Both present Joseph as the legal father of Jesus, without being his physical father. Both are more concerned with the present identity of Jesus than with the precise details of the genealogy. Attempts at harmonizing the lists or appeals to a Marian genealogy at Luke's disposal are not convincing.

Pastoral-Liturgical Tradition

The Matthean genealogy of Jesus is read on the Vigil of Christmas. It places Jesus within the Jewish tradition reaching from Abraham through David and the Exile to

Joseph. Thus it brings out the Jewish heritage of Jesus and the common spiritual heritage that Jews and Christians share (see Vatican II's Declaration on the Relationship of the Church to Non-Christian Religions, no. 4). It also recognizes the place of women in the history of salvation and places before us a peculiar array of saints and sinners, heroes and unknowns, who constitute the ancestors of the Messiah (and the Church today).

Without slighting the Jewishness of Jesus, the Lucan genealogy of Jesus "the son of Adam, the son of God," expresses his solidarity with all of humankind, a perspective brought out in the remaining parts of Vatican II's Declaration on the Relationship of the Church to Non-Christian Religions and in the Pastoral Constitution on the Church in the Modern World.

See: ANCESTORS, FAMILY

DANIEL J. HARRINGTON, S.J.

GETHSEMANE

Gethsemane is the location for Jesus' final prayer before his arrest, mentioned in Mark 14:32 and the parallel in Matthew 26:36. The name itself means in Aramaic "oil press." Mark seems to envisage this retreat as on the way to the Mount of Olives (14:26). Luke does not refer to Gethsemane but retains Mark's location for the prayer on the Mount of Olives (22:39), a detail that fits nicely into Luke's theology since he portrays the passion as the moment of the great eschatological "test" of Jesus (see 22:39-47, 53) and from this same Mount of Olives Jesus would give final instruction to his disciples and ascend victoriously to heaven (Luke 23:50-53; Acts 1:6-12). John has transposed the scene of Jesus' final prayer (see John 12:27-33) but similar to the Synoptics has Jesus leave the supper room to go "across the Kidron valley" to a "garden" where the arrest will take place (18:1).

For most Christians this entire complex of Gospel scenes (and perhaps a similar tradition in Heb 5:7-10) is known as Jesus' prayer in Gethsemane, a haunting moment of Jesus' life that has great drama and force. Gethsemane takes place in the final moments of Jesus' freedom with his disciples before his arrest. He prays with intensity, asking God to deliver him from death yet faithfully submitting his life and destiny to the will of the "Abba" or "Father" he intensely loves and trusts. Luke introduces the note of "agony"—presenting Jesus like an athlete straining with exertion before the challenge of his life. Each Gospel also gives attention to the disciples who, particularly in Mark's account, seem unable or unwilling to grasp the meaning of this fateful moment and the need for prayer and, therefore, will prove unprepared for the onslaught of violence and death.

The Gospels use this scene as an instruction on prayer, particularly earnest prayer for deliverance from the awful test of the end time which, ultimately, only the power of God can endure.

See: AGONY, PASSION, PRAYER

DONALD SENIOR, C.P.

GIFTS (FROM GOD, TO GOD)

The Scriptures speak of "gifts" in several different ways: gifts that one person gives to another, gifts that come from God, and gifts that are offered to God. In the OT mention is made of God's gifts to the people of Israel and the gifts of the people of Israel to God. In the NT, especially in the letters of Paul, the gifts of God to the baptized are highlighted. The Spirit of God is both the source of these gifts or charisms* and the actual gift. The liturgy of the Church underlines the two-fold nature of gifts offered to God and God's gifts given to the baptized in the Eucharist where bread and wine are offered and the Body and Blood of Christ is received.

Old Testament

In the OT, people valued the gift of life* itself and all that is needed to sustain and prolong it as God's most basic gift to them (e.g., Psalms 23; 27; 100; 104). As a religious people, they esteemed primarily the gift of

God's self-revelation to them, and the covenant* which bound them to God in a unique relationship (e.g., 2 Sam 7:18-29; Psalm 105). They loved the gift of God's law, sign of God's abiding care and presence among them (see Psalm 119). Finally, they rejoiced and gave thanks for the gift of God's unfailing mercy, and forgiveness of their sins and failures (e.g., Psalms 51; 103; 130). As a response of gratitude for God's gifts, an elaborate system of gifts, offerings, and sacrifices was prescribed (see Leviticus 1–7). These sacrificial gifts could be free-will offerings (Ezra 3:5) or sacrifices for sin or other reasons. One does not come into God's presence without a gift: "Bring gifts and enter his presence; worship the LORD in holy attire" (1 Chr 16:29). God's gifts to the people are manifold and are signs of divine favor: "the LORD's gift remains with the just" (Sir 11:17).

New Testament

In the NT gifts that come from God are given a more prominent place than those that are offered to God. The latter are mentioned in Matthew 5:23-24: "If you bring your gift to the altar, and there recall that your brother [or sister] has anything against you, go first and be reconciled with your brother [or sister], and then come and offer your gift." The original reference is to the sacrificial offerings of the Temple, but in the later Christian context Christ's words will be seen as referring to the gifts offered at the celebration of the Eucharist. By far the largest number of references to gifts are to those that come from God. God's gifts are given by the Spirit and, in fact, the holy Spirit is often the gift that is given. "He [Jesus] does not ration his gift of the Spirit" (John 3:34). God's gift is freely given and we need only ask: "If you knew the gift of God . . . you would have asked him" (John 4:10). Christ himself is the recipient of God's gifts: "this glory of mine which is your gift to me" (John 14:24); and he in turn shares God's gifts with his followers: "my peace is my gift to you" (John 17:27). Acts speaks of the gift that Christ promises to

leave the Church as being the holy Spirit given in baptism, when Peter says: "Repent and be baptized every one of you, in the name of Jesus Christ for the forgiveness of sins; and you will receive the gift of the holy Spirit" (Acts 2:38). The largest number of references to gifts given by God are found in the letters of Paul. For Paul the great gift that has been given by God in Christ Jesus is justification through faith (see Rom 3:21-26). It is through the "grace of God and the gracious gift of the one person Jesus Christ" (Rom 5:15) that those who "receive the abundance of grace and the gift of justification come to reign in life through the one person Jesus Christ" (Rom 5:17). Paul also speaks of the effect of this gift of God on those who receive it: "The gift of God is eternal life in Christ Jesus our Lord" (Rom 6:23). Thus the gift of justification through faith in Christ leads to eternal life in Christ. The individual believer is not the source of God's gift of faith and justification, rather "it is the gift of God" (Eph 2:8). This primary gift is manifested in the Christian through specific gifts given by God to each person (Rom 12:3-6). These individual gifts are: prophecy, ministry, teaching, exhorting, contributing, authority over others, and doing acts of mercy (see Rom 12:6-8). Because of the charismatic nature of the Church in Corinth, Paul goes into greater detail regarding the spiritual gifts of God and their proper exercise for the good of the community in his first letter to the Corinthians. He reminds the Corinthians that they are not lacking in any of the spiritual gifts (1 Cor 1:7). Chapter 12 speaks of these gifts: "Now in regard to spiritual gifts, brothers [and sisters], I do not want you to be unaware" (1 Cor 12:1). The one Spirit is the source of all the spiritual gifts (1 Cor 12:4). "To each individual the manifestation of the Spirit is given for some benefit" (1 Corinthians 7). Among these gifts are: the expression of wisdom, the expression of knowledge, healing, mighty deeds, prophecy, the discernment of spirits, variety of tongues, interpretation of tongues (1 Cor 12:8-10). Paul uses the analogy of the human body to show that each of these gifts is for the common good and serve the one body, the Church (see 1 Cor 12:12-31). He notes that these gifts are not to be seen as private possessions, but are to be used in the service of all (1 Cor 14:1-40, on the use of tongues). The greatest of all these spiritual gifts is love (see 1 Cor 13:1-13). In 2 Timothy 1:6 Paul reminds Timothy "to stir into flame the gift of God that you have through the imposition of my hands." This "gift of God" is the grace given to Timothy through the conferral of an office in the Church (see also 1 Tim 4:14).

Pastoral-Liturgical Tradition

The term "gifts" takes on a different usage in the post-apostolic and subsequent periods. Whereas in the NT the term is applied to God's gift of faith through justification and the individual gifts given by the Spirit, the word is later used to refer to the offerings of the people and the Eucharist itself.

The Gifts of the People. The practice of the people bringing bread, wine, and other gifts for the celebration of the Eucharist is very ancient. Justin Martyr mentions it in the second century, as does Hippolytus in the third century. The Latin words *dona* (gifts), *munera* (presents or gifts), and *oblatio* (offering) are used in reference to the gifts of the people (see Roman Canon, *Te igitur*). It is also clear from many of the prayers over the gifts that, in addition to the bread and wine, the gifts also include the prayers and lives of those who make the offering.

The Eucharist. The liturgical texts of the ancient sacramentaries speak of an exchange *(commercium)* of gifts taking place in the Eucharist: God receives our gifts (bread and wine) and transforms them into the Body and Blood of Christ so that by receiving the Eucharist in Communion we may be transformed. This concept is expressed by the prayer used for the preparation of the wine and water during the Mass, and which was originally the opening prayer for the Christmas liturgy in the Sacramen-

tary of Verona: "O God, you wondrously ennobled human nature in creating it and even more wondrously restored it. Grant that through the mystery of this water and wine we may be made partakers of his divinity, who condescended to share our humanity." This is expressed in the Syriac Maronite liturgy in a similar way: "You have united, O Lord, your divinity with our humanity and our humanity with your divinity; your life with our mortality and our mortality with your life. You have assumed what is ours, and you have given us what is yours for the life and salvation of our souls." These transformed Eucharistic gifts are "God's holy gifts to his holy people" that are received with thanksgiving (Rite of Anointing outside Mass, invitation to communion, B).

See: CHARISM, EUCHARIST, JESUS CHRIST, SPIRIT

ALAN F. DETSCHER

GLORY

While glory implies a wondrous or splendid manifestation of God's presence in human life, nonetheless glory also calls upon important aspects of faith: a realization that God is acting out of loving concern; a confidence that God reenacts the great acts of redemption in the liturgy; a prophetic determination to share God's glorious presence with the poor through social justice. The NT sees God's glory manifest in Jesus, especially in his miracles of healing and in his cross/resurrection. The OT prophetic vision reveals itself again in the documents of Vatican II, which call for an integration of human and religious values, so as to lead to a glorious manifestation of God's hopes in the final, eschatological age of the world.

Old Testament

Glory theologically does not so much reflect a glow of majestic wonder around God as it announces the extraordinary way that God impacts our human existence with the weight of divine holiness and redemption. In the OT Israel experienced this marvelous presence of divine glory in the great moments of salvation,* like the Exodus out of Egypt or the return from Exile, moments that were relived liturgically in the Temple and would envelop the world in its final, eschatological age. In no case was the glory so visible to the naked eye as to eliminate the need of faith. One must believe that at times within unlikely human circumstances God was accomplishing a remarkable feat in salvation. Even when the externals were impressive, to the point of being miraculous, faith was necessary to recognize the personal care of God Savior within the glorious events, as well as God's concern for justice and peace at these times.

Kabed or Kabod, the Principal Hebrew Word for Glory. This word denotes a quality of being heavy, whether with weight, wealth, or nobility, with exceptional goodness or with a heavy burden of sorrow, and so is variously translated. The patriarch "Abram was very rich in livestock, silver and gold" (Gen 13:2). Priests vest themselves with glorious adornment (Exod 28:2, 40). The noun designates "nobility" (Isa 5:13) or strong persons (Isa 17:4); the verb requires us to "honor" our parents (Exod 20:12; Deut 5:16) and "respect" the Sabbath day (Isa 58:13). The Hebrew root for "glory" occurs in all these cases; it indicates a way of relating with others and impressing others. This relationship depends upon a common set of values or ways of measuring what is honorable and prized. In the religious order faith provides this norm; God inspires the attitude or reveals the rules and ideals to judge what is rightly considered glorious.

Kabod denotes a quality that impresses us and influences us, either positively as in the previous examples, or more negatively. This Hebrew word can bespeak difficulty or laziness in responding and interacting; it is translated "slow [or heavy] of speech" (Exod 4:10), "eyes dim [or heavy] from age" (Gen 48:10), ears that are "dull" (Isa 6:10), a heart that is "obdurate" (Exod 9:7). From this negative use, the word came to refer to sinfulness: a people "laden [or heavy] with wickedness" (Isa 1:4). Therefore "the hand of God had been very heavy" upon the Philistines for having seized and profaned the ark of the covenant (1 Sam 5:11). The prophet Isaiah threatens the unfaithful kingdom of Judah with "the king of Assyria and all his power" (Isa 8:7), weighted with anger and revenge.

Kabod, therefore, indicates how someone or something weighs in upon another with unusually good or bad effects. While *kabod*, or glory, most often reflects wonder or majesty in a positive way, it can also bring the weight of God's demand for holiness and justice into our lives and so be a punishing and purifying force in a sinful situation. It is not glory for glory's sake but for the purpose of moral and religious transformation.

Priestly and Liturgical Uses. The word occurs frequently in what is called the Priestly (or "P") tradition in the Pentateuch, passages concerned with priesthood and worship. Prophecy also made a special use of it in challenging religious or civil leaders and their ritual, too "heavy" with pomp and sham.

According to P, the Lord Redeemer manifests divine "glory" in bringing Israel out of Egyptian slavery and caring for this elect people in the Sinai wilderness. Manna is the divine response when Moses promised a hungry people that "in the morning you will see the glory of the Lord" (Exod 16:7). One of the key moments came at Mount Sinai, where God descended amid "peals of thunder and lightning, and a heavy cloud . . . and a very loud trumpet blast" (Exod 19:16). In concluding the covenant, "the glory of the Lord settled upon Mount Sinai. [It was] seen as a consuming fire on the mountaintop" (Exod 24:16-17). Only Moses or a very select few could climb the mountain and enter the cloud of glory. These chapters of Exodus already evince a strong influence from Israel's later sanctuary ceremonies: the manifold use of light, fire, incense, and trumpets as well as the areas of the Temple restricted to priests and even the high priest. These sections of the Bible were composed to accompany the liturgy, so that later liturgical celebrations merge with historical remembrances of the original event. The glory of the Lord, according to the Book of Exodus, will reside upon the altar and make it sacred, so that all Israel "shall know that I, the LORD, am their God who brought them out of the land of Egypt, so that I, the LORD, their God, might dwell among them" (Exod 29:43-45). This same glory, the marvelous sign of God's care for the Israelites in the wilderness and of God's covenant with them, will fill the meeting tent, the forerunner of the Temple (Exod 40:34-38). "Glory" reflects Israel's faith that God accomplishes again and again within the liturgy the great, redemptive deeds from the days of Moses.

Glory, as we shall see, also included the paradoxical phenomenon of shielding the invisible, almighty God from Israel and simultaneously revealing the intimate bonding of God with Israel. When Moses asked of God: "Do let me see your glory" (Exod 33:18), God first responded that "no [one] sees me and still lives" (v. 20). God then proceeded to call Moses again to the top of Mount Sinai and there passed before him, calling out the divine name, "Yahweh, Yahweh," who is "a merciful and gracious God, slow to anger and rich in kindness and fidelity, . . . yet not declaring the guilty guiltless" (Exod 34:6-7). This intimacy with the divine person was to reach out and influence a just and merciful way of living. Yet such wholesome morality toward one's neighbors not only sustains but also feeds upon a contemplative approach toward God. At the end of chapter 34 we are told that whenever Moses left the presence of God within the tabernacle, such glory shone from his own face that he had to cover it with a cloth (Exod 34:29-35).

This glorious divine presence would not tolerate deliberate sinfulness in the people (Num 14:10-12), not even a slight sin of hesitation in Moses (Num 20:2-13). God's glory embraced a demanding holiness, severely punishing those Israelite priests who rebelled against Aaron (Num 16:19), those other Israelites who lost their confidence in Yahweh at the report about giants in the Promised Land (Num 14:20). This aspect of the Lord's glory, interfaced with justice and fidelity, will surface again in prophecy, as prophets challenge the Temple liturgy in the name of the poor and oppressed people of Israel.

Israel remembered, as mentioned already, the glorious redemptive deeds of the Lord particularly in liturgical celebrations. Therefore at the consecration of Solomon's Temple a dark cloud is said to have filled the Temple with the Lord's blinding glory (1 Kgs 8:10-12). This glory is synonymous with the Lord's wonderful deeds in the days of Moses. The psalms praise God whose glory in the Temple reflects the glory shining across the heavens and the earth (Pss 8:2; 19:2), thundering out fearfully in the midst of storms (Ps 29:2, 3, 9), mystically perceived during night vigils in the Temple (Ps 63:3, 7, 12), seen coming from Sinai and Teman by the prophet Habakkuk (Hab 3:3), magnificently entering the Temple once again during a procession with the ark of the covenant (Ps 24:7-10), enthroned with impregnable might and mystic wonder (Psalms 46–48). The passage of Habakkuk is important in that it follows an earlier statement that just persons live because of their faith (Hab 2:4). One must believe to appreciate God's personal, glorious presence in the Temple as well as across the universe; one must believe that God repeats now what once occurred in the days of Moses or David. Without faith glory vanishes!

Prophetic Presence. The glorious ritual of the Temple, reenacting the great moments of Israel's redemption through the ages, as recounted for instance in Psalm 68, must respect God's holiness and its demands of righteousness and justice in people's lives. Isaiah, while praying in the Temple, hears the seraphim proclaim, "Holy, holy, holy is the LORD of hosts" and sees that "the earth is filled with . . . glory" (Isa 6:3). As later verses in chapter 6 indicate, God's glory comes with a holiness that repudiates sin and sluggishness, in such a fearful way that only a stump is left standing of the once glorious Temple and city. Prophets lashed at Israel's conscience when the people lapsed repeatedly into sins profaning the Temple (Isa 1:10-17; Micah 3; Jeremiah 7). The prophets' words even seemed blasphemous and made the prophets guilty of death, for were they not denying God's eternal promises that glory always resides in the Temple (Jeremiah 26)?

Finally Ezekiel sees the glory of the Lord departing the Temple because of its abominations (8:3-10; 10:4-6, 18-23). This glory, as in the days of Moses, is not confined to any place but will appear to Ezekiel in the so-called unclean land of exile (Ezek 1:28). This "glory" is displayed in the punishment of Israel for its sins as well as in their purification through the pouring out of God's Spirit (Ezek 39:21-29). The second part of Isaiah's prophecy (chs. 40–55), also from the time of the Exile, declares that all Israel, scattered among the nations, will see the revelation of the glory of the Lord in a foreign land (Isa 40:5). From the sea and the coastlands, the steppes and villages, "let them give glory to the LORD!" (Isa 42:10-12). All Israel will be created anew, God says, "for my glory," when God tenderly brings sons and daughters from the ends of the earth (Isa 43:1-7). The lowly, persecuted servant who accomplishes these wonders will become "glorious in the sight of the LORD, [for] my God is now my strength" (Isa 49:5). Certainly faith, the intuitive insight to see as God sees, is required to recognize glory in the repudiated servant and in a people tired and depressed (Isa 40:28-31; 42:18-21).

The end of the Exile comes when Ezekiel sees "the glory of the Lord [entering] the [rebuilt] Temple by the gate that faces east." God then announces that "I will dwell in their midst forever" (43:4, 9). Just as the Lord's glory had punished Israel in the wilderness but led the next generation into the Promised Land and dwelt with them in Solomon's Temple, this same glory leveled a fearsome execution against a sinful people at the time of the Exile, led them back from the foreign lands and, as we shall see, came to dwell again in their Temple.

A New Prophecy. A new kind of prophecy appeared in the early postexilic period, not condemning the Temple because of the people's immorality, but proclaiming its necessity to sustain the people's faith. The prophet Haggai sees a marvelous trembling of the heavens and the earth, as the treasures of the nations flow into the new Temple, which God says, "I will fill . . . with glory. . . . Greater will be the future glory of this house than the former" (Hag 2:7, 9). In a similar strain the contemporary prophet Zechariah announces in God's name: "I will be for her an encircling wall of fire, . . . and I will be the glory in her midst" (Zech 2:9). The Temple, in this way of thinking, replaces the Messiah as the sign of God's final, glorious blessing upon Israel. Another prophetic tradition, that of Isaiah 56–66, is more expansive than Haggai and Zechariah, calls foreigners into the Temple, which is now "a house of prayer for all peoples" (Isa 56:7). Those who "have never heard of my fame, or seen my glory . . . shall proclaim my glory among the nations. . . . Some of them I will take as priests and Levites, says the LORD" (Isa 66:19, 21). In this new Jerusalem "nations shall behold your vindication, and all kings your glory" (Isa 62:2). Prophecy, we see, is still insisting upon justice, a key word in other parts of the third section of the Book of Isaiah (chs. 58–59), as a prerequisite for the Lord's glory at the Temple. Late, postexilic psalms also link God's glory with the demand for social justice: "The heavens proclaim God's justice, and all people see God's glory" (Ps 97:6). Prophecy also sounds a special call to disabled people. "They will see the glory of the LORD, the splendor of our God," and as a result "will the eyes of the blind be opened, the ears of the deaf be cleared; then will the lame leap like a stag, then the tongue of the dumb will sing" (Isa 35:2, 5-6).

Lest these magnificent visions of the glory of the Lord remove us too far from reality, the Wisdom literature, as in Proverbs and in many psalms, grants that this "honor [the Hebrew word is *kabod*, or glory] is the possession of the wise" (Prov 20:3), given to "the humble of spirit" (Prov 29:23b). Again faith is necessary to recognize God's transforming strength and special honor with humble, wise people. The gauge for judging true glory comes from God.

See: CLOUD, COVENANT, ESCHATOLOGY, FAITH, HOLY/HOLINESS, JUSTICE, LIGHT AND DARKNESS, MIRACLES, PEACE, REDEMPTION/REDEEMER

CARROLL STUHLMUELLER, C.P.

New Testament

The Glory of God. Glory is used in the NT in much the same way as in the OT. Primarily, glory refers to God's nature, honor, and power. As in the OT (e.g., Exod 24:17; 33:18-23; Num 12:8), God cannot be seen directly by human beings; rather, it is the divine glory that can be perceived. Sometimes a person glimpses the glory of God that resides in the heavenly sphere. Stephen, for example, "looked up intently to heaven and saw the glory of God" (Acts 7:55). God's glory is evident in creation. Paul denounces those who do not discern this and exchange "the glory of the immortal God" for other images (Rom 1:23). The Temple is also a locus of divine glory. In a description that echoes 1 Kings 8:10 and Isaiah 6:3-4, the visionary of Revelation 15:8 tells that, "the temple became so filled with the smoke from God's glory and might that no one could enter it." Similarly, in the vision of the new Jerusalem the city "gleamed with the splendor [glory] of God . . . the city had no need of sun or moon to shine on it, for the glory of God gave it light, and its lamp was the Lamb" (Rev 21:11, 23). In such descriptions the literal meaning of the Greek word for glory, *doxa,* comes to the fore: "brightness, splendor, radiance." When Acts 22:11 tells of "the brightness [*doxa*] of that light" from the sky that blinded Paul on the road to Damascus, the reference is to God's glory. Glory, then, is the manifestation of God that is able to be perceived by humankind. Consequently, God is known as "the God of glory" (Acts 7:2).

Throughout the NT people extol God's glory. Phrases such as "glorify God," "glory to God," or "give glory to God" can also be translated "give thanks to God" or "praise God." Giving God glory adds nothing to God, but rather acknowledges God's magnificence and power, thus praising and thanking God. Liturgical formulae such as "To the king of ages, incorruptible, invisible, the only God, honor and glory forever and ever" (1 Tim 1:17) are scattered throughout the NT (e.g., Gal 1:5; Rom 11:36; 16:27). Such expressions are similar to those found in the OT, e.g., Isaiah 42:12. Human praise of God parallels the way the heavenly court extols God, e.g., "Worthy are you, Lord, our God, to receive glory and honor and power" (Rev 4:11; similarly, Rev 7:12; 19:2).

The command "Give glory to God!" is used as an oath formula in John 9:24. As in Joshua 7:19, the expression stresses God's unique claim to worship and is invoked to urge a person to admit their guilt before God.

Those who do not give God the proper glory suffer dire consequences. Because Herod "did not ascribe the honor [*doxa*] to God," he was struck dead (Acts 12:23). Paul condemns those Gentiles who have known God through creation, but who "did not accord him glory as God or give him thanks" (Rom 1:21).

The Third Gospel is especially permeated with expressions of glory to God. For Luke, Jesus' birth is a particular moment for extolling God's glory. The heavenly host proclaims, "Glory to God in the highest" (Luke 2:14) and the shepherds "returned, glorifying and praising God for all they had heard and seen" (Luke 2:20). Jesus' mighty deeds of healing evoke the same reaction: the man who was paralyzed "picked up what he had been lying on, and went home, glorifying God" (Luke 5:25), as did all who witnessed the healing (Luke 5:26). When Jesus encountered the woman who was bent for eighteen years, "He laid his hands on her, and she at once stood up straight and glorified God" (Luke 13:13). The Samaritan leper, "realizing he had been healed, returned glorifying God in a loud voice" (Luke 17:15). In like manner, the blind beggar, upon receiving his sight, followed Jesus "giving glory to God" (Luke 18:43). At Jesus' entrance into Jerusalem, the beginning of his passion, death, and resurrection, the multitude of disciples cry out, "glory in the highest" (Luke 19:38). And at Jesus' death, "the centurion who witnessed what had happened glorified God" (Luke 23:47). Not only in the Gospel of Luke, but in the whole NT Jesus is the supreme revelation of divine glory to humankind.

The Glory of Christ. The NT takes a significant step by using glory in relation to Christ in much the same way that it had earlier been used of God. Hebrews 1:3 asserts that Christ "is the refulgence of his [God's] glory, the very imprint of his being." Paul makes a similar statement, "God who said, 'Let light shine out of darkness,' has shone in our hearts to bring to light the knowledge of the glory of God on the face of [Jesus] Christ" (2 Cor 4:6). In the NT not only is Jesus said to manifest God's glory, but glory is ascribed to Jesus himself.

The Synoptic Gospel writers refer to Jesus' glory primarily as a future manifestation at the parousia: "then they will see the Son of Man coming in the clouds with great power and glory," (Mark 8:26; similarly Mark 13:26; Matt 24:30; 25:31; Luke 9:26; 21:27). A foretaste of this eschatological glory is given the disciples at the transfiguration (Luke 9:32).

The Gospel of John has the greatest emphasis on the glory of Jesus. For the fourth evangelist, this glory is not to be awaited in the future but is already revealed. According to John 17:5, Jesus had glory with God before the world began. This glory is revealed on earth in the incarnation: "the Word became flesh and made his dwelling among us, and we saw his glory, the glory as of the Father's only Son, full of grace and truth" (1:14). The earthly Jesus further re-veals his glory through mighty deeds, just as God had done in the OT. The account of the first of these powerful acts, the changing of water into wine, concludes, "Jesus did this as the beginning of his signs in Cana in Galilee and so revealed his glory, and his disciples began to believe in him" (John 2:11). Similarly, the final sign, the raising of Lazarus is explained, "This illness is not to end in death, but is for the glory of God, that the Son of Man may be glorified through it" (11:4). The ultimate manifestation of Jesus' glory comes at his passion, death, and resurrection: "The hour has come for the Son of Man to be glorified" (12:23; similarly 12:28; 13:31; 17:1, 5; cf. 7:39; 12:16).

Throughout the Fourth Gospel there is a close connection between God's glory and that of Jesus. It is God who glorifies Jesus (8:54; 17:1, 5, 22, 24); but Jesus also glorifies God (13:31, 32; 14:13; 17:1, 4). Jesus' powerful deeds are for the glory of God, but at the same time the Son of God is glorified through them (11:4). A similar juxtaposition is found in Luke 9:26: "Whoever is ashamed of me and of my words, the Son of Man will be ashamed of when he comes in his glory and in the glory of the Father and of the holy angels." (See also Titus 2:13; 1 Pet 4:11.)

Many NT writers connect Jesus' glory with the resurrection. Paul asserts that "Christ was raised from the dead by the glory of the Father" (Rom 6:4). Here the resurrection is seen in terms of God's glory, or mighty act. The same act also gave glory to Christ (1 Pet 1:21). Paul speaks of the glory of the resurrected Christ being evident in his transformed or "glorified body" (Phil 3:21). Another aspect of Christ's movement back from the earthly realm to the heavenly is described in 1 Timothy 3:16 as Jesus being "taken up in glory."

In a few instances, Jesus' glory is connected with his suffering. Hebrews 2:9 declares that Jesus is now "crowned with glory and honor because he suffered death." Similarly, the resurrected Jesus asks the disciples on the way to Emmaus, "Was it not necessary that the Messiah should suffer these things and enter into his glory?" (Luke 24:26). 1 Peter 1:11 speaks of the "sufferings destined for Christ and the glories to follow them."

Just as God was known as "the God of glory" (Acts 7:2), so too Christ is termed "the Lord of glory" (1 Cor 2:8); or "our glorious Lord Jesus Christ" (Jas 2:1). It follows that just as God's glory had been extolled in doxologies or liturgical formulae, so too would such acclamations be made to Christ: "Worthy is the Lamb that was slain to receive power and riches, wisdom and strength, honor and glory and blessing" (Rev 5:12; similarly Rev 1:6; Heb 13:21).

Believers and Glory. In the OT the promise to believers was that they would *see* God's glory (e.g., Isa 35:2; 66:18). Although there is mention of seeing the glory of God (Acts 7:2; John 11:40) as well as that of Christ (John 1:14; 17:24), there is much more emphasis in the NT on the *participation* of believers in glory. The origin of this concept is found in apocalyptic writing, e.g., Daniel 12:3, which expects the radiance of the righteous at the resurrection. Matthew 13:43 reflects this notion: "Then the righteous will shine like the sun in the kingdom of their Father." Similarly, Colossians 3:4 states, "When Christ your life appears, then you too will appear with him in glory." The very vocation of Christians is put in terms of being called into the glory of God and of Christ (1 Thess 2:12; 2 Thess 2:14). This glory is eternal (2 Cor 4:17; 2 Tim 2:10; 1 Pet 5:4, 10) and is the object of hope* (Rom 5:2).

The glory of the faithful is patterned on that of Jesus. As with Jesus, the believer's glory is connected with the resurrection. Paul says that Christ "will change our lowly body to conform with his glorified body" (Phil 3:21). Similarly, "it is sown dishonorable; it is raised glorious" (1 Cor 15:43). As Jesus' glory was connected with his suffering, so too is that of believers. Paul assures, "if only we suffer with him . . . we may also be glorified with him. I con-

sider that the sufferings of this present time are as nothing compared with the glory to be revealed for us" (Rom 8:17-18). By contrast, those who inflict suffering and do not obey the gospel "will be separated from the presence of the Lord and from the glory of his power when he comes to be glorified among his holy ones" (2 Thess 1:9-10). Sin deprives a person of the glory of God (Rom 3:23).

Glory is not entirely futuristic for Jesus' followers. In the prayer for believers Jesus says, "I have given them the glory that you gave me" (John 17:22). Furthermore, Jesus has been glorified in believers (John 17:10). God too is glorified in that Jesus' followers bear much fruit and become his disciples (John 15:8). The death of a believer glorifies God (John 21:19). The prayer in Ephesians 4:16, "that he may grant you in accord with the riches of his glory to be strengthened with power through his Spirit in the inner self," implies that glory is at work already in the life of the believer. Likewise, there is the assurance in 1 Peter 4:14 to those suffering persecution, "the Spirit of glory and of God rests upon you." Another indication that glory is already realized for believers is found in Paul's discussion in 2 Corinthians 3:7-18 of the glory of the new covenant that surpasses that of the former. Perhaps the best illustration of the tension between the glory that is already present for the believer, and that which is yet to come is Paul's description in 2 Corinthians 3:18, "All of us, gazing with unveiled face on the glory of the Lord, are being transformed into the same image from glory to glory, as from the Lord who is the Spirit."

Heavenly Beings. Everything in the heavenly realm shares in God's glory. Thus, glory or radiance accompanies heavenly beings that appear on earth. When the angel of God appears to the shepherds to announce Jesus' birth, "the glory of the Lord shone around them" (Luke 2:9). Similarly, when an angel comes down from heaven in Revelation 18:1, "the earth became illumined by his splendor [glory]." So too in the Lucan story of the transfiguration, the heavenly figures Moses and Elijah "appeared in glory" (Luke 9:31). In several instances, angelic powers are simply referred to as doxai, "glorious beings" (2 Pet 2:10; Jude 8).

Human Glory. On a human level, *doxa* also denotes "splendor, honor," and is used to refer to anything that catches the eye. Several such examples are found in the NT. In the temptation story in Luke 4:6, the devil offers Jesus the "splendor" *(doxa)* of all the kingdoms of the world. Solomon's magnificence is also referred to with this term (Luke 12:27; Matt 6:29). There is also the "honor" *(doxa)* of being invited to a higher place at table (Luke 14:10). The fourth evangelist contrasts human praise *(doxa)* and the glory of God, "How can you believe, when you accept praise from one another and do not seek the praise that comes from the only God?" (John 5:44; also 12:43).

See: ANGEL, HEAVEN, POWER, PRAISE, RESURRECTION, TRANSFIGURATION

BARBARA E. REID, O.P.

Pastoral-Liturgical Tradition

As in the Scriptures, early Christian literature employs glory to describe the appearance of divine light,* brilliance, and splendor during moments of God's gracious self-revelation to human beings. In Patristic writings and in the liturgy, the recognition of God's glory, especially that glory revealed to humanity in Christ, is the foundation for all Christian worship, and leads to salvation* since it is through this recognition that both the Church and individual believers participate in the divine life and are transformed into the very image of God. Through faith in the manifestation of the holy One in Christ celebrated at baptism, believers also reflect that same divine glory and share in its saving power both in this world and at the end of time when God's glory will be completely revealed in all creation.

Glory as an Attribute of God and Christ. Glory, as the usual translation for the Hebrew word *kabod* and the Greek term *doxa*, enters the English language through the Latin noun *gloria*. Both Greek and Latin Patristic authors employ *doxa-gloria* to speak of the overwhelming holiness and power of the presence of God as it manifests itself to human beings. An example of this use of glory is found in the "Holy, Holy, Holy" acclamation of the Eucharistic liturgy which is based on Isaiah's vision of God in the Temple: "Holy, holy, holy Lord, God of power and might, heaven and earth are full of your glory" (Isa 6:3). While alluding to the visual experience of brightness and light, *doxa* was the word of choice in early Greek Patristic literature and preferred over the cognate terms epiphany or theophany because it had never been used in the context of the pagan mystery religions. In the shift from Greek to Latin, *gloria* as a translation of *doxa* was a later development. The earliest versions of the Latin Bible usually use either *maiestas* or *claritas* to translate *doxa* in order to convey a sense of the majestic or resplendent presence of the Holy One; both of these words are more consistent with the biblical meaning of *kabod-doxa* as light, brilliance, and power. This seems to point to a Jewish influence in these early Latin translations.

Gradually, however, *gloria* becomes the ordinary translation for *kabod-doxa*. Rather than exclusively emphasizing light and brightness, *gloria* in Latin Patristic literature conveys a nuance of military victory and prowess. The Exultet's ecstatic call for earth and all believers to rejoice because of the resurrection reflects this use of glory as an outcome of Christ's victory over death: "Christ has conquered, glory fills you! . . . Rejoice O Mother Church! Exult in glory! The risen Savior shines upon you!" Moreover, it is through the paradoxical image of the glorious cross that liturgical texts attribute glory to martyrs and saints—those who have most closely imitated Christ by offering their lives in testimony to the Savior's glory and are in turn sharers in God's glory.

Recognition of God's Glory as the Heart of Worship. Doxology or "words of glory" is a synonym for worship itself. Giving glory to God is basically confession and praise of the divine presence by human beings who recognize the resplendent presence of God in creation, in Christ, and in the Church. Both the greater doxology, the angelic hymn of the Eucharistic liturgy "Glory to God in the Highest," and the lesser doxology, "Glory to the Father and to the Son and to the holy Spirit," which concludes the psalmody of the Liturgy of the Hours, posit glory as that which is due God.

The way in which glory or divinity is ascribed to the persons of the Trinity becomes a hallmark of what comes to be known as orthodox or "right-worshiping" Christianity. The conclusion of the Eucharistic Prayer therefore was composed very carefully to speak of our relationship to God through the attribution of glory to the Father "through Christ, with Christ, and in Christ" and "in the unity of the holy Spirit." It is therefore because of Christ and his paschal mystery that Christians are able to recognize the glory of God and worship the divine majesty.

Glory also serves as a way of expressing our participation in the divine life through the saving power of the paschal mystery. In much the same way that martyrs and saints have attained the glory of God through imitating the victory of the Lord of Glory, so we also, through the sacraments, exhibit God's glory which radically changes our relationship with God and the world. In this sense, the acknowledgement of God's glory in Christ in worship informs all aspects of human life. Thus, Vatican II exhorts Christians "to integrate human, domestic, professional, scientific and technical enterprises with religious values, under whose supreme direction all things are ordered to the glory of God" (*Gaudium et spes* 43). It is in achieving this integration

that we attain true freedom and are called to the life that God intends for us; a life which also redounds to God's glory. Conscious of this life in Christ, then, St. Irenaeus could say in the second century, "The glory of God is a human being fully alive" (*Adv. Haer.* IV 20.7).

Glory as the Eschatological Hope* of All Who Believe in Christ. Finally, glory is used to describe the ultimate destiny of the world and those who believe. Christ's second coming will bring the world to perfection through the universal manifestation of his glory. We pray at Christmas Midnight Mass that, as we wait for the consummation of the world, that God might "give us a foretaste of the joy that you will grant us when the fullness of [Christ's] glory has filled the earth." It is in this sense that the Dogmatic Constitution on the Church (48) speaks of those who believe in Christ as a pilgrim people who "have not yet appeared with Christ in glory (see Col 3:4) in which we will be like God, for we will see him as he is (see 1 John 3:2)."

Pastoral Notes. It is obvious from the examples cited above that "glory" conveys a range of meanings depending upon its context. In the Church's tradition glory does not convey simply the static majesty and splendor of God, but is a way of speaking about how God dynamically communicates God's very life to humanity and to the world. While this presence is communicated in a variety of ways, some of which are quite dramatic, for example, in the awesome power of nature that accompanies the theophanies in the Hebrew Scriptures, for Christians, the glory of God is most perfectly revealed in the humanity of one like us, in Jesus Christ. Christian revelation contends that because of the incarnation of Jesus Christ, God's glory is present and active in human life and is a dynamic force for good in transforming those who recognize that glory into people who can attain to the very perfection of God. Thus, an utterly transcendent attribute of divinity is made immanent and accessible through faith in the one who suffered, died, and rose again. This underlines the dignity of all human beings and serves as the basis for not only "worship in spirit and in truth" but also Christian ethics.

See: ANGEL, CLOUD, FIRE, LIGHT AND DARKNESS, LORD, POWER, REDEMPTION, TRANSFIGURATION

MARK R. FRANCIS, C.S.V.

GOD

Belief in one God is the basis of the entire Judeo-Christian tradition. However, this God has been understood and worshiped in a variety of ways at different times in history. This diversity has resulted both in a wealth of traditions and in periodic confusion.

Old Testament

The common word for God in Semitic languages is *El.* Sometimes the plural *Elohim* is used. In the Bible the God of the Hebrews can be referred to with both the singular and the plural forms, although the plural is more common. Grammarians have called the plural usage "a plural of majesty."

God is also referred to in the Bible as Yahweh. This late Hebrew name became so common that its supposed historical origin was ignored and the name was included in writings that predated the use of the term. Perhaps the northern tribes favored the use of El or Elohim and the Judeans preferred Yahweh.

Other names such as El Shaddai (translated "The One of the Mountain"; Gen 49:25) and Adonai ("my lord") were used less frequently. The ancestral compounds El Elyon ("God most High"), El Olam ("God Eternal") also appear in the Bible.

God of the Ancestors. The ancient national traditions of Israel begin with the story of Abraham. It tells how God suddenly appeared to Abraham. "The LORD said to Abram: 'Go forth from the land of your kinsfolk and from your father's house to a land that I will show you'" (Gen 12:1). We learn from this early theology that God

was depicted anthropomorphically (in human form): God spoke as a person, gave instructions as a person, had concern as a person. God made certain ethical demands, such as complete faith and circumcision of male children, and gave promises about a future time of peace and blessing. This is quite unusual in comparative religion.

In the ancestral period God was invoked principally as a patron and protector. As in pastoral societies generally, God was called upon to protect the tribe from the common dangers of ferocious animals, natural disasters, and human enemies. In return for such protection God was praised for God's wondrous deeds and was clung to with unquestioned faith.

Mosaic Religion. In the story of the Exodus from Egypt, God is pictured as the great liberator. God alone does the wondrous deeds that bring the people into the land of promise. The great covenant experiences related in various different places all emphasize the total initiative of God. The ethical demands made are also escalated. As God has freed this people simply because God willed it, so they must choose freedom because they will it. The recognition of freedom, both in God and in human beings, has become a central point of Israelite religion. The freedom is not without its responsibilities; love, fidelity, and understanding are recognized as mutual obligations. The sermons of Deuteronomy, especially Deuteronomy 6, make these responsibilities central to the mutual understanding. Just how much of this was in the original understanding of the Mosaic covenant is not clear. It is unlikely that the final documents have misinterpreted the original understanding.

In the story of the call of Moses (Exod 3:1-14), God is called Yahweh for the first time and the American Bible translation renders this as "I AM." The precise meaning of this word is not entirely clear. Undoubtedly, it has something to do with the origin of Israel as a chosen people.

God was never described by the Israelites

as distant. God was known only in relational terms. This is sometimes depicted in surprising stories. God could be argued with and blamed, sometimes reversed decisions and sometimes repented of what had been done. This is, indeed, the crux of the stories of Moses as he tries to see God (Exodus 32–33). We read that when the people made the molten calf, God reproved Moses for the conduct of "your people." Moses objected that he was not getting much help from the Lord in dealing with the people and the Lord responded somewhat peevishly: "Let me alone" (Exod 31:10). But Moses pressed on and demanded a change. "So the Lord relented in the punishment he had threatened to inflict on his people" (Exod 32:14). This clash did not interfere with the relationship between God and Moses. Indeed, as the commentator says, "The LORD used to speak to Moses face to face, as one man speaks to another" (Exod 33:11). These anthropomorphisms show that the basic experience of the biblical authors was of a relationship.

The OT tradition of God relenting or repenting endured for a long time. It implies that God does not admit moral guilt in repentance, but God does change decisions. Judges 2:18 sums up the theme of the entire book as that of God relenting; 1 Samuel 15:11 and 35 report that God repented that Saul had been made king; 2 Samuel 24:16 has God regretting the calamity of the plague sent after David took up a census; 1 Chronicles 21:15 repeats this story; frequently in Jeremiah (Jer 18:8, 10; 20:16; 26:3, 13, 19; 31:19; 42:10) and in the other prophets (such as Joel 2:13, 14; Amos 7:3, 6; Jonah 3:9, 10; Zech 8:14) God repents or at least relents. The converse point of the Lord not repenting is made in Psalm 110:4; Jeremiah 4:28; Ezekiel 24:14.

Other characters in later stories challenge God's way of acting. Job quite clearly calls upon God to explain the evil that has befallen him, and Qoheleth complains that God has withheld the explanation of all things. This way of speaking of God had divine approval. We read that God commended Job for his integrity: "You have not spoken rightly concerning me, as has my servant Job" (Job 42:7).

El or Yahweh is quite clearly perceived as a warrior God. The Song of the Sea in Exodus 15 (one of the earliest pieces of poetry in the Bible) begins exuberantly:

> I will sing to the LORD, for he is gloriously triumphant;
>> horse and chariot he has cast into the sea.
> The LORD is a warrior, LORD is his name
>> (Exod 15:1, 3).

God, the protector of the people, is a loving God. The love theme begins with the giving of the Decalogue (Exod 20:6; Deut 6:5; 11:1, 13, 22), is stressed in the great commandment (Lev 19:18, 34; Deut 10:12; 19:9; 30:6, 20), becomes a constant reminder of God's attitude toward the people (Deut 4:37; 7:13; 15:16) and is constantly stressed in the psalms (see Pss 25:6; 36:7; 63:3; 148:2; etc.).

Monarchy. During the times of the monarchy (tenth century BCE to sixth century BCE), an exceedingly strong portrait of God as conquering Warrior is painted. Thus the much later Psalm 68 uses these traditions to invoke God during a liturgical procession when the ark was carried into the Temple. It begins with the war cry used at the beginning of battle: "God arises; his enemies are scattered, and those who hate him flee before him" (Ps 63:2). This psalm uses memories of past victories to exalt this God whom the people are placing in the holy of holies on Mount Zion. Sometimes the imagery is disconcertingly vengeful. "The LORD said: 'I will fetch them back from Bashar; I will fetch them back from the depths of the sea, so that you will bathe your feet in blood; the tongues of your dogs will have their share of your enemies'" (Ps 68:23-24). This is a harsh note of relentless justice.

The monarchial establishment itself elevated worship of God in the Temple on Mount Zion to the highest duty of the Israelite. Many psalms are directed toward the presence of God within the Temple. There was a consistency in the wish:

One thing I ask of the LORD;
  this I seek:
To dwell in the house of the LORD
  all the days of my life
                    (Ps 27:4).

What is most impressive about this picture is God's intimacy with the people. God is also consistently the savior in all troubles both national and personal; God is the shepherd, the defender, the consoler. Peace and prosperity are divine gifts; God is clothed with majesty and splendor.

Prophets. Most notable in the prophets, despite their denunciations, is the tendency to personalize the relations between God and the people, especially to emphasize divine love. Hosea introduces the picture of God as the faithful spouse of unfaithful Israel who calls her back from her wayward ways (Hos 2:1-25). "On that day, says the LORD, she shall call me 'My husband' and never again 'My baal'" (Hos 2:18). God is also the loving parent: "When Israel was a child I loved him, out of Egypt I called my son" (Hos 11:1). Isaiah and Zechariah also have this vivid imagery of God as the lover and spouse of Israel.

In Deutero-Isaiah the protective action of God tends to shift to feminine imagery. So the great hymns to Zion the Holy One of Israel (Isa 60:1-22), the Lord's bride (Isa 62:1-12), Jerusalem my delight (Isa 65:17-25), and especially the almost final poem to Mother Zion:

Rejoice with Jerusalem and be glad of her,
  all you who love her;
Exult, exult with her,
  all you who were mourning over her!
Oh, that you may suck fully
  of the milk of her comfort,
That you may nurse with delight
  at her abundant breasts!
For thus says the LORD:
Lo, I will spread prosperity over her like a
  river,
  and the wealth of the nations like
  an overflowing torrent.

As nurslings you shall be carried in her
  arms,
  and fondled in her lap;
As a mother comforts her son,
  so will I comfort you;
In Jerusalem you shall find your comfort
                    (Isa 66:10-13).

"Mother Jerusalem" becomes a stand-in for God, as some of the later rabbis assert. It is mother Jerusalem who hovers over her children as a hen protects her brood; it is mother Jerusalem who showers them with comfort and with wealth; it is mother Jerusalem who calls them back. The Hebrews had no female god; they had no word for such. God was both mother and father.

The tendency to take a final refuge in the Warrior God imagery is often quite strong. The prophecy of Obadiah is a blood-curdling curse against Edom and Nineveh. The Book of Ezekiel also includes denunciations of Tyre and Sidon which appear later in the Book of Revelation as a taunt song against the new Babylon, Rome. Justice was applied against all evil-doing with fine indifference; retribution at times seemed almost the principal job of God. Yet the ideal retribution theology was never achieved. The prophetic messages were never simply threats of condemnation. They were assurances of consolation and love as well. The freedom of God could not be coerced within a human and manageable system.

Central to this perception of monarchial times was the re-emerging picture of God as the free and loving creator of all things. This wisdom motif had been stressed in as early a tradition as the prophetic book of Amos. It is also the linchpin between the First and Second Isaiah.

Late Judaism. The postexilic period (fourth century BCE to the time of Christ) is notable for the wisdom writings. They were simply called "the other writings" by the Jews; they had lesser authority and were not expressed as words from God but as human reflections. Still, they were so apposite and so practical that they became part of Israel's lore. One of the central images of Wisdom writing is God the good creator. The central need is the quest for order in life. What worked and what did not work in personal relations was duly recorded. Here the national scene and the covenant are not first and foremost. The good life is. This is a life based on doing what is most effective with the least stress. When the achievement is impossible of attainment (as in Job and Ecclesiastes), the recourse is made to the mystery of God. This wisdom of God is almost equated with God's own self; it is a spirit, mobile and pure, which governs all things (Wis 7:22-27).

The most noticeable characteristic of the postexilic concept of God was its practiced monotheism. "I shall be your God; you shall be my people" (Lev 26:12) came to identify the Jew. At a time in late Judaism when the proliferation of gods occurred among the Romans and Greeks, Judaism pursued its unquestioned assertion that God is one.

There were divergent nuances about this one God however. Among the Pharisees at the time of Christ God was a God whom one blessed for all the salvation and order that had been wrought. Then there is Paul who denounces an obliging God who rewards obedience to the Law. In addition to this, the Qumran secretaries seemed to emphasize the holiness of God with a rigid asceticism and an emphasis on an unworldly coming war of good and evil. Finally, a still more divergent view was held by the Sadducees, who thought that God did very little rewarding and certainly none in the future life, as popular belief seemed to hold.

See: APOCALYPTIC, EL/ELOHIM, ISRAEL, YAHWEH

JAMES A. FISCHER, C.M.

New Testament

Revelation of God. The God of Jesus and the early Church is the God of the ancestors, "the God of Abraham, the God of Isaac and the God of Jacob" (Mark 12:26; Matt 22:32; Luke 20:37; Acts 3:13; 7:32, see

Exod 3:6). The sweep of human history unfolds from a God, who creates the universe and humanity by his word (Genesis 1–3) and who is involved in human history, and in the lives of Israel and the Church to God reigning with the holy ones in the new creation (Rev 22:5). The Bible disavows any contrast between the merciful or loving God of the NT and the wrathful God of the OT. God's self-disclosure in history, in law and wisdom, and in the praise and worship of the people of Israel is the OT's legacy to the NT and the nascent Church (Rom 9:4-5). Radical monotheism is the foundation of NT faith. When asked about the "first" of all the commandments, Jesus quotes the *Shema'*, the classic expression and daily affirmation of Jewish faith: "Hear, O Israel: The Lord our God, the Lord is one" (Mark 12:29, *et par.*). Christian converts "turn from idols to serve the living and true God" (1 Thess 1:9) and confess, "for us there is one God, the Father from whom all things are and for whom we exist, and one Lord, Jesus Christ, through whom all things are and through whom we exist" (1 Cor 8:6).

Attributes of God. When trying to describe God, "we see through a glass darkly" (1 Cor 13:12) and his "invisible attributes of eternal power and divinity" (Rom 1:20) transcend the descriptive power of language. There is always a dialectic of affirmation and of denial, e.g., God is like a human parent, father or mother, but unlike, in a transcendent way, our experience of a father or mother. Also, opposing human attitudes are reconciled in God. God shows his mercy from age to age (Luke 1:50) and pours wrath on "every impiety and wickedness" (Rom 1:18). God's folly is wiser than human wisdom (1 Cor 1:25).

The OT attributes of God prevail in the NT. God is eternal (Deut 33:27; Rom 1:20) and powerful (Ps 29:4; Heb 4:12), creator of heaven and earth (Genesis 1–3; Isa 40:28; Mark 13:19), the holy one who forms a holy people (Isa 6:3; 57:15; Rev 4:8; Lev 11:44; 1 Pet 1:15-16), savior (Ps 27:1; Isa 43:3; Luke 1:47; 1 Tim 1:1), compassionate and merciful

(Exod 34:6-7; Luke 1:50; Mark 5:19), yet standing in judgment over idolatry and human arrogance (Isa 2:8-10; 45:18-25; Rom 1:18-32). The divine saving actions are expressed in a special way by a series of genitives where God effects the quality mentioned: God of hope (Rom 15:3), of peace (Rom 15:33; 1 Cor 14:33; 1 Thess 5:23), of comfort (2 Cor 1:3-4), of grace (1 Pet 5:10), and of love (2 Cor 13:11). These attributes of God are to determine human conduct: "be imitators of God and walk in love" (Eph 5:1-2). Christians upon whom the love of God is poured out (Rom 5:15) are to show this love to others, so much so that in 1 John whoever does not love a brother or sister can not love God (3:11-18) and "God is love, and whoever remains in love, remains in God" (4:16).

Jesus and God. The ministry of Jesus in the Synoptic Gospels is theocentric. He is primarily the herald of the reign of God (Mark 1:14-15), i.e., God's active claim upon human life which will be manifest in his ministry. Jesus' mighty works are done in the Spirit of God (Matt 12:28; Luke 11:20), and evoke praise of God (Mark 2:12). When criticized for violating the Law, Jesus invokes a God who desires mercy, not sacrifice (Matt 9:13; 12:6 see Hos 6:6). Jesus proclaims a God who is on the side of the poor, the mourners, the meek, the merciful, the peacemakers, and those who hunger and thirst for justice (Matt 5:3-11), and teaches his followers to forsake anxiety and have trust in a "heavenly Father" whose lavish care for the birds and the flowers is an image of the care he has for them (Matt 6:25-34). His followers are to pray that God's name be hallowed and that God's will be done (Matt 6:9-13); he himself follows this will even to death (Mark 14:36); his final words are a cry to God (Mark 15:34). God does not desire only obedience, for Jesus summarizes the whole Law by the precept to love God with whole heart and mind and soul, and the neighbor as one's self (Mark 12:38-42, *et par*). This love, when extended even to enemies who are under

God's care, makes a person perfect, even as God is perfect (Matt 5:43-48).

The God and Father of Our Lord Jesus Christ (2 Cor 11:31). In the OT, God is described as "father" relatively infrequently, and not in the context of dominating power, but of communicating life in becoming a "father" to the people or by care for them (e.g., Exod 4:22; Deut 32:6; Jer 3:19; Isa 45:9-11; 64:8; Mal 2:10). In the NT, as well, saving history provides the context for calling God "Father." God has been revealed in a new way in the Christ event, i.e., the teaching, life, death, resurrection and abiding presence of Jesus, expressed by the phrase "the gospel of God" (Mark 1:14; 1 Thess 2:2; Rom 15:16; 1 Pet 4:17). This comprises the gift of his own Son in whom all people have access to God (Gal 4:4; Rom 8:32; Acts 2:21; 4:12). God's initiative unfolds in three "moments": "sending" of his son (Gal 4:4; Rom 8:3; see John 3:16), "handing over" his son to death for the sake of human salvation (Rom 8:32) and "raising him up" to be Lord and Messiah (Acts 2:32-36), and establishing him as a Son of God in power through the resurrection from the dead (Rom 1:2-5).

Though Jesus called God "father," and though "Son of God" of itself does not always designate divine status, the post-resurrection faith of the early Church expressed a deep unity between God and Jesus. While God is normally the subject of saving action (e.g., God gave his Son; God handed Jesus over and raised him from the dead), Jesus himself is also the subject: "Christ, while we were still helpless, yet died at the appointed time for the ungodly" (Rom 5:6-8), Paul states that Christ has redeemed us (Gal 3:13) and says that we will appear before the judgment seat of Christ (2 Cor 5:10, normally God is the sole judge). Paul speaks of Christ sending him (1 Cor 1:17) and of his faith in Christ, which brings salvation (Gal 2:15-21). The benefits of salvation, grace, and peace come from both "our Father and the Lord Jesus Christ" (Rom 1:7; 1 Cor 1:3; 2 Cor 1:2). Jesus comes from God with divine authority; God is with him (John 3:2; Matt 1:23); he is the image of the invisible God (Col 1:15); in him the fullness of God dwells bodily (Col 2:9) and he and the Father are one (John 10:30; 14:10; 17:11, 21).

Such expressions have created the classical problem of the Christian understanding of God: how to reconcile a virtual unity and harmony in speech and action between Jesus and God, while maintaining strict monotheism, and a clear distinction between "Father" and "Son." Equally challenging are a series of "triadic" texts in which Father, Son, and Spirit are closely related. These often reflect a baptismal context, e.g., 1 Corinthians 6:11, "But you have had yourself washed, you were sanctified, you were justified in the name of the Lord Jesus Christ and in the Spirit of our God"; "But the one who gives us security with you in Christ and who anointed us is God; he has also put his seal upon us and given the Spirit in our hearts as a first installment" (for other triadic texts see, Gal 4:4-6; Rom 5:1-5; 8:9-11; 15:30; 1 Cor 12:4-6; 2 Cor 13:14). Baptism (Matt 28:19) was to take place in the name of the Father, the Son, and the holy Spirit. In Ephesians 4:1-4, the threefold unity is the basis of the unity in the Church: "one body and one Spirit, as you were also called to the one hope of your call; one Lord, one faith, one baptism; one God and Father of all, who is over all and through all and in all." The Gospel and Letters of John also speak of the most intimate relation between Jesus, the Father, and the "Advocate" (Paraclete), "whom I [Jesus] will send you from the Father, the Spirit of truth that proceeds from the Father" (John 15:26; 14:26). What these texts show is that the early Christians saw God revealed both in the Christ event and in the manner in which the power and Spirit of God shaped their lives (see esp. 1 Cor 12:1-4). Such texts will provide both the "raw material" and the exegetical battleground for the evolution of the later doctrine of the Trinity.

God and the Salvation of All Humanity. The NT contains hints that God's will could be known apart from its revelation to Jews and Christians (Acts 17:22-32; Rom 1:19-21) and affirms that "God wishes everyone to be saved and to come to the knowledge of the truth" (1 Tim 2:4; see 2 Pet 3:9; Rom 11:32). Though the OT and late Jewish intertestamental literature contain elements of God's rule over "the nations" (Ps 86:9; Rev 15:4), salvation for the Gentiles involved becoming a member of the elect people of God, which was ratified by circumcision. One of the major struggles of the early Church was to claim that the heritage of Israel and the Christ event broke through the bounds of ethnic and religious identity. The conversion of Cornelius in Acts 10 and the Jerusalem Council (Acts 15:1-29) are moments which set the all-inclusive course of Church history.

The letters to the Galatians, and especially to the Romans, represent Paul's struggle with a Jewish Christian theology of election, which would have forced Gentiles to become Christians only after adopting Jewish law and practices. At stake is a fundamental understanding of God, expressed by a series of dilemmas. How could a just God who rejects "Gentile sinners" (Gal 2:15) seem to change? How can God's law which was to have eternal validity not be obeyed (Romans 7)? How can the elect people turn away from the love of God manifest in the gift of his son (Romans 9–11)? Such problems become the stimulus for profound theological insights, especially in Romans. All human pretense and sin stand under the judgment of God, "all have sinned and are deprived of the Glory of God" (Rom 3:23), and, paradoxically then, "all are justified [i.e., made upright before God] by God's grace [i.e., not by human effort] through the redemption in Jesus Christ" (Rom 3:24). While the Law had an important saving function, Abraham, "our ancestor," was justified by faith apart from the Law (Rom 4:1-24), and now access to this redemption is not through Law or circumcision but through faith, a faith that at the appointed time Christ died for the ungodly (Rom 5:1-11). Therefore, for Paul no human is outside the pale of God's loving concern. After spelling out the effects of the Christ event as freedom *from* sin, Law, and death, and freedom *for* life in the Spirit, Paul struggles with the apparent rejection of his Jewish brothers and sisters and concludes that in the mystery of God their apparent alienation from God is temporary and for the sake of the salvation of the Gentiles (Romans 9–11, esp. 11:25-36).

Pastoral Notes. The Bible does not contain systematic doctrines about God but testimonies to God as a living personal being, reaching out for human response throughout history. As the great Jewish theologian Abraham Heschel reminded us, the Bible does not present the "unmoved mover" of Aristotle but "the most moved mover" (*Between God and Man* [New York: Harpers, 1959] 24). It contains equally a vast diversity of responses to God, ranging from praise of the creator and liberator through joy in the presence of God, to agonizing cries to a seemingly absent God. The Bible itself sanctions a plurality of responses to the mystery of God's existence and love.

The tension between strict monotheism and "binatarian" statements in the NT (i.e., two agents of salvation, God and Jesus), as well as with "triadic" statements, is a constant warning against a "Christomonism" which forgets that Jesus points beyond himself to the hidden God, or a "tritheism" which treats Father, Son, and Spirit as independent agents.

In speaking of the NT today, the cultural context of its language presents a major problem. God is most often "Father" and Jesus, "the Son." Feminist exegesis and hermeneutics has raised acutely the problem of the viability of "androcentric" language for faith today. One response is always to keep in mind both the historical contingency of revelation in a definite social milieu, and the inadequacy of all human language about God. Also, the description of God as "Father" in the NT shatters the images of a dominating father which were a cultural commonplace in the first century. Nor is Jesus' "sonship" particularly connected with maleness, but with trust, fidelity, and a unity of purpose with his Father in giving his life for others.

By rejecting literalism and fundamentalism, Roman Catholic teaching on the interpretation and authority of Scripture, and on the role of the community of faith in expressing the substance of revelation (Tradition), has recognized that non-Scriptural language can often better express the substance of revelation than biblical terms (e.g., in the case during the Arian controversy of *homoousios*, "of one substance," for the relation between the Son and Father in the Godhead). The Church is constantly summoned to find ways of speaking about God (e.g., God as friend) which, while supplementing NT language, may help to enter more deeply into the mystery of God.

While the NT does not address directly either the contemporary problems of the relation of Judaism and Christianity, nor of salvation of non-Christians and unbelievers, it contains the seeds of future reflection. The NT claims that the Christ event that took place at a definite time and among particular people has universal significance in that the human condition has been radically changed by Jesus, the "last Adam" (1 Cor 15:20-28, 45-49; Rom 5:15-21), who reconciles humanity to God. How this takes place among particular Christians—or non-Christians—is as mysterious as how the created world came from God and how Christ is to hand over God's reign to his God and Father (1 Cor 15:24). These are part of what Paul called "the unsearchable ways" of God's salvation (Rom 11:33). The self-disclosure of God in the NT is an invitation. Who is to determine the shape of the answer?

JOHN R. DONAHUE, S.J.

Pastoral-Liturgical Tradition

Early Christians shared the monotheistic faith of the people of Israel and faced a complex series of challenges in interpreting this faith in relation to creation, to the experience of God in Jesus Christ, and to Hellenistic religions. Debates over the relationship of Jesus to God and over the nature of the Spirit led eventually to the articulation of the Trinitarian faith of the Church.

One God the Creator. The belief in one God, the creator of the universe and source of all reality, had deep roots both in the Hebrew Bible and in the teaching of Jesus. According to the Gospel of Mark, Jesus explicitly accepted the traditional call: "Hear, O Israel! The Lord our God is Lord alone!" (Deut 6:4; Mark 12:29). In continuity with the Hebrew Bible, the parables of Jesus present God as the creator and the mysterious and watchful caretaker of the universe (e.g., Matt 6:26-30; Mark 4:26-29).

Some early Christian groups, however, distinguished the God of creation, who was often viewed as merely just or as evil, from the God of redemption who had sent Jesus Christ to rescue humans from an evil world. In denying that the God of Christians is creator of the universe, both Christian Gnostics and followers of Marcion of Pontus (ca. 85–ca. 160) expressed a deep sense of alienation from the world. In response, the early Church affirmed that the one God is the absolute source of all reality, creating all things from nothing.

In affirming the identity of the God of creation with the God of Jesus Christ, the early Church acknowledged a close relationship between the universal presence of God in all creation and the concrete historical revelation of God in Jesus Christ (see 1 Cor 8:6; John 1:3; Col 1:16; Eph 4:6). This had important implications for relations between Christians and non-Christians in the Hellenistic world.

Jesus Christ as God. The most distinctive claim of early Christian witness and worship was that Jesus himself is to be addressed as and thought of as God. At the beginning of the second century Ignatius of Antioch expressed his faith in "our God, Jesus the Christ" (Letter to the Ephesians 18:2; see also Ignatius, Epistle to the Romans 3:3; 6:3). About the same time, the Roman provincial governor, Pliny, informed the Emperor Trajan that Christians sang hymns to Christ as to God (Letter to the Emperor Trajan, 7; Epistle 10, 96, 7). Moreover, the earliest extant Christian sermon outside of the NT advised its audience that "we ought to think of Jesus Christ as we do of God" (2 Clement 1:1).

The pastoral witness and the liturgical practice of addressing Jesus Christ as divine arose from the experience of God's presence in Jesus, transforming those who encountered and accepted him. The acclamation of Jesus Christ as God (John 20:28), however, had to be related to the monotheistic faith of the Church. This challenge called forth both intense reflection and bitter controversy from Christians. Debate over this issue would propel the Church into the Trinitarian decisions of the fourth century.

God and Hellenistic Religions and Culture. Hellenistic culture was filled with competing religious traditions and with influential philosophical schools. Early Christians approached the pressing pastoral task of communicating their understanding of God to non-Christians through a twofold strategy. On the one hand, they insisted on the uniqueness and oneness of God and reaffirmed the biblical rejection of all other gods and goddesses as idols. Even when threatened by death, many bore witness to their faith, steadfastly refusing to worship the Roman Emperor or the protecting deity of the Emperor as a god.

On the other hand, Christians also stressed links between their faith and Hellenistic experience and culture in order to proclaim the God of Jesus Christ to the Hellenistic world in a way that non-Christians could more easily understand. This process begins already in NT times. According to the Acts of the Apostles, Paul attempted to persuade the Athenians that the God of Christianity was in fact the "unknown God" already worshiped in Athens (Acts 17:23), and even quoted pagan poets as witnesses of God (Acts 17:28).

Early Christian apologists such as Justin Martyr (ca. 100–ca. 165) continued this strategy of proclaiming the one God who is universally present and thus already experienced by the non-Christian world. Justin stressed that the God of Jesus Christ is the same as the God of the best Greek philosophers (1 Apology, 46), and claimed that all truth everywhere comes from God through the Word (or *Logos*), which is present in all human experience.

In continuity with this tradition, the Declaration on the Relation of the Church to Non-Christian Religions of Vatican II acknowledges that God offers a ray of truth to enlighten all people and that elements of truth and holiness are found in non-Christian religious traditions (no. 2).

God as Triune. The early Church not only addressed Jesus as God, but also celebrated the role of the Spirit in worship and in guiding and building up the Christian community. The Christian Scriptures do not offer an explicit doctrine of the Trinity, but they do include triadic formulas, especially in liturgical contexts such as baptism (Matt 28:19) and in the greetings of letters (2 Cor 13:13; see also 1 Pet 1:2).

The liturgical practice of praying to Jesus Christ as divine and the threefold baptismal invocation of God impelled Christians to reflect more explicitly on the reality of God as triune. Much confusion, however, arose from the variety of language used about God and Jesus and the Spirit in the Christian Scriptures themselves. If Jesus Christ is addressed as God, this could suggest a simple identity between Jesus and God without specifying any distinction of persons (see John 10:30); some early Christians, such as Sabellius (ca. 220), concluded from this that God is one and only appears in a threefold way in the work of creation and salvation. For Sabellius, the Word and the Spirit were simply modes of God's external self-expression, and not eternal realities in God.

On the other hand, many passages in the Bible implied a distinction between God and Jesus. Jesus prays to God in the second person and distinguishes his will from God's (Mark 14:36). The Gospel of John presents Jesus as affirming that "the Father is greater than I" (John 14:28). Some Christians, such as Arius (ca. 256–336), believed these passages implied a subordination of Jesus to God, and concluded that Jesus Christ was the greatest of all creatures but was not fully divine.

The decisive steps in the formation of the Christian doctrine of God occurred in the fourth century. At the Council of Nicaea in 325 the Church rejected Arius's teaching and declared that Jesus Christ is one in being *(homoousios)* with God. In the vigorous debates that followed the council, the most influential interpreter and defender of the Council of Nicaea was Athanasius, the bishop of Alexandria (ca. 295–373). For him, the decisive issue is determined by the experience of redemption in Christ. The heart of Christian faith and experience is that God became human so that we might become divine. The experience of salvation in Jesus Christ impelled Athanasius to defend the full divinity of Christ as of the same essence or substance as God.

Athanasius also drew the further conclusion that the Spirit who sanctifies us is also fully divine. In the fourth-century debates over the divinity of the Spirit, the liturgical practice of the baptismal formula, initiating Christians into the faith "in the name of the Father and of the Son, and of the holy Spirit" (Matt 28:19) was of decisive importance. Athanasius and Basil the Great (ca. 330–379) argued that if Christians baptize in the name of the Spirit to welcome people into the Church, then the Spirit must be fully divine. Basil saw the Spirit as empowering Christians to see Jesus Christ as the revelation of God. For Basil, we would not have faith in God at all without the Spirit (*The Holy Spirit*, 27).

With the affirmation of the Spirit's divinity at the First Council of Constantinople in 381, the central articulation of the Church's faith in the triune God was established.

See: BAPTISM, CREATION, JESUS CHRIST, REDEMPTION, SPIRIT, WORD

LEO D. LEFEBURE

GOOD NEWS/GOSPEL

The term "gospel" or "good news" can refer to the entire reality of the message proclaimed and embodied in Christ or, more specifically, to the four accounts of Jesus' life and message contained within the New Testament canon.

Good News as the Christian Message

The good news in the NT announces God's action to save the world in and through his Son, Jesus Christ. Jesus Christ is God's good news because his life, death, and resurrection make salvation available to all, both the Jewish people and the Gentile world. The Synoptic Gospels tell how God's Spirit anointed Jesus to announce in word and action the good news about God's reign to the people of Israel, especially God's concern for the poor and the outcasts. When God revealed the Son to Paul, Paul preached to Jews and Gentiles outside Palestine that their salvation is in Jesus Christ crucified and raised from the dead.

"Good news" translates "gospel," which derives from the Anglo-Saxon "god-spell," "good tidings." It also translates the Greek *euangelion*, "good tidings," and *euangelizesthai*, to "announce good news." These terms in the NT are no doubt influenced by the Hebrew *bsr* and its derivatives as used in Isaiah 40:9; 41:27; 52:7 to designate the good news of the salvation to Zion, and especially in Isaiah 61:1, which describes the same salvation as comforting the afflicted and releasing captives. The use of *euangelion* in classical and Hellenistic Greek to designate good news, particularly the news of a victory, is not clearly reflected in the NT; but it is altogether probable that the NT reflects the use of the word *euangelion* in Roman times for the news that an heir of Caesar has been born or that a new Emperor has acceded to the throne. Against this good news the NT places its own good news of the birth of the one true savior and the coming of God's reign. Paul uses the noun *euangelion* far more frequently than do the other NT authors taken together.

Paul and the author of Luke-Acts use the verb *euangelizesthai* more than twice as much as the other NT authors. Nowhere in the NT does "good news" designate the four writings which we call Gospels.

Paul

Euangelion as "the good news of Jesus Christ" is a specifically Christian meaning of the word, and as such was almost certainly developed by Paul within the early Christian community. Paul uses the word forty-eight times in his uncontested letters (it occurs eight times in the Deutero-Paulines, and four times in the Pastorals). In general, it designates Paul's own personal presentation of the Christ-event. *Euangelion* sometimes denotes the activity of evangelization (Gal 2:7; Phil 4:3, 15; 1 Cor 9:14, 18; 2 Cor 2:12; 8:18), as does the verb *euangelizesthai* (used by Paul nineteen times; it occurs twice also in the Deutero-Paulines). Normally however, *euangelion* denotes the content of his apostolic message—what he preached, proclaimed, announced, spoke about.

Paul realized that his message, having its origin in God, was "God's gospel" (1 Thess 2:2, 8-9; 2 Cor 11:7; Rom 1:1; 15:16). Succinctly, its content was for him "the gospel of Christ" (1 Thess 3:2; Gal 1:7; Phil 1:27) or "the gospel of his Son" (Rom 1:9), which is normally understood as "the good news about Christ" or "the good news about his Son." In some instances we may detect the nuance that Christ originates the gospel (2 Cor 5:20; Rom 15:18-19). More specifically, the gospel is "the good news of the glory of Christ" (2 Cor 4:4), that is, the message about the risen Christ: "We do not preach ourselves, but Jesus Christ as Lord!" (2 Cor 4:5). Sometimes the content is expressed simply as "the faith" (Gal 1:23), "the word" (1 Thess 1:6), or "the word of God" (2 Cor 2:17).

Euangelion became Paul's personal way of summing up the meaning of God's action in Jesus Christ crucified and risen from the dead, the meaning that the person and lordship of Jesus of Nazareth had and still has for human history and existence. Hence Paul could speak of "my gospel" (Rom 2:16), "the gospel that I preach" (Gal 2:2; see also 1:8, 11; 1 Cor 15:1), or "our gospel" (1 Thess 1:5; 2 Cor 4:3), because he was aware that "Christ did not send me to baptize, but to preach the gospel" (1 Cor 1:7). Paul was fully aware that his commission to preach the good news of God's Son among the Gentiles (Gal 1:16) was not a message wholly peculiar to himself or different from that preached by those "who were apostles before me" (Gal 1:17); "whether it be I or they, so we preach and so you believed" (1 Cor 15:11). Paul recognized himself as the "servant" of the gospel (Phil 2:22), aware of the special grace of being called to be an apostle. He thought of himself as set apart like the prophets of old (Jer 1:5; Isa 49:1) from his mother's womb for this task (Gal 1:15; Rom 1:1), being "entrusted" with the gospel as with some prized possession (1 Thess 2:4; Gal 2:7). He experienced a "compulsion" (1 Cor 9:16) to proclaim it and considered his preaching of it as a cultic, priestly act offered to God (Rom 1:9; 15:16). He was never ashamed of the gospel (Rom 1:16), and imprisonment because of it he considered a "grace" (Phil 1:7, 16).

Paul received the "good news" about God's action in Jesus Christ: "God revealed his Son to me" (Gal 1:15-16); "have I not seen the Lord?" (1 Cor 9:1); "the risen Lord appeared also to me" (1 Cor 15:9). Paul accepted God's call to preach the good news about Jesus Christ to the Gentile world, and his journeys took him to Asia Minor, Macedonia, Greece, and finally to Rome where he died. He wrote letters to the communities he founded to instruct them about the meaning of his message of salvation.

Paul reminds the Corinthians of his preaching: "For the word of the cross is foolishness to those who are perishing, but to us who are being saved it is the power of God" (1 Cor 1:18). Paul preached the paradox of the cross, the mystery of power in apparent weakness, of wisdom in apparent foolishness: "we proclaim Christ crucified" (1 Cor 1:23). Most Jews and Gentiles, finding Paul's words anything but "good news," dismissed both the man and his message. It was a stumbling block to Jews; it was folly to the Gentiles (1 Cor 1:23). But God called those who became the Corinthian community to let Paul's message disclose a hidden truth about God's power and wisdom. These Jews and Gentiles saw through the apparent contradiction of a crucified Messiah to the mystery that "the foolishness of God is wiser than human wisdom, and the weakness of God is stronger than human strength" (1 Cor 1:25). Paul also experienced God's power working in and through his own human weakness (1 Cor 2:1-5; 2 Cor 12:7-10).

Paul also used an earlier traditional formula to recall what he had preached to the Corinthians and what they had come to believe: "Now I am reminding you, brothers and sisters, of the gospel I preached to you which you indeed received . . . For I handed on to you as of first importance what I also received that Christ died for our sins in accordance with the Scriptures; that he was buried; that he was raised on the third day in accordance with the Scriptures; that he appeared to Kephas, then to the Twelve . . . So we preach and so you have believed" (1 Cor 15:1, 3-5, 11).

Paul preached the good news, and the Corinthians believed. Faith included hearing Paul's message about Jesus Christ and heeding its call for a response, committing themselves to what they heard and submitting to it in obedience. The Corinthians trusted Paul and let his good news begin to inform and influence their lives. They also trusted God and Jesus Christ who died and was raised from the dead. Faith also meant that the Corinthians received this good news as a pure, undeserved gift. God's love had been revealed in the death and resurrection of Jesus Christ. Faith opened them to the mystery of that event and to its power.

The "story of the cross" is "the power of God," a salvific force (dynamis) unleashed in the world of human beings for the salvation of all (Rom 1:16). The good news includes the statement, "Jesus is Lord" (1 Cor 12:3; Rom 10:9) to which believers are called to assent. But it involves much more, because it proclaims a Son who was crucified, whom God raised from the dead, who delivers us from the coming wrath" (1 Thess 1:10). It is thus good news that comes "not in words alone, but with power and the holy Spirit" (1 Thess 1:5), it is "the word of God, which is at work among you who believe" (1 Thess 2:13; see also 1 Cor 15:2). It is God's power for the salvation of "everyone who has faith, the Jew first and also the Greek" (Rom 1:16; similarly, 10:12).

Mark and Matthew

Mark introduced his story of Jesus by calling it "the good news [gospel] of Jesus Christ" (Mark 1:1). The term "good news" occurs seven times in Mark (1:1, 14, 15; 8:35; 10:29; 13:10; 14:9). Apart from Mark 1:1 and 1:14 ("the gospel of God") the absolute *to euangelion* is characteristic of Mark and is found only on the lips of Jesus. For Mark, as for Paul, the good news is centered on and closely linked to the person of Jesus Christ. It is the news about the crucified and risen Lord, as it is told throughout the story of Jesus. His followers can leave their family and even give their life for the good news because it is identified with Jesus himself (Mark 8:35; 10:29). The saving power of Jesus himself is present in the gospel.

Mark described the beginning of Jesus' public ministry: "After John had been arrested, Jesus came to Galilee, proclaiming the gospel of God: 'This is the time of fulfillment. The kingdom of God is at hand. Repent, and believe in the gospel'" (Mark 1:14-15). Jesus preaches "the good news from God," the Christian message of salvation (recall Paul in 1 Thess 2:2, 8-9; 2 Cor 11:7; Rom 1:1; 15:16). His preaching calls his hearers to receive the good news and begin a process of conversion by believing in salvation through Jesus Christ.

Matthew summarizes Jesus' work in Galilee: "He went around all of Galilee,

teaching in their synagogues, proclaiming the good news of the kingdom and curing every disease and illness among the people" (Matt 4:23; 9:35). What John the Baptist announced at the Jordan (Matt 3:2), Jesus now announces in Galilee: "Repent, for the kingdom of heaven is at hand" (Matt 4:17). He preaches, heralds, proclaims the good news that God has seized power and has begun his definitive rule over the world. As preacher, Jesus announces God's action in the world; as teacher, he will speak of what people are to do, how they are to live in the light of that good news (5:1–7:28); as healer, he will reveal God's rule over evil in the world (8:1–9:34).

Matthew's Jesus, predicting the end of the age, tells his disciples: "And this gospel of the kingdom will be preached throughout the world, as a witness to all nations, and then the end will come" (Matt 24:14). Despite persecution from outside and betrayal from within his followers must continue Jesus' mission, proclaiming the good news about God's kingdom throughout the entire inhabited world (see Matt 28:19). Their preaching and their message will be a witness for or against "all nations," depending upon how they respond (Matt 25:31-46).

Luke-Acts

At Nazareth, Luke's Jesus announces that he has been anointed by the Spirit "to bring glad tidings to the poor" and "to proclaim liberty to the captives and recovery of sight to the blind, to let the oppressed go free" (Luke 4:18-19 = Isa 61:1). Luke repeatedly uses the verb "preach good news" *(euange-lizesthai)* to describe Jesus' ministry and summarize his activities with the verb "proclaim" *(kerysso)* as its synonym. Jesus was sent to preach good news to the poor, that is, above all to people without economic resources, to the outcasts and sinners who receive special attention in Luke. The description of Jesus' message as good news to the poor presents Jesus as carrying out the mission from a God especially concerned with helping the poor and hungry (Luke

6:20-21, 24-25). The good news promises an eschatological reversal in which God's reign will belong to the poor and in which the hungry will be satisfied. It challenges the rich to share their resources now to relieve the poor as well as gain their own salvation.

As the crowd attempts to prevent Jesus from leaving Capernaum after a day and night of teaching and healing, Jesus restates his mission: "To the other towns also I must proclaim the good news of the kingdom of God, because for this purpose I have been sent" (Luke 4:43). Luke makes clear that Jesus must continue the work announced in Nazareth in the whole Jewish land. The verb "preach good news" is a key term to describe Jesus' mission: the noun *euangelion* is never used in Luke and appears only twice in Acts, while the verb *euangelizesthai* occurs ten times in Luke and fifteen times in Acts. Luke's usage may show the influence of Isaiah 61:1 (LXX) and other passages in Isaiah 40–66. Isaiah's time of "release," the "acceptable year of the Lord," is closely associated with the "reign of God" in the rest of Luke-Acts.

Luke has characterized Jesus' mission as preaching good news to the poor, proclaiming release to captives, and preaching the good news of God's reign. Jesus also names these activities when he responds to the question from John the Baptist: "the blind regain their sight, the lame walk, lepers are cleansed, the deaf hear, the dead are raised, the poor have the good news proclaimed to them" (Luke 7:22). These words declare that the mission announced in Nazareth (Luke 4:18-19; Isa 61:1) is now to be carried out in all that Jesus has said and done in Galilee.

In Luke 8:1 we are told that Jesus was preaching the "good news of God's reign," as he said he must do (Luke 4:43). Luke's statement that he was traveling "from one city and village to another" broadens the earlier reference to "the other cities." The notice that the Twelve were with Jesus recalls the appointment of the Twelve (Luke 6:12-16) and prepares for their role as partners in Jesus' mission: "and he sent them to proclaim the kingdom of God and to heal. . . . Then they set out and went from village to village proclaiming the good news and curing diseases everywhere" (Luke 9:2, 6). The Twelve extend Jesus' mission when they proclaim God's reign, preach good news, and heal. Women also traveled with Jesus and the Twelve in Galilee (Luke 8:2-3). Three women are named, but many others were also "serving them" from their possessions.

Luke 4:18-19 and Luke 4:43-44 have summarized Jesus' entire ministry. Jesus makes still another summary statement: "The law and the prophets lasted until John; but from then on the kingdom of God is proclaimed as good news" (Luke 16:16). Here "preaching the good news of God's reign" marks the time of Jesus' ministry, a new time that Jesus differentiates from the old time of the Law and the prophets. Finally, in Jerusalem Jesus "teaches" and "preaches good news" in the Temple (Luke 20:1).

Peter's summary of Jesus' ministry in Acts 10:36-38 echoes these passages from Luke and their themes. God's message is the word which was sent to Israel through Jesus' "preaching good news of peace" (Acts 10:36). He also describes the same geographical area as in Luke 4:43-44 ("throughout the whole of the Jewish land, beginning from Galilee after the baptism of John," Acts 10:37). Peter clearly recalls Luke 4:18 ("how God anointed Jesus of Nazareth with the Holy Spirit and with power," Acts 10:38).

See: CONVERSION, EPISTLE/LETTER, FAITH, GIFTS, GLORY, GRACE, LOVE, MINISTRY, MISSION, PAUL, POOR, POWER, PROPHET, REIGN OF GOD, SALVATION, SPIRIT, TRUTH

WILLIAM G. THOMPSON, S.J.

Pastoral-Liturgical Tradition

In Christian usage the heading of Mark's Gospel, although it did not describe the piece of writing to follow, probably contributed strongly to the designation of this kind of writing as a gospel. The one "gospel of Jesus Christ" according to Matthew, Mark, etc., at the head of each of the four was a late second or third-century development.

For Paul and his fellow workers the gospel is the tidings in their entirety about what God has accomplished through Christ's death and resurrection (see 1 Cor 15:1). In the seven letters that are indisputably his, the word occurs forty-one times; in the deutero- (2 Thessalonians, Colossians, Ephesians) and trito- (1 and 2 Timothy, Titus) Pauline writings, "gospel" occurs in fifteen verses, sometimes more than once. When Paul writes, it may be the gospel "of God," "of Christ," "of [God's] son," "my" gospel, or "the gospel proclaimed by me." Once it is contrasted by way of rejection with "another gospel" (2 Cor 11:4). In a well-known passage on the division of apostolic labor it is the gospel "of the uncircumcision" (literally "foreskin") and "of the circumcision" (Gal 2:7).

In the writings of Paul and his followers the gospel never means the teachings Jesus proclaimed (as it does in Matt 4:23; Mark 1:14) but always the proclamation made about him. The same is true in Acts 20:24, where Luke has Paul as the speaker. Contrariwise, in Matthew 24:14; 26:13; and Mark 8:35; 13:10; 16:14 the gospel is ambivalently Jesus' teaching and the teaching about him. The non-appearance of the noun "gospel" in Luke and John is noteworthy but the verb form is a Lucan favorite, both to describe the good tidings about Jesus (Luke 1:19; 2:10) and Jesus' own proclamation of the good tidings (Luke 4:43; 8:1; 9:6; 20:1). In Acts 5:42 and a dozen other places it can mean "to proclaim the good news" absolutely or "to proclaim the word of the Lord," "Jesus," "Christ Jesus," "the Lord Jesus," "peace," or "Jesus and resurrection." The connotations of the word "gospel" cited above are often found in "word" (*lógos* and *rhēma*) in the Synoptic Gospels, John, and Acts, the second of these is used particularly in John to convey the utterances of Jesus and scriptural "words" uttered by God that, for John, are about Jesus.

Each of the four Gospels is in biographical form but none is a biography, strictly speaking. They are four distinct literary products, despite a measure of interdependence, each with its own creative religious purpose. Drawing on written and oral sources that contain sayings and stories of Jesus and accounts of his miracles and exorcisms, and culminating in his death and resurrection, the four evangelists address their contemporaries on how to live as his disciples in light of this knowledge. The account of his earthly days is secondary to this existential purpose. Tatian, writing in Syriac circa 175, misconstrued the Gospels' purpose as biographic and wove them into one continuous narrative known as the *Diatesseron* ("as through four").

In the third through the fifth centuries many spurious or "apocryphal" gospels were produced, usually to support a doctrinal position about Christ. Some are fanciful, others amusing, all are intended to edify. The best collection of NT apocrypha in English is that of Hennecke-Schneemelcher (Philadelphia, 1963), which also contains the 1945 find at Nag Hammadi in Upper Egypt, the collection of 114 sayings of Jesus. It is erroneously called "The Gospel of Thomas" because a Gospel, by convention, is composed of narrative elements. The earliest papyrus fragments (second and third centuries) are predominantly of the Gospel. The Gospels are likewise found in the six earliest parchment codices (fourth through sixth century). Illuminated books of Gospels were produced, in emulation of those of the East, in Durrow (675), Lindisfarne (toward 700), and Kells (toward 800). The Gospels and the Psalter in vernacular languages preceded the first complete vernacular Bibles of the sixteenth century.

The earliest mention of the reading of the Gospels at the Eucharistic liturgy occurs in Justin's *First Apology* (ca. 155) where he writes: "The memoirs of the apostles or the writings of the prophets are read" (66). The practice is a constant in the next two centuries whenever the mode of celebration is specified. Thus, Ambrose (d. 397), commenting *On Psalm 118* (17.10), mentions that the "prophets, the Apostle, and the Gospel" are proclaimed at the Eucharist. Books of pericopes (selections) begin to appear in the fifth century; 397 different ones are recorded between the eighth and the seventeenth centuries, some "evangelaries" among them. The ceremonial attached to the singing of the gospel in the Roman rite is first found in the *Ordo Romanus* dating from the eighth century (J. Mabillon, ed., *Musaeum Italicum*, Paris, 1689; crit. ed., M. Andrieu, Louvain, 1931). Bringing the gospel book into the sanctuary aloft in procession, doing the same as the deacon prepares to read it, censing it, and tracing the sign of the cross upon it are all part of the preparation for chanting it in specified tones.

See: JESUS CHRIST, LIGHT AND DARKNESS, PREACHING, PROPHET, TEACH/TEACHING, WORD, WAY

GERARD S. SLOYAN

GRACE

Grace means favor, God's favor toward us. It can be creative, redemptive, or eschatological.

Old Testament

The basic Hebrew verb that is translated "grace" in the Bible literally means "to incline oneself favorably toward another," and the Hebrew noun literally is "favor." The Mediterranean cultural experience that lies at the base of these ideas is patronage. When a centralized government is ineffective in providing for the basic necessities of its citizens, people seek help from others who can. Mediterranean patronage is one such avenue of help. It is a social institution involving a relationship between a person of higher status and a person of lesser status. This relationship does not exist between equals. The higher status person not only is able to help people of lesser means to meet their needs, but the culture expects such a person to play that role.

The person of higher status, the patron, makes a free and arbitrary choice of a client or clients from among people of lesser status. Needy clients do their best to win a patron of their choice, but clients know they have no rights in this strategy.

Once the choice is made, the patron leans favorably toward or shows favoritism to these clients. The advantage of such favoritism for a client is a new ability to obtain favors otherwise not available, or the ability to obtain favors on more advantageous terms than elsewhere. The benefit of being a patron is that it entitles one to honorable acclaim. A person of means who does not share surplus is greedy and selfish, exceedingly shameful descriptions. It is this Mediterranean cultural experience that provides our ancestors in the faith with an analogous way of thinking about the manner in which God relates to and behaves toward them: "God is like a patron."

The mind-boggling basic experience in the OT is that God elected Israel. God freely decided to be patron for Israel as client. "Did any god venture to go and take a nation for himself from the midst of another nation?" (Deut 4:32-34). The Deuteronomist reminds them that it was "for the love of your fathers" that God did the favor or bestowed the benefaction of liberation from bondage in Egypt, a favor nowhere else available and better than any they might imagine.

God became patron to Noah (Gen 6:8), Jacob (Gen 19:17-22; 31:5), and Moses (Exod 33:12-13), among others in the OT. The operative "grace" word in all these stories is "favor." These leaders "found favor" with God the patron. The specific stories relative to each favored one describe the specific favor received. One "favor" or grace God bestowed on Israel consisted in making the Egyptians show "favor" to them (Exod 3:21; 11:3; 12:36).

In the patron-client relationship, however, favors are not "free." Though the patron "freely" bestows gifts according to personal pleasure, the patron's gift contains a "hook." These gifts come with strings attached. The patron expects a response. Minimally, the patron expects that the client will display good will and openness to the gift even when it was not sought and perhaps not even wanted.

The Deuteronomist reminds Israel of its obligations: "fear the LORD, your God," follow his ways, love and serve him, keep the commandments (10:12-22; 11:1). Israel the client is also cautioned not to forget the identity of the one who led them out of slavery in Egypt (6:12), a very great favor.

The history of Israel's relationships with God its patron, particularly as recounted in the Prophetic books, indicates that Israel frequently forgot or abandoned its patron and the gifts it received. Sometimes it refused to make the proper response, to consecrate its life and heart to the patron as the Deuteronomist urged.

Isaiah compared his compatriots unfavorably with dumb animals (1:1-4). The ox and ass recognize their master and know who feeds and sustains them, but Israel has disowned, forsaken, and spurned its patron. Hosea similarly laments that God's people have been disloyal to their patron, a very basic obligation for a client (4:1).

Jeremiah observes that Judah's lack of loyalty (faithlessness) to its patron, God, is shameful enough, but God's clients have compounded the shame by acting dishonorably toward one another. They lie, deceive, are perverse toward other clients of the same loving and devoted patron God. Remember that in patronage, the patron treats clients "as if" they were kin, members of the family. Clients of the same patron are expected to treat each other as if they were members of the same family. Judah's failure to behave like this shames God and his prophet, Jeremiah.

In such circumstances, however, God amazingly demonstrates the qualities of an extraordinary and unusual patron. Like many other human patrons, God too is tempted to abandon the clients (Hos 1:1–2:15), never to show favoritism again. But unlike human patrons, God remains faithful to his promises* (Deut 6:10, 18), to his covenant.* God's love for his clients does not diminish or vanish.

On the contrary, God demonstrates the true qualities of patron by providing the clients with something they could not do for themselves or obtain anywhere else. Isaiah's lyric poetry praises the benefactions of this powerful patron (1:18-26). Though the people's sins be like scarlet, God the patron will make them white as snow. Though Jerusalem has proved faithless, and has sunk to low levels of injustice, bribery, and all sorts of corruption, God the patron will restore its identity as a city of justice, a faithful city.

Jeremiah is even more assertive about the favor God the patron can do for the clients (Jer 31:31). He will initiate a new and better covenant (relationship of patronage). Or as Ezekiel phrases it, God will take utterly rebellious hearts and turn them into hearts once more capable of knowing and loving their patron as they ought (Ezek 36:26-27). To facilitate this response, God will aid his clients with his very own spirit.

Throughout the OT, therefore, God behaves like an outstanding patron toward his client-people. He bestows favors ("grace") upon them without end. He gives and forgives (Exod 34:6; Num 14:18; Pss 51:3; 86:15; Joel 2:13; Jonah 4:2; Neh 9:17). God surpasses every human hope and expectation. His favor is indeed everlasting.

New Testament

In the NT, the greatest "favor" that God the patron gave to his clients is the divine Son: "For God so loved the world that he gave his only Son, so that everyone who believes in him might not perish but might have eternal life" (John 3:16). By trusting in and pledging loyalty to the God the patron's Son, God's clients are no longer "as if" members of the family but are "real" members of the family through baptism (Gal 3:26; 4:6; Rom 8:15).

The NT vocabulary of favoritism includes the Greek words customarily translated as reward, gift, and grace. The word for grace occurs mainly in Paul and 1 Peter, less so in Luke-Acts and Hebrews, and very rarely elsewhere. Of course, Bible readers know that word studies and word counts can be deceptive. The reality behind "grace" understood as "favoritism" describing the relationship of God with human beings is present everywhere in the Bible from beginning to end.

In the NT, the Greek noun underlying the word "grace" describes the patron-client relationship between God and his people in general. The gospel is "the good news of God's grace" (Acts 20:24) that is, the good news that God wills to be patron with all the benefactions that role entails. This relationship of "favoritism" with God is a gift Paul personally experienced (Gal 1:15) and the same gift that he wishes for the recipients of his letters: "grace to you and peace from God" (Rom 1:7; 1 Cor 1:3; 2 Cor 1:2; Gal 1:4; Eph 1:2; Phil 1:2; Col 1:2; 1 Thess 1:1; 2 Thess 1:2; Philemon 3).

God's favor or grace, of course, takes different form with different people. The churches of Macedonia were moved by God's favoritism to imitate that same behavior by sharing their surplus with the needy (1 Cor 8:1-15). Such sharing between equals, Macedonia and Jerusalem, is not a patron-client relationship, but rather a mutual kind of exchange that the benefits of a patron-client relationship are intended to make possible and to encourage. The wicked servant in Matthew 18:24-35 is condemned because he failed to forgive a fellow servant as the patron-king had forgiven him.

Paul identifies the Philippians as recipients of the same "favoritism" (grace) from God that he has received: confirming the good news and willing to suffer for it (Phil 1:7). Indeed, Paul's total ministry is his response to the favoritism that God the patron has extended to him (Rom 1:5; 1 Cor 3:10; Gal 1:15; Eph 3:2).

The Greek verb underlying "grace" describes the activity of a patron, one who "gives in" to others, who yields to their entreaties, and who gives benefactions freely in the sense of liberally. The key ideas reflecting this kind of "giving-in" activity in the NT are "giving and forgiving." The point of Matthew's parable about the workers in the vineyard is that God freely chooses to treat some people with favoritism (Matt 20:1-15). Others should not display the "evil eye" because God the patron chooses to give generously to some rather than to others.

As a broker between God the patron and the people who are God's clients, Jesus acts just like his patron as he cures diseases and suffering and casts out evil spirits (Luke 7:21). After the shipwreck on Cauda, Paul assures the travelers that the rest of the trip will be safe because for the sake of Paul God has given safe passage to all who sail with him (Acts 24:20). Paul is able to obtain gifts for others from his patron (God) just as he himself has received gifts from him. God the patron is expert at giving: not only did he not spare his own son, but he gives everything else besides (Rom 8:32).

Forgiving is also a favor, a grace, from God to human beings which they in turn ought to imitate. This was Jesus' object lesson for Simon the leper (Luke 7:42-43), and Paul's exhortation to the Corinthians (2 Cor 2:1-11). The Ephesians, too, are reminded not to frustrate the patron, but to forgive "one another as God has forgiven you in Christ" (Eph 4:32). Clearly without the good example and benevolence of the institution of patronage, the subsistence population in this culture might be even more cut-throat in survival than it often is. This cultural background of "grace" in the context of patronage casts it in a fresh light.

A third "grace" word that occurs fairly frequently in the NT translates its Greek counterpart as *"charism."* In the cultural scenario of patronage, a charism* is a gift that definitely has strings attached. Every patron including God expects a return. A familiar Middle-Eastern proverb states: "Don't thank me, you will repay me."

The minimal return for God's gift is good will and openness to the gift. This is what Paul means when he urges the Corinthians "not to receive the grace of God in vain" (2 Cor 6:1). This would be equivalent to turning down "an offer one shouldn't refuse." Paul boasts that he is not such an ingrate (1 Cor 15:10).

Paul, who develops the grace vocabulary extensively in the NT, is the first one in antiquity to give the word charism a technical meaning. It describes the specific part or gift that God gives an individual Christian in the lordship and glory of Jesus. This charism manifests itself in a specific service. Every Christian has a personal and distinct charism from God (1 Cor 7:7). A charism is never given for personal enrichment but is always intended for the service and benefit of others. "As each one has received a gift [lit. charism], use it to serve one another as good stewards of God's varied grace" (1 Pet 4:10).

Further, charisms are services or functions, but definitely not states of life. Since they can be prayed for (2 Cor 1:11), strived for (1 Cor 12:31), neglected (1 Tim 4:14), rekindled (2 Tim 1:6), and are distributed by one and the same Spirit to each one individually as the Spirit wills and when the Spirit wills (1 Cor 12:11), any given charism in a concrete individual need not be permanent. Everything depends on the Spirit: one charism may go, and another may come. In the final analysis, however, God never fails to show favoritism, to bestow grace.

See: BAPTISM, CHARISM, COVENANT, ELECTION, GRACE, JEALOUSY, JUSTICE, PROMISE, SIN, SPIRIT

JOHN J. PILCH

Pastoral-Liturgical Tradition

The early Christian community used the term grace *(charis)* to express the many dimensions and effects of the gift of God's own self in Jesus Christ (John 1:17). The English word "grace" is a translation of the Latin word, *gratia,* which is the usual translation of the Greek word, *charis.* In both Greek and Latin the term can mean either (1) graciousness, attractiveness, charm, or (2) a favor granted to someone, or (3) the gratitude due to someone in response to a gift. Moreover, in both Greek and Latin the term can designate either the source of a gift in the giver or the effect of the gift in the recipient. All of these meanings influenced the Christian usage of the term. Grace came to mean the source of the Christian life, and in this sense was called uncreated grace,

namely, God. The term could also mean created grace, i.e., the created effect of God's loving presence upon human beings.

Grace as Present Gift and Future Pledge. In the early Church grace *(charis)* had a special connection with the Eucharist *(eucharistia),* which celebrated God's presence in the Christian assembly, expressed the community's gratitude to God, and anticipated the fullness of union with God in the future. One of the earliest Christian liturgies recorded outside the NT prays for grace as a future eschatological gift: "Let grace come and let this world pass away" (Didache 10:6). Whether grace in this context is understood as sacramental grace or as a title for Christ or as an equivalent to "your kingdom come" in the prayer of Jesus (Matt 6:10), the prayer of the Didache expresses the community's understanding of the present experience of grace in Jesus Christ as a pledge and foretaste of the consummation of God's gift in the future.

Grace as Universal Offer of God's Love. While the early Church celebrated its own experience of grace in the sacraments, it wrestled with the question of grace in relation to those outside the Church. Cyprian of Carthage (ca. 200–258) saw the effective offer of God's grace as limited to those receiving the sacraments in the Catholic Church and taught that outside of the Church no one could be saved (*On the Unity of the Church,* 6).

Justin Martyr (ca. 100–ca. 165), however, had already expressed the foundations of a broader view of God's offer of grace. Justin saw the Word *(Logos)* of God as active throughout all human experience. According to Justin, Christ is the Word of God and all who live in accordance with the Word are Christians even though they may not have explicitly accepted the God of Israel and Christianity (First Apology, 46). Thus, according to Justin, pagans such as Socrates and Heraclitus lived in accord with the Word of God and were friends of God. Only those who live in opposition to the Word are ungracious.

While the view of Cyprian was dominant in Catholic teaching for centuries, Justin Martyr's affirmation of God's universal offer of grace has found recent expression in the Pastoral Constitution on the Church in the Modern World of Vatican II, which declares that God extends an effective offer of grace to all humans (no. 22).

Grace as Transforming the Sinner. Western theology, both Catholic and Protestant, has been profoundly marked by the debate between Augustine of Hippo (354–430) and Pelagius (ca. 360–after 418). Pelagius, an ascetic spiritual guide from England or Ireland, held that human nature as created by God is good and thus is capable of performing the good apart from any special added gift of God. While Pelagius acknowledged that the natural capacity to do good comes from God as a free gift, he insisted that humans have the power to will and do good themselves. In debate with Augustine, Pelagius did acknowledge a certain necessity of grace, but he saw grace simply as an external aid, like Christian teaching, the law of God, and the moral example of Christ.

Appealing to Paul's Letter to the Romans, Augustine argued strenuously that we cannot be saved by our own good works apart from grace. Rejecting Pelagius's understanding of grace, Augustine saw grace as a special gratuitous gift from God beyond the capacity of human nature, a gift that moves the will internally to do the good. This grace is given by God apart from any consideration of our merits and it is absolutely efficacious in transforming the sinner into a righteous person empowered to love. Apart from grace, human freedom is a freedom to choose only within a horizon of evil. Only God's grace, received in faith, makes us righteous and allows us to find the meaning of our existence in the self-sacrificing love centered on God.

Later in his career, Augustine also came to see that humans need an added grace of perseverance, which guides a person to the final state of being at peace with God with no possibility of falling, a state reached only in heaven.

Grace as Participation in the Divine Life. While the Eastern Christian communities accepted the condemnation of Pelagius's disciple Celestius at the Council of Ephesus in 431, the Eastern tradition pursued its own distinctive approach to grace, little affected by the controversy between Augustine and Pelagius. While aware of the necessity of grace in forgiving sin and empowering virtue, Christian writers in the East thought of grace primarily as the experience of participation in God's own nature, as adoption as children of God, and as becoming a new creation. At the center of Eastern thought on grace was the notion of divinization. For Athanasius of Alexandria (ca. 295–373), this is the central meaning of the incarnation: God became human so that humans could share in God's own life and become divine. Similarly, Cyril of Alexandria (d. 444) viewed grace as a state of communion with God, a state in which we become partakers of the divine nature.

See: ESCHATOLOGY, EUCHARIST, GOD, JESUS CHRIST, WORD

LEO D. LEFEBURE

GREEK

The term "Greek" does not arrive on the biblical scene until after the Exile. It then takes on a variety of meanings throughout the OT and NT. In the postbiblical period the Christian community often used it to signify all non-Jews. Understanding the term has been further complicated in English translations of the Bible over the years where the term sometimes has been distinguished from "Grecians" (reserved for Greek-speaking Jews) and sometimes not.

Old Testament

The Hebrew term *yawan* is rendered in many translations as "Greek" even though it might more appropriately be translated as "Ionian." This is true of the Septuagint and the Latin Vulgate editions, both widely influential in the framing of the classical Catholic tradition. Examples are Ezekiel 27:13; Isaiah 66:19; Daniel 8:21; Joel 3:6; and Zechariah 9:13.

Trade or commerce likely provided the initial impetus for Hebrew contacts with the Greek community (Joel 3:6). In his vision of the ram (i.e., the king of the Medes and Persians) and the goat (i.e., king of the Greeks), the prophet Daniel appears to anticipate the existence of the future Graeco-Macedonian Empire headed by Alexander the Great to which reference is made in 1 Maccabees 1:1ff. The Seleucids, who later took over a part of Alexander's vast empire, also became known as Greeks (1 Macc 8:18). The cultural tradition that developed after Alexander's death throughout the Middle East and Mediterranean regions was called Hellenism. It had an impact on Jews as well as non-Jews. Some Jewish scholars such as the historian Ellis Rivkin feel that Hellenism seeded the Pharisaic revolution within Second Temple Judaism, which eventually gave rise to both the Jesus movement and rabbinic Judaism.

New Testament

As a general term, Greek in the NT refers both to people who were native to Greece itself or its island possessions (Acts 17:4; 18:4) and to all those non-Jews, whatever their place of residence, who had in some way embraced Greek culture and its language (John 7:35; Acts 11:20; 1 Cor 1:22). Greeks were normally distinguished from "barbarians" who clearly were not on the same plane as them. The term Hellenists (Grecians in some English translations) was used to signify Jews who had been imbued with the Greek cultural heritage. There is extant manuscript evidence to prove the presence of Hellenistic Jews in Jerusalem around the time of Jesus. Their challenge to Palestinian Judaism may account for Jesus' rather strong reaffirmation of his personal commitment to Torah observance since some Hellenists at least seemed to be urging Jews to let go of their particularistic identity and submerge themselves into the larger Greco-Roman society (Matt 5:17-19).

There are instances, however, when Greeks may refer to Greek-speaking Jews rather than to non-Jews, complicating the correct interpretation of the text. This is especially true of the famous passage in Galatians 3:28 abolishing all distinctions between "Jew and Greek." Greek here has usually been interpreted as inclusive of all Gentiles by subsequent Christian commentators. The author, however, may have had in mind only mainstream Jews and Hellenistic Jews. Other uncertain passages include Colossians 3:11; Acts 14:1; 11:20.

Pastoral-Liturgical Tradition

The terms Greek and Hellenist fall out of use after the period of the early Church. They tend to be replaced by the broader term Gentile, which glosses over the various distinctions retained by the authors of scriptural texts. Greek eventually became a virtual synonym for the Eastern Christian tradition after the split between the Eastern and Western churches, even for those churches not specifically using the Greek language. Recently, with the appearance of Vatican II's Declaration *Nostra Aetate* in 1965 and the developments it has spawned in Christian-Jewish relations, Greek has tended to take on a negative connotation in the Western Church for those promoting Christianity's return to its Jewish roots. It has been taken to signify the loss of the heart and soul of Jesus' teaching by its transference from a fundamentally Jewish religious context into Greek philosophical categories by Church councils and theologians.

See: EXILE, PHARISEE

JOHN T. PAWLIKOWSKI, O.S.M.

GUILT

Old Testament

In the OT, guilt is a consequence of a sinful act (Gen 3:10). For the Israelites the link between sin* and guilt, between an abnormal act and an abnormal state, was so self-evident that guilt as such was not frequently mentioned. The terms 'āwôn, "bowed down, turned aside" (occurs 231 times), and 'āšām, "guilt, guilt-obligation" (occurs 46 times), are used to highlight the consequences of "missing the mark" or "failing to realize the norm" (ḥaṭṭā't).

Sins could be either deliberate or unintentional; in both cases guilt was incurred. The bloodguilt linked to an unintentional homicide illustrates the objective character of guilt (Exod 21:13). The guilty one had to flee to a city of refuge in order to forestall the ironclad link between sin and punishment until the elders could hear his case. If an unidentified corpse was discovered near a town, the elders had to conduct a purificatory ritual with the ashes of a red heifer in order to free the populace from the danger of bloodguilt (Num 19:11-13). Unintentional adultery was a breach of the moral order; it was an action that produced guilt. In the patriarchal stories, a foreign king or his courtiers (Pharaoh [Gen 12:18-19] or Abimelech [Gen 20:9; 26:10]) could have had relations with Sarah or Rebekah. Such an adulterous action would have been regarded as automatically bringing guilt. In response to the catastrophe of the Exile, Israel increased its expiatory offerings (especially the ḥaṭṭā't and the 'āšām) to atone for inadvertent sins, for they were objectively guilty ('āšēm) for their failures (Lev 4:13, 22, 27).

Experiences of subjective guilt ranged from self-centered regret to true contrition. Cain lamented before God, "My punishment is too great to bear" (Gen 4:13). Such self-absorption contrasts markedly with the psalmist who confessed his sins after feeling pressured by God (Ps 32:3-5). In the psalmist's case the burden of guilt translated in his consciousness into a broken relationship with the Lord, whereas Cain's guilt took the form of the punishment suffered by a perpetual fugitive.

Sins committed by one individual could incur guilt for the entire community and for succeeding generations. The Israelite community took strict measures to remove an offender from its midst. Capital punishment was meted out to such sinners as those who cursed their father or mother (Exod 21:17) or who sacrificed to other gods (Exod 22:19). The aura of evil unleashed by such evil actions could pollute the entire community unless swift, severe punishment eliminated the evil. Cultic violations, such as the unauthorized eating of sacrificial food, likewise brought guilt upon the community, which demanded expiation (Lev 22:16).

For inadvertent cultic sins, the ḥaṭṭā't and 'āšām sacrifices remedied the guilty situation by purging the sanctuary of the sin or by repaying God for the offense. The 'āšām, "guilt-offering," in origin seems to have been a compensatory payment for a sin or failure (Lev 5:6-7, 15b). But the 'āšām also appears to have been conceived of as a propitiatory sacrifice (Lev 5:15b). The need to propitiate an angry deity explains the guilt-offering of golden tumors and mice sent by the Philistines when they returned the ark (1 Sam 6:3, 4, 8, 17). The guilt-offering also played a significant role in the cleansing of a leper. Even though a leper with small material resources could reduce his holocaust and sin-offerings to two turtledoves (Lev 14:21-22), he had to offer a lamb for a guilt-offering, for it provided the blood* for his cleansing (Lev 14:24-29).

The severity of the problem of guilt in the postexilic community is evident in the solemn rituals of the Day of Atonement (Leviticus 16). A significant development in the exilic community modeled on the expiatory sacrifices is the vicarious suffering of the Servant. Like a sacrificial lamb, he gave his life as an expiatory offering ('āšām) to bear away others' guilt ('āwôn, Isa 53:10-11).

New Testament

In his ministry, Jesus removed the guilt and punishment from sinners who believed in his power to forgive sins (Matt 9:5-8). In his teaching and through his exorcisms, Jesus invited sinners to enter into God's reign (Mark 1:38-39). Their entry into the sphere of his rule severed the connection between their sins and the calamities that weighed on them. Their faith in him brought them reconciliation with the Father.

Jesus predicted the destruction of the Temple and the sacrificial system. According to the Marcan and Johannine accounts of Jesus' cleansing of the Temple, Jesus replaced the expiatory offerings with his own person as the meeting point between God and humans.

In Matthew's account of the Last Supper (Matt 26:26-30), Jesus proclaims that his "blood, the blood of the covenant, is to be poured out in behalf of many for the forgiveness of sins." Like the blood of the expiatory sacrifices of the Temple, Jesus' blood was to remove the guilt of humans so that the relationship with the Father could be restored. Paul explains that Jesus' blood remits sins committed in the past so that believers might stand upright before the Father's tribunal (Rom 3:25-26).

Paul teaches that Jesus' death freed believers from the bondage to sin under which all labor as children of Adam (Rom 5:12-14). The condition or state of sinfulness of humans in the world can be described as an objective state of guilt. Drawing upon personal experience, Paul laments that the alien force of sin is at work within him through particular sinful actions (Rom 7:23).

In John's Gospel, Jesus teaches that those who become his disciples will be freed from the bondage of sin (8:31-34). The Pauline and Johannine conceptions of objective guilt resulting from "original sin" converge around the notion that sin is an enslaving power.

In the Gospels, Jesus refutes the view that illness is necessarily a consequence of an individual's sin: i.e., an outward sign of the individual's guilt (Mark 2:1-12; Luke 13:1-5; John 9:2-3, 34).

Pastoral-Liturgical Tradition

Guilt is the state or feeling of having departed from objective norms of truth and goodness. Theologically, guilt is a consequence of knowingly sinning against God. Although some inadvertent actions can adversely affect others, such involuntary actions can never legitimately cause guilt.

Guilt feelings can be inauthentic. As social beings, we humans must go outside of ourselves to God and others in order to realize ourselves. This common world, which we both receive and help to construct, is the arena within which we sort out those facets of our self-images that belong most properly to ourselves against those imposed from without. The ambiguous authority of these internal and external voices of conscience can be constructively managed by accepting the uncertainty about oneself and submitting oneself unconditionally to God. To absolutize one's self-image is to turn it into an idol; this sinful act will lead to inauthentic guilt feelings which in turn distort the structure of one's own personhood and one's proper relationship to God and others.

In Christian communities, the uncertainties and ambiguities of walking before God receive special assistance through the sacraments of Eucharist and penance. These sacraments of reconciliation address us symbolically with a message of forgiveness in the midst of our individual and collective struggles. Our sense of alienation from God, others, and ourselves can be remedied only by entering the realm of God's love where we can accept the gift of God's forgiveness and thus refrain from tormenting ourselves with irrational fears and unrealistic expectations.

See: ATONEMENT, BLOOD, DAY OF ATONEMENT, RECONCILIATION, REPENTANCE, SACRIFICE

DALE LAUNDERVILLE, O.S.B.

H

HAND

While hand appears in numerous biblical passages simply designating a part of the body, on many other occasions it is used metaphorically. In most of these instances hand occurs as a symbol of power. This is clearly the intent when the reference is to the hand of God. When the right hand is mentioned it may be simply to distinguish it from the left hand. However, on many occasions mention of the right hand suggests a position of power or honor. The word also appears with reference to the imposition of hands, a ceremony with various contexts and meanings in both the OT and NT and in Pastoral-Liturgical tradition.

Old Testament

In many instances hand simply refers to a part of the body. Reference to hand or hands on other occasions conveys a variety of different meanings. Silence is suggested when one reads, "Look at me and be astonished, put your hands over your mouths" (Job 21:5). Prayer seems to be in the mind of the psalmist who writes: "lifting up my hands, I will call upon your name" (Ps 63:5). Clapping the hands is a sign of rejoicing (Ezek 25:6).

In the OT, as in antiquity in general, greater value is attached to the right hand than the left. "But Israel, crossing his hands, put out his right hand and laid it on the head of Ephraim, although he was the younger, and his left hand on the head of Manasseh, although he was the first-born" (Gen 48:14). "The LORD said to my Lord: 'sit at my right hand till I make your enemies your footstool'" (Ps 110:1).

Of the many metaphorical uses of hand, most numerous are those in which it occurs as a symbol of power. In fact, frequently the English word power is used to translate hand. "They assured Joshua, 'The LORD has delivered all this land into our power [i.e., hands]'" (Josh 2:24). "So the LORD allowed them to fall into the power [i.e., hands] of the Canaanite king" (Judg 4:2). At other times the word hands, meaning power, occurs in the English translation. "Therefore I have come down to rescue them from the hands of the Egyptians" (Exod 3:8).

When the OT mentions the hand of God, as it does over two hundred times, the reference is normally to divine power. "Remember this day on which you came out of Egypt, that place of slavery. It was with a strong hand that the LORD brought you away" (Exod 13:3). "That all may see and know, observe and understand, That the hand of the LORD has done this" (Isa 41:20). The reference to divine power is especially evident when mention is made of the right hand of God. "Your right hand, O LORD, magnificent in power, your right hand, O LORD, has shattered the enemy" (Exod 15:6).

"The joyful shout of victory in the tents of the just: 'The right hand of the LORD has struck with power'" (Ps 118:15). Those who flee from their persecutors can find refuge at God's right hand (Ps 17:7). "My soul clings fast to you; your right hand upholds me" (Ps 63:9).

One cannot end a discussion of the OT use of hand without mentioning the ceremonial imposition of hands. This gesture has a variety of contexts and meanings:

Laws of Sacrifice. In connection with the laws of sacrifice, presiding officials lay hands on the offering (Exod 29:10; Lev 1:4; 4:4, 24, 29, 33; 8:14; Num 8:10, 12; 2 Chr 29:23). In the case of a scapegoat, the transfer of guilt is involved (Lev 16:21). In most instances, however, this action represents a setting apart for a sacred purpose (Lev 24:14) and seems to set up a relationship between the offering and the one making the offering. If the sacrifice is acceptable, then the individual making the sacrifice also is acceptable.

To Impart a Blessing. Laying on of hands also is used to impart a blessing. Jacob blesses the children of Joseph (Gen 48:14). By the lifting up of outstretched hands a blessing is invoked on a group (e.g., the priestly benediction in Lev 9:22).

Transfer of Power. On several occasions, this action suggests a transfer of power such as would take place when instituting someone into an office. In Numbers 27, the Lord directs Moses to lay his hand upon Joshua and Moses "laid his hands on him and gave him his commission" (Num 27:23; see also Deut 34:9). This action is usually seen as an outward sign that recognizes Joshua's spiritual qualifications and gives him authority to exercise the office of leadership among the people.

In later times this gesture was adopted for ordination to the rabbinate and may well have been the source of the Christian rite of ordination.

New Testament

The uses of hand in the NT are similar to those found in the OT. On numerous occasions hand simply refers to a part of the body. Often, however, it is used metaphorically as a symbol for power. Jesus was "fully aware that the Father had put everything into his power [i.e., hand]" (John 13:3). Peter knew that the Lord had sent his angel and rescued him "from the hand of Herod and from all that the Jewish people had been expecting" (Acts 12:11).

Reference to the hand of God is relatively rare in the NT. The phrase occurs most frequently in Luke and Acts where it is clear that OT expressions are being adopted (Luke 1:66; Acts 4:28, 30; 7:50; 11:21; 13:11). The hand of God is active in creation (Acts 7:50; Heb 1:10), it protects and guides (Luke 1:66; Acts 11:21), but it also punishes (Acts 13:11).

The imposition of hands in the NT, like in the OT, has a variety of contexts and meanings.

To Heal. Numerous times in the NT Jesus touches the sick with his hand and they are healed. This gesture is also a common feature of miracle stories in antiquity. A typical NT example is when the synagogue official Jairus pleads with Jesus, "My daughter is at the point of death. Please, come lay your hands on her that she may get well and live" (Mark 5:23). The followers of Jesus demonstrate that they too have this power to transfer spiritual and physical wholeness to those in need. Ananias lays his hands on Paul so that Paul may regain his sight (Acts 9:12, 17) and Paul heals the father of Publius by laying hands on him (Acts 28:8; see Mark 16:18).

To Impart a Blessing. Hands are also imposed in order to impart a blessing. Jesus blesses little children in this manner when they are brought to him (Mark 10:16). This is also the method by which the holy Spirit is imparted at baptism (Acts 8:17-19; 19:6).

Ministry or Mission. On several occasions hands are laid on an individual as a way of conferring on that person some ministry or mission. It invokes on the individual a divine blessing and the power to perform some special task. When the apostles "laid hands on" the seven Hellenists (Acts 6:6), they were designating them for a specific function. In a similar fashion, Paul and Barnabas were commissioned for their missionary journey by prophets and teachers at Antioch (Acts 13:3).

In the Pastoral Letters, the laying on of hands is associated with the installation into an office. In 1 Timothy 4:14 we read, "Do not neglect the gift you have, which was conferred on you through the prophetic word with the imposition of hands of the presbyterate." Whether it is the presbyterate or the apostle (see 2 Tim 1:6) who ordains, it is clear that the gifts needed to carry out the office are being imparted by means of this ceremony.

See: BLESSING, BODY, GIFTS, HEALING, MINISTRY, MISSION, POWER, SACRIFICE, SIGN

DENNIS M. SWEETLAND

Pastoral-Liturgical Tradition

As in the Scriptures, hand indicates both a part of the body and metaphorically an extension of the self. Thus the hand can convey both the intentions of the heart and the way that the hand will be used in salvation. The hand can refer to God's action in creation, in delivering, in correcting, and in blessing. To sit at the right hand (Ps 110:2) can indicate one's special role and the trustworthy nature of the one so placed. Jesus as the risen Lord and Christ is described as sitting at the right hand of his Father in order to indicate his intercessory role as high priest who has won salvation for the Church.

Jesus' Use of Hands. Before Jesus was handed over to those who would crucify him, he took bread and cup into his hands at the Last Supper. This final meal that Jesus would hand over to his disciples as a perpetual memorial of himself was in continuity with his entire life. The Gospels of Mark and Luke note the times Jesus deliberately took initiative and laid hands on the sick and suffering in order to heal them (Mark 5:23; 6:5; 16:18; Luke 4:40; 13:13). Thus the power of God both to heal and to offer salvation in faith were expressed through the hands of Jesus. Jesus blessed the little children and offered them as models of faith (Matt 19:15; Mark 10:13, 16). After his resurrection Jesus led the disciples out to Bethany and lifted up his hands in blessing. While blessing them, he parted from them (Luke 24:50).

The Church's Use of Hands. The power of the Spirit continues to be conveyed and communicated by the laying on of hands. This gesture is the basic rite in all the sacraments. Through the use of hands spiritual power flows from God to the Christian Churches. Hands touch those whose senses will be signed by presider and sponsors as they are admitted into the catechumenate. Clergy and catechist lay hands on the catechumens often so that the toxants of sin may be emptied out and the Spirit may fill the person. Hands are placed on the elect as they go down into the waters of the font in baptism and as they are anointed with the chrism of salvation. Hands are also extended over the gifts of bread and wine in the Eucharist to express the role of the Spirit in changing the elements into the Body and Blood of Christ and as the Spirit transforms the assembly into the body of Christ. Hands impart blessing as the assembly concludes its liturgical action.

As in the Scriptures, hands are laid on those called to leadership and service at ordination and in moments of commissioning for specific ministries. Hands are joined as a man and a woman enter into the covenant of marriage. The sick experience the healing and compassion, the mercy and consolation of God when hands are placed upon their heads in silence. The gesture speaks for itself. Hands are also placed upon the head of penitents as they are reconciled with God and with the Church.

Just as the pillars of the Jerusalem Church gave the right hand of fellowship to Paul and Barnabas, so also the handclasp of peace conveys unity within the body of Christ and the desire for unity among Christian Churches.

See: BLESSING, HEALING, HEART, PEACE

JOHN J. O'BRIEN, C.P.

HARDNESS OF HEART

One of the most important words in the vocabulary of biblical anthropology is "heart." The heart, not the brain, was thought to be the source of a range of feelings, of desires and longings, of understanding and of decision. Just as conversion was regarded as an change of mind or heart, so closing one's mind or heart to change resulted in hardness of heart.

Old Testament

The first instance of hardness of heart is found in the story of the Exodus. Having been called by God to lead the people out of Egypt, Moses is forewarned by the Lord of the obstinacy of Pharaoh (Exod 7:13f., 22; 8:15, 28; 9:7, 34f.). The Egyptian ruler will be deaf to the cries of the oppressed people and to the demands of their God. In fact, the narrative states again and again that this hardness of heart was actually caused by the God of the Israelites (Exod 4:21; 7:3; 9:12; 10:1, 21, 27; 11:10; 14:4, 8, 17). This hardness of heart can be explained in several ways. First, Pharaoh's resistance provides an opportunity to devise a stage on which the drama of conflict can unfold. This is a contest of power. It will decide who determines the destiny of this people: the powers of Egypt or the God of the wilderness.

Furthermore, the tenacity of Pharaoh's resistance, despite the mounting evidence of the mysterious powers of Israel's God, adds to the buildup of narrative tension created by the storyteller. The rivalry demands higher and higher stakes. Pharaoh disregards the price that he and his people will have to pay, for his heart remains hardened. Finally, the fact that it was the Lord who hardened Pharaoh's heart does not absolve the Egyptian ruler from responsibility. Rather, it underscores the authority that Israel's God exercised even over Israel's enemies. To believe that a God, who came out of the wilderness and who was aligned with a motley group of forced laborers, could challenge and prevail over the forces of the great power of Egypt was heady thinking.

Hardness of heart is not the same as ignorance. It always presumes that the will of God is somehow communicated and that people with open minds and hearts will try to conform to this will. In the Exodus tradition God's will for the people was made known through the mediation of Moses. In the story of the people's search for a way of entrance into the land of Canaan, messengers were sent to Sihon, the hard-hearted king of Heshbon (Deut 2:26-30). Both of these traditions relate the opposition posed by foreign rulers to God's plan for God's people.

Such opposition was not universal. The Philistines, considered mortal enemies of Israel, appear to have heeded the warning not to harden their hearts against God's people. Having defeated the Israelites at Aphek, they captured the ark of the covenant and carried it from place to place within their own realm. Wherever the ark resided the people were ravaged and afflicted. Advised by priests and fortune-tellers not to harden their hearts as had the Egyptians, the Philistines returned the ark to the Israelites (1 Sam 6:1-16).

Israelites themselves are warned against becoming hard-hearted. The community-centered laws of Deuteronomy include a concern for individuals in need of land. The fortunate are admonished not to harden their hearts against those less fortunate (Deut 15:7). A puzzling reference to this disposition of heart is found in the prophet Isaiah (6:9f.). The prophet is told to make the hearts of the people, if not hard, at least sluggish so that they will not understand the warnings of God. Along with the other references to God's role in hardening hearts and closing minds, this passage is difficult to understand. It may be a way of saying that the punishment for closing themselves from God was necessary in order to break open the callous hearts of the people. God allowed them to sink to such depths in order to draw them up again, chastened and repentant.

Perhaps the best-known example of hardness of heart is found in Psalm 95:

Oh, that today you would hear his voice:
"Harden not your hearts as at Meribah,
as in the day of Massah in the desert"
(v. 7d).

The reference is to an incident that occurred during the early wandering in the wilderness. The people quarreled about water and there put God to the test (Exod 17:1-7; Num 20:8-13). The names of the sites mean "place of contention" and "place of testing," respectively. The murmuring of these wilderness wanderers was perceived as evidence of their hardness of heart. They did not try to understand the will or the ways of God and so they closed their minds to it. The Israelites who might recite this psalm were reminded of the stubbornness of their ancestors and warned not to follow their bad example lest they suffer similar consequences. Inevitably, hardness of heart will lead to evil (Prov 28:14).

New Testament

Hardness of heart and blindness of mind refer to the same inner disposition. A person so described is closed to the will of God as announced by another or perceptible in the events of life. Since Christians believe that the will of God is revealed in Jesus, to be closed to Jesus is to spurn the will of God. The Gospels all embrace this teaching.

When, in Matthew's Gospel (13:10-15; see Mark 4:10-12; Luke 8:9f.; John 12:37-40), Jesus is asked why he speaks in parables, he identifies his strategy as a way of fulfilling the prophecy of Isaiah mentioned above (Isa 6:9f.). The people's hearts had hardened so that they no longer understood their religious tradition (Matt 19:8; Mark 10:5). How could they be expected to be open to Jesus, his works, or his message? When he healed the man with the withered hand, he was met with hardness of heart (Mark 3:5). Even his own disciples reacted with disbelief. "They did not understand the incident of the loaves. On the contrary,

their hearts were hardened" (Mark 6:52). Even after he had risen from the dead and appeared to some, those who had not yet seen him did not believe and he rebuked them for their hardness of heart (Mark 16:14). The early Christians, like their ancient Israelite ancestors, were frequently close minded and hard hearted. Still, God never rejected them.

See: CONVERSION, HEART, SIN, TEMPTATION

DIANNE BERGANT, C.S.A.

HARVEST

In the agricultural economy of the biblical period, the harvest was a most significant time. It was the culmination of intensive labor over several months. A good harvest meant plenty and prosperity. A poor harvest meant hunger and poverty. The completion of the harvest was celebrated by important religious rituals whose purpose was to share the harvest with God to ensure a good harvest the next year.

Old Testament

Farmers have worked the land of Canaan for ten thousand years. Each of these years the quantity and quality of the harvest marked the success or failure of their efforts. The Gezer Calendar, the oldest Hebrew text in existence (tenth century BCE) gives some information about the sequence of harvesting in Canaan. Olives and other fruit were harvested at the beginning of the year (September–October). Flax was harvested near the end of Passover (March–April) by cutting the stalks and laying them out to dry. The barley harvest took place in April or early May; the wheat harvest seven weeks later in May or June. Farmers picked their summer fruit (figs, grapes, and pomegranates) in late August or September.

Reapers harvested grain with a hand-held curved sickle made of stone or metal with an attached wooden handle. Early sickles were made by placing serrated flints into a rounded wooden frame. Other early sickles were made from jawbones of large animals. These were sharpened to serve as a primitive sickle. (This would make the "jawbone of an ass" in the Samson story a formidable weapon [Judg 15:15-16].)

First to go through the fields of grain ready for harvesting would be the cutters with sickle in hand. Following them came the gatherers who bound the cut grain into sheaves. Egyptian tomb paintings illustrate the harvesting of grain in great detail since Egypt was famous for its abundant grain harvests. The Bible asks the Israelite farmer to practice a type of studied inefficiency when harvesting his fields (Lev 19:9; 23:22; Deut 24:17-22). Leaving some grain to be gleaned by the poor will allow them to survive without being dependent on obvious charity. They will have to work for their own support. The biblical tradition expects Israelite farmers to have compassion on those who do not own land and therefore have no share in the wealth that God gave to the community.

From the field the sheaves went to a threshing floor where farmers separated the grain from the chaff. In Canaan these threshing floors were usually outcroppings of bedrock on a high point where the prevailing winds could help the process of winnowing. The community owned threshing floors, although sometimes large landowners had their own. (The site chosen for the Temple was Araunah's threshing floor that was just north of the Jerusalem of David [2 Sam 24:16-25].) During the harvest, farmers slept on the threshing floor to guard the newly harvested grain (Ruth 3:7) since freshly harvested grain was valuable and therefore highly prized booty (1 Sam 23:1). Another method of threshing involved driving oxen over the sheaves (Deut 25:4). A third method made use of a threshing sledge: a wooden implement imbedded with sharpened stones or pieces of metal that was weighted down and driven over the sheaves (2 Sam 24:22; Isa 41:15; Amos 1:3). A fourth method involved the use of a wagon whose wheels separated the grain from the chaff (Isa 28:27-28). The choice of which method to use depended on the type of grain that was being harvested.

The harvesting of olives involved beating the trees with sticks and letting the olives fall to the ground (Deut 24:20; Isa 17:6). Other fruit, like grapes, was simply picked. Deuteronomy also expected the Israelite farmer to leave some fruit to be picked by the poor.

Harvest time was a time of rejoicing. Isaiah compares the joy at victory in battle with the joy at harvest time. The joy that will come with the restoration following the Exile is like the joy that comes with the harvest after months of difficult work (Ps 126:5-6). It is no wonder that the principal OT feasts (Passover, Weeks, and Booths) were originally festivals that celebrated the completion of the barley, wheat, and fruit harvest respectively. During these feasts, the Israelite farmer and his family went on pilgrimage to offer God a portion of the harvest and to offer a prayer of thanksgiving (Deut 26:1-11).

The Bible refers to this offering as a tithe, i.e., ten percent of the harvest (Lev 27:30; Deut 14:22-24). The figure of ten percent was chosen probably because scribes could compute such a figure easily. Originally the tithe was a tax given to the royal administration that supported ancient Israel's official cult. After the end of the monarchy, the tithe went directly to the Temple to support its personnel (Num 18:21, 24; Lev 23:10). According to Deuteronomy, however, after the farmer presented his tithe in the Temple, the priest returned it to him so that he could celebrate the harvest and God's bounty with his entire household (Deut 14:26). Every three years, however, this tithe was to be given to the poor (Deut 14:28-29; 26:12). The discrepancies between the legislation in Numbers and Deuteronomy regarding the tithe led the scrupulous to insist that Mosaic legislation required two tithes. This double burden led most people to abandon the practice of tithing by the time of Jesus. Another reason for the abandonment of tithing is that it is an inherently recessive form of taxation. It demands more of the poor than it does of the rich. The Pharisees considered their careful observance of the law of tithing a special mark of their strict observance (Luke 18:12), though the early Church* considered the laws of tithing to be of minimal importance (Matt 23:23; Luke 11:42). Some of the Fathers of the Church considered tithing an objectionable practice because the Jews observed it.

In a culture where farming is the occupation and support of most people, naturally religious language is going to use agricultural metaphors. Harvest or reaping is such a metaphor. The Book of Proverbs makes use of this metaphor several times to inculcate forethought and prudence (Prov 6:8; 10:5; 20:4). The pattern of sowing and reaping describes the inevitable consequences that follow from embarking on a certain path in the moral realm (Prov 22:8; Job 4:8). Hosea uses this metaphor when he predicts Israel's judgement (Hos 8:7) and when he offers a promise of redemption (Hos 10:12).

New Testament

In the NT, this metaphor has an eschatological dimension (Matt 9:37, 38; 13:30; Mark 4:29; Luke 10:2; John 4:35). The harvest is not grain or fruit but people to be gathered into the reign of God. The harvest becomes an image of the coming judgment (Matt 13:39). An angel stands ready with a sickle to execute that judgment (Rev 14:15-16). The kernels of grain will be sifted to remove every bit of straw (Luke 22:31). The grain will be bagged for storage, but the straw will be burnt (Matt 3:12).

Pastoral-Liturgical Tradition

In Western societies the number of people directly involved in agriculture is significantly less today than in the biblical period. Still the metaphor of the harvest can speak to people. It is a powerful reminder that once people choose a certain pattern of behavior, specific and inevitable consequences follow, just as reaping inevitably follows sowing. God then does not punish immoral behavior; such behavior carries with it the seeds of destruction that will come on those who choose to act contrary to the divine will.

Older patterns of Catholic liturgical observance were tied to agricultural cycles. For example, the Ember Days that were observed in the fall prayed for a good harvest. The Ember Days are no longer a part of the liturgical calendar. In certain forms of popular piety, however, celebration of the harvest continues. For example, in some cultures the Feast of the Assumption (August 15) takes on the character of a harvest celebration.

See: FEASTS, LAND

LESLIE J. HOPPE, O.F.M.

HATE

The very strong emotion of hate is described in the Bible, sometimes as an expected interhuman relationship, other times as human behavior to be condemned. Such attitudes are most often put into a religious context: God hates sinful human beings and their sin; sinful human beings hate God; the righteous hate what God hates; the righteous are hated by those who also hate God. The NT does not attribute hatred to God and is more rigorous in condemning hatred between human beings.

Old Testament

While there is a selection of Hebrew words related to the expression of hatred (e.g., cursing, rejecting, showing hostility, rising up against, crushing), and while the Septuagint sometimes translates these terms by the Greek verb for hate (*misein*), the principle verb and the object of our study is *sanay* with its derivatives meaning "to hate," "hatred," and "enemy."

The Hebrews were matter-of-fact about use of these terms to express human relations, sometimes taking such strong feeling for granted in human life. Thus, King Abimelech hated Isaac and sent him away when Isaac's family became too numerous (Gen 26:27); Joseph's brothers hated him because his father loved him best and because of his dreams (Gen 37:4, 8); David hated the Jebusites who possessed Jerusalem (2 Sam 5:8); Joab accused David of loving those who hated him and hating those who loved him (2 Sam 19:6-7). The strong connotation of hate, however, must be qualified, at least in some instances, since some passages show that the word simply means to dislike or to like less: "If a man with two wives loves one and dislikes ["hates"] the other . . ." (Deut 21:15; see also 22:13, 16; 24:3; Gen 29:31, 33; Sir 7:26); "He who spares his rod hates his son" (Prov 13:24); "Let your foot be seldom in your neighbor's house, lest he . . . hate you" (Prov 25:17). Nevertheless, the OT is fully aware that hatred can harbor deep resentments against others. The Law required a distinction between accidental killing and murder with hatred (Deut 4:42; 19:4, 6, 11-12). It is also clear that the law of Israel condemned hatred for a fellow Israelite and commanded love* of neighbor as its opposite (Lev 19:17-18).

The moral judgments on hate derive from the religious context within which human relationships exist. This gives a positive and a negative cast to hate. Put in a favorable light, God is said to hate all evildoers (Ps 5:6; Sir 12:7). The OT does not know the subtle distinction between loving the sinner and hating the sin. Nevertheless, God's hatred is not to be read as divine emotion against persons, but as the absolute incompatibility between God and evil. Moreover, the biblical text balances God's hatred with God's forgiveness (see Hos 9:15-17; 11:9-11). Just what is the evil that the Lord hates is occasionally spelled out in more specific morality: being like the other nations and practicing idolatry (Deut 12:31; Wis 12:3-7); externalism in worship (Amos 5:21; Isa 1:14); lack of justice (Isa 61:8; Jdt 5:17), especially on the part of the rulers of Israel (Mic 3:2) who are haughty and presumptuous (Amos 6:8); deception and false oaths (Zech 8:17). Many of these evils are gathered together when Proverbs says, "There are six things the LORD hates, yes, seven are an abomination to him" (6:16-19). This positive view of hate as a divine quality gives rise to a negative mirror image. Those who succumb to these evils that God hates become in turn enemies of God, i.e.,

those who hate God (Pss 68:2; 83:3) and will receive God's punishment (Exod 20:5; Deut 5:9; 32:41).

The favorable and unfavorable reflections on hate transfer from God to the righteous who fear the Lord. What God hates will not befall them (Sir 15:13) and, in fact, they will hate the same evil things (Amos 5:15; Prov 8:13) and evil persons (Ps 139:21-22). Here again, it is not so much a question of emotional aversion to persons as the commitment to disown evil. Conversely, the enemies of God will hate the righteous, who will need to be delivered by God (Isa 66:5). These enemies may be religious (Ps 38:18-20), political (Pss 18:17, 40; 89:23), personal (Prov 17:9), or communal (Ps 129:5). Finally, while there is strong sentiment to hate evildoers, there is, as noted above, explicit command not to hate one's own people, but to love neighbor as self.

New Testament

The NT provides more basis for distinguishing the sinner from the sin. It never speaks of God's hatred for persons, though one text (Rev 2:6) says that Christ hates the works of the heretical Nicolaitans. The NT also extends the command of love to embrace even the enemy (Matt 5:43-44; Luke 6:27).

The Gospels. Not unexpectedly, John's Gospel, which probes most deeply the meaning of love, also highlights the deepest aspects of love's opposite. John speaks most explicitly of the hatred of Jesus by his enemies (7:7; 15:18). Those who hate are persons of immoral behavior. They prefer to remain in the darkness, and hate the light that Jesus brings (3:20). Hatred of Jesus is, in turn, hatred of God (15:23-25). The other Gospels make only one direct reference to hating God, when they warn that love of worldly goods will mean hatred of God (Matt 6:24; Luke 16:13). Otherwise, both the Synoptic Gospels and John speak of the hatred that evildoers have for the disciples of Jesus, those who belong to God. They will be hated on account of their belonging to Jesus (Matt 10:22; 24:9; Mark

18:13; Luke 21:17; John 15:18; 17:14), but God will save them from these enemies (Luke 1:71; 6:22). Nevertheless, to remain true disciples, they must hate themselves and all other human ties that keep them from Jesus (Luke 14:26; John 12:25). In these last passages we see carried over the OT understanding of hate as "loving less" (see Luke 14:26; Matt 10:37).

The Letters. The rest of the books of the NT mention only once the hatred of the world for those who are righteous children of God (1 John 3:13). Instead, these books concentrate on the demand for the righteous to hate evil and to overcome hatred by their love for others. Indeed, hatred is seen as characteristic of the world that the Christians renounced at their conversion (Titus 3:3; Rev 17:16). This means that Christians must hate sin in others, even while striving to save these people (Jude 23). The hatred of evil is an interior process only gradually achieved. Paul lamented his not doing what he wanted, and his doing the very things he hated, but rejoiced in new possibilities through Christ (Rom 7:15, 24-25). Interior hatred of evil must show itself in actions, especially of love that counters hate. This may be in the love of husbands for wives based on the tendency to love self rather than to hate (Eph 5:28-29). It will be above all in communal love, a hatred of hatred itself. The Johannine community once again makes the strongest point in this regard by observing that one who hates brother or sister is the equivalent of a murderer (1 John 3:15), lives in darkness (1 John 2:9, 11), and is a liar against the Spirit of truth and under demonic powers (1 John 4:20).

Pastoral-Liturgical Tradition

The definition and characteristics of hate are in many ways parallel to that of love, which is its opposite. Hate may be seen as a passion of hostility or strong aversion. With or without this emotion it is also an act of the will, expressing repugnance for what is perceived as evil. Hate is a vice when what is perceived and rejected as evil are the very things that perfect one's being. In that case, as love is outgoing and is received only by being given away, hate is a pursuit of selfish interests, keeping all and repelling others as a threat to those interests. In the same way that love of God is expressed in love of neighbor, so hatred of neighbor is also a hatred of God. Ultimately, rejection of these relationships is a form of self-hatred, for it repels what is really best for oneself. Nevertheless, the commitment of love entails a repugnance for genuine evil. Hate is a quality of the virtue of love when it is directed toward what is genuinely evil.

As contemporary theology has stressed the relationship of love to justice, so it has also seen injustice as the expression of hatred in the sense of alienation. Oppressors hate the oppressed and create conditions in which the oppressed come to be alienated from—or to hate—everything, even themselves. The oppressed must transform this destructive hatred into a creative hatred for what is genuinely unjust, so that they might begin the achievement of justice as the first expression of genuine love.

See: FEAR, JUSTICE, LOVE, NEIGHBOR, RECONCILIATION, SIN

ANTHONY J. TAMBASCO

HEALING

This entry consists of three parts. The OT section compares the contemporary world's understanding of healing with that of the ancient Mediterranean world. The NT section examines the healing stories of the Gospels with those differences in mind. The section on the Pastoral-Liturgical Tradition considers the consequences of believing that Christians are to continue the healing work of Jesus.

Old Testament

The ancient biblical world's understanding of healing differs radically from that of the modern, scientifically oriented western culture. Science is rooted in the conviction that human beings can control and manipulate nature and its processes. The ancient world believed only God could control and manipulate nature. Human beings had no choice but to submit to nature and its seemingly whimsical operation. Sickness was one such experience.

Medical anthropology, a contemporary social science, offers Bible readers helpful ideas and distinctions for understanding healing and related questions in the ancient world. According to this science, the human experience of non-well-being is best called sickness. A modern, science-based view of sickness is called disease, that is, a biological (or psychological) disorder caused by a germ, virus, or other "single" culprit. The science-based view of the remedy is called "cure," that is, the process of identifying the single-cause of the disease and removing, destroying, or controlling it.

The ordinary, human (and non-science based) interpretation of sickness is called illness, that is, the experience of some biological or psychological disorder along with its many and complex social consequences for the individual, the family, and community. Healing is the strategy of managing illness by addressing the symptom in some satisfying way and by regaining or finding new meaning in life.

In the ancient Mediterranean world long before scientific medicine came into existence, sick people sought to be healed. Sometimes they may even have been cured, but since the evidence for disease in individual cases is no longer available, this determination cannot be made from a scientific point of view.

Bible translations will not reflect these distinctions because Bible translators are unaware of this important insight from medical anthropology. Guided by this insight, however, the critical Bible reader should be able to read and interpret each passage with respect for its cultural context and with confidence that the text will be understood as its author and original readers understood it. Such an understanding also helps to grasp the theology of healing reflected in biblical texts.

If human beings have no control over nature, then only God is in control, and any human being who seemed to heal a sick person was normally viewed as empowered by God to do so. When Elisha's instructions proved effective in cleansing Naaman of his skin condition (called leprosy in the Bible), the Syrian exclaimed, "Now I know that there is no God in all the earth, except in Israel" (2 Kgs 5:15). Naaman recognized the God of Israel as his benefactor or patron. Elisha was God's broker.

This common cultural belief is reflected in Exodus 15:26: "'If you really listen to the voice of the LORD, your God,' [God] told them, 'and do right in his eyes: if you heed his commandments and keep all his precepts, I will not afflict you with any of the diseases with which I afflicted the Egyptians; for I, the LORD, am your healer.'" The Israelites had no theory of secondary causality. God causes illnesses and removes them. Prophets like Elijah (1 Kgs 17:17-24) and Elisha (2 Kgs 5:1-19) acted on God's behalf in healing sick people.

The story of Naaman also shows other gods were viewed as healers, too. Though he takes dirt from Israel with him back to Syria where he will construct an altar at which to worship Yahweh, Naaman admits he will also have to continue attending the Temple of Rimmon to please his master (vv. 16-18). The ancient Egyptians sought healing from Serapis, while the ancient Greeks sought healing from Asclepius.

Later in Israelite history, after secular Greek medicine had been spread throughout the ancient world by the armies of Alexander the Great, worshipers of Yahweh faced a new challenge. Should sick people turn to human beings (physicians) or to God for healing? The reflections found in Sirach 38 (second century BCE) reflect that challenge.

At face value, the passage seems ambivalent toward physicians. It advises consulting this healer but reminds the sick person that God gave healing power to this person, and God is responsible for the success or failure of the venture (vv. 1-8). Sirach points out that both patient (v. 9) and physician (v. 13) rely on God through prayer. Although a sick person consults a physician, traditional remedies of repentance, purification, and offerings (vv. 10-11) should not be neglected.

At the time Sirach was written, Palestinian Jews were beginning to learn about human healers (whom some might identify as "professional" at that time) in Hellenistic culture with curiosity and admiration. Sirach attempted to promote respect for tradition while not entirely squelching the opportunities for learning from Hellenism.

Modern scholars rely upon a variety of tools to investigate, understand, and interpret the sicknesses that were healed in the ancient world. The history of medicine approach with rare exceptions uses modern medicine as the measuring stick of information presented in biblical and other ancient texts. For instance, these specialists believe that "true" leprosy (Hansen's Disease) was first introduced to the Middle East from India by Alexander's armies. For this historical reason true leprosy is probably not the concern of Leviticus 13–14. Philology appears to support this historical judgment since the Hebrew and Greek words used there are not the ones that typically identify true leprosy. From this perspective, the condition was probably a self-limiting skin problem.

Paleopathology studies ancient disease in humans and in animals from archeological remains such as bones, fecal matter, dried blood, and the like. Paleopathologists have still not found any evidence of true leprosy or syphilis in human bones from the ancient Middle East that can be dated earlier than the sixth century CE.

Medical anthropology views sickness in its cultural setting and seeks to learn the cultural interpretation of a sickness condition. It was an anthropologist who pointed out that biblical personalities interpreted what they called leprosy as a condition to be feared because it was polluting ("dirty") rather than because it was contagious ("catchy"). Victims of biblical leprosy were isolated from the holy community because they defiled it and not because they were spreading germs. The concern was purity rather than sickness, and the desired outcome was cleansing rather than cure. Healing of lepers always included restoration to full membership in the holy community.

The history of medicine documents that blindness was very common in the ancient Middle East. Perhaps this explains in part why the blind and the deaf were guaranteed special protection in the Torah (Lev 19:14). Most cases of blindness were due to trachoma, a contagious infection of the inner mucous lining of the eyelids (the conjunctiva) and of the cornea. The disease was transmitted by flies and by poor hygiene.

It was not until the nineteenth century that the Scottish surgeon, Joseph Lister, succeeded in convincing physicians that washing one's hands was a major step toward preventing the spread of disease. Before that, surgeons went directly from dissecting cadavers in the morgue to treating patients in the hospital, causing a high mortality rate. In antiquity, scarcity of water prompted many peasants to omit even required ritual ablutions (possibly the case in Mark 7).

There were other reasons for loss of sight in antiquity. Some were congenitally blind (John 9). Sorrow was blamed for some eye problems. Job lamented: "my eye has grown dim with sorrow" (17:7), and the psalmist echoes this belief: "my eye grows dim through sorrow" (Ps 88:9). Old age was blamed for others. "Now Eli was ninety-eight years old and his eyes were set, so that he could not see" (1 Sam 4:15). Still other cases sound to modern ears like cataracts (Tob 6:8).

A widely recognized and accepted cure for blindness in antiquity was gall, a bitter greenish fluid secreted by the liver and stored in the gall bladder. The angel Raphael, whose Hebrew name means "God is my healer," advised Tobias to use the gall of a fish to cure a person with "white films in his eyes" (Tob 6:8). With this remedy, Tobias restored his father's sight (Tob 11:7-15).

One historian of medicine, a physician,

believes blindness was considered the ultimate disaster among biblical people because it caused total dependence on others. This explanation is culturally appropriate to highly individualistic western culture with its emphasis on independence and self determination. In the Mediterranean world, where people are group-oriented and personalities are other-directed, the explanation is unsatisfactory.

The real bane of blindness in ancient Israel was the awareness that God who bestows this gift also withholds it or takes it away (Exod 4:11). In some though not all instances, loss of sight was associated with displeasing God, i.e., sin (Gen 19:11; Deut 28:28; 2 Kgs 6:18; Acts 13:11). Tobit and the man-born-blind in John 9 illustrate exceptions to this belief.

Yet despite the pain deriving from knowing that for some mysterious reason God has deprived one of sight, a blind person did not feel cursed. In Genesis (1:3-5), God existed in darkness before creating light. Darkness therefore symbolizes the presence of God. To live in darkness, that is being unable to see, means one lives in the presence of God. Such intimacy with God compensates the blind person who can interact with but not see other human beings who are created in the image and likeness of God (Gen 1:26).

Concerning longevity, the psalmist's observation that "seventy is the sum of our years, or eighty if we are strong" (Ps 90:10) is familiar to all Bible readers. Presuming the ancients counted the way we do and used the same calendars that we possess, this is an impressive life-expectancy. The presumptions, of course, are erroneous.

Study of skeletal remains suggests that life expectancy in the ancient world averaged between thirty and forty-five years depending on the specific location and period. In ancient cities, almost thirty percent of live births were dead by the age of six. Another sixty percent of live births would have died by mid-teens. By the mid-twenties, seventy-five percent would be dead. Only ten percent might have

lasted until the mid-forties, and perhaps as few as three percent made it to their sixties.

The death of the twelve-year-old girl whom Jesus restored to life (Mark 5:21-24, 35-43) is therefore a very common experience in his day. The Gospel record does not indicate the cause of her death, but we can make at least three plausible suggestions.

She may have died of natural causes, or more likely she may have died of some childhood sickness or disease. But a third cause is conceivable and plausible, namely a culture-specific syndrome. Perhaps the girl was a victim of the "evil eye." (The word "evil eye" appears in Prov 28:22; 23:6-8; Tob 4:7, 16; Matt 20:15; Mark 7:22; and elsewhere, but is often translated envy).

There is a pervasive belief in Mediterranean cultures that some people can cause misfortune (sickness, deformity, death, crop-failure, and other tragedies) by a mere "glance" described in the contemporary Middle East as "the fierce look." Frequently these people have an eye ailment like the modern "lazy eye" or weak muscular control of one eye.

Their glance is considered damaging by itself, but the glance is also considered to be linked with a desire to destroy whatever they behold with "envy." In the Mediterranean world, a person envies a precise object like this lovely child, but since it cannot be possessed it must be destroyed. The agents of destruction are invariably any of the capricious and malicious spirits who inhabit the atmosphere and spy on human beings ever ready to interfere in their lives.

Children, particularly if attractive or gifted, are common targets of the evil eye and malicious spirits. A common preventive measure against the evil eye and its consequences (sickness and death) is to wear something blue or red in color (ribbons, tassels). Special amulets can thwart the evil eye.

It is also a custom to spit, sometimes three times. This is how the Galatians reacted to Paul whom they suspected of having such powers (see Gal 4:14). Others bite the knuckle of the index finger.

Tragedies and deaths believed to be caused by the evil eye were so common and so commonly known in the Middle East that Mark's Jesus did not even have to mention it concerning the twelve-year-old girl. Nor would he want to "risk" the consequences that might result from even saying the words. The unfortunate girl may not have been adequately protected.

Possessing the evil eye is not a sickness in the ancient world. People suspected of having it ordinarily go out of their way to be kind and generous to avoid accusations.

Setting aside contemporary medical knowledge allows for a better appreciation of healing as reported in the Bible. Lacking a theory of secondary causality (germs, medicines), the ancient Israelites viewed God as the cause and remedy of human health problems. Humans (prophets or others) who brokered healing to sick human beings always acted in the name of God. When faced with the possibility in Hellenism that human beings might actually have greater mastery over nature and some of its problems than traditionally acknowledged, early Jewish sages insisted on God as the ultimate source of all healing.

See: LEPROSY

JOHN J. PILCH

New Testament

The Mediterranean cultural tendency to personify nature always looks for a personal agent behind the human experience of well-being or misfortune. Life is good because God or other spiritual beings have not disturbed the basically good order of creation. Misfortunes are blamed not on germs, erratic weather patterns, or natural disasters but rather on some personal agent who has deliberately disturbed or thwarted a good situation. Human beings are personally helpless in remedying the misfortune, though they can and must intervene with the proper super-human agent who can restore well-being. Mediterranean human beings are convinced they do not control nature but must simply suffer it or yield to it.

Clearly the Bible interprets human misfortunes very differently than modern Western believers do. Since ancient peoples could not see or know the existence of germs and viruses, they could not know diseases and therefore were not interested in cures. Disease is a pathological state that involves only the afflicted individual. These concepts—germs, diseases, cures—are very modern. They derive from a culture that believes in and actually has accomplished an impressive mastery of nature viewed in a very impersonal way. A cure attacks a germ, defeats a disease, and restores biological well-being.

Our ancestors in the faith ascribed their misfortunes such as a loss of well-being to personal agents—either to capricious or malicious spirits, or to offended spirits who inflicted punishment upon the offending individual. Here the operative concepts are socially interpreted difficulties, illness, and healing. Illness is a socially disvalued state, and it involves others even beyond the confines of the family. These concepts—social evaluation, illness, healing—relate to meaning in life. A culture that does not believe nature can be mastered or controlled and which also personifies nature perceives health-related misfortunes as illness, that is, as a loss of human meaning, and seeks healing, that is, a restoration of meaning to life. Cure of a disease is always a rare occurrence, but healing of an illness happens always, infallibly, since everyone ultimately regains old meaning in life or achieves a new meaning.

Because of this cultural understanding, the NT does not provide sufficient evidence to identify germs, diseases, or cures, but it definitely offers more than enough evidence of socially interpreted misfortunes, illnesses, and healing.

At the beginning of Mark's Gospel, Jesus astonishes people with his teaching in the synagogue (1:22), drives an unclean spirit out of a possessed person (1:25-26), and dispels the fever of Simon's mother-in-law (1:30-31). Then follows the first of six statements summarizing Jesus' ministry: he healed many who were sick and drove out many demons (1:32-34; see also 1:39; 3:10-11; 6:5, 7-13, 56).

These summary statements frequently join mention of healing sick people with driving demons out of possessed people. Though the modern mind tends to distinguish these two activities, the Mediterranean world sees both as indicative of a loss of well-being and understands that both require a remedy. Jesus' strategy is effective in both cases, and people recognize that he is a mighty broker who can intervene with God the patron who is able to afflict enemies as well as clients, and to heal both also. "I, the LORD, am your healer," said God to Moses (Exod 15:26).

The illnesses that Mark reports Jesus to have healed include a fever (1:29-31); a repulsive, scaly skin condition (1:40-45); paralysis (2:1-12); withered hands (3:1-6); death (5:21-24, 35-43); menstrual irregularity (hemorrhage, 5:25-34); hearing loss and speech impediment (7:31-37); and blindness (8:22-26; 10:46-52).

We do not know the diseases these stories describe, and in some instances like leprosy we are positive it is not the leprosy we know, but the illnesses Mark describes clearly affect the entire person as perceived and understood by first-century Mediterranean culture. Jesus restored the ability to gather information (heart-eyes, e.g., blindness) and to share information (mouth-ears, e.g., being deaf or mute) as well as the ability to act upon that information (hands-feet, e.g., paralysis, death). These human activities are essential for discovering and creating meaning.

By remedying the woman's menstrual irregularity Jesus removed her from the category of "unclean" (see clean/unclean) and restored her to full membership in the community and unhindered participation in the community efforts to make sense out of life. Jesus' success in casting out demons (1:21-28; 3:20-30; 5:1-20; 7:24-30; 9:14-29; 9:38-40; 19:9-20) demonstrates his superior power to that of demons. Such a person is welcome and honored in a world that feels itself battered by and at the mercy of mischievous spirits and demons. Moreover, such a mastery over the spirit world is convincing evidence that the reign of God has arrived and is present in the ministry of Jesus.

Many people in Mark's Gospel address Jesus as teacher, but a distinctive feature of this Gospel is Mark's presentation of Jesus as a teacher-healer (see 1:21, 22; 2:13; 4:1; 5:2, 6, 30). This confirms the contemporary insight that healing in antiquity was indeed a response to the quest for meaning in life especially by people who had lost it in a health-related misfortune, that is, an illness.

Matthew's portrait of Jesus as healer differs from Mark's. Matthew has clustered ten mighty deeds or miracles of Jesus in chapters eight and nine. By including Jesus' calming of the storm while he and the disciples are at sea among nine healing and exorcism stories, Matthew highlights Jesus' entire wonder-working activity precisely as people of that culture would perceive it: as an extraordinary and quite unusual ability to control nature in all its dimensions.

These same chapters also highlight another difference between Matthew's and Mark's portraits. Both highlight Jesus' compassion, but in different contexts. Mark notes that Jesus was moved by the crowd to compassion because they seemed like sheep without a shepherd. In response, Jesus taught and fed them (Mark 6:34-44). Matthew's report of this same incident states that the sight of the crowd moved Jesus to compassion with the result that he "healed their sick" in addition to feeding them all (Matt 14:13-20). Matthew concludes his cluster of Jesus' ten mighty deeds with a similar reference to his compassion. The effective broker with God the healer deals with God's needy clients out of a sense of compassion rather than from a position of arrogant superiority. Healing includes both instruction and restoration to a proper state of being.

While Mark presents Jesus as a teacher-healer, Matthew presents Jesus as one whose power and mastery over nature is not magic but quite superior to it. Uniquely in the NT, Matthew uses a Greek word literally translated as "moon-struck" to describe one category of sick people whom Jesus healed (4:24; 17:14-18). The moon is brighter in the East than in northern latitudes, and its most noticeable feature easily seen by the naked human eye is its changing phases and continually varying relation to the constellations. Its most common name in Hebrew means "the wanderer." Moon-struck people behave unpredictably and erratically.

Though Israel's neighbors worshiped the moon, she herself did not. Job protests his innocence by affirming that he has not been swayed by the moon (Job 31:26-27), and the saint is described as a person who is not smitten by the moon (Ps 121:6). Jesus' ability to heal the "moon-struck" demonstrates he is immune to the alleged power of the moon and much more powerful than magicians and others who worship the moon as servants of that deity. This is another way affirming the ancient faith that God alone heals (Exod 15:16).

The single author of Luke's Gospel and Acts of the Apostles presents yet another distinctive portrait of Jesus as healer. Here blindness and its healing holds a central position in the ministry of Jesus. Luke assures us that Jesus bestowed sight on "many that were blind" (7:21-22), yet there is only one specific report in the Gospel (18:35-43)! A modern believer too narrowly focused on physical blindness and the restoration of physical sight will miss the point of these miracle-signs.

No one minimizes the gift of sight, but in a geographical region like the circum-Mediterranean countries where blindness (most often due to trachoma) and poor vision were quite common in antiquity and eye-glasses were not yet invented, and in a culture where lying and deception are accepted as legitimate strategies in the service of preserving honor and avoiding shame, it is easy to understand that sociocultural blindness and vision were an equal if not stronger concern.

This is the central concern in Luke-Acts. Jesus reminds believers to improve their own sight and understanding before seeking to improve that of another believer (Luke 6:39-42). The parable of the sower and seed (8:1-15) is "illuminated" by the image of a lamp whose light should be seen. Jesus exclaims: "Blessed are the eyes that see what you see" (10:21-24), criticizes the evil generation for refusing to see the sign it seeks (11:29-32), and urges people to get an "eye check-up" (11:33-36)!

Unless one's eyes work well, one will not be able to see and interpret what one sees (Luke 12:54-56). Those who want to see the revelation of the Son of Man may actually miss it (17:22-37). Herod misses his opportunity to see (23:8). In contrast, the crowds that witnessed Jesus' death and its circumstances returned home beating their breasts (23:48). They saw and understood.

Within this context, the blind man who addresses Jesus as "Son of David" and wins back his sight (Luke 18:35-43) underscores the evangelist's point: it is often easier for physically blind people to regain sight than for sighted people to truly understand Jesus and the miracle-signs that he works. Many in the Gospel refuse to listen to and understand Jesus, while the healed man immediately follows Jesus and glorifies God.

Acts of the Apostles continues this emphasis on seeing (1:8; 2:19), especially in the contexts where the phrase "wonders and signs" appears almost as a refrain. This is what people are expected to see and understand. During his ministry, Jesus empowered the apostles to heal and exorcise and sent them on mission with this purpose (Matthew 10; Mark 3; Luke 9; 10). Acts reports this activity by the apostles in general (2:43; 5:12), Peter and John and others (4:30), Stephen (6:8), and Paul and Barnabas (14:3; 15:12).

Luke concludes Acts of the Apostles on a relatively sad note but one that demonstrates how much more remains for disciples to do to help others see. As Paul preaches in Rome, some were convinced and others did not believe (Acts 28:24).

Paul's final statement is a citation from Isaiah 6:9-10, which he applies to some of his stubborn Roman audience. They have closed their ears and eyes and refused to understand and be converted, and have not allowed God to heal them.

All of this meshes well with the specific image in which Luke presents Jesus as healer, namely: Jesus is an authorized, spirit-filled prophet who vanquished unclean spirits and illness associated with them (7:16; 9:8, 19; 14:19).

John's careful selection of seven of Jesus' mighty deeds and his specific characterization of them as signs is yet another portrayal of Jesus as a genuine, Mediterranean healer, that is, one who specializes in meaning in life and in helping others to find it in God. This is the clear thrust of his healing ministry.

In all the Gospels, but especially in John, details of the healings that are not abbreviated are omitted. Instead, more attention is devoted to explanatory comments, which in John become fairly lengthy narratives. The healing of the man-born-blind is recounted in two verses (John 9:6-7), but the seven-scene dialogue involving alternating groups of characters fill the remaining thirty-nine verses of this chapter. Frustrating as the two verses may be to scientifically oriented Western readers, John's readers and all first-century Mediterranean readers would have found more than enough to think and talk about in the thirty-nine verses.

Healing, after all, is a process of restoring meaning to life along with some kind of an ameliorated physical condition. We know that people born blind who regain sight are so bombarded by visual sensations, they must close their eyes for long periods of time in order to avoid confusion. They have yet to learn how to select the significant sensations from the millions that bombard them. This is a process that early-childhood socialization teaches in each culture. Jesus therefore very appropriately controls the dialogue and includes the healed man in the dialogues so that all might learn how to focus on the really important things to see and understand.

See: CLEAN/UNCLEAN, MAGIC AND DIVINATION, MIRACLE, MOON, REIGN OF GOD, SIGN, STARS

JOHN J. PILCH

Pastoral-Liturgical Tradition

Healing and the Mission of the Church. The mission of the Church to be a mediation of healing in the world flows from its task of proclaiming the reign of God. This rule of God's love, inaugurated by the ministry, death, and resurrection of Jesus, entails a state of affairs in which people discover the fullness of salvation. Because the Christian community experiences the presence and the power of the risen Christ in its midst, it is called to continue the work of Jesus in making present this reign of God that brings wholeness to broken people. Christians believe that their faith and identity are intimately connected with human wholeness.

The Christian approach to healing is based on the fundamental convictions that creation is essentially good, that life itself is a gift from God, and that God has acted in Christ to redeem creation. It is also grounded in a biblical anthropology that understands the human person to be a unity of body and spirit, of physical and spiritual dimensions. Sickness and disability are viewed as consequences of a disruption in the human condition caused by sin. While Christian writers of every age have expounded on the spiritual growth and other blessings that can come to the believer through the endurance of physical and emotional suffering, Christian theology understands sickness and disability in themselves to be contrary to the purposes of a loving God. In the second century, when Ignatius of Antioch depicted Christ as the divine Physician (Eph 7:2), he was echoing the biblical testimony that Christ reveals a God who offers life for humanity and who is active in opposing the forces of death that are at work in the world.

Ministry to the sick has always held a significant place in the life of the Church. The practice of praying for the sick and dying in the liturgy and of bringing the Eucharist to them began in the early Church. There are numerous accounts of physical healing experienced through prayer and anointing of the sick by the Desert Fathers, though the bulk of early Christian literature addressed to the sick stresses the opportunity for spiritual growth and purification that illness affords. The charism of healing that Paul lists among the gifts of the holy Spirit (1 Cor 12:9) has been evident throughout the history of the Church and has become part of the testimony about the lives of holy women and men. The perduring phenomenon of pilgrimages to shrines like Lourdes manifests the faith of the Christian people in the power of God to grant physical, emotional, and spiritual healing. From its earliest days, the Church has endeavored to distinguish between authentic and inauthentic claims to healing, and believers have discovered that the healing sought in prayer is something more profound than merely physical cure. Ultimately, healing is a process that takes place throughout life and which culminates in the new life of the resurrection.

The Church retained the lesson of Matthew 25:31-46 and placed the visitation and care of the sick among the corporal works of mercy. It played a leading role in the West in the founding of hospitals and hospices, occupying a virtual monopoly on care for the sick up until the French Revolution. Much of this work has been carried out by religious communities of women and men that were founded for the specific purpose of ministry to the sick. This tradition lives on in the many health care facilities sponsored by the Church today. It represents one important dimension of the Christian vocation to proclaim and make present the healing power of Christ.

The Sacraments of Healing. The grace of Christ communicated in the celebration of the sacraments* is a source of healing for body and spirit. The Eucharist is the principal sacrament of healing for the Christian community. Faith in the healing effects of the Eucharist is expressed by the community in the prayer before reception of communion that recalls the Gospel words of trust spoken by the centurion (Matt 8:8-9). Through remembrance in the intercessory prayer of the liturgy and by reception of the Eucharist brought by the Church's ministers, the sick are included in the Eucharistic celebration of the community. The participation of lay persons today in bringing the Eucharist to the ill and infirm has enriched and broadened this aspect of the healing ministry of the Church.

In the sacrament of reconciliation, believers celebrate the healing power of Christ's forgiveness. Those who are alienated from God, others, and themselves through sin are enabled to know the pardon and peace offered by the risen Jesus and to be reconciled with the Christian community. This sacramental experience of being forgiven and being called to forgive can be a source of profound spiritual and emotional healing.

The practice of anointing the sick with oil, commended in James 5:14-15, was adopted by the early Church and eventually developed into an official sacrament. The *Apostolic Tradition* of Hippolytus contains an ancient reference to this practice, prescribing a prayer of consecration that asks God to endow the oil with the power of healing (no. 5). In the early Church, this rite of anointing was not restricted to the dying, nor does it appear that only clergy administered it. This anointing was understood to have both physical and spiritual effects. After the period of the Carolingian Reform in the eighth century, the ministry of anointing was restricted to the ordained, greater emphasis was placed on the forgiveness of sin and other spiritual effects of the sacrament, and the rite became more associated with the dying. Today, the ritual for this sacrament, renewed after Vatican II, declares that the whole person, in his/her bodily and spiritual dimensions, is helped by the grace of the holy Spirit. Any who are seriously ill are encouraged to receive it. The sacrament is a celebration of the Christian community, meant to give the sick their rightful place within the community and to help in overcoming the isolation brought on by illness.

Contemporary Challenges. There are special challenges and opportunities for the Church in its mission of continuing the healing of Jesus in the world today. The advances in medical technology that have done so much to improve health care can sometimes result in the depersonalization of the sick. In its care for the ill, the Christian community must continue to minister to the whole person and to advocate medical and pastoral methods which respect the dignity of the infirm. One essential component of its ministry of healing is the Church's ongoing reflection on the increasingly complex ethical questions surrounding the care of the sick.

The social dimension of healing represents another significant challenge in the Church's effort to mediate the healing of Christ in the contemporary world. Persistent illness and low life expectancy among the poor of the world, often due to malnutrition, inadequate sanitation, and the scarcity of ordinary medicines, is a situation that calls out to believers for action. If they wish to be faithful to the task of proclaiming God's reign, Christians must be concerned about sociopolitical reforms that will increase the availability of health care to all. Jesus' compassionate response to the pleading of the man with leprosy in the Gospel, of one left impoverished and ostracized because of his illness, must also be the response of Christians in their efforts to extend the healing touch of Christ to the poor and marginalized of our world (see Mark 1:40-45).

See: ANOINTING, EUCHARIST, MIRACLE, MISSION, PASSION, PRAYER, RECONCILIATION, REIGN OF GOD, RESURRECTION, SUFFERING

ROBIN RYAN, C.P.

HEART

A most important term in biblical psychology, the heart is at the center of an individual's human life. The word's range of meaning embraces both the physical organ and a wealth of psychic, emotional, intellectual, and moral powers attributed to it. Thus, as practically equivalent to a person's "inner life" and personality, the heart is the seat of the desires, emotions, thoughts, and plans that determine the human character and its activities. For the same reason it is also the primary arena in which one meets God, and in which God works to cause change, enlightenment, and a new life. For all practical purposes the OT and NT uses of heart are the same, with the latter especially emphasizing God's power to work through the human heart.

Old Testament

The Hebrew words for heart, *lēb, lēbāb,* appear some eight hundred times. The physical organ or its activity is rarely mentioned (2 Sam 18:14; 2 Kgs 9:24; 1 Sam 25:37, where the stopped heart is equivalent to paralysis from fear). Eating can strengthen the heart (Gen 18:5; Judg 19:5) and help the heart recover (1 Kgs 21:7); wine can make the heart joyful (Ps 104:15). Even these last examples carry overtones of psychological well-being.

In a few cases, the heart just represents the person, the "self," and is best translated by the pronoun. So, in Psalm 27:3, "my heart will not fear," "my heart" is equivalent to "I." In Genesis 8:21 the Lord "says to his heart," that is, he "says to himself." Sometimes the heart can simply stand for the person (by synecdoche): "the wise of heart" = the wise person (Prov 10:8; 11:29), = experts (Exod 31:6). There is also the idiom where heart means "center/innermost part of," such as "the heart of the sea" (Exod 15:8; see also Deut 4:11; Jonah 2:4; Ps 46:3; Matt 12:40).

Most often the heart is used figuratively to refer to a person's inner life. This is often conveyed by distinguishing it from physical realities or physical organs: the flesh (Pss 73:26; 84:3; Prov 14:30), one's clothes (Joel 2:13), the tongue (Pss 28:3; 78:18), the ears (Ezek 3:10), the hands (Ps 73:13). It can be equivalent to *rûaḥ,* "spirit" (Pss 51:12, 19;

143:4; Ezek 11:19). In cases, the heart represents the deepest and most personal secrets and thoughts of the person (Judg 16:17; 1 Sam 9:19). It is that part of a person that God alone can see (1 Sam 16:7) and that alone reveals who the person is. God alone can change the heart, i.e. "give a new heart" (Ezek 36:26). In this figurative understanding of heart the OT parallels similar usage in other Semitic literatures. The Septuagint follows this usage as does the NT. What, then, is represented by this inner life of the heart?

It is from the heart that come all emotions, feelings, passions, and moods. The heart can be joyful (Deut 28:47; Job 29:13; Zech 10:7), sad (Neh 2:2), discouraged (Num 32:7), troubled (2 Kgs 6:11), grief-stricken (Ps 13:2; Jer 4:19; Isa 65:14), ill-disposed (Deut 15:10), full of courage (2 Sam 17:10; Ps 27:14) or fear (Deut 20:3). It can be moved to envy (Prov 23:17), love (Deut 6:5), or hatred (Lev 19:17). It is the seat of loyalty (2 Sam 15:13), care (1 Sam 9:20), pity (Hos 11:8), and desire (Ps 21:3). The description of these emotions can be graphic: the heart sinks (Gen 42:28), becomes numb (Gen 45:26), gets sick (Lam 5:17), trembles (1 Sam 28:5), melts (Ps 22:15), breaks (Ps 69:21), throbs (Ps 38:11), reels (Isa 21:4), and becomes "withered and dried up" (Ps 102:5). "Greatness of heart" (Isa 9:8) is a heart swollen with pride.

The heart is also the seat of the intellectual life and has functions other cultures would ascribe to the mind. Thus, it can think, although the concreteness of Hebrew expression would phrase this idea as "say, devise in the heart" (Gen 27:41; Pss 4:4; 140:3). The heart understands (Deut 8:5; 29:3; 1 Kgs 3:12; Prov 14:10; 22:17; Eccl 7:22; Jer 24:7), remembers ("bring back to the heart" Isa 44:19; 46:8; "place on the heart" 1 Sam 21:13; Isa 42:5; 47:7; Jer 12:11; "come to the heart" Isa 65:17; Jer 3:16; 19:5), and considers things carefully (Prov 15:28; 16:9; Isa 33:18). The heart is equivalent to intelligence. The one who has heart understands (Job 34:10), but the "lack of heart" is folly (Prov 6:32; 10:21; Hos 7:11). To "get

heart" is to gain understanding (Prov 15:32). The heart is the source of skills (Exod 31:6), the storehouse of wisdom (1 Kgs 10:24), the repository for memories (Prov 7:3), and the origin of thinking (Judg 5:16). The heart has depths that are seemingly limitless (Prov 25:3), except to the all-seeing vision of God (Ps 33:15; Jer 11:20).

It is just a small step to move from the heart as the setting for human intelligence and thought to the heart as the place for the will, the source of decisions, plans, attitudes, and therefore the center for the moral life. The heart has its own intentions (1 Kgs 8:17; Isa 10:7; Jer 23:20), acts as one's conscience (2 Sam 24:10; Ps 51:12), and impels the person to act (Exod 36:2; Num 16:28). Because of this close connection with human thought and action, therefore, the heart readily takes on moral and religious implications. The person of "twisted heart" (Prov 11:20) is an abomination to God. The heart can be faithless (Isa 29:13; Ezek 6:9), hypocritical or a "double heart" (Ps 12:3), godless (Job 36:13), or turned away from God (1 Kgs 11:2), hardened against God (Exod 4:21; Deut 2:30; Zech 7:12), "uncircumcised" (Jer 9:25). The return of such a heart to God requires "circumcision" (Deut 10:16) and the offering of the "whole heart" (Joel 2:12). The good heart is completely devoted to God (1 Kgs 8:61), perfect (Ps 119:80), and upright (Ps 32:11). A person can strive to keep his heart clean (Ps 73:13), renew his heart (Ezek 18:31), or "guide it in the right way" (Prov 23:19).

The heart is the center of one's relationship with God. It is the heart that speaks to God (Ps 27:8), that trusts in God (Ps 28:7), and receives God's word (Deut 30:14). God knows the secrets of the heart (Ps 44:22), is the tester of hearts (Ps 17:3), and can inspire hearts to action (Neh 2:12). God can give hearts understanding (1 Kgs 3:9) or even take it away (Job 12:24). Ultimately, then, real renewal of the heart will depend on God's action, when God writes the Law on human hearts (Jer 31:33), or replaces hardened human hearts with new malleable hearts (Ezek 36:26).

New Testament

The Greek word *kardia,* rare in ancient Greek secular literature, is the common Septuagint and NT translation for *lēb* and *lēbāb* and has the same range of meaning as its Hebrew counterparts. It never refers to a physical organ in the body, but to the center of physical life (Acts 14:17; Jas 5:5). Most especially it represents the inner self (1 Pet 3:4). As in the OT, it is the seat of the emotions. It is the source of one's deepest motivation and desires (Matt 6:21; Luke 12:34). It can be troubled (John 14:1), full of grief and anguish (John 16:6; Rom 9:2; 2 Cor 2:4), full of sinful desires (Matt 5:28; Rom 1:24), jealousy, and ambition (Jas 3:14). On the other hand, the heart can also rejoice (John 16:22; Acts 2:26), and be resolute (Jas 5:8) and sincere in disposition (Eph 6:5; Heb 10:22). It can be filled with a burning love (Luke 24:32), affectionate love ("hold in the heart" Phil 1:7; 2 Cor 7:3), longing (Rom 10:1), and be moved to conversion (Acts 2:37).

The heart is also the source of thinking and speaking (Mark 2:6; 7:21; Matt 12:34) and could at times be equated with the mind (2 Cor 4:6; Eph 1:18; 2 Pet 1:19). The act of thinking is expressed by the phrase "say/consider in one's heart" (Matt 24:48; Luke 12:45; Mark 2:6); a thought occurring to a person is expressed by a phrase that recalls a similar Hebrew expression, "comes into the heart" (Acts 7:23; Luke 24:38). The heart stores memories (Luke 1:66; 2:19) and all kinds of evil (Matt 15:19; Mark 7:21). The heart can have doubts (Mark 11:23), lack understanding altogether (Rom 1:21; 2 Cor 3:15), be slow to accept the truth (Luke 24:25), or even be hardened against it (Mark 6:52; Eph 4:18). The heart is also the source of decisions (2 Cor 9:7; Luke 21:14) and can be influenced to act by the devil (John 13:2) or by God (Rev 17:17). It can become practiced in greed (2 Pet 2:14) and distract itself from attending to the judgment (Luke 21:34). A stubborn heart that refuses to repent stores up wrath (Rom 2:5); an evil and unfaithful heart abandons God (Heb 3:12). Yet God's law to guide human decisions is written in the human heart (Rom 2:15; 2 Cor 3:3). Indeed, the heart can act like the conscience and condemn us (1 John 3:20-21); it can also be cleansed from an evil conscience (Heb 10:22).

It is in the heart that the person first meets God and comes under God's influence. God sees and tests what is in the human heart (Luke 16:15; 1 Thess 2:4; Rom 8:27) where there can be found either faith (Mark 11:22-23; Rom 10:8-10) or doubts (Luke 24:38) or a "darkened" heart and unbelief (Rom 1:21). But God can open the heart (Luke 24:45; Acts 16:14) and shine his revealing light on it to bring it to knowledge and faith in the glory of Christ (2 Cor 4:6). The same kind of enlightenment brings the newly baptized's heart to hope in the heavenly inheritance (Eph 1:18). The downpayment of the Spirit dwells in the heart (2 Cor 1:22) and furthers that hope while also bestowing the love of God (Rom 5:5; 2 Cor 1:22). Christ lives in the heart to fill it with knowledge and love of himself (Eph 3:17). It is faith (Acts 15:9) and baptism (Heb 10:22) that purify the heart and love that strengthens it to lead a blameless and holy life (1 Thess 3:13). Only in this way can the heart grow in the love of God and neighbor (Mark 12:30; Luke 10:27).

See: BODY

THOMAS P. MCCREESH, O.P.

HEAVEN

The biblical concept of heaven extends literally from the opening book of the OT to the final book of the NT. In Genesis the first creation account begins with the words, "In the beginning, when God created the heavens and the earth" (Gen 1:1). And the opening words of the final vision of the Book of Revelation states, "Then I saw a new heaven and a new earth" (Rev 21:1). Heaven begins as the spatial sphere of God which encompasses all reality above the earth—stars, moon, sun, and rain. Gradually throughout the books of the OT the concept of heaven expands symbolically to refer to the relationship of the righteous believers to God. And finally, from the Intertestamental literature to the books of the NT heaven evolves into the final destiny of the righteous believers, the kingdom of heaven, the place of everlasting paradise and spiritual fulfillment, the new creation where righteous believers will be united body and soul with God and all the angels and saints. In our own day the term heaven continues to symbolize the ultimate hope of faithful believers. That hope longs for the coming of a new creation, for the time of salvation, for the experience of everlasting unity and oneness with God (Pastoral Constitution on the Church in the Modern World 45, 93).

Old Testament

Heaven as Part of God's Created Universe. The Hebrew understanding of the structure of the universe was influenced by many ancient oriental ideas. The universe was a huge cosmic structure consisting of three basic areas. In the middle of the structure was the earth, a flat disk-like area surrounded by water and supported by big columns. Below the earth was the underworld, the place of sheol and hell, which was also surrounded by waters referred to as the abyss. Above the earth was heaven or the firmament. From the earth, this firmament looked like an inverted bowl. It rested firmly on columns, known to us as mountains (Job 26:11; 2 Sam 22:8). Immediately over this inverted bowl were the waters above the firmament or the ocean of heaven (Gen 1:7; Ps 148:4-6). Heaven contained windows and floodgates through which at the proper times pass the rain, snow, hail, and wind, all retained in their heavenly storehouses (Gen 7:11; 2 Kgs 7:2; Mal 3:10; Job 38:22; Jer 49:36). Certain celestial bodies were located in the firmament— sun, moon, and stars (Gen 1:14-16). Beyond this firmament the ancients believed there were many other heavenly spheres and thus the early use of the plural, "heavens" (Deut 10:14; 1 Kgs 8:27).

Heaven as the Dwelling Place of God. The OT clearly asserts that God created heaven (Gen 1:1; 2:4; Isa 42:5; 45:18; Ps 33:6; Prov 3:19; 8:27). However, not only did God create heaven, God also dwells there (Gen 11:5; Ps 18:10). "The LORD is in his holy temple; the LORD's throne is in heaven" (Ps 11:4; Mic 1:2; Hab 2:20; Isa 66:1). From this throne in heaven God convenes the heavenly council and issues directives for the entire universe. "Therefore hear the word of the LORD: I saw the LORD seated on his throne, with the whole host of heaven standing by to his right and to his left" (1 Kgs 22:19; Isa 6:1f.; Job 1:6-12). It is especially in the theology of the Book of Deuteronomy that God resides almost totally in heaven and speaks exclusively from there (Deut 4:36; see also, 12:5, 11, 21; 26:15). Heaven was the sphere of God's activity; thus it was only natural for people to regard it as the source of all divine blessings (Gen 49:25; Deut 33:13; 1 Kgs 8:35).

Heaven in Postexilic Judaism. With the experience of the exiles of 721 BCE and 586 BCE, the hope for redeeming this world quickly eroded. The apocalyptic movement looked forward to the total destruction of this world and the coming of a totally new world ruled by God (Isa 24–27; 66:17-25). With the apocalyptic movement there also emerged the theological concepts of the final judgment and the resurrection of the dead. Those who had maintained their covenant loyalty to God were considered righteous and deserving of eternal life in communion with God (Dan 12:1-3). Eternal life lived out in the new age ushered in by God ultimately became the destiny of the righteous believer. Exactly how all this would take place was the subject of much speculation carried out by various Apocalyptic and Intertestamental authors.

New Testament

Heaven as the Future State of Bliss. The NT is the heir to much of the ancient Near Eastern thought concerning heaven and the eschatological age to come. However here there is no interest shown in cosmological structure. That has been superseded by theological and soteriological concerns. The imagery of heaven permeates the Gospel of Matthew from the initial preaching of John the Baptist (Matt 3:2) to Jesus' final commissioning of the disciples (Matt 28:18). The kingdom of heaven is a key concept for Matthew and replaces the expectation of a messianic kingdom hoped for in earlier Jewish writings (Matthew 13). We can expect our reward to be in heaven and therefore it is in heaven that we should strive to store up treasures where they will be secure (Matt 5:12; 6:20). Paul teaches that "our citizenship is in heaven, and from it we also await a savior, the LORD Jesus Christ" (Phil 3:20). This is our Christian hope. Heaven is also described in the Book of Revelation as a community made for us and designated the new Jerusalem (Rev 3:12; 21:3, 10ff.). Heaven is a new creation, "Then I saw a new heaven and a new earth. The former heaven and the former earth had passed away, and the sea was no more" (Rev 21:1). Here there will be everlasting happiness and joy. Our earthly dwelling shall be taken away but "we have a building from God, a dwelling not made with hands, eternal in heaven" (2 Cor 5:1ff.).

Jesus and Heaven. The Son of Man came from heaven to become incarnate in Jesus (John 3:13). After the resurrection he ascended into that same heaven to sit at the right hand of God (Luke 24:50f.; Acts 1:6-12; Matt 26:64; Acts 7:56). A unique aspect of the preaching of Jesus was that, with the very announcement of the reign of God and the new life of salvation it promised, its presence was already being established. "For behold, the kingdom of God is among you" (Luke 17:21). Nevertheless, its fulfillment was still in the future (Matt 16:20).

Perhaps the place where the vision of Jesus and the reality of heaven are best united is in the Lord's prayer (Matt 6:9-13). Addressing God who is in heaven, Jesus very boldly requests the immediate advent of the future reign. This is all to be modeled on what goes on in heaven. Unlike his Jew-ish predecessors, Jesus wants the reality of heaven to be present now. Jesus who is from heaven can request this from God his father who is in heaven. However, it is precisely this heavenly relationship that is handed on to the disciples and all followers of Jesus as he says, "This is how you are to pray" (Matt 6:9).

Pastoral-Liturgical Tradition

Heaven the Hope of Christians. From NT times to the present, heaven has always been the epitome of Christian hope. Whether it was understood as place, vision, or relationship, heaven always expressed the belief that the risen Christ was victorious over death, and therefore those who are faithful to Christ will share in that same resurrection and enjoy a future life of glory with him. Death could never be the final answer for the faithful Christian.

Heaven and the Celebration of the Liturgy. Heavenly existence, however, was not totally relegated to the future. This was clear even in the Letter to the Hebrews (Heb 6:4; 11:3; 13:22). The continual presence of Christ in the world through Spirit, word, and sacrament allows Christians to share spiritually and partially in that heavenly reality whose fullness would only come with the end of time. Nowhere is this experience more pronounced than in the Christian celebration of the liturgy. "In the earthly liturgy we take part in a foretaste of that heavenly liturgy which is celebrated in the Holy City of Jerusalem toward which we journey as pilgrims, where Christ is sitting at the right hand of God, Minister of the holies and of the true tabernacle" (The Constitution on the Sacred Liturgy, 8). It is as the body of Christ that Christians come together to commemorate the paschal mystery in the celebration of the Eucharist. Following the words of institution the whole congregation proclaims the mystery of faith, "Dying you destroyed our death, rising you restored our life, Lord Jesus, come in glory." This liturgical language captures the Christians' longing for heaven.

Heaven as a Personal Relationship with God. The scholastic and neo-scholastic theologians often discussed heaven in terms of the beatific vision. This described a relationship between the person and God. Its uniqueness was that it allowed for no mediation; it was perfect contemplation of the glory of God. Contemporary theologians, although they use a different language, also understand heaven in terms of a personal relationship with God through and in Christ. This relationship implies a mutuality of love between God, Jesus, and the faithful Christian. It is symbolized in the doctrine of the Trinity and lived out in terms of charity and justice for all.

See: ANGEL, APOCALYPTIC, COVENANT, DISCIPLE, ESCHATOLOGY, EUCHARIST, GOD, HELL, HOPE, JESUS CHRIST, JOHN THE BAPTIST, REIGN OF GOD, RESURRECTION, SAINTS, SALVATION

EUGENE HENSELL, O.S.B.

HEBREW

The term "Hebrew" refers to a people and to the language they spoke. As a reference to people, the term "Hebrew" usually appears when the text is concerned with the relationship of Israelites* to non-Israelites. It is almost exclusively confined to the story of Joseph (Genesis 37–50), the story of Israel in Egypt (Exodus 1–15) and 1 Samuel. Apart from these larger units, the term "Hebrew" appears in just a few texts. Jonah 1:9 is the only time an Israelite describes himself as a Hebrew. In all other instances, other people speak of Israelites as Hebrews.

Many historians believe that the term *ibri* or "Hebrew" comes from the semitic word *abiru* (sometimes transliterated as *apiru* or *habiru*). This word appears in more than two hundred ancient Near Eastern texts from the eighteenth to the eleventh centuries BCE. In these texts the *abiru* were not members of a national or ethnic group. They were a social type: migrant or stateless persons.

The *abiru* were those people who left their villages and families to seek a better life elsewhere. The pressures that led to their taking such a drastic step included heavy taxation, personal problems, excessive debts, lack of economic opportunity, war, famine—motivations similar to today's migrants.

Apparently some *abiru* banded together for mutual benefit. Also some *abiru* groups became raiders or extortionists. Others became mercenaries hiring themselves to local rulers. During the period of Egyptian hegemony in Canaan (1550–1150 BCE), *abiru* became a disparaging term for rebels against Egypt. With the decline of Egyptian power, the *abiru* were among those who attempted to fill the political vacuum.

While some of the *abiru* formed themselves into what the Bible describes as the tribes of Israel, not all *abiru* were Israelites. The Bible, however, understands the term "Hebrew" as the name of a people and not as a designation of social status. According to Genesis 11:21, a certain Eber (his name contains the same letters as "Hebrew") was a descendant of Shem, the son of Noah from whom the Israelites descended. First Chronicles 1:24-27 explicitly states that Eber was an ancestor of Abraham.

If contemporary historians are correct about the association of the Israelite tribes with the *abiru*, evidently some shift in meaning occurred. Still, the term "Hebrew" in the Joseph story refers to a group of refugees from famine in Canaan. Similarly, when the Philistines call David a Hebrew in 1 Samuel 29:3 it is likely because he and some associates withdrew their loyalty from Saul to become Philistine mercenaries.

In the Greco-Roman period, the term "Hebrew" became a common way to speak of Jews. The NT uses this term three times: Acts 6:1; 2 Corinthians 11:22; Philippians 3:5. In Acts the term refers to Jewish Christians. In the Pauline texts, Paul uses the term to identify himself as a Hebrew-speaking Jew in contrast to Greek-speaking ones.

The language spoken by the people who lived in the Israelite kingdoms was a northwest semitic language known as Hebrew. It is the language of the OT except for portions of Ezra and Daniel that are written in Aramaic, another semitic language, and the deuterocanonical books that were written or have survived only in Greek.

In addition to Hebrew, many ancient Israelite royal officials knew Aramaic, the international language of the ancient Near East (see 2 Kgs 18:26). During the Persian period, the general population began using Aramaic and by Jesus' day it became the vernacular in Roman Palestine. Hebrew became a language used almost exclusively for worship and study. A century ago, Eliezer ben Yehuda reintroduced Hebrew as a spoken language for the Jews from around the world who were settling in Palestine. It and Arabic are the official languages of the modern State of Israel.

See: ISRAELITE, JEW

LESLIE J. HOPPE, O.F.M.

HELL

Hell is the English word frequently used to translate the biblical Hebrew terms, sheol* and gehenna,* and the biblical Greek term hades. However, there is no one biblical word that fully captures all the various nuances contained in the theological concept of hell. In the Bible hell is generally described in terms that refer to the underworld (Isa 14:9; Ezek 31:15; Wis 1:4; Bar 3:19; Matt 11:23; Luke 16:23). The word itself derives from the Old English *helan*, whose root meaning is "hide," "cover," or "conceal." This term proved to be quite fitting since ultimately hell came to be understood as a fiery abyss of anguish and suffering located somewhere below the earth (Matt 5:22; 18:9; Luke 16:23). The biblical concept of hell underwent change and development during the course of Judeo-Christian history although not in a clear systematic way. Its understanding, however, continued to be linked to and shaped by the shifts in the biblical understanding of afterlife, resurrection,* and personal responsibility for sin.*

Old Testament

Preexilic Understanding of Hell. Prior to the Babylonian exile of 597 BCE, the OT did not manifest a strong interest in an afterlife or a resurrection from the dead. All notions of rewards and punishments were confined to the present world experience. At death everyone went to the same place, sheol, the realm of the dead. The psalmist asks, "What man shall live, and not see death, but deliver himself from the power of the nether world?" (Ps 89:49). It was the common plight of all humanity (Isa 14:9-15; Job 3:11-21). Sheol was understood as something resembling a universal tomb and thus existence there was nebulous, obscure, and shadowy. It was a place without value and without joy (Gen 44:29-31; Prov 30:16). Sometimes it was portrayed as "a hole," "a pit," or "a ditch," located deep within the bowels of the earth (Ps 30:10; Ezek 28:8; Deut 32:22). At other times it was referred to as a chaotic watery abyss confined deep beneath the earth (Job 26:5; 2 Sam 22:5). Nothing reigned there but deep obscurity and darkness (Ps 88:7, 13; Job 10:21f.). No one ever escaped. "As a cloud dissolves and vanishes, so he who goes down to the nether world shall come up no more" (Job 7:9). Those in sheol are unable to remember God or to hope in God's justice and kindness (Pss 6:6; 88:11-13; 30:10; Isa 38:18). Ultimately sheol signified total destitution (Ps 88:6).

In addition to being a place, sheol was also characterized as an insatiable monster whose jaws were ever ready to consume the living. "Therefore the nether world enlarges its throat and opens its maw without limit" (Isa 5:14; Prov 30:15f.). It enmeshed and numbed its victims (Pss 18:6; 88:4f.). Nevertheless, even though sheol was inevitable and all consuming, it was not understood to be a place of punishment.*

Postexilic Understanding of Hell. After the Exile several significant changes occurred that directly influenced the biblical concept of hell. First, Judaism developed a belief in the resurrection of the dead (2

Macc 7:20-23; Dan 12:1-3). Second, they began to move from an exclusive understanding of corporate personality to a new concept of personal responsibility for sin and repentance (Jer 31:31-34). Third, beginning about the third century BCE and due largely to the Diaspora, Greek thought penetrated traditional Hebrew thought patterns. An important result of this was the development throughout Diaspora Judaism of a belief in the immortality of the soul. Eventually these three developments played a crucial role in shaping the belief that at the end of the world everyone would be summoned to a general resurrection. God would then pronounce a solemn judgment on each person. Those who had remained good and faithful would go to live with God in eternal bliss, but those who had been evil would be condemned to everlasting damnation.

A further development took place as hell came to be understood as the permanent realm of the damned. Neither sheol nor hades carried with them this notion of punishment or permanency. Gehenna became the place of eternal fiery damnation. The imagery surrounding gehenna was developed quite boldly in the Intertestamental writings (1 Enoch 18:11-16; 103:3-7, 15; 2 Esdr 7:36-38). Hell, therefore, became the permanent habitation for the unrepentant sinner.

New Testament

Hades and Gehenna in the NT. Hades and gehenna are the two terms the NT employs to speak about the realm of the dead and the place where sinners will be eternally punished. In general, however, the NT understanding of hell is influenced by and similar to that of intertestamental Judaism. A good example of this is the parable of the rich man and Lazarus (Luke 16:19-31). Lazarus at death is carried away to the bosom of Abraham, but the rich man suffers torment in hades (Luke 16:22f.). For the most part, however, hades serves only an interim purpose until the time of the general resurrection (Acts 2:27, 31). After the resurrection on the last day, hades is replaced by gehenna and becomes the final place of punishment (Matt 5:22, 29, 30; Mark 9:43-46).

Jesus and the Fires of Hell. Jesus spoke very harshly when referring to the place of eternal damnation. "The Son of Man will send his angels, and they will collect out of his kingdom all who cause others to sin and all evildoers. They will throw them into the fiery furnace, where there will be wailing and grinding of teeth" (Matt 13:41-42). It is the place where "their worm does not die, and the fire is not quenched" (Mark 9:48). And the only person who is to be feared is "the one who can destroy both soul and body in Gehenna" (Matt 10:28). Those who are condemned at the final judgment will be destroyed by everlasting fire (Matt 5:22; 23:33). This is graphically reconfirmed by the Book of Revelation (Rev 19:20; 20:10, 14-15). A watery abyss, fire, and harsh everlasting punishment—these are the images that informed the NT Christians' understanding of hell.

Pastoral-Liturgical Tradition

The concept of hell has always been informed by the reality of human sin. Retributive justice, fear of punishment, and faith in God's forgiveness evolve around the seriousness of sin and the possibility of human failure. Ultimate failure to respond to God's offer of saving grace is hell. From the Patristic writers, Origin, Ambrose, and Jerome, through the Middle Ages and Dante's *Divine Comedy*, right up to the present time, hell remains a terrifying thought. Choosing total alienation from God is always a human possibility, and that fact alone makes the reality of hell always a possibility. Jews and Christians do not deny this possibility, they simply continue to hope in God's saving grace and to trust in God's reconciliation.

See: DIASPORA, GEHENNA, JUDAISM, JUSTICE, RESURRECTION, SHEOL, SIN

EUGENE HENSELL, O.S.B.

HOLY/HOLINESS

The notion of "holy" and "holiness" spans the entire biblical and Christian tradition.

Old Testament

Experience of the Holy. The basic experience of the holy is the numinous presence of God. The aesthetic, ethical, and spiritual aspects of the holy are derivative from this fundamental theophanic experience. In the OT, the holy is expressed by words derived from the root *qdš*, among which the most frequently attested are: *qōdeš* (469 times), *qādôš* (116 times), and *miqdāš* (74 times).

Standing before the majestic, glorious Other gives rise to feelings of awe, dread, fascination, and vitality. The paradoxical or conflicting nature of the human response arises from the life-and-death encounter with the totally Other. This numinous experience of the holy is attested throughout the religions of the world and as such is not a unique feature of the Israelite religion. Nevertheless, throughout Israelite history among priests, prophets, and sages alike, holiness communicated a central dynamic of Israel's relationship to the Lord: the holy One enthroned on high turns toward humans. This glorious, majestic Being who belongs to a totally distinct sphere of being is zealous for the human covenant partner (Exod 20:4-5). The paradoxical mode of the revelation of holiness, in which manifestation and concealment accompany one another, is appropriate for God's communicating the divine transcendence and immanence.

Human Response. The place at which God chose to overwhelm a particular individual or group became a holy site where the memory of the glorious encounter was kept alive (e.g., Gen 28:10-22). The cult which became institutionalized on that site performed rituals in which the holy convocation acknowledged the majesty and graciousness of its sovereign Lord and pledged obedience. This type of covenant ritual before a numinous Deity was exemplified well in the Sinai theophany of Exodus 19. God instructed Moses to have the people sanctify themselves for two days (Exod 19:10); boundaries were to be established so that the people would not touch the mountain, for such an action merited capital punishment (Exod 19:12); they were also to refrain from sexual relations (Exod 19:15). Thus, the line between the sacred and the profane at the holy mountain of Sinai was clearly drawn. When the theophany occurred in the form of a thunderstorm and a volcanic eruption (Exod 19:16-18), the people were terrified (Exod 20:18) and requested that Moses serve as their mediator (Exod 20:19-21). Later, within a sacrificial ritual, Moses mediated the Law to them and sealed the covenant relationship (Exod 24:3-8). This account of the Sinai theophany sketched the essential features of the cultic response to the numinous presence of God: (1) a life-and-death experience of the awe-inspiring, terrifying God; (2) the establishment of boundaries to highlight symbolically the radical distinction between the divine and human; (3) an encounter initiated by God in which humans were granted a glimpse of the divine reality. Sinai became a holy place because God manifested his holiness there; Israel was to become "a kingdom of priests, a holy nation" (Exod 19:6) because it met the Lord there.

Attribute of God. Holiness is an essential characteristic or attribute of God. When people, places, or things are regarded as holy, it is due to God's bestowing holiness on them. As the source of holiness, God is the Incomparable One: "There is no Holy One like the LORD; there is no Rock like our God" (1 Sam 2:2; see Exod 15:11; Isa 40:25). As the sovereign ruler enthroned on the holy Mount Zion and ruling with justice and equity, God is repeatedly praised as "holy" (Ps 99:3, 5, 9), and God's house is acknowledged as one to which "holiness is fitting for length of days" (Ps 93:5).

As a personal Deity, the God of Israel does not unleash power anonymously but rather acts to promote justice and righteousness; the religious and ethical aspects of God's Being are essentially intertwined.

Isaiah's vision of God enthroned in the Temple supports the essential connection between holiness, purity, and uprightness. Isaiah saw seraphim crying out: "Holy, holy, holy is the LORD of hosts" (Isa 6:3). This heavenly liturgy linked praise of the holy One of Israel with the overwhelming awareness of the distinction between sinful humanity and God (Isa 6:5). To make possible Isaiah's standing before God, one of the seraphim purged his lips with a glowing ember (Isa 6:6-7). The purification of sinfulness cannot be done painlessly. The rituals enacted in the Temple were intended to reach to the heart of the worshiper or to the roots of the human will where actions originate. Those who scorn the holy One of Israel have doomed themselves: "Woe . . . to those who say, 'Let him make haste and speed his work, that we may see it; On with the plan of the holy One of Israel!'" (Isa 5:19). Those who make light of God's word sever their connection with holiness and merit blazing wrath (Isa 5:24-25).

Separation between Sacred and Profane. The essential connection between cult and ethics is evident in priestly ritual and theology. The in-breaking of the holy into human experience demands a separation between the sacred and the profane. Out of reverence for the holy One of Israel, the priest monitored the boundaries between the spheres of holiness in the Temple: e.g., the high priest could enter the holy of holies only on the Day of Atonement (Lev 16:2, 29-34). The priests could enter the inner Temple court, but the people of Israel were not allowed beyond the outer Temple court. Only in later prophetic works is it even suggested that foreigners could legitimately enter the Temple courts (Isa 56:6-8). The privilege of drawing closer to the Lord carried with it the obligation to observe a more rigid code of behavior. Just as the priest had to be observant of special regulations in the sanctuary (Lev 22:9, 15-16), so also the Israelites were to be faithful to the deepest kinds of ethical and humanitarian concerns: e.g., leaving grain in the field for the poor, avoid-

ing vindictiveness, being sensitive to the handicapped (Lev 19:9-10, 14, 17-18). The separation into spheres of holiness promoted reverence for the Holy One of Israel who is the source of well-being and uprightness; by leaving free gleanings (Lev 19:9-10), by granting interest-free loans (Lev 25:35-37), and by promoting equality in civil justice (Lev 20:2; 24:16, 22), the Israelites concretized the law of love (Lev 19:18) and thereby proved themselves holy by imitating God.

To draw near to the holy of holies, a symbol of the hidden realm of danger and death, the priests had to undergo ordination as a rite of passage. The oil of anointing was placed upon the priest's head and upon his garments; the blood of the ordination ram was placed upon the priest's right ear, the thumb of his right hand, and the large toe of his right foot. These rites of consecration and cleansing were accompanied by rites of clothing and offering sacrifice (Lev 8:1-35). These symbolic preparations for ministering at the altar did not release a priest from the obligation of carrying out the sacrificial rituals with reverence and sincerity. For example, when Nadab and Abihu offered incense with profane, unauthorized fire, they were consumed by fire from God (Lev 10:1). Presumptuous disregard for the holiness of God merited death.

The seriousness of the obligation to respect the holiness of God is evident in the stories concerning the transfer of the ark. When the Philistines returned the captured ark to the Israelites, the descendants of Jeconiah did not join the people of Bethshemesh in welcoming the ark; for their indifference, seventy of them were struck down (1 Sam 6:19-20). Later, during David's transfer of the ark to Jerusalem, Uzzah inadvertently trespassed the boundary of holiness when he tried to steady the ark on the cart; the Lord then struck Uzzah down (2 Sam 6:7). Because from a human perspective this punishment seems unfair to the well-intentioned Uzzah, the distinction between a God-centered approach to holiness and a human-centered one reminds us of the serious attention which must be paid to God's holiness.

In the Priestly sections of the Pentateuch, the materialistic conception of the holy as contagious is applicable to consecrated objects but not to persons. For example, whatever object touches the consecrated altar also becomes sacred (Exod 29:37), or whatever object touches the consecrated furniture of the sanctuary becomes holy (Exod 30:29). But in Ezekiel's restored cultic community, not only objects but also persons would be sanctified through contact with holy objects (Ezek 44:19; 46:20).

Sanctified objects became the property of the sanctuary. Categories of persons or objects that belonged to the Lord were: (1) the first-born males of humans and animals (Exod 13:2, 12-15), the first-fruits of the field and orchard (Neh 10:36), the first batch of processed foods (Num 15:20), and the fourth year's yield from the fruit trees after entry into the land (Lev 19:24); (2) tithes (Deut 26:12-15; Lev 27:30-33); (3) votive dedications (Lev 27:1-25). For those persons or objects that could not be sacrificed on the altar, substitutes were to be provided (cf. Exod 13:13).

In addition to setting aside persons, objects, and space as sacred, the Israelites also observed sacred time. The Sabbath, of course, was the most important time the Israelites were commanded to observe: "Take care to keep my sabbaths, for that is to be the token between you and me throughout the generations, to show that it is I, the LORD, who make you holy" (Exod 31:13). Observing the Sabbath was a significant way to pay homage to God as king of creation. Further arrangements of the calendar to dedicate time to God in addition to the Sabbath took the form of feast days and special convocations: festivals (Lev 23:1-25, 33-44; Neh 8:9-12), the Jubilee year (Lev 25:8-22), solemn gatherings and fasts (Joel 1:14; 2:15-17).

Priests, prophets, and sages developed rituals, exhortations, and teachings to guide the Israelites in imitating the holy One of Israel. The priests directed the Israelites to become holy by maintaining inner integrity,

fostering humanitarian conduct, and observing ritual purity. The prophets preached the importance of reverence for God, the link between social justice and cleanness, and the purposive and purgative character of God's holiness. The sages emphasized the significance of fear of the Lord, the mystery associated with divine omniscience, and the requirement of purity of mind and heart for holiness. In a comparison of these three groups of leaders, holiness figured most prominently in the thought of the priests.

As more emphasis was placed upon the conception of the Israelites as a holy people, the boundaries of the sacred were extended so as to "democratize" access to the holy. A few references to God's holy Spirit (Isa 63:10; Ps 51:13) describe a mode of God's numinous presence that is not sheltered by the cult and which, of course, foreshadows the pneumatology of the NT.

See: ANOINTING, ARK OF THE COVENANT, CLEAN/UNCLEAN, CONSECRATION, FEAR OF GOD, FEASTS, FIRE, JUBILEE YEAR, ORDINATION, SABBATH, VISITATION OF GOD

DALE LAUNDERVILLE, O.S.B.

New Testament

Terminology. Christians adopted the ideas and language of holiness present in Judaism, although the cultic aspects of this term are downplayed or transformed in Christian usage. Instead, there is a greater emphasis on the moral and ethical connotations of holiness. The NT speaks of "holiness" (*hagiasmos, hagiosyne*) with reference to God and those things associated with God (viz., law, Temple, angels, covenant, etc.), with reference to Christ, to the Spirit, and to Christians themselves, each of which can be called "holy" (*hagios*). As in the OT, holiness derives from a participation in the holiness that is proper to God alone. Related concepts such as purity, blamelessness, exaltation, majesty, glory indicate that holiness places one in the orbit of God's transcendent presence, so that God's holiness is transferred to them. Holiness is, furthermore, a calling and a grace bestowed by God, not something we achieve for ourselves.

The Holiness of God. Although there are surprisingly few explicit references in the NT to the holiness of God, Revelation 4:8, echoing the words of Isaiah 6:3 and the images of Ezekiel 1, repeats the Trisagion hymn celebrating God's holiness. This vision of the seer in the Book of Revelation depicts the thought world of Christians and their conception of God's holiness.

Elsewhere, Jesus addresses God as "Holy Father" (John 17:11). Moreover, God is the one who has the power to consecrate others in holiness. God, first of all, consecrates Jesus (John 10:36) who is the beloved Son sent into the world. Jesus then prays that God will also consecrate the disciples (John 17:17, 19) who, like Jesus, are sent to the world to carry on Jesus' mission.

In her canticle, Mary praises the One whose name is holy, the mighty One, savior, and helper of Israel (Luke 1:47, 49). God's holiness is manifest in beneficence and care for all creation. The canticle of Zechariah praises the holiness of the prophets, and of the covenant made with Israel (Luke 1:70, 73). God's angels are holy (Mark 8:38) as is God's law (Rom 7:12) and the new Temple, God's holy people (1 Cor 3:17).

The first petition of the Lord's Prayer, "Hallowed [holy] be your name" (Matt 6:9; Luke 11:2) recalls the identification in Jewish tradition between the name and the very person. The second petition specifies how this hallowing of the name is to be manifest, viz., in the coming of God's reign, in the accomplishment of God's will on earth, when the whole of creation incarnates the holiness of God.

Jesus the Holy One. Only Jesus, the Christ, shares perfectly in the holiness of God who consecrated him (John 10:36). From the beginning, Jesus has been the holy One of God (Mark 1:24; Luke 4:34; John 6:69), the true child of the Most High (Luke 1:35; Matt 1:18), the one who was with God, sharing in God's very being (John 1:1). As the Son who was sent, Jesus received at his baptism the anointing of the holy Spirit, and its fullness took possession

of him (Luke 3:22; Acts 10:38). His holiness was manifest in extraordinary powers and miraculous deeds, and in teaching that displayed unique authority.

In the Acts of the Apostles, there is a special connection drawn between Jesus' holiness and his identity as the Servant of God (Acts 3:14; 4:27, 30). Jesus' role as servant places him in a unique relationship to God, as the one chosen and beloved by God. His holiness is marked by sinlessness and righteousness; his fidelity to God caused him to suffer death, while bearing our infirmities and sufferings (Isa 53:4) so that we might be healed (Isa 53:5).

The early Christian hymn that Paul quotes in Philippians 2:6-11 proclaims that Jesus' obedience unto death led to his exaltation. The risen One is revealed, in a definitive way, as Son of God "according to the spirit of holiness" (Rom 1:4).

The Letter to the Hebrews reflects on Jesus' role as mediator between God and creation. As the Temple and priesthood of old, with their sacrificial offerings and cultic practices, had provided a way of access to God, a way of approaching the holy One, so Christ, through his obedience and sacrificial death, established a new covenant in his blood, a new and eternal way of access to the holy God.

The Holy Spirit. It is by means of the Spirit that God communicates holiness, that very share in the divine life, to the created world. As the breath of God's Spirit hovered over the waters at creation, so God's continued gift of the Spirit sanctifies those open to receive it. The Spirit is *holy*, because it is God's own Spirit, a Spirit that accomplishes God's designs.

The holiness associated with the Spirit is manifest in a number of ways: in power to proclaim the gospel, to announce the good news (Luke 4:18-22), in the establishment of peace and unity among Christians (Eph 4:3-6), in forgiveness and reconciliation (John 20:22-23), and in truth and wisdom to discern the ways of God in the world (John 16:8-11).

433

The Holiness of the Christian Community
The Christian community has inherited the elect and holy status of the covenant people (1 Pet 2:9), and has received the same imperative given their Israelite ancestors: "as he who called you is holy, be holy yourselves in every aspect of your conduct, for it is written, 'Be holy because I [am] holy'" (1 Pet 1:15-16 = Lev 19:2).

Because the Spirit of God has been poured out among them (Acts 2:4; Gal 4:6), Christians share in the holiness proper to God and to Jesus, God's anointed One. They, too, have become children of God (Gal 4:6; Rom 8:14; John 1:12; 20:17) who are able to say with Jesus, "Abba!" They are, furthermore, temples of the holy Spirit (1 Cor 3:16-17; 6:11, 19).

Christians have been anointed with the "anointing that comes from the holy one" (1 John 2:20) and are, thereby, made holy and strengthened to live a holy life (1 Cor 1:30; Eph 5:26). They are not set apart from the world, but are sent into the world to share in Christ's mission of salvation (John 17:15-19; see John 3:17). Holiness demands of Christians that they put off "the old self with its practices" (Col 3:9-10) and "put on then, as God's chosen ones, holy and beloved, heartfelt compassion, kindness, humility, gentleness and patience" (Col 3:12-14).

By means of faith and baptism, Christians are incorporated into the new covenant community. They share in the passion, death, and resurrection of Jesus (Rom 6:3-4) and enter into the newness of life promised to those who believe. Instead of the cultic sacrifices of the Temple service, Christians are encouraged to offer their very selves. In Paul's words, they should offer their "bodies as a living sacrifice, holy and pleasing to God" (Rom 12:1). The whole of Christian life, therefore, should itself be a means of sanctification, a means of "making holiness perfect in the fear of God" (2 Cor 7:1).

Finally, as Paul knew so well, Christian holiness is a life long process of transformation in which we become more and more conformed to Christ, so that Christ lives in us, by faith (Gal 2:20). It is because Christ has taken possession of us that we continue to strain "forward to what lies ahead . . . toward the goal, the prize of God's upward calling, in Christ Jesus" (Phil 3:13-14).

See: ANOINTING, BLESSING, CLEAN/UNCLEAN, CONSECRATION, SAINTS, SPIRIT OF GOD, TEMPLE

BARBARA E. BOWE, R.S.C.J.

Pastoral-Liturgical Tradition

Perhaps no other word is more identified with religious experience than the term "holy." It is used in both the liturgy and in theological commentaries as a kind of shorthand describing a reality that is essentially impossible to put into words: the divine presence and how that presence affects human life. When directly attributed to God who is holiness itself, this term also encompasses such referents as glory, majesty, awe, power, splendor, light, incomprehensibility, and purity. Although holiness is of the very essence of God, the Judaeo-Christian tradition has always maintained that it is not something that God jealously guards. On the contrary, God graciously and lovingly seeks to communicate to the world and to human beings that holiness which is most part of the divine nature.

For a Christian, the incarnation of Jesus Christ is the paradigm or model for the way by which God "shares holiness" or "graces" the world and humanity. The Church, in turn, as Christ's continuing presence in the world, perpetuates this action of sanctification through both its liturgical remembrance of Christ's suffering, death, and resurrection—a remembrance made possible by the holy Spirit—and through its mission of proclaiming God's reign in the world. Thus, "making holy" or "sanctifying" can be said to be the very heart of both Christian worship and Christian life.

Holiness as an Attribute of God. The most obvious place in the liturgy where holiness is attributed to God is in the *Sanctus* acclamation, or "Holy, Holy, Holy," which forms part of the Eucharistic prayer. The acclamation is based on Isaiah's awe-inspiring vision of God in the Temple described in Isaiah 6. These verses are also used liturgically in the worship of the synagogue where it is known as the *kedushat hashem,* or sanctification of the Name. The Byzantine Rite also proclaims God's holiness through a prayer recited at the Eucharistic liturgy prior to the Scripture readings known as the *Trisagion* or "thrice holy"—"Holy is God! Holy the Mighty One! Holy the Immortal One! Have mercy on us!" These invocations emphasize divine transcendence—and our human recognition that God is "totally other" and beyond our limited ability to understand, describe, or control.

Sanctification as a Description of Christ's Ministry. While various liturgical acclamations emphasize God who "lives through all eternity in unapproachable light" (Eucharistic Prayer IV), the very purpose of the incarnation of Jesus and of his ministry is seen as one of bridging the gap between humanity and God by sharing that which is most part of God's nature: God's holiness. The announcement of the Feast of Christmas in the Roman Martyrology expresses this particular understanding of salvation. The whole purpose of the incarnation is seen as reestablishing God's accessibility to the human race and to all of creation by making holy or sanctifying the world: "Jesus Christ, the eternal God, and Son of the eternal Father, desiring to sanctify the world by his most merciful coming." This same idea underlines the private prayer of the priest at the commingling of the water and the wine during the preparation of the gifts—a prayer inspired by a Christmas collect written by Pope Leo the Great: "[By the mystery of this water and wine] may we come to share in the divinity of Christ who humbled himself to share in our humanity."

Holiness as an Attribute of the Church and of Christians. One of the most ancient affirmations of Christians is that the Church is holy insofar as it is Christ's presence in the world. In the Niceno-Constantinopolitan creed we acknowledge that we believe in "one, holy, catholic and apostolic Church." The Second Vatican Council explains this affirmation in the Dogmatic Constitution on the Church (39): "The Church whose mystery is set forth by this sacred Council, is held, as a matter of faith, to be unfailingly holy. This is because Christ, the Son of God, who with the Father, Son and Holy Spirit is hailed as 'alone holy.'" Although the Church itself is sinful and in constant need of renewal and purification, Christ's promise of the Spirit's presence guarantees that the Church's mission of "making holy," of sanctification—by healing and reconciling humanity to God through its ministry of word and sacrament—will always be effectively carried out.

It is for this reason that the entire fifth chapter of the Dogmatic Constitution on the Church emphasizes that holiness is the condition to which all Christians are called. "The followers of Christ, called by God not in virtue of their works but by his design and grace, and justified in the Lord Jesus, have been made sons [and daughters] of God in the baptism of faith and partakers of the divine nature, and so are truly sanctified" (Dogmatic Constitution on the Church, no. 40).

See: GLORY, GRACE, LIGHT AND DARKNESS, POWER, PURITY, SPIRIT OF GOD

MARK R. FRANCIS, C.S.V.

HOPE

Old Testament

Mediterranean peasants are primarily oriented to the present moment. They are much too concerned about subsistence (food to eat, rain and sun for the crops, a decent harvest or sufficient catch of fish, etc.) to think beyond today. Landowners and other elites can ease that concern for some peasants by establishing a distinctive benevolent relationship with them. They become patrons and these "chosen" peasants become their clients. In return for the patron's assurance that the client's needs will always be taken care of, the client sings the praises of the patron far and wide. Such a caring patron is the peasant-client's hope for survival and for the future. This human, Mediterranean experience guides and shapes the way Mediterranean peasants think about and perceive God.

In making promises and establishing covenants with the first parents (Gen 3:15), Noah (9:1-17) and Abraham (Gen 12:1), among other leaders and their descendants, God takes the initiative to become a divine patron to Israel, the clients. God is all powerful, and God alone knows the future. If God the all-powerful patron promises a good future for the clients, that is a solid basis for the clients' hope, trust, and confidence. If God should fail to keep the promises, God will reap shame because other nations will see that the patron let the client-nation down (Joel 2:17).

The chief object of hope is peaceful possession of the land (Gen 15:7; 17:8) flowing with milk and honey (Exod 3:8, 17) and numerous posterity (Gen 12:1-2; 15:5). These earthly goods are blessings (Gen 39:5; 49:25) and gifts (Gen 13:15; 28:13) from God the patron demonstrating faithfulness to the covenant promises.

Unfortunately, some clients lost sight of God (Hos 2:10; Ezekiel 16) and placed their hope in idolatry, formal and legalistic cult, and treaties with foreign nations. Prophets like Hosea, Isaiah, and others denounced this blatantly shameful behavior by God's clients and warned that God the patron would cease to look after them. "Cursed is the man who trusts in human beings, who seeks his strength in flesh, whose heart turns away from the LORD. . . . Blessed is the man who trusts in the LORD, whose hope is the LORD" (Jer 17:5, 7).

The warnings fell for the most part on deaf ears. To those who did listen the prophets preached and fostered hope in a subsequent redemption and restoration. Israel the client was exhorted to repent and repair its relationship with God the patron who is "a merciful and gracious God, slow to anger and rich in kindness and fidelity,

continuing his kindness for a thousand generations" (Exod 34:6-7). God faithfully keeps the promises made and does not renege (Num 23:19; Tob 14:4).

It was ironically after the destruction of both kingdoms that hope was at its highest in Israel (Jer 31:31-34; Ezek 16:59-63). Even as the future seemed bleak, the prophets preached that God the patron would save at least a remnant (see Amos 9:8-15; Isa 10:19). God the patron would forgive client unfaithfulness just as a parent forgives a wayward child (Hosea 11).

The prophet Hosea's use of kinship imagery to describe the relationship of God to Israel fits well with the Mediterranean social institution of patron and client that supports hope. In the OT, there is no other basis for believers to consider themselves as kin to God except through patronage. The essence of the patron-client relationship is that the patron elects to treat the client "as if" that person were a family member. In the Mediterranean world, the family never fails a family member. Fittingly then do the prophets interject family imagery into the patron-client relationship between God and Israel, especially when Israel has been unfaithful. Such imagery reminds Israel the client of its proper obligations to God the patron.

Even though rooted in God's promise of blessings and all good things, hope weakens when innocent people suffer, evil people prosper, and death seems to end everything. In response to such experiences, the prophets sought to shore up hope by proposing the redemptive value of suffering: "by his stripes we were healed" (Isa 53:5). The just person who suffers innocently will see "that the will of the LORD shall be accomplished through him" (Isa 53:10) and will receive from God the patron "his portion among the great" (Isa 53:12). Not all were convinced by this line of thinking. At the dawn of the NT era, Israel's hope took many different forms. For the most part, however, Israel still hoped that God would somehow keep the promises made.

New Testament

Though the word "hope" is a rare occurrence in the Gospels, the reality is not. Those with eyes to see realized that the promises made by God the Patron to Israel were perfectly fulfilled in Jesus Christ the Son. For this reason, the author of 1 Timothy calls Christ Jesus "our hope" (1:1).

In Jesus, the promised and long awaited reign of God is made present and has already begun. "For behold, the kingdom of God is among you," says Jesus to his contemporaries who were still looking for it (Luke 17:21). Hope, which always involves a future dimension, is so rarely spoken in the Gospels because there the future is now!

In John's Gospel, hope rests upon the possession of life eternal given already now to the believer (3:15; 6:54) who is already risen (11:25) and judged. The passage of the Christian to eternity will only be a visible marker of a reality that already exists.

How does Jesus fit into the understanding of hope as an attitude culturally rooted in God as patron? Throughout the Gospels, Jesus is presented as a "broker," one who is able to solicit new clients for the heavenly patron and who can put all the clients in touch with his Father, God the all-powerful patron, with ease. This was in stark contrast to his compatriots the Pharisees whose 612 commandments and enforcement of "the traditions of the elders" effectively weakened hope by making God more remote and access to God more difficult. Such strategies fostered elitism and did not build hope among the non-elite, the peasant majority in the population.

It is especially Paul who helps us understand that hope is but one element in a single but complex cultural concept that includes faith, trust, love, and hope. Faith in the Mediterranean world—whether faith in God or in a human being—is understood as unswerving loyalty no matter what. It is the social glue that holds people together. "God is faithful," writes Paul to the Corinthians, "and will not let you be tried beyond your strength" (1 Cor 10:13). Because God is faithful in this manner, a believer can reciprocate with similar faithfulness and loyalty.

Moreover, a believer can trust God in the same way Abraham trusted him when God requested the sacrifice of Isaac (Gen 22:8-14; Heb 11:17-19). Matthew's Jesus, the broker for God the patron, recommends that God's clients place a similar trust in God by not even worrying about daily food and drink (6:24-34). Further, Jesus expects a similar trust, loyalty, and allegiance to himself (Mark 9:42). "Come to me, all you who labor and are burdened, and I will give you rest" (Matt 11:28).

The word we usually translate as "love" is better understood in the Mediterranean context as attachment to a person and/or to a group. The individual who makes promises and keeps them wins loyal supporters who stick with the patron no matter what. "Serve one another through love," Paul urges the Galatians (5:13), which means remain attached to one another through devoted service. For in Christ Jesus, what counts above all is "loyalty working itself out in attachment to the community as well as attachment to Jesus" or, as the traditional translations put it, "faith working through love" (Gal 5:6).

Paul demonstrates the unity of this complex of attitudes with his familiar triad: faith, hope, and love. He recalls with gratitude the Thessalonians' "work of faith and labor of love and endurance in hope" (1 Thess 1:3). He advises them to "put on the breastplate of faith and love and the helmet that is hope for salvation" (1 Thess 5:8). Paul's well-known hymn to love in 1 Corinthians 13 lists ten examples of how love can be identified. The entire list describes values that contribute to and strengthen one's attachment to another person as well as to a group.

Finally, though Christian hope expressed in the NT did indeed find fulfillment in the present, it is important to remember that the Mediterranean view of present time is considerably wider than the western view. It includes tomorrow and perhaps a bit more. In addition, forthcoming events are viewed as already contained in a present realization. Paul echoes this understanding when he writes: "We know that all creation is groaning in labor pains even until now; . . . and we also groan within ourselves as we wait for adoption, the redemption of our bodies" (Rom 8:22-23). There are elements of God's promises that still await fulfillment. In loyalty, secure trust, and unswerving commitment, believers affirm the conviction of the author of Revelation that Jesus will return soon, sometime in this extensively understood present moment. And they echo his prayer of hope: "Amen! Come, Lord Jesus!" (Rev 22:20).

See: ADOPTION, BLESSING, CONFIDENCE, COVENANT, FAITH, LOVE, PROMISE, PROPHECY/PROPHET, REDEMPTION

JOHN J. PILCH

Pastoral-Liturgical Tradition

Hope is a fundamental disposition of human beings whereby we have trust and confidence that goals difficult to achieve can be reached. Even more so, hope ought to be a characteristic attitude of Christians, a perduring orientation to believe in promising possibilities for life, especially the promises of God. In this respect, hope enables us to be oriented to a fulfillment not yet achieved while still acknowledging the finitude, incompleteness, and fragility of life. The basis of hope is the bedrock Christian conviction that God wants all things to live and is constantly at work to lead us to fulfillment. Thus, despite the suffering and diminishment that is part of a world not yet fully redeemed, the person of hope knows that life will be fulfilled, that existence is blessed, and that since we are held fast by divine love, trust and confidence befit us far more than despair.

Moreover, as an indispensable quality for meeting the trials and challenges of life, hope respects the historical and contingent nature of human existence. It is the disposition or virtue that best honors our status as wayfarers in the world. Hope is the heart of a life that is essentially pilgrimage and fortifies one who makes progress toward blessedness but never completely comprehends it. Nothing so well captures the essence of our creatureliness as hope because it holds in tension two inescapable facts: to live is to be oriented to fulfillment, but, short of death, never to embrace it completely. Hope knows that we are forever on the way, but that our confidence in an ultimate blessedness will not be betrayed.

As a theological virtue, the focus of hope is not worldly bliss but supernatural happiness in God. A virtue strives to enhance human beings in the way most befitting our nature. The special power of any virtue is to reach for our most perfecting possibilities, and in the Christian framework of the theological virtues, hope envisions our ultimate potential to be nothing less than everlasting intimacy with God. This is why the theological virtue of hope is similar to but also something more than merely human hope. Hope is a matter of confidence, and the theological virtue of hope assures us that the utmost fulfillment of our nature is friendship, life with God, and of such peace and blessedness we shall not be denied. The theological virtue of hope vastly extends the parameters of what we can be confident about. It takes the general orientation of our nature to fulfillment and specifies that fulfillment as the perfection of our being in God. If to be hopeful is to be turned toward completion and fullness of life, biblically inspired hope testifies that our proper fulfillment is in God and that thanks to grace, Christ, and the Spirit, nothing less than that unsurpassed perfection awaits us.

It is because the vision of Christian hope is grand that magnanimity ought to characterize a life of discipleship. Magnanimity is a species of hope and describes a person who aspires to greatness and refuses to settle for mediocrity. A magnanimous person remains undaunted before the tribulations of life and has the courage to seek what is best and most promising. Despite obstacles and disappointments, he or she refuses to be misled by the temptation that God's grandest promises cannot be ours. Amidst times of struggle and adversity, it is easy to lose hope, to lower our vision, and to despair of greatness in goodness and holiness;* however, the magnanimous person steadfastly chooses what is best because his/her confidence is rooted not in oneself but in God.

Hope as an Emotion and as a Virtue. Thomas Aquinas treated hope both as a passion or emotion and as a virtue. As regards the first, he classified hope among the "irascible" or "spirited" emotions, those which come into play when the good we seek is difficult to attain or evil hard to avoid (S.Th., I-II, 23, 1 and 4). As the word suggests, these emotions are engaged when we grow dispirited, whether from adversity or tedium, and tire in our desire to do good. In the Christian story, life is an ongoing pilgrimage to God, but there are things both within us and outside us that hinder our progress to God and sometimes discourage us to the point of defeat. We are summoned to keep focused on the glory* God has in store for us, but there is much in life that frustrates that single-mindedness. Whether from our own weakness, our divided hearts, or the misfortunes that powerfully undermine any confidence that what we desire can truly be had, there is much that turns us away from magnanimous aspirations and kills our belief that grand possibilities are worthy of pursuit.

That is why hope is crucial. If life is a pilgrimage and we are wayfarers, we need something to empower us to continue on when misfortune tempts us to despair. Hope is the emotion that enables us to be resolute in our pursuit of goodness and glory when difficulty urges us to turn toward mediocrity or sin. When misfortune convinces us we cannot achieve the purposes with which we have identified our lives, hope rekindles our zeal. As an empowering emotion, hope is indispensable to any pilgrimage life in which success depends on finishing the journey undertaken. In Christian language,

hope is the quintessential passion that carries us forward to God at precisely those moments we begin to question God's pledge of blessedness. Hope is the passion that protects us from the disenchantment which inevitably accompanies any quest for a grand but arduous goal. In this respect, it is interesting that Aquinas says hope lies midway between love and joy (S.Th. I-II, 25, 3), suggesting that hope connects the start of the Christian life in love with its completion in joy. Hope is the link between love and joy, the connection between what we desire and therefore seek, and our final possession of it. Thus, even though love empowers hope, love lives through hope and in hope never despairs of joy.

As a theological virtue, Aquinas defined hope as the conviction that a difficult good is nonetheless possible to attain either through our own efforts or with the help of others (S.Th., II-II, 17, 1). The key to the theological virtue of hope is that fullness of life with God is available to us not primarily through our own efforts or merit, but through the abiding assistance of God. This is why Aquinas said God is both the basis of our hope and the object of our hope. God is the basis of Christian hope because we absolutely depend on grace to attain eternal life, but God is also the object of our hope because God represents the most excellent of all goods. For Aquinas, the good for which we hope should be commensurate with the power that enables us to hope; thus, our hope should be immeasurable because the power on which it rests is the unfailing goodness of God. As Aquinas wrote, "the good we should rightly and chiefly hope for from God is an unlimited one, matching the power of God who helps us. For it belongs to his limitless power to bring us to limitless good" (S.Th., II-II, 17, 2). This "limitless good" is "life eternal, consisting in the joyful possession of God" (S.Th., II-II, 17, 2). Christian hope expects to find God, indeed it is confident of happiness with God, because it is empowered not by human goodness but divine.

The paradox at the heart of the theological virtue of hope is that we can be confident of possessing God because at every moment we rely on God and live from the goodness of God. "Hope, in turn, is a cleaving to God as source of absolute goodness," Aquinas wrote, "since hope is reliance on God's help to bring us to blessedness" (S.Th., II-II, 17, 6). In short, we can seek God with confident wholeheartedness because we live by God's love; that is why God is both the greatest object of hope and its unshakable foundation. "Hope makes us tend towards God," Thomas says, "both as the ultimate good sought after and as an unfailing source of help in attaining thereto" (S.Th., II-II, 17, 6).

In the Christian life we are called to hope for what lies beyond our capacities because of the help available to us from God. Our hopes should never be puny; rather, they should be daring and extravagant because they rest not on our own virtues or powers, but on the unsurpassable goodness of God. We are summoned to hope for nothing less than eternal life because that grand hope best squares with the truth about God. Aquinas argues that authentic hope must reflect true judgment about God, but then concludes it is precisely because the truth about God is God's enduring benevolence that we should never hope for anything less than union with God. One who hopes for absolute beatitude with God judges rightly—he or she has a hope that squares with the facts—because if "we are most inclined to be hopeful when we have friends to rely upon," how much greater is our hope when we "expect something from God as from a friend" (S.Th., II-II, 17, 8).

Sins Against Hope. There are two sins against hope: despair and presumption. To despair is no longer to believe a share in the divine happiness is possible for us; however, the absolute truth about God is that God "grants pardon to sinners" and brings all to salvation (S.Th., II-II, 20, 1). Despair misunderstands God by doubting God's mercy and tenderness of heart, and by failing to believe that God desires nothing more and works for nothing less than the reconciliation and redemption of all. For Aquinas, despair rests on a "false opinion" about God because it "envisions God as denying pardon to the repentant sinner, or as not converting sinners to himself through justifying grace" (S.Th., II-II, 20, 1).

Similarly, despair sins against hope because to despair is "to set personal fault above the divine goodness or mercy," and thus to claim that God's forgiveness is not limitless (S.Th., II-II, 20, 2). From this perspective, to despair of God's mercy on account of our sin is to claim that our sin is greater and more powerful than God's capacity to forgive, but that is to blaspheme the unconditional love of God. Thus, we can sin against hope by having exalted notions of our sinfulness and insufficient confidence in God's goodness. As Aquinas reasoned, "Despair is precisely this, i.e., the placing of one's own fault beyond divine goodness or mercy. So, the person who despairs is guilty of faithlessness" (S.Th., II-II, 20, 2). Such faithlessness is morally perilous because to despair of God's pardon is to believe that goodness is no longer possible for us; thus, having lost hope in our restoration, we may more fully embrace evil out of despair for the good. This is why Aquinas said that "through hope we are dissuaded from pursuing evil things and induced to seek after good, so that the loss of hope has as its consequence that [people] plunge into evil without restraint and abandon their efforts to do good" (S.Th., II-II, 20, 3).

Sadness and depression can also engender despair. Discouragements can choke our hope. Too much disappointment can bring a heaviness of heart, depressing us in the literal sense of weighing us down, sometimes making it extremely difficult, if not impossible, to find the energy we need to act. Sadness immobilizes for it robs us of the hope we need to believe something good is possible. The term in classical Christian spirituality for such life-robbing sadness is *acedia*, a paralyzing sorrow specifically linked to our greatest possibility. To be oppressed by *acedia* is to despair of the glory to which God calls us. It is sorrow born from a loss of hope in achieving what God's love wants for us. *Acedia* shrivels our vision of life's possibilities. To suffer this loss of hope is to lose the courage and trust necessary to pursue the grand promises of the Christian life; it is to reject as no longer possible the fullness of life to which God's love constantly calls us and God's grace enables us. In this respect, to fall into the control of *acedia* is to settle for so much less than what God wants for us. This is why Aquinas says those in the grip of *acedia* "look upon some worthwhile good as impossible to achieve, whether alone or with the help of others," and that this extreme depression and listlessness of spirit "can dominate someone's affections to the point where he begins to think that he can never again be given aspirations towards the good. Because *acedia* is a kind of sadness having this depressive effect upon the spirit, it gives rise to despair" (S.Th., II-II, 20, 4).

Presumption is the second sin against hope. There are two kinds of presumption. In the first, persons have excessive confidence in their own capabilities and thus believe that by themselves they can achieve a salvation only God's goodness can give. With this type of presumption we exaggerate our own power and contend that by relying on our virtues alone we can achieve a glory that infinitely surpasses us. To sin against hope in this way is to deny our absolute need for the assistance of God by attempting of ourselves a salvation which lies completely beyond our competency (S.Th., II-II, 21, 1).

The second kind of presumption focuses not on our own abilities, but the mercy of God. We can sin against hope by presuming upon God's mercy or abusing it. This occurs when we presume God's pardon without repentance or eternal life without any attempt to turn from sin (S.Th., II-II, 21, 4). Aquinas describes presumption as an "excess of hope" or "as a sort of twisted hope" rooted in false judgment about God. "Just as it is erroneous to believe that God refuses to pardon those who repent or that he does not turn sinners to repentance," Aquinas writes, "it is equally erroneous to imagine that [God] gives pardon to those who persist in their sins or leads those to glory who shirk from an upright life. But this is the kind of attitude behind the act of presumption" (S.Th., II-II, 21, 2). Nonetheless, Aquinas agrees there is a thin line between legitimate hope and this second type of presumption. It is precisely because of the abundance of God's mercy and the magnitude of God's love that the genuinely limitless nature of Christian hope can seem like presumption. As Aquinas wisely observes, "'Presumption' is sometimes used to describe what really is hope, because genuine hope in God when looked at from the vantage point of the human situation almost seems like presumption; whereas it really is not presumption at all, when the immensity of the divine goodness also is kept in the picture" (S.Th., II-II, 21, 3).

Pastoral Applications. The Eucharist is the primary setting for cultivating the disposition of hope. There we listen to the stories of salvation recounting God's constant offer of love to us in covenant, Christ, and the Spirit. There we commemorate and share in the love of a God who did not abandon us "to the power of death" but again and again taught us "to hope for salvation" (Eucharistic Prayer IV). Confident that God will "bring us the fullness of grace," we pray that we may "enter into our heavenly inheritance" where "we shall sing your glory with every creature through Christ our Lord" (Eucharistic Prayer IV). Through the Eucharist, we live not by the hope of a world that is passing away, but by the hope of a kingdom dawning; thus, we are convinced that everything does not have to go on as before, that life can be different, and that the world can be what God calls it to be. This is why deep resilient hope leads to works of justice and commitment to social and political change.

But hope is nurtured and confirmed through all the sacraments. Through baptism we become sharers in God's hope. Through confirmation we are sealed and fortified in the Spirit, pledge of our salvation. In matrimony a man and a woman find hope in knowing that their deep love for one another is God's saving love for them. In the sacrament of reconciliation our hope is renewed as barriers to God's life are removed from our hearts and we learn once more the depth of God's love. And in the sacrament of anointing of the sick our attention is called to God's reign where "every tear will be wiped away" and we "shall see you, our God, as you are" (Eucharistic Prayer III).

But the Eucharist is the preeminent sacrament of hope for another reason. We do not come to Eucharist alone, we come as a community of faith. We come not only to feed on the one who is the bread of life and the hope of the world, but also to be sacraments of hope for one another. Just as Aquinas said we often have hope not in ourselves but through others, we are called to support, strengthen, and encourage each other in hope. The hope that comes to us in Christ should be a hope we share. If the Eucharist is food for those with a journey to make, we should remember that people on pilgrimage travel together and arrive at their destination only when all are willing to offer consolation and hope to one another. In this respect, the Eucharist teaches us that hope is not a private virtue, but sign of a community's love.

See: CONFIDENCE, EUCHARIST, GRACE

PAUL J. WADELL, C.P.

HOSANNAH

Hosannah in the Scriptures

Hosannah is a Greek transliteration of a Hebrew petition, *hoshioh no* (save now), used to invoke a blessing as, for example, in Psalm 118:25: "Save us, we beseech thee, O Lord! O Lord, we beseech thee, give us success." Originally a word of supplica-

tion, hosannah was a word adopted and adapted by the crowds during the joyous processions of the Feast of Tabernacles. Particularly on the seventh day of the feast, the assembly waved ceremonial branches, known as lulov, and circled the altar singing psalms of praise interspersed with the cry "hosannah," now become a liturgical acclamation. From above—from God's vantage point, or so they understood—they were not humans, but a forest of trees shaking in the wind and beseeching God's favor.

It was instinctive in the crowd who received Jesus at his triumphal entry into Jerusalem that they should adopt a familiar ritual such as the waving of the lulov together with its acclamation to greet the one whose royal messianic presence they recognized and celebrated: "They took branches of palm trees and went out to meet him, crying, 'Hosannah! Blessed is he who comes in the name of the Lord, even the King of Israel!'" (John 12:13; see Matt 21:9, 15; Mark 11:9-10).

Pastoral-Liturgical Reflection

At a very early stage "hosannah" entered the Christian liturgy, as the Didache, a late first-century document, attests. At the end of the Didache's table prayer we find: "Let grace come and let this world pass away. Hosannah to the God of David! If anyone is holy, let him come. If not, let him repent. Our Lord, come! Amen."

The annual commemoration of Jesus' triumphal entry into Jerusalem probably dates from the third century, a celebration that to this day includes recognition of Jesus' messianic role at the beginning of Holy Week, each year commemorating anew his dying and rising.

Hosannah, both as acclamation and invocation, continues to find a place at the very heart of the vernacular liturgy. In every celebration of the Eucharist, before beginning the great prayer of praise and thanksgiving, the community prays: "Holy, holy, holy Lord, God of power and might, heaven and earth are full of your glory.

Hosannah in the highest. Blessed is he who comes in the name of the Lord. Hosannah in the highest." While we regularly refer to these words as an acclamation, "hosannah in the highest" may well function also at this most solemn moment to invoke God that what we are about to do we do well.

Christian hymnody also regularly incorporates the word hosannah, most familiarly in the classic hymn of Palm Sunday: "All glory, laud, and honor to you, Redeemer, King! To whom the lips of children made sweet hosannahs ring."

See: SALVATION

KATHLEEN HUGHES, R.S.C.J.

HOSPITALITY

To the people of the ancient world, providing hospitality—especially to strangers*—was a religious act. The Greeks and the Romans, for example, saw a mysterious link between a helpless stranger and the gods themselves. This is illustrated in several Greco-Roman myths that recount the gods traveling disguised as helpless wayfarers seeking shelter and food. The fate of the mortals who receive them depended on the quality of their hospitality. Writers as diverse as Homer, Plato, Plautus, and Ovid praise hospitality as one of the most important virtues—a sign of civilization and source of blessing for those who practice it.

Exhortations to hospitality appear prominently in the pages of the Hebrew Scriptures, undoubtedly because of Israel's memory of being both a nomadic people and an exiled nation in Egypt. Divine hospitality itself also becomes an eloquent metaphor for God's care of Israel. The Christian Scriptures continue this traditional Jewish reverence for hospitality by highlighting the reception of the poor and outcast. Affording them hospitality is a moral imperative because in receiving them, one receives Christ. Therefore, concern for hospitality becomes a prized virtue of Christianity and is an important characteristic of later monastic spirituality. Fi-

nally, hospitality to God's people ought to be a crucial concern for those involved in preparing the worship of the Church.

Old Testament

Hospitality to Strangers. Reflection on Israel's state of servitude in Egypt serves as the basis for hospitality toward strangers found not only in the Law but in the rest of the Hebrew Scriptures as well. "When an alien resides with you in your land, you shall not oppress the alien. The alien who resides with you shall be to you as citizens among you; you shall love the alien as yourself, for you were once aliens in the land of Egypt" (Lev 19:33-34; see also Exod 22:20; Deut 10:19; Jer 7:6-7; Zach 7:10; Mal 3:5; Wis 19:13-16).

The Hospitality of Abraham. The Old Testament story of hospitality par excellence is that of Abraham's reception of the three mysterious strangers at the Oak of Mamre in Genesis 18:2-8. Because of Abraham's swift and generous welcome of these travelers, it is revealed that his posterity is to become a great and mighty nation and all the nations of the earth will be blessed in him (Gen 18:18).

God's Hospitality to Israel. Many biblical texts describe the covenant between God and Israel as one of hospitality. Even before Yahweh gave Israel the land, God "spread a table for them in the wilderness" (Psalm 78). The figure of the banquet offered by Wisdom in Proverbs 9:1-5 echoes the image of being lavishly welcomed into God's house expressed in Psalm 23:5-6, "You prepare a table before me in the presence of my enemies; you anoint my head with oil; my cup overflows. Surely goodness and mercy shall follow me all the days of my life, and I shall dwell in the house of the Lord my whole life long."

New Testament

Hospitality as a Means of Entering into God's Presence. Throughout the NT, hospitality toward the outcast and helpless is not only presented as virtuous conduct, but as a means of entering into the very presence of God. From the beginning of Luke's Gospel where Mary and Joseph search for hospitality in Bethlehem (Luke 2) to the exhortation contained in the Book of Revelation to admit Christ who stands at the door knocking (3:20), willingness to be hospitable is not only described as an ethical imperative but as an essential attitude of the Christian believer. Those who welcome the poor, the crippled, the lame, and the blind precisely because they cannot repay this hospitality (Luke 14:12-14) will find recompense at the resurrection of the righteous (Luke 14:12-14). Indeed, in welcoming those who are in need and helpless—those who are strangers or children—one welcomes Christ himself (Matt 25:35-36; also 10:40-41; 18:5; Mark 9:37; Luke 9:48; John 13:20).

Jesus as Host. Paradoxically, although "the Son of Man has nowhere to lay his head" (Matt 8:20) the Gospels present Jesus as a generous host. Significantly, references to Jesus' hospitality appear in unmistakably Eucharistic contexts. This becomes evident in the feeding stories found in all four gospels where Jesus lavishly satisfies the hunger of the multitudes (Matt 14:13-21; 15:32-39; Mark 6:30-38; 8:1-10; Luke 9:10-17; John 6:1-14). Jesus acts as a host at the Last Supper narratives (Matt 26:20-29; Mark 14:17-25; Luke 22:14-38), as well as in various post-resurrection appearances where he is recognized in the breaking of the bread on the road to Emmaus (Luke 24:13-35) or in preparing a meal of bread and fish on the lakeshore for the disciples (John 21).

Pastoral-Liturgical Tradition

Given the emphasis placed on hospitality in both the Hebrew and Christian Scriptures it is not surprising that the early Church would prize the reception of the alien and the outcast as an important characteristic of Christian life and ministry. That this hospitality would be reflected in their Eucharistic worship would be considered natural for a community that envi-

sioned itself as the "household of God" animated by the Spirit of unity and love.

The Patristic Church (Second to Sixth Centuries). In the second century, Justin Martyr proclaims that Christians, through their leaders, offer help and hospitality to orphans, widows, the sick, prisoners, and strangers (*Apology* I, 62, 5). Three centuries later, the apostate Roman Emperor Julian would complain that it is precisely the hospitality offered by Christians to the sick and helpless that makes their "superstition" attractive to the people of the Roman Empire (see Gregory of Nazianzus, *Oratio IV, 111, Contra Julianum*, PG 35, 648).

The reception of wandering charismatic prophets as Christ himself also figures prominently in the writings of the first several Christian generations, though at the beginning of the second century, the Didache places a common sense limit to this hospitality that could prove disruptive of the order in local communities after a certain length of time. But nowhere else was hospitality to be better modeled than in the Eucharist—for once baptized all are considered radically equal at the table of the Lord. The advice given to bishops in the fourth-century *Didaskalia Apostolorum* poignantly (and surprisingly) expresses this concern for the Eucharistic assembly being hospitable toward God's poor: "If a poor man or woman comes, whether they are from your own parish or from another, and especially if they are advanced in years, and if there is no room for them, make a place for them, O bishop, with all your heart, even if you yourself have to sit on the ground. You must not make any distinction between persons if you wish your ministry to be pleasing before God" (12).

The Middle Ages (Seventh to Fifteenth Centuries). The evolving monastic movement of the early Middle Ages emphasized hospitality to strangers and especially pilgrims as a hallmark of a monk's spirituality. St. Basil also speaks of the care his monks should give to the sick who present themselves at the door of the monastery. It is St. Benedict, though, who devotes two chapters of his rule to hospitality: chapter 61 dealing with the reception of fellow monks from other monasteries and chapter 53 spelling out in great detail the ministry of hospitality that should be afforded all who come to the monastery. It is from this Benedictine tradition of offering disinterested hospitality to pilgrims and other travelers in search of miraculous cures at places of pilgrimage that religious hostels and hospitals develop, the immediate forerunners of our modern health care facilities.

Pastoral Notes. Hospitality as a work of mercy is paradigmatic of any act of charity shown toward our brothers and sisters: in acting toward others as Jesus has taught us we come into the very presence of God. It is not surprising, then, that our liturgies—where we celebrate that presence of God in our world and our lives—are most expressive of God's Spirit when they reflect the same hospitality lovingly praised in the pages of both the OT and NT. The U.S. Bishops' document *Environment and Art in Catholic Worship* well describes the importance of hospitality for the liturgy. "As common prayer and ecclesial experience, liturgy flourishes in a climate of hospitality: a situation in which people are comfortable with one another, either knowing or being introduced to one another; a space in which people are seated together, with mobility, in view of one another as well as the focal point of the rite, involved as participants and *not* as spectators" (EACW 11).

Just as hospitality should be extended to those with disabilities, the stranger, the poor, and the socially marginalized, inviting them to participate actively in liturgical celebrations by making necessary structural changes in the church building (ramps, etc.) or by providing celebrations in the languages of the minorities of the parish, so Christians should be at the forefront extending a hand of welcome to those who are "different" in their own local communities, thus continuing the practice of hospitality that is at the heart of Judaeo-Christian spirituality.

See: EUCHARIST, FAMILY, HOUSE, MEAL, STRANGER

MARK R. FRANCIS, C.S.V.

HOUSE/FAMILY HOME/HOUSE CHURCH

House has a number of important connotations in biblical tradition. In the OT it is a term applied to a people as well as the locale of their dwelling in family units. The home is a locus for worship, as was the Temple, as the house of God. In NT tradition, although Jesus often appears to be homeless, many of his followers did not leave their homes. Rather, these became the gathering places for the early Christians, who formed networks of house churches. Some contemporary movements in the Church try to recover the familial sense of church that prevailed in the first centuries of Christianity.

Old Testament

The biblical Hebrew word for house or household, *bayit,* has a broad sense ranging from race to dwelling. At times the word emphasizes the people of the house, at other times the physical structure. Hence 2 Samuel 7:5-11 could play on the word *bayit* depicting God as refusing the offer of a house (temple) to be built by David and in turn promising David a house (dynasty).

Inevitably the word "house" suggested a union or companionship of people sharing shelter and essential services. An invited entry into someone's house meant receiving a sacred pledge of security and care. Although apparently the word "hospitality" does not exist in the OT, stories abound about this sacred duty (Gen 18:1-15; 19:1-11; Job 31:32).

The sanctuaries of Israel (Gen 28:17) and later the Temple (Ps 27:4) were each "the house of God" *(beth elohim* or simply *beth-el).* Such a structure implied both the relative stability of God's presence on earth as well as the possibility of companionship with God by entering God's house. Similarly divine Wisdom built her "house" precisely to extend to human beings a sharing in her blessings (Prov 9:1-5). The Temple as "God's house" was also "a house of prayer" (Isa 56:7; 60:7 LXX). Entering the house of God implied specific duties on the part of God's guests. The OT emphasized especially the moral aspect of those duties (Psalm 15).

No biblical Hebrew word existed for "family" in the modern sense of the word, but the concept was expressed by one's "father's house" *(bet ab)*. This entity was the smallest social unit in Israel, out of which the clan and the tribe were made up. Larger than the modern nuclear family, this unit was composed of the father as head, his wife or wives and concubines, his children, slaves and servants, many of his clients, and his guests. The Passover was celebrated within this unit (Exod 12:1-28). The sense of solidarity of this "house" appears in the matter of fact accounts of God punishing whole households—for multiple generations—because of the sin of one member (Exod 20:5; Josh 7:24). Only with the Babylonian exile appeared the revolutionary view of individual responsibility precisely in contrast to family solidarity (Ezekiel 18).

The expression "house of Israel" *(bet Israel;* Isa 5:7; Hos 5:1) describing the Jewish people is an extension of this full sense of "house." This extension reflects the ancient idea that a nation received its identity and perhaps even its name from a common ancestor. It was with this whole "house of Israel" that God consistently forms covenants (Jer 31:31). Members of Israel were therefore brothers and sisters (Lev 10:4; Deut 15:3).

New Testament

The Gospels. One level of the Gospels—especially Q material—portrays a break with the Jewish and OT emphasis on one's house and household. Jesus appears as a homeless itinerant (Matt 8:20; Luke 9:58). The disciples are called upon to imitate this rupture with one's home, even as regards the most sacred duties toward one's parents (Matt 8:21-22; Luke 9:59-60). One's home could well be the site of hostility to the believer (Matt 10:34-36; Luke 12:52-53). This level of the Gospel expresses the most radical apocalyptic aspects of Jesus' teaching and stresses discontinuity between the approaching reign of God and the present life.

On another less apocalyptic level, the Gospels reaffirm the role of the house and household. The logistics of Jesus' own mission as well as that of the earliest disciples required hospitality and support by those who did not join Jesus in his lifestyle of propertyless itinerancy (Luke 8:1-3; Mark 6:10-11). Furthermore the followers of Jesus quickly established social ties among themselves that followed the model of the house and household. They were brothers, sisters, mothers, and children to each other (Mark 10:29-30). No one among them, however, was to be their father, most likely since Jesus had instructed them to direct their "abba" sentiments to God (Matt 23:9).

Even in Jesus' mission, especially as portrayed in Mark, a house or home unexpectedly shows up at crucial moments of instruction. After teaching the crowds outside in the fields, on the hillsides, or along the shore, Jesus gives special instructions to the Twelve "at home" *(en oikô;* Mark 1:14-23; 9:14-27; 10:2-12). The *diwan* or living room of the Palestinian home is the setting for Jesus' most dramatic offer of divine mercy to sinners (Mark 2:15).

Acts. In the Acts of the Apostles, the two contrasting life styles of homelessness and home ownership continue. In its idealized form the Jerusalem community was one where members sold all they possessed and gave the proceeds to the poor—yet met at each other's homes (Act 2:42-47). The home was the place of prayerful gathering (Act 12:12; 20:7-8). The expansion of the church occurs especially by the conversion of key persons in a city along "with all his/her house" (Acts 11:14; 16:15, 31-32; 18:8). This converted household then becomes the basis of operations for an extended mission in the city.

Paul. Paul speaks four times explicitly of "house churches" (*hê kat' oikon ekklêsia*; 1 Cor 16:19; Rom 16:5; Phlm 2; Col 4:15). These churches appear to be in contrast to a city-wide church and hence seem to be the units federated within a Pauline city church.

Whether meeting as a smaller house church or gathering as a whole city church, the Christians evangelized by Paul met in private homes and specifically in a Hellenistic *triclinium* or dining room (see 1 Cor 11:18-22). The consequences of such an early setting were far reaching. For one thing, the household provided a conducive atmosphere in which the Christians could express the bonds of brotherhood and sisterhood as well as maternity and paternity that linked them together. Throughout his letters Paul addresses or refers to his fellow Christians as "brother" and "sister." Several times Paul describes his own work as that of a "father" (1 Thess 2:11; 1 Cor 14:14-15) or even as a "mother" (Gal 4:19; 1 Thess 2:7; 1 Cor 3:2).

Ministries within this home-based church more than likely reflected the functions of the Jewish/Hellenistic household. The gifts shared at the gathering included those of "assistants" and "administrators" (1 Cor 12:28) as well as those of the one "who gives alms," "who rules" (better translated as "the patron") and the one "who shows mercy" (Rom 12:8)—all functions proper to a powerful head of a household. The conspicuously frequent mention of women in regard to house churches, sometimes along with their husbands (1 Cor 16:19; Rom 16:5; Phlm 2), sometimes as a single head of a house church (Col 4:15), suggests the active participation of the mother of the house in the gathering, a participation parallel to her role in the household at other times.

The house *triclinium* obviously promoted the sense of the Lord's Supper as a family meal, yet Paul had to insist that this family meal be open to the larger community. For Paul the greatest challenge of this celebration was to convince his readers to be willing to share with all present. Celebrating the Lord's Supper meant recognizing the household in which one gathered as "the church of God," seeing the food served as not simply one's own supper but a Supper meant to be shared by rich and poor together (1 Cor 11:17-22). Given the intense loyalties that ancient families evoked even to the point of divisive hostility, we can understand the forcefulness of Paul's instructions.

Later Writings. The difficulties faced by Paul eventually led the early Christians to distinguish far more clearly the Christian home from the Christian gathering. For the author of the Pastoral Letters (1–2 Timothy, Titus), the home was the place where dangerous teachings could arise, especially under the influence of women (1 Tim 5:13; 2 Tim 3:6). The chief local officers, elders/overseers, who had assumed the teaching, managing, and presiding roles in the Church, had to prove their abilities in their homes, but functioning in the Church was distinct from operating in their homes. They were given this Church role by an official Church appointment (1 Tim 5:22; Titus 1:5). In this "household of God" (1 Tim 3:15) removed from the household, the role for women is effectively eliminated, reduced to instructing other women about domestic affairs (Titus 2:4-5).

Architecture would soon catch up to this new understanding and churches would soon be built or remodeled as dedicated sanctuaries, separated from the family.

See: CHURCH, MEAL, MISSION, PRAYER, TEMPLE

VINCENT P. BRANICK

Pastoral-Liturgical Tradition

Both home and synagogue as they were regarded by Jews during the first century became models for Christian reflection on both the place where the assembly came together and the very nature of the Church. The synagogue was viewed as a house of assembly, a house of prayer, and a house of study. After the destruction of the Temple, the synagogue became the main focus of Jewish worship. The family home was always a place of religious observance, even when the Temple was in existence. It was the place of daily prayer, especially before and after meals. The Sabbath was celebrated in the home, as was the Passover and other festivals; of course there were temple and synagogue services as well. The home was a place for religious teaching and example of holy living.

The term house church or its equivalent occurs four times in the NT letters: "Aquila and Prisca, together with the assembly that meets in their house, send you cordial greetings in the Lord" (1 Cor 16:19); "Give my greetings to Prisca and Aquila. . . . Remember me also to the congregation that meets in their house" (Rom 16:3, 5); "Give our best wishes to the brothers at Laodicea and to Nympha and the assembly that meets at his house" (Col 4:15); "Paul . . . to our beloved friend and fellow worker Philemon . . . and to the church that meets in your house" (Phlm 1:2).

In its idealistic picture of the very early days of the Christian Church in Jerusalem Acts 2:46 recounts: "They went to the temple area together every day, while in their home they broke bread." Outside of Jerusalem, Christians worshiped in the synagogue and then retired to their homes. At a later date relationship with the Jewish community deteriorated and Christians no longer went to the Temple or synagogue but worshiped by themselves in their own homes.

Private dwellings of members of the local Christian community formed the environment for the house churches, as well as for the religious life of individual households. Christians living in a town or district gathered around one family in the family's home. The building still remained the domicile of the host family, who welcomed others at the time of worship and other gatherings of the community. A city such as Corinth or Rome might have more than one house church.

It was only natural for Christians to gather in larger homes in order to accommodate more persons. The wealthy members of the community thus provided a service to the others, and also probably acquired a particular leadership role as well. The dining room or atrium provided an environment that was congenial to the early churches. This setting reflected the upper room chosen by Jesus for the last supper, and contributed to the quasi familial relationship that existed among church members. House churches helped the community economically and were a starting place for missionary work, a setting for leadership, and probably enabled the greater participation of women.

At a later date the house church began to decline. Toward the end of the second century Christians began to dedicate entire homes for the assembly and worship of the local church community. The building ceased to be a private residence, and modifications were made to better accommodate larger numbers of people as well as specific liturgical needs such as baptism. Though resembling a house, the building in fact became a church. After 314 CE Christians were allowed to construct entire church buildings, and the first basilicas arose.

In addition, problems of orthodoxy, discipline, leadership and authority, and communication had arisen in the small gatherings that had assembled in homes. The increasing size of local churches also made gathering in private homes inconvenient.

In early Christianity, church buildings were called the house of the church; later they became known as the house of God. This shift reflects a lowered appreciation of the whole baptized people as Church, a decreased awareness of the baptized person as temple of the holy Spirit, and diminished consciousness of the Trinitarian life of the baptized.

In the rite of dedication of a church, the church building is clearly an icon or symbol of the people who comprise the local church community: they are really the Church, not the building. Today people within the Christian community are divided with respect to their image of Church. Some define Church in terms of baptized people, others in terms of buildings and other features of an institutional model, others in terms of clergy and church authorities, others in terms of Christian living and prophetic preaching.

Today households are sometimes referred to as the domestic church. This indicates that those who live together, whether traditional or single-parent families or single persons, are valued as valid religious individuals and groups. It suggests that they are to express their religious lives in their private homes, and hence that they do not have to "go to church" to be in Church, to worship, or to study. Of course they are also expected to take part in the worship and work of the entire community on Sunday and other occasions.

The Catholic Worker Movement founded by Peter Maurin and Dorothy Day in the 1940s and the growth of "Base Christian Communities" in Latin America and in North America in the past several decades also attests to the desire on the part of many Christians to envision church in a familial context that inspires relationship and commitment. These new forms of "house church" draw much of their inspiration from the house churches of the early Christian Church.

See: CHURCH, COMMUNITY, FAMILY, SYNAGOGUE, TEMPLE

J. FRANK HENDERSON

HUMANKIND

The Bible views the human person first and foremost as a creature of God living in a relationship with God, with other human beings, and with the rest of the created world. Although, like other creatures, they are made of the substance of the world, human beings have unique abilities that set them apart. They can think and imagine and decide. They can love and praise God, but they can also make mistakes and sin.

Old Testament

The biblical accounts of the creation* of Adam and Eve (Genesis 1 and 2) sketch the way ancient Israel characterized humankind. Although the two accounts differ, they both attest to humankind's affinity with the natural world (dust) as well as its uniqueness within that world (image of God). In addition to these narrative sketches, examination of some vocabulary can provide a fuller picture of the biblical perception of humankind. Four words are pivotal in this understanding: body, soul, spirit, heart. The word *bāśār*, translated "body" or "flesh," is used of both humans and animals, reenforcing the notion of affinity. Since this body is made of dust, it is subject to death. The Israelites did not have any concept of soul as did the Greeks. Instead, the life-giving force within the human being was called the *nepeš*, a word also translated as "throat," the source of human breath (*neśāmā*). Breath and spirit (*rūah*) are frequently used interchangeably and are closely connected with the force of life that comes from God.

Nowhere in the first eleven chapters of Genesis are the people identified as Israelites. These are the stories of Everyman and Everywoman. They tell of the universal need of human companionship (2:18, 24); movement toward development and civilization (4:20-22); propensity toward hubris (3:5; 11:4); envy and violence (4:5-8), wickedness of every kind (6:5), drunkenness (10:20f.). Human beings universally are capable of applying their creative talents to improving the conditions of life for themselves and for others, or of turning and directing them solely to their own benefit and against God, others, or the natural world. All human beings need social institutions that will direct their energies in ways that are true to the nature created by God and that will benefit themselves and others.

All societies have at least four basic social institutions: kinship structures, political systems, economic systems, and religious systems. Anthropological analysis challenges us to understand the social structures of the biblical societies in order to understand the theology that the biblical texts might yield.

Kinship provides the context and the idiom for many different kinds of social relationships. The place of residence, group and community membership, lines of authority and obedience, designation of friends and enemies, marriage practices, and lines of inheritance are determined by one's status in the kinship system. It is clear from the stories of early Israel that the tribe was the fundamental building block of the society. Although some women seem to have been quite influential (Exod 15:20f; Judges 4–5), power within the tribe was patriarchal (father-headed), and the biblical genealogies show that descent was patrilineal (through the father's line, Numbers 1). Marriage was usually endogamous (within the family, clan, or tribe, Gen 24:3; 28:2).

Politics provides an orderly system of social relationships. Authority is the legitimate exercise of power. It implies a shared system of values, the acceptance of social and political institutions through which authority is exercised, and agreed upon grounds for its legitimation. The tribal organization within which Israel originated soon gave way to a monarchical system of governing. However, the fundamental social values shared by the society remained the same. All Israelites, whether identified according to tribal loyalty or national allegiance, endorsed the Law of the covenant. Within the tribal structure, authority was legitimated through patrilineal descent and group endorsement; within the monarchy it was through a divinely established dynasty. The Bible recounts numerous examples of how the prophets spoke out against the abuse of this political power (Isa 28:7-15; Jer 21:11-14).

Economics is concerned with the production and distribution of goods. Since labor plays such a vital role in the production of goods, the control of the labor force is also a concern of economics. Ancient Israel was involved in both herding and agriculture and its material wealth was defined in terms of both means of production. Abraham (Gen 13:2) and Job (Job 1:3) were both known for the size of their flocks. Israel itself was called a "land of milk and honey" (Deut 8:7-9). This wealth was seen as fulfillment of God's promise to the ancestors (Gen 12:1-3) and a sign that God was rewarding them for their obedience to the laws of the covenant (Deut 28:1-6).

Ideally, everyone was to have access to the riches of this land of promise. Too frequently, however, greed and exploitation ruled and the society suffered economic stratification. The theory of retribution mentioned above served to reenforce social divisions, for prosperity and poverty were considered sent by God as reward and punishment respectively. Still, the laws found in Deuteronomy (15:1-18) insist that wealth be distributed and that the poor be given opportunities to better their circumstances.

Religion is concerned with the ultimate meaning of things. Its values are embedded within the social fabric of the group. It influences the way kinship, politics, and economics are related to each other and to the ultimate reality. Israel believed that the underlying order of reality was established by God and that God holds all things in existence. Believing that God had intervened in a special way in its history (e.g., the liberation of the Exodus, the punishment of the Exile), it commemorated these historical events as moments of sacred time. It also revered certain natural places (e.g., mountains, springs) as sacred space, as sites of some experience of God. In the course of its history, Israel devised an elaborate system of religious laws to regulate its relationship with its God (Holiness Code, Leviticus 17–26).

Finally, the entire Wisdom tradition (in particular Proverbs, Job, Ecclesiastes or Qoheleth, Wisdom, and Sirach) springs from concern for what is human. Every aspect of human life, not merely the significant national events, was believed to be under the control of God. Israel maintained that it encountered God *through* human experience not *in addition* to it. The question now became: What kind of specific role does God play in human life?

The sages were humanists. Attentive to human welfare, values, and dignity, they taught that whatever benefitted humankind was a good to be pursued and whatever was injurious should be avoided and condemned. Training of any kind (e.g., within the family, the court, or in preparation for a profession) sought to impart whatever ability was needed to achieve the respective goal. Success or happiness was the criterion for judging the value of the project. It was also considered concrete evidence of the wisdom of the person who succeeded. Although the ancients did believe that there was a right way of behaving, they did not insist on a rigid standard that would apply to every instance. Each situation called for its own response. The wise person was the one who, having a vast store of experiential wisdom, knew which avenue of conduct was suitable.

See: CREATION, DEATH, MAN/MEN, SALVATION, WOMAN/WOMEN

DIANNE BERGANT, C.S.A.

New Testament

General. The NT does not use the word "humankind"; such an abstraction does not fit comfortably with Semitic attitudes expressed in concrete and personal terms. The NT uses two terms for the reality. *Aner*, man, is male specific and is also the usual word for husband; it is paired with *gune*, woman or wife. The other word *anthropos* is usually generic in referring to all human beings.

So Paul writes: "How do you know, wife, whether you will save your husband" (1 Cor 7:16); here he uses the proper *gune* and *aner*. In the usual expression "men and women," *aner* is paired with *gune*, woman or wife, in Acts 5:14; 8:3, 12; 9:2. Paul usually employs *anthropos* in referring generically to all people. This is particularly true in Romans and is usually found in the later Letters called Pauline. Paul states his basic thesis in Romans thus: "We consider that a person [man] is justified by faith apart from works of the law" (Rom 3:28). The context clearly indicates that the meaning is without sexual preference. The NAB translation quoted above uses inclusive English language to achieve the same effect.

Unfortunately, the rule of thumb in Greek is not always observed. About one fifth of the uses of the specific *aner* in the NT are generic, although many of them occur in conventional sayings such as "O men of" or "blessed is the man" where the context clearly indicates a generic application. John, however, uses the two words almost interchangeably.

Anthropos also is sometimes used of an individual male where we would expect the specific *aner*. Matthew 9:9, for example, uses *anthropos* in the phrase "a man named Matthew." Paul occasionally surprises by shifting the connotation as in "it is a good thing for a man not to touch a woman," where he uses *anthropos* (1 Cor 7:1).

Woman. The feminine *gune* is never used generically for all people. This seems to be mostly a question of social usage. However, when it came to the theological explanation of what salvation was all about, the need arose for a word that was both concrete and yet which included all human beings. The Greek language did not have such a word and neither does English.

Redemption. Many of the uses, especially in the Gospels, refer to a character in the story. The introduction is often, "There was a certain one [man]." These clearly have no deep theological implication. On the other hand, the generic uses generally do. "Whoever breaks one of the least of these commandments and teaches others [men] to do so will be called least in the kingdom of heaven" (Matt 5:19). The saying obviously applies to all human beings. However, it does so in a way that is difficult for us to capture. The word used is generic

451

and yet concrete. It does not refer to an indefinite group whom one influences, but to individual humans. This is sometimes crucial theologically. "But to those who did accept him he gave the power to become children of God, to those who believe in his name, who were born not by natural generation [of men] nor by human choice nor by man's decision but of God" (John 1:12-13). Here a theological point is being made. Our likeness to God depends on being children of God not born as Adam, the earthy creature. Abstract terminology detracts from the theological meaning.

When the word is used in the Gospels in a generic sense, it is more apt to be in an admonition than a promise (see Matt 4:4; 6:1, 5, 15; 10:17, 33; 12:31, 45; 15:9, 20; 16:23; 17:22; 18:7; 19:6, 26; 23:4, 5, 7, 13, 28 to give a sampling from one Gospel). These negative comments are not abstractions but references to actual conduct that the readers had experienced.

The original stories of Jesus were not strong on the interpretation of the meaning of his life and death. It was Paul who first brought out of the original tradition the central interpretative point. This appears especially in Romans 5, 1 Corinthians 15, and the later development of the tradition in Ephesians, Philippians, and Colossians. In Romans 5 Paul's objective is to explain that we are connected with Jesus not as an example of admirable living, not because he is a hero of ours, but because he is much more our progenitor than the traditional Adam who stood at the beginning of the story. "For just as through the disobedience of one person [anthropos] so through the obedience of one the many will be made righteous" (Rom 5:19). In 1 Corinthians 15 the whole explanation depends on Christ being the first fruits of a resurrection which necessarily will determine our resurrection. "For since death came through a human being [anthropos], the resurrection of the dead came also through a human being [anthropos]" (1 Cor 15:21). In the later letters Christ is the "icon," the model, the head who makes our union with him inevitable (see Col 1:15 and 3:10 in context especially).

The crux was not a male salvation myth, but rather a need to think of sinfulness and salvation in concrete terms which affected all individuals. Mankind did not sin and receive redemption through mankind. Adam sinned and Jesus redeemed us through his cross (Rom 5:12, 15, 17, 19; see also 1 Cor 1:18-24 for Paul's protest against an abstract approach). It is this same attitude that causes the NT to use "body" and "flesh" to refer to the whole human race in its total state as a creature.

Son of Man. The phrase "Son of Man" appears frequently in the Gospels, especially the Synoptics. The rest of the NT does not use it. It may well have been the actual way in which Jesus referred to himself. The repetitive expression is a Semitic way of designating a person as belonging to some group, as in "sons of Abraham" or "daughters of Zion." So Jesus would have been affirming his solidarity with all people who have lived or will live. However, there also seems to be a deliberate reference to the figure in Daniel 7:13, "one like a son of man coming, on the clouds of heaven." Jesus solemnly affirms this connection with that apocalyptic figure during his questioning at the time of the Passion (Matt 24:30; Mark 14:62; Luke 22:69). In that sense the title draws attention to the victory of all of us in our struggle with evil.

Story-telling. These explanations need to be seen within the context of the story-telling in which they occur. They do not enable us to diagnose how humankind is constituted or how it can be made to work as we want. That would be a philosophical or scientific approach and we are tempted to use such diagnoses in order to control actions. Instead, the NT is basically a story. The people who first came out to hear Jesus heard him telling their story. It was a story with a rich tradition, but it was also their personal experience of failure and frustration. They came to Jesus because he offered hope. He did not tell them how to be a success; he demanded faith that he could give them a power which they did not possess.

Paul, the first interpreter of the story, frequently recalls to his readers what their experience of salvation had been and how it had been grounded in faith. "The one who is righteous by faith will live" (Rom 1:17). Then follows a social critique on how everything else has failed. To Paul and his readers faith in Jesus was not simply faith in another human being, even in a superior human being; it was faith in one who somehow summed up everything that we were and had experienced. He was the new Abraham (Rom 4:1-3) and the new Adam (Rom 5:12-21). He too had experienced injustice, failure, humiliation, the oppression of the Law, the temptation of Satan. But his story did not end in the common human disaster. He rose from the dead and lives as the triumphant Savior whom mankind had awaited over the centuries. He unites us all in the potential of his victory.

We can abandon the old self and receive a new one (see Eph 3:16; 4:22, 24 for expressions such as "inner self, old self, new self," which translate the Greek *anthropos*). The new self has the potential of making us somehow like Jesus himself, even to the extent of a bodily resurrection. The story of the NT as canonically arranged ends with the Book of Revelation. It must be so. The victory is total; the goodness which was put into us at creation has been liberated and we now truly realize in our lived experience what it means to be the children of God.

We are all equal. The story does not work without a constant reference to the concrete circumstances of our history as a people, our own personal experiences, and the reality of the human and divine Jesus. "There is neither Jew nor Greek, slave nor free person, there is not male and female, for you are all one in Christ Jesus" (Gal 3:28).

See: LIFE, MAN/MEN, WOMAN/WOMEN

JAMES A. FISCHER, C.M.

Pastoral-Liturgical Tradition

Three considerations precede a discussion of the pastoral-liturgical use of "humankind": the effects of language on speaker and hearer, contemporary issues and concerns relating to "humankind," and the nature of liturgical language.

The importance of language and the power of a turn of phrase, long known by public speakers and poets, has been emphasized anew by modern philosophers and those involved in human rights and feminist movements. Words and phrases participate in the creation of consciousness, in the formation of identity, in evaluating people and groups as well as actions, and in creating conflict and in healing divisions. In the case of a religious community, a carefully chosen word or a well-crafted phrase can move a people to a deepened sense of its proper place before God; other words or phrases can maintain the status quo or deepen alienation. Contemporary ministers are challenged to be conscious of the mysterious power of language of words, phrases, syntax, and context. Those who wish to further the reign of God rather than cause frustration and alienation are cautioned to watch their language.

A second group of concerns that heightens the contemporary minister's awareness of correct speech is the growing awareness of the human dignity and rights of all men and women. Doctrinal and moral theologians have traditionally been concerned with expressing themselves in correct and precise words and phrases. Those involved in pastoral ministry were often allowed more liberty in their self expression. An increasingly educated laity and a growing cultural awareness of issues of human identity and equality no longer allows that license. In North America words like "Indians," "Negroes," "girls," and "foreigners" carry with them a pejorative connotation. At a time in history when the fundamental dignity and equality of all people presses itself on our consciousness such words are no longer appropriate in many quarters.

"Humankind" is an attempt to express the Christian belief in the universal dignity and value of all men and women as creatures of God while avoiding the perceived subtle exclusivity of the earlier words "man" or "mankind." "Humankind" refers to all men and women regardless of sex, race, political, social or economic status, state of health, or stage of development. It is an inclusive, non-sexist, non-evaluative word developed in order to convey the heightened consciousness of human dignity and equality.

Consciousness of the power of language in the shaping of human consciousness and affairs and a developing awareness of the issues of human rights and feminism leaves those involved in pastoral and liturgical settings many difficulties. Language which may be appropriate for a parish meeting, the classroom, a pastoral gathering, or casual conversation may be inappropriate for liturgy and prayer. The thoughtful and skilled pastor must make important decisions as to proper linguistic usage.

A third preliminary consideration—liturgical language. The language of liturgy and public prayer must be theologically correct and pastorally appropriate. It should also be beautiful. It should be remembered that liturgy is art and poetry. It should not be reduced to theological and political correctness or pastoral solicitude. Teachers or administrators working in prosaic contexts may use prosaic language. Those preparing and leading liturgy, however, are attempting to move the heart and soul as well as the mind and the hands. Poetry and elegance of speech together with truth and sensitivity must be the norm. Words that are trendy or politically motivated have a place in ministry, but that place is not public liturgy. Liturgists face the challenge of expressing contemporary insight and concerns in a language that beautifully transcends the moment.

The word "humankind" presents a problem. Its use will vary. For some educational settings, in social justice work, and in pastoral gatherings and similar situations where human dignity, equality, and solidarity should be emphasized, "humankind" may well help create that consciousness and reality. While the word may meet resistance and cause questions, the use of "humankind" rather than "mankind" or "all men" can be understood as another expression of the prophetic mission of the Church. If the first of the above assumptions is correct, in time, the use of "humankind," along with other movements of culture, will eliminate the unnecessary and sinful distinctions between men and women, the franchised and disenfranchised. The use of "humankind" will contribute to the creation of human solidarity. Those who use the word will develop a more universal consciousness and those who hear "humankind" being used will be challenged to think in more universal categories. Moreover, they will feel affirmed in their commitments to universal human dignity and value.

There are also difficulties in the use of "humankind." The word intentionally ignores the differences between men and women. In creating a generic "humanity," gender differences are overlooked. While this may be desired in some theological and pastoral contexts, in other situations the elimination of gender differentiation is a mistake. At a time in Western history when the distinctive contributions of women to consciousness and civilization are being highlighted, the use of "humankind" overlooks those emphases. If an important pastoral priority is for women to become more proud of their womanhood and for men to come into greater contact with and appreciation of their feminine dimension, and if men are challenged to discover their deep manhood while women are to affirm their manly characteristics, the use of the generic "humankind" seems inappropriate. When the pastoral setting calls for a study and appreciation of the unique contributions of men and women to human life, "humankind" is not the word to use.

It is important for contemporary Christians to develop a consciousness that affirms both the universality of human dignity and value, as well as the distinctiveness and value of men and women. "Humankind" is useful in some contexts. Other situations demand that gender distinctions be maintained.

The use of "humankind" in liturgical contexts presents special challenges. Liturgy and liturgical language are to express and deepen Christian faith and move people to prayer. Consequently, the liturgy planner might question the fittingness of "humankind" in the liturgical life of the local community. How will the word be heard? Does "humankind" express the faith and hope of those at liturgy? Will the use of "humankind" promote unity and prayer or will it polarize the community? Is the word beautiful? elegant? Or is "humankind" provocative and crass to the community assembled? Language that draws attention to itself or to an idea rather than moving the faithful to prayer is usually liturgically inappropriate. A question must be addressed: Will the use of "humankind" (or any other word for that matter) move its hearers to prayer?

If the minister decides that the use of "humankind" is inappropriate for the liturgy of the local community, the challenge becomes one of finding other words to express the Christian faith in human dignity and universality. Based on a criteria that includes theological precision, pastoral sensitivity, and beauty of language, phrases like "the entire human family," "all men and women," "every man and woman," "all God's people," or "people of every race and sex, language and way of life" may be judged more appropriate for liturgical usage in a specific community. Some may complain that the liturgy becomes too verbal when such formulations are used. Excessive verbalization is a problem in Western liturgy, but it is not uncommon for poetry to use more words than prose in expressing an idea. While avoiding wordiness, the liturgical planner must find the language of the local community that accurately, sensitively, and beautifully expresses Christian faith. Critical care and creativity are needed in finding the fitting turn of phrase for a liturgical celebration.

Thinking and imagination, hard work, and a sense of language is needed if "humankind" is to be used well and if one intends to correct the historically conditioned sexist language of Scripture and traditional formulae.

See: MAN/MEN, WOMAN/WOMEN, SEXUALITY

JAMES R. HALSTEAD, O.S.A.

HYPOCRITE

Old Testament

Definition. The Greek term *hypocrites* denotes an actor, one who plays a role on stage. Its metaphoric sense connotes a pretender or dissembler, and this is the meaning that prevails in the Bible. A hypocrite is one who displays an exterior piety without interior devotion, one whose actions conform to ritual obligations but whose heart is without intention. In the context of NT polemic (Matt 15:7), Isaiah's description of hypocrisy is quoted (Isa 29:13): "This people honors me with their lips, but their hearts are far from me."

In OT usage, "hypocrite" typically translates the Hebrew root *haneph*, which is joined in synonymous parallelism with such terms as "evildoer" (Isa 9:17), "sinners" (Isa 33:14), "the wicked" (Job 20:5). Apart from the two occurrences in Isaiah, OT usage of this term is restricted largely to the Wisdom tradition (eight times in Job, once in Proverbs) and generally refers to an intense hostility to God and the ways of God. This very negative connotation contrasts with the meaning of hypocrite in the NT, which seems to underscore the quality of deception and dissimulation. The prophetic denunciations of empty religion, however, condemn hypocritical religious practices that lack an interior motivation (Mic 6:8; Isa 1:11-17).

New Testament

Definition. The term hypocrite appears in the NT primarily in the polemic ex-

455

changes between Jesus and the Jewish opponents (see especially Matthew 6 and 23). We find hypocrisy equated with malice and craftiness (see Mark 12:15; Matt 22:18; Luke 20:23). And in Galatians 2:13 Paul accused Peter of hypocrisy in Antioch because of the insincerity with which he changed his mind in order to please those "who were aligned with James and the circumcision party" when they came to Antioch. In addition, the incident described in Acts 5:1-11 involving Ananias and Sapphira, although it does not use the term hypocrite, concerns nevertheless the same willful deception associated with this term hypocrite as it is used elsewhere in the NT.

Polemic Setting for Denunciations. Empty displays of piety are labeled hypocrisy in Matthew 6:5 because they serve only to impress others and lack sincerity of heart. Christians are urged instead to "pray in secret" so that God alone will hear their prayer. The strongest denunciations of hypocrisy in the NT are found in Matthew 23, and these occur in the context of bitter debates between Jesus and the Pharisees. These harsh exchanges probably reflect the situation prevailing in Matthew's Church during the decade of the 80s when Christianity came into intense conflict with the Pharisaic leadership of Judaism. But these Gospel passages also challenge *Christians* within the Matthean community who display similar hypocritical attitudes in their legal casuistry (Matt 23:24) and external religious observance.

Hypocrisy in the NT stems from religious formalism and displays of religion, from blindness and self-deception (Matt 15:3-14), and from self-satisfied arrogance that hardens one to the possibility of conversion. All, Christian as well as Jew, run the risk of becoming hypocritical, and hypocrisy is a danger especially to those in leadership roles who must teach others. It is even possible to become a hypocrite without being aware of our hypocrisy (Matt 7:20-23).

Pastoral Notes

Hypocrisy is a perennial risk to all who practice formal religion. Religious ritual and practice must flow from an inner attitude of the heart dedicated to God and to God's people. Only when our words and deeds flow from this interior disposition can we avoid the danger of hypocrisy.

See: PHARISEE, PRIDE

BARBARA E. BOWE, R.S.C.J.

I

IDOLATRY

Idolatry, the worship of some visible model of a higher power, is a constant temptation. The great myths generally begin with a creation account which tries to explain our inability to control the basic life forces. This is true of the OT that begins with the story of creation. The early stories in the OT often depict Israel's fierce combat with the pagan versions of the myths. Loyalty to state and community often went hand in hand with the worship of a god or an image of a god. The prophets were inclined to pour scorn on the worship of lifeless gods. Eventually monotheism conquered and after the Babylonian Captivity there was no major falling away from it to idolatry.

The NT takes monotheism as the accepted norm. The Pauline writings continue the prophetic attitude that pagan gods are "nothingnesses." These writings also take advantage of pagan idolatry to develop further that we are created in the image of God by using Jesus as the very icon of God.

In the pastoral care of the Church today our combat is more subtle and the images more seductive. Materialism and superstitious practices are our temptations.

Old Testament

The canonical text of the OT begins with the story of creation. There God is portrayed as one who is free. God's last act of creation is that of human beings in God's own divine image (Gen 1:28). The Hebrew word *selem*, "image" or "statue," suggests that there is some recognizable form.

The likeness referred to in the Genesis text probably implies the abilities to multiply and to have dominion. Life and power are at the basis of these abilities. Being like God is the goal of life, and this is expressed as holiness. In the Holiness Code of Leviticus the fundamental commandment is: "Be holy, for I, the LORD, your God, am holy" (Lev 19:2). It is repeated incessantly in the Torah and used most effectively by the prophets. The only real image of God is the human being, free, life-giving, and powerful. The worst sin is to deny such dignity and so deny the existence of the sole God, Yahweh.

On the other hand, the supreme enemy is the pagan idol. This is especially true in agricultural societies in which the continuance of the desired, known life depends on the orderly succession of the seasons and the begetting of children. The higher powers, or the gods, seem to have created humans to serve their own purposes. However, the gods of war and of love, of fertility and pleasure, of protection of the family hearth, and of wisdom serve human needs as well as divine.

The Bible both encounters idolatry as enemy and embraces some of its inevitable conclusions. Humankind is created in the image and likeness of God. In this story the human being is not a puppet; the human being is a free person who can choose to grow in the image of God.

Endless stories are told of the combat of Israel with the pagan gods around them. The most seductive idolatry in Palestine was the fertility cult, especially that of Baal and his consort Asherah. This cult concentrated attention on the reproductive ability of human beings and of agriculture. In order to control such a basic force, the higher power was worshiped in ways that visually presented the kind of power desired. These powers were seductive because they seemed to be effective and their dramatic presentations were pleasurable. We have abundant evidences of such worship from archaeological digs in Palestine.

The story of Gideon, among many others, illustrates the courage needed to attack this idolatry (Judg 6:1–8:28). It took wondrous signs from God to convince Gideon that he could destroy his father's altar to Baal. Power and the will to act came only from Yahweh.

The dramatic story of Elijah's contest with the pagan priests of Baal on Mount Carmel also records the severity of the conflict (1 Kgs 18:1-46). What is at stake there is the people's images of God and of themselves. The biblical religion demanded total fidelity to being imitators of God and yet being free to live up to it.

There were other idols which exerted great influence on Israel, particularly warrior gods. It was not only seductively human to worship a conquering nations' gods, but it sometimes seemed the only politically expedient thing to do. For this reason, the war gods of Syria and especially Mesopotamia were worshiped. Sometimes, as in the reign of Manasseh, they practically displaced the altar of Yahweh in the Temple of Jerusalem (2 Kgs 21:7-9). Prophets such as Jeremiah and Isaiah poured scorn on this idolatry. Isaiah, in his great summons to judgment, derides the idols which must be fashioned by artisans and then carried on their shoulders (Isa 44:18). In the so-called Letter of Jeremiah against idolatry, the idols are mercilessly derided for not being able to keep themselves clean or to feed themselves (Bar 6:64).

After the bitter experiences of the Babylonian Captivity Judaism no longer seemed tempted to adopt outright paganism. There were temptations to conform to pagan religions, but they were much more subtle. The worship of the one true God had become the accepted norm of life; the pagan gods were scorned as "nothingnesses."

New Testament

Idolatry is much less a concern in the NT. The Jewish setting of the Gospels, where monotheism was taken for granted, helps to explain this. Only in the story of the tribute due to Caesar does the word image occur in the Synoptics (Matt 22:20; Mark 12:16; Luke 20:24).

However, idolatry is a major consideration for Paul since most of his dealings were with Gentiles. For him Jesus was the true image of God (2 Cor 4:4). This is clearly evident in the later Letter to the Colossians. "He is the image of the invisible God, the firstborn of all creation" (Col 1:15). We too are in the image of Jesus and of God (see Rom 8:29; 1 Cor 15:49; Col 3:10). These are not peripheral texts; they are at the heart of Pauline theology. He teaches that our access to the Father is through Christ. We grow into the image of Jesus, into his suffering image and his resurrected and glorious image, by being united with him. We do not worship some human image, but the image of God within us which becomes accessible to us through faith.

Paul takes the same scornful attitude toward idolatry in the Gentile world as did the prophets. "We know that 'there is no idol in the world'" (1 Cor 8:4). In Paul's world of reality they simply do not exist. However, he knows the power of idolatry. Romans 1–2 is a devastating social commentary on the power of idolatry to destroy the Roman world. So he writes: "although they knew God they did not accord him glory as God or give him thanks. Instead, they became vain in their reasoning, and their senseless minds were darkened. While claiming to be wise, they became fools and exchanged the glory of the immortal God for the likeness of an image of mortal man or of birds or of four-legged animals or snakes" (Rom 2:21-23).

Pastoral-Liturgical Tradition

The making of images of gods does not seem to be a major problem today and so we are inclined to think of it as a practice of the past. However, we live in an image-filled society and we have the same instincts. We often say that we worship the almighty dollar.

On the other hand, the need for an image which unites us is still essential. The Church's liturgy is full of visual images of God and of ourselves.

The Church has always contended with problems relating to visual representations of higher powers. The basic temptation remains, sometimes crudely in superstitious practices of worship of patron saints and sometimes in sophisticated dependence on secular science. We are always trying to control life and to keep the control for ourselves. Such an attitude is divisive of the race since it separates us in the pursuit of personal gain. Both the United States Bishops' Conference and Vatican II have frequently identified materialism as the supreme vice of the culture of the first world. That is our idolatry.

See: IMAGE OF GOD

JAMES A. FISCHER, C.M.

IMAGE OF GOD

An image is a material representation of something, often a deity. However, one of the creation narratives claims that humankind was made in the image/likeness of God, and another story states that Adam begot Seth in his likeness/image. In the NT, Jesus is seen as the image or divine prototype of God.

Old Testament

Creation. The first account of the creation of humankind consists of two short verses (Gen 1:27f.). There, humankind, male and female, is created in God's image and according to God's likeness. A reference to this statement is found in Genesis 9:6: "For in the image of God has man been made." Although the definite article appears in the Hebrew in this latter verse (the man), the literary context indicates that this is not an allusion to the first man but to all of humanity. All, including both male and female, are made in the image of God.

The Hebrew word for image refers to some kind of physical representation. It usually designates a molten image, painted picture, or some other form of material expression. The word for likeness denotes some less tangible representation. By juxtaposing these two words, the author has softened the material character of image with the less concrete nuance of likeness. This would suggest that the image/likeness of God should not be understood either as a purely spiritual entity (the soul) or as something simply material (physical resemblance). It transcends the physical/spiritual alternative without denying either. Hebrew thought seldom separated the physical and the spiritual, but usually considered the human being in entirety. It was the whole human being that was created in the image and according to the likeness of God, and the whole race, both male and female, was so created.

In this creation account, all of the other living things are said to be made "according to their kind" (a better translation than "every kind" or "all kinds," vv. 11f., 21, 24f.). Human beings are unique in that they were created in God's image, according to God's likeness (v. 26f.). This feature, along with the use of a verb that expresses direct and deliberate action on the part of God ("Let us make. . ." , v. 26a), clearly sets humankind apart from the rest of creation.

Very diverse interpretations of image of God have been advanced through the years. The most common understanding

459

has been that of the spiritual soul. Other explanations insist that the image is realized in sexual differentiation or in upright posture, or in the human ability to think, to decide, to love, or to create. Many contemporary scholars link the special commission given by God to human beings, that is, authority over the earth and the animals (v. 26), with this unique aspect of human nature. Such an understanding is probably closest to the ancient point of view. It sees the significance of image, not so much as the possession of some divine ingredient, but rather as a partner in relationship with the divine creator.

Vice-Regent. Most likely Israel, like its neighbors, understood image/likeness in relational terms. An ancient ruler was often considered the image of the god, a direct descendant of the god. This ruler was thought to exercise sovereign control in the place of the god as ruler in the land and over the land. When a particular image was installed, its location represented the locale and extent of the sovereignty of the deity and the jurisdiction of the ruling monarch. This kind of royal authority was provisional and contingent on the good will of the god.

The creation account in Genesis 1 depicts the man and the woman in just such a capacity. They were not menial slaves of the gods, created to bear the yoke of the gods, ministering to them and relieving them of the burden of daily work, as human beings are characterized in some other ancient Near Eastern myths. In Israel's tradition, they did indeed exercise dominion, but they did it in virtue of God's authority, not their own. They were images or representations of God; they were not sovereign in their own right. Actually, no ancient monarch really was.

This image/likeness defined not only the human couple's relationship with God but also their relationship with the animals and with the land. Though intimately linked to the land animals at creation (human beings seem to have appropriated the blessing that should have been given to the animals [v.

28, see v. 22]), the couple was commissioned to dominate them along with all the other living creatures and to subdue the earth. This charge clearly denotes authority over others, but it was not without limitation or restriction. Such restriction is implicit in the idea of image/likeness. Human beings are portrayed as representatives of, but not identical with, the true sovereign. Women and men were appointed vice-regents of the sole legitimate ruler. They were to be responsible to God for the earth and the things of the earth.

New Testament

There is a section of 1 Corinthians that preserves some of Paul's attempt to settle problems that existed in the liturgical assemblies. In order to reestablish the practice of head coverings for women, he utilized the theme of the image of God. However, he misrepresented its original meaning significantly. Where the early tradition maintained that both male and female were made in the image of God, Paul claimed that only the man is the image and glory of God, while the woman is the glory of the man (v. 7). He does this in order to reenforce gender distinctions, apparently a problem in that particular community.

The second significant reinterpretation of the theme is found in Paul's designation of Jesus as the image of the invisible God (Col 1:15, also see 2 Cor 4:4). It is clear that here Paul is using the metaphor in a way different from the Genesis use. The poetic construction links "image of God" with the phrase "the firstborn of all creation" in a way that the phrases interpret each other. Here Christ is perceived as the divine prototype, the one through whom all else was created.

See: CREATION, HUMANKIND

DIANNE BERGANT, C.S.A.

INHERITANCE

The laws of inheritance in ancient Israel attempted to ensure that land* and property remained within the family of origin.

A widow could not inherit the property or land of her deceased husband because that land would pass from the control of the deceased man's family since a widow normally returned to her father's family. Her husband's family would then lose claim to the land that was its means of economic sustenance.

Old Testament

Legal Practice. Only sons inherit and the eldest son receives a double portion (Deut 21:15-17). When there are no sons, daughters may inherit with the proviso that they marry within their clan or tribe so that the property they inherit does not pass outside the family (Num 36:6, 11). When there are no daughters to inherit, the deceased man's closest male relatives inherit (Num 27:8-11).

Laws such as these were to ensure that an equitable distribution of land remained intact. This was important in an agricultural society. Ownership of land was the basis of economic survival. By ensuring that families maintained control of land, this legislation helped guarantee that acquisition of extensive land holdings by a few to the detriment of the many would be difficult. The story of Naboth's vineyard (1 Kings 21) shows how seriously the ancient Israelites took the obligation to transmit the inheritance of their family intact. They were not free to alienate their family's real property that they received and were to hand on to the next generation.

By contemporary standards the ancient Israelite laws of inheritance are biased in favor of the male. The provision of Israelite law allowing a daughter to inherit was not the general practice in the ancient Near East. While it is unclear what rights daughters had in Babylon, the Assyrians positively excluded them from inheritance. Such bias was not based on sexism, but on the insistence that land and property do not pass from one family to another.

Though inheritance was an important concern in ancient Israel, biblical legislation is rather meager, though it is possible to make some inferences based on various narratives. For example, apparently all a man's sons could inherit, including sons born to slaves (Gen 21:10) and to prostitutes (Judg 11:1). According to the Code of Hammurabi (art. 170–171) the right of the sons of a concubine to inherit along with the sons of a man's wife was dependent on the man's recognition of them as his children. This procedure may have been operative in Israel too. The social status of the heir's mother was not an issue. Apparently the ancient Israelites were not as concerned about legitimacy as they were about preventing poverty, for a man without land was condemned to poverty or slavery.

Religious Metaphor. More significant than the legislation regarding inheritance is the use of this idea as a religious metaphor. In particular, Deuteronomy describes the land as the inheritance Israel has from Yahweh. God promised the ancestors of Israel that their descendants would come to possess Canaan (Deut 4:21, 38; 12:10; 15:4; 19:10; 20:16; 21:23; 24:4; 25:19; 26:1). Each tribe was to receive its portion of this inheritance (Josh 13:7; 14:2; 19:49). The land of course belonged to Israel's God and is called therefore "the inheritance of Yahweh" (1 Sam 26:19; 2 Sam 21:3). God fulfilled this promise when Joshua led the people across the Jordan to take possession of the land.

The point of this metaphor is that Israel's acquisition of its land was not its own achievement. It was a gift of God. Though the Deuteronomistic tradition describes the battles that the Israelite tribes had to fight and win before they controlled Canaan, the tradition also remembers that the land was God's gift to Israel. Israel's military achievements did not give it title to the land (Deut 8:17-18).

There is a problem with this metaphor. If the land is Israel's inheritance, one could argue that it was Israel's by right. That is precisely what the Deuteronomic tradition does not want to say. It wants to affirm that the land is God's gift to Israel—a gift that Israel did not merit and a gift to which Israel had no right.

The OT also describes Israel as God's inheritance. This is clearly an extension of the metaphor. It shows the closeness of God to Israel (Deut 9:26, 29). The psalms use this image frequently (Pss 33:12; 74:2). Israel then "belongs" to its God. Israel is not to act independently but in conformity to the divine will.

New Testament

In the OT inheritance refers to something quite tangible: the land. Ownership of the land was crucial to the peace and prosperity of the ancient Israelites. The NT gives up this land-based theology, but does not abandon the metaphors associated with it. In the NT what believers inherit is no longer the land but salvation (Heb 1:14), eternal life (Titus 3:7), a place in the reign of God (1 Cor 6:9-10; Gal 5:21); therefore, their inheritance is incorruptible (1 Pet 1:4). Believers receive their inheritance in view of their adoption as children of God and the identification with Jesus who is the true son and heir (Matt 21:38; Mark 12:7; Luke 20:14; Heb 1:2). The believer becomes a co-heir with Christ (Rom 8:17; Gal 3:29; 4:7).

A significant part of the NT's reinterpretation of this metaphor is its extension. The inheritance is not limited to those physically descended from Abraham to whom God made the promise. The gospel extends the promise and therefore the inheritance to the Gentiles as well (Gal 3:26-29; Eph 3:6). Galatians 3–4 uses this motif in speaking about the rights of the Gentiles to be heirs along with the Jews. The reason Paul uses this metaphor is the original OT assumption behind the idea of inheritance. Just as Israel had no claim on the land, believers have no claim on grace. The land was a gift that God gave to Israel as an inheritance, and grace was a gift that God gives to people through Jesus. No one can earn or merit it but can only gratefully receive it as a pure gift. The inheritance of believers does not come to them as a right (Gal 3:18). They share in the inheritance of believers through faith.

Paul continues with this metaphor when he asserts that while heirs are minors, they are no better than slaves who have no claim on the inheritance. Under the Law, the Jews were like minors. The coming of Christ brings them into their majority if they recognize that they will gain the inheritance promised when they are united to the true son (Gal 4:1-7). Paul's final point is homiletical. The Apostle says that Abraham's son by the slave Hagar did not inherit that which his son by Sarah did. Christians will come to their inheritance by rejecting slavery to sin (Gal 4:21–5:1).

Pastoral-Liturgical Tradition

This metaphor underscores the priority of what God does in establishing and maintaining a relationship with the believer. What is important here is that believers recognize that their relationship with God is not their own achievement, but is the consequence of God's gift to them—a gift that they could not earn. Reflection on this metaphor ought to prevent a Pelagian self-assurance that considers the believers' relationship with God as a by-product of their moral striving. Paul insisted that the Law was no longer in force for Christians. He did not mean that Christians reject the Law as a moral standard, but as a means of salvation. Obedience to the Law does not save Christians. The quality of their moral lives ought to be a testimony to the salvation they have as an unmerited gift of God given through Jesus.

Believers celebrate the liturgy not as a ritual that compels God's blessing, but as an act of praise and gratitude to God who is so generous with blessings. Baptism identifies the believer with Christ, the true heir. Through faith Christians open themselves to receive the gifts that God offers them as an inheritance. The Eucharist is not a reward for a good moral life, but it is a communion with God who is the inheritance of believers. This is why believers receive communion from the ministers of this sacrament rather than take it from them. God's forgiveness comes not because of an integral confession, but because of God's desire to be reconciled with believers and their grateful reception of this gift.

The OT used the metaphor of inheritance to help ancient Israel recognize that the land that was the basis of its prosperity was not theirs by right of conquest, although the tradition remembered that Israel got its land at least in part by violent means. The land belongs to God. It was God who gave it to Israel as an inheritance—not as a right. God recognized Israel as God's heir. The NT uses this metaphor to remind believers of the priority of God's action. It is through their baptismal identification with Jesus, the true son, that Christians become heirs with him.

See: GIFTS, LAND

LESLIE J. HOPPE, O.F.M.

ISAAC

Despite the richly developed pastoral traditions about Isaac, the OT itself knows Isaac only as a name, not as a fully developed character. Not even the name of Isaac's God, *The Fear of Isaac* (Gen 31:42, 53), is explained.

Old Testament

Isaac as a Main Character. OT traditions with Isaac as the main character are all retellings of stories about other ancestors. The story of Isaac and Rebekah at Gerar (Gen 26:1-11) retells the story of Abram and Sarai in Egypt (Gen 12:10-20) and the story of Abraham and Sarah at Gerar (Gen 20:1-18). The covenant between Isaac and Abimelech (Gen 26:26-33) retells the covenant between Abraham and Abimelech (Gen 21:22-34).

Isaac as a Minor Character. In none of the OT traditions without parallels is Isaac himself the main character. In the story of Isaac's birth (Gen 18:1-15; 21:1-8), Sarah is the protagonist. In the story of the sacrifice of Isaac (Gen 22:1-19) and the story of Isaac's marriage (Gen 24:1-67), Abraham and his slaves are the protagonists. In the story of Esau and Jacob's birth (Gen 25:19-

26) and the story of Isaac's blessing (Gen 27:1-45), Rebekah is the protagonist. Even the obituary of Isaac (Gen 35:28-29) is part of the genealogy of Jacob (Gen 35:22-29). These stories characterize Isaac neither as passive, nor manipulated. They either simply cast him in a minor role or as the antagonist who is overcome.

Consequently, the Isaac tradition never speaks for itself. Isaac is a phantom, seen only through the stories of Sarah, Abraham, Rebekah, Esau, and Jacob in which he appears without definition or development.

The Sacrifice of Isaac. Key words and key themes shared by the Hagar and Ishmael story (Gen 21:9-21) and the story of the sacrifice of Isaac (Gen 22:1-19) suggest that they were originally closer parallels than they appear now. In one story, the ordeal or sacrifice which Sarah demands (Gen 21:9-11) would have been conducted by Hagar (Gen 21:12-16), in the other by Abraham (Gen 22:1-10). Ishmael would have been the only victim placed helpless before Elohim (Gen 21:15-16; 22:9-10), who resolves the dispute by decreeing a covenant promising Ishmael land and children comparable to those of Isaac (Gen 21:17-21; 22:11-19).

Even though the identity of the victim has changed, the symmetry between the stories remains critical for understanding important aspects of the story of the sacrifice of Isaac. First, in no version of the story is Ishmael or Isaac a contender. The protagonists are Sarah, Hagar, and Abraham. They initiate the ordeal to clarify Elohim's covenant with them. Second, the protagonists struggle to resolve an external legal claim, not to resolve an interior crisis of faith. In contrast to modern literature, the Bible has little interest in the internal emotions of its characters; only external actions move the plot. And third, in contrast to modern characterizations of both the story of the sacrifice of Isaac and the Book of Job, the Bible understands God as intervening on behalf of the helpless to protect them from harm, not as tormenting them to see how they will react. Consequently, neither story celebrates Sarah, Hagar, and Abraham for blind obedience to a God who toys with their feelings by giving and then taking away. They are remembered for their struggle for freedom—for land and children of their own in a world where slavery seemed inevitable. And in both the story of Hagar and Ishmael and the story of the sacrifice of Isaac, Elohim is an ally, not an enemy in their pursuit.

The story of the sacrifice of Isaac also reflects Israel's struggle with the widespread practice of human sacrifice in the ancient Near East. Human sacrifice was not seen as barbaric. On the contrary, it demonstrated complete dependence upon God for life. Thus the story asks: "How else could Israel show its faith in Yahweh as the giver of life?" Abraham models the believer who seeks to offer a human sacrifice and then learns patience. The willingness to wait for land and children regardless of how long it might take and how unlikely it seemed that the promises could be fulfilled became Israel's demonstration of its complete dependence upon Yahweh for life.

New Testament

Genealogies in the NT continue the OT tradition merely of naming Isaac as God's covenant partner without comment (Matt 1:1-17; Luke 3:23-38; Acts 7:8). Elsewhere quite new understandings of Isaac appear in connection with the fundamental Christian teachings on salvation. On the one hand, the tradition in the Pauline Letters cites the story of Isaac's birth as an example of salvation by faith alone. For Romans 9:1-24 and Galatians 4:21-31, it is no easier to explain God's choice of Christians over Jews than it is to explain God's choice of Isaac over Ishmael. Both share a common human ancestry, but only one receives the divine promise. Salvation is not earned during life, it is given at birth. The tradition in the Pastoral Letters, on the other hand, cites the story of the sacrifice of Isaac as an example that "without works faith is idle . . . and that Abraham [was] justified by his works" (Jas 2:14-26).

Pastoral-Liturgical Tradition

The Lectionary is fascinated by how God's power endows the powerless in the Isaac stories. A barren woman, a condemned man, and a weakling are all called to do God's work. The power by which Jesus makes the sick well (Matt 8:5-17) is identified with the power by which Yahweh made Isaac's barren mother fertile. Likewise, Jesus lifts up the paralytic from his mat (Matt 9:1-8), just as Elohim lifts up Isaac from the altar. And finally, Jesus' choice of disciples who do not fast over those of John the Baptizer who do (Matt 9:14-17) is paralleled with Isaac's choice of the delicate Jacob over the hardier Esau.

The Church Fathers turned the lack of character definition in the OT Isaac into an enduring pastoral model of complete obedience to the will of God. The story of the sacrifice of Isaac became a prototype for the story of Jesus' passion. Jesus goes to the cross of Mount Golgotha as unquestioningly as Isaac goes to the altar on Mount Moriah (*The Epistle of Barnabas* 7:3; Clement of Alexandria, *Paedagogica* I.5.1; Strom. 2.5; Irenaeus, *Against Heresies* 4.4; Origen).

See: ABRAHAM, JACOB, SARAH

DON C. BENJAMIN, O.CARM.

ISRAEL

Old Testament

Origins of the Name. The etymology and meaning of the name Israel is uncertain. The etymology given in Genesis 32:28-29 implies that the name means "he who contends with God." The form suggests otherwise: "let God contend." Though the precise meaning of the name is unknown, it is a theophoric name, i.e., a personal name, a component of which is the name of a god. In this case, the divine name is "El," the chief god of the Canaanite pantheon. Though this name and the prerogatives of this god are ascribed routinely to the national God of the Israelites, the presence of the element "El" in the name for the worshipers of Yahweh* is surprising.

There are many names in the Bible with a theophoric element from Yahweh, e.g., *Elijah* (My God is Yahweh); *Jonathan* (Yahweh had given), and *Jehoahaz* (Yahweh grasps). Why does the name Israel contain a theophoric element connected with El instead of one associated with Yahweh?

One suggestion is that originally Israel was the geographic name. It referred to that part of the highlands located in the center of Canaan.* This area was known as Israel. Those who lived there were *bene Israel*, literally "the sons of Israel." Modern English translations render this phrase as "the Israelites" just as they render *bene Ammon* as "the Ammonites." The latter phrase refers to the people who live in the territory of Ammon. The God worshiped by the *bene Israel* was Yahweh. This God was not associated with the territory "Israel" but with the desert. This may explain why the name Israel does not contain a Yahwistic theophoric element. When the people who worshiped Yahweh moved beyond the central highlands, they continued to be called *bene Israel*, perhaps in recognition of the importance that the people living in Israel had among the rest of the worshipers of Yahweh.

The biblical tradition understands *bene Israel* literally. These were the physical descendants of Jacob* who, according to Genesis 32:21-29, was renamed Israel after his struggle with "the man" after crossing a ford of the River Jabbok on his way back to Canaan with his wives and children. The Book of Genesis is not as consistent with this name change as it is with the name change from Abram to Abraham in Genesis 17:5. After that verse the name Abraham appears consistently. After the name change in Genesis 32, Jacob and Israel occur with about the same frequency.

The name *bene Israel* or simply Israel refers to the worshipers of Yahweh who lived in Canaan. It is not likely that all these people were the physical descendants of Jacob. The origins of Israel were much more complicated. Israel was a more ethnically diverse group than would be possible were all the people descended from a single ancestor.

When and under what circumstances Israel came to existence is also not easy to determine. The first time the name occurs in a non-Biblical text is in the stele of Merneptah: "Israel is stripped bare, wholly lacking seed; Hurru has become a widow, due to Egypt." This monument celebrates the Pharaoh's victory over the Libyans in 1207 BCE. The stele lists all opponents over whom the Pharaoh was victorious. All the names in the stanza where Israel's appears are accompanied by a hieroglyphic sign that defines the names as referring to a town or a city-state e.g., Gaza, Ashkelon, and Gezer. Before the name Israel is a sign that appears to mean "people." Also the name Israel is masculine while the other names are feminine. According to this Egyptian inscription Israel related to Hurru (an Egyptian name for Canaan) as a husband to a wife. The scribe who composed this text did not understand Israel as a territory but as a group of people descended from a common ancestor.

Ethnic Designation. The association of the benê Israel with Jacob is understandable since tribal relationships were expressed in terms of blood relationship. Conceiving relationships in this way created a sense of equality between all descendants at a given level of descent. The political purpose of tribal identity was to mobilize power in view of some threat from a state political organization. One of the earliest biblical texts where the name Israel occurs is in Judges 5, a poem that celebrates a victory by several Israelite tribes over the forces of Hazor, a Canaanite city-state. Here Israel does not refer to a centralized political organization but to a loose confederation of tribes. These tribes opposed the attempt by Hazor to impose a uniform political order in Galilee. The tribal idea of social order centered on the loyalty of the heirs of a common ancestor. The loyalties to the tribe came before the loyalties due to the state—in this case the city-state of Hazor.

The stories of the tribes as related in the Book of Judges appear in an "all Israel" framework since the final shape of this book occurred much later than the events they purport to relate. The impression intended is that all the ancestors of the later Israelites took part in every conflict of the Israelite tribes. A careful reading of these stories shows that they were all local affairs. The idealized notion of "Israel" characteristic of a later period is imposed on stories that come from a time when the intertribal organization known as Israel was not very strong.

The National State. In a sense, tribal identity opposed the national identity that the state tried to foster. David established a national state in Canaan. The transition from an intertribal confederation to a national state was a process that extended over a long time. Saul was the first king of Israel. Saul took the first steps to make the transition. His military achievements brought him the loyalty of people of a large area. How extensive his kingdom was is not clear. The establishment of a national state was a personal achievement of David though it did not happen without some tension. The tension that this action caused is clear from the revolts that opposed David's rule (2 Samuel 15–18; 20:1-4). In the first instance the text says that Absalom was "stealing away the loyalties of the men of Israel" (2 Sam 15:6) and in the second the rallying cry of the revolt is "Every man to his tent, O Israel" (2 Sam 20:1).

David and Solomon were able to hold the Israelite tribes together in a personal union. This union collapsed immediately after the death of Solomon. The tribes rejected the Davidic national state with the cry: "To your tents, O Israel!" (1 Kgs 12:16). The national state established by David and maintained by Solomon was replaced by two rival kingdoms. The northern kingdom was known as Israel and the southern kingdom as Judah.

The Ideal Israel. The ancient Israelite literature that has survived in the Bible reflects the perspectives of Judah for the most part. Accordingly it does not recognize the legiti-

macy of the Kingdom of Israel, although its existence was foretold by a prophetic oracle (1 Kgs 11:26-32). Especially in the prophets then, Israel stands not for the historical reality of the northern kingdom, but of the "ideal" Israel in which all the elements of the nations would be united under the rule of the Davidic dynasty. After the fall of the northern kingdom to the Assyrians in 721 BCE, the more inclusive meaning of Israel became dominant. Josiah (640–609) attempted to reestablish the rule of the Davidic dynasty over the territory of the former northern kingdom by extending his "reform" into cities north of Jerusalem (2 Kgs 23:16-20). It was difficult for the kings of Judah to give up on the claims of the Davidic dynasty to rule over all Israel as promised in Nathan's oracle. Josiah was able to act on this dream because Assyria, troubled by internal problems, was no longer able to control its vassal states.

Israel is more than an ethnic or political term. It is a fundamental theological idea in the Bible. Central to this idea is that of election:* Israel is the chosen people of God. Israel is chosen to live in the land promised to its ancestors. The principal story line in the Books from Genesis to Joshua is how God chose Israel's ancestors, promised that their descendants would live in the land, and fulfilled those promises. This is the story that begins with Abraham and his immediate descendants. It reaches its climax with the miraculous deliverance of the Israelite slaves in Egypt and concludes with their victory over the indigenous population of Canaan and the settlement in their land. The promise is fulfilled.

Bound up with the story of the promise of the land and its fulfillment is another story line whose climax is not in the land of Israel, but at Sinai. In this story line, Israel is chosen to receive the Law. The story also begins with Abraham, whose descendants God chooses to be a source of blessing for all nations (Gen 12:3). God gave the descendants of Abraham commandments to order their lives so that they could fulfill their calling to be a blessing to the nations.

The association of Israel with the land comes from pre-exilic Israel, while its association with the Law comes from the postexilic situation. Still the exilic prophet Ezekiel does not describe the restoration of Israel apart from restoration to its land. He envisions a redistribution of the land and a retribalization of the people (Ezek 47:13–48:35).

A variation on the theme of Israel as a blessing to the nation also emerges in the prophets of the Exile. Ezekiel makes the same point when he asserts that God is vindicated through God's dealing with Israel. God's purpose in both punishing and restoring Israel is to show the power of God's justice and mercy to the nations (Ezek 36:22-23; 39:21; 37:28; 38:23). According to Isaiah 43:10, 12 and 44:8, Israel acts as a witness to the nations. Because of what God is doing for Israel, all nations will recognize the unique character of Israel's God.

The prophets see Israel as a political unity with a religious foundation. When they speak of a restoration following the fall of the two Israelite kingdoms, they envision a restoration that will embrace "all Israel." This probably meant the restoration of the national state established by David in its full territorial extent (Isa 49:5-6; 56:8; 66:20; Jer 30–31; Ezek 36:1-15; 37:15-28). The dream of restoring "all Israel" never faded since it was apparently the plan of the Hasmonean dynasty. Alexander Yannai (103–76 BCE) brought most of the territory of what was Solomon's kingdom under Jewish rule again. No wonder that he was the first Hasmonean to use the title "king" on his coins.

New Testament

Not every Jew was pleased with the achievements of the Hasmoneans to restore the kingdom. They saw Israel's identity in the observance of the Law rather than in a political state. Some of these people believed that the universal reign of God was immanent. They believed that their devotion to the Law would make possible the reign of God. The people of Qumran believed that their observances were laying the foundation of God's reign. Jesus proclaimed that his preaching was establishing the reign of God. The early Christians therefore thought that they were the legitimate heirs of ancient Israel and sometimes used the archaic language of the old tribal confederation to refer to itself (e.g., Gal 6:16; Jas 1:1; 1 Pet 2:9).

See: JACOB, LAND

LESLIE J. HOPPE, O.F.M.

ISRAELITE

Modern English translations of the Bible use the term "Israelite(s)" to translate the Hebrew expression *bene Israel*, i.e., "the sons [children] of Israel." The origin of this group is still a matter under study. The main problem in settling this question is matching the biblical accounts of a family arriving from Mesopotamia (Genesis 12–50) or a group of freed slaves from Egypt (Exodus–Joshua) with the evidence of archaeology. A related question is how the ancient Israelites may be identified culturally. What is distinctive about early Israelite material culture that can serve to mark the presence of the Israelites at a particular site?

The archaeological evidence supports the suggestion is that the *bene Israel* began as a tribal confederation in Canaan during the final period of Egyptian rule, which lasted from 1550 to 1150 BCE. The only written reference to early Israel outside the Bible is an inscription from a stele found in the mortuary temple of the Pharaoh Merneptah, who ruled Egypt at the end of the thirteenth century BCE. The stele contains a series of hymns celebrating Merneptah's victory over the Libyans in 1207 BCE.

Analysis of the Merneptah stele leads to several important conclusions. First, Israel was a military force to be reckoned with in the thirteenth century BCE. Second, Israel was not named for a town or a city-state. (The other political entities mentioned on the stele are geographical regions, towns, or city-states.) Finally, since the central highlands of Canaan witnessed a spurt of village settlement in the twelfth and eleven centuries, the Israelites were politically established *before* their settlement in the highlands.

Apparently at the end of the thirteenth century, the *bene Israel* were an important tribal confederacy of transhumant shepherds and perhaps some farmers in the territory of Canaan then ruled by Egypt through their Canaanite vassals. The Israelite tribal confederation began as an alternative to this two-tiered political system.

Supporting both the Egyptians and their Canaanite vassals was difficult for the villagers of the region. They were subsistence farmers, who were able to raise barely enough food for their needs. Taxation to support both the local and foreign political hierarchies was so heavy that it led many of the farmers to abandon their settlements and convert to pastoralism. The Israelite tribal confederation began as groups of these shepherds joined for mutual protection.

The collapse of Egyptian rule in Palestine in the twelfth century allowed the Israelite tribes to gain some control over the region and reestablish village settlements and farms. They were, however, not the only group that tried to supplant the Egyptians. Their chief rivals were the Philistines who came into Canaan from Europe and Anatolia. The Philistines and the Israelites vied for supremacy until David successfully neutralized the Philistine threat and established a small empire along both sides of the Jordan River. The Israelite tribes that emerged as a result of the economic and political oppression of the Egyptian monarchy found themselves part of a new monarchic system, though one ruled by an Israelite.

The Bible presents the Israelites as descendants of Jacob,* who receives the name Israel in Genesis 32:29. Each tribe is named for one of the sons of Jacob/Israel, though this is not consistent. For example, Ephraim and Manasseh are sons of Joseph. Judges 5:14-18 speaks of Machir and Gilead as if they were among the Israelite tribes. Neither is a son of Jacob.

Relating all the members of the confederation to a single ancestor may reflect tribal tradition, but it is as much ideological as real. Those who formed the Israelite tribal confederation withdrew their loyalty from a political, social, and economic system that they experienced as oppressive. They wanted to have nothing to do with the hierarchical political systems of Egypt and its client Canaanite city-states. By asserting that all members of the Israelite confederation were descended from a common ancestor, it made them all into brothers and sisters. While this did not eliminate all distinctions, it supported a more egalitarian way of conceiving social and political relationships.

The Israelite tribes began in response to the oppressive social and political system of Canaanite and Egyptian rule. They withdrew their loyalty from systems that they experienced as oppressive and developed a tribal confederation ruled by their own elders. The *bene Israel* (the "Israelites"), then, owed their origins to the impulse to resist oppression and to reject the absolute supremacy of the state. After the introduction of the monarchy under Saul and David, the kings of Israel experienced opposition from the prophets who likewise rejected the absolute supremacy of the Israelite kingdoms.

After the death of Solomon at the end of the tenth century BCE, the Davidic empire split into two separate kingdoms: Israel (also known as the northern kingdom) and Judah (also known as the southern kingdom). Before that split the term "Israelite" signified all the descendants of the former tribal confederacy. After that event, the term sometimes referred solely to the citizens of the Kingdom of Israel. In the eighth century BCE, the Assyrians incorporated the territory of the northern kingdom into their provincial system. As a political entity, the northern kingdom ceased to exist in 721 BCE. Many of its leading citizens were taken into other parts of the Assyrian Empire for resettlement. After the southern kingdom fell to the Babylonians in 587 BCE, some hoped that remnants of the two former northern and southern kingdoms would reunite (e.g., Ezek 37:15-22). This did not happen and the term "Israelite" became synonymous with the term "Judahite" or Jew.

Authors of the NT spiritualized the term "Israelite." They reflect the tendency in early Judaism to make distinctions within the Jewish community on the basis of observance. For example, Paul notes a difference between those who are Israelites by physical lineage and those who are Israelites by faith in Christ (Rom 2:28-29; 9:6). The single appearance of the word in the Gospel of John makes a similar differentiation. When Jesus describes Nathaniel as a "true Israelite" (1:47), he implies that one may be an external member of the people of God without being a genuine Israelite.

Though the usual use of the term "Israel" or "Israelite" in the NT refers to the historic people of ancient Israel and their descendants (e.g., Acts 2:29; 5:35; 13:16), it does not necessarily have negative connotations. Paul calls himself an "Israelite" (Rom 11:1; 2 Cor 11:22).

The term "Israelite" underwent several transformations. It began as a name for the people of Late Bronze Age Canaan who rejected hierarchy in favor of equality. It then served as the name of those who were citizens of the Davidic Empire and later of one of the kingdoms that was its successor. After the Exile, it became synonymous with Jew or Hebrew as a name of those who considered themselves adherents of the religion of Yahweh. The NT uses "Israelite" in one of two ways. It refers to the members of the historic people of God though it can also refer to those who have become part of that people through adoption in Jesus Christ.

See: CANAAN, HEBREW, ISRAEL, JEW

LESLIE J. HOPPE, O.F.M.

J

JACOB

The Stories of Jacob, Leah, and Rachel (Gen 25:19–36:43) are a window through which to view Israel's struggle for survival in the hostile world of 1250–1000 BCE. Israel remembered them the way it understood itself—as survivors who compensated for lack of power by an ability to manipulate the power of others.

Old Testament

Jacob or Israel was the favorite ancestor of a Middle (2000–2500 BCE) or Late (1500–1250 BCE) Bronze Age people who appear both in the Bible and in documents from Mesopotamia and Egypt. They lived north of Jerusalem and on both sides of the Jordan. Jacob's rivals all lived along the frontiers of this area—Esau lived in Edom along the south; Laban in Aram along the north, and Shechem along the west. Jacob's encounters with God took place at Jabbok and Bethel (Gen 28:10-22), important sanctuaries in the area.

The villages where Jacob's stories were told were always threatened by rivalry from within and invasion from without. Similarly, Jacob was always embroiled in conflict—with Esau his brother, with Laban his uncle, with Levi and Simeon his sons, and even with Yahweh, his god. Jacob is remembered, not as a trouble maker, but as a survivor. His position was never secure and had to be continually defended.

Early Israel was a people on the margins of society and, like all marginal people, it admired the clever who improved themselves at the expense of the establishment. (Cleverness is the wisdom of the poor.) Jacob tricked Esau into selling him his birthright (Gen 25:19-34), Isaac into designating him as his heir (Gen 27:1-45), Laban into selling him his sheep (Gen 30:25-43) and his land (Gen 31:1–32:3), and even Yahweh into letting him cross the Jabbok (Gen 32:23-33).

Jacob was not an outlaw, but he knew how to work the system to his own advantage. Cuneiform tablets from Nuzi, an important Mesopotamian city around 1500 BCE, now document Jacob's legal sophistication by showing that birthrights could be bought and sold; oral wills, even when conferred on the wrong beneficiary, were irrevocable; citizens like Laban who had no natural heirs could adopt an heir like Jacob (Gen 29:1-30) and title to property belonged to whomever could produce the *teraphim* statues of a household's gods (Gen 31:19-35).

Jacob, Leah, and Rachel not only could manipulate society, but also could use nature to their advantage as well. Leah used mandrake plants to conceive a child (Gen 30:14-21). (Mandrakes are only one plant which the clever in traditional societies use to help the childless conceive.) Jacob built a breeding corral from multicolored poles so that his sheep would conceive multicolored lambs. Traditional societies have a wonderful inventory of techniques like this for priming nature to imitate human behavior.

Nonetheless, the Bible is quite balanced in its assessment of cleverness, which is, at best, only a temporary challenge to the establishment. The clever are fugitives at risk. Jacob was always on the run, a wandering Aramean (Deut 25:5-10). Esau (Gen 27:30-45), Isaac (Gen 27:46–28:9), and Laban (Gen 31:1-24) all exiled Jacob when they discovered their losses. And the Jacob who outwitted Isaac was eventually outwitted by Simeon and Levi (Gen 34:1-31) and Joseph (Gen 47:27–48:22).

The Bible does not celebrate cleverness to teach that it is all right to lie, cheat, and steal to get ahead, nor even to say that it is all right for ancestors, but not for ordinary people. Biblical cleverness celebrates the tenacity with which the poor struggle to survive and honors Jacob's God for helping the poor, rather than supporting the powerful.

New Testament

Luke's Gospel particularly continues the traditions of Jacob, Leah, and Rachel by highlighting *anawim,* or marginal people, like Mary of Nazareth for whom God unseats the powerful (Luke 1:50-53). John's Gospel (John 1:51; 3:31-36) portrays Jesus as the new Jacob who reunites heaven and earth just as Jacob did by founding Bethel. Also, on the principle that the clever like Jacob are always at risk, Romans 9:1–11:36 argues that Christians are as justified in laying claim to the blessings of Jews as Jacob was in laying claim to the blessings of Esau.

Pastoral-Liturgical Tradition

In the Lectionary, Christians toast their designation as the new and unexpected heir to Israel's blessings with wine (Matt 9:14-17) just as Isaac toasted Jacob, his new and unexpected heir (Gen 27:1-45). Jesus

awakens an official's daughter from death (Matt 9:18-26) and candidates from the waters of baptism, just as El awakened Jacob at Bethel.

See: ABRAHAM, ISAAC, ISRAEL, JOSEPH

DON C. BENJAMIN, O.CARM.

JEALOUSY

Jealousy is a passionate devotion to good, either one's own good or that of another. Both the OT and the NT have a single word group to express this devotion. The biblical notion includes both jealousy, which implies vice, and zeal, which implies virtue.

Old Testament

In the OT jealousy is associated more with God than with humans. "I, the LORD, your God, am a jealous God" (Exod 20:5; Deut 4:24; 5:9; 6:15; Josh 24:19; Nah 1:2). This prelude to the Decalogue becomes a conventional formula. God is even named "The Jealous One" (Exod 20:5; 34:14; Deut 4:24; 5:9; 6:15). An opposing pagan idol is called "the statue of jealousy" by Ezekiel (Ezek 1:14; 8:2, 3, 5; 23:25; 36:5, 6).

In the distinctive Israelite faith there was only one God. Any attack on this monotheistic belief endangered everything in the religious code. God claimed to be a jealous God and threatened with the severest punishment those who gave worship to any other god. Hence his anger blazed up against Zion for worshiping false gods (Zech 8:2). Jealousy is a fire (Ezek 36:5; 38:19; Zeph 1:18; 3:8); it is divine anger (Deut 29:19; Ezek 35:11); it is characteristic of God as a warrior (Isa 42:13). God is wrapped in it (Isa 59:17). The heroes in the sacred stories from Moses to the Maccabees were always those who had zeal to resist worship of another god even at the danger to their own lives. The standard condemnation for the Kings of Israel was that they had committed the "sin of Jeroboam." At first, that sin was worship of God in the form of a bull; later it was seen as outright idolatry. So God is acknowledged as jealous both by the prophets (1 Kgs 19:10, 14;

Isa 12:13; Zeph 1:18; 3:8; Zech 1:14; 8:2 [jealous for Zion]) and by the Wisdom writers (Ps 79:5).

God's jealousy, however, is also protective. God is jealous for the land (Joel 2:18), for the people (Isa 26:11), and for God's own name that has been challenged because the people have not been restored to their land (Ezek 39:25). God owns this people and has plans for them; those who oppose God face divine anger and jealousy for this people.

Only rarely is the human emotion of jealousy the focus, and then the Hebrew word is often translated anger, wrath, devotion for it. Numbers recounts the curious test of bitter waters for a woman whose husband is overcome by jealousy that she might have committed adultery (Num 5:14, 15, 18, 25, 29, 30). Phineas is said to have been jealous for the Lord (Num 25:11). Proverbs states that a cuckold husband can be dangerous. "For vindictive is the husband's wrath [jealousy], he will have no pity on the day of vengeance" (Prov 6:34). The Canticle of Canticles observes at its climax that "stern as death is love, relentless as the nether world is devotion [jealousy]; its flames are a blazing fire" (Song 8:6). True love is jealous; it will not allow the beloved to be taken away.

New Testament

The NT has much less to say about jealousy. The jealousy of God is not emphasized since polytheism among Jews or Christians, at least of a blatant sort, was not a crucial problem. Nothing is said about God being a jealous God.

Jealousy as a human emotion is mentioned among the ethical considerations. Paul remembered the lesson of history when he asked himself why his Jewish co-religionists had not listened to the good news. He saw it as a repetition of what had happened in the past. "But I ask, did not Israel understand? First Moses says, 'I will make you jealous of those who are not a nation; with a senseless nation I will make you angry'" (Rom 10:19). God used this human jealousy for a good result. "But through their transgression salvation has come to the Gentiles, so as to make them jealous" (Rom 11:11). Jealousy in the sense of a virtuous drive is found in one passage: "For I am jealous of you with the jealousy of God, since I betrothed you to one husband to present you as a chaste virgin to Christ" (2 Cor 11:2). This statement seems to emulate the protective jealousy of God and the human love spoken of in the Song of Songs.

Pastoral-Liturgical Tradition

Jealousy, both good and bad, has always played a role in the Church's history and liturgy. Perhaps Cyprian was right in seeing human jealousy as the most dangerous and often secret evil in the life of Christians. Since so much power is concentrated in any organized religion, it is normal that there should have been power struggles for control of the papacy, of bishoprics, of material wealth and social privilege. Perhaps most upsetting have been the stories of all the founders of religious orders, such as Francis of Assisi; Alphonsus Ligouri, the founder of the Redemptorists; Jean Jugan, the foundress of the Little Sisters of the Poor, who were deposed from leadership by lesser people who were jealous of their influence and authority. In our imitation of the saints we put particular emphasis on humility. They were consumed, as Paul was, with a pure zeal that did not take account of human self-profit. It is not an easy or common virtue.

So the Church in its liturgy has emphasized that all glory and honor belong to God. In the Eucharistic Prayer we have added the ancient Byzantine liturgical acclamation to the Our Father: "For thine is the kingdom and the power and the glory." Much of our struggling in the present-day Church is a question of jealousy over powers and privileges. We forget the central teaching that there is but one God who demands that all honor be paid to him.

See: IDOLATRY

JAMES A. FISCHER, C.M.

JERICHO

Jericho is a city located in the Jordan Valley twenty-three miles east of Jerusalem* and six miles north of the Dead Sea. There is evidence of human occupation in the region from the Mesolithic period (9000 BCE). What made the site so attractive is a bountiful spring that waters the plain where Jericho is found. During the Neolithic period (8000–4000 BCE) a stone wall surrounded the city. Its most distinctive feature was a circular tower rising twenty-five feet above the city. The period witnessed the transition of Jericho's inhabitants from food gatherers to food producers. Canaan* went through a period of urbanization in the Early Bronze Age (3200–2000 BCE), and Jericho shows evidence of the intense building activity at that time. It was destroyed and rebuilt several times, but in the Late Bronze Age (1500–1200 BCE) that witnessed Israel's entrance into Canaan, Jericho was a small unwalled settlement.

The Bible asserts that the Israelites entered Canaan by crossing the Jordan River at a ford near Jericho (Josh 3:14-16). The Book of Joshua describes a miraculous victory over a heavily fortified Jericho (Joshua 6). This story reads more like the description of a liturgical procession than a military maneuver. It is a theological reconstruction of the fall of the city rather than an account based on a living memory of any conquest of Jericho. For those who insist on the historicity of every biblical story, Jericho was an interesting test case. Archaeological excavations have not helped bolster their cause. The archaeological evidence does not support the story in Joshua 6.

The Israelites did not settle in Jericho in any large numbers until the ninth century. It may be that Jericho's spring became polluted because of the intense occupation of the site from the Mesolithic period and could no longer support a large urban population during the period of Israel's monarchy. It was during this four-hundred-year abandonment of the site that much of the Late Bronze Age material eroded, leaving scant material for the archaeologist to recover.

After the Babylonian invasion of Judah in the sixth century, Jericho was abandoned again. Subsequent occupation shifted the site of the settlement away from the old mound closer to the spring where the modern city is located. The Seleucid general Baccides fortified the new site of Jericho (1 Macc 9:50). It was where Simon Maccabee was assassinated (1 Macc 12:11-17). Alexander Yannai (107–76 BCE) built a palace at the Wadi Qelt a little more than a mile south of ancient Jericho. Herod the Great (33–4 BCE) renovated and expanded the royal buildings. These served as a convenient winter retreat.

Jericho played no significant role in the ministry of Jesus or in the history of the early Church. Jesus was baptized near Jericho (Matt 3:17). He passed through the city on his way to Jerusalem (Matthew 20). He healed Bartimaeus there (Mark 10:46-50) and was welcomed by Zacchaeus (Luke 19:1-11). The road that linked it to Jerusalem provided the setting for the parable of the good Samaritan (Luke 10:30). Hebrews 11:30 is the only text outside the Gospels that mentions Jericho. It is a homiletic allusion to Joshua 6.

See: CONQUEST, JOSHUA

LESLIE J. HOPPE, O.F.M.

JERUSALEM

The biblical and liturgical traditions treat Jerusalem as both a concrete and symbolic reality. In the OT, Jerusalem is the city that became the capital of the Davidic dynasty and the earthly throne of the Divine Monarch. In the NT, Jerusalem represents those who accept Jesus and those who reject him. The liturgy recognizes Jerusalem as a historical place and as a heavenly goal.

Old Testament

The Geography and History of Jerusalem. Jerusalem means "foundation of Shalem," a god found in the Ugaritic texts. However, the more popular understanding links *shalem* with *shalom,* the Hebrew word for "peace." An ancient city, Jerusalem is mentioned already during the mid third millenium BCE. Melchizedek,* who blessed Abraham, is identified as the "king of Salem" (Gen 14:18-20). Although Joshua captured its king (Josh 10:1-11), the city's natural fortifications left it intact until David took it from the Jebusites for his capital.

Situated on the watershed of Palestine, Jerusalem overlooked the north-south trading routes along the high ridge as well as the east-west routes from the Mediterranean to Jericho. Its geographical location consists of two hills separated by a shallow valley. This quadrangular area is bound on the west and south by the steep valley of Hinnom and on the east by the valley of the Kidron brook. Although the western hill was more strategic because of its height, the only perennial source of water flowed from the Gihon Spring in the southeast corner. Thus the earliest habitation and fortification were made on the southern spur of the eastern hill, Mount Zion. Even so, the spring lay beyond the natural fortification, and a shaft was sunk to meet a tunnel that provided access during war.

According to 2 Samuel 5:6-10, David used this tunnel to enter and conquer Jerusalem, which he named the City of David. The captured town, a bit more than ten acres, was triangular, reflecting the shape of promontory projecting south from the main ridge. Jerusalem served David well as a capital, for it belonged neither to the north nor the south but to the king alone. David brought the ark of the covenant with its tent to Jerusalem and thereby made the royal city the center of worship (2 Samuel 6; Psalm 132). David's proposal to build a temple was rejected by God who instead made David a house, that is, a dynasty "forever" (2 Samuel 7). Still David acquired as a place for the ark the threshing floor of Araunah the Jebusite, situated just north of the Davidic city on the top of Mount Zion (2 Sam 24:15-25; 1 Chronicles 21). Here Solomon built the Temple with a palace complex in the style of Phoenicia and Syria, and he extended the city walls northward to sur-

round Mount Zion (1 Kgs 5–7; 10:14-21; 2 Chr 3:1). Solomon built a separate house for Pharaoh's daughter, as well as temples for gods of his other foreign wives (1 Kgs 9:24; 11:7-8). With the division of the kingdom after Solomon's death, Jerusalem remained the capital of Judah, the southern kingdom. Though poorer than its northern counterparts, Jerusalem enjoyed the stability of a single dynasty with a descendant of David sitting on the throne until its destruction in 586 BCE.

Various kings continued the fortification and glorification of the city (2 Chr 26:9-10; 27:3-4). After the fall of the northern kingdom, Hezekiah further strengthened the fortifications and routed waters of the Gihon Spring through the famous Siloam tunnel, which continues to carry water even to this day (2 Chr 32:4-5). This foresight, presumably, contributed to the city's ability to withstand, if barely, the seige of Sennacherib in 701 BCE. As Assyrian power began to wane, Josiah (630–609 BCE) was able to extend the state's boundaries and carry out a religious reform. He refurbished the Temple and removed the sanctuaries of foreign cults whose existence in Jerusalem has been confirmed by archaeology. The city had by then spread west to include the valley and western hill of what is now the Old City.

After the death of Josiah, the city suffered its greatest tragedy. Its leaders looked to Egypt and rebelled against the new eastern power, Babylon. The city fell in 597 BCE to Nebuchadnezzar, who deported the upper class with the new king Jehoiakin. Zedekiah, left as titular king, rebelled again ten years later. Nebuchadnezzar laid seige to the city for eighteen devastating months. When Jerusalem fell in 586 BCE, Babylon burned the Temple, tore down its walls, and led more into exile. The fall of Jerusalem was one of the most significant events in the history of Israel. It challenged many theological assumptions and caused its theologians to look deeper into the mystery of God.

Following the conquest of Babylon in 539 BCE, Cyrus, the Persian king, granted permission for the rebuilding of the Temple, which was dedicated in 515 BCE. The city, however, did not become viable again until Nehemiah rebuilt its wall around 450 BCE (Neh 2:11–3:32). Both he and Ezra bring about a religious reform based on Jewish law and the centrality of Jerusalem with the high priest taking the dominant religious and political role.

Alexander the Great conquered Palestine in 332 BCE and brought the influence of Greece. Hellenization continued after his death under the Ptolomies, and after them under the Seleucids of Syria who took control in 200 BCE. The most famous of these rulers, Antiochus IV, sought to press the Hellenization of the country and erected in the Temple a statue of Zeus, the famous "abomination of desolation." The ensuing Maccabean revolt ended the Seleucid rule with the purification of the Temple celebrated by the festival of Purim.

The Theology of Jerusalem. As the city of the divine and human king, Jerusalem reflected its ancient Near Eastern counterparts, and the theology developed in Jerusalem, typically called the Zion theology, bears marks of the surrounding cultures with a focus on the image of God as king who is both warrior and judge. Just as Baal was master of the chaotic waters, so "the LORD is enthroned above the flood . . . as king forever" (Ps 29:10).

The stability of the Davidic dynasty contributed to the development of this theology. Both Psalms 46:6 and 48:9 suggest the inviolability of Jerusalem, which is bound up with the eternal promise of the Davidic covenant (1 Samuel 7; Ps 89:37) and the invincibility of the "LORD SABAOTH" over both cosmic and human enemies (Pss 46:6; 48:4; 76:5-6; 93:3-4). The common images for kingdom from the ancient Near East form an interrelated whole: throne, house, city, and mountain.

The cherubim throne serves as an image of royal presence and the giving of law and judgment (Ps 122:5). The Zion theology emphasizes the dwelling of God in the holy of holies (1 Kgs 8:12-13) and divine kingship which, perhaps, was celebrated at the autumn Feast of Booths (Psalms 47; 93; 96–100). The insistence upon God's presence and "dwelling" in Jerusalem is balanced by the absence of any image for God upon the cherubim throne. Psalm 11:4 expresses this paradox of the immanent and the transcendent: "The LORD is in his holy temple, the LORD's throne is in heaven."

During the reform of King Josiah (630–609 BCE; 2 Kings 22–23), the Deuteronomistic theology attempted with some success to purify the Jerusalem cult of all foreign influence by centralizing the sacrificial cult in Jerusalem (Deut 12:13-14). This theology also moved away from the anthropomorphic idea of God enthroned in Jerusalem; the city became instead the dwelling place for God's name (Deut 12:11; 1 Kgs 8:16-20). The "ark of the covenant" was transformed from the footstool of the throne into the box containing the tablets of the Ten Commandments and the focal point for the Torah, the Teaching of Moses. This movement toward transcendence gathers strength with the destruction of Jerusalem and is reflected also in the Priestly theology that speaks of God's glory dwelling in the Temple (Ezekiel 10–11; 43). Before the destruction of the city, Ezekiel sees God's glory rise out of the city, and later in a vision of the new Jerusalem, the prophet sees God's glory return (Ezek 10; 43:1-9). The vision underlines the independence of God's power from the city.

The Hebrew word for "city" is feminine, and the ancient cities, encircled by their walls, offered womb-like safety of a mother to their inhabitants. Given this, the metaphors for the city explore the images of women, both positively and negatively. As the faithless city, God condemns Jerusalem as a harlot (Isa 1:21). Raped by the nations in punishment, "she" is left as a widow to weep (Lamentations 1–2; 4). Even so, the larger tradition expects the repentance and transformation of the city (Zechariah 3).

Jeremiah 2:1-3 describes the city as the innocent bride of old. Second Isaiah takes up the image of the barren and bereaved mother who becomes the fruitful mother miraculously receiving her children because God is not a mother who forgets (Isa 49:14-21; 54). Psalm 87 expands this notion and presents the city as the birthplace of all people and nations. In Psalm 48:13-15, Jerusalem with "her" many towers and ramparts becomes a manifestation of God. Isaiah 66:7-14 transfers the image of the Jerusalem as mother to God and makes the city thereby the manifestation of God as mother.

Finally, Sinai gives way to Zion as the central mountain of Israel's religion. Though only a hill, Zion takes on the dimensions of strength and mystery in the theology of Jerusalem. In Psalm 48:3, Mount Zion is identified with Mount Saphon (meaning "north"), the seat of the Syro-Phoenician pantheon (see also Isa 14:13-14) and serves as the connecting point with the heavens (Ps 78:68-69; 76:3, 9). With this, Jerusalem takes its place in cosmic space and time. As Isaiah 2:2 says, "In days to come, the mountain of the LORD's house shall be established as the highest mountain and raised above the hills. All nations shall stream toward it."

In summary, Jerusalem, as the throne, house, city, and mountain of the Davidic king and Divine Ruler, served as a part used for the whole in many ways. The positive and negative imagery, its earthly and cosmic connections made the city a symbol of the people's tragedy and triumph. As the city chosen by God, Jerusalem became and remains the holy city in and through which God is made manifest.

See: ARK OF THE COVENANT, ASSYRIA, BABEL/BABYLON, CHERUBIM, FEASTS, GLORY, MELCHIZEDEK, SOLOMON, TENT, WORSHIP

HARRY HAGAN, O.S.B.

New Testament

In the NT, no apparent significance is to be attached to the two spellings for Jerusalem, *Hierosolyma* and *'Ierousalēm*. The city is likewise called "Sion." Geographically one has to go up to the city or come down from it. While the Synoptics report that Jesus only once went up to Jerusalem, John, who probably is more accurate, speaks of three such journeys. The center of Jewish religious and political life and associated with the Temple for good or ill, Jerusalem for Jesus and the earliest Church was most important. In 70 CE the city underwent a terrible siege and ultimate destruction by the Romans.

Jerusalem in the NT has many symbolic associations. Positively, people from Jerusalem listened to Jesus, and women from Galilee followed him all the way up to Jerusalem (Mark 15:40-41). Jerusalem remains sacred; no one is to swear by it (Matt 5:35). Jesus wanted to benefit it and says, "How often would I have gathered your children together as a hen gathers her brood under her wings, and you would not" (Matt 23:37; see also Luke 13:34). All four gospels speak of Jesus' riding on an ass and entering Jerusalem as her king. There he cleanses the Temple and celebrates the Last Supper.

On the other hand, opponents of God's prophets and messengers and of Jesus come from Jerusalem. Jerusalem kills the prophets, stones those who are sent to her, and rejects Jesus' efforts to touch its heart. The Temple stands under the judgment of desolation (Matt 23:37-38; Luke 13:34-35). Jesus himself must travel there to suffer and die (Mark 10:32; par.). Some NT writers treat Jerusalem in more detail.

Since he records no resurrectional appearances there, is Mark anti-Jerusalem? Luke develops what he finds in his sources and gives special import to Jerusalem. Four scenes in Jerusalem may provide a framework for Luke-Acts (Luke 1:5–4:13; 19:45–24:53; Acts 1:4–7:60; 21:18–26:32). Jesus is presented in the Temple, and only Luke has the Great Insertion (9:51–19:28), Jesus' extended journey to Jerusalem filled with instructions for the disciples. This "way" imitates that of Moses and the chosen people through the desert and later becomes a name for Christianity. For Luke Jesus is a prophet who must die in Jerusalem. More than the other Synoptics, Luke describes Jesus' entry into Jerusalem in terms of Zechariah 9:9: the arrival of her king; and with historical details, he expands on the prediction of Jerusalem's fall (Luke 19:41-44; 21:20-24). Jerusalem rejects Jesus and there he endures his passion and death, to which the weeping "daughters of Jerusalem" furnish the correct response (Luke 23:27-31). Yet for Luke in Jerusalem Jesus is also raised from the dead, appears to his disciples and ascends into heaven.

Jerusalem helps to link Luke's Gospel and Acts. The disciples are not to leave the city but to await the reception of the Spirit and be Jesus' witnesses, "beginning from Jerusalem" (Acts 1:8; see also Luke 24:47). This they begin at Pentecost. The life of the early Christian community in Jerusalem (Acts 1–5) constitutes a model for later Christians. Nonetheless, persecution of Christians begins in Jerusalem; Stephen (Acts 7:60) and James (Acts 12:2) are even killed. The first Church council occurs in Jerusalem (Acts 15:1-35; see also Gal 2:1-10), and Paul sees a missionary vision there (Acts 22:17-21). Although persecution awaits him, Paul resolves in the Spirit to go up to Jerusalem for the feast of Pentecost (Acts 19:21; 20:16, 20-24; 21:10-14). Like Jesus, the innocent Paul must suffer and be rejected there. With the activity of Paul Luke portrays how, in accord with God's will, Christianity moves from Jerusalem to Rome. In summary, in Jerusalem Jesus (and his followers) ministers, worships (e.g., Luke 2:41-43; Acts 8:26-27; 22:17; 24:11), saves, but is rejected, suffers, and is killed. In Acts, Luke lets Jerusalem little by little fade into the background.

In the Fourth Gospel each of the three times that Jesus travels to Jerusalem relates to a Jewish feast (John 2:13; 5:1; 7:10; see also 11:55; 12:12). Twice, Jesus' healings there relate to pools (5:2-18; 9:7), to whose existence archaeological evidence testifies. According to John, true worshipers will worship God in spirit and truth and not on Mount Gerizim or in Jerusalem (John 4:19-24).

To defend his apostleship, Paul corrects a misunderstanding about when he first went up to Jerusalem (Gal 1:17–2:2), and so his statement about beginning his mission there (Rom 15:19) needs to be nuanced. He dedicates considerable energy to the collection for the poor in Jerusalem, and apparently is the first Christian to distinguish between the present Jerusalem in slavery with her children and the Jerusalem above who is free and our mother (Gal 4:25-27).

Later NT writings expand on this latter idea. For the author of Hebrews, Christians have come to the city of the new covenant and of the living God, the heavenly Jerusalem (Heb 12:22-24). The Book of Revelation sees Mount Sion as the throne of the Lamb (Rev 14:1-3) and the heavenly Jerusalem as his bride. The heavenly Jerusalem possesses the glory of God and the radiance of a rare jewel. On its gates are the names of the twelve tribes, and on her twelve foundations the names of the apostles. God and the Lamb are her temple, and the glory of God her light, the Lamb her lamp. She gives light to all the nations and is the center to which the kings of the earth bring the splendor of the whole world. Since there is no night, her gates are never shut. Nothing unclean nor any irreverent person can enter, but only those written in the Lamb's book of life. From the throne of God and the Lamb, whose reign lasts forever, flows a life-giving, healing river, and the Lamb's servants worship him (Rev 21:9–22:5).

See: APOSTLE, CITY, COVENANT, DEATH, MISSION, PASSION, REIGN OF GOD, RESURRECTION, SALVATION, SUFFERING, TEMPLE, TRIBES, WAY, WITNESS, WORSHIP

ROBERT F. O'TOOLE, S.J.

Pastoral-Liturgical Tradition

Jerusalem as Historic Place. Jerusalem appears as the final goal of Jesus' journey in the celebration of Passion (Palm) Sunday.

Jerusalem, of course, has a special place in both OT and NT. In the OT it is the Lord's city, the site of the Temple.* In the NT it is the final goal of Jesus' journey; this latter theme is especially prominent in Luke's Gospel. It is the final goal of all religious yearning. The ascent psalms, written to accompany the actual journey of pilgrims to Jerusalem, also serve as texts for those who cannot make the journey physically. The city that the Deuteronomic reform placed at the center of Jewish worship becomes the final goal of Jesus' life, the place of the final consummation of his life of obedience to God.

The liturgy of Lent, especially, sees Jerusalem as associated with the historic events of Jesus' life, death, and resurrection: "Now we must go up to Jerusalem where all that has been written about the Son of Man will be fulfilled" (Sunday I of Lent, antiphon for Psalm 110 at Evening Prayer II).

As the site of Jesus' passion, death, and resurrection, Jerusalem becomes a key site of Christian pilgrimage. The pilgrim Egeria wrote a diary in which she shares her journey through the Holy Land, and spends an enormous amount of space describing Jerusalem and the elaborate liturgy celebrated there. Jerusalem remained an important pilgrimage site; the Crusades, at least in part, had the goal of keeping the Holy Land accessible to pilgrims.

The celebration of the procession with palms on Passion (Palm) Sunday is a ritual participation in this final journey of Jesus to Jerusalem.

This importance of Jerusalem as a concrete, historical, physical site is crucial to the tradition and to modern piety: ours is an incarnate faith. But it is primarily as a symbol that Jerusalem forms a part of the liturgy.

Jerusalem as Heavenly Goal and Messianic Fulfillment. The Book of Revelation, in line with many of the apocalyptic writings of the Intertestamental period, presents Jerusalem as the site of the final fulfillment. This theme from Revelation is picked up by the liturgy and used for reflection on several feasts and other celebrations.

The season of Advent in particular has this use of the symbol of Jerusalem. The constant refrain at Morning Prayer in response to the reading is: "Your light will come, Jerusalem; the Lord will dawn on you in radiant beauty. You will see his glory within you." The emphasis on "glory," "light," "radiance," captures the sense that Jerusalem is the site of the dwelling of God's majesty. The coming of Christ, both the first coming, historically and in time, and his second coming in judgment at the end of time, bring to mind the imagery in Ezekiel and the Book of Revelation that Jerusalem will be transformed to be that dwelling perfectly. The antiphons for the liturgy of the hours especially delight in using the imagery of Zion and Jerusalem to speak of the intensity of our expectation and longing: "Rejoice, Jerusalem, let your joy overflow; your Savior will come to you, alleluia" (Advent Sunday III, antiphon for Psalm 113, Evening Prayer I).

The theme comes up as well during Lent, and as one would expect, on Passion (Palm) Sunday at the Commemoration of the Lord's Entrance into Jerusalem. Here the blessing of palms (A) says: "May we reach one day the happiness of the new and everlasting Jerusalem by faithfully following him who lives and reigns for ever and ever."

One last example of this type of reflection on Jerusalem as the final goal of our life and as the symbol of having arrived at our destination, God's dwelling, is found in the funeral liturgy. It is the well-known antiphon for accompanying the body of the deceased from the church to its final burial place, *In paradisum*: "May the angels lead you into paradise; may the martyrs come to welcome you and take you to the holy city, the new and eternal Jerusalem" (*Order of Christian Funerals* no. 176).

Jerusalem as Heavenly Community, Symbol of Mary and the Church. Jerusalem is also seen as the new City of God where all the saved will dwell. This understanding is found particularly in the celebration of the dedication of a church and in feasts of Mary. For instance, the preface for the Anniversary of the Dedication of a Church says: "Here you build your temple of living stones, and bring the Church to its full stature as the body of Christ throughout the world, to reach its perfection at last in the heavenly city of Jerusalem, which is the vision of your peace." The prayer after Communion makes the point explicit: "Father, you make your Church on earth a sign of the new and eternal Jerusalem."

This symbolism is also applied to Mary, through use of Galatians 4:26 ("But the Jerusalem above is freeborn, and she is our mother"). The antiphon for the Canticle of Zechariah at morning prayer on the solemnity of the Assumption refers to Mary: "This daughter of Jerusalem is lovely and beautiful as she ascends to heaven like the rising sun at daybreak." The connection is made even more explicit in the antiphon for Psalm 127, evening prayer II for the solemnity of the Immaculate Conception: "You are the glory of Jerusalem, the joy of Israel; you are the fairest honor of our race."

Conclusion. Jerusalem is a powerful symbol in the liturgy. It is the site of the unfolding of the events of our salvation, the dwelling place of God. It is a symbol of the final disposition of salvation history, when all will be gathered and made new at the end of time. It is the image of the community of believers who dwell in the light of God's presence. Jerusalem stands as a beacon that draws us all from the sin and darkness of this world to the bright promise of life in communion with Mary and the saints, with God, in the reign of love and peace for all eternity. And where that community of believers is, there is the new and eternal Jerusalem!

See: ISRAEL, MESSIAH, PRIESTHOOD, TEMPLE

MICHAEL G. WITCZAK, S.J.

JESUS CHRIST

Introduction

The name Jesus Christ confronts us with a mystery and paradox. Jesus (Hebrew *Yešûa'*, Yahweh helps or saves), relatively common in the first century, is proclaimed as "the anointed one" (Greek *christos* or Hebrew *mašiaḥ*), Lord and Son of God. Human exis-tence and transcendent power merge. Born near the end of the reign of Herod the Great (37–4 BC), his mother's name was Mary and he grew up in Nazareth in Galilee where his putative father was a *tektōn*, an artisan or carpenter (Mark 6:3; Luke 4:22). His ministry of itinerant preaching, much in the reformist vein of John the Baptist, began circa 29 CE and, after a short public ministry of teaching, exorcizing, and healing, he was executed as a criminal at the order of Pontius Pilate, near the end of his term as Roman Prefect of Judea, 26–36 CE. Jesus' first followers proclaimed that he was raised from the dead and became Lord and Messiah (1 Cor 15:4; Acts 2:36).

The NT offers a rich tableaux of descriptions of Jesus that developed in an extraordinarily short period. The matrix of this development is the proclamation of the Christ event by the early followers of Jesus and its impact in their lives. "Christ event" is a shorthand description of the saving significance of the life, teaching, death, resurrection of Jesus of Nazareth as well as his continuing presence in the Church through the gift of the Spirit. However diverse, the early Christian communities comprised individuals who, under the conviction that human salvation is found in the Christ-event, responded to it in faith and love and were driven by a desire to share their faith.

Though we normally distinguish Christology (who Jesus is) from Soteriology or redemption (what he did for us), early Christians moved from the experience of the power and salvation of God to questions of person and nature. Paul offers a panoply of effects of the Christ event. Principal among these are: *justification*: an acquitting of human beings whereby they enter a "right relationship" with God (Gal 2:16; Rom 3:26-28; 4:25; 5:18); *salvation*: a restoration to health, wholeness, or integrity from a state of danger, sickness, corruption, or sin (2 Cor 6:2; Rom 1:16; 10:10; 13:11); *ransom/redemption*: an emancipation or manumission bringing about human liberation through a "ransom" whereby God acquires a people in a new sense (1 Cor

1:30; Rom 3:24, cf. Rom 8:32, Eph 1:14); *freedom:* a liberation that gives men and women new rights (as citizens of a heavenly commonwealth) and an outlook freed of the anxiety of self, sin, death, and law, (Gal 5:1, 13; Rom 8:1-2, 21; 2 Cor 3:17).

A number of terms describe the new conditions of the Christian: *sanctification:* creation of a holy people who are the locus of God's presence and dedicated to God's service (1 Cor 1:2, 30; 6:11); *reconciliation:* a restoring of humanity and the world *(kosmos)* to a status of friendship to God and fellow humans (2 Cor 5:18-20; Rom 5:10-11; 11:15; cf. Col 1:20-22); *new creation:* a creating of a new life and of a new humanity of which Christ is the head as the "Adam" of the final age through his life-giving Spirit (Gal 6:15; 2 Cor 5:17; Rom 6:4; 1 Cor 15:45); *transformation:* a gradual reshaping of human beings by the glory of God reflected in the face of Christ (2 Cor 3:18; Rom 12:2; cf. Eph 4:22-24); and *glorification:* Christians beginning to share in this life the power and glory of the risen Jesus (Rom 8:30). These terms attempt to put into words life-transforming experiences of both Paul and his communities (summarized from J. A. Fitzmyer, "Pauline Theology," *NJBC* 82:68-80).

Early Expressions of Christian Faith

In confessing Jesus as "the Christ," the early Christians turned to a wide variety of texts, descriptions, and figures from both their heritage and their environment. Since they shared with other Jews a conviction that Scripture contained God's infallible word, to overcome the scandal of the cross and the curse of Deuteronomy against one who was hung on a tree (Deut 21:23, see Gal 3:10-14), they turned to the OT as storehouse of apologetic texts. The Servant Songs of Isaiah portray a beloved servant of God, who was rejected and suffered, and who suffered for the people (Isa 42:1-4; 49:1-6; 50:4-9; 52:13–53:12). The figure of the suffering just one who was tested by God, rejected by humans, and yet vindicated, influenced the early formation of the account of the passion and death of Jesus (Wis 2:10-24; 5:1-23). Psalm 22 offers many details of the crucifixion narrative. Any Christology that is to remain faithful to its roots must see what God has done in Jesus in continuity with God's saving action in the OT.

The earliest expressions of Jesus as the Christ are proclamations of the resurrection (esp. 1 Cor 15:1-11), the kerygmatic sermons of Acts (e.g., 2:32-36; 4:10-12; 5:30-32; 10:36-41; 13:26-40), and fragments of creeds or hymns (e.g., Phil 2:5-11; 1 Tim 3:16; 1 Pet 3:18-22). God raised Jesus or exalted him, which constitutes God's vindication of the life of Jesus and his exaltation of Jesus to glory and power. The resurrection also involves the "second calling" of the disciples to continue Jesus' mission of proclaiming God's mercy and summoning people to conversion (Acts 2:1-39). The setting for early Christian confession of Jesus is worship, and the driving force, the experience of joy and power which comes from a conviction (faith) that the love and mercy of God has been revealed in Jesus.

The Titles or Names of Jesus

The Jewish and Hellenistic environment of early Christianity offer a wealth of titles and descriptions which are both adopted and radically transformed when applied to the Christ event.

Christ (Messiah) and Son of David. Though quickly becoming a proper name, strictly speaking, "Christ" refers to a human "anointed" by God (usually a king) for a special purpose. While the prime messianic hope was for a Davidic king (Son of David) who would free the people from foreign rule and restore a theocracy (2 Sam 7:8-17), there were various "messianic" figures expected at the time of Jesus. For example, Qumran expected two (or three) messiahs, the messiah of Aaron (a priestly messiah), the messiah of Israel, and a "prophet" (1QS 9:11). The term was extended to other figures who were agents of God's eschatological salvation, e.g. the Son of Man as "messianic." While Jesus rejected a political messiahship, the early

Church saw him as God's anointed agent of that salvation which was to usher in the final age (eschatology).

Son of God. Although in light of subsequent theology "Son of God" seems the most obvious key to the identity of Jesus in the Bible, it does not necessarily suggest a divine figure. In the OT it is used of angels (Job 1:6; 2:1; 38:7; Ps 29:1; Dan 3:25; Gen 6:2); as description of God's love for the collective people of Israel (Exod 4:22; Deut 14:1; Hos 2:1; 11:1; Isa 1:2; 30:1; Jer 3:22; Wis 18:1-3); it is a title of adoption for a Davidic ruler (2 Sam 7:14; Pss 2:7; 89:27), for judges (Ps 82:6), and a just person, especially one remaining faithful amid trial and suffering (Wis 2:18; Sir 4:10; 5:1-23). The unifying themes of the different usages of "Son of God" are divine election and fidelity to a God-given task. In the NT, through adoption, Christians are sons and daughters of God (Gal 4:7) or the gift of the Spirit (Rom 8:14, see Gal 3:26; 4:1-7), as are peacemakers and those who love their enemies (Matt 5:9, 45).

In Romans 1:3-4, Paul adopts an early Christian confession: "the gospel about his Son, descended from David according to the flesh, but established as Son of God in power according to the Spirit of holiness through the resurrection from the dead." Jesus is God's Son in a dual sense, according to the flesh of David's line (therefore the royal son), but through the resurrection established as "Son of God" in power. The resurrection, conceived as the exaltation of Jesus to the realm of divine power and as his enthronement in glory as God's vice-regent, is the seed of later Christological developments (see esp. Acts 2:36, "God has made him both Lord and Christ, this Jesus whom you crucified" and Acts 3:15; 4:10; 5:30-32; 13:32-33).

Lord. Along with this "resurrection Christology," other moments of Jesus' existence took on Christological significance. Building on Jewish eschatology where God and God's agents (e.g., Enoch) ushered in the end time, there is a "second coming Christology" (see 1 Cor 15:22-28, where the risen Jesus will hand over the kingdom to "his God and Father"). One of the earliest uses of "Lord" is in the prayer of 1 Corinthians 16:22, *marana tha,* come, Lord Jesus (see Rev 22:20). In 1 Thessalonians 4:17, Paul consoles his community with the thought of the second coming, when "we who are left will be caught up together with them in the clouds to meet the Lord [*kyrios*] in the air." In the hymn of Philippians 2:5-11, which may have been part of an early baptismal ritual, Jesus who was "in the form" of God, and who "emptied himself unto death is greatly exalted by God and given a name above every name, so that every tongue should confess that Jesus is Lord." When applied to Jesus, "lord" loses the sense of dominant and distant power current in the first century, and evokes the saving Lord of the OT.

"Pre-existent Son." The major OT text behind the "Son" Christology is Psalm 2:7, "You are my son, this day I have begotten you." Though originally used in reference to the resurrection, divine sonship was quickly applied to different aspects of Jesus' career: his baptism and earthly ministry (Mark 1:11), his birth and conception (Luke 1:35), and finally his pre-existence (see below under the Gospel of John).

Son of Man. The enigmatic title "Son of Man" is used originally in the context of a "second coming" Christology. This phrase derives from Daniel 7:13-14 where, in the context of judgment over arrogant earthly kingdoms, one "like a son of man" (lit. a human being), coming on the clouds of heavens, approaches the "Ancient One" and receives dominion, glory, and everlasting kingship. In Daniel 7:27 this "son of man" represents the "saints of the most high" (7:22).

With minor exceptions (Acts 7:56; Rev 3:3; 14:14), Son of Man appears only in the Gospels and always (with the possible exception of Mark 2:10) on the lips of Jesus. Jesus uses it in speaking of his earthly ministry (Mark 2:10, 28), his suffering and death (Mark 8:31; 9:31; 10:33; 10:45), and his return at the end of history (Mark 13:26; 14:62). Though it is debated which are authentic sayings of the historical Jesus, the Son of Man Christology is important for understanding the picture of Jesus in the Gospels.

From Daniel onward it became a symbol for an individual or group that was vindicated by God after persecution. If Jesus used it in reference to Daniel 7:12-14 (as many scholars increasingly believe) it captures strongly the two aspects of his life. He lives in solidarity with the human condition (one like a human) and simultaneously hopes for vindication by God. It also integrates the moments of his career. The one who shared the human condition through suffering and death (Mark 10:33-34, 45) and manifested on earth the forgiving power of God (Mark 2:10) will appear to vindicate his suffering brothers and sisters (Mark 13:26-27).

The Historical Jesus and Christology

Before the rise of historical criticism there was little difficulty in turning to the NT for an understanding of Christ. The words and deeds of Jesus, authentically handed on in the Gospels, were the starting point for Christology. The Christ of faith was the Jesus of history, who spoke of himself as God's anointed, performed mighty works, and was aware of his impending death and resurrection. However, a century of source, form, and redaction criticism has shown that the Gospels comprise many layers of material and that the early Church did not distinguish the words of the risen Lord proclaimed by inspired teachers and prophets from those of the earthly Jesus which had been handed on by "eye witnesses and ministers of the word" (Luke 1:1). Scholars today tend to locate the continuity between what Jesus proclaimed and the proclamation about Jesus in an implicit Christology based on reconstruction of central aspects of his life and teaching. Such a Christology might take the following form.

Jesus proclaims that in his teaching and ministry the reign of God is imminent and he calls for faith and conversion (Mark 1:14-15). He gathers disciples who were "to be with him" and to do the things he did (Mark 3:13-19). He performs "works of power" (miracles), specifically exorcisms and healings as signs of the breaking in of God's reign (Mark 1:21-45).

He teaches "with authority" and radically reinterprets the Law in service of suffering humanity (Mark 2:27), and summarizes the Law in the command to love God with whole heart, mind, and soul and the neighbor as one's self (Mark 12:38-40; Matt 22:34-40; Luke 12:25-29; John 13:34-35). In the familial language of love and trust, Jesus calls God "Abba" (Mark 14:36) and teaches his disciples to do the same (Luke 11:1-4; Matt 6:9-14, the "Our Father," cf. Gal 4:6, "God sent the spirit of his Son into our hearts, crying out 'Abba, Father!'"). He is ready to follow his Father's will completely, even to death (Mark 14:32-42).

His characteristic teaching is in parables, short, realistic, concrete sayings and narratives that capture the hearer by their vividness and strangeness, and yet metaphorically point to the action of God in the lives of the hearers. For example, in the Prodigal Son (Luke 15:11-32), this very untypical father images a God who both welcomes back the restless son who squanders his property and invites the dutiful to the feast of life. In the Unmerciful Servant (Matt 18:23-35) God summons us to embody in our own lives the undeserved forgiveness we have received or risk the loss of the gift. In the story of the persistent widow, a woman's courageous struggle for justice offers a model of prayer (Luke 18:1-8).

The offer of unrestricted love and mercy manifest in his teaching (Mark 2:1-12) is enacted by table fellowship with tax collectors and sinners (Mark 2:13-17; Matt 11:19; Luke 15:1-2). Like the OT prophets, Jesus is on the side of the powerless groups of his time: the widow (Luke 7:11-17), children (Mark 10:13-16), the poor (Luke 4:18=Isa 61:1-2; 58:6; Luke 6:20-26), and the stranger in the land (Luke 17:11-19, the Samaritan).

Jesus' activity and teaching evoked strong opposition from certain Jewish leaders (esp. the Jerusalem Temple priesthood, Mark 14:10-11). In the heritage of the prophets and, like other reformers within Judaism itself (e.g., John the Baptist, the Qumran movement), Jesus does not reject all Jewish law and tradition, but attacks interpretations and customs which distort the real meaning of the Law (Mark 3:1-6; 7:1-8, "You disregard God's command, but cling to human tradition"). On the fourteenth of Nisan, shortly before his death, which took place during the celebration of Passover (most likely ca. 32 CE), Jesus eats a final meal with his disciples. This meal was both the culmination of the many meals he shared with his followers and the anticipation of the eschatological banquet he would share with them (Mark 14:20-25; Matt 26:26-29; Luke 22:14-23; 1 Cor 11:23-25). In its Passover context (Exod 12:1–13:16) it also symbolizes the liberating action of God which forms people into a new covenant relationship (Jer 31:31). His mission will continue in the work of disciples who share this meal and who will continue to celebrate it in his memory.

Jesus is executed, along with two revolutionary bandits (lēstai), by a mode of death reserved to political threats. Jesus' claim of intimacy with God and of God's sovereignty over all of human life, along with his criticism of the misuse of Israel's religious institutions (e.g., the cleansing of the Temple), as well as his association with "unclean" outsiders, alienated both Temple authorities and Roman rulers.

Though the prophecies of his death and resurrection (e.g., Mark 8:31; 9:31; 10:33-34) most likely arise after his resurrection and are read back into the Gospels, during his ministry Jesus probably foresaw the possibility of his own death. His Jewish heritage offered examples of martyred prophets (Matt 23:37-39) and suffering and vindicated just people (see above). The parable of the wicked vineyard tenants (Mark 12:1-12) ends with the murder of the son and heir who was sent. The death of John the Baptist, whose preaching is similar to Jesus' brought home to Jesus the potential cost of his own mission (Matt 11:1-15). Yet, in the face of rejection and lethal opposition, Jesus continues to proclaim and enact God's merciful love. He is truly the one who lives for others.

The Christology of the Gospels

The Gospels both record authentic events from the time of Jesus and offer interpretations of this same life from a post-resurrectional perspective. They present "narrative Christologies," each with a distinctive emphasis.

Mark is characterized by mystery and paradox, and leads inexorably to the cross. Jesus simultaneously represents human vulnerability and divine power. He experiences strong emotions: anger (3:5), indignation (10:14), surprise at unbelief (6:6), compassion (1:41; 6:34), and love (10:14). He is addressed by a heavenly voice as God's beloved son (1:11; 9:7) and as Son of God by "otherworldly figures" such as demons (3:11; 5:7). He constantly tries, somewhat unsuccessfully, to conceal his identity (the "messianic secret," e.g., 1:44) and only at the Centurion's statement at the cross ("truly this was the Son of God"; 15:39) do the readers understand that Jesus is Son of God, not simply as a figure of power, but as one who faithfully follows his Father's will even to death.

The Matthean Jesus is introduced as a "Son of David, and a Son of Abraham"; his birth of a virgin mother takes place through the power of God's spirit (Matt 1:18-25, see Isa 7:14). His names anticipate his ministry: Jesus (1:21, he will save his people from their sins) and "Emmanuel" (1:23, "God with us"). Distinctive of Matthew's Christology is his stress on Jesus as authoritative teacher, manifest in the collection of his major teachings into five great blocks (chs. 5–7; 10; 13; 18; 24–25), recalling the Pentateuch of Moses. Salvation comes through fidelity to the teaching of Jesus, and handing it on to others (Matt 28:16-20).

Most distinctive to Luke is his presentation of Jesus' life as a saving model for his Church. There is a broad parallelism between the Gospel and Acts. Both Jesus and his Church are born of the Spirit and are led by the Spirit (Luke 1:35; Acts 2:1-4). Both manifest God's love through acts of power that heal human suffering (e.g., Luke 5:17-26; Acts 5:12-15). When martyred both Jesus and his followers beg forgiveness for their executioners (Luke 24:33-38; Acts 7:54-60). The Lukan Jesus also is a model of broad social concern by his care for the poor and warnings against wealth (esp. 4:18-19; 6:20-26; 12:16-21; 16:19-31).

Historically and from a literary perspective John's Gospel is complex. It contains extensive early sayings and deeds of Jesus not found in the Synoptic Gospels and yet reflects theological developments at the end of the first century. While accenting the humanity of Jesus—the word made "flesh" (1:14), John's Jesus is both pre-existent and described in language normally reserved to God (10:33; 14:1; 20:28; "my Lord and my God").

He is the Word with God from the beginning (1:1) who has come from God (1:9-14) in order to make known the Father (1:18). The bond between Jesus and the Father is closer than in any other NT writing ("I and the Father are one" [10:30] and the Johannine Jesus speaks very often of "my Father"). Jesus reveals the Father and is the way to the Father. John's theology is summed up in the statement of Jesus: "I came from the Father and have come into the world; again I am leaving the world and going to the Father" (16:28). After his return Jesus will send to his community from the Father a "paraclete" who will bear witness to him, and enable the community to give the kind of testimony to the world that Jesus gave in his life (15:26-27). John, nonetheless, carefully distinguishes Jesus from the Father. Though Jesus says, "I am in the Father and the Father in me," he also adds "the words I say to you I do not speak on my own authority, but the Father who dwells in me does these works" (14:10), and later in speaking of his return to the Father he says, "the Father is greater than I" (14:28).

Very influential on the Christological development which bore fruit in John are the Wisdom traditions of Judaism (esp. Prov 1:20-33; 8:1-36; Sir 24:1-31; Wis 7:1-22). In Proverbs wisdom is the first born of God, existing prior to creation (8:22) and assisting God at creation (8:30); she calls out to humans to learn from her and those who find her find life. In Sirach 24:8, wisdom pre-exists creation ("before all ages, in the beginning he created me") and will exist forever (24:9). People are summoned to eat and drink of wisdom (cf. John 6:1-51) and to obey her precepts (24:18-21). Early Christians, then, interpreted the life of Jesus as the revelation of God's wisdom ("I am the way, the truth and the life"), and the Wisdom traditions gave them the concepts by which to describe the pre-existence of Jesus (see also Col 1:15-20; Eph 1:18-23).

Pastoral Notes

Despite our faith that God has been revealed in the life, teaching, death, and resurrection of Jesus, the person and work of Jesus remain a mystery in the strictest theological sense, i.e., "understandable" only through faith, where language can better describe the parameters of misunderstanding than adequately exhaust its meaning. One enduring effect of the Enlightenment is a tendency to rationalism, even in our most religious expressions. The statement "Jesus is divine or God" can be based on the assumption that we know what "God" means, which then can be applied to Jesus. Rather it is in and through Jesus that we discover what "God" means.

The diversity of presentations of Jesus in the NT is a constant warning against selecting any "one Jesus" to the exclusion of all others. NT documents themselves contain diverse Christologies. In Hebrews Jesus is the son through whom God created the universe, the "refulgence of his glory and the very imprint of his being" (1:1-3). He is also the son who shared flesh and blood with his brothers and sisters, (2:14) who is tested in every way, yet without sin (5:15), and who learns obedience from what he suffered (5:8). To describe Jesus, John combines philosophical language from Wisdom traditions (1:1-14) with concrete images of everyday life: Jesus is bread (6:35), light (8:12), the gate for the sheep (10:7, 9), the vine (15:1).

The "many Christs" of the NT speak to different people and differently to individuals throughout their lives. The stark reality of the cross in Mark with its picture of Jesus begging God to spare him from suffering and dying with a cry of abandonment may well speak to people facing the enigma of suffering. People seeking guidance in a troubled world repeat again and again the rhythmic cadences of Matthew's Sermon on the Mount. Socially sensitive Christians find in Luke a model of compassion in whom God's care for the poor and marginal becomes incarnate. John's Gospel, long the favorite of Christian mystics, draws its readers into the inner life of God.

For Paul the Christ-event breaks through every attempt to constrain God's action by human law or custom or to limit God's mercy to any one group. Paul fought to extend the beauty of his Jewish heritage to Gentiles and agonized over the unbelief of his Jewish brothers and sisters (Romans 9–11). In Paul also the life of Christ is played out again in the community and in individuals. The baptized Christian has put on Christ (Gal 3:27), and the community is Christ's body, where there is neither Jew nor Greek, slave nor free, male and female (Gal 3:28). Scorn of other Christians is a wound to the brother or sister for whom Christ died (1 Cor 8:11-13). What Paul proclaimed, he experienced in his own life. He knows of a human Jesus who was raised up in power (Rom 1:1-3), and amid his own sufferings, states that "power is made perfect in weakness" (2 Cor 12:9). Simply put for Paul (and for all baptized Christians), "I live no longer, but Christ lives in me" (Gal 2:20).

Persecuted Christians who hunger after justice turn to Revelation with the confidence that the world is ultimately not subject to the brutal power of evil overlords, and that the just will dwell in unending joy with the Lamb who suffered for them (Revelation 18–22). People concerned about the destruction of God's creation can be drawn to a Jesus who spoke of God's care for the lilies of the field and the birds of the air (Matt 6:25-30), and see all creation as an expression of God's eternal Word (John 1:1-3; see Col 1:15-16).

Amid this diversity a constant is that Jesus lived a human life in total solidarity with the human condition, and yet was a unique revelation of God. In confronting this mystery and in response to pastoral questions alive in their communities, the NT authors combined fidelity to tradition (e.g., 1 Cor 11:23-26; 15:1-7) with adaptation to pastoral needs. They joined traditional language to daring new images. No lesser challenges face the Church of every age.

JOHN R. DONAHUE, S.J.

Pastoral-Liturgical Tradition

After the close of the Apostolic Age, reflection on the life, death, and resurrection of Jesus continued among his followers. That reflection process was intensified by the shift of the center of gravity of the Jesus movement out of a largely Semitic context into a largely Hellenistic setting. When such cultural shifts are made, two things happen. First of all, the narratives that carry the story take on different meanings since everything that was implied in the context of the narrative is largely lost on the new readers. Second, readers in the new context are likely to ask different questions than those posed earlier.

This happened also as the early Jesus movement changed its cultural context. In its Semitic setting, to call Jesus "the Christ" summoned up a rich history of God's acting again and again for the sake of Israel by anointing figures who would speak God's message or rescue Israel from its enemies. In the new context, among Gentiles not steeped in Israel's traditions, "the Christ" became almost a surname attached to "Jesus." Israel's story was told, but that narrative would never have the power it carried for Jews. Thus the stories about Jesus, already set forth for a variety of different audiences in the four Gospels, would be reread in yet other ways by later generations of followers.

These same generations would also pose new questions and make attempts to situate Jesus in settings more familiar to them. A prominent set of questions that came to the fore tried to specify more clearly just what was Jesus' relationship to God. The early Greek apologists, rereading the Prologue to John's Gospel, saw Jesus as the Logos (Word) who was the principle of world reason, by which the whole cosmos is governed and held together. The Logos in some strands of Hellenistic thought was also the creator of the world, the mediator between God and material creation. These meanings began to accrue to the more Semitic understanding of the Word in John 1. Thus, original understandings set forth in the books of the NT came into contact with another cultural world, creating new and complex understandings.

Of particular interest was the relation of the Logos to God. If more Semitic understandings focused upon the passion, death, and resurrection of Jesus as a New Exodus, a new paschal event, the Hellenistic mind was fascinated by John 1:14, the Word becoming flesh. Attention fastened upon the incarnation as defining the Jesus event. The reflection (and the struggles) that ensued culminated in the Council of Nicaea in 325, further refined by the deliberations of the Council of Constantinople in 381. There Jesus was defined as the Son, begotten before all time, one in being with God (DS 125). The Council of Chalcedon in 451 struggled to define the relation of the divinity of Christ to his humanity, and stated that Christ possessed both a divine and a human nature, united in one *hypostasis* or person. Because of that coming together in a single hypostasis, Christians speak of the hypostatic union. The Council of Chalcedon was careful to balance the two natures as coming together "without mixture, without change, undivided, inseparable"

(DS 301), but the balance was hard to maintain in practice. Consequently, the divinity of Jesus came to be emphasized without denying his humanity. The understandings of Jesus set forth in the Johannine literature and the letters of Paul came to predominate for Christians.

These understandings were affirmed by the experience of the worshiping community, but they did not exclude other understandings. The iconography of the early Church points to images of Christ as the Good Shepherd and Christ the teacher as favorite ways of portraying Christ. After Christianity was no longer persecuted and went on to become the official religion of the Roman Empire at the end of the fourth century, images of Christ as the all-powerful *Kyrios* or Lord began to appear in the apses of the newly built basilicas. The Eucharist, in which Christ becomes present in a special way, carried with it its own images of Christ. The Eucharistic banquet became a favorite image of Christ and the soon-to-be realized reign of God. In one ancient Syrian text, Christ is portrayed as the Life-Giver, who is "the fire in the bread, the glow in the wine."

Every age and culture have given their own expression to the story of Jesus. To help the recently converted Franks in northern Europe understand the Jesus story, an eighth century monk in Magdeburg composed the *Heliand*, in which the life and teaching of Christ is set forth as the teaching of a local lord to his twelve vassals.

In the Middle Ages, other images came to prevail. Christ became identified with the judge of Matthew 25:31-46, and appeared seated in judgment above the principal doorway into churches. Devotion to the infant Jesus took on special importance in this period as well, one that persisted in the Mediterranean rim and in countries colonized by Spain and Portugal. The infant is a sign of new life and hope, and Jesus signifies this for a world always in need of new possibilities and a second chance. The high Middle Ages saw the beginning of an intense devotion to the passion of Christ in all its aspects, perhaps in part to answer the acute sufferings of that time. The stations of the cross and passion plays date from this period, as do devotions to the wounds and pierced heart of Christ. These images of the suffering Christ continue to be a source of comfort to those who suffer today.

Devotion to the heart of Christ continued to take on a variety of meanings from the Middle Ages down to modern times, first as a symbol of the Catholic Reformation, then associated alternately with Jansenism and anti-Jansenism. Christ as *Kyrios* resurfaces in the twentieth century as Christ the King in response to the crumbling of monarchies in Europe. And the *Logos* once again holds the world together in the Christogenesis of Pierre Teilhard de Chardin's mystical view of the convergence of all creation in Christ.

The modern period has seen no dogmatic redefinition of Christ; its confession still rests on the Creed of Nicaea and Constantinople and the declaration of Chalcedon. But two movements have done much to shape contemporary sensibility about the meaning of Jesus Christ. The first movement has been called the quest of the historical Jesus. It began in the late eighteenth century as an attempt to get behind the dogmatic confessions of the Church about Jesus in order to uncover the historical Jesus of Nazareth. In its origins it had a distinctly anti-Church bias. But devout Christians, too, wished to know whatever could be discovered about the historical Jesus. The Gospels, of course, did not pretend to be historical documents. While they do contain fragments of history, their principal intent is to bring their readers to faith. So no full historical portrait of Jesus of Nazareth is possible, or at least none completely satisfying to the Western contemporary mind. This quest of the historical Jesus has continued, off and on, from the 1770s down to the present time. The focus has changed in the course of this period, especially as historical methods have become more refined. But the attitudes of those who undertake the quest, motivated by faith or eager to debunk, inevitably shine through. By the end of the twentieth century, Jesus of Nazareth has emerged as a wandering preacher and teacher who also had powers as a healer. But what remains clear in the quest is that the historical Jesus that we perceive dimly through the fragments of history comes alive to us only in faith.

The second movement that has shaped contemporary sensibility about Jesus Christ is the emergence of Christianity as a worldwide faith. As more and more peoples in a wide variety of the world's cultures have embraced Christ, the process of cultural encounter with the Gospel message has only intensified. Images of Jesus that are emerging both recapitulate earlier Church history and suggest new emphasis on the Jesus story. The interest in healing as a religious activity has motivated Christians to look more closely at the stories in the Gospels of Jesus as a healer and wonder-worker. The vibrant links that most African cultures have with the ancestors, those previous generations that have died, have led many Africans to see Christ as Ancestor, echoing the New Adam image from Romans 5. Feminist thinkers in North America and Europe and Asian theologians following different pathways have rediscovered the strands of the wisdom traditions submerged in the Gospels. They see Christ as *Sophia* (wisdom) incarnate. For feminists, it links Christ to a female personification of an attribute of God; for Asian theologians, it links Christianity to the wisdom traditions of their continent. Beginning among the poor in Latin America and spreading among the poor and oppressed of every continent, Christ has come to be seen as friend and liberator of the poor and oppressed. This image is a variant and development of the NT understanding of redemption, and has become a powerful source of hope for poor Christians, who make up the majority of the Church.

All this ferment, caused by so many more Christians of ever increasingly diverse cultural backgrounds reflecting on the meaning of Jesus for their lives, has not resulted in new dogmatic definitions about the nature of Christ. But it has caused a decided shift in focus toward the understandings of Jesus found in the Synoptic Gospels and portrayed in the ministry of Jesus. For secularized Christians, who have difficulty with the lofty images of Jesus in John and Paul, the images of the first three Gospels likewise exercise a certain fascination. How all this ferment will eventually deepen Christian understanding of Jesus is still being worked out, but it surely seems to bespeak a lively presence of the Spirit among Christians around the world today.

With Christianity now being a worldwide Church, and with the unprecedented migration of peoples, the Christian message about Jesus Christ is coming into encounter with the other great religious traditions of the world as never before. What this will mean for Christian self-understanding and for preaching the message of Jesus remains a point of struggle, and may be the single most important question Christian theology faces as Christianity begins its third millennium.

See: ATONEMENT, REDEMPTION, SALVATION

ROBERT J. SCHREITER, C.PP.S.

JEW

This entry is composed of two parts. The first summarizes the meanings and use of the term "Jew" in the Bible. The second traces the history of Jewish-Christian relationships with particular focus on the Roman Catholic tradition.

The Biblical Tradition

Jew is the translation of the Hebrew term *yᵉhudi* and the Greek term *ioudaios*. When used in the preexilic books of the OT, the Hebrew term refers to a member of the tribe of Judah. In those cases it is best translated as Judahite. In postexilic books, the term refers to the inhabitants of the Persian subprovince of Judah that consisted of the city of Jerusalem* and its immediate surroundings. In most English translations of the

OT, the term Jew as a translation for *yᵉhudi* is almost entirely limited to postexilic texts such as Ezra, Nehemiah, and Esther.

The term Jew had political and ethnic connotations as it designated members of a people beginning with the late sixth century in Palestine. Its religious equivalent was Israel.* In the Diaspora, Jew was both an ethnic and religious term.

The word Jew is rare in the Synoptic Gospels. It occurs only sixteen times. All but four occurrences (Matt 28:15; Mark 7:3; Luke 7:3; 23:51) are placed on the lips of Gentiles. The Synoptics understood the term as a secular designation. The Gospel of John understands the term this way (see John 2:6; 5:1; 6:4). But the Fourth Gospel also uses "Jews" to designate the opponents of Jesus in situations when the Synoptics would use the terms scribes and Pharisees. The Acts of the Apostles sometimes parallels John's usage (e.g., 9:23), but at other times the term designates members of the Christian community (e.g., 14:1). There is some archaeological evidence to support the hypothesis that Jewish Christianity existed in Palestine until the fourth century CE when the more dominant Byzantine Christian community absorbed it.

Paul also uses the term Jew to designate members of the Christian community (Gal 2:12-14). Usually though he uses the term to refer to a type of person rather than to individuals. For Paul, a Jew is a person who lives under Torah with hopes for salvation through it (Rom 3:1; 9:4).

John's distinctive use of the term Jew has had the most influence on Christian thought and practice. Though not intended by the evangelist, his use of the word "Jew" to designate a person who refuses to accept Jesus because it demands the abandonment of Jewish belief and practice has led to the development of anti-Semitism among Christians. To avoid any hints of anti-Semitism today, some suggest the substitution of other terms such as "religious authorities" or "scribes and Pharisees" for "Jews" when the Gospel of John is read in a liturgical setting. Such sensitivity is especially important on

Good Friday when the John's passion story is proclaimed.

See: JUDAISM

LESLIE J. HOPPE, O.F.M.

The Pastoral Response

The early Church inherited from parts of the NT, especially the Pauline corpus and John's Gospel, the generic use of the term Jew. Loss of the distinction among the various Jewish groups of Jesus' time, particularly the Sadducees and the Pharisees, resulted in the globalization of Christian attitudes toward Jews, particularly negative attitudes. Jews increasingly became stereotyped and cast as villains in the unfolding drama of human salvation that reached its culmination in Christ. This process was enhanced by three factors in particular: (1) the rapid gentilization of Church membership with the virtual disappearance of the Jerusalem Christian community after the disastrous Jewish war with Rome (64–70 CE); (2) the cultural antisemitism that many Gentile converts to the Church brought with them; (3) the formal expulsion of the Christian Jews from the synagogue in the late first century. By the beginning of the second century the pieces were in place for the formalization of a negative theology of Jews and Judaism.

The *Adversos Judaeos* Tradition. Scholars usually credit Marcion, writing in the second century, with having given the original impetus to the framing of a comprehensive anti-Jewish theology during that period of Christian theology. Marcion apparently lived in the midst of a Christian community that strongly affirmed its sense of newness. It pointedly refused to abide by the major provisions of Jewish law such as circumcision, Sabbath observance, abstention from certain foods, and temple sacrifice. Nonetheless this second century Christian community retained a great respect for the OT. This situation created tension for Marcion. How could Christian faith remain faithful to the God of the Hebrew Bible while rejecting out of hand so many of the specific practices associated with this belief? Marcion's response to this tension was to urge the complete abandonment of the OT as religiously authoritative. At best, it served as an account of an inferior vision of God through which Christians were totally liberated in the newness of Jesus Christ.

Few Christian writers of the period followed completely Marcion's lead in the matter of the Hebrew Scriptures. Yet many of them found it necessary to respond to his challenge. Tertullian, for example, wrote a five volume rebuttal to Marcion's basic thesis. He staunchly defended the continued importance of the God of the OT for Christian faith. But in so doing, intentionally or not, Tertullian helped lay the foundations for an anti-Judaic myth that had a direct role in centuries of Christian anti-Semitism and its sorry legacy of human suffering and death. His argument was that while the God of the Hebrews was not inherently inferior to the God revealed in Jesus Christ, as Marcion had claimed, nonetheless the Jewish people were inherently inferior and hence their religious practices could be safely discarded by Christians. Tertullian thus salvaged the God of the Hebrew Bible by generating the myth of inherent Jewish inferiority, a myth that would become a permanent fixture of the Church's preaching and teaching until the Second Vatican Council.

Tertullian also used the anti-Jewish myth to build up a picture of Jesus as standing staunchly in opposition to the Jewish community in which he lived. Not only was there an emphatic heightening in Tertullian's writings against Marcion of the anti-Jewishness supposedly endemic to Jesus' preaching, but we find as well the introduction of the notion that God had opposed Israel for some time and in fact was looking for ways to break the original covenant with the Jews for something new and better.

Tertullian did not produce his response in a vacuum. Others before and after him continued to play on the same anti-Jewish themes that were central to his attack on

Marcion. Justin, in his famous *Dialogue with Trypho*, put forth many of the same ideas, though not in as developed a form, a half-century or so before Tertullian. And a generation afterwards Irenaeus offered yet another response to Marcion's attack on the God of the OT. He portrayed the God of Sinai as a good and powerful God, but then went on, relying on the parables of the wicked husbandmen (Matt 21:33-44) and the wedding feast (Matt 22:1-14), to argue that this same God had replaced the unresponsive Jews with Gentiles in the covenantal relationship. Finally, well into the third century, Origen picked up in part on this same "replacement of the Jews by Gentiles" theme based on these parables and introduced the notion that a new spiritual sense of the Scriptures, possible only after the Christ Event, enabled Christians to see aspects of this God hidden to Jews. Thus, for the better part of a century, for the four writers who dominated the scene, theological discourse on God, Christ, and Scripture developed in a fundamentally anti-Jewish mode that would set the basic tone for the Church's approach to the Jewish people until the papacy of Pope John XXIII.

Medieval Developments. The thirteenth century marked a new turning point in the Church's relationship to Jews. A strong desire began to grow for an intensified missionizing campaign targeted specifically at them. When this new missionizing campaign was actually put into effect, it was marked by an unprecedented seriousness of purpose. The resources of a powerful Church were marshalled in support. The Dominican and Franciscan orders became the specialists in this endeavor with valuable assistance from converted Jews. Church leaders enlisted the support of important secular authorities for the campaign, thereby ensuring that the Jews would be regularly exposed to the outreach. Considerable work went into the formulation of new lines of argumentation that would move beyond the original *Adversos Judaeos* tradition while retaining its

central features. There was even a sustained effort to master the Rabbinic style of interpretation in the hope that arguments presented in this mode might become attractive to Jewish audiences.

The new thirteenth-century argumentation consisted of an intensification of prior approaches and an attempt to launch out in new directions. The former involved the claim that empirical data alone suggested the moral superiority of Christianity. The wretched conditions of Jews and the relative success of Christianity were in fact a reflection of theological truth. God obviously dispensed success to those who are correct in their beliefs while at the same time punishing those pursuing erroneous paths. So went the claim.

The distinctive aspect of the thirteenth-century argumentation against the Jews came in the turn toward Rabbinic exegesis. By focusing on Rabbinic exegesis, the new missionizing created the following options: either Jewish interpretation corroborated Christian claims or it did not. In the latter instance, Christianity as a faith suffered no harm. This was a definite advance in the minds of the thirteenth-century preachers over biblical, philosophical, or especially empirical grounds that could be turned against the truth of Christianity. Use of Rabbinic materials, on the other hand, was seen as a foolproof way of establishing Christianity's inherent superiority over Judaism.

Contemporary Catholicism's Response to its Anti-Judaic Legacy. The *Adversos Judaeos* theology forged by the major figures of the Patristic period and given new intensity during the thirteenth century continued to define the image of Jews and Judaism for Catholics until the time of the Second Vatican Council. It had become deeply imbedded in popular Catholicism as well as in the Church's liturgy and catechesis. It played a direct role in generating social anti-Semitism throughout Europe, especially in the late nineteenth century and first half of the twentieth when it often combined with rising political nationalism among Catholics. The ultimate event in the history of antisemitism, the Nazi Holocaust, while it was a distinctly modern phenomenon in many ways, nonetheless was conditioned by the historic Christian degradation of the Jews. On a popular level, Christian anti-Semitism played a significant role in support for the Nazi attack on the Jews by many within the Church.

In 1965, with the approval of *Nostra Aetate* by the Second Vatican Council, the *Adversos Judaeos* tradition was formally repudiated as acceptable Catholic teaching. Instead, in chapter four of that document, the Church proclaimed the continued validity of the Jewish covenantal tradition and emphasized that the Church remains tied to it in a profound manner. Subsequent Vatican documents in 1975 and 1985 amplified this theme by stressing the need for greater sensitivity in handling the term "the Jews" in John (especially those passages where "Jews" are linked to diabolic forces), and in presenting Jesus' positive links with Pharisaic Judaism that the 1985 document presents as the Jewish movement to which Jesus was the closest. Pope John Paul II, in a number of major public statements, including one delivered during his historic visit to the Rome synagogue (1986), has underscored the Church's continuing linkage to the Jewish people, a linkage he describes as affecting the Church's fundamental identity. Finally, the U.S. Catholic Bishops' Liturgy Commission in 1988 issued a document *God's Mercy Endures Forever* which lays out preaching and liturgical suggestions for the major seasons of the Church year in the light of *Nostra Aetate* and its companion documents.

Slowly the curtain is coming down on the *Adversos Judaeos* tradition and its centuries-long legacy of anti-Jewish hatred and Christian superiority. In its place is emerging an understanding of Jews as inherent partners with Christians in God's work of human salvation, a partnership that will enable the Church to understand more profoundly the message of Jesus whose teachings were thoroughly rooted in the Judaism of his day.

See: CIRCUMCISION, ISRAEL, PARABLE, PHARISEES, SABBATH, SACRIFICE, SADDUCEES, TEMPLE

JOHN T. PAWLIKOWSKI, O.S.M.

JOB

Structure of the Book

The outline of the Book of Job is clear enough: prologue, Chapters 1–2; dialogue, 3–31; speeches of Elihu, 32–37; speeches of the Lord and reaction of Job, 38:1–42:6; epilogue, 42:7-17. However, the meaning is quite subtle, as the history of its interpretation shows. This is a literary work, not a description of a specific historical debate between Job and his friends. The unknown author has chosen as the protagonist a famous holy man (cf. Ezek 14:14), a non-Israelite who suffered without cause but remained faithful to God. In chapters 1–2 the reader is transfixed by the depth of Satan's question: "Is it *for nothing* that Job is God-fearing?" (1:9). Yes, why does anyone serve God? What are their motives? The great St. Bernard of Clairvaux took up the question again in his book on the love of God, and no human being can escape it.

The dialogue between Job and his three "friends" is clear-cut: the three defend the justice of God as they understand it (and therefore consider Job wrong and even sinful). They continually lecture Job. Job replies to them, but also directs bitter complaints to God. Chapter 28 seems to say that the wisdom to explain Job's plight is beyond human ability. Job lays down the gauntlet to God (the specific Israelite name, Yahweh, is used only in chs. 1–2 and 38–42) in chapters 29–31.

Elihu (chs. 32–37) seems a brash interloper who adds little to the debate. When the Lord finally answers Job out of the whirlwind, there is little abatement in the mystery of Job's suffering. Job (and the reader) doubtless realize more fully the mystery of God's dealings with human beings; all are drawn more deeply into that mystery but no rational explanation of suffering is given; it remains a mystery. Job himself, who has been a hardheaded theologian in dealing with the three friends, now submits to the Lord (42:5). That he is restored is neither surprising nor contrary to the ideas of the book; sometimes God does reward the good according to the mysterious divine will.

Message

This brief description of contents does not convey the power and the depth of the book's message. Job is not a book about patience (cf. Jas 5:11, for his steadfastness or endurance), nor is his suffering a vicarious healing of others (as in the Suffering Servant of Isaiah 53). It is a test, analogous to the testing of Abraham in Genesis 22:1-12. Job comes through this testing with all the strength and weakness of human beings, with a mixture of faith and despair as he contends with the hidden God. Indeed, the Bible provides us with a theological basis for the right to quarrel with God; the psalms of lament, the "confessions" of Jeremiah, and Job are eminent examples.

There is no one point to the message of Job. It puts before the reader the existential question of disinterested piety (Why do I love God? cf. 1:9). It breaks through any rigid interpretation of divine justice, as if God has to reward the good and punish the evil (according to our standards of justice). God cannot be stereotyped or put in a box; the Lord is free to lead followers through mysteries in life, to win their allegiance by the gift of freedom, not by the seduction of reward. When Job is "restored" in chapter 42, it is not simply a restoration to the fortune he formerly enjoyed, but a restoration to the friendship of a God who had seemingly deserted him (see the "dark night of the soul" expressed in ch. 23). His cry in 42:5 is a cry that underlines the importance of a true experience (expressed here in terms of vision, "my eyes have seen") of God. Although this is a high point in the book, it has been overshadowed in the past by such stirring lines as "I know that my redeemer lives,"—lines that are colored by Handel's *Messiah*. Indeed one finds a great affirmation of faith in 19:25-27 (even if the

translation of the text is quite uncertain). Job affirms that his "vindicator" (not "redeemer") will somehow eventually come to his aid. He will be proved right by no less than God, in whom he has kept faith throughout his trials.

Pastoral-Liturgical Tradition

The message of the book and its powerful literary expression form the true basis of its pastoral use for those who suffer adversity. However, the utilization of the book in the Roman Catholic liturgy has been minor and sometimes even misleading. For centuries it was used in the liturgical "Office" for the Dead, and 19:25-27 was seen as a conquest of death—it is not at all the equivalent of 1 Corinthians 15:54-57! Even in the new lectionary that came from Vatican II it must be confessed that the book does not receive the share of readings that it deserves.

The history of interpretation of the work has been influenced by the triumphant translation that Jerome gave in the Vulgate rendition of 19:25-27. The *Moralia* of Gregory the Great (d. 604 CE) was very influential throughout the ages, but it is more of a handbook of spirituality than an explanation of the book itself. The attraction of the biblical poem has nonetheless prevailed down to our own day, as can be exemplified in the brilliant poem by Robert Frost, "The Masque of Reason."

See: JUSTICE, RETRIBUTION, SUFFERING, WISDOM

ROLAND E. MURPHY, O.CARM.

JOHN THE BAPTIST

John the Baptist fulfilled OT expectations of a chosen messenger to announce the messianic age. His message and baptism were a means of repentance and preparation for this. The Gospels present him as baptizing Jesus and announcing him as the Messiah who will baptize with the holy Spirit.

In biblical tradition, a special new intervention of God called for a messenger to prepare the way (Mark 1:2-3; Isa 40:3). John first appeared in the Judean desert in the spirit and garb of the prophet Elijah (Mark 1:6) who was expected to return before the last days (Mal 3:23). The Baptist proclaimed that this day was imminent and preached repentance. His disciples confessed their sins and underwent baptism* in the river Jordan. It is quite possible that the Baptist originally was a member of the Qumran community situated near the Jordan. However, his invitation to the outcasts of Israel, tax collectors and sinners, was not characteristic of Qumran. John's approach was stern and ascetic, providing his disciples a regimen of prayer and fasting (Mark 2:18). His preaching attracted a wide following. Finally, king Herod had him imprisoned and executed because he denounced the king's marriage with his brother's wife (Mark 1:14; 6:17-29).

Jesus began his messianic career after John baptized him. After the Baptist's execution by Herod, many of his disciples joined Jesus in a much wider apostolate. The NT has two principal concerns about the relationship between Jesus and the Baptist. First, by the time of the Gospel writings there were disciples of the Baptist scattered about the ancient world who still followed the teachings of their master (Acts 18:24-26; 19:1-7). It was important to show that Jesus was indeed superior to the Baptist even though he was baptized by him. Thus Matthew has the Baptist protest Jesus' request for Baptism (3:14-15). Luke carefully contrasts the birth stories of both to show Jesus' superiority (chs. 1–2). The Fourth Gospel even omits Jesus' baptism and states that Jesus as Word of God came before the Baptist (1:15).

The second NT concern was to present the Baptist as a herald and witness of Jesus. The Baptist announced that one greater than himself was coming to baptize with the holy Spirit (Mark 1:7-8). In the "Q" source, John in prison sent his disciples to Jesus to confirm that Jesus was indeed the one to come (Matt 11:2-19; Luke 7:18-23). Finally, John's Gospel has further "educated" the Baptist to proclaim Jesus' saving death with the

words, "Behold the Lamb of God who takes away the sins of the world" (1:29).

In Church tradition, John the Baptist's person gradually fades into that of the preaching and saving word of God pointing to Christ. Every preacher of the gospel becomes another John the Baptist called to bear witness to the prophetic word of God. Especially in the seasons of Lent and Advent, John appears on the scene in the chosen liturgical readings as the ever-present prophetic voice proclaiming the urgency of repentance.

See: BAPTISM, PROPHET, REPENTANCE

JOSEPH A. GRASSI

JORDAN

The Jordan River, etymologically "the river that rushes down" or "the descender," is the largest in Palestine. Formed from the convergence of four sources near the city of Caesarea Philippi, it is a twisting, circuitous waterway through the Sea of Galilee to the Dead Sea. The Jordan has played less a role in agriculture—its low level makes it virtually useless for irrigation much beyond its own fertile banks—than as a natural divide between settled and nomadic peoples on east and west.

Jordan in the Scriptures

OT references to the Jordan, though certainly including the simple geographical reality of the river, tend more to make of it a mythic place of passage and theophany. It was through the Jordan, whose waters divided miraculously, that the Hebrews passed dryshod into the promised land (Josh 3:14-17), although Moses was denied passage and could only gaze across at the good land beyond its banks (Deut 3:23-27). There was a parting of the Jordan's waters through which Elijah and Elisha passed immediately before Elijah's ascent in the chariot of fire (2 Kgs 2:6-12). Apparently, the news of such miraculous features did not reach the ears of Naaman the Syrian who nearly refused the suggestion of the holy man, Elisha, to wash in its waters and be cleansed of his leprosy (2 Kgs 5:1-14). Other significant references to the Jordan in the OT include Lot's choice of land on its banks (Gen 13:10f.), Jacob's reference to his crossing (Gen 32:10), David's passage and return over the Jordan (2 Sam 10:17; 17:22, 24; 19:15-39) and Absalom's flight across the Jordan (2 Sam 17:24).

The Jordan achieves a new significance in the NT as the place of John the Baptist's* preaching (Matt 3:5; Mark 1:5; and Luke 3:3) and the location of the baptism* of the Lord (Matt 3:13ff.; Mark 1:9-11; Luke 3:21-22). It was to John that crowds flocked from all the country of Judea, and they were baptized by him in the river Jordan after confessing their sins. To those who questioned him John proclaimed: "For this I came baptizing with water, that he [the Lamb of God] might be revealed to Israel" (John 1:24-31). When Jesus, the Lamb of God, presented himself to John for baptism "in order to fulfill all righteousness," he went down into the waters of the Jordan and as he emerged, "the heavens were opened and he saw the Spirit of God descending like a dove, and alighting on him; and lo, a voice from heaven, saying, 'This is my beloved Son, with whom I am well pleased'" (Matt 3:16-17).

Pastoral-Liturgical Reflections

The Jordan thus is the place of revelation, of spiritual encounter, of confirmation of God's election and favor. It is a place of signs and wonders as described in the Preface for the Feast of the Baptism of the Lord. The Jordan, as symbol, finds its way into the blessing of water* at the Easter Vigil and perdures in the Christian imagination in hymnody and even popular folk music.

See: BAPTISM, LAND

KATHLEEN HUGHES, R.S.C.J.

JOSEPH

Old Testament

A Joseph is named in the Moses stories (Num 13:7), in the David stories (1 Chr 25:2-9), and in the Ezra and Nehemiah stories (Ezra 10:42; Neh 12:14), but only two are fully developed in the Bible.

During the period of early Israel (1250–1000 BCE), Joseph is the name of a people who live in the regions of Ephraim, Manassah (Judg 1:22-29), and Benjamin (2 Sam 19:21) between the cities of Bethel and Megiddo. After the death of Solomon (925 BCE) they secede from Judah to become the kingdom of Israel (Amos 5:6-15). This biblical people developed traditions about Jacob, Moses, the Exodus, and the ark of the covenant, but their most artistic traditions appear in the story of Joseph (Gen 37:1–45:28) for whom they were named.

Unlike the traditions that celebrate Abraham, Sarah, Isaac, Rebekah, Jacob, Rachel, and Leah, the traditions that celebrate Joseph are not ancestor stories, but wisdom or teaching stories. They remember Joseph not so much as an ancestor, but rather as a wise man.

The Wisdom tradition, in contrast to other biblical traditions, was based on human observation, not divine revelation. In the ancient Near East, teachers used analogy to hand on their judgments. Analogies could be as short as an adage (Prov 9:17) or a proverb (Prov 10:1), or as long as the episodes that make up the Joseph story. The wise, like Joseph, followed these teachings and excelled in every aspect of life (Prov 31:10-31). Joseph knew his strengths (Gen 45:8-9) and his weaknesses (Gen 41:16). He knew when to speak (Gen 41:22), when to keep silent, the significance of meals (Prov 23:1; Sir 8:1; 31:12) and how to deal with women (Gen 39:6-9). He made the right friends to whom he was loyal (Gen 39:9). Joseph governed with subtlety (Gen 42:9; 44:15) and pleased his king.

Wisdom is Yahweh's hidden providence which guided the observant Joseph safely through one life-threatening situation after the other. The story of Joseph meticulously weaves and reweaves events, symbols, and dialogue around him to demonstrate how such wisdom can turn rivals into partners, the least into the greatest, famine into plenty, and death into life. It became a textbook for monarchs in Israel, especially those who, like Joseph, rose to power over older candidates and who, like Joseph, struggled to build and maintain unity in the face of rivalry, famine and war. Like the Books of Daniel (Daniel 1–6) and Esther, this story became an inspiration for Jews living in foreign lands who, like Joseph, wanted to survive, to succeed, to understand their exile as a call to take God's blessings to foreign lands.

New Testament

At least eight persons in the NT are named Joseph—the husband of Mary (Matt 1:16) and three of his ancestors (Luke 3:26-34), a brother of Jesus (Matt 13:55), one of the Twelve (Acts 1:23), the rich man who buried Jesus (Luke 23:50-53), and a missionary companion of Paul (Acts 4:36). But it is Jesus himself and the husband of Mary who are most closely modeled on the Joseph in the Book of Genesis.

In Genesis, Joseph is repeatedly put down and raised up—he is put to death and then raised from the dead. When his brothers throw him down into a cistern (Gen 37:24), nomads save his life. When the nomads sell him down into slavery (Gen 37:25-28; 39:1), Potiphar saves his life. When Potiphar throws him down into prison (Gen 39:20), Pharaoh saves his life. In the story of the passion Jesus likewise goes down into prison and down into the tomb, before being raised up from the dead and taken up into the heavens (Acts 1:1-14). Like Joseph, Jesus is the wise man whom God continues to protect in order to turn violence into peace, rivalry into unity.

Joseph, the husband of Mary, is remembered as a just or wise man (Matt 1:19) because he does not judge by appearances and divorce his pregnant wife-to-be for adultery. Like Joseph in Genesis, he does not act with cynicism or betrayal, but looks beyond the superficial crisis and wisely observes a divine plan for deliverance.

Pastoral-Liturgical Tradition

The Lectionary reads the Joseph story together with the parable of the foolish tenants (Matt 21:33-46) who like Joseph's brothers try to murder the only son who can save them. It also understands the power that Jesus confers on the Twelve "to expel unclean spirits and to cure sickness and disease of every kind" (Matt 10:1-7) in terms of the power Pharaoh confers on Joseph. The twelve are to use their power to reunite Jews with one another just as Joseph used his power to reconcile himself to his brothers.

See: JACOB

DON C. BENJAMIN, O.CARM.

JOSHUA

There are two men by this name who have important roles in the life of ancient Israel. (The Books of Ezra and Nehemiah use the Aramaic spelling Jeshua.) Joshua, son of Nun, was the leader of the Israelites as they entered Canaan following the wandering in the wilderness. Joshua, son of Jozadak, is a high priest who was a prominent leader in Judah following the Exile.

The biblical tradition's memory of Joshua, son of Nun, makes him larger than life. He is a military leader (Exod 17:9-14), an assistant to Moses* (Exod 32:17), a guard at the tent of meeting (Exod 33:11), one of the scouts who reconnoitered Canaan (Numbers 13–14), the successor to Moses (Deut 1:38), and the conqueror and distributor of the land (Judg 2:8-9). Later Jewish tradition builds on this memory when it designates Joshua as a prophet (Sir 46:1), a judge (1 Macc 2:55), and an intercessor (2 Esdr 7:107). The NT mentions Joshua only twice: Acts 7:45 and Hebrews 4:8.

Joshua is not only Moses' successor, he is another Moses (Joshua 24) whom the people honored as they did Moses (Josh 4:14). The historical value of the traditions about Joshua are limited. More important is the theological image that the biblical tradition sustains.

The traditions surrounding the settlement as preserved in the Book of Joshua are the most significant. The image of Joshua that the book projects is that of the ideal Israelite leader whose faith and obedience help him accomplish the mission that God gave him. This portrait is consistent with the homiletical tone of the Deuteronomistic History that wishes to commend the example of Joshua to Judah and its leaders. The violence that Joshua wrecks on the Canaanites according to the tradition needs to be seen in this light. This violence is evil—not edifying, but the aim of the Book of Joshua was not to edify but to move its readers to obedience to the God who can bring good out of evil.

Joshua, son of Jozadak, was a priest who returned to Jerusalem in 537 BCE following the end of the Exile (Ezra 2:2, 36; Neh 7:7, 39). This period is very poorly documented, but clearly Joshua was a leader of the newly returned Judahites. Haggai calls upon him to rebuild the Temple and serve in it following its reconstruction (Hag 1:1; 2:2, 4). In Zechariah 3:1-10, the prophet envisions Joshua as embodying the rehabilitation of the priesthood as Joshua exchanges his "filthy garment" for "rich apparel."

Another leader of the community was Zerubbabel, with whom Joshua is associated in several texts (Ezra 3:2, 8-9; 5:2). Hopes for the restoration of the native Judahite dynasty probably centered on Zerubbabel. Those hopes never came to fruition and the high priest took on the role of leadership in the community in Jerusalem. The oracle in Zechariah 6:9-15 was probably first spoken about Zerubbabel. When it became clear that Persians would not allow the restoration of the Judahite monarchy, Joshua replaced Zerubbabel as the subject of the oracle (v. 11).

See: CONQUEST, EXILE

LESLIE J. HOPPE, O.F.M.

JOY

While the expression of joy in the Bible is variegated, the cause of joy is both God's gifts and God's self. Joy is central to the faith experience throughout Church history and is one of the most recurrent motifs of the liturgy.

Old Testament

Joy is often portrayed as part of domestic life: it is said to thrive between husband and wife (Prov 5:18-23; Sir 26:1, 2, 13; Cant 1:4), is caused by a (wise) child (1 Sam 2:1-5; Ps 113:9) and is produced by wine (Ps 104:15; Judg 9:13; Eccl 8:15). Lack of joy accompanies loss of marriage and of the fruit of the vine (Jer 7:34; Isa 16:10).

Israel's historians associate joy with landmarks in their history: David's victories (1 Sam 18:6), the transfer of the ark of the covenant (2 Sam 6:14, 15), the coronation of Solomon (1 Kgs 1:40), the assembly's celebration anticipating the Temple's construction (2 Chr 29:22) the dedication of the walls of Jerusalem after the Exile (Neh 12:27). Repeated celebrations are also to be characterized by joy: holocaust offerings (Deut 12:7; 2 Chr 23:18; 29:30), as well as the harvest (Deut 26:11). Although the tone of the injunction to celebrate Passover is solemn in Deuteronomy 16:18, it is complemented by the Chronicler's description of the Passover celebrated with Hezekiah which was accomplished "with great rejoicing" (2 Chr 30:21-25). Other joyous feasts include Pentecost or the Feast of Weeks (Deut 16:11), Booths or Tents (Deut 16:15), Purim (Esth 9:17, 22), and New Moon (Ps 81:2-4).

Psalmic piety runs the gamut in describing various sources of joy: creation is a source of joy for the creator (Ps 104:31) as well as for all creation, human and non-human (Pss 92:5; 96:11). "Let the children of Zion rejoice in their King" (Ps 149:2) is representative of those psalmic texts which call the faithful to rejoice because of the special gifts given to Israel: the Law (Pss 1:2; 19:9; 119; see also Jer 15:16) and the Temple (Psalms 42; 100; 122) for example. Even when the psalmist calls out, "This is the day the LORD has made; let us be glad and rejoice in it" (Ps 118:24), the context makes clear that the faithful are being urged to celebrate the election of Israel in the security of the Temple sanctuary. God's acts of justice are a source of joy (Ps 146:7). The return from exile is so celebrated (Ps 126:2) as is the gift of forgiveness (Ps 51:9, 11). The people who are formed by this God have reason to rejoice in what is being accomplished among them: The meek are those who "shall delight in abounding peace" (Ps 37:11) and "the just rejoice and exult before God; they are glad and rejoice" (Ps 68:4). The Lord's people have every reason to "be glad in the Lord" (Ps 104:34; see also Neh 8:10). This joy comes to physical expression in a variety of ways: the sea "resounds" and the trees "exult" (Ps 96:11, 12). "Sing joyfully to the LORD, all you lands" (Ps 100:1) is indicative of the frequent interplay between joy and song. The only joy castigated in the psalms is that unjust joy of the enemies of the righteous person (Pss 13:5; 35:26).

In the Prophetic corpus, we sometimes find expressions of expected joy intermingled with denunciations of the nation's failures: during Josiah's reign (Zeph 3:17, 18) and immediately preceding the fall of Jerusalem (Hab 3:16, 18). In the exhilaration of the return from Babylonian exile, the words of Second Isaiah are filled with joy: Isaiah 44:23 rejoices over the fact that the Lord has "brushed away your offenses like a cloud" (see also Isa 49:13). Joy is present even amidst the difficult task of restoration after the Babylonian exile (Isa 61:10). Indeed, Isaiah 65:14, 17 portrays the restoration and its joy as part of an entirely new act of creation.

As Israel turned its attention to a Greek world adulating wisdom in the Hellenistic period, it too proclaimed itself to have been given a wisdom, and one in which it rejoiced: "For association with her [wisdom] involves no bitterness, and living with her no grief, but rather joy and gladness" (Wis 8:16).

New Testament

Matthew associates joy with the reign of God (13:44; 25:1, 21, 23). Even Matthew 5:12, which links joy to persecution of prophets, may be seen as deriving its rationale from the tradition of prophetic announcement of God's reign and its claims. Luke links joy to the announcement of the good news. It is an announcement destined especially for the lowly and poor (1:47, 48, 52, 53) and in which the rich may choose to participate (19:6). The gifts given to the former and shared by the latter proceed from the divine initiative in sending Jesus to give an array of gifts. One such gift is forgiveness of sins and resultant table companionship with sinners at which joy is appropriate (15:11-32). The most important gift of course is that of the holy Spirit. Indeed, it is "in the holy Spirit" that Jesus rejoices when he thanks the Father that these things are revealed "to the childlike" (10:21). And it is in the actions initiated by the Spirit that the apostles, other disciples, and new converts rejoice as the good news spreads (Acts 2:46; 8:8; 8:39; 13:48; 16:34; 13:52; 11:23; 15:3). Luke may contain an implicit critique of joy which is preoccupied by "mighty deeds" apart from their ultimate purpose in catalyzing conversion (10:17; 23:8) or which is insufficiently appreciative of the cross of Jesus by which these gifts are effected (24:41). John's Gospel associates joy with participation in the fate of Jesus the Word who, like a seed that dies, produces much fruit (12:24). The evangelist may be presupposing the image of joy at the harvest (Deuteronomy 26; Psalm 126). That would explain why joy is so often linked to Jesus speaking and others hearing him as prerequisite to joy (3:29; 15:11; 17:13) and why the disciples' joy is fully appropriate as response to Jesus' cross, because by that very act Jesus returns to the Father and breathes forth the Spirit of life on them (14:28; 20:20-22) initiating a cycle of petition and response which draws them deeper into the joyous new life (16:24).

Paul makes explicit the link between joy and conversion, calling joy a "fruit of the Spirit" (Gal 5:22) as distinguished from a gift of the Spirit. His joy therefore increases in proportion to the Corinthian openness to his exhortations to live the new life (2 Cor

7:9; 13:9). Second only to love as a fruit of the Spirit (Gal 5:22), joy also persists through hope (Rom 12:12) and flows from faith (Rom 15:13; Phil 1:25). Other NT letters preserve the assertion that Christian joy is not jeopardized by confiscation of property (Heb 10:34) or various "trials" (Jas 1:2) if the faithful see themselves as "sharing in the sufferings of Christ" (1 Pet 4:13) who "for the sake of the joy that lay before him endured the cross, despising its shame" (Heb 12:2). They anticipate the cry of the elect "Let us rejoice and exult . . . for the marriage of the Lamb has come" (Rev 19:7).

Pastoral-Liturgical Tradition

Francis of Assisi is perhaps one of the better known representatives of the experience of Christian joy; he defined perfect joy as having endured humiliation, beating, hunger in the cold and rain as gifts through which one might conquer oneself for the love of Christ. Francis de Sales warned against giving in to excessive sadness; he reasoned "how can it help holy charity, since joy is ranked next to holy charity?" Therese of Lisieux said that while the perception of her life as filled with consolation was inflated, she did admit that she found continuing joy in the love of God. Not long before his assassination, Oscar Romero meditated on the coffee groves of his beautiful land, whose economic exploitation by a few wealthy families contributes to the injustice in that country. He looked forward to a time when "God will free nature from sinful hands, and along with the redeemed it will sing a hymn of joy to God the Liberator." Among the recent Popes, John XXIII is noted for stressing the joy of incorporation into the Body of Christ. In an encyclical on ecumenism, he said, "Through that life [in the body of Christ] those who faithfully obey all the precepts and demands of our Redeemer can enjoy even in this mortal life that happiness which is a foretaste and pledge of heaven's eternal happiness." The Constitution on the Sacred Liturgy (106) urges that the faithful be taught about the Lord's day and the importance of gathering

to celebrate His resurrection in such a way that the Lord's day "in fact becomes a day of joy." The note of joy is particularly prominent in the liturgies for Easter and Christmas but is present as well in two of the four Eucharistic prayers available for use on any day: we hope to enjoy forever the vision of your glory, through Christ our Lord" (#3) and "To the poor he proclaimed the good news of salvation, to prisoners freedom, and to those in sorrow, joy" (#4).

See: APOSTLES, FAITH, FEASTS, GOOD NEWS, HOLY SPIRIT, HOPE, JUSTICE, LOVE, MEEKNESS, POOR, REIGN OF GOD, WISDOM

MARK C. KILEY

JUBILEE YEAR

A late development in Israelite law, the Jubilee year was designed to bring about economic and social justice in Israel. The law freed Israelite slaves and returned ancestral land to its original owners. Although the law may never have been practiced, the Jubilee became a symbol of hope in late OT literature and in the Gospel of Luke.

Old Testament

The Jubilee year refers to the fiftieth year following seven cycles of seven years. During the Jubilee all Israelite slaves were to be freed, the land was to lie fallow, and ancestral lands that had been sold during the fifty years were to be redeemed by their original owners. The Jubilee law (Lev 25:8-55) appears only in the Levitical Holiness Code (Leviticus 19–26), which took its final form sometime after the Exodus, that is, after 516 BCE.

The Jubilee year was to begin on the Day of Atonement.* This was an appropriate inaugural day because on the Day of Atonement the community sought release from its sins. The Jubilee celebration attempted to redress some of Israel's sins against its own people.

The year's beginning was to be proclaimed by the blowing of a particular kind of ram's horn, known in Hebrew as a *yobel*, from which the word jubilee derives (Lev 25:9). At the beginning of the Jubilee, the community was commanded to "let the trumpet resound . . . the trumpet blast shall re-echo throughout the land. This fiftieth year you shall make sacred by proclaiming liberty in the land for all its inhabitants" (Lev 25:9-10).

Economic Background. To understand the stipulations of the Jubilee law it is first necessary to grasp some of the economic realities facing the people of Israel. Most people lived with little economic security. Even when a family owned land, they were in danger of falling into an escalating cycle of debt. Droughts, wars, insects could destroy crops and interfere with harvests, requiring that the family borrow in order to plant crops the following year. Because there were no external controls over debts in the ancient world, lenders could demand any interest they wished and exact repayment at any time.

When debts could not be met, families would attempt to meet lenders' demands by selling their land, by becoming day laborers, or in the worst circumstances, by indenturing themselves as slaves until their debts were met. It is in the face of such punishing economic and social arrangements that Leviticus proclaims, "It shall be a jubilee for you, when every one of you shall return to his own property, every one to his family estate" (Lev 25:10).

Stipulations. Like any Sabbatical year in Israel, the Jubilee was to be a year of rest for the land (Lev 25:1-7, 18-22). The land would lie fallow and the community would eat by taking directly from the field (vv. 11-12).

During the Jubilee everyone was to return to their family property (Lev 25:13). The land was not simply to be given back to the original owners but repurchased according to a just price (vv. 13-17). Underlying this stipulation was the recognition that the land was the property neither of individuals nor of families, but belonged to God alone. "The land shall not be sold in

perpetuity; for the land is mine, and you are but aliens who have become my tenants" (v. 23).

When Israel entered the land, the land was parcelled out equitably to the tribes (Joshua 13–22). Economic conditions caused the sale of some tribal lands, causing some people to become large landholders and others to be displaced from the land. The Jubilee was to redistribute land by returning the tribal heritage to the original owners. Similarly, the Jubilee made special provision for the return of houses to the Levites (Lev 25:32-34), a priestly tribe that never received a land inheritance (Joshua 21).

The third concern of the Jubilee law was with the circumstances and release of slaves (Lev 25:35-55). The law enjoins Israelites to treat the poor among them with dignity and justice, neither charging them interest on debts nor making a profit on food sold to them (vv. 35-37). The law further insists that when Israelites do enslave themselves to other Israelites, their owners are to treat them, not as slaves, but as hired servants until the Jubilee release. Should Israelites become slaves of aliens in Israel, the slaves retain the right of redemption by which one of their kin could buy them back even before the Jubilee.

Purpose. The purpose of the Jubilee laws was to ensure justice within the community. Compliance with the Law would prevent the development of a permanent landless class. By redistributing the land, the community would share it equitably, and theoretically, at least, no one would be deprived of home and/or livelihood.

The Jubilee celebration would also prevent a permanent class of slaves from developing in Israel. The Law taught Israel the dignity of all its members, though it did not extend that dignity in the same way to aliens (Lev 25:44-46). Nor did it outlaw slavery, though it did insist upon compassionate treatment of the lowliest in the society. The Law reminded the community of its origins in slavery and of the activity of its God who "brought you out of the land of Egypt" (Lev 25:38, 42, 55).

Observance. There is no firm evidence that Israel actually kept the Jubilee. Some texts suggest that it did (Num 36:4; Ezek 46:17), but the Book of Isaiah uses the Jubilee only symbolically (61:1-2). Nehemiah 5:1-5 indicates that during the period of restoration after the Exile the Jubilee law was not followed. Yet the Nehemiah text reveals the very conditions that may have given rise to the Law.

Even if the laws were not actually practiced, their promulgation instructed the community about its responsibilities to the poorest among them. Moreover, the Jubilee would live in Israel's imagination, giving it hope, as it struggled under oppressive regimes, that one day there would be a "year of liberty" (Isa 61:1-2).

New Testament

For Christians, the year of Jubilee has already arrived. In Luke's Gospel, Jesus begins his ministry by announcing the Jubilee. "The Spirit of the Lord is upon me, because he has anointed me to bring glad tidings to the poor. He has sent me to proclaim liberty to captives . . . to let the oppressed go free, and to proclaim a year acceptable to the Lord" (Luke 4:18-19).

Pastoral Notes

The consequences of Luke's depiction of Jesus for Christians is that the Christian life should be characterized by the spirit of Jubilee, of rejoicing in our freedom, in celebration of justice among us. It means that the Christian community should be marked by insistence upon the dignity of the poor and the oppressed and by its active work for economic and social justice. It means that the community is not fully Christian where these are lacking.

See: FEASTS, SABBATH

KATHLEEN M. O'CONNOR

JUDAISM

Judaism refers to the religious beliefs and practices of the people in postexilic Judah who worshiped Yahweh,* the national God of ancient Israel,* and have chosen to pattern the behavior according to the Torah, which they believed to be the revelation of Yahweh's will for them.

The national religion of ancient Israel underwent a profound transformation following the fall of Jerusalem, the end of the monarchy, and the rise of Persian hegemony in the ancient Near East. Usually historians of Judaism credit Ezra with effecting this transformation. The Bible remembers Ezra as an emissary of the Persian emperor who sent him to restore the worship of Yahweh in the territory of the former Southern Kingdom. The Book of Nehemiah describes a ceremony during which Ezra read the Torah aloud to the assembled people who accepted the Torah as God's will (Nehemiah 8). It was at this time that the religion of ancient Israel, a Temple-centered religion, became Judaism, a religion of the book.

In Judaism, the national God of ancient Israel became a universal deity though belief in the election of Israel persisted. The NT (Matt 23:15) and Rabbinic literature speak about a missionary drive among some Jews. The Temple* of Jerusalem was the setting of its official worship. Though it is difficult to be certain about its exact origins, the synagogue developed in early Judaism to respond to the religious needs of people for whom regular access to the Temple was difficult or impossible. The synagogue became the most important institution of early Judaism. Its non-sacrificial pattern of worship focused on the reading of the Torah and prayer. The synagogue was subject to administration by laity and did not require the presence of a priest for its worship. While the concern of the sacrificial cult of the Temple continued to be the fertility of the land, the concern of the synagogue was on the salvation of the individual. The synagogue provided a setting for the study and interpretation of the Torah. This study became the central focus of Judaism.

In its formative period, Judaism exhibited an amazing variety. The NT mentions the Pharisees and Sadducees. Josephus mentions the Essenes. The Roman authorities considered the early Christian movement as just another Jewish religious group. These groups differed with one another regarding both belief and practice. For example, the Sadducees considered only the Pentateuch as authoritative while the Pharisees also accepted the Prophets and the Writings. The Christians accepted the Septuagint version of the OT and produced their own religious texts. The Essenes too produced their own distinctive religious literature that along with the OT guided the lives of the people of Qumran. The Pharisees and Sadducees followed a lunar religious calendar while the Essenes used a solar calendar. This means that these groups celebrated the same religious festivals on different days. It was only after the unsuccessful Jewish revolts against Rome in the first and second centuries CE that Rabbinic Judaism became dominant.

There are two sources of knowledge about early Judaism. The first are the literary sources. These include the Intertestamental literature, the NT, the writings of Josephus, and Rabbinic literature. There are problems with each of these. Rabbinic Judaism abandoned the Intertestamental literature. Its preservation was the achievement of various Christian churches. Before these texts can provide information about the development of Judaism, it is necessary to identify any Christian interpolations in them. The NT takes a polemical stand against some Jewish beliefs and practices. This does not give confidence that it provides objective information. Josephus' intention was apologetic so his description of early Judaism needs to be evaluated accordingly. Finally the Rabbinic literature dates from at least 200 CE. It too takes a polemical stand against Jewish beliefs and practices that it considers illegitimate. The value of its information for the early period of Judaism is a matter of debate. Of course, some Jewish groups may not have produced any literature or it may be that none of their literature has survived.

The other source of knowledge about early Judaism is the archaeological record. Though more work is being done at sites that date from the Jewish period, there is not enough to make firm conclusions. Inscriptions at these sites are rare and this leaves the matter of the interpretation of the archaeological data critical. For example, there is no consensus about the identification of buildings as synagogues. There is no building in Palestine built before the third century CE that is unanimously identified as a synagogue. The identification of first-century structures at Gamla, Magdala, Masada, and the Herodion as synagogues is a matter of debate. More excavation needs to be done before one can confidently use the archaeological data to help reconstruct the shape of early Judaism.

At one time scholars spoke of a "normative Judaism" in the Judaism's formative period. "Normative Judaism" was generally taken to be the precursor of Rabbinic Judaism. Other types of Judaism in the early period were considered "sects." The model for such a characterization of early Judaism comes from the history of the Church that was fragmented into orthodox Christianity and a maze of heretical groups. Christianity placed a great store by correctly formulated doctrinal statements so that orthodoxy and heresy are suitable categories for the interpretation of early Christianity. Judaism, however, had no comparative concern. The interest of early Judaism centered on correct patterns of behavior by its adherents. Correctly formulated statements of belief were less important.

Finally, though the center of early Judaism was Jerusalem and the land of Israel, important Jewish centers developed elsewhere. For example, in Egypt there were settlements at Elephantine and Leontopolis with each having its own temple. The Jewish community in Alexandria produced the Septuagint. There was a vibrant Jewish community in Babylon. In the sixth century CE the Jewish sages there produced the only complete Talmud.

The relationship between Judaism and Christianity in their formative years was not a happy one. More research needs to be done on the hypothesis of "Jewish Christianity," i.e., a form of Palestinian Judaism that professed Jesus as the Messiah. Once Christianity became the dominant religion of Palestine in the Byzantine Period (fourth to the seventh centuries CE), the relationship between Christianity and Judaism deteriorated tragically. The anti-Jewish legislation of the Byzantine emperors was the beginning of an anti-semitism that Christians have found difficult to eliminate despite the stance taken by the Vatican Council's *Declaration on the Relationship of the Church to Non-Christian Religions (Nostra Aetate)* (art. 4). Here the Church states that there is a spiritual bond between Jews and Christians, that the Church received the revelation of the OT from the Jews, and, above all, that the Jews are not responsible for the death of Jesus.

See: ISRAEL, JEW

LESLIE J. HOPPE, O.F.M.

JUDGES

The judges were the leaders of the Israelite tribes in the transition period between the ages of ancient Israel's great leaders. They emerged after both Moses and Joshua died. The period of ancient Israel's ascendancy under David and Solomon was yet to come. The judges led Israel at a crucial time when a new community was arising out of the disparate groups that were trying to create an entirely new pattern of life in Canaan. This new community was to be one in which all people had an equal range of opportunities. The creation of a new community meant a rejection of the oppressive Canaanite political and social systems and the religious beliefs that were their foundation and legitimation. The new people led by the judges would offer their allegiance only to Yahweh.

The creation of this new society was an immense struggle. The Israelite tribes were not the only groups that were trying to gain a foothold in Canaan. The Book of Judges remembers the judges as military leaders who helped the tribes resist the peoples that were threatening Israel's continued existence in the land. During distressful times, there arose individuals whose personal initiative inspired the Israelite population. They set a course of action for the people and undertook the task of eliminating the military perils posed by the Canaanites. Personal initiative by the judges, followed by popular acceptance of the judges' leadership, justifies the description of the judges as "charismatic" leaders. The Book of Judges describes the source of the judges' charisma as the "spirit of the LORD" (3:10; 6:34; 11:29; 13:25; 14:6, 19; 15:14).

The charismatic leadership characteristic of the judges is strictly personal and not hereditary. The one attempt at establishing a dynasty during the era of the judges failed (Judges 9). It was also independent of social status, age, or sex. Jephthah was a prostitute's son (Judg 11:1), Gideon was the youngest member of his family (Judg 6:15), and Deborah (Judges 4–5) was a woman. In addition the judges did not derive their authority from any association with places of special status among the tribes such as Bethel, Shechem, or Shiloh. Their emergence from fringe areas or insignificant places underscored the personal nature of their charismatic authority. Finally their leadership did not depend on coercion. Voluntary militia composed the armies raised by the judges.

There were two principal shortcomings of the charismatic leadership provided by the judges. First, no judge was ever able to unite all the tribes in any common effort. Deborah managed to assemble the largest tribal league according to the Book of Judges. Still it included only six tribes. Second, the effectiveness of the judges' leadership was temporary. With the death of a particular judge, the tribes had to face a recurrence of military and political insecurity. The representatives of the tribes tried to give a more permanent form to the charismatic leadership provided by the judges (Judg 8:22), but these attempts were not successful. The Philistines posed the most serious threat to Israel's existence. The tribal militia led by charismatic leaders was no match for them. It was under pressure brought to bear by the Philistines that a permanent, centralized leadership in the form of the monarchy established itself in Israel.

See: CANAAN, CONQUEST, JOSHUA, PHILISTINES

LESLIE J. HOPPE, O.F.M.

JUDGMENT

The notion that human beings bear responsibility for individual and corporate attitudes and actions undergirds the biblical concept of judgment. There is always a disparity between God's will and the human response to it. In the OT the covenant is the measuring rod of fidelity to God. In NT traditions, the basis of judgment is one's response to Jesus. From an initial focus on God's judgment being exercised in the present, there develops the idea that a future judgment will take place after death.

Old Testament

The criterion for judgment by God in the OT is not an abstract, philosophical notion of justice considered as valid throughout the world, but rather the concrete reality of covenant which brought with it mutual obligations of fidelity. Historically, Israel was conscious of the Exodus and Sinai experience as the establishment of a covenant between God and the nation. God would be faithful to the covenant by bringing Israel victory, salvation,* justice, and guidance, and the people would uphold their side by obedience, faith, worship, and keeping of the commandments. The activity of the prophets helped to clarify the nature and importance of social justice as a norm of divine judgment, and also enlarged the place of the foreign nations in this regard. Initially, foreign nations were simply thought of as the enemy of God and Israel, yet prophets such as Amos held foreign rulers also bound by the requirements of social justice. Of course the early conception of God as creator of all humanity, as shown in the Yah-

wistic account of creation of Adam and Eve, Fall, Flood, Tower of Babel, and election of Abraham as a blessing for "all nations," already betrays a positive interest in the relationship of non-Israelites to God (Genesis 2–12), but the full flowering of this theological inquiry did not take place until the prophetic preaching taught the centrality of social justice as the hallmark of fidelity to God's will, through the covenant for Israelites, and simply as divine demand in the case of the Gentiles. The ambivalence of Israel toward outsiders, considered primarily as enemy, remained strong throughout its history, though universalism, the hope that all nations would worship God in harmony and peace, was periodically expressed, especially in the "swords to plowshares" text of Isaiah 2:2-4, Micah 4:1-4, and in the future vision of Trito-Isaiah (Isa 56:1-8; 60:5-14). The criteria regarding judgment became more personal, more individual, and eventually moved, in apocalyptic thought, to reward and punishment beyond the grave.

Hebrew Words. Judgment is described by many Hebrew words, all of them applicable to God as well as to human judges. *Shaphat* refers to the restoration of order that has been disturbed. When this is accomplished by the exercise of power, *shaphat* means to "rule" (Pss 96:13; 98:9); when order is restored by the singling out and disposing of the disturbing factor, it means "to judge" (Gen 16:5; 1 Sam 24:13, 16) or "to condemn" (1 Sam 3:13; Ps 51:6).

The verb *din*, "to judge," is used variously of God, who "tries" Israel in court (Isa 3:13; Ps 50:4), condemns sinful nations (Gen 15:14), and helps the oppressed attain their rights (Gen 30:6; Deut 32:36; Ps 54:3).

Hebrew *rib* means "to quarrel" (Gen 26:20) or "litigate" in court (Isa 1:17) and can be said of people versus God (Job 9:3; Isa 45:9; Jer 12:1), God versus people (Amos 7:4; Isa 3:13; Mic 6:1; Hos 4:4), but is often applied to God as defender of those in need (Jer 50:34; 51:36; Prov 22:23; 23:11).

Naqam signifies "to avenge," in human contexts (Josh 10:13) and divine (Ps 99:8; Isa

1:24; Jer 5:9; 9:8; Nah 1:2). As a noun it means "vengeance" and may be used apropos of God (Deut 32:35; Isa 34:8; Jer 20:12).

The causative Hiphil form of *yakah* can be predicated of God, who "judges" (Isa 2:4 = Mic 4:3; Job 16:21) or "chastises" (2 Sam 7:14; Ps 6:2; 38:2; Jer 2:19).

Paqad signifies "to be concerned about," "to visit." God "visits" to bring a blessing (Gen 21:1; Ruth 1:6; Ps 65:10; 106:4; Jer 29:10), or punishment (Isa 13:9-11; 24:21; 26:14; Jer 6:15; Zeph 1:8f.; Zech 10:3).

Pentateuch and Historical Books. God as judge is primarily concerned about fidelity to the Mosaic covenant, a covenant that also serves as the background to the Yahwist's account of Israel's pre-history with its divine judgments about Adam and Eve, Cain and Abel, the Flood, the Tower of Babel (Genesis 2–11). As covenant partner, God granted Israel *sedaqa*, "justice," which included victory ("just deeds," Judg 5:11; "acts of mercy," 1 Sam 12:7), but also the demand for honesty (Lev 19:36; Deut 25:15) and the threat of judgment (1 Sam 26:23). Like any good judge (see Deut 25:1) God is fair, acquitting the innocent and punishing the guilty (1 Kgs 8:31f.), but especially liberating the oppressed (Judg 11:27; Deut 10:18; 32:36). On their part, the Israelites were to act with "righteousness" in relation to God (Gen 15:6; Deut 6:25) and one another, judging justly (Lev 19:15; Deut 1:16) and with special concern for their exploited fellow citizens (Exod 23:6).

Psalms. Hymns often praise God as a "ruler" (Ps 96:10) who is just (Pss 98:9; 96:13), punishes the wicked (Ps 9:17), and defends the oppressed (Pss 68:6; 76:10; 103:6; 135:14). Laments call upon God to judge in favor of the innocent (Pss 7:9; 17:2; 26:1; 43:1) and punish the guilty (Ps 94:2f.). They express confidence that in spite of injustice, God is ultimately judge (Ps 67:5) and will defend those in need (Pss 10:18; 140:13). Prophetic psalms portray God as judge (Pss 50:4f.; 82:2f., 8), as do historical psalms (e.g., Ps 105:5-7). Royal/messianic psalms see just judgment and defense of

the afflicted as characteristics of the king who is to come (Pss 72:2, 4; 110:6).

Prophets. Most of the preexilic prophetic texts about divine judgment are condemnations of sin, with relatively little room for promises of salvation. The typical prophetic literary form is the judgment-speech, which includes an accusation, messenger-formula, and announcement of punishment (Amos 7:16f.; Isa 8:6-8; Mic 3:9-12). The Babylonian Exile (587–538 BCE) was seen as a major judgment because of sin, and was followed by new emphasis on oracles of salvation, especially by Jeremiah, Ezekiel, and Deutero-Isaiah.

Among the preexilic prophets, Amos inaugurates the concept of the Day of the Lord* as a time of judgment and condemnation (Amos 5:18-20) because of the people's great social injustices (Amos 2:6-8; 4:1-3; 5:7-12) and hypocritical worship (Amos 5:21-24). Threats include war (Amos 3:11; 6:14), exile (Amos 5:27; 6:7; 7:11), destruction of the kingdom (Amos 5:1; 7:9; 9:8), and death (Amos 5:16f.; 6:9f.; 8:3). Hosea indicts Israel for sins against the covenant decalogue (Hos 4:1-2) and for worship of Baal (Hos 2:7, 10; 4:11-14; 8:4-7), but offers hope of repentance and a new intimate relationship with God through the purification of punishment (Hos 2:1-3, 10-25; 11:8-9; 14:5-9). For Isaiah God is the holy One whose sanctity is manifested in divine justice (Isa 5:16), but against whom the people have sinned (Isa 1:4). God summons Judah to court (Isa 1:2f.; 3:13f.), accuses it of empty worship (Isa 1:10-17; 29:13f.), corrupt legislation (Isa 10:1-4), pride (Isa 3:16), oppression of the poor (Isa 3:14; 5:8), and threatens divine punishment (Isa 13:11). Hope is expressed that a future Davidic king would come to rule "by judgment and justice" (Isa 9:6; see 11:3-5). Micah also sees God calling Israel and Judah to account (Mic 6:1f.), lists their social evils (Mic 2:1-11; 3:1-11), and threatens the utter destruction of Jerusalem (Mic 3:12), in a warning that was remembered over one hundred years later (Jer 26:18). Jeremiah announces a "time of punishment" (Jer 6:15; see 5:9; 9:8; 21:14) for the evil of Judah's citizens (Jer 5:2-9; 7:1-15). Yet the people's enemies shall also be judged and condemned (Jer 25:31), for God is the defender of those in need (Jer 50:34; 51:36), and will establish a "new covenant" of grace in place of the old one which had been "broken" (Jer 31:31-34).

In preexilic Israel, evil was threatened with punishment and good deeds promised reward, but with the understanding that both would take place in this life. A new emphasis on personal responsibility by Jeremiah and Ezekiel, with reward or punishment on an individual basis, (see Ezekiel 18) helped the Israelites notice more clearly glaring inequities in this life, where the wicked often prosper and the good suffer. The possibility of judgment and justice that reaches beyond death was then envisioned in Job 14:13-15; 19:25-27; probably also Psalm 49:15, and became explicit in Daniel 12:1-3; 2 Maccabees 7, and Wisdom 2–5.

See: APOCALYPTIC, COVENANT, JUSTICE

JOSEPH F. WIMMER, O.S.A.

New Testament

In the NT traditions there are several new notions concerning God's judgment. Response to Jesus becomes the basis of judgment. Moreover, Jesus shares in God's activity of judgment. In defining "judgment" in the NT three distinct issues arise: (1) whether the divine judgment takes place in the present or future; (2) whether judgment is upon an individual or a group; and (3) whether God judges directly or only through an agent, such as Jesus. There is a diversity of opinion among the NT authors in their answers to these theological questions.

Krisis. *Krisis* (the etymological root of the English word "crisis") is the Greek noun translated as "judgment." The word in NT Greek carries the juridical connotation of a courtroom verdict or sentence. God's judgment results in vindication for the righteous (e.g., 2 Thess 1:5); but for the unjust it ends in condemnation and punishment (e.g., Heb 10:27).

The Synoptic Gospel Authors. Surprisingly the word "judgment" does not occur in the Gospel of Mark. This evangelist apparently understood Jesus as having little to say directly about judgment. However, Mark's narrative does include the so-called "little apocalypse," in which Jesus warns of several events imminent in human history that will inaugurate divine judgment on a national scale: destruction of the Jerusalem Temple, a coming persecution, a great tribulation, and an arrival of a heavenly figure called the "Son of Man" (Mark 13). Jesus says, "Woe to pregnant women and nursing mothers in those days. Pray that it does not happen in winter. For those times will have tribulation such as has not been since the beginning of God's creation until now, nor will ever be" (Mark 13:17-19). These words echo the preaching of John the Baptizer that "the kingdom of God is at hand" (Mark 1:15). They express ancient Jewish national apocalypticism, which hoped for the judgment of God on cities and nations during the present course of human history. This idea finds articulation in the OT (Daniel 7) and Jewish noncanonical Intertestamental literature (such as *1 Enoch, 4 Ezra*, and some works from the Dead Sea Scrolls).

Matthew and Luke also present Jesus preaching the judgment of God, but they use the actual word *krisis.* In his reproach to unrepentant towns, the Synoptic Jesus laments: "Woe to you, Chorazin! Woe to you Bethsaida! For if the mighty deeds done in your midst had been done in Tyre and Sidon, they would long ago have repented, sitting in sackcloth and ashes. But it will be more tolerable for Tyre and Sidon at the judgment than for you. And as for you, Capernaum, 'Will you be exalted to heaven? You will go down to the netherworld'" (Luke 10:13-15; par. Matt 11:21-23). This reproach amounts to a curse and quotes OT prophetic language taunting a foreign king (Isa 14:13-15). The reproach of

Jesus is against cities and not individuals; the residents share collective accountability, and so suffer on a municipal and even national level. In the Acts of the Apostles, Luke continues this theme by including it in the speeches of Stephen (Acts 7:7), Peter (Acts 10:42), and Paul (Acts 17:31; 24:25). Evidently, the judgment of God was an important theme in early Christian preaching.

But who will do the actual judging? Matthew writes: "When the Son of Man comes in his glory, and all the angels with him, he will sit upon this glorious throne, and all the nations will be assembled before him. And he will separate them one from another, as a shepherd separates the sheep from the goats" (Matt 25:31-32). The judgment of God will be done by an agent, the heavenly figure called the "Son of Man," and by the apostles themselves who will "sit on twelve thrones, judging the twelve tribes of Israel" (Matt 19:28). One tribe will be separated from another tribe. This is not what later Christians would call the Last Judgment of the Second Coming, but the first (and, presumably, only) judgment of the first (and, presumably, only) coming of the apocalyptic "Son of Man" (equated with the Lord Jesus).

The Fourth Gospel. The Gospel of John expresses a view of divine judgment different from that of the Synoptics. The Johannine Jesus says: "Now is the time of judgment on this world; now the ruler of this world will be driven out" (John 12:31); "Whoever believes in him [God] will not be condemned, but whoever does not believe has already been condemned, because he has not believed in the name of the only Son of God" (John 3:18). The author of John claims that the judgment of God has already taken place, effectively enacted in the earthly life of each human being. Judgment is not the future historical event the Synoptic authors describe. In the Fourth Gospel, the judgment of God is based not on a national but an individual level, on each person's attitude toward Jesus. Since the judgment of God has already taken place,

the Fourth Gospel does not need to show conflict between divine and demonic powers. This helps explain why John omits all exorcism stories. The devil, as the prototype of unbelief, has already lost the contest before the Gospel narrative begins. Additionally, in one of the most extraordinary passages in the Bible, the Johannine Jesus claims to have been given, as God's son, the twin powers traditionally reserved to God alone, the power of judgment and the power of bestowing life (John 5:22-27; John Ashton, *Understanding the Fourth Gospel* [Oxford: Clarendon Press, 1991] 322; see also 220–226). Such statements stand in tension with the theology of OT authors, who view God as the exclusive maker of judgment and life.

Paul. Contrary to John, Paul clearly understands the judgment of God to be a future event, and here he is steeped thoroughly in Jewish apocalyptic eschatology. Throughout Romans 2, Paul argues that humans in the present age must not attempt judgment, especially of outsiders, since that right belongs to God. The apostle asks the rhetorical question, "Do you suppose . . . that you will escape the judgment of God?" (Rom 2:3) and declares, "By your stubbornness and impenitent heart, you are storing up wrath for yourself for the day of wrath and revelation of the just judgment of God" (Rom 2:5). Judgment is a technical term for Paul, which differs from communal discipline in a congregation (1 Corinthians 5). While Paul insists that "God will judge outsiders," he also exhorts that the Corinthian Church should "Purge the evil person from your midst" (1 Cor 5:13). Interestingly, this expulsion ritual is for the *benefit* of the offender, "so that his spirit may be saved on the day of the Lord" (1 Cor 5:5). For Paul, church discipline works in increasing the chances for an individual to receive a favorable verdict in the divine judgment that occurs at the end of time and before the throne of God.

Paul insists that "we shall all stand before the judgment seat of God" (Rom 14:10). At the end of time, every individual will be judged: Jews according to Torah (Rom 2:12-13) and Gentiles according to their interior law of conscience (Rom 2:14-16). Yet it was Paul's constant hope that all Israel as a national group would eventually receive the positive judgment of God and that Israel's current disbelief in Christ was only part of God's plan to delay their salvation until the "full number of Gentiles" have entered (Rom 11:25-35).

1–2 Timothy, Hebrews, James, 1 Peter. These letters depart from the national apocalyptic eschatology of a Paul who believed that all Israel would eventually be saved by God's judgment. This is not surprising since these NT letters reflect Christian belief of the second generation (ca. after 100 CE), when reconciliation between Jews and Gentile Christians became an unlikely, even undesirable, event. Previously apocalyptic statements about the judgment of God become domesticated and incorporated into literary household codes that contain rules of conduct in the family, the Church, and the wider Greco-Roman society. For example, under the rule of behavior for presbyters the deutero-Pauline author of Timothy writes: "Do not lay hands too readily on anyone, and do not share in another's sins. Keep yourself pure. . . . Some people's sins are public, preceding them to judgment; but other people are followed by their sins" (1 Tim 5:22, 24). Here we find the idea of the Last Judgment, which (the author believed) will occur outside history, not in the political course of human events, and on individuals, not nations.

The author of Hebrews shares this view of a future Last Judgment, when God will render either a positive or negative verdict on individuals, even those who have died previously: "Just as it is appointed that human beings die once, and after this the judgment, so also Christ, offered once to take away the sins of many, will appear a second time, not to take away sin but to bring salvation to those who eagerly await him" (Heb 9:27; see also 6:2 and 10:26-31;

1 Pet 4:5-6). The domesticated eschatology is evident when the author exhorts a household code: "Let marriage be honored among all and the marriage bed kept undefiled, for God will judge the immoral and adulterers" (Heb 13:3). The Letter of James repeats this notion that fear of the Last Judgment has a pedagogical, domestic function in the Church: "Not many of you should become teachers, my brothers, for you realize that we will be judged more strictly" (Jas 3:1; see also 2:13; 4:12; 5:9). First Peter continues this vein: "For it is now time for the judgment to begin with the household of God; if it begins with us, how will it end for those who fail to obey the gospel of God?" (1 Pet 4:17; see also 1:17; 2:23).

2 Peter, Jude, and Revelation. When modern Christians speak of the "Judgment Day," they mainly refer (whether consciously or not) to the imagery found in these latter letters of the NT, as well as the Intertestamental literature upon which they depend (Jude 14–15 even makes a direct citation of *1 Enoch* 1.9; found in James H. Charlesworth, ed., *The Old Testament Pseudepigrapha* [Garden City, N.Y.: Doubleday] 1:13-14). The biblical reader is presented with a startling apocalyptic vision of the judgment of God as a cosmic catastrophe, with bizarre imagery of chained angels, horned dragons, armed horsemen, and heavenly thrones. John, apparently in exile on the island of Patmos, narrates his terrifying vision: "When he broke open the fifth seal, I saw underneath the altar the souls of those who had been slaughtered because of the witness they bore to the word of God. They cried out, 'How long will it be, holy and true master, before you sit in judgment and avenge our blood on the inhabitants of the earth?'" (Rev 6:9-10). John continues: "Then one of the seven angels who were holding the seven bowls came and said to me, 'Come here. I will show you the judgment on the great harlot who lives near the many waters. The great kings of the earth have had intercourse with her, and the inhabitants of the earth became drunk on the wine of her harlotry'"

(Rev 17:1-2). This wicked prostitute is later identified as the Harlot of Babylon (Rev 17:5), meaning the city of Rome as the capital of the Roman Empire, whose hour of judgment has come (Rev 18:10). The reference to wine refers to the blood of martyred Christians persecuted by Greco-Roman officials. The author calls upon God to bring divine wrath upon the political enemies of the Church. In John's visions, angels in heaven continually emphasize that the judgment of God is just (Rev 16:5, 7; 19:2). In all these examples, the judgment (*krisis*) of God occurs in the negative sense of condemnation following a cosmic crisis.

In Jude and 1 Peter, the judgment of God is said to convict not only humans, but also disobedient divinities: "The angels too, who did not keep to their own domain but deserted their proper dwelling, he has kept in eternal chains, in gloom, for the judgment of the great day" (Jude 6; see also 2 Pet 2:4, which uses Jude as a literary source). No creature on earth or heaven can escape the just judgment of God.

See: APOCALYPTIC, CONSCIENCE, DAY OF THE LORD, ESCHATOLOGY, HOPE, NATIONS, POWER, RECONCILIATION, REIGN OF GOD, SALVATION, SIN, SON OF MAN, THRONE OF GOD, WRATH OF GOD

J. ALBERT HARRILL

Pastoral-Liturgical Tradition

In general, the notion of judgment is related to the sense of disparity between God and humanity, and with the sense that this unfortunate condition involves human decisions and responsibility. It assumes that there is an ethical order which is ultimately grounded in divine reality, and that human beings, through their ethical decisions, have failed to live in a way that is appropriate to this ethical order.

Early Tradition. The theological tradition has consistently maintained the biblical sense of a final judgment for all human beings at the end of history. The early Christian creedal formulas contain this idea from the beginning (DS 10; 42; 44; 76; 125; 150).

Less clear is the understanding of individual judgment which is associated with the death of each human person and decides each person's eternal destiny. While some patristic authors like Jerome, Augustine, and John Chrysostom hold firmly to the idea of individual judgment, others like Lactantius seem to be less convinced or at least give no explicit witness to the teaching. While there has never been a dogmatic definition on the matter, the notion of personal judgment seems to be presupposed in the Medieval teachings concerning the necessary purgation of souls between the death of individuals and their entrance into glory (DS 838–839; 857–858; 1305–1306).

Current Developments. The meaning of general judgment is well summarized by K. Rahner. This symbol speaks "of the fact that humankind and its history as a collective unity comes under God's judgment" (*Sacramentum Mundi* III, 275). It is, therefore, the symbol of God's ultimate victory with respect to the whole of humanity and its history. It is within this whole that one must situate the question of individual destiny.

Medieval and later representations of individual judgment tended to envision it in terms of a courtroom scene and created the impression that judgment came as an act of God that was totally external to the person under judgment. Recent interpretations have taken a more anthropological approach and see judgment to rest in the fact that the human person comes to know itself fully in the light of the divine reality and in the light of the deepest potential of human nature. What one has actually made of one's life for oneself and for others is seen against the backdrop of what might have been through a more generous response to God's grace. In this sense, judgment is not simply external but internal, for it is the deepest personal awareness of what one has become in one's personal relation with God. It is not merely a future reality but an element of present experience as well.

Recent developments in the understanding of human death as the moment of final decision lead to the position that personal judgment is an element intrinsic to the experience of death. If the theory of final decision is taken in its strong form, it follows that the personal judgment involved in the experience of death is irrevocable and final. The mainline of Christian tradition does not envision any form of reincarnation.

Many current treatments seek to recover the Christological dimension of judgment as it appeared in the NT. The criterion of judgment is embodied in the human-divine mystery of Jesus Christ who represents the full realization of human potential in its relation to God.

Pastoral Dimensions. In general, the significance of the metaphor of "judgment" consists in the way it underscores the significance of human responsibility and the reality of a norm for ethical decisions that transcends the level of personal taste.

See: DEATH, JUSTICE

ZACHARY HAYES, O.F.M.

JUSTICE

Justice is part of the moral fiber of a society. In the Bible, the covenant relationship that the people have with God is the basis of the responsibility of justice that they have toward each other. Human justice is a mirror of divine justice.

Old Testament

Justice is a word that has far-reaching dimensions in the OT. On the one hand, it can refer to the legal systems of government and the expectations of societal relations. On the other hand, it is part of the moral fiber of a religious people who act in a particular way because they have discovered their God to be just and faithful. It is no exaggeration to say that the theme of justice is central to the theological message of the Hebrew Scriptures and weaves its way through almost every book of the OT.

The two most common Hebrew terms used to describe justice are *mišpaṭ* and *ṣedaqâ*. The word *mišpaṭ* appears over four hundred times in the OT, referring primarily to deeds of justice and the execution of judgment. Most often this term relates to legal situations where decisions are made according to a judicial procedure (Exod 21:31; 1 Kgs 3:28). This word is also used to describe the actions of God, who is known as the "God of justice" (Isa 30:18). Divine judgments came from God's love, faithfulness, and mercy (Pss 37:28; 146:6-7). The other term, *ṣedaqâ*, means "to be straight, true, righteous and just." One of the important nuances of the word suggests an element of relationship in the practice of authentic justice. Whether it is God or a person who is practicing justice, its perfect expression is founded on an understanding of "right relationship" between the involved parties. God demonstrated the way of right relationship to creation in the way that all things and creatures were made and are supported and sustained by their Creator (Genesis 1; Pss 104:24-30; 106:1-5). As God has established a mode of right relationship with human beings, so Israel was to respond in a right manner by obedience, reverence, and faithfulness to their God. It is also true that the right relationship God established demonstrates the way of justice for human beings in dealing with one another. The implications of such a notion of justice are far-reaching, indeed.

The Torah/Pentateuch. From the very beginning, divine justice is seen in primeval salvation history. God established a way for mortal beings to respond to the gifts that were given them. When the human response was disobedience, God's justice was seen in both punishment (Gen 3:16-19, 23; 4:11-12; 6:7; 11:7-9) and mercy (Gen 3:21; 4:15; 6:8; 9:1-7).

In the event of the Exodus, the gifts of the covenant and the Law were perceived as further manifestations of divine justice. As the Initiator of the covenant, God provided for the well-being and safety of the people of Israel (Exod 19:3-6; 20:2). Israel's response needed to be faithful adherence to the commandments and laws (Exod 19:5; 20:1-17) which were given to them. The stipulations of the covenant set up a treaty of "right relationship" in which God's word of promise called forth a response of obedience and trust on the part of Israel.

The Book of Deuteronomy shows another dimension of divine justice. The mercy, compassion, and love which God showed to Israel and to all people in need are the same as that which Israel was to practice within its own community and toward foreigners (Deut 10:17-19). The Initiator of the intimate relationship of covenant expected Israel to practice divine justice. In this expectation of the covenant relationship, we see how justice took on a dynamic character: justice lives on in the world both by divine action and through those who fulfill the obligations of their covenant relationship with God.

The Prophets. The classical prophets raged at the injustice which they saw present in their life situations. They were keenly aware of the demands of the covenant and were infuriated by the elected people's lack of responsiveness. Similarly, the prophets realized the depth of God's gracious offer of salvation to Israel and they lamented a half-hearted acknowledgement of it. They warned Israel of the judgment which awaited their injustice (cf. Isa 1:11-20; Amos 2:4-16).

Among the preexilic prophets, Amos railed the fiercest against the injustices of Israel. "They sell the just man for silver, and the poor man for a pair of sandals" (Amos 2:6). God promised blessing to the just and poor, yet Israel thwarted the divine word of promise by shrewd calculations and selfish gain. God wished the exaltation of the lowly in Israel, but the wicked defied the divine word by crushing the poor. Amos reminded the people that justice would prevail "on that day" (Amos 2:16; 3:14; 5:18, 20; 6:3; 8:3, 9, 11, 13), a time of judgment for those who have mocked the justice of God rooted in care, compassion, and steadfast kindness.

The prophet Hosea used the image of marriage to describe the covenant relationship between God and Israel. "I will make a covenant for them on that day. . . . I will espouse you to me forever: I will espouse you in right and in justice, in love and in mercy; I will espouse you to me in fidelity, and you shall know the LORD" (Hos 2:20-22). The qualities which make up a right relationship with God include: righteousness, justice, compassion, and steadfast kindness. God revealed what would be bestowed upon Israel for all eternity in the restoration of the covenant. God's gift of justice to Israel was an act of re-creation, a return to the state of paradise where justice once reigned.

The Isaian tradition presents yet another aspect of the meaning of justice. Throughout the corpus of the book of Isaiah, the words *mišpaṭ* and *ṣedaqâ* appear with frequency. There are numerous examples of where they appear together as a pair of terms to denote justice in an emphatic way (Isa 1:27; 5:7, 16; 9:6; 16:5; 26:9; 28:17; 32:1, 16; 33:5). These references to justice in the first section of Isaiah (chs. 1–39) rehearse this essential quality of life according to the covenant which was absent from Israel's way of life. Because of this, Israel was a nation without hope (Isa 1:3-7, 16). However, there is hope that justice will renew the world through the coming Messiah (Isa 9:6; 32:1) or on the day of eschatological judgment (Isa 16:5; 26:9, 32:16; 33:5).

In the second section of Isaiah (chs. 40–55), the day of justice is described as a salvific event. On six occasions, the word *ṣedaqâ* is found in tandem with the word for salvation—(see Isa 45:8; 45:21; 46:13; 51:5, 6, 8). "I will make my justice come speedily; my salvation shall go forth" (Isa 51:5; cf. vv. 6-8). The renewal of justice by God will be a redemptive experience for Israel in which they will be restored to their status as a covenant people. The descriptive language and imagery used in Second Isaiah shows that the gift of salvific justice restored peace (i.e., well-being), prosperity, and victory to a once-defeated people.

The third section of Isaiah (chs. 56–66) begins with the theme of justice in its dimensions of both right living and salvation: "Observe what is right, do what is just; for my salvation is about to come, my justice, about to be revealed" (Isa 56:1). These final chapters of Isaiah show a glimpse of the struggle existing in the community of Israel, even after their restoration, to live in right relationship with one another. The priestly class and the prophetic visionaries disputed over who would provide the new leadership for the people restored to their land. The establishment of justice took a back seat to other issues (Isa 57:1-2, 12-13; 58:2; 59:4). The absence of justice is described as an experience of utter darkness and futility: "right is far from us and justice does not reach us. We look for light, and lo, darkness; for brightness, but we walk in gloom! Like blind men we grope along the wall, like people without eyes we feel our way" (Isa 59:9-10). However, darkness will be transformed into light with the advent of God; God will clothe the people of the covenant in the garments of justice and salvation (see Isa 60:1-3; 61:10; 62:1). The Isaian corpus thus teaches that the practice of justice led the covenant people of God toward the experience of salvation.

The Writings. The prayers of Israel, the psalms, reflect the understanding that God's justice far exceeds what the human mind can even comprehend (Pss 65:6; 71:15-16, 19; 103:6, 17; 111:2-4; 145:7). God's blessing of justice promised Israel well-being and security. Though God also executed punishment as Israel's judge (Ps 129:4), Israel knew well that mercy, kindness, and compassion characterize the divine reign (Ps 116:5). The psalmist cried out for vindication from false accusation (Pss 7:9; 26:1; 35:24; 43:1). The psalmist expressed the belief that God's justice is shown in the demise of the wicked (Pss 129:4; 143:11-12). The psalmist also knew well that human attempts to attain the justice of God are so futile that one must ask for divine assistance to be righteous (Ps 143:1-2). Even the king prayed that he might be able to judge the people with God's own justice (Ps 72:1-2). Everyone, from the royalty to the poor, spoke to God of the divine justice they desired in their own lives.

In the Book of Proverbs justice is seen in its day-to-day setting of business transactions and payment for services rendered (Prov 11:15, 26; 16:11; 17:18; 20:10). All of these seemingly mundane activities are part of the way in which divine justice is incarnated in the human sphere.

In the Book of Job justice is a key theme: how can a just God allow a just person to suffer? In the book, Job's friends try to place human justice on the same footing with divine justice, but Job knows well that there is no way that the transcendent One can be made to be like mortals (Job 9:11-15, 32-33). In the end, Job learns that God's justice can be understood best in relation to the unfathomable movement of the universe, the splendor of the cosmos, and the wisdom of creation's order (Job 38–42).

The author of the late sapiential writing, the Book of Wisdom, encouraged the pursuit of justice, for it brings forth the fruit of moderation, prudence, righteousness and fortitude, "and nothing in comparison with her" is more useful (Wis 7:8).

See: COVENANT, ESCHATOLOGY, FAITHFULNESS, JUDGMENT, LAW, PEACE, SALVATION

GREGORY J. POLAN, O.S.B.

New Testament

Dikē (right, penalty), *dikaiosynē* (righteousness, justification), and *krisis* (judgment) are the Greek words translated as "justice." The linguistic decision depends on the specific context in which the word occurs and the theology of the particular translator. "Justice" has a wide semantic range in Greek, covering both jurisprudence and ethics. The topic will be divided into three categories: (1) justice from human courts; (2) justice from God; and (3) justice from the Church. In general, the NT writers take a pessimistic view on the ability of human courts to render justice. However, they take an optimistic view on the abilities of God to act justly and of the Church to effect positive social change.

Justice from Human Courts. The trials of Jesus and Paul share a similar cast of characters: conspirators, perjurers, and corrupt magistrates. Neither human courtroom renders justice, but allows innocents to be punished while criminals go free. The Synoptic Gospels are quite clear on this point. Concerning Jesus, Mark writes: "So the chief priests and the scribes were seeking a way to arrest him by treachery and put him to death" (Mark 14:1; par. Matt 26:5; Luke 22:2 tones down Mark's language, leaving the Jewish leaders simply unsure what to do). During Jesus' trial before the Jewish high council (the Sanhedrin), "Many gave false witness against him, but their testimony did not agree" (Mark 14:56; par. Matt 26:59). In their accounts of Jesus' trial before Pilate, Mark and Matthew narrate that the prefect knew that it was the envy of the Jewish leaders that had brought this case to trial (Mark 15:10; Matt 27:18); Matthew writes that Pilate washed his hands of the matter (only in Matt 27:24); and Luke tells that not only the prefect but also a Roman centurion openly declared Jesus to be innocent (Luke 23:22; Luke 23:41). All three evangelists report the prefect's release of Barabbas, a bandit guilty of murder, in place of the innocent Jesus (Mark 15:15; Matt 27:26; Luke 23:25). The jurisprudence of both Jewish and Roman private law fails to render a just verdict.

This failure of human law to render justice is not surprising, since it is foreshadowed in the sayings of Jesus against the hypocrisy of Jewish leaders, especially the scribes and Pharisees. Matthew writes: "Woe to you, scribes and Pharisees, you hypocrites. You pay tithes of mint and dill and cummin, and you have neglected the weightier things of the law: judgment and mercy and fidelity. [But] these things you should have done, without neglecting the others" (Matt 23:23; par. Luke 11:42). Jesus accuses the Pharisees and scribes of having a self-righteous and so distorted view of justice and the law. In his Sermon on the Mount (the Sermon on the Plain in Luke), Jesus corrects Pharisaic views of justice and the law, by replacing retribution, vengeance, and the OT law of talion with the ethical imperative to love enemies (Matt 5:38-48; Luke 6:27-36).

The public street theater of the Pharisees and scribes trumpeting their goodness before them, similar to a performance of thespians masked as in Greek drama to win the praise of others, becomes a caricature of justice gone bad. It is small wonder that the Pharisees and scribes become instrumental in twisting Jewish and Roman justice toward their own selfish ends as the plot of Gospel narrative develops. True justice is described to be divine in origin, achievable through private observance of love of enemies, almsgiving, and prayer done for the sight of God, not humans (Matt 6:1-8).

Acts continues this theme. Repeatedly, the apostles suffer false accusations by Jewish leaders and receive miscarriages of justice before Roman magistrates. Peter and John denounce the injustice of their Sanhedrin proceedings by saying: "Whether it is right in the sight of God for us to obey you rather than God, you be the judges" (Acts 4:19). In another place, Stephen comes before the Sanhedrin and his accusers "presented false witnesses who testified, 'This man never stops saying things against [this] holy place and the law. For we have heard him claim that this Jesus the Nazorean will destroy this place and change the customs that Moses handed down to us'" (Acts 6:13-14). The high priest asks whether these things are so, and rather than defend himself before the council Stephen recounts Israel's history. They stone Stephen, and Saul (soon to be renamed Paul) consents to the execution, which is based on false testimony. This is hardly justice.

The rest of Acts is devoted to the deeds of Paul, who finds himself numerous times before judicial magistrates, on trumped-up charges. In the city of Philippi, Paul exorcises an oracular spirit from a slave girl and incites the anger of her masters, who used her fortune telling abilities to yield a large profit. The masters seize Paul and Silas, drag them to the public square, and enlist on-looking crowds and local authorities to join the fracas (Acts 16:16-24; a similar situation occurs in Acts 19:23-40, the riot of the Ephesian silversmiths).

Mob activity continues to follow Paul and Silas into Thessalonica. After preaching in a synagogue and gaining some prominent converts, the Jewish leaders become jealous, recruit derelicts loitering in the public square, and set the entire city in turmoil. These Jews ironically accuse the apostles with the very crime they themselves are doing: creating a disturbance. Again, the local Greek magistrates are not much help in rendering justice (Acts 17:1-9).

When Paul finally faces Roman imperial magistrates, he is bounced back and forth in a game of judicial ping pong. The Roman proconsul Gallio acts like a referee in the dispute between Paul and the Jewish leaders. The Jews bring Paul to the tribunal, saying, "This man is inducing people to worship God contrary to the law" (Acts 18:13). But which law? Jewish law. Gallio discovers the dispute to be a Jewish and not a Roman matter and refuses to be the judge (Acts 18:14-15). The Jews, not to be deterred, continue to follow Paul from city to city and to incite riots among the crowds against him. Such is the case in Jerusalem, when "the Jews from the province of Asia noticed him in the Temple, stirred up the whole crowd, and laid hands upon him" (Acts 21:27). A riot ensues, which starts the process of Paul's final trial before the Sanhedrin (Acts 22:30–23:11), his transfer to Caesarea (Acts 23:12-35), trial before the proconsul Felix (Acts 24:1-23), and the proconsul Porcius Festus (Acts 25:1-12). During this process, the Jews regularly encourage gang violence and make murder conspiracies and false accusations.

On the whole, Paul gains fairer treatment from Roman authorities than he did from local Greek and Jewish authorities, as the examples of the Roman cohort commander (Acts 22:29), Felix (Acts 24:22-23), and Festus illustrate (Acts 25:12). Because Paul is discovered to be a Roman citizen, he receives just treatment from Roman soldiers. Yet just treatment under arrest and detention is not the same thing as justice. In the narrative, Paul never gets his trial before

Caesar (who at this time would have been the Emperor Nero). Acts ends with Paul sitting in an apartment in the city of Rome. Human justice fails to deliver on its promises. Believers must rely on divine, not human, justice.

Paul sounds a similar theme in his letters. In 1 Corinthians 6:1-6, he tells the believers in that congregation not to seek justice in Greco-Roman courts. Apparently the Corinthian Christians were settling their differences by suing one another. Believers must settle their disputes before the congregation, which acts under divine justice and judgment. Paul, in Romans, argues that humans cannot achieve justice by their own actions through the law (Rom 9:30-33, with *dikaiosynē* translated as "righteousness"). In their attempt to establish their own justice, humans did not submit to the justice ("righteousness") of God (Rom 10:3). Justice ("justification") comes not from Torah, but Christ (Gal 2:21; 3:11; 3:21; Phil 3:9). Human justice is at best inexact and at worst evil. In 2 Corinthians, Paul accuses his opponents with the charge of hypocrisy, disguising themselves as ministers of justice ("righteousness") while being in actuality "false apostles, deceitful workers, who masquerade as apostles of Christ" acting as agents of Satan (2 Cor 11:14-15). Such language is similar to the sharp criticism that the Gospel writers would later report Jesus leveling against the street theater of the Pharisees.

Justice from God. Despite early Christian claims that pagan law was a human invention, such was not the belief in Greco-Roman polytheism. Even the NT acknowledges this understanding. In the sea voyage of Acts, Paul becomes a castaway on the island of Malta. The locals observe a viper bite Paul: "When the natives saw the snake hanging from his hand, they said to one another, 'This man must certainly be a murderer; though he escaped the sea, Justice has not let him remain alive'" (Acts 28:4). The original Greek word translated as "Justice" is *Dikē*, which ancient mythology personified as a Greek goddess (e.g., Sophocles, *Antigone* 538). Therefore, in the history of ancient Mediterranean religions, early Christianity did not introduce the idea that justice has a divine origin.

In addition, OT narratives that told of divine justice influenced the theology of the NT writers, especially in explaining the problem of evil (theodicy). Echoing God's response to the complaint of Job that God's justice appears to humans unfair, Paul writes: "But who indeed are you, a human being, to talk back to God? Will what is made say to its maker, 'Why have you created me so?'" (Rom 9:20; see Job 38:1–42:6). God's justice is not as arbitrary as appearances might suggest; is not reducible to the level of human justice. Paul asks the rhetorical question: "Is God unjust, humanly speaking to inflict his wrath? Of course not! For how else is God to judge the world?" (Rom 3:5). Here the apostle connects divine justice with divine judgment.

While the NT writers tell believers not to exact vengeance or retribution, it nonetheless retains this right of an "eye for an eye" to God, quoting the OT. Paul writes: "Beloved, do not look for revenge but leave room for the wrath; for it is written, 'Vengeance is mine, I will repay, says the Lord'" (Rom 12:19; see also 2 Thess 1:6-10; Heb 10:30; Luke 18:8; Jas 1:20). In these passages divine justice seems to rule by the law of talion, whereas human justice is to be governed by the love ethic. The deaths of Judas Iscariot, Ananias, Sapphira, and King Herod Antipas are illustrative of the former (Matt 27:3-10 [cf. Acts 1:18-20]; Acts 5:1-6; 12:20-24). Yet because of Jesus Christ, God's wrath is tempered by forgiveness, love, and mercy. God will judge the world in justice, through Christ (Acts 17:31; Rom 2:25; 5:17, 21; 14:21; 1 Cor 1:30; Phil 1:11; 2 Pet 3:13; Rev 19:11 [God will wage a "just war"]).

Justice from the Church. From the early Jesus movement, some early Christian preaching taught concern for the less fortunate in society: persons who are poor and disabled, those widowed or orphaned, and other marginalized, lowly segments of the rural and urban population. This call for social justice finds it fullest expression in Luke-Acts. In the canticle of Mary, Luke quotes Jewish Scripture: "He has thrown down the rulers from their thrones / but lifted up the lowly. / The hungry he has filled with good things; / the rich he has sent away empty" (Luke 1:52-53). In another place, Luke repeats his theme of concern for the poor, using a passage from the OT on the lips of Jesus: "'The Spirit of the Lord is upon me, / because he has anointed me / to bring glad tiding to the poor. / He has sent me to proclaim liberty to captives / and recovery of sight to the blind, / to let the oppressed go free" (Luke 4:18). Jesus tells the messengers of John the Baptist to report that "the poor have the good news proclaimed to them" (Luke 7:22). The first beatitude in the Sermon on the Plain mentions the economically poor: "'Blessed are you who are poor, / for the kingdom of God is yours" (Luke 6:20; cf. Matt 5:3, which changes the beatitude to read "the poor *in spirit*," reflecting a theology different from that of Luke-Acts). Luke continues this theme in Acts. He describes the first Christian community as a collective: "All who believed were together and had all things in common; they would sell their property and possessions and divide them among all according to each one's need" (Acts 2:44-45; see also 4:32-37, which approaches a description of an early Jewish monastic group called the Essenes).

Alms to the poor goes in hand with the NT ideal of social justice. Luke argues that the Church should follow the examples set in the narratives of the earliest Christians. Jesus' charge to his disciples was, "Sell your belongings and give alms. Provide money bags for yourselves that do not wear out, an inexhaustible treasure in heaven that no thief can reach nor moth destroy. For where your treasure is, there also will your heart be" (Luke 12:33). The NT authors—especially Luke— are optimistic about the ability of the Church to ameliorate social injustice while awaiting the coming of the reign of God.

See: ALMSGIVING, JUDGMENT, LAW, LOVE, MERCY, SIN, WITNESS, WRATH OF GOD

J. ALBERT HARRILL

Pastoral-Liturgical Tradition

One of the four cardinal virtues* essential to the moral life, justice governs our relations with others by ensuring that we give them their due. Justice means there is something we owe others; it not only underscores the indebtedness at the heart of life, but calls our attention to the debt we must pay in respecting others and responding to their needs. As a virtue, justice is both a quality of character and a rule of action. As a quality of character, justice habitually disposes us to take the needs and well-being of others into account, and as a rule of action it insists that the principal element to any genuinely moral act be to render the debt we owe another. In this respect, justice focuses an act not primarily on the well-being of the agent, but on the flourishing of one's neighbors. It is through justice that all our actions are informed by a fundamental and enduring concern for others; indeed, the opposite of selfishness, it is through the virtue of justice that our will is set not on our own needs, but on the needs of our neighbors. There is then an outward direction to acts of justice, and hence all moral behavior, because justice orients us to the welfare of others and the community. In this respect, justice is the virtue of human togetherness, the virtue which both enables and sustains community, first by respecting the social nature of our humanity, and second by ensuring that each person has access to the goods and opportunities essential for human flourishing.

The obligation of justice is derived from the nature of God and the dignity of human beings. As regards the first, Scripture cites justice as a quintessential quality of God, so much so that the being and nature of God is primarily revealed through acts of justice, especially on behalf of the weak and abandoned. Since we are called to live faithful to the ways of God, justice should character-ize all our relationships and be the soul of our behavior. But the justice of God also, paradoxically, reminds us of a debt we can never adequately repay. If God's justice is expressed through God's covenant faithfulness, it reminds us of the indebtedness at the heart of life, an indebtedness that infinitely surpasses the power of human justice. To be human is to be indebted, to be conscious of an obligation we can never repay. This awareness of the unbridgeable disparity between God's goodness and our merit ought to cultivate the thanksgiving and gratitude necessary to enrich, deepen, and sustain our justice toward others; in short, only those who know they are indebted can truly be just.

But justice is also based in the dignity of every human being as a child of God and an expression of God's love. Justice is derived from a vision of the fundamental equality of all people before God. Christian justice argues that because all of us are created in the image and likeness of God, no person is more important than any other, none more valuable, none more precious. As the handiwork of God's love, everyone who lives matters. Justice grows from the discovery of the inalienable value of other persons, and testifies that everyone has worth, no one is expendable, and the dignity of some can never be sacrificed for the enhancement of others. Justice reminds us that there are centers of life outside ourself that we must take into account, and justice chastens egotism by telling us that these others do not exist to serve our needs, but have value in themselves; our debt to them is a result of their autonomous worth. By contrast, injustice suggests that some people do not matter, some need not be loved, and some can be forgotten. The core of injustice is the lie that some persons lack value and are due nothing. Injustice requires perceiving persons as worthless, but that is not only to sin against them, but to blaspheme the God who made them. Put differently, to treat persons unjustly is to dishonor them by denying their dignity as human beings, and in light of that denial to harm them by depriving them of the basic conditions for life that are their due (S.Th., II-II, 72, 1).

Justice is entailed by basic human rights that are owed all human beings as creatures of God. Human rights are prior to justice because we only know what is due another when we know why something is due them at all. It is because every person has rights that we have duties to them in justice. In the Catholic social tradition, not only do we have an obligation not to infringe on the rights of others, but more positively, we have an obligation to ensure that those rights are not being denied. Part of the responsibility of justice is both to respect the rights of others and to help create the conditions in which those rights can be realized (*Pacem in Terris*, nos. 31, 32).

Justice Seeks Solidarity and Community. In the Catholic social tradition, justice reflects a relational understanding of the self based on the principle of the common unity of humanity; in short, from a Catholic perspective community precedes individuality. Human beings are meant to be community—we are all members one of another—and it is this solidarity that justice ought to seek and protect. Justice demands a deep sensitivity of human solidarity, a felt awareness of the kinship we have with people everywhere. Justice is impossible unless we appreciate that all men and women are our brothers and sisters, not outsiders or strangers but members of the family of God (*Mater et Magistra* 157). We are meant to be one, each person contributing to the well-being and flourishing of others, but injustice destroys this oneness by fostering the selfishness that fractures and divides. Community is the truth about humanity, but injustice frustrates and diminishes humanity by structuring a world that keeps us from being one. Thus, injustice is dehumanizing for everyone, not only the poor. If the poor are harmed by injustice, the wealthy are too. In *Populorum Progressio* Paul VI cites avarice and greed as the "most evident form of moral underdevelopment" and speaks of such people as "mutilated by selfishness"

(21). Too much wealth diminishes the spirit because it denies the responsibility we have toward others and is blind to the community we need in order to stay human.

It is because of the solidarity we have as children of God that we are obliged to be responsible for one another. Justice argues that we are our sisters' and brothers' keeper. If the human family is one, we have a responsibility to the disinherited and forgotten as one of our own; justice demands that we give them their due precisely because they belong to us and we belong to them. In this respect, injustice is essentially betrayal, it is to turn our backs on one of our own. It is the essential equality of all people in God that accounts for the debt we owe one another in justice and stands behind Aquinas's insistence that the fundamental rule of justice is that we harm no one and fulfill our obligations to all (S.Th., I-II, 100,5). Similarly, it is because justice is for the sake of community that it works to preserve the conditions for both individual and communal well-being by establishing at least a rough equality among people as regards the fundamental needs of life (S.Th., II-II, 66,7).

Justice determines the proper relationship between the common good and an individual's good. In the Catholic social tradition, one's personal good is not contrasted with the common good, but intrinsically connected to it; in fact, though distinct, they are inseparable. What genuinely enables personal well-being contributes to the common good and, correspondingly, what preserves and enhances the community's good serves individuals' good. The interrelationship between individual and communal good is such that each requires the other; thus, the measure for authentic personal well-being is that it contributes to the common good, and the measure for authentic communal well-being is that it benefits all members of society equitably. The balance between personal good and the common good is maintained insofar as each respects and nurtures the other. If the well-being of society sometimes demands adjusting or even sacrificing individual good, it is also true that a just community is impossible without steadfast regard for the welfare of all its members.

Nonetheless, because of the social nature of human existence, the Catholic social tradition has consistently argued that the demands of the common good can override an individual's immediate good. As a way of ensuring justice, or most often to remedy injustice, individuals may have to subordinate their good to the common good. Since the common good embraces all the things necessary to guarantee the flourishing of every member of society, particular individuals may have to be disadvantaged in order to overcome past injustices and restore the basic equality necessary for justice. This is why, for instance, the Catholic social tradition sets limits on the right to private property. Since God intended the goods of creation for all people, private property ought to serve the divine intention, not impede it; thus, when the surplus property of a few becomes a source of injustice for the many, the state may legitimately appropriate and redistribute property, even by force, for the sake of the common good (S.Th., II-II, 66,5,8; *Gaudium et spes*, no. 71). More generally, the state is to be an agent of the common good and has a responsibility to intervene in unjust situations to ensure that every person has access to the basic goods of society. If the common good is being violated through injustice, the duty of the state is to create the structures and conditions which will restore it by respecting the welfare of each member of society. This is why the state has a special responsibility to the poor and vulnerable members of society (*Rerum Novarum*, nos. 48, 52, 54).

That justice seeks to establish or restore community indicates that every understanding of justice is informed by some vision of what the world should be; therefore, the work of justice is measured by the discrepancy between what the world is now and what it needs to become. Justice is the transformative power that restores a disordered world by putting things in proper relationship and by creating the structures in which community is possible. In theological language, Christian justice works to transform the world according to God's original plan for creation. Justice works from a memory of God's dream for the world and seeks to recapture in deeds and structures God's fundamental desire that all may know life; in this respect, the power of justice is to retrieve the community lost through sin and to create the conditions necessary for the full and proper development of life. Justice seeks human flourishing, and a just society is one that makes it possible for all people to grow to their full stature before God. If injustice is an affront to God because it violates what God wants the world to be, the most radical transformative power of justice is to remake the world according to the plans and purposes of God. There is nothing middling to Christian justice because it is fired by the kind of moral imagination and gospel vision that is unwilling to concede the world cannot be other than it is. Christian justice challenges our sense of possibility and resists any resignation to injustice. The antithesis of fatalism, Christian justice is utopian insofar as it steadfastly believes the world can be remade according to God's dream for it (*Octogesima Adveniens*, no. 37).

Three Types of Justice. There are three kinds of justice that correspond to the three basic relations or structures of social life: commutative justice, distributive justice, and social justice. Commutative justice focuses on relationships between members of the community. It is sometimes called "reciprocal" justice because it orders relationships between individuals. Its specific task is to regulate interactions between persons, especially exchanges, contracts, or agreements. Restitution from one person to another would be an example of commutative justice. Through restitution a relationship that had been thrown out of balance by injustice would be restored to equilibrium through some act of recompense.

Distributive justice orders the relationship between society and its members. Its specific function is to ensure an equitable distribution of the goods, benefits, and burdens of society; it is through distributive justice that all persons receive their share of the common good. Distributive justice describes how the agencies of society, particularly the government, must allocate goods and resources so that all persons receive their due. This is the justice that "distributes" the economic, political, and cultural goods of the community and which enables an equitable participation of each person in the life of the society. Concretely, confronted with an unjust distribution of goods, opportunities, and services, the task of distributive justice is to rearrange or restructure the patterns of distribution for the sake of the common good. Thus, distributive justice is often a corrective; it works to remedy injustices by reshaping the flow of goods and opportunities in a society.

The third type of justice, social justice, entered the Catholic social tradition in Pius XI's 1931 encyclical *Quadragesimo Anno*. Pius described social justice as the set of moral principles needed to inform economic, political, and social structures if they are to serve instead of hinder the common good (*Quadragesimo Anno*, no. 88). There is a relationship between distributive justice and social justice inasmuch as social justice effects the kind of social order necessary for distributive justice; put differently, social justice makes distributive justice possible because it structures the institutions of society so that the demands of distributive justice can be met. More recently, the definition of social justice has been broadened to include how individuals relate to community. If distributive justice focuses on the relation of society to individuals, social justice focuses on what each person owes the common good. The thrust of recent understandings of social justice is the contribution each person ought to make for the well-being of society. Individuals practice social justice when they make the social order as a whole one in which the just desserts of every person are met.

Pastoral Applications. Justice is not only a cardinal virtue, but is also "a constitutive dimension of the preaching of the Gospel" and the mission of the Church (Justice in the World 6). This means that action on behalf of justice is not only a distinguishing characteristic of a gospel life, but is also the activity that brings the discipleship community into being. There can be no gospel life without a commitment to justice; indeed, both the gospel and the Church live through justice. Justice is integral and essential to the life of the Church because the Christian community is defined through its fidelity to the healing and liberating actions of God on behalf of the poor. If we are called to live in keeping with the character of God, faithful discipleship requires working for the liberation and wholeness of all peoples. Justice is an elementary responsibility and definitive characteristic of the Church because the gospel is misconstrued and impotent without it.

The absolute centrality of justice in a gospel life is grasped when we understand the relationship between justice and salvation, and between God's activity and human activity. God's salvation works through justice, that is why there is no authentic conversion that is not expressed outwardly in acts of justice. A truly regenerated heart should lead to a regenerated world. Similarly, the relationship between God's activity and human activity is that redemption continues through justice. It is through the virtue of justice that God redeems. Salvation is carried forward through human agency because when we act justly we become God's instruments in the re-creation of the world.

The Eucharist is central in cultivating gospel justice because it is there we encounter the God who has given "all peoples one common origin" and whose will is to "gather them as one family in yourself." There we are summoned to share "the good things you give us" so that we "may secure justice and equality for every human being, an end to all division, and a human society built on love and peace" (Mass for the Progress of Peoples). The Eucharist reminds us that our first task is to become people of justice ourselves. Calls for justice are hollow, even dangerous, without the profound and radical change of heart that signals a conversion to God's justice. If the work of justice is to rearrange the world according to the purposes of God, the power of the Eucharist is to remind us our hearts too must be purified, transformed, and rearranged by God; otherwise we have the rhetoric of justice, but not the virtue of justice.

That Christ came to proclaim "the good news of salvation" to the poor, freedom to prisoners, and joy to all who are sorrowing (Eucharistic Prayer IV) reminds us that all human beings are meant to give adoration and praise to God. Our lives are to be an endless liturgy of praise and thanksgiving; however, such doxology is impossible without justice. Injustice hinders worship because injustice kills. We are the Mystical Body of Christ, a people who collectively form one person giving thanks, but injustice mutes that splendid worship by leaving the body of Christ fractured and misshapen. Thus, authentic worship is inseparable from a steadfast commitment to justice.

See: COMMUNITY, CONVERSION, LOVE, POOR, POWER, REDEMPTION, WORSHIP

PAUL J. WADELL, C.P.

JUSTIFICATION

The concept of justification is found in the OT, but there is a distinctively new turn with Paul's formulation of justification by faith. Both the Hebrew term *ṣĕdāqâ* and the Greek word *dikaiosynē* denote a state of right relation. These terms are also translated as "righteousness," "uprightness," and "justice." In biblical usage justification refers to the right relationship between human beings and God. It has its roots in legal language: one is "justified" when proven right or innocent before the law. In the NT it is one of many metaphors for the effects of the Christ-event.

Old Testament

In the OT righteousness is understood in terms of covenant faithfulness. The word is applied to both God and Israel. When God is said to be upright, however, it is not solely an intrinsic quality of the godhead that is described. Rather, God's righteousness is always manifest in relation to human beings. Divine uprightness is revealed in God's saving deeds toward Israel and God's absolute faithfulness to the covenant. The psalmist appeals to God's justice (*ṣĕdāqâ*) when pleading for rescue from distress (Pss 31:2; 71:2; 143:1, 11). Likewise, the praise psalms exult in the justice of God made known in saving deeds (Ps 98:2).

As a just judge God will save "the upright of heart" (Ps 7:11-12). Even if the petitioner has fallen short of covenant fidelity, he or she can yet maintain confidence that God will act uprightly, making appeal to God's own honor: "for your name's sake" (Ps 143:11). Indeed, the psalmist pleads with God "enter not into judgment with your servant, for before you no living person is just" (Ps 143:2). In passages cast as lawsuits between Israel and Yahweh, Israel is always the guilty party (e.g., Isa 43:25-26; Jer 12:1). God's justice results not in a declaration of Israel's innocence, but rather a guilty verdict followed by acquittal. Saving righteousness, then, is not dependent on human ability to be just, but rather, on God's covenant fidelity.

Nonetheless, there are a few individuals in the OT who are said to be righteous. In Genesis 15:6 Abraham, who enters into covenant relationship with God, is said to have "put his faith in the LORD, who credited it to him as an act of righteousness." This text will be important to Paul's argument in Romans 4:3-8. Others who are said to be upright include: Noah (Gen 6:9); Tamar (Gen 38:26); Job (Job 1:1); Daniel (4 Macc 16:21); Ishbaal, the son of Saul (2 Sam 4:11); the Servant of God (Isa 53:11).

In the context of the Exile, where God's saving justice seemed not presently manifest, it is spoken of as an eschatological hope (e.g., Isa 51:4-5; 59:15-20). The expectation is that once again it will become evident that "There is no just and saving God but me [Yahweh]" (Isa 45:21).

New Testament

It is Paul who develops the concept of justification by faith in Jesus Christ. His most extensive exposition is found in the Letter to the Romans; it is also a central theme of Galatians and Philippians. Paul's theology of justification is worked out in the polemical context of refuting those who preached circumcision and observance of Jewish dietary regulations as necessary for Gentile converts. Paul's position is most clearly stated in Romans 3:21-31, which begins, "But now the righteousness of God has been manifested apart from the law, though testified to by the law and the prophets, the righteousness of God through faith in Jesus Christ for all who believe." He demonstrates in the first chapters of Romans that all, Jew and Gentile alike, "have sinned and are deprived of the glory of God" (Rom 3:23). No one can achieve right relation with God by their own doing, through observance of works of the law (Rom 3:20; Gal 3:11). Justification is a free gift from God, accomplished by Christ Jesus, and appropriated by the believer through faith. In the Letter to Titus justification is linked with baptism and emphasizes again that it comes by "the kindness and generous love of God . . . not because of any righteous deeds we have done" (3:4-7).

In both Romans and Galatians Paul appeals to the example of Abraham, whose faith in God "was credited to him as righteousness" (Rom 4:3, quoting Gen 15:6). He argues that since Abraham was declared righteous before the law was given, so too may all the other uncircumcised who believe be reckoned righteous (Rom 4:9-12). Thus, Abraham can be considered "father of all the uncircumcised who believe, so that to them [also] righteousness might be credited, as well as the father of the circumcised" (Rom 4:11-12; see also Gal 3:1-14).

The righteousness effected by Christ is more than moral rectitude. It results in freedom for the believer from sin and death (Rom 5:12-21), from the old self (Rom 6:1-23), and from the law (Rom 7:1-25) through the power of the Spirit (Rom 8:1-39). This freedom can in no way be interpreted as license to libertarianism. Nor does it mean that no actions are demanded of a person beyond that of believing. As Paul says most explicitly in Galatians 5:6, faith must be manifest in deeds; it is "faith working through love." The famous passage in James 2:14-26 has been read by some as a contradiction of Paul's doctrine of justification by faith. The assertion, "a person is justified by works and not by faith alone" (Jas 2:24) corrects a misreading of Paul. Paul never says that justification is by faith *alone*. Paul and James both hold that faith must be manifest in righteous deeds.

Elsewhere in the NT justification is not a major theme. In Matthew *dikaiosynē* is human conduct that strives for right relation with God. The Beatitudes declare blessed those who hunger and thirst for righteousness and those who are persecuted for the sake of righteousness (Matt 5:6, 10). When one's foremost seeking is for righteousness and the reign of God, everything else is given besides (Matt 6:33). Jesus instructs his disciples that their righteousness must surpass that of the scribes and Pharisees (Matt 5:20). That is, their life must overflow with just action, making visible the abundant self-gift of God in Christ. One is to take care, however, "not to perform righteous deeds in order that people may see them" (Matt 6:1).

In Luke and Acts the adjective *dikaios*, "upright," "innocent," is significant. Luke changes the climactic declaration of the centurion at the death of Jesus from, "Truly this man was the Son of God!" (Mark 15:39) to "Certainly this man was innocent [*dikaios*]" (Luke 23:47). And in his second volume, "the Righteous One" (*ho dikaios*) becomes a title of Jesus in three key speeches (Acts 3:14; 7:52; 22:14). Elsewhere Jesus is described as "righteous," as in Matthew 27:19; 27:24 (some mss); 1 Peter 3:18; 1 John 2:1, 29; 3:7. God is called righteous in Romans 3:26; 2 Timothy 4:8; 1 John 1:9, and is addressed as *pater dikaie*, "Righteous Father," by Jesus in John 17:25. Other individuals who are said to be righteous in the NT are: Joseph (Matt 1:19); John the Baptist (Mark 6:20); Zechariah and Elizabeth (Luke 1:6); Simeon (Luke 2:25); Joseph of Arimathea (Luke 23:50); Cornelius (Acts 10:22); Abel (Heb 11:4; 1 John 3:12); and Lot (2 Pet 2:7).

See: ABRAHAM, CIRCUMCISION, COVENANT, FAITH, GRACE, JUDGMENT, JUSTICE, LAW, LIBERTY, PAUL, SALVATION

BARBARA E. REID, O.P.

Pastoral-Liturgical Tradition

While the meaning of the doctrine of justification by faith had always been implicit in Christian tradition, especially in theologies of grace, it was Martin Luther who gave it its first articulation at the beginning of the sixteenth century. As he developed the notion, justification is an act whereby God renders sinners righteous, i.e., forgiving their sins in a way that sinners could never achieve for themselves. This puts sinners in right relation with God because of faith, not because of anything that sinners could do for themselves.

Luther developed this insight in reaction to the "works-righteousness" of the medieval Church, wherein it was taught that human beings could perform all kinds of works to expiate their sins and come into right relation with God. Pilgrimages, acts of penance, Mass offerings, and indulgences were propagated widely as means to secure God's favor. Luther thought that such earning of one's salvation went against the very center of the message of God's salvation in Christ: salvation comes to us by justification by faith, not by anything we do or can do. For Luther, this insight, gained from his reflection and study of the Letter to the Romans, was not merely a perspective on sal-

vation, but was the center of Christian belief, the article of faith on which the Church stands or falls.

The Council of Trent took up Luther's challenge, and sought to reform many of the abuses of works that had become part of religious practice. They addressed squarely too Luther's position on justification (DS 1520-83). While agreeing with Luther that the grace of Christ is the sole means of justification, and that it is in faith that sinners become acceptable before God, the council went on to say faith must be followed by hope and charity, and that everlasting life in heaven may be seen as a reward for works done in faith, as well as being a freely given grace of God.

Because of the council's insistence on these two latter points, Catholics and Reformers have remained divided. However, more recent historical research on both positions has revealed that the two sides may be far closer than it has seemed. And in the Lutheran-Roman Catholic bilateral discussions in the 1970s and 1980s, the participants concluded that the teaching on justification need no longer divide the two communions. Differences remain, however. Roman Catholics accept the importance of the doctrine of justification, but would not make it the litmus test for judging everything the Church says or does. Nor would Roman Catholics accept that means of grace given to the Church by God are null and void. But it is without doubt that Lutherans and Roman Catholics have come closer together on their understandings of justification by faith than was the case at the time of their separation.

See: FAITH, SALVATION

ROBERT J. SCHREITER, C.PP.S.

K

KNEELING

The symbolic meaning of kneeling derives from the physical posture itself. Kneeling before others reduces us in stature before them and renders us powerless to act without great effort. In the Judaeo-Christian religious tradition of kneeling in prayer* before God, the meaning of act is transformed into one of adoration,* supplication, and penitence.

Biblical Practice and Meanings

In both Testaments kneeling before others is used to express the homage due to those who have authority and power (Gen 42:6; Esth 3:2-5; Matt 18:29; Acts 10:25), and its inverse in mockery (Matt 27:28). To kneel before God is an act of worship of the "one who made us" (Ps 95:6; also Eph 32:14), a confession of divine sovereignty and power (Isa 45:23; Phil 2:10). The correlative human powerlessness finds expression in supplication, as when Solomon knelt to pray to God at the dedication of the Temple (1 Kgs 8:22-54; 2 Chr 6:13-42) and when petitioners knelt before Jesus to request a healing (Matt 17:14; Mark 1:40; 10:17). Jesus' own prayer in the garden of Gethsemane, said kneeling, is a supreme expression of supplication (Luke 22:41). Kneeling for prayer not only bespeaks human need and dependence; it can also embody an acknowledgement of sin and a plea for forgiveness (Ezra 9:4-15).

Though standing seems to have been the more ancient posture for ordinary prayer in Judaism (Dan 6:10; Matt 6:5; Mark 11:25), kneeling had also become customary by NT times. Early Christians are frequently depicted as kneeling for prayer (Acts 7:60; 9:40; 20:36; 21:5).

Pastoral-Liturgical Tradition

The biblical practice and meanings of kneeling for prayer continued on through the history of Christianity. Standing is commonly said to have been the most primitive posture for Christian prayer. However, the relative frequency with which Acts mentions kneeling suggests that both postures were customary from the beginning. Kneeling for prayer came to be the rule for fast days, while the Council of Nicaea (325) forbade kneeling on Sundays and during Eastertide. Accordingly, writers like St. Basil (379) saw kneeling as a symbol of our human sinfulness and standing as a symbol of the resurrection and an image of the world to come.

Though kneeling has been connected with various acts of liturgical and non-liturgical prayer through the centuries, its meanings have remained quite constant: adoration, petition, penitence. Those in the order of penitents were at times required to kneel in the liturgical assembly. At times all the members of the assembly knelt for the great prayers of intercession, as we still do on Good Friday. Similarly, for a time all knelt for silent prayer during the opening prayer of the Mass, a posture eventually kept for the whole Liturgy of the Word. In the early Middle Ages the change to unleavened hosts eventually led to reception of communion kneeling at a low railing in a posture of unworthiness, rather than standing at the altar. The medieval custom of kneeling in adoration during the consecration was later extended to the entire Eucharistic Prayer. Kneeling in adoration before the Blessed Sacrament flourished in the period after the Middle Ages. During that same period kneeling for confession increased with the introduction of the confessional. Until recently the bridal couple also knelt during the wedding ceremony and nuptial Mass. And finally, kneeling has been used as a meditative posture for private prayer during most of Christian history.

Though kneeling is not as frequent in the revised liturgy of Vatican II, it is retained in significant moments, e.g., by the assembly during the words of institution; by penitents during the general confession of sinfulness in the communal rites of reconciliation; by the elect during the scrutinies; and during Eucharistic adoration. In addition to the traditional meanings of kneeling still embodied in these practices, the revised rites occasionally speak of the power of bodily postures to express the unity of the assembly and to evoke the spiritual attitudes appropriate to each.

Current pastoral practice might well look beyond the rubrics regarding kneeling to ask two more important questions. How can the biblical tradition of God's sovereignty and of our neediness before God enshrined in the practice of kneeling for prayer be made our own in the modern world? And how can a prayer posture such as kneeling serve to foster and express that attitude toward God? To accomplish this, kneeling will have to be as authentic and prayerful a gesture as we can make it, transforming the inarticulate meanings already inherent in the physical act itself into a fully embodied profession of our belief in God's reign* over us and of our dependence on God to bring it about.

See: POWER, PRAYER, REIGN OF GOD, RESURRECTION, TEMPLE, WORSHIP

GILBERT OSTDIEK, O.F.M.

KNOWLEDGE

The Biblical tradition emphasizes the relational quality inherent in knowledge of God. The NT in particular presents Christ as the sum and summit of knowledge of God and resists incipient attempts to grant knowledge any independent salvific status. Subsequent pastoral/liturgical emphases similarly suggest the purpose of knowledge as enhancing persons in relationship, and advises that human persons pass through periods of knowing God characterized by love, study, prayer, and recognition of the limits of human theologizing.

Old Testament

God's knowledge is often focused on people and implies an interest in them and willingness to assist them: "the LORD has compassion on those who fear him; for he knows how we are formed, he remembers that we are dust" (Ps 103:13, 14). At the time of the new Exodus, the prophet proclaims "all flesh shall know that I, the LORD, am your Savior" (Isa 49:26). Similarly, "know that I am the LORD" occurs over seventy times in Ezekiel, in conjunction with salvific activity (see also Deut 4:32-39; Pss 59:11, 14; 78:6).

Knowing God's "ordinances" (Ps 147:19, 20) is a privilege not shared by the nations, and coming to know God's "ways" (Ps 25:4) requires certain behavior, as seen for example in Jeremiah's proclamation of Josiah's knowledge of God "Because he dispensed justice to the weak and the poor, it went well with him; is this not true knowledge of me?" (Jer 22:16). The struggle to know God's ways is not always successful either (Ps 95:10). Hosea laments the fact that there is "no knowledge of God in the land," a knowledge which is more important than holocausts, because the land is rife with lying, stealing, murder, and adultery (Hos 4:1, 2; 6:6). The fact that we deal here not with propositions about God, but relationship with God, is perhaps best summed up in two statements: "the fear of the LORD is the beginning of knowledge" (Prov 1:7) and in the fact that Jeremiah's anticipation of a time when "all, from least to greatest, shall know me" is part of his expectation of a new covenant (Jer 31:31).

Later prophetic teaching about knowledge of God focuses on there being only one God who can be known (Isa 45:6); and wisdom speculation suggests not only that "where there is no knowledge, there is no wisdom" (Sir 3:24) but also that God's pleasure and counsel would have remained unknown had not the Lord sent Wisdom and the holy Spirit from on high (Wis 9:9-18).

New Testament

Matthew records a saying of Jesus which focuses on the mutual knowing of Father and Son (11:25-30), into which Jesus the meek invites those who would learn this relationship. John also portrays a mutual knowing of Father and Son (neither John nor the Matthean saying uses the noun "knowledge") that does not involve a dissolution of their respective identities into each other. Rather, Jesus knows and obeys the Father's word (8:55). Through Jesus the disciples see and know the Father (14:7), which knowing is eternal life (17:3). Knowing is associated with believing (10:38).

Paul presents the cross as an undercover operation when he portrays the "rulers of this age" as not knowing God's wisdom, when they crucified the Lord of Glory (1 Cor 2:7-9). He will accept the Corinthian slogan that "we have knowledge" that there is only one God (1 Cor 8:1). But he insists that such knowledge is secondary to their being known by God, an experience operative when they love God (1 Cor 8:3). At present, he knows only partially, and while waiting for that time when he will know even as he is fully known, he hopes

to know Jesus and the power of his resurrection (1 Cor 13:12; Phil 3:10). He asserts that the creator has "shone in our hearts to bring to light the knowledge of the glory of God on the face of Jesus Christ" (2 Cor 4:6). He laments that when the Gentiles, though knowing God from creation, refuse to "accord him glory as God or give him thanks," they fall into prideful behavior (Rom 1:21, 30). And with the salvific act of God on behalf of creation primarily in view, he proclaims a foreknowledge on God's part of those being conformed to the image of the Son (Rom 8:29). Other epistolary authors celebrate Christ as the one in whom God's original intentions for creation are being brought to consummation by proclaiming that in him "are hidden all the treasures of wisdom and knowledge" (Col 2:3).

The literary evidence for full-fledged gnosticism is much later than the NT, but it is possible that some of the NT traditons are aimed at an incipient gnosticism. Some of the emphases in Paul and in John can be seen as attacking claims that saving knowledge reinforces one's awareness that one *is* divine and proceeds from a redeemer antagonistic to the creator.

Pastoral-Liturgical Tradition

Origen encourages especially pastors and teachers to increase their knowledge of the origin and destiny of humanity. Dionysius, the Pseudo-Areopagite, suggests that rejecting all knowledge leads to a kind of knowledge exceeding understanding, the Darkness of Unknowing. And in the same vein, Richard Rolle's *Fire of Love* suggests that "he knows God perfectly who understands him to be incomprehensible." Erasmus said that one's prayer is enhanced by the gift of knowledge that discriminates and selects ideas worthy of desire. Wesley asserted that the gift of following Christ to Calvary is itself, and even the knowledge of it, given only "through faith in the Son of God."

The Pastoral Constitution on the Church in the Modern World (59) reasserted the teaching of the First Vatican Council that both faith and reason are sources of knowledge. And the Decree on the Ministry and Life of Priests (19) urges priests to "develop their knowledge of divine and human affairs aptly and uninterruptedly." A contemporary service for the blessing of students and teachers prays in part "For teachers, that they may share their knowledge with gentleness, patience and concern for their students," and "For those who seek knowledge of the things of this world, that they may always pursue God's wisdom."

See: COVENANT, CREATION, GLORY, HOLY SPIRIT, LIFE, LOVE, MEEKNESS, OBEDIENCE, PRAYER, PRIDE, REDEMPTION, WISDOM

MARK C. KILEY

L

LABOR

A constant of human experience, labor figures prominently in both the biblical and Church tradition.

Old Testament

Labor is found in the OT in various contexts and is used to translate a variety of Hebrew words. In general the terms indicate service, physical or mental toil, or exertion. Thus, labor is that activity which humans do every day. "So [it is] with the potter sitting at his labor" (Sir 38:29). According to Ecclesiastes, for such labor one may expect to receive "a good wage" (4:9) and to "drink and enjoy all the fruits" which result (5:17).

From that same labor, however, the Israelites were to rest on the Sabbath. "Six days you may labor and do all your work" (Exod 20:9; Deut 5:13). At the same time, the command to desist from work did not thereby devalue it in Hebrew thinking; rather, the Sabbath is established in recognition of a complementarity between labor and rest and as a sign of the Israelites' covenant with their God (Exod 31:12-17). The command to rest was indeed for one day a week only. Idleness was perceived as leading to trouble. "When hands are lazy, the rafters sag; when hands are slack, the house leaks" (Eccl 10:18). And, in the words

of Proverbs 10:4, "The slack hand impoverishes, but the hand of the diligent enriches." This Hebrew honor and respect for manual labor stood in contrast to Greco-Roman disdain for physical work and elevation of mental activity.

In many instances labor is the especially hard forced work done by slaves, which the Israelites themselves had experienced during their oppression in Egypt (see e.g., Exod 1:11; 2:11; 5:4-5; 6:6-7; Deut 20:11; 26:6). They in turn imposed the same upon their own captives or each other, as in the period of Solomon (e.g., 1 Kgs 4:6; 9:15; 2 Chr 8:8; 10:18). In these texts the underlying Hebrew words for labor, *mas* and *sebel*, refer to the institution known as the levy or *corvée*, by which captives of war were forced to work for their captors or some Israelites themselves were forced into a modified, temporary work force. The *corvée* was implemented most often for special projects like road building and constructing large edifices.

Labor is also used in many texts to refer to the travail of childbirth, as in Genesis 35:16, "Rachel began to be in labor." Hebrew terms translated as such are, for example, *yālad* (Gen 35:16; Ps 48:7; Isa 13:8; 21:3; 42:14) and *ḥûl*; *ḥîl* (Isa 54:1; 66:7). By way of analogy, this same image functions in describing people's terror in the face of great destruction: "Pangs and sorrow take hold of them, like a woman in labor they writhe" (Isa 13:8). To compare the dread of calamity to the labor of giving birth reflects the fear, anxiety, and tremendous physical struggle connected with childbirth in OT thinking.

New Testament

As with the OT, the NT likewise contains numerous words that can be rendered in English translations as labor. Paralleling OT usage, many references to *labor* in the NT, specifically those using terms based on the verb *ōdinō,* refer to giving birth (e.g., Gal 4:27; Rev 12:2) or draw a comparison with the massive exertion of childbirth. In Mark 13:8 and Matthew 24:8 signs of the eschatological end such as earthquakes and famines are described as "the beginnings of labor pains." And, in 1 Thessalonians 5:3 the arrival of the Day of the Lord is compared to sudden disaster which would come "like labor pains upon a pregnant woman." In a related vein, apparently with the thought in mind of the endurance the labor of birth requires on the part of one human being to bring forth another, Paul describes himself to his converts in Galatians 4:19 as being "in labor until Christ be formed in you."

As was noted with respect to various OT passages, so in these representative NT texts it is evident that the labor of childbirth was perceived as potentially disastrous as well as strenuously self-sacrificial. To comprehend this broadly used biblical understanding of labor, modern readers may have to prescind consciously from their own experience or witness of childbirth as a generally safe, perhaps even anesthetically aided, process.

Elsewhere in NT usage, employing words based on such verbs as *kopiaō* and *ergazomai,* labor refers to one's daily work (e.g., Matt 20:1, 8; Jas 5:4). That work is variously qualified as manual labor (e.g., 1 Cor 4:12; Eph 4:28), as honest work, which contrasts, for example, with the activity of a thief (Eph 4:28). In the view of the writer of Ephesians, since "we are members of one another" (4:25) we ought to labor in order to "have

something to share with one in need" (4:28). In a saying of Jesus found only in Matthew 11:28 Jesus beckons: "Come to me, all you who labor and are burdened, and I will give you rest."

Likewise drawing on the same root words, but using also the term *synathleō,* the NT reflects an understanding of the work of ministering within the churches as labor. In Philippians 4:3 Paul describes Clement and various others of his co-workers such as Euodia and Syntyche as having "labored side by side" (RSV) with him in promoting the gospel (see also Phil 1:27). And, in Romans 16:6 he sends greetings to Mary who had "worked hard" for the Roman believers as well as in 16:12 to "those workers in the Lord, Tryphaena and Tryphosa" and to one "beloved Persis" whom Paul characterizes also as having "worked hard in the Lord." The terminology used with respect to these four ministering women is used by Paul elsewhere to designate his own activities in teaching and evangelization (1 Cor 15:10; Phil 2:16; Col 1:29; 1 Tim 4:10; 5:17). For example, in his exasperation with the Galatians Paul states, "I am afraid on your account that perhaps I have labored for you in vain" (4:11). In 1 Thessalonians 5:12 he beseeches his readers to respect those, who as he had done, were "laboring among you and who are over you in the Lord and who admonish you" (see also 1 Cor 16:16).

The Gospels of Matthew, Luke, and John share Paul's perception of ministry as labor. "The harvest is abundant but the laborers are few; so ask the master of the harvest to send out laborers for his harvest" (Matt 9:37-38; Luke 10:2). It is also observed that the laborer, i.e., the minister, deserves payment (Luke 10:7; Matt 10:10; 1 Tim 5:18). In a tradition found only in John 4:38, Jesus reminds his disciples of one of the puzzling complexities of evangelizing: "I sent you to reap that for which you did not labor; others have labored, and you have entered into their labor" (RSV).

See: COVENANT, DAY OF THE LORD, ESCHATOLOGY, MINISTRY, SABBATH, SLAVERY

FLORENCE MORGAN GILLMAN

Pastoral-Liturgical Tradition

Labor in the Post-Biblical Tradition. The Christian in the early Church was expected to work for a living so as not to be a burden on the community but instead contribute to the support of those who could not earn a living. Indeed, labor's redemptive value lay in its power to provide for the indigent. The mutuality of charity and the conviction of Christian equality invested slaves with new dignity, and manual labor was esteemed as the fruitful activity of a child of God. Nevertheless, too much labor would afford one little time to serve the Lord and neighbor while a Christian who refused to work at a craft was considered, a *christotemporos*, one who traffics in Christ.

The rule of charity made it a task of the community to provide the unemployed with their needs: if unemployment resulted from abandoning a forbidden craft, they were to be supported and trained in a new craft; if skilled but lacking sufficient capital to start a trade, this was to be provided; if working but not earning enough to support a family, their income was to be supplemented by the Church. From earliest times, this ecclesiastical system of welfare became the special charge of deacons who worked directly under the bishop.

The monastic movement (fourth century) valued labor not only for the ancient motives of self-sufficiency and charity but also for ascetical reasons: physical work is the best weapon against idleness and even the most humble of tasks contributes to the common good. The Apostle's injunction to "pray without ceasing" (1 Thess 5:17) and still "work for your bread" (2 Thess 3:10) inspired every monastic rule in East and West until the two ideals were carefully balanced in the Benedictine maxim *"ora et labora"* ("prayer and work"). Benedict's flexible, compassionate Rule (ca. 540) regulated times for common prayer—which he termed *opus Dei*, i.e., "the work of God"— and manual labor, and included time for reflective reading each day. The talents and abilities of the individual monk were taken into consideration when assigning "tasks" in the community's prayer as well as its manual labor.

In the course of the Middle Ages, the careful balance between prayer and work was lost as monastic properties increased and communities were clericalized. Numerous devotional accretions to the hours of prayer and the addition of two or more celebrations of the Mass to the daily round gave rise to a form of monastic life devoid of any but liturgical work. The *opus Dei* became the *onus dei* ("burden of God") while the necessary manual labor was supplied by *conversi* (=second class monks or "lay-brothers") and serfs from the monastery's lands. The call to return to manual labor was at the heart of every monastic reform movement.

In the meantime, the waning of feudalism and the rise of the towns saw the appearance of guilds of skilled craftsmen. Inside the cities the guilds maintained equal opportunities, regulated quality, trained members, and functioned as benefit societies, social organizations, and religious associations. Members cared for sick colleagues, attended funerals, paid ransoms, raised bail, assumed responsibility for other members' debts. The feasts and seasons of the year were celebrated together, each guild participating in the major festivals and sponsoring great fairs in honor of their own patron saints. Liturgy and life, prayer and work were inextricably connected.

As for interregional or international trade by land or sea the guild system was totally inadequate. With the rise of the merchant class, the majority of laborers became wage earners. Working conditions— though never glorious in the guilds— deteriorated rapidly. Working families suffered considerably at the hands of the more powerful merchants who, with the help of the aristocracy and hierarchy, crushed every strike and named heretical any religious who supported their claims. Pastors exhorted workers to trust in divine providence, and to practice Christian resignation, invoking always the *theologia crucis* ("Theology of the cross").

In theory, the Church could not countenance the capitalistic tendencies of medieval society. Theologians, moralists, and canon lawyers continued to insist upon a "just price" which would cover raw materials, wages, and sufficient profit to maintain the worker's family. But nothing more: everything beyond one's genuine needs belonged to the poor. Those who were in the business of making money and nothing else (usurers) were excluded from the kiss of peace while alive and refused Christian burial when they died.

In the long run, the Church succeeded no better in prohibiting usury than in forbidding excessive wealth. Loopholes were found in the canons, and not only Christian merchants, but clergy, prelates, and popes were soon in the business of borrowing and lending with interest due. The accumulation of debt by the Roman Curia and its attempt to raise revenues through the "sale" of indulgences ignited the Reformation. The resultant shift from monastery to marketplace as the focus of the Christian vocation was irrevocable. Calvinism's new form of interior asceticism gave rise to the "Protestant" work ethic and Wesley's "Gain all you can, save all you can; give all you can" emphasized thrift and the rewards of hard work as a sign of divine favor.

The industrial revolution, while increasing production, meant that even more workers would be engaged in mindless repetition, regulated by machines and clocks. Labor, like raw materials and machines, was regarded as just one more manufacturing cost. Real profits became the private property of the owners while the living and working conditions of laborers remained abysmal.

In 1891, Leo XIII's *Rerum Novarum* addressed the new conditions of workers and called for a real partnership between management and labor. In *Quadragesimo Anno* (1931), Pius XI valued labor for developing natural talents, enunciated the principle of subsidiarity, and demanded the recognition of the social and individual nature of work. John XXIII, *Mater et Magistra* (1961), in-

sisted that work is endowed with dignity since it is an expression of the human person and is the locus for human cooperation and fellowship. The Constitution on the Church in the Modern World (1965) noted that while labor humanizes nature and joins laborers in service and charity yet the work itself must suit the needs of the workers and enable them to develop themselves and participate in the running of the enterprise. In *Populorum Progressio* (1967) Paul VI warned that development cannot be limited to economic gain. The "world is sick" precisely because of selfishness and a lack of solidarity. Finally, John Paul II's *Laborem Exercens* (1981), quoting from the Book of Genesis, emphasized that the one who labors is a co-creator of the world with God and collaborator "with the Son of God for the redemption of humanity."

Labor in the Liturgy. In its use of vessels, furnishings, books, objects, and especially bread, wine, and oil, the liturgy has always connected the worship of God and the work of human hands. Labor itself is highlighted in embertide, rogation days, certain feasts and votive celebrations.

By the middle of the fifth century, special fasts on Wednesdays, Fridays, and Saturdays at the beginning of the four seasons were associated not only with the perennial need for penitence, but with "abstinence offered to God the Giver in gratitude for the now completed harvest of all the fruits of the soil" (Leo I, *Sermo* 13). Ember days soon became the preferred days for preparing (Wednesday and Friday) and celebrating (at the end of Saturday's fast) ordinations to the diaconate and presbyterate. These agricultural observances acquired the additional significance of "ordering" the life and work of the Church by ministries.

Rogation days, observed until 1969 on April 25 (Greater Litanies—Roman origin) and on the three days before Ascension Thursday (Lesser Litanies—Gallican origin), also have agricultural roots: intercession for blessing and protection of the crops. Many rural dioceses and parishes maintain the custom of blessing seeds and praying for favorable weather and fruitful harvests on one or more days each spring. In response to the May Day celebrations of the Workers, Pius XII established the feast of St. Joseph the Worker in 1955 to give the observance a Christian dimension. In countries that celebrate Labor Day, communities may choose the votive Mass of St. Joseph the Worker or the votive Mass for the blessing of human labor.

Liturgy as Labor. At root *(leitourgia)*, liturgy is the work that the people of God do together for the building up of the body of Christ and the salvation of the world. It envisions and ritualizes a communal life of unity, harmony, equality, patterned on the self-giving life of Christ whose saving work continues in the community that shares his Spirit and bears his name. The various tasks of this common "labor" are done by various members gifted for those tasks. The members of the assembly put themselves at the service of God and of each other and thus they repeat the taking, blessing, breaking, and sharing of all they have been given in imitation of Christ who did so with bread and wine as sacrament of his very self. The unity formed through sharing this Eucharistic meal requires them to defy every injustice and inequality created by divisions of clan or nation, power or possessions.

The liturgy is therefore a model for all human labor in as much as a variety of talents are employed for the life of the community. Labor—even the most mundane task is valuable, because it contributes to the growth and unity in love of actual communities. We do not need to attribute ultimate value to labor in and of itself, for we know that work can estrange as easily as it can unify. It is holy and good and valuable in so far as it helps sustain the lives of other people. Through the liturgy the members of the Church are formed into a group of actual people who can rely and depend on one another. Gathering time and again to remember our origin in the self-giving life and death of Christ, the Church is the community whose unity can see us through the conflicts and division, the boredom and frustration, that our interaction in work can so easily entail.

See: ADAM AND EVE, ALMSGIVING, CALL/VOCATION, LIBERTY, JUBILEE YEAR

JOHN K. LEONARD

LAMB OF GOD

Though there is no use of the phrase "Lamb of God" in the OT, only two occurrences in the NT, and just three instances of its use during the Eucharistic liturgy, this invocation nonetheless has a rich and varied meaning within the Judeo-Christian tradition. Drawing on the imagery and function of shepherds and sheep and their offspring, we can glean not only an understanding of the phrase but also why it has come to be a liturgical formula.

Old Testament

Several different and not unrelated meanings can be identified as to the use of the image "lamb" in the OT. Preeminent among these meanings is that of sacrificial victim, especially abundant in the ritual descriptions of Exodus-Leviticus-Numbers. This meaning included not only the well-known Passover* lamb (Exod 12:3-9), but also the lamb of the daily morning and evening sacrifice as well as the Sabbath sacrifice. The cultic requirement of a sacrificial lamb is closely connected to the meaning of oblation and atonement: the OT mentions the two yearling lambs sacrificed during the priestly ordination rites (Exod 29:38-41) and its octave day (Lev 9:3), the lamb presented to the Most High as a Peace Offering (Lev 3:6-11), that of the sin offering (Lev 4:32), and numerous circumstances under which a lamb is offered to make pure what was impure.

Other OT meanings attached to the figure of lamb are especially apparent in the prophet Isaiah. They include the lamb as a figure of innocence (Isa 53:7), as one who needs care and nurturing (Isa 40:11), and as a sign of gentle and serene peace (Isa 11:6) and prosperity (Isa 65:25).

New Testament

All of these OT images take on new meaning in the NT where the lamb often refers specifically to the person Jesus Christ who bears the sins of humanity as his redemptive mission (Acts 8:32; 1 Pet 1:19) in a typological application of the suffering servant of Isaiah. Moreover, in the NT for the first time we encounter from the lips of John the Baptist the phrase "Lamb of God" (John 1:29, 36). Its accompanying qualifier "who takes away the sins of the world" suggests the evangelist was probably referring to the Isaian suffering servant.

This initial Johannine picture of the Lamb of God as suffering servant shifts radically when we consider the abundant reference to Christ as the lamb that is so central to the Book of Revelation. Here, the Lamb is the blessed One who sits at the throne of God and in whose redemptive blood we are purified. Furthermore, the followers of Jesus are also referred to as lambs, those whom the shepherd is to feed (John 21:15) and who are sacrificial victims as they go out as disciples (Luke 10:3).

Pastoral-Liturgical Tradition

Aside from readings and homilies and images in the psalter, specific use is made of Lamb of God as a liturgical formula in the Eucharistic rite.

The revised Roman Rite of Vatican II has three occurrences of "Lamb of God": at the *Gloria*, during the fraction rite, and at the *Ecce agnus Dei* immediately preceding the Communion procession. However, its liturgical use and meaning are clearly Eastern in origin.

Gloria. Also known as the "great doxology," the *Gloria* originally was part of the eastern Church's morning prayer. By late seventh century it had found its way into the Eucharistic liturgy at Rome and was universally used in the western Church by the eleventh century. The first part of the hymn is addressed to God, but the second part is addressed to the Lord Jesus Christ. It is here where we find among the attributes of Christ that of Lamb of God which is followed by a short litany consisting of two invocations and responses. The first is redemptive in character, requesting that the Lamb of God "take away the sin of the world" followed by the response "have mercy on us." The second invocation acclaims the Lamb's victorious place at the right hand of the Father followed by the response "hear our prayer," one reminding us of Christ's ever constant intercession on our behalf. The entire third part of the hymn is a litany of attributes of Christ, concluding with a trinitarian formula. It is unusual for the prayers of a Eucharistic liturgy to address Christ rather than God, which underscores perhaps the morning prayer origins of this hymn which is a celebration of resurrection during which we address Christ the risen One.

Fraction Rite. In the East, the breaking of the bread is a symbol of the Lord's passion and death, and it is no surprise to find the Greek fathers using *arnion*, lamb, to refer to the Eucharistic bread. In the West, however, the Latin fathers referred to the Eucharistic bread as *hostia*, the sacrificial gift. These two complementary images merge in the West when the Lamb of God found its way into the Roman liturgy by the late seventh century as a litany sung during the fraction rite, repeated as many times as needed until the fraction was completed. When, during the eleventh-twelfth centuries, the Roman rite required unleavened bread, the fraction rite lost its meaning and the Lamb of God was reduced to three invocations. Later, it was separated from the (much reduced) fraction rite and accompanied the kiss of peace; hence, the final ending "grant us peace." Another variation was introduced during *Requiem* Masses where the responses were changed from "have mercy on us" to "give us rest" and from "grant us peace" to "give us eternal rest." This latter innovation is now suppressed.

Ecce Agnus Dei. The third use of "Lamb of God" during the Eucharistic liturgy occurs immediately before the Communion procession begins. The presider raises the bread and cup and says "This is the Lamb of God who takes away the sins of the world. Happy are those who are called to his supper." This formula clearly addresses Christ in the Eucharist and identifies Eucharist as a sacrificial offering. The *"ecce,"* behold, of the earlier sixteenth-century formula has been changed to a demonstrative adjective, "this," quite in keeping with our contemporary Communion practice of not gazing in spiritual Communion but really partaking in Christ our Passover sacrifice.

See: MISSION, PASSOVER, SERVANT, SHEPHERD, SUFFERING, SYMBOL, TYPE

JOYCE A. ZIMMERMAN, C.PP.S.

LAMENT

The lament is a form of speech that cries out against any form of suffering or loss whether personal or public. In the Bible it is found as a prophetic mourning, an official lawsuit, a funeral dirge, or a psalm of lament.

Prophetic Mourning

While many of the oracles of the early prophets contain speeches of warning, from the time of Jeremiah the harsh pronouncements often gave way to prophetic laments. This is particularly evident in the laments over Judah (8:18-22) and over Zion (9:9-21). The sentiments voiced in the first passage are rather complex. The prophet's grief over the suffering of the people is clear and unabashed. However, their misfortune is the consequence of their own transgressions. Jeremiah's own agony results from his own complicated involvement in their predicament. He genuinely loves and sympathizes with his people, but it was his own message that foretold their doom. This conflict will well up later in his own personal laments.

The second passage is a composite of a lament over the ruin of the land (vv. 9-10), reasons for the devastation (vv. 11-15), and a call for the professional mourners (vv. 16-21). Much of this passage seems to be divine first person, a characteristic of prophetic speech regarded as the word of God. In such cases, it is not always helpful to try to separate the sentiments of the prophet from those of God. The point is, both Jeremiah and God mourn the devastation of the land.

Another group of oracles (11:18–12:6; 15:10-21; 17:14-18; 18:18-23; 20:7-18) contains Jeremiah's complaints against his personal enemies and also against God. These complaints share many of the characteristics of the psalms of lament and were most likely derived in great part from them. Still, the "confessions" probably expose the profound inner struggles of this tragic man. Not only were his hopes dashed by the ill-fated death of the righteous king Josiah, but he had to deal with Judah's national blindness, knowing that disaster was imminent.

Most of the "confessions" are really prayers to God. (In three of them the Lord appears to reply [11:21-23; 12:5-6; 15:19-21].) They reveal a man who was by nature sensitive, introspective, and reluctant to assume the role of "prophet of doom." Not only had he been chosen for a mission that seemed opposed to his natural disposition, but he was denied the support one might hope for from a marriage companion (16:1-13). His solitary life itself proclaimed the devastation and isolation that infidelity was to wreak on the nation. Grief arose naturally in his soul.

Official Lawsuit

Mention of a lawsuit, a formulation brought by God against Israel or the nations, is found in several passages of the Book of Job. Here, the complaint is proposed by Job against God. In places, Job's complaint takes on the character of a legal dispute (9:2-24). The vocabulary suggests a court scene where the charge of injustice is brought. The plaintiff, Job, hopes to bring the accused, God, to justice. Job realizes that his case is hopeless, for God is the judge and he, Job, is powerless to force a verdict of "guilty." Although he accuses God, it is Job who is on trial. Thus his initial lament is compounded by a second complaint.

Job longs for some kind of patron whose authority is powerful enough to vindicate him. He rues the fact that there is no umpire who can rule without prejudice (9:3). Later he pleads for an arbitrator who can act impartially (16:19). Both of these passages presume a court scene where judgement might be passed in his favor. While the tenor of the first lament is quite disconsolate, the second one contains an element of hope. There is a witness, a defender in heaven who will hear Job's innocent cries and will intervene. However, no sooner does Job articulate this claim than he takes up his lament anew.

Funeral Dirge

The best example of a funeral dirge is found in the description of David's lament over the deaths of Saul and Saul's son Jonathan ("Ah, how are the heroes fallen," 2 Sam 1:17-27). There the form is explicitly identified as a qînâ and preceded by the characteristic dirge expression "ah, how!" ('êkâ). The funeral dirge, which originated with the death of an individual, came to be applied to the demise of tribes, cities, and whole peoples. The Book of Lamentations, which derives its name "Ah, How!" from 'êkâ, exemplifies this. Chapters 1, 2, and 4 of Lamentations all begin with this opening word and, although the literary style changes throughout the chapters, parts of these poems can still be regarded as a form of a funeral dirge. As with actual funeral dirges, these poems recall the former beauty of the city even as they describe its present desolation.

Psalm of Lament

The type of psalm that occurs most frequently in the Psalter is the lament. Nearly one-third of all the psalms belong to this category. Depending upon the speaker, they are further classified as community laments (e.g., Psalms 12; 44; 58; 74; 80) or laments of the individual (e.g., Psalms 3–7; 25–28; 38–40; 51).

The structure of the lament is not exactly the same in every case. Not all laments ap-pear to be complete, and even when the most common elements are present, they do not seem to have any fixed order. Still, laments are usually comprised of an invocation similar to the hymnic introduction; the actual lamentation which describes the suffering endured by the one(s) praying; a plea for deliverance from this misfortune; some kind of praise of God, often an expression of confidence that God will come to the rescue of the community or the individual; a vow to perform an act of worship in gratitude for God's intervention. Some laments also include an acknowledgment of guilt or an assertion of innocence. Finally, there is frequently a curse hurled against the one(s) believed to be responsible for the intolerable situation that precipitates the lament.

See: PSALMS

DIANNE BERGANT, C.S.A.

LAND

Old Testament

There are two commonly used Hebrew words for "land" in the OT, aretz and adamah. Both of these words can mean land as "country" and land as "earth" or "soil," but to speak of the land of promise, the Bible chiefly uses aretz.

The ancient peoples thought of the land not as private property or as an investment or as disposable capital, but as life itself. Access to land provided the possibility for the survival of the community. The land gave sustenance. It offered a place where the community could plant its crops, care for its flocks, and flourish as a people. Land struggles were, and are today in many parts of the world, battles for the future of the people. It is not surprising, then, that Israel tells its story from the perspective of its relationship to the land.

The subject of the land is so important in the OT that it emerges as a central theme of the literature. From God's promises to the ancestors in Genesis to the last book in the OT canon, Israel's relationship to the land is a major theological concern and in some respects a historical conundrum.

Settlement of the Land. From a historical point of view, Israel's story of the land begins after it takes up residence in Palestine, the geographical name for Canaan and, later, Israel. Accounts of the settlement appear in the historical Books of Joshua and Judges. These two books, however, do not agree about how the people of Israel came to the land.

The Book of Joshua describes a military conquest led by Joshua who gathered the twelve tribes behind him and, with the direct assistance of God, defeated the native Canaanites and took control of their land (Joshua 1–12).

In the Book of Judges, however, and even in later chapters of Joshua, a different picture emerges. Instead of a swift military invasion by all the tribes, Judges reports that much of the land remained in Canaanite hands after Joshua's death (Judges 1). In the Judges' account, the twelve tribes were not united but operated independently of one another. Some Israelites intermarried with local Canaanites (Judg 3:5-6), and some were defeated by Canaanites (Judg 1:34).

The fact that the authors of Joshua and Judges had different theological purposes in writing their stories explains some of the differences between these two accounts. Nonetheless, the contradictions in their descriptions of events create problems for historians. For a long time, modern interpreters gave priority to the Joshua account, understanding the settlement to be the result of a full-scale invasion of Canaan by a united Israel. Later, another group of scholars favored the Judges version of the settlement. They argued that the early Israelites were nomads who came in from the desert and clashed with some of the settled Canaanites and intermarried with others.

More recently, an American scholar has proposed that Israel gained control of the land through an internal revolution. In this view, a small band of slaves escaped from Egypt and made their way through the desert to Palestine. There they were joined by many native Canaanites who were themselves oppressed by the city-state system. They joined the Israelites because they were attracted to the liberating God whom the escaped slaves worshiped. Together these peoples formed new tribal groups and successfully overthrew their Canaanite overlords.

Whatever actually happened—some scholars think a mixture of the above interpretations is correct—Israel's relationship to the land became a prominent element in the way it conceptualized its relationship with God. The land symbolized, in a most intimate way, the divine covenant with the chosen people (Gen 15:7-12).

The Promise of Land. Only after Israelites settled in the land did they look back to tell their story. When they did so, they understood the past as preparation for life in the land. The Pentateuch, the first five books of the Bible, focuses on God's promise to give them the land, a "land flowing with milk and honey" (Deut 11:9).

The narrative thread that ties the complex materials of the Pentateuch together relates how Israel's ancestors migrated from Mesopotamia to a land God promised to show them (Gen 12:1). In Genesis God promises to make the descendants of Abraham and Sarah into "a great nation" on that land (Gen 12:2). In the Book of Exodus God rescues the people from bondage to a cruel and tyrannical government (Exodus 1–15) to bring them at last to the land of promise (Numbers 33). It is this promise of land that propels the story of the Pentateuch forward.

How to Keep the Land. The rest of the Pentateuch contains instructions and exhortations about how the community of freed slaves should live in the land. The Book of Deuteronomy, for instance, is an exhortation, placed on the lips of Moses, about the attitudes and the behavior that was required if the people were to remain on the land.

Moses enjoined the community to recognize that the land was a gift of God, given to them out of love for their ancestors (Deut 4:37). It was a lush land of prosperity and peace, "a land with streams of water, with springs and fountains welling up on the hills and valleys, a land of wheat and barley, of vines and fig trees and pomegranates, of olive trees and of honey, a land where you an eat bread without stint and where you will lack nothing" (Deut 8:7-9).

Hence, for the writer of Deuteronomy, the Israelites would stay in the land only if they remained obedient to the covenant which God had made with them (Deut 8:1). They must live with justice toward one another (Deut 24:6-22), and in the midst of their prosperity, they must remember to "love the Lord your God with all your heart, with all your soul, and with all your strength" (Deut 6:5).

Whereas the Deuteronomist argued that God had freely given Israel the land, later priestly writers would claim that God alone owned the land; Israel was merely a tenant (Lev 25:23). In proposing the celebration of the Jubilee year (Leviticus 25), the priestly compilers of the holiness code (Leviticus 19–26) were elaborating on the tradition of tribal land inheritance found in the Book of Joshua. That book reports that after entering the land, Joshua himself equitably apportioned the land among the tribes (Joshua 13–22) according to the numbers in each group (Num 26:53). The holiness code claims that the tribal heritage gave only the right of stewardship to each tribe. "The land shall not be sold in perpetuity, for the land is mine, and you are but aliens who have become my tenants" (Lev 25:23).

God's ownership of the land formed the motivation for the jubilee law that tribal lands must be resold to their original owners. Through this legal stipulation, no one individual or group would be able to accumulate permanently large tracts of land at the expense of the poor. At least theoretically, the jubilee provided for the redistribution of land and, hence, for a certain equalizing of wealth among the people.

Threats to the Land. Like the Deuteronomists and Priestly writers, preexilic prophets also believed that Israel's continued life on the land was dependent upon the people's fidelity to the covenant. The story of the seizure of Naboth's vineyard (1 Kings 21) illustrates the prophetic critique of the monarchy's attitudes toward the land.

King Ahab wanted to buy Naboth's vineyard to plant a vegetable garden. Naboth refused the king saying, "The Lord forbid . . . that I should give you my ancestral heritage" (1 Kgs 21:3). Angered at this, Queen Jezebel arranged for two "scoundrels" to contrive a charge against Naboth that resulted in his death by stoning. Besides murdering an innocent man, the royal family had violated Israel's law of ancestral inheritance of the land. For this offence, the prophet Elijah cursed king and queen, promising them that "the dogs shall lick up your blood" (v. 19).

Isaiah decries similar abuses of the laws of ancestral inheritance. "Woe to you who join house to house, who connect field with field" (Isa 5:8), he shouts at those who had become wealthy by displacing the land's original owners.

For the prophets, particular land abuses were only a symptom of greater infidelity. They were concerned about Israel's very existence on the land because the people could remain there only if they lived justly. Infidelity to God and mistreatment of neighbors would result in expulsion.

Amos warned that God would exile them from the land, if they did not "let justice surge like water and goodness like an unfailing stream" (Amos 5:24-27). He threatened them with exile, if they continued their luxurious lifestyle without concern for the collapse of the nation (Amos 6:4-7). Jeremiah announced, "All Judah is banished in universal exile" (Jer 13:19).

In the prophetic view, the fate of the land was inextricably bound up with the fate of the people. Humans are not separate from the land and cannot live as if their actions had no effect upon it. Because of their falsehood, the land itself was dying. Jeremiah asked, "How long must the earth mourn, the green of the whole countryside wither? For the wickedness of those who dwell in it beasts and birds disappear" (Jer 12:4). Micah promised, "The land shall be a waste because of its citizens" (7:13). For Hosea, God gave "the grain, the wine and the oil" or took it back depending upon the fidelity of the people (Hos 2:10).

The Loss of the Land. When Israel lost the land as the prophets had warned, its identity, its faith, and its future were in doubt. Many Israelites became prisoners of war in Babylon where they endured exile for nearly fifty years. In Babylon they grieved for their lost land, "How could we sing the song of the Lord in a foreign land?" (Ps 137:4). Like most exiles, they kept the hope of a return to the land alive among them.

The great prophets of the Exile began to look to the future and to anticipate a renewal of life on the land. In a section of the Book of Jeremiah dated after the fall of the nation, God announces the people's return to the land in a great procession. "Behold, I will bring them back from the land of the north; I will gather them from the ends of the world, with the blind and the lame in their midst, the mothers and those with child; they shall return as an immense throng" (31:8).

Similarly, Second Isaiah promised that God would lead the people back to their land through the desert. It would be a new exodus but this time the desert too would be transformed. "I will pour out my spirit upon the thirsty ground, and streams upon the dry land" (Isa 44:3). The people would return to their land and life would be restored. Their lives there would be "like watered gardens, never again shall they languish" (Jer 31:12).

After the Persian emperor Cyrus defeated the Babylonians, he issued an edict by which the Jews in Babylon were permitted to return to Jerusalem (Ezra 1:1-4). A small group returned under the leadership of Ezra and Nehemiah and began life again on the land.

New Testament

In the NT land is no longer a central issue in a literal sense. Instead, the primary concern of the NT writers is with Jesus' message and with life in the communities of his followers. The subject of the land does not disappear completely in the NT, however. Jesus' announcement that the Reign of God is at hand includes in it nuances of the sense of the land, that is, political, historical, and physical life of the people. With the coming of the reign of God in Jesus, old social arrangements are overturned; life in the land is characterized by justice and by care and honor for the afflicted and the downtrodden. In the sense that Jesus' message concerns actual human life, not only spiritualized afterlife, OT concerns for land and for justice for the peoples of all lands are reiterated and fulfilled in the New.

Pastoral-Liturgical Tradition

Land is as great an issue in the struggles of peoples today as it was in biblical times. Many communities around the globe struggle for the right to live on their ancestral lands. In some countries, small groups of rich families control most of the arable land. In others, foreign powers determine who will use the land and how. The biblical literature does not justify land-grabbing by individuals or nations. The Bible sees the land as belonging to God alone. The peoples are its tenants and stewards whose religious duty it is to care for it and for each other.

The law and the prophets teach that God gives the land for the use of everyone. In the OT land symbolizes access to life, to food, to community, joy, and prosperity. These are not for the few but for all, those living and those not yet born. Hence, the prophet's recognition of the interrelationship of land and people and their cries for justice on the land is as timely as ever.

See: BABYLON, CANAAN, EXILE, JUBILEE YEAR

KATHLEEN M. O'CONNOR

LAW

This entry consists of three parts. The OT section reviews the development of the idea of the law in Isarel's relationship with God. The attitude toward the law that characterizes the OT is that the law is God's gracious guidance for Israel's life. The NT section centers its attention on the Pauline understanding of the law while also considering its occurrences in the Gospels, Acts, and Hebrews. The Pastoral-Liturgical section examines the historical development of canon law.

Old Testament

In the OT the idea of law is inseparable from the idea of election* and the idea of covenant.* It rests upon the initiative of God who out of love chose a particular people, Israel,* entered covenant with them, and in grace provided the basic terms of this covenant relationship in the covenant law. The context of covenant stresses the intimate connection between God's gift to Israel on the one hand and the requirement of Israel's proper conduct, its willing obedience to God's law, on the other. Within this framework the law is not seen as a burden but as God's gracious guidance through the uncertainties of life. It is a lamp to the feet and a light to the path (Ps 119:105).

The OT has many Hebrew words to describe various types of law, such as those referring to judgments, statutes, testimonies, words, and commandments. The most common Hebrew word for law, however, is *torah*, which the Septuagint regularly translates as *nomos*. Its basic meaning is instruction or guidance. Eventually the word Torah was extended to refer to the first five books of the Bible, the Pentateuch.

Moses and the Law. The Pentateuchal narratives, which grew out of different oral and literary traditions, all unequivocally assign to Moses a unique role in the promulgation of covenant law. It was to Moses that God spoke face to face, to Moses that God revealed the law. He is God's spokesman, the mediator of God's law who is without equal. So strong is this assessment that all subsequent laws that developed over the centuries are traced back to Moses and to the Sinai events. One speaks of the whole Pentateuch as "the law of Moses." The theological implication is clear: God's deliverance from Egypt, the covenant between God and Israel enacted at Sinai (Exodus 19–20; 24), form the basis for all Israelite law. All laws from whatever period are thus grounded in this initial event. God chose Israel to be the people of God; Israel acknowledged God to be its God. The laws are then an expression of God's claim to reign over the whole life of the people in virtue of this choice.

The Ten Commandments. From the earliest period of interpretation the Ten Commandments (in Hebrew phrasing, "the ten words") have been considered the foundation of Israelite law. They provide the basic stipulations of the covenant relationship. The Ten Commandments are recorded in two places in the Pentateuch (Exod 20:2-17; Deut 5:6-21) with only slight variations between them. They begin with the self-identification of this God who has acted to save the people and to enter a relationship with them: "I, the LORD, am your God, who brought you out of the land of Egypt, that place of slavery" (Exod 20:2; Deut 5:6). God's redeeming action provides the context for the commandments that follow. This opening sentence also makes clear that the commandments are intended to be Israel's response to God's saving deed and not a condition for it. The first, the "religious" commandments, clarify what is to be Israel's stance before God. They are to have dealings with no other gods; they are not to make images; they are to respect God's name; they are to consecrate the Sabbath to

God. All the general moral precepts and prohibitions that follow are linked to the will of God. The uniqueness of these latter precepts does not lie in their content. Prohibitions against murder, adultery, theft, etc., are characteristic of all social organizations. Rather it lies in the connection established between these moral precepts and the religious commands that have preceded them. For Israel, moral action is inseparably linked to the worship of God. Indeed, not only the worship of God but the whole of life stands under God's law. The fact that the commandments are formulated without any mention of specific punishment for their transgression forcefully illustrates the absolute nature of the law. Forbidden is any intention or act that is not in harmony with the covenant between Israel and its God. Furthermore, the negative expression of most of these commandments leaves open the future development of their positive implications. These commands are addressed to each individual Israelite and therefore to the whole Israelite community of which each Israelite is a member.

The Covenant Code. Two typical types of law are found in the Pentateuch. The first is absolute, or apodictic, law. It is straightforward and is stated in sharp, succinct form. "You must not do this." No stipulation about enforcement is given. The Ten Commandments are characteristic of this type. A second is conditional or case law, which suggests the procedure for dealing with particular issues. Its pattern is, "If that happens, then this will be the legal consequence." This was the common formulation in the legal codes of the ancient Near East, the best known of which is the Code of Hammurabi. It is also the type that predominates in the collection of laws known as the Book of the Covenant or Covenant Code that immediately follow the Ten Commandments in Exodus (Exod 20:22–23:33).

The laws of the Covenant Code reflect the new agricultural situation faced by the Israelites when they left the desert and settled in Canaan, although some elements may go back to the earlier time of the patriarchs. It is clear that the various tribal groups that existed before Moses had laws to govern such things as tribal relations, adoption procedures, marriage customs, etc. Such customs and regulations are reflected in the patriarchal narratives of Genesis. In this period, as well as in the laws that developed after Sinai, there is obvious influence of non-Israelite bodies of laws, but what is most noteworthy is the extent to which both the laws retained from the early period and those that developed after the Sinai experience are unmistakably appropriated into the context of the covenant. Indeed, all Israelite law had but one purpose: to maintain the vitality of the covenant community.

Another remarkable feature of the Covenant Code may be seen in the laws that protect the weak and the poor. Nothing like them exists in any of the laws proper to the Mesopotamian law codes. For example, there is a prohibition against exacting interest from a poor Israelite and a command to return every evening a neighbor's cloak taken in pledge, because it is his only source of covering (Exod 22:24-26). Along with widows and orphans, foreigners also are to receive special concern. The motivation for this is made clear: "You well know how it felt to be an alien, since you were once alien yourselves in the land of Egypt" (Exod 23:9). The covenant relationship between God and Israel was renewed at various periods in subsequent history (Josh 8:30-35; 24; Deut 27; 31:9-13), and on these occasions the laws were read aloud and the people reaffirmed their commitment to obey.

Law Under the Monarchy. The introduction of the kingship into Israel caused a marked change in Israel's life. Although there is some dispute about this, it seems that while the king eventually came to exercise the function of supreme judge in legal matters (2 Sam 15:2-6), the structures of Israelite law were so firmly established that no king was ever looked upon as lawgiver, nor did any king attempt to set up his own law. Furthermore, when necessary, the king was firmly reminded that, although king, he was not above the law but was bound by the same covenant stipulations as the people (2 Samuel 11–12; 1 Kings 21).

The preexilic prophets seldom mention the law specifically, but the context of all their preaching is the realty of the covenant and consequently the legal requirements by which it is to be sustained. In the name of God they constantly remind the people of their covenant obligations and warn them of the dire consequences that will result from their violation of these stipulations (Amos 2:4-5: Hos 8:1, 12).

The Book of Deuteronomy. Deuteronomy presents itself as a long speech addressed by Moses to the people of Israel as they prepare to enter Canaan and settle there. In an exceedingly forceful manner Deuteronomy explains the meaning of God's law for Israel. To love God and to keep God's commandments will bring life and blessing (Deuteronomy 6; 30; 20). To forget God, to go after other gods will result in death and a curse (Deut 8:19; 28:15-69; 30:17-18).

The primary command to love God is repeatedly set in the context of God's own love for Israel. A pleading summons is issued to the people to choose life over death (Deut 30:19). The body of laws incorporated into Moses' speech (Deuteronomy 12–26) had gradually developed over the centuries following his death, but, as in the case with all Israelite law, they are attributed to Moses himself. In this way the ancient covenant law was applied and adapted to the ever-changing circumstances of life.

Deuteronomy repeatedly stresses that the covenant law continues to be valid for each generation up to the present day: "Moses summoned all Israel and said to them, 'Hear, O Israel, the statutes and decrees which I proclaim in your hearing this day, that you may learn them and take care to observe them. The LORD, our God, made a covenant with us at Horeb; not with our fathers did he make this covenant, but with us, all of us who are alive here this day'" (Deut 5:1-3; 26:16-19; 29:13-14).

A highly distinctive feature of Deuteronomy is its laws seeking to alleviate the lot of the poor. In its attempt to outline a world where poverty will no longer exist, it goes even beyond the laws found in the Covenant Code (Deuteronomy 15). God's covenant blessings are to be available to every individual.

Exilic and Postexilic Law. In 587 BCE Nebuchadnezzar attacked Jerusalem. The city and the Temple were destroyed; the people were deported from their land and taken into captivity in Babylon. In many ways the loss of land, kingship, and Temple seemed to signal the death of Israel, but in remarkable fashion Israelite faith and Israelite law gained new vitality in the Exile. The priests, who had always been the chief interpreters of the law, began at this time to study and elaborate it with new intensity, for they saw it as the primary means of preserving the Israelite community within a hostile environment. Their collection of laws is known as the Priestly Code. It is not found in one place, as is the case with the Covenant and Deuteronomic Codes, but is scattered throughout the "P" or Priestly source of the Pentateuch. Its primary emphasis is on proper worship. While the relationship between worship and the observance of God's law had been recognized from earliest times, it received particularly strong emphasis from the priests. Responsible both for worship and for the legal tradition, they were able to reinforce for the people the intimate connection between these two aspects of life. References to this connection abound also in the psalms, of which Psalm 119 is a fine example. Here, as well as in other psalms, the Israelite worshiper expresses delight and gratitude for God's law that teaches one how to live before God in faithfulness.

Another characteristic of the "P" account is to attach all laws to some historical event. It begins with the very creation of the world. God is portrayed as the divine lawgiver whose word alone brings about the ordered structure of the world and gives a universal command to all human beings to "be fertile and multiply; fill the earth, and subdue it" (Gen 1:28). "P" then traces the development of the law through the decisive events in Israel's own history, particularly the Sinai experience. God gives a command to Moses to build a sanctuary that will mediate God's word and will thus become for all time the center of Israel's life. In this way "P" presents the law as the foundation of renewal for a defeated people in Exile.

Within "P" is a distinguishable collection of laws known as the Holiness Code (Leviticus 17–26). Its general concern is to maintain holiness and purity. Israel is to be distinctly different from the other nations and is not to engage in religious and social practices like those of other peoples. The reason for this is repeatedly emphasized, "To me, therefore, you shall be sacred; for I, the LORD, am sacred, I, who have set you apart from the other nations to be my own" (Lev 20:26). Like the Covenant Code and the Deuteronomic legislation, the Holiness Code emphasizes the importance of caring for the underprivileged of society, giving as an all-embracing expression the idea of love: "You shall love your neighbor as yourself" (Lev 19:18).

As the exilic prophets reflected on what was asked of Israel as God's people, they were acutely aware that the whole of Israelite history was one of constant failure to live up to the covenant obligations. They were, however, able to look beyond the past and the present and to emphasize that what God had intended for the people would be achieved in the future. The term used to describe this fulfillment is eschatology. The law receives prominence in this vision for the future. In "those days" God will make Israel truly faithful and obedient, and God's law will be taught to all the world (Isa 42:1-4). Jeremiah posits that God will make a new covenant with Israel. "This is the covenant which I will make with the house of Israel after those days, says the LORD. I will place my law within them, and write it upon their hearts; I will be their God, and they shall be my people"

(Jer 31:33). The law, perfectly lived, will thus be at the essence of Israelite life.

An edict of Cyrus the Great in 538 BCE made it possible for the exiles to return from Babylon to Jerusalem, and the Temple was rebuilt. Throughout the Exile the perception had grown that Israel had been punished for its disobedience to the covenant. So now, after the return, the predominant concern was to carry out God's will. Exact fidelity to the law was seen as the means to do this. Although the intention may have been good, there were negative results as obedience to the law gradually eclipsed all other concerns. Separated from its context of covenant relationship, observance of the law became almost an end in itself, a supposedly guaranteed means of winning God's favor, rather than as an expression of Israel's grateful response to God's gracious and delivering acts. This distorted understanding was a prelude to a doctrine of merit.

Despite this late development, the dominant OT view is that the law is God's gracious guide to Israel, the means by which it lives out its willing response to God's covenant love.

See: COVENANT, ELECTION, ESCHATOLOGY, HOLY/ HOLINESS

MARILYN M. SCHAUB

New Testament

In the NT the term "law" has multiple meanings; some repeat OT usages and some do not. Over half of all the NT occurrences of the word are in the letters of Paul, especially Galatians and Romans. Because of its complexity in meaning and its controversy in the history of biblical interpretation, the term generates extensive discussion and debate in the study of Pauline theology.

Jewish and Hellenistic Background. *Nomos* is the Greek word translated as "law," although "custom" or "norm" more accurately conveys how non-Jews in the ancient world would have heard the term. Gentiles would have had little familiarity with OT Hebrew notions of law. This lack of familiarity created the potential for confusion, as

Paul himself discovered to his horror. First Corinthians 5 describes the case of a Greek convert who had heard the Pauline gospel message that those in Christ were no longer under *nomos*, but who apparently thought *nomos* meant Greco-Roman social conventions, including prohibitions against incest. So he acted accordingly and began to have sex with his stepmother. Paul had to correct this gross misunderstanding of his theology and to pass judgment on the Gentile believer. This episode illustrates just one of the cross-cultural challenges Paul faced in his preaching Jewish concepts to non-Jews.

Depending on the specific context and rhetorical intent, Paul, like any other first-century Jew who knew Greek, used *nomos* to mean at least four different things: (1) Scripture, meaning the whole Jewish Bible as the Word of God (Hebrew: *Torah*); (2) the Pentateuch, meaning the writings on the parchment scrolls of the five biblical books by Moses, the "Law" in the technical literary sense, as opposed to the "Prophets" (*Nevi'im*) and "Writings" (*Kethuvim*); (3) *halakah*, a Hebrew word meaning the guidelines for ritual action to produce purity and separation from Gentiles, found in Deuteronomy and the Holiness Code of Leviticus 17–26; and (4) the Decalogue, meaning the Ten Commandments that Yahweh gave to Moses during the divine revelation on Mount Sinai. In addition to these, the NT era saw the beginnings of *Torah* being expanded to mean not only the written but also an "oral" law, especially among the teachings of the Pharisees (which eventually formed the basis of the Talmud and Mishnah of later rabbinic Judaism).

Paul and the Law. We find the earliest Christian discussions of the law in the Pauline letters. Paul believed that Jewish law came from heaven, and that this fact made *Torah* superior to pagan legal traditions, which (he believed) had merely human origins. Yet Paul also believed that God's law was no longer binding on Gentiles. As a Christian missionary, then, Paul

had to explain why a law from God was no longer valid. He faced questions such as: Why then did God give the law in the first place? Did God's mind change? Did God lie to Israel? Or did Israel just misunderstand the revelation on Mount Sinai? Paul answered negatively to all these questions. For Paul, the crucifixion of Jesus shattered and recast Jewish tradition into a new mold. Because of the Cross, Paul's whole understanding of God and the world had changed (Gal 6:14). To understand this transformation, we need to look closely at the events of his life.

Paul's view of the Jewish law changed dramatically after he received his call to the Christian mission. He presents his autobiography in the following manner: "Circumcised on the eighth day, of the race of Israel, of the tribe of Benjamin, a Hebrew of Hebrew parentage, in observance of the law a Pharisee, in zeal I persecuted the church, in righteousness based on the law I was blameless" (Phil 3:5-6; cf. Acts 22:3; 26:5). Paul describes himself as an observant Jew who lived under *Torah*. Yet after his call, Paul changed some—but not all—of his opinions about *Torah*, primarily the Holiness Code that frustrated his Gentile mission. Openly attacking *kashrut* and circumcision,* the Christian Paul never saw such a law as an absolute requirement for admission into the people of God (e.g., Gal 2:3-5; 3:28; 5:2-12). In this view, he disagreed sharply with Peter, especially on the circumcision and kosher issues; Paul even "opposed him to his face because he was clearly wrong" (Gal 2:11).

Paul did not, however, change completely, and it is wrong to caricature Paul as preaching that Judaism was a "legalistic" and therefore dead religion. Paul does not attack a claim that works of the law achieve salvation, but argues over the role of works of the law as the grammar of the covenantal relationship between God and Israel. Throughout his mission, Paul maintained that he was still a pious and righteous Jew whose efforts to gain Gentile belief in Christ were not annulling the law but supporting it (Rom 3:31). He makes many positive statements about the law, saying that "what matters is keeping God's commandments" (1 Cor 7:19) and that "the law is holy, and the commandment is holy and righteous and good" (Rom 7:12; see also Rom 8:4). While making these positive statements, nonetheless Paul also speaks negatively about Jewish law as tool of sin, something without which sin would lie dormant (Rom 6:12-14; 7:5-6).

How do we reconcile these seemingly contradictory claims? The answer lies in understanding the law like a first-century Jew, as a broad term that refers to many different parts of Jewish ancestral tradition. Generally, when Paul refers to the Decalogue (Rom 13:8-10; Gal 5:14) or the Pentateuch (1 Cor 9:9-10; 14:21-22), he speaks favorably of the law, even quoting it as authoritative for Christians. But when Paul refers to circumcision, dietary restrictions, and other parts of the Holiness Code, he talks negatively of the law. Among the positive statements, we find a recurring call to obey the Golden Rule. He writes: "Whatever other commandments there may be, are summed up in this saying, [namely] 'You shall love your neighbor as yourself.' Love does no evil to the neighbor; hence, love is the fulfillment of the law" (Rom 13:9-10; see also Gal 5:14 and Jas 2:8). Paul does not say that he received this love ethic from any particular source (e.g., the teaching of Jesus). Because the ethic was commonplace in first-century Judaism, he could have learned it from childhood.

For example, there is an anecdote about one of the greatest rabbis of Jewish tradition, Hillel (ca. 80 BCE–10 CE). A Gentile once came to Hillel and asked him whether he could teach him the whole *Torah* while standing on one foot, apparently in the hopes that the instruction would be brief. Hillel answered him, "What is hateful to you, don't do to your neighbor; that is the whole *Torah*, and the rest . . . is just a commentary" (The Babylonian Talmud, tractate *Shabbat* 31a; see Yitzhak Buxbaum, *The Life*

and Teachings of Hillel [London: Jason Aronson, 1994] 95–102).

Although he rarely quoted OT commandments directly to his congregations, Paul did exhort them to obey *Torah* epitomized in the Golden Rule as their guiding principle not only in ethical but also ritual behavior (e.g., the Pauline assessment of conscience in the ritual practice of the "strong" sacrificing meat to pagan idols, 1 Corinthians 8 and 10). He recognized the Rule's importance in pastoring a church. He believed that the Gentiles should keep at least some of *Torah*. The applicability of this Jewish love ethic to the Gentile mission explains Paul's positive statements about the law.

To understand Paul's negative statements about the law, we need to examine Paul's letters in the light of the historical struggle among first-century Jews on the controversial issue of whether membership into the people of God required circumcision. In Galatians, Paul attacks the claim of unnamed opponents that he is a religious fraud who has trimmed the gospel to please humans. The opponents appear to be Jewish-Christian missionaries who bring "another gospel" mandating Gentile converts to become circumcised and keep Jewish festivals. The Jewish-Christian missionaries told the Galatians that Paul had made it too easy for them; yes, the Galatians took the first step by accepting God and Christ, but to complete the conversion the Galatians must be circumcised according to Jewish ancestral custom. Paul retorts that his gospel is not expedient but a new revelation from God to Israel. Why is circumcision such a hotly contested issue in Galatians and other Pauline writings?

A helpful clue is found in the writings of another Jewish author, Josephus (born ca. 37 CE, a late contemporary of Paul). Josephus recounts a story of a certain Izates, who was a Gentile king attracted to the Jewish religion. One Jew, Ananias, told the king that he could become Jewish and worship God *even without being circumcised* (the Pauline argument). Yet another Jew, Eleazar from Galilee, told the King the opposite, namely, that

Torah (i.e., *halakah*) mandates circumcision. If the King practiced Judaism uncircumcised, then he would be guilty of the greatest offense against the law and against God (the argument of Paul's opponents). This story helps to locate the Pauline mission within the internal Jewish debate over inclusion of Gentiles into the people of God (Josephus, *Jewish Antiquities* 20.38-48; found in Hans Dieter Betz, *Galatians: A Commentary on Paul's Letter to the Churches in Galatia* [Hermeneia series; Philadelphia: Fortress, 1979] 328).

Both sides of this debate understand law as part of a covenant. But which covenant? Paul writes: "Now the promises were made to Abraham and to his descendant. It does not say, 'And to descendants,' as referring to many, but as referring to one, 'And to your descendant,' who is Christ. This is what I mean: the law, which came four hundred and thirty years afterward, does not annul a covenant previously ratified by God, so as to cancel the promise" (Gal 3:16-17). Here, Paul compares the covenant of Abraham (who was from Mesopotamia, not a Hebrew but a pagan) with the covenant of Moses, and finds the first prior and so superior to the second.

The Mosaic covenant is conditional, containing obligations for Israel to obey God and *Torah* (specifically by the membership requirements embodied in the Holiness Code). The Abrahamic covenant is unconditional, simply a promise that God makes with Abraham without conditions or membership requirements attached. The two covenants are contradictory to Paul. The question then becomes: "Why, then, the law?" Paul answers: "It was added for transgressions, until the descendant came to whom the promise had been made; it was promulgated by angels at the hand of a mediator" (Gal 3:19). The covenant of Moses did not even come from God, but angels (cf. Acts 7:53).

Does Christianity then replace Judaism (as, for example, the authors of Matthew and the Fourth Gospel maintain)? No, says Paul: "Is the law then opposed to the promises [of God]? Of course not! For if a law had been given that could bring life, then righteousness would in reality come from the law. But scripture confined all things under the power of sin, that through faith in Jesus Christ the promise might be given to those who believe" (Gal 3:21-22). No further explanation is given in Galatians. Paul will develop this theology later in his last extant letter, to the Romans (esp. chs. 9–11).

In Romans, Paul makes statements about the law that seem to contradict what he had said previously in Galatians. Paul writes: "The law entered in so that transgression might increase but, where sin increased, grace overflowed all the more, so that, as sin reigned in death, grace also might reign through justification for eternal life through Jesus Christ our Lord" (Rom 5:20). The law only harasses human beings and causes them to sin: "For up to the time of the law, sin was in the world, though sin was not accounted when there was no law" (Rom 5:13). The law is said to come directly from God; no longer do we hear of angels or mediators giving the law.

Why then did God give the law? According to Romans, God originally gave the law as a true expression of the divine will (Romans 2), but sin used the law to harm people (Romans 7), and thus the law was too "weakened" to deal with sin (Rom 8:3). The law was, in effect, a *catalyst* for sin. Paul had argued in Galatians that "Before faith came, we were held in custody under law, confined for the faith that was to be revealed. Consequently, the law was our disciplinarian for Christ, that we might be justified by faith. But now that faith has come, we are no longer under a disciplinarian" (Gal 3:23-25). Why was the law given? According to Galatians, it was given to keep sin in check, under lock and key. The law was a "disciplinarian" (or "pedagogue" in the original Greek), which acted as a *hindrance* for sin. Because *Torah* was not considered a human construct, it was a problem for Paul to explain away.

This comparison of Galatians with Romans reveals that Paul sets up two possibilities for why the law was given to humans. He argues that the law has two opposite functions. In Romans, God gave a law too weak to deal with sin, in order to increase sin. In Galatians, the law is given by angels to bridle transgressions, in order to diminish sin. This tension shows that Paul lacked a singular—or systematic—theology of the law.

Paul came to his theology of the law not through empirical observation of sinning in the world; he did not first believe that all humans are heinous sinners and then learned that people covet only because they heard the commandment *not* to covet. Instead, after his call to be an apostle, Paul reinterpreted all of his Jewish traditions and values in the light of the crucifixion and resurrection of Christ. Paul reckoned that because God saves only through Christ, the law therefore could not have the salvific value he once thought it did.

Synoptic Gospels and Acts. The Synoptic Gospels postdate the writings of Paul and reflect a later stage of development in the life of the Church. The evangelists wrote after Christianity began to define itself as a movement distinct from Judaism, which was not the case in Paul's day. (Paul does not know the word "Christian," for example.) Consequently, we cannot assume that the Gospel or other NT authors shared the Pauline understanding of the law.

All three evangelists attribute the Jewish love ethic to Jesus. When a Jewish scribe asks Jesus which commandment of *Torah* is the greatest, Jesus replied, "The first is this: 'Hear, O Israel! The Lord our God is Lord alone! You shall love the Lord your God with all your heart, with all your soul, with all your mind, and with all your strength.' The second is this: 'You shall love your neighbor as yourself.' There is no other commandment greater than these" (Mark 12:29-31; par. Matt 22:34-40; Luke 10:25-28). Here Jesus speaks like Hillel and Paul, which is understandable since they all were Jews. (The Golden Rule proper is found only in Matt 7:12 and Luke 6:31.)

Jews divided *Torah* into two tablets: (1) laws governing behavior between humans (epitomized as Lev 19:18); and (2) laws governing behavior between humans and God (epitomized as Deut 6:4-5). The Synoptics report Jesus in agreement with both tablets of the law. In his Sermon on the Mount, the Matthean Jesus says: "Do not think that I have come to abolish the law or the prophets. I have come not abolish but to fulfill" (Matt 5:17). Here the term "law" refers to the Pentateuch of Moses, which together with the "Prophets" constitutes Jewish Scripture (see also Matt 11:13; 12:5; Luke 2:22-27; 16:16-17; 24:44; Acts 13:15; 15:5; 28:23).

While Jesus fulfilled the law, he nonetheless did not always obey it, at least according to his Pharisaic critics: "So the Pharisees and scribes questioned him, 'Why do your disciples not follow the tradition of the elders but instead eat a meal with unclean hands?'" (Mark 7:5; par. Matt 15:2). Jesus responds: "Woe to you, scribes and Pharisees, you hypocrites. You pay tithes of mint and dill and cummin, and have neglected the weightier things of the law: judgment and mercy and fidelity. [But] these you should have done, without neglecting the others" (Matt 23:23). The Synoptics report that Jesus and his followers regularly ignored Jewish dietary restrictions and even ate with tax-collectors, sinners, and other unclean—and marginalized—people, in apparent belief that they were indeed following *Torah* in a sense greater than did the Pharisees. Jewish law centers on many of the Synoptic controversy statements about Jesus, but these episodes may reflect later Christian debates with their Jewish contemporaries as much as actual events in the ministry of the historical Jesus.

The same is reported of major characters in the Book of Acts, such as Stephen (Acts 6:13) and especially Paul (Acts 21:28; 23:29; 25:8). For example, Luke writes: "But when Gallio was proconsul of Achaia, the Jews rose up together against Paul and brought him to the tribunal, saying, 'This man is inducing people to worship God contrary to the law'" (Acts 18:12-13). Such a passage reflects early Christian apologetic attempts to defend itself against outside accusations that it operates as an illegal and subversive religion under both Jewish and Roman law. Christianity, the author of Acts argues, is open and friendly to the Roman Empire: "this was not done in a corner," meaning in secret (Acts 26:26). All major Christian characters are presented as pious in relation to Jewish law and innocent in relation to the state.

The Fourth Gospel. The author of John identifies law exclusively with the Jewish Scriptures, specifically the law of Moses. The Johannine Jesus speaks disparagingly of the Jews and their ability to understand their own law: "Did not Moses give you the law? Yet none of you keeps the law. Why are you trying to kill me?" (John 7:19). The law operates as a literary device, even a character, in the narrative to propel the plot. At the trial scene before Pilate, the Jews scream that "We have a law, and according to that law he ought to die, because he made himself the Son of God" (John 19:7). With these words, the author of the Fourth Gospel expresses dramatic irony: the Jews speak more wisely than they could possibly realize. Indeed, the law of Moses does state that Jesus must die, but not for the reason the Jews think. Jesus must die precisely in order to realize God's plan to glorify Christ. The Johannine Jesus says: "But in order that the word written in their law might be fulfilled, 'They hated me without cause'" (John 15:15; quoting parts of Pss 35:19 and 69:4).

The true meaning of the law is the opposite of its literal meaning. The "Jews," operating as a singular character in the narrative, strive to oppose Jesus for his so-called breaking of the law, but by their own actions they paradoxically help Jesus to fulfill the law. As the author has Jesus say: "And just as Moses lifted up the serpent in the desert, so must the Son of Man be lifted up, so that everyone who believes in him may have eternal life" (John 3:14-15). The phrase "lifted up" (i.e., on the cross) functions as a literary pun, playing on both the positive and negative connotations of Jesus' death as demanded by the law of Moses. In this way, the author demonstrates how the Jews do not even know their own law.

Hebrews. The author of Hebrews generally understands "law" to be the law of Moses (Heb 10:28), but as a rule he narrows the term to mean the rules of OT priesthood orders, especially cultic rites governing animal blood sacrifice (e.g., Heb 9:22; 10:8). Hebrews argues that Christ's sacrifice exposes the inadequacy of previous priestly blood sacrifice as a route to perfection. Yet despite this claim, the author of Hebrews does view the law positively: it came, after all, from God and always possessed a shadow of the coming good in Christ. The author writes: "Since the law has only a shadow of the good things to come, and not the very image of them, it can never make perfect those who come to worship by the same sacrifices that they offer continually each year" (Heb 10:1). Christ, as the new high priest, brings an end to levitical priestly law: "When there is a change of priesthood, there is necessarily a change of law as well" (Heb 7:12). In strong language, the author avers that "a former commandment is annulled because of its weakness and uselessness, for the law brought nothing to perfection" (Heb 7:18-19).

Christ shatters OT cultic categories and recasts them into a new law, a new covenant that declares the old obsolete (Heb 8:7-13). Christians must now worship in a new mode, following the new law written in our hearts, which is conscience* (Heb 10:16-25). Such a statement modifies Pauline thinking of the law, especially the notion that the law was written on the hearts of Gentiles *even before* the death and resurrection of Christ (Rom 2:14-16). Hebrews anticipates later Christian thought in seeing OT law as allegorical anticipation of Christ.

James. The letter of James exhorts believers to follow the Jewish love ethic: "If you fulfill the royal law according to scripture,

'You shall love your neighbor as yourself,' you are doing well" (Jas 2:8). This love ethic is the measure of proper behavior and the basis of judgment: "So speak and so act as those who are to be judged by the law of liberty" (Jas 2:12), that is the law that renders one truly free. The author of James argues that believers must exhibit consistency in their obedience to the *entire* law of God, which he cites as the Decalogue (Jas 2:10-11). This citation suggests that the author of James may have identified God's "whole law" in a limited sense.

See: CIRCUMCISION, CLEAN/UNCLEAN, CONSCIENCE, COVENANT, FAITH, FULFILLMENT, GRACE, HOLY/HOLINESS, ISRAEL, JEW, JUDAISM, JUDGMENT, JUSTIFICATION, LIBERTY, LOVE, MEDIATOR, MOSES, OBEDIENCE, PAUL, PEOPLE OF GOD, PROMISE, SACRIFICE, SALVATION, SIN, WORD

J. ALBERT HARRILL

Pastoral-Liturgical Tradition

Like all human societies, the Christian Church from the beginning has been organized and governed by law *(ius)*, if not always in the strict sense of written legislation *(lex)*, at least in the broad meaning of the term which includes customs or other rules for ordering and structuring the community.

The first Christian communities were ordered by Jewish laws, moral teachings of philosophers, and by established conventions and customs. The leaders of the community felt free, under the guidance of the holy Spirit, to change established practices when faced with new circumstances and cultural differences (e.g., Acts 15, esp. 28–29).

Early examples of ecclesiastical discipline are found in the pseudo-apostolic Church orders beginning about 100 CE. These manuals, claiming apostolic authority, contained disciplinary rules, liturgical prescriptions, moral duties, and legal ordinances in force in the community. Some of the better known are the Didache (ca. 100), the Apostolic Tradition of Hippolytus (ca. 225), and the Apostolic Constitutions (ca. late fourth century).

From the fourth century onward, a principal source of Church law and organization were the canons enacted by local and ecumenical councils. The word "canon" comes from the Greek, meaning a rod or straight rule, from whence it came to mean a rule for life. The first canons were promulgated by local councils. The first ecumenical council in Nicea in 325 enacted twenty canons dealing with practical matters such as the dignity of clergy, public penance, the readmission of schismatics, and the regulation of the liturgy. Many councils adopted canons dealing with doctrinal as well as disciplinary matters.

The canons enacted by local and ecumenical councils were compiled into various collections from the fourth to the twelfth centuries. In addition to the conciliar canons, sources of medieval canon law included Roman law, papal decretals, the Irish penitentials, the pseudo-Isidorian decretals, and the customs and laws of the Germanic tribes. The definitive canonical collection was the *Concordia discordantium canonum* of John Gratian, also called the *Decretum* (ca. 1140). Gratian is known as the father of canon law. The dissemination of his *Decretum* gave rise to much scholarly activity, and schools of canon law flourished in the great medieval universities.

Prior to the twentieth century, the chief source of canon law for the Western Catholic Church was the *Corpus Iuris Canonici* consisting of Gratian's *Decretum* and five collections of papal decretals assembled between 1234 and about 1500. The disciplinary decrees of the Council of Trent (1545–1563) and later papal legislation, notably that of Benedict XIV (1740–1758), also were important sources of canon law.

All this represented an immense body of law which was difficult if not impossible for bishops and pastors to know and implement. Several bishops at Vatican I (1869–1870) pleaded for a manageable codification of Church law. In the pontificate of Pius X in 1904, a commission of cardinals began the laborious process of reducing most of canon law to a slim code.

The work was continued under Pius' successor, Benedict XV, who promulgated the first *Codex Iuris Canonici* on Pentecost Sunday, 1917.

In 1959 Pope John XXIII called for a revision of the first code and for a second ecumenical council at the Vatican. The reforms mandated by Vatican II (1962–1965) made many parts of the old law obsolete. The conciliar agenda necessitated many new laws governing the liturgy, religious life, the powers of bishops, ecumenical relations, Church structures, and other areas of Church life. These legal reforms were implemented for the most part during the pontificate of Paul VI (1963–1978) and were reflected in the new Code of Canon Law, promulgated by John Paul II in 1983.

The 1983 Code of Canon Law is divided into seven parts: general norms, the people of God (the rights and obligations of the faithful, Church offices and organizational structures, religious law), the teaching office (the magisterium, preaching, education, missions, the media), the sanctifying office (sacraments and other acts of divine worship, sacred times and places), temporal goods, sanctions, and processes.

Another major body of canon law, not found in the code, are the rubrics and introductions in the liturgical books. There are also many papal and curial documents that are sources of universal canon law. The Eastern Catholic Churches have their own code, liturgical traditions, customs, and particular laws. Although they are not subject to the Latin rite discipline, they recognize the bishop of Rome as their highest superior.

The canonical system is unlike other legal systems in a number of respects. It is, first of all, largely noncoercive. Relatively few laws are specifically sanctioned by penalties. There is no effective way to enforce many Church laws that directly touch the conduct of the faithful other than by appealing to the believer's own faith and commitment (e.g., the law requiring participation at Mass on Sundays and holy days).

Unlike other legal systems, many provisions of canon law are not even worded as preceptive norms—commanding what must be done—but rather are expressed as exhortations, as what the individual Christian should strive to do, or what the community ought to do ideally. Moreover, it is not unusual to find in canon law statements that are doctrinal rather than juridical in nature; these frequently are compressed expressions of theological principles which form the basis for subsequent disciplinary norms.

The canonical system is also different from other legal systems by its considerable flexibility. The canons themselves not infrequently allow for causes which may excuse from observance of the law. Or a qualified superior may give a dispensation from the observance of most disciplinary laws. The code also permits the toleration of long-standing customs contrary to the law, and provides a mechanism for the development of future customs, even contrary customs. Well established in the canonical tradition, moreover, are the principles of equity and *epikeia* which urge the law's implementers to temper justice with mercy and to mitigate the law's strict observance when special circumstances and conditions warrant it.

Canon law is a unique system of law because its nature and purpose are unique. Canon law reflects the incarnational, sacramental nature of the Church. The Church's laws and customs, its structures and procedures, are all part of its visible dimension which gives expression to its inner, spiritual reality. The visible order of the Church, the living practices of the community, constitute an important way that God's word is enfleshed by successive ages of Christian people.

A chief purpose of canon law is to provide for the harmonious ordering of the community while protecting individual rights. Ideally the law should ensure the unity of the Church in the essentials of its life, while fostering the development of legitimate customs and adaptations in keeping with the diversity of peoples and cultures. Because of its theological nature and purpose, canon law is better understood as a theological rather than a strictly legal discipline. Generally it can be understood and implemented by someone who has no knowledge of legal theory, but rarely could it be interpreted adequately by someone who is not sufficiently grounded in the teachings and life of the Church.

See: CHURCH

JOHN M. HUELS, O.S.M.

LEAVEN

Leaven is a fermenting agent which causes the expansion of dough and batters by the release of gases, producing baked products with porous structure. Yeast (a number of species of single cell fungi) is the most common baking agent, as well as fermenting agent for alcoholic beverages.

In the OT both leavened and unleavened bread were common food which took on symbolic and ritual significance. Only unleavened bread was allowed during the seven-day Feast of Unleavened Bread which began with the Passover sacrifice and meal at which unleavened bread was eaten (Exod 12:14-20; 13:6-10). The removal of all leaven from the house for this feast (Exod 12:15) probably originated in an agricultural festival celebrating the new crop year in which old leaven from the previous year was forbidden. In Israel the eating of unleavened bread became a memorial of the Hebrews' hasty departure from Egypt while their dough was still unleavened (Exod 12:34).

In Israel agricultural products were regularly offered on the altar and eaten by the priests and participants in sacrifice. Leaven was forbidden as part of the meal offering (Lev 2:4, 11; 6:10) and peace offering of thanksgiving (Lev 7:12) because leaven cannot be burned on the altar. (Amos' invitation [4:5] to burn leavened food as a thanksgiving sacrifice is an ironic invitation to the Samaritans to sin even more.) The reason for the prohibition of leavened bread is not given, though perhaps the living nature of yeast caused the sharp distinction between leavened and unleavened bread. Leavened loaves played a part in some rituals not involving fire. They were to be eaten by the participants in the peace offering (Lev 7:12-15) and two leavened loaves were to accompany the wave offering of first fruits at Pentecost (Lev 23:17).

In the NT leaven's power to make dough rise is used as a symbol of growth in one parable of the reign of God (Matt 13:33; Luke 13:20-21). All other references to leaven utilize it as a negative symbol for decay and evil, an allusion to yeast's ability to cause fermentation and decay in fruit and other food. Paul twice quotes the proverb that "a little yeast leavens the whole batch of dough" (Gal 5:9; 1 Cor 5:6) as a warning against evil behavior. Mark has Jesus warn against the leaven of the Pharisees (8:15) which Matthew interprets as their teaching (16:12) and Luke as hypocrisy (12:1). Paul uses the Feast of Unleavened Bread as a metaphor for becoming Christian. The old yeast of malice and wickedness has been cleansed and the community, new and unleavened, should celebrate with the unleavened bread of sincerity and truth (1 Cor 5:6-8).

Ignatius of Antioch draws on both meanings of leaven when he contrasts the old, sour leaven (Judaism) with the new leaven, Jesus (Mag 10:2). Rabbinic literature uses leaven as a symbol for decay and sin. Leaven is one of a group of common, familiar food products basic to physical life which gained wide usage as symbols for both growth and decay in the spiritual life.

See: PASSOVER, PENTECOST

ANTHONY J. SALDARINI

LEPROSY

In 1871 Armauer Hansen of Norway identified the bacterium that causes leprosy. Consequently, medicine began referring to the condition as "Hansen's Disease," the healthy stopped sentencing lepers to remote colonies like Molokai, Hawaii, and the persecution of lepers, fueled by a misunderstanding of the world of the Bible, came to a close.

Old Testament

Leviticus. There is no hard evidence for Hansen's Disease in the world of the Bible until after 333 BCE when Alexander's armies returned from India. None of the symptoms in Leviticus (Lev 13:9-23; 14:54-57) is exclusively associated with the condition, and descriptions in Hippocrates and Polybius are equally inconclusive. In the OT, "leprosy" refers to psoriasis, eczema, seborrhea, or ringworm. To some extent, Leviticus views these conditions as diseases, but it primarily treats them as social disorders.

Lepers break out. Rashes, flakes, scales, and boils on human skin, as well as molds on the walls of houses and on clothes, were symptoms of chaos or the misuse of power. Reactions to these conditions reflect Israel's sense of social organization, more than its medical knowledge. Skin, clothes, and walls are social surfaces or borders that mark the frontiers between cosmos where life is possible and chaos where it is not. Any disorder on these frontiers is like a hole in the dike, which would quickly spread. Lepers were the incarnation of households aggressively misusing power in a village that must establish and maintain certain clearly defined codes of honor to survive. Households who conformed and those who deviated from these norms must be clearly labeled. Otherwise, social organization would disappear, everyone would be out of place, and life would become impossible.

The procedure for diagnosing and treating leprosy was neither hasty nor cruel. When symptoms appeared, priests examined patients for changes in skin and hair color. After a seven-day waiting period patients were reexamined (Lev 13:12-17). One cure for leprosy was humility. Confirmed lepers were treated with a protocol of ritual degradation. They were allowed to die and to be reborn. They dressed like corpses, shrouded their faces, did not cut their hair and wailed like mourners (Lev 13:45; Num 5:18; Mic 3:7; Isa 52:11). When the symptoms of leprosy subsided and they were ready to use their power to care for, rather than abuse, other households, priests readmitted lepers to their places in the village.

Samuel-Kings. Relinquishing power for powerlessness also heals strangers like Naaman, a great warrior and a royal advisor from Syria (2 Kgs 5:1-27). Naaman begins his therapy by seeking advice from his own Hebrew slave, who refers him to the prophet Elisha in Israel. Naaman complies and goes into voluntary exile foolishly carrying a letter from the ruler of Syria to the ruler of Israel and gifts for the prophet. Rulers, their letters, and their gifts are powerless. Prophets, who say long prayers and lay hands on their patients, are also powerless. These monarchs and prophets use power to abuse villages. They are lepers. Naaman is cured only when he follows the advice of Gehazi, yet another slave, and bathes seven times in the Jordan River.

New Testament

By the time of Jesus, Hansen's Disease had been added to the OT conditions labeled "leprosy," and was treated similarly as a social disorder. The Gospels portray Jesus (Matt 8:1-4; 11:2-6; Mark 1:40-45; Luke 5:12-16; 7:18-35; 17:11-19) and his disciples (Matt 10:5-15) treating lepers. The miracles emphasize both his vocation as a suffering servant and the social consequences of his way of life. Jesus humbles himself in the incarnation to become human, and accepts death in the passion to restore Israel to life. Lepers in ancient Israel followed a parallel ritual of degradation to restore their households to life. The protocol for the healing of lepers in the OT was a model for the paschal mystery of bringing life from death. Power is acquired by becoming powerless.

The repatriation of lepers from the margins of society by Jesus was also a first step signaling that the reign of God was being established. In this new world, everything would be upside down. The powerless, like the lepers, would be powerful. The reign of monarchs and prophets who exploit and marginalize the poor was ending. These lepers would be followed by the blind, the lame, the deaf, and the dead.

Pastoral-Liturgical Tradition

The Lectionary reads the story of Naaman the leper with the sermon of Jesus in the synagogue at Nazareth (Luke 4:24-30) to emphasize that strangers will benefit from the blessings that Israel ignores. Crisis and critical illness are the great democracies which not only threaten boundaries, but cross them and dissolve the distinctions between friends and enemies.

The Lectionary reads the cure of a leper (Mark 8:1-4) that introduces the ten Moses-like (Exod 7:8–11:10) miracles of Jesus in Mark (Mark 8:1–9:34) with a covenant between Yahweh, Abraham, and Sarah (Gen 17:1-22) and the entry from the annals of Zedekiah describing the destruction of Jerusalem (2 Kgs 25:1-12). The leper confesses Jesus as Lord (Mark 8:2), because he recognizes in him the same compassion for the poor which draws Yahweh to protect and provide for the old, like Abraham and Sarah (Gen 17:1), and for refugees, like the people of the land who survive the destruction of Jerusalem.

Finally, the Lectionary reads Jesus' testimony to John the Baptist that because "lepers are cured (Matt 11:4)," he is "the one who is to come" (Matt 11:3), with a creation story from Isaiah (Isa 35:1-10) that describes human creation as healing: "the eyes of the blind [will] be opened, and the ears of the deaf cleared; then the lame [will] leap like a stag, and the tongue of the dumb will sing" (Isa 35:5-6). To heal is to create. To cure is to bring the old world of disease to an end, and the new world of health into being. As a healer of lepers, Jesus is the creator of a new world called "the reign of heaven" (Matt 4:17; 10:7).

See: HEALING

DON C. BENJAMIN, O.CARM.

LIBERTY

Liberty or freedom is a notion that touches the heart of the biblical experience, from the foundational experience of the Exodus to the Pauline theology of freedom from sin and death. Liberty is a word that denotes freedom from constraint or control.

Old Testament

In the OT, the liberty of the people of God is a theological theme that is foundational for understanding the basis for Israel's faith. The fact that God rescued and sustained Israel against the forces of Egypt served as evidence through which the Hebrew people came to understand their history as charged with salvation and redemption. Israel's remembrance of its liberation from the power of Egypt nourished their faith in God over the years. Each time the people of God found themselves in an experience of captivity or bondage, they looked to their God for an experience of liberation in a new and ever more powerful way.

The Torah/Pentateuch. In the account of the covenant made with Abraham, God tells of a future time of bondage for Abraham's descendants, but in this encounter there is also a divine promise announcing liberation and prosperity: "Know for certain that your descendants shall be aliens in a land not their own, where they shall be enslaved and oppressed for four hundred years. But I will bring judgment on the nation they must serve, and in the end they will depart with great wealth" (Gen 15:13-14). Motifs of enslavement, oppression, alienation, service, and departure in wealth echo in the early chapters of the Book of Exodus (see Exod 1:11-14; 2:23-24; 3:7-9, 22). Thus, the God of the promise is also to be understood as the God of liberation. In a moment of dire need, God will come to the rescue of this people called through divine election.

In Exodus 6:6, God speaks to Moses and tells him of the promise once made to his ancestors and promises that redemption will come to the children of Israel. In this passage the Hebrew verb that is used to describe the act of redemption is *ga'al*. This verb is found in contexts explaining the liberation of some family member from a situation of crisis or difficulty. This act of liberating is part of the responsibility of a blood-relative toward another member of the family or clan. Some examples of this act of liberation drawn from everyday life in Israel are found in Leviticus 25:23-34; Numbers 35:12ff.; Deuteronomy 25:5-10; Ruth 4:1-12. The use of this verb in the setting of Exodus 6:6 sets a tone for understanding the kind of liberation which God offered Israel: God will take on the role of a family member. God chooses to bind the Divinity to an elected people in an act of faithful love, of familial bondedness.

In Leviticus 25:8-17, 23-35, we hear about the Jubilee year. This celebration was to occur every fifty years at the end of seven weeks of years. It was a general emancipation for everyone. Lands were restored to those who had lost or mortgaged them. Prisoners went free. Debts were remitted to those who couldn't fulfill their obligations, and slaves were emancipated. All of this was intended to remind the people that they were only caretakers of the land, because the land belonged to God alone (a scriptural foundation for ecological stewardship today). Furthermore, since God had once emancipated the Israelites from slavery in Egypt, there was to be no slavery among them. They were to liberate one another as God had liberated them. The Jubilee year was to be an experience of liberation, redemption, and re-creation. There is no record in the Hebrew Scriptures that this marvelous event ever took place. The Jubilee year was a dream; it was a Utopian law; it was a vision of liberation one-day to be realized.

In Deuteronomy 7:8; 9:26; 15:15 and 24:18, the Hebrew verb *padah* is used to describe the rescue or ransom of Israel by God in the experience of the Exodus from Egypt. This verb is most often found in a commercial context of payment for ownership of something or someone. "It is because the LORD loved you and because of his fidelity to the oath he had sworn . . . that he brought you out with his strong hand from that place of slavery, and ransomed you from the hand of Pharaoh, king of Egypt" (Deut 7:8). The subsequent verses of this passage go on to explain that this ransom of Israel is in line with the covenant promise of steadfast mercy for the elected people of God.

The Prophets. In Ezekiel 46:17, the prophet uses a new term to speak of liberty *(deror)*. This is probably a reference to the Jubilee year discussed above. What is important to note here is the spiritualizing of something economic or commercial (e.g., the sale of property, the right of inheritance) for the purpose of showing God's desire that all people experience freedom and liberation in the age to come.

In the second part of Isaiah (chs. 40–55), the unknown prophet of the Exile primarily used the verb *ga'al* to describe the experience of liberation from Babylonian forces in terms of both a new exodus and a new creation. "See, I am doing something new! Now it springs forth, do you not perceive it? In the desert I make a way, in the wasteland, rivers" (Isa 43:19). Drawing from the image of a rejuvenated desert and the act of bringing something new into being, the prophet claimed that, with the salvific act that was about to take place, there would be something totally new. It would supercede the previous acts of redemption in the creation of the world and the exodus from Egypt. In its moment of crisis, beloved Israel came to a new experience of liberation through a God described as a partner in the covenant.

In the third part of Isaiah (chs. 56–66), the postexilic prophet looked both to an anointed person (Isa 61:1) and to the community (Isa 58:6-7, 9b-10a) to engage in the work of liberation. "The spirit of the LORD God is upon me, because the LORD has anointed me; He has sent me to bring glad tidings to the lowly, to heal the brokenhearted, to proclaim *liberty* to the captives and release to prisoners" (Isa 61:1-2). Here God's anointed one carries on the work of God's redemption by bringing freedom to those held bound, just as was done for the Hebrew slaves in Egypt. In describing authentic fasting to the community, the prophet's words are a clarion call of liberation: "This, rather is the fasting that I wish: releasing those bound unjustly, untying the thongs of the yoke; Setting free the oppressed, breaking every yoke; sharing your bread with the hungry, sheltering the oppressed and the homeless; Clothing the naked when you see them, and not turning your back on your own" (Isa 58:6-7). Here it is made clear that the task of divine liberation of all people comes through an informed and sensitive commitment by those who count themselves among God's people.

The Psalms. The laments of the Psalter are prayers for liberation. "Cleanse me of sin with hyssop, that I may be purified . . . Free me from blood guilt, O God, my saving God" (Ps 51:9, 16). An individual prays for divine assistance in being freed from the power of sin. "Save me, O LORD, from the hands of the wicked; preserve me from violent men Who plan to trip up my feet" (Ps 140:5). A common plea in the individual laments is the supplication for God's help against the enemy in a variety of situations. "Rouse your power, and come to save us. O LORD of hosts, restore us; if your face shine upon us, then we shall be safe" (Ps 80:3b-4). The whole community calls for divine intercession, knowing that the God of Israel, faithful and just, is the only One to liberate them.

See: COVENANT, CREATION, ELECTION, EXODUS, JUBILEE YEAR, LAMENT, MERCY, REDEMPTION

GREGORY J. POLAN, O.S.B.

New Testament

Eleutheria. *Eleutheria* is the Greek noun for "liberty, freedom." In ancient private law, the term in the context of Athenian democracy denotes the condition of enfranchised citizenship (the highest rank) as opposed to *douleia*, the condition of chattel slavery (the lowest rank). Additionally, *eleutheria* (and later its Latin equivalent, *libertas*) carries the public meaning of constitutional liberation from domestic or foreign tyrannical domination. The ancient philosopher Aristotle criticizes the false idea of *eleutheria* as equivalent to "doing whatever one wants" in polity and private life (*Politics*, Book 5.9 [1310a]). According to him and other ancient thinkers, liberty is not absolute or unrestricted license; it also brings a responsibility to live in justice, according to the rule of the civic constitution. This belief that freedom and responsibility go hand in glove appears in the NT most often in the writings of Paul. Paul's theology of liberty arose from both Hellenistic philosophy and Jewish apocalypticism.

Paul. By far Paul uses *eleutheria* more than any other NT writer; his letters contain the first known witness to an understanding of Christian faith as freedom. Although Paul's thinking on liberty is habitually discussed in terms of freedom from the Law, freedom from sin, and freedom from death, many scholars no longer follow this habit. "This trifold schema is based less on an examination of the passages on freedom than on the assumption that since law, sin, and death are the main enslaving entities in Paul's thought, freedom must consist of the inverse of these elements" (F. Stanley Jones, "Freedom," *Anchor Bible Dictionary* 2 [1992] 857).

We first encounter *eleutheria* in Paul's advice to baptized slaves who might be offered an opportunity for liberty through manumission (1 Cor 7:21-24). Paul argues in verse 21 that Christian slaves should indeed take such manumission offers and become freedmen/women. Liberty in this case carries a legal definition: the freed (as opposed to freeborn) social order in Greco-Roman society. Paul then in verse 22 turns to address the freeborn social order. With a wordplay on *eleutheria*, Paul writes that both a freeborn person and a chattel slave (legally, a nonperson) gain new identities by accepting a call to be Christian. The chattel turns into a freedman/woman in the Lord, rendering legal manumission according to the customs of Greco-Roman society of no consequence in theory, and the freeborn person turns into a slave of Christ. With a paradox, Paul claims that baptism subverts the three social orders of free, freed, and slave, thus exploding old categories and creating new ones (see also 1 Cor 12:13; Gal 3:28; Col 3:11). The slave does not need legal manumission in order to obtain liberty in the Lord; likewise, the freeborn man or woman may not presume that his or her secular status of freedom (or even enfranchised citizenship) automatically denotes religious liberty in Christ. As a model for his parishioners to imitate, Paul offers himself as an example of a freeborn man downgraded to a "slave to all" (1 Cor 9:19).

A second major use of liberty occurs in the controversy over eating meats butchered in shops within pagan temples (1 Corinthians 8 and 10). There, Paul argues that "strong" Christians must yield to "weak" Christians. By "strong" and "weak" Paul employs what we would call sociological categories: those few who have education, socio-political power, and aristocratic birth, as opposed to those many who have nothing (see 1 Cor 1:26; 8:21-22; essentially, a tale of "the haves" versus "the have-nots"). The liberty of the "strong" must not degenerate into license to do whatever one wants. "Strong" Christians, who have knowledge, must use their liberty responsibly, taking careful consideration of the conscience of "weak" Christians, who lack (in Paul's estimation) the ability to gain knowledge (1 Cor 8:7; 10:29). Personal liberty exercised responsibly is a central imperative of Pauline ethics (see also Gal 5:13).

The centrality of the notion of freedom is especially evident in Galatians. Paul writes, "For freedom Christ set us free; so stand firm and do not submit again to the yoke of slavery" (Gal 5:1). Christ's death on the cross enables the possibility of redemption

(a technical term at root meaning the manumission of a slave). For Paul, Spirit and liberty are equivalent concepts (Gal 2:4). The experience of the Spirit corresponds to a liberation from the "elemental powers of the universe" and their tyrannical regime of evil (Gal 1:4; 4:1-10). *Eleutheria*, then, is the central theological concept that epitomizes the Christian situation before God as well as in this world. According to Paul, "to be free" means to participate in Christ's crucifixion and resurrection. Christ is the liberator. This theme of Christ as liberator occurs only here in Galatians; it is not found in Romans.

Paul employs allegory to strengthen his point about liberty in Christ. The apostle's overarching aim in the letter is to dissuade the Galatians from accepting circumcision and those who preach it. He writes, "For it is written that Abraham had two sons, one by the slave woman and the other by the freeborn woman" (Gal 4:22; referring to Genesis 21). Paul presents a revisionist reading of OT Scripture that reverses Jewish tradition about Hagar's son Ishmael symbolizing the Gentiles and Sarah's (circumcised) son Isaac symbolizing Israel. He argues that contrary to standard Jewish belief, Hagar's son in fact symbolizes present Israel and Jerusalem, while Sarah's son symbolizes the heavenly Jerusalem (Gal 4:21–5:1). Since circumcision does not secure the inheritance promised to Abraham, Paul argues, opponents who advocate circumcision are enemies not only of Paul but also of freedom.

In contrast to Galatians, Romans presents a more restrained use of the liberty language. Paul describes the Christian existence in a strikingly balanced way: "Freed from *sin*" (Rom 6:18 and 22) is offset by "you were free from *righteousness*" in the pre-baptismal state (Rom 6:20; emphasis added). The phrase "freed from the law" appears for the first time in Romans 7:2-3, meaning a new bond imposed on the Christian; Paul may have coined the phrase at the time he wrote Romans, adapting from his earlier Corinthian discussion concerning marriage regulations (1 Cor 7:39-40). Romans 8:2-4 argues that the Christian, by definition one who has true liberty, will fulfill the law. This usage is similar to preaching by Hellenistic philosophers (particularly, the Stoics) who maintained that liberty must be practiced within the bounds of a constitution; otherwise it degenerates into license. Eventually, Paul locates the realization of liberty for all in the future. Final Judgment will occur as an eschatological event, which will liberate the whole of creation from its bondage of corruption (Rom 8:21). This passage illustrates Paul's apocalyptic outlook on liberty.

Non-Pauline Usage. Outside the Pauline corpus, the Greek term for liberty (in its nominal and verbal forms) occurs infrequently. It is found in Matthew 17:26, where it refers to exemption from taxation. In John 8:32, 33, 36 it describes the liberating effects of truth. The expression "law of freedom" in James 1:26; 2:12 recalls the claims of many ancient Jewish teachers that the Law (Torah) was not a constraint, but rather an agent of true freedom. 1 Peter 2:16 exhorts Christians, although living as free people, "not to use your freedom as a pretext for evil." In 2 Peter 2:19 is found a polemic against false teachers who promise freedom from divine judgment. And finally, in Revelation 6:15; 13:16; 19:18 are eschatological forecasts that both slave and free will suffer the wrath of the Lamb on Judgment day.

See: DEATH, FAITH, JESUS CHRIST, LAW, PASSION, SIN, SLAVERY, SPIRIT OF GOD

J. ALBERT HARRILL

Pastoral-Liturgical Tradition

In the final analysis, human liberty or freedom is a mystery that fundamentally situates the divine-human interaction. Historically, freedom has been understood in a psychological and moral sense in which a person possesses the capacity to choose a particular object (freedom of choice or *libertas arbitrii*). Consequently, freedom of choice was considered an inalienable and essential part of human nature. More recently, however, theologians like Karl Rahner have pointed to the fact that there is a more fundamental capacity within the human person (transcendental or basic freedom) whereby the person determines the self as a whole toward or away from God as the origin and end of human freedom.

Freedom and the Grace of God. It is impossible to speak of human freedom without at the same time speaking of the enabling and healing grace of God. One who is truly free is one who has already accepted the free gift of God's love and reconciled the self with God. In a strict sense, then, when Christian theology speaks of freedom it is the freedom that has been healed and restored through and in Christ's saving acts.

The Catholic Church teaches that in principle we are free even when we are under the influence of original sin. However, we must consent to the free gift of God's love that preveniently floods our hearts and enables us to accept divine grace. Without the grace of God we remain incapable of any salutary act in our moral lives, and our freedom is only truly free when we have been set free by the absolutely gratuitous grace of God's love.

Basic Freedom as the Capacity to Decide About the Self. Whereas freedom of choice is concerned with choosing this or that particular object or aspect of the good, basic freedom is concerned with the capacity to decide about the self as a whole before God. To choose and therefore to commit the self freely to a particular aspect of the good always entails a certain limited capacity to determine the self. At the level of freedom of choice, then, one does not determine the whole self toward goodness as the ground or horizon of particular values. It is at the level of basic freedom, where the person possesses the radical capacity to determine the entire self, that one freely chooses either goodness or evil, God or sin. Thus, basic freedom stands as the condition or ground of freedom of choice, and it is this former type of freedom that must be considered moral freedom in its highest sense.

Freedom and the Fundamental Option. A proper grasp of fundamental option relies upon an adequate understanding of the nature of human freedom and of the unity of the self. Persons are a moral unity, and therefore they are more than merely the sum total of individual acts of freedom of choice. This unity of the self is achieved and expressed in and through the fundamental option of the person. Over a period of time and under the influence of the grace of the holy Spirit, a person's exercise of basic freedom both unifies and directs the self in a stable orientation toward or away from God. The option that results from the exercise of basic freedom toward the ultimate good of human life is free in the sense that the option is within our power and is our responsibility. Though the option cannot be consciously objectified in the way that particular choices of the good can, nonetheless, a person can be consciously aware of the basic orientation of one's life. Conscious awareness of one's option, however, does not result in certitude about how one ultimately stands in relation to God, but it is possible to look upon one's choices of particular goods or values as symbolic representations of what is occurring at a deeper level of one's existence. For if one's fundamental orientation both underlies and is manifested in particular choices, then whenever this option is engaged at the deepest levels of the human subject those choices embody one's true and real disposition before God. It is possible to say, then, that one's exercises of freedom of choice are never fully as good or as evil morally as one's fundamental option is good or evil.

Pastoral Implications. This understanding of human freedom and fundamental option has important pastoral applications. First, the moral life should be viewed as a growth process. It is really a gradual and dynamic unfolding of ourselves as Christians. Rather than understanding and assessing our moral lives through discrete acts of choice, the perspective presented above offers the possibility of construing morality more properly as a progressive dedication to or withdrawal from God. What we choose and how we act are indeed important, but these choices and actions are really signs and symbols of a deeper commitment to or refusal of God's offer of salvation.

Second, conversion, as one of the central themes of the biblical witness, is restored to its rightful place in the Christian life. The radical turning away from sinfulness and the turning toward God are the principal features of all conversion, and this call to conversion is surely the central moral message of Jesus. When one withdraws from sinfulness and not merely withdraws from individual acts of sin, one's acts are not only changed but the person is changed. Such continual conversion, achieved through personal exercises of basic freedom in response to God's grace, is embodied and manifested in the fundamental option, which in turn tends to reveal itself in particular choices.

Finally, the distinction between mortal and venial sin in this perspective is not primarily concerned with the "matter" in itself and with whether the matter is serious or light. Rather, the distinction is concerned with whether one's basic freedom and evil fundamental option were actively implicated in a particular choice and action. It is true that a person will dispose totally of the self only in instances in which he or she knows the "matter" to be serious and therefore knows that one's relation to God is involved. However, it is more accurate to speak of mortal sin in terms of the person's self-disposition at the level of basic freedom where the fundamental option is a radical refusal of God's love.

See: DISCIPLE/DISCIPLESHIP, FAITH, HOPE, REDEMPTION, SIN

JAMES J. WALTER

LIFE

Old Testament

The OT uses the concept of life primarily in the ordinary sense of earthly existence. It variously employs the noun "life" the verb "to live," or the adjective "living" to describe all living beings, whether plant, animal, or human.

Physical Existence. A most frequent use of life is a reference to the span of human existence. This is sometimes seen in the listing of the number of years that one lived, as in Genesis 25:7, where it is said, "The whole span of Abraham's life was one hundred and seventy-five years." Longevity and good health and happiness were considered a sign of a good life. Expressions like "as long as you live" (Deut 4:9), "all my life" or "while I live" (Ps 146:2), and "all the days of his [your] life" (Deut 17:19; see 6:2) all refer to one's life-span on earth. Human existence itself is sometimes designated "the land of the living" (Ezek 32:23, 26; Ps 116:9).

The OT also acknowledges that human life is especially precarious and brief in the eyes of God. Job complains that life can be dreary and cries out, "Is not man's life on earth a drudgery? . . . Remember that my life is like the wind" (Job 7:1, 7). The psalmist, too, acknowledged that human life is fleeting: "Seventy is the sum of our years, or eighty, if we are strong, and most of them are fruitless toil, for they pass away quickly and we drift away" (Ps 90:10). Yet, human life is deemed worth preserving, as made plain in the frequent pleas of those who feel oppressed. We read in the laments: "Hear, O God, my voice in my lament; from the dread enemy preserve my life" (Ps 64:2); "Men lay snares for me seeking my life" (Ps 38:13). God was seen as a refuge for preserving one's life or the life of a people threatened by enemies (Ps 116:1-4).

The king was also looked to for protection. The people exclaimed "Long live the king!" (1 Sam 10:24; 2 Kgs 11:12), for the king was a source of life for his people (Prov 16:15). The life of a people, along with their power and success, was tied to that of their king.

Life, God, and Creation. The OT clearly ties life to God and to *creation.** The well-known Genesis stories of creation (Genesis 1–2) depict God as the source of all life, whether plant, animal, or human. God created "all kinds of living creatures" and pronounced them "good," mirroring God's own divine goodness. The text says that when God created the first human being, God "blew into his nostrils the breath of life, and so man became a living being" (Gen 2:7). God is often called "the living God" (Ps 42:3; Isa 37:17; Jer 10:10) both to emphasize God's dynamism and power over all creation and to draw contrast with pagan gods who are ineffectual. The OT views God as both the source of life and the sustainer of it. God is "the fountain of life" (Ps 36:10) who "has given life to our souls" (Ps 66:9) and who alone has the power to "revive" us in times of distress (Ps 71:20).

Two special expressions occur in the OT to connect life with God and creation. First, "the tree of life" appears in the creation story (Gen 2:9; 3:22, 24). It was placed in the middle of the garden and it represents the source of immortality. In the Wisdom literature, personified *Wisdom** herself is called "the tree of life" (Prov 3:18), for partaking of wisdom leads to a proper life. The second expression, "the book of the living" (Ps 69:29; see Ps 139:16), suggests that God is a record keeper, whose "book" contains our names and the account of our deeds on this earth.

Life and Death. The OT also makes special use of the juxtaposition of life with death,* the end of earthly life. A more intriguing use of the contrast is found in the choice that is placed before Israel when challenged to accept God's *covenant* (Deut 30:15-20). The choice is made explicit in Deuteronomy 30:19-20: "I have set before you life and death, the blessing and the curse. Choose life, then, that you and your descendants may live by loving the LORD, your God, heeding his voice, and holding fast to him. For that will mean life for you, a long life for you to live." The contrast between life and death is thus tied to obedience to God's laws. One of the prophets also sets forth the options in even starker tones and tied it to the presence of God: "Seek good and not evil, that you may live; Then, truly will the LORD, the God of hosts, be with you as you claim!" (Amos 5:14).

This attitude is also reflected in the Wisdom literature. There the path of the wicked, which leads to death, is contrasted with the path of the righteous, which leads to life (Prov 2:18-19; 4:13; 6:23). Discipline, study of the Torah, and obedience to God's commandments are the elements of a good life, but laziness and doing unrighteous deeds leads to destruction. In this contrast the choice is left open-ended, yet the consequences of making the wrong choice are also made very clear: "In the path of justice there is life, but the abominable way leads to death" (Prov 12:28). The contrast of death and life can also be used figuratively to describe possible consequences of one's words or deeds, as in Proverbs 18:21, "Death and life are in the power of the tongue."

Fullness of Life. While most of the OT associates life with physical reality, there is a deeper aspect to the Hebrew understanding. Life is associated with light, peace, blessing, health, victory, success, faithfulness, restoration to health, repentance, and happiness, as well as with longevity. Reaching old age was seen as a special blessing and a reward for a life well lived.

Concepts like "soul" or "spirit" are used synonymously for one's life (e.g., Pss 33:20; 66:9). Ezekiel 37:1-14 paints the picture of God breathing new life into the old, dry bones of a whole people. This powerful image fed the fires of hope of the survivors of the Exile assuring them that their nation could be reborn. While this picture portrays a renewed earthly life of an entire people, other late OT works imply interest in an individual resurrected life (e.g., Dan 12:2, 13). This latter idea developed under the influence of apocalyptic hope, but the idea did not find full expression until the NT time.

For the Hebrews, life can never be experienced apart from God. God is both source and sustaining force of all life. "Seek the LORD that you may live" (Amos 5:6) summarizes the basic OT stance that life cannot be lived in any qualitative manner apart from the one who created it.

See: CREATION, DEATH, RESURRECTION, WISDOM

RONALD D. WITHERUP, S.S.

New Testament

The OT affirmation that life is from the "living God" is consistently upheld in the NT (see Acts 14:15 and Rom 9:26), as is the view which links the concept of life with being in right relationship to God. Thus Jesus quotes Deuteronomy in Matthew 4:4, "One does not live by bread alone, but by every word that comes from the mouth of God." The decisive difference between the testaments on the understanding of life lies in two areas. First, the belief in eternal life, which comes to the fore only at the very end of the OT period (see Dan 12:2; 2 Macc 7:9; Wis 2:22-23), is central to the NT teaching. Second, and closely related to this, is the pivotal place given to the risen Christ who is not simply the Messiah but also "the Son of the living God" (Matt 16:16) and "the author of life" (Acts 3:15).

The Synoptic Gospels. Life is not extensively treated as a theological concept in the Synoptic tradition, though the concern with life and "eternal life" is very present. The people Jesus encounters wish to know the way to eternal life (see Mark 10:17) and he speaks to them about what is necessary in order to "receive eternal life" (Mark 10:30) or to "enter into life" (Matt 18:8). In these examples there is a future orientation and the gift of eternal life is dependant on living in accordance with the demands of the gospel which are presented in a very uncompromising way. This serves to remind believers that "life is more than food" (Matt 6:25) and that "one's life does not consist of possessions" (Luke 12:15). The connection between life and discipleship is forcefully driven home when a would-be follower of Jesus is told: "Follow me, and let the dead bury their dead" (Matt 8:22). The implication here is that though one may be physically alive, one may still be spiritually dead. There is a strong emphasis on the necessity of choosing life and on the fact that this presents a challenge: "How narrow the gate and constricted the road that leads to life" (Matt 7:14). The offer of life however is not only to be seen as a challenge, it is a generous gift of God embodied in the ministry of Jesus. In Mark 5:23 Jairus pleads with Jesus to come and lay hands on his daughter, "that she may get well and live," and in 5:41 Jesus shows his power over death by raising the girl to life. In this section of the Gospel (Mark 5:21-43) there is a strong connection made between life, salvation (being made well), and the need for faith (5:34, 36). The life-giving, healing ministry of Jesus is symbolic of God's desire to save us from evil, sin, and death (see also Mark 2:3-12; 3:4-5).

Paul. For Paul life means life in Christ and he understands this as rooted in the mystery of the death and resurrection of Jesus. The believer, through baptism, is joined to this mystery, baptism being symbolic of dying and rising to a new life with the risen Christ. Life, therefore, does not refer primarily to life after death but is about the lived Christian experience in the here and now. "We were indeed buried with him through baptism into death, so that, just as Christ was raised from the dead by the glory of the Father, we too might live in newness of life" (Rom 6:4). This life that is "the gift of God" is contrasted with "the wages of sin which is death" (Rom 6:23). It is also the work of the Spirit and this in turn leads to another metaphor to explain it: the contrast between flesh and spirit. The life which the believer now lives is contrasted with a life in "the flesh" (sarx), one lived at a purely natural level and dominated by sinful tendencies. The struggle of this existence is graphically portrayed in Romans 7:19-24,

but Paul rejoices that because of Christ and the gift of the Spirit all that is changed: "The concern of the flesh is death, the concern of the spirit is life and peace" (Rom 8:6). Such is the transformation that Paul can say, "I live, no longer I, but Christ lives in me" (Gal 2:20) and so the Christian life is not to be lived for oneself but for God (Rom 14:7), for "our lives are hidden with Christ in God" (Col 3:3). This life involves a dynamic process of becoming more and more rooted in Christ so that "you may be filled with the utter fullness of God" (Eph 3:14-19). Even though he had such a keen understanding of life in Christ in the here and now, Paul experienced the tension between his life here on earth and his desire to be with Christ in heaven: "For me to live is Christ, and death is gain . . . I long to depart this life and be with Christ" (Phil 1:21-23).

John. In John 20:31 the purpose of the Fourth Gospel is stated in these terms: "These things are written that you may [come to] believe that Jesus is the Messiah, the Son of God, and that through this belief you may have life in his name." In this Gospel the sense in which life is "now" is even more radical than in Paul. Most often life is spoken about in the present tense and refers to what is operative now through faith and the indwelling of Jesus in the disciples. John presents Jesus as the pre-existent Word, "through him was life and this life was the light of the human race" (1:4). That everyone should have eternal life is the commandment of God (12:50) and Jesus has come that "they may have life and have it more abundantly" (10:10). The reader is made to understand that this life is present now to the believer and will continue into eternity: "For this is the will of my Father, that everyone who sees the Son and believes in him may have eternal life, and I will raise him up on the last day" (6:40). The symbols of water and bread are used to highlight this depiction of Jesus as the source of life: "The water that I shall give will become in him a spring of water welling up to eternal life" (4:14), and, "I am the bread of life; whoever comes to me will never hunger" (6:35). Jesus sustains the life that he offers through the gift of the Eucharist which is life-giving to the believer just as his relationship with the Father is life-giving to Jesus (see 6:53-57).

In his confrontation with death at the raising of Lazarus Jesus prepares his disciples for his own death and resurrection and urges them to understand that he is "the resurrection and the life" (11:26). In this chapter there is a sustained play on the difference between physical and spiritual death. What Jesus offers is life in God, a life which is indestructible, based on faith and expressed in love. Jesus as "the way, the truth and the life" (14:6) makes God manifest and just as he is sustained in his life by the Father (5:26), so too the disciples will be sustained by their union with Jesus (15:1-7). This union is based in mutual love, that very love which led Jesus to lay down his life for his friends (15:14). In the final prayer of Jesus eternal life is defined thus: "that they should know you, the only true God, and the one whom you sent, Jesus Christ" (17:3). This knowledge is not merely intellectual but is based on a living faith relationship by which the believer shares in the love of the Father and the Son.

See: DEATH, ESCHATOLOGY, SALVATION

SEAN GOAN

LIGHT AND DARKNESS

In most religions light is a natural sign of divine power and presence, and darkness is a sign of divine absence and even of forces hostile to the gods and to society. In the Bible the same basic symbolism is found. This article concentrates on the polarity of light and darkness.

Old Testament

Light and darkness play varied roles in the religions of the ancient Near East. Egyptians imagined their world as a finite "box" of light, space, and order within an infinite expanse of dark, formless waters. Across the surface of the waters above the sun, the

sun god "Re in his daytime," sails during the day. The greatest determinant of creation is the daily cycle of the sun. The sun's first rising is the act that prompted and concluded the creation. In Mesopotamia the primordial state was usually conceived as limitless waters or negation of social order rather than as darkness. When heavenly luminaries—sun, moon, and stars—are mentioned in Mesopotamian cosmogonies, they mark times for temple ritual rather than illuminate the world. Mesopotamian gods were endowed with *melammu,* "awe inspiring radiance." In Canaanite religion, according to the Ugaritic texts, solar elements did not play an important role. Baal Hadad appears in the thunderstorm rather than in brilliant light.

In the majestic opening chapter of the Bible, light *(or)* and darkness *(hoshek)* are central. Before creation there is only "formless wasteland" and "darkness," which make human life (the pinnacle of creation) impossible. God's very first act is to place darkness, the obstacle to order, where it can become part of the universe—night. God also relegated the waters to the sea so that dry land can appear. The same rearrangement of chaos, waters, and darkness is found in Psalm 104; God overcomes the evil of darkness by making the beneficial sequence of day and night: "You bring darkness, and it is night; then all the beasts of the forest roam about; . . . When the sun rises, they withdraw . . . Man goes forth to his work and to his tillage till the evening" (vv. 20-23). To control primordial light and darkness is proof of divinity, as the divine speech in Second Isaiah shows: "I am the LORD, there is no other; I form the light, and create the darkness, I make well-being [*shalom*] and create woe [lit. "evil"]; I, the LORD, do all these things" (Isa 45:6b-7). Psalm 139:11-12 shows similar divine mastery: "If I [the psalmist] say, 'Surely the darkness shall hide me, and night shall be my light'—For you darkness itself is not dark, and night shines as the day."

Light is imagined as an entity in its own right and, hence, more than the rays of the sun. In Genesis 1 it is created on the first day, whereas the sun is created on the fourth day. In Job 38:19, God asks Job: "Which is the way to the dwelling place of light, and where is the abode of darkness?"

The temple (or the temple-city) in ancient Near Eastern cultures was built on the day of creation and was the memorial of divine victory over chaos. The Israelite Temple displays to the world the light of divine victory: "Rise up [Zion] in splendor! Your light has come, the glory of the LORD shines upon you. See, darkness covers the earth, and thick darkness the people; But upon you the LORD shines, and over you appears his glory" (Isa 60:1-2). The temple-city memorializes creation light; outside all is darkness. Similarly Ezekiel sees the return of God's glory* to the Temple: "I heard a sound like the roaring of many waters, and the earth shone with his glory" (43:2).

God's intervention was imagined as light. The prophet Amos counters the popular expectation that God would always intervene in favor of Israel no matter how unfaithful they were: "What will this day of the LORD mean for you? Darkness and not light! . . . Will not the day of the LORD be darkness and not light, gloom without any brightness?" (5:18-20). God's effective presence was light and brought blessing, as in the famous blessing of Aaron: "The LORD let his face shine upon you, and be gracious to you!" (Num 6:25).

Light signifies the presence of God as it does in the surrounding cultures, and is especially frequent in the image of God leading Israel in safety. In the escape from Egypt, "The LORD preceded them, in the daytime by means of a column of cloud to show them the way, and at night by means of a column of fire to give them light. Thus they could travel day and night" (Exod 13:21). God's leading Israel is expressed in a variety of ways: "Send forth your light and your fidelity; they shall lead me on and bring me to your holy mountain, to your dwelling place" (Ps 43:3); "Even though I walk in the dark valley I fear no evil; for you are at my side" (Ps 23:4); "I will turn darkness into light before them, and make crooked ways straight" (Isa 42:16).

The metaphor of conscious life as two competing paths is common, especially in the Wisdom literature. Individuals are declared happy or unhappy according to whether they walk in the way of the just or in the way of the wicked (Psalm 1; Prov 4:11-14) and it was natural that people asked God to illuminate their path: "For the bidding [i.e., commandment] is a lamp, and the teaching is a light" (Prov 6:23).

God's law or teaching (torah) is a light to individuals and the nation. Psalm 19 suggests that the divine wisdom of the beautifully ordered universe and of the all-seeing sun is distilled in the Torah, and the psalmist prays for a share of that wisdom. Psalm 119:105 praises the law and declares that, "A lamp to my feet is your word, a light to my path."

The sectarians of Qumran (late second century BCE to the mid-first century CE) used the light-darkness distinction and metaphor of the two ways to create an ethical dualism. They were "sons of light, each according to his lot in God's design" and pledged themselves to hate all the sons of darkness, i.e., their enemies. The same terminology shows up in NT writings, especially in the children of light in the letters of John.

See: CREATION

RICHARD J. CLIFFORD, S.J.

New Testament

As in the OT light (in Greek, *phōs*) and darkness (in Greek, *skotos, skotia*) are frequently set in antithesis in the NT. Light is associated with Christ and the faithful, whereas darkness is connected with the cosmos and unbelievers. The pairing of light and darkness is used figuratively to describe the dichotomy between acceptance and rejection of Christ. This dichotomy shows itself in conduct, so that an ethical dualism is present in the NT, especially in the Johannine and Pauline literatures. In addition to a symbolic or

561

figurative use of light and darkness, the individual terms are also used frequently in their literal meanings.

Christological Significance. Light is a symbol of the person of Christ and the divine life he offers (Matt 4:16; Luke 1:79; 2:32). Christ is a light to Jews and Gentiles alike (Acts 26:23). The Word entered into the world as its light (John 8:12) in order to save it from sin and darkness. Darkness strives to overcome the light (John 1:5). This antithesis between light and darkness is a metaphorical way of describing the hostility of the cosmos to Christ and his truth. The Word's entrance in human history forces humankind to make a decision about him. Those who respond positively to Christ are children of light (John 12:36). Likewise, those who reject Christ are said to be in darkness. They are never described, however, as children of darkness; the dualism is not ontological.

For John, the light of Christ is inseparable from the truth. Christ is described as the true light which gives light to humanity (John 1:9). His self-designation as the light of the world suggests exclusivity: he alone is the one true light (John 8:12; 9:5). As the light Christ offers the light of life (John 8:12). Christ promises those who follow him that they shall never walk in darkness but possess the light of life, namely, a share in his own divine life. By implication, those who reject Christ will walk in darkness and possess death. The aim of Christ's revelation is to bring the world to life in Christ. Faith is the proper response to the light of the world. Unbelief is nothing but darkness (John 12:46).

Christ calls humankind out of the darkness of unbelief. There is an urgency to accept him, the light, and walk accordingly; revelation will not always be available (John 12:35-36). Moreover, those who reject the light are in danger of being overcome by darkness (John 12:36). Humanity can freely choose to remain in darkness, which is its natural state without Christ (John 12:46); without his light the world is in a continual state of darkness, blind, and without direction (1 John 2:8-11). In fact, humankind loves this darkness (John 3:19).

The Dichotomy of Light and Darkness. As indicated above, light and darkness are seen in relation to one's response to divine revelation. The presence of Christ in the world forces a lived decision, demonstrated in conduct, which determines whether one is either in darkness or in light. There is no in-between condition. This ethical dualism is most often described figuratively in terms of how one "walks." Those who lie or do falsehood are said not to walk in the light (1 John 1:5-10), which is possible only because the true light shines (1 John 2:8-11). The truth of light is set in contrast to the falsehood of darkness. Those who do evil deeds hate the light and fear it (John 3:19-21). By contrast, those who act in truth are in the light and do not fear it. The wicked prefer darkness because they do not wish their evil deeds to be brought to light. Those who walk in light act in accord with the truth and God, who is light, in whom there is no darkness (1 John 1:5). This description of God as light is not a metaphysical one, but rather a symbolic one that describes God's holiness. It has ethical implications. If God is light, Christians have a clear duty to live accordingly and to have no part of darkness. They are to be set apart. As a result they will have true community (1 John 1:7). They are not to act in accord with darkness, hating their fellow Christians (1 John 2:8-10). To walk in darkness is to walk apart from God and other Christians. Thus a lived decision that shows itself in moral conduct is emphasized by this dualism of light and darkness.

In the Pauline Letters the faithful are urged to cast off deeds of darkness and put on armor of light (Rom 13:12; Eph 6:12). This suggests that Christians must be vigilant not to let darkness overcome them. The Ephesians are exhorted to live as children of light, that is, in goodness, justice, and truth (5:8-9). In contrast are the deeds of darkness that are not even named (Eph

5:12). Thus light and darkness are evident in one's deeds. The light of Christ gives life (Eph 5:14). The light of Christ also brings to manifestation what is now hidden in darkness (Matt 10:27; Luke 12:3-4; 1 Cor 4:5; Eph 5:13).

The antithesis of light and darkness is also used as a metaphor for conversion. The unbeliever moves from darkness into light upon coming to faith in Christ; such a one has moved from Satan to God (Acts 26:18). The darkness of the cosmos is antithetical to life in Christ. Unbelievers are blind, whereas believers have experienced the light that shines out of darkness (2 Cor 4:4-6). Likewise a faithful disciple is a light to the world (Matt 5:14-16; Phil 2:15). God calls humanity out of darkness into his marvelous light (1 Pet 2:9). Christ has rescued the faithful from darkness and brought them into his reign. The Thessalonians are called children of light (1 Thess 5:5) and are reminded of their duty in that regard. The Christian must stand fast because darkness is powerful and deceptive (Luke 22:53; 2 Cor 11:14; Eph 6:12; Col 1:13). The faithful will share "the lot of the saints in light" (Col 1:12-13). The heavenly reign is a place of light, which is provided by God and the Lamb. Moreover, it has no darkness of night (Rev 21:22-27; 22:5).

Light is a gift from God that dispels the darkness of this world. The pairing of light and darkness expresses a significant NT soteriology: light is associated with life in Christ and divine truth, whereas darkness is associated with death and the falsehood of sin.

See: COSMOS, DEATH, FAITH, HOLY/HOLINESS, JUSTICE, REIGN OF GOD, SIN, TRUTH, WORD, WORLD

SUSAN FOURNIER MATHEWS

Pastoral-Liturgical Tradition

The themes of light and darkness found in the Bible were given ritual expression in the liturgical and devotional life of the Church. Light is associated with God and with Christ, and the realm where they dwell, heaven. Darkness is experienced as the utter absence of God, and the pangs of separation from God. Darkness is the realm of demons and the lost souls.

The second article of the Nicene-Constantinopolitan Creed describes the procession of the Son from the Father in the Trinity as "light from light, true God from true God." Christ, the "light of the world" (cf. Matt 5:14) inspired Clement of Alexandria to speak of Christ as the "eternal light," and Tertullian and Lactantius to speak of him as the "illuminator." The paschal candle, lit in the darkness of the Easter Vigil, carried into the church and the source of its illumination, remains one of the most powerful symbols of the presence of Christ in the Christian assembly.

Baptism has been especially associated with light. Justin Martyr was the first of a long line of Church Fathers to refer to Baptism as illumination or enlightenment. The symbolism of the white garment conferred in Baptism is that of a garment of light. The baptismal candle is lit from the paschal candle and given to the newly baptized with the admonition "Receive the light of Christ," and an allusion to being watchful for the Lord until he comes (cf. Matt 25:1-13).

The blessing of candles has long been associated with the feast of the purification of Mary on February 2. The angels and those in heaven are frequently depicted as having a nimbus or halo of light surrounding their heads. Votive candles have long been a popular practice in Catholic and Orthodox Christianity. The lighted Christmas tree, taken into Christianity from the Germanic peoples, celebrates the birth of Christ. In some European countries fires are lit to celebrate the birth of John the Baptist (June 24), and also the birth of Christ.

Light has also been associated with the dead. The prayer for them in the Roman Canon asks for them a place of "light, happiness and peace." A common prayer for the dead asked that "perpetual light shine upon them."

Darkness, as the opposite of light, signifies the absence of Christ, the light of the world. The celebration of Tenebrae ("darkness") commemorated the death of Christ in the liturgical rites of Holy Week prior to the reform of Vatican II. Similarly, the snuffing of a candle was part of an excommunication rite. Although hell is frequently imagined as a place of unending fire, it is also portrayed in the tradition as a place of darkness.

See: BAPTISM, HELL

ROBERT J. SCHREITER, C.PP.S.

LORD

In the OT "lord" is a title that indicates the rightful authority of one over another; it is applied both to human beings and to God. It is used in the same way in the NT, but is most common as a title for Jesus. Early Christian talk of Jesus as lord contributed to an increasingly exalted understanding of Jesus. In the centuries following the composition of the NT, the Church found it necessary to define the precise relationship between Jesus and God, ultimately by means of the doctrine of the Trinity.

Old Testament

"Lord" is the English translation of the Hebrew word ʾādôn. Use of this title for someone is an acknowledgment of the rightful authority of a superior over an inferior. In the OT ʾādôn is frequently used as a title for human beings. It can be applied to anyone who has authority over something. In Genesis 45:8-9 Joseph says that Pharaoh has made him "lord of all his household" and "lord of all Egypt." It can also be applied to the recognized leaders of Israel: priests (e.g., 1 Sam 1:15), prophets (e.g., 1 Kgs 18:7), and most of all kings (e.g., 1 Sam 22:12).

In addition to its use as a title for human beings, ʾādôn is also frequently used in the OT as a title for God. Exodus 23:17 sums up the law regarding the pilgrimage festivals by saying, "Thrice a year shall all your men appear before the LORD God." Other examples of the use of this title for God can be found in Exodus 34:23; Isaiah 1:24.

In the time after the OT was written, use of the title "lord" for God became even more important than it had been in the OT. In the OT God is frequently given the name Yahweh. In the years after the writing of the OT, it became the custom to avoid pronouncing the name of God and to substitute the title "lord" for the name. This had the effect of associating the title with God even more closely than it had been in the OT.

This substitution is indicated in the Masoretic text of the OT (dating from about the ninth century CE) by combining the vowels for the word *adonai* (= my lord) with the consonants of Yahweh. What this was intended to indicate is that the reader should read *adonai* instead of Yahweh.

It is not clear how early this replacement of Yahweh with *adonai* is. It seems likely that the earliest Greek translations of the OT (dating from the third century BCE) retained the name Yahweh in some form. However, in the first century BCE Philo of Alexandria uses a Greek translation of the OT in which Yahweh is translated *kyrios* (= lord).

New Testament

In the NT also "lord" is used as a title for any human being who has authority over someone or something (e.g., Matt 25:19) and as a title for God (e.g., Acts 4:29). But "lord" is most often used in the NT as a title for Jesus. It is the second most common title for Jesus in the NT, though it is absent from the Letter to Titus and the First, Second, and Third Letters of John. The NT writings show evidence of several different ways in which the title "lord" was given to Jesus. First, during his lifetime Jesus was probably called "lord" by his followers and others. Second, the earliest Christians believed that Jesus was the Messiah,* and this made "lord" an appropriate title for him. Third, "lord" proved to be a very useful title for Jesus when the early Church proclaimed Jesus in the Gentile world. Fourth, "lord" became the vehicle for an increasingly exalted understanding of Jesus.

Jesus. The title "lord" is frequently given to Jesus in the Gospels. In part this reflects the later faith of his followers that Jesus is lord. However, it seems quite likely that Jesus was called "lord" during his lifetime. In the Gospels Jesus is called "lord" by those who are asking for his help (e.g., Mark 7:28; Matt 15:27) and by his disciples (e.g., Mark 11:13; Matt 21:3; Luke 19:31). It seems entirely likely that both of these groups would acknowledge his authority by calling him "lord."

Messiah and Lord. An even more important reason for the early Church's use of "lord" as a title for Jesus was their faith that he was the Messiah. The Messiah was the eschatological king of David's line; the king is frequently called "lord" in the OT; thus the eschatological king would also be "lord" (see Luke 2:11).

Use of the title "lord" for Jesus as Messiah can be seen in the interpretation of Psalm 110:1 as applying to him. This psalm originally applied to the king of Israel. The psalmist begins, "The LORD [i.e., God] said to my Lord [i.e., the king]." Later this was understood as something that God said to the eschatological king, i.e., the Messiah (see Mark 12:35-37; Matt 22:41-45; Luke 20:41-44). When the early Church believed that Jesus was the Messiah, they also believed that this passage applied to him (see Acts 2:34-36).

The most striking confirmation that Jesus was called "lord" by the earliest Church is the Aramaic phrase *marana tha* (= Our Lord, come). This phrase is found in the Greek text of 1 Corinthians 16:22 and Didache 10.6 (see also Rev 22:20). This is probably a prayer used in the earliest, Aramaic-speaking Church and retained in the Greek-speaking Churches to which Paul writes and from which the Didache derives. This prayer was probably used in the Christian celebration of the Lord's Supper. It requests the second coming of the Lord (= Jesus, the Messiah), and his anticipatory presence among his followers as they celebrate the Lord's Supper.

The Usefulness of "Lord" in the Gentile Mission. When the early Christians began to proclaim the gospel of Jesus to Gentiles, they found that proclaiming him as the Messiah communicated very little. Since this title embodied the basic belief of the early Christians about Jesus, it could not be abandoned. So they attached it to Jesus' name almost as a second name, and relied on equivalent titles like "lord" to say who Jesus was.

The early Christians could do this because "lord" was a title used by Gentiles with a meaning very close to the meaning it had for Christians. In fact it was used in the same two ways in which it was used in the OT—as a title acknowledging the authority of human beings and as a title acknowledging the authority of the gods.

In saying that Jesus was lord the earliest Christians intended to say something close to what it meant to say that Jesus was the Messiah, i.e., that he was the eschatological king sent by God to save the world. What Gentiles spontaneously understood by "lord" was not identical to this, but it was close enough to be useful. In proclaiming Jesus as lord, the early Christians would have needed to clarify the meaning of the term as they used it. It meant that Jesus was something like the human beings and gods acknowledged as lords by the Hellenistic world, but with important differences. The usefulness of "lord" for saying who Jesus is to non-Jews accounts partly for the prominence of the title in the NT.

Further Developments. Early Christian use of the title "lord" in proclaiming Jesus, especially in the Gentile world, was one factor which encouraged development in the early Christian understanding of Jesus. Use of this title, which also applied to heavenly beings and divinities, made it easy to think of Jesus as something like them. This, along with the early Christians' present experience of Jesus in their midst, moved them to think of Jesus as lord in the sense that he was a heavenly being. And they saw Jesus as a heavenly being in two distinct ways. First, they saw his resurrection as God's exaltation of Jesus to heaven and God's enthronement of Jesus at God's right hand, where he rules over heaven and earth. Second, they believed that Jesus had been a heavenly being even before his birth as a human being. Having been with God from the beginning, he was sent by God to become a human being, to die, rise, and return to God from whom he came. Thus, "lord," which was originally synonymous with Messiah as applied to Jesus, came to mean something more than Messiah.

This is explicit in 1 Corinthians 8:4-6. In this passage Paul indicates the points of contact, and the differences, between the Christian belief that Jesus is lord and Hellenistic use of this title. For Paul Jesus clearly is lord in somewhat the same sense that others are recognized as lord in the Hellenistic world. In particular he mentions Jesus' role in creation ("through whom everything was made") and his present activity ("through whom we live"). The main point of difference is that Jesus is the one lord; all others who are given that title are undeserving of it. And likewise, there is only one God; the many gods recognized in the Hellenistic world are not truly gods.

An important factor in the development of this understanding of Jesus as lord was the application of OT passages which originally referred to God as lord, to the lord Jesus (e.g., Rom 10:12-13, quoting Joel 3:5). This had the effect of attributing to Jesus God's present reign over the universe and his existence from the beginning of the world. This interpretation of OT passages was undoubtedly encouraged by the early Christians' use of Greek translations of the OT in which Yahweh was rendered "lord." However, at least in some cases they interpreted passages in this way, knowing that they were applying to Jesus something which originally spoke about Yahweh.

Pastoral-Liturgical Tradition

We have seen that the NT writings reflect early Christian use of "lord" as the vehicle for an increasingly exalted understanding of Jesus. Originally to say that Jesus was lord was virtually synonymous with saying that he was Messiah. But within a short time "lord" and other titles for Jesus, such as son of God, come to express a belief about Jesus which goes beyond the belief that he was the Messiah whose reign would begin at his second coming. "Lord" and other titles come to express the belief that Jesus presently rules over heaven and earth at God's right hand, and that he was with God from the beginning.

This raised the question of Jesus' precise relationship with God. This question was resolved definitively by the council of Nicea (325 CE), which declared that Jesus was of the same substance (*homoousios*) as the Father. This was the foundation for the doctrine of the Trinity, i.e., that God is three persons who are the one divine nature or substance. This doctrine explains how it can be true that there is only one God and at the same time that Jesus can be so much like God. Jesus and the Father are two of the persons of God. As such they are distinct, yet are of the same substance. The status of Jesus was further clarified at the council of Chalcedon (451 CE). This council declared that Jesus was a single person, i.e., the second person of the Trinity, in two natures—the divine and the human—which exist in this one person without confusion, change, division, or separation. Thus Jesus is fully God and fully a human being.

The title "lord" was not an important element in this ongoing attempt to understand the status of Jesus. Throughout this time and since, "lord" has simply been taken for granted as a title for Jesus, expressing the believer's recognition of Jesus' authority for him or her.

In recent times Christians (and others) have become concerned to avoid gender-specific language where it is not necessary, in order to avoid giving the impression that the masculine gender is paradigmatic. This concern makes the title "lord" problematic because it is a masculine noun. As applied to God it suggests that God is male, or can only or best be visualized as male, neither of which is true. For this reason many now minimize the use of this title for God.

See: FAITH, MESSIAH, NAME, PAROUSIA, REIGN OF GOD, RESURRECTION, SON OF GOD

TERRANCE CALLAN

LOVE

As in modern society, the biblical concept of love has many and varied dimensions, such as sexual love, love of family, friendship, loyalty, compassion, graciousness, desire, and delight. It embraces God's love for humanity and all of creation, humanity's love for God, and human love of others and of things. In the OT the experience of human love with all its passion and desire gave a base for understanding God's love, but Israel experienced a divine love that surpassed all human qualities. This love from God elicited a response of love that included also love of neighbor. The NT does not initiate the concept of God's love, but deepens it, coming ultimately to defining God as love, to showing divine love and human response in Jesus, and to enlarging love of neighbor to embrace even enemies.

Old Testament

The occasionally proposed stereotype of the God of the OT as a God of fear in contrast to the God of the NT as a God of love is to be avoided, since there is more continuity between testaments than discontinuity. The words to describe God's love are the same as those describing human love, and there are several words. The most common OT word for love, the verb *'āhab* and its related noun forms, are used most frequently for love between the sexes (e.g., Gen 24:67; 29:18; Judg 16:4; 1 Sam 1:5) and may etymologically come from a root meaning "to desire." Another important word for love is *ḥesed*, which is difficult to translate directly because it embraces several qualities of love all at once, such as loving kindness, graciousness, steadfastness, and loyalty. This word always indicates some kind of relationship and deep, lasting affection, whether between sexes (Esth

2:17), in kinship (Gen 24:49), or through some social bond (2 Sam 2:5). Other words are infrequently translated as love or have traits closely associated with love, e.g., *raḥamim*, which means "mercy" or "compassion" (Gen 43:30); *ḥašaq*, which means "to be lovingly attached to" (Gen 34:8); *yādîd* and *dôd*, which mean "beloved" (Ps 84:1; Cant 6:3); *ḥāpheṣ*, which means "to delight in" (1 Sam 18:22); *ḥānan*, which means "to favor" (Job 19:21).

Pentateuch and Historical Books. The narrative texts of the OT use the vocabulary of love, as just presented, to describe various human experiences. If there are any minor differences, they would be found in frequency of usage. Both the Pentateuch and the historical books depict sexual love. Besides that, the Pentateuch speaks most often of family love, while the historical books accentuate the love between friends. When this vocabulary is used theologically to speak of God's love, one can turn to several texts in the historical books which speak of individuals, such as God's love for Solomon (2 Sam 12:24; Neh 13:36), but most often God's love for individuals is seen within God's love for the community of Israel as a whole: "In his enduring love for Israel, the LORD has made you king to carry out judgment and justice" (1 Kgs 10:9). In any case, there are not many references to God's love in the historical books, while the Pentateuch offers significant passages, especially in Deuteronomy.

In texts such as Deuteronomy 7:6-8, the entire relationship of God with Israel, the covenant relationship, is described as a relationship of love. This covenant begins with the choice of Israel to be God's people, not because Israel merited or deserved that election, but because of God's generous and gratuitous love: "It was not because you are the largest of all nations that the LORD set his heart [*ḥāšaq*] on you and chose you. . . . It was because the LORD loved [*'āhab*] you" (See Deut 4:37-38; 10:15). As love founded the covenant, so love sustains it. In this steadfastness and loyalty of God

Israel discovered a love far superior to any human love. The OT expresses this especially by the word *ḥesed*: "The LORD, your God, is God indeed, the faithful God who keeps his merciful covenant [lit. "covenant and steadfast love"] down to the thousandth generation" (Deut 7:9; see also Jer 31:3). In the Pentateuch as elsewhere, *ḥesed* is used most often of God rather than of humans; such love is the ideal for humanity, the reality for God. In Psalm 136, the word recurs in the refrain of every verse, so that as God's achievements in covenant are depicted, the chorus proclaims, "His mercy [lit. "steadfast love"] endures forever."

Such love from God should elicit a like response of love from Israel, hence the great commandment of Deuteronomy 6:5, "You shall love the LORD, your God, with all your heart, and with all your soul, and with all your strength," meaning total love of God with one's deepest life (soul), all of its rational choices and commitments (heart), and with one's external achievements and possessions (strength). This response of love is seen as the true accomplishment of the Torah or law. Moreover, since God's love forms a community, both love and the Torah are to be patterned on that love and activity. Thus, the Torah emphasizes social ethics, especially justice for the poor and oppressed, and therefore love must embrace these same concerns: "The LORD, your God, . . . executes justice for the orphan and the widow, and befriends [*'āhab*] the alien, feeding and clothing him. So you too must befriend [*'āhab*] the alien, for you were once aliens yourselves in the land of Egypt" (Deut 10:17-19). Leviticus picks up this same theme (19:33-34) and also frames it in more general terms, "You shall love your neighbor as yourself" (19:18), with neighbor understood as one within the borders of Israel, as the preceding part of verse 18 shows.

Prophets and Poetic Books. What is expressed as duty and command is likewise presented with all the spontaneity, passion, and intimacy that can also characterize the experience of love. Thus, in addition to the word *ḥesed* and sometimes linked with it, the word *raḥămîm* is used in the OT, and more often of God than of humans. But whereas *ḥesed* implies duty or obligation, *raḥămîm* suggests only spontaneous compassion, mercy, or forgiveness (Ps 51:3; Deut 13:18).

Especially in the Prophetic literature the passionate experiences of human love are used to describe God's love for Israel and Israel's response, all in such a way as to show also how divine love surpasses the human. Thus, Hosea, in his first three chapters, uses the imagery of intimate marital love and even the example of his own marriage. He shows how God chose Israel as spouse, but Israel did not respond with love. The rejection of God for idols, the inordinate love of created things, the consequent injustices, and the lack even of neighbor-love are all described as adultery and infidelity. God's steadfast love, in contrast to this human infidelity, is expressed by the command to Hosea to take back his prostitute wife, even as God takes back the adulterous people and calls them again to love that embraces justice and social ethics: "I will espouse you to me forever: I will espouse you in right and in justice, in love [*ḥesed*] and in mercy [*raḥămîm*]" (Hos 2:21; see Isa 62:1-5; Ezek 16:23). Hosea also uses the image of father-love to show God's constancy and forgiveness. Even though Israel is like a rebellious child, God embraces the nation: "How could I give you up, O Ephraim. . . . My heart is overwhelmed, my pity is stirred" (11:8). Second Isaiah uses mother-love to show how deep is God's love and how far surpassing the human: "Can a mother forget her infant, be without tenderness for the child of her womb? Even should she forget, I will never forget you" (49:15).

Among the other writings of the OT the Canticle of Canticles offers the most elaborate treatment of the passionate, spontaneous, and intimate qualities of love, especially of sexual love. Here the word *dôd* is used frequently for human love, as the young man and woman of the text speak of each other as "beloved" or "lover." Some scholars read the entire book as an allegory of the love of God for Israel. It may serve that function, but it is also a splendid encomium of real human love without which we would have no vocabulary or experience for understanding divine love.

New Testament

The early Christians adopted the OT insights as they were filtered through the Septuagint. This Greek OT continues the tradition of the Hebrew text, but along with a greater emphasis on the transcendence of God, it stresses divine love even more and shows it as pure gift out of God's compassion. Thus, it sometimes uses "to love" (agapaō) as translation, not only of the corresponding Hebrew verb 'āhab, but of other verbs as well. It also often translates as "compassion" or "mercy" (eleos) the Hebrew words for "steadfast love" (hesed) and "favor" (hēn). In addition, it contains new books that reinforce the thought, "thus will you be like a son to the Most High, and he will be more tender to you than a mother" (Sir 4:10). In describing love, philia, the love of friendship, was the prevalent classical Greek term, but the Septuagint uses it only occasionally and, when speaking theologically, almost always uses the verb agapaō, and infrequently the noun agapē, originally somewhat neutral or colorless words. The NT picks up this trend. It even makes more use of the noun agapē than the Septuagint. Most scholars tend to downplay any real distinctions between agapē and philia. While this is probably true and the word agapē did not of itself have a distinct meaning, nevertheless a growing concept may have led to the use of this distinct word. In other words, the NT builds on the Septuagint's insight into the theological meaning of love and emphasizes the importance of God's love. This stress on divine love may have been what led the Septuagint and NT authors to choose a new verb and the NT authors to add a noun not common in the literature before them. In any case, both Septuagint and NT

avoid the Greek word eros, which bespeaks passionate, possessive, and often carnal love drawn by the attractiveness of the object loved. God's love is, rather, freeing and generous, loving even the unlovable, though the intensity and passion of divine love warns us against too sharp a contrast even between agapē and eros.

Jesus and the Synoptics. The Synoptic Gospels rarely speak of love, but when they do, they concentrate on the great commandments of love received from Jesus himself. All three Gospels present the story of Jesus quoting the love commands from Deuteronomy and Leviticus (Matt 22:34-40; Mark 12:28-34; Luke 10:25-28). The further mention of neighbor-love in the conversation with the rich young man also shows continuity with the OT (Matt 19:16-22). A new dimension brought by Jesus is that love is the response to the arriving reign of God to which human beings must submit themselves wholeheartedly. As Jesus words it, "No one can serve two masters. He will either hate one and love the other, or be devoted to one and despise the other. You cannot serve God and mammon" (Matt 6:24; see Luke 16:13). Another fresh development in Jesus' citation of the love commands is his using the law to love neighbor as also a summation of the Torah and his joining in tighter fashion this command with that of loving God. A further new insight is the explicit universal understanding of the term neighbor beyond the boundaries of the community. It entails even love of enemy (Matt 5:43-48; Luke 6:27-36). The parable of the good Samaritan (Luke 10:30-36) further illustrates this universal application.

The Letters and John. Paul rarely speaks of love for God (e.g., Rom 8:28) and does not cite the command from Deuteronomy, but he dwells on God's love for humanity which elicits that response of love. God's love is so strong that "neither death, nor life, nor angels, nor principalities, . . . nor any other creature will be able to separate us from the love of God in Christ Jesus our

Lord" (Rom 8:38-39). The unique aspect of God's love in Paul and the NT is that it is manifest in Christ. Moreover, the gratuity and undeserved generosity of that love is shown in that, "while we were still sinners Christ died for us" (Rom 5:8; see also Gal 2:20; Eph 2:4-5; 5:2). Sometimes Paul stresses that the love of God is poured into our hearts through the Spirit (Rom 5:5; 15:30), thus suggesting a Trinitarian dimension to divine love.

Since "the love of Christ impels us" (2 Cor 5:15), since we have been taught by God to love (1 Thess 4:9), and since we must be imitators of God, loving as Christ loves (Eph 5:1-2), Paul (and his school) put great stress on love of neighbor. This should show itself in communities of one mind and heart (Phil 2:2) who are able to bear with one another in unity and peace (Eph 4:1-3; Col 3:12-14), in families in which husbands and wives love and respect each other (Eph 5:33; Col 3:19), in churches giving generously for the poor in other churches (2 Cor 8:8, 24), in households in which masters receive slaves as brothers and sisters (Phlm 5, 7, 9), among preachers who proclaim the gospel out of good will for others and not out of envy or selfish ambition (Phil 1:15-17), among groups who realize that subtle distinctions may occasion scandal and who therefore respect the consciences of others (1 Cor 8:1), and in many other ways. Such deeds are possible, not out of human initiative, but because of the grace given by God through Christ and in response to God's love for us in Christ (Phil 1:9-11; 2 Thess 2:16-17). Thus, Paul joins love with faith and hope (Rom 5:1-8; 1 Cor 13:13; Gal 5:5-6; 1 Thess 1:3; 5:8), with faith because love is grounded on Christ's love (Gal 3:20; Eph 3:17), and with hope because love anticipates the Spirit's final work in us. Love is the working out of genuine faith (Gal 5:6) and love verifies hope (Rom 5:5). Therefore, the greatest and enduring gift is love (1 Cor 13:13). Paul sees love of neighbor as central to his own life, even when it requires self-sacrifice (2 Cor 6:6; 11:11; 12:15), and even

when he must reprimand a community (2 Cor 2:4), and he sets himself as an example for his communities of forgiveness and reconciliation (2 Cor 2:6-11; 5:14-20). Love is the principal fruit of the Spirit (Gal 5:22). Paul bequeaths us an elegant hymn to love (1 Corinthians 13), showing that all is meaningless without it. Finally love is, as Jesus himself taught, the fulfillment of the entire law (Rom 13:8-10; Gal 5:13-14).

Other NT texts pick up themes similar to the Synoptic and Pauline thought, especially concerning love of neighbor (Heb 10:24; 1 Pet 2:17; 4:8; 2 Pet 1:7). James 2:8 even repeats the teaching that love of neighbor fulfills the law. It is, however, in the Johannine school of thought that the teaching about love, while reaffirming NT traditions, also reaches its heights. A summary may be found in 1 John 4:7-12, where the author defines God as love itself, shows God's love as incarnate in Christ, especially in his death, and establishes divine love as the principle of Christians' own love of one another (see also 4:16). The Gospel of John centers on love, showing first of all the incarnation of divine love in Christ. The Father loves Christ: "The Father loves the Son and has given everything over to him" (3:35); Christ loves the Father: "The world must know that I love the Father and that I do just as the Father has commanded me" (14:31). This relationship of love overflows into both the Father's and Christ's love for humanity: "God so loved the world that he gave his only Son, so that everyone who believes in him might not perish but might have eternal life" (3:16); "As the Father loves me, so I also love you. Remain in my love" (15:9). The love between the Father and Christ is underscored by the death and resurrection of Christ (10:17). Since no greater love is shown than in one's dying for another, divine love for humanity also reaches its culmination in Christ's laying down his life in order to take it up again (13:1; 15:13; see also 1 John 3:16).

This love of Christ even unto death becomes model and means of love for one another, so that Christ can offer a "new" command to love one another (13:34; 15:12; see also 1 John 3:16, 23). The newness is in loving as Christ loves, not simply following Christ's example, but drawing from the power of Christ's love which abides within each one (14:20-23). This power of love may also be described as the holy Spirit, the Advocate (14:15-17). In this way love marks the true disciple (13:35): such a one is beloved of Christ (19:26; 20:2; 21:7, 20), loves Christ (14:15, 21, 23, 28; 21:15-17), and therefore keeps the command to love others (14:15; 15:9, 17). 1 John 4:20 shows the practical, concrete dimensions of love to be such that one cannot truly love God without loving neighbor. Ultimately, love bespeaks a unity in which the Father is one with Jesus in love, loves the community with that same love, and empowers the community to love in the same way, so that the Father, Jesus, and the community might abide together (John 17:23, 24, 26). It is frequently observed that John's Gospel narrows the command of love to the closed circle of Christians. Such commands are understandable when the author is concerned primarily with preserving a threatened community (17:9-19; see also 1 John 4:1-7), but in any case, one must not forget the claims that God sent Jesus because God so loved the entire world (3:16) and that Jesus prayed that the entire world be one (17:20-21).

Pastoral-Liturgical Tradition

The idea and necessity of love in the Christian life has seemed so basic that more often than not it has been presumed and implicit in Christian theology rather than the object of extensive and explicit treatment. This is not to say, however, that the concept of love is not complex and that there have not been different approaches to the subject over the course of Christian tradition. Much discussion seems to have revolved around questions of definition. Is Christian love for others *eros* or *agapē*? Does it seek the good for self (value-recognizing love or love of concupiscence) or does it will good to the other (value-bestowing love or love of

benevolence)? Is divine love essentially the same as human love? Can human love for God be the same as love for neighbor? Other discussion revolves around the practice of love. Can love really be commanded and still be genuine love? How is love related to norms and principles and to the other virtues? How is love related to justice?

The Essence of Love. St. Augustine's theology of love has been the prominent paradigm in Christian tradition. In explaining love for others he sought to relate *eros* to *agapē*, seeing *eros* as love in what Augustine called the "City of Man," characterized by self-interest and desire for the good perceived in the other, while *agapē* was patterned on God's love in the "City of God," characterized as disinterested, unmerited, and creative of good in the other. For Augustine, *eros* became the means of discovering *agapē*, as the human quest for happiness would find its rest only in finding God. In modern times Anders Nygren brought the discussion to the fore in challenging Augustine's attempt to relate the two kinds of love and in opposing human *eros* to Christian *agapē*. In Nygren's scheme of things, purely human love for others can only be value-recognizing as it seeks what is good for self, while genuine Christian love—like God's— must be value-bestowing, as it seeks totally the good of the other. Nygren's thesis of benevolent Christian love for others is founded on the gratuity of God's love for humanity based on no merit or desert, and reflects Luther's emphasis on justification by grace. Nevertheless, it must be complemented by Catholic stress on free cooperation with grace which founds a love of others as response to what in them truly perfects us. In summary, Christian love for others embraces and perfects human love by melding both giving and desiring.

Love of benevolence and love of concupiscence become the focus of debate when moving from our love for others to God's love for us or our love for God. Can God's love for us be anything other than benevolence, bestowing value? Can our love for

God be other than concupiscence, recognizing value? If gift and desire are complementary, then both have place in both God's love for us and our love for God. God's love not only creates goodness in humanity, but desires communion and forms a covenant with those so created in the divine image. Likewise, human beings not only seek union with God as their ultimate good, but in their yearning enable God to become fully the Creator and Savior.

The Practice of Love. If the essence of love is thus to be freely bestowed and freely received, can it be commanded? If a command is understood as purely external law and coercion, then love cannot be commanded. But in that case, neither can any other moral virtue or moral activity, which must all come from the heart, and the absence of which would be the basis for legalism or hypocrisy. The commandment to love ultimately expresses the absolute necessity of love for authentic human existence. It reminds us that, while love presupposes freedom, true freedom is found in love. By the same token, love is not just interior, but manifests itself in the external actions of human life, thus warranting further reference to commandments. In other words, love in its exterior manifestation requires obedience to law properly understood.

Just how love relates to law has been the object of painful and still unresolved discussion among Catholics since Vatican II. Catholic teaching has consistently resisted "situation ethics" and the view that there are no absolute laws and that one must decide what is loving in each case. Classical Catholic teaching has maintained that norms and principles have general and universal applicability, since there are some things that can never be loving and are always intrinsically evil. Debate has arisen over whether past tendencies within the tradition have over-extended absolute rules and over whether and how one can test the tradition to find which rules should remain exceptionless and which should not.

As another way of dealing with this problem, authors have shifted the focus away from relating love to norms and principles for action and onto the Catholic tradition of relating love to virtues which form character and attitudes. Love is described as the mother, basis, root, and form of all the virtues. Each virtue communicates a different dimension of love, but is drawn from its narrow scope to become a vital force of the entire person when infused by love and joined by love to the other virtues. This centrality of love, developed by Aquinas, received less emphasis over time until the renewal encouraged by Vatican II. Now there is further emphasis also in the relationship of justice to love, with less contrasting of justice with love and more recognition that justice is the first expression of love.

See: DISCIPLE, ELECTION, FRIENDSHIP, GRACE, MERCY, SPIRIT

ANTHONY J. TAMBASCO

M

MAGI

The Greek historian Herodotus tells us that the *Magoi* or Magi were members of a Persian tribe *(genea)*, some of whom interpreted dreams and heavenly portents and acted in priestly roles at sacrifices (*History* I, 101, 107, 120, 132, 140; VII, 37). In the Septuagint, the Book of Daniel knows the Magi as wise men who interpret dreams and visions (Dan 1:20; 2:2; 4:4; 5:7). Philo knows Magi as magicians and writes also of a counterfeit magic practiced by charlatans (*Special Laws* 3:100-101).

Magi appear three times in the NT, unfavorably in two instances. Simon, a convert to the Lord at Samaria, practiced magic before his conversion and is traditionally known as Simon Magus. His attempt to buy from Peter the power to confer the holy Spirit has given the name "simony" to such attempts to buy the spiritual gifts of God (Acts 8:9-25). At Paphos on the island of Cyprus, Paul and his fellow missionaries encountered Elymas, also known as Bar Jesus, a false prophet and magician, who attempted to turn the Roman proconsul Sergius Paulus from the faith preached by Barnabas and Paul. But Paul struck Elymas with temporary blindness, and this miracle led to the conversion of Sergius Paulus (Acts 13:6-12).

In Matthew's Gospel (Matt 2:1-12), the Magi appear more favorably. They represent the Gentiles who come to Jesus through the Jewish community, represented here by Herod and the Sanhedrin, who direct the Magi to Bethlehem by citing the prophet Micah (Mic 5:1; Matt 2:5-6). Led by the star "they had seen at its rising" (Matt 2:9), the Magi arrive at the star arising out of Jacob (Num 24:17), the Davidic King, Jesus.

Because the Magi's point of origin is not stated in Matthew, various attempts have been made to locate their home country. For some scholars, the Magi's astrological observation marks them as coming from Babylonia, where astrology was highlighted. Other scholars point to the gifts of the Magi—gold, frankincense, and myrrh—and see the Magi's origin in the Arabian peninsula (see Isa 60:1-6; Ps 72:15). Still other scholars place the Magi in Persia, because Magi functioned as wise men and priests of that region. In any case, it is clear from Matthew's text that the Magi are not Jews and are representative of Gentiles.

Christian tradition, picking up the scriptural allusions in the visit of the Magi, has turned the Magi into kings (Ps 72:10-12; Isa 49:23; 60:6) and has numbered them as three because of their three gifts. Eastern and Western Christians have given different names to the Magi. The West has known them since the sixth century as Balthasar, Gaspar, and Melchior. In recent times, the statuary of the traditional Christmas crib is inclined to show the Magi as representatives of various branches of humanity, a trend that accords well with the teaching of Matthew's Gospel.

See: BETHLEHEM, DREAMS, EPIPHANY, MAGIC AND DIVINATION, POWER, STARS, VISIONS

NEIL J. MCELENEY, C.S.P.

MAGIC AND DIVINATION

Magic is the art that attempts to reach into the realm of the divine or the unknown and to gain control of powers outside the influence of human beings. It is occult, known only to a few, and it acknowledges no power higher than itself. Magic was practiced in Mesopotamia where it was merged with religion through the rites, gestures, and incantations that were used. It thus came into the realm of the priestly class in temple worship. Egyptians also were devoted to magic and used it both for overcoming evils and for bringing about positive effects. Divination is a form of magic and uses pseudo-scientific means of predicting the future. It attempts to read natural events, entrails of animals, and other such phenomena, and it sometimes resorts to necromancy. All forms of magic and divination were forbidden in Hebrew law codes where they were punishable by death. Those practices were considered heinous vices and were classified with idolatry.

Magic and divination were both prevalent in the NT period since people believed that they provided the means to gain knowledge about the future and to control the forces that determined it. The pastoral tradition of the Church has always opposed magic and divination as inconsistent with the Christian faith despite their popularity.

Old Testament

Magic in the Old Testament. The Bible attests that magic was present in cultures of the ancient world which touched the life of Israel. When Pharaoh had dreams* magicians and sages of his country were called upon for aid, but they could not help him (Gen 41:8). Joseph was called to interpret the dreams, and the sacred writer immediately subjected the interpretation to the power of God (Gen 41:16). That pattern is seen again at the time of the plagues in Egypt. Pharaoh's magicians could do many wonderful tricks, but when they turned their staffs into snakes, Aaron's staff swallowed their staffs. Thus the power of Egyptian magicians was subject to the word of the Lord. The plagues worked against the Egyptians and ultimately to the good of Israel (Exod 7:11-12).

If the rituals of magic were adopted by Israel in some way, it was only after they had been changed and purified to suit the religious stance of Yahwism. For instance, the use of blood was prohibited, for it symbolized life that was under the power of God alone. In the name of the Lord blood was used in rites of expiation and of the covenant and thus in a new context it had a new meaning. The ceremony showed that the entire life of the people was dedicated to God.

In time Israel lost the true perspective of some of its rituals and magic asserted itself. The prophets denounced it as a vice for which the Lord would punish his people (Isa 2:6; Jer 29:8-9). Ezekiel denounced the sorceresses who believed they could command power over people by magical practices; God's power would triumph over such entrapment (Ezek 13:18-21). Malachi speaks of the Lord's swift judgment against sorcerers and all who do not fear the Lord (Mal 3:5).

Condemnation of magic was rooted in its prohibition in the three Mosaic law codes. The people were forbidden the use of mediums and fortune tellers (Lev 19:31). Those who acted in such a role were punished by death (Lev 20:27; Exod 22:17). When Israel came into their land they were warned not to imitate the abominations of the inhabitants. Among vices to be avoided were works of magic (Deut 18:9-12). This was not always faithfully observed, and Manasseh was known to use magical practices that provoked the Lord to anger (2 Kgs 21:6). It was his grandson Josiah who took positive action against such practices (2 Kgs 23:24), and there was none after him who could compare with him (2 Kgs 23:25).

Divination in the Old Testament. Closely tied in with magic is the practice of divination, which is sometimes mentioned in the same texts with other forms of magic. Essentially divination attempts to foretell the future by occult or supernatural means using special rituals, spells, or charms. Divination is identified by the use of lots, or signs in natural objects such as animal entrails (hepatoscopy), phenomena of nature, or observation of heavenly bodies (astrology). It was forbidden in Israel and considered to be as wicked as idolatry, for only God is master of time and events. Human beings were given dominion over the earth, and their relationship with God was to be one of obedience with dignity.

Divination existed in Israel and it was listed among the sins for which the nation was punished. Samuel called divination rebellion and spoke of it in the same breath with idolatry* (1 Sam 15:23). Kings often fell into the same trap (2 Kgs 17:17) and led the nation into corruption and disintegration. Jeremiah condemns lying visions and foolish divination for which God would pour out upon the people their own wickedness (Jer 14:14). The great purification God would work in the exiles in Babylon was described in part as eradication of false visions and deceitful divinations. Thus a return to the true word of God would triumph in the nation, for God's word is final (Ezek 12:24). In contrast the divining practices of the king of Babylon were called lying oracles.* In these things lay Babylonian guilt (Ezek 21:23-28). Most of the Prophetical books have oracles against false prophets, sometimes called false diviners. Micah ridiculed those whose oracles are determined by venal motives (Mic 3:5-6). Later on, Ben Sira would call divination and dreams unreal (Sir 34:5). Those who believe in them are fools, for what a person already expects the mind depicts. The hopes of the sense-less are empty and false. The inherent contradiction of seeking wisdom in emptiness is an unmistakable mark of a fool.

In time some of the religious rites established for the well-being of the nation became the object of superstitions, and then they were abolished. Hezekiah smashed the bronze serpent that Moses had made because the Israelite had been burning incense to it (2 Kgs 18:4). The prophet Micah preached an oracle about the abolition of idolatry in the land. Destruction of the means of divination and soothsaying were included in the list of proscribed practices (Mic 5:11). Among the people Israel, God's power was to be absolutely sovereign. Thus anything that attempted to insinuate itself above God's power was inconsistent with that religious faith stance.

See: ATONEMENT, BLOOD, DREAMS, EXPIATION, IDOLATRY, LAW, ORACLE

BETTY JANE LILLIE, S.C.

New Testament

One prevalent, cultural belief in the first-century Mediterranean world of the NT is that people have no control over nature and little to no control over life. Daily experience confirmed the validity of this belief. Peasants, who constituted more than ninety-five percent of the population, were battered by powerful forces, notably stars,* perceived to be in control of nature.

As peasants learned how to manipulate the elite through the institution of patronage, they also sought to learn how to manipulate the forces that controlled nature through magic. An alternative to manipulation was divination, a strategy for gaining knowledge of forthcoming events from the suprahuman beings (deities or spirits) who possessed it.

Divination attempts to "influence" the knowing being to reveal something unknown to the human petitioner. Divination does not intend to alter these events but merely to learn about them.

The underlying idea is that those who know future matters or events can reveal them under proper circumstances or if the petitioner uses the proper strategy. Casting lots, sometimes accompanied by prayer, is one very common way of learning divine intent. The Roman soldiers sought divine intent on who among them should take Jesus' seamless inner tunic (John 19:24). By a similar casting of lots, the Eleven determined that God intended Matthias to replace Judas (Acts 1:26).

Another common way of probing divine intent is by interpreting signs* presumed to have originated with the deity. Probing livers or other entrails of sacrificial animals is one widely known example, though in the NT Jesus both works signs (e.g., John 2:11) and is himself a sign (John 20:23).

In Mediterranean culture, dreams* are a favorite and frequent vehicle for learning God's will. Though some dreams are presumed to be spontaneous, many are requested and/or induced. Joseph learned God's will about his wife, Mary (Matt 1:20-21), as well as his will about Jesus (Matt 2:13), in a dream. The astrologers learned about Jesus in a dream (Matt 2:12), and a dream gave Pilate's wife some insight into Jesus while her husband was conducting Jesus' trial (Matt 27:13). The rich man's request in Jesus' parable to return from the dead to warn his brothers could have taken place in a dream or in a response to necromancy, another favorite ancient Mediterranean strategy for seeking information known only to God.

Of course, certain gifted human beings like prophets, mystics, and seers also served as vehicles of divine communication with other human beings. Jesus is presented and acts like a prophet in the Gospels. People understandably ask him about future events (Mark 13:4) but in one instance he admits he doesn't know (Mark 13:32). The Father has not revealed it to anyone.

In Acts 16:16, Luke tells the story of a slave girl with the gift of divination ("a spirit of Python") who earned a good living for her masters with her skills. She knows and tells the truth about Paul and his companions. Paul, however, becomes annoyed with her repeated pronouncements and demonstrates that his source is more powerful than her source: "I command you in the name of Jesus Christ to come out of her" (16:18). With that, the spirit left her and she fell silent.

This latter incident reflects the repeated NT condemnation of divination in its many variations (Gal 5:20; Rev 9:21; 21:8). Believers have direct access to God and need not go through intermediaries. Ask, seek, knock, and God will answer you (see Matt 7:7).

Though related, magic differs from divination in that it is rooted in "power." It relies on strategies to "force" those who control nature and life to respond according to the wishes of the petitioner. The contrast between magic and divination is the difference between doing and knowing. In the Bible, those whose strategies involve magic are shamans, magi* (astrologers), and liturgical ministers. Their strategies include prophetic-symbolic actions, divinely-directed techniques, and sacraments in a very broad sense.

Magic and magicians were found all over the Greco-Roman world. Luke reports that the magic books burned in Ephesus by just a few magician-converts to Christianity had an estimated value of 50,000 silver pieces (Acts 19:19).

The Book of Revelation, directed to believers in Asia Minor, bears the strongest and most numerous traces of magic in the NT. The author may well have been battling against beliefs in the likes of Hecate who possessed the keys to the gates of Hades, was honored as patron goddess of magic and sorcery, was known for her revelatory magic, and whose cult flourished in southwest Asia Minor. He counters her popularity by identifying the risen Jesus as the one who holds "the keys to death and the netherworld" (Rev 1:18).

The author's point is that God works the greatest magic of all, for his magic protects and empowers his group of believers against a magic-enamored society as a whole. Moreover, the "Alpha and Omega" phrases (Rev 1:4, 8, 17; 21:6; 22:13) are common magical formulas, but it is Christ himself and not some human manipulator that utters this and other formulas as self-predicates. Thus does Jesus show that he is Lord of the cosmos who will not be manipulated or controlled by any human being.

A magician gained power from knowing the names of powerful deities. His admirers named Simon the Magician "the 'power of God' that is called 'Great'" (Acts 8:10). Yet Simon's desire to obtain from the apostles the power to impart the holy Spirit "upon whom I lay my hands" (Acts 8:19) expresses the very reason why magic was viewed as deviant behavior throughout the entire Mediterranean world. It manipulated power to serve individual and private interests rather than the common good. In group-oriented Mediterranean culture, such selfishness is the worst failing imaginable.

To thwart the curiosity of magicians, the author of Revelation notes that Jesus has "a name inscribed that no one knows except himself" (Rev 19:12). Believers have no need of magic, for they are baptized in the power of the name of God and Jesus (Matt 28:19), people are healed in Jesus' name (Acts 3:6), and every knee should bend at the name of Jesus (Phil 2:10) who does good for all those who believe in him.

See: APOSTLE, COSMOS, DREAMS, PROPHECY/PROPHET, SIGN, STARS

JOHN J. PILCH

Pastoral-Liturgical Tradition

As was true in biblical times, Church history reveals both the pervasive popularity of magic and divination and staunch opposition to it. Within the wider context of common religious phenomena, these practices can be understood as expressions of a basic human yearning to know and/or predict the future or any aspect of the unknown, and to channel and/or manipulate a power* beyond oneself, divine or otherwise, for one's own purpose. The Church repeatedly opposes magic and divination as being inconsistent with Christian faith, in that these practices presume the knowledge and power which are God's alone.

Christians of the early Church were accused of practicing magic by such critics as Celsus of the second century, who charged that Christians got power by using incantations and the names of demons (Origen, *Cels.* 1.6). Within the Church, Justin Martyr, Hippolytus, Tertullian, and others pointed out that through baptism, Christians turned their backs on the world of demons, magic, and immorality, and Ignatius of Antioch wrote that Jesus' incarnation dissolved the powers of magic (*Eph.* 19.3). Also such people as John Chrysostom (*Jud.* 8.5-7) and Augustine (*Serm.* 9.3; 56.12; 88.25) spoke against the incorporation of magic into Christian practice in Antioch and North Africa. Likewise, throughout its history, the Church spoke against various forms of divination, such as augury, palmistry, and spiritualism.

To a great part due to the Protestant reaction to certain sacramental practices of the Roman Catholic Church during and after the Reformation of the sixteenth century, magic became associated with the concept of *ex opere operato,* whereby ritual words and procedures are considered automatically effective simply by being recited or performed. Eventually, magic and religion were understood as strictly dichotomous, according to a basic relationship with the divine, whereby magic (and divination) was equated with manipulation and religion with supplication.

During the twentieth century, a more in-depth study of non-Western religions and cultures has shown the difficulty and inaccuracy of maintaining such a dichotomous understanding of magic and religion, so that today many scholars of religion prefer the term "magical-religious phenomena." Others avoid using the term "magic" completely, and rather speak only in terms of "ritual," and then distinguish between various types of ritual, such as group and individual, or beneficial and harmful.

This latter distinction between benevolent and malevolent ritual indicates that perhaps the best way of understanding magic and divination is in terms of deviancy. From this perspective, magic is associated with means that are not usually sanctioned by the dominant religious institution, and those goals which are practically considered assured through the use of divine powers. Therefore, magic and divination are judged as religiously deviant from the perspective of particular religious and cultural values and norms. Therefore, back to the situation of Christianity, the Church continues to oppose certain events and rituals associated with magic and divination, because they are inconsistent with Christian faith, which places knowledge of the unknown and control over divine power solely in God's hands.

See: FAITH, POWER

ROGER P. SCHROEDER, S.V.D.

MAMMON

Mammon is an Aramaic word found in several sayings of Jesus. Its precise derivation is unknown but it means "wealth" or "possessions" and, at least in the sayings of Jesus, seems to have the implication of ill-gotten wealth. Some have suggested that the word may come from the Hebrew root *'aman* which means "reliable"; thus wealth upon which one relies.

The term is used in the NT only in sayings of Jesus and reflects his strong and distinctive teaching about not relying on wealth for the ultimate meaning and security of one's life. In Matthew 6:24 (see also Luke 16:13) the disciples are warned that they cannot serve both God and "mammon." In Luke 16 where Jesus instructs the disciples on the danger of wealth, the conclusion to the parable of the shrewd manager (16:1-8) advises them to "make friends for yourselves by means of mammon" (16:9); that is, the disciples should follow the example of the manager and distribute their wealth as alms, thereby equipping themselves for eternal life. The saying in

16:11—"If then you have not been faithful with mammon, who will entrust to you the true riches?"—moves in a similar vein.

See: POOR, RICH

DONALD SENIOR, C.P.

MAN/MEN

The biblical understanding of humankind* is grounded in the traditions embodied in the narrative accounts of creation and sin (Genesis 1–3). There the man and the woman* are depicted as created in the image of God with both privilege and responsibility in relationship to the rest of the natural world. Despite their fundamental goodness, the first couple sinned and were subsequently punished. Their relationship with God was altered and the harmony that they originally enjoyed with each other and with the world was dashed. The biblical portraits of man and woman, as well as the religious and social roles that each played in the narratives preserved in the Bible, must be understood against this basic anthropological point of view.

Old Testament

Terms. There are four major Hebrew words that translate as "man." Each one characterizes a particular aspect of Israelite anthropology. The first of these words, and the one that plays the most prominent role in the creation narratives, is 'ādām. The word comes from the same root meaning "to be red" as does 'ªdāmâ, the reddish clay from which God fashioned the first man (Gen 2:7), the trees (2:9), and the animals (2:19). This etymological link is probably the author's way of highlighting the affinity of this earth-creature with other creatures of the earth and with the earth itself. The word serves as a collective noun distinguishing humankind from non-human creation (Gen 1:26), and it also refers to a male individual (the man, 2:8). Since Hebrew does not have a corresponding word identifying an individual as both human (as distinct from animal) and female (as distinct from male), some linguistic scholars maintain that the language itself demonstrates a male bias which is reenforced by certain interpretations of the narrative depicting the woman's creation from the man. The word usually appears with the article in prose and without the article in poetry and occasionally serves as a proper name (Adam, 5:1).

Another word for man found in the second creation narrative is 'îš (Gen 2:23f.). This word, which is probably a primary noun (not based on a verbal root), denotes male sex and, for this reason, is also translated "husband," thus emphasizing the relational dimension of the human being. It carries this meaning when marriage is used as a metaphor for the union of God and Israel and the word is used to characterize God as Israel's husband (Hos 2:18; Isa 54:5). Like the word 'ādām, which is better known to most people though less frequently used in the Bible, this word also yields the meaning "humankind." Thus, it too identifies the entire species as well as the male member of that species.

A third word, 'ĕnôš, is used infrequently and then almost exclusively in postexilic poetic texts (Job 4:17a; Ps 8:4; Isa 51:12). It is probably derived from the verb meaning "to be weak" and is thus often translated "mortal." The weakness that it implies stems from the inherent limits of human nature and not from any lack of moral integrity. A counterpart of this word is geber. Derived from the verb meaning "to be strong," it suggests a kind of courage under duress and it came to imply impressive military bearing (Exod 10:11; Job 4:17b; 38:3; 40:7). There is a fifth word, mat, but it is used only occasionally and then solely in the plural.

Family Roles. Even a cursory examination of the roles that men played in ancient Israelite families reveals a well defined and firmly maintained patriarchal social system. The man or father of the house was considered its master, baal, exercising vast control over the lives and fortunes of the other members, including wives, concubines, children, and slaves. This control even extended at times to decisions regarding matters of life and death (Genesis 22). The word baal is also rendered "husband," thus indicating the nature of the control that men exercised over women within the marriage. The family itself was referred to as the father's "house" (e.g., Abraham left his father's house [Gen 12:1] and established his own [Gen 14:14]), and genealogies were traced through the father's line (Genesis 10–11). Inheritance was also usually patrilineal and the right to inheritance belonged to the sons (Deut 21:15-17). Daughters could only inherit in the absence of a male heir, and then those same daughters were required to marry within the father's tribe in order to ensure the tribal possession of the father's property (Num 27:1-11; 36:1-9).

The notion of patriarchal house was also applied to kin in a wider sense: to the clan (Judg 5:15f.); to the tribe (Num 13:2); and even to the entire nation (Isa 58:1; Jer 3:18). When a census was taken, it was done house by house (understood as clan and/or tribe), registering only the men (Num 1:1-44). Accordingly, the patriarchal structures and practices that prevailed in the family also governed society at every level.

The husband had control over the reproductive powers of his wife, since descendants, particularly male descendants, were essential for the survival of his family and his name. Polygamy and concubinage grew out of the need to ensure such descent (Gen 16:1f., 29-30). The custom of levirate (from the Latin levir, brother-in-law) was another means of safeguarding the name of a childless man, in this case a man who had died. A brother or nearest male relative of the deceased was obliged to act as surrogate husband of the widow. The child born of this union was considered the legal heir of the deceased man, assuming his name and inheriting his property (Deut 25:5-10; see also Gen 38:6-11; Ruth 4:1-12).

It was because of the nature of his relationship with the father of the household that the second most important member of the family was the son. Perpetuation of the father's name, disposition of the family property, and questions concerning descent were determined through the son. As a child, he would be under the care and control of his mother, but when he had grown and been accorded the status of an adult male, he would be in a social position superior to hers. Among the sons, the first-born enjoyed special privileges called the birthright (Gen 25:31-34). He occupied a position of honor among his brothers (Exod 6:14), had claims on the father's special blessing (Gen 27:1-4), and received a double portion of the family inheritance (Deut 21:17). Sons were carefully trained in both the religious traditions of the community and in the proper behavior for social interaction (Deut 6:20-25; Prov 1:8-15; 3:1-12; 10:1-5; 23:15-25), so that they would be prepared to take their fathers' places in leadership roles when the appropriate time came. As seen above regarding the meaning of patriarchal house, so the word son was also used within the context of extended family. It referred to a member of a clan (Num 4:41), a tribe (Num 16:10) or the nation as a whole (Ps 105:6).

Brothers also exercised a certain amount of power in the lives of their sisters. There seems to be question about the nature of the household within which Rebekah resided when the servant of Abraham went in search of a bride for Isaac. The text indicates that it is her mother's household (Gen 24:28). It is unclear whether her father was dead or this arrangement was common in polygamous unions. What is clear, however, is the role played by her brother Laban in settling the marriage arrangements (Genesis 24).

Two other narratives recount fraternal intervention in the lives of women. In each case a young woman is raped and vengeance for the violation is meted out by her brother(s) and not by her father. In the first incident, after Shechem had raped Dinah, her brothers Simeon and Levi retaliated by massacring all of the men of Shechem's city (Genesis 34). The second incident occurred within the very household of David. Tamar was assaulted by her half-brother Amnon and sought refuge with her brother Absalom

who then avenged her by having Amnon murdered (2 Sam 13:1-29). In both cases, the fathers were alive and acting patriarchs in their respective families, but it is the brothers who stepped in on their sisters' behalf.

These narratives should be read less as examples of fraternal sentiment than as illustrations of political intrigue wherein the reproductive capability of the family is at stake. It is in the brothers' interests that their sisters' sexual potential be safeguarded so that family property either remain within their jurisdiction or be allocated judiciously.

The Broader Society. Circumcision was the sign of membership in the people of God (Gen 17:10-14). It conferred upon men both social and liturgical rights and responsibilities (Exod 23:17). Women were incorporated into the community as part of the household of their respective patriarchs—first their fathers, then their brothers (if they had not married) or husbands, and finally their sons. The earliest division of labor developed quite naturally out of the demands of agricultural work and the procreation and rearing of children. (The punishments pronounced against the first couple reflect this reality, see Gen 3:16-19). The physical demands that accompanied recurring times of pregnancy, delivery, and lactation, along with the need to safeguard the new life which would perpetuate the name and property of the patriarchal family, may explain some of the relational dynamics that developed between men and women. What in all probability began as consideration for and a kind of guardianship over women during such periods of physical vulnerability developed into a presumption of innate male power and superiority and resulted in universal domination of all women by all men. Since clan and tribe are normally an extension of family, such a perspective and the structures that flow from it inspired the social patterns that are reflected in the Bible.

Men were the judges, both judicial and military. They were the priests, rulers of the monarchy, and the official prophets and sages. Indeed, the Bible does include examples of women functioning in some of these roles (Deborah the prophet and judge [Judges 4–5], Athaliah the monarch [2 Kings 11], Miriam and Huldah the prophets [Exod 15:20; 2 Kgs 22:14], and wise women [2 Sam 14:1-20; 20:14-22]). However, these women were probably either surrogates who stepped in when no qualified man was available (e.g., Athaliah) or they were exceptions to the rule, and the stories that described them and their feats most likely were included in the tradition to show that the power of God can work through even the weak members of the community.

Throughout Israel's history, municipal power and governance were in the hands of the elders of the people (Exod 3:16; Deut 27:1; 1 Sam 8:4; 2 Kgs 23:1; Ezra 6:7). These were probably adult men, perhaps the heads of prominent families, who formed a ruling council in their respective villages. At times they appear to have been officials at court, men of importance who were sometimes referred to simply as "the great ones" (Jer 5:5) or nobles (Jonah 3:7). In addition to the elders, the principal officials of the king were men who served as commander of the army, commander of the guard, royal herald, royal secretary, authorized priests or prophets, and partisan sages. The Davidic dynasty was believed to have been founded on divine promise (2 Sam 7:12-17) and, therefore, the patriarchal organization enjoyed a kind of sacred legitimation.

The Wisdom writings of Israel, which include the books of Proverbs, Job, Qoheleth, Sirach, and the Wisdom of Solomon, are described by some as anthropological rather than historical or theological. This is probably due to the fact that they concentrate on universal questions related to human welfare, values, and dignity rather than the distinctive events in Israel's history or elements of its religion. They teach that whatever benefitted humankind was a good to be pursued and whatever was injurious should be avoided and condemned. Training of any kind (e.g., within the family, the court, or in preparation for a profession) sought to impart whatever ability was needed to achieve the respective goal. Since the society was patriarchal and the perspective was androcentric, these values and pursuits were considered from a male point of view. The descriptions of the Wisdom Woman (Proverbs 8–9; Sirach 24; Wisdom 7–10), the woman of folly (Prov 6:20–7:27), as well as the worthy wife (Prov 31:10-31) were formulated from this point of view.

Religious Language. Since religious language grows out of and gives evidence of the experiences and perception of people, it is understandable that a patriarchal society with an androcentric bias would develop male images for its primary metaphors for God. Whether the God of Israel actually *was* a male deity or was so perceived because of the nation's androcentric worldview is a point of current theological debate. What cannot be denied is the preponderance in the Bible of male representations of God. God is depicted anthropomorphically in some of the roles described above. Although it is found very rarely in the First Testament, the characterization of God as father occasionally does appear in prophetic poetry (Isa 63:16; Jer 3:19). Other male images appear more frequently, thus suggesting that they were more representative of Israel's theology. Foremost among these depictions is the image of the divine warrior whose victory resulted in the orderly creation of the world (Ps 24:1-2, 8, 10) and who fought to release the people from their bondage in Egypt (Exod 15:3). God is also praised as the consummate monarch who alone rules over the heavens and the earth (an entire category of psalms attests to this representation—Pss 24; 29; 47; 93; 96–99; 149). As already mentioned, God is also seen as husband of the entire people.

See: ADAM AND EVE, FAMILY, FATHER, HUMANKIND, IMAGE OF GOD, MARRIAGE, WOMAN/WOMEN

DIANNE BERGANT, C.S.A.

Pastoral-Liturgical Tradition

As a word used in the social sciences, man refers to a subset of biological males who have achieved the status of manhood. Many contemporary anthropologists, sociologists, social-psychologists, and pastoral theologians understand manhood as a socially constructed, earned psychosocial reality. While maleness is a biological given, manhood is earned by those boys who (1) pass a series of culturally mandated tests and who (2) make a contribution to the general welfare of the society.

Cross-cultural studies reveal several common themes in the earning of manhood. First, a boy must meet and courageously respond to a variety of challenges in order to earn the status of manhood. Boys must be willing to compete with others and with life itself in a fearless and confident manner in order to earn manhood. Boys are protected from life; men confront it. Men take risks. They defy failure, even death. A man must be courageous and strong in facing the challenges that life in the given society offers. Failure to pass the culturally mandated test—failure as a hunter in some societies or as a farmer in others, failure as an athlete, a student, or in facing the neighborhood bully—leaves the boy a male, but less than a man in the eyes of the society and, usually, in his own eyes as well. While victory over opposition is not always required, courageous struggle is.

Potential for violence is a closely related characteristic of manhood noted by anthropologists. While a man does not need to actually engage in physical violence, the threat of violence in the defense of one's family, property, or social group is a common characteristic of manhood.

In addition to personal competence, courage, and strength, a boy earns manhood by being productive for the wider society. Society demands that true men contribute to the common good. Selfishness is a disvalue. As a minimum, man must provide the basic necessities of life for his family and himself. After this, respected men contribute something to the common welfare. They lead, nourish, and protect the broader society. Even in capitalistic societies, the fullness of manhood includes philanthropy.

Sexual virility and self-control is a part of one's social responsibility and an essential test in the earning and maintenance of manhood. While the good ordering of society forbids sexual excess—rape or adultery in its many different understandings are forbidden—sexual competence is important. Men are those males who are successful in sexual matters. The actual fathering of children is not an absolute requirement in order to enjoy manhood status, but most societies link the attainment of manhood to success in sexual relations with women. For the Roman Catholic Church clergy of the Latin Rite, biological fathering is replaced with spiritual fathering and leadership. In some cultures the manhood and the celibacy of these clergymen remain problematic.

Two other characteristics of manhood are briefly noted: boys are frequently forced to become men and the social status of "manhood" is tenuous—it is easily lost in either the public eye or in the eyes of the man himself.

Since childhood/boyhood is a relatively easy life, many boys prefer to remain boys and some men seek a second boyhood. In traditional societies, boys are often kidnapped by the man and subjected to ritual initiation. In Western societies it is not uncommon for boys and some men to be forced to confront studies, work, and adult responsibilities. Moreover, manhood, even when attained, is tenuous. The loss of a job, loss of sexual potency, sterility, aging and the loss of strength, and retirement threaten the status and self-confidence of many Western males.

Some Christian and much of feminist thought criticizes the construction of manhood outlined above. Objecting to a perceived emphasis on achievement, independence to the point of disconnectedness, control and domination of others and the environment, and limited emotional and spiritual responsiveness, feminist critics call upon males to develop the skills of interdependence, mutuality, and cooperation, as well as the cultivation of a wider range of emotional responsiveness, gentleness, and tenderness. The new man, a man appropriate for contemporary society, is said to be communicative and egalitarian, interpersonal and socially responsible. Abandoning a spirituality said to be based on obedience to law and the attainment of reward, the modern man is called upon to develop a new life vision and interior life based on the mystery and wonder of creation.

In reaction to this "feminizing of the Western male," another movement attempts to construct manhood in a third fashion. For these critics, manhood is defined not in terms of achievement, strength, and virility, or in terms of cooperation and communication, but in the integration of "masculine" and "feminine" characteristics. Traditional masculine virtues of strength, courage, competence, sexual prowess, and individuality are to be developed, but gentleness, tenderness, mutuality, receptivity, wonder, and aesthetic appreciation are also characteristic of the fully developed man. Those males without these later personal characteristics are considered less than fully men. The men's liberation movement urges Western men to move beyond the anemic manhood of contemporary society and the feminized manhood of the women's liberation movement to discover the "deep male" that abides in the depths of the male soul.

These thinkers postulate a uniquely male way of being in the world. From a deep well of male energy, men are to create, destroy, and recreate their culture, bond with and care for their loved ones, and be in communion with the God who creates and hallows the cosmos.

Like the feminist critique, the contemporary men's movement criticizes the modern understanding and experience of Western manhood. Manhood has become domineering, isolated, disconnected, and emotionally, morally, and spiritually bankrupt. Since the rise of capitalism and the Industrial Revolution, men have left their natural lives—hunting, planting and harvesting, working, mentoring and storytelling, and celebrating with other men in cross-generational settings—to live the life of urban factories and offices. Human relationships have withered, work has become meaningless, and men's interior lives have become grossly underdeveloped. Consequently, men are a mess. Their life span is about seven years shorter than women's and an essential quality of those lives is quiet desperation.

The solution to men's dilemma, according to these theorists, is discovery of manhood in multi-generational and multi-ethnic groups. A return to male bonding and mentoring and the honoring of other men is required. A renewed connection to the natural world is another characteristic of the men's movement. Awareness of one's own body and the body of others is important, as is appreciation and respect for the environment. While flight from modern economic and social realities is not demanded, a renewed understanding of work and the cultivation of new forms of relationships with men, women, and God are characteristic of the movement. Among the virtues of the new manhood are wonder, empathy, heartful thinking, enjoyment, friendship, husbanding and fathering, communion, moral outrage, and "wildness" or passion.

The pastor trying to make sense of manhood in the contemporary Church must steer a critical middle ground. The gospel calls us beyond all social forms and every contemporary movement. Many of the critiques of the cultural ideal of manhood are also biblical critiques. God is the master of creation, not males. The human family was given Eden for cultivation and care, not for exploitation. Harmonious relationships between men and women are modeled by Jesus and the women of the NT. And the commandment to honor one's father and mother is not revoked in the New Law. The full range of human/male passions can and should be understood, embraced, and integrated into Christian spirituality. Jesus and Paul are outstanding examples of male "wildness" put in service of the reign of God.

On the other hand, some feminist ideas and some of the ideas of men's liberation can be interpreted in ways contrary to the gospel and sacred Tradition. A return to nature can ignore the reality of sin in the world. The Noble Savage is a literary ideal whose practical reality is non-existent. A return to an idealized time of manly innocence is just that: an idealized time and innocence. Egalitarianism can overlook rightful differences, inexperience, education, and responsibility. Moreover, to the degree that feminism and the men's movement are simply white, middle-class reactions to contemporary Western society, they lose their catholicity. Conversion of heart and human cooperation in the establishment of the reign of God involve more than the personal enrichment of an already blessed elite. Pastoral leadership in the Christian community requires a careful discernment of the various voices that would shape the contemporary vision of manhood.

See: HUMANKIND, SEXUALITY, WOMAN/WOMEN

JAMES R. HALSTEAD, O.S.A.

MANNA

Manna is the honeylike dropping from the tamarisk tree of Sinai and Palestine. The Bible has expanded this rather limited food to make it the regular diet of all Israel during the sojourn in the desert (see Deut 8:3, 16).

Old Testament

Exodus 16:1-36. The principal author of this passage elaborates a certain "spiritual" aspect of the manna. Whether one gathers a small amount or a large amount, there is just enough. Manna kept over for the next day automatically becomes wormy and rotten (Exod 16:17-21). On the sixth day one is permitted to gather twice as much in order to observe the Sabbath rest (Exod 16:22-27). The people are to preserve some of the manna to show later generations and an amount is to be preserved in the ark of the covenant (Exod 16:32-33). This tradition originally underlined the concern of Yahweh for the people in the desert.* "In the morning you shall have your fill of bread, so that you may know that I, the LORD, am your God" (Exod 16:12).

Wisdom 16:16-29. In this passage the first-century BCE Book of Wisdom speaks of a plague of rains that punishes the Egyptians during the Exodus and of fire (thunderbolts) that devastates their crops. By contrast the Israelites enjoyed the manna that resisted the fire and did not melt. The author thus teaches that God works in and through creation for good or for ill.

The author describes the manna as "food of angels and . . . bread from heaven, ready to hand, untoiled-for, endowed with all delights and conforming to every taste" (Wis 16:20; Ps 78:24 calls the manna "heavenly bread" and Ps 105:40, "bread from heaven"). This food reveals God's sweetness to the Israelites and assures every imaginable flavor (Wis 16:21). Although similar to hoarfrost and ice, the manna is not melted by the fire (Wis 16:22; see Exod 16:23).

New Testament

John 6:22-58. In this section of John that builds on the multiplication of loaves and fish (John 6:1-15), the crowd wants Jesus to perform some new sign like the manna in the desert. Jesus responds that his Father gave the Israelites the manna, not Moses (John 6:32). Indeed, the real heavenly bread is Jesus himself. After presenting himself as "the bread of life," Jesus reveals the difference between the manna and himself. The crowd's ancestors ate the manna and died but "this is the bread that comes down from heaven so that one may eat it and not die" (John 6:50; see also 6:58). Later Jewish writings suggest that in the eschatological age the manna would reappear.

Pastoral-Liturgical Tradition

Lectionary. On the eighteenth Sunday in Ordinary Time (cycle B) the liturgy uses Exodus 16:2-4, 12-15 and connects it thematically with the Gospel, viz., John 6:24-35. On the Feast of Corpus Christi (cycle A) the liturgy uses Deuteronomy 8:2-3, 14-16 (God's providing in the desert, especially the manna) and links it thematically with the Gospel, viz., John 6:51-58. In both instances the liturgy sees both a link between God's providential care for the desert community and the Eucharist and a difference, viz., the Eucharist surpasses the manna.

Eucharist and Communal Responsibility. Building upon God's providing of food for the desert community, one may legitimately view the Eucharist as a relentless call to communal action. To share the bread is to be like a God who meets the concrete needs of a hungry people, e.g., in the manna tradition. Eucharist is calculated to thrust the believing community into the real situations where bread, whether literal or figurative, is wanting. To that extent Eucharist forces the body of Christ to search modern desert communities, communities that yearn for food in whatever form.

See: ARK OF THE COVENANT, BREAD, DESERT, EUCHARIST, EXODUS, SIGN

JOHN F. CRAGHAN

MARANATHA

The word *maranatha* is found in the NT only once: in Paul's greeting at the end of 1 Corinthians (16:22). It is also found at the conclusion of a thanksgiving prayer prescribed for the community meal in the Didache (10:6). In Paul's closing greeting to the Corinthians he directs the community to greet one another with a holy kiss (v. 20), and then admonishes, "If anyone does not love the Lord, let him be accursed. *Maranatha*" (1 Cor 16:22). One is surprised to find an untranslated Aramaic phrase in a Greek letter to a Greek church. There are, however, other instances in which Aramaic words appear in the NT: *Abba* (Gal 4:6; Rom 8:15; Mark 14:36), *Alleluia* (Rev 17:1, 3, 6), *Amen* (2 Cor 1:20), and *Hosanna* (Matt 21:9; Mark 11:9-10; John 12:13).

Evidently the meaning of *maranatha* was familiar to Paul's Corinthian audience.

Linguistic analysis offers three possible meanings for the Aramaic phrase, depending on whether it is read *marána tha*, "Our Lord, come," or *marán athá*, "Our Lord has come." The former is a prayer for Christ's second coming. The latter can be understood either as a credal confession of Christ's having come into the world or as an acclamation of his coming in the Eucharistic celebration. Most recent scholars, because of an Enochic text that has come to light from Qumran Cave 4, have favored the imperative "Our Lord, come." *Maranatha* was evidently a liturgical invocation that originated in a Palestinian context. The expression *maranatha* then made its way into Hellenistic churches that proclaimed "the death of the Lord until he comes" (1 Cor 11:26).

In 1 Corinthians 16:22 the admonition to love lest one be *anathema*, juxtaposed with the acclamation *maranatha*, reminds the community that love is the gauge for authentic discipleship while awaiting the parousia. The Eucharistic meal, as an anticipation of the parousia, may have been the occasion for pronouncing accursed anyone who does not love the Lord.

Some scholars conclude that the end of the Book of Revelation likewise reflects the Eucharistic liturgy with its structure of curse, *maranatha*, and concluding benediction. "Amen! Come, Lord Jesus" (Rev 22:20) seems to be a direct translation of *maranatha*. A similar context in Didache 10:6 suggests a warning against participation by the unholy in the Eucharist.

Pastoral-Liturgical Tradition

The prayerful cry *maranatha* is similar to the Christian prayer, "Thy Kingdom come." However there seems to be a rather subtle change from the common Jewish expectation of the full manifestation on earth of the reign of God to the personal return of Jesus in judgment. It is remarkable that early on Christians referred to Jesus as "Lord" (*mārê'* in Aramaic), the title used of Yahweh, and also attributed to him the saving acts of God.

As Paul uses it, *maranatha* is clearly an acclamation of the Lord's coming. However, in later tradition, from the fourth century onward, this original meaning was lost and *maranatha* was used in formulas of excommunication or cursing.

See: BLESSING, CURSE, DAY OF THE LORD, EUCHARIST, MEAL, PAROUSIA, REIGN OF GOD

SEAN P. KEALY, C.S.SP.

MARRIAGE

A fundamental institution such as marriage was inevitably entwined with the evolving culture, history, and theological expressions of the biblical peoples.

Old Testament

Genesis 2:24. This text, that a "man leaves his father and mother and cleaves to his wife, and they become one flesh," has been traditionally associated with marriage, and is often quoted in Christian contexts as the origin of the sacrament of marriage. It should be noted that usually it is the woman who leaves father and mother to cleave to her husband. Fathers give daughters to approved husbands (e.g., Exod 2:21; Josh 15:16-17) and often, if not always, the exchange involves "a marriage price" (e.g., Exod 22:16; Deut 22:29; Josh 15:18-19).

The Importance of a Future Wife's Family. A man's choice of woman for a wife was significant. Thus, Abraham is concerned lest his son Isaac marry outside the family. He sends a servant to secure a wife for Isaac from among his own relatives (Gen 24:4). Likewise, Rebekah persuades Isaac to be concerned lest their son Jacob marry outside the family (Gen 27:46); Isaac sends Jacob to his mother's family to secure for himself a wife (Gen 28:1-2). These texts, when combined with Numbers 12:1 (Aaron and Miriam reprimand Moses for taking a Cushite woman as a wife), suggest that at a particular time there was a strong prohibition in Israel against marriage to foreign women.

Foreign women were associated with idolatry. Marriage to foreigners in general was problematic (Josh 23:12-13), but marriage to foreign women was especially prohibited. Foreign women were more likely to be taken alive as spoils of war than were their male counterparts. If they continued to worship the gods and goddesses of their respective peoples, then their children, children of Israelite fathers who should grow up to believe in "the God who brought us out of Egypt," would grow up believing in the gods and goddesses whom their mothers worshiped. Many of these deities were fertility figures, and in a not-so-fertile land where people desperately needed successful harvests to survive, the temptation was strong to worship them. Prohibiting marriage to foreign women was one effort, though probably not a very successful one, to curb idolatry (e.g., 1 Kgs 11:1-8).

The effort was not totally successful, for several of the ancient Israelites are cited as taking foreign wives and the text does not judge them as evil for having done so. God does not reprimand Moses for having taken a Cushite wife (Numbers 12); David is not reprimanded for taking foreign wives (e.g., Was Bathsheba a Hittite? 2 Sam 11:3); Solomon is not reprimanded for his Egyptian wife (1 Kgs 3:1). At certain periods in Israel's history more attention was paid to marriage within the group than at other times. Also, different attitudes toward foreign women were held contemporaneously by different people. Marriage to certain foreign women was tolerated, for example, marriages which were intended to strengthen political alliances (e.g., 1 Kgs 3:1; see 1 Kgs 11:19).

Levirite Marriage. If a man died without having begotten a son, the dead man's brother was supposed to take as his wife his dead brother's widow. The first child born of that union was to succeed to the name of the dead husband to prevent that man's name from being blotted out in Israel. If the brother did not wish to take his dead brother's widow as a wife, the widow was to go to the elders at the city gates and describe her situation, in which case the elders would talk to the brother of the dead man. If the man was still unwilling to take his dead brother's widow to raise up a son for his dead brother, then the widow, in front of the elders, was to pull off the sandal of her dead husband's brother, and spit in his face. His house would henceforth be known in Israel as "the house of him that had his sandal pulled off" (Deut 25:5-10).

The law suggests the appropriateness of marriage within the family—for the woman, the same family to which she had come to belong in marriage—but even more importantly, it suggests the significance of a man becoming a father. If such had not been accomplished during his married life, provision was made so that it could be accomplished after his death. In the Book of Ruth, Ruth's husband died without having begotten a son; Boaz performs the duty of "the next of kin," marries Ruth, and they have children.

Other Marriage Laws. The marriage laws contained in the OT legal material are intended to protect certain persons, either because of their vulnerable or their venerable status. For example, certain laws provided for a woman's continued material support by guaranteeing that a man either had to marry her, or that he could not divorce her all her days. A man was expected to marry a not-yet-betrothed virgin whom he had raped and he was not permitted to divorce her (Deut 22:29). A husband who had falsely accused his wife of shameful conduct was prohibited from ever divorcing her all her days (Deut 22:13-19). A man could not take for himself his father's wife (Deut 23:1). A man could not remarry a woman whom he had divorced if, in the interim of their separation, she had been married to another man (Deut 24:1-4). A newly married man was excused from military obligations and business responsibilities (Deut 24:5). Priests had certain restrictions placed on whom they could marry; they were to marry virgins of their own people, not divorcees or defiled women or harlots (e.g., Lev 21:13-15). Although it was legal for a husband to divorce his wife (Deut 24:1), the Book of Malachi encourages husbands to be faithful to the wives of their youth (2:14-16).

Widows. Because Israel's was a patriarchal society and property passed from father to son, a woman who had been given by her father to a husband and whose husband had subsequently died was relatively powerless within the society. Unless it was possible for her to return to her father's house, she was dependent on her sons, and if her sons were too young, on the generosity of the Israelite king and people. The Elijah-Elisha material contains many narratives which detail acts of divine power accomplished through a prophet for the well-being of widows (e.g., 1 Kgs 17:7-24; 2 Kgs 4:1-7). The Prophetic writings often admonish Israel to defend the widow (e.g., Isa 1:17; Jer 7:6; 22:3) and they denounce disregard for widows on the part of leadership and/or people (e.g., Isa 1:23; 10:2; Ezek 22:7; Mal 3:5). In the Book of Lamentations Judah is compared to a widow who is separated from her husband, Yahweh, and whose children have been taken from her into exile (cf. Isa 50:1; Jer 3:8).

Song of Solomon. Many biblical scholars identify the original settings of this book's literary units as wedding celebrations. Though the lovers are explicitly identified neither as newlyweds nor as wife and husband, and though some recent feminist scholarship has challenged that assumption, traditional interpretation has accorded them this relationship. The couple are presented as interdependent, each responding to the other with desire and longing. Theirs is a mutual love.

See: FAMILY, FATHER, MOTHER

ALICE L. LAFFEY

New Testament

Jewish Background. The case of Mary and Joseph in Matthew 1:18-25 provides an entry into Jewish marriage customs in the first century. The marriage was usually arranged through the elders in the two families. The parties to be married were generally young by today's Western standards. In rabbinic times the minimum ages were thirteen for the male and twelve for the female. It was customary to marry within tribes or families, but outside the forbidden degrees of kinship (Leviticus 18).

The engagement took place at the home of the bride's father, where she stayed after the betrothal ceremony. At the betrothal ceremony the husband presented the wife (and her father) with the marriage contract and the bride-price. Engagement was understood to have legal consequences (see Deut 20:7; 22:23-27). One or even several years might separate the engagement ceremony from the marriage ceremony. When reading Matthew 1:18-25 we are to imagine that the betrothal ceremony between Joseph and Mary had taken place and that they were awaiting the marriage ceremony. Mary remains at her parents' home, and Joseph visits from time to time.

On discovering that Mary was pregnant before the actual marriage ceremony, Joseph had to choose between making a public example of Mary in accordance with Deuteronomy 22:23-27 or simply going through the private divorce procedure outlined in Deuteronomy 24:1. According to Matthew 1:19 Joseph planned to give Mary the written notice signed by two witnesses that he had divorced her and she was free to marry someone else.

Jews in Jesus' time understood marriage more in terms of a civil contract than as a religious ritual or a sacrament. The marriage ceremony consisted in the transfer of the bride from her father's home to that of her husband or her husband's father. A vivid picture of this transfer appears in the parable of the ten virgins in Matthew 25:1-13 in which the young women go out from the groom's house to meet the groom and his new bride as they come toward the groom's house. The bride's arrival at her new home was marked by several days of festivities. The story of the wedding feast at Cana in John 2:1-11 illustrates this custom and serves as the occasion for Jesus' first public "sign" in the Fourth Gospel.

Jesus' Teaching. Jesus' teaching about marriage occurs in the context of a debate with the Pharisees about the legality of divorce in Mark 10:1-12. While acknowledging that divorce is lawful since Moses in Deuteronomy 24:1 permitted it, Jesus contends that this law was simply a concession to human weakness ("because of the hardness of your hearts," 10:5). He argues then on the basis of Genesis 1:27 ("God made them male and female") and 2:24 ("the two shall become one flesh") that God's original intention in creation was "no divorce." The positive thrust of this teaching is that the man and woman constitute "one flesh" and therefore their union cannot be dissolved.

The negative side of Jesus' teaching is the absolute prohibition of divorce: "Whoever divorces his wife and marries another commits adultery against her" (Mark 10:11). Likewise, a wife who divorces her husband commits adultery (Mark 10:12). The source Q contains a variant form of this prohibition (Luke 16:18; Matt 5:32), but the conclusion remains the same: Divorce and remarriage constitute adultery.

Jesus' teachings about marriage ("one flesh") and divorce (= adultery) were radical in his own day. The debate among Jews of the time concerned the ground for divorce, not the possibility of divorce. The debate concerned the interpretation of the enigmatic phrase 'erwat dabar ("something indecent") in Deuteronomy 24:1: Is the proper ground for divorce the woman's sexual misconduct (Shammai) or something more general (Hillel)? Matthew 19:1-9, which is a rewriting of Mark 10:1-12, stands within this Jewish debate by virtue of the Pharisees' question to Jesus: "Is it lawful for a man to divorce his wife for any cause whatever?" (19:3). Jesus' answer is basically that of Mark 10:11: "whoever divorces his wife . . . and marries another commits adultery" (Matt 19:9). But Matthew 19:9 (and 5:32) introduces an exception *me epi porneia* (and *parektos logou porneias* in 5:32). The interpretation of these phrases is much debated. Some take them as referring to marriages within the degrees of kinship forbidden by Leviticus 18 (see Acts 15:20, 29). Others view them as siding with Shammai that the only basis for divorce is sexual misconduct on the woman's part.

Paul. It is rare for Paul to appeal directly to Jesus' teaching. But with regard to marriage and divorce he does so in 1 Corinthians 7:10-11: "A wife should not separate from her husband—and if she does separate she must either remain single or become reconciled to her husband—and a husband should not divorce his wife." Yet Paul, like Matthew, allows an exception to this general rule. The exception (the so-called Pauline privilege) concerns the case of a Christian whose unbelieving spouse wishes to separate: "The brother or sister is not bound in such cases" (1 Cor 7:15).

In the rest of his reflections on marriage and related topics Paul assumes that most Christians will marry. He rejects the Corinthian slogan "It is a good thing for a man not to touch a woman" (1 Cor 7:1) and insists on the mutual responsibilities that spouses have (7:3-4). Though Paul regards celibacy as superior to the married state (7:8, 32, 38), he nonetheless considers marriage also to be good and indeed necessary for many. He urges married converts to stay as they are (7:27) but does not forbid unmarried Christians from getting married (7:28). His major misgiving seems to be the anxiety (7:28) and afflictions (7:32-34) that marriage entails and the consequent distraction from the concerns of the Lord (7:35). But he insists that marriage is no sin (7:36) and allows widows to remarry (7:39).

Paul's ambivalent instructions about marriage should be read in their context. In 1 Corinthians 7 he was responding to attitudes and aberrations that had grown up among the Corinthian Christians, and was cutting a path between the excesses of puritanism ("It is a good thing for a man not to touch a woman") and libertinism ("everything is lawful," 10:23). Moreover, Paul had a strong sense of living in a time of transition before God's reign would come in fullness: "the time is running out . . . the world in its present form is passing away" (7:29, 31). Paul was responding to the Corinthians' problems, not writing a treatise on marriage. He wrote out of the conviction that the present age was passing away and looked forward to a time when "they neither marry nor are they given in marriage" (Mark 12:25).

Household Codes. The basic social stance of the "household codes" (Col 3:18–4:1; Eph 5:22–6:9; 1 Pet 2:18–3:7) is conservative. They accept the social institutions of marriage, family, and slavery as "givens" and seek to guide Christians on how to behave within this social framework. They embody ideas and assumptions that were current in Hellenistic philosophy (especially Stoicism)—attitudes that had equivalents among Palestinian and Diaspora Jews.

In Colossians 3:18-19 wives are urged to be subordinate to their husbands and husbands are told to love their wives. This advice is expanded in Ephesians 5:21-32 into a teaching on the relationship between Christ and the Church. Both texts stress that the relationship between husband and wife is "in the Lord" and that it demands mutual responsibility. In 1 Peter 3:1-6 wives are urged to be subordinate to their husbands as part of their duty to give good example as Christians. The simplicity and modesty of their lifestyle will win over their non-Christian husbands. Likewise in 1 Peter 3:7 husbands are exhorted to live in understanding with their wives and to remember that "we are joint heirs of the gift of life" (3:7). All social institutions are relativized to some extent by the reality of Christ, the source of "life" in his resurrection.

Symbolic Uses. At several points in the NT marriage imagery serves to teach about spiritual realities. In the parable of the ten virgins (Matt 25:1-13) the need to be always on guard for the (second) coming of the Son of Man is expressed by those women who were unprepared for the bridegroom's return home. The reason why Jesus' disciples do not fast during his earthly ministry is explained as a consequence of Jesus' presence as the bridegroom (Mark 2:19-20). The intimacy between Christ and the Church is spelled out in terms of the husband-wife relationship in Ephesians 5:21-32. And in Revelation 19 the fullness of God's reign is described as the "wedding day of the Lamb" (19:7) and the "wedding feast of the Lamb" (19:9).

Challenges and Questions. There is no treatise on marriage in the NT. Most of its teaching on the topic is indirect, made in connection with some other issue or topic or as part of a larger debate. Nevertheless, the radical character of Jesus' teaching about marriage making man and woman "one flesh" (Mark 10:8) is clear. From this principle derives the prohibition against divorce: "what God has joined together, no human being must separate" (Mark 10:9). With these teachings Jesus not only challenged the assumptions of his Jewish and Gentile contemporaries but also a permission granted by Deuteronomy 24:1.

Yet Jesus' emphasis on the absolute indissolubility of marriage raises many questions—matters that have been taken up throughout Christian history and remain controversial today. How is Jesus' prohibition of divorce to be interpreted—as an ideal to be sought, or as a law to be observed? How is Jesus' teaching best made effective—by leaving it as an ideal, or enshrining it in ecclesiastical and/or civil law? How are the "exceptions" to be taken (see Matt 5:32; 19:9; 1 Cor 7:15)—as concessions due to "hardness of heart," or as a genuine part of the biblical teaching on a par with Jesus' teaching about indissolubility?

Another set of questions concerns the cultural assumptions underlying the NT marriage texts. In the Palestinian Jewish context the wife appears as something like property or chattel. In the household codes the wife is assumed to be subordinate to the husband. Part of Paul's ambivalence about marriage stems from his conviction

that the present world is passing away. How is the NT teaching on marriage to be applied in cultural settings where these assumptions do not hold? How closely is this teaching bound to first-century Mediterranean society?

Though Ephesians 5:32 uses the word "mystery" with regard to marriage, it hardly calls marriage a "sacrament" in the theological sense in which that term developed in Patristic times. How did Catholics come to look upon marriage as a sacrament?

DANIEL J. HARRINGTON, S.J.

Pastoral-Liturgical Tradition

The Tradition's Understanding of Marriage. The Church's understanding of marriage has developed as a pastoral response to particular theological and cultural challenges. The early development of the Church's understanding of marriage was the result of attacks on the institution originating from Gnosticism and Manichaeism. These schools of thought held that marriage was evil because it was part of the material sector of the universe, which itself was evil. Paradoxically, some Gnostic sects also held that sexual intercourse was a value in itself and should be freed from its material element, which was procreation. The orthodox response was both to acknowledge marriage as a good and also to acknowledge a necessary link between sexual intercourse and procreation. God's command to "fill the earth" (Gen 1:28) was a central argument demonstrating that marriage had a purpose beyond itself, that of populating the world. Similarly, in defending this orthodox position, the Church increasingly depended upon Stoic and neo-Platonic philosophy to explain that the sole purpose of intercourse was that of producing offspring.

The most developed theology of marriage in the Western Church at this time was that of St. Augustine. In this theology, he combined biblical reflection, especially on Genesis and 1 Corinthians 7, with the thought of his neo-Platonic and Stoic Christian predecessors. Augustine maintained that all functions and faculties of the person must be ordered under the control of reason. To use the sexual faculties for any purpose other than procreation was immoderation. Nevertheless, marriage itself is *good*, both because it was created by God and because within marriage there exist three other goods. The good of offspring includes not only the begetting of children but also their proper nurture. The good that is fidelity is both a general attitude and, more particularly, the exclusive commitment of each spouse to those sexual acts apt for procreation. The good that is sacrament designates the permanence of the marriage commitment and unbreakable character of the marital bond.

In the generations after the migrations of the Germanic peoples into the Roman Empire, conflicts arose between conceptions of marriage common among these tribes and Roman understandings. Not only did the Church assume increasing jurisdiction in the area of marriage, but theologians and canonists were called upon to define the nature of marriage and to explain what constituted a marriage as such. By the thirteenth century, it was generally understood that marriage was to be understood as a natural institution defined by its purposes: on the one hand, the procreation and nurturing of children, something impossible without the stable union of mother* and father,* and on the other hand the mutual help which the spouses need for such nurturing. That which creates a marriage is the consent of the spouses consummated in first intercourse. Thomas Aquinas suggested that this mutual consent exhibits the *contractual* nature of marriage.

By the time of the Council of Trent, these notions formed an essential part of the Church's theology of marriage. The Catechism of the Council of Trent, for example, defines marriage as "the conjugal and legitimate union of man and woman, which is to last during life. . . . The original institution of marriage, as a natural contract, had for object the propagation of the human race." It further emphasizes that "the marriage contract is not a mere promise, but a trans-

fer of right, by which the man yields dominion of his person to the woman, the woman the dominion of her person to the man." It is this contractual understanding that forms the basis of the understanding of marriage in the 1917 Code of Canon Law, which adds that "the primary end of marriage is the procreation and nurture of children; its secondary end is mutual help and the remedying of concupiscence" (canon 1013).

Sacramentality of Marriage. In the early Church there was little concern for the sacramental nature of marriage, though several Church Fathers, following 1 Corinthians 7, did acknowledge that marriage itself could be a way of holiness. Tertullian spoke of marriage as a *sacramentum*, but for him this meant that the promise between husband and wife was an image or a prefiguring of the relation between Christ and the Church. It was Augustine's investigation into the nature of this *sacramentum* that lay the groundwork for the traditional understanding of the sacramentality of marriage. One of the three goods of marriage was the good of the sacrament. Although Augustine never systematically articulated his meaning, he demonstrated on several occasions that it referred to the nature of the marital union which rendered it indestructible. This indestructibility of the marriage union made it the great sacrament of the union of Christ and the Church (Ephesians 5). Centuries later, theologians would try to work this into a coherent teaching on the sacramentality of marriage.

In the early Middle Ages, marriage came to be accepted among the Church's seven sacraments. Returning again to Ephesians 5:21-23, theologians acknowledged the marital relationship between husband and wife as a sacred sign of the relationship between Christ and the Church. Marriage was a sign of a sacred reality and a means of grace for the spouses. This acknowledgement of marriage as a sacrament, however, led to other questions that defined the work of theologians in the high Middle Ages: the matter and form of this sacrament, its institution, its minister(s), how grace co-exists with the fact that in part marriage depends upon the act of sexual intercourse.

The Reformers rejected this understanding of the sacramentality of marriage. Both Luther and Calvin maintained that there was no record in the NT that Jesus instituted marriage as a sacrament; that it does not grace the spouses; nor was it a divinely instituted sign. In its decree, *Tametsi*, the Council of Trent merely reaffirmed the sacramentality of marriage, its institution by God in the garden of Eden, and its confirmation by Christ in his words "Therefore what God has joined together, no human being must separate" (Matt 19:6). They concluded that Christ merited the grace which confirms the natural love of husband and wife, thus making it a sacrament. Later generations of theologians would be called upon to show more convincingly that marriage is a grace-conferring sacrament.

Early in the twentieth century, theologians began to challenge an overly juridical understanding of marriage and began to describe it in more personalist and biblical terms, showing a positive understanding of marital love within the sacrament. Heribert Doms, for example, began his theology of marriage with a description of the sexual nature of human beings. In themselves, both male and female are incomplete. Only in the mutual giving of each to the other can they find their completion. This desire for union arises from the depths of the person and enables each spouse to become gift to the other in a marital union which completes both. This goal of complete union is a task which lasts a lifetime. Thus the purpose of intercourse within a marriage is to realize this union in which each spouse gives to the other and receives from the other. This union in turn is directed to the mutual fulfillment of the spouses and the begetting of children. The work of Edward Schillebeeckx in sacramental theology also emphasized the mutual love of husband and wife. Spousal love, linked to love of Christ, is sacramental. As God's love for humanity through Christ is covenantal, so too the love of spouses is covenantal.

The Second Vatican Council. Although the work of theologians such as Doms and Schillebeeckx was not accepted at first by those in authority in the Church, it became the basis for a debate which continued for decades and found fruition in the Second Vatican Council. The "Pastoral Constitution on the Church in the Modern World" devoted a single chapter to marriage, but in light of what has been said above, what it does say is significant in that it accepts in principle the personalist and biblical understanding put forth by theologians such as Doms.

The Constitution actually outlines a spirituality of marriage, describing it as a community of love (47), a sharing in life and love (48), and a vocation (49). The Council returns to the biblical notion of covenant in describing marriage and claims that the kind of act which creates a marriage is personal, self-giving consent which pervades the entire life of the spouses. It replaces the contractual language of the rights over one's body with a more spiritual language, reminiscent of Doms, of giving and receiving of self. Lacking from the Constitution is the language of procreation as the primary end of marriage. In its place is an acknowledgment that the very nature of marital love is oriented toward and fulfilled in children.

Since the time of the Vatican Council, theologians and Church leaders have debated the meaning of these paragraphs and their relation to the tradition which had gone before. Older questions have reoccurred, such as what constitutes a sacramental marriage or whether divorce can ever be acceptable. Acknowledging the fact that the mutual bestowal and receiving of the entire self seems more like a goal than something accomplished at a wedding or first intercourse, some theologians have begun to suggest a theory of *gradualness*, the notion that marriages only gradually become sacramental and therefore indissoluble. In response to these and other concerns, Pope John Paul II issued his Apostolic Exhortation on the Family, in which he both reiterated the personalist notions of Vatican II and defended the sacramentality and indissolubility of all marriages among Christians.

Liturgical Developments. Marriage in ancient Rome consisted of four elements: (1) the will to be married, (2) manifested by some reciprocal consent that could be verified, (3) the taking of the wife into the home of the husband, and (4) cohabitation. To these basic elements, other ceremonies could be added, such as the consulting of auguries, sacrifices at particular shrines, or an offering to the household god. When Christians married, they kept the major elements, adding invocations to God or to Christ and a blessing bestowed by the parents, similar to the Jewish model described in the Book of Tobit. If a bishop or presbyter was present for the wedding ceremony, he might be asked to bestow the blessing. This, however, was not seen as an act of ecclesiastical authority.

By the time of Pope Damasus (366–384), a truly liturgical celebration of first marriages had developed. Constitutive to these liturgies was the blessing by the priest, often accompanied by his veiling of the bride and groom. By the beginning of the fifth century, these ceremonies took place in the church building, though marriages were still governed by familial custom and under the jurisdiction of the state.

It was not until the end of the first millennium that marriages came under the jurisdiction of the Church. By the Middle Ages, the formal liturgical ceremony began at the entrance of the church building with the priest asking the bride and groom to state their consent. The parents of the bride then handed their daughter to the groom and the dowry was given, followed by the giving of the ring and the blessing of the couple by the priest. The wedding party then entered the church and celebrated the nuptial Mass. The priest then gave the couple a second blessing and exchanged the kiss of peace. This was frequently followed by the blessing of the wedding chamber.

Because of the growing incidence of clandestine marriages, the Council of Trent introduced the law that for validity marriages must be celebrated according to the proper ecclesiastical form, that is, in the presence of a priest and at least two witnesses. Thus it established the basic form of celebrating the sacrament which has survived to the present.

See: FAMILY, SACRAMENT

THOMAS NAIRN

MARY, MOTHER OF JESUS

Given the large role that Mary has played in Christian devotional life, particularly for Roman Catholics, it is surprising how little there is about her in the Scriptures. The Gospels focus on Jesus and his ministry, and where Mary appears, it is in a secondary role. Nonetheless, believers have seen in Mary, particularly as portrayed by Luke, the model of one who responds perfectly to God's will. Some OT texts can also be seen to point forward to her. Vatican Council II has reemphasized the place of Mary at the center of the Church, as seen in Acts of the Apostles.

New Testament

The primary NT source of information about Mary, mother of Jesus, is Luke 1–2. Other sources are Matthew 1–2, as well as short but significant references in Mark and John.

Luke 1–2. The first chapter of Luke's Gospel describes two annunciations, first for John the Baptist and then for Jesus, followed by the visitation of Mary to Elizabeth, the *Magnificat,* the birth of the Baptist, and Zachary's *Benedictus.* Chapter 2 describes the birth of Jesus, the reaction of the shepherds, the circumcision, and the presentation in the Temple, followed by the return to Nazareth and, finally, a separate story about the boy Jesus in the Temple.

In this exceedingly rich and variously interpreted mosaic of stories about the infancy of Jesus, certain features may be highlighted. First of all, the central figure is clearly Jesus; all other actors, including Mary, play supporting roles. Secondly, in regard to the role of Mary, the central and most carefully developed element is the annunciation. This story declares the divine choice of Mary and announces that she will be the mother of the long-awaited Messiah. This announcement is eclipsed by the far more surprising declaration that she will be, by special divine intervention and virginal conception, the mother of "the Son of God" (1:35). After this display of divine power and love, Mary is at her finest when she responds: "Behold, I am the handmaid of the Lord. May it be done to me according to your word" (1:38).

The Gospel portrait of Mary is therefore, first and foremost, that of one who responds unconditionally to the word of God—a word that is freighted with both promise and mystery. Her response is an act of faith and establishes her as a perfect believer. All of her wonderful and well-deserved privileges, including her choice as mother of God, derive from her obedience to God's word. In sum, she is the model Christian disciple.

The *Magnificat* celebrates this exemplary faith. It expresses a sense of wonder and joy at being offered such an opportunity and it praises God's goodness reflected in the effects of such a meeting of divine grace and human generosity. Most scholars agree that it was originally a hymn about salvation in general which was later adapted by Luke and attributed to Mary as the one who most perfectly experienced that salvation.

This basic biblical story is profoundly enriched by *symbolic interpretation*. All major human actors in the biblical drama of salvation acquire a symbolic resonance that is derived from but greatly transcends their historical appearance. This is particularly true in the case of Mary and it represents a recognition of the perennial meaning that her historical reality has for Christians.

Mary's symbolic significance is attached primarily to her identity as mother and vir-

gin.* As mother, she is a living example of the profound truth that wherever the divine word is received with wholehearted generosity there will be a life-giving and nurturing fruitfulness that transcends all the categories of sex and age. All Christian believers are thus invited to imitate as much as possible Mary's incredibly fruitful motherhood.

As virgin, Mary not only experienced a miraculous biological event but, even more so, is a living reminder that wherever one responds generously in faith to the divine word there will be a "virginal" witness to hope that will be able to challenge effectively the powerful forces of cynicism and despair. For virginity, understood in its spiritual sense, dramatically witnesses to promise. A young virgin represents promise in a biological sense and thus becomes a symbolic representation of promise in every sense. Accordingly, all believers, regardless of age or gender, are invited to emulate Mary in her symbolic virginal witness to the victory of divine promise in ordinary and constantly threatened human life.

Mark, Matthew, and John. Mary rarely appears in the public ministry of Jesus. In Mark 3:31-35, she provides the occasion, somewhat obliquely, for an assertion by Jesus about the preference of spiritual over natural family bonds. In Matthew 1–2, the infancy story is told from the perspective of Joseph and the imagery, borrowed mainly from the OT, anticipates reactions to Jesus, both hostile and favorable, in his public ministry. It is significant that Matthew and Luke, whose infancy stories are so different, nonetheless agree completely on the central facts of the virginal conception and the birth of Jesus.

Mary appears twice in John's Gospel (2:3-5 and 19:25-27). She is identified only as the mother of Jesus and is addressed in both cases with the surprising title of "woman." In the first instance, Mary's request is declared inappropriate because the "hour" of Jesus has not yet come. However, in 19:25-27, having participated personally in the "hour" of Jesus' passion, she is declared to be "woman" again, possibly in the radical sense of the first woman, Eve, who was called the "mother of all the living" (Gen 3:20). Mary has now become the mother of all who live by faith. It would be in this sense that she can be understood to be mother of the Church, since she has shared in the birth pangs of the new creation and has become, in a sense, the "mother" of all who have been renewed by participation in the Christian suffering of unselfish love.

Marian Allusions. Because of the profound symbolic meaning inherent in the terms "mother" and "woman," many biblical texts that reflect these meanings have been associated with Mary. Thus, in the OT, texts about Eve or Wisdom (e.g., Prov 8:22-31) evoke the special creative and life-giving role of Mary as "woman." Other OT texts have been seen as allusions to her role as "virgin" (e.g., Cant 4:12) or "mother/protector" (e.g., Jdt 15:9-10). These texts do not, of course, refer to Mary in their literal sense, but they are appropriate on the symbolic level.

A similar evaluation can be made in regard to the application to Mary of the image of the "woman clothed with the sun" in Revelation 12:1. This woman, whose son is snatched up to heaven and who is pursued by the dragon, represents the new Israel, the Christian Church, but the image may also be applied to Mary in her symbolic identification with the community of believers. In all these instances, the symbolic meaning is based on and presupposes the historical meaning of Mary as virgin and mother.

See: DISCIPLE, FAITH, HOPE, JESUS CHRIST, MESSIAH, PROMISE, VIRGIN, VISITATION OF MARY, WISDOM, WORD

DEMETRIUS R. DUMM, O.S.B.

Pastoral-Liturgical Tradition

Mary has played a key role in the pastoral-liturgical life of the Christian community since its very beginnings. The first chapter of Acts (1:14) highlights Mary, the mother of Jesus in that first group of Christians devoted to "constant prayer" as they waited in the upper room for the coming of the holy Spirit. Details are not given about the prayer itself during that critical time in the life of the infant Church. But Mary is identified as the mother of Jesus in a prayerful context of major pastoral significance.

The Lucan author, responsible for both the Third Gospel and Acts, wants subsequent generations of Christians to understand Mary's pastoral significance in preparing the first Christians for the coming of the holy Spirit. From experience, Mary, the mother of Jesus, knew how God's own life found new expression through the empowering of the holy Spirit. In the annunciation account (Luke 1:26) Mary is overshadowed by the power of the Most High when the holy Spirit comes upon her. In Acts, Mary is helping a nascent Church prepare for the coming of that same holy Spirit.

At the Second Vatican Council, a Council that ushered in a time of New Pentecost, Mary was given a new official title, Mother of the Church. A major scriptural text supporting this title is the text from Acts. "Together they devoted themselves to constant prayer. There were some women in their company, and Mary the mother of Jesus and his brothers" (Acts 1:14). In addition to this scriptural text, the entire tradition of the Church witnesses to a belief that Mary the mother of Jesus continues to nurture life in the members of Jesus, who are the Church. Long before this official title was conferred on Mary, Christians have understood her to be Mother of the Church as well as Mother of Jesus.

The question might be raised as to why Mary as mother has had such a powerful influence on Christians in every century and in all cultures. Surely the fifth-century clarification of another Marian title, *Theotokos*, meaning God-bearer or Mother of God, placed a great emphasis on Mary's role as mother. This clarification at the Council of Ephesus in 431 not only highlighted Mary's motherhood, but also helped clarify Mary's unique relation to God.

The deliberations and conclusions at Ephesus had far-reaching liturgical implications. Christians were encouraged to pray to Mary as Mother of God. In popular devotion prayer to Mary became ever more important. Particularly when Christians labored under a pastoral orientation that overemphasized the majesty and power of God and the divinity of Jesus, the people of God found ways to relate to Mary as a compassionate mother. Mary was seen as one who knew from experience the needs of her children. Christians knew that Mary, Mother of God, would always find ways to intercede for them no matter what their predicaments, struggles, and sufferings happened to be.

Devotion to Mary as compassionate mother has inspired some of the most beautiful art in the history of the Christian people. In this regard, icons deserve special mention, particularly those classified as images of Our Lady of Tenderness. Probably the famous Vladimir Madonna is best known for this pastoral orientation. This icon portrays total confidence and trust in Mary through the figure of Jesus embracing his mother who presses him to her cheek.

Although a madonna is not the only way Mary has been pictured in Christian art, it is clearly one of the most frequent. Whether the art form was an icon, a stained glass window, a carving, or a cathedral, the artists' portrayal of Mary's compassionate understanding as mother exerted a profound influence on the faith life of Christians.

Gradually other Marian devotions developed which made considerable impact on the pastoral life of the Church. Places of special prayer experiences became places of pilgrimage, such as Lourdes in France and Guadalupe in Mexico. Processions became more frequent and new titles for Mary developed, many of which were gathered in the Litany of Loretto. Many of these devotions did not focus primarily on Mary's motherhood, although that reality was always acknowledged and cherished.

Perhaps no devotion to Mary has been more widespread than the rosary. One of the greatest blessings of this prayer form is its scriptural orientation. The mysteries of the rosary can help Christians meditate on the lives of Mary and of Jesus. For many persons this prayer has become a way of contemplation.

By the time the Second Vatican Council was called, a certain imbalance had developed with respect to Marian devotions. The nineteenth and twentieth centuries had witnessed two dogmatic definitions regarding Mary: the Immaculate Conception and the Assumption. Within the decade before Vatican II, the entire Church had celebrated a Marian Year. The Council faced a major decision with respect to the Church's ongoing Marian emphasis. Many bishops were keenly aware that for some Christians, Marian devotions were more important than the celebration of the Eucharist.

One of the most heated debates of the entire Council was the debate over the placement of the teaching on Mary. Some bishops held out for a separate document which would highlight Mary's privileges. Others wanted the Marian doctrine to be inserted in the Dogmatic Constitution on the Church. By a slim margin of forty votes, the decision prevailed to include the Second Vatican Council's teaching on Mary within the latter document. The impact of that decision was far-reaching.

However, for many Catholics Vatican II's orientation to Mary has been puzzling, if not downright disappointing. So many familiar, well-loved devotions have all but disappeared. The implications of the Council's teaching on Mary is neither understood nor appreciated by those persons who have little or no education regarding the teachings of Vatican II. But for those Christians who have moved with the Council, a growing realization of Mary's ongoing role in the life of the Church has been a most welcome sign of authentic renewal and reform.

The Marian emphasis of the Second Vatican Council is in beautiful harmony with its biblical and liturgical emphases. An awareness of Mary's strong faith as seen in the Gospels has become a focal point for a devotion much more in tune with the liturgical renewal. Once again, Advent and the Christmas season have become Mary's special time in the liturgical year. The feast of the Maternity of Mary is now celebrated on the octave of Christmas.

Two Marian documents issued after Vatican II have followed this Conciliar orientation: Devotion to the Blessed Virgin Mary, promulgated by Paul VI in 1974; and Behold Your Mother, promulgated by the United States National Conference of Catholic Bishops in 1973. Both documents speak of Mary's strengthening role in the lives of today's Christians faced with the manifold challenges of life in contemporary times.

The United States Catholic Bishops' Challenge of Peace deserves special mention because of the way it can relate Mary to Vatican II's Pastoral Constitution on the Church. The first sentence of The Challenge of Peace begins with a quotation from that Council document. "The whole human race faces a moment of supreme crisis in its advance toward maturity" (Pastoral Constitution on the Church, no. 77). The final section on "The Pastoral Challenge and Response" calls attention to Mary's intercessory power. "We call upon Mary, the first disciple and the Queen of Peace, to intercede for us and for the people of our time that we may walk in the way of peace. In this context, we encourage devotion to Our Lady of Peace" (The Challenge of Peace, no. 292).

This explicit focus on Mary in The Challenge of Peace clearly situates her in the midst of the Church's pastoral outreach to the entire human family. The ecumenical and interfaith developments of Vatican II make this pastoral thrust a realistic one. Largely because of recent biblical scholarship, all Christians are coming to understand Mary better as the first disciple of Jesus. Mary is seen as the one who witnesses first and foremost to authentic discipleship. Furthermore, recent emphasis on the genuine humanness of both Jesus and Mary has called attention to their Jewish religious and cultural roots. This awareness is providing new possibilities for Jewish/Christian cooperation.

The progress made thus far in ecumenical and interfaith dialog and reconciliation is a hopeful sign of the Church's ongoing mission of peacemaking. In this mission as in all others, Mary, Mother of the Church, continues to play a major role. Well might it be said that the historical Mary, the mother of Jesus known in Acts, is the Mary of faith truly active in the midst of the Church's life throughout all generations who continue to call her blessed.

See: DISCIPLE, FAITH

CAROL FRANCES JEGEN, B.V.M.

MEAL

This entry consists of three parts that discuss the significance of eating in the Bible and the pastoral-liturgical tradition. The first deals with important meals in the OT. The second describes meal as an important motif in the NT. The last part discusses meal as a sacred event in early Rabbinic and Christian tradition and the development of this idea in the Christian liturgy.

Old Testament

Meals, even banquets, are usually quite simple events, but even the simplest is rich in symbolism and profound in personal, social, and religious implications. Meals are an expression of hospitality, a source and sign of reconciliation, peace, unity, community, and solidarity. Oftentimes, as in the case of a marriage, meals are joyous, festive celebrations. In the context of worship, they are sacred events, often associated with sacrifice. Bound to their Lord by a covenant of grace, the Israelites were prohibited from participating in the cultic meals of other peoples (Num 25:2-4) or imitating them (Exod 32:6). Solemnly celebrated on the feasts of Passover (Exod 12:1-14, 21-28) and Unleavened Bread (Exod 12:15-20), meals are a memorial (Exod 12:14) of God's mighty signs and wonders, a celebration of liberation, and an act of thanksgiving.

Some of the most important meals in the OT are associated with historic events. One of these is the hospitality meal offered by Abraham and Sarah for three mysterious visitors by the terebinth of Mamre (Gen 18:1-15). After a gracious gesture of welcome and respectful greetings, a generous meal is prepared and set before the visitors, and Abraham personally waits on them. The hospitality of old Abraham and Sarah is rewarded with new life in the person of a son, Isaac (Gen 21:1-3), the first-born of divine promise (Gen 15:4-5).

Equally historic are the Passover meal shared by the people on the eve of their liberation from Egypt (Exodus 12) and the meal taken in the presence of God by Moses, Aaron, Nadab, and Abihu, together with seventy elders of Israel, ratifying and celebrating the covenant (Exod 24:9-11; see also Deut 27:7). Sharing a meal together establishes a bond of trust which increases the gravity of a subsequent betrayal. "Even my friend who had my trust," says Psalm 41:10, "and partook of my bread has raised his heel against me."

Meals can be joyous celebrations to welcome visiting relatives. Such is the reception given Tobiah, who came a great distance and wished to marry his kinswoman Sarah (Tob 7:9-11). At the reception, the marriage was agreed upon, the contract signed (Tob 7:11-13), and the welcome reception became a wedding feast (Tob 7:14-17).

Festive meals such as Tobiah's reception called on the participants to "eat and drink and be merry" (Tob 7:10) and could be quite extravagant (see 1 Kgs 10:5; Esth 1:5-8; Jdt 1:16). Accordingly, the Wisdom literature warns readers to "consort not with winebibbers, nor with those who eat meat to excess" (Prov 23:20) and provides a set of general rules for table etiquette (Sir 31:12-31) as well as special rules for presiders and guests at dinner (Sir 32:1-13).

New Testament

Meals constitute a major theme in the NT, which abounds in stories of meals with Jesus and presents meals as a dominant motif in Jesus' teaching. Having played an important role in Jesus' ministry, meals maintain their importance in the early Christian communities and provide some of the NT's basic imagery.

Meals with Jesus. Every Gospel tells of meals with Jesus. Of these, the most significant is the Last Supper, where the Synoptic Gospels associated the Lord's Supper of the early Church with the final supper of Jesus' historical life, thereby presenting it as the institution of the Eucharist* (Mark 14:17-26; Matt 26:20-30; Luke 22:14-38). In the Synoptic Gospels, where the Last Supper is a Passover meal (see Mark 14:1-2, 12-16; Matt 26:2, 17-19; Luke 22:1, 7-13, 15), it also shares in the festive, sacred, and memorial character of the Israelite Passover. For John, the Last Supper was a great preparatory event in which Jesus gave his disciples "a model to follow" (John 13:15) by washing their feet (John 13:1-11), for "no slave is greater than a master nor any messenger greater than the one who sent him" (John 13:16).

As the climactic meal of Jesus' life, the Last Supper presupposes many other meals with Jesus, including the breaking of bread where Jesus nourishes vast crowds in deserted places with a few loaves of bread and a few fish (Mark 6:34-44; 8:1-9; Matt 14:13-21; 15:32-38; Luke 9:10-17; John 6:1-15). These stories emphasize the mission and ministry of Jesus and his disciples in nourishing the crowds.

More than any other evangelist, Luke exploited the tradition of meals with Jesus and showed their relationship to most facets of Jesus' ministry. Meals are teaching and healing events in which Jesus fulfills the role of prophet. In a series of seven meals leading up to the Last Supper, Jesus challenges current practices and deals with important issues, such as that of inclusivism and exclusivism. Who is to be invited and included at a meal with Jesus? Is anyone to be excluded?

There is the meal at the home of Levi, where the Pharisees and their scribes complain about the disciples eating and drinking with tax collectors and sinners (Luke 5:27-32). Jesus responds that he came as a physician for the sick to call not the righteous but sinners to repentance *(metanoia)*. Is anyone righteous? Are they not all sinners? Then there is the meal at the home of a Pharisee, where a sinful woman comes to Jesus, demonstrating her great love and showing that her sins are forgiven (Luke 7:36-50). When the Pharisee questions Jesus' authenticity as a prophet, Jesus confronts him with his own meager love. Next there is the breaking of bread for the five thousand in a deserted place, which Luke resituates in the city of Bethsaida (Luke 9:10-17; see Mark 6:34-44). When the Twelve ask Jesus to dismiss the crowd, he tells them, "Give them some food yourselves" and shows them how to do it.

The next meal, the first of four on the journey to Jerusalem, is in the home of Martha, who was "burdened with much serving *[diakonia]*." When she protests that her sister Mary is not helping her, Jesus responds that unlike Martha, who is "anxious and worried about many things," Mary attends to the one thing needed, listening as a disciple to the word of the Lord (Luke 10:38-42). The next two meals are in the homes of Pharisees. In the first, Jesus confronts his host and others with the hypocrisy of attending to external cleanness while neglecting the interior (Luke 11:37-54). In the second, Jesus challenges those opposed to his healing on the Sabbath and addresses the greater illness of guests seeking places of honor at table and of a host inviting those alone who can repay him in kind (Luke 14:1-24). Finally, there is the meal, not explicitly mentioned but implied, when Jesus comes to the home of Zacchaeus. With this last meal, Luke shows how Jesus comes as a guest with the gift of salvation (Luke 19:1-10).

After Jesus' death and resurrection, there are two more meals with Jesus, one at Emmaus with two disciples who had left Jerusalem in discouragement (Luke 24:13-35), and one before the ascension with the whole community in Jerusalem (Luke 24:36-49). The Emmaus story shows how Jesus the Nazarene (Luke 24:19) was the suffering Christ manifested at the Last Supper (Luke 24:26) and the Lord who "has truly been raised and has appeared to Simon" (Luke 24:34). The story deals with the recognition of Jesus Christ the Lord "in the breaking of the bread" (Luke 14:35). The meal during Jesus' final appearance addresses the reality of the risen Lord. The wounded humanity of Jesus eating before the disciples introduces the mission "to all the nations, beginning from Jerusalem" (Luke 24:47), once they have been "clothed with power from on high" (Luke 24:49).

Besides the Last Supper and the breaking of the bread for the five thousand, John's Gospel presents two great meals with Jesus, the wedding feast of Cana, the first of Jesus' signs (John 2:11), and the breakfast by the Sea of Tiberias (21:9-14). At Cana, Jesus changes water into wine, showing the absolute newness and the great superiority of the wine of the new dispensation over that of the old (2:1-10). In the Gospel's epilogue, Jesus invites the disciples to a post-resurrection breakfast prepared for them after they have demonstrated themselves great missionary fishermen by an extraordinary catch of fish (21:1-14).

Jesus' Teaching about Meals. Much of Jesus' teaching about meals is done while Jesus is at a meal and usually bears on issues raised by the attitudes and behavior of those present. In Luke, Jesus presents a farewell discourse at the Last Supper and addresses the matter of betrayals and denials both at the end of his life and in the life of the early Christian community (Luke 22:14-38). At the house of Levi, he takes up the matter of feasting and fasting, in which his disciples stand in sharp contrast with those of John the Baptist and of the Pharisees (Luke 5:33-39). Jesus' disciples are like wedding guests who do not "fast while the bridegroom is with them" (Luke 5:34) but will fast "when the bridegroom is taken away from them" (Luke 5:35) in the passion. But the fasting of the passion will be followed by the feasting of the resurrection and the beginning of Passover fulfillment in the reign of God (Luke 22:16; see 22:18), announced by the beatitude of an enthusiastic guest, "Blessed is the one who will dine in the kingdom of God" (Luke 14:15).

The beatitude elicits the parable of one who "gave a great dinner to which he invited many" but from which many excused themselves (Luke 14:15-24). Their places were taken by "the poor and the crippled, the blind and the lame" (Luke 14:21), showing the nature and scope of Jesus' messianic mission (see Luke 4:18; 7:21-22; 14:13). The Lukan parable has a parallel in Matthew in the parable of the wedding feast (Matt 22:2-14), where a guest is found without a wedding garment and cast "into the darkness outside, where there will be wailing and grinding of teeth" (Matt 22:13). The wedding garment is symbolic of the new identity required to join in the banquet. For the banquet of the Church, Christians need a new identity.

The Matthean version of the parable of the wedding feast (Matt 22:2-14; see Luke 14:15-24) is not told at a meal with Jesus. Luke also has such parables, notably that of the lost younger son (Luke 15:11-32), where the father offers a feast at the son's return but the older son refuses to attend. Attending would mean welcoming the younger son, being reconciled with him and recognizing him as a brother. Then there is the parable of the rich man "who dressed in purple garments and fine linen and dined sumptuously each day" (Luke 16:19) and poor Lazarus, "who would gladly have eaten his fill of the scraps that fell from the rich man's table" (Luke 16:21). The parable (Luke 16:19-31) has obvious implications for all situations where "a great chasm" separates rich and poor. The chasm is maintained in the resurrection.

Early Christian Community. The meal stories in the Gospels and the presentation of Jesus' teaching there were written for the early Christian communities and reflect the practices and concerns of those communities. As such, they already say much about the place and significance of meals in the apostolic and post-apostolic communities. To round out the picture, we also have Luke's second volume, the Acts of the Apostles, which presents the Christian meal, here called "the breaking of bread," as one of the distinguishing characteristics of a Christian community, along with "the teaching of the apostles," "the communal life," and "the prayers" (Acts 2:42; see Luke 24:35). Besides the community breaking of the bread, which was associated with the first day of the week (see Luke 24:35; Acts 20:7), the members of the community also broke bread daily in their homes (Acts 2:46), and this too had religious significance. Later in Acts, meals became a critical issue in the Church's opening to the Gentile mission. The credentials of the witnesses in Jesus' universal mission were that they "ate and drank with him after he rose from the dead" (Acts 10:40-42).

The letters of Paul show the complexity of the issue of meals for communities composed of both Jews and Gentiles. In a personal apologia for his apostolic credentials, Paul appeals to an event at Antioch when Peter and the other Jewish Christians, who ordinarily ate with Gentile Christians, withdrew from the Gentile table when people came on visit from Jerusalem (Gal 2:11-13).

There was also the recurrent question of eating meat that was offered to idols and subsequently sold in the market. Since the idols are really nothing, there is nothing intrinsically wrong in eating such meat, but Christians should refrain from doing so when there is danger of scandal (1 Cor 8:1-13; 10:23-33; Rom 14:1–15:6). Even more important, Christians must not participate in idol worship by joining in pagan sacrifices. Again it is not that the idols are anything, but the act would disassociate Christians from the table of the Lord (1 Cor 10:14-22). Partaking of the table of the Lord had profound implications for the behavior and relationships of Christians (1 Cor 10:1-13), as is extremely clear from Paul's message regarding divisions among those who claim to eat the Lord's Supper but in fact eat their own supper (1 Cor 11:17-34).

See: COMMUNITY, COVENANT, EUCHARIST, PASSOVER, PEACE, RECONCILIATION, WINE

EUGENE LAVERDIERE, S.S.S.

Pastoral-Liturgical Tradition

The Experience of Eating. Despite the obvious differences among human beings occasioned by factors such as culture and geography, there is at least one activity common to all people: human beings eat to live. Although eating is universal and biologically based, the *way* in which human beings eat and drink as well as *what* they consume differ greatly from one culture to another—and it is these socially established customs surrounding table etiquette that constitute one of the principal expressions of human culture. One need only consider the dietary laws prescribed by religions as diverse as Judaism and Hinduism to see that both social values and religious meaning are attached to taking food—especially in common. In traditional human groupings as well as in "modern" societies, meal customs not only help a culture express its identity, they also aid in handing down deeply held convictions about relationships within the group as well as the inter-relatedness of all life and life's ultimate source in God.

However, due to progress in technology and changing customs of food distribution, an important dimension of dining together has been obscured over the past century. Our ancestors more readily understood the intrinsic connection between eating and the cycle of life and death. For human beings to survive—even those who are "peaceful" vegetarians—a living being must die. Very few of us, in examining neatly wrapped cuts of meat in a refrigerated counter at the grocery store, spend much time thinking about the origin of these packets of protein. However, not many hours before these convenient bits of pig, cow, or lamb arrived in the grocery store they were parts of living organisms. The same is true, of course, of the vegetables and fruits that we consume.

This relationship was obvious to our forebears. It was a common custom in most simple hunting societies to thank the deity and/or the animal itself for giving its life that humans might live. After killing the animal it was also common to offer a part of the animal to the gods in thanksgiving. In many agricultural communities, governed by its rhythm of seed time and harvest, it was also common to offer the "first fruits" of both field and flock to the gods by means of sacrifice. A portion of these first fruits were offered and a meal was then held with the remainder. It was therefore believed that the gods took part in this meal, having shared in the same food. Therefore, in the ancient mind there was not a hard and fast distinction between meal and sacrifice, and Paul's parallel use of the images of "altar"* and "table" in 1 Corinthians 10:21 becomes perfectly understandable.

Just as our technology separates us from the fact that we always eat in the presence of death as well as life, we in the modern world are also very far from really experiencing what it means to be hungry or thirsty. Much like driving into a service station to fill up the car with gas, we easily "tank up" by going to a fast food restaurant or our nearest grocery store where food in quantity and variety unimaginable to our ancestors is readily available. Most of us have never experienced hunger—other than a vague twinge of the stomach at dinner time. As a result, it is hard for us to sympathize (= feel with) those who are truly hungry, even when we see their plight graphically portrayed on the evening news. As a consequence, it is hard for us to imagine the full impact of the biblical expressions such as "hunger and thirst for righteousness" (Matt 5:6).

An essential aspect of Eucharistic worship—our Christian ritual meal—is rooted in both the human need for nourishment and the culturally determined modes of dining together. Any attempt at sketching a theology of the Eucharist,* then, must take into account its matrix in a Jewish sacred meal as well as in the larger context of Jesus' table ministry and dining-as-sacred-activity in the Judaism of the first century.

Meal in Early Christianity. The prominence in both the Hebrew and Christian Scriptures of a joyous banquet at the end of time as an image of bliss in God's presence highlights the religious significance of meal in the Judeao-Christian tradition: a tradition that insists that a relationship with God is not simply a matter of individual salvation but necessarily involves a horizontal relationship with the human community and the world itself. For Christians the religious significance of meal as a place where God is encountered is further accentuated by the Gospels, which recount Jesus' eating and drinking with sinners and outcasts both before and after the resurrection. Thus, this table ministry of Jesus dramatically proclaims the coming of the immanent reign of God—a reign characterized by God's gratuitous and reconciling invitation to all people to come to the banquet and eat and drink in the presence of the risen Christ.

It would be hard to overemphasize that the meal as a locus of the sacred is firmly rooted in the Jewish attitudes—and that this attitude directly influenced early Christian practice. Many scholars see an organic progression between the Jewish thanksgiving prayer after meals (the *Birkat Ha-Mazon*) and our own Eucharistic Prayers. In fact, after the destruction of the Temple in 70 CE by the Romans, when the sacrificial worship of Judaism has to be discontinued, it was to the humble table in the homes of faithful Jews that the rabbis attributed much of the benefits of sacrifice. This is well expressed in the Talmud, a document that dates from the early centuries of the common era. Since sacrifice could only be offered at the Temple in Jerusalem, with its destruction in 70 CE by the Romans, the rabbis had to develop an alternative to the animal and cereal sacrifices for the forgiveness of sins offered in the Temple. For some of the rabbis it was natural to substitute actions at table for those

once practiced at the altar. Rabbi Yohanan (+279), and Rabbi Eleazar (+ ca. 270) noted that "As long as the sanctuary existed, the altar expiated the sins of Israel, but now it is the human table of hospitality that expiates sin" (Tractate Berakhot, IX, f. 55a, in *Der Babylonischer Talmud*).

Given this background of dining-as-sacred-activity in Judaism it is not surprising that the most characteristic rite of the emerging Christian Church finds its origin in Jesus' reinterpretation of the Jewish ritual meal held at Pesach or Passover.* Familiarity with the religious significance of this meal for first-century Jews is very important for our contemporary understanding of the Eucharist. The Passover is replete with many themes that will later be incorporated into the Eucharist: sacrifice (the paschal lamb), the life-giving quality of blood (the blood of the lamb), liberation from oppression (freedom from slavery in Egypt), and eschatological expectation of God's definitive liberation of Israel through the promised Messiah. Jesus' identification of himself with the two most basic elements of a festive Jewish meal—the bread* and the wine*—quickly took on the gamut of associations connected with the Passover, however now interpreted Christologically.

There is abundant evidence to suggest that during the early Christian period the celebrations of the Eucharist took place in the context of a full meal. In addition to the NT witness to this practice (Acts 2; 1 Corinthians 11) one of the earliest extra biblical documents, the Didache (ca. 100 CE) describes the celebration of the Eucharist in the context of a full meal, with blessings beginning and ending the dinner. While some scholars hold that these chapters (9 and 10) are describing an *agape* or fellowship meal and not a Eucharist proper, it is likely in this early period (the first century of the Church's existence) a hard and fast distinction between the two cannot be made. It is not until the *Apostolic Tradition* of Hippolytus (ca. 215 CE) that a formal distinction in made between Eucharist and an *agape* that looks much like the later Eastern practice of distributing bread blessed but not consecrated at the end of the Divine Liturgy called *eulogía* or *antídoron*. There is evidence to suggest that the *agape* lasted until the fifth or sixth century in the West—toward the end of this period associated with the dinner given at funerals to which the poor of the town or village would be invited.

Meal and Later Christianity. It is likely that the Eucharist and the community's meal or *agape* separated at a relatively early date: both to avoid abuses such as the ones criticized by Paul in 1 Corinthians and because of the logistical problems of feeding larger numbers of people. As the intimate communities grew larger, a meal of this nature also became impractical. The official recognition of Christianity as the religion of the Empire also had important implications for the liturgy and its relationship with meal. A process of "sacralization" took place during the high Patristic period (fourth through seventh centuries) and beyond which promoted an emphasis on the hieratic and awe inspiring nature of Christian worship and tended to downplay the fact that the basic symbols of the liturgy (bread, wine, oil, water) are derived from everyday life.

The disassociation of the basic Eucharistic symbols from its origin in a sacred meal became even more pronounced in the West because the liturgy was celebrated in Latin; a language that was becoming increasingly incomprehensible to the people. Preoccupation with sinfulness and unworthiness also seriously limited the number of communicants at an average Eucharist in both East and West. For these reasons, a growing movement to interpret the Mass as an allegory of the life of Christ and the liturgy of the Eucharist almost exclusively as a reenactment of Christ's sacrifice on the cross began to overshadow the earlier emphasis on the Eucharist as sacred meal.

However, while the meal dimension of the Eucharist was obscured during the Middle Ages, the basis of the Mass in a human meal was never completely lost. This is reflected in some of the hymnody written during the middle ages. A famous example of which is *"O Sacrum Convivium"*

> O sacrum convivium in quo Christus sumitur
> recolitur memoria passionis eius
> Mens impletur gratia et futurae gloriae
> nobis pignus datur.

> O holy meal in which Christ is received,
> his passion remembered,
> our being filled with grace, and given
> the pledge of future glory.

The reforms of the Second Vatican Council recovered this universally familiar human activity of sharing nourishment as the principal referent to the Eucharist. Many of the liturgical changes revolve around accentuating the Mass as a sacred meal of the community gathered around the "table of God's word" and the "table of the Eucharist." Far from rejecting the understanding of the Mass as the sacrament of the sacrifice of Christ, the liturgy of Vatican II seeks to balance the richness of this later medieval understanding with the earlier Eucharistic traditions of the Church which, based on the Jewish-Christian matrix of sacred meal, emphasize that it is in the action of sharing in the Eucharistic bread and wine that we become one in Christ Jesus. In his instruction *Eucharisticum mysterium* (1967), Pope Paul VI discusses the grounding of the Eucharist as a sacred banquet, in addition to its sacrificial and memorial (sacramental) dimensions. Thus the Mass or Lord's Supper is:

> the sacred banquet in which, through the communion of the body and blood of the Lord, the people of God share the benefits of the paschal sacrifice, renew the new Covenant with us made once and for all by God in Christ's blood, and in faith and hope foreshadow and anticipate the eschatological banquet in the Father's kingdom as they proclaim the death of the Lord "until he comes" (Paul VI's Instruction *Eucharisticum mysterium 3 a.*).

See: BLOOD, BREAD, ESCHATOLOGY, EUCHARIST, FU-
NERAL CUSTOMS, HOSPITALITY, MEAL, REMEMBRANCE,
SACRIFICE, WINE

MARK R. FRANCIS, C.S.V.

MEDIATOR/INTERCESSOR

The terms mediator and intercessor are correlative. In religious usage, a mediator is one who stands between God and the human community. The mediator speaks God's word to the human community and represents the community to God. In Jewish and Christian understandings, the mediator is designated by God. Because the mediator has been so designated and favored by God, the mediator is the prime intercessor on behalf of the community to God for the community's well-being and safety. Mediation is therefore the condition that makes effective intercession possible.

Some form of mediation is found in most every religion. It is because of the profound qualitative difference between the divine and the human that mediation becomes necessary. Intercession reminds us of the needs of the human community and creates a special solidarity between those who intercede and those who need help.

In the history of Israel Moses is the prototype of the mediator. Moses is designated by God to lead the Hebrew people out of Egypt. It is through Moses that God gives the law and initiates the covenant. The early kings of Israel are also mediators inasmuch as they too are designated by God and speak to God as the representatives of the people. The prophets speak God's word for the sake of the people and even rebuke the king. The suffering servant of Isaiah 53 has become a special mediator in the eyes of Christians because he not only takes upon himself the sins of the people, but also, through his death, wins favor before God.

In the NT, Jesus is the supreme mediator between God and humanity, superseding all previous mediators. The Gospels portray Jesus as being anointed with God's Spirit at his baptism as God's favored Son. Likewise, the Gospels depict Jesus as being in intense communication with God throughout his ministry. Jesus' prayer for his disciples in John 17 reveals especially his mediating role. 1 Timothy 2:5 states it most explicitly: "For there is one God. There is also one mediator between God and the human race, Christ Jesus, himself human." This quotation, stressing the one God and the one mediator, implies the universality of Jesus' mediation. The uniqueness and the universality of Jesus' mediation is a recurrent theme in the Letter to the Hebrews where Christ's sacrifice is offered up once for all (see Heb 8:6; 9:15; 12:24).

That the Word, the second person of the Trinity, became human, and in dying offered a perfect sacrifice to God in atonement for all human sin, makes Jesus the perfect mediator between God and humankind. It is in and through this mediation that any mediation of God's grace by the Church takes place. The Church as the Mystical Body of Christ continues that mediation. The intercession by the Church is efficacious only because it is taken up in the intercession of Christ.

The Church becomes the prime place of that mediation of Christ. Revelation in the Holy Scriptures and in the Tradition has been entrusted to the Church. The sacraments too are expressions of that mediation, especially in baptism by which new members are incorporated into the body of Christ and are given new life, and in the Eucharist where Christ's mediation is again made present.

Because Christ has mediated Word and sacrament to the Church, the Church is able to intercede for those in need. Thus the general intercessions at the conclusion of the Liturgy of the Word, and the intercessions for the living and the dead in the Eucharistic Prayer, represent part of the Church's necessary activity in virtue of its mediating role. These intercessions are not just pious acts of altruism; they are constitutive of what the Church is.

Those members of the Church whose lives are most closely modeled on that of

Christ—the saints, and preeminent among them, Mary—share in a special way in the intercessory power of Christ. It is for that reason that Christians have called upon Mary and the saints to intercede before God on their behalf. Through the centuries customs grew up that associated certain saints with particular efficacy in certain situations. Thus, St. Gerard is associated with safety in childbirth; St. Anthony, with finding lost articles; St. Joseph, with a happy death. Mary, as mother of Jesus, has been seen as having intercessory power that surpasses that of all the saints.

The sixteenth-century reformers objected strenuously to the abuses that had grown up around intercessory practices in the Church. They insisted that intercession through Mary and the saints obscured the unique mediating role of Christ. Much of the mediating practice of the Church was also condemned, since it appeared to promote a works-righteousness rather than a focus on faith. The claims of the reformers had considerable justification at the time. Intercession can become obsessive and even coercive in the minds and hearts of some. Mary and the saints can take on more practical significance than Christ. While the Church took steps to reform the abuses and check the hybris to which intercession is sometimes subject, it did not abandon its claim to a mediating role. That is still evident in the understanding of the Church set forth at the Second Vatican Council in the Dogmatic Constitution on the Church.

Understandings of mediation and intercession are frequently heavily influenced by cultural practices of patronage. The mediator or intercessor is seen as someone with power and influence who can win favors for those who approach them. By entering into relations with the patron, it becomes possible to coerce the patron into doing one's bidding. This all too human way of acting often spills over into the relations Christians have with God in Christ. But interceding understood religiously is not coercion. Nor is it a simple cause-and-effect activity. In intercession we become mindful of our own needs and those of others. Intercession thus creates a certain solidarity in the human community. Intercession acknowledges too our finitude and our dependence upon God. It places our needs and hopes with God in an act of trust that commends them to God's care.

Of special importance are the intercessory prayers for the dead. Prayers for the dead are part of nearly all cultures, and represent the continuing link between generations that death does not entirely sever. By praying for the dead we keep them in memory and gain some comfort in our loss as we commend them to the care of God. An older piety and the frequent celebration of weekday Requiem Masses focused upon the release of the souls of the dead from the punishment due their sins. Such intercessory prayer was seen to contribute to their purification process prior to entering heaven. The revised funeral rites emphasize more our hope in their sharing in Christ's new life, begun in baptism and now to be consummated in a fuller share in Christ's resurrection. As already noted, intercessory prayer for the dead both comforts those who mourn and represents a solidarity between those still alive and the "great cloud of witnesses" (Heb 12:1) that have gone before us.

See: PRAYER, SACRIFICE

ROBERT J. SCHREITER, C.PP.S.

MEEKNESS

The Greek adjective *praus* and its nominal adjunct are translated only a few times by the NAB as "meek(ness)." Elsewhere the root is translated by words such as humble, afflicted, lowly, humility, gentle(ness), graciousness, kindness, courtesy. The meek are those totally reliant on God to save them, often from socioeconomic situations of oppression. That trust allows them to suffer wrongs to themselves, but their very rootedness in God and God's justice motivates their action on behalf of others to endure injustice. The pastoral tradition of the Church preserves the outline of this little understood, and much ignored, phenomenon.

Old Testament

The meek are the recipients of God's action on their behalf: they "shall possess the land" (Ps 37:11). They are those who will be taught (Ps 25:9), saved (Ps 76:10), sustained (Ps 147:6), and given victory (Ps 149:4). Moses, after being criticized by Aaron and Miriam, is described as "by far the meekest man on the face of the earth" and is defended by the Lord as one with whom God speaks face to face (Num 12:3). They are the ones who can expect that their present oppression will come to an end: "the thrones of the arrogant God overturns, and establishes the lowly in their stead" (Sir 10:14).

Those who are meek are described by Zephaniah as part of the remnant whom God will leave the disintegrating nation, those who, unlike the proud braggarts who are doomed, "shall do no wrong and speak no lies" (Zeph 3:12, 13). The ideal wife of Sirach 36:23 has speech which is "kindly."

The author of Sirach exhorts his readers to "give a hearing to the poor man, and return his greeting with courtesy" (Sir 4:8). This exhortation is juxtaposed with one to "deliver the oppressed from the hand of the oppressor, let not justice be repugnant to you" (Sir 4:9). This association of meekness with justice is repeated in the portrait of the expected meek king of Zechariah 9:9 who is also a "just savior."

New Testament

Apart from three occasions in Matthew, the epistolary literature of the NT is the major proponent of the phenomenon of meekness.

Meekness is often enjoined in an unjust situation and meekness seems to function here as part of a program to promote the presence of justice/righteousness. Christians in Asia Minor who suffer "because of justice," presumably for the violent reaction evoked by just behavior, are enjoined to "always be ready to give an explanation to anyone who asks you for a reason for your hope, but do it with gentleness and reverence" (1 Pet 3:15). The addressees of James, in a situation torn by tensions between rich and poor, are told to be slow to wrath, "for the wrath of a man does not accomplish the righteousness of God" (Jas 1:20). And they are exhorted to a humility which forswears jealousy and selfish ambition and to cultivate rather the "fruit of righteousness" (Jas 3:14, 18).

However, these admonitions, so focused on a personal discipline willing to suffer in an unjust situation, do not mean that the meek are unable to act decisively on behalf of others in the cause of justice. The Matthean portrait of Jesus outlines one who is "meek and humble of heart" and who offers rest (11:29). But in the very next pericope, he is shown twice publicly breaking the Pharisaic interpretation of Sabbath law in order that he might feed and heal, arguably illustrating the kind of rest Sabbath was meant to sanctify, and as part of a program of "bringing justice to victory" (12:20). Similarly, the one who enters Jerusalem "meek and riding on an ass" (Matt 21:5) is the one who in the immediately following scene destroys property in defense of people's access to the house of prayer (21:13). Jesus defines in his person what it is to be meek, and as such reaps the reward of "inheriting the land" promised by God (5:5; 20:18).

In the Corinthian correspondence, Paul expresses the hope that he can come to the community in "gentleness" (1 Cor 4:21) and appeals to them by the "gentleness of Christ" (2 Cor 10:1) but threatens to come to the community "with a rod" and act "boldly" against some. These sentiments drive a wedge between meekness and aggressive behavior, and do not reflect the full range of activity associated with Matthew's meek Christ. This may simply be another indicator that Paul's contact with the Jesus tradition was partial, perhaps devolving on the passion-resurrection as well as select sayings and traditions.

Pastoral-Liturgical Tradition

The concern to foster meekness is apparent in many contexts throughout the history of the Church's care for souls. Anthony, a fourth-century desert ascetic, suggested that the demons are in dread of ascetics because of the ascetic "fasting, their vigils, their prayers; their meekness, calmness, contempt of money, lack of conceit, humility, love of the poor, almsgiving, freedom from anger, and most of all, their loyalty to Christ." Francis of Assisi, after hearing how rudely a fellow brother had treated robbers begging food from their house, scolded the brother, reminding him that more sinners are led back to Christ by holy meekness than by cruel scolding. To illustrate, Francis sent the brother to pursue the robbers, feed them, and apologize for his earlier behavior; whereupon they were converted. Francis de Sales suggested that a certain meekness even toward ourselves is necessary for growth in the love of God.

Meekness was enjoined by Pope Paul VI when he envisioned the ideal circumstances under which the gospel is to be communicated. Our dialogue must be accompanied by that meekness which Christ bade us learn from Himself: "Learn of me for I am meek and humble of heart." It would indeed be a disgrace if our dialogue were marked by arrogance, the use of barbed words, or offensive bitterness (*Ecclesiam Suam*, On the Church 81.2).

Oscar Romero saw in the exhortation of James a word which his fellow Salvadorans needed to hear: "St. James exhorts us to accept with meekness the word planted in us that is able to save us. Only this word is able to save us. To believe, to hope: this is the Christian's grace in our time. When many give up hope, when it seems to them that the nation has nowhere to go, as though it were all over, the Christian says: No, we have not yet begun. We are still awaiting God's grace. With certainty, it is just beginning to be built on this earth, and we will be a blessed nation and will escape from so much evil."

See: HOPE, JUSTICE, PRAYER, PRIDE, REMNANT

MARK C. KILEY

MELCHIZEDEK

Melchizedek, popularly understood to mean "King of Justice," was king of Salem ("peace") and priest of God Most High who met Abraham at the gates of his city. This mysterious figure is cited in Psalm 110 as "priest forever" and taken up in the Letter to the Hebrews as a type of the priesthood of Christ. He becomes an image of the Eucharistic sacrifice in the tradition, appearing in Eucharistic Prayer I (the Roman Canon).

Old Testament

Encounter with Abraham. Melchizedek appears in Genesis 14:18-20. Abraham is just returning from a victory over the Canaanite kings (Gen 14:13-17). The passage appears without reference to what comes before and after it and may be an interpolation. Melchizedek, whose name means "King of Justice" or "my king is Sedeq" (a divine name), is King of Salem, usually identified with Jerusalem (see Ps 76:3). He is also priest of God Most High (*El Elyon*). Melchizedek brings out bread and wine and, as priest, pronounces a blessing over Abraham, which praises God as creator and savior. Abraham responds by giving a tithe of all he has.

According to the Order of Melchizedek. Psalm 110 recalls this encounter of Abraham and Melchizedek. The king of Israel is reminded that he is both king and priest under the Lord, "a priest forever, according to the order of Melchizedek." The Hebrew text is unclear, and is generally translated according to the Septuagint. What "according to the order of Melchizedek" means is itself unclear. Later Christian tradition will see it as referring to Christ.

Ideal Priestly King and Heavenly Judge. Melchizedek remains a fascinating figure for the Jewish tradition: he appears in the Qumran literature (11QMelch) and the OT pseudepigrapha (2 Enoch 71–72). The Qumran material presents Melchizedek as the heavenly prince who acts as an agent of redemption in the last days. The apocalyptic 2 Enoch tells the story of Melchizedek's miraculous birth and subsequent removal to paradise.

New Testament

A Priest Forever. The Letter to the Hebrews uses Psalm 110 extensively to reflect on the priesthood of Jesus Christ. In Hebrews 5:6 the author uses Psalm 110:4 for the first of several times to indicate that Jesus' priesthood establishes a special relationship between Jesus and God. This eternal high priesthood of Melchizedek which Jesus shares is part of his perfection and the source of eternal salvation for all who obey him (Heb 5:9-10). Melchizedek as a type of Christ is developed in most detail in Hebrews 7. A key part of the interpretation is in verse 3: "Without father, mother, or ancestry, without beginning of days or end of life, thus made to resemble the Son of God, he remains a priest forever." This mysterious quality of Melchizedek thus makes him an apt type for Jesus whose origins and ancestry are likewise shrouded in mystery. Abraham admits his superiority by tithing (vv. 4-10). Jesus is the establishment of a new and more effective priesthood (vv. 11-25), which replaces the levitical, Aaronic priesthood. We have that priest in Jesus Christ, who intercedes for us and offers the once for all sacrifice for us before God.

The gnostic literature from Nag Hammadi develops this understanding (*Melchizedek [IX, 1]*) and actually sees Melchizedek as having returned in Jesus Christ!

Pastoral-Liturgical Tradition

The Typology of Bread and Wine. The Patristic reflection sees the image of Melchizedek bringing out (*ekpherein*) bread and wine as a type of the Eucharist. First the elements are considered to be established by the figure of Melchizedek (see Clement of Alexandria, *Strom* 4,25; Cyprian, Ep. 63,4). Ambrose develops the typology in a number of places, focusing both on Melchizedek as type of Christ and the actions of offering (now understood as *prospherein*) and blessing as types of Christ's actions in the Eucharist.

Melchizedek's "Sacrifice" as a Type of Eucharistic Sacrifice. Ambrose gives a version of the Eucharistic Prayer very similar to what has come down to us as the Roman Canon, in which the figure of Melchizedek is seen in this typological sense: "take up this offering . . . just as you were graciously pleased to receive the gifts of your just servant Abel, the sacrifice of our father Abraham, and the offering the high priest Melchizedek made to you" (*De Sacr.* 4,27; tr. in Yarnold, *The Awe-Inspiring Rites of Initiation* [Slough, England, 1971], pp. 139–140). The same phrase is found in the current Roman Canon: "accept them as once you accepted . . . the bread and wine offered by your priest Melchizedek." A more exact translation of the Latin text would be: "what your high priest Melchizedek offered you, a holy sacrifice, an immaculate victim." The only other place in the celebration of the Eucharist where Melchizedek is mentioned is in the Entrance Antiphon for the votive Mass of the Holy Eucharist. In the opening prayer the theme is continued: "you appointed Christ eternal High Priest."

"Messianic Fulfillment" in the Liturgy of the Hours. Evening Prayer II of every Sunday and every solemnity and feast of the Lord uses Psalm 110. Sunday is the Lord's Day and it is appropriate that this messianic psalm reminds us of how Jesus Christ fulfills God's will to offer himself for the salvation of all. Two antiphons pick up the use of Melchizedek as the type of Christ: the antiphon for Psalm 110 for Sunday Evening Prayer II of Week II of the Psalter; and the antiphon for Psalm 110 for Evening Prayer II for the solemnity of Corpus Christi. The intercessions from Morning Prayer on Corpus Christi also pick up the typology: priest of the new and eternal covenant; king of justice and peace.

Conclusion. The figure of Melchizedek serves as a means of reflecting on the meaning of Christ: priest and king who, bringing forth bread and wine, blesses Abraham. We are called to share in the priestly reality of Christ, partaking of the bread and wine which form the ongoing celebration of our covenant with God Most High who loves us and draws us to himself through the priestly mediation of Jesus Christ.

See: KINGSHIP, MEDIATION, PRIESTHOOD, SACRIFICE

MICHAEL G. WITCZAK, S.J.

MERCY

New Testament

The Mission of Jesus as the Manifestation of a Merciful God. Among several manifestations of the divine presence, God is known in the OT as one who responds to the suffering* and need of petitioners. God's rescue of the Israelites begins with witnessing their affliction and knowing what they are suffering (Exod 3:7). God is experienced as eternal, unending *hesed* or mercy (Pss 86:15; 136:2, 3, 4), *rachamim* or tender compassion (Ps 103:4), and as *hanan* or graciousness (Ps 57:2). In the OT, God's kindly presence is the opposite of punishing wrath and fearful judgment. God is a helper who gives people hope. God's merciful power is benevolent, and makes a faithful and enduring commitment. God's mercy is not reserved for a heavenly future, but takes the form of practical action in relieving the suffering of this life. God brings about justice for the poor, feeds the hungry, sets captives free, gives sight to the blind, straightens those stooped over, affirms upright people, protects aliens, and supports orphans and widows (Ps 146:5-9).

Luke's Gospel opens with a celebration of God's mercy. Like Hannah, the mother of Samuel (1 Sam 2:1-10), Mary sings a song of praise in which she remembers God's history of merciful actions on behalf of downtrodden people (Luke 1:50, 54). John the Baptist's birth is evidence of God's mercy to Elizabeth (Luke 1:58). Zechariah's canticle also affirms God's covenant, understood as a history of God's mercy (Luke 1:72, 78). Thus, Mary, Jesus, John the Baptist, Elizabeth, and Zechariah are all interrelated because of a long history of God's compassion. Compassion is the name for the unbroken covenant which links God's actions in the OT and their continuity in the NT era.

This manifestation of God is incarnated in Jesus who understands that his own prophetic mission is primarily one of compassion and relief of suffering. The synonyms of *hesed*, *rachamim*, and *hanan* are translated in the NT in various contexts as the tender yearning of Jesus *(splagchnizomai)*, his disposition to show mildness and kindness *(eleeō)*, and to have pity *(oikteirō)*. Jesus will preach to the poor, offer liberation to the oppressed, give sight to the blind, and assure people of God's kindly disposition and season of favor. He announces that all this is taking place in the present moment, not reserved for a future fulfillment (Luke 4:18.21).

The mercy of Jesus expresses itself during his public ministry as an abiding readiness to acknowledge the needs of the poor and politically oppressed, sympathy for partnerless women, inclusion of social outcasts in his company, forgiveness of repentant sinners, healing of those sick in mind and body, consolation of his followers when they are sad or afraid, and patience toward those who do him violence. The pity of Jesus is aroused by the presence of crowds who are like sheep without a shepherd and he is inspired to teach them many things before feeding five thousand of them (Mark 6:34). Jesus is moved with sympathy and yearning when he sees how tired and hungry the crowds are (Mark 8:1-10; Matt 15:32). His sympathy moves him to find a way to feed four thousand people. Thus, the compassion of Jesus inspires both his teaching to relieve spiritual confusion, and his determination to relieve physical hunger.

Two blind men follow Jesus and call out for mercy (Matt 9:27). Jesus asks if they believe he can heal them. Their faith in the mercy of Jesus is rewarded by their recovery of sight. The following of Jesus precedes their healing, and afterwards, they spread the word about what he has done (Matt 9:31). A similar, insistent prayer of two other blind men, "Lord, Son of David, have pity on us!" evokes the deeply felt pity of Jesus who touches them. After they are healed, they follow Jesus. Thus, the experience of mercy empowers them to be disciples (Matt 20:30, 31). The story of Bartimaeus who twice invokes the mercy of Jesus (Mark 10:47-48; Luke 18:38-39) is the healing story that concludes the public ministry of Jesus in Mark. The experience of God's mercy is to be the content of the good news the Gerasene man shares with those closest to him. "Go home to your family and announce to them all that the Lord in his pity has done for you" (Mark 5:19). Thus, the experience of mercy enables people to be disciples, and is the foundation of what they say about Jesus.

The mercy of Jesus shows no partiality to insiders and does not exclude outsiders. One of the ten lepers who cries out for pity, "Jesus, Master! Have pity on us!" returns to give thanks, and he is a Samaritan (Luke 17:11-19). The Canaanite woman, a social and religious outsider, begs Jesus to heal her daughter. "Have pity on me, Lord, Son of David! My daughter is tormented by a demon" (Matt 15:22). Her prayer for mercy is actually an intercession on behalf of someone else. The scorned Jewish tax collector, socially compromised by his need to make a living through cooperation with Roman occupation, asks for God to be merciful to him as a sinner (Luke 18:13). His consciousness of need and his readiness to receive God's benevolent love make him the model for believers.

The mercy of Jesus responds both to direct and indirect appeals from those suffering. A father shares the torment of his son and begs Jesus to cure his possessed child, "If you can do anything, have compassion on us and help us" (Mark 9:22). In another version, he prays only for his child, "Lord, have pity on my son, for he is a lunatic and suffers severely" (Matt 17:15). A disposition of faith enables the merciful response of Jesus to be effective in responding to the seeker, whether the petitioner asks for himself or herself, or on behalf of someone else. The prayers for mercy addressed to Jesus by petitioners in the Gospels echo the appeals for mercy which sufferers make to God in the psalms.

Jesus raises the widow's only son at Naim because he is moved with pity for her (Luke 7:13). She does not ask him for anything. Her need is dramatized by her grief, the fact that she is now a childless widow, and the consequence of her social vulnerability as a woman left with no means of economic support. The same initiative inspires Jesus to cure a crippled woman on the Sabbath (Luke 13:10-17) and defend her dignity and right to be cured since she is a daughter of Abraham (Luke 13:16). The anonymous woman who anoints the feet of Jesus does not use words, but her actions prompt Jesus to defend her by telling a parable about debtors who are forgiven what they owe. The debtors are assured of forgiveness, just as she is (Luke 7:40-43).

The parable of the lost son (Luke 15:11-32) equates the father's longing for reunion with God's loving and attentive waiting for sinners to repent. God's forgiving mercy, the parable consolingly suggests, is an interior movement of tender yearning (*splagchnizomai*), gracious welcome, and generous embrace of a wayward child (Luke 15:20). Mercy is equivalent to forgiveness, pardon, and the beginning of a new season of celebration, symbolized by the feast. The merciful disposition of Jesus manifests itself even when violence is done to him. When he is nailed to the cross he says, "Father, forgive them, they know not what they do" (Luke 23:34). The repentant thief who acknowledges Jesus' innocence is assured that he will be in God's reign with Jesus (Luke 23:40-42).

Imitating the Compassion of Jesus as Disciples. Since the outflow of God's goodness on the world, like rain, is not conditioned by people's justice or injustice, neither should love of neighbor be extended only to friends, relatives, and those who can reciprocate (Matt 10:44-47). Imitation of God means being perfect as God is perfect (Matt 5:48). However, this perfection is made equivalent with mercy in "Be merciful just as your Father is merciful" and is essentially the same unconditional love God shows toward even the ungrateful and the wicked (Luke 6:36). In the parable of the unforgiving servant (Matt 18:21-35) mercy is equivalent to forgiveness of another's debt. Just as one's own debts have already been forgiven by God, so should a person extend that pity and forgiveness to others (Matt 18:33).

The disciples of Jesus are blessed and assured of receiving God's mercy when they themselves are kind, *eleeō* (Matt 5:7). The Good Samaritan (Luke 10:29-37) exemplifies mercy as the response that characterizes the person who keeps the greatest commandment, "You shall love the Lord, your God, with all your heart, with all your being, with all your strength, and with all your mind, and your neighbor as yourself" (Luke 10:25-28). The Samaritan is moved with compassion at the sight of the man victimized by robbers and acts toward him as a neighbor, that is, shows him mercy (Luke 10:33, 37). Thus, a Samaritan is a keeper of the greatest commandment, to love God wholeheartedly and one's neighbor as oneself, precisely because he has acted compassionately toward someone in dire need. In the parable of the rich man and Lazarus, the rich man's appeal for mercy comes too late (Luke 16:24). He did not notice the needs of the impoverished at his doorstep and show mercy during his lifetime. Thus, a great chasm separates him from those like Lazarus who receive God's consolation (Luke 16:26).

In the final days of sorting sheep from goats (Matt 25:31-46), the measure by which all people will be judged by God, even Gentiles, will not be their status as believers or unbelievers. Rather, their compassionate action to relieve the suffering of those in dire need will sort the righteous from the unrighteous. It does not matter whether or not they have been inspired by love for Jesus, but only that they acted mercifully toward others, concretely meeting the survival needs of the dispossessed: feeding the hungry, giving drink to the thirsty, welcoming strangers, clothing the naked, caring for the sick, and visiting the imprisoned.

The Community Formed by Receivers of Mercy. Paul and other writers of Pastoral Letters greet their congregations with an invocation of God's benevolent mercy or *eleos* (2 Cor 1:3; 1 Tim 1:2; Titus 1:4). The blessing of mercy concludes their message (Gal 6:16). The person who receives the divine mercy feels joyful and secure in God's presence. God's merciful graciousness actually creates a new community and is a universal gift to all people, Jews, Gentiles, those near, and those far away (Rom 11:31; 15:9). Mercy is the way God acts toward people, independent of their efforts. The appropriate way to name God's kindliness and choice of those to love is mercy, not injustice. God's pity is the divine prerogative, not a matter of human will (Rom 9:15, 16, 18). Mercy is God's invitation of relationship extended to anyone who is alienated and disobedient. Whether Jew or Gentile, all receive God's mercy (Rom 11:30, 31, 32). Identification with human beings makes it possible for Jesus to be a merciful high priest expiating the sins of the people before God (Heb 2:17). Believers can confidently approach God's throne of grace and there receive mercy (Heb 4:16).

Within the Christian community, the performance of acts of mercy is considered a distinct personal charism that enriches the entire body of Christ. Some have gifts for prophetic pronouncement, ministerial service, teaching, exhortation, providing financial support, or performing administrative duties. As though completing the series of charisms, others have a specific gift for doing acts of mercy, and they should be accomplished cheerfully (Rom 12:6-8). Compassion and mercy inspire members of a community to be united in intention, love, heart, and thoughts, and this union is the opposite of attitudes of self-interest, self-importance, and status-seeking (Phil 2:2). Unlike attitudes of jealousy and ambition among community members, it is possible to act out of a heavenly wisdom which is "pure, then peaceable, gentle, compliant, full of mercy and good fruits, without inconstancy or insincerity" (Jas 3:17).

The new community is one which thankfully knows it has received God's mercy, and experiences a profound change of identity from anonymity, disgrace, sinfulness, and darkness, for it is now a chosen race, a royal priesthood, a holy nation (1 Pet 2:9). "Once you were 'no people' but now you are God's people; you 'had not received mercy' but now you have received mercy" (1 Pet 2:10).

See: CHARISM, COMPASSION, COVENANT, FAITHFULNESS, HEALING, JUDGMENT, JUSTICE, PRAYER, SUFFERING, TEACH/TEACHING

MARIE-ELOISE ROSENBLATT, R.S.M.

Pastoral-Liturgical Tradition

The rich biblical vocabulary of mercy with its multiple understandings flowed over into early Christian writings. Thus, Clement of Rome depicts God as a God of kindness who longs to show mercy, and he exhorts the Christians of Corinth to beg for that mercy (1 Clement 9; 23). In the Didache (15) Christians, who are the recipients of God's gracious mercy, are exhorted to show mercy in turn.

As prayer texts of the early Church increasingly came to be written down in the third and fourth centuries, the mercy of God was a recurring motif. These prayers, especially the opening prayers and other such collects, often begin: "God of mercies," "almighty and merciful God." The petitionary section of the prayers frequently asks for God's mercy ("have mercy on your people") or it associates a proclamation of God's mercy with the saving action requested of God ("in your mercy, hear us," "mercifully grant," etc.). The *Kyrie eleison* ("Lord, have mercy") developed in fourth-century Jerusalem as a spoken response to the community's prayers of intercession and soon spread to other parts of the Christian world. These ways of addressing God are still part of the Church's prayer vocabulary.

Though the biblical vocabulary of mercy has survived in liturgical tradition, there has been at times a drift in its meaning. For example, some biblical ways of speaking image mercy as the tender, responsive love felt in the very center of one's body (*rahamim,* womb-love; *splanchna,* a spontaneous outward movement of one's heart and entrails in compassion), like the feelings of a mother and father for their child. These images found a reflection in some early prayers which ask God's favor *per viscera misericordiae tuae.* Recent translations, however, tend to leave behind these graphic biblical images and render them simply as "mercy." More significantly, the play on fidelity, mutuality, and response found in the biblical vocabulary *(hesed; eleos),* implying that those who have received the mercy of God are to engage in merciful actions toward others (Luke 6:36), has been overshadowed by a stress on the gratuity and unearned favor of God's gift of mercy *(hen)* to a sinful people. Thus, Medieval and subsequent tradition became preoccupied with a more legal image of mercy as forgiveness of the debt/offense of sin, as amnesty. In that context theologians had to wrestle with the difficulty of reconciling God's mercy and justice.

The presider now faces the assembly and prays to God in their name. That seemingly simple liturgical reform intimates that the God we address is among us and that all in the circle of prayer have a responsibility to each other. The Church is thus being called not only to new ways of imaging and addressing the God who is among us in Christ Jesus and who is partner to us in our world, but also to a new way of living out the justice and mercy of that God in our relationships to one another and the world. Recovery of the fuller biblical imagery of the mercy can help us on both scores.

SEE: JUSTICE, LOVE, SIN

GILBERT OSTDIEK, O.F.M.

MERIT

Pastoral-Liturgical Tradition

Merit is the reward or commendation an act is said to deserve in virtue of its excellence. In general, a good work or deed was said to be meritorious if its virtuous quality entitled a person to some kind of recognition, usually a reward. Specifically, Catholic theology has traditionally spoken of merit as the spiritual reward due a person, usually in terms of eternal life, because of the inherent worth or value of their actions. A meritorious act was any deed, freely chosen and done under the influence of grace, that was directed to God and meant to honor God. Too, even though an act might have a more immediate purpose, such as justice, compassion, or generosity to one's neighbor, if it was also intended to give glory to God, it was considered meritorious. Nonetheless, does God owe us anything for the good we do? Even with a lifetime of virtue, can we merit eternal life through good works if these are nothing more than giving what we owe to God?

Protestant and Catholic Teaching on Merit. These questions illumine the differences between traditional Protestant and Catholic approaches to merit. In general, classical Protestant theology argues that human beings cannot be justified or made righteous by virtue of their good works, but only through the healing, reconciling grace of God. It is the redeeming goodness of God in Christ, not personal virtue, that saves and justifies, and such goodness is wholly a gift of God's mercy, never an achievement of human merit (Rom 1:16-17; Eph 2:8-10). Rooted in the Reformation, the Protestant approach sees God as the agent of justification, and grace as the gift that justifies through forgiveness of sins and sanctification; thus, what makes us new creatures in Christ is not our own goodness, but the entirely unmerited mercy of God. It is through grace, not personal merit, that we become children of God and heirs of eternal life. Too, since justification is comprehensive and enduring, good works add nothing to the assurance of salvation, but are expressions of gratitude for a blessedness already won. The strength of the Protestant position is that it avoids a Pelagian perfectionism that would

suggest human beings, through good works done without the assistance of grace, could be agents of their own righteousness.

Catholic teaching on merit is more complex and nuanced. Catholic theology maintains that virtuous acts are meritorious, but not without prior justification. Justification through grace is a prerequisite for merit because the very possibility of an act being pleasing to God is contingent on a person being reconciled to God. The principal reconciliation between God and ourselves occurs through the justifying and sanctifying powers of grace in baptism, which frees us from original sin and makes us a new creation in Christ. Through this grace, which is purely a gift of God's love, we are transformed from sin to righteousness and made capable of deeds pleasing to God (S.Th., I-II, 113,1).

Meritorious acts flow from and are made possible by the prior grace of justification; indeed, that we can merit anything is solely because of what grace enables us to do. Without grace, we remain infinitely far from God and utterly incapable of acts worthy of God; in fact, in sin there persists an absolute inequality between God and ourselves. That our acts can give glory to God is only because God first and always enables us to do what otherwise would be impossible for us (S.Th., I-II, 114, 1,2).

Our capacity for virtuous acts requires grace for two reasons. First, even if we had not sinned we would be incapable of acts adequate for salvation. Strictly speaking, in order to merit eternal life we must practice virtues whose goodness is proportionate to the goodness of God; however, this is impossible for us because the supreme goodness of God is infinitely superior to our own. Left to ourselves, we are not capable of acts of supernatural goodness, they are utterly beyond the powers of human nature. To have eternal life with God is to be transformed in the goodness of God, but such a drastic conversion* of ourselves cannot be the work of our own virtue alone; rather, for virtuous acts to be meritorious they must be rooted in and respond to grace. Grace empowers virtue by bestowing on our human nature a capacity for goodness pleasing to God, and in this sense gives our actions supernatural possibilities: "Now eternal life is an end which lies beyond the proportionate scope of human nature," Aquinas writes. "And so by his natural endowments man cannot produce meritorious works proportionate to eternal life, but a higher power is needed for this, which is the power of grace" (S.Th., I-II, 109,5).

Second, meritorious acts are impossible without grace because of human sinfulness. Sin, whether original or actual, brings disorder to our nature. If disease weakens our bodies, sin is an illness of the spirit leaving us infirm in our ability to do good; Aquinas describes it as a "congenital defect" affecting our whole person and diminishing our capacity for virtue (S.Th., I-II, 82,1). If in the state of original justice our wills were set firmly on God, with original sin came a corruption and disordering of our nature that leaves us divided and distracted, often attached to goods other than God. Overall, sin represents a wounding of our nature. Because our whole self is debilitated by sin, grace is necessary to rehabilitate us for goodness. Consequently, truly meritorious deeds are impossible without grace not only because of the limited powers of our nature, but also because of the deep roots of sin that divide us from God; thus, grace abides as the principle and source of any good work (S.Th., I-II, 114,5). In this respect, Catholic and Protestant teaching on merit are virtually the same.

But if the Catholic position agrees that the primary cause of merit is God's grace and mercy, it goes beyond Protestant teaching by holding that the secondary cause of merit is a person's free choice (S.Th., I-II, 114,3). Unlike other creatures who do God's will by instinct, and thus give glory to God simply in virtue of their existence, human beings do God's will by choice. Though we depend on grace to live virtuously, our acts of goodness are freely chosen, not determined. We have intelligence and free will; thus, we can actively choose either to act in accordance with grace or to sin. It is the element of choice that gives our good deeds merit (S.Th., I-II, 114,1). Put differently, if grace enables virtue, virtue is our freely chosen and intentional response to grace. Unlike other creatures who have no choice but to be what they are, we can choose to be other than human by embracing dehumanizing behavior. Virtue is meritorious because it is an act of free will whereby we respond gratefully and deliberately to what God's love enables us to do.

The Relation between Charity and Merit. Of all the virtues, charity is quintessential for meritorious behavior. The perfecting activity of charity is to turn our hearts to God in an expression of friendship which loves God and seeks what is best for God (S.Th., II-II, 23,1). Persons of charity are wholeheartedly devoted to God as the supreme good and seeks to give glory to God through all their behavior. If charity, as the virtue which represents the steadfast love of our life, is in our heart, this desire to please God will be expressed in everything we do, and it is this that makes our actions meritorious. Traditionally this has been described by saying charity directs the acts of all the virtues to God and makes them serve its primary intention of giving glory to God (S.Th., I-II, 114,4). As the principal theological virtue whose purpose is to center us on God, charity gathers all the activities of our lives and puts them in the service of God (S.Th., II-II, 23,4).

This is why charity is called the "form" of all the virtues, and why there can be no true virtue or genuinely meritorious act that is not born from charity's love. An act is meritorious only if it helps us achieve the ultimate purpose of our lives, union with God. The special efficacy of charity is that it empowers every act to reach its maximum excellence by forming it in friendship and love for God. If love of God is the intention that abides in our hearts, then it will be impressed upon everything we do. Just as a mother conceives through another, every genuinely virtuous act is conceived through charity's love (S.Th., II-II, 23,8). It is in being quickened by charity that any act becomes meritorious. The power of charity is that through the influence of its love every other virtue reaches its highest possible excellence (S.Th., II-II, 23,7); indeed, through charity anything we do, no matter how mundane or seemingly insignificant, has supernatural bearing. Charity makes all our deeds incalculably valuable, indeed, acts of worship, by charging them with love for God and placing them in the service of God.

Pastoral Applications. If it is true that justification through grace and the forgiveness of sins are necessary for our deeds to be meritorious, then it is also true that Christians have merit not in themselves but only in and through Christ. Ultimately, only Christ is wholly pleasing to God, and thus can merit our salvation. It is through the incarnation of Christ, especially his passion, death, and resurrection, that justice is restored between God and ourselves. If a meritorious act is one which is pleasing to God, the passion and death of Jesus is most perfectly meritorious because through this offering all are cleansed of sin and made a new creation (S.Th., III, 22,3). Insofar as we are members of the body of Christ and participate in his saving life, principally through the sacraments, our life and actions are pleasing to God. It is through our sharing in the priesthood of Christ, especially in the Eucharist, that our sins are forgiven and we are made holy. Thus, we merit salvation not through the efficacy of our own virtue, but through Christ's passion and death (S.Th., III, 48,1).

It is in union with Christ and thanks to Christ, the source of all life and holiness (Eucharistic Prayer III), that we who were alienated from God become the people of God. The offering of Christ is the offering of the Church, and it is through Christ, the source of all merit, that we become an acceptable offering to God (Eucharistic Prayer I). Along with baptism, the Eucharist is the sacrament of merit because insofar as we join ourselves to the priesthood of Christ we become rec-

onciled to God, filled with the holy Spirit, and summoned to share the inheritance of all the saints (Eucharistic Prayer III). Thus, it is through the paschal mystery that our peace is made with God and salvation is brought to the whole world (Eucharistic Prayer IV). To realize that we are "freed from the corruption of sin and death" (Eucharistic Prayer IV) and able to sing God's glory only because of the redemption Christ has won for us is to understand why our most meritorious acts are gratitude and praise.

See: GRACE, JUSTIFICATION, REDEMPTION, RETRIBUTION

PAUL J. WADELL, C.P.

MESSIAH

This article will explore the idea of messiah evident in the writings of the NT, the range of messianic expectations in early Judaism,* their emergence under the impact of the Babylonian Exile, and their roots in ancient Israelite and ancient Near Eastern royal traditions. In the "Lord's Anointed" ancient Israel saw its legitimate leaders. It perceived God at work in and through them though ancient Israel was always aware of the limitations of institutionalized patterns of leadership. Early Christianity inherited these messianic traditions and reinterpreted them so as to comprehend the person and work of Jesus of Nazareth.

The Use of the Old Testament in the New

In the NT "messiah" is the most frequently used title for Jesus. (*Christós* is the Greek translation of the Hebrew word *mashiach*. Both derive from words that mean "anoint.") The problem that early Christianity had to face in appropriating this title centered on the manner of Jesus' death. None of the messianic expectations of early Judaism inherited by the Church envisioned a messiah who would suffer and die a humiliating death. One text that probably helped the early Church to find a link between suffering and messiahship was Psalm 89. The psalm speaks about the humiliation of the king, God's anointed (messiah; Ps 89:38-39). It makes an appeal for the king by recalling God's promise to David (Ps 89:49). The psalm concludes with an appeal by the anointed (messiah) himself (Ps 89:50-51). While the psalm says little about the nature of the suffering and humiliation, it provides a link to texts that do. In verse 39, the psalm calls the king "thy servant" and so justifies the use of servant as a messianic designation. This allows the NT to use texts such as Isaiah 53 to explain the suffering of Jesus the Messiah as according to the Scriptures.

The NT association of suffering with the Messiah is clear from Peter's confession (Mark 8:27-33; Matt 16:13-23; Luke 9:18-22). Each Synoptic associates this confession with a prediction of the passion. The one time in Mark that Jesus unambiguously accepts the title of Messiah comes during the trial before the Sanhedrin (14:53-62). Here there is no possibility that anyone could misunderstand the type of messiah that Jesus was to be. Mark portrays Jesus' ministry in non-messianic categories, but royal imagery dominates the story of his trial and death. Jesus is condemned because he accepts the designation of "Messiah, the Son of the Blessed One" (14:61). Pilate tries Jesus because some accuse him of being "the King of the Jews" (15:2, 12). The soldiers mock Jesus because of the same title (15:18). The bystanders at the cross jeer at Jesus while calling him "the Messiah, the king of Israel" (15:32).

Luke goes beyond Mark by asserting that scriptural necessity of the Messiah's death and resurrection (Luke 24:46-47). In Acts 2:24-31, Luke has Peter cite Psalm 16 as proof that the Messiah was not to experience corruption. Paul's speech in Acts 13 uses Psalm 16 and Isaiah 55:3 to argue that the Scriptures speak of the Messiah's death and resurrection.

In the Gospels, "the Messiah" refers to the expected king from the line of David. Still Matthew illustrates the complexity of messianic expectations. In Matthew 22:41-46 Jesus tests the Pharisees' exegetical skill by asking them how they could teach that the Messiah was David's son when David called him "Lord." The text implies that the Pharisees are not competent religious teachers since they cannot solve this problem. How could anyone believe that they know anything about the Messiah since they cannot explain an obviously messianic text?

For the author of the Letter to the Hebrews, the Messiah was a priest as well as a king. Though Jewish thought separated priestly and royal functions, Hebrews describes Jesus as both Messiah and high priest. According to Hebrews, Jesus offered the unique sacrifice of himself and has qualified for the position of heavenly high priest to make expiation for sin. God has designated Jesus a high priest after the order of Melchizedek (5:5-6). The union of the royal and priestly functions in the person of the king was not an innovation of Hebrews. In the royal ideology of the ancient world, such union was quite usual. In the traditions of ancient Israel, there was a high priest alongside the king. The way Hebrews presents Jesus as Messiah is another example of the Christian transformation of Jewish messianic expectations.

The Dead Sea Scrolls

Contemporaneous with Jesus and the development of the traditions that emerged in the NT, there was another Jewish movement that had strong and explicit messianic expectations. This is the Qumran community that produced the Dead Sea Scrolls. In the Scrolls the theme of messianism is prominent, though the scrolls do not treat this theme systematically. What these texts reveal is a complex and unique messianism that envisages two and perhaps three messianic figures. There is a "Messiah of Israel" (1QSb 5:21, 28, 28). This figure is also known as the "Branch of David," "the Prince of the Congregation," and "the Scepter." The Messiah of Israel was to establish the "kingdom of his people." This he would do by defeating the nations and destroying the forces of evil.

A second messianic figure was to be a priest. This was the "Messiah of Aaron" also known as the "Priest" and the "Interpreter of the Law" (1QSa 2:20). The "Messiah of Aaron" appeared to have precedence over the "Messiah of Israel" (4QpIsa 8-10:23). He led the liturgy that preceded the final battle with the powers of darkness (1QM 15:4; 16:13; 18:5).

There is a third messianic figure who is mentioned only once (1QS 9:11). This is the prophet whose arrival was anticipated along with the Messiahs of Aaron and Israel. The precise identification of this prophet is unclear. He may be an Elijah-figure who is to return as a precursor of Messiah (see Mal 4:5; 1 Enoch 90:31; Matt 11:13; 17:12). He may be the promised "prophet like Moses" (Deut 18:15-18; Acts 3:22-23; 7:37). Some interpreters hold that the people of Qumran believed that this prophet had already come in the person of the Teacher of Righteousness.

Because the reconstruction of Qumran messianic beliefs is based on the interpretation of isolated passages from several Qumran documents, there is no consensus on the exact contours of Qumran messianism. This much can be said: the people of Qumran believed that they were living in the eschatological age that would witness the victory of God's people over the powers of darkness. The final act of this eschatological age would be marked by the coming of a messiah or messiahs who would inaugurate the new age.

Intertestamental Literature

There were other Jews beside the people of Qumran who were looking forward to the coming of a messiah. Their expectations survive in a collection of non-canonical texts known collectively as the Intertestamental literature or the Apocrypha and Pseudepigrapha of the OT. These texts date from approximately 200 BCE to 200 CE. There are about fifty-one books in this collection. Of these only five contain explicit statements about "the Messiah." These texts mention other ideal figures of the eschatological age, but occurrences of the term "Messiah" are relatively infrequent. What is most surprising is that three documents (the Apocalypse of Moses, the Life of Adam and Eve, and the Lives of the Prophets) that are contemporaneous with the early life of Jesus of Nazareth contain no references to a messiah.

The Psalms of Solomon. The first of the Intertestamental texts to mention "the messiah" is the Psalms of Solomon that come from the middle of the first century BCE. In Psalms of Solomon 17:21-33 there is a description of the Messiah who will be a descendant of David. He will purge Jerusalem and defeat its enemies by "the word of his mouth" rather than by armed might. This Messiah is not a political revolutionary. This Messiah simply presides over the kingdom that God will establish.

Psalm of Solomon 18 looks back to the Davidic kings of Judah who reigned as God's anointed. It looks forward to the day when God will bring back a king like David. The ideal king will embody all the hopes that ancient Israel had for David and his dynasty. It is important to note that it is God who will accomplish all this.

Second Baruch. The second document with references to the messiah is Second Baruch. This text was written sometime during the second half of the first century CE. The specific texts include 2 Baruch 29:3; 30:1; 39:7; 40:1; 70:9; and 72:2. According to Second Baruch the days of the Messiah will be days of plenty. The Messiah will capture and execute the leader of the peoples arrayed against Israel (2 Baruch 39–42). The Messiah will execute harsh judgment on the nations that oppressed Israel but spare those that have not (2 Baruch 72–74). After the Messiah fulfills his task, he will return to his glory and the souls of the righteous will rise (30:1-2). The Messiah of Second Baruch takes an active role in leading the forces of Israel in a military defeat of their enemies.

Fourth Ezra. Fourth Ezra is the third Intertestamental text that mentions the Messiah. It is contemporaneous with Second Baruch. The most significant text in this book is its chapter seven. The author of

617

Fourth Ezra divides the "world to come" into three periods. The first begins with the coming of the Messiah (7:28-29). What is most significant about this text is the idea that the Messiah will come and die. The messianic age then is not the eschaton. Following the Messiah's death comes the second period: a return to primeval silence for seven days (7:30). The last period is a time of judgment that will last for seven years (7:31-44). Following the judgment, the present world will come to its end.

The second messianic section of Fourth Ezra is 11:37–12:34. Here the text describes the Messiah as a lion who comes as a warrior and a judge. Still the Messiah fulfills his task not by means available to human beings but by the power of God. He defeats God's enemies by supernatural power and not by weapons of war. The text states explicitly that the Messiah is preexistent and of Davidic descent. The Messiah's kingdom is temporary and will last only until the day of judgment.

First Enoch. The fourth document that explicitly mentions the Messiah is First Enoch, one of the more important Jewish apocalyptic works. The book's date is a matter of controversy, but the messianic passages apparently are contemporaneous with the rise of Christianity. It is a lengthy work that contains only two passages about the Messiah: 48:10 and 52:4. The Messiah of First Enoch is an earthly, human king. This Messiah does not inaugurate any type of messianic kingdom. He has no important functions and has no apparent association with the Davidic dynasty. God fulfills the usual messianic tasks.

Third Enoch. The final early Jewish text that mentions the Messiah is Third Enoch. It is a composition that dates from the third century CE. What is significant about this text is that it mentions two messiahs. One will be a "son of Joseph" and the other a "son of David" (45:5). This passage describes a battle with the powers of evil that Israel will win only when God takes an active part. A second text (48:10) takes its inspiration from three OT texts (Isa 52:10;

Deut 32:12; Zech 14:9) as it describes the celebrations with the Messiah after God frees Israel from its enemies.

What these texts show is that some Jews of the second century BCE to the third century CE believed that God's intervention on Israel's behalf was immanent and that the coming of the Messiah will mark the beginning of Israel's redemption. There were other Jews who looked for God to act directly and had no explicit expectations about the coming of a messiah. The fact that only five texts outside of the Dead Sea Scrolls explicitly mention a messiah raises the question about the extent of messianic expectations in early Judaism.

Three of the references to the Messiah in Intertestamental literature occur in apocalyptic texts (Enoch, 4 Ezra, and 2 Baruch). The time of the Messiah is one of peace and prosperity, but the apocalyptic setting places the appearance of the Messiah in the period before an apocalyptic judgment. This literature then joins two motifs in its presentation of the Messiah. The first is the OT belief that the restoration of the Davidic dynasty will be a time of peace and prosperity for Israel (Isa 9:2-7; Jer 23:5-6; 33:15-16). The second is unique to the apocalyptic tradition: good and evil are engaged in a struggle that will continue until God makes a final resolution on the day of judgment.

Postexilic Texts. The matrix for the speculation about the Messiah in the Intertestamental literature is the hope held by some Jews for the restoration of the native Judahite dynasty following the return from the Exile in 539 BCE. The purpose of restoring Judah's native dynasty was to reestablish political and economic independence. In view of the power of the Persian empire such goals were unrealistic.

Zerubbabel. While this period is not well documented, clearly hopes first centered on Zerubbabel (Hag 2:21, 23; Zech 4:6-7). There was probably a messianic movement in Judah following the death of the Persian ruler Cambyses in 522 BCE. A period of political and military unrest usually followed the death of an imperial ruler in the ancient Near East. Judah's messianic movement was one part of the disturbances that plagued the whole empire. Some people in Judah probably thought that Cambyses' death opened the way for the restoration of Judah's native dynasty. Darius was able to restore order throughout the Persian empire in 520 BCE. What happened to Zerubbabel is not clear. What we do know is that there was no restoration of a native Jewish monarchy.

Nehemiah. There is some evidence of a second attempt to restore a native dynasty. This time hopes centered on Nehemiah. Again the attempt proved to be futile. Nehemiah himself denied any royal ambitions and repudiated the prophets that supported him (Neh 6:6-9). Hopes for a restoration of Judah's monarchy diminished to the point that people gave up on the present world as the scene of the resurgence of the Davidic dynasty. The Messiah will be part of the eschaton, God's final act of deliverance for Israel.

Not all Jews were looking for the restoration of the native monarchy. In particular the upper levels of the priestly hierocracy may not have been anxious for the return of royal rule in Judah since they replaced the royal bureaucracy and the high priest functioned as the *de facto* leader of the Jewish community though he had to acknowledge the Persian hegemony. Their subservience to the empire was so complete that they were able to invest the high priest with the traditional raiment of the king and install him with a ritual of anointing without alarming Persian authorities. The priests believed that their administration, while subject to the Persians, was the best hope for conserving and maintaining the worship of Judah's ancestral deity and the distinctive way of life that followed from that worship.

The Exile

The Exile was the crucible in which messianism was forged. The defeat of the Kingdom of Judah and the exile of many of its leading citizens following the fall of Jerusalem to Nabuchadnezzar in 587 BCE meant the end of most of the institutions that gave Judah its identity. The last years of the Judahite state were tumultuous. Babylon* deposed and exiled one king and set up another whose rebellion against his patrons sealed his doom and that of Judah and Jerusalem. When the exiled king, Jehoiachin, died in Babylon, some saw this as the end of the one dynasty that ruled in Judah for more than four hundred years. Clearly any hope for restoration of an independent Judah involved plans to reintroduce the monarchy and have a member of the Davidic family as king (Jer 33:14-26).

Not all exiles were so committed to the Davidic dynasty and the restoration of the old system. In Ezekiel's vision of a resurrected Judah, the king becomes a prince with no real political power (Ezek 46:1-18). His principal duty is to be a patron of the Temple and its rituals. It is difficult to describe Ezekiel's "prince" as a messiah. More explicit regarding the shape of the hoped-for restoration is Deutero-Isaiah who calls Cyrus the Persian God's messiah (Isa 45:1). The prophet calls a non-Jew the Messiah. This prophet and his followers did not consider the restoration of the Davidic dynasty an essential component of Judah's restoration.

Israel's Royal Ideology

The roots of exilic and postexilic messianism lie in ancient Israel's royal traditions. Israel came into existence without a monarchy much less with the idea of a messiah. The Israelite tribes had no central political power from the time of the settlement (thirteenth century BCE) until the rise of Saul (ca. 1040 BCE). Saul was the first Israelite to be installed as king with an anointing. Saul was, in effect, Israel's first messiah. His rule over the tribes was modest even by Israelite standards. It was David (1000–970 BCE) who created an absolute, centralized political power in Canaan. The elders of Judah and then Israel anoint David as their king (2 Sam 2:4; 5:3). Solomon's accession to the throne involved a solemn ritual of anointing led by a priest (1 Kgs 1:39). The ritual of anointing apparently symbolized the unique relationship between God and Israel's king. It endowed the king with "the spirit of Yahweh" that brought with it the talents necessary for leadership over the tribes (1 Sam 16:13).

Ancient Israel's royal ideology that emerges in the royal psalms envisions the Lord's anointed as a victorious military leader (Ps 2:8-9), an impartial judge (Ps 72:2, 12-13), and even a "son of God" (Ps 2:7). The fact was that the claims made for the king and the reality of the Israelite monarchy did not coincide. While the reigns of David and Solomon were bright periods in the political history of the monarchy, the Israelite kingdoms were minor players in the ancient Near East. Both Israel and Judah lived in the shadow of the Mesopotamian imperial powers. Against this background, claims made in the royal psalms seem ludicrous (e.g., Psalm 2). Even if the rhetoric of those psalms implied nothing more than a peaceful political existence for Israel under its anointed king (messiah), it was little more than a vain hope.

Ancient Near Eastern Royal Ideology

The roots of Israel's way of thinking about its kings ultimately derive from ancient Near Eastern kingship ideology. The king was the one who stood between two worlds: the world of the gods and the world of humans. The monarchy was the basis of civilization. In Egypt, the king was a living God who ruled in the human world. His word was law because it was the embodiment of the divine will. In Mesopotamia the king was a human being, but one with a unique relationship to the gods. Monarchy then was not a political institution; it was a religious one. Its function was to maintain harmony between the visible world and the powers that rule nature. Ancient Israel thought of its kings in a similar fashion. That is why the hope for an ideal king (messiah) continued in some circles after the end of the Davidic dynasty.

See: MONARCHY

LESLIE J. HOPPE, O.F.M.

New Testament

In the writings that comprise the NT, which are written in Greek, the Hebrew word *messiah* is translated *christos*. In English translations of the NT *christos* is usually transliterated as Christ. This title is applied to Jesus in every writing of the NT except the Third Letter of John, which makes no reference to Jesus. This is the title that the early Christians associated most closely with Jesus. It expresses their basic faith in Jesus, i.e., that he was the Savior God had promised to Israel.

The Problem Involved in the Use of Christ for Jesus. The early Christians' use of the title Christ to express their fundamental belief about Jesus is puzzling for two reasons. The first is that Jesus did not closely resemble the Messiah expected by Israel. One description of the expected Messiah can be found in the Psalms of Solomon, a Jewish writing composed in mid-first century BCE. Psalms of Solomon 17 describes the Messiah as a righteous king who will free Jerusalem from those who oppress her and establish hegemony over the nations of the earth. There are points of similarity between this description and Jesus, but more differences. Jesus was not a universal king in the ordinary sense of these words. Because of this the Christian claim that Jesus is the Messiah has always been incredible to most Jews.

Not only did Jesus differ from what the Messiah was expected to be, he also does not seem to have made the claim to be the Messiah a central element of his teaching. It does seem clear that during his lifetime the followers of Jesus and others thought that he might be the Messiah. However, it seems likely that Jesus refrained from affirming this idea. There are a few NT passages in which Jesus unambiguously calls himself the Messiah (Mark 14:61-62; John 4:25-26; 17:3). Usually Jesus seems more reserved about the title. Mark 8:27-33; Matt 16:13-23; Luke 9:18-22 is characteristic. In this passage Jesus asks his disciples who they say he is, and Peter answers, "You are the Messiah." In response Jesus orders his disciples not to tell anyone about him. Then Jesus goes on to teach his disciples about his coming passion (v. 31); Peter rebukes him (v. 32); and Jesus rebukes Peter, calling him Satan (v. 33). From this it is not clear whether or not Jesus accepted the identification of himself as Messiah. Very likely he was hesitant to do so because he realized that his mission differed from what the Messiah was expected to do. Other passages in which Jesus seems reserved about the title "Messiah" include Matthew 26:63-64; Luke 22:67-70; and John 10:24-25.

A Solution. Because Jesus did not greatly resemble the expected Messiah, nor make a strong claim to be the Messiah, it is at first unclear why this was the title that the early Christians used as the basic expression of their faith. Several explanations of this have been proposed; the most satisfactory is that of N. A. Dahl. Dahl observes that according to the Gospels, Jesus was crucified as "King of the Jews," i.e., messianic pretender (Mark 15:26; Matt 27:37; Luke 23:38; John 19:19). This is very likely to be historically accurate. Coming after his crucifixion by the Romans as a false Messiah, God's resurrection of Jesus from the dead was understood by Jesus' followers as God's declaration that Jesus truly was the Messiah. By raising him from the dead, God vindicated Jesus, showing that the human judgment of him was wrong. Thus the resurrection of Jesus is the reason for the faith of the early Christians that Jesus was the Messiah.

Consequences. If this explanation of the faith of the early Christians that Jesus was the Messiah is correct, then this faith did not rest either on Jesus' resemblance to what was expected of the Messiah or on Jesus' claim to be the Messiah. Rather, it rested on God's own declaration, in the resurrection of Jesus, that Jesus was the Messiah. Beginning with this assurance that Jesus was the Messiah, the early Christians were able to reinterpret the expectation of the Messiah which Jesus fulfilled. Since they knew that Jesus was the

Messiah, they also knew that, correctly understood, the Scriptures must have foretold him. And they were able to find many scriptural anticipations of Jesus. Their reinterpretation was so successful that most Christians today are not even aware that such a reinterpretation has occurred. To most it seems very obvious that Scripture predicted just the sort of Messiah that Jesus was.

Not only was it necessary for the early Christians to support their belief that Jesus was the Messiah by showing that Scripture had predicted the kind of Messiah he turned out to be; it was also necessary to explain *how* Jesus was the Messiah. They needed to explain how Jesus did the work of the Messiah, how he saved the human race and established the reign of God. The earliest and most important explanation was that Jesus would come again and at that time do all that the Messiah was expected to do. At his second coming* Jesus would free all from oppression and establish a righteous order that would last forever. However, in addition to this explanation the early Christians developed other explanations of how Jesus was the Messiah. Since the belief that Jesus was the Messiah preceded the explanation of how he was the Messiah, the history of Christianity has seen many explanations of what it means to say that Jesus is the Messiah.

Later Developments. The belief that Jesus was the Messiah arose among Palestinian Jewish followers of Jesus who thus became the earliest Church. Within twenty years the Church had expanded to include Gentiles. These Gentiles were unfamiliar with the expectation of the Messiah. Because of this, the missionaries who preached Christianity to the Gentiles depended on titles other than "Messiah" to communicate who Jesus was to the Gentiles. They proclaimed Jesus as the Messiah but let "Messiah" serve almost as a second name for Jesus. The titles "Lord" and "Son of God," which were familiar to Gentiles, were much more useful for expressing who Jesus was. NT writings such as the letters of Paul, written to largely

Gentile Christian Churches, reflect this development. The titles "Lord" and "Son of God" have become more important, though not more fundamental, than Messiah.

See: LORD, NAME, PAROUSIA, PASSION, REIGN OF GOD, SATAN, SON OF GOD

TERRANCE CALLAN

MILLENARIANISM

Millenarianism is the Christian belief in the reign of Christ upon the earth that will last for one thousand years. The word derives from the Latin word for one thousand. The millennium will be a time of peace and prosperity that will precede the end of the world and the final judgment. Belief in the soon-to-come millennium is an important part of the eschatological scenario of evangelical Christians.

Old Testament

While the Christian expectation of a millennium derives from the NT, there are some roots in Judaism. The OT itself knows nothing of a thousand year reign of God on earth. Psalm 90:4 suggests that a thousand years "are as yesterday" in God's sight. This poetic declaration may have inspired the author of the Pseudepigraphical work 2 Enoch who conceived of human history as a week whose days consisted of one thousand years. At the end of human history there will come an eighth day, but it would be endless (33:1-2).

New Testament

Some early Christians convinced themselves that they were living in the "last days" before the return of Jesus and the beginning of the reign of God. When year after year passed without Christ's return, there was some discouragement. It is difficult to maintain excitement about an "end" that does not come. The author of 2 Peter tries to speak to this discouragement not by denying that Christians were living in the last days but by reminding his readers that for God one thousand years is the same as a day (3:8).

The millennium occupies a significant place in the eschatology of the Book of Revelation. The author of this book was convinced that God would not allow the evil perpetrated against the Christians by the Roman Empire to continue for long. He believed that Rome was under the control of evil powers and that God will destroy these powers (Rev 17:1–18:24). The destruction of evil on earth will pave the way for the one-thousand-year reign of Christ (Rev 20:1-6). Faithful Christians will reign with Christ on earth during this time.

Pastoral-Liturgical Tradition

The Book of Revelation is a testimony of faith in God's victory over the power of evil. To read it as a script for events that are yet to occur has stimulated the overactive imaginations of Christians who find existence in this world as meaningless. A most attractive image for these people is the prospect of ruling the world with Christ for one thousand years. That is why the millennium is an alluring image for some Christians.

At the end of the last century most evangelical Christians believed that the thousand-year reign of Christ would begin *after* Christians establish a new world through social, economic, technological, and scientific progress that would come to the world through the spread of Christian civilization. The optimism of these "postmillenialists" ended with World War I. It became clear that human progress focused on ways to take life rather than to enhance it.

In the aftermath of the war and the social change that began with it, there developed a strain of Protestant evangelicalism that was pessimistic about the possibilities of human progress. They were convinced that the world was becoming more corrupt and evil. The only way that the world could be saved from self-destruction would be for Christ to return and destroy the powers of evil that threaten the Church and the world. Christ must return *before* there can be hope for any true peace and progress. This is the view of the "premillenialists."

The premillenialist view was popularized in America by Cyrus I. Scofield through his notations to the King James Version of the Bible. His *Scofield Reference Bible* published originally in 1909 continues to sell in large numbers. In these notes Scofield weds American evangelical premillenialism to the dispensationalism of Nelson Darby, a British evangelical.

Darby divided human history into a series of "dispensations." In each dispensation God tests people's fidelity. If they pass the test, they are saved. According to Darby, the Bible shows a consistent pattern of human failure. That is why Jesus came to offer a new way to salvation. In the "Church Age" that began with the death of Jesus and continues to the present, the test that humans must pass to be saved involves their acceptance of Jesus as their Savior. Unless they accept Jesus, people will be damned.

The "Church Age" will end when the "Kingdom Age" begins, i.e., when the thousand-year reign of Christ begins. That is why evangelicals believe that we are living in the final days. According to their dispensationalist schema, there are no more dispensations before the millennium. Dispensationalists, however, differ among themselves about exactly how much time is left before the "Church Age" ends. The vagueness of the biblical scenario of the last days provides ample room for the wildest speculations. Some people have set precise dates and have made detailed preparations for the end of the age that never happens.

Some form of premillenial dispensationalism is characteristic of fundamentalist Christianity. There are differences among those who hold such views simply because of the intended vagueness of the biblical imagery and the failure to understand the apocalyptic world view and literary forms.

The first Christians lived in anticipation of Christ's imminent return. They lived this way without the pseudo-biblical schemas propounded by premillenial dispensationalists. Living with the conviction of Christ's certain victory over evil allows believers to live in hope. The liturgical readings of the final weeks of Ordinary Time and the first week of Advent remind Catholics that reflection on the Lord's return is an authentic part of the Christian life. Unfortunately the affluence of most Christians in Europe and North America has dulled the expectation that Christians ought to have regarding the coming reign of God. It is a mistake to hand this part of the biblical heritage to the premillenialists and dispensationalists whose futile speculations lead to trivializing this important part of the biblical tradition.

See: ESCHATOLOGY

LESLIE J. HOPPE, O.F.M.

MINISTRY

Ministry, or service, is a predominantly Christian notion, although it has some roots in the OT. Jesus speaks of his own mission* in terms of service, and bids his followers minister in the same manner. As Christian tradition developed, ministry, once seen as encumbent on all the baptized, came to be understood as the purview of professionals. A renewed vision of all Christians called to exercise their gifts in diverse ministries has been emphasized since Vatican II.

Old Testament

Ministry in the Christian sense is not a developed idea in the OT. Its meaning is generally interchangeable with the idea of service, and confined to the liturgical service of the Tabernacle, and later the Temple. It is therefore normally applied to men of priestly families who took turns performing the various services connected with Temple sacrifice. Several texts also suggest the ministry of women at the Tabernacle or Temple gates and perhaps in the choir: Exodus 38:8; 1 Samuel 2:22; perhaps Psalm 46:1 and 1 Chronicles 15:20. Their roles, however, are obscure.

New Testament

In the early Church, *diakonia* as service in the name of Christ becomes a major concept. Jesus himself says that he has come not to be served but to serve, and is among his disciples as one who serves (Matt 20:28; Mark 10:45; Luke 22:26-27). He stresses that the one who would be a minister must also be a disciple (John 12:26), and illustrates the saying by washing the disciples' feet, taking the role of a servant, and telling them he has done it as an example for them (John 13:1-17). This ideal sets the pace for Christian service.

Done by others, this ministry takes the form of hospitality and table service as modeled by Martha (Luke 10:40) and the apostles in the early years in Jerusalem, until they think it necessary to choose seven men to take their place (Acts 6:2) so they can devote themselves to other duties. Because of the memory of Jesus' significant actions and admonitions in the context of a common meal, it continues to carry rich overtones of association with meals and thus with Eucharist.

This kind of ministry is performed by the women who accompany Jesus from Galilee to Calvary (Matt 27:55; Mark 15:41; Luke 8:3). Increasingly it becomes associated with preaching and teaching (Acts 6:4), and for Luke, with official witness to the resurrection of Jesus (Acts 1:17, 25). In the Pauline churches, *diakonia* is one of the large categories for describing spiritual gifts given for the building up of the community (Rom 12:7; 1 Cor 12:7). It can take many forms, all aimed at the nurturing of the community's life of faith: wisdom, knowledge, healing, prophecy, speaking in tongues, interpretation, and discernment of spirits (1 Cor 12:4-11). There are also people designated with the title of *diakonos*, minister or deacon of particular churches: Phoebe at Cenchrae near Corinth (Rom 16:1), and the collegial group who lead the Church at Philippi, the *episkopoi* and *diakonoi*, "overseers and ministers" (Phil 1:1), as well as some of the Church leaders in 1 Timothy 3:8, 12.

Paul often calls his own work *diakonia* (e.g., 2 Cor 4:1; 5:18; 6:3), and himself *diakonos* or minister of Christ, the gospel, or the new covenant (Rom 15:8; Eph 3:7; 2 Cor 3:6).

NT ministry is service to the community in the name of Christ, whether through the performance of hospitality and physical nurturing at meals, or through the spiritual nurturing of teaching and the exercise of leadership.

See: DEACON, EUCHARIST, GIFTS, SACRIFICE, SERVANT, TEMPLE

CAROLYN OSIEK, R.S.C.J.

Pastoral-Liturgical Tradition

The Inclusive Character of Christian Ministry in the Earliest Sources. One of the most striking features of the NT's usual term for ministry (Greek, *diakonia*) is its broad inclusivity. *Diakonia* covers an impressive range of both human needs/satisfactions and Christian services: (1) Bodily sustenance and table-supervision (see Acts 6:1-2; Luke 10:40); (2) Financial support (the collection of money for needy Christians in Jerusalem is *diakonia*; see Acts 11:29-30; Rom 15:31); (3) The itinerant preaching and Church-founding ministry of an apostle* like Paul (see Rom 11:13 where Paul calls his mission to the Gentiles *diakonia*); (4) The local leadership ministry of a woman like Phoebe (who is a *diakonos*, according to Rom 16:1); (5) The ministry of preachers who offer the gospel as bread of life and leaven of reconciliation (see Acts 6:4; 2 Cor 5:18). The earliest Christian traditions thus viewed the whole body of believers as gifted with grace and so equipped "for the work of ministry [*diakonia*], for building up the body of Christ" (NRSV, Eph 4:12). For Paul, indeed, no one in the community can be excluded from ministry precisely because no one is excluded from charism (which in Pauline thinking means something quite specific, viz., the eschatological gift of God in Christ, the "eternal life" that claims us now in our very history and bodily existence). In every member of the community, charism is manifest in "spirit"* (our present participation in eternal life) and "power"* (Christ acting as lord to bring us into the "captivity" of his service). So a "Church," as Paul understood it, is nothing more or less than an interplay of charismatic ministries—expressions of spirit and power in the actual being and doing for others in word and deed.

Ordained Ministers as a Class of Religious "Professionals."

In the Pauline vision of Church as charismatic community, *all* members are ministers—and all are ministered to. While authority and power exist in the community, there is no special "caste" of ministerial professionals. The political and social models of "ruler" versus "subject" or "superior" versus "inferior" (as ways to categorize people and stratify society) seem to have been consciously rejected by Christians like Paul (see Gal 3:28).

By the third century, however, this picture had begun to change. Borrowing Jewish biblical categories, influential teachers and writers like Cyprian, bishop of Carthage (+258), regularly used images of sacrifice for the Eucharist and priesthood for those who preside (bishops, usually; presbyters, occasionally). (See Cyprian, Letter 63, where Melchizedek* and his "sacrifice" of bread and wine are explicitly interpreted as prefigurements of the Christian Eucharist and its priesthood. See also Letter 66, where the bishop's "sacerdotal honor" is likened to that of Israel's high priest.) Similarly, *The Apostolic Tradition* of Hippolytus (written ca. 215) spoke of the Christian bishop as "high priest" and—more importantly for later theology and praxis—drew a line between priesthood (restricted to bishops and presbyters) and ministry (the kind of service rendered by "lesser" officials like deacons). Here we can see the roots of the tradition that gained such widespread allegiance in the West—viz., that the priesthood of professionals (= the ordained clergy) is different in essence—and not merely in degree—from the priesthood of the baptized faithful. We can see, too, a tendency to regard priesthood as superior to "mere" ministry.

The way was thus paved for the gradual "ontologization" of priesthood as a permanent state that imprints a uniquely sacerdotal character (= conformation to Christ's priesthood) and imparts awesome powers (chiefly, the power to consecrate the Eucharistic elements). The emerging status of the ordained as a class of ministerial professionals was further enhanced in the fourth century, when bishops took over the traditional civic rights and privileges of the "order" of priests in the Roman Empire. After Roman culture collapsed during the fifth to eighth centuries, a new social and political order emerged in Europe—the feudal system—which also shaped Church life and ministry. Because feudalism found it difficult to separate the secular and religious sectors, a kind of homogenizing exchange took place between the rites and symbols of ecclesiastical authority and those of accession to temporal power. The institution of monarchy came to be viewed in quasi-sacramental terms, with the anointed monarch a sacred minister similar to a priest. Similarly, just as monarchs were invested with symbols of their power (crown, scepter, orb), so priests were likewise invested (with stole and chasuble, chalice and paten). (Until 1947, this ritual investiture was considered essential to sacramental orders; Pius XII finally clarified the matter by reasserting the ancient tradition of laying-on hands and prayer as the essential "matter" and "form" of ordination.)

Despite this tendency to equate ministry with a professional priestly class, other (non-ordained) forms of ministerial service continued throughout the Middle Ages and in the post-reformation era. Missionary work and evangelization, education and care of the sick, spiritual direction and counsel—all these ministries have been performed by non-ordained men and women living either in religious communities or "in the world." Clearly too, women like Theresa of Avila in the sixteenth century—or Mother Theresa in the twentieth—have exercised ministries of leadership and pastoral care that influence the life of the whole Church, even though they do not belong to the class of priestly professionals.

The Servant Church of Vatican II. While the vision of ministry as basically "clerical" dominated the official Church's thinking from the Council of Trent to the mid-twentieth century, the documents of Vatican II reflected a return to earlier Christian sources. Thus, for instance, the Constitution on the Church notes that in the body of Christ all the members are endowed by the Spirit with "gifts of ministries through which . . . we serve each other unto salvation . . . carrying out the truth in love" (no. 7). Even more remarkable is what Vatican II's Decree on the Apostolate of Lay People has to say. Lay people, the Council implies, are true successors of the apostles: "From the fact of their union with Christ the head flows lay people's right and duty to be apostles" (no. 3). The laity's apostolic ministry is a true sharing in the prophetic, royal, and priestly ministry of Christ Jesus (ibid.). Moreover, the holy Spirit gives every one of the faithful "special gifts" (= charisms), so that "from the reception of these charisms, even the most ordinary ones, there arises for each of the faithful the right and duty of exercising them in the Church and in the world for the good of humanity and the development of the Church" (ibid.). The Council thus affirmed that the whole Church is a servant community—a Church created for ministry and constantly renewed by its service on behalf of the world.

See: APOSTLE, BODY OF CHRIST, CHARISM, ORDINATION, POWER, PREACHING, SPIRIT

NATHAN D. MITCHELL

MIRACLE

The first part of this entry considers the idea of the miracles in ancient Israelite experience. The second part examines this notion in the culture of the NT period. The biblical concept offers a challenge to modern believers as they try to recognize the presence of God in their experience.

Old Testament

The great cultural gap that exists between the biblical and modern worlds is no more obvious than when speaking of miracles. For some people miracles, understood as events that transcend natural causes to such a degree that they can be explained only as an intervention of God, are impossible. For them events that the Bible describes as miracles are susceptible to some rational explanation. For other people, miracles help prove the reasonableness of their religious faith. Those who produced the Bible would not feel at ease holding either position.

People in the ancient Near East explained what people today call "natural phenomena" in terms of divine personal activity. For the Canaanite farmer, it rained not because of a high pressure system over the Mediterranean Sea, but because Baal, the god of the storm, sent his thunder bolts across the skies. For the Israelite farmer, it was Yahweh who brought the rain (Pss 68:9; 135:7; 147:8). Phenomena that today can be explained in terms of ordinary cause and effect by most people with an elementary education in science were great wonders to the people of the ancient world. For the people who wrote the Bible a miracle was not the surpassing of the laws of nature because there were no such laws. Whatever happened in what we describe as the world of nature happened because of the personal activity of their gods.

Second, accounts of what contemporary believers understand as miracles are embedded in texts that display a variety of literary forms. The apologetic use of miracles ignores this variety and usually considers accounts of the miraculous events as historically valid eye-witness accounts. The first step in any responsible use of the biblical tradition requires that interpreters recognize the type of literature that they are reading. One cannot read the stories of Moses, Samson, Elijah, Elisha, Daniel, and Jonah as if they were objective third-party accounts of events that happened in the lives of these individuals.

This is not to imply that the ancient Israelites did not recognize the miraculous or that they did not recognize cause and effect in natural phenomena. They simply had a keener and more direct insight into God's presence and power in nature than we have today. Also the Israelites simply did not identify the miraculous with what happened in the realm of nature. All creation and all natural phenomena were wondrous (Job 4:8-10; 9:5-10; 26:5-14; 36:26–37:18; 38:1–41:26). *The* miracle in the biblical tradition was the Exodus. What was wondrous was not Yahweh's control over the forces of nature, but the exercise of that control to effect Israel's liberation from slavery. The miracle was that Yahweh took the side of slaves against their masters. While the gods of ancient Near Eastern religions supported the status quo in which a few ruled and oppressed the many, the God of Israel chose to save a band of slaves. That is the mystery, the wonder, the miracle that lies at the heart of the biblical tradition.

There is no single Hebrew word that is the equivalent of the English word "miracle." Hebrew uses three different words to designate what modern readers consider miracles. First is the word "sign," i.e., something that attracts attention. This word is used to speak about the plagues through which God moved Pharaoh to free the Israelites. It occurs twenty-five times in the biblical story of the plagues (Exod 7:14–12:36). The same word describes the significance of Isaiah's name and those of his children (Isa 8:18) and the prophet's eccentric behavior in walking about naked in Jerusalem for three years (Isa 20:3).

A second word is "portent." Often this is a sign of the future event. It too is used of the plagues of Egypt (nineteen times). It is also used to describe the significance of Ezekiel's mourning for his deceased wife (Ezek 24:24, 27). The third word is "wonder." Here the emphasis is on the unexpected, that which surpasses what people have come to expect. This word is used generally to describe the marvels of God in creation (Pss 107:24; 136:4; Job 5:9; 9:10). It describes the crossing of the Jordan (Josh 3:5). What is important to note about each word is that none of the three refers to the miraculous per se. They can and do refer to

ordinary events of life such as naming a child, mourning for one's wife, and admiring creation. The "miraculous" element in the signs, portents, and wonders described in the Bible is that God accomplished them for the sake of Israel.

Only rarely do individuals in the OT work miracles. Since Moses was God's chosen instrument to free the Israelites from slavery in Egypt, it was through him that God worked "the signs and wonders" that effected their freedom. The Elijah/Elisha stories contain a cluster of miracles that the prophets work. These stories reflect the notion that the best way to portray the importance of a religious leader is to show him to be a worker of miracles. These signs legitimate the prophet as a chosen instrument of God. The wonders that God performed on his behalf put a divine seal of approval on him.

This pattern repeats itself in the noncanonical Letter of Aristeas that describes the origin of the Septuagint, the Greek translation of the Hebrew Bible (ca. 200 BCE). The letter describes the work as the result of efforts made by seventy-two translators working independently over seventy-two days. When they came together, their translations agreed word for word. This is an obvious attempt to legitimate the translation of the Old Testament into Greek. The Jews of Alexandria—even those for whom Hebrew was a dead language—had to be convinced that translating the Bible was God's will. A "miracle" convinced them.

Contemporary readers of the Bible sometimes believe that they must reject the miraculous elements in biblical stories if they want to know "what happened." Others simply assume that the contemporary notion of the miraculous is the same as that in the Bible. Both views are mistaken. The OT stories about the miraculous affirm a faith not in the miraculous as such, but in the God who chose to save Israel. For the Israelites that choice was miracle enough.

See: SIGN

LESLIE J. HOPPE, O.F.M.

New Testament

Already at the turn of this century, biblical scholars observed that the English word "miracle" was a "somewhat unfortunate translation" of the wide variety of Hebrew and Greek words that the Bible utilizes to describe a single reality: visible signs of God's presence, power, and love for his people. Also disappointing has been the long-standing and still-popular tendency to draw upon gospel "miracles" as "proofs," an aspect of these events which was never primary in the life of Jesus nor in the Gospels.

Recent pastoral practice reflects a healthy move away from this latter perspective. The Holy Father and his Commissions have promoted candidates like Kateri Tekakwitha and Maximillian Kolbe to the rank of "Blessed" and "Saint" without evidence that these holy persons have been instrumental in working specific "miracles." More in line with the biblical view, the Church now urges that "other 'signs'" of personal holiness should be accepted. Moreover, instead of concentrating on one or two "spectacular" events, the Church now accepts the "well-established belief" by ordinary people that miracles or extraordinary favors have been obtained through these candidates for sainthood.

The opinions of ordinary people in every culture are always key in interpreting the reality known as "miracle," whether in the Bible or in the modern world. Different understandings of and relationships to nature lie at the root of the difficulty that modern, Western, post-enlightenment, post-industrial revolution cultures experience trying to respect the beliefs of first-century Mediterranean culture. The Mediterranean world personifies nature and sees God—and no one else!—in absolute control over it. God is responsible for everything that happens, and because God is omnipotent everything is possible.

Since God determines the rhythms of nature (Gen 8:22; Jer 5:24), the course of the stars (Ps 148:6; Jer 31:35; 33:20, 25), rules over the seas (Job 38:10) and earth (Jer 33:25), it is not so much the extraordinary nature of God's intervention that stirs awe and amazement but rather the fact that he intervenes. Thus, marvelous, wonderful, and awesome deeds are seen as signs of God's mercy and revelations of his infinite power and majesty. From this biblical perspective, a miracle might be defined as an "act of power through which God gives a sign to human beings who are always astonished by it even though they recognize it as quite in keeping with God's nature."

In contrast, the modern Western world separates nature from God, objectifies it, and perceives it to operate by independent "laws." Having gained a "scientific" understanding of these laws and then having developed appropriate technologies to control, manipulate, and even imitate nature and many of its processes, Western believers view God as someone who is distantly removed from the world and its operation but who should act as a facilitator for human activity when called upon (in prayer) to do so. From this perspective, a miracle is defined as a happening "contrary to or above the laws of nature" as they are presently known and understood by human beings. Irregularities in nature are baffling. When these irregularities are particularly damaging, insurance companies call them "acts of God."

In the NT era, Jesus lived among those disappointed descendants of the returnees from Exile (537 BCE) whom Sirach 36:1, 6 described as praying: "Come to our aid, O God of the universe . . . Give new signs and work new wonders." The first-century world believed that it was time once more for God to intervene impressively in nature and history on their behalf and demonstrate thereby that God is really in charge.

In his person, life, and ministry, Jesus was perceived by those who believed in him as a person commended by God "with mighty deeds, wonders, and signs, which God worked through him" in the midst of those among whom he lived (Acts 2:22). Skeptics and non-believers who witnessed these same occurrences were unmoved and sometimes even indignant (Matt 21:15). Divided judgment over the miracles of Jesus was as common in his day and culture as it is in ours.

The Greek word most often translated "miracle" in the Synoptic Gospels is literally *"mighty deeds,"* a word that implicitly aligns such activity with the mighty deeds of God (Deut 3:23). Familiar mighty deeds or miracles in the NT are various healings and exorcisms, instances of mastery over nature such as taming winds and storm or increasing food supply, and the like.

Herod uses this Greek word to describe the activity of John the Baptist (Matt 14:2), and Jesus uses the word to identify the activity of others both favorably (Mark 9:39) and unfavorably (Matt 7:22) as well as his own activity (Matt 11:20-21, 23). The chief priests and elders, among others, were unimpressed by Jesus' mighty deeds (Matt 21:15).

At issue in these diverse assessments of miracles viewed as mighty deeds is their link with the mighty deeds of God. Who among these individuals is acting like God, doing the kinds of things God does, working in God's name and with his power, and who is an imposter, a fraud, a deceiver, or a pretender? That is the challenge to everyone who perceives a miracle, whether it is a healing, an exorcism, the calming of nature, or the like.

Equally striking in all these NT cases is the apparent acknowledgment that human beings can indeed perform mighty deeds, do have some control over nature. But this power is not widely distributed, and it always derives from a higher, other-than-human source. In the Gospels, this higher source can be either God or Beelzebul (Matt 12:22-28). In the NT, therefore, miracles are definitely possible and happen often. Their origin, however, is a riddle much more difficult to solve.

Two other items emerge relative to miracles viewed as mighty deeds. One, in the Synoptic Gospels faith is a prerequisite for a miracle to occur. The people of Jesus' native place were skeptical about his wisdom and his ability to perform mighty deeds. As a consequence, Matthew notes that Jesus "did not work many mighty deeds there because of their lack of faith" (13:58).

Two, when God empowers Jesus to perform mighty deeds, a response is expected. In the Gospels, Jesus stands between God and the people as a Mediterranean broker intervenes between a patron and the clients. Patrons bestow gifts that are either not available elsewhere, or not available in this way or on such advantageous terms. Though these gifts are "freely" given, they are not "free." Each carries a price, that is, it requires a response.

Patronage is the appropriate Mediterranean cultural context for interpreting the miracles of Jesus. Miracles in the NT are precisely gifts with a "hook," gifts that require a response. Jesus obtains favors of healing and the like from the Father for a variety of needy petitioners. Jesus' complaint that Chorazin and Bethsaida failed to respond to the mighty deeds with repentance (Matt 11:20-24) indicates that they insulted and dishonored their God, their heavenly patron, and Jesus as broker. They accepted the gifts but did not reciprocate as they should. In "theological" language, they had accepted God's grace offered through Jesus "in vain!"

One way in which the recipient should not respond to a gift is by saying "thank you." This terminates a relationship and effectively says the recipient no longer has need of the benefactor. The healed Samaritan leper who came to thank Jesus (Luke 17:16) recognized how fortunate he was to be in the right place at the right time and in the right company. He is willing to terminate the relationship because Jesus might not pass through Samaria again. The other nine know that they might need another of Jesus' mighty deeds in the future, and so they continue to the Temple where they will meet the priests and glorify and thank God, as is appropriate in the Temple. Luke's theology of the Samaritans has reinterpreted the cultural elements of this story to cast the Samaritan in a favorable light. But he makes the very same point!

Another Greek word commonly translated as miracle is, literally, "sign." In the Synoptic Gospels, Jesus refuses to offer any signs other than his exorcisms, healing, and preaching (Matt 12:38-42; 16:1-4). In fact, Jesus scolds those who ask for signs.

In John's Gospel, Jesus is presented as acknowledging that signs can be "missed" or even misconstrued (6:26). Still, John finds the word "sign" especially apt to describe Jesus' mighty deeds of which he reports just seven.

The significance of these seven miracles interpreted as signs is that John deliberately describes them also as "works." Jesus claims to be doing his Father's works (10:37) with a Greek word used in the Greek OT to describe God's two greatest works: creation and redemption. With creation, God gives life; in redemption, God restores meaning to life or puts new meaning in life.

The seven signs of Jesus, the "works" of the Father that Jesus does, can easily be divided into two such groups. In raising Lazarus, saving the royal official's son from death, and feeding the hungry crowds, Jesus definitely gives life. Restoring sight to the blind man, walking calmly on an agitated sea, healing a cripple, and providing fresh wine for a wedding are instances of restoring meaning to life or putting new meaning in life. Giving life and restoring meaning to life in these seven works, Jesus continues God's creation and redemption. As such, these works are very definitely signs, biblical miracles understood as acts of power pointing to the loving, caring, omnipotent presence of God which never fail to impress and astonish human beings. And whoever believes in Jesus will do these same works and far greater still (14:10)!

For John, Jesus' signs should normally lead to recognizing Jesus as the one sent by God (3:2; 9:16; 10:36), as a prophet (4:19), as the Christ (7:31), as Son of Man (9:35-38). In fact, Jesus' word alone should be sufficient as it was for the Samaritans whose curiosity, first aroused by the woman at the well,

was finally resolved by hearing from Jesus for themselves (4:40-42). The case was similar with the royal official whose son lay ill in Capernaum. He believed what Jesus said to him and at that moment his son gained a new hold on life (5:46-54).

Not everyone responded to the miracles of Jesus in such a positive and edifying manner (5:36-38). These people are spiritually immature (6:14-15, 26) or suffer from a paralyzing legalism (5:16; 7:49, 52). After Jesus restored sight to a blind man, some people said: "This man is not from God, because he does not keep the Sabbath," while others said: "How can a sinful man do such signs?" (9:16).

How tragic it is to read the response of the chief priests to the raising of Lazarus. They plotted to kill Lazarus along with Jesus, because "many of the Jews were turning away and believing in Jesus because of Lazarus" (12:9-10).

In summary, the NT view of miracle challenges the modern, Western believer to reevaluate scientific skepticism about the very possibility of miracles in general and to temper justifiable self-confidence with an increased sensitivity to God's loving and caring presence in nature and history. The signs are still there for those who have eyes to see.

See: CREATION, FAITH, GRACE, HEALING, POWER, PREACHING, REDEMPTION, SATAN, SIGN

JOHN J. PILCH

MISSION

While many consider mission to be a uniquely Christian phenomenon, a full understanding of the biblical roots of the Church's mission must take into account the entire expanse of the Scriptures.

Old Testament

In general terms, mission involves the sending of a representative of a deity for the purpose of presenting a message or performing a task. Thus many of the important personalities of the OT could be said to have participated in mission. The prophets and other charismatic leaders of Israel especially recognized that they were *sent* by God with a specific purpose in mind (Exod 3:10; Judg 6:14; Isa 6:8; Jer 1:7; Ezek 2:3-4). With few exceptions their mission was directed toward Israel. But Israel too had a mission. It was chosen by Yahweh to be a kingdom of priests and a holy nation (Exod 19:6). Its mission was to worship and live out a covenant relationship with God.

In more specific terms, mission includes all those activities of a religious community dedicated to spreading its faith to others. This necessitates the crossing of political, cultural, linguistic, and religious frontiers. If mission then means going out to the Gentiles to convert them to the true God, the OT knows little or nothing about it. There is no divine commission to go to the Gentiles, no deliberate witness to foreigners, no conscious outreach to the nations. Yet the OT is fundamental for the understanding of mission in the NT. For what it has to say about God and about other nations has influenced the concept of mission.

Israel's understanding of God is important for mission. Yahweh, the God of Israel, is fundamentally different from the gods of the other nations. Originally seen as a warrior God favorable to Israel (Exod 15:3), Yahweh was subsequently recognized as the only God (Ps 86:80; Isa 44:6-20; 45:5, 21). Eventually all peoples were invited to acknowledge this (Psalms 96; 97). The holy One of Israel was not only self-revealing but also active in history, intervening in human affairs. God chose Israel from all the nations, and the purpose of election is service (Deut 7:6; 14:2; Isa 43:1; 44:2, 21, 23; 45:4). The power of Yahweh is not limited to a certain territory nor to a particular group (Exodus 7–12; Isa 43:5-6; 45:1-6, 12; Jer 27:5-8; Amos 9:7; Nah 2:14). In fact, God expects all nations to live up to certain moral standards (Isa 14:4b-21; Amos 1–2). God's compassion and concern extends beyond Israel to the other nations.

Every culture and every people must deal with outsiders or foreigners—those who do not belong. Israel was no exception. Its relationship with the nations exhibits a dynamic tension between two opposing tendencies. On the one hand, an inward or particularistic movement focused Israel's attention on itself and its own needs. On the other hand, an outgoing or universalistic movement attempted to expand Israel's horizons. Israel's history can be seen as an attempt to balance these two movements or tendencies. At times it absorbed the customs and ideas of its neighbors. At other times it rejected or challenged their practices and values. Too much accommodation to other nations could mean a loss of identity or a betrayal of Yahweh; too much hostility toward others could mean narrow sectarianism.

Israel valued its election and its special relationship with God (Deut 4:7-8). Other nations and ethnic groups were often viewed as either military and political threats or as religious temptations and sources of corruption (Deut 7:3-4; 12:29-31; 2 Kgs 17:8, 11, 15, 23; Ezra 10; Neh 13:23-31). Thus Israel was often hostile to other nations and spurned them, especially when they were seen as wicked.

However, an outward movement or universalistic tendency kept Israel from turning in on itself. It borrowed much of its culture, politics, and religion from the Canaanites. Aliens were frequently integrated into society or played important roles (Exod 12:38; 2 Sam 11:6-11; Ruth). Foreign rulers and armies could be viewed as instruments of Yahweh (Isa 10:5-6; Jer 27:5-8). Without doubt the concept of election played a much more important role in the OT than that of universalism. Yet this did not mean that Yahweh had rejected the nations or had uniformly condemned them. God's activity was not confined to Israel. The chosen people's existence and redemption affected others. Thus the relationship between Israel and the nations has important consequences for the concept of mission.

In the OT outsiders were not always viewed as enemies. Other images or understandings occur as well:

A. In a few places the nations are seen as *servants* or subjects of Israel or of its king (Gen 27:29; Josh 9:27; Ps 72:11; Isa 14:1-2; 45:14; 60:10-14).

B. Sometimes the Gentiles were simply accepted as *worshipers of other gods.* Yahweh was the God of Israel, but other nations might serve other gods without necessarily incurring guilt or condemnation (Deut 4:19; 32:8; Judg 11:24; Mic 4:5).

C. The OT often recognizes that *Yahweh is also the God of the nations* and of all the world (Jer 32:37; Ps 47:3, 8-9). Yahweh directs and guides all peoples, not only Israel (Isa 14:26-27; Jer 18:6-10; Amos 9:7). Genesis 1–11 expands Israel's view to include all the earth. God's presence and activity may even qualify non-Israelites as holy or as instruments of Yahweh: Melchizedek (Gen 14:18-20), Jethro (Exod 18:13-27), Balaam (Numbers 23–24), Achior (Judith 5–6), Job, and Cyrus of Persia (Isa 44:28–45:6).

D. Significant for mission is Israel's understanding that it serves as a *witness* to the nations. In and through the chosen people others see and hear about the divine saving activity (Num 14:13-16; Josh 4:24; 1 Kgs 8:60; Ps 98:2-3; Isa 49:26; 52:10; Ezek 38:23; Zeph 3:20). Israel serves as a witness in both positive and negative ways, for Yahweh not only performs wonders and receives worship but also punishes this people when they are sinful. Both aspects have witness value.

E. At times the OT knows of the possibility that *the nations will share in the blessings of Israel* and in the salvation that God promises (Isa 49:6; 60:3). This may take place through a purification or a conversion of the Gentiles (Tob 14:6-7; Jer 16:19; Zeph 3:9). Zion is seen as the universal mother of all people (Ps 87:4-7), while the powerful and hostile nations of Egypt and Assyria shall be equal partners with Israel (Isa 19:24-25). Generally speaking, these situations will occur in a distant future.

F. Perhaps the most important image for mission is that of the nations in *pilgrimage.* Jerusalem is seen as the center of the world, and the nations will one day have the privilege of going there to be instructed, to worship, to bring tribute, and to share in Israel's blessing (Tob 13:11; Ps 72:10; Isa 2:2-4; 60:5-7; Hag 2:6-8; Zech 8:20-22). Not only do the nations come in pilgrimage to Zion, but they also participate in a special feast or banquet (Isa 25:6-8). Jerusalem in the future will become an international religious center, attracting all peoples to itself because of Israel's special relationship with God.

G. Finally, in a few places we learn that *the nations will acknowledge, praise, or even worship Yahweh,* the God of Israel. Sometimes this is part of a liturgical invitation to praise God (Pss 98:4; 117:1; 148:11). But elsewhere the OT seems to indicate that at some future time the nations will revere God, acknowledge Yahweh's name, and worship (Pss 22:28-30; 86:9; Isa 17:7-8; 19:19-22; 45:14-17; Zeph 2:11; Zech 8:23; Mal 1:11).

The final three understandings of Israel's relationship with the nations envision a future when the Gentiles will somehow participate in the blessings promised to Abraham (Gen 12:3). But this is a distant future, an eschatological age. Thus they point to the days of the Messiah and to the NT.

Israel's universalistic tendencies can be found throughout the OT. But they are most obvious in the Prophetic literature and in the psalms.

It was the responsibility of the prophets to announce God's word. Their focus was primarily on Israel. Yet they also concerned themselves at times with foreigners. Often enough their oracles were condemnations of other nations (Isaiah 13–23; Ezekiel 25–32; Amos 13–2:3; Zeph 2:4-15). But the prophets could also extend God's message of warning and promise to non-Israelites.

Jeremiah was the only prophet who was specifically commissioned as "a prophet to the nations" (Jer 1:5). He did pronounce oracles condemning other nations (Jer 25:14-38; 46–51) much like other prophets. On at least one occasion Jeremiah may have directly contacted foreign ambassadors (Jer 27:3-11) in order to deliver a message to them from God. He also traveled to Egypt (probably brought there by force) where he prophesied to Judahites living in exile (Jer 43:8-13; 44:1-30). His main audience then was his own people.

It is worthy to note that universalistic tendencies appear frequently in the Book of Isaiah. This is especially true for Second Isaiah (chs. 40–55). With the recognition that there is only one God comes a new mission for Israel: "I will make you a light for the nations, that my salvation may reach the ends of the earth" (Isa 49:6). This is certainly the mission of the Servant of Yahweh, who at times seems to represent the nation of Israel (Isa 44:21; 49:3). The Servant is charged with providing justice and instruction *(torah)* to other peoples (Isa 42:1, 4). Since the salvation of Israel has implications for the entire world, the Servant is responsible for communicating God's work of judgment and redemption to all the nations. However, this task is not yet missionary in the sense of public proclamation to the Gentiles. Rather the life and sufferings of this Servant of Yahweh are mute testimony of God's salvific activity.

Third Isaiah (Isaiah 56–66) continues the universalistic tradition found throughout the Book of Isaiah. Once again the focus of these chapters is on Israel as a renewed people of God. However, openness to the nations is an important characteristic of a renewed Israel. "Nations shall walk by your light, and kings by your shining radiance" (Isa 60:3). For they witness what Yahweh has done for Judah, and they willingly offer tribute and service to this redeemed people (Isa 60:5-7, 10-16; 61:5-6). There are some indications that the nations will tremble or be punished (Isa 63:1-6), but otherwise they serve as witnesses to Israel's salvation and want to share in its blessings.

Jonah is the only prophet who is actually sent to another nation with the specific purpose of converting it. When he finally goes to Nineveh, he is successful beyond his wildest dreams (and fears). The city repents, and all turn to God. But Jonah is a parody of a prophet, one who tries to escape his mission and who resents the results. This tale of a successful if sour missionary underscores the irony of the conversion of a wicked city after a brief oracle when Jerusalem too often rejected the message of numerous prophets. The book demonstrates God's concern for the nations (Jonah 4:11). But it is no call to overt missionary activity.

The psalms too have universalistic overtones. Many invite foreigners to praise God: "Praise the Lord, all you nations! Give glory, all you peoples!" (Ps 117:1). But nature too can be exhorted to praise God (Pss 96:11-12; 98:4-8; 148:3-4, 7-10), so it would be difficult to see in this liturgical invitation a missionary mandate.

A few psalms urge the proclamation of God's deeds among the nations (Pss 9:12; 105:1). Psalm 96 declares: "Tell God's glory among the nations; among all peoples, God's marvelous deeds" (v. 3). The nations are commanded to bring gifts to the Temple and to worship God in fear (vv. 8-9). In yet other psalms the poet promises to praise God among the Gentiles (Pss 18:50; 57:10; 108:4).

Israel's cult tended to reinforce the separation between the elect and the non-elect. Yet its public prayer not only acknowledged the nations but also included them in the call to worship. This was especially true in the hymns of praise. The references to the nations may be stereotyped liturgical formulas, but they also recognize the impossibility of limiting God's field of action and sphere of influence (Ps 22:28-30).

The mission of Israel was simple: to be God's people. Thus it was responsible for communicating divine revelation and for witnessing to God's sovereignty. However, there is no real centrifugal mission (a deliberate outreach to foreigners) in the OT. Rather there is a centripetal mission, a mission of drawing others to Israel, one that would take place in the distant future. The knowledge of God and the blessings of Israel would be shared by those nations which came to Jerusalem. Mission in the OT is not what it would become in the NT.

But it provides the context and preparation for it.

See: NATIONS

TIMOTHY A. LENCHAK, S.V.D.

New Testament

The experience of being sent by Jesus is an essential component of discipleship,* for one cannot follow Jesus without also sharing in his vision for the world and his program for proclaiming the good news. Mission can take many forms, however, and need not be limited to formal preaching or work in foreign lands. Nevertheless, from the earliest years there was an outward movement to spread the message to new hearers, so that from the very beginning Christianity faced the challenge of reinterpretation in new contexts. The experience of mission is described and developed in different ways by the four evangelists and later NT writers.

Matthew. The Synoptic Gospels all portray Jesus as sending out the disciples during his lifetime in rather organized forays of preaching and healing. The Gospel of Matthew puts the sending out of the Twelve at the beginning of his second great discourse, the so-called missionary discourse (10:1-15). The disciples are given Jesus' own authority to exorcise demons and to heal. In keeping with Matthew's depiction of Jesus' intended ministry during his lifetime as limited to Israel (see Matt 15:24), they are instructed to avoid pagan and Samaritan towns. They are given exact information about what they may not take along, including money and a change of clothing, for they are to depend on the hospitality of those who receive them.

The missionary instructions quickly move, however, from practical instructions for the disciples' behavior on mission to more serious discussion about what to do in a situation of persecution, perhaps indicating the real issues of concern for Matthew's community, and their experience of where mission leads. Of course, chapter ten is not the first place in which the theme of mission occurs in Matthew. Jesus himself, firmly rooted in his Jewish identity by birth as son of David and son of Abraham (Matt 1:1), already as a child demonstrates his openness to all by receiving the Magi who have been guided to him by God's plan (Matt 2:1-12). Likewise, at the very end of the story, the risen Christ is no longer bound by his earlier intentions, and now tells his disciples to go into the whole world preaching and baptizing (Matt 28:16-20). These two stories of the Magi and the command of the risen Christ serve as "bookends" to frame the focus on the mission to Israel during Jesus' ministry.

Mark. The Gospel of Mark also portrays Jesus as one sent to preach the good news and to back it up by healing and exorcising. From the beginning of his public ministry, he seems eager to reach out to as many people as possible: "For this purpose have I come" (Mark 1:38; par. Luke 4:43). For Mark, however, Jesus' mission is never limited to Israel, for he is constantly moving back and forth across the Lake of Galilee, from Jewish territory on the west side to Gentile territory on the east, performing healings and miracles on both sides (e.g., first on the east side, then the west in ch. 5; a miraculous feeding first on the Jewish side, 6:34-44, then on the Gentile side, 8:1-10). He even moves far north to the area of Tyre and Sidon in southern Syria (7:31).

The disciples, too, are sent out on mission. The Twelve are hand-picked by Jesus to be with him but also to be sent, as in Matthew, with authority to preach and exorcise demons (Mark 3:13-19). They are to go to the surrounding villages—with no prohibition against pagan or Samaritan ones as in Matthew—and to stay to perform good deeds for those who would receive them (Mark 6:6-13). Curiously, in the midst of practical instructions almost the same as Matthew's, this time they are allowed a pair of sandals (Mark 6:9; cf. Matt 10:10).

John. Although the Gospel of John lacks a scene in which Jesus officially sends out the disciples on a missionary tour during his lifetime, it is the Fourth Gospel that most profoundly explores the reality of what it is to be sent by God in Jesus. It is John the Baptist who is first of all sent to bear witness (John 1:6-7). Jesus' self-consciousness is formed by the reality of having been sent by God into the world (e.g., 3:16-17; 6:38-40, 51; 12:44; 13:3; 18:37). His mission is to bear witness to the truth (18:37). When Jesus has completed his work and can no longer be present, he passes on this responsibility to the disciples: "Peace be with you. As the Father has sent me, so I send you" (20:21). This is the ultimate moment of mission for John, the point at which the disciples—all disciples, for they are an indefinite number present at the scene—receive from the risen Jesus not only his work but his identity as those sent by God into the world to witness to God's presence and love.

John's Jesus gives no practical instructions for mission, and does not send out the disciples as he does in the Synoptics. There are, however, two persons in the Gospel who model what mission is: they witness to what they have seen and heard. The first is the unnamed Samaritan woman who has encountered Jesus at her village well, believed what she has heard, and gone back to the village to spread the word. Because of her witness, other villagers come to meet Jesus and also believe (4:4-42). The second model of mission is Mary Magdalene, not to be confused with Mary of Bethany who anointed Jesus' head the week before (12:1-8), much less with the "sinful woman" of Luke who anointed his feet much earlier (Luke 7:36-50). Mary Magdalene is among the first women (and in John, the only woman) to arrive at the empty tomb on Easter morning, and thus the first witness to the resurrection. At the conclusion of her encounter with the risen Jesus in the garden, she is sent by him to tell the other disciples what she has seen and heard (John 20:1-18).

Luke-Acts. The Gospel of Luke portrays the mission of Jesus as one of proclaiming and doing justice. In the Acts of the Apostles, the sequel volume, the author is able to show how that mission continued beyond the immediate years after Jesus' death, and how it began to be carried to the ends of the earth (Luke 24:47; Acts 1:8). The infancy narrative of the gospel begins by depicting Jesus as savior of his people Israel. In the appearance of Jesus, God's promises to Israel are being fulfilled (Luke 1:55).

While Matthew brings Gentile Magi to worship the newborn Messiah, even though the adult Jesus will concern himself more with a mission to the Jews, Luke's infancy story brings Jewish shepherds (2:15-20). Jesus is circumcised and Mary fulfills the ritual of purification according to the Law (1:21-24). Jesus and his family are in every way devout Jews. Thus Luke begins with Jesus' origins. It is clear, however, in his "inaugural speech" in the synagogue at Nazareth that Jesus' mission is to be in the realm of justice to people who are poor, disabled, and oppressed. Using the words of Isaiah, he proclaims: "The Spirit of the Lord . . . has anointed me to bring glad tidings to the poor . . . to proclaim liberty to captives and recovery of sight to the blind, to let the oppressed go free" (4:18-19; see Isa 61:1-2; 58:6). Consistently Luke portrays Jesus throughout his ministry as faithful to that originating purpose.

Like Matthew and Mark, Luke's Jesus chooses the Twelve (Luke 6:12-16), and sends them out on an organized mission of preaching, healing, and expelling demons (9:1-6). (This time sandals are not even mentioned!) Unlike Matthew and Mark, Luke sees the mission during Jesus' lifetime taking on even larger dimensions: in addition to the Twelve, Jesus sends out seventy(-two) more disciples in pairs to go ahead and prepare the way for him in towns that he intends to visit (10:1-12). Their instructions are quite similar to those given elsewhere to the Twelve, and in fact some of them are sayings that Matthew's Jesus addresses to the Twelve (cf. Matt 10:8, 13-15; again, as in Matthew, no sandals allowed). Later, when the seventy(-two) return, Jesus rejoices in the fact that they have been able to use the power he gave them to have significant victory over evil spirits (10:17-20).

Just as Luke's Gospel orients Jesus at a certain point on a conscious journey to Jerusalem (Luke 9:51), so his second volume, Acts of the Apostles, has a definite geographical progression of the early Christian mission. Beginning from Jerusalem as Jesus had foretold (Acts 1:8), it moves from there north to Samaria with the mission of Philip when persecution breaks out in Jerusalem (ch. 8). Leaving Philip in Samaria, the story jumps further north to the road to Damascus where Saul/Paul encounters the risen Jesus on the road (ch. 9).

From then on, the story belongs to Paul. Peter is persuaded through his vision and the surprising conversion of the Roman centurion Cornelius that, indeed, God is calling Gentiles as well as Jews to faith in Jesus (ch. 10). Paul and Barnabas, through prophetic inspiration, begin their first mission to Cyprus and southeastern Asia Minor (13:1-3). Once Paul has seen that the gospel is to be preached to Gentiles as well as Jews, and once agreement is reached with the Jerusalem authorities (ch. 15), Paul is on his way through various adventures to his final destination, Rome. Once he has reached the capital, Luke's schema is complete, for the Christian message has indeed reached to the ends of the earth. Even though Luke knows that there are already Christians in Rome before Paul (Acts 28:14-15), it is Paul's arrival that creates the link with the beginnings in Galilee and Jerusalem.

Paul. Paul is the New Testament's missionary par excellence, largely because he was such an effective letter writer and because we know so little about the many other missionaries who were his contemporaries: Barnabas, Titus, Prisca and Aquila, Andronicus and Junia (Rom 16:7), etc. He repeatedly calls himself an apostle, notably at the beginning of nearly every letter. Tradition assigns the title to the Twelve, espe-

cially because of Luke's usage, and to Paul, almost by way of exception and because it is so evident that he used the term of himself. In reality, there were many who bore the title, e.g., Barnabas (Acts 14:4, 14); Andronicus and Junia (Rom 16:7); some unnamed coworkers (2 Cor 8:23).

For Paul, mission meant the proclamation of the wonderful news that in Christ the God of Israel has reached out to save all. In the second Temple period, prophetic vision like that of Second Isaiah struggled with some way in which Israel could be graced and salvific presence for the world. With Paul, salvation by the one true God is no longer only on Israel's terms, but on universal terms, for faith in Christ saves apart from the Law that is the heart of Israel's response (Rom 3:28). Jesus had all his life been a faithful Jew. Similarly, Paul never renounced his Jewish heritage and identity. But he recognized that the redemptive meaning of Jesus' death and resurrection reached far beyond the boundaries of Judaism to embrace the whole world, not to repudiate Judaism, but to continue and spread its promises.

One of the most powerful symbols for mission in the Pauline letters is the Church as agent of reconciliation for the world. In 2 Corinthians 5:11-21, Paul speaks of his own ministry and that of all Christians as continuation of God's act of reconciling the world in Christ. Likewise, the Letter to the Ephesians 2:11-22 speaks of Christ as the one "who made both one and broke down the dividing wall of enmity, through his flesh" in order to create "one new person in place of the two, thus establishing peace." It is the message that life according to Christ can overcome alienation and bring about reconciliation and peace. Wherever and however mission is undertaken, there can be no better goal.

See: ABRAHAM, APOSTLE, BAPTISM, BETHANY, COMMUNITY, DISCIPLE/DISCIPLESHIP, GALILEE/SEA OF GALILEE, GOOD NEWS, HEALING, HOSPITALITY, ISRAEL, JESUS CHRIST, JEW, JUDAISM, JUSTICE, LAW, LOVE, MAGI, MESSIAH, MINISTRY, NATIONS, PAUL, PERSECUTION, PETER, POOR, PREACHING, RECONCILIATION, RESURRECTION, ROME, SAMARIA/SAMARI-

TAN, SHEPHERD, SPIRIT, SYNAGOGUE, TEMPLE, WIT-
NESS, WORLD

CAROLYN OSIEK, R.S.C.J.

Pastoral-Liturgical Tradition

The importance of the missionary impulse and expansion of the Church so
strongly evidenced in Acts and the letters
of Paul continued through the first millennium of the Christian Church. Efforts were
focused first on the regions of the Roman
Empire, although the Churches of Syria
and Persia moved also into China and even
Southeast Asia. In the West, the focus was
upon the Germanic peoples of the North
and the Slavic peoples to the East. Missionary activity was more intermittent between
1000 and 1500, with attention to consolidating the foothold of Christianity in the
northernmost parts of Europe and forays
into China and the Mongol Empire. Missionary activity increased again with Spanish and Portuguese expansion at the end of
the fifteenth century. Protestants became
active as missionaries beginning especially
in the eighteenth century. Both Protestants
and Roman Catholics intensified their missionary efforts throughout the nineteenth
and through the middle of the twentieth
centuries.

The theology which underlay missionary
motivation has varied considerably through
the centuries. The Great Commission of
Matthew 28:19-20, so important in the modern missionary movement, did not achieve
such central status as the reason for mission
until the sixteenth century. The twentieth
century has been a period of intense theological reflection on the meaning of Christian mission, especially in Roman Catholic
circles. This has been prompted by the success of the missions of the nineteenth and
twentieth centuries, which has resulted in a
Church wherein the majority of Christians
now live in the southern hemisphere. These
southern Churches now are providing the
majority of new members of religious orders and are already themselves sending
out missionaries to other countries. The end

of the colonial period raised abiding questions about the relation between state and
Church, imperialism and mission. And
changing understandings of the Church itself, particularly in the documents of the
Second Vatican Council, required a rethinking of the meaning of mission.

The beginning of this rethinking began
with Pope Benedict XV in his 1919 encyclical *Maximum Illud*. Amidst the ruins of a
Europe devastated by World War I, he
called for a renewed missionary effort, but
one that clearly uncoupled colonialism and
the spread of the Church, one that would
lead to indigenous Churches staffed by
their own people. Pius XI reiterated this by
ordaining indigenous bishops to many
countries for the first time. Pius XII and
John XXIII carried this line forward with
additional encyclicals on mission, emphasizing the need for sensitivity to local situations and for promotion of laypeople as
agents of mission. These papal initiatives,
as well as the work of theologians, set the
stage for a new missionary theology to be
presented at Vatican II.

The context for the new mission theology
at Vatican II was an expanded understanding of the Church. Rather than continuing
the notion of the Church as a bulwark
against the world, the Dogmatic Constitution on the Church presents the Church as a
sacrament, offering God's salvation to the
world. Thus for the Church to be Church, it
must be making this offer to the world at all
times. Missionary activity as constitutive of
the Church itself was to be underscored as
presented in the Decree on the Church's
Missionary Activity. The understanding of
the Church as a pilgrim people, when connected with Church as sacrament, made it
clear that missionary activity was incumbent upon all the baptized, not just the hierarchy or specialized missionaries.

The Pastoral Constitution on the Church
in the Modern World, in expressing appreciation of the nature of human culture (nos.
58-62), helped give expression to what it
means to be sensitive to local cultures, as
well as according dignity to each culture as

a shaper of the human. All of these perspectives come together in the Decree on the Church's Missionary Activity. Here mission is rooted first and foremost in the mission of the Trinity, the sending forth of the Son and the Spirit for the sake of the redemption of the world and its reconciliation to God. The Church becomes the visible presence of the Trinity's mission, although that mission is not restricted to it. The whole Church is called into mission to carry forth the message of God's coming reign.

Three themes have been especially formative of the understanding of mission since the Second Vatican Council. The first appeared especially at the 1971 Roman Synod. There, in a way consistent with earlier teaching but never so forcefully set forth, justice came to be proclaimed as constitutive of preaching the gospel. Preaching the gospel could not be reduced to the struggle for justice in concrete political and social situations, but a genuine preaching of the gospel was now impossible without it.

The second theme was inculturation. Respect for cultures was already raised up especially by Pius XII, but was taken considerably further by Paul VI, especially in his missionary journeys to Africa. The term inculturation, paralleling incarnation, first involved planting the seed of the gospel in new cultural soil, or grafting its shoot on new cultural stock. The resulting plant would be both authentically Christian and authentically true to the best of the local culture. John Paul II was the first pope to use the term inculturation, and it has now become part of official Church vocabulary.

The third theme is evangelization. Developed most clearly and effectively by Paul VI in his *Evangelii Nuntiandi* in 1975, it was to become the hallmark of the pontificate of John Paul II. "Evangelization" has to some extent come to replace the word "mission," since it intends to cover the same understanding, only in a broader and more holistic way. As it has come to be understood, evangelization is directed not just to individuals but also to entire cultures. It is a movement to all peoples: those who have

not heard the gospel, those whose faith needs strengthening, those who no longer believe. And it employs a variety of means: direct proclamation, dialogue of words and of life, inculturation, and the struggle for justice.

See: GOOD NEWS/GOSPEL, SALVATION

ROBERT J. SCHREITER, C.PP.S.

MONARCHY

Monarchy in the biblical tradition, as in other ancient Near Eastern texts, is depicted as kingship. Kings are overlords and their peoples vassals. However, more powerful kings are at times also overlords to lesser monarchs who are treated as vassals.

Parallels and contrasts have been drawn between Israel on the one hand and Egypt and Mesopotamia on the other. In the latter, kings were responsible for maintaining a divinely established timeless social and political order. The king was a principle of order in the eternal struggle between chaos and order. Kings were responsible for law, war, and cult, which, like kingship itself, were divine creations. Societies were highly stratified and individual rights were practically unknown. In some societies, the monarchs enjoyed divine filiation and were treated accordingly in life and in death.

Against this comparative background scholarship has devoted a great deal of attention to the origins and role of Yahwist, i.e., Israelite, monarchy. Its emergence is treated ambivalently and with hesitation in the OT. The so-called law of the kings in 1 Samuel 8:11-18 is an entirely negative description of ancient Near Eastern totalitarian regimes. The characterization eventually became a reality in Israel as well.

The Books of Samuel contain evidence for more than one attitude toward monarchy. These are best described on the one hand as "resisting" and on the other hand as "reluctantly accepting" the new institution. The ambiguity extends to the date of origin that in turn relates to the division and dating of the sources of the biblical story. Samuel personifies the quandaries by appearing as both favorably (1 Sam 9:1-10; 16:11) and unfavorably (1 Sam 8; 10:17-27) disposed toward the institution. Earlier attempts to explain the inconsistency in terms of earlier and later sources are increasingly abandoned. Although caution is advised in attempts to assess the popular mind in ancient societies, the uncertainty attributed to Samuel is now generally thought to reflect confusion or dissension among Yahwists. The cause of such disagreement has been warmly debated among scholars. The Book of Judges (chs. 8–9) with the ambiguity in Samuel suggests that the Yahwists made abortive attempts to centralize before finally establishing monarchy. Such passages led earlier scholars to suggest that Yahwist monarchy was an organized response to threats from external enemies. This led many to conclude that the institution was alien to Yahwism and was introduced without regard for Yahwist religious values.

Recent studies drawing on comparative sociology and archaeology have challenged this interpretation by expanding biblical interpretation. These studies have shown that the Yahwists' embracing of monarchy was a more gradual and prolonged process than the Bible suggests, and that factors internal to the community account for much of the development. Current portrayals show the Yahwists to be strongly committed to covenant ideals but initially pragmatic enough to accept political and economic changes necessary for preserving the community. This flexibility did not endure.

Several studies have assumed that Yahwist statehood and monarchy were achieved in the late tenth and the ninth centuries BCE. The date has been challenged based on archaeological indicators of centralization. One proposal suggests the eighth century, or possibly the seventh or sixth, for the earliest Yahwist monarchy. While the thesis has not compelled broad consensus, it offers a valuable critique of standard scholarship and invites continuing research on important issues.

Several short-term and long-term pressures within Israel and Judah appear to have moved the community toward centralization. In the tenth–ninth centuries, monarchy would have emerged while the eastern Mediterranean basin enjoyed a relative power vacuum that enabled the Yahwists to exercise exceptional self-determination. Developing agriculture and trade, movement into and exploiting marginally productive agricultural areas, pacification that enabled investment in labor-intensive terrace farming, discovery of new technologies such as iron working, and a shared general ideological (religious) base provided a politically, socially, and religiously stable environment needed for economic development and a corresponding need for administrative structures. Yahwist monarchy in this scenario emerged as a companion to other developments within Israelite and Judahite society.

The monarchs' role in the cult was multiform and long standing. The urge to build a temple is traced to the stories of David (2 Samuel 7 and 24). The obstructions are credited to the Yahweh who expresses displeasure through Nathan the prophet. In 2 Samuel 24, David's continuing desire to build is revealed when he purchases the threshing floor as a site. Scholarship sees similar signs in the census that presumably would enable taxation and conscription for forced labor, resources that were needed for the project. Divine displeasure was expressed this time in the plague that in effect eroded the resources and sabotaged the project.

Solomon is credited with building the First Temple, appointing priests, and regulating the cultic calendar (1 Kings 5–8). Kings offer sacrifices (1 Kgs 8:5), blessings (1 Kgs 8:14), and cultic reforms (2 Kings 23). Several studies have argued that the psalms celebrated kingship's rituals (Psalm 2). In every instance, however, the king does not displace Yahweh as the ultimate monarch over the Yahwists.

The negative attitude toward political monarchy grows within the biblical tradition. Authors describe callous indifference toward Yahwist covenant values giving way to military conscription, forced labor, and privilege for an elite ruling class. Yahwist kings, like their neighbors, appeared to own all properties and could administer with impunity. The so-called Schism of the North and South following Solomon's reign (1 Kings 12) and Amos' condemnation at Bethel (Amos 7:10-16) are examples of the depth, breadth, and endurance of such attitudes. This persistence has led some to argue that much early Yahwist narrative represents attempts of monarchists to reconcile the institution with the covenant tradition. This applies to pre-Deuteronomic Samuel, but becomes more clear in the writings of the Deuteronomists and Chroniclers. They are major literary efforts to understand, explain, and correct the problems associated with monarchy.

The monarchic period (ca. 1150–587 BCE) is usually divided between the United Monarchy and the Divided Monarchy, assigning Saul, David, and Solomon to the former and the separate monarchies of Israel and Judah following Solomon to the latter. The division assumes monarchy as early as the mid-eleventh century, the time usually attributed to Saul. Reasons have already been cited for questioning such an early date. Similarly, the Samuel texts do not explicitly affirm Saul's dominion over Judah, and it is possible that he was leader only of a federation of northern tribes. David simultaneously led Judah (2 Samuel 3) in a separate if not fully independent development of a second similar federation. The two moieties were not joined politically in the stories either of David or Solomon. This is probably an accurate portrayal. Hence, the "schism" in which Israel and Judah chose separate leaders realized the longstanding independence of the two regions rather than the breakup of an earlier unity.

The Books of Kings record a long series of separate successions in Judah and Israel. A dynastic principle of primogeniture seems to have developed but was not rigidly applied. The period as described in the OT was characterized by external and internal conflicts often over seemingly petty and personal matters. As in similar societies, such tensions often arose around questions of succession and inheritance. Many institutions that comprise the Yahwist and biblical tradition, such as prophecy and wisdom, took root and flourished during this era. Their stances were sometimes supportive and sometimes hostile to monarchy and individual monarchs. The so-called "E" or "Elohist" source was compiled during the Divided Monarchy. The sixth-century Deuteronomic reform and writings credited to the reign of Josiah attempted but failed to provide a religious basis for reuniting Israel with Judah under Jerusalemite leadership. The northern kingdom failed finally with its collapse in 721 BCE. Judah endured longer until the destruction of Jerusalem in 587 BCE and the beginning of the Babylonian Exile.

The causes for failure were both political and economic, although the biblical tradition assigns theological categories by crediting ineptitude and moral decay. Undoubtedly the tradition is at least partially accurate, but the theology was not independent of the politics and economy. The societies' religious values and the region's capacity to support overpowering, expensive elites are interrelated. Without the aid of new technologies or infusions of capital from abroad, with notable exceptions, the eastern Mediterranean Basin has rarely been able to sustain long-term the habits and tastes of elaborate bureaucracies. Like the circumstances depicted in the Exodus stories, the Yahwists fell victim to excesses they could not afford. This led to neglect, indifference, exploitation, the loss of a cohesive support base. Yahwist monarchy paid for its excesses by its own demise.

In the wake of the collapse of political monarchy left, the community further developed alternate uses for the kingship metaphor. Three that rest on earlier traditions can be cited: kingship of Yahweh, enhanced priesthood, and messianism.

Like other nations, by depicting Yahweh as king, Israel and Judah affirmed the deity's absolute sovereignty and expressed their belief in their vassalhood. The date of the origin of this belief is uncertain, but Yahweh is called king in both the Pentateuch and Deuteronomic History (e.g., Exod 15:18; Num 23:21; Judg 8:23; 1 Sam 8:7). The theme is explicit in the psalms and elsewhere where Yahweh is called king and credited with custody over creation and the people (Pss 98:6; 99:1-2; 24:1; 74:15-17; Jer 10:7-10).

With the end of political kingship, many aspirations were transferred to the priests who then served as leaders of the community. Priesthood was an ancient institution that assumed new prominence in the wake of monarchy and the Exile. Then and during the second Temple period, aspirations associated with royal theology were affixed to priesthood and priestly institutions and environments. The confidence and hope that monarchy had provided was now supplied by the priests as leaders of surviving remnants of the Yahwists. The theme of this transferring is continued in the NT where the believing community is described as a priestly nation (Hebrews).

The question of messianism rooted in the David stories, especially in the so-called Davidic Covenant (2 Samuel 7; Ps 89:1-38), is widely debated. Many Christian scholars, of course, see messianic hopes fulfilled in the NT. Recent scholarship has produced massive works on messianism and the Messiah. Earlier, McKenzie, however, was among those who insisted that the messianism of the OT was political and that reading Christian significance into those stories and hopes was the result of a Christian reader's bias.

Applying kingly metaphors to Jesus in the NT does not imply the regal politics of Israel's earlier age. Identifications such as in the dialog with Pilate (Matt 27:11; Mark 15:2; Luke 23:3) stress the other worldly, nonpolitical character of Jesus' kingly role. Scholars have insisted that his reign is religious and eschatological rather than political. In modern scholarship the distinction is not so easily maintained. Newer hermeneu-tics based in multicultural experiences and practices recommend reconsidering the terminologies and distinctions.

See: SOLOMON

JAMES W. FLANAGAN

MONOTHEISM

It is certain that Israel believed in the existence of only one God and worshiped that one God from the latter part of the sixth century BCE. What is a matter of some conjecture and dispute is the nature of ancient Israelite religion before that date. If one takes the evidence of the Bible at face value, the religion of ancient Israel was always monotheistic in theory. It is important to remember that the Bible reflects an elitist view of ancient Israelite religion. Also, though ancient traditions have found their way into the Bible, the text as a whole represents a relatively late conception of that religion. The popular religion of the Israelites was polytheistic up to the Exile.

The polytheistic religions of the ancient Semitic world followed a regular pattern. Clans and families honored the god responsible for the clan's prosperity and health. Hannah prayed for a son during the annual pilgrimage to the clan shrine at Shiloh (1 Samuel 1). There were gods who had areas of competence such as fertility, rain, and war. Like their neighbors, Israelite farmers prayed to Baal for rain (1 Kgs 8:21-22) and to Dumuzi for fertility (Ezek 8:14). Then there was the national god. The Moabites had Chemosh, the Ammonites Molech, the Assyrians Ashur, and the Israelites Yahweh.* 2 Kings 17:30-31 gives a list of national gods. As Micah 4:5 affirms, Yahweh's position as the national God of Israel was never in question, even amid the polytheism of preexilic religion. National gods could be worshiped outside their own territory. For example, Solomon built shrines to Chemosh and Molech on the Mount of Olives (1 Kgs 11:7).

One feature that made Israelite worship of Yahweh different was that Israel's God was not depicted with an image. There were attempts to symbolize Yahweh's power as a bronze serpent (Num 21:9), golden calves (1 Kgs 12:28), or a sacred wooden pole (1 Kgs 16:23). Later these would be considered inappropriate (2 Kgs 18:4), but at one time some Israelites believed them to be legitimate parts of their ancestral religion. In fact, Moses is credited with fashioning the bronze serpent (Num 21:9). The results of recent archaeological work at Kuntillet 'Aǧrud have raised the possibility that some Israelites did depict Yahweh with images and may have given a female consort to Yahweh.

Despite the similarity of Israelite religion with its counterparts in the rest of the ancient Near East, it is possible to trace a movement to monotheism. In the ninth century there was a fierce conflict with Baalism in the northern kingdom. Elijah has a significant role in this conflict. Jezebel, who was a Tyrian princess before becoming Ahab's (874–853 BCE) queen, began killing the prophets of Yahweh (1 Kgs 18:4, 13). Elijah retaliated by slitting the throats of 450 of Baal's prophets (1 Kgs 18:22, 40). Ahab's successor, Jehoram (852–841 BCE) removed the stone monument to Baal that his father had raised in Yahweh's temple in Samaria. Jehu (841–813 BCE), who assassinated Jehoram, destroyed the temple of Baal and has all the priests and prophets of Baal killed (2 Kings 9–10). Though these conflicts had political and economic roots, some people perceived them as a religiously motivated revolution that rejected Baal in favor of Yahweh, the ancestral God of the Israelites.

About one hundred years later (ca. 750 BCE) the prophet Hosea who repudiated the violence of Jehu's coup (Hos 1:4) moved the conflict between Baal and Yahweh to the religious plane. The prophet asserts that Israel should worship Yahweh alone because there is no other god but Yahweh (Hos 13:4). The prophet makes this proclamation with passion precisely because Israel does serve other gods (Hos 2:13, 17; 3:1; 11:2). The prophet is not simply opposing the worship of the Baal introduced by Jezebel, but the popular worship of the Baals that was endemic in the region before Israel entered Canaan.

Following the fall of the northern kingdom in 722 BCE refugees from the north came to Jerusalem and provided the stimulus for a movement to the exclusive worship of Yahweh in the south. They portray the fall of their kingdom as a direct consequence of their people's failure to worship Yahweh alone. This no doubt inspired the modest reforms of Hezekiah (739–699 BCE; 2 Kgs 18:4). The political and military crisis that resulted from Sennacherib's invasion of Judah and siege of Jerusalem in 701 BCE inspired a greater concern for the loyalty that Judah owed to its national God.

The reign of Josiah (641–609 BCE) was the setting for the ministry of the prophet Zephaniah whose preaching called for the elimination of all Baal worship (Zeph 1:4-6). The king supported the movement that called for the exclusive service of Judah's ancestral God. 2 Kings 22–23 describes the action that Josiah took. First he closed local shrines. They were the sites of significant abuse. Legitimate worship of Yahweh took place only in Jerusalem. This centralization of the worship of Yahweh would have had little value without the purification of the worship that took place in the Temple at Jerusalem. This the king ordered (2 Kgs 23:4). Control of worship in Judah by those who wanted the people to worship Yahweh alone became institutionalized by making the contents of the Book of the Law national policy (2 Kgs 22:8–23:3).

The policies of Josiah did not outlive him. He died in battle against the Egyptians in 609 BCE. The words of Ezekiel prove that the images of foreign gods returned to the Temple (Ezekiel 8). Even after the fall of Jerusalem to the Babylonians, there are some who were convinced that the worship of non-Israelite gods should continue (Jer 44:17).

The movement to monotheism shifted into another gear after the Exile. With the return from Babylon, those who wished to serve Yahweh alone were no longer a minority. The allure of Baal was gone. Contact with Persian religion provided stimulus for conceiving the unity of divinity, though Persian religion itself was dualistic. The ideology for this movement toward monotheism was provided by Deuteronomy (4:35, 39; 6:4) and Second Isaiah (45:21, 22; 43:10). Ezekiel provides a constitution for the renewed Judah engaged in the exclusive service of Yahweh (Ezekiel 40–48).

The Israelite religion of the postexilic period gave expression to the monotheism that was an undercurrent of ancient religions—even that of Egypt. Already two hundred years before the entrance of the Israelites into Canaan, the Pharaoh Ikhnaton (Amenopis IV, 1364–1347 BCE) recognized the fundamental unity of the divine. Israel came to monotheism after a long struggle culminated by the experience of the Exile. The best answer to the theological problems created by the Exile was provided by monotheism: the God of Israel was the only God who is the Creator and Ruler of the earth.

See: GOD

LESLIE J. HOPPE, O.F.M.

MOON

Old Testament

The moon has been created and set in place by God along with the sun and the stars (Ps 8:4) to provide light in the night sky (Ps 136:9). In Genesis 1:4-9, it is described as the lesser light that governs the night to distinguish it from the sun that rules the day. It also marks the seasons (Ps 104:19). As a part of the created universe, it is called upon to praise its creator (Ps 148:3; Dan 3:62). The movement of the moon has been determined by divine command (Jer 31:35; Bar 6:59); only because he acts as the Lord's agent can Joshua halt the sun and the moon during his battle with the Amorites (Josh 10:12-13). In Canticle 6:10 and Isaiah 30:26, the moon is "the white lady," a reference to the white luminosity of its light.

First-generation ancestors of Israel, Abraham and Sarah, are linked with Ur in southern Mesopotamia; Rebecca, Leah, and Rachel, wives of the second- and third-generation Isaac and Jacob, were from Haran in northwestern Mesopotamia. Both places were major centers for the worship of the Babylonian moon god Sin. In the popular imagination, the god manifested in the moon controlled the fertility of the flock, the field, and the marriage bed. Inhabitants of Beth-Yerach, "Shrine of the moon" (modern Khirbet Kerak at the southern end of the Sea of Galilee) and of Jericho probably worshiped this god.

Such worship undoubtedly continued alongside worship of the Israelite God. Behind the declaration of faith in the Lord's protection in Psalm 121:6 is the popular belief that the moon was a deity who in certain circumstances could harm human beings. Worship of the moon received state sanction when King Manasseh (2 Kgs 21:3, 5) came under the sway of the Assyrian Empire. Jeremiah 8:1-2 identifies the moon as "part of the whole army of heaven which [the kings and princes of Judah] loved and served." According to 2 Kings 23:5 the model king Josiah commissioned the priest Hilkiah to outlaw this worship. Deuteronomy 4:19 judged such worship to be a rejection of the Lord as the only god for Israel. Those who engaged in it were punished by death (Deut 17:3-5). Job notes that had "my heart been secretly enticed to waft [it] a kiss with my hand this too would be a crime for condemnation, for I would have denied God above" (Job 31:27-28).

In biblical Israel, the phases of the moon determined the calendar. The major fall and spring festivals, Passover and Sukkoth, began with the full moons of Nisan and Tishri respectively. Months were measured from new moon to new moon. The day of the new moon was a day of rest (Amos 8:5), as well as a day on which people consulted the "man of God" at local shrines or sanctuaries (2 Kgs 4:23). The timing of this practice Israel shared with its neighbors; e.g., Isaiah 47:13 criticizes Babylonian stargazers who make their predictions at each new moon. Special sacrifices were offered (Num 28:11-15), and the shofar, the ceremonial trumpet, was to be blown to remind the Lord of his people (Num 10:10; Ps 81:4). According to some prophets, the Lord disdained these sacrifices when the needs of the poor were being neglected (Hos 5:7; Isa 1:13).

These preexilic rituals are echoed in the Chronicler's idealized presentation in which the Levites are charged with offering new moon sacrifices. Solomon built the first temple to provide a place for these sacrifices (2 Chr 2:3) and himself offered them (2 Chr 8:13). The ruling king was obligated to use some of his own wealth to finance such sacrifices (2 Chr 31:3). New moon sacrifices are also mentioned in Ezekiel's blueprint for postexilic temple liturgy. On that day the gates of the inner court would be thrown open; princes (46:6) would offer special sacrifices (45:17).

The darkening of the moon is part of the imagery associated with the Day of the Lord tradition, an eschatalogical event in which the Lord would appear at the head of the heavenly army to destroy the enemies of faithful Israel. This visitation would coincide with the arrival of abundant winter rains for Jerusalem and its environs. The Day of the Lord thus inaugurates a new age of agricultural plenty and political security for Jerusalem. This imagery mirrors the meteorology of the fall interchange period, the alternating dust-bearing storms from the eastern *Deserta Arabia* and the rain-bearing storms from the western Mediterranean. The dust clouds of hyperbolic east wind storms blot out the natural light of the moon (Isa 13:10; Ezek 32:7; Joel 2:10). Moonlight filtered through the reddish-brown dust cloud takes on the color of blood (Joel 3:4).

In Qoheleth 12:2, Qoheleth advises his audience to remember God "before the moon darkens," a metaphor for the failing eyesight associated with approaching death. It is also used as a symbol of permanence (Ps 72:5, 7; 89:38). However, in Sirach 27:11, its waxing and waning suggests instability and changeableness.

New Testament

References to the moon here occur in the citation of OT passages. Mark 13:24 and parallel passages (Matt 24:29; Luke 21:25-26) describe the arrival of Jesus as the Son of Man in imagery related to the Day of the Lord tradition. The moon will not shed its light (Matt 24:29); signs will appear in the sun, the moon, and the stars (Luke 21:25). Acts 2:20 claims that the day of Pentecost fulfills Joel 3:4. Revelation 6:12 uses the same imagery, "the moon turning blood red," when the Lamb breaks open the Sixth Seal. The great sign, "a woman clothed with the sun," has the moon under her feet (Rev 12:1). The New Jerusalem will have no need of natural light; the glory of the Lord will be its lamp (see Isa 60:19-20).

Two miracle stories suggest the harmful effects of the moon on human beings. In Matthew 4:24, Jesus heals people who are "moon-struck," i.e., "lunatics." In Matthew 17:15, the boy cured of epilepsy is described in the same way.

Paul appeals to the unique quality of light provided by the moon to distinguish the peculiar glory that will be proper to the resurrected body when the Lord will return to awaken those who sleep in death (1 Cor 15:35-44).

See: DAY OF THE LORD

KATHLEEN S. NASH

MOSES

The Bible presents Moses as the leader chosen by God to deliver the descendants of Jacob from bondage in Egypt* and the chosen instrument to transmit the Torah to these liberated slaves. As such, Moses has a very prominent role in the religious traditions of ancient Israel. That is why the relatively few references to Moses outside the Pentateuch are so surprising. Books of the Hebrew Bible outside the Pentateuch mention Moses only fifty-eight times, and most of these occur in Chronicles, Ezra, and Nehemiah. By contrast, the NT mentions Moses seventy-eight times.

The name "Moses" is an Egyptian word that means "has been born." It is usually appended to the name of a god thought to be the new child's protector as in "Tutmoses" (= "[the god] Tut is born"). The Book of Exodus asserts that Moses was named by Pharaoh's daughter who rescued him after he had been set adrift on the Nile by his Hebrew mother to save him from Pharaoh's command to kill male Hebrew newborns (Exod 1:22–2:6). Despite asserting that an Egyptian gave Moses his name, Exodus derives the meaning of the name from the Hebrew word meaning "to draw out" (*mashah*; Exod 2:10).

The historical value of the story about birth and adoption of Moses as well as the other stories about him in the Pentateuch is part of the larger question of the origins of ancient Israel. While there is no consensus about this issue, it is clear that Moses is not a historical figure in the same sense as David and Solomon. Still, there can be no question about the significance of the figure of Moses for the theological traditions of ancient Israel.

Moses represents the tradition that sees ancient Israel's relationship with God as a consequence of the Sinai covenant that bound Israel to obedience (see Exod 19:5-6). This idea stood in some tension with the covenant tradition that centered on the Davidic dynasty. According to the latter tradition, God's choice of David was not only an act of unmerited kindness; it was also eternal (see 2 Sam 7:8-17). It is through the Davidic dynasty that Israel can maintain its relationship with God.

The prophets only rarely mention Moses by name (five times in the entire prophetic corpus). Still, they operate out of the suppositions of the Mosaic tradition, viz., that the barometer of Israel's relationship with God is the quality of its obedience to the norms of traditional Israelite morality. The prophets criticized Israel for its infidelity and spoke words of judgment in the name of God. In spite of Israel's failures, the prophetic tradition was convinced that judgment was not God's last word. Israel can look forward to a new Exodus (Isa 41:17-20; 51:9-11).

When the people began to recognize the importance of obedience to Torah for their future, Moses' role as lawgiver began to overshadow his role as the deliverer from Egyptian slavery. The Book of Deuteronomy reflects this as it focuses on Moses' role in transmitting the Torah from God to Israel (Deut 5:22-27). Still, the enhancement of Moses' importance was gradual. For example, in his praise of Israel's great ancestors, Sirach devotes five verses to Moses but three times as many to Aaron (Sir 44:1-22).

By the time of Jesus, Moses' role as lawgiver was secure. The centrality of the Torah in early Judaism enhanced the role of Moses, who transmitted the Torah from God to Israel. This is clear from non-canonical Jewish religious literature. For example, in the *Book of Jubilees*, Moses becomes a great miracle worker. The miraculous events associated with his death and burial are the subject of *The Assumption of Moses*.

The great prestige of Moses caused a serious problem. By the Greco-Roman period, it became clear that the laws of ancient Israel needed updating. Still, to have any validity, legal traditions had to have a Mosaic pedigree. That is why the Pharisees of Jesus' day claimed such a sanction for their traditions. Later Rabbinic writings made explicit the claim that an "oral law" (actually the Rabbinic updating of the Torah) as well as a "written law" (the Pentateuch) was given by God to Moses on Sinai. Jesus did not accept the Pharisees' claims about the "oral law" and regarded it as simply human tradition with no divine authority (see Mark 7:1-23). Jesus, therefore, did not feel himself bound to observe these traditions, though he never violated any prescription of the written Law of Moses.

When the Samaritan tradition looked forward to the future, it did not see a royal, messianic figure as did some Jewish expectations. The Samaritan eschatological figure was "the prophet like [Moses]" of Deuteronomy 18:15. Acts 7:37 reflects the Christian belief that Jesus fulfilled this expectation as well as the Jewish ones regarding a Messiah.

In view of Moses' role in early Judaism and perhaps also because of the Samaritan expectations, the Gospels attempt to establish parallels between Jesus and Moses. For example, some interpreters have seen Matthew's description of Jesus teaching from the mountainside (5:1-2) as a deliberate analogy with Moses on Sinai. Though Moses is not mentioned by name, Matthew tells the story of Jesus' birth by making obvious allusions to the birth of Moses, e.g., the slaughter of the innocents by Herod (Matt 2:16-18) and the Pharaoh's command to kill the newborn male Hebrews (Exod 1:23). Often the purpose of these allusions to Moses is to express the superseding of Judaism by Christianity as when John makes the comparison between the manna given by Moses and the "true bread from heaven" (John 6:32).

Unfortunately, Christians have been guilty of caricaturing the approach to religion represented by the Mosaic tradition as minimalism and legalism without the Spirit. A more informed view of the Mosaic tradition recognizes this approach to God as one of responsibility. Moses calls Israel to respond to the blessings it has received from God—most notably the blessing of freedom. Moses represents an approach to religion that seeks to have believers imitate God. As God is faithful, righteous, just, and loving, so believers are to be the same.

See: EGYPT, LAW

LESLIE J. HOPPE, O.F.M.

MOTHER

In the patriarchal societies of biblical times, the mother played an important but secondary role in the family. Within a polygamous culture, there was often a hierarchy among the wives, which added to the complexity of the kinship structure.

Old Testament

Extraordinary Births. Bearing children was highly valued in the ancient Near East where survival was precarious and where patriarchy dominated. Both the OT and NT texts contain illustrations of how God overcomes obstacles so that a mother can bear a son and bring him to fulfill the mission for which God has destined him. Sarah, barren and elderly, bears Isaac (Gen 21:2) and becomes a mother of nations (Gen 17:16). Rebekah, barren until God opens her womb, bears twin sons, Esau and Jacob (Gen 25:21-23). Rachel, barren alongside her fertile sister Leah, eventually bears Joseph (Gen 30:22-24) and then Benjamin (Gen 35:17). Manoah's unnamed barren wife learns through a messenger from God that she will bear a son, Samson, who is to be a Nazarite (Judg 13:3). Hannah, barren alongside Elkanah's fertile wife Peninnah, bears the prophet Samuel (1 Sam 1:20). The prophet Elisha intercedes with God for his generous but barren hostess whom God then blesses with a son (2 Kgs 4:17).

Other women, in extraordinary circumstances though not barren, bring forth sons who themselves promise to be extraordinary. For example, through ingenuity despite the risk, the mother of Moses saves her infant son from death (Exod 2:1-10).

Despite the patriarchal culture in which men were valued more than women, several laws indicate that mothers and fathers received equal treatment with respect to their children. For example, children were to honor their mother (as well as their father, e.g., Exod 20:12; Lev 19:3; Deut 27:16). A person who struck his mother (or his father, Exod 21:15) or cursed his mother (or his father, Exod 21:17) would be put to death (see Deut 7:16). A woman's daughters were considered of lesser value than her sons, though they would eventually rise in esteem as they bore someone else's sons. When a mother undertook purification after childbirth the duration of her purification was determined by the sex of her new offspring. For a son she would purify herself a total of forty days; for a daughter, eighty days (Lev 12:2-5).

Surrogate Motherhood. Surrogate motherhood is one indication of just how important ancient Israel viewed the bearing of sons. Though Abraham had been promised a son, Sarah was thought to be too old to bear children and consequently barren. She gave Abraham her maidservant Hagar through whom Abraham begot Ishmael (Gen 16:2-3). When Rachel seemed unable to bear sons, she gave her maid Bilhah to her husband Jacob (Gen 30:3-5); likewise, when Leah feared that she had ceased bearing children, she handed over her maidservant Zilpah to Jacob (Gen 30:9-10).

Queen Mothers. A major source of women's prestige was the sons whom they bore. For this reason, the mothers of kings are given special mention in the OT texts. Though they both were wives of David, Bathsheba is remembered over Abigail because she was the mother of King Solomon (1 Kgs 1:28-31). The Books of Kings specify by name the mother of a new king on the throne of Judah. This naming may have been done to distinguish the new king from his half-brothers, who were also his father's sons. Her name specified which of the former king's several wives had borne the new king (e.g., 1 Kgs 15:2, 10; 1 Kgs 22:42).

The Mother-Child Relationship. "Can a mother forget her infant, be without tenderness for the child of her womb? Even should she forget, I will not forget you" (Isa 49:15). The prophet's assumption is that mothers do not forget the children they have borne, and in like manner, God will not forget the people. Examples from the OT narratives bear this out. Sarah protects her son Isaac's place as the heir of God's promise to Abraham (Gen 21:10). Rebekah secures Isaac's blessing for her favored son Jacob (Gen 27:10), and then later protects him from his brother Esau (vv. 43-45). Moses' mother risks her well-being to keep her son safe from the Egyptians who would kill him (Exod 2:1-3). King Saul's wife Rizpah remains day and night with the bodies of her dead sons to protect them, lest they become prey to birds and wild animals (2 Sam 21:10). King David's wife Bathsheba intercedes with her husband to secure his throne for her son Solomon (1 Kgs 1:17).

Proverbs 31:10-31 depicts an ideal woman who is also an ideal mother. Among her virtues are strength and dignity, wisdom and kindness. She is industrious, providing her household with food and clothing.

The Hebrew word for "womb," *rehem*, is etymologically bound to the Hebrew verb, *rihhem*, meaning "to be compassionate." Children are the product of women's wombs; mothers have compassion for the children of their wombs. God, who is compassionate (e.g., Isa 14:1; 49:13; 55:7; Mic 7:19; Pss 86:15; 103:8), is like those who have wombs; God behaves like mothers behave.

New Testament

Extraordinary Births. In the NT, Elizabeth, like Sarah, has been barren and is elderly when she bears the son whom God promises to her husband (Luke 1:13-18). Mary, through the overshadowing of the holy Spirit, becomes the mother of Jesus (Luke 1:30-35).

The Mother-Child Relationship. Consistent with the texts of the OT, the NT depicts mothers as having compassion and concern for the children of their wombs. In Matthew 20:20-21 the mother of Zebedee's sons asks Jesus to allow her sons to sit on either side of him when he comes into God's reign; that she would seek her sons' best interest would be a widely accepted cultural assumption. In another text Jesus himself was touched by the sorrow of the widow who was burying her only son, and responded with compassion (Luke 7:11-13). Moreover, Jesus himself is portrayed as caring for the people of Jerusalem as a mother hen is concerned for her offspring: "Jerusalem, Jerusalem, you who kill the prophets and stone those sent to you, how many times I yearned to gather your children together as a hen gathers her brood under her wings, but you were unwilling!" (see Luke 13:34).

Contrary to what one might expect, Mary, the mother of Jesus, is given very little attention in the NT texts. As with OT mothers of extraordinary sons, there are wondrous circumstances surrounding Jesus' birth.

Both Matthew's and Luke's Gospels contain an account of Jesus' infancy in which Mary is featured (Matthew 1–2; Luke 1–2). Yet careful attention to the relevant chapters of each of these gospels reveals very different emphases. In the Matthean narrative Joseph dominates; in the Lucan account Mary's role, in cooperation with the holy Spirit, is central. Though John's Gospel lacks an infancy narrative, it depicts Mary as central to the performance of Jesus' first miracle, at the Cana wedding (2:1).

The NT texts seem to reprioritize and enlarge the mother-son relationship developed in the OT texts. One is to love Jesus even more than one's father or mother (Matt 10:37; cf. Luke 14:26). Jesus promises those who have given up their mothers and fathers for his sake or the sake of the gospel that they will receive a hundred-fold payment in the present age and eternal life in the age to come (Matt 19:29; Mark 10:29-30).

Jesus uses the occasion of a visit from his family to ask, "Who are my mother and my brothers?" with an intent to enlarging his "family:" "Whoever does the will of God is my brother and sister and mother" (Mark 3:33-35). Consequently, one should not be surprised to discover that Jesus does not accept the request of the mother of Zebedee to award her sons special favor (Matt 20:23). It is curious that in each of the Synoptic accounts of Jesus' crucifixion, though mothers are explicitly mentioned as being present, Jesus' own mother Mary is not mentioned (Matt 27:55-56; Mark 15:40-41; Luke 23:49). In the Johannine account Mary is present; Jesus uses the occasion to give John to Mary as her son, and Mary to John as his mother (John 19:25-27). Whereas society legitimated an intimate relationship between a mother and her natural son, Jesus extended that intimacy to everyone.

Offspring in the New Testament: Faith and Love. Having children is not necessarily less important to first-century Christians than it was to the ancient Israelites. However, the NT texts are not very concerned with that phenomenon (despite the fact that, except for early Pauline texts, the parousia was not expected immediately). Elizabeth and Mary are the only women who become mothers in the narratives, and there are comparatively few references to other mothers. On the other hand, the Genesis command to "increase and multiply" (1:22), with children understood to be a blessing from God, is channeled in the NT to prayers that faith and love may increase (e.g., Luke 17:5; Phil 1:9), that good works may multiply (e.g., Col 1:10). These are gifts of God, fruits of the holy Spirit which the entire Christian community is to bear (cf. Gal 5:22; Heb 12:11).

See: FAMILY, FATHER, MARRIAGE

ALICE L. LAFFEY

Pastoral-Liturgical Tradition

Notion of Motherhood. In the ancient Greco-Roman world, the roles of mother and father* were based on philosophical understandings of biological differences. For example, using an agrarian model of human conception, Aristotle taught that the father provided in his semen (lit. "seed") the homunculus or the complete "form" of the human person, and therefore was the "principle" of the child. The mother, on the other hand, was considered the passive partner, her womb furnishing the "fertile field" in which the seed was planted and her menstrual blood providing the "matter" to aid in the growth of the homunculus into a person. Women thus needed a greater amount of the elements of earth and water, as opposed to air and fire which were more prevalent in the male. While these elements aided in her fertility, they also made her more emotional and consequently less apt for rational endeavors. Thus mothers were expected to be the "heart" of the home, while, in accordance with natural law, fathers were properly the head of the household.

The tradition of the Church, based on a similar understanding of natural order, has virtually identified the vocation of woman with that of mother. In his encyclical On the Condition of Labor (*Rerum novarum*) Pope Leo XII stresses that "women are not suited for certain occupations. A woman is by nature fitted for home work, and it is this which is best adapted to preserve her modesty and to promote the good bringing up of children and the well-being of the family."* Similarly, Pope John XXIII suggested that the "end for which the Creator fashioned woman's whole being is motherhood."

Contemporary society has created many pressures for the contemporary family, and the roles of both mother and father have changed accordingly. It is much more likely that both parents work outside the home and both divide the domestic responsibilities. Thus the Church's teaching has also developed in response to this change. In his Apostolic Exhortation on the Family, Pope John Paul II emphasizes the equal dignity of women and men. He adds that this equality "is realized in the reciprocal self-giving of each to the other and by both to the children which is proper to marriage* and the family." Nevertheless, he adds that "the true advancement of women requires that clear recognition be given to the value of their maternal and family role," exhibiting the ambiguity with which the Church has viewed these contemporary developments in domestic relations.

Motherhood of Mary. One of the most ancient titles of Mary is that of *Theotokos,* the Bearer or Mother of God. The earliest known instance of the term is in a letter of Alexander of Alexandria against the Arians in 324, but its use in devotion is likely much earlier. Dogmatically, this understanding of Mary arises from a context of Christology. It is a statement of faith in the incarnation of Christ. Mary was the Mother of Jesus, but since Jesus was also God without division between human and divine, she also had to be the Mother of God.

As the title has been used in Marian devotion, there seem to be two distinct traditions. One sees Mary, the Mother of God, as the model of Christian living, inviting the

Christian to "bring forth Christ" in his or her life. The story of the Annunciation is central to this understanding. Mary is the model for Christian living because of her obedience to the Word which then took flesh in her. Christians are to model her faithfulness, and repeat her words, "Be it done unto me according to your Word" in their lives. In the early Middle Ages, St. Francis of Assisi, for example, could ask his followers to become "mothers of Christ" by receiving God's Word, which is Christ, in faith; by allowing the Word to develop within them; and finally by "begetting Christ" in their holy manner of living.

There is a second way in which this understanding has been used in popular devotion. Since Mary is the Mother of Christ, she is also Mother of the mystical body of Christ, that is the Church. As such she is the mediatrix between the faithful and Christ. An example of this reasoning can be found in the Dogmatic Constitution on the Church which states: "By reason of the gift and role of her divine motherhood, by which she is united with her Son, the Redeemer, the Blessed Virgin is also intimately united to the Church. As St. Ambrose taught, the Mother of God is a type of the Church in the order of faith, charity, and perfect union with Christ."

Although devotion to Mary as Mother of God began early in the Church's tradition, the feast of the Maternity of the Blessed Virgin Mary was not added to the universal calendar until 1931. At that time, the feast was celebrated on October 11. Pope Paul VI changed the feast to January 1.

Church as Mother. The term "Mother Church" is already present in the writings of St. Cyprian of Carthage. The development of this notion is similar to that of Mary as Mother of God and Mother of the Church. On the one hand, the Church was seen in terms of the maternal roles of nourishing and teaching the faithful. On the other hand, as the Dogmatic Constitution on the Church also shows, the Church becomes herself a mother by accepting the

Word of God in a manner reminiscent of Mary at the Annunciation.

God as Mother. In recent years, theologians, influenced at least in part by feminist concerns, have begun to retrieve from the tradition more feminine aspects of the Church's understanding of God. The imagery of God as mother and even of Jesus as mother is present in theological and mystical writings throughout the Middle Ages. It is present in the work of both men and women mystics. Contemporary theologians have also suggested that female metaphors, especially that of giving birth, may be more beneficial in explaining God's relation to the world than the traditional masculine metaphors. In doing so, they are actually returning to an ancient theological tradition that maintains that one needs many names to describe God.

See: FAMILY, MARRIAGE

THOMAS NAIRN

MOUNTAIN

Mountains have a natural religious significance in that they seem to bring us closer to the transcendant, to ecstasy, to God. They are also a fitting symbol of the power and permanence of God. God can, of course, be experienced in other marvelous, natural settings: deserts, the sea, and in other cultures, in forests—any quiet place. Mountains become important in the OT not only because of major revelatory events which occur on them, but also because they become the magnets or points of attachment for clusters of memories and theological associations and traditions. The traditions then remain tenaciously attached to these sacred places. OT usage occurs against a rich background of Canaanite and other ancient Near Eastern mountain traditions and religious symbols. In the NT Jesus performs foundational acts on mountains: the call of the Twelve, prayer, and the transfiguration. This tradition is then developed by the later evangelists and reflected upon by the letter writers.

Old Testament

The ordinary Hebrew word for mountain is *har.* Others are *harar, matzab,* and, as we are coming to see, *tzur,* traditionally translated "rock" (see Job 14:18; also *gibeah* [Num 23:9]). Aramaic uses *tur, tura,* and Greek *horos* (*charax* for seige mounds or ramparts, Luke 19:43). Mountains are present as two ridges in the Holy Land, on either side of the Jordan. On the left or western side are the Judean, Samaritan, and Galilean hills. On the right or eastern side are the bluffs of Moab, Gilead, and Bashan (Jordan, ancient Ammon). To the north are the mountains of Lebanon and the anti-Lebanon (Hermon), to the south the mountains or rugged terrain of the Negev (Edom) and the Sinai peninsula. Some of the great mountains of the Holy Land in order of height are Hermon (9,230 ft.), Horeb-Sinai (Jebel Musa, 7,500 ft. called in Exod 3:1 the mountain of God), the twin peaks of Samaria, Ebal (3,084 ft.) and Gerezim (2,890 ft.), Nebo (2,630 ft.), Tabor (1,930 ft.), Carmel (1,818 ft.), Jerusalem (= Zion and Moriah 2,711 ft.), and the Mount of Olives (actually higher than Jerusalem but since waterless not the city center in antiquity).

Mountains serve many functions in antiquity. Since *tzur* serves as a title for the God of Israel (2 Sam 23:3; 22:32; Ps 78:35, and esp. Deut 32:4, 15, 18, 30), connoting the divine protective power and ability to strike dread in the hearts of God's enemies, mountains can be said to be objects of worship at least abstractly, and certainly as places of worship. They provoke awe at the majesty of creation and thus of the creator. They serve as boundaries, as places for ambushes, as battle grounds, as dwellings for goats, rock rabbits, and birds. For humans they can serve as places of refuge and of spiritual retreat (1 Kgs 19:18). Metaphorically they represent stability (even eternity), obstacles, power over nature.

Theologically, the most important mountains in the OT are Sinai and Zion. They are roughly related to the diverse theological traditions of the northern and southern kingdoms respectively, Israel and Judah. In any case, Sinai is associated with Moses, the Exodus from Egypt, the gift of the Law, and several appearances of God both to Moses and to Elijah. Theophanies to Moses begin with his experience of the burning bush. The word for the bush in Exodus 3:2 is *sĕneh*, which could itself be related to the name of the mountain, Sinai (though the mountain is called Horeb in the chapter, 3:1, and Sinai beginning in 16:1). Sinai appears in early poetic texts like Deuteronomy 33:2 and Judges 5:5 (echoed in Ps 68:9, 18). The term *Mount* Sinai occurs in Exodus especially in contexts of the great theophanies connected with the giving of the Law (Exod 19:11, 18, 20, 23; 24:16; 31:18; 34:2, 4, 29, 32). The term *"wilderness* of Sinai" occurs especially in Numbers. The mountain of the covenant and the Law is called Horeb throughout Deuteronomy (in chs. 1; 4; 5; 9; 18; 29), but also in the prayer of dedication of the Temple (1 Kgs 8:9; 2 Chr 5:10) and especially in the wonderful theophany to Elijah in 1 Kings 19:8. There Horeb is again called the mountain of God, as in Exodus 3:1. The idolatrous worship of the golden calf at Horeb is recalled in Psalm 106:19. The prophet Malachi (3:22) endorses the Law given at Horeb and links this with the prophet Elijah at the very close of the OT. Symbolically then, Sinai-Horeb is the mountain connected with the covenant of the Law.

With Mount Zion comes a different circle of associations. Apart from a few mentions in the historical and Wisdom books (2 Sam 5:7; par. 1 Chr 11:5, a stronghold and City of David, 1 Kgs 8:1; in parallel with Jerusalem, 2 Kgs 19:31; Cant 3:11), this is a name that belongs to the prophets and to the psalms. Isaiah is the prophet of Zion par excellence and this includes all three parts of the long book that bears his name. Zion is called holy in Isaiah 4:3-4. Often Zion is paralleled with Jerusalem (e.g., Isa 2:3) because it seems to have been the name of the little hill (now the village of Ophel or Silwan) which David chose as his capital, named Jerusalem by its Jebusite inhabitants. Solomon then built the Temple on the topmost part, as David had built his palace above the village. The city was supplied with water from the pool of Siloam and the spring of Gihon at the bottom of the hill, and this water was made available even during a seige after Hezekiah's tunnel was built (2 Kgs 20:20). Because it is the city of David, Zion is the city of all the kings of Judah, the royal city. Since the kings were anointed, they were *messiahs* (anointed ones). Because the Temple was on Zion, it becomes the city of God (Isa 60:14) and thus itself holy (Ps 2:6; Zech 8:3). Theologically, therefore, Zion is associated not primarily with the Law, but with royal messianism (for Christians this points toward Christology), with Temple and priestly ritual of sacrifice, for Christians the Eucharist, within the Pentateuch to the Priestly cult traditions and laws, and with the prophets whom God raised up as a check and balance to the kings, and with the Temple songs, the psalms.

Christians are therefore confronted with a basic decision: Sinai or Zion, Moses or David, law or prophecy? Sometimes this is answered simply in terms of the second option: Zion, David, prophecy, because Jesus is the Messiah or Christ, spirit-filled, who came to free us from the Law. A more balanced perception of NT revelation however suggests that a both-and answer is appropriate. Jesus in the Sermon on the Mount does not abolish all of the Law but centers it on love and justice, frees it from imperfections, and radically reinterprets and deepens it in the light of the imminently coming reign of God. He is "the prophet like Moses" of Deuteronomy 18:18 as well as the son of David. He is the great high priest as well as the victim. He fulfills and perfects all parts of the OT faith and expectation: Sinai as well as Zion, Mosaic as well as Davidic, legal as well as prophetic. Still, it would probably be correct to say that in Jesus Christ the Sinai-Moses-legal line is integrated into and thus in a way subordinated or sublated to the Zion-David-messianic line.

New Testament

Mountains in the NT serve as places of isolation (in conjunction with deserts) for prayer, or as places of revelation or eschatological authority. Matthew is the main thematizer of mountains in the NT, but he builds on Mark. Mark, followed by Luke, has Jesus appoint the Twelve on a mountain (Mark 3:13). Strangely, Matthew does not place this scene on a mountain. The Gerasene demoniac cried out on the mountains (Mark 5:5). Jesus prays on the mountain after the feeding of the five thousand, and just before he walks on the water to rejoin his disciples (Mark 6:46). But theologically, the event by far the most pregnant with meaning is the transfiguration. "After six days Jesus took Peter, James, and John and led them up a high mountain apart by themselves. And he was transfigured before them" (Mark 9:2). The way this story is told shows that Mark chooses to echo Sinai events where Moses and Elijah saw or heard God (Exod 24:15-18; esp. 34:29-30; 1 Kgs 19:8-18) and where the chosen people first celebrated the feast of booths or tents (Lev 23:33-43; Num 29:12-38; Deut 16:13-17; Exod 23:16; Mark 9:4-5). Uprooting mountains and casting them into the sea becomes a symbol of a powerful faith and prayer (11:2). The same image, uprooting Mount Sinai, was used in Rabbinic literature to describe the powerful, hard intellects of the rabbis of Babylonia (in contrast with the smoother ones of Palestine).

Jesus settles on the Mount of Olives just across the Kedron valley from the Temple on Mount Zion at the beginning of his final Jerusalem ministry (Mark 11:1). There he delivers his apocalyptic discourse (13:3), wherein he predicts the destruction of the Temple (13:2) and warns those in Judea to flee to the mountains (13:14). There too Jesus returns after the Last Supper (14:26). In the garden of Gethsemane on the slopes of the Mount of Olives he prays in struggle and agony and is arrested. The crucifixion itself takes place at the Place of the Skull, Golgotha (15:22). This is not said to be a mountain in the Bible, but was early identified with a little knoll just outside the old western city gate, now inside the Renaissance Ottoman city walls and covered by the Church of the Holy Sepulcher.

The mountain becomes a deliberate motif in Matthew. It is not random but a pattern. "*Horos* serves as a literary motif with the aid of which Matthew develops several of his distinctive theological themes," (T. L. Donaldson, *Jesus on the Mountain* [Sheffield, 1985] 196–197). Besides parallels to many of the passages in Mark, Matthew has six major mountain scenes: the temptation of Jesus (4:8); the great inaugural discourse known as the Sermon on the Mount (5:1; 14; 8:1); the healing of many people (15:29-31); the transfiguration (17:1-9); the apocalyptic discourse on the Mount of Olives (chs. 24–25); and the final great commissioning (28:16-20). The fourth and fifth of these are parallel to Mark. As well as serving as places of isolation or revelation, mountains in Matthew function "as eschatological sites where Jesus enters into the full authority of his Sonship, where the eschatological community is gathered, and where the age of fulfillment is inaugurated" (Donaldson). But mountains for Matthew are not important in themselves; Jesus himself is the Christian replacement for the holy mountain, as he is the new and greater prophet-revealer like Moses, bringing the Sinai law to perfection.

Luke adds little on mountains as such to the Marcan tradition: the fuller quotation of Isaiah 40:3-5 in Luke 3:5 includes the lowering of the mountains; at the conclusion of Jesus' inaugural discourse in Nazareth, his fellow-citizens intend to hurl him over the hill on which their town was built (4:29). But Luke greatly develops the importance of Jerusalem, making it a theme of his two-volume work, along with the word for city, *polis*. Luke places the ascension of Jesus on the Mount of Olives (Acts 1:12), and Mount Sinai is twice mentioned in Stephen's discourse (Acts 7:30, 38).

Apart from a few minor references (6:3, 15; 8:1; 12:15), John's Gospel contains one major theological use of mountains: the dialogue between Jesus and the Samaritan woman (4:20-21). Here the woman refers to the traditional conflict between the cult centers of Judea and Samaria, the northern and southern kingdoms of Israelite antiquity: Mounts Gerizim and Jerusalem (i.e., Zion). This prepares for Jesus' great announcement of the Trinitarian universal worship of the future: God will be worshiped in Spirit and in truth, that is, in the holy Spirit and in Jesus Christ who is the truth incarnate. This passage transforms the concept of sacred places to locate it in persons, in Jesus, and in those who live in him, as a vine and its branches.

The Book of Revelation mentions mountains in three different contexts. Mountains are moved as a sign of endtime troubles (6:14-16; 8:8; 16:20). The seven hills of Rome are the seven heads of the beast, the idolatrous state (17:9). But the Lamb stands on Mount Zion (14:1) and the seer is taken in spirit to a great high mountain to view the holy city, the new Jerusalem (21:10), the supreme symbol of salvation, the reign of God come to earth.

Theologically the two most powerful uses of OT mountain theology in the NT come from the letters. Paul, in Galatians 4:24-25, in an allegory on Christian freedom which expresses for him the essence of his gospel that Christ's death on the cross frees us from the ceremonial laws of the OT, contrasts two covenants. Each is symbolized by a woman (Sarah or Hagar) and a mountain (Mount Sinai, boldly identified by Paul with the present Jerusalem, as opposed to Zion, identified with the "Jerusalem above"). This contrast between mountain covenants is then developed magnificently by the author of Hebrews, 12:18-24. Here the fearful revelation at Sinai is sharply opposed to the joyful festival on a new Mount Zion. "You have approached Mount Zion and the city of the living God, the heavenly Jerusalem, and countless angels in festal gathering, and the assembly of the firstborn enrolled in heaven, and God the judge of all, and the spirits of the just made perfect, and Jesus, the mediator of a new covenant" (Heb 12:22-24).

The two mountains Sinai and Zion, with their two covenants, moral and messianic, remain the heritage of the Christian, for whom Jesus is "the prophet like Moses" (Deut 18:18) and the royal son of David. These two accents can also be symbolized by the different accents of Matthew and Paul, yet both have more in common than their disagreements.

Pastoral-Liturgical Tradition

Mountains continue to have religious significance for Christians. They are connected with the theology of pilgrimages to sacred shrines. The great mountains of biblical revelation continue to be visited by Christian pilgrims, as Melito of Sardis and Egeria attest. The Christian emperors and empresses built mosaic-laden basilicas on them. Justinian's on Sinai is well preserved. But the Greek Christians found a sacred mountain closer to home in St. Nilus' monastic republic on Mount Athos (963). In the West, St. Benedict founded the abbey of Monte Cassino in 529. The Irish have an annual pilgrimage up Croaghpatrick (2,510 ft.) in County Mayo, in honor of St. Patrick (d. 461). Mont St. Michel was founded by the bishop of Coutances in Normandy in 966. St. Bruno set up his mountain hermitage in what became La Grande Chartreuse in the French Alps. The Swiss have a sacred site at Einsiedeln associated with St. Meinrad (835), and the Catalans have Montserrat devoted to Mary (880). The Germans have a mountain castle shrine at the Wartburg, where St. Elizabeth of Hungary/Thuringia cared for the poor as her husband fought the Crusade; the Austrians, a shrine to Mary at Mariazell. The mendicant orders of the thirteenth century associated mystical happenings with Mount Alverno (the stigmata of St. Francis), Fanjeaux (the vision of St. Dominic), and of course, Mount Carmel. In the new world the Christ of Corcovado stretches out his arms in blessing from Sugarloaf Mountain over Rio de Janeiro, Brazil. American Catholics have mountain shrines at Holy Hill in Wisconsin, Snowmass Abbey (Colorado), Mount Angel (Oregon), St. Martin's Abbey in Washington state's Olympic peninsula. But anyone who has ever taken a vacation in the mountains has felt closer to God. The natural religious symbolism gives one perspective.

The liturgy frequently invokes mountain revelations: the Sanctus at Mass daily recalls Isaiah's experience on Mount Zion. The Transfiguration gospel is read on the second Sunday of Lent, and on the feast August 6. The great Sinai theophanies are invoked on the vigil of Pentecost, on Trinity Sunday, and on the feast of Corpus Christi (B), as well as on the nineteenth Sunday in Ordinary Time (A). The Sermon on the Mount and the Great Commission in the lectionary occur so frequently, especially in the A Cycle, that one may say that they form the ordinary temper of the liturgy and thus of Christian life.

See: COVENANT, DESERT, JERUSALEM, LAW, POWER, TEMPLE

BENEDICT T. VIVIANO, O.P.

MUSIC, BIBLE AND

Introduction

There is no generic word in biblical Hebrew or Greek for music. That linguistic fact underscores the difficulty in accurately outlining the place and function of music in the Bible. While there are innumerable references to song, dance, and musical instruments in the Scriptures, these provide a limited introduction to the role of music in the Bible. As in many ancient civilizations, the peoples of the Bible did not always make clear distinctions between singing and speaking. The lyrical character of their public speech, reading, praying, and preaching encompassed certain rhythmic and melodic features which migrated toward song. Thus it is not always possible to discuss music as an isolated element in their cultures or worship.

Fundamental to understanding the musical strata of the Scriptures and emerging Christian worship is an awareness of the primacy of audition in Judaism and primitive Christianity. While visual and other sense imagery abound in both testaments, hearing is clearly the primary form of sense perception in the Bible. The Scriptures present a God who communicates primarily through the word. This translated into a heightened auditory environment for the people of the Bible, who were capable of innumerable sound shadings between the polarities of speech and music. The explicit musical references in the Scriptures are but one part of the lyricism that permeated the lives of Jews and early Christians. The people of the OT and NT lived in an auditory environment very different from our own.

Old Testament

The Bible traces the origins of music to a descendant of Cain, Jubal, "the ancestor of all who play the lyre and harp" (Gen 4:21). This unadorned myth and the lack of other specific musical references in the earliest strata of the OT suggest that music played a minor role in the life of Israel before the conquest of Caanan (ca. 1200 BCE). During the period of the monarchy (ca. 1020–587) this situation changed dramatically. Both biblical and extra-biblical evidence from this period suggest that the Jews were an exceptionally musical people. Archaeological evidence, for example, demonstrates that among the tributes which Hezechiah (d. 687) offered to his conqueror, Sennacherib of Assyria, were Jewish musicians.

Music played an important role in Jewish culture after the "conquest." This music was generally of a non-professional nature. Musical expression commonly took the form of social merrymaking (Exod 32:17-18), dirges and laments (2 Sam 1:19-27), martial noisemaking (Judg 7:18-20), songs of warfare (Num 21:14-15), songs of victory (Exod 15:1-18, 20), acclamations of heroes (1 Sam 18:6), magical incantations (Josh 6:4-20), working songs (27:2-5), and worship (1 Sam 10:5-6). Women played a major role in the amateur musical life of ancient Israel.

As in neighboring Egypt and Assyria, there was a strong connection between professional musicians and the monarchy in ancient Israel. The cultivation of professional musicians in Israel seems to have begun during the time of David, who was remembered as a talented lyre player (1 Sam 16:16-18) and an inventor of instruments (Amos 6:5). David is also remembered as having established professional temple music (1 Chronicles 15), placing Levites in charge (1 Chronicles 25). The earliest accounts of the Temple (2 Samuel 6), however, do not mention professional temple musicians, which may have been a post-Davidic development. Music of the first Temple included the singing of religious texts accompanied by instruments (Amos 5:23) and possibly trumpet flourishes (Ps 98:6).

Evidence of second temple music is more abundant. Under the direction of the descendants of the Levitical musicians (Ezra 2:41), it included instrumental signaling of ritual events as well as choral music accompanied by instruments that would have reproduced the vocal line of the singers with slight ornamentation. Texts would have included the psalms, a variety of canticles and other poetic texts from the Bible, and possibly even non-biblical texts. Although professional singers and instrumentalists were the dominant musical force in temple worship, the people were not totally excluded from the ritual song. Numerous psalm texts (e.g., 136, 148–150) suggest how people could have added refrains or "Hallelujah" to the song of the professionals.

Vocal music dominated in the OT, especially in the many synagogues that arose after the Exile. No choirs or instrumentalists functioned in the synagogue. This word-centered worship continuously migrated back and forth between contemporary categories of speech and song. The oldest consistent element of synagogue worship was the *Shema* (Deut 6:4-9; 11:13-21; Num 15:37-41), which could have been chanted in unison by the whole assembly. The musical building blocks for the *Shema* probably derived from chants that had developed for the cantillation of Scripture. Cantillation was a method of chanting that

employed a series of set melodic formulas. The scrolls from which one chanted were marked with signs that indicated the appropriate formula. Cantillation generally respected the structure and sense of the text. While vocal music dominated the OT, there is ample evidence of the use of instruments outside of synagogue worship, including percussion (bells, cymbals, and tambourine), woodwinds (flutes, oboes, and shofar), and strings (lyre and harp).

New Testament

Although the NT does not contain as much musical data as the OT, it does offer some information about the content and performance of emerging Christian music. There are, for example, a number of short, lyrical praise-formulas in the NT, like the doxology sung by the angels at the birth of Jesus (Luke 2:14). Based on Jewish models, such doxologies eventually led to the development of Christological doxologies (Rom 16:27). The NT also contains a significant number of lyrical fragments borrowed from Judaism but given a distinctively Christian treatment, such as "Amen" (Gal 6:18), "Alleluia" (Rev 19:1), "Hosanna" (Mark 11:9), and "Maranatha" (1 Cor 16:22). Larger lyrical forms include the infancy canticles (e.g., Luke 1:46-55) and hymns to Christ (Col 1:15-20), also based on Jewish models. Although lyrical texts are not the same thing as musical settings, their consistent appearance throughout the NT confirms that the followers of Jesus embraced the lyrical heritage of Judaism and carried it with them into an urban and Gentile world.

Paul's words about public worship are helpful in understanding something of the form and style of early Christian singing (1 Cor 14:13-19). Although Paul recognizes a place for solo expression in worship—like the gift of tongues—his overriding concern is for the engagement and prayer of the whole community. His emphasis that all gifts should serve the common good would extend to the musical elements of worship as well. This suggests a preference for responsorial rather than solo forms, a leaning toward dialogue rather than monologue in worship, and a constant respect for the community's "Amen." This implies a style of liturgical-musical leadership akin to that which would be found in the synagogue rather than that of the Temple. While undoubtedly there were talented musicians in the early community, these did not dominate the lyrical landscape of first-century worship which strove for single voiced praise. The emphasis on vocal music in the NT suggests that references to musical instruments (e.g., 1 Cor 14:7; Rev 18:22) are simply metaphorical and do not substantiate the use of instruments in early Christian worship.

While the NT notes that the followers of Jesus continued to frequent the Temple (e.g., Acts 3:1) and the synagogue (Acts 9:19-20) after his death, it was especially in the home that the distinctive rituals and music of the early Christians developed. Some of the simply chanted blessings before and after meals (see Luke 22:19-20), the singing of psalms and other traditional home songs (Eph 5:18) were probably indistinguishable from those of other Jewish households. As the fledgling community began to reshape its prayer in the memory and example of Jesus, certain variations on these homespun prayers, songs, and chants emerged. Variation eventually gave way to more distinctive Christian texts, forms, and melodies.

Pastoral-Liturgical Tradition

The history of Christian music in general, and worship music in particular, is a long and complex subject. Two major issues that arose within the worship music of the OT and NT can provide us with a framework for considering some of the musical development within Christian liturgy. These are: (1) the relationship between amateur and professional musicians, and (2) the relationship between texts and their musical settings.

Amateur vs. Professional Musicians. As previously noted, there was a strong connection between the monarchy and profes-

sional musicians in ancient Israel. The former seems to have provided the rationale and impetus for the establishment of the latter. The rise of professional temple musicians had two notable effects on official worship. The first was the gradual elimination of women from the ranks of official musical leadership. Even though women had played a central role in the amateur musical life of ancient Israel, including its worship, with the rise of the Levitical caste women were barred from musical leadership in worship. A second effect was the gradual shift in musical performance from the people to the professionals: the more defined the role of the professional musicians, the less ordinary people shared in the music of the Temple.

Parallel developments can be noted in the history of Christian worship music. There is no evidence of any musical specialist or professional in Christian worship before the fourth century. With the wedding of Christianity to the empire in the fourth century, however, there appear musical specialists who, like the Levites before them, hold a specific place in the Church's developing hierarchy. The rise of the musical specialist in Christianity is accompanied by the two developments noted in ancient Israel: the elimination of women from the ranks of official musical leadership and the gradual shift in musical performance from the people to the professionals. Through the centuries various groups of musical specialists have come to dominate the music of the Church. Women have virtually never been included in their ranks. In addition, the continued existence of such professionals has usually been at the expense of the community's voice in the Church's music. It is only by exception that Christianity has known musical specialists who attempt to engage the laity instead of other professionals in liturgical music making. Contemporary reforms have attempted to correct these developments by noting that one key role of the professional musician is to support the song of the assembly, which is essential to the Church's music. Women, thus, cannot be excluded from leading or joining in the Church's worship music.

Texts and Their Musical Settings. Christianity inherited its appreciation of the word from Judaism. Christian music at its core is vocal music, and its primary purpose has been to serve the word. Instrumental music was generally disallowed until the Middle Ages. Various types of texts were supported by musical settings, including improvised and fixed prayers, scriptural readings, biblical and non-biblical psalms, and hymns. While melismatic or florid musical outbursts in the midsts of such settings were not unknown, in general the vocal music of the Church for almost the first millennium was word centered and crafted so as to serve the meaning of the text. As a body of music, Gregorian chant is one of the Church's premier expressions of this word-centered music.

By the early Middle Ages two developments helped to weaken this tradition of music in service of the text. First was the tendency, apparent by the ninth century, for priests to recite chant texts. Eventually it was possible for priests to celebrate an entire Eucharist without any singing or music. This development contributed to the eventual dissolution of the fundamental link between liturgical texts and music. Before this development it was unthinkable to employ a text in public worship without some degree of lyricism. After this change, it was possible to distinguish between a "sung" and a "read" Mass.

A second notable development that helped to weaken the tradition of music in service of the text was the emergence of polyphony, which helped to obscure the text through the addition of two or more lines of texted music. Sometimes this meant that a single liturgical text was sung by a variety of voices at different pitches and rhythms; at other times multiple texts were sung by multiple voices in varying pitches and rhythms. Both phenomena undercut the traditional role of music as servant to the text. From the viewpoint of the assembly this situation was aggravated by the fact that official texts were sung in Latin. Recent reforms have reiterated traditional Christian principles, calling for intelligibility in liturgical texts, and underlining music's role to serve and not obscure liturgical texts.

See: BLESSING, LAMENT, PRAYER, PRAISE, PSALMS, WORSHIP

EDWARD FOLEY, CAPUCHIN

MYSTERY

A profound sense of "mystery" (*mystērion*) characterized religion in the Hellenistic Age, as people lived with political chaos and cultural confusion. In esoteric mystery cults, participants communed deeply with gods hidden in the cosmos. Jewish prophets and apocalyptic visionaries sought to know God's secret plan to save the world; and Christians understood that plan to be finally and definitely revealed in the life, death, and resurrection of Jesus Christ.

Greek Mystery Cults; Old Testament; Qumran

In profane Greek, *mystērion*, "mystery," appears most frequently in the plural to designate religious rites, and this may be the source from which the more general meaning of secret or mystery is derived. The mystery cults became extremely popular in the Hellenistic and Roman worlds because their exotic foreign elements fascinated people whose religious hunger was no longer satisfied by the classical religions of Greece and Rome. All the mystery cults were esoteric: the participants were bound by an oath not to reveal the rites. Hence we must reconstruct the mysteries from scattered allusions. These cults include the Eleusinian mysteries near Athens; the mysteries of Dionysius in Thrace; the Orphic mysteries; the mysteries of the Great Mother and Attis in Asia Minor, of Adonis at Byblos in Phoenicia, of Isis and Osiris in Egypt, and of Mithra in Iran.

The term "mystery" (*mystērion*) is used in the Septuagint twice of the mystery cults (Wis 14:15, 23) and several times with the meaning of secret (Sir 22:22; 27:16, 17, 21; 2 Macc 13:21). "The secret of the king" (Tob 12:7; Jdt 2:2) is the plan or decision of the king; this meaning is certainly reflected in the Pauline use of the word. "The mysteries of God" (Wis 2:22) are the saving designs of God; this use also is reflected in the NT.

The Aramaic and Hebrew *raz* occurs more than forty times in the texts of Qumran. In Daniel (2:18-19, 27-30; 4:6) it designates the secret meaning of a dream that God reveals to Daniel. Mystery is a key word in these sectarian writings. God reveals the mystery to certain persons, such as the Teacher of Righteousness. It often concerns the plans or decisions of God concerning salvation and judgment in the end-time. The mystery in Jewish Prophetic, Apocalyptic, and Wisdom writings is associated with the visions by which God introduced ancient prophets into the heavenly assembly where they learned God's secret plans for history. Hence mystery refers to the divine plan of history, not to cosmic, metaphysical, or philosphical secrets as in the Greek mystery cults. This Jewish use seems a better background for the NT than either profane Greek or the Greek OT.

New Testament

The NT uses mystery exclusively in religious senses, most often closely connected with the revelation of the divine plan, concealed from all except the recipients of revelation, or concealed until God's good time. It is a divine secret, but designed by God to be revealed, an "open secret." Mystery thus is almost equivalent to the Christian "good news." In the Synoptic Gospels the word occurs only in Mark 4:11 and its parallels (Matt 13:11; Luke 8:10). The disciples have been given to know "the secret of the rule of God," whereas to others it is hidden in parables. The secret being communicated to this inner circle is that Jesus himself reveals God's rule in and through his words and actions, but people recognize it only by being given a divine revelation.

Paul. Paul views God's plan to save the world as a mystery, secret, hidden in God for long ages and now revealed—a new revelation about God's salvation in the new, eschatological age. Paul equates God's mystery with "Jesus Christ . . . crucified" (1 Cor 2:1-2), just as he equates his gospel with Christ crucified (1 Cor 1:17, 23-24). Paul viewed himself as a steward, dispensing the wealth of the mystery (1 Cor 4:1). It now reveals to Christians the plan conceived by God and hidden in him from all eternity (1 Cor 2:7) to share with all humanity, Gentiles as well as Jews, the salvation of Israel now realized in Christ Jesus. This mystery even includes Israel's insensitivity to Paul's good news (Rom 11:25). For the divine plan, as Paul sees it, includes the partial eclipse of Israel until the Gentiles are won to Christ. Paul also implies that his message as mystery is fully made known not by ordinary communication but only by God's revelation; and its divine wisdom, known now only by faith, will be fully known at the end-time.

Elsewhere Paul uses mystery with different meanings. He seems to speak of mysteries as secrets, probably known by divine revelation: "in the spirit he speaks mysteries" (1 Cor 14:2; also 13:2). He makes an explicit statement about the change of the body in the resurrection, a truth known to him by revelation, which he apparently has not uttered before to the Corinthians (1 Cor 15:51).

Colossians and Ephesians. In Colossians the mystery, hidden for ages but now revealed to the saints, is "Christ in you" (Col 1:26-27). Christ, in whom are hidden all the treasures of wisdom and knowledge, is the divine mystery, the mystery of God (Col 2:2-3). In contrast to the esoteric mysteries with their cosmic or religious secrets available only to privileged initiates, the mystery here is a universal revelation available and open to all, the word of God, Christ among you, the glorious hope (see also 1 Tim 3:9; 3:26).

In Ephesians, the author uses mystery in the sense that God has revealed to the apostles the mystery that all things will be brought under one head in Christ (Eph 1:9-10). This mystery, unknown to former ages but revealed by the Spirit to the apostles and prophets, concerns God's hidden, "wonderful plan" to make all nations equally joint heirs, members of the same body, and partakers of the promise in Christ, so that all are saved through the death of Jesus (Eph 3:3-6, 9).

Elsewhere, the author speaks of marriage: "This is a great mystery, and I take it to mean Christ and the church" (Eph 5:32). The apostle is to make known this mystery (Eph 6:19). In Jewish tradition, God reveals mysteries hidden in Scripture to chosen interpreters. Hence the true, hidden meaning was not to be found in the original, literal setting but in their interpretation either in the present or at the end of time. God now reveals that the mystery of the two becoming one flesh in marriage (Gen 2:24) means the union of Christ and the Church, and that union models the union between husbands and wives. Near to this sense may be Revelation 1:20: "As for the mystery of the seven stars . . . the seven stars are the angels," and 17:5: "On her forehead was written a name of mystery: 'Babylon the great.'"

See: APOCALYPTIC, GOOD NEWS, NATIONS, PARABLE, PAUL, REVELATION, SALVATION, TRUTH, VISIONS, WISDOM

WILLIAM G. THOMPSON, S.J.

Pastoral-Liturgical Tradition

The contributions to liturgical scholarship and renewed pastoral practice of the liturgical movement are incalculable, and this is especially apparent with respect to the notion of "mystery." A storm of controversy was unleashed by Dom Odo Casel, a monk of the Abbey of Maria Laach in Germany, which is yet to completely subside. The storm, however, rather than wreaking havoc has instead worked much like John XXIII's opening the window to let a fresh breeze into the Church. The controversy over the relationship of Christian and pagan mysteries has been significant, but even more consequential is the liturgical research and scholarship it precipitated resulting in a deeper understanding of the Paschal Mystery.

Christian and Pagan Mysteries. At least three stages can be detected in the relationship of Christian and pagan mysteries (Bouyer and Jungmann). Though ancient in origin, the pagan mystery cults were not prevalent in the geographic locations where Christianity had its origins. Thus during the apostolic era (roughly the first century) Christianity developed its self-understanding and worship more from within its Judaic ancestry and shaped it according to its own unique Christian experience. With the Dorian invasions the mystery cults were introduced to Roman territories and began to mingle with Christianity. During the second and third centuries patristic evidence (especially from the works of Clement of Alexandria, Justin, and Tertullian) indicates that there was scant acceptance of this influence; the apologists lost no time in condemning mystery cults such as that of Eleusius and Dionysius. By the fourth century the influence of these cults had waned and, during a time when Christian rituals were free to develop, terminology and practices entered into Christian ritual that had formerly been proper to the pagan mystery cults: initiates, mystagogia, purification, enlightenment, parallels in the initiation process, *disciplina arcani.*

Casel's Position. Casel's thesis is that the pagan mystery cults prepared for and suggested a framework for the Church's sacraments; that is, the ancient mysteries point to Christian mystery as a type. He asserted that every sacrament is a "cult-mystery" of Christ and the Church. In this Casel made a radical stance against any passive or intellectualized understanding of liturgy. Liturgy is the remembrance of God's plan of salvation as carried out by Christ. This, not as a mental act by which one goes back to the historical act of redemption but the saving act of Christ, is truly and wholly present and enacted in the liturgical celebration. The substance of Casel's position is that liturgy is a very engaging human/divine activity whereby the community actually enters into the death/resurrection mystery of Christ.

Scholars' Responses. The wave of reaction to Casel's position lies in his making Christian sacraments dependent upon Hellenistic precursors. Rather, claim Casel's opponents, Christian sacraments are uniquely Christian in origin, being grounded by the actual historical events of Christ's passion, death, and resurrection. Nonetheless these scholars still allow for a certain (limited) relationship between the mystery religions and Christian sacraments which are a gain in understanding not only the origins of sacramental rites but also are a gain in meaning.

The mystery cults were nature religions that celebrated the dying and rising cycle of the natural seasons upon which the ancient agrarian cultures were so dependent. Their central rites were an enactment of the myths which tell of the gods' dying and rising. They were performed by an esoteric group of initiates who received mystic knowledge which they might communicate to others. The very acting out of the myth enabled the initiate to share in the dying/rising cycle of the gods. Any notion of salvation is a truncated one: the gods are not salvific but receive salvation when they rise to new life as a result of some intervention in the natural cycle in a recurring cycle of nature (Prümm).

The Christian mystery, however, is the object of revelation: the Christian God is a saving God who offers redemption. Though the Christian and pagan mysteries may share a common cultural apparatus (Hugo Rahner; Jungmann: but not a common tradition), Christianity is more than a religion of emotion which promotes a human participation in the "other" world and addresses the problem of a dark future (Prümm). Christianity makes ethical demands on in-

dividuals who actually play a determinate role in working out their salvation. While the salvific God who authors the Christian plan of redemption can never be completely known, nonetheless in liturgy Christians encounter the presence of God and God's saving deeds.

Meaning of Christian "Mystery." The overall theological orientation of Christian liturgy, entering into the saving mystery of Christ, is a radical departure from the intent or meaning of the pagan mystery religions. Likewise, liturgists today would reject any numeric "representation" (Casel) or reenactment of the historical circumstances of Christ's salvific act. The contemporary gains in understanding the concepts of time and historicity as well as advances in exegesis do sensitize us to the pastoral concerns of Casel and his disciples. They also enable us to bridge the gap between Casel's concerns and the objections of his challengers.

Vatican II's Constitution on the Sacred Liturgy called for "full and active participation" in the liturgy (nos. 11, 19, 30, 50) by all the faithful. Though there is no clear response to the problem on re-presentation or reenactment in the Constitution, its implication is that more is happening than simply receiving the fruits of the Paschal Mystery. Paragraph 7 in particular, which outlines the presences of the resurrected Christ in the Church and goes on to say "liturgy is considered as an exercise of the priestly office of Jesus Christ" and "in the liturgy full public worship is performed by the Mystical Body of Jesus Christ, that is, by the Head and His members," implies that the liturgical assembly actively enters into the ongoing mystery of Christ's redemptive act. True, the historical circumstances of the Paschal Mystery cannot be repeated; what is available is the meaning of those actions which constitutes the content of human/divine history.

Liturgical participation collapses past, present, and future into a single moment pregnant with meaning. The whole of the meaning of the past historical events and the future promise of fulfillment are encountered in the saving presence of Christ which renders thanks to the Father through the dynamism of the Spirit. This is the essence of the Christian mystery and in this it is wholly unique.

See: KNOWLEDGE, MYTH, REDEMPTION, REMEMBRANCE, SALVATION, TIME, TYPE, WORSHIP

JOYCE A. ZIMMERMAN, C.PP.S.

MYTH, MYTHOLOGY

From the Greek word *mythos* (tale, story, legend, fable), the very etymology of this word points to both its richness and its snares. Too often referring to something untrue when used both in Scripture (e.g., 1 Tim 1:4; 4:7) and in colloquial speech, a negative and narrow connotation eclipses the depth meaning myths try to convey. Found in almost all primitive and modern cultures, myths are a way for a people to deal with the origins of the world and themselves and their relationship to the divine, with the origins of culture and societal institutions which incorporate a people's ideals and aspirations, with life and suffering and death.

Post-Enlightenment, rationalist humanity decried myth as an unscientific way primitive peoples dealt with their world, especially insofar as it was controlled by beings from another world. Allegedly radically dualistic in nature, a mythical explanation of the world was rejected in favor of *logos* (argumentation and analysis). The twentieth century has seen a decided change in attitude (though not without its critics), recognizing a mythical-poetic view of reality (Northrop Frye's first stage of language, following Vico) as simply a different universe of discourse. Myth, then, is not opposed to the real or to history, but it is a different mode of expression with its own inherent validity. Respectful of the truth-reality of their content, both mythic and scientific language are different linguistic forms that seek to express content. A basic problem from a religious perspective is how to deal linguistically with the irruption of the transcendent. Myths are an alternative linguistic form that express those mysteries of life not readily at hand and therefore not able to be examined according to the rigors of scientific discourse.

Myths address the critical questions of life and enable a people to live mystery at its most profound depths. This is particularly true when the myth is concretized in specific cultic celebrations, rituals. It is no surprise, then, that we find myth in both the OT and the NT as well as throughout the tradition of pastoral practice.

Old Testament

Scant use of the word "myth" is made in the OT (e.g., Sir 20:19 where it is translated and used in the sense of "proverb"); nonetheless extensive use is made of myth as a literary genre (contrary to some scholars' positions, e.g., Gunkel, who contend there is no myth in the OT because myth by its very nature is polytheistic). Noteworthy about OT mythical material is the insight we get into the relationship among ancient cultures. The sacred writers felt free to draw on their neighbors' myths, especially those of Mesopotamia and Canaan, to fashion their own accounts of sacred origins. Perhaps best known are the creation (see *Enuma elish*) and the fall and deluge (see *Gilgamesh Epic*) accounts.

The interest in OT myth is not so much to sort out the relationship of these myths to the literary forms from which the sacred writers obviously borrowed. For it is inconceivable that Israel and her literature could be isolated from the cosmogony of the cultures surrounding her. Rather, the interest in OT myths lies in the unique history and theology that is contained therein and renders myth in the OT qualitatively different from that of Israel's contemporaries. Because of this some scholars properly speak of myth in the OT.

The Hebraic use of myth is consistent with that of the neighboring cultures in terms of literary characteristics, but OT myth is remarkably different in content and purpose. We are familiar with the systematized accounts of myths of ancient cultures, particularly those of Rome and Greece. These myths weave a comprehensive mythology (Frye notes that it is this relationship one to another that makes myth different from other stories), an account of the gods and their deeds and interrelationships that depict all aspects of life both human and divine. Israel, on the other hand, did not evolve a mythology as such because her monotheism portrayed the ongoing and consistent deeds of the One True God who was in relationship to Israel as a people. While employing myths in order to deal with non-sensible reality, Israel transformed the literary forms and infused them with its own perception of God and how God relates to humanity. Rather than simply a cosmogony and/or anthropology, OT use of myth discloses a theology as well. In Israel the correspondence pattern of mythology, whereby the gods depart divine qualities to humanity, was broken in favor of a divine-human relationship whereby God is radically transcendent, and human qualities are interpreted in the light of Israel's experience of God (Barr).

OT myth is always woven into a larger unit of salvation history. Even when it is an interpretation of a known myth the new interpretation is always from within Israel's unique self-understanding: a people chosen by God and intimate with God. Basic to Israel's self-understanding is that, unlike the other gods who are unknowable and unpredictable, God reveals self to Israel as present. In this God is both transcendent and immanent.

New Testament

The mythical waters of NT scholarship were stirred by the publication of Rudolf Bultmann's 1941 essay "New Testament and Mythology." Defining myth as "the use of imagery to express the other worldly in terms of this world and the divine in terms of human life, the other side in terms of this side," Bultmann decried this mythical-poetic thought as not befitting the thought of scientific humanity. Since a "mythical

view of the world is obsolete," Bultmann sought to address this archaic approach to the questions of life by what he considered to be scientific methods. Recognizing a number of mythical elements contained in the NT corpus such as the virgin birth, redemption, resurrection, atonement, eschatology, and the apocalyptic, Bultmann called for answers not from beyond the text but from within the interpretive method applied to the text. Therefore he set an exegetical agenda that "demythologizes" the NT. That is, Bultmann called for an interpretation of the NT in existential terms that liberates the message from its mythical language. Wishing to recover the kerygma that is the proper content of the NT, Bultmann's demythologizing project was directed to the question, "Can we recover the truth of the kerygma for men who do not think in mythological terms without forfeiting its character as kerygma?" His answer is an existentialist interpretation of the NT that begins with the Christian's life of faith as the self-understanding that informs a critique of the Jesus event rendering it meaningful for Christians today. Bultmann's suggestion is that the NT kerygma points to a new understanding of human existence. Thielicke criticizes Bultmann for lacking a sensitivity to history that renders a philosophy instead of a theology. New self-knowledge, according to Thielicke, comes from encountering God's working in history and not from exegetical methods that bring a contemporary understanding to bear on the meaning of a text.

Though many scholars and exegetes in particular call Bultmann to task for his radical agenda, most acknowledge the important issues that he raised and which NT exegesis can no longer ignore. To overcome a radically dualistic approach to the secular and sacred, to seek the truth of the content of history, and to acknowledge the relevance of the Jesus event for today and its demand for a new understanding of human existence all have their exegetical demands.

Rather than abandoning mythical discourse solely in favor of scientific discourse, scholars in the wake of Bultmann recognize the contribution both discourses can make to human knowledge. Authentic interpretation leaves the myth intact and at the same time discloses the divine/human history and kerygma that is the reality-content of the myth. Indeed, "every interpretation preserves the text: the text is not only its material, but the master which it endeavors to serve" (Ernst Lohmeyer). These universes of discourse are not mutually exclusive, but rather they are complementary.

Even in a post-Bultmann era, some proponents assert that the only valid revelation of reality is the mythical (Mircea Eliade). Scientific discourse is an indispensable tool in the interpretation and critique of the content of the myths. The various schools of hermeneutics bearing on exegesis especially in the latter part of this century recognize this value. Yet Bultmann's exegetical agenda of demythologization continues to surface in other areas of human interaction (e.g., some feminists call for a "reconstruction" of the NT not dissimilar in intent to Bultmann's demythologizing), which suggests that dualism and the relationship of discourses are questions that still have not been resolved.

Pastoral-Liturgical Tradition

The myth is a sacred story that endeavors to preserve and increase the quality of life among peoples; it endeavors to integrate reality and experience. To the extent that it has to do with human action, we may expect myth to be concretized in some kind of enactment. When this is so, ritual comes to be.

Since NT times Christians have enacted their originary myth in ritual; specifically, we call this Christian liturgy. Christian liturgy is distinctive in that its manner of ritual integrates both the myth (telling the story) and ritual action (living out the story) into a single celebration. Liturgical celebrations concretize or manifest the myth through a particular liturgical tradition which focuses on one or the other aspect of myth. Liturgy both enacts the Paschal Mystery—the Jesus event—in every liturgical celebration as well as tells the story in a cycle unfolding throughout the liturgical year.

Very early liturgical evidence points to liturgy's drawing on elements of myth as a means of bringing the assembly into the ritual action. The apostolic Church made extensive use of vigils in order to recite and keep alive the Christian story. Chief among these is the Great Vigil of Easter with its yearly recitation of salvation history. In some cases the homilies of this early period approach an unfolding of the Christian story as myth, especially the mystagogic homilies of the fourth–fifth centuries where the use of typology, especially of the Alexandrian school (see, for example, the mystagogical homilies of John Chrysostom), is rich in its use of symbols and images, which are two literary elements proper to myths.

The use of symbols as images to concretize the story is an element of myth used to great advantage throughout the liturgical tradition of Christianity. Malinowski claims that myth in itself is not symbolic, though it often uses symbols as a means of expression. To the extent that Christian liturgy claims an immediate access to a trans-historical and transcendent reality, symbols are an indispensable aid. Throughout Christian tradition sacraments have been described as signs/symbols and have used water, oil, bread, wine, imposition of hands, and other symbols to give access to the meaning of the Christian story.

Today there may be a pastoral tendency to so focus on liturgical celebration as praise and thanksgiving, often with a heavy didactic dose of "relevancy," that we may lose sight of the mythical-poetic characteristics constitutive of narratives that have the power to form a people into a living tradition of faith. Some liturgical scholars are urging a greater sensitivity to narrative as one of liturgy's organizing principles (Stevick).

A number of narrative elements are constitutive of Christian liturgies. In the Eucharistic rite, the blessing of the water in the rite of sprinkling, the central portion of the Creed, and much of the Eucharistic Prayer are but a few examples of the use of narrative. The *Exultet* of the Easter Vigil is a high point of the whole liturgical year which eloquently narrates the Judaeo-Christian story. The Psalter, the backbone of the Liturgy of the Hours, is a kind of mythical-poetic recitation of Israel's relationship to God. Even the semi-continuous proclamation of the gospel during the Sundays of the year may be construed as being mythical-poetic in intent.

Throughout the history of religions there have been three linguistic forms of religious expression: symbol, ritual, and myth. Christianity has woven all three expressions together in its liturgy. In contrast to other linguistic forms that analyze or deduce, myth presents or discloses reality that is otherwise unknowable. When understood in this deeper sense, myth affords Judaeo-Christian tradition a unique immediacy to a God who has always chosen to be intimately present and celebrated.

See: APOCALYPTIC, ATONEMENT, ESCHATOLOGY, MYSTERY, REDEMPTION, RESURRECTION, SALVATION, TRADITION

JOYCE A. ZIMMERMAN, C.PP.S.

N

NAME

Name, in the biblical world, carries the nuance of being an expression of identity, whether that be of God, persons, or even places. From the first chapter of Genesis to the last of Revelation, the act of naming and the designation of names reveal persons and places that make up the drama of human redemption in a way that shows the hand of God at work in the created world. Also, by means of names and titles, the Bible shows how God is spoken of and addressed. The names of persons often offer an insight into their mission, calling, or state in life. Sometimes significant individuals have their names changed to indicate a shift in calling or the acceptance of a special task for God or for the community of faith. Among the people of the ancient Near East, knowing the name of someone or something was a means of possessing power over them. Throughout the Bible there are examples of people and of places that are given a particular name for a special reason: to reveal the plan of God, to explain the background of a particular moment in history, or to distinguish a God-given aspect of a person's personality or identity.

Old Testament

Names of God. The people of the ancient Near East both chose their gods and gave them names; but with Israel it was different. In Judaism God revealed the divine name (Exod 3:13-15). It is within the call-narrative of Moses that the divine name, Yahweh, was revealed. What is of significance to note in that context is how both a transcendent (Yahweh) and an immanent name (the God of Abraham, the God of Isaac, the God of Jacob) were given by God to Moses. Thus God reveals the divine identity as something which is both beyond the limits of ordinary experience and as near as the descendants of Israel's ancestors in the faith.

One of the most common ways of referring to God in the Hebrew Scriptures is El. While not actually a divine name, it is a way of citing the Divinity, sometimes used with other designations of places or religious expressions: El of Bethel (Gen 35:7); El of the covenant (Judg 9:46); El of Jacob (Ps 146:5); El of your ancestors (Gen 49:25). A derivative of El is Elohim. This designation of God is a plural form, suggesting an intensification of the splendor and greatness of the God of Israel. The name El-Elyon (God the Most High) indicates the God of Abraham (Gen 14:22), who is also Yahweh, and the God of Melchizedek, "priest of God Most High" (Gen 14:18). References to God as El-Shaddai (God Almighty) represent an early identification that is believed to belong to the patriarchal (Gen 17:1; 28:3; 35:11; 43:14) and Mosaic times (Exod 6:3; Num 24:4, 16); El-Shaddai is associated with the God of the covenant, the pact made with Abraham (Genesis 17) and Moses (Exod 6:2-8). Another common designation of God was Adonai (my Master), though this word in Hebrew could refer to the deity or to an earthly ruler. The name Adonai was also significant since the Massoretes used the vowels of this name with the tetragrammaton (YHWH) to signal another pronunciation of Yahweh (i.e., Jehovah), so sacred had the name of Yahweh become over the course of time.

The psalmist attested to the redemptive power of God's name when saying, "O God, by your name save me" (Ps 54:3), and "the name of the God of Jacob defend you" (Ps 20:2). The young David, with the name of the Lord of hosts, came against the warrior Goliath and defeated him (1 Sam 17:45). The prophets made present the divine word of judgment or salvation when they spoke in God's name, using the messenger formula, "Thus says Yahweh" (Isa 7:7; Jer 4:3; Amos 1:3). The psalmist affirmed that those who honor God's name act in trust (Ps 9:11). And to "praise the name of the Lord" (Ps 113:1, 2, 3) is to offer homage and reverence to God, whose wondrous deeds fill the whole earth (Ps 72:18-19).

Personal Names. Examples abound in the Hebrew Scriptures to show how significant names were in biblical times. As part of his prophetic message, Isaiah named two of his sons Shear-jashub (meaning, a remnant will return) and Maher-shalal-hashbaz (meaning, quick the spoils, speedy the plunder) (Isa 7:3; 8:1); the mere sight of them told of the coming lamentable fate of the nation. Likewise, as these names signaled a time of judgment, Isaiah's announcement of one who would be named Immanuel (Isa 7:14) looked forward to a redemptive intervention that was hopeful. Another example of symbolic names is

found in the opening of the prophecy of Hosea (Hos 1:4, 6, 9). A lifetime reminder of the capture of the ark of the covenant was the naming of Phinehas' son, Ichabod (meaning, gone is the glory) (1 Sam 4:21-22), when also his father and grandfather were killed in battle. Others who are given names of significance at birth include Moses (Exod 2:10), Gershom (Exod 2:22), Samson (Judg 13:24), Samuel (1 Sam 1:20), and Solomon/Jedidiah (2 Sam 12:24-25).

When a person's name was changed, a transformation took place in his or her life. Abram (meaning exalted father) becomes Abraham (meaning father of a host of nations). The name of Jacob is closely associated with the narrative telling of his birth (Gen 25:26) and life (Gen 27:36). At birth, Jacob held tight his brother's heel (in Hebrew, 'āqēb) as he followed Esau from his mother's womb. In his earlier life, Jacob cheated (in Hebrew, 'āqab) his brother Esau of both his birthright (Gen 25:33-34) and his blessing (Gen 27:27-29, 36). Then Jacob's name was changed to Israel (Gen 32:29; 35:10) to designate one who had "contended with God." It is from Jacob that his ancestry take their name: the house of Jacob (Exod 19:3), the children of Israel (Exod 1:1; 28:9). Others whose names are changed include Sarai to Sarah (Gen 17:15), Ben-oni to Benjamin (Gen 35:18), and Eliakim to Jehoiakim (2 Kgs 23:34).

An expression of destruction was that a person's name be destroyed or blotted out (1 Sam 24:21-22; 2 Kgs 14:27; Pss 41:6; 109:13). And likewise, blessing came to individuals when their names were pronounced, and thus they live on in their name (Sir 44:14). People call upon the name of the Lord in praise (Ps 148:13), in petition (Ps 119:55), in trust (Ps 9:11), in thanksgiving (Ps 116:17), and in hope (Ps 124:8).

Names of Places and Creatures. Places that are given special names in the Bible tell the stories-in-brief of events that happen in Israel's sacred history. Babel (Gen 11:9) and Bethel (Gen 28:19) demonstrate this phenomenon. The renewed city of Zion would be given new names (Isa 60:14, 18; 62:2, 4, 12) to express her new destiny as the spouse of Yahweh in an age of divine blessing.

In the creation account, God gave Adam the freedom to name the animals (Gen 2:19-20), a reference to his authority and power over them. In contrast to this, it was God who named the elements of creation (Gen 1:5, 8, 10) exercising divine dominion over the world and all within it.

New Testament

Names of God. There are some clear lines of connection between the names, titles, and designations of God found in the OT and what is in the NT. With the authors of the Septuagint having translated the Hebrew names and titles of God into Greek, there was a basis for their use in the early Christian texts, which eventually became the NT. Yahweh was translated *Kyrios* (Lord); *El* and *Elohim* became *Theos* (God).

A distinguishing characteristic of the NT is the revelation of God as Father. While used a few times in the OT to speak of God, it had not been common. But when Jesus taught his disciples to pray to God, he told them to address God as (our) Father (Matt 6:9; Luke 11:2). In the Johannine Gospel, the farewell discourse emphasizes the relationship of Jesus as Son to God as Father, with the understanding that those united to Jesus share in an intimate relationship with the Father (John 14:20-21, 31; 17:1-2, 20-25). The Pauline literature also witnessed to this teaching of Jesus by speaking of the power of the Father that raised Jesus from the dead (Gal 1:1), the same God to whom we cry out as *Abba* (Rom 8:15; Gal 4:6).

The NT attested to the divinity of Jesus in attributing to him fitting names and titles that possessed divine power. At the outset of the gospel, the angel of the Lord announced to Joseph that the child to be born to Mary is to be named Jesus, "because he will save his people from their sins" (Matt 1:21). Given the name above all other names, Jesus Christ is acclaimed as Lord (Phil 2:9). The messiahship of Jesus, called the Christ, enables us to be called children of God (Gal 3:26-29). The

apostles "left the presence of the Sanhedrin, rejoicing that they had been found worthy to suffer dishonor for the sake of the name" (Acts 5:41). In the power of the name of Jesus, the apostles performed miracles and spoke new languages (Mark 15:17-18; Luke 10:17; Acts 3:6; 4:12).

Names of Persons. As in the OT, the NT has persons for whom change of name signaled a new mission and destiny. Simon son of Jonah was called Peter (i.e., Rock) upon which the Church was to be built (Matt 16:17-18).

Jesus showed power and authority over the demon in the man from Gerasene when he called him by name, Legion, and restored the man to full healing (Mark 5:9-10, 15).

See: ABRAHAM, JACOB, PETER, YAHWEH

GREGORY J. POLAN, O.S.B.

NATIONS

Capturing the imagination and attention of readers and listeners throughout the centuries, the OT, specifically the Book of Genesis, relates the story of the divine origin of all creation and tells how humanity, part of God's creation (Gen 1:27; 2:7, 21-23), develops into nations that eventually become known as non-Israelites (*goyîm*) and Israelites (*'am, 'ammîm*). To the Israelites, the non-Israelites are "foreign nations" who are often a threat and a temptation.

The Israelites, however, are at times forgetful of and unfaithful to God and God's ways. Yet, despite the shortcomings of both sets of nations, the OT text makes clear that all nations have a common origin, have the same dignity, are blessed by God through Abraham, Sarah, and their descendants (Gen 17:15-16; 18:18), have a relationship with God and with each other, and are included in God's universal plan of salvation (Isa 25:6-8).

Old Testament

In the Pentateuch, Genesis 1–11 focuses on the divine creation of the world. It includes the creation of the first human beings (Gen 1:27; 2:7, 21-23) and relates the story of subsequent primeval events. These chapters also feature a series of genealogies. Most important are those found in Genesis 5: the generations from Adam and Eve to Noah; Genesis 10: the descendants of Noah who populate the whole earth; and Genesis 11:10-26: the descendants of Shem to Terah.

In addition to providing a chronological and historical human lineage, these genealogies also portray the evolution of peoples into nations, of which Israel is part through Abraham, the son of Terah (Gen 11:26). Israel plays a significant role in relation to the other nations. Through Abraham, Sarah, and their descendants, hence "Israel," all nations are divinely blessed (Gen 17:15-16; 18:18).

The two genealogies most pertinent to the evolution of the idea of "nations" are Genesis 10 and Genesis 11:10-26.

In Genesis 10 the term "nations" appears for the first time. The nations that issue from Noah's sons include the Medes, the Greeks, the Kittim who are the inhabitants of Rhodes (Gen 10:2-3), the Ethiopians (Cush), the Libyans (Put), the Canaanites (Gen 10:6), and the peoples of Elam, Assyria, and Aram (Gen 10:21-23). These nations are distinguished one from another partly by their language, partly by their geographic locations, and partly by their political affiliations (Gen 10:31), but not by their origin.

Genesis 11:10-26 outlines the descendants of Noah's son Shem. This genealogy is significant because Terah is the father of Abram (later Abraham), Nahor, and Haran (Gen 11:26). Abraham is the link between the primeval stories (Gen 1:1–11:26) and the ancestral stories (Gen 11:27–50:26).

The ancestral stories open with Abraham and Sarah who, landless and childless, set out under God's direction (Gen 12:1) and promise (Gen 12:2-3). God promises to make Abraham "a great nation" (Gen 12:2), a father of a host of nations (Gen 17:5), and that to his descendants that land will be given (Gen 12:7). Both he and Sarah will be blessed (Gen 12:2; 17:15-16) with a son

(Isaac) who "shall give rise to nations, and rulers of peoples shall issue from him" (17:16). God also promises that all the nations (NAB, "communities") of the earth will be blessed in Abraham (Gen 12:3).

God's promises are fulfilled. Abraham and Sarah beget Isaac; Isaac and Rebekah beget Jacob; Jacob and Rachel, Leah, Bilhah, and Zilpah beget twelve sons, one of whom is Joseph. Israel emerges as a nation from among nations (Gen 41:50; Exod 12:38; 18:11; Lev 24:10; Num 10:29ff.; Deut 26:5; Josh 9:3ff.; Judg 1:16; 4:11) as a result of call, election, covenant, and promise (Genesis 12; 17).

Although Israel is distinct, it continues to have a place among the other nations because of its common divine origin and common human ancestral lineage. As a nation among nations, Israel has a natural kinship with other nations: Ishmael (Genesis 16), the Midianites (Gen 25:1-6), the Moabites and Ammonites (Gen 19:30-38), the Arameans (Gen 29:1-14), and the Edomites (Genesis 36). Thus, Israel's story as a nation is part of the nations' story as a whole which is, essentially, the story of the human race and its relationship with God.

The Israelites' particular story as a nation continues with the migration of Jacob's descendants into Egypt (Exod 1:1-7) where they increase in number and grow strong to the dismay and threat of a non-Israelite nation, Egypt, whose leadership and people oppress them (Exod 1:8-14, 15-22) to the point that they cry out to God (Exod 2:23-24). Subsequent OT texts, particularly Exodus, Deuteronomy, the Prophets, and the Psalms, describe the relationship that God has with all the nations, the tension that exists between Israel and the other nations, and how, despite differences and tensions, all are destined for salvation.

The distinctive relationship that Israel shares with God on account of call, election, covenant, and promise, as seen in the Genesis ancestral stories, deepens in the Exodus account of Israel's oppression and liberation. Just as God called Abraham and Sarah and chose them to begin the evolution of a great nation, Israel, so now God, remembering the covenant with Abraham (Exod 2:24), Isaac, and Jacob (Exod 6:2-5), calls Moses to liberate their descendants, the Israelites, from Egyptian bondage and then enters into covenant with them at Sinai (Exodus 19–20). The Israelites are to be God's own chosen people (Exod 6:7a) and Israel is to take God as their God (Exod 6:7b-8).

Thus, the Mosaic Covenant expresses the distinctive faith of Israel as the people of God and places them under obligation to be faithful to the covenant. Deuteronomy 7:7-8 makes clear why God chose Israel.

Abraham and Sarah, Isaac and Rebekah, Jacob and Rachel, Leah, Bilhah, and Zilpah and all their descendants not only evolve into a nation but also become God's nation—a holy nation (Exod 19:6) among nations.

The latter prophets show that Israel does not always remain faithful to its relationship with God. Many members turn to other gods (Jer 5:1-6; Mic 1:5-7), and conspire and perform unjust deeds against their own members (Amos 2:4-8; Mic 2:1-2). Covenant and law are broken; Israel's relationship with God suffers; and the nation becomes the object of God's anger (Amos 3:2). It experiences God's chastisement for its faithlessness and injustices (Mic 1:2-7; 3:12) and becomes a reproach among the other nations (Joel 2:19).

Yet, God does not abandon Israel or break covenant (Hos 11:8-11). Through the prophets, God calls the nation to repentance (Ezek 18:30-32), announces plans for a new covenant (Jer 31:31-34), assures deliverance from the threat and power of the other nations (Isaiah 43), and promises healing, forgiveness (Jer 33:6-8), and restoration (Jer 30:18-22). Israel will be called "blessed" by the nations (Mal 3:12) and will become a sign for them (Jer 4:1-2a) and a blessing (Isa 19:24-25). The nations, in turn, will use God's name "in blessing" and "will glory in him" (Jer 4:2b). Thus, the promise made to Abraham is fulfilled.

The latter prophets, the writings, specifically the Psalms, as well as other OT books, also show that unlike the nation Israel, the other nations do not enjoy the same kind of personal relationship with God. They conspire against God (Ps 2:1) and become God's laughingstock (Ps 59:8); they are the object of God's rebuke (Ps 9:6), wrath (Isa 24:7-13; Hab 3:12; Ps 149:7), judgment (Amos 1:3–2:4; Isaiah 13–19), and chastisement (Ps 59:5). God brings the nations' counsel to nothing (Ps 33:10) and drives them out of Canaan (Deut 7:1-2; Josh 24:18). To Israel, the foreign nations are a political threat on account of their military power (Isa 30:1-5; 31:1-3) and strength (Ezekiel 38; Jer 50:1-3). They are a religious temptation because of their idols (Deut 29:15-16; Ezek 20:32). Yet, God reigns over them (Ps 47:8-9) and guides them (Ps 67:4).

Despite the shortcomings of all the nations, there are members among them, e.g., Melchizedek (Gen 14:18-20), Jethro (Exod 18:12), and Naaman (2 Kgs 5:17), who offer acceptable sacrifices to God. Others are incorporated into Israel, e.g., Tamar (Genesis 38), Rahab (Josh 6:25), Ruth (Ruth 1:16).

Finally, the nations are included in God's message to all peoples (Jer 1:5-10). Through Israel, they have knowledge of God (1 Kgs 8:60) and God's works (Ezek 37:28). Like Israel, they too are the recipients of God's promise and favor (Isa 42:1; 66:18-19) and have a place in the divine plan for universal salvation (Isa 2:1-3; 25:6-8; Mic 4:1-4).

In summary, the OT makes several theological assertions about the nations. First, the basic family unit of all the earth as it existed in primeval times and as it exists today has a common divine origin. Second, all the nations past and present belong to the human race. Third, as members of the human race with a divine origin, all are blessed and preserved by God. Fourth, the history and stories of the different nations intersect because of their common divine origin, the ancestral ties among them, and the bond that God has made with them. Fifth, all nations—those closest to and those at a distance from God—share in God's justice and mercy and the divine plan for universal salvation.

See: ADAM AND EVE, ANCESTORS, CALL, COVENANT, CREATION, ELECTION, FAMILY, GENEALOGY, ISRAELITE, JUDGMENT, LAND, NOAH, POWER, PROMISE, REPENTANCE, SACRIFICE, SALVATION

CAROL J. DEMPSEY, O.P.

New Testament

In the New Testament, nations is one of three terms used to translate the plural Greek term *ta ethnē*. Generally nations refers to *all* nations, including the Jews (Matt 24:10, 14; 28:19; Luke 21:25; Rev 2:26; 12:5). This meaning is often made clear by the adjective "all" (*panta*), as in "all the nations" (Matt 28:19). The second and most frequent translation for *ta ethnē* is "Gentiles" (from the Latin *gentes*, "nations"), a name given to non-Jews by the Jews. This usage was later taken over by Christians (see e.g., the "Jew-Gentile" contrast in Rom 3:29; 1 Cor 1:23). This is the sense found in the numerous OT quotations in the NT where *ta ethnē* occurs (see Acts 4:25; Rom 15:9-12). A third rendition for *ta ethnē* is "pagans," non-Jews who do not know how to pray (Matt 6:7), who are led astray to mute idols (1 Cor 12:2), and whose activity is to be avoided by Christians (Matt 5:47; 1 Cor 5:1; Eph 4:17).

The Gospels and Acts. In the Gospels Jesus is presented before his death as living among, ministering to, and renewing his own people, the Israelites. Jesus' general practice was not to go out on mission to the Gentiles (although see Mark 7:24-30 where "he went off to the district of Tyre" [v. 24] and there healed the daughter of a Syrophoenician woman), nor does he instruct his disciples to do so. Rather, in Matthew 10:5 he instructs his disciples: "Go nowhere among the Gentiles and enter no town of the Samaritans." His vision of a renewed Israel did include, however, Gentiles coming to participate in the reign of God (Matt 11:8). Jesus himself does minister to Gentile people who come into contact with him, performing exorcisms and working miracles (Mark 5:1-20 par.; 7:24-30 par.; Matt 8:5-13 par.; Luke 17:11-19). In a stern saying to his listeners, Jesus affirms that Gentile villages will fare better at judgment than unrepentant Israel (Matt 11:20-24). Further, Jesus makes clear that people from outside Israel will participate in the eschatological banquet of the patriarchs (Luke 13:28-30). While Jesus is not presented as going on mission out to the nations, they are definitely included in God's plan of salvation. In the prophecy of Simeon, Jesus is indeed a "light for revelation to the Gentiles" (Luke 2:32).

There is a shadow side, also, to the nations. They "babble" in their prayers, thinking "that they will be heard because of their many words" (Matt 6:7); the disciples "will be hated by all the nations because of my [Jesus'] name" (Matt 24:10). Faced with cataclysmic signs preceding the coming of the Son of Man, nations "will be in dismay, perplexed by the roaring of the sea and the waves" (Luke 21:25). At the coming of the Son of Man "all the nations will be assembled before him" (Matt 25:32) to be separated into two groups, the sheep and the goats.

Entrusted with the mission to the *nations* are the disciples. The risen Jesus commissions them with the instructions: "Go, therefore, and make disciples of all nations, baptizing them in the name of the Father, and of the Son, and of the Holy Spirit" (Matt 28:19). They are to be baptized and taught everything Jesus has commanded. This universal mission to carry on Jesus' teaching ministry applies to all peoples, including the Jewish people who are not yet disciples. This commission is formally announced as the programmatic theme in Acts 1:8: "You will be my witnesses . . . to the ends of the earth," and then chronicled in the ensuing story of the early Church, particularly in the drama of its two main figures, Peter and Paul. The first sustained ministry to the Gentiles comes with Peter's witness to Cornelius and his household, Gentiles who received "the gift of the Holy Spirit" (Acts 10:45). After these "Gentiles . . . had accepted the word of God" (Acts 11:1), Peter successfully persuaded the "circumcised believers" in Jerusalem to stop objecting. When Peter told his story, the

Jerusalem gathering glorified God, saying: "God has then granted life-giving repentance to the Gentiles too" (Acts 11:18). Peter's personal account of how he had been led by the Spirit and of how the Gentiles had received the Spirit convinced those who heard this to acknowledge what God was doing among the nations.

Each of the three times that Luke narrates Paul's call story in Acts, Paul's mission to the Gentiles is affirmed. In the words of the Lord, Paul "is a chosen instrument of mine to carry my name before the Gentiles, kings and Israelites" (9:15; see 22:21; 26:20, 23). The missionary pattern of Paul and his companions was to preach first to the Jews, but when opposition was encountered they would then "turn to the Gentiles" (13:46; see 18:6; 28:17-28), who in turn "were delighted when they heard this and glorified the word of the Lord" (13:48). To them God "had opened the door of faith" (14:27). However, the Gentiles were not always receptive (14:5).

The conversion of the Gentiles came to a crisis with the question of entrance requirements. This precipitated the "council" of Jerusalem, where some from the party of the Pharisees demanded: "It is necessary to circumcise them and direct them to observe the Mosaic law" (Acts 15:5). After an exchange of views it was decided to accept the Gentile converts without requiring circumcision. At a later visit to Jerusalem Paul related to the believers "what God had accomplished among the Gentiles through his ministry" (21:19). Having heard this the believers "praised God" (21:20). Acts concludes with the prophetic announcement from Isaiah 6:9-10 which reflects the experience of Luke's generation that the conversion of the Jewish people at large had failed. The Church was becoming predominantly Gentile. Thus, the prophetic message of Isaiah was being realized: "This salvation of God has been sent to the Gentiles; they will listen" (Acts 28:28).

The Pauline Letters. It is clear from his self-presentation in the letters that Paul understands himself as "a minister of Christ Jesus to the Gentiles" (Rom 15:16). Indeed, the very purpose of God's revelation of the Son to Paul was that he might proclaim Jesus "to the Gentiles" (Gal 1:16, see 2:9). This is what Paul did, traveling predominantly to Gentile urban areas in the eastern Mediterranean, founding churches, and, during times of physical absence, maintaining his apostolic presence there by sending letters and personal emissaries. It is certainly appropriate that Paul refers to himself as "the apostle to the Gentiles" (Rom 11:13).

The relationship of the Gentiles to the Jews from the perspective of salvation is treated most extensively in the Letter to the Romans. Paul affirms that, even though the Gentiles are without the Mosaic Law, they are still held accountable for their "sins" and will be punished. From their knowledge of the regular, natural order of things, the Gentiles can derive rules of conduct for themselves that are absolute and objective. The reflective thought process in the Gentiles' conscience indicates to them the moral quality of their actions. Hence Paul can say that "the demands of law are written in their hearts" (Rom 2:15).

Although the Gentiles are without the Mosaic Law, those who believe can claim Abraham as their father in faith. Paul argues that just as Abraham had faith (personal confidence) in Yahweh, and thus was justified apart from deeds (Rom 4:3), so also, all Christians, whether Jew or Gentile, are children of Abraham and are justified by faith in Christ. In this sense, Paul can say: "Scripture, which saw in advance that God would justify the Gentiles by faith, foretold the good news to Abraham, saying, 'Through you shall all the nations be blessed'" (Gal 3:8).

Further comment on how Gentiles will be saved is taken up in Romans 9–11. Paul reflects that Israel's failure to recognize (literally, their stumbling over) Christ was providential, because then the apostle went out to bring salvation precisely to the Gentiles (Rom 11:11). The Gentiles are warned, however, not to be smug about their favored situation, but to remember that they are "a wild olive shoot" (11:17), which has been grafted into the root, i.e., Israel, that supports them. The Gentiles are warned: "Do not become haughty, but stand in awe" (11:20), because as grafted branches they can be lopped off if they are unfaithful, just as some of the natural branches (unbelieving Israel) had been (11:21). According to the divine plan or mystery, God's mercy is to be shown to all. After "the full number of the Gentiles comes in" (11:25), then "all Israel will be saved" (11:26).

The Book of Revelation. John, the visionary of the Book of Revelation, gives considerable attention to the salvation of all the nations. He is instructed to prophesy about the nations (10:11) and their salvation. The nations are not an absolute power unto themselves but are to be ruled by the male child of the woman clothed with the sun (12:5). Some nations of the earth, lured by riches and power, have failed to recognize this and have been led astray by Babylon's (i.e., Rome's) claims to quasi-divine status and sovereignty (14:8; 18:3). However, God, not Babylon, is acclaimed as "the king of the nations," the Lord whom "all the nations will come and worship" (15:3-4). The glory of God is acclaimed as the light of a majestic city, a symbol of the community. By this light, "the nations will walk"; to this city "the kings of the earth will bring their treasure" (21:24). The faithful who conquer adversity are promised a share in Christ's messianic rule over the nations: "To the victor, who keeps to my ways until the end, I will give authority over the nations" (2:26).

See: APOSTLE, CIRCUMCISION, IDOLATRY, ISRAEL, JUDGMENT, LAW, MISSION, PAUL, PEOPLE OF GOD, PETER, SALVATION, SAMARIA/SAMARITAN

JOHN L. GILLMAN

Pastoral-Liturgical Tradition

The Christian tradition shows the same wide range of understandings of the relation of "the nations" to those most directly related to God's saving history as do the biblical traditions. Indeed how one understands the nations is somewhat reflexive; i.e., it depends on how one understands Israel or the Church. The nations are "the other" and more often than not a generalization is made about the nature or the quality of this other. If one follows the perspective of the Wisdom literature, for example, Israel is wise and the nations are foolish. Early urban-dwelling Christians in the Roman Empire saw the nations as pagans (Latin *pagani* = rustic unlettered rural dwellers at a lower cultural level). "Heathen" ("dwellers in the open heath") is the Anglo-Germanic equivalent. All of these designations see the nations as inherently inferior. Jews and (at times) Muslims were excluded from the nations since they had embraced the true God. The ambivalence toward Muslims arose from how "different" they seemed to the Christians encountering them. From the time of John of Damascus (ca. 675–ca. 749) Islam was mostly seen as a Christian heresy—false ideas about the true God.

Throughout a good deal of Christian history no distinction was made between culture and belief. Hence if the nations were to embrace belief in the Christian God, this also meant abandonment of cultural ways and embracing the evangelizers' culture. This became especially so where evangelization and colonialization by an imperial power went hand in hand. When that happened, to "Christianize" meant also to "civilize." This reached its height in the nineteenth century, especially in Africa.

Alongside this identification of belief and culture, which saw cultures other than Christian ones as "lower" in need of redemption into "higher" Christian cultures, movements to recognize the dignity and autonomy of the cultures of the nations began to grow from the late nineteenth century. To be sure, there had been such attitudes at times earlier in Christian history: Pope Gregory the Great's instructions to Augustine in evangelizing England at the end of the sixth century or Matteo Ricci's efforts in the Chinese Court in the sixteenth century come to mind. But most of these were not sustained or were directly suppressed. By the middle of the twentieth century, more and more calls were being made to respect the cultures of the non-Christian nations, calls by missionaries and popes alike.

The Second Vatican Council laid the groundwork for a new understanding of the nations—those who had not heard the gospel and those who had only recently accepted it. Three elements especially emerged, the full consequences of which are still not entirely worked out.

The first had to do with the nature of the Church itself. The Dogmatic Constitution on the Church reintroduced into the Western Church the concept of the particular or local church. The fullness of the Church could be had and experienced in the gathering of a local Church around its bishop. To be sure, such local Churches still needed to be in communion with all local Churches and with the Church of Rome. But the local Church possessed its own integrity, and was not just a branch office. Consequently its local expression of faith (always of course in communion with other Churches), embedded in its own culture, could be seen as an authentic expression of Christian faith.

The second element was a new appreciation of the dignity of cultures. This is worked out for the first time in the Pastoral Constitution on the Church in the Modern World (nos. 58ff.). Different ways of organizing human culture are recognized, and these cultures needn't be ranked on a scale from lower to higher. Through creation and the mysterious work of the holy Spirit, God is already active in these cultures before missionaries arrive. A central task of the missionary preaching the gospel is to acknowledge and identify those good and noble aspects of culture where God is already at work as possible "seeds of the gospel" already planted in the culture. These should be lifted up and nourished so that the gospel preached might truly become part of, and help transform, the culture.

This is a much different attitude from that of civilizing the nations, i.e., making them over in our own image and likeness. The attitudes that made this change possible only began to emerge in the late eighteenth century, so earlier generations cannot be faulted for not having had them. This teaching of Vatican II laid the groundwork for understanding the mission to the nations as an inculturation of the gospel, the full implications of which are still being worked out.

The third element is the emergence of dialogue with other religions as a value. If cultures have a certain dignity and integrity as works of God's creation and the activity of the holy Spirit, then the religions represented within them need new consideration as well. The Dogmatic Constitution on the Church (no. 16) talks about the possibilities for salvation of individuals who lead upright lives outside Christianity. The Decree on the Church's Relations with Non-Christian Religions addresses religions as systems (specifically, the world religions of Islam, Judaism, Hinduism, and Buddhism). The Decree acknowledges the dignity of their search noting that, even when their teachings differ from those of Christianity, they "nevertheless often reflect a truth that enlightens all men" (no. 2). The Decree then urges members of the Church to enter into discussion and collaboration with adherents of these religious traditions: "Let Christians, while witnessing to their own faith and way of life, acknowledge, preserve and encourage the spiritual and moral truths found among non-Christians, also their social life and culture" (ibid.).

While this according of respect and acknowledgment of (some) truth does not diminish the mandate to preach and witness to the gospel, the relation between proclamation and dialogue is still not clear. In Vatican documents of the 1990s, both are seen as integral parts of evangelization. However such relations may be clarified in

673

the future, it is clear that the attitude toward the nations is no more a mere reflex opposite of how Christians identify themselves; it is gaining its own integrity within a more consistent understanding of God's creative and redemptive work in our world.

See: CHURCH, CULTURE, SALVATION

ROBERT J. SCHREITER, C.PP.S.

NEIGHBOR

Old Testament

General. Our English word "neighbor" suggests first of all physical or geographical proximity—the one whose house adjoins or is close to our own. The emphasis on propinquity is original, while the friendly quality implied in "good neighbor," "neighborliness" seems to take its origin from biblical usage. In terms of vocabulary the OT often does not make a distinction between "friend" and "neighbor"; our English translations often render the same Hebrew term *(rea')* now with one, now with the other, depending on the force the word has from the context in each particular passage. Other Hebrew terms, however, do suggest the idea of dwelling *(shaken)*, of comradeship *('amith*—a term used several times in Leviticus but not in earlier books), or of being close *(qarob)*; such terms may be used interchangeably, without apparent distinction in meaning (Ps 15:3). "Friend" can sometimes be equated with "brother" (Lev 19:17; Ps 35:14; 122:8; cf. Jer 34:15 with v. 17).

Distribution and Import. The concept appears quite often in the legal tradition, the prophets, the psalms, and the Wisdom literature, but relatively infrequently in narrative. The reason is that in most occurrences of the term, the concern is with the treatment of others, and "neighbor" already suggests something about what sort of treatment that should be. In part this is no doubt because the one who lives or stands nearby is the one we are most likely to have contact with and therefore the most occa-

sions to help or harm. However, the expression used in parallel with "neighbor" in Proverbs 3:29, one "who lives at peace with you," may be instructive: "neighbor" implies a relationship and creates certain expectations as to behavior. Thus it is no surprise that in the great majority of instances, the context says something about how the neighbor is to be treated; but since behavior toward others ought to be based on something other than mere physical proximity, the injunctions tend to become universal in application and so the term, in its turn, tends to be general rather than particular in its reference: the "neighbor" comes to be any fellow human being with whom we may have more than casual contact.

Legislation. In the legal tradition there are prohibitions against bearing false witness against the neighbor (Exod 20:16; Deut 5:20), coveting house or wife (Exod 20:17; Deut 5:21), committing adultery (Lev 18:20; 20:10), slaying (Deut 27:24), defrauding or deceiving (Lev 5:20), removing a boundary stone (Deut 19:14; 27:17), and regulations concerning cities of refuge for the one who slays a neighbor (Exod 21:14; Deut 4:42; 19:4-13), and dealing fairly for the Sabbatical or Jubilee year (Lev 25:14-15; Deut 15:2). While these provisions are negative in content in that they simply prohibit doing harm, many others are very positive, having to do with merciful treatment of debtors (Exod 22:25), just judgment (Lev 19:15), and, especially, loving one's neighbor as oneself (Lev 19:18). This last provision is often said to extend only to fellow Israelites, but in fact verse 34 says very much the same with reference to the resident alien. Deuteronomy 15:2-3, however, enjoins the relaxation of debts to a neighbor who is a "brother" (probably any Israelite) in a Sabbatical year but allows one to demand repayment from a foreigner.

Wisdom and Prophets. The Wisdom and Prophetic traditions often reflect the same concerns as legislative texts (Prov 3:29; 6:29; 25:18; 26:19; Jer 5:8; 29:23; Ezek 18:6, 11, 15; 22:11-12). Wisdom texts advise wise conduct toward the neighbor (Prov 3:28; 25:9, 17; 27:10), and urge truth and right judgment (Jer 7:5; Zech 8:16). Jeremiah condemns Jehoiakim for enslaving "his neighbor" in his policy of forced labor (Jer 22:13; see 34:15, 17), thus placing the king on a level with those in the corvee.

New Testament

General. "Neighbor" is referred to in a relatively neutral way a couple of times in the parables: the shepherd calls friends and neighbors together to rejoice with him over the sheep brought back in safety, as does the housewife over the coin lost and then found (Luke 15:6, 9). Jesus tells us not to invite friends and neighbors to the banquet we give but to invite the poor who cannot repay us (Luke 14:12). The influence of the OT exhortation to love of neighbor is obvious in that about half of the NT occurrences refer directly or indirectly to Leviticus 19:18. Jesus contrasts the OT command to love the neighbor as oneself with its sometimes harsh attitude toward enemies (Matt 5:43). Matthew (though not Mark and Luke) lists this commandment as one to be kept, along with several provisions of the Decalogue, in response to the rich young man's question concerning the way to eternal life (Matt 19:18-19; cf. Mark 10:19; Luke 18:20). But special import is given to it when Jesus, in answer to the question "which is the greatest commandment" first cites Deuteronomy 6:4-5 (the opening words of the "Shema") as the "first commandment" and then says of the command of love of neighbor "the second is like it"; thus love of neighbor is approximated to love of God in importance (Matt 22:39; see Mark 12:31). In Luke's version it is a lawyer who lists love of God and love of neighbor in response to his own question about inheriting eternal life; but he then asks "and who is my neighbor?" and so provides the occasion for Jesus' parable of the good Samaritan (Luke 10:25-37). Any tendency to interpret "neighbor" in a restricted sense is rejected by the identification of the Samaritan as the one who was "neighbor" to the one in need. Paul cites Leviticus 19:18 as summing up all the other commandments and as, therefore, the fulfillment of the Law (Rom 13:8-10; see Gal 5:14; Jas 2:8).

Pastoral-Liturgical Tradition

The whole biblical tradition clearly indicates that the neighbor is not simply the one who dwells near us nor even the one who stands near us in the liturgical assembly. The neighbor is any one to whom we can do good, especially the one most in need of our help. The help that is needed may not always, or even usually, be ministering to physical needs; more frequently it will have to do with welcoming the other into our love, with bringing the other into the community. Those in the same community become "neighbors," and the concept of community is multi-leveled, from parish to diocese to Church in the ecclesial sense, and from local to national to world in the broader secular sense. The Bible teaches that the concept of "neighbor" embraces all.

See: FRIEND, LOVE, STRANGER

JOSEPH JENSEN, O.S.B.

NOAH

Noah was the righteous man through whom both the human race and the world of the animals were saved from the flood.* He has become symbolic of the person of exceptional virtue (see Ezek 14:14, 20; Sir 44:17; Heb 11:7; 2 Pet 2:5).

The story of the flood begins with the notice of Noah's birth. Whether the name itself means "comfort" or "rest," the explanation that follows its announcement has strong links with the report of the punishment of Adam in the story of the first sin (see Genesis 3). Noah was to bring relief from the toil that was so burdensome since the ground was cursed. This is the identical language used in the sentencing of the sinful Adam. It seems that Noah would reverse the punishment that Adam merited for his transgression (see Gen 3:17). If Adam can be considered the first father of the race, Noah can be regarded as the second. In addition to reversing Adam's punishment and, thereby, providing a second chance for the human race, Noah too received the divine commission, "Be fertile and multiply; abound on the earth and subdue it" (Gen 9:7). Thus life begins anew.

In the midst of total depravity, only Noah "found favor with the LORD" (Gen 6:8). According to the story, his devotion to God was such that he followed God's directions to build the ark even without knowing God's intention to destroy the world (see Heb 11:7). Because of his unquestioning righteousness, his wife, his sons, and their wives were saved along with him. Just as Adam's family would have to endure the consequences of his sinfulness, so Noah's family profited from his righteousness. The story not only identifies him as righteous, it also portrays him as such. He obeyed God's command regarding clean and unclean animals (Gen 7:2-3; 8), and when the waters finally receded and the occupants of the ark were able to disembark, the first act he performed was the construction of an altar and the offering of holocausts (8:20). It was the sweetness of Noah's sacrifice that prompted God to promise never again to destroy all living things. Again, it was the righteousness of one person that saved all of the others.

The covenant that God made with Noah (9:8-17) was really a covenant between God and all living beings. Since nearly everything had been destroyed, henceforth everything remaining would have to be safeguarded. This covenant embraced not only Noah's generation but every succeeding generation; it included not only human beings but every living creature on earth, even the earth itself. The sign of this covenant, the bow in the sky, was to be a reminder to God of the promise made: "The waters shall never again become a flood to destroy all mortal beings" (9:15).

Those saved from the devastation of the flood went on to repopulate the world. Although actual descent is difficult to trace, genealogies suggest that Shem was the ancestor of the Israelites, Ham was the forebear of the Canaanites, and Japheth, of the Philistines (10:1-32). The story of Noah's drunkenness may be an etiological tale justifying Israel's animosity toward the Canaanites. According to Israelite perception, the Canaanites, like their forebear, were always ready to take advantage of the vulnerabilities of others.

See: ADAM AND EVE, FLOOD

DIANNE BERGANT, C.S.A.

NUMBERS

Biblical numbers have both literal value and symbolic connotations. Here the focus will be on the latter, e.g., completeness, totality, immeasurability.

Old Testament

Three. In some instances it is hard to determine whether three merely means a small round number. However, in other cases it suggests some notion of completeness. Thus, Abram offers a three-year-old heifer, a three-year-old she-goat, and a three-year-old ram (Gen 15:9). Likewise Daniel prays three times a day (Dan 6:14). The third day is the day for covenant-making or renewal of covenant (Exod 19:11, 16; Hos 6:2).

Four. This number implies totality, probably deriving from the four cardinal points. Thus the four rivers of paradise irrigate the whole world (Gen 2:10-14). God punishes Jerusalem fourfold (Ezek 14:21). Four chariots patrol the earth (Zech 6:1-8).

Seven. This number connotes completeness/fullness. There are seven days of creation (Gen 2:3). Ruth is worth more than seven sons (Ruth 4:15). The Israelites march around Jericho for seven days with seven priests carrying rams' horns (Josh 6:4). (See also the Sabbatical year in Deut 15:1-11 and the Jubilee year* in Leviticus 25.)

Ten. This figure can imply simple completeness. There are Ten Commandments (Exod 34:28; Deut 4:14). In Sodom Yahweh would be satisfied with only ten righteous men (Gen 18:32). "Ten" may also mean a fairly large number, e.g., Job's friends have reviled him ten times (Job 19:3; see Num 14:22).

Twelve. This number suggests fullness, probably being connected with the twelve months. There are twelve tribes of Israel (Gen 49:28). Ishmael is the father of twelve chieftains (Gen 17:20). At Elim there are twelve springs of water along with seventy palm trees (Exod 15:27).

Forty. This number conjures up a fairly long period of time. Israel is forty years in the desert (Exod 16:35; Num 14:33). David reigns as king for forty years (2 Sam 5:4). Forty days is the common duration in critical situations of punishment (Gen 7:17), fasting (Exod 34:28), and repentance (Jonah 3:4).

Seventy. This is a product of ten times seven, hence a round number with a hint of unknown dimensions. At the entrance into Egypt there are seventy sons of Israel (Gen 46:27). According to Jeremiah there are seventy years of exile (Jer 25:11). The ideal life span is seventy years (Ps 90:10).

One Thousand. This suggests a very large group or entity, particularly one so large that it is beyond numbering. Thus God's mercy extends to a thousand generations (Deut 5:10). One day in Yahweh's courts is better than a thousand days elsewhere (Ps 84:11). In military contexts the Hebrew word for one thousand (*'elep*) may imply a unit of rather variable size mustered from the tribes of Israel.

New Testament

Three. This figure suggests some notion of completeness. In the context of the death-resurrection of Jesus, reference is made to Jonah who spent three days and three nights in the belly of the whale (Matt 12:40). The earliest creedal tradition about the resurrection states that Jesus was raised on the third day according to the Scriptures (1 Cor 15:4). Later Jewish tradition regarded the third day as the day of salvation.

Four. This number connotes totality. There are four horsemen who spread calamity on earth (Rev 6:2, 4-5, 8) and four angels who bring destruction (Rev 9:13-15).

Seven. This figure again implies completeness/fullness. Mary Magdalene is possessed by seven demons (Mark 16:9; Luke 8:2). Peter's question about forgiving seven times (Matt 18:21; see Luke 17:4) recommends a certain number beyond which the obligation is fulfilled. Jesus' response about forgiving seventy times seven (Matt 18:22) means an unlimited number of times.

Twelve. The Twelve called by Jesus bring to mind the twelve sons/tribes of Jacob/Israel and connotes completeness. Thus the Twelve are the ancestors of the new Israel, the new people of God. For Luke this number is so significant that a replacement must be found for Judas (Acts 1:15-26). In Luke's view the Christian Church is the reconstituted Israel. In Revelation 7:4-9; 14:1-5 there is mention of 144,000, i.e., $12 \times 12 \times 1000 = 144,000$. This figure has symbolic connotations, i.e., the Church as the fullness of Israel. In Revelation 14:1-5 these 144,000 are special. They do not simply follow the Lamb but go wherever he goes, viz., unto death.

Forty. As in the OT, this points to a fairly long period of time, e.g., Jesus' temptation in the desert (Matt 4:2; Mark 1:13; Luke 4:2). In Acts 1:3 forty days is the length of Jesus' sojourn on earth after the resurrection. For Luke this symbolizes a sufficient space of time for preparing the witnesses (Acts 1:8).

Seventy. It is not clear whether Jesus sends seventy or seventy-two disciples on mission (Luke 10:1). In the Bible seventy reflects a round number with possible unknown dimensions (see Gen 10:2-31 in the Hebrew Bible—the Greek Bible reads seventy-two). In Luke seventy may be an approximation for a more original seventy-two.

One Thousand. In Revelation 20:1-6 an angel binds Satan for a thousand years. After this period Satan is to be released for a short time. The number has symbolic value, depicting a long period of time between Christ's conquest of death and the forces of evil (the binding of Satan) and the end of the world. During this time God's people enjoy his glorious reign.

Gematria. This is a pattern in which the numerical value of the Hebrew consonants reveals the hidden sense of the text. The number "fourteen" in Matthew's genealogy (Matt 1:17) may stand for David (D=4; V=6; D=4). The meaning of Israel's history would thus be: Jesus Christ, the son of David (Matt 1:1). According to this pattern the number of the beast in Revelation 13:18, viz., 666, may mean "Nero Caesar."

Pastoral-Liturgical Tradition

Symbolic Value. In approaching numbers in the Bible, one cannot always press for exact mathematical equivalents. In its use of numbers the Bible often attaches a symbolic value that demands an understanding on the part of the interpreter of the connotation of numbers. Thus the Bible is not an exact timetable that predicts the precise occurrence of future events.

Feast of All Saints. The first reading for this feast is Revelation 7:2-4, 9-14 with its mention of the 144,000. In this context the number suggests the Church as the fullness of Israel. While the 144,000 are special in the text, there is no indication that the number to be saved is this exact figure. It is especially in Apocalyptic literature (e.g., Daniel 7–12 and the Book of Revelation) that the symbolism of numbers, not their precise mathematical equivalent, is implied.

See: ANGEL, APOCALYPTIC, JUBILEE YEAR, RESURRECTION

JOHN F. CRAGHAN

O

OATH

An oath is a solemn statement by a person who appeals to God in witness of the truthfulness of what is being affirmed. It may either be declaratory, referring to a past or present fact, or it may be promissory, relating to one's intention regarding some future course of action. In both the OT and the NT oaths are taken either by God or a person. The truthfulness or the fulfillment of oaths brings blessings; violations of an oath bring curses. In the Code of Canon Law (1983) oaths are included as acts of worship along with vows (see cc. 1199-1204). The Code defines oaths, affirms their obligatory nature, and treats the cessation of the obligation of oaths.

Old Testament

In the ancient Near East oaths were commonly taken in the name of a god or the king, e.g., "as the king my lord lives" or "may the god live for me" as a way of guaranteeing the truthfulness of one's affirmation, the sincerity of one's promise. The most common type of oath in the OT was unconditional, as in Genesis 47:28-31 where Joseph takes an oath to fulfill his father's wish to bury him not in Egypt but with his fathers ("So Joseph swore it to him," v. 31). Conditional oaths are also attested. Under certain circumstances, exemptions are allowed, e.g., Abraham exempted his servant from bringing back from Mesopotamia a wife for Isaac if the woman was unwilling to return with him (Gen 24:8; see also Josh 2:17). Oaths could be taken before the priest in a sanctuary to proclaim a person innocent (Exod 22:8), and could even involve an ordeal to ascertain guilt or innocence (Num 5:16-28). There were also oaths taken between two parties, as illustrated by the mutual oath of David and Jonathan to remain friends: "We two have sworn by the name of the Lord" (1 Sam 20:42).

Two common terms used for oath are *šĕbûʿâ* (which has the same root as the number seven) and *ʿālāh* (which literally means "curse"). These terms are used together for the woman suspected of adultery who is told to take "the oath of imprecation [lit. curse]" (Num 5:21). Oaths were sometimes followed by curses that would be incurred if the oath was not fulfilled (Ruth 1:17; 1 Sam 3:17; 14:44; 2 Sam 3:35; 2 Kgs 2:23).

God is presented as taking oaths by God's own name, promising either blessings or punishment. Frequently God swears concerning the promise of the land, as God does to Abraham: "I swear by myself, declares the Lord, . . . I will bless you abundantly and make your descendants as countless as the stars of the sky" (Gen 22:16-17). In some cases God's oath has a threatening character, promising destruction (Num 32:10-15; see Amos 6:8).

New Testament

The fulfillment of God's sworn promises from the past is recounted in the NT. God remembers "the oath he swore to Abraham our father" (Luke 1:73); God did indeed set one of David's descendants (Jesus) on his throne as "God had sworn" (Acts 2:29-31).

In the Sermon on the Mount, the Matthean Jesus reminds his listeners what their ancestors were told ("Do not take a false oath, but make good to the Lord all that you vow"), and then affirms: "Do not swear at all; not by heaven, for it is God's throne; nor by the earth, for it is his footstool; nor by Jerusalem, for it is the city of the great King" (Matt 5:33-34). The negative command about swearing is balanced by the positive command about correct speech that follows: "Let your 'Yes' mean 'Yes,' and your 'No' mean 'No'" (v. 37). Jesus affirms that a person shall not swear by God's name or any substitute for it, but rather speak the truth in a straightforward way. Some groups, e.g., the Baptists, Mennonites, and Quakers, take this passage as prohibiting all oaths, but others usually understand this section more generally as prohibiting the use of God's name for false statements, subterfuge, or trivial, frivolous matters, and not as an absolute prohibition against oath-taking. See also James 5:12.

On several occasions Paul uses an oath formula to attest the truth of his speech, e.g., "God is my witness" (Rom 1:9; see also 2 Cor 1:23), "I speak the truth in Christ, I do not lie" (Rom 9:1; see also 2 Cor 11:31; Gal 1:20).

Pastoral-Liturgical Tradition

The new Code of Canon Law treats oaths along with vows under the section entitled "acts of worship" (see cc. 1199-1204 for oaths). Oaths are only to be taken "in truth, in judgment and in justice" (c. 1199). The oath taken has to fulfill what has been affirmed "by a special obligation of religion" (c. 1200). The code also lays down several conditions that can nullify the obligations of an oath, e.g., if the thing sworn "be-comes either evil or entirely indifferent or, finally, if it would impede a greater good" (c. 1202).

See: BLESSING, CURSE, FULFILLMENT, GUILT, NAME, PROMISE, TRUTH, VOW, WITNESS, WORSHIP

JOHN L. GILLMAN

OBEDIENCE

The English word obedience derives from the Latin for "to listen to." Similarly in the NT, the basic Greek word for obedience is a verb for listening. The same is true for the Hebrew OT. In the Bible then, obedience has something to do with listening to the call of God. In both the OT and NT, the assembly which responds to the call is described with words meaning call: OT—*qahal*, from *qol*, voice; NT—*ekklesia*, from "to call-out." As followers of Christ, obedience embraces our openness to hear the Word of God and our wholehearted response to its call in our lives.

Old Testament

Whole-hearted Obedience. In Hebrew, the idiom for "to obey" means "to listen to the voice of." Repeatedly throughout the OT, Israel is exhorted to "listen/obey" (e.g., Deut 6:4). But there is more to this listening than meets the ear. Moses called on Israel to hear "with all your heart" (Deut 11:13; 13:4; 30:2). In the Bible, the primary organ of hearing is not the ear, though this is where the sound enters, but the heart. If the word goes in one ear and out the other, we have not truly "heard." On becoming king, Solomon prayed for "a listening heart" (1 Kgs 3:9). When we turn away our hearts, we do not listen (Deut 3:17); in the same way, if our heart is hardened, the word cannot enter and take effect (Ps 95:7b-8; Jer 4:4). In our popular understanding, the heart is the seat of the emotions; in the Bible it is much more than that. The heart is the very center of the person. To hear with the whole heart means that we allow the word of God to enter deeply into our inner selves, to the very core of our persons. As a result, we are changed; our "obedience" is manifested in our changed lives.

Obedience in Creation. In the very first chapters of Genesis (1:1–2:4), God created the universe and humans by calling them into existence. As images of God (Gen 1:26-28), humans are called to accept their condition of imagehood, and to reflect God by sharing in the divine activities of life-giving and dominion over chaos. Unfortunately, humans disobeyed. Preferring to be God (Gen 3:5), Adam and Eve, representing all humans, rejected imagehood and spawned death, injustice, and brokenness (Genesis 2–3). God's purpose for life and blessing will, however, be heard, and the call of Abraham marks the turning point. Abraham heard God's call to leave behind land and family and to set out into an unknown future (Gen 12:1-3). His obedience reached its final testing in the sacrifice of Isaac (Genesis 22). In the biblical story of Abraham we can see how obedience and faith are very closely connected.

In the Wisdom literature, another aspect of God's call and of human obedience appears. We learn wisdom in and through our experience of the natural world and of our life with others in society. God, personified in the figure of the Wisdom Woman, calls to us at the crossroads of our lives (Prov 1:20-33; 8:1-36), and our obedience is a matter of life and death (8:35-36). In the context of wisdom, we often meet the expression "fear of the Lord." This attitude, the beginning of all wisdom, encompasses our obedient and faithful response to God (Prov 1:7; 9:10; 14:26, 27; Job 28:28; Ps 111:10; Eccl 5:6; 12:13; Sir 1:9-18).

Obedience and the Covenant. When the Israelites were enslaved in Egypt and cried out to God in their distress, God responded and delivered them from oppression. Coming to Sinai, the Israelites recognized Yahweh as the source of their life and entered into a covenant. "If you listen to my voice ["obey"] . . . you shall be a holy nation" (Exod 19:5-6). Before sealing the covenant, the people affirmed, "We will do everything that the LORD has told us" (Exod 24:3). Obedience to the covenant was to be manifested in two directions: (1) they must worship only this God, and (2) they must live this out in their behavior toward each other. An intrinsic connection exists between the nature of Yahweh as a God who frees from oppression and the demands of social behavior. All of the laws now found in the Torah can be subsumed under one of these two headings. Thus we can understand why it is that in Deuteronomy, the call to Israel "to hear" is so often closely joined to expressions like "and carefully observe the commandments and statutes" (5:1; 6:3; 7:12; etc.). Israel's very existence depended on their obedience to the covenant; it was a matter of life and death (Deut 30:1-20), but all too often, they failed.

Obedience to Humans. In the OT, the call of God does not come directly to each individual, but is mediated through others in the community (e.g., children should obey parents [Deut 21:18-21]). Especially important are the civil and religious leaders (kings, priests, prophets, and the wise [Jer 18:18; Ezek 7:26; Deut 17:14–18:22]) who have the obligation, each in their own way, of speaking and transmitting God's word to the people. However, obedience to them is not absolute. The OT recognizes that these leaders can fail in their duty and lead the people astray (Jer 5:31; 6:13-15; 8:8-9; Mic 3:1-12). As the issue of prophetic conflict illustrates (Jeremiah 28), discernment is called for and is not easy.

New Testament

The Obedience of Jesus. The whole life of Jesus was marked by obedience to the will of God. "When he came into the world, he said: . . . 'Behold, I come to do your will, O God'" (Heb 10:5-7). As a twelve year old, Jesus stayed behind in Jerusalem because he must be about God's will, thus causing Mary and Joseph anxiety (Luke 2:49). At the very beginning of his public ministry, he, like Israel of old, went into the wilderness to be tested (Matt 4:1-11; Mark 1:12-13;

Luke 4:1-13). The three temptations he faced there can actually be reduced to one: would he be led astray from the obedient following of his call by God? These temptations characterized his whole ministry (e.g., Matt 16:23; John 6:14-15), and, unlike Israel of old, throughout Jesus was obedient.

Jesus "came down from heaven, not to do my own will but the will of the one who sent me" (John 6:38), and that will was manifested in Jesus' preaching of and working for the reign of God, a reign marked by justice, peace, and love. The disobedience of Adam was reversed by the obedience of Jesus (Rom 5:19) who, as full image of God, reconciled everything in heaven and on earth (Col 1:15-20). As he approached the end of his life, Jesus faced another temptation, in the garden of Gethsemane, but again, "not as I will, but as you will" (Matt 26:39). Finally, he was obedient even to death on a cross (Phil 2:8), and through his death, achieved the will of God, the salvation of all (John 6:40). Jesus taught his followers to pray to God, "your will be done, on earth as in heaven" (Matt 6:10), and he was in his person the fullest embodiment of this prayer.

Obedience of Disciples. During his life on earth, Jesus called disciples* to follow him and be one with him in doing God's will (Matt 7:21; 12:50; 18:14; 21:28-31), and after his resurrection he continues, through the preaching of the gospel, to call disciples to respond in obedient faith (Acts 6:7; Rom 1:5; 16:26; 2 Thess 1:8) and to continue his work on earth. The narratives of the calling of the disciples (e.g., Mark 1:16-20) show them responding with obedience, ready to leave all and follow Jesus wherever he might lead. Whoever would follow Christ must be prepared for radical obedience (e.g., Luke 14:25-33). In Luke's Gospel especially, the model of Christian discipleship can be seen in Mary. She is the one who truly heard the word of God, "May it be done to me according to your word" (1:38); she "kept all these things/words in her heart" (2:51). When she was praised simply

for being his biological mother, Jesus corrected this: "My mother and my brothers are those who hear the word of God and act on it" (8:21). Mary was so truly open to listen to God's word, to obey, that she was able to bear that word into the world.

Obedience to Humans. Like the OT, the NT also recognizes that obedience is due to human authority such as parents (Col 3:20), masters (Col 3:22), religious (Matt 23:3), and civil authorities (Mark 12:17; Rom 13:1-7). Also, like the OT, it recognizes that this kind of obedience is not absolute. Jesus often came into conflict with the religious authorities of his day. We need only recall his cleansing of the Temple (John 2:13-22), breaking of Sabbath laws (Mark 2:23-28), challenging the traditions of the elders (Mark 7:1-8), and associating with publicans and sinners (e.g., Matt 9:10-13). Peter and John would have to decide whether they should obey God rather than humans (Acts 4:19), and Stephen would become the first Christian martyr at the hands of the religious leadership (Acts 7). The Book of Revelation is a sustained warning against the idolatrous potential of civil authority.

Pastoral-Liturgical Tradition

The basic Christian obedience is that of the individual to the call of God in one's life: to what am I called? How do I live that call out in my life? Early in Christian history, that call often led to martyrdom. However, during the fourth century, the Church went from being persecuted to receiving official acceptance. Responding to God's call in their lives, individuals then would leave society to find God in the desert, either alone or in communities. Religious orders began to develop, and with them a new context in which to view obedience. Initially the young members placed themselves in obedience under a mother or father director for guidance in the spiritual life. Later, obedience was seen as a requisite for orderly communal life together, thus becoming a dimension of Christian love. Still later, from the twelfth century on, obedience came to be connected with availability for a particular mission or apostolic activity within the Church. Certain other developments in the concept of obedience (e.g, renunciation of self, the superior as speaking for God) were open to severe distortions which could lead far from the biblical understanding.

Since obedience is most basically our response to the call of God in our lives, where is it that we hear this call? Certainly the Scriptures play an important role; a deep, prayerful, and continuous meditation on this Word of God would seem an essential component of obedience. But we do not listen to the Scriptures alone; we are, rather, part of a community, a Church, in which the Scriptures are proclaimed, passed on, and interpreted. The call of God also comes to us through the life of the Church, its leadership, and its liturgy. The call of God further comes to us, as the biblical wisdom traditions attest, through everyday life and experience—our own, with our unique gifts, talents, insights; and that of others, in our society and in our world. Vatican II spoke of the need of the Church to be attentive to "the signs of the times" (Pastoral Constitution on the Church, no. 4) in order to respond to God's call today. None of these sources for hearing the call of God can be identified simply with God. As both OT and NT testify, they must not be absolutized, but must be approached with both humility and discernment.

Christian obedience is not something negative, externally imposed, or slavishly demanded. It is rather a whole-hearted listening to the call of God, a God who has first loved us (Deut 4:37; 7:8; 10:15; 1 John 4:19) and whose will is the fullness of life for all (John 10:10). Our obedience is manifested in our lives as images of God, disciples of Christ, and servants of the reign of God.

See: CALL, COVENANT, DISCIPLE, FAITH, FEAR OF GOD, HEART, JUSTICE, LOVE, MARY, MISSION, PEACE, PRIEST, PROPHET, REIGN OF GOD, WISDOM, WORSHIP

MICHAEL D. GUINAN, O.F.M.

ORACLE

Old Testament

An oracle is a message or word from God to the people. The most common terms for "oracle" in the OT are *maśśâ'*, which also means "burden" or "load," and *ne'um*, usually found in the phrase *ne'um YHWH*, "oracle of the Lord." *Maśśâ'*, "burden," conveys the sense of an oracle. The message of God is a burden borne both by the messenger, usually a prophet, and by the people to whom it is addressed. Often the *maśśâ'* is a message of doom, whether against Israel's kings (2 Kgs 9:25), foreign nations (Isa 13:1; 14:28; 15:1; 17:1; 19:1; 21:1, 11, 13; 23:1; 30:6; Nah 1:1), or against Jerusalem (Isa 22:1; Ezek 12:10). Jeremiah makes a pun on the double meaning of *maśśâ'*: "When this people, or a prophet or a priest asks you, 'What is the *burden* [*maśśâ'*] of the LORD?' you shall answer, 'You are the *burden,* and I cast you off, says the LORD.' If a prophet or a priest or anyone else mentions 'the *burden* of the LORD,' I will punish that man and his house. Thus you shall ask, when speaking to one another, 'What answer did the LORD give?' or, 'What did the LORD say?' But the *burden* of the LORD you shall mention no more. For each man his own word becomes the *burden* so that you pervert the words of the living God, the LORD of hosts, our God" (Jer 23:33-36; see 23:38).

The phrase *ne'um YHWH*, "oracle of the LORD," is used most frequently in the prophets. The prophet Jeremiah alone uses the phrase over 160 times. It is usually translated as a verbal phrase, "says the LORD." This phrase is often referred to as the messenger formula, a way in which the prophet legitimates the message about to be delivered. The few instances where the phrase is used outside the Prophetic books are passages of great importance: God's promise to Abraham after the sacrifice of Isaac (Gen 22:16); God's declaration that the Exodus generation will die in the desert (Num 14:28); the oracle of doom against Eli's house (1 Sam 2:30). Many of these uses have to do with the words of a prophet: the fulfillment of Elijah's oracle against Ahab (2 Kgs 9:26); Isaiah's prediction concerning Sennacherib's siege against Jerusalem (2 Kgs 19:33); Huldah's words to Josiah after the discovery of Deuteronomy (2 Kgs 22:19; 2 Chr 34:27); the messianic oracle to David (Ps 110:1).

The passage in Deuteronomy concerning true and false prophecy uses the Hebrew word *dâbâr*, "word," in the sense of oracle: "'But if a prophet presumes to speak in my name an *oracle [dâbâr]* that I have not commanded him to speak, or speaks in the name of other gods, he shall die.' If you say to yourselves, 'How can we recognize an *oracle* which the LORD has spoken?' know that, even though a prophet speaks in the name of the LORD, if his *oracle* is not fulfilled or verified, it is an *oracle* which the LORD did not speak" (Deut 18:20-22). In 2 Samuel 16:23 Ahithophel's counsel is true as an oracle *(dâbâr)* from the LORD.

The oracles of Balaam, in which he blesses Israel against the wishes of the Moabite king, are called *mâšâl* (Num 23:7, 18; 24:3, 15, 20, 21, 23), a word usually used to refer to proverb or parable.

New Testament

The proper term for oracle in the NT is *logion*, "utterance." It occurs only four times. Stephen in the Acts of the Apostles describes Moses as a prophet and the Law given to him on Mount Sinai as "living oracles" *(logia)* to be handed on to later generations (Acts 7:38). In Romans Paul too describes the law as oracles *(logia)* of God which were entrusted to the Jews (Rom 3:2). The author of the Letter to the Hebrews scolds his audience for not understanding the Christian proclamation: "Although you should be teachers by this time, you need to have someone teach you again the basic elements of the utterances *[logia]* of God" (Heb 5:12). The author of 1 Peter exhorts his preachers to preach only with the words *(logia)* of God (1 Pet 4:11), i.e., the good news in Christ.

The Greek word *hrema*, which is one Septuagint translation of the Hebrew word

maśśâ' when it is used in the sense of oracle, sometimes connotes oracle, message of God, in the NT as well. Mary responds to Gabriel's announcement: "May it be done to me according to your word *[hrema]*" (Luke 1:38). The shepherds reflect that the message given to them by the angels concerning the child is indeed an oracle (Luke 2:17). Simeon too has received a message from God: "You may let your servant go in peace, according to your word" (Luke 2:29). The disciples do not understand Jesus' oracle concerning his passion (Luke 9:45; 18:34). After denying Jesus the repentant Peter remembers his oracle: "Before the cock crows you will deny me three times" (Matt 26:75; Mark 14:72; Luke 22:61). *Hrema* in the Gospel of John almost always suggests oracle (e.g., John 3:34; 6:63, 68; 14:10). Peter introduces his Pentecost speech as an oracle (Acts 2:14). In his final speech in the Acts of the Apostles, Paul introduces a citation from Isaiah as *hrema* (Acts 28:25).

See: PROPHET, WORD

IRENE NOWELL, O.S.B.

ORDINATION

Ordination is one of the oldest, most controversial issues surrounding service and ministry,* office and leadership in the Church. The NT shows that, in some cases at least, it was customary to connect the beginning of a ministry with community actions of choice/election, prayer and fasting, and ritual gestures. Such is the picture in Acts 13:1-3, where the Christians of Antioch (an important interracial community with a vigorous missionary outreach) confirm the Spirit's choice of Paul and Barnabas as missionaries ("election") through communal prayer and fasting, followed by a "laying on of hands" ("ritual gesture"). This three-part pattern of election, prayer, and laying on of hands came to be regarded as the classic and quintessential shape of ordination by virtually all Christian Churches that are served by formally recognized ministers. Among Roman Catholics, there is a long-standing tradition that connects the ordination of deacons, presbyters, and bishops with the "ordination" of Israel's priests and levites (a connection which, as will be seen, is problematic for a variety of reasons). This article begins, then, with the question of ordination in the literature of the Hebrew Bible. An analysis of evidence for ordination in the NT follows, as well as a discussion of the ways this evidence has been interpreted by the Church's pastoral-liturgical tradition.

Old Testament

The descriptions of "ordination" found in Exodus (28:1–29:35; 39:1-31; 40:12-15) and Leviticus (8:1–10:20) are not really primitive in character, in spite of their references to Moses, Aaron, and Aaron's sons. Rather, these rituals represent the interests—theological and political—of postexilic writers attached to the circle of priestly professionals at the second Temple in Jerusalem. In their basic shape, these "ordinations" (to "ordain" in biblical Hebrew means "to fill the hands," probably with sacrifices) involved three major elements: the investiture and anointing of the priest(s) (Lev 8:1-13); the offering of sacrifices (Lev 8:14-36); and an octave-day ritual involving further sacrifices, solemn blessings, and a theophany showing God's approval of the proceedings (Lev 9:1-24).

A number of points should be made about these rites. First, the OT priesthood was not "vocational" (based on the discernment of a call from God) but genealogical. Preexilic Israel's priests originally came from the tribe of Levi, but many Levites found themselves "reduced in status" after David succeeded in establishing a single, national sanctuary in Jerusalem staffed by a royal Zadokite priesthood (so called after Zadok, whom David had appointed priest in 2 Sam 8:16). Second, by the time of the Exile the Israelite priesthood had become primarily a cultic and functional office. It was not a "pastoral ministry." Functions which may have accrued to priests at an earlier stage of Is-

rael's history—e.g., prophetic interpretation of events, teaching (torah)—had long since been co-opted by others. Third, in the postexilic era, the Israelite priesthood (especially the high priesthood, an office for which there is no evidence prior to the Exile) became increasingly linked to a small circle of conservative, wealthy, aristocratic families who dominated politics and religion in Jerusalem. Such was certainly the case by the time of Jesus. Indeed, in the first century CE, the economic stability of Jerusalem depended upon the Temple with its regular pattern of worship, its revenues, tithes and tax exemptions, and its prominence as a pilgrimage center.

It should be clear, then, that the ordinations described in the Pentateuch had nothing to do with recognition of a "charism" for service or with the creation of any "bond" between priest and people for the sake of pastoral care or with any commission to preach or teach God's Word. In some ways, the postexilic ordinations of Israel's priests functioned as surrogates for the anointing and investiture of a monarch, which the nation no longer had. Such ordinations were thus similar to coronations, a fact that was to have fateful consequences when Christians began assimilating the vocabulary of Israelite priesthood in the second and third centuries CE.

New Testament

In a real sense, the question "Does ordination exist in the NT?" is misleading. It would be better to ask how Christian communities of the first two or three generations recognized their leaders, and then to show how those leaders gained authoritative status through faithful service. After all, those figures in the NT who either claimed the greatest authority (e.g., Paul) or had it claimed for them (e.g., the "Twelve" in the theology of Luke/Acts) did not appeal to rites of ordination but to God's own choice and election in Christ. Thus Paul argues, loudly and often, that his status and ministry as an apostle came directly from God, not from any human source or ecclesiastical mandate (see Gal 1:1, 15-19; 2 Cor 3:4-6; 10:1–12:18). Similarly, the authoritative witness of the Twelve (as interpreted by Luke/Acts) came from their status as Jesus' "privileged companions" from the time of his baptism by John until "he was taken up from us" (see Acts 1:21-22).

At the same time we know that some rudimentary rituals for designating or commissioning ministers were known by some of the NT writers. Several passages in Acts and in the pastorals speak of "laying on of hands" (Greek, *epitithemi tas cheiras*) within the context of choosing someone for a ministry (see Acts 6:6; 13:1-3; 1 Tim 4:14; 5:22; 2 Tim 1:6). Elsewhere, presbyters (Acts 14:23) and a missionary's traveling companion (2 Cor 8:19) are said to be "appointed" (Greek, *cheirotonein*, a verb that originally signified the expression of choice by a "show of hands"—and thus "to vote for" or "to elect").

Do such passages "prove" that ministers in the NT were ordained? To answer this question accurately requires some careful analysis. First, the NT does not use language like "laying on hands" or "appoint" with the precision and consistency of later Christian theology. Thus, the phrase "laying on of hands," in addition to its uses in ministerial contexts, was also employed in the NT to describe Jesus' deeds of healing the sick (Mark 8:23) and blessing children (Matt 19:13-15). The same gesture, in Acts 8:17 and 19:6, signifies giving the Spirit to new converts. So in the NT, the language linked to the choice, appointment, and/or ritual designation of ministers was still fluid; it had not yet acquired the technical precision of a later era. Second, the precise nature of the ministries to which Christians were being "appointed" in the NT is far from clear. Take Timothy as a case in point. Although it is often assumed that he served as a kind of early "bishop" (Greek, *episkopos*) or "presbyter/elder" (Greek, *presbyteros*), in fact Timothy is never called either of these. Instead, he is described as a "minister" of Jesus Christ (Greek, *diakonos*; 1 Tim 4:6), as a "co-worker" for God in the gospel of Christ (Greek, *diakonos*; 1 Thess 3:2), or as an "evangelist" (2 Tim 4:5). None of these descriptions of Timothy's ministry tallies exactly with the "ordained offices" that emerge later in the second century (bishop, presbyter, deacon).

So the NT fails to provide us with unambiguous evidence for either ordination (as a ritual act) or orders (as a clearly defined, hierarchical set of offices in the Church). After the first generation of Church leaders (e.g., Paul; the Twelve) began to die out, the question of who could legitimately claim a mandate to minister grew more troublesome. Wandering prophets and preachers, who had doubtless been part of the Jesus movement from its earliest stages, were a source of increasing anxiety to those concerned to fix and preserve the "purity" of Jesus' teaching. Sources from the second (Luke/Acts) and third (the Pastoral Letters) generations of Christians reveal a tendency to limit or control the innovative impulses linked with charismatic preachers. Paul himself, certainly an innovator in his views about the mission to the Gentiles, is thus pictured by Luke as "ritually approved" for his job through a laying on of hands (Acts 13:1-3). Paul's companion Timothy is similarly depicted in the Pastorals (1 Tim 4:14).

The emerging picture of "ordination" in the NT should be viewed, therefore, in relation to the pastoral problems and leadership crisis that Christians of the second and third generations had begun facing. One cannot speak of a general custom of "ordaining" Church leaders at this period, though some persons chosen for special tasks (e.g., missionary work) did apparently receive a laying on of hands within the liturgical context of communal prayer and fasting.

Pastoral-Liturgical Tradition

During the century that followed the writing of the final NT documents, both the structures of Christian ministry and the liturgical rites of ordination underwent enormous development. By the beginning of the third century (ca. 215 CE), a full complement of prayers and rites for ordaining bishops, presbyters, and deacons is found in the *Apostolic Tradition* of Hippolytus of Rome. Although this document did not represent universal practice or consensus on the matter of ordination, it clearly signaled a crucial stage in the development of the tradition that limits the major Church leadership categories to three (bishop, presbyter, deacon) and links access to those ministries to communal rituals of prayer and laying on of hands. At the same time, in the work of Latin theologians like Tertullian (ca. 225 CE), the term "order" had begun to acquire the more technical and restricted meaning of "clergy."

Equally significant was an evolution in the interpretation of what ministry among Christians meant. In the NT the dominant image of ministry is mutual service, *diakonia*, in imitation of the One who "did not come to be served but to serve" (Mark 10:45). The language of priesthood in the NT is limited to Jesus (see Heb 3:1) and the Christian people (see 1 Pet 2:9); it is never used of individual ministers. But by the end of the first century, in sources outside the NT (such as the "Letter of Clement of Rome to the Corinthians," written ca. 96 CE), a new trend began to appear. Increasingly, Christian ministers were likened to Israelite priests of the second Temple, especially in their roles as leaders of the sacrificial cultus. Thus, the *Apostolic Tradition* of Hippolytus of Rome (written ca. 215 CE) speaks of the bishop as exercising the "high priesthood" and specifically links ordination to liturgical duties. In Hippolytus, bishops, presbyters, and deacons have already begun to monopolize *leitourgia*, even though they do not yet completely dominate *diakonia* (mutual service, ministry). St. Cyprian of Carthage (ca. 258) likewise emphasized the bishop's "high priestly" role, especially in relation to the liturgical functions of baptism, Eucharist, ordination, and the reconciliation of penitents.

Thus, by the beginning of the fourth century, the basic patterns for the ordination of bishops, presbyters, and deacons were well established in the West. The liturgical functions of these ministers were paramount, and (with the possible exception of the diaconate) women were excluded from the ranks of the ordained.

See: BISHOP, DEACON, MINISTRY, PRIEST

NATHAN D. MITCHELL

P

PARABLE

Old Testament

The use of parables reflects an ancient, culturally universal method of teaching an ethical lesson applicable to everyday life, by using symbolic stories with concrete characters and actions. Parables refer to open-ended metaphors, allegorical parallels to historical events, or short stories about God's covenantal fidelity and the community's way of being God-like in the world. The Hebrew *mashal* or figurative form of expression refers to a variety of non-literal material in the OT. *Meshalim*, which require imaginative interpretation, can be relatively short sayings, comparisons, or riddles. Longer units include allegorical reflections, a series of metaphors interspersed with commentary, and fiction-like teaching stories. What parables and parabolic expressions have in common are their metaphoric base, their application to specific theological, historical and ethical concerns, and the multiplicity of possible meanings for the believing community then and now. Parables should not be analyzed as separable, isolated literary forms. Rather, they should be contextualized within the pastoral vision of a particular biblical writer's entire work.

Ezekiel relies heavily on parabolic language, using metaphors of the burned wood of the useless grape vine (Ezek 15:1-8), and the uprooted vine which is re-planted in dry desert (Ezek 19:10-14). These describe the sad fortunes of exiled Israel, once God's chosen vine. In longer allegorical reflections that include commentary, Ezekiel takes as images for the consequences of Israel's religious infidelity an eagle which tears the crest off a cedar tree (17:1-24), a woman's adulterous betrayal of her faithful spouse (16:1-62), and the fortunes of two harlot sisters Oholah and Oholibah, representing Jerusalem and Samaria (23:1-49). Parabolic action or mime is performed by Ezekiel to warn Israel of the coming political disaster, as the building of a miniature siege-works around a tablet representing Jerusalem (4:1-8), and the cutting and ritual burning of his hair and beard (5:1-15).

Parabolic stories express warning and the call to conversion: e.g., Nathan's confrontation of David with the story of the rich man who seized the poor man's lamb (2 Sam 12:1-11) and the story of fratricide told to David by the woman of Tekoa (2 Sam 14:1-20). Telling the story, making its application, and David's conversion of heart all belong to a single narrative event. Isaiah's parable of the vineyard expresses both the possibility of Israel's fruitfulness and its production of sour grapes (Isa 5:1-7). The parable cannot be confined to the consoling description of what the vinedresser has done to ensure fertility, for the context of Isaiah 1–5 describes a scenario of invasion and woe.

Parabolic discourse can also instruct and console the community. The potter at the wheel confirms a promise that the house of Israel remains in the hand of the Lord (Jer 18:1-6). Two baskets of figs, one of them the early-ripening kind, illustrate the survival of Judah's exiles (Jer 24:1-10). The parable of the shepherd coming to rescue his sheep from irresponsible leaders consoles the community (Ezek 34:1-31), as does the surrealistic story of reassembled dry bones, signifying the house of Israel which comes back to life at the prophet's words (Ezek 37:1-14). Hosea takes as wife a known adulteress, a foolish choice enacting a living parable of God's loving commitment to Israel. God is waiting for the people to turn back and seek the one who is faithful (Hos 3:1-5; 2:1-3).

Restoration after exile is communicated through a variety of parabolic images. The desert itself miraculously begins to bloom like a garden, bursts open with rivers, and produces a highway upon which all the disabled can easily walk and sing their way to Jerusalem (Isa 35:1-10). Israel becomes a bride decked out for a wedding with God (Isa 61:10-11; 62:1-5), and Jerusalem is a birthing mother nursing many newborn children in comfort and safety (Isa 66:7-16). The final vision of Ezekiel is an elaborate parable of hope in the reconstruction of people and the city. Like an architect's master plan, the design of Jerusalem is redrawn and the new Temple measured by a man from heaven in the presence of the prophet (Ezek 40:1–48:35). Instructive in all these parabolic descriptions is the presentation of a rescuing God whose love transcends disaster, whose saving initiative is determined neither by the power nor impotence of the enemy, and whose continuing covenant bypasses seasons of the community's infidelity.

Are parables understood by the community to which they are addressed? Heard, spoken, or enacted, parables confront a community with a different picture of God or a more inclusive social vision than ones they have cherished. This can provoke resistance. Isaiah's entire prophetic message is to be parabolic. "Go and say to this people: Listen carefully, but you shall not understand! Look intently, but you shall know nothing! You are to make the heart of this people sluggish, to dull their ears and close their eyes. Else their eyes will see, their ears hear, their heart will understand, and they will turn and be healed" (Isa 6:9-10).

The NT writers use this passage in Isaiah 6 to comment on the mixed reception, often negative, that Jesus and the apostles meet in carrying out their prophetic mission to preach and teach (Matt 13:14; Mark 4:12; Luke 8:10; Acts 28:26; John 12:40). The challenge of Jesus at the end of a teaching session is double-edged, "Whoever has ears ought to hear" (Matt 13:9). True disciples of Jesus are those who are ready to receive wisdom and can think symbolically. The indirectness of parables makes the wisdom of Jesus inaccessible to hostile literalists. "The disciples approached him and said, 'Why do you speak to them in parables?' He said to them in reply, 'Because knowledge of the mysteries of the kingdom of heaven has been granted to you, but to them it has not been granted'" (Matt 13:10-11).

New Testament

When the Hebrew *mashal* is translated into Greek as *parabolē*, the term becomes more narrow, referring to Jesus' teaching stories, often about the reign of God. In retelling parables attributed to Jesus, evangelists echoed the imaginative use of language in the OT more than they drew on Hellenistic rhetorical usage of parabolic expression. It is unlikely that each of the forty or so parables in the Gospels was actually told by Jesus. Matthew and Luke reworked stories received from oral tradition, Mark and Q, adjusting them to suit the needs of their own communities.

The social setting of the parables reflects the first-century Mediterranean experience of a largely agrarian society. Such an audience would recognize the economic implications of losing a sheep (Matt 18:12-14), and the social shame endured by a father with a wayward son who runs off and squanders his inheritance (Luke 15:11-32). They would know how unthinkable it was to slight the honor of a king by refusing his invitation to dinner (Matt 22:1-14), and how dangerous the road from Jerusalem to Jericho for a man traveling alone, at the mercy of strangers who turn out to be thieves (Luke 10:29-37).

Some parables are common to all three Synoptics, such as the sower who went out to sow seed (Mark 4:1-12; Matt 13:1-9; Luke 8:4-10), describing four possible responses to hearing the message of Jesus. The sober message for disciples is that only one in four hearers will respond in a way that makes the preaching fruitful for their lives. The paradoxical story of tenants who resist the master's servants and kill the master's son is also a shared Synoptic tradition (Mark 12:1-11; Matt 21:33-46; Luke 20:9-19). It reflects an intense atmosphere of hostility between the Christian community and oppositional Jewish communities. The great feast or wedding banquet to which many were invited and some refused (Luke 14:16-24; Matt 22:2-10) also reflects the hostility between Jewish and Christian groups struggling for survival in a post-70 CE era after the destruction of Jerusalem.

Some parables are unique to Luke, who preserves the story of the good Samaritan (10:29-37), a commentary on the magnanimity of neighborly compassion. This sort of love reaches out to relieve suffering, despite violation of religious rules, social risks, and economic inconvenience. The dramatic scene contrasting the Pharisee and the tax collector (18:9-14) also calls attention to the exemplary disposition of the social outsider. The tax collector is acceptable to God, not because of his performance or status, but because he is receptive and vulnerable before God. A widow, desperate for a financial settlement of her estate, pesters the unwilling judge so persistently that the judge fears she will eventually get so mad she will

strike him (18:1-8). The message is both about persistence in prayer and the certainty of response from a God who hears prayers and sees that those who suffer injustice are requited.

While it is true that NT parables are dominated by men and male activities, women are also models for the true character of God. Their actions portray what the reign of God means. The yeast a woman kneads into dough makes everyone in the community, as it were, rise and be capable of satisfying the hunger of others (Matt 13:33). Like the searching shepherd, the woman is also a figure for God, who searches for the one missing coin needed to complete the monetary unit of ten pieces, much like a deck of cards that is useless if one is missing (Luke 15:8-10). A woman's world of ten lamp-carrying virgins (Matt 25:10-13) is offered as metaphoric parallel to the story of the three male servants given talents (Matt 25:14-30). Like the third servant who buries his money, five of the women prove to be foolish and unprepared for delay. Both parables describe how to live wisely and self-responsively in the world. Awaiting the arrival of the last day is imaged both by the master's judgment on men's productivity and the opening of the door to the wedding banquet, bringing joy to those women who endured to the end.

By parables, Jesus attempted to convey the true nature of a loving and benevolent God. God is like a merchant who sells everything in order to possess the single pearl, a people dearly loved and cherished (Matt 13:44-46). God is like a shepherd who rejoices at finding the stray, and doesn't punish it for wandering off (Matt 18:12-14). As a sign of hope* for a struggling community, Jesus' parables assure believers that the future of the reign of God is inevitable. The seed in the earth has a life of its own (Mark 4:26-29). A grain of mustard seed grows from insignificance to a supportive bush that welcomes all the birds of the air (Mark 4:30-32). The worrisome and threatening presence of evil in the midst of good is ameliorated by a farmer's wisdom that weeds and wheat grow together until harvest (Matt 13:34-30).

Parables reinforce the sayings of Jesus on community ethics, such as forgiveness. A negative example is the servant forgiven a huge debt by his master, who then refuses to forgive a small debt owed by a fellow servant (Matt 18:23-35). The ending of a parable may threaten the worst of consequences, exclusion from the community (Matt 5:26; 22:11-14). Self-interest, if not gratitude or compassion, is commended if it motivates a person to correct injustice. The steward calls in the master's debtors and reduces their debt by sacrificing his high commission on their loans, still assuring that his master will be paid the amount actually due. He trades his own financial gain for the longer-term support of people who will owe him favors after he loses his job (Luke 16:1-8). The story of the rich man who refuses to pay attention to the poor man Lazarus at his door states important values of the community: attention to the poor rather than avoidance of them, justice to those right at one's doorstop, and sharing of wealth with the needy (Luke 16:19-31).

While the Fourth Gospel does not preserve parables in the form of the Synoptic teaching stories, John does attribute OT parabolic language of covenant and restoration to Jesus. Jesus is described in the messianic image of the bridegroom by the Baptist (John 3:28-30), and he speaks of the mission to the Samaritans as a field white for harvest (John 4:35-38). Jesus is the good shepherd (John 10:1-8), reminiscent of Ezekiel 34, and speaks of himself as a living vine (John 15:1-7).

See: CONVERSION, COVENANT, DISCIPLE/DISCIPLESHIP, FEASTS, JUSTICE, MYSTERY, PRAYER, SEED, SHEPHERD, VINE, WISDOM

MARIE-ELOISE ROSENBLATT, R.S.M.

PAROUSIA

The Greek word *parousia,* meaning "presence" or "coming," was the normal word used for a person's presence or arrival (1 Cor 16:17; 2 Cor 7:6-7; Phil 1:26; in the LXX:

Jdt 10:18; 2 Macc 8:12; 15:21). It was used in the Greco-Roman world to describe official visits of a king or governor to a province of his empire (Latin *adventus*). It could also denote a helpful appearance of a god in authority and power.

New Testament

The word parousia appears twenty-four times in the NT; the concept is found in all strands of the NT. Parousia denotes Jesus' second coming in glory and is associated with the full completion of Jesus' work, the final coming of the reign of God, the resurrection from the dead, and the day of judgment. Other words used for the same idea include the passive form of the verb *phaneroun* ("to reveal"), used twenty-two times in the Johannine literature (e.g., 1 John 2:28; 3:2, 5, 8); *epiphaneia* ("epiphany") in Titus 2:13; 2 Timothy 4:1; 2 Thessalonians 2:8; and *apokalypsis* ("revelation") in 1 Corinthians 1:7; 2 Thessalonians 1:7; and 1 Peter 1:7.

Much of the NT imagery of the parousia is drawn from Jewish apocalyptic descriptions of the last things, such as the coming of the Son of Man in Daniel 7:13-14. The basic notion of a second coming derives from the OT idea that Yahweh was the Lord of history directing all to a goal, a reign of peace (Gen 49:8; Num 23:21). For the prophets there would be a day of reckoning for the Jewish people, a Day of Yahweh. This was eventually extended to embrace all history when Yahweh would finally conquer all evil powers and establish a reign that is extended to include not just Israel but the whole world (Isa 2:2-5; 9:2; 11:6-16; Jer 23:6; Hos 2:21-25; Zech 11:10).

With the coming of Jesus, OT expectations changed radically so that for Christians it is Christ's second coming that is now anticipated. Although in the Gospels the term parousia is found only in Matthew 24:3, 27, 37, 39, there are numerous sayings on the lips of Jesus about the coming of the Son of Man (Matt 10:23; 16:27-28; 24:30, 36-51; 25:31; 26:64; Mark 8:38; 9:1; 13:26, 35, 36; 14:62; Luke 9:26; 12:40, 46; 17:20-37; 18:8; 21:27). All three Synoptic evangelists describe signs in the heavens preceding the parousia (Matt 24:29; Mark 13:24; Luke 21:25-27).

In the Acts of the Apostles the expectation of Christ's return is articulated by the two heavenly messengers at the ascension, who explain to the disciples, "this Jesus who has been taken up from you into heaven will return in the same way as you have seen him going into heaven" (Acts 1:11).

Paul uses the term parousia in a variety of ways. Five times it refers to the expected coming of Christ (1 Cor 15:23; 1 Thess 2:19; 3:13; 4:15; 5:23). It also is used of the lawless one, the antichrist, who by his miracles tries to imitate Christ's parousia (2 Thess 2:9). It also denotes Paul's own outward appearance and the presence or arrival of his colleagues or of himself among his churches (1 Cor 16:17; 2 Cor 7:6-7; 10:10; Phil 1:26; 2:12).

The author of Hebrews asserts that Christ "offered once to take away the sins of many, will appear a second time, not to take away sin but to bring salvation to those who eagerly await him" (9:28).

The Time of the Parousia

Given our modern approach to logic and to time, the attitude of the early Church toward the time of the parousia is not easy for us to appreciate. In the Synoptic Gospels Jesus affirms that to the end we will be ignorant of the exact time of the parousia (Matt 24:36; Mark 13:32; Luke 12:40). Yet a number of texts such as James 5:7-8 suggest that it is near. Early Christians would have made a connection between the parousia and the destruction of Jerusalem, a symbol of the final judgment.

During the last hundred years of biblical exegesis there has been much emphasis on the delay of the parousia as problematic for the early Christians. Clear evidence from the NT is quite meager. The author of 2 Peter, who mentions the first parousia of Jesus in reference to the transfiguration (1:16), deals with criticism of the delay of the second coming in 3:4. The scoffers, seeing that nothing even in the second or third generation of Christians seemed to have changed radically could ask, "Where is the promise of his coming?" In answer, the author insists on the creative power of God's word, that God had already destroyed the world with the flood and that God does not measure time as humans do. Furthermore, God's slowness is a merciful opportunity for repentance. He then reasserts the traditional doctrine of the suddenness of the parousia.

A common opinion is that Luke, in his twofold volume, is dealing with the delay of the parousia (e.g., Luke 12:45; 19:11; 20:9; Acts 1:7). These quotations and the addition of a second volume with Acts show Luke's focus on the present interests of the Christian community, which pushes the focus on imminent parousia from center stage. Luke does not have Paul's concern about Jesus' preexistence or John's emphasis on the incarnation. Luke develops the time between the ascension and the parousia.

The realized eschatology* that is so prominent in John's Gospel seems to be the answer of the fourth evangelist to the indefinite delay of the parousia. Belief in the future eschatological events is rooted in the whole thinking of John and in the explicit future tests of John 5:27-29; 6:39-57; 12:48. But for John the beginning of these final events is already set in motion as victory, judgment, and eternal life are already present with Jesus' first coming (John 3:19; 5:24). In 1 John the parousia seems to be clearly assumed with a hope for the coming judge (2:28). The Book of Revelation does not use the term parousia, but its basic theme is one of ardent hope (1:1; 22:20). In 3:11 and 22:20 the glorified Jesus insists that he is coming quickly (cf. 1 Pet 1:5-9). Profound and beautiful portrayals are provided in such texts as 14:14-16; 19:11-16. In the last analysis the Book of Revelation is an invitation to pray "Come, Lord Jesus."

Pastoral-Liturgical Tradition

The doctrine of the parousia gives an essential biblical teaching that history has meaning and purpose and that Christ ultimately triumphs over evil. The various descriptions of signs of the end time (e.g., 1 Thess 4:15-18) are not intended to provide factual information about what the parousia will be like, but rather, employ symbols that evoke hope and give encouragement to believers in the interim. For those who anticipate it and eagerly await the parousia with love, it can make a profound difference to their behavior (1 Thess 5:23; Jas 5:7-8; 2 Pet 3:4, 12; 1 John 2:28). For a Christian it is no "pie-in-the-sky" escape but a challenge to be sober (1 Pet 4:7), to grow in holiness (1 Thess 3:13; 5:23; Rom 13:11-14), to use one's given time well in love, mutual encouragement, hospitality, and forgiveness (Heb 10:24-25), and, above all, to abide in Christ (1 John 2:8).

See: APOCALYPTIC, DAY OF THE LORD, ESCHATOLOGY, GLORY, HOPE, JUDGMENT, REIGN OF GOD, RESURRECTION, SIGN, SON OF MAN, TIME

SEAN P. KEALY, C.S.SP.

PASSION

The word "passion" derives from the Latin verb *patior*, to "bear" or "suffer." The Greek equivalent is *pascho*. The word has preeminently been used to refer to the suffering and death of Jesus as described in the passion narratives of the four Gospels.

The events surrounding the final hours of Jesus' life dominate the four Gospels. In Mark's Gospel, probably the first of the Gospels to be composed, the passion comprises the whole of chapters 14 and 15 and the forthcoming arrest, trial, torments, and death of Jesus are alluded to early in the Gospel story. Matthew and Luke follow Mark's lead. The passion takes up chapters 26–27 in Matthew, who follows essentially the same sequence of events as in Mark. In Luke the passion story covers chapters 22–23 and, along with the resurrection appearance stories, forms the pivot between the ministry of Jesus (= the Gospel) and the beginning of the church (= Acts). As in Mark, both evangelists reference the up-

coming events of the passion early in their Gospel stories and direct the "plot" of the Gospel toward this climactic event.

Not unexpectedly the Gospel of John has a passion story somewhat distinct from that of the Synoptics, yet here, more than anywhere else in the four Gospels, there are strong similarities among the four passion narratives. If anything, the passion plays a more dominant role in John's Gospel, commanding the whole of chapters 13 through 19, if one takes into account the long discourse of chapters 14–17. Frequent allusions to the passion also characterize the Fourth Gospel presentation of the public ministry of Jesus.

Although Paul gives scant attention to the narrative details of the passion, the sufferings and death of Jesus play a capital role in the theological vision of his letters. The death and resurrection of Jesus form the core redemptive event as well as the pattern for authentic discipleship. Through baptism one experiences the salvific death and triumphant resurrection of Jesus. This also holds true for such deutero-Pauline works as the Letter to the Ephesians. The suffering and death of Jesus also figure significantly in the distinctive theologies of other NT writings such the Letter to the Hebrews, the First Letter of Peter, and the Apocalypse.

Historical Causes of the Death of Jesus

Current biblical scholarship debates the precise historical circumstances that led to the arrest and crucifixion of Jesus of Nazareth. While knowledge about the history of this period of Palestinian Judaism has greatly advanced, it is still fragmentary.

Not unexpectedly the passion narratives themselves focus more intensely on the religious significance of Jesus' death and, therefore, the role of the Jews. The Gospels accurately report that Jesus was ultimately condemned by Roman authorities and publicly executed by crucifixion, which is a Roman form of capital punishment. However, in the body of the Gospel narratives leading to the passion stories, the evangelists focus on the mounting opposition of the religious leaders to the ministry of Jesus. It is not surprising, therefore, that within the passion narratives themselves, the role of the Jewish religious leaders is presented as more active than that of Pilate and the Romans.

Several historical factors probably led to the decision to arrest and execute Jesus.

The Style and Force of Jesus' Ministry. First of all, there is little doubt, as the Gospels themselves report, that Jesus' own ministry and teaching stirred opposition among some of the religious leaders of his time. Aspects of his interpretation of law, what may have been perceived as too liberal an association with marginalized Jews, his prophet-like critique of some religious leaders, and the vigorous emotions and reactions stirred by his dramatic powers of healing and preaching may have guaranteed Jesus some determined opponents among his contemporaries.

It is also likely that Jesus, in the eyes of some religious Jews, may have been perceived as claiming undue personal authority in his manner of interpreting the Law and the traditions of Israel.

The Increasingly Volatile Social and Political Atmosphere of First-Century Palestinian Judaism. In 70 CE, some thirty years after the death of Jesus, the Jews of Palestine would revolt against Roman rule. However, scholars caution against transposing the high tension of this later period back into the time of Jesus. While Palestine was under Roman domination during Jesus' lifetime, much of day to day civil administration was still in the hands of Jewish officials, as it had been in the days of Herod the Great (ca. 33–3 BCE). In most of the areas where Jesus exercised his ministry Jewish kings still ruled (Herod Philip in upper Galilee; Herod Antipas in lower Galilee), even though they were subservient to the Romans. Only in Judea and Samaria did the Romans exercise direct rule over Jewish subjects. But even here actual Roman presence in the form of troops or public officials was not dominant. In Judea and its capital city, Jerusalem, day to day administration was still overseen by the priestly aristocracy.

While there was no clear cut revolutionary movement during the time of Jesus, things were by no means tension free. Josephus reports a number of instances in which public disturbances broke out in Judea and Samaria in the early part of the first century. It is likely that for the sake of good public order the religious authorities of Jerusalem would not welcome a popular and possibly radical Jewish preacher whose message seemed to stir unrest and who was perceived as critical of traditional institutions and values.

Many scholars agree that Jesus' symbolic action against the Temple, reported in all four Gospels, may have been a dangerous step that galvanized the opponents of Jesus and brought some of the Jewish leaders and Roman authorities into an uneasy alliance to arrest him. The Jewish leaders would have been reluctant to give the Romans any excuse, however convenient, to crucify a Jew. At the same time, Roman rule, while firm, did not incline to rash or purely arbitrary violence. Only in the case of someone perceived to be actually or potentially dangerous to social order and only in circumstances and at a time when tensions were high and the possibility of a serious public disturbance acute, is it possible to conceive of this type of interaction.

The Role of the Romans. It is probable, therefore, that from a purely historical perspective, Jesus was arrested and handed over to the Roman authorities for trial and capital punishment because of a convergence of circumstances. The Synoptic Gospels identify the religious authorities as the driving force behind the arrest of Jesus, with Pilate assuming a somewhat reluctant and passive role (although the passion narratives ultimately present Jesus as formally condemned by Pilate, tortured by Roman soldiers, and executed by crucifixion).

What on the part of the Jewish authorities may have been an interrogation or a strategy session to determine what to do with Jesus takes on characteristics of a formal trial in the Gospel tradition.

Assessing the historical accuracy of this portrayal is difficult. John's Gospel seems to imply that Roman soldiers were also present when the Temple police arrested Jesus (18:3), suggesting to some scholars that the collusion between the Roman and Jewish authorities, if it existed, may have been in place prior to Jesus' arrest.

Debate about these issues is driven by more than academic historical interest. The Gospels' emphasis on the role of the Jewish authorities in the events leading to the death of Jesus has been used over the centuries as a justification for virulent anti-Semitism, a toxin that ultimately exploded in the genocide of the Holocaust. It is imperative that Christian interpreters of the Gospels be aware of the complexity of first-century history that stands behind the Gospel narratives. Whatever may have been the degree of involvement on the part of some first-century Jews in the now largely irretrievable historical circumstances leading to Jesus' death, it is clear that Judaism as a whole does not in any way bear that responsibility.

Evolution of the Passion Narratives

Some awareness of how the passion narratives may have been formed can assist in understanding their theological message.

Jewish Background. Although the Gospel passion accounts have a distinctive character of their own, some precedent for their literary style and basic theological motifs can be found in Jewish tradition.

Popular accounts of heroic Jews persecuted and tormented by their enemies and yet vindicated by God are already found in the Bible and in Jewish literature. The innocent and chaste Susannah threatened by death yet ultimately vindicated (Daniel 13), and the stories of Jewish heroes in the Maccabees who are horribly tortured yet remain steadfast and are promised vindication by

God (2 Maccabees 6–7), are some vivid examples. The relative sobriety of the Gospel accounts of the passion of Jesus contrast with the sometimes bloody stories of heroic Jewish martyrs, yet undoubtedly the tradition of the martyr helped the early Christians understand one dimension of the meaning of Jesus' death for others.

Another important tradition is that of the just Israelite who is innocent and faithful but has to endure ridicule and torment by persecutors. This powerful motif of suffering and vindication is exemplified in some chapters of the Wisdom of Solomon (chs. 2–5) and in the psalms, and both find echoes and even direct quotation in the passion stories themselves.

Another variation on this is the mysterious figure of the suffering servant as found in Isaiah 53. Here, too, an innocent Israelite, who may have been the King or some representative figure, bears suffering and rejection on behalf of Israel and through that suffering ultimately finds vindication with God and atonement for the people.

The psalms of lament are also an important biblical tradition that had influence on the passion story. The psalmist suffers physical and spiritual anguish, crying out to God for deliverance, and ultimately finding peace and triumph with God. The great lament, Psalm 22, for example, is mined by the passion stories and has had a strong influence on the crucifixion scenes in Mark and Matthew's passion stories.

These OT sources rest on a fundamental biblical conviction: that the God of Israel was a faithful, redeeming God who would bring the people and its faithful leaders from death to life, from slavery to freedom, from humiliation to exaltation. That fundamental creed, expressed in a variety of literary forms in the Bible, provides the starting point for early Christian reflection on the death of Jesus.

The Early Church. Scholars debate to what extent there was a formally shaped passion narrative prior to the writing of Mark's Gospel. It seems probable that the early

Christians remembered the basic information about the circumstances of Jesus' death (arrest; interrogation and trial before the Romans; crucifixion; burial) and used this fund of memory as the catchpoint for their reflection on the meaning of Jesus' death in the light of resurrection faith. Some scholars suggest that the passion story would have taken on personality in a liturgical setting similar to our Holy Week triduum if psalms, OT reflections, and prayer were woven into a remembrance of Jesus' final hours. Through this means, as well as in the preaching and catechesis of the community in other settings, the early Church developed a rich theology of the Cross, variations of which undoubtedly found their way into the Gospels themselves.

The Theologies of the Evangelists

Each evangelist tells the story of the passion in accord with the particular theological perspective and style of his Gospel as a whole.

Mark. Mark's account was most likely the first. The arrest, trial, and crucifixion of Jesus (chs. 14–15) are the climax of his powerful account of Jesus' ministry. Two major currents move through the account: Mark's portrayal of Jesus, and his portrayal of the disciples and other key characters in the story.

Mark's portrayal of Jesus within the passion is stark and gripping. Earlier in Mark's Gospel, Jesus had proclaimed his messianic mission as that of giving his life on behalf of the many (10:45) and had alerted his disciples to his impending passion (8:31; 9:31; 10:32-34). Now in the events of the passion, his messianic destiny would be fulfilled. At the Last Supper he reaffirms that his body would be broken and his blood shed "for the many" (14:22-24). In Gethsemane he prays for deliverance, yet that God's will may be done. Interrogated as a prisoner by the High Priest, Jesus breaks his silence only to affirm that he is, indeed, the Christ, the Son of the Blessed One, and the Son of Man who would come in triumph at the end of time (14:62). Faced with Pilate's questions,

Jesus' response to the question, "Are you the King of the Jews?" (15:2) is ambiguous ("You say so."), and then he falls silent.

The rest of Mark's account is grim, as Jesus submits to torment and ultimately crucifixion and death. Probably drawing on earlier traditions, Mark uses Psalm 22 ("My God, My God, why have you forsaken me?") as the final words of Jesus, suffusing the climactic scene of the passion story with this wrenching lament of the faithful Israelite under deadly assault. Jesus dies with a wordless scream (15:37).

Even within this stark passion story, Mark's theology of resurrection makes itself felt. At the moment of Jesus' death, the temple veil is torn in two—seeming to bring judgment on the Temple as Jesus' prophetic actions had threatened (11:15-19; see 14:58)—and the Roman Centurion who had led the execution detail, upon seeing the manner of Jesus' death, acclaims that indeed he truly was "the Son of God" (15:39). These marvelous portents prepare the reader for the discovery of the empty tomb where the "young man," a heavenly messenger, will proclaim the Easter message to the women: "Do not be amazed! You seek Jesus of Nazareth, the crucified. He has been raised; he is not here" (16:6). Thus God has raised Jesus and vindicated his messianic mission.

Parallel to this portrayal of Jesus in the passion is Mark's description of the disciples and other witnesses. Here the evangelist gives us a subtle portrayal of the meaning of the passion for discipleship. In chapter 13, immediately before the passion account, Jesus had warned the community of the persecutions and travails it would experience as it carried out its mission in history. In a sense, the passion of Jesus is a foretaste of the "passion" the community itself would have to endure.

The comportment of the disciples in Mark's account is not exemplary. Judas betrays Jesus, Peter denies his discipleship, and all of the disciples ultimately flee. Only a few characters respond faithfully: the woman who anoints Jesus in Bethany (14:3-

9); the Centurion at the cross (15:39); Joseph of Arimathea who provides Jesus with a fitting burial; the faithful women who stand by at the cross, witness his burial, and become the first messengers of the resurrection (16:1-8). Thus Mark demonstrates that suffering and persecution are a withering test for the community and must be met with faithful prayer and watchfulness (see 13:9-10; 14:38).

The final outcome for the disciples is predicted but not narrated in the original form of Mark's Gospel (16:1-8). As Jesus had prophesied at the supper (14:27-28), they would all fall away but after his resurrection he would go ahead of them to Galilee and there renew their discipleship. Thus resurrection in Mark also means a reconciliation with the fallen disciples and the restoration of the community's mission to the world.

Matthew. Matthew follows closely the storyline and much of the theological perspective of Mark yet leaves his own distinct imprint on the passion narrative. Some of the starkness of his portrayal of Jesus is relieved in that Jesus' prophetic knowledge of the impending events is more pronounced: he solemnly predicts the beginning of the passion (26:1-2) and he is in firm command even as he is arrested (26:50-56). The events that follow the death of Jesus are greatly expanded: cosmic signs erupt, signaling God's vindication of Jesus and the beginning of the final age (27:51-54). And Matthew sees the guiding principle of scriptural fulfillment in the passion story, as he does in the body of the Gospel (26:56; 27:9-10). For Matthew, Jesus is the obedient Son of God who was already tested in the desert as well as in the conflicts of his ministry, and who in the face of suffering and death remains faithful to God and thereby enacts his messianic mission.

As he is throughout his Gospel, Matthew is preoccupied with the response of the Jewish leaders. They decisively reject Jesus and choose Barabbas, even as Pilate (and his wife, 27:19) declare Jesus' innocence. The people as a whole take responsibility

for his death while Pilate attempts to wash his hands of guilt (27:24-25). This is part of Matthew's theology of history: Jesus is the fulfillment of God's revelation to Israel (5:17), bringing the law and the prophets to their intended purpose and ushering in the new age of salvation for all peoples. The death of Jesus is the turning point of history for Matthew; now the triumphant Son of God and vindicated Son of Man can charge his community to proclaim the good news to the nations (28:16-20). Thus, for Matthew, the rejection of the Messiah by Israel and the death of Jesus are one side of a divine paradox that now opens God's saving message to the whole world (including Israel if it is willing to welcome its Messiah, see 23:37-39).

Luke. Luke, too, draws on Mark's account but adapts it more freely to his own portrayal of Jesus. At the Last Supper, Luke extends Jesus' discourse to the disciples, introducing typical themes of his theology. Jesus' death models servant leadership in contrast to oppressive leadership (22:24-27). Satan, who tests Jesus in his public ministry and now returns for the events of the passion (22:3), would like to "sift" Peter and the community, but Jesus' sustaining prayer for them will rescue them from ultimate infidelity and confirm their role of leadership in the Easter community (22:28-32). Consequently in the passion story Luke downplays the failures of the disciples, not mentioning their flight, having Jesus look at Peter the very moment the disciple publicly disavows Jesus (22:61), and hinting at their distant presence at the moment of the crucifixion (23:49). This prepares for the story of Acts where Luke will present the Twelve apostles as the link between the story of Jesus and the emergence of the Spirit-filled Church.

As the passion story unfolds in Luke, Jesus is presented as the faithful Israelite who suffers unjustly but with great majesty and virtue. He prays with anguish and resolve on the Mount of Olives (22:39-46), heals the ear of the High Priest's servant at the moment of the arrest (22:51), forgives his executioners at his crucifixion (23:34), forgives the sin of the repentant criminal on the cross (23:43), and dies with words of resignation drawn from Psalm 31 (23:46). The Centurion who witnesses his death affirms Jesus' identity as the "just one" (23:47).

Luke's portrayal of Jesus in this manner also fits his casting of Jesus as a prophet-martyr in the body of his Gospel. Jesus witnesses to God's mercy and justice (4:16-30) and, like the prophets of Israel, must endure rejection and persecution (13:31-35). But through Jesus' resurrection and ascension, God's prophetic word is vindicated and the power of the Spirit will be unleashed on the world.

John. As one might expect, the passion narrative of John has unique features. Although the general cast of the narrative is similar to Mark's (arrest, interrogation and trial, crucifixion, burial), the tone and style are distinctive, reflecting John's theology as a whole.

The passion is the final moment in the exaltation of Jesus, the Incarnate Word, as he completes his mission of revealing God's love for the world and returns to his Father in glory. The long discourse (preceded by the footwashing in ch. 13) of chapters 14–17 is laden with Johannine themes, recapitulating his portrayal of Jesus as the one sent from God to reveal the Father's love for the world, to confront and judge evil, to gather a community of disciples who would give witness to Jesus' love command, and, finally, to send God's Spirit to the community and the world once Jesus has returned through death to God.

When John turns to the arrest of Jesus and the subsequent events, this powerful resurrection theology is close to the surface of the narrative. Thus Jesus seems fully in command, even though a prisoner: captors fall to the ground at his word (18:6); he dismisses his disciples rather than them fleeing (18:8-9); he challenges his interrogators (18:20-21); and in the dominant Roman trial scene (18:28–19:16), Jesus stands captive but majestic in his bearing before Pilate. In

fact, motifs of "kingship" dominate this scene and Jesus' crucifixion becomes a paradoxical kind of enthronement in which the "King of the Jews" is indeed "lifted up" in exaltation to proclaim his abiding love for humankind (19:18-22). Jesus' last words in John's Gospel are "it is finished" (19:30)—affirming that Jesus has indeed finished the work he was sent to accomplish (see 13:1).

John also plays upon Passover symbolism. Jesus is indeed the "lamb of God" (1:19, 35), his condemnation taking place at the very moment the Passover lambs are slain in the Temple. When the soldiers decide not to break his bones to assure death (thus unwittingly fulfilling Scripture) one of them drives a lance into Jesus' side, drawing out blood and water (19:34), haunting symbolism typical of John that suggests that from the crucified Jesus comes the power of the Spirit and the redeeming blood of the lamb.

The disciples do not figure prominently in John's narrative. As in the Synoptics, Judas betrays Jesus and Peter denies him, but the rest are absent from the narrative after the arrest scene. The important exception is the Beloved Disciple who ushers Peter into the courtyard of the High Priest (18:15) and, more importantly, stands as a witness at the foot of the cross along with the Mother of Jesus (19:26-27). In this famous scene unique to John, the crucified Jesus entrusts the mother to the son and the son to the mother, a final act that creates new community rooted in history yet constituted by faith in the Johannine Jesus such as is exemplified by this faithful disciple.

The Gospel passion narratives are, therefore, rich in theology and diverse in expression. No doubt the evangelists intended them to be a source of reflection for their own communities as they pondered the meaning of Jesus' death and the experience of that passion in the sufferings and losses of the community itself. The passion stories strong affirm Christian faith in Jesus as the redeeming Christ, whose death atoned for the sins of the world and who serves as the exemplar of authentic faith before the mystery of suffering. In the comportment of the disciples the community undoubtedly was meant to see a mirror reflection of its own weakness, both as warning and, ultimately, as a source of hope. Even though Peter and the disciples failed in the crucible of suffering they were not abandoned by the Risen Christ; his gracious love healed and restored their relationship with him.

See: DEATH, SUFFERING

DONALD SENIOR, C.P.

Pastoral-Liturgical Tradition

The Suffering of Jesus and His Mission. Contemporary theologians incorporate the findings of biblical scholarship concerning the relationship between the suffering* and death* of Jesus and his mission of proclaiming the reign of God. Reflection on the meaning of the passion of Christ for the life of the Church must keep in mind this connection between the Cross of Jesus and his fidelity to his mission. Jesus was executed as a criminal because his proclamation of the reign of God in word and deed was offensive to the religious and political authorities. Jesus would have recognized the hostility mounting against him, though he continued to offer the good news of salvation. Because of his inviolable trust in God, he was able to integrate the prospect of his own death into his self-understanding and his mission. Though his last hours were marked by intense suffering and powerlessness, the passion became Jesus' ultimate act of commitment to God and of loving service to others.

The Redemptive Significance of Christ's Sufferings. In the history of the Christian tradition, writers have consistently expounded the NT teaching about the redemptive significance of Christ's sufferings. Such an affirmation is possible only from the vantage point of the resurrection. It is because the person and mission of Jesus have been vindicated by God in the resurrection

that Christians can proclaim the salvific meaning of the passion. In the second century, Justin Martyr wrote that Christ's death procures the remission of sins and redemption from death (*Dialogue With Trypho,* 41, 111). Augustine understood the essence of redemption to consist in the expiatory sacrifice offered for us by Christ in his passion (*Enchiridion,* 41). In Medieval theology, Anselm worked out a detailed theology of redemption that centered on the satisfaction offered to God by Jesus through his obedient death (*Cur Deus Homo*). Anselm's thought influenced Thomas Aquinas, who elaborated on the fittingness of redemption through the sufferings and death of Christ (*Summa Theologiae,* III, Q. 46). This theory of satisfaction has played an important part in the thinking and the worship of the Church up to the present day.

There is a positive meaning to the sacrificial nature of Christ's sufferings, which is an essential part of the Christian tradition. Jesus' offering of salvation from God culminates in his self-offering on the cross. Christians believe that it is by means of this self-offering of Jesus in his passion, which is accepted and vindicated by God in the resurrection, that sin and death are overcome. This tradition about the sacrifice of Christ does not warrant an understanding of the passion as the appeasement of a wrathful God who was ready to condemn humanity. The ministry, passion, and resurrection of Jesus are embraced by the loving providence of God and are expressions of God's will that all people find salvation. The salvation of humankind by Christ has its source in the redeeming love of God.

The Memory of the Passion in Christian Liturgy and Devotion. The Christian tradition views the suffering, death, and resurrection of Jesus as the central mystery of the faith. It is this Paschal Mystery that is celebrated in the liturgy of the Church. Thus, the passion of Jesus is not simply an event of the distant past; it is a mystery that must be entered into by every believer. In baptism, Christians are immersed into the dying of Jesus so that they might also be raised to new life (Rom 6:3-5). In the celebration of the Eucharist, the community of faith "proclaims the death of the Lord until he comes" (1 Cor 11:26-27). It is the self-offering of Jesus in his passion that is remembered and made present in the Church's Eucharistic liturgy. All of those who participate in the Eucharist are drawn into union with Christ in offering themselves to God.

The memory of the passion of Christ has also been an important part of the preaching and popular devotion of the Church. In the second century, Melito of Sardis preached on the passion and marveled at the sufferings of Christ (*Homily on the Passover*). Egeria, a fourth-century pilgrim to Jerusalem, reported on the veneration of the cross on Good Friday. In the Middle Ages, Francis of Assisi was influential in the spread of popular devotion to the suffering Christ. The Medieval passion plays, beginning in the vernacular in France and Germany in the fourteenth century, became effective and influential ways of retelling the story of Christ's passion and resurrection. Devotion to the stations of the cross developed from the fourteenth century on, and this form of prayer continues today in a variety of cultural expressions.

The memory of the passion has also been a significant element in the mystical tradition of the Church. Women and men who have chronicled the way toward union with God have consistently taught the necessity of loving contemplation of the sufferings of Christ. They have held up the contemplation of Christ in his passion as the means by which believers can catch a glimpse of the indomitable love of God and can find the strength to offer their lives in loving service to God. In the eighteenth century, Paul of the Cross founded a religious community specifically committed to this memory of the passion of Christ, which he called "the greatest and most overwhelming work of God's love."

The Contemporary Passion of Christ. Christian theology and spirituality affirm that the passion of Christ is not merely an event of the past; Christ continues to be present in all of those who undergo suffering throughout history. Knowing that what is done for one of these least ones is done for Christ (Matt 25:40), believers are exhorted to recognize and respond to those who today experience the passion of Christ. It is the memory of the passion that impels believers to seek to alleviate the suffering around them. It is faith in the Christ who was condemned unjustly that leads Christians to express their solidarity with victims of injustice and to strive to change those social and political structures which cause suffering. Faith in the crucified Christ even leads to the recognition of the suffering of the earth, which has become a victim of the carelessness of humanity. The rich Christian tradition of the memory of Jesus' sufferings and death is a source of inspiration to believers in their mission to the crucified of today.

See: DEATH, JUSTICE, REDEMPTION, RESURRECTION, SACRIFICE, SALVATION, SUFFERING

ROBIN RYAN, C.P.

PASSOVER

This entry consists of three parts. The OT section considers the treatment of Passover in the liturgical calendars of ancient Israel and in the Deuteronomic, Chronistic, and Priestly traditions. It also examines the origin of this festival. The NT section studies the influence of imagery connected with the Passover on the Christian understanding of Jesus' death and resurrection. The pastoral-liturgical section describes the Passover as shaping the theology of the Eucharist and the Christian liturgical year.

Old Testament

Although the feast of Passover is important in the NT and in post-biblical Judaism, information about the feast during OT times is sparse and ambiguous. This information is found in such liturgical material as the descriptions of the ritual in Exodus

12, Numbers 28:16-25, and Ezekiel 45:21-24; the calendars of pilgrimage feasts in Exodus 34:25; Deuteronomy 16:1-8; Leviticus 23:5-8; and a narrative that legitimates observing the feast in the second month (Num 9:1-14). Some historical texts also contain descriptions; the first Passover (Exodus 12); the Passover of Joshua in Canaan (Josh 5:10-12); the Passover of Josiah (2 Kgs 23:21-23 [= 2 Chron 35:1-18]); a postexilic Passover (Ezra 6:19-22); and the Passover of Hezekiah in 2 Chronicles 30.

Liturgical Calendars. The oldest calendars (Exod 23:15; 34:18) mention a feast of Unleavened Bread but not the Passover. The Passover is mentioned in Exodus 34:25, but not in a listing of pilgrimage feasts. According to this text leavened bread was not to be offered along with the Passover sacrifice, nor was any part of the Passover sacrifice to be reserved for use the following day. The restriction against leavened bread harmonizes with the tradition that made unleavened bread a part of the Passover meal. The mention of unleavened bread in the account of the Passover celebrated by Joshua (Josh 5:10-12) should not be construed as evidence that the feasts of Passover and of Unleavened Bread were combined at an early date.

Deuteronomy. Deuteronomy 16:1-8 describes two distinct observances: one is Passover (vv. 1, 2, 4b-7), and the other, Unleavened Bread (vv. 3, 4a, 8). Passover is to be celebrated during Abib (March–April), but no specific date is given. The animal sacrificed could be from the flock or the herd, hence a calf, a sheep, or a goat. It was to be slaughtered at sunset, roasted, and eaten that same night. All of this was to take place "in the place which he [the Lord] chooses as the dwelling place of his name" (16:2), i.e., Jerusalem, not "in any of the communities which the LORD, your God, gives you" (Deut 16:5). Participants were then to return home.

The Feast of Unleavened Bread, a separate observance, lasted for seven days. During this time, the people ate the "bread of affliction" as a reminder of the night that marked the end of their oppression in Egypt (Deut 16:5). The final day was the occasion of rest and solemn assembly (Deut 16:8).

The description of the Passover ritual in Deuteronomy 16 undoubtedly governed the observance of the Passover directed by Josiah (2 Kgs 23:21-23). Missing from Josiah's Passover, however, is any mention of the feast of Unleavened Bread. Thus these two feasts were still being celebrated separately at this stage of the tradition. 2 Kings 23:21-23 does insist that there was a novelty about Josiah's passover. That novelty is the fact that Josiah made Passover a pilgrimage feast and required all participants to journey to his newly renovated Temple in Jerusalem for its observance; this was essentially the intent of Deuteronomy 16:1-8. Before Josiah's politically motivated religious reforms, Passover was observed in a family context (Exod 12:21-23). When Josiah tried to centralize worship in Jerusalem in order to solidify his hold on the nation, observance of Passover, along with that of the Feast of Unleavened Bread, was transferred out of this local context to Jerusalem and thus given the status of a pilgrimage feast.

The Chronicler retrojects the combination of the two feasts and the pilgrimage status for Passover into his description of Hezekiah's Passover (2 Chronicles 30).

Priestly Tradition. By the time this material (Exod 12:1-20, 40-51; Lev 23:5-8; Num 28:16-25) achieved its present form in the postexilic period, the feasts of Passover and Unleavened Bread had been combined. According to these texts, Passover was celebrated on the occasion of the full moon of the first month (March–April) of the year. On the tenth day, each family group selected an unblemished male yearling lamb. Four days later, "between the two evenings," i.e., at twilight, the lamb was slaughtered and its blood sprinkled on the doorposts of the house. During this night of full moon, the lamb was roasted whole and eaten. Care had to be taken that none of its bones were broken. Unleavened bread and bitter herbs were eaten along with the roasted lamb. Slaves and resident strangers could participate in the meal as long as they were circumcised. Any meat left over had to be burned.

The next day, the fifteenth day of the month, the seven days of Unleavened Bread began. Prior to that day, all leavened bread was destroyed. During the ensuing week only unleavened bread was eaten. On the first and the seventh day, both days of rest, there were religious gatherings.

Ezekiel 45:21 and Ezra 6:19-22 both connect the Passover and the Feast of Unleavened Bread. The 419 BCE "Passover Papyrus" from the Jewish colony in Elephantine, Egypt, reflects the same pattern.

Origin of Passover. According to Exodus 12, "Passover" refers to the Destroyer passing over the Hebrew homes during the tenth plague. The feast is thus given a historical setting and connected with the liberation of the Hebrew slaves from Egypt. Linguistic links have been suggested between Hebrew *pesaḥ*, an Akkadian verb meaning "to appease," and an Egyptian noun meaning "a stroke" or "a blow." But removal of sin is not the aim of the ritual. The Egyptian connection would commemorate the death of the firstborn of Egypt, an unlikely association for an Israelite feast.

The ritual itself suggests a pastoral setting, shepherds and their flocks. It required neither priest nor altar; its central symbol is the blood of the sacrificed animal. Behind the feast is a springtime ritual observed by shepherds. Originally, a young animal was sacrificed to secure fertility for the entire flock; its blood was put on tent poles to ward off demons and evil spirits. The narrative of the tenth plague in Exodus may have been designed to link this custom to the liberating action of Israel's God and to provide a historical basis for the feast. The original ritual would have been celebrated in the spring when shepherds left winter headquarters in search of new pastures. Many features support this view: the lamb was roasted, eaten with unleavened bread and bitter (= wild) herbs; participants were

dressed ready for an early departure. The later texts that set a date for the festival, fourteenth–fifteenth Abib (later Nisan), the brightly lit night of the full moon, also reflect the pastoral origins of this feast.

Passover, then, derives from pastoralist tribes who eventually became part of Israel. It pre-dates the Exodus and is probably the feast for which the Hebrew slaves petition Pharaoh for permission to observe (Exod 5:1).

The Passover took precedence over Unleavened Bread in determining the date on which the feast would begin. On whatever day of the week the full moon occurred, Passover was celebrated. The feast of Unleavened Bread began on the next day and lasted a week. Both springtime feasts were eventually reinterpreted as a commemoration of the Lord's liberation of his people from Egypt.

See: EXODUS, FEASTS

KATHLEEN S. NASH

New Testament

The Jewish feast of Passover has exercised a dominant influence on the Christian understanding of the meaning of Jesus' death and resurrection. Because Jesus died during the Passover Festival in Jerusalem, Jesus' saving sacrifice is associated with the Passover sacrifice and meal and thus with God's primordial act of saving Israel from slavery in Egypt (Exodus 11–13). In the Synoptic Gospels Jesus' last supper with his disciples is the Passover meal (Matt 26:17; Mark 14:12; Luke 22:7). Matthew introduces the passion narrative with an explicit connection between Passover and Jesus' crucifixion: "You know that in two days' time it will be Passover, and the Son of Man will be handed over to be crucified" (26:2). Luke too dwells on the special and final significance of this Passover meal by having Jesus say to his disciples: "I have eagerly desired to eat this Passover with you before I suffer, for, I tell you, I shall not eat it [again] until there is fulfillment in the kingdom of God" (22:15-16).

Jesus' giving of his body and blood in the blessing of the bread and wine of the meal (Matt 26:26-29; Mark 14:22-25; Luke 22:19-20) both identifies him with the lamb sacrificed at Passover and symbolizes his unity with his followers in a sacred, sacrificial meal like that of Passover. The mention of the covenant in the account of the Last Supper (Matt 26:28; Mark 14:24; Luke 22:20) recalls God's fidelity to Israel in Egypt and Israel's salvation both through the blood of the lamb on their doorposts (Exod 12:21-23) and the death of the first-born Egyptians (Exod 12:29-32). This complex of OT symbols is focused by Matthew specifically on salvation from sin through forgiveness (26:28). All the Synoptics bind together past and future into the present. The Eucharistic formula embedded in the Gospels requires that the followers of Jesus do this (the special Passover meal) in remembrance of Jesus. Thus the OT Passover, Jesus' Passover, death and resurrection, and the community's celebration are experienced and understood as one. Likewise, the future messianic banquet that the saved will enjoy with God and Jesus in the reign of God is foreshadowed by Jesus' meal with his disciples.

In the Gospel of John Jesus eats his meal with his disciples and dies before the feast of Passover (13:1; 18:28) begins, rather than on the feast of Passover as in the Synoptics (Mark 14:12). However, John embeds Jesus' death in the Passover ritual. Jesus dies on the Preparation Day for the Passover, when the Passover lambs were being sacrificed in the Temple. Jesus' legs are not broken so that like the Passover lamb, "not a bone of it will be broken" (John 19:36; Exod 12:46). The branch of hyssop used to offer a wine-soaked sponge to Jesus recalls the hyssop branches used to smear blood on the doorposts during the original Passover (Exod 12:22).

References and allusions to the Passover and Exodus are frequent in John. In the introductory hymn John alludes to the first Passover when he says that the "Word became flesh and made his dwelling [lit. "tents"] among us" (1:14), recalling the presence of God in the Tent of Meeting in the desert (Exodus 40). Jesus is introduced as the Lamb of God by John the Baptist and is compared to Moses several times (1:17; 5:45-47; 6:31). Both the manna (6:31; Exodus 16) and water from the rock (7:38-39; Exodus 17), which sustained Israel in the desert, are used to explain Jesus' effect on believers. The bread of life discourse (ch. 6), given during the Passover season (6:4), anticipates the symbolic meaning of Jesus' death and its remembrance in the Christian sacred meal through Jesus' command to eat his body and drink his blood in order to gain eternal life. Jesus' final instruction and encouragement of his disciples (chs. 13–17) binds up communal unity, union with God, resistance to evil, and love with Jesus' death for us and service of one another (the washing of the disciples' feet, 13:1-20).

Allusions to Passover imagery occur elsewhere in the NT. In the Book of Revelation the paradoxical symbol of a "Lamb that seems to have been slain" (5:6 and twenty-seven more times) is the dominant metaphor for Jesus. The Lamb has triumphed over evil by his sacrificial death, and those who have been saved by him "have survived the time of great distress; they have washed their robes and made them white in the blood of the Lamb" (7:14). The sacrifice of the Passover Lamb, the death of Jesus on the cross, and the deaths of Christian martyrs all contribute to the defeat of evil and the salvation of the faithful. The Lamb has ransomed humans by his blood (5:9) and the saved conquer their accusers (12:11). Jesus' death as ransom from the slavery of sin is explicitly recalled in the exhortation found in 1 Peter as well: "Do not act in compliance with the desires of your former ignorance, but, as he who called you is holy, be holy yourselves in every aspect of your conduct. . . . Conduct yourselves with reverence during the time of your sojourning, realizing that you were ransomed from your futile conduct, handed on by your ancestors, not with perishable things like silver or gold but with the precious blood of Christ as of a spotless unblemished lamb" (1 Pet 1:14-19). The holiness of the Temple and people, the sojourning in the desert and the Passover sacrifice are all mobilized to throw light on what is at stake in daily Christian life. Finally, Moses' faith in God during the first Passover is invoked in the Letter to the Hebrews (11:28) as a model for Christian faith in Jesus.

See: PASSION, SACRIFICE, TEMPLE

ANTHONY J. SALDARINI

Pastoral-Liturgical Tradition

While there is no clear resolution to the question of whether or not the Last Supper was a Passover meal, there is no doubt that it occurred within a Passover context. This Passover context was determinative for the shape of the Christian liturgical year and the theology of Christian Eucharist.

Many scholars believe that an annual observance of the death of Jesus was celebrated by the primitive community from the very beginning. Such a celebration would have taken its cue from the annual Jewish Passover, which was remembered as the context for Jesus' death and resurrection. The Exodus images of liberation, covenant, and redemption, combined with the various sacrificial and memorial rites that comprised the Jewish Passover celebration of the first century, would have provided an exceedingly rich setting for the remembrance of the death of Jesus.

The Passover meal itself took place on the evening of the first full moon of Spring. Since the Jewish day begins at sundown, the meal would have begun after sundown on the fifteenth of Nisan. Jews observed a brief fast before the Passover festival. This fast, begun in the late afternoon on the "day of preparation" (about 3:00 p.m. on the fourteenth Nisan), ended with the Passover meal after sundown. Scholars conjecture that while the Jews celebrated the ritual meal, the followers of Jesus continued the fast, keeping vigil through the night (Thomas Talley, *The Origins of the Liturgical Year*). There is no clear evidence what these early believers did during the vigil, though it is possible that they retold the stories of Jesus' passion, death, and resurrection. Toward dawn they may have celebrated Eucharist which, from early on, was interpreted through the prism of Jewish sacrifices, especially Passover.

Clear evidence for an annual celebration of the death of Jesus at Passover first appeared in the second century. The Ethiopic version of the *Epistula Apostolorum* (ca. 140–160 CE) contains this apocryphal address of the risen Christ to the apostles, "And you therefore celebrate the remembrance of my death, i.e., the Passover" (ch. 15). The late second century was also the time of a celebrated dispute concerning this annual celebration in Rome. Some second-century Asian Christians living in Rome remembered their tradition of annually commemorating the death of Jesus on the fourteenth Nisan (thus their name: *quartodecimans*). Rome did not have such a custom. The Asian Christians complained about this lacuna to their bishop, Polycrates of Ephesus, who wrote to the Victor (+198) bishop of Rome hoping to correct this error (Eusebius, *Ecclesiastical History* 5.24). Polycrates, who was at least sixty-five years old at the time, noted that he had always celebrated Pascha on the fourteenth Nisan, and he cited numerous precedents for this practice, suggesting its apostolic origins.

It thus appears that in the second century the ancient tradition for annually celebrating the death of Jesus beginning on the preparation day for Passover (which could have fallen on any day of the week) came into conflict with a more recent tradition of celebrating this annual festival on a particular Sunday. Talley suggests that the Roman church may have introduced this annual Sunday festival around the year 165 CE, though there is evidence that a Sunday "*Pascha*" was established in Palestine and Alexandria earlier.

This history illustrates that the annual celebration of the Christian *Pascha* is rooted in the Passover memory of the death of Jesus, and wedded to traditional Passover

705

images of sacrifice, exodus, and liberation. This focus on Jesus' death, central to primitive understandings of the Eucharist, is already reflected in Paul (1 Cor. 11.26). It is also at the heart of the Paschal homily of Melito of Sardis (ca. 165 CE) who wrote, "It is he [Christ] who endured every kind of suffering in all those who foreshadowed him. In Abel he was slain, in Isaac bound, in Jacob exiled, in Joseph sold, in Moses exposed to die. He was sacrificed in the Passover lamb, persecuted in David, dishonored in the prophets" (no. 99).

It is ironic that, although Passover was the context for the central events of our redemption, Christians lost esteem for this great festival. Anti-semitism undoubtedly contributed to the establishment of an annual date for Easter that would never coincide with the first day of the Jewish Passover. Holy Week rituals of the Church grew increasingly anti-semitic, slandering the Jewish community at the core of the Good Friday liturgy. Christians and their worship intentionally ignored their Jewish roots. In medieval Europe, Passover became synonymous with persecution of the Jews. At Passover Jews were particularly accused of "blood libel," i.e., of murdering non-Jews, especially Christians, in order to obtain blood for Passover and other rituals. Numerous massacres of Jews occurred during the Middle Ages around Passover time because of such false allegations.

One aspect of this century's ecumenical and liturgical movements has been acknowledgement of our common bond with Judaism. As Vatican II decreed, "Since the spiritual patrimony common to Christians and Jews is . . . so great, this sacred Synod wishes to foster . . . that mutual understanding and respect which is the fruit above all of biblical and theological studies and of brotherly dialogues" (*Nostra Aetate*, no. 4). Liturgical scholarship has made great strides in demonstrating the Jewish roots of many of our worship practices. The influence of the Passover on the emerging Christian Eucharist and liturgical year has received particular attention.

Pastorally we have changed the solemn intercession on Good Friday from a prayer for "the faithless Jews" to a prayer for "the first to hear the word of God." Official directives also note that the Good Friday "Reproaches" are particularly susceptible to anti-semitic interpretation, and for this reason substitute music is suggested. In general, the reformed Triduum respectfully acknowledges the importance of Passover for understanding and celebrating what the exsultet calls "our passover feast."

One consequence of Christians' reappropriation of their Jewish roots has been the growing custom for Christians to celebrate the Passover meal during Holy Week. While well intentioned, such celebrations could be interpreted as inappropriate or even sacrilegious by Jews, especially if the rites are adapted for Christian usage. Official directives note: "When Christians celebrate this sacred feast among themselves the rites of the *haggadah* for the seder should be respected in all their integrity. The seder . . . should be celebrated in a dignified manner and with sensitivity to those to whom the seder truly belongs. The primary reason why Christians may celebrate the festival of Passover should be to acknowledge common roots in the history of salvation. Any sense of 're-staging' the Last Supper of the Lord Jesus should be avoided" (*Bishops' Committee on the Liturgy Newsletter* 16 [1980] 204). More appropriate than Christians celebrating Passover amongst themselves is accepting the invitation to celebrate this sacred rite with Jews. Such offers us an unrivaled experience for discovering the richness of this ancient festival.

See: EUCHARIST, EXODUS, MEAL, MOON PASSION

EDWARD FOLEY, CAPUCHIN

PAUL

In Paul contemporary Christians meet a man of extraordinary knowledge and love of what it means to be human. He loved his sisters and brothers, and he lived in them. He felt their pain, and he turned to them for comfort. He rejoiced with those who were rejoicing, and he wept with those who were weeping. Paul was born in the Diaspora Jewish community of Tarsus, and he later moved to Jerusalem to be trained as a Pharisee. His experience of the risen Lord changed his life with its call to become a missionary to the Gentile world. He founded base communities throughout Asia Minor, Macedonia, and Greece. A letter writer and a man of prayer, Paul may also be, as some have called him, the second founder of Christianity.

I. LIFE AND LETTERS.

Diaspora Jew in Tarsus: Pharisee in Jerusalem

Paul was born some time between 4 BC and 10 CE in Tarsus, the capital of the Roman province of Cilicia in Asia Minor. He was raised in a minority Jewish community away from Palestine, like those that Jews established across the Roman Empire. Paul received his early education in Tarsus, a center of Hellenistic culture, philosophy, and education, whose schools surpassed those of Athens and Alexandria. Paul learned Greek, was exposed to philosophy, and absorbed the Hellenistic religious view of the world. Within the Jewish community Paul became deeply convinced that he was "of the race of Israel, of the tribe of Benjamin, a Hebrew of Hebrew parentage" (Phil 3:5). In the synagogue each Sabbath, Paul learned that observing the Mosaic Law was more important to Jews in the Diaspora than the Temple sacrifices in Jerusalem. His religious formation as a Jew, combined with an appreciation of Hellenistic culture, laid a foundation for Paul's mission to the Gentile world.

As a young man, Paul moved to Jerusalem where he was formed, trained, and educated as a Pharisee to teach and interpret the Mosaic Law. Paul found Jews whose piety was grounded in the land of Palestine and centered in the Temple sacrifices. With them he celebrated the Jewish feasts: Passover, Tabernacles, Pentecost, Atonement, Dedication. As a dedicated Pharisee, Paul strove to understand and live the Mosaic Law: "in observance of the law a Pharisee, in zeal I persecuted the church, in righteousness based on the law I was blameless" (Phil 3:5-6). Paul's right relationship with the God of Abraham, Isaac, and Jacob was based on doing the works of the law, and Paul persecuted Christian-Jews because he saw them as a threat to the law (Gal 1:13; 1 Cor 15:9; Phil 3:6).

Experience of the Risen Lord

About 35 CE, God was pleased to reveal the Son to Paul so that Paul might preach Christ among the Gentiles (Gal 1:13-17); the risen Lord appeared to Paul (1 Cor 15:8-11); Paul saw the Lord (1 Cor 9:1-2). Paul's experience was a "conversion" in that Jesus Christ replaced the Mosaic Law as the center of his life with the God of Israel. Remaining a convinced Jew, Paul began to know that the God of his ancestors now intended to save the world in and through Jesus Christ crucified and risen from the dead.

God took the initiative in revealing the Son to Paul, and Paul heard, trusted, and received God's revelation as an unearned, undeserved, and unexpected gift. His greatest asset was no longer the Jewish Law but that he "may gain Christ and be found in him, not having any righteousness of my own based on the law but that which comes through faith in Christ, the righteousness from God, depending on faith to know him and the power of his resurrection and the sharing of his sufferings by being conformed to his death, if somehow I may attain the resurrection from the dead" (Phil 3:7-11).

Missionary to the Gentiles: Martyr in Rome

God also revealed that Paul was to preach Jesus Christ to the Gentile world, and Paul dedicated the rest of his life to founding communities in Asia Minor, Macedonia, and Greece. He was convinced that he was as much an apostle as the other apostles because like them he had seen the risen Lord (1 Cor 15:8-10). For the first three years Paul's activities centered around Damascus and the area to the southeast (Gal 1:17). He then went to Jerusalem to meet with Peter (Gal 1:19-20).

With Antioch in Syria as his base Paul worked to establish communities in Syria and Cilicia. Subsequently he struck across Asia Minor, and founded his first churches in Europe. He stayed eighteen months in Corinth (Acts 18:11) where he wrote 1 Thessalonians, probably in the summer of 50 CE. Paul then went to Jerusalem with the delegation from Antioch to resolve the conflict about whether the Mosaic Law continued to be valid (see Gal 2:1-10; Acts 15:1-35). Shortly afterwards, Paul confronted Peter in Antioch about his hypocritical behavior. Peter did not observe Jewish dietary laws when he first came to Antioch, but he later withdrew from table fellowship with Gentiles because of pressure from Jerusalem (see Gal 2:11-14).

As Paul preached the good news about Jesus Christ, he understood his experience of the risen Lord. Successes and failures, as well as struggles within the communities he founded, led Paul to the comprehensive view of the Christian life that we find in his letters. From Ephesus, where Paul stayed for over two years (Acts 19:10), he wrote Galatians, Philippians, Philemon, 1 Corinthians, and part of 2 Corinthians. These letters disclose the controversies in which Paul was involved. Jewish-Christian missionaries attempted to persuade the communities in Galatia and Philippi that Gentile members had not only to believe in Jesus Christ but also to be circumcised and observe the Mosaic Law. Different factions in Corinth claimed a special wisdom that so transformed them that they were already leading the life of the resurrection.

During his stay at Corinth (winter, 55–56 CE) Paul wrote Romans in anticipation of his visit to that capital city. The next spring, with a delegation of fellow Christians, Paul left Corinth for Jerusalem carrying a collection for the Jewish-Christian community. When Paul visited the Temple, some Jews from Asia Minor, aware that he preached belief in Jesus Christ without observing the Mosaic Law, seized Paul and threatened to kill him. Roman authorities sent him to Felix, the Roman procurator in Caesarea Maritima, who kept Paul in prison for two years (56–58 CE). When Paul appealed to Caesar, Porcius Festus, the new procurator, sent him to Rome. Arriving in Rome in early 59 CE, Paul was kept under house arrest for two years (59–60 CE). Paul was martyred in Rome around 60–61 CE or after a second imprisonment under Nero around 64–65 CE.

Pastoral-Liturgical Tradition

Within twenty years after Paul's death different strains of his thought developed within the communities he influenced. Colossians (ca. 62–70 CE) and Ephesians (date uncertain) honored Paul as one who speaks with the authority of the apostles on whom the Church is founded (Eph 2:20). The wall of hostility between Jews and Gentiles has broken down, since both are reconciled to God as one body through the cross (Eph 2:11-22). Second, the author of Luke/Acts (ca. 85 CE) idealized Paul as embodying God's plan to spread Christianity from Jerusalem to Rome and to the ends of the earth. But the author showed no knowledge of Paul's letters. In Rome, Luke's Paul indicates that Jews are permanently closed off from the gospel and that salvation is for the Gentiles (Acts 28:25-28). Finally, the author of 1–2 Timothy and Titus (ca. 100/110 CE) insisted on church structure and the appointment of church officials. Such various interpretations of Paul are found in writings that were attributed to Paul in the time after his death.

This process has continued down to our own day. After Vatican II we stand at a great distance from Paul in personality and temperament, in historical situation, in background and culture, in our experience of God, and in our call to mission. But when we listen to Paul's letters in our liturgy and dialogue within our prayer, we let him inform and influence how we live today as Christians in our unique historical situation.

See: APOSTLE, COMMUNITY, CONVERSION, EPISTLE/ LETTER, FERTILE, GOOD NEWS, NATIONS, PHARISEE

WILLIAM G. THOMPSON, S.J.

PEACE

Peace is more than the absence of strife. It is the state of fulfillment that results from harmony and well-being. It comes to us as a blessing from God, but it is also the goal toward which we strive.

Old Testament

Peace (*šālôm*) in the OT refers to the harmony a person experiences when relationships with God, with community, and with self are properly ordered. Peace is a dynamic reality that persons may receive (Ps 85:9) or pursue (Ps 34:15). Even though human acts and decisions are significant factors in the presence or absence of peace, peace is more a consequence of right ordering of one's life with God, others, and nature than a reality that one can construct through correct procedures and plans. This right ordering or obedience to God results in the idyllic scene of peace such as God promises in Leviticus 26:3-7:

> If you live in accordance with my precepts and are careful to observe my commandments, I will give you rain in due season, so that the land will bear its crops, and the trees their fruit; your threshing will last till vintage time, and your vintage till the time for sowing, and you will have food to eat in abundance, so that you may dwell securely in your land. I will establish peace in the land, that you may lie down to rest without anxiety. I will rid the country of ravenous beasts, and keep the sword of war from sweeping across your land. Your will rout your enemies and lay them low with your sword.

This picture of peace as a gift from God is confirmed by the multitude of factors (e.g., weather, absence of foes, freedom from faults) which need to converge for the creation of a comprehensive and lasting peace.

But even for the peace that the OT regards as normal or minimal for everyday life, this harmony or equilibrium is fragile. The hope for peace then rests with God: "I will appoint peace your governor, and justice your ruler" (Isa 60:18). Only such divine oversight and assistance can assure the proper ordering of creation which the OT refers to as *šālôm*, "peace."

Everyday Life. Israelites typically greeted one another by asking about each other's *šālôm*. An equivalent greeting in English would be, "How is it going?" Such a conventional greeting often expects the response, "fine," where the primary intention of the greeting is to communicate mutual concern. Nevertheless, such a greeting can open the way to a more extended exchange of information about one another's welfare. For example, when Moses returns to his father-in-law Jethro in Sinai after the Exodus from Egypt, Jethro and Moses "asked after one another's *šālôm*" (Exod 18:7). When Elisha saw the Shunammite woman coming from a distance, he sent his servant Gehazi: "Hurry to meet her, and to ask if all is well with her, with her husband, and with the boy, and she replied, '*šālôm*'" (2 Kgs 4:26). This conventional greeting then opened the way for the woman to present her plea to Elisha on behalf of her deceased son (see also Gen 29:6; 1 Sam 25:6).

Blessings or best wishes upon departure also took the form of statement about a person's *šālôm*. When Hannah departs from the sanctuary at Shiloh, the priest Eli says: "Go in peace, and may the God of Israel grant what you have asked of him" (1 Sam 1:17; see Exod 4:18). Such blessings communicate not only the current harmonious relationship of the individuals but also their wishes for well-being and wholeness in new environments.

Peace in the Face of Conflict. In conflict situations, the well-being (*šālôm*) of an individual or of one group or nation is perceived to be at odds with the well-being of another. The attitudes or intentions of individuals promote either peace or conflict as the psalmist says: "Too long did I live among those who hated peace. When I spoke of peace, they were for war" (Ps 120:6-7). The rivalry between Joseph and the sons of Jacob for their father's esteem led to a murderous conflict in which the brothers could not even greet Joseph (i.e., ask about his *šālôm*, Gen 37:4).

When conflicts break out into violence, the combatants focus upon winning and define their well-being accordingly. When the warrior Gideon speaks of a victory in battle over the Midianites, he refers to his triumph as coming back in *šālôm*, "in well-being." Gideon perceives his well-being and that of the Midianites to be incompatible. After the quelling of Absalom's revolt, David asks of the messenger reporting the outcome: "Is Absalom safe [*šālôm*]? (2 Sam 18:32). Because the revolt was a life-or-death struggle, David's army could not conceive of Absalom's *šālôm* coexisting with David's *šālôm*. Absalom was slain immediately upon his capture (2 Sam 18:14).

The Israelites regularly made treaties with their neighbors so that the well-being of each might be protected (Deut 2:26; Josh 9:15; Gen 26:31). The Deuteronomic law states: "When you march up to attack a city, first offer it terms of peace" (Deut 20:10).

The Israelites hoped that a king would secure their well-being (Ps 72:7). However, their kings were usually not able to meet the demands of the people's *šālôm* and so the hope for an ideal king arose, a "prince of peace" (Isa 9:5; see Mic 5:4; Zech 9:10).

God's Gift of Peace. The Israelites increasingly came to understand peace as a gift from God whereby they came into harmony with God's will for them and all creation. The psalmist proclaims this truth simply and directly, "In peace I shall both lie down and sleep, for you alone, Lord, make me secure" (Ps 4:9). Through the trauma and chastisement of the Exile, the Israelites were challenged to bring their lives into harmony with the will of the creator, for Yahweh brought them both their peace and their troubles (Isa 45:7). Yahweh chastised the

people of Jerusalem in order to bring them a lasting peace, as spoken in Trito-Isaiah: "I will spread well-being [shalom] over her like a river, and the glory of nations like an overflowing river" (Isa 66:12; see Job 25:2).

Those who are faithful acknowledge that their peace comes from trust in Yahweh (Isa 26:3; see 26:12). Jeremiah envisions the Lord saying to a restored Jerusalem: "Behold, I will treat and assuage the city's wounds; I will heal them, and reveal to them a lasting peace" (Jer 33:6). Yahweh has fought against Jerusalem and punished her (Jer 12:12; 25:7), but such judgment was, according to Jeremiah, aimed at increasing the *šālôm* of the exiles (29:11). In a more radical attack upon a nationalistic, inward-looking view of peace, Jeremiah exhorted the exiles to pray for Babylon since he saw that the *šālôm* of the exiles was linked to the *šālôm* of Babylon. Jeremiah was regarded as a traitor by many Jerusalemites for claiming that Yahweh would work for his faithful people apart from Jerusalem and Zion (Jer 38:4).

The upright will walk in peace (Isa 57:2), but the wicked "do not know the way of peace" (Isa 59:8). Because the people of Jerusalem rebelled against Yahweh's rule, they were taken into exile. Then Yahweh promised to enter into a "covenant of peace" (Ezek 34:25-30) which mirrors the paradisiacal harmony described in Leviticus 26:3-6. This covenant of peace was a pledge by Yahweh to turn aside from wrath and to dwell with the offspring of Jacob and David forever (Ezek 37:26-27; see Isa 54:10). Hezekiah's life-threatening illness, which reflected in personal terms the trauma of Jerusalem besieged by the Assyrians, was turned aside by Yahweh, and so Hezekiah could claim that he experienced bitterness for his own well-being (Isa 38:17). In other words, a chastening illness brought him into greater harmony with God, with others, and with himself. The figure of the Servant in Isaiah 53 highlights the transformative role of suffering in producing wholeness or harmony: "Upon him was the chastisement that makes us whole *[šālôm]*, by his stripes we were healed" (v. 5).

The understanding of *šālôm* by Hezekiah and the Servant of Isaiah 53 stands in stark contrast with the complacency and deceit of the false prophets of peace denounced by Micah (Mic 3:5), Jeremiah (Jer 4:10; 6:14; 8:11; 14:13), and Ezekiel (Ezek 13:10, 16). These false prophets were telling the people what they wanted to hear and what would promote the self-interest of the prophets. God punishes such injustice and falsehood.

The everyday meaning of *šālôm* was deepened and widened to cosmic dimensions of harmony as the Israelite tradition came to a clearer understanding of the interconnected nature of all persons and things. *Šālôm* refers to this interconnected, harmonious reality where God, people, and nature stand in proper relationship to one another: a dynamic, restful scene "where the calf and the young lion shall browse together, with a little child to guide them" (Isa 11:6).

See: BLESSING, GIFTS

DALE LAUNDERVILLE, O.S.B.

New Testament

The word for peace, *eirēnē,* though signifying simply the absence of war in customary Greek usage, takes on wider meaning in the NT under the influence of the Septuagint. In fact, it has the same rich and diverse meanings as the Hebrew concept of *shālôm,* signifying general wholeness or well-being, and describing in varied contexts physical health (Mark 5:34), economic prosperity (Luke 11:21), military security (Luke 14:32; Rev 6:4), political stability (Acts 12:20), spiritual unity (Eph 4:3), and/ or eschatological salvation (Luke 2:29). Like its Hebrew counterpart it can be a blessing, a greeting, a farewell, a statement of fact, a hope for the future, a prayer, a virtue, or other such manifestation of a relationship in which all is well with God, with others, with self, and even with creation. In the NT a specifically Christological dimension is added, and the particular historical situation of the militarily enforced peace of the Roman empire (the *Pax Romana*) provides the setting within which the concept is elaborated.

The Gospels and Acts. While the teaching of Jesus in the Synoptics never directly links *eirēnē* with the proclamation of the reign of God, nevertheless the early Church understood peace as both the present effect and future goal of the reign of God. The title "children of God," which identifies Christians who are peacemakers in the Sermon on the Mount (Matt 5:9), also identifies them as those who love their persecutors (Matt 5:44-45), and the eighth beatitude tells us that those who suffer persecution for righteousness are participants in the kingdom of heaven (Matt 5:10). Since peace is the product of the reign of God, it is not a human achievement and is not merited, but is a gift from God fully bestowed in Jesus Christ. The Gospel of Luke, which has more than half the gospel references to *eirēnē,* frames the entire book within the hymn of the angels at the nativity and the hymn of the disciples at the palm procession before the death of Christ, both proclaiming that with Christ comes God's glory and a peace that begins on earth but ends in heaven (2:14; 19:38). Zechariah and Simeon recognize this peace (Luke 1:79; 2:29), but Jerusalem leaders do not (Luke 10:42). Within the Gospel, Luke identifies this peace with the wondrous signs of the reign of God: forgiveness (7:50) and healing (8:48). In a sermon in the Acts, Peter sums up the gospel as the proclamation of peace through Jesus Christ (Acts 10:36). Ephesians says the same (6:15) and even more pointedly says, "He [Christ] is our peace" (2:14). The link of the reign of God to peace is explicitly confirmed by Paul: "The kingdom of God is not a matter of food and drink, but of righteousness, peace, and joy in the holy Spirit" (Rom 14:17).

The final achievement of peace is effected by the resurrection of Christ, so that in the apparition stories, when Christ uses the traditional greeting, it has much deeper resonance: "Peace be with you" (Luke 24:36; John 20:19, 21, 26). This wholeness and well-being empowered by the risen Lord has the

Pax Romana pale in significance, so that Christ says he gives a peace that the world cannot give (John 14:27). Still, while peace is a gift, Christians are not to remain passive. Thus, missionaries are to proclaim the reign of God (Matt 10:7) by first offering peace, and the offer must be received by the hearers (Matt 10:13; Luke 10:5-6). Christians must maintain witness to the reign of God, and this will show itself in the peace it brings (Mark 9:50). Unfortunately, not everyone is open to this gift of peace, so that its establishment is ultimately eschatological and paradoxically entails, in the present, warfare and violence against evil. In this sense, Jesus can claim that he brings not peace, but the sword (Matt 10:34; Luke 12:51), and can counsel his disciples that they will have peace in him even while they experience trouble in the world, because he has conquered the world (John 16:33). Nevertheless, it is important to stress that in the NT, peace is almost never opposed simply to war, but to enmity in relationships; violence is against evil, but not the persons who do evil. The peacemaker fights and conquers evil not by hostility against his or her persecutors, but by love (Matt 5:43-48; Luke 6:27-36).

The Letters. Almost every letter in the NT begins with a greeting of "grace and peace" from God and Jesus Christ. Grace accompanying peace indicates once again that peace is a gift and that God is the giver through Christ, themes indicated also in a number of closing wishes in the letters (Rom 15:33; 2 Cor 13:11; Phil 4:9; 2 Thess 3:16). Paul specifies that peace is conferred by the holy Spirit and overcomes hostility toward God (Rom 8:6-7). As a fruit of the Spirit, peace is often associated with love and with joy (Rom 15:13; 2 Cor 13:11; Gal 5:22), and occasionally with mercy (Gal 6:16; see also 2 John 3). Paul stresses the theological and spiritual dimensions of peace by describing it as the result of justification in such a way as practically to identify it with reconciliation (Rom 5:1-11). In the same vein, peace is interchangeable with holiness (2 Thess 3:16). There are a few passages that speak of peace in the personal and psychological sense of peace of mind (Phil 4:7; Col 3:15), but the predominant concern of the NT letters is the wholeness of relationships between human beings. The Letter to the Ephesians centers on the theme of peace as the unity of the Church, reconciling Jew and Gentile (2:14-18). Indeed, Christ died in order to effect that peace (2:13, 16; see also Col 1:20). Therefore, all should strive to preserve that peace (4:3). Other letters describe some specific aspects of peace within the ecclesial community: unity in marriage (1 Cor 7:15); order in worship (14:33); agreement that overcomes factions (2 Cor 13:11); acceptance of leaders in ministry (1 Cor 16:11). While the focus of peace is on wholeness of relationship with God and within the Church, the letters do call for the wholeness in relations with all humanity (Rom 12:16; Heb 12:14) and even with all of creation (Col 1:15-20). There is also, of course, an eschatological dimension that calls for one to strive in hope (Rom 15:13; 1 Thess 5:3, 23; 2 Pet 3:14).

As the above would indicate, the NT dwells primarily on the theological foundations and the spiritual dimensions of peace and less on its socio-political or material aspects. Still, the actual living of the gospel of peace had to be dangerous to the superficial *Pax Romana*, while love of enemies encouraged nonviolent resistance to such evil. Among the letters, 1 Peter's counsel to "seek peace" (3:11) was undoubtedly to affect the political and social institutions around his community, and James makes it clear that biblical peace is not authentic if it does not translate into genuine economic and social well-being (2:14-17; 3:13-18).

See: HEALING, JOY, LOVE, RECONCILIATION, REIGN OF GOD, SPIRIT

ANTHONY J. TAMBASCO

Pastoral-Liturgical Tradition

As in the Scriptures, the Christian tradition understands peace to mean far more than the absence of conflict or violence;

rather, peace or *shālôm* describes the condition of wholeness and well-being that God intends for all creation, and which reflects the harmony that is the achievement of justice. In this respect, the focus of *shālôm* is not exclusively human well-being, but that cosmic wholeness reminiscent of the original harmony of creation. Similarly, such peace is inherently communal. While it involves personal fulfillment, it never envisions individual flourishing apart from or at the expense of communal well-being; indeed, in the Catholic social tradition one's personal good and the common good are interrelated. Finally, although *shālôm* may be centered on one's relationship with God, its meaning is far richer than spiritual well-being. Genuine peace embraces all the conditions necessary for human living: food, clothing, employment, respect, shelter, friendships, freedom of conscience, freedom of religion.

Peace as the Antithesis of Chaos. Peace works to restore the integrity of creation sundered by sin. If the original intention of God was to fashion a universe in which human beings were to live in harmony with one another and the rest of creation, then the strategy of peace is to achieve the reconciliation in which that original harmony is restored. The intention of creation is *shālôm*; this means not only that every creature lives in community with every other creature, but also that the prospering of one creature depends on justice being done to all creatures, a theme echoed in the opening prayer for the Mass of Peace and Justice: "Help us to work without ceasing for that justice which brings true and lasting peace."

The antithesis of peace is chaos, the disorder and brokenness brought to the world by sin, especially sins of selfishness and injustice. The world was created out of chaos and is called to move from the disorder of chaos to the harmony and beauty of *shālôm*; however, the grip of chaos is tightened through individual acts or social structures that rupture the bonds of life and deprive others of the well-being due them. War is the epitome of chaos and the principal enemy of peace, but any behavior that undermines the harmony God's love intends unleashes forces of chaos in the world and participates in the work of sin, which is essentially a decreation.

Biblically, God's abiding intention is *shālôm*, which is why God never accepts the resurgence of chaos in the world and continually works through history to overcome it. God's peace is restored through justice, and justice is the power that vanquishes the forces of chaos by putting the various elements of creation back in their proper relationship. In this respect, justice is the most fitting expression of moral behavior because it is through just deeds that human beings work in harmony with God's intention to reestablish *shālôm* for the whole of creation. As the U.S. bishops stated in their pastoral letter "The Challenge of Peace," we are called "to seek for ways in which to make the forgiveness, justice and mercy, and love of God visible in a world where violence and enmity are too often the norm" (55).

For God's peace to prevail there must be a deep appreciation for the inter-connectedness of all life and a deep sensitivity of human solidarity. *Shālôm* depends on living the truth that every creature is in community with every other creature; peace flows from recognizing and responding to the kinship we have with all life (*Mater et Magistra*, no. 157). The moral sensitivity that is required for peace is dulled through selfishness, materialism, and greed. Similarly, the peace that entails well-being and wholeness for all creation is thwarted by a lack of respect for the fundamental rights due human beings and all created life, including the earth. These rights are derived from an understanding of the dignity of all creatures as expressions of the life and love of God and called to a fullness and perfection that gives glory to God (*Pacem in Terris*, nos. 11-34, *Sollicitudo Rei Socialis*).

The Church Is Called to Witness and Embody *Shālôm*. Jesus Christ is the incarnation and perfection of God's peace; as the

Eucharistic Prayer for Masses of Reconciliation II testifies, "He is the way that leads to your peace." In his passion and death Jesus surrenders to the disintegration and chaos of the world, and in his resurrection he overcomes them; in Jesus, a broken world is made whole. The mission of the Church, and the task of every follower of Jesus, is to carry forward the reconciling, healing ministry he began. The purpose of the Church is to do what God wants done in history. God's abiding intention is the restoration of *shalôm,* and the primary mission of the Church is to be the community whose faithfulness to the ways of God mediates that healing, reconciling love to the world. In the words of *Gaudium et spes,* Christians are to be "artisans of peace" (77) whose fidelity to Jesus enables them to be "a leaven and . . . a kind of soul for human society as it is to be renewed in Christ and transformed into God's family" (40). In this way the Church models the wholeness and harmony possible in the world when men and women live in correspondence with God's redemptive plan. As the Eucharistic Prayer for Masses of Reconciliation II says, "We celebrate the memory of his death and resurrection and bring you the gift you have given us, the sacrifice of reconciliation."

Bringing God's peace to the world is an implication of discipleship. If Christ's mission was to offer God's reconciling love to the world, followers of Christ are to participate in that same ministry of *shalôm.* For Christians, the responsibility to be peacemakers is derived from the disciple's duty to imitate and embody the ways of God revealed to us in Christ. Christians are peacemakers working to reconcile all men and women in Christ because it is through that activity that they best imitate God and carry forward what God began in Christ and continues in the Spirit. This is why in "The Challenge of Peace" the U.S. bishops said that "peacemaking is not an optional commitment. It is a requirement of our faith. We are called to be peacemakers, not by some movement of the moment, but by our Lord Jesus" (333).

The Eucharist is the setting where the habits and practices of peace ought to be learned. The Eucharist is *shalôm* inasmuch as it is through the broken body of Christ that creation is healed and the death of chaos is transfigured into community and life. In the Eucharist, the Church remembers the healing, liberating love of God whose tender mercy freed all humanity from sin and ransomed the world from the bondage of death. In Eucharist, Christians are called to do their lives in the power of a memory that refused to let enmity prevail and insisted that ultimately love is stronger than hatred and peace more promising than division: "We do this in memory of Jesus Christ, our Passover and our lasting peace" (Eucharistic Prayer for Masses of Reconciliation I). Because it is the gift of God's *shalôm* that gives humanity hope, the peace Christians pledge to practice is foremost an expression of gratitude and indebtedness to a God who wants nothing more than that all may live.

See: CHAOS, HEALING, JUSTICE, MERCY, RECONCILIATION, VIOLENCE

PAUL J. WADELL, C.P.

PENTECOST

Pentecost, originally an agricultural feast, celebrating the end of the grain harvest, came to be associated in OT traditions with the Exodus and the giving of the covenant. In the NT it takes on new significance as the day in which the Spirit is given to Jesus' disciples. Eventually Christians separated into three distinct feasts the fifty-day period of celebration of Resurrection-Ascension-Pentecost.

Old Testament and Later Jewish Tradition

Pentecost (from Greek for "fiftieth") is the Greek name for the Israelite feast of Weeks (two texts in the LXX explain the name in this way, Tob 2:1 and 2 Macc 12:32). The second of the three classical pilgrim feasts of Israel—Unleavened Bread/Passover, Weeks, and Booths (Exod 23:14-17; 34:22; Deut 16:16)—Weeks was called "fiftieth" in

Greek because it occurred seven weeks, or fifty days, after Unleavened Bread. All three were originally agricultural feasts: Unleavened Bread celebrated the beginning of the cereal harvest, Weeks the end of the grain harvest, and Booths the vintage. Eventually each of these agricultural feasts became a commemoration of a specific moment of Israel's sacred history. Unleavened Bread (linked early with the feast of Passover) became the time to remember the deliverance from Egypt. Once that Passover/Exodus link was forged, it was almost inevitable that Weeks should be associated with the event that Exodus 19:1 places "in the third month after their departure," that is, the giving of the Law at Sinai, which is indeed the meaning of the feast in post-biblical Judaism.

Did Jews celebrate Weeks/Pentecost to commemorate the Sinai covenant already in the first century CE? Several facts suggest that such was indeed the practice of at least some Palestinian Jews. The users of the Qumran *Manual of Discipline* and the non-canonical *Book of Jubilees* celebrated the Feast of Weeks in the middle of the third month as the renewal of the Sinai covenant. It is not impossible that the covenant renewal celebrated by King Asa in the third month (2 Chr 15:10-12) was a celebration of Weeks with Sinai in mind. (The recently discovered Temple Scroll, found in Qumran Cave 11, indicates that the users of that document celebrated *three* Pentecosts— New Grain, New Wine, and New Oil.)

The liturgical readings for Weeks recorded by rabbinical sources, though they date from post-NT times, surely reflect tradition and provide important background for the Christian understanding of Pentecost. These readings include Genesis 11 (the tower of Babel), Exodus 19–20 (the Sinai theophany and covenant), and Psalm 68 (interpreted as referring to Moses' mediation of the Law).

New Testament

Pentecost is mentioned three times in the NT. The references to the feast in 1 Corinthians 16:8 and Acts 20:16 tell us only that the feast was important to Paul. For the Christian interpretation of Pentecost we depend on the famous account of Acts 2, one of the richest theological narratives in the whole of Luke-Acts.

The Pentecost events are told in words and images that evoke the giving of the Law at Sinai. The reconstituted Twelve (and the 120) are gathered like the twelve tribes at Sinai. The sound from heaven, the filling of the *whole* house (like the shaking of the *whole* mountain in Exod 19:18), and the fire recall the theophany at Sinai. The tongues of fire symbolize the reality that the powerful presence of God (like fire) will find expression in human words, the prophetic ministry of the disciples (tongues). In the broader sweep of the narrative, the Moses typology is evident in that Jesus ascends with a cloud (1:9) and then mediates the gift of the word of God for his people (2:4, 11, 18, 33). On the feast of the giving of the Law (the privileged communication of God's word) comes the endtime gift of the holy Spirit to empower the new expression of the divine word in the ministry of the apostles.

The list of the nationalities of the Jewish pilgrims symbolizes the future implications of what occurs here. By highlighting this inclusive gathering, Luke proclaims that this is in fact the fulfillment of the endtime ingathering of Israel. The Pentecostal gift is destined for Jews first, but then for the "ends of the earth" (Acts 1:8), "those far off" (2:39; Isa 57:19).

Some see in this account a reversal of the story of the tower of Babel. Whereas Genesis 11 tells of a sinful people who wish to make a name for themselves and are scattered in confusion and lose their ability to communicate, Acts 2 tells of a people of many languages, gathered, "confused" by a new ability to receive communication, and enabled to become a new community as they repent from their sin and call upon the name of the Lord.

The full narrative of Luke-Acts itself may be the best guide to Luke's interpretation of the Pentecost event. The message of the angel in Luke 1:32b-33 looks back to Isaiah 49:6 (the servant who raises up the tribes of Jacob and becomes a light to the nations) and to 2 Samuel 7:12-13 and Psalm 132:11 (about the heir of David). The announcement also looks forward to Acts 2:30-32, where we learn that Jesus' "reign" over the house of endtime restored Israel as its risen Lord. The reality of an apostolic share in the kingship of Jesus was prepared for in the Lucan farewell discourse at the Last Supper: "And I confer a kingdom on you, just as my Father has conferred one on me, that you may eat and drink at my table in the kingdom; and you will sit on thrones judging the twelve tribes of Israel" (Luke 22:29-30). In Luke's understanding, this is fulfilled in the renewed community enlivened with the Pentecostal gift. The Church is the rebuilt "hut of David" ready for the next step, the ingathering of the Gentiles (Acts 15:16-17 using Amos 9:11-12).

John the Baptist's reference to the coming one who will "baptize with the holy Spirit and fire" (Luke 3:16) evokes such prophetic OT texts of endtime renewal and purification as Ezekiel 36:25-27; Malachi 3:2-3; and Joel 3. This prepares the reader to see Jesus' baptism (Luke 3:31-32) as an anointing* for prophetic ministry (Luke 4:18 with Isaiah 61 and Acts 10:38, which describes the baptism as the anointing of Jesus "with Spirit and power"). The words of Jesus just before the ascension link John's prophecy with the approaching event of Pentecost: "While meeting with them, he enjoined them not to depart from Jerusalem, but to wait for the 'promise of the Father' about which you have heard me speak [a reference to Luke 24:49]. And I am sending the promise of my Father upon you; but stay in the city until you are clothed with power from on high." They will, in other words, be given the prophetic anointing that Jesus had been given.

The speech of Peter to the Church in Jerusalem (Acts 11:15-17), in which he reflects on the "Gentile Pentecost" that had occurred on the household of Cornelius (10:44-47), makes further connections between the prophecy of the Baptist and the experience of Pentecost: "As I began to speak, the holy Spirit fell upon them as it had upon us at the beginning, as I remembered the word of the Lord, how he had said, 'John baptized with water but you will be baptized with the holy Spirit.' If then God gave them the same gift he gave to us when we came to believe in the Lord Jesus Christ, who was I to be able to hinder God?" This is given further refinement in the speech of Peter in 15:8-9, which is an interpretation of both the Jewish Pentecost of Acts 2 and the "Gentile Pentecost" of Acts 10 as fulfillment of Ezekiel 36:25-29 (outpouring of God's Spirit, cleansing and renewal of hearts).

All these Lucan texts, anticipating and following the Pentecost account, help the implied reader follow the meaning of the narrative and speech of Acts 2. This Christian experience on the Jewish feast of Weeks is a major "wonder and sign" of the unfolding of the endtimes, the creation of the prophetic community (Acts 2:17-21 [Joel 3:1-5]) continuing the mission of the risen Lord Jesus (Acts 2:22-47 [using Ps 16:8-11; 2 Sam 7:12; Pss 110:1; 132:11]). The rest of Acts unfolds the story of this Spirit-led mission of the Church.

See: ANOINTING, ASCENSION, BABEL/BABYLON, BAPTISM, CHURCH, CLOUD, COMMUNITY, COVENANT, FEASTS, JUDAISM, LAW, MOUNTAIN, MOSES, MINISTRY, NATIONS, PASSOVER, PROPHECY/PROPHET, SERVANT, SPIRIT OF GOD, TRIBES, WORD OF GOD

M. DENNIS HAMM, S.J.

Pastoral-Liturgical Tradition

Although Acts 1–2 offers a precise chronology for the sending of the holy Spirit* ten days after the ascension and fifty days after the resurrection, the early Christian community did not introduce parallel celebrations to commemorate these as historical events. For the early Church, Resurrection-Ascension-Pentecost was a unitive feast of unbroken joy, celebrating Christ's once and for all victory over death. The early community did not share the tendency of a later period to divide this fifty-day feast into three feasts, each with its own season. Until the end of the second century, notices about Christians celebrating Pentecost refer to their keeping of the Jewish agricultural festival (e.g., *Epistula Apostolorum* 17).

Tertullian (ca. 225) offers the first clear evidence for a celebration of Pentecost with a Christian content, both as a fifty-day festal period (*De Corona* 3) and as a feast day appropriate to baptism (*De Baptismo* 19). Origen (254) explains the feast by noting that "if a man is able to say truthfully 'we are risen with Christ,' and also that 'he raised us up and made us sit with him in the heavenly places in Christ,' he is always living in the days of Pentecost . . . [and] he becomes worthy also of some share in the fiery tongue given by God" (*Contra Celsum* 8.22). The Council of Nicea recognizes Pentecost as a season during which no fasting or kneeling were allowed (can. 20). In general, the sources from the first four centuries know Pentecost both as a day intimately wed to Easter and as a season without internal thematic development that ends where it began (Patrick Reagan, "Fifty Days and the Fiftieth Day," *Worship* 55 [1981] 203).

The first evidence of a distinctive content for Pentecost comes from Egeria (ca. 384 CE), who noted that the Jerusalem Church celebrated the outpouring of the Spirit and the Ascension together fifty days after Easter (ch. 43). The Jerusalem liturgy shares the tendency of the early Church to understand Pentecost and Ascension as intimately related theologically: Ascension as the triumphant completion of Christ's earthly ministry, with the missionary outpouring of the holy Spirit as the unavoidable result. Thus they were celebrated on the same day. This tradition harkens back to John 20 that suggests that the resurrection, the sending of the Spirit, and the end of Christ's earthly ministry all occurred on the same day.

Between the time of Egeria's visit and the appearance of the *Armenian Lectionary* (415–439 CE), Jerusalem's liturgy experienced an important shift in its Pentecost celebration. As the antiphon (Ps 142:3-10b), reading (Acts 2:1-21), and gospels (John 14:15-24, 25-31) for various prayer gatherings during the day demonstrate, the Pentecost liturgy in fifth-century Jerusalem more narrowly commemorates the original Pentecost event. Henceforth, Pentecost diminishes as a Christological feast, and is transformed into a celebration of the holy Spirit. It is not surprising that such should occur in the decades following the first Council of Constantinople (381 CE) that decisively defined the divinity of the holy Spirit (*Symbolum of the First Council of Constantinople*).

The sermons of Augustine (430) and Leo the Great (461) illustrate this fifth-century development of Pentecost, with its singular focus on the holy Spirit. Leo writes, "The hearts of all Catholics are fully aware that this day's solemnity is to be venerated among the greatest of the feasts. We have no uncertainty as to the reverence due to this day, made sacred by the Holy Spirit in the surpassing miracle of the gift of himself" (Sermon 75.1).

The separation of Pentecost from the Christological feasts of Easter and the Ascension is amplified by consequent structural developments in the evolving liturgical year. A vigil for Pentecost, patterned after the Easter vigil, is evident in the *Apostolic Constitutions* (5.20.14; ca. 380? CE), suggesting that by the late fourth century Pentecost was already an established baptismal day. This ancient baptismal connection provides an explanation for the Old English synonym for Pentecost, i.e. Whitsunday (Latin: *Dominica in Albis*). The epithet "white" is generally taken to refer to the ancient custom of the wearing of white robes by the neophytes after their baptism on Pentecost.

The seventh-century *Gelasian Sacramentary* (n. 81) offers the first indications of an octave after Pentecost. Counting Sundays according to their occurrence after Pentecost soon follows. The seventh-century

Comes of Würtzburg lists two Sundays after Pentecost, seven after the feast of Saints Peter and Paul (June 29), five after the feast of St. Lawrence (August 10), and seven after the feast of St. Cyprian (September 16). Eventually all but the first Sunday are enumerated as "Sundays after Pentecost." The octave of Pentecost became a feast of all saints and finally a feast of the Most Holy Trinity, first noted in the tenth-century *Sacramentary of Fulda.*

The cumulative effect of these developments was to weaken severely the ancient unity of the Easter-Ascension-Pentecost celebration. Instead of various facets of a single paschal mystery, Ascension and Pentecost developed independently. Though an implicit link with Easter continued during the Middle Ages, the evolution of a separate "Pentecost cycle" in the liturgical year seriously weakened this link.

Contemporary reform of the celebration of Pentecost began in 1955. In an attempt to make the Easter Vigil more prominent, Pius XII abolished the series of lessons and blessing of baptismal water prescribed for the Pentecost vigil. The result was to reduce Pentecost to a feast of the holy Spirit with its octave intact. The reform of the calendar, mandated by the Second Vatican Council (Constitution on the Sacred Liturgy, no. 107), has taken further steps to restore the ancient linkage between Pentecost and Easter. The octave of Pentecost has been suppressed, the "Sundays after Pentecost" changed to "Sundays in Ordinary Time," and the fifty days from Easter to Pentecost restored as "one feast day" (*General Norms for the Liturgical Year and the Calendar*, no. 22). Today's Lectionary and Sacramentary texts for Pentecost, however, generally continue the centuries-old tradition of focusing on the holy Spirit. While there are many implicit connections between Pentecost and the Easter mysteries in these texts, few are as explicit as the Pentecost preface: "Today you sent the Holy Spirit on those marked out to be your children by sharing the life of your only Son, and so you brought the paschal mystery to its completion."

See: BAPTISM, CHURCH, GIFTS, PASSOVER, SPIRIT OF GOD

EDWARD FOLEY, CAPUCHIN

PEOPLE OF GOD

This entry consists of three parts. The OT section focuses on the choice and formation of ancient Israel as the people of God. Although this motif is not as prominent in the NT, the second part of the entry shows how the NT reinterpreted it to include all human beings. The third part of the entry examines this motif in the history of theology, its importance in the ecclesiology of Vatican II, and its continuing impact.

Old Testament

General. "People" is itself a problematic term, for it is not immediately clear what constitutes a people, whether race, territory, government, or some other factor(s). Although the OT uses several terms, the two most common are *'am* and *goy*. These two often seem to have approximately the same meaning, sometimes being used synonymously or in parallel (e.g., Exod 33:13; Deut 4:6; Ps 33:12), but *goy* tends to stress the territorial and political aspects and is more often translated "nation" than "people," while *'am* regards rather the concept of blood relationship. Although Israel* could be, and often was, described as a nation (especially during the period of the monarchy), this term did not seem apt for expressing its unique character; thus while the expressions "people [*'am*] of Yahweh" or "my people" (said by Yahweh) are frequent, equivalent expressions with "nation" do not occur. However, especially in the later OT period, the term "nations" (*goyim*) came to stand in contradistinction to Israel, as not sharing Israel's high religion, morals, or election. And from this arose the Talmudic usage of using "goy" to designate an individual non-Israelite, often in an unfavorable sense.

Formation of a People. Since God is the creator and sustainer of all peoples, the belief that one group is *the* people of God in some special way necessarily relates to the concept of election. Election, in the case of Israel, begins with one man. The call of Abraham involved, from the beginning, the promise that God would make of him a great nation (Gen 12:1-3). That promise was repeated several times, sometimes giving reference to the extraordinary number of his offspring, at times compared to the sands of the seashore or the stars of the sky as to number; the promise sometimes included possession of the land of Canaan as well (13:14-17; 15:5-7; 22:15-18; etc.); it was renewed to Isaac (26:2-5) and Jacob (28:13-14; 46:3). Thus, as seen through the eyes of the biblical authors, it was not a question of a preexistent people being called or chosen by God; rather, Israel's ancestors were chosen by God as the means by which a special people were to be brought into being. Nevertheless, the concepts of call and election continue to be important throughout Israel's history because of the supposition that Israel was called into existence for some purpose on the part of God.

Exodus. Historically speaking, the birth of Israel as a people owes more to the Exodus experience than to any other factor. The dual concepts of choice and formation continue together here, as God intervenes by calling Moses and commissioning him to deliver the people from bondage and slavery, besting the Egyptian rulers and their gods, and overcoming pharaoh's obstinacy by means of the signs and wonders worked through Moses. In this context, God repeatedly refers to Israel as "my people" (Exod 3:7, 10; 5:1; 7:16; 8:16, 17, 19; etc.) and Israel is designated as God's child ("Israel is my son, my firstborn"—Exod 4:22). To the experience of the Exodus is added the experience of Mount Sinai, as God calls the people into a still closer relationship. Upon their arrival at Mount Sinai, the Lord who led them out of Egypt tells them "you shall be my special possession, dearer to me than all other people, though all the earth is mine. You shall be to me a kingdom of priests, a holy nation" (Exod 19:5-6).

Covenant. This promise is given under the condition "if you hearken to my voice and keep my covenant" (Exod 19:5). God's love for Israel as a special people is confirmed in the covenant relationship granted to them. The covenant gives form and substance to the relationship by providing a note of permanence and a context for Israel's response (Exod 24:3-8). The enacting of a covenant implied the inauguration of a relationship similar to that of blood kinship; it involved a sharing of blessing, of peace and fullness *(shālôm)*, and of mutual loyalty. Israel, as the weaker partner, would enjoy God's protection, but would also be expected to manifest obedience to God's will as revealed in the Law and in the teaching of the prophets. "Covenant" and "people of God" are inseparable concepts; the classical formulation of the central provision of the covenant is "I will be your God and you will be my people" (Jer 11:4; 24:7; 30:22; 31:33; 32:38; Ezek 14:11; 36:28; 37:27; Zech 8:8; see Exod 6:7). This formulation expresses the bond between God and the people and points to covenant as its basis. No better formula is found, even in the NT, though it is capable of being understood and lived ever more deeply.

Obedience and Disobedience. Covenant, at least as understood in this context, involves an obligation of response to God in obedience. Yahweh is designated as "God" of the people Israel (Exod 5:1; 6:7; 7:16; 8:23; 18:1). One of the severest forms of punishment is to be "cut off from the people" (Gen 17:14; Exod 30:33). Both Israel's call as a people and the formulation of the covenant are found in the context of Sinai, where we find also virtually all of Israel's legislation; thus obedience to the laws is one form of Israel's response to election and covenant, one way of finding identity as God's people (Exod 19:5). Many times the Lord has occasion to blame the people; they are stiff-necked (Exod 32:9) and rebellious (Isa 30:9; 65:2; Ezek 2:3-8), lack faith (Num 14:11), do not understand (Isa 1:3). Nevertheless, they are a people formed as God's very own (Isa

43:21), God's inheritance (Pss 28:9; 33:12) and sheep (Pss 95:7; 100:3). This is not because they are the largest or most numerous of people, since they are in fact the smallest, but because God loved them (Deut 7:7-8). They are called to be holy (Lev 20:26; Deut 14:2, 21; 26:19), to be God's special people (Deut 7:6; 10:15; 14:2; 29:12; 1 Kgs 8:53), distinct from all other peoples (Exod 33:16; Lev 20:24, 26; Num 23:9).

God's History with Israel. The implications of Israel's election as God's people are carried on in its history. In addition to rescuing them from Egypt, God brings them into the land promised to Abraham, Isaac, and Jacob, raises up charismatic leaders to deliver them in times of need (Judg 3:9, 15; 1 Sam 9:16) and prophets to lead them into ways of truth and away from those sins which would bring about their ruin. God's special concern for Israel is seen in the way God treats them vis-à-vis other peoples. Thus God thwarts the plan of Balak, king of Moab, to have Balaam curse Israel, going so far as to open the mouth of his donkey, and replacing the curse with a blessing (Num 22:2–24:25); God's choice of Israel over Edom is expressed in terms of "love" for the one, "hate" for the other (Mal 1:2-5; cf. Gen 25:28). Other nations are instruments in God's hands to be used to carry out the divine plans for the people. Assyria is used to chastise Israel (Isa 5:26-29; 7:18-20; 10:5-6) and Babylon to destroy the nation and lead them into exile (Jer 32:28-38); Persia, under Cyrus, is God's instrument for bringing them back from exile and restoring them to their own land (Isa 44:24–45:8); prophetic vision sees foreign nations transporting them back from exile and even flooding their country with riches (Isa 49:22-23; 60:4-9).

Universal Potential. Although strictly speaking the concept of "people" resides more in the concept of blood relationship than in any other factor (see above), the introduction of the covenant concept ultimately began to suggest that membership in God's people was not simply a matter of physical descent but could be extended to those who were willing to choose Yahweh as their God, to hold fast to the covenant, and to do the things God commands (Isa 56:3-8; cf. Jdt 14:10)—though deuteronomic legislation placed some restrictions upon people with certain physical deformities or who had won Israel's special enmity (Deut 23:2-9). On the other hand, some prophetic passages, remarkable for their universalistic spirit, speak of peoples other than Israel being reckoned as God's people, as when Zechariah 2:15 says that "many nations shall join themselves to the LORD . . . and they shall be his people" or Isaiah 19:25 sees Egypt, Assyria, and Israel, inveterate enemies throughout their history, ranking as, respectively, God's people, "the work of my hands," and "my inheritance."

See: ABRAHAM, ASSYRIA, BABEL/BABYLON, COVENANT, ELECTION, EXCOMMUNICATION, EXODUS, FIRSTBORN, HOLY/HOLINESS, INHERITANCE, ISRAEL, LAW, NATIONS, OBEDIENCE

JOSEPH JENSEN, O.S.B.

New Testament

In the OT, the people of God represented a special people, chosen by God and constituted as one people in a covenant of grace. Israel's being a people ('am in Hebrew, laos in Greek) stemmed from a common ancestry and history and transcended geography, language, and every political and social structure, including that of being a nation (goy in Hebrew, ethnos in Greek). As the people of God, Israel was not just a nation among other nations. Being "the people of God" was a fact of revelation, faith, and historical consciousness. It was profoundly influenced by Israel's history among other peoples, but it also expressed the identity of Israel* in a way that transcended every phase of its long and complex history. As a reality of history, the people of God was a particular people, distinct and set apart from other people, and it was God's people in a way no other people could claim. As a reality of eschatological hope, the history of the people of God was situated in the context of creation and envisioned in the universal terms associated with God's work as creator.

The theme of the people of God is not as prominent in the NT as in the OT, but it does remain important in several books of the NT, beginning with the Pauline writings. As in the OT, the notion transcends every political, social, geographical, and linguistic limitation. In referring to the people of the second covenant, however, it also transcends having a common ancestry and history and is a reality of revelation, faith, and historical awareness open to all human beings. This universality stems from the people's relationship to the person of Christ who died and rose in a great Passover event to be Lord of all, as well as from the creative Spirit of God manifested on Pentecost. The NT saw this universal people of God as the beginning of eschatological fulfillment. What the OT envisioned eschatologically, the NT therefore saw as its historical agenda for a universal mission.

Pauline Writings. The Pauline writings often refer to the people of God as an important element in Paul's theology of history, but nearly always in a quotation from the OT or with reference to one. The theme, which is very close to that of the *ekklēsia* or Church, appears in four distinct but closely related contexts.

First, Paul refers to Israel as God's people, a "disobedient and contentious people" (Rom 10:21; see Isa 65:2), but adding that "God has not rejected his people whom he foreknew" (Rom 11:1-2; see Ps 94:14). So it is that, as in the days of Elijah, there was again a remnant of God's people, chosen by grace (Rom 11:2-5). Paul also cites Deuteronomy 32:43 and Psalm 117:1, inviting Gentiles to rejoice with God's people and all the peoples to praise God (Rom 15:10-11). In these passages, Paul associates the Gentiles with the people of God but does not view them as an actual part of it.

Second, Paul applies OT texts, referring to the people of God to the NT people. In this context, he cites Hosea 2:25, "Those who were not my people I will call 'my people,'" and Hosea 2:1, "And in the very place where it was said to them, 'You are not my people,'

there they shall be called children of the living God" (Rom 9:25-26). In the context of Hosea, these texts referred to the origins of Israel as God's people by God's gracious choice. In Paul's use of these texts, they extend the gracious choice of God to those "whom he has called, not only from the Jews but also from the Gentiles" (Rom 9:24) who have achieved righteousness from faith (Rom 9:30). To show how "the believers" are "the temple of the living God" and must not associate with unbelievers, Paul cites Leviticus 26:11-12: "I will live with them and move among them, and I will be their God and they shall be my people" (2 Cor 6:16). In these passages, Paul clearly includes the Gentiles among the people of God, which is viewed as open to all through faith.

Third, Paul warns the Corinthians against behavior and attitudes found at one time among God's OT people (1 Cor 10:7 and 14:21; see Exod 32:6 and Isa 28:11). In a biblically inspired theology of history, Paul sees the people of God in the NT as related by faith to those in the OT in a common heritage and history. The universal people of God is related to a particular people of God at a new stage of history.

Fourth, the Letter to Titus presents the Church as the special people "of our savior Jesus Christ, who gave himself for us to deliver us from lawlessness and to cleanse for himself a people as his own, eager to do what is good" (Titus 2:13-14). By reason of the redemption, the people of God is consequently the people of Jesus Christ as well.

The Gospels and Acts. The theme of the people of God is not very prominent in Mark (but see Mark 7:6 and 14:2) and John, who preferred imagery such as that of the vine and the branches (John 15:1-10) and the shepherd and the flock (John 10:1-18; but see John 11:50-52 and 18:14). The theme has a rather meager role in Matthew, almost exclusively in reference to the people of Israel. The angel of the Lord appeared to Joseph in a dream and announced that Mary would bear a son, whom he was to name Jesus "because he will save his people from their sins" (Matt 1:21). Jesus belongs to that people and they can consequently be referred to as "his people," but without necessarily implying that "his people" is the people of God. That Israel is God's people is expressed later when Matthew applies Micah 5:1 to Jesus, the ruler who would shepherd God's people Israel (Matt 2:6).

Later in the course of Matthew's Gospel, references to Israel as a people appear in several OT quotations: "the people who sit in darkness have seen a great light" (Matt 4:16; see Isa 9:1); "gross is the heart of this people" (Matt 13:15; see Isa 6:10); and "this people honors me with their lips" (Matt 15:8; see Isa 29:13). Many of these references to Israel as a people reflect Matthew's negative view of the synagogue following the Christian community's exclusion from it.

The theme received a far more extensive and positive development in Luke-Acts, where it is related both to the history of salvation and to the challenges of universality. The Lucan prologue shows the whole assembly of the people in the Temple at prayer (Luke 1:10) as Gabriel announces to Zechariah that he and Elizabeth would have a son whose mission would be "to prepare a people fit for the Lord" (Luke 1:17). Seen from this point of view, the people were consequently seen as lacking but not as outside God's concern. Later, at John's birth, Zechariah would sing in the *Benedictus* of the coming of Jesus in whom "the Lord the God of Israel . . . has visited and brought redemption to his people" (Luke 1:68), and of his son John who would prepare his way and "give his people knowledge of salvation through the forgiveness of their sins" (Luke 1:77).

The theme of universality, in which both Jews and Gentiles are included in the people of God, is suggested in the angel's proclamation to the shepherds of the "good news of great joy that will be for all the people" (Luke 2:10). It is almost explicit in Simeon's canticle, the *Nunc Dimittis*, singing of God's salvation "prepared in sight of all the peoples, a light for revelation to the Gentiles, and glory for your people Israel"

(Luke 2:30-32). The canticle gathers peoples together in one event revealing salvation, but it still distinguishes between other peoples and Israel, the people of God. So it is that when Jesus raised the widow of Nain's son, those present glorified God, announcing that "A great prophet has arisen in our midst . . . God has visited his people" (Luke 7:16), that is, the people of Israel.

In the early chapters of The Book of Acts, "the people" and "the people of God" continue to refer to Israel as a particular people (see Acts 3:23, Deut 18:19; Acts 4:10, 17; 7:34, Exod 3:7; Acts 13:17). The change comes after Peter's decisive discourse on how God "who knows the heart, bore witness by granting them," that is, the Gentiles, "the holy Spirit just as he did us." As such, God "made no distinction between us and them, for by faith he purified their hearts" (Acts 15:8-9). James then responded, interpreting Peter's discourse as a description of "how God first concerned himself with acquiring from among the Gentiles a people for his name" (Acts 15:14). In support of Peter's experience, he cited Amos 9:11ff. a text that dealt with Israel's conquest of the nations around it, but rephrased it to include rather than conquer the Gentiles. God would rebuild the fallen hut of David and raise it up again, "so that the rest of humanity may seek out the Lord, even all the Gentiles on whom my name is invoked" (Acts 15:16-17).

The Gentiles would therefore be included along with the Jews as integral members of the people of God. As the Church's mission unfolded, it happened that Jews were not able to hear and understand what in effect was a proclamation of the reign of God (Acts 28:25-27, 30-31) and that the salvation of God was sent to the Gentiles, who would listen (Acts 28:28), but the invitation for Jews to join with the Gentiles in one people of God would never be withdrawn.

Other Writings. Two additional letters, the Letter to the Hebrews and the First Letter of Peter, as well as the Book of Revelation, also contribute to the pastoral theology of the people of God in the NT. The Letter to the Hebrews, which was written for Jewish Christians, was keenly interested in the history of the Israelite people and its institutions and frequently referred to the people of God who preceded the coming of Jesus. It did this especially in relation to the office of the high priest or the levitical priesthood (Heb 5:3; 7:5, 11, 27; 9:7) and the story of Moses and the Mosaic covenant (9:19; 11:24-25). It is in this historical and theological setting that it presented the life and high priesthood of Jesus, who became like us "in every way, that he might be a merciful and faithful high priest before God to expiate the sins of the people" (Heb 2:17). The people of God, redeemed by Christ's self-offering (Heb 7:27) and consecrated by his own blood (Heb 13:12), thus stands in continuity with the people of God under the Mosaic covenant. So it is that the ancient institution of the Sabbath still remained for them (Heb 4:9-11). Like Paul (Rom 9:25-26; 2 Cor 6:16), the Letter to the Hebrews also applied OT texts concerning the people of God to the Christian community (Heb 10:30; see Deut 32:36), living under the second (Heb 8:7) covenant, the new covenant in which God's people would have the law written upon their hearts (Heb 8:8-12; see Jer 31:31-34). With the second covenant, the first became obsolete (Heb 8:13) but the people of God perdured (Heb 8:10).

The First Letter of Peter, which was addressed to Gentiles, includes a highly developed theology of the people of God in relation to those who had received "new birth to a living hope through the resurrection of Jesus Christ" (1 Pet 1:3). Being the people of God is part of the very identity of those who were born anew (1 Pet 1:23) and are "a chosen race, a royal priesthood, a holy nation, a people of his own" (1 Pet 2:9). Being "a people of his own," an expression steeped in the OT (see Exod 19:6; Mal 3:17), is the fourth and climactic element in this extraordinary proclamation of the Christian identity.

The First Letter of Peter was written to people of vastly different backgrounds and belonging to various nations and peoples

(1 Pet 1:1). Prior to their rebirth, they represented not one but many peoples. Now they were not only one people but the people of God. The message of Hosea could be applied to them: "Once you were 'no people' but now you are God's people; you 'had not received mercy' but now you have received mercy" (1 Pet 2:10; see Hos 1:6, 9; 2:3). They were chosen like living stones to be built into a spiritual house or temple and a holy priesthood to offer spiritual sacrifices (1 Pet 2:4-5) and announce the praises of him who called them from darkness into his wonderful light (1 Pet 2:9).

The Book of Revelation, with its strong awareness and concern for universality, often refers to "every tribe and tongue, people and nation" (Rev 5:9; 7:9; 10:11; 11:9; 13:7; 14:6; 17:15) without speaking of a particular people or of all peoples as the people of God. There is reference to God's people, however, in the vision of the fall of Babylon (Rev 18:1-19:4), when a voice from heaven orders God's people to depart from Babylon "so as not to take part in her sins" (Rev 18:4). Later, in the vision of the new creation (Rev 21:1–22:5), when salvation history is finally fulfilled, God's dwelling will be with the entire human race. "He will dwell with them and they will be his people" (Rev 21:3).

See: COVENANT, CHURCH, REIGN OF GOD, SALVATION, SHEPHERD, VINE

EUGENE LAVERDIERE, S.S.S.

Pastoral-Liturgical Tradition

Introduction. The Dogmatic Constitution on the Church promulgated by the Second Vatican Council is the contemporary focal text for the use of the symbol, people of God. In the choice of this term the Council names the Church in direct relation to the covenant made between God and the people of Israel.* Christians interpret that foundational relationship as their own ultimate source, renewed in Jesus and his Spirit and opened to all the people of earth. This theology of a renewed covenant and an extension of the intimate relation of God to all people, beyond the specific nation of Israel, is part of Paul's thought as he works out the meaning of Christ, the Law, and the gospel, especially in his Letter to the Romans. Thus the Council appropriated an ancient symbol, rooted in Scripture and repeated in the history of the Church.

People of God in the History of Theology. The early Church struggled with its relationship to Israel. They were of Israel, but were not Israel the people, the nation. They were a religious entity. Christians already began this struggle with their identity in the NT; apologists, like Justin, the Church Fathers, and Irenaeus, continued to work this out, though not always using the term "people of God." They wrote about the Church as the true Israel that now took the place that the Jews had once held. They described Israel as having forsaken God, thus the Gentiles became heirs of the covenant in their stead. Yet in keeping with the NT, the theologians of the early Church modified this trenchant theology; the Church grew out of Israel, and so was in some way continuous with it. This continuity was embraced by Augustine with his "ecclesia ab Abel" theme that connects the Church to God's first engagement with humanity. Augustine sees the Church on its way, from this first moment of creation toward its eschatological realization when the Church's journey culminates in life with God in heaven.

During the Middle Ages the political and ecclesial spheres were so intertwined that little theological attention was given to the identity of the Church per se. Even Thomas treats only briefly of the Church under the heading of Christ, and then in terms of the body of Christ, not the people of God. The Reformers do direct attention to the Church because it has become an issue. However, they too do not appropriate the symbol, people of God, but look to the communion of the saints, the invisible communion of believers who are the true Church. Neither does Robert Bellarmine's Catholic Reformation ecclesiology use the symbol. Rather, he uses the perfect society, hierarchically ordered, whole in itself. The emphasis on the visible and external responds to the Reformers' emphasis on the internal and invisible.

It is not until the nineteenth century that the theology that leads to Vatican II begins to take shape, particularly in the work of Johann Adam Mohler. Here the Romantic interpretation of the spirit of a people binding them together as a community works to retrieve the symbol of the body of Christ to describe the organic unity of the Church, through the enlivening presence of the holy Spirit. This dynamic theology met Rome's perfect society to produce the famous encyclical *Mystici Corporis* in 1943. In it the communitarian aspects of the symbol meet uneasily with the complementarity of the body parts that give a place to Bellarmine's rigidly ordered church.

Between 1937 and 1942 Catholic attention to biblical resources for theology reclaimed the symbol people of God, and with it the location of the Church in the process of salvation history. In the thirty years prior to the Council, the ecclesiologies of the perfect society, mystical body, and people of God continued to interact while biblical studies widened the meaning of the people of God. The symbol was used to critique the other two, but it also absorbed the insight into the priority and bondedness of the community that was Mohler's gift, and wedded it to the covenant theology it contained. By 1962 the symbol had gained widespread attention in European ecclesiology.

People of God at Vatican II. The symbol appears first in the cornerstone document of the Council, The Dogmatic Constitution on the Church. Its second chapter is devoted to it. The location of the symbol is important. It appears after the opening chapter on the mystery of the Church, and prior to the chapters that treat the hierarchical structure of the Church and the laity. Thus its location indicates both that it interprets the mystery of the Church, and it takes priority as an identification of the Church before its division into ranks of hierarchy and laity.

The word "people" is derived from the Greek *laos*, which translates the Hebrew term *'am*. It does not mean "laity" in the modern sense of "non-specialists" vis-à-vis the expertise and abilities of another group. That notion would be covered by the term *laikos*. The term *laos* formally indicates a whole people who are bound together as a corporate entity. In the case of Israel, it indicates the nation bound together through their covenant with God. Thus all members, without distinction, together form the one people of God.

Together this people shares the election of God, who chooses to call them all into relationship with the Divine self, and has accepted their common response of faith. Thus participants include not only members of the Roman Catholic Church, but all baptized Christians, and indeed all whose minds and hearts incline to God. It is in and through this whole people that God chooses to work out the mystery of salvation among us. The redemptive ministry, death, and resurrection of Jesus are effective for the whole people. The entire people that is swept up into the mystery of the work of Jesus is enlivened and gifted by his Spirit. This people is finally called into the eternal life of God when human history finds its fulfillment in the echatological mystery. In this way the symbol, people of God, interprets the mystery of the Church because it points to the ways we are sourced, supported, and finally drawn into God.

Clearly, this people is not a static entity. It is a people on its way, a pilgrim people, caught up in the historical mystery of salvation. This theme is part of the Catholic rediscovery of biblical eschatology. This has two implications for the Church. One, it is a changing entity with a goal. Two, that very goal, its eschatological fulfillment in the experience of the reign of God, works as both a lure and a horizon against which the Church can measure its own partial realization of that to which it is called. The people is not perfect. Called to holiness, and able to mediate God's holiness, it is nevertheless the home of sinners and is sinful itself. The people is called into conversion and ongoing transformation.

Here the symbol of the pilgrim people is linked to the symbols of the mystical body and the Church as universal sacrament of salvation for all humanity.

In Christ this whole people shares his triple office of priest, prophet, and king. These are the roles related to sacrament, teaching, and governance. This naming gives priority to the whole community's share in the offices of Christ that belong to the Church. Yet this grace and activity in which the whole people participate is immediately limited by the division between hierarchy and laity. The one grace that funds the common priesthood, for example, contrasts with the hierarchical priesthood that is different "in essence and not only in degree" (10). This demonstrates the fact that the theology of the people of God was laid down right next to alternative ecclesiological voices (here the Dionysian hierarchy mediated through Bellarmine and later subsumed into *Mystici Corporis*) without resolving their differences. These two theologies move in entirely different directions. This theological division, directly related to the use of the ranks in the body of Christ, is repeated in relation to teaching and receiving what is taught, and to exercise of authority in relation to role. This unresolved tension in the ecclesiology of the Constitution is extended throughout the text, and is present in many of the other Council documents and has continued in subsequent Roman documents. The symbol of the people of God is used to fund the practice of episcopal collegiality as well as other new collegial forms of institutional conversation within the Church (e.g., bishops' conferences, diocesan councils, parish councils). However, the symbol of the body of Christ is also persistently drawn upon to fund the theology of hierarchical retention of decision-making authority. This symbolic and political conflict is the legacy of Vatican II, and it has been interpreted differently in the subsequent theology and practice of the Church since 1965.

People of God Since Vatican II. The theology of the people of God has been variously received in the emerging multi-cultural world church of the post-Vatican II era. In the United States Vatican II coincided with the presidency of John F. Kennedy, an event that marked the arrival of the Catholic descendants of European immigrants as fully fledged, mainstream American citizens. The Council's liturgical reforms together with the proclamation that we are all the people of God sounded like the announcement of a long-awaited enlightenment, a democratic turn in the institution, to moderate and liberal American Catholics. Altars turned around and parish councils, school boards, diocesan councils, and new lay ministries that engaged both men and women sprang up. Religious orders began to reform, vocations changed; in short, the Catholic world became transformed. The people of God was heard as "we the people, who are baptized, we are the Church." What many people sought was to realize that identity in practice. Others, however, found this new Church uncongenial; thus the conflict in ecclesiologies is played out in the United States in terms of enacting the hierarchical Church out of the perfect society theology, or enacting an American democratic interpretation of the people of God.

In Latin America, despite differences in national situations, there is a widespread movement to build Church from among the poor and marginalized peoples. A grassroots church of basic Christian communities is taking shape. Thus a church of the people, embracing its own interpretation of the people of God, has come into being. It is a church in which people are engaged in study of the Word, witness to the reign of God, and transformation of Church and society toward God's reign. Leonardo Boff suggests that each community of people can be understood as a realization of the people of God, a local church that instances the universal Church in a Church of local churches. These churches are agents of change, on their way, churches wrestling with eschatological hope. More than pilgrims, these men and women have taken the responsibility to become revolutionaries. They are a people

of God working for justice and love in their own situations on behalf of themselves and their fellow citizens. As elsewhere, this ecclesiology is not accepted by all, but it has become a critically important event on the Latin American continent and for the international Catholic Church.

In Europe, political theologians, like Johannes Baptist Metz, who are in conversation with the basic Christian communities of Latin American and those developing in their own countries, and who are informed by the developments in socialist philosophy, have enhanced the theology of the people of God. Metz talks about the Church as the situation in which people are called to become subjects, to become fully who they are created to be, before God. At issue is the fact that we are not simply a people, but are enabled to become the subjects of our own history. Being the people of God is a project, not a fact. This enlarges the influential theology of Karl Rahner, who understood the people of God who are the Church to be the sacrament of God's saving activity in and for the world. He envisioned a conversation among the peoples of the Church and the peoples of our many nations for the sake of making the gospel available globally. Metz adds the notion that the work of the Church is to make humanity more possible. The Church should be engaged in the challenge of growth toward human wholeness in history and in our social, political situations.

In parts of Asia and Africa the impact of Vatican II's people of God is mixed. In the Philippines, for example, it is expressed in the base community movement and the struggle for social transformation. However, in some nations, like Cameroon, still wrestling with a neo-colonial relationship to industrialized nations, it has had little effect. On the contrary, the Church is still aligned with neo-colonial concerns that continue practices of oppression.

In the changing ecclesiologies of the late twentieth century the people of God is both lending its power to and being critiqued by the recent symbols of the discipleship of equals, notably with its feminist content, and the symbol of the *communio,* the Church as a community of communities and a communion of communions.

See: CHURCH, BODY OF CHRIST, SIGN

ANN E. GRAFF

PERSECUTION

The mistreatment and oppression of individual believers and the community of faith is a consistent theme in the Hebrew and Christian Scriptures. In the OT, faith in Yahweh calls for the courage to be loyal to the demands of the covenant in the face of opposition. The NT is clear in its teaching that disciples of Jesus must be willing to undergo persecution if they are to be genuine followers of the crucified one. The witness of those who have suffered and died for the faith forms an integral part of Christian liturgy, spirituality, and theology. Underlying Christian reflection on persecution and martyrdom is the conviction that, through the death and resurrection of Jesus, God has overcome the powers of evil in the world and is faithfully active in offering new life to those who suffer for the faith.

Old Testament

The Hebrew Scriptures narrate experiences of persecution undergone by the people of Israel, by some of its prominent leaders and prophets, and by individuals within the community. The principal Hebrew word for persecute is *radaph.* It denotes the action of pursuing another with hostile intent. The psalmist takes refuge in God and prays, "Save me from all my pursuers and rescue me" (Ps 7:2).

Persecution of the People of Israel. The nation of Israel was born out of the event of being saved from the oppression of slavery in Egypt. The Pentateuch depicts God as witnessing the affliction of the people and resolving to rescue them from their forced labor (Exod 3:7-10). It is this formative experience of liberation from oppression by Yahweh that is at the heart of Hebrew faith and which the covenant community will

continue to recall in subsequent times of persecution.

Two key moments of persecution of Israel by foreign powers were the invasion of Jerusalem by Babylon (588 BCE) and the brutal persecution of the Jews by Antiochus IV (168–165 BCE). The siege by the Babylonians resulted in the destruction of the Temple, the burning of the city, and the Exile of important segments of the population (2 Kgs 25:8-12). Convinced of the sovereignty of God over human history, Jeremiah interprets this moment of persecution as God's punishment of the people for their infidelity to the covenant, though this prophet also proclaims the vision of a new covenant in which the community will be restored (Jer 31:31-34). A few decades later, Second Isaiah will proclaim the return of the exiles as a new exodus in which Yahweh delivers the people from captivity and from guilt (Isa 40:1-11). The story of the attempts by Antiochus IV to abolish the Jewish faith is told in the Books of Maccabees and in the apocalyptic Book of Daniel. This Seleucid king outlawed the practice of the faith, burned copies of the Torah, and erected an altar to Zeus in the Temple court. The visions depicted in the Book of Daniel express confidence that, even in these moments of severe trial, God has not abandoned the people and divine providence is still at work within history. Yahweh will pronounce judgment over Israel's persecutors, removing their power and restoring justice (Dan 7:25-27). The account of the torture and execution of a mother and her seven sons (2 Maccabees 7) is a classic OT story of loyalty to the Torah in the face of persecution and of trust in God's vindication of the just.

The experience of the persecution of the nation is articulated in prayer in those psalms known as community laments (see Psalms 12; 44; 74; 79). In these prayers, the people bring their situation before God at a time when it is difficult to believe that God is still present to them. God's past saving deeds are hymned and trust in the divine power is reaffirmed. God is implored to remember the covenant and to defend the chosen people against their enemies (Ps 74:20-23).

The Persecution of Individuals. The Hebrew Scriptures show that those who are charged with leading the people or proclaiming the word of God were often the objects of persecution by the community. Moses has to endure the complaints of the people in the desert (Exod 14:11-14), David is pursued by Saul (1 Samuel 19–24), Elijah has to escape to the wilderness to avoid the sentence of Ahab and Jezebel (1 Kings 19), and Amos is forced by the priest Amaziah to flee the northern kingdom (Amos 7:10-17). Jeremiah is perhaps the preeminent OT figure of persecution, and we are given an insight into his experience in those autobiographical sections of his prophecy known as the "confessions" (Jer 11:18–12:6; 15:10-21; 17:14-18; 18:18-23; 20:7-13, 15-18). Despised as a traitor because of his denunciations of the conduct of the people, the prophet is persecuted from all sides, even by members of his own family. He brings his complaints before Yahweh, protesting his innocence and his faithfulness to the prophetic vocation and asking that his enemies be defeated. Like the confessions of Jeremiah, the individual laments in the Book of Psalms also express the prayer of those undergoing persecution (see Psalms 3; 4; 22; 31; 71). Motivated by faith in a God who is close to people in their need, these psalms present the distress of the individual, confess confidence in the power of God, and sometimes express thanksgiving for deliverance from the enemy.

New Testament

Persecution because of faithfulness to the gospel is a central theme of the NT. Like its Hebrew equivalent, the principal Greek words for persecute (*diôkô*) and persecution (*diôgmos*) denote the experience of being pursued by the enemy (see Matt 5:10-12; 10:23; John 15:20; Acts 7:52; Phil 3:6; 2 Thess 1:4; 2 Tim 3:11). The word *thlipsis* is sometimes employed to refer to persecution (Rom 12:12; Rev 2:10), though this is a more general term that has shades of meaning that vary from slight affliction to the great tribulation of the last days.

Jesus as the Model for Persecuted Believers. In the NT, Jesus serves as the model and inspiration for those who endure persecution for their faith in the gospel. Like the prophets of the OT, Jesus is rejected by his own people. This rejection and the suffering* that ensues from it is not to be avoided but courageously faced. Jesus sets his face for Jerusalem, aware that opposition is building and confrontation with the religious and political authorities awaits him (Mark 8:31-33). He remains faithful to the mission of proclaiming the good news of salvation, convinced of the fidelity of God and of the victory of God's purposes to effect salvation, even through suffering. Luke's portrayal of Jesus' forgiveness of his enemies from the cross and his trustful handing over of his spirit to God depicts Jesus as the paradigm for Christians who suffer persecution (Luke 23:34, 46).

Persecution of the Disciples. The Gospels relate Jesus' warnings to his disciples that they, too, will encounter severe opposition. In the Sermon on the Mount, Jesus numbers the persecuted among those who are blessed and who experience the eschatological joy of the saved (Matt 5:10-12; cf. Luke 6:22-23). Jesus' commission to the disciples to proclaim the reign of God includes a warning about persecutions to come (Matt 10:16-33). As the disciples share in the authority of Jesus, so they will also participate in his sufferings. In John's account of the Last Discourse, Jesus warns his disciples that the "world" (those who reject faith in Jesus) will hate them just as it has hated him (John 15:18-27). The disciples are assured that when they are brought to trial for their faith the Spirit will be able to use them to bear witness to Jesus.

The reality of persecution is evident throughout the NT descriptions of the first Christian communities. In his portrayal of the origins of the Church in Acts, Luke narrates the sufferings of the community and of leaders such as Stephen, Peter, and Paul.

Instances of persecution are enveloped in the designs of God, who is able to effect the spread of the gospel and the growth of the Church through these trials. In their interrogation before the Sanhedrin and subsequent scourging, Peter and the apostles are witnesses (*martyres*) to the resurrection and exaltation of Jesus (Acts 5:29-42). The theology of martyrdom that developed in the early Church derived from this notion of "witness" (*martys*; see Acts 1:8, 22) to the risen Jesus, originally applied to the apostles and later extended to all those who lay down their lives for their faith.

The various NT letters and the Book of Revelation offer counsel and encouragement to Christians who are experiencing persecution. Referring to his apostolic ministry, Paul tells the Corinthians about his patient endurance of persecution (1 Cor 4:12). It is God's power, not his own, that is operative in moments when Paul is persecuted (2 Cor 4:7-9). In the First Letter of Peter, the author extols the blessings of undergoing persecution, teaching that these trials are purifying and that they provide Christians an opportunity to share in the sufferings of Christ (1 Pet 4:12-19). The author of the Book of Revelation uses the apocalyptic genre to encourage several Christian communities who are suffering persecution to remain steadfast in faith and to assure them that God is ultimately victorious over the powers of evil.

In general, the NT writings understand the suffering of persecution to be one aspect of the believer's dying with Christ. Those who have been baptized into the death of Christ must be willing to share the lot of the master. Believers are called to trust that God's power is at work through their own human weakness and to recognize that moments of persecution can become moments of eloquent testimony to the gospel. Through fidelity to Christ in suffering, believers are assured of participation in his resurrection.

Pastoral-Liturgical Tradition

Persecution and Martyrdom in the Early Church. The experience of systematic persecution and martyrdom of Christians under the Roman Empire was a threat to the very existence of the Church, yet it also became formative of Christian identity and spirituality. Tertullian's remark that the blood of Christians is seed for the Church (*Apology*, 50, 13) proved to be true. Christians were often viewed as politically subversive because of their refusal to engage in the cult of the emperor or to sacrifice to the Roman deities. After a great fire that destroyed much of Rome, Nero inaugurated the first great persecution of Christians (64 CE), making the profession of the Christian faith a crime punishable by death. The deaths of Peter and Paul have traditionally been associated with this persecution. Subsequent persecutions under Domitian (95 CE), Trajan (112 CE), Septimus Severus (202 CE), Decius (250 CE), and Diocletian (303 CE) resulted in extensive suffering and numerous deaths. The final, severe persecution under Diocletian was ended by an edict of religious toleration signed by Galerius (311 CE) and a proclamation of the equality of rights to all religions issued in Milan by Constantine and Licinius (313 CE).

The willingness to suffer for the faith became a favorite topic of great Christian writers and a source of inspiration for the entire Church. The epistles of Ignatius of Antioch (d. ca. 110 CE), written to several Christian communities in Asia Minor while Ignatius was being taken under guard to Rome, are important for the theology of martyrdom that developed in the early Church. Ignatius understands martyrdom as an opportunity to imitate the suffering Christ (*Romans* 6, 3). The story of the martyrdom of Felicity and Perpetua (d. 203 CE) also became famous and influential for early Christian thinking about martyrdom. As those who actually suffered death for the faith, martyrs gradually became distinguished from confessors, who suffered some lesser punishment for their profession of Christianity. Confessors were often granted the rights and privileges of the presbyterate (see Hippolytus, *Apostolic Tradition*, 9), though abuses in this practice eventually had to be addressed. Imprisoned Christians who were awaiting their execution had the right to receive back into the Church those who had lapsed from the faith under the pressures of persecution.

Commemoration of the martyrs became an essential part of the liturgy of the Church. Martyrs were believed to have the power to intercede for the living. The graves of martyrs were viewed as holy places and their relics were treasured. Augustine tells of the healing of a blind man through Ambrose's use of the relics of the martyrs Protasius and Gervasius (*City of God*, 22, 8). The practice of celebrating the Eucharist at the tomb of a martyr, particularly on the anniversary of his or her death, became widespread. Martyrologies—lists of the martyrs in the order of their feasts—were composed and became significant for later liturgical development within the Church. Churches were erected over the tombs of some of the martyrs, and cities adopted particular martyrs as patrons.

Persecution as a Constant Factor in the Life of the Church. Suffering and death for the faith have continued to inform the life and the tradition of the Church through the centuries. The persecution of Christians under the Goths and Vandals in the fifth and sixth centuries, the Muslims in the seventh and eighth centuries, and leaders of the French Revolution at the end of the eighteenth century are only a few examples. Study of these moments in the history of the Church reveals that religious persecution was usually entangled with political strife, particularly as the Church itself became a political power.

It must also be acknowledged that, as the Church's power in society grew, it sometimes became involved in the persecution of others. Individual Christians, as well as the official Church, bear some of the responsibility for the recurrent persecution of Jews throughout the course of history, particularly during the First and Second Crusades. The establishment of the Inquisition by Pope Gregory IX (1231) led to the persecution of dissident groups within late medieval society. Originally directed against the Cathari and Waldenses, this tribunal was used against a variety of groups and individuals who were accused of heresy.

Vatican II taught that Christians will always be called upon to offer their lives as a supreme testimony of faith and, in so doing, to be transformed into the image of the master (Dogmatic Constitution on the Church, no. 42). In the recent past, some direct persecution of Christians for religious reasons has occurred, particularly under Communist regimes. Many Christians in the Third World suffer for their social and political convictions, sometimes at the hands of authorities who identify themselves as Christians. While such persecution is not usually directed at the profession of faith in Christ, it is the result of action for justice taken by believers who are convinced that their witness to the gospel requires the building of a more just society. This suffering and martyrdom for God's reign is usually more anonymous than the martyrdom of believers in the early Church. Though one must be careful not to ascribe martyrdom to every person who dies for a social or political cause, it is clear that witness to Christ includes and demands active striving for justice.

See: APOCALYPTIC, DEATH, EXILE, EXODUS, JUSTICE, PASSION, PROPHECY/PROPHET, SLAVERY, SUFFERING

ROBIN RYAN, C.P.

PETER

Peter's original name was Simon. Jesus gave him the label "The Rock"* (Aramaic, *kefa*); "Peter" comes from the Greek form of the latter.

The NT is full of evidence of Peter's unique leadership role both before and after the resurrection. Frequently he was the disciples' spokesman. His name always occurs first in lists of the disciples (Mark 3:16; Luke 6:14; Matt 10:2, where "first" is added to Peter's name). Along with James and John, he was singled out for special revelations of Jesus' divinity, such as at the transfiguration.

As the one who was to function as a "Christian rabbi," interpreting the traditions of Jesus, Peter had special understanding of that teaching. He was the one who requested clarification about the saying by which Jesus declared all things clean (Matt 15:15; in Mark 7:17 it is simply "the disciples" who ask). Peter dealt with the authorities on the question of paying the Temple tax and then received further instruction from Jesus, who significantly provided for both himself and Peter (Matt 17:24-27). Peter also received special instructions on forgiveness within the Christian community (Matt 18:21-22).

In John 21:15-17, the risen Jesus elicited from Peter a threefold protestation of love, corresponding to an earlier threefold denial, before commissioning him to feed Jesus' sheep. These passages suggest that Peter's leadership among the disciples in the post-Easter Church was based on his having been the first disciple to see the risen Lord (e.g., Luke 24:34; Mark 16:7). Our earliest testimony to the resurrection, the creedal passage in 1 Corinthians 15:3-5, places an appearance to Peter before all the others.

Paul tells us that Peter was one of the leaders of the Jerusalem community when he went there to "visit" two or three years after his conversion (Gal 1:18-19). At this time Paul's gospel and mission were subject to some authority from the Jerusalem community. The overall picture of Peter as one of the chief leaders responsible for an expanding Christian mission, first to the Jews then to interested Gentiles, is confirmed by the picture of Peter in Acts 1–15. In a heavenly vision God revealed to Peter that "all things are clean" and thus paved the way for Peter to baptize the first Gentiles (Acts 10:16). Peter may also have been responsible, as Acts 10–11 suggests, for some sort of compromise by which Gentiles were considered "clean" and acceptable members of the Christian community.

Paul castigated Peter for encouraging Jewish Christians at Antioch to separate from their Gentile brothers and sisters lest visiting Jewish Christians be scandalized.

Yet Peter's attitude of compromising with the visitors may have won out, since Paul left Antioch at about this time.

Peter and Rome

Peter, traveling as a missionary (Acts 9–10), enjoyed considerable prestige among the Corinthians, some of whom claimed special allegiance to him (1 Cor 1:12; 3:22). A letter from Rome, 1 Peter, is directed to churches in rural Asia Minor, reflecting Peter's reputation there. These churches were predominantly of Gentile origin and were probably the fruit of Petrine missionary work in that area.

Traditionally the Gospel of Mark has been associated with Rome, Peter, and John Mark. After having been subjected to every kind of criticism and investigation, these opinions are reasserting themselves. In 1985, M. Hengel, a luminary of German critical exegesis, stated flatly that Mark was written in Rome in 69 CE, where John Mark, a Jewish Christian from Palestine, wrote for a sorely tried community, which a few years earlier had to suffer the first cruel persecution under Nero.

It is quite certain that Peter spent his last years in Rome. The first of the two letters ascribed to him was written from "Babylon," a code name for Rome. Peter was martyred in Rome in 69 CE during the persecution of Nero. The earliest Church Fathers, starting with Clement of Rome, 95 CE, and followed by Ignatius of Antioch a few years later, bear witness to Peter's martyrdom in Rome. In the first half of the second century Papias wrote that Mark's Gospel was a record of Peter's Roman preaching.

Around 200 CE, a Roman writer invited his opponent to come to Rome to inspect the trophies (triumphal tombs) of St. Peter on the Vatican and St. Paul on the Via Ostia. The excavations made between 1940 and 1949 under the "confession" in St. Peter's at Rome have given strong confirmation to the ancient tradition that Peter was buried there.

Peter had a personality as big as his leadership role, and impetuosity is a trait that stands out in the NT accounts. Immediately after his confession of Jesus' messiahship and his receiving words of praise from his master, Peter rebuked Jesus for what seemed to him negative thinking, drawing Jesus' sharp reply, "Get behind me, Satan!" (Matt 16:21-23). When he asked Jesus to allow him to walk on water he began to sink through fear. At the transfiguration he was rebuked for suggesting that they build booths for Moses and Elijah as well as for Jesus (Matt 17:1-5).

Again, at the Last Supper, it was Peter who first refused to let Jesus wash his feet (John 13:6-9). On this same occasion Jesus predicted that all the disciples would fall away but again Peter was ready to argue with Jesus and to declare that he would never fall away. Jesus then foretold Peter's denial of the one he so loved. This threefold denial occurred only a few hours later in the courtyard of the high priest,* and when Peter realized what he had done, Matthew records that he "went out and began to weep bitterly" (26:75). This, and the events of the next couple of days, deeply affected Peter. The later picture is that of a humbler man, willing to wait for God to use him.

Fully aware of this side of Peter's character, Jesus could hardly have foregone an ironic smile when he conferred the name "The Rock" on Peter. All too soon this lovable aspect of the Jesus/Peter relationship would be covered over by the demands of "dignity of office." This process began already with Luke, who "rehabilitated" Peter through Jesus' prayer that "your own faith may not fail" (Luke 22:31-32). Peter was "the perfect man for the job," but only as Jesus would understand that term, i.e., not flawless, but wholehearted. Peter was much loved by Jesus and his fellow disciples, as he is by the faithful today.

See: BABEL/BABYLON, MISSION, ROCK/STONE, SATAN, TRANSFIGURATION

AUGUSTINE STOCK, O.S.B.

PHARISEE

Old Testament

The OT itself does not mention the Pharisees. From a first-century CE Jewish histo-

rian named Josephus it is known that the Pharisees constituted one of several important Jewish groups who wielded considerable influence in the Judaism of that time. The origins of this group of pious, law-observant Jews are obscured in the mists of history. It is believed that they came into existence during the second century BCE in the context of the identity crisis among Jews caused by the pagan influence of the Seleucid empire. Although the precise meaning of the term "Pharisees" is uncertain, it probably means "the separate ones," referring to their attempt to maintain the purity of Jewish traditions by avoiding contact with impure cultural influences.

Josephus, who wrote in Greek to explain Jewish traditions and history to a non-Jewish audience, labels the Pharisees a "philosophy," emphasizing their religious character, but they were also a potent political force in their early history. They struggled to preserve the Jewish traditions, which they believed were being eroded by external political influences and internal lax observance of the Law (Torah) among Jews. Contrary to popular modern belief, the Pharisees were mostly a lay movement within Judaism; they opposed corruption in the priestly aristocracy in Jerusalem as well as the increasing Hellenization (pagan Greek cultural influence) of their society. Furthermore, they attempted to make daily legal observance more attainable by validating both the written Torah and its oral interpretation, and by promoting the synagogue as a place for prayer and study apart from the Temple. Other important characteristics of this group included cultic ritual purity (especially associated with meals), tithing, fasting, and promoting an innovative belief in life after death.

New Testament

Christians have become familiar with the Pharisees mostly through the NT, especially the Gospels. Outside of the Gospels the Pharisees are mentioned only in Paul and Acts. Paul proudly refers to himself as a Pharisee "in observance of the law" (Phil

3:5) in the context of an autobiographical passage defending his impeccable Jewish heritage. This positive context is reinforced by his recollection of the zealous desire to preserve the traditions of his ancestors (Gal 1:14). Acts paints a somewhat ambivalent portrait of Pharisees. Although they are seen trying to enforce the strict requirement of the Law on the question of circumcision (Acts 15:5), one Pharisee named Gamaliel is portrayed as widely respected and wisely calling for caution among the Jews with regard to their treatment of the Christians (Acts 5:34-35). Paul is even said to have been a disciple of this Gamaliel (Acts 22:3). Acts 23:6-8 shows Paul shrewdly referring to his Pharisaic background to divide his accusers before the Sanhedrin over the issue of the Pharisees' belief in the resurrection of the dead, a doctrine vehemently opposed by another Jewish group, the Sadducees. Nicodemus is another Pharisee who receives favorable treatment in the NT. Though he comes to Jesus only "at night" (John 3:1), he tries to defend him (John 7:50) and assists at Jesus' burial (John 19:39).

This relatively neutral or positive portrayal of the Pharisees is overshadowed by the sharply negative images in the Gospels. All four Gospels show the Pharisees as archenemies of Jesus and the disciples, allied to others, such as Sadducees, scribes, and chief priests (e.g., Matt 15:1; 16:1; 27:62). If at times the NT acknowledges a distinction between these Jewish groups, the norm is more often a historically inaccurate presentation of the Pharisees as conspirators with other Jewish groups in continual opposition to Jesus. Matthew, for example, curiously combines Pharisees with Sadducees (3:7; 16:1) as if they were friendly allies, when in fact they were bitter enemies. Pharisees are portrayed pejoratively as legalistic (Luke 6:1-5), petty (Matt 23:23-24), and arrogant (Luke 18:11-12). The very word Pharisee becomes synonymous with "hypocrite," one who says one thing but does the opposite. The most vehement portrait of all is that of Matthew 23:3-36, where the Pharisees are excoriated, along with the scribes, in a series of condemnations. They are hypocritical blind guides, a self-indulgent "brood of vipers," who have their priorities entirely mixed up, who lay upon others burdens they themselves cannot bear, and who "are like whitewashed tombs, which appear beautiful on the outside, but inside are full of dead men's bones and every kind of filth" (v. 27). This fiery portrait is compounded by numerous scenes of confrontation in which Pharisees either accuse Jesus and his disciples of breaking Jewish traditions (Mark 7:5; John 9:16), try to entrap Jesus on legal technicalities (Mark 10:2; 12:13; Matt 22:34-35), or improperly seek signs (Mark 8:11).

For his part, Jesus warns against the "teaching" of the Pharisees (Matt 16:11-12) and associates them with those who have rejected God's prophets through the ages (Matt 23:31). Though he dines at the house of a Pharisee (Luke 7:36), he also admonishes him for his lack of proper hospitality (Luke 7:44-46). If Jesus seemingly upholds their general teaching authority, he nonetheless negates many of their specific actions, "For they preach but they do not practice" (Matt 23:2-3).

Although Pharisees are said to participate in the plot against Jesus (Matt 12:14; John 7:32; 11:57; 18:3), they do not figure prominently in the Gospel passion narratives. From a historical perspective, the intensely pejorative presentation of the Pharisees in the Gospels reflects more the late first-century conflict between the early Christians and the Pharisees who survived the fall of Jerusalem in 70 CE than to a conflict between themselves and Jesus.

Pastoral-Liturgical Tradition

A sad fact of Christian history is that the NT view of the Pharisees led to many anti-Jewish actions and to blatant antisemitism. Early Patristic interpreters of Scripture often subsumed the figure of the Pharisee under a stereotyped caricature of Jews, heightening their evil ways and responsibility for the death of Jesus. Modern biblical study has begun to correct this unfortunate development. Not only does contemporary Judaism trace its lineage to the Pharisaic Judaism that survived the destruction of Jerusalem, but it is recognized that the NT image of the Pharisees emerged in the heat of virulent disagreements in the first century CE when the Church was struggling to establish its own identity in relation to Judaism. Vatican II (Declaration on Non-Christian Religions, no. 4) indicates that Christians and Jews should acknowledge their common heritage and promote dialogue in order to understand one another from a non-polemical standpoint. No longer should the Pharisees or Pharisaism be synonyms for hypocrisy. Historically, they were devout reformers who fostered the preservation of Judaism. Christian preachers and teachers especially need to exercise caution when discussing the role of the Pharisees in the NT.

See: HYPOCRITE, JUDAISM, PASSION, RESURRECTION, SADDUCEES, SCRIBE, SYNAGOGUE, TEMPLE

RONALD D. WITHERUP, S.S.

PHILISTINES

The Philistines were ancient Israel's chief rival for the control of Canaan. In the thirteenth century BCE the Israelite settlement was confined to the central highlands of Canaan. About the same time, the Philistines, who migrated from the Aegean region, settled along the southern Mediterranean coast of Canaan. As the Philistines and Israelites began expanding their territorial holdings conflicts were inevitable. Though the Philistines had a more advanced material culture and a stronger military organization than the Israelite tribes, they were not able to dislodge the Israelites. David, who was a very capable military leader, was able to check the Philistines who were never again a serious threat to Israel. As a political entity Philistia disappeared during the Babylonian conquest in sixth century BCE. The Romans named the territory of the former Israelite kingdoms Palestina. This word derives from *Palaistinoi,* a Greek name for the descendants of the ancient Philistines. Per-

haps the Romans intended an insult to their restive Jewish subjects by naming their homeland after their ancient rivals. This name survives in its modern English form "Palestine."

A principal problem of ancient Near Eastern history and archaeology is identifying the Philistines and their place of origin. What makes this identification difficult is that soon after the Philistines arrived in Canaan, they abandoned their own culture, language, and religion and adopted that of the indigenous population. For example, the Bible mentions three Philistine deities: Dagon (Judg 16:21-30), Astarte (1 Sam 31:10), and Baal-zebub (2 Kgs 1:2). These names are Semitic. Analysis of the material remains of the Philistines shows a similar phenomenon. Early Philistine pottery shows the influence of Aegean forms, but by 1000 BCE these forms disappear and local Canaanite forms dominate. Excavations at Philistine sites are still in process and preliminary analysis is beginning to establish a profile of the distinctive Philistine culture.

The current consensus is that the Philistines were part of the massive movement of refugees from Greece and the Aegean islands that surged into the eastern Mediterranean region in the thirteenth century. They overcame the Hittites and the city-state of Ugarit. When they struck at Egypt, they were not as successful. Rameses III describes a battle he fought with them in 1190 BCE. Following his victory over the Philistines, he settled them along the southern Mediterranean coast of Canaan. The Bible appears to reflect a similar view of Philistine origins since it asserts that the Philistines were descendants of the Caphtorim [people of Crete?] (Gen 10:14).

The Philistines prospered in Canaan. They developed a confederation of autonomous city-states, the most famous of which were Gaza, Ashkelon, Ashdod, Ekron, and Gath. From these cities the Philistines began expanding their holdings to the north and east. This brought them into direct conflict with the Israelites who wanted to move beyond the central highlands into coastal plain to the west because of its great agricultural potential. The first reference to the conflict between these two peoples is the isolated reference to Shamgar, who is credited with killing six hundred Philistines (Judg 3:31).

At first the Philistines held the upper hand in the conflict. The political relations between the Philistine cities made an efficient military organization possible. The Bible asserts that the Philistines had a technological edge because of their monopoly on the forging of iron (1 Sam 13:19-22). The Philistine turned these advantages to early victories. The story of Samson assumes their conquest of Israelite territory (Judges 13–16). Eventually they forced the Danites to leave their settlements near Philistine territory and move to the north (Judges 18). When the Israelite began to resist the Philistine pressure, the Philistines defeated them soundly and captured the ark of the covenant (1 Samuel 4–6). While Saul led the Israelites to a victory over the Philistines early in his career (1 Samuel 13–14), it was not a decisive win and the conflicts continued through the rest of Saul's reign. Saul killed himself on Mount Gilboa when it became clear that the Philistine routed his army (1 Samuel 31).

Israel's fortunes changed with David. He gained fame as a member of Saul's army that contested Philistine incursions into Israel (1 Sam 17:41-54). When Saul's jealousy of the acclaim that came to David turned into murderous rage, David sought refuge among the Philistines and became a vassal to the king of Gath (1 Sam 27:1–28:2). After Saul's death, David broke his alliance with the Philistines. They attacked him (2 Sam 5:17-25), but failed to defeat their former ally. David defeated them and ended the Philistine threat (2 Sam 8:1). In Solomon's time, the Philistine city-states were paying tribute to the Israelites. The breakup of the Davidic-Solomonic Empire meant that the Philistines faced a weakened enemy in the Southern Kingdom. Conflict between Judah and the Philistines continued into the eighth century.

The prophets of the eighth century made use of this conflict in their preaching. Amos condemned the Philistines because of their involvement in the slave trade (Amos 1:6-8). Isaiah asserted that God used the Philistines to punish Israel for its infidelity (Isa 9:2) and he warned the Philistines that they would have to face divine judgment meted by the Assyrians (Isa 14:28-31). The Philistines survived the Assyrians but not the Babylonians (Jer 25:20; 47:2-7; Zech 9:5-6). The Philistines made the mistake of supporting Egypt in an anti-Babylonian alliance. The Babylonians exiled a sizeable portion of the Philistine population and ended the political existence of the Philistine city-states.

This did not end the animosity that the Jews felt toward the Philistines. Ben Sira, writing in the second century BCE, includes the Philistines on his enemies' list.

See: CANAAN, ISRAELITE

LESLIE J. HOPPE, O.F.M.

PILGRIMAGE

Of the three great monotheistic religions, Christianity is the only one that does not mandate pilgrimage as a religious duty. The OT reflects the intention to make Jerusalem the goal of pilgrimage. The NT recounts pilgrimages made there by Jesus. Because Christianity does not require the making of pilgrimage, this notion undergoes important transformation in the pastoral and liturgical traditions.

Old Testament

Pilgrimage is a journey to a holy place for some religious purpose. It is a feature of religions across the boundaries of time and culture. In the ancient Near East, shrines were built at sites because some manifestation of divine activity reportedly took place at that site (e.g., the story of Jacob's vision at Bethel in Gen 28:10-22 may have served to explain the existence of a Yahwistic shrine there). A shrine often became the goal of pilgrimages (e.g., the Book of Amos testifies that Bethel was still a pilgrimage center in the eighth century BCE).

The Bible mentions several pilgrimage centers in addition to Bethel. Shiloh was the goal of an annual pilgrimage (Judg 21:19-21; 1 Sam 1:3-7). The destruction of the town by the Philistines ended the pilgrimages there. Other places of pilgrimage included Gibeon, where Solomon went after his accession to pray for wisdom (1 Kgs 3:4); Beersheba, where the Israelites remembered Abraham (Gen 21:22-34; Amos 5:5; 8:14); and Gilgal, where they celebrated their entrance into the land (Josh 4:19–5:12; Hos 4:15: Amos 4:4-5; 8:14). There were other "high places" that attracted pilgrims as well (1 Sam 9:12-19, 25). The Bible looks down at these early pilgrimage sites because the final form of the text represents the perspectives of those who wished to promote Jerusalem as the only pilgrimage site for Israel.

David and Solomon initiated the process that led to Jerusalem's unique status in Israel. David made the city the religious center of his empire (2 Sam 6:12-19). Solomon built a Temple there (1 Kings 6), which enhanced the city's attractiveness as a center for pilgrimage. When the Davidic empire split into two smaller kingdoms following the death of Solomon, Jeroboam I established temples at Bethel and Dan to rival that of Jerusalem (1 Kgs 12:26-30).

Though it was royal policy in Judah to foster pilgrimage to Jerusalem, other shrines continued to attract worshipers. Both Hezekiah (2 Kgs 18:4) and Josiah (2 Kgs 23:8-9) made special efforts to centralize all sacrificial activity in the Temple of Jerusalem. They dismantled the "high places" and dispersed their priests. The attractiveness of these old shrines for the people is evident in the failure of the two kings' centralizing efforts to outlive them.

After the return from Exile, Judah was hardly able to support one shrine. The economic circumstances at the end of the sixth century BCE made the restoration of Jerusalem's Temple very difficult and that of other shrines almost impossible. Even with the financial support of the Persian Empire, Jerusalem's Temple was not rebuilt until 515 BCE—some twenty-four years after the return from Exile. This, together with the ideological support from the Deuteronomic tradition, secured the position of Jerusalem's Temple as *the* shrine of Judaism.

This status was enshrined in the Book of Deuteronomy, which required pilgrimage to the place "where the Lord will make his name dwell there" (=Jerusalem) three times a year. The three pilgrimage festivals are Passover/Unleavened Bread, Weeks (Pentecost), and Booths (Tabernacles) (Deut 16:16). It is improbable that every male Israelite made a pilgrimage to Jerusalem for each of these feasts as this law required, but the Deuteronomic legislation did establish the custom of these annual visits to Jerusalem and its Temple.

Though the members of the Qumran community rejected the priesthood of the Jerusalem Temple and considered that the rituals they led there illegitimate, the Qumran people did not reject Jerusalem or its Temple. They believed that one day, the wicked priests in Jerusalem will be expelled and the priests of the Qumran community will take their place, ensuring the holiness of the prescribed rituals.

New Testament

The NT observes that Jerusalem attracted large crowds for the pilgrimage feasts (Luke 2:41-45; John 12:20; Acts 2:1-10). Apparently, the objections of the Qumran people to the priesthood and rituals of the Jerusalem Temple were not taken seriously by most Jews. Jesus himself made several pilgrimages to Jerusalem according to the Gospel of John (John 2:13; 5:1; 7:2-10). The Synoptic Gospels record just one such pilgrimage during Jesus' ministry when he came to Jerusalem for the celebration of the Passover Festival during which he died.

Journeys to Jerusalem from elsewhere in Palestine and from the Diaspora were arduous. Pilgrims then usually traveled in groups for support and safety (Pss 42:4; 55:14; Luke 2:44). The Book of Psalms has preserved some of the songs pilgrims sang during their journey. These songs are marked by anticipation and joy (Psalms 24; 84; 118; 120–134). Excavations south of the Temple area in Jerusalem have uncovered some of the facilities for the many pilgrims that descended upon the city for the feasts. Among these facilities are the ritual baths that pilgrims used to enable them to enter the Temple courts.

Although the destruction of Jerusalem and its Temple by the Romans in 70 CE made it impossible for Jews to fulfill all the requirements of pilgrimage, the centuries have witnessed a continual procession of religious Jews to Jerusalem. The goal of these pilgrimages has been to pray at the Western Wall, which is the only architectural feature of the Herodian Temple precincts to remain after the Roman destruction.

The NT has spiritualized the idea of pilgrimage. It portrays the Christian life as a journey to the heavenly home (Heb 11:13-16; 1 Pet 1:17; 2:11). Unlike the Hebrew Bible, the NT does not require pilgrimage as a religious duty. Despite this, Christian pilgrims have been coming to the Holy Land as pilgrims from the beginning of the second century CE. In the fourth century CE, Constantine the Great had churches built on places associated with the life of Jesus. These churches became magnets drawing great numbers of Christian pilgrims to Jerusalem and Galilee. In the Middle Ages, the Crusades began as an attempt to maintain the rights of Christians to visit these pilgrim sites after Palestine passed into Muslim control. The desire for Christians of almost all ecclesial traditions to visit the Holy Land remains unabated.

See: FEASTS, JERUSALEM, TEMPLE

LESLIE J. HOPPE, O.F.M.

Pastoral-Liturgical Tradition

The term pilgrimage, designating a practice common to many religious experiences, but especially notable in Semitic cultures (Hebrew and Islamic), has taken on three different connotations in Christianity.

On a deep level, strongly influenced by certain biblical texts, pilgrimage designates the common condition of all Christians who have their true citizenship in heaven (Phil 3:20), groan and long for their heavenly dwelling (2 Cor 5:2), and must therefore live as pilgrims and exiles, struggling against the flesh (1 Pet 2:11).

Augustine spoke of the whole Church as a pilgrim living in a foreign land (City of God, 18, 51.2, cited in Dogmatic Constitution on the Church, no. 8). In the Eucharist, the Christian community sacramentally anticipates the banquet to be celebrated in the heavenly city. In its Dogmatic Constitution on the Church, Vatican II often uses the same image of pilgrimage, sometimes alluding to the Exodus story, in speaking of the eschatological orientation of the Church (Dogmatic Constitution on the Church, nos. 8, 10, 44, 48). The Council also uses the expression "the pilgrim Church" to designate God's people in its present earthly stage (Dogmatic Constitution on the Church, no. 50). Yet Christians have an earthly task, and it belongs mainly to the laity to permeate social structures with the spirit of the Gospel (Dogmatic Constitution on the Church, no. 36). The whole Church is concerned with "the joys and hopes, the griefs and anxieties" of humankind (Pastoral Constitution on the Church in the Modern World, no. 1).

Monasticism and later forms of religious life have arisen in the Church as a living, challenging parable that aims at expressing the main aspects of common Christian life. Hence from the beginning, monks and nuns undertook to express through their renunciation the eschatological thrust of Christian life (Athanasius, Life of Antony, 14), and therefore included "being a pilgrim" among the main features of their call. The practice seems to have begun in Syria and then spread to the rest of the Hellenistic world, where the terms xeniteia (the condition of being foreign) and xenos (foreign) were often used to denote this idea. In Syria, there were also pilgrim monks who took as their rule walking from dawn to sunset in order to manifest their pilgrimage to heaven. The pilgrimage of Israel's wandering through the desert was often taken as a source of inspiration.

It belongs to pastoral action to impress upon the faithful both the need to orient their life toward final fulfillment in heaven and at the same time a sense of responsibility for what needs to be done on earth. The texts of Vatican II trace a clear line for pastoral ministry in both senses. There is a need for a balanced lay spirituality that will take into account both dimensions of Christian life. In the past, the monastic calling exerted too strong an influence on common Christian spirituality. In contrast, however, the eschatological orientation of Christian life has never been more endangered than it is in today's consumerist and materialistic society.

Pilgrimage has also denoted the inner itinerary through which believers travel toward their encounter with God in mystical union.

Gregory of Nyssa took up the Exodus story as an inspirational image of the Christian's way to perfection (*Life of Moses*, nos. 112, 120, 228). John of the Cross speaks of the Ascent, but also of the wandering of the soul in search of Christ (*Canticle*). Today, the idea of stages and phases in Christian life is quite alive, owing to the fact that different forms of humanistic psychology emphasize the dynamic aspects of human growth and development. Human beings are always "on the road."

At this level, pastoral action takes two forms. The first form is to inculcate in sermons and homilies the call to ceaseless growth in faith, hope, and love. The Gospel of the Beatitudes and the call to love God with all our heart do not speak of a minimum we must keep, but a goal toward which we must tend. The second form is spiritual direction. The spiritual director is a companion on the road to Christian maturity.

Pilgrimage, in its usual and proper sense, refers to a journey made from one's home to a distant, sacred place. Egyptians, Greeks, and Romans made visits to remote shrines,

as Hindus do today, but it was in Semitic societies that pilgrimage became an important religious practice. In Israel there were periodic journeys to the "house of God" in Jerusalem, similar to temple visits in classic paganism. But in an isolated instance, Elijah made a famous visit to Mount Horeb, where God was revealed to Moses. In this case, the journey was made in order to commemorate and recreate a historical event. In Islam, the *hajj*, or pilgrimage to Mecca (a sacred duty for all Muslims), is also motivated by historical events.

In Christianity, pilgrimages are made in two different contexts. They are either visits to a prestigious shrine (e.g., of the Blessed Virgin or of a Saint) or visits to a place where historical events have or are supposed to have occurred.

Trips to a place (or associated places) where religious events have occurred were the earliest and most common form of pilgrimage. According to Eusebius, Bishop Melito of Sardis (ca. 160) and Bishop Alexander of Cappadocia (ca. 216) went on pilgrimage to the Holy Land (*Hist. Eccl.*, 4.26.14 and 6.11.2). But it was the pilgrimage of Emperor Constantine and his mother Helena to the Holy Land (where they built basilicas) that found the greatest echo among Christians. Toward the end of the fourth century some Fathers attribute to Helena the finding of the true cross. A text from the first half of the fourth century describes the stations where pilgrims stopped on their way from Gaul to Jerusalem and back to Rome. The most famous pilgrims of this time were the Spanish lady, Egeria, who narrated her trip and described a liturgy celebrated in Jerusalem (ca. 384), and Jerome, who remained in the Holy Land as a monk. On their way to the Holy Land, many pilgrims made side visits to monastic sites in Egypt, Palestine, and Syria (Egeria and Basil the Great). John Chrysostom spoke of pilgrimages as a means for arousing devotion (*In Phil.*: PG 62, 702-703), yet he and other Fathers warned about abuses taking place during pilgrimages.

The Crusades and the establishment of a Latin Kingdom in Palestine once again made pilgrimages to the Holy Land a popular expression of piety and penance. It is surprising to note how many medieval women famous in the history of spirituality (Bridget of Sweden and her daughter Catherine, for example) made pilgrimages to the Holy Land. For Ignatius Loyola, his pilgrimage to the Holy Land was an expression of his strong devotion to the humanity of Christ.

Another popular form of pilgrimage since Patristic times have been visits to the Apostles Peter and Paul in Rome, and of James in Compostela. The route of Saint James began in Germany, passed through France, and traversed Northern Spain. Civilization traveled with it, leaving monuments of romanesque and gothic art along its route. Francis of Assisi, Bridget, and Catherine of Sweden made their way to the tomb of Saint James. Saint Bona of Pisa, ever on the move, went first to the Holy Land and then made the pilgrimage to Compostela nine times, acting as an expert guide for others. There were also visits to the tomb of Mary Magdalene and to other shrines. Chaucer's comic masterpiece, *The Canterbury Tales*, is told in the context of a pilgrimage to the shrine of Thomas à Becket.

In recent times, pilgrimages to places where the Mother of the Lord has shown her power of attraction and intercession (Lourdes and Fatima) have equaled trips to the Holy Land in popularity. Compostela is still a popular place of pilgrimage, especially during a St. James' Holy Year (a year when his feastday, July 25, falls on a Sunday).

In our days of rapid transportation, pilgrimages are much easier than they were in Patristic and Medieval times, when people had to leave their homes for months and had to walk or go on mule-back through dangerous territory. This is why it is important for us to keep alive the penitential attitude that has been an essential part of the spirituality of pilgrimages for centuries.

To leave home means nothing if it does not involve the intention of leaving behind one's sinful past and pushing on to an encounter with God's grace. The sacrament of reconciliation at the shrine (Saint Peter's, Lourdes, or Fatima) is even now an important part of any pilgrimage. In the Middle Ages, pilgrimages were in some sense equivalents to long retreats. The interruption of normal activities and social relationships was a means of immersing oneself in a spiritual atmosphere. Today, the same spirit will be kept if times for silent prayer and communal celebrations are included. Finally, in the past pilgrimages were occasions for exercising solidarity with the poor who often waited at the gates of shrines to beg alms from the pilgrims. Setting something aside for donations to the needy will make modern pilgrimages more Christian.

See: DESERT, EXODUS

JOHN MANUEL LOZANO

PLAGUES

People and nature of the ancient world were often afflicted with plagues. Some plagues, namely, highly contagious epidemics, were thought to be caused by natural circumstances, i.e., poor sanitary conditions or the neglect of sanitary precautions. Certain diseases and ailments, i.e., leprosy* (Lev 13:1-45, 47-49; 14:33-57) and hemorrhages (Mark 5:25), were also associated with plagues. Other plagues were thought to be caused by divine intervention and thus understood as calamities that God imposed upon certain people for specific reasons. Both the OT and NT contain examples of plagues. The texts also show how plagues can be a means of divine chastisement for sin and injustice as well as the impetus for salvation and liberation.

Old Testament

The OT uses a variety of Hebrew words to express the notion of plague, e.g., *deber*, "pestilence," "plague"; *maggēpâ*, "plague"; *makkâ*, "blow," "wound," "stripe," "plague";

nega^c, "stroke," "wound," "plague," "mark"; and *negep*, "blow," "plague," "pestilence." Plagues affect Israelites, non-Israelites, the environment, and creatures. Plagues often have a theological function.

In Genesis 12:17 God strikes Pharaoh and his household with "severe plagues" to protect Sarai from being taken into Pharaoh's harem, an act that would jeopardize the divine covenant that God made with Abram that he and Sarai would have an heir, hence descendants, who would possess the promised land (Gen 12:2-3; 15:2-6, 7-21; 17:15-22).

The Egyptian plagues (Exod 7:14–12:36) include: the pollution of the Nile River and all other Egyptian water supplies (7:14-24), frogs (7:25–8:11), gnats (8:12-15), flies (8:16-28), pestilence (9:1-7), boils (9:8-12), hail and thunder (9:13-35), locusts (10:1-20), darkness (10:21-29), and death of the first-born among the Egyptians and their animals (11:1-10; 12:29-36). These plagues affect not only the Egyptian people (8:28-29; 11:29) but also their water (7:19), land (8:2, 9, 20; 9:25b; 10:14, 22), crops (9:31; 10:15), and animals (7:21; 8:13; 9:3, 9, 10, 25a, 29). The worst plague is the last. Exodus 11:1-10 and 12:29-30 portray God directly planning and executing this disaster.

The historicity of the plague phenomenon in Egypt continues to interest scholars. Reading the accounts from a synchronic and literary perspective, one can see that the plagues have a theological function. Together, they are (1) a means of divine chastisement; (2) an acknowledgment of divine power (Exod 8:15) and sovereignty (Exod 8:18; 9:29); and (3) an attestation that God is a God of liberation who does indeed hear and answer the cry of the oppressed (Exod 3:7-8). They also provide an opportunity for one to acknowledge one's sinfulness, to ask for forgiveness (Exod 9:27-28; 10:16-17), and to experience a change of heart (Exod 10:10; see 10:24a). Thus, the plagues show that God interacts in history and people's lives, in particular the lives of the oppressed, for the sake of transformation, liberation, and salvation.

Other OT texts, particularly the Prophets and the Psalms, also feature plagues in relation to divine power. God uses plagues to chastise the Israelites for their faithless or unjust deeds. God sends a plague upon the Israelites because they grumbled against Aaron and Moses (Num 17:11-15). Angry at the Israelites and David, God inflicts a pestilence upon them for three days (2 Sam 24:1-9, 10-17).

Plagues are also used as a divine threat. God warns the Israelites that if they do not observe all the commandments that were given to them, then they will be divinely struck with sickness and defeat (Deut 28:21, 58-62). Part of their suffering will be a "pestilence" that will exterminate them. Through the prophets God warns the Israelites continually that "they shall fall by the sword, by famine, and by pestilence" on account of their wicked deeds (see e.g., Jer 14:12; Ezek 6:11).

An angel of God uses a plague to assist the Israelites against the Assyrian army (2 Kgs 19:35; Isa 37:36). For the Israelites, the plagues serve as a reminder of God's goodness despite their ingratitude (Ps 78:43-55). Faithful Israelites are also assured of God's protection against "the destroying pestilence" (Ps 91:3) and "the devastating plague at noon" (Ps 91:6). The prophet Habakkuk implies that pestilence and plague reside with God (Hab 3:5).

Thus, with few exceptions, plagues in the OT are associated with divine power and God's plan for justice, mercy, liberation, and salvation.

New Testament

The Greek word for plague is *plēgē*, which means "bruise," "wound, "calamity," "plague." By extension plague is associated with a physical affliction, e.g., a hemorrhage in Mark 5:25-34. Here the Gospel writer depicts Jesus healing a woman of her affliction. This deed liberates her from pain and suffering.

Specific references to plagues are used throughout the book of Revelation (see Rev 9:18, 20; 11:6; 15:1, 5–16:21). Several of these plagues resemble those of Egypt, e.g., sores (16:2), darkness (17:10), hail (16:21), and like the Egyptian plagues, the ones in the Book of Revelation are inflicted by God. They are a sign of God's wrath, judgment, and chastisement (15:1; 16:21; 22:18), and strike both humankind and the natural world.

While the NT does not contain many examples of plagues, those cited above do show that, like those of the OT, these plagues are used in conjunction with a divine purpose, be it liberation or chastisement.

Pastoral-Liturgical Tradition

From a historical and literary perspective, one can see how plagues function theologically in the culture and setting of the ancient world. Even though there may be historical evidence to support the existence of the various plagues mentioned, one needs to be careful not to interpret or understand them in an excessively literal way. The ancient Judeo-Christian people and writers were highly imaginative when they told and wrote the stories.

From an ethical, pastoral, and hermeneutical perspective, plagues interpreted as calamities resulting from divine intervention raise certain contemporary theological questions, e.g., Why must the natural world—fish (Exod 7:18), livestock (Exod 9:3), trees (Exod 9:25), etc.—suffer affliction because of humankind's sin and injustice and for the purpose of demonstrating that divine power surpasses human strength? Or, what theology is expressed by such a punitive portrait of God? Questions like this call for ongoing scholarly and theological discussion as well as pastoral reflection and comment.

See: DEATH, EGYPT, JUSTICE, LEPROSY, LIGHT AND DARKNESS, MERCY, MOSES, POWER, SALVATION, SIN, SUFFERING, WRATH OF GOD

CAROL J. DEMPSEY, O.P.

POOR

Attempting a synthesis of what the biblical tradition says about the poor is difficult because this tradition developed over more than one thousand years. It reflects varying circumstances of time and place. It is the product of very different types of experience and exhibits an amazing variety of ways of reflecting on that experience.

Old Testament

The Book of Deuteronomy. Of the legal traditions in the OT, Deuteronomy pays the most attention to the poor. Deuteronomy never intimates that there is any positive value in poverty. On the contrary, Deuteronomy asserts that poverty is something that does not belong in the Israelite community (Deut 15:4). It is a curse on a disobedient Israel (28:29b). Deuteronomy calls upon the Israelites who have the means to relieve the burdens of the poor and to direct their community's life to combat the causes of poverty.

The first step in accomplishing these goals involves a call to the wealthy to renounce their rights and claims upon the poor. They are to take no interest on loans (Deut 23:19-20), they are to release the poor from the debts periodically (15:1-6), they are to release their bond servants with generous provisions (15:12-18), and part of the harvest should be left for the poor (24:17-22). Deuteronomy asks people of means to follow a course of action that is contrary to their self-interest but one that assures them that the results of such behavior will be of ultimate benefit because it will be God's blessings and continued possession of the land. Deuteronomy recognizes that unmitigated self-interest breeds injustice. The only way to secure God's blessings is to share them.

The Deuteronomistic History. The narratives in Joshua to Second Kings derive their theological inspiration from Deuteronomy. This Deuteronomistic history of Israel tells a sad story. What begins with so much promise ends with tragedy and despair. At both the beginning and end of the story of Israel in its land stand the poor and dispossessed. At the beginning of the story stand the people who escaped slavery in Egypt. With only the promise of land ahead of them, they enter Canaan and join with the disaffected poor of that land to establish a new social and economic order. It was to be one without great class distinctions. Its foundation was the service of Yahweh who gave Israel its land, the means of their support.

Unfortunately, attempts at subverting the divine plan for Israel's well being mark the rest of Israel's history. The people themselves ask for a monarchy that accelerates this process of subversion. In the end, Israel loses its land because some of its people were not content with their share of Israel's inheritance and sought to accumulate as much as possible for themselves. It was these people who created poverty in Israel as they took over more of the land. In the end, however, only the poor remained in the land while the people of means, power, and position found themselves in exile from the land that was to be Israel's everlasting inheritance.

The Prophets. The oracles of Israel's prophets also describe how people of means rejected the divine plan and by that created poverty. The prophets strongly criticize the monarchy and the judiciary for offenses against the poor (Amos 5:7; Isa 5:23; Mic 3:9-11; Jer 22:13-17). The objects of scathing criticism were the wealthy landowners and creditors who foreclosed on peasants who had owned their own land. The result was the concentration of the land in the hands of a few and the creation of many landless farmers (Isa 5:8; Mic 2:1-3; Ezek 22:29; Hab 2:5-6). Then there were merchants who exploited their customers (Hos 12:8; Amos 8:5; Mic 6:10-11; Isa 3:14; Jer 5:27). The prophets believed that poverty then was the creation of the rich who oppressed the poor (Amos 3:9; Isa 5:8; Mic 2:1; Hab 2:9; Ezek 45:9; Mal 3:5).

The prophets were not economic theorists or simply social critics. What they did was to show Israel the consequences of its behavior from their own understanding of the covenant that bound Israel to God.

They did not regard poverty as the result of chance, destiny, or laziness. Poverty was simply the creation of the rich who have broken the covenant because of their greed. The wealthy used their resources not to enhance the community's life but to support their own purposes. In this way they violated the covenant, they destroyed the unity of Israel, and created poverty. This called for the divine judgment that the prophets announced.

One basis for the prophetic attitude toward the poor was the common ancient Near Eastern belief that the gods were the protectors of the poor (Isa 41:17; 51:21; 54:11). There are several prophetic texts that call for an attitude of confidence of God using the vocabulary of the poor (Zeph 2:3; 3:12). Still the prophets do not idealize poverty as a state of special closeness to God. For the prophets, poverty is an evil created by the wealthy who engage in immoral practices to enrich themselves. In accomplishing this, they consume the poor. The prophets see this as one reason for divine judgment upon Israel. In their visions of a restored Israel, some prophets see an end to injustice that breeds poverty (Isa 61:1-2).

If the prophets view the poor in any consistent way it is not as people who are in some way closer to God because of their poverty. The prophets see the poor as victims. Their fellow Israelites victimized them by violating the most fundamental stipulations of the covenant. There is only one legitimate response to this and that is divine judgment. The prophets speak the words of judgment against the people who created the conditions that breed poverty and make it part of the Israelite social system.

The only way that the Bible can effect social change in the world today is if people again hear the prophetic protest against poverty and those who cause it. Focusing on isolated texts from certain prophets leads to a spiritualization of poverty. What is damaging about such an approach is that it leads to an acceptance of poverty and a failure to follow the prophets to protest against the existence of poverty that calls divine judgment on those who allow it to exist.

The Wisdom Literature. Except for the psalms, most of the statements made in the Bible about the poor occur in the Wisdom literature of the OT. Its views of poverty are realistic, for this tradition recognizes that poverty may at times be one's own fault— an idea not found in the prophets or psalms. According to the Book of Proverbs, poverty is the inevitable result of an undisciplined life (Prov 6:10-11). In evaluating the attitude of this tradition about poverty it is important to remember that it was not trying to explain the origins of poverty. Its goal was to describe the consequences of a life-style that is without self-control (e.g., Prov 13:18). The assumption behind much of the wisdom's traditions views is that the poor choose their own lot.

Still the sages did not believe that poverty was only the result of the way some people choose to live. They urged compassion for the poor (Prov 21:13). They sought to motivate people to compassion by teaching that a kindness to the poor is a kindness done to God (Prov 19:17). This would not make much sense if poverty were simply the choice that undisciplined people make.

The Wisdom tradition also recognizes that the rich and powerful are responsible for creating and perpetuating poverty. Ecclesiastes focuses on the corruption of Israel's judicial system (Eccl 5:8). The book contains a parable (Eccl 9:14-16) that shows how the system keeps the poor in their poverty. The parable asserts that even when a poor person does something extraordinary, people forget because the poor are not supposed to distinguish themselves—or at least that is what the wealthy tell themselves to rationalize poverty. The poor are trapped. They cannot extricate themselves from their poverty.

Some characterize the approach of the Wisdom tradition toward poverty as neutral. It traces the origins of poverty to both laziness and folly and to oppression and injustice. What the tradition is not neutral

about is the responsibility of the rich. Poverty calls for action from the wealthy to alleviate the burdens of the poor.

The Psalms. The Psalter is replete with references to the poor. Here the poor are idealized. In the psalms poverty takes on an aura of sanctity as if it possessed a religious character. The poor are meek, lowly, humble, faithful, righteous, dependent, hopeful. The poor have surrendered themselves completely to God. This is especially evident in psalms of lament (e.g., Psalms 3; 5; 6; 44; 74; 79; 83). The form that these psalms follow reflects a liturgical pattern. An invocation of God is followed by the psalmist's petitions for deliverance.

The psalm concludes with an expression of trust in God. The psalmist turns to God because God is the protector and refuge of the poor. God combats those who would prevent the poor from securing their rights. Others may fall, but God will always be help to the poor in need.

In the psalms the poor individual is contrasted with those who are unrighteous. The poor person has the quality of authenticity. Since the rich are the oppressors, the poor person is always presented as the "righteous one." The traditional ancient Near Eastern idea of God as the protector of the poor takes on an added dimension here since the poor are equated with the righteous and therefore they deserve divine protection.

The psalms are, after all, prayers; therefore, a certain amount of "spiritualization" is to be expected. Still the psalms do not ignore the realities of a corrupt social system. The psalms of lament make it clear that the situation in which the poor find themselves is caused by "enemies" (9:4, 7; 35:19; 65:5, 19). While sometimes vague terms are used to describe these enemies, such as "the wicked" (10:4; 12:9; 140:5, 9), other times specific terms are used that make it clear that these enemies are the wealthy who take advantage of the poor: "despoilers" (35:10), "plunderers" (109:11), "creditors" (109:11), and perjured witnesses (35:11;

109:31). While these psalms use a variety of terms to describe the "enemies" of the poor, clearly some of these terms reflect a situation of socio-economic conflict within the Israelite community. This conflict is described as one involving the very survival of the poor (37:14; 109:16).

The psalms give an insight into how the poor handled the conflict. They had none of the power possessed by the wealthy. All they had was prayer. The poor were, however, to have more than just a prayer for justice. The king was to be God's instrument for securing justice for the poor and oppressed. Psalm 72 is a prayer for divine blessing on the king. It asks that God's justice be given to the king so that the king may, in turn, judge the people in righteousness. This means nothing less than the poor receiving their dues (vv. 1-2). The psalm asserts that it is the king who was to defend the poor and deal with their oppressors (v. 4). If the king is faithful to this responsibility, he will be rewarded with universal dominion (vv. 8-14). This text certainly reflects social conflict within Israel. Here again the "poor" are the economically marginal who are in danger of exploitation and who are to be protected by the king.

Most often words for "the poor" in the psalms are singular, except in some later psalms when the plural form 'anawim begins to appear (Pss 9:19; 10:16; 22:26; 34:2; 37:11; 69:32; 76:9; 147:6; 149:4). Some interpreters see the 'anawim as a group forming the religious nucleus of the nation in contrast to their opponents who are ready to abandon their ancestral religion. What is clear from the reading of the psalms in which the word 'anawim appears is that allusions to material poverty or the problems of the poor are missing. Here the primary social conflict is no longer simply on an economic level but it moves to the religious level. While poverty still existed, the conflict with the wealthy was seen to be determined not by their economic practices but by their approach to their ancestral religion. In the eyes of the 'anawim, the wealthy were not true believers—they were

evil. Observant Jews, no matter what their economic status, considered themselves to be among the poor. The words for "poor" become functionally equivalent to "pious" or "humble" and the opposite of "evil" and "wicked."

Although one may speak of a type of "spiritualization" of poverty and the poor in the Book of Psalms, these prayers nevertheless do not detach themselves completely from earlier perspectives on the poor and they do not idealize the state of poverty as such. The intensity of the language in the psalms of lament make it clear that the "poor" did not accept their situation as the divine will. They beg for deliverance. They ask for the defeat of their enemies. They pray for vindication. They hardly resign themselves to the situation that they experience as oppressive. Second, those who pray these psalms fully expect that they will be vindicated by God. Submission does not mean the quiet acceptance of oppression. It refers to the confidence that the expected deliverance will take place in accord with the divine good pleasure. The "humility" of the 'anawim consisted in the acknowledgment that only God was able to save them. Indeed the 'anawim understand and totally accept God's justice, providence, and will because they understand that God's will is for the vindication of the just. The reason that some observant Jews reinterpreted the cries of the poor in their own conflicts with those whom they considered the "wicked" was precisely because the poor fully expected justice from God.

The Apocalyptic Literature. Apocalyptic literature reflects a continuing social and economic conflict between the poor and the wealthy within the Jewish community as well as the problems the Jewish community faced because of its lack of political independence. It may very well have been that apocalyptic emerged as a way for the dispossessed within the Jewish community to deal with their experience of oppression. Apocalyptic literature exhibited a point of continuity with earlier biblical tradition when it presented God as the defender of the oppressed. What made apocalyptic unique was its belief that God's intervention for the oppressed was imminent and that this intervention will usher in a new world. In that new world God's justice will reign and therefore the poor will experience a reversal of fortunes, and by that finally receive the reward for their fidelity in the midst of oppression.

The one apocalyptic work in the OT is the Book of Daniel. This book deals with questions of justice from an apocalyptic perspective—one that looks for the imminent intervention of God to reverse the fortunes of the faithful. It offers no practical advice on overcoming injustice since it sees the future as controlled by God alone. There is no justice in this world. Oppression, persecution, poverty are only passing realities as are the kingdoms of this world. What is so critical is that people remain faithful to God despite the problems they face as they struggle to maintain their fidelity. The book's faith in the power of God to control the future enabled those who accepted its message to defy the forces of oppression. There are no practical suggestions for resisting the powers of evil; therefore, a materialist and positivist analysis of Daniel would regard its approach to the problem of oppression as an illusion. Those who first heard its message, however, experienced it as life-giving and liberating. The problem comes when contemporary readers try to make Daniel's approach a universal ethic. Among religious Jews of the day there were striking differences of approach to the persecution of Antiochus. Daniel represents one view. Though the book offers no "practical" advice on overcoming oppression, it obviously regards it as an evil which calls forth divine judgment. The "people who know their God" (11:31) are praised not because they suffer persecution but because they remain faithful to their God despite the suffering that they have to endure. Daniel affirms that this suffering will end by the power of God.

New Testament

The Gospels. The Gospels portray Jesus of Nazareth as a poor man. Jesus, however, belonged to a family that was not poor. His legal father, Joseph was a skilled laborer. But Jesus left his family and occupation. He asked the same of those who wished to follow him. In Jesus' inaugural sermon, Luke has Jesus proclaim a year of jubilee (4:18) when the poor have their debts forgiven. During his ministry he had no place where he could lay his head (Matt 8:20; Luke 9:58). Throughout his life Jesus was able to dissociate himself from possessions because they accounted for nothing in terms of the reign he was called to proclaim. He challenges his followers to trust in God implicitly (Matt 6:25-34). His solidarity with the poor became complete during his passion when he died the death of a criminal. Paul calls this act of solidarity the taking on the form of a slave (Phil 2:7). It is among the least important members of the Christian community that Jesus is to be found today (Matt 25:31-36). Because of his own poverty, Jesus' call for detachment from every care and for complete trust in God (Matt 6:25-34; Luke 12:22-32) has an air of authenticity about it.

The Gospels of Mark and Matthew are not directly concerned with poverty, but the theme of the rich and the poor is a significant one for Luke. This evangelist has nine separate pericopes in which the poor are mentioned, and of these five are unique to Luke: Mary's Song (1:39-54); Jesus' inaugural sermon at Nazareth (4:16-22); the parable of the great supper (14:16-24); the parable of the rich man and Lazarus (16:19-31); and the story of Zacchaeus (19:1-10).

The Pauline Corpus. Paul's attitude toward the poor was probably colored by his expectations regarding the parousia. The apostle's eschatological orientation does not allow him to deal at any great length with socioeconomic problems. If people work, the lack of a comfortable life will at least be tolerable. Paul sets himself up as a model (2 Thess 3:7-9). The apostle reflects his Greco-Roman background that considered dependence upon the charity of others as repugnant. He was unwilling to live off alms though he had a right to do so because of his position as a minister of the Gospel. In Philippians 4:10, Paul implies that his independence is important to him. He does not wish to be dependent upon the Philippian church. To do so he has learned how to be content with little. Paul is willing to make the necessary renunciations not because he values poverty in and of itself but because he values his independence more than a comfortable existence.

When the NT speaks of "the poor," it refers to the materially poor. It praises the actions of some poor people but it does not idealize poverty as a state that gives a person special access to God. The most that can be said about poverty is that it eliminates one type of temptation to dismiss Jesus' call to repentance—the temptation that comes through the self-sufficiency that wealth provides. One way for people of means to give a tangible sign of their repentance is for them to distribute their wealth to people in need. Despite its eschatological orientation, nothing in the NT leads to the conclusion that material poverty is something that can be ignored or that its existence ought to be accepted fatalistically. Indeed the Gospels present Jesus as one of the poor so that any observations Jesus makes about poverty and the poor need to be understood as statements of a poor person. Responding to Jesus' call for conversion enables the disciple to hear the call of the biblical tradition for justice. It impels the disciples to sell what they have to give to the poor. Paul gives no evidence of any transvaluation of poverty into some sort of a spiritual reality. He advises people to work to support themselves and to be happy with a less than comfortable existence. The apostle also asks people to support the poor of the Church in Jerusalem (2 Corinthians 8–9).

The NT does not speak with the passion of the Hebrew prophets regarding social injustice except in a few places, such as James 2:1-6 and 5:1-6. It does, however, speak quite a lot about a kind of solidarity within the community of faith that makes social injustice unthinkable. Above all, it presents the life and teaching of one who was able to live without the security of possessions and power. It challenges his followers to do the same.

See: RICH

LESLIE J. HOPPE, O.F.M.

POWER

The English term power has been used for a variety of Hebrew and Greek words and phrases. In general it means the ability to do something. Included here is the idea of adequate strength, skill, resources, energy, etc., to effect the intended result. Power can be something possessed and something exercised. It does not necessarily imply an ordered situation in which might is exercised. However, at times, it may include the idea of rightful authority. Strictly speaking, there is no real power or authority but that which belongs to God (Ps 62:12; John 19:11). However, God has given power to others, some of whom possess the ability to perform acts contrary to the will and commandments of God. One finds the term used for physical strength, human will, political, economic, or military power, and spiritual power.

When one speaks about power it is also necessary to mention authority, because it is sometimes difficult to separate power and authority. Certain authority is illusory unless it is backed by real power. Perhaps the best distinction is between the authority one has to issue a command and the external power one can bring to bear, if necessary, to ensure that the command is carried out. Authority can be said to be the capability, freedom, and right to do what one wills in a given instance. It refers especially to the right one has, by virtue of office, position, or relationship, to command obedience.

Old Testament

In the OT power is usually used to refer to right, authority, permission, or freedom in the legal or political sense. In the later writings it denotes the power of the king or of God, power that decides in authoritarian relationships. According to the OT, "power belongs to God" (Ps 62:12). "Yours, O LORD, are grandeur and power, majesty, splendor, and glory. For all in heaven and on earth is yours; yours, O LORD, is the sovereignty; you are exalted as head over all. Riches and honor are from you and you have dominion over all. In your hand are power and might; it is yours to give grandeur and strength to all" (1 Chr 29:11-12). The Almighty is "preeminent in power" (Job 37:23).

Nature and History. God's power is manifested in a variety of ways and places. It is manifested in nature, especially in the act of creation. Jeremiah refers to God as "He who made the earth by his power, established the world by his wisdom, and stretched out the heavens by his skill" (Jer 10:12). Later in the same Prophetic book God says, "It was I who made the earth, and man and beast on the face of the earth, by my great power, with my outstretched arm" (Jer 27:5).

God's power is manifested also in history, especially in the Exodus events by means of which God saved the Israelites "for his name's sake, to make known his power" (Ps 106:8). "Why, O LORD, should your wrath blaze up against your own people, whom you brought out of the land of Egypt with such great power and with so strong a hand?" (Exod 32:11). The power of God, manifest in the liberation of the chosen people from Egyptian bondage, is seen as directed against those who stand in the way of this liberation. "Your right hand, O LORD, magnificent in power, your right hand, O LORD, has shattered the enemy" (Exod 15:6).

God Intervenes on Israel's Behalf. Because God's power unfolds in nature and history, the people of Israel have recourse to it whenever they find themselves in need or in danger. "It is God who has the power to reinforce or to defeat" (2 Chr 25:8). In God's hand is "power and might," which no one can withstand (2 Chr 20:6).

The psalmist informs us that God will save the just: "But God will redeem me from the power of the nether world by receiving me" (Ps 49:16). God is asked to provide defense against the wicked: "O God, slay them, lest they beguile my people; shake them by your power, and bring them down" (Ps 59:12). And God is asked to intercede on behalf of condemned prisoners: "Let the prisoners' sighing come before you; with your great power free those doomed to death" (Ps 79:11).

God Gives Power to Others. While God is the source of all power, the OT indicates that God has given power to others. Power is given to the nation: "Confess the power of God! Over Israel is his majesty; his power is in the skies. Awesome in his sanctuary is God, the God of Israel; he gives power and strength to his people" (Ps 68:35-36). And God gives power to human beings like Balaam and Moses. Balaam, a prophet hired to curse the Israelites, says to Balak, the king of Moab, "Well, I have come to you after all. But what power have I to say anything? I can speak only what God puts in my mouth" (Num 22:38). The Lord said to Moses, "On your return to Egypt, see that you perform before Pharoah all the wonders I have put in your power" (Exod 4:21). In Deuteronomy one reads about "the might and the terrifying power that Moses exhibited in the sight of all Israel" (Deut 34:12).

At times the power of the Lord manifests itself in Israel's prophets. When "the power of the LORD came upon Elisha" (2 Kgs 3:15), he began to prophecy. Micah notes, "But as for me, I am filled with power, with the spirit of the LORD, with authority and with might" (Mic 3:8).

Power to Do Evil. Sometimes God gives power to those who possess the ability to perform acts contrary to the will and commandments of God. This includes Satan and various individuals and nations. Speaking to Satan about Job, God first says, "Behold, all that he has is in your power; only do not lay a hand upon his person" (Job 1:12). Later, "The LORD said to Satan,

'He is in your power, only spare his life'" (Job 2:6).

Power is given also to individual human beings who then have the ability to work at cross purposes with God. Daniel tells King Nebuchadnezzar, "You, O king, are the king of kings; to you the God of heaven has given dominion and strength, power and glory" (Dan 2:37). Susanna concludes that she cannot escape the power of the elders who wish to lie with her, but adds, "it is better for me to fall into your power without guilt than to sin before the Lord" (Dan 13:22-23). Micah notes, "Woe to those who plan iniquity, and work out evil on their couches; in the morning light they accomplish it when it lies within their power" (Mic 13:14). And in Job's sixth reply Job asks, "Why do the wicked survive, grow old, become might in power?" (Job 21:7).

At other times, power is given to nations who use this might to perform acts contrary to the will of God. In the Book of Daniel the reader learns that no one can withstand the power of the two-horned ram, symbolic of the combined kingdom of the Medes and Persians (Dan 8:4, 7). The Lord was angry with the Israelites and "He allowed them to fall into the power of their enemies" (Judg 2:14). Later, the Lord raised up judges to deliver the Israelites "from the power of their despoilers" (Judg 2:16).

Power Not Used. God also chooses, on various occasions, not to use the power he has. The Lord says to Moses, "But this is why I have spared you: to show you my power and to make my name resound throughout the earth" (Exod 9:16). Ecclesiastes speaks of the evil that exists when someone lacks nothing "yet God does not grant him power to partake of them" (Eccl 6:2).

New Testament

In the NT the term power is used to refer to God's very self (Matt 26:64): "From now on you will see 'the Son of Man seated at the right hand of the Power.'" As in the OT, all power comes from God. Pilate says to

Jesus, "'Do you not know that I have power to release you and I have power to crucify you?' Jesus answered [him], 'You would have no power over me if it had not been given to you from above'" (John 19:10-11). The author of Ephesians recognizes this fact as well when he says, "I became a minister by the gift of God's grace that was granted me in accord with the exercise of his power!" (Eph 3:7).

The power of God is seen in nature and the spiritual world: there is power that Satan exercises and imparts, and the power given to Jesus, and by him to his disciples. Jesus receives his power from the anointing by the Spirit (Luke 4:14; Acts 10:38), while his authority is more closely linked by God to his mission.

Creation and Redemption. The power of God can be seen in all God's works, especially those of creation and redemption. Paul says of God, "Ever since the creation of the world, his invisible attributes of eternal power and divinity have been able to be understood" (Rom 1:20). Paul also notes that, "The message of the cross is foolishness to those who are perishing, but to us who are being saved it is the power of God" (1 Cor 1:18). "For I am not ashamed of the gospel. It is the power of God for the salvation of everyone who believes" (Rom 1:16). In Luke's Gospel the angel Gabriel tells Mary that, "The holy Spirit will come upon you, and the power of the Most High will overshadow you. Therefore the child to be born will be called holy, the Son of God" (Luke 1:35). And in the Corinthian correspondence one learns that Christ "lives by the power of God" (2 Cor 13:4) and that "God raised the Lord and will also raise us by his power" (1 Cor 6:14). The power remains God's, however, as Paul testifies: "But we hold this treasure in earthen vessels, that the surpassing power may be of God and not from us" (2 Cor 4:7).

God Gives Power to Others. God has given power to others, some of whom possess the ability to perform acts contrary to the will and commandments of God. In 2

Thessalonians one reads about the lawless one "whose coming springs from the power of Satan in every mighty deed and in signs and wonders that lie" (2 Thess 2:9). Likewise, Hebrews 2:14 speaks of the devil as the one who has "the power of death." "We know that we belong to God, and the whole world is under the power of the evil one" (1 John 5:19). Jesus, the risen Lord, says to Paul, "I shall deliver you from this people and from the Gentiles to whom I send you, to open their eyes that they may turn from darkness to light and from the power of Satan to God" (Acts 26:17-18).

Secular rulers also possess power. Pilate has power: "They watched him [Jesus] closely and sent agents pretending to be righteous who were to trap him in speech, in order to hand him over to the authority and power of the governor" (Luke 20:20). "So Pilate said to him, 'Do you not speak to me? Do you not know that I have power to release you and I have power to crucify you?'" (John 19:10). And kings have power: "The ten horns that you saw represent ten kings who have not yet been crowned; they will receive royal authority along with the beast for one hour. They are of one mind and will give their power and authority to the beast" (Rev 17:11-12).

Manifest in the Career of Jesus. The power of God was made manifest in the life and deeds of Jesus. "For with what authority and power he commands the unclean spirits, and they come out" (Luke 4:36). One day Jesus was teaching "and the power of the Lord was with him for healing" (Luke 5:17). "Everyone in the crowd sought to touch him because power came forth from him and healed them all" (Luke 6:19).

While God is the highest authority in heaven and on earth, he has also given the "Son of Man . . . authority on earth to forgive sins" (Matt 9:6). The "Son of Man" will come "upon the clouds of heaven with power and great glory" (Matt 24:30). In John's Gospel Jesus, speaking about his life, says, "No one takes it from me, but I lay it down on my own. I have power to lay it down, and power to take it up again. This command I have received from my Father" (John 10:18). And after his resurrection Jesus, the risen Lord, declares that "All power in heaven and on earth has been given to me" (Matt 28:18).

Power Given to Jesus' Disciples. The power of the Spirit is linked especially with the apostolic witness in Acts: "But you will receive power when the holy Spirit comes upon you" (Acts 1:8). "With great power the apostles bore witness to the resurrection of the Lord Jesus" (Acts 4:33).

Jesus gives power and authority to his disciples. "He summoned the Twelve and gave them power and authority over all demons and to cure diseases" (Luke 9:1). "Behold, I have given you power 'to tread upon serpents' and scorpions upon the full force of the enemy and nothing will harm you" (Luke 10:19). In John's Gospel the Word "gave power to become children of God" (John 1:12) to those who accept him. Before his ascension, Jesus tells his disciples to stay in Jerusalem "until you are clothed with power from on high" (Luke 24:49). In Acts he says to them, "But you will receive power when the holy Spirit comes upon you, and you will be my witnesses in Jerusalem, throughout Judea and Samaria, and to the ends of the earth" (Acts 1:8). Paul notes that he came to Corinth in weakness and fear and much trembling, "but with a demonstration of spirit and power, so that your faith might rest not on human wisdom but on the power of God" (1 Cor 2:4).

Miracles. Power is often associated with the miraculous activity of Jesus and his disciples. After the cure of the crippled beggar, Peter asked the Israelite audience, "Why are you amazed at this, and why do you look so intently at us as if we had made him walk by our own power or piety? (Acts 3:12). On the next day the Jewish leaders asked Peter and John, "By what power or by what name have you done this? (Acts 4:7). The connection between power and miracle can be seen also in the Stephen story: "Now Stephen, filled with grace and power, was working great wonders and signs among the people" (Acts 6:8). Simon the magician says to the apostles, "Give me this power too, so that anyone upon whom I lay my hands may receive the holy Spirit" (Acts 8:19).

See: CREATION, GLORY, HEALING, LIGHT AND DARKNESS, MIRACLES, MISSION, OBEDIENCE, REDEMPTION, SATAN, SIGN, SPIRIT, WEAKNESS, WILL OF GOD, WISDOM

DENNIS M. SWEETLAND

Pastoral-Liturgical Tradition

In general terms for theology, power first names the fact of being. There is power in the sheer fact of sustaining existence. Given that, one can then distinguish diverse forms of being, and indicate the dependence of some on others. Second, power names the ability to act, or to withhold action, and again, degrees can be distinguished, and situations. Thus power appears as both a natural and a political fact. These problems have been worked out in a multitude of metaphysical, social scientific, and psychological frameworks, *inter alia*, and theologians have been in conversation with them. This brief article can only indicate some of this richness in relation to the key topics of God, human beings, and the natural world.

Power in Relation to God. Within a general understanding of power as the power to be, God is usually understood as Being Itself, the Being that sources and sustains all beings. Thus God's creative and providential powers immediately appear. In reference to the second general definition, Thomas Aquinas tells us that the Divine essence is fully realized in act. This is infinite in form and so is infinitely powerful. Thomas goes on to tell us (ST I, q. 25, a. 3) that this omnipotence means that God can do all things that are absolutely possible. God, however, cannot act in contradiction to the Divine nature, because of the necessary relation between a cause and an effect.

With these classical formulations, the problem of theodicy appears. The God who is all-powerful is also all-good, all-loving, all-knowing: how can there be evil and suffering? This introduces both problems caused by nature and by human choice. The classical theologians made proposals regarding these issues. Three emerge as noteworthy. (1) They insisted that evil was not anything substantive, but always nonbeing, a loss or defect. (2) They agreed that "all things work together for the good," but that we do not always recognize the good of the greater whole in the events that occur. (3) They recognized that human freedom allows us to choose lesser goods rather than greater ones, and to use the goods we have in selfish ways.

Contemporary theology has been rethinking the issue of God's power in relation to evil, and the problem of evil itself. Process theologians, for example, continue to see God as the source, support, and goal of all that is, but do not describe God as having power over the process of the coming to be and passing away of all things. God does not coerce or intervene. Rather God grounds and sustains what is and offers new possibilities in the arising of each moment to each entity. Every entity, natural or human, may or may not incorporate the life-giving possibilities offered to it by the Divine. God acts to lure the process into love and life, but does not control it. Other theologies, including some post-Holocaust Jewish theologies, describe the self-limitation of God in order that humanity and the cosmos might be free. They talk about the risks God took in this dialectic of self-limitation and the granting of authentic freedom. Others look to the incarnation as the example of that risk, that offer of love to us in our freedom, that decision to make the Divine self-gift available in and through, not over against, the human. Far from a vision of a God "in charge," God is vulnerable and limited by the very gifts God gives in creating. God's power is in persuading us to love and to seek life, in opening the new, in affirming hope, not in control.

Power in Relation to Human Beings. Once we grant that human beings participate in the powers to be and to act, the interesting problems about power are social and political. Today theologians are wrestling with the issue of power in both the public and the ecclesial arenas, particularly in Catholic circles where the older paradigm is in question.

The worlds of the late Roman Empire and of the European Middle Ages were committed to a notion of power as control over others, and they lived in hierarchically ordered societies. In the Neo-Platonic hierarchy of being that informs much of the Christian tradition from the third century to the present, higher forms of being generate lower, lesser forms of being and these lower, derivative forms need to participate in those above in order to be fulfilled. This theology came to serve as an ideology when hierarchical institutional forms of Church leadership solidified, first with the approval of the emperor in the East, and later with the necessities of the political collapse of the empire in the West, and the subsequent reconfiguration of politics and economics in Europe. This theology supported the distribution of power from the top of the ecclesial and secular hierarchies downward, and reinforced the dependence of the lower ranks upon the higher. While the Church maintained a theology of separate spheres of power vis-à-vis the state, it struggled to maintain its own position above secular rulers because the Church held the keys to eternity, while the secular ruler governed only temporal affairs. Thus, life-giving grace flowed downward toward the faithful, especially through the doors of the sacraments, while power and responsibility accumulated upward following the echelons of the hierarchy. Whether we read the Pseudo-Dionysius in the sixth century or Robert Bellarmine in the sixteenth or Vatican I in the nineteenth, the power commitments are the same.

Today it is a commonplace in post-Enlightenment political theory that power comes from below, not from above. In social contract theory, people designate particular people to hold specific kinds of governing powers. Moral theology has joined this view with its language about the dignity and rights of persons. Second, as in the problem of God, power as coercion, domination, or control over people is viewed not only as problematic, but even as a kind of impotence when it means the one attempting this control has no consensual approval and no other option than force. Thus power emerges as a factor in our social relations, both personal and institutional. We retain responsibility for how we structure it. Therefore, theologians today are examining power as empowerment of people to become fully human within social systems that work to sustain justice for all.

The notion of authority has undergone a similar transformation. It is no longer understood as given from above, or inherent in offices or even texts like the Bible. Rather, people authorize particular persons, offices, texts because they authentically reflect our experience and meet our needs.

The grassroots liberation movements, including feminist and base communities, are locations in which new kinds of social arrangements of power can be tried, and in which the old dialectics of oppressor and oppressed can be transformed so that a more humane world emerges for everyone. Christians involved use the gospel to give voice to and expose social injustice as well as to nourish and empower each other with the good news that they share. This solidarity flows over into action for transformation of the situation toward the vision of the gospel, and so a cycle of empowerment is built. Thus power wears the face of enabling, love, voice, vision, community, and transformative action, and discards the mask of control among the makers of today's theology.

See: LIBERTY

ANN E. GRAFF

PRAISE

Praise is the human response to God's glory, power, mercy, and love. It consists largely of (1) an acknowledgment or confession of God's existence and grandeur; and (2) the rendering of honor and glory to God. Praise is thus a response to the experience of God's grace and power and a proclamation that bears witness to that experience. It is also a primary human activity that occurs spontaneously and naturally. Praise is especially associated with joy, delight, jubilation, and a sense of wonder. Encountering the divine automatically gives rise to emotions such as awe, fear, desire, and exaltation. Praise attempts to articulate the feelings stirred by God's presence and power.

Old Testament

It is often difficult to distinguish between praise, blessing, and thanksgiving in the OT. The ancient Hebrew language had no special word for "to thank." The word normally translated in this way, *hodah*, could also mean "to bless" and "to praise." The Hebrew verb used most often in the OT to mean "praise" is *hillel*. From this word is derived the English term "Alleluia" (from Hallelu-yah, "praise Yahweh").

Praise is often expressed in song, and its most common manifestation in the OT is the hymn. An invitation to the community to sing is frequently found at the beginning of these hymns (Exod 15:21; Isa 42:10; Ps 105:2). Hymns of praise were found throughout the ancient Near East, yet Israel's hymns were distinctive in that they were not manipulative. They acknowledged the power and greatness of God, who had already accomplished wonderful things for the Chosen People. But they did not attempt to flatter Yahweh in order to get something. Hymns of praise focus on God, not on human needs.

Praise was especially associated with Israel's liturgy, for hymns of praise were eminently suitable for the cult. They could easily become ritualized expressions of worship in the sanctuary:

> Hallelujah! Praise the name of the LORD!
>   Praise, you servants of the LORD,
> Who stand in the house of the LORD,
>   in the courts of the house of our God!
> Praise the LORD; the LORD is good!
>   Sing to God's name; it is gracious!
>   (Ps 135:1-3).

Solemn cultic celebrations in Israel regularly included communal acclamation of praise (1 Chr 16:36; Neh 8:6; Pss 96:1-4; 147:12; Isa 12:4-6). Asaph and other Levites were appointed "to minister before the ark of the LORD, to celebrate, thank, and praise the LORD, the God of Israel" (1 Chr 16:4). Many of the hymns of praise found among the psalms were undoubtedly composed to be used in public worship. It is noteworthy that the Hebrew name for the psalms is *tehillim*, which literally means "praises."

While the hymn of praise shows great variety, it follows a basic pattern: (1) a declaration of praise or call to praise; and (2) the reason for praise. The hymn first invites or commands some audience to praise God. Then it explains why this response is appropriate. Praise makes sense, for there are good reasons to glorify God.

This pattern is readily apparent in Psalm 117:

> Praise the LORD, all you nations!
>   Give glory, all you peoples!
> The LORD's love for us is strong;
>   the LORD is faithful forever.
> Hallelujah!

The psalm begins with a call to praise God in the imperative; the audience includes all peoples and nations; the reason for praise is God's love and faithfulness. The motivation in Psalm 117 is rather general, for there is no reference to any particular historical context. So it is suitable for any joyful liturgical celebration. This is descriptive praise, for it focuses on God's nature or on divine attributes.

Declarative or confessional praise, usually associated with thanksgiving, tends to locate the reasons for praise in God's saving activity in human history. An example of this occurs in the Song of Miriam:

Sing to the LORD, for he is gloriously triumphant;
    horse and chariot he has cast into the sea
                  (Exod 15:21).

This hymn does not even use the word "praise," yet that is the nature and purpose of the song. Here the reason for glorifying God takes up most of this brief hymn.

Praise of God occurs as well in certain blessing formulas normally expressed in the third person. These are generally embedded within biblical narratives. Such blessing formulas are simple sentences which consist of (1) the passive participle *baruk*, "blessed (be)"; (2) an identification of God as the recipient of praise; and (3) a reason that is usually introduced by the relative pronoun "who." Examples of such blessing formulas are: "Blessed be the LORD . . . who has rescued his people from the hands of Pharaoh and the Egyptians" (Exod 18:10); "Blessed be the LORD, who did not leave us to be torn by their fangs" (Ps 124:6).

Praise in the OT is confessional and theological. It makes an attempt to describe God's nature, attributes, and activity. In fact praise was important in Israel's attempt to theologize. It was also part of Israel's witness to the Gentiles, especially after Yahweh the God of Israel was identified as the awesome presence behind every manifestation of the divine. In praise Yahweh was seen as the One who created and shaped the world, intervenes in history, saves the poor, and controls the elements of nature. Other nations and even cosmic elements are called upon to praise Israel's God (1 Chr 16:23, 28-30; Pss 68:33-36; 148:1-13; Dan 3:58-89). Thus praise tends toward universalism and is the beginning of mission, for it calls upon all peoples and forces to acknowledge God.

Prayer in the OT revolves around two focal points. One is lament, which is closely linked to petition or supplication. Worshipers remind God of their needs and beg for help. This kind of prayer is centered around human concerns. The second focal point is praise, which is centered on God. Praise is given to God for God's own sake and not for any human advantage. These two types of prayer are in constant tension and balance. For God's answer to petition and lament leads to praise; and praise gives the worshiper confidence to address God with complaint and supplication.

Praise of God is scattered throughout the OT. Many of the psalms, of course, are hymns of praise. These include Psalms 8; 19A; 29; 33; 47; 65; 93; 96; 97; 98; 99; 100; 103; 104; 105; 106; 111; 113; 117; 134; 135; 145; 146; 147; 148; 149; and 150. Outside the Psalter some examples of hymns of praise are Exodus 15:1-18 (the Song of the Sea); Deuteronomy 32:1-43 (the Song of Moses); Judges 5:1-31 (the Song of Deborah); 1 Samuel 2:1-10 (the Song of Hannah); 2 Samuel 22:2-51 (the Song of David); and 1 Chronicles 16:8-36 (the Song of the Levites).

New Testament

Praise is essentially the same in both the OT and the NT. In the NT it is both confession and the rendering of honor and glory to God, but these now include the special role of Christ. The coming of the Messiah is an event for which both angels and human beings praise God (Luke 2:13-14, 20). So praise is not only a human response but also an angelic one.

In the NT the concepts of blessing, confession, honor, and glory are all closely related to praise and sometimes indistinguishable from it. Praise is especially associated with feelings of joy and delight. Although there may be special times to praise God, the whole of Christian existence should somehow be dedicated to it. God's wonders should be proclaimed and praised not only with the voice but with one's entire life. In fact praise of God seems to be an important part of worship and a prime purpose of Christian existence (Acts 2:47; Eph 1:12; 1 Pet 2:9). The NT recognizes that Gentiles will also participate in this obligation and privilege to praise and worship God (Acts 10:46; Rom 14:11; 15:9-11; Phil 2:11; Rev 15:4). The failure to give glory to God is a sign of the stubbornness of the wicked (Rom 1:21). Praise seems to be one of the chief activities in heaven. There vast multitudes will sing hymns of praise (Rev 19:1-8) in a celestial liturgy.

NT praise is based on Christ and imitates the prayer of Jesus, who acknowledged God's wisdom and greatness (Matt 11:25; Luke 10:21; John 17:1-5). Praise is directed not only to God but also to Christ: "To the one who sits on the throne and to the Lamb be blessing and honor, glory and might, forever and ever" (Rev 5:13; see also vv. 9-10, 12; Matt 21:9; Acts 19:17; Heb 13:21).

Christian worship involves both giving thanks and also rendering praise to God. The NT describes it in terms of "addressing one another in psalms and hymns and spiritual songs, singing and playing to the Lord in your hearts" (Eph 5:19; see 1 Cor 14:26; Col 3:16). A number of hymns were composed by the early Church, and fragments of these have been incorporated into the NT. Some include descriptions of Christ that are confessions of faith and indirect accolades, such as Philippians 2:6-11 and Colossians 1:15-20. Canticles such as the *Magnificat* (Luke 1:46-55) and the *Benedictus* (Luke 1:68-79) are also hymns of praise. Doxologies resemble the blessing formulas of the OT: "Blessed be the God and Father of our Lord Jesus Christ, who has blessed us in Christ with every spiritual blessing in the heavens" (Eph 1:3; see also vv. 4-14). In the Book of Revelation the heavenly choir sings "Alleluia" when praising God (Rev 19:1-8). This Hebrew expression has now become the paramount Christian exclamation of praise and joy.

See: PRAYER, PSALMS

TIMOTHY A. LENCHAK, S.V.D.

Pastoral-Liturgical Tradition

It is evident in both the OT and the NT that praise is an essential part of the human response to all the wonders God has done for us. The Church has inherited many of the liturgical forms used to express praise: the hymns of praise of the Temple and synagogue (the psalms) and the basic structure of praise and thanksgiving of Jewish prayer *(berakoth),* which often begins and ends with praise of God. The Church has also taken the other hymns and songs of the OT, as well as those of the NT, and has incorporated them into the liturgy. Following the example of the early Pauline communities, the Church in our own time has seen a revival of charismatic or ecstatic praise in the context of prayer groups. Praise lies at the center of the Church's prayer and is the duty and privilege of all the baptized.

Use of the Psalms. The early Church continued to use the psalms of Temple and synagogue, and psalmody continued for some time to comprise the greater part of the songs sung by the Church. In the Eastern Churches the use of psalmody gave way to poetic hymns. The Roman Church, however, continued the tradition of singing psalms during the Eucharist and the hours of the divine office. Psalms were frequently sung with brief refrains or antiphons during the entrance procession, the procession of the gifts to the altar, and during the procession of the faithful to the altar for the reception of Communion. In common practice, these psalms are most often replaced by hymns. A psalm of praise may be sung after the completion of the distribution of Communion. In the ancient Roman liturgy, a psalm (gradual) was sung after the first reading and was eventually reduced to an antiphon and one verse of the psalm. The reformed Mass of Paul VI has restored the gradual psalm, under the name of "responsorial psalm," to its more ancient form and purpose. The responsorial psalm is related to the first reading and may or may not reflect the element of praise, depending on the content of the first reading. The alleluia verse before the reading of the Gospel is often one or more verses of a psalm, and clearly is an acclamation of praise before the gospel. The use of a psalm of praise is specifically required as a part of the psalmody of morning prayer and it follows the morning canticle from the OT. Psalms 144–150 are frequently used as the morning psalm of praise.

Canticles. In addition to the psalms of the OT, the Church has taken other poetic passages of Scripture from both the OT and the NT for use as songs of praise in the divine office or Liturgy of the Hours. The three Gospel canticles, i.e., *Benedictus* (Luke 1:68-79), *Magnificat* (Luke 1:46-55), and *Nunc Dimittis* (Luke 2:29-32) are given the place of honor in morning prayer, evening prayer, and night prayer respectively. The Liturgy of the Hours appoints an OT canticle at morning prayer, e.g., Daniel 3:52-57, 56; Daniel 3:57-88; Exodus 15:1-4a, 8-13, 17-18; Judith 16:2-31, 13-15; Isaiah 45:15-25. A NT canticle from Paul or the Book of Revelation is appointed for evening prayer, e.g., Philippians 2:6-11; Revelation 19:1-7; Revelation 4:11 and 5:9, 10, 12; Colossians 1:12-20. By using these scriptural canticles, the Church joins itself to the praise of the great men and women of the OT and the NT and makes their praise of God its own.

Hymns. In the post-apostolic period poets and theologians began to write hymns or songs to be sung to a metered melody. These reflected the Scriptures or were a meditation on the truths of the faith. One of the earliest authors of such hymns was St. Ephrem of Syria, who was given the name "harp of the holy Spirit" because of his songs of praise and thanksgiving. In the East, ecclesiastical hymnody tended to overshadow and displace the use of psalmody in the liturgy. The Roman Church remained more conservative in this area and allowed hymns in the divine office, but tended to reserve psalmody for the Eucharist. In the middle ages many new hymns were written for liturgical use. The Protestant Reformation saw the introduction of vernacular hymnody into the Eucharistic liturgy to the detriment of the use of the psalms. As a result of the Conciliar liturgical reforms of Vatican II, hymnody has taken on a new importance in the Catholic Church. The processional psalms of the Mass generally have been replaced by hymns. Outside the season of Lent, the use of hymns of praise is most appropriate in the Liturgy of the Hours and in the celebration of the Eucharist. There are two ancient hymns that have a special place in the liturgy of the Roman Church: the *Gloria,* and the *Te Deum.* The *Gloria* came from the Syrian Church into the Western liturgy. It was an office hymn in the Syrian tradition and was later adopted by the West, for use in the papal Masses of Christmas and Easter. Eventually its use at Mass was extended to Masses celebrated by bishops and priests outside Advent and Lent. It is now used only on non-penitential days and major feasts. It begins with the hymn of the angels (Luke 2:14) and is directed to the Father and Son. The *Gloria* is also known as the greater doxology (hymn of praise) and the *Gloria Patri* (Glory to the Father, and to the Son, and to the holy Spirit) is called the lesser doxology. The *Te Deum* is a fourth-century hymn of praise that begins with the words: "We praise you, God." The hymn is used for occasions of solemn thanksgiving. In this hymn the Church joins itself to the praise given by the angels and the whole company of the saints. The second half of the hymn is a profession of faith in Christ and his redemptive acts.

Alleluia. The word "alleluia" means praise to YHWH, and is used in the liturgy outside of the season of Lent. During the season of Easter, Alleluia is added to the refrains (antiphons) of the psalms, to canticles, and other liturgical texts. It is chanted in a solemn form as a part of the gospel acclamation that accompanies the procession of the Book of Gospels to the ambo in all the liturgical seasons, except Lent. Alleluia is sung in the Eastern Churches throughout the year.

Eucharistic Prayer. The Eucharistic Prayer (anaphora, canon) is the central prayer of the Liturgy of the Eucharist. It has its origin in the Jewish prayers of blessing for the evening meal of the Sabbath and Passover and the blessings of the synagogue liturgy. The Eucharistic Prayer contains elements of praise, thanksgiving, invocation, and intercession. Praise and thanksgiving are often so intertwined that it is difficult to make a clear distinction between the two. The first part of the prayer is called the preface, a term that comes from the Latin word for proclamation. The preface and the hymn that concludes it (*Sanctus*) contain the clearest expressions of praise within the prayer. In keeping with the themes found in the prayers of blessing of the synagogue liturgy, the prefaces of the early anaphoras of the Eastern liturgies praise God for the gift of light and creation. These themes are also found in the Roman fourth Eucharistic Prayer: "it is right that we should give you thanks and glory. . . . Through all eternity you live in unapproachable light. Source of life and goodness, you have created all things, to fill your creatures with every blessing and to lead all . . . to the joyful vision of your light." The preface of the first three Roman Eucharistic Prayers is variable. It is addressed to the Father and gives thanks to the Son for some aspect of the paschal mystery of salvation. The prayer concludes by uniting with the praise of the angels and saints, e.g., "May our voices be one with theirs [the angels and saints] in their triumphant hymn of praise," and the *Sanctus* follows. The first part of the *Sanctus* is taken from Isaiah 6:3, and is also used in the synagogue liturgy; the second part of the *Sanctus*, also called the *Benedictus*, is taken from Matthew 21:9 and Psalm 17:25f. The notion of praise as the central theme is also found in the Roman Canon (Eucharistic Prayer I), which begins after the *Sanctus* with the words: "We come to you, Father, with praise and thanksgiving, through Jesus Christ your Son." The Roman Canon also speaks of the Eucharist as a "sacrifice of praise." Praise is thus seen to lie at the heart of the Church's most solemn prayer. The Eucharistic Prayers end with a doxology that reassumes the praise that characterizes the beginning of the prayer: "Through Christ, with him, and in him, in the unity of the holy Spirit, all glory and honor is your, almighty Father, for ever and ever."

Exsultet. The *Exsultet* or Easter Proclamation is the solemn hymn of praise sung by the deacon at the beginning of the Easter Vigil. Its origins lie in the evening blessing of light as the lamps are lighted. It is sung before the easter candle that has been lighted and represents the light of the risen Christ. The deacon begins by asking the heavenly powers, the earth, and Church to rejoice and exult, and he begs the prayers of the assembly that he may be worthy to sing God's "Easter praises." The rest of the proclamation is in the form of a Eucharistic preface: "It is truly right that with full hearts and minds and voices we should praise the unseen God, the all-powerful Father, and his only Son, our Lord Jesus Christ." The deacon recalls the great themes of the Passover and Christ's redemption of sinners. At the conclusion of the proclamation, the deacon asks God to accept the burning candle as an "evening sacrifice of praise." The Latin text of the *Exsultet* and its accompanying chant is one of the most beautiful texts of the Roman liturgy.

Charismatic Praise. The past two decades have seen a reemergence of charismatic prayer among Catholics. Charismatic prayer groups have been formed that emphasize the gifts of the Spirit enumerated by Paul in his first letter to the Corinthians (1 Cor 12:27-31). The prayer of these groups reflects the advice of Paul to the Colossians (Col 3:16): "Let the word of Christ dwell in you richly, as in all wisdom you teach and admonish one another, singing psalms, hymns, and spiritual songs with gratitude in your hearts to God." Songs of praise based on biblical texts are sung, acclamations and shouts of praise are frequent, and singing is often done in tongues (see 1 Corinthians 13–14).

See: BLESSING, CANTICLE, EUCHARIST, PRAYER, PSALMS, SACRIFICE

ALAN F. DETSCHER

PRAYER

Prayer has often been described as communication, communion, or dialogue with God. It is the human response to God's revelation and activity in the world. A variety of forms of prayer are represented in the Bible. The development from Jewish to distinctively Christian practices can be traced in liturgical, devotional, and private prayer.

Old Testament

In the OT turning to God in prayer seems to be a normal and natural human activity. It may be private or public, spontaneous or planned, voiced or mute, intensely personal or highly ritualized. Prayer was not the exclusive concern of priest, prophet, or king, for anyone could pray.

Various types of prayer can be found in the OT. Above all there is petition, which asks God to fill some need or to come to a person's aid. Intercession is prayer on the behalf of others. Lament is a complaint or description of difficulty, distress, or affliction. Praise is the proclamation of God's goodness, power, and mercy. Closely associated with praise is thanksgiving. There are also confessions of sin, confessions of faith, and expressions of confidence in God.

OT prayer is marked by certain features. First, it is pervasive. Prayer appears not only in the Psalter but throughout the OT. It is also recognized as a daily obligation (Pss 55:18; 119:164; Dan 6:11). Second, prayer is personal. It involves the whole person, including one's history, culture, and emotional life. Third, OT prayer tends to be simple and direct. Certainly there were long and complicated prayers in ancient Israel. However, the prayers recorded in the OT are normally short, plain, and to the point (Exod 32:11-13; Josh 7:7-9; Judg 16:28). Fourth, OT prayer tends to be completely immersed in the history and life of Israel. It addresses a God who is actively involved in the history of a particular people, for prayer occurs in the context of the covenant* relationship between Yahweh and Israel. Fifth, prayer is effective. Israel rejected the notion that prayer was magical and that God had no choice but to respond positively. Yet it also recognized that God heard prayer and was powerful enough to change situations. Sixth, OT prayer is flexi-

ble. Although cultic expressions of prayer were often fixed in ancient Israel, there was a great diversity of prayer forms and styles. The sanctuary was certainly a favorite place for prayer, yet Israelites could pray anywhere and at any time.

In ancient Israel physical posture during prayer was limited to standing (1 Kgs 8:22; Neh 9:2; Jer 18:20), kneeling (1 Kgs 8:54; 2 Chr 6:13; Ps 95:6; Dan 6:11), and prostration (Gen 17:3; Josh 7:6; 1 Chr 29:20; Neh 9:3). Although standing seems to be the normal prayer posture in NT times, kneeling and prostrating seem to have been more common in the OT. Standing and kneeling were often accompanied by raised hands (1 Kgs 8:22, 54; Ps 28:2; Lam 2:19). After the Exile Jews turned toward Jerusalem and the Temple when they prayed (Dan 6:11).

In the Pentateuch it can be difficult to distinguish between prayer and conversation with God. The first conversation between God and human beings took place in the Garden of Eden after Adam and Eve ate the forbidden fruit (Gen 3:9-19). The dialogue between God and Cain (Gen 4:9-15) also resembles normal human conversation. Abraham and Sarah spoke directly with God as well (Gen 18:1-33). Making use of questions, expressions of courtesy, and hypothetical propositions, Abraham interceded for the city of Sodom (vv. 23-32). Jacob's prayers are more like bargaining (Gen 28:20-22; 32:10-13); yet his wrestling with an unknown opponent (Gen 32:24-31) seems to symbolize the struggle that prayer can be.

Undoubtedly the model of prayer in the Pentateuch is Moses. He is celebrated as someone who could speak face-to-face with God (Deut 34:10; see Exod 3:4–4:17). Moses dared to argue with and challenge God, even citing Yahweh's own words and questioning God's justice (Num 11:11-15, 21-22; 12:13; 14:13-19). These prayers of Moses appear in a conversation format, where Moses is both intercessor and God's partner in dialogue.

In the Deuteronomistic History (Deuteronomy–2 Kings) we find the prayers not only of political and military leaders and prophets but also of the lowly. Joshua imitated Moses' prayer with questions and rational argument when Israel was defeated at Ai (Josh 7:7-9). Deborah sang a victory song after the battle with Sisera (Judg 5:2-31). Gideon tested God with a fleece before setting out on his mission (Judg 6:36-40). The Israelites confessed their sinfulness and begged for help when the Ammonites oppressed them (Judg 10:10, 15). Manoah, the father of Samson, petitioned God for the return of the angel who had appeared to his wife (Judg 13:8). Samson himself begged for the strength to avenge himself on the Philistines (Judg 16:28; see also 15:18). Hannah prayed silently for a child (1 Sam 1:10-13). When this prayer was granted, she sang a song of praise and gratitude to God (1 Sam 2:1-10). Samuel, like Moses, functioned as God's dialogue partner (1 Sam 3:10-14; 16:1-3, 6-7). He also interceded for the people, and his prayers were effective (1 Sam 7:9; 8:6; 12:16-19, 23).

From the institution of the monarchy until the fall of Jerusalem various royal prayers were recorded. The prayers of David that appear in 2 Samuel 7:18-29 and 1 Chronicles 29:10-19 are largely praise and petition. There is also David's confession of sin in 2 Samuel 24:10, 17. Solomon requested wisdom from God (1 Kgs 3:6-9) and offered a long petition at the dedication of the Temple (1 Kgs 8:23-53). Kings Hezekiah (2 Kgs 19:15-19; 20:2-3; Isa 38:10-20), Asa (2 Chr 14:10), and Jehoshaphat (2 Chr 20:6-12) are also remembered for various prayers of lament and petition.

Likewise various prophets have prayers recorded in the OT. In his contest with the prophets of Baal Elijah's petition for divine favor (1 Kgs 18:36-37) was granted. He also interceded successfully for the son of the widow of Zarephath (1 Kgs 17:20-21). Later Elijah prayed for death (1 Kgs 19:4) and lamented his lonely and perilous situation (1 Kgs 19:10, 14). Twice Amos prayed on behalf of Israel (Amos 7:2, 5). These prayers of intercession were effective, for God relented from punishing the people.

Three prayers are recorded in the book of the prophet Habakkuk. Two of these are laments (Hab 1:2-4, 12-17) that seem to accuse the Almighty of responsibility for the present situation of affliction. The third prayer (Hab 3:1-19) is a hymn of thanksgiving. Twice the prophet Jonah prays. In Jonah 4:2-3 he expresses anger and begs for death, much like Elijah did. The prayer in Jonah 2:3-10 is a thanksgiving hymn. However, Jonah's prayers are parodies, for they are self-centered and unrealistic. The prayer of the pagan sailors (Jonah 1:14) seems much more sincere. Third Isaiah sees the Temple becoming "a house of prayer for all peoples" (Isa 56:7). A communal lament also appears in Isaiah 63:7–64:11. This recounts God's saving deeds in the past, describes the community's present distress, and asks for help.

Jeremiah was especially known as a prophet of prayer. On numerous occasions he addressed God on behalf of Judah (Jer 14:7-9, 19-22; 16:19-20), although he was eventually commanded to stop interceding for the people (Jer 7:16; 11:14; 14:11). A number of distinctive prayers or conversations with God are the so-called "confessions" of Jeremiah (Jer 11:18-23; 12:1-6; 15:10-21; 17:14-18; 18:18-23; 20:7-18). Largely laments or complaints featuring strong emotional outbursts, they are concerned with the difficulties of Jeremiah's prophetic ministry. The prophet demands vengeance on his enemies (Jer 11:20; 12:3; 15:15; 17:18; 20:12), curses the day of his birth (Jer 20:14-18), and even rebukes and accuses God (Jer 15:18; 20:7). These prayers acknowledge the divine presence, yet at the same time lament God's absence. For Jeremiah everything was subject to prayer—even personal feelings, doubts, and temptations.

Postexilic prayer was especially characterized by the remembrance of Yahweh's saving deeds in the past and the confession of Israel's guilt. Ezra prays two laments (Ezra 9:6-15; Neh 9:6-37) that acknowledge God's goodness and the people's sinfulness. Nehemiah's prayer (Neh 1:5-11) is a short petition that also confesses the sins of Israel.

The prayers of Tobit and his future daughter-in-law Sarah are laments requesting death (Tob 3:2-6, 11-15). Tobiah combined praise and petition on his wedding night (Tob 8:5-7), while his father-in-law Raguel recited a psalm of praise and thanksgiving when he learned that Tobiah was still alive (Tob 8:15-17). Tobit too can praise God at the end of the story (Tob 11:14-15; 13:1-18). In this prayer the history of Israel's sinfulness is recalled, and a glorious future is proclaimed for Jerusalem.

Judith's prayer of petition both appeals to history and describes the present crisis (Jdt 9:2-14). She asks God for strength before beheading Holofernes (Jdt 13:4-5, 7) and later leads all Israel in a hymn of praise and thanksgiving (Jdt 16:1-17). In the Book of Esther both Mordecai (Est C:2-10) and Esther (Est C:14-30) petition God for help, confessing Israel's sinfulness and God's power.

Daniel is presented as a model of the wise and devout Jew who is faithful in prayer even under adverse circumstances (Dan 6:11). When God revealed King Nebuchadnezzar's dream to him, Daniel responded with a hymn of praise (Dan 2:20-23). While fasting and doing penance, Daniel recounted the shameful history of Israel (Dan 9:4-19). This confession becomes a petition for God's pardon and help. The Book of Daniel also records the long prayers of Azariah (Dan 3:26-45) and of the three young men in the fiery furnace (Dan 3:52-90). The prayer of Azariah begins as a hymn of praise but also contains elements of lament, for it describes at length the distress of Israel and asks for help. The song of the three young men is a hymn of praise that focuses largely on creation.

The Book of Psalms* consists mostly of prayers. There is no other book of the Bible quite like it. Although God's words are cited occasionally, the Psalter is basically a human response to God. Every type of OT prayer can be found here: wisdom reflections, hymns of praise, songs of thanksgiving, prayers of confidence, confessions, laments, blessings, and curses. They reflect both individual and communal needs and aspirations.

Some psalms dwell on the glory of God as reflected in nature (Psalms 8; 19:2-7; 29); others praise God's activity in human history (Psalms 105; 114; 135). The Torah (Psalms 1; 19:8-15; 119), Yahweh's reign (Psalms 96–99), the Temple (Psalms 24; 84; 122), Jerusalem (Psalms 46; 48; 87), wealth and poverty (Psalms 37; 49; 73), and even royal coronations and weddings (Psalms 2; 45; 110) are all subjects of the psalms. There are psalms that deal with national crises (Psalms 44; 60; 79), serious illness (Psalms 6; 38; 88), old age (Psalm 71), sinfulness (Psalms 32; 51; 130), and personal distress and persecution (Psalms 22; 42–43; 140).

Most of the psalms probably originated in Israel's public worship. The cultic recital of the psalms not only expressed the needs and emotions of ancient Israelites but also helped to incorporate them into the covenant community. By means of the regular communal recitation of the psalms Israel encountered God and reenacted its history. Through prayer the individual became part of the reality of the covenant relationship.

Wisdom literature does not contain many prayers, yet a few are recorded. Solomon petitions God for the gift of wisdom in Wisdom 9:1-18. The lengthy reflection on the Exodus experience and on idolatry (Wisdom 11–19) takes on the form of a prayer, since God is occasionally addressed. A short petition for self-discipline appears in Sirach 22:27–23:6. A longer petition for new signs and wonders on behalf of Jerusalem is recorded in Sirach 36:1-17. Sirach 39:12-15 resembles the beginning of a hymn of praise, although it does not address God; a hymn of thanksgiving is found in Sirach 51:1-12.

The Book of Job might be described as an extended lament. Job's friends do not actually pray, but they address the topic of prayer. Job's way of praying is opposed to what they believe is appropriate. The friends hold that Job must turn to God by confessing and renouncing his sinfulness (Job 11:13-14; 22:23). Job insists on his innocence and refuses to link righteousness with prosperity and wickedness with punishment. He questions and challenges God's justice (Job 6:8-10; 7:11-21; 9:19-24; 10:1-3, 7; 13:14-15). God's response eventually silences Job, who in prayer acknowledges the divine power and his own ignorance (Job 42:2-6). Job then intercedes on behalf of his friends so that they will not be punished (Job 42:8-9).

Prayer is the human response to God's revelation. In the OT it occurs in the context of the covenant, that special dynamic relationship between Yahweh and Israel. The purpose of biblical prayer was not manipulation but communication. Therefore it was not limited to flattery, submission, and begging. Rather OT prayer reflected Israel's historical experiences, both positive and negative. No human emotion was excluded. Thus OT prayer was capable of questioning and challenging the Almighty; it was also open to God's questions and challenges. The divine-human relationship was affected not only by God's revelation and activity but also by Israel's response. The prayers of the OT are an important part of that human response.

See: PRAISE, PSALMS

TIMOTHY A. LENCHAK, S.V.D.

New Testament

In the NT the example of Jesus' prayer becomes the model for his followers. The Gospels portray Jesus habitually at prayer, seeking God at all major turning points in his life and ministry. Jesus specifically teaches his disciples to pray. As in the OT, a variety of prayers are found in the NT. A number of early Christian prayers and hymns are imbedded in the Pauline letters and later NT writings.

The Example of Jesus. Jesus' observance of the traditional Jewish prayer rituals is assumed, though the evangelists make no comment about it. For example, the only mention of meal prayers is at the Last Supper and in meals with Eucharistic over-

tones, such as the multiplication of the loaves (Mark 6:41) and the post-resurrection meal at Emmaus (Luke 24:30). Similarly, little is said about Jesus' participation in public worship, but synagogue and Temple are often the setting for his teaching, healings, and exorcisms.

A distinctive note in the prayer life of Jesus was his practice of going away from the crowd and his disciples to pray in solitude. Though he might do this anytime (Luke 5:16), the evidence shows that he preferred the pre-dawn hours before the work of the day began (Mark 1:35-38), or night after the crowds had gone away (Luke 6:12). Jesus sought communion with God, whom he addressed as Father with the intimate term "Abba," for refreshment and renewal in his hectic pace and for peace and direction at critical moments.

Matthew and Luke record a joyful prayer of Jesus, praising God for the revelation of his will. In Matthew, this prayer is especially striking as it is set in a context dominated by Jesus' disappointment at the unbelief he is encountering (Matt 11:25-27; Luke 21:22). The Synoptics preserve the scene of Jesus' prayer at Gethsemane the night he was betrayed (Mark 14:32-42; Matt 26:36-46; Luke 22:39-46). The core of this prayer is submission to the Father's will. Jesus prayed on the cross, using Psalm 22 in the accounts of Matthew and Mark, and in the account of Luke again expressing his submission to the Father's will (Luke 23:46).

The Gospel of John portrays Jesus speaking personally to his Father in the midst of a crowd, expressing thanks and seeking God's glory (John 11:41; 12:28). In the great prayer of intercession at the Last Supper, Jesus prays to be glorified and seeks protection for his disciples (17:4-11).

More than the other evangelists, Luke focuses on practices and habits of prayer in his portrayal of Jesus. Jesus is at prayer after his baptism when the holy Spirit comes upon him (Luke 3:21). He prays all night before making the important choice of the Twelve (6:12), and has been praying when he asks them their view of his true identity

(9:18). The transfiguration on the mountain took place "while he was praying" (9:29). He prays for Peter (22:32) and for those who put him to death (23:34). The submission expressed in the prayer at Gethsemane reappears in Jesus' final words on the cross, a prayer of self-offering (23:46). In Luke's story of the Lord's Prayer, the disciples' request for instruction in prayer is prompted by Jesus' example of prayer (11:1).

The Teaching of Jesus. Jesus directly addresses the issue of "how to pray" when he gives his disciples the Lord's Prayer (Matt 6:9-13; Luke 11:1-4). The versions of Matthew and Luke are different because of their liturgical conditioning, but contain the same basic elements. Jesus' disciples are to follow his example in addressing God as Father, and to seek the submission of all creatures in reverence to God and in furtherance of the divine purpose and plan. Bodily needs are to be mentioned, and the spiritual needs of forgiveness and protection from failing the ultimate test of fidelity.

Several of these points are mentioned in other contexts in the course of Jesus' teaching about prayer. The emphasis on seeking first the reign of God, for example, is presented dramatically in the admonition: "Seek first the kingdom of God and his righteousness, and all these things will be given you besides" (Matt 6:33). Prayer is not a matter of informing God of our needs. God is a loving father who knows our needs; in prayer we express confidence in God's loving care and try to conform our wills to the divine will. Our prayer must be animated by faith and trust and free of anxiety. The faithful disciple is glad to see signs of the Father's care, but does not depend on them for security (John 4:48).

The emphasis on praying with a forgiving heart is highlighted by verses appended to the Lord's Prayer in Matthew's version (Matt 6:14-15; see Mark 11:25-26). Elsewhere Matthew records the saying about leaving one's gift at the altar (Matt 5:23-24), making lack of forgiveness the one block to the efficacy of prayer cited by Jesus. At Gethsemane Jesus urges Peter to watch and pray, "that you may not undergo the test" (Mark 14:38).

Elsewhere Jesus gave other indications of what to pray for and how to pray. God is to be thanked for his favors. The Samaritan leper was praised when he returned to thank Jesus for his cleansing, but Jesus asked, "Where are the other nine?" (Luke 17:17). Prayer is needed in difficult cases of exorcism (Mark 9:29), and for an increase of harvest-workers for the reign of God (Matt 9:37-38).

Prayer is not to be ostentatious, and it is not better because it is eloquent or long (Mark 12:40). Jesus urges secret prayer, "in your inner room" (Matt 6:6), but also group prayer (18:19-20); in both cases the Father will listen. The attitude in prayer is the important thing; the contrast of right and wrong attitudes is given in the parable of the Pharisee and the tax collector (Luke 18:9-14). Prayer is to be persistent: ask, seek, knock (Matt 7:7). The parables of the importunate friend (Luke 11:5-8) and the persistent widow (18:1-8) do not mean to imply that God is worn down by prayer, but that, unlike the sleeper and the judge, God is always ready to be approached by his children. Our asking from now on is to be in the name of Jesus (John 16:24). Prayer is a way of life, a constant communion with the Father through Jesus, so we can "pray always without becoming weary." (Luke 18:1).

Paul. Paul has had a powerful impact on the Christian understanding of prayer through that body of NT literature written or influenced by him. He customarily begins his letters with a prayer of thanksgiving for something concerning his readers: "your faith" (Rom 1:8); spiritual gifts (1 Cor 1:4-7); "your partnership for the gospel" (Phil 1:5); your faith, love, and hope (1 Thess 1:3; Phlm 5). These same prayers often continue with spiritual petitions for his readers: "that your love may increase ever more and more in knowledge and every kind of perception" (Phil 1:9; Phlm 6; see Eph 3:14-19). He asks that his friends may be united and respectful of one another (Rom 15:5), and filled with joy and peace (Rom 15:13), love and holiness (1 Thess 3:12; 5:23). Paul also seeks their prayers for him and his mission (2 Cor 1:11; 1 Thess 5:25). Occasionally he prays for a personal intention: "that somehow by God's will I may at last find my way clear to come to you" (Rom 1:10).

Our confidence in prayer is based on the faithfulness of God (1 Cor 1:9) and the riches God wants to share with us in Christ (Phil 4:19). Prayer is not something we must generate by our own power, however. We are able to pray because of the gift of the holy Spirit, who frees us from slavery and empowers us to address God as "Abba" (Gal 4:6) and to approach Jesus as the Lord (1 Cor 12:3). We do not need to be able to articulate clearly the deepest desires of our heart, because the Spirit knows what we mean and perfects our prayer (Rom 8:26-27).

Paul says little about his own prayer practices. From his admonition to "pray without ceasing" (1 Thess 5:17) we may infer that he felt the need to pray with regularity so as to establish a constant prayerful attitude. He had the gift of praying and prophesying in tongues (1 Cor 14:14, 18). His references to "visions and revelations" and a personal mysterious experience (2 Cor 12:1-4) hint of a mystical dimension in his prayer. In the same passage he shows that God may "answer" a petition without granting the request (vv. 7-9).

Later NT writings on prayer reflect ongoing Church experience and interpretation. The Pastorals, in encouraging prayer for public officials and for universal salvation, list the types of prayer familiar to the community, "supplications, prayers, petitions, and thanksgivings" (1 Tim 2:1-4). The Letter to the Hebrews emphasizes the mediation of Jesus, our "merciful and faithful high priest" (Heb 2:17), who gives us confidence because he is one of us and knows what it is to cry out to God in time of need (5:7). The Letter of James describes prayer responses for several situations: in suffering, in good spirits, when one is sick, for forgiveness, for community healing (Jas 5:13-16). This letter stresses a fervent spirit, confidence, and right motives as the proper context for prayer (1:6; 4:3). The theme of confidence is echoed in 1 John, based on a clear conscience, obedience, and praying according to God's will (1 John 3:21; 5:14).

The First Letter of Peter urges a serious and sober spirit of prayer because "the end of all things is at hand" (4:7); but the author then tempers this stern attitude with the beautiful admonition: "Cast all your worries upon him because he cares for you" (5:7). Though the prayer described in the Book of Revelation is generally the worship of the heavenly community, the prayers of Christians on earth are symbolized in the image of the "gold bowls filled with incense, which are the prayers of the holy ones" (Rev 5:8). This scene presents the clearest NT evidence for the intercession of the saints.

See: GETHSEMANE, HOLY/HOLINESS, JOY, LOVE, PEACE, SPIRIT, SYNAGOGUE, TEMPLE, TRANSFIGURATION, WORSHIP

JEROME KODELL, O.S.B.

Pastoral-Liturgical Tradition

Prayer is a basic part of human religious activity in which a person or community seeks to communicate with God, conceived as a person. In the OT much of the prayer of the people of Israel is prayer of praise, thanksgiving, or intercession (see Book of Psalms). Individuals such as Moses talk directly to God, Judith prays to God for the deliverance of her people; the prophets make intercession with God to spare a sinful people; the three young men sing praise to God in the midst of the furnace. Unlike the magical formulas used by the pagans who seek to compel their gods to do what they desire, the prayers of the Israelites try to persuade God to act on their behalf, but they are well aware that God is free to ignore their prayers.

In the NT we see that Jesus attends the synagogue and Temple and would, as a consequence, be well aware of prayers and rites used in them. He celebrates the Passover with his disciples and acts as the head of the family in praying and performing the required ritual acts. Yet Christ also frequently engages in personal prayer with God, whom he addresses as Father and *Abba.* The early Christian Church, being born out of the context of the people of Israel, was also aware of these same patterns of individual, communal, and liturgical prayer. It took the prayer forms of Judaism and transformed them in order to express its growing understanding of Jesus Christ as Messiah, Son of God, Savior, and God. The early Church also had to deal with forms of charismatic prayer that were both individual and communal, such as those originally found in many of the Pauline communities (see 1 Cor 14:26-40). As the Church expanded, personal and communal forms of prayer were developed in the early monastic communities. These would influence the development of the divine office, and what would later be called meditation and contemplation. In the Middle Ages meditation and contemplation were given greater emphasis and became more and more divorced from the ancient notion of liturgical prayer as the center of the life of the Church and of individual piety. The Second Vatican Council has restored the place of liturgical prayer as the source for personal prayer and piety.

Prayer in the Early Church. In the early days of the Church, there was little in the prayer life of the Jerusalem Church that distinguished it from Jewish prayer. At the time of Christ and during the apostolic period, Jewish prayer and liturgical forms were still undergoing change. It should not be surprising that Christian liturgy and prayer were still very Jewish in their external form. The followers of Jesus continued to go to the Temple and synagogue to pray. When they were no longer welcome there they continued to follow the pattern of the synagogue service. The early forms of the Christian liturgy of the word have much in common with the synagogue service. Justin Martyr

(ca. 100–165) gives the earliest description of the liturgy of the word: the memoirs of the apostles (gospels) and the writings of the prophets are read, a homily is given by the bishop, all stand up to offer prayers. In the synagogue the Torah and the Prophets were read, an explanation of the readings was given (see Luke 4:16-21), and all stood for a series of eighteen prayers of blessing and intercession. The early Church also took the structure of the Sabbath and paschal meals and, following the example of Jesus, blessed the bread and cup. However, it is clear from Paul (1 Cor 11:17-34) that the meal was quickly dropped out of the Eucharistic celebration and only the prayers of blessing and thanksgiving remained. In this regard, the early Church transformed the prayers connected with the blessing of the bread and cup of the Sabbath and paschal meals into the great prayer of thanksgiving that would later be called the Eucharistic Prayer. The Syrian Didache (ca. 75–125) gives texts of thanksgiving prayers over the bread and cup (scholars are divided whether or not the celebration described is the Eucharist or an agape meal). The hymn, *Father, we thank thee,* is metrical version of these most ancient Christian prayers.

The most significant change manifested in early prayers was the new understanding of the person and role of Jesus. Within the framework of traditional Jewish concepts there was inserted the growing understanding of Jesus as child/servant *(pais)*, Lord, and God. Early Christian prayer is essentially Jewish prayer adapted to the new Christian understanding of Jesus and his role in the history of God's saving acts for the Jews. The Church continued to read the Scriptures of the OT: Torah, the Prophets, and the Writings. And it also continued to sing the OT psalms and canticles while, at the same time, it began to read the writings and memoirs of the apostles (letters of Paul, Peter, James, and John, the Acts of the Apostles, and the Gospels of Matthew, Mark, Luke, and John).

The Church used the prayer given by Christ (the Lord's Prayer), itself based on

Jewish forms of prayer, as the Christian prayer par excellence. This is evident from the instruction in the Didache: "You most not pray like the hypocrites, but 'pray as follows' as the Lord bids us in his gospel: Our Father. . . . You should pray in this way three times a day." The Church replaced the Jewish daily practice of saying the *Shema Israel*, "Hear, O Israel" (Deut 6:4-9; 11:12-21; Num 15:37-41), with the prayer of Christ. The Christian practice of praying three times a day eventually developed into the divine office with its two main hours of prayer in the morning (lauds) and in the evening (vespers). These two hours of prayer consist mainly of the recitation or singing of psalms. In later periods Scripture readings were added as well as prayers of intercession. Under the influence of the growing monastic communities, a midnight or early morning office (matins) was added, as well as prayers before going to bed (compline), and for the first (prime), third (terce), sixth (sext), and ninth (none) hours of the day. This total of eight hours of prayer was seen to be a reflection of Psalm 118:164: "Seven times a day I praise you for your just ordinances." In the early Church liturgical or communal prayer and personal or individual prayer were seen as interrelated. Personal prayer took its inspiration from Scripture and the liturgy. Liturgical prayer involved the whole community, each person participating according to his or her role in the community of the baptized.

Prayer during the Middle Ages. By the Middle Ages the liturgy of the Church had become the province of the clergy. It was in a language the people did not understand and much of it could not be heard. As a consequence of this, devotional forms of prayer arose for use by the people, while the clergy celebrated the liturgy, especially the Mass. Devotions to the Blessed Virgin Mary, such as the rosary, flourished, as did prayers to the saints. The liturgy became the background for prayer, but it was not perceived as being the prayer of the assembly. In content, the liturgical prayers of the Church were directed to God, through Christ, and the holy Spirit, whereas, devotional prayers were more frequently directed to Jesus, the Blessed Virgin Mary, or the saints. Allegorical interpretations of the Mass developed that had little to do with the actual celebration of the Eucharist, and these in turn had an effect on devotional prayers that were composed for use during the Mass. A frequent theme was the passion of Christ, and every action of the priest was explained as relating to some aspect of the passion and death of Christ. Especially under monastic influence, individual and personal prayer centered more and more on meditation and contemplation. Meditation or mental prayer, as it was often called, is centered on the mysteries of the faith. Mental images are used to reflect upon and enter into the mystery. The purpose of meditation is to lead the individual to make resolutions based on the virtues or to make acts of faith, hope, and love. Needless to say, during the Middle Ages the passion of Christ was most frequently the subject of meditation. Contemplation is a higher form of mental prayer, the object of which can be a mystery of Christ or the very being of God. In its highest form, contemplation leads to communion with God in which words and images are no longer used.

Prayer after the Second Vatican Council. The Constitution on the Liturgy, *Sacrosanctum Concilium* (CSL) of the Second Vatican Council had a profound effect on the prayer life of the Church and its members. The Council set in motion a reform of all the liturgical rites of the Church that is ongoing. The Council called for a reform of the liturgy that would be both a restoration of the ancient from of the rites and prayers of the Church and a renewal that would adapt them to the needs of the Church today. The Council says, "The liturgy is the summit toward which all the activity of the Church is directed; at the same time it is the fount from which all the Church's power flows" (CSL no. 10). The liturgy is the prayer of the Church gathered in faith and love. Each liturgical celebration is itself a prayer, and those who participate in the celebration themselves pray in word and song. However, the Council also reminds us that "The spiritual life, however, is not limited solely to participation in the liturgy. Christians are indeed called to pray in union with one another, but they must also enter into their chamber to pray to the Father in secret" (CSL no. 12). The Council also speaks about devotions when it says, "devotions should be so fashioned that they harmonize with the liturgical seasons, accord with the sacred liturgy, are in some way derived from it, and lead the people to it, since, in fact, the liturgy by its very nature far surpasses any of them" (CSL no. 13). The conciliar reform clearly sees the liturgy as the center of the prayer life of the Church. For, in fact, it is the prayer of the Church. And yet, the prayer of the community gathered in faith must also be nurtured by the personal prayer of each of the faithful. This personal prayer should center on Scripture and the texts of the liturgy and lead the individual back to the communal celebration of the liturgy. For this reason, the reform of the *Lectionary for Mass* is one of the most important results of the conciliar reforms that has influenced not only the Roman Church, but also many other Christian Churches in this country and elsewhere.

See: CANTICLE, CHURCH, EUCHARIST, MEAL, PRAISE, PSALMS, THANKSGIVING

ALAN F. DETSCHER

PREACHING

Preaching is an activity that no one biblical word or phrase describes, although good news (gospel),* teach,* and word* are entries to consult in these pages. The English term "to preach" is sometimes understood to be the best translation of *kerússein*, literally "to proclaim" or "announce" as heralds do. But the verb in our tongue encompasses many more types of sacred discourse than the proclamation of tidings new to the hearer. Among these are the homily, properly a comment on biblical material that has just been read, usually with a hortatory purpose; the catechesis or in-

structional discourse; the eulogy or praise of the dead (more fittingly than of the living); the appeal either for money (see 2 Corinthians 8 and 9 for two such) or for other resources such as support of the missions, food for the needy, etc; the sermon, an extended discourse on some doctrinal theme or Christian occasion; and the admonition, to be delivered more sparingly and thoughtfully than is normally done.

Preaching has had a bad name in Christian circles almost from apostolic times. There are a number of reasons for this. The basic one is that God and the things that pertain to God are ineffable; therefore, when words about the divine are multiplied they attempt to do the impossible. More practically, preachers have numerous faults that can make the word of God unpalatable. They depart from the biblical word and deliver a merely human word; they do not sufficiently prepare what they mean to say; they deal in clichés, thereby rendering their remarks predictable and otiose; they preach too long. The latter is not a chronological judgment so much as the perceived disproportion between the number of words spoken and the ideas expressed.

Choosing a mode of discourse is not an easy matter. Preachers may not know their congregations well enough to judge correctly either their readiness for the message, their own verbal style, or how much of the gospel a congregation can bear. People's needs differ sharply from one locality to the next. A preacher can miss the mark as regards the occasion, the temperament of hearers, or their educational level. Another factor is the variety within a congregation. Oratorical skill may be suitable for one person, plain speech and down-to-earth illustration for another. Some listeners can handle subtlety and not be affronted by irony. Others cannot, being baffled by the first and taking the second literally.

The chief requirement of effective preaching is that it be sincere. Preachers must themselves be convinced of the truth and the importance of their message. They must be prayerful. Trafficking in sacred things, they may not deal with them lightly. Just as Jesus passed on to those who heard him all that he had received from his Father, so the preacher must hand on the main matters of the apostolic tradition to which the Scriptures testify. Rough-hewn speech is not a sign of sincerity, certainly not brutal or offensive speech. Conversely, carefully crafted speech can be utterly sincere. Matter and manner must be coordinated, the one not being confused with the other. Since all preaching is an attempt to use language effectively, they will preach best who are docile to the Spirit and employ the best human speech they are capable of. The conversational tone may mark it, but not the casual manner. Preaching is too serious for that. It must at all times be done with power, the power that the Spirit of Christ alone can give.

Old Testament

The two testaments are testified to in written sources. It is all but impossible to identify what portions had their origin as oral presentations. The Hebrew and Hellenistic cultures were both predominantly oral, although the learned in each were skilled in written composition. In the bardic or Homeric era and similarly the pre-Davidic days of the judges, much would have been not only committed to memory but first presented orally. Writing down what had long been recited marks a turning-point in human history, but we cannot date it. The closest we can come to identifying OT preaching is cite blocs of material with a hortatory purpose that give evidence of having been spoken many times. Confining the search in the first four Mosaic books to exhortation eliminates large portions of etiological cult legend; narrative, with its interspersed folk wisdom; law; ritual prescription; and genealogy. This leaves as the material that was probably often preached the instructions God gave to Moses and Aaron about how to eat the meal commemorative of deliverance from Egypt (Exod 12:1-27; 43-49), the stipulations about consecrating the first

born (ch. 13) and gathering the manna (ch. 16). If all the instructions God gave to Moses for transmission to the people are reckoned sermonic because they were delivered orally with frequency, much in Exodus, Leviticus, and Numbers will fall into that category. The oracles of Balaam and similar poetic works are perhaps to be categorized as homiletic (Num 23:7-10, 18-24; 24:3-9, 15-24); likewise, blessings and snatches of praise-songs (Num 6:24-26; 10:35-36; 12:6-8; 21:27-30). But song is not preaching, so it may be unwise to attribute to it a homiletic character. Perhaps only Moses' charges to the Israelites about their lack of trust in God should be designated as pentateuchal "preaching," not because it is admonitory but because these parts are exhortations to fidelity to a faithful God.

All of Deuteronomy 1–33 is cast as Moses' deliverance of the Law to Israel, the thirty-fourth and final chapter being a description of his death on Mount Nebo. This literary convention should not be confused with his preaching. Within the book, however, there are some excellent homiletic excursions: thus, all of Deuteronomy 28–30 spells out the blessings the people may expect in Canaan if they are faithful and the miseries that are in store (the "curse") if they are not. Joshua is similarly awarded a farewell speech that consumes the last two chapters of that book (23–24). Like Moses' final words in Deuteronomy it is a charge of fidelity to God with promises and threats attached. The people respond to the appeal by saying: "We will serve the LORD, our God, and obey his voice" (24:24).

Samuel's warning to the elders of Israel about the unpleasant consequences they may expect if they choose a king is called "delivering a message of the LORD in full" (1 Sam 8:10-18). The aged Samuel preaches to "all Israel" on the eve of his death, claiming a lifetime of integrity and declaring that the people, despite the evil of having asked for a king, must still worship with their whole heart (ch. 12). Saul and David do not qualify as preachers, but David is credited with a poetic eulogy of Saul and Jonathan

(2 Sam 1:19-27), even as a marvelous prayer for wisdom is attributed to Solomon that is, in effect, a homily of petition (1 Kgs 8:23-53). Elijah and Elisha deliver some striking challenges to Ahab, Jezebel, and the prophets of Baal but it is not to be called preaching.

The entire books of the "writing prophets" are the proclamation of the word of God to the southern or northern kingdom. Lengthy poetic stretches reported as visions are oracular in tone, which is to say revelatory (Isaiah 13–23). The house of Jacob is addressed (Isa 2:5-6), more especially its greedy and acquisitive upper class (10:1-4). Kings are admonished and told to make right choices (7:10–8:23), Jerusalem and Judah are charged with their sins (22:1-14; 28:7-29). God speaks in the second segment of Isaiah (chs. 40–55), concerned now not with the eighth-century Syrian threat but the sixth-century return of the exiles from Babylon (see 40:1-5; 41:1–44:8). The power of God to deliver Judah from captivity begins to be praised as creative power in a manner that the book of Job will take up (see Isa 40:12-31, esp. v. 28: "Do you not know or have you not heard? The LORD is the eternal God, creator of the ends of the earth.").

Again, the problem everywhere asserts itself: are the lengthy poetic portions of Jeremiah, Hosea, Amos, and the rest who speak as if with the voice of God to be accounted preaching? The answer seems to be an unequivocal yes. Regardless of how much was spoken before or after the writing, the literary genre of the Prophetic books is sacred discourse calculated to elicit in the hearer the response of covenant fidelity.

At times the prophets indulge in prose speech, enjoining on their hearers a course of action such as abjuring seers "who prophesy their own thoughts" or engage in magical practices (Ezek 13:3-9; 17-23). "Like foxes among ruins are your prophets, O Israel! Their visions are false and their divinations lying" (vv. 4, 6). Ezra the postexilic priest is unequivocally a preacher as he expresses anger and shame at the Israelite men who have taken foreign wives (Ezra 9:6-15). "Do not give your daughters to the sons [of the pagans] in marriage. . . . Never promote their peace and prosperity; thus you will grow strong, enjoy the produce of the land, and leave it as an inheritance to your children forever" (v. 12).

The writers of the Wisdom books acted as moralists rather than expositors of Israel's history in searching for motives for faithfulness, but preachers they certainly were: "Hear, O children, a father's instruction, be attentive that you may gain understanding!" (Prov 4:1). "In swaddling clothes and with constant care I was nurtured. For no king has any different origin or birth, but one is the entry into life for all; and in one same way they leave it" (Wis 7:4-6). "Rely not on your wealth; say not, 'I have the power.' / Rely not on your strength in following the desires of your heart. / Say not, 'Who can prevail against me?'" (Sir 5:1-3a). Qoheleth, whose literary name can mean "convoker of an assembly," is known from the Authorized Version tradition as the Preacher.

New Testament

Jesus' proclamation of the kingship of God in the Synoptic Gospels is the paramount example of NT preaching. It is not easy to know what his extended discourses were actually like since the evangelists bunch his aphorisms and parables (e.g., Matthew 5–7; Luke 12). This creates the problem of whether he spoke in any of the ways ascribed to him. As his preaching reaches us, we can conclude that he employed simple examples out of daily life to illustrate the things of God. He suited action to word and word to action. He never became so involved rhetorically that he lost his hearers. In the Gospel telling of it, Jesus did not belabor a point. Often repetition of phrasing in the Oriental manner is reported of him (e.g., Matt 25:31-46 in Greek), but he never becomes tedious or a bore in his preaching. He knows when to stop. He alternates stern warnings with words of comfort; praise, as of John the Baptist, with reproach for not heeding the Baptist's teaching. In his preaching, Jesus does not concentrate on himself, his own reminiscences, or his reflections. His style is objective. He has all of Scripture ready to hand as his chief book of reference—that and the book of the world. He rebuffs the palpably insincere but willingly engages in exchange with any who have something to say. He loves dialogue. Hearers must be on their toes, however, if they wish to dialogue with him. The most evident thing about the preaching of Jesus is that it is not dull. Boredom does not overtake the listeners no matter what the length of his discourses (which may have gone on for hours). He found the things of God supremely interesting but was no less concerned with human affairs. That is why people hung on his words as he related the one to the other.

When discussing the Lucan parables of mercy (e.g., those in Luke 15), the sermons in Acts (2:14-36; 10:34-43; 17:22-31), or the discourses of Jesus in John we are wise to concentrate on the preaching styles that were put in the service of the words of Jesus for, indeed, each Gospel is a proclamation of the one gospel. Luke is the consummate story-teller; John, the master of sonorous, poetic-sounding prose put freshly a second (or third) time. It is impressive to see how he reworks material found in the Synoptics even though he may not have access to any one of these Gospels. John illustrates perfectly the rhetorical axiom, *Non nova sed nove*, "Not new but newly expressed." The skill of both evangelists lies in their not making explicit anything that can be conveyed implicitly. Each is a master of allusion.

The Pauline corpus, meaning Paul's letters and those of his imitators, are filled with materials that have been preached many times. The apostle himself has proclaimed the gospel often, yet seems perfectly capable of presenting the old message in a new way while writing (i.e., dictating) at high speed. The "gospel of God" he proclaims is summarized at the very outset of Romans (1:2-6). The thanksgivings with which his letters usually open contain packaged summaries of the effect on people's lives of waiting for the revelation of Jesus Christ at the end (1 Cor 1:4-9; 2 Cor 1:3-7; Gal 1:1-5; Phil 1:6-11). These thanksgivings contain a reminder of the believers' central faith commitment; prayer for their perseverance; encouragement; and an expression of hope—all of them elements of effective preaching. Many think that Paul uses a preformed formula in whole or part at Romans 3:24-26, where he speaks of Christ's blood as the means of expiation redeeming all who believe. In chapter 6 he faces the problem of whether being dead to sin in baptism and emerging alive to God provides new freedom to sin. Paul answers heatedly that the bodies of believers have now been made slaves to justice as once they were to impurity and license. This is not his ultimate homiletic application, which will come in chapters 12–14, but is one he feels he must make having spelled out the new freedom of believers.

The paraenetic sections at the end of a Pauline letter are powerful preaching, even though much may have preceded it in the body. See the applications of the mystery of the new life in Christ Paul has been proclaiming that occur in 2 Corinthians 13:1-9; Galatians 5–6; Philippians 4; 1 Thessalonians 5. Similarly, Colossians 3:1–4:6 and Ephesians 5–6 exhort to virtuous living, using the device of "household tables [of duties]" that Paul does not employ. The Pastoral Letters contain many preachments, some of them flicked with censure like the various disapprovals of Ben Sira.

It is widely held that the early portion of 1 Peter, 1:3–2:10 is taken from the sermon at an early baptismal liturgy to which have been appended admonitions about conduct in various states of life. Importantly, the sufferings of Christ are proposed as a model for enduring injustice and hardship (2:21-25; 3:18; 4:12-14). 2 Peter, Jude, and the three Johannine letters are exhortations to steadfastness in the received teaching and warnings against false teachers. The second-century writings, with which the last-named NT books are so closely cognate, contain many elements of NT preaching (e.g., 1 Clement, the letters of Ignatius, the Epistle to Diognetus). It is not until mid-century, however, with the work of another author than 1 Clement called 2 Clement, that we have "the first Christian sermon." It proposes in general terms the nature of Christian life and the duty of repentance.

Pastoral-Liturgical Tradition

Preaching has always striven for relevance to worshipers' lives, even when it is adjudged most irrelevant. It has variously been an exercise in cajoling, threat, consolation, entertainment, instruction, panegyric, flight of fancy, and scolding. At times it uses illustration and example so memorably that the main point is lost. Christian preaching has as its primary purpose reminding believers of God's mercy and justice and calling them to respond by living lives motivated by the Christ-life within them. When it stays close to biblical patterns of preaching—which is not the same thing as citing the Bible copiously—it can be at its most effective.

See: GOOD NEWS, JESUS CHRIST, PAUL, PROPHECY/ PROPHET, TEACH/TEACHING, WISDOM, WORD

GERARD S. SLOYAN

PREDESTINATION

Etymology: *prae-destinare* (Latin); *pro-orizein* (Greek). The Latin means "to appoint, to ordain beforehand." The Greek seems to mean essentially the same and in fact is translated into Latin as "prae-determinare" or "prae-destinare." In its broadest theological sense, the term is used to designate the general salvific will of God that gratuitously determines a supernatural goal for creation. Predestination is not identical with God's foreknowledge but, while presupposing this, includes the reality of the divine will as that which turns knowledge into reality in the order of creation and history.

Old Testament

Strictly speaking, this formulation of predestination is shaped by post-biblical tradition. But there are statements already in the OT that suggest relations between God and human freedom that raise important questions for the attentive reader. God is described as hardening the heart of the Pharaoh (Exod 9:12) and as using human agents as instruments of divine judgment (Isa 10:5, 15) or mercy (Isa 45:1). One might ask whether these obviously anthropomorphic formulations can be adequately dealt with in strictly literary terms, or whether they raise questions concerning the relation between God's activity and human activity that can be drawn out only later in the light of a more philosophical framework.

New Testament

In the NT the Pauline and deutero-Pauline letters use the term predestination six times. In general the term refers to that act whereby God's love, from all eternity, determines the principal moments of salvation history. Classical formulations of the Pauline understanding are found in Romans and in Ephesians. The text of Romans 8:29ff. seems to contain the basic elements of the later doctrinal formulations: the divine knowledge, the divine will, and the execution of that will in history through the stages of call, justification, and glorification. Ephesians 1:3-11 speaks of those who were chosen by God "before the foundation of the world" to be holy and blameless before God. The text speaks explicitly of God's plan for salvation in Christ and of those who have been "destined and appointed" to live for the glory of Christ. Perhaps the most emphatic biblical statement about the execution of God's will is found in Romans 9:14-18. God "has mercy upon whomever he wills," and "hardens the heart of whomever he wills."

In the Pauline context, the language of predestination seems to be concerned primarily with a salvific plan and with a possibility for salvation that is open to all rather than with the predestination of particular individuals. This plan is the salvific mystery embodied in Christ.

Theological Tradition

Texts such as these provided the basis for later theologians to develop the understanding of predestination. Important in this area was the thought of Augustine who wrote two works that bear directly on the problem: *On the predestination of the blessed* and *On the gift of perseverance*. Augustine's thought was developed in the context of his understanding of original sin and included not only the biblical sense of a general predestination but the notion of individual predestination as well. The latter included the possibility of a positive predestination to glory as well as the possibility of reprobation, both of which must be related to the divine will in some way. While his concern was to defend the Church's tradition against the Pelagians who seemed to deny the reality of predestination, Augustine's formulation led eventually to the theory of a predestination to evil and reprobation rejected by the Council of Orange (DS 397) and by the Council of Trent (DS 1556, 1567). It also gave an emphasis to the primacy of God that would be problematic in later history, especially at the time of the Reformation.

While the Magisterium has never formally defined the existence of predestination as a dogma, it presupposes predestination in a number of important statements. In the year 853, a local synod at Quiercy-sur-Oise in France stated clearly that, although God wills that all people be saved (1 Tim 2:4), it does not follow that all are actually saved. The fact that someone is saved is a gift of God's salvific love. On the other hand, the fact that someone is lost must be blamed on the free decisions of that person (DS 623). God does not create particular people for the express purpose of condemning them to eternal punishment (DS 621). In its response to the teaching of the sixteenth-century Protestant theologians, the Council of Trent rejected the claim that one could be certain of one's personal predestination (DS 1540). According to Roman Catholic theol-

ogy, the question of one's personal salvation remains an object of hope not an object of knowledge.

The problem of understanding the primacy of God's will in relation to human freedom led to the classical debates and theories *De auxiliis* in the post-Tridentine period, the Jesuits favoring the system of L. Molina (d. 1600) and the Dominicans favoring that of D. Banez (d. 1604). The Magisterium has never resolved the issue in favor of either school. From a speculative viewpoint, the problem is a specific case of understanding the universal relation between primary and secondary causality that is part of the doctrine of creation. The matter is confused when these are placed on the same level as a kind of team-operation in which each partner provides a portion of what is needed for the final result. Here, as in the doctrine of creation, the activity of God is at a fundamentally different level than that of the creature. The ultimate ground of grace and salvation is the mystery of God's creative, forgiving, and self-communicative love (primacy of God). Only because of this is there created existence and human freedom. On the other hand, it is the freedom with which the creative activity of God has endowed us that makes it possible for human beings to respond either positively or negatively to God's offer of grace and salvation.

It is perhaps useful to think of the relation between God and humanity by way of analogy with human, interpersonal relations. If some sort of loving mutuality between God and creatures is the divine aim in creating, this can be accomplished only by give and take from both sides. Love cannot be demanded; it can only be freely given and received. Hence, the language of grace (gift) is most appropriate for speaking of the love-relation between God and creatures. Because of God's ontological priority, God's initiative is always the first element or the basis of this relation (the primacy of God). The human initiative is always of the nature of reception and response to the prior action of God (human freedom and responsibility). While God's offer is first, it does not reach home (gratia efficax) until there is a positive human response. God makes it possible for us to love God humanly. But God does not do what only we can do; that is, actually love God humanly in response to God's loving presence. While God's agency is primary, it is not the only agency involved in this relationship. Human agency is real though dependent. The classical formulations often obscure this fact.

See: GRACE

ZACHARY HAYES, O.F.M.

PRIDE

Pride is only one of the English words used in the NAB to describe phenomena evaluated differently according to the source in which one "takes pride": such terms include haughtiness, arrogance, insolence, pretension, openness, confidence, glory (vb.), or boasting. Depending on context, the last two terms are not always negative. It is probably fair to say that God and God's actions alone are the source of just pride, and that this righteous pride degenerates into something less worthy when humans alone become "the measure of all things." The pastoral tradition of the Church tends to use the term pride per se for this vice and warns against its potentially lethal results.

Old Testament

Pride has various sources and associated characteristics. We hear of the boast of a warrior (1 Kgs 20:1). Jeremiah laments the deafness of the proud (13:17). The boasting of the prince of Tyre is evidenced in his claiming "I am a god," in part due to his beauty (Ezek 28:2, 17). Some boast in their wealth (Ps 49:7) and the proud of Sodom are those who "gave no help to the poor and needy" (Ezek 16:49).

The consequences of the vice of pride are disastrous, whether on a national or personal scale. Isaiah portrays the proud being "abased" (2:6-22) and portrays the Lord

about to degrade the pride of majesty of Tyre (23:9). The deaf pride condemned by Jeremiah leads the prophet to weep secret tears over their imminent exile (13:17). Zephaniah looks forward to the "removal" of the proud braggarts from the people's midst (3:11-13). The Lord promises to desecrate the sanctuary, the "stronghold of your pride" in Ezekiel 24:21. Following the Exile, the priests writing the nation's history portray the punishment of past kings for offenses against the cult: for making an offering on the altar of incense, the Lord is shown visiting "destruction" (leprosy) on proud King Uzziah (2 Chr 26:16). The Chronicler portrays the "anger" of God being visited on the pride of Hezekiah as long as he fails to discharge a debt of gratitude for answered prayer (2 Chr 32:25). And in the Hellenistic period, Daniel explains that the pride of Nebuchadnezzar was punished by the king's being "deprived of his glory" (Dan 5:20).

The Psalter and Wisdom literature also depict the sorry results of haughtiness, arrogance, and pride. The haughty are "brought low" (Ps 18:28), and the Lord "will not endure" them (Ps 101:5). The arrogant "may not stand" (Ps 5:5). The psalmist prays that the proud will receive their just deserts (Ps 94:2). The author of Proverbs knows that "pride comes before disaster, and a haughty spirit before a fall" (16:18). Pride leads to "disgrace" (Prov 11:2). And "the LORD overturns the house of the proud" (Prov 15:25). "For the affliction of the proud man there is no cure" (Sir 3:27).

The positive side of this phenomenon is also known in the OT. A head of grey hair that represents a life of virtue is one's "glory" (Prov 16:31). "Give not your glory to another" is an appeal to Israel not to forfeit the blessings of her election (Bar 4:2-4). The Servant whose help is the Lord will not know shame or disgrace (Isa 50:7). The just one boasts of God as Father (Wis 2:17) and will at the last confront persecutors "full of assurance" (Wis 5:1-5). The basis of this confidence is God who "is your glory" (Deut 10:21). Indeed the only sure basis for boasting is God, "Let not the wise man glory in his wisdom, nor the strong man glory in his strength, nor the rich man glory in his riches; But rather, let him who glories, glory in this, that in his prudence, he knows me" (Jer 9:22-23).

New Testament

Mark 7:22 condemns "arrogance" but Jesus speaks "openly" about the necessity of the cross (Mark 8:32). John's Jesus speaks "openly" (7:25; 18:20) and is a model for a community explaining its faith to its persecutors. In the Spirit of the resurrection, the apostles preach the Word with "boldness" (Acts 4:29, 31; 9:27).

The knowledge of God in Jeremiah 9:22, 23, quoted above, is fundamental to understanding Paul's frequent treatment of the theme of boasting. Paul partly quotes it at 1 Corinthians 1:30, but omits any explicit mention of "knowing," perhaps because knowledge had become such a problem in Corinth. (He has no difficulty discussing knowledge of Jesus with the Philippians; see Phil 3:8.) He laments that when the Gentiles deny their knowledge of God, they become "haughty, arrogant, boastful" (Rom 1:21, 30). He expects to boast about the Thessalonians at Jesus' coming (1 Thess 2:19) and boasts now about the Corinthians (2 Cor 7:14; 8:24; 9:2, 3) because of what God is now and will finally accomplish among them. He allows no boasting in the Law that breaks the Law (Rom 2:23) or boasting in works (Rom 4:2), but counsels the Gentiles to abjure boasting and stand in awe of God's Christ-event (Rom 11:20). When he counsels boasting in what look to be negative experiences, he does so precisely because he sees in them evidence of God's activity. He boasts in the cross because it reveals the new creation (Gal 6:14, 15). He boasts in trials because they produce a trustworthy hope (Rom 5:4, 5) and in his weakness because it reveals the "power of Christ" (2 Cor 11:30; 12:9). Even when Paul does not use the language of boasting and speaks instead of an "open" declaration of the truth, such openness is propagated by the impress of his glorious ministry (2 Cor 3:1-18; 4:2).

Other epistolary literature divides its attention between pretension and confidence. James 3:5 derides the pretensions of the tongue and 1 John 2:16 castigates an (economically) pretentious life. On the other hand, the author of Hebrews claims "pride in our hope" for the future (3:6) and "confidence of entrance into the sanctuary" in the present for those who have been exposed to abuse and affliction and deprived of their possessions (10:34). The author of 1 John proleptically claims a confidence at the judgment in face of the claims made by those who have gone out from us (1 John 2:19, 28; 4:17).

Pastoral-Liturgical Tradition

John Cassian lists eight principal faults: gluttony, fornication, pride, vainglory, covetousness, anger, spiritual sloth, and dejection. Richard Rolle warns that human presumption produces vainglory, pride of self, and confusion. Teresa of Avila was wary of the self-delusion, pride, and (unbalanced) zealousness that can result from the graced period of infused prayer. Benedict Canfield was sure, however, that prayer was a necessary part of the project of destroying pride. And Wesley asserted that grace can free Christians from pride, even in this life.

The Pastoral Constitution on the Church in the Modern World (25) asserts that social unrest occurs in part from the natural tensions of economic, political, and social forms. But it goes on to say that such unrest flows "at a deeper level, from man's pride and selfishness, which contaminate even the social sphere." Oscar Romero, who spent much of his episcopate working to alleviate the imbalances in his society, was not blind to this deeper dynamic: "Holy Week is a call to follow Christ's austerities, the only legitimate violence, the violence that he does to himself and that he invites us to do to ourselves: 'Let those who would follow me deny themselves,' be violent to themselves, repress in themselves the outbursts of pride, kill in their hearts the outbursts of greed, of avarice, of conceit, of arrogance . . . so that out of it a new person my arise, the only one who can build a new civilization, a civilization of love."

See: CREATION, GLORY, HOPE, JUDGMENT, KNOWLEDGE, POOR, RESURRECTION, SERVANT, WEAKNESS, WEEPING

MARK C. KILEY

PRIEST

Priests in the Bible perform special roles and functions, but they differ from a contemporary understanding of priest, whose ministry derives from the presbyters of the NT. The English word "priest" derives from the French *pretre*, and ultimately from the Greek, *presbytes* (presbyter). Yet some issues and struggles concerning priests in the OT and Judaism parallel those of contemporary Christians: changing roles and functions, adaptation to altered socio-political milieux, and struggles over identity and inclusion.

Old Testament

To be a priest is not a personal response to a call from God (more appropriate to prophets); rather, persons are either appointed or born into a hereditary priestly family.

Priestly Functions. First, they served God and cared for the sanctuary, as Eli at Shiloh (1 Samuel 1–3), Ahimelech at Nob (1 Samuel 21–22), Jonathan, son of Gershom, at Dan (Judg 18:30), and Zadok and the Aaronites at Jerusalem. Cultic service included offering of sacrifices, burning of frankincense (Exod 30:7-9), care of the lamps (Exod 27:20-21), setting out the showbread on the table (Lev 24:5-9), as well as sounding the trumpets on feasts and New Moons, and carrying the ark. They prepared and examined sacrificial materials, managed the business of the sanctuary in terms of donations, upkeep, inspections, purifications, and maintenance.

Second, priests manifested God's mind: in oracular consultation, by a process of consulting the Urim and Thummim to gain a "yes" or "no" answer (1 Sam 14:18-19), or to determine innocence or guilt (1 Sam 14:41-42); reporting God's ordinances or decisions (Deut 33:8-10), especially in separating holy from profane. At the sanctuary doors priests probably engaged in liturgical dialogue (Introits) with worshipers seeking admission; priests articulated the requirements for entry, an elementary form of Torah (Pss 15:2-5; 24:4; Isa 33:15-16); priestly Torah refers both to judgments and to teaching. In preexilic days, Torah generally was expounded at the sanctuary (Isa 2:3; Mic 4:2; Deut 31:10-11), probably by priests.

Third, Aaronite priests performed therapeutic functions, especially in regard to certain skin diseases where they combined medical procedures (diagnosis, quarantine, and observation) with magical and sacrificial rites (Leviticus 13–15).

Fourth, in lamentation rituals priests may have pronounced a type of salvation oracle (e.g., Pss 12:6; 85:9-14), a function carried out by Levites in postexilic days (2 Chr 20:13-17).

Difficulty Interpreting Priestly Texts. The complex nature of the Pentateuchal texts, with various layers of tradition folded in during several centuries, makes a history of the priests difficult to describe. Followers of the documentary hypothesis (JEPD) and its chronological scheme argue that descriptions of priests in J and E come from the early monarchy, those of D from the seventh century, and P materials were postexilic. References to priests in the historical books seem more reliable and useful for interpreting the various portraits in J, E, and D; the result is an evolutionary view, with a developing priesthood: priests were unimportant in early (JE) Israel, since heads of families offered sacrifice; later, kings appointed priests for the royal sanctuary, but after Babylon destroyed the Temple, priestly activities ceased. When Jews returned to the land, priests assumed previous royal leadership roles in addition to their functions in the second temple. This view is evolutionary, implying that pristine Hebrew religion was superior to postexilic Judaism, dominated by Law, temple rituals, and preservation of political detente. This hypothesis is criticized for overemphasizing a reconstructed history and naive view of early times.

Another view of JEDP sees them as traditions deriving from different social settings, perhaps from various priestly houses (e.g., Levites, Aaronites, Zadokites). When various layers of description appear together, interpreters must struggle to separate different images, not only as indicators of historical development but also of geographical and sociological variety. In an alternative scheme, the same literary data (JEDP) point to priestly groups struggling for leadership and identity. If P's portrait of Aaron's family were the "latest," in the sense that it prevailed in the canon, that fact does not necessitate a postexilic origin of the traditions. For example, only sacrifices made at a sanctuary required a priest (1 Sam 2:12-17), so before the time of Aaron and the tent, people made their own sacrifices. Later, priests played an expanded role at the central sanctuary, so the priestly organization represented in P traditions may have emerged by the time of D, which stressed the single sanctuary. In that case, D—with little concern for Aaron's family—and P—focusing on Aaron's priesthood—could represent diverse preexilic positions until the Aaronites prevailed after the return from exile. No matter the source, priests were required for sanctuary sacrifice.

History of Priesthood. Eli was priest at Shiloh, where the young Samuel stayed (1 Samuel 1–3). Later, his descendant Abiathar was sole survivor of Saul's slaughter of the priests at Nob (1 Sam 22:20-23); he took refuge with David and functioned as priest for him (1 Sam 23:6, 9; 30:7). After David captured Jerusalem, Zadok appeared as priest alongside Abiathar, and in the struggle for succession to David, he supported Solomon over Adonijah, Abiathar's candidate. Solomon banished Abiathar to Anathoth (1 Kgs 2:26-27) and Zadok became priest par excellence (1 Kgs 2:35). Since Zadok had no ge-

nealogy, a hypothesis about his origin arose: he was a Canaanite/Jebusite priest whom David retained in his attempt to meld disparate factions. Recently, some have linked Zadok's ancestors to an Aaronite family in Hebron, where David first reigned (Zadok and the Aaronites were related to David through marriage; Exod 6:23; Num 2:3). Since the priests in P traditions and Chronicles were Aaronite, it may be that Hezekiah, a hero in Chronicles, was the king when the P traditions originated.

After the fall of Jerusalem, most Zadokites were exiled, but many lower-class Levites remained in Palestine. Among the returnees from Babylon, Zadokite priests far outnumbered Levites, whose exclusion from significant roles in the Temple provided little incentive to return. During the Persian and Hellenistic eras, Judah resembled a theocracy, where a priest usually assumed leadership; Ezra's significance is an example. Eventually Zadokite priests took charge of temple sacrificial ritual, while Levites became a lower clergy (singers, doorkeepers, and interpreters of Torah). The number of priests grew too large (10% of the males in Judah) for all of them to be on duty at the Temple and to be supported by offerings, so they divided into twenty-four divisions, sixteen Zadokite and eight Levite, which rotated week-long periods of service (1 Chr 24:4-19). When they were not ministering at the Temple, they supported themselves like other Judahites.

During the Hellenistic era the Zadokite high priests represented the people to their foreign monarchs. Some of them exercised great spiritual influence over the people, like the high priest Simon, son of Onias II (219–196 BCE), who contributed much for public worship and welfare; Sirach described the Yom Kippur liturgy and gave all the details of Simon's role (Sir 50:1-21). When Hellenization began in Palestine in the early second century, Onias III was ousted from the high priesthood by his brother Jason; he was later replaced by a non-Zadokite, Menelaus, during the rule of Antiochus Epiphanes (175–164 BCE). After the Maccabean revolt, one Aaronite was made high priest, Alcimus (162), then Hasmonean rulers took over the high priest's role (Jonathan in 152, Simon Maccabee in 142). The Hasidim broke off from the Maccabees (ca. 160 BCE) and they probably divided into two sects striving for holiness: the Pharisees, a lay movement, and the Essenes, a priestly movement. While Sadducees, a priestly group of the Zadokite line, grew in social-economic status, Pharisee scholars emerged as spiritual leaders of the people. The Essenes who considered their priests as the legitimate heirs of the Aaronite/Zadokite priesthood and their calendar of feasts and order of worship as correct, struggled against Jerusalem. Political machinations continued during the Roman era and the number of priests increased so that in the time of Herod the Great many priests belonged to the upper classes and the conservative Sadducee party and played an important role in the Sanhedrin. So Jewish priests in NT texts do not resemble the Aaronite priests of old, but comprise a new caste in competition with sectarian groups who had undertaken many functions originally performed by the priests (e.g., teaching Torah passed from priest scribes to the Pharisees).

Women in the Priestly Cult. While there is no clear evidence that women functioned as priests, they did belong to priestly families. There are clues to a lost history: the "ministering women" at sanctuaries (1 Sam 2:22; Exod 38:8). One theory is that women officiated in early Israel, but historical circumstances (famine, plague) occasioned their restriction to child-bearing and the hearth; later, priestly theology elaborated a purity/holiness code that excluded women from the cult. But the important texts and their dating are disputed, so it seems safer to claim that some women ministered at early sanctuaries, while P traditions (representing both pre- and postexilic life) have some indications of women present in the cult.

In P women do participate in some sanctuary rituals, so purity issues cannot explain their exclusion from officiating. Women became Nazirites (Num 6:2) and made offerings at the sanctuary (Exod 35:22; Numbers 30; also 1 Sam 1:11; Prov 7:14). Women participated in some preexilic cultic celebrations (Deut 12:12; 31:10-12), while postexilic writers envision women as active in the Temple (servants and singers in Ezra 2:65 and Neh 7:67). One passage in Chronicles lists three daughters of the Levite Heman, who may have been Levitical singers (1 Chr 25:5); another speaks of male and female lament singers (2 Chr 35:25). Moreover, characteristic P language for the worshiper is inclusive: *nephesh*, "person," and *adam*, "human or person" (Lev 1:2; 2:1; 4:2, 27; 5:1, 17, 21). Such factors negate the claim that women had no roles in Israel's cult, even in priestly circles.

A Theology of Priesthood. Many factors militate against a wholesome view of Israel's priestly life. Although first-century Jewish priesthood had suffered scandals and was negatively viewed in the NT, many priests in earlier ages exercised great religious influence, e.g., Simon and Ezra. In the Torah several important aspects of priestly theology and spirituality emerge. They represent and protect Israel's holiness, revealed to Moses at Sinai: "You shall be to me a kingdom of priests, a holy nation" (Exod 19:6). Closely related is the motivation in Leviticus 19, the ethical high point of the Holiness Code: "Be holy, for I, the LORD, your God, am holy" (Lev 19:2). This text responds in a priestly way to Micah's question: What does the Lord require of Israel (Mic 6:8)? Priestly traditions emphasized the pursuit of holiness and proper worship of God, which only occurred in a sanctuary and society guided by religious law. Justice and compassion are aspects of holiness (Leviticus 19); here priestly and prophetic responses coincide, though priests focused more on celebrating holiness, preserving purity, and creating a religious community.

Two texts demonstrate the close connection of priests to the altar. At Aaron's ordination (Leviticus 8–9), the high priest's anointing and consecration resemble the consecration of the altar, another source of holiness (Lev 8:6-12); so the high priest appears as a human counterpart to the altar. Elsewhere Aaron's two sons Nadab and Abihu made improper incense offerings, so fire from God consumed them (Lev 10:1-2). In Moses' explanation to Aaron that his sons had violated God's word about priests, he said: "Through those who approach me I will manifest my sacredness" (Lev 10:3). Priests are those who approach God, but God's self reveals the holiness; they function only as mediators and guarantors of divine holiness—they are not its initiators.

Finally, the priestly blessing in Numbers provides another aspect of their theology and spirituality (Num 6:24-26); it concludes with God's word: "So shall they invoke my name upon the Israelites, and I will bless them" (Num 6:27). The prayer contains an expansive notion of God's gifts to Israel, but the blessing comes from God, not from the priests.

See: AARON, ALTAR, ANOINTING, CLEAN/UNCLEAN, CONSECRATION, ELDERS, HOLY/HOLINESS, LAMENT, MELCHIZEDEK, PHARISEE, SACRIFICE, SADDUCEES

JOHN C. ENDRES, S.J.

New Testament

There is an ambivalence in the NT literature surrounding the word "priest," as well as "high priest," a term closely allied with it. According to the gospel stories, Jesus himself is not of priestly descent but his teachings and ministry bring him into conflict with the groups in Jerusalem bearing these titles. None of his immediate followers are priests and there is no order of priesthood evident among the more structured types of ministry that were beginning to emerge toward the end of the first century. Only within one stream of early Christian tradition, namely that evident in the Letter to the Hebrews, is Jesus' life and ministry interpreted symbolically through the lens of priesthood, and in a few brief references, the life of Christians is similarly interpreted.

Tensions within the Gospel Stories and Beyond. The order of priesthood within the Judaism of Jesus' day is evident in the Gospel stories. Zechariah is said to be "of the priestly division of Abijah," indicating that he belonged to the tribe of Levi. He was a priest, therefore, by way of heredity, and carried out his priestly function of offering incense in the outer sanctuary according to the time allotted to his division (Luke 1:5, 9). Jesus himself is seen to recognize the juridical role of the priests when he sends the leper whom he heals to the priest to be pronounced ritually clean (Matt 8:4; Mark 1:44; Luke 5:14; see Lev 14:1-4). He is also depicted in Matthew's Gospel as using the example of the Sabbath exemption given to priests who had to serve in the Temple in order to encourage an application of the law that did not deny genuine human need or mercy for the sake of sacrifice (Matt 12:1-9). In that same scene, on the other hand, he claims that something greater than the Temple is here in his ministry in a way that points to the Temple being obsolete, a vision which finds a more graphic expression in prophecy (Matt 24:1-2) and in the early Christian apocalyptic (Luke 21:20-24). Similarly, in his story of the good Samaritan, Jesus would seem to critique priestly practice that fulfilled all the purity laws and yet denied compassion to another human person (Luke 10:31). In the eyes of many interpreters, therefore, Jesus' repudiation of the Temple symbolizes a rejection of the entire socio-political order associated with it, including the cultus.

Within the gospel stories, Jesus is presented as a prophetic figure. He is not from the priestly family of Levi but is of Davidic descent. He is anointed for his ministry with the power and spirit of God (Matt 3:13-17; Luke 4:18), and that ministry is predominantly one of preaching like the great prophets whose oracles are preserved within the Scriptures and of healing in line with the early prophets Elijah and Elisha (1 Kgs 17:8-24; 2 Kgs 4:8-37). It is this very mission that brings Jesus into conflict with the administrative authorities within Judaism among whom the priestly and high priestly families exercised significant power. In the Matthean gospel story, by way of example, this conflict runs from beginning to end like a thread (Matt 2:4; 28:11). It is foreshadowed in the passion predictions (Matt 16:21; 20:18) and becomes explicit when Jesus enters Jerusalem (21:15, 23) and teaches in the Temple area (21:46). Finally, the entire passion narrative is then presented under the banner of Matthew 26:3-4: "Then the chief priests and the elders of the people assembled in the palace of the high priest who was called Caiaphas, and they consulted together to arrest Jesus by treachery and put him to death."

This same tension is presented by the Lucan writer as continuing beyond the life of Jesus into the story of the early Church. The priests together with the captain of the Temple and some of the Sadducees arrest Peter and John as they teach in the Temple area following the healing of a man who was crippled (Acts 4:1-3). Stephen is brought to trial before the Sanhedrin, questioned by the high priest as leader of this body (Acts 6:12; 7:1) and presumably stoned to death by its members (Acts 7:54). Paul, too, who like these early preachers of the Jesus story has his ministry presented in a way that parallels that of Jesus, is brought before the council and the high priest Ananias (Acts 23:2, 4, 5) and they plot to kill him (Acts 25:1-3, 15). Within the same story, however, there is a passing reference that "even a large group of priests were becoming obedient to the faith" (Acts 6:7).

A Different Perspective: Jesus as High Priest. In a stream of early Christian tradition considered by some to be much less central than that of the Gospels examined above, or the Pauline tradition in which there is no reference at all to priests or high priests, the death and resurrection of Jesus is interpreted through a sacerdotal lens. The Letter to the Hebrews presents Jesus who is designated "son of God" as "a great high priest who has passed through the heavens" (Heb 4:14) and explores this image by way of various OT allusions and citations in a manner typical of the writer's style.

We are introduced to the imagery early in this literary work which has more of the characteristics of a homily or sermon than of a letter. Jesus' solidarity with humanity, an aspect of interpretation already familiar in the Gospel and Pauline traditions, is emphasized as the basis for his becoming "a merciful and faithful high priest before God to expiate the sins of the people" (Heb 2:17). In the subsequent verse and in the further development of the imagery in chapter 5, this solidarity is explicated in terms of Jesus being "tested through what he suffered" (2:18) and being "beset by weakness" (5:2), although an earlier verse added the qualification "yet without sin" (4:15). It forms the basis of the compassionate high priesthood that the homilist then develops as characterizing Jesus.

An aspect of the high priestly construct within Judaism, namely mediation on behalf of the people, is first explored. The high priest was the one who offered both prayer and sacrifice to God on behalf of the people and hence obtained for them mercy and forgiveness. The homilist presents Jesus acting on behalf of humanity with God especially in relation to their liberation from the effects of sin (5:1, 9). Since such mediation even for the earthly high priest was a sacred task, within Judaism an authentic holder of this office did not choose this role for himself but was seen as "called by God" (5:4). So too was Jesus called, an interpretation founded on Psalm 2:7: "You are my son; this day I have begotten you," a text used in various ways with messianic connotations within the early tradition (Acts 13:33 and closely related to Matt 3:17; Mark 1:11; Luke 3:22). The compassionate mediation of Jesus is therefore already ordained by God and hence will be acceptable to God for the sake of humanity.

The scriptural mosaic that forms the backdrop for the homilist's continuing development of the image of Jesus as high priest is enhanced by drawing on Psalm 110. Like Psalm 2, it was a text used widely within early Christian reflections on the messianic nature of Jesus' life and ministry (Matt 22:44; Mark 12:36; Luke 20:42-43; Acts 2:34-35; Heb 1:13). Here, however, the homilist cites verse 4 rather than verse 1, introducing into this messianic reflection the almost mythic figure of Melchizedek as a type for the priesthood of Jesus: "You are a priest forever according to the order of Melchizedek." This brief reference then needs to be supplemented for the richer exploration of the fundamental image in relation to Jesus, and so the homilist provides an excellent midrash on the only other reference to Melchizedek in the OT, Genesis 14:17-20 (Heb 7:1-10).

First, the homilist provides a foundation for the priestly aspect of Jesus' messianism within the more commonly accepted royal tradition by translating the name and designation of Melchizedek—"king of righteousness" and "king of peace"—two central tenets of royal messianism (7:1-2; Psalm 72). Second, the lack of information provided in Genesis in relation to the origin/birth or departure/end of Melchizedek is interpreted as a prefiguration of the eternal priesthood of the risen Jesus (7:3). A third aspect developed by way of agile rabbinic exegesis is the superiority of the priesthood of Melchizedek to that of the Levitical priests (7:4-10). In this way the homilist provides a profound critique of one of the central elements of Judaism, its priesthood, and allied with that its Law and covenant (7:12, 18, 22), and may even be said to be suggesting its obsolescence or complete repudiation in a way similar to that seen earlier in the Matthean tradition. The need for the ongoing offerings of the high priests is replaced by the "once for all" offering of Jesus of himself (7:27; 9:26; 10:10, 12). The order of Levi and the law of Moses in relation to levitical priests have not brought perfection, but perfection or completion occurs in Jesus "who has been made perfect forever" (7:28; 10:14).

A climactic point in the unfolding logic of our homilist is reached in the acclamation: "we have such a high priest, who has taken his seat at the right hand of the throne of the Majesty in heaven!" (8:1). From this high point it can be claimed emphatically, by citing Jeremiah 31:31-34 extensively, that the old covenant with its law and priesthood has indeed become obsolete and is repudiated. Relationship with God, access to God is now through "the mediator of the new covenant," Jesus.

In true homiletic style, the hearers are exhorted to allow their lives to be shaped by this understanding of Jesus as the great high priest. They are to "approach with a sincere heart and in absolute trust" (10:22), to "hold unwaveringly to our confession that gives us hope," and to persevere in lives of compassion and in the suffering that comes (10:32-39).

The Christian Life as Priestly. The early Christian critique of priests and the order of priesthood as responsible for the death of Jesus and also inadequate in effecting lasting salvation, as well as the presentation of Jesus as the great high priest who brought to completion the priestly work begun by the levitical priests, meant that neither the followers of Jesus nor Christian missionaries or ministers were designated in priestly terms. Only in 1 Peter 2:5 and Revelation 1:6; 5:10; 20:6 do we find the family of words used metaphorically or symbolically in relation to the members of the Christian community. In 1 Peter, the metaphorical sense is made explicit by the use of "like": "like living stones, let yourselves be built into a spiritual house to be a holy priesthood to offer spiritual sacrifices acceptable to God through Jesus Christ." The inextricable link between priesthood and Temple within Jewish tradition enables the writer of this letter to encourage disparate communities to see themselves as the place where God dwells with humanity (1 Cor 3:16; 6:19). The totality of the lives of the members of these communities then become like "sacrifices" within the temple of God's presence in the world (Rom 12:1). In the context of the eschatological vision of the seer who speaks out of the text of Revelation, the priestly and kingly roles of the believing community are symbolically linked, pointing toward the final perfection of the community at the end of the age. In both instances, the Christian community is given roles similar to those fulfilled in Jesus and so it is each member of the community who must bear witness in the world to what has, in fact, been accomplished in Jesus. Within the NT, therefore, the only priesthood attributed to members of the human community is that of the symbolic priesthood of all believers.

See: COMPASSION, COVENANT, HEALING, JUDAISM, LAW, MELCHIZEDEK, MERCY, MESSIAH, MISSION, PRAYER, PREACHING, PROPHECY/PROPHET, SACRIFICE, SADDUCEES, SALVATION, SIN, TEMPLE

ELAINE M. WAINWRIGHT

Pastoral-Liturgical Tradition

The Second Vatican Council and ecclesial developments since then have set the context for the contemporary understanding of priesthood in the Roman Catholic Church. Changed relations with other Christian churches and increased participation of the laity in ministry have also considerably shaped that context. Since the late Middle Ages the sacrament of Orders has been explained above all in terms of priesthood and the power to offer the Eucharistic Sacrifice. In fact ordination* to the priesthood was generally equated with ordination to the presbyterate, the second rank of the hierarchical order; the episcopacy was looked upon as an appointment to an office with special jurisdiction but not as a stage in sacramental ordination.

The Constitution on the Church affirmed that the sacrament of Orders includes the threefold ministry of bishop, presbyter, and deacon, and that each of these ranks includes a right and responsibility to proclaim the Word of God, to minister liturgically, and to engage in pastoral care. As NT studies affirm, the names for Christian ministers varied in the apostolic period of the Church, but during the second century the presbyter came to be identified as a minister of second rank. He was part of a college whose primary task was to give advice to the *episkopos*

who was the leader of the community. By the end of the second century, the ministry of the presbyter was linked with the Jewish and Greek exercise of priesthood; hence liturgical presidency became the foundation for Church leadership rather than community leadership being the foundation for liturgical leadership.

It is in the *Apostolic Tradition* of Hippolytus (early third century) that we find the oldest known ritual for ordination to the presbyterate. The rite makes no mention of liturgical leadership; giving pastoral advice to the *episkopos* is the presbyter's responsibility. Gradually presbyters became pastors and liturgical ministers in communities that were supervised by a bishop. Hence their ordination came to involve pastoral care, sacramental ministry, and to some extent ministry of the Word. Throughout the Middle Ages the number of presbyters increased dramatically, above all in monasteries. Their function was primarily liturgical, often limited to the consecration of the Eucharist. The priest was above all one commissioned to act *in persona Christi*, mediating divine grace through the offering of the Sacrifice of Christ's Body and Blood and the absolution from sins.

In the sixteenth century, the Protestant Reformers objected that the ordained priesthood appeared to obstruct the freedom of God's mercy and neglected the priesthood of all believers and the ministry of God's Word. In response the Council of Trent asserted an essential distinction between the baptized and the ordained, affirmed the institution of the priesthood and hierarchy by Christ, and defined the priesthood in terms of the power to consecrate and offer the Body and Blood of Christ and to remit and retain sins.

Counter-Reformation theology of the priesthood tended to be defensive, but there is no doubt that as a result of the development of seminaries and improved academic programs, priests were better educated and formed spiritually, though culturally and socially they were usually distanced from the faithful who were looked upon simply as the beneficiaries of priestly ministry.

In developing a contemporary theology of priesthood that supports both effective pastoral ministry and liturgical leadership, one must try to retrieve important aspects of the history of the ordained priesthood which have been neglected. That is precisely what the Second Vatican Council tried to do. The Council devoted three documents exclusively to the sacrament of Orders, one to bishops, *Christus dominus,* and two to priests, *Presbyterorum ordinis* and *Optatam totius.* These texts focus primarily on the pastoral responsibilities of the ordained. The primary theological treatment of the sacrament of Orders is found in the Constitution on the Church, *Lumen gentium.*

The Second Vatican Council retrieved the priestly identity of all the baptized (1 Pet 2:9) while maintaining that the common priesthood and the ordained priesthood "differ from one another in essence and not only in degree" (Dogmatic Constitution on the Church, no. 10). In order to free the ordained priesthood from the tendency to identify it with liturgical cult, it retrieved the scriptural term "presbyter." Whereas the Council of Trent dealt with the priesthood primarily in Eucharistic terms, the Second Vatican Council speaks of priesthood more broadly in Christological and ecclesial terms. It begins with the mission of the Son of God. Just as Jesus was sent by the Father, so he in turn sent his apostles and their successors, the bishops, whose ministry is shared in a limited degree by presbyters (Decree on the Ministry and Life of Priests, no. 2).

Trent viewed the priesthood above all as finding its identity in the power to confect the Eucharist, whereas the description of the priesthood in the documents of Vatican II takes in a wide field. "Those who are consecrated by holy orders are appointed to feed the Church in Christ's name with the Word and grace of God" (Dogmatic Constitution on the Church, no. 11). Within that broad framework there is scope for the preaching of the gospel, pastoral work on

behalf of God's people, and celebration of the liturgy (Dogmatic Constitution on the Church, no. 28). Priests are not ordained for their own sanctification but for the service of the people of God (Dogmatic Constitution on the Church, no. 18). Hence the ordained priesthood, contrary to the view of the Protestant Reformers, does not intrude between God and the priesthood of all believers, but rather serves the latter so that it achieves its own proper fulfillment.

As mandated by the Constitution on the Sacred Liturgy, revised rites of ordination were promulgated by Paul VI on June 18, 1968, in his apostolic constitution *Pontificalis Romani.* A revised edition was promulgated on June 29, 1989. The three ordinations of bishop, presbyter, and deacon are identical in structure and are celebrated between the Liturgy of the Word and the Liturgy of the Eucharist. The ordination of a presbyter begins with his call and presentation to the bishop, who in turn asks whether the candidate has the requisite qualifications. The bishop's homily, first addressed to the community and then to the ordinand, speaks of the functions proper to presbyters and of their relationship to the bishop. His service involves ministry of the Word, celebration of the liturgy, especially the Eucharist, and union with the bishop and his successors. After the litany of the saints has been sung over the prostrate candidate, the bishop imposes hands on his head, then all the presbyters present do the same. With the presbyters gathered around him, the bishop recites the ordination prayer, which makes it clear that the presbyteral ministry is both ecclesial and missionary. The new presbyter is then vested in stole and chasuble, his hands are anointed with chrism by the bishop, he is given the paten containing the bread and the cup containing the wine and water, which will be consecrated in the Liturgy of the Eucharist. The bishop then gives the kiss of peace to the new presbyter; the other priests present do the same. In the concelebration of the Eucharist the new presbyter takes first place after the bishop.

A number of important questions concerning ordination to the priesthood continue to be raised. These include the possibility of ordaining women to the priesthood, the introduction of optional celibacy and the ordination of married men, the mutual recognition of ordained ministries among the Christian churches, the formation and spirituality of diocesan priests, and the distinctive character of priests in religious institutes.

The disciplinary matters concerning the priesthood are treated in Book IV, Title VI of the code of canon law, canons 1008-1054.

See: APOSTLE, CALL/VOCATION, COMMUNITY, MINISTRY, MISSION, PREACHING, SACRIFICE

R. KEVIN SEASOLTZ, O.S.B.

PROMISE

A promise is an oral or written assurance to be faithful to one's word. The Bible only rarely calls attention to human promises, vows, or oaths, sometimes in positive contexts (Deut 23:24; Neh 5:12-13) and sometimes in negative ones (Mark 14:11; 2 Pet 2:19). The most frequent mention of promise in the Bible refers to God's fidelity to promises. The OT focuses on God's faithfulness to covenantal promises while the NT reiterates this stance and points to new promises made in and through Jesus Christ. The concept of promise, both human and divine, remains an important aspect of the Church's contemporary life.

Old Testament

Despite the pervasive influence of the notion of promise in the OT, the Hebrew language surprisingly has no specific word for promise. Other concepts express this notion, such as making a covenant or swearing an oath. Yet the overwhelming orientation of the entire OT is one of promise, emphasizing God's desire to make promises to people and to keep them. The God of Israel is a God of promise, and promise is intimately bound to fulfillment. The very concept of promise produces expectation which, in turn, anticipates fulfillment or accomplishment. These two concepts remain in a constant theological tension in the OT.

The promises of God to the patriarchs (Genesis 12–50) are particularly important in the OT because they establish a pattern. God's promises are quite concrete. To Abraham God promises continual blessing (Gen 12:2), a son even in his old age (Gen 17:16-17), fertility in the form of innumerable descendants (Gen 17:6), a land for permanent possession (Gen 17:8), and an ongoing personal relationship (Gen 17:7). These promises are repeated throughout the stories of the patriarchs and are often recalled as testimony to God's fidelity. Although God always initiates promises through covenants, Abraham, for his part, also enters into a promise: "On your part, you and your descendants after you must keep my covenant throughout the ages. . . . every male among you shall be circumcised" (Gen 17:9-10). Obedience and fealty to this command is Abraham's commitment to God's promise (Gen 17:23-27).

The patriarchal promises of blessing, posterity, land, and relationship reappear through-out the OT (e.g., Exod 12:25; Deut 12:20; 19:8). The greatest act of faithfulness in the OT is God's remembrance of the chosen people in their suffering as slaves in Egypt. When God appears to Moses, God's identity is revealed as the same God of the patriarchs with whom God had a special relationship. God recalls that relationship and affirms it as the basis for the extraordinary intervention of the Exodus event: "I have witnessed the affliction of my people in Egypt and have heard their cry of complaint. . . . Therefore I have come down to rescue them" (Exod 3:6-8). The great king Solomon much later recalls the covenant with Moses with somewhat exaggerated praise: "Blessed be the LORD who has given rest to his people Israel, just as he promised. Not a single word has gone unfulfilled of the entire generous promise he made through his servant Moses" (1 Kgs 8:56).

God makes further promises to the kings of Israel. God tells Nathan the prophet to give David the promise of a dynasty through the ages: "Your house and your kingdom shall endure forever before me; your throne shall stand firm forever" (2 Sam 7:16; Ps 89:4-5). David's son and successor, Solomon, also recalls God's promise when he dedicates the Temple in Jerusalem: "Blessed be the LORD, the God of Israel, who with his own mouth made a promise to my father David and by his hand has brought it to fulfillment" (1 Kgs 8:15). These royal promises find further life in later prophetic promises of a messiah in the line of David, who will come to God's people with salvation (Isa 11:1; Acts 13:22-23).

The psalms especially recall God's faithfulness to the great promises to Israel in poetic recitals of testimony and remembrance (e.g., Psalm 105). Promise is tied closely to the concept of remembrance. The verb "remember" (*zakar*) often expresses God's faithfulness; the God of Israel is not one to forget promises. The psalmist gives assurance that God always remains faithful: "He remembers his covenant which he made binding for a thousand generations. . . . For he remembered his holy word to his servant Abraham" (Ps 105:8, 42). At times, God's fidelity is contrasted with the infidelity of the people of Israel who often strayed from their part of the promises. Psalm 78, for example, is a lengthy recounting of God's faithfulness to Israel even though Israel time and again wandered away from its relationship with God. When the OT drives home God's commitment to promises it is sometimes in the form of poignant questions. God cries out in a prophecy in Isaiah: "Can a mother forget her infant, be without tenderness for the child of her womb? Even should she forget, I will never forget you" (Isa 49:15; see also Ps 77:9-10).

This testimony to the ceaseless fidelity of God to words and actions of promise forms the foundation for later prophetic assurances of God's action on behalf of the chosen people. Indeed, God's fidelity to promise undergirds the biblical perspective on faith and hope. The hopeful visions of Deutero-Isaiah are rooted in the fact that the people of Israel are "offspring of Abraham my [i.e., god's] friend" (Isa 41:8). The prophet Jeremiah also speaks of a new age of promise and hope based upon the previous promises of God to the chosen people: "The days are coming, says the LORD, when I will fulfill the promise I made to the house of Israel and Judah" (Jer 33:14; see also 32:42). This open-ended vision of promise ultimately renders the OT a book of promise which, from a Christian perspective, only finds its true fulfillment in the NT and in the person of Jesus Christ, the Messiah and Son of God.

New Testament

If the OT is primarily a book of promise, this is not to say that the NT is only a book of fulfillment, for it also recalls the promises of the patriarchs and speaks of God's further promises through Jesus. The NT frequently uses the Greek word "promise" as both a verb (*epaggellō*) and a noun (*epaggelia*) and exclusively relates it to divine promise (except Acts 23:21, which refers to a human oath). As in the OT, the NT also connects promise with fulfillment (Acts 7:17; 13:32-33), referring primarily to the fulfillment effected in Jesus Christ.

The NT sometimes recalls the promises made to Abraham and to the patriarchs (e.g., Rom 15:8) or to the Davidic promise of a messiah (Acts 13:23). Paul particularly refers to God's promise to Abraham (Galatians 3). Two factors make Abraham crucially tied to the image of promise. First, Paul views God's promises to Abraham as an unconditional, free, and absolute commitment on God's part. Second, Abraham serves as a model of faith for the Christian community because "Abraham 'believed God, and it was credited to him as righteousness'" (Gal 3:6; Rom 4:20). Paul contrasts the value of promise with that of the Law (Rom 4:13-16). Though the Law is not opposed to the "promises of God" (Gal 3:21), nevertheless those who belong to Christ are "children of the promise" (Gal 3:29; Rom 9:8) who are no longer bound by the Law but live in the freedom of Christian faith. Paul sees Christ as the descendant of Abraham (Gal 3:16) who brings to fulfillment the patriarchal promise of descendants "that the blessing of Abraham might be extended to the Gentiles through Christ Jesus" (Gal 3:14). Paul consistently sees the broad patriarchal promises as having their fulfillment in Christ, with the implication that the Gentiles, and by extension the Church as the new people of God, have become coheirs of these eternal promises (Eph 3:6).

The NT also applies the word "promise" to the holy Spirit. Jesus explicitly refers to the holy Spirit as "the promise of my Father" (Luke 24:49; Acts 1:4) and this promise is poured out on believers at Pentecost (Acts 2:33) as the abiding presence of the risen Lord in the midst of the Christian community. In applying this notion to the holy Spirit Ephesians designates this gift to Christians as "the first installment of our inheritance toward redemption as God's possession" (Eph 1:14). The presence of the Spirit in the community becomes a significant reminder of the fidelity of God who never abandons the chosen people.

The Letter to the Hebrews conceives of promise from a slightly different angle. While Hebrews utilizes the promises to Abraham and the patriarchs as an example of fidelity (7:6; 11:17, 33), the fulfillment of these promises pales in comparison to the new promise that has come in Jesus Christ, the new High Priest, who brings a better promise and a better covenant (8:6; see 11:13). Consequently, the NT also emphasizes the new promises rooted in the person of Jesus Christ. In Jesus God has acted in a final, definitive manner to fulfill all the hopes of Israel's covenants and to expand the promise to encompass those who were once perceived as outsiders to God's promises (Eph 2:11-13). If God acts in Jesus to remain true to the promises of the patriarchs (Luke 1:72-73), this action also yields a new promise that provides an eternal hope. "And this is the promise he made us: eternal life" (1 John 2:25; 2 Tim 1:1). This new life in Christ is God's ultimate fidelity to the promises witnessed in the Bible. The NT also includes a vibrant sense of ceaseless expectation to the new promises made in Christ. The figure of the parousia, the second coming of Christ in glory, is the primary focus of this expectancy. The early Christians felt the tension of this unfulfilled hope and sometimes doubted it (e.g., 2 Pet 3:4), "But according to his promise we await new heavens and a new earth in which righteousness dwells" (2 Pet 3:13). The NT exhorts Christians to remain firm in their confidence that God will one day accomplish the promises made through Jesus Christ precisely because God is faithful and never abandons the word of promise.

Pastoral-Liturgical Tradition

Modern life ascribes a human, ethical, and pastoral dimension to promise which continues to call people to strive for fidelity and commitment to their own words and actions. In an age where people find permanent commitments difficult to make, there is a crying need for an integrity that strengthens people to be faithful to their own promises. Jesus' simple exhortation concerning oaths still needs to be heeded: "Let your 'Yes' mean 'Yes,' and your 'No' mean 'No.' Anything more is from the evil one" (Matt 5:37).

As with the biblical teaching, however, the power of this concept is centered not on human fidelity but on God's. Any possibility of the people of God remaining faithful to the gospel of Jesus Christ is rooted firmly in God's own prior, irreversible commitment to be faithful to covenantal promises. That this faithfulness is bound to hope is made clear in Vatican II: "Advancing through trials and tribulations, the Church is strengthened by God's grace, promised to her by the Lord so that she may not waver from perfect fidelity, but remain the worthy bride of the Lord until, through the cross, she may attain to that light which knows no setting" (Constitution on the Church, no. 9).

Liturgically, the Church continues to celebrate God's fidelity through the ancient memorial of the Eucharist, which recalls God's greatest act of faithfulness in Jesus Christ. Though every Eucharist memorializes this eternal gesture of love, the celebration of the Easter Vigil, in particular, recalls the great paschal mystery we commemorate. The nine readings of the Vigil constitute a sacred history, an eternal testimony to God's continual response to people when they cried out in need. These readings rehearse the Bible's witness to God's keeping of promises through the ages, despite the frequent failures of the chosen people to keep their part of the bargain. The Church, as the new people of God and the new inheritors of the ageless promises, is continually called to remember the great deeds of God and to repent of its own periodic infidelity. As a community of hope, the Church also remembers the promise of Jesus Christ to return in glory and to establish the promised reign of his heavenly Father. The Church thus remains a people of promise, bound to one another in faith and sustaining one another in hope. The preface of the Eucharist for Christ the King Sunday, the final Sunday of the liturgical year, expresses the hope of this promised kingdom well: "a kingdom of truth and life, a kingdom of holiness and grace, a kingdom of justice, love, and peace" (*Sacramentary*, p. 475). In short, the pastoral and liturgical life of the Church continues to thrive on the promises of God. Through these promises we remember the great, salvific deeds of God through history, and, consequently, remain true to the hopes of our ancestors in faith.

See: ABRAHAM, BLESSING, COVENANT, EXODUS, FAITH, FULFILLMENT, HOPE, LAND, MESSIAH, MOSES, OATH, PEOPLE OF GOD, SPIRIT, VOWS

RONALD D. WITHERUP, S.S.

PROPHET/PROPHECY

The term prophet has rich biblical connotations in both testaments.

Old Testament

Terms and Definition. The most common word for "prophet" in the Old Testament is *nabi'*, which is found almost three hundred times in the Hebrew Bible. The meaning of *nabi'* is doubtful; the probable meaning is "one called." A prophet is also referred to as a "seer," *ro'eh* (e.g., 1 Sam 9:9, 11, 18, 19; Isa 30:10), or a "man of God," *'ish 'elohim* (1 Kgs 17:18, 24; 2 Kgs 1:9-13). The English word "prophet" comes from the Greek *prophêtês*, meaning "one who speaks for/before/in favor of."

The terms indicate the meaning. The prophet is one called by God to be a messenger to God's people. The prophet is a visionary, who sees the life of the people from God's perspective and who understands the consequences of their actions. The prophet is "God's person," who speaks to the people for God and who pleads with God in favor of the people.

Prophetic Call and Vision. The prophet is "one called." There is a stereotypical form for the narration of a call* experience which consists of all or some of the following parts:

1. Confrontation with God;
2. Introductory words, ordinarily from God;
3. Commission of the prophet by God;
4. Objection by the prophet;
5. Reassurance by God, usually the promise, "I will be with you";
6. Gift of a sign to confirm the call.

The form can be illustrated with the call of Moses in Exodus 3. First, God appears in the form of a burning bush (3:2). There is some introductory dialogue, including an acknowledgement by God that the chosen people are suffering and a statement of the divine decision to come to their aid (3:4-9). The commission follows in 3:10: "Come, now! I will send you to Pharaoh to lead my people, the Israelites, out of Egypt." Moses has several reasons to object. In 3:11 he says, "Who am I that I should go to Pharaoh and lead the Israelites out of

Egypt?" God reassures Moses with a promise of the divine presence and promises him a sign: When he brings the people out of Egypt they will return to Mount Sinai to worship God (3:12). The call of Moses is characterized by several repetitions of the final parts of the form: further objections in 3:13; 4:1, 10, 13; additional expressions of reassurance in 3:14-15; 4:11-12, 14-15; and further signs in 4:2-9.

Other examples of prophetic call narratives are found in Isaiah 6:1-13; Jeremiah 1:4-10; Ezekiel 1:1–3:15.

Prophets receive the message they are to convey in various ways. Early prophets are characterized by experiences of ecstasy and trance (1 Sam 10:5, 10-12, 20-24; 1 Kgs 18:28-29). The prophet is sometimes described as clairvoyant, knowing what has happened at a distance (1 Sam 9:16-20; 1 Kgs 14:5-13). There is frequent mention of visions. Some visions are extraordinary, like Ezekiel's vision of the living creatures around God's throne (Ezek 1:4-28). Some visions are ordinary, but the prophet sees a significance that others do not see. Amos sees a basket of ripe fruit and sees that the people are ripe for judgment (Amos 8:1-2). Jeremiah sees a bubbling cauldron turned to the north and recognizes that the threat to the people will come from the north (Jer 1:13-15). The word of God, however, is the most significant experience for the prophet. The visions are always in the service of the word.

Prophetic Words and Actions. The prophet is a messenger for God. The function of a prophet is to convey to the people God's desire for them. This task involves two kinds of persuasion: criticizing and energizing (see W. Brueggemann, *The Prophetic Imagination* [Fortress, 1978]). The prophet criticizes the people for departing from God and God's covenant. This departure is found in worship of other gods (see Hos 2:7-15) and reliance on the works of their own hands (see Mic 5:9-14; Jer 7:3-4). It is also found in their treatment of one another. The rich exploit the poor by raising prices (Amos 8:4-7), by taking their land (Isa 5:8-10; Mic 2:2-3), by condoning violence (Isa 1:15), by perverting justice (Isa 59:1-15). The prosperous do not care about the desperation of the poor (Amos 6:1-7). Such contempt for God's covenant will bring devastation upon all the people.

The prophets are also called to energize the people, to make it possible for them to imagine a different present and a different future. Active promotion of God's rule will result in a world so characterized by peace that the wolf will lie down with the lamb (Isa 11:6-9). Food will be so abundant that wine and milk will run down the hills (Amos 9:13; Joel 4:18). All nations will come to worship God (Isa 56:1-8; 66:18-23). God will fling human sin into the depth of the sea (Mic 7:19-20) and there will be a new creation (Isa 65:17-25).

Both prophetic tasks, criticizing and energizing, are directed primarily toward the prophet's own time. The prophet criticizes the institutions of the present—political, economic, religious. The prophet energizes by stirring the imagination of a different present. The prophet refers to the past actions of God and the people as support for the message. The prophet presents a vision of the future as motivation for present action. The primary focus of the prophetic message, however, is the present time.

Prophets carry out their task by preaching. There are several books in the OT that represent the written memory of their words. They also carry out this task by becoming themselves the message. They act out God's word. Isaiah walks around barefoot and naked for three years to dramatize the situation of exile that threatens the people (Isa 20:2-4; see Mic 1:8). Jeremiah smashes a pot (19:11) and buries his underwear (13:1-11) to illustrate the rupture of the relationship between God and the people. Ezekiel begins by eating the scroll, thus literally internalizing God's word (3:1-3). He lies on his side for several days (4:4-9), builds a little wall (4:1-3), packs his belongings (12:1-16), burns and scatters his hair (5:1-15), all to visualize for the people what is going to happen to them as a result of their actions.

The prophet functions within the community of God's people (see C. Stuhlmueller, *Thirsting for the Lord* [Doubleday, 1977] 35–48). Ordinarily prophets arise from the community to whom they preach. Amos may be considered an exception to this rule; he originates in the southern kingdom of Judah and is called to minister to the people of the northern kingdom, Israel. The prophet also remains within the community. Whatever consequence results for the people as a result of their actions will also be experienced by the prophet. Jeremiah warns the people of impending exile if they do not repent. He too ends his life in a foreign country because of the disaster that overtakes Judah (Jer 43:4-7).

The people discern the truth of a prophet's message in several ways. The simplest test is to wait and see whether the prophet's words come true (see Deut 18:21-22). This test, however, is not enough. In some instances the prophetic message does not come to fulfillment for centuries. In the eighth century Micah proclaimed the destruction of Jerusalem (Mic 3:12), which did not happen until 587 BCE. Some prophetic messages were reinterpreted if they did not happen exactly as stated. In Zechariah 6:9-15, the prophet seems to think that Zerubbabel will become king and restore the Davidic dynasty in postexilic Judah. Zerubbabel, however, disappears from history and the prophecy is reinterpreted to show the leadership of the priests (Joshua).

Other tests of a prophet's validity include the measuring of the message against the tradition of God's law and the people's experience of God in the past (Deut 13:2-6). Sometimes a prophet can be identified by specific clothes or a specific mark (1 Kgs 20:35-42; 2 Kgs 1:8; Zech 13:4-6). Prophets who preach a message that results in their own benefit are suspect (1 Kgs 22:6-23; Jer 28:1-17).

For a prophet to function well there are also conditions that must be present regarding the community (see R. R. Wilson, "Early Israelite Prophecy," *Interpreting the Prophets.* Ed. J. L. Mays and P. J. Achtemeier [Fortress, 1987] 6–9). First of all, there must be a community that has a certain degree of cohesion and identity. Prophets function more effectively in times of strong leadership. In the OT the prophets flourish in the time of the kings. Prophecy begins to wane when the monarchy disappears. Second, the community must believe in the possibility of prophecy. The community must be prepared to acknowledge that God might have a message for them and might convey that message through someone in their midst.

The office of prophet is institutionalized in some cases. Gad and Nathan are court prophets of David (1 Sam 22:5; 2 Sam 7:1-17; 12:1-15, 25; 24:11-19; 1 Kgs 1:8-45). Isaiah appears to have recognition at the court of Ahaz and Hezekiah (Isa 7:1-12; 37:21; 38:1-8, 21-22; 39:3-8). In other instances the prophet is marginalized. Elijah is pursued by the queen (1 Kgs 18:4, 7-14; 19:1-2). Jeremiah is threatened with execution (Jer 26:7-15; 38:6-13; see 26:20-24). Other prophets criticize both political and religious leadership (Hos 4:4–5:7; Mic 3:1-12; Mal 1:6–2:9).

Prophetic Traditions Outside of Israel. Outside of Israel there is evidence of prophetic traditions. In the Amorite city-state of Mari (eighteenth century BCE) tablets were discovered describing prophetic activity. These prophets are both men and women. They deliver messages from the gods to the king concerning political and cultic affairs. Some of the prophets were cultic personnel; some seem to have no official position. Their messages are received through dreams, visions, or in ecstatic trances.

Prophecy is also found in Canaan. The story of Elijah (1 Kings 18) describes the prophets of Baal who gash themselves in order to fall into an ecstatic trance. The story of Balaam (Numbers 22–24) gives evidence of a tradition of ecstatic prophecy in Moab.

Prophetic Traditions in Israel Before the Ninth Century. Within Israel itself there is mention of prophets before the great prophetic legends of Elijah-Elisha. In the

Elohist version of the wife-sister story (Gen 20:1-18), Abraham is named a prophet who will intercede for the king (20:7; see Ps 105:15). Moses is identified as the model prophet in Deuteronomy 18:15-19 (see Deut 34:10-12). The story of his call in Exodus 3 is in the traditional form of the call of a prophet. In contrast to other prophets who receive the revelation through dreams and visions, the Lord speaks to Moses face to face (Num 12:6-8).

When Moses' responsibilities become too burdensome, God sends a share of the Spirit upon the seventy-two elders and they begin to prophesy (Num 11:16-17, 24-30). In response to Joshua's jealousy concerning the two who received God's spirit without going to the tent Moses says, "Would that all the people of the LORD were prophets!" (11:29).

Miriam is named a prophet in Exodus. She functions as a messenger for God in leading the victory dance after the crossing of the sea (Exod 15:20). Later she challenges Moses' exclusive exercise of the role of prophet: "Is it through Moses alone that the LORD speaks?" (Num 12:2). Her identification as a prophet may conceal other leadership roles such as priest.

During the period of the judges (1200–1020 BCE) Deborah is called both prophet and judge. She sat regularly under a palm tree settling disputes and pronouncing judgment for the people (Judg 4:4-5). It is the word of God coming through her that instigates the battle in which the army of Hazor is defeated (Judg 4:6–5:31). Samuel is also identified as both prophet and judge. After his experience of the Lord in the shrine at Shiloh (1 Sam 3:7-18), Samuel is acknowledged as "an accredited prophet of the LORD" (3:20). "The LORD was with him, not permitting any word of his to be without effect" (3:19). Samuel is also named a "seer" in his encounter with Saul (1 Sam 9:9-11).

When Saul is anointed king, one of the signs given him by Samuel that his anointing is legitimate is that he will "meet a band of prophets in a prophetic state" and that "the spirit of the LORD will rush upon [Saul] and [he] will join them in their prophetic state and will be changed into another man" (1 Sam 10:5-6; see 10:10-13; 19:18-24).

There are two prophets who seem to have an official position in the court of King David: Nathan and Gad. Gad's relationship with David begins already when David is being pursued by Saul (1 Sam 22:5). Gad advises David where to flee. Gad also brings God's judgment to David after the census and advises him concerning the purchase of the threshing floor which later becomes the site of the temple (2 Sam 24:10-25). Nathan appears after David is settled in his kingdom. Nathan brings the oracle to David informing him that he is not to build a house (temple) for God but rather that God will build a house (dynasty) for him (2 Sam 7:1-17). Upon this prophetic word all the hopes of the Davidic messiah rest. Nathan also challenges David after his sin with Bathsheba and brings an oracle of judgment on his house (2 Sam 12:1-12). Nathan, along with Bathsheba, arranges that David name Solomon as his successor and Nathan witnesses the anointing of Solomon (1 Kgs 1:11-40).

Prophets continue to influence the political life of the country. During the reign of Solomon the prophet Ahijah announces to Jeroboam that the kingdom will be divided and Jeroboam will rule over ten of the twelve tribes (1 Kgs 11:29-39). Ahijah also prophesies the death of Jeroboam's son (1 Kgs 14:1-18). The prophet Jehu predicts the fall of Baasha's dynasty (1 Kgs 16:1-13).

Ninth-Century Prophets. Two prophets dominate the ninth century: Elijah and Elisha. Their stories form a cycle of prophetic legends (1 Kgs 17:1–2 Kgs 13). Elijah and Elisha are leaders of a guild of prophets. The stories about them are full of miracles such as multiplying food (1 Kgs 17:12-16; 2 Kgs 4:2-7, 42-44), purifying inedible food (1 Kgs 2:19-22; 4:38-41), curing diseases (5:1-27), and raising people from the dead (1 Kgs 17:17-24; 2 Kgs 4:18-37). Elijah protests against false worship (1 Kgs 18:18-40) and against unjust kings (1 Kgs 21:17-29). Like Moses, he receives a revelation at Mount Sinai/Horeb (1 Kgs 19:8-18). Elisha, who is commissioned to follow Elijah, has a major effect on the politics of his time. He is instrumental in the change of power in Syria (2 Kgs 8:7-15) and in the anointing of Jehu king of Israel (2 Kgs 9:1-15). Jehu takes power with a bloodbath that destroys most of the royal families in both Israel and Judah (2 Kgs 9:16–10:17).

Micaiah ben Imlah is another prophet of the same period. When the king of Israel is planning a campaign against Syria, several prophets bring oracles of good news (1 Kgs 22:1-12). The king, however, does not trust them. He calls Micaiah, who, after some persuading, prophesies that the king will be killed and the people scattered (22:13-28). He is thrown into prison until the king shall return. The king, however, is killed as the prophet predicted.

One other prophet mentioned in the Books of Kings deserves mention. During the reign of Josiah (640–609 BCE) a book of the law is found in the Temple. The priests bring the book to the king who instructs them to send it to a prophet concerning its authenticity (2 Kgs 22:8-13). They take the book to the prophet Huldah, who declares that all the words of the book will indeed happen (22:14-20). The book is the major section of Deuteronomy.

Classical Prophets. Beginning in the eighth century the primary prophetic witness is represented in books of the prophets' preaching. Three of these books are named the major prophets because of the length of the book: Isaiah, Jeremiah, and Ezekiel. The other prophetic works, called the minor prophets, are contained on a single scroll called the Book of the Twelve: Amos, Hosea, Micah, Zephaniah, Nahum, Habakkuk, Haggai, Zechariah, Joel, Jonah, Obadiah, and Malachi. The oracles in the Book of the Twelve range from the eighth century until the fifth or fourth century BCE.

Two works are commonly classified with the prophets although, strictly speaking, they belong in a different category. The Book of Daniel, found among the prophets in Christian Bibles but with the writings in the Hebrew Bible, is an apocalyptic work. The Book of Jonah, found in the scroll of the Twelve, is a short story that illustrates the point of God's universal forgiveness by using the tale of a reluctant prophet.

See: APOCALYPTIC, CALL/VOCATION, DREAMS, ELIJAH/ELISHA, MOSES, ORACLE, VISIONS, WORD

IRENE NOWELL, O.S.B.

New Testament

Prophecy in Judaism at the Dawn of Christianity. Genuine prophecy (*prophēteia*) was lacking in Israel in late OT times, as several scriptural passages and some pseudepigraphical works testify. Not long after the fall of Jerusalem (587 BCE), Psalm 74:9 lamented, "there is no prophet now." And in the second century before Jesus, there was again no true prophet to tell Judas Maccabeus and his followers what to do with the defiled altar of holocausts (1 Macc 4:46) or to guide the people in choosing a leader (1 Macc 14:41). For at least one current of Jewish thought at that time, prophecy had simply ceased (1 Macc 9:27). This cessation helped spawn pseudonymous literature issued in the name of a prophet, such as the *Apocryphon of Ezekiel*, and books about the prophets, such as the *Martyrdom and Ascension of Isaiah* and *The Lives of the Prophets*.

But prophecy was expected to return. Joel 3:1-2 foretold an outpouring of God's spirit that would result in widespread prophesying. And in Malachi 3:1, God promised a messenger who would prepare the way for God's intervention. A later hand adding to Malachi's prophecy identified this messenger as Elijah returning to life (Mal 3:23-24; see 2 Kgs 2:1-18). Expectation of prophecy's resumption can be found also in *Testament of the Twelve Patriarchs*, written in the second century before Jesus (*T. Levi* 8:15; *T. Benj.* 9:2).

Writing in the first Christian century, the Jewish historian Flavius Josephus ascribed the gift of prophecy to the Hasmonean Jewish ruler John Hyrcanus (134–104 BCE) (*J. W.* 1:68) and said also that two messianic pretenders closer to his own day—Theudas (ca. 44 CE) (*Ant.* 20:97; see Acts 5:36) and "the Egyptian" (ca. 58 CE) (*Ant.* 20:169; *J. W.* 2:261; see Acts 21:38)—had declared themselves to be prophets.

New Prophets Appear. With John the Baptist,* who personally declined the title of prophet (*prophētēs*) when asked if he were a prophet, and described himself merely as a voice crying out in the wilderness (John 1:9-23), prophecy returned to Israel. Although he would not declare himself a prophet, John nevertheless functioned as one. He set forth the will of God for the people by preaching a baptism of repentance for the forgiveness of sins (Mark 1:4). And he spoke of what God was about to do. John was held in high regard as a prophet by his contemporaries (Mark 12:32) and was revered as a martyred prophet after his death. Jesus identified John as the Elijah whose return was expected (Matt 17:9-13), no doubt basing this identification on the similarity of John's work to that predicted for the returned Elijah. Acting as his prophetic predecessor was expected to act, John worked to prepare a reformed people, a community worthy of participating in the blessings of the new age that was soon to appear. Through reception of the baptism of repentance administered by John, a reformed Israelite signified an interior disposition of sorrow for sin. Mark's Gospel adds to this picture of John as Elijah when it describes John in the hairy garment of a prophet like Elijah (Mark 1:6; 2 Kgs 1:7-8). And Luke 1:17 makes this Christian identification of the Baptist with Elijah crystal clear.

Jesus, too, functioned as a prophet, although he was much more than a prophet. He announced in the synagogue at Nazareth that he had received the prophetic task of proclaiming to the lowly God's salvific activity (Luke 4:16-22). Yet his townspeople did not accept and honor their local prophet, but took offense at him and rejected him (Mark 6:1-4; Luke 4:24).

While lack of acceptance limited Jesus' miraculous activity in his own home town, elsewhere Jesus was gladly acclaimed as a prophet for his mighty deeds, as when he brought the widow's son back to life at Nain (Luke 7:11-17) or opened the eyes of the man born blind (John 9:17). Other aspects of Jesus' ministry also showed him to be God's spokesman. The Pharisee Simon's expectation that a prophet would know the secrets of the mind were more than met when Jesus knew the heart of the penitent woman who anointed his feet and read Simon's heart as well (Luke 7:36-50). A similar discernment of spirit evoked the Samaritan woman's, "Sir, I can see that you are a prophet" (John 4:16-19).

In time, "Jesus the prophet from Nazareth in Galilee" (Matt 21:11) grew so popular that John the Baptist sent to him to inquire whether Jesus was "the one who is to come" or not (Matt 11:3). A number of scholars say John was puzzled, because he thought of Jesus as the awaited Elijah (Mal 3:1, 23-24), and when Jesus did not act as John had expected Elijah to act—with fiery and judgmental decisiveness—John needed assurance. In his reply to John, Jesus referred to another prophetic book, describing himself as restoring sight to the blind, curing the lame, cleansing lepers, healing the deaf, raising the dead, and evangelizing the poor (see Isa 26:19; 29:18-19; 35:5-6; 61:1).

Before long, Jesus' enemies feared to arrest him openly, because the crowds "regarded him as a prophet" (Matt 21:46). Nevertheless, they plotted his death. In Luke's Gospel, Jesus moves inexorably toward the Holy City, "for it is impossible that a prophet should die outside of Jerusalem" (Luke 13:33). After his death (and resurrection), the disciples on the road to Emmaus are heard mourning Jesus as "a prophet mighty in deed and word before God and all the people" (Luke 24:19).

Prophecy in the Early Church. After Jesus' ascension to his Father, Peter proclaimed the fulfillment of Joel's prophecy in the outpouring of God's prophetic Spirit upon Jesus' disciples at Pentecost (Acts 2:14-21). And the prophetic charism continued to flourish in the early Church along with other charisms, as Paul's correspondence with the Christians at Corinth makes abundantly clear. Indiscriminate use of the charisms while Christians met for worship, however, could lead to confusion and disorderly conduct in the liturgical assembly. To forestall and correct such abuses in the Christian assembly at Corinth, Paul established regulations for the exercise of the prophetic and other charisms (1 Cor 14:29-33). But he insisted on the excellence of the prophetic charism, "Pursue love, but strive eagerly for the spiritual gifts, above all that you may prophesy" (1 Cor 14:1). For "whoever prophesies builds up the church" (1 Cor 14:4).

At some point, the prophetic charism was institutionalized in the early Church. Paul, when listing charisms found among the Corinthians, begins his enumeration with three offices held by charismatics, "Some people God has designated in the church to be, first, apostles; second, prophets; third, teachers. . . . Are all apostles? Are all prophets? Are all teachers?" (1 Cor 12:28-29). The full extent and function of the prophetic office in the early Church is not known, but prophets obviously proclaimed the will of God for the Christian community and its members.

Various figures in the early Church exercised this office of prophet, being gifted with the charism of prophecy. Agabus, a prophet from the Christian community at Jerusalem, foretold a famine, which occurred in the reign of the Roman emperor Claudius (41–54 CE) (Acts 11:27-29). Fulfillment of this prediction can be seen in Josephus, who speaks of a great famine in Judea in 46–48 CE (*Ant.* 20:101). Agabus also predicted Paul's captivity and suffering in Jerusalem, dramatizing his prophecy by symbolically binding his own hands and feet with Paul's belt (Acts 21:7-14). The prophets of the Church at Antioch passed on the holy Spirit's commissioning of Barnabas and Saul for mission (Acts 13:1-3).

Later, Judas and Silas, prophets sent from Jerusalem, exhorted and strengthened the Christians at Antioch (Acts 15:22-33). At Caesarea Maritima, the deacon Philip had four daughters "gifted with prophecy" (Acts 21:8-9).

The early Church had its share of false apostles (2 Cor 11:13), false teachers (2 Tim 4:3), and false prophets (Matt 7:15; 2 Pet 2:1; 1 John 4:1). Among these false prophets, a certain "Jezebel" was misleading the Church at Thyatira (Rev 2:20-23). To avoid being deceived by false prophets, the faithful are to "test the spirits to see whether they belong to God, because many false prophets have gone out into the world" (1 John 4:1).

The Use of OT Prophets in the NT. Besides making many allusions to prophetic writings of the OT, the NT writers often explicitly cite particular prophets to show "fulfillment" of specific passages in the life and works of Jesus. Matthew, to give only one example, has several fulfillment citations in his early chapters. These generally have a formula similar to that in Matthew 1:22, "All this took place to fulfill what the Lord had said through the prophet." Fulfillment citations occur in Matt 1:23; 2:5-6, 15, 17-18; 3:3; etc. The general purpose of such citations is to show that in Jesus the hopes and expectations of the OT community were realized.

See: APOSTLE, ASCENSION, CHARISM, CORINTH, DEACON, ELIJAH/ELISHA, FULFILLMENT, GIFTS, JOHN THE BAPTIST, PENTECOST, PROMISE, SPIRIT, TEACH/TEACHING, WILL OF GOD

NEIL J. MCELENEY, C.S.P.

PROSELYTES

The English term proselyte is a transliteration of the Greek *proselytos,* a word found often in the Septuagint. *Proselytos* was the Septuagint's usual rendering for the Hebrew term *gēr,* which denoted a foreign stranger or sojourner who through some unfortunate circumstances had taken refuge with the Israelites. In the Hellenistic and Roman periods, however, both the terms *gēr* and *proselytos* underwent an evolution. Due to the missionary spirit that developed in Judaism in the postexilic era, the meaning of the words moved from signifying a resident alien to describing a non-Jew who had converted from paganism to Judaism. It is in the latter sense that *proselytos* is found in the NT. Apart from these biblical sources and other Jewish and Christian documents, the term is not found elsewhere in ancient writings.

Old Testament

In the OT the *gēr,* as a foreigner settled among the Israelites, was differentiated from the *nākrî,* the alien who was only temporarily in the land. While the *gēr* was usually attached as a client to the head of a house, tribe, or locality, a person in this position was not enslaved. And, although not allowed to own land, the *gēr* nevertheless stood under the jurisdiction of Israel and was therefore obliged to observe the Sabbath. Such immigrants normally became adherents of the patron's beliefs, i.e. worshipers of Yahweh.

According to Exodus 22:20 the Israelites were forbidden to "molest or oppress an alien" since they had once been aliens themselves in the land of Egypt. Exodus 12:48 stipulated that males among the *gērîm* who wished to observe the Passover "must first be circumcised, and then they may join in its observance just like the natives." In this example it is evident how *gēr* eventually came to mean a convert to Judaism.

The Septuagint translated the Hebrew *gēr* some seventy-eight times as *proselytos*. Since that Greek term is not found in classical writers, it has been concluded that the Septuagint translators borrowed it from colloquial speech. Generally *proselytos* bears the same meanings throughout the Septuagint as *gēr* does in the Hebrew Bible, i.e., in many instances it denotes an immigrant, while in other texts that immigrant is evidently a convert.

The development of meaning that *gēr* and *proselytos* underwent occurred in the postexilic, particularly the Intertestamental, period due to the missionary movement which developed especially in the Hellenistic Jewish Diaspora. Via the Dispersion, vast numbers of Gentiles were exposed to the God of Israel. Of particular attraction for the Gentiles were the Jews' monotheism and their high ethical ideals. Jewish proselytism in the Intertestamental period achieved some success, although the requirement of circumcision deterred many males from full conversion if they were unwilling to undergo a painful operation. Those pagans who nevertheless did join themselves with the Jews by circumcision were called in Hebrew *gērîm* or in Greek *proselytoi*.

According to Rabbinic texts, conversion followed upon circumcision (in the case of males) and immersion in some instances. Thereafter the convert was considered a Jew and seen as equivalent to a newborn; his or her former pagan life, including relationships and marriage (if the partner had not converted) counted as nothing. Only children born after a male proselyte's conversion could be his heirs. And, since female proselytes were suspected of having been promiscuous in their Gentile lives, a female proselyte could not marry a Jewish priest.

For each pagan who became a full convert, however, there were many more who, apart from agreeing to circumcision, held to the theological and ethical beliefs of Judaism, attended the synagogue, and observed various Jewish laws and ceremonies. While Jews themselves discussed the absolute necessity of circumcision for their converts, with some holding it could be waived, a majority held firm to the requirement. Thus, these partial adherents remained technically pagan, although they were a closely allied group. In Hellenistic Judaism such quasi-converts were called *sebomenoi*, "God worshipers," or *phoboumenoi ton theon*, "God fearers."

New Testament

Reference to proselytes is made directly only four times in the NT (Matt 23:15; Acts 2:11; 6:5; 13:43; rendered as "convert(s)" by the NAB). They are first mentioned in Matthew 23:15 where Jesus, in denouncing the scribes and Pharisees as hypocrites, charges, "You traverse sea and land to make one convert, and when that happens you make him a child of Gehenna twice as much as yourselves." This passage reflects that, while many proselytes were converted by their Hellenistic Jewish neighbors, others came to Judaism through the missionary efforts of Palestinian Jews. That the Gentile converts were twice as worthy of punishment as their mentors could be an observation that the zeal of converts was even more noteworthy than that of those who preached to them. It is possible that as Christianity launched its own proselytizing efforts beyond Judea, various of its missionaries had previously been emissaries for Judaism.

The other NT references to proselytes are each found in Acts. In 2:11 the phrase "both Jews and converts to Judaism" qualifies the relation to Judaism of all the peoples from the Dispersion listed as present in the crowd at Pentecost. In 6:5 an individual, Nicholas of Antioch, one of the seven, is identified as "a convert to Judaism." And, in 13:43, with respect to the preaching of Paul and Barnabas in Pisidian Antioch, the narrative observes that "after the congregation had dispersed, many Jews and worshipers who were converts [polloi tōn Ioudaiōn kai tōn sebomenōn proselytōn] followed Paul and Barnabas."

The latter example in particular occasions discussion because of the qualification of proselytes as sebomenoi, a linkage of terms not found elsewhere. In light of the distinctions noted above, the combination does not seem to make sense. Many suspect that proselytōn in 13:43 must be an ancient gloss in the text or a slip on the part of Luke and that the group indicated as accompanying the Jews are in fact partial proselytes, i.e., those who frequented the synagogues yet had not accepted the whole of the Law.

The latter group, referred to now in most discussions as the God-fearers, are themselves elsewhere mentioned in the NT, most notably in Acts. Included within this general designation are all those Gentiles who, with varying degrees of commitment to Judaism, were attracted to the synagogues but were unwilling to become full proselytes. One such individual was Cornelius, identified in Acts 10:2, 22 as a phoboumenos ton theon, literally a "fearer of God." While such persons felt themselves attached to the synagogue to some degree, it is clear from 11:2-3 where Peter is criticized for having eaten with Cornelius, that Jews felt compelled to retain a degree of separation between themselves and their partial converts.

Another person categorized by Acts similarly with Cornelius is Lydia, described in 16:14 as a sebomenē ton theon, literally a "worshiper of God." While one might assume that Cornelius had not become a proselyte because of the requirement of circumcision, with female God-fearers it is more difficult to assess the degree of their immersion in Judaism.

In recent discussions the very existence of God-fearers has come under close scrutiny. Some have proposed that the presence of such people in the synagogues as described in Acts was actually a Lucan invention, introduced for the purpose of showing how Christianity was legitimately extended to the Gentiles without losing its Jewish roots. Such scholars point out that the Rabbinic sources noted above, which also mention the God-fearers, actually postdate the NT (although the oral tradition upon which they are based may not). But, a consensus has rather clearly emerged which ascertains the existence of the God-fearers not only on the basis of a breadth of literary references or allusions but also on the evidence of a recently published insiption.

Pastoral-Liturgical Tradition

While the term "proselyte" has come to refer to a full convert to any religion, since the biblical usage exclusively denotes converts to Judaism, the pastoral-liturgical remarks here will be confined to the latter centuries of Jewish proselytizing in the post-NT era, particularly as that proselytizing related to the spread of Christianity.

On the part of the Jews, opposition to proselytizing was probably caused by heightened anti-foreign feelings arising during both rebellions against Rome as well as the destruction of Jerusalem and the rise of Christianity. To be noted especially is that after the second revolt, during which many proselytes became traitors to the Jewish cause, Judaism's fervor for making conversions turned to fear and hostility toward such people.

On the part of the Romans, both conflicts resulted in a period of disfavor toward the Jews and Judaism. The emperor Hadrian is known to have outlawed circumcision, as a type of castration, and possibly even proselytism altogether. Under Antoninus pius Jews could circumcise Jewish children again, but circumcising Gentile converts remained illegal and dangerous.

In the meantime, Christianity's missionary activities met with great success, no doubt to a great extent since it had set aside any insistence on circumcision or observance of the Jewish Law. Christianity, in proclaiming a universal faith, with no requirement for initiation other than baptism, appears to have been especially attractive to the ranks of the God-fearers. Alienated from their Gentile past, yet not fully Jews and not completely accepted by the Jews, they found it dangerous both surgically and at times politically to become Jewish converts. Such people welcomed the new faith.

In sum, conflict with Rome and competition with Christianity severely undermined Jewish proselytism, although the impulse to convert was not lost entirely. To a great extent that impulse also survived in being handed on to Christianity, which in turn preached to the Gentiles its parent tradition's rejection of polytheism and idolatry.

See: CIRCUMCISION, COVERSION, DIASPORA/DISPERSION, ISRAELITE, JUDAISM, LAND, LAW, NATIONS, PHARISEE, SABBATH, STRANGER, SYNAGOGUE

FLORENCE MORGAN GILLMAN

PROSTITUTION

In the ancient Near East the practice of prostitution was common, and in pagan cultures it apparently received little or no censure. In Mesopotamia and Canaan a unique expression of the practice was ritual prostitution, which supposedly brought those who engaged in it into communion with the divine principle of fertility. Israel's association with those cultures brought her into confrontation with prostitution and it was known to exist within the nation. Even so, Israel's response was one of moral condemnation of the practice. The notion of prostitution or harlotry was also used as a metaphor for unfaithfulness to Yahweh. The relationship between the Lord and his people was sometimes referred to under the image of marriage, and thus involvement with any other gods was described as harlotry. In NT times the mentality of the Hellenistic-Roman world impacted on the Christian way of life and necessitated a strong countercultural stand against any form of licentiousness.

Old Testament

The story of Judah and Tamar attests to the presence of prostitution in Israel (Genesis 38). A harlot was readily approached and fees were paid for her services. Whereas Judah was censured for his role, Tamar was acknowledged as more right than he was because of the institution of levirate marriage. Another early example was the revenge of the brothers of Dinah for her rape by Shechem (Genesis 34). The extreme extent of their retaliation reflected the strength of their conviction that Dinah should not have been treated like a harlot.

The Holiness Code of Leviticus 17–26 emphasizes the holiness required of Israel as God's chosen people. All aspects of life came under consideration, and improper sexual expression was censured (Lev 19:20-22). Further, it was not permitted to give a daughter into prostitution, for that would bring corruption and lewdness into the land (Lev 19:29). With regard to priestly marriages, a woman who had been a prostitute or a divorcee was an unfit spouse, and even a widow was not acceptable lest the priest bring forth base offspring (Lev 21:7, 14). Bastards and their descendants were not allowed membership in the assembly of the Lord (Deut 23:3). This provision was harsh retaliation on children for the offenses of parents. The very harshness of the punishment emphasizes the severity with which sexual aberration was judged, at least officially.

On entering Canaan Joshua's spies lodged in Rahab's house (Josh 2:1), and it was this harlot who assisted the Israelite spies and provided for their safety. Thus her family was saved in the siege of Jericho (Josh 6:17). Among the judges of Israel were Jephthah, the son of a harlot (Judg 11:1), and Samson who visited one in Gaza (Judg 16:1). Jephthah was driven out of his home by the legitimate sons of his father, and the men of Gaza proposed to kill Samson. King Solomon was called upon to judge between two harlots regarding maternal possession of an infant (1 Kgs 3:16-28). Solomon himself had an enormous number of wives and concubines who turned his heart away from the Lord (1 Kgs 11:3).

Among other evils that the land of Judah was charged with were idolatry and cult prostitution (1 Kgs 14:22-24). It was incumbent upon the kings to foster pure Yahwism, and some of them attempted to remove idols and banish temple prostitutes (1 Kgs 15:12; 22:47). Josiah's reform measures included destroying the apartments of cult prostitutes where garments were woven for the Asherah (2 Kgs 23:7). No sons or daughters of Israel were to engage in cult prostitution.

The prophets of Israel mentioned prostitution or harlotry among evils punishable by God, or they spoke of it symbolically as perversion of the covenant relationship between the Lord and his people. Amos (2:7) condemned it as social sin and Hosea (4:12-14) included it among the crimes of Israel that distorted religious observance. In Hosea's marriage (Hosea 1–3) the unfaithful wife was a paradigm for Israel's infidelity, punishment, purification, and restoration. Isaiah followed the symbolic approach in referring to the faithless city as adulteress (Isa 1:21). In the postexilic section of Isaiah the people are referred to as an adulterous race (Isa 57:3) because of idolatry and general lack of covenant morality. Jeremiah strongly reproached the people for turning away from the Lord, running after many lovers, and showing no sense of shame (Jer 3:1-8). Their blatant insolence in the face of their sin (Jer 5:7-8) was at once a departure from true morality and an expression of infidelity to Yahweh. The Book of Baruch portrays Jeremiah warning the exiles not to fall into the Babylonian practice of idolatry, and ridiculing their priests who took wealth from gods to pay harlots (Bar 6:10). Ezekiel proclaimed long oracles about abominations of the faithless spouse and crass violations of covenant morality. Two oracles, Ezekiel 16 and 23, condemn liturgical perversion and the sinfulness of Samaria and Jerusalem. They contain images of dire distress, terror, and plunder as punishment for lewdness and adultery. He hoped they would begin to take seriously the word of God calling them to fidelity through an upright way of life. Perhaps the experience of exile would reinforce the warning.

In the Wisdom literature of the OT sages revealed their developing reflection on this subject. Proverbs warned against the destructiveness of adultery (Prov 5:3) and entrapment of one man with another man's wife (Prov 6:26). A realistic picture was painted of the harlot's wiles and the stupidity of one who succumbed to them (Prov 7:7-27). In the end such activity led to the squandering of one's wealth (Prov 29:3). Ben Sira gave similar advice concerning women and cautioned against their snares (Sir 9:1-9). Wine and women make the mind giddy and harlotry brings on recklessness. A whoring husband and an unfaithful wife sin against their own flesh and do not go unseen by the all-knowing God (Sir 23:16-27). Wisdom's emphasis on a right way of life opens the way for discussion of the NT teaching about sexual morality.

New Testament

From references in the NT we know that prostitution was present in the time of Jesus (Matt 21:31). While Judaism had held a strict censure against it, Hellenistic influence in the area presented a challenge to that position. In the Graeco-Roman mentality sexual involvement was considered a natural part of life, and prostitutes were thought to provide a needed and respected service for which fees were paid. This position was totally rejected in NT teaching, which did not allow for any extramarital or unnatural sexual relations. This stance follows in the line of OT instruction and goes beyond legalism to a deeper formation of the attitudes and dispositions of the heart.

The Gospel Message. In the teaching of Jesus a new attitude toward women raised them to equal dignity with men. The fact that they were no longer considered possessions of men casts new light on their involvement with men in all areas. In the discourse of Matthew 5 the sixth commandment is repeated. For Jesus' hearers the legal implications of Judaism would have come to mind, but Jesus' teaching does not stop there. Not only the act of illicit sexual relations is forbidden, but even the lust of mind and heart is disallowed (Matt 5:27-28). Implicitly respect for women is demanded. However, even though a demanding standard of integrity is presented, the condemnation of sinfulness does not call for punishment by death, transference of guilt to children, or expulsion from the community. From Luke's story of the repentant sinner (Luke 7:36-50) we see that forgiveness of sins was possible and faith in Jesus allowed for membership in the community of salvation. The demand for total integrity in morality was preached in the context of a human situation in which upright people struggled to rise above aspects of their culture that were inconsistent with the Christian way of life.

The Christian Missionary Movement. Preaching missions out of Jerusalem and into the Graeco-Roman world found new difficulties in the establishment of the Christian way of life in those parts of the world. As differences of opinion arose, even among preachers, the contours of the Christian commitment had to be clearly explained. In contrast to some Gentile practices, abstinence from illicit sexual union was considered essential for Christians (Acts 15:20). From early in his ministry Paul had made that clear (1 Thess 4:3). The apostle also made a strong case against idolatry, which he believed was at the root of an irreligious and perverse spirit and delivered people to disgraceful degradation and every kind of wickedness (Rom 1:18-32). The Letter to the Colossians refers to sexual sins and idolatry as formerly their very way of life, but now they are called to be formed anew in the image of the creator (Col 3:5-11). This amounted to complete transformation of their whole outlook on life. Again, in Ephesians Paul identified fornication and sexual sins with idolatry, and all lewdness and promiscuity in word and deed was ruled out of the Christian lifestyle (Eph 5:3-6). The vices of an earthly way of life include the lusts of the flesh, whereas one who lives by the spirit crucifies those desires and passions and takes on the virtues of the Christian life (Gal 5:16-26). Not surprisingly Paul worried over the expression of Corinthian faith in a culture notedly pagan. He feared that they would revert to the sensuality of their former way of life (2 Cor 12:21) and be excluded from the community of believers in this world and ultimately lose the kingdom of God (1 Cor 6:9-10). The motive he offered for fidelity to Christian moral standards was that our bodies are members of Christ, and temples of the holy Spirit. Thus they are joined with the Lord, and giving themselves to fornication would prostitute that relationship. The Christian commitment calls for a total dedication involving the whole person. Thus to live in union with him is to glorify God in our bodies (1 Cor 6:15-20).

The Book of Revelation. While the thrust of this book is eschatological, the book speaks of the struggle of Christ and his followers against Satan. In the letter to Pergamum the Nicolaitans were accused of leading the congregation astray into idolatry and fornication (Rev 2:14-15). To Thyatira is addressed the charge of allowing a self-styled prophetess to seduce them into lewdness and idolatry (Rev 2:20). Chapters 17–19 offer a description of the city of Rome, the counterpart of Babylon, under the image of a harlot as symbolic of its absolute degeneracy. She offered her lewd deeds from a golden cup, and on her headband wore the title, "mother of harlots" (Rev 17:5). Traitors to the faith who followed her wicked ways would come to the second death, there to receive final punishment. They would not enter the new Jerusalem, for only the Lamb is worshiped there and only the faithful community would inherit his gifts (Rev 21:7).

Pastoral-Liturgical Tradition

Current thinking in the area of sexual expression attempts to integrate psychology with theology and understand human behavior in terms of developmental maturation of the person. This can throw light on the degree of guilt or innocence in the subjective orientation to morality. It also helps us think in terms of the whole person in growth toward an adult expression of faith and integration into the Christian way of life. However, this approach is susceptible to cultural influences, and it is vulnerable to the same kind of social pressures that religious people have confronted in various cultures throughout history. In many ways contemporary culture does not support a quest for abstinence from much of anything, and certainly takes sexual promiscuity lightly. The biblical identification of illicit sexual involvement with idolatry is seldom mentioned. The call for a faith commitment to the Lord or to the message of Jesus in this life, and an orientation toward a heavenly kingdom in the next, can present a motive toward refinement of sexual ethics and integrity in daily living. It is necessary to find a proper ground between extremes of puritanism and libertinism and establish stability in life direction. Our biblical heritage can offer this direction and motivation in support of convictions about upright behavior.

See: COVENANT, FERTILITY, HOLY/HOLINESS, IDOLATRY, MARRIAGE, SEXUALITY, WIDOW

BETTY JANE LILLIE, S.C.

PROVERBS

Composition and Origins

The Book of Proverbs is not a simple, unified work. It consists of collections, as the several titles within the work clearly suggest (cf. 1:1; 10:1; 24:23; 25:1; 30:1; 31:1). This suggests that it has had a long history of composition and it is likely that the older material (preexilic) is the two line sayings that dominate chapters 10–31, while the wisdom poems found in chapters 1–9 are postexilic. In any case, the title of "Proverbs of Solomon" (1:1; 10:1; 25:1) is to be understood merely in the sense of the attribution of the Wisdom books (see Wisdom) to this famous king (see 1 Kgs 5:9-14; NRSV 4:29-34).

The origins of these aphorisms have been sought in an alleged Jerusalem (court) school, for which we have no hard evidence, and also in the family and tribe, where parents and elders would have passed on the fruits of their experience. Whatever be the origins, the whole material has been assembled in one work that is introduced by the strong moral emphasis evident in 1:1-6. These verses state the purpose of the book, and they are followed by the astonishing claim in 1:7 that the beginning of knowledge or wisdom is "fear of the Lord." The wisdom of the OT is not theoretical but practical: how to cope with life, and in virtue of 1:7 it has an obvious religious thrust.

The Message

Chapters 1–9 consist of long consecutive poems that are heavy in moralizing content: doing good and avoiding evil. One of the most striking characteristics of this section is the personification of wisdom as a woman, with the trappings of an OT prophet (chs. 1; 8; 9). Particularly important is her description of her origins from Almighty God before the creation of the world. This is asserted repeatedly in 8:22-31. She even seems to have some role in creation (if the problematic 'amon in 8:30 is translated as craftsman; see Wis 7:22). In any case, Lady Wisdom is a singular literary personification in the Bible. She is open to the world, finding "delight in human children" (8:31) and making the astounding promise that the one "who finds me finds life" (8:35).

Life, which is the "kerygma" of the book (see 8:35), is the good life, as it is in most of the OT, which knew of no blessed immortality with God after death until just before the Christian era (see 1 Maccabees 12; Wis 1:15). The good life is prosperity and well-being, a large family that continues a kind of "immortality" in the transmission of the memory of the ancestors. In this respect it forms an invaluable ballast to the thoughts and desires of the average Christian that are often so eschatologically oriented (i.e., life beyond death to the neglect of the importance of a relationship with God in *this* life). The OT view is that the only life one knows is life in the here and now, and beyond that lies a bleak existence, if it can even be called that, in Sheol where one is no longer in loving contact with God (e.g., Pss 6:6; 30:10). Therefore life with God must be lived in the present, in loving loyalty to the Lord of the covenant. The Book of Proverbs provides practical counsels toward that end.

In harmony with the rest of Wisdom literature, there is no explicit reference in Proverbs to the Exodus or Sinai events, covenant, and Torah. Nonetheless the spirit of the moral teaching of the work is in harmony with the ethos of Israel. Proverbs is definitely not a book of moral theology, of do's and don'ts. Rather, it is primer of moral formation; the wisdom ideal is the person who is master of all human appetites, from tongue to sex, who is diligent and also concerned for neighbor, who is responsible and in control of life's situations.

The teaching is expressed subtly—in terms of the "saying" of two lines that are parallel, and often paradoxical and challenging. The object of the sayings is to provoke thought, not merely to exhaust it with a moral dictum. Sometimes the sayings are experiential, telling it "the way it is"; at other times, they are laden with moral values. It is often a challenge to the reader to figure out the exact meaning of what seems at first to be a simple "proverb" (e.g., 18:21). The sages of Israel have often been scored as being conservative and simplistic (a mentality clearly evidenced in Psalm 37). However, such sayings as Proverbs 16:2, 9; 21:31 show that they were aware of their limitations, or better, aware of the mysterious ways of God. They believed that the justice of God had to be made manifest somehow, but at the same time they had to live with the mystery of God's dealings (e.g., Prov 3:11-12).

The sayings of Proverbs have been found to be an echo of the older wisdom of the ancient Near East, where "wisdom literature" was also cultivated, especially in Egypt. The most striking resemblance has been found between Proverbs 22:17–23:11 and the teaching of the Egyptian sage, Amenemope (whose name is restored by a bold emendation in the NAB version of Prov 22:19). There can be little doubt that the author of these sayings in Proverbs was very much influenced by the work of the Egyptian, but at the same time, the author operated without slavish dependence. The international character of wisdom is also manifested in the words of Agur (30:1) and of Lemuel (31:1) who seem to be from Massa.

Pastoral-Liturgical Tradition

The liturgical use of the book centers mainly on 8:22-31, as an anticipation of the mystery of Christ. This passage played an important role in the Arian controversy of the early Church. The figure of the valiant women 31:10-31 is also used. By and large, Proverbs is not used much in the lectionary, although it is very popular in the religion of the people. The popularity is due to the pungent sayings concerning human conduct. It should be remembered that these sayings are not absolutes; their truth is relative to the situations in which humans find themselves; see, for example, 17:27-28; 26:4-5. But they are a distillation of the practical insights of a people who lived a life under God. The book is perhaps best absorbed in two ways: chapters 1–9 can be read consecutively, since their thoughts flow somewhat logically, but in chapters 10–31, one must read with greater attention since very little context is provided for the disparate sayings. In this way the goal of character formation intended by the sages is more easily attained.

See: WISDOM

ROLAND E. MURPHY, O.CARM.

PROVIDENCE

God's supreme power and authority over the universe are often affirmed in the OT (e.g., Ps 115:3; Prov 19:21; Deut 32:39), as is divine care for both individuals and community. God's role in the world is a providential one, beginning with creation. If humans sin and are rightly punished, God always steps in with mercy, clothing Adam and Eve with animal skins, putting a sign on Cain to protect him, and mitigating the ravages of the Flood by preserving Noah and his family in the ark. The call of Abraham is accompanied by a promise of divine guidance, as is the vocation of Moses to liberate captive Israelites from Egypt. It is God who liberates (e.g., Exod 3:8; Deut 7:8), gives Israel "a land which you had not tilled and cities which you did not build" (Jos 24:13), takes David from the pasture "to be commander of my people Israel" (2 Sam 7:8), and appoints Jeremiah a prophet to the nations before he was born (Jer 1:5).

"Providence" in the OT is not limited to mercy;* justice* is part of it too. The primary word, *paqad,* to "visit," can refer to

salvific or punitive interventions, but the purpose of divine chastisement is the restoration of relationship with God. The ideal is order, as opposed to chaos, not only in the physical world, stabilized at creation, but also in the realm of society, where God often needs to guide the human heart.

Though divine efficacy is unchallenged in the biblical world, human responsibility is given due prominence, beginning with the sin and punishment of Adam and Eve. God's purposes are always achieved, sometimes through the sinful acts of humans who are nevertheless punished for them.

Issues of the problem of evil are faced courageously in the Book of Job, in Qoheleth (Ecclesiastes), and in part of the Psalter, but the only real answer is silence drawn from one's own personal experience of God's majesty (Job 42:1-6).

The NT leaves little doubt about the supreme sovereignty of the "LORD of heaven and earth" (Matt 11:25), but that same God is portrayed as a loving Father who feeds the birds in the sky, clothes the wild flowers in great splendor, and knows the number of hairs on our head (Matt 6:25ff.; 10:29f.). Jesus promises, "ask and it will be given to you" (Matt 7:7). Paul asserts that "all things work for good to those who love God" (Rom 8:28), and John quotes Jesus as saying, "No one can receive anything except what has been given him from heaven" (John 3:27).

Old Testament

Divine providence is expressed by several Hebrew words, especially *paqad,* "to attend to with care," "visit"; *zakar,* "be mindful of," "remember"; and *nabat* (in Hiphil), "to gaze down" (from heaven). The needy can trust that God will notice their plight and come to their aid, but sinners will find God's "visit" uncomfortable. According to ancient belief, God is "merciful and gracious. . . . slow to anger and rich in kindness and fidelity . . . for a thousand generations . . . yet not declaring the guilty guiltless, but punishing children and grandchildren to the third and fourth generation for their fathers' wickedness" (Exod 34:6-7); Ezekiel later introduced the idea of strict personal responsibility, threatening punishment only for the guilty individual (Ezekiel 18). We must cooperate with God in order to attain proper results.

Historical Tradition. God's care is directed to those in need, individuals like Sarah or Hannah (Gen 21:1; 1 Sam 1:19-20), or the whole community, such as Israel stranded in Egypt (Gen 50:24-25; Exod 3:16; 4:31) or later in Babylon (Jer 29:10; Zech 10:3). Joseph was allowed to be sold into Egypt so that his whole family should be providentially cared for in time of famine (Gen 45:8; 50:20). It was wrong of his brothers to sell him, and they were punished (Gen 42:21). God's purpose was achieved through a sinful human act which was nevertheless punished. That this involves a mystery may be deduced also from texts about God's hardening of Pharaoh's heart. At times it is said that "the LORD made Pharaoh obstinate" (Exod 9:12; 10:1f., 20, 27; 11:9f.), but also that Pharaoh "became obdurate" (Exod 8:28; 9:34). The difference in language may result from separate traditions (priestly and Yahwist respectively), but the editors had no difficulty in joining the two ideas and in holding Pharaoh responsible (see the later redactional text of Exod 10:1f.); similarly Sihon (Deut 2:30).

God also "tests" (*nissah*) to see if people are faithful in difficult circumstances: Abraham (Gen 22:1), the Israelites in the desert (Exod 16:4), before false prophets or dreamers (Deut 13:4), before powerful nations (Judg 3:4). According to 2 Samuel, God "prompts" (*nissah*) David to take a census of the people, and then punishes him for doing so (2 Sam 24:1ff.). In retelling the story, 1 Chronicles asserts that it was "Satan" who "enticed" (*nissah*) David (1 Chr 21:1); evidently it was no longer proper in the time of Chronicles (ca. 400 BCE) to attribute such temptation directly to God. Yet the existence of both texts in the one Bible points to the mystery of the relationship between divine omnipotence and human freedom.

Prophets. The good things of life—grain, wine, oil, even silver and gold—are gifts from God, but are sometimes the occasions of sin, forcing God to withhold them in hopes of bringing about repentance (Hos 2:10; Jer 6:23-25). Ultimately God is in charge and controls the destiny of Israel as well as that of its neighbors (Amos 9:7-8; Jer 27:6). Individuals and nations are instruments used by God to attain a certain end, even without their awareness, often to punish Israel (Isa 10:5-27) but also to save it (Isa 41:2-5; 45:1-7). With trust in God's providence Jeremiah pleads in his time of trial, "Remember me LORD, visit me" (Jer 15:15). He can also promise that God would "visit" and bring the exiles in Babylon back home at the proper moment (Jer 29:10; similarly Zeph 2:7). But if the people are sinful, that same God will "visit" in punishment (Amos 3:14; Hos 9:9; Jer 5:9).

Psalms and Wisdom Literature. The created world is stable and intelligible (e.g., Job 38:8-11; Ps 104:5-9; Prov 8:29), but is still in need of God's continuing care. The threat of chaos is ever present, both in nature and in human life. Psalm 104 praises God not only for having set limits to the ocean (v. 9) but also for continuing to give all living creatures "food in due time" (v. 27); "when you hide your face they are lost, when you take away their breath they perish" (v. 29; see Pss 65:6-14; 145:15-16; 147:8-9). Job can assert: "your providence has preserved my spirit" (Job 10:12). The author of the Book of Wisdom speaks about the hazards of a merchant ship at sea, and exclaims: "But your providence, O Father! guides it . . . showing that you can save from any danger" (Wis 14:3-4). The psalmist marvels at God's wondrous concern for us: "What are humans that you are mindful of them, mere mortals that you care for them?" (Ps 8:5), and in times of difficulty calls upon God to "remember me . . . come to me with your saving help" (Ps 106:4), or, in the name of the people, "look down from heaven . . . attend to this vine" (Ps 80:15). In general: "Unless the LORD build the house, they labor in vain who build. Unless the LORD guard the city, in vain does the guard keep watch" (Ps 127:1).

New Testament

Synoptic Gospels. Jesus not only experienced God as his loving, providential Father whom he called Abba, "Papa," he also encouraged others to think of God in that way: "Not one [sparrow] falls to the ground without your Father's knowledge. Even all the hairs of your head are counted" (Matt 10:29f.; Luke 12:6f.; see Luke 21:18). The same attitude of trust is expressed in the beautiful image of the birds in the sky and the lilies in the field: "do not worry about your life . . . look at the birds in the sky . . . your heavenly Father feeds them. . . . Can any of you by worrying add a single moment to your life span? . . . Learn from the way the wild flowers grow . . . will [God] not much more provide for you, O you of little faith? . . . Seek first the kingdom of God and his righteousness, and all these things will be given you besides" (Matt 6:25-34; Luke 12:22-32). Jesus reminds his audience that instead of being anxious they are to seek God's kingdom, and the basic necessities of life will be given them as well.

In both the Matthean and especially Lucan context, the fundamental attitude inculcated is one of trust in God, coupled with a life of simplicity, generosity, service of neighbor, and the formation of community. God's providence will then be experienced not least through mutual service and support. In Matthew: seek treasure in heaven (6:19-21), do not serve mammon (6:24), and more generally, feed the hungry (25:31-46); in Luke: the Magnificat ("he has filled the starving with good things," Luke 1:53), call to compassion and generosity (6:36-38; 12:33), the good Samaritan (10:29-37). Mark's Gospel also teaches these ideals: parable of the measure (Mark 4:24f.), cup of cold water (9:41), reward of renunciation (10:29-31).

Trust in God must permeate our prayer of petition: "Ask, and it will be given to you; seek, and you will find; knock, and the door will be opened to you. . . . If you, who are wicked, know how to give good gifts to your children, how much more will your heavenly Father give good things to those who ask him" (Matt 7:7-11; Luke 11:9-13). And elsewhere: "Your Father knows what you need before you ask him" (Matt 6:8). Of course, every prayer of petition must repeat the words of Jesus at Gethsemane: "not what I will but what you will" (Mark 14:36; see Matt 6:10).

Acts. "God . . . gives to everyone life and breath and everything"; "in him we live and move and have our being" (17:26; 28). God's providence is concretized by the ideal community in which everyone shares completely, without holding back (Acts 2:42-47; 4:32-35).

Paul. The Greek world believed in fate, Paul in the personal care and guidance of God, especially for our salvation in Christ. "We know that all things work for good for those who love God" (Rom 8:28-30); "If God is for us, who can be against us? . . . [nothing] will be able to separate us from the love of God in Christ Jesus our Lord" (Rom 8:31, 39). Paul says of God that "from him and through him and for him are all things" (Rom 11:36; see 1 Cor 15:28), and urges the Philippians to work out their salvation with fear and trembling "for God is the one who, for his good purpose, works in you both to desire and to work" (Phil 2:12f.). In 1 Timothy 6:17-19, the wealthy are reminded that it is God who "richly provides us with all things for our enjoyment," and that they are therefore to rely on God, be generous, share, and thus to accumulate treasure that leads to true life.

John. God's sovereign guidance of the world, especially of human salvation, is clearly stated several times: "No one can receive anything except what has been given him from heaven" (John 3:27); the man was born blind "so that the works of God might be made visible through him" (9:3), and Lazarus was allowed to die "for the glory of God, that the Son of God may be glorified through it" (11:4). When Pilate demanded answers from Jesus on the basis of his authority, Jesus replied: "You would have no power over me if it had not been given to you from above" (19:11). Even the betrayal of Judas fulfills a divine purpose: "so that the scripture might be fulfilled" (13:18; 17:12). Nevertheless, this does not excuse Judas; he acted on his own and was guilty of betrayal (see 12:4-6; 18:2f., 5). The world is sinful and under the power of sin (7:7; 15:18f.; 17:14)—even neutral passages about the world prepare for the mention of sin (1:10; 3:16-19), but humans are called to repentance and faith (4:13ff.; 7:37f.; 12:24-26;), and are threatened with punishment if they don't (8:21-24; 15:22). They can free themselves from the power of a sinful world, but only with the saving grace of Christ. They must be born anew (3:19-21), be in the world but not of it (17:11, 14ff.), and abide in Christ (6:56) like branches in the vine (15:4). "Without me you can do nothing" (15:5).

See: CREATION, FREEDOM, JUSTICE, MERCY

JOSEPH F. WIMMER, O.S.A.

PSALMS

Psalms are songs that express religious piety. Examples of psalms appear throughout both testaments of the Bible, but they are usually associated with the biblical book by the same name. Their variety and range reflect the history and religious insight of the people.

Old Testament

The word psalm comes from the Greek word *psalmos,* which is a translation of the Hebrew word *mizmor,* a song accompanied by instrumental music. The Hebrew title for the Book of Psalms, however, is *tehillim,* which means "praises." The Psalter begins that part of the Hebrew Bible known as the Writings. It contains 150 psalms that vary in length, theme, style, and mood.

Poetry. The psalms are poetic expressions of religious experience. Poetry has a tendency to be concrete and imaginative, to explore frontiers, and to link together what may seem contradictory. It makes use of rhythm, sound, and figures of speech. The psalms as poetic prayer can draw on images and feelings in order to escape literal language and to express what is otherwise ineffable in religious experience.

Ancient Hebrew poetry was marked by repetition, especially by parallelism. This occurs when the thought of a line is repeated (in the same or different words), contrasted, or built up in one or more successive lines. This type of repetition may seem monotonous to us, but it was appreciated by the Hebrew ear.

Some of the psalms are acrostic poetry. These are alphabetic poems where each new line, verse, or stanza begins with the next letter of the Hebrew alphabet. Psalm 119, the longest psalm in the Bible, is an acrostic poem. So are Psalms 9–10; 25; 34; 37; 111; 112; and 145.

Liturgy. It is likely that at least some, if not most, of the psalms found in the OT had their origin in Israel's liturgical practice. Not every psalm was composed for use in the cult, yet the majority of psalms are appropriate for public, communal worship. Even today they are used extensively in both Jewish and Christian liturgy.

The Bible does not provide much information about the use of the psalms in Israel's worship. However, a number of psalms allude to various ritual acts: "But I can enter your house because of your great love. I can worship in your holy temple" (Ps 5:8). "I will wash my hands in innocence and walk round your altar. . . . LORD, I love the house where you dwell, the tenting-place of your glory" (Ps 26:6, 8). Psalm 66:13-15 mentions holocausts and vows, while in Psalm 63:3 the poet looks toward God in the sanctuary. A few notations in some of the psalms' titles may be liturgical notations (Psalms 38; 70; 92; 100).

Some of the psalms express an ardent longing for the Temple in Jerusalem. The Psalms of Zion (Psalms 46; 48; 76; 84; 87; 122) associate God's presence with the holy City. Pilgrimage to the Temple was therefore an occasion of great joy. Liturgical processions are presupposed in Psalms 68:25-28; 100; 118:19-20, 26-27; 132:7-8. Psalms 15 and 24 seem especially appropriate for greeting pilgrims with a recital of requirements for entering the Temple. They may have served as entrance rites that combined an examination of conscience with a confession of faith. The Psalms of Ascents (Psalms 120–134) may have formed a kind of hymnal for pilgrims on their way to Jerusalem.

Literary Categories. Scholars have classified the psalms under a number of different literary categories: royal psalms, wisdom psalms, liturgical psalms, prophetic psalms, psalms of confidence, psalms of thanksgiving, hymns of praise, and laments. Often these may be subdivided into individual and communal types. Royal, liturgical, prophetic, and wisdom psalms are not actually literary categories, since their classification depends on specific themes rather than on form.

Contemporary scholarship tends to divide most psalms into two general categories: hymns (or praise) and prayers (or laments). Psalms of confidence are usually classified as prayers, since they are closely related to laments. Psalms of thanksgiving are sometimes classified as hymns and sometimes as prayers, for thanksgiving is often a spontaneous response to deliverance from distress (the subject of laments). Yet thanking and praising are closely related to one another. In fact, ancient Hebrew had no specific word to distinguish "to thank" from "to praise."

If the psalms are poetic expressions of religious experience, then the hymn articulates the feeling of wonder and the overwhelming sense of God's power and presence. The hymns of praise were probably composed for specific cultic ceremonies and for the great religious feasts of Israel. That they were meant to be sung by the community is indicated by refrains ("God's love endures forever" in Psalms 118 and 136) and responses ("Amen" in Pss 41:14; 72:19; 89:53; 106:48; and "Halleluia" in Psalms 111–113; 115–117; and 146–150). The hymns also tend to follow certain general themes: praise of the creator, praise of Yahweh as the One who reigns, longing for God, praise of God's presence in the cult, and praise of God's activity in history and in the Torah.

If the hymns express the experience of God's power and presence, then the laments express those moments of pain, sorrow, and disorder—moments when God seems absent, helpless, or distant. Laments acknowledge that the individual or the community is not in control but that God can change the situation, for the laments call on God to bring order out of chaos and to restore wholeness in times of disorientation and trouble.

Laments usually describe some crisis situation, plead for relief, and express confidence that God will help. A transition from complaint to confidence in God is the normal pattern. An exception is Psalm 88, which ends on a despairing note. The Psalter contains both individual and communal laments. Communal laments are concerned with national issues, and most likely were offered on public days of fasting and prayer. Individual laments often deal with serious illness, old age, sinfulness, or personal distress and persecution.

The cursing psalms are a particular group of laments that may embarrass us. For these psalms express anger, rage, and even the human propensity toward violence: "Break the arms of the wicked and depraved; make them account for their crimes; let none of them survive" (Ps 10:15); "LORD, avenging God, avenging God, shine forth! Rise up, judge of the earth; give the proud what they deserve" (Ps 94:1-2); "Happy those who seize your children and smash them against a rock" (Ps 137:9); "If only you would destroy the wicked, O God" (Ps 139:19). Such statements challenge the way things are, for enemies are cursed and vengeance is demanded. Disorder was seen as dangerous and contrary to the divine plan, so God was asked to do something about it. However, the cursing psalms have been eliminated from the lectionary and the Liturgy of the Hours.

Emotions. The psalms are prayers and confessions of faith. They arose from ordinary, concrete experiences—both positive and negative. Although they often became fixed formulas dictated by liturgical use, they managed to express a variety of human emotions, such as wonder, joy, confidence, thanksgiving, sorrow, despair, and fear.

The ancient Israelites were not afraid to express anger and rage in their prayers—even toward God. They had no reservations about venting frustration, resentment, and revenge. The shadow side of human life was not denied. Challenging the Almighty and expressing strong feelings in prayer was a part of biblical tradition. When the world became disoriented, Israel went to God and demanded redress. It was actually a way of affirming God's existence and of expressing confidence in God's power and concern.

The psalmists did not limit their prayers to moments of loss, rage, and frustration. They also delighted in moments of blessing, joy, and peace. Confidence is actually the most widespread mood in the psalms. Israel could feel confident and unafraid, since God's faithfulness was beyond doubt.

It should be noted that the Book of Psalms as a whole moves from lament to praise. Hymns of praise, psalms of confidence and thanksgiving, and laments are scattered throughout the Psalter. However, laments are especially prevalent in the first half, while hymns of praise dominate the second half. So the very shape of the Psalter emphasizes the movement from complaint and distress to wonder and awe.

New Testament

Scholars recognize as many as ninety-three citations of sixty different OT psalms in the NT. The psalms were part of the Jewish liturgical tradition during the lifetime of Jesus, so most likely Jesus and his early followers recited them regularly in prayer. The only indication of this, however, occurs in Mark 14:26 and Matthew 26:30: "Then, after singing a hymn, they went out to the Mount of Olives." The "hymn" probably was the Hallel (Psalms 113–118), which was sung at the Passover meal.

Psalms are frequently quoted or alluded to in the Synoptic Gospels. For example, the devil quotes Psalm 91:11-12 in the narrative of Jesus' temptation in the desert (Matt 4:6; Luke 4:10-11). The Sermon on the Mount refers to Psalms 6:9; 37:11; 48:3; 145:15-16; and 147:9. God's words at Jesus' baptism and transfiguration may be an allusion to Psalm 2:7.

The narratives describing Jesus' last few days refer frequently to the psalms. Psalm 118:25-26 is part of the acclamation of welcome when Jesus enters Jerusalem (Matt 21:9; 23:39; Mark 11:9-10; Luke 19:38). In the debate over the identity of the Messiah, Jesus quotes Psalm 110:1 (Matt 22:44; Mark 12:36; Luke 20:42-43). Twice Jesus quotes psalms from the cross: "My God, my God, why have you forsaken me?" (Matt 27:46; Mark 15:34) comes from Psalm 2:2; and "into your hands I commend my spirit" (Luke 23:46) is from Psalm 31:6. The division of Jesus' clothes and the casting of lots recalls Psalm 22:19. Matthew 27:43 also cites Psalm 22:9: "He trusted in God; let him deliver him now if he wants him."

The Gospel of John adds other quotations from the psalms. For example, John 2:17 ("Zeal for your house will consume me") cites Psalm 69:10. In John 6:31 Jesus paraphrases Psalm 78:24: "He gave them bread from heaven to eat." Psalm 41:10 ("The one who ate my food has raised his heel against me") is paraphrased in John 13:18.

The first chapter of the Acts of the Apostles connects two cursing psalms (Pss 69:26; 109:8) with the defection of Judas. A section of Peter's Pentecost sermon (Acts 2:25-35) makes reference to Psalms 16:8-11; 110:1; and 132:11. In other sermons and speeches both Peter and Paul demonstrate their knowledge of the psalms.

Paul frequently refers to the psalms in his letters. Four are found in his Corinthian correspondence and more than a dozen in his Letter to the Romans. For example, in his description of the wicked in Romans 3:10-18, Paul links together portions of

Psalms 5:10; 10:7; 14:1-3; 36:2; 53:2-4; and 140:4. In Romans 4:7-8 he describes the righteous in terms of Psalm 32:1-2. Psalm 44:23 is used to portray the difficulties that result from following Christ (Rom 8:36). Psalm 19:5 is applied to the spread of the gospel in Romans 10:18, while Psalm 69:23-24 is applied to unbelievers within Israel in Romans 11:9-10.

A number of citations from eleven different psalms are to be found in the Letter to the Hebrews. In the first two chapters of this letter nine references to the psalms are used to prove the superiority of Christ over the angels. Hebrews 3:7–4:11 cites various portions of Psalm 95 in an attempt to encourage obedience to God. Psalm 2:7 ("You are my son; this day I have begotten you") is quoted twice in the letter (Heb 1:5; 5:5), while Psalm 110:4 ("You are a priest forever, according to the order of Melchizedek") is cited three times (Heb 5:6; 7:17, 21).

Prayers and hymns of various kinds are scattered throughout the NT, but Christianity never wrote its own book of psalms. The early Church regarded the psalms of the OT as Scripture, and it saw no need to replace them with a specifically Christian work. It did not hesitate to apply the psalms directly to the Church's situation, for passages from Scripture were read as prophecy and were assumed to refer to Jesus and to the Christian community. The royal psalms were especially suitable for messianic applications.

Certain psalms are quite popular in the NT. Psalm 2 is cited or alluded to six times in contexts of conflict between Christ the exalted king and the hostile Gentile nations. The NT interprets this psalm in the light of Christ's resurrection. Psalm 110 is also quoted extensively. It is applied to Jesus as Messiah and high priest. The Church reads Psalm 118 as a prophecy of the death and resurrection of Jesus. Psalm 22 is the most popular psalm in the NT, for it is cited thirteen times, nine of which occur in the passion narrative. After Psalm 22, Psalm 69 is the most extensively cited psalm. Both were interpreted in a mes-

sianic sense, prophesying the sufferings of Christ.

See: PRAYER, WORSHIP

TIMOTHY A. LENCHAK, S.V.D.

Pastoral-Liturgical Tradition

The Use of the Psalter in the Early Church. Following the example of the NT, the primitive Church continued to see in the psalms numerous prophecies fulfilled in Christ. They obviously understood the messianic psalms (e.g., Psalms 2; 45; 89; 110; and 132) in this way, and on the basis of typology, expanded this Christianization to include the entire Psalter. Thus, the words of Psalm 3, "I lie down and sleep comes at once—and I arise, for the Lord upholds me" became for Justin, Irenaeus, Hippolytus, and Cyprian not only David's morning song of joy, but the exultation of the risen One on Easter morning. Of Psalm 141 with its famous "Let my prayer rise before you like incense; the lifting of my hands like an evening sacrifice," Augustine said, "This evening sacrifice is the passion of the Lord, the cross of the Lord, the oblation of the victim that brings salvation, the holocaust acceptable to God. In his resurrection he made this evening sacrifice a morning sacrifice" (*Enarr in Ps.* 140,6). For Origen, the joy of Israel at its liberation in Psalm 124, "Our soul, like a sparrow, has been delivered from the snare of the fowler; the snare has been broken and we are set free," is also the song of the Church rejoicing in salvation won by Christ.

By way of symbolic association, the "righteous one" (Psalms 1; 35; 37; 112; etc.), the "shepherd" (Psalms 23; 100), and the "one unjustly accused" (Psalms 31; 35; 41; 55; 68; 142) are psalmic references to Christ. Even non-human images pointed to him: "the sun comes forth like a bridegroom coming from his tent" (Ps 19:6) was in fact the "Sun of righteousness" (Mal 4:2) and the "Orient from on High" (Luke 1:78) coming forth in splendor from the tomb; "in the shelter of your wings I rejoice" (Ps 63:7) called to mind the outstretched arms of the crucified and, simultaneously, the image of Jesus as a hen with outstretched and gathering wings (Matt 23:37).

It was not difficult for the Christian to see the cross imaged in every "tree" (Psalms 1; 37; 52; and especially the early Christian gloss to Psalm 96: "Tell it among the nations, the Lord has reigned from the wood!" which Justin [ca. 150 CE] considered an authentic part of the text). Likewise, baptism was prefigured in "water" or "the Red Sea" (Psalms 1; 42; 63; 66; 77; 78; 104; 105; 106; 107; 114; 136); the Spirit of Jesus in "God's power" and "holy spirit" (51; 63; 65; 68; 80; 104; 118; 139; 143); the Eucharist in the "banquet table," "food" or "bread" (23; 34; 78; 104; 132); the Word-Made-Flesh in the many synonyms for Torah—word, laws, decrees, precepts, statutes, promises (Psalms 1; 19b; 119); and the Church itself in "Jerusalem," "Mt. Zion," the "Holy City" (Psalms 48; 87; 122; 125).

Finally, because the Septuagint Greek version of the Hebrew Scriptures had translated the sacred name, YHWH with *Kyrios* and in the NT Jesus Christ is *Kyrios* (see Phil 2:11), every occurrence of *Kyrios* in the Psalter could refer to Christ (especially Psalms 93–100). Thus it was possible to hear in the Psalter not only the voice of Christ speaking to God and the voice of the Church speaking about Christ, but also the voice of the Church speaking to (or about) Christ *as* God!

Use of the Psalter in the Liturgy. Although the Psalter was probably first used in Christian liturgy as one of the principal books of prophecy, its adoption in the course of the third century as *the* book of songs for Christian worship cannot be explained apart from the process of Christianization described above. It is quite possible that the Psalter replaced non-scriptural hymns and canticles (*psalmoi idiotikoi*) when these became tools of certain heretical sects precisely because the psalms had already been thoroughly Christianized through catechesis and the writings of the apologists. Because they had been inspired by the holy Spirit, the psalms were free from heresy; Augustine would say: "So

that God might be praised correctly by humankind, God has praised himself in the psalms" (*Enarr in Ps.* 144,1).

In spite of second-century evidence that psalms were in fact sung at public worship, it is only fourth-century records that indicate which psalms were sung, when, and in which churches. At morning and evening prayer in cathedral churches—for centuries the center of all liturgical life—only certain psalms or sections of psalms were chosen for their suitability to the hour or service (e.g., Psalms, 63 and 148–150 in the morning, Psalm 141 in the evening); in monastic communities all 150 psalms were read in numerical order with little or no reference to the time of day. When cathedral and monastic traditions merged in parts of the East and West in the sixth and seventh centuries, the monastic ideal with regard to the entire Psalter was adopted while psalms for morning prayer and feasts continued to be matched to the hour or day.

The variable chants for Eucharist in the West consisted of psalms sung with antiphons or refrains—some being a verse from the psalm or another part of the Scriptures; others being "ecclesiastical compositions," i.e., written for the feast or taken from some other post-apostolic source. The earliest collections of chants for Mass, which for Rome date from the eighth century, indicate that psalms were assigned to feasts of the Lord and the strong seasons (Advent, Christmas, Lent, Easter) according to the focus of the feast, the mystery being celebrated, or even the stational church where the Mass on that day was celebrated each year. But, because all the psalms were understood to be prayers of the body of Christ—head and members, it was considered quite natural to assign them in numerical order when there was no obvious reason for choosing one over the other as was the case with the communion psalms on the weekdays of Lent and the entrance psalms on the Sundays after Pentecost.

The Psalms as Prayer Today. Many commentators have rightly pointed to the universal appeal of the psalms—their capacity for expressing the full range of human experience: angers, fears, joys, pleasures, hopes, desires, regrets, thanks, and praise. Bringing all these before God in prayer is offering one's very self. Christians know intuitively that this self-offering is done through, with, and in Christ who not only prayed these psalms before us, but through his Spirit joins the prayer of all creation through our prayer to the praise which he sings eternally before the Throne of Grace. This would be reason enough for Christians to pray the psalms both in private and liturgical prayer. However, current liturgical documents still consider the Christian sense of the psalms useful and necessary (see General Instruction on the Liturgy of the Hours, 100-109; the Order of Christian Funerals, 25-26, 355). If, in addition to their literal sense, the psalms are reread in the light of the Paschal Mystery, the voice of Christ and his Body is heard, the continuity of God's self-revelation in the life of Israel, the life of Christ, the life of the Church, and the life of the individual is perceived, and Christians find themselves praying these texts in a way that is not only liturgically correct and traditional, but rooted in the NT itself.

See: PRAISE, PRAYER, TIME, TYPE, WORSHIP

JOHN K. LEONARD

R

RECONCILIATION

Terms for reconciliation are infrequent throughout the Bible. Israel was sometimes affected by pagan religious ideals including that of appeasement of the divinity. Because of human sin, reconciliation necessarily implied human unworthiness. Making things right again involved a very high cost from a human standpoint. A sin-offering or guilt-offering had to involve sacrifice, the price of a life or equivalent of a ransom. God is never the subject of the verb in the OT, but according to the NT, it is God who changes us and reconciles us in Jesus. Human beings are "covered" or "changed thoroughly" so that reconciliation can be achieved. Reconciliation between humans is emphasized as an integral and essential part of Jesus' message. And Paul perceives reconciliation as the thorough change brought about by God's saving action in Jesus.

Old Testament

In the OT, the context for the idea of reconciliation is usually cultic, that is, it refers to the priestly sacrifice as a sin or guilt offering and is related to the substitution of something valuable as the "price" of ransom owed because of sin. The terms signifying reconciliation and related to the cultic notion of purifying or making worthy an otherwise unworthy thing or person are borrowed from the language of finance.

Reconciliation was part of fiscal parlance; it meant to bring into harmony, to add or subtract or manipulate, so that the columns are balanced. When people sin, something is "due" before reconciliation can be achieved. Sin and guilt cry out for remedy. So, for example, Samuel, testifying to his own integrity, asked his people rhetorically, "From whom have I accepted a bribe and overlooked his guilt? I will make restitution to you" (1 Sam 12:3). The people answer that Samuel has not overlooked anyone's guilt and thus wronged them. Since there is no guilt to be remedied or debt to be repaid, there is no need for Samuel to be reconciled.

The Hebrew root *kaphar,* meaning "to cover, or to make atonement" (see Lev 6:30; 8:15; Ezek 45:15, 17, 20), and the term *ratsah* can be translated "reconcile" (see 1 Sam 29:4). All creatures are subject to sin and thus purification is required, even for inanimate objects involved in the true worship of Israel's God. So, for example, according to the ordinances of Leviticus, Moses put blood of the slaughtered bullock on the altar, "thus purifying the altar." Moses also made atonement for the altar when he consecrated it (Lev 8:15).

Similarly the reform introduced by Ezekiel renewed the covenant and its priestly emphasis on codes and rituals. The Israelites are instructed: "One sheep from the flock for every two hundred from the pasturage of Israel, for sacrifice—holocausts and peace offerings and atonement sacrifices, says the Lord God. . . . On the first day of the first month you shall use an unblemished young bull as a sacrifice to purify the sanctuary. . . . thus you shall make atonement for the temple" (45:15, 18, 20).

New Testament

In the NT, reconciliation sometimes refers to relations between people. For example, reconciliation can refer to the repair of an estranged relationship between husband and wife. Thus Paul urges married Christians to be reconciled (*katallageto:* 1 Cor 7:11). The fact that this demand was necessary indicates that baptism was experienced by at least some early Christians as disruptive of family life. Yet the goal of Christianity is unity, not division. In cases where a wife has separated from her husband because of her new freedom as a baptized person, she should be reconciled with her husband, even if he is unbaptized.

The gospel message may be summed up as a message of peace. As our estranged relationship with God is healed, so too is there peace and healing among people. The NT speaks of reconciliation as the experience of the new relationships we enjoy with God and among ourselves.

The Gospels emphasize that many different facets of human experience need to be healed as a result of hearing the gospel. For example, in the Sermon on the Mount, Jesus commands Christians to be reconciled not only with one another but with their enemies, that is, with people who are persecuting them. The demands of Christian love are unconditional and unlimited. Before the believers pray at the altar, if they remember that anyone has a grudge against them, they should leave their offering and go to make peace, and only then return to make their offering to God (see Matt 5:23-24). A disciple of Christ cannot claim to love God and ignore the demands of love of neighbor and even of enemy.

Only in Paul does the term reconciliation refer to our relations with God, and then it is initiated by God and achieved through Christ. In Romans 5, reconciliation is practically equivalent to justification, which is for Paul the supreme act of God in Christ. Paul writes: "God proves his love for us in that while we were still sinners Christ died for us. How much more then, since we are now justified by his blood, will we be saved through him from the wrath. Indeed, if, while we were enemies, we were reconciled to God through the death of his Son, how much more, once reconciled, will we be saved by his life. Not only that, but we also boast of God through our Lord Jesus Christ, through whom we have now received reconciliation" (5:8-11). Reconciliation, like justification, is usually in the past tense. Reconciliation is already achieved through Christ's death and already obtained through baptism. So Paul says, "we are at peace with God through our Lord Jesus Christ" (5:1).

The social implications of reconciliation are emphasized by Paul, especially in speaking to the Corinthians who not only had a number of quarrels with Paul, but experienced major divisions among themselves. Paraphrasing 1 Corinthians 1–4, for example, Paul stresses that, because of their common baptism, the divisions among the Corinthians are groundless, even absurd. The unity of their common faith makes reconciliation among the factions imperative.

Reconciliation also has a mission dimension to outsiders. Paul is insistent: "All this [i.e., new creation] is from God who has reconciled us to himself through Christ and given us the ministry of reconciliation, namely, God was reconciling the world to himself in Christ, not counting their trespasses against them and entrusting to us the message of reconciliation. So we are ambassadors for Christ, as if God were appealing through us. We implore you on behalf of Christ, be reconciled to God" (2 Cor 5:18-20). For Paul, then, God is the source of human reconciliation. The divine power enables the ministry of reconciliation in the world, extended to all areas where divisions remain. God is in us, saying to the world, "Be reconciled."

The Deutero-Pauline literature contains just a few references to reconciliation. The term itself, with the meaning "to change thoroughly," occurs only in Colossians and Ephesians. In both letters the image of a glorified Christ is used to describe the cosmic peace won by the cross: "For in him all the fullness was pleased to dwell, and through him to reconcile all things for him, making peace by the blood of his cross. . . . And you who once were alienated and hostile in mind because of evil deeds, he has now reconciled . . . through his death, to present you holy, without blemish, and irreproachable before him" (Col 1:19-22).

Ephesians, which is a kind of expansion of Colossians, uses the same idea of the social harmony brought about by the complete transformation of believers through the death of Christ. The author of Ephesians speaks of Christ as "our peace" (2:14) who created "in himself one new person" (2:15) in place of the two (i.e., Jew and Gentile), thus establishing peace that he might "reconcile both with God, in one body, through the cross, putting that enmity to death by it" (2:16).

In the Bible, as in modern usage, reconciliation means a deep improvement in relationships, not only between God and human beings, but among human beings. From a biblical standpoint, the empowerment to develop healing and growth-producing relationships among people, however, is given by God. According to the NT, reconciliation is the supreme gift of God expressed in the saving death of Jesus who thereby won for us redemption and salvation. Reconciliation continues to be offered and sustained through the Church. Reconciliation in the NT is not so much the cultic matter that it is for the OT. It is the sum and essence of God's work in Christ, and the expression of grace in our relationships with one another.

See: BAPTISM, JUSTIFICATION, PEACE, REDEMPTION, SACRIFICE, SALVATION, SIN

MARY ANN GETTY

Pastoral-Liturgical Tradition

In Paul's letters reconciliation is used more as a theological master-image for what God has done in Christ to save us (2 Cor 5:18-19) than as a name for a particular set ritual practice of the early community. To be sure, there are biblical traces of inchoate procedures for dealing with sinful disciples in the early Church, e.g.: a step-by-step correction process (Matt 18:15-18; Gal 6:1-2), public reprimand (1 Tim 5:20), a form of shunning (2 Thess 3:14-15), and practices of isolating sinners from the community (1 Cor 5:1-5) and reconciling them with the community (2 Cor 2:5-11). Nevertheless, baptism for the forgiveness of sins (Acts 2:38), the Eucharistic memorial of the Lord who was given in death for the forgiveness of sins (Matt 26:28), and seeking pardon of one another (Matt 5:23-24) would have been the more important ways of ritualizing the experience of forgiveness and reconciliation in the early community.

Clearer evidence of a more patterned process of reconciliation appears in the late second and early third centuries. In that period the community faced the pressures of persecution and the need to come to terms with repentant apostates and others who had seriously compromised their discipleship and wished to be reinstated in the community. An intermediate process of pastoral care and reform, to accompany the sinner from isolation to readmission, gradually took shape. This process was marked ritually in several ways by the fourth century. There was an opening ritual of public admission into the order of penitents, still vestigially preserved in the distribution of ashes on Ash Wednesday. A time of penance followed, during which the prayer of the community supported the penitents as they undertook practices of penance designed to help them retrace the process of baptismal conversion. Those practices were

809

the forerunners of today's lenten prayer and penance. The process concluded with a public rite of reconciliation that restored the sinner to community, and they were then readmitted to the Eucharistic table at the Holy Thursday celebration of the Lord's Supper. This full-blown pastoral-ritual process developed in tandem with the catechumenate, which it mirrored in many ways. Theology of that period even named reconciliation a "second baptism." Such "canonical penance" could be received only once in a lifetime.

As canonical penance came to impose more severe and lasting demands on penitents, however, the way was opened in the early Middle Ages for another form of the process of reconciliation introduced to Europe by the Irish monks. This "Irish penance" was characterized by the personal guidance through a journey of conversion that it provided for the sinner, a process that could be repeated as often as one wished. As in canonical penance, a liturgical rite of pardon eventually brought the process to a close, though this rite was celebrated individually.

However, this form of reconciliation, also called "tariff penance," required a detailed confessing of one's sins and the performance of complex, severe penances. This led in turn to the general disuse of reconciliation. Penance was simply postponed until one's deathbed, when it could be celebrated as a continuous rite without the arduous process of penance and satisfaction. To this medieval form of the rite, the forerunner of the modern "confession," the scholastic theologians applied the courtroom analogy of crime, judgement, sentence, and punishment. That theological understanding is still familiar in the experience of many today.

Vatican II decreed that the sacrament should be revised to express more clearly its nature and effects (Constitution on the Sacred Liturgy, no. 72). The revision has provided three forms of the rite. In each of them the celebration of reconciliation is still telescoped into a single, continuous liturgical rite. However, the council did reintroduce the ancient thematic of the journey in the introduction to the rite, where conversion is described as "a profound change of the whole person by which one begins to consider, judge, and arrange [one's] life according to the holiness and love of God, made manifest in his Son in the last days and given to us in abundance" (*Rite of Penance*, Introduction no. 6a). Whether the revision will be effective remains to be seen.

The drop-off in the use of the sacrament of reconciliation has been a cause of concern in contemporary pastoral practice. Two considerations may be of help in reflecting on those concerns. First, the history of the sacrament suggests that reconciliation, more than any other sacrament, has served as an accurate barometer to indicate those times when the Church is living through a significant time of change. Rituals of reconciliation function as one of the most personal ways for Christians to name the reality of sin and forgiveness, of alienation and healing in their lives. In times of change when those realities were not so clear, the faithful have historically abandoned the existing form of the sacrament and opted for new forms of experiencing forgiveness and reconciliation, whether sacramental or non-sacramental.

Second, the biblical understanding of what reconciliation is and how it is experienced by Christians offers a way to move beyond the narrow ritual limits in which the experience of reconciliation has been confined in recent times. The crucified and risen Lord is our peace and reconciliation (Eph 2:14-16). Christian initiation first sets disciples on a journey of dying and rising with the Lord. Whenever and wherever people enter into that mystery, whether in living it out in their lives or in rehearsing it in all the liturgical moments of remembering Christ's death and resurrection, the reconciliation God has accomplished in him is being worked out. One of the signs of the times may be that believers are again beginning to find pardon and reconciliation in a variety of ways. Recovery of a more biblically-based understanding of reconciliation and of the many ways in which the early Christians ritualized it can provide a fresh and healthy perspective for pastoral practice today.

See: BAPTISM, CONVERSION, HEALING, REPENTANCE, SIN

GILBERT OSTDIEK, O.F.M.

REDEMPTION/REDEEMER

In the Bible God is seen as one who liberates from oppression and enslavement, both at the concrete political and physical level as well as on a more spiritual plane. One of the metaphors used to portray this divine action is "redemption," a concept that stems from the OT world of indebtedness and the legal obligation of the next of kin to provide a resolution.

God's act of saving the Israelites from slavery in Egypt or Babylon could be described as a redemption, but whenever God was viewed as redeemer there was no mention of payment or ransom. The metaphor of redemption was applied to God only partially, with emphasis on the covenant* relationship as a result of which God exercised the function of next of kin. Although redemption by God in the OT usually referred to liberation from human situations of oppression and danger, it was also applied to deliverance from sin.

Indeed a primary concern of the OT priesthood and sacrificial system was the removal of sin and its consequences, as exemplified in the rites of the Day of Atonement.* The prophets dealt with the same issue by their call for repentance and by their special function as intercessors for others. It was a prophet who developed the idea of the Suffering Servant, probably a personification of Israel itself, who voluntarily offers his life in vicarious atonement for the sins of others, bringing about their conversion and salvation.*

The life—and especially death—of Jesus in the NT was interpreted as having varied significance. It included the idea of "redemption" from enslavement to sin, in the larger context of the establishment of a new covenant in the blood of Christ and the inauguration of the reign of God, which was effective already in this life but would reach its consummation in the resurrection.

Contemporary reflection on the metaphor of redemption seeks to be faithful to the dual nature of the reality expressed by the imagery of enslavement to sin. Sin is both personal and communal. It has a this-worldly dimension of personal and corporate alienation and oppression, but it also consists in a turning away from God that merits eternal condemnation. Redemption from oppression implies political and economic liberation, but it also symbolizes God's wonderful initiative in bringing about the possibility of renewed friendship and divine reconciliation. Redemption envisages both this life and the next, but becomes definitive only in eternity.

Old Testament

The biblical concept of redemption is rooted in family law. If someone was forced to enter service in someone else's household as a slave, or if someone had to sell property in order to pay a debt, it was the task of the nearest male relative to "redeem" or "buy back" (Hebrew *ga'al*) that person or family property by paying a price to the master or owner (Lev 25:23ff.). The purpose of this duty placed on the "redeemer" (Hebrew *go'el*) was to reestablish the former integrity of family membership and property. The image of "redemption" is also found in matters pertaining to sacrifice. Leviticus 27 treats gifts (usually farm animals) vowed to God, and regulates the circumstances according to which they were able to be "redeemed" by the payment of money in their stead.

Another verb used figuratively of God's liberating action is *padah*, "to ransom." In the context of Israel's sacrificial worship, *padah* referred primarily to the ransoming of the firstborn who belong to God by substituting an animal or money in their place (Exod 13:13; 34:19-20; Num 18:15-18). But when God "ransomed" the Israelites from some enemy, there was never any mention of payment; the verb then meant much the same as "to free" (Deut 7:8, from Egypt; Isa 35:10, from Babylon; Psalm 130:8, from sin).

Historical Traditions. Besides "leading out" or "bringing up" the Israelites from slavery in Egypt, God was said in Deuteronomy to "ransom" them (Deut 9:26; 13:6; 15:15). This was a new way of expressing the idea of liberation, and probably occasioned the further image of divine "redemption." Like a next of kin because of the covenant established with the Israelites, God "redeemed" them from slavery in Egypt (Exod 6:6; 15:13).

Psalms and Wisdom Literature. "Redemption" from Egypt is commemorated in Psalms 74:2; 77:16; 106:10. God is recognized as "redeemer" also in other situations, as liberator from death (Ps 103:4), from "fraud and violence" (Ps 72:14), from enemies (Ps 69:19), in aid of orphans (Prov 23:10-11), of the afflicted who seek divine help (Ps 119:154), and in general (Ps 19:15). In a dramatic expression of hope for vindication and a moment of life after death, Job sees God as his "redeemer" (Job 19:25).

God also "ransomed" from Egypt (Ps 78:42), from enemies (Ps 55:19; 119:134), from "all distress" (Ps 25:22), from dying (Job 5:20; Ps 69:19), and from death, with perhaps the hope of resurrection (Ps 49:9, 16). In a special way, God will "ransom" Israel "from all their iniquities" (Ps 130:8).

Prophets. The return from exile in Babylon (538 BCE) was seen as a new Exodus, and God was hailed "redeemer" (Isa 41:14; 43:14; 49:26). The Israelites were also th-ought to be "ransomed" from Babylon (Isa 35:10; Jer 31:11), but never for a price. Isaiah 52:3 states that no money was paid in the redemption: "You were sold for nothing, and without money you shall be redeemed." Cyrus, the human agent who freed the exiles, did so "without price or ransom" (Isa 45:13).

Redemption of the individual from mortal danger is found in Lamentations 3:58;

the same must be said of Hosea 7:13; 13:14, though 1 Corinthians 15:54f. quotes the latter in a different sense (life after death).

During the Exile Deutero-Isaiah developed the idea of the Suffering Servant, probably a personification of Israel itself, who voluntarily offers his life in vicarious atonement for the sins of others (Isa 52:13–53:12, esp. vv. 6, 12). The same idea can be found in other texts of the OT and Intertestamental period: "Be merciful to your people and let our punishment be a satisfaction on their behalf. Make my blood their purification and take my life as a ransom for theirs" (4 Macc 6:28f.); "Through the blood of these righteous ones and through the propitiation of their death the divine providence rescued Israel" (4 Macc 17:22; see also 2 Macc 7:37f.). These texts prepared the way for a deeper NT understanding of redemption.

New Testament

The death of Jesus on the cross was interpreted variously in the NT; it revealed him as a suffering Messiah (Luke 24:25-27), but it also bore a special soteriological significance. As a Suffering Servant (Isaiah 53), Jesus freely offered his life in vicarious atonement for the sins of others (Mark 10:45). In the OT God had "redeemed" Israel from Egypt and established a covenant in blood; now God "redeemed" all humanity from the power of sin and established a new covenant in the death ("blood"), but also in the life, and indeed in the resurrection, of Jesus. If the forces of evil and sin brought about the death of all humanity, then in Jesus God "redeemed" humanity from the power of those same forces: "[The Father] delivered us from the power of darkness and transferred us to the kingdom of his beloved Son" (Col 1:13). Elsewhere we read that the risen Jesus "delivers us from the coming wrath" (1 Thess 1:10).

Synoptic Gospels. A key text is Mark 10:45: "For the Son of Man did not come to be served but to serve and to give his life as a ransom for many" (par., Matt 20:28). The word "ransom" *(lutron)* is associated with "liberation" or "redemption" *(lutrosis)* and indicates the cost involved in the process of freeing those enslaved. In the Greek secular world "ransom" referred to a sum of money given for the release of prisoners of war, slaves, or booty seized in war, but as in the OT, there is never mention in the NT of anyone to whom the "ransom" would be paid; the focus is on the generous free and loving service of Jesus. Mark 10:45 alludes to the institution of the holy Eucharist, Mark 14:24, "this is my blood . . . shed for many," which itself is an allusion to the Suffering Servant of Isaiah 53:12. The expiatory death of Jesus vicariously for others is here presented as a paradigm for Christians, urging them to love one another as Jesus had loved them, and to be willing to give their lives for their neighbor (see John 15:12-13; 1 John 3:16). Humans were subject to death because of their sins; Jesus became their redeemer, their liberator. The "redemption" spoken of in Luke 1:68 and 2:38 has various levels, hope of political liberation from the Romans, but also liberation from sin through the person of Jesus. In the Our Father concern for liberation from the power of sin is expressed eschatologically: "deliver us from the evil one" (Matt 6:13); "redemption" at the end time in Luke 21:28 is associated with the second coming of Christ, the Son of Man.

Pauline Letters. Romans 3:24-25 states that "all have sinned and are deprived of the glory of God. They are justified freely by his grace through the redemption in Christ Jesus, whom God set forth as an expiation, through faith, by his blood." This means that sinners are put in right relationship with God as a free divine gift; they are liberated from the power of sin ("redeemed") by Christ Jesus; their sin is removed by the vicarious efficacy ("expiation") of the death of Christ, with allusion to the OT Day of Atonement (Leviticus 16). In 1 Corinthians 1:28-31 Paul urges the Christians not to boast, for their new life in Christ Jesus who had become their "re-

demption" is a gift of God; this passage demonstrates the close relationship between the salvific activity of Jesus and of God the Father; also Colossians 1:13-14. Although Christ's redemptive act for the forgiveness of sin is often associated with his death (Eph 1:7; 1 Tim 2:6; Titus 2:14), the emphasis is on his generous gift of self, "the riches of his grace that he lavished upon us" (Eph 1:7), with no mention of coercion or recipient of a ransom.

The definitive and cosmic phase of redemption is expressed in Romans 8:22-23, referring to the "redemption of our bodies" in our resurrection to eternal life. In similar fashion, Ephesians 1:14 speaks of our final "redemption as God's possession," the definitive state of belonging to God.

Hebrews. The idea of Christ as the one mediator between God and ourselves is emphasized in 1 Timothy 2:6 and Hebrews 9:11-15. "He entered once for all into the sanctuary, not with the blood of goats and calves but with his own blood, thus obtaining eternal redemption" (Heb 9:12). This text contrasts the means of mediation between OT and NT. The sacrificial cult of the OT was unable to bring about mediation between God and the human race. Christ "offered himself" to God (Heb 9:14), and in him sinful humanity was transformed into a new humanity, because Christ, as sinless, could present himself before God with assurance of not displeasing him. All of Christ's acts were done in the Spirit, including his death, and so his whole life was a perfect offering acceptable to God. Christ's offering of self consisted in a perfect act of love, as expressed in John 13:1: "he loved them to the end" (see Heb 2:14-18; 4:15-16).

Catholic Epistles. 1 Peter 1:18-19, "you were ransomed from your futile conduct . . . not with silver and gold but with the precious blood of Christ as of a spotless unblemished lamb," focuses once more on the generosity of Christ's redemptive death and alludes to the paschal lamb of Exodus 12:5. Even here no one receives the ransom; "ransomed" means liberated, the general thrust of this concept as it appears in the Bible.

See: ATONEMENT, COVENANT, DAY OF ATONEMENT, LIBERTY, SALVATION

JOSEPH F. WIMMER, O.S.A.

New Testament

The term redemption, which is so meaningful in the OT and in the writings of the Church Fathers, appears relatively rarely in the NT. The OT background is rich in history and significance. The notion of redemption includes the ideas of rescue, liberation, payment of a price (no matter how high), and even sometimes the value of a life with payment in blood. It implies also ownership or responsibility of the redeemer for the redeemed who is now considered dependent, although perhaps undeserving. In the family-centered culture of Israel, the father or eldest male usually represented the redeemer while the children and wives were sometimes placed in situations where they needed to be redeemed. God is portrayed as the redeemer of Israel, the one who rescues Israel from peril, debt, sin, who avenges Israel's foes and continues to acts responsibly and powerfully on Israel's behalf.

The Gospels. In a saying ascribed by Mark to Jesus, the death of the Son of Man is understood as a redemption or "ransom for many" (Mark 10:45). This saying is reminiscent of the role of the Servant of the Lord described by Isaiah (see 42:7; 49:8-13, 22-26). The redeemer is sent to open the eyes of the blind, to bring freedom to prisoners and light to those in darkness. God is "the Lord, the redeemer and the Holy One of Israel" (Isa 49:7). And God sends his servant to be a "light to the nations" so that salvation may "reach to the ends of the earth" (49:6).

The many trials of the just and sinless Servant appear to be a scandal for the faithful and a challenge to God's own justice. But when the redeemer is God's Son, these same trials show the extent of God's care for the people, who are thus "ransomed" from their sins and purchased or redeemed for God (Isa 53:1-13). According to Mark, Jesus predicts his own death and interprets it as a redemption or a liberation of "the many," a phrase denoting the inclusion of the Gentiles as well as Jews in God's plan of salvation.

This ancient saying recorded by Mark is repeated in Matthew, but does not occur in Luke. Nevertheless, it is especially Luke and Paul who most develop the NT notion of redemption, drawing on the OT. In the infancy narrative, Luke portrays Zechariah praising God on the occasion of John's birth: the people of Israel are about to witness their "redemption" (Luke 1:68). Similarly, Anna, the prophetess, gives thanks to God and speaks of what she has witnessed "to all who were awaiting the redemption of Jerusalem" (2:38).

In his eschatological discourse just before the passion, Jesus predicts the ominous signs of the last days, but interprets them very positively for his hearers, saying, "But when these signs begin to happen, stand erect and raise your heads because your redemption is at hand" (Luke 21:28). The disciples walking the road to Emmaus and explaining the events of the previous days to Jesus longingly exclaimed, "we were hoping that he would be the one to redeem Israel" (24:21). Jesus then had to show them how the Scriptures had indeed been fulfilled through these events, including his death.

Paul. It is Paul who further advances the notion of redemption, describing it as the vicarious nature of Jesus' death "for our sins," that is, for our liberation from sin and freedom to live for God. In Galatians, Paul says that "Christ ransomed us from the curse of the law" (3:13), having been "born under the law, to ransom those under the law" (4:4-5). The notion of ransoming or delivery is also conveyed by the Greek term *apolytrosis* found in Romans 3:24; 8:23; 1 Corinthians 1:30; Ephesians 1:7; 4:30; and Colossians 1:14.

Redemption includes the price of Jesus' death as a ransom "for us," and our liberation now to live "for God." So, Romans 3:24 says that all "are justified freely by his grace, through the redemption in Christ Jesus." Drawing on the story of the fall of humankind described in Genesis 3 and the sinful condition that wreaks havoc in all creation, Paul refers to the awaited eschatological fulfillment of the promises uttered even before the curse (see Gen 3:15). He says in Romans 8:22-23, "We know that all creation is groaning in labor pains even until now; and not only that, but we ourselves, who have the firstfruits of the Spirit, we also groan within ourselves as we wait for adoption, the redemption of our bodies."

Although nowhere in the NT is Christ called "Redeemer," Paul speaks of him in 1 Corinthians 1:30 as one "who became for us wisdom from God, as well as righteousness, sanctification and redemption." This redemption or ransom involves the "forgiveness of transgressions" (Eph 1:7; Col 1:14), so that now we are free to live without sin. Yet the fulfillment of our liberation can only be realized on the coming "day of redemption" (Eph 4:30).

The Deutero-Pauline Letters. Similarly the author of the Letter to Titus reminds us that "we await the blessed hope, the appearance of the glory of the great God and of our savior Jesus Christ, who gave himself for us to deliver us [*lytrosetai,* lit. "redeem us"] from all lawlessness and to cleanse for himself a people as his own, eager to do what is good" (2:13-14).

According to the author of Hebrews, the fact that Jesus, the high priest, is also himself the offering in blood, demonstrates the superiority of the new covenant over the old. By "his own blood" (Heb 9:12), Jesus won an eternal redemption, not a renewable sacrifice: "For this reason he is mediator of a new covenant: since a death has taken place for deliverance from transgressions under the first covenant, those who are called may receive the promised eternal inheritance" (Heb 9:15).

Conclusion. Perhaps some of the Fathers of the Church over-allegorized the image of Christ the Redeemer, pushing too far some aspects of this notion. The question of ransom could cause one to ask to whom the price was paid as well as who would demand such a price. If, for example, ransom is owed to Satan, one may wonder how he had become so powerful, and why forgiveness is so easily granted by Jesus in the Gospels; and if demanded by God, we may wonder how this is consistent with the God of mercy portrayed throughout the Scriptures.

Redemption itself is a very mercy-full concept. The biblical person always expects God to work in his or her life, to intervene on his or her behalf, whenever necessary. And it is frequently necessary since the biblical person is often powerless and dependent only on God. Redemption addresses the real needs of those who are defenseless, who have been disenfranchised and who long for salvation although they do not think of themselves as "deserving" salvation. Redemption is the sure intervention of an all-powerful God who has come to save. Both God's power and will to use it to save the powerless are reliable certainties from a biblical viewpoint.

See: GOD, JUSTICE, SALVATION, SERVANT, SIN

MARY ANN GETTY

Pastoral-Liturgical Tradition

Redemption is one of the chief ways of speaking about God's activity in Christ. In redemption, Christ has freed us from bondage and brought us back into communion with God. In the use of the term in the Pauline letters, it means freeing from the bondage of slavery. In the course of the Christian tradition the two dimensions of redemption, bondage and the emancipated state, have been construed in various ways. The state of bondage has been described as sin, death, the devil, darkness, the world, the flesh, or oppression. The emancipated state has been described as forgiveness, righteousness, new life, eternal life, light, divine heirship, or liberation. From these enumerations one can get the sense of the variety of different ways our bondage is imagined, and the kinds of possibilities that the emancipated state present.

The Church has never made solemn pronouncements on how we are to understand redemption in any fixed ways, but there are certain elements that need to be present in any talk about redemption. First of all, redemption is the work of God, not something that we humans can do or achieve or merit. This work is done through the agency of Jesus Christ—through his incarnation, his life and ministry, but especially through his death and resurrection. While redemption has been won for us in Christ, we do not experience its fulfillment entirely in this earthly life; full redemption will be manifest with the coming of God's reign. The posture of the Christian toward God's offer of salvation is one of faith.

In the contemporary period, reflection has focused upon expressing redemption in terms appropriate to human experience today, terms that are more holistic, and terms that speak both of present and of future realities. Thus feminist theologians have suggested that the sin from which we are redeemed—mainly pride and disobedience—reflect a male-centered view. The experience of women has often been a lack of self-esteem and submission. These are the sins from which women must be redeemed. Karl Rahner tried to explore the nature and experience of human freedom.

To other theologians talk of the redemption of our souls or of individuals has seemed too narrow a focus. We are embodied beings who are constituted as individuals in communities and in societies. The totality of our realities have to be taken into account. Feminist theologians again have taken the lead in speaking of the redemption of our whole selves, including our bodies. Edward Schillebeeckx in his concept of our "well-being" tries to mediate both embodiment and our sociohistorical relatedness.

It has been especially liberation theologians who have examined the social and political structures of oppression and seek out the redemptive action of God in the concrete present time. They have been on occasion accused of neglecting the spiritual side of redemption and focusing too much on the here and now, but they have provided an important corrective to a sometimes spiritualized and other-worldly view of redemption.

See: ATONEMENT, JUSTIFICATION, LIBERTY, SALVATION

ROBERT J. SCHREITER, C.PP.S.

REIGN OF GOD/REIGN OF HEAVEN

A motif with deep roots in biblical history and Jewish theology, the expression "reign of God" would ultimately become a central metaphor within Jesus' preaching and take on multiple meanings with Christian tradition.

Old Testament

The closest the OT comes to this phrase is the expression "the reign of the LORD" and related phrases in some of the latest material in the OT (1 Chr 17:14; 28:5; 29:11; 2 Chr 13:8) where its reference is an idealized Israel or a restored Davidic kingship. In numerous passages, however, Israelite writers gave their God the title "king." The metaphor represents Israel's beliefs about its God in relation to both history and nature.

The OT God is king of history, having freed the Hebrew slaves from political bondage in Egypt, adopted them as his people in the Sinai covenant, and given them a homeland in Israel. Other passages portray a warrior God, performing a central duty of ancient Near Eastern rulers, destroying enemies or leading armies in battle. The destruction of Jerusalem and its Temple, the demise of its kingship, the exile of the upper classes, and the return of some Jews to Jerusalem a generation later are all interpreted as evidence that this God controls not only Israel's history but also the histories of other nations.

Israel's God is also king of creation, establishing and maintaining order in the universe and using natural phenomena (e.g., winter rains, locust, drought) to bless or punish Israel or Israel's enemies. This aspect of divine kingship may be rooted in ancient Mesopotamian creation mythology where a divine kingship may be rooted in ancient Mesopotamian creation mythology where a divine warrior destroys forces of chaos hostile to a new order he is establishing (e.g., *Enuma Elish*) or in Canaanite mythology where gods and goddesses are responsible for the alternating seasons of desiccation and regeneration that make up the Palestinian agricultural cycle (the Baal myths). The successful beginning of a new agricultural year, sufficient winter rains, heralded the divine king's continued defeat of death and disorder for another year so that the economic and political order could continue.

In a similar fashion, some of the Israel's "Enthronement Psalms" (e.g., Psalms 93; 95–99), with their refrain "The LORD has become king" or "The LORD reigns," link kingship, creation, and history. Psalm 93 asserts that "the Lord reigns . . . he has made the world firm; it shall never be moved" (vv. 1-2). Psalm 97 connects God's rule over non-Israelite nations with God's efforts on Israel's behalf, declaring, "All who worship graven things are put to shame, who glory in empty things" (v. 7). The psalms also connect the Davidic monarchy and God's reign over Israel. In fact, the successful coronation of a new king announced God's enduring victory over political disorder (Psalm 2). This new king was tangible evidence that God remained with the people (e.g., the throne name Immanuel, "God is with us").

Other OT traditions, however, indicate a different view. The king, like everyone else, was clearly subject to divine law (Deut 17:14-20). Furthermore, the themes of opposition to the very establishment of the monarchy (1 Sam 8:1-18), the critical commentaries on individual kings in Samuel (2 Samuel 11–12) and Kings (1 Kings 11; 12; 21; 2 Kings 21), the prophetic indictments against those courts for their domestic policies (Amos; Jeremiah 27; 34) and excessive life-styles (Isaiah 10) indicate

that, in the eyes of the theologians who compiled most of the OT after the Babylonian exile, the Lord's reign was not necessarily dependent upon the old Davidic kingship (Obad 17–21). Others (Amos 9:11; Jer 23:5-6) hoped for a restoration of that kingship in the person of an ideal figure who would launch a true reign of God. This divine reign, a symbol for a glorious historical future for Israel, marked by political security and economic prosperity for those Jews faithful to God, would appear at some future time (Isa 43:14-21; 52:7-10; Zeph 3:14-16). In the Book of Daniel (ca. 165 BCE), for example, God, the Ancient of Days, establishes the book's first-century BCE audience as an eternal, earthly kingdom and confers on "the Holy Ones of the Most High" a personification of that audience, an everlasting heavenly kingdom to which all other earthly kingdoms are subjected (7:9-14).

KATHLEEN S. NASH

New Testament

The imminent kingdom or reign of God is the central message of Jesus from the beginning of his public ministry to the Last Supper. At the beginning he says: "Repent, for the kingdom of heaven is at hand" (Matt 4:17). At the end he says: "I shall not drink this fruit of the vine until the day when I drink it with you new in the kingdom of my Father" (Matt 26:29).

In many respects the expression "kingdom of God" is original with Jesus. No other biblical teacher makes it the center of his message. It is true that the OT frequently speaks of God as king. Indeed, the Book of Daniel not only portrays God as the Ancient of Days giving the kingdom to the Son of Man (Dan 7:13-14), but also makes the kingdom the theme of the entire work. This passage doubtless influenced Jesus; it further induced early Christians to think of Jesus as the Son of Man sent from the Father to bring the kingdom to his people.

The term *basileia/malkut* in the Bible has two references: it refers to the political government of a territory (as in modern English), or to the personal activity of ruling by a king, which may also be called a king's reign. It is important to retain both connotations. The territorial sense makes the term concrete and earthly. The personal sense is a reminder that this kingdom is God's.

Mark. Tracing the term through a single Gospel, Mark, provides a sense of the manner in which Jesus employed the concept. His first public preaching runs: "This is the time of fulfillment. The kingdom of God is at hand. Repent, and believe in the gospel" (Mark 1:15). This kingdom constitutes the content and the purpose of the parables (Mark 4:11, 26, 30). It is the goal of death and the motive for ethical practice (Mark 9:1, 47). It must be approached as a child and is far from the rich (Mark 10:14-15, 23-25). One who knows that the great commandment is to love is near to it (Mark 12:34). The Eucharistic meal anticipates it and looks forward to it (Mark 14:25). The man who takes care of the dead body of Jesus is one who seeks the kingdom (Mark 15:43). Thus the kingdom of God is the ultimate horizon of the preaching of Jesus, the highest value, the goal of history, and a symbol of eternity.

Matthew. In Matthew the meaning of the kingdom of God in the preaching of Jesus may be listed under five characteristics. First, the kingdom of God is a social reality; it is not individualistic. This is evident from an analysis of the term. A kingdom is a territory and a people over which a king rules, a society ordered by a king; the kingdom is something one enters (Matt 5:20; 7:21).

Second, the kingdom preached by Jesus is intended to be an earthly as well as a heavenly political reality. Thus he teaches the prayer: "your kingdom come, your will be done, on earth as in heaven" (Matt 6:10). His will is a will for justice and peace: "But seek first the kingdom [of God] and his righteousness" (Matt 6:33).

Third, the kingdom of God is personalistic, not tyrannical or insensitive. It respects human dignity and the need for human rights and political freedom: "the kingdom of God is among you" (Luke 17:21).

Fourth, the kingdom is universal, intended to all men and women, all peoples and nations: "make disciples of all nations" (Matt 28:19). All are invited to the feast (Matt 22:9). All stand under judgment (Matt 25:32).

Fifth, the kingdom of God is God's kingdom. In this sense it is connected with spiritual life and religious faith. It is a divine gift of grace, i.e., it cannot be dissolved into purely human political arrangements. The best short definition of the kingdom is by Paul: "For the kingdom of God is . . . righteousness, peace, and joy in the holy Spirit" (Rom 14:17).

The kingdom is Jesus' future hope and promise for this world just as the resurrection is the hope he offers for the next world, for heaven. This is why he prayed, "Your kingdom come."

Matthew and Luke have added their own redactional developments to the more primitive depiction of Jesus in Mark and the Q tradition. The phrase, "kingdom of God" or "kingdom of the heavens" occurs 104 times in the Synoptic Gospels: fifty-one times in Matthew, fourteen times in Mark, and thirty-nine times in Luke. From these statistics it is plain that Matthew had a special interest in this theme. Indeed, one could unify the entire content of his Gospel by means of this theme, especially as it is related to the Christological theme of Jesus as king or royal Messiah.

An example of this systematizing tendency can be seen in the parables. Although both Mark (4:26, 30) and Luke (13:18, 20) each contain two parables about the kingdom, it is Matthew above all who gives the impression that the parables of Jesus were usually cast in the form, "the Kingdom of heaven is like . . ." (13:24, 31, 33, 44, 45, 47; 18:23; 20:1; 22:2; 25:1), ten times in all. He does this because it makes the sometimes homely parables more dignified in tone, in keeping with his royal Christology; because of his fondness for stereotyped, easily learnable formulae; and because, along with the story of Jesus as the Christ, the kingdom is his unifying theme.

The last and greatest of Matthew's parables of the kingdom, the parable of the sheep and the goats (25:31-46), illustrates another of the evangelist's redactional emphases, namely, right conduct as a condition for entrance to the kingdom: "Then the king will say to those on his right, come you who are blessed by my Father. Inherit the kingdom prepared for you from the foundation of the world. For I was hungry and you gave me food, I was thirsty and you gave me drink, a stranger and you welcomed me, naked and you clothed me, ill and you cared for me, in prison and you visited me" (25:34-36). It is not that Matthew is legalistic or lacking in compassion for sinners. What he is concerned about is warning Christians against complacency and encouraging them to live their faith.

Still another aspect of Matthew's theology of the kingdom is his explicit attempt to relate it to the post-Easter reality of the Church. He does this most directly in the famous "You are Peter" passage (16:17-19). These verses assert that there is a connection between Church and kingdom, that leaders in the Church hold the keys to the kingdom and, implicitly, that our relationship to them has some bearing on our eternal destiny. The Church is not the kingdom, nor is it heaven, but it is the path to them, that is, a gathering of those who look forward to them. As for ministry, there are eunuchs for the sake of the kingdom (19:12), children are welcome (19:14), but the rich will enter it with difficulty (19:23-24). The entrance to it is shut by the scribes and Pharisees (23:13), but the harlots and sinners will enter it ahead of them (21:31).

Luke. One feature of Luke's handling of the kingdom theme is its relation to preaching. There are seven passages in his Gospel (4:43; 8:1; 9:2, 11, 60, 62; 16:16) that have the character of general summaries wherein the kingdom of God is presented as the object of preaching. These passages are quite general, even vague, as to when or how the kingdom

will be concretely realized. Some authors understand the kingdom in these cases as meaning the Christian Church, others as Christian preaching and teaching, but many others as the eschatological reign of God. Probably the best understanding of the matter is that while in these cases the kingdom does refer to the future reign, there is also a strong concern in Luke that the preaching of the kingdom contain an appeal to the hearers to make a present decision of faith. But that the kingdom is central and the ultimate goal of the early Christian mission becomes magnificently plain in the very last verse of Acts, which speaks of Paul in Rome, the heart of the empire, where "with complete assurance and without hindrance he proclaimed the kingdom of God and taught about the Lord Jesus Christ" (28:31).

John. The kingdom theme is replaced by the concept of eternal life in the Gospel of John. The two concepts had already been linked in the Synoptic Gospels (e.g., Mark 9:43-47; Matt 25:34, 46). The kingdom emerges at only two points in John. In the dialogue with Nicodemus, Jesus insists on a rebirth in baptism and the holy Spirit as a condition for entering (or seeing) the kingdom (John 3:1-5). In the Revised Standard Version text of John 18:36, Jesus says: "My kingship is not of this world; if my kingship were of this world, my servants would fight, that I might not be handed over to the Jews; but my kingship is not from the world." This common translation gives the casual reader the impression that Jesus' kingship has nothing to do with this world, but in fact the Greek text shows that it has no other meaning than the common Synoptic doctrine, since the Greek preposition is *ek*, meaning from. Thus, the verse should read: "My kingdom is not of this world. . . ." That is, it does not come from here, does not originate here, a possibility directly taught and prayed for in the Synoptics.

The danger of the RSV translation lies in the fact that it tends to diffuse the powerful promise of Jesus for this world into a purely heavenly, mystical, and spiritual idea of the kingdom. Another frequently abused passage, often twisted to justify social injustice and indifference to the poor, is Jesus' reply during the anointing at Bethany: "The poor you will always have with you" (Matt 26:11). The corrective appears in the earliest form of the story (Mark 14:7) and in its OT source (Deut 15:11).

Paul. It could appear that the kingdom is not an important theme for Paul since the term occurs only fourteen times in his letters. But we should remember that in studying Paul's eschatology we must notice his use of the verb, "to reign," as well as the noun. It will then be seen that the kingdom forms the apocalyptic horizon of Paul's every thought (excepting 2 Corinthians) as much as it is true for Jesus and the Synoptic Gospels.

In his earliest letters, Paul speaks in terms of God's invitation to the kingdom and of our required conduct in order to be worthy of an invitation (1 Thess 2:12; 2 Thess 1:5). In other words, the kingdom functions as the basis of ethical exhortation. A series of later texts continues this approach by speaking of evil-doers who will not inherit the kingdom (1 Cor 6:9-10; 15:50; Gal 5:21; Eph 5:5; see Jas 2:5). In 1 Corinthians 4:8, Paul ironically teases those Christians who think that they are already living in the full realization of the kingdom of God on earth and are thus "reigning" with Christ. Paul needs to expose this view as a monumental illusion in order to save the early churches from the pomposity and folly to which that view usually leads.

In 1 Corinthians 4:20, Paul coins the immortal line: "For the kingdom of God is not a matter of talk but of power." The enthusiasts of Corinth have become inflated with a baseless pride and so need to be brought down to earth. By contrast with their over-realized eschatology, Paul expresses his own nuanced view that the Christian stands at present "between the times" (Rom 5:14, 17, 21). Christ has overcome death, but the Christian does not yet reign with Christ. That remains for the future, as is evident from verse 17: "For if, by the transgression

of one person, death came to reign through that one, how much more will those who receive the abundance of grace and of the gift of justification come to reign in life through the one man Jesus Christ." As we have noted above, Paul defines the moral content of the kingdom in Romans 14:17 as "righteousness, peace and joy in the holy Spirit."

In Colossians 1:13, God is said to have transferred us to the kingdom of his beloved Son, presumably here meaning the Church. In Colossians 4:11, an unusual formula appears: "my co-workers for the kingdom of God. . . ." This is an important but potentially dangerous phrase. Positively, it shows that Paul thought that Christians (and others) could work for the coming of the kingdom. The danger is that Christians may begin to identify their current project too easily with the kingdom. They may begin to speak of their own "building" of the kingdom. (This word incidentally never occurs in the Bible in connection with the kingdom.) This amounts to the error of Pelagianism (that we can save ourselves) and causes the kingdom to cease to be fully God's. These errors become not only theoretical but practical when Christians, for example, identify a particular political regime or system with the kingdom. In this connection, the best we can do is to prepare the way of the Lord (Matt 3:3) and to hasten the day of God (2 Pet 3:12), but not build the kingdom.

This kingdom is unshakable (Heb 12:28) and eternal (2 Pet 1:11). James asks: "Did not God choose those who are poor in the world to be rich in faith and heirs of the kingdom. . . ?" (2:5). It is out of our poverty, not our strength, that we will receive it, though we must continue, through trial and error and struggle, to be co-workers for it.

Revelation. The Book of Revelation returns to the OT ideal of a priestly kingdom (1:6; 5:10), based on Exodus 19:6 and Isaiah 61:6. By contrast, there are the kingdoms that have been given over to the Beast (16:10; 17:12, 17, 18). This realm of the great

Adversary is similar to the "kingdom of Satan" in the Gospels (Mark 3:25 and parallels; Luke 4:6) and related to the Johannine idea of the "ruler of this world" (John 12:31; 14:30; 16:11; see also Eph 2:2; Luke 22:53; Col 1:13). After the angel Michael defeats Satan in the cosmic battle there is a song of victory that includes the verse: "Now have salvation and power come, and the kingdom of our God and the authority of his Anointed" (Rev 12:10). A similar idea is found in 11:15: "The kingdom of the world now belongs to our Lord and to his Anointed, and he will reign forever and ever."

The most important kingdom text in Revelation concerns the millennium, that is, the thousand-year reign of the martyred saints on earth with Christ (Rev 20:1-10). Curiously the noun "kingdom" does not occur in this passage. The weight is carried by the verb in the two key verses. In verse 4, the saints "came to life and they reigned with Christ for a thousand years." In verse 6, "they will be priests of God and of Christ, and they will reign with him for [the] thousand years." This passage teaches that, after the return or arrival of Christ in glory, these saints will reign on earth for a millennium with him, in a kingdom of peace and justice. This will take place on the threshold between history and eternity, but on this side of the boundary. It would represent an intra-historical fulfillment of God's plan for God's people in this world, a world that is God's creation, fallen and redeemed.

What should we think of this vision and promise? If God is indeed the lord of history, he must bring history to fulfillment before its end. The question of the exact number of years may be left, in the light of 2 Peter 3:8, to pious speculation. But the seriousness with which Jesus, Paul, and John preached the kingdom of God, as well as the anguished need of the world for justice, peace, and joy, would seem to require some kind of early realization of the divine plan, notwithstanding all the philosophical and moral obstacles to such a plan. With heaven, then, the kingdom of God on earth remains part of the larger horizon of hope in the Scriptures.

See: CHURCH, ESCHATOLOGY, HOPE, JUSTICE, LIFE, MESSIAH, PARABLE, PEACE, SON OF MAN

BENEDICT T. VIVIANO, O.P.

Pastoral-Liturgical Tradition

The biblical metaphor of the "reign of God" has had a complex history in post-biblical Christianity. The tradition commonly translates the term as "kingdom" or as "rule" of God. Specific meanings given to the metaphor are conditioned by political and philosophical circumstances of particular periods of history.

Early Non-political Interpretations. Around the turn of the first century CE, the prayer of the Didache expressed an urgent sense of near-expectation similar to the scriptural apocalyptic texts when it prayed that the Lord might gather the Church from the four winds into the reign of God (Didache 10,5ff.). This apocalyptic sense is totally absent from the later formulation of Origen, who described Christ himself as the very reign of God in person *(autobasileia)*. Here the reign of God symbolizes a spiritual condition that can be identified with the presence in human life of virtues such as wisdom, justice, and truth. In his attempt to move away from a belief in the thousand-year reign of Christ on earth, Augustine *(City of God,* 20,7-10) allegorized the apocalyptic symbolism of the tradition in such a way that the "thousand-year reign" of Revelation 20:4ff. is identified with the historical time of the Church stretching from Christ's first coming to his return at the end of history. All true members of the Church can be said to be already "in the kingdom" at least in a limited sense. But in its fullest sense, the "kingdom" symbolizes the fullest perfection of that community of love (the city of God) that has been brought about in the course of Church history.

Politicized Interpretations. The tendency to interpret metaphors such as rule, reign, and kingdom in terms of political realities surfaced more clearly in the Constantinian Church. Important for later history is the tendency to associate a period of political peace with the presence or anticipation of God's reign and the tendency to see the "mon-archy" of the empire as a reflection of the rule of the only God (mono-theism). The implications of this conjunction of monarchy and monotheism would remain with Christianity for centuries and would play a signif-icant role in the theological assessments of the political revolutions that replaced monarchical forms of government with vari-ous republican and democratic forms in the modern world. Also, the tendency to sim-plify the Augustinian vision would lead to a naive identification of the Church as the kingdom of God on earth. This would be corrected by Vatican II's clear vision of the Church as the historical instrument of the kingdom and not the kingdom in itself (Dog-matic Constitution on the Church, no. 7).

Modern Interpretations. While originally a religious metaphor, the idea of a "king-dom" appears in a secularized form in the philosophy of Karl Marx and in much con-temporary utopian thought. It symbolizes that future condition in which the painful dialectic of historical experience will be brought to a peaceful resolution. While the biblical tradition had emphasized the role of God, the secularized vision emphasizes the role of human beings in creating this utopian situation. Various forms of "political theology" and "liberation theology" cur-rently attempt to relate the divine and the human dimensions in some form of dialecti-cal framework that does not identify the rule of God with particular political or ecclesias-tical configurations and yet argues for the positive importance of human engagement in the social and political orders. While the "reign of God" cannot be directly translated into any specific political or ecclesiastical program, it elicits a vision of a future in the light of which present political and ecclesial reality may be critiqued.

ZACHARY HAYES, O.F.M.

REMEMBRANCE

Old Testament

In the OT, the process of remembering is ac-tive, personal, and rooted in a relationship that may be positive or negative. For exam-ple, Abigail asks David to remember her when he becomes the leader of Israel (1 Sam 25:31). David's subsequent marriage proposal (vv. 40-43) fulfills that request. Abimelek asks the citizens of Shechem to "re-member that I am your own flesh and blood" (Judg 9:2). They respond by financing the assassination of all his half-brothers ex-cept Jotham. To the high priest Jonathan, Demetrius writes about Alexander, the son of Antiochus Epiphanes, "Let us be the first to make peace with him . . . since he will remem-ber all the wrongs we have done to him" (1 Macc 10:4-5). In the first two instances, the plea for remembrance carries with it an im-plied request for a response that benefits or advances the cause of the speaker. In the last instance, an offer of peace is intended to neu-tralize future revenge for past behavior.

As these examples indicate, remembrance is not, in itself, a purely religious activity. Nonetheless, given the peculiar concerns of most of the literature in the OT, the vocab-ulary of remembrance ("to remember," "memorial," "token offering") occurs most often in a theological context.

Divine Remembrance. Psalm 88:6 sug-gests that being remembered by God is a metaphor for being alive, since the dead are those "whom you remember no longer." Elsewhere, God's remembrance is double edged. It can bring blessing or misfortune. When God remembers Noah (Gen 8:1), the flood waters recede and order reemerges from chaos. God's remembrance of Rachel and Hannah opens their wombs so they bear sons (Gen 30:22; 1 Sam 1:11, 19-20). Samson's strength is renewed so he can de-stroy the Philistines assembled in their tem-ple because God remembers him (Judg 16:28-30).

Similarly, when God remembers the covenant (Exod 2:23-25; Ps 105:5-11; Ezek

16:60; 1 Chr 16:15), he removes whatever obstacles prevent the realization of its promises. That remembrance is objectified in the defeat of the Egyptians and the Exodus from Egypt so that the Hebrew slaves can become God's people and possess the land (Ps 105:42-45). In Exodus 32:13-14 and Deuteronomy 9:27-29, remembering the ancestors overrides God's anger about the Golden Calf. Nehemiah asks God to consider the promises over the people's disobedience, to accept their repentance, and to bring them back to Jerusalem (Neh 1:8-10; see Bar 2:34-35). Mordecai interprets Haman's destruction as evidence that God "has remembered his people and rendered justice to his inheritance" (Esth VF:9). When God remembers his mercy, his loving kindness, his compassion (Ps 25:6), he acts with these qualities and makes them effective in his dealings with human beings (cf. Jer 31:20).

For this reason, remembrance plays an important role in the prayers of Israel, especially in the psalms. There God is asked to remember and act appropriately toward the king (Pss 20:4; 106:4), the enemies of the speaker (Ps 9:13) or of Israel itself (Ps 137:7). In taking action, the psalmists ask God to remember, i.e., to take into account, Israel's lowly status (Pss 89:48; 103:14), God's own mercy (Ps 98:3); similarly, he should not remember sin (Ps 89:51).

God's remembering can also bring destruction. The plea that the Lord remember the guilt of the ancestors of an oppressor is a plea for the punishment of that individual (Ps 109:14; see 1 Macc 7:38; 2 Macc 8:1-4). Hosea warns that when the Lord remembers the guilt of Israel, he will punish the northern kingdom and return the people to the slavery of Egypt (Hos 8:13; cf. 9:9). Jeremiah connects the destruction done by the Babylonians to the Lord remembering that the people had offered incense in Jerusalem (Jer 44:20-21). Ben Sira teaches that "the vengeful will suffer the Lord's vengeance, for he remembers their sin in detail" (Sir 28:1).

Similarly, the Lord's failure to remember sin means that those sins are forgiven (Isa 43:25-26; Jer 31:34). Thus the psalmist prays, "Remember not against us the iniquities of the past; may your compassion quickly come to us for we are brought very low" (Ps 79:8).

Human Remembrance. Just as God is expected to express his remembrance in right action, so, too, Israel is encouraged to remember what the Lord has done on its behalf (1 Chr 16:12; Pss 77:12-13; 105:4-5) as the basis for its worship and its covenant living.

This is particularly true in the book of Deuteronomy where Israel's remembrance of the Lord, perhaps in the form of periodical narration of God's saving acts, approaches an act of worship. The content of this remembrance is the past (Deut 32:7), Israel's enslavement in Egypt (Deut 15:15; 16:12; 24:18, 22), the Exodus (Deut 5:15; 11:1-9), God's care and nourishment during the wilderness journey (Deut 8:2-4). Remembrance of the experience of slavery in Egypt is motivation for protecting the rights of the stranger, the orphan, and the widow (Deut 24:17-18); for leaving a portion of the crop unharvested in the field and vineyard (Deut 24:22); for observing the law of release of slaves during the Sabbatical year (Deut 15:15); and for keeping the Sabbath (Deut 5:15).

Deuteronomy emphasizes remembrance because this activity is directly related to obedience. When Israel did not remember the Lord, it broke the covenant (Isa 57:11). This failure to remember was rebellion (Ps 106:7) that brought punishment (Ezek 16:43) and disaster (Isa 17:10).

This emphasis on remembrance is found throughout the OT. Many psalms catalogue God's wondrous deeds (e.g., Psalms 18; 44; 78). Nehemiah's prayer mentions these deeds (Neh 9:6-15). This suggests that such remembering was a central activity of the cult; it formed the basis for thanksgiving and nourished the faith of Israel that in moments of national crises, particularly the postexilic period, God might intervene again in similar ways. It strengthened confidence in the Lord (Deut 8:18-19; Josh 1:13) and in divine providence (Deut 8:2) and restored hope (Lam 3:21). Remembrance of God's goodness in conjunction with sinfulness brought confusion and disgust, especially in Ezekiel (Ezek 6:9; 16:60-63; 20:43-44; 36:31-32), and could lead to conversion (Ps 22:28-30; Jer 51:50; Bar 2:33; Zech 10:9).

The Wisdom tradition recognized that remembrance is important for living well in society and family. Tobit and his son Tobiah exemplify Deuteronomy's theology of remembrance; in his deathbed speech, Tobit advises Tobiah to command his children "to be mindful of God" (Tob 14:9). Ben Sira frequently urged his students to remember their inevitable death in order to cultivate the virtue proper to the wise (Sir 7:36; 14:12; 28:6; 38:22; 41:3). For the Preacher, such remembrance brought the command, "Therefore, rejoice in life" (Qoh 11:8-9).

Memorials. To ensure that the Lord remembers and pays attention at times of worship, Israel is commanded to sound the trumpet (Lev 23:24; Num 10:10). Inscribed on the breastplate of decision worn by the high priest are the names of the tribes of Israel (Exod 28:12). In Isaiah 62:6, watchers on the walls of Jerusalem remind the Lord to restore Jerusalem and bring the exiles home. In the Priestly tradition, "token offerings" burned with incense make the individual present to the Lord in their sweet smell (Lev 2:2, 9, 16; 5:15; 6:8; 24:7; Num 5:26). Similarly, tassels on clothing recall the obligation of obedience to the law (Num 15:37-40). The pilgrimage feasts, i.e., Passover, Unleavened Bread, and Weeks, enshrine the memory of God's saving deeds and allow each generation to participate in their effects.

New Testament

The use of remembrance in the NT is much the same as in the OT. The birth of Jesus of Nazareth is evidence that God has remembered, i.e., fulfilled, the promises made to Israel's ancestors (Luke 1:54-55, 69-75). As in Leviticus, prayers and good deeds remind God to act favorably (Acts 10:4, 31). The author of Hebrews uses OT passages that connect forgiveness of sin with God's failure to remember them (Heb 8:12; 10:7). Where the enemies of the people are concerned, however, God's remembrance of their wickedness means judgment and destruction (Rev 16:19; 18:5).

Here, too, human remembrance completes itself in action. Immediately after his denial, Peter remembers the words of Jesus and is overcome with grief (Matt 26:75; Mark 14:72; Luke 22:61-62). Christians should remember their teachers (1 Thess 2:9; Col 4:18); they should pray for and imitate them (Heb 13:7). Jesus himself commends the nameless woman who anoints him in preparation for his enthronement upon the cross as Messiah (Matt 26:13; Mark 14:8-9); her memorial is the gospel, remembered in preaching and right living.

Just as Israel is commanded to remember the saving deeds of its God and live properly, so the early Christians are encouraged to remember the life and preaching of Jesus, delivered in the gospel preached by the apostles, especially Paul. Paul praises the believers at Corinth because "you remember me in everything and hold fast to the traditions, just as I handed them on to you" (1 Cor 11:2). Here remembrance of Paul means adherence to the gospel as he preached it as well as imitation of him (cf. 1 Cor 4:17; Jude 5). In Galatians 2:10, the command to remember the poor is met by taking up a collection for the Christian community at Jerusalem. Elsewhere, believers are urged to remember "these things, even though you already know them" (2 Pet 1:12-13), "the words previously spoken by the holy prophets and the commandments of the Lord and savior through your apostles" (2 Pet 3:2), "Jesus Christ raised from the dead" (2 Tim 2:8). Such remembrance compels each community to rededicate itself to the correct gospel preached by its apostles and to live by the demands of that preaching (Acts 20:35).

Although Jesus urged his disciples to remember in order to understand the purpose of his preaching and his miracles, authentic understanding occurs only after his resurrection. Thus, the two apostles on the road to Emmaus gain new insight into the teaching of Jesus from their encounter with the risen Christ (Luke 24:5-9). This motif occurs several times in the Gospel of John. For example, the narrator notes that "when he was raised from the dead," his disciples remembered Jesus' saying, "Destroy this temple and in three days I will raise it up" and understood its true meaning (John 2:19-22; cf. 12:16; 16:4). Such understanding is unique to the Christian community; it is the work of the Spirit who "will teach you everything and remind you of all that [I] told you" (John 14:26).

The memory of what Jesus of Nazareth did and preached is maintained not only in the activity of the apostles and in the everyday life of the Christian community. Encounter with the risen Christ and the opportunity to believe and understand his life and message more fully is available to the community each time it obeys his command delivered at the meal he celebrated with his apostles the night before he died: "Do this in memory of me" (Matt 26:26-28; Luke 22:17-20; 1 Cor 11:23-26; cf. Mark 14:22-23). This breaking of bread and sharing of wine, like Israel's Passover, is the remembrance of God's saving power manifested in Jesus the Christ; it makes that power present and available to the celebrating community.

See: BLESSING, EUCHARIST, WORSHIP

KATHLEEN S. NASH

Basic to the NT use of remembrance as a noun *(anamnesis, hupomnesis)* or the action of calling to mind, remembering *(anamimnesko, mimnesko)* is the underlying understanding of the Jewish concept of *zikkaron:* the notion of remembering in such a way as to make a past event a present experience by means of words and actions—to re-actualize what has already taken place. Also basic to *anamnesis* is the simultaneous evocation of the past, present, and future dimensions of human reality. Those who "make memorial"—especially with others in the context of religious ritual like the Passover—not only call the past into the present, but in doing so are affected by that past in such a way that their future is also changed.

In the NT, the use of *anamnesis* or memorial finds paradigmatic expression in the Pauline and Lucan accounts of the Last Supper when Jesus gives God thanks, breaks bread, and shares wine in the context of a Passover celebration. By identifying his body and blood with these elements and by commanding his disciples to "do this in memory *[anamnesis]* of me" (see 1 Cor 11:24-25; Luke 22:19), Jesus reinterpreted the Passover celebration that commemorated God's dramatic intervention in human history by freeing Israel from slavery and death in Egypt described in the Book of Exodus. Now, to this celebration of God's liberation-in-history of Israel is added another event that, like the Exodus, is to be remembered in such a way that the event has relevance to the present moment—the suffering, death, and resurrection of Jesus commemorated by sharing a sacred meal. Like the Passover, which makes real God's merciful dealings with Israel for each generation—each time Jesus' suffering, death, and resurrection is recalled in this ritual meal, Christ's work of redemption is made accessible to all subsequent believers no matter how separated they are by time and place from the historical event—and calls disciples of every age to a more faithful witness to this paschal mystery by their witness to God's love through their own suffering until the end of time, when Christ will come in glory. It is this on-going, ethical dimension of Eucharistic remembrance that Paul describes in 1 Corinthians 11:26: "For as often as you eat this bread and drink the cup, you proclaim the death of the Lord until he comes."

While remembering is described in the NT as an important human activity, this action is also something predicated of God in continuity with the use of the concept of remembrance in the OT. The NT also reflects the characteristic Jewish petition asking God "to remember" God's mercy and God's people, i.e., asking God to continue to care for the people and not to forget them, since God's forgetting would be tantamount to letting Israel slide into oblivion. Thus we see in Mary's song of praise in Luke 1:54 "He [God] has helped Israel his servant, remembering his mercy." God's remembering of us guarantees our future. Some scholars have suggested that Jesus' command at the Last Supper (do this in memory of me) could also be understood in the sense that his disciples should pray so that "God may remember me."

Pastoral-Liturgical Tradition

Liturgical Remembrance—The Paschal Mystery. The idea of formal ritual remembrance or *anamnesis* inherited from the Scriptures continues to be an important part of our understanding of the dynamics of worship. The Constitution on the Sacred Liturgy makes this point very strongly in an initial paragraph that explains the nature of the liturgy and its importance in the life of the Church. It begins by citing the prayer over the gifts for the Evening Mass of the Lord's Supper on Holy Thursday.

> For the liturgy, "making the work of our redemption a present actuality" most of all in the divine sacrifice of the Eucharist, is the outstanding means whereby the faithful may express in their lives and manifest to others the mystery of Christ and the real nature of the true Church (CSL no. 2).

The way in which "our redemption is made a present actuality" is through remembering since the basis for Jewish and Christian prayer is the invocation of God who is not conceived of as distant and disinterested in human life but a God passionately involved with us and our world; a God who has worked marvels throughout our history. That is why we usually call upon God in light of God's past record of dealing mercifully with humankind. We confidently call upon the holy One who is

"full of mercy," "abounding in loving kindness," "who sent the Son to be our Savior." Whether it is remembering God as the creator of the universe or as the prime-mover in the two primordial redemptive events recounted in the Bible—the Exodus from Egypt or the Paschal Mystery—we remember that our approach to God here and now is possible and appropriate. For ultimately, Christian "making memorial" of Jesus Christ is not about long-past events, but about the way God continues to move and act with and through Jesus Christ today in our lives and in our world—almost two thousand years after the unrepeatable event we call the paschal mystery.

The Relationship Between Remembering and Sacrifice. The intrinsic link between remembering and worship understood metaphorically as sacrifice is well illustrated in what is technically known as the "anamnesis-offering" section of the Eucharistic Prayer, which occurs right after the assembly's acclamation of the mystery of faith—an acclamation whose various forms are anamnetic or rememorative in nature. After this acclamation, what we remember and what we are doing in so remembering is specified by all of the Eucharistic Prayers of the Roman Sacramentary. One of the most expansive versions of the anamnesis/offering is found in the classic Roman Canon (Eucharistic Prayer I), which makes it clear that it is all present who are participating in the memorial of Christ. It is by virtue of this remembering of Christ that we can approach God in thankful prayer with our offering, which is in reality what God has already given us—the memorial of the passion, death, and resurrection of Jesus Christ now sacramentalized in the elements of bread and wine.

> Father, we celebrate the memory of Christ, your Son.
> We your people and your ministers, recall his passion, his resurrection from the dead,
> and his ascension into glory;

and from the many gifts you have given
us
we offer to you God of glory and majesty,
this holy and perfect sacrifice:
the bread of life
and the cup of eternal salvation.

The traditional Catholic notion of Eucharistic sacrifice is an important part of this section of the prayer. It is only in remembering Christ's sacrifice on the cross that we approach God in prayer; that we can even use the term sacrifice to describe the Liturgy of the Eucharist. It is by virtue of this sacrifice and ability to make formal memorial of it that we can offer our sacrifice of praise to the Father. This is the point of the anamnesis/offering section of the second Eucharistic Prayer, based on the ancient Eucharistic Prayer from the *Apostolic Tradition* (ca. 215).

In memory of his death and resurrection,
we offer to you, Father, this life-giving
bread,
this saving cup.
We thank you for counting us worthy
to stand in your presence and serve you.

Thus, what is presented in this section of the Eucharistic Prayers of the Sacramentary is the solemn memorial or remembrance made of Christ's entire work of salvation. It is this remembrance—conceived of in the full richness of the biblical understanding of *zikkaron/anamnesis*, a remembering that re-presents a past event—which brings about the sacrament of the sacrifice of the cross celebrated in the Eucharist. It has been the recovery of the underlining dynamic of formal, ritual remembering as it is understood in the biblical texts that has led to new areas of ecumenical agreement on the use of the term "sacrifice" as it is applied to the Eucharist, especially among Catholic, Lutherans, and Anglicans.

Remembering the Future. Finally, any prayer that remembers in order to make the paschal mystery present will call forth a change in those who remember and influence their future. The transformative nature of the Eucharist is underlined by remembering the mystery of faith celebrated. In the words of one of the anamnetic acclamations addressed to Christ: "Dying you destroyed our death, rising you restored our life. Lord Jesus, come in glory." We acknowledge the effect of Christ's work of redemption in such a way that we have been given new life—but a life that is not yet complete, for even our sacramental celebration is provisory—until the final and glorious coming of Jesus Christ at the end of time. It is thus that we "remember the future" by anticipating in our Eucharistic celebrations that presence of God in Christ which will be fully accessible to us at the final, joyous eschatological banquet.

See: COVENANT, ESCHATOLOGY, EUCHARIST, EXODUS, MEAL, MEDIATOR/INTERCESSOR, MYSTERY, SPIRIT OF GOD, WORSHIP

MARK R. FRANCIS, C.S.V.

REMNANT

The remnant motif served the people of the ancient Near East in expressing their hope for the preservation of life. This term came to have specifically Israelite theological connotations as it served to express Israel's hope for the future. The remnant was the bearer of the community's future existence. It became an important motif in the Book of Revelation.

Old Testament

Ancient Near Eastern Background. This motif appears in many ancient Near Eastern texts that reflect on the many threats to human existence. It surfaces first in the Sumerian flood story, the prototype of later Mesopotamian, Ugaritic, and Israelite versions. The story tells of the destruction of humankind and the survival of a remnant. Though this remnant was small, it made possible the survival of human beings. The remnant idea is the way that these texts speak about the possibilities of the renewal and restoration of human existence. The survival of the remnant means the survival of human life.

This becomes clearer in the way the Assyrian Chronicles use this motif. The Assyrians boast that their military campaigns were so successful that not even a remnant of the enemy survived. Occasionally these chronicles note that a remnant managed to escape but later they were caught and destroyed. It is clear then that the remnant motif emerges from circumstances in which human existence of at least a whole people's existence is threatened with extinction.

The remnant motif also appears in Hittite and Egyptian literature. Its appearance in these ancient Near Eastern texts proves that this literary motif antedates the Bible. It speaks to the variety of circumstances that seriously threaten human existence: war, flood, famine, plague, and death. The origin of this motif lies in a basic concern of human existence: the preservation of life when its continuation comes under serious threat. If no remnant survives the threat, there is nothing but total destruction and the end of life. If a remnant survives, the future is secure. No remnant means death; a surviving remnant means life and a future.

Ancient Israel. In some OT texts remnant has no special theological connotation. For example, in Isaiah 37:4 and 2 Kings 19:4 Hezekiah asks Isaiah to pray for what remained of his kingdom following Sennacherib's invasion. In Ezekiel 9:8 and 11:13 "that which is left of Israel" is the rump Judahite state that managed to survive the first Babylonian assault in 597 BCE. The term has this neutral sense when the OT uses it to speak of other peoples. Isaiah speaks of the remnant of Philistia (Isa 14:30), Moab (Isa 16:14), and Aram (Isa 17:3) that like Israel had to face the Assyrian onslaught.

Remnant as a theological motif carries with it connotations of both judgment* and salvation.* This is clear from the stories of Noah (Gen 7:23) and Lot (Gen 18:16-32). Fearing revenge from Esau, Jacob divided his possessions so that at least some people from his household could escape as a remnant (Gen 32:9). Joseph tells his brothers that God directed his life and fortunes to ensure that their father's family would be kept alive as a remnant (Gen 45:7). The judgment of God devastates the unfaithful, but God's mercy brings salvation on the nucleus of the people who remained faithful. The survival of this nucleus is essential to OT hope and eschatology.

The Prophetic Tradition. An important shift in emphasis occurs in the Elijah cycle. The prophet hears the news about the seven thousand Israelites who remained faithful to Yahweh and did not serve the Baals (2 Kgs 19:18). The text says that God "caused seven thousand to remain." They became a new and significant group within Israel. They became the harbingers of later, similar groups that survived the destruction of the Judahite state, its monarchy, and cult.

Amos attacked the misappropriation of the remnant motif (Amos 3:12; 5:3; 6:9; 9:1) because it became an expression of self-confidence and not a summons to conversion. The survival of the nation depends on Israel's response. According to Amos 9:11-12, the "remnant of Edom" will participate in the blessing that come to Israel as part of the promise made to David. The remnant motif in Amos does not aim merely at national survival, but it has a religious function.

The importance of this motif for Isaiah is clear from the name he gave to his eldest son: "A remnant shall return" (Isa 7:3). Nonetheless for the prophet, the remnant motif involves a proclamation of judgment on unfaithful Judah: Isaiah 10:19; 17:5-6; 30:17. Faith and conversion are necessary before the remnant can experience God's salvation. This will lead God to restore the remnant to the land from the nations where they have been exiled (Isa 11:11). Most of the occurrences of remnant language in Isaiah reflect political usage in which remnant describes what remained of a people who managed to survive a military campaign that aimed at their total destruction.

There are several texts from the Book of Isaiah in which the remnant idea is defined clearly: 4:3; 10:20; and 38:5. Here the remnant is a miraculously preserved minority. This idea meshes with a principal Isaianic theme: Zion threatened but ultimately delivered. In Isaiah the remnant motif is part of the prophet's call for repentance and faith. Still Isaiah says practically nothing about who this remnant is. Zephaniah is not so reticent and identifies the remnant with the poor (Zeph 2:3; 3:12-13). They will survive the judgment and by the nucleus of a new people of God. God will reign the remnant, the basic element of a new people, in Jerusalem (Mic 4:7).

Jeremiah and Ezekiel speak in terms of a total judgment on Israel for its infidelity. In their oracles remnant has little positive role. God will glean the remnant of Israel (Jer 6:9) and treat it like bad figs (Jer 24:8). The people who survive divine judgment will find death preferable to their continued existence (Jer 8:3). God threatens to destroy the remnant that has fled to Egypt (Jer 42:15, 19). God will scatter the remnant to the winds (Ezek 5:10). In these prophets survival following divine judgment involves no promise of salvation.

In some postexilic texts, the remnant becomes the purified core of the restored people of God. Those who survived the judgment of the Exile identify themselves as this purified remnant, though Haggai insists that the community restored to Judah is not simply the hoped-for remnant (Hag 1:12-14; 2:2). There is still need for purification (Zech 13:8-9; 14:2). This term could sometimes become an elitist self-designation that points to a portion of post-exilic Judah as existing on some higher spiritual plane because of its experiences. The prophets warn against this elitism that ignored their call to conversion.

In the OT the motif of the remnant expressed the future hopes grounded in Israel's faith in its God. The idea of a remnant purified by divine judgment helped Judah secure its existence when the institutions that supported that existence were destroyed. The prophets used this motif to support their urgent call for repentance. Without repentance there could be no rem-

nant. Conversion then is the only basis for survival.

Intertestamental Literature. In the Intertestamental literature the remnant motif reappears because Judaism was threatened again (Enoch 83:8; 4 Ezra 12:34; 2 Bar 40:2). The literature uses this motif because of its implied promise of salvation. The people of Qumran thought of themselves as the remnant of the true Israel (1QM 14:8-9; 1QH 6:8). The elitist possibilities of this idea reassert themselves here. In Rabbinic literature, the idea of the remnant recedes before the idea that all Israel will be saved (M. Sanhedrin 10:1).

New Testament

The remnant motif also makes no appearance in the preaching of Jesus who called all people to repentance though he could expect that only a few people would accept his teaching (Matt 7:14). Still Jesus clearly intended to create a community that thought of itself as a remnant of true Israel, though the Gospels never use "remnant" to speak for the community of Jesus' disciples. In Romans 9–11 Paul makes use of the remnant motif as he discusses Judaism. He maintains that the Jews who accept Jesus are the true remnant of Israel (Rom 11:5). Finally in the Book of Revelation, the remnant idea is a prominent theme. The book reflects the circumstances of a Church whose first fervor is diminishing because of internal disagreements (Rev 2:4) and the threat of persecution (Rev 11:13; 12:17; 13:11-18; 19:21).

Pastoral-Liturgical Tradition

The question of human survival is as real as it ever was. Technology has made it possible for human beings to bring an end to human existence. The insecurities reflected in the ancient Near Eastern myths have a genuine basis in fact. There is the threat of nuclear annihilation, the specter of mass starvation, the devastation of the environment, social and political unrest caused by poverty and racism. The biblical motif of the remnant offers people the alternative of security that comes from a confident trust in the God who saves. The response that the remnant motif evokes is the response of conversion. When human life is threatened with extinction and these threats are real and immediate only a return to God can provide security, peace, and hope. Faith and repentance give people the assurance that they are part of the remnant.

See: CONVERSION, EXILE, REPENTANCE

LESLIE J. HOPPE, O.F.M.

REPENTANCE

Repentance has a range of meanings in the Bible, from regret or relentment on the part of God, to change of heart by human beings. For human beings, such change involves shifting one's whole stance away from sin and toward God. This turnabout demands both inner transformation and visible reformation of one's manner of living.

Old Testament

Terms. The most common root for repentance in the OT is *niham*. In its various verb forms this root can mean to be sorry or repent, to console or to be consoled, or to comfort oneself (by vengeance). Thus the root has the sense of changing not only one's mind but also one's feeling. When it is used in the sense of repentance, the word is translated "repent," "regret," "relent." The Hebrew word *shub*, "turn," is also used for the notion of repenting. One turns away from evil and turns toward reconciliation* and mercy.*

The most common term for repentance in the Septuagint is *metanoeō/metanoia*, "to change one's mind or heart." Various forms of the root *strephō*, "to turn," are also used in the Septuagint.

God. In the Hebrew Bible God is spoken of as repenting/not repenting almost twice as often as the people are. Sometimes God regrets the divine action. God regrets having made human beings and so begins the flood (Gen 6:6). God regrets having made Saul king of Israel and so turns to David (1 Sam 15:11, 35).

Sometimes God does not repent. When Saul pleads with Samuel for forgiveness,* Samuel will not take back God's rejection of Saul: "The Glory of Israel neither retracts nor repents, for he is not man that he should repent" (1 Sam 15:29). In his misery Job declares his helplessness before the power of God who does not relent (Job 9:13, *shub*). God does not repent of the decision to consecrate the king-messiah as priest forever (Ps 110:4). In his despair Jeremiah curses the man who brought the news of his birth: "Let that man be like the cities which the LORD relentlessly *[lo niham]* overthrew" (Jer 20:16). When the people continue to sin and do not themselves repent, God does not repent of the Exile (Jer 4:28; Lam 2:8; Ezek 24:14; Zech 8:14).

Most often, however, God relents of punishment. After the people have made a golden calf in the desert, Moses pleads with God and God repents of punishing them (Exod 32:12-14). In the settlement stories when someone breaks the ban and takes booty, God punishes the people by defeat. After they have removed the offender, "the anger of the LORD relented" (Josh 7:26). God regrets the suffering brought on the people and stops the pestilence that came upon them as a consequence of David's census (2 Sam 24:16). In the eighth century the prophet Amos sees four visions of God's wrath coming against Israel. After the first two visions Amos pleads with God, "Forgive, O Lord GOD! How can Jacob stand? He is so small!" (Amos 7:2; cf. 7:6). And God repents: "It shall not be" (Amos 7:3, 6). In pleading with the nation to repent so that the Exile might not overtake them, Jeremiah delivers the message that God may threaten to do evil, "but if that nation which [God] has threatened turns from its evil, [God] also repents of the evil" which had been threatened. On the other hand, if God promises to build up a nation and "that nation does what is evil in [God's] eyes, [God] repents of the good" which has been promised (Jer 18:7-10). Consistently Jeremiah repeats the message: Repent, and God may repent of the evil that threatens us (Jer 26:3, 13). Jeremiah is saved from execution because at least some of the people recognize the truth of his message. Once before in the time of the prophet Micah the people repented and God did repent of punishment (Jer 26:19).

This hope for God's repentance, God's change of heart, becomes a consistent element in Israel's prayer. The prophet Joel calls for a day of fasting and penance, a day of true repentance because God is "gracious and merciful, . . . slow to anger, rich in kindness, and relenting in punishment" (Joel 2:13-14; see Exod 34:6; Num 14:18; Neh 9:17; Pss 86:15; 103:8; 145:8; Wis 15:1; Nah 1:3). The prophet Jonah knows this too. He knows God will relent of punishing the Ninevites: "I beseech you, LORD," he prayed, "is not this what I said while I was still in my own country? This is why I fled at first to Tarshish. I knew that you are a gracious and merciful God, slow to anger, rich in clemency, loathe [niham] to punish" (Jonah 4:2; see 3:9-10). Psalm 106 tells the history of God's people from the Exodus to the entrance into the land. The plea that ends the psalm is based on the memory that over and over again God remembered the covenant and repented of punishment (Ps 106:45). The psalmist can pray once more: "Save us, O LORD" (106:47).

God's People. God's people are consistently exhorted by the prophets to repent. God will not fail to turn to the people who themselves turn in repentance. In every section of the Book of Isaiah there is a call for repentance and a promise that God will redeem the repentant (1:27; 31:6; 44:2; 45:22; 55:7; 59:20). In Hosea the people cannot repent (shub) because of their wicked deeds. They make a feeble, short-lived attempt (6:1). God resolves to destroy them because they will not repent (11:5-7) but cannot give them up because of love for them (11:8-9). In the final chapter of the book the prophet calls them again to return to the Lord (14:2-3).

The concept of return and repentance is a key message of the prophet Jeremiah. He complains about the people's unwillingness to return (3:7; 5:3; 8:4-5; 23:14) or insincere return (3:1, 10). He complains that the birds "know their time of return," but God's people do not know how to repent (8:6; cf. 9:4). He holds out God's promise to restore them if they return (3:12, 14, 22; 4:1; 18:8; 31:19) and God's threat of exile if they refuse (18:9-17). Even Jeremiah himself is called to repent of his despair (15:9) and in return God will restore him. Throughout the book the hope persists that the people will finally repent, turn away from evil and back to God (24:7; 25:5; 26:3; 36:3, 7).

Ezekiel preaches personal responsibility for repentance. If the wicked turn away from sin, God will grant them life. On the other hand, if the virtuous repent of goodness, turn away from virtue, and do wrong, they will die (18:21-29). It is the prophet's responsibility to warn the people of this (3:18-21; 33:7-20) and to proclaim God's call: "Turn and be converted from all your crimes, . . . for I have no pleasure in the death of anyone who dies, says the Lord GOD. Return and live!" (18:30, 32). The later prophets continue the call to turn back to God (Joel 2:12-13; Zech 1:3-4; Mal 3:7).

Solomon's prayer at the dedication of the Temple reveals the hope for God's constant mercy toward the repentant through a persistent repetition of the root shub, "return":

> If your people Israel sin against you and are defeated by an enemy, and if then they *return* to you, praise your name, pray to you, and entreat you in this temple, listen in heaven and forgive the sin of your people Israel, and *bring them back* to the land you gave their fathers. If the sky is closed, so that there is no rain, because they have sinned against you and you afflict them, and if then they *repent* of their sin, and pray, and praise your name in this place, listen in heaven and forgive the sin of your servant and of your people Israel (1 Kgs 8:33-36; see 46-50).

Repentance is a wise thing to do. Wisdom psalms repeat the call to "turn from evil and do good" (Pss 34:15; 37:27). Ben Sira exhorts us not to shame a repentant sinner because we are all in need of repentance (Sir 8:5). The sage recommends repentance whenever one has sinned (Sir 18:21). One who fears the Lord is known by repentance (Sir 21:6). Ben Sira attributes the Exile to the fact that the people did not repent (Sir 48:15). But he is in awe at the mercy of the Lord who forgives those who return (Sir 17:24). The Book of Wisdom asserts that it is God's grace that gives people the ability to repent. God overlooks sins that people may repent (11:23), gives them space for repentance (12:10), permits repentance for their sins (12:19).

See: CONVERSION, COVENANT, GRACE, MERCY

IRENE NOWELL, O.S.B.

New Testament

In the NT repentance is not spoken of as something that God does. It is central to John the Baptist's preaching and to Jesus' initial proclamation of the reign of God. Repentance and forgiveness of sins continued to be preached in the early Church, as is seen in Acts of the Apostles. Later NT tradition takes up the painful question of whether there can be repentance following apostasy.

Repentance Is at the Heart of Christian Faith. Three principal Greek terms convey the idea of repentance in the NT. *Metanoia* (twenty-four times), *metanoeō* (thirty-four times), meaning "repentance" and "to repent," denote, literally, a change of mind *(nous)*. But it is clear that the idea of repentance is not simply an intellectual shift, but a change of thinking and of attitude, a change of one's whole stance toward the divine that affects the person in a total way. The less frequent term *metamelomai* (six times) carries an added nuance of remorse or regret for what one has left behind. A third word group in the NT, *epistrephō, epistrophē* (to turn, return; conversion) and its related synonyms, underscore the notion that repentance involves the turning of the whole person away from one thing and toward another. From its earliest formulation the content of the gospel invitation

called for persons to "turn from darkness to light, from the power of Satan to God" (Acts 26:18). In the case of each of these terms, Christian repentance entails leaving behind a way of thinking and being or acting that is marked by sinfulness and separates a person from the one, true God.

The Gospel Tradition. In essence the story of Jesus begins with the sudden appearance of John the Baptist proclaiming "a baptism of repentance for the forgiveness of sins" (Mark 1:4; Luke 3:3). The urgency of John's preaching reflected his certainty that "the kingdom of heaven [was] near" (Matt 3:2). Repentance was the only proper response to, and preparation for, this imminent arrival of God's reign. His baptism was a baptism of water, but one which would later be sealed in a baptism of the Spirit which only "the one to come after him" could give. John saw, furthermore, that a change of mind and heart must show itself in concrete deeds: "Produce good fruits as evidence of your repentance," he said (Luke 3:8). And in his view, no one was exempt from this call to repentance; there was no room for smugness or self-satisfaction (Luke 3:8-9). All were summoned to a change of life in preparation for God's coming reign.

Jesus, too, echoed in his earliest preaching the message of repentance that John had proclaimed (Mark 1:15). For Jesus, however, the time had *already* come, the good news was indeed present, and repentance demanded belief in the gospel (Mark 1:15). Repentance and faith became in Jesus' preaching two dimensions of the same response. Together they would signal a person's entire response to the invitation of God, given now, once and for all, in the person and ministry of Jesus. All relationships and priorities must be reordered in light of the call to repentance (Luke 14:26-33). Repentance demands a fundamental change of heart and attitude, and it calls us to an ongoing perseverance to "seek the kingdom." It is not merely a once and for all response. We must become "like little children" (Matt 18:3) assuming a stance of complete openness and dependence on God. In his ministry, Jesus sought out, moreover, all those in special need of God's mercy and forgiveness. He came to call "not the righteous but sinners" to repentance (Luke 5:32). Only John's Gospel fails to include this important dimension of repentance as a requisite element in following Jesus. But for John, one assumes, repentance is implicitly present in one's affirmation of faith in Jesus.

The call to repentance placed persons in the Gospel at a moment of decision. They could decide to either respond or not to God's call. And the outcome of their decision had ultimate consequences for either life or destruction. Repentance in the NT, therefore, is set within an eschatological context in which one's response ultimately brings either reward or punishment, life or death. There is more "joy in heaven" (Luke 15:7), we are told, over one sinner who repents than over ninety-nine righteous who have no need of repentance. Similarly in Luke, Jesus warns his hearers, "If you do not repent, you will all perish" (Luke 13:3). In these stern warnings there is an echo of the OT challenge to "Choose life" in the context of blessing and curse (Deut 30:19-20), or to "Harden not [our] hearts" if the voice of God summons us to repentance today (Ps 95:7).

The Early Christian Mission. The post-resurrection challenge to the followers of Jesus in Luke's Gospel underscores once more the centrality of repentance in the ongoing proclamation of the gospel message. "Repentance and the forgiveness of sins must be preached in his name to all the nations" (Luke 24:47). In Acts, the apostles take up this charge, beginning with the programmatic speech of Peter in Acts 2:38 which reaffirms the Baptist's call to repent and be baptized into the forgiveness of sins. The link between repentance (*metanoeō*) and conversion (*epistrophē*) is reiterated in Peter's speech in Acts 3:19: "Repent, therefore, and be converted, that your sins may be wiped away." Jew and Greek alike received the same call to repent and were baptized (Acts 2:38; 3:19;

5:31; 11:18). Once embraced, moreover, repentance leads to eternal life (Acts 11:18).

Pauline Tradition. Paul only rarely uses the Synoptic terminology for repentance (2 Cor 12:21; Rom 2:4; 2 Tim 2:25). Instead, his profound notion of faith, understood as an active adherence of one's whole life to the person and message of Jesus Christ ("the obedience of faith" [Rom 1:5; 16:26]), seems to contain of its very essence an implicit act of repentance. According to Paul, in the act of faith the believer surrenders anything that might hinder his or her complete adherence to Christ. In one important passage, however, Paul is at pains to distinguish between "godly regret" (*metamelomai*), which leads to repentance (*metanoia*), and "worldly regret," which leads not to repentance but to death (2 Cor 7:8-10). This text illustrates, therefore, that true repentance, in the Pauline sense, demands one's wholehearted surrender to God.

Repentance and Apostasy. In some of the later NT documents, such as Hebrews and the Book of Revelation, one finds the beginnings of a debate that raged among Christians in the second and third centuries over the question of repentance, and the possibility (or impossibility) of repentance following apostasy. The author of Hebrews argues that if a believer abandons the life of faith after his or her initial repentance and baptism, there is no possibility of a "second repentance" (Heb 6:4-8). The Book of Revelation, on the other hand, begins with a stern charge to the Churches of Ephesus, Pergamum, Thyatira, and Laodicea. The author calls upon each of these Churches to "Repent" and to return to the Lord in order to escape punishment (Rev 2:4-5, 14-16, 20-23; 3:19). In the author's mind, repentance was clearly possible if only these Churches would heed the warning given them.

In the ensuing debates over the possibility, or impossibility, of post-baptismal repentance, the *Shepherd of Hermas* (*Vis.* II.ii. 1-6) reiterated the conviction that God's mercy continues to invite sinners to repentance throughout their lives. In the third century,

Cyprian (d. 258), Bishop of Carthage, and Novatian (d. 257) in Rome again espoused the rigorist view that post-baptismal repentance was impossible and apostates were doomed to eternal punishment. Alternatively, Cornelius (d. 253), Bishop of Rome, adopted a more lenient position offering pardon to all those whose repentance was sincere.

Belief in God's forgiving mercy in response to the repentance of sinners, therefore, stands as the foundation of Christian faith. Moreover, the image of the shepherd leaving the ninety-nine to search for the one who has strayed captures the essence of the NT teaching on repentance. Not only does God forgive and welcome back the repentant one, God continues to pursue us calling us to repentance at every moment of our lives.

See: BAPTISM, FAITH, MERCY, RECONCILIATION, SIN

BARBARA E. BOWE, R.S.C.J.

Pastoral-Liturgical Tradition

In English, repentance and conversion can be used almost interchangeably to translate the radical change in attitudes and behavior imaged in the biblical vocabulary of *metanoiein* and *epistrephein* (see Acts 3:19). In keeping with the Latin root of the word *(paenitere/paenitentia),* these few paragraphs will consider repentance from the limited perspective of repenting or doing penance for sin, rather than under the aspect of the process of conversion* or sacramental reconciliation.*

In the early Christian community, sin* was seen as more than a purely personal and private matter. Early Christian writers understood that sin affects the holiness of the Church in a very real sense, and that repentance entails not only an inner change of heart, but also a visible change in one's way of living as a member of that community. By doing penance, the sinful disciple manifested that transformation to the community. Repentance was an ethical and communal concern, and through its leaders the community focused its concern on the

pastoral question of how to sustain its members in their conversion to the Christian way. In the time of the persecutions, for example, the discussion over whether and how often lapsed members could receive forgiveness stemmed from a deep pastoral concern for the holiness of the community and the authenticity of the original conversion of the lapsed adult convert. Doing penance continued the process begun in baptism and was part and parcel of all Christian living. These perspectives remained in force even when the doing of penance was organized into the order of penitents in the third and fourth centuries.

After the development of tariff penance (early Middle Ages) and medieval confession, stress focused more exclusively on the inner attitudes needed for true repentance. High on the list of the confessor's sacramental responsibilities was judging whether the penitent possessed true sorrow for sin and a firm purpose of amendment. It was also the confessor's duty to assign the repentant sinner the proper penance to atone for the temporal punishment due to sin. Doing penance, i.e., continuing on the journey of *metanoia*, thus gave way to performing "penances" in satisfaction for one's sins. Practices of piety centered on making reparation for sin still draw on this theology of expiation.

As a result of the biblical movement, as also the work of the liturgical renewal in the areas of the catechumenate and sacramental reconciliation, it is now possible to reinsert repentance into a larger, more integrated biblical and liturgical context. In that context, repentance for sin is not ultimately distinct from conversion, but rather one way of seeing the journey begun in baptism and continued throughout life. In addition, the doing of penance is more than an individual believer's response to the reality of sin; it is the shared response of the community to the gospel call to "repent and believe," a response to be lived out in common. Finally, though there are ritual moments of naming and celebrating repentance, a life of repentance is essential to

Christian discipleship. Pastoral care for repentance must be equally comprehensive and constant.

See: CONVERSION, RECONCILIATION, SIN

GILBERT OSTDIEK, O.F.M.

RESURRECTION

Resurrection refers to persons whom God raises up from death, usually in a bodily form. The resurrected may be exalted to a heavenly life with the angels, brought before God's judgment, or return to live in the new creation after the end of the present evil age. Although the resurrected never die, resurrection is not identical with the philosophical belief that what is characteristically human is a non-material soul* that never dies. Nor should resurrection be confused with the resuscitation of a person who appears to have died. The resurrected do not return to the life that ended in death. Miracles in which a dead person is restored to life, as in the healing of the widow's son (by Elijah, 1 Kgs 17:17-24; by Jesus, Luke 8:11-17), are not examples of resurrection.

Old Testament

The term "resurrection" appears only once in the Hebrew Bible, in Daniel 12:1-3. Generally the OT holds that an individual's relationship to God terminates with death. The basis of this relationship can be described in cultic terms as the opportunity to offer praise to God. The dead no longer do so: "It is not the dead who praise the LORD, nor those who go down into silence" (Ps 115:17). The OT in the Catholic canon contains an additional reference to resurrection in 2 Maccabees 7 and a strong affirmation of the immortality of the righteous in Wisdom 2 and 5. All three examples depict resurrection as vindication for the righteous who have been persecuted in this life.

Confidence in God's Saving Power. Though
human life is generally viewed as ending in death, one does find in the Hebrew Bible expressions of confidence in God's saving power that depict the individual or the na-

tion as near death, yet rescued and sustained by God: "But God will redeem me from the power of the nether world by receiving me" (Ps 49:16; see also Ps 16:10). Prophetic texts spoke of a time in which the weak, suffering people of Israel would be restored: "But your dead shall live, their corpses shall rise; awake and sing, you who lie in the dust. For your dew is a dew of light, and the land of shades gives birth" (Isa 26:19).

Ezekiel 37:1-14 paints a dramatic picture of the people as a valley of dry bones revived by a new outpouring of the Spirit: "Then you shall know that I am the LORD, when I open your graves and have you rise from them, O my people!" (Ezek 37:13). Once an explicit belief in resurrection had developed, these passages were understood to be confirmation of that teaching.

Vindication of the Faithful. Both Daniel and
2 Maccabees were written during the persecutions of the second century BCE when the Syrian king Antiochus IV attempted to force Jews to adapt their ancestral religion to pagan practices. Though the ensuing wars waged by the Maccabees threw off the persecutor, some had given up their lives as martyrs rather than comply with the decrees requiring Jews to give up their ancestral faith.

2 Maccabees 7 tells the story of a mother and her seven sons who suffer a heroic martyrdom rather than renounce their faith. When the torturers taunt the victims with the pain they can inflict on the body, the martyrs affirm their faith in God as the true king who can raise them up to eternal life (2 Macc 7:9, 11, 14, 23). They are willing to offer the bodies God had created in the womb because the same creator can give them life again. In this account, bodily resurrection provides a just reward for the faithful martyrs. The wicked are not raised.

Daniel 12:1-3 describes the appearance of the angel Michael at the end of the world and the resurrection of the dead. Verse 2 is somewhat unclear. When it says that "those who sleep in the dust of the earth shall wake," this resurrection may apply only to those who have been faithful even as they were being slaughtered by the invading forces (see Dan 11:33-35). By contrast, those who "shall be an everlasting horror and disgrace" are the wicked who may simply remain among the dead. Others, however, have read the verse as affirming a general resurrection after which the nations are judged (see Matt 25:31-32). Verse 3 turns to a group that had played a special role in keeping Israel faithful, "the wise." They are exalted to celestial glory. The star imagery probably implies that they are among the angels.

Eternal Life for the Righteous. Wisdom 2 and 5 present a more general picture of the suffering and vindication of the just person. The tale of how the wicked skeptics who think that there is nothing after death persecute the good person is introduced by an appeal to seek life rather than death (Wis 1:12-16). This tale of patient suffering by one close to God—"[he] boasts that God is his Father"—(Wis 2:16b) provided material for the Gospels' portrayal of Jesus.

Wisdom depicts the reward of the innocent as eternal life with God (2:22-23). When it is too late, after death, the wicked discover the righteous person exalted among the angels of God (Wis 5:5). Their reward is to vanish into the nothingness that their erroneous philosophy had led them to consider the end of life. The Daniel and 2 Maccabees traditions affirm the value of the sacrifices made by those who did not give way in the persecutions of the mid-second century BCE. Bodily resurrection is an appropriate reward for persons who sacrificed their lives. Wisdom makes a universal case of the good person persecuted and killed by the wicked. Eternal life with God is contrasted with the complete oblivion that comes upon the wicked.

New Testament

Belief in resurrection or eternal life as God's vindication of individual or communal suffering for the sake of righteousness was not commonplace in Jesus' day. NT authors refer to controversy over the point be-

tween Sadducees, who reject the doctrine, and others who accept it (Jesus in Mark 12:18-27; Pharisees in Acts 23:6-8). Christian belief in resurrection is not simply a development of the convictions expressed in some Jewish circles or an adaptation of philosophical teaching about the immortality of the soul. The NT understanding begins with the Easter kerygma that God raised the Jesus who was crucified (see Acts 2:30-33; 3:15).

The Resurrection Kerygma. Our earliest examples of Christian belief in the resurrection are the kerygmatic formulae proclaiming that the crucified has been exalted to God's right hand (see Rom 4:24-25). These formulae are sometimes complemented by references to those who had seen the risen Lord (see 1 Cor 15:3-5).

Though we sometimes say that "Jesus rose" at Easter, the NT kerygma emphasizes the fact that God is the one who raised Jesus from the dead (Acts 3:7, 15; 5:30; Rom 4:24; 2 Cor 1:9; Gal 1:1). Resurrection is not a special power or achievement of Jesus. It is God's confirmation and vindication of Jesus' faithfulness. Consequently, NT Christians could speak of their faith in a God who raises the dead: "It is through him [Jesus] that you are believers in God, the God who raised him from the dead and gave him glory. Your faith and hope, then, are centered in God" (1 Pet 1:21).

The early confessions also speak of Jesus' exaltation at God's right hand. This pattern of righteous suffering followed by exaltation in God's presence was used in the eternal life tradition of Wisdom 2. But, unlike Wisdom 2, the NT holds that Jesus occupies a special place in relationship to God. He is invested with God's own name, "Lord" (see Phil 2:6-11). Unlike the martyrs whose resurrected bodies are the just reward for what they have suffered, Jesus' resurrection is not personal recompense for the pain of crucifixion. Rather, it represents the new conviction that the one who had been crucified now participates in the very rule and power of God. Paul uses an early creedal formula in Romans 1:3-4: "the gospel concerning his Son, who was descended from David according to the flesh but was made Son of God in power according to the spirit of holiness, by his resurrection from the dead, Jesus Christ our Lord."

1 Corinthians 15:3b-5 contains the core of an early creed that Paul says he received from others and handed on in the churches. It includes Jesus' death as atonement for sin, Jesus' burial, Jesus' resurrection, and the testimony of those who had seen the risen One. As in the shorter formulae that speak of the resurrection of the crucified One (Rom 4:25), this creed makes it clear that the risen/exalted Christ is to be identified with the Jesus who actually died on the cross. The risen Christ is not some inner essence or immortal soul that did not participate in the reality of death. Jesus is not like the semi-divine beings of mythology.

Appearances of the Risen One. The creed in 1 Corinthians 15:3-5 is supplemented by reference to others who had seen the risen Christ, including Paul himself (vv. 6-10). Nothing is said about the content of such appearances. Paul's other references to his own experience suggest a revelation from heaven that is in part an internal experience (Gal 1:16; 2 Cor 4:6). Somewhat later, narrative accounts of Jesus' appearances not only gave shape to that witness but also included commissioning of Jesus' followers for their future mission as a community and to the world (see Matt 28:9-10, 16-20; Luke 24:13-49; John 20:11-29; 21:1-23).

There are two types of narrative about Jesus' appearances: a concise, commissioning type and a more expanded tale, which often develops apologetic or catechetical concerns. The commissioning type, like Matthew 28:16-20, or the appearances to the women, like Matthew 28:9-10 and John 20:11-18, resemble the divine commissioning of prophets or the appearances of angelic messengers. The risen One appears, the recipient's reaction is described, some word of reassurance or self-identification is

spoken, the recipient is given a divine commission, and there is a departure. Paul speaks of his own experience as a divine commission to preach Christ among the Gentiles (Gal 1:10-11). The other examples also include this type of mission to convey the kerygma to others.

While this element can also be found in the longer stories, they often include elements that are related to the life of the community: demonstration that the risen one really is identical with the Jesus who had died (see John 20:24-29; Luke 24:38-42); teaching that Scripture had predicted the death and resurrection of the Messiah or recollection of Jesus' words (Luke 24:6b-7, 25-27, 44-46). These stories also ground later Church practices, such as recognizing Christ's presence in the communal meal (Luke 24:30-31; John 21:9-13), forgiveness of sin (Luke 24:47; John 20:23), and the Trinitarian baptismal formula (Matt 28:19b). This type of story is sometimes spoken of as a "church founding" story. It affirms characteristics of the community of believers gathered in Jesus' name. The function of appearance traditions was not simply to quell the doubts that some felt about whether or not Jesus had been raised. Rather, these stories point to fundamental realities of Christian life as founded on the word of the risen Jesus.

The Empty Tomb. Since resurrection was always understood as "from the dead" or "from the grave," accounts of the discovery that Jesus was no longer in the tomb (Mark 16:1-8a; Matt 28:1-8; Luke 24:1-12; John 20:1-13) were joined with both the Easter kerygma and appearance stories. These stories may also be formulated to ward off anti-Christian polemics (see Matt 27:62-65; 28:11-15). The empty tomb traditions have more elements in common than the appearance stories do, in part because Matthew and Luke are variations of the earlier version in Mark.

As John indicates, an empty tomb itself proves nothing (20:2, 13). The body could have been moved or stolen and such a false rumor may have circulated among the Jews to discredit Christian preaching (Matt 28:13). (The "they" in John 20:2, 13 might refer to Jesus' enemies.) Archaeological evidence of secondary burial, the reburial of a person's bones in an ossuary, indicates that a person's remains could easily be removed to another location. Consequently, the Easter kerygma has to be announced to the women by an angel (Mark 16:6; Matt 28:7; Luke 24:5-7) or by the risen Jesus (Matt 28:10; John 20:17).

However, unlike immortality of the soul, resurrection was felt to imply transformation of the person buried in the tomb. Matthew 27:52-53 preserves a curious legend that the power of Jesus' resurrection also awakened other holy persons from the grave. It would be difficult to imagine that God could raise Jesus and yet leave his remains in the tomb. Acts 2:24-31 uses Psalm 16:8-11 and the fact that David's tomb was venerated to show that David had been abandoned to the netherworld and corruption. Therefore, the psalm must have been a prophecy that the Messiah would be raised. This argument shows that resurrection was understood to imply that Jesus' body no longer remained in the grave. Some scholars think that the empty tomb tradition found in Mark 16:1-8 was shaped by an early Christian liturgical practice of worship at the tomb.

The Resurrection of Believers. Since Christians are united with Christ in baptism and through the Spirit, they should also expect to share Christ's resurrection (Rom 6:3-5). Paul's letters indicate that the skepticism with which many greeted the resurrection message (see Acts 17:32) was also evident among Christians (see 1 Cor 15:12; 1 Thess 4:13-14). It was possible for people to separate their belief in the resurrection and exaltation of Christ from their conception of the fate of believers. At the same time, other passages in the NT employ the imagery of an end time resurrection for judgment (see Rev 20:11-15).

The OT images are sparse and diverse. One might conclude that all are raised for judgment at the end time; that only those martyred for God's sake are resurrected; that only the righteous or those who have led others to righteousness are to be raised up. Many Jewish converts might not have believed in any of these views. Gentile converts did not even have that prior tradition to fall back on. Since Jesus' resurrection involved exaltation to a unique status with God, it would be even easier to believe that Jesus had been raised without drawing any conclusions at all about what would happen to the faithful.

Paul faces two different examples of Christian disbelief. The Thessalonians (1 Thess 4:13-18) are unsure what to think about the fate of members of their community who had died. They anticipated the early return of Jesus as judge (1 Thess 1:9-10). Divine judgment would vindicate them for what they had suffered on behalf of the gospel (1 Thess 1:6-7). Would those who had died miss out? Paul assures the Thessalonians that the dead will come with Jesus and the community will be restored to the unity which seems broken by death.

In 1 Corinthians 15, Paul faces a more deliberate polemic against belief in resurrection. The opponents may have held that some core of the person is immortal but not the individual in all of his or her personal, bodily individuality. Such a view would be coherent with the over-emphasis on wisdom and spiritual gifts as signs of perfection that Paul criticizes earlier in 1 Corinthians. Paul accuses them of holding the same view as many ancient skeptics, a view also found inscribed on tombstones, that you should get what you can in this life because when you die nothing will remain (1 Cor 15:19, 32-33). Resurrection of the faithful constitutes the core of Christian faith. As in the Jewish tradition, this resurrection occurs at the final judgment when death is defeated and all things return to God's rule.

Paul gives several arguments to support Christian belief. God's creative power will transform what we know as the material body into a spiritual one. Consequently, the absurdities that follow from supposing that God would simply take the dead and put them back into the flesh they had in this life do not apply (1 Cor 15:35-44; note a similar argument in Mark 12:18-27, based on the idea that the resurrected become like angels). Resurrection is also suited to the plan of salvation, since Christ has become the life-giving, spiritual Adam (1 Cor 15:20-21, 45-49). Finally, Paul includes practical arguments. Without hope in the resurrection, the suffering he has endured to preach the gospel would be absurd (15:14, 30-32) and the new life of reconciliation and forgiveness the Corinthians experience would be impossible (15:17). In addition, the Corinthians know that in Christ their ties to the dead are preserved (15:29).

Resurrection and the Spirit. The kerygma, appearance stories, and incorporation into Christ are not the only basis for NT belief in resurrection. The resurrection and exaltation of Jesus are the basis for powerful new experiences of God's presence. The risen Jesus is present to his followers (Matt 28:20; John 14:19-24). The Spirit experienced in the community is associated with the risen One (Rom 1:3-4; 8:9-10). The formula in Romans 1:3-4 attributes the resurrection and exaltation of Christ to the power of the Spirit. Romans 8:9-10 shows that Paul thinks of the activity of the holy Spirit as that of the risen Christ. As Romans 8 shows, there could be no Christian life at all without the transforming and sustaining presence of the Spirit.

Other NT authors pick up the theme of resurrection as the presence of Christ. For Matthew, the promise, "I am with you always, until the end of the world!" (28:20) reminds the reader of the name that the angel gave the expected child: "'and they shall call him Emmanuel,' which means, 'God is with us'" (Matt 1:23). In John, the guiding presence of the Spirit-Paraclete, who comes after Jesus' return to God, is complemented by the promise that Jesus and the Father will come to dwell with the disciples (John 14:19-24). As Luke 24:29-31 indicates, this presence came to be associated with the Eucharistic action of blessing, breaking, and distributing the bread. The Church-founding appearance stories and other references to words of Christ in the NT suggest that early Christian prophets sometimes spoke words that had their source in the risen/exalted one. The most dramatic picture of this process occurs in the opening of Revelation. The prophet/author conveys words of warning and encouragement to Christians in Asia Minor as letters from the risen Christ (Rev 1:5–3:21).

From a NT perspective, there is no facet of Christian life that has not been shaped by the conviction that God raised Jesus, the crucified, from the dead. The ultimate goal of Christian life is not merely surviving death but transformation into the image of God, which is the risen Christ (1 Cor 15:49; 2 Cor 3:18).

See: ADAM AND EVE, ATONEMENT, BAPTISM, DEATH, EUCHARIST, IMAGE OF GOD, JUDGMENT, SOUL, SPIRIT OF GOD

PHEME PERKINS

Pastoral-Liturgical Tradition

The proclamation of the resurrection has been the principal constant of the Christian tradition from the earliest generations. It is found in the earliest creedal formulae, the liturgy, and the writings of Christian authors of all ages. In the ancient Church, however, resurrection is not seen in isolation but generally within the context of an incarnational model of Christology. The mystery of salvation is the real communication of divine reality to creation, and the transformation of creation in that relation with God which Christians believe has taken place in the incarnation of the divine Word in Jesus of Nazareth. God enters into human life so that human beings may enter into the divine life. This is the mystery of the salvific incarnation. The resurrection, then, is a crucial stage in this incarnational mystery.

In liturgical usage, the resurrection is commonly seen as indissolubly related with the mystery of Christ's death, and the death-resurrection model offers Christians a way of understanding their own life and liturgical experience as an entrance into the mystery of death and new life. The OT experience of Passover is seen as an anticipation of the Passover of Christ which, in turn, provides the clue to the Christian understanding of the spiritual journey to God.

The liturgical connection is seen early in the celebration of the "Lord's Day" (Ignatius, *Magn* 9,1) and the "Eighth Day" (*Barnabas*, 15, 8ff.) as a memorial of the resurrection. The celebration of baptism, especially in the context of the Easter Vigil, became the principal locale for developing the creedal formulae of the early Church (Hippolytus, *Apostolic Tradition*, 21ff.), and the Eucharistic celebration was seen as the memorial of the death and resurrection of Christ. It was particularly in the controversy with the spiritualizing tendencies of Gnosticism that emphasis was given precisely to resurrection of the body.

In the Medieval period, the question of the resurrection gave rise to extensive speculation about the nature of the glorified body of Christ and of all the redeemed. Post-Reformation Catholic theology tended to treat the resurrection not so much as a salvific mystery, but more as an apologetic one. The resurrection was crucial in the proof of the divinity of Christ. From this base, it could readily be shown that the Christian revelation was true, and that the Roman Catholic Church was the authentic instrument carrying that revelation through history.

Drawing from the insights of contemporary biblical and historical studies, liturgy and theology at the present time have regained a sense of the salvific nature of the resurrection. In the development of the liturgical renewal of this century, this recovery has been of central importance in giving a significant shape and interpretation to the liturgical experience of the community. In doctrinal theology, the development of the implications of the resur-

rection has come more slowly but is now noticeable in every major Christological study. Particular concerns are:

(1) Rather than think of the resurrection as a mystery that has no relation to human experience, contemporary theology tends to search for the roots of human hope as a point in human experience that is addressed in a specific way by the Christian claim of the resurrection. In broad terms, then, resurrection theology becomes a framework for interpreting human hopes and expectations in relation to the biblical vision of hope.

(2) The resurrection is a crucial moment in the historical revelation of God. If the resurrection is God's decisive salvific act in Jesus, God is revealed as the "God who gives life to the dead" (Rom 4:17). God is then seen to be truly the Lord of the living and the dead whose life-giving power transcends the power of death. God's final word to creation is not one of rejection but one of forgiveness and acceptance. This lies at the heart of the Christian hope for a positive outcome for life.

(3) The resurrection is a Christological mystery. The resurrection does not mean that Jesus becomes God. Rather it means that the deepest potential of his human nature has been brought to fulfillment in that relation with God that began already at the start of his human life. The affirmation of the resurrection as a statement about Christ's destiny with God provides a perspective from which Christians can look back to his life and interpret its significance. In as far as his personal resurrection is the anticipation of the collective resurrection of all the redeemed, the claim that Jesus is indeed the Christ is simultaneously a claim that his destiny embodies the mystery of human salvation.

(4) If the language of resurrection is finally a metaphor of salvation, it is a Christian statement about the nature of the reign of God preached by Jesus. The metaphor opens a vision of the ultimate possibilities of human existence. It suggests a vision of a transformed world that will find its fulfill-

ment only when the requirements of love have thoroughly penetrated all human reality and human relations. The call of love lies at the heart of all dreams of a world characterized by peace, justice, and the fullness of life.

(5) To speak of the resurrection of the body is to be reminded of the tie between individual destiny and the collective destiny of the human race, as well as the tie between human destiny and cosmic destiny. Traditionally the Christian hope for the final condition has been expressed not by a vision of disembodied souls but by a formula that expresses a dialectical relation between the spiritual soul and the risen body. By naming both of these dimensions of human reality, theology elicits the sense of the eternal significance of the universe in both its material and spiritual dimensions. That which is the object of God's creative love is also the object of God's redemptive activity.

(6) The mystery of Christ's resurrection is understood not as a movement to another world but as the beginning of a new relation of Christ to this world. Some systematic theologians prefer to use personalistic categories to explain this (e.g., K. Rahner, W. Kasper), while others attempt to employ categories of a more cosmological sort (e.g., J. Barbour, R. Pendergast). Both attempt to speak of the world of material creation as the object of God's salvific activity.

(7) If the resurrection has the basic revelatory and salvific meaning that is claimed for it, then it must provide key insights into the understanding of God, creation, church, sacraments, history, and eschatology. These implications remain to be worked out for the other areas of theology.

See: BODY, DEATH, JESUS CHRIST, SOUL

ZACHARY HAYES, O.F.M.

RETRIBUTION

A biblical consideration of retribution is progressive and developmental, moving from descriptions of reward and punishment in the OT to the vision of a new creation and redemption through Christ in the NT. The texts of the Hebrew and the Christian Scriptures contain theological reflection on the meaning of both reward and punishment. Similarly both testaments portray God as a just judge in the drama of salvation history.

Old Testament

Retribution, if properly understood, refers to a payment in the form of reward or punishment. The idea of retribution is most often associated with punishment for deeds that are perceived as evil; the recompense for crimes and sins is a penalty or disciplinary action. In early civilizations outside of Israel, where the deity was believed to be the bestower of blessings and punishments, there was an understanding that divine justice rested in the hands of the gods. A community that fell into hard times believed that it had offended the deity, and it sought to remedy the situation by obeying the deity's commands. The situation was similar in the ancient world of the Bible. There is a clear line of connection between God's wrath and the sin of humanity. The God of Israel was not capricious in inflicting punishment or in judging harshly. Nonetheless, it is true that the Hebrew Scriptures reveal God as a warrior and a judge, one whose authority is cosmic in dimension and whose power is eternal. The Hebrew Scriptures also tell of retribution that is exacted by one person on another. It is sometimes described as a "law of symmetry" in which equal punishment is inflicted on others as they had first delivered it.

The perspective on retribution, both divine and human, that is found in the OT is sometimes difficult for us to understand and appreciate today; it is foreign to our contemporary belief of the way that God responds to the human situation and the way that neighbor should respond to neighbor. Nonetheless, retribution represents a certain perspective on such important topics as divine justice, covenant, and redemption.

Torah/Pentateuch. We can only understand the meaning of retribution from within the full understanding of what is entailed in the covenant relationship. The divine initiative in Israel's covenant with God was the source of relationship. God had offered protection, security, and blessing to a people who were called to live in communion with their God by obedience to a set of precepts and laws. When Israel departed from the path of the covenant, God withdrew the protection and care which were part of the covenant treaty (Exod 20:2-6). Although there was wrath and vengeance expressed in the divine response to human frailty, God's covenant love remained open to receive back the wayward Israel who wished to renew the ruptured relationship (Exod 34:6-9).

The "retribution theory," or what is sometimes called the "deuteronomic principle," underlies Deuteronomy's basic teaching. "I set before you here, this day, a blessing and a curse: a blessing for obeying the commandments of the LORD, your God, which I enjoin on you today; a curse if you do not obey the commandments of the LORD, your God, but turn aside from the way I ordain for you today, to follow other gods, whom you have not known" (Deut 11:26-28). This teaching, set in very clear language, states that if the people expect to experience God's blessings and protection, they will have to follow the demands of the law; if they disobey the precepts and commandments, they can expect to know God's wrath and punishment for their infidelity to the covenant. The retribution theory includes both the notion of reward and punishment in response to the covenant.

There are examples of retribution that distinguish a way of relating to one's neighbor. "Life for life, eye for eye, tooth for tooth, hand for hand, and foot for foot" (Deut 19:21). This example of equal retribution is traditionally referred to as the Law of Talion. While it appears excessive and harsh to our contemporary social codes, scholars have suggested that it was probably a diminishing of earlier practices which were more brutal in nature and unlimited in the extent of a person's wrath to a situation. With the Law of Talion, boundaries were established for deciding upon a punishment for a particular crime: the punishment could not be greater than the crime that had been perpetrated.

The Deuteronomic History. It is worth noting that the retribution theory spoken of in Deuteronomy is also at work in the Books of Joshua, Judges, 1–2 Samuel, and 1–2 Kings. The story of Israel's defeat at Ai in Joshua 7:1-26 demonstrates this theory. Achan had kept some of the booty that was under the ban (i.e., dedicated to God); this act of disobedience brought misfortune and defeat to Israel. Only after Achan admitted his sinful deed and was punished was Israel able to defeat Ai and continue the victorious conquest of the land.

Similarly, there is a set of stereotypical expressions found in the Book of Judges that reveals the Deuteronomic principle at work in that period of Israel's history: "Because the Israelites had offended the LORD by forgetting the LORD, their God, and serving the Baals and the Asherahs, the anger of the LORD flared up against them. . . . But when the Israelites cried out to the LORD, he raised up for them a savior, Othniel, . . . who rescued them. . . . The land then was at rest for forty years, until Othniel, son of Kenaz, died" (Judg 3:7-11; see also 3:12-30; 6:1–8:28). These narratives from the book of Judges show young Israel's struggles to live in accord with the covenant demands, as they were adjusting to a new way of life in a new land.

The Prophets. The teaching of the prophets had an impact on the development of Israel's understanding of divine retribution. For the prophets, the day of judgment was drawing near when, "on that day," God would reward those who were loyal and punish those who were wicked (see Isa 2:11-17; 27:12-13; Jer 30:8-11; Amos 8:9-13). The day of God's retribution would also be a day of purification when punishment and chastisement would lead to the establishment of justice upon the earth (see Isa 29:17-24; 32:1-8; Zeph 3:11-20).

The Book of Lamentations presents a perspective on the notion of retribution consonant with the Deuteronomic and Prophetic position. Its unique perspective shows that in the midst of suffering, Israel proclaimed God's justice, awaiting healing and restoration (Lam 1:18; 3:22-26).

The Writings. The retribution theory of the Deuteronomic and Prophetic traditions is thrown into question with the searching questions of Job. While his friends keep reciting to him the religious theories of old, Job pleads his innocence (Job 4:2-6, 7-11; 29:18-20). While Job does not provide an answer to the question of divine retribution, he shows that there is more mystery than there are clear-cut answers in understanding the ways of God. God shows the friends of Job that suffering in the human experience is not easily explained (Job 42:8-9).

The Book of Wisdom opens a new doctrine of retribution in its references to life after death for those who are just (Wis 3:1-11; 4:7-19). Death is given a new meaning, and reward for a just life is eternal peace.

New Testament

What distinguishes the understanding of retribution in the New Covenant from that of the Old Covenant is the revelation of God's love in the person of Jesus Christ. While the image of God as Judge is still operative in the NT writings, its overriding message is a development of the new commandment of love and the implications of its exemplification in the lives of Jesus' disciples. It is also true that some of the OT thought about justice, eschatology, and recompense for one's deeds is still important in defining retribution in the Christian Scriptures.

Pauline Literature. For the apostle to the Gentiles, the sacrificial blood of Christ put an end to all vengeance among persons and established an eternal justice between God and humanity (Rom 3:24-26). The community of the faithful is to live in mutual love and respect, realizing their oneness in the Body of Christ. "Beloved, do not look for revenge but leave room for the wrath; for it is written, 'vengeance is mine, I will repay, says the Lord.' Rather, 'if your enemy is hungry, feed him; if he is thirsty, give him something to drink; for by so doing you will heap burning coals upon his head.' Do not be conquered by evil but conquer evil with good" (Rom 12:19-21). Just recompense still resides in God, who both rewards and punishes people according to their deeds.

In speaking about the final coming of Christ, Paul notes that God's creatures are not destined for wrath but for salvation. God wills that all people live according to the plan of divine justice and experience the effects of salvation brought about in Jesus Christ.

The Gospels. In the Sermon of the Mount, the moral teaching of Jesus provides a corrective to the instruction of the law. "You have heard that it was said, 'An eye for an eye and a tooth for a tooth.' But I say to you, offer no resistance to one who is evil. When someone strikes you on [your] right cheek, turn the other one to him as well" (Matt 5:38-39). Jesus overturned the Law of Talion, which guided the punishment for crimes in the law (cf. Exod 21:24; Lev 24:20; Deut 19:21). There is now a morality for a new age that puts an end to any kind of retaliation or retribution based on human standards or logic. Instead, Christian dealings with any person are to be based on a love that guides toward perfection according to God's reign (Matt 5:48).

The second coming of Jesus is portrayed as a judgment scene in which the righteous are separated from the unrighteous, according to their response to their brothers and sisters in need (Matt 25:31-46). This passage expresses the understanding of retribution as a system of both reward and punishment.

The Book of Revelation. The Book of Revelation shows the souls of the just at the end-times crying out for the vindication promised them for their witness to the word of God: "How long will it be, holy and true master, before you sit in judgment and avenge our blood on the inhabitants of the earth?" (Rev 6:10). The closing chapters (Revelation 21–22) paint a portrait of the new creation established in the end-times; there will be no need for retribution for "nothing accursed will be found there anymore" (Rev 22:3). Darkness will be overcome by light and eternal death will be replaced by everlasting life. "Behold, I am coming soon. I bring with me the recompense I will give to each according to his deeds. I am the Alpha and the Omega, the first and the last, the beginning and the end" (Rev 22:12-13).

See: COVENANT, ESCHATOLOGY, JUDGMENT, JUSTICE, REDEMPTION, WILL OF GOD, WRATH OF GOD

GREGORY J. POLAN, O.S.B.

New Testament

Antapodoma (noun: "repayment"), *antapodōmi* (verb: "I repay"), *misthos* ("pay, wages, reward," with both positive or negative connotations—as in receiving one's due reward for a crime), and *misthapodosia* ("payment of wages") are the basic Koine Greek terms translated as "retribution" (or recompense, vindication, vengeance, penalty, wrath, a return, compensation). Negative retribution is punishment that retaliates in kind, similar to the OT Law of Talion. Positive retribution is favor that rewards in kind. Either way, retribution in the NT is an ethical category naturally connected to justice,* judgment,* and mercy.* In this regard, many NT authors teach that negative retribution remains the sole prerogative of God; God can avenge, but people may not. Believers are urged instead to practice positive retribution (even toward enemies): to repay with kindness and mercy, not hate.

Divine Retribution. Several NT writers allude to or directly quote from OT passages speaking about the vengeance and wrath of God upon sinners. However, unlike the OT narratives of God's wrath falling promptly upon sinners, the NT doc-

uments describe divine retribution remaining a future act of God, occurring only at the end of time—the parousia of Jesus Christ—during the Last Judgment. Christians suffering injury are told to be patient for this delayed, eschatological justice. For example, the author of Hebrews exhorts: "Do you not think that a much worse punishment is due the one who has contempt for the Son of God, considers unclean the covenant blood by which he was consecrated, and insults the spirit of grace? We know the one who said: 'Vengeance is mine; I will repay,' and again: 'The Lord will judge his people.' It is a fearful thing to fall into the hands of the living God" (Heb 10:29-31; the citations are paraphrases, the first taken loosely from Deut 32:35, the second from Deut 32:36 or Ps 135:14). The author continues: "You even joined in the sufferings of those in prison and joyfully accepted the confiscation of property, knowing that you had a better and lasting possession. Therefore, do not throw away your confidence; it will have great recompense. You need endurance to do the will of God and receive what he has promised" (Heb 10:34-36).

Divine justice saves and damns: "For if the word announced through angels proved firm, and every transgression and disobedience received its just recompense, how shall we escape if we ignore so great a salvation?" (Heb 2:2-3). Paul echoes this warning of divine retribution. He writes: "By your stubbornness of heart, you are storing up wrath for yourself for the day of wrath and revelation of the just judgment of God, who will repay everyone according to his works" (Rom 2:5-6; see also 2 Thess 1:6-9).

In the Gospels, we find similar retribution language associated with judgment day. The author of Matthew has Jesus warn: "'Woe to you, scribes and Pharisees, you hypocrites. . . . Thus you bear witness against yourselves that you are the children of those who murdered the prophets; now fill up what your ancestors have measured out! You serpents, you brood of vipers, how can you flee from the judgment of Gehenna?" (Matt 23:29, 31-33; see also 11:20-24; 13:40-43).

Several parables of Jesus tell of divine retribution, such as the parable of the unjust slave (Matt 18:23-35). This parable teaches mercy and warns of eschatological judgment. Although the master forgives the debts of the slave, the slave refuses to act in kind to his fellow slaves. Upon discovery, the master shouts: "'You wicked servant! I forgave you your entire debt because you begged me to. Should you not have had pity on your fellow servant, as I had pity on you?'" Matthew reports Jesus explaining how the parable is an illustration of divine retribution: "Then in anger his master handed him over to the torturers until he should pay back the whole debt. So will my heavenly father do to you unless each of you forgives his brother from his heart" (Matt 18:32-35). The parable of the great dinner further illustrates this biblical principle (Matthew 22:1-14 = Luke 14:15-24). There will be disastrous consequences for refusing an invitation to enter the reign of God. Divine retribution occurs in the future, at the final day of reckoning, which is the Jewish theological concept of apocalyptic eschatology. Notice that believers are admonished to behave toward one another with mercy, leaving retributive punishment to God. This leads into the next issue to consider, namely the appropriateness of human retribution.

Human Retribution. Many NT writers demand that believers never avenge themselves. Christians are to leave negative retribution to God, practicing instead positive retribution. In Christian conduct, Paul tells his major rule: "See that no one returns evil for evil; rather always seek what is good [both] for each other and for all" (1 Thess 5:15). In another place, Paul repeats this ethic: "Do not repay evil for evil; be concerned for what is noble in the sight of all. If possible, on your part, live at peace with all. Beloved, do not look for revenge but leave room for wrath; for it is written, 'Vengeance is mine, I will repay, says the Lord.' Rather 'if your enemy is hungry, feed him; if he is thirsty, give him something to drink; for by so doing you will heap burning coals upon his head.' Do not be conquered by evil but conquer evil with good" (Rom 12:17-21; citing Deut 32:35 and Prov 20:22; 25:21-22). As any good pastor, Paul was constantly concerned with successful or at least agreeable relationships within his congregations. Punitive behavior damaged the concord that he tried so urgently to instill in his churches.

We see a similar plea from the author of 1 Peter, who writes: "Do not return evil for evil, or insult for insult; but, on the contrary, a blessing, because to this you were called, that you might inherit a blessing" (1 Pet 3:9). Later Christian preachers connected this communal ethic back to the teachings of Jesus himself. In the sermon on the mount, Jesus is reported to say: "You have heard that it was said, 'An eye for an eye and a tooth for a tooth.' But I say to you offer no resistance to one who is evil. When someone strikes you on [your] right cheek, turn the other one to him as well. If anyone wants to go to law with you over your tunic, hand him your cloak as well. Should anyone press you into service for one mile, go with him for two miles. Give to the one who asks of you, and do not turn your back on the one who wants to borrow." (Matt 5:38-42). This is a patent rejection of the OT Law of Talion.

In summary, then, negative retribution is unacceptable Christian behavior, according to these NT authors. God retaliates in both positive and negative ways; people may retaliate only in positive ways.

See: APOCALYPTIC, ESCHATOLOGY, GEHENNA, GRACE, HATE, JUDGMENT, JUSTICE, MERCY, PAROUSIA, SALVATION, SIN, WRATH OF GOD

J. ALBERT HARRILL

RICH

In the early traditions of the OT, wealth is simply the gift of God. Riches were not a social or moral problem. It is with the social division that arose within Israelite society between rich and poor* that this issue came to the fore. The Prophetic and Wisdom traditions focus on this issue. Jesus calls not only for a correct attitude by the wealthy toward their possessions but also expects that they use them to benefit the poor. Paul and James both insist that rich Christians do not allow social and economic distinctions to affect their relationships with their poorer brothers and sisters.

Old Testament

The Book of Amos.
Of the prophets Amos directed his attention specifically to the rich. Perhaps the most dramatic accusation of Amos directed at the rich occurs in 4:1 in which the prophet says that the lifestyle of the rich results from their robbing the poor. The prophet makes the same accusation in 5:11: "you trample upon the poor and take from them exactions of wheat, you have built houses of hewn stone." In 8:4 the prophet makes it clear that the rich are crushing the poor and killing them.

The prophecy of Amos is an uncompromising attack on the social evils of the eighth century BCE in Israel. The prophet excoriates the wealthy because they seize the land of the poor, because they pervert the traditional legal system that is to protect the poor, and because they corrupt the economy for their own benefit. His words describe the actions of the wealthy as heartless and dishonest.

It almost appears as if Amos is describing a class conflict as if he were a contemporary Marxist analyst. For Amos, however, the poor do not form a "class." The poor are so because they are alone and defenseless. They are not in any way organized against the rich in some sort of a struggle. On the other hand, Amos sees the rich not as isolated individuals but as a group. They are rich precisely because they are able to marshall the forces at their disposal, especially the judicial system, to undercut the poor and by that increase their own wealth. Amos does not see some class conflict in all this. According to the prophet, Yahweh and Yahweh alone will bring vengeance upon the wealthy.

The Book of Proverbs.
Very often the sages responsible for ancient Israel's Wisdom tradition are presented as those who sought success, prosperity, and happiness. In a sense that is true, though it is perhaps better to say that the sages as those who sought to find effective ways to cope with the problems of life rather than those who sought to find the solution to those problems in wealth and success. They were realistic enough to know that wealth brought its own set of problems as did poverty. Just as they did not idealize the poor, the sages did not idolize the rich (Prov 29:13). The sages prayed that God would protect them from the pitfalls that come with both poverty *and* wealth (Prov 30:7-9). Wealth can blind people to the real source of their prosperity. They can believe that it is the result of their own effective planning and careful judgments when, in fact, it is due to the goodness of God (Prov 19:21). Poverty and wealth are the kinds of extremes that are dangerous because they can lead people to be forgetful of God.

The Book of Sirach.
The Book of Sirach engages in a striking polemic against a hectic concern for earning money characteristic of the merchant class of second-century BCE Palestine (Sir 26:29–27:3). The author probably considered traditional agricultural pursuits to be the more acceptable way of earning a living (7:15; 20:28). He evidently had a problem with the emerging merchant class that had more occasions to deal with Hellenists and to compromise Yahwistic traditions than the peasants who followed agrarian occupations. More serious is the author's intimation that the rich take advantage of the poor to enrich themselves. He condemns those who use what they have taken from the poor as a sacrifice, those who deprive the poor of their most basic needs, and those who withhold the wages of the poor (Sir 34:20-22). In 13:19 Sirach graphically describes how the poor are at the mercy of the rich.

The words of Sirach point to a social climate that was marked by observable social conflict between the rich and poor: "What peace is there between a hyena and a dog? And what peace between a rich man and a poor man?" (13:18; see also 13:20). What made this conflict so acute was the perception by the poor and those who sympathized with them, like Sirach, that the rich were ready to compromise traditional values for economic and social gain. Sirach notes the penchant the rich had for exploiting the poor (13:4a). Despite the social conflict that marked Sirach's experience, he did not condemn riches as such. He values wealth that people have gained honestly because it guarantees a secure life (10:27; 13:24a; 40:18a). But Sirach also warns against the dangers of riches (8:2; 13:15-24). He advises the wealthy to respond to the cries of the poor (4:8; see also 4:1-5; 29:8-9).

Sirach repeatedly returns to the topic of wealth. He compares generosity and niggardliness (14:3-8). He calls people of means to be generous with their help to the needy (4:4-6; 7:32-36; 29:9-13). Because the poor need loans to survive at times, he asks the wealthy to be forthcoming though there are many problems connected with loans (29:1-7, 14-20). According to Sirach wealth is not wrong but he sharply criticizes undeserved profit (4:1-3; 5:8; 21:8) and warns that it is difficult for the rich to remain honest and faithful to God (26:29–27:2; 31:1-11).

New Testament

The Gospel of Luke. The Gospel of Luke deals with the rich explicitly several times. One significant pericope is the parable of the rich man and Lazarus (16:19-31). In the parable there is no indication of any special guilt on the rich man's part except that he did not care for Lazarus. Similarly there is no special merit on Lazarus' part. The parable implies that the reign of God belongs to the poor while the rich may share in it if they treat the poor with kindness and benevolence. Although this parable is about the after-life, its purpose is to describe how the rich ought to lead their lives in the present.

The story of Zacchaeus (19:1-10) illustrates the truth of this parable. The rich man Zacchaeus (v. 2) asserts that he will give half his wealth to the poor (v. 8). This is tangible evidence of his repentance. Zacchaeus is the only rich man who is saved in Luke. Apparently Luke believed that people of means can be saved only by a kind of repentance that shows its sincerity by giving to the poor.

Zacchaeus was willing to forego his wealth for the sake of the reign of God. Luke, however, knew of another man who was not so willing. The tradition behind 18:18-30 (the rich ruler) is common to the Synoptics (see Matt 19:16-30 and Mark 10:17-31). Luke was not unique in pointing out the dangers to salvation that wealth brought with itself. He, however, accentuated the warning regarding the proper use of wealth. But did Luke call for a total renunciation of possessions by those who wished to be disciples of Jesus? Luke is probably quite close to Jesus' own teaching here because total renunciation is most compatible with the eschatological orientation of Jesus' message, yet renunciation is only half the story. The rich man was called to place all his trust in God by selling his possessions. Jesus also asked him to use the profits from the sale to benefit the poor. Jesus was not merely looking for a proper attitude toward wealth; he deemed proper action equally important. In explaining the failure of the man to pick up on the challenge offered by Jesus, Matthew and Mark note that the young man "had many possessions." Luke, however, states that he was "very rich" (v. 23). Luke keeps the social distinction between rich and poor quite clear. A striking contrast to the rich man is the poor widow whose gift of two copper coins to the Temple's treasury was "all the living she had" (21:1-4). Luke then uses the contrast between the wealthy and the poor as an indicator of people's attitudes toward Jesus and the message he brings from God.

The Pauline Corpus. There is one place where Paul speaks directly to the rich when he wrote to the Church at Corinth. Evidently there were social differences among the members of that community. The Hellenistic world was quite class-conscious, and the divisions within Corinthian society spilled over into the community of faith: "when you assemble as a church, I hear that there are divisions among you" (1 Cor 11:18). Wealthy members of that community kept to themselves, feasted on their own food at the Lord's Supper, and neglected the hungry. Paul condemns such behavior because it disrupted the unity of the body of Christ (1 Cor 11:22, 29). The wealthy Corinthians were introducing their unjust social system into the Church. This Paul had rejected by describing how God acts toward the poor: "God chose what is low and despised in the world, even things that are not, to bring to nothing things that are" (1 Cor 1:28). Paul says that the community of faith represents God's decision to overturn the existing unjust social order. The social tensions of Corinthian society must not be allowed to spill over into the Church.

The Letter of James. James 2:1-7 is a caustic rebuke to the rich. It reflects a situation in which the poor were not being held in very high esteem because of the entry of wealthy people into the community. This James regarded as detestable. To bolster his argument he observes that "God has chosen the poor in the world to be rich in faith" (2:5). James insisted that the social differentiation between poor and rich within the community must stop. In 5:1-6 James launches another scathing attack on the rich. This time he describes their role in general society. He accuses them of unjust activity with an intensity that rivals even Amos.

See: JUSTICE, POOR

LESLIE J. HOPPE, O.F.M.

ROCK/STONE

The image of "rock" (*'eben, sûr, sela'*) appears frequently in both Testaments. Most prominent is its use as a title for God. The "Rock of Israel" (Gen 49:24; 2 Sam 23:3; Pss 40:2; 62:7) is the one whose might and steadiness shields from all harm. As "a rock

of refuge" (2 Sam 22:3; Pss 31:2; 71:3; Isa 17:10), God is like a "a strong fortress" (Pss 18:2; 31:2, 3; 62:6; 71:3; 144:2; 2 Sam 22:2). To establish a position in the rocky heights (Isa 33:16) was an ancient means of protection. The psalmist asserts that "in the day of trouble" God will "set me high upon a rock" (Pss 27:5; 61:2). As rock, God also trains hands for battle (Ps 144:1).

God is "rock of salvation" (Deut 32:15; 2 Sam 22:47; Pss 18:46; 62:6; 89:26; 94:22; 95:1; 2 Sam 22:47), "rock and redeemer" (Pss 19:15; 78:35). As rock, God's deeds are faultless (Deut 32:4), just (Ps 92:16), and powerful (Hab 1:12). God is invoked as Rock to hear pleas (Ps 28:1) and not forget a petitioner (Ps 42:10). One may securely trust in God forever, "for the LORD is an eternal Rock" (Isa 26:4). God alone is rock (2 Sam 22:32; Pss 18:32; 62:3, 7), there is no other (Deut 32:31; Isa 44:8; 1 Sam 2:2).

God's word is so powerful that it is "like a hammer shattering rocks" (Jer 23:29). When God's fury is poured out "the rocks are rent asunder before him" (Nah 1:6). One should "speak not haughtily against the Rock" (Ps 75:6).

In Deuteronomy 32 two images for God are juxtaposed: Rock and birthing mother. Moses upbraids the Israelites, "You were unmindful of the Rock that begot you, You forgot the God who gave you birth" (Deut 32:18). Isaiah also employs the metaphor of progeny from rock: "Look to the rock from which you were hewn, to the pit from which you were quarried" (Isa 51:1-2). Here, however, it is not God who is the rock, but Israel's ancestors.

The famous incident during the Exodus in which God provided water from a rock for the Israelites (Exod 17:1-7; Num 20:2-13) is recalled numerous times (Deut 8:15; Neh 9:15; Pss 78:16, 20; 105:41; 114:8; Isa 48:21; 1 Cor 10:4). God also gave Israel honey (Deut 32:13; Ps 81:17) and oil from the rock (Deut 32:13; Job 29:6). These are not miraculous provisions, but rather are a description of the land where wild honey can be found among the rocks and oil is produced from olives that grow in the stony soil.

Rock provides security in its clefts, as in Exodus 33:22, where God shields Moses from direct exposure to the divine countenance. The cleft of a rock gave protection to Samson from the Philistines (Judg 15:8; see also 1 Sam 13:6) and to David from Saul (1 Sam 23:25). The prophet Isaiah likens just rulers to "the shade of a great rock in a parched land" (Isa 32:2). Those who pursue idols "will go into caves in the rocks" to hide from the terror of the Lord (Isa 2:19; similarly Jer 48:28).

In the Bible there are many uses for rock and stone. The Law given to Moses was inscribed on two tablets of stone (Exod 24:12; 31:18; 34:1, 4; Deut 4:13; 5:22; 9:9, 10, 11; 10:1). Tombs were carved from rock (Isa 22:16; Matt 27:60) and sealed with large rolling stones (Matt 27:66; 28:2; John 11:38, 39, 41; 20:1). Stone slabs sealed the mouths of wells (Gen 29:2). Rocks served as tables on which to lay sacrifice offered to God (Judg 6:20-21; 13:19; 1 Sam 6:14). Altars were to be made of unhewn stones (Exod 20:25; cf. Ezek 40:42). Jacob used a stone for a pillow (Gen 28:11).

Vessels were made of stone (Exod 7:19; John 2:6). Precious stones were found in Eden (Gen 2:12; Ezek 28:13). They adorned crowns (2 Sam 12:30) and sacred vestments (Exod 39:10). Weights were made of stone (Lev 19:36; Deut 25:13; Prov 16:11; 20:10, 23). Rocks served as boundary markers (Josh 15:6; 18:17). Walls (Prov 24:31), pavements (John 19:13), and houses (Amos 5:11) were constructed with stone. For the temple "fine, large blocks were quarried to give the temple a foundation of hewn stone" (1 Kgs 5:31; see also 1 Kgs 6:7; 7:12). Facing the temple Jesus prophesies that "there will not be one stone left upon another" (Mark 13:2 and par.).

Stones were used in warfare. When slung they could be deadly, as in the famous encounter between David and Goliath (1 Sam 17:40-49; see also Judg 20:16; 1 Chr 12:2). Stoning to death was prescribed as punishment for various offenses (Lev 24:14, 16; Num 15:35; 35:17; Deut 13:10; 17:5; 21:21; 22:21; 22:24; John 8:5). Some Jews at-tempted to stone Jesus for blasphemy (John 10:31; 11:8). The first follower of Jesus to be stoned to death was Stephen (Acts 7:58).

A memorial stone was set up by Jacob at Bethel (Gen 28:22). He set up another when he entered into a treaty with Laban (Gen 31:45, 46). Joshua marked the spot of Israel's crossing into Canaan with twelve memorial stones (Josh 4:1-9; see also 1 Sam 7:12). And when renewing the covenant with the people he set up a "stone of witness" (Josh 24:26-27).

There are repeated admonitions to Israel against idols of wood and stone (Deut 4:28; 16:22; 28:26, 64; 29:17; Dan 5:4, 23). Jeremiah derides those "who say to a piece of wood, 'You are my father,' and to a stone, 'You gave me birth'" (Jer 2:27). He insists that the wooden posts and erect stones, cultic objects of the Canaanites, were totally ineffectual.

Stone is used as an image of intransigence, a refusal to convert. Jeremiah complains to God, "They set their faces harder than stone, and refused to return to you" (Jer 5:3). God promises restoration to the exiles, "I will remove the stony heart from their bodies, and replace it with a natural heart, so that they will live according to my statutes, and observe and carry out my ordinances" (Ezek 11:19-20; see also Job 41:24).

Stone, particularly a cornerstone, is a metaphor for the firmest of foundations. Isaiah prophesies, "See, I am laying a stone in Zion, a stone that has been tested, A precious cornerstone as a sure foundation"; whoever puts faith in it shall not be shaken (Isa 28:16). Christians understand this prophecy as fulfilled in Christ (Rom 9:33; Eph 2:20; 1 Peter 2:6-8). Also applied to him is Psalm 118:22, "The stone which the builders rejected has become the cornerstone" (Matt 21:42; Mark 12:10; Luke 20:17; Acts 4:11). Yet this stone can be a cause of stumbling. Just as God "shall be a snare, an obstacle and a stumbling stone to both the houses of Israel" (Isa 8:14), so is the crucified Christ to many (Rom 9:32; 1 Cor 1:23).

See: COVENANT, EXODUS, FAITH, IDOLATRY, REDEMPTION/REDEEMER, SALVATION, SCANDAL, WITNESS

BARBARA E. REID, O.P.

ROME

The turmoil accompanying the century-long death throes of the republic came to an end in 31 BCE when the Roman world was united under the undisputed leadership of Octavian, who on 16 January 27 was given the title Augustus. The climate of stability and security which ensued greatly facilitated the spread of Christianity. It must have been brought to Rome by Jews converted when on pilgrimage to Jerusalem (Acts 2:10). The closeness of the connection between the two cities is underlined by the presence in Jerusalem of a synagogue of the "libertini" (Acts 6:9), who can only have been Roman freedmen.

In the fourth decade of the first century Jews in Rome numbered between forty and fifty thousand. The names of between ten and thirteen synagogues are known. It was in this soil that Christianity first took root, but not without difficulty. The details are disputed, but the most plausible explanation of references in Suetonius (Claudius, 24), Dio Cassius (History, 60:6.6), and Philo (Leg. to Gaius, 156–157) is that in 41 there was a disturbance in a Roman synagogue concerning Christ. Claudius reacted by expelling the Judaeo-Christian missionaries who were not Roman citizens, and temporarily withdrew from that community the right of assembly. Luke's use of this event to date Paul's arrival in Corinth reflects a misunderstanding of its nature and timing, but he is probably correct in imply-ing that Aquila and Priscilla had been converted in and through a Roman synagogue (Acts 18:2).

Fifteen years later the composition of the community had changed. When Paul wrote to Rome in 56, it seems clear that the majority in the Church were Gentile converts (Rom 11:13-32; 15:7-12). The knowledge of the OT presumed by Paul suggests that they had originally been attracted by the austerity of Judaism and had attended synagogue sermons. From the names in Romans 16 it has been deduced that most of the community were slaves or freedmen/women, nearly half of whom were well off. There were certainly three house-churches (Rom 16:5, 14-15), possibly more (16:10-11). One indication of the quality of their Christian life is their avoidance of Paul when he came to Rome as a prisoner in the early 60s (cf. Acts 28:16, 30 with 27:3).

Such lack of charity had more terrible consequences in the summer of 64. "First, Nero had self-acknowledged Christians arrested. Then, on their information, large numbers of others were condemned" (Tacitus, Annals, 15:43-44). The savage persecution thus unleashed by Nero lasted until his death in 68. At some point, the date is uncertain, he had Paul decapitated and Peter crucified; the latter was buried on the Vatican hill, the former on the road to Ostia (Eusebius, Church History, 2:25.5-8).

See: JEWS, HOUSE CHURCH, PAUL, PETER, SYNAGOGUE

JEROME MURPHY-O'CONNOR, O.P.

S

SABBATH

The historical origins of the Israelite celebration of the Sabbath are not certain, but the Sabbath was and continues to be immensely important in Jewish religious practice. The Sabbath is mentioned in all three pentateuchal law codes, and it became particularly important during and after the Exile. It served as a sign of Israel's covenant with God and as a vehicle to remind the community of its identity through rest and worship. The early Christian community gradually shifted its day of worship to Sunday but brought with it many of the practices of the Jewish Sabbath.

Old Testament

The Hebrew word for Sabbath, *shabat*, means "to cease" or "to desist." On the Sabbath the members of the community cease or desist from labor. A secondary meaning of the Hebrew word is "to rest" (Exod 21:19; Lev 26:34-35; 2 Chr 36:21), the obvious result of the cessation of labors. The Sabbath is celebrated on the seventh day of the week, a celebration that gains significance from God's rest on the seventh day after six days of creation (Gen 2:3).

Origins. The historical antecedents of the celebration of the Sabbath in Israel are unclear. Biblical scholars have tried to connect the Israelite observance of the Sabbath with ancient Babylonian practices. The Babylonians rested on the fifteenth day of each month, the day of the full moon. The Akkadian title for the day is similar to the Hebrew word for Sabbath. The Babylonians, however, understood the day to be an "evil day" because on that day gods who were hostile to humans took control. Humans abstained from certain labors to pacify the gods or to avoid drawing down their ire.

Another possible connection with Israel's celebration of the Sabbath appears in the Babylonian creation myth known as *Enuma elish*. In this story the Babylonian gods rest after the creation of humankind as does the God of Israel after creation (Gen 2:3).

Even if Israel drew its ideas for the Sabbath from Babylonian antecedents, Israel's own practices and perceptions of the meaning of the Sabbath were distinctive. For instance, in the Genesis 1 account of creation God rests in contentment and satisfaction because everything is "very good" (Gen 1:31). In the *Enuma elish*, by contrast, the gods rest because they are liberated from labors that humans can now do for them. Another difference is that Israel's observance of the Sabbath was weekly and not monthly, and Israel's Sabbath was a day of joy and praise of God and not of appeasement of the deity.

Importance. Whatever its origins, Sabbath observance was central to Israel's religious practice. The presence of Sabbath laws in the major legal codes found in the Pentateuch reveal the antiquity of Israel's Sabbath celebration. In the Ten Commandments given to Moses on Mount Sinai, God commands the community: "Remember to keep holy the sabbath day. Six days you may labor and do all your work, but the seventh day is the sabbath of the Lord, your God" (Exod 20:8-10). This commandment prohibits work by anyone in the family, by slaves, beasts, or by aliens who might live with the family (v. 10c; see Exod 23:12).

The Deuteronomic version of the Ten Commandments repeats the Sabbath injunctions of the Exodus law but gives more attention to the rest by slaves (Deut 5:12-15). "Your male and female slaves should rest as you do" (Deut 5:14).

Another Exodus collection of laws also associated with Mount Sinai testifies to the seriousness with which the observance of the Sabbath was treated, at least at a certain period of its history. The Israelites should keep the Sabbaths "as a token" between them and God "throughout the generations" (Exod 31:12-13). But in addition to refraining from work (vv. 14-15), the community was to "keep the sabbath as something sacred." Anyone who violated the Sabbath by working was to be put to death (vv. 14-15).

Purpose. Although the Pentateuchal texts agree about the importance of keeping the Sabbath, the purpose of the Sabbath differs from law code to law code. This variation indicates that the significance of the Sabbath expanded and developed as the people's circumstances changed.

In one group of texts the reason for keeping the Sabbath is that God rested on the seventh day after creation. "That is why the Lord has blessed the sabbath day and made it holy" (Exod 20:11). In this text, as in Genesis 1:1–2:4, the community is to observe the Sabbath because their creator made the day holy and rested on it. They are to imitate God and celebrate their place in the creation by keeping the Sabbath.

Exodus 31:12-17 provides the same motivation for keeping the Sabbath, but expands the theological significance of the practice. Israelites are to observe the Sabbath "throughout their generations as a perpetual covenant" (v. 16). Between God and the Israelites, it is to be "an everlasting token" (v. 17). Here observance of the Sabbath becomes a sign and reminder of the everlasting covenant Israel has with its God.

By contrast, the Deuteronomic commandment derives its motivation from the concerns of justice. Its emphasis is not exclusively theological. Rather, its theology arises from its concerns for suffering human beings. Slaves are to rest just like everyone else because "you too were once slaves in Egypt and the Lord, your God, brought you from there with his strong hand and outstretched arm" (Deut 5:15). This understanding of God as the one who frees slaves did not lead Israel to reject the institution of slavery that was generally accepted among the ancients, but it did require that Israel treat slaves with compassion. In the Deuteronomic view the Sabbath was to remind the community of its own origins as a people freed from slavery who now have responsibilities of justice toward the enslaved.

Leviticus 23:3 develops the law to keep the Sabbath in yet another way. To the command to abstain from work, it adds that the Sabbath is a day "for sacred assembly." The Priestly writers of Leviticus make liturgical worship an explicit feature of Sabbath observance that "the sabbath shall belong to the Lord wherever you dwell" (Lev 23:3).

Sign of Identity. Over the course of time, the Sabbath became a vehicle to express and to solidify Israel's self-understanding as God's people. The theological understanding of the Sabbath expanded greatly during the period of Exile when large portions of Israel's population became prisoners of war in Babylon. Exile not only caused great suffering, it also deprived the community of its traditional supports for its faith.

During this crisis Israel's priests urged the exiles to celebrate the Sabbath "wherever you dwell" (Lev 23:3). The observance of the Sabbath as a day of rest and of sacred assembly would bring the people together and remind them of their identity as God's people in an alien land. This may explain why the Holiness Code of Leviticus (19:3, 30; 23:3; 26:2) gives special emphasis to Sabbath laws, and why the Sabbath became an essential sign of the covenant (Exod 31:12-17).

The prophets also place added importance on the Sabbath at the time of the Exile and after. For Jeremiah, the fate of the nation would hinge upon the nation's fidelity to Sabbath observance (Jer 17:19-27). Ezekiel understood the Sabbath as a sign of God's relationship with the people (Ezek 20:20). Like Jeremiah, Nehemiah asserted that profaning the Sabbath brought "all this evil upon us and upon this city" (Neh 13:17-18). Third Isaiah declared that the one who keeps the Sabbath will be "happy" (Isa 56:2-5), and promises that "If you call the sabbath a delight . . . then you shall delight in the Lord" (Isa 58:13-14).

Sabbath Regulations. Just as the theological significance of the Sabbath varied during the OT period, so Sabbath regulations changed and expanded. The Sabbath was to provide rest for humans and animals (Exod 20:10; 23:12; Deut 5:14), and so certain work was prohibited. It was forbidden to gather wood (Num 15:32), to light fires (Exod 35:3), to prepare food (Exod 16:23), to move unnecessarily from place to place (Exod 16:29), or to engage in business (Amos 8:5). In a more positive vein, the Sabbath was a time for sacred assembly (Lev 23:3), for offering of sacrifices (Num 28:9-10), and for setting out fresh showbread by the priests (Lev 24:8).

So important was the observance of the Sabbath that during the sojourn in the desert God sent manna from heaven for six days only. On the sixth day God sent a double portion so that Israel could refrain from gathering manna and thus keep the Sabbath (Exod 16:4-36). During the Maccabean war some Jews would not bear arms on the Sabbath even in self-defense (1 Macc 2:32-38). In response to the massacre of these pious Jews, Mattathias, the leader of the Maccabees, insisted that fighting in self-defense was according to God's will (1 Macc 2:39-41).

Sabbath observance united Israel as a people, celebrated their identity, and symbolized their relationship with God. It was characterized by a concern for justice to slaves and was celebrated liturgically. It may be significant that Psalm 92, described in the text as "a song for the sabbath day" (Ps 92:1), is a great hymn of thanksgiving. It captures the Jewish spirit of the Sabbath. "It is good to give thanks to the Lord, to sing praise to your name, Most High" (Ps 92:1).

New Testament

Christians do not celebrate the Sabbath or seventh day of the week. They celebrate Sunday or the Lord's Day, the day Jesus Christ rose from the dead. In actual practice, however, Christians transferred the spirit and many of the observances of the Jewish Sabbath to their celebration of Sunday.

Jesus and the Sabbath. Jesus did not cancel the celebration of the Sabbath. Indeed, he was a faithful adherent of its spirit, and he celebrated it liturgically. Luke presents him in Nazareth going to the synagogue on the Sabbath day, "according to his custom" (Luke 4:16). According to Luke's Gospel, it was on the Sabbath that Jesus inaugurated his public ministry. He participated in worship by reading publicly from the Scriptures, and he dramatically announced his mission to proclaim "glad tidings to the poor" (Luke 4:18).

From the point of view of some Jews of his time, however, Jesus did appear lax in his observance. He allowed the disciples to pick grain on the Sabbath because they were hungry (Matt 12:1-8). He healed the bent over woman in the synagogue on the Sabbath (Luke 13:10-17). He confounded his opponents by curing a man with dropsy on the Sabbath (Luke 14:1-6). He claimed that God does not cease working on the Sabbath, so neither would he (5:1-18).

What Jesus rejected was not the Sabbath but the legalism regarding the Sabbath observance that had crept in among some of his contemporaries. Jesus set believers free from religious legalism for all time by declaring that the Sabbath was made for humans and not humans for the Sabbath (Mark 2:27). For Jesus, as well as for some of his other Jewish contemporaries, love, compassion, and justice took precedence over religious law.

The Disciples and the Sabbath. That Jesus did not oppose the celebration of the Sabbath is further supported by the fact that his disciples continued to observe the Sabbath after the resurrection (Matt 28:1; Mark 15:42; 16:1; John 19:42). The Acts of the Apostles relates that the disciples attended synagogue services and preached to the congregation (Acts 13:14-15). They used the Sabbath as a time to make contact with devout believers like Lydia and to preach to them about Jesus (Acts 16:13-15). Acts particularly presents Paul celebrating the Sabbath. "Following his usual custom" Paul met with others to discuss the Scriptures and to preach the good news to them (Acts 17:2).

Gradually, however, Christians shifted the day of solemn rest and worship to Sunday, the day of resurrection and the first day of the week. Christian liturgical heritage, nonetheless, has its roots in the Jewish celebration of the Sabbath.

Pastoral Notes

In many parts of the United States today, Sunday appears to be little different from other days of the week. Many people have to go out to work, malls and shops are open, necessary chores around the home must be done. This raises the question of how to celebrate the day of worship when its traditional practices receive little support from the society itself.

In such a setting, attendance at liturgy and time for rest happen only as the result of a conscious choice. This is probably good because it requires clear decision on the part of Christians, a circumstance that has always faced Jewish communities in their observance of the Sabbath.

The reasons for observing Sunday today are no less compelling than they were for the celebration of the Sabbath in biblical times. To set time aside to worship together on the same day of every week can remind Christians of our common identity in Jesus and of our unity as a people. At least theoretically, such worship renews our life in the crucified and resurrected One, nourishes our spirit of thanksgiving for our participation in creation, and reminds us of our commitment to justice for all peoples.

Then there is the simple fact that a day of rest, or at least a more restful day, enables us to return to our usual work refreshed and alive. Among the middle classes in the United States this is a particularly important reason for observing the Sabbath, because stepping aside from our work can show us how work and its monetary reward can become our idol. It can also remind us of our duty of justice to those around the globe and in our neighborhood who have no work from which to rest or who cannot take a day of rest because of their economic conditions.

Moreover, our celebration of Sunday can remind Christians of their Jewish origins. Throughout history Christians have forgotten their Jewish roots with deadly consequences for the Jewish community. Jews have become victims of the murderous hatred of Christians, and Christians have lost their humanity and denied their faith in the process. Sometimes Christians perpetuate themes of this sad history in subtle ways.

For instance, in seeking to show the uniqueness of Christianity, Christians often describe Judaism as an inferior religion that has been completely replaced by Christianity. One way this has been done has been to denigrate Jewish observance of the Sabbath as nothing more than legalism, pure and simple. But such remarks are false and dangerous.

It is true that at times in their history, some Jewish groups stressed external aspects of Sabbath celebration, becoming excessively legalistic. Yet this is the fate of every religious group at some time or other in its history. Especially during uncertain economic or political times, all religions have a tendency to fall into rigidity and formalism. To find a parallel Roman Catholics need only remember their excessive legal scrupulosity before Vatican II.

Some groups of Pharisees among Jesus' contemporaries emphasized externals and lost the underlying spirit of the Sabbath. But neither Jesus nor his disciples turned away from celebrating the Sabbath. Jesus was a reformer of Judaism, reminding his contemporaries of the true spirit of the Sabbath. Christians and Jews worship the same God, the one God, the creator of all. Sundays will be truly hallowed if Christians raise their voices in repentance for the sins of the past and join with their Jewish sisters and brothers to praise the God who made us all.

See: FEASTS, JUBILEE YEAR

KATHLEEN M. O'CONNOR

Pastoral-Liturgical Tradition

The Sabbath can be adequately understood in the Christian experience only in terms of its relationship to Sunday. Many Christians continued to observe the Sabbath for most of the first century. These included Jewish-Christians, even after their expulsion from the synagogues at the end of that century, as well as some Gentile groups, although the latter does not appear to be a widespread phenomenon. Despite such continuity with Jewish practice, significant questions about the place of the Sabbath in the new dispensation already arose in NT times. While the Sabbath is mentioned more often than Sunday (the first day of the week) in the NT, and the practice of Jewish and even some Gentile followers of Jesus demonstrates continued observance of the Sabbath law, various developments in this period foreshadow the eventual eclipse of Sabbath by Sunday.

Originally Christians gathered constantly for those things articulated in Acts 2:42. Besides irregularly scheduled gatherings, they also inherited the custom of gathering on particular days of the week. The Jews held regularly scheduled services on Sabbath as well as the market days of Monday and Thursday. Jewish Christians adapted these practices to their own needs. By the end of the first century adaptation was giving way to replacement: Sunday in place of the Sabbath, and Wednesday-Friday as fast days [Didache 8] to replace the Monday-Thursdays of the Jews.

The reasons why Sabbath was replaced by Sunday are complex. The three major theories explaining this change suggest that Sunday superceded the Sabbath because (1) the Christian community remembered Sunday as the day of Christ's resurrection (C. Mosna, *Storia della domenica*), (2) Christians gathered for Eucharist on Sunday (W. Rordorf, *Sabbath und Sontag*), or (3) the growing rivalry between Christians and Jews gave rise to an anti-semitism that compelled Christians to distinguish themselves as much as possible from Jews, including an intentional distancing from Sabbath observance (S. Bacchiocchi, *From Sabbath to Sunday*). It is probably a combination of all of these elements, especially the memory of Sunday as the day of resurrection, that led to the eventual triumph of Sunday over Sabbath in Christianity.

The early second century provides evidence for the gradual abandonment of the Sabbath observance in various Christian communities. Ignatius of Antioch (d. ca. 107), for example, remarked about some Gentile communities who abandoned their Sabbath observance (*Letter to Magnesians* 8-9). In the course of the second century many Gentile writers attacked the Sabbath observance. Noteworthy are the vehement condemnations of Justin Martyr (d. ca. 165) who, for example, wrote, "We, too, would observe your circumcision of the flesh, your Sabbath days, and in a word, all your festivals, if we were not aware of the reason why they were imposed upon you, namely, because of your sins and your hardness of heart" (*Dialogue with Trypho* 18.2).

Some Jewish Christians continued to observe the Sabbath until the end of the second century. Residual signs of respect for the Sabbath also remained in Gentile communities. Tertullian (d. ca. 225), for example, noted that people refused to kneel on the Sabbath (*On the Soldier's Chaplet* 3) and he condemned the practice of fasting on the Sabbath (*On Fasting* 14). The tradition not to fast on the Sabbath extended to fourth-century Jerusalem, which calculated a forty-day Lent by observing eight weeks of fasting Monday through Friday ($8 \times 5 = 40$; *Egeria*, 27.1).

During the Patristic period, the idea if not the observance of the Sabbath remained an issue. Like the NT, early Patristic writers mentioned Sabbath more often than Sunday, indicative of the continuing influence of this ancient tradition. Christians needed to justify why they did or did not observe the Sabbath. Early writers agreed that the Sabbath was fulfilled in Jesus, and that the Sabbath was a type of the eschaton. Although the Sabbath had been fulfilled, many writers did not conclude that the Sabbath command had been eliminated, but only spiritualized. Thus even Justin Martyr could write, "The New Law demands that you observe a perpetual Sabbath. . . . If there be a perjurer or thief among you, let him mend his ways; if there be an adulterer, let him repent; in this way he will have kept a true and peaceful Sabbath" (*Dialogue with Trypho* 12.3).

Throughout the Patristic period the Sabbath served as an image of (1) the Christian life, (2) rest from sin, and (3) eschatological hope. This typological treatment of the Sabbath continued despite vigorous condemnation of the Sabbath observance. The Council of Laodicea (ca. 360), for example, explicitly condemned the veneration of the Sabbath and enjoined working on that day in order to show special respect for Sunday. "Christians must not judaize by resting on the Sabbath, but must work on that day, honoring rather the Lord's day by resting,

if possible, as Christians. However if any shall be found judaizing let them be anathema from Christ" (can. 29).

Gradually, Christians transferred many Sabbath customs and observances to Sunday. The Council of Elvira (ca. 306), for example, instructed that Sunday be a day of rest (can. 21). The second commandment of the Decalogue was frequently interpreted in Christian terms. Explicit legislation mandating attendance at Sunday Eucharist arose in the sixth century (Council of Agde, 506 CE). The prescription to avoid "servile work" (see Lev 23:7-8) on Sunday grew in strength over the centuries. The great Dominican scholar Cajetan (d. 1534) was instrumental in giving this practice the force of law for the universal Church (1917 Code, can. 1238; 1983 Code, can. 1247).

The *General Norms for the Liturgical Year and the Calendar* note the centrality of Sunday in Roman Catholic worship without any attempt to demean or displace the honor Jews accord to the Sabbath. Contemporary scholarship as well recognizes the unique role of the Sabbath in faith and history, a weekly celebration of the first covenant. Thus Abraham Heschel could rightly contend that the Sabbath is "a palace in time" and "the day on which we learn the art of surpassing civilization" (*The Sabbath*).

See: CREATION, EUCHARIST, JESUS CHRIST, PASSOVER, RESURRECTION

EDWARD FOLEY, CAPUCHIN

SACRIFICE

Throughout the OT sacrificial offerings represent the primary means of worship of God. Various types of sacrifice were offered for different occasions and reasons. During the first and second Temple periods, sacrificial rituals were centered in Jerusalem, under the direction of priests and Levites. After the destruction of the Temple, prayer replaced sacrifice and Temple worship. When the term appears in the NT it usually has a metaphorical or spiritual sense. In Christian tradition both Christ's death and the Eucharist are spoken of as sacrifice.

Old Testament

Origins. Sacrifice is the form in which God was worshiped during the period of the first and second Temples. This included the slaughter, roasting, and eating of animals, as well as offerings of grain, bread, and incense. The sacrificial structure is most completely described in the Books of Leviticus and Numbers, and in the last chapters of the Book of Ezekiel.

Through sacrifice, priestly theology transformed pagan and Temple worship to its own needs. In pagan religion the gods were seen as dependent on realms beyond the divine, which spawned benevolent and malevolent entities. Humans tapping into these entities could influence the gods. These premises were negated by priestly theology. There was only one supreme God, the world of demons was abolished, and all that remained of demonic powers was in humans, and this had to be controlled in relation to the Divine.

The purpose of the Temple was to house God, to feed God in exchange for God's protection. By their actions, humans could defile the Temple and drive out God's presence. Reordering this disorder was the primary rationale for sacrifice and the sacrificial cult. After the destruction of the second Temple in the year 70 CE, sacrifices and Temple worship ceased, and this was replaced in Judaism by prayer.

In the Bible. Various Hebrew verbs are used to designate the act of sacrifice. They include: *shahat* and *tevah*, i.e., slaughter of animals for both secular and sacred purposes; *zevah*, the slaughter of animals for sacrifice. The terms *olah* and *korban* are used to denote sacrifice only. The former term means "that which goes up" (burnt offering). It is this term that is used most often to denote sacrifice, perhaps because of its root meaning ("to draw near"). In fact it is probably correct to suggest that the idea of sacrifice as an act of worship was in fact an act of drawing near to God.

Meal offerings and wine libations played a prominent part in the rituals, but the most important sacrifices were those of animals. The surrender of a living thing was a major factor in nearly every kind of sacrificial ritual. This was achieved by the extraction of the animal's blood, "for the life of the flesh is in the blood and I have given it upon the altar to make atonement for your souls" (Lev 17:11). Hence the prohibition for eating blood.

The core sacrifice, to atone for the sins of the people as a whole, was a burnt offering known as *olat tamid*, made twice each day throughout the year. The end of the sacrificial process came in the year 70 CE, when, because of the war and the sacking of Jerusalem and the Temple, the Tamid ceased.

There was a wide range of offerings in the sacrificial structure. They included: propitiatory offerings (Lev 4:3 and 5:17) involving guilt and sin offerings; meal offerings, usually taking the form of loaves of bread (*hallot*) or wafers (Lev 6:7-16); libations (Num 15:1-10); fellowship offerings (Lev 23:19-20); peace offerings (Leviticus 3) culminating in a communal meal; thanksgiving offerings (Lev 7:12-13); freewill offerings (Lev 7:16); ordination offerings (Lev 8:22-32); wave offerings (Lev 23:19); and votive offering (Lev 7:16-17).

It should be noted that nowhere in the Hebrew Bible is worship regulated by prayer, although prayers are frequently referred to. According to Deuteronomy, formal worship of God could be only in one place, Jerusalem, and by one principal method, sacrifice. Since you could not offer sacrifices outside of Jerusalem, you prayed, wherever you were. It has been suggested that the contrast between sacrifice and prayer was the contrast between elitism and populism. When the Temple was destroyed the popular consensus expressing worship through prayer surfaced.

Biblical Tradition and History. The traces of the existence and development of the system of worship through sacrifice come through clearly in a reading of the biblical record. Cain and Abel bring offerings to

God (Gen 4:4ff.), and after the flood Noah shows his gratitude with a burnt offering (Gen 8:20ff.). Job's piety and uprightness was underscored by the fact that he made frequent offerings to God (Job 1:15; 42:7-9).

The patriarchs "call on the name of God" by building an altar* for sacrifice. We learn this in connection with Abraham (Gen 12:8) and Isaac (Gen 26:55). In the case of Jacob, the place where he built an altar undergoes a name change from Luz to Beth El (Gen 33:20). The most unusual sacrifice associated with the patriarchs is the ritual of the divided carcasses (Gen 15:4ff.) and the account of the almost-sacrifice of Isaac (Gen 22).

With Moses, the account of God's covenant with Israel is sealed by a sacrifice rite (Exod 24:3-8). In the period of the Judges, sacrifices are performed in various places: Bochim (Judg 2:1-5), Ophrah (Judg 6:24), and the episode of the sacrifice of Jephtha's daughter is told with a sense of horror (Judg 11:30-40).

Cult centers for sacrifice existed at Shiloh (1 Sam 1:3), Mizpah (1 Sam 7:9), Beth Shemesh (1 Sam 6:14-15), Gilgal (1 Sam 10:8), and at Nob (1 Sam 1:21) until King David moved the ark of the covenant to Jerusalem and Solomon built the Temple. The Deuteronomic reform made Jerusalem the exclusive site for worship and other surviving centers were finally destroyed.

During the period of the second Temple we have evidence from sources in the Mishnah and Talmud (see esp. Tamid) that liturgical prayers were included in the actual sacrificial rites. We learn that after the sacrifice was made and the incense burnt, the priestly blessing, the Shema and its blessings, the Ten Commandments, and concluding paragraphs of the Amida were recited (Tamid 6).

While priests and Levites performed their rites, a supportive system known as Maamadot provided groups of Israelite laity who each stood for an hour each day throughout the day in the vicinity of where the sacrifices were performed and uttered appropriate prayers. In this significant development of the Temple rites during the Second Commonwealth, we can see the link between sacrifice and prayer, and the germs of transition from the one to the other when the Commonwealth was finally destroyed. How many came? We have a few interesting clues. A count was taken in the reign of King Agrippa (first century) of pilgrims one Passover, and it totalled 600,000 (Talmud, Pesahim 64b). According to Josephus (Wars 2:280 and 6:425) more than 3,000,000 gathered in Jerusalem for the Passover of 65 CE. Clearly the Mecca pilgrimage had its antecedents.

Interpretations. As Judaism developed, efforts to find a spiritual meaning for sacrifice were made. Philo (De Victimis, Spec. 1:112-256) saw, in the fact that only domesticated animals and gentle birds could be used, a paradigm that the offerers must be wholesome in body and in soul, ready to approach the altar purged of all passion and viciousness.

The Rabbis of the Talmud noticed that the type of animals permitted for sacrifice indicated that God is on the side of the pursued and not the pursuer (Lev. R. 27:5). The Medieval poet Judah Halevi suggested that the fire on the altar was a divine sign that the people of Israel had found favor in God's sight (Kuzari 2:26).

Others took a juridical approach. The eleventh-century Spanish Jewish commentator Abraham Ibn Ezra, commenting on Leviticus 1:1, observed that the life of the sinner was forfeited to God. However, through God's grace, that sinner was permitted to offer a surrogate (the sacrifice) to atone for the sin and thus receive absolution from the Divine Court.

The Medieval philosopher Maimonides took a rational position, rejecting the symbolists. His position was that sacrifice needed to be perceived as of pagan origin, a system of worship used by all peoples at the time of Moses. Since the people had been brought up in that atmosphere, God realized that they could not totally abandon it. It was limited to one place in the world, with the goal of ultimately weaning them away from it. Just as they were led to the Promised Land by a circuitous route, because they were not ready for the direct short journey, so it was in the evolution of worship from sacrifice to prayer (Guide 3:32).

This position was already implicit in the decisions by the Rabbis of the Synod of Yavneh (after 70 CE) that prayer was to take the place of sacrifice. Nostalgia was served by inserting into the liturgy a description of the Temple sacrifice liturgy, and by the addition of a Musaf (additional) prayer to the Amida of Sabbath and festivals as a reminder of the musaf sacrifice. Similarly, discussions about the sacrificial rites in one section of the Talmud were designed for the same end. It can be argued that once prayer replaced sacrifice for divine worship, there was no real desire that it be restored despite the nostalgia.

Conclusion. In contemporary Judaism, in Orthodoxy and right wing Conservative Judaism, the liturgy about sacrifice is included. In moderate Conservatism, in Reform, and in Reconstructionism it is excluded. The symbolists and the rationalists continue to have their differences.

See: ALTAR, ATONEMENT, PRIEST

HAYIM GOREN PERELMUTER

New Testament

The most common term for "sacrifice" in the NT is *thysia*. It alludes to the sacrifices offered to God in the Jerusalem Temple, but often there is a reference to Christ's death understood as a sacrifice and to the worship and good deeds of Christians as "sacrifices." Thus in the NT the metaphorical or spiritual uses of the term predominate.

Jewish Background. The Lucan infancy narrative places the announcement of the birth of John the Baptist at the time when Zechariah was offering incense in the Temple (Luke 1:8-9). At the purification Joseph and Mary offer the sacrifice of "a pair of turtledoves or two young pigeons" in accord with Leviticus 12:2-8 (Luke 2:24), and

the young boy Jesus teaches "in my Father's house" (Luke 2:49). Thus the Temple and the sacrifices performed in it are taken for granted as part of Jewish life in the land of Israel.

Jesus' saying in Matthew 5:23-24 ("If you bring your gift to the altar and there recall that your brother has anything against you . . .") assumes the smooth running of the sacrificial system in the Jerusalem Temple. Likewise, the early chapters in Acts portray the apostles and other early Christians as frequenting the Temple and participating in its rituals (Acts 2:46; 3:1–4:3; 21:26; 22:17).

Alongside the basic acceptance of the Temple and its sacrifices there is also a critical perspective captured by Jesus' use of Hosea 6:6 in Matthew 9:13 and 12:7: "I desire mercy, not sacrifice." Though not a criticism of sacrifice itself, this prophetic saying insists on the importance of good deeds and intentions along with sacrifice. An even more critical attitude is captured in the saying attributed to Jesus at his trial: "I will destroy this temple made with hands and within three days I will build another not made with hands" (Mark 14:58; Matt 26:61; John 2:19; Acts 6:13). Standing in the Prophetic tradition of Jeremiah (see 7:1-15; 26:1-8), this saying looks to the coming of God's reign as bringing in a new kind of worship that will render the Jerusalem Temple obsolete (see John 4:21-24). Stephen goes so far as to suggest that the Temple service is idolatrous (Acts 7:41-50).

In Jesus' time worship at the Jerusalem Temple was part of Jewish life in Israel. For Gentile Christians in Asia Minor and Greece, however, that Temple had little meaning. And its destruction in 70 CE and the abolition of the sacrificial system there meant that the door was open to metaphorical or spiritual interpretations of sacrifice.

Christ's Death. In writing to the Corinthians Paul speaks of Christ's death as a sacrifice in such a way as to indicate that he was calling upon the common faith of the early Church: "For our paschal lamb, Christ, has been sacrificed" (1 Cor 5:7). The same Passover lamb symbolism is applied to Jesus' death in John 18–19 (see especially 19:14). Abraham's sacrifice of Isaac in Genesis 22 (a topic of great interest and development among Jews) may be behind famous sayings such as Romans 8:32 ("He who did not spare his own Son but handed him over for us all") and John 3:16 ("God so loved the world that he gave his only Son"). The themes of Jesus' death as both a bloody sacrifice and as having value for others appear in his words over cup at the Last Supper (Mark 14:24; Matt 26:28; Luke 22:20; 1 Cor 11:25), and thus endow the Eucharist with its sacrificial dimension. There may also be an element of sacrifice in the saying about Christ's mission "to give his life as a ransom for many" (Mark 10:45; Matt 20:28). This application of "sacrificial" themes to the life and death of Jesus clearly reflects the influence of the Suffering Servant of Isaiah 53 ("he was pierced for our offenses . . . the Lord laid upon him the guilt of us all"). In the Book of Revelation Christ is often portrayed as "the Lamb that was slain" (5:6, 9, 12; 13:8).

The most extensive and systematic NT reflection on Christ's death as a sacrifice appears in Hebrews. There Christ is both the high priest and the sacrifice: "It was fitting that we should have such a high priest . . . he did that once for all when he offered himself" (7:26-27). The author of Hebrews goes to great lengths to identify Jesus as the high priest superior to all Jewish high priests (4:14–5:10) who presides at a heavenly liturgy with better sacrifices than those offered at the Jerusalem Temple (9:23). The sacrifice that he offered was his own life. If Temple sacrifices had any effect, how much more does the blood of Christ achieve (9:13-14)! His death is the truly effective sacrifice for sins: "now once for all he has appeared at the end of the ages to take away sin by his sacrifice" (9:26). Hebrews 10 contrasts other priests and other sacrifices with Christ and his sacrifice: "This one offered one sacrifice for sins" (10:12), and so "there no longer remains sacrifice for sins" (10:26). Through Christ's perfect sacrifice the priesthood and sacrifices of the Jerusalem Temple were superseded.

Christian Life. In describing his apostolic ministry Paul sometimes used the imagery of sacrifice: "even if I am poured out as a libation upon the sacrificial service of your faith" (Phil 2:17); "in performing the priestly service of the gospel of God, so that the offering up of the Gentiles may be acceptable" (Rom 15:16). Since the recipients of Paul's letters were not frequenters of the Jerusalem Temple and probably knew about sacrifices mainly from pagan temples, Paul was therefore appealing to his readers' everyday experience of sacrifice. Paul himself regarded pagan sacrifices as at best nothing and at worst made to demons (1 Corinthians 8–10).

Behind Paul's use of sacrificial imagery was the idea of the everyday life of Christians as a sacrifice to God: "I urge you, therefore, brothers, by the mercies of God, to offer your bodies as a living sacrifice, holy and pleasing to God, your spiritual worship" (Rom 12:1). Now God's temple is the world, and the proper sacrifice ("living . . . spiritual") is life in response to what God has done through Christ. Thus Romans 12:1 serves as the bridge between the Christ-event described in chapters 1–11 and the ethical instructions in the rest of the letter. Likewise, the Gentiles addressed in 1 Peter who had become part of God's "royal priesthood" (2:9) are exhorted to let themselves "be built into a spiritual house to be a holy priesthood to offer spiritual sacrifices acceptable to God through Jesus Christ" (2:5). These "spiritual sacrifices" are no longer the material offerings of the Israelite priesthood, but worship of God in "Spirit and truth" (John 4:24) and good deeds.

Hebrews 13:15-16 defines the nature of Christian sacrifice as "a sacrifice of praise, that is, the fruit of lips that confess his name . . . to do good and to share what you have; God is pleased by sacrifices of that kind." Similar texts about the nature of worship under the new covenant appear in Hebrews 10:19-25 and 12:18-28. While Christ continues to preside at the heavenly liturgy, Christians on earth worship God by praise and good deeds.

Whereas Romans 12:1 appears to identify the world as God's temple, other texts suggest that the community functions as the temple; that is, the place where fitting worship is offered to God. Such an approach was already current among the Jewish sect of Essenes that produced the Qumran scrolls. The Manual of Discipline describes the Essene community as "a House of Holiness for Israel, an assembly of the holy of holies for Aaron . . . who shall atone for the Land" (1QS 8:5-10). Their prayers and actions are reckoned to "obtain loving kindness for the land more than from the flesh of burnt offerings and the fat of sacrifice" (1QS 9:3-5).

The understanding of the Christian community as God's temple appears in 2 Corinthians 6:16 ("we are the temple of the living God"), Ephesians 2:21-22 ("a temple sacred in the Lord . . . a dwelling place of God"), and 1 Peter 2:5 ("a spiritual house"). The logical consequence of imagining the world or the Church as God's temple is that the worship and good deeds of Christians constitute the sacrifices offered in that temple. Thus the proper worship for Christians takes place not in a single building at an appointed time but everywhere and at all times.

The interpretation of Christ's death as a sacrifice appeared early in Christian theology, as the pre-Pauline formula incorporated in Romans 3:25 shows: "whom God set forth as an expiation . . . by his blood . . . because of the forgiveness of sins previously committed." Reflection on Christ's death as a sacrifice and his willing embrace of that death for sinners (Rom 5:6-9) led to the conviction developed systematically in Hebrews that Christ's priesthood and sacrifice supersede all other priesthood and sacrifices. Because the Jerusalem Temple was far away or (after 70 CE) destroyed, Christians began to look upon the world or the Christian community as God's true temple and their communal worship and good

deeds as "spiritual sacrifices acceptable to God" (1 Pet 2:5).

See: PASSOVER, PRIEST, TEMPLE, WORSHIP

DANIEL J. HARRINGTON, S.J.

Pastoral-Liturgical Tradition

"Sacrifice" as Key to Christ's Death and to the Eucharist. Sacrifice becomes one of the key ways to understand both the death of Christ and the celebration of the Eucharist that he left as his memorial. The Letter to the Hebrews began this reflection with its extensive interpretation of Jesus as the fulfillment and replacement of OT priesthood. Clement of Rome's *First Letter to the Corinthians* (ca. 95 CE) picks up this OT priestly, sacrificial language: "Those who make their offerings at the appointed time, therefore, are acceptable and blessed, for they err not, following the ordinance of the Lord. For the High Priest has been allotted his proper ministrations, and to the priests their proper place has been assigned, and on the Levites their own duties are laid. The lay [person] is bound by the lay ordinances" (c. 40; *The Fathers of the Church* [Washington, DC, 1947] 1:41).

Cyprian of Carthage (+258 CE) in his famous *Epistle* 63 also uses this kind of sacrificial terminology: "And since we make mention of his passion in all sacrifices, for the passion of the Lord is, indeed, the sacrifice which we offer, we ought to do nothing other than what he did" (Ep. 63, 17; cited in A. Hamman, *The Mass* [New York, 1967] 195).

An important part of the Patristic reflection on the Eucharist is the use of OT typology. Melchizedek, Abel, and Abraham are figures who are used to reflect on the meaning of the Eucharistic sacrifice. This was further reflected in the iconographic tradition: see the mosaics in the city of Ravenna at the Churches of S. Apollinare Nuovo (Abel, Abraham, and Melchizedek) and of S. Vitale (Abel and Melchizedek). The innocence of Abel, the bread and wine of Melchizedek, the offering of his only son Isaac by Abraham, all are seen as ways of understanding what is happening when the Eucharist is celebrated.

Eucharist Praying as Sacrificial. The Eucharistic Prayer tradition has strong sacrificial overtones. The first prayer to come down to us, from the *Apostolic Tradition* of Hippolytus of Rome, speaks of what we are doing in the Eucharist within the context of God's salvific will manifested in Jesus Christ. Then after the narrative of the institution of the Eucharist, the prayer continues: "Remembering therefore his death and resurrection, we offer to you the bread and the cup, giving you thanks because you have held us worthy to stand before you and minister to you" (cited in *Prayers of the Eucharist*, 3rd ed., ed. Jasper and Cuming [New York, 1987] 35). This prayer is very complex, combining memorial, offering, ministering, thanksgiving, the death and resurrection of Jesus, and our action of this celebration. Is it this complex that is the sacrifice? A similar prayer is found in Eastern Eucharistic Prayers, many of the Western prayers, and especially the Roman Canon (Eucharistic Prayer I).

The Roman Canon, after the preface and *Sanctus,* introduces a series of prayers that have a highly sacrificial content: language of acceptance, offering, the sacrifice of praise. The prayer following the institution narrative is similar to that of Hippolytus above: "Father, we celebrate the memory of Christ your Son. We, your people and your ministers, recall his passion, his resurrection from the dead, and his ascension into glory; and from the many gifts you have given us we offer to you, God of glory and majesty, this holy and perfect sacrifice: the bread of life and the cup of eternal salvation." Note again the complexus of ideas: memorial; ministering; Jesus' passion, resurrection, ascension; offering of sacrifice; bread and wine: Christ's action and our action. This same dynamic is to be found in all the new Eucharistic Prayers.

The Sacrifice of Praise. The celebration of the Liturgy of the Hours (LOTH) offers another understanding of sacrifice. The use of the psalms in the LOTH sets in strong relief the idea of the spiritual sacrifice so emphasized by the prophets (e.g., Isaiah 1). The traditional evening psalm (Psalm 141) used on Evening Prayer I of Sunday of the first week of the Psalter sets the tone: "Let my prayer come like incense before you; the lifting up of my hands, like the evening sacrifice" (v. 2). Our prayers are an incense offering (see Exod 30:7-8). Our uplifted hands are the evening sacrifice. Another psalm that takes up the theme of spiritual sacrifice is Psalm 51, recited every Friday morning prayer: "for you are not pleased with sacrifices; should I offer a holocaust, you would not accept it. My sacrifice, O God, is a contrite spirit; a heart contrite and humbled, O God, you will not spurn" (vv. 18-19). This same theme is repeated in several of the prayers of the LOTH (e.g., Monday Evening Prayer, week II; Tuesday Evening Prayer, week I; Thursday Evening Prayer, week II; Wednesday Evening Prayer, week IV: "keep in mind your holy covenant, sealed with the blood of the Lamb"; Friday Evening Prayer week IV: ". . . you brought salvation to all [hu]mankind through the suffering of Christ your Son. May your people strive to offer themselves to you as a living sacrifice").

Pastoral Notes. The notion of sacrifice includes the covenantal reality of OT sacrifices: holocaust, total commitment to God; communion sacrifice, sharing of the life of God; expiatory sacrifice, recognizing the sinfulness that threatens the covenant and which God forgives. The ritual is a symbol of the interior reality of commitment that the covenant implies. This is at the heart of the Prophetic and Wisdom critique of sacrificial ritual. The whole OT reality is transformed in Jesus Christ. In him Temple, altar, and sacrifice find their replacement and fulfillment. Christian life is a living sacrifice, the Eucharist is the ritualization of the sacrifice of Christ and of his body, the Church. Our lives are lived in Christ in obedience to the salvific will of the Father. This we live every day and every time we celebrate the thanksgiving sacrifice of the Eucharist.

See: ABEL, ABRAHAM, ISAAC, LAMB OF GOD, MELCHIZE-DEK, OFFERING, PRIESTHOOD, TEMPLE, WORSHIP

MICHAEL G. WITCZAK, S.J.

SADDUCEES

Frequently mentioned in the Gospels as opponents of Jesus, the origin, nature, and history of the Sadducees are very difficult to determine with precision. They are mentioned in Josephus and later Rabbinic writings as well as the NT, but on some points it is hard to reconcile the various portraits.

The name "Sadducee" probably derives from "Zadok," the name of the high priest during David's reign (1 Kgs 1:26), and harmonizes with the general identification of the Sadducees as belonging to the priestly and aristocratic groups of Jerusalem. They appear to originate in the first century BCE and fade from sight after the destruction of the Temple and Jerusalem in the wake of the Jewish revolt in 70 CE.

They were probably not a strictly defined group but a movement or association among the varied factions of Jewish religious leadership in the turbulent context of the times. Although the Gospels tend to lump the Sadducees together with the Pharisees as among the principal opponents of Jesus, the Gospels also make clear that they had distinctive stands of their own and that Jerusalem, not Galilee, was their power base (see Mark 12:18; Matt 22:23, 34; Luke 20:27; Acts 4:1; 5:17; 23:6). Unlike the Pharisees, the Sadducees did not believe in the resurrection of the dead (Mark 12:18) or in angels and spirits (Acts 23:8). These were innovations in Jewish doctrine supported by the Pharisees (and Jesus) but not by the Sadducees and probably indicates the latter's more conservative religious bent. Josephus may be right in describing them as strongly under the influence of Hellenistic culture. It is not difficult to understand how Jesus and the Sadducees would not see eye to eye.

See: PHARISEE

DONALD SENIOR, C.P.

SAINTS

This entry describes how the Bible understands the words that are commonly translated as saints or holy ones. It also explores how the Church came to reserve these terms for people considered to be exceptional models of the Christian life.

Old Testament

"Saints" or "holy ones" is the usual translation in the OT for two different Hebrew terms, *hasidim* and *qᵉdeshim*. Both terms reflect human qualities that mirror or imitate properties of God. A *hasid*, "saint," is one who is bound in faithfulness to the God of the Covenant, the God who shows *hesed* (lit. faithfulness, covenant loyalty, loving kindness). The other term, *qᵉdeshim*, identifies persons who share in God's holiness (*qodesh*) and who are thereby set apart, kept from profane use, and dedicated for the service of God.

Yahweh, the Holy One. In the OT, God is the holy One above all others. But, because God is holy, people, places, things, actions, and times can also be holy in so far as they are dedicated to God. Nowhere is this conviction more simply put than in the stark imperative of the Holiness Code in Leviticus 19:2: "Be holy, for I the LORD your God am holy."

God's Holy Ones. God was envisioned as surrounded by a host of "holy ones," who shared in the holiness of the divine realm (Ps 89:6, 8). These saints of God were to accompany the Lord in the final coming on the last day (Zech 14:5).

Israel, a Holy Nation. In the context of Israel's covenant relationship, God chose Israel as God's own possession to be "a people sacred to the LORD . . .; a people peculiarly his own" (Deut 7:6; see Exod 19:6). In this sense, every Israelite was a "saint," called to be holy as God is holy. In a few instances, special individuals are singled out for this designation: Aaron (Ps 106:16) and priests in general (Ps 132:9, 16; 2 Chr 6:41).

The blessing of Moses (Deut 33:3) refers to all Israel as God's holy ones whom God had carried on pinions through the desert ordeal and would soon establish in the land. The psalmist, in Psalm 16:3, praises the faithful "saints" in Israel who have inherited the land. Other psalms call upon the Israelites as "saints" (NAB: "faithful ones") to love the Lord (Ps 31:24), to sing to the Lord (Ps 30:5), or to fear the Lord (Ps 34:10), that is, to live out faithfully their obligations as members of God's covenant community, God's holy assembly (Pss 50:5; 149:1).

The Holy Remnant. In a special way, the remnant, those who remain faithful and are found to be among the elect at the end time, are designated as the saints of God (Isa 4:3). In the prophecy of Daniel, the prophet refers repeatedly to the "saints of the Most High." They are the faithful Israelites, the pious upholders of the law, to whom the kingdom will be given in the day of judgment. Daniel hears a conversation between two such saints discussing how long the time will be before the end.

New Testament

Hagios, in Greek, denotes a person or thing dedicated or reserved for God's service. "Saints" is the translation in the NT for *hagioi* (lit. holy ones, the NAB translation), a term that normally refers to Christians, as distinct from those who have not accepted Jesus, the holy One of God (Mark 1:24; Luke 1:35; 4:34; Acts 3:14). But Matthew 27:52 and 1 Thessalonians 3:13 can speak of the faithful who have died before the coming of Christ as "saints," reiterating the promises of Daniel 7 regarding God's righteous elect. These saints will be manifest at the day of judgment, judging the world (1 Cor 6:2) and sharing in the glory of the Lord's power (2 Thess 1:10).

Jesus, the Holy One. In the same way that Israel understood its holiness as a participation in and reflection of the holiness of God, so Christians saw themselves as sharing in the life of the risen Jesus, God's holy One, by virtue of their faith and their baptism

into Christ. They were the people of the New Covenant, bound together as God's holy people (1 Pet 2:9), "called to belong to Jesus Christ . . . called to be holy" (Rom 1:6, 7). It is Christ who sanctifies, consecrates, his faithful followers "in the truth" (John 17:17, 19) by bestowing on them the Spirit of truth and holiness (John 14:16-17; 16:13).

Saints in Christ Jesus. Paul takes pains to remind Christians of their calling as saints, their vocation to be a consecrated people (1 Cor 1:2). Their sanctity derives from their being "in Christ" (Phil 1:1); they have been incorporated into the one Body of Christ (1 Cor 12:13) and thereby share his Spirit. Gentiles as well as Jews share in this vocation to be saints (Eph 2:19); all are called to the same holiness.

For Paul, *hagioi* becomes a common designation for "Christians" who are members of local congregations (Rom 1:7; 1 Cor 1:2; 2 Cor 1:1; 13:12; Phil 1:1), or who are identified with a particular house church (Rom 16:15; NAB "holy ones"). Moreover, the saints in Jerusalem (2 Cor 8:4; 9:1) are the special object of concern in the Pauline mission, a concern demonstrated by Paul's desire to make a collection of funds for their relief, in keeping with his agreement at the Jerusalem Council (Gal 2:10).

Saints as Martyrs. The Book of Revelation refers to the Christian martyrs as saints or "holy ones" in 16:6; 17:6; 18:24. Together with the saints and prophets of old, the Christian martyrs demonstrate by their faithfulness that they are holy and share in the promises for God's elect.

See: CONSECRATION, HOLY/HOLINESS

BARBARA E. BOWE, R.S.C.J.

Pastoral-Liturgical Tradition

While the NT first applied the term "saints" to all followers of Christ, the Church community eventually recognized some of its members as exceptional. For these it came to reserve the name saints, holy ones, and they serve as exemplars or paradigms of Christian life. The Church also believes that they intercede for the community before the throne of God in heaven.

The Development of the Cult. The cult of the saints first developed in early Christianity around those who bravely suffered martyrdom for their faith. The narratives of the martyrs' passions indicated the exemplary way in which an individual entered into the death and resurrection of Christ. The stories also reinterpret the liturgies of the Church in the martyr's death. For example, one of the earliest stories, that of Polycarp, bishop of Smyrna, who was burned to death in 156, not only follows the gospel details of Christ's passion, but also inserts the Eucharistic prayer as he is burned, like "bread baking" in the fire. Similarly, in the tale of the martyrdoms of Perpetua and Felicitas (203), each young woman has recently given birth, and this serves as a metaphor for the new birth and the baptism in blood that they undergo in the jaws of the beasts in the arena. Thus the early martyrs die and are raised with Christ, they intensify the meaning of the sacraments, and become vital links between the Church on earth and in heaven.

This connection is made more real by the treatment of the bodies, clothing, and jewelry of the martyrs after death. Relics were kept and honored. Their burial place became the site of annual celebration of the birth of the martyr into heaven. In time, relics were placed in altars, and some were built over tombs themselves.

When martyrdom ceased, it was a short step for the Church to honor the dead who had lived impressively holy lives without experiencing violent death. These saints were recognized as witnesses, confessors of the faith. The holy ones who went before the Church into death were understood as near and living connections to the next world. They could act as intercessors, friends, and patrons who could aid one past the terrors of judgment and plead one's case with God.

Given the important work of the saints on behalf of the living, shrines sprang up at their tombs. Continuing the practice begun with the martyrs, altars were built over some graves; relics were treasured and placed in altars elsewhere. Eschewing the horror death evokes, people felt that the body and spirit were so closely intertwined that to touch a relic or go to the tomb was to allow the holiness of the saint to touch oneself. Thus miracle stories multiplied as the saint increased her/his good works or offered friends a taste of paradise.

Canonization. Because cults proliferated in late antiquity and into the Middle Ages, bishops came to exercise control over which individuals were deemed worthy of the Church's devotion and which were not. Moreover, the saints were not to be equated with God. They were accorded veneration, *dulia*, not adoration, *latria*, which was reserved for God alone. From the tenth century on the papacy played an increasing juridical role in identifying or canonizing legitimate saints, and this solidified in papal law by the mid-twelfth century.

The procedure that takes place before canonization entails extensive review of testimony, documentary or oral as available, regarding the sanctity of the individual. If the person's holiness seems sure, he/she is pronounced "venerable." Then evidence of miracles performed through the person's intercession is sought. This can lead to beatification, and further miracles to final canonization.

Sanctity. It has been suggested that saints disclose the interplay of mystical holiness and virtue. In the Catholic tradition the emphasis tends to be on the former. It is the mystical link with God, both before and after death, that draws devotion. Perhaps this is the reason that miracles weigh so heavily in the Church's assessment of sainthood. While they seem a crude or unwieldy measure in the contemporary secularized world, they remain a bald symbol of the human relation to the extraordinary, to the transcendent. In ages prior to our own, miracle working may even have exceeded virtue in authenticating a saint.

Yet the saints tend to exemplify both moral heroism and intense personal holiness in a public way. These people who have gone before us are now public property, public paradigms of how it is possible to live humanly and gracefully. The two most recent doctors of the Church, Catherine of Siena and Teresa of Avila, illustrate this combination of holiness and virtue in lives replete with prayer, courage, love, neuroses, and, indeed, miracles. They are human beings who knew God in such a way that the Church, too, knows that they knew God. And so we also trust that it is possible for us as well.

See: CHURCH, HOLY/HOLINESS

ANN E. GRAFF

SALT

Old Testament

Long valued in the ancient world for its capacity to preserve food, salt was used in the Scriptures as a symbol for permanence and preservation. In 2 Kings 2:21 the prophet Elisha throws salt into a spring of water near Jericho to purify it for the inhabitants of the town who were in need of wholesome water. Scholars of Semitic religion and culture have also pointed out that salt was also a sign of friendship and solidarity uniting diners at a banquet in a sacred bond. Thus, in Numbers 18:19, to underscore the permanence and inviolability of the convenant relationship between God and the people of Israel, the expression "covenant of salt" is employed (see also 2 Chr 13:5).

New Testament

It is likely that Jesus used the metaphor of salt as a way of speaking about the need for steadfast faith before the judgment of God. In Matthew 5:13 Jesus compares believers to the "salt of the earth." For all intents and purposes, just as salt is a symbol of stability, friendship, and permanence, believers are permanently related to God. But even here, the Gospels turns "common sense" on its head by insisting that even salt can lose its flavor. Technically speaking this is impossible. Salt that is no longer salty is obviously no longer salt. However, in the context of the Judaism of Jesus' day salt can become ritually unclean and then it is to be thrown out. The fate of this salt is an image of divine judgment and for not taking for granted one's relationship with God (see also Mark 9:50; Luke 14:34).

Pastoral-Liturgical Tradition

Not surprisingly, the early Church used ordinary salt to symbolize the preservation from evil of those preparing for baptism. In a letter written around the year 500 we read that "the catechumen receives blessed salt . . . to signify that just as all flesh is kept healthy by salt, so the mind that is drenched and weakened by the waves of the world is held steady by the salt of wisdom and of the preaching of the word of God: so that it may come to stability and permanence, after the distemper of corruption is thoroughly settled by the gentle action of divine salt" (John the Deacon, *Letter to Senarius* 3). The use of salt continued in the baptismal liturgy until the most recent reform. In the old rite of baptism, a small amount of blessed salt was placed on the tongue of the child accompanied by the words, "Receive the salt of wisdom. May it win for you mercy and forgiveness and life everlasting."

Although salt is no longer used in the rite of baptism, it may still be used in the blessing of holy water. The biblical image invoked in the present prayer of blessing found in the *Sacramentary* is appropriately that of the prophet Elisha. "Almighty God, we ask you to bless + this salt as once you blessed the salt scattered over the water by the prophet Elisha. Whenever this salt and water are sprinkled, drive away the power of evil, and protect us always by the presence of your Holy Spirit."

See: WATER, WISDOM

MARK R. FRANCIS, C.S.V.

SALVATION

Salvation is one of the most fundamental concepts of the Bible. It was out of the saving act of deliverance from Egypt that the nation of Israel was born, and Christian faith is rooted in the salvation realized through Christ.

Old Testament

The word "salvation" comes from the Hebrew *yāshaʿ*, which means "to make wide" or "to make sufficient." What is wide or sufficient is unrestricted and able to pursue its own objectives. The salvation usually comes from the outside. In the OT, the distress that requires salvation can be either individual or national, economic, social, or spiritual. Although the word is sometimes found in situations describing human endeavor (e.g., the men of Gibeon plead with Joshua to save them [Jos 10:6]), it normally has strong religious meaning, for it is usually the Lord who brings salvation.

Military Intervention. In the OT the focal point of God's acts of salvation is Israel's deliverance from the bondage of Egypt. This experience is the basis for understanding God's concern for Israel and involvement in its history. One of the central characterizations of God is derived from this event. In it, God is the one who brought them out of Egypt with a mighty hand and an outstretched arm (Deut 4:34; 5:15; 7:19; 11:2; 26:8; also 9:29; Ps 136:12), and who acts on their behalf at other decisive moments in their history as well (Ezek 20:33f.). Although deliverance is clearly a political or military undertaking, it was perceived as an act of God with profound religious implications.

The narratives recounting the occupation of the land feature military leaders known as judges. These were local or tribal leaders who fought mightily to defend their respective groups from the encroachment or assaults of rival parties. The majority of the conflicts between Israel and its neighbors resulted from territorial disputes. The claim that God had promised and was now giving the land of Canaan to Israel lay at the heart of these conflicts (see Josh 1:6). With the exception of Deborah who was both a judicial arbiter and a leader in war (Judg 4:4-5), most of the judges are depicted as charismatic leaders who, when impelled by the spirit of the Lord, delivered Israel from its enemies.

Most of the stories of the judges follow a simple literary pattern, which also contains an important theological message: (1) The people sin by forgetting their God and worshiping the gods of the land; (2) God is angered and delivers the people into the hands of their enemies; (3) The people repent and cry out to God for release; (4) God raises up a savior to deliver them. This pattern demonstrates the principle of retribution: Sin will be punished; fidelity, in this case repentance, will be rewarded. It also shows that it is really God who saves, even though it may be through the agency of some human leader. Frequently, in order to underscore that it is indeed God who saves, the human limitations of the judge are made quite evident. For example, Gideon was reluctant to assume this burdensome role (Judg 6:15), and Samson was subject to sexual naivete (Judg 14:1-20) and violent rages (Judg 15:1-20). Despite these weaknesses, the spirit of the Lord would come upon these men, filling them with the power of God and enabling them to save the people from whatever endangered them at the moment (Judg 3:10; 6:34; 11:29; 13:25; 14:6, 19; 15:14).

Eschatological Expectation. The experience of past deliverance raised the hope of salvation in the future. Several prophets spoke of this future time of salvation for the Israelites. The nation's return from captivity was envisioned using language of salvation (Jer 30:10; 31:7; Ezek 34:22). At some future time the people would be saved from their impurities (Ezek 36:29) and brought back to the land originally promised to their ancestors (Jer 31:7-9). Second Isaiah speaks of salvation as being eternal (45:17; 51:6, 8), but only if the people return to fidelity to God (45:22). Again and again, this prophet calls

God by the title Savior (43:3, 11; 45:15, 21; 49:26); Third Isaiah uses the same title (60:16; 63:8).

Many of the prophetic passages tell of an extraordinary figure who will not only proclaim the advent of this time of salvation but will usher it in as well (see Isa 9:2-7; 11:1-9; Jer 23:6). They instructed Israel to look forward to the time when an "anointed one," a messiah, would be the vehicle of God's salvation of the people. A second mysterious figure, distinct from yet often closely associated with the messiah, is the servant of the Lord. In the second of the four servant songs, the Lord declares that the servant will be given as a light to the nations so that salvation might reach the end of the earth (Isa 49:6). This theme of universal salvation is found elsewhere in Isaiah. Since salvation comes from the Lord, it is extended to all (Isa 45:22; 52:10).

Prayer for Salvation. Just as the basis of Israel's salvation was its experience of release from Egyptian bondage, so the earliest song of praise (Exod 15:1-21) celebrates God's deliverance (14:30). There are actually two songs here, one attributed to Moses (vv. 2-18) and the other, a refrain, to Miriam (vv. 1, 21). In this ancient hymn of thanksgiving, God is portrayed as the divine warrior who, as a storm-god, battles the enemies of Israel with wind and thunder and lightning and emerges victorious. This victory is also celebrated in several psalms (78:12-13; 105:37; 106:9-12). Here, salvation has been won through battle.

While many narratives recount Israel's plea to God for salvation, it is in the psalms themselves that this appeal becomes explicit. Communal and individual laments, psalms of confidence, and psalms of thanksgiving are replete with cries for help, reminders of past deliverance and divine promises for the future, and gratitude for rescue realized. It is clear that salvation comes from God and God alone (18:2; 25:5; 27:1; 51:14; 62:1-6; 68:2; 89:26). The psalmist pleads to be saved from enemies (7:1; 18:3; 37:40; 44:7; 59:2; 106:10;

109:31) and from all manner of trouble (22:21; 34:6; 69:1). There is a note of confidence in these prayers because God has been known to be loving (31:16; 34:18; 72:13; 109:26) and faithful (7:10; 22:5; 28:8; 31:2; 54:1; 71:3; 76:9; 86:2; 106:8; 119:94). The psalms maintain that God saves the upright (7:10; 34:19; 36:10; 37:39; 119:155), the poor (109:39) and humble (18:27; 116:60), and all those who fear God (145:19).

Spiritual Meaning. Salvation, as found in the OT, is usually physical rather than spiritual, accomplished in this life rather than in some kind of afterlife. Still, there are references to salvation from evil of any kind. The psalms ask to be delivered from bloodguilt (51:14) and sin in general (79:9). Jeremiah prays for internal healing (17:14), and Ezekiel states that the new Israel will be saved from uncleanness (36:29) and apostasies (37:23).

Even in those passages which envision a restored nation, there is a presumption that this is really a new Israel, a new creation purified of the sins that caused the suffering in the first place. This regeneration is expressed as a new covenant (Jer 31:31), a new heart and a new spirit (Ezek 36:26), a new heaven and a new earth (Isa 65:17; 66:22). Just as the original covenant was the foundation of Israel's salvation, so this regeneration is the basis of all of the blessings that are promised. This notion of interior regeneration gives rise to the idea of the reign of God.

Although this expression is itself rare in Jewish literature, it has very old and treasured roots in the tradition of biblical Israel. It signifies the actual sovereignty or rule of God rather than the territorial sphere or realm within which God rules. From the beginning it had both political and religious significance. It would be established in history, but in a way not limited to the usual geographic or political boundaries. Its presence would be characterized by righteousness and love.

There was also a temporal dimension to the reign of God. Israel looked for a future that would fulfill every hope. The Prophetic writings contain several poetic descriptions of this ideal time (e.g., Isaiah 11–12). Before the reign of God could be brought to final completion, all of the enemies of God and of Israel would have to be conquered. The righteous would have to be saved from harm. The royal roots of this notion are obvious, and connections between the reign of God and a future messiah can be easily drawn. It will take the mystery of Christ and Christian development of biblical themes to bring these various strands of tradition together.

See: CANAAN, EGYPT, ESCHATOLOGY, JUDGES, MESSIAH, NATIONS, SERVANT, SPIRIT OF GOD

DIANNE BERGANT, C.S.A.

New Testament

Salvation is such a familiar concept that it may be surprising to learn that the term appears relatively infrequently in the NT. The verb "to save" occurs more often than the noun "salvation." But the noun does appear, especially in Paul. It is found only once in John and occasionally in Luke-Acts, as well as in the later letters and in Revelation. The basic nuances of both the verb and the noun are essentially the same in both secular Greek and the NT.

In ordinary Greek, the word "salvation" means "preservation in life." In this sense, the author of Hebrews refers to Noah as the one who "with reverence built an ark for the salvation of his household" (11:7). This is also the meaning implied in the question of the jailer who, fearing that his prisoners Paul and Silas had escaped when an earthquake opened the doors of the prison, and that his own life was at risk either from the apostles or from his superiors, asked: "Sirs, what must I do to be saved [i.e., to preserve or spare my life]?" (Acts 16:30). In fact, the apostles were in prison because they were preaching the "way of salvation" (16:17).

Salvation applies especially to the inner life or being of a person. Thus, Jesus' enig-matic saying about "saving" or "losing" one's life refers not only to physical life but to the innermost being of a person (see Luke 9:24). Such a meaning is consistent with usage in Greek philosophy about the deepest meaning of life and how that meaning can be preserved.

The term "savior" can refer in secular Greek to a benefactor. Salvation can likewise mean reinforcing and maintaining a sense of well-being. In the OT, salvation was understood as ultimately coming from God who creates and maintains human life. In the NT, the benefit or blessing known as salvation is found in Jesus. As Peter said, according to Acts 4:12: "There is no salvation through anyone else, nor is there any other name under heaven given to the human race by which we are to be saved."

The Gospels. In the Synoptic Gospels, the term salvation occurs uniquely in Luke and then primarily in quotations from the OT. So, for example, in the *Benedictus* Zechariah gives praise to God who "has raised up a horn for our salvation . . . from our enemies" (Luke 1:69, 71). John the Baptist is recognized as the instrument by which God grants people "knowledge of salvation through the forgiveness of their sins" (1:77). Likewise, Simeon acknowledges that in Jesus he has seen salvation (2:30). John the Baptist himself echoes the promise of Isaiah that "all flesh shall see the salvation of God" (3:6). The only time the word "salvation" is put on the lips of Jesus is in his announcement to Zacchaeus, "Today salvation has come to this house" (19:9).

In John's Gospel, the single occurrence of the noun is in the saying of 4:22, that "salvation is from the Jews."

Paul and Deutero-Paul. It is Paul and Deutero-Paul who develop the meaning of salvation in its most distinctively Christian sense. Salvation encompasses the whole person, the physical as well as the spiritual. Salvation is from something, for something. According to Paul, salvation is from judgment. It is God's victory over sin. Paul consistently describes salvation as an act of God through Jesus Christ (see Rom 1:16-17). Salvation is proclaimed by the gospel and received through faith understood as a response to God's action and initiative. Salvation is the goal of the gospel and of faith. It is achieved through the power of God (Rom 1:16) and is the hope of all the faithful; it is inclusive of all, Jews and Gentiles, slave and free, male and female (Rom 10:1, 10; 11:11; see Gal 3:28).

According to Paul, salvation usually refers to the future, although it begins in the present. Paul urges the Romans to acknowledge what time it is, saying, "it is the hour now for you to awake from sleep. For our salvation is nearer now than when we first believed" (Rom 13:11). Salvation is a process to be finally realized rather than a single act. Although this process is initiated by God, it requires cooperation with God's grace, as Paul warns the Philippians: "work out your salvation with fear and trembling" (2:12).

The opposite of salvation is perishing (1 Cor 8:11; see 1:18). Speaking of his and the community's opponents, Paul describes his imprisonment as "proof to them of destruction, but of your salvation" (Phil 1:28). To clarify further what salvation means, Paul makes use of several traditional contrasts: light and darkness, sobriety and drunkenness, wakefulness and sleep, day and night. He writes: "since we are of the day, let us be sober, putting on the breastplate of faith and love and the helmet that is hope for salvation. For God did not destine us for wrath, but to gain salvation through our Lord Jesus Christ" (1 Thess 5:8, 9; see 2 Thess 2:13).

Righteousness, similar to salvation in meaning, is Paul's preferred term for expressing God's action in Christ. But when these terms occur together in the same context, justification usually refers to what is already achieved and salvation to the final outcome (see Rom 5:9).

The Church is entrusted with preaching the "gospel of your salvation" and is thus "sealed with the promised holy Spirit" (Eph 1:13). Believers are urged to clothe themselves with "the helmet of salvation and the sword of the Spirit, which is the word of God" (Eph 6:17). The imprisoned Paul speaks with honesty and candor about the uncertainty of his fate, whether he will be released from prison or put to death, in his Letter to the Philippians. Yet, for all this uncertainty, one thing Paul knows for sure: "for I know that this will result in deliverance [i.e., salvation] for me through your prayers and support from the Spirit of Jesus Christ" (Phil 1:19).

Later Letters. For the author of Hebrews, even the angels are destined to serve the salvation of all humankind (1:14). The hope of salvation was announced through angels (2:3), but it is Jesus who is the "leader" of our salvation (2:10). The author of Hebrews points out to his church, suffering persecution for the faith and in need of encouragement, that Jesus himself was "made perfect through suffering" (2:10). If he is the pioneer and leader of our salvation and he had to suffer, we are to expect a similar fate. And when he was made perfect, Jesus became the "source of eternal salvation for all who obey him" (5:9) and follow him. These are those who await his glorious return when he will "bring salvation" (9:28).

The author of 1 Peter also writes to a church suffering the throes of persecution for the faith. According to this letter, believers are promised salvation after persevering in their baptismal commitment, although salvation has already begun in the present (1 Pet 1:5, 9-10; 2:2). Jude 3 also speaks of the "common salvation" of believers.

Book of Revelation. The noun "salvation" occurs three times in the Book of Revelation where it basically retains the OT meaning of God's ultimate victory over sin. The great multitude of the saved chant their belief that "Salvation comes from our God, who is seated on the throne, and from the Lamb" (Rev 7:10), that is, Jesus Christ. After the war between Michael and the dragon, a loud and powerful voice from heaven proclaims that "Now have salvation and power come, and the kingdom of our God and the authority of his Anointed" (12:10). Finally, God is praised in jubilant song when the multitude again cry out, "Alleluia! Salvation, glory and might belong to our God" (19:1).

Thus, the reality of salvation is certainly central to the story of God as revealed in the Scriptures. But God's saving action is only occasionally described explicitly as "salvation." It is with a rich and varied vocabulary that the biblical writers tell of the many ways that God is present with us to save us.

See: FAITH, GOOD NEWS/GOSPEL, JUDGMENT, JUSTIFICATION, PEACE, RECONCILIATION, SIN

MARY ANN GETTY

Pastoral-Liturgical Tradition

Salvation is one of several concepts used to communicate the work of God for us in Christ. With the concept of redemption, it carries the implication of rescue. Its distinctive contribution, however, is its sense of healing and health. This dimension of God's activity on our behalf has been emphasized especially in the Eastern Church, where salvation is healing, and the sacraments, especially the Eucharist, medicine for our souls.

But there are two other questions of importance today in understanding salvation: does God wish the salvation of all people? And what of the salvation of those who have not heard and accepted Jesus Christ and his gospel?

While most Christians would answer the first question with a "yes," citing 1 Timothy 2:4, the further question arises: but what of those who are condemned in the Last Judgment? Does their loss to the love of God represent something less than complete victory over sin in Christ? Christian thinkers have struggled with this question, trying to balance God's all-encompassing love on the one hand, and God's respecting our freedom not to choose God on the other. Eternal punishment for a decision that may have been made under unfortunate or oppressive circumstances seems for some too much. But God also takes our experience and decisions seriously.

From the point of view of Catholic teaching, the concept of eternal punishment has been affirmed repeatedly since the fifth century. But while the Church has proclaimed many people now to be in heaven, it has never declared any single individual to be in hell. Thus Catholics believe that hell exists, but there is no certainty that anyone has ever been condemned to it.

The second question, the fate of those who have not accepted Christ, has become a burning issue in the last part of the twentieth century. It has become so with the much closer contact many Christians have with people of other religious traditions. In an earlier age, the answer to the question was simple: outside the Church there is no salvation, sometimes called the exclusivist view. That is no longer the view of the Roman Catholic Church. The Church holds that there are people who are not part of the Christian Church, nor who have accepted Christ, but somehow, through the agency of Christ and the holy Spirit, are deemed righteous before God. This position, sometimes called inclusivism, was affirmed by the Second Vatican Council (Dogmatic Constitution on the Church, no. 16). A third position, called the pluralist position, holds that all religions can be ways of salvation. This goes beyond the current teaching of the Roman Catholic Church, but recommends itself to some because it seems to offer the respect to other religious traditions that the Church also calls for. The inclusivist position wants to maintain the primacy of salvation in Christ, but does not account well for the relation of salvation in Christ to salvation in other religions. Consequently, many believers find themselves struggling between an inclusivist and pluralist position. It is one of the great theological dilemmas at the end of the twentieth century.

See: ATONEMENT, JUSTIFICATION, REDEMPTION

ROBERT J. SCHREITER, C.PP.S.

871

SAMARIA/SAMARITAN

Idolatry and an indifferent wealthy class characterized Samaria of the OT, where a heterodox Yahwism and consequent hostility with the Jews developed. In the NT there is a Christian mission to the Samaritans, who become heroes of stories and examples of Christian virtues and of being disadvantaged. Throughout much of their later history Samaritans have endured persecution, and, because they oppose intermarriage, today probably number less than five hundred persons.

Old Testament

Strategically located Samaria (*šômᵉrôn*, probably "guard" or "watch") was the capital of the northern kingdom, Israel, for most of its existence. The historical writers and prophets viewed it as corrupt. Ahab built a temple and altar to Baal there (1 Kgs 16:32), and Samaria should also be associated with the false worship at Bethel (see Amos 3:13-15; Hos 8:6; 10:5-7). Isaiah (10:9-11; see also 8:3-4; Amos 8:14; Mic 1:5-7) connects the fall of the city with idolatry surpassed only by that of Jerusalem (e.g., Ezek 16:46-47, 51-55; 23:1-39). The rich of Samaria enjoyed luxury but cared little for the poor, and so Amos calls their wives "cows of Bashan" (Amos 4:1-3; see also 3:9-12; 6:1-7; 8:4-6). The inhabitants of Samaria are likewise called arrogant (Isa 9:8-17) and full of evil deeds and rebellion (Hos 7:1-7; 13:16).

As part of the Assyrian (721–612 BCE) and Persian (539–332 BCE) empires, Samaria designated both the province (Jer 31:5-6) and its capital, and Samaritans, mentioned only once in the OT (2 Kgs 17:29) in connection with false worship, are the inhabitants of both. The Assyrians brought in foreign colonists and deported much of the native population; others fled to Judea. A heterodox Yahwism based on the Pentateuch and influenced by other religions soon developed (2 Kgs 17:24-41; 2 Chr 30:1-9) and provoked Jewish antipathy. In the Persian period the governor of Samaria and his allies badgered those restoring Jerusalem (Neh 2:19-20; 4:1-16; 6:1-14), and the Jewish refusal to permit Samaritans to help rebuild the Temple led to further hostility (Ezra 4).

A revolt against the Macedonians forced the population of Samaria to flee to Shechem, and these refugees supposedly built the controversial temple to Yahweh on Mount Gerizim. The Hellenistic city constructed by the Macedonians was destroyed by John Hyrcanus in ca. 108 BCE, but was magnificently rebuilt by Herod the Great and named Sebaste in honor of Augustus.

New Testament

Samaritans and Samaria play a more positive role in the NT. "Samaria," as always in the NT, designates the district immediately north of Jerusalem (e.g., Acts 15:3). Although Jesus may have charged the Twelve not to enter any Samaritan town (Matt 10:5), Luke includes Samaritans among the disadvantaged whom Jesus particularly saves. Nor will Jesus call down fire from heaven to consume the Samaritan village that does not receive him because he is headed to Jerusalem (Luke 9:52-56). In contrast to the priest and the Levite, the good Samaritan truly understands love of the neighbor and to whom one should be a neighbor (Luke 10:29-37). Through his faith and thankful praise of God the Samaritan leper responds correctly to Jesus' saving action (Luke 17:11-19). Among other places Jesus sends his witnesses to Samaria (Acts 1:8), and during the persecution in Jerusalem some Christians flee there. In Samaria Philip proclaims Christ and works signs and wonders, and the multitudes and even Simon the magician, who later learns that the gift of the Spirit cannot be bought, believe (Acts 8:1-25; see also 9:31). Church tradition sees the sacrament of confirmation in the laying on of hands by Peter and John, which is followed by the reception of the Spirit (Acts 8:14-17), but more importantly for Luke the authorities in Jerusalem approve the mission to Samaria.

In John 4:1-42, although it was not the Jewish custom, Jesus speaks with a Samaritan woman at the well of Jacob near Sychar. The woman functions as a foil for John to show that true worship of God will not occur on Mount Gerizim or in Jerusalem but in spirit and truth, and that Jesus is a prophet, the Christ and Savior of the world. Some of the Samaritans believe in Jesus because of the woman's words; others because they hear for themselves. Jews, however, despised Samaritans (John 8:48).

Pastoral-Liturgical Tradition

Although generally accepted by the Romans, the Samaritans were persecuted by Trajan, and subsequently by Christians and Moslems. Up to the fifteenth century CE a diaspora of considerable size existed, but later history remains somewhat vague. Presently a self-contained religious community, the Samaritans adhere to Yahweh, Moses, the Law (the Pentateuch), Mount Gerizim, and the Day of Recompense. Based in modern Nablus and Holon, they are sadly reduced in numbers.

See: ASSYRIA, BAAL, BETHEL, IDOLATRY, ISRAEL, JERUSALEM, JESUS CHRIST, MISSION, PERSECUTION, POOR, RICH, TEMPLE, WORSHIP, YAHWEH

ROBERT F. O'TOOLE, S.J.

SARAH

Old Testament

The Bible remembers Sarah or Sarai both as ancestor and adversary.

Ancestor. Sarah is buried with Abraham* at Machpelah (Gen 23:1-20) not simply because she is his wife, but because both are ancestors (Gen 11:27–13:18; 17:1-27) called to teach the poor how to cross the threshold from death to life. They do not hand on wealth or power, but alternative skills for survival. She is good-looking, he is fast-talking—traits the poor in every folk tradition use to trick the powerful into letting them have land and children (Gen 12:9–13:1). Sarah is not sexually abused or seductive, but resourceful in setting her household free. The results are extraordinary. Normally, only after six years, slaves

pay owners to set them free to enjoy citizens' rights (Exod 21:1-5), but Pharaoh pays Sarah's household to leave immediately and enjoy royal privileges!

Hospitality to strangers also confers extraordinary blessings (Gen 18:1-33). Sarah's guests summon her for an official announcement (Gen 18:9): she and Abraham will have a child. She laughs, not out of misunderstanding, irreverence, or fear, but out of reticence to accept such a gift. Late-life pregnancy is an *isaac*, a surprise! Protocol demands that candidates like Sarah (Gen 18:12-15), Moses (Exod 4:10-17), Isaiah (Isa 6:5-7), Jeremiah (Jer 1:6-10), Mary (Luke 1:34-37), and even the centurion (Matt 8:5-13) politely protest divine calls in one way or another. The refusal is always denied, the invitation repeated.

Sarah is remembered as an ancestor both in life and death. Her hospitality brings her household children, and her body buried at Machpelah gives them legal claim to the land.

Adversary. Sarah is also the antagonist who blocks Hagar's struggle for land and children (Gen 16:1-16; 21:9-21). Nonetheless, her reactions are neither impulsive nor cruel. Even in the traditions of her adversary, Sarah is law-abiding and god-fearing, carefully following the prescriptions of Mesopotamian law and trusting in Yahweh to protect her household.

Law required a wife to bear children; if she could not, to arrange for a surrogate. Only a wife could choose a surrogate and only from her own household. Like a man chosen as *levir* or brother-in-law (Deut 25:5-10), a woman chosen as surrogate must be known and remain part of the household. Therefore, Sarah who cannot have children chooses her slave Hagar as a surrogate.

Like the slaves who plot an exodus from Egypt, Hagar plots escape from Sarah. Law allowed Sarah to punish or demote a surrogate, but not sell her (Exod 21:1-6). Sarah, however, submits Hagar to a desert ordeal and allows Yahweh who promised her the child to decide the case.

SATAN

New Testament

As adversaries, Hagar and Sarah became metaphors for the prejudice that scarred relations between Jews and Christians. In Galatians 4:21-31 Hagar is the slave forever—Sarah, the slave set-free. The contrast understands conversion from Judaism to Christianity like manumission that changes one's status from Hagar to Sarah, from slave to free.

Romans 4:13-25 and 9:6-24, on the other hand, celebrate Abraham and Sarah as ancestors-who-persevered, which is how both testaments understand a faith that waits patiently through disappointment and delay without despair (Heb 11:1-40).

Pastoral-Liturgical Tradition

Liturgies for baptism (1 Pet 3:1-7) and marriage (see nuptial blessing) see Sarah as an obedient and, therefore, a model wife—a tradition shared with the Book of Tobit (Tob 3:1–4:1).

In the Lectionary the hospitable like Martha and Mary (Luke 10:38-42) are presented as the descendants of Sarah and Abraham.

See: ABRAHAM, ISAAC

DON C. BENJAMIN, O.CARM.

SATAN

In our day the most likely conception of Satan is the head of the demons who are organized under his leadership. This spirit may also be called Mastema or Beliar, though the last two names are less commonly used. This identification was only arrived at through centuries, and it underwent transitions as time went on. In the OT the Hebrew verb *satan* has such meanings as to harass, to accuse, to hold a grudge, or to assail. As a noun it is generally used with the article, "the satan," with meanings such as adversary, accuser, or one who tests human beings. In the Septuagint the Hebrew word is rendered as *diabolos* from which is derived the English word "devil." Only in later traditions did the word become a proper name, Satan, and the function moves to that of tempter and destroyer of right relationship with the Lord.

Old Testament

The basic meaning for the Hebrew word *satan* is to accuse someone of wrong, as in a case against the person in a law court. From this meaning a metaphorical sense is derived in the expression "adversary." An adversary is a human being who accuses others by slander or accusation and thus harasses them by attacking their lives at the level of their good intentions and the good they actually do. The psalmists could pray to the Lord against those who attacked their lives by speaking falsely in an attempt to bring them down. The prayer was for ignominy and disgrace to fall upon the attackers so they would be put to shame (Ps 71:13). In the third Penitential Psalm the sinner called to God for help to sustain the grief experienced because of those who repay evil for good and harass those who pursue virtue (Ps 38:21). A sense of the relentlessness of such harassment can be understood from a complaint against enemies whose persecution caused the sufferer to rock with grief and be deeply troubled (Ps 55:4). The harassment added to the pain of the afflicted person and the adversary became an impediment to the well-being of the one striving for goodness of life. This type of harrying or attacking can be seen again in the wrongs done to Joseph as mentioned in Jacob's testament (Gen 49:23). After their father's death the brothers feared that the tables would be turned on them and that Joseph would hold a grudge against them, thus himself becoming a kind of adversary to them (Gen 50:15).

The noun with the article, "the satan," refers to the person who is the accuser, adversary, or tester of human beings. When David was among the Philistines they were apprehensive that in battle David would turn and become a military or political adversary to them (1 Sam 29:4), so they wanted him removed from their ranks. Later on as king, David remonstrated with

Abishai, son of Zeruiah, for becoming a hindrance or adversary to him in calling for the death of Shimei (2 Sam 19:23). There had been enough trouble in Israel at that point without creating further enmity. In time, David's son Solomon came to a period when there was neither adversary nor evil hindrance in the land. Then he made plans for the building of the first Temple (1 Kgs 5:18). Ultimately the peace was not lasting, for Edom became a political and military adversary as also did Rezon of Damascus (1 Kgs 11:14, 23, 25). These instances in the realm of government do not stand alone in their use of the noun "the satan" as an obstruction to the smooth course of events. The psalmists also spoke of an adversary who falsely accused another person and brought guilt upon the person through slander (Ps 109:6). Thus personal events also became the object of "the satan" or adversary against the cause of good. This can be seen in the personal incident in the life of Balaam when an angel of the Lord was his adversary on his way to see Balak (Num 22:22). Thus the adversarial function was linked to God.

In later thinking the concept of "the satan" as a specific figure was further developed. The opening chapters of the Book of Job show the heavenly court assembled with God and Satan the adversary came among them (Job 1:6-12). This figure had the position of a prosecutor whose function was to test the genuineness of Job's virtue. For this purpose he was allowed certain powers, which nevertheless remained subject to the authority of God. The notion at work in this instance is that virtue is not authentic unless it is tested and triumphs over the challenge (Job 1:6-12; 2:1-7). Satan had the same sort of function in the Book of Zechariah as he made accusations against Joshua the high priest to the angel of the Lord (Zech 3:1-2). However, the angel triumphed over the adversary/satan and restoration became the message. The references from Job and Zechariah show evils previously attributed to Yahweh now being attributed to the satan.

Demonology was prohibited in Hebrew law, but a few instances of superstition did persist. Though Saul drove mediums and fortune tellers out of the land, he himself consulted a medium to conjure up the ghost of Samuel (1 Sam 28:8-11). A psalmist bemoaned the sacrifice of children to demons (Ps 106:37) when Israel mingled with the nations. Some think the language of demonology perdures in Psalm 91:5-6 where Yahweh is praised for protecting the faithful people from the terror of the night, the arrow that flies by day, the pestilence that roams in darkness, and the devastating plague at noon.

As time went on Satan became a proper name for one who instigated evil in order to bring people to catastrophe. In a later text the Chronicler (1 Chr 21:1) attributed the plague that came upon David to this agent of evil, rather than to God as had been done in earlier writing (2 Sam 24:1). In this same vein the sage of the Book of Wisdom attributed the entrance of death into the world to the devil, and thus he identified the serpent of Genesis with the adversary angel who had come to be named Satan (Wis 2:24). At that point NT thought took up the theme.

See: ANGEL, TEMPTATION

BETTY JANE LILLIE, S.C.

New Testament

Satan appears thirty-six times in the NT. Its background is those OT uses of the Hebrew *satan* that refer to an adversary or accuser belonging essentially to the celestial realm. As in the OT, Satan's activities sometimes have positive results, as when they test someone and thereby purify or show the worthiness of the one so challenged.

The main synonyms of "Satan" in the NT are "the devil" (*ho diabolos*, see Rev 20:2; Matt 4:1-8, 11; and Rev 20:10 in the light of, respectively, Matt 4:10 and Rev 20:7); less frequently, Beelzebul (Matt 12:24, 27; cf. 12:26) or "the evil one" (*ho ponēros*, Matt 13:19; at the corresponding place in the explanation of the parable of the sower, Luke

8:12 has "the devil" and Mark 4:15, "Satan"); and "ruler of this world" (John 14:30; 16:11).

In the NT as a whole, Satan is an intelligent being who tests Jesus and is the adversary against whom his ministry is primarily directed; this ministry is successful and Satan's power is broken by Jesus' death and resurrection, but Satan is allowed to retain some scope for action, for the sake of the elect. In the Book of Revelation, Satan's ultimate defeat is associated with the judgment that immediately precedes the establishment of the new heaven and new earth.

The Gospels. In the Synoptic Gospels Jesus' ministry is bounded and defined by a life-and-death contest with this adversary. Thus, Satan comes on stage immediately after Jesus' baptism, and Jesus' ministry is depicted as a struggle to overcome Satan, although his human opponents think otherwise. In Luke, Satan reappears to play a key role in the passion narrative. The resurrection proves that Satan was not, after all, the victor.

Jesus' ministry opens with him implicitly (Mark 1:13) or explicitly (Matt 4:1-11; Luke 4:1-13) rejecting Satan's plans for him and choosing instead God's way. For Luke, this concludes Satan's testing of Jesus (Luke 4:13) until the passion narrative (22:3). At a key point in Mark's story, however, Peter suggests that suffering is not part of Jesus' destiny and is, therefore, told, "Get behind me, Satan!" (Mark 8:33; see also Matt 16:23). The contrast is between God's way of thinking and Peter's human way, the latter being satanic when it conflicts with the former.

The Synoptic account of Jesus pits him against Satan's power over human beings. Thus, Jesus tacitly interprets his cures as "driving out Satan" (Mark 3:23; Matt 12:26), which Luke expresses in narrative form by telling how Jesus cures a woman "whom Satan bound for eighteen years" (Luke 13:16). Furthermore, Luke sees as part of the same strategy the mission of the seventy [-two] disciples whom Jesus sends out: on their return, Jesus tells them, "I saw Satan fall like lightning from heaven"

(Luke 10:18). So they, too, are involved in the defeat of Satan that Jesus' ministry sets in motion (Acts 10:38 offers a similar interpretation of Jesus' ministry).

By contrast, the religious authorities claim that Jesus acts not against, but in league with, Satan (Mark 3:22-30 and parallels). Jesus vehemently rejects this: to attribute to Satan what is done through God's Spirit is to commit the "unforgivable sin" of putting oneself outside the sphere of the Spirit (Mark 3:29-31). In reply, Jesus suggests that whatever the authority behind his exorcisms, their effectiveness shows that, one way or another, Satan is finished: either because his "house is divided against itself" or because the "strong man" who owns the house has been "tied up" (Mark 3:25-27). The reader knows which is the case.

Satan remains active throughout Jesus' life. Luke and John depict Judas' treachery as due to Satan's influence: Satan "entered into Judas" just before the latter arranged to hand Jesus over to the religious authorities (Luke 22:3; John 13:27, the only mention of "Satan" in this Gospel; see also John 13:2; 14:30). In Luke's passion narrative Satan is further implicated: at the Last Supper, Jesus reveals that Satan's demand "to sift [the apostles] like wheat" will be granted. This refers, of course, to the effect on them of Jesus' passion and death. Like Job before them, they will survive the test, in their case because Jesus has prayed that Peter's faith will not fail, and has made him responsible for strengthening the others, once he has "turned back" (Luke 22:31-32). Presumably all emerge stronger from the ordeal.

NT Books Other than the Gospels. Even the resurrection does not end Satan's influence over humanity. Thus, Acts 26:18 regards Gentiles as still under Satan's power and in need of Paul's ministrations. Those who have been evangelized are far from safe: Satan can steal God's word from them (Mark 4:15), fill their hearts and then induce them to act deceitfully (Acts 5:3), or tempt those who are taking asceticism too far (1 Cor 7:5). Paul knows all about Satan's efforts at gaining advantage over Christians: "We are not unaware of his purposes," he says in 2 Corinthians 2:11, and recognizes that "even Satan masquerades as an angel of light" (11:14). Paul does not doubt God's power to "crush Satan" under the feet of those who are "wise as to what is good and simple as to what is evil" (Rom 16:19-20). But fulfilling these conditions is another matter: the writer of 1 Timothy notes that "some have already turned away to follow Satan" (1 Tim 5:15).

Satan's activity can have positive effects, however: as Jesus' resolve to do God's will was made evident by his encounter with Satan in the desert, so Paul's tendency to pride is kept in check by his "thorn in the flesh, . . . an angel of Satan" (2 Cor 12:7) who is obviously carrying out God's intention in Paul's regard (12:8-10). Satan's repeated thwarting of Paul's plans to visit the Thessalonians may be similarly within God's design, although the apostle obviously does not see it as such in 1 Thessalonians 2:18. An understanding of "handing people over to Satan" (i.e., excluding them from the community) as having a potentially salutary effect is evident in 1 Corinthians 5:1 and 1 Timothy 1:20.

Nevertheless, the emphasis is on the negative character of Satan's work, particularly in the Book of Revelation, which lacks any hint of a positive role for Satan. Deception is here, as in Paul, a prominent feature of Satan's activity. Thus, just as in 2 Thessalonians 2:9-10, Satan's power is to be recognized behind "every mighty deed and . . . signs and wonders that lie and . . . every wicked deceit" (2 Thess 2:9-10; see also *T.Dan.* 3:6; *T.Job* 6:4), so John sympathizes with the Christians of Smyrna, slandered by false Jews from "the assembly [or synagogue] of Satan" (Rev 2:9), and offers hope of final vindication to the Philadelphians, who are similarly troubled (3:9). Christians in Pergamum live "where Satan dwells," and John's reference to "Satan's throne" there (2:13) expresses succinctly his view of the empire's religious demands; later chapters of Revelation will reveal the extent to which imperial pomp totally misrepresents the underlying reality. Perhaps the "deep secrets of Satan" known in Thyatira (Rev 2:24) were professedly satanic, but the expression may be sarcastic and thus not reflect terms used by the promoters of the teachings.

It is not surprising, then, that the Book of Revelation goes on to tell of Satan's defeat. The first stage occurs in 12:9 (and see also 12:10: behind the Greek word "the accuser [of our brothers]" lies the Hebrew *Satan*); in 20:2 Satan is "tied . . . up for a thousand years," before being definitively defeated, punished, and thereby rendered incapable of further deception (20:7-10).

See: ANGEL, DEATH, DESERT, JUDGMENT, LIGHT AND DARKNESS, MINISTRY, SIGN, TEMPTATION, WAY

PATRICIA M. MCDONALD, S.H.C.J.

Pastoral-Liturgical Tradition

The early Church continued the beliefs found in apostolic times in Satan and demons. It must be said, however, that popular demonologies have always been more elaborate than the somewhat spare lines of Church teaching. Not infrequently in European territories that were Christianized in the first millennium, local deities came to be incorporated into the ranks of demons.

The Book of Enoch and other Apocryphal writings influenced the speculations of the Church Fathers regarding the fall of the angels and the origins of demons. Justin Martyr, Tertullian, and Cyprian believed that the demons were the offspring of fallen angels and human mothers. The fall of the angels was caused by the envy of humans. Later the view came to prevail that the demons and their leader, Satan, fell from grace out of pride—either pride in their own capacities or because they envied God. In all of this, there is a clear sense that the demons were originally created good, but fell from grace by their own accord. Since that fall, they have been implacable enemies of the good, wreaking havoc where they might and constantly attempting to lure human beings away from good into sin. Popular, pre-Christian beliefs about demons melded with those in early Christian tradition to create extensive and often graphic representations of evil throughout early Christianity down to early modern times. Accusations of evil persons making pacts with the devil to gain power over others were frequently made throughout this period, most frequently against women, Jews, and other marginalized persons. The story of Faust, a scholar who makes a pact with the devil and then loses his soul, was a popular literary figure from the sixteenth century down to the present. Sightings of demons and of Satan were reported, especially in the Medieval and early Modern period. One of the most famous was that of Martin Luther, who reportedly threw his inkpot at the demon while working in his study.

Fascination with and worship of Satan are reported down into the present time. During the period following the French Revolution the so-called "Black Mass" was purportedly celebrated, which was a blasphemous parody of the Eucharist that was offered to Satan. The chief purpose of such a rite was to mock the Church. Periodically interest in Satanism resurges. When encountered among adolescents, it is usually an act of rebellion and search for an autonomous identity over the world of their elders. The small Churches of Satan found in the United States claim to be benevolent, dualist worshipers of the transcendent. Dangerous and malevolent, however, are small, secretive groups of so-called "generational Satanists" who do indeed worship Satan and try to bring others under their power. They pass their beliefs onto their children, often through a process of repeated traumatization.

The Church has developed no specific teaching on Satan and the demons, other than to affirm their existence, maintain that they were created good, and that they seek the ruin of creation and of human beings. There are only three passing references in the documents of Vatican II (Pastoral Constitution on the Church in the Modern World, nos. 2, 13; Decree on the Church's Missionary Activity, no. 9). The Vatican has, however, insisted on the existence of personified evil in the world against modern scepticism.

Closely allied to belief in the power of Satan is the practice of exorcism, or the expelling of demons and resistance to their power. Exorcism was practiced widely in the early Church, but it covered a range of phenomena from what today would be called mental illness to actual encounter with Satan. The exorcisms practiced today in the Scrutinies that form part of the Rite of Christian Initiation of Adults focus on the need for strength to resist the powers of temptation to sin rather than possession by demons. Similarly, the (optional) rite of exorcism in the Rite for Baptism of Children is concerned with deliverance from original sin. There is a rite of exorcism specifically directed at demon possession that may be performed by a priest who has been delegated by the diocesan bishop. Its use, however, is very infrequent.

Central to Christian understanding of Satan and demons is the overwhelming victory over evil and sin by Christ. It is always within that context that they must be seen. While they might continue to wreak havoc in our world, in whatever way or form, they can be and will be overcome in the power of the redeeming activity of Jesus Christ.

See: ANGEL, SPIRIT

ROBERT J. SCHREITER, C.PP.S.

SCANDAL

The Hebrew words behind this concept are usually either *kāśal* (to stumble, totter) or *môqēš* (a trap or, originally, some part of one, such as a trigger). In our context, the terms are mostly used metaphorically. The Greek OT translates most of them as *skandalon,* the source of the English word "scandal," although occasionally (e.g., Ezek 3:20 and 14:3) it uses other Greek words *(basanos; kolasis)* conveying the idea of trial by torture ("touchstone"). The cognate verb, *skandal-*

izein, is rare in the OT, being found only three times in the Book of Sirach and once in some versions of Daniel. In the NT *skandalon* is used fifteen times, and *skandalizein* twice as often.

In English Bibles, a variety of terms are used to translate these words. In the NAB they include "stumbling block" (Lev 19:14; Ps 119:165; Rom 11:9; 1 Cor 1:23; Gal 5:11; Rev 2:14); "trap" (Josh 23:13); "snare" (1 Sam 18:21; Ps 106:36); "roadblock" (Jdt 5:1, one of the rare literal usages); "ruin" (Sir 27:23; Judg 8:27); "occasion of sin" (Ezek 7:19; 44:12); "obstacle" (Matt 16:23; Rom 16:17); "hindrance" (Rom 14:13); and various other phrases conveying the idea of things that cause people to sin (e.g., Matt 18:7; Luke 17:1) or fall (1 Pet 2:8; 1 John 2:10). In the NT the verb *skandalizein* is translated by such expressions as "to cause [someone] to sin" (Mark 9:43-47 and par.); "to take offense at" Jesus (Matt 11:6; Mark 6:3; Luke 7:23); "to shock" or "offend" someone (John 6:61; Matt 15:12; 17:27); "to lead into sin" (Matt 24:10); "to shake [someone's] faith" (Mark 14:27 and par.); "to fall away" (John 16:1); "to become a stumbling block" (Rom 14:21); "to cause (or lead) [someone] to sin" (1 Cor 8:13; 2 Cor 11:29).

Old Testament

Very occasionally, the word denotes an object over which one might literally fall. Thus, Leviticus 19:14 insists "You shall not curse the deaf or put a stumbling block in front of the blind, but you shall fear your God." See also Judith 5:1 and 1 Maccabees 5:4. Mostly, however, scandal is that which, when set in place by a malicious enemy, causes a metaphorical downfall: death, disgrace, or apostasy. For example, when Saul discovers that his younger daughter, Michal, loves David, he decides to give her to him in marriage "to become a snare for him, so that the Philistines may strike him": the bride price will be the foreskins of a hundred Philistines, and Saul is confident that obtaining them will cost David his life (1 Sam 18:21). More typically, the gods of other nations constitute a hazard for Israel: a trap into which they probably will fall (e.g., Josh 23:13; Judg 2:3; 8:27; Ezek 14:3-4, 7).

The scandal is not always set up by enemies, however; it can arise through one's own riches, desires, or speech (Ezek 7:19; Sir 9:5; 23:8), or even, for the hypocrite, through studying the law (Sir 35 [32]:15). Indeed, in the textually problematic Isaiah 8:14-15, the Lord himself is to be "a snare, an obstacle and a stumbling stone to both the houses of Israel," and God supplies the stumbling block for one who forsakes virtue in Ezekiel 3:20.

New Testament

The NT takes up the OT notion of *skandalon* as that which (metaphorically) prevents one from continuing on the right road. Jesus finds Peter an "obstacle" (*skandalon*) because the disciple refuses to countenance that Jesus must suffer (Matt 16:23). Similarly, Christians will have to face "things that cause sin" (e.g., Matt 18:7; Luke 17:1), sometimes from other Christians (Mark 9:42 and par.; Rom 14:13, 21; 16:17; 1 Cor 8:13), or even from their own bodies (Mark 9:43-47 and par.; Matt 18:8-9). In these instances, "scandals" function as temptations, which are to be recognized as such and overcome, albeit with difficulty. Sometimes they prove to be too much for people; then, "to be scandalized" means "to be led [in]to sin" (Matt 24:10; 2 Cor 11:29) or "to fall away" (Mark 4:17 and par.).

Paradoxically, Jesus himself is a source of scandal, for some people reject his claims as outrageous. During his ministry, those scandalized by him include his relations (Mark 6:3; Matt 13:57), Pharisees (Matt 15:12; cf. 17:27), and "many of his disciples" (John 6:61). According to Matthew and Mark, Jesus predicts at the Last Supper that the Twelve will be scandalized (NAB: "have their faith shaken") by what happens to him (Mark 14:27, 29 and par.). John uses the same verb on the same occasion, but in a positive sense: Jesus' purpose in telling his disciples about future persecution of the Church and the role that the Spirit will play is so that they "may not fall away" (lit. "be scandalized"; John 16:1).

More profoundly, Paul recognizes that for Jews, the crucified Christ is a stumbling block (1 Cor 1:23) and, indeed, one that is somehow a necessary part of God's design (Gal 5:11). The latter notion is taken up in 1 Peter 2:4-8 in a complex passage that presents Jesus as the cornerstone, "chosen and precious" (Isa 28:16), but nevertheless rejected by the builders (Ps 118:22) and therefore being "a stone that will make people stumble" (Isa 8:14). This stumbling results from their refusal to obey God's word (1 Pet 2:8).

Pastoral-Liturgical Tradition

That Christians preach a crucified Christ has been a central stumbling block throughout Christian history, and remains so.

In the moral sphere, "giving scandal" has two main thrusts: toward those outside the community and within the community itself. The first of these occurs when Christians' conduct is such as to discredit their religion; its effect is to put off (or at least confuse) those who might otherwise have found their way to God. The second is a leading astray of one's fellow Christians: to induce them to do wrong by means of teaching that, while good in itself, is not profitable to them in their particular situation. Sometimes, the fault lies in the ones so scandalized, because the offense results from their culpable lack of good judgment about the situation; if, however, they are merely weak or immature, one who scandalizes them is at fault.

See: FAITH, HYPOCRITE, SIN, TEMPTATION

PATRICIA M. MCDONALD, S.H.C.J.

SCRIBE

Originally secular functionaries, scribes came to prominence as religious leaders in postexilic times. As skilled writers and interpreters of the biblical texts, they became invaluable when the focus of religious life shifted to the Law.* In the NT scribes continue to appear as influential. The majority of NT references to scribes are pejorative, painting them in contrast to Jesus and his teaching.

Old Testament

Active throughout the OT period, the scribes appear first as public officials whose skills as writers make them indispensable. Without necessarily losing this official function, their talents eventually give them access to high government positions and, in the later biblical period, to roles as religious leaders as well.

Scribe translates the Hebrew word *sōpēr*, derived from the root meaning "count, relate." Originally the root probably referred to a written document. The word describes not merely the ability to read and write, but covers a wide range of activities from copying documents to serving as officials in government, roles that can change over time. The word "secretary" in our own culture is probably the closest parallel since it can refer to a typist, a file clerk, and a high official in government, for example, the "Secretary of Education." The ancient scribe usually had competence in some area, such as law or finance.

Scribes were active throughout the ancient Near East, but the most information about them comes from Egypt and Mesopotamia. They served at the court and in temples administering and preserving records on taxes, correspondence, forced labor crews, military activities, various kinds of goods, building projects, and such. They were also responsible for preserving religious traditions and training future scribes. Because of their access to such learning, it is not surprising that scribes became high government officials and counselors.

Little is known about scribal training, but evidently some general education, a knowledge of particular subjects such as law, and expertise in languages was required. This presumes a whole system of training and schools. The biblical Wisdom literature reflects some kind of scribal and school activity as is found in Egypt and Mesopotamia though direct evidence is lacking.

When scribes first appear in the Bible, they are functioning at high levels in the government at Jerusalem. The post of "royal secretary" was in the king's palace and the scribes appointed to this office had charge of policy, administration, and finance (2 Kgs 18:18; 22:3-10; Jer 36:12). Baruch was a scribe who served as Jeremiah's secretary and had access to government officials (Jer 36:8-10). He also was given charge of legal documents (Jer 32:12). Shebna, during the time of Isaiah, was probably demoted from the post of "master of the palace" (Isa 22:15-16) to royal secretary (Isa 36:3) because of the prophet's denunciation. During the period before the Exile, therefore, it seems the scribe was a secular functionary.

It is in postexilic times that the scribe takes on religious significance as well. Without land, king, and Temple, the Law became a special focus of religious life for the exiles. The study, preservation, and transmission of the Law and Israel's other religious traditions became important for the identity and survival of the exilic community. Thus, Ezra is described as a priest and a scribe "well-versed in the law of Moses" (Ezra 7:6). Whatever his official status, Ezra had enough standing in his community and among the Persians to obtain permission to bring a party of Jews back to Jerusalem and be commissioned to appoint the magistrates and judges for the new community (Ezra 7:21-26). He also led the community, along with other Levites and priests, in prayer and fasting, though he does not officiate at the altar (Ezra 8–10). He proclaimed the Law, which was then explained by Levites to the people (Nehemiah 8). Ezra, thus, represents those early teachers of the Law who helped expand the role of scribes. But even then purely administrative functions were not abandoned. Zadok the scribe is appointed, along with others, to be in charge of the tithes collected for the Temple (Neh 13:12-13).

At this time scribes were among the leadership group of the Jewish community, but they were not necessarily a distinct group. Roles overlapped. There were priests and Levites who were scribes as well (1 Chr 24:6; 2 Chr 34:13). Scribes were active in prophetic and other leadership circles. Their activity also included the editing, transmission, and interpretation of biblical texts.

During the Hellenistic period evidence for Temple scribes appears in a letter of Antiochus III exempting them (along with other groups) from certain taxes. During the Maccabean revolt scribes joined in the struggle, and the biblical text seems to associate them with the Hasideans (the "pious ones") when they attempt to make peace at the accession of Demetrius I (1 Macc 7:11-14; see 1 Macc 2:42). These scribes evidently joined those who were defending the traditional patterns of Jewish life. The fact that sixty of them were killed by those with whom they were trying to make peace (1 Macc 7:16) reflects the position and influence they held within the Jewish community, which ended with their assassination. How much these scribes had to do with the formation of the group, later known as the Pharisees, is not clear. Finally, 2 Maccabees narrates the martyrdom of Eleazar, "one of the foremost scribes" (6:18), as an example of courage and religious virtue.

It was during this period, as well, that an abundance of Jewish literature appeared, including some biblical Wisdom books, Qoheleth and Sirach, plus Daniel. So much writing must testify to the existence of a well-educated class of Jews, among whom surely would be scribes. The Enoch literature, which had its origins around this time, refers to the hero Enoch as a scribe and later Rabbinic literature attributes some of its teachings to the scribes. But it is questionable whether all this activity suggests a cohesive class with a consistent body of teaching. A most famous portrait of the scribe is found in the second century BCE work of Sirach (39:1-11). According to this text, the scribe is a scholar in all areas of knowledge including the biblical writings. Also, he is a counselor, a high official, and ambassador for the government. His wise teaching, guided by the Lord, will bring lasting fame. The scribe is no longer just a public official, but a religious leader who belongs in the circle of the wise.

See: LAW, PHARISEE

THOMAS P. MCCREESH, O.P.

New Testament

The NT rarely mentions a scribe individually but most often refers to scribes collectively, usually in association with other groups like the Pharisees,* Sadducees,* or chief priests. In the first century CE the scribes were well-educated professionals whose ability to read and write placed them in the powerful position of transmitting and interpreting the oral and written traditions of Judaism. They were the legal scholars and theologians of their day (see Matt 2:4-6). As members of the aristocracy, scribes held influential positions in the Sanhedrin, where the majority of scribes were also Pharisees. The four Gospels most frequently mention the scribes in connection with other official Jewish groups who plotted against Jesus. There are neutral, positive, and polemical senses to the concept of scribe in the NT.

Neutral Sense. The neutral sense of the Greek word for "scribe" (*grammateus*) appears only at Acts 19:35, where the term is translated "town clerk," reflecting standard secular usage for one who is literate and professionally trained to keep official records. 1 Corinthians 1:20 uses the word "scribe" in the neutral sense of an educated person, but it is found in the context of Paul's denigration of human learning when contrasted with God's wisdom.

Positive Sense. Mark 12:28-34 presents a sympathetic portrait of a scribe. Although the scene is one of a series of confrontations between Jesus and various Jewish leaders in Jerusalem, the interchange between Jesus and this particular scribe lacks the intensity of opposition seen in the surrounding passages. The scribe asks Jesus a fair question, in light of contemporary Jewish disputations about the Torah: "Which is the first of all the commandments?" Jesus' famous re-

sponse, which lays out the greatest commandment and its corollary—wholehearted love of God and neighbor—is commended by the scribe. He reacts positively to Jesus' teaching: "Well said, teacher. You are right . . . [These commandments are] worth more than all burnt offerings and sacrifices." But it is Jesus' response to the scribe which is most interesting: "And when Jesus saw that [he] answered with understanding, he said to him, 'You are not far from the kingdom of God.'" Though this passage is less than an outright commendation of the scribe, it presents an image of one seeking a deeper understanding of God's Law* and receiving encouragement from Jesus for this search.

The most striking example of the positive use of the term "scribe" is found in Matthew 13:52. This verse concludes the great parable chapter of Matthew. Once the disciples have responded affirmatively to Jesus' query of whether they have understood his teaching, Jesus says: "Then every scribe who has been instructed in the kingdom of heaven is like the head of a household who brings from his storeroom both the new and the old." Many Matthean scholars see in this passage a virtual autobiographical signature of the author. The Christian writer takes a traditional concept from Israel (scribe) and transforms it into a special role for his own community. This is confirmed in the list of authoritative positions apparently extant in the Matthean community, where scribes are listed along with "prophets and wise men" (Matt 23:34). These specially trained scribes have the responsibility to teach the community, combining insights from old traditions (the Law and the Prophets) with new traditions (the teachings of Jesus).

Pejorative Sense. The overwhelming portrait of the scribes in the NT is, however, not positive. Rather, the scribes are seen as part of the mass of opposition to Jesus and the disciples, which culminates in his passion and death.

In the Synoptic Gospels the scribes are most frequently seen in polemical contexts concerning teaching authority, or participating in the plot to entrap Jesus. Mark 1:22 explicitly commends Jesus' teaching, "for he taught them as one having authority and not as the scribes." This attitude would have been very offensive to those professionally trained in the interpretation of God's Law. Yet the contrast between the authoritative teaching of Jesus, seen in words and in miraculous deeds, and the traditional interpretation of the Law of Israel is an essential part of the gospel message that God has acted uniquely in Jesus Christ.

Matthew and Luke have a tendency to ally the scribes with the Pharisees in their opposition to Jesus (Matt 15:1; Luke 11:53). Historically, scribes were not limited to the Pharisaic party. The occurrence of the description "scribes who were Pharisees" (Mark 2:16; Acts 23:9) implies that scribes could belong to other groups within Judaism as well as to the Pharisees.

The scribes participate in the plot against Jesus in various ways. They question his authority (Luke 20:1-2), accuse Jesus of blasphemy (Matt 9:3), improperly seek signs (Matt 12:38), and plot outrightly to kill Jesus (Luke 22:2). They receive explicit mention in the passion predictions (Mark 8:31), where they are portrayed as part of the established religious authorities of the Temple in Jerusalem who are threatened by Jesus' teaching and actions and thus seek to destroy him. Acts also indicates that their opposition extended to the disciples after the resurrection (Acts 4:5).

Jesus himself only rarely singles out any teaching on the scribes alone in the Gospels. He calls his disciples to exceed in the righteousness of both the scribes and the Pharisees (Matt 5:20). He warns strongly against the scribes' reliance on the trappings of authority while doing dishonest deeds (Luke 20:45-47), and vehemently denounces them along with the Pharisees for hypocrisy, lack of integrity, and misplaced priorities (Matt 23:3-36).

By the time of John's Gospel, the scribes apparently did not warrant specific mention, for they do not appear in this Gospel. Instead, the generic term "the Jews" is most frequently used to describe the opposition to Jesus.

As with the case of other Jewish groups mentioned in the NT, it is necessary to separate images shaped by late first-century CE Jewish and Christian polemics from other historical concerns. If some Jewish scribes merited the deep enmity of Christians for having played a role along with some other officials in opposition to Jesus, scribes were nonetheless an essential factor in the preservation of Judaism and the birth of Christianity. Early Christian scribes had to preserve and develop the same skills in education as their Jewish counterparts in order to transmit faithfully the traditions that came to be known as the NT.

See: JUDAISM, LAW, PHARISEE, PRIEST, SADDUCEES, TEACH/TEACHING, TEMPLE

RONALD D. WITHERUP, S.S.

SEA

The term sea designates a body of salt or fresh water, and can also have a symbolic meaning, usually a threat to order and life.

Old Testament

There are two terms for sea, *yam* (390+) and *tehom* (33); the latter term is often translated "the deep." Sea, *yam,* can be used generally as the watery part of the universe, e.g., "the heavens and the earth, the sea and all that is in them" (Exod 20:11). It can refer to a specific sea: the Mediterranean (the Great Sea or the Western Sea); the Dead Sea or Sea of Salt; the Sea of Galilee or Sea of Chinnereth; the Red Sea or Sea of Reeds. The term sometimes means simply the West (Gen 13:14). It can also mean a large river like the Nile (Isa 19:5). The term occasionally designates the waters that were thought to encircle the earth above and below, e.g., "For you cast me into the deep, into the heart of the sea, and the flood enveloped me" (Jonah 2:4); "He gathers the waters of the sea as in a flask; in cellars he confines the deep" (Ps 33:7).

The word for sea or cosmic waters is *tehom* (sometimes "waters," *mayim*). Before

God created, "the earth was a formless wasteland and darkness covered the abyss" (Gen 1:2). When God decided to end the Flood, "The fountains of the abyss and the floodgates of the sky were closed, and the downpour from the sky was held back" (Gen 8:2). *Tehom* is cognate to Ugaritic *tihamatu* and Akkadian *tamtu*, which have the same semantic field, and to Akkadian Tiamat, the personified salt sea and enemy of the gods in the Akkadian epic *Enuma elish*. The storm god Marduk slays her in battle and from her corpse creates the world.

In Ugaritic texts Sea is an enemy of the storm god Baal Hadad, who brings fertility* and social order to the world. After a long battle Baal defeats Sea, builds a palace with El's blessing, and proclaims his kingship at a great banquet of the gods. The same scenario appears in the Bible. Sea is the enemy of Yahweh who appears in the storm. Ancient Near East creation was concerned primarily with the world of gods and human beings rather than with the physical universe as in modern scientific conceptions. Sea, the obstacle to life, had to be destroyed or tamed. In Genesis 1, sea is tamed by the appearance of dry land (days 2 and 3). In Psalm 77:11-20 it is defeated by Yahweh making a way through it for Israel to cross. Psalms 18:5-6, 16-20; 29:3, 10; 65:8; 89:10; 93; 104:5-18; 114 also tell how sea's threat to the people was removed by God.

In its cosmogonic sense sea is important in Second Isaiah's preaching. Just as in olden times sea kept Israel from entering the Promised Land until Yahweh made a way through it, so the desert is keeping Israel from entering Zion: "Thus says the LORD, who opens *a way in the sea*, and *a path in the mighty waters*. . . . See, I am doing something new! Now it springs forth, do you not perceive it? *In the desert* I make *a way, in the wasteland, paths* [Qumran manuscript]" (Isa 43:16, 19). Language of creation complements and deepens language of exodus-landtaking: "Was it not you [God] who dried up the sea, the waters of the great deep, Who made the depths of the sea into a way for the redeemed to pass over? Those whom the LORD has ransomed will return, and enter Zion singing" (Isa 51:10-11).

Because sea in many ancient cosmogonies was the enemy of human community, it became a general symbol of evil. In the apocalyptic vision in Daniel 7, the four great beasts that symbolize the oppressive world empires came up out of the great sea (7:2-3). The sea symbolizes the abiding evil behind each empire.

In the OT, then, sea is part of an ordered world, a universe of "heaven, earth, and sea." In that universe, sea is not only lakes and seas but also the waters surrounding the hollow center, earth. The deep can symbolize the menace of pre-creation chaos. Yahweh conquered sea to introduce order and existence. In Genesis 1 and Psalm 104, sea is not destroyed but is made part of a beautiful universe. Some psalms as well as Second Isaiah describe God creating Israel by defeating the sea that separates Israel from its land.

New Testament

Sea in NT, *thalassa*, can be general (Mark 9:42) or refer to bodies of water like the Sea of Galilee and the Mediterranean. Sea, as a symbol of the primeval disordered state, may be behind Jesus' taming of the sea (Mark 4:35-41; Matt 8:23-27; Luke 8:22-25) and walking on the water (Matt 14:22-36; Mark 6:45-52; John 6:16-21) but the acts take place on the non-mythic Sea of Galilee.

In the apocalyptic Book of Revelation sea symbolizes the residual evil in the world, as in Daniel 7. In chapters 12–21, the dragon who commissions the beasts (the Roman Empire and its priesthood) lives in the sea. In chapter 20 the dragon itself is destroyed, and John writes: "Then I saw a new heaven and a new earth. The former heaven and the former earth had passed away, *and the sea was no more*" (Rev 21:1). Evil will not exist in the new creation.

Pastoral-Liturgical Tradition

The earliest baptismal tradition, especially the Holy Saturday readings, saw the waters of baptism both positively and negatively, and justified both attitudes by appealing to the OT. Just as the waters of creation brought forth life (Gen 1:20), so the waters of baptism bring forth life. The most common analogy, however, is the Flood. Just as the Flood waters brought judgment and removed sin, so the baptismal waters wipe away sin.

As the symbol of the mysterious evil within the universe, sea is in the biblical tradition and should not be neglected. Christians have so stressed the once for all divine victory over primordial chaos that they sometimes forget that in the Bible something of that chaos lingers at the edge of life. Jeremiah preached the possible return of chaos (Jer 4:23-28). God reminds Job that Leviathan, magnificent but evil, still lives (Job 41). Empires that oppress God's holy people represent a residual malevolence as in Daniel 7 and Revelation.

See: CHAOS, WATER

RICHARD J. CLIFFORD, S.J.

SEAL

Three Pauline letters speak of the Christian as one who enjoys the "seal of the Spirit." The Corinthians are taught that it is God "who anointed us and sealed us, thereby depositing the first payment, the Spirit, in our hearts" (2 Cor 1:21-22). The teaching is repeated in the Letter to the Ephesians, who are reminded that when they heard and believed in the glad tidings of salvation, they were "sealed with the Holy Spirit who had been promised" (Eph 1:13). Again the Spirit is called "the first payment against the full redemption." The image recurs in an exhortation later in the same letter: "Do nothing to sadden the Holy Spirit with whom you were sealed against the day of redemption" (Eph 4:30). These texts are the biblical source for the liturgical formula that presently accompanies the anointing with chrism in the Roman rite of Christian initiation, "N., be sealed with the Gift of the Spirit."

Paul's use of the image of a "seal" against the day of redemption has its own cultural and religious background. Persons and things were sealed with the insignia of their owner to lay a claim on them and to protect them. Official and private documents were "sealed" with impressed wax. The flesh of soldiers and slaves as well as animals was tattooed or branded with such proprietary insignia. Bodily marking was also practiced by religious devotees, and scholars have noted that the ancient Jewish practice of circumcision as a mark of covenant membership is to be understood in this context.

Such culturally familiar physical marking or sealing, not unlike contemporary cultural interest in name-brands, gave rise to metaphors of spiritual sealing or marking in the writings of the prophets. In Ezekiel's vision of God's wrath turned against evildoers, God sends an advance man to mark the letter *tau*, a cross-mark, on the foreheads of those who are to be saved from destruction (Ezek 9:4). The author of the Book of Revelation picks up this image to give a dramatic account of the last days in which four messengers of God will "imprint [the seal of the living God] on the foreheads of the servants of God" (Rev 7:2-4). Like Paul, this author understands Christians to be sealed in anticipation of their redemption.

In every instance cited, the outward seal is an indicator of a relationship, and the relationship signified is what has meaning. Thus Jesus' spiritual identity as the beloved son of the living God was manifested in his anointing by the holy Spirit at his baptism in the river Jordan. Analogously, disciples of Jesus who receive this gift of the holy Spirit in baptism are, according to Paul, "sealed" by this holy Spirit for future glory.

Liturgical rites of anointing with chrism and consignation (marking with the sign of the cross) have a long history that gives tangible, visible, and olfactory expression to this inner mystery: the Christian is one who is sealed now with the first fruits of the Spirit and marked for the glory that is yet to be revealed. The Eastern and Western liturgical traditions exhibit diversity in their enactment of rites of Christian initiation that give expression to their common faith in this saving relationship with the holy Spirit. Most problematic in their history was the splitting of the post-baptismal anointing from the water bath in the Western Church to create two separate events, one called baptism and the other confirmation. The 1972 Roman Rite of Christian Initiation of Adults corrects this historical disjunction, reconnecting the "seal of the spirit" with baptismal anointing at the time of the water bath.

See: ANOINTING, BAPTISM, CHRISM, CIRCUMCISION, GIFTS, SPIRIT

MARY COLLINS, O.S.B.

SEED

Old Testament

Several meanings of seed or *zera* exist in the OT. The literal agricultural context refers to the individuality and fruitfulness of plants, trees, and fruits. As commanded by a benevolent God on the third day of creation, each propagates according to its own kind of seed, and plants and fruits with seed are given to human beings for their nourishment (Genesis 1; 11; 12; 29). Joseph's fortunes in Egypt turn on his anticipation of a short-fall in the grain supply when he interprets the Pharaoh's dream. Seven years of famine are sustained because of Joseph's foresight in gathering grain and storing it in towns prior to the disaster (Gen 41:35-36). It is because of the famine and their need for grain that the family of Jacob, the brothers of Joseph, are eventually reunited (Gen 42:1; 45:6).

The seed that is harvested, i.e. wheat or barley, marks the passage of seasons and years. For six years the soil may be sown, but the seventh year is a sabbatical for the earth (Exod 23:10-11). Seeds, understood as the harvest of grain, are linked to feasts of the Jewish liturgical year. After the harvest, a sheaf of first-fruits is offered to God (Lev 23:9-11). Pentecost is the festival held fifty days after the wave offering of first fruits (Lev 23:15-17) and involves cereal offerings

of bread. In accord with laws governing the leaving of stray grain in the field at harvest (Lev 23:22), Ruth gleans barley in the field of Boaz (Ruth 2:1-23). The time for threshing of the sheaves is decisive for Ruth's success in propelling Boaz to formalize their marriage (Ruth 3:1-18). Restoration after exile is metaphorically represented by a harvest image. The people who went forth weeping, carrying the seed to be sown, shall come back rejoicing, carrying their sheaves (Ps 126:6).

A second meaning of seed refers to human procreation, one's immediate children and long-term descendants. Abraham is promised that his seed shall be given the land (Gen 12:7; 13:15), that his seed will be as numerous as grains of dust (Gen 13:16) and as uncountable as the stars or sands of the seashore (Gen 15:5; 22:17). The physical descendants of Abraham fulfill God's promise and are the people chosen to keep the covenant, ritualized by circumcision (Gen 17:9-10), identifying them as a distinct religious community and ethnic population. Jacob is promised that his seed shall have universal extension and be a blessing for all the nations of the earth (Gen 28:4, 13, 14).

A physical and national meaning of seed is linked with David and his offspring. God shows kindness and victory to David and his seed forever (2 Sam 22:51; Ps 18:51). David is the recipient of the covenant, and the throne of David and his posterity will last forever (Ps 89:4-5, 29-30). His seed is the nation of Israel and its political continuity, endlessly renewed and vital.

A third meaning of seed involves the spiritual likeness both to one's ancestors and to one's own descendants in fidelity to the covenant. God pledges fidelity to individuals and to their descendants (Gen 17:7-19) as well as to the descendants because of their predecessors. Those who survive the wandering in the desert experience themselves as inheritors of the election and love God had for the patriarchs and matriarchs (Deut 10:15). Those who are lovingly obedient to God's commandments will have their hearts and the hearts of their own descendants circumcised and dedicated to God who has chosen them. The choice of a life of obedience by one generation ensures that one's seed will also live and have blessing, just as Abraham, Isaac, and Jacob received it (Deut 30:6, 19-20). Seed now implies the propagation of spiritual fidelity to God. The opposite is a community that represents "bad seed," a people laden with iniquity, the seed of evil (Isa 1:4).

New Testament

The three meanings of seed in the OT, agricultural, physical descent, and spiritual descent, cross in the literal and metaphoric applications of *spora* and *sperma* in the NT. In addition, seed becomes a metaphor of transformation in resurrection.

The parable of the sower and the seed (Matt 13:1-23) has an agricultural setting, but it refers to Jesus' teaching about the reign of God and the receptivity of hearers. The same may be said for the grain of mustard seed (Mark 4:31), which signifies the growth of the community from seeming insignificance. The sowing of good wheat and the appearance of weeds suggests the vulnerability of the community to evil in its immediate environment, but the moral distinctions will eventually be clear to all in due season (Matt 13:24-30). The reign of God has life and determinacy of its own, suggested by a farmer who scatters seed that grows of its own accord in a mysterious way, yet produces a field of grain (Mark 4:26-29).

Jesus and his challengers speak at cross purposes on the matter of who is really seed of Abraham. One level of meaning refers to physical Jewish descent and circumcision. Jesus insists that this is not enough to confirm that a person is a keeper of Torah and true descendant of Abraham. In fact, those who want to kill him, even though Jewish by blood, are neither seed of Abraham, nor children of God, but seed of the devil and illegitimate descendants of Abraham (John 8:39-47).

Paul also deals with several meanings of covenantal identity. He himself claims physical Jewish descent as seed of Abraham (2 Cor 11:22), but argues that God counts as children those who were elected and promised as descendants to Abraham, not only those who were actually born to him in the flesh (Rom 8:1-13). This is part of his argument for counting believing Gentiles as descendants of Abraham and sharers in God's election. Physical descent from Abraham cannot be the ultimate norm for election, for it was Abraham's faith that made him acceptable to God. The Gentiles' descent from Abraham is established by their faith in God (Gal 3:6-10). Zechariah praises God for covenantal fidelity to the seed of Abraham, which has been realized in the birth of John the Baptist, a fidelity that will continue (Luke 1:73). Luke understands this fidelity to embrace not only devout Jews but the believing Gentiles as well.

Pastoral-Liturgical Tradition

The events of the paschal season, suffering, and death transformed in resurrection are metaphorically expressed by the image of seed. Jesus describes his passage as a grain of wheat which falls into the earth and dies, then produces much fruit. The meaning of the hour, discipleship, union with Jesus, service, death, and glorification are all suggested by this growth process, in which the seed is hidden and buried in the ground (John 12:23-26).

Paul, struggling to answer what sort of body the resurrected person will have, uses the image of the body as a seed. On the third day of creation in Genesis, plants and fruit trees were brought forth from the earth bearing the seeds of reproduction. Likewise, one's body is seed, a beginning of what will emerge from the earth incorruptible, glorious, powerful, a body given by God that is unique to the "seed" or person (Gen 1:11-12). This spiritual body will transcend all the limits of the seed's original nature (1 Cor 15:35-44). For the Christian, this resurrection has already taken place, for rebirth is being experienced not from receiving the seed of a perishable message but from receiving an imperishable seed that is the abiding word of God proclaimed to the community (1 Pet 1:23).

See: CIRCUMCISION, COVENANT, CREATION, DISCIPLE/DISCIPLESHIP, ELECTION, FEASTS, ISRAEL, RESURRECTION

MARIE-ELOISE ROSENBLATT, R.S.M.

SELF-DENIAL

Although the term "self-denial" is not found in the OT, this entry discusses patterns of behavior found in the OT that reflect the desire to forego one's inclinations to follow the divine will. The NT further specifies the following of the divine will as commitment to Christ. The final section of this entry discusses various patterns of Christian asceticism.

Old Testament

Self-denial in the biblical sense is the submission of one's will to the will of God. The terminology is not typical of the OT, but the theme of self-denial is present in the desire to forego one's own inclinations in order to pursue the path set out by God. Israel the nation saw its national aspirations dashed by destruction and exile; survival came through those who were able to accept and adapt to the unglamorous reality of the postexilic age, which they came to understand as the design of God.

Following the Lord. Subordination of personal plans to God's will is implied in vocation stories in the Hebrew Scriptures, beginning with the call of Abram (Gen 12:1). But it is explicit in the history of some key figures. Moses was astonished by the revelation of God in the burning bush, but not so overwhelmed that he did not try to maneuver out of the program God had planned for him. Four times he questioned his appointment as the savior of the people, ending finally with the desperate plea: "If you please, Lord, send someone else" (Exod 4:13). But he did accept the mission, at great personal cost to himself and to his dreams of retirement in Midian. This denial of himself did not put to rest all his doubts and problems. The history of the wilderness trek tells the daily cost in terms of agonizing decisions and the constant complaints of the people.

The prophet Amos was called away from his flocks and sycamore trees. His reply to Amaziah the high priest shows that a prophetic career was not his idea, but something he accepted as a divine vocation (Amos 7:14-15). Probably the most poignant example of self-denial in pursuit of God's will is the prophet Jeremiah. He pleaded his inability at the beginning and at later junctures, especially in his "confessions" (12:1-5; 15:10-21; 17:14-18; 18:18-23; 20:7-18). Jeremiah complains about the evil of the people he has agreed to serve; he says that his expectations have not been met; he is not able to live a normal life "in the circle of merrymakers" (Jer 15:10-19). But he does not run away and eventually his self-denial will lead him to imprisonment in a cistern and to death in Egyptian exile. Other figures striking for their acceptance of God's design at the expense of their own plans are Gideon, Hosea, and Tobit.

Jeremiah is our source for the example of the Rechabites, an Israelite clan who believed that the sedentary ways that had developed with the settlement of the kingdom were a perversion of God's plan, and that faithfulness to the covenant meant maintaining the original nomadic conditions of Israel's early life (Jer 35:5-10). They lived in tents, refusing to build houses or own vineyards and fields, or to drink wine. Jeremiah did not necessarily agree with these reactionaries, but he praised them for their obedience to God's command as they interpreted it.

Religious Practices. Various religious practices of the ancient Israelites were in the nature of self-denial as going against natural habits and feelings; their meaning was interpreted in different ways. A Nazarite vow restricted one from cutting hair from the head or beard and from drinking alcoholic beverages (Num 6:1-8). This act suggested the strength of one's devotion and was probably connected frequently with a special prayer intention.

Fasting was practiced for several reasons. First of all, it did not imply a dualistic rejection of material things; the Hebrews considered food a gift from God. Often fasting was meant to intensify prayer before a difficult task (Judg 20:26), before an important decision, or in time of great need (2 Sam 12:16). It was part of a plan for forgiveness of sins (1 Kgs 21:27) or a sign of mourning (2 Sam 1:12). Moses fasted when he went to meet the Lord on Mount Sinai (Exod 34:28). Implied in the practice of fasting is the purpose of humbling oneself before God, who is master and lord of life.

The above examples are of devotional fasting undertaken on personal initiative. On the occasion of national need or calamity, a public fast might be proclaimed, as when the returning exiles sought protection for their journey (Ezra 8:21). There is only one ritually prescribed fast in the OT, that connected with the autumn Day of Atonement *(Yom Kippur)*: "On the tenth day of the seventh month every one of you, whether a native or a resident alien, shall mortify himself and shall do no work" (Lev 16:29). The verb translated "mortify himself" (NAB) or "afflict yourselves" (RSV) means "to be humbled by fasting." Fasting on that day was considered a mark of the true Israelite, by which God's sovereignty and direction were again acknowledged and accepted. Fasting also seems to have been prominent in the asceticism of the Essenes who lived at Qumran and produced the Dead Sea Scrolls.

New Testament

Christian self-denial focuses on the person of Jesus Christ; it is the decision to give up every personal plan and inclination in order to commit oneself to the following of Christ. The terminology comes from Jesus' saying in the Synoptic Gospels: "Whoever wishes to come after me must deny himself, take up his cross and follow me" (Mark 8:34; Matt 16:24; Luke 9:23). As becomes clear from the larger context, this statement does not imply a killing of the ego or the abolition of one's personality. Rather, it means a turning away from the natural preoccupation with one's own interests, needs, and desires in order to become united to the divine will in a life for God and others. This brings not self-annihilation, but discovery of the true self created in God's image: "Whoever finds his life will lose it, and whoever loses his life for my sake will find it" (Matt 10:39).

The Call of Jesus. Jesus' call to self-denial is connected directly to his own example. He shows the disciples what he expects of them by what he is doing himself. The call to deny oneself and take up the cross follows the first prediction of his own passion, which expresses his clear understanding of what his destiny will be and his desire to carry this divine plan to fulfillment. The disciple's self-denial will not necessarily involve martyrdom, but will be a carrying of the cross ("daily" is added in Luke's version) as a participation in Jesus' sacrificial death. After the third prediction of the passion, the question of James and John shows how little their minds have penetrated Jesus' message about the cross. He reiterates his own example: "the Son of Man did not come to be served but to serve and to give his life as a ransom for many" (Mark 10:45). This attitude of service is dramatized in the footwashing scene at the Last Supper in John's Gospel (John 13:1-17).

The disciples' first act of self-denial was to respond to the call of Jesus at the lakeshore by leaving their father and their nets or, as Luke has it, "everything" (Luke 5:11). The everything was later specified as "house or wife or brothers or parents or children" (18:29). This implies indifference toward one's own life, relations, property, and welfare to be completely at the disposal of the reign of God proclaimed by Jesus.

The consequences of the Christian vocation are sprinkled through Jesus' teaching. The disciple is to forego retaliation and even protection of property and self, ready to love enemies and persecutors (Matt 5:38-48). When Jesus' followers give alms or fast, they are to deepen the self-denial of these actions by performing them in secret (Matt 6:1-4, 16-21). The greatest in God's reign will be "the last of all and the servant of all" (Mark 9:35). The disciple of Jesus, like the master, must become a grain of wheat falling into the earth (John 12:24).

In two statements regarding sexuality, Jesus made difficult demands on the disciples. They bridled when he told them that divorce amounted to adultery, responding petulantly, "It is better not to marry" (Matt 19:10). Instead of softening the challenge he makes an even more difficult statement, speaking favorably of those who have renounced marriage for the sake of God's reign (Matt 19:12). This invitation to celibacy is only for those who feel called to such a witness: "Whoever can accept this ought to accept it" (19:12).

Paul. Both by example and by teaching Paul has become a major influence in Christian understanding of the life of self-denial. His own life changed abruptly when he met the Lord on the road to Damascus (Acts 9:1-22). His carefully laid plans were changed in an instant. Paul's willingness to be led by the hand of God is graphically demonstrated in his adoption of a new creed and a new way of life, which cost him loss of friends and a familiar pattern of life, as well as high prestige in the Jewish community. For all intents and purposes, Paul began his life all over again at the beckoning of God.

The development of the Gentile mission is presented in Acts as the unfolding of the plan of God through disciples willing to listen, to follow, to change their own plans under the leading of the holy Spirit. Thus the Samaritans, the Ethiopian eunuch, and the house of Cornelius were admitted to the Church despite the precedent that seemed to forbid this openness to non-Jews. While at worship and while fasting (an expression of availability before God), the community at Antioch received the inspiration to send Barnabas and Saul on the Gentile mission (Acts 13:2). Later, the readiness of the missionaries to adapt their plans

is expressed by divine guidance through visions (Acts 16:6-10; 18:9-11).

In his writings, Paul does not use the precise terminology of self-denial, but in many ways he expresses his understanding of the Christian life as the acceptance of a new existence, involving consequently the loss of what was possessed or planned before. In defending his mission against critics at Philippi, he writes: "For his sake I have accepted the loss of all things and I consider them so much rubbish, that I may gain Christ and be found in him" (Phil 3:8-9). In the preceding chapter he had presented the example of Jesus "taking the form of a slave, coming in human likeness" (2:7). Such self-emptying echoes Jesus' words about "losing life for my sake" (Mark 8:35). Paul imitates Jesus by "forgetting what lies behind but straining forward to what lies ahead" (Phil 3:13) under God's leading.

Christian life is a "living sacrifice," a continuing liturgy (Rom 12:1). Paul speaks of a union in the death (or dying) of Jesus begun in baptism (Rom 6:3). Hence the practice of referring to religious acts of self-denial as "mortification," putting to death. Using a favorite expression, Paul writes in Galatians: "Those who belong to Christ Jesus have crucified their *flesh* with its passions and desires" (Gal 5:24). The "flesh" means human disobedience and independence from God; it corresponds to the (false) self in Jesus' call to "deny oneself" (Mark 8:34). The Christian profession is a death to self: "I have been crucified with Christ; yet I live, no longer I, but Christ lives in me" (Gal 2:19-20).

The dying with Christ begins at baptism, but it is a commitment renewed in the daily struggle: "We who live are constantly being given up to death for the sake of Jesus" (2 Cor 4:11). As the "flesh" or false self dies, the new life grows; death and life become entwined in the dynamic process of the Christian journey. Twice in 2 Corinthians Paul lists the costs of his apostleship—the suffering, the anxiety, privations—which he understands as validating his ministry (6:4-10; 11:16-33). He "endangers" himself and "faces death every day" because of

Christ and the people (1 Cor 15:30-31). Even beyond the self-denial imposed on him by the demands of the ministry, Paul sees the need for personal asceticism, for he realizes that even suffering can be twisted to give new life to the false self (1 Cor 9:27). Paul does not dwell on his own celibacy as a form of self-denial, though he does mention periodic sexual abstinence within marriage for the sake of prayer (1 Cor 7:5).

Other NT Writings. The Pauline school reflects the insights of the apostle on self-denial. "You were buried with him in baptism" (Col 2:12); "If we have died with him we shall also live with him" (2 Tim 2:11). The ongoing nature of this death with Christ is developed in the Letters to the Ephesians and the Colossians. The disciple should "put away the old self of your former way of life" and "put on the new self, created in God's way in righteousness and holiness or truth" (Eph 4:22-24). The terms are literally "old person" and "new person" (*anthropos*). The individuals who are thus renewed become corporately a "new person" (Eph 2:15).

Jesus handed himself over for us as a "sacrificial offering" (Eph 5:1); we imitate his sacrificial spirit by living as children of the light, trying to learn "what is pleasing to the Lord," not to ourselves (6:10). In fact, in the exalted view of these letters, we have passed through death with Christ and have been raised to a heavenly life, "hidden with Christ in God" (Col 3:3). But Christian life is not therefore ethereal; it is very firmly life in this world. We are called to cut the bonds of sin and flesh that render our life merely "earthly" (3:5). Self-denying mortification is not an end in itself, however. We are warned against acts of asceticism that cause pride but do not kill the "flesh" (2:23), and against dualism-inspired calls for abstinence from marriage and particular foods (1 Tim 4:3). Here motive and understanding will determine whether a particular ascetical discipline will produce liberation or more bondage.

The Letters of James and 1 Peter speak to Christians as people placed by God in a hostile environment, in the "dispersion" (Jas 1:1), as "aliens and sojourners" (1 Pet 2:11). In order to remain faithful to the pattern established by Jesus, his disciples must break with many practices of the surrounding society, living by different values so as to remain "unstained by the world" (Jas 1:27; see 1 Pet 4:1-2). Besides molding the disciples in the pattern of the innocent Savior, this self-sacrificing conduct may have the added blessing of bringing others to salvation (1 Pet 2:12).

See: BAPTISM, CALL/VOCATION, CELIBACY, DEATH, FLESH, MISSION, OBEDIENCE, PASSION, REIGN OF GOD, SACRIFICE, SIN, SUFFERING, VOWS

JEROME KODELL, O.S.B.

Pastoral-Liturgical Tradition

Under this term we will discuss the various forms of Christian asceticism, admittedly a rather complex subject.

The term "self-denial" is a Christian one, coming directly from Mark 8:34 and parallels ("let them deny themselves, take up their cross and follow me"), which is echoed in a secondary variant in Matthew 10:38 and Luke 14:27. Jesus placed utter dedication to the reign of God above family ties and possessions. He was not asking for self-hate or, as a rule, for a material abandonment of one's family or goods (Peter, for example, kept his wife and the fishermen their boats), but rather, such a strong orientation of the heart that nothing would stand as an obstacle between a disciple and the great, in-breaking grace of God's reign. He was asking for a spiritual freedom that implied a readiness to lose everything, should that prove necessary.

Whenever the Church preaches the two-fold commandment of loving God with all our heart and our neighbor as ourselves, we are being asked to avoid self-centeredness and to go out of ourselves. Friendly or benevolent love, as the Fathers and Thomas Aquinas (following the Greek philosophers) tell us, means looking for what is good for others. Love itself, then, implies a certain self-denial. But love makes us alive: it is both a death and a resurrection. The essential core of Christian asceticism is implied in love.

From the time of Ignatius of Antioch (d. 110), the Church used the Gospel texts on renunciation with reference to martyrdom. One must be prepared to lose one's family, possessions, and even life itself, in order to follow Christ until death. This interpretation is still very close to the original meaning of the sayings on self-denial. It happened, however, that these same Gospel sayings and stories were soon to be read in a cultural context in which material renunciation was very important. From the dynamic dualism of Jesus (God's "tomorrow" as opposed to the "now" of sin and suffering), Christianity entered the world of the static dualism of Hellenistic spirituality (the "high" level of God, eternity, and spirit, as opposed to the "low" level of the world, time, matter, and body). It seemed obvious, in this early form of gospel inculturation, that the only way to reach the divine in contemplation lay in turning away from the lower and toward the higher plane of reality. The Gospel sayings received a pronounced ascetical interpretation in Origen (d. 250) and in monasticism. Origen both practiced and taught that renunciation was an efficacious means for reaching perfection. Early Christian ascetics vied with one another in all forms of bodily mortification: fasting, abstinence, vigils, and the sufferings that came from poverty. Even chastity was perceived as a form of fasting, rather than in the positive and liberating sense that celibacy has in 1 Corinthians 7:32-34. This ascetical bent acted as a challenge to a Church that had, as many of the Fathers (Basil and Jerome) lamented, lost its first fervor. Later ascetics would invent new forms of bodily mortification: immersion in cold water among the Celts, and hairshirts and disciplines imported from the East by Peter Damian (d. 1072).

In general, bodily mortification was much esteemed in rural societies, which were in closer contact with the earth and where the body was more relevant. Among Medieval women mystics, we can see that bodily penances were generally more important for laywomen and Beguines than for nuns. It was their way of being regarded as religious women, a condition that nuns did not need to affirm. Some of these women drove themselves to exhaustion and early death. But bodily mortification tended to lose its prominence in urban societies. Basil, Macrina, Augustine, Benedict, and Scholastica (all of them fourth–sixth-century urbanites) moderated the extreme bodily asceticism of the Desert. Later, the *Devotio moderna* of the Low Countries (fourteenth–fifteenth centuries), the Reformation, the Society of Jesus and other Clerks Regular, and the French School emphasized spiritual mortification and self-discipline. This new approach responded in part to a more spiritualistic anthropology. However, there was a return to the body in the Reformed Order (Discalced Carmelites, Capuchins) and, in keeping with their devotion to Christ's sufferings, among the Passionists.

Mortification is practiced in yet another context. First, in a liturgical setting. Early on, until the third century, Christians began fasting for one or two days in preparation for Easter. A penitential orientation was soon added: catechumens fasted in preparation for baptism and many Christians fasted in atonement for their sins. From the practice of the catechumens, a longer period of fasting was adopted by all. During the fourth century a forty-day fast began to be observed in the East, and was enacted into law at the Council of Laodicea (360). Later, a ritual fast was observed by a whole community in preparation for the consecration of their church. For centuries, beginning in the fifth century, ritual fasting was very strict: only one meal per day was allowed, initially in the evening. Meat and fish, and in most places also eggs and dairy products, were forbidden. Fasting implied abstinence. In the thirteenth century a light snack (*collatio*) was added, even by religious. It is significant that since the early days of the Church, prayer and the works of mercy went together. Penance inflicted on the body had a deeper, more Christian meaning: it must bring us closer to God and to our neighbors in need. In our own century, because of present living and working conditions, fast and abstinence have gradually been mitigated. This trend received legislative expression in the Bull *Poenitemini* (1966), in which Paul VI reaffirmed the ancient bond of fast and abstinence with prayer and works of solidarity with the poor.

In our times, too, there has been a rediscovery of the body (diets, exercises and physical fitness programs), and there is much talk about holistic, overall spirituality, in which soul and body are integrated. Hence there is still room for some form of bodily penance. Though we celebrate Easter with a good meal, we begin our Lent by reaffirming our repentance by fasting symbolically on Ash Wednesday and associate our bodies with the commemoration of Christ's death by fasting on Good Friday. Many Christians fast to show their solidarity with the hungry and thus experience their physical want. But fasting is not a purely bodily affair. We must fast with our whole person, by getting closer to God and to our neighbor through prayer and solidarity with the poor. Israel's prophets had already insisted on this more general and radical interpretation of fasting.

See: BODY, PRAYER

JOHN MANUEL LOZANO

SERPENT

Serpents or snakes were common in the biblical lands. Given their mysterious and sometimes toxic nature, it is not surprising that they often became symbols of evil or cunning.

Old Testament

Snakes of various kinds are mentioned frequently in the OT. Serpents were often worshiped in the ancient world (especially in Egypt), and there is some archaeological evidence of the cult of a snake goddess in Canaan and early Israel. The story of the bronze serpent in Numbers 21:4-9 is in-

triguing in this regard. Moses allegedly made a bronze serpent and mounted it on a pole, and whenever anyone who had been bitten by a serpent looked at it, he was healed. An object, which was supposed to be this bronze serpent made by Moses, was extant in the eighth century BCE, but it was destroyed by King Hezekiah during a religious reform (2 Kgs 18:4). Whatever the origin of this object, it was evidently regarded as idolatrous by the reforming king.

The Jewish attitude to snake worship in the late OT period is vividly portrayed in the story of Bel and the Dragon, which appears as chapter 14 of the Book of Daniel in the Greek and Latin Bible and in the Catholic canon, but is not included in the Hebrew Bible and is regarded as apocryphal by Protestants. According to this story the Babylonians worshiped a snake (Greek *drakon*, hence "dragon") that they regarded as a living god. The Jewish hero Daniel tells the king that he can kill this "god" without sword or club. He then feeds the snake a mixture of pitch, fat, and hair, which causes the snake to burst asunder. The Babylonians force the king to have Daniel thrown into the lions' den, but he is miraculously preserved. The king then acknowledges the God of Daniel. This story is hardly a fair representation of Babylonian religion. (Live snakes were worshiped in some places in Greece, and there was a tradition of snake worship in Egypt, but not, to our knowledge, in Babylon.) The story is a parody of idol worship, which holds all kinds of idolatry up to ridicule.

The importance of the serpent in the OT lies primarily in its symbolism in certain narratives. The most conspicuous use is in the story of Adam and Eve. There the serpent is more cunning than all the other animals, and it tempts Eve to eat the fruit. As a result it is cursed by God: "On your belly shall you crawl and dirt shall you eat all the days of your life. I will put enmity between you and the woman and between your offspring and hers. He will strike at your head while you strike at his heel" (Gen 3:14-15). Later tradition would identify the serpent as Satan or the devil, but no such supernatural figure was envisaged by the author of Genesis. The story is a fable that uses the device of a talking animal, well known from Aesop. The serpent symbolizes temptation, whether it comes from within the human person or from another source. It is quite clear, in any case, that Genesis places the responsibility for sin squarely on the shoulders of humanity. The curses of serpent, woman, and man are essentially descriptions of life as the author understood it. The author was evidently no herpetologist: snakes do not eat dirt. The enmity between serpent and woman is simply the enmity between snakes and human beings and their tendency to hurt each other. Christian theology later gave this passage a richer meaning, identifying the woman as Mary, the mother of the Messiah, and the snake as the Devil, but this must be considered a secondary, allegorical interpretation of the text.

Serpents also appear in the OT as mythological beings, opposed to the creator God. In the poetic passages of the OT we find references to a battle between God and a serpent—e.g., Job 26:13: "His hand pierces the fleeing serpent [NAB: the fugitive dragon] as from his hand it strives to flee" (cf. Ps 74:13-14; Isa 51:9). There is no narrative about a battle with a serpent or dragon in the Hebrew Bible, but such stories figure prominently in other ancient Near Eastern cultures. A Canaanite myth from about 1500 BCE mentions a serpent called Lotan and another called Shalyat of the seven heads. Lotan appears in the Bible as Leviathan. In Isaiah 27:1-2 the confrontation between God and Leviathan is still in the future: "On that day the Lord will punish . . . Leviathan, the fleeing serpent, Leviathan the coiled serpent, and he will slay the dragon that is in the sea." Here the serpent becomes a symbol for the eschatological enemy of God, which sums up everything that is opposed to the creator.

New Testament

The serpent or dragon as eschatological monster figures prominently in the Book of

Revelation. In Revelation 12 a great sign appears in heaven, a woman clothed with the sun, with the moon under her feet, wearing a crown of twelve stars. The woman is about to give birth. She is confronted by "a huge red dragon, with seven heads and ten horns." Then a war breaks out in heaven and the archangel Michael casts the dragon down to earth. The passage explicitly identifies the dragon as "the ancient serpent, who is called the Devil and Satan." Revelation here brings together the mythical dragon, represented in the OT by Leviathan, and the snake of Genesis (the ancient serpent) and identifies both as Satan or the Devil. This identification would remain standard in Christian tradition. In Revelation 20 the Devil/serpent is cast into the abyss for a thousand years. Then after the final battle he is cast into the lake of fire.

A rare positive use of serpent imagery is found in the Gospel of John 3:13 "as Moses lifted up the serpent in the desert, so must the Son of Man be lifted up." Exceptional as this passage is, it may serve as a reminder that serpents in themselves are not evil, and that their symbolism depends on the context in which it is used.

Pastoral-Liturgical Tradition

In the Catholic Church the serpent is most commonly associated with the traditional statue of the Virgin Mary with a snake under her feet. This imagery combines the woman of Revelation 12 with the snake of Genesis, and provides a succinct summary of traditional Christian belief. The representation is deficient in some respects, especially if Christ is left out of the picture, and for that reason it has declined in popularity since Vatican II. Even the use of Genesis 3 and Revelation 12 is selective: it hardly does justice to the raging dragon of the NT book and suggests perhaps too facile a victory over evil. It is important to bear in mind that this traditional representation of Mary is not an accurate interpretation of either biblical passage, but it is not invalid for that reason. Biblical passages can feed the imagination of future generations in ways that go far beyond anything the original authors could have intended.

See: SATAN, SPIRIT

JOHN J. COLLINS

SERVANT

The Judeo-Christian religion is one of service. Members are considered servants of God, and they in turn are to be of service to others.

Old Testament

Servants. In the OT, many different people are called "servant of God" by others. However, there are very few who are referred to as "my servant" in divine speech itself. The entire nation is so identified in the Book of Leviticus, where the enslavement of Israelites is prohibited. Brought out of the land of Egypt, these people are servants of God and are to be slaves to no one (Lev 25:42, 55).

Normally, this designation is reserved for a few individuals, who were either major figures in the religious history of the people or models of righteousness and fidelity. The list begins with Abraham. A promise of blessing and descendants is made to Isaac, but it is made for the sake of "my servant Abraham" (Gen 26:24). This servant is the source of blessing for others (see Gen 12:3). Moses, the mediator of the covenant (Jos 1:7; 2 Kgs 21:8), is also called "my servant." His place of privilege in the community arises from his unique relationship with God (Num 12:7, 8). Caleb's fidelity in the wilderness, when the rest of the people lost faith in God and revolted (Num 14:24), earned him the title "my servant," as well as the privilege of entering the land of promise. The other man celebrated for his constancy was Job. It should be noted that each time the Lord mentions Job's name, it is as "my servant," and it is accompanied by a description of him as "blameless, upright, fearing God, and turning from evil" (Job 1:8; 2:3; also 42:7, 8).

The person most frequently referred to in this way is David. It is at the hand of "my servant David" that God will save the people from the threatening Philistines (2 Sam 3:8). It is to "my servant David" that Nathan delivers God's wishes concerning the construction of the Temple and God's promise about the establishment of a royal dynasty (2 Sam 7:5, 8). It is because of this promise to "my servant David" that the kingdom of Judah will survive, although in a significantly diminished form (1 Kgs 11:13, 32-38), and the royal city of Jerusalem is saved (2 Kgs 19:34; 20:6).

The Servant in Isaiah. The Book of Isaiah contains allusions to a godly figure who will come in the near future to inaugurate the righteous reign of God. This figure, known as the Servant of the Lord, is distinct from, but in later religious thought often associated with, the royal messiah. Mention of this servant is found in four passages referred to as Servant Songs (Isa 42:1-4; 49:1-6; 50:4-9; 52:13–53:12). Although these four separate passages are quite similar in tone and content, they do not form a single unit. They are not only independent of their respective contexts, but also independent of each other. Yet, together they have generated a portrait of a pious agent of God's compassionate care. The image that they project and the promise that they contain have inspired people in their religious longing and have sustained them in their patient waiting.

The Poems. The speaker in the first poem (42:1-4) is God, who presents the anonymous servant chosen to be the agent of justice to the nations. Like the prophets, he is endowed with the spirit of God. From the outset, his mission is marked by tenderness rather than brute force and by constancy in the face of opposition. Furthermore, the servant's mission is not merely to a reconstituted or rejuvenated Israel; it is to the nations, universal in its scope.

The servant speaks in the second poem (49:1-6). Addressing his far-flung audience, he first claims a prenatal calling reminiscent of Jeremiah's (Jer 1:5) and he then describes how his uncommon gifts of speech were sharpened so that his prophetic mission might be effective. There is confusion in this poem about the identity of the servant. He is designated as Israel itself (v. 3) yet has the task of bringing that rebellious nation to repentance. Scholarly attempts to resolve this disparity have failed and the ambiguity remains. This has led to several different interpretations. However the identity of the servant is understood, the expansion in his mission is clearly stated. Unsuccessful in his original efforts to gather Israel to the Lord, he is made a light to the nations so that God's salvation might reach the ends of the earth.

The oratorical competence of the servant mentioned in the second song is repeated in the third song (50:4-9). The difficulties that the servant must endure, alluded to earlier, are made specific here. The servant not only accepts abuse, but does so without defense. In the face of such treatment, he relies on the assistance of the Lord God.

The fourth song (52:13–53:12) presents more problems than any of the other three. It consists of speeches of the Lord (52:13-15) and of unidentified bystanders (53:1-12). The servant prospers, is exalted and lifted up, but in shame and disgrace rather than in the triumph and glory that is normally associated with exaltation. He not only suffers because of his mission, but he does so for the sake of the very ones inflicting the suffering. It seems that the effectiveness of the servant lies not in his preaching but in the suffering that results from the rejection of that preaching. Such a concept is exceptional in Israel's theology.

The identity of the servant that emerges from this fourfold composite has always been a mystery to interpreters. Is this an individual (49:1) or does it represent the entire people (49:3)? Is the mission of the servant to Israel itself (49:5) or to the nations outside of the confines of Israel (42:1)? One thing is quite clear: the servant will have to suffer (50:6), and this suffering will be both in the place of others (53:4-6) and for their deliverance (53:10).

The servant appears to behave as both king and prophet. First, and perhaps most importantly, he is endowed with the spirit of God (42:1). Like a king he establishes justice (42:1, 3-4), and like a prophet his ministry is a ministry of the word (49:2; 50:4). However, the servant is no ordinary king or prophet. He is an innocent man whose anguish seems itself to be his principal service. It is not primarily through his judging or his teaching that he effects the transformation of others, but rather it is through his suffering that he himself becomes the reparation for their sin.

The Identity of the Servant. There are several theories that attempt to identify the servant. If he is an individual, he could be either a historical or a fictitious person. If historical, the most obvious person would be the prophet Second Isaiah himself. The mission of the servant is clearly prophetic and includes a call to repentance. However, the fourth song challenges this interpretation. There is no evidence that Second Isaiah suffered the kind of rejection, shameful and violent death, and ostensible resurrection depicted in this song. In fact, belief in resurrection arose much later during the postexilic period. The servant most likely was not this anonymous prophet.

Some scholars suggest that the servant was a prophet later than but influenced by the school of Isaiah. This could account for the similarities with, but the further development of, Isaian theology. Others maintain that the figure of the servant is idealized and not entirely historical. To date, no theory regarding the past historical identity of the servant is without serious problems.

If not a person of the past, perhaps the servant is a historical person yet to appear. This kind of predictive reading was taken up by various Jewish sects, including the Christian community. One theory identifies the servant with the Messiah. The title "Messiah" could refer to anyone who was chosen by God to realize the destiny of Israel. The word itself is derived from the Hebrew for "anoint." The Messiah was "the anointed one." Since kings, prophets, and priests were among those anointed at different times in Israel's history, messianic figures were envisioned as being royal, prophetic, and often cultic leaders. Among these characterizations, the most prominent is the royal messiah. Such a person appears in the teaching of the prophet Isaiah (Isa 9:2-7; 11:1-9). Still, despite the similarities, the servant himself demonstrates no explicit royal traits. The figures of the royal messiah and the servant of the Lord do not really converge. Rather, they are juxtaposed.

A third theory maintains that the servant is an ideal figure fashioned out of elements of Israel's religious imagination and represents several of its richest beliefs and most profound aspirations. An ideal figure possesses traits of both the past and the future without being limited to either or both. It becomes a standard after which individuals will model themselves, as well as a characterization that provides religious interpretation of an actual person. For example, individuals with prophetic ambitions might be inspired by this portrait. It has been proposed that some of the community at Qumran perceived their leader in terms of this ideal figure. The early Church certainly understood Jesus in this way, and it placed this figure before its members as a model for discipleship.

See: ISRAEL, JUSTICE, MESSIAH, PRIEST, PROPHET, REIGN OF GOD, RESURRECTION, SALVATION, SPIRIT OF GOD

DIANNE BERGANT, C.S.A.

New Testament

This is an ambiguous and sometimes misleading term in English because it translates three different Greek words used in the NT: *diakonos,* more properly "servant" (e.g., Mark 10:43) or in later contexts, "deacon"; *pais,* "child," a condescending word for servant, something like the English "boy" (e.g., "boy" at Luke 2:43; "servants" at Matt 14:2); and *doulos,* "slave" (e.g., Matt 10:24 in RSV), the word "servant" probably being thought more acceptable to modern readers than slave.

The terminology would have been inexact in NT times as well, in a society somewhat based on slave labor and familiar with the degradation of slavery, yet also familiar

with slave-stewards in wealthy households and businesses who had far more power and prestige than free peasants and small householders. The NT knows slaves as personal and household servants (e.g., Luke 7:2, 7-8; John 4:51), agricultural laborers (Matt 13:27; 21:34-36), social representatives (Matt 22:3-10), and financial managers (Matt 25:14-30), in all of these passages represented by the word *doulos.* Slave women are owned by the high priest (Matt 26:69 and par.), a householder (Luke 12:45), a Christian matron (Acts 12:13), and profiteers (Acts 16:16), each called *paidiske,* a feminine diminutive of *pais.* A presumed runaway slave, Onesimus, is the occasion for Paul to write his Letter to Philemon. The modern reader must realize that any of the terms for servant when used literally usually refer to someone legally living in slavery, though not necessarily therefore in abuse; when used figuratively, the connotations of slavery were inescapable. Yet servant language can be used in other ways even outside the Christian context, e.g., Paul speaks of civil authorities as servants of God (Rom 13:3-6).

Jesus as Servant. The Isaian Servant of the Lord undoubtedly exercised a profound influence on NT interpretations of Jesus' role, and perhaps on Jesus' own self-understanding, though the degree of that influence is debated. The so-called Servant Songs, especially Isaiah 52:13–53:12, provide the image of the innocent one who proves his worth through a suffering that is redemptive (see esp. 53:10-12). At 52:13 the use of *pais* in the Septuagint enables a sustained play on the meanings of servant and child that is retained in the Gospel portrayal of Jesus in relation to God, even though the Greek terminology may differ.

The baptism of Jesus in the Synoptic Gospels features the heavenly voice that confirms Jesus as Son of God in whom God delights (Matt 3:17; Mark 1:11; Luke 3:22); it echoes Isaiah 42:1. There are undoubted allusions to portions of Isaiah 53 in reference to Jesus in such NT texts as Mark 9:12;

10:45; Acts 3:13, 26; 4:27-30 (Acts even uses *pais* here, the same word used by the Septuagint at Isa 52:13). Luke 22:37 explicitly quotes a portion of Isaiah 53:12 to explain why Jesus could have been seen and treated as a criminal. 1 Peter 2:22-25 weaves quotes and allusions to Isaiah 53:4-6, 9, 12 into its description of Jesus as innocent sufferer who should be a role model to slaves abused by their owners—a difficult text that unfortunately has been used to justify both slavery and harsh treatment of slaves. To be understood, it must be seen in its context of providing encouragement to Christian slaves of cruel pagan owners, against whom both slaves and author were powerless (see Eph 6:7).

Jesus is the model servant of God whose will is to do the will of the one who sent him (John 5:30), as any faithful servant-representative would do. He describes his mission as that of serving rather than being served (Matt 20:28; Mark 10:45; Luke 22:27), even to the point of giving his life in ransom. As a dramatic illustration of what he has been talking about, he performs the servant role at his final meal with the disciples by washing their feet (John 13:1-15).

Disciples as Servants. The usual domestic serving role of women (Mark 1:31 and pars.) becomes an act of discipleship on the part of those women who follow Jesus as did the male disciples (Luke 8:3; Matt 27:55; Mark 15:41). In the case of Martha of Bethany (Luke 10:40) and the seven chosen to replace the apostles in table service at community meals so that the apostles can devote themselves to another kind of service, that of the word (Acts 6:1-7), serving becomes a special responsibility. Soon after Jesus' death, Matthias was chosen to replace Judas, joining the other apostles in their role of service (*diakonia*, Acts 1:17, 25). In the Pauline Churches, there are persons designated to certain service roles, though their exact function is not clear: Phoebe the *diakonos* in Romans 16:1; the "overseers and ministers" (*diakonoi*) at Philippi and in 1 Timothy (Phil 1:1—see note in revised NAB; 1 Tim 3:8-13).

The role of serving begins to be transformed into the language and function of ministry, so that it is often a translator's judgment call whether to render the Greek word as slave, servant, or minister in a given passage, though in English the three words have very different connotations. The translator's bias can therefore determine how a passage in translation will be understood.

Paul and His Co-workers as Servants. Paul often describes his labor as service/ministry, and himself and his companions as servants/ministers (*diakonoi*) of God (2 Cor 6:4); of Christ (2 Cor 11:23); of a new covenant (2 Cor 3:6); of reconciliation (2 Cor 5:18); of the gospel (Eph 3:7); of the Church (Col 1:25). He identifies himself as slave (*doulos*) of Christ (Rom 1:1; Phil 1:1; Gal 1:10) or of God (Titus 1:1; see James 1:1; 2 Pet 1:1; Jude 1), and even of his intractable congregation at Corinth for the sake of Jesus (2 Cor 4:5). Paul and Apollos are servants/ministers through whom they have come to faith (1 Cor 3:5). Acts refers to two of Paul's co-workers, Timothy and Erastus, as servants/ministers together with Paul (Acts 19:22); the NAB wisely renders them as "assistants." Likewise, Tychichus is a fellow servant/minister in Ephesians 6:21. Here it is quite clear that service has become ministry.

The Ideal of Service. The disciples are admonished not to become slaves of sin (John 8:34; cf. Rom 6:17, 20), and are frequently warned by Jesus that, in imitation of him, those in leadership are to be as servants (Luke 22:26), aware that no slaves are greater than their master (Matt 10:24; John 13:16; 15:20). It is therefore extremely significant that in spite of these reminders of the disciples' servant status, Jesus, in his Last Discourse in the Gospel of John, changes that status from servants or slaves (the NAB translator of the Gospel of John rightly prefers the word "slave" [John 15:15]) to friends, thus evoking a wealth of connotations for the original hearers, for friends are those who can always depend on good will, patronage, and protection from the one granting friendship.

Nevertheless, the ideal of Christian life as service remains. There is some evidence that the ideal of placing oneself at the service of others was considered virtuous and ennobling in the Graeco-Roman context in which the NT developed. It is a quite clear NT teaching that community leadership is a kind of service and a special spiritual gift (Rom 12:7; Eph 4:12). But the ideal of service extends to all Christians, who are to turn from serving other gods to serve the one God (1 Thess 1:1), and to live together in the spirit of service to one another (Gal 5:13; 1 Pet 4:10), after the example of Jesus who, after performing the role of servant, explicitly bid his followers to do the same (John 13:12-17).

See: DEACON, FAMILY, FRIEND, HOUSE, JESUS CHRIST, LIBERTY, MINISTRY, REDEMPTION/REDEEMER, SLAVERY

CAROLYN OSIEK, R.S.C.J.

From the beginning of their history, Christians have borrowed key words and ideas from secular sources, reinterpreting them in light of God's revelation and self-bestowal in Christ. This phenomenon is nowhere more evident than in the use of a term like "servant" (covering the Greek words *diakonos, doulos,* and *pais,* as well as the Latin words *servus, famulus,* and *minister*). The carefully calibrated social structure of the Greco-Roman world gave rise to a richly varied vocabulary for types and degrees of service: the attentive, personal service of one individual for another (expressed by the Greek verb *diakonein,* "to wait at table"); the involuntary service of a master by a slave *(doulouein);* service rendered for wages *(latreuein);* willing service expressing concern and respect *(therapeuein);* and finally, official public service of the people or the state *(leitourgein).*

As used of secular officials (see Rom 13:4), "servant" implied a pattern of human relationships based on superior/inferior status. But this implication was subverted by Christian usage, where "servant" no longer meant subjugation, inferiority, or diminished status—but rather the privilege of helping others hear and respond to God's gracious Word in the life of the Church. The inner content of the word "servant" was thus transformed: a Christian servant is one who fully surrenders self in order to belong wholly to God and to the ministry of the gospel.

Servants as Worshipers of God

In the Church's liturgical tradition, therefore, a "servant" is, first and foremost, one who worships God in spirit and truth. Thus, the early second-century "table prayers" of the Didache refer to Jesus, God's "servant" *(pais),* who leads believers in authentic worship by revealing divine knowledge, faith, and immortality (Didache 10:2). Though the "servant of God" epithet for Jesus did not long survive in the liturgical tradition (perhaps because it suggested to some a low or adoptionist Christology), such a vocabulary did flourish as a designation for the worshiping assembly. The sixth-century collection of Latin prayers known as the Verona ("Leonine") Sacramentary regularly uses "servants" in reference to the baptized faithful gathered for worship.

Significantly, this "servant" vocabulary supplied a comprehensive common denominator for *all* worshipers, whatever their rank in the Christian community. Thus, the "old Roman canon" (=Eucharistic Prayer I), uses the same word, servant *(famulus),* to designate the pope; the living corps of worshipers who surround the altar and offer the "sacrifice of praise"; the liturgy's presider and ministers; and all those men and women "who have died and have gone before us marked with the sign of faith." "Servant" thus expresses our common vocation in faith, as well as the communion signified and celebrated in the Eucharist.

Ordained Ministers as Servants

Of further interest in the liturgical tradition is the persistence of the "servant" *(famulus)* vocabulary within the prayers of the Roman rite for the ordination of deacons, presbyters, and bishops. Among our oldest examples of such prayers are those found in the Verona Sacramentary (mentioned above). There, the candidates chosen to serve as ordained ministers are identified by the same comprehensive term—"servants" *(famuli)*—used for all members of the Christian assembly. The theological impact of this should not be overlooked, for it signifies that the ordained are, first of all, worshipers, members of the praying assembly. This fact—more than any distinction or "status" attached to holy orders—is the fundamental basis, theologically and liturgically, for the Church's ministry. Although the interpretation of holy orders as a "series of honors" *(cursus honorum)* that "advanced" the candidate from lower to higher rungs on the hierarchical ladder was already present in the Verona Sacramentary (and so continued to dominate theology up through the twentieth century), the image of minister as servant/worshiper quietly persisted as a corrective counterpart even in prayers which seemed to approve triumphalism and status-seeking.

Servant in the Theology of Vatican II

Vatican II's ecclesiology presented the Church itself as a servant whose mission is the renewal of human persons "whole and entire, body and soul, heart and conscience" (The Church in the Modern World, no. 3). For the Church, like Jesus, came "to rescue and not to sit in judgment, to serve and not to be served" (ibid.). By linking a servant ecclesiology to a servant Christology, the council also laid the foundation for a renewed theology of ministry. This theology affirms the uniqueness of Jesus' priesthood and sees both the priesthood of the baptized and that of the ordained as participating in the one priestly mission of Christ (see Vatican II's Decree on the Ministry and Life of Priests, nos. 2-3). In spite of such sound theological background, however, the revised Roman rites for ordaining deacons, presbyters, and bishops seem to lack a coherent focus. Their prayers, ritual gestures, and "model homilies" seem unable to decide whether the candidates for ordination are being called to service or to status and "advancement." Greater reflection at both pastoral and theological levels is needed if these rites are genuinely to model the Church and its ministers as servants of the Word and servants of the world.

See: CHURCH, MINISTRY, ORDINATION

NATHAN D. MITCHELL

SEXUALITY

Biblical Reflections

Sexuality is a word used in contemporary parlance to refer to a number of related human realities. Depending on its context, sexuality may refer to (1) those dimensions of one's affective life that promote or make difficult warm and loving relationships with oneself and others, including one's physical and emotional attractions and fantasies, (2) sexual orientation, (3) genital sexual activity, or (4) socially constructed gender roles. Conditioned by historical realities including the limited vision of the sacred author and the communities that received and canonized the texts, the Scriptures address many of the concerns summarized by the modern term "sexuality" without using the word itself.

Any understanding of sexuality as well as the living of one's sexual life occurs in a context. In specific historical situations, people develop world views, perspectives on the meaning and purpose of human life. The Christian Scriptures and Tradition teach that human beings were created to live in loving covenant with God, one's self, one another, and all creation. There is a basic thrust throughout the Judeo-Christian tradition: people are not to live as isolated, individualistic entities, but as vibrant men and women, creatures of a loving God, relating to God, self, others, and nature in ever-deepening bonds of justice and love. Covenants with Noah, Abraham, Moses, and the Hebrew people, and the New Covenant who is Jesus reflect a deepening understanding of human life. While covenant life and its demands are always in the process of being more fully understood and imperfectly lived, the fundamental human situation—relatedness to God, to self and others, and to nature—is constant.

Human sexuality is to be exercised in such a way that covenant life is developed and deepened. One's affective life, sexual orientation and activity, and the gender roles society constructs are to contribute to just and loving relationships with God, self, others, and the natural world.

Assuming a divine-human covenant, the Scriptures teach the fundamental goodness of human sexuality. As elements of the creation, which is "good," the realities of maleness and femaleness and heterosexual attraction, affection, and bonding are given positive evaluation. The creation stories of Genesis (1:2–2:4a and 2:4b-25) reflect a faith that sees men and women equally manifesting the divine image and likeness. Humanity is not a cause for shame; human life is good. Maleness and femaleness, physicality and interiority are gifts of God. Sexual differentiation makes possible complementarity and procreation. When the contemporary reader considers other creation stories of the ancient world and their theologies, Genesis faith is remarkably optimistic.

Included in the goodness of creation is human affectivity. The Song of Songs is an outstanding example of Scripture's positive evaluation of human longing and desire, and a celebration of erotic attraction. The goodness of friendship and emotional bonding is assumed in the relationship between David and Jonathan (2 Sam 18:1ff.), Naomi and Ruth (Ruth 1:15ff.), John and Jesus (John 13:23), Paul and his comrades (2 Tim 1:1ff.) and churches (Phil 1:3ff.; 1 Thess 2:7ff.). Jesus is tender and compassionate as well as a wonder-worker and charismatic teacher (Luke 13:34-35). Even righteous anger and jealousy are attributes of the God involved in covenant with his people (Exod 20:5; Deut 6:15).

For all the positive evaluation of human affectivity, the Scriptures are full of stories of attraction and affection gone errant. Samson loses his greatness (Judges 16),

Saul's love for David turns to jealousy (1 Samuel 18), King David goes astray (2 Samuel 11), and the sins of Judah are, in part, sexual (2 Kings 21). The Wisdom authors realize that the gift of sexuality must be carefully trained (Prov 6:20-35; Sir 9:1-9). Paul warns that some modes of sexual conduct lead to a forfeiture of the reign of God (1 Cor 6:9-11).

In summary, Scripture presents and tradition affirms a complex view of affective life: human affectivity is a great blessing and a reflection of God. It is part of covenant life. But affective life can also lead one away from proper relationships with God and others. Wisdom and discipline are needed to direct one's affective life, one's sexuality, properly.

Sexual orientation is a second major issue in contemporary reflection on human sexuality. The Scriptures do not seem to discuss this issue. Heterosexual attraction and bonding is considered the common human experience. Heterosexual expression is normative. Bisexuality and constitutional homosexuality, contemporary psychological concepts, are not a subject of theological or moral reflection. While warm and loving same-sex relationships are valued in the Bible, to assume that these relationships were understood as homosexual relationships in the modern sense is mistaken.

The 1975 Congregation for the Doctrine of the Faith's "Declaration on Certain Questions Concerning Sexual Ethics" and the American bishops' 1976 joint pastoral letter "To Live in Christ Jesus" present the most important official Catholic teachings on sexual orientation. While homosexual activity is said to be objectively immoral, homosexual orientation is called morally neutral. This relatively new theological position on homosexual orientation will need the reflection of the Christian community over time before it can be fully affirmed or rejected.

A third meaning of sexuality in contemporary usage is genital sexual activity. Experience teaches that genital activity is an important element in the lives of both individuals and the community. Sexual activity can enrich and ennoble. It can also degrade and manipulate. Sometimes sexual activity enslaves. Genital activity can enhance the community by ennobling its members as well as by enriching the community with children. Other genital activity (e.g., rape or adultery) can be a source of communal conflict.

Among the difficult questions men and women of the covenant constantly face is the best context for genital activity. Under what conditions does genital sexual expression help individuals and communities grow in covenant life? Over the centuries an answer emerged. Heterosexual, permanent, public, monogamous marriages, open to the gift of children, understood to be reflections of and participation in God's own love for creation, are the most fitting context for genital expression of human attraction and affection. Any other context falls short of the ideal and endangers the welfare of individuals or the community.

Certain behaviors are explicitly condemned in Scripture. The Bible condemns bestiality (Exod 22:18; Lev 18:23), homosexual activity (Lev 20:13), and incest (Deut 27:20-23; Lev 20:10-21). Adultery was also condemned (Exod 20:14), though the precise definition of adultery evolved over time. In time, fornication became equally objectionable. For Paul, heterosexual marriage was the human ideal (1 Cor 6:9–7:16).

Gender roles and the arrangement of power between the sexes is a fourth usage of the modern word sexuality. Scripture presents an inconsistent portrait of appropriate gender roles for a covenant people. The Christian Tradition is equally uneven. On the one hand, there is a positive picture of women painted and an egalitarian ethic implied. Genesis creation stories teach that men and women are companions and helpmates in the Garden of Eden. The first story says that men and women were simultaneously created in the image and likeness of God and are together to increase and multiply, to tend to the earth and to subdue it (Gen 1:27-28). In the second creation account, woman is created from the rib of Adam to be his companion (Gen 2:22). Improper interpretation of this story creates a traditional problem. Many have used this text to legitimate the inferior social status of women. Women can be treated as inferiors because they are, in fact, inferior. While it is with the woman that Adam would find fulfillment, it is the man whose happiness is primary. Interpreting the Genesis story as an indicator of women's inherent inferiority is mistaken.

Respectful portraits of Naomi and Ruth, Judith, Queen Esther, the woman in the Song of Songs, Mary (Luke 1:26-38), the faithful women at the foot of Jesus's cross (Matt 27:55-56; Mark 15:40-41; Luke 23:49; John 19:25-27), the women in the Gospel of Luke, and Paul's greetings to prominent women in the early Church all indicate a positive biblical evaluation of women.

But the Scriptures accept a different condition as well. Women are not among the Levitical priests. Women, as well as men, can be bought and sold as slaves (Exod 21:7ff.; Deut 15:12ff.; Col 4:1). Sirach expresses an understanding of women that is sexist to modern sensibilities (Sir 19:2; 25:12–26:18; 42:9-14). While women proclaim the resurrection to men (Matt 28:1ff.; Luke 24:1-12), women are not listed among the Twelve. In summary, it is accurate to say that while Scripture at significant moments affirms the holiness, dignity, and equality of women, there is also a subtext in which the inferior status endured by women for centuries is permitted and even legitimated.

Pastoral Perspectives

Those working with issues of sexuality in pastoral ministry need to keep in mind several principles: (1) The issues around sexuality are enormously complex psychologically as well as intellectually. Sexuality is often difficult to discuss. What appears to be a question of sexual activity can really be a matter of affectivity. When a person appears to be dealing with questions of gender roles, the real issues could be sexual orientation. In dealing with sexuality, one issue is usually related to several others. (2) Affectivity, sexual orientation, sexual activity, and gender roles are greatly influenced by culture. Biblical insights and norms evolved over the course of centuries and in specific cultural settings. The Judeo-Christian tradition developed and continues to evolve. While Scripture and tradition are invaluable to the Christian community as it lives and discusses its sexual life, the sources do not give the last word. (3) The evolution of the tradition around questions of sexuality happens in a covenantal, communal context. Attention must be paid to the impact of affectivity, sexual orientation and behavior, and gender roles on the community. That which helps the community grow in love is good. As a covenant people, our history, hierarchical leaders, experts, the common experience of the faithful and the experience of the poor and the outcast need to be in prayerful, respectful, and honest dialogue in discerning the good—in the development of a spirituality and theology of sexuality and a morality for sexual activity appropriate for the contemporary Christian.

See: HUMANKIND, MAN/MEN, WOMAN/WOMEN

JAMES R. HALSTEAD, O.S.A.

SHADDAI

Shaddai is an ancient title for God that appears in English translations as "the Almighty." In many of its occurrences (the Priestly narratives of the Pentateuch: Num 24:4, 16; Ruth 1:20, 21; Isa 13:6; Ezek 1:24; 10:5; and Pss 68:14; 91:1), the term Shaddai follows the word El, the general Semitic word for God, to create the title "God Almighty." But in the Book of Job where Shaddai appears most abundantly, the word Shaddai appears alone.

A key text for interpreting the title is Exodus 6:3 where God reveals the divine name to Moses. "As God the Almighty I appeared to Abraham, Isaac, and Jacob, but my name, Lord, I did not make known to them." This verse indicates that God was once known as Shaddai but after the Exodus became

known by the name Lord (Yahweh). From this observation scholars conclude that the priestly writer of Exodus was combining two distinct traditions about God, perhaps to join the theological traditions of two different communities within Israel.

The origin and meaning of the title are uncertain. Some scholars argue that the root word is the Hebrew *shadad,* which means "to overpower," "to destroy," or "to be strong." This is the usual understanding, expressed by the translation, "the Almighty." Other interpreters maintain that Shaddai derives from the Assyrian root, *shadu,* which means mountain. Hence, El Shaddai is "the God of the Mountains," or "the God who resides in the mountains." Still others believe that the root word is *shaddayim,* meaning "breasts." This etymology suggests a connection between Shaddai and an unknown fertility goddess who may have been known to Israel's ancestors when they departed from Mesopotamia.

The latter interpretation receives some support from a number of Genesis passages that mention Shaddai in relation to the blessings of offspring. Shaddai blesses a patriarch (Gen 17:1; 35:11); a patriarch prays for a blessing (43:14); a patriarch relates that God has blessed him (48:3), or a patriarch prays for blessing on his son (49:25). These "blessings of the breasts and the womb" (49:25) ensure the survival of the people. The significance of the interpretation of Shaddai as a term associated with breasts and offspring is that it may point to an ancient memory of God as female.

Outside of Genesis, however, procreation is no longer an obvious part of the context of Shaddai. Many instances of the title require the meaning of power and majesty, and though these attributes may derive from a female fertility deity, fertility nuances are not obvious. El Shaddai appears in visions to Balaam (Num 24:4, 6) and to Ezekiel (Ezek 1:24; 10:5). El Shaddai punishes and destroys (Isa 13:6; Joel 1:15; Ruth 1:20, 21). El Shaddai disperses kings (Ps 68:15) and provides protection and refuge to the one in distress (Ps 91:1).

By far the most frequent occurrence of Shaddai is in the poetry of the Book of Job where it appears twenty-nine times, always without El. It seems likely that the author of the book used the ancient title precisely because it was ancient and, therefore, avoided the overly used and more familiar term, Yahweh, that occurs in the book's prologue (chs. 1–2) and epilogue (42:7-17). In Job the title conveys the notions of transcendent power and majesty, but the title Shaddai may also promote a sense of divine otherness.

See: MOUNTAIN

KATHLEEN M. O'CONNOR

SHEOL

Sheol is a Hebrew word, perhaps related to the verb *ša'al* ("ask, request"). It refers to the place where the dead go and maintain a shadowy existence. In the NAB the word is usually translated "nether world," since many statements about it presume that it is beneath the earth.

Old Testament

Sheol is the abode of the dead. Those who go to Sheol include Jacob (Gen 37:35; 42:38; 44:29, 31), Dathan and Abiram (Num 16:30, 33), David (2 Sam 22:6), and Joab (1 Kgs 2:6, 9). It is not so much a place of punishment as it is of shadowy existence beyond the grave. The reality of Sheol is assumed by the biblical writers, and so they give no extended description of it.

The most illuminating biblical text about Sheol is the taunt song against the king of Babylon in Isaiah 14:9-11. At the defeat and death of the king of Babylon, Sheol will prepare for his coming to the abode of the dead. Sheol is the "nether world below," that is, beneath the earth. It is populated by the "shades" (*rĕpa'îm*), including those of great leaders and kings. These beings have real existence but in diminished form: "You too have become weak like us, you are the same as we." There is a connection between Sheol and the grave: "The couch beneath you is the maggot, your covering, the worm."

In the psalms Sheol is the place to which the wicked will go (Pss 9:18; 31:18; 49:15; 55:16; 141:7). In the thanksgiving psalms God's rescue of the speaker is often expressed as a deliverance from Sheol (Pss 16:10; 30:4; 86:13; 116:3; Jonah 2:2-3). What makes Sheol such a gloomy place is that God is not worshiped there: "For among the dead no one remembers you; in the nether world who gives you thanks?" (Ps 6:6). Nevertheless, God has ultimate power over Sheol (1 Sam 2:6) and therefore can be said to be there: "if I sink to the nether world, you are present there" (Ps 139:8). There is no escaping the sovereignty of God, even in Sheol.

As he laments the sufferings that befall him, Job looks to Sheol as a place of rest (Job 3:17). He recognizes it as the end of earthly existence (7:9), the abode of the dead (17:13, 16; 21:13), and under God's ultimate control (26:6). But as Job fantasizes about escaping his torments and wishes that they will last only for a short time, he turns Sheol into a symbol of hope, a refuge from his troubles: "Oh, that you would hide me in the nether world and keep me sheltered till your wrath is past" (14:13). The Wisdom books Proverbs and Sirach agree with the basic Hebrew traditions regarding Sheol. The grimmest picture appears in Ecclesiastes 9:10: "there will be no work, nor reason, nor knowledge, nor wisdom in the nether world where you are going." The worst that a wisdom teacher can say about Sheol is that there is no wisdom there.

New Testament

What the OT calls Sheol, the NT names "Hades." The Greek word *Hades* derives from the name of a Greek god ("the unseen one") who is master of the nether world. But there are few, if any, pagan mythological associations in the NT use of the term. In Peter's quotation of Psalm 16:8-11 ("you will not abandon my soul to the nether world") and the interpretation of it in Acts 2:31 as applying to Jesus ("neither was he abandoned to the nether world") the OT idea of Sheol is maintained. Likewise in Jesus' warning to Capernaum in Matthew 11:23 and Luke 10:15 ("Will you be exalted to heaven? You will go down to the nether-world") the language is taken from the taunt against the king of Babylon (Isa 14:13-15). In Revelation 6:8; 20:13, 14, Hades is personified alongside Death. In Luke 16:23 Hades is the place of torment for the rich man who failed to share with the poor Lazarus during their lifetimes; a great chasm separates those in Hades from those enjoying happiness with God and those still living on earth (16:26).

The biblical doctrine of Sheol is presup-posed by the statement in 1 Peter 3:19 that Christ "also went to preach to the spirits in prison." Since these spirits are said to have been "disobedient" (3:20), there is contro-versy over who they were: fallen angels, sinners who died in the flood, etc. And there is also debate whether there is a con-nection between 1 Peter 3:19 and 4:6 ("the gospel was preached even to the dead"). Of course, the central NT proclamation that God raised Jesus from the dead as-sumes that the "saints" who had died be-fore Christ's coming will also share in his resurrection (Matt 27:51-53), and thus they are freed from their shadowy existence in Sheol. The risen Christ has the power over the gates of the nether world (Matt 16:18; Rev 1:18), that is, over the abode of the dead.

Pastoral-Liturgical Tradition

According to Vatican II's Pastoral Consti-tution on the Church in the Modern World, no. 18, the mystery of human existence be-comes most acute in the face of death. We are troubled by a dread of perpetual extinc-tion and repudiate the "absolute ruin and total disappearance" of our own person. The OT's doctrine of after-life is shadowy and inchoate. Yet it does bear witness to the conviction that human existence is not to-tally ended by physical death. Belief in Christ's resurrection transforms our con-victions about life after death. Neverthe-less, the restraint with which the ancient

Hebrews described the life after death pro-vides a salutary warning about letting the human imagination run wild regarding the precise conditions of life after death.

The biblical teachings about Sheol/Hades are the basis for Christian traditions about hell,* purgatory, and limbo. And the Chris-tian proclamation of Christ's descent into "hell" (1 Pet 3:19) assumes the existence of an abode of the dead like Sheol.

See: DEATH, RESURRECTION, WISDOM

DANIEL J. HARRINGTON, S.J.

SHEPHERD

The image of the shepherd was a common one in the biblical world, since sheep and goats provided the staples of the diet (meat and milk) and clothing (wool), and their skin and horns had other uses as well, in-cluding tents and writing material. They were also necessary for sacrifice. Being en-trusted with the family's flocks was a crucial responsibility, often filled by the children of the family. Flocks generally grazed in un-fenced ground and, in the arid countryside, needed an expansive space to provide suffi-cient good pasture. Sheep are virtually de-fenseless against swift predators, hence the need for a personal guardian to accompany them at all times. The shepherd and his dog were necessary for the survival of the herd, and so shepherding became a natural image for ministry.

The ancestors of Israel were all shep-herds: Abraham, Isaac, Rachel, Jacob, and their descendants. Moses and David were also shepherds when called to use their pastoral skills to lead God's people. God, first and foremost, is "Shepherd of Israel." The protection and devotion of a shepherd toward his or her sheep provides an apt metaphor for God's care for Israel. God raises up leaders that are entrusted with shepherding the people. More often, Is-rael's shepherds fail, and God must again rescue the flock.

For Christians, promises of a future shep-herd are realized in Jesus. He is the good shepherd who seeks out the lost sheep, and whom the sheep follow because they know his voice. He pays the ultimate price, laying down his life for them. In liturgical tradition, the Good Shepherd theme is particularly highlighted in the Easter season. Pastoral language and imagery for ministry remains strong.

Old Testament

A number of important OT figures were shepherds. Abel was "a keeper of flocks," whereas his brother Cain was "a tiller of the soil" (Gen 4:2). The perennial tension between herders and farmers is represented in the animosity of the two brothers that results in murder. Abraham was a shepherd when called by God (Genesis 12). Abraham and Sarah lived as nomads, moving with the seasons, taking their flocks in search of pasture. Abraham was very rich in livestock (Gen 13:2; 24:35). Genesis 13 tells of how he and Lot, who also had numerous flocks and herds, had to part ways because there was not sufficient land to support both herders. Isaac inherited all his father's wealth in flocks and herds (Gen 24:35-36).

A frequent biblical motif is the meeting of future brides and grooms at a well while watering their sheep. Rachel, who tended her father Laban's sheep, met Jacob in just such an encounter (Gen 29:9-14). In Genesis 30:25-43 is the incident where Jacob outwits Laban by taking all the dark sheep and the spotted goats as his payment. These increased so that Jacob became more prosperous than his father-in-law. His descendants, too, would be shepherds.

It is perhaps the familiarity of shepherds and pastoral life that gives rise to the frequent biblical metaphor of God as shepherd. Jacob, at his deathbed, blesses his sons Ephraim and Manasseh by "the God who has been my shepherd from my birth to this day" (Gen 48:15; see also Gen 49:24). Probably the most famous use of the metaphor is Psalm 23, beginning, "The LORD is my shepherd; I shall not want." One who is led by God does not hunger or thirst, but rather is refreshed in "verdant pastures," "beside restful waters" (v. 2). There is no need for fear because the Shepherd walks alongside with a rod to ward off beasts and a staff to guide the flock "in right paths" (vv. 3-4).

This image recurs in Psalm 28:9, "Save your people, and bless your inheritance; feed them [lit. "shepherd them"], and carry them forever!" (see also Ps 80:1). The metaphor is used negatively in Psalm 49, where the upright are reassured about the fate of the unrighteous who seem to prosper: "Like sheep they are herded into the nether world; death is their shepherd, and the upright rule over them" (Ps 49:15).

In the OT God chooses leaders for Israel who are shepherds, whose skills of care and enduring hardship for the flock transfer to compassionate ministry to God's people. Moses was tending the flock of his father-in-law Jethro when God called him (Exodus 3). David was a most valiant shepherd, who relates to Saul how, when he was tending his father's sheep, "whenever a lion or bear came to carry off a sheep from the flock, I would go after it and attack it and rescue the prey from its mouth. If it attacked me, I would seize it by the jaw, strike it, and kill it" (1 Sam 17:34-35). It is these skills he employs in his encounter with Goliath to rescue the people. The psalmist recounts how God "chose David, his servant, and took him from the sheepfolds; From following the ewes he brought him to shepherd Jacob, his people, and Israel, his inheritance. And he tended them with a sincere heart, and with skillful hands he guided them" (Ps 78:70-72).

Most other references in the OT to shepherds of God's people are denouncing the failure of these leaders to act as good shepherds. Ezekiel rails against the shepherds of Israel who have been pasturing themselves instead of the sheep (Ezek 34:2). He lists their shortcomings: "You did not strengthen the weak nor heal the sick nor bind up the injured. You did not bring back the strayed nor seek the lost, but you lorded it over them harshly and brutally. So they were scattered for lack of a shepherd, and became food for all the wild beasts" (Ezek 34:4-5).

And so, God vows to come against these shepherds and claim the sheep from them, saying, "I myself will look after and tend my sheep" (34:11). God will "rescue them from every place where they were scattered" (v. 12); will "lead them out from among the peoples and gather them from the foreign lands," will "bring them back to their own country" (v. 13) and pasture them in good pastures (v. 14). Shepherding rightly, God will give them rest, seek out the lost and bring them back, bind up the injured, and heal the sick (vv. 15-16). Second Isaiah elaborates the same theme: "Like a shepherd he feeds his flock; in his arms he gathers the lambs, Carrying them in his bosom, and leading the ewes with care" (Isa 40:11).

A motif emerges of a divine promise to raise up new shepherds. Jeremiah prophesies that God will gather the remnant of the flock and "will appoint shepherds for them who will shepherd them so that they need no longer fear and tremble; and none shall be missing" (Jer 23:3-4). This promise takes on messianic significance in Ezekiel, who prophesies, "I will appoint one shepherd over them to pasture them" (34:23; see also 37:22, 24). Zechariah's prophecy, "Strike the shepherd that the sheep may be dispersed" (13:7) is interpreted by Matthew (26:31) and Mark (14:27) as referring to the death of Jesus.

BARBARA E. REID, O.P.

New Testament

The NT effectively builds upon and expands OT imagery of shepherding. As in the OT, shepherd (*poimēn* in Greek) is used in two ways: literally and metaphorically. The literal sense is restricted to Luke 2:8-20, where shepherds watching over their flocks in the night are recipients of the heavenly message about Jesus' birth in Bethlehem. Shepherds appear in this passage for two reasons. The first is that they are part of the pastoral or rural setting for Jesus' birth, emphasizing his lowly origins. Second, they fit with a major theme in Luke's Gospel that the lowly are favored recipients of revela-

tory messages and divine favors (Luke 1:48-52). This image is ironically made all the more effective by the common first-century CE view of shepherds as conniving and dishonest.

Far more frequent in the NT is the use of shepherd in a metaphorical sense, in similar fashion to the OT. It is often tied to the related concepts sheep, lamb, or flock. Mark relates that Jesus, in the presence of crowds of people during his Galilean ministry, takes pity on them, "for they were like sheep without a shepherd" (Mark 6:34). The combination of shepherd, representing Jesus as one who watches over, guards, and guides, with sheep, representing people in need of this care, is also found in the passion traditions. At the Last Supper Jesus uses a passage from Zechariah to indicate that he, as shepherd, will be struck down, while the faith of his "sheep," the disciples, will be sorely tested, to the point that they will be scattered (Mark 14:27; see also Matt 26:31; Zech 13:7).

Matthew develops the shepherd image even further through various allusions. Not only does Matthew view Jesus as a compassionate shepherd of his people (Matt 9:36), but he extends the shepherding action to the final judgment. "As a shepherd separates the sheep from the goats" so Jesus, as a royal messianic shepherd, will separate the righteous from the wicked on the judgment day (Matt 25:31-45). Goats were as highly prized as sheep for their milk, flesh, and long hair used for weaving. Thus the action of sorting is the focus of this part of the parable, rather than a disparagement of goats in comparison with sheep by associating the wicked with them. Goats, however, have much more independent personalities than sheep; this may be why the parable is told as it is. Shepherding is, thus, an exercise in earthly compassion and heavenly judgment.

Matthew makes it clear from the beginning of his Gospel that Jesus is the fulfillment of Israel's hope for a messianic shepherd. He directly applies an OT quote to Jesus with regard to his birth in Bethlehem, "since from you shall come a ruler, who is to shepherd my people Israel" (Matt 2:6). Moreover, only in Matthew does one find a restriction to Jesus' earthly ministry. He insists, "I was sent only to the lost sheep of the house of Israel" (Matt 15:24). Jesus also extends this ministry of shepherding his lost people to his own disciples (Matt 10:5-6). Despite the apparent narrowing of Jesus' shepherding function to Israel, Matthew portrays Jesus as a gentle, humble shepherd whose joy is boundless when he seeks out and finds even one lost sheep (Matt 18:12-14; see also Luke 15:3-7) and whose seeking as risen Lord ultimately extends even to the ends of the earth (Matt 28:18-20).

It is the Fourth Gospel that carries the shepherd image to a new height in an extended metaphorical passage on Jesus "the Good Shepherd" (John 10:1-30). In this passage, Jesus is both the sheepgate (v. 9) and the Good Shepherd (v. 11). He is the proper way into the sheepfold, not a thief. He is not like the hireling who lacks the courage to defend the sheep in time of danger (vv. 12-13; cf. Ezekiel 34). He is like one of the family who depend on the sheep for their livelihood. Jesus is the model, caring shepherd who truly tends his sheep.

The closeness between the shepherd and the sheep represents the closeness between Jesus and his followers. Just as sheep will respond only to the voice of their own shepherd, so will Jesus' followers know his voice and follow after him (v. 27). The Good Shepherd is defined not only as one who cares for the sheep and sees that they do not get lost, but also as one who willingly lays down his own life to save them from marauders (vv. 11, 15). The image is thus connected to Jesus' sacrificial death, not as a helpless victim of injustice, but as love incarnate, who shares the intimate love he experiences in full union with his heavenly Father (v. 30) with his disciples. That this death is not defeat but victory, and entirely voluntary, is made clear as Jesus says, "I lay down my life in order to take it up again" (vv. 17-18). This shepherd is no ordinary protector of his people, but one who will bring them eternal life (v. 28).

John's Gospel forcefully presents the image of the Good Shepherd as the new way God has chosen to come to the aid of people. In Jesus, all model shepherding reaches its apex. But John also extends the metaphor of the shepherd to one particular disciple, Peter. The appendix to the Fourth Gospel includes a poignant scene between the risen Jesus and Peter, in which Peter, too, is called to be shepherd. Three times in response to his affirmation that he loves Jesus, Peter is told "feed my lambs" and "tend my sheep" (John 21:15-19), actions of a devoted shepherd. This passage is traditionally seen as a rehabilitation of Peter who had denied the Lord three times. It also shows Peter's role in the community. He who had shared intimately with Jesus as a disciple in the unified love between Jesus and his Father is also called to guide and watch over the "flock" of the Church.

The rest of the NT reaffirms the image of the Good Shepherd. Jesus is explicitly called "the great shepherd of the sheep" (Heb 13:20) and "the chief Shepherd" (1 Pet 5:4; see also 2:25). The image is also applied to presbyters who lead and instruct the community (1 Pet 5:1-4) in a pattern reminiscent of the way Peter, in the appendix of John, is told to tend the flock. Minor allusions to the shepherding and pastoring function of church leaders appear periodically in other parts of the NT (e.g., Eph 4:11, where the Greek term is translated "pastors"), but these do not depart from the main lines of thought outlined above. One interesting twist on the shepherd image in the NT is the use in Revelation of the "lamb" image for the victorious risen Jesus (Rev 7:14; 17:14). It is intimately tied to blood, the life-giving fluid that the Lamb shed for the sake of his people: "For the Lamb . . . will shepherd them and lead them to springs of life-giving water and God will wipe away every tear from their eyes" (Rev 7:17). The function of the shepherd and the lamb merge into one for the purpose of giving hope to a suffering people. Because Jesus was victorious in his death, by the sacrifice of his own body and blood, so will his faithful followers share in that ultimate victory over evil and death.

While being compared with sheep does not seem very complimentary to people, it must be remembered that most flocks belonged to families, were guarded by family members, and were carefully secured at night as close as possible to the family's sleeping quarters, so that the relationship between shepherd and sheep was very close.

In the urban context of early Christianity beyond the ministry of Jesus, many people may have had no direct experience of shepherding, yet the figure of the young shepherd with a lamb or kid over his shoulders was ubiquitous in Greco-Roman art as a conventional motif. It was soon adopted by Christians as well, and some of the earliest Christian catacomb art portrays this figure.

Because the shepherd was so widespread in prior non-Christian art, it is uncertain whether the earliest Christian representations of the shepherd are consciously meant to portray Jesus under the guise of shepherd, or are simply repeating a familiar symbol. Soon, however, the shepherd became a popular Christ figure in art as well as literature.

In literature, too, the shepherd appears in some Greco-Roman writings as initiator into secret mysteries and agent of heavenly revelation. This literary motif is also represented in Christianity by the second-century Jewish Christian revelation from Rome, the *Shepherd of Hermas*, in which one of the two principal revelatory agents is an angel dressed as a shepherd, clothed in white goatskin, carrying sack and staff. He announces to Hermas, recipient of the vision, that he has been sent to remain with him for the rest of his life (Vision 5.1-2). Here the Shepherd, who is really an angel in disguise, performs the double role of revealing and protecting.

See: BETHLEHEM, BLOOD, CHURCH, COMPASSION, DEATH, DISCIPLE, FAMILY, HOPE, JESUS CHRIST, JUDG-MENT, LAMB OF GOD, MESSIAH, MINISTRY, PASSION, WATCH

CAROLYN OSIEK, R.S.C.J., AND
RONALD D. WITHERUP, S.S.

Pastoral-Liturgical Tradition

The NT consistently links the image of Jesus as shepherd to his death, understood as a selfless sacrifice for the life of his flock. Thus in the tenth chapter of John's Gospel, Jesus repeats—no less than five times!—his conviction that "A good shepherd lays down his life for the sheep," and that he surrenders his life "on his own" (see John 10:11, 15, 17, 18a, 18b). So intimately united are shepherd and sheep that the shepherd takes upon himself all the weakness and vulnerability, all the pain and suffering of the "little ones" entrusted to his care. This imagery reappears in the First Letter of Peter, where Jesus, "the shepherd and guardian of your souls," is said to bear "our sins in his body upon the cross" so that his wounds become our healing (1 Pet 2:24, 25). Supporting all these NT images of Christ as the Good Shepherd is the powerful text of Isaiah 53 (explicitly cited in 1 Peter), which celebrates that mysterious Servant (= Shepherd) of God who "bore our sufferings" even though we had all "strayed like sheep" (see Isa 53:4-6).

Soteriological Value of Jesus' Death. The early Christian proclamation of Jesus as shepherd thus represented a significant Christological development, for it signaled the triumph of a specific interpretation of Jesus' death. Time and experience had gradually convinced Christians that Jesus had not simply suffered the predictable fate of a faithful prophet (rejection, martyrdom), but that his death had a unique soteriological value. It was a death freely accepted "for the many" (i.e., for all), a sacrificial death so complete in its power and efficacy that it brought the long history of alienation between God and humans to a close. This interpretation was already present in Paul's thought (see e.g., Gal 2:19-21; 3:13-14), and it permitted him to argue that since Christians had been incorporated into Jesus' efficacious death by baptism, they shared as well in his resurrection destiny: "We were indeed buried with him through baptism into death, so that, just as Christ was raised from the dead by the glory of the Father, we too might live in newness of life" (Rom 6:4). By the time John's Gospel was written (a generation or two after Paul's time), the soteriological interpretation of Jesus' death had been enriched by further reflection on the great images and themes of the Hebrew Bible. Thus Jesus was not only the Good Shepherd ready to "lay down his life for the sheep" (John 10:11), but the very "Lamb of God, who takes away the sins of the world" (John 1:29). In John's Gospel, Lamb and Shepherd are one; the One who prepares the great paschal sacrifice is himself the victim offered for all (see John 17–19). Thus too, the risen One, in the perspective of John's Gospel, can invite his closest disciples and witnesses to share his own role and destiny as Shepherd: "Simon . . . do you love me? . . . Feed my lambs" (John 21:15-17).

Liturgical Use of the Shepherd Theme. The soteriological interpretation of Jesus' death fits quite naturally into the Church's liturgical celebration of the paschal mystery. It is not surprising, therefore, that the liturgy makes use of the Johannine theme of the Good Shepherd during its celebration of the Easter season. Presently, the Fourth Sunday of Easter (in both the Lectionary/Sacramentary and the Liturgy of the Hours) is devoted to the Good Shepherd. The gospel assigned to be read at Mass on this Sunday is always taken from the tenth chapter of John: John 10:1-10 (cycle A); John 10:11-18 (cycle B); and John 10:27-30 (cycle C). This custom of reading the Good Shepherd gospel during paschaltide is quite ancient. The "Lectionary of Würzburg," which dates from the middle of the seventh century CE and provides a list of gospels read in the Roman liturgy throughout the year, assigns John 10:14-16 ("I am the good shepherd . . .") for the sec-

ond Sunday after Easter. But it is possible that use of the Good Shepherd gospel goes back even further, for among the homilies of Pope Gregory the Great (bishop of Rome from 590 to 603 CE) is one on John 10:11-16 for the second Sunday of Easter. (A portion of Gregory's homily is included in the Office of Readings for the fourth Sunday of Easter in the Liturgy of the Hours as revised by Vatican II.) And earlier still, from the time of Pope Leo the Great (bishop of Rome from 440 to 461 CE), we possess a homily preached probably on the Wednesday before Easter (19 March 452), in which the Good Shepherd gospel is cited. Wrote Leo, "He [Christ] is the One who . . . brings all nations under heaven into one single flock, thereby fulfilling daily what he had promised, 'I must lead, and they will hear my voice, and there will be one flock, one shepherd'" (John 10:16). Indeed, so intimately linked are Shepherd and sheep, in Leo's thought, that what happens to the one happens also to the other. Thus, in the paschal sacraments of baptism and Eucharist, a real transformation occurs: "When people reject Satan and put their trust in God, when they exchange an old life for an utterly new one, . . . they really participate in Christ's death and resurrection. Those who have been baptized are changed—the body of those reborn in the waters becomes the flesh of the Crucified One. . . . And this is how Christ's Passover is truly celebrated with 'the unleavened bread of sincerity and truth'. . . . For these newly baptized creatures are filled and fed by their Shepherd—since to participate in Christ's body and blood is to become, in fact, what we consume."

The liturgical use of the Good Shepherd texts during the Easter season is thus a tradition that stretches back some 1500 years, from the time of Leo and Gregory, through the Middle Ages and the 1570 Missal of Pius V (the "Tridentine" liturgy), down to our own day.

Christian Pastors as Shepherds. In the Patristic tradition the image of Christ as the Good Shepherd willing to go to any lengths—including death—to nourish, protect, and save his flock was soon applied to Church leaders. In fact, this Patristic reflection on biblical texts like John 10 gave birth to the adjective "pastoral" as a description for those charged with the task of nurturing Christians by Word and sacrament. Augustine's great sermon on pastors (read at the Office of Readings during weeks 24 and 25 in the Liturgy of the Hours revised by Vatican II) reminds Church leaders that they are first of all Christians, members of the assembly of faith, and that their role reflects God's greatness rather than personal merit. Another noteworthy Patristic work, Gregory the Great's *Regulae Pastoralis Liber*, might justly be called the Church's first attempt to formulate a pastoral theology. Like the liturgy and the earlier Church fathers, Gregory links Jesus' role as shepherd to his cross and passion: "He refused to be a king, freely embracing the cross; he fled all glory and exaltation" (*Regulae Pastoralis Liber*, Pt. I, ch. 3). With that model in mind, Gregory counsels, pastors must guard against pleasing people at the expense of truth or "hiding themselves in silence when the wolf appears" (ibid., Pt. II, ch. 4). In a word, one who serves by leading has to be a "neighbour in compassion to everyone," able by the heart's love to take on the infirmities of others. The pastor's highest goal, Gregory asserts, is that charity which bonds one to the highest and the lowest alike, which lets one be "weak with others in their weakness," after the example of Paul (see 2 Cor 11:29; *Regulae Pastoralis Liber*, Pt. II, ch. 5).

These biblical and Patristic images of shepherding had a strong impact on the Second Vatican Council's theology of pastoral ministry. In the Constitution on the Church, no. 6, the Johannine images of flock and Shepherd are invoked to support the view that the Church is a communion born of Christ's sacrifice on the cross, enlivened by the Spirit, and nourished by the paschal sacraments. Similarly, the council's documents on the Bishops' Pastoral Office in the Church, nos. 2, 16, and on the Life and Ministry of Priests, no. 3, interpret ordained ministry by reference to Christ the shepherd, who freely surrendered his own life that others might live.

See: SACRIFICE, SERVANT

NATHAN D. MITCHELL

SIGN/SYMBOL

In the OT, signs are manifestations of God's presence and power. As vehicles of communication, they require interpretation by God. In the NT, the signs that Jesus worked guide people toward accepting Jesus as the one sent from God. The Church's pastoral and liturgical tradition makes extensive use of signs and symbols.

Old Testament

A sign is a vehicle of communication—an action, condition, quality, occurrence, visible object, or linguistic unit—that conveys meaning. In the Bible, a tattoo or other body-disfigurement is a sign marked on a slave publicly identifying the owner (Exod 21:6; Deut 15:17). Some signs manifest devotion to a deity (Isa 44:5; Gal 6:17), while others indicate affiliation with an evil spirit (Rev 13:16; 14:9; 16:2; 19:2). Signs or marks like an "X" or something similar on one's forehead can save a person from harm or divine punishment (Ezek 9:4; Rev 7:3-8).

Most commonly in the Bible, however, a sign is any significant deed, event, or other vehicle of communication that speaks God's presence or intention. Unlike modern, western believers who distinguish between primary and secondary causality and who interpret nature as a free-standing element of the cosmos following its own inflexible and impersonal laws, Mediterranean peasants in the OT see God's hand everywhere and in everything.

Thus all creation (Ps 65:9) and many of its elements are perceived as signs that symbolize God: the rainbow (Gen 9:13), the cloud (Exod 13:21), fire (Exod 3:2; Gen 15:17), thunder during a storm (Exod 19:6; Psalm 29), and a gentle breeze (1 Kgs

19:12). The meaning of these signs so clear to believers was missed by pagans (Wis 13:1-19). They considered the signs to be themselves gods rather than the handiwork or evidence of the one true God.

Life-events constitute another group of signs that are common in the Bible. Physical disfigurement like circumcision (Gen 17:11) or even a person's life-situation like being a prophet and giving one's children symbolic names (Isa 7:3; 8:18; Hosea 1–2) are signs that convey a message from God. Certain deeds of prophets known as "prophetic symbolic actions" (e.g., Jer 27:2) are also signs that are drawn from daily, humdrum life but are invested with special meaning because they spring not from the prophet's creative imagination but rather from a direct command and interpretation by God. From this perspective, various life-events are indeed the visible dimension of God's plan of salvation.

The principal signs of the OT, however, are God's mighty deeds that abound and loom large in the Exodus and again in the Elijah-Elisha stories (1 Kgs 17:1–2 Kgs 2:18). As a sign to Pharaoh that the Lord did indeed appear and speak to him, God helped Moses turn his staff into a snake then back into a staff (Exod 4:1-5). As a sign to Pharaoh that it was indeed the Lord who was protecting and planned to liberate his people from Egypt, Moses directed Aaron to use that same staff to make the waters of the Nile undrinkable (Exod 7:14-25). Gradually the signs in Exodus, such as the plagues, truly accomplished what they pointed to. God was acting with love and power to free his people.

In the final analysis, proper understanding of the signs as manifestations of God's presence and power requires an interpretation from God himself. Historians, prophets, psalmists, and sages vie with one another to gain this proper understanding that derives from God whose word explains and interprets the real events which he wills and directs. "The Lord God does nothing without revealing his secret to his servants the prophets" (Amos 3:7). By manifesting God's

power, these mighty signs interpreted by God's word strengthen faith, trust, thanksgiving, memory, humility, obedience, fear of God, and hope in believers.

Signs demand loyal and unswerving trust. The OT offers many instances where this was lacking. Israel lacked this trust in the desert (Ps 78:32) when it responded to God's test by testing God (Exod 17:2; Ps 95:9). It was also lacking in Achaz who hid behind Mediterranean cultural humility in refusing to request a sign when he knew he had already trusted in national alliances rather than wait on divine deliverance (Isa 7:12). In each of these instances, deficient trust blinded potential beneficiaries from seeing their prospective blessing in signs.

New Testament

Just as the OT, so too does the NT describe a variety of signs. People know how to interpret the appearance of the sky as a sign predicting the weather (Matt 16:1-4). The shepherds who are told of the Savior's birth are also given a sign that will confirm the announcement: "And this will be a sign for you; you will find an infant wrapped in swaddling clothes and lying in a manger" (Luke 1:12). In betraying Jesus to his enemies, Judas arranged a sign that allowed them to single Jesus out of the crowd in the dark garden: "The man I shall kiss is the one; arrest him" (Matt 26:48). Letter-writers frequently appended a personally selected sign to the end of their letters (see 2 Thess 3:17) to confirm their authenticity.

Mediterranean culture's acknowledged inability to "read hearts" (1 Sam 16:7) and consequent lack of interest in the matter of what other people are thinking leave its natives entirely dependent on external indicators such as signs to confirm insights or information. But this reliance often turned into a search for a guarantee or a proof that a sign was never intended to be. And beyond that, humdrum daily existence in antiquity stimulated a desire for the extraordinary or the sensational so that there might be something exciting about which to gossip and argue.

It is very likely for that reason that Jesus in the Synoptic Gospels refuses to give a sign (Mark 8:11-12; Matt 12:38-39), and in John 4:48 he denounces the quest for signs. Impatiently he points out that he himself is the sign of God's power and love in their midst: "An evil and unfaithful generation seeks a sign, but no sign will be given it except the sign of Jonah the prophet" (Matt 12:39; 16:4).

Even so, the Synoptics interpreted Jesus' miracles* as mighty deeds, and John interpreted them as "signs." These mighty deeds stand in continuity with God's mighty deeds of creation and redemption. In John, Jesus' signs become the major focus of early missionary propaganda. Their purpose is to guide people toward accepting Jesus as God's legitimate and authorized prophet or covenant leader. Jesus changed water into wine "as the beginning of his signs in Cana in Galilee and so revealed his glory, and his disciples began to believe in him" (John 2:11). At the end of the Gospel, John again notes: "Now Jesus did many other signs in the presence of his disciples that are not written in this book. But these are written that you may come to believe that Jesus is the Messiah, the Son of God, and that through this belief you may have life in his name" (John 20:30-31).

The seven signs reported by John reflect God's mighty deeds of creation and redemption. Saving from death (John 4:46-54; 11:38-44) and feeding hungry crowds (John 6:1-15) are life-giving deeds echoing creation. Replenishing the failed wine supply at a wedding (John 2:1-11), healing a lame man (John 5:1-18), taming the sea (John 6:16-21), and restoring sight to a man congenitally blind (John 9:1-41) give new meaning to human life which echoes redemption.

All of Jesus' signs inchoatively realize what they signify. With these deeds, Jesus effectively and decisively repels sickness, conquers death, and tames the hostility of nature toward human beings. The final victory, of course, will come at the end of time. Jesus' signs were only the beginning.

These signs mean nothing to skeptics or unbelievers. Like Pharaoh, they harden their hearts to God's communication. Yet one must not judge such people harshly because signs are difficult to interpret even in cultures where they are familiar and common. Scripture warns believers not to be deceived by false signs. "False messiahs and false prophets will arise, and they will perform signs and wonders so great as to deceive, if that were possible, even the elect" (Matt 24:24; see also 2 Thess 2:9; Rev 13:13; 16:14; 19:20).

Jesus' warning merely repeats what is very obvious to everyone in Mediterranean culture wherein secrecy, deception, and lying are commonly practiced strategies routinely pressed into service to preserve and safeguard honor. Yet believers, the elect, are fully expected to be able to see through deceptions and to identify authentic signs and other forms of communication from God. When authentic signs are identified, believers respond with conversion (or reconversion) and faith, which in the Bible is best interpreted as unswerving loyalty (to God) no matter what.

See: CONVERSION, CREATION, FAITH, MIRACLE, REDEMPTION, REVELATION, SALVATION, SYMBOL, THANKSGIVING

JOHN J. PILCH

Pastoral-Liturgical Tradition

At the very heart of the Church's pastoral-liturgical tradition is an extensive and rich use of signs/symbols. In liturgy (water and oil, bread and wine, extending hands) as well as popular piety (holy pictures and medals and statues) signs and symbols fashion the tangible means by which the Christian community renders thanks and praise and invokes God's favor. These obvious truisms, however, come through a long and arduous road of understanding and application.

Both modern scholarship and research as well as sacred Scripture's use attest to a plurality of meanings for sign and symbol, sometimes using the two interchangeably and sometimes making a sharp distinction between them. Generally agreed is that both sign and symbol represent or point to a reality beyond themselves. Variances in meaning derive from the relationship of the sign or symbol to the human or religious experience or reality to which it points.

Psychologists, philosophers, theologians, and linguists all share a common interest in signs/symbols, albeit each with her/his own stake in the question. Freud reduced sign/symbol to a representation as denotation; each image in a dream has a specific referent and these are universal. Jung, a student of Freud and influenced by his interpretation of dreams and theory of the unconscious, proposed a theory of archetypes that are shared symbolic forms pointing to fundamental sets of relationships and residing in the unconscious. Symbols, for Jung, are windows into the unconscious. They give an access to the deepest core of human experience.

Ernst Cassirer's philosophy of symbolic forms pushes the discussion into another realm. Struggling with what makes humans really human—as opposed to merely animal—Cassirer linked symbols to culture, values, art, and religious experience, which are uniquely human concerns. Denotation is limiting; symbols open up an ideal world to humankind. Suzanne Langer, a disciple of Cassirer, approaches symbol as that which is concerned with functional aspects of human life. She explores symbols in terms of how they react on the symbol-user and enable control over non-objective aspects of life. In this way humankind can perfect their humanity without altering or renouncing science and its language and methods. Both of these philosophers made enormous contributions to sign/symbol theory, especially in terms of relating symbol to life experiences. Neither of them, however, dealt with what is ultimately an ontological question: How do symbols disclose the real?

For theologians, delving into sign/symbol is necessarily an ontological task. At this point a differentiation between sign and symbol is especially helpful. While both point beyond themselves, signs are human conventions that are completely un-

derstood. Traffic lights and stop signs are good examples. Thus, a first distinction: signs are completely known, but symbols are a tangible manifestation of mystery,* that which cannot be completely known (Rahner). Further, a second distinction: while signs are arbitrary and their meaning is known by convention, symbols participate in the reality to which they point (Tillich). Symbols, then, cannot be created by a people but come out of the collective history and experience of a community. Symbols are a people's response to who and how they are. This is particularly critical when considering religious symbols because by their very nature they cannot be arbitrary since they disclose a communal transcendent experience which is mystery.

Paul Ricoeur is a philosopher of language who bridges the concerns of the psychologist, philosopher, and theologian. The early Ricoeur (*The Symbolism of Evil*) approached symbol as that which is polyvalent in meaning. That is, there is a hidden meaning couched in a literal, apparent meaning. While this polysemic approach allowed the symbol to disclose mystery, it fell short of gaining an (ontological) access to human experience. The later Ricoeur (*Interpretation Theory* and subsequent works) abandoned polysemy in favor of polyreference. That is, symbols incorporate a "split" reference: one reference is to the immediately sensible object or discernible human activity to which the symbol obviously points; the other (hidden) reference is to a disclosure of an alternative human experience that can be appropriated into a new self-understanding. To interpret a symbol is to interpret self.

The implications of these developments in sign/symbol theory are substantial when we turn to consider the use of sign/symbol in Christian pastoral-liturgical tradition. We divide our remarks into two considerations: popular devotions and liturgical prayer.

Popular Devotions. At first glance we might hastily relegate devotional images, processions, pilgrimages, and other such objects and practices to the category of sign and dismiss them as religiosity that does not disclose a God-experience (though under certain circumstances they may be just that). Closer examination suggests caution.

At the heart of our discussion has been a question of the relationship of the visible and invisible. A symbol works in two ways. On the one hand a symbol is a concrete manifestation which gains access to that which is not immediately grasped; in other words, symbol allows an encounter with mystery or, particularly, religious experience. In addition, a symbol by this very disclosure invites a new self-understanding. Any encounter or interpretation of a symbol includes the potential for transformation. In a religious context, this suggests that symbols not only open us to the Holy, but also make us holy.

If the means of popular devotion do not lead to the transformation of lives then they function as signs. They may be nice decorations on a living room wall but they are not disclosures of divine presence. A recent and growing respect for popular devotions reminds us that the objects and actions of popular devotions have not always functioned in so limited a way. For example, the golden age of mysticism flowered during a time some would consider liturgical decadence (at least with respect to celebration and the assembly). In these cases the creative and powerful symbols of popular devotion were the means of encounter with God and transformation of self into images of that divine presence for others. Holiness was manifest.

The means of popular devotion, when deployed as a complement to the liturgical experience, can truly be symbols engendering encounter with the divine.

Liturgical Prayer. That liturgy incorporates symbols can hardly be denied. Indeed, sacraments themselves for centuries have been defined as "outward signs" (symbols). Our human experience of water and oil, food and touch opens the way for interpreting these symbols more expansively in terms of divine activity. This has been the traditional way of understanding sacramental signs/symbols. Rich and rewarding though this approach has been, modern scholarship invites us to other considerations that more adequately relate the visible and invisible and implicate self in symbol-use.

Speech-act theory (Austin and Searle) has suggested that the very utterance of certain speech forms (called "performatives") results in a required consequent activity on the part of one of the interlocutors. For example, to say "I believe" implies an existential faith stance; "I vow" demands a certain subsequent behavior. These kinds of linguistic utterances, too, are symbolic activities. Modern liturgical scholarship suggests that liturgical symbolism includes more than the established objects the Christian community has customarily associated with specific sacraments. All words and actions said and performed by the liturgical assembly during its ritual expression are inherently symbolic. This expands the notion of liturgical symbol to include the entire composite of the various rites. It gives new meaning to the concept of "participation." Not only the objects which may be the immediate focus of a sacramental rite but all the words and gestures—the very "participation"—of the assembly have symbolic import. That is, every aspect of the liturgical celebration cooperates in an integrity of the rite that is symbolic as a whole. As such, the entire rite and all that takes place (not just the hallowed objects) disclose the salvific activity of the divine presence and transform the assembly more perfectly into God's holy people.

Not to be forgotten nor undermined is the liturgical assembly itself as symbol of the presence of the risen Christ. This is a radical departure from much of liturgical tradition where the priest as *alter Christus* mediated God's presence for the assembly and represented that assembly before God. This narrow delimitation of liturgical roles has the unfortunate consequence of skewing the relationship of liturgy and life, which an adequate understanding of symbol places into perspective. With the recovery of the assembly as symbol of the presence of the risen Christ, the assembly itself exercises its priestly function in the celebration of liturgy and recovers the essential relationship between liturgy and Christian living so evident in the caritative activity of the early Christians. Thus the daily activities of Christians are extensions and recurring expressions of liturgical celebration. Only so understood as symbol can the assembly's participation in liturgy be "full and active." The ultimate stake in the assembly as symbol of the presence of the risen Christ is their ongoing participation in the reality of the Paschal Mystery.

The shift in liturgical theology from sign to symbol is more than semantics. It is an attempt to grasp the implication of what Paul proclaimed so long ago: "I have been crucified with Christ, and the life I live now is not my own; Christ is living in me" (Gal 2:19b-20).

See: COMMUNITY, HOLY, MYSTERY, PRIEST

JOYCE A. ZIMMERMAN, C.PP.S

SIN

Steeped in human experience and having a profound sense of God's holiness, the Bible is fully aware of the reality of sin and its various dimensions. The notion of sin finds diverse expression across the span of the Old and New Testaments.

Old Testament

Sin is part of our story as a race. Although numerous words are used to express the idea, the basic term means "missing the mark." A character in a story who misses the mark is always a contender, but never the hero. Sin, then, is like a character who lives with us or within us and impels us to arrogate to ourselves notions of the image of God that are foolish and ineffective. This concept is crucial to understanding the role

sin plays in the story of salvation. We must look for sin as a *persona dramatis*.

Stories. Stories define sin as a character. The canonical OT begins with two stories of creation. Both stress that Adam was like God in some ways. The second story (the Yahwist's, Gen 2:4b–3:24) describes how Adam and Eve attempted to be like God in their own way. Sin enters the story through the agency of the character of "the serpent [who] was the most cunning of all the animals that the LORD God had made" (Gen 3:1). The plot centers on whether the new human creatures will attain knowledge properly, through an acceptance of God's supreme wisdom and power, or they will attempt it on their own as the serpent suggested. In this way sin entered the world.

The rest of the collection of stories in Genesis 4–11 gives a picture of how all the prominent social sins we know began and how they ended in failure. Cain, the first descendant of Adam and Eve, took God's power over life and death into his own hands in order to kill his rival Abel. Sin is mentioned by name for the first time when God admonishes Cain: "Why are you so resentful and crestfallen? If you do well, you can hold up your head; but if not, sin is a demon lurking at the door; his urge is toward you, yet you can be his master" (Gen 4:6b-7). Freedom and responsibility are stressed, but sin has entered the story as a demon or wild animal.

In many of the later stories sin manipulates human actions. The stories also show that the opposite of sin is faith. Faith is the key to understanding the stories and God's promise. "Abraham believed God and it was credited to him as righteousness" (Rom 4:3), as it was later summarized.

The tradition retold how Moses led the people out of Egypt. Yet despite the wondrous deeds of the Lord, the people murmured, murmuring about the lack of water and food or the authority of Moses (see especially Exodus 15–17 and Numbers 14–16). The multiple references to these sins are sometimes called the "murmuring tradition." Numbers 14:11 has Moses disputing with the Lord about the punishment for a mutiny of the people. "And the LORD said to Moses, 'How long will this people spurn me [sin against me]? How long will they refuse to believe in me, despite all the signs I have performed among them?'" The sin here is the lack of faith, a desire to control their own future.

After David had become the hero who established the Israelite kingdom in glory, his successors were tempted to manipulate cult and war to their own advantage. This became the "sin of Jeroboam, king of Israel, who made Israel to sin." All the kings of the north were condemned for this sin. Of Jehu, a quite successful king, the formula runs: "But Jehu was not careful to observe wholeheartedly the law of the LORD, the God of Israel, since he did not desist from the sins which Jeroboam caused Israel to commit" (2 Kgs 10:31). The sins of the king affected the whole people. In the final summary of the destruction of the Kingdom of Israel, the commentator says: "When he [Jeroboam] tore Israel away from the house of David, they made Jeroboam, son of Nebat, king: he drove the Israelites away from the LORD, causing them to commit a great sin. The Israelites imitated Jeroboam in all the sins he committed, nor would they desist from them" (2 Kgs 17:21-22).

In the south, after Manasseh, king of Judah, had become a virtual pagan and eliminated the worship of Yahweh in Jerusalem, his successors were measured by his sinfulness. When roving bands of Chaldeans, Arameans, Moabites, and Ammonites threatened Jerusalem, it was said of Jehoiakim, the king, "He [the LORD] loosed them against Judah to destroy it, as the LORD had threatened through his servants the prophets. This befell Judah because the LORD had stated that he would inexorably put them out of his sight for the sins Manasseh had committed in all that he did" (2 Kgs 24:2-3). The incessant repetition of these phrases define the plot of this particular history. The sin of pride of one man, initiated to control events himself, had forced all the people to commit the same sin. There was no hope in that misunderstanding of the creative plans of God.

The Prophets. Despite the different messages and literary techniques of the prophets, one fact is constant: true prophets spoke of both condemnation and consolation. The condemnation was for community sin. It was almost a formula for Jeremiah to say, "we have sinned" (Jer 3:25; 8:14; 14:7, 20; 40:3; 44:23; 50:7). The community sin was basically the abandonment of the worship of the true God for that of idols. Pagan gods seemed easier to control. Such control was seen as very pragmatic as demonstrated by sins of power seeking, oppression of the poor, bribery, lying, murder, etc. The conviction that these sins endure from generation to generation permeate the history.

Despite this there is a growing, or perhaps recuperative, understanding of personal responsibility (see Exod 20:5; Deut 5:9 for the original insight). Jeremiah and Ezekiel challenge the traditional sayings that the younger generations are punished for the sins of their ancestors. "What is the meaning of this proverb that you recite in the land of Israel: 'Fathers have eaten green grapes, thus their children's teeth are on edge?' As I live, says the LORD God: I swear that there shall no longer be anyone among you who will repeat this proverb in Israel. For all lives are mine; the life of the father is like the life of the son, both are mine; only the one who sins shall die" (Ezek 18:2-4). It is repeated in Ezekiel 33:10-20 and is found in Jeremiah 31:29-30.

The consolation is found not in the hope that the people will become righteous and so merit forgiveness, but in the gracious action of God. "It is I, I, who wipe out, for my own sake, your offenses; your sins I remember no more" (Isa 43:25). This message of hope emerges most clearly in the Servant of Yahweh canticles of Deutero-Isaiah. "He shall take away the sins of many, and win pardon for their offenses" (Isa 53:12).

The Law. The cultic legislation illustrates well the notion of sin as "missing of the mark." In Leviticus 4 and 5 a number of sin and guilt offerings are prescribed for those who inadvertently contracted cultic uncleanness and so were barred from worship. No moral guilt was involved, but, when cultic impurity was present, the ceremony did not achieve its effect; it simply missed the mark. More serious were crimes of rebellion, infidelity, sexual misconduct, which disturbed community or family order. These were severely condemned and appropriate reparations mandated. Finally, there was the most serious crime of all, revolt against God (Lev 24:15). For such a violation there was no other remedy than exclusion from the community (which the culprit had already affected) and death. In these instances, sin was not seen as a demonic force, but as perverse human action. This notion is much more akin to our idea of sin.

The Wisdom Tradition. The sages struggled with the problem of personal sin or folly. Hosea, who was influenced by this thinking, says: "My people perish for want of knowledge" (Hos 4:6). The orderliness of life which could be observed in human affairs was the greatest good. To espouse disorderliness was the greatest folly. The great poem on Lady Wisdom concludes: "For he who finds me [wisdom] finds life, and wins favor from the LORD. But he who misses me harms himself; all who hate me love death" (Prov 8:35-36). Such was conventional wisdom.

The Book of Job introduces the problem of suffering unmerited by sinning. According to the hypothesis of the story, Job was without sin (Job 1:22). When he was accused of sin by his friends, he claimed that even if he were guilty God was being unfair both in searching out his petty sins and in refusing to forgive such an insignificant sinner. "Though I have sinned, what can I do to you, O watcher of men? Why do you not pardon my offense, or take away my guilt?" (Job 7:20-21; so also in 10:14). Eventually Job came to admit that he had not known enough to understand the relation of good and evil, prosperity and sin. God praised him for trying.

Ecclesiastes observed that all the alternating vices and virtues that we observe inevitably succeed one another—war and peace, hate and love, etc. This defies understanding. "He has made everything appropriate to its time, and has put the timeless into their hearts, without men's ever discovering, from beginning to end, the work which God has done" (Eccl 3:11). The sages acknowledged the endless drive to know, but they had the wisdom to admit that there was sin in trying to know as much as God.

Psalms speak of this kind of sin and there are many prayers for forgiveness of such sin. David's prayer for forgiveness in Psalm 51 is most notable. The psalmists also know of the good effect that a struggle with evil can have. "To you all flesh must come because of wicked deeds" (Ps 65:3). Folly is in trying to forgive one's own sins. The awareness of sinfulness must lead to the hope for a savior whom God alone can send.

Apocalyptic Writings. The literature of the final centuries of Judaism do not use the word sin frequently, but the idea of personified evil dominates the thought. Apocalyptic writings indulge in wild visions of great heavenly battles between armies of good and evil, of falling stars and suns, of terrifying beasts and dragons. This is imagination run riot in the service of faith. The purpose of this exuberant imagery was to proclaim the final word on the story's outcome. In his great prayer for forgiveness in chapter 9 Daniel first confesses the sins of his people throughout history. Then the vision opens up and Gabriel proclaims to him:

Seventy weeks are decreed
  for your people and for your holy city:
Then transgression will stop and sin will
    end,
  guilt will be expiated,
Everlasting justice will be introduced,
  vision and prophecy ratified,
  and a most holy will be anointed
                              (Dan 9:24).

The final word on sin belongs to the Lord: "I have overcome." The sin that was a demon lurking at the door will finally be tamed.

See: APOCALYPTIC, APOSTASY, CLEAN/UNCLEAN, IDOLATRY

JAMES A. FISCHER, C.M.

New Testament

The NT meaning of sin is derived from its religious sense in the OT rather than from classical Greek. The common or generic term is *hamartia* and its derivatives. This term means to "miss the mark" or, in a religious sense, to fall short of God's will for us. In the NT, the term can refer to a single act or actions, as is sometimes the case in the Synoptic Gospels where it appears in the plural. But more often, especially in John and Paul, sin designates a state or condition or even a power. The idea that Jesus is the victor over sin is unique to the NT.

There is very little emphasis in either the OT or NT on sin as an interior disposition or the act of an individual. What is more at issue is the community dimension of sin. Even though its sense is religious (i.e., having to do with our relationship to God), sin usually also involves relationships among people. Sin has an effect on others: on our neighbors, our brothers and sisters, one another, even our enemies. The community dimension that is stressed with regard to the virtues, such as faith, hope, charity, and forgiveness, is likewise present in NT descriptions of sin.

The Synoptic Gospels. In the Synoptic Gospels, sin appears often in contexts that speak of the forgiveness brought by Jesus. Jesus associates with sinners whom he calls to repentance* and conversion (Matt 9:10, 13; 11:19; Luke 7:34; 15:1-2, 18, 21; 19:7). Jesus does not condone sin but he loves sinners. Unlike the Pharisees and other religious people of his time, Jesus shows kindness toward sinners. Jesus' solidarity with sinners is one of the ways God touches human hearts. Yet Jesus also recognizes the evil of sin. Sin is in the human heart and defiles people (Matt 15:18-19; Mark 7:20-22). The disciples proclaim the gospel as the forgiveness of sins, a forgiveness received by belief and repentance (Acts 2:38). In this sense, the gospel is salvation from sin.

The social dimension of sin is also emphasized in the Synoptic Gospels. So, for example, Peter asks Jesus about how many times to forgive the "brother who sins against me" (Matt 18:21). All of Matthew 18 has to do with the social repercussions of sin. Matthew's church was threatened with apostasy and those who were renouncing their faith were scandalizing the others. Jesus speaks of the children of the reign of God as "little ones" and warns that anyone who causes one of these little ones to sin would be better off drowned in the sea (18:6). But the repentance and conversion of a sinner causes celebration in heaven.

According to Luke, in Jesus' farewell address at the Last Supper, Peter is encouraged by the prediction that, while the sin symbolized by his denial is a failure hurtful to the other disciples, Peter's "turning back" or reconversion will "strengthen your brothers" (Luke 22:32).

John. In John's writings, the notion of sin as power is more explicit. The one who sins is born of the devil (1 John 3:8) and is a slave to sin (John 8:34). Sin is lawlessness or unrighteousness (1 John 3:4; 5:17). Those "in sin" choose darkness over light, blindness over seeing, falsehood over truth (John 3:19-20). The result of sin is death.

In John, the world is the forum for the battle between good and evil. When Jesus overcomes the world, he conquers sin. Jesus is the Lamb of God who takes away the sin of the world (John 1:29; see 1 John 2:2; 3:5; 4:10). Because he is the Christ, Jesus conquers sin by his death (1 John 3:5). Those who believe may confess their sin and find forgiveness in repentance. Believers are born of God through baptism; in community they profess their faith, grow in love, and persevere in the hope of Jesus' glorious return to judge the world.

Paul. It is Paul who develops the most complete NT theology of sin. Paul sometimes refers to acts of sin, but more often he describes sin as a state or power. In the first eight chapters of Romans, where Paul's theology of sin is most clearly and systematically expressed, sin represents the universal state of all humankind. In three ways Paul develops this notion of universality. In Romans 1–3, Paul describes the sin of all people, Gentiles and Jews alike. His description in these three chapters depicts sin as idolatry, that is, offering to creatures the respect and obedience worthy of God alone. "Gentiles and Jews" together represent all humankind. Paul's emphasis is that all people are in need of God's saving power to liberate and to save them.

Sin is personified as well as universalized by Paul in Romans 5:12-21. With Adam, Paul says, sin came into the world. Paul is suggesting that sin is a power that "entered" the world with the first human act of defiance against God. Adam provides an image by which Paul relates the universality of sin. Adam is not so much a historical figure as a symbol of all humankind.

The third way Paul depicts the universality of sin in Romans is by way of an illustration that uses the first person singular, "I," to show how all humans sin (cf. Rom 7:7-25). Drawing on an experience that everyone, upon reflection, would be able to identify with, Paul says, "For I do not do the good I want, but I do the evil I do not want. Now if [I] do what I do not want, it is no longer I who do it, but sin that dwells in me" (Rom 7:19-20).

This experience is true not only for Paul but for everyone: knowledge of what is right does not of itself empower humans to do what is right. Rather, the "sin" that dwells in us impels us to do evil. Paul is neither rationalizing away human responsibility nor is he interested here in making everyone admit to individual acts of sinfulness. Rather Paul is illustrating the universality of sin by observing the great power of sin contrasted with our powerlessness to

redeem ourselves. We rely on God's action in Christ to save us from this dilemma.

Christ brings saving grace to this universal situation of sin. Although he himself is free from sin, God "made him to be sin" (2 Cor 5:21) in order to destroy sin. Christ represents humanity as he undergoes death on the cross "for our sins" (1 Cor 15:3; Gal 1:4). And Christ is revealed the victor over sin through the resurrection. God raised Jesus from the dead and, in doing so, nullified the judgment of sin and death by going beyond them. Resurrection is more than restoration; it is a re-creation. It is in Christ that we are created anew (Gal 6:15).

Of course, believers sometimes fail and sin again, even after baptism. But they are freed from the state of alienation from God and from the power of sin. Christ's death and resurrection provide the ultimate sign of our new communion with God.

Other NT Writings. The remaining NT writings likewise take for granted the universal power of sin. Hebrews examines the cultic dimension of sin; that is, Hebrews presents Christ as the high priest whose mediation and sacrifice effected atonement and redemption (Heb 1:3; 9:28). Hebrews, like much of the rest of the NT, was written for churches struggling with the danger and fear of apostasy. Many who initially believed later wavered in their faith when they faced persecution. In time, many renounced their faith. That is sin.

The Letter of James stresses sin as specific actions and sometimes as failure to act in certain ways (Jas 4:17). Taking seriously the gospel mandate to love and serve others, James warns against the sin of trying to have faith without good works. The works of mercy toward others are an integral part of Christian life. To claim to be a disciple of Christ without performing such works is sin.

The First Letter of Peter was written for a church struggling to keep faith despite persecution. In solidarity with Christ, who has conquered sin by his death, Christians are urged to avoid sin by persevering in a new way of life that distinguishes them from the world in which they live. Christians are exhorted to suffer faithfully, to endure without losing hope, to persevere even in the midst of trial. 1 Peter is a kind of baptismal homily, but it does not represent a one-time sermon so much as an exhortation to faith over the long and difficult journey of life. For the author of 1 Peter, to give up faith is to sin.

Conclusion. Sin represents several aspects of estrangement from God according to the NT writers. Whether it is depicted as individual acts or as a universal power threatening all humankind, sin is everywhere prevalent and is overcome only in union with Jesus through a faith that confesses him to be the Christ. Sin is, therefore, the opposite of faith, and faith, for the NT, is centered in Jesus' messiahship, which involves his victory over sin.

See: ADAM AND EVE, APOSTASY, FAITH, REDEMPTION, REPENTANCE, SALVATION

MARY ANN GETTY

Pastoral-Liturgical Tradition

The early Church had a strong sense of sin, but it was the challenge of Gnosticism that prompted more direct reflection upon it. A dualistic view that saw the good in the spiritual and evil in the material led to the belief that sin was something embedded in the material creation. Such thinking went squarely against the belief that God had created the world good, and that evil had come into the world through the misuse of the freedom given by God to the angels and to human beings. Thus the Church Fathers were led into a deeper reflection on the meaning of sin and how it relates to the choices of the will.

Augustine mapped out, as it were, the terrain for this reflection on sin. On the one hand, he spoke of sin as a violation of the divine law. Legal metaphors for speaking about sin and forgiveness of sin are rooted in the Scriptures (images of a tribunal, of transgression, of forgiveness as a verdict of acquittal) and have enjoyed a long history in the Christian tradition, especially in the

West. The eternal law here does not mean primarily a legal code of do's and don't's, but rather the loving plan God has for creation in order that it might be brought to the fulfillment in Christ which God has intended for it. To go against God's plan is really to deviate from our own being, since in sinning we go against what God intends for us—our restoration as the image of God. To sin, then, is first and foremost not about infractions of a divinely sanctioned code, but rather a posture against the redemptive plan of God.

On the other hand, Augustine spoke of sin as the turning away from God and turning toward the creature ("aversio a Deo et conversio ad creaturam," *De Libro Arbitrio*, II, 53). By saying this, Augustine was not reverting to the dualist heresy that saw sin embedded in creation. Rather, what sin means is turning away from God to something or someone who is not God, and therefore according that creature the honor due God. Sin is a mismeasure of things, an idolatrous act. In sinning, we confide in finite things when we should be directing ourselves to God. For Augustine this was most evident in our disordered desire, or concupiscence. Such disordered desire was the seat of sin in the human being, through which the human will replaced God with creaturely pleasure.

The reformers in the sixteenth century tried to recover a stronger biblical sense of sin and, at the same time, focus on the personal experience of sin. In their reflection on the immensity of God's justifying grace they contemplated also the deep sinfulness of humankind that had called forth such dramatic action from God. In so doing, there was a tendency to become so pessimistic about the human condition that sinfulness was sometimes seen as having corrupted the human being and the human powers of will and freedom completely. While the deep shadows of human sinfulness only looked darker in the bright light of grace, to root sinfulness so deeply in the will runs the risk of so impairing human freedom that sin ceases to be a free act of rebellion against God. The moderate optimism of the Catholic tradition about human freedom seems better to maintain that in sinning we turn freely against God.

The reformers were right, however, in emphasizing that we can only plumb the depths of sin by understanding the remedy that God put against it: the incarnation, death, and resurrection of Christ. It was Christ's free act of self-emptying that restored us to the freedom of the sons and daughters of God. Our sin was such that only God could overcome it.

Sin can therefore be seen in the following fashion: as a denial of God, a destruction of the self, and as damage to the community. Sin is a denial of God because it is a choice against God and God's plan for us. By turning away from God we go against the very nature of our own being which, as creatures, is meant to be related and connected deeply to our creator. We were created in God's image (Gen 1:26), and so to turn away from the One we image is actually a destruction of ourselves by making ourselves into something we were not intended to be. And because our very selves are formed by and embedded in communities, such a denial of God and destruction of self damages the community as well. This last dimension of sinfulness has received much attention in recent years, especially by theologians of liberation. It is often called social sin. Social sin represents, as it were, the accumulation of sinful acts that create environments of oppression, racism, and sexism, environments of sinfulness so powerful and so pervasive that no one can escape them. Social sin only feeds the human propensity to turn away from God.

Already in the Bible and throughout the tradition it has been recognized that not all sin is of the same degree. The name "sin" belongs in the first place to the kind of sin discussed thus far in this entry: a fundamental turning away from God. This is usually called mortal or grave sin. That such sin was possible was reflected already in the penitential practice of the early Church, where it was felt that such sin could be forgiven only once after baptism. Christian belief and practice down to the present day holds that mortal sin, by its fundamental alienation from God, excludes the sinner from the Eucharist. But it has always been recognized that there are also lesser infractions that do not result in a fundamental turning away from God—shortcomings, failings, temporary lapses. These have been called venial or lighter sins. Such venial sins do not carry the same burden of alienation from God, although they too require God's forgiveness.

The reformed penitential practice in the sacrament of reconciliation reflects contemporary theological thinking about the nature of sin. Sin is more than individual acts of transgression; it speaks of the basic orientation of one's life. The sacrament is an opportunity to reflect about one's overall relationship to God and not only specific acts of wrongdoing. The communal dimension of sinfulness—both how social sin leads us into sinfulness and how our sin affects others—is more clearly manifested in the revised rites.

All of this has led contemporary theologians to the awareness that mortal sin is not as easily committed as once thought. Mortal sin, as a fundamental turning away from God, does not occur as readily as once thought. To be sure there are single acts that are mortally sinful, but those acts are usually part of a longer history that led up to them. Contemporary psychology suggests also that our freedom can be impaired by our previous histories and by unconscious urges. Some theologians have even suggested a threefold distinction between a fundamental option against God, grave acts, and lesser acts. While this seems more consonant with modern Western understandings of the person as a self that is gradually created, the distinction between the fundamental option and the grave acts is sometimes blurred. Such an understanding of sin, however, does emphasize that our relation to God, grounded as it is in God's infinite grace and love, is not easily broken.

See: ATONEMENT, GRACE, JUSTIFICATION, REDEMPTION

ROBERT J. SCHREITER, C.PP.S.

SLAVERY

A curious anomaly in both Testaments and in the history of the Church is the apparent acceptance of the institution of slavery. The ownership of one human being by another was economically and socially integral to the ancient Near Eastern and Greco-Roman world. The biblical tradition did not explicitly challenge this despite the origins of that tradition in the liberation of the descendants of Jacob from slavery in Egypt.

While slavery was socially acceptable, it was not economically necessary or even profitable. Small land owners held most agricultural land. They worked their land with the aid of the families and required no outside help, slave or free. There were large estates but the workers on these were sharecroppers or tenant farmers. Slave labor had little role in the agriculture economy into the Roman period. Slaves were too expensive to buy and support. The slave was a luxury of the rich. Slaves were domestic servants who made life easier for the wealthy. This should have made the condemnation of slavery easier, but the biblical tradition simply accepted this institution. Church authorities and moral theologians continued to accept this institution until society itself abolished it.

Old Testament

Most slaves in the ancient world were captives taken during war. Human beings were the most valuable booty of war. Solomon made slaves of the Canaanites who lived within the territory he controlled (1 Kgs 9:20-21). The rich acquired their slaves by purchasing them. Prophetic texts condemn the nations that engaged in the slave trade (Amos 1:6, 9; Ezek 27:13; Joel 3:6). Leviticus forbids Israelites from enslaving their fellow Israelites but they could possess foreigners as slaves (25:39-46). Despite these prophetic strictures the Israelites participated in the slave trade at least as buyers.

A second source of slaves was the economic difficulties of the poor. Overwhelming debt could lead a person to sell himself into slavery. This is the type of slavery envisioned by Exodus 21:1-6 and Deuteronomy 15:12-18. These laws put a six-year limit on a debtor's slavery. At the end of the six years, slaves can reclaim their freedom or choose to remain in the service of their masters. Slavery was the fate of a thief who could not make restitution (Exod 22:2).

Another source of slaves was the natural increase of those in slavery. The children of slaves were the property of their owners. If a slave was married when entering the service of his master, he could take his wife and children upon becoming free. If the slave married a woman given him by his master, the slave's wife and children remained the property of the master when the male slave acquired his freedom (Exod 21:4-5). The only way a slave in such a situation could keep his family would be to give up his freedom (Exod 21:6). Apparently slaves born into the household enjoyed a status different from those that were purchased. They were considered members of the Israelite religious community and the males were circumcised (Gen 17:12-13, 23, 27). They were treated as members of the family and entrusted with important tasks (Genesis 24). Their advice was sought and respected (Judg 19:11; 1 Sam 9:5-10; 25:14-17; 2 Kgs 5:2-3). They could inherit the estate of their owner if he died without an heir (Gen 15:2; Prov 17:2).

Special laws applied to female slaves whom rich men bought for their sexual pleasure. These slaves could not look forward to release after six years. Only if the master married and did not provide for his slave could she claim her freedom. A man who bought a slave as a concubine for his son had to treat that slave as a daughter (Exod 21:7-11). An Israelite could not make a concubine out of a female war captive. He had to marry her or free her (Deut 21:10-14). In the patriarchal narratives (Genesis

12–50), there are instances of a wife giving a concubine to her husband from the female slaves that she owned (Gen 16:1-2; 30:3, 9).

Ancient Near Eastern law codes dealt severely with runaway slaves and even more severely with those who abet their escape. Deuteronomy is unique because it forbids the return of fugitive slaves, but this is a late text. There are several texts that are not aware of this legislation: Genesis 16:6; 1 Samuel 25:10; 1 Kings 2:39.

Though the OT does not challenge slavery as an institution, its law codes try to make the institution more humane. For example, Deuteronomy orders a master to provide support for slaves released after six years of service. Since economic problems forced people into slavery in the first place, some sort of support is necessary to prevent the cycle of poverty and slavery from repeating itself. Also a master who injures or maims his slaves must give them their freedom (Exod 21:26-27). Slaves were to enjoy rest on the Sabbath (Exod 20:10; 23:12) and participated in the celebration of religious festivals (Exod 12:44; Deut 12:12, 18; 16:11, 14).

More than any other legal code Deuteronomy admonishes Israelites to deal humanely and compassionately with their slaves: Deuteronomy 5:15; 15:15; 16:2; 24:18, 22. After all, the favorite Deuteronomic word for a fellow Israelite is "brother." The Israelite community was to transcend social boundaries since both the king and the slave were included in this relationship (Deut 17:15; 15:12). Joel believes that a sign of God's final intervention on Israel's behalf will be the pouring out of the Spirit on slaves as well as their masters (Joel 2:29).

The approach of the OT then toward slavery is paradoxical. It accepts an inhumane institution but tries to humanize it. Nowhere is this paradox stated more clearly than in Sirach 33:25-33. This text advises masters to keep their slaves busy with hard work or else they will become lazy, and recommends harsh punishment for slaves that are not fulfilling their responsibilities. The same passage urges masters to treat slaves like brothers.

New Testament

The NT also takes a neutral attitude toward slavery. It too accepts slavery as a social fact. In the stories about and the parables of Jesus, slaves appear in typical roles and situations (Matt 18:23-35; 24:45-51; 26:51; Luke 7:1-10; 12:37-39, 45), but Jesus never condemns slavery. Some texts do condemn facets of this institution. For example, the Book of Revelation condemns that slave trade (18:13). 1 Timothy denounces the kidnappers of slaves (1:9-10). In the Letter to Philemon, Paul advises this Christian to receive Onesimus, his runaway slave—also a Christian—as a brother. This may have been Paul's subtle way of suggesting that Philemon free Onesimus.

The NT condemned the mistreatment of slaves (Eph 6:9; Col 4:1) but not the institution of slavery (Eph 6:5-9; Col 3:22–4:1; 1 Tim 6:1-2; Titus 2:9-10). It offers Jesus as a model for slaves suffering from harsh masters (1 Pet 2:18-25). The only group contemporaneous with the early Church known to have condemned slavery as such was the Essenes. The benevolent attitude of the NT toward slaves may be due to the number of slaves that became Christians and the influence of Stoicism.

Slavery as a Metaphor

In view of the existence of slavery and the number of slaves in ancient Israel and the early Church, it is not surprising that the Bible frequently uses the term "slave" as a metaphor. In some texts it serves as the way an inferior speaks of himself to a superior (Gen 32:18; 43:28; Ruth 3:9). While some of those called "the slaves of the king" (1 Sam 16:17; 18:22; 21:8; 28:27; 2 Sam 11:13; 1 Kgs 1:47) may have been slaves, others were important advisors. Israelites are to be the slaves of Yahweh as are the prophets (Jer 25:4; Amos 3:7). Isaiah 40–55 speaks of the servant, i.e., the slave of the Lord.

Jesus demands that those who have roles of leadership should become the slaves of all (Matt 20:27). Jesus takes the role of a slave when he washes the feet of the disciples

(John 13:1-20). Paul asserts that Jesus took on the form of slave (Phil 2:7). Acts call the apostles the slaves of the Lord (4:29; 16:17). "Slave of God" or "slave of Jesus Christ" occurs in the titles of some letters (Jas 1:1; Titus 1:1; Rom 1:1; Phil 1:1; Jude 1:1). People can choose to become slaves to sin (Rom 6:17, 20) or slaves to God (Rom 6:22). Still the dominant metaphor in the NT for the believer's relationship with God is adoption. Paul contrasts the circumstances of an adopted child with those of a slave (Gal 4:1-7).

Pastoral Dimensions

The paradoxical attitude of the biblical tradition toward slavery shows that the people who produced the Bible were not always aware of the full implications of their own words. What they wrote should have led them to assert that the one relationship that must not exist between human beings is that of slave and master. The freedom Yahweh gave to the Israelites, and that purchased by the death of Jesus, should make it impossible for the believer to regard another human being as a slave.

Because the biblical tradition did not explicitly condemn slavery some people actually believed that slavery was in accord with the will of God and that God destined some people to be slaves. Fortunately there were others whose reflection on this same tradition led them to believe that it is impossible that a Christian regard another person as a slave without betraying the gospel.

See: FREEDOM

LESLIE J. HOPPE, O.F.M.

Pastoral-Liturgical Tradition

An Ambiguous Term. Wherever it was practiced, slavery was marked by inner contradictions. On one hand, slaves were chattel property that could be alienated by sale, will, gift, or legal seizures. They could be traded or mortgaged, rented or wagered. They were often likened to beasts of burden and penalties for harming them were usually closer to those laid down for injury to animals. Yet few societies were able to ignore totally that slaves in the end were human beings. Thus laws were generally in force against capricious killing of slaves. Slaves were also deemed capable of committing "human" crimes.

Slavery and Christianity. Christians shared in the general ambiguity of the larger society regarding slavery. Prior to Constantine the nascent Church tried to ignore a slave's status as far as possible in its internal framework without speaking out against public policy on the matter. But when Christianity became the religion of the Roman Empire it could no longer remain neutral with regard to the public dimensions of slaves. Hence there arose a body of theology and Church law that justified and protected slavery while asserting the essential humanity of slaves.

Augustine, in the early fifth century, was the principal architect of the Church's theological approach to the slave question. For him, slavery was the direct result of the sin of Adam and Eve, which in turn necessitated establishment of instruments of coercion such as slavery. People became slaves in the Augustinian perspective as a direct consequence of some sin. The slave master, acting as the representative of God, was in fact serving the slaves by protecting them from further sinfulness. In exercising their "protective" role masters were to act kindly.

The Augustinian approach to slaves as both property and persons persisted through the Middle Ages. Others did reflect on the issue, but did not deviate greatly from the original framework laid out by the Bishop of Hippo. St. Gregory the Great as well as many canon lawyers regarded slavery as against the natural law even though necessary at times. Thomas Aquinas, on the other hand, suggested it was part of the governing pattern of nature. Despite these occasional philosophical differences on the question, there was widespread willingness on the part of Church leaders and theologians to support slavery as a societal institution. History shows that, on the whole, Christian societies produced neither improvement nor deterioration in the condition of slaves as compared with other societies.

U.S. Catholicism and Slavery. Catholic attitudes toward the vibrant slave trade in early America ranged from supportive to non-committal. The Maryland Jesuits were slave owners themselves. When public efforts to abolish slavery began, Catholic leaders stayed on the sidelines, generating considerable anti-Catholic feeling among abolitionists. The official Catholic position was that slavery, a principle of social organization, was not in itself sinful even though Pope Gregory XVI had condemned the organized slave trade in 1839. Bishop Kenrick of St. Louis, considered the leading American theologian figure of the period, argued that since slavery was an accepted public institution in the United States the Catholic Church should not advance any policies that would cause the slaves to "bear their yoke unwillingly."

After the Civil War, the Second Plenary Council of Baltimore (1886), at the urging of the then apostolic delegate Bishop Martin Spalding, passed legislation to assist the plight of four million newly emancipated slaves. But little was done to implement this legislation in local areas due to the hostility of clergy and laity alike. The Catholic Church was to remain with the legacy of slavery until after World War II when Cardinal Ritter of St. Louis began the process of internal Catholic desegregation by opening his schools to African-American students.

See: ADAM AND EVE

JOHN T. PAWLIKOWSKI, O.S.M.

SLEEP

Old Testament

Sleep has both a literal and figurative meaning in the OT. It is the common human experience that sleep brings sweetness and refreshment to the weary person (Jer 31:25-26). Peaceful sleep is a sign that one is living as a faithful servant of God and trusts in God's protection (Ps 4:9). One who finds Wisdom experiences "sweet" sleep (Prov 3:24). The psalmist advises, "It is vain for you to rise early, or put off your rest, You that eat hard-earned bread, for he gives to his beloved in sleep" (Ps 127:2).

Sleeplessness can result from sickness or worry. "The care of wealth drives away rest. Concern for one's livelihood banishes slumber; more than a serious illness it disturbs repose" (Sir 31:1-2; see also Sir 40:5). Sin also keeps one awake until it is acknowledged (Ps 32:4-5).

On the other hand, not to sleep at night is a mark of a faithful servant. Jacob recalls his service of twenty years, for Laban, "How often the scorching heat ravaged me by day, and the frost by night, while sleep fled from my eyes!" (Gen 31:40). Sleep may also be eschewed for meditation on the Law (Ps 1:2).

Diligent sleeplessness imitates God, who "neither slumbers nor sleeps, the guardian of Israel" (Ps 121:3-4; see also 1 Kgs 18:27). The sense of God's absence, however, causes one to cry out, "Awake! Why are you asleep, O LORD? Arise! Cast us not off forever!" (Ps 44:24; similarly Ps 78:65-66).

Sleeping too much indicates culpable indolence, "Laziness plunges a man into deep sleep, and the sluggard must go hungry" (Prov 19:15; similarly, Prov 10:5). Sleep may also accompany disobedience, as when Jonah lay fast asleep in the ship while fleeing God's call to go to Nineveh (Jonah 1:1-6).

In some episodes, God induces sleep so as to accomplish the divine purposes. In Genesis 2:21 God cast a deep sleep on the first human being, then took one of his ribs to build it into a woman. The sleep renders the man inactive to emphasize that the creation of woman is God's action. In 1 Samuel 26:12 Saul and his men are put into a deep sleep by God so that David was able to make his escape without Saul knowing.

The time of sleep is opportune for receiving divine communication. Samuel's call comes while he is asleep in the temple (1 Sam 3:1-15). Revelations from God occur in the dreams* of sleepers such as Jacob (Gen

28:10-15), Joseph (Gen 37:5, 9), Solomon (1 Kgs 3:5-15), and Daniel (Dan 7:1-28).

Finally, sleep is a metaphor for death, as in Daniel 12:2, "Many of those who sleep in the dust of the earth shall awake; some shall live forever, others shall be an everlasting horror and disgrace."

New Testament

Sleep has similar connotations in the NT. It is part of the rhythm of life (Mark 4:26-29). When the hour grows late, one naturally succumbs to sleep, as do the ten virgins (Matt 25:5) and Eutychus (Acts 20:9-10).

As in the psalms, the ability to sleep peacefully indicates one's uprightness and faith in God. Jesus, in contrast to his disciples who have little faith, sleeps soundly during a great storm on the Sea of Galilee (Matt 8:23-27; Mark 4:35-41; Luke 8:22-25).

On the other hand, Jesus' sleeplessness during nights of prayer (Mark 1:35; Luke 6:12) is to be emulated. Before his arrest at Gethsemane, Jesus reproves his disciples for sleeping while he remains awake, praying (Mark 14:37; Matt 26:41; Luke 22:46). Their sleep is a sign of weakness (Mark 14:38; Matt 26:41) or sorrow (Luke 22:45). Similarly, Peter, John, and James sleep at the transfiguration while Jesus discusses his coming "exodus" with Moses and Elijah (Luke 9:32).

There are frequent exhortations in the NT not to be found sleeping at the second coming of Christ: "Be watchful! Be alert! . . . May he not come suddenly and find you sleeping" (Mark 13:33, 36; similarly Matt 25:13; Rom 13:11; 1 Thess 5:6). One must beware since sleep provides an opportunity for one's enemies to accomplish their purposes (Matt 13:25; 28:13).

Sleep is also a euphemism for death in the NT. Paul reassures the Thessalonians who are concerned about "those who have fallen asleep" before the second coming that "whether we are awake or asleep" all will "live together with him" (1 Thess 5:10; see also Matt 27:52; Acts 7:60; 13:36; 1 Cor 7:39; 11:30; 15:6, 18, 20, 51; 2 Pet 3:4). In Ephesians 5:14 sleep is a metaphor for the death that is life without Christ. The baptismal hymn exhorts, "Awake, O sleeper, and arise from the dead, and Christ will give you light."

Sleep is mistaken for death in the story of the raising of Jairus' daughter (Matt 9:24; Mark 5:39; Luke 8:52). In John 11:11-13 the opposite error is made. Jesus tells his disciples, "'Our friend Lazarus is asleep, but I am going to awaken him' . . . Jesus was talking about his death, while they thought that he meant ordinary sleep."

Sleep as a time for God's communication in dreams is found in Matthew 1:20-24; 2:12, 13, 19, 22; 27:19. God reveals the divine plan regarding Jesus' birth to Joseph, diverts the Magi away from Herod, directs the sojourn of the holy family to Egypt and Galilee, and makes known to Pilate's wife that Jesus is a "righteous man."

Pastoral-Liturgical Tradition

Sleep continues to be used as a metaphor for death in Christian tradition. In the opening prayer of the Christian funeral liturgy, Christ is addressed as "the firstfruits of all who have fallen asleep." Likewise, Eucharistic Prayer I commemorates the dead as "all who sleep in Christ."

There are a number of Christian legends of saints who slept for years and then awoke. One such is associated with Ephesus, dating to the latter part of the fifth century. According to the legend, there were seven young men who refused to offer sacrifice to the Emperor Decius. They took refuge in a cave, where they fell asleep for two hundred years. Upon awakening they were amazed to discover not only the length of their sleep, but also that Christianity had spread throughout the whole empire. When Emperor Theodosius II heard of the incident, he is said to have accepted it as evidence of resurrection. At their death, the seven sleepers were buried in their cave, on which a church was later built. It was surrounded by several hundred graves, dating to the fifth and sixth centuries, as Christians regarded the seven as holy.

927

See: DEATH, DREAMS, DRUNKENNESS, LIGHT AND DARKNESS, RESURRECTION, WATCH

BARBARA E. REID, O.P.

SODOM AND GOMORRAH

The story of Sodom and Gomorrah (Gen 19:1-38) is a story about hospitality: strangers appear, Lot's household protects them, and they bless it with life.

Old Testament

Hospitality. Hospitality tests strangers to see if they are friends or enemies. The visitors pass their first test by declining Lot's initial invitation; protocol demands they accept only a repeated invitation. Passing makes them guests to which foot washing promotes them. Lot's household tests them again with a meal. Their table manners will show how well they understand their host's culture.

Before the assessment is finished, however, the men of the city convene. This is a technical term for a city assembly made up of young warriors and older legislators. It unanimously decides the strangers are enemies and plans to rape them, just as the Ammonites shaved off half the beard of each and cut off their garments in the middle, at their hips (2 Sam 10:1-5), before sending David's envoys away.

Sexual Behavior. Biblical cultures were concerned about personal sexual behavior, but not to the extent that we are today. They considered sexual behavior like marriage and rape from the point of view of social justice and as part of their social and economic institutions. Marriage established full diplomatic relations. Solomon had seven hundred wives and three hundred concubines (1 Kgs 11:3), because in his day Israel had treaties with at least one thousand countries. Rape, homosexual or heterosexual (Judges 19–20), cut diplomatic relations. Shechem's rape of Dinah (Gen 34:1-31) and David's rape of Bathsheba (2 Sam 11:1-27), were not only acts of sexual violence, but were hostile bids for economic and political power (2 Sam 13:1-22; 16:21-22).

Lot's Daughters. Lot offered his daughters to protect the strangers. We are understandably shocked by Lot's treatment of them, and their later treatment of him. We do not expect the Bible to endorse sexual abuse, drunkenness, and incest, but we are not sure what Lot's gesture meant. More than likely, Lot offered his daughters precisely because they *were* his life, not in order to protect his life. The ancients believed that parents who die live on in their children; children who die leave their parents to starvation and extinction. Lot accepts death by poverty and without heirs in order to defend his guests.

Certainly, the world of the Bible is patriarchal, and sexist interpretations of this and other biblical stories continue to put women today at risk. Nonetheless, the role of Lot's daughters may be much more noble than we realize. In at least three ways, the Bible portrays them as hosts willing to lay down their lives to protect their guests (Gen 19:1-29) and as ancestors willing to risk their lives to save their households (Gen 19:30-38), not as victims of sexual abuse and women guilty of incest. First, Lot is not an isolated individual, but a corporate personality, whose actions combine the actions of the entire household. Everything that can be said about Lot's hospitality should be said about his daughters' as well. Second, the hospitality of Abraham and Sarah recorded in Genesis 18:1-15 and that of Lot and his daughters found in Genesis 19:1-29 are comparable. Third, the strangers reward both Lot and his daughters, as well as their families, by offering to save them from the assembly and from Sodom's destruction.

Homosexuality. The Sodom and Gomorrah story is often read as a cry against homosexuality. Although slavery (Exod 2:23), idolatry (Judg 10:10), and murder (Jonah 1:14) cry out to God in the Bible, homosexuality never does. The story itself does not specify the outcry (Gen 18:20), and elsewhere the cry is against the unjust for mistreating the widow, the orphan, and the stranger, not against the homosexual.

New Testament

Implicitly and explicitly, the NT echoes the Sodom and Gomorrah story. In the stories of the Samaritan woman (John 4:4-42) and the anointing at Bethany (Mark 14:3-9) two women, like the daughters of Lot, are saved by their hospitality. In John 13:1-20, Jesus plays Lot's role and promotes disciples from strangers to guests by washing their feet. Matthew 10:14-15 remembers the cities as inhospitable; in Matthew 11:23-24 and Luke 10:13-16 they are unrepentant; in Luke 17:22-37 they ignore the signs of the times. 2 Peter 2:4-10 remembers Lot as an example of how God can deliver the righteous from the midst of the godless; Jude 5–16 indicts the cities for sexual promiscuity and unnatural vice.

Pastoral-Liturgical Tradition

In post-biblical teaching traditions Sodom and Gomorrah become symbols of sexual depravity in non-biblical societies. The liturgy, however, remains more biblical. The Lectionary parallels Genesis 19:15-29 with Matthew 8:23-27 to emphasize that virtues like hospitality and faith bring life not only in the present world, but in the world to come as well. The Holy Thursday liturgy offers the host as a model for ministry and the protocol for a guest as a pattern for biblical morality.

See: ABRAHAM, HOSPITALITY, SEXUALITY

DON C. BENJAMIN, O.CARM.

SOLITUDE

Religious solitude is not loneliness. It is the aloneness that helps us to realize that we are meant for God, and only in God will we find rest.

Old Testament

The Hebrew people viewed isolation from others as a dangerous and unnatural condition. To be "cut off from the people" (Num 9:13) was a curse and perhaps a death sentence in a nomadic society. That was the tragedy of one diagnosed as an incurable leper and forced to dwell outside the camp, more like an animal than a human (Lev 13:46). The creator had said in the beginning: "It is not good for the man to be alone" (Gen 2:18).

Still, the OT does express a positive attitude toward some kinds of aloneness. In his farewell blessing, Moses sees God's care in separating Israel from the other nations (Deut 33:28); Balaam's oracle speaks favorably of this "people that lives apart and does not reckon itself among the nations" (Num 23:9). Later, this isolation will turn bitter: "How lonely she is now, the once crowded city!" (Lam 1:1).

The ambivalence here is roughly equivalent to the difference between loneliness, a negative, and solitude, a positive, in today's language. Loneliness is like being a sparrow alone on the housetop (Ps 102:8); it makes one "alone and afflicted" (Ps 25:16). But when aloneness is presented positively, as above, there is the sense of being alone with God. Solitude is Moses on the mountaintop (Exod 24:2), or the people being shepherded by God "apart in a woodland" (Mic 7:14). It is what the prophets longed for in a romantic view of the desert, where the young bride, Israel, had been alone with God (Jer 2:2; Hos 2:16).

New Testament

Jesus experienced the kind of loneliness that is isolation in the midst of a crowd. Time and again his closest associates failed to understand what he was doing: "Do you have eyes and not see, ears and not hear?" (Mark 9:18). He could not satisfy his critics, whom he compared to mocking children in the marketplace (Matt 11:16-19). Once he cried out: "How long will I endure you?" (Mark 9:19).

But Jesus also sought solitude for communion with his Father. After a long day preaching and ministering in Capernaum, he rose before dawn "and went off to a deserted place, where he prayed" (Mark 1:35). It became his habit to stay outside the towns, changing a dangerous and forbidding place into a place of ministry (1:45).

He invited the disciples to join him in retreat after their mission: "Come away by yourselves to a deserted place and rest a while" (6:31).

In Luke's Gospel, Jesus is engaged in private prayer when important events occur: after his baptism (3:21), at the transfiguration (9:29), when asked about prayer (11:1). Before calling the Twelve he spent the night in prayer on the mountain (6:12). Even when others are present, he is said to be "praying in solitude" (*kata monas:* 9:18). The difference between the isolation of loneliness and the peace and strength of solitude is the awareness of communion with the Father (John 6:29).

Jesus promised that he would not leave us orphans, cast adrift in our loneliness (John 14:18). He would send us a Paraclete and he would come back to us. The Book of Revelation expressed the security of the Church in the midst of a hostile environment by the symbol of the woman being taken to the desert, where a safe place had been prepared by God (Rev 12:6). Early Christians who felt themselves to be "aliens and sojourners" in the Roman Empire (1 Pet 2:11) were supported by the nearness of God, "the shepherd and guardian of your souls" (2:25).

See: DESERT, MISSION, PRAYER

JEROME KODELL, O.S.B.

Pastoral-Liturgical Tradition

Solitude has two different meanings: (1) psychological and spiritual isolation imposed as a burden on a person (loneliness) and (2) a situation willingly embraced by persons in search of rest or inwardness. The first is often a dehumanizing factor, the second, an enriching one.

As regards the first—solitude leading to loneliness—the need for a ministry of companionship is becoming ever more urgent in a society of lonely people (divorced, widowed, broken and battered persons). Married couples can also suffer from isolation. Marriage encounters can help them escape from or at least cope with their solitude.

In the second sense, in Christian spirituality solitude has for centuries been the ideal milieu in which to experience God. Early solitaries and nuns fled to the desert or built their own solitudes outside towns. It became something of a commonplace to say that a minimum of solitude was necessary for Mary, the contemplative, while a minimum of company was unavoidable for Martha, the prototype of Christians in ministry. A problem arose when Christians undertook solitude as a permanent situation. It was soon realized that total seclusion could be borne only by mature persons, so that candidates for the solitary life were required to remain for a few years under an elder's guidance. In Palestine, this led to the creation of *lavras,* where solitude, reserved to mature members, was periodically tempered by community life.

Friars began to blend solitude with ministry. With the *Devotio Moderna* (fourteenth-fifteenth centuries), solitude became an interior disposition rather than a material situation. Catherine of Siena spoke of building an "interior cell" in her heart, an expression often repeated by the Jesuits. In fact, Ignatius Loyola, emphasizing the need for interior prayer and examination, made inner solitude a prerequisite for intense ministry. His Spiritual Exercises were extended to people from all walks of life, and eventually gave rise to periodic retreats.

Among us in our own times, Thomas Merton often spoke of the value of solitude, initially in a rather naive way: "escape as often as you can." But this was a luxury that few workers or parents could afford. Later, he changed his teaching, so that solitude became a way of "listening to the heartbeats of the world."

The whole Christian life is a tension between involvement and solitude. Christians are called to proclaim, to heal, and to share at table. But, like Jesus, they also need to retire to an out-of-the-way place in order to deepen their faith experience. This two-sided orientation reflects the twofold dimension of human existence, characterized as a self-in-solitude (which Sartre's existentialism pushed to an extreme) and self-with-others.

Christians retreat for a while from time to time in order to empower themselves for service and relationships. Moreover, a certain inner solitude must be kept even in the midst of the hubbub of life, since activity without solitude makes us superficial. A permanent contemplative solitude is fully legitimate. But as Teresa of Jesus, Therese of Lisieux, and Thomas Merton have shown, a solitary life is Christian only as a way of entering into a deeper communion with the rest of the Church and the world.

See: DESERT

JOHN MANUEL LOZANO

SOLOMON

Solomon is known only from the OT where he is portrayed as son and successor to David as simultaneous leader of Israel and Judah. He is the second offspring of the David-Bathsheba liaison (1 Sam 12:24; 2 Chr 14:4) who succeeds after elder contenders eliminate themselves and after Bathsheba and the prophet Nathan intercede for him (1 Kings 1–2). Although the length of his term, forty years (1 Kgs 11:42; 2 Chr 9:30), is thought to be symbolic, scholars have persisted in placing it approximately 960–922/918 BCE.

Solomon is credited with great wisdom and becomes the paramount figure in that tradition (Prov 1:1). He is also the Temple builder, an international trader, and the diplomat who forged or forced alliances on his neighbors. His administration reportedly established twelve territorial districts that reflected but did not follow exactly earlier tribal boundaries (1 Kgs 4:7-19). This is accepted as a strategy for weakening older allegiances without sparking rebellion. Such maneuvers for consolidating administrative and cultic power in Jerusalem were costly and led to taxation and hardships, including forced labor, practices that earlier traditions insisted were alien to the Yahwist (i.e., Israel's) values (1 Kgs 11:28). Therefore, later writers' judgment of Solomon is mixed. He is seen as the fulfillment of the aspirations of David and the Davidic line (1 Kgs 9:10-14), but also as the person who introduced foreign elements, practices, and personnel into his court thereby weakening or ignoring Yahwist religion (1 Kings 11).

This paraphrase of the Bible follows a tradition of interpretation primarily rooted in European scholarship of the 1930s. Source and historical critics who work within it accept the essential accuracy of the story-line in the Books of Kings and modify it in light of evidence internal to the biblical tradition. They see Jerusalem's power increased, at least in part, as a reaction against foreign enemies.

Recent studies have challenged both the portrayal and the approach that leads to such "Big Man" history, a view that credits sociopolitical change to aggressive nearly solitary leadership. Newer readings of the archaeological record and analyses that draw on social scientific models suggest that many claims are exaggerations if not distortions. Later royal theologians writing with political and religious motivation idealized centralization and attributed to characters roles and endeavors beyond those substantiated by history.

The march toward monarchy and statehood now appears more gradual and less certain. In the 1980s, social world critics applied anthropologist Elman Service's 1962 evolutionary model of successive stages of bands, tribes, chiefdoms, and statehood to tenth-century BCE ancient Israel. In that scheme, the period was transitional, a time when tribal organization was giving way to—but had not yet been fully replaced by—statehood. Accordingly, Solomon was at best the first monarch, not the second or third, and the Saul and David stories represent an earlier stage or stages in the evolution. Jamieson-Drake goes further by arguing that monarchy was not established in Israel before the eighth or possibly the seventh or sixth century BCE. The theory has not gained strong support, and its implication for Solomonic studies has not been explored.

Solomon's proverbial wisdom and power is known in the NT (Matt 6:29; 12:42) where he is also listed among the ancestors of Jesus (Matt 1:6-7).

See: MONARCHY

JAMES W. FLANAGAN

SON OF DAVID

Son of David is a frequent title of Jesus that has messianic connotations. Although it does not occur in this sense in the OT, its roots can be found there. Its ongoing liturgical use in the church can serve to emphasize God's saving action in a continuous history of redemption.

Old Testament

The phrase "son of David" is used infrequently in the OT to designate immediate male children of David (2 Sam 13:1; 1 Chr 3:1-9), including Solomon, who succeeded him as king of Israel (Prov 1:1; see Eccl 1:1). It is also used to designate more distant descendants of David (Ezra 8:2). Likewise David is referred to as the father of Solomon (frequently in 1 Kings 2–11) and of later kings of Judah: Hezekiah (2 Kgs 18:3; 20:5; Isa 38:5) and Josiah (2 Kgs 22:2).

In the OT "son of David" is not used to designate an expected figure. However, several passages promise the coming of a "branch" of David (e.g., Jer 23:5). Mid-first-century BCE Psalms of Solomon 17 does refer to the coming Messiah* as son of David. In the Dead Sea Scrolls the Messiah is called "branch" of David (4QFlor).

New Testament

In the Synoptic Gospels Jesus is frequently called the Son of David. Undoubtedly, the Gospels emphasize this because they proclaim Jesus as Messiah, and a messiah was expected to be the son of David. The expectation that a messiah would be the son of David is reflected in Mark 12:35; Matt 22:42; Luke 20:41. According to John 7:42 the Messiah was to be the seed of David.

One of the main purposes of the genealogies in Matthew (1:1-17) and Luke (3:23-38) is to establish that Jesus was the Son of David. Likewise the stories of Jesus' birth (Matt 1:18–2:23; Luke 1–2) emphasize that Jesus was the Son of David.

Elsewhere in the Synoptic Gospels Jesus is addressed as Son of David by those who ask for his help (Mark 10:47-48; Matt 20:30-31; Luke 18:38-39). This is particularly true in Matthew (9:27; 15:22). Matthew also says that in response to one of Jesus' miracles people asked if Jesus might be the Son of David (12:23), and that at Jesus' entry into Jerusalem the people cried out, "Hosanna to the Son of David" (21:9, 15).

Outside of the Gospels Jesus is not called Son of David, but we do find equivalent expressions. In 2 Timothy 2:8 Jesus is said to be of the seed of David, and in Revelation 5:5; 22:16 Jesus is called the root of David.

Many of the passages that refer to Jesus as Son of David reflect a concern to make it clear that Jesus is also more than the Son of David. This concern is probably most explicit in Romans 1:3-4. Here Paul summarizes the gospel as being about God's son, "descended from David according to the flesh but established as Son of God in power according to the spirit of holiness through resurrection from the dead." In this passage Jesus' descent from David is clearly affirmed, but the passage suggests that at his resurrection Jesus became something more than Son of David, namely, Son of God in power. Paul probably understands this to mean that at his resurrection Jesus was enthroned at the right hand of God as a cosmic ruler, surpassing the expectation that the Messiah would be a universal king on earth.

See: GENEALOGY, ISRAEL, MESSIAH, NAME, RESURRECTION, SOLOMON, SON OF GOD

TERRANCE CALLAN

Pastoral-Liturgical Tradition

The use of the title Son of David in the liturgical traditions of the Church closely follows the NT usage. It is a means of linking Jesus to the continuation of God's saving work, exemplified so strikingly in the establishment of the monarchy in Israel. What the liturgical tradition has done is to draw out the parallels between the David story and the Jesus story in more detail. This became especially important in iconography as a way of instruction and catechesis. Thus in illustrations in the Breviary, in frescoes and in stained glass, and in the block-printed picture Bibles *(biblia pauperum)* of the Middle Ages the stories of David and Jesus are paralleled.

In the liturgical tradition, the prominence given to the Psalms of David, particularly Psalm 110, underscores the Church's efforts to link the two stories. The connection is perhaps most clearly drawn in the blessing and procession with palms on Passion (Palm) Sunday, whose rites begin with Matthew 21:9.

In the iconography of the Eastern Church, a favorite image is David greeting Christ as he descends among the dead after his death on Good Friday.

The renewed sensitivity of Christians' relationship with Jews since the time of Pope John XXIII and the Second Vatican Council has caused focused attention on the meaning of Jesus as Son of David as a continuation of God's working a single history for our salvation. Previously there would have been more attempts to read "Son of David" as meaning a superseding of God's work through David and his descendants.

ROBERT J. SCHREITER, C.PP.S.

SON OF GOD

This entry explores the transformation of the expression "Son of God." In the OT, the use of this term shows that the person so designated has a special relationship with God. The second part of the entry discusses the specific meanings of this term as applied to Jesus in the NT. In the Church's tradition, this term became a vehicle for describing the nature of Jesus' unique relationship with God.

Old Testament

In Semitic languages "son of" is an idiom that indicates a relationship, but not exclusively or even primarily that of physical descent. Thus, in the OT many persons are called sons of God in order to indicate their special relationship with God. Most uses of the title fall into one of three groups.

First, members of the heavenly court, or angels, are called sons of God. Deuteronomy 32:8 says that when God divided the human race into distinct peoples, "He set up the boundaries of the peoples after the number of the sons of God." Other examples of this use of son of God to apply to heavenly beings can be found in Genesis 6:2; Job 1:6; etc.

Second, the people of Israel are frequently called son(s) of God. When sending Moses to Pharaoh, God told Moses to say, "Thus says the LORD: Israel is my son, my first-born" (Exod 4:22). Israel is also called son of God in Hosea 11:1; Jeremiah 31:9, 20. The people of Israel are called sons, daughters, or children of God in Deuteronomy 14:1; Isaiah 43:6; etc.

Third, the king of Israel is called son of God. This is related to the use of son of God for the people of Israel because the king was regarded as the representative of the people. Through the prophet Nathan God promised David that God would establish David's descendants securely on the throne of Israel. God said "I will be a father to him, and he shall be a son to me" (2 Sam 7:14). Psalm 2 is probably a psalm used at the enthronement of the king. In verse 7 the king says that God has declared to him, "You are my son; this day I have begotten you." This probably reflects the view that at his enthronement the king became son of God.

In post-biblical Judaism the title son of God was applied to the Messiah.* Just as kings had earlier been sons of God, so would the Messiah, the expected eschatological king, be son of God. We can see this in 4QFlor, one of the Dead Sea Scrolls, which quotes 2 Samuel 7:14 and explains that it refers to the shoot of David, i.e., the Messiah, "who will appear . . . in Zion at the end of days."

New Testament

Jesus is frequently called Son of God in the NT. The NT writings show evidence of several different ways in which the title Son of God was given to Jesus. First, Jesus seems to have regarded himself as Son of God. Second, the earliest Christians believed that Jesus was the Messiah and thus that he was also Son of God. Third, Son of God proved to be very useful to the early Church as it proclaimed Jesus in the Gentile world. Fourth, Son of God became the vehicle for an increasingly exalted understanding of Jesus.

Jesus. In the Gospels Jesus frequently calls God his father (e.g., Matt 7:21) and less often refers to himself as son or Son of God. To some extent this presentation of Jesus as saying that he was the Son of God undoubtedly reflects the later belief of his followers that he was the Son of God. But that the historical Jesus spoke of God as his father is very likely. One thing that supports this is the presence of *abba*, an Aramaic word meaning father, in the Greek text of Mark 14:36. This may go back to the historical Jesus and may have been used by Greek-speaking Christians (see Gal 4:6; Rom 8:15) because of that.

It is not clear what self-understanding is implied by Jesus' use of "father" for God and "son" for himself. In the Gospels Jesus also frequently calls God the father of those to whom he is speaking (e.g., Matt 5:45). It is possible that Jesus regarded himself as Son of God in the same sense that many others were children of God. On the other hand, some passages suggest that Jesus saw himself as Son of God in a unique sense. Most important is Matthew 11:25-27; Luke 10:21-22. In addition, an understanding of Jesus as Son of God in a unique sense pervades the Gospel of John (e.g., John 1:18). In the light of this it seems possible that Jesus saw himself as Son of God in the sense that he had a special mission to reveal God to the world.

Messiah and Son of God. The connection between Messiah and Son of God was even more important as a reason for the early Church to call Jesus Son of God. The most basic belief of the early Church about Jesus

was that he was the Messiah. Since the Messiah would be Son of God, the belief that Jesus was the Messiah implied that he was also Son of God. This equivalence is clear in several NT passages. In Matthew 16:16 Peter confesses that Jesus is "the Messiah, the Son of the living God." In Mark 14:61 and Matthew 26:63 the high priest asks Jesus, "Are you the Messiah, the Son of the Blessed One?" (see also Mark 1:1; John 11:27; 20:31).

The Usefulness of "Son of God" in the Gentile Mission. When the early Christians began to proclaim the gospel of Jesus to Gentiles, they found that proclaiming him as the Messiah communicated very little. Since this title embodied the basic belief of the early Christians about Jesus, it could not be abandoned. So they attached it to Jesus' name almost as a second name, and relied on equivalent titles like Son of God to say who Jesus was.

The early Christians could do this because son of God was a title used by Gentiles with a meaning fairly close to the meaning it had for Christians. First, son of god designated divine and semi-divine offspring of Zeus and other gods. Second, for the Stoics all human beings were by nature sons of god, since they shared in the divine reason that orders the cosmos (see Acts 17:28). Third, the Roman emperors from Augustus onward called themselves sons of god, meaning that they were the sons of their divinized predecessors.

In saying that Jesus was the Son of God the earliest Christians intended to communicate something close to what it meant to say that Jesus was the Messiah, i.e., that he was the eschatological king sent by God to save the world. What Gentiles spontaneously understood by son of God was not identical to that, but it was close enough to be useful. In proclaiming Jesus as son of God, the early Christians would have needed to clarify the meaning of the term as they used it. It meant that Jesus was something like those acknowledged as sons of god by the Hellenistic world, but with important differences. Most of all it was necessary to make it clear that Christians acknowledged only one God, and that Jesus would be fully revealed as Son of God when he came again (see 1 Thess 1:9-10).

Further Developments. Early Christian use of the title Son of God in proclaiming Jesus, especially in the Gentile world, was one factor that encouraged development in the early Christian understanding of Jesus. Use of this title, which also applied to heavenly beings and divinities, made it easy to think of Jesus as something like them. This, along with the early Christians' present experience of Jesus in their midst, moved them to think of Jesus as Son of God in the sense that he was a heavenly being. And they saw Jesus as a heavenly being in two distinct ways. First, they saw his resurrection as God's exaltation of Jesus to heaven and God's enthronement of Jesus at God's right hand, where he rules over heaven and earth. Second, they believed that Jesus had been a heavenly being even before his birth as a human being. Having been with God from the beginning, he was sent by God to become a human being, to die, rise, and return to God from whom he came. Thus, Son of God, which was originally synonymous with Messiah as applied to Jesus, came to mean something more than Messiah.

This development is clear in Romans 1:3-4. In this passage Paul contrasts Jesus' descent from David according to the flesh with his being made Son of God in power according to the spirit of holiness by his resurrection from the dead. At the earliest stage, to call Jesus Son of David and to call him Son of God were two ways of saying the same thing, i.e., that he was the Messiah. But Paul here sees Son of God as saying much more than Son of David. By saying that Jesus became Son of God in power at his resurrection, Paul means that he was enthroned in heaven to rule at God's right hand.

In other passages we see that Son of God not only refers to the exaltation of Jesus after his resurrection, but also to his pre-existence. The Letter to the Hebrews begins by saying that God "spoke to us through a son . . . through whom he created the universe," who "sustains all things by his mighty word. When he had accomplished purification from sins, he took his seat at the right hand of the Majesty on high" (1:2-3).

See: ANGEL, FATHER, MESSIAH, NAME, POWER, RESURRECTION, SON OF DAVID

TERRANCE CALLAN

Pastoral-Liturgical Tradition

As the early Church moved out of its predominantly Semitic context and into the predominantly Hellenistic context of the Mediterranean world, its understanding of addressing Jesus as Son of God underwent a corresponding shift. In that Semitic cultural context, to address Jesus as Son of God was to draw attention to his role in God's saving activity, how he acted on God's behalf as God's emissary. In that role, Jesus held special status with God. This line of thinking continued in the Semitic contexts of early Christianity, and saw Jesus of Nazareth, as Son, as having been adopted by God. This approach, however, seemed unsatisfactory and even insufficient to express the experience of the risen Jesus in the community.

In Hellenistic Christianity the focus shifted from looking at Jesus' role in God's saving plan to a greater focus on the nature of the relation of Jesus to God. Both the inadequacy of the so-called "adoptionist" approach in Semitic Christianity and the Hellenistic preoccupation with metaphysics prompted this. The early Church Fathers, picking the strands of the biblical traditions of the Image of God, of Wisdom, and of the *Logos* (Word), began to build a position whereby Jesus' relation to God went much further than adoption. Jesus came to be seen as sharing divinity fully with the Father as Son. Since this seemed to contradict the monotheism of the Jewish tradition, it was resisted in some quarters. These latter suggested that, while partaking in divinity, the Son must still somehow be subordinated to the Father. Most notable among this group was the priest Arius. At the Council of Nicaea in 325, it was declared that the Son was begotten of the Father before time began, but not as a creature, and is one in being with the Father (Greek: *homoousios*) (DS 125). This formula appears in the Nicene-Constantinopolitan Creed and has been the teaching of the Church ever since.

Related to Jesus' being Son of God is the filiation (sonship and daughtership) of all who are taken up into the Body of Christ by baptism. This understanding of the destiny of Christians grew out of the Eastern understanding of divinization, whereby human beings are called to share in divinity. Our filiation to God occurs through Christ by dying and rising with him in baptism. Traditionally this understanding of sonship and daughtership has been elaborated in a theology of grace.

See: JESUS, MESSIAH

ROBERT J. SCHREITER, C.PP.S.

SON OF MAN

In the OT son of Man is a synonym for human being. In Daniel 7:13 Son of Man is used to indicate that a symbolic figure of the last days is human in appearance. In the NT Jesus seems to have used Son of Man in two different ways: as a way of referring to himself, and in reference to Daniel 7:13. After Jesus' death and resurrection, his followers expressed their expectation that he would come again by identifying him with the Son of Man of Daniel 7:13. Outside of the gospel tradition Son of Man was little used by the first-century Church. It was revived in the Patristic era as an expression of Jesus' humanity.

Old Testament

The phrase Son of Man embodies one idiomatic use of "son of" in Semitic languages, namely its use to indicate membership in a group or class. "Man" in this phrase translates *ʾādām*, which means "human being."

Thus Son of Man means "member of the human race" or simply "human being."

"Son of Man" or "sons of man" is found rather frequently in the OT, mainly in poetic passages. It is often used as a parallel expression for man, presumably in order to provide variety. Numbers 23:19 is typical: "God is not man that he should speak falsely, nor [a son of man], that he should change his mind." For other examples of this see 2 Samuel 7:14; Isaiah 51:12; etc. In other passages "sons of man" is used in speaking of the human race in relationship to God. This is especially common in the psalms (e.g., Pss 11:14; 12:2; etc.).

In the Book of Ezekiel "Son of Man" is used ninety-three times as God addresses the prophet (e.g., 2:1). In Daniel 8:17 Gabriel uses "Son of Man" to address Daniel.

The single most important OT occurrence of "Son of Man" is found in Daniel 7:13. Daniel 7 recounts a vision in which Daniel first sees four beasts (vv. 3-8); then he sees the Ancient One judge the four beasts (vv. 9-12) and give dominion to "one like a son of man" (vv. 13-14). This vision is interpreted in verses 17-18. The four beasts and the "one like a son of man" are symbolic figures. The beasts represent four kingdoms; the "one like a son of man" represents the holy ones of the Most High. He is described as "one like a son of man" to indicate that he is human in appearance, unlike the four beasts. The holy ones of the Most High are probably the faithful people of Israel.

It is currently debated whether or not subsequent to the composition of Daniel 7, i.e., in post-biblical literature, Son of Man became the title of an expected eschatological figure. It is clear that by the first century CE Daniel 7:13 was understood as referring to an individual who would play a part in the final judgment. However, it is not certain that the Son of Man had become an expected figure in people's minds such that even when they were not thinking of Daniel 7:13 they would understand the phrase as referring to that figure. It seems more likely that it was only when Daniel

7:13 was in view that Son of Man would have this meaning. At other times Son of Man would have its ordinary sense in Hebrew or Aramaic. Son of Man is used in this ordinary sense in the Dead Sea Scrolls (see 1QS 11.20; 1QH 4.30).

New Testament

Apart from Acts 7:56; Hebrews 2:6 (quoting Ps 8:5); Revelation 1:13; 14:14, "Son of Man" is found in the NT only in the Gospels, and there only in sayings of Jesus. But it is very common in the sayings of Jesus. This probably means that the title Son of Man was used by Jesus himself and expresses a very early understanding of Jesus, even though it is not found in the NT writings which antedate the Gospels. However, the many occurrences of the title Son of Man in the sayings of Jesus present a somewhat complicated picture. As yet there is no general agreement among scholars about what Jesus meant by using this title, or about its meaning for the early Church. I propose to begin answering these questions by asking whether "Son of Man," as used in the sayings of Jesus, refers to Daniel 7:13 or not, and whether it refers to Jesus or not.

Does "Son of Man" Refer to Daniel 7:13? In many sayings of Jesus the Son of Man he refers to is clearly the figure of Daniel 7:13. For example in Mark 13:26; Matt 24:30; Luke 21:27 Jesus says, "Then they will see 'the Son of Man coming in the clouds' with great power and glory." (See also Matt 13:41; 16:27-28; 25:31; and perhaps John 5:27.)

On the other hand, "Son of Man" in many sayings of Jesus does not seem to refer to the figure mentioned in Daniel 7:13. This is true first of all in sayings where "Son of Man" seems to have no content. For example, in Matthew 16:13-15 Jesus asks his disciples, "Who do people say that the Son of Man is?" The disciples respond, "Some say John the Baptizer, others Elijah, still others Jeremiah or one of the other prophets." Then Jesus asks, "Who do you say that I am?" This exchange presupposes that "Son of Man" is equivalent to "I" and

communicates nothing about the person called the Son of Man, certainly not that he is the one mentioned in Daniel 7:13. The person called Son of Man must be further identified as John or a prophet. (See also John 9:35-36; 12:34.)

Second, "Son of Man" does not seem to refer to the figure mentioned in Daniel 7:13 in sayings in which Jesus says something about the Son of Man that is not related to the description in Daniel 7. For example, in Mark 2:10; Matthew 9:6; Luke 5:24 Jesus says that "the Son of Man has authority on earth to forgive sins." In Matthew 8:20; Luke 9:58 Jesus says that "the Son of Man has nowhere to lay his head." (See also Matt 11:19; Luke 7:34; 19:10.)

Third and most emphatically, "Son of Man" does not seem to refer to the figure mentioned in Daniel 7:13 in sayings in which Jesus speaks about the suffering and death of the Son of Man. This seems to have no relationship to the Son of Man of Daniel 7:13. In passages like Mark 14:21; Matthew 26:24; Luke 22:22 and elsewhere Jesus speaks of the betrayal of the Son of Man. In Mark 8:31; Luke 9:22 and many other passages Jesus predicts the suffering and death of the Son of Man. In John 3:14; 8:28; and 12:34 Jesus says that the Son of Man will be lifted up. This refers to crucifixion, but sees crucifixion as the first stage in being lifted up to rejoin the Father.

Does "Son of Man" Refer to Jesus? In some sayings of Jesus it is fairly clear that "Son of Man" refers to Jesus himself. This is clearest in a passage like Matthew 16:13 where "Son of Man" is equivalent to "I." But it is also fairly clear in Mark 2:10 and parallels where Jesus, having forgiven the sins of the paralytic, says that he will show the bystanders that the Son of Man has authority to forgive sins by healing the paralytic. It is also clear in Mark 14:21 and parallels where Jesus, after speaking of his own betrayal, talks about the betrayal of the Son of Man.

However, in many sayings of Jesus it is possible that "Son of Man" refers to someone other than Jesus. This possibility results largely from the fact that "Son of Man" is grammatically third person and would most naturally refer to someone other than the speaker in any saying. No doubt the evangelists understand "Son of Man" as referring to Jesus every time it occurs; and this interpretation is always possible. But considered in themselves, many of these sayings can be seen as references to someone other than Jesus. And in some cases, this even seems most likely to be the original meaning of the saying. For example, in Luke 18:8 Jesus asks, "But when the Son of Man comes, will he find any faith on the earth?" Jesus could be referring to himself, but it would be most natural to see this as a reference to someone else.

Further, "Son of Man" most clearly refers to Jesus in sayings where it does not seem to refer to the figure mentioned in Daniel 7:13. And conversely "Son of Man" seems least likely to refer to Jesus where it does seem to refer to the figure mentioned in Daniel 7.

The Meaning of "Son of Man" for Jesus. One way to account for this is to suppose that Jesus used "Son of Man" in two different ways. Sometimes he used it to refer to himself, with a meaning equivalent to "I." In doing so he might either have been coining his own term for himself, or making use of an idiom according to which "Son of Man" was a circumlocution for "I." At a later time this idiom was an established usage in Aramaic; it is not yet certain that this was already so in the first century. When Jesus used "Son of Man" in this way, he simply spoke about himself; he intended no allusion to the figure mentioned in Daniel 7:13.

However, at other times Jesus used "Son of Man" in order to speak of the figure mentioned in Daniel 7:13. In these cases it is not clear whether Jesus identifies himself with that figure or not. But it is clear that Jesus sees a close connection between himself and that figure. For example in Mark 8:38; Luke 9:26 Jesus says, "Whoever is ashamed of me and of my words in this faithless and sinful generation, the Son of Man will be ashamed of when he comes in his Father's glory with the holy angels." It seems fairly clear that "Son of Man" here refers to the figure mentioned in Daniel 7:13. It is not clear whether "Son of Man" refers to Jesus or not, though the latter might seem most likely. But what is entirely clear is that one's reaction to Jesus determines the reaction one will receive from the Son of Man. If someone is ashamed of Jesus, the Son of Man will also be ashamed of him or her. If Jesus is not the Son of Man, at least his mission is intimately connected to the coming of the Son of Man. (See also Luke 12:8; Matt 19:28.)

The Meaning of "Son of Man" for the Early Church. After the death and resurrection of Jesus, his followers came to believe that he was the Messiah.* But because Jesus did not greatly resemble the expected Messiah, it was necessary to explain *how* he was the Messiah, how he did the work of the Messiah. The earliest and most important explanation of this was that Jesus would come again and at that time do all that the Messiah had been expected to do. The followers of Jesus arrived at this explanation partly by identifying Jesus the Messiah with the coming Son of Man.

One reason they were able to do this was that Jesus used the term "Son of Man" in reference to himself; he also spoke about the Son of Man in Daniel 7:13 as a figure closely connected to his own mission. This made it easy for his followers to understand Jesus' references to the Son of Man in Daniel 7:13 as references to himself. Interpreted in this way, these sayings were Jesus' own predictions of his second coming in glory.

Another factor was that, as Messiah, Jesus fulfilled Psalm 110:1. This passage was seen as predicting the enthronement of the Messiah at God's right hand. And this in turn was connected to the enthronement of the Son of Man in Daniel 7. Thus the link between Psalm 110 and Daniel 7 also made it possible to look for a second coming of the Messiah. This view is reflected in Mark 14:62; Matt 26:64; Luke 22:22. When the high priest asked Jesus if he was the Messiah, Jesus said, "I am; and 'you will see the Son of Man seated at the right hand of the Power and coming with the clouds of heaven.'"

The title "Son of Man" continued to be an important way of expressing the expectation that Jesus would come again in the gospel tradition, even in its Greek form, perhaps because of its conservatism. But outside the gospel tradition, "Son of Man" ceased to be an important title for Jesus once his followers proclaimed him in the Greek-speaking world. The reason it is not found elsewhere is probably that in Greek (as in English) the phrase "Son of Man" makes little immediate sense because the Semitic idiom embodied in the phrase is lacking. Therefore, when the early Church proclaimed Jesus to the Greek-speaking world, they did not use "Son of Man" to express who Jesus was. Outside of the gospel tradition, the expectation that Jesus would come again was expressed by using the titles "lord" and "son of God."

Pastoral-Liturgical Tradition

After the first century, "Son of Man" once again became an important title for Jesus. This happened partly because the title was prominent in the NT. But it was also because the title was useful for explicating the nature of Jesus, a concern that loomed very large in the Patristic era. Patristic writers used "Son of Man" in conjunction with "son of God." "Son of Man" was seen as an expression of Jesus' humanity, "son of God" as an expression of his divinity. For example, in Tertullian's treatise *Against Praxeas* (ca. 213 CE) he says, "Of these Jesus is composed, of flesh as man and of spirit as God: and on that occasion [i.e., the annunciation] the angel, reserving for the flesh the designation Son of Man, pronounced him the Son of God in respect of that part in which he was spirit" (27.14). This usage is also found in the *Divine Insti-*

tutions (4.8.1) of Lactantius (ca. 250–317 CE), in the 229th *Letter* (ca. 418–421) of Augustine, and elsewhere.

In recent times, realization that "Son of Man" in the NT is not mainly an expression of Jesus' humanity has made the use of the title in this sense rather uncommon among theologians. However, this probably still seems to be the obvious meaning of the title for those who are not familiar with NT usage.

At the present time Christians (and others) have become concerned to avoid gender-specific language where it is not necessary, in order to avoid giving the impression that the masculine gender is paradigmatic. This concern makes the title "Son of Man" problematic. Obviously this phrase is no longer an acceptable synonym for "human being"; nor is it satisfactory as a way of referring to an expected eschatological figure. Even as applied to Jesus, "Son of Man" presents a problem. Although Jesus was male, calling him "Son of Man" seems to emphasize his gender unnecessarily. For these reasons many now minimize the use of this title.

See: DEATH, HAND, HUMANKIND, JUDGMENT, LORD, MESSIAH, PAROUSIA, PASSION, RESURRECTION, SON OF GOD, SUFFERING

TERRANCE CALLAN

SOUL

The notion of "soul" draws on both biblical and philosophical sources and has a variety of connotations in Christian tradition.

Old Testament

When one finds the term soul in an English translation of the OT, the underlying Hebrew word is generally *nefesh*. *Nefesh* comes from a root word meaning "to breathe." The noun form *nefesh* thus fundamentally means the neck or throat. An instance of this use is in Isaiah 5:14, "the nether world enlarges its throat." Insofar as the neck or throat is central to breathing, *nefesh* also means "breath" or "breath of life." Job 41:13 says of Leviathan, "His breath sets coals afire." A similar usage is evident in Genesis 35:18 where the dying Rachel names her son "with her last breath." And, in Genesis 1:30 God gives green plants for food to "everything that has the breath of life" (RSV).

To have lost one's *nefesh* is to have died. In 1 Kings 17:21 Elijah prays for the widow's son, "Let the life breath return to the body of this child." The absent or lost breath of this child, however, would not have been construed by an Israelite as having embarked upon an existence apart from the child; Hebrew thought did not conceive of a disembodied *nefesh*. In this respect, it is interesting to note that the term could also be used to speak of the deceased, "Do not lacerate your bodies for the dead" (Lev 19:28).

As various of the texts already cited reflect, because it is breath that is the ultimate demarcation between the living and the dead, *nefesh*, thus soul, in OT thinking came to be understood as the vital principle of a person's life. In Genesis 2:7 it is explained that God blew into the nostrils of the man who had been formed out of dust and how that dust then became enlivened with a *nefesh*, i.e., "man became a living being." According to Leviticus 17:11, the seat of one's *nefesh* is in the blood (see also Gen 9:4; Deut 12:23).

A tremendous fluidity of use for *nefesh* throughout the OT can be noted even in addition to the range of meanings illustrated in the few texts mentioned above. For example, in many instances *nefesh* refers to a person's matrix of emotions or experiences as in the phrases, "Why are you so downcast O my soul?" (Ps 42:6), "My soul weeps for sorrow" (Ps 119:28), "Was not my soul grieved for the destitute?" (Job 30:25), "My soul is surfeited with troubles" (Ps 88:4), "In my God is the joy of my soul" (Isa 61:10). *Nefesh* also has the meaning "life." In Job 27:8 "God requires [the impious person's] life"; in Proverbs 29:10 "the upright show concern for [the honest person's] life."

There are other instances where *nefesh* has the meaning "person," as in Genesis 12:5, "the persons . . . in Haran," and in Genesis 46:18, "she bore . . . sixteen persons." The same Hebrew term can indicate what is most individuating about a person, that is, the ego, and therefore sometimes functions as a synonym for personal pronouns. So, one finds in Genesis 27:25, "that I [lit. "my *nefesh*"] may . . . bless you."

Given the wide sampling of translations for *nefesh* noted here, it is evident that the OT notion of soul is embedded in a field of terms which do not betray any Hebrew anthropological perception of a dichotomy between body and soul as is found in much Greek thought. Rather, Israelite anthropology was monistic. Hebrew thinking saw things concretely, in their totality; human beings were not viewed as composites subjected to the dualism of body and soul which permeated Hellenistic views. Consequently, even though *nefesh* is in many instances translated into English by *soul*, the reader ought not to envision an entity that is capable of an existence distinct from or opposed to the body. In contrast, the OT sees the soul as essentially the animating principle of a body, the living being, the very self that makes a body into a living being. In the Hebrew view, then, one does not have a body or have a soul; he or she is a soul-body unity.

By way of possible exception to the general OT view of soul summarized above, the Book of Wisdom contains a few passages that seem to illustrate that the idea of soul therein is wholly Greek. In this book, originally written in Greek and included in the Septuagint, the term used for soul is the Greek *psychē*. While in some passages the word is used with the same meaning as the Hebrew *nefesh*, i.e., "life" (12:6; 14:5; 16:9), elsewhere it clearly expresses a body-soul antithesis, as in 9:15: "For the corruptible body burdens the soul." Wisdom 3:1, "the souls of the just are in the hand of God," may envision that the soul lives on in the hereafter, although it would not thereby necessarily imply that immortality is an inherent quality of human nature. Commentators have observed that while the author of Wisdom has accommodated to Greek thought, one must be cautious about extending that assimilation further than he did.

New Testament

As compared with *nefesh* in the OT, the NT Greek term for soul, *psychē*, is found relatively infrequently. Since the Septuagint had used *psychē* to translate *nefesh*, when the Greek term is used in the NT it normally carries most of the basic meanings of the Hebrew word. Thus, it can mean the vitalizing principle of life, life itself, or the living being. For example, in 1 Corinthians 15:45 Adam is said to have become a living *psychē*, "a living being." Mark 10:45 and Matthew 20:28 state that the Son of Man came "to give his life [*psychē*] as a ransom for many." *Psychē* evidently describes his mortal life. The use of the same term to denote individual lives can be recognized in, for example, Acts 2:43, "Awe came upon everyone [*pasē psychē*]." Finally, as with *nefesh*, *psychē* may also be the seat of emotion, as is clear in John 12:27, "My soul is troubled now."

Some have argued that while the Hebrew understanding of *nefesh* is present in the NT instances of *psychē*, such as those cited above, that under Greek influence *psychē* gradually became opposed to the body and was used for the immortal principle of a human being. A text that has been cited to suggest this is Matthew 10:28: "And do not be afraid of those who kill the body but cannot kill the soul [*psychē*]; rather, be afraid of the one who can destroy both soul [*psychē*] and body in Gehenna." Others, however, argue that *psychē* here points to one's inner life or true personhood that cannot be killed by others. A similar usage is apparent in Mark 8:37 and Matthew 16:26 where Jesus teaches that the *psychē* is priceless. Those who try to save it will lose it, but those who lose their *psychē* for Christ's sake will find it (Matt 16:25; Mark 8:36; Luke 9:25).

It is clear that Paul's use of *psychē* does not reflect the Greek notion of opposition between soul and body. For Paul, while *psychē* expresses the vitality, consciousness, intelligence, and volition of the self, it remains only an earthly, natural aspect of the human. While he does not usually use *psychē* in a derogatory sense, he nevertheless sees it as the life of the flesh, the *sarx*, not life dominated by the Spirit. Thus Paul calls whoever lives without the Spirit by the adjective *psychikos*, "natural" or "material," not *pneumatikos*, "spiritual."

The Pauline threesome of *pneuma*, *psychē*, and *sōma* in 1 Thessalonians 5:23, "May you entirely, spirit, soul, and body, be preserved blameless," likewise does not support a di- or trichotomization of humans. Rather, the three terms together describe the human being under different aspects. (*Pneuma* in this instance does not refer to the Spirit, and as such is not easy to distinguish from *psychē*.)

This brief survey suggests that in general the NT view of *psychē*, as with the OT understanding of *nefesh*, reflects a holistic anthropology. There is a text in 1 Peter 2:11, however, that is often quoted as exceptional in its implication that the author viewed the *psychē* as standing in antithesis to the *sarx*, "Keep away from worldly desires that wage war against the soul." Here it appears one's own fleshly attractions are understood as being capable of conflict with the *psychē*.

See: BLOOD, BODY, DEATH, FLESH, GEHENNA, HUMANKIND, LIFE, RESURRECTION, SPIRIT

FLORENCE MORGAN GILLMAN

Pastoral-Liturgical Tradition

The concept of the soul in post-Scriptural tradition is heavily influenced by Hellenistic philosophical thought that was impressed by the difference between empirical things, which seemed very transient, and the realm of ideas, thoughts, and judgments, which seemed to have a validity that was at least relatively independent of space and time. Hellenistic thought tended to relate these to two distinct principles of being: the material body and the spiritual soul. The Platonic tradition tended to emphasize the difference between body and soul and envisioned a loose relation between them in the human person. On the contrary, the Aristotelian tradition tended to think of a much closer relation between body and soul conceiving of the soul as the very form of the body. The Platonic tradition suggests a way of conceptualizing an independently existing soul with a natural immortality whereas the Aristotelian tradition suggests a concept of a soul that seems to cease when the human person dies.

While Christian theology found the Platonic tradition relatively congenial for its concerns for many centuries, it never accepted the concept of a naturally immortal soul as an adequate account of salvation. The idea of an immortal soul that survived death was always juxtaposed with the idea of the resurrection of the body. Only when both were involved was the concept of salvation satisfactory. The entire human person, and not one or the other part of the person, is the object of God's salvific will. In the Middle Ages, when theology engaged Aristotle as its primary dialogue partner, the theological definition of the soul could be given as "forma corporis" (see Thomas Aquinas, *Summa Theologiae* I, 1a, q. 76, a. 1, resp), but it was necessary to make adjustments in Aristotle's philosophy to make such an understanding of the soul amenable to the Christian understanding of salvation. The definition of the soul as the form of the body together with its implications would be accepted by the Magisterial teaching of the Church at the fourteenth-century Council of Vienne (DS 902).

While this Scholastic formulation emphasizes the unity of the human person and does not envision a fundamental opposition between body and soul, the philosophy of R. Descartes at the beginning of the modern era would radicalize the Platonic vision and would envision soul and body to be basically opposed realities incapable of interacting with each other. Here an un-

fortunate dualism was introduced into the question which had the disastrous effect of isolating the soul from the body and seeing religion as exclusively an affair of the soul. The implications of this body-soul dualism on Christian spirituality remain to the present time.

Contemporary philosophies and cosmologies frequently tend to forms of materialistic monism in which all human spiritual functions are interpreted as forms of chemical interaction. And even theology and pastoral care today in many instances seem more concerned with human persons than with souls. But the traditional concern of classical philosophy and theology for a genuinely transcendent dimension in human reality, which is the fundamental issue in the question about the soul, cautions against the temptation to be too easily satisfied with such reductionistic formulations.

See: BODY, HUMANKIND

ZACHARY HAYES, O.F.M.

SPIRIT, HUMAN

Old Testament

The Hebrew word *ruah* is generally rendered spirit in English translations of the OT. The original Hebrew signifies both wind and breath, and consequently, the breath of life by which all living beings exist. This breath of life, though temporarily resident in living humans and even animals, belongs to God alone. In creating the human race, God is said to have fashioned Adam from the earth and breathed the breath of life into the inanimate form, thus rendering it a living being (Gen 2:7). It is clear that although this breath or spirit is the force by which humans exist, it is always God's breath and not the equivalent of the human soul; it has no personal existence apart from God to whom it returns at death (Gen 6:3; Isa 42:5; Job 27:3; 34:14-15; Eccl 12:7; Tob 3:6).

Spirit in the OT also connotes the seat of emotions and of all human experiences (Prov 16:18; Eccl 7:8-9), not because these are immaterial realities but because they produce concrete and observable changes in the pattern of respiration. So it is that spirit is associated with anger and temper (Exod 6:9; Prov 14:29ff.; 16:22; 25:28; Judg 8:3; Mic 2:7). The spirit of Pharaoh became agitated when he awoke from a troubling dream (Gen 41:8). The spirit can be daunted or disturbed (Ezek 21:12) or even stirred up or enlivened for action (Jer 51:11). Behavioral traits and personal character are also described as expressions of spirit. It is a spirit of harlotry that plagues those against whom Hosea prophesies (Hos 4:12) and a spirit of justice that makes right judgment possible for the people to whom Isaiah announces salvation (Isa 28:6). There is a spirit of arrogance (Dan 5:20), of jealousy (Num 5:14), and even of anguish and despair (Job 7:11).

The workings of the intellect, especially in later writings, are also matters of spirit. The spirit of wisdom is given to Joshua for the proper guidance of the people (Deut 34:9) and to Solomon in answer to his prayer (Wis 7:7). Daniel's cleverness and mental powers are due to his possession of an extraordinary spirit (Dan 5:12; 6:4).

For all its association with what seems immaterial, spirit is a concrete reality. It cannot be said that spirit, in its usual OT meaning, is the immaterial dimension of living beings. Nor is spirit, when linked with a substantive (as we have seen above), an independent living being. The OT uses the term to indicate subjective attitudes or intellectual abilities, not immaterial creatures capable of causing these. Though spirit is distinct from flesh, this distinction has to do with its divine origin, not with its immateriality. It is different from flesh as divinity and humanity are separate entities. Spirit is divine while flesh is frail, sinful, and mortal.

Thus, what the OT names spirit can be spoken of as human only in a highly nuanced sense. While it makes human life possible, it has no independent and personal existence once separated from human flesh, nor does it contribute anything distinctly human to the existence of its possessor. The same spirit, which comes from God and gives life, is found in all animate beings (Gen 6:17). Animals as well as humans live as a result of being infused with the divine spirit, but a spirit that is distinctly human does not appear to have a place in the mainstream of OT anthropology.

The concept of a human spirit as the immaterial and personal dimension of human existence emerges only in late Judaism under the influence of Persian and Greek philosophy, appearing in Rabbinic writings and in the Books of Wisdom and 2 Maccabees. The existence of a multiplicity of intelligent spirits is found in the Book of Wisdom (Wis 7:22), and Wisdom herself "passes into holy souls from age to age, she produces friends of God and prophets" (Wis 7:27). In 2 Maccabees, God is the "Lord of spirits" (2 Macc 3:24). Not only does late OT literature and Intertestamentary writing speak of the existence of many spirits or human souls, but they also bear witness to a belief in good and evil spirits that can influence human beings and persuade them to act in one way or another.

New Testament

Spirit is the word used to translate the Greek "pneuma" of the NT books. As is true of the Hebrew *ruah*, the root meaning of "pneuma" is wind or breath, but in the NT it is seldom used with this basic meaning. It is more likely to signify the breath of life as the principle of human existence, a personal human spirit, and even good spirits and demons. Spirit as the inner identity of human beings or the life principle that departs at death appears in the Gospel of Luke and in the Acts of the Apostles (Luke 1:47, 80; 8:55; 23:46; Acts 7:59). Matthew also uses the word in this way (Matt 27:50). The OT opposition of spirit, the source of good inclinations, to the flesh, from which come evil designs, may be found in the NT as well (Matt 26:41; Mark 14:38). While this opposition between spirit and flesh does not imply that spirit is the immaterial component of human life and flesh the corporeal, the NT does develop this meaning for spirit. In fact, the spirit survives after death so that Christ is said to have preached to the "spirits in prison" who died prior to his own passion (1 Pet 3:19), and "the spirits of the just made perfect" reside in the heavenly Jerusalem (Heb 12:23). This is a meaning that goes well beyond the OT notion.

The Pauline letters employ the term "spirit" in several different ways. Paul seems not to identify it with a single specific philosophical or theological concept. In some cases it is used to connote the seat of consciousness in which reside the psychic functions of human existence (1 Cor 7:34; 16:18; 2 Cor 7:1; Phil 1:27). In other instances, Paul indicates that spirit does not belong to the human person but is lent by God to the Christian (Rom 8:15). While this may seem terribly contradictory, Paul's use of the term is not to be confused with the purely anthropological spirit or soul, which would be a necessary component of human existence. It is often that gift of God residing within the Christian which becomes the believer's innermost self so that one lives now by God's Being within rather than by one's own being. Thus it is possible for him to speak of spirit as extrinsic to human life and at the same time intrinsic to the life of the believer. The NT sometimes uses spirit (*pneuma*) and soul (*psyche*) interchangeably. When Paul writes of spirit, soul, and body (1 Thess 5:23), he is probably not making a statement about philosophical anthropology.

Another use of the word spirit found in the NT but only rarely in the OT is as a designation for good and evil immaterial beings. By far the more frequent references of this sort in the NT are to evil spirits or demons. In fact, the expulsion of such is an important part of the ministry of Jesus (Luke 4:33; 8:27; Matt 9:33-34). These evil spirits often know Jesus' identity but are forbidden to reveal it to others and are expelled (Mark 1:23-28).

Pastoral-Liturgical Tradition

The Human Spirit in the Liturgy. In the liturgical books of the Roman Rite, the Latin term *spiritus* is seldom used to designate the human spirit. This meaning is generally communicated by the words *anima* and *mens*. *Spiritus* is most often used with a substantive to express some inner state or subjective attitude, such as a spirit of adoption, humility, charity, truth, courage, etc. It is sometimes used with the name of the saint whose celebration is being observed. In such cases God is asked to give the participants the spirit of Paul or Augustine or Margaret Mary so that they might imitate their virtues. Otherwise, *spiritus* is used of the third person of the Trinity.

The word spirit is also found in the Latin text of the people's response to the liturgical greeting of an ordained minister. In this response, "and with your spirit" (now translated "and also with you"), the spirit is the charism of order resident in the minister; it does not refer to the personal soul. The only instance in the Sacramentary in which *spiritus* is clearly contrasted to body (*corpus*) is in the blessing of water for Sunday Mass. Here the blessed water is expected to counter every evil of spirit and body (*ab omni malo spiritus et corporis*). Ordinarily, this distinction is made by using the genitive couplets "*corporis et animae*" or "*corporis et mentis*." While both Hebrew and Greek Scripture texts use one word *ruah* or *pneuma* for the many meanings of spirit, the Latin liturgical tradition retains a stricter distinction of vocabulary.

The liturgical books use *spiritus* almost exclusively to mean an immaterial being that has no corporeal dimension. So the immaterial dimension of human existence is *anima* or *mens*, while *spiritus* designates either the divinity or demons, bodiless spirits. Angels are referred to directly as angels and not as good spirits. In the catechumenal and scrutiny rites, the evil One and the demons are called spirits. They are personal beings that can affect the candidates and they are driven away by the holy Spirit. The texts make it clear that the candidates are not possessed by such spirits but merely, that apart from the holy Spirit's power by which we are initiated into

Christ, all people stand to be influenced by them. Thus, we find here references to the existence of evil spirits but no references to demonic possession.

Discernment of Spirits. The pastoral exercise of the discernment of spirits has its roots in the epistolary literature of the NT. The ability to discern one spirit from another is a charism granted by the holy Spirit about which Paul instructs the Corinthians (1 Cor 12:10). Putting the spirits to the test is advised as a way to discern false prophets lest they lead believers astray (1 John 4:1-3). The basis for making such judgments is the observance of the fruits of the spirits in question. The acknowledgement of "Jesus Christ come in the flesh" is a sign of the trustworthy spirit (1 John 4:2). Paul's list is longer and has more to do with moral rectitude and personal qualities: "love, joy, peace, patience, kindness, generosity, faithfulness, gentleness, self control" (Gal 5:22-23).

The testing of spirits is further developed much later by St. Ignatius of Loyola, who applies the principle to the discernment of God's will in the life of the Christian. Personal decisions that can affect the life of the Christian should be arrived at only after a process of discernment of God's presence and activity in one's life. To be examined are the ordinary and extraordinary events of one's experiences as they might shed light on the interior life and, above all, the narrative of the Gospels, which, held next to these personal experiences and phenomena, illumine them and produce true discernment. Decisions arrived at by way of such discernment of spirits are likely to produce growth in the Christian life and conformity to God's Will.

See: GRACE, HOLY, SOUL, SPIRIT OF GOD, VISIONS

DOMINIC SERRA

SPIRIT OF GOD/HOLY SPIRIT

In biblical tradition the Spirit is God's animating presence in all creation. The Spirit creates and renews, giving capabilities to human beings, especially gifts for leadership. In the NT Jesus is conceived by and continually acts in the power of God's Spirit. Jesus, ministering by the Spirit of God, confronts and defeats evil spirits. A consequence of Jesus' death and resurrection is the pouring out of the Spirit upon his disciples, which empowers and directs them in continuing Jesus' mission. Christians continue to invoke the Spirit to give vitality and power to the life and prayer of the Church.

Old Testament

The underlying meaning of the Hebrew word for spirit, *rûăḥ*, is wind, movement of air, breath. *Rûăḥ* is the dynamic entity by which God achieves the divine purposes. It is the principle of life and of power. The expression "spirit of God" occurs ninety-four times in the OT, primarily in connection with God's power in creation and in animating Israel's leaders. The juxtaposition of "holy"* (*qōdeš*) with "spirit" occurs only twice in the OT: Isaiah 63:10 and Psalm 51:13.

The "spirit of God" (*rûăḥ 'ĕlōhîm,* also translated "a mighty wind" [NAB], or "a wind from God" [NRSV]) sweeping over the waters initiates the divine creative action in Genesis 1:2. In the second story of creation (Gen 2:4b-25) God gives spirit, the life power, to created beings. The first human becomes a living being by God blowing into its nostrils the "breath [*rûăḥ*] of life" (Gen 2:7; see also Job 27:3). Animals, too, have in them "the breath of life" (Gen 6:17; 7:15, 22). The Spirit of God both creates and sustains life (Job 33:4). When prophesying new manifestations of God's creative power, Isaiah recalls God's initial creation of the heavens and earth, and the gift of "breath to its people and spirit to those who walk on it" (Isa 42:5; similarly, Zech 12:1).

Spirit, though given by God to humans, continues to belong to God. The mother in 2 Maccabees 7:20-41, who saw her seven sons perish ahead of her, reminds them, "it was not I who gave you the breath of life." She encourages them to rely on the creator of the universe to give them back "both breath and life" (2 Macc 7:22-23). In Wisdom 15:11 a potter who makes clay idols is denounced "because he knew not the one who fashioned him, and breathed into him a quickening soul, and infused a vital spirit."

God's Spirit does not remain forever in mortals (Gen 6:3). A human being is one to whom "spirit has been lent" (Wis 15:16). God it is who preserves spirit (Job 10:12) and who takes it back at death (Bar 2:17; Eccl 12:7). The psalmist says, "if you take away their breath [*rûăḥ*], they perish and return to their dust. When you send forth your spirit [*rûăḥ*], they are created, and you renew the face of the earth" (Ps 104:29-30; similarly, Jdt 16:14; Job 34:14).

God's Spirit is what gives a person particular capabilities. In Exodus 28:3 God speaks of "the various expert workers whom I have endowed with skill" (*rûăḥ hokmah*, lit. "a spirit of wisdom"). Bezalel is endowed with "a divine spirit of skill and understanding and knowledge in every craft" (Exod 31:3; 35:31). Daniel, having the spirit of God in him, possesses "brilliant knowledge and extraordinary wisdom" (Dan 5:14). Solomon's prayer acknowledges that his wisdom is of divine origin (Wis 7:7; see also Prov 1:23). It is not age that gives one wisdom, but it is a "spirit" in a human being, "the breath of the Almighty," that gives understanding (Job 32:8; similarly Neh 9:20).

The Spirit of God gives "justice to him who sits in judgment and strength to those who turn back the battle at the gate" (Isa 28:6). Prophesying a reign of justice, Isaiah tells of when "the desert will become an orchard" after "the spirit from on high is poured out on us" (Isa 32:15). God's Spirit gives courage (Hag 2:5). The restoration of the Temple will be accomplished, "not by an army, nor by might, but by my spirit" (Zech 4:6). It is God's "good spirit" that teaches people to do the divine will and guides them on level ground (Ps 143:10). Rebellion against God is characterized as grieving God's holy Spirit (Isa 63:10). Repenting, Israel looks for God "who put his holy spirit in their midst" (Isa 63:11).

God's Spirit is what inspires and empowers Israel's leaders. Moses leads by God's Spirit (Num 11:17, 25). The Spirit of God raises up judges: Othniel (Judg 3:10), Gideon (Judg 6:34), Samson (Judg 13:25; 14:6, 19; 15:14) and comes upon the chieftain Jephthah (Judg 11:29). The Spirit of God rushes upon Israel's kings, Saul (1 Sam 11:6) and David (1 Sam 16:13). Isaiah prophesies of the messianic king, "The spirit of the LORD shall rest upon him: a spirit of wisdom and of understanding, a spirit of counsel and of strength, a spirit of knowledge and of fear of the LORD" (Isa 11:2). In the servant songs, Deutero-Isaiah speaks of "my chosen one . . . upon whom I have put my spirit," who will bring forth justice to the nations (Isa 42:1). Even a foreign ruler, Cyrus, can claim, "God has sent me, and his spirit" (Isa 48:16), as he is carrying out God's saving plan for Israel.

The spirit of God possesses prophets, moving them to speak and act on behalf of the divine. When God took some of the spirit that was on Moses and bestowed it on the seventy elders, "as the spirit came to rest on them, they prophesied" (Num 11:25). It is by the Spirit of God that Balaam utters his oracles (Num 24:2). Saul joins a band of prophets in their prophetic state when the Spirit of God rushes upon him (1 Sam 10:6, 10). David's last words are uttered through the spirit of God (2 Sam 23:2). The spirit of the Lord carries off Elijah (1 Kgs 18:12; 2 Kgs 2:16). Trito-Isaiah prophesies, "The spirit of the Lord GOD is upon me, because the LORD has anointed me; he has sent me to bring glad tidings to the lowly, to heal the brokenhearted, to proclaim liberty to the captives and release to the prisoners" (Isa 61:1; see also Luke 4:18). Ezekiel recounts how God called him to prophesy to Israel: "As he [God] spoke to me, spirit entered into me and set me on my feet" (Ezek 2:2; similarly Mic 3:8). Ezra recalls how, when Israel was rebellious, "You were patient with them for many years, bearing witness against them through your spirit, by means of your prophets" (Neh 9:30; similarly Zech 7:12).

Joel (quoted by Peter in his Pentecost speech in Acts 2:17-21) promises an outpouring of the spirit on all humankind in the messianic age: "your sons and daughters shall prophesy . . . Even upon the servants and the handmaids, in those days, I will pour out my spirit" (Joel 3:1-2). Isaiah also prophesied the pouring out of the spirit on the whole people in the messianic age (Isa 32:15). Similarly, Zechariah declares, "I will pour out on the house of David and on the inhabitants of Jerusalem a spirit of grace and petition" (Zech 12:10; similarly Ezek 39:29). This expectation of a future outpouring of the spirit on Israel, at times connected with the coming of a messianic figure, is found also in Intertestamental literature (e.g., *Pss. Sol.* 17:37; 18:7; *T. Levi* 18:7; *T. Judah* 24:2).

The prophet Ezekiel spoke to the exiles of the action of God's spirit in renewing Israel: "I will give them a new heart and put a new spirit within them" (Ezek 11:19; similarly 36:26). Thus, will they again be able to live according to God's statutes. Israel must, however, take responsibility to respond to God's action, making for themselves "a new heart and a new spirit" (Ezek 18:31). In his vision of the dry bones, God says to the bones, "See! I will bring spirit into you, that you may come to life" (37:5). The sinews and flesh cover the bones, but only when the spirit comes into them do they come alive and stand upright (Ezek 37:10). Thus does God promise Israel, "I will put my spirit in you that you may live" (Ezek 37:14). Psalm 51:12 speaks of repentance and conversion similarly, "A clean heart create for me, O God, and a steadfast spirit renew within me." This is possible when one has "a contrite spirit" (Ps 51:19).

God's empowering Spirit is passed from one leader to another. At Moses' plea for assistance, God takes some of the Spirit that is on him and bestows it on the seventy elders (Num 11:17, 25). At the death of Moses, "Joshua, son of Nun, was filled with the spirit of wisdom, since Moses had laid his hands upon him" (Deut 34:9). When the Spirit of God comes upon the newly anointed David it departs from Saul (1 Sam 16:13-14). When Elisha succeeds Elijah, he requests from him "a double portion of your spirit" (2 Kgs 2:9). After Elijah is taken up to heaven in a whirlwind the guild prophets remark, "The spirit of Elijah rests on Elisha" (2 Kgs 2:15).

To the ancient Israelites, everything that happened, both good and evil, was attributable to God's action. Thus, when Saul is tormented by an evil spirit (1 Sam 16:14-16, 23; 18:10; 19:9), this, too, is sent by God. A lying spirit is put in the mouths of false prophets by God (1 Kgs 22:21-23). In the Qumran literature a frequent theme is the struggle between the good spirit and the evil spirit.

Isaiah 31:3 contrasts the spirit to the flesh in speaking of Egypt's horses. This highlights that spirit is powerful, immortal, of divine origin, as opposed to what is weak and corruptible. There is no notion in the OT of a dualism between spirit and body, as is found in Greek thought. Nor is there to be found in the OT the idea of the spirit as a personal being separate from the creator. God's Spirit is the divine presence that permeates the whole world. As the psalmist says, "Where can I go from your spirit? from your presence where can I flee?" (Ps 139:7; similarly Wis 1:7).

See: BODY, CREATION, FLESH, GOD, GRACE, HOLY, LIFE, POWER, PROPHET, SOUL

BARBARA E. REID, O.P.

New Testament

As in the OT, the Spirit continues to be represented in the NT as God's presence and power. The Greek word for spirit, *pneuma*, has the same basic meaning as the Hebrew *rûăḥ*: "breath, movement of air." In the Gospels, the work of God's Spirit centers on the life and ministry of Jesus. At his death and resurrection, the Spirit is given to his followers to empower them to carry his mission forward.

Mark. In Mark, the Spirit of God or holy Spirit is mentioned at moments that are sparse but key.

John the Baptist says, "I have baptized you with water; he [the one who is coming—i.e., Jesus] will baptize you with the holy Spirit" (1:8). Here the image of immersion in the Spirit of God evokes such prophetic OT texts as Joel 3:1; Ezekiel 36:25-27; and Isaiah 44:3. To call Jesus the one who will "baptize in the Spirit" is to say that Jesus will mediate the endtime gift of the Spirit of God to renew the people of God.

Before that can happen, the Spirit baptizer must himself be baptized in the Spirit, the very thing that Mark next describes in 1:10-11. This description recalls at least three OT passages: (1) Psalm 2:7b, "The Lord said to me, 'You are my beloved Son,'" asserting that Jesus fulfills this messianic psalm: he is the expected king; (2) Isaiah 42:1, "Here is my servant whom I uphold, my chosen one with whom I am pleased, Upon whom I have put my spirit; he shall bring forth justice to the nations"— that is, Jesus is identified with the Servant of Yahweh portrayed in the scroll of Isaiah; he is the Spirit-endowed person who will restore the house of Jacob and be a light to the nations; (3) the detail about the heavens being "torn open" for the release of the Spirit evokes an OT fulfillment: it recalls Isaiah 63:19, "Oh, that you would rend the heavens and come down," words occurring in the middle of the prophet's prayer for a repetition of Exodus, when God "put his holy spirit in their midst" (Isa 63:11) and "the Spirit of the Lord" guided them (63:14). With these allusions, Mark celebrates the baptism of Jesus as the debut of the Messiah, the advent of Isaiah's Servant of YHWH, and the dawn of a new Exodus bringing about a fresh creation of the people of God.

That Exodus note having been sounded, "At once the Spirit drove him out into the desert, and he remained in the desert for forty days, tempted by Satan" (1:12-13). Jesus recapitulates the story of Israel's being tested in the desert. The rest of the Gospel of Mark will unfold the implications of this baptism of the holy Spirit until

it issues in the baptism (10:38) of the Passover events of the Cross.

The first healing act that Jesus does under the impulse of this holy Spirit (in Mark) is the deliverance of a man oppressed by an *unclean* spirit (1:23-27), a conflict that will typify his ministry (3:11; 5:2, 8, 13; 6:7; 7:25; 9:25) and receives direct commentary on the famous "blasphemy against the holy Spirit" statement of 3:29-30. Mark's understanding of the holy Spirit posits its operation both prior to the time of Jesus (12:26, inspiring David as psalmist) and afterward (speaking through arrested disciples in the post-Easter Church, 13:11). In the Gospel of Mark, then, the Spirit of God is mainly the animator of the endtime prophetic ministry of Jesus and the Church confronting the power of evil.

Matthew. Matthew's theology of the Spirit of God affirms Mark's and develops it slightly. The child that Mary bears has been conceived by the holy Spirit (Matt 1:18, 20). Matthew's account of the baptism of Jesus says it is the "the Spirit *of God*" that Jesus saw coming down upon him (3:16). When Matthew transfers Mark's material about persecution during the post-Easter mission from the endtime discourse (Mark 13:9-10) and makes it part of his version of the mission charge (Matt 10:17-22), he specifies that it is "the Spirit *of your Father speaking through you*" (10:20), words that fit Matthew's penchant for speaking of God as Father and focusing on the divine presence operating in the context of Church life and mission. When Matthew introduces his special formula quotation of Isaiah 42:1-4 at Matthew 12:17-21, he is making explicit a reference already inherent in the statement of the divine voice at the Jordan baptism scene. The full Servant-song quotation at 12:17-21 serves to comment on Jesus' nonviolent withdrawal from hostile opposition (12:14), his healing ministry, and the eventual outreach of that ministry to the Gentiles (12:21). When the hostile challenges of the Pharisees resume (12:22-24), Jesus identifies his healing/deliverance ministry with the inauguration of the reign of God: "But if it is by the Spirit of God that I drive out demons, then the kingdom of God has come upon you" (12:28). His healing/deliverance work, then, is a sign of both the Spirit of God and the reign of God, an early expression of the idea, to be developed later by Paul, that the Spirit of God is indeed the manifestation and the primary agent of the reign of God. The final reference to the divine Spirit in Matthew occurs in the baptismal formula of the risen Christ at 28:19. This is the perfect completion of a gospel that has announced Jesus as the one who will baptize in the holy Spirit (3:11), specified that it was the Spirit of God that came upon him at his baptism at the Jordan when he was publicly announced as God's Son (3:16-17), identified him as the Servant of Yahweh of Isaiah 42:1-4 (12:17-21) whose Spirit-led ministry would one day touch the Gentiles, and promised that the "Spirit of the Father" would speak through them on the mission (10:20).

Luke. Luke's two-volume work has rightly been called "The Gospel of the Holy Spirit." The phrase "holy Spirit" occurs fifty-six times in Luke-Acts.

Luke's infancy narrative concurs with Matthew's in asserting the divine conception of Jesus by the holy Spirit (Luke 1:35; Matt 1:18, 20). The holy Spirit of prophecy anticipates its powerful work in the ministries of Jesus and the Church by exploding already in the infancy narrative. Elizabeth (1:41), Zechariah (1:67), and Simeon (2:25-27) are each in turn "filled by the holy Spirit" in a way that issues in canticles that celebrate the good news of Jesus in the language of OT fulfillment. Even the unborn John the Baptist is said to be filled with that same prophetic Spirit (1:15, 41).

By means of holy Spirit references, Luke weaves a strong thread of continuity through the early chapters of Jesus' public ministry. Having been announced by John the Baptist's Q saying about the Coming One baptizing in the holy Spirit and fire (3:16), Jesus is said to experience the descent of the holy Spirit "in bodily form" (3:22).

Luke is aware that Jesus was conceived by the holy Spirit, making this a manifestation of what Jesus already possesses through divine Sonship rather than a new endowment. The genealogy, expressing sonship that is both divine and in solidarity with all Adam's children, leads to the Spirit-led encounter of the desert testing and, following that, the Spirit-powered teaching ministry in the synagogues of Galilee (4:14), right into the revelation of the sermon at Nazareth. There Luke uses Isaiah 61:1-2 and 58:6 to interpret the descent of the holy Spirit at the Jordan as the anointing ("christ-ing" in Greek) of Jesus as Isaiah's Servant of Yahweh (precisely the point made in Acts 10:38). At 10:21, Luke says that Jesus "rejoiced in the holy Spirit" when he praises the Father for revealing "these things" to the childlike. At 11:21, preparing the reader for the celebration of the gift of the holy Spirit to the Church, as presented in Acts, Luke alters the Q saying found in Matthew 7:11 to read: "how much more will the Father in heaven give *the holy Spirit* to those who ask him?" After recording two further holy Spirit sayings of Jesus already present in Mark and Matthew (12:10, blasphemy against the holy Spirit, and 12:12, holy Spirit teaching the persecuted what to say), the Third Gospel becomes silent on the topic, until the pneumatic explosion of Luke's sequel, Acts.

Acts. Just before the ascension, Acts 1:5, Jesus instructs the disciples to wait in the city to receive the "promise of the Father" (Luke 24:49). Here the promise is explained as the fulfillment of John the Baptist's word about Jesus' baptizing in the holy Spirit (Luke 3:16), a gift of power that will animate their mission of witness "to the ends of the earth." In Acts, Luke states clearly that it is the same holy Spirit that had already spoken through David (1:16) and Isaiah (28:25).

On the Jewish feast of Pentecost, amidst sounds and sights recalling the giving of the Law at Sinai, the community of the disciples received the promised gift of the holy Spirit, expressed through speech that was understood in many languages as proclamation about the mighty acts of God. The ensuing speech of Peter interprets all of this as a fulfillment of Joel 3:1-5, i.e., the end-time outpouring of the Spirit of God on the whole people of God, transcending barriers of age, gender, and class (Acts 2:16-18). Acts 2:33 explains the Pentecostal prophetic ministry of the Twelve as a sign of the resurrection of Jesus and the fulfillment of promises about Jesus ruling over the house of David and bestowing the promise of the Father.

The number of believers grows quickly from 120 to 3000 to 5000, and the power of the Spirit comes by way of repeated infillings that facilitate the prophetic ministry of word and healing: Peter before the Sanhedrin (4:8-12), the gathered community praying for God to continue the endtime Exodus in their ministry (4:24-30) and experiencing an "aftershock" of Pentecost (4:31), Stephen confronting the Synagogue of the Freedmen (6:5, 10) and facing his death with words that parallel his master's (7:55-60), Barnabas rejoicing when he saw the grace of God in Antioch (11:22), Paul confronting the magician Elymas bar-Jesus (13:9), Paul and Barnabas rejoicing after expulsion from Pisidian Antioch (13:51).

The holy Spirit is sometimes experienced in the community through its leadership. Ananias and Sapphira discover this in a powerfully negative way; their financial deception of the apostles is called lying to and testing the very Spirit of God (5:3, 9). And those who resist the Jerusalem Christians are said to oppose the holy Spirit (7:51). Positively, the decision of the Jerusalem Council to hold Gentiles only to the Mosaic rules for resident aliens is described as "the decision of the holy Spirit and of us" (15:28). Paul, in his farewell speech at Miletus, can speak to the elders and refer to the "flock of which the holy Spirit has appointed you overseers" (20:28).

One of the primary effects of Christian conversion and baptism is the gift of the holy Spirit (2:38; 5:32; 9:17). By exception, sometimes the endowment of the Spirit is delayed, as in the cases of Philip's Samaritan converts (8:15, 17) and the Ephesian twelve (19:2-6).

Prompted by visions and an impulse of the Spirit (10:19), Peter is led to preach the word to the Gentile household of Cornelius, whose response is confirmed by another "Pentecost," the gift of the Spirit expressed in speaking in tongues and glorifying God (10:44-47). When Peter reports this experience to the Jewish Christians of Jerusalem, he says that this was every bit as much a fulfillment of the Baptist's prophecy about the coming baptism in the Spirit as the gift of Pentecost (11:15-16) that the disciples had received. Indeed, in the later retelling before the Jerusalem Council, Peter uses words that allude to both Pentecost and to Ezekiel 36:25-26, "He made no distinction between us and them, for by faith he purified their hearts" (15:9).

Luke sometimes describes missioners' movements as suggested or prevented by the Spirit (8:29; 10:19; 13:4; 20:22-23). Usually this seems to be a shorthand way of referring to advice mediated by a Christian prophet, as it is spelled out at 21:4, 11.

Hebrews. Twice the author of Hebrews mentions the holy Spirit in connection with descriptions of the Christian experience in language very much that of Luke-Acts. "God added his testimony by signs, wonders, various acts of power, and distribution of the gifts of the holy Spirit according to his will" (Heb 2:4; see also 6:4-5). Three times the author refers to OT passages as spoken by the holy Spirit, 3:7 (LXX Ps 94), 9:8 (Exodus' description of the desert tabernacle), and 10:15 (Jer 31:33, 34).

Paul. In Paul, kingdom-talk becomes Spirit-talk. Paul apparently found it more congenial to his largely Hellenized readership to speak of the Christian experience more in the language of the Spirit of God than in the language of the reign of God. Writing to the Christians of Thessalonica, he thanks God for their response to God's initiative; for the gospel came to them not "in word alone, but also in power and in the holy Spirit and much conviction . . . with joy from the holy Spirit (1 Thess 1:5-6). In his exhortation, he reminds them that failure in the call to holiness in sexual matters is a disregard of God "who gives his holy Spirit to you" (4:8). He can describe their conversion being chosen by God for salvation "through sanctification by the Spirit and belief in truth" (2 Thess 2:13). Writing to the Philippians from prison, he alludes to the Spirit of Jesus Christ (see Rom 8:9) as the support that will eventually deliver him from chains. He refers to the "participation [koinōnia] in the Spirit" as one of the elements of community life which facilitate the putting on the mind of Christ he celebrates with the "emptying out" hymn of Philippians 2:6-11. Contrasting the spiritual gift of his relationship with Christ with his "fleshly" Hebrew pedigree, he insists that he worships "through the Spirit of God" (3:3).

To the Gentile Christians of Galatia who were being seduced by the "Judaizers," the conversion/initiation experience was so vivid and so closely identified with the gift of the Spirit of God that Paul has only to allude to it to make his point: "Did you receive the Spirit from works of the law, or from faith in what you heard? Are you so stupid? After beginning with the Spirit, are you now ending with the flesh? [A contrast also reflected in the OT at Isa 31:3.] Did you experience so many things in vain? . . . Does, then, the one who supplies the Spirit to you and works mighty deeds among you do so from works of the law or from faith in what you heard?" (Gal 3:2-5). Paul can interpret the blessing of Abraham extended to the Gentiles (see Gen 12:3) as the "promise of the Spirit" received through faith (Gal 3:14). Perhaps Paul's most memorable expression of the new life of the convert is the image that describes the convert, male or female, as adopted into the very "sonship" of Jesus Christ and is thereby enabled to pray Jesus' Abba prayer (4:6). For Paul the Spirit-versus-flesh contrast is not a matter of warring aspects of the human person but of trying to live on one's own power as opposed to living out a graced relationship with God. The first way issues only in "works of the flesh" while the second bears the "fruits of the Spirit" (Gal 5:16-25). Christian morality is a matter of "walking in the Spirit," living out that new covenant relationship.

Galatians turned out to be a kind of "rough draft" for Romans. The theology of the Spirit worked out in passionate exhortation in Galatians Paul developed at greater leisure in Romans. Christian hope is grounded in present experience: "because the love of God has been poured out into our hearts through the holy Spirit that has been given to us" (Rom 5:5). Elaborating the thoughts of Galatians 4 and 5, Paul presents his fullest pneumatology in the famous eighth chapter of Romans. What has released the Christian from the frustrating slavery to sin sketched in Romans 7:13-25 is the indwelling of "the Spirit of the one who raised Jesus from the dead" (v. 11)—also described as "the Spirit of Christ" (v. 9) or simply "Christ in you" (v. 10). Here Paul expands on the "adoption" image of Galatians 4:6 by adding the dimension of suffering with Christ so as to be glorified with him (8:17), a process of joining in the groaning of all creation until the full revelation of the children of God (8:18-25). Meanwhile, the Spirit intercedes for us with inexpressible groanings (8:26-27). In his conclusion, Paul describes his ministry as gathering a priestly offering of the Gentiles "sanctified by the holy Spirit," and as "What Christ has accomplished through me to lead the Gentiles to obedience by word and deed, by the power and signs and wonders, by the power of the Spirit of God" (Rom 15:16-18).

In his correspondence to that most charismatic of his communities, the Corinthians, Paul has, of course, much to say about the Spirit. He reminds them that his ministry took its power not from his personal talents but from the Spirit and power of God (1 Cor 2:4-5), that what Isaiah 64:3 had hinted about "what eye has not seen" God "has revealed to us through the Spirit" (2:9-10), that the gift of the Spirit of God has given them a "supernatural" understanding of spiritual things, an understanding that is nothing less than the "mind of Christ" (vv. 10-16).

Paul employs the image of temple of the Spirit both communally and individually. Speaking of the destructive nature of factions, he asks them, "Do you not know that you [plural] are the temple of God and that the Spirit of God dwells in you?" (3:16). Later, warning against sexual abuse, he refers to the body of the individual person as the temple of the holy Spirit (6:19).

Taking up the issue of competition regarding the "spiritual gifts" *(charismata)*, Paul runs through a sample list of the spiritual gifts (healings, tongues, etc.) to illustrate how the variety of gifts all come from one and the same Spirit of God (1 Cor 12:4-11). He then introduces the body-of-Christ image to urge that Christians use their special and diverse gifts as members of an organic body, working for the common good of that body (vv. 12-31). Later, in his extended discussion of the risen body, Paul distinguishes between a body animated by natural life-principle *(psychē)* and a body animated by a higher life-principle *(pneuma)* and climaxes in the contrast between the first Adam and "life-giving being" and the last Adam, Christ, "a life-giving spirit" *(pneuma zōopoioun)* (1 Cor 15:42-49).

In the second Corinthian letter, aiming to alert his flock to the distractions of the "outside agitators" he calls "the super-apostles," Paul calls the community to reflect on how they have experienced the gift of the Spirit of God that was mediated through his ministry. They had received the gift of the Spirit as a "first installment" of further messianic blessings to come (2 Cor 1:22; 5:5). The best "letter of recommendation" in support of the authenticity of Paul's ministry is the Spirit-filled life of the community itself, which he proceeds to describe as the realization of the promises of Jeremiah 31:31-33 and Ezekiel 36:26 (2 Cor 3:1-6). Further, improvising on a theme from Exodus 34:34, he celebrates their conversion experience as a lifting of a veil from their hearts and a turning to "the Lord who is the Spirit" (2 Cor 3:12-18).

Ephesians. It is fitting in this letter, which focuses on the universal community of communities, that the author should also speak of the holy Spirit mainly as the animator of that universal unity: Gentiles as well as Jews have been "sealed with the promised holy Spirit" (Eph 1:13), "have access in one Spirit to the Father" (2:18), and "are being built together into a dwelling place of God in the Spirit" (2:22). That Jews and Gentiles are coheirs of this promise is something revealed by the Spirit to the prophets and apostles (3:5). Growth in that vocation is a matter of being "strengthened through the Spirit" of the Father (3:16), being part of one body animated by one Spirit (4:4), and, consequently, immoral behavior is understood as "grieving the holy Spirit" (4:30).

John. If Jesus' kingdom-talk becomes Spirit-talk in Paul, this reflection of the Church comes to full narrative expression in the Fourth Gospel. Here John the Baptist speaks of getting a revelation from the Father about the identity of Jesus: "He on whom you see the Spirit descend and remain, this is he who baptizes with [the] holy Spirit" (1:33). The final reference to the holy Spirit in John occurs on Easter Sunday evening, when the risen Jesus breathes upon the disciples and says, "Receive [the] holy Spirit. Whose sins you shall forgive are forgiven them, and whose sins you retain are retained" (20:22). Much in the intervening episodes and discourses unfolds the rich meaning of that Spirit baptism. When Jesus tells Nicodemus that no one can see the reign of God without being born *anōthen* (meaning both "again" and "from above") and Nicodemus takes that on the literal, physical level, Jesus explains that he is referring to being born of "water and Spirit," an allusion to Christian baptism sealing conversion (John 3:3-16). To the Samaritan woman at the well (John 4), Jesus first mysteriously promises a gift of "living water" welling up to eternal life, which she misunderstands as a reference to well water, and then he moves on to conversation about worshiping "in Spirit and truth" the God who is Spirit. The connection between "living water" and the Spirit of God becomes more explicit in Jesus' utterance at the close of the feast of Tabernacles, where he promises rivers of living water to those who come to him to drink—which John explains as a reference to the Spirit those who came to believe in him were to receive after the hour of glory (7:38-39). When the man born blind is healed in the waters of "the sent one" (Jesus), though Spirit is not mentioned in this episode, the reference to Christian baptism and the healing of living waters is unmistakable.

Four times in the Last Supper discourses Jesus calls the promised Spirit *parakletos*, a Greek word that can mean comforter and advocate. The *parakletos* will be a "Spirit of truth" sent by the Father (14:16-17), a holy Spirit that will remind them of everything Jesus had taught them (14:16) and testify concerning Jesus, facilitating their own witness (15:26-27), an advocate that will vindicate Jesus, condemn the unbelieving world (16:8-11), the teacher who will interpret for them all they need to know about Jesus and the endtime things (16:12-15).

When the fourth evangelist describes the death of Jesus, he uses the curious phrase, "He handed over the spirit" (19:30). Another example of John's solemn wordplay, the words mean both that Jesus died (expired) and that this hour of glory (death/resurrection) is the source of his gift of the holy Spirit (recall 7:39). This is confirmed by the emphatic reference to the outpouring of water from the side of Jesus (19:34), a sign of the promised "living water" (4:10-14; 7:38) that is the Spirit (7:39). For John, the death and resurrection of Jesus is the Pentecostal moment and this is expressed in the creative breathing and commissioning of the risen Lord at 20:21-23. Thus, in his own way, the fourth evangelist illustrates how it is as crucified and risen Lord that Jesus becomes the Spirit baptizer.

The Pastoral Letters. In their muted way, the Pastoral Letters reflect the same sense of the Spirit operating first in Christ ("vindicated in the Spirit," 1 Tim 3:16) and in the community's prophets (1 Tim 4:1) and the general faithful (2 Tim 1:7, "For God did not give us a spirit of cowardice but rather of power and love and self-control"; 1 Tim 1:14, "the help of the holy Spirit that dwells within us"), who are all saved through the "bath of rebirth and the renewal by the holy Spirit, whom [God] richly poured out on us through Jesus Christ our savior" (Titus 3:5-6).

The Catholic Letters. The author of 1 Peter can speak of "the Spirit of Christ" speaking through the Hebrew prophets (1 Pet 1:11) and, more conventionally, of the preaching of the good news "[through] the holy Spirit sent from heaven" (1:12). Just as Christ was "brought to life in the spirit" (3:18), the dead are meant to "live in the spirit" (4:6) and persecuted Christians experience the blessing of Jesus' last beatitude as an endowment of the Spirit (4:14).

Like Paul to the Galatians, the author of 1 John points to the experience of the Spirit as evidence of God's presence (3:24 and 4:13). The context of these statements suggests that Christian prophecy is the experience he means. The criteria for discerning the spirit of true prophecy is whether the prophet holds that Jesus Christ "came in the flesh" (4:2).

Revelation. Four times the author speaks of the seven spirits of God (1:4; 3:1; 4:5; 5:6). Since seven is an apocalyptic convention symbolizing fullness, this is an apocalyptic way of referring to the fullness of spirit, i.e., the Spirit of God. The "seven spirits before the throne" of God (1:4), also described as "seven flaming torches" burning in front of the throne (4:5), are also identified as the possession of the Risen Jesus (3:1). This symbolism comes together in the description of the Lamb "standing as if slain": "He had seven horns and seven eyes; these are the [seven] spirits of God sent out into the whole world" (5:6). That is, the strength and wisdom of the risen Lord are now present in the world through the gift of the Spirit of God. This expresses in apocalyptic language what Matthew, Mark, Luke, John, and Paul said, each in his own way.

See: ANOINTING, BAPTISM, BODY OF CHRIST, CHURCH, COMMUNITY, CONVERSION, CREATION, GIFTS, GLORY, GOOD NEWS, HEALING, JORDAN, LAW, MISSION, PENTECOST, PEOPLE OF GOD, PROPHECY, REIGN OF GOD, SERVANT, SON OF GOD, TEMPLE, TONGUES, WITNESS

M. DENNIS HAMM, S.J.

Pastoral-Liturgical Tradition

The Holy Spirit and the Church. The coming of the holy Spirit upon the apostles at Pentecost* is often thought of as the event that gave birth to the Church, since the presence and operation of the Spirit is essential to the Church's existence. The gift of the Paraclete is the result of the Lord's death and resurrection. After rising from the dead, Christ breathes upon the apostles and communicates to them the holy Spirit who is the guarantor of the remission of sins (John 20:22-23). Christ's victory over death is brought to believers throughout all of history by the working of the holy Spirit sent by the risen One. Participation in the mystery of Christ comes through the operation of the Spirit poured out upon the Church.

The very same dynamic by which the mission of the Spirit results from the passion and resurrection of Christ for the establishment of the Church and for the salvation of the world is operative in every celebration of the Church's liturgy. This is most clearly observable in the Eucharist. As a result of the liturgical remembrance of the Lord's passion, the Spirit is poured out upon the assembly, establishing it as the body of Christ by transforming the oblation into a sacrament of the Lord's Supper. That is why the most perfect manifestation of the Church occurs when the Spirit-filled community gathers for liturgical worship (Constitution on the Sacred Liturgy, no. 2). In fact, the operation of the Spirit as made explicit in the texts of the Eucharistic liturgy is paradigmatic of the pneumatic function that animates all of the Church's liturgy and life.

The Holy Spirit and the Eucharist. Much of Christian liturgical prayer is based upon the remembrance of the great deeds of salvation wrought by God in Christ. This remembrance is at the very heart of Eucharistic thanksgiving. It provides, at the same time, both the motive for our giving thanks and the encouragement that gives birth to our supplications. Such liturgical remembrance, or anamnesis, is the work of the Spirit who reminds us of the words and deeds of Jesus (John 14:26). Anamnesis unleashes the power of the Spirit who makes our commemoration a participation. We become participants in the mystery we commemorate and so enter into salvation. Our anamnesis is no pious daydreaming or wistful longing for a past golden age of God's powerful deeds. It is itself a divine deed by which we become one with the redeemed of history. Remembrance is anamnetic participation in salvation when it is the act of the Spirit-filled community of Christ's Church. Thus the remembrance is both a participation in the mystery of salvation and a motive for giving thanks, in which act of thanksgiving the remembrance becomes itself an offering. This offering of thanksgiving, inspired by divine deeds for which there can be no adequate reciprocation, carries with it the worshipers' supplication for the continuation of God's mercy in the present and for its perfection in the future. This pattern of grateful remembrance and supplication is common to the liturgical practice of both Judaism and Christianity. It is the very heart of sacramental worship and of liturgical prayer.

The pattern of prayer described here is the action of God's people, yet it is possible only through the operation of the holy Spirit. It is the Spirit who inspires our remembrance and it is the Spirit who renders our memorial effective and powerful for us in the present and the future. For this reason, the Church's Eucharistic Prayers so often include an invocation of the holy

Spirit upon the oblation. Such an invocation is a natural outgrowth of the anamnesis. It makes explicit what is implied by our making memorial of the *mirabilia Dei*, the wonders God has wrought.

The earliest type of epiclesis appears in the form of a petition for the coming of the holy Spirit upon the oblation so that all who partake of it may be united in Christ. Just such an epiclesis may be found in the early third-century anaphora of the *Apostolic Tradition* of Hippolytus (*Ap Trad* 4). The unity in Christ, which is sought in the epiclesis, is not only the fullness of the sacramental effect of the Eucharist but also the hoped for culmination of all Christian life; it is the eschatological perfection of the *mirabilia Dei* of Christ's death and resurrection. After all, every celebration of the Eucharist is a proclamation of the Lord's death until he comes again (1 Cor 11:26). The holy Spirit, then, makes our anamnesis possible, the Spirit's presence brings about the sacramental effects, and produces in the celebration a prolepsis of the glorious life to be enjoyed in the eschatological reign of God.

Later Eucharistic Prayers make the operation of the Spirit more explicit still as they petition for the descent of the Paraclete for the transformation of the elements of bread and wine into the Body and Blood of Christ. Thus the communicants receive the elements that are a pledge of future glory and participate in a ritual meal which is made by the Spirit a sacrament of the Lord's Supper. The development of what is commonly called the consecratory epiclesis from the so-called communion epiclesis was an inevitable unfolding of the meaning of the celebrated mystery.

Although the Roman Canon does not include a pneumatic epiclesis, each of the Eucharistic Prayers approved for use in the Roman Rite since the Second Vatican Council does make use of this prayer form. An invocation of the Spirit for both the consecration of the elements and for the sanctification of the communicants may be found in all other families of Eucharistic Prayers. The East Syrian, the West Syrian (from which the Byzantine prayers evolved), the Alexandrian (from which the Ethiopian and Coptic prayers developed), and many of the non-Roman Western prayers of Gaul and Spain bear witness to the pneumatic epiclesis as a significant component of the Eucharistic Prayer.

Even the Roman Canon, which lacks an explicit pneumatic epiclesis, does exhibit some of the essential dynamism of this prayer form. The Canon makes intercession for the sanctification of the gifts and for the acceptance of the sacrifice without invoking the holy Spirit. Such intercessions make it clear that whatever is accomplished in the Eucharist happens by God's power alone. Our supplication, however, is not hubris, since it flows from the remembrance of God's deeds of promise; it is a petition at once humble and confident.

The power of the Spirit in liturgical prayer makes anamnesis both possible and fruitful. The Spirit is the harbinger of the eschaton, making present for us a foretaste of the banquet of God's reign. It is the holy Spirit who brings about in the present moment of celebration both the past events of salvation and the glory they promise for the future. This is true not only of the Eucharist, but of all liturgical prayer.

The Holy Spirit in Other Liturgical Celebrations. What is true of the operation of the Spirit in the Eucharistic Prayer is simply paradigmatic of that action in all liturgical prayer in the Christian tradition. It is always by the power of the holy Spirit that the sacraments achieve their purpose, and always by the operation of the Spirit that Christian worship is perfected. An examination of the major blessings of the Roman Rite will reveal to what extent this is true. The blessings of water and of oil, the consecratory prayers pronounced over ordination candidates, virgins, abbots, abbesses bear out the fact that blessing comes through the operation of the holy Spirit. The pattern too is always the same. Thankful remembrance of the deeds of salvation in Christ calls forth supplication for the continuation of God's gracious gift in the present and for its perfection in the future. The supplication is usually made by requesting the coming of the holy Spirit upon the person or element being blessed. It is the Spirit that guarantees the present application of the mystery of salvation.

Just as the Eucharistic assembly is established as the body of Christ by the power of the Spirit, so are individuals incorporated into Christ by the Spirit at work in the sacraments of initiation. Born again of water and the Spirit, the neophyte is anointed in the holy Spirit and led into the Eucharistic assembly to become a member of Christ's body by the reception of the holy gifts sanctified by the Spirit.

In the celebration of penance, the declaration of absolution announces that God has "sent the Holy Spirit among us for the forgiveness of sins." The prayer that accompanies the anointing of the sick asks: "Through this holy anointing may the Lord in his love and mercy help you with the grace of the Holy Spirit." And when oil is blessed for this anointing, God is asked to "Send the power of the holy Spirit, the Consoler, into this precious oil." Marriage is to be celebrated during Mass, whenever possible, because a couple is united by the power of the Spirit who effects the union of all in the Eucharist. The Liturgy of the Hours manifests the communion of the Church, which is itself a sign of the holy Spirit's presence. The descent of the holy Spirit still gives birth to the Church by making our liturgy a fruitful participation in the mystery of Christ.

See: BAPTISM, CHURCH, EUCHARIST, PENTECOST, REMEMBRANCE

DOMINIC SERRA

STARS

In the OT, stars are persons, a category of God's beautiful creatures. People who worship stars instead of God err. On the other hand, star gazing, so popular among shepherds and navigators, provided the ancients in both the OT and NT with useful information for daily life. While recognizing some

value in star gazing, the Church Fathers condemned star worship and astrology. Various subsequent Church councils repeated this condemnation. Contemporary Christians place their faith in a loving and omnipotent God rather than in their horoscope published daily in many newspapers.

Old Testament

The throne of God is set high above the stars (Job 22:12) symbolizing the fact that God possesses unlimited power over them (Ps 147:4; Job 9:7; Sir 43:9-10). The stars are God's creatures (Gen 1:16; Job 9:9; Ps 8:3; Isa 30:25-26; Amos 5:8). In spite of that, the Hebrews and neighboring nations often worshiped stars, chiefly because Mediterranean peasants personify nature and its forces. To the peasant, stars are persons who have power greater than humans possess. Because peasant daily experience confirmed that human persons are totally subject to nature and incapable of controlling it at all, these powerful star-persons were divinized and worshiped (2 Kgs 17:26; 21:3, 5; Amos 5:25). One aspect of Job's righteousness (31:26) is that he has not broken the prohibition in Deuteronomy 4:19 and 17:3 against worshiping the sun, moon, or any star.

New Testament

Belief in star-persons continued into the NT period (Rev 1:17, 20; 2:1; 3:1), but at the turn of the era the practice of seeking in the stars an explanation of one's fate or destiny became closely linked with astrology, which until then had been synonymous with astronomy. The astrologers who followed a star to visit Jesus at his birth (Matt 2:9) represented the tendency of that time and culture to cast horoscopes of famous leaders and extraordinary individuals.

Paul and Revelation show signs of familiarity with astrology and astronomy (Gal 4:2, 3; Rom 8:38; Col 1:16; 2:15; Eph 1:20; 3:10; meteors in Rev 8:12; 12:4). The commonly held belief that celestial phenomena had influence upon or were signs of the events that happened on earth seems to be reflected in the visions of Revelation. Still, both authors are critical of star worship (Gal 4:10).

Alpha Draconis was the North Star (Polaris) when the Babylonians began observing the heavens, but because of the earth's movement it was no longer the North Star in NT times. This explains Revelation's comparison of Satan with "the huge dragon [*draco*] who deceived the whole world" (Rev 12:9).

Pastoral-Liturgical Tradition

The Church Fathers and those they opposed agreed that stars were persons and not inanimate objects. Some Fathers believed that star gazing was useful for determining time, different events, and probable weather (Justin, Clement of Alexandria, John Damascene). Most condemned astrology, star worship, and belief in astral determinism (Minucius Felix, Tertullian, Origen, Gregory of Nyssa). Human beings understandably yearn to know about God's plans, but belief in astral determinism and astrology obliterate faith in God's providence and goodness as well as faith in the effectiveness of prayer and repentance.

See: PROVIDENCE, THRONE OF GOD

JOHN J. PILCH

STRANGER

The OT remembers that the Hebrews were strangers in Egypt. It shows special concern for aliens who later came to live among the Israelites. The NT continues this concern for the outsider. Moreover hospitality is a fundamental virtue across cultures. Responding to strangers then involves thinking of them as guests rather than enemies.

Old Testament

Summary. The word "stranger" suggests, basically, someone who is out of place where he/she currently is, whether as guest or intruder; or it may indicate someone who does not "belong," as being unacquainted or uninitiated, at least in a particular group.

These and other nuances are found in the OT, though they are expressed in various terms in the several English translations. Examples dealt with are the patriarchs, Israelites before their settlement in Palestine, resident aliens in Israel, foreigners, and God's people in general as only wayfarers on earth.

Patriarchs and Israel. Abraham, the other patriarchs, and their descendants, whether in Palestine or Egypt, and all of Israel during the oppression in Egypt, lived as strangers and aliens, until they were able to take possession of the Promised Land (e.g., Gen 23:4; 47:9; Exod 6:4; Ps 105:12). These are simply special cases of the "resident alien."

Resident Alien. The term "resident alien" can apply to anyone abiding in a place in which he/she is not permanently located or at least is not a full citizen, although the term has different nuances in different literary and chronological contexts; in some matters the resident alien was treated much like a native, in others like a foreigner. Different groups in Israel came to rank, at one time or another, as resident aliens, e.g., the native Canaanites after the conquest, those who fled to Judah from Israel at the fall of the northern kingdom, and some scholars think that in some later texts the term designates proselytes. Without full citizenship the resident alien lacked most legal rights and therefore was in need of special protection, which some of Israel's laws were designed to supply; thus the Israelites were commanded not to molest or oppress an alien (Exod 22:20; 23:9; Lev 19:33); the alien was to enjoy the same Sabbath rest as natives, work animals, and slaves (Exod 20:10; 23:12; Lev 16:29). Because they were often economically disadvantaged, gleaning rights were extended to them as they were to the poor (Lev 19:10; 23:22), and they are often classed with the widow, the orphan, the Levite, and other disadvantaged individuals. The motivation given for this special treatment is that the Israelites themselves had once been strangers in the land of Egypt and knew what it was like (e.g., Lev 19:34, which provides also that the alien is to be loved as oneself). They were allowed to share in the Passover meal, providing they were circumcised (Exod 12:48-49), and were allowed to offer sacrifice (Num 15:14, 15-16, 26, 29). In some cases it is specified that the same law applies to the resident alien as to the native (Exod 12:49; Lev 24:22; Num 9:14; 15:15-16). They were to be present for the solemn reading of the Law (Deut 31:12), which indicates they were understood to be subject to it—at least in part. They are specifically included in the Sabbath rest (see above). They were to observe the law of unleavened bread (Exod 12:19), the Day of Atonement (Lev 16:29), and to abstain from blood (Lev 17:10, 12, 13). They enjoyed the privilege of the cities of refuge for inadvertent homicide (Num 35:15; Josh 20:9). Yet provisions in Deuteronomy and P are sometimes at variance, which no doubt reflects changing customs and the fact that the term applied at various times to different groups. The OT distinguishes between the resident alien *(ger)* and the sojourner *(toshab*—foreign peoples working among the Israelites as merchants and artisans, according to M. Noth); the latter could not partake of the Passover (Exod 12:45) and could be bought and held as slaves (Lev 25:45).

Foreigner. The foreigner, distinguished from the resident alien in Deuteronomy 14:21, did not enjoy the same status and was often the subject of suspicion or even hostility. Unlike the resident alien he was not to share in the Passover (Exod 12:43). Foreign wives were the downfall of Solomon (1 Kgs 11:1, 8), and Ezra and Nehemiah strove to drive away foreign wives (Ezra 9:1-2; 10:1-44; Neh 13:23-30). Illicit cult was often designated as the worship of "foreign" gods (Deut 31:16; Josh 24:20, 23; Judg 10:16. See below on the "strange" woman.) Foreigners, unlike Israelites, could be charged interest (Deut 23:21) and pressed for debts even in the Sabbatical year (Deut 15:3). Nevertheless, Trito-Isaiah sees foreigners as helpers in the restoration of Israel (Isa 60:10; 61:5)

and even as being admitted to the people of God (Isa 56:3-8); and Ruth, though a foreigner (Ruth 2:10), was shown to be a model woman who became ancestress of David.

Stranger. The term "stranger" *(zar)* can be applied to a foreign invader (Isa 29:5; Ezek 7:21), or it may simply be one who is an outsider with reference to any group, such as the family (Deut 25:5), the worshiping community, the nation, a particular circle (e.g., the layman with reference to priestly privileges: Exod 29:33; Lev 22:12; etc.), or even outside accepted ways of behavior. For example, false gods are "strange gods" (Deut 31:16), just as they are "foreign" gods (see above). In Wisdom literature the young man is warned of the "strange woman" who seeks to seduce (NAB: "adulteress"; RSV: "loose woman"—Prov 2:16; 5:3, 20; etc.), who is called also "foreign," both terms sometimes being used in the same context (2:16; 5:10, 20; 6:24; etc.). Such usage does not betray xenophobia so much as it reflects values that are cherished by those who have oriented their ways toward God, unlike those "outside."

New Testament

Kindness toward Strangers. The NT continues many of the usages found in the OT. It may be the OT's insistence on consideration for the resident alien that led the early Christians to look upon kindness to strangers as a good deed especially to be practiced, but no doubt Jesus' account of the last judgment, in which the sheep will be separated from the goats on the basis of what they had done "for one of these least brothers of mine" had much to do with it; among the works listed was: "I was . . . a stranger and you welcomed me" (Matt 25:31-41). For a woman to be on the Church's roll of widows, she should, among other good works, have shown hospitality to strangers (1 Tim 5:10); 3 John 5 speaks of "brothers even though they are strangers" as those to whom hospitality is shown, and Hebrews 13:2, no doubt reflecting Genesis

18:1-15, speaks of entertaining angels unaware in looking after strangers.

Outsiders. The sense of "outsider, unfamiliar" is found in Jesus' shepherd/sheepfold allegory in John's Gospel: the sheep flee from the stranger because they do not recognize his voice (John 10:5). Of the ten lepers cleansed by Jesus, only the Samaritan, the outsider and foreigner, returned to give thanks to God (Luke 17:18). The same meaning lies behind Paul's contrast of Gentiles' former state of being non-participants in Christ, Israel, the covenant and its promises, with their present state as Christians, being no longer "alienated from the community of Israel and strangers to the covenants of promise," but "fellow citizens with the holy ones and members of the household of God" (Eph 2:12, 19).

Sojourners All. The NT expresses clearly a thought found germinally in the OT (see Pss 39:13; 119:19), that somehow this earth provides no final home for us, so that we must consider ourselves strangers and sojourners wherever we may be (Heb 11:13; 1 Pet 2:11). It is probably in line with this that 1 Peter 1:1 refers to the addressees as "sojourners."

See: ABRAHAM, COMMUNITY, HOSPITALITY, IDOLATRY, ISRAEL, NATIONS, PEOPLE OF GOD, POOR, PROSELYTES, SHEPHERD

JOSEPH JENSEN, O.S.B.

Pastoral-Liturgical Tradition

The Challenge of the "Stranger" for Christians. "Come, you have my Father's blessing. . . . I was a stranger and you welcomed me" (Matt 25:34, 35). Christians have understood this as Jesus identifying himself as a stranger and calling us to seek him out and *offer* hospitality: as hosts therefore, we will be blessed. But this is only part of the implication, since hospitality is a motif that recurs frequently in Jesus' life and culture, and it implies reciprocity; if there are hosts there must also be those who receive hospitality: guests or strangers. We only need think of Martha and Mary (Luke 10:38-42),

the woman at Bethany who washed Jesus' feet with her hair (Mark 14:3-9), Zacchaeus (Luke 19:1-10), or the disciples on the way to Emmaus (Luke 24:13-35) to recall occasions when Jesus was a *recipient* of hospitality: the guest or stranger. We are called to be the same.

Hospitality is a fundamental virtue and obligation across cultures, and some knowledge of its manifestations and demands can be a helpful spur to a Christian pastoral response. We know the phrase, "hospitality to the stranger," yet we are also aware that hospitality is not limited to people we do not know. In many languages a single word designates both "stranger" and "guest"; people treat strangers and guests similarly, whereas we might think of them and treat them very differently. Having two very different words may have assisted us in separating notions that other cultures combine. Furthermore, to show hospitality to a stranger/guest is rather different from actually being the stranger/guest. We may have overlooked the model of Jesus as a stranger/guest in our rush to position ourselves as hosts.

The Stranger in Cross-cultural Perspective. Every culture must produce institutionalized responses to strangers, since they may not always be peaceful and congenial but may constitute a threat. Strangers are those who come from beyond one's own boundaries, who do things differently, whose ways are unknown; by extension, they are "weird," "odd," "irrelevant." Hospitality is sometimes overruled and xenophobia practiced, usually as a result of previous bad experiences with strangers. Even when welcomed, there is no immediate and unconditional absorption of strangers but rather a culturally determined pattern of behavior, comprised of conventional stages through which the stranger must pass.

We are probably familiar with cases of extreme hospitality to strangers, like that offered by inhabitants of Tahiti to the crew of the "Bounty"; but this is only part of the story since hospitality may be as short-lived as it is intense. Proverbs tell us that a stranger is sweet on the first day, insipid on the second, and distinctly sour on the third; or that the welcome accorded the stranger lasts only a limited time and then turns to hostility unless the latter becomes productive and useful. So if the stranger is more than simply a transient there will tend to be fairly clear expectations.

The Stranger as "the Other." When we think of other people as strangers, we adopt the perspective of host. Sociologically speaking, "stranger" is a category defined by another: the "host." Though strangers may be unknown and sometimes inconvenient, so long as the host maintains the initiative the stranger can be rather readily "defined," that is, "limited," "specified," and thereby controlled.

Typically the stranger is initially treated in rather formal ways and not expected to take initiatives. There follows a period of scrutiny and a process of "domestication." Now the stranger must acquiesce, surrender privacy, be vulnerable, trust; things will be wildly unpredictable and sometimes quite uncomfortable. This is essential to being a stranger. If stranger and host satisfactorily negotiate this phase, it gradually gives way to a third aspect of the process, during which some real incorporation takes place. But if one or the other party is not committed to the process it will abort. Unless the stranger is willing to be patient, vulnerable, and trusting, assimilation is impossible.

The Stranger as Oneself. The host is considerably more comfortable and in control than the stranger. This may sometimes be pleasant for a stranger who is being indulged, and irksome for a host who is put-upon (like Martha: Luke 10:40-42). To undertake to be a stranger is quite difficult for people who can ensure that they retain initiatives and avoid situations of vulnerability. But in other cultures, or wherever people undertake to cross boundaries and entrust themselves to others, it becomes

important to learn how to be a stranger. Such is part of the Christian mission, since every Christian is called to cross boundaries. But most of us prefer to be in control of social situations, privacy, and decision making: to be *host* rather than *stranger*. We even make a virtue of this, not noticing how ungracious it can be to those who have the right to be our hosts! Willingly to be a stranger is to choose vulnerability, to surrender initiatives, to suspend decisions; which brings us to the heart of a pastoral consideration of our topic.

To follow the Great Commission found in Matthew 28:19 and to "Go!" is to be propelled *as stranger* into a context that preexisted us and about which we may know little or nothing. However much we consider the other to be so, it is we ourselves who are "strange." We are marginal to the worlds in which we arrive, and not part of their history; their members are familiar to each other, but we are unfamiliar.

Jesus as Stranger. Jesus is an example to anyone who wishes to embrace this essentially ambiguous position. He had nowhere to lay his head (Matt 8:20). He received hospitality graciously. He entrusted himself to others, even when this was a source of pharisaical scandal. But in so doing he was showing a fundamental respect to others, refusing to lord it over them.

Jesus knew how to be a stranger and how to relate to other strangers. He was drawn to outcasts whose social identity was almost non-existent; by offering them hospitality (being host) he was also helping create a social identity for them. But he was also drawn *as a stranger* into the lives of others: tax collectors, women in prostitution, sinners of all kinds; and by allowing them to show him hospitality, he was massively endorsing them as persons and affirming their goodness.

Jesus was able to ask for advice as well as to dispense it, to receive as well as to give, to listen as well as to speak, to react as well as to act. He was gracious. These are features of a good stranger or guest.

Pastoral Applications. Strangers may be, literally and culturally, the life-blood of communities. Any society not touched by the presence of strangers will soon run out of creativity. Not only do strangers have a socio-biological function, but they can be culturally and spiritually crucial, bringing new perspectives, gifts, insights, resources; they are catalysts for change. Furthermore, the stranger prepared to undertake the process of being assimilated *as stranger* will receive a social identity from the host and the host's group; the stranger who refuses to undertake that process will be an "alien" and not a "guest," the interloper but not the invited one, the threat and not the opportunity. The implications for mission and evangelization are obvious.

But likewise, the gracious stranger enhances the host's status, since the gratitude of the stranger becomes a significant reward to the host and the basis for further cooperation. Both stranger and host engage in mutually respectful relationships. The churlish or ungracious or unneedy stranger is not only an anomaly but a disgrace; the host whose hospitality is spurned or belittled is personally demeaned.

The words "I was a stranger and you welcomed me" (Matt 25:35) may have endorsed the ways we have *offered* hospitality. But there remains a whole meditation on our possible self-identification as strangers in the spirit of Jesus. Are we sometimes more prepared to be hosts than to be strangers, to give rather than to receive? Then it follows that we take initiatives and hold power but are less prepared to surrender them. And then we confront a crucial pastoral issue: such an attitude is fundamentally disrespectful of the *actual* hosts. Unless we are prepared to enter unfamiliar contexts as did Jesus the stranger, we will be stripping our hosts of their rights to lead, to give, and to act! This is incompatible with true evangelization.

Strangers/guests are as necessary as hosts; without them there are no hosts! If we think of the stranger only as an alien or an enemy, perhaps we should consider the implications of "guest" as a synonym for "stranger." This, I believe, is what the gospel and Jesus calls us to do. We will be "blessed" to the extent that we succeed, both in treating strangers as we would treat guests and in allowing ourselves to be strangers so that others may have the dignity of behaving as hosts.

See: COMMUNITY, HOSPITALITY

ANTHONY J. GITTINS, C.S.SP.

SUFFERING

Suffering in all its aspects pervades the life experience of all people. The biblical writers had to deal with it in an effort to explain why it is present in the world, and how faith copes with it in living out a relationship with God. Throughout the OT many types of affliction beset the nation as a whole and also individuals in their personal lives. Sickness, death, loneliness, misfortune, and derision are among the trials that extend to every facet of human existence, and thus it was incumbent upon the religious leadership and the sages to offer theological approaches to the understanding of suffering. Various solutions were offered beginning from the early literature and continuing into the Intertestamental period, but ultimately the mystery of suffering remains even to our day.

Old Testament

In the biblical accounts of creation the sacred writers clearly showed their belief that God's work was good, and it was ordered to the happiness and comfort of all creatures. Human beings were created in dignity and given dominion over creation to rejoice in its productivity through enjoyment of its fruits and of their own sense of achievement and security (Genesis 1–2). Suffering was not the destiny of human beings, and eventually it will be abolished in the new heaven and the new earth (Rev 21:4; Isa 65:17-18). However, the end time is a long way off, and the present time continues to witness to the universality of suffering. The author of Job complains that life is short and full of trouble (Job 14:1). Ben Sira has a similar comment on the miseries of life which pursue a person day and night, the more so even for the wicked (Sir 40:1-8). Since suffering seemed not to be in God's original plan, the question arose as to how it came into the world and how faithful people were to deal with it. Disorder in creation was not attributed to God, but it was seen as the result of evil powers that worked against human beings and caused a rupture in their participation in God's destiny for them. The first couple succumbed to the suggestion of evil and the fall was the result of their disobedience to God's commands (Genesis 3). It was human limitation that was the cause of the sinful situation in which suffering abounds.

The Deuteronomic theologians present temporal retribution as a solution to the problem (Deuteronomy 28). Lacking a clear teaching about an afterlife with eternal rewards and punishments for behavior, they looked for retribution in this world. The traditional stance was based on God's justice. If the nation or individual were good, blessings would come from God. If people sinned, punishment would come to them in this life. In application, this theory led to judgmentalism that brought condemnation on those who suffered sickness or any natural misfortune, even though they knew they were innocent of blame. Thus, Job's counselors believed him to be sinful, whereas Job was convinced that he had not transgressed the commands of the holy One (Job 6:10). The same conundrum existed with regard to those who enjoyed good fortune, for sometimes their evil lives were obvious to others who realized their prosperity did not follow on their virtues. The prophets pointed to the lack of covenant morality as the cause of impending doom for Israel. Both the fall of the northern kingdom and the fall of the southern kingdom were attributed to infidelity to Yahweh (Hosea 4; Jer 13:15-27). They realized that in the destruction some good people would suffer, but the evils of the nation were so great that God's chastisement had to come upon it. Faith prompted them to believe that some-

how some good would come to those who walked in God's way.

From early in their history (Judg 2:13-15) and throughout the OT (Sir 9:11) suffering was theologically interpreted as punishment for sin. A milder form of the chastising value of suffering was taught in Proverbs 13:24 by a sage who believed that a loving parent chastises his son. Suffering in that case took on a corrective or educative character from which good things would accrue in a person's life. Thus some saw suffering leading to a greater good. Joseph in Egypt followed this line of thought in rationalizing the suffering he experienced from his brothers as God's way of saving lives and ensuring the survival of the remnant of Jacob. He reasoned that God brought good out of evil circumstances (Gen 50:20). A similar solution was offered to Job by Eliphaz who saw God's chastisement leading to healing (Job 5:17-18). Elihu also took such an approach in seeing the affliction of God's correction as a means of turning one back to fidelity and bringing the person to a lifetime of prosperity and happiness (Job 36:8-11).

Among the wonderful works of God a psalmist included giving life to souls by testing them and bringing them to refreshment (Ps 66:9-12). This made affliction God's work (Ps 39:10-12), which thrust the psalmist into a crisis until the fate of the wicked was considered and the counsel and blessing of the Lord was seen as the ultimate good (Psalm 73). The sufferer came to a new understanding of dependence on God and strength of conviction in forging a new relationship in faith (Ps 119:67-72).

Another facet of the issue was handled theologically by positing that virtue could not be considered authentic without testing by adversity. Abraham's faith was tested by a call to sacrifice Isaac (Genesis 22). Presumably, a person in so important a role in salvation history had to have great faith proved only by a great test. Job was represented as blameless and upright, fearing God and avoiding evil (Job 1:8). If Job's virtue were authentic it would withstand severe trial. In Tobit's case an explanation of the test was given by Raphael, who not only tested Tobit but healed Tobit and Sarah (Tob 12:11-15).

In the faith of Israel there was the ability to find comfort and healing in prayer. We get an insight into intimacy with the Lord in psalms of lament in which the sufferers spoke freely and directly about their affliction and called to God for help. The seeming exaggeration of a person brought down to death who suffers the mockery of evildoers along with physical pain gives a strong sense of authenticity to the lament (Psalm 22). The nation as a whole expressed its bitter suffering after the exile and had no hope except in the Lord (Psalm 137). The faithful servants of the Lord who depended on God for all their needs found a shield and a refuge in all necessities (Ps 18:28-31). The theme of temporal retribution often surfaced in the laments, for sickness and misfortune were considered the results of sin. The sufferer became the object of mockery and rejection that added to the intensity of the suffering. Even in the laments there was dissatisfaction with the traditional stance on retribution, for those slandered realized the incongruity of such a theory (Psalm 109). What is important to note is that Israel freely cried to the Lord and expressed pain and fear, for God alone was their rescuer. This is shown clearly in the great laments of Jeremiah in which he confronts God with what he thought was unfair suffering in his prophetic ministry (Jer 12:1-6).

The election and call of Israel to serve the redemptive plan of God in salvation history brought the people into the work of divine mercy. Israel looked also for the love of God to reach into their lives and help the affliction and reproach that came to them as they attempted to follow the call. A new understanding appeared in the Songs of the Suffering Servant in Second Isaiah. The fourth song (Isa 52:13–53:12) especially spoke of vicarious suffering of the faithful servant who bore infirmities and chastisement that made others whole. By his stripes others were healed. In this instance suffering did not come simply as a result of righteousness. It became central to the ministry of servanthood for others, and the will of God would be accomplished through the suffering servant. Thus the idea of vicarious suffering became operative in the faith of Israel.

In the Wisdom tradition the sages reasoned that well-being came through following the Law, and the counsel of the wicked led to destruction (Psalm 1). Living in a wise way brought good health (Prov 3:8) and it was to God's benefit that people were alive to sing praise (Sir 17:28 [NAB 17:22]). Nevertheless, there were short-lived persons. The beginning of belief in life after death allowed the sage of the Book of Wisdom to approach the problem from a different perspective. A short life could be a blessing by which a person was saved from sin and wickedness (Wisdom 4). The souls of the righteous are in the hand of God who saves them from the derision of the foolish (Wisdom 3).

Amidst all the considerations and theologizing the mystery of suffering remained. Israel had no conclusive solution. Faith in God and acceptance of unfathomable wisdom remained the commitment of those who followed God's way.

See: CREATION, ESCHATOLOGY, FEAR, JUSTICE, LAMENT, RETRIBUTION, SERVANT, WISDOM

BETTY JANE LILLIE, S.C.

New Testament

The suffering of Jesus gives profound coloration to the NT views of suffering. Jesus' own suffering and death become the pattern for understanding the true meaning and potential of all human suffering. The Gospels indicate that some outside forces were responsible for inflicting suffering on Jesus: the hostility of the religious leaders; the unjust condemnation by the Roman authorities; the machinations of Satan (particularly in Luke's passion story, see Luke 22:3). But ultimately God's own providence stands behind the reality of the passion of Jesus. The death and resurrection reveal that by enduring suffering for the sake of the many Jesus brings new life to the world.

The Gospels do not hesitate to emphasize Jesus' profound suffering. While his physical sufferings of scourging and crucifixion are evident, the focus of the passion stories falls primarily on his spiritual anguish. He prays for deliverance from the fearful power of death in Gethsemane (Mark 14:34 and pars.) and, in the accounts of Mark and Matthew, cries out in near despair on the cross with the words of the lament Psalm 22 on his lips (Mark 15:34; Matthew 27:46). Thus Jesus absorbs the full power of death on the cross and is vindicated by God through resurrection. This gives new meaning to the redemptive power of human suffering.

Paul's theology moves in a similar vein, even though he does not dwell on the historical details of Jesus' sufferings. For Paul the movement from death to life effected in Jesus' passion and resurrection is the basic pattern of all redemption. Through baptism the believer is plunged into the mystery of Jesus' own death and resurrection, dying to sin and coming alive to God (Rom 6:3-11). Thus for the Christian, suffering is a participation in the passion of Jesus (2 Cor 4:7-11).

Pauline theology is also aware of the exemplary value of suffering. Just as the Gospels present Jesus as the model for all suffering born in faith, so Paul's own letters as well as the deutero-Pauline letters present the apostle himself as suffering nobly on behalf of the community. His apostolic sufferings are on behalf of the Church, helping them come to life (already in Paul's own letters; see 1 Cor 4:9-13; 2 Cor 4:7-11; Phil 2:17; 2 Tim 1:9-14; 3:10-17; 4:6-8).

While the Bible recognizes value in the experience of suffering, neither the OT or the NT romanticize suffering. It remains an "evil" that afflicts the children of God. Thus Jesus' own ministry is presented as an energetic assault on human suffering; through his healings and his critique of injustice and exclusion, the Jesus of the Gospels clearly demonstrates that human suffering is not to be tolerated. As proclaimed in the inaugural discourse at Nazareth in Luke's Gospel (4:16-30), Jesus' mission is to liberate humans from suffering and to have them experience the joy and bounty of God's merciful rule. Yet, at the same time, the NT recognizes that suffering borne in faith can also lead to new life as demonstrated in the paschal mystery itself.

The biblical views on suffering suggest some sound pastoral wisdom. First of all, the full span of the biblical literature demonstrates that there is no single orthodox view on the origin or meaning of suffering. So profound a human experience escapes any naive explanation, and faithful response to suffering can be multiple. The Bible also testifies that lamenting suffering and feeling distress about its meaning are not incompatible with strong faith. The psalmist, Job, Paul, and Jesus himself all rail against the agonies of suffering and death. Some suffering is no doubt caused by individual sinfulness as well as the failings of the community as a whole; in warfare, for example, the innocent suffer as well as the guilty. Only turning to God in repentance will alleviate some forms of suffering. On the other hand, many experiences of human suffering elude any credible explanation. The Bible testifies that when suffering is endured with faith it can have redemptive value both for oneself and for others. In such experiences, the Christian is invited to unite him or herself with the mystery of Christ's suffering and to believe that God's power can bring new life even from the most abject of human distress. Such a conviction is not based on logic but is rooted in the experience of Jesus and the lived testimony of generations of believers.

See: DEATH, GETHSEMANE, REDEMPTION, RESURRECTION

DONALD SENIOR, C.P.

Pastoral-Liturgical Tradition

Suffering in Patristic and Medieval Theology. The early Christian writers reflected on the experience of human suffering in light of the biblical witness and in dialogue with the philosophies of the Graeco-Roman world.

Confronted with various forms of dualism, which posited two absolute principles, one good and one evil, Christian theologians reaffirmed the biblical belief in the one God who is creator and redeemer* and who is the source of all life and goodness. Human suffering is understood as a consequence of the evil introduced into the world by sin. It is a result of the disruption of the harmony in creation caused by the misuse of human freedom. Augustine, whose investigation into the mystery of evil and suffering formed an essential part of his quest for truth, articulates the doctrine of the unchanging goodness of God and views the reality of suffering as part of the corruption of a good creation by sin. Concerning the suffering of individuals, Augustine cites Romans 11:33 as evidence that God's providential judgments are inscrutable, making it impossible for human beings to understand why some suffer more than others (*City of God*, 20,2). Jerome adduces the sufferings of just persons in the OT and the gospel story of the man born blind (John 9:1-41) in counseling a blind man not to believe that his disability is the outcome of his own personal sin (Letter 68). In general, early Christian writers understood suffering to have a corrective and educational function. They viewed suffering as a test and a teacher of virtue, a source of strength and purification, and an opportunity to share in the Cross of Christ.

Thomas Aquinas strongly affirms the intrinsic goodness of God's creation. The reality of evil, which Thomas defines as the lack of some good that should be present, is the consequence of the sin of the first parents in which all human beings have a share. Suffering is the result of the encounter with this evil in the world. God permits the existence of evil and the suffering that results from it in order to bring good out of them. Employing the philosophical categories of Aristotle, Thomas holds that God cannot suffer in the divine nature (*Summa Theologiae* III, q. 46, a. 12). Through the incarnation, however, God really takes on the suffering of humanity. In the person of Jesus, who is truly human and truly divine, God becomes one with all suffering people and is victorious over suffering through the cross and resurrection.

The Contemporary Experience of Suffering. Contemporary believers are continually confronted with the presence of massive suffering throughout the world. The stark reality of this suffering is daily brought before their eyes through the electronic and print media. The phenomenon of apparently meaningless human suffering on a vast scale, like the systematic persecution undergone by the victims of the Nazi Holocaust, brings all people face to face with this intractable mystery. Many contemporaries who espouse atheism do so as a protest against the suffering that is so prevalent in the world. In his Apostolic Letter on the Christian Meaning of Human Suffering, Pope John Paul II reminds believers that suffering is a universal theme which accompanies humanity at every point on earth and demands to be constantly reconsidered. The pope notes that, in the attempt to plumb the depths of the "why" of suffering, Christians are always conscious of the insufficiency and inadequacy of their explanations (no. 13).

Pastoral Considerations. Christian faith offers no solution to the mystery of human suffering. As a mystery, suffering defies even the most subtle and refined attempts at a reasoned explanation. Confronted with the experience of suffering in themselves and others, believers are impelled to look to the person of Jesus. It is Jesus who reveals the God who is not distant from the plight of the human family but who chose to become one with humankind in the incarnation. The ministry of Jesus manifests a God who is compassionate toward those who suffer, who is present to them in their suffering, and who offers healing and life. In the cross and resurrection, Christians believe that God has acted from within creation to conquer suffering and death. It is faith in the presence and power of the risen Christ that enables the Christian to affirm that God is faithfully active in bringing good out of the evil which we and others endure.

965

In the liturgical life of the Christian community, both solidarity with human suffering and faith in the redemptive power of God are expressed. Through baptism, believers are immersed into the redemptive mystery of Christ's dying and rising, called and empowered to unite their own sufferings with the sufferings of Christ. When the community remembers and makes present Christ's self-offering to God in the celebration of the Eucharist, believers offer their own sufferings with the faith that God is able to transform them, just as the gifts of bread and wine are transformed. The intercessory prayers of the Eucharistic liturgy express the community's concern for and union with its own suffering members and with those who suffer throughout the world. The anointing of the sick is the sacramental moment in which the Church, through family, friends, and ministers, seeks to be present to those suffering from serious illness and to mediate to them the healing of Christ. In their personal and communal prayer, Christians are called to take seriously the concrete reality of suffering in themselves and others, to make memory of the death and resurrection of Jesus, to open themselves to the compassionate presence of Christ, and to nurture hope in the redemptive power of God.

The Christian attitude toward suffering also entails obedience to God's summons to struggle against the causes of human suffering. Striving to be faithful to the way of Jesus, who welcomed the outcast and opposed all of those powers that were oppressive to people, Christians are called to be active in efforts to alleviate suffering and to eradicate those structures which cause human suffering. In the Pastoral Constitution on the Church in the Modern World, Vatican II teaches that Christians must seek to make their faith credible through actions of justice and love (no. 21). The Church's concern for social justice flows immediately from its vocation to affirm its faith in a loving God, to communicate God's compassion to those who suffer, and to actualize its faith in the redemptive power of Christ's death and resurrection.

See: ANOINTING, CREATION, HEALING, JUSTICE, PASSION, PERSECUTION, RECONCILIATION, REDEMPTION/REDEEMER, RESURRECTION, SALVATION

ROBIN RYAN, C.P.

SUICIDE

Suicide in the Ancient World

Suicide was accepted in ancient societies for a variety of reasons: (1) to escape too much evil in life. The earliest text known is Egyptian from the twenty-second century BCE, "A Dispute over Suicide" (ANET 405–407), and argues it is better to go to the afterlife than put up with the evil in this one. (2) To avoid shame. According to Homer, both Jocasta, the mother of Oedipus who discovers she has married her own son, and Ajax, the warrior friend of Achilles who was denied the great hero's armor at his death, committed suicide. (3) To express grief at the tragic death of a loved one. Aegeus, father of Theseus, jumped to his death when he falsely thought his son had been killed by the minotaur; Hero leapt into the ocean to join her lover Leander when he was found drowned; Cleopatra and Mark Antony both killed themselves when they heard the other had died. (4) To end a hopeless and unrequited love. Dido kills herself when Aeneas leaves her for good. (5) As a form of execution. Socrates forced to take hemlock as a condemned criminal is the most famous ancient suicide; but Nero and other Roman emperors frequently forced courtiers who displeased them to kill themselves or be killed. (6) To avoid capture or dishonor in battle. The hero Cato the Younger died when defeated by Julius Caesar; and Hannibal killed himself rather than fall into the hands of the Roman enemy.

All of these were well-known both in literature and perhaps in life to Romans, Greeks, and Egyptians. But as a rule, ancient thinkers, except for the Stoics and the Roman philosopher Seneca, condemned suicide because it usurped the rights of the gods over life and death and was an act of human hubris. They allowed it only if there were clear signs the gods might want a person's death or at least accept it.

Old Testament

Suicide is noted in the OT in only six places: (1) Abimelech (Judg 9:54) was a usurper and oppressive king who was mortally wounded in an attack on the town of Thebez when a woman threw a millstone on his head. To avoid the shame of death at the hands of a woman, he had his armor-bearer kill him with the sword. (2) Samson (Judg 16:28-31) is able to pull down the Temple in which he is a prisoner to kill the Philistines who had both captured and blinded him to make him helpless. His death is seen both as an act of vengeance and a last heroic deed by a man who fought as a warrior against these enemies. (3) Saul (1 Sam 31:1-4) is wounded in battle, and to avoid being captured and degraded by the Philistines, orders his armor-bearer to kill him by the sword. (4) Saul's armor-bearer (1 Sam 31:5) then takes his own life by falling on his sword to be equal in service to his master the king and to atone for the "wrong" of killing a royal figure (see this very argument made in the following passage, 2 Sam 1:1-16). (5) Ahitophel (2 Sam 17:23) was the royal advisor of David who joined the revolt of Absalom. When he saw his wise counsel to capture David spurned in favor of the advice of Hushai, who was deceiving Absalom, he hanged himself. The text does not condemn him but says he even was buried in the tomb of his ancestors, thereby receiving honor. (6) Zimri (1 Kgs 16:18) rebelled against King Elah of Israel and declared himself king. But the army, under Omri, opposed him and when defeat was imminent, Zimri burned himself to death in his palace to avoid capture.

None of these deaths are judged to be wrong or the persons condemned. No one grieves the loss of Abimelech or Zimri because of their evil ways; but David praises Saul for his bravery at the time of his death and deeply laments his loss (2 Sam 1:17-27). The accounts of Samson and Ahitophel are silent on people's reactions, but the editor certainly praises Samson for winning a great victory against Israel's enemies in his act of self-destruction. These examples suggest three reasons for which suicide would be permitted: to avoid dishonor or a crueler death at the hands of enemies in war, to escape life when your entire job or honor has been taken from you (Ahitophel), and to be united to a loved one or master in his or her untimely death (the armor-bearer).

A few other passages might suggest that a person might contemplate suicide if his or her whole life was ruined, such as Job (Job 2:9; 7:15; and 13:19). But the significant point in Job is that he does not kill himself but places trust in God to deliver him.

New Testament

The only suicide recorded in the NT is that of Judas (Matt 27:3-5; Acts 1:18-20). It is not condemned by either account, but both Matthew and Acts see its shameful and bitter end as a fitting punishment for the betrayer. Later tradition held that Judas' suicide compounded his sin of betrayal, but this is not implied in the NT itself. There are still other mentions of suicide: in John 8:22, many in his audience think Jesus may be planning suicide when he says he is going where they cannot come; and Paul stops the suicide of his Philippian jailor (Acts 16:27-28). Paul himself muses on the possibility of hastening or permitting his own death so he can be with the Lord sooner (Phil 1:21-26; 2 Cor 5:1-8), but rejects the option. However, Paul's thought may fit more readily in the category of Christian longing for the fullness of life in the next world.

Analyzing the Ancient Attitude to Suicide

Rabbinic Judaism in the Talmud argued strongly against suicide on the basis of Genesis 9:5, "I will require for your own life-blood a reckoning." But although they considered this to make suicide worse than murder, pastorally they buried the person with honor unless it was clear that the death was premeditated and not done in

967

dire straits (Gen Rab 34:13). This attitude dates to after the biblical period, but the very infrequency of biblical examples and the fact that each one came in a situation in which the person was alienated from God or needed to make amends (e.g., Samson) suggests that suicide was frowned on, if not forbidden. The true biblical approach saw life as a gift from God and under God's decision to give it or take it away (Job 1:21). One rather poured out his or her troubles to the Lord and sought divine help and deliverance. In general, OT texts see God as a god of life and goodness (Gen 1:31; Pss 16:10-11; 30:4; 36:10). The lament psalms in particular give voice to many moments of despair that are transformed to hope by relying on the love of God.

Pastorally we can learn the lesson from Scripture that suicide is not offered as an option for times of trouble; suffering can be an important part of God's will for individuals, and we need to turn to God's love and care in dire troubles when death might seem preferable (Tob 3:10-15). However, we also learn that no suicide should be condemned or dishonored: it is in God's hands to judge, and in ours to proclaim divine compassion and divine life-giving love.

See: DEATH, SUFFERING

LAWRENCE BOADT, C.S.P.

SUN

The Hebrew word for sun is *shemesh,* a word that exists in various forms in other Semitic languages. In many places in the ancient world the sun was worshiped as a deity. A peculiar feature of the Hebrew word is that sometimes it appears in both masculine and feminine forms. This may indicate that the solar deity was depicted in both male and female forms.

That sun worship existed in Israel is clear from a number of texts. For one thing, laws condemning it indicate that it was practiced. "And when you look up to the heavens and behold the sun or the moon or the stars among the heavenly hosts, do not be led astray into adoring them and serving them" (Deut 4:19). It was considered so serious an offense in Israel that it was punishable by stoning (Deut 17:3-5).

Nonetheless, the wicked King Manasseh worshiped "the whole host of heaven" (2 Kgs 21:3-5), and apparently King Josiah's reforms (2 Kgs 23:5) did not succeed in eradicating the practice (Ezek 8:16). The prevalence of sun worship is reflected in the occurrence of the word for sun in place names such as Beth Shemesh, "house of the sun" (Josh 15:10; 1 Sam 6:9; 1 Kgs 4:9) and En Shemesh, "spring of the sun" (Josh 15:7; 18:17).

Although sun worship existed in Israel, the creation account of Genesis 1 states unequivocally that the sun is not God. Israel's God created the sun, not on the first day with the creation of light (Gen 1:3-5), but on the fourth day with the creation of the heavenly luminaries (Gen 1:14-16). Most interpreters understand the delay in the sun's creation to be a subtle statement of Israel's monotheism, not an indication of Israel's ignorance of the sun's role in producing light.

In view of the sun's theological demotion in Israel from deity to mere heavenly body, its primary role in OT literature is symbolic. In some passages the sun represents permanence and stability. The psalms pray that the king may "endure as long as the sun" (Pss 72:5; 89:37); they praise the regularity of its benefits to humans (Ps 104:19-23), and they personify the sun as a bridegroom and a giant "who joyfully runs his course" (Ps 19:5-7).

In other texts the sun symbolizes God's involvement in the events of human life. A poetic passage in the book of Joshua uses a common solar motif of ancient literature. In the course of battle "the sun stood still, and the moon stayed, while the nation took vengeance on its foes" (Josh 10:13). Similarly, as a sign to King Hezekiah that God's word is reliable, the prophet Isaiah promised that the shadow of the sun would regress ten steps on a stairway. "So the sun came back the ten steps it had advanced" (Isa 38:8; 2 Kgs 20:8-11).

The sun also figures in the promises of God's eschatological intervention in the future. In the punishment to come upon Israel's conqueror, Babylon, the sun will be dark when it rises (Isa 13:10). And in the new and glorious age to come, "The light of the sun will be seven times greater than the light of seven days" (Isa 31:26).

See: LIGHT, MOON

KATHLEEN M. O'CONNOR

Pastoral-Liturgical Tradition

The early Christians inherited many of the attitudes toward the sun and stars that were part of their larger Mediterranean environment. The sun and the moon ruled over the day and the night, respectively. They were the cosmic lodestones, as it were, that guaranteed the order of things. Thus the Synoptic Gospels all portray the death of Jesus as being accompanied by the darkening of the sun at what would ordinarily be the brightest time of the day.

The stars, too, provided orientation for individual and social life. Dependence upon astrological readings was frowned upon by the early Church, but nonetheless continued to be practiced on a popular level.

While much of the symbolism surrounding the sun and stars was part and parcel of early Christian experience, identification (and worship) of the emperor with the sun was strongly resisted. Indeed the Church at Rome deliberately celebrated the birthday of Jesus on December 25 from as early as the year 336 to counteract the celebration of the birthday of the sun *(sol invictus)* on that same day. Christ was proclaimed the "sun of righteousness" *(sol iustitiae)* against the cult of the *sol invictus.*

Christ and the sun have been identified at various times in Christian history, not to foster sun worship, but to underscore Christ as the light of Christians and source of life. In the Counter-Reformation period, the Eucharist came to be identified with the sun in Baroque architecture and ornamentation. Monstrances for the exposition of the Blessed Sacrament were oftened fashioned with rays emanating from the Eucharistic Host.

The sun has also come to be associated with apparitions of Mary, from at least the sixteenth century onward. Again, the sense seems to be Mary as being at the center of the religious universe and experience.

Following popular understandings, the stars were understood to adorn the heavens and attest to the power and grandeur of God, as exemplified in Christian hymns, such as *"Creator alme siderum"* ("Creator of the Starry Skies"). Astrology, as has been noted, has enjoyed a following at many points in earlier Christian history. Renaissance popes, for example, often set the dates for consistories on the basis of astrological calculation. The advent of the telescope, however, led to astrology's demise, at least in official and intellectual circles.

See: MOON, STARS

ROBERT J. SCHREITER, C.PP.S.

SYNAGOGUE

There are three parts to this article. The first considered the origins of the synagogue as an institution in Judaism according to written sources. The second reviews archaeological data that can shed light on this issue. The third examines the development of this institution.

For the last two millennia, the synagogue has been *the* central institution of Judaism, yet it is quite doubtful that the synagogue had any place within the religion of ancient Israel. Toward the end of the biblical period legitimate worship became confined to the Temple* of Jerusalem. The development of the synagogue marked a genuine religious revolution. Because of the synagogue, worship was no longer centralized at a single site. The synagogue brought the liturgy to every Jewish village in Palestine. The divinity was symbolically present in the assembly of lay worshipers who followed a standard ritual that included prayers and readings from the Scriptures but without sacrifice. The goal of worship in the synagogue was centered on the salvation of individual worshipers who were praying for the grace of resurrection in the messianic age.

Origins

Despite the pivotal importance of the synagogue in the transition from the religion of ancient Israel to that of early Judaism, the origins of the synagogue are a subject of continued controversy. Rabbinic tradition located the beginnings of the synagogue in the Mosaic period. Literary hypotheses locate the origins of the synagogue anywhere from the late seventh century BCE to the first century CE.

A preexilic date for origin of the synagogue focuses on the practical difficulties involved in making pilgrimages to Jerusalem and the proscription of sacrificial worship outside its Temple. The local shrines where Josiah forbade sacrificial worship (2 Kgs 23:8) became places of communal pilgrimage. The exilic hypothesis sees Ezekiel 11:16 as proof that synagogues became part of Jewish life during the Exile. There are others who agree that the beginnings of the synagogue ought to be located in the Exile but its consolidation was due to Ezra who urged the returning Jews to establish synagogues in Judah.

The hypothesis of a postexilic origin for the synagogue locates its beginnings in the secular assemblies of Jews who gathered in their towns and villages to deal with the social and economic problems. As these meetings became more regular, the rabbis introduced the public reading of the Law for the benefit of those assembled. The Pharisees divided the people into twenty-four divisions that enabled the daily sacrifice in the Temple to be a communal sacrifice provided, in turn, by each division. Previously the daily sacrifice was a private offering made by wealthy Jews who could afford the purchase of the animals prescribed for the sacrifice. When a particular division was responsible for the daily sacrifice, not all its members were able to go to Jerusalem for the ritual. Those who could not make the trip remained in their towns and assembled at the time of the sacrifice for prayer and reading the passage of Torah relating to the sacrifice. When the Temple was destroyed the divisions continued to meet for prayer and Scripture reading. Thus what originally was a secular meeting dealing with social and economic questions became, over the years, a time for prayer with a standardized liturgy.

Another hypothesis assumes that the synagogue cannot refer to a place of formal worship in Judea before the destruction of the Temple in 70 CE because it is only after that date that the term "synagogue" appears in connection with a formal liturgical service. Before this time the city square was the locus of public worship outside the Temple. The city-square was not only a locus of economic and social life but also it was a center of religious life as well. The destruction of the Temple provided the catalyst for the metamorphosis of the city square into the institution of the synagogue.

The problem with the theories regarding the origin of the synagogue is that they are all based on arguments from silence. The Hebrew Scriptures never mention a synagogue. The Septuagint never uses the term "synagogue" to refer to a building but to a liturgical or secular assembly of the people. Even a second-century BCE source like Ben Sira does not mention synagogues. Synagogues are well-attested in Josephus and the NT, both first-century sources, but it is not certain that these texts refer to a single-purpose building or a multi-purpose community building that was used for worship.

Archaeological Data

Since written sources do not provide conclusive data about the origins of the synagogue, one recourse is to consider the material remains that archaeology has revealed. Before one can appreciate archaeology's contribution to resolving this issue it must be noted that there are two fundamental problems of methodology in the archaeology of ancient synagogues in Palestine: (1) the identification of a particular structure as a synagogue and (2) dating the structure. Sometimes a building will be identified as a synagogue based on the architectural form or its decorative motifs. This evidence, in turn, is used to establish the date of the building. Very few synagogues in Palestine are dated with certainty from inscriptions, and none before the sixth century CE. Despite these difficulties, archaeological evidence supports the conclusion that distinct synagogue buildings existed by the third century CE. These buildings were adaptations of the Roman basilica.

To identify a particular ruin as the remains of an ancient synagogue, its architectural fragments must be decorated with common Jewish motifs such as the Torah shrine or the menorah. Sometimes it is possible to make this identification on the basis of inscriptions that confirm the building's use as a place for liturgical assembly.

Though both Josephus and the NT speak of synagogues as a building or place of Jewish assembly, no building dating from the first century CE has been positively identified as a synagogue based on the above criteria. Structures at Masada, Gamla, Magdala, and the Herodion that were in use during the first century have been identified as synagogues based on architectural characteristics that the buildings in question share with synagogues of a later era. These buildings were probably no more than examples of the various kinds of assembly halls in which the Jewish people would gather to conduct community business.

It may be that the buildings used as synagogues in the first century cannot be identified since they are not distinguishable from domestic architecture. A better conclusion would be to assert that before the third century CE, synagogue buildings as single-purpose structures with a recognizable architectural form did not exist. Jews in Palestine met for communal prayer and reading of the Scriptures in private homes that may have been modified for that purpose or in public buildings that were built to fit many communal functions. Single-purpose structures built to house the wor-

ship that replaced that of the destroyed Second Temple was a later development.

At the present, no firm date for the origins of the synagogue can be established on archaeological grounds. Though written sources from the first century such as the Gospels show that the Jews worshiped in synagogues, it is not clear that these buildings were, in fact, monumental buildings used for worship. In all likelihood, these "synagogues" were not distinguishable from ordinary domestic architecture. At times, the community may have assembled for prayer in a public building that was erected for other public purposes. Before the destruction of the Temple in Jerusalem, it is unlikely that any structure was intended to replace or supplement the Temple and its rituals. Once the Temple was destroyed and the probability of its restoration appeared remote, then the synagogue could develop as a liturgical institution and structure. The question of the origin of the synagogue as a Jewish institution and the date when synagogue buildings were first erected remain controverted topics.

See: PRAYER

LESLIE J. HOPPE, O.F.M.

Later Developments

The synagogue developed within Judaism to make possible Jewish survival after the destruction of the Temple and to help spread Judaism through the Diaspora. It was not a place that possessed inherent sanctity: it had no sacrificial or sacramental ritual, and did not require the mediation of a specially chosen priesthood. It was essentially a fellowship of worshipers seeking both community and God, and eager to study God's Torah.

The synagogue as it developed had a threefold function. It was a House of Assembly (*Beth-ha-Knesset*), a House of Prayer (*Beth-ha-Tefilah*), and a House of Study (*Beth-ha-Midrash*).

The term itself is the Greek translation of the Hebrew for House of Assembly (*synagogos*). In medieval Germany it was referred to as *Shul* (see the German *Schule* = school), and this designation is still widely used. In the Greek world it was often termed *proseuchē* (House of Prayer). In the contemporary United States, it is often designated as Temple, particularly by the Reform movement, which does not look forward to the rebuilding of the ancient Temple. And as a way of emphasizing both the House of Assembly and the interdenominational aspect, it is referred to as Center on the American Jewish scene.

As was indicated above, both from textual and archaeological evidence, the exact origins of the synagogue are obscure. By the first century, however, it is clearly on the scene. Besides references in Philo and the NT (e.g., Matt 13:54; Mark 1:21), another source indicated that there were some 480 synagogues in Jerusalem at the time of the destruction of the Temple (Talmud *Ketubot* 105a). If this sounds exaggerated, it should be noted that there are at least that many in Jerusalem today.

While there are indications in the Gospels and other books of the NT corpus that there was a mutual antagonism between Jews and the followers of Jesus, this tension should not be interpreted as indication of a universal and decisive break on the part of the early Christians with the practices of Judaism. Indeed, it can be said that the Church took the already existing institution of the synagogue and adapted it to its needs, as it did other forms and structures of Judaism such as Hebrew Scripture, the sermon as a means of communication, and the priesthood itself. There is also reason to believe that Christians—even Gentile converts to Christianity—continued to worship in synagogues not only in the period of the primitive Church (see Acts 6:9; 22:19) but well into the fourth century. John Chrysostom, in a series of eight homilies entitled "Against the Jews" written in Antioch in 386–387, condemns Christians who continue to follow Jewish practices, especially attendance at synagogue (MG 48:843-942).

The continued influence of the synagogue on the Christian Church and its liturgy in the Semitic regions of the Roman world is also well illustrated in the design of early Syrian churches. These Christian prayer spaces are essentially modified synagogues. They generally contain a *bema* or raised reader's desk in the center of the building for the proclamation of the Scriptures. In place of the ark in the eastern apse of the building where the Torah scrolls were enshrined, Syrian Christian churches locate the altar table, a liturgical symbol for Christ, and move the ark—the place where the Scriptures are housed—to the *bema* itself. This basic design perdures to this day in the traditional design of those churches in the Middle East that follow the Eastern Syrian Rite, a rite still celebrated in Aramaic.

The synagogue was the successor to the Temple, and prayer was the surrogate for sacrifice. In the Temple there were morning, afternoon, and evening daily sacrifices, and on Sabbaths and festivals there was the additional *(musaph)* sacrifice. In the synagogues, therefore, there were morning, afternoon, and evening prayers. The focus, however, is on the Sabbath. On Friday nights in most Reform congregations, and on Saturday mornings in Conservative and Orthodox synagogues, there is the full service, including the reading of the Torah portion of the week and from the Prophets.

It should be stressed that, in the final analysis, the essence of the synagogue is its purpose rather than its form or structure. The Temple in Jerusalem came to be the centralizing force in ancient Israel, bringing together a disparate people after they found their home in the Promised Land. In the long period of Diaspora it was the decentralized, highly mobile, and adaptable institution of the synagogue that made it possible to reconstitute the spiritual body of the Jewish people wherever they cast their roots. And in this sense it represents the core of Jewish communities throughout the world and, with the reestablishment of the Jewish State, its alternate central force.

HAYIM GOREN PERELMUTER

T

TABOR

Old Testament

Tabor is a relatively low mountain,* with an elevation of 1850 feet, and is located in the northeast corner of the Plain of Esdraelon (or Jezreel). In ancient Israel, it was the boundary marker of the territories of Issachar (Josh 19:22), Zebulun (Josh 19:12), and Naphtali (Josh 19:34). Rising steeply from the plain, Mount Tabor gives a commanding view of Mount Hermon to the north, the Jordan Rift Valley to the east, the Plain of Esdraelon and the mountains of Samaria to the south, and Nazareth and the heights of Mount Carmel beyond to the west. Its imposing presence in contrast to the surrounding plain is reflected in Psalm 89:13, where Tabor is paired with Mount Hermon, the highest peak in the Levant (1968 feet). The psalmist extols Tabor and Hermon as representative of the great mountains created by the mighty God: "North and south you created; Tabor and Hermon rejoice at your name." Similarly, in Jeremiah 46:18 Tabor is set in parallelism with Carmel, as an impressive mountain, a symbol of strength and power: "Like Tabor among the mountains he shall come, like Carmel above the sea."

In addition to its commanding view, Tabor's strategic importance is due to its location along the ancient north-south route from Damascus to the coastal plain, and the east-west road from Megiddo to the Sea of Galilee. So it is that in the time of the Judges Deborah sends Barak and his army of ten thousand Naphtalites and Zebulunites (Judg 4:6) to encamp on Mount Tabor. At Deborah's command, they descend upon the Canaanite Sisera, where "the LORD put Sisera and all his chariots and all his forces to route before Barak" (Judg 4:14-15).

In another instance, Mount Tabor is the sight of the slaying of Gideon's brothers by the Midianites (Judg 8:18).

One final reference to Tabor is found in Hosea 5:1, where the prophet decries priests who were "a net spread upon Tabor." Using hunting imagery, Hosea denounces priests who trap the people and lead them astray from proper worship of God to the pagan gods, who were presumably worshiped atop Tabor.

New Testament

There is no reference to Mount Tabor in the NT, but from the fourth century CE on it has been venerated by Christians as the site of Jesus' transfiguration* (Jerome mentions it in letter 46, which dates to 386). The evangelists simply locate the event "up a high mountain" (Mark 9:2; Matt 17:1). Josephus (*War* 4.54-61) tells that Tabor was fortified by the Jews in 67 CE, during the first revolt against Rome. The first church was built on Mount Tabor in the early fifth cen-

973

tury and it was a bishopric from 533. In the twelfth century a Crusader fortress stood atop Tabor. It was taken by Saladin in 1187 and was destroyed in 1263 by the Mameluke sultan Babars. The summit today is shared by the Greek Orthodox and the Franciscans. The Greek Orthodox Church of Elijah was built in 1911. The presence of the Franciscans dates to 1631, and their current church was built in 1924.

See: MOUNTAIN, POWER, SAMARIA, TRANSFIGURATION

BARBARA E. REID, O.P.

TEACH/TEACHING

The passing on of tradition from one generation to the next is essential for the preservation of culture and religious faith. It is a task encumbent upon family members as well as professional ministers. In Jewish tradition teaching centered on Torah, both written and oral. Christians see Jesus as the teacher par excellence. Furthermore, his person, words, and deeds become the content of Christian teaching. This remains an extremely important ministry in the Church.

Old Testament

In the ancient Near East, there were many ways in which teaching was done. Within the family, storytelling was one of the important ways of socializing new members. Children were trained in the craft or occupation passed down from one generation to the next, and both male and female children were trained by their elders to fulfill the economic and familial roles that they would someday inherit. Parents and all adult relatives assumed the role of teacher to the next generation.

Beyond the family circle, religious training may have originally been in the hands of professional religious scholars connected with the Temple, but increasingly with the Diaspora expansion of Jewish life and the Babylonian Exile, that responsibility had to be more widely shared. By the last few centuries before Christ, strong local traditions of ongoing religious education were forming in Jewish communities everywhere, es-

pecially in Babylonia. In the absence of Temple worship, weekly gatherings focused on Scripture reading, prayer, and instruction through commentary on biblical texts. Those interested in more advanced learning would assemble daily for study and reflection. These centers of learning were to grow into the synagogues of the Christian era. Here the collected wisdom of the elders was preserved and passed down. Religious teaching was education in Torah, not only the written Law, but also the oral tradition and the faithful way of life of the devout Jew.

Scribes were the professional secretaries and scholars in many cultures, including Israel. Their responsibilities could range from local village secretarial service for the illiterate masses to high-level court officials entrusted with vast administrative powers. A good example is Ezra, a high-ranking official at the Persian court who was also learned in Jewish Law, and was given sweeping powers by the king of Persia to investigate and reform Jewish life in Jerusalem in the late sixth century BCE. The Book of Ezra 7–10 and that of Nehemiah 8–10 portray him not only as a capable royal administrator, but a capable teacher of the Jewish Law as well.

The Wisdom literature, especially the brief, pithy axioms such as those in Proverbs, may represent the kinds of practical education to faith and character given by scribal scholars to the children of court and well-to-do families.

New Testament

Jesus. One of the best highlighted roles of Jesus in the Gospels is that of teacher. In a traditional Jewish setting, teaching and learning center around the Law: to learn to read and write is to learn Torah. Combined with the title "rabbi," which is nearly synonymous, "teacher" is the title most frequently ascribed to Jesus, often with a great deal of respect and admiration (e.g., Mark 10:17; Matt 22:16). Jesus' teaching is astonishing, with authority (Matt 7:28; Mark 1:27; Luke 4:32); it is the sign that he truly comes from God (John 7:17). One of his favorite settings for teaching was the synagogue (Matt 4:23; Mark 6:2; Luke 6:6; 13:10; John 6:59), and in Jerusalem of course, the Temple. While in Galilee, he also favored outdoor settings: a mountain (Matt 5:1-2); by the sea (Mark 4:1); on the plain (Luke 6:17).

Jesus' teaching is not confined to exposition of the Law. In the Synoptic Gospels he tells stories called "parables" (meaning either illustrative examples or riddles). Sometimes these are given in collected form (Mark 4; Matthew 13). Elsewhere they are found scattered through a Gospel, as in Luke, where after chapter 14 a number appear that are proper to this Gospel and may owe as much to Luke's artistry as to Jesus' inspiration. Many of these stories that illustrate either God's coming rule or kingship, or the behavior that befits those who await it, are comprehensible on a hearing, but some are cryptic, challenging the hearers to puzzle over the meaning the tale has for *them*. Much of Jesus' teaching was in the form of gnomic sayings that the evangelists group, giving the almost certainly wrong impression that they were delivered orally in that sequence (see Matt 5:13-16; 7:1-20; Luke 16:9-13).

Jesus is not reported to have taught in the manner of the later Rabbinic period, balancing the opinions of teachers of the Law against each other and reconciling apparent contradictions in the Scriptures. He lodges the claim God makes on persons, expecting them to decide for or against God's will. His teaching, while highly intelligent and insightful, cannot be called intellectual. It contains no speculative element, no abstraction, no search for essences. It is always concerned with human behavior, although the Godward dimension is never absent. At times Jesus will throw out questions as he teaches, but the dialectic is chiefly an interior one in the hearers' minds.

The Synoptics have Jesus addressed as "Teacher" (*didáskalos*) by friend, foe, and stranger alike twenty-seven times (including parallels). The Baptist is thus addressed once (Luke 3:12). In John, Jesus is addressed by the Semitic equivalent of *didáskale* three times, *rabbi* and *rabboni*. The textually interpolated passage calls Jesus *didáskale* at John 8:4. In the third person "teacher" comes in for about fifteen uses, including parallels, generally to describe both Jesus and teachers of the Law or the gospel.

In John, the Father is named as the teacher of Jesus (8:28), as the one who speaks a word to him which he in turn utters (14:24). The Spirit-Paraclete whom the Father will send in Jesus' name will act as a teacher, recalling to the disciples' minds all that he has said to them (v. 26). It is probably this same holy Spirit who is called "the anointing" in 1 John 2:27 and abides in believers, ensuring that they need no one to teach them (an echo of Jer 31:34).

The noun for "teaching" (*didachē*) occurs in the Septuagint only once (Ps 59 [60]:1; not in the MT). The Hebrew has many words to convey it, however, chief among them *lᵉmmᵘd*. Ten times the Gospels refer to the "teaching" of Jesus and once to that of the Pharisees (Matt 16:12). Acts employs the word four times to describe the apostles' message about "the Lord." In Romans, Paul speaks of the *didachē* at 6:17 and 16:17, the first time with the interesting turn of phrase, "the pattern of teaching to which you were entrusted." He employs the word twice in 1 Corinthians (14:6, 26) in a discussion of comprehensible speech (*propheteía*) as preferable by far to "speaking in tongues (or a tongue)." There, *didachē* is contrasted to both, and also to "revelation," "knowledge," and "interpretation." This results in its usually being translated "instruction." The term has a dynamic meaning rather than a static in 2 Timothy 4:2, where the addressee is charged to "proclaim [*kēruxon*] the word persistently . . . encouraging through all patience and teaching." The epistle to Titus (1:9) enjoins "holding fast in accord with the teaching [*didachē*] of the true word" but immediately speaks of sound "doctrine" (*didaskalía*). Other appearances of *didachē* are in Hebrews 6:2; 13:9; 2 John 9–10; Revelation 2:14, 24. It is false teaching in the latter two cases, and elsewhere can be either the act of teaching or what is taught.

When the teaching act is at issue translators tend to render it "instruction." "Teaching" as content is also rendered "doctrine" or "message." There is nothing, however, to distinguish *didachē* from *didaskalía* in the NT. The latter word occurs in Mark 7:7 (par. Matt 15:9) as a quotation of Isaiah 29:13, contrasting human precepts with "doctrines" *(didaskalías).* Colossians 2:22 couples the same two nouns (the word for precepts is *entálmata)* but dismisses both as of human origin. For Paul *didaskalía* is teaching or instruction (Rom 12:7; 15:4). The same is true of Ephesians 4:14, although the teaching mentioned there is not good. Whoever wrote the letters to Timothy and Titus favored this word over *didachē,* for it occurs no less than fifteen times, all but once descriptive of sound apostolic teaching. The word's translation as "doctrine" can give the impression that it is teaching somehow formulated as contrasted with *didachē,* but there is no difference, any more than there is between "teaching" (Anglo-Saxon) and "instruction" (Latin).

Some have distinguished sharply between the NT use of "proclaim" *(kēryssein)* and "teach" *(didáskein)* as if it were clear that the first of these and its cognate noun *kērygma* describe the first presentation of the gospel to unbelievers while the second means the exposition of a faith already held. It is true that the work of proclamation is often done in the midst of pagans, e.g., among the Ninevites or the Diaspora Gentiles to whom Paul brings the gospel, but the word connotes a mode of speech (like its cognate, *krázein,* to "shriek" or "cry out") more than the content of speech. Matthew 11:1 may illustrate this, where Jesus "goes to teach and to preach in their towns." Note the order of the words. Different persons (the Baptist, Jesus, the disciples) "proclaim" thirty-six times in the Gospels and Acts; Paul uses the word fourteen times and other NT writers six. The translation of *kēryssein* as "preach" (Lat. *praedicare)* more often than "proclaim" is without serious significance. The first English word means, at root, "to speak before an audience" while "proclaim," as has been said, describes a mode of speech: the herald's announcement, the messenger's public word.

Pastoral-Liturgical Tradition

Modern catechetic and homiletic literature has built on the presumed verbal distinction. While the philological foundation is not there, there is a different mode of art in each type of gospel presentation. In catechizing, the first presentation of Christian faith is done differently from the exploration of the various mysteries and practices of faith, whether with adults or children. In preaching, too, the pulpit is the place for motivating believers to persevere in gospel living, not for the careful exposition of doctrines or moral distinctions. Despite this, long familiarity with the vocabulary and phenomena of Christianity is not the same as having *heard* the gospel for the first time and responded to it. Consequently, all instruction or teaching retains a proclamational element. Similarly, the pulpit is the only place where any instruction of most worshipers may be done. This means that the homily cannot cease being informative and the instructional situation must at all times be motivational.

"Catechesis" is a word with which the NT is unfamiliar, whereas its cognate verb *katēchein* occurs six times. The latter is made up of a prepositional prefix and the verb "to sound" (as in "echo" or "sounding brass," 1 Cor 13:1), yielding the basic meaning "make to hear," but in context *"teach* or instruct *orally."* Luke's Gospel begins (1:14) with a promise to Theophilos of confirmation of "those matters in which you have been instructed *[katēchethēs]."* The same writer uses this verb to describe Apollos as "instructed" (Acts 18:25) and James and all the Jerusalem presbyters as "informed" (21:21) or "able to learn" (v. 24). Paul speaks of a Jew as "instructed" by the Law (Rom 2:18) and says he would prefer to speak five intelligible words to "instruct" others than ten thousand words in a tongue (1 Cor 14:19). Toward the end of Galatians he requires a person "instructed" in the word to share it all with the "instructor" (6:6). In the Romans and Galatians passages the person instructed is a *katēchoúmenos,* yielding the third-century term *"catechumen,"* one who undergoes a two- or three-year period in preparation for baptism.

There are thus a number of words and phrases among which no fine lines can be drawn, employed by NT writers to describe the way the gospel is transmitted. They are the ways in common use to say things like spreading the news, delivering a message, or teaching hearers what they need to know. The vocabulary takes on certain meanings from its new Christian settings. All these words and phrases are understood to describe oral transmission. For epistolary or other written communication there is another language group. Yet, with centuries of use, one can become the other. Thus, the Latin word *catechismus* is simply the Greek *katēchēsis* translated. For centuries it described the oral teaching of the faith. The question-and-answer form dates from Charlemagne's time (ca. 800). With the sixteenth-century invention of printing, the catechism became a book in question-and-answer form, but still something intended for oral recitation.

See: DISCIPLE, JESUS, KNOWLEDGE, PARABLE, PROPHET, SYNAGOGUE, WORD, WISDOM

CAROLYN OSIEK, R.S.C.J., AND
GERARD S. SLOYAN

TEMPLE

A temple was a necessity for the religion of ancient Israel. For Israel and for all the people of the ancient world, religion was essentially a social phenomenon. It was expressed through communal participation in specified rituals that could only take place in a temple. In the ancient world, the notion of a private religion independent of a temple

and its priesthood was just not available.

While the NT continues to speak of the Temple of Jerusalem as an important venue of Jesus' activity, the entry of Gentiles into the Christian community makes that structure less relevant. Temple becomes a metaphor for the body of Christ. Early Christians become increasingly ambivalent toward the Temple. Still, it is an important image in the liturgy.

Old Testament

The goal of the rituals in the Temple was the survival of the nation Israel guaranteed through success in its agricultural pursuits. The three main feasts, Passover/Unleavened Bread, Weeks, and Booths were harvest festivals. A system of sacrifices was the centerpiece of ceremonies connected with these festivals. Through the sacrifices made during the feasts, a portion of the land's produce was given to God as a thanksgiving for the successful harvest (see Deut 26:1-10). The underlying assumption of this system was that God, if properly thanked, will continue to grant prosperity. This will, in turn, lead to additional thank offerings in a continuing cycle that benefitted both God and the people.

The most famous of ancient Israelite temples was that built by Solomon in Jerusalem (1 Kings 6). The Bible presents the building of Solomon's Temple as an act of piety through which the young king fulfilled the intention of his father David (1 Kgs 8:15-21). The project was more likely the final step in securing Jerusalem's place as the principal city of the Davidic-Solomonic Empire and associating David's dynasty with the religious traditions of the Israelite tribes by providing a shrine to house the ark of the covenant that David brought to Jerusalem (2 Samuel 6).

Though the Bible presents Solomon's structure as the first Israelite Temple, archaeology has uncovered several earlier Israelite shrines. Some were large open-air cult places and others were smaller household shrines. Among the former are a twelfth-century BCE site with a large altar-like installation near Dothan and another altar complex in use from 1225 to 1100 BCE on Mount Ebal above the Shechem pass. Among the latter is a household shrine found at Megiddo. Dating from the time of Solomon, the shrine included two stone horned altars, ceramic cultic stands, and other vessels. These indicate that food, drink, and incense offerings were made there. Not far from Megiddo is Taanach. A household shrine dating from Solomon's time also turned up there. Among its cultic artifacts was a square terra cotta offering stand with an image of Astarte, the Canaanite goddess of fertility.

The First Book of Kings describes in some detail Solomon's Temple in Jerusalem (chs. 6–7). Ezekiel's dream of the restored Temple (chs. 40–43) provides additional details, though the prophet's vision provides an idealized picture of the Jerusalem edifice. Though there have been attempts to excavate in the area where this building was thought to have stood, no trace of it has ever been found.

It is unlikely that excavation could ever succeed in finding any elements of the Solomonic structure. The Babylonians destroyed it in 587 BCE. Supported by the Persian government, the Jews rebuilt the structure in 515 BCE, but Roman engineers employed by Herod the Great razed it to bedrock before building a new temple. This Herodian building was, in turn, destroyed by Romans during their sack of Jerusalem in 70 CE.

The Bible asserts that Babylonians "burned the house of the Lord" (2 Kgs 25:9). What they probably did was to set immense fires in the building. The limestone used in its construction simply disintegrated upon reaching a certain temperature and the building literally turned into powder. The Romans probably used the same procedure when they destroyed the second Temple.

The platform on which both Solomon's and Herod's Temples stood is now the site of two important Islamic structures, the Dome of the Rock and the al-Aqsa mosque. Any excavation in the area would threaten these buildings. Also many Orthodox Jews proscribe any activity in the area for fear of profaning the location of the holy of holies. In deference to Jewish and Muslim religious sensibilities, international law has made any systematic excavation of the site of Jerusalem's Temple an impossibility.

In the absence of direct archaeological evidence, we are dependent upon biblical texts and the excavation of other ancient Near Eastern temples in reconstructing the Temple of Solomon. The ground plan of the Temple divided the building into three parts arranged on a central axis: a vestibule, a central court, and the holy of holies. Archaeology has shown that the architects of the Temple borrowed a local Canaanite temple style that went back almost a millennium. Temples with similar tripartite floor plans were found at Middle Bronze Age Shechem and Late Bronze Age Hazor.

The superstructure and decoration of the Solomonic Temple also have parallels in similar structures from pre-Israelite temples in the region. These archaeological data serve to confirm the note in 1 Kings that Solomon consulted with the Phoenician king Hiram when he decided to build his temple and that Solomon's and Hiram's builders worked together on the project (1 Kgs 5:15-20, 32).

In the ancient Near East, temples were considered the earthly dwellings of the gods. As such, they were not buildings to shelter worshipers. Only the king and senior priests were allowed within temples at specific times for specified purposes. Ordinary worshipers gathered outside the temple in adjacent courtyards. That is one reason for the emphasis on the exterior decoration of the building. It was to impress worshipers whose homes were modified caves or simple four-room homes.

Sacrifices were offered outside the Temple on an altar erected for that purpose. Animal sacrifice was an especially messy process that required plenty of water to keep the area clean. That is why several large pools were located in Jerusalem and its vicinity. The sacrificial worship of the Temple required an immense volume of readily available water.

The only Israelite temple found by archaeologists is located in a small fortress south of Jerusalem at Arad in the Negev. This temple was much smaller and more available to the worshiper than its counterpart in Jerusalem. The Arad temple was in use from the time of Solomon to the late eighth century BCE. At that time, Hezekiah tried to centralize all sacrificial worship in Jerusalem (2 Kgs 18:3-4) by closing temples like the one at Arad.

The finds associated with an eighth-century BCE shrine at Kuntillet Ajrud in the south give some evidence that the Israelites who worshiped there honored not only Yahweh but Asherah, whom they may have conceived as his consort. Finally, a large, stone platform from the ninth century BCE was discovered at Dan. This platform could have supported a temple, but there is no certain evidence of that as yet. According to 1 Kings 12:25-31 Jeroboam established a place of worship at Dan to rival the one at Jerusalem.

This apparent diversity among Israelite temples and shrines shows that there never was a single pattern for the religion of ancient Israel. There existed side by side various strands from the religion of the Jerusalem Temple to that of Kuntillet Ajrud. The Bible, however, portrays Israelite religion as being handed down from Moses with little subsequent change. This is an idealized picture. Part of that picture was painted by the Book of Deuteronomy.

An important aspect of Deuteronomy's view of religion was the necessity of worshiping at the place God "will choose" (Deuteronomy 12). This, of course, was Jerusalem though Deuteronomy could not specify this location by name since Jerusalem was a Jebusite city until David conquered it. Deuteronomy presents itself as "the words spoken by Moses to all Israel beyond the Jordan" (1:1). By the time of the restoration (late sixth century BCE), when Deuteronomy took the form it now has, Jerusalem became by default the only place where the dispirited and destitute population of Judah could afford to support a sacrificial cult. Deuteronomy's choice of Jerusalem as the place of the only legitimate temple was dictated by necessity rather than theology.

Despite Jerusalem's exclusive claims that the Deuteronomic tradition supported, two Jewish communities in the Diaspora worshiped in temples. A Jewish military colony located in Upper Egypt built a temple on Elephantine Island in the fifth century BCE. During the Hellenistic period, another Jewish community at Leontopolis in the Nile Delta was given use of an ancient pharonic temple for the worship of Yahweh. Rabbinic tradition considered both these temples as illegitimate.

The teaching of the early rabbis enabled Judaism to survive the destruction of the second Temple. They completed the process that transformed the communal religion of ancient Israel into the religion of early Judaism. The former was a Temple-based, priestly-led religion whose principal goal was securing the blessing of fertility for the land through a system of sacrifices. The latter was an assembly-based, lay religion whose goal was the salvation of individuals through a life lived in obedience to Torah. The synagogue more than the Temple nourished religious life of rabbinic Judaism through a service of prayer and the reading of Scripture.

There were two attempts in antiquity to rebuild Jerusalem's Temple. The first one was sponsored by Julian the Apostate, but it ended with his death in 363 CE. The Persians who temporarily gained control of Jerusalem from the Byzantines in 614 CE sponsored the second attempt. It came to naught when the Byzantines regained control of Jerusalem in 629 CE. Today many religious Jews regard the reestablishment of sacrificial worship at a temple a step back into another age. Others are content to wait for the coming of the Messiah to renew worship in a temple. There is, however, a significant minority of ultra-Orthodox Jews who want to build a "Third

Temple." To do this will require the destruction of the Muslim shrines on the Temple Mount. They find support among many evangelical and fundamentalist Christians for whom a Third Temple is an indispensable part of their eschatological scenario.

See: SOLOMON, WORSHIP

LESLIE J. HOPPE, O.F.M.

New Testament

The Temple of Jerusalem. As in the OT, no edifice in Jerusalem was more prominent than the Temple, recognized by Jews and Christians as the house of God. The Temple was a house of worship, prayer, and sacrifice, accomodating vast crowds on feasts such as Passover and Pentecost. The Temple of the NT stood on the site of a first Temple built in the tenth century BCE by Solomon,* destroyed in 587 BCE in the Babylonian invasion, but restored as the second Temple early in the postexilic period. The NT structure was a grand edifice, rebuilt and much enlarged by Herod the Great. Its construction began in 19 BCE and was completed in 64 CE, six years before its destruction by the Romans in 70 CE. The Temple played an important part in the story of Jesus and the apostolic Church. Its very structure, its walls, gates, courts and porticoes, and its sanctuaries, inner and outer, was the setting for many important events and provided the NT with a fine set of theological images.

Some of the climactic events of Jesus' life took place in the Temple at Jerusalem. According to the Synoptic Gospels, when Jesus arrived at Jerusalem, he went to the Temple area and cleansed it (Mark 11:15-19, par.), driving out "those selling and buying there" and overturning "the tables of the money changers and the seats of those who were selling doves" (Mark 11:15). Jesus' prophetic action was inspired by Isaiah 56:7, declaring God's house a house of prayer, whereas they had made it a den of thieves (Mark 11:17).

In John, the event is at the beginning of Jesus' ministry (John 2:13-22), where it re-calls Psalm 69:9: "Zeal for your house will consume me." John presents the cleansing after the wedding at Cana as a second great event showing the passing of an era and the beginning of another. The time for sacrifices and the need for animal stalls and money changers were over. The hour had come when "true worshipers" would "worship the Father in Spirit and truth" (John 4:23).

Once cleansed, the Temple was the site of Jesus' teaching. In Mark, he addresses key issues affecting various parties, beginning with the chief priests, the scribes, and the elders (11:27–12:12), and continuing with the Pharisees and Herodians (12:13-17), the Sadducees (12:18-27), one of the scribes (12:28-37), people in general (12:38-40), and the disciples (12:41-44).

On leaving the Temple, one of the disciples expressed amazement at its buildings and stones (Mark 13:1), prompting a prophecy of the Temple's total destruction. In Luke, the same prophecy reflects the Gospel's concern with wealth and poverty and refers to the Temple's costly stones and votive offerings (Luke 21:5-6).

Jesus and the disciples then went to the Mount of Olives opposite the Temple for the great eschatological discourse (Mark 13:3-37; Matt 24:3–25:46) in which the Temple's destruction is connected with the persecution and the great tribulation heralding the coming of the Son of Man. The sign for these things would be the Temple's profanation by "the desolating abomination" (Mark 13:14). Luke's version of the eschatological discourse says nothing of the Temple's desecration and separates the destruction of Jerusalem from the final cataclysm, which will not be "until the times of the Gentiles are fulfilled" (Luke 21:24).

The Temple is a major theme in Luke, which begins with a scene in the Temple (1:5-25) and ends with a summary showing the disciples "continually in the temple praising God" (24:53). The prologue includes a first visit to the Temple for Jesus' presentation (2:22-38) and a second when he was lost but then found teaching in the

Temple after three days (2:41-52), evoking Jesus' final journey to Jerusalem to fulfill the necessity that he be in his Father's house (2:49). The earthly Temple was a symbol of the Father's heavenly dwelling and Jesus' ultimate destiny, embraced anew when he refused to cast himself down from the Temple parapet. Testing God was not compatible with openness to the will of the Father (4:9-12). In Jesus' final moment, when "the veil of the temple was torn down the middle," the earthly symbol gave way to the heavenly reality, and Jesus committed his spirit into his Father's hands (23:45-46).

The Acts of the Apostles speak of the Christians as gathering every day in the Temple area (2:46). Once, Peter cured someone by the "Beautiful Gate" (Acts 3:1-10) and addressed the people in "Solomon's Portico" (3:11-26). For many years, the Temple remained for the Christians a symbol of the Father's dwelling, and the early Christians fulfilled all the observances regarding it (21:26; see Luke 2:22-24). Paul's coming into the Temple area with some Greeks for the purpose of purification provoked a riot and required military intervention (21:27-36). The Temple was a place of prayer for all the people (22:17), both Jew and Greek.

The New Temple. Because of its importance for Judaism, for Jesus' ministry, and the apostolic Church, the Temple of Jerusalem loomed large in early Christian consciousness, raising problems when the Church welcomed Gentiles and after the Temple's destruction. But with time the Christians saw in Jesus' death an image of the destruction of the Temple and in his resurrection an image of its rebuilding. The body of Christ was a new temple replacing the Temple of Jerusalem as a sign of God's presence.

In Mark's passion account, Jesus is accused of having said: "I will destroy this temple made with hands and within three days I will build another not made with hands" (Mark 14:58; see 15:29). The only record we have of Jesus having said this is in John's account of the cleansing of the Temple (John 2:19). John explains that Jesus "was speaking about the temple of his body" (2:21), and this is something his disciples remembered when he was raised from the dead (2:22).

A similar theme appears in Paul, where it refers to Christians, the Church, forming the body of Christ and the people of God (2 Cor 6:16-18). Christians constitute the temple of God, the dwelling of God's Spirit, rising on the foundation that is Jesus Christ. Being God's temple assures them of divine protection (1 Cor 3:10-17) and has implications for Christian living (2 Cor 6:14-18). The finest development of the theme is in Ephesians 2:19-22. Both Jews and Gentiles are made one in the body of Christ (Eph 2:11-18), where they are "members of the household of God, built upon the foundation of the apostles and prophets, with Christ Jesus himself as the capstone" (Eph 2:19-20). The temple is still being built. Through Christ "the whole structure is held together and grows into a temple sacred in the Lord; in him you also are being built together into a dwelling place of God in the Spirit" (Eph 2:21-22). There is a similar development in 1 Peter who asks that Christians, like living stones, allow themselves to be built into a spiritual house, for which Jesus Christ is the cornerstone (1 Pet 2:4-6). Paul also extended the image of the Temple to each Christian's body, making sexual sins against their own body sins against the very temple of God (1 Cor 6:15-20).

The Heavenly Temple. Besides the Temple of Jerusalem and the new temple of Christ's body, the NT also speaks of a heavenly temple patterned on God's earthly dwelling. The heavenly temple imagery appears in the Letter to the Hebrews and in the Book of Revelation.

In the Letter to the Hebrews, Jesus is the unique high priest who already has passed "through the greater and more perfect tabernacle not made by hands, that is, not belonging to this creation" and "entered once for all into the sanctuary . . . with his own blood, thus obtaining eternal redemption" (Heb 9:11-12). The earthly counterpart for this heavenly tabernacle is not the Temple of Jerusalem but the Mosaic tabernacle (see Exod 25:1–31:18), which was but an earthly "copy and shadow of the heavenly sanctuary." The copy was built by human beings according to the pattern shown Moses on the mountain. It is there in the heavenly sanctuary, which is the true tabernacle set up by the Lord, that God has his throne and that Jesus has taken his seat at the right hand (8:1-5). The heavenly tabernacle belongs to the second (8:7) or new covenant (8:13) and is "greater and more perfect" (9:11) than the tabernacle of the first covenant (9:1-5).

The Book of Revelation is also concerned with the superiority of the heavenly over the earthly temple, but the earthly temple is not that of Jerusalem or the Mosaic tabernacle, which belonged to the first covenant, but that of the Church, belonging to the new. The heavenly temple is seen in visions as the dwelling of God, with God reigning from a great throne on which the Lamb that was slain is seen standing. The heavenly liturgy, with its hymns and incense, is one of praise (4:1–5:14) and supplication (7:9-17). During the time of the Church, there is also an earthly temple, which is the Church itself, with its outer court handed over to the Gentiles. It too has an altar and worshipers, but it is also a place for prophesying (11:1-3). At the end of time, God will make all things new and dwell with the entire human race, which will then constitute the people of God (21:1-4). At that time, there will be no temple in the city, for its temple will be "the Lord God almighty and the Lamb" (21:22). With God and Christ present throughout the Church and the Church throughout the human race, there will be no need for a special divine dwelling.

See: BODY OF CHRIST, COVENANT, HEAVEN, PEOPLE OF GOD, WORSHIP

EUGENE LAVERDIERE, S.S.S.

Pastoral-Liturgical Tradition

The Image of Temple in the Patristic Period. The early generations of the Church manifested ambivalence toward the Temple and its cult. This ambivalence seems to be rooted in Jesus' own attitude. While the NT reports that Jesus taught in the Temple and regarded it as God's house and a house of prayer, he also suggests that in the fulfillment of his mission he will himself surpass the Temple (John 2:18-22; cf. Matt 24:2; Mark 13:2; Luke 21:6).

After the resurrection the early Christian community is slow to distinguish itself from Judaism, a posture expressed in part by their participation in Temple worship (Acts 2:46; 3:1; 22:17). Against this must be viewed Jesus' identification of his body with the Temple and Paul's subsequent identification of Christ's body with the Church, a living Temple (1 Cor 12:27; 3:16-17; Eph 2:19-22). God dwells now in Christ and in his body, the Church.

All of salvation history finds its fulfillment in Christ and in his paschal mystery. A distinctive feature of Christian worship is that it "memorializes" the salvation already accomplished in Christ. Christian worship is distinguished from Jewish worship not simply by the appearance of its cult, its liturgy, but by its content. The victory of Christ animates Christian liturgy with its eternally present reality of salvation already accomplished. In our celebration of the sacred mysteries Christ acts in us, head with body, in offering worship pleasing to the Father. In turn, that which the Temple symbolizes, God dwelling with us, is fulfilled and perpetuated.

One must be wary, therefore, of too facile an identification of Christian churches with the Temple. The post-apostolic Church continued to convene in the homes of members for the breaking of bread. There seems to be no early cultic reverence for the building in which the Church gathered, often referred to simply as the *domus ecclesiae* or "house of the assembly."

After the Edict of Milan in the fourth century Constantine initiated the erection of basilicas, in and around Jerusalem, at the sites of the "holy places." These efforts expressed and encouraged a devout fascination with the geography of Christian history. Not only the locations at which the events of Christ's own life, death, and resurrection transpired, but the burial places of the early apostles and martyrs were so honored, especially at Rome.

Basilicas also served to accommodate the larger number of worshipers that resulted from the "peace of the Church." In places where the size of homes was no longer adequate to these swollen assemblies, especially the large urban communities, the basilica was an apt accommodation.

It must be remembered that the basilica was originally a civic gathering space without explicit cultic associations, unless insofar as these came over from Judaism, which had already pressed into service the basilican architecture for synagogue worship. By the fourth century, however, this connection would have been no more than tenuous and unconscious, owing to the Church's antipathy toward things Jewish and pagan. Although the Fathers of the Church may have borrowed the imagery of the Temple as a typological referent in their preaching, the allusion was not to the building in Jerusalem, which had lost its sacred significance and, in any event, had long since been destroyed. As Clement of Alexandria (d. ca. 215) explains, "What I am calling a temple is not a building but a gathering of the elect" (*Stromata* 7.5).

Rather, an organic adaptation unfolded, which invested old forms with new meanings. Perhaps this can be seen at the architectural level in the shift of orientation from synagogue to Christian basilica. The cultic significance of the synagogue derived from the Jerusalem Temple, even after the latter's destruction in 70 CE. This was expressed in the custom of "orienting" synagogues toward the Temple and the holy of holies in Jerusalem. When Christians began to build their own churches according to the basilica model they too "oriented" them, though not toward the earthly Jerusalem, but toward the East.

As the station from which the sun rose and the day dawned the eastern sky symbolized the Church's hope of Christ's return from the heavenly Jerusalem. The Christian basilica derived its meaning not from the precedent of the Jerusalem Temple, or if so only secondarily. Rather, Christians gathered in *anamnesis*, "in memory" of Christ's promised return. This custom did not change even after the erection of basilicas by Christians in fourth-century Jerusalem, when it might be supposed that a restoration of Jerusalem orientation would have been thought fitting. Later, especially in the West, this custom did break down for apparently practical reasons: as the liturgy itself evolved or due to topographical requirements. The earlier preference is instructive, though, in the relationship of church to Temple.

Temple in the Rite for the Dedication of a Church. This ancient understanding of the relationship between Church and Temple informs the Rite for the Dedication of a Church and an Altar (1977). In the decree of promulgation itself we read:

> A church is the place where the Christian community is gathered to hear the word of God, to offer prayers of intercession and praise to God, and above all to celebrate the holy mysteries; and it is the place where the holy sacrament of the eucharist is kept. Thus it stands as a special kind of image of the Church itself, *which is God's temple built from living stones.*

"Temple" here clearly refers not to the structure we call "church," but to the assembly of the baptized, for which the structure "stands as a special kind of image."

The word "temple" occurs numerous times within the Rite, in rubrics, antiphons, instructions, and prayer texts. The Rite's uses of the word describe Christ himself, the Church, that is, the assembly, or the two in union. Only secondarily does the Rite use the word "temple" to refer to the building being dedicated.

In paragraph 6 of the "Prayer of Dedication" the word evokes Ephesians 2:21-22:

> The Church is favored,
> the dwelling place of God on earth:

> a temple built of living stones,
> founded on the apostles
> with Jesus Christ its cornerstone.

Here the "temple" is the assembly of the Church, founded on the apostles, built on Christ, and the dwelling place of God. The building that houses the Church becomes a sacrament of the heavenly Temple, established in Christ and manifested in the Church.

Perhaps the richness of the Temple image is expressed most fully in the proper Preface provided for the Rite of Dedication. Here "temple" serves as the primary metaphor for the entire text and the word itself is used three times with three different referents. "Temple" is an image for the whole of creation, for God's heavenly city, and for the incarnate Christ, "born of the Virgin." Secondarily in the text it is also an image for the whole assembly of the Church, living and dead, "enlivened by the Spirit and cemented together in love." The preface concludes, "In that holy city you will be all in all for endless ages, and Christ will be its light for ever."

The Temple can be seen, therefore, to be an organizing metaphor for the Christian vision of space and time, with Christ himself, his body the Church, the *"domus ecclesiae,"* and the kingdom of heaven each among its referents.

See: CHURCH, HOLY, PRIEST/PRIESTHOOD, VIRTUE

BRIAN J. FISCHER

TEMPTATION

The experience of being seduced by evil or being severely tested by contrary spirits is a recurring motif of the Bible and Christian spiritual tradition.

Old Testament

The Bible is filled with stories about temptation. Sometimes the people are tempted, and sometimes the people tempt God.

God Tempts. The story of the garden of Eden (Gen 2:4b–3:24) centers on what is commonly called the temptation, although that word is not found in the canonical text. According to the story, God created the tree of knowledge and the tree of life. Then he told Adam and Eve that they could not eat of the tree. The temptation was not, as we think of temptation, an urge to violate an ethical law, but an attempt to depend on themselves. As the early Church writers said, it was a sin of pride. God tested them to find out what mettle they had, whether they were willing to take the risk of depending on God. Here temptation is a test.

So also God tempted Abraham. "Some time after these events, God put Abraham to the test" (Gen 22:1). Then follows the story of the sacrifice of Isaac. What God is asking seems unreasonable and unethical; namely, a human sacrifice. Within the traditional story of Abraham, the patriarch had willingly enough left his own country and accepted the promise of blessings. He had received a good measure of reward. But had he really believed? The final test came in this incident. Both God and Abraham learned the true meaning of this man's faith.

The Exodus is interpreted by the later sermons in Deuteronomy as a series of tests by God. "[God] fed you in the desert with manna, a food unknown to your fathers, that he might afflict you and test you, but also make you prosperous in the end. Otherwise, you might say to yourselves, 'It is my own power and the strength of my own hand that has obtained for me this wealth'" (Deut 8:16-17; see also 13:4; 33:8). So also God warned them that they might be tested by false prophets (Deut 13:4). When the people failed to believe the original scouts sent into the Promised Land God sentenced all of them to die in the desert. "Of all the men who have seen my glory and the signs I worked in Egypt and in the desert, and who nevertheless have put me to the test ten times already and have failed to heed my voice, not one shall see the land which I promised on oath to their fathers" (Num 14:21-23). It is noteworthy in these reflections of the sacred authors that temptation is a test of understanding and of faith in the power of God.

In the tribal stories recounted in the Book of Judges there is a theme that God tested the people by allowing more powerful neighbors to ravage them. "Through these nations the Israelites were to be made to prove whether or not they would keep to the way of the LORD and continue in it as their fathers had done" (Judg 2:22; see also 3:1, 4; 6:39).

This sense of learning something from temptation is present throughout and grows in importance in the Wisdom tradition. Solomon was famed for his wisdom. The early story of the Queen of Sheba says: "The queen of Sheba, having heard of Solomon's fame, came to test him with subtle questions" (1 Kgs 10:1; 2 Chr 9:1). Later in the second century BCE Ben Sira observes concerning Wisdom:

She walks with him as a stranger,
  and at first she puts him to the test;
Fear and dread she brings upon him
  and tries him with her discipline;
With her precepts she puts him to the proof,
  until his heart is fully with her.
Then she comes back to bring him happiness
  and reveal her secrets to him
                              (Sir 4:17-18).

So on a more pedestrian level he says later:

A man with training gains wide knowledge;
  a man of experience speaks sense.
One never put to the proof knows little,
  whereas with travel a man adds to his
    resourcefulness
                              (Sir 34:9-10).

The Book of Wisdom, which is late and written in Greek, observes of the wise,

Chastised a little, they shall be greatly blessed,
  because God tried them
  and found them worthy of himself.
As gold in the furnace, he proved them,
  and as sacrificial offerings he took them to
    himself.
. . . Those who trust in him shall understand
    truth,
  and the faithful shall abide with him in love
                              (Wis 3:5-6, 9).

Temptation in all these texts is always a question of probing true understanding and taking a gamble on faith in God.

We Tempt God. Conversely, we tempt God to see if God will be faithful to us. In the story of the Exodus occurs the "murmuring tradition." The people frequently complained that God was not providing them with the means necessary for living comfortably in the desert (Exod 15:25, the water at Marah; 16:4, the quail and manna; 20:20, the convocation at Sinai). In all these cases it is said that God tempted them. But the people also tempted God (Exod 17:2) and so that place was called *Massah*. It was remembered later in the psalms as the Day of Massah (Ps 95:8). Those psalms, which most frequently mention this tempting of the Lord, exhort the people to seek forgiveness for their lack of trust.

But they sinned yet more against him,
  rebelling against the Most High in the
    wasteland,
And they tempted God in their hearts,
  by demanding the food they craved.
Again and again they tempted God,
  and provoked the Holy One of Israel.
But they tempted and rebelled against God
the Most High,
  and kept not his decrees
                              (Ps 78:18, 41, 56).

See: SIN, TRUST

                              JAMES A. FISCHER, C.M.

New Testament

The underlying Greek word here is nearly always the noun *peirasmos* and its cognate verb, *peirazein*; together, these occur a total of sixty times in the NT, mostly with theologically significant meanings. Four times (Matt 4:7; Luke 4:12; 10:25; 1 Cor 10:9) the related compound verb *ekpeirazein* is used. In the revised NT of the NAB, both verbs are translated by "to tempt," "to test," or "to put to the test"; instances where words of this group are used in a non-theological sense (in Acts 9:26; 16:7; 24:6; 2 Cor 13:5; Gal 4:14) will not be treated here. In the RSV, "temptation" is occasionally used to translate other Greek terms, but this has been changed in the revised edition of 1989.

Behind the NT understanding of temptation lie two OT experiences: that God (sometimes through Satan) tested Israel or individual Israelites to prove their steadfastness or expose their lack of it; and that Israel, quite inappropriately, was inclined to do the same to God. Although the NT never depicts God as the tempter (except in a reference to Abraham in Heb 11:17), it does speak relatively frequently of people's character being tried or tested by others, sometimes under explicitly satanic influence. The presumption is that this state of affairs is permitted by God. We shall begin by considering examples of this in the Gospels and then in the rest of the NT. The second understanding of temptation, that of tempting God, will be dealt with in section 2.

The Testing of Individuals. This testing may be recognized in three contexts in the Gospels. In two of these Jesus is tested: first, by Satan in the desert and then by the religious establishment, which tries to discredit him by showing in one way or another that his power cannot come from God. The third kind of reference is to the temptation that Christians will have to undergo, a testing expected to become particularly acute in the "last days."

Jesus' own testing by Satan is found in Matthew 4:1-11; Mark 1:12-13; and Luke 4:1-13; John has no equivalent. All three evangelists state that Jesus, immediately after his baptism, was led by the Spirit into the desert, where he stayed for forty days; in each of these Gospels it is evident that Jesus does not succumb, although this is only implicit in Mark. The principal idea is this: whereas Israel, during forty years in the desert, repeatedly failed to measure up to the standard required of God's people, Jesus proves himself faithful to God. Mark's brief account conveys little more than this, but what he says is highly significant, for it begins Mark's specification of the kind of Messiah (Mark 1:1) that Jesus is to be.

In contrast to Mark, Matthew and Luke (presumably in reliance on their non-Marcan source, Q) give details of three acts of tempting by Satan, including the accompanying dialogue. The order of the second and third of these is reversed in the two accounts. Most scholars think that Matthew gives the original order, in which the story's horizon expands from the desert, to the holy city, and then to all the kingdoms of the world; Luke probably changed this so as to make this story, like his Gospel as a whole, climax in Jerusalem and thereby reflect Jesus' subsequent deliberate movement to that city.

Matthew and Luke thus show Jesus resisting three temptations. These have been understood as enticements to: (1) provide himself (and the people?) with bread; (2) to make a name for himself by a highly spectacular feat; and (3) to use illicit means to gain power over human institutions. More convincingly the temptations have been shown: (1) to surrender to the evil inclination; (2) to test God; (3) to give in to the seduction of wealth (see B. Gerhardsson, *The Testing of God's Son,* Lund: Gleerup, 1966). In this way, they amply demonstrate (at least in a provisional way) what it means for Jesus to be Son of God, the title applied to him by the voice from heaven in the baptism story (Matt 3:17; Luke 3:22). Luke concludes his account with the note: "When the devil had finished every temptation, he departed from him for a time" (4:13); that Jesus was comprehensively tested is reflected also in Hebrews 4:15, where he is the high priest and Son of God "who has [like Christians] been tested in every way, yet [unlike Christians] without sin."

There are some indications that, more consciously than the other evangelists, Luke may be presenting the tempted Jesus as a model for Christians. Thus in 4:13, a verse that is clearly editorial, he alone uses the noun "temptation" to refer to what happened to Jesus in the desert, and he uses it again in the explanation of the parable of the sower: in distinction from his source,

Mark, Luke says it is "in time of temptation" that those sown on rocky ground fall away (8:13; cf. Matt 13:21; Mark 4:17). In line with this, whereas in Gethsemane Mark and Matthew have Jesus once exhort the disciples to pray lest they enter into temptation (Mark 14:38; Matt 26:41; Luke 22:46), Luke has an earlier, unparalleled example of the same thing (22:40). Finally, in Luke alone does Jesus commend and promise to reward the disciples for having stood by him in his "trials" (Greek: *peirasmos*, in the plural; Luke 22:28). Evidently, Luke saw coping with temptation as an area in which those for whom he wrote needed help and encouragement.

The second use of "temptation" in the Gospels is in those sections where various religious officials either (1) challenge Jesus to prove the source of his authority, usually by asking for a heavenly sign, or (2) make him answer questions intended to ensnare him. The details vary with each Gospel, but the first type of testing is worked out in Mark 8:11-13 and Luke 11:16-17 (where Jesus refuses to give such a sign) and in Matthew 12:38-40; 16:1, 4; and Luke 11:29-33, where Jesus offers the "sign of Jonah." In Luke 12:54-56 (and in some, though not the best, manuscripts of Matt 16:2-3) Jesus does indeed offer a sign from heaven: the weather!

Each of the Synoptic Gospels also shows the second type of testing: where religious authorities ask Jesus trick questions. Thus, all three portray Jesus as recognizing the question about tribute as such a test (Mark 12:15 and par.). When, in Mark 10:2-12 and Matthew 19:3-12, Pharisees ask Jesus about divorce, each evangelist observes that their intent was to test him, while Matthew (22:35) and Luke (10:25) present in the same terms the scribal question about the greatest commandment of the Law. Similarly, in John 8:1-12 (which is unlikely to be the work of this evangelist), scribes and Pharisees bring the adulterous woman to Jesus for judgment "to test him, so that they could have some charge to bring against him" (8:6). There is one other use of this verb in the Fourth Gospel: in 6:6 Jesus tests Philip by asking him where they are to get food for the hungry crowds; Philip fails the test, of course.

The third sense of "temptation" in the Gospels is the use of the noun in the Synoptics to refer to temptation that Christians must undergo. In the tradition of texts such as Daniel 12:10, it is probably right to understand all such instances (except possibly Luke 8:13) as part of the heightened testing that occurs with the end time. Jesus tells the sleeping disciples in Gethsemane, "Watch and pray that you may not undergo the test. The spirit is willing but the flesh is weak" (Mark 14:38; Matt 26:41; Luke 22:46 is briefer). This was certainly an appropriate message for them at that point, but is no less so for readers of the Gospels, who, whenever they pray the prayer that Jesus taught them, are to say, "And lead us not into temptation" (Matt 6:13; Luke 11:4).

In the NT outside the Gospels there is much about temptation. Mostly, the blame is put on Satan/the tempter/the devil (1 Cor 7:5; 1 Thess 3:5; Rev 2:10). James is insistent that God is not responsible for temptations: rather, people are seduced by their own desire (Jas 1:13-14; see also 1 Tim 6:9). However, at least in Paul, the question of God's involvement remains open: in 1 Corinthians 10:13 Paul notes that "with the trial [God] will also provide a way out, so that you may be able to bear it." This would be consistent with the situation envisaged in the Book of Job, where God allows Satan to test people and in this way carry out God's deeper (and sometimes quite inscrutable) designs.

The general assumption of NT writers is that temptation is, if not inevitable (Jas 1:2, 12; 1 Pet 1:6; 4:12), at least an ever present possibility for Christians (Gal 6:1). As in Daniel, it is characteristic of the "end time" in which people now live (see above, in the section on the Gospels). Such trials should lead to joy, says James, because they enable people to demonstrate their love for God.

Readers of 2 Peter 2:9 and the Philadelphian community addressed in Revelation 3:10 are reassured that God will not allow them to be overcome by such trial. According to the writer of Hebrews, Christ's own experience makes him prone to help here: "Because he himself was tested through what he suffered, he is able to help those who are being tested" (Heb 2:18; see also 4:15). Throughout the NT, God ultimately remains in control, even though "testing" (sometimes of a very prosaic sort—e.g., Acts 20:19) may loom large in the Christian consciousness. The providence of God is always more encompassing than such trials.

People Who Test God. There is a radical difference between trusting in God (as Israel was required to do) and putting that same God to the test by taking foolish risks to see how far God's protection extends. (No parent of a small child needs to be told this.) Jesus knows it well. Thus when, in Matthew and Luke, the devil suggests that he throw himself from the pinnacle of the Temple, to force God to send angels to catch him and thereby "prove" that he is indeed the Son of God, Jesus responds by quoting Deuteronomy 6:16: "You shall not put the Lord, your God, to the test" (Matt 4:7; Luke 4:12). As we saw in the first part of section 1 above, the underlying issue here is what it means for Jesus to be God's Son. The issue of someone testing God does not arise elsewhere in the Gospels.

Temptation as "testing God" comes up several times in the rest of the NT. There are two examples in Acts. In chapter 15, at his description of the Jerusalem Council, Luke depicts Peter as saying that to make Gentile converts keep the whole Jewish Law constituted just such a temptation. For one thing, they would not be able to do it (v. 10) and, besides, it was unnecessary, because salvation is "through the grace of the Lord Jesus" (v. 11). Earlier, in chapter 5, Ananias and Sapphira came to a bad end because they had agreed "to test the Spirit of the Lord" (v. 9) by giving to the apostles only part of the money from the sale of their piece of property, while pretending to donate the whole amount. In doing this, they were not merely trying to deceive human beings, as they apparently thought, but were rather testing God by trying to win divine favor by deceitful means, which God will not allow.

The other two instances of this concept are warnings to Christians about putting God to the test in the way that Israel did in the desert. Thus, Paul tells the overconfident Corinthians that they must not test Christ (and, presumably, his power to save) by immoral behavior, as did Israel (see 1 Cor 10:9). Similar warnings about testing God come from the writer of the Letter to the Hebrews, who reminds his readers about the dire fate of the desert generation, "your ancestors [who] tested and tried" God (Heb 3:8-9, quoting Ps 95:8-9).

For NT writers, then, temptation refers to the testing of human or divine character. In the former instance it may lead to sin, and to put God to the test always indicates a lack of faith; however, the NT concept is far richer than the common contemporary understanding of temptation as a simple lure or enticement to sin.

See: ANOINTING, BAPTISM, BODY OF CHRIST, CHURCH, COMMUNITY, CONVERSION, CREATION, GIFTS, GLORY, GOOD NEWS, HEALING, JORDAN, LAW, MISSION, PENTECOST, PEOPLE OF GOD, PROPHET/PROPHECY, REIGN OF GOD, SERVANT, SON OF GOD, TEMPLE, TONGUES, WITNESS

PATRICIA M. MCDONALD, S.H.C.J.

Pastoral-Liturgical Tradition

Temptation as understood in the Christian tradition draws its understanding from two sets of meanings in the Bible. The first set has to do with the factors and agents that lead persons away from God's law and the dictates of their conscience to choose against God. The second set of meanings is temptation in a quite different sense: God's putting us to the test for the sake of our own moral and spiritual advancement. This latter sense is evidenced in the request in the Lord's prayer ("lead us not into temptation").

Temptation in the first sense, temptation to sin (q.v.), has its roots in the effects of original sin. The prototypical story told in Genesis 2–3 portrays the misuse of human freedom. The possibility to misuse our freedom—to choose those things that are to our detriment and bring about our diminishment—is further complicated by the confused and disordered nature of human desire, called in the tradition "concupiscence." This concupiscence is played upon to make an object of temptation appear attractive, desirable, even good. Even though such disordered desire runs up against the dictates of conscience, the desire may in some instances overwhelm conscience in our choice to sin. The Christian tradition insists upon resistance to temptation from its first stirrings, and goes further to urge avoiding situations in which temptation is likely to arise. The tradition recommends further developing habits of prayer and exercises of self-denial to strengthen the will against acquiescing to the lures of temptation.

In exploring the origins of temptation, there are three possible sources that the tradition identifies which may interact in a number of ways. The first source is Satan. Drawing upon the story of the serpent with Adam and Eve in the Garden in Genesis 2–3 and the stories of Christ's temptation in the desert, this fallen angel or personification of evil is seen as the adversary of the good and thus of God. Satan tries to lure human beings away from their communion with God in the good. At times, and in some cultures, the action of Satan has been depicted most graphically, such as the case of the temptations of St. Antony (d. 356) in the desert. Western medieval iconography made much of Satan and the demons. Contemporary Western cultures, emphasizing the individual and individual responsibility, have played down the role of Satan as an active agent in human temptation. The image of Satan, however, as personified evil (the phrase favored in Vatican II's Pastoral Constitution on the Church in the Modern World) is an important antidote against an optimism about the self-perfectibility of human nature.

The preferred contemporary mode in Western theology to speak of the origins of temptation is to explore the workings of the human person. Such an approach has, of course, a long history in the tradition, both in theological and in spiritual writings. This possibility examines how disordered desire works upon a human person willing to lead him/her away from the good, through a seduction into believing that the object desired really is the good, or an accumulation of previous acts into a habit that the will finds difficult to resist. How one understands the working of the human person in this regard depends upon a prior understanding of how the human being is constituted in the first place. The early Modern period, for example, employed a faculty psychology that saw different psychic functions as separate entities or working units, an idea that seems somewhat foreign today. Contemporary psychological understandings of this process accord a greater role to the workings of the unconscious and to prior individual history.

A third source is the social environment in which the individual operates. The environment, tainted by social sin, can contribute to the malformation of the individual conscience or ingrain habits of acting that are only partially available to rational control. An example of malformation of conscience would be a child who grows up unloved and comes to act out of anger and protectiveness rather than love or trust. How does one explain the process of encountering temptation, and the possibility of acquiescing to it, in such circumstances? An example of ingrained habits is racism. Even those who hold conscious, anti-racist attitudes will still find themselves succumbing to racism. To say that persons in either of these circumstances are not entirely culpable for their actions only gets at part of the point. While they may not be personally guilty for their actions, their actions nonetheless contribute to an increment of separation from God in the world. Latin American liberation theologians and African American theologians have contributed to our better understanding of this.

As the last comment indicates, being subject to temptation is not in itself sin. As human beings we are all so subject, and the Scriptures indicate that even Jesus did not escape temptation. But how we respond to temptation in each instance affects also our ability or failure to resist in future encounters.

God's putting us to the test is something quite different, since its intent is to lead us closer to God rather than away from God. This way of speaking uses the language of temptation to explain how encounter with adversity moves us beyond human incapacity and failing to acknowledge our deep dependence upon God. In so recognizing our contingency and our right relation to God, we are offered an opportunity to draw closer to God.

As already noted, the Church urges Christians to a life of prayer, whereby the habit of communion with God can help overcome habits of giving in to temptation. Habits too of self-restraint and self-denial help with the ordering and controlling of disordered desire. Desire in itself is not evil; it might be considered a kind of life-force. But through sinfulness it has become disordered and needs guidance to achieve its true ends, away from sin and conversion to God.

See: CONSCIENCE, WEAKNESS

ROBERT J. SCHREITER, C.PP.S.

TENT

Old Testament

As a human abode, tent (*'ohel*) is the portable dwelling used by the Israelites when they were nomadic shepherds. Not until after the settlement in Canaan did they begin to construct houses (*bayit*). In Genesis 4:20 Jabal is said to be "the ancestor of all who dwell in tents and keep cattle." The Song of Songs (1:5) refers to the dark color of tents, probably woven from black goats' hair, as are Bedouin tents today. Animal skins were also used.

The E and P strands of the Pentateuch describe the tent of meeting (*'ōhel mô'ēd*), the place where God would speak with representative Israelites (Exod 33:7-11; Num 11:16-17, 24-30) during the period of wilderness wandering. God was not thought to reside there permanently, but rather the divine presence was manifest there whenever Moses entered to speak with God. The Priestly sources of the Pentateuch depict the tabernacle of God's dwelling (*miškān*), the portable sanctuary made by the Israelites (Exodus 25–30; 35–40) and used during the wilderness period. Whenever they would move on, the Levites would dismantle the tabernacle and reerect it in the new place of encampment (Num 1:50-51).

Another kind of temporary shelter are the *sukkôt*, or booths, made for the feast of Tabernacles (Exod 23:16; 34:22; Deut 16:13-15). Dwelling in booths during this joyous autumnal harvest feast was a reminder of God's protection of Israel during the wilderness wandering (Lev 23:39-43; John 7:2, 10).

Tent is used metaphorically as an image of security and protection. In the day of trouble, God will conceal one "in the shelter of his tent" (Ps 27:5). Tent also connotes one's life, "the tent of the upright will flourish" (Prov 14:11). Jeremiah laments, "My tent is ruined, all its cords are severed. My sons have left me, they are no more: no one to pitch my tent" (10:20). God's promise of restoration in Amos 9:11 is, "On that day I will raise up the fallen hut [*sukkôt*] of David."

New Testament

In the NT tent (*skēnē*) is also used in the figurative sense. Paul, a tentmaker by profession (Acts 18:3), mixes tent and clothing imagery to contrast the earthly body with the resurrected body, "For we know that if our earthly dwelling, a tent, should be destroyed, we have a building from God, a dwelling not made with hands, eternal in heaven. For in this tent we groan, longing to be further clothed with our heavenly habitation" (2 Cor 5:1-3). Similarly, Luke refers to everlasting life as "eternal tents" (16:9).

The author of Hebrews, in comparing Jesus' priesthood and that of the Levitical priests, contrasts the former sacred place, the tent of meeting set up by Moses, with the "true tent that the Lord, not any mortal, has set up" (Heb 8:2 [NRSV]). The tent of the Israelites was "a copy and a shadow of the heavenly sanctuary" (8:5); but Christ passed through "the greater and perfect tent (not made with hands, that is, not of this creation)" (9:11 [NRSV]).

In John 1:14 tenting is an image for Jesus' incarnation, "And the Word became flesh and made his dwelling among us" (lit. "pitched his tent among us"). At the transfiguration, Peter proposes setting up three tents, one each for Jesus, Moses, and Elijah (Mark 9:5; Matt 17:4; Luke 9:33).

See: BODY, ELIJAH/ELISHA, FEASTS, HOUSE, MOSES, TRANSFIGURATION

BARBARA E. REID, O.P.

THANKSGIVING

Thanksgiving permeates both testaments of the Bible. In the OT it is public expression in song and sacrifice of gratitude to God for rescue and favor. In the NT thanksgiving is so constitutive of Christian life that the very name of their central act of worship, "Eucharist," derives from the Greek verb that means "to give thanks." Almost every letter of Paul opens with a formulaic thanksgiving for the faith of the community to whom he writes. Christians phrase their thanksgiving to God through Jesus Christ, who is the supreme expression of God's graciousness to humankind.

Old Testament

In the OT giving thanks *(tôdâ)* is not a private expression of gratitude of one person to another, but rather is a public acclamation of God's saving action. This is manifest in songs and sacrifices of thanksgiving.

Psalms of Thanksgiving. Thanksgiving psalms are closely related to psalms of lament, and may have developed from these. Psalms of lament, after describing the need of the petitioner(s) and the reasons why God should respond, always conclude with grateful praise or the promise of thanksgiving (e.g., Pss 57:9; 79:13; 86:12). When the gratitude overshadows the expression of distress, the psalm may be classified as a psalm of thanksgiving.

Psalms of thanksgiving may be collective (Psalms 67; 124; 129; 136) or individual (Psalms 9; 10; 30; 32; 34; 40; 41; 66; 92; 103; 107; 116; 138). Their typical structure is: (1) an introductory address; (2) a narration of the need experienced by the individual or community, often with a mention of the petition made; (3) a recitation of how God has acted as deliverer; (4) a conclusion that may express confidence, invite all to praise God, or contain a promise of future praise.

Motives for thanksgiving include: deliverance from mortal illness (Psalms 30; 107; 116); forgiveness of sins (Psalms 32; 103); rescue from the dangers of desert and sea (Psalm 107); the overthrow of hostile nations (Psalm 9); deliverance from prison (Ps 142:7); God's creation and omnipotent rule (Pss 95:3-5; 97:12; 147:7), including divine judgment (Pss 75; 140:13-14); God's enduring kindness and faithfulness (1 Chr 16:34; 2 Chr 5:13; 20:21; Pss 100:4; 106:1; 107:1; 108:3; 118:1; 136:1-3; 138:2); God's grandeur and power (1 Chr 29:10-13); and God's favor in general (Psalm 34).

David set apart Levites for liturgical service of singing thanks. Asaph and his brothers and descendants were first given this ministry (1 Chr 16:18; 25:1-8; 2 Chr 5:11-13). They "sang inspired songs to the accompaniment of a lyre, to give thanks and praise to the LORD" (1 Chr 25:3). After the Exile, Mattaniah was appointed director of the psalms, "who led the thanksgiving at prayer" (Neh 11:17; 12:8). Hezekiah reestablished these levitical ministries in his liturgical reform (2 Chr 31:2). In one instance in the psalms not only human beings are said to give thanks, but all God's works do so (Ps 145:10).

Songs of thanksgiving are also found outside the psalms. David sings his thanks after collecting offerings for the Temple (1 Chr 29:10-13). A hymn of thanksgiving for promised salvation is found in Isaiah 12:1-6. Jonah, while yet in the belly of the fish, utters a psalm of thanksgiving just prior to his rescue (Jonah 2:3-10). Daniel sings thanks to God for giving him wisdom in interpreting the king's dream (Dan 2:23). Both Jeremiah (30:19) and Deutero-Isaiah speak of the joy and gladness that will be found in restored Zion, "thanksgiving and the sound of song" (Isa 51:3). When the newly rebuilt wall of Jerusalem was dedicated, the Levites were sought out and brought to the holy city "to celebrate a joyful dedication with thanksgiving hymns and the music of cymbals, harps, and lyres" (Neh 12:27).

The cultic setting of the psalms of thanksgiving is the thanksgiving sacrifice. In Psalm 42:5 the psalmist remembers his past participation in the cult, "When I went with the throng and led them in procession to the house of God, Amid loud cries of joy and thanksgiving, with the multitude keeping festival." And in Psalm 26:6-8 the one praying alludes to thanksgiving offered in the temple: "I go around your altar, O Lord, giving voice to my thanks, and recounting all your wondrous deeds. O Lord, I love the house in which you dwell, the tenting-place of your glory." Psalm 122, a hymn sung by pilgrims upon arrival at the Temple, speaks of the tribes going up "to give thanks to the name of the Lord" (Ps 122:4).

Thanksgiving Sacrifices. Sacrifices of thanksgiving are a subdivision of peace offerings (Lev 3:1-17), along with votive offerings and free-will offerings. The prescriptions for thank offerings are found in Leviticus 7:11-18. The substance of the offering is as follows: "When anyone makes a peace offering in thanksgiving, together with his thanksgiving sacrifice he shall offer unleavened cakes mixed with oil, unleavened wafers spread with oil, and cakes made of fine flour mixed with oil and well kneaded. His offering shall also include loaves of leavened bread* along with the victim of his peace offering for thanksgiving" (Lev 7:12-13). One portion from each of the offerings is presented to God; this belongs to the priest who splashes the blood of the peace offering (Lev 7:14). All of the meat of the sacrifice of thanksgiving must be eaten on the day on which it is offered (Lev 7:15; 22:29-30). By contrast, what is not eaten of a votive or free-will offering on the day it is offered may be consumed the next day (Lev 7:16).

A thank offering may accompany an avowal of sin (Ps 107:22). Thanksgiving sacrifices are offered to God out of gratitude for rescue from dire circumstances (Pss 56:13; 116:17). In the case of Manasseh, his sacrifice of thanksgiving was made after his restoration to Jerusalem following his deliverance from the hands of the Assyrians (2 Chr 33:16). In the lament psalms one finds the promise of a thank offering in anticipation of deliverance from enemies (e.g., Ps 54:6). The prophet Amos condemns the thanksgiving sacrifices offered at Bethel and Gilgal (Amos 4:5) because they are substitutes for authentic hearing and obeying the word of God. Jeremiah lists thank offerings among those sacrifices that people will bring to the restored Jerusalem (Jer 17:26; 33:11). Psalm 69:31-32 advocates offering songs of thanksgiving in place of thanksgiving sacrifices. This, the psalmist says, "will please the Lord more than oxen or bullocks with horns and divided hooves." It is probable that this psalm is postexilic, when temple sacrifice was no longer possible (similarly, Ps 50:14, 23).

Qumran Thanksgiving Hymns. Among the scrolls found in Qumran Cave 1 were texts of nonbiblical hymns that are predominantly songs of praise. Because of the oft-repeated phrase, "I shall praise you, Lord," these hymns have been called the *Hōdāyôt* ("praise," from the same Hebrew root as *tôdâ*) Psalms. These are similar to the OT psalms of thanksgiving. They exult in the glories of creation and God's omnipotence. The emphasis in these psalms is not so much thanksgiving for rescue from distress or from sickness as it is God's saving action toward the one who has endured persecution for speaking God's message. It is thought that the Teacher of Righteousness is the beleaguered individual behind these psalms.

See: FAITHFULNESS, JERUSALEM, JOY, LAMENT, PRAISE, PRAYER, PSALMS, SACRIFICE, SALVATION, TEMPLE

BARBARA E. REID, O.P.

New Testament

Much of religious expression in the Greco-Roman world outside the NT was inspired by awe, fear, guilt, and need, calling for adoration, propitiation, purification, and petition, and these are present in the NT as well. But like the OT, the NT introduces something quite special, namely thanksgiving, which transforms them all. Thanksgiving is a personal response to a personal act. It presupposes a relationship in which God personally and graciously enters into human life and history, as we find in the OT. In the OT and the NT, as well as in the life of the Church, everything is seen as gift of God, even when it is something "which earth has given and human hands have made," or the "fruit of the vine and work of human hands." In the NT, as in all of biblical religion, the most characteristic response to a personal God, who is creator, giver of life, provider, and savior, is thanksgiving. So it is that, for Paul, thanksgiving is what distinguishes believers from those who know God but do not accord glory or give thanks to God (Rom 1:21).

Thanksgiving is a major theme especially in the Pauline letters, beginning with 1 Thessalonians, where expressions of thanksgiving dominate fully three of the five chapters. Already from this very first of Paul's letters, thanksgiving constitutes a distinct literary unit (1 Thess 1:2-10), immediately after the letter's greeting or prescript (1 Thess 1:1). Present in all the letters save Galatians, 1 Timothy, and Titus, the thanksgiving unit witnesses to the importance of thanksgiving in all of Christian life and situates it in the totality of the Christian response to God. The theme of thanksgiving is also developed elsewhere in the Pauline letters as well as in the Gospel narratives of Eucharistic institution and in allusions to these in accounts of the breaking of the bread.

Grace and Blessing. The Pauline thanksgiving units (Rom 1:8-15; 1 Cor 1:4-9; 2 Cor 1:3-11; Eph 1:3-14; Phil 1:3-11; Col 1:3-8; 1 Thess 1:2-10; 2 Thess 1:3-12; 2 Tim 1:3-5; Phlm 4-6) show how thanksgiving is the first and most fundamental Christian response, presupposing a strong sense of grace and life as graced, in every respect but sin. Thanksgiving is the Christian response to grace (see 1 Cor 1:4). So close is the relationship that the early Christians and Paul drew upon a new term to express it. Grace, in Greek *charis*, calls for thanksgiving, in Greek *eucharistia*, a term all but absent from the Septuagint, where a closely comparable term, blessing, in Greek *eulogia*, appears very frequently. In the OT, to bless the Lord is the proper response to the Lord's blessing, and a pervasive sense of blessing is present also in the NT, often in close association with giving thanks (Mark 14:22; Matt 26:26) or as an alternative for it (2 Cor 1:3; Eph 1:3; 1 Pet 1:3). But the characteristic and specifically Christian response is thanksgiving, so much so that the Christians are seen as men and women who give thanks in everything they do, "in word or in deed," and Paul calls them to be faithful to that (Col 3:17). In the NT, a Christian is essentially a graced person who gives thanks.

The relationship of thanksgiving to divine grace is so close that in the NT thanksgiving is addressed exclusively to God, whereas blessing is addressed to other persons (see Luke 2:34) as well as God (see Luke 2:28). In the one apparent exception, where thanksgiving seems to be directed to Christ Jesus our Lord (1 Tim 1:12), the terms thanksgiving or giving thanks are not used, but another expression, which is well-rendered as "I am grateful."

Remembrance, Confession, and Proclamation. Addressed to God, the ultimate source of all gifts, thanksgiving is given through Jesus Christ, the ultimate gift (Rom 1:8; 5:15; 7:25; Col 3:17) and "in the name of the Lord Jesus Christ" (Eph 5:20). Just as grace comes from God in and through Jesus Christ, so does thanksgiving return to God in and through Jesus Christ. The central act of grace is that of salvation effected in and through the person, death, and resurrection of Jesus Christ. Such is the "grace in which we stand" (Rom 5:2). God's love was clearly proven to us "in that while we were still sinners Christ died for us" (Rom 5:8). God's grace abounds and overflows in the gracious gift of the person of Jesus Christ (Rom 5:15). Jesus Christ is grace incarnate, the personal expression of divine grace for the human race. Accordingly, our central act of thanksgiving is the celebration of his life, death, and resurrection in the Lord's Supper, where Christians eat bread which is Christ's body and drink the cup of the new covenant in his blood, thereby joining their love to his and taking part in his unique act of thanksgiving.

The Christian response of thanksgiving flows from the act of remembrance, whereby Christians recall and make present the wonders done for us and for all in and through Jesus Christ. This remembrance and all that flows from it is the foundation and first expression of faith and the object of the celebration of the Lord's Supper, where Christians remember how the Lord Jesus gave thanks by offering his body and blood (1 Cor 11:23-25). By our thanksgiving remembrance, we enter into what God has done for us in and through Christ's gift of his life, and are taken up into his unique gift.

Christians give thanks by remembering the grace of God offered and realized in Christ by confessing their faith, much as the Israelites did when offering the first-fruits of the harvest (Deut 26:5-10) and celebrating with all the good things the Lord had given them (Deut 26:11). Christian remembering and confessing come together in the traditional creed, where Christians profess "that Christ died for our sins in accordance with the scriptures; that he was buried; that he was raised on the third day in accordance with the scriptures; that he appeared to Kephas, then to the Twelve" (1 Cor 15:3-5). The two also come together in the Eucharistic event when the participants both remember and do what he did "on the night he was handed over" (1 Cor 11:23).

Thanksgiving, and in particular that of the Lord's Supper, is not only a remembering and confessional celebration of the great events of grace that have made us who we are but also a proclamation of those deeds and words of grace, inviting all to join in Christ's perfect act of thanksgiving: "as often as you eat this bread and drink the cup, you proclaim the death of the Lord until he comes" (1 Cor 11:26). As a proclamation, thanksgiving looks to the future, announces the gospel of hope, and calls on all to join in that hope which will be fulfilled in the final return and manifestation of Christ in glory (see 1 Cor 1:7-8; Eph 1:14; Phil 1:10; 1 Thess 1:10; 2 Thess 1:10). And this hope, which flows from remembering the works of grace in faith and its confessional expression in love, is the ground of Christian prayer (Phil 1:4, 9; 1 Thess 1:2-3).

See: EUCHARIST, FAITH, GOOD NEWS/GOSPEL, HOPE, LOVE, PRAYER, REMEMBRANCE

EUGENE LAVERDIERE, S.S.S.

Pastoral-Liturgical Tradition

Thanksgiving is at the heart of any spirituality that claims to be Christian. While a natural response to God's on-going action in creating and sustaining the world, Christian thanksgiving is ultimately centered around praise* and thanks to God for the mighty work of redemption carried out through, with, and in Jesus Christ in the paschal mystery. For this reason, the Church's celebration of the Lord's Supper or Mass seen from its traditional optic as the Eucharist—"thanksgiving"—expresses the Christian attitude of thanks and praise in a paradigmatic way.

Thanksgiving as Confession and Self-transcendence. Thanksgiving has much to do with acknowledging the giver as much as the gift. It is part of the capacity we have as human beings to relate to God in such a way as we go out of ourselves and transcend our own particular concerns by expressing in words and actions our inner feelings of gratitude for a gift received. Thanksgiving as self-transcendence allows us to open ourselves to God's grace. Part of thanksgiving is also recognizing the reality of who we are, especially the fact that we are contingent creatures who are not complete in ourselves. We need God to fulfill our deepest needs and longings for wholeness. Thus, when thanksgiving is directed to God, there is also a recognition that our response can never "pay back" the gift received since we are ultimately thanking God for life itself. The only thing that remains for us to do is to express our love and our thanks—not only out of a sense of duty but because we need to witness the reality of God's love to the world. This confession of God's love is itself transformative of who we are and our own attitudes. It serves to help us put things into perspective, thus changing our vision of the world and others. The transformative power of giving thanks is beautifully expressed in the Sacramentary's fourth preface for weekdays, which acknowledges our creaturehood and total dependence on God:

> You have no need of our praise,
> yet our desire to thank you is itself your gift.
> Our prayer of thanksgiving adds nothing to your greatness,
> but makes us grow in your grace, through Jesus Christ our Lord.

Thanksgiving as the Basis for Communal Prayer. We are a redeemed people—redeemed not by our own actions but by God's gratuitous love for us in Christ Jesus.

There is simply no surer foundation for liturgical prayer than in contemplating the *mirabilia Dei*—the marvels God has done on our behalf—wonderfully accomplished in the passion, death, and resurrection of Jesus Christ. For this reason, in the Eucharistic liturgy, we recount God's mighty deeds described in the Scriptures, reflect on those stories of God's love in such a way as we recognize that these words are not just part of a long past historical record, but indicate how God continues to marvelously deal with us today, here and now. The entire Liturgy of the Word is so arranged that it inexorably leads us to thanksgiving and praise for what God has done and continues to do for us. In short, it leads to Eucharist.

For that reason, the Eucharistic prayer models our prayer of thanks. Each of the ordinary prefaces begins with the standard line: "It is our duty and our salvation always and everywhere to give you thanks through your beloved Son, Jesus Christ." All that had preceded in the celebration as well as in our own lives in Christ allows us to say with conviction at the beginning of the Eucharistic prayer, "We come to you Father with praise and thanksgiving through Jesus Christ your Son" (Eucharistic Prayer I).

See: EUCHARIST, HOSPITALITY, MEAL, MYSTERY, PRAISE, PRAYER, SALVATION, WORSHIP

MARK R. FRANCIS, C.S.V.

THRONE OF GOD

New Testament

Thronos is the Greek noun translated as "throne" and a cognate of the English term. As the large ceremonial chair (with footstool) of a sovereign, the throne in the OT and other ancient Near Eastern literature (Persian, Egyptian, Assyrian, Babylonian, Aramaean, Sumerian) is so closely associated with the royal office that it becomes the very symbol of the height, pageantry, and power of kingship. (The footstool refers to the practice of victorious rulers placing their feet on the back of captured enemies; see Ps 110:1.) The throne rests on a raised platform, or dais, in a large hall or room, which serves as the monarch's public space where one might have an audience with the king or queen. It is from the throne that a monarch renders judgment. Therefore, another Greek noun, *bēma* ("judgment seat"), deserves consideration.

In OT usage, the throne of the Israelite king becomes equated with the throne of God. For example, King Solomon inherits David's throne, which is called the "Throne of the LORD" (1 Chr 29:23). The Davidic throne is a piece of heaven on earth. The OT and Jewish tradition describe God enthroned in heaven upon the cherubim, angelic courtiers who guard and support the divine seat (1 Sam 4:4; Pss 80:2; 99:1; Isa 37:16). One human observer of the heavenly court is reported to say: "'I saw the LORD seated on his throne, with the whole host of heaven standing by to his right and to his left'" (1 Kgs 22:19). The throne symbolizes God's sovereignty. These OT images continue into the NT.

Book of Revelation. Three-fourths of all NT instances of *thronos* occur in the Apocalypse, also known as Revelation. This book is a series of carefully constructed visions, woven together to form a narrative of what a certain John, on the isle of Patmos likely in political exile, sees. Many of the visions draw on OT themes and images, especially from Ezekiel, Daniel, and the "enthronement" psalms.

In the narrative, the author portrays events in heaven determining events on earth. Several visions of the heavenly throne room precede other visions of destructive judgment on earth (cf. Ps 11:4-7). In the first heavenly throne room scene, John peeks beyond an open door to heaven and hears the "trumpetlike voice" of Christ beckoning him to enter. At once he is "caught up in spirit" and envisages a "throne there in heaven" on which sat "one whose appearance sparkled like jasper and carnelian. Around the throne was a halo as brilliant as an emerald" (Rev 4:1-3). The images here reflect the vision found in 1 Kings 22:19 quoted above.

The colored, translucent stoneware that ornament the description of God's splendor can also be found in Ezekiel's inaugural vision of God (Ezek 1:16, 26, 27). The colored halo (Greek: *iris*, "rainbow") can also be found in Ezekiel's description: "Upward from what resembled his waist I saw what gleamed like electrum; downward from what resembled his waist I saw what looked like fire; he was surrounded with splendor. Like the bow that appears in the clouds on a rainy day was the splendor that surrounded him. Such was the vision of the likeness of the glory of the LORD" (Ezek 1:27-28).

John not only sees, but also hears the throne of God. It is a full sensory experience: "From the throne came flashes of lightning, rumblings, and peals of thunder. Seven flaming torches burned in front of the throne, which are the seven spirits of God. In front of the throne was something that resembled a sea of glass like crystal" (Rev 4:5-6). Compare this to the OT verbalization of theophany scenes: "On the morning of the third day there were peals of thunder and lightning, and a heavy cloud over the mountain, and a very loud trumpet blast, so that all the people in the camp trembled" (Exod 19:16); "And the LORD thundered from heaven, the Most High gave forth his voice; He sent forth his arrows to put them to flight, with frequent lightnings he routed them" (Ps 18:14-15); "Then suddenly, in an instant, / you shall be visited by the LORD of hosts, with thunder, earthquake, and great noise, / whirlwind, storm, and the flame of consuming fire" (Isa 29:6). The "sea of glass" is the celestial dome that separates creation from watery chaos, apparently functioning as a kind of glass floor beneath the throne of God. This is an image taken from OT cosmology: "Then God said, 'Let there be a dome in the middle of the waters, to separate one body of water from the other.' And so it happened: God made the dome, and it separated the water above the dome and the water below it. God called the dome 'the sky'" (Gen 1:6-7).

John envisages the heavenly throne room populated by singing creatures who perpetually glorify God (Rev 4:6-8), angelic courtiers taken directly from OT literary accounts of the cherubim. From this evidence, one can reasonably conclude that the OT directly influenced the literary description of the heavenly throne of God found in Revelation (see also the other preparatory heavenly throne scenes in Rev 7:9-17; 8:2-5; 11:15-19; 14:2-3; 19:1-10; 21:3-8).

Throne of Christ. An important occupant of the heavenly dais envisaged in Revelation is the Lamb; near the end of the series of visions, John envisages the "throne of God and of the Lamb" (Rev 22:1, 3). This imagery symbolizes the enthronement of Christ on the final day of judgment when the conquering Lamb will topple Satan from his throne and rule of earth (Rev 2:13; a possible reference to Caesar or his legate and imperial Roman occupation of the ancient Mediterranean world, specifically the city of Pergamum).

Christians will also sit in judgment. The voice of Christ says: "I will give the victor the right to sit with me on my throne, as I myself first won the victory and sit with my father on his throne" (Rev 3:21; note imagery from Daniel 7:9-10). This is an allusion to Psalm 110:1, understood as the heavenly enthronement of the resurrected Christ on his judgment seat. Reference to the throne of Christ (or, alternatively, the heavenly apocalyptic figure called "Son of Man") is also found in Mark 14:62; Matthew 22:42-44; Acts 2:34-35; Ephesians 1:20; and Hebrews 8:1; 12:2. The resurrected Christ ascends as the rightful heir to the throne of David. From his heavenly bench, Christ judges as the agent of God. Paul, in this connection, speaks interchangeably of the judgment seat of God and Christ (Rom 14:10; 2 Cor 5:10).

See: ANGELS, CHERUBIM, EPIPHANY, GLORY, HEAVEN, JUDGMENT, LAMB OF GOD, MONARCHY, POWER, SON OF MAN, VOICE OF GOD

J. ALBERT HARRILL

Pastoral-Liturgical Tradition

The early Christian tradition understood a number of realities in light of the biblical image of the throne of God, experiencing in each the majestic presence of God. The Epistle of Barnabas warned that humans erred by putting their hopes in the building of the earthly temple and quoted Isaiah's affirmation that heaven is God's throne (Barnabas 16:2; see Isa 66:1; Matt 5:34; 23:22; Acts 7:49). Barnabas also stressed that "God truly dwells in us, in the habitation which we are" (16:8), thus associating the Christian community itself with the temple and throne of God.

Ignatius of Antioch (d. ca. 110) saw the bishop presiding in the Christian assembly in the place of God (Epistle to the Magnesians 6:1), and the early Christian tradition interpreted the bishop's throne, from which he preached, as representing the throne of God.

Christians also viewed Mary, the bearer of God, as the throne of God, an image important for Medieval art. Andrew of Crete (660–749) described Mary in the image of Isaiah 6:1 as the exalted throne in which God is seen. John of Damascus (675–749) hailed Mary as the throne lifted up on high in glory, representing in herself the throne of God. Peter Damian (d. 1072) described God establishing the divine throne in the Virgin's womb.

Symeon of Thessalonica (d. 1429) interpreted the altar in the sanctuary as representing the throne of God, which must be viewed from afar.

See: ALTAR, BISHOP, GOD, HEAVEN, MARY, TEMPLE

LEO D. LEFEBURE

TIME

To understand OT concepts of time, modern people in industrialized nations generally have to put aside their own notions about time. For the ancients, time was not money, nor was it closely measured or scrupulously followed. It was not perceived in an abstract way, as if it were a vast empty space stretching forward into the future. Instead, time represented concrete events of life in which the community participated, year in and year out, day in and day out. Time could not be separated from the events that filled it. In the OT there are, in addition to the notion of moments of time, concepts of enduring, appointed, and liturgical time. Measuring time was by movements of heavenly bodies and agricultural seasons. Notions of time in the NT distinguish between ordinary calendar time and opportune time. For Christians time is measured as before or after Christ's coming. Furthermore, they look to the eschatological time of the second coming of Christ.

Old Testament

A consideration of the Hebrew verbal system highlights the differences between ancient and modern western notions of time. Biblical Hebrew contains only two tenses—the perfect tense to describe completed action, and the imperfect tense to describe incomplete action. While it was possible, through various verb forms, to express the sense of past and future, the very structure of the language reveals the relative unimportance of strict expressions of time in the ancient culture.

Moments of Time. The commonly used Hebrew terms for time continue to point out the differences between modern and ancient perceptions of time. There is no Hebrew word for time in general. The most frequently used word for time in the OT is *'et*. This word does not mean time as duration but time as the moment or period during which something happens.

The prophet Amos uses *'et* to mean a particular set of events. "Therefore, the prudent man is silent at this time, for it is an evil time" (5:13). Similarly, Jeremiah promises that "in their time of punishment, they shall go down" (8:12). In the book of Daniel *'et* refers to an eschatological event. "At that time there shall arise Michael, the great prince, guardian of your people" (12:1). In the Book of Exodus the same Hebrew word appears in a phrase that means literally "in all times," but in the context of Exodus 18 means legal events or "cases." "Let these men render decisions for the people in all ordinary cases" (Exod 18:22).

In the Book of Job the term *'et* appears in a slightly different way. God speaks to Job from the storm and asks him if he knows the "time" when the mountain goats bring forth (Job 39:2). Here time conveys the sense of usual or repetitive events. Likewise in Deuteronomy God promises to send the rain "in its time." "I will give the seasonal rain to your land, the early rain and the late rain, that you may have your grain, wine and oil to gather in" (Deut 11:14). This point is repeated in a passage in Jeremiah where God is addressed as the one "who gives us rain early and late in its time" (Jer 5:24).

For the Hebrew writers, human life was a series of many times. This is nowhere more evident than in the famous passage from Ecclesiastes (3:1-9). "There is an appointed time for everything and a time for every affair under the heavens. A time to be born, and a time to die; a time to plant and a time to uproot the plant. A time to kill and a time to heal; a time to tear down and a time to build" (Eccl 3:1-3). As this carefully balanced poem continues, it catalogues major events and activities of life and speaks of them as appropriate times, suitable activities, that compose human existence. For Ecclesiastes, human life participates in cyclical time; it consists of repeated events that occur over and over again in each generation.

Enduring Time. Ecclesiastes used another Hebrew word, *'olam*, to contrast the times of human life with "enduring time," time that stretches from beginning to end, time that approaches the more abstract notion of "eternity." God "has made everything appropriate to its time, but has put the timeless [*'olam*] in their hearts" (Eccl 3:11). This wisdom writer claimed that the times God has created for humans are beautiful and appropriate, but humans long for more, for "the timeless," for knowledge of God's work "from beginning to end," but that they cannot grasp it.

The Israelites did not have a concept of a timeless eternity. Instead, they used the word *'olam* to speak of a long duration of time, of ancient times, of continuous future times. For instance, Third Isaiah spoke of how God redeemed the people, "lifting and carrying them all the days of old" (Isa 63:9). Jeremiah cursed the day of his birth by wishing that he would have died in his mother's womb, "confining me forever" (Jer 20:17). The psalmist proclaimed that God has founded the earth "forever" (Ps 78:69).

In each of these examples, current times or events are perceived as stretching backward or forward or as continuing indefinitely, but this is not the same as later notions of eternity, as a life or event outside of time.

Appointed Time. Between the two concepts of time as an event or moment and time as enduring or continuous lies the notion of appointed time. The Hebrew word *mo'ed* comes from a verb that means "to appoint." With this word the people could express the ideas of an appointed meeting or an assembly (Isa 14:13), or of an "appointed time" for any event (Gen 18:14). Perhaps the most important use of this word was to identify the times of prescribed feasts (Deut 31:10; Hos 2:13; Lam 2:6).

Liturgical Time. The word *mo'ed* was used to identify sacred or festive time, time marked out for remembering or celebrating (Lev 23:2, 4; Deut 31:10; Hos 2:13; Lam 2:6). Sacred or liturgical time in Israel created a kind of synchrony between the past and the present. Liturgical celebrations reenacted past events, not simply to remind the community of the past but to enable participants to experience the events as if they were happening to them. For example, with the celebration of the Passover, each generation could say that, not only their ancestors, but they were set free from bondage (Exod 13:8). Past time and present time merge by dramatic reenactment during liturgical ritual.

Measuring Time. The Israelites understood that God created time at the creation of the world. God separated day from night (Gen 1:3-5) and established the seasons and the times of assemblies and feasts by creating the heavenly lights (Gen 1:14). The function of sun, moon, and stars was to "mark the fixed times, the days and the years, and serve as luminaries in the dome of the sky" (Gen 1:14). The heavenly bodies made possible the measurement and division of time.

The day began in the evening, not in the morning, and was counted from sunset to sunset. "Thus evening came and morning followed—the first day" (Gen 1:5). Hence, the Jewish and Christian feasts begin with the sunset. The night comprised three watches (Exod 14:24; Judg 7:19; Lam 2:19), and the days also seem to have had three divisions, not our familiar morning, noon, and night, but evening, dawn, and noon (Ps 55:18).

Biblical Hebrew lacks a word for "hour," but it could specify the smallest division of time with a word that means a "moment" (Lam 4:6). It also has a word for "week," a word that also means literally "seven." The week ended, rather than began, with the Sabbath, a sacred day of rest because God rested on the seventh day (Gen 1:2-3). Israel followed the lunar calendar. Its words for "month" come from the Hebrew words for "moon" and "new moon."

Israel's sense of time derived from its agricultural way of life and from its observations of the heavenly bodies, but always it considered God the creator and sustainer of time (Ps 104:19-23). Gradually Israel developed a sense of historical time. This probably came about through the activity of its storytellers and writers, who put together sequentially events that were originally experienced as isolated. In the retelling of these events, they created the story of the community's interaction with its God and they pointed toward a historical future in which God would continue to be present in the life of the people. Still, when Israel recounts its history it does not tell it in the modern sense. Even its chronological lists of the kings of Judah and Israel do not form an accurate chronological line.

Pastoral Notes. Many people in industrialized countries are prisoners of time. They perceive it as a tyrant that squeezes life from them as they try to meet its ever-present demands to accomplish more activities, make more money, meet more goals. The OT sense of time challenges this view. Time belongs to God. Time is the span of life that people are given to live in justice and peace with others and to praise God. It is a mysterious aspect of human life, no more understood by moderns than by the ancient peoples. Reflection on the mystery of time invites people to consider what is important and to decide how to conduct their lives. Such reflection may invite people to savor the life they have and to live it in God's presence.

See: FROSTS, SABBATH

KATHLEEN M. O'CONNOR

New Testament

The NT gives no treatise or speculative analysis of time. For awhile Lucan scholars thought that the third evangelist came the closest to providing a comprehensive timeline of salvation history. H. von Baer (*Der heilige Geist in den Lukasschriften*, BWZNT 39; Stuttgart: Kohlhammer, 1926) and H. Conzelmann (*The Theology of St. Luke*, Tübingen: Mohr, 1953) formulated the thesis that in his two-volume work Luke construes salvation history in three eras: the OT; the time of Jesus, which is the center and turning point of time (see Luke 16:16); and the apostolic history of Acts. More recently, scholars see in Luke's work a two-fold outline of time: the Old Age, that is, the time of Israel as the time of preparation, prophecy, and promise; and the New Age inaugurated by the Christ event and now awaiting final consummation.

The NT remarks about time, its terms, and concepts should be read in continuity with those of Judaism. Modern readers may, for example, be surprised to learn that the Last Supper and the crucifixion took place on the same day—for a day in Judaism begins at sundown and ends with the next sundown. One must also keep in mind that during the

time of Christian beginnings there was a distinctive circum-Mediterranean conception of time that was quite different from our own (see Bruce J. Malina, "Christ and Time: Swiss or Mediterranean?" *CBQ* 51 [1989] 1–30). Even Jewish and Greek concepts of time (*pace* Oscar Cullman, *Christ and Time*, Philadelphia: Westminster, 1946) have more in common with one another than with our own rather abstract, future-oriented, mathematically based, and chronologically sensitive approach. Malina insists that there was no tension between the now and the not yet. Rather, in the NT period there was "only emphasis on a rather broad now," whereas future oriented societies such as ours stress the not yet.

Three Greek words are generally used to express the different dimensions of time in the NT: *aiōn*, from which our "eon" derives (Hebrew *ʿôlām*), describes the wider sweep of time; *chronos*, ordinary calendar time as a quantity; and *kairos*, a particular quality of time, the psychological moment or opportunity.

Aiōn. The NT probably developed the concept of *aiōn* from Jewish apocalyptic speculation, which often separated time into the present (evil) world (Matt 12:32; Eph 1:21) and the future world (Mark 10:30; Eph 2:7; Heb 6:2). When applied to God it suggests eternity in the proper sense (Rom 16:26; 1 Tim 1:17). The plural (*aiōna*) is frequently translated "forever," although scholars dispute whether the meaning is "time without end" or "time which stretches beyond what we can imagine" (see Matt 21:19; John 12:34; Rom 16:27; Heb 1:8). The adjective (*aiōnios*) is normally translated "eternal" or "everlasting." It is applied to the results of the final judgment, but most importantly, to eternal life. It is used of the eternal covenant of which Jesus is the mediator (Heb 13:20); the eternal habitation and glory into which the Christian shall enter (Luke 16:9; 2 Cor 5:1; Heb 9:15; 2 Tim 2:10; 1 Pet 5:10); the eternal kingdom (2 Pet 1:11); the everlasting good news (Rev 14:6); hope of eternal life (Titus

3:7); the fire of punishment (Matt 18:8; 25:41, 46); eternal judgment (Heb 6:2); and of the sin that separates one from God (Mark 3:29).

To understand *aiōnios* merely as "lasting forever" is to oversimplify and even to distort the word completely. Because words such as "eternal" are most properly used of the divine they can also be applied to those who share in the divine life, to emphasize the quality of a Christian life. With the coming of Jesus and his resurrection in particular, the Jewish hopes and expectations of time have been fulfilled, albeit in a surprising way, because no one expected a messiah to die and return again. Practically speaking, this fulfillment means that the believer is already redeemed from this present time (Gal 1:4) and already tastes the powers of the future (Heb 6:5). Luke, for example, places great emphasis on the "today" and the "now" of salvation (e.g., 4:21; 19:9; 23:43). In contrast to the Synoptic evangelists, who emphasize future time, John stresses that eternal life begins now, as soon as one turns to Jesus in faith, which is the key moment of time in one's life. The fact that Jesus is the resurrection and the life (John 11:25) means that already, even now, he raises a person from death and gives life to the full.

Chronos. The Greek word *chronos* is used for a determined length of time, and is usually accompanied by an adjective such as "short" or "long" (Matt 25:19; Mark 9:21; Luke 8:27; John 5:6; Acts 14:3; Heb 5:12). Somewhat rarely it can be used for a specific time (Luke 1:57; Acts 7:17; Gal 4:4). *Chronos* is normally translated "time" in the NAB, although it has been rendered variously as "span," "set time," "delay," "term," "point of time" (Matt 2:7, 16; Luke 1:57; Acts 1:6-7; Rev 2:21). The famous text in Revelation 10:6 (lit. "time will be no more") is rightly translated, "There shall be no more delay."

Kairos. This is the time word with the deepest theological significance. It is, however, used in some instances, simply as a generic time marker, as in Luke 4:13, "for a time," and Luke 21:36, "at all times" (see also Matt 11:25; 12:1; 14:1; Luke 8:13; 13:1; Acts 7:20; 13:11; Rom 3:26; 1 Cor 7:5; Eph 6:18; Heb 9:9). *Kairos* also connotes "the right, proper, or favorable time" (Matt 24:45; Luke 12:42). It can mean "opportunity" (Acts 24:25; Gal 6:10; Eph 5:16; Col 4:5; Heb 11:15). It is used to speak of definite, fixed times, such as the time of harvest (Matt 13:30) or the season for figs (Mark 11:13). In Galatians 4:10 "seasons" *(kairous)*, listed with "months" and "years," refers to ritual observances.

The great theological significance attached to *kairos* comes from the instances in which it refers to the critical moments of Jesus' coming, his inauguration of the reign of God, his passion and death, and his parousia. The author of the Letter to Titus speaks of "the proper time" when God decisively revealed the word (Titus 1:3). Mark headlines Jesus' public ministry with his proclamation of the time of fulfillment, the coming of the reign of God, and the invitation to repent and believe in the good news (Mark 1:15). There is a sense of urgency and shortness of time in the Gospel of Mark, as the narrative is punctuated forty-two times with the word *euthys*, "immediately." The "appointed time" of Jesus' passion and death is designated as *kairos* in Matthew 26:18 and Romans 5:6. Christ's second coming will happen "at the right time" (1 Tim 6:15).

In the Gospel of John the word *kairos* rarely appears (only 7:6, 8). The fourth evangelist develops, instead, a theology of the "hour" *(hōra)*. In the Synoptic Gospels "hour" refers most often to the hour of the day (e.g., Mark 6:35; Luke 13:31). It also denotes a time of persecution of the disciples (Mark 13:11; Luke 12:12). In a few instances it refers to Jesus' approaching passion (Matt 26:18, 45; Mark 14:35) or to the timing of the parousia (Matt 24:36; Mark 13:32; Luke 12:40). In the Gospel of John "the hour" or "my hour" is the time of Jesus' passing "from this world to the Father" (13:1) that encompasses his passion, death, resurrection, and exaltation. In John 2:4;

7:30; 8:20 Jesus' "hour" has not yet come. In John 12:23 Jesus declares, "The hour has come for the Son of Man to be glorified" (similarly 13:1; 17:1). He does not ask the Father to save him from this hour, because "it was for this purpose that I came to this hour" (12:27). Several Johannine passages speak of the effects of Jesus' "hour" on believers: with regard to worship (4:21, 23), resurrection (5:25, 28-29), persecution (16:2; 17:32), and plain speech about God (16:25).

For the Christian the *kairos* inaugurated with Jesus is the time for doing good. It is a time of which to make profit (Eph 5:16; Col 4:5). It is the hour to awake from sleep, for salvation is nearer, to conduct oneself properly (Rom 13:11-14; Gal 3:10). The length of these "times of refreshment . . . until the times of universal restoration" (Acts 3:20) is unknown (Mark 13:33; Acts 1:7; 1 Thess 5:1; 1 Pet 1:5). The Christian time should be marked by watching, waiting, and praying for Christ's return (Luke 21:36; 1 Cor 4:5; Eph 6:18; 1 Tim 6:14; 1 Pet 4:17-18; Rev 11:18). Jesus' followers are not to follow the example of Jerusalem, who did not recognize the time of its visitation (Luke 19:44). "Seize your opportunities" was Paul's timely advice to the Romans (12:9-13). God's delay is intended to be helpful to Christians. When 2 Peter 3:8 asserts, "with the Lord one day is like a thousand years and a thousand years like one day," the stress is on the mercy of God's delay, since God has all eternity for the divine plans. The times have been established by God's own authority and God has not made available detailed information about the end (Matt 24:36; Mark 13:33; Acts 1:7; 1 Thess 5:1-2). Just as Jesus urged the crowd in Luke 12:54-59, disciples must learn how to interpret the signs of the times (similarly Matt 16:1-4).

Thus what is distinctive in the NT view of time is that it is centered on Christ. All history from Adam and Abraham onward, as the genealogies of Matthew and Luke attest, is significant in that it prepares the way and finds its fulfillment in him. For Christians, all history is measured against the example that was Jesus' life. Not unlike their Jewish predecessors, who waited in expectation for the Day of the Lord, Christians look forward to the parousia, the second coming of Christ. Thus the center of history and time is identical with the final point. Life is lived in tension between the present and the future. The future is already inaugurated with the Christ event, but is not yet completed. Through the resurrection Christ is present everywhere giving his followers, through his Spirit, the power to follow his example. Christians are challenged to live in the present age temperately, justly and devoutly being trained by God's grace to reject godless ways and worldly desires (Titus 2:12; 2 Tim 4:10).

Later Christians would draw the deeper consequences of the historical *kairos* of Jesus' coming by placing him at the center point of the calendar. In 525 Denis the Small fixed the date of Jesus' birth in the year 753 of the foundation of Rome. Venerable Bede (+735) popularized the use of this Christian era. Charlemagne imposed it on Europe. But the custom of counting before the birth of Christ seems only to have begun with Bossuet in 1681.

See: APOCALYPTIC, DAY OF THE LORD, FEASTS, FULFILLMENT, JUDGMENT, LIFE, PAROUSIA, PASSION, REIGN OF GOD, SABBATH, WATCH

SEAN P. KEALY, C.S.SP.

Pastoral-Liturgical Tradition

Judaism distinguished itself from other religions by affirming that time has a beginning and an end. This linear (rather than cyclic) view of time emerged with their belief that God had intervened in history. Each historical intervention by God was a unique and determinative event for the Jews. Although these events could not be repeated, they could be appropriated by each succeeding generation through remembering (*zikkaron*). More than a simple act of recollection, remembering was a way for Jews to actualize past events rendering them effective for each succeeding generation.

Christianity valorized historical time

even more through its belief in the Incarnation in which divinity and humanity were united at a specific place and time in history. The non-repeatable birth, life, and death of the historical Jesus represent a new focal point in time for Christians. The gospel is to be proclaimed in this interim between Jesus' death and his final coming in glory.

From the beginning Christians have believed that Jesus' passion and death was the pivotal event in human history, perfectly revealing Jesus' infinite love for the One he called the Father. Jesus' once and for all sacrifice revealed a love that could not be contained by human history. Thus the death of Jesus was neither the beginning nor the end of his love for the One he called Father. Rather, Jesus' death was the perfect manifestation of an infinite, trans-historical relationship of love confirmed in resurrection. This belief is called the paschal mystery.

Christians are invited into this continuing relationship between Christ and the "Father" in the holy Spirit. This relationship is a present reality. Since, however, the most perfect revelation of Jesus' love for the "Father"—manifest in the cross—occurred at a specific time in human history, Christians are obliged to remember the death of Jesus. This remembering (*anamnesis*, akin to the Jewish notion of *zikkaron*) is more than re-calling a completed historical event. Rather, Christians remember the historical circumstances of Jesus' passion and death as explications of his total surrender to the "Father" and as a model for their own surrender to the same "Father" in Jesus' spirit. Christians remember Jesus' passion and death in order to become a part of the loving relationship that motivated Jesus' sacrifice in the past, that continues today, and that will continue eternally.

The first Christians were aware that they were living in the interim between Christ's resurrection and his final coming in glory. This awareness deterred them from giving much attention to special calendars or daily horaria. Since Jesus' return could be at any moment, it was not the keeping of particular schedules of feasts that was significant. Rather it was important to live in the presence of the paschal mystery. The NT injunction to pray always (Eph 6:18) expressed well this spirit.

The early community viewed all reality through the prism of Christ's death and resurrection and they reinterpreted the world through this belief. Hellenistic Judaism possessed a sophisticated yearly calendar and framework for daily prayer that Christians reinterpreted in view of the Lord's death and resurrection. The times of Temple sacrifice (morning and evening) were reinterpreted as symbols of Jesus' own sacrifice. The setting of the sun became a special memorial of his death and eschatological hope; the rising of the sun was a daily symbol of resurrection. Yearly festivals, like Passover, were similarly reinterpreted as metaphors for Jesus' death and resurrection.

Christians inherited from the Jews the custom of observing particular days of the week. The Jews regularly scheduled services on Sabbath as well as on market days: Monday and Thursday. Jewish Christians adapted these practices to their own needs. By the end of the first century adaptation gave way to replacement. Sunday replaced Sabbath as the primary day for communal worship. Monday and Thursday were similarly replaced by Wednesday and Friday, which became new fast days [Didache 8], though there is no evidence that worship was regularly scheduled on these days in the early community. With the exception of the annual *pascha*, Sunday was the only regularly scheduled day for Christian worship in the first two centuries.

Christians did not take a literal approach to time or its organization. While the stories of Jesus' passion and death were recounted by the early community, the only annual celebration commemorating any of these was the yearly *pascha*. Similarly, although Jesus was remembered as accomplishing specific activities at certain times of the day or night, there is no evidence that the early community regularly observed set times for prayer or other activities in imitation of Jesus. There is almost a total absence of directives for the observance of times of prayer or regularly occurring festivals for Christians of the first two centuries.

The third century demonstrates a change in this pattern. The reasons for this change are complex. They include a growing awareness by the Christian community that the return of Christ Jesus was not imminent, as well as the need to organize cultic patterns for a Christianity definitively separated from Judaism and established as an independent religion. These changes contributed to a shift in the Christian community's perspective on and organization of time.

The most notable change in the third century is the substantial evidence for observing particular times of the day and night for prayer. Tertullian (d. ca. 225), for example, specifies six different times for prayer in his treatise *Concerning Prayer*, sometimes with particular reasons for each. Thus Christians are to pray in the morning, in the evening, at the third hour because the gifts of the holy Spirit were given at that time (Acts 2:15), at the sixth hour because Peter prayed on the housetop at that time (Acts 10:9), at the ninth hour because Peter and John went to the Temple at that hour (Acts 3:1), and at midnight. Tertullian and his contemporaries also repeat the injunction to pray always, and his references to particular times of day and night for prayer seem to provide a symbolic structure for fulfilling that ideal.

Eventually this symbolic approach yielded to a more literal interpretation of prayer times. While authors repeated the call to pray always, this ideal was increasingly interpreted in terms of particular prayer formulae at predetermined hours of the day. By the sixth century, monastic communities had established eight fixed times for prayer during each twenty-four hour period. Through the early Middle Ages a variety of accretions developed around these hours of the Divine Office. The cumulative effect of these developments was de-

creased awareness of the movement of the sun as a metaphor for the paschal mystery, and increased emphasis on reciting fixed numbers of prayers each twenty-four hours. The total disjunction between time and this prayer form emerged with the breviary. The obligation to recite the eight hours of prayer each day did not require that these hours be observed at any particular time. Consequently it was frequent practice for clerics to recite these hours of prayer at any time.

Similar developments occurred in the yearly cycle. The early Christian community only observed a yearly *pascha* and the weekly Sunday celebration. The third century provides evidence for Epiphany as well as various commemorations of martyrs. The fourth century provides further evidence for annual celebrations of the Nativity, Ascension, Pentecost, and many more martyrs. At their inception these feasts were unitive feasts, each embracing the whole paschal mystery through the prism of a particular faith symbol or event. Thus Augustine (d. 430) could call them sacraments. Eventually, however, the unitive symbolism of these feasts gave way to a more literal commemoration of a single event in salvation history.

This tendency to interpret time in a literal rather than symbolic manner finds particular expression in the work of Dionysius Exiguus (d. ca. 550), who (inaccurately) calculated that 753 A.U.C. was the year of Christ's birth. The resulting system he devised is still in place today, numbering each year in relationship to Christ's birth. This system contributed to a literalist interpretation of time that no longer treats the cycle of the day or the year as a metaphor for the paschal mystery, but rather as markers in linear time.

Recent reforms have attempted to reemphasize that for Christians, the natural rhythms in time are important metaphors for the paschal mystery. Like Augustine, current Church teaching recognizes that the daily rhythm of darkness and light, and the constellation of festivals that constitute the liturgical year, exert "a special sacramental power and influence which strengthens Christian Life" (Pius XII, *Maxima Redemptionis nostrae mysteriis*). Rather than simply marking time, these temporal symbols mirror the paschal mystery in the rhythm of light and darkness, and in the cycle of feasts and season. These symbols are reminders for Christians that they live in the interim between resurrection and the parousia, and that time is a vehicle for our journey to the day of Christ Jesus.

See: CHURCH, FEASTS, JUDAISM

EDWARD FOLEY, CAPUCHIN

TONGUES

This entry consists of two parts. The first examines the gift of tongues in Acts and First Corinthians. The second examines its value for private and common prayer.

New Testament

The gift of tongues is a spontaneous stream of articulate phonemes. Apart from some texts of the late addition to Mark (16:17), the gift of tongues is primarily described in Acts of the Apostles and in 1 Corinthians. The presentation of the phenomenon in these texts bears some affinities with various ecstatic phenomena in antiquity. And interpreters still debate the precise range and meaning of the texts relevant to the phenomenon. But we may fairly say that Luke and Paul are concerned to demonstrate that tongues function in tandem with intelligible discourse in the communities.

Like the Bacchanalia, tongues could be perceived as a kind of frenzied or mad activity, and were also associated with a community claiming liberation from social mores (Livy 39.13; 1 Cor 14:23; 6:12). Like Plato, Paul asserts that the one who utters things in a frenzied state should be complemented by one who can utter an interpretive prophecy of the contents of that utterance (Timaeus 72 a-b; 1 Cor 14:27, 28). And if Paul thought of tongues as the "language of the angels" (1 Cor 13:1), then we may have a parallel phenomenon described in the *Testament of Job* (48) in which one of Job's daughters speaks "ecstatically in the angelic dialect." She is followed in this activity by her two sisters, speaking in the language of the "archons" and "cherubim" about the work of the heavens and the glory of the heavenly powers (chs. 49, 50).

In Acts 10:46 and 19:6, the descent of the Spirit is accompanied by the recipients speaking "in tongues." However, the Spirit's coming on others in Acts is not always so attested (2:41; 9:18, 19). In Acts 2:4, the Apostles, Mary, and others are gathered together, and, after hearing a sound like wind and seeing tongues of fire, they begin "to speak in different tongues, as the Spirit enabled them to proclaim." What follows is a report from the linguistically diverse crowd: "we hear them speaking in our own tongues of the mighty acts of God" (2:11). Interpreters are not agreed on whether this involved a miracle of the apostles' speech or of the crowd's hearing. But while Luke does not identify the apostles' speech in 2:4 with intelligible discourse, he does bring the apostles' speech into association with intelligible discourse. The verb "to proclaim" used at the end of 2:4 is used only two other times in Acts: at 2:14, where it describes Peter's discourse, in part defending the apostles against the charge of drunkenness, and at 26:25, where it introduces Paul's comments defending himself against the charge of madness. Whatever the precise mechanism of the different tongues, Luke seems concerned for the ultimate intelligibility of their content.

In Corinth, the speaker in tongues speaks "mysteries" to God alone (1 Cor 14:2). Paul exercises the gift and tells the Corinthians that he "should like all of you to speak in tongues" (1 Cor 14:5). However he sees a need to complement the gift with the prophecy, which makes it intelligible and stresses its Spirit-inspired function in edifying all of Christ's Body. Whereas the community treated tongues as a "sign for [recognizing] believers" (1 Cor 14:22), as a sure sign of the person's having the Spirit, Paul stresses instead that an outsider's re-action to the community's prophecy is a better guideline for recognizing believers (1 Cor 14:22-26). He feels that tongues function to convince unbelievers of the Spirit's presence (1 Cor 14:22). In asserting the need for interpreters, he says that the one praying in tongues is not being guided by the mind, and that he prefers prayer, which engages his mind as well (1 Cor 14:13-15). Since the rational mind is not the primary force behind tongues, some commentators have said that the sounds which emerged may have expressed an ambivalence of the speaker toward the Christian message: in the midst of repeatedly proclaiming "Come Lord (Jesus)," MARANATHAMARANA-THA (1 Cor 16:22), one could also be heard to proclaim a curse (anathema) on Jesus (1 Cor 12:3). And Paul strenuously defends only the former as Spirit-inspired. Whereas the community may have seen themselves as "spiritual" because of the gift, Paul places a variety of gifts, including administration, ahead of tongues (1 Cor 12:8-10, 28, 29-30). He underscores their equal inspiration by the Spirit as well as the mutual interdependence of all members of Christ's Body so animated (12:4-30) and implies that love is the superior coordinator of all such temporary gifts (1 Corinthians 13). Thus the gift of tongues is to be shared in an orderly way that edifies (1 Cor 14:26-28). Whereas the tongues-speakers may have seen themselves as "mature" (vis-à-vis non speakers) he calls them childish in their thinking until they have appropriate understanding (1 Cor 14:20).

At present, interpreters debate whether or not the Spirit's "inexpressible groanings" (Rom 8:26, 27) are to be identified with tongues. Some insist not, because tongues are both audible and articulate (even if unintelligible). Others see Paul discussing tongues here and suggest that he proclaims the role of tongues as a phenomenon by which the Spirit-speaker both petitions for a (sure) acquittal as well as laments the Fall that makes such petition

necessary; an experience by which one celebrates the birth of the new creation as well as one's share in the pain of that birth.

See: APOSTLE, BODY OF CHRIST, LOVE, MARY, MYSTERY, PROPHET/PROPHECY, SPIRIT

MARK C. KILEY

Pastoral-Liturgical Tradition

The charisms by which one prays in ecstatic unintelligible speech or speaks hitherto unlearned languages are often identified as the gift of tongues, although they are quite distinct phenomena. The term, however, generally refers to ecstatic speech as an expression of prayer. As such, it benefits the speaker and gives glory to God, but requires the companion gift of interpretation if it is to edify the assembly (1 Cor 14:1-19). Paul's discussion of this gift leaves us with the impression that he recognizes it as a valid expression of prayer, but of secondary worth in communal worship. The inability of the hearers to understand the ecstatic speech makes them outsiders to the prayer, no matter how fervent the speaker. Their inability to understand renders them incapable of responding with their "Amen" (1 Cor 14:16). Thus, the pattern of communal prayer leaves little room for speaking in tongues unless one can interpret for the congregation's edification.

The contemporary reappearance of the gift of tongues or *glossolalia* challenges us to recognize the value of this gift and to seek a proper avenue for its use. While its benefit to the speaker and as a glorification of God is undeniable, its use without interpretation seems unsuited to communal or liturgical worship. In such instances, the pattern of communal prayer must take precedence. This pattern requires active and intelligent participation rather than vicarious involvement.

See: GIFTS, HUMANKIND, SPIRIT OF GOD, VISIONS

DOMINIC SERRA

TRADITION

The purpose of Scripture is the preservation of tradition. Tradition is carried through the generations both orally, as Psalm 78:3-8 describes, or in writing, e.g., the books of the Bible. Tradition lives in the people's experience as old stories are retold and reshaped to fit current situations. See, for example, the retelling of the story of the plagues in Exodus 7–12; Psalms 78; 105; and Wisdom 11–19. The passing on of tradition and its significance are mentioned in many biblical passages.

Old Testament

God and God's Covenant. God's name, Yahweh, is for all generations (Exod 3:15; Ps 135:13). If the exiled people learn again to swear by this name, they will be built up; otherwise they will be destroyed (Jer 12:16). God's covenant is for Abraham's descendants forever (Gen 17:7; Ps 105:8-10). Every generation is to be told that God alone is to be worshiped; idols are forbidden (Deut 6:4-9; Jdt 8:18).

Telling the History. The story of God's actions in the people's history is told and retold for many reasons. The people remind God of covenant responsibility to care for them: "O God, we have heard with our own ears; our ancestors have told us the deeds you did in their days. . . . But now you have rejected and disgraced us. . . . Redeem us as your love demands" (Ps 44:2, 10, 27; see Pss 77:6-13; 143:5). When the angel of the Lord says to Gideon, "The Lord is with you," Gideon responds, "Where are [God's] wondrous deeds of which our [ancestors] told us?" (Judg 6:12-13). The eighth-century prophet Micah cries, "As in the days when you came from the land of Egypt, show us wonderful signs" (Mic 7:15). An exilic prophet echoes, "Awake as in the days of old" (Isa 51:9; see Isa 63:7-16).

The people are also called to covenant responsibility through the stories of their tradition.

> What [God] commanded our ancestors,
> they were to teach their children;
> That the next generation might come to know,

children yet to be born.
> In turn they were to recite them to their
> children, that they might put their trust
> in God,
> And not forget the works of God,
> keeping his commandments (Ps 78:5-7;
> see Deut 32:7).

If the people do not keep God's commandments they will go into exile and the land will be destroyed. This too will be told as part of the tradition (Deut 29:21-28).

The tradition is told to encourage the people to trust in God. Micah declares God's covenant fidelity, "You will show faithfulness to Jacob and grace to Abraham, as you have sworn to our [ancestors] from days of old" (Mic 7:20). Amos promises God's fidelity to the covenant with David (Amos 9:11). Centuries later, when the people are fighting for their lives and their traditions (1 Macc 2:40), Judas Maccabeus encourages them by telling them "of the times when help had been given their ancestors: both the time of Sennacherib, . . . and the time of the battle in Babylonia against the Galatians" (2 Macc 8:19-20). A second-century sage tells the story of Israel's holy ancestors both to praise God and to exhort the people to live holy lives (Sirach 44–50).

Traditional Wisdom. The study of the tradition, of the stories of generations long past, teaches one how to live wisely:

> Reject not the tradition of old [people]
> which they have learned from their
> [ancestors];
> From it you will obtain the knowledge
> how to answer in time of need (Sir 8:9;
> see 2:10).

The ancient tradition has authority to explain present experience (Job 8:8; Lam 2:17). Sirach, the sage, "explores the wisdom of the men of old" and "treasures the discourses of famous men" (Sir 39:1-2). As a teacher of wisdom he intends to carry on the tradition, to "pour out instruction like prophecy and bestow it on generations to come" (Sir 24:31).

Specific Traditions in the Life of the People. The life of the people is shaped by tradition. Liturgical activity is based on tradition. The Sabbath is to be observed "throughout the generations" (Exod 31:13, 16; cf. 2 Macc 6:6). Feast and fast days are kept according to tradition: Passover (Exod 12:14, 17, 42); Unleavened Bread (Exod 12:17); Day of Atonement (Exod 30:10); Purim (Esth 10:13). Sacrifices are offered in the Temple (Deut 12:1-14; Tob 1:4-7) according to prescribed customs (Exod 29:42; 30:8; 1 Sam 2:16). Priests and Levites are anointed according to custom and their way of life is governed by tradition (Exod 40:15; Lev 7:36; 10:9; Num 18:23). Various purifications and washings are required by custom (Exod 30:21; 2 Macc 12:38). Even private prayer is eventually regulated by the custom of facing Jerusalem (Dan 6:11; Tob 3:11). There are also some traditions of women's prayer outside the regular liturgical cycle: the memorial of Jephthah's daughter (Judg 11:39-40), the offering to the queen of heaven (Jer 44:15-19).

Diet is regulated by the traditions of clean and unclean food (Leviticus 11; see Daniel 1). The custom of removing a sandal seals a contract of exchange (Ruth 4:7).

There are several war customs. During the period of entrance into the land, war is regulated by the custom of *herem*, the destruction of all booty and the killing of all living things in a conquered city (Joshua 7; 1 Sam 15:4-22). Later, when the taking of plunder is approved, David establishes a custom of sharing the spoil between soldiers in battle and soldiers who guard the camp (1 Sam 30:24).

Marriage is also regulated by tradition. Laban claims a marriage custom of marrying the older daughter before the younger (Gen 29:26). A postexilic marriage custom requires marriage within the clan (Tob 1:9; 4:12-13).

See: MARRIAGE, PASSOVER, PRIEST, SACRIFICE, TEMPLE

IRENE NOWELL, O.S.B.

New Testament

Jewish Tradition. Like the people of the OT and the Jewish people, the early Christians were a people of tradition. They had their own traditional values, practices, teaching, creeds, hymns, and liturgical formulas, many of which were specifically Christian. They also had deep respect for traditional values originating in the OT and Judaism. But that does not mean they accepted everything that was handed down as traditional. As in the synagogue, it often happened that ancient values and traditions conflicted with the demands of new situations. Among the early Christians, such conflicts usually involved Jewish traditions that were incompatible with values and practices flowing from the universality of the Church.

Some practices that were deemed traditional by segments of the Jewish community were rejected outright by the early Christians. A good example can be found in Mark 7:1-23 and Matthew 15:1-20, where Jesus deals with "the tradition of the elders" regarding purifications in the preparation of meals. These traditional practices were not genuine and had to be set aside. They were not "the tradition of the elders" but of the Pharisees and the scribes who clung to them while disregarding the commandment of God.

In the life of Jesus, the criterion for rejecting those traditions came from Jesus' prophetic stance against their imposition on ordinary people by leaders who exalted them over the word of God. In the Marcan and Matthean communities, the criterion came from the need to open the Christian table to all peoples, Jewish as well as Gentile. Traditions that prevented or inhibited the participation of Gentiles at the Christian table had to be set aside because they prevented the Church from reaching out to all peoples and welcoming them as Christians.

Some traditional teachings and practices, especially those that sprang from the Law and the Prophets, were not abolished or set aside but fulfilled (Matt 5:17-20). Fulfillment did not mean maintaining the status quo but developing the traditions further, extending and refining them, as in the case of the commandments governing anger (Matt 5:21-26), adultery (Matt 5:27-30), divorce (Matt 5:31-32), oaths (Matt 5:33-37), and retaliation (Matt 5:38-42). It could also mean purifying traditional attitudes of elements that distorted the Law and its intent, as when tradition assumed that the command to love one's neighbor implied hating one's enemy. Purified and developed in the Christian tradition, the command to love one's neighbor included loving one's enemies and even one's persecutors (Matt 5:43-48). Finally, besides developing and purifying a tradition, fulfillment could mean transforming it, as in the case of Passover and Pentecost, whose origins were told in the OT (Exod 12:1-51; Deut 16:1-9; Lev 23:15-22; Deut 16:9-12) and which had an important place in Judaism. When these feasts became associated with Christian events, they acquired a new and specifically Christian meaning in the early Church.

Apostolic Tradition. The NT witnesses to the origins and development of Christian tradition, distinct from Jewish tradition. We call that tradition "apostolic" because of its development in the apostolic community. It is in that tradition that the life, teaching, death, and resurrection of Christ and their meaning for Christians were transmitted. Luke witnesses to this tradition when he announces his intention (Luke 1:3) "to compile a narrative of the events that have been fulfilled among us, just as those who were eyewitnesses from the beginning and ministers of the word have handed them down to us" (Luke 1:1-2).

Studying the Gospels and Acts, we see how the early Christians left aside some of their own traditions as incompatible with new situations (see Luke 22:35-36; cf. Luke 9:3; 10:4; Mark 6:8-9). We see also how they developed traditional stories and adapted them for new contexts. In Luke 9:10-17, for example, we see how the setting for the breaking of bread has been transferred from a deserted place in the countryside (see Mark 6:34-44) to the city of Bethsaida and adapted to the urban circumstances of Luke's readers. In their transmission and adaptation, such stories reveal a process of tradition that was sensitive to what was handed down and intent on maintaining its dynamism.

We learn much about early Christian tradition from Paul. In his very first letter, 1 Thessalonians, he asks the Christians to conduct themselves according to what they had received from him (1 Thess 4:1), that is, according to the "instructions we gave you through the Lord Jesus" (1 Thess 4:2). For Paul, the Lord Jesus was both the ultimate source of tradition (see 1 Cor 7:10; Gal 1:11-12) and the principal agent of its transmission. Second Thessalonians refers to Paul's instructions as "the traditions that you were taught, either by an oral statement or by a letter of ours" (2 Thess 2:15).

The importance Paul placed on tradition is obvious from 1 Corinthians, where he praises the Christians of Corinth: "I praise you because . . . you hold fast to the traditions, just as I handed them on to you" (1 Cor 11:2). Later Paul addresses matters in which he cannot praise them, especially the way they behave at what is intended to be the Lord's Supper but which in reality has become each one's private supper (1 Cor 11:18-21). By way of response and exhortation, Paul appeals to the liturgical tradition of the Lord's Supper that he himself had given them: "I received from the Lord what I also handed on to you" (1 Cor 11:23a). He then quotes a traditional liturgical text (1 Cor 11:23b-25) and applies it to the situation at Corinth (1 Cor 11:26-34). In his teaching and exhortation, Paul thus calls the people to be faithful to the tradition and he develops its implications for Christian attitudes and behavior at the Lord's Supper.

Later in 1 Corinthians, Paul again appeals to tradition (1 Cor 15:1-3a) and cites a traditional creed: "that Christ died for our sins in accordance with the scriptures; that he was buried; that he was raised on the third day in accordance with the scriptures; that he appeared to Kephas, then to the Twelve" (1 Cor 15:3b-5). This time he invokes tradition to show the inconsistency of those who deny the possibility of resurrection in general while confessing their belief in that of Christ. Paul's appeal to liturgical and credal tradition in 1 Corinthians 11 and 15 tells us much about the content, transmission, and implications of apostolic tradition for pastoral theology.

See: COMMUNITY, TEACH/TEACHING

EUGENE LAVERDIERE, S.S.S.

Pastoral-Liturgical Tradition

Tradition is the common English translation of *parádosis*, being composed of the same elements as the word in Latin and Greek: to "give over" or "hand on" (see Ezra 7:26, LXX, in a passage quite unlike the MT). When Paul speaks in 1 Corinthians 15:3 of "having handed on" *(parédōka)* what he "also received" *(parélabon)* he is understood to be reflecting the two verbs *masar 1ᵉ* and *qibbel min*, rabbinic usage for the faithful transmission of teaching received from a master. In this case the content of the tradition is Christ's death, burial, resurrection, and appearances to "Cephas . . . James . . . and all the apostles" (vv. 3-7). Paul uses the same two verbs earlier in this letter to describe the way he has transmitted what the Lord Jesus did and said at the supper table on the night he was betrayed (11:23). He employs one of the two verbs, "I handed on [to you]" (11:2), with "traditions" *(paradóseis)* as its object, to describe the practices he requires regarding the headdress and hair styles of women and men in Corinth (vv. 3-16).

This use of the word and the description of the way tradition is handed on illustrates a later development in Church life. Some matters that were received from the first witnesses, like the resurrection of Christ

and the Lord's Supper, were taken to be of the core of Christian faith and practice while others, usually practices rather than beliefs, were allowed to languish (see, e.g., 15:29 on being baptized "for the dead" and the hair styles). Several traditions like male circumcision, Sabbath observance, and abstention from pork continued among Semitic Gentile churches for many centuries, while the central "tradition" of faith and moral practice was held in common in all the churches—although much debated theologically.

Paul writes of having lived out with excessive zeal all the "traditions" of his ancestors (Gal 1:14), something he does not regret. The whole thrust of his Galatian letter, however, is that his Gentiles need not, indeed must not, observe them if they think this a necessary complement to their faith in Christ. The letter to the Church at Colossae, of Pauline inspiration if not composition, warns the people there against the "empty deception of human tradition" (Col 2:8), meaning in context the vain "philosophy" of being under the influence of cosmic powers rather than relying on Christ. The above two are examples of traditions to which believers in Jesus Christ may not adhere.

A letter to Thessalonica likewise exhorts the Church in that city, first to eschew baseless rumors and letters purporting to come from Paul (2 Thess 2:2), then to "hold fast to the traditions that you were taught, either by an oral statement or by a letter of ours" (v. 15). The injunction is repeated with "tradition" in the singular (3:6).

Mark is familiar with the "*tradition*" of the Pharisees and, indeed, all Jews of washing their hands, food bought in markets, and kitchenware before preparing and eating food (Mark 7:3-5). In this matter Matthew follows but abbreviates him (15:2). Similarly, Mark has Jesus accuse "the Pharisees and scribes" of nullifying God's commandment to honor father and mother by replacing it with a dedication of all possession to God and doing nothing further for parents, thereby putting "the traditions you have handed on" in place of "God's word" (Mark 7:13; see Matt 15:6).

The verb meaning to "hand over," "deliver up," or "transmit" (*paradídonai*) occurs frequently in the NT and the Septuagint. It can be used for the transmission of anything, but it often describes the handing over of captives in war or slaves, sometimes of innocent victims like Jesus and John the Baptist. It is the verb for Judas' betrayal of Jesus (Matt 26:21). Jesus says in one place: "All things have been handed over to me by my Father" (Matt 11:27; par. Luke 10:22). Similarly, the devil claims: "[Authority] has been handed over to me and I give it to whomever I wish" (Luke 4:6). In the "great commission" at the end of Matthew where we might expect this verb, the simple word for "give" is used: "Full authority has been given [*èdóthē*] to me" (Matt 28:18b).

A NT word similar to "tradition" is *parathēkē*. Its usual translation, "deposit," connotes the giving and receiving of something that is not expected to be passed on. This is unfortunate, deriving as it does from the fact that in the three places where it occurs there is an injunction to keep safe "what has been entrusted to you" (1 Tim 6:20; 2 Tim 1:12, 14). This says nothing, however, about not transmitting it further. The cognate verb, *paratithénai*, which is employed eighteen times, can mean "entrust," "present," and "propose," but also "distribute [bread]" (Mark 6:41), "hand on [teachings]" (2 Tim 2:2), and "apply [biblical texts]" (Acts 17:3). Unfortunately, "commit for safekeeping" has prevailed over the more dynamic meanings of this word-group, as if this were its only meaning. The treasures of the gospel are not for hoarding but for passing on.

Because both terms can mean the best and the worst of what is transmitted, the question arises as to how the kerygma of the NT became the "apostolic tradition" of the second century. Credal statements on the incarnation begin to occur in St. Ignatius of Antioch (ca. 110) to the Ephesians (7.2; 18.2) and more fully in Trallians (9) and Smyrnaeans (1). A *Letter to Diognetus*, probably the work of Quadratus from as early as 130, contains a summary of God's offering the Son as a ransom for us—Jesus' righteousness covering our sins—that seems to derive directly from Romans 5:8-11 and 8:32-33. The concluding chapters 11 and 12 of this document, while close in spirit to 1–10, apparently come from another hand. They speak of "the pledge of [believers'] faith," probably meaning the baptismal promises, and "the faith of the gospels made secure, the tradition of the apostles maintained" (11.5-6). The tradition thus spoken of is presented by St. Justin Martyr in diffuse fashion in his *1 Apology* (ca. 155), chapters 12, 13, 33, 35, 61, 65.

The consolidator of the concept of apostolic tradition is St. Irenaeus, bishop of Lugdunum (Lyon) in Gaul, writing in his five books entitled *The Refutation and Overthrow of the Knowledge So-Called (Adversus Haereses)*. There he gives a credal summary (I.10.1) and later a presentation of the tradition that derives from the apostles and how it is arrived at (III.1.1-2; 2–5). It is "guarded by the successions of elders in the churches" but resisted by Gnostic heretics who "oppose the tradition" and "will not agree with either Scripture or tradition" (III.2.2). "The tradition of the apostles, made clear in all the world, can be clearly seen in every church by those who wish to behold the truth." Following this, Irenaeus chooses as prototypical "that very great, oldest and well-known Church, founded and established at Rome by those two most glorious apostles, Peter and Paul," in having received that tradition from the apostles and handed it down "through the successions of bishops" (ibid.).

Rome's tradition of orthodoxy, namely choosing the side that ultimately became the faith of the Church, is unbroken except for Pope Honorius' espousal of the monothelete (one will in Christ) position in 634, in an effort to heal the monophysite (one nature) heresy. He was formally condemned at III Constantinople in 681. Pope Vigilius probably signed the condemnation of the "Three Chapters," which he opposed, under duress at II Constantinople (553), thereby placing in some doubt, at least from the West's point of view, the binding force of the Cyrillian theory of the hypostatic union.

The Dogmatic Constitution of II Council of the Vatican (*Dei Verbum*, Nov. 18, 1965) discusses at length the relation of sacred Scripture and sacred Tradition without bringing to a vote the question debated since the Council of Trent (Sess. IV, DS 1501) as to whether they constitute one source of knowledge of faith or two (II.8-9). Trent refers to "written books and unwritten traditions." The carefully worded statement of *Dei Verbum* describes Scripture and tradition as together "flowing from the same divine wellspring and in a certain way merging into a unity and tending toward the same end. For sacred Scripture is the word of God . . . [while], to the successors of the apostles, sacred tradition hands on in its full purity God's word. . . . [Since] these successors can in their preaching preserve this word of God faithfully, explain it, and make it more widely known . . . it is not from sacred Scripture alone that the Church draws its certainty about everything that has been revealed" (II.9).

Distinguishing between apostolic tradition and human traditions (e.g., the modes and languages of the celebration of the Christian mysteries; Eucharistic bread with or without yeast) will always be a problem in the Church. Claims for that which is the Church's "tradition" are often made for matters no more than two, four, or nine hundred years old. All such traditions are reformable. Even the constant and unbroken tradition of the responsibility of Jews of all the ages for the death of Christ, a teaching of the Church Fathers of East and West from the third century onward, could be reprobated at II Vatican (Declaration on Non-Christian Religions, no. 4). The apostolic tradition is, in fact, the central core of matters of faith, many doctrinal but some moral and liturgical.

See: ANCESTORS, CHURCH, ELDERS, PAUL, TEACH/ TEACHING, WITNESS, WORD

GERARD S. SLOYAN

TRANSFIGURATION

New Testament

The concept of *metamorphōsis* or transfiguration was a common one in the Greco-Roman world. There are two separate ideas found in Hellenistic mystery religions: (1) that gods could transform themselves and appear in visible form to human beings; (2) that human beings could achieve a change from earthly to supraterrestrial appearance by a process of deification or regeneration. Neither concept corresponds to the transfiguration of Jesus in the NT.

The Gospels of Mark (9:2-10), Matthew (17:1-8), and Luke (9:28-36) relate the transfiguration as an event that took place near the end of Jesus' Galilean ministry in which his visible appearance changed. In all three Gospels the account follows directly upon Peter's confession of Jesus as the Messiah. The incident is said to have taken place atop a mountain* in the presence of Peter, James, and John. In addition to a change in Jesus himself, his clothing became white. Then Moses and Elijah appeared and spoke with Jesus. Peter remarks how good it was to be there and suggests that they make three tents: one for Jesus, one for Moses, and one for Elijah. Then a cloud overshadowed them and a voice came from the cloud identifying Jesus as the Son of God and giving the command, "Listen to him." While this basic story line is found in each of the Synoptic accounts, each evangelist presents the transfiguration story with a slightly different theological interpretation.

In the Gospel of Mark the transfiguration is presented as a revelation directed to the disciples to further their understanding of Jesus. Throughout Mark's Gospel the question of Jesus' identity arises again and again (e.g., Mark 1:24, 34; 3:11; 4:41; 6:3, 14-16; 8:27, 29). Coming on the heels of Peter's confession of Jesus as the Messiah and Jesus' first prediction of his passion, the transfiguration serves to unfold Mark's Christology further. It affirms Jesus' identity as the Son of God (9:7), the Messiah (8:29), and the coming Son of Man (8:38;

9:9). This revelation was intended to call forth from the disciples a response of obedience (9:7), even though they do not fully understand (9:6).

Matthew presents the transfiguration event more as a vision directed to the three disciples: "As they were coming down from the mountain, Jesus charged them, 'Do not tell the vision to anyone until the Son of Man has been raised from the dead'" (Matt 17:9). Matthew also stresses the apocalyptic nature of Jesus as the Son of Man by adding details from Daniel 10: "his face shone like the sun" (Matt 17:2; Dan 10:6); "they fell prostrate" (lit. "they fell on their faces," Matt 17:6; Dan 10:9); "Jesus came and touched them, saying, 'Rise, and do not be afraid'" (Matt 17:7; Dan 10:10, 12); and "the disciples raised their eyes" (Matt 17:8; Dan 10:5). Matthew also emphasizes Jesus' lordship (Matt 17:4). Throughout his Gospel, Matthew portrays Jesus as the one greater than Moses. So too, at the transfiguration, with the appearance of Moses and Elijah, Jesus is shown to be the fulfillment of the Law and the Prophets, yet he supersedes them. As in Mark, so also in Matthew, the transfiguration occurrence is for the sake of the disciples. Throughout his Gospel, Matthew emphasizes the necessity that the disciples hear and understand Jesus' words (Matt 13:13-15, 19, 23, 51) and then obey them (Matt 7:24-28; 21:6, 28-32; 28:20). Thus, in his version of the transfiguration, Matthew eliminates the misunderstanding of the disciples (Mark 9:6) and the climax of the story is the command, "Listen to him" (Matt 17:5).

In Luke's account (9:28-36) the transfiguration is seen as both an experience for Jesus and the disciples. Luke, in accord with his emphasis on prayer, says that Jesus "went up the mountain to pray" (9:28) and that "while he was praying his face changed in appearance" (9:29). Luke does not use the language of transfiguration (*metemorphōthē*) to describe what happened to Jesus as do Matthew (17:2) and Mark (9:2). Luke alone tells the content of the conversation between Jesus, Moses, and

Elijah: "they spoke of his exodus that he was going to accomplish in Jerusalem" (9:31). The two heavenly figures point to Jesus' "exodus" as being the new redeeming action for his people, as was the Exodus of old. Like the angel Gabriel announcing the births of John the Baptist (Luke 1:8-23) and Jesus (Luke 1:26-38), and the "two men" at the resurrection (Luke 24:1-12) and the ascension (Acts 1:10-12), the "two men . . . who appeared in glory" (9:30-31) are harbingers of an event of great significance for salvation. Like Moses and Elijah, Jesus is a prophet mighty in deed and word. Like them, Jesus too would suffer persecution and rejection, but would be vindicated by God. As eschatological figures, Moses and Elijah are heralds that in Jesus the end time is inaugurated. The disappearance of Moses and Elijah (9:33) signals that it is now in Jesus that salvation is to be found and he is the one to be heeded (9:35). In Luke's Gospel, the transfiguration is one of the episodes that answers Herod's question in 9:9, "Who is this?" The transfiguration both affirms Peter's recognition of Jesus as the Messiah (9:20) and spells out what that messiahship entails: an "exodus" through suffering and death into glory. For followers of Jesus, the path is the same as his, and it is he alone that the disciples must heed and follow (9:35).

The Gospel of John does not contain a narrative account of the transfiguration; John portrays Jesus' whole life as lived in glory. However, John 12:27-35 does contain many similarities to the Synoptic story.

In 2 Peter 1:16-18 the transfiguration is interpreted as a prefigurement of the parousia. Because of its delay, there were those who challenged the tradition of the parousia. The author of 2 Peter invokes his supposed eyewitness experience of the transfiguration to authenticate the teaching about the parousia as grounded in God's sure prophetic word and not in "cleverly devised myths" (2 Pet 1:16) of human beings.

In Paul's letters, there are two passages that speak of metamorphosis: "All of us, gazing with unveiled face on the glory of the Lord, are being transformed [metamorphoumetha] into the same image from glory to glory, as from the Lord who is the Spirit" (2 Cor 3:18); "Do not conform yourself to this age but be transformed [metamorphousthe] by the renewal of your mind, that you may discern what is the will of God, what is good and pleasing and perfect" (Rom 12:2). In both instances Paul speaks of the process of inward transformation of the Christian that is effected by God's indwelling Spirit.

See: ANGEL, ASCENSION, CLOUD, DEATH, DISCIPLE/ DISCIPLESHIP, ELIJAH/ELISHA, EXODUS, GLORY, LAW, MESSIAH, MOSES, MOUNTAIN, PAROUSIA, PASSION, PRAYER, PROPHET, SON OF GOD, SON OF MAN, SUFFERING, TENT

BARBARA E. REID, O.P.

TREE

Visitors to the State of Israel today come away with the impression that the land has few forest resources. That is why it may be surprising that the Bible mentions at least thirty-one species of trees, though the Bible was not concerned with describing ancient Israel's plant environment. The Bible does not mention many common forest trees because it had not occasion to bring them into its narratives or poems. On the other hand, the Bible mentions the cedar tree more than seventy times, though it is not native to Palestine. Cedar wood was a component of monumental projects like the Temple (1 Kgs 6:9) and became a symbol of grandeur (Ps 92:12; 2 Kgs 14:9).

Old Testament

The presence of trees in the land of the Bible depends upon two considerations: the climate and human activity. Palestine is subject to a wide range of climactic conditions. About one half the region falls into the subtropical desert belt. The survival of trees or any other vegetation depends on the moisture of the soil and its salt content. Only some grasses and thorny shrubs can tolerate this climate. Mediterranean forests covered about forty percent of ancient Pa-

lestine. Some species characteristic of these forests include the oak and terebinth. The Jordan Valley, especially near perennial streams, is a savannah with tall grass and scattered trees like the acacia. The forests of ancient Israel (1 Sam 22:5; 2 Sam 18:6; Ezek 20:46-47; Neh 2:6) have been subject to a constant process of destruction because of the use to which people have put the wood products of these forests. Trees were a source of fuel and building material. Also trees were cleared for agricultural purposes. The limited resources of the region cannot support all these enterprises. Recent attempts at reforestation have not been able to restore the original forests.

Trees sometimes serve as metaphors in the OT. When the trees seek a king, they turn to fruit trees all of which reject the offer. It is the bramble who agrees to be king (Judg 9:8-13). Trees with deep roots that enable them to keep their green foliage throughout the dry summer are images that speak of commitment, endurance, and life (Ps 1:3; Isa 65:22). A stately and majestic tree is an apt image of power and might (Ezek 31:3; Dan 4:10-12). Perhaps this is a reason trees marked sites for worship in the region. God appeared to Abraham at the terebinth of Mamre where the patriarch built an altar (Gen 12:6-7). Later the prophets would consider worship at such places to be unacceptable (Jer 3:6).

An extended metaphor that involves trees occurs in the story of Eden (Genesis 2–3). Here the Bible adapts a common ancient Near Eastern motif to express Israel's understanding of God and the human condition. Ancient Near Eastern mythology sometimes thought of life as a material substance that one can possess through eating. The tree of life (Gen 2:9; 3:22) reflects this belief. It stands in the middle of the garden apparently as a source of eternal life for the people who eat its fruit. God expelled Adam and Eve from the garden so they could not eat of the fruit of this tree because they chose to eat of the fruit of the tree of knowledge though God had forbidden them to do so (Gen 3:3, 5).

There are no parallels to the image of the tree of knowledge in ancient Near Eastern literature. The introduction of this tree into the story shifts the emphasis away from the loss of the tree as the reason for death to the disobedience of the man and woman. The Bible transforms the ancient myth that is concerned with life and death. In Genesis the primary concern is with the relationship of the man and woman with God. The tree of life reappears in the Book of Revelation (2:7; 22:2, 14, 19). The righteous will be able to eat from the tree of life that is in paradise.

The ancient Israelites valued trees for more mundane purposes beyond their usefulness as literary metaphors. The shade that tree provided was a welcome relief for people who spent most of their waking hours out of doors in the Mediterranean sun. Highly prized for the shade it provided was the fig tree. The image of a person sitting under the shade of a fig tree is a proverbial portrait of a person enjoying prosperity and peace (1 Kgs 4:25; Mic 4:4). Leafy trees provided the best place to pitch a tent (Gen 13:18) or to judge disputes (Judg 4:5). Farmers prized fruit trees that they cultivated for the value of the fruit they produced. The olive tree was the most important of these. Olive trees were cultivated in Palestine from the Bronze Age (3200–3000 BCE). Its fruit was part of the daily diet, and it had other uses as well. The olive is about fifty percent oil. People extracted its oil as fuel for lamps, medicine, a component of perfume and soap. The fruit of some other trees like the fig also had medicinal properties (2 Kgs 20:7; Isa 38:21).

A fruit tree that was cultivated in Palestine from the prehistoric age was the date palm. The fruit's sugar content makes it ideal as an energy source. Their presence at oases was a boon to travelers (Exod 15:27). Its fruit was eaten fresh, dried, or in cakes that travelers could carry conveniently. The leaves of the date palm covered the roof, and its trunk often supported the roof. The palm as a decorative motif in the Temple (1

Kgs 6:29, 32; Ezekiel 40–41) is testimony to the importance of the palm in the life of the ancient Israelites. The importance of trees is also evident from the directions on the proper way to observe the Feast of Booths in Leviticus 23:40. The Israelite is to bring foliage from various trees (myrtle, palm, and willow) to the Temple to celebrate the fruit harvest.

New Testament

In the NT trees serve as metaphors in the teaching of Jesus. Most often the tree and its fruit serve as a metaphor for actions as revealing the character of an individual (Matt 3:10; 7:17-19; 12:33). Paul uses the practice of grafting as a metaphor for the salvation of the Gentiles (Rom 11:17, 24). Several texts use the term tree to speak about the cross of Jesus: Acts 5:30; 10:39; 13:29; Galatians 3:13; 1 Peter 2:24.

LESLIE J. HOPPE, O.F.M.

TRIBES

The most common Hebrew words for tribe are *šebeṭ* and *maṭṭeh*, both translated as "staff," "branch," "tribe." The idea of "staff" and "branch" implies authority associated with a social unit. The Greek word is *phylē*, "tribe," "nation," "people."

In the ancient world, tribes were part of a social structure that took care of people's basic needs and performed various religious and legal functions. Princes often ruled tribes instead of kings. Both non-Israelite and Israelite* peoples were organized into tribes, but when settlement and agriculture took hold in the land, tribal organization eventually faded away.

The OT mentions the existence of non-Israelite tribes but focuses on the Israelite tribes. The Pentateuch describes the Israelite tribes in detail; the Former and Latter Prophets and the Writings also highlight aspects of Israel's tribal life. The NT specifically mentions the twelve tribes of Israel.

From a theological perspective, the development of peoples into tribes reflects a sense of order inherent in all of creation (see Gen 1:1-2a). The formation of the Israelites into tribes shows that even though they are a people special to God, they are not an entity unto themselves. They are, in fact, part of a larger social structure—the tribe—to which many people belonged. But as a distinct group of people, the tribes of Israel show how God is intimately involved in a community's life and is ultimately responsible for shaping that life. The Israelite tribes become a symbol of hope for future generations and provide a historical and literary link between the OT and NT canons and the Jewish and Christian traditions.

Old Testament

In the OT, the Pentateuch mentions the names of various tribes of people and focuses specifically on the Israelites who become a great tribal unit among all other tribes.

The Book of Genesis traces the historical origins of the tribal units. Abraham is the father of Ishmael (Gen 16:1-4, 15) and Isaac (Gen 21:2). Ishmael's mother is Hagar, Sarah's maidservant; Sarah is Abraham's wife and Isaac's mother. Both sons are the recipients of God's divine blessing (Gen 17:16, 20) but with Isaac God maintains the Abrahamic Covenant (Gen 17:1-14).

Genesis 25:13-16 lists the names of Ishmael's children who became known as the Ishmaelites. Abraham and another wife, Keturah, also bear children whose descendants became known as prominent Arabian or Aramean tribes (Gen 25:1-4). From Abraham's and Keturah's loins also sprang another group, the Midianites (Gen 25:1-2).

Isaac marries Rebekah who gives birth to two sons, Esau and Jacob, Abraham's grandsons. God maintains covenant with Jacob whose sons shall inherit the Promised Land. Esau's descendants are the Edomites (Gen 36:1, 15-19). Jacob, whom God renames Israel, and his wives Rachel and Leah and his concubines Bilhah and Zilpah give birth to twelve sons (Gen 35:22b-26) who, in turn, become known as the twelve tribes of Israel. Genesis 49:1-28 lists the

names of these tribes: Reuben, Simeon, Levi, Judah, Zebulun, Issachar, Dan, Gad, Asher, Naphtali, Joseph, Benjamin.

According to patriarchal lineage, Jacob's twelve sons are Abraham's great-grandsons. Thus, in the ancient world there are both non-Israelite and Israelite tribes. The above examples show that, from a literary and historical perspective, the Israelite tribes are united to some of the non-Israelite tribes through a common ancestor and bloodline—Abraham. But it is God's election, covenant, promise and its fulfillment, and the personal, intimate relationship with God who chose Israel that makes the Israelites distinct from all other tribes.

Following the historical origins of the tribal units, the Books of Exodus, Leviticus, Numbers, and Deuteronomy trace the development of the Israelite tribes and God's care and predilection for them. The tribes' story begins with Jacob's and his sons' migration to Egypt to join Joseph who was already there (Exod 1:1-5). Despite the eventual death of Jacob and his sons, their descendants were prolific and continued to thrive (Exod 1:1-7) in the midst of Egyptian oppression (Exod 1:12b-14). Through Moses, God frees them from bondage (Exod 12:51), and they continue to live under divine guidance and promise (Exod 19:1–24:18; see also Deuteronomy 7).

In Exodus 25:1-9 Moses is commanded to build a sanctuary so that God might dwell in the Israelites' midst (see also Exod 29:45-46). God chooses from among the Israelite tribes artisans and assistants to perform the task (Exod 31:6a), and the work is completed (Exod 38:22-23). God's desire to dwell among the Israelite tribes and the building of the Dwelling reflects the mutual relationship that God and the tribes of Israel enjoy.

After the erection, anointing, and consecration of the Dwelling and all its equipment, the Israelite tribes, through their princes, make offerings before the Dwelling (Num 7:1-3).

Under God's further direction, Moses takes a census of the Israelite tribes, enrolls them in companies (Num 1:1-3, 19b-46), and prepares them for their departure from Sinai. God appoints from each tribe various heads of the ancestral houses to assist Moses in his task. Numbers 1:5-15 lists the names of the appointees. Other OT lists of the Israelite tribes show variations in names that may be due in part to geographical locations, genealogical relationships, and status changes that affected the tribes over a period of time. A second census is taken later (Num 26:1-51).

Numbers 1:47-54 states that the Levite tribe is not registered with the other tribes. They are set aside and dedicated especially to God for the purpose of carrying out the tasks associated with the Dwelling (Num 3:21-39; see also Deut 10:8-9). It is only after the general census is taken that God commands Moses to take a census of the Levites (Num 3:14-20; see also 26:57-65).

The Israelite tribes, under the continued direction of God and Moses' and Aaron's leadership, are arranged in camps around the meeting tent (Num 2:1-34). Encamped on the east side are Judah, Issachar, and Zebulun, the first on the march to Canaan (Num 2:3-9). On the south are Reuben, Simeon, and Gad, the second on the march (Num 2:10-16); in the middle of the line are the Levites (Num 2:17); on the west are Ephraim, Manasseh, and Benjamin, the third on the march (Num 2:18-24); and on the north are Dan, Asher, and Naphtali, the last on the march (Num 2:25-31).

Numbers 10:11-28 and 33:1-56 outline the Israelite tribes' systematic march toward Canaan as they move in stages under divine protection (Num 10:33-36).

Commanded by God, Moses sends out leaders from among the Israelite tribes to act as scouts to reconnoiter the land of Canaan (Num 13:1-16). They inform Moses about the non-Israelite tribes residing in the land and express their fear of them (Num 13:25-33). However, God gives Moses instructions that help to reassure the Israelites of the divine promise (Num 33:50-56).

After God establishes boundaries in Canaan (Num 34:1-13), God then names men,

one from among each Israelite tribe, to apportion the land to the different tribes (Num 34:16-29). The Levites are to receive cities and pasture lands around the cities (Num 35:1-8).

In the Book of Deuteronomy, Moses instructs the Israelite tribes on how to worship God in the land (Deut 12:5-14). In Deuteronomy 16:18-20 God instructs Moses to appoint judges and officials throughout his tribes "to administer true justice for the people in all the communities" that God is giving them. In Deuteronomy 33:1-29, the tribes receive Moses' blessing before he dies. Here he extols God's greatness and reminds the tribes of how fortunate they are to be under divine care and favor (Deut 33:26-29).

Finally, within the Pentateuch one also sees the Israelite tribes in another light. Some rebel against Moses' leadership (Num 16:1-11, 12-15) and then suffer God's chastisement (Num 16:16-24, 35; 16:25-34). Thus, the Israelite tribes experience not only God's care and promise but also God's wrath. Hence, obedience to God and God's servant, in this case Moses, is extremely important.

The Former Prophets also make reference to the Israelite tribes. The Book of Joshua focuses on the tribes' conquest of the land of Canaan (Josh 1:1–12:24) and how it is divided up among them as their heritage (Josh 13:1–24:34). Joshua 7:1 also records the story of Achan, of the tribe of Judah, who disobeys God's commands (Josh 6:16-19; 7:1) and causes God to be angry with all of Israel. Under the leadership of Joshua, the Israelites, in turn, stone Achan to death, and God's anger relents (Josh 7:24-26). Again, obedience to God is intrinsic to the life of the Israelite tribes.

1 Samuel 9:14–10:27 features the story of how Saul, a Benjamite, becomes God's anointed one and eventually the Israelite tribes' first king (1 Sam 10:17-24).

The Latter Prophets also refer to the Israelite tribes. Addressed to Israel in exile, Isaiah 49:6 speaks of restoration of the tribes/survivors of Jacob/Israel. In Isaiah

63:17 a reference to the tribes is used as part of a plea for God's mercy. Ezekiel 47:13-20 outlines the boundaries of the restored land and lists several of the Israelite tribes who are to receive the land (Ezek 48:1-29). Unlike the former boundaries that provided land to the tribes according to their size (Num 26:52-56), these boundaries provide for an equal portion of land to be allotted to each tribe. Hosea 5:9 portrays the Israelite tribes as the object of God's wrath, while Zechariah 9:1 designates the tribes as God's.

Finally, in the Writings, the psalmist reminds one of God's goodness toward the Israelite tribes (Ps 78:55) despite their ingratitude (Ps 78:56-58) which caused God to become angry (Ps 78:59-60). Later God exerts care for the people (Ps 78:65-72) who eventually go up as tribes to Jerusalem to give thanks to their God (Ps 122:4).

In summary, the use of tribes in the OT seems to have a fourfold purpose. First, as a social structure, tribes reflect a sense of order inherent in the divine plan of creation. Second, the evolution of the Israelites into tribes shows how they have a common lineage yet are distinct from the other tribes of their day because of covenant and their relationship to God. Third, the development of Israel's tribal unit under God's care, promise, and even chastisement shows how God is intimately involved in forming and shaping a community's life and history. And finally, the fulfillment of the promise and covenant made to Abraham that the Israelite tribes would indeed inherit the Promised Land attests to the love and faithfulness of God who desires that people walk in the divine ways only to be blessed again and again.

New Testament

The NT does not refer to tribes as extensively as does the OT. However, many people in the NT world are concerned with tribal connections, e.g., Anna, of the tribe Asher (Luke 2:36); Barnabas, a Levite (Acts 4:36); Paul, of the tribe of Benjamin (Rom 11:1); and Jesus from Judah (Heb 7:14). Ref-

erences to the specific tribes seem to be used for identification purposes or to stress a particular point.

In the Gospels, Jesus promises his disciples that when all things are renewed, they will sit on twelve thrones judging the twelve tribes of Israel (Matt 19:28). Those who have left all to follow Jesus will, in the end, share in his glory and authority. The fulfillment of this promise begins in the time of the early Church. Jesus makes a similar promise to those disciples who have stood by him in his trials (Luke 22:30). Hence, both uses of tribes are associated with the promise of a reward.

In Acts, Paul stands before the Jewish king Agrippa and expresses hope in connection with the twelve tribes. In the Letter of James, James addresses his message of hope and exhortation to "the twelve tribes in dispersion" (Jas 1:1). Finally, in the Book of Revelation, the Israelite tribes are associated with the promise of salvation and the new Jerusalem (Rev 7:4-8; 21:12).

Thus, in the OT tribes are related to the fulfillment of God's promise to Abraham; in the NT they are related to hope and promise for a future time.

See: ABRAHAM, BLESSING, CANAAN, COMMUNITY, COVENANT, FAMILY, GENEALOGY, ISAAC, ISRAELITE, JACOB, JOSEPH, JUDGES, LAND, PROMISE

CAROL J. DEMPSEY, O.P.

TRUTH

In our contemporary Western culture, truth is something that is sought after a rational process of discernment. In the biblical world, truth is something quite different. There, discovered through experience, it is perceived as giving rise to belief and to a moral order of conduct. The Hebrew word for truth, 'met, comes from the Semitic root 'aman, which denotes something reliable, faithful, constant, certain, secure, permanent, and honest. In the liturgical assembly, we express our belief in what we hold to be true, secure, and reliable with the response, *amen,* a derivation of the Semitic word.

Old Testament

In the world of biblical times, the experience of something that was faithful and certain came to be associated with truth: God, a person, a word, a relationship, a treaty, a judgement, a law, a way of living. The creator of the world gave all things their place and function. The sun and the moon, the light and the darkness, the animals in the water and those on the land—all have their roles in manifesting God's fidelity in a harmonious and reliable plan for earthly existence. The movement of creation reveals a God who is true. God's people did not always acknowledge or respond to the truth that surrounded them. The Scriptures are filled with voices that lament the absence of truth in human experience (Ps 12:2-3; Wis 5:6; Isa 59:14-15; Jer 9:2, 4-5). In the face of Israel's inconstancy, God remained forever faithful.

Human Truth. When an exchange between persons was found to be honest and reliable, it was said to be true (Gen 47:29-31; Josh 2:14). "There is no fidelity, no mercy, no knowledge of God in the land" (Hos 4:1). Hosea lamented the fact that the people of Israel were the nation of the covenant and yet they were unfaithful both to God's word and to their own word. Truth had departed from them because they were disloyal and unreliable in what was expected of them.

In the Sapiential tradition, truth is deemed something that should be sought after and pursued by every person. "Get truth and sell it not—wisdom, instruction and understanding" (Prov 23:23). This proverb holds up truth as one of life's treasures, which is precious and necessary for living life fully. Truth is not something a person can buy; it has to be pursued and then given a place in the heart, in a person's interior self, where it gives focus to both attitudes and deeds (Prov 3:3).

Truth was associated with the biblical notion of justice, which touched on the level of relationship with one's neighbor. "These are the things you should do: Speak the truth to one another; let there be honesty

and peace in the judgments at your gates, and let none of you plot evil against another in his heart, nor love a false oath. For all these things I hate, says the LORD" (Zech 8:16-17). Despite the difficulty in translating and interpreting the biblical notion of truth, these passages show how truth is woven throughout the personal fabric of human existence. Truth can be seen both as a compass and as a pathway to the living out of justice.

Divine Truth. In the experience of God's covenant and promise, the elected community of Israel came to know truth as trust, exemplified in God's reliable and stable love. God remains faithful to the word of promise given in covenant (Deut 7:9; 32:4). "Withhold not, O Lord, your compassion from me; may your kindness and your truth ever preserve me" (Ps 40:12). This selection from Psalm 40 is one example, among many, where the word "truth" is associated with the term for covenant love. As God's kindness is understood to be stable, permanent, and steadfast, so is divine truth (see also Pss 25:5, 10; 26:3; 43:3; 86:11). "With his pinions he will cover you, and under his wings you shall take refuge; his faithfulness is a buckler and a shield" (Ps 91:4). Here God's covenant faithfulness/truth is described in images of strength and protection. Divine truth is also associated with the ways of peace, that is, well-being, prosperity, and blessing (Isa 39:8; Jer 33:6).

God's word is always steadfast and true (Pss 119:86, 138, 142, 151, 160). "The fear of the LORD is pure, enduring forever; the ordinances of the LORD are true, all of them just" (Ps 19:10). Likewise, God's law is true. It is a stable set of precepts that have guided people in the pathway of blessing down through the ages. To this day, God's law remains true.

God is the origin of truth and people must seek God's assistance in walking in the ways of divine truth. "Guide me in your truth and teach me, for you are God my savior, and for you I wait all the day" (Ps 25:5). Here the psalmist prays for the fidelity that will enable mortal beings to respond to the covenant demands with readiness of heart and joy of spirit. Not only can "walking in the truth" keep a person in faithful response to the covenant, but it can also draw the individual into deeper personal relationship with God: "The LORD is near to all who call upon him, to all who call upon him in truth" (Ps 145:18).

The power and impact of truth is uniquely expressed through a personification of justice, covenant love, and peace in the final age: "Kindness and truth shall meet; justice and peace shall kiss. Truth shall spring out of the earth, and justice shall look down from heaven" (Ps 85:11-12). Here the psalmist speaks of a mystic union of earth and heaven, the human and the divine, which will have the effect of bringing forth blessing (an abundant harvest, v. 13) and salvation (justice in the hearts of God's people, v. 14). Truth, both human and divine, is an aspect of salvation; God's truth in the human heart can draw people to a life of blessing and hope. "Those who trust in [God] shall understand truth, and the faithful shall abide with him in love: Because grace and mercy are with his holy ones, and his care is with his elect" (Wis 3:9).

See: COVENANT, FAITHFULNESS, JUSTICE, LAW, LOVE, PEACE, WORD

GREGORY J. POLAN, O.S.B.

New Testament

Hebrew and Greek Roots of NT Truth. The Hebrew Scriptures, reflecting Hebrew mentality, used *'emeth* in its various forms to affirm the constancy, dependability, fidelity, reliability, and thus the "truth" of both God and human beings. And this Hebrew notion that God (and, dependently on God, any human) is one in whom a person can, and should, place trust continues to be an important aspect of truth in the NT. The basis for placing such confidence is the reality and constancy of God. To the Hebrew way of thinking, one *accepts* or *chooses* the truth by putting confidence in the person who is trustworthy.

In the last three centuries before Jesus Christ, the spread of Greek culture and thought to the Middle East strongly influenced the chosen people's concept of truth, particularly through the Septuagint's most frequent translation of *'emeth* (reliability, solidity) as *alētheia* (truth). For the Greeks, truth is something *known*. They *assent* to truth as something intellectually apprehensible.

The Synoptic Gospels and Acts. Both Hebrew and Greek notions of truth appear as the Synoptics and Acts use *alētheia*. Jesus' enemies say to him, "Teacher, we know that you are a truthful man," i.e., one who is reliable and in whom one can place confidence. "You . . . teach the way of God in accordance with the truth" (Mark 12:14; Matt 22:16). In another situation, the woman cured of a hemorrhage admits "the whole truth," i.e., what happened (Mark 5:33). In the Lucan writings, the expression "of a truth" often means no more than "indeed" (Luke 4:25; 20:21; 22:59; Acts 4:27; 10:34).

The Pauline Corpus. In the unquestionably Pauline literature, the apostle reflects both Hebrew and Greek views of truth. He says, "Christ became a minister of the circumcised to show God's truthfulness," i.e., God's reliability and fidelity to the promises made to Israel (Rom 15:8). And Paul reassures his Roman audience, "I speak the truth in Christ, I do not lie" (Rom 9:1). At times, Paul seems to equate truth with the divine plan for salvation and with life in Christ. Paul informs his Galatian converts that he resisted false brethren at Jerusalem, "so that the truth of the gospel might remain intact for you" (Gal 2:5). Once one is a Christian, he points out to them, one must remain "on the right road in line with the truth of the gospel" (Gal 2:14; see 5:7). The believer will not do deeds of wickedness but of truth (see 1 Cor 5:8; 13:6).

The link between "truth" and the divine plan of salvation is even clearer in works whose Pauline authorship is disputed or now generally denied. The author of Ephesians says, "In him [Christ] you also, who have heard the word of truth, the gospel of your salvation, and have believed in him, were sealed with the promised holy Spirit, which is the first installment of our inheritance toward redemption as God's possession, to the praise of his glory" (Eph 1:13). Again, Christians are urged to remain in this way of salvation as they put away the old self and "put on the new self, created in God's way in righteousness and holiness of truth" (Eph 4:24). One consequence of their doing so is that they will "speak the truth, each one to his neighbor, for we are members one of another" (Eph 4:25). For the author of Colossians, too, the word of truth is the gospel (Col 1:5). And 2 Thessalonians threatens those "who have not accepted the love of truth" (2 Thess 2:10). "All who have not believed the truth" are headed for condemnation (2 Thess 2:12). The preacher of Hebrews warns his hearers, "If we sin deliberately after receiving knowledge of the truth," there is the fearful prospect of judgment and a flaming fire (Heb 10:26).

In the Pastoral Letters (1 and 2 Timothy, Titus), truth seems to take on the connotation of a way of life, and even a deposit of faith to be passed on. God "wills everyone to be saved and to come to knowledge of the truth" (1 Tim 2:4; see 4:3; 6:5; 2 Tim 3:7-8; 4:4; Titus 1:1, 14). Timothy is exhorted to impart the word of truth without deviation (2 Tim 2:15). Appointed preacher and apostle, Paul speaks the truth and teaches the Gentiles in faith and truth, i.e., reliably (1 Tim 2:7). Christians should know how to behave in "the church of the living God, the pillar and foundation of the truth" (1 Tim 3:15).

The Catholic Letters. In these letters, the "truth" again is a correct way of life according to the divine plan: "if anyone among you should stray from the truth and someone bring him back," the one who "brings back a sinner from the error of his way will save his soul from death and will cover a multitude of sins" (Jas 5:19-20). The disciples are purified by "obedience to the truth" (1 Pet 1:22), but as 2 Peter warns, though they are "established in the truth" (2 Pet 1:12), false teachers will arise to lead some astray and bring revilement upon "the way of truth" (2 Pet 2:1-2).

The Johannine Literature. For the Johannine school, God is ultimate reality or truth. This truth is revealed by, and in, Jesus Christ, who is himself "the way, and the truth, and the life" (John 14:6). Jesus testifies to the truth (John 18:37), which he has heard from God (John 8:40). Whoever accepts Jesus comes to a knowledge (i.e., experience) of the truth (= reality) of God, whose "word is truth," i.e., the way of salvation (John 17:17), and this knowledge liberates from sin. "You will know the truth, and the truth will set you free" (John 8:32). One who believes in Jesus, accepts this truth, and keeps the commandments of Jesus has "the Spirit of truth" residing in him/her (John 14:15-17) and guiding him/her to all truth (John 16:13). That person will then worship God "in spirit and in truth," i.e., appropriately (John 4:23). But some will not accept the truth, the revelation that Jesus brings (see John 8:45-46) and, rejecting Jesus, will risk condemnation on the last day (see John 12:48).

Thus, it is imperative to keep the commandments of Jesus Christ in order to possess the truth (1 John 1:6, 8; 2:4). One must love "not in word or speech but in deed and truth," i.e., in solid, dependable action (1 John 3:18).

See: KNOWLEDGE, OBEDIENCE, PROMISE, TEACH/ TEACHING, WAY

NEIL J. MCELENEY, C.S.P.

Pastoral-Liturgical Tradition

Truth obtains when our thoughts, words, and actions correspond to reality. The opposite of truth is the duplicity "by which a person holds one thing inwardly, and outwardly expresses something else" (S.Th., II-II, 109, 3); to truth belongs the simplicity and integrity characteristic of goodness. God is both the source and principle of all truth, and human beings participate in the truth insofar as they live in keeping with the character of God and conform their lives to the goodness of God.

Truthfulness makes life together possible. Society collapses where there is flagrant and widespread disregard for the truth because when people no longer trust each other even the most minimal cooperation necessary for society is impossible. Trustworthiness is essential in order to work together on the projects and tasks constitutive of social living; indeed, without a shared commitment to truth the most blessed and enriching human relationships such as friendship and marriage are impossible. Truthfulness establishes the confidence we need for relationships and assures the order and tranquility necessary for society to flourish. As an indispensable virtue for society, it bonds us together with the certainty that others, like ourselves, are basically trustworthy and honorable, that their words and deeds portray what is in their hearts, and because of this we can entrust ourselves to them and they to us for the well-being of the community. By contrast, when regard for the truth breaks down chaos ensues. People do not mean what they say, promises are glibly made and flippantly broken, and language is used to distort and disguise instead of illumine. When falsehood prevails community life is impossible because people no longer hold each other in respect. This is why lying shows contempt for persons and disdain for the common good.

Truth is part of justice and an expression of justice. Justice governs our relations with others by insisting on fairness and equity in our dealings with them. By its nature justice tempers our relationships by ordering them to the common good and by correcting them when they frustrate or jeopardize that good. As a species of justice, truthfulness safeguards relationships by ensuring that our communication with others is straightforward and not duplicitous. If justice is the quintessential virtue of social living, then truthfulness is justice fostering the communication that makes community possible. Moreover, if it is through justice that the virtuous person, with a firm and constant will, renders to everyone all that they deserve, then truthfulness is the "debt of honor" we owe others in virtue of their dignity and worth as persons (S.Th., II-II, 109, 3); it is in this respect that to lie is to dishonor another.

There is also a connection between living truthfully and goodness. Our behavior flows from our perceptions, and this means right behavior or virtue is impossible without a just and truthful vision of reality, especially other people. Virtue depends on vision because how we act in a situation turns largely on how we see it; our behavior reflects the quality of our perceptions. If we live locked in a vision of fantasy and self-deception, our behavior, however unintentionally, will do harm. An inability to perceive and appreciate the truth prevents moral goodness because it falsifies our reading of the world. If fantasy and falsehood become stronger than the truth, goodness is impossible because we are not able to perceive reality with the clarity and humility necessary for virtue. Only persons of truthfulness can be good because they alone are able to see things as they are, not as they need them to be. Truthfulness is intrinsic to goodness because a just and virtuous act is rooted in a reverent grasp of reality.

Sins Against the Truth. Lying is the vice most directly opposed to truthfulness. A lie is an intentional deception, normally uttered in speech, meant to mislead others by conveying an impression contrary to what we know or believe to be true. Thomas Aquinas defined a lie as an act of speech in which there is falsehood in what is expressed, the willingness to express it, and the deliberate intention to deceive (S.Th., II-II, 110, 1). But not all kinds of lies are equally serious. Aquinas distinguished three categories of lies: the useful, the humorous, and the malicious. Of the three, only the malicious lie could never be justified because its formal purpose was to inflict injury on another. Slander is an example of the malicious lie, for to slander a person is deliberately to misrepresent their character, deeds, or actions before others for the sake of doing them harm. The other types of lies were of "lesser sinfulness" because they were not intended to harm another and could even have good effects. The useful lie described falsehoods that were stated for the sake of protecting another from harm, and the humorous lie referred to statements told in jest, either clear exaggerations or evident falsehoods that were uttered for the sake of entertainment. The malicious lie was always sinful because its sole intent was to harm another, but the other types of lies need not be morally serious, especially if the intent was either good (the useful lie) or morally indifferent (the humorous lie). As Aquinas reasoned, "Clearly, the better the good intended, the lighter the blame of a lie" (S.Th., II-II, 110, 2).

More recently, Christian ethicists have questioned whether it is proper to characterize every falsehood a lie, stressing that a lie occurs only when the truth is denied someone who has a rightful claim to it. Thus, what Aquinas called a useful lie later Catholic moralists called a "mental reservation," and other ethicists a "saving deceit," an act of speech that did not disclose the truth completely for the sake of protecting a greater good, e.g., to save a life. Even though there is a basic duty to state the truth, it can be overridden by a more pressing duty or greater good, particularly when a full disclosure of the truth would bring unjustified harm to individuals or a community. Nonetheless, since lying cannot be justified by trivial reasons, such as a lie told merely for the sake of convenience, it is only the person of truthful character who is able to discern when the normal obligation of truthfulness ought to be superceded for the sake of a more pressing moral concern.

In Catholic moral theology, defamation and detraction are sins directed specifically against the truth of another person. Defamation is an act by which injury is done to another by depriving them of their good name. We defame others when we say something misleading or prejudicial about them for the sake of lowering them before others. Aquinas describes defamation as "taking away somebody's character" by denying or misrepresenting their goodness (S.Th., II-II, 72, 1). Defamation is an act against the truth because it is to misde-scribe someone for the sake of shaming them. But defamation is also a kind of thievery because it robs others of their good name or takes from them the excellence of character that is rightfully theirs. As Aquinas reasoned, "Since the notion of insult or defamation implies a certain taking away of a person's character, words uttered with the intention of taking away another's character amount to insult or defamation in the strict sense. And such utterances would constitute mortal sin as much as theft or robbery would, since a person is no less attached to his reputation than to his material possessions" (S.Th., II-II, 72, 2).

Detraction is a sin against the character of another that is distinguished from defamation by being secretive and surreptitious. To defame others is to insult or belittle them openly, while detraction is to ridicule them behind their back. Both constitute sins against the truth of another person, and thus are acts of injustice, and both are designed to diminish others by attacking their character or reputation. "Now detraction is of its nature calculated to blacken another's reputation, so that, simply speaking, any one who tells tales behind another's back in order to blacken his [or her] reputation is committing detraction" (S.Th., II-II, 73, 2).

Duties of Confidentiality. Since truthfulness is a species of justice, our obligation to disclose the truth is determined by the kinds of relationships we have with others. The debt of truthfulness cannot be figured apart from the status of different relationships in our lives. This is why confidentiality is not opposed to truthfulness, but is the trustworthiness we owe others in light of the special relationship we have with them. Traditionally, confidentiality has been understood to belong to professions such as ministry, counseling, medicine, and law because of the relationship of trust that arises between the professional and a client. In the context of these distinctive relationships, confidentiality is not something other than truthfulness, but is the form truthfulness must take if the client is not to be betrayed. In this respect, to withhold the truth from others outside the relationship is what remaining truthful and loyal to the client demands.

Duties of confidentiality to those who entrust themselves to our care indicate how special obligations are entailed by institutional roles. For instance, that a priest never break the seal of the confessional illustrates the extreme importance of trust in the priest-penitent relationship. That confidentiality be an obligation of justice in special relationships demonstrates the connection between particular duties of our lives and the distinctive roles we assume. We expect certain behavior from persons not only in light of their character, but also in light of the primary roles by which they are identified. Spouses, for instance, ought not to betray one another's secrets not because of general notions of promise keeping, but because to disclose what each other has asked not to be revealed would be to violate a behavioral norm crucial to the well-being of marriage. In such special relationships confidentiality is not an exemption from truthfulness, but what the duty of truthfulness demands. That the truth ought not to be disclosed to everyone indicates that withholding facts from others is not necessarily to do them an injustice, but is what being faithful to those most closely connected to us means.

It is essential that those to whom we entrust ourselves are trustworthy, especially those in caring and helping professions. These are institutional roles in which the professionals are trustees of our well-being. We give them power over our lives because we are confident that they are both skilled and willing to help us. To abuse the trust we place in them is a grievous injustice and a violation of our person. This is why the duty of confidentiality can be overridden only for the most serious of reasons, most notably if great harm would come to a person or others if something is not revealed. Still, because of the extreme importance of maintaining trust in these relationships, the possibility of breaching confidentiality should never be presumed and only rarely seen as justified; indeed, one should give the benefit of the doubt to preserving confidentiality.

Pastoral Applications. The task of the Christian moral life is to embody and witness the truth that comes to us in Jesus, for to do this is to be redeemed. But it is not a truth we easily embrace; sometimes it is even a scandal to us. The truth that comes to us in Christ involves nothing less than dying to one understanding of life and taking up another; to live this truth is to cross over to a new way of seeing and thinking, it is to become a new creation. It is a truth that affirms trust instead of betrayal, community instead of division, generosity and service instead of domination and violence. Confronted with such liberating truth, we often choose to remain with the lies and deceits of a world that is passing away.

Part of the human condition is for fantasy to become stronger than the truth. Fantasy is a kind of falsehood that overpowers people who see the world strictly in terms of their preferences and needs. Fantasy is a skewed and self-serving reading of the world that reflects a deep lack of reverence for the inherent value and goodness of all things apart from how they may serve our needs. As a constant tendency to distort and manipulate reality for self-centered aims, fantasy destroys the justice and respect necessary for truthfulness, and without the enlightenment that comes from the truth, it is impossible to be good. If fantasy is such a powerful impediment to goodness, there must be some way that we can be freed from it in order to see and embrace the truth.

The Eucharist is one setting in which the conversion from fantasy to truthfulness can occur. The Eucharist is the ritual activity through which a people's vision is cleansed and healed, a sacrament that nurtures the truthfulness necessary for goodness. Unlike fantasy, in the Eucharist we do not retreat from reality, but enter more deeply into all that is not ourselves, particularly the ultimate otherness of God. Through the Eucharist we respond to the call for a more radical engagement with the world, other people, and God. In this way the Eucharist edges us beyond the limited and often prejudiced boundaries of our own perceptions. By opening our hearts to the God who comes to us in bread and wine, our whole orientation to reality changes. We begin to see the world truthfully because we view it not through the falsifying lens of fantasy, but through the one we say is the light and truth of the world. Through the proclamation and reception of the Word, the darkness of fantasy is scattered by the light of the one through whom everything is truthfully and lovingly seen. When we eat the body and drink the blood of Christ, we are nourished in the truth; indeed, to feed on Christ is to live his truth. When this occurs, the falsifying powers of fantasy are overcome and we witness the truth whose most perfect expression is holiness.

See: EUCHARIST, JUSTICE, VIRTUE

PAUL J. WADELL, C.P.

TYPE

This word is used frequently in the Bible in the usual sense of mark, impression, or model. However, it is given a special meaning in Romans 5:14 and 1 Corinthians 10:6 where it refers to an OT person or event that foreshadows a NT reality. Finally, its usage in Hebrews 8:5 is concerned with a comparison of the liturgy of Israel with the heavenly liturgy inaugurated by Jesus.

In the Church's pastoral and liturgical tradition typology emphasizes the continuity between the Testaments. It also underscores the abiding presence of God among those who believe.

New Testament

Type as Mark or Model. The word "type" is a translation of the Greek *typos* (from *typtein*, to strike) and means either the blow itself or, more commonly, the impression or

mark left by a blow. This is its meaning in John 20:25 where it refers to the marks of the nails in Jesus' hands. Its meaning is extended then to include the spiritual impression or mark left by faith and which becomes an example or model of faith and behavior for others, as in 1 Thessalonians 1:7: "so that you became a model for all the believers in Macedonia and in Achaia." (See also Phil 3:17; 2 Thess 3:9; 1 Tim 4:12; Titus 2:7; 1 Pet 5:3.)

Type as a Hermeneutical Term. Paul uses "type" in a unique, biblical sense when, after describing the experiences of Israel in their desert journey, he writes: "These things happened as examples [lit. types] for us, so that we might not desire evil things, as they did" (1 Cor 10:6). It is clear from the context that Paul wants to remind the Corinthians about the disastrous consequences that befell the sinful Israelites and to warn them that they will suffer the same fate if they are not more obedient. The Corinthians must be careful not to imitate the Israelites' idolatry or immorality or grumbling (10:7-10). They must learn from that bad example: "These things happened to them [the Israelites] as an example [lit. type], and they have been written down as a warning to us, upon whom the end of the ages has come" (10:11).

There is more to this correspondence, however, than a mere surface similarity between the situation of the Israelites and the Corinthians. For Paul sees in the experience of Israel a type or model that is valid for all subsequent eras of history. He claims that faith allows us to discern God's action in human history as it reveals a special story line that binds together all the segments of history. Thus, by divine intention, what happens in the first chapter of the story (Israel in the desert) has significance for a later chapter (the Christians at Corinth).

It is important to note that this typology is not based on the words but on the events of the Exodus period. Because of a divinely provided "excess of meaning" in the events, one can speak of a more-than-literal sense also in the words that describe those events. In other words, God intended more in those events than the people of that time could have understood. The events were not theirs alone but were also types of greater events to come. In this way, the old and new events enrich and explain each other as the admirable unity of God's plan in human history is affirmed and illustrated.

Paul uses type in the same special sense in Romans 5:14, where he refers to Adam as "the type of the one who was to come." The correspondence here is between persons rather than events, but it functions in the same way. From the context, it is clear that Paul viewed Adam, reputed father of a human race burdened by sin, as a type or foreshadowing, antithetically, of Christ, the progenitor of a new race of humans delivered from sin and death. This "new Adam" thus fulfills the loving plan of God that existed at the time of the first Adam but whose realization had been delayed by human sinfulness. Once again, the continuous and consistent plan of God is illuminated by the insight that discovers this fruitful correspondence between events and persons of the Hebrew Scriptures and the NT.

Type as a Heavenly Model. Another uniquely biblical use of "type" is found in Hebrews 8:5, where the type is not a person or an event in the OT but a heavenly model of God's dwelling-place to which Jesus now gives access in a way that could not have been imagined in the world of the OT. Those who offer gifts in accordance with the Law "worship in a copy and shadow of the heavenly sanctuary, as Moses was warned when he was about to erect the tabernacle. For he says, 'See that you make everything according to the pattern [lit. type] shown you on the mountain'" (Heb 8:5; see Exod 25:40).

The implication of this passage is that no OT dwelling place, whether tent or temple, fulfilled this ideal but that it has been fulfilled only now in the ministry of Jesus: "Now he [Jesus] has obtained so much

more excellent a ministry as he is mediator of a better covenant, enacted on better promises" (Heb 8:6). The correspondence between OT and NT has now reached beyond the merely earthly ministry of Jesus to penetrate the eschatological and heavenly realm. However, there is the same awareness of the continuity and consistency in the divine plan as it is realized in the deepest currents of human history.

Stephen refers to the same text (Exod 25:40) in his sermon in Acts (7:44), accusing the Jews of settling for an imperfect earthly temple when they should have been open to the new heavenly model offered by Jesus.

Summary. The significance of the biblical use of type is not limited to the few passages in which this word is found. Rather, as suggested above, this usage opens up a dramatic new vision of the continuity and consistency of God's work which reveals the golden thread that runs through the fabric of human history. Suddenly a whole world of correspondences between the OT and the NT opens up. These are centered primarily in the persons and events associated with the Exodus and creation. No doubt these correspondences have at times been exaggerated but the net effect has been an extraordinary richness, particularly for the liturgical tradition of the Church.

See: ADAM AND EVE, CREATION, EXODUS, FAITH, TEMPLE

DEMETRIUS R. DUMM, O.S.B.

Pastoral-Liturgical Tradition

Since typology is a method of interpretation of Scripture and a way to relate the OT and NT, its use in the pastoral-liturgical tradition of the Church is within this context. Particularly, three categories of early Christian writings are replete with typological material: apologetical works (especially those used against Jews and Gnostics concerning the unity of the two testaments; e.g. Justin's *Dialogue with Trypho*), sacramental/catechetical works (especially the mystagogical catecheses), and homilies.

Given the (neo)Platonic mind of early

Christian writers with their concern for transcendent reality and humankind's ability to know that reality only partially as a shadow, typology was a natural literary way to express the Christian mysteries. Especially Paul's use of type was an encouragement for the Patristic use of this method of interpretation. Even Thomas and the scholastic theologians, working from Aristotelian philosophy, made (more reserved) use of typology. Post-conciliar revised liturgies still include typological material in the texts.

Patristic Typology. It was generally accepted in Christian antiquity that even though a nonbeliever could make a literal interpretation of the text of Scripture, only believers could distinguish deeper meanings of Scripture by means of typology. A type is the antecedent of a proposed figurative relationship between two objects, concepts, images, persons, events, etc. The antitype, the second term of the relationship, was considered a more perfect realization of the type. Some Patristic examples include Adam as a type for Christ, the flood as a type of baptism, and the Exodus as a type for the sacraments (baptism and Eucharist). By knowing something of both type and antitype, it was thought that one who was further advanced in Christian perfection could more completely (though never perfectly) grasp the mystery being expressed.

Origen was the first Christian writer to set forth principles governing the use of typology vis-à-vis Sacred Scripture, though he made no clear distinction between type and allegory. However, by the fourth century two distinct schools of interpretation had evolved. The Alexandrian school (to which belonged, for example, Ambrose) was much more literal in its drawing connections between OT and NT. They employed a very one-to-one relationship that was not very controlled, often drawing on mere material details or likenesses. For example, Ambrose (in *De Sacramentis*) likens the baptistry to a second tabernacle, the font to a sepulchre, and the anointing on the head to myrrh. For the Alexandrian school, Scripture had all the meaning the interpreter could extract from it. On the contrary, the Antiochene school (John Chrysostom, Theodore of Mopsuestia) rejected this literal and exaggerated speculation in favor of a more reserved, spiritual approach. In his first baptismal instruction, for example, John Chrysostom calls baptism a spiritual marriage.

Both schools of interpretation were wholly pastoral in their approach. Their homilies during liturgies as well as their various explanations of rites, feasts, and theological/doctrinal points were largely catechetical, ethical, and spiritual in nature. An understanding of the Christian mysteries was not so much directed toward an intellectual gain as toward a deepening of their life in Christ.

Thomistic Typology. In the *Summa Theologica* Aquinas explicitly lays bare his Aristotelian epistemology and is consistent with it in his argument for the use of figurative (typological) language: "But in the present state of life, we are unable to gaze upon the Divine Truth in Itself, and we need the ray of Divine light to shine upon us under the form of certain sensible figures" (I-II, 101, 2); and, "Accordingly the reasons for the ceremonial precepts of the Old Law can be taken in two ways. First, in respect of the Divine worship which was to be observed for that particular time: and these reasons are literal. . . . Secondly, their reasons can be gathered from the point of view of their being ordained to foreshadow Christ: and thus their reasons are figurative and mystical" (I-II, 102, 2). If we accept the tradition that Thomas Aquinas is responsible for the beautiful *Corpus Christi* texts and hymns, we have concrete evidence of his specific use of typology. Especially in the sequence *Lauda Sion Salvatorem* is this evident: "Now the new the old effaces, Truth away the shadow chases, . . . Truth the ancient types fulfilling, Isaac bound, a victim willing, Paschal lamb, its life blood spilling, manna to the fathers sent."

Liturgical Use Today. The post-conciliar liturgy takes a much more reserved approach to typological use, mostly as images and metaphors and usually not typology in the sense of a method of Scripture interpretation. A notable exception to this is the inclusion of an interpretive passage (often from the NT) at the beginning of each psalm in the Psalter.

Not a surprise, the most extensive use of typology in a single renewed liturgy is at the Easter Vigil. From the proclamation of the *Exultet* (Christ paid the price for Adam's sin, Passover feast whereby Christ's blood consecrates the homes of believers, pillar of fire destroyed the darkness of sin, Christ is the morning star), through the readings (made explicit in the prayers: redemption is a new creation, Red Sea is a symbol of baptism, preaching of the prophets proclaimed the Easter mysteries, old made new), and at the blessing of the baptismal water (deluge and Red Sea are signs of baptism)—almost the entire feel of the liturgy is the fulfillment/completion of the Old dispensation in the New.

Other sacramental liturgies also have typological elements. The blessing of water at baptism corresponds to the deluge and Red Sea typology of Holy Saturday. The opening prayer, preface, and nuptial blessing of the marriage rite all speak of marriage as a type of the relationship of Christ and his Church. The ordination rite mentions the priesthood of the Levites and of Melchizedek as well as the high priesthood of Christ. The Eucharistic liturgy uses some typological images. The typology of The Rite of Blessing and Sprinkling Holy Water and Eucharistic Prayer I (offerings of Abel, Abraham, and Melchizedek) is easily recognized. In addition, many prefaces (especially for particular occasions) contain typological material as well as do entrance antiphons: Church as a temple of living stones, earthly and heavenly Jerusalem, manna from the desert and Eucharist, twelves tribes of Israel and the twelve apostles, to mention but a few examples.

While today there is a growing tendency among Christian exegetes to accept the OT on its own terms and not only in reference to the NT, typology nonetheless reminds us of at least two important liturgical/pastoral principles. First, salvation is a sacred *history* in continuity with the past, played out in the present, and completed only in the future. Second, the dynamism inherent in typological interpretation reminds us that all Scripture and liturgy is ultimately a proclamation of an abiding and ever-faithful presence of God.

See: FEASTS, JEWS, MYSTERY, RITES

JOYCE A. ZIMMERMAN, C.PP.S.

TYRE AND SIDON

Old Testament

Tyre and Sidon were the two leading cities of ancient Phoenicia and are frequently mentioned together in the Bible. They were founded in the third millennium BCE and are situated on the coast of present-day Lebanon. Tyre, whose name derives from the Hebrew ṣôr, "rock" (today called ṣur), is twenty miles south of Sidon. Sidon ("fortified," from the Hebrew ṣîdôn), named for the eldest son of Canaan, son of Ham (Gen 10:15), is situated twenty miles south of modern Beirut and today is called Saida.

From the late Bronze Age there are Egyptian, Ugaritic, and Hittite references to Tyre. Correspondence from the kings of Tyre and Sidon with the Egyptian Pharaoh Akhenaton during the fourteenth century BCE has been preserved in the Amarna letters. In the twelfth century BCE Tyre and Sidon, along with other coastal cities, were destroyed by the Philistines. They were rebuilt in the same century and gained preeminence among the Phoenician cities in the eleventh century. Both cities were assigned to the tribe of Asher, but were never occupied by the Israelites. Having resisted onslaughts from the Assyrians in the eighth century BCE and the Babylonians in the sixth century BCE, these cities were taken in 333–332 BCE by Alexander the Great.

They continued to be prosperous commercial centers throughout the Hellenistic and Roman periods.

The riches of these two port cities were notorious in antiquity. Ezekiel 27:9 says of Tyre, "Every ship and sailor on the sea came to you to carry trade." Ezekiel 27 lists numerous nations who did business with Tyre and the kinds of goods they brought in exchange for Tyre's wares. Among these trade partners was Israel, who in the days of David and Solomon had a very amicable relationship with Tyre. Hiram, the king of Tyre, furnished David with cedar wood, carpenters, and masons to build his palace (1 Sam 5:11; 1 Chr 14:1). 1 Kings 5:1 asserts that Hiram "had always been David's friend." This friendship continued with Solomon, whom Hiram also supplied with cedars and craftsmen for the building of the Temple (1 Kgs 5:1-32; 7:14; 2 Chr 2:3-15). In return, Solomon sent wheat and oil to Hiram (1 Kgs 5:25). Ezra 3:7 describes this same kind of exchange between the Israelites and the Sidonians and Tyrians in the building of the second Temple.

In the psalms there are three references to Tyre. Psalm 87:4 lists Tyre among all the places of the earth that count Zion as their spiritual home. Psalm 45:13, a nuptial ode for the messianic king, speaks of the gifts brought by the city of Tyre. But in Psalm 83:8 Tyre is listed among the league of hostile nations against whom the psalmist implores divine assistance.

It appears that Israel's close relation with Tyre ended with the revolution of Jehu. The latter put to death Jezebel, the Tyrian wife of the Israelite King Ahab, who had promoted the cult of the Baal of Tyre. In the remaining OT references to Tyre and Sidon in the prophetic books, the two cities are excoriated along with the other pagan nations. Isaiah (23:1-18), Jeremiah (25:22; 27:3; 47:4), Ezekiel (26:1–28:26), Joel (4:4), Amos (1:9-10), and Zechariah (9:2-3) all include Tyre and Sidon in their oracles of judgment upon the nations. Nehemiah (13:16) denounces the Tyrians resident in Jerusalem who were profaning the Sabbath with selling fish and merchandise to Judahites.

New Testament

In the NT, one of Jesus' sayings presumes this same hostility toward Tyre and Sidon on the part of the Israelites. In his denunciation of unrepentant towns, Jesus compares Chorazin and Bethsaida to the pagan towns Tyre and Sidon. He warns them, "if the mighty deeds done in your midst had been done in Tyre and Sidon, they would long ago have repented in sackcloth and ashes. But I tell you, it will be more tolerable for Tyre and Sidon on the day of judgment than for you" (Matt 11:21-22; Luke 10:13-14).

A favorable reference is found in Mark 3:8 (par. Luke 6:17) where people from Tyre and Sidon formed part of the multitude who came to hear Jesus and be healed. And on one occasion it is related that Jesus withdrew to the region of Tyre and Sidon, where a Canaanite woman persuaded him to heal her daughter (Matt 15:21-28; Mark 7:24-30). This is a significant incident in the Gospels in that it takes place on the frontier of Jewish and Phoenician territory, thus setting the stage for an extension of Jesus' mission to Gentiles.

Acts 12:20-23 tells of a dispute between Herod Agrippa and the people of Tyre and Sidon. The latter, dependent on Herod for grain and oil, came to seek an economic peace, perhaps from a grain embargo enforced by Agrippa. When the Tyrians and Sidonians succeeded in obtaining an audience and a favorable outcome, they acclaimed Herod's was "the voice of a god, not of a human" (Acts 12:22). Herod's acceptance of this adulation resulted in his immediate and awful death.

In Acts of the Apostles, Paul's travels take him to the two port cities. In his final journey to Jerusalem, Paul stays a week in Tyre, one of the port stops at which the ship was to unload cargo. Meanwhile, Paul sought out the disciples in Tyre, who kept trying to persuade him not to go on to Jerusalem (Acts 21:1-6). He continues from

Tyre to Ptolemais (Acts 21:7), then Caesarea (Acts 21:8), and, finally, to Jerusalem. In Paul's last journey, as a prisoner from Jerusalem to Rome, there is a stopover in Sidon, where Julius, the centurion to whom Paul had been handed over, "was kind enough to allow Paul to visit his friends who took care of him" (Acts 27:3).

See: CITY, DAVID, JUDGMENT, MISSION, NATIONS, REPENTANCE, SOLOMON, TEMPLE

BARBARA E. REID, O.P.

V

VEIL

Symbolic use of veils appears in the Bible and in continued Christian practice. There are traditions relating to the veiling of women. Both the OT and NT speak of Moses having to veil his face after his encounter with God on Sinai. Paul sees a metaphorical meaning in this. The veil of the Jewish Temple, described in the OT, takes on a symbolic meaning related to the saving death of Jesus in the NT. Veils have continued to be used to shroud sacred objects and spaces in liturgical tradition.

Old Testament

Ornamental Coverings. Veil refers to ornamental coverings worn by women in the OT. Mention of veils occurs in a variety of circumstances. There is no one meaning attached to the wearing of veils. It appears from Genesis 12:14-15; 24:15-16; 26:7 that Israelite women did not customarily wear veils. In Genesis 24:65 Rebekah covered herself with her veil when she saw Isaac, her husband-to-be, approach. This may be part of the wedding ceremony, during which Rebekah would have been veiled until she and Isaac retired to the bridal chamber. So, too, in the Canticle of Canticles during the wedding procession the bridegroom extols the beauty of his veiled beloved: "your eyes are like doves behind your veil" (4:1); "Your cheek is like a half-pomegranate behind your veil"

(4:3; 6:7). In the case of Tamar, who "veiled her face by covering herself with a shawl" (Gen 38:14), her veiling concealed her identity from Judah. "He mistook her for a harlot, since she had covered her face" (Gen 38:15). In Isaiah 3:19, veils are listed among the finery of rich women that the Lord will do away with because it is "loot wrested from the poor" (Isa 3:14). So, too, in the description of the fall of "virgin daughter Babylon" her veil is removed (Isa 47:1-2), thus stripping the once glorious city of her elite existence.

Cultic Significance. Ezekiel prophesied against the women of Jerusalem "who prophesy their own thoughts" and who "sew bands for everyone's wrists and make veils for every size of head so as to entrap their owners" (Ezek 14:17-18). The wristbands and veils appear as fetishes worn when one pronounced magic spells. God promises to tear off the veils and rescue the Israelites from their power (14:20).

The wilderness dwelling for the ark of the covenant was constructed with a series of veils or curtains. The innermost sanctum, the holy of holies, was separated by a veil "woven of violet, purple and scarlet yarn, and of fine linen twined, with cherubim embroidered on it" (Exod 26:31). It was hung on four gold-plated columns of acacia wood. Behind it were set the ark of the commandments and the propitiatory (Exod

26:32-34). Another veil, only slightly less fine, covered the entrance to the holy place, separating it from the outside court (Exod 26:36-37; Num 3:26).

In the ritual prescribed for sin offerings for priests and for the community the priest brought some of the blood of an animal sacrifice into the holy place and sprinkled it seven times toward the veil of the sanctuary (Lev 4:6, 16, 17). In Numbers 18:7 it is prescribed that only the Levitical priests were to "have charge of performing the priestly functions in whatever concerns the altar and the room within the veil." The priests were also charged with taking down the veil when the Israelites broke camp (Num 4:5). Later, only the high priest was allowed to enter the holy of holies, once a year, on the Day of Atonement (Lev 16:1-19).

In Solomon's Temple, a similar veil separated the holy place and the holy of holies. It was made "of violet, purple, crimson and fine linen, and had cherubim embroidered upon it" (2 Chron 3:14).

Veil of Moses. Exodus 34:29-35 describes how the skin of Moses' face became radiant after his encounter with God on Mount Sinai. After relaying to the Israelites all that God had told him, he put a veil over his face. He would remove it whenever he entered into the presence of God. In the text the ostensible reason for veiling his face was so that the divine radiance reflected on his face would not cause fear in the Israelites. It is possible that this explanation is a later popular explanation of a rite whose meaning had been lost. The veil may have been the equivalent of the mask worn by prophets to conceal their own identity when speaking in the name of a god.

New Testament

The Veil of Moses. In 2 Corinthians 3:13-16 Paul gives two other interpretations of the veil on the face of Moses. Paul is contrasting the fading glory of the Mosaic ministry with the enduring glory of Christian ministry (2 Cor 3:7-11). Moses, he says, "put a veil over his face so that the Israelites

could not look intently at the cessation of what was fading" (2 Cor 3:13). Paul then shifts the metaphor, so that in verses 14-16 veil refers to an inability on the part of those without Christ to perceive the meaning of the Scriptures. He says, "To this day, in fact, whenever Moses is read, a veil lies over their hearts, but whenever a person turns to the Lord the veil is removed" (vv. 15-16).

1 Corinthians 11:2-16. The interpretation of this passage is notoriously difficult, compounded by the various English translations. The Greek word for veil, *kalymma*, which Paul uses in 2 Corinthians 3:13-16, is not found in 1 Corinthians 11:2-16. Nonetheless, some scholars, believing the issue under discussion is the wearing of veils by women, translate as does the NAB: "any woman who prays or prophesies with her head unveiled [*akatakalyptō*] brings shame upon her head" (v. 5); "for if a woman does not have her head veiled [*ou katakalyptetetai*] . . . she should wear a veil (*katakalyptesthō*)" (v. 6); "is it proper for a woman to pray to God with her head unveiled [*akatakalypton*]?" (v. 13). The literal meaning of the Greek verb, *katakalyptō* (v. 6), is "to cover"; as it is translated in verse 7: "A man, on the other hand, should not cover [*katakalyptesthai*] his head." The adjective *akatakalyptos* (vv. 5, 13) means "uncovered." It is not clear that the covering Paul refers to is a veil; some believe it refers to hair. In an earlier version (1946), the RSV also translated *exousia* in verse 10 as veil: "That is why a woman ought to have a veil [*exousia*] on her head." Elsewhere *exousia* means "power, authority." Thus the NRSV (1989) translates, "a woman ought to have a symbol of authority on her head" (similarly, NAB).

The Veil of the Temple. According to the Synoptic Gospels, at the death of Jesus the veil (*katapetasma*) of the Temple "was torn in two from top to bottom" (Mark 15:38; similarly Matt 27:51; Luke 23:45). Probably the reference is to the veil that separated the holy of holies from the holy place. Some interpret this rending of the veil as a sign of judgment against the Temple. Others see it as a symbol of the new access to God made possible by the death of Jesus. The author of Hebrews expands on this symbol. In 6:19-20 he speaks of Christian hope as an anchor that "reaches into the interior behind the veil, where Jesus has entered on our behalf as forerunner." The holy of holies is described as the earthly counterpart of God's heavenly abode, into which Christ has entered, by his atoning sacrifice (Heb 9:1-14). In Hebrews 10:20 the metaphor shifts once again, as entrance into the sanctuary is by the new and living way Christ "opened for us through the veil, that is, his flesh."

See: ATONEMENT, MAGIC AND DIVINATION, MARRIAGE, MOSES, POWER, PRIEST, TEMPLE, VESTURE

BARBARA E. REID, O.P.

Pastoral-Liturgical Tradition

The symbolic veiling of people, places, and objects continues to this day.

People. In both sacred and secular wedding rituals, across a variety of cultures, the head of the bride is covered, usually with a veil, in a color dependent on the ritual code of the specific culture. The veil indicates the change of ritual status of the woman who is leaving single life behind and is now beginning a new existence as a married woman. Similarly, until recent times veiling has figured prominently in the liturgies of solemn consecration of virgins and of religious profession of women. Whether in ceremonies of solemn or simple vows, veiling has acted as a ritual code, designating the status of these women as set apart and consecrated in a life of chastity. More recently, in communities where religious garb is no longer adopted, ritual change of status is communicated in the prayer of consecration and the public profession of vows.

Places. Since the fourth century the veiling of sacred space, like the veiling of the holy of holies, has been a practice of Eastern Churches. A curtain, a veil, and/or the iconostasis screen separates the sanctuary and its ministers from the assembly of the faithful. In the West, with the exception of the Medieval rood screen, the practice of

setting the sanctuary apart was accomplished not by veils or screens but by low communion railings.

Objects. A variety of veils have figured in the liturgy—the chalice veil which covered the chalice when not in use; the humeral veil used to pick up the blessed sacrament in exposition and benediction; the tabernacle veil which designates a holy of holies in miniature. Until the reforms of Holy Week and the liturgical year, veils were also used to shroud all crucifixes, statues, and pictures during Lent—a kind of visual fast until the triumphant joy of the Easter vigil, a latter day rending of the veil of the Temple.

KATHLEEN HUGHES, R.S.C.J.

VESTURE, PRIESTLY

Old Testament

The most elaborate descriptions of liturgical vesture are found in passages from the Priestly tradition (Exodus 28–29; 39; Leviticus 8). Although these passages reflect the usage of the second Temple, there are also links to earlier periods. In part, this is clear because the basic liturgical vestments for priests were the same as those worn by the general population.

The Vestments of the Priests. The priests, like everyone else in OT and NT times, wore a tunic gathered with a sash and a turban (Exod 28:40; Lev 8:13). While wool served as the main fabric for clothing, priestly garments were made primarily of linen, which was common in Egypt where flax grew in abundance. These vestments were decorated with gold thread and with yarns of violet, purple, and scarlet. Such special work, not limited to liturgical vestments, helped to set these garments apart from ordinary clothing. In addition to these common garments, priests wore long shorts "to cover their naked flesh from their loins to their thighs" (Exod 28:42).

The Vestments of the High Priest. The high priest wore the same basic garments, although they were more elaborate (Exod

1033

28:1-39; 39:1-31; Lev 8:7-9). Instead of the priest's turban, the high priest wore a special headdress, sometimes translated "miter," which differed perhaps only in design and fancy work. Over the basic garments the high priest wore a robe as was the custom in the larger culture. However, the high priest's robe, also called the robe of the ephod, differed from the general fashion, which was just a squarish piece of material wrapped over one or both shoulders, in that it had a hole for the head in the center of the garment surrounded by a selvage to prevent its tearing. Woven entirely of violet or blue yarn, according to Exodus 39:22, the robe was finished at the hem with alternating bells of gold and pomegranates made of the colored yarns.

The most distinguishing features of the high priest's vestments were the breastpiece and the ephod, and both had links to the ancient priestly function of giving oracles.

The ephod is found mainly in the Books of Samuel and seems to designate two different things. The linen ephod was clearly a garment worn around the waist, perhaps as a loin cloth, by the boy Samuel, the priests of Nob, and also by David as he danced before the ark (1 Sam 2:18; 22:18; 2 Sam 6:14). Some believe this to have been the sole priestly garment in the earliest period. In other texts, the ephod appears as an object; Gideon's, perhaps the most famous, was made of gold (Judg 8:27; see also Judg 17:5; 18:14, 18, 20; 1 Sam 2:28; 14:3; 21:10; 23:6, 9-10; 30:7-8). In these texts the ephod is connected to the giving of oracles, seemingly as a receptacle for sacred lots: the Urim and Thummim. Perhaps the two meanings were really one: the ephod may have been a waist cloth worn by a priest which also held the sacred lots.

The Urim and Thummim were sacred lots, perhaps dice or stones or sticks. When someone came to consult with God, a priest would employ the lots to obtain an answer of "yes" or "no" to a question. According to Deuteronomy 33:8, Moses handed over these instruments of divination to the sons of Levi as part of their priestly function. In Numbers 27:21, Eleazar, the son of Aaron, had received them from his father. While the text from Deuteronomy represents the more ancient tradition, the text from Numbers indicates the importance of their connection to the priesthood into the period of the second Temple, even though no one knew how to use them at that point (Ezra 2:63).

The high priest's ephod, worn over the robe of the ephod, was made of linen with gold threads and colored yarns; it was fastened around the waist with an attached sash and held up with shoulder straps. The breastpiece was essentially a square pouch attached to the shoulder straps of the ephod with gold chains, and it held the Urim and Thummim. More important than these vestiges of oracles were the precious stones. To the shoulder straps of the ephod were fixed two great onyx stones into which were cut the names of the twelve tribes of Israel. On the breastpiece were fixed twelve precious stones, one for each of the tribes. The garments, therefore, came to represent the nation of Israel that the high priest carried into the presence of God.

The high priest also wore on his "miter" a golden plate, called the "sacred diadem," on which was inscribed "Sacred to the Lord" (Exod 28:36; Lev 8:9). During the consecration of priests, Moses used the oil for anointing priests and blood from the sacrifice to sprinkle Aaron and his sons and also their vestments (Lev 8:30). The ritual set apart both the individuals and their clothing for holiness. The vestments identified the priests as consecrated for holiness, and they were commanded to wear them when serving in the sanctuary "lest they incur guilt and die" (Exod 28:43). Likewise they had to take them off before going into the outer court (Ezek 44:15-19).

Thus the priestly vestments of the second Temple represented both holiness and the nation.

See: ANOINTING, BLOOD, MAGIC AND DIVINATION, ORACLE, PRIESTS, TEMPLE

HARRY HAGAN, O.S.B.

Pastoral-Liturgical Tradition

The Origin and History of Special Christian Liturgical Vesture. Because the first generations of Christians worshiped in domestic settings rather than in temples, the vesture of those who presided at Christian prayer differed very little from the clothing worn in ordinary life. It was not until the legalization of Christianity and its eventual establishment as a state religion at the end of the third century that Christian officials began to dress in a distinctive or at least more formal manner when presiding at prayer. Since bishops were granted the rank of magistrates by the Emperor Constantine, much of this distinctiveness stemmed from articles of clothing worn by officials of the late Roman Empire. The worship of the large basilicas also dictated more formal liturgical vesture, although much of what was worn by liturgical ministers was not really different from their "secular clothing": the alb, a white tunic worn as an undergarment by people of all social classes; the chasuble, a poncho-like garment worn both in church and outside of church during the late Empire; the stole, a scarf that may have originated as a symbol of magisterial office; the dalmatic, a formal version of the alb associated with the imperial court and hence limited to bishops and those who directly serve them, the deacons; the miter, headgear originally worn by imperial officials, it was naturally worn by bishops who were magistrates of the late Empire.

With the fall of the Empire, at least in the West, and the gradual change of secular clothing brought about by the barbarian invasions of the fifth through the seventh centuries, the leaders of the Church maintained their traditional vesture for public religious functions. Now, however, their manner of dress was decidedly different from that of everyday life. The tendency to sacralize both the vesture of liturgical ministers and the place where the rites were celebrated by finding antecedents for sacerdotal ritual attire in the OT became a characteristic of the late Patristic and early Medieval periods. Associating bishops' clothing with the attire of the high priest of the OT, for example, became a concern for many theologians of the early Middle Ages. The consecration of vestments and other objects of cult as wholly dedicated to liturgical use also began during this period and continues to the present day.

Christian Liturgical Vesture Today. Since the Second Vatican Council, reforms in liturgical vesture have been characterized by a return to simplicity. The General Instruction on the Roman Missal, for example, states that "the beauty of a liturgical vestment should derive from its material and design rather than from lavish ornamentation" (GIRM 306). While there has also been a reevaluation of the inherent sacrality of the garments worn by liturgical ministers, the function of the traditional vestments to enhance the prayer of the assembly and to link our celebrations with those of previous generations remain important considerations in maintaining their use by leaders of prayer.

See: PRIEST/PRIESTHOOD, TEMPLE

MARK R. FRANCIS, C.S.V.

VINE

Along with the olive (see Josh 24:13; 1 Sam 8:14; 2 Kgs 5:26) and the fig tree (1 Kgs 5:5; Jer 5:17; Hos 2:14), the grapevine is typical of the cultivated, fruit-bearing plants in the biblical world. Although the wood of the vine is worthless (Ezek 15:2-5), its fruit was much appreciated for sustenance and well-being. Abundant vineyards were part of the plenty provided in the promised land (Deut 8:7-10), and their vines would be even more fruitful in messianic times (Amos 9:13-14). Rich vineyards were a sign of the Lord's blessing and called for blessing the Lord in return. To be deprived of their fruit was a sign of the Lord's curse (Amos 5:11). Little wonder that the vine and all that was associated with it became a rich source of imagery for the OT, the NT, and the life of the Church.

Old Testament

In the OT, the vine is a major prophetic image for Israel, the people of God, and God is its vinedresser. Along with many other images, including that of the kingdom, the shepherd and the flock, the spouse and the bride, it restates the various relationships in the Mosaic covenant with a different set of images.

One of the recurrent themes is that of a fine vineyard that has been devastated or produced a bad crop. The theme appears in Isaiah's song of the vineyard, where a friend carefully prepares a vineyard and plants it with the choicest vines only to have it yield wild grapes (Isa 5:1-7). Isaiah's song provided some of the inspiration for Jesus' parable in Mark 12:1-12 (see Matt 21:33-46; Luke 20:9-19). The theme, which can be described as the unfaithful vine, appears in different forms and with a variety of emphases in many of the prophets. Hosea refers to Israel as "a luxuriant vine" whose abundant fruit has led to corruption (Hos 10:1-2). Jeremiah describes Israel as "a choice vine of fully tested stock" which has become "a spurious weed," obnoxious to the Lord who planted it (Jer 2:21). For this, her tendrils will be torn away (Jer 5:10), and there will be "no grapes on the vine" (Jer 8:13).

Ezekiel laments the fate of Judah, the vine of David, a vine once planted by the water, with "one strong branch she put out as a royal scepter," which has been torn up and planted in the desert (Ezek 19:10-14). Ezekiel's genius for imagery appears also in his parable of the vine whose wood, fit only to be "fuel for the fire," is an image of Jerusalem (Ezek 15:17), and in the allegory of the eagles and the vine (Ezek 17:1-10), describing the history of Israel in the early sixth century BCE (Ezek 17:11-21; see Jer 12:10). In Psalm 80, Israel is a vine transplanted from Egypt which once prospered but is now devastated (Ps 80:9-14), but here, unlike in the Prophets, the emphasis is not on judgment but on prayer for the vine's restoration and the vinedresser's care (Ps 80:15-20) in view of the messianic day announced by Isaiah when the vine-yard would be pleasant, with the Lord its keeper watering it and guarding it from harm (Isa 27:2-4).

New Testament

The NT refers to the song of the vineyard that yielded wild grapes (Isa 5:1-7), but changes its focus from the vineyard to the tenants and transforms it into a historical allegory. It is the tenants who are unfaithful, not the vineyard. After killing the owner's servants, they even kill his son when he comes for the harvest (Mark 12:1-9; Matt 21:33-41; Luke 20:9-16). In Matthew, this parable is preceded by that of the two sons sent to work in the father's vineyard. Both agree to go, but only one actually does so (Matt 21:28-32). In yet another Matthean parable, the focus is on the generous owner of the vineyard and the workers, all of whom receive the same pay, irrespective of the time of day they went to work in the vineyard (Matt 20:1-16).

The theme of the vine reaches its NT climax in Jesus' discourse at the Last Supper in John, which as in the OT is about the vine and the vinedresser (John 15:1-8), not the tenants or the workers. "I am the true vine," says Jesus, "and my Father is the vine grower" (John 15:1). He tells also of the severing of branches in him that do not bear fruit and of the pruning of the other branches. In Jesus' discourse, the vine imagery illumines the nature of the Church and the life it draws from Christ the vine. In the Synoptic account of the Last Supper, the fruit of the vine is related to the eschatological banquet when Jesus announces that he would "not drink again of the fruit of the vine" until he drinks it new in the kingdom of God (Mark 14:25; Matt 26:29; Luke 22:18). Each of these themes, whether ecclesiological, Christological, or Eucharistic, reappears in the life of the Church.

Pastoral-Liturgical Tradition

In the life of the Church, the vine motif tends to be overshadowed by related images such as the shepherd and the flock, and the head and the body, but it does play a part, beginning with the Didache, giving thanks "for the holy vine of David your servant which you have made known to us through Jesus your Servant" (Did 9:2), and in the Eucharist's offertory prayer where we bless God for his goodness, through which "we have this wine, fruit of the vine."

In modern times, Pius XII referred to "the vital union of branch and vine" along with the "chaste union of man and wife" and "the cohesion found in one body" to describe "our union with Christ in the Body of the Church" (*On the Mystical Body of Christ*, no. 67). While all three images refer to "our union with Christ," each highlights a different aspect of it. The image of the vine emphasizes the life and vitality which flow into the Church from the person of Christ.

In a brief synthesis of biblical theology, Vatican II's Dogmatic Constitution on the Church, no. 6, presents the vine as a biblical image of "the inner nature of the Church," which is "a tract of land . . . cultivated by the heavenly Vinedresser as his choice vineyard" (Matt 21:33-43 par.; see Isa 5:1 ff.). The true vine is Christ who gives life and fruitfulness to the branches, that is, to us. Through the Church, we abide in Christ, without whom we can do nothing (John 15:1-5).

See: BODY OF CHRIST, COVENANT, EUCHARIST, PEOPLE OF GOD, WINE

EUGENE LAVERDIERE, S.S.S.

VIOLENCE

People who expect the Bible to be a collection of edifying stories are unpleasantly surprised at the level of violence in the Bible. What is even more disconcerting is that God not only countenances the violence but approves and even orders it (e.g., Josh 6:1-5). This violence is not confined to the OT. Jesus says that the reign of God suffers violence and the violent are taking it (Matt 11:12). Ananias and Sapphira, who try to deceive the apostles, are struck dead (Acts 5:1-11). Paul curses those who preached a gospel that differs from the one he preached (Gal

1:8). He also condemns those who do not love the Lord (1 Col 16:22). The Book of Revelation describes a final great battle between the forces of good and evil (Rev 17:1–20:15). Though Augustine developed a "just war" theory, a pacifist strain survived in Christianity. Still, some see pacifism as a fundamental deviation from Christian tradition.

Old Testament

The violence that is a part of the biblical tradition is understandable once contemporary readers understand that this tradition developed in a region where conflict over political hegemony was endemic. The tradition remembers that the ancestors of the Israelites entered the land as migrants. Canaan was attractive to other peoples who found it a refuge in time of political and economic problems. The Israelites found that they had to contest for the land that was to be the scene of their subsequent history. They had to face the powers in control of the Canaanite city-states, the Philistines, and the other national states (Ammon, Edom, Moab, Aram) that arose in the region. Also, bedouin raiders were a continuing threat to Israelite farmers.

The myths of Canaanite religion reflect these conflicts over hegemony. This literature portrays Baal as a divine warrior who fights against the forces of chaos. His victories bring order to nature and the human community. Ancient Israel adopts and reinterprets this tradition. Yahweh fights for the people Israel against oppressive political powers that threaten Israel's control over the land that God promised to their ancestors. The cosmic war functions typical of Baal became less important than Yahweh's historical role as Israel's defender.

The Bible affirms that wars of conquest ordered and directed by Yahweh were the means by which Israel acquired its land. The term "Holy War" is used to describe the Israelite belief that holds that it was God who fought the battles against Israel's enemies. (The term "Holy War" does not occur in the Bible.) The land then was not acquired by Israelite military prowess but was a gift given by God to fulfill the promises made to Israel's ancestors.

The descriptions of the battles in Joshua and Judges are more ideological statements than historical reports. There have been attempts to diminish the harshness of those battle reports. For example, it has been suggested that the word that is usually rendered as "thousand" referred to the village muster. This number was hardly ever larger than twenty. The numbers of those who fought and died in the wars of conquest must be revised downward. Similarly some consider the *herem* (the massacre of all enemy people by the victorious army) to have been a measure to control plague. Third, some have described the wars of conquest as social revolutionary movements that aimed to overthrow the oppressive leadership of the Canaanite city-states. The worshipers of Yahweh who escaped from Egypt became the catalyst for this revolution since their escape from the Pharaoh proved that it was possible to be victorious in the face of seemingly insurmountable odds. Eventually these successful revolutions came to be seen as victories of Yahweh.

While these attempts to explain the apparent harshness of early Israel's wars as misunderstandings of the actual historical circumstances may be quite convincing, they cannot eliminate the fact that ancient Israel did get its land, in part, through violent means. While this may offend some believers' sensibilities, it cannot be ignored without ignoring the bulk of Joshua and Judges. The question then shifts: how can this violence be justified theologically? The ideology of Holy War (see Deut 20:1-4) is not any more difficult to explain than the necessity of Jesus' death. Both reveal the mysterious ways by which God uses human folly and sin as a means of salvation. The basic message of the Bible is summed up in Joseph's response to his brothers who feared his retribution for their crime against him: "Even though you intended to do harm to me, God intended it for good, in order to preserve a numerous people, as he is doing today"

(Gen 50:20). The wars that took place while Israel was trying to secure the land of Canaan were evil. There is no denying that the identity and culpability of the human agents responsible for that evil is another question. What the Bible does affirm is that God's purpose was served even by this violence. Admittedly, reading some episodes of ancient Israel's history does not make for pleasant reading. The Bible, however, was not written to edify but to lead people to obedience and faith.

The monarchy arose in Israel to secure Israel's hold on the land, but the monarchy brought its own violence: plots over succession (2 Samuel 9–20; 1 Kings 1–2), revolutions (2 Kings 9–10), assassinations (2 Kgs 11:1-3), and oppression (1 Kings 21). When the resurgent Assyrian and Babylonian Empires began to set their sights on the territory of the Israelite kingdoms, the violence experienced by Israel and Judah led to the destruction of the kingdoms, their political and religious institutions, and the dispersal of their populations.

In the midst of the crises caused by Assyria and Babylon, the Israelite prophets assert that Yahweh is no longer Israel's defender. On the contrary, Yahweh fights against Israel through the Mesopotamian powers (Amos 2:4-16). The prophets claim that the reason for this change is the oppression of the poor. Yahweh, who formerly fought against foreign powers, now fights again the Israelite state and the people of means. The prophets of the Exile often use dire predictions of evil against the nations as a prelude to the promise of redemption for Israel (e.g., Ezekiel 25–32). Again the image undergoes reinterpretation. Yahweh takes Israel's side against the nations.

During the restoration conflicts arose within the community over control of the community's life. With the arrival of the Greeks in the fourth century, the split within the community became more pronounced. There were some who wanted to remain loyal to their ancestral religion. Others were ready to compromise their traditions for the sake of economic prosperity (1 Macc 1:10-15). When the Seleucids proscribed the observances of Judaism, violence was the way that some Jews chose to resist their persecutors (1 Maccabees 2). The Maccabees were successful in their revolution against the Seleucids, but the kingdom that their descendants established was guilty of the usual oppression that follows from an absolutist political rule.

The Book of Daniel represents the views of those who did not regard violence as an acceptable response to the persecution of the Jews by the Seleucids. The perspective of the book is that the real conflict is not on the earthly plane but on the heavenly. When Antiochus IV persecuted the Jews, he was actually rebelling against God. This was enough to guarantee his fall and the end to the violence he brought to bear upon the Jews; therefore, the Book of Daniel does not have a high regard for the militancy represented by the Maccabees. While the Jews are to resist Antiochus, their resistance is to be passive and therefore non-violent. The quality of their resistance expresses itself in a willingness to undergo suffering and even death. The actual warfare against the forces of evil is left to God (Dan 12:1). The victory over the Seleucids belongs to God and the faithful do nothing more than prepare themselves for the day of victory by accepting suffering and death that will come their way because of their non-compliance with Antiochus' laws. The Book of Daniel can offer non-violent resistance as an option because of its explicit belief in resurrection (Dan 12:2-3).

Besides the violence on this national level, the Bible describes violence on an individual level. The economic exploitation of the poor led to the threats against their oppressors by the prophets who believed that they were speaking in the name of God. The psalms contain imprecations of the poor who call for God's retribution against their persecutors. Imprecations such as Psalm 109 and the passages in Jeremiah where the prophet curses his enemies (Jer 11:21; 18:19-23) are not simply expressions of anger.

They reflect a formal pattern of speech in the ancient Near East: the curse.

Ancient people believed that a curse once uttered would pursue its object until the doom pronounced in the curse took place. It was impossible to annul a curse once it was spoken. At most one may neutralize it by speaking a blessing on the person cursed (Judg 17:2). A person cursing another followed a ritual pattern. That people believed such rituals were effective is clear from Balak's hiring of Balaam to curse the Israelites (Num 22:2-8). A solemn ritual of cursing those who break the Law occurs in Deuteronomy 27:14-26. Ancient Near Eastern treaties and law codes contain similar curses. The Book of Numbers provides an example of how a ritual of cursing proceeded (Num 5:11-28). Here a woman suspected of adultery drinks water into which a written curse has been washed. If she is guilty of adultery, she will suffer miscarriages and be unable to bear children.

When the liturgy chooses texts for Christian worship, it avoids imprecations or at least edits out offending sections. For example, the lectionary uses Psalm 137 three times as a response (fourth Sunday of Lent B; Friday of the Twelfth Week of Year II; Wednesday of the Twenty-sixth Week of Year I). The editors omitted verses 8-9 for each of these selections. They believed the psalmist's cry, "Happy the one who shall seize and smash your little one against the rock!" to be offensive to modern worshipers. One theological reason Christians find these words offensive is that suffering can become a positive value in Christian theology. Resignation and acceptance of suffering and evil are important in some types of Christian spirituality. The religion of ancient Israel did not find positive value in suffering.

The presence of evil in the world is a testimony to the disruptive power of sin. Violence entered the world after sin (see Gen 4:1-16). It remains part of human experience because of sin. More than anything else, violence in the Bible and in the contemporary world makes it impossible to trivialize sin. The power of sin is manifest more clearly in violence than in any other way. The Bible is explicit and realistic about the power and presence of sin in the world. It also sees the power of redemption as greater than the power of sin.

See: PEACE, SIN

LESLIE J. HOPPE, O.F.M.

New Testament

Jesus sets the pattern for the NT teaching by bringing new attitudes and approaches toward violence, yet in a realistic though complex fashion. He rejects physical violence as illusory, so that the NT teaching could be summed up in his saying, "All who take the sword will perish by the sword" (Matt 26:52). Nevertheless, violence is a fact of human existence and must be countered. Moreover, it can take many forms besides the physical. Thus, the NT builds on the model of a Jesus who, while not physically violent, is actively resistant to injustice. This can be seen as a different kind of violence, i.e., a revolutionary stance against the established (and unjust) order. Ultimately, this struggle is beyond the political and is an eschatological quest for the time when all violence gives way to peace* and reconciliation. This NT message on violence is intimately related to teaching on war, cursing, and victory. The NT is realistic about the persistence of war in the world, but transports it into an eschatological struggle. Victory is neither military nor necessarily an immediate political one, though there begins some mastery of this world, but it is the final conquest of the evil powers by Jesus and the Church. In the same way cursing is channeled into blessing while yet presaging the final condemnation of evil.

The Gospels. The only place in the Gospels where Jesus actually uses the verb "to act violently" *(biazomai)* is in Matthew 11:12 and its parallel in Luke 16:16, and both texts present violence as an inevitable consequence of the reign of God. The realism and the complexity of Jesus' teaching is captured well by the ambiguity of the saying in Matthew. It could mean negatively that the reign of God "suffers violence" (the verb understood as passive) and violent people attack it ("are taking it by force"). It could also mean positively that the reign of God "does violence" (the verb understood as middle voice) and that fiercely dedicated people attain it only by discipline and rigorous commitment ("the violent are taking it by force"). Commentators favor the former meaning for Matthew, but point out that Luke seems to favor the latter in the way he has changed his version: "The kingdom of God is proclaimed, and everyone who enters does so with violence." The combination of both interpretations highlights the recognition of violence as an evil force that persists against the reign of God, the implicit condemnation of such violence by Jesus, and the call for a different kind of violence that stands up to evil and conquers it.

While Jesus uses the term violence only in this text, his life is lived out in relation to this complex word. He speaks of war and military victory in matter-of-fact fashion in parables, as an expected part of human life (Matt 22:7; Luke 11:21-22; 14:31). Soldiers are an accepted part of society (Matt 8:10; Luke 3:14). At the same time, Jesus relinquishes use of physical force or resistance in response to violence in society: "Offer no resistance to one who is evil. When someone strikes you on [your] right cheek, turn the other one to him as well" (Matt 5:39). In the same way, Jesus turns people from the harsh tradition of cursing: "Bless those who curse you" (Luke 6:28); still, he uses curse when confronting his hearers with the reality of evil and when guaranteeing its demise (Matt 25:41). He lives such a program from the very beginning of his ministry, when he refuses the temptations* to bring the reign of God by human manipulation and force (Matt 4:1-11; Luke 4:1-13; see also Mark 8:27-33; John 6:15). He continues this attitude in the face of rejection, refusing to send fire on the Samaritans (Luke 9:52-56), blessing the meek, the peacemakers, and those who endure persecution (Matt 5:5, 9-10), and encouraging his disciples not to be as the Gentiles who lord it over others (Matt 20:25). Finally, his death on the cross is supreme example of his refusal to counter physical violence with physical violence (Luke 22:49-51).

Scholars still debate whether the teaching and example of the physically non-violent Jesus demand strict pacifism from his disciples, or show examples of response that may apply in some cases but not in others, or provide an ethic for individuals but not governments or societies. Certainly, Jesus speaks little about politics, probably because he had no political power, and his teaching was not to offer a detailed political program. Whatever the case, it is clear that his physical non-violence should not be understood as passivity to evil forces. He cleanses the Temple (Matt 21:12-17; Mark 11:15-19; Luke 19:45-48; John 2:14-22), brings not peace but the sword of division between those who accept the reign of God and those who do not (Matt 10:34-36), counters worldly rulers (Luke 13:31-33; John 18:28-38), convicts the world (John 16:7-11), and offers a peace that the world cannot give (John 14:27). This very active non-violence of Jesus is the beginning of the eschatological victory, which is not a temporal military or even necessarily a political success, but is war against the conquest of Satan and all of his evil minions (Matt 24:6-14; Luke 11:14-23; 22:53; John 13:2; 14:30). The eschatological victory may be anticipated in the partial successes of those who live the beatitudes and turn the other cheek (Matthew 5). In any case all evil power has already been subverted and Christ offers ever new possibilities for exposing the hollow external trappings that remain of this power, even while his disciples await the final overthrow. Jesus has already "conquered the world" (John 16:33) and prays that we be protected even while we are still in the world (John 17:15-16).

Acts, Letters, and Revelation. The other NT books take up principally the eschatological dimensions of Jesus' teaching on vio-

lence, war, cursing, and victory, and this predominantly in the Book of Revelation. There are a few texts that once again assume the existence of war as part of human reality (1 Cor 14:8; Heb 11:32-34), and Acts explicitly mentions physical violence in relation to Paul's experiences of the Roman government and of his accusers (5:26; 21:35). In a famous text, however, James mimics the attitude of Jesus by condemning war: "Where do the wars and where do the conflicts among you come from? Is it not from your passions that make war within your members? . . . Do not speak evil of one another" (4:1, 11). Still James himself does not remain passive to the violence of war and unjust oppression throughout the letter (1:9-11; 2:1-4, 11; 5:1-6), and Paul also resists his persecutors and their evil (Acts 25:6-12; 26:2). Yet it was all without physical violence, after the example of Jesus himself (1 Pet 2:21-24). It takes over Jesus' practice regarding cursing: it blesses those who persecute, and does not curse them (Rom 12:14), yet it condemns the evil of infidelity to the true gospel and to the love of Christ (1 Cor 16:22; Gal 1:8). Acceptance of suffering should not be seen, then, as passivity to this world's problems, but rather as part of an eschatological struggle. It is not being conquered, but conquering evil with good (Rom 12:21). Evil powers are behind political and physical persecution (1 Cor 2:7-8; Eph 6:12). Christians are to wage war with the armor of virtue and not physical weapons (1 Thess 5:8; Eph 6:13-17), but they do "fight a good fight" (1 Tim 1:18) as soldiers of Christ (1 Cor 9:7; 2 Tim 2:3). In fact, belonging to God, with faith in Christ, they have already conquered the world (1 John 2:13-14; 4:4; 5:5), because Christ through his death and resurrection has despoiled the powers (Col 2:15), even if the final dismantling of their empire is eschatological.

This final eschatological victory over war and violence is highlighted especially in the Book of Revelation. This last NT book is filled with images of violence, yet is a book of hope. Oppression and even physical persecution by the Roman empire is seen as representative of powers of evil greater than human. They require God's intervention for an eschatological conquest. Thus, evil is described as a dragon (ch. 12) and Rome as its beast (ch. 13). Evil sought to destroy Christ (12:4), was unsuccessful (12:5), so it wars now against the Church (12:13) and her children (12:17). That evil resides in the Roman empire, which wages war and conquers the holy ones (13:7; see 11:7). Some even capitulate to the empire and its religion, fascinated by them: "Who can fight against it?" (13:4). But their victory is hollow and not decisive. This struggle is played out against the backdrop of, and as a scene within, the eschatological battle in which God's forces have already begun to, and will finally, crush totally the forces of evil. Michael wages war against the dragon (12:7-8), and Christ's death shows that even martyrs are victorious and that the devil has but a short time before defeat (12:10-12). Until the end of time kings will assemble under the aegis of demonic spirits to wage war against the Lamb and his disciples; but the Lamb, who is faithful and true, will conquer (16:14-16; 17:12-14; 19:11-21; 20:7-10; see 5:5; 6:2; 9:7-11). This imagery is the anticipated development completing the general exhortations to the churches of the first chapters of the Book of Revelation. In these early chapters the author encourages those communities who are experiencing violence in varied forms. He assures them that if they remain faithful, they will be the real victors. Among other things, they will eat from the tree of life (2:7), will not be harmed by final death (2:11), will have their names enshrined forever (2:17; 3:5), and will sit with Christ on a throne of victory forever (3:21). In the same vein, Revelation can end with the note that finally nothing accursed will be found anymore (22:3).

See: PASSION, PERSECUTION, POWER, SATAN, SUFFERING, WORLD

ANTHONY J. TAMBASCO

Pastoral-Liturgical Tradition

Traditionally the term violence has been related in Christianity to issues of war and peace. Only recently has the Church become far more sensitive to other forms of violence (e.g., child abuse, spouse abuse, homophobia, rape, exploitation of workers, etc.) as its awareness of personal dignity and human rights has grown in the light of Vatican II and papal encyclicals by Popes John XXIII and John Paul II. Hence in our day a discussion of violence could properly take several turns. The present observations will be confined, however, to the more classical discussion of violence within the context of armed military struggle by a nation-state.

Christianity and War Before Augustine. For the first two centuries of its existence violence was not a paramount issue for the Church. Christians generally lived on the fringes of the social order and there was little or no demand for them to join the ranks of the military. The Church felt no immediate responsibility for the destiny of the state. The writings of the early Church Fathers such as St. Clement of Rome and St. Justin deny any Christian obligation to engage in warfare. On the other hand, however, neither is there any evidence of a clear commitment to pacifism as a religious ideal in their thought.

After 180 CE a pronounced change occured. First of all, the Church was making great strides numerically despite unrelenting persecution. At the same time the Roman Empire was increasingly threatened by foreign forces enhancing the drive for military conscription. The Church Fathers thus tried to address this new challenge of increasing numbers of Christian military personnel. A strong pacifist strain marked many of the responses. This is especially evident in Hippolytus' influential *Apostolic Tradition*, as well as in the writings of Tertullian and Origen. All proclaimed a doctrinal pacifism rooted in the judgment that Jesus' teachings were fundamentally incompatible with the resort to violence. Others, such as St. Cyprian, spoke out forcefully against war as an evil, but he acknowledged the necessity of the armies for the safety of the Empire.

The whole tenor of the discussion on violence within Christianity changed with the decree at Milan by Constantine in 313 CE. Church writers suddenly ceased speaking about the pacifist orientation of Jesus' message. Instead they began to emphasize the notion that to fight for the Emperor is to fight for God. Athanasius, Basil, and Ambrose began the process of reconstructing Christian thought on the question of violence, a process brought to completion in the writings of Augustine.

Christianity and War in Augustine. Augustine took all those to task who were critical of either the OT or the NT with regard to war. In the Hebrew Bible warfare was a direct disposition of Almighty God. The NT, Augustine insisted, not only did not condemn war, but in fact produced positive justification for military service.

Augustine did not glorify armed violence. On the contrary, he considered war a plague upon humanity. Christians must look upon it as a trial for their patience, humility, and general discipline. Since war is contrary to the natural order in Augustinian thought, anyone wishing to initiate military violence must have a just cause. In order to ascertain whether a just cause was present, Augustine developed a set of criteria that have remained the basis for the classical "just war" theory. These criteria included a formal declaration of war, right intention, reasonable hope of success in battle, and reliance on war as a last resort. In addition, other criteria were established for the actual conduct of the war. A generally "just war" could be declared "unjust" in terms of some of its features (e.g., in the modern era, saturation bombing).

No understanding of Augustine's approach to military violence would be complete without some reference to his ideas on peace, which he considered the crowning point of all his teaching on this subject. There is so much lively anti-war material in Augustinian thought that, taken out of context, he could easily be transformed into a staunch advocate of pacifism. For Augustine peace was such a value that a Christian ruler, under certain conditions, could wage a war in order to restore or preserve peace. His "just war" theory was not intended as a guide for ordinary citizens. Rather, it was meant to guide Christian kings who alone had the authority to order the use of military force.

The Persistence of Non-Violence. Pre-Constantinian Christianity's pacifist strain, though greatly diminished after Augustine, survived throughout Christian history. It was reaffirmed by some in the monastic tradition and by the historic "peace churches" such as the Mennonites. Evidence of a pacifist outlook are to be found in Catholic America in the early nineteenth century in the works of Isaac Hecker and Orestes Brownson, though Brownson eventually came around to support the Civil War. The two world wars of the twentieth century each saw some pacifist manifestations on the part of Catholics. Included in this non-violent witness were Ammon Henancy, Dorothy Day, the Catholic Pax group, Archbishop John T. McNicholas of Cincinnati, and Professor Gordon Zahn.

The development of atomic and nuclear weaponry in recent decades, as well as the actual use of weapons of mass destruction in World War II, has generated a new discussion on military violence within Catholic Christianity. Pope John XXIII (particularly in *Pacem in Terris*), Paul VI (at the United Nations), and John Paul II have questioned the moral validity of modern warfare. The U.S. bishops in their pastoral letter gave highly conditioned approval to warfare and legitimated pacifism as a moral option for individuals within the Church. And biblical scholars increasingly have brought to light Jesus' strong insistence on "love of enemy."

It is too early to tell how strong the pacifist viewpoint will become in contemporary Catholicism. Certainly there are Catholic scholars who feel that pacifism represents a fundamental deviation from the tradition. And some in the peace and justice movement, particularly with roots in the Third World, regard pacifism as naive and ultimately supportive of an exploitative status quo in the political realm. The debate goes on and will likely continue in the foreseeable future. What is clear is that the rather easy acceptance of the Augustinian synthesis is breaking down as Christianity begins a major reexamination of its attitudes toward violence in light of the mass destruction capabilities of twentieth-century civilization.

See: PEACE

JOHN T. PAWLIKOWSKI, O.S.M.

VIRGIN

Old Testament

In traditional Middle Eastern cultures, a woman's virginity at marriage* is of immense importance to the honor of her family* (Deut 22:13-21); its loss is not only a disgrace but economic disaster as well, for her bride value will suffer. Hence the sentence of capital punishment was meted out for the adultery of a married or engaged woman, along with her lover. Payment of a fine was required by the offender to the father of a virgin not yet engaged who is raped, as well as forced marriage without possibility of divorce (Deut 22:22-29).

The most common term for virgin in the Hebrew OT, *bethulah,* comes from a root meaning "to separate," indicative of the watchfulness of family over unmarried girls. Sirach frets over the worries of the father of an unmarried daughter (Sir 42:9-11), and the first-century Jewish philosopher Philo describes the women of Alexandrian Jews kept in seclusion in their houses, the young virgins not even allowed to approach the outer doors (*Against Flaccus* 2.89). Occasionally other words are used: *na'ărah* (Gen 24:14, 16, 55; 34:3), a maiden or girl; or *'almah* (Gen 24:43; Isa 7:14), meaning a young woman* capable of bearing children who has not yet done so, even though she may have had sexual intercourse. All three were translated into Greek in the Septuagint as *parthenos,* causing later difficulty in Matthew 1:23 (see below).

The virgin is also a symbol of youth and promise, often applied to Israel (e.g., Jer 18:13; 31:4, 21; Amos 5:2), but occasionally to other nations: e.g., Babylon (Isa 47:1) and Egypt (Jer 46:11).

New Testament

Matthew 1:23 quotes Isaiah 7:14 to indicate that a virgin (Greek, *parthenos*; Hebrew, *bethulah*) will conceive and bear Emmanuel. The Isaian text as understood in Hebrew refers to a young woman who has not previously borne a child; the Greek text, to a woman who has not previously had sexual intercourse. Matthew takes it one step further by understanding it to prophesy the virginal conception of Jesus. It is important to realize the predicament in which Joseph found himself in Matthew's narrative. The dire penalties of Deuteronomy 22:23-27 were legally applicable, but Joseph would not invoke them (Matt 1:19). The NT has nothing to say about Mary's sexual status after the birth of Jesus.

All reliable early traditions seem to suggest that Jesus did not marry or have a sexual partner, though they have nothing to say about whether he was ever sexually active, since this was not a significant question for men until well into the Christian era. Within the same generation, however, Paul's Corinthian community has raised the question of possible advantages of not marrying, perhaps because of the teaching of Paul himself, who seems to prefer the unmarried state because of eschatological expectation (1 Corinthians 7). Still, however, the emphasis is not on a physical understanding of virginity as total absence of sexual activity, but on the freedom of being either unmarried or emotionally uninvolved in order to devote oneself more fully to prayer. The four prophesying daughters of the evangelist Philip were known to be unmarried (Acts 21:9). Paul could refer figuratively to the Corinthian community as a virgin betrothed to Christ (2 Cor 11:2-3).

Matthew's parable of the ten *parthenoi* (virgins or maidens; Matt 25:1-12) features young, unmarried women taking a role in a marriage feast, without reference to their sexual history. Since our knowledge of rural Palestinian wedding customs is minimal, it is difficult to say how unusual their behavior is. Because the parable lent itself so readily to eschatological teaching on preparedness (see already the editorial comment in Matt 25:13), once the Christian positive valuation of prolonged virginity was in place, it became a prime symbol of the role of virginity as eschatological paradigm and even mystical marriage. It would seem that by the early second century there were groups of women or men in some Christian communities who did not marry. The Christian fascination with virginity as precursor of the heavenly life or imitation of angelic life (an interpretation of Mark 12:25 and pars.) developed over the first centuries of the Christian era into a major phenomenon that symbolized non-compromise with the material world of birth and death. It is important, however, not to read a later view into the NT texts.

Pastoral-Liturgical Tradition

As a symbol, virginity can evoke the archetypal power of the uncompromised and unspoiled, of that which is authentically what it claims to be: e.g., virgin forest. As a social institution, it revolutionized economics, politics, and family structures in the West from the fourth century to the Reformation. For countless women, the institutionalized virginity of monasticism provided the only means of escape from oppressive marriage structures and patriarchal power.

In contemporary society, with its affirmation of the positive values of sexuality,* marriage, responsible intimacy, and childbearing, chosen virginity is frequently the object of humor or of pity. The theology of virginity in the past focused too narrowly on women as sexual beings seen as a threat to men rather than as full persons, so that today's social analysts see how it has also functioned not to free but to control women's lives.

The present Rite for the Consecration of Virgins flows with traditional and poetic imagery. It is careful to avoid any claim that virginity is superior to marriage, as was done for many centuries. Yet since it can be used only for women and is filled with spiritualized marital imagery, it still places the emphasis on women's sexuality, and thus is still inherently sexist. Rites of religious profession and consecration written for women still stress purity and the overcoming of weakness, while those for men highlight service to the community. Until rites of consecration to celibacy* (not to be confused with virginity) are fully respectful of both women and men as both sexual and interpersonal beings, virginity will remain a powerful symbol whose potential has been subverted.

See: ESCHATOLOGY, FAMILY, MARY, PRAYER, VOWS, WOMAN/WOMEN

CAROLYN OSIEK, R.S.C.J.

VISIONS

From the biblical perspective, the world of the supernatural was close to the surface of the human arena. It is not surprising that visions and portents are an integral part of the biblical story from God's appearances to the Patriarchs to the specters that put fear into the hearts of Israel's enemies in the book of Daniel. Within the New Testament, angelic visitations and the appearances of the Risen Christ guide the course of history and are particularly important.

New Testament

Visions and revelations are especially common in Apocalyptic* literature, but are by no means limited to it. The ancient belief that the spirit* world could break through into human consciousness in dreams meant that what we would call waking visions were not clearly distinguishable from dreams. The value given to dream visions in the NT world is exemplified by the second-century pagan author Artemidorus of Ephesus, who traveled extensively collecting the dream accounts of others, and wrote a long treatise on their interpretation.

Visions usually contain both visual and auditory components, and serve various purposes: identification of the one who appears (Acts 9:3-7); encouragement (Acts 27:23-25); communication of information (Rev 4:1); or giving directives (Matt 2:13). NT visions can be divided into angelophanies (revelation through a divine messenger or intermediary, e.g., the annunciation, Luke 1:26-27) and theophanies (revelations of the glory of God or Christ, e.g., the transfiguration,* Mark 9:2-8 and par.).

Attitudes toward visions varied in early Christianity. In prophetic and apocalyptic circles they were highly prized. Where ecstatic and charismatic manifestations were held in some suscipion, so too were visions.

Gospels and Acts. Matthew's infancy narrative portrays Joseph as recipient of visions by which he is led to protect his family from danger during Jesus' early years (Matt 1:2-24; 2:13, 19-20, 22), and even the Magi are so guided (Matt 2:12). Luke's infancy narrative depicts the angelophanies of Zechariah's vision in the Temple (Luke 1:11-20) and Gabriel's appearance to Mary (Luke 1:26-38).

The baptism and transfiguration visions of Matthew and Luke identify Jesus as Son of God. In the baptismal scene of Matthew and Mark, only Jesus sees the Spirit descend, but the confirming voice is perhaps public (Matt 3:16-17; Mark 1:10-11), while Luke implies that both dove and voice are public theophany (Luke 3:22), and in John, only John the Baptist sees the vision (John 1:32-33). The transfiguration accounts contain both theophanous vision of Christ's glory and identifying voice, that of God (Matt 17:1-8; Mark 9:2-8; Luke 9:28-36).

The Synoptic Gospels all depict Jesus as recipient of both angelic and diabolic visions during his time in the desert (Matt 4:1-11; Mark 1:12-13; Luke 4:1-13). Later, Jesus has a vision of the defeat of Satan through the disciples' preaching (Luke 17:18). Even John, who does not emphasize visions and does not include the transfiguration scene, has a heavenly voice confirm Jesus' purpose, heard but not properly identified by the crowd (John 12:28-30). At the death of Jesus, apocalyptic events like an earthquake and the appearance of some of the dead (Matt

27:52-53) signal the cosmic significance of the event. The Synoptic versions of the empty tomb all feature a heavenly messenger or messengers who convey the proclamation of the resurrection to the women (Matt 28:2-7; Mark 16:5-7; Luke 24:4-7).

In Acts, Paul first encounters the risen Christ in a vision of light and an overpowering voice (Acts 9:3-6); those with him hear the voice, but see nothing. Later, the apostle crosses over from Asia to Europe to begin a new ministry there because of a vision (Acts 16:9-10), and is encouraged in the midst of shipwreck by the vision of an angel who promises he will survive to go to Rome (Acts 27:23-25).

There are two separate double visions in Acts, in which two parties receive complementary visions that will bring them together for God's purposes. Paul and Ananias are connected in Damascus for Paul's healing after his encounter with the risen Christ on the way (Acts 9:10-12), and Peter is brought to the house of the Roman centurion Cornelius to evangelize and baptize his household (Acts 10).

This brief survey shows that all three Synoptic writers value visions as communication from God. For them, Jesus is both subject and recipient of visions.

Appearances of the Risen Christ. The appearances of the risen Christ are visions of a unique kind, involving a risen body that can be grasped (Matt 28:9; John 20:17), firmly touched (John 20:27), that eats (Luke 24:39-43), and even cooks breakfast (John 21:9), yet is not limited by closed doors (John 20:19, 26). Despite the corporeality implied in some of these passages, Paul, our earliest and most direct witness, understands these events as appearances, to which the recipients witness: to Cephas, the Twelve, five hundred at one time, James, and all the apostles (1 Cor 15:5-7).

For Paul, the most important element of the resurrection appearances is not their nature or content, but the testimony of those who say they saw Jesus alive after his death. Paul's expression is not that Jesus appeared, but that he "was seen by" the witnesses. Paul himself goes on to claim to be a recipient of a similar appearance on the same terms (1 Cor 15:8-9), by which he was constituted an apostle (Gal 1:15-16). Looking back from the perspective of fourteen years later, he describes an ecstatic "heavenly journey" that was probably different from the original encounter with the risen Christ and apostolic call: he was caught up to the third heaven and heard secret or incommunicable utterances (2 Cor 12:1-4)—a prototypical mystical experience of a kind later recognizable in Jewish "kabbalah" mysticism.

Revelation. The NT book in which visions feature most extensively is of course the Book of Revelation. Here, apocalyptic visions of cosmic scope announce the present crisis and the projection of the future. The visions come to the author John not in a dream, but in ecstasy: he is "in the Spirit" one Sunday (Rev 1:10). The first, terrifying vision is of the risen, glorious Christ, described in cosmic terms: he holds the stars and is of dazzling appearance (1:9-16). Whereas it is usual in Apocalyptic literature for some kind of heavenly intermediary to convey the message to the seer, here the intermediary is the risen Christ himself. He holds the power over life and death (1:18), and dictates to the recipient the letters to the seven churches, in relation to which John apparently holds some authority (2:1–3:22).

The rest of the book consists of a series of visions that reveal in figurative form the true significance of present events and what is soon to come, much of it worked around the cosmic number seven: the throne of God, the lamb, the opening of the seven seals, the blowing of seven trumpets, the beasts and the whore of Babylon, seven plagues, seven bowls, and finally, the triumph of God in the new Jerusalem. This tightly woven sequence of apocalyptic visions spans the projected future and destiny of the world, as imagined by a first-century Jewish Christian caught up in the oppression of the Roman Empire.

Because many of the visions recounted in the NT are in fact dream experiences, there is no need to see all of them as miraculous happenings of a totally different order than God's communication with human beings in other stages of church history and even today.

See: APOCALYPTIC, APOSTLE, BABYLON, BAPTISM, DEATH, FAMILY, GLORY, JERUSALEM, JESUS CHRIST, JOHN THE BAPTIST, LAMB OF GOD, LIFE, RESURRECTION, SATAN, SON OF GOD, SPIRIT, TEMPLE, TRANSFIGURATION

CAROLYN OSIEK, R.S.C.J.

Pastoral-Liturgical Tradition

Visions often are associated in the Scriptures with the revelation of truth or with the mediated manifestation of God's presence. When such ecstatic phenomena occur after the scriptural era, they can be validated only in relationship to these others. Such visions may be of great value for individual persons, but even when recognized by the Church, are not considered to be universally binding on the faithful.

These phenomena of individual revelation are seldom alluded to in liturgical texts. In such documents, it is far more common to find vision used as a metaphor for salvation. In the Eucharistic Prayers of the Roman Rite we pray that the departed may be brought into the light of God's presence (E.P. II), and that we enjoy forever the vision of God's glory (E.P. III). The eschatological event is spoken of as the day on which "we shall see you, our God, as you are" (E.P. III). God's purpose in creating humanity is to lead us to the "joyful vision" of God's light where the angels eternally look upon and praise the divine glory (E.P. IV).

In the prayer texts of the Roman tradition, vision as a metaphor for salvation is mutual. Not only is our vision of God's glory the essence of redemption, but God's looking upon us and upon our offerings is equivalent to the divine acceptance that guarantees our participation in Christ's sacrifice. This mutual gaze is expressive of the future relationship between God and the redeemed, for "now we see indistinctly, as in a mirror; then we shall see face to face" (1 Cor 13:12).

See: APOCALYPTIC, GLORY, SALVATION

DOMINIC SERRA

VISITATION OF GOD

The Bible contains many accounts of appearances of God despite ancient Israel's belief that God could not be represented by any image and that no one who sees God can live (Exod 33:20). Some of these appearances come to individuals as a sign* of God's favor. Others are manifestation of divine power* to frighten Israel's enemies. The NT asserts that Jesus is God's decisive self-disclosure. In some sense, the Gospels are a continuous narrative of God's visitation. Still the NT describes specific experiences of God's presence.

In the stories of ancient Israel's ancestors, God appears to them to announce or reaffirm promises of land and posterity. Sometimes the person receiving the visitation builds an altar as a memorial of the appearance (Gen 12:7; 26:24-25; 28:12-19; 35:1-15). These stories usually give few details about the appearance itself since the main focus is on the promises God makes. Sometimes divine beings (or angels) appear in human form to be received as guests (Gen 18:1-15; Judg 6:11-18; 13:2). The point of these stories is usually to announce that a previously barren woman will have a child.

A second function of the stories of God's appearances is to announce the commissioning of individuals who have a special role to play in Israel's life. Such individuals include Moses (Exodus 3), Samuel (1 Sam 3:10), and Solomon (1 Kgs 3:5; 9:2). The appearance of God on Mount Sinai (Exod 19:16-25) serves to commission Israel as the people of God. Volcanic eruptions and thunderstorms accompany the coming of Yahweh to Sinai. They are of such intensity that the people ask Moses to mediate for them. The appearance of God ends with the giving of the commandments. The visitation of God is an expression of the divine will. As a response the people construct a sanctuary in the wilderness and begin a regular form of worship.

Yahweh accompanies Israel through the wilderness as a pillar of cloud and fire (Exod 13:21-22; 14:19-20). Ritual activities provided a conventional context for God's visitation of Israel. Yahweh is present at the tent of meeting (Num 11:24-25; Deut 31:14-15). The priest signals God's presence in Israel's worship when he says "I am Yahweh" (Pss 50:7; 81:10). The Temple is the place where one can encounter the Divine and find asylum. Another purpose of God's visitation is to save Israel by causing panic among its enemies. God comes as a warrior (Judg 5:4-5; Isa 40:10-11; Sir 16:18-19).

Yahweh, the divine warrior, is usually surrounded by fire or other spectacular manifestations (Deut 33:2; Pss 18:8; 104:2; Ezek 1:27-28; Hab 3:4). When God appears nature trembles (Exod 19:18). A pattern that appears in texts like Psalm 18:8-16 and Habakkuk 3:3-15 shows a combination of a violent thunderstorm with the effects of an earthquake. Here the OT descriptions of the manifestation of Yahweh's power and presence are similar to those of Sumerian, Akkadian, and Ugaritic hymns. These hymns also describe a warrior god who is surrounded with radiance. The earth trembles at their appearance. The OT, while accepting and reinterpreting this ancient Near Eastern pattern, asserts that the actions of God go beyond natural phenomenon. God's power is manifest in the world through the experiences of Israel.

A remarkable recasting of the link between God and the phenomena of nature occurs in 1 Kings 19:11-13. Here the manifestation of God to Elijah abandons what was conventional language to describe an experience of God's presence. The prophet learns that God is not present in the earthquake, wind, or thunder. Elijah recognizes God's presence in a barely perceptible breeze. This text affirms God's power is effective even when there is no spectacular display accompanying it exercised.

The prophets introduce a new reason for God's visitation of Israel: judgment (Amos

1:2; Isa 26:21). In a strict sense, God does not appear to execute judgment. Only the consequences of that judgment are visible. Here God's power is manifest not to reveal who God is or what God wants. The manifestation of God's power brings confusion and destruction. Amos insists that Israel will hear the voice of God, but that voice is not the thunder that brings rain and fertility. The sound of God's voice will wither vegetation and bring death.

In the Intertestamental literature the earth is no longer a locus for the visitation by God. Heaven is the usual place that people encounter God. That is why it is necessary for seers to be transported into the heavenly realms (1 Enoch 14:8-25). The apocalyptic world view of much of this literature believes that God has largely abandoned to the power of evil. The Book of Revelation follows this pattern. The seer has a vision of heaven in Revelation 4:1-11.

The rest of the NT follows more conventional patterns in describing the visitation of God. In Jesus' baptism, the Spirit of God descends on Jesus as a dove (Matt 3:17). The accounts of the Easter appearances in the Gospels probably were influenced by the stories of the appearances of God in the OT. The accounts of Paul's vision on the Damascus Road (Acts 9; 22; 26) are meant to convey the impression of a visitation of God that transformed the apostle.

Accounts of God's visitation have two basic elements: a reference to God's appearance and a description of the consequences of that appearance. The stories of God's visitation attempt to describe God's relationship to the world and to the believer. They assume a distinction between God and the world of nature. They speak of God because they speak of the effects of God's presence.

See: JUDGMENT, PROMISE

LESLIE J. HOPPE, O.F.M.

VISITATION OF MARY

In the infancy narrative of Luke's Gospel, Mary is pictured visiting her cousin, Elizabeth, who is pregnant with John the Baptist (1:39-45). The narrative element in the account is intended to provide both women an opportunity to praise and thank God for the blessings they have received. Mary's hymn of praise is highlighted and is known as the *Magnificat.*

New Testament

The story of Mary's visit to Elizabeth is more concerned with theology than with history. It is intended to reflect and reinforce the relationship of Jesus and John the Baptist where the Baptist's role is significant but clearly subordinate. Here too, Elizabeth is pregnant through a special intervention of God, who delivers her from barrenness, whereas Mary is pregnant by a far more dramatic intervention in the form of virginal conception. Both women have experienced God's mercy, but Mary's gift surpasses Elizabeth's as much as Jesus' gift eclipses that of the Baptist.

The stirring of John the Baptist in the womb of his mother (1:41) is a hint of the joy that will accompany the messianic age. Elizabeth takes this as her cue to praise God's goodness to her. She does this by declaring the blessedness, not of herself, but of Mary, just as her son will later declare the superiority of Jesus. Her brief canticle of praise recalls the experience of Deborah and Judith, two OT women who were agents of God's power in history. Deborah sang, "Blessed among women be Jael" (Judg 5:24) because she had prevailed over Sisera, while Judith, who beheaded Holofernes, is declared blessed "above all the women on earth" (Jdt 13:18). Mary, however, is declared blessed, not for military prowess, but because the child she bears is destined to save his people.

The final words of Elizabeth are particularly significant: "Blessed are you who believed that what was spoken to you by the Lord would be fulfilled" (Luke 1:45). This certainly implies that Mary's biological motherhood derived from her faith in God's word, but it goes far beyond that and matches those passages from the public ministry in which Jesus declares that the ultimate relationship to him is spiritual rather than physical: "whoever does the will of God is my brother and sister and mother" (Mark 3:35). Mary's ultimate beatitude is thus attributed to her exemplary faith.

The Magnificat. After Elizabeth has praised God for what has happened in Mary, it is Mary's turn to proclaim her gratitude for God's gracious gift to her. The *Magnificat* is modeled after the classic biblical hymn of praise in which there is an opening declaration of praise to God, followed by reasons for such gratitude and, in conclusion, a new proclamation of praise.

In the opening statement (Luke 1:46-47), "my soul" and "my spirit" are, in Semitic usage, synonyms for "I." In parallel fashion, God's greatness or magnificence is recognized in the divine work of salvation that is realized in Jesus. These words are appropriate for any follower of Christ but never more so than for Mary.

The first reason for praising God refers to Mary herself who, like Hannah, mother of Samuel (1 Sam 1:11), is conscious of her lowly condition in the presence of God and is therefore radiant with joy when she discovers that this is no obstacle to divine election. In fact, God's favor is so special that people of every age will celebrate her good fortune.

The subsequent reasons for praising God are expressed in more generic terms and could apply to any Christian. In fact, it is very probable that this hymn was composed originally in the early Jewish-Christian community at Jerusalem, to which Mary also belonged, to express their general gratitude for God's mercy. It should be noted that the verbs in Luke 1:48-54 are all in the historical tense, which would indicate that they were written after the resurrection of Jesus to celebrate the salvation that had already been accomplished. In this case, verse 45 would have been inserted when the author of the Gospel attributed and adapted the hymn to Mary.

In this review of God's saving activity, one notes in particular the reversal of for-

tunes that was so obvious to these first Christians as they saw the suffering and dying Messiah revealed as risen Lord. In this sense, the "arrogant" and the "rulers" and the "rich" are cast down, whereas the "lowly" and the "hungry" are noticed and lifted up. This is classic gospel theology that places salvation in the humble reception of God's gift rather than in human effort and pride.

Finally, this wonderful work of salvation in Jesus Christ is declared to be in accordance with God's "promise to our fathers, to Abraham and to his descendants forever" (1:55). In this way, the entire history of salvation is made the subject of this hymn of praise. It all began with God's gracious and unconditional promise to Abraham and reached its climax in the presence and loving sacrifice of Jesus, who is the fulfillment of that promise.

Therefore, the message of the Visitation is not to be sought in an analysis of the details of the story or in the psychology of the participants. Rather, this story is to be recognized as a setting for the *Magnificat*, which is in turn an expression of wonder and praise for the mercy of God revealed in Jesus for all humankind. The fact that this hymn is attributed to Mary suggests most fittingly that every Christian who praises God in these words does so in union with Mary, the perfect disciple.

Pastoral-Liturgical Tradition

Luke's account situates Mary's visit to Elizabeth in the "hill country" of Judea (1:39). Eventually, 'Ain Karim was identified as the precise location, but there is little solid evidence for this tradition.

The feast of the Visitation was first celebrated among the Franciscans in the thirteenth century, and was then extended to the universal Church by Urban VI in 1389 in gratitude for the end of the Western Schism. When the Roman liturgical calendar was reformed in 1969, this feast was transferred from July 2 to May 31 so that, in keeping with the biblical sequence of events, it would follow the Annunciation (March 25) and precede the feast of John the Baptist (June 24).

See: ABRAHAM, JOHN THE BAPTIST, MARY, MESSIAH, PRAISE

DEMETRIUS R. DUMM, O.S.B.

VOICE OF GOD

Old Testament

God's voice *(qôl)* is divine revelation in audible form. "Hearing the voice of God" is a stereotyped expression for true obedience to God. The benefits of such obedience are declared to Abraham, "I will bless you abundantly and make your descendants as countless as the stars of the sky and the sand of the seashore; your descendants shall take possession of the gates of their enemies, and in your descendants all the nations of the earth shall find blessing—all this because you obeyed my command [lit. "my voice"]" (Gen 22:17-18). Through Moses God also promises, "if you hearken to my voice and keep my covenant, you shall be my special possession, dearer to me than all other people" (Exod 19:5). Alternatively, if Israel does not heed God's voice, disaster results in the form of affliction with diseases (Exod 16:26), not seeing the promised land (Num 14:22-23; Josh 5:6), defeat in battle (1 Sam 12:15; 28:18; 2 Kgs 18:12), and death (1 Kgs 20:36).

The paradigmatic revelation of the voice of God was at Sinai. Moses rehearses for Israel, "the LORD spoke to you from the midst of the fire. You heard the sound of the words, but saw no form; there was only a voice. He proclaimed to you his covenant, which he commanded you to keep: the ten commandments" (Deut 4:12-13). Divine encounters always evoke fear. Just as they believed that one could not see God and live (Deut 33:19-20), so too the Israelites feared for their lives as recipients of an auditory revelation, "For what mortal has heard, as we have, the voice of the living God speaking from the midst of fire, and survived?" (Deut 5:26). Thus they charged Moses, "Go closer, you, and hear all that the LORD, our God, will say, and then tell us what the

LORD, our God, tells you; we will listen and obey" (Deut 5:27). Accordingly, Moses would go into the tent of meeting to speak with God and he would hear "the voice addressing him from above the propitiatory on the ark of the commandments, from between the two cherubim" (Num 7:89).

The voice of God is often described as thunder (Exod 19:19; 2 Sam 22:14; Pss 18:14; 29:3; Job 37:2, 4, 5; 40:9). Not only mighty in sound, it is also equated with saving deeds: "Again his voice roars—the majestic sound of his thunder. He does great things beyond our knowing; wonders past our searching out" (Job 37:4-5; see also 1 Sam 7:10; Psalm 29; Isa 30:30-31; Joel 2:11; cf. 1 Kgs 19:11-13).

Isaiah (6:8) and Ezekiel (2:1) received their prophetic call by means of the voice of God. Although the word *qôl* is not always used, divine communication with God's chosen instruments is often expressed in terms of God speaking to the person or the word of God coming to them (e.g., Gen 15:1; Jer 1:2; Jonah 1:1; Mic 1:1; Zech 1:1). A frequent charge of the prophets is that Israel has not obeyed the voice of the Lord (Jer 3:13, 25; 25:30; 40:3; 42:21; Dan 9:10, 14; Zeph 3:2).

Rabbinic Judaism

One concept that developed with the rabbis is that of *bat qôl*. Believing that the holy Spirit departed from Israel with the last prophets, the rabbis maintained that in its place God sent the *bat qôl*, "a daughter of the voice," from heaven. It was not on a par with prophecy or the holy Spirit; the revelation of God in the Torah and prophets was considered closed.

New Testament

At the baptism of Jesus and at the transfiguration, a heavenly voice is heard. That it is to be understood as the voice of God is clear from the message and the context. At Jesus' baptism, the voice from the heavens declares, "You are my beloved Son; with you I am well pleased" (Mark 1:11; Luke 3:22; cf. Matt 3:17). At the transfiguration the voice comes from a cloud, "This is my beloved Son" (Mark 9:7; Matt 17:5; Luke 9:35 has "This is my chosen Son"; see also 2 Pet 1:17-18). It further enjoins, "Listen to him." For the people of the new covenant God's voice is heard through the Son. Obedience to God consists in heeding the voice of Jesus.

Although the Gospel of John has neither the baptism story nor that of the transfiguration, there is a voice from heaven in John 12:28. Jesus prays, "Father, glorify your name" and the voice responds, "I have glorified it and will glorify it again." It is the fourth evangelist who reflects more fully on the importance of heeding the voice of Jesus. In John 5:37-38 Jesus charges the Jewish leaders, "you have never heard his [the Father's] voice nor seen his form, and you do not have his word remaining in you, because you do not believe in the one whom he has sent." The figure Jesus the Good Shepherd illustrates his relationship with believers: "the sheep hear his voice, as he calls his own sheep by name and leads them out . . . the sheep follow him, because they recognize his voice" (John 10:3-4). Before Pilate Jesus declares, "Everyone who belongs to the truth listens to my voice" (John 18:37). The eschatological aspect is highlighted when Jesus proclaims, "Amen, amen, I say to you, the hour is coming and is now here when the dead will hear the voice of the Son of God, and those who hear will live" (John 5:25). As the voice of God in the OT grants life and judges, so in the NT the voice of the Son does the same.

In two key episodes of the Acts of the Apostles a heavenly voice is heard. At his conversion, Paul* heard the voice of the resurrected Jesus saying to him, "Saul, Saul, why are you persecuting me?" (Acts 9:4). Peter, too, heard a voice when he fell into a trance, "Get up, Peter. Slaughter and eat" (Acts 10:13). When Peter objected, it spoke to him a second time, "What God has made clean, you are not to call profane" (Acts 10:15). This revelation leads to the inauguration of the Gentile mission.

The author of Hebrews recalls the Sinai traditions (Heb 3:7-8, 15; 4:7; 12:19, 26), while exhorting his Christian audience to heed the voice of Jesus. Quoting Psalm 95:7-8, he adjures, "Oh, that today you would hear his voice, Harden not your hearts as at the rebellion" (Heb 3:7-8, 15).

Throughout the Book of Revelation voices from heaven issue commands (1:1-11; 16:1; 19:5) and interpret the eschatological happenings (11:15; 12:10-12; 16:17).

See: ABRAHAM, BAPTISM, BLESSING, COVENANT, CURSE, EPIPHANY, EXODUS, FACE OF GOD, FEAR OF GOD, FIRE, HEAVEN, ISRAEL, MOSES, NAME, OBEDIENCE, PROPHET, SPIRIT, TRANSFIGURATION, TRUTH, WORD

BARBARA E. REID, O.P.

VOWS

A vow is a solemn promise made to God to perform some act of devotion or to refrain from some action. Whether public or private, vows are always an act of worship.

Old Testament

The Hebrew root used seems to mean "to separate from profane usage; to consecrate to God." A vow is then an act of worship. It is a conditional promise to give something to God if God first grants some favor: "If God does X for me, then I will do Y." Almost always (Ps 132:2 seems to be an exception), the vows in the OT have a bargaining quality about them.

As Jacob left Bethel for Haran, he promised that if God would protect him on this journey, would give him food, and would bring him back safely, "of everything you give me, I will faithfully return a tenth part to you" (Gen 28:20; 31:13). As Israel was about to enter the land, they faced the king and army of Arad. Israel vowed that if God would deliver this people to them, they would "doom" (consecrate completely to God) them and their cities (Num 21:2-3). In exchange for victory over the Ammonites, Jephthah promised to sacrifice to God whoever first came out of the doors of his house to greet him. When this turned out to be his daughter, he was stricken with grief, but fulfilled his vow (Judg 11:30-39). The childless Hannah promised that if she would bear a child, she would consecrate him to the service of God (1 Sam 1:11; see also Prov 31:2). Absalom, while in Aram, made a vow to worship God in Hebron if God would return him safely to Jerusalem (2 Sam 15:7-8).

Vows then were made above all in situations of need and distress. "I will bring holocausts to your house, to you I fulfill the vows which my lips uttered, and my words promised in my distress" (Ps 66:13-14). The sailors were frightened of the great storm that had come upon them because of Jonah's disobedience, and they sacrificed and made vows to God (Jonah 1:16). Similarly, Jonah, in the belly of the fish, promised to sacrifice to God and fulfill the vows he had made (Jonah 2:10). During the Babylonian attack on Jerusalem, some of its inhabitants forsook Yahweh and offered sacrifices and made vows to the queen of heaven (Jer 44:25). In the psalms, the promise to fulfill vows is often found in contexts of lamentation in which the psalmist had prayed in some way for deliverance (22:26; 50:14; 56:13; 61:6, 9; 65:2; 66:13-14; 76:12; 116:14, 18).

Vows include a variety of things: a tithe (Gen 28:20), conquered peoples and cities (Num 21:2), a person (Judg 11:30-31; 1 Sam 1:11), worship (2 Sam 15:7-8). The most frequent vows seem to have involved the offering of sacrifices. One could vow holocausts (Lev 22:18-20; Ps 66:13) or peace-offerings (Lev 7:16; 22:21-22; Prov 7:14; Mal 1:14; Pss 50:14; 56:13); either could be accompanied by secondary cereal offerings and libations (Num 15:3, 8). Such vows are summarized in Numbers 29:39. Further, certain things could not be the object of vows: (1) things that already belonged to God (the first-born of cattle) or things consecrated ("doomed") to God (Lev 27:26); (2) things offensive to God's holiness, such as revenue from sacred fertility rites (Deut 23:19).

In special cases, one might vow oneself to God for a determined period of time. The vow of a Nazarite and the rules for it are given in Numbers 6:1-21. The nazir was to abstain from wine and all fermented drinks, to allow the hair to grow uncut, and to avoid all contact with dead bodies. At the end of the determined time, prescribed sacrifices were offered, and the nazir could return to normal life. Indications within the OT suggest that the nazir originally represented a life-long call by God (Amos 2:11-12); Samson would represent such a nazir (Judg 13:3-5). While the term is not used, Samuel would also seem to be a life-long nazir, but this was the result of a vow by his mother (1 Sam 1:11). Later, anyone, man or woman, could make a temporary nazir vow (Num 6:2).

Once made, a vow should be fulfilled. The word used in Hebrew for "to fulfill" (some translations, "to repay") a vow is *shillem*, from the same root as *shalom*. It means "to be whole, entire, complete," and indicates that the vow hung in the air incomplete until brought to wholeness by the performance of the vow. Thus fulfilling the vow should not be delayed (Qoh 5:3-4) or left until the day of death (Sir 18:22-23). Later legislation provided that certain objects of vows (persons, animals, house, land) could be redeemed by paying amounts of money determined by law or the judgment of a priest (Lev 27:1-25). Some vows, within strict limitations, could be annulled (Num 30:1-17). Making a vow to God represented a serious commitment and was not to be undertaken lightly (Deut 23:22-24; Prov 20:25).

New Testament

In the NT, a vow is mentioned only two times, both times in Acts of the Apostles. In the first, as Paul is traveling from Corinth back to Antioch, he stops at Cenchreae where "he had his hair cut because he had taken a vow" (Acts 18:18). In the second, after his third missionary journey, Paul has returned to Jerusalem where he joins with four other men and pays the expenses of having their hair cut and offering the purification sacrifices (Acts 21:23-26). Both of these seem to be examples of the nazirite vow (Num 6:1-21). The taking of vows continued as an important part of Jewish religious life as witnessed to by a whole tractate in the Misnah devoted to vows (Nedarim).

See: HOLY/HOLINESS, LAMENT, OATH, REDEMPTION, SACRIFICE

MICHAEL D. GUINAN, O.F.M.

Pastoral-Liturgical Tradition

From the twelfth century until recently, Christian reflection on vows focused primarily on the nature and role of vows of poverty, chastity, and obedience as they shape the lives of canonically-professed religious. Today, however, as a result of both historical research and new developments in philosophy and theology, focus has shifted to "vowing" as an act that originates in the deepest human interiority and may find expression in a plurality of social and ecclesial forms.

When the term "vow" is used in a theological context, at least four distinct levels of meaning may be intended. These are:

(1) An interior decision of total self-giving in response to the call of the Word of God.
(2) An ecclesially-situated, ritually expressed self-offering or consecration of one's life to God.
(3) A public commitment to behave in specific ways and/or to shape one's life according to specific values, as a way of following the gospel of Christ.
(4) A legal contract with a person or community, witnessed formally by the institutional Church and implicitly by God.

In the early history of religious life, these four meanings emerged to prominence more or less sequentially. The desert tradition (for example, the *Life of Antony*) emphasized the *pròthesis* or firm decision as the root of the monks' radical Christian way of life. Gregory of Nyssa and others of the Greek tradition found the center of Christian dedication in *euchè*—a ritual act of self-offering that is both the deepest form of prayer and a vow to God. The theology of "the vows" as public acts binding one to a specified lifestyle developed from the Latin concept of *votum* (vows), which had its roots in Roman notions of social obligation. As religious life became thoroughly institutionalized, the need for a clearly defined contractual formula (to protect both the institution and the individual) came to the fore.

With Vatican Council II, recognition that Christian discipleship is essentially one (rather than a hierarchy in which "vowed" or religious life is superior to lay life) has grounded a renewed theology of Christian vowing. The root of vowing is rediscovered as an exercise of the very root of humanness: namely, the free capacity to give oneself in responsive love to God and human beings. While this root has an essential character of interiority and solitude (so that no human forum can fully judge the nature or quality of another's vowing), it also is intrinsically oriented to social and public expression.

The most profound dimension of the latter is that named as level two above: namely, an ecclesial and ritualized act of self-offering. This is the anthropological ground of each of the events that Roman Catholics identify as sacraments, as well as of the event of canonical religious profession. It is important to recognize, however, that there is not a one-to-one identity between these institutionally-recognized events and the Christian act of vowing. While Roman Catholic theology affirms that God always acts in a sacrament, the *human* commitment manifested in baptism, marriage, holy orders, religious profession, etc., may or may not have the depth of a full interior vow. Moreover, it is possible that other, non-sacramental and non-canonical events (a family resolving a crisis, a decision taken in a basic Christian community, etc.) may in some cases manifest both the fullness of depth and the basic theological character of ecclesial and ritual expression that can qualify them as acts of Christian "vowing."

In sum, references to "vowing" today require careful nuancing. Christian vowing is a profoundly human, ecclesial, and God-centered act that may find expression in a plurality of concrete lifestyles. While at its deepest root the act of vowing does entail a total and permanent self-offering from which the vower cannot turn back without serious spiritual peril, in the complex and rapidly shifting circumstances of modern life it is not uncommon to encounter people who have become convinced that fidelity to their core vowing necessitates significant and unforeseen changes at the level of lifestyle. In light of this, the theology, spirituality, and pastoral care of "vowing" continue to be a growing edge in the Church today.

See: DISCIPLE/DISCIPLESHIP

MARY E. FROHLICH

W

WATCH

To watch over human beings is one of God's functions. As messengers of God, the prophets in the OT and Christian leaders in the NT watch for and warn the people of impending danger. Their watching may also result in an announcement of good news. Jesus' followers must be watchful for his final coming. Such vigilance is intimately linked with prayer.

Old Testament

In antiquity, sentries were stationed on the walls of a city (2 Sam 18:24; Isa 5:2; Cant 5:7), at the city gates (Neh 11:19), or in a watchtower (2 Chr 20:24; Matt 21:33; Mark 12:1) to watch for and warn of approaching danger (Ezek 33:2-6). Watchers guarded flocks (Luke 2:8), fields, and vineyards, particularly during the time of harvest (Job 27:18). Watching was done in shifts. There are references to the morning watch (Exod 14:24; 1 Sam 11:11; Ps 130:6), the middle watch (Judg 7:19), and watches of the night (Pss 90:4; 119:148; Isa 21:8). However vigilant, no human watcher alone could ensure protection: "Unless the LORD guard the city, in vain does the guard keep vigil" (Ps 127:1).

God it is who watches over humanity (Job 7:20; Ps 66:7; Prov 15:3). This task is entrusted to the prophets,* who are frequently dubbed God's "watchmen." Ezekiel describes the word of God that came to him: "I have appointed you a watchman for the house of Israel. When you hear a word from my mouth, you shall warn them for me" (Ezek 3:17). This is a great responsibility. A watcher who fails to sound the warning is the one held responsible for the consequent disaster (Ezek 33:6).

Oftentimes, the message of the prophetic watcher is one of impending punishment for Israel (e.g., Hos 9:8). God's complaint in Jeremiah 6:17-19 is, "When I raised up watchmen for them: 'Hearken to the sound of the trumpet!' they said, 'We will not hearken.' Therefore hear, O nations . . . I bring evil upon this people. . . . Because they heeded not my words, because they despised my law."

At other times, the watchers announce good news, as in Isaiah 52:8, "Hark! Your watchmen raise a cry, together they shout for joy, For they see directly, before their eyes, the LORD restoring Zion." In Isaiah 62:6-7 the watchers stationed on the walls of Jerusalem "are to remind the LORD, take no rest and give no rest to him, until he reestablishes Jerusalem and makes of it the pride of the earth."

There is only one instance of a heavenly watcher in the Bible, although such appear frequently in later Jewish literature. In Daniel 4, the holy sentinel communicates in a dream to King Nebuchadnezzar God's sentence on him, which the prophet Daniel interprets.

New Testament

Frequent warnings are found in the NT to watch out for moral danger. In the Gospels Jesus advises his disciples, "Watch out, guard against the leaven of the Pharisees and the leaven of Herod" (Mark 8:15; Matt 16:6). Paul gives a similar admonition to the Corinthians to watch out not to fall if they think they are standing (1 Cor 10:12). Comparable alerts to the dangers of the present time are found in 1 Corinthians 16:13 and 1 Peter 5:8.

During his ministry, Jesus was watched by his opponents for any misstep. "The scribes and the Pharisees watched him closely to see if he would cure on the sabbath so that they might discover a reason to accuse him" (Luke 6:7; see also Luke 14:1; 20:20). At his crucifixion, a centurion kept watch over Jesus (Matt 27:54) and sentinels were placed at his tomb (Matt 27:36). Ironically, these watchers do not perceive rightly the one upon whom they have fixed their attention.

The most frequent references to watchfulness in the NT are exhortations not to be caught off guard at Christ's coming. Because no one knows the day or the hour, one must be constantly vigilant (Mark 13:32-37; Matt 24:36-44; 25:13; Luke 21:36; Rev 3:2). One must beware of "carousing and drunkenness and the anxieties of daily life" because they make the heart "drowsy" (Luke 21:34). Paul advises sleepless sobriety, the armor of faith, love, and hope, and mutual encouragement while awaiting "that day" (1 Thess 5:4-11). One is to pray while watching (Luke 21:36; Col 4:2; Eph 6:18), as Jesus does at Gethsemane (Matt 26:41; Mark 14:38; Luke 22:46).

Like the prophets of the OT, Christian leaders are also God's watchers over the people. In his farewell speech to the elders at Miletus, Paul exhorts, "Keep watch over yourselves and over the whole flock of which the holy Spirit has appointed you overseers, in which you tend the church of God that he acquired with his own blood"

(Acts 20:28). In the final chapter of Hebrews is a similar exhortation, "Obey your leaders and defer to them, for they keep watch over you and will have to give an account, that they may fulfill their task with joy and not with sorrow, for that would be of no advantage to you" (13:17).

See: CITY, DAY OF THE LORD, GOOD NEWS, HARVEST, HOPE, PAROUSIA, PRAYER, PROPHET, TIME

BARBARA E. REID, O.P.

Pastoral-Liturgical Tradition

The early community remembered that Jesus kept watch and invited his followers to do the same. Keeping watch, in memory of Jesus, was more than remaining awake from the setting until the rising of the sun. Rather, as J. Ellul asserts, keeping watch is indissolubly linked with prayer, for "prayer is an act of vigilance and vigilance is a consequence of prayer" *(Prayer and Modern Man)*.

The first followers of Jesus were Jewish and calculated the day from sunset to sunset. Particular practices in the early community, however, contributed to an evolution in their perspective on the beginning of the day and on their practice of keeping watch. One determinative practice was associated with the Passover of Jesus. Jesus died in a Passover context. Scholars conjecture that after the death of Jesus, when the Jews celebrated the annual Passover meal, Jesus' followers fasted, keeping vigil through the night (Thomas Talley, *The Origins of the Liturgical Year*). Toward dawn, they may have celebrated Eucharist.

The rituals for remembering the death of Jesus offered an alternative to the Jewish custom of reckoning sunset as the time of beginning. Sunset did not, in this instance, signal the beginning of the feast, but a time of fasting, prayer, and vigil until the dawn. Although Christian Eucharist was at first an evening phenomenon, with increasing frequency it and baptism were celebrated at dawn. The symbolism of the rising sun, with its overtones of resurrection and new creation, easily wed itself to these rites.

When the annual *pascha* moved to Sunday, the preparatory fast and vigil moved to the Sabbath. This institutionalized the first Sabbath fast and prepared later generations to observe a Saturday vigil in anticipation of Sunday morning Eucharist. It is also possible that the primitive paschal vigil provided the model for the ember days. These four fasts, falling every three months through the year, could have been a primitive attempt to shape the year with regularly scheduled commemorations of Christ's death. Although unambiguous evidence for these quarter-tense days does not surface until the fourth century, they may have been of primitive origins. The distinctive characteristic of these observances was the Saturday night vigil, culminating in Sunday morning Eucharist.

The custom of praying through the night has many third-century witnesses. Clement of Alexandria (d. ca. 215) exhorts people to pray during the night as a sign of eschatological hope in Christ's return, "At night we ought to rise often and bless God. For blessed are they who watch for him, and so make themselves like the angels, whom we call 'watchers'" (*Pedagogue*, 2.9). The *Apostolic Tradition* (ca. 215) of Hippolytus calls believers to prayer at midnight and at cockcrow (ca. 2:30 a.m.); Tertullian (d. ca. 225) speaks of midnight prayer (*Concerning Prayer*, 29); Origen (d. 254) knows of prayer at night (*Concerning Prayer*, 12.2); and Cyprian (d. 254) encourages people to pray through the night (*The Lord's Prayer*, 36). Many of these exhortations to night prayer were practical suggestions for fulfilling the dominical command to pray always. The call to ceaseless prayer was the impetus behind every injunction to pray, no matter what the time of day.

Much of the early evidence about keeping watch or praying at night concerns individuals, and does not prove that communities kept watch together. The evidence for communal vigils before the fourth century is limited. Tertullian (*To His Wife*, 2.2) speaks of "nocturnal assemblies," and the *Apocryphal Acts of the Martyrdom of St. Saturninus of Toulouse* (ca. 300 CE) testifies to vigils in honor of martyrs. By the fourth century communal vigils were widespread. Some were connected to particular feasts, in imitation of the annual paschal vigil. Besides these particular vigils, Jerusalem had a weekly Saturday vigil in preparation for Sunday (Egeria 24.8). The people of Cappadocia occasionally celebrated night vigils (Basil, Letter 207).

Monastic communities introduced vigils into their daily cursus of prayer. Originally such communities celebrated only morning and evening prayer. Some communities, like those of Scetis in Lower Egypt, celebrated one office at cockcrow; this was not so much a vigil as their equivalent to morning prayer (Robert Taft, *The Liturgy of the Hours in East and West*). Eventually monastic communities combined this early morning prayer with a later morning prayer. The earlier prayer, celebrated during the night, took on more of a vigil character; it is alternately called nocturns, vigils, or matins. Besides this regular prayer at night, monastic communities like those of Palestine added all night vigils on Friday.

As vigils were becoming an ordinary part of the daily monastic cursus, the number of public vigils tied to major festivals increased. The Easter Vigil, the "mother of all vigils" (Augustine, Sermon 219), which traces its origins back to the dawn of Christianity, was complemented by a Pentecost vigil (fourth century), a Christmas vigil (fifth century), and an Ascension vigil (eighth century). These and innumerable vigils for local saints and feasts involved the laity as well as members of monastic communities and clergy in nights of prayer, fasting, and song. Many vigils, however, eventually lost their all night character, and were reduced to evening prayer sometimes with the addition of a vigil Mass. This ritual reduction yet witnesses to the ancient tradition of calculating the beginning of the liturgical day from sunset (Vespers) to sunset (Vespers).

The central Christian mystery is the death and resurrection of Jesus. The cycle of darkness and light is one metaphor that the Christian community has adopted for entering this mystery. While Christians put special emphasis on the dawn as a symbol of resurrection and thus the traditional time for Eucharist and baptism, the setting of the sun is yet an important marker for Christians, calling them to watch hopefully through the darkness that Christ will be revealed in each new day and in his return at the end of time.

See: FEASTS, HOPE, PRAYER

EDWARD FOLEY, CAPUCHIN

WATER

Water can cause destruction as well as life and cleansing, lending itself as a symbol of God's judgment as well as of life and forgiveness. The NT points to the fulfillment of this symbol in Christ as source of living water/Spirit through the baptismal waters.

Old Testament

Water, especially as the ocean or in floods, can be destructive and chaotic. Examples are the creation account (Genesis 1–2) and the great flood (Genesis 6–9). God overcame the chaotic primeval waters over the earth (1:1-10). He unleashed the deluge as a punishment for sin and then brought it to an end, saving Noah, the Hebrew ancestor.

Water as a Source of Life. It can also be a source of life and therefore a gift of God as author of life. God gave the first humans the garden of Eden with its life-giving streams (Gen 2:10-14). Both meanings can be simultaneous. When God brought Israel out of Egypt and across the sea, he drowned Pharoah and his chariots in the water and thus rescued his people Israel (Exod 15:5). The crossing of the dangerous waters of the Jordan enabled God's people to enter the promised land of covenant (Joshua 3–4). The miraculous crossing of the Jordan by the people confirmed their role in new beginnings of Israel. As a gift, rain water can be taken away in punishment for sin and then restored when repentance takes place (Deut 11:14-17). Water as

life-source symbolizes God's creative presence. Thus Jeremiah announced, "Two evils have my people done: they have forsaken me, the source of living waters; they have dug themselves cisterns, broken cisterns that hold no water" (2:13).

Water as Cleansing and Purifying. As a means of cleansing and purification, water also represented a deeper meaning when used in accord with God's command. The enormous bronze laver before the Temple altar of sacrifice served this function as well as being a continual reminder to the people (Exod 30:17-21). Water was frequently used to obtain ritual purification before taking part in community or personal religious ceremonies (see Num 19:11-22). However, full purification and forgiveness of sin could only come through inner repentance and God's special action (Isa 1:16). Thus the psalmist prayed, "Cleanse me of sin with hyssop, that I may be purified; wash me and I shall be whiter than snow" (51:9).

The prophets used water symbols as they looked to the future for a time of full forgiveness: "There shall be open to the house of David and to the inhabitants of Jerusalem, a fountain to purify from sin and uncleanness" (Zech 13:1). This purification involved the action of the Spirit and a transformed heart (Ezek 36:25-26). The future temple will have a mysterious hidden water source underneath its altar. This will become a continually growing stream that will flow down into the Dead Sea and make it a new garden of Eden (Ezekiel 47).

New Testament

The Synoptic Gospels. The Gospels signal a new beginning in salvation history that takes place at the Jordan river. John the Baptist is dressed like Elijah (Matt 4:4; Mark 1:6) to identify him with God's chosen herald who was expected to return to announce the Day of the Lord (Mal 3:24). In the role of Elijah, John at the Jordan called Israel to a new beginning by requiring repentance accompanied by confession of sins and baptism (Matt 3:1-6; Mark 1:4-5;

Luke 3:3). It is not enough to be circumcised children of Abraham (Matt 3:7-11); a new beginning, like the baptism of Gentile proselytes, is necessary.

However, the Gospels look back on the baptismal waters of John as only a preparation for a new baptism of water infused with the holy Spirit and mediated by Jesus. John says, "He [Jesus] will baptize you with the holy Spirit and fire" (Matt 3:11; see Mark 1:8; Luke 3:16; John 1:33). Except for the miraculous calming of the storm when Jesus walked on water (4:35-41; 6:45-52), Mark makes little further use of water symbolism. He does state in effect that the water purifications of the OT are no longer necessary (7:2-3, 19). The longer ending of Mark carries Jesus' words about the necessity of his baptism (16:16), but this is a second-century addition.

Matthew, however, has the whole gospel drama lead to a final mountain enthronement scene where Jesus commands his disciples to go out, teach the whole world, and baptize disciples: "Go, therefore, and make disciples of all nations, baptizing them in the name of the Father, and of the Son, and of the holy Spirit" (28:16-20). Thus, after Jesus' resurrection and at his command, water takes on a new meaning of incorporation into Jesus' own experience at his baptism where the Spirit descended upon him and the voice from heaven declared him to be God's son (3:16-20).

Acts of the Apostles. Luke's Acts of the Apostles contains frequent references to water in connection with the holy Spirit and baptism. On Pentecost day, Peter told the assembled crowds, "Repent and be baptized every one of you, in the name of Jesus Christ for the forgiveness of your sins; and you will receive the gift of the holy Spirit" (3:38). The expression "in the name of Jesus Christ" is an old baptismal formula.

Philip the evangelist baptized Samaritans (8:13-16). Luke here separates water and the holy Spirit, for Peter and John later came to lay on hands so that they might receive the Spirit. Perhaps this separation was intended to bring out communion and continuity with the Jerusalem community. Philip also led an Ethiopian eunuch into water for baptism (8:38-39). Ananias baptized Paul (9:17; 22:16), and Peter ordered Cornelius and his Gentile friends to be baptized after the holy Spirit fell on them following Peter's sermon (10:44-49). Paul "rebaptized" former disciples of John the Baptist who had only received the latter's baptism (19:1-5). The sequence or separation of the holy Spirit and water baptism in Acts is probably not a logical order but is meant simply to indicate the various aspects of the whole baptismal process.

The Gospel of John. The Fourth Gospel makes extensive use of water symbolism. At the Cana wedding feast, obedience to Jesus' word makes possible the changing of water into wine. The six jars of water represent the old purification waters of the OT. The new wine, never tasted before, signifies the Spirit made available through Jesus' "hour" of death and resurrection (1:1-11). Jesus told Nicodemus that he must be born again of water and the Spirit in order to enter the reign of God (3:5). This signified a whole new beginning and lifestyle under the Spirit. Jesus asked a Samaritan woman for water and led her to understand that he would give a new water, the Spirit, which would completely quench the thirst of believers and bring eternal life (4:1-26).

At the feast of Tabernacles, which recalled God's miraculous gift of water to his people in the desert, Jesus promised that he would be the new source of living water. The evangelist explains that Jesus was speaking of the Spirit who will come after Jesus' glorification (7:37-39). Jesus tells the man born blind to go and wash in the pool of Siloam. Obedience to Jesus' word thus gave water a new power to cure the blind man and also to provide new vision to all who believe in Jesus (9:1-41). Jesus' washing of his disciples' feet is a sign of hospitable welcome into his community as well as an indication of forgiveness and humble service which Jesus' disciples are to continue (13:1-20).

After Jesus' death, the evangelist understood that the water and blood issuing from Jesus' side was a very special sign. It meant that his death was a sacrifice, since flowing blood was necessary for this. Jesus' sacrifice was that of a new paschal lamb offered for the sins of the world as John the Baptist had foretold (19:34-37; 1:29, 36). The water from Jesus' side was a sign of the fulfilment of Jesus' promise to provide a new source of water, the holy Spirit (7:37-39). It was also a sign of the fulfillment of OT prophecy of a new fountain of water and forgiveness through one who was pierced (Zech 12:10; John 19:37). The essence of Jesus' sacrifice was obedience to his Father's word (19:28). In turn, obedience to Jesus, as in the Cana sign, will enable disciples to accomplish the same results in themselves and in others.

See: BAPTISM, CLEAN/UNCLEAN, CREATION, FLOOD, JOHN THE BAPTIST, LIFE, SPIRIT

JOSEPH A. GRASSI

Pastoral-Liturgical Tradition

When the turn of a tap brings water in abundance, it takes a leap of the imagination to understand why water figures so prominently in Scripture (it is the natural resource cited most frequently) and to appreciate how it has functioned and can continue to function as such a powerful symbol of life, wisdom, fruitfulness, prosperity, and, indeed, of God's gracious favor. Yet the Scriptures are the product of Near Eastern peoples whose constant experience was that of insufficient water supply, of infrequent rainfall, and even occasional droughts. These people were necessarily preoccupied by water because they lived always in the fragile space between thirst and satisfaction, aridity and fruitfulness, the desert and the springs. In their experience water was blessing and curse, misfortune and benefice, a source of physical cleanliness and refreshment. Its absence spelled death.

Water participates in the *tremendum et fascinans,* the fearful and the fascinating, because it reveals the God of Mystery who is its source and faithful dispenser. It is thus a many-layered natural symbol of the sacred whose liturgical uses include blessings, dedications, exorcisms, anointings, burials, ceremonial cleansing, and acts of hospitality and servanthood.

Those who would try to recover the symbolic power of water might well first remember that water remains a matter of life and death for millions in places like Ethiopia, Somalia, the Sudan, and Chad. The multivalency of water, given lyric expression in the Blessing of Water at the Easter Vigil, takes on a new symbolic expression when the natural symbol itself is reappropriated.

See: LIFE

KATHLEEN HUGHES, R.S.C.J.

WAY

In both the OT and the NT "the way" is a common figure of speech for many aspects of human life and conduct, and the activity of God. As such, it is part of some of the most central religious statements contained in the Bible. Still, the varied nuances and insights represented by "the way" are veiled by its literal meanings. The significance of each occurrence of the word must be determined from an examination of the context in which it appears. In the pastoral-liturgical tradition, "the way" becomes a metaphor for the Christian Life understood as a journey.

Old Testament

"The way" translates several Hebrew words that have a range of meaning. It is common to refer to the concept's literal sense (way as spatially and physically conceived, i.e., a road) as distinct from its figurative use (way as "custom, conduct, behavior, venture"). But with some words it is often difficult to distinguish a physical sense completely from a figurative one in an actual text. In practice, it is best to regard these words on a spectrum that ranges from the literal to the figurative. Sometimes both aspects are in view in the one occurrence.

The most common term in Hebrew for way is *derek,* occurring some seven hundred times in the OT. Usually its usage is figurative, referring to various aspects of human and animal activity (conduct of life: Josh 1:8; Job 17:9; Ps 37:5, 7, 23; the habits of creatures: Prov 30:19; Gen 18:11; 31:35; moral conduct: 1 Kgs 2:4; 2 Chr 27:6; Pss 5:9; 50:23). But even in a more literal rendering of the term it often designates the movement or direction on a road, rather than the road itself (Num 21:4; Deut 1:19, 40). By way of exception, there are also some texts where *derek* probably means "power, dominion," rather than "way" (Hos 10:13; Jer 3:13; Prov 8:22; 31:3).

The next most important word is *'orah,* often translated as "path," which appears frequently in synonymous parallelism with *derek* (Gen 49:17; Prov 2:8; 3:6; 9:15). But this word is not simply to be equated with *derek.* It denotes the route taken (Pss 8:9; 19:6; 142:4; Isa 33:8) and, more figuratively, the condition or state of the one on the road (Job 8:13; 13:27; 19:8; 34:11; Prov 3:6). In the latter sense, *'orah* is used for the expression "way of life" (Prov 2:19; 5:6; 10:17; 15:24; Ps 16:11; see also Prov 12:28) or "way of righteousness, justice" (Prov 2:8, 13; 8:20; 12:28; 17:23; Isa 40:14). There are also paths of evil (Prov 22:25; Ps 17:4).

Less frequently used words are *ma'gāl,* "track," and *nĕtîbâ (nātîb),* "path." The former has the figurative sense of a course or habit of life that can be determinative of good or evil for the person (Prov 2:9, 15, 18; 4:11, 26; 5:6, 21; Ps 23:3; Isa 26:7; 59:8). The latter, like *'orah,* can refer figuratively to one's condition or state in life (Job 19:8; 30:13; Pss 119:105; 142:4) and can have moral overtones (Prov 1:15; 3:17; 7:25; 8:20; Job 24:13; Isa 59:8; Jer 6:16). Another word, *mĕsillā,* usually means "raised way, highway"; but in a few instances it refers to the paths of stars (Judg 5:20) or locusts (Joel 2:8), and to personal conduct (Prov 16:17). Other words, such as *hûs* ("the outside;

street") and *šûq* ("street") are always used in their literal sense.

In the discussion that follows it is the more figurative understanding of these terms that is important, and much of what is said will be based mainly on the various uses of *derek*—given the overwhelming number of times it occurs.

In the earlier biblical period way (mostly *derek*) generally represented one's undertakings or direction in life, either self-determined (Josh 1:8) or as set by others (1 Sam 18:24; 24:20). Usually it is without any moral implications. In the Psalms, on the other hand, the words for way take on the notion of one's moral conduct or behavior (Pss 1:1; 25:4, 8, 10; 37:5, 14, 23; 101:2, 6; 119:1) and appear in contexts that ask for divine guidance on one's life (Pss 25:4; 37:5). There is a choice involved, since an alternate way, that of the wicked, is also possible (Pss 1:6; 37:7; 119:104, 128; 146:9).

In the Wisdom literature, Proverbs develops the idea of the individual's way, that is, the complex of choices and actions that determine one's life. The heart is the origin of one's way (16:9; 23:19) and thought should be given to the consequences of embarking on the way (4:19; 14:14; 16:17; 21:29); one can easily be deceived (14:12; 16:25). Instruction is necessary and highly esteemed in Proverbs for understanding the way (4:10-14; 6:20-23; 15:10). Wisdom promises life to those who receive her instruction and "keep her ways" (8:32). Again, choice is a prominent reality since there are two basic ways that present themselves to the individual: the way of justice and wisdom that leads to life and peace or the way of evil and folly that leads to death (2:9, 12-15, 20; 11:20; 13:6; 28:10; see also Pss 1:6; 101:2; Jer 18:11). Among the prophets Ezekiel emphasizes the possibility and need for individuals to turn from evil ways and return to God (3:18-19; 18:25, 29, 30; 24:14; 33:17, 20).

Prominent in the early biblical narratives, the way refers to the Exodus (Exod 13:21; 23:20) and to the divine protection and guidance along that journey (Josh 24:17). Here, the way is God's alone, and is not one humanly determined. Nonetheless, the people do rebel against God's way (Exod 32:8). The journey of the people on God's way recurs in some collective psalms (Pss 44:19; 81:14; 95:10). Another aspect of this is that the individual's way should be oriented toward the community and its prosperity (Pss 1:1; 101:6; 119:1). On the other hand, the "community" of the wicked will suffer the consequences of their ways (Pss 1:4-6; 146:9). Similarly, in Proverbs, one does not follow one's way alone (Prov 21:16, 29).

The prophets address the people to point out their evil ways in the hope they will repent (Jer 4:18; 5:4-5; 6:16; 10:2). Despite the people's sins, Jeremiah has hope in a future where God will give the people "one way" (32:39). Ezekiel also speaks of the ways of the people that call down divine judgment (7:3-4; 36:17); but he sees a time when they will finally come to loathe their ways (36:31). The way of the Exodus reappears in Second Isaiah as a promise of return from exile (43:16, 19; 48:15; 51:10). But this physical return also implies an interior return to God's ways (55:6-9). Finally, in Deuteronomy the way is the Exodus (1:31, 33; 8:2). But this forms a backdrop against which is displayed a deeper sense of the way, which is the following of God's command (5:32-33; 8:6; 11:22). The physical journey is assured only by guarding the ways of the heart in obedience.

When used concerning God, the way can mean either God's own ways of acting or the ways that God teaches humanity to go. But ambiguity arises since this distinction is not always clear in texts. The latter sense is found where divine help is acknowledged in prayerful petition or thanksgiving (Gen 24:27, 48; 28:20; 35:3). The Psalms, especially, recognize the need for divine help on the way (Pss 91:11; 107:7; 119:26; 139:3, 24). The same idea is also found where divine approval is awaited for something already done or which accompanies an individual (God "makes prosper / successful," as in Gen 24:21; Judg 18:5; 1 Sam 18:14; or God can hinder or change one's way, as

in Num 22:22; Ps 107:40). Way is almost synonymous with command in some texts (Jer 7:23; Pss 18:22; 119:15; Job 23:11). But here the meaning becomes ambiguous. God's own ways are more clearly indicated when there is an explicit or implied contrast with human ways (Deut 32:4; Job 26:14; 40:19; Isa 55:8-9; Ezek 18:25).

THOMAS P. MCCREESH, O.P.

New Testament

"Way" (generally, *hodos*) appears in the NT in the literal sense but can describe divine or human reasoning and actions. The ways of God are unsearchable (Rom 11:33), yet just and true (Rev 15:3). Ruin and misery characterize the way of unredeemed humankind who know not the way of peace (Rom 3:16-17; see also Acts 13:10; 14:16; Heb 3:10). Timothy will remind the Corinthians of Paul's ways in Christ, which he teaches everywhere in every church (1 Cor 4:17), and Paul introduces his treatment of love with "But I shall show you a still more excellent way" (1 Cor 12:31).

All four Gospels provide a similar OT description of John the Baptist's ministry, "Behold, I am sending my messenger ahead of you; he will prepare your way. A voice of one crying in the desert: 'Prepare the way of the Lord, make straight his paths'" (Mark 1:2-3; par.; see also Matt 11:10; Luke 1:76; 7:27). The Synoptics report the ironical flattery of Jesus as truthfully teaching the way of God (Mark 12:13-17; par.).

Mark probably initiates the theological understanding of the way to Jerusalem, for Jesus goes ahead, and the disciples follow in amazement and fear. Jesus then predicts for the Twelve his passion for the third time (Mark 10:32-34). The story of Bartimaeus, right before the entry into Jerusalem, furthers this understanding because after the cure Mark writes, "Immediately he [Bartimaeus] received his sight and followed him [Jesus] on the way" (Mark 10:52).

According to Matthew, on their mission the Twelve are not to go the way of the Gentiles but only to the Jews (Matt 10:5). Jesus teaches that the gate is wide and the way broad that leads to destruction, and many enter through it, but narrow the gate and constricted the way that leads to life, and few find it (Matt 7:13-14; see also Luke 13:24; Acts 16:17). Later, Jesus admonishes the high priests and elders because John the Baptist came in the way of righteousness and they did not believe him, but tax collectors and prostitutes believed (Matt 21:32).

"Way" and travel motifs (e.g., Luke 24:47; Acts 1:8) permeate the whole of Luke-Acts, for the mission of Jesus and of his disciples brings them to many places. Jesus guides our feet on the way of peace (Luke 1:79), and his journey to Jerusalem (Luke 9:51–19:28) and to his subsequent passion, death, and resurrection functions as an example for Christians and includes much didactic material for the disciples. This journey imitates the Exodus (see Luke 9:31, 51) and Moses' leading the people to the promised land. Twice in short passion narratives Jesus appears as "leader" (archēgos).

Luke says of Jesus' resurrection, "You have made known to me the paths of life" (Acts 2:28 [Ps 16:11]), and names Jesus "leader of life" (Acts 3:15). Jesus was exalted to God's right hand as "leader and savior to grant Israel repentance and forgiveness of sins" (Acts 5:31). Paul's journey to Jerusalem (Acts 20:22-24; 21:13-14) and then to Rome (Acts 19:21; 23:11) are modeled on that of Jesus. In fact, Luke calls Christianity "the Way" (Acts 9:2; 16:17; 18:25-26; 19:9, 23; 22:4; 24:14, 22; cf. 8:39).

In two Lucan stories, "The Walk to Emmaus" (Luke 24:13-35) and "Philip and the Ethiopian Eunuch" (Acts 8:25-40), "way" plays a dominant role. The first story reminds one of the Eucharist: service of the word and communion itself. In both stories, as the characters move along the way, they are joined by someone who explains that the Scriptures are fulfilled in the Christ-event; each journey then stops and there is the recognition of Jesus in the breaking of bread and in the baptism of the eunuch; Jesus and Philip then miraculously disappear. So our Christian journey is guided by the Scriptures fulfilled in Jesus still present

in them and in the breaking of bread, and a true understanding of the Scriptures leads to baptism.

Several interpretations are offered of Jesus' statement "I am the way and the truth and the life. No one comes to the Father except through me" (John 14:6). Most probably, the emphasis falls on "the way" since this accords best with the rest of the verse and as a response to Thomas' question in verse 5. Thus, Jesus is the way because he is the revelation of the Father and so "the truth" according to which the Spirit of truth "will lead" (hodēgēsei) the disciples (John 16:13) and through which "life" is obtained. Much the same idea appears in John 10:9: "I am the gate. Whoever enters through me will be saved."

The author of Hebrews writes of our access to God, "Therefore, brothers and sisters, since through the blood of Jesus we have confidence of entrance into the sanctuary by the new and living way he opened for us through the veil, that is, his flesh . . ." (Heb 10:19-22; see also 4:14-16; 6:19-20; 9:6-8, 11-28). Whether "flesh" refers to "way" or the "veil," Jesus, our high priest, by his sacrificial death, removed all barriers between humankind and God.

A person unstable in all of his or her ways is double-minded and should expect nothing from God (Jas 1:7-8), but whoever brings sinners back from an erroneous way will save their souls from death and cover a multitude of sins (Jas 5:20). The author of 2 Peter refers to Christianity or the gospel as "the way of truth" (2 Pet 2:2) and accuses false teachers of abandoning the true way and following the way of Balaam, who accepted payment for wrongdoing but was rebuked and prevented from his madness by a mute beast (2 Pet 2:15-16; see also Jude 11). It would have been better for these false teachers not to have known the way of righteousness than to turn away from its holy commandment (2 Pet 2:21).

Judas guides (Acts 1:16: hodēgos) those who arrested Jesus. Jesus himself calls the Pharisees "blind guides" (Matt 23:16-24; see also 15:14; Rom 2:19-23) probably because of their erroneous teachings. On the other hand, the Lamb leads the martyrs to springs of life-giving water (Rev 7:17).

See: BAPTISM, BREAD, DEATH, DESERT, EXODUS, JERUSALEM, LIFE, MINISTRY, MISSION, PASSION, RESURRECTION, TEACH/TEACHING, TRUTH, VEIL

ROBERT F. O'TOOLE, S.J.

Pastoral-Liturgical Tradition

The Christian Life as a Pilgrimage. The term "way" (Latin *via*) signifies a road or path or route, and therefore implies the ideas of movement, travel, voyage, and progress. In Christian usage, it suggests that the spiritual life be symbolized as a journey or pilgrimage. Indeed, as a means of describing the unique qualities, obstacles, and ends of the Christian life, few metaphors have been more popular in Christian tradition than that of pilgrimage. Augustine's *City of God* and John Bunyan's *Pilgrim's Progress* (1678), however much they differed in other ways, both used pilgrimage as their principal image. Both meant to suggest at least three things by using it. The first is that the Christian is an alien in this world. (The Latin word *peregrinus*, used by Augustine and translated into English as "pilgrim," literally means "foreigner" or "stranger.") The second is that this world is not ultimately real, and its goods, which are few, are proximate rather than ultimate. The third is that the Heavenly City—itself a metaphor for salvation or beatitude—is the supreme end and happiness of the pilgrim. The popularity of both books is persuasive testimony to how deeply shared were these assumptions by Christians in pre- and early-modern Europe.

The Way of the Pilgrim: Religious Journeys. The religious journey, or pilgrimage, was used as a way to ritualize or actualize the Augustinian theological view of life-as-pilgrimage. (However, the practice of pilgrimage, that is, of a religious journey to holy places, is actually common to Islam, Hinduism, and Christianity.) In Christianity, pilgrimages were undertaken to see the places (e.g., the Holy Sepulcher) associated with Christ, Mary, and the apostles; to venerate the saints

at shrines that preserved their physical remains; to gain the intercessory help of the saints or to do penance (sometimes involuntarily). Already in the third century, pilgrims began to travel to Jerusalem and to other parts of Syro-Palestine. In the West, Rome quickly gained a place of preeminence as a pilgrimage site, largely because of its unrivaled collection of relics, including, purportedly, the remains of Peter, Paul, and many third-century martyrs. Beginning in the ninth century, Santiago de Compostela (Spain), alleged to be the site of St. James' burial tomb, emerged as the second great pilgrim goal in the Middle Ages, while Lourdes and its curative waters have enjoyed unparalleled popularity in the last two centuries. While open to abuse and harshly criticized by churchmen of the caliber of Jerome and Erasmus, pilgrimage, involving as it did suffering and hardship for the sake of penance and worship, was an effective way for the laity and clerics alike to satisfy the ascetical appetite.

The Two Ways: Active and Contemplative. Whether *theoria* (lit. "watching") or *praxis* (action, practice) is at the core of the ideal life is a question with deep roots in pre-Christian Greek philosophy. Most Greek philosophers in the Hellenistic era made supreme the life of contemplative vision and discouraged or even disparaged the life of action and politics. Because of the impact of Greek philosophy (especially of Neoplatonism) on early Christianity, this dichotomous and hierarchical vision had an enormous impact on the Church's theology and life. Nowhere is this more evident than in the writings of Clement (d. 215) and Origen (d. ca. 254). Origen maintained that, before Adam's sin, the unfallen intellect was entirely consumed in contemplating God the Father. In this way, the life of *praxis* was interpreted as the result of sin. While both Clement and Origen encouraged works of charity, it is quite clear that the life devoted primarily or exclusively to prayer is the more eminent. This is quite evident in Origen's influential interpretation of Jesus' visit to Bethany (Luke 10:38-42), when

Jesus praises Mary, for Origen the symbol of the contemplative life, over Martha, the type of the active life. While most forms of organized asceticism have made some provision for the practice of charity, the rise of monasticism in the fourth century institutionalized the Origenistic privileging of contemplation over action and assured its triumph for roughly another millennium. Over the succeeding seven centuries and even to our own day, the relationship of action and contemplation has become very complex. Nonetheless, the general trend has been toward a reversal and even criticism of the ancient hierarchy.

The Three Spiritual Ways: Purgative, Illuminative, Unitive. The purgative, illuminative, and unitive ways are three stages or orientations in the spiritual life usually said to culminate in union with the divine and, for some, deification *(theosis)*. The classic expression of the three ways is found in the writings of Pseudo-Dionysius (ca. 500). Though probably written by a Syrian monk in the early sixth century, the Dionysian writings were attributed in the sixth century to an Athenian follower of Paul (Acts 17:34), and the ascription was not seriously challenged until the fifteenth century.

While many medieval theologians considered the three ways to be simultaneous activities, Dionysius thought of them as successive stages of mystical progress. As the terms themselves clearly suggest, the mystical aspirant seeks to purify himself or herself of sin in the purgative phase, to achieve enlightenment and virtue in the illuminative stage, and to realize union with God in the final, unitive stage. Medieval writers, like the thirteenth-century Carthusian Hugh of Balma, would correlate these stages with different categories of seekers: beginners, proficients, and the perfect. Whether mystical experience begins in the illuminative or only in the unitive stage is an issue on which there is much variety in the tradition. Because of its putative subapostolic origin, the Dionysian corpus exerted a profound influence on the subsequent history of spirituality, and the purgative-illuminative-unitive scheme became the starting point for many medieval and modern mystical treatises.

Pastoral Note. There is obviously a considerable richness and diversity associated with the use in Christian tradition of the term "way." Nonetheless, there is one assumption that has always governed it use, namely, that the Christian life is one of perpetual movement, struggle, labor, suffering, and imperfection rather than of rest, triumph, sinlessness, peace, or satisfaction. So pervasive has this assumption been that many in the tradition have simply said that to be Christian is to be "on the way" *(in via)*.

See: APOSTLE, JERUSALEM, JESUS CHRIST, MARY, PETER, PILGRIMAGE, SALVATION

KEVIN MADIGAN

WEAKNESS

In the Hebrew and Greek bibles there are several words that signify weaknesses of one kind or another. In the OT these terms are often used to mean weakness in a physical sense. Frequently, however, the OT translates these words as "to stumble," which can be understood either in a physical or a moral sense. Less often, the OT uses weakness to refer to sickness or poverty. In the NT this word group is sometimes used in a physical sense, but more often it either refers to the human condition, sickness, moral weakness, or is used figuratively for poverty.

Old Testament

Physical Weakness. Perhaps the most obvious use of these terms is when OT authors use weakness in the physical sense. In 2 Chronicles there is a story about Ephraimite leaders who help captives who have been left behind by some soldiers: "All of them who were naked they clothed from the booty; they clothed them, put sandals on their feet, gave them food and drink, anointed them, and all who were weak they set on asses" (2 Chr 28:15). In a similar fashion one reads about the blacksmith who works so hard fashioning false gods that he "is hungry and weak, drinks no water and becomes exhausted" (Isa 44:12). The question Moses asks of those sent to scout Canaan also suggests that weakness is understood in a physical sense: "Are the people living there strong or weak, few or many?" (Num 13:18).

To Stumble. Translators often suggest that this word group means "to stumble." At times this is used in a physical sense. "The swift cannot flee, nor the hero escape: There in the north, on the Euphrates bank they stumble and fall" (Jer 46:6). "The many slain, the heaping corpses, the endless bodies to stumble upon!" (Nah 3:3). At other times these words have the overtone of moral failing. "You shall stumble in the day, and the prophets shall stumble with you at night" (Hos 4:5). Ephraim stumbles in his guilt, and Judah stumbles with them" (Hos 5:5). "For the just man falls seven times and rises again, but the wicked stumble to ruin" (Prov 24:16). In criticizing the priests, the prophet Malachi says, "You have turned aside from the way, and caused many to falter by your instruction" (Mal 2:8).

Sickness. These words suggesting weakness can also be used to refer to sickness. Antiochus writes, "Now that I am ill, I recall with affection the esteem and good will you bear me. On returning from the region of Persia, I fell victim to a troublesome illness . . . . Actually, I do not despair about my health, since I have great hopes of recovering from my illness" (2 Macc 9:21-22).

Economic Need. The weakness spoken about can also be understood as economic need or poverty. "He who shuts his ear to the cry of the poor will himself also call and not be heard" (Prov 21:13). "Injure not the poor because they are poor, nor crush the needy at the gate" (Prov 22:22). The mother of Lemuel, king of Masa, tells him that rulers should not drink wine or strong drink, "Lest in drinking they forget what the law decrees, and violate the rights of all who are in need" (Prov 31:5). She also tells her son, "Open your mouth, decree what is just, defend the needy and the poor!" (Prov 31:9).

Inner Poverty. At times inner poverty or a lack of ability is what is meant. "There followed a long war between the house of Saul and that of David, in which David grew stronger, but the house of Saul weaker" (2 Sam 3:1). Isaiah speaks the word of the Lord to Sennacherib, king of Assyria, and states that he will reduce fortified cities into heaps of ruins, "While their inhabitants, shorn of power, are dismayed and ashamed" (2 Kgs 19:26).

New Testament

In the NT this word group signifying weakness is sometimes used in a physical sense, but more often it refers to the human condition, sickness, moral weakness, or is used figuratively for poverty.

Physical Weakness. Weakness is used in a physical sense in the NT, but to a lesser degree than in the OT. Paul comments on his physical state when he says, "For someone will say, 'His letters are severe and forceful, but his bodily presence is weak, and his speech contemptible'" (2 Cor 10:10). This is probably what Paul intends to refer to when he says that he came to Corinth "in weakness and fear and much trembling" (1 Cor 2:3). On other occasions, however, weakness occurs in texts that speak more comprehensively of the whole person. In 1 Peter 3:7, for example, we read that "you husbands should live with your wives in understanding, showing honor to the weaker female sex."

Part of the Human Condition. Weakness is spoken about as part of the human condition, at times with moral overtones. In Romans 8:26 the opposite of the weakness of the flesh is the power of the Spirit: "In the same way, the Spirit too comes to the aid of our weakness; for we do not know how to pray as we ought" (Rom 8:26). Earlier in the same letter Paul states, "I am speaking in human terms because of the weakness of your nature" (Rom 6:19). In another letter he makes this same point when speaking about the human body: "It is sown dishonorable; it is raised glorious. It is sown weak; it is raised powerful" (1 Cor 15:43). At times weakness is caused by fear, timidity, or caution. Paul confesses, "To my shame I say that we were too weak!" (2 Cor 11:21).

The Jewish high priest is said to be "beset by weakness and so, for this reason, must make sin offerings for himself as well as for the people" (Heb 5:2). In the Letter to the Hebrews one learns that in Jesus, himself, "we do not have a high priest who is unable to sympathize with our weaknesses, but one who has similarly been tested in every way, yet without sin" (Heb 4:15). Jesus comments in Gethsemane that, "The spirit is willing, but the flesh is weak" (Matt 26:41; Mark 14:38). And Paul concludes that Jesus was crucified as a result of the weakness of human nature: "For indeed he was crucified out of weakness, but he lives by the power of God" (2 Cor 13:4).

In the NT, weakness can be the place where divine power is revealed on earth. "For what the law, weakened by the flesh, was powerless to do, this God has done: by sending his own Son in the likeness of sinful flesh" (Rom 8:3). In another letter Paul says, "I will rather boast most gladly of my weaknesses, in order that the power of Christ may dwell with me" (2 Cor 12:9). "I am content with weaknesses, insults, hardships, persecutions, and constraints, for the sake of Christ; for when I am weak, then I am strong" (2 Cor 12:10). He adds that, "God chose the foolish of the world to shame the wise, and God chose the weak of the world to shame the strong" (1 Cor 1:27; see 2:3).

Moral Weakness. Alongside a weakness that is accepted as part of the human condition, there is also a religious or moral weakness which must be overcome. The Greek words used in these texts are found only rarely prior to the NT. Paul, especially in Romans and in the Corinthian correspondence, is the NT author who most often uses these words in this manner. "We who are strong ought to put up with the failings of the weak" (Rom 15:1). "Welcome anyone who is weak in faith, but not for disputes over opinions" (Rom 14:1; see 14:2; 4:19; 1 Cor 8:9-13, 9:22; 2 Cor 11:29-30). The weak lack the knowledge of the strong Christian: "But not all have this knowledge. There are some who have been so used to idolatry up until now that, when they eat meat sacrificed to idols, their conscience, which is weak, is defiled" (1 Cor 8:7). "When you sin in this way against your brothers and wound their consciences, weak as they are, you are sinning against Christ" (1 Cor 8:12).

Sickness. The same terms are used to speak of bodily weakness in the sense of sickness or disease. In fact, these terms are the most common NT expressions for sickness. Paul reminds the Galatians, "you know that it was because of a physical illness that I originally preached the gospel to you" (Gal 4:13). Mark reports that whatever villages or towns Jesus entered, "they laid the sick in the marketplaces and begged him that they might touch only the tassel on his cloak" (Mark 6:56). In the famous last judgment scene in Matthew, the "son of man" sitting in judgment speaks about when he was "ill and in prison" (Matt 25:43-44).

Jesus instructs the seventy-two that he is about to send on their missionary journey to "cure the sick" (Luke 10:9; see 5:15; 8:2; 13:11-12). In a letter to the Christian community at Corinth Paul recognizes that "many among you are ill and infirm" (1 Cor 11:30). The fourth evangelist also uses weakness in this fashion when he writes that, "One man was there who had been ill for thirty-eight years" (John 5:5; see also 11:4).

A connection between sin and illness can be seen in Matthew's citation of Isaiah 53:4 in which the prophet speaks about the Servant of the Lord who suffers vicariously for the sins of others. Matthew takes the infirmities not as sins, but as physical afflictions. Thus his version of Isaiah 53:4 reads, "He took away our infirmities and bore our diseases" (Matt 8:17).

Economic Need. On occasion one encounters these terms used of economic weakness or poverty. "In every way I have shown you that by hard work of that sort we must help the weak, and keep in mind the words of the Lord Jesus" (Acts 20:35).

Inner Poverty. This word group can also be used figuratively to refer to inner poverty or incapacity. In Galatians Paul asks, "Now that you have come to know God, or rather to be known by God, how can you turn back again to the weak and destitute elemental powers?" (Gal 4:9). In Hebrews one reads, "On the one hand, a former commandment is annulled because of its weakness and uselessness" (Heb 7:18).

See: BODY, FLESH, HEALING, POOR, POWER, SIN, SPIRIT, TEMPTATION

DENNIS M. SWEETLAND

Pastoral-Liturgical Tradition

Weakness (and its correlate, strength) has been understood at two distinct levels in the Christian tradition. At one level, it refers to an incapacity caused by a lack of strength or a deprivation of ordinary resources ordinarily considered to be available. Physical disabilities, diminished strength caused by illness or old age or injury would be examples of such lack of strength. Diminished resources, caused by poverty, upbringing, or forms of oppression (gender, political, social) would be examples of the latter. These types of weaknesses would all be considered as remediable in a better order of things or with a better distribution of resources and the goods of the earth.

A second level of weakness refers to a deeper level of existence. This kind of weakness becomes apparent in the acknowledgement of our being created beings, dependent first on God our creator and then upon one another. God is the source and continual sustainer of our lives. Without God's constant attention we would not exist. As human beings, we are constituted as individuals within community, and must rely on communities to sustain and develop our identities. Seen in this manner, we are contingent beings, i.e., part of a network of connections and relations without which we would not be human and would cease to exist. The fact of the inevitability of death underscores that fact every moment of our lives.

Christian spirituality has dealt with both of these levels. At the level of lack of strength or deprivation, it has mandated special attention and care for those who lack strength, since they are special in God's eyes, even when looked down upon in human settings. In the case of deprivation, Christians are called to struggle to bring about justice as a constitutive part of the Christian vocation. Weakness is in this latter sense not the source of virtue, but is an injustice that is to be combatted.

Weakness at the deeper level of existence is not seen as something to be overcome as much as invitation to embrace more closely the right set of relations with God and with the human community. Increasingly also it involves getting in right relation with the earth and its resources. Christians believe that this embracing of our contingency opens up possibilities for dealing with suffering and for healing. Such an embrace is focused especially in entering more deeply into Jesus of Nazareth's embrace of the poor and the weak, and in his voluntary undertaking of suffering in his passion and death. This latter identification with the suffering Christ opens the Christian up to the power and strength drawn from the love and the union that marks the persons of the Trinity.

Weakness, then, can become for the Christian a source of strength. It is not to be confused with acquiescing to oppression. Its strength is found especially in the suffering and in the Cross of Christ.

See: DEATH, SUFFERING

ROBERT J. SCHREITER, C.PP.S.

WEEPING

Shedding tears is usually an expression of heightened emotions and is a normal human response to many situations in life. Weeping takes its specific meaning from the particular context.

The Bible

In the Bible weeping expresses a variety of human emotions. It is often associated with mourning, e.g., at parting (Acts 20:37; 2 Tim 1:14), over someone's death (Luke 23:28; John 11:33), over the destruction of a city (1 Sam 1:5; Jer 14:17). Jesus himself wept over the death of Lazarus (Luke 19:41) and the future destruction of Jerusalem (John 11:35). Hannah wept because of her bitter sadness over not having children (1 Samuel 7–8). In contrast, tears of joy marked the reunion of lost relatives (Tob 7:6) and the reading of the law after the restoration of Jerusalem in the time of Nehemiah (Neh 8:9).

There are several biblical contexts in which the shedding of tears takes on religious significance. Weeping is a sign of particularly intense petition and supplication, as in the cases of Judas Maccabeus (2 Macc 11:6; 13:12) and Esther (Esth 4:3). These descriptions often reinforce the feeling of the intensity of the prayer by linking weeping with other actions, such as mourning, groaning, lamentation, prostration, and fasting. The intensity of Jesus' prayer is described with these same phrases: "In the days when he was in the flesh, he offered prayers and supplications with loud cries and tears to God, who was able to save him from death" (Heb 5:7). The passage concludes: "and he was heard because of his reverence" (Heb 5:7). Prayers in which one's need is poured out like tears seem especially apt to gain a response from the God who "hears prayers and sees tears" (2 Kgs 20:5; Isa 38:5).

Another context in which weeping has religious meaning is that of repentance. God summons people to "return to me with your whole heart, with fasting, and weeping, and mourning" (Joel 2:12). The tears of the penitent woman who knelt at Jesus' feet to wash them speak eloquently of sorrow and repentant love (Luke 7:38, 44). In the

wake of his denial, Peter "went out and began to weep bitterly" (Matt 26:75).

Weeping also serves to describe the pain and sorrow of our time on earth: "A time to weep, and a time to laugh, a time to mourn, and a time to dance" (Eccl 3:4). In that context, tears are often used as a graphic way to describe not only God's corrective interaction in human life: "You have fed them with the bread of tears and given them tears to drink in ample measure" (Ps 80:6), but especially the liberating and saving acts of the God of the endtime who reserves human misfortunes, exchanging weeping and laughing (Luke 6:21; Ps 126:5), and "who will wipe away the tears from all faces" (Isa 25:8; Jer 31:16; Rev 7:17; 21:4), so that even now those who weep can live "as though they were not weeping" (1 Cor 7:30).

Pastoral-Liturgical Tradition

Writers of the later Christian tradition, commenting on biblical passages like those above, have taken the biblical meaning of weeping into their own pastoral and spiritual vocabulary. For example, there are exhortations to pour out not only prayers but also one's tears during the hours of the night. Drawing on the analogy of baptismal waters, ancient writers speak of the shedding of tears as another, post-baptismal repentance and cleansing. In a somewhat unique Christian development, the spiritual tradition has also adapted the image to speak of the gift of tears, given to us, like all gifts, through the Spirit sent by Christ. And finally, the image of a time when God will wipe away every tear from our eyes has become one of the most consoling images in the liturgical texts for Christian burial.

Though weeping is no longer a common religious image today, the understandings behind the biblical image might still be of pastoral use: the need to be whole-hearted and repentantly honest in prayer, God's readiness to hear such prayer, and especially the vision and the task to which God calls us, to believe in and work toward that new heaven and earth in which all human suffering and sorrow are overturned.

See: FASTING, JERUSALEM, LAMENTATION, LAW, PRAYER, REPENTANCE, SUPPLICATION

GILBERT OSTDIEK, O.F.M.

WIDOW

Old Testament

Since in most ancient cultures a woman's status was entirely dependent on that of her father or husband, a widow with no male protector had no social standing and was especially vulnerable to all kinds of exploitation. Hebrew law, therefore, was careful to see that the rights of widows were safeguarded (e.g., Exod 22:21-23). Their clothing is not to be taken in pledge for a loan (Deut 24:17). At festivals they are to be invited to join family celebrations, along with strangers and orphans (Deut 16:11, 14). Elijah's reception of hospitality in the home of a widow, and his miraculous preservation of her and her son from starvation, is indicative of the way in which widows are portrayed as needy, and at the same time as recipients of God's special attention (1 Kgs 17:7-24; see also Luke 4:25-26; Pss 68:6; 146:9; Isa 1:17). One of the characteristics of the wicked is their injustice toward widows, orphans, and strangers (e.g., Ps 146:6; cf. Mark 12:40; Luke 20:47).

Widows and orphans frequently appear together in these texts because an orphan was understood to be a fatherless child, but not necessarily motherless. The children of widows shared in the ambiguous status of their mothers because they too lacked a male protector. So important was the felt need of continuing the patrilineal descendants of a man that a widow without a son was expected to claim her right to marriage with her dead husband's brother, and any sons born from their union would bear the name of their mother's deceased husband (the so-called Levirate Law; Deut 25:5-10; Mark 12:18-27). For the surviving brother to refuse brought social disgrace. The story of Judah and Tamar in Genesis 38 is about the same concern.

The experience of widowhood is used symbolically to convey desolation: Babylon boasts that she will never be widowed (Isa 47:8; cf. Rev 18:7); destroyed Jerusalem is an abandoned widow (Lam 1:1-2). Widows are objects of pity, one of the special kinds of suffering people for whom God looks out in a special way.

New Testament

Jesus has compassion on the widow bereft of her only child at Nain (Luke 7:11-17), and holds up for praise a poor but generous widow in the Temple (Mark 12:41-44; Luke 21:1-4). He tells a parable of a persistent widow denied her rights by a recalcitrant judge, echoing from the OT not only the social plight of widows but also God's wrath on those who oppress them (Luke 18:1-8).

In the early Christian churches, widows continued to be the needy objects of charity and justice (Jas 1:27). The dispute that arises between the Hebrew-speaking and Greek-speaking contingents of the Jerusalem church has to do with daily food distribution to widows, and probably to their children as well (Acts 6:1). Soon, however, another picture emerges: widows become the special group of church members counted on for prayer and spiritual aid. Those who are sufficiently affluent provide hospitality in their homes to travelers as well. In 1 Timothy we see discussion of both groups of widows. Those supported by the Church are to be without other familial means, and living examples of virtue (1 Tim 5:3-8). Those who are to be "enrolled," or officially accepted for a ministry of service, are to be at least sixty years old and proven examples of virtue as well (1 Tim 5:9-13).

Paul himself had earlier stated in answer to an inquiry from the Corinthians that a widow was free to remarry "in the Lord," that is, to marry a Christian, but in his own opinion she would be better off not to (1 Cor 7:39-40). The later author of 1 Timothy specifies on the contrary that he wants younger widows to marry and raise children so as not to give scandal to outsiders (1 Tim 5:14). This attitude is much more in keeping with the surrounding Greco-Roman culture, in which, because of low population growth, there were heavy expectations for childbearing placed on women (see 1 Tim 2:15).

In the discussion of widows in service ministry in 1 Timothy 6:9-13, we see the beginnings of the order of widows which, in certain times and places (e.g., early third-century Carthage and fifth-century Syria), seems to have been considered part of the clergy.

Pastoral-Liturgical Tradition

If today widows are not an identifiably needy group, the feminization of poverty and the neglect of the elderly that are part of our society still caution us to give them special attention as God's poor ones who are often deprived of income and always of affection, companionship, and emotional support. Ministry *to* widows and widowers in their bereavement should be an important part of any pastoral ministry program.

At the same time, the ministry *of* widows is often not utilized as it might be. Many widows face an emptiness in their lives that could be lightened by knowing that they are of help to someone, that they matter to someone. Widows are a nearly untapped source of rich experience and love that could be shared much more effectively with the people of God.

See: CHRISTIAN, CHURCH, COMPASSION, FATHER, HOSPITALITY, JUSTICE, LAW, LOVE, MINISTRY, PARABLE, PEOPLE OF GOD, POOR, PRAYER, SERVANT, STRANGER, WRATH OF GOD

CAROLYN OSIEK, R.S.C.J.

WILL AND TESTAMENT

In the OT, the Hebrew word used most often to convey the ideas of will and testament is *berît*, "covenant";* in Greek it is *diathēkē*. In Hellenistic times, *diathēkē* meant "last will and testament." But as a parallel to *berît*, "covenant," *diathēkē* loses its sense of "will" and "testament" since God cannot ask for the life of the testator in order to implement the "will" or "testament." However, both *berît* and *diathēkē* are concerned with the declaration of a person's will and not just an agreement or pact between two parties. When God established the "covenants," God willed certain conditions. Thus, *diathēkē* in the Septuagint and the NT can be interpreted as *berît*, "covenant." The exceptions are Galatians 3:15 and Hebrews 9 where *diathēkē* is understood as "will."

Throughout the OT there are many examples of covenants. Important ones are the Mosaic Covenant and the "new covenant" that the prophet Jeremiah announces. These two covenants figure in the NT understanding of *diathēkē*. Both the Mosaic Covenant and Jeremiah's vision of the "new covenant" are fulfilled in Jesus Christ who extends God's salvation to all nations. The "new covenant" established by Christ concerns a change of heart, has the Spirit as its mark, and is based on faith; the Mosaic Covenant is based on keeping the letter of the Law.

With respect to *berît* and *diathēkē*, what is begun and foreshadowed in the OT is brought to completion and fulfilled in the NT and gives hope for future generations.

Old Testament

In the OT, *berît*, "covenant," understood as *diathēkē*, "will," "testament," and "covenant" in the NT, is an important theological concept central to the relationship that exists between God and all of creation. This concept is at the heart of Israel's faith, its self-identity, and its future life.

In the Pentateuch, *berît* is used in relation to several kinds of covenants. There are covenants or "pacts" made between two people, i.e., Abraham and Abimelech (Gen 21:27), Laban and Jacob (Gen 31:44). However, the meaning of *berît* as "covenant," "will," and "testament" becomes clearer in covenants that involve a divine commitment in which God is bound. Three such covenants are the Noachice Covenant (Gen 9:8-17), the Abrahamic Covenant (Genesis 15 [J]; 17 [P]), and the covenant made with Phinehas (Num 25:10-13).

The Noachice Covenant is made between God, Noah, his descendants, and every living thing (Gen 9:9). Initiated by God, this covenant is a unilateral promise whereby

God pledges never again to destroy creation by a flood (Gen 9:11). The sign of the covenant is the bow (Gen 9:13).

Like the Noachice Covenant, the Abrahamic Covenant binds only God; it too is initiated by God and is unilateral. By this covenant God is obligated to give descendants and land to Abraham. God promises to be his God and his descendants' God (Gen 17:3-8). The sign of the covenant is circumcision (Gen 17:11).

The covenant made with Phinehas is also initiated by God and is unilateral. Here God pledges friendship with Phinehas "which shall be for him and for his descendants after him the pledge of an everlasting priesthood" (Num 25:12-13).

There is another type of covenant that perhaps best expresses the relationship between *berît* and *diathēkē* as "covenant," "will," and "testament." Initiated by God, this covenant is bilateral in which Israel is bound; hence, it is a covenant of human obligation. An example of this kind of covenant is the Mosaic Covenant (Exod 19:1–24:11), which is central to the OT.

Unlike the Noachice and Abrahamic Covenants, the Mosaic Covenant is a mutual one between God and the Israelites. It expresses God's choice of Israel and Israel's choice of God. Israel freely chooses to be obedient and faithful to God. Different from the Noachice and Abrahamic Covenants, the Israelites, though bound to God, are free to be faithful to God, to serve only God, and to act justly. Even though this covenant began with God's election, it can be terminated by the people's disobedience. Hence, the stability of the covenant depends on the people. As part of this covenant, the people are entrusted with God's law, the Decalogue (Exod 20:2-17), written on stone tablets. The Decalogue is to help preserve covenant and relationship.

Unlike the earlier covenants, the Mosaic Covenant is sealed by blood and a meal (Exod 24:1-2, 9-11 [J]; 24:3-8 [E]). The blood of the covenant is significant. A synchronic reading of Exodus 24:3-8 shows Moses sprinkling the blood of sacrificed bulls on the altar (Exod 24:6) and on the people (Exod 24:7) while saying, "This is the blood of the covenant which the Lord has made with you in accordance with all these words of his" (Exod 24:8). Blood, a constitutive element of life in the OT, binds God with the people and the people with their God. The people now have an obligation to keep the ordinances that God has given them. Soon after the Mosaic Covenant is ratified, the Israelites break the covenant (Exodus 32). Moses has to intercede to God on their behalf (Exodus 33), and the covenant is renewed (Exodus 34). Both the blood and the meal of the Mosaic Covenant are significant for the covenant that Jesus establishes in the NT.

In the Former Prophets, *berît* is used in connection with a "pact" between two people, e.g., Jonathan and David (1 Sam 18:3), David and the Israelite elders (2 Sam 5:7). More importantly, *berît* is also used for other covenants of human obligation, e.g., Joshua renews the Mosaic Covenant by means of making a covenant with the Israelites (Josh 24:16-18); Josiah makes a covenant between God, himself, and the Israelites (2 Kgs 23:1-3). David also enters into covenant with God (2 Sam 7:8-29; see also 2 Sam 23:5; Ps 89:4), which means that God's bond to the people is now through a line of monarchs.

In the Latter Prophets, the prophets speak of a future covenant that God will establish with the people (Isa 61:8; Jer 31:31-33; 32:40; Ezek 16:60; 34:25; 37:26). The covenant is "everlasting" (Isa 61:8; Jer 32:40) and "new" (Jer 31:31). The "new covenant" that Jeremiah speaks about will not be like the Mosaic Covenant. The law will not be on tablets; it will be written within people's hearts. God will be their God and they will be God's people. They will instinctively know God and God's law without instruction from others. This covenant speaks of direct intervention instead of intervention through intermediaries, i.e., Moses.

Both the "old" Mosaic Covenant and the "new" covenant are fundamentally the same: both are initiated by God and both pertain to God's people. But the "new" covenant has as its focus the inner nature of humanity, namely, the heart, that will be transformed. The covenant for Jeremiah becomes a symbol and a hope that he does not expect to see in his day. Jeremiah's covenant foreshadows the "new covenant" that Jesus will make. Through Christ, Moses' and Jeremiah's covenants are fulfilled.

New Testament

In the NT *diathēkē* means "covenant," "will," and "testament." In the Synoptic Gospels, Jesus at the Passover Meal speaks of the blood of the "new covenant" (Luke 22:20). The idea of "new covenant" contrasts with the "old covenant." The blood of the old, Mosaic Covenant was that of bulls; in the "new covenant" it is that of Jesus himself (Heb 9:12; 1 John 1:7) shed for the reparation, purification, and forgiveness of faults (Rom 3:25; Eph 1:7; Heb 9:22) and for justification, reconciliation, and liberation (Rom 5:9; Col 1:20; 1 Pet 1:18-19). Liturgically, the blood of Christ is sacramentally present on the altar and is not sprinkled on it. The blood is offered to God's people as nourishment and as a sign of union and communion with all of God's community.

In the Pauline Letters, Paul uses *diathēkē* in relation to covenant and stresses that with the "new" covenant sins are taken away (Rom 11:27). God dwells among people (2 Cor 6:16), transforms hearts, and places his Spirit within them. The "new" covenant is of the Spirit and not the letter of the law. However, in his argument on inheritance, promise, and law (Gal 3:15-18), Paul uses *diathēkē* to mean "covenant," "will," and "testament."

The author of the Letter to the Hebrews also understands *diathēkē* as both "covenant" and "will." The "new covenant" announced by Jeremiah is realized through Christ (Heb 8:8-12; cf. Jer 31:31-34). In Hebrews 9:15-17 *diathēkē* (v. 16) clearly means "will." Here, the "new covenant" is a "will" that requires the death of the testator. Thus, Jesus Christ is the one who establishes the "new covenant" and his death puts his "will" into effect.

In summary, *diathēkē* in the OT has the same nuance as *berît*. However, in the NT, *diathēkē* means not only "covenant" but also "will" and "testament." Furthermore, with respect to the covenants with Moses and Jeremiah, what is begun and hinted at in the OT is brought to fulfillment by God through Christ in the NT.

See: ALTAR, BLOOD, COVENANT, DEATH, ELECTION, HEART, HOPE, JUSTIFICATION, LAND, LAW, LIFE, MEAL, MOSES, OBEDIENCE, PASSOVER, RECONCILIATION, SALVATION, SIN

CAROL J. DEMPSEY, O.P.

WILL OF GOD

The will of God has been revealed and is still in the process of being made known to us. The discovery of God's will remains for the spiritual person a life-long pursuit. It is marked both by the uncertainty of knowing authentically the divine will and by the peace of discovering it. The search for the will of God, both by the community of faith and by the individual believer, is a mysterious journey of discerning the ways in which God is revealed in human experience and the ways that experience is to be interpreted.

Old Testament

In the Hebrew Scriptures, it is clear that God wills certain things to happen. In fact, some of the most important elements of theological reflection on the Scriptures come from the belief that God has an overarching intention, a divine will. This will includes: the election of the people of God, the saving acts of redemption toward Israel, the just punishment of sinful deeds, the gift of the law, the promise of a messiah. All of these manifestations of the divine will show a God who is in close relationship with a people who are chosen, loved, and offered a marvelous destiny.

The Hebrew vocabulary used in speaking of the will of God is not extensive, but understanding it is helpful in gaining an insight into the biblical mind. The most common verb used to describe the act of "God willing" something is ḥapeṣ. In most of its uses, this verb carries the nuance of a desire that is positive and pleasurable. Thus, God's desire for something to happen carries the sense of an affirmative and agreeable wish. This is well exemplified in the prophet Ezekiel where God says: "For I have no pleasure [wish] in the death of anyone who dies, says the LORD God. Return and live!" (Ezek 18:32). Thus God's will for humanity is geared toward life and vitality, not toward punishment or death.

The Torah/Pentateuch. In the early chapters of Genesis, God's will is expressed to Adam and Eve in the command not to eat of the fruit of the tree in the middle of the garden. A breach of this order would result in their death (Gen 3:3-5). Despite their disobedience, God relents and only banishes them from the garden. Yet, the fullness of blessing has been transformed into a curse. From the beginning, the Scriptures point out that God's will is to foster life (Gen 3:21-24), in spite of human weakness and frailty which impede the free reception of the gifts of life.

The will of God is manifested in the signs and wonders worked on behalf of Israel in the experience of the Exodus from Egypt. In the book of Exodus, God says: "tell the Israelites: You have seen for yourselves how I treated the Egyptians and how I bore you up on eagle wings and brought you here to myself. Therefore, if you hearken to my voice and keep my covenant, you shall be my special possession, dearer to me than all other people, though all the earth is mine. You shall be to me a kingdom of priests, a holy nation" (Exod 19:4-6). This covenant* formula recounts God's saving deeds to Israel and further expresses the dimension of the love that comes out of this relationship. God's desire to enter into covenant with Israel bespeaks a relationship directed toward the security, safety, and total well-being of the people. Israel must fulfill its part of the treaty by a faithful observance of God's laws. If the people heed God's voice, they can expect divine kindness in abundance.

God's will for Israel is contained in the laws and precepts of the covenant. With the guidance of the law, God's people can walk in the way of the divine will.

The Deuteronomic tradition further develops the idea that God's will can be known in the law. "For this command which I enjoin on you today is not too mysterious and remote for you. It is not up in the sky, that you should say, 'Who will go up in the sky to get it for us and tell us of it, that we may carry it out?' . . . No, it is something very near to you, already in your mouths and in your hearts; you have only to carry it out" (Deut 30:11-14). The precepts of the covenant dwell in the heart and mind of the chosen people. While fulfilling God's will appears to be something difficult, far-off, and enigmatic, it is really something that has already been given to them; their task is to put into practice the attitude and word which already dwells within them. The gift of the law is another sign of God's love for Israel, inviting them to cling ever more closely to the One who has brought them into being and has formed them as a people.

The Prophets. The prophetic writings teach that God's will for blessing in Israel is sometimes manifested in destructive and harsh ways. When called to the prophetic mission, Isaiah is told that the pronouncement of God's word to the people will only steep them deeper in their sin until their land is leveled and they are left desolate (Isa 6:9-13). This will be the message of other prophets as well (see Jer 1:9-10; Amos 7:11). Destruction and death are not the final word, for God brings restoration after the experience of desolation (Isa 66:22-23; Jeremiah 31; Amos 9:8b-15). The story of Jonah gives us an example of God's change of heart (Jonah 3:10). After threatening to destroy Nineveh, God sees their conversion and repents of the earlier threat. God's graciousness and mercy, slowness to anger, and plenitude of mercy demonstrate the divine will (Jonah 4:3).

The Writings. The divine will is also described as a plan in which God directs the progression of history and the peoples and events connected with it. This plan is eternal, bringing blessing to the good and thwarting those opposed to Israel (Ps 33:10-12).

The Wisdom tradition holds Job as an example of the person par excellence in search of God's will. Although Job errs in his beliefs, in his self-righteous indignation, and in his questioning, God brings him to a new knowledge of the divine will (Job 42:1-3, 5-6). In the end, Job experiences rich blessings. Similarly, through numerous trials young Tobiah is reminded by Raphael of God's will to bless him with a good and prosperous life: "When I came to you it was not out of any favor on my part, but because it was God's will. So continue to thank him every day; praise him with song" (Tob 12:18).

See: BLESSING, COVENANT, CURSE, LAW

GREGORY J. POLAN, O.S.B.

New Testament

In the NT God's will that all creation have life and be transformed in love is manifest fully in Jesus. He is the perfect revelation of God's will and leads his followers to work to establish God's will on earth through their lives.

Thelema, in Greek, denotes "will, purpose, intention, desire, rule." It is used in the NT with reference to God, Christ, the devil, those in authority, or human beings in general. It expresses something that one wishes to happen, what one wishes to communicate or to bring about by one's own action, or by the activity of others, to whom one assigns a task.

God's will is expressed in the singular because, though there are many different aspects to God's intention for creation, many commandments and obligations incumbent upon the people of God, the will of God is a unity. Therefore, an understanding of God's will is grounded, ultimately, in the initial act of creation: the breath of life bestowed on all creatures. This breath of life is a sharing in the very life of God. God's will for creation, therefore, is that it have life,

eternal life, as the Gospel of John rightly understands it (John 6:40).

God's will is manifest, above all, in love for creation, and in the divine desire that all creation be transformed in love. Nowhere is the character of God's loving will more explicit than in the proclamation of John 3:16—"For God so loved the world that he gave his only Son, so that everyone who believes in him might not perish but might have eternal life." Christian tradition affirms, above all, that God wills to save the world, so that not one of the "little ones" is lost (Matt 18:14). This divine purpose is a "mystery" hidden in ages past but revealed, once for all, in the coming of Christ (Eph 1:5-11).

Christ, the Perfect Revelation of God's Will. God's will is manifest to the world in all its fullness only in Christ, the beloved, the one sent by God. John's Gospel especially acknowledges this truth again and again. "No one has ever seen God. The only Son, God, who is at the Father's side, has revealed him" (John 1:18). The Word made flesh discloses to the world the heart and intentions of God.

Jesus' union with the One who sent him means that the will of God is identical with that of Jesus, "My food is to do the will of the one who sent me and to finish his work" (John 4:34; see also 5:30; 6:38). Jesus' consciousness of doing the Father's will was present, according to Luke, even in his childhood (Luke 2:49). And the prayer of Jesus in Gethsemane, "not what I will, but what you will" (Mark 14:36; Matt 26:39; Luke 22:42), attests to his fidelity to the end.

God's Will Expressed in the Vision of the Reign of God. In the Synoptic Gospels, Jesus' proclamation of the reign or kingdom of God announces the inbreaking of God's will on earth: the power of the evil one, with his destructive will, has been overcome, the reign of God is "at hand" (Mark 1:15), and we await its fulfillment still in our time. The signs of the reign, which is God's will established on earth, are many, but often they are imperceptible.

The will of God is manifest when all those things that keep us less than human are overcome by God: sickness, poverty, hunger, hatred, divisions of all kinds. In Jesus, God reveals a divine will that wishes to heal and to reconcile, to break down the barriers that separate people from God, as well as to lavish blessings upon all creatures. The parable of the laborers in the vineyard (Matt 20:1-15) captures well this bountiful will of God.

Christians and the Will of God. In the Lord's Prayer, Christians, too, pray that God's will be established "on earth, as in heaven." They echo in these words the prayer of Jesus in Gethsemane: "not my will, but yours be done." Mary's "Fiat" offers the example of one's total cooperation with God's will in fidelity and trust (Luke 1:38). Discerning and doing the will of God is, moreover, the fundamental requisite of Christian discipleship (Mark 3:35 and pars.).

Discernment of God's will, in Paul's view, demands nothing less than a "transformation" by the "renewal of the mind" (Rom 12:2). Paul prays fervently that this transformation may continue in the communities to which he writes (Col 1:9-12; Eph 3:14-21). For the Johannine community, it is the Paraclete who "teaches everything" and reminds them of all that Jesus had taught them (John 14:26; 16:12-15). To recognize God's will is not only to know the commandments as revealed and interpreted by Jesus (Matt 5:17-20; John 14:21), but it also demands an adherence to the person of Jesus and a following of his way.

Discipleship is not a matter only of knowing God's will, of saying "Lord, Lord," it demands that we put into practice God's will in our lives (Matt 7:21; 21:28-31; Luke 12:47). The whole of Christian life is to be lived in accordance with God's will for our holiness (1 Thess 4:3). It calls us to put aside human desires and to embrace instead the will and desires of God. The power of the Spirit (Rom 8:26-27) is at work in us inspiring both our prayer and our actions so that they might be in accord with the mind of God.

God's invitation to act according to the divine will is given freely; we are not compelled, but invited, to conform our actions to the will of God. Yet we can be confident that God is with us, enabling us to live according to God's designs, as Paul says, "For God is the one who, for his good purpose, works in you both to desire and to work" (Phil 2:13).

See: CONSCIENCE, LAW, OBEDIENCE, PROVIDENCE

BARBARA E. BOWE, R.S.C.J.

Pastoral-Liturgical Tradition

Subsequent reflection about the will of God in Christian tradition centered on questions about the nature and the freedom of the divine will and its relation to evil. The stuggle human beings experience to try to do the will of God leads to the doctrine of grace.

The Existence of the Divine Will. None of the Fathers of the Church doubted the existence of the divine will. Yet none wrote about it except in connection with other theological themes (e.g., creation). Indeed, there is no explicit teaching about the existence of the divine will until the seventh century, and that teaching is given in connection with the Monothelite Christological controversy. Six centuries later, Thomas Aquinas made explicit the assumptions of the preceding tradition. While Thomas assumed, as did the Fathers, that the existence of the divine will was revealed by the Scriptures, he taught that it was given by reason as well. Beginning with the premise that intelligent creatures possess wills, Thomas Aquinas argued that, since God is an intelligent creature, God must have a will (*Summa* 1.19.1).

Nature of the Divine Will. The nature of the divine will can be known in part by analogy to the human will. Nonetheless, it is even better known by how it *differs* from the human will. The human will is a faculty that strives for that which it desires, needs, and lacks. Human volition is, therefore, an illustration of human dependence on powers the will cannot control and on goods it did not create. On the other hand, the divine will lacks nothing; it has no unrealized potentialities. It is, moreover, affected by and dependent on nothing outside of itself. Accordingly, reflection on the divine will leads the theologian to posit several divine perfections, including omnipotence, aseity (God's being is self-derived), and freedom.

Freedom of the Divine Will. The freedom of God's will has usually been connected in Church tradition with the doctrine of creation. Was God free to create? Or was creation in some sense necessary? Generally, Catholic tradition has affirmed that God did not need creatures. Instead, God created in a free and gracious act so that creatures might partake of the goodness of God. Thus, reflection on the nature of the divine will leads ineluctably to the doctrine of *grace*, or the unmerited goodness of God in creating, sustaining, and redeeming human creatures.

The Divine Will and Evil. More problematically, it also invites meditation on how the infinite goodness and power of the divine will can be reconciled with the massive reality of evil. The Catholic tradition is extremely complex on this issue. Some have taught that God freely restrained the divine will in creation. Others have stressed that freedom is a necessary condition of genuine human progress and that, given human finitude, freedom must lead to evil. Some have argued that evil is an illusion of temporal experience, while others have been frustrated by the problems inherent in all of these proposals and have pronounced the problem an insoluble mystery.

Knowing and Doing the Will of God. Even while affirming with Paul that we know now "through a glass darkly" (1 Cor 13:12), Catholic tradition has unanimously affirmed, nowhere more vigorously than in the thought of Augustine (d. 430), that it is more difficult to do the will of God than to know it. Many Catholic theologians have recognized as the problem of everyone Paul's confession (Rom 7:19) that he could

not do the will of God, which he clearly knew. Once again, reflection on the will of God leads back to the doctrine of grace, for all Catholic theologians have taught that only divine help can bring the human will into harmony with the divine.

See: CREATION, GRACE, MYSTERY

KEVIN MADIGAN

WINE

Wine, one of God's blessings (Prov 3:10), is life for those who take it with moderation (Sir 31:27) but a harbinger of violence (Sir 31:30-31) and debauchery for those who overindulge (Sir 19:2-4; Eph 5:18). Rulers in particular were warned against wine lest they forget what the law decrees (Prov 31:4-5), but it was recommended for those who were perishing precisely to forget their misery (Prov 31:6-7). Wine could be a mixed blessing, and this ambivalence is found even in the story of Noah, "the first to plant a vineyard" (Gen 9:20-28).

Old Testament

Wine, the fruit of the vine,* comes as a blessed reward for fidelity to the covenant and observing its commandments. With infidelity, on the other hand, comes the curse of heavens withholding their rain and soil refusing to yield its crop (Deut 11:16-17), or of locusts devouring the crop and grubs eating the vines clean so that "you will not drink or store up the wine" (Deut 28:38-39). But after a period of infidelity (Hos 2:11), repentance suffices to restore the blessing of wine along with grain and oil (Hos 2:24). In Israelite worship, wine, the blood of the grape, was poured out as a sacrificial libation (Deut 32:14, 38; Hos 9:4), and it was part of the firstfruits* given to the priests (Deut 18:4).

The wine imagery is especially brilliant in the prophetic writing on retribution. In Isaiah, God treads the winepress and tramples Israel's enemies as grapes of wrath and their blood spurts out, staining God's garments red (Isa 63:1-6). In Jeremiah, the Lord asks the prophet: "Take this cup of foaming wine from my hand, and have all the nations to whom I will send you drink it" (Jer 25:15). The natural effects of excess, the drunkenness, the sickness, the staggering (Jer 25:27), the convulsions, and the madness (Jer 25:16) are signs of God's wrathful judgment. On the other hand, wine and the abundance of wine is the image of messianic times, when "the juice of grapes shall drip down the mountains, and all the hills shall run with it," and God's people will again "plant vineyards and drink the wine" (Amos 9:13-14; see Jer 31:12). The messianic banquet itself will be a "feast of rich food and choice wines" (Isa 25:6). In those days, their king and savior will come, "meek, and riding on an ass," bringing salvation to God's people (Zech 9:9, 16) and with it new wine: "What wealth is theirs, and what beauty! grain that makes the youths flourish and new wine, the maidens!" (Zech 9:17).

New Testament

The fruit of the vine remains a strong image in the NT, where emphasis is on the new wine of eschatological fulfillment, notably in the accounts of Eucharistic institution. All three accounts included a closely related form of Jesus' solemn announcement, "Amen, I say to you, I shall not drink again the fruit of the vine until the day when I drink it new in the kingdom of God" (Mark 14:25; see Matt 26:29; Luke 22:18). This announcement must be kept in mind later when Jesus ignores the wine offered him as he is dying on the cross (Mark 15:36; Matt 27:48; Luke 23:36).

The Synoptic theme of the old and the new wine was well prepared earlier in each Gospel when Jesus defended his disciples' feasting while those of John and of the Pharisees fasted. While the wedding guests have the bridegroom with them they do not fast. Later when the bridegroom is taken away, they will fast. But there is no pouring of new wine into the old wineskins (Mark 2:18-22; Matt 9:14-17; Luke 5:33-39). It was not time yet for the new wine, which would require new wineskins (see Mark 14:25; Matt 26:29; Luke 22:18). Luke adds that "no

one who has been drinking old wine," the wine of the Pharisees and John the Baptist, "desires the new" wine (Luke 5:39), offered in the kingdom of God (Luke 22:18) in the cup of the new covenant (Luke 22:20).

In John's Gospel, where Jesus' hour comes in his exaltation on the cross (see John 2:4; 4:23; 5:25; 13:1), Jesus cries "I thirst," accepts the offer of common wine, and announces, "It is finished," as his dying words (John 19:28-30). Jesus has fulfilled the old covenant, and the new begins. This closing scene of Jesus' life in John's Gospel responds to the opening scene of his ministry and the beginning of his signs, when during the wedding at Cana the wine ran out (John 2:1-11). Jesus' hour had not yet come to provide the good wine of the eschatological wedding banquet (John 2:4), but Jesus nevertheless provided superior wine drawn from water (John 2:7-10) as a sign of the new covenant to be inaugurated in the hour of his exaltation.

Pastoral-Liturgical Tradition

Along with bread,* wine is a key element in the Eucharistic liturgy. Poured with a little water into the chalice, it evokes the mystery of Jesus' divinity and humanity as presented in an ancient hymn quoted in Philippians 2:6-11. The first part of the hymn sings of Christ Jesus who was "in the form of God" but "emptied himself, taking the form of a slave" and "humbled himself, becoming obedient to death" (Phil 2:6-8). While pouring the water, the celebrant prays that we "come to share in the divinity of Christ who humbled himself to share in our humanity."

Like the bread, the wine is then offered with a blessing to the "Lord, God of all creation," through whose goodness "we have this wine, fruit of the vine and work of human hands." This wine "will become our spiritual drink." The expression "fruit of the vine" recalls the words of Jesus at the Last Supper that he would "not drink again of the fruit of the vine until the day" he drank "it new in the kingdom of God" (Mark 14:25; see Matt 26:29; Luke 22:18).

Wine is also referred to in Eucharistic Prayer IV in the narrative of Eucharistic institution: "In the same way, he took the cup, filled with wine." The Eucharistic Prayers I, II, and III focus exclusively on the cup,* symbol of Christ's commitment to pour out his life, while Eucharistic Prayer IV draws attention to the wine that fills the cup as a symbol of divine blessing and rejoicing.

See: BLESSING, COVENANT, CURSE, EUCHARIST, MEAL, REIGN OF GOD, RETRIBUTION, THANKSGIVING, VINE

EUGENE LAVERDIERE, S.S.S.

WISDOM

Biblical wisdom (Hebrew, *hokmah;* Greek, *sophia*) is essentially a practical instruction about how to live properly and successfully (e.g., Prov 1:1-6; Jas 3:1–4:17). There are five Wisdom books in the OT: Proverbs, Job, Ecclesiastes, Sirach, and Wisdom of Solomon. While Proverbs, Ecclesiastes, and Wisdom have been attributed to Solomon, it is generally recognized that this tradition is not historical. Most of these works (certainly Ecclesiastes, Sirach, Wisdom, and probably Proverbs 1–9) were produced in the postexilic period. In the NT the letter of James is marked by many wisdom counsels, and the sayings and parables that are characteristic of the teachings of Jesus are cast in the Wisdom tradition of his ancestors (Matt 12:34b; Luke 6:45b; Matt 6:34b). This entry will deal with (1) the literary and doctrinal characteristics of OT wisdom, (2) the figure of Jesus as a sage or rabbi, and (3) the liturgical and pastoral implications of biblical wisdom.

Old Testament

Literary and Doctrinal Characteristics. The Wisdom literature is characterized by distinctive literary forms, among them the following: the saying or aphorism, the wisdom poem, the disputation speech (in Job; actually several individual forms are used in the speeches), reflections (characteristic of Qoheleth), and diatribe (Wisdom of Solomon).

The two-line saying is distinctive of all Hebrew wisdom. This consists of parallel lines whereby the second line can repeat or intensify the idea of the first line, either positively (synonymous parallelism, e.g., Prov 16:18) or negatively (antithetic parallelism, e.g., Prov 10:1). Sometimes there is a third line, and the parallelism is called synthetic, in that the idea of the verse is developed at greater length, often without obvious parallelism (e.g., Prov 23:5).

The wisdom saying is deceiving in that it often means more than it seems to say (e.g., Prov 18:21). The sages prized artful speech (Prov 15:23) and they were aware of the ambiguities of existence (Prov 17:27-28; 21:30-31). They were relentless in pressing home their insights into life: the rewards of justice, the value of diligence and self-control, and so forth. It is said that they were in pursuit of the order that governed the world, but it can equally be maintained that they pressed against the mysteries of creation. Even the Book of Proverbs, usually so secure and final in judgment, is aware of the problems of existence (3:11-12; 30:1-4). The optimism of this book, while supported by Sirach, is vigorously disputed in Job and Qoheleth. It is helpful to distinguish between the content and style of the wisdom teachers. Their content is sometimes short-sighted and necessarily limited (as all sayings are), but their style is ever probing and seeking new insights. Job and Qoheleth extend and purify the efforts of wisdom to understand God and the world.

The reach of the sages is also indicated by the lively variety of other forms they use. Comparisons are often sharp: "By patience is a ruler persuaded, / and a soft tongue will break a bone" (Prov 25:15) or, "like the wheel of a cart is the mind of a fool; / his thoughts revolve in circles" (Sir 33:51). Admonitions are frequent, especially in Proverbs and Sirach ("Accept whatever befalls you, in crushing misfortune be patient; for in fire gold is tested, and worthy people in the crucible of humiliation," Sir 2:4-5).

When "pleasing sayings" are attributed to Qoheleth (Eccl 12:10; see Prov 16:24), the reference is not to words that might make a person feel better, but words that are well chosen and carry a punch: "the sayings of the wise are like goads" (Eccl 12:11). Their literary dress is appropriate to their message. Frequently some traditional values can be overturned in favor of higher values, as in the "better" sayings. Thus Proverbs 16:8, "Better a little with virtue, / than a large income with injustice," or Sirach 40:25, "Gold and silver make one's way secure, / but better than either, sound judgment." The numerical saying, favored also by the prophets (Amos 1:3–2:8), is a popular form. It usually consists in a number, x, followed by another digit (x plus 1):

> Three things are too wonderful for me, yes, four I cannot understand: The way of an eagle in the air, the way of a serpent upon a rock, The way of a ship on the high seas, and the way of a man with a maiden (Prov 30:18-19).

The formula x and x plus one is found also in other Wisdom books, such as Sirach 26:28; Job 5:19-22. The blessing is frequent: "Happy the one who finds wisdom, / the one who gains understanding" (Prov 3:13). This formula corresponds to the well-known beatitudes of the NT. Especially in Proverbs, Job, and Sirach there are lengthy wisdom poems that incorporate other forms such as sayings and questions. Noteworthy are those that play on the number of letters in the Hebrew alphabet, such as the strict alphabetic acrostic (Sir 51:13-30; Psalm 37), or the 22/23 line poem that can be identified in Proverbs 2:1-22 and Sirach 1:11-30. Such a structure underlies the Book of Lamentations 1–5.

The doctrinal characteristics of biblical wisdom can be defined positively and negatively. Negatively, these works do not deal with the characteristic themes of the rest of the OT. Thus, there is no mention of the patriarchal promises, the Exodus and Sinai covenant, or the promise to David. Instead, the sages sound the depths of experience, the events of everyday life. Their goal is to help one to gain life (Prov 8:35, Lady Wisdom declares: "whoever finds me finds life"). This is the life of body and spirit: material prosperity, renown, and dignity, the good life that was a sign of divine blessing. A relationship to the Lord (see Prov 1:7 and 9:10 on fear of the Lord) colors the entire wisdom enterprise.

A particular issue deserves to be singled out since it is often misunderstood: retribution. The theory has been advanced that the Israelite mentality was one of deed-consequence. That is to say, an evil deed begets an evil result (punishment) and a good deed begets a good result (reward), and God watches over this divinely established order as a kind of midwife. It is true that the language of many sayings reflects a kind of mechanical correspondence between act and consequence (e.g., Ps 7:16, one falls into the pit one has dug for another; see Prov 26:27). But it is obvious that this is not a strict rule. Moreover, the direct agency of God is featured even more often and emphatically. Nothing happens, but that the Lord has done it (Job 1:21; Amos 1–2; 3:6; Isa 45:7). It was precisely this activity of God that made the problem of evil and suffering so acute, as the Book of Job shows.

Although the mystery of divine freedom was recognized, there was an understandable tendency to judge God by human standards of justice. It is worth noting that this becomes the great problem in Wisdom literature rather than in the prophets (but see Habakkuk and many psalms, such as 37 and 73). The sages relied upon the insights of human experience, admittedly an area fraught with insecurity and uncertainty but impossible to neglect. Qoheleth could even say that experience did not tell him whether God loved him or hated him (Eccl 9:1-2). The author of Psalm 73 seems to have understood that a personal relationship to the Lord was ultimately indestructible, if humans chose to preserve it (73:23-28). Certainly the author of the Book of Wisdom was of that mind. For him justice (or righteousness) was undying (Wis 1:15). The right relationship to God was no longer subject to the awful interruption of a shadowy existence in Sheol. Humans might destroy this relationship and ultimately "be in grief" (Wis 4:19), but otherwise it is destined to go on. The just "are in the hand of God, and no torment shall touch them" (Wis 3:1), because they are accounted among the children of God, the holy ones (see 5:5). The solution concerning eternal life is arrived at in the wisdom movement in terms of relationship to God, not in terms of the human composite (the soul that is immortal, or the body that rises from the grave). Although the author of the Wisdom of Solomon was probably aware of Greek ideas about the soul and immortality, he did not reason to a blessed afterlife by means of these ideas.

The most striking personification in the OT is that of Lady Wisdom. There are other personifications (e.g., Prov 20:1), but nothing like this one. The personification emerges in Job 28: one can find precious stones in the earth, but where is wisdom to be found (vv. 12, 20)? The answer is clear: with God (vv. 23-27). Lady Wisdom adopts the accents of a Hebrew prophet in Proverbs 1:20-33; 8:1-33, and in 9:1-6, where she is contrasted with Dame Folly (9:13-18). The most famous passage is Proverbs 8:22-31 that describes wisdom as begotten of God before the beginning of creation, beside God as an 'amon (artisan or nursing), and her delight is to be with humankind. She makes the extraordinary promise that the one who finds her finds life (8:35). In contrast, the invitation that Dame Folly issues is one that leads to Sheol and death (9:18; see 7:27). The divine origins of Wisdom suggest that she is another aspect of the divinity, the Lord who issues a summons to all human beings through Wisdom's presence in nature and in the world of experience. She is somehow in a mysterious manner a communication from God.

The personification of Wisdom is taken up again in Sirach 24, which is deliberately modeled on Proverbs 8. Wisdom describes her divine origin (v. 3, "from the mouth of the Most High") and her wandering through the world seeking a resting place. The creator ordered her to pitch her tent in Jacob, specifically in Jerusalem where she "ministered" (liturgically) before God. Her description ends with an invitation to all to come to her ("whoever drinks of me will thirst for more" v. 20). Sirach explicitly identifies Wisdom with the Law of Moses: "the book of the Most High's covenant" (24:23).

In the Book of Wisdom, Solomon is pictured as praying for wisdom, a gift from God (9:1-19; see 1 Kgs 3:1-14). Chapters 7–9 are a description of the marvelous attributes of Lady Wisdom. She is an artisan in creation (7:22; see Prov 8:30) and knows all things (7:15-21) because she pervades all things (7:24; 8:1). The relationship that Solomon seeks is one of marriage (8:2, "I sought to take her for my bride"). She surpasses any kind of riches because she brings to him the treasure of God's friendship (7:14). The most remarkable description is given in 7:25-26, where Wisdom is described as intimately related to God:

> She is an aura of the might of God and a pure effusion of the glory of the Almighty; therefore nought that is sullied enters into her. For she is the refulgence of eternal light, the spotless mirror of the power of God, the image of his goodness.

New Testament

Jesus as a Teacher of Wisdom. Although it is obvious that Jesus is a teacher, that his teaching abounds in *logia* (or sayings) and parables, and that he is called rabbi or teacher, still not very much attention is paid to him as a sage. His person and life and moral ideals tend to overshadow the practical every-day wisdom that is recorded so fully in the Gospels. The parables are very well known, but their association with OT wisdom is not often remarked. As he stood in the line of the OT prophets, Jesus also was solidly formed in the tradition of the OT sages.

The apocryphal Gospel of Thomas is a collection of the sayings of Jesus, most of which have some parallel in the Synoptic Gospels, and it underscores the importance that the early Church attached to the sayings of Jesus. When read from the point of view of wisdom, the gospel message presents new accents to its readers. Matthew 6:19–7:23 (see 6:22, "The lamp of the body is the eye . . .") is an outstanding example of wisdom within the Sermon on the Mount. Several famous contrasts of Jesus are cast in the wisdom form: "Whoever wishes to save his life will lose it, but whoever loses his life for my sake and that of the gospel will save it" (Mark 8:35). And the beatitudes are a continuation of the "Happy"-sayings of the OT: "Blessed are those who hear the word of God and observe it" (Luke 11:28). It is no wonder that people marveled at his wisdom (Mark 6:2); truly, "there is something greater than Solomon here" (Luke 11:31). And Jesus, like personified Wisdom, issued an invitation to learn from him: "Take my yoke upon you and learn from me . . . and you will find rest for yourselves" (Matt 11:29; see Sir 51:26). While the term "wisdom" is not used in the Johannine literature, there is no mistaking the wisdom background to John 1:1-18. Here Jesus is presented as the *Logos*, analogous to *Sophia*, who preexisted all creation, while also being a mediator of creation ("all things came to be through him," 1:3). OT Wisdom (Proverbs 8; Sirach 24) has become incarnate in Christ.

A lengthy argument between Christian and Greek wisdom is presented by Paul in 1 Corinthians 1–2. He criticizes the "worldly" (and yet, theological) wisdom of the Corinthians because they neglected the doctrine of the cross, a "foolish" wisdom. No longer is there question of God merely being wise or making wise; Christ is identified as the wisdom of God (1 Cor 1:30). Similarly in Colossians 1:15, he is described as "the image" (see Wis 7:25-26) of God, "the firstborn of all creation" (just as Wisdom was created before all else, Prov 8:22; Sir 24:9).

Thus the NT makes particular use of practical wisdom, as it came from the mouth of Jesus, and the OT development of Lady Wisdom serves as background to the incarnation.

Pastoral-Liturgical Tradition

First, the theological development of Christology owes much to the doctrine of personified Wisdom, as Patristic discussions show. This approach to the incarnation is simply taken for granted today, and the humanity of Jesus is more emphasized. In this "Christology from below," the general body of OT wisdom teaching is important, because it shows how Jesus was a child of his time, and formed by distinctively Jewish wisdom.

Second, the approach of the OT sage to morality carries pedagogical lessons for the modern Christian. The sage did not preach with the obvious force of the Decalogue—commands and prohibitions in the name of the God of the covenant. But it may be said that the various forms used by the sages—sayings and aphorisms, paradoxes, well-chosen expressions—can turn out to be more convincing than a curt command or prohibition. It is true that the motives are self-centered, but who will deny that such motives are without effect? In sum, one may say that the persuasiveness of the sage was all the greater for the low-key appearance of the teaching. The variation in intensity is remarkable. One may contrast the preaching tone of Proverbs 1–8, which yields nothing to the intensity of Deuteronomic preaching, with the deft and oblique style of most of the discrete proverbs in Proverbs 10–31. The purpose is to provide moral formation of the youth across a broad spectrum of action. Modern educational methods have something to learn from the venerable sages.

Third, in view of the inescapable fact of suffering the Book of Job assumes increased importance. Of course other portions of the OT have value in this respect, such as the psalms, Qoheleth, and Isaiah 53, as well as the "confessions" of Jeremiah. But the earthiness and humanness of the literary character of Job has tremendous power. So strong is this that the readers find themselves speaking of Job as a real and current person, forgetting that he is ultimately a literary character. That is precisely the measure of his success; he is *real*.

Fourth, it has been said that Wisdom theology is Creation theology. This is true because of the role that nature and human experience have in the development of the teachings. They alert us to the religious potential of everyday life. Most of human life is spent precisely in this area, not in church or in formal liturgical celebration. The Wisdom literature answers to a great need in the religious life of a human being.

Finally, a feature that at first seems to be a drawback to a Christian may turn out to be a salutary reminder. The reference is to the characteristic OT limitation to this life, with the attendant dim prospect of Sheol (Eccl 9:10) after death. In other words, the Wisdom literature provides a much needed ballast to Christian eschatology. Israel lived without any significant personal eschatology. The believing Israelite found God in this life, in the here and now, and that was all there was to be had. This did not eliminate the desire for divine blessings or even "reward" for the good life, or the immortality of name one could find in a long line of descendants. Life within that purview was realistic: faith, hope, and love were not only possible, but they could even be enhanced by the absence of the motivation of eternal life. So may it also be for the Christian who lives in a different time frame. We can receive much purification of life from a deepening of faith, hope, and love in the Israelite mode, and live for the glory of God. It has been remarked that the kerygma of wisdom was life, life in the here and now. Ultimately that kerygma proclaimed life eternal (Wis 1:15). The path that wisdom trod was the path we must all walk: from this life into the next, and wisdom underlines that continuity in a helpful way.

In the current lectionary more readings are taken from Sirach than from any other Wisdom book. This is perhaps in harmony with the usage this book received in the early Church. Its other name, "Ecclesiasticus," is perhaps because it provided a sort of *vademecum* for the catechumens. It was a "church book." However, the lectionary is badly in need of revision since the other Wisdom writings are represented in a totally inadequate manner.

See: BEATITUDES, JOB

ROLAND E. MURPHY, O.CARM.

WITNESS

This article is composed of two parts. The first will illustrate how the biblical tradition took what was a juridical term to describe the calling of believers to testify to their beliefs, even when this testimony results in suffering or death. The second part of the article examines the pastoral-liturgical development of this idea from martyrdom to asceticism. It concludes with suggestions about the type of witness that is appropriate to the Church today.

Old Testament

The "witness" complex (verb, person, thing) comes from a root meaning "to be in mind." A witness *(martys)* is "one who remembers and can tell about something." In nonbiblical Greek, the proper sphere of the terms is the legal one, i.e., in trials or legal transactions. The witness gives personal testimony to events, relations, persons, etc. In a more general use, witnessing may also refer to truths or views that are proclaimed with conviction but cannot be verified empirically (Aristotle).

In the Septuagint, the legal use is still primary, but the religious use is of particular significance. Thus in Isaiah 43:9-11; 44:7ff. God arranges a trial that will show who is truly God. The nations are spectators but they are also witnesses on behalf of their various candidates. Idols, however, are impotent and will thus be put to shame. In contrast, the people of Israel are God's witnesses (Isa 43:10, 12; 44:8). On the basis of God's acts of calling and redemption Israel will declare the reality and uniqueness of her God. The content of this witness is God's saving work; this may not be demonstrable to unbelief (Isa 43:8) but it is an incontestable certainty to faith.

The witness as martyr emerges in later Judaism, e.g., Josephus, and Philo. In this period, Judaism is portrayed as a religion of martyrdom, borne out of the sufferings of the Maccabean age. Indeed, even prior to this time, the figure of the prophet or the righteous person who suffers calumny and even death is familiar in Israel (see Elijah in 1 Kgs 19:10 or Uriah in Jer 26:20-21). The prophets have to preach whether they are heard or not, and the righteous maintain their integrity even in persecution (Ps 44:22). This experience comes to a climax in the Maccabean period. The author of 4 Maccabees reads the whole of the OT as a series of examples of the martyr spirit. Later, Josephus extolled the Essenes for their patient acceptance of suffering, and various rabbis display the same loyalty to the faith in persecution or death. Yet the "martyr" word group is nowhere used in this connection, for the suffering of persecution is seen as a work of piety rather than of witness.

New Testament

The Greek word *martys* occurs thirty-five times in the NT. Like the corresponding Hebrew word *'ed* of the OT, it is usually used in its ordinary sense of anyone who gives testimony to some fact because of what he or she has seen or heard, i.e., an eyewitness or earwitness, particularly in the juridical sense of one who gives testimony in a court trial (see Matt 18:16).

A specifically Christian connotation is found in *Luke/Acts*. The apostles are the specially commissioned witnesses appointed by God (Acts 1:22; 5:32; 10:41; 26:16). Several different elements are included in this concept. First of all, as with the general use of the term, each of the apostles is an eyewitness and an earwitness of what he has seen and heard, i.e., he can testify to the historical facts (Luke 24:48; Acts 1:8). But here the object of this testi-

mony is something special. At first it was particularly concerned with the resurrection of Christ (Acts 1:21; 4:33), which is understandable in light of the profound spiritual change that the sight of the risen One produced in the apostles, as also later in Paul. Indeed, without the resurrection of Jesus their preaching about him would have been in vain (1 Cor 15:14-17).

Soon the object of the apostles' witnessing broadened. Already in Acts 1:21 it is demanded as a requisite for the apostleship that a candidate for this office must have lived with Jesus from his baptism in the Jordan until his ascension into heaven. An apostle, therefore, had to be able to give testimony to the whole earthly life of Jesus—in fact, to the whole salvific reality resulting from Christ's passion, death, and resurrection.

In Acts, the term "witness" also includes a certain juridical meaning: the apostles are witnesses *for* Christ (Acts 1:8; 2:32; 3:15; 13:31). The apostles take their stand as witnesses in defense of Christ and against the Jewish law as well as the people who brought about his death (Acts 3:14-15). For this purpose they, as witnesses, were given a special charism of the Spirit (Acts 1:8; 2:14), which had been foretold for the messianic age (Acts 1:7-10). This assistance of the Spirit would inspire them about what to say when they would be dragged before the tribunal (Luke 12:11-12; Matt 10:18; see Acts 6:10). They do not testify alone, but the holy Spirit is a witness with them (Acts 5:32). From the Spirit comes the strength *(dynamis)* and the courage *(parresia)* with which they give their testimony (Acts 4:13, 33) in the persecutions that characterize the messianic age (Matt 10:18; Mark 13:9; Luke 21:13), which the Christian community at Jerusalem regarded as already here.

The "cloud of witnesses" in Hebrews 12:1 compares the multitude who have suffered but retained their faith to the great crowd of spectators at a Greco-Roman athletic contest, whose presence spurs the contestants to give their best efforts.

The verb *martyreo* has a special use in *John*. Witness is especially that testimony which is given, not specifically to the facts of Jesus' history, but to the person of Jesus as the eternal Son of God (1:15, 34). Thus the Baptist has come to bear witness to the incarnate *Logos* as the light (1:8; see 8:12). As the Son, Jesus is the truth, so that to witness to the truth is to witness to him (3:26). Witness is given to him by the Baptist (1:7-8), by Scripture (5:39), by God (5:32), by his works (5:36), by himself (8:13-14), and later by the Spirit (15:26) and by his disciples (15:27).

The three that bear witness in 1 John 5:7 seem to be baptism, the crucifixion, and the Spirit, though possibly with an allusion to John 19:34-35, which shows that the conviction about the death of Jesus goes back to the beloved disciple. Witness in John is confession. Hence witness can still be given even by those who are not eyewitnesses, i.e., by those who confess who Jesus was and what he signified. The term is in no way reserved for those who are put to death for their witness.

The noun *martyria* is used thirty times in the Johannine writings and a Christian use dominates. The reference is to evangelistic witness to the nature and significance of Christ. This is the active bearing of witness in John 1:7 and Revelation 11:7, but in all the other instances it is the witness that is given, e.g., by the Baptist (John 1:19), by Jesus (3:11), by God (5:32), or by the author (19:35). God's witness is also the point in 1 John 5:9-11, with the conclusion: "And this is the testimony: God gave us eternal life, and this life is in his Son."

The Book of Revelation also speaks about the witness of Jesus (1:2, 9; 12:17; 19:10; 20:4), which is identical to the word of God. In 1:2, the testimony of Jesus refers to the book, and this is perhaps the point in 19:10 as well: the testimony to Jesus is their witness as Christian prophets. Elsewhere this testimony is revelation in general. Because of this witness the author is exiled (1:9), the martyrs are slain (6:9), and the dragon fights against them (12:17).

The persecutions of the second century added a new depth to the concept of witness. The ordinary use lives on, as does the NT use for evangelistic witness. But full witness now becomes witness under threat. Witnessing becomes a special term that is reserved for the one who seals the seriousness of witness with death.

The beginnings of the postbiblical usage can be seen in Acts 22:20 where Paul, in ecstasy, speaks to Christ of "the blood of your witness Stephen." In the same sense the apocalyptic Christ speaks to the Christians at Pergamum of "Antipas, my faithful witness, who was martyred among you" (Rev 2:13). Similarly, Christ's "two witnesses" (Rev 11:3) of eschatological times, "when they have finished their testimony," will be slain by the beast (Rev 11:7); so also, the woman on the scarlet beast "was drunk on the blood of the holy ones and on the blood of the witnesses to Jesus" (Rev 17:6). Finally, because the early Church regarded Jesus as the first and greatest of the martyrs, in Revelation 1:5 and 3:14 Jesus himself is called "the faithful witness," i.e., martyr.

The concept of a struggle with the devil also enters into the idea of martyrdom. This is an imitation and continuation of Christ's sufferings, and Christ himself will provide support. Some may even have a vision of his glory. Such thoughts originate in the NT (see Matt 5:11-12). The martyrological sense is in fact a consequence of the suffering that the Church actually experiences in bearing its witness.

See: APOSTLE, CHARISM, FAITH, PROPHET/PROPHECY, RESURRECTION, SPIRIT, SUFFERING

AUGUSTINE STOCK, O.S.B.

Pastoral-Liturgical Tradition

In the idiom of the courtroom, a witness is one who gives testimony under oath in such a way that the integrity of the person as a whole is implicated in his or her testimony. To give false testimony is not only to expose another to unjust penalties; it is also to destroy one's own access to the trust, honor, and respect that are the lifeblood of human community. In a true sense, life and death—both for the accused and for the witness—may hang in the balance of a witness's testimony. In the Christian tradition the witness is, in a yet more radical sense, one who is wholly implicated in his or her testimony. Placed on trial by the most extreme manifestations of evil, suffering, absurdity, and death, the Christian witness testifies that the love of God in Christ is here and now victorious.

Although the original Greek concept of witness (*martyria*) did not necessarily include physical death as a constitutive component, the association of witness with violent death for the faith developed very early in Christian history. During the first three centuries of the Christian era persecutions were frequent, and many Christians were placed in circumstances where fidelity to a witness to Christ led directly to a bloody death. More and more frequently, the term "martyr" came to refer primarily to this form of Christian witness.

The earliest written accounts of the martyrs, such as the *Letters* of Ignatius of Antioch, *The Martyrdom of Polycarp*, and *The Martyrdom of Saints Perpetua and Felicitas*, emphasize the eagerness and joy with which they embraced their charism of physical participation in Christ's suffering and death. Even as a gruesome and humiliating death overtakes them, each of these martyrs testifies in word and deed that he or she is already sharing in the divine life, light, and power of the risen Christ. In these accounts the martyr is often depicted as both a supremely vigorous athlete or gladiator who heroically conquers the evil powers, and a frail creature of flesh who can achieve nothing without the grace of Christ. This seeming paradox of wholehearted human effort combined with radical reliance on divine grace is a mark of Christian witness.

The testimony of the martyrs made a powerful impression on the early Church. Even their physical remains were regarded as bearing a special relationship to the divine presence; a cult of relics soon developed, with the bones of martyrs especially prized for placement in altarstones. Their names and stories were held in the highest honor as models of Christian life. In some cases martyrs were believed to share in the unique powers of Christ; Perpetua, for example, implied that her prayers could deliver her long-dead brother from his eternal suffering, while Origen asserted that the blood of martyrs is an additional ransom beyond that of Christ.

Even more significant than the effect of the martyr's witness on the Church was its impact on those who were not yet Christians. It was often reported that those who had observed Christians serenely undergoing deprivation, torture, and death for their faith soon thereafter wanted to become Christians themselves. Tertullian went so far as to proclaim that "We multiply whenever we are mown down by you; the blood of Christians is seed" (*Apologeticus*, 50). The conviction that the suffering and/or death of Christians, when it is a willing sharing in the kenotic passion of Christ, is transformed in God into a fount of divine life for others has remained a constant of Christian spirituality through changing eras and circumstances.

Even during the initial era of persecutions, Christians who had been faithful under the threat of death, yet had survived, were sometimes regarded as equal to the martyrs. Given the honorific title of "confessor," in some locales they were accorded the status of the baptized or even of the ordained without having to receive the sacraments in the usual way. By adhering to Christ under the most stressful circumstances they had enacted the living essence of the sacraments, namely, a total self-offering in concert with the crucified and risen Lord; hence it was not necessary for them to receive the sacraments in the form of signs. In subsequent theological development the "baptism of blood," in which an unbaptized person who dies as a result of witnessing to faith in Christ is regarded as baptized, has been affirmed. For those who survive, however, contemporary theology and practice require reception of the sacraments in the usual manner.

Although the initial era of persecution came to an end with the peace of Constantine in 313, the call to give witness through physical martyrdom has reappeared frequently throughout Church history. Yet the vast majority of past and present Christians have not actually experienced a threat to their survival because of being Christian. For them the witness to resurrection joy in the face of contrary evidence must take place in the midst of the more ordinary trials of life and mortality.

The tendency to link intense Christian witness with an ascetical lifestyle began early and has reappeared in many variations through the centuries. A typical example is Gregory of Nyssa's fourth-century *Life of St. Macrina*, in which Gregory finds a Christian ideal in the way Macrina severely minimized both her use of material things (such as food and clothing) and her emotional response to temporal events (such as the deaths of her brothers). From that period until recently, ascetical practices such as celibacy, voluntary poverty, strict obedience to a religious superior, fasting, and other forms of self-denial were often regarded as a normative manner of witnessing to the priority of eternal values over earthly ones.

As a model of Christian witness for today, this ascetical ideal must be given a balanced evaluation. On the one hand, its roots lie within a Hellenistic cultural and philosophical milieu that tended to polarize the physical and the spiritual, to the detriment of what today is understood as a holistic and humanizing way of life. On the other hand, the best of the ascetical tradition highlights a perennial component of Christian witness—namely, the development of a graced and disciplined capacity to live from a center of compassionate and joyful faith even as one experiences the suffering and loss that are endemic to the human condition.

While the ascetical impulse focuses on the inner discipline undergirding Christian witness, the missionary thrust of Christianity focuses on generous proclamation of that witness to others. Convinced that the gospel offers unique access to salvation and that God desires it to be offered to all human beings, Christian missionaries of every generation have given up possessions, comfort, and even their lives to preach the gospel to those who have not yet received it. As Christianity moves toward its third millennium, however, awareness has grown that Christian mission must divest itself of many long-held assumptions—for example, that acceptance of the gospel also requires acceptance of Western culture, or that non-Christians are spiritually inferior to Christians. Since the Spirit of God has preceded the missionaries, all parties come to the encounter able to testify to God's presence in their lives. Hence, missionaries are discovering that the gospel of Jesus is more genuinely proclaimed when they begin from an attitude of deep and respectful listening than when they proceed too hastily to speaking.

Expectations in regard to normative models of Christian witness continue to evolve in other respects as well. While many past models emphasized witness to God as "above and beyond" the everyday world, the emphasis today is more often on witness to God's desire to be among us in the incarnation and to transform human life here and now. In light of this, a much clearer recognition of the potential witness value of a life of Christian marriage, parenthood, and secular work is beginning to emerge. To enter marriage with trust that, with the grace of God, a full-hearted commitment to lifelong love and fidelity can be sustained is a striking witness in a world where superficial relationships and constantly shifting loyalties are the norm. The faithful love of Christian spouses and parents can offer a profound image of God's love, proclaimed through everyday life in family, neighborhood, and workplace.

Struggles for social justice, peace, and the environment are another developing realm of Christian witness. Increasingly, the intensely lived Christian life is marked by the willingness to significantly change one's lifestyle, accept reduction in privilege or status, or give time and talent toward efforts to change the conditions of human life on earth. Fidelity to a witness to the priority of life and justice in these struggles has even led some to physical martyrdom.

Although the cultural, political, and philosophical contexts of Christian life have changed many times through the centuries, the heart of Christian witness remains the same: a wager of the whole person, in every act during life and in the moment of death, on the saving truth of the gospel of Jesus Christ.

MARY FROHLICH

WOMAN/WOMEN

The biblical understanding of humankind* is grounded in the traditions embodied in the narrative accounts of creation and sin (Genesis 1–3). There the woman and man* are depicted as created in the image of God with both privilege and responsibility in relationship to the rest of the natural world. Despite their fundamental goodness, the first couple sinned and were subsequently punished. Their relationship with God was altered and the harmony that they had originally enjoyed with each other and with the world was dashed. The biblical portraits of man and woman, as well as the religious and social roles that each played in the narratives preserved in the Bible, must be understood against this basic anthropological point of view.

Old Testament

Terms. There is one principal Hebrew word, 'iššâ, that translates as "woman." Although some claim that it is derived from 'nš, meaning "to be weak," others believe that, like 'îš (man or husband), it is probably a primary noun (not based on a verbal root). The linguistic relationship between 'iššâ and 'îš is most likely based on the similarity of sound rather than on linguistic etymology. Because the word means woman (in contrast to man), it is sometimes translated "wife." Unlike the word for female, which merely denotes sex, this word connotes relationship between the woman and

her man, although the word itself does not indicate the nature of this relationship.

Family Roles. The biblical tradition shows that the familial roles of the woman were always secondary to corresponding roles of the man. The wife was subservient to her husband (in one version of the Decalogue she was even listed among his possessions [Exod 20:17]); the mother was subordinate to the father; sisters were dependent on brothers; widows were among the most vulnerable members of the society because they were bereft of a male protector. Even when women appear to have exercised a certain amount of authority and responsibility, they did so as an exception to the patriarchal norm or with the consent of men.

Israelite women were expected to marry and thus pass from the control of their fathers or brothers to that of their husbands and fathers-in-law. Since it would be through them that the husband's bloodline would be transmitted, it was imperative that the women be virgins at the time of marriage and faithful to their husbands ever after. Wives were valued primarily for their reproductive powers. (Exceptions to this can be found in Gen 29:18 and 1 Sam 1:8.) Since children, particularly sons, carried forward the family name and ensured possession of the family property, the fertility of the wife was of utmost importance not only to the husband but also to the entire family, clan, and tribe. The tensions between Sarah and Hagar (Gen 16:4-6), Rachel and Leah (Gen 30:1f.), and Hannah and Peninnah (1 Sam 1:2-8) were precisely over the barrenness of the former woman and the fruitfulness of the latter in each pair. The stories about the earliest ancestresses recount how they often circumvented their own inability to provide their husbands with heirs by offering their maidservants as surrogates. Thus Hagar became Abram's concubine and bore him a son (Genesis 16), and Bilhah, the maidservant of Rachel, and Zilpah, the maidservant of Leah, augmented the family of Jacob in the same way (Gen 30:3-14).

In each of the cases mentioned above, the legitimate wife exercised significant control over the lives and sexual activities of their maidservants even after these latter women became the concubines of the husbands. This suggests that a certain hierarchy of power did exist among the women within the patriarchal family. Most prominent in this hierarchy was the legitimate wife who, depending upon the prosperity of her husband, managed her own maidservants. These maidservants may have been taken in payment of debt (Lev 25:39-41), acquired by purchase from poor Hebrew families (Exod 21:1-11), or captured in war (Deut 21:10-13). If they became concubines of the husband they acquired a status that was higher than other servants but still not equal to that of the legitimate wife.

During the period of the ancestors, the practice of concubinage ensured the succession of the paternal bloodline and patrilineal descent. During the time of the monarchy, however, it became a sign of power and prestige. Since ancient treaties often included the marriage of the daughter of the weaker member of the agreement to the stronger member, the size of a royal harem might act as a gauge of the international station of the king (1 Kgs 11:1-3).

As influential as may have been the legitimate wife and the queen-mother (1 Kgs 2:19f.), the social structure of ancient Israel was not matriarchal (mother-rule) nor was descent normally matrilineal (mother-line). However, a few passages suggest remnants of matrilocal (mother-located) marriage practices. The claim that "a man leaves his father and mother and clings to his wife" (Gen 2:24a) does not correspond to ancient patriarchal marriage custom. Neither does the marriage of Samson. He is described as visiting his wife rather than bringing her into his own family (Judg 14:1–15:1). The account of Jacob's fourteen-year residence in the household of Laban (Gen 29:14b-30) also reflects a custom of matrilocal marriage.

Marriage itself was a social arrangement wherein women were exchanged by the male members of the family (fathers [Gen 29:14b-30] or brothers [Gen 24:29-54]). These men were responsible for devising marriages that would enhance the economic condition of the family. This was done through the exchange of property, which constituted a integral element of the marriage. The women brought a dowry and the man paid a bride price (called bridewealth). The dowry served as the woman's portion of the family inheritance. It was administered by her husband and might significantly alter his economic status, but did not by rights belong to him. It offered the woman some degree of protection against domestic abuse, since it had to be returned to her family in the event of divorce. The bridewealth, on the other hand, was a sample of the man's productive ability (Jacob worked seven years for each of his wives [Gen 29:18, 27]). It compensated the woman's family for the loss of her reproductive capacity. Rape was seldom regarded as a violation of the woman, but rather of her husband, or father and brother. Since it jeopardized the patriarchal bloodline, rape undercut the economic advantage that the woman's family might have realized through a substantial bride price.

Despite the fact that in the patriarchal family the mother was subordinate to the father, the law dictated that respect and love be given to her as well as to the father (Exod 20:12; 21:15, 17; Lev 19:3; 20:9; Deut 5:16; 21:18-20; 27:16). The Wisdom tradition further exhorts the young man to heed the teaching of both his father and his mother (Prov 1:8; 6:20) lest he become a fool and, as such, a disappointment to them both (Prov 10:1; 15:20).

The plight of the widow was a matter of public concern. If her deceased husband left her without children, his family might provide her with a levirate marriage. In this situation, a brother or nearest male relative of the deceased was obliged to act as surrogate husband of the widow. The child born of this union was considered the legal heir of the deceased man, assuming his name and inheriting his property (Deut 25:5-10; see also Gen 38:6-11; Ruth 4:1-12). Although the practice was concerned primarily with the perpetuation of the name and property rights of the deceased, it did afford the widow considerable security.

Daughters were valued in as much as they might augment the family resources by commanding substantial bridewealth. They could inherit only in the absence of a male heir, and even then, when they would marry, they were required to do so within the father's tribe in order to ensure the tribal possession of the father's property (Num 27:1-11; 36:1-9). A notable exception to this inheritance custom is found in the epilogue of the Book of Job, where his three daughters receive a share of the estate along with their brothers (Job 42:13-15).

The Broader Society. In a patriarchal society, positions of authority are normally held by men. This does not mean that Israelite women were not powerful. Quite the contrary is true. Only the priesthood was closed to women, and this was most likely because of the mysterious reproductive powers of the female body as well as the blood taboo. Women did exercise significant influence in both the family and broader social circles.

Early Israelite households, like those of other ancient Near Eastern societies, were quite self-sufficient. This meant that all members of the household were required to contribute to the economic survival of the family. The production, gathering, preparation, and storage of food were domestic responsibilities that frequently fell to the women. In addition, the mother played an important role in the education and socialization of the young, a responsibility that was critical for the vitality of the community. The portrayal of the virtuous wife found in the Book of Proverbs depicts a woman who not only manages the family household but also is engaged in business transactions outside of the home (31:10-31).

There is additional biblical evidence that women were active outside of the home. Although they were prevented from functioning as priests, women still participated in the cultic life of the people. They served at the entrance of the meeting tent (Exod 38:8; 1 Sam 2:22) and as singers in the postexilic community (Ezra 2:65; Neh 7:67). It appears that Israelite society did not accept its king's wife as ruler in her own right. However, it did recognize her as a regent or temporary care-taker monarch (2 Kings 11). On the other hand, it seems to have acknowledged the legitimacy of queenship for foreign lands (e.g., Jezebel [1 Kings 21] and Esther [Esther]). It also endorsed the prophetic activity of Deborah (Judg 4:4), Miriam (Exod 15:20), Huldah (2 Kgs 22:14), Noadiah (Neh 6:14), and the wife of Isaiah (Isa 8:3). Finally, the David saga includes accounts of two different wise women who were able to influence the lives of their respective communities and, thereby, save them from disaster (2 Sam 14:1-20; 20:14-22). Unlike the rule of monarchs and priests, which were fixed institutionalized organizations, the roles of prophet and sage were more charismatic and, thus, more open. This may explain why women were more easily accepted in some roles than in others.

Finally, women are depicted exclusively as sexual partners, either as legitimate lovers or as harlots. Secular or commercial prostitution seems to have been accepted at certain times in Israel's history (e.g., Tamar [Genesis 38], Rahab [Joshua 2], the two harlots who came before Solomon [1 Kgs 13:16-28]) and condemned at other times (Lev 19:29). Cult prostitution, whether performed by men or by women, was always condemned (Deut 23:18). The principal depiction of a woman as a lover, equal to her male partner, is found in the Song of Songs. Although most of the OT is clearly androcentric in its perspective, these love lyrics embody no gender stereotypes, nor are the erotic inclinations of the woman depicted here filtered through a male lens. When she speaks, it is clearly from a woman's point of view.

Religious Language. When the Bible depicts God anthropomorphically with male imagery, it is usually in some political role (e.g., warrior or creator, king, and husband—in the sense of covenant partner, not sexual partner). When female imagery is ascribed to God, it usually refers to some kind of maternal role. God is depicted as having given birth to Israel (Deut 32:18) or as comforting it as a mother would comfort (Isa 66:13). In the process of restoring the people, God is said to cry out as a woman in labor (Isa 42:14).

One religious image, the female personification of wisdom, stands out. The identity and nature of this figure is an enigma, for at times she appears to be at home at the crossroads and by the gates of the city (Prov 8:1-5), and at other times she is on the stage of creation itself, watching and participating in the marvels of divine activity (Prov 8:22-31). This Wisdom Woman is clearly described as having originated from and being other than God (Prov 8:22; Sir 24:23), but she speaks in the way that God speaks (see divine speeches in the I-style in Exod 3:4-10 and Isa 43:1-7), and she seems to possess divine qualities in her own right (Wis 7:22-30). She is not God, but she is an intimate companion of God, acting as God would act. Some claim that this characterization of wisdom is a remnant of ancient Near Eastern (even Israelite) worship of a goddess of wisdom. Others see it merely as a development from the feminine form of *hokmâ*, the Hebrew word for wisdom.

See: ADAM AND EVE, FAMILY, HUMANKIND, IMAGE OF GOD, MAN/MEN, MARRIAGE, MOTHER

DIANNE BERGANT, C.S.A.

Pastoral-Liturgical Tradition

A new understanding of women and women's place in social and ecclesial life has been developing for more than a century. In his 1963 encyclical letter "*Pacem in terris*," Pope John XXIII summarized the progress:

It is obvious to everyone that women are now taking a part in public life. This is happening more rapidly perhaps in nations of Christian civilization, and, more

slowly but broadly, among peoples who have inherited other traditions or cultures. Since women are becoming ever more conscious of their human dignity, they will not tolerate being treated as mere material instruments, but demand rights befitting a human person both in domestic and public life (*Pacem in terris*, no. 41).

Since the Renaissance, Western society has seen a gradual recognition of and respect for the human rights of all people. Pope John wrote "*Pacem in terris*" conscious of this historical movement. Along with the liberal political and social movements of the past four centuries, and the contemporary civil rights movement, gay and lesbian liberation movements, and Third World liberation theologies, the various forms of the women's movement can be seen as part of a reaction against a socially constructed patriarchal system.

Feminist thought begins in social analysis. It proceeds to call for a new understanding of the nature of women, a rethinking of the demands of justice in relationship to women, and a critical understanding of the place of women in the highly important world of symbolic and ritual life.

When feminist writers begin their analysis of women and the understanding of women in society, they frequently critique the social structures that interpret and evaluate women's lives and experience, as well as the interpretation and evaluation itself. Male-dominated economic, social, political, and religious institutions, and male-dominated linguistic and symbolic systems tell women, children, and other men that women and their contribution to human existence is of secondary value. (The reality of maleness and the activities of males are more highly prized.) Being judged inferior, women can then be relegated to a sphere of life other than the male. The domestic world becomes the proper place for women, and care for home and children becomes properly women's work. When value is placed on home and child-rearing, home and child-rearing become second class activities, male protestations to the contrary notwithstanding. Economic, political, and social structures reinforce the male interpretation and evaluation of women and their experience as secondary though essential. Linguistic, symbolic, and ritual systems further solidify male dominated interpretations. Finally, religious institutions give divine legitimization to the resultant construction of the meaning and value of womanhood and female experience.

The place where the secondary status of women can be most easily seen in America is in economic life. The inferior economic condition of women in America has been noted by many feminist authors and the feminization of poverty has been substantiated by governmental studies. Women are paid a fraction of the wage men are paid for the same or similar work. Women in the child-bearing years are less likely to be hired or promoted for managerial or professional positions. The expectation that women are primarily responsible for child care, combined with the lack of child-care facilities in many workplaces, leaves women at a disadvantage in the workplace. Lack of adequate child-care facilities interrupts, shortens, or makes unduly difficult the careers of many women. All of these conditions lead to households headed by women finding themselves increasingly impoverished.

Contemporary reflection on the meaning and value of women and women's experience, a reflection engaged in by both women and men, yields a different vision. First and fundamentally, both women and men are the subjects of human dignity and human rights. Popes, bishops, and feminists agree that both men and women share the same human dignity and rights articulated in the United Nations Universal Declaration of Human Rights and in *"Pacem in terris."* The intelligence and wisdom, sensitivity and power of women is similarly affirmed. The appropriateness of women making personal decisions as to vocation, occupation, living situations, and child-

bearing and rearing is also widely asserted. Finally, a female spirituality that experiences, celebrates, and deepens the experience of God and divine life in women, in her body and its cycles, and in the uniquely feminine experience of childbirth and nurture is increasingly discussed. No longer is the female body seen simply as a temptation to men or its rhythms interpreted as a problem for women in the living of the Christian life.

Recognition of the inherent dignity of women results in a more positive evaluation of those things traditionally associated with women and the feminine: domestic life, nurture of children, closeness to nature, intuition, cooperation, and tenderness, to name a few. Conversely, some of the things typically associated with men— aggression, domination, control, abstract thought, and excessive independence—are also reevaluated, usually in a less positive light.

In psychological and moral literature, one finds research and speculation on particularly feminine patterns of psychological, social, and moral development and experience. Though most scholars agree that further research is needed to properly understand the relationship between culture and biological determinants in the development of the female psyche, tentative acceptance and a positive evaluation is given to the fact that there are different ways of experiencing, knowing, judging, and deciding.

A changed understanding of women and women's relationship to God and to men demands a new understanding of the requirements of justice in relationship to women. A new realization of women's giftedness, freedom, and responsibility requires men and women to find new ways by which women's gifts can be respected, cultivated, and used for the common good. Justice demands that free and competent people be given maximum opportunity for choice in accord with their human dignity. If women are understood to share in the fullness of human dignity and human rights, women must also be permitted and encouraged to share in and be responsible for the fullness of private, public, and ecclesial life. Access to education, employment, and advancement, and a share in influence, authority, and power, must be assured. The Church, as a model of justice for human communities, ought to be particularity sensitive and responsive to the legitimate place of women in society, especially in the Church's internal life.

As our understanding of the nature of women continues to develop and as the demands of justice continue to be more deeply understood, the symbolic and ritual life of society and Church must change. The use of inclusive language in both the secular and ecclesial worlds is a reflection of deep insights: the power and importance of language in shaping consciousness and the dignity and proper place of women in the divine ordering. A mutually reinforcing system can be expected to develop. As more and more men and women experience the complementarity and equality of men and women, a language will evolve that will reflect that experience. Likewise, as inclusive language becomes more widely used in society and in the Church, consciousness of the human dignity of both men and women will be raised.

Liturgical changes including women in ritual functions also reflect an understanding of women and their place in society and Church. The inclusion of women in those roles charged with symbolic social importance—e.g., police officers, judges, doctors—will enhance the status of women in society. To the degree that women are incorporated into religious rituals, women's position in human life will be enhanced. In those institutions and communities where men deny women a full and equal place in ritual life, women can be expected to be looked upon as inferior and those societies will deal with the consequences.

See: HUMANKIND, MAN/MEN, SEXUALITY

JAMES R. HALSTEAD, O.S.A.

WORD

The spoken word, along with the other modes of language, is a uniquely human characteristic. Words reveal our innermost selves, shape and express our understanding of reality, and help establish our relationship with others. Accordingly, one of the most important and frequent metaphors in biblical and Christian tradition used to describe God's self-revelation and the communication of the message of salvation is that of "word."

Old Testament

God's Word. The power of God's word appears immediately in the first chapter of the Book of Genesis. God says "Let there be light" and there is light (Gen 1:3). Through the rest of the chapter God continues to speak in order to bring the world into being. Psalm 33 declares, "By the word of the LORD the heavens were made; by the breath of his mouth all their host" (33:6). Ben Sira's hymn to creation is also a hymn to the word of God (Sir 42:15–43:35). God's word brings creation into being (42:15; see Wis 9:1), marks out the path for the lightning (42:13), and drives the winds (42:17). All things happen according to God's word (43:27).

The offer of covenant, which is the creation of Israel, is brought to the people as the word of the Lord. They respond, "Everything the LORD has said, we will do" (Exod 19:8; 24:3, 7). The covenant charter, the Ten Commandments, are referred to as the Ten Words which the Lord has spoken (Deut 10:4; see 5:5, 22). Those who break the commandments despise the word of the Lord (Num 15:31). When the covenant is renewed after the incident of the golden calf Moses enjoins on the Israelites all that the Lord has told him (Exod 34:32). Israel is exhorted to remember that at Sinai they saw no form representing God; God's revelation came to them through the word (Deut 4:15).

The word of the Lord represents God's promise to the people. The word of the

Lord reveals the promises to Abraham of land and descendants (Gen 15:1, 4). God's word reveals to Abraham's servant that Rebekah is Isaac's future wife (Gen 24:51), the mother of Abraham's future descendants. The spying out of the land (Deut 1:21) and the eventual taking of the land happen "as the LORD has said" (Deut 9:3; 27:3). Israel will prosper in the land according to the word of the Lord (Deut 6:3, 19). Joshua leads them in the land (Deut 31:3), they defeat their enemies, and settle in the land just as God said to their ancestors. "Not a single promise that the LORD made [said] to the house of Israel was broken; every one was fulfilled" (Josh 21:45; 23:14).

God's Word Spoken Through the Prophets. Most often God's word is brought to the people through a prophet. Moses, the premier prophet to whom God speaks face to face (Exod 33:11; Num 12:8; Deut 34:10; Sir 45:5), is sent to speak the word of the Lord to Pharaoh (Exod 6:28-30) and the plagues happen in the way and at the time that the Lord has said through Moses (Exodus 7–12). Pharaoh's heart is hardened, just as the Lord had said (7:13, 22; 8:11, 15; 9:12, 35). Moses' prophetic office is challenged by Miriam and Aaron, "Is it through Moses alone that the LORD speaks?" (Num 12:2), and God defends his right to speak the word of the Lord.

As a young man the prophet-judge Samuel hears the voice of the Lord in the night (1 Sam 3:7-14) and from that time on God is revealed to Samuel through the divine word (1 Sam 3:21; see Sir 46:13). The word of the Lord comes to Samuel instructing him to appoint Saul as king (1 Sam 9:16-17) and to reject Saul because Saul has rejected God's word (15:10, 23, 26; see Prov 13:13; 19:16). God speaks to Samuel again, instructing him to anoint David king in place of Saul (1 Sam 16:4).

Two prophets bring the word of God to David. Nathan brings the word that David's house and kingdom will endure forever (2 Sam 7:8-17; see 1 Chr 17:3). Nathan also brings God's word of rebuke after David's affair with Bathsheba (2 Sam 12:1-12). David too has despised God's word (12:9) and God speaks the consequences to him. The word of the Lord came to Gad after David had taken the census offering him a choice between three afflictions (2 Sam 24:11).

In the stories of Elijah and Elisha the word of the Lord is always at the forefront. The word of the Lord instructs Elijah in his mission (e.g., 1 Kgs 17:2, 5, 8; 18:1; see Sir 48:3). The widow whose son he raises from the dead recognizes him as a minister of the word, "The word of the LORD comes truly from your mouth" (17:24). At Horeb, the word of the Lord encourages him and gives him a new commission (19:9; see 19:14). Elisha too is identified as one who "has the word of the LORD" (2 Kgs 3:12; see 7:1; Sir 48:12).

An important element in the Deuteronomic history (Joshua–Kings) is the fulfillment of the prophetic word. What the prophet has said is as good as done. The word Samuel hears in his inaugural vision, the rejection of the house of Eli, is declared fulfilled at the death of Abiathar (1 Kgs 2:27). Nathan's word to David concerning his kingdom and the building of the Temple is fulfilled in Solomon (1 Kgs 5:19; 8:20). The prophecy of Ahijah the Shilonite that the kingdom would be divided is fulfilled at the failure of Rehoboam to win over the northern tribes (1 Kgs 12:15). Abijah's word to Jeroboam's wife concerning the death of her son comes to pass (1 Kgs 14:18; see 15:29). Elijah's prophecy that the house of Ahab would fall and the dogs lick up the blood of Jezebel is fulfilled in Jehu's bloodbath (2 Kgs 9:36; 10:17; see 1 Kgs 22:38). The mention of fulfillment of the word of God through a prophet becomes a regular refrain throughout the history (see, e.g., 1 Kgs 13:5, 26, 32; 16:12, 34; 17:16; 20:35-36; 2 Kgs 1:17; 4:44; 7:16; 14:25). Finally, Nebuchadnezzar's destruction of Jerusalem and the beginning of exile come about according to the word foretold by the Lord (2 Kgs 24:2, 13).

Each of the three major prophets—Isaiah, Jeremiah, and Ezekiel—and nine of the twelve minor prophets (all except Obadiah, Nahum, and Habakkuk) introduce their oracles with the phrase: "The word of the LORD came to . . ." (e.g., Isa 38:4; Jer 1:2, 4; Ezek 1:3; 6:1; Hos 1:1; Joel 1:1; Jonah 1:1; 3:1; Mic 1:1; Zeph 1:1; Hag 1:1; Zech 1:1; Mal 1:1) or "Now hear the word of the LORD" (e.g., Isa 1:10; 39:5; Jer 7:2; Ezek 6:3; Hos 4:1; Amos 7:16). The whole message of the prophet is the word of the Lord.

God speaks through non-Israelite prophets as well. Balaam, the prophet hired by Balak, king of Moab, is charged to say only what God tells him (Num 22:35). His oracles represent the word of the Lord (Num 23:17; 24:4, 16).

The Power of the Human Word. Not only God's word has power; the human word once spoken takes on a life and reality of its own. Isaac, although he intends to bless his elder son Esau, is tricked into blessing his younger son Jacob (Gen 27:1-29). When Esau arrives for his blessing, Isaac realizes his mistake. He declares "I blessed him. Now he must remain blessed!" (27:33). The word has been spoken and has already taken effect.

In his eagerness to win a battle against the Ammonites, Jephthah rashly vows to sacrifice to the Lord whoever comes first out of the doors of his house to meet him (Judg 11:30-31). When the first to appear turns out to be his only daughter, Jephthah tears his garments and says to her, "Alas, daughter, you have struck me down and brought calamity upon me. For I have made a vow* to the LORD and I cannot retract" (11:35). The word has been spoken and cannot be taken back.

Wisdom, Psalms and the Word. Proverbs declares that "every word of God is tested" (30:5). God's word can be trusted (Sir 33:3; Ps 130:5); God's word is faithful (Ps 145:13). The author of the Book of Wisdom sees God's word as the agent of all good things that happen to God's people and all bad things that happen to their enemies. God's word heals those stung by the serpents (Wis 16:12) and feeds the people with manna (16:26; see Deut 8:3). "When peaceful stillness compassed everything and the night in its swift course was half spent, [God's] all-powerful word from heaven's royal throne bounded, a fierce warrior into the doomed land bearing the sharp sword of [God's] inexorable decree" to destroy the firstborn of Egypt (Wis 18:14-16).

In Psalm 119 "word" is one of the eight terms for the law that is repeated in every stanza. The psalmist sings that God's word gives life (Ps 119:25, 107), strength (119:28), light (119:130), and hope (119:74, 81, 114, 147). God's word is the assurance of God's goodness (119:65). God's word endures forever, as firm as the heavens (119:89). How great is the word of the Lord!

See: COVENANT, ORACLE, PROPHET

IRENE NOWELL, O.S.B.

New Testament

"Word" (*logos*) is used 331 times in the NT and in most of the same ways in which it is used in the Septuagint and in Greek literature in general. It can mean a statement (Luke 20:20), an assertion (Matt 15:12), a command (Luke 4:36), a report or story (Matt 28:15), a proverb or saying (John 4:37), an oracle or prophecy (John 2:22), a speech (Matt 15:12), or the matter under discussion (Mark 9:10). In the plural "words" (*logoi*) can refer to speeches of various sorts (Matt 7:24; 13:37; 26:1; Mark 10:24; 13:31; Luke 1:20; John 14:24). It can be used of written words and speeches, as well as of the separate books of a larger work (Acts 1:1; Heb 5:11). It can also be used, although not often, to mean "ground" (Acts 10:29) or "reason" (Acts 18:14) for something. With the exception of Johannine Literature, however, *logos* is not used in the NT in the more philosophical senses.

What characterizes the use of *logos* in the NT is not some new meaning for the word beyond what is found in the Septuagint but its reference to the divine revelation of God, specifically the revelation through Jesus Christ and his messengers. In many cases the "word of God" is simply the Christian message, the good news. Apostles and preachers are said to "speak the word of God" (Acts 4:31), to "proclaim the word of God" (Acts 13:5), or to "teach the word of God" (Acts 18:11). Because it is the word of *God*, it is also efficacious (Heb 4:12; 1 Thess 2:13), to be received (1 Thess 1:16; Acts 8:14; 11:1), and to be acted on (Jas 1:21). Since Christ brings the word of revelation, the "word of the Lord," the "word of Christ," or the "words" of Jesus can be used in the same sense as the "word of God" (John 5:14; 12:48; 18:32; Acts 8:26; 12:24; 13:44, 48-49; Col 3:16). Other phrases often qualify *logos*, such as "the word of the kingdom" (Matt 13:19); "the word of salvation" (Acts 13:26); "the word of reconciliation" (2 Cor 5:19); "the word of the cross" (1 Cor 1:18); "the word of righteousness" (Heb 5:13). But "word" is also often used simply to refer to the Christian message as such (Matt 13:20-23; Mark 2:2; Luke 8:12-13; Acts 6:4; Gal 6:6; Jas 1:21).

Prologue of John (1:1-18). The most striking use of the term *logos* is found in the Johannine literature, specifically in John 1:1-18 and 1 John 1:1-4. While some scholars think that the Prologue of John (John 1:1-18) is a unified whole and entirely the work of the evangelist, most are convinced that behind the Prologue lies a hymn that has been commented on and added to in order to be used as the beginning of the Fourth Gospel. The references to John the Baptist (John 1:6-8, 15) were later additions to incorporate the hymn into an already existing narrative that began with episodes about John. Also, the explanatory comments (John 1:12c-13, 17-18) were added to the original hymn.

While the structure of the original hymn is debated, it seems to have consisted of three strophes. In the first (John 1:1-5), the *logos* was with God at the beginning and was God and was the means through which God created the universe and life. In the second strophe (John 1:10-12b), the *logos* came to its own people, was not received by them, but gave power to become children of God to those who did receive the

logos. In the final strophe (John 1:14-16, 19), the *logos* became flesh in Jesus of Nazareth and the glory of the *logos* was experienced by those who believe.

How Christians understand the meaning of *logos* in this hymn depends on its religious and intellectual background. Various backgrounds have been suggested. Some scholars understand the *logos* against the background of Jewish targums and midrashim, that is, the Aramaic translations of the Bible and certain kinds of Jewish interpretation. For example, in the midrash of the Four Nights, the first night is that of creation. The Word of the Lord seems identified with the primordial light which shone at creation, an identification that resembles that found in the Prologue: "The first night: when the Lord was revealed over the world to create it. The world was without form and void and darkness was spread over the face of the abyss and the word [*memra*] of the Lord was the light, and it shone; and he called it the First Night" (*Targum Neofiti I* to Exod 12:42).

R. Bultmann (1971) situated the background for the *logos* in the Johannine hymn in Gnosticism. According to Bultmann, the hymn in its original form was a Gnostic hymn to John the Baptist. It was later Christianized to become a hymn to Jesus as the incarnate *logos*, becoming part of the polemic against followers of John the Baptist. Behind the hymn to John the Baptist was a pre-Christian Gnostic myth about a heavenly redeemer figure. According to the myth an Original Man (*Urmensch*) first dwelt in the realm of light, but he later became scattered about in the world of darkness below in the form of human souls. God then sent a heavenly redeemer to awaken the human souls below, revealing to them their true identity and so bringing them once more into the world of light above.

Gnostic documents discovered at Nag Hammadi have stimulated further interest in how the Gospel of John, particularly the Prologue, is related to Gnosticism. The most striking parallel to the Prologue is found in *Trimorphic Protennoia:* "I revealed myself to them in their tents *(skēnē)* as the Word and I revealed myself in the likeness of their shape. And I wore everyone's garment and hid myself within them" (*Trim. Prot.* 47.14-18).

Jewish Wisdom literature, however, provides the closest parallels to the use of *logos* in the Johannine hymn (Proverbs, Sirach, Baruch, and the Wisdom of Solomon). The various attributes and activities ascribed to "wisdom" *(sophia)* are ascribed to the "word" *(logos)* in the Johannine hymn.

Both the *logos* of the Johannine hymn and wisdom in the Jewish literature are with God in the beginning (John 1:1; Prov 8:22-23, 27, 29-30; Sir 24:9; Wis 9:9); both are involved in the creation of the world (John 1:3-4; Wis 7:22; 8:13; 9:9; Prov 8:35); both are associated with light (John 1:4-5; Wis 6:12; 7:29-30; 8:26); both seek to find a place among humans (John 1:10-14; Prov 8:30-31; Sir 1:15; 24:8; Wis 7:27; 8:1; 24:10; Bar 3:37–4:1).

Both the Wisdom literature and the Prologue stand within the Jewish tradition of speculation about the deeper meaning, the hidden mystery, in the early chapters of Genesis. And many of the parallels between the *logos* in the hymn and the figure of wisdom occur in poetic passages such as Proverbs 8:22-31:

> The Lord begot me, the first-born of his ways,
>   the forerunner of his prodigies of long ago;
> From of old I was poured forth,
>   at the first, before the earth.
> When there were no depths I was brought forth,
>   when there were no fountains or springs of water;
> Before the mountains were settled into place,
>   before the hills, I was brought forth;
> While as yet the earth and the fields were not made,
>   nor the first clods of the world.
> When he established the heavens I was there,
> when he marked out the vault over the face of the deep;
> When he set for the sea its limit,
>   so that the waters should not transgress his command;
> Then was I beside him as his craftsman,
>   and I was his delight day by day,
> Playing before him all the while,
>   playing on the surface of his earth;
>   and I found delight in the children of men.

Jewish Wisdom literature differs from the Johannine hymn, however, in that the *logos* never displaces the figure of wisdom. This striking difference indicates that the speculation found in the hymn has moved beyond Proverbs, Sirach, Baruch, and the Wisdom of Solomon. The displacement of wisdom by *logos* is found, however, in the works of the Alexandrian Jewish exegete Philo of Alexandria (first century CE). Both Philo and the hymn use *logos* as the equivalent of wisdom in Jewish Wisdom literature. In both, *logos* overshadows the figure of wisdom. Both Philo and the hymn (John 1:1-2) understand the *logos* as existing with God before creation; both connect the *logos* with the "beginning" *(archē)* of Gen 1:1; both think of the *logos* as the instrument through which God created the universe; both associate the *logos* with light; both connect the *logos* with becoming children of God.

While the parallels between Philo and the Johannine hymn are striking, the concept of *logos* in Philo is more philosophical than *logos* in the hymn. Nor is the parallelism close enough to think that the author of the hymn was acquainted with the works of Philo. Nevertheless, the similarities strongly suggest that the Johannine hymn must be seen against both the background of Jewish Wisdom literature and the background of Jewish speculation about *logos*/wisdom which extended beyond Jewish Wisdom literature and included the speculative traditions reflected in Philo of Alexandria. Both the Johannine hymn and Philo belong to the larger movement of Hellenistic Jewish wisdom/*logos* speculation.

Logos in the Prologue of John, however, moves beyond that Hellenistic Jewish speculation to identify this *logos* with Jesus of Nazareth. Neither Jewish Wisdom literature nor the kind of Hellenistic Jewish speculation represented by Philo ever sought to identify either wisdom or *logos* with a specific human being. The hymn in the Prologue is the clearest example in first-century Christian literature of both an incarnation and a preexistence Christology. It affirms both that the *logos* has become flesh in the person of Jesus of Nazareth and that Jesus of Nazareth existed before the incarnation, indeed before the creation of the world, as God's divine *logos*. This development in the hymn and in the Gospel of John as a whole is most characteristic of the Johannine tradition.

This development, however, was not without the ambiguity reflected in John 1:14:

And the Word became flesh
and made his dwelling among us,
and we saw his glory,
the glory as of the Father's only Son,
full of grace and truth.

The hymn affirms both that "the Word [*logos*] became flesh" and that "we saw his glory, the glory as of the Father's only Son." The first statement identifies the "word" with the human being Jesus of Nazareth; the second statement identifies Jesus with the *divine word*. This statement created a tension between a more incarnational Christology and a somewhat more docetic Christology that did not value the earthly life of Jesus including his crucifixion and death. Such ambiguity is not surprising, given the religious and intellectual background of the hymn in Hellenistic Jewish speculation.

First Letter of John. The same ambiguity seems to have surfaced in the Johannine community shortly after the completion of the Gospel of John (ca. 90 CE). Some members wanted to emphasize the incarnational intent of the Prologue (and the Gospel) more than the divine *logos*, while others wanted to emphasize the divine aspect of Jesus as the *logos* more than the incarnation (see 1 John 4:1-3; 2 John 7). These differences created tensions and conflicts that resulted in a schism. Disputes about the interpretation of *logos* appear in the opening verses of the First Letter of John (1 John 1:1-4):

What was from the beginning,
  what we have heard,
  what we have seen with our eyes,
  what we looked upon
  and touched with our hands
  concerns the Word [*logos*] of life—
for the life was made visible;
  we have seen it and testify to it
  and proclaim to you the eternal life
  that was with the Father and was
    made visible to us—
what we have seen and heard
  we proclaim now to you,
  so that you too may have fellowship
    with us;
  for our fellowship is with the Father
  and with his Son, Jesus Christ.
We are writing this so that our joy may
    be complete.

The author spoke for those in the community who stressed the incarnation, the reality of the Word's earthly identification with Jesus of Nazareth. He emphasized that the "word of life," the *logos* of the Prologue, was the same one who was from the beginning and whom the correct interpreters of the Johannine tradition had heard, seen with their own eyes, looked upon, and touched with their own hands. It ultimately derived from the source of their tradition, the Beloved Disciple (see John 13:23-26; 19:25-27; 20:2-10; 21:7; 21:20-23; 21:24). Against his opponents, the author of 1 John wanted to emphasize that the correct interpretation of *logos* in the Prologue affirmed the significance of the earthly life of Jesus, the word of life.

In the end, the author's interpretation of Johannine tradition was probably absorbed into the churches represented by the Pastoral Letter, Acts, Matthew, and 1 Peter. The other more docetic interpretation may have been absorbed into various second-century

Christian Gnostic groups, accounting for the fact that the first commentary on the Gospel of John was by the Valentinian Gnostic, Heracleon (ca. 160 CE). In the end, the message in the Prologue (John 1:1-18) and in the First Letter of John (1 John 1:1-4) is that Jesus of Nazareth can be approached in many ways, but he can only be understood on Christian terms and from the perspective of Christian faith.

The "word of God" in Christian usage is both the "word become human" or "enfleshed" of John's Gospel and the way God speaks to the Church: in self-disclosure to Israel culminating in Jesus, to which the Scriptures testify; in the prophetic word of preachers and teachers; in the events of our lives, the "signs of the times" (Matt 16:3; "the present time," Luke 12:56); in our sisters and our brothers; and in the book of the world around us. The Roman liturgy for many recent centuries proclaimed that *verbum caro factum est*, with genuflection at that point, at the end of every Eucharist (John 1:1-18), to celebrate the incarnation of the Word; likewise in the devotional prayer the "Angelus." Within the liturgy proper there are admonitions before the Bible is read to "hear the word of the LORD" and a solemn affirmation, as the book is reverenced with a kiss, that, "[This is] the word of the LORD."

See: GOOD NEWS, JESUS CHRIST, MYSTERY, POWER, PROPHET, SALVATION, SPIRIT OF GOD, WISDOM

WILLIAM G. THOMPSON, S.J., AND
GERARD S. SLOYAN

WORLD

While in the OT there is no single term that is used for the world there are ways in which this reality is expressed in relation both to God and humanity. The Greek OT differs in its usage from the Hebrew Scriptures. The NT continues both usages, but goes beyond them by focusing on the tension between the world and the people of God. The early Patristic outlook was characterized by Christian abandonment of the world, while the modern concern is marked by a call for the Christian to transform the world by living within it.

Old Testament

In the Hebrew Scriptures heaven and earth* is the normal designation for the universe, which the Lord created. The pairing of these two opposites simply refers to the totality of the cosmos.* Thus Genesis 1:1 uses heaven and earth to indicate the world as a whole and its entire order. The world was created to be lived in by humans in space and time. In the Hebrew Scriptures the world as a whole is situated within the context of salvation history so that the world is seen primarily in relation to humanity. As with humanity, the world as a whole is understood in terms of its genesis; it is not viewed as nature but as creature. Furthermore, its creatureliness is bound up with that of humanity (see Genesis 1–11). Moreover, the relationship of humanity to the world is viewed in terms of the Exodus: the creation of heaven and earth in six days contextualizes the world in terms of the covenant between the Lord and his people. The creation of heaven and earth, therefore, is the first of the saving deeds of the Lord of the Covenant. The world is not divine, but it is good (Gen 1:1–2:4). It is the work of a God who is beyond it.

The world as creature stands in close connection with God and has an existence clearly dependent on God for continuation (e.g., Psalm 104). It is God's fidelity to the world that guarantees its preservation. The eschatological hope for a new world is expressed in terms of a new heaven and a new earth (e.g., Isa 65:17; 66:22). In cosmological terms the world is understood to have a threefold division of heaven, earth, and sea (e.g., Exod 20:11; Ps 146:6).

The Hebrew term *tēbēl* (a poetic synonym of *'ereṣ*, "earth") is sometimes translated as "world" in the sense of the expanse of the earth (e.g., Job 18:18; 37:12 [NRSV]; Prov 8:31 [RSV]; Isa 27:6). It also refers to the foundation of the world (e.g., Pss 18:16; 93:1; 96:10). The world is the object of the Lord's just judgment (Ps 9:9), and it is punished for its evil (Isa 13:11). *Tēbēl* can refer to the inhabited world (Isa 14:17). The whole world belongs to the Lord (Pss 24:1; 33:8; 50:12).

In the Greek OT cosmos is used to speak of the world. The concept is a Hellenistic one, and so it only appears in the late Greek books of Wisdom (nineteen times) and Maccabees (five times). Here world corresponds to the visible universe, its inhabitants, or humanity. God created the world from nothing (2 Macc 7:23; 13:14; Wis 9:9; 11:17). God rules it (2 Macc 12:15), but humanity is to govern it in holiness and justice (Wis 9:3). The unifying principle of the world can be observed by humans because of the cosmos' cohesiveness and order (Wis 7:17-22). Because the goodness of God is reflected in the world, it fights on behalf of the just (Wis 5:20; 16:17). Adam is the first-formed father of the world (Wis 10:1); Noah, its hope (Wis 14:6); and the wise, its safety (Wis 6:24). By envy of the devil death entered the world (Wis 2:24). Idols came into the world because of humanity's vanity (Wis 14:14).

New Testament

The pairing of heaven and earth is also used occasionally in the NT to speak of the world, which will pass away (e.g., Mark 13:31). The eschatological hope for a new world is expressed in terms of a new heaven and a new earth where the justice of God will reside (2 Pet 3:13; Rev 21:1). As in the OT the sea together with the heaven and earth comprises the cosmos (e.g., Acts 4:24; Rev 10:6). God created the world (Acts 17:24).

The Greek term *oikoumenē* is used fifteen times in the NT to refer to the world in the sense of the inhabited world, humanity, or civilization (e.g., Matt 24:14; Acts 11:28; Rev 3:10). God has set the day when the world will be judged with justice (Acts 17:31). *Oikoumenē* refers to "Asia and the whole world" (Acts 19:27), the Roman empire (Acts 17:6; 24:5), and every political realm (Luke 4:5). Satan leads the whole world astray (Rev 12:9).

The Greek term *aiōn* can refer to the world as the universe created by God through the Son (Heb 1:2) and his word (Heb 11:3). *Aiōn* carries a pejorative sense when it is used of the people or things of the world in opposition to God (Luke 16:8; Eph 2:2). The rulers of this world crucified Christ (1 Cor 2:8). In Romans 12:2 Paul warns Christians not to conform to this world. It has its own transitory wealth (1 Tim 6:17), which is a source of temptation to Christians (2 Tim 4:4). *Aiōn* is used further to mean the cares of this world (Mark 4:19; Matt 13:22) as well as worldliness in general (1 Cor 1:20; 2:6; 3:18). This world has its own god opposed to Christ (2 Cor 4:4; 1 Cor 2:6-8).

Aiōn is also used to refer to this world in contrast to the world to come. The present world is corrupt, whereas the one to come is not (Matt 12:32; Mark 10:30; Luke 18:30; 20:35; Gal 1:4; Eph 1:21; Heb 6:5). *Aiōn* can denote the duration of the world (Matt 13:39-40, 49; 28:20). This world is of limited duration, with a beginning (foundation) and an end (Matt 25:35; Luke 11:50; 1 Cor 10:11; Heb 4:3).

The Greek term most commonly translated as world in the NT is *cosmos*. This term is both spatial and temporal in its meaning, and is especially used to refer to the world of humanity in opposition to God. While the world, which was created by God, is not evil in itself, it is fallen and in need of the redemption of Christ,* who has been sent by the Father into the world to save and illuminate it. Primarily, then, the world is the locus of salvation, where the *logos* has become flesh and entered into human history (John 1:14; 4:42). The world is thereby shown to be loved by God (John 3:16).

The conflict between Christ and the world is carried over into tension between Christians and the world. Although the world was created in Christ (John 1:3-4), it is at enmity with him and does not recognize him (John 1:10-11). Paul has died to the world (Gal 6:11-18) where sin and death have entered (Rom 5:12). While Paul himself is free of the cares of this world (1 Cor 7:33) he recognizes that Christians cannot escape the world (1 Cor 5:10). Yet they are not bound by it (Col 2:20).

Accordingly, Christians are to keep separate from the world (1 Cor 11:32) because their spirit is not like that of the world (1 Cor 2:12). In faith Christians conquer the world opposed to Christ (1 John 4–5). Christians are counseled to reject love of the world (1 John 2:12-17) because it is filled with evil desires that are incompatible with a life in God. Those allied with the world become enslaved to evil desires, which are transitory. Through God's grace Christians are said to have fled a world corrupted by lust (2 Pet 1:4; see 2 Pet 2:20). They are to remain unspotted by the world (Jas 1:27). The saints will judge the world (1 Cor 6:2). Christians are likened to stars shining in the cosmos (Phil 2:15).

Pastoral-Liturgical Tradition

The Apostolic Fathers encouraged Christian flight from the world because it was viewed as fundamentally opposed to life in Christ and a source of temptation. Ignatius of Antioch was convinced that the prince of this world sought to corrupt Godward desires. He counseled Christians not to have Christ on their lips but the world in their hearts (Ep Rom 7:1). Clement of Rome also encouraged Christian abandonment of this world, which is opposed to the will of God. He believed that life in this fleshly world is transitory; it is in contrast to the great and wonderful promise of Christ of everlasting life. He exhorted Christians, therefore, not to regard the things of this world as their own, nor to desire them. He argued that a Christian cannot desire the things of this world and remain righteous. Because this world and the world to come are opposed to one another a Christian must bid farewell to this world and consort instead with the world that is to come. This world is corruptible, the other is not (2 Clem 5:6f.; 6:6).

Later Ambrose likewise taught that Christians ought to flee from the world so as to come from evil to good, from death to life. Because this life is subject to the world and its wickedness, the Christian ought to flee it

relentlessly. The point of such flight is to unburden oneself of the fleshly world. To die to the elements of this world is to hide one's life in God (*Flight from the World*, 7.37-39).

Augustine, in opposition to the Manichees, taught that the material world was created by a good God, and as such is good, but fallen. Augustine believed, however, that the human heart could not find happiness in this world, but rather in God alone.

Still later, the fundamental principle of the *Spiritual Exercises* of Ignatius Loyola taught that all things in this world are gifts of God, created for humanity, to be the means by which it can come to know God better, love God more surely, and serve God more faithfully. Accordingly, the things of this world are to be embraced if they lead one to loving union and service of God, and to be avoided if they lead away from that goal.

The Second Vatican Council recognized that the expectation of the world to come must not weaken, but rather stimulate Christians' concern for cultivating this one. It understood the Church and the world to be mutually related, for the Church is in the world as a leaven and a kind of soul (The Church in the Modern World, nos. 39, 40). The primary sphere of the laity is in the world; its mission is to work for the world's salvation. Thus the laity are called to consecrate the world to God. It is they who, in their daily lives, perform a work of great value for the evangelization of the world. It is also the laity's task to see that the world is permeated by the spirit of Christ so that it may more effectively fulfill its purpose in justice, charity, and peace (Constitution on the Church, nos. 33-36).

See: COSMOS, COVENANT, CREATION, DEATH, EARTH, EXODUS, GIFTS, HEAVEN, HOLY/HOLINESS, HOPE, JUDGMENT, MISSION, PEOPLE OF GOD, REDEMPTION/REDEEMER, SAINTS, SALVATION, SATAN, SEA, SPIRIT, STARS, TIME, WILL OF GOD

SUSAN FOURNIER MATHEWS

WORSHIP

Worship is essentially those actions and words of human beings that define and acknowledge and reestablish their relationship to God. For Israel, worship focused on the one God who was revealed to them on Mount Sinai. During the first and second Temple periods sacrifice at the Temple in Jerusalem was central to Israelite worship. Prayer, Sabbath observance, and celebration of festivals were other forms of worship that took on even greater significance when Temple sacrifice was no longer possible. Christians, who first worshiped as Jews, reinterpreted Jewish ritual and terminology in light of the Christ event. The Lord's Supper holds primacy of place among Christian forms of worship.

Old Testament

Israel's Relationship to the Ancient Near East. Although some scholars have attempted to work out a neat framework for development of worship in ancient Israel, the evidence admits no simple progression from the primitive to the complex. Still there was change. As the social context of the people changed, the forms of worship shifted to meet new situations.

The relationship of Israel's worship to the religions of the larger culture of the ancient Near East has been an important focus of scholarship. One pole of this inquiry has stressed the similarity of Israel's religion to that of its neighbors. For them the autumn New Year festival celebrated the universal renewal of life and fertility ushered in by the enthronement of YHWH, similar to that of the god Marduk in Babylon. The other pole has stressed Israel's uniqueness and described the New Year festival as a covenant renewal unlike anything found in the dominant culture. The truth would seem to lie somewhere in the middle. With the development of kingship in Jerusalem, motifs of the surrounding Canaanite religion found a place within the Temple liturgy and songs. Still covenant with its roots on Mount Sinai remained a dominant metaphor for Israel's relationship to its God.

Sinai and the Relationship of Covenant. The tops of mountains and hills, called the "high places," were the natural location in the ancient Near East for sacrifice and worship. The Canaanite god, Baal, had his mountain, Saphon, in northern Syria, and the Promised Land was dotted with many "high places" sacred to Israel, Canaan or both. Mount Sinai is, of course, the place of Israel's foundational religious experience. There Moses and the people confront the God who brought them out of Egypt, and this God makes with them a covenant with its stipulations or laws defining that covenantal relationship between sovereign and servant which holds the promise of blessing.

The Ten Commandments open with prohibitions against the worship of any other deity and also the making of any image (Exod 20:2-6; Deut 5:7-10). These prohibitions focus Israel's worship only on the God who brought them out of Egypt. Psalm 115 sums up the dominant theme: "Our God is in heaven; whatever he wills, he does." Their gods, however, are the work of human hands, unable to speak or act. Furthermore, the psalm insists that all who make idols become like them, unable to speak or act, and are therefore "dead" and reduced to silence. Life, on the other hand, is equated with praise, and only those who praise God have life.

Although Israel's stories and liturgy are full of anthropomorphic images such as warrior, shepherd, king, etc., the commandment against the making of images also undercuts every metaphor of God and insists on the primacy of God's mystery and transcendence represented most graphically by the invisible God enthroned on the cherubim. The call to worship this God, who both transcends time and space and also acts within it, is summed up in Deuteronomy 6:4, "Hear, O Israel! The LORD is our God, the LORD alone. Therefore, you shall love the LORD, your God with all your heart, and with all your soul, and with all your strength." The key word "love" belongs both to the world of human affection and also to the language of covenant where it describes the relationship between sovereign and servant.

Sacrifice. Exodus 24:1-11 records two instructive rituals that sealed the covenant. In one, Moses sprinkles both the altar as the image of the divine and then the people with the blood of the sacrifice. Blood was understood as liquid life belonging only to God. The ritual thus joined the people to their God by bringing them into contact with the holy. All sacrifice, in some sense, sought to establish this union. In the second story, Moses and the elders see God and then seal the covenant by eating and drinking.

The communion sacrifice of various kinds represents one whole branch of the sacrificial system. In these sacrifices, the people eat part of offering and thereby are linked to God. In the holocaust, the other large branch of sacrifice, the gift is burned whole and entire as an acknowledgement that the gift belongs completely to God.

Royal Worship. Beginning with King David, the mediocre height of Mount Zion in Jerusalem, transformed by language and imagination, supplants Sinai as the mountain of revelation and worship. It becomes the place for Solomon's Temple, the house where God dwells (2 Samuel 6; 1 Kings 8). The cult grows with the monarchy and takes on religious dimension from the surrounding culture. This poses an ever present threat to the injunction against the worship of false gods (1 Kings 18). Late in the monarchy, the deuteronomistic theology brought a new transcendent thrust to the religion and also banned all sacrifice outside of Jerusalem in an attempt to preserve the worship of the One God free of foreign influence (Deuteronomy 12; 2 Kings 23). The keeping of the first commandment, however, was not enough. Justice was the precondition of worship (Psalm 50; Isa 1:12-17; Amos 5:21-25; Sir 34:18-26). Likewise the external action of cult should reflect interior obedience and love of the worshiper (Ps 51:17-19; Hos 6:6; Mic 6:6-8). According to the ideal, the outside and the inside should function together as one, and so the psalmist prays, "Let the words of my

mouth and the thought of my heart win favor before you, O LORD, my rock, and my redeemer" (Ps 19:15).

Forms of Prayer. The psalms contain three basic forms of prayer: songs of petition, hymns of thanksgiving, and hymns of praise. The songs of petition (often called "laments") ask the help of God in time of trouble caused either by the sin and oppression of others or by one's own sin. Thanksgiving hymns acknowledge God's help. The hymns of praise proclaim God as God; they confess God's transcendent mystery and recount the deeds of the divine in this world. Each form, in its own way, clarifies the relationship between the human and the divine.

Passover, Sabbath, and Torah. Although the Temple, destroyed by the Babylonians in 587 BCE was rebuilt by 515 BCE, the world of Israelite religion was shifting. The Passover, essentially a family feast celebrated in the home, became the central festival. While the priestly theology of the postexilic period put great stress on the Temple cult, it also exalted the place of the Sabbath by linking it to creation (Gen 2:1-3) and by designating it as the sign of the Sinai covenant (Exod 31:12-17). With the people now scattered throughout the ancient world, a new institution, the synagogue, emerged and brought prominence to the written text of the Torah, which served as the new focus for worship.

See: ALTAR, PASSOVER, PRIEST, PSALMS, SABBATH, SACRIFICE, SYNAGOGUE, TEMPLE

HARRY HAGAN, O.S.B.

New Testament

Christian Worship. The first Christians were faithful Jews, nurtured in the rich ceremonial of Jewish family life, Temple,* and synagogue.* After the death and resurrection of Jesus they continued to worship as Jews for years (Acts 3:1). With the passage of time, historical developments, and reflection, Christian worship gradually took on distinctive forms and emphases. The focus on Jesus as the risen Messiah and Lord affected everything.

The Jewish heritage left its stamp on Christian worship in terminology and ritual. The "temple" was no longer a building in Jerusalem, but the community of believers (2 Cor 6:16; Eph 2:21) or the body of Jesus (John 2:21). The institution of the priesthood with the sacrifice of animals was replaced by Jesus, the eternal high priest whose once-for-all sacrifice abolished all other sacrifices (Heb 6:20; 10:11-14). He is the new Passover lamb (John 1:36). The synagogue service of the word became the basic pattern for the Liturgy of the Word in the Christian Eucharist. Christians continued to use the psalms and prophecies in their assemblies (Acts 4:24-26), never doubting that the Jewish Scriptures still belonged to them, even after the split between synagogue and Church* late in the first century.

Christian worship expressed its distinctive character especially in the rituals of baptism and the Lord's Supper. At first there was some confusion with John's baptism (Acts 18:25), but soon specific formulae were developed (Matt 28:19). Paul spoke eloquently of baptism as a plunge into the death and resurrection of Christ (Rom 6:3-4). 1 Peter, which was influenced by homiletic and hymnic elements of an early baptismal ritual, further connected the dying of daily suffering with the sharing of new life in Christ (1 Pet 1:3-7). A baptismal hymn in Ephesians 5:14 stresses the resurrection theme: "Awake, O sleeper, and arise from the dead, and Christ will give you light."

Assemblies. From the beginning, the followers of Jesus assembled for worship; even daily, to judge from Acts 2:46. Later, the special day for Christian assembly was Sunday (Acts 20:7; 1 Cor 16:2), which replaced Saturday as the day for Sabbath* observance and became known as "the Lord's day" (Rev 1:10).

The believers came together for the Lord's Supper, but also for other prayer assemblies. The synagogue service of proclamation of the word, preaching, and psalm-singing was adapted to Christian use: "you teach and admonish one another, singing psalms, hymns, and spiritual songs, with gratitude in your hearts to God" (Col 3:16). Charismatic gifts of prophecy and tongues had their place (1 Cor 14:1-5). Proper decorum became an issue when Christianity moved into Greek society and Jewish practices were no longer normative (1 Cor 11:13-16; 14:26-28).

Much can be learned both about early Christian liturgy and the nature of Christian worship by an examination of a distinctive creation of the NT Church, the Christ-hymn. One of these, Ephesians 5:16, has already been noted. The ancient hymn in 1 Timothy 3:16 calls Christ the "mystery of devotion," and summarizes his mission:

> Who was manifested in the flesh,
> vindicated in the spirit,
> seen by angels,
> proclaimed to the Gentiles,
> believed in throughout the world,
> taken up in glory.

Heavenly and earthly realities are artfully entwined in three sets of antithetical couplets, hailing Christ as the one reconciling the divine and the human. Discernible elements of the proclamation are the incarnation (line 1), the resurrection (2), universal salvation (3-4), and the ascension. The first line also implies a belief in Christ's divine preexistence.

Two other hymns have been influential in Christian liturgy and theology down to the present day. Philippians 2:6-11 may have been used originally in the baptismal ceremony. It has a descending and ascending movement (imitating the steps of the font?) pivoting at bottom on the death and resurrection (vv. 8-9), and climaxing in the exaltation of Christ as Lord (v. 11). Unlike Adam who grasped for equality with God, Jesus emptied himself in humility for our sake.

In Colossians 1:15-20, the theme is Christ and creation. Christ has an exalted role as God's agent in the creation of all things, "in heaven and on earth, the visible and the invisible" (v. 16). The terminology here reflects wisdom themes of the OT (Prov 8:22-31), but also shows the influence of the vocabulary of Greek gnosticism as the community's liturgy began to reflect the issues of a new world. The forceful expressions describing Christ as God's image, head of the Church, and firstborn of creation bear witness to the energy and vitality of Christian reflection and worship during the early period.

The Lord's Supper. Jesus' meal with his disciples the night before he died became the pattern for the unique and central act of Christian worship called the "Lord's Supper" by Paul (1 Cor 11:20), the "breaking of the bread" by Luke (24:35; Acts 2:42), and the Eucharist in later usage (from the verb "to give thanks" in the institution narratives). There are four accounts of the Eucharist in the NT: Paul's description is of a liturgical ritual based on the Last Supper; the narratives of the three Synoptic evangelists are descriptions of the Last Supper influenced by liturgical usage.

All four Gospels relate the Last Supper to the Jewish Passover. Paul does not do so, though elsewhere he refers to Christ as "our paschal lamb" (1 Cor 5:7). The Christian Eucharist may be a "passover meal" as a sharing in salvation and liberation by joining in the banquet of Jesus as lamb, but the parallel is not strict. The new ritual is not a once-yearly ceremony. The disciples understood "Do this in memory of me" (Luke 22:19; 1 Cor 11:25) to require a regular reenactment of the Lord's Supper on the first day of the week (Acts 20:7) and even daily (Acts 2:46).

The Supper ritual is not merely a ceremony remembering the past. Jesus, now the risen Lord, becomes present and offers himself to the worshipers in an intimate sharing that bonds them to one another. "The cup of blessing that we bless, is it not a participation in the blood of Christ? The bread that we break, is it not a participation in the body of Christ? Because the loaf of bread is one, we, though many, are one body, for we all partake of the one loaf" (1 Cor 10:16-17). The realism of this communion was a scandal from the beginning (John 6:52) and remains a source of division among Christians.

See: BAPTISM, EUCHARIST, LAMB OF GOD, PASSOVER, PRIESTHOOD, SABBATH, SACRIFICE, SYNAGOGUE, TEMPLE

JEROME KODELL, O.S.B.

Pastoral-Liturgical Tradition

The English word worship comes from the Old English "worth" and the suffix "scipe," which means the adoration, reverence, and honor paid to God or to a sacred person. It is the word used in English to translate the Latin word "cultus." Worship involves not only an interior attitude of adoration, but is also manifested by exterior signs of reverence. In Greek the word usually used for the worship of God is *latria*. The worship given to God is distinct from that which may be given to the saints or to the Blessed Virgin Mary, which is called *dulia* (in the case of the saints) or *hyperdulia* (in the case of the Blessed Virgin Mary). In English it is more common to refer to the "cultus" of Mary, and the saints as "veneration," reserving the use of the term "worship" to God alone. The Christian acts of worship and adoration are expressed in the liturgy of the Church (the sacraments, sacramentals, and other rites) and by actions and prayers of the individual believer. The Second Vatican Council has restored the worship offered by the Church in its liturgy to clearer and more ancient form and made provision for adapting it to the needs and cultures of the people.

Worship in the Early Church. Worship in the early Church is rooted in the rites and prayers of the Jewish people. The followers of Christ used the prayers and songs of the Temple and synagogue and transformed them to reflect their understanding that Christ was both Lord and God and therefore due the worship and adoration reserved to God. From the worship of the

Temple the Church took the psalms and continued to use them as expressions of praise, thanksgiving, and intercession. The psalms became the core of the divine office or, as it is now known, the Liturgy of the Hours. The Church also took the notion of various times of prayer during the day that eventually helped to shape the Liturgy of the Hours with its two "hinge" hours of morning prayer (lauds) and evening prayer (vespers). Even the concept of the liturgical day beginning at sundown has its origins in Jewish liturgical practice. The Christian celebration of the Eucharist, which is divided into two parts, the Liturgy of the Word and the Liturgy of the Eucharist, was profoundly influenced by the synagogue liturgy and the family home celebration of the Sabbath meal and the Passover. The early Church continued to employ elements of the synagogue service, i.e., Scripture readings, homily, and prayers of intercession, when Christians were no longer able to participate in the worship of the synagogue. The prayers and rites associated with the Sabbath and Passover formed the context of the Last Supper and continued to influence the Christian celebration of the Eucharist. This is especially true of the Eucharistic Prayer or anaphora (prayer of offering), which quickly evolved into a distinctively Christian prayer of praise, thanksgiving, and intercession. As the Church began to spread outside of Palestine it incorporated customs from local cultures that led to the development of distinct liturgical families or rites that shared a common basis but manifested different manners of praying and celebrating the sacraments.

Worship in the Middle Ages. By the time of the Middle Ages, there were great differences in worship between the Eastern Churches and the Churches of the West. The Eastern Churches used the languages of the people or an older form of the vernacular. The Western Churches used Latin, which was no longer understood by the people. The Eastern Churches understood the Eucharistic celebration as a participation in the heavenly liturgy, whereas the Latin Church saw the Eucharist in terms of the representation of the sacrifice of the cross. In the Latin Church, the ancient roles of the faithful in the celebration were assumed only by the clergy, and the people became content with praying devotional prayers as the clergy conducted the Church's worship. In the eyes of the laity, veneration of Mary and the saints was much more accessible than actual participation in the rites and prayers of the Mass. Because of widespread abuses in the liturgy and in order to respond to the attacks of the Protestant reformers, the Council of Trent (sixteenth century) attempted to reform the worship of the Church and a four hundred year period of liturgical uniformity began. Many abuses were corrected, but the liturgy remained the worship carried out by the clergy with minimal participation of the laity.

Worship and the Second Vatican Council. The first document of the Second Vatican Council to be promulgated was the Constitution on the Sacred Liturgy, *Sacrosanctum concilium* [CSL] (December 4, 1963). It enunciated a principle that lies at the heart of liturgical reform: "The Church earnestly desires that all the faithful be led to that full, conscious, and active participation in liturgical celebrations called for by the very nature of the liturgy. Such participation by the Christian people as 'a chosen race, a royal priesthood, a holy nation, God's own people' (1 Pet 2:9; see 2:4-5) is their right and duty by reason of baptism" (CSL, no. 14). The Council reaffirms that public worship of the Church, the liturgy, is a right and obligation of every Christian that flows from the very nature of baptism. And it further declares that participation of the baptized in the Church's liturgical worship is to be full, active, and conscious. Hence, the Council restored the various roles or ministries in the liturgy that had existed in the early Church: ". . . liturgical services involve the whole Body of the Church; they manifest it and have effects upon it; but they also concern the individual members of the Church in different ways, according to different orders, offices, and actual participation" (CSL, no. 26). The Constitution on the Liturgy also reminds us: "Rightly, then, the liturgy is considered as an exercise of the priestly office of Jesus Christ. In the liturgy, by means of signs perceptible to the senses, human sanctification is signified and brought about in ways proper to each of these signs; in the liturgy the whole public worship is performed by the Mystical Body of Jesus Christ, that is by the Head and his members" (CSL, no. 7).

See: EUCHARIST, JESUS CHRIST, PRAYER, PRIEST, TEMPLE

ALAN F. DETSCHER

WRATH OF GOD

The wrath of God is God's response to sin and disobedience on the part of human beings. Several Hebrew words express the idea, while in the Greek NT *orge* and *thymos* are the chief terms. God's wrath is a corollary of the divine mercy (and justice and love). In early Judaism and the NT the expression appears in connection with the last judgment and the coming of God's reign.

Old Testament

The Hebrew Bible contains many words for expressing anger: *'ap, ḥēmâ, ḥārôn, 'ebrâ,* etc. These terms apply not only to human beings but also to God. In almost all cases God's wrath is an appropriate response to human sinfulness. Moreover, there is an insistence that "mercy and anger alike" are with God (Sir 5:7; 16:11) and that the God of Israel is "a merciful and gracious God, slow to anger and rich in kindness and fidelity" (Exod 34:6).

The episode of the golden calf in Exodus 32 in which Israel engages in idolatry ("make us a god who will be our leader") evokes the wrath of God. Recognizing the infidelity of the wilderness generation, God tells Moses: "Let me alone, then, that my wrath may blaze up against them to con-

sume them" (32:10). Thus God's wrath is assumed to be the fitting response to the people's sin. Nevertheless, when Moses points out that for God to destroy the wilderness generation would give the Egyptians cause to gloat and would imperil the promises to the patriarchs (32:11-13), "the LORD relented in the punishment he had threatened to inflict on his people" (32:14). Thus God's mercy overwhelms God's wrath.

But in some cases God's wrath takes its effect. The objects of God's wrath are the enemies of Israel, great sinners, or Israel itself. It may fall upon the representatives of Israel (see Exod 4:14; Num 12:9; Deut 9:20; 1 Sam 15:28, etc.) for the people's sins, or upon the whole people for the sins of individuals (Josh 7:1; 2 Sam 24:17). God's wrath may come in the form of fire, storms, or plagues, or (more commonly) the enemies of Israel who function as instruments of God (Isa 42:24-25).

The prophets Jeremiah and Ezekiel give particular attention to God's wrath. They appeal to it to explain the misfortunes that had already taken place in Judah before and during the Exile in the early sixth century BCE. They use it to warn Israel to repent of its sins and pull itself together lest even worse things happen, and they promise that at the right time God's wrath will punish Israel's enemies. So close is the relation between the people's sin and God's wrath that Job assumes that he is the victim of God's wrath (Job 16:9; 19:11) but cannot understand this since he has not sinned. Though Lamentations 4:11 claims that in allowing Jerusalem to be destroyed "the LORD has spent his anger," the prophet Malachi looks forward to the day of God's wrath "when all the proud and all evildoers will be stubble" (Mal 3:19; see Zeph 1:15, 18; 2:2, 3).

New Testament

The theme of a final, or eschatological, day of wrath appears in the preaching of John the Baptist: "Who warned you to flee from the coming wrath?" (Matt 3:7; Luke

3:7). John refers to the divine judgment that will come upon unrepentant sinners as part of the scenario of events connected with the coming of God's kingdom in its fullness. Those who remain obdurate in their evil deeds "are storing up wrath" for the "day of wrath" (Rom 2:5); thus God's eschatological wrath is part of the divine justice or righteousness that both rewards and punishes. Those who do deeds that deserve God's wrath are aptly called "children of wrath" (Eph 2:3).

The Christian conviction that through Jesus' resurrection God's reign has been inaugurated has the effect of moving God's wrath back into the present. Using a pre-Pauline formula, Paul celebrates Jesus as the one "who delivers us from the coming wrath" (1 Thess 1:10). Just as in Christ God's righteousness has been made manifest, so also according to Romans 1:18-32 the wrath of God is being revealed against every impiety and wickedness in the present time. Likewise, the enemies of the gospel fall victim to God's wrath (1 Thess 2:16), and those who fail to believe and obey God's Son remain under God's wrath (John 3:36). Nevertheless, the eschatological dimension of God's wrath remains prominent, especially in the Book of Revelation.

Jesus in his earthly ministry shows anger at those persons and things that oppose God: Satan, demons, disease, opponents, obtuse disciples, sin, etc. In his displays of anger he enacts God's wrath. Thus Jesus' anger affirms not only his humanity but also his divinity.

Pastoral-Liturgical Tradition

Many people find the wrath of God to be an unworthy or even offensive idea. They cannot (or do not want to) imagine an angry God. But what kind of person would someone be who was totally unable to summon up righteous indignation and anger in the face of obvious injustice and sinfulness? God's mercy and wrath belong together (see Sir 5:7; 16:11); God's wrath is the obverse of grace. A God incapable of wrath would also be incapable of mercy and justice and grace.

The stereotype of the OT God of wrath and the NT God of love does not fit the evidence of Scripture. In both Testaments God displays love and wrath, with love being the predominant force. The God of the Hebrew Scriptures is the God of Jesus, despite the claims of Marcion and the gnostics in antiquity and of anti-Semites throughout the ages.

Perhaps due to the influence of the hymn *Dies irae* ("Day of Wrath"), Catholics often relate God's wrath to the particular judgment after death. While this identification is not wrong, the Bible's approach to God is more communal (affecting God's people or all humankind) and eschatological (pertaining to the last judgment).

See: JUDGMENT, JUSTICE, LOVE, MERCY, SIN

DANIEL J. HARRINGTON, S.J.

Y

YAHWEH

Yahweh is the proper name of Israel's God. In the Hebrew text, which consists solely of consonants, it is spelled YHWH. Thus the name is sometimes called the Tetragrammaton, the four letters.

Old Testament

Gift of the Name. In Exodus 3 in the midst of God's call of Moses, Moses asks: "'When I go to the Israelites and say to them, "the God of your fathers has sent me to you," if they ask me, "What is his name?" what am I to tell them?' God replied, 'I am who I am.' Then he added, 'This is what you shall tell the Israelites: I AM sent me to you.' God spoke further to Moses, 'Thus shall you say to the Israelites: The LORD, the God of your fathers, the God of Abraham, the God of Isaac, the God of Jacob, has sent me to you. This is my name forever; / this is my title for all generations'" (Exod 3:13-15).

This short dialogue between Moses and God describes the gift of God's proper name, Yahweh, to the people of Israel. From this point Israel is on a first name basis with God.

Meaning of the Name. The name Yahweh is a verb. Yahweh has revealed the dynamism of the divine nature in the revelation of a name that is neither noun nor adjective but verb. The root of the name seems to be the verb connoting being, *hyh* or *hwh*. (He-brew roots consist of consonants only.) Thus the revelation of the name indicates that God's nature is intimately related to being itself.

There are several interpretations of the meaning of the name. Exodus 3:14 indicates that the meaning is simply to be: "I AM." It is God's essence to be. Existence is the very nature of God. God *is* by very definition. All other beings exist only by analogy. The existence of all other creatures is limited by beginnings and endings. God is, always was, and will be forever.

The vowels of the name, however, suggest a further nuance to the meaning of the name. The "a" vowel in the first syllable indicates a causative meaning. God not only is, God causes to be. God is the origin of all else that is. God creates and sustains all other beings. When the name is used in conjunction with another term, for example, Yahweh Sabaoth, the meaning is that God is the one who causes the hosts of heaven to be.

Hebrew verbs have two basic forms: a form that indicates a completed action or final state and another form which indicates an action in progress, whether repeated, incomplete, future, continuing, or conditional. The name Yahweh is in the latter form. God is continually coming to be. God is a god of the living. God is future. This form also demonstrates the freedom and mystery of God: "I will be who I will be."

The future sense gives rise to a final nuance in the interpretation of the name. God is not only the one who will be, rather God is the one who will be present. God is the one who will be there for the people when they are in need. God's very name says, "I will be there."

All the interpretations of the name are true. All contribute to an understanding of the divine nature: God is; God causes to be; God is free and incomprehensible to human minds; God is the one who is faithful forever. The final interpretation, however, is probably closest to the original meaning. The gift of the name occurs in the midst of God's call to Moses. This call follows the standard pattern for the call of a prophet. In the midst of the call, there is usually an objection by the person being called. This objection is followed by God's reassurance, ordinarily a pledge by God to be with the prophet (see Jer 1:8; Exod 3:12). Moses has objected, "Who are you?" God responds, "I AM; my very name promises that I will be with you." A second indication that the original meaning is "I will be with you" is found in the Exodus story itself. Throughout the plague narrative there is a continual repetition of the phrase, "This is how you will know that I am Yahweh" (see Exod 7:17; 8:6, 18; 9:29; 10:1-2). At the sea, Israel is told, "Even the Egyptians shall know that I am Yahweh" (Exod 14:18; see 14:4). The message is clear: this god is one who will be present to deliver the people. This interpretation becomes a part of the name itself. God is continually identified not only as Yahweh, but as Yahweh who brought Israel out of Egypt (see Exod 20:2-3; Lev 11:44-45; 22:32-33; Deut 6:12-13; Judg 6:8). (See also Elijah and the prophets of Baal in 1 Kings 19. Yahweh is present; Baal never arrives.)

Significance of the Gift of the Name. The gift of God's name is a gift of power. The people can now call upon God's name and enjoy God's intimacy. The psalms illustrate the use of the name in prayer. The faithful call upon the name when they are in need and praise God's name in thanksgiving for deliverance: "O God, by your name save me . . . then I will . . . praise your gracious name, Yahweh" (Ps 54:3, 8; see also Pss 5:12; 69:31; 80:19; 106:74; 116:4; 140:14). Yahweh's name is the greatest defense; therefore it is worthy of complete trust: "Some rely on chariots, others on horses, but we on the name of Yahweh, our God" (Ps 20:8; see also Pss 9:11; 44:6; 124:8). Because the name itself is the assurance of God's love and fidelity, it is worthy of all praise. Psalm 148 calls on all creation—angels, sun and moon, sea and land, storms, mountains and hills, animals and human beings—to praise the name of Yahweh (148:5, 13; see also 7:18; 8:2, 10; 29:2; 66:2, 4; 68:5; 103:1; 115:1).

Pentateuchal Traditions. The name Yahweh is found throughout the Pentateuch, appearing as early as Genesis 2. In Genesis 4:26 Enosh is reported to have called on the name of Yahweh. In the chapters between Genesis and Exodus 3, however, the name is used by only one of the early sources of the Pentateuch. This source is named the Yahwist because of this consistent use of Yahweh as the name of God. The other sources of the Pentateuch, particularly the Elohist and the Priestly source, avoid the use of the name Yahweh until the gift of the name in Exodus 3. The Priestly source attempts historical consistency by using the name for God that would have been known to the people of the time. In Exodus 6:2-3, according to the Priestly source, God said to Moses, "I am Yahweh. As God the Almighty [El Shaddai] I appeared to Abraham, Isaac and Jacob, but my name, Yahweh, I did not make known to them" (see Gen 17:1; 35:11). The Elohist, so called because of a preference for the generic name for God, Elohim, is the source for the story of the gift of Yahweh's name to Moses in Exodus 3:13-15.

The sources are each pursuing a different accuracy. The Priestly source and the Elohist are historically accurate. The name

Yahweh seems to have been unknown to Israel until the Mosaic period. It is only with the Mosaic period that names honoring Yahweh begin to appear, such as Joshua (Yahweh is salvation), Elijah (Yahweh is my God), Isaiah (Yahweh is salvation). The Yahwist source, on the other hand, is theologically accurate. Whether the proper name of God was known or not, it is the same God who creates in Genesis and delivers in Exodus. The revealed name of this God is Yahweh.

Yahweh Cult. Several attempts have been made to determine the origin of the cult of Yahweh before Moses. One hypothesis traces the worship of a god named Yahweh to the Midianites. Tent shrines have been discovered in the Sinai desert but without images suggesting a cult which forbade images. Mount Sinai is a sacred mountain in Midianite territory. According to this theory Moses would have learned the name Yahweh through his father-in-law, the priest of Midian (Exod 2:15-22). The origin of the name, however, is insignificant in comparison to the development of understanding of Yahweh in Israelite faith and worship. Yahweh is the God who delivered Israel from Egypt, who is always active in the history of the chosen people, whose love endures forever.

Reverence for the Name. After the Babylonian exile in the sixth century BCE, reverence for the holy name of God becomes evident in several Jewish practices. The Qumran scrolls leave evidence of this reverence. Wherever the name is found the letters are in archaic script and the scrolls indicate that different ink and pens were used. This reverence also led the people to cease pronouncing the name aloud lest somehow they dishonor it. Rather they substituted the title 'adonai, "lord." Whenever the Scripture was read, 'adonai was read in place of Yahweh.

In the third–second century BCE when the Hebrew Scriptures were translated into Greek, the translation of 'adonai (lord), kyrios in Greek, was ordinarily used wherever Yah-

weh was found in the Hebrew text. Most English translations also translate 'adonai rather than use the name Yahweh. In order to indicate that the original is Yahweh, small capital letters are used thus: LORD.

The substitution of 'adonai for Yahweh led to an interesting aberration that has persisted into modern times. When later scribes added vowels to the Hebrew text they added the vowels of 'adonai to the consonants for Yahweh in order to help readers remember that the word they were to pronounce was 'adonai. Thus the four consonants, YHWH, were supplemented with the vowels "a" (short a or schwa), "o," and "a." The resulting combination appeared to be "yehowah," or in languages such as German that have no "y" or "w," "jehovah." Thus the name Jehovah never existed as a Hebrew word. It is a misunderstanding of the scribal addition of the vowels for 'adonai to the consonants YHWH.

New Testament

There are implications for Christology both in the meaning of the name Yahweh itself and in the substitution of "lord" for the sacred name. Several times in the Gospels, especially in the Gospel of John, Jesus says simply, "I am," *ego eimi* (John 6:20; 8:24, 28, 58; 13:19; 18:5). Some of these statements are directly connected to faith: "Unless you believe that I AM, you will surely die in your sins" (8:24; cf. 8:28; 13:19). One is an expression of reassurance. When the disciples are terrified because of the storm, Jesus says, "I AM; do not be afraid" (6:20; cf. Luke 24:36). In the parallel passage in Matthew the disciples respond, "Truly, you are God's son!" (Matt 14:27; see also Mark 6:50). After Jesus says, "before Abraham even came into existence, I AM" (John 8:58), his hearers threaten to stone him. At his arrest, when the soldiers say that they are seeking Jesus of Nazareth and he responds, "I AM," the soldiers fall to the ground. At his trial, when he responds to the question of his identity as Messiah and Son of God with "I AM," he is charged with blasphemy

(Mark 14:62; Luke 22:70). These instances suggest that I AM is being used as a claim to divine status, as a reference to the name Yahweh.

Jesus is also called "Lord." The hymn in Philippians 2 describes first his obedience: "Though he was in the form of God, he did not think equality with God something to be grasped at . . . but was obedient unto death." As a result God exalts him, giving him the title at which every knee shall bow, the name "Lord." The hearers would immediately connect the title *kyrios* with the title for God in the Septuagint. Jesus Christ, the Son of God, is *Kyrios*.

Pastoral-Liturgical Tradition

Modern liturgical texts and most modern English translations of the Bible use the title "Lord" for God rather than the proper name "Yahweh." This usage flows from the reverential treatment of the name by Jews throughout the centuries. The gift of God's name, however, remains a treasure for God's people. The gift is a gift of power and of intimacy with God. The gift of the name is a revelation of God's identity. Our God is the one whose very name proclaims: I will be with you.

See: EL/ELOHIM, GOD, MOSES

IRENE NOWELL, O.S.B.

Contributors

Don C. Benjamin, O.CARM, Ph.D., is a scholar in residence at Rice University, Houston.

Dianne Bergant, C.S.A., Ph.D., is professor of Old Testament studies at Catholic Theological Union, Chicago.

Lawrence Boadt, C.S.P., S.S.D., is associate professor of biblical studies at the Washington Theological Union.

Barbara E. Bowe, R.S.C.J., Th.D., is associate professor of biblical studies at Catholic Theological Union, Chicago.

Vincent P. Branick, S.S.D., is a professor of religious studies at the University of Dayton, Ohio.

Terrance Callan, Ph.D., is academic dean and professor of biblical studies at the Athenaeum of Ohio.

Richard J. Clifford, S.J., S.T.L., Ph.D., is professor of Old Testament at Weston Jesuit School of Theology, Cambridge, Massachusetts.

John J. Collins, Ph.D., is professor of Old Testament at the Divinity School of the University of Chicago.

Mary Collins, O.S.B., Ph.D., is associate professor of religion and religious education at The Catholic University of America.

John F. Craghan, Th.D., is professor of religious studies at St. Norbert College, De Pere, Wisconsin.

Carol J. Dempsey, O.P., Ph.D., is assistant professor of biblical studies and theology at the University of Portland, Oregon.

Alan F. Detscher, S.L.D., is executive director, Secretariat for the Liturgy of the National Conference of Catholic Bishops.

John R. Donahue, S.J., Ph.D., is professor of New Testament at the Jesuit School of Theology, Berkeley, California.

Demetrius R. Dumm, O.S.B., is professor of New Testament at St. Vincent Seminary, Latrobe, Pennsylvania.

John C. Endres, S.J., Ph.D., is associate professor of Sacred Scripture (Old Testament) at the Jesuit School of Theology at Berkeley/Graduate Theological Union.

Brian J. Fischer, S.L.D., cand., is instructor of Liturgy at St. Mary of the Lake Seminary, Mundelein, Illinois.

James A. Fischer, C.M., S.T.L., S.S.L., served as professor of New Testament studies at St. Thomas Seminary, Denver.

James W. Flanagan, Ph.D., is Paul J. Hallinan professor of Catholic studies at Cast Western Reserve University.

Edward Foley, Capuchin, Ph.D., is professor of liturgy and music at Catholic Theological Union, Chicago.

Mark R. Francis, C.S.V., S.L.D., is associate professor of liturgy at Catholic Theological Union, Chicago.

Mary Frohlich, Ph.D., is assistant professor of spirituality at Catholic Theological Union, Chicago.

Mary Ann Getty, S.T.D., Ph.D., is an associate professor at St. Vincent College, Latrobe, Pennsylvania.

Florence Morgan Gillman, S.T.D., is associate professor of biblical studies at the University of San Diego.

John L. Gillman, Ph.D., is lecturer in religious studies at San Diego State University.

Anthony J. Gittins, C.S.SP., is professor of theological anthropology at Catholic Theological Union, Chicago.

Sean Goan, S.T.L., conducts biblical courses and education programs for the Archdiocese of Dublin.

Ann E. Graff, Ph.D., is assistant professor of theology at Seattle University.

Joseph A. Grassi, S.S.L., is professor of religious studies at Santa Clara University.

Michael D. Guinan, O.F.M., Ph.D., is professor of Old Testament and Semitic languages at the Franciscan School of Theology, Berkeley.

Harry Hagan, O.S.B., S.S.D., is an associate professor of Scriptures at St. Meinrad School of Theology, St. Meinrad, Indiana.

James R. Halstead, O.S.A., S.T.D., is associate professor of religious studies at De Paul University, Chicago.

M. Dennis Hamm, S.J., Ph.D., is professor of New Testament at Creighton University, Omaha.

J. Albert Harril, Ph.D., is assistant professor of theology at Creighton University, Omaha.

Daniel J. Harrington, S.J., Ph.D., is professor of New Testament at Weston Jesuit School of Theology, Cambridge, Massachusetts.

Zachary Hayes, O.F.M., Dr.Theol., is professor of systematic theology at Catholic Theological Union, Chicago.

J. Frank Henderson is a scholar who resides in Edmonton, Alberta.

Eugene Hensell, O.S.B., Ph.D., is associate professor of Scripture at St. Meinrad School of Theology, St. Meinrad, Indiana.

Leslie J. Hoppe, O.F.M., Ph.D., is professor of Old Testament studies at Catholic Theological Union, Chicago.

John M. Huels, O.S.M., J.C.D., is an expert on canon law and liturgy.

Kathleen Hughes, R.S.C.J., Ph.D., is professor of liturgy at Catholic Theological Union, Chicago.

Carol Frances Jegen, B.V.M., Ph.D., is senior professor emerita at the Institute of Pastoral Studies, Loyola University, Chicago.

Joseph Jensen, O.S.B., S.T.D., is associate professor of religious studies at The Catholic University of America and executive director of The Catholic Biblical Association, Washington, D.C.

Sean P. Kealy, C.S.SP., is professor of New Testament at Duquesne University, Pittsburgh.

Mark C. Kiley, Ph.D., is assistant professor of philosophy and theology at St. John's University, Staten Island, New York.

Jerome Kodell, O.S.B., S.S.L., is abbot of Subiaco Abbey, Arkansas.

Alice L. Laffey, S.S.D., is associate professor of religious studies at the College of the Holy Cross.

Dale Launderville, O.S.B., Ph.D., is dean of the School of Theology, St. John's University, Collegeville, Minnesota.

Eugene LaVerdiere, S.S.S., S.T.L., S.S.L., Ph.D., is adjunct professor of New Testament at Catholic Theological Union, Chicago.

Leo D. Lefebure, Ph.D., is professor of systematic theology and dean of the Ecclesiastical Faculty of Theology at the University of St. Mary of the Lake.

Timothy A. Lenchak, S.V.D., S.T.D., is assistant professor of Old Testament at Catholic Theological Union, Chicago.

John K. Leonard, Ph.D., is assistant professor of religious studies at Edgewood College, Madison, Wisconsin.

Betty Jane Lilly, S.C., Ph.D., is professor of biblical studies at the Athenaeum of Ohio/Mount St. Mary's Seminary in Cincinnati.

John Manuel Lozano, S.T.D., recently retired as professor of spirituality at Catholic Theological Union, Chicago.

Kevin Madigan, Ph.D., is assistant professor of Church history at Catholic Theological Union, Chicago.

Susan Fournier Mathews, Ph.D., is associate professor of Doctrinal Theology at the University of Scranton, Pennsylvania.

Thomas P. McCreesh, O.P., Ph.D., is a professor and president at Dominican House of Studies.

Patricia M. McDonald, S.H.C.J., S.S.L., Ph.D., is assistant professor of Scripture at Mount St. Mary's College, Emmitsburg, Maryland.

Neil J. McEleney, C.S.P., M.A., S.T.L., S.S.L., is adjunct professor at The Catholic University of America, Washington, D.C.

Nathan D. Mitchell, Ph.D., is associate director for research, Center for Pastoral Liturgy, University of Notre Dame, Indiana.

Roland E. Murphy, O. CARM., S.T.D., S.S.L., is George Washington Ivey Emeritus professor of biblical studies at Duke University.

Jerome Murphy-O'Connor, O.P., Th.D., is professor of New Testament at the École Biblique, Jerusalem.

Thomas Nairn, Ph.D., is associate professor of Christian ethics at Catholic Theological Union, Chicago.

Kathleen S. Nash, Ph.D., is associate professor of Hebrew Bible/Old Testament studies at Le Moyne College, Syracuse, New York.

Jerome H. Neyrey, S.J., Ph.D., is professor of New Testament studies at the University of Notre Dame.

Irene Nowell, O.S.B., Ph.D., is director of community formation, Mount St. Scholastica, Atchison, Kansas.

John J. O'Brien, C.P., M.A., M.L.S., is a graduate student at Weston Jesuit School of Theology, Cambridge, Massachusetts.

Kathleen M. O'Connor, Ph.D., is professor of Old Testament at Columbia Theological Seminary, Decatur, Georgia.

Carolyn Osiek, R.S.C.J., Th.D., is professor of New Testament at Catholic Theological Union, Chicago.

Gilbert Ostdiek, O.F.M., S.T.D., is professor of liturgy at Catholic Theological Union, Chicago.

John T. Pawlikowski, O.S.M., Ph.D., is professor of social ethics at Catholic Theological Union, Chicago.

Hayim Goren Perelmuter, D.H.L., D.D., is professor of Jewish studies at Catholic Theological Union, Chicago.

Pheme Perkins, Ph.D., is professor of New Testament theology at Boston College.

Jamie T. Phelps, O.P., Ph.D., is associate professor of Doctrinal Theology at Catholic Theological Union, Chicago.

John J. Pilch, Ph.D., is visiting assistant professor of biblical studies at Georgetown University, Washington, D.C.

Gregory J. Polan, O.S.B., S.T.D., is professor of Scripture and biblical languages at Conception Seminary College, Missouri.

Barbara E. Reid, O.P., Ph.D., is associate professor of New Testament studies at Catholic Theological Union, Chicago.

Marie-Eloise Rosenblatt, R.S.M., S.T.L., Ph.D., is assistant professor of religious studies at Santa Clara University, California.

Susan A. Ross, Ph.D., is associate professor of theology at Loyola University, Chicago.

Robin Ryan, C.P., Ph.D., is professor of systematic theology at St. John's Seminary, Brighton, Massachusetts.

Anthony J. Saldarini, Ph.D., is professor of biblical studies at Boston College.

Marilyn M. Schaub, Ph.D., is professor of biblical studies at Duquesne University, Pittsburgh.

Robert J. Schreiter, C.PP.S., Dr.Theol., is professor of doctrinal theology at Catholic Theological Union, Chicago.

Roger P. Schroeder, S.V.D., D.Miss., is assistant professor of cross cultural ministry at Catholic Theological Union, Chicago.

R. Kevin Seasoltz, O.S.B., J.C.D., is professor at the School of Theology, St. John's University, Collegeville, Minnesota.

Donald Senior, C.P., S.T.D., is professor of New Testament at Catholic Theological Union, Chicago.

Dominic Serra, S.L.D., is assistant professor of liturgy and sacramental theology at the St. Paul Seminary School of Divinity, University of St. Thomas, St. Paul, Minnesota.

Gerard S. Sloyan, S.T.L., Ph.D., is professional lecturer at The Catholic University of America, Washington, D.C.

Augustine Stock, O.S.B., S.T.L., is professor of Sacred Scripture, Conception Seminary, Conception, Missouri.

Dennis M. Sweetland, Ph.D., is professor of theology at St. Anselm College, Manchester, New Hampshire.

Anthony J. Tambasco, Ph.D., is professor of theology at Georgetown University, Washington, D.C.

William G. Thompson, S.J., is associate professor of New Testament studies at the Institute of Pastoral Studies at Loyola University, Chicago.

Benedict T. Viviano, O.P., Ph.D., is professor of New Testament at the University of Fribourg, Switzerland.

Paul J. Wadell, C.P., Ph.D., is professor of ethics at Catholic Theological Union, Chicago.

Elaine M. Wainwright, Ph.D., is lecturer in biblical studies at the Brisbane College of Theology.

James J. Walter, Ph.D., is professor of Christian ethics at Loyola University, Chicago.

Joseph F. Wimmer, O.S.A., S.T.D., is assistant professor at Washington Theological Union, Washington, D.C.

Michael G. Witczak, S.L.D., is associate professor of liturgical studies at St. Francis Seminary, Milwaukee.

CONTRIBUTORS

Ronald D. Witherup, S.S., Ph.D., is professor of Sacred Scripture and academic dean at St. Patrick's Seminary, Menlo Park, California.

Joyce A. Zimmerman, C.PP.S., S.T.D., is professor and director of seminary liturgy at Conception Seminary College, Missouri, and director of the Institute for Liturgical Ministry at Maria Stein Center, Ohio.

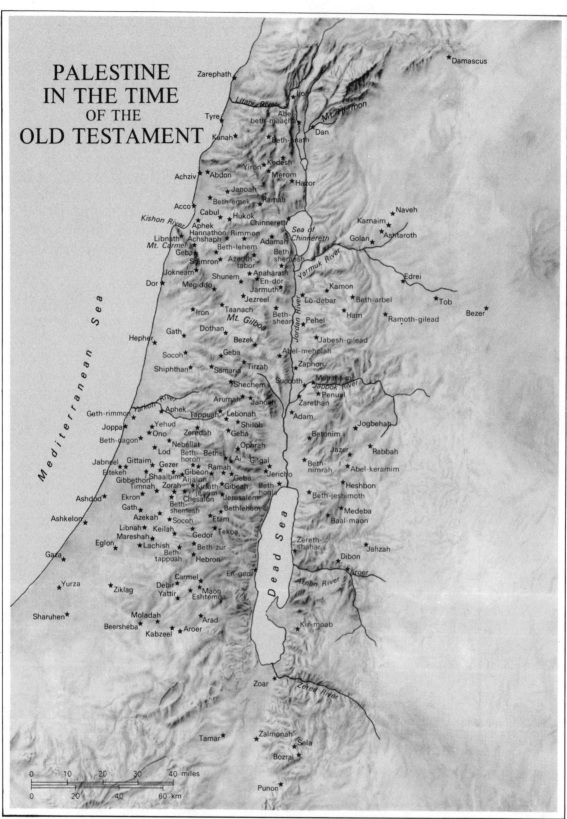

PALESTINE
IN THE TIME
OF THE
OLD TESTAMENT

Damascus

Zarephath

Litani River

Ijon

Tyre

Abel
beth-maacha

Mt. Hermon

Kanah

Beth-anath

Dan

Achziv

Abdon

Yiron

Kedesh

Merom

Hazor

Janoah

Beth-emek

Ramah

Acco

Cabul

Hukok

Chinnereth

Karnaim

Naveh

Kishon River

Aphek

Hannathon

Rimmon

Sea of
Chinnereth

Golan

Ashtaroth

Libnath

Achshaph

Beth-lehem

Adamah

Mt. Carmel

Geba

Azmoth-
tabor

Beth-
shemesh

Yarmuk River

Edrei

Shimron

Jokneam

Shunem

Anaharath

En-dor

Kamon

Dor

Megiddo

Jarmuth

Jezreel

Lo-debar

Beth-arbel

Tob

Iron

Taanach

Mt. Gilboa

Beth-
shean

Ham

Ramoth-gilead

Bezer

Gath

Dothan

Bezek

Pehel

Hepher

Geba

Abel-meholah

Jabesh-gilead

Socoh

Tirzah

Zaphon

Shiphthan

Samaria

Succoth

Mahanaim

Shechem

Jabbok River

Penuel

Arumah

Janoah

Zarethan

Yarkon River

Aphek

Tappuah

Lebonah

Adam

Geth-rimmon

Yehud

Shiloh

Betonim

Jogbehah

Joppa

Ono

Zeredah

Geba

Jazer

Rabbah

Beth-dagon

Nebellat

Ophrah

Lod

Beth-
horon

Bethel

Ai

Gilgal

Beth-
nimrah

Abel-keramim

Jabneel

Gittaim

Gezer

Ramah

Geba

Heshbon

Eltekeh

Shaalbim

Gibeon

Aijalon

Jericho

Gibbethon

Timnah

Zorah

Kirjath-
jearim

Gibeah

Beth-
hogla

Beth-jeshimoth

Ashdod

Ekron

Chesalon

Jerusalem

Gath

Beth-
shemesh

Bethlehem

Medeba

Ashkelon

Azekah

Socoh

Etam

Baal-maon

Libnah

Keilah

Gedor

Tekoa

Zereth-
shahar

Jahzah

Mareshah

Beth-zur

Eglon

Lachish

Beth-
tappuah

Hebron

Dibon

Aroer

Gaza

En-gedi

Arnon River

Yurza

Ziklag

Debir

Carmel

Yattir

Maon

Eshtemoa

Sharuhen

Moladah

Arad

Kir-moab

Beersheba

Kabzeel

Aroer

Mediterranean Sea

Jordan River

Dead Sea

Zoar

Zered River

Tamar

Zalmonah

Sela

Bozrah

Punon

0   10   20   30   40 miles

0   20   40   60 km